Canadian Master Tax Guide

.CCH

a Wolters Kluwer business

68th Edition, 2013

DISCARDED

CCH Canadian Limited
300-90 Sheppard Avenue East
Toronto Ontario
M2N 6X1
1 800 268 4522
www.cch.ca

336.2 (71)
C73
00119082 RL

Published by CCH Canadian Limited

Important Disclaimer: This publication is sold with the understanding that (1) the authors and editors are not responsible for the results of any actions taken on the basis of information in this work, nor for any errors or omissions; and (2) the publisher is not engaged in rendering legal, accounting or other professional services. The publisher, and the authors and editors, expressly disclaim all and any liability to any person, whether a purchaser of this publication or not, in respect of anything and of the consequences of anything done or omitted to be done by any such person in reliance, whether whole or partial, upon the whole or any part of the contents of this publication. If legal advice or other expert assistance is required, the services of a competent professional person should be sought.

A cataloguing record for this publication is available from Library and Archives Canada.

All rights reserved. No part of this work covered by the publisher's copyright may be reproduced or copied in any form or by any means (graphic, electronic or mechanical, including photocopying, recording, taping, or information and retrieval systems) without the written permission of the publisher.

A licence, however, is hereby given by the publisher:

(a) to a lawyer to make a copy of any part of this publication to give to a judge or other presiding officer or to other parties in making legal submissions in judicial proceedings;

(b) to a judge or other presiding officer to reproduce any part of this publication in any decision in judicial proceedings; or

(c) to anyone to reproduce any part of this publication for the purposes of parliamentary proceedings.

"Judicial proceedings" includes proceedings before any court, tribunal or person having authority to decide any matter affecting a person's legal rights or liabilities.

Explanation of Footnotes

Footnotes throughout the book cite the authorities for the conclusions given and unless otherwise indicated refer to the following:

Sec.	Indicates a section of the Income Tax Act, R.S.C. 1985 (5th Supp.) c. 1, as amended.
ITAR	Indicates a section of the Income Tax Application Rules, 1971.
Reg.	Indicates a section of the Income Tax Regulations.
Interp. Bul.	Refers to an Interpretation Bulletin issued by the Canada Revenue Agency. The full text of each Interpretation Bulletin is reproduced in the CCH CANADIAN TAX REPORTER.
Inf. Cir.	Refers to an Information Circular issued by the Canada Revenue Agency. The full text of each Information Circular is reproduced in the CCH CANADIAN TAX REPORTER.
CCH	This reference is to fuller coverage of the subject in the CCH CANADIAN TAX REPORTER. The numbers following such references are to paragraphs of the Reporter.
DTC	This reference is to the CCH DOMINION TAX CASES where the cases cited are reported in full text.

ISBN 978-1-55496-557–1

© 2012, CCH Canadian Limited

Typeset by CCH Canadian Limited.

Printed in Canada.

Table of Contents

	Paragraph
Foreword	100

Tax Charts

Tax Calendar	250
Indexed Personal Income Tax Parameters for 2011 and 2012	300
Personal Income Tax Key Amounts — 2012	400
2012 Combined Marginal Tax Rates	410
Top Marginal Rates — A 17-Year History/Deferred Income Plan Contribution Limits — 2007–2013	415
Personal Income Tax Rate Components — 2012	425
Federal and Provincial Income Taxes Payable by Individuals at Various Levels of Taxable Income — 2012	430
Federal Corporate Tax Rates — 2006–2012	460
Corporate Income Tax Rates by Province — 2012	465
Canadian-Controlled Private Corporation (CCPC) Income Tax Rates	470
Prescribed Interest Rates	475
Automobile Rates and Limits	477
Foreign Exchange Rates	480
Capital Tax Rates and Exemptions for 2012	485
Payroll Tax Rates for 2012	490
Provincial Health Insurance Premiums	495
Rates of Withholding Tax under Income Tax Agreements Signed by Canada	520
Chapter I Introduction to Income Taxation in Canada	700
II Taxation of Individuals	2000
III Income from Business or Property	3000
IV Capital Cost Allowance	4000
V Capital Gains and Losses	5000
VI Corporations and Their Shareholders	6000
VII Partnerships and Trusts	7000
VIII Tax Rates, Averaging, and Credits	8000
IX Special Cases	9000
X Deferred and Special Income Arrangements	10,000
XI Tax Exemptions	11,000
XII Returns, Assessments, Payments, and Appeals	12,000
XIII Special Transactions Taxes	13,000
XIV Non-Residents, International Income, and Tax Agreements	14,000
XV Administration, Enforcement, and Interpretation	15,000
XVI Miscellaneous Taxes	16,080
XVII Tax Planning	17,010
Topical Index	18,000

Foreword

¶100

The 68th edition of the CANADIAN MASTER TAX GUIDE is designed both to assist in the preparation of income tax returns and to serve as a convenient reference source on federal taxation.

This book is a complete, accurate, and up-to-date guide to Canadian federal taxation. It includes comprehensive commentary on the *Income Tax Act* and Regulations, including all amendments to the Act and Regulations to October 22, 2012, as well as references to pertinent official Interpretation Bulletins, Information Circulars, and court decisions received to that date.

In addition, the CANADIAN MASTER TAX GUIDE includes highlights of the Canada–U.S. and Canada–U.K. Income Tax Conventions (Chapter XIV), an overview with respect to GST and HST (Chapter XVI), and a wide range of tax planning opportunities (Chapter XVII).

Footnote references in this book are to sections of the present *Income Tax Act* (R.S.C. 1985, c. 1 (5th Supp.)), as amended; the *Income Tax Application Rules, 1971*; the Income Tax Regulations; Canada Revenue Agency Bulletins and Circulars; paragraphs in the CCH CANADIAN TAX REPORTER; and cases reported in CCH DOMINION TAX CASES. See page ii for an explanation of the footnotes.

To keep abreast of the latest changes and issues in Canadian tax, professionals also rely on the wide array of content provided by CCH Canadian Limited via the Internet, DVD, and loose leaf print:

- The CANADIAN TAX REPORTER reports, integrates, and comments on the very latest changes in income tax law in continual updates on the Internet, monthly updates on DVD, and weekly reports in loose leaf print format.

- The CANADA INCOME TAX GUIDE reports on income tax law in continual updates on the Internet, monthly updates on DVD, and in monthly reports in loose leaf print format.

- The CANADIAN INCOME TAX RESEARCH INDEX locates written articles, papers, or cases on specific tax problems or concepts, published on the Internet and DVD. This indispensable tool compiles references to relevant items and arranges those references both by topic and by section number of pertinent tax legislation.

- TAX PROFILE provides insightful analysis of important federal and provincial tax issues in a monthly newsletter on the Internet, DVD, and print.

- The GOODS AND SERVICES TAX REPORTER provides complete coverage of all GST/HST developments, including full coverage of legislation and proposed legislation, detailed commentary and analysis, and all related government documents. It is available on the Internet with continual updates, on DVD with monthly updates, and in loose leaf print format with monthly reporting.

- The CANADIAN ESTATE PLANNING GUIDE offers detailed commentary on legal and tax issues concerning estate and retirement planning in Canada, and includes case comments, digests of recent cases, and a brief summary of in-depth topical articles. It is available on the Internet, on DVD, and in loose leaf print format.

- TAX PLANNING FOR SMALL BUSINESS examines tax matters of particular interest to small businesses, and is available on the Internet and DVD.

CCH Canadian Limited   October 22, 2012

Tax Charts

¶250

Tax Calendar

The following calendar embraces the principal dates provided by general law or regulation for filing returns or paying federal income tax.

This day each month

Monthly Requirements

10th — Date by which employers with an average monthly withholding of $15,000 or more but less than $50,000 (for the second calendar year preceding a particular calendar year) must remit the income tax withheld from the renumeration paid after the 15th of the previous month (ITR s. 108(1.1)(a)(ii)) .... ¶12,110

15th — Date by which employers with an average monthly withholding of under $15,000 must remit the income tax withheld from the remuneration paid for the previous month (ITR s. 108(1)) .... ¶12,110

25th — Date by which employers with an average monthly withholding of $15,000 or more but less than $50,000 (for the second calendar year preceding a particular calendar year) must remit the income tax withheld from the remuneration paid before the 16th of the current month (ITR s. 108(1.1)(a)(i)) .... ¶12,110

Last day — Date by which corporations must make income tax instalments. No instalments are required if a corporation's first instalment base or total taxes payable under Parts I, VI, VI.1 and XIII.1 of the Act is $3,000 or less (ITA ss. 157(1) and 157(2.1)) .... ¶12,210

Quarterly Requirements

15th — (March, June, September, December) — Dates by which income tax instalments must be made by individuals whose expected tax liability for the current year or each of the two preceding years exceeds their source deductions by $1,800 of federal income tax for a Quebec resident or $3,000 of combined federal and provincial income taxes for a non-Quebec resident (ITA ss. 156(1), 156.1(1) "instalment threshold" and 156.1(2)(b)) .... ¶12,200

15th — (April, July, October, January) — Dates by which employers who have an average monthly withholding of less than $3,000 for the first or second preceding calendar year and no compliance irregularities for the preceding 12 months must remit the income tax withheld from the remuneration paid for the previous quarter (ITR s. 108(1.12)) .... ¶12,110

Last day of fiscal quarter Date by which a small Canadian-controlled private corporation may pay its tax instalments if: (1) it has a perfect income tax, sales tax, EI, and CPP compliance history; (2) it claimed the small business deduction in the current or previous year; and (3) it had a taxable capital employed in Canada of $10 million or less and a taxable income of $500,000 or less in the current or previous year where those two limits are calculated on an associated basis (ITA ss. 157(1.1), 157(1.2)(*b*), 157(1.3), and 157(1.4)(*b*)) .... ¶12,210

Annual Calendar

Feb. 14 — Date by which employees must reimburse their employer for all the operating costs incurred in the previous year for the personal use of an employer-provided automobile. Otherwise, an automobile operating cost benefit will be included in their income (ITA s. 6(1)(*k*)) ¶2085

Feb. 29 — Last day for individuals to make their RRSP contribution for a year preceding a leap year (ITA s. 146(5)) .... ¶10,336

Feb. (last day) — Date by which a T4, T4A or T4A-RCA information return is due to report an employee's remuneration and benefits (ITR ss. 200 and 205(1)) .... ¶12,050

Date by which a T4A information return is due to report patronage payments (ITA s.135; ITR ss. 205(1) and 218) .... ¶12,050

Date by which a T4RSP information return is due to report amounts included in a taxpayer's income under an RRSP, HBP or an LLP (ITA ss. 146, 146.01 and 146.02; ITR s. 205(1) and 214) .... ¶12,050

Date by which a T4RIF information return is due to report amounts included in a taxpayer's income under a RRIF (ITA s. 146.3; ITR ss. 205(1) and 215) .... ¶12,050

Date by which a T5 information return is due to report interest, eligible or non-eligible dividends, capital gains dividends, or other investment income (ITR ss. 201 and 205(1)) .... ¶12,050

Date by which a T5003 information return is due to report the acquisition of an interest in a tax shelter. If the business in respect of which the form is required was discontinued, the form is due by the earlier of the last day of February or 30 days after the discontinuance of the business (ITA ss. 237.1(7), (7.1) and (7.2))... ¶15,250

Date by which a T5008 information return is due to report proceeds paid in respect of securities transactions (mostly dispositions) (ITR ss. 205(1) and 230) .... ¶12,050

Date by which a TFSA annual information return must be sent to the CRA by each TFSA issuer to report the contributions, withdrawals, and other amounts in respect of a tax-free savings account (As per current ITR s. 205(1) and proposed ITR s. 223) .... ¶12,050

Mar. 1 — Last day for individuals to make their RRSP contribution for a year preceding a non-leap year (ITA s. 146(5)) .... ¶10,336

Mar. 31 — Date by which an NR4 information return is due to report income like interest, dividends, royalties, trust income, etc. paid to or received for the account of a non-resident in the preceding calendar year (ITA s. 212; ITR s. 202) .... ¶12,050

| | Date by which a T1-CP information return is due to report the ownership of an interest in a certified film or video tape (ITR s. 225) | ¶12,050 |

Date by which a T5013 partnership information return is due if, throughout the partnerships fiscal period, all partners were individuals, trusts, or professional corporations, or if the partnership was a tax shelter (ITR s. 229(5)(*b*)) .... ¶12,050

Apr. 30 — Date by which the balance of tax owed by any individual (including one having until June 15 to file his/her T1 income tax return) is due (ITA ss. 156.1(4) and 248(1) "balance due day") .... ¶12,180

Date by which individuals not carrying on a business in the year and whose cohabiting spouse or common-law partner is not carrying on such a business either must file their T1 income tax return (ITA s. 150(1)(*d*)(i)) .... ¶12,050

June 15 — Date by which individuals carrying on a business in the year or whose cohabiting spouse or common-law partner is carrying on such a business must file their T1 income tax return (ITA ss. 122.6 "cohabiting spouse or common-law partner" and 150(1)(*d*)(ii)) .... ¶12,025

June 30 — Date by which the T2 income tax return of a corporation operating on a calendar-year basis is due (ITA s. 150(1)(*a*)) .... ¶12,010

Date by which persons with a TFSA account must file a TFSA Return (Form RC243) and pay Part XI.01 Tax owed for the preceding year for any excess TFSA amount, non-resident contribution, non-qualified investment, prohibited investment, or advantage received in respect of their TFSA account ITA s. 207.07(1) states that persons liable to Part XI.01. Tax have only 90 days after year-end to file their return and pay their tax but, under administrative policy, the CRA extends the deadline to June 30 (ITA s. 207.07(1)) .... ¶13,517

Dec. 31 — Date by which the income tax instalment payable by a farmer or fisherman for a particular year is due. The instalment is only required if the farmer's or fisherman's net tax owing for the particular year or either of the 2 preceding years exceeds $1,800 of federal income tax for a Quebec resident or $3,000 of combined federal and provincial income taxes for a non-Quebec resident. (ITA ss. 155(1), 156.1(1) "instalment threshold", and 156.1(2)(*a*)) .... ¶12,190

Contingent Calendar

The principal tax requirements which do not fall upon fixed dates but are instead related to some other event or duty are listed below under two categories: tax collection and tax filing.

Tax Collection

- Employers with an average monthly withholding of $50,000 or more (for the second calendar year preceding a particular calendar year) must remit the income tax withheld from the remuneration paid in each of the following periods within 3 days (excluding Saturdays or holidays) from each period: (i) the first seven days of the month; (ii) the period after the 7th and before the 15th day; (iii) the period after the 14th but before the 22nd day; and (iv) the part of the month after the 21st day. The remittances must be made to the account of the Receiver General at a designated financial institution or directly to the Receiver General on the day before the normal due date (ITA ss. 153(1) and 153(1.4); ITR ss. 108(1.1)(*b*) and 110)) .... ¶12,110

- Employers required to remit their deductions twice a month by virtue of ITR s. 108(1.1)(*a*) or four times a month by virtue of ITR s. 108(1.1)(*b*) in respect of a given calendar year may elect to remit them only once a month or twice a month respectively if they qualified for this decelerated remittance in the immediately preceding calendar year (ITR s. 108(1.1)(*b*)) .... ¶12,110

• Employers ceasing to carry on their business on a given date have only seven days
  after that given date to remit their deductions (ITR s. 108(2)) . . . .   ¶12,115

• Taxpayers owing amounts of taxes, interest or penalties may be informed, by a
  registered letter sent by the Minister to their last known address, that their goods,
  chattels or moveable properties will be seized and sold unless those amounts are
  paid within 30 days (ITA s. 225) . . . .   ¶15,055

• Taxpayers owing amounts of taxes, interest or penalties and leaving (or intending to
  leave) Canada may be asked, by a notice served personally or a registered letter
  sent by the Minister to their last known address, to pay those amounts immediately
  (ITA s. 226) . . . .   ¶15,060

• Taxpayers having filed a return within three years from the end of a taxation year
  have three years from the earlier of the sending date of the original notice of
  assessment or notification that no tax is payable to apply for a refund. Under the
  "Taxpayer Relief Provisions', the Minister may decide to grant a refund to a taxpayer
  beyond the 3-year period but within 10 years from the end of the taxation year. No
  refunds will be made under those relief provisions unless all returns required under
  the Income Tax Act, the Excise Act, 2001, the Excise Tax Act, and the Air Travellers
  Security Charge Act have been filed by the taxpayer. Non-residents having been
  withheld non-resident tax from fees or commissions paid for services rendered in
  Canada or from amounts paid for the sale of certain properties would also qualify
  for the above favorable treatment provided their Part I income tax return was filed
  within two years from the date the person who withheld the tax was reassessed (ITA
  s. 152(3.1), 152(4), 152(4.2), 164(1)(a)(iii), 164(1)(b), 164(1.5), 164(2.01), 164(7),
  227(10), and 227(10.1) . . . .   ¶12,345

• Taxpayers holding amounts of unclaimed dividends, interest or sales proceeds at
  the end of their taxation year for the account of unknown beneficial owners must
  withhold and remit a tax on those amounts within 60 days from the end of the
  taxation year (ITA s. 153(4)) . . . .   ¶12,185

• Taxpayers objecting to an assessment must generally mail their notice of objection
  within 90 days from the sending date of the notice of assessment. For individuals
  other than trusts and testamentary trusts, notices of objection from assessments
  concerning Part I and I.2 taxes must be served on or before the later of 90 days
  after the sending of the notice of assessment or one year after the taxpayer's filing-
  due date for the year (ITA s. 165(1)) . . . .   ¶12,380

• Taxpayers appealing to the Tax Court of Canada must serve their notice of appeal
  within 90 days from the sending date of the reassessment or confirmed
  assessment, or after 90 days have elapsed from the service date of the notice of
  objection if the Minister never replied to that notice (ITA s. 169(1)) . . . .   ¶12,380

• Taxpayers receiving a notice of assessment showing an amount of tax assessed
  but remaining unpaid must pay the remainder immediately (ITA s. 158) . . . .   ¶15,035

• Corporations with interest refunds and interest arrears have 90 days after the latest
  of the following dates to apply for an offset of the two amounts: (1) sending dates of
  original notices of assessment giving rise to the interests; (2) sending dates of
  Minister's notifications where notices of objection were filed; and (3) issue dates of
  court decisions if appeals were filed (ITA ss. 161.1(2) and (3)(c)) . . . .   ¶12,267

• The Minister has normally four years after the sending of the notice of original
  assessment for a mutual fund trust or corporation other than a Canadian-controlled
  private corporation (CCPC), and three years for an individual, a CCPC, or any other
  person, to reassess the taxpayer. The time limits may be extended in various
  circumstances (including when the taxpayer filed a waiver, or carried back or
  claimed a loss, gift, credit, or other eligible deduction in a preceding taxation year)
  and do not apply for taxpayers having made some misrepresentations attributable
  to neglect, carelessness, or wilful default. If a corporation has received a provincial
  income tax reassessment caused by a reallocation of its taxable income earned in
  a province, the normal reassessment period is extended by one year after the later
  of: (1) the date the Minister is advised of the reassessment; and (2) 90 days after
  the sending of the provincial reassessment notice (ITA ss 152(3.1) and 152(4)) . . . . . .   ¶12,080

- The Minister must wait 90 days after the sending of the notice of assessment to commence actions to collect a tax debt if a notice of objection was not filed by the taxpayer and 90 days after the sending of the notice confirming or varying the assessment if a notice of objection was filed by the taxpayer (ITA ss. 225.1(1), and (1.1) and (2)) . . . . ¶15,025

- The Minister has 10 years from the day that is 90 days after the mailing of the notice of assessment concerning a tax debt, to commence an action to collect the tax debt but this 10-year period can be restarted in certain circumstances (ITA ss. 222(3), (4) and (5)) . . . . ¶15,020

- The Minister has two years after an individual has ceased to be a director of a corporation to commence an action to recover amounts that were not deducted or remitted by the corporation (ITA s. 227.1(4)) . . . . ¶15,085

- Corporations with a balance of tax due after having paid their instalments must pay that balance as follows: (1) Within three months after year-end for Canadian-controlled private corporations who claimed the small business deduction in the current year or preceding year, and had a taxable income calculated on an associated basis not exceeding $500,000 in the preceding year; and (2) Within two months after year-end for all other corporations (ITA 157(1) and 248(1) "balance due today") . . . . ¶12,210

- Trusts governed by a deferred profit sharing plan that acquire a non-qualified investment or use a trust property as a security for a loan must pay the Part X tax within 10 days from the day of its acquisition or use (ITA s. 198(2)) . . . . ¶13,440

Tax Filing

- Registered charities must file a T3010-1 information return within six months from the end of their fiscal period (ITA s. 149.1(14)) . . . . ¶11,648

- Persons involved in construction activities providing their primary source of business income and making payments to subcontractors for construction services must file a T5018 information return (which includes a summary and statements of contract payments) within six months from the end of their business period (i.e., calendar or fiscal year). If they cease their operations, they have 30 days to file that return (ITR s. 238) . . . . ¶12,050

- Corporations must file a T2 income tax return within six months from the end of their taxation year if they have Part I tax payable for the year or if, at any time in the year, they are resident in Canada, carry on business in Canada, have a taxable capital gain or dispose of a taxable Canadian property (ITA s. 150(1)(a)) . . . . ¶12,010

- The legal representative of a deceased taxpayer must file his/her T1 return (1) by the return's normal filing due date if the date of death is before November; (2) by the later of the normal filing due date and six months after the date of death if the date of death is after October but before the filing due date (ITA s. 150(1)(b)) . . . . ¶12,015

- Taxpayers discontinuing a business must file the T3, T4, T5, T5008, NR4, and other information returns required under Part II of the Income Tax Regulations within 30 days from the date of dicontinuance of the business (ITR s. 205(2)) . . . . ¶12,050

- Trustees, estate administrators, or any other persons controlling and receiving trust income (including interest, dividends, capital gains, or other profits) in a fiduciary capacity for the account of trust beneficiaries must file a T3 information return within 90 days from the end of the trust's taxation year. However, this reporting obligation does not apply to a registered charity, cemetery care trust, or trust governed by a deferred profit sharing plan, employee profit sharing plan, eligible funeral arrangement, registered education savings plan, or tax-free savings account. Public trusts must post prescribed financial information on the CDS Innovations Inc. website no later than: (1) 67 days from the end of the calendar year during which their fiscal period ends if they are considered public investment trusts; and (2) 60 days from the end of their fiscal period if they are not considered public investment trusts (ITR ss. 204(3) and 204.1) . . . . ¶12,050

- A T600 Ownership Certificate must be filed on or before the 15th day of the month following the month of payment or negotiation by: (1) a financial company paying accrued interest on transfers of bonds, debentures or similar securities; (2) a debtor or encashing agent negotiating bearer coupons or warrants representing interest or dividend paid by any debtor or cheques representing interest or dividend paid by a non-resident debtor (ITA s. 234 and ITR ss. 207 and 211) .... ¶12,050; ¶15,200

- Registered amateur athletic associations must file a T2052 information return within six months from the end of their fiscal period (ITR s. 216) .... ¶12,050

- Corporations and trusts wanting to certify for a taxation year that their shares, units, or interests are qualified investments for the purpose of an RRSP, RESP, RRIF, DPSP, RDSP, and TFSA must file a T3F information return within 90 days from the end of their taxation year (ITA s. 146(1) "qualified investment", 146.1(1) "qualified investment", 146.3(1) "qualified investment", 204 "qualified investment", 205(1) "qualified investment", and 207.01(1) "qualified investment"; ITR s. 221(2)) .... ¶12,050

- Partnerships or SIFT partnerships composed exclusively of corporations (other than professional corporations) must file a T5013 information return within five months after the end of their fiscal period. Tax shelter partnerships and partnerships composed exclusively of individuals, trusts, or professional corporations must file the T5013 on or before March 31 of the calendar year following the calendar year in which their fiscal period ends. Other partnerships must file the T5013 on or before the earlier of five months after the end of their fiscal period and March 31 of the calendar year following the calendar year in which their fiscal period ends. Publicly traded partnerships must post prescribed financial information on the CDS Innovations Inc. website no later than: (1) 67 days from the end of the calendar year during which their fiscal period ends if they are considered public investment partnerships; and (2) 60 days from the end of their fiscal period if they are not considered public investment partnerships (ITR ss. 229(5)(*a*), (*b*) and (*c*), and 229.1)) ¶12,050

- Partnerships discontinuing their business must file the T5013 on or before the earlier of their normal filing due date and 90 days after the discontinuance of their activities (ITR ss. 229(5)(*a*), (*b*), (*c*) and (6)) .... ¶12,050

- Corporations renouncing their Canadian exploration or development expenses for the benefit of investors having bought their flow-through shares must file a T101A information return before the end of the first month after the month in which the renunciation was made (ITA s. 66(12.7)) .... ¶12,010; ¶12,055

¶300

Indexed Personal Income Tax Parameters for 2011 and 2012

	2012 ($)	2011 ($)
Tax bracket thresholds		
Taxable income above which the 22% bracket begins	42,707	41,544
Taxable income above which the 26% bracket begins	85,414	83,088
Taxable income above which the 29% bracket begins	132,406	128,800
Amounts relating to non-refundable tax credits		
Basic personal amount	10,822	10,527
Age amount	6,720	6,537
Net income threshold	33,884	32,961
Spouse or common-law partner amount (max.)	10,822	10,527
Spouse or common-law partner amount		
(max. if eligible for the family caregiver amount)	12,822	N/A
Amount for an eligible dependant (max.)	10,822	10,527
Amount for an eligible dependant		
(max. if dependant eligible for the family caregiver amount)	12,822	N/A
Amount for children under age 18 (max. per child)	2,191	2,131
Amount for children under age 18		
(max. per child eligible for the family caregiver amount)	4,191	N/A
Canada employment amount (max.)	1,095	1,065
Infirm dependant amount (max. per dependant) **(See Note below.)**	6,402	4,282
Net income threshold	6,420	6,076
Caregiver amount (max. per dependant)	4,402	4,282
Caregiver amount		
(max. per dependant eligible for the family caregiver amount)	6,402	N/A
Net income threshold	15,033	14,624
Disability amount	7,546	7,341
Supplement for children with disabilities (max.)	4,402	4,282
Threshold relating to allowable child care and attendant care expenses	2,578	2,508
Adoption expenses (max. per adoption)	11,440	11,128
Medical expense tax credit — 3% of net income ceiling	2,109	2,052
Refundable medical expense supplement		
Maximum supplement	1,119	1,089
Minimum earnings threshold	3,268	3,179
Family net income threshold	24,783	24,108
Old Age Security repayment threshold	69,562	67,668
Certain board and lodging allowances paid to players on sports teams or members of recreation programs		
Income exclusion (max. per month)	329	320

	2012 ($)	2011 ($)
Tradesperson's tools deduction		
Threshold amount relating to cost of eligible tools	1,095	1,065
Goods and Services Tax/Harmonized Sales Tax credit		
Adult maximum	260	253
Child maximum	137	133
Single supplement	137	133
Phase-in threshold for the single supplement	8,439	8,209
Family net income at which credit begins to phase out	33,884	32,961
Canada Child Tax Benefit		
Base benefit	1,405	1,367
Additional benefit for third child	98	95
Family net income at which base benefit begins to phase out	42,707	41,544
National Child Benefit (NCB) supplement		
First child	2,177	2,118
Second child	1,926	1,873
Third child	1,832	1,782
Family net income at which NCB supplement begins to phase out	24,863	24,183
Family net income at which NCB supplement phase-out is complete	42,707	41,544
Canada Disability Benefit (CDB)		
Maximum benefit	2,575	2,504
Family net income at which CDB supplement begins to phase out	42,707	41,544
Children's Special Allowances (CSA)		
CSA Base Amount	3,582	3,485

Note:

Includes family caregiver amount of $2,000.

¶400

Personal Income Tax Key Amounts — 2012

The two tables below contain information concerning select non-refundable personal tax credits. The first table contains the federal and provincial/territorial rates used in the calculation of personal tax credits. The second table shows the value of the credits. Provinces and territories use their own prescribed amounts to determine their personal tax credits.

Personal tax credit rates
(See table below for some limitations)

		Federal	Alt.	B.C.	Man.	N.B.	Nfld. & Lab.	N.W.T.	N.S.	Nun.	Ont.	P.E.I.	Que.¹	Sask.	Yukon
General factor²															
Charitable donations	First $200	15%	10%	5.06%	10.8%	9.1%	7.7%	5.9%	8.79%	4%	5.05%	9.8%	20%	11%	7.04%
	Amount over $200	29%	21%	14.7%	17.4%	17.95%	13.3%	14.05%	21%	11.5%	11.16%⁵	16.7%	24%	15%	12.76%
Dividend tax credit³ (on grossed-up amount)	Eligible	15.02%	10%	10%	8%	12%⁴	11%	11.5%	8.85%	5.51%	6.4%	10.5%	11.9%	11%	15.08%
	Non-eligible	13.33%	3.5%	3.4%	1.75%	5.3%	5%	6%	7.7%	4%	4.5%	1%	8%	4%	4.51%

Maximum value (before surtaxes) of credits that are based on prescribed amounts

	Federal Amounts	Federal	Alt.	B.C.	Man.	N.B.	Nfld. & Lab.	N.W.T.	N.S.	Nun.	Ont.	P.E.I.	Que.¹	Sask.	Yukon
Basic				$575		$837	$634				$475	$755	$2,185¹		
Spouse	$10,822⁶	$1,623	$1,728	$504	$932	$711	$518	$784	$745	$488	$403	$642		$1,644	$762⁶
Equivalent to spouse												$617			
Age 65	$6,720	$1,008	$482	$220	$403	$409	$405	$383	$364	$366	$232	$369	$470¹	$501	$473
Disability — Basic	$7,546	$1,132	$1,333	$369	$667	$678	$428	$635	$645	$488	$384	$675		$497	$531
Disability — Under 18 supplement									$303			$394			
Infirm dependant (18 or over)	$4,402⁶	$660	$1,000	$215	$389	$396		$201	$260	$246	$176	$224	N/A¹	$968	$310⁶
Caregiver						$395			$431			$240			
Pension income	$2,000	$300	$133	$51	$108	$91	$77	$59	$103	$80	$66	$98	$418¹	$110	$141
Child	$2,191⁶	$329	N/A	N/A	N/A	N/A	N/A⁷	N/A	N/A⁸	N/A	N/A	N/A⁸	N/A	$623	$154⁶
Adoption	$11,440	$1,716		$579	$1,080	N/A	$856	N/A	N/A	N/A	$579	N/A	N/A¹	N/A	$805
Children's fitness	$500	$75	N/A	$25¹³	$54⁹	N/A	N/A	$44	N/A	N/A¹⁰	N/A¹⁰	N/A	N/A¹¹	N/A¹¹	$35
Children's arts			N/A	$25	$54	N/A	N/A	$44	N/A	N/A	N/A	N/A	N/A	N/A	$35
Canada Pension Plan (CPP)	$2,307¹²	$346	$231	$117	$249	$210	$178	$136	$203	$92	$116	$226	N/A	$254	$162
Quebec Pension Plan (QPP)	$2,342¹²	$351	N/A	N/A	N/A	N/A	N/A	N/A	N/A	N/A	N/A	N/A	N/A¹	N/A	N/A
Employment Insurance — not in Quebec	$840	$126	$84	$43	$91	$76	$65	$50	$74	$34	$42	$82	N/A	$92	$59
Employment Insurance — in Quebec	$675¹	$101	N/A	N/A	N/A	N/A	N/A	N/A	N/A	N/A	N/A	N/A	N/A¹	N/A	N/A
Canada Employment	$1,095	$164	N/A	N/A	N/A	N/A	N/A	N/A	N/A	N/A	N/A	N/A	N/A	N/A	$77
Education — Full-time (per month)	$400	$60	$67	$10	$43	$36	$15	$24	$18	$16	$26	$39	$403¹	$44	$28
Education — Part-time	$120	$18	$20	$3	$13	$11	$5	$7	$5	$5	$8	$12	N/A	$13	$8
Textbook — Full-time (per month)	$65	$10					N/A			$3					$5
Textbook — Part-time	$20	$3					N/A			$1					$1
Factors¹⁴											× 1.2 or × 1.56	× 1.1			× 1.05

Factors at bottom of table increase value of credits to reflect surtaxes.¹⁴

Notes:

1. See below for Quebec's special credits and rules.
2. The general factor, multiplied by the federal (or provincial/territorial) amount, yields the value of the federal (or provincial/territorial) credit.
3. Eligible dividends are designated as such by the payor. They are grossed up by 38% and include dividends paid by:
   - public corporations or other corporations that are not Canadian-controlled private corporations (CCPCs), that are resident in Canada and are subject to the federal general corporate income tax rate (i.e., 15% in 2012); or
   - CCPCs, to the extent that the CCPC's income is:
     - not investment income (other than eligible dividends from public corporations); and
     - subject to the federal general corporate income tax rate (i.e., the income is active business income not subject to the federal small business rate).

   Non-eligible dividends are grossed up by 25% and include dividends paid out of either income eligible for the federal small business rate or a CCPC's investment income (other than eligible dividends received from public corporations).
4. According to New Brunswick's 2010 and 2011 T1 individual tax returns (and confirmed by a New Brunswick Finance official), the province will maintain its eligible dividend tax credit rate at 12% for 2010 and subsequent years.
5. Ontario's top charitable donation credit remains 11.16%, although Ontario's new top rate is 12.16% (13.16% after 2012) on incomes over $500,000.
6. Commencing 2012, caregivers of dependants with a mental or physical infirmity can claim the Family Caregiver Tax Credit. This credit increases the spouse/equivalent to spouse, infirm dependant, caregiver or child tax credit by $300 (i.e., $2,000 x 15%; to be indexed). Only one Family Caregiver Tax Credit can be claimed for each infirm dependant. The Yukon has paralleled this credit, with an increase of up to $148 (i.e., $2,000 x 7.04% x 1.05; to be indexed).
7. In Newfoundland and Labrador, parents can claim a non-refundable tax credit amount equal to the child care expenses that are deductible from their income.
8. A non-refundable tax credit for children under six is available in Nova Scotia (up to $105 per year), in Nunavut ($48 per year) and Prince Edward Island (up to $129 per year).
9. In Manitoba, individuals up to age 24 can claim the fitness credit.
10. In Ontario, a refundable tax credit provides up to $53 for a child under 16 (up to $105 for a child under 18 with a disability) for fitness and certain non-fitness activities.
11. In Saskatchewan, a refundable tax credit provides up to $150 per child aged six to 17 (to 14, before 2012), for cultural, recreational and sports activity fees.
12. Commencing 2012, CPP and QPP amounts differ.
13. In British Columbia, tax credits for children's fitness and for children's arts can be claimed, starting 2012.
14. For taxpayers affected by provincial/territorial surtaxes, the value of the credits shown will be higher by the factors indicated. For example, to a taxpayer in Ontario's top bracket, the $475 shown for the basic Ontario credit would be worth $741 (i.e., $475 × 1.56).

Quebec's Special Credits and Rules — 2012

The following special rules apply to Quebec's non-refundable tax credits:
- the minimum basic personal credit, the Quebec Pension Plan (QPP), Employment Insurance (EI), Health Services Fund and Quebec Parental Insurance Plan (QPIP) credits are combined into a single basic personal credit equal to $10,925;
- employees, employers and the self-employed must contribute to the QPIP, from which maternity, adoption and parental leave benefits are paid. As a result, federal EI premiums are lower for Quebec employees than for other employees ($675 instead of $840). A federal credit is available to individuals for QPIP premiums;
- an adult student can transfer the unused portion of the basic personal credit to a parent, but if this transfer is made, the other dependant (18 or over) credit of $586 cannot be claimed for that student;
- most non-refundable credits, such as the basic personal credit and the age credit, can be transferred to a spouse, if not used by the taxpayer;
- the age, pension and living alone credits are reduced if net family income exceeds $31,695;
- a person that lives alone or with a dependant can claim a credit of $256;
- a person that qualifies for the living alone credit and lives with an eligible student is eligible for an additional $317 credit;
- the maximum education credit of $403 per term (maximum two terms per year) can be claimed by a supporting Quebec parent (but is not transferable) for a child under 18 who attends post-secondary school full-time (part-time for infirm dependants);
- a student can transfer the unused portion of the tuition and examination tax credits to a parent or grandparent; and
- the medical expense credit is based on the amount by which qualifying expenses exceed 3% of net family income (see below for details on the refundable medical expense credit).

Select Quebec refundable tax credits are listed in the table below.

	Details
Adoption	50% of eligible adoption expenses (maximum credit of $10,000)
Child care	26% to 75% of qualifying child care expenses (limits apply)
Caregivers[1,2]	Maximum credit of $700 plus supplement of $497, which is reduced if the dependant's income exceeds $22,075
Respite expenses for informal caregivers	30% of eligible respite expenses paid for the care of a person who resides with the caregiver and has a significant disability; maximum credit of $1,560 is reduced if family income exceeds $53,465
Informal caregivers	Maximum credit of $500 for each care recipient can be allocated to a volunteer who provides home respite to informal caregivers of the care recipient
Home support for seniors[2]	30% of eligible expenses; maximum credit of $4,680 for independent seniors, and $6,480 for dependent seniors, aged 70 and over, is reduced if family income exceeds $53,465; expenses eligible for this credit will not qualify for the medical expense credit
Medical	25% of medical expenses eligible for the non-refundable credit and 25% of amount deducted for impairment support products and services; maximum credit of $1,103 is reduced if family income exceeds $21,340

1. The informal caregivers credit consists of separate credits for:
   - informal caregivers who house, in the strict sense of the term, an eligible relative;
   - informal caregivers who cohabit with an eligible relative unable to live alone; and
   - certain informal caregivers caring for an elderly spouse (credit is not affected by the spouse's income).
2. The maximum credit will increase annually to 2016 for the caregivers credit and to 2017 for the home support for seniors credit.

Personal Tax Credits: Federal Limitations and Other Information — 2012

This table presents additional information related to federal credits. Other restrictions may also apply. The provinces/territories may have comparable thresholds and rules.

	Limitations	To whom the credit may be transferred	Carry-forward
Tuition	Credit available only if at least $100 is paid in fees to an institution	Spouse, parent or grandparent (Maximum combined tuition, education and textbook credits transferable is $750)	Indefinite
Education	Credit is $60/month for full-time students and certain disabled part-time students; $18/month for other part-time students		
Textbook	Credit is $10/month for full-time students and certain disabled part-time students; $3/month for other part-time students		
Medical	Credit is based on amount by which qualifying medical expenses exceed the lesser of $2,109 and 3% of net income (generally, expenses for any twelve-month period ending in the year can be claimed)	Either spouse may claim	
CPP/QPP and EI	For employees, maximum credit is $472 (in Quebec, $452); self-employed persons deduct 50% of CPP/QPP premiums paid for their own coverage (maximum deduction of $2,307; in Quebec $2,342) and claim a credit for the non-deductible half of premiums paid (maximum credit $346; in Quebec $351); self-employed persons do not pay EI premiums	N/A	
Canada Employment	Credit is based on employment income		
Transit pass	Public transit passes (monthly or longer) and certain weekly and electronic payment cards for travel are eligible	Spouse or parent	
Student loan interest	Interest must be paid on qualifying student loans	N/A	5 years
Charitable donations	Eligible donations are limited to 75% of net income	Either spouse may claim	
Spousal and equivalent to spouse	Reduced by any net income of the spouse or qualifying dependant		
Infirm dependant	Reduced if dependant's income exceeds $6,420	N/A	
Caregiver	For providers of in-home care for an adult relative (reduced if relative's income exceeds $15,033)		
Age	Reduced if income exceeds $33,884		
Pension	Maximum credit is $300	Spouse	
Child	Credit available for each child under 18		
Adoption	Must be claimed in the year the adoption period ends		
Children's fitness	Maximum credit is $75 for children under 16; $150 for children under 18 who qualify for the disability tax credit	Either parent may claim	
Children's arts			
Disability	Basic For individuals with severe and prolonged impairment	Spouse, parent, grandparent, child, grandchild, sibling, aunt, uncle, niece or nephew	
	Under 18 supplement Reduced if child care expenses and attendant care expenses (claimed as a medical expense for child) exceed $2,578		

¶410

2012 Combined Marginal Tax Rates

These tables show combined federal and provincial (or federal and territorial) marginal tax rates – the percentage of tax paid on the last dollar of income, or on additional income.

| | Taxable income $10,822[1] to $42,707 | | | | | Taxable income $42,707 to $85,414 | | | | |
	Brackets	Ordinary income & interest	Capital gains	Canadian dividends Eligible[2]	Non-eligible[2]	Brackets	Ordinary income & interest	Capital gains	Canadian dividends Eligible[2]	Non-eligible
Federal only	$10,822	15.00%	7.50%	(0.03%) to 0%	2.08%	$42,707	22.00%	11.00%	9.63%	10.83%
Alberta	$17,282	25.00%	12.50%	(0.03%) to 0%	10.21%	$42,707	32.00%	16.00%	9.63%	18.96%
British Columbia[1]	$37,013	22.70%	11.35%	(3.20%) to 0%	7.46%	$84,993	34.29%	17.15%	12.79%	21.95%
	$11,354	20.06%	10.03%	(6.84%) to 0%	4.16%	$74,028	32.50%	16.25%	10.32%	19.71%
	$10,822	15.00%	7.50%	(0.03%) to 0%	2.08%	$42,707	29.70%	14.85%	6.46% to 9.63%	16.21%
Manitoba[1]	$31,000	27.75%	13.88%	6.53% to 6.56%	15.83%	$67,000	39.40%	19.70%	22.60%	30.40%
	$10,822	25.80%	12.90%	3.84% to 3.86%	13.40%	$42,707	34.75%	17.38%	16.19%	24.58%
New Brunswick[1]	$38,190	27.10%	13.55%	0.11% to 0.14%[3]	10.58%	$76,380	34.40%	17.20%	10.18%[3]	19.71%
	$10,822	24.10%	12.05%	(4.03%) to 0%[3]	6.83%	$42,707	34.10%	17.05%	9.77%[3]	19.33%
Newfoundland and Labrador[1]	$32,893	27.50%	13.75%	2.04% to 2.07%	11.46%	$65,785	35.30%	17.65%	12.81%	21.21%
	$10,822	22.70%	11.35%	(4.58%) to 0%	5.46%	$42,707	34.50%	17.25%	11.70%	20.21%
Non-resident[4]	$10,822	22.20%	11.10%	(0.04%) to 0%	3.08%	$42,707	32.56%	16.28%	14.26%	16.03%
Northwest Territories	$38,679	23.60%	11.80%	(4.03%) to 0%	5.33%	$77,360	34.20%	17.10%	10.60%	18.58%
	$13,280	20.90%	10.45%	(7.76%) to 2.08%	1.96% to 2.08%	$42,707	30.60%	15.30%	5.63% to 9.63%	14.08%
	$10,822	15.00%	7.50%	(0.03%) to 0%	2.08%					
Nova Scotia[1]	$29,590	29.95%	14.98%	8.39% to 8.42%	11.15%	$59,180	38.67%	19.34%	20.42%	22.05%
	$10,822	23.79%	11.90%	(0.11%) to 0%	3.45%	$42,707	36.95%	18.48%	18.05%	19.90%
Nunavut	$40,721	22.00%	11.00%	2.03% to 2.06%	5.83%	$81,442	31.00%	15.50%	14.45%	17.08%
	$12,211	19.00%	9.50%	(2.11%) to 0%	2.08%	$42,707	29.00%	14.50%	11.69%	14.58%
	$10,822	15.00%	7.50%	(0.03%) to 0%	2.08%					
Ontario[1]	$39,020	24.15%	12.08%	3.77% to 3.80%	7.90%	$80,963[6]	39.41%	19.70%	19.88%	23.82%
	$10,822	20.05%	10.03%	(1.89%) to 0%	2.77%	$78,043	35.39%	17.70%	17.52%	20.82%
						$68,719[6]	32.98%	16.49%	14.19%	17.81%
						$42,707	31.15%	15.58%	13.43%	16.65%
Prince Edward Island[1]	$31,984	28.80%	14.40%	4.53% to 4.55%	18.08%	$63,969	38.70%	19.35%	18.19%	30.46%
	$10,822	24.80%	12.40%	(0.99%) to 0%	13.08%	$42,707	35.80%	17.90%	14.19%	26.83%
Quebec	$40,100	32.53%	16.26%	11.16% to 11.18%	16.74%	$80,200	42.37%	21.19%	24.74%	29.05%
	$13,656	28.53%	14.26%	5.64% to 5.66%	11.74%	$42,707	38.37%	19.19%	19.22%	24.05%
	$10,822	12.53%	6.26%	(0.02%) to 0%	1.74%					
Saskatchewan	$42,065	28.00%	14.00%	2.73% to 2.76%	13.33%	$42,707	35.00%	17.50%	12.39%	22.08%
	$14,942	26.00%	13.00%	(0.03%) to 0%	10.83%					
	$10,822	15.00%	7.50%	(0.03%) to 0%	2.08%					
Yukon[1]	$10,822	22.04%	11.02%	(11.12%) to 0%	5.25%	$81,501[6]	32.16%	16.08%	1.81% to 9.63%	17.62%
						$42,707	31.68%	15.84%	2.18% to 9.63%	17.30%

Individual Marginal Rates for 2012 (continued)

Taxable income $85,414 to $132,406

	Brackets	Ordinary income & Interest	Capital gains	Canadian dividends Eligible(2)	Canadian dividends Non-eligible
Federal only	$85,414	26.00%	13.00%	15.15%	15.83%
Alberta	$85,414	36.00%	18.00%	15.15%	23.96%
British Columbia	$103,205	40.70%	20.35%	21.64%	29.96%
Manitoba	$85,414	38.29%	19.15%	18.31%	26.95%
New Brunswick	$85,414	43.40%	21.70%	28.12%	35.40%
	$124,178	40.30%	20.15%	18.33%(3)	27.08%
Newfoundland and Labrador	$85,414	38.40%	19.20%	15.70%(3)	24.71%
Non-resident(4)	$85,414	39.30%	19.65%	18.33%	26.21%
Northwest Territories	$85,414	38.48%	19.24%	22.43%	23.43%
	$125,771	40.05%	20.03%	18.67%	25.90%
Nova Scotia	$85,414	38.20%	19.10%	16.12%	23.58%
	$93,000	43.50%	21.75%	27.09%	28.08%
Nunavut	$85,414	35.00%	17.50%	19.97%	22.08%
Ontario	$85,414	42.67%	21.34%	25.94%	27.05%
	$98,143(6)	43.41%	21.70%	25.40%	28.82%
Prince Edward Island	$85,414	44.37%	22.19%	24.56%	37.42%
	$85,414	42.70%	21.35%	23.71%	35.46%
Quebec	$85,414	45.71%	22.86%	29.35%	33.22%
Saskatchewan	$85,414	39.00%	19.50%	17.91%	27.08%
	$120,185	41.00%	20.50%	20.67%	29.58%
Yukon	$85,414	38.01%	19.01%	9.88% to 15.15%	24.93%

Taxable income over $132,406

	Brackets	Ordinary income & Interest	Capital gains	Canadian dividends Eligible(2)	Canadian dividends Non-eligible
Federal only	$132,406	29.00%	14.50%	19.29%	19.58%
Alberta	$132,406	39.00%	19.50%	19.29%	27.71%
British Columbia	$132,406	43.70%	21.85%	25.78%	33.71%
Manitoba	$132,406	46.40%	23.20%	32.26%	39.15%
New Brunswick	$132,406	43.30%	21.65%	22.47%(3)	30.83%
Newfoundland and Labrador	$132,406	42.30%	21.15%	22.47%	29.96%
Non-resident(4)	$132,406	42.92%	21.46%	28.55%	28.98%
Northwest Territories	$132,406	43.05%	21.53%	22.81%	29.65%
Nova Scotia	$132,406	46.50%	23.25%	31.23%	31.83%
	$150,000	50.00%	25.00%	36.06%	36.21%
Nunavut	$132,406	40.50%	20.25%	27.56%	28.96%
Ontario	$132,406	46.41%	23.20%	29.54%	32.57%
	$500,000(5)	47.97%	23.98%	31.69%	34.52%
Prince Edward Island	$132,406	47.37%	23.69%	28.70%	41.17%
Quebec	$132,406	48.22%	24.11%	32.81%	36.35%
Saskatchewan	$132,406	44.00%	22.00%	24.81%	33.33%
Yukon	$132,406	42.40%	21.20%	15.93% to 19.29%	30.41%

(1) The table does not take into account the low-income tax reductions in British Columbia, New Brunswick, Newfoundland and Labrador, Nova Scotia, Ontario, Prince Edward Island and the Yukon, or the Manitoba Family Tax Benefit (for low-income taxpayers), which may affect the rates shown.

(2) When two dividend rates are indicated, the lower rate has a negative federal and/or provincial/territorial component. A negative federal component shelters other income from federal tax and a negative provincial/territorial component shelters other income from provincial/territorial tax. As a result, the combined federal and provincial/territorial rate that applies depends on the level of the taxpayer's other income, with the higher rate applying if the taxpayer has no other income.

(3) New Brunswick's rates reflect a 12% provincial eligible dividend tax credit rate. According to New Brunswick's 2010 and 2011 T1 individual tax returns (and confirmed by a New Brunswick Finance official), the province will maintain its eligible dividend tax credit rate at 12% for 2010 and subsequent years.

(4) A non-resident who does not qualify for the federal personal basic credit of $10,822 will pay tax on taxable income below $10,822. A non-resident can claim the personal basic credit only if all or substantially all (i.e., 90% or more) of the non-resident's worldwide income is included in his or her taxable income earned in Canada for the year.

Non-resident rates for interest and dividends apply only in limited circumstances. Generally, interest (other than most interest paid to arm's length non-residents) and dividends paid to non-residents are subject to Part XIII withholding tax.)

(5) The table reflects Ontario's new tax on incomes over $500,000.

(6) The bracket relates to surtaxes levied by Ontario, Prince Edward Island or the Yukon, and assumes that only the basic personal credit is available.

¶415

Top Marginal Rates — A 17-Year History

Top Marginal Rates — A 17-Year History
(Prepared from information available as of June 28, 2012)

		1996	1997	1998	1999	2000	2001	2002	2003	2004	2005	2006	2007	2008	2009	2010	2011	2012
Federal rates (including surtaxes)		31.32			30.89	30.45	29.00											
Combined rates (%) (including surtaxes and flat taxes)	**Alberta**	46.07		45.60	45.17	43.71	39.00											
	British Columbia	54.17			52.27	51.26	45.70	43.70										
	Manitoba	50.40		50.11	48.95	48.08	46.40											
	New Brunswick	51.36	51.05	50.43	49.68	48.77	46.84							46.95	46.00		43.30	
	Newfoundland and Labrador	53.33			52.90	51.31	48.64						47.04	45.00	43.40		42.30	
	Non-resident	46.40			45.97	44.37	42.92											
	Northwest Territories	44.37			43.94	43.50	42.05			42.55		43.05						
	Nova Scotia	50.30	49.98	49.66	49.23	48.79	47.34					48.25				50.00		
	Nunavut	(Nunavut came into existence on April 1, 1999)			43.94	43.50	42.05	40.50										
	Ontario	52.92	51.64	50.29	48.75	47.86	46.41											47.97 [1]
	Prince Edward Island	50.30			49.55	48.79	47.37											
	Quebec	52.94	53.01	52.61	52.18	50.67	48.72	48.22										
	Saskatchewan	51.95		51.58	50.79	49.73	45.00	44.50	44.00									
	Yukon	46.55			46.11	45.37	43.01	42.40										

[1] For Ontario, the 47.97% rate reflects Ontario's new highest tax bracket on incomes over $500,000.

Deferred Income Plan Contribution Limits — 2007–2013

The maximum amount deductible RRSP, DPSP and money RPP contribution limits for 2007 to 2013 are shown in the table below:

	2007	2008	2009	2010	2011	2012	2013
Dollar limits:							
RRSP	$19,000	$20,000	$21,000	$22,000	$22,450	$22,970	$23,820
DPSP	$10,000	$10,500	$11,000	$11,225	$11,485	$11,910	Indexed*
Money Purchase RPP	$20,000	$21,000	$22,000	$22,450	$22,970	$23,820	Indexed*

* The Money Purchase limit is increased by increases in the Average Wage. See the definitions in s. 147.1(1) of the *Income Tax Act*.

¶425

Personal Income Tax Rate Components — 2012

		Basic Tax		Surtax
		Rates	Brackets	
Federal[1]		15.00%	$0	
		22.00%	$42,707	
		26.00%	$85,414	
		29.00%	$132,406	
Provincial or Territorial	Alberta	10.00%	$0	
	British Columbia	5.06%	$0	
		7.70%	$37,013	
		10.50%	$74,028	
		12.29%	$84,993	
		14.70%	$103,205	
	Manitoba	10.80%	$0	
		12.75%	$31,000	
		17.40%	$67,000	
	New Brunswick	9.10%	$0	
		12.10%	$38,190	
		12.40%	$76,380	
		14.30%	$124,178	No surtax
	Newfoundland and Labrador	7.70%	$0	
		12.50%	$32,893	
		13.30%	$65,785	
	Northwest Territories	5.90%	$0	
		8.60%	$38,679	
		12.20%	$77,360	
		14.05%	$125,771	
	Nova Scotia	8.79%	$0	
		14.95%	$29,590	
		16.67%	$59,180	
		17.50%	$93,000	
		21.00%	$150,000	
	Nunavut	4.00%	$0	
		7.00%	$40,721	
		9.00%	$81,442	
		11.50%	$132,406	
	Ontario	5.05%	$0	
		9.15%	$39,020	20% of tax above $4,213
		11.16%	$78,043	+ 36% of tax above $5,392
		12.16%[2]	$500,000[2]	
	Prince Edward Island	9.80%	$0	
		13.80%	$31,984	10% of tax above $12,500
		16.70%	$63,969	
	Quebec[1]	16.00%	$0	
		20.00%	$40,100	
		24.00%	$80,200	No surtax
	Saskatchewan	11.00%	$0	
		13.00%	$42,065	
		15.00%	$120,185	
	Yukon	7.04%	$0	
		9.68%	$42,707	5% of tax above $6,000
		11.44%	$85,414	
		12.76%	$132,406	
Non-residents[3]		7.20%	$0	
		10.56%	$42,707	No surtax
		12.48%	$85,414	
		13.92%	$132,406	

Notes:

1. In Quebec, federal tax is reduced by 16.5% for Quebec's abatement of basic federal tax.

2. The table reflects Ontario's new tax on incomes over $500,000. The rate is 13.16% after 2012.

3. Instead of provincial or territorial tax, non-residents pay an additional 48% of basic federal tax on income taxable in Canada that is not earned in a province or territory. Non-residents are subject to provincial or territorial rates (in this table) on employment income earned, and business income connected with a permanent establishment, in the respective province or territory. Different rates may apply to non-residents in other circumstances.

¶430

Federal and Provincial Income Taxes Payable by Individuals at Various Levels of Taxable Income — 2012

This table shows the combined federal and provincial (or territorial) income taxes payable, including surtaxes, assuming only the basic personal tax credit is claimed (except for non-residents see footnote 3, below), and that all income is either interest or ordinary income (such as salary). When income includes at least $1,095 of salary, the Canada Employment Credit, described under Personal Tax Credit — 2012 (see table), will reduce the results shown by $164 ($137 in Quebec). Depending on the types of income and deductions, the alternative minimum tax (AMT) may apply.

2012	Alberta[1]	British Columbia[1]	Manitoba[1]	New Brunswick[1]	Newfoundland and Labrador[1]	Non-resident[3][4]	Northwest Territories[1]	Nova Scotia	Nunavut[1]	Ontario[1][8][9]	Prince Edward Island	Quebec[10]	Saskatchewan	Yukon
$1,000,000	$376,270	$417,365	$447,346	$416,427	$408,259	$413,840	$411,559	$478,390	$386,349	$451,427	$456,170	$465,132	$423,110	$406,281
$500,000	$181,270	$198,865	$215,346	$199,927	$196,759	$199,240	$196,309	$228,390	$183,849	$211,579	$219,320	$224,057	$203,110	$194,291
$400,000	$142,270	$155,165	$168,946	$156,627	$154,459	$156,321	$153,259	$178,390	$143,349	$165,169	$171,950	$175,842	$159,110	$151,893
$300,000	$103,270	$111,465	$122,546	$113,327	$112,159	$113,401	$110,209	$128,390	$102,849	$118,760	$124,581	$127,627	$115,110	$109,495
$250,000	$83,770	$89,615	$99,346	$91,677	$91,009	$91,941	$88,684	$103,390	$82,599	$95,555	$100,896	$103,519	$93,110	$88,296
$200,000	$64,270	$67,765	$76,146	$70,027	$69,859	$70,481	$67,139	$78,390	$62,349	$72,350	$77,210	$79,412	$71,110	$67,097
$150,000	$44,770	$45,915	$52,946	$48,377	$48,709	$49,020	$45,634	$53,390	$42,099	$49,145	$53,525	$55,304	$49,110	$45,898
$100,000	$26,242	$25,115	$30,718	$28,158	$28,531	$28,999	$25,558	$31,113	$23,652	$26,911	$30,812	$32,009	$28,486	$26,120
$90,000	$22,642	$21,286	$26,378	$24,318	$24,601	$25,151	$21,836	$26,788	$20,132	$22,572	$26,511	$27,437	$24,586	$22,319
$80,000	$19,259	$17,763	$22,255	$20,695	$20,888	$21,623	$18,334	$22,737	$16,877	$18,486	$22,458	$23,055	$20,902	$18,842
$70,000	$16,059	$14,626	$18,315	$17,274	$17,358	$18,367	$14,979	$18,870	$13,977	$15,141	$18,587	$19,218	$17,402	$15,674
$60,000	$12,859	$11,656	$14,700	$13,864	$13,874	$15,111	$11,919	$15,002	$11,077	$12,002	$14,832	$15,381	$13,902	$12,506
$50,000	$9,659	$8,686	$11,225	$10,454	$10,424	$11,855	$8,859	$11,294	$8,177	$8,887	$11,252	$11,544	$10,402	$9,338
$40,000	$6,649	$5,905	$7,940	$7,234	$7,164	$8,880	$5,980	$7,788	$5,488	$5,962	$7,863	$7,870	$7,133	$6,431
$30,000	$4,149	$3,820	$5,184	$4,769	$4,552	$6,660	$3,863	$4,793	$3,558	$3,917	$5,061	$5,017	$4,533	$4,227
$20,000	$1,649	$1,814	$2,604	$2,359	$2,282	$4,440	$1,773	$2,389	$1,688	$1,912	$2,581	$2,165	$1,933	$2,023
Top marginal rates:														
Canadian dividends														
(eligible)	19.29%	25.78%	32.26%	22.47%[2]	22.47%	28.55%	22.81%	36.06%	27.56%	31.69%	28.70%	32.81%	24.81%	15.93% to 19.29%[11]
(non-eligible)	27.71%	33.71%	39.15%	30.83%	29.96%	28.98%	29.65%	36.21%	28.96%	34.52%	41.17%	36.35%	33.33%	30.41%
Capital gains	19.50%	21.85%	23.20%	21.65%	21.15%	21.46%	21.53%	25.00%	20.25%	23.98%	23.69%	24.11%	22.00%	21.20%
Other income	39.00%	43.70%	46.40%	43.30%	42.30%	42.92%	43.05%	50.00%	40.50%	47.97%	47.37%	48.22%	44.00%	42.40%
Dividend tax credit														
(eligible)[5]	25.02%	25.02%	23.02%	27.02%[2]	27.02%	22.23%	26.52%	26.52%	20.53%	25.00%	26.57%	24.44%	26.02%	30.85%
(non-eligible)[6]	16.83%	16.73%	15.08%	18.63%	18.33%	19.73%	19.33%	21.03%	17.33%	20.35%	14.43%	19.13%	17.33%	18.07%
Maximum value of additional credits[7]	25.00%	20.06%	25.80%	24.10%	22.70%	22.20%	20.90%	23.79%	19.00%	22.88%	25.78%	32.53%	26.00%	23.39%

1 These provinces and the Yukon have low-income tax reductions, which may decrease some amounts shown.

2 New Brunswick's rates reflect a 12% provincial eligible dividend tax credit rate. According to New Brunswick's 2010 and 2011 T1 individual tax returns (and confirmed by a New Brunswick Finance official), the province will maintain its eligible dividend tax credit rate at 12% for 2010 and subsequent years.

3 This table assumes the non-resident will not qualify for the federal basic personal tax credit of $10,822. Non-residents can claim this credit only if all or substantially all (i.e., 90% or more) of the non-resident's worldwide income is included in his or her taxable income earned in Canada for the year. The non-resident amounts apply to income taxable in Canada that is not earned in a province or territory.

4 Non-resident rates for interest and dividends apply only in limited circumstances. Generally, interest (other than most interest paid to arm's length non-residents) and dividends paid to non-residents are subject to Part XIII withholding tax.

5 Taxpayers in top brackets (i.e., taxable income above $132,406/$150,000 for Nova Scotia and $500,000 in Ontario) who receive Canadian eligible dividends can determine their tax by multiplying the dividend tax credit by the amount of eligible dividends (grossed up by 38%) and subtracting the result from the amount of tax shown in the table. For example, a Manitoba resident with $200,000 taxable income consisting of $186,200 salary plus $13,800 of grossed-up eligible dividends ($10,000 actual dividends) will pay the $76,146 tax shown, less 23.02% of $13,800, yielding $72,969.

6 Taxpayers in top brackets (i.e., taxable income above $132,406/$150,000 for Nova Scotia and $500,000 in Ontario) who receive Canadian non-eligible dividends can determine their tax by multiplying the dividend tax credit by the amount of non-eligible dividends (grossed up by 25%) and subtracting the result from the amount of tax shown in the table. For example, an Alberta resident with $250,000 taxable income consisting of $240,000 salary plus $10,000 of grossed-up non-eligible dividends ($8,000 actual dividends) will pay the $83,770 tax shown, less 16.83% of $10,000, yielding $82,087.

7 When provincial tax credits in addition to the basic personal tax credit are available, the results in this table are too high. For taxpayers in the top tax bracket, the amounts can be adjusted by subtracting the product of the percentage indicated (maximum value of additional credits) and the amount of the additional credits. Charitable donations over $200 have a higher maximum value.

8 Amounts do not include the Northwest Territories and Nunavut employee payroll taxes and provincial health levies (e.g., the Ontario Health Premium).

9 For Ontario, the taxes payable amounts and top marginal rates in the table reflect Ontario's new tax on incomes over $500,000.

10 Taxable income may differ for federal and Quebec purposes, in which case the amounts shown in the table may require adjustment.

11 For the Yukon, the lower eligible dividend rate has a negative Yukon component, which shelters other income from Yukon tax. As a result, the combined federal/Yukon rate that applies depends on the level of the taxpayer's other income, with the higher rate applying if the taxpayer has no other income.

¶460

Federal Corporate Tax Rates — 2006–2012

The rates shown are in effect for 12-month taxation years ended December 31. All rate changes must be prorated for taxation years that straddle the effective date.

The rates shown are in effect for 12-month taxation years ended December 31. All rate and threshold changes must be prorated for taxation years that straddle the effective date.

			2006	2007	2008	2009	2010	2011	2012
General and manufacturing & processing (M&P) income		Basic rate	38						
		Less: provincial abatement	10						
		Rate after abatement	28						
		Plus: federal surtax[1]	1.12		n/a				
		General federal rate (before deductions)	29.12		28				
		Less: general rate reduction or M&P deduction[2,3]	7		8.5	9	10	11.5	13
		General federal and M&P rate[4]	**22.12**		**19.5**	**19**	**18**	**16.5**	**15**
Canadian-controlled private corporations (CCPCs)	**Active business income up to threshold**	Threshold	Small business deduction threshold[5]	$300,000		$400,000	$500,000			
		General federal rate (before deductions)[3]	29.12		28				
		Less: small business deduction[5]	16		17				
		CCPC small business rate	**13.12**		**11**				
	Investment income	General federal rate (before deductions)[3]	29.12		28				
		Additional refundable tax[6]	6.67						
		CCPC investment income rate	**35.79**		**34.67**				

Notes:

1. The federal surtax was eliminated on January 1, 2008, resulting in a 1.12% decrease in income tax rates.

2. Recent changes to the general rate reduction and manufacturing and processing (M&P) deduction are shown in the following table.

	Changes effective after December 31, 2007		
	From	**To**	**Effective**
General rate reduction and M&P deduction	7%	8.5%	January 1, 2008
	8.5%	9%	January 1, 2009
	9%	10%	January 1, 2010
	10%	11.5%	January 1, 2011
	11.5%	13%	January 1, 2012

3. The general rate reduction and M&P deduction do not apply to: income benefiting from the small business deduction; investment income of CCPCs; income of certain corporations (e.g., mutual fund corporations, mortgage investment corporations and investment corporations); and, until taxation years beginning after 2006, resource income. For taxation years beginning after October 31, 2011, proposed legislation disallows income from a personal services business from being eligible for the general rate reduction.

4. The resource income tax rate was 24.12% before January 1, 2007. Commencing January 1, 2007, the rate is the same as the general and M&P rate.

5. The small business deduction applies to active business income earned in Canada of associated CCPCs, up to a threshold. As a result of a clawback, the small business deduction is reduced if taxable paid-up capital employed in Canada, on an associated basis, exceeded $10 million in the preceding year.

   Recent changes to the small business deduction and threshold are shown in the following table.

	Changes effective after December 31, 2007		
	From	**To**	**Effective**
Small business deduction	16%	17%	January 1, 2008
Threshold up to which CCPC rate applies	$400,000	$500,000	January 1, 2009

6. A 6⅔% additional refundable tax on investment income applies to investment income (other than deductible dividends) of CCPCs. It is refundable through the refundable dividend tax on hand (RDTOH) mechanism.

Other Federal Corporate Tax Rates for 2012

	Rate	Corporations affected	Description	Special rules
Income not earned in a province or territory	25%[1]	All corporations	Income tax for 2012 is calculated as follows: Basic federal rate 38% Less: General rate reduction -13% General federal rate 25% Therefore, the federal rate is 25%, instead of 15%.	Corporate income not earned in a province or territory is neither: • eligible for the provincial abatement; nor • subject to provincial or territorial tax (exceptions apply).
Branch tax	25%	Non-resident corporations, except: • transportation, communications and iron-ore mining companies; and • insurers (other than in special circumstances).	Applies to after-tax profits that are not invested in qualifying property in Canada.	The 25% rate may be reduced by the relevant tax treaty (generally to the withholding tax rate on dividends, which is usually 5%, 10% or 15%). Some treaties prohibit the imposition of branch tax or provide that the tax is payable only on earnings exceeding a threshold.
Part III.1 Tax on Excess Eligible Dividend Designations	20% or 30%	Canadian-resident corporations	Applies if: • a CCPC has designated as eligible dividends during the year an amount that exceeds the corporation's general rate income pool (GRIP) at the end of the year; or • a non-CCPC pays an eligible dividend when it has a positive balance in its low rate income pool (LRIP).	A corporation subject to Part III.1 tax at the 20% rate (i.e., the excess designation was inadvertent) can elect, with shareholder concurrence, to treat all or part of the excess designation as a separate non-eligible dividend, in which case Part III.1 tax will not apply to the amount that is the subject of the election.
Refundable Part IV tax	33⅓%	Private corporations and certain public corporations	Payable on taxable dividends received from certain taxable Canadian corporations.	Refundable to the corporation when it pays dividends, through the refundable dividend tax on hand (RDTOH) mechanism, at a rate of $1 for every $3 of taxable dividends paid.
Refundable Investment Tax	6⅔%	Canadian-Controlled Private Corporations (CCPCs)	Increases the total federal rate that applies to investment income of a CCPC to 34.67%. Generally, 26⅔% of a CCPC's aggregate investment income is added to its RDTOH.	
Large Corporations Tax (LCT)	Nil	All corporations	Before 2006, imposed on taxable capital employed in Canada over $50 million. (The threshold was shared by related corporations; associated corporations in the case of CCPCs.)	A notional LCT, calculated as if the LCT rate and capital tax threshold were 0.225% and $10 million, respectively, is relevant for certain purposes (e.g., a CCPC's small business limit). Before 2008, the portion of the federal surtax liability that was the corporation's Canadian surtax liability reduced any LCT liability for the year or the previous three years (and, before 2006, the next seven years).
Part VI Financial Institutions Capital Tax	1.25%	Banks Trust and loan corporations Life insurance companies	Applies to banks, trust and loan corporations and life insurance companies with capital employed in Canada over $1 billion. The threshold is shared by related corporations.	Reduced by the corporation's federal income tax liability. Any unused federal income tax liability can be applied to reduce Financial Institutions Capital Tax for the previous three years and the next seven.

Notes:

1. Recent changes to the federal rate for income not earned in a province or territory are shown in the following table:

	Changes effective after December 31, 2007		
	From	To	Effective
Income not earned in a province or territory	32.12%	29.5%	January 1, 2008
	29.5%	29%	January 1, 2009
	29%	28%	January 1, 2010
	28%	26.5%	January 1, 2011
	26.5%	25%	January 1, 2012

¶465

Corporate Income Tax Rates by Province — 2012

All rate changes must be pro-rated for taxation years that straddle the effective date. Use the rate changes to determine rates for taxation years ending on December 31, 2008 or later.

Tax holidays may reduce or eliminate provincial tax.

In addition to income tax:

- one province (Nova Scotia) imposes general capital tax on corporations that have a permanent establishment there (see **Capital Tax Rates and Exemptions for 2012**); and

- financial institutions may also be subject to Part VI Financial Institution Capital Tax (see **Other Federal Corporate Tax Rates for 2012**) and provincial capital taxes (see **Capital Tax Rates and Exemptions for 2012**).

General and M&P Corporate Income Tax Rates
(for December 31, 2012 year end) (%)

The percentages shown in the table below reflect the combined federal and provincial/territorial corporate rates (general and manufacturing and processing (M&P)) for a 12-month taxation year ended December 31, 2012, on income allocated to provinces or territories. For Canadian-controlled private corporations (CCPCs), this table does not apply to:

- the first $500,000 ($400,000 in Manitoba and Nova Scotia) of active business income; and
- investment income.

For more CCPC rates, see table **Canadian-Controlled Private Corporation (CCPC) Income Tax Rates**.

		General and Manufacturing & Processing (M&P)	
Basic federal rate		38	
Provincial abatement		(10)	
4% federal surtax[1]		n/a	
Federal rate (before deductions)		28	
General rate reduction[3] or M&P deduction[3]		(13)[2]	
Federal rate		15[2] ↓	
	Provincial/Territorial	Combined	
Alberta	10	25	
British Columbia[4]	10	25	
Manitoba[5]	12	27	
New Brunswick[6]	10	25	
Newfoundland and Labrador	General	14 H	29
	M&P	5 H	20
Northwest Territories	11.5	26.5	
Nova Scotia	16	31	
Nunavut	12	27	
Ontario[7, 8]	General	11.5 H	26.5
	M&P	10 H	25
Prince Edward Island	16 H	31	
Quebec[9]	11.9 H	26.9	
Saskatchewan[10]	General	12	27
	M&P	10[11]	25
Yukon	General	15	30
	M&P	2.5	17.5

H = Tax holidays are available to certain corporations in the provinces indicated.

Notes:

1. The 4% federal surtax was eliminated on January 1, 2008. See footnote 1 to the table, **Federal Corporate Tax Rates**.

2. Footnote 3 to the table, **Federal Corporate Tax Rates** indicates when the general rate reduction and M&P deduction do not apply.

3. For recent changes to the general rate reduction and M&P deduction, see footnote 2 to the table, **Federal Corporate Tax Rates**.

4. Recent and planned British Columbia changes are shown in the following table:

	British Columbia changes effective after December 31, 2007		
	From	To	Effective
General and M&P	12%	11%	July 1, 2008
	11%	10.5%	January 1, 2010
	10.5%	10%	January 1, 2011
	10%	11%*	April 1, 2014

* British Columbia's 2012 budget describes the increase to the 11% rate on April 1, 2014, as a temporary measure to be triggered only if the province's fiscal situation worsens.

Corporate Income Tax Rates by Province — 2012 (%) (continued)

5. Recent and planned Manitoba changes are shown in the following table:

Manitoba changes effective after December 31, 2007		
From	To	Effective
14%	13%	July 1, 2008
General and M&P 13%	12%	July 1, 2009
12%	11%*	To be determined

   * The rate reduction is subject to balanced budget requirements.

6. Recent New Brunswick changes are shown in the following table:

New Brunswick changes effective after December 31, 2007		
From	To	Effective
13%	12%	July 1, 2009
General and M&P 12%	11%	July 1, 2010
11%	10%*	July 1, 2011

   * New Brunswick repealed the legislated corporate income tax rate of 8% that was to apply on July 1, 2012.

7. Recent and planned Ontario changes are shown in the following table:

Ontario changes effective after December 31, 2007		
From	To	Effective
General 14%	12%	July 1, 2010
12%	11.5%*	July 1, 2011
M&P 12%	10%	July 1, 2010

   * Ontario's 2012 budget froze the general income tax rate at 11.5%, until the province returns to a balanced budget (scheduled for 2017-18). The rate was to drop to 11% on July 1, 2012, and to 10% on July 1, 2013.

8. Corporations subject to Ontario income tax may also be liable for corporate minimum tax (CMT) based on adjusted book income. The minimum tax is payable only to the extent that it exceeds the regular Ontario income tax liability. Recent Ontario CMT changes are shown in the following table:

	Ontario changes effective after December 31, 2007		
	From	To	Effective
Corporate Minimum Tax (CMT) rate	4%	2.7%	July 1, 2010
Thresholds for CMT to apply* Total assets	> $5 million	≥ $50 million	Taxation years ending after June 30, 2010
	or	and	
Annual gross revenues	> $10 million	≥ $100 million	

   * Thresholds apply on an associated basis.

9. Recent Quebec changes are shown in the following table:

Quebec changes effective after December 31, 2007		
From	To	Effective
General and M&P* 9.9%	11.4%	January 1, 2008
11.4%	11.9%	January 1, 2009

   * For financial institutions (other than insurance corporations) and oil refining companies, the rate is 11.9% and the combined rate is 31.4% for December 31, 2008 year ends. However, deposit insurance corporations are not financial institutions and were subject to a rate of 5.75%, which increased to 11.9% on June 23, 2009.

10. Recent Saskatchewan changes are shown in the following table:

Saskatchewan changes effective after December 31, 2007		
From	To	Effective
General 13%	12%	July 1, 2008

11. The general rate (12% in 2012) is the maximum Saskatchewan rate. A rebate of up to the difference between the general rate and 10% (2% in 2012) of manufacturing profits allocated to Saskatchewan is available.

¶470

Canadian-Controlled Private Corporation (CCPC) Income Tax Rates (for December 31, 2012 Year End) %

	Active business income of CCPCs[1] up to $500,000[2]		Investment income[3]	
Federal rate (before deductions)	28		28	
Small business deduction[2]	(17)		n/a	
Refundable investment tax	n/a		6.67	
Federal rate	11 ↓		34.67 ↓	
	Provincial/ Territorial	Combined	Provincial/ Territorial	Combined
Alberta[4]	3	14	10	44.67
British Columbia[5]	2.5	13.5	10	44.67
Manitoba[6]	Nil* or 12*	11* or 23*	12	46.67
New Brunswick[7]	4.5	15.5	10	44.67
Newfoundland and Labrador[8]	4 H	15	14 H	48.67
Northwest Territories[9]	4	15	11.5	46.17
Nova Scotia[10]	4* H or 16*	15* or 27*	16	50.67
Nunavut[11]	4	15	12	46.67
Ontario[12, 13]	4.5 H	15.5	11.5 H	46.17
Prince Edward Island[14]	1 H	12	16 H	50.67
Quebec[15]	8 H	19	11.9 H	46.57
Saskatchewan[16]	2	13	12	46.67
Yukon[17] M&P	2.5	13.5	n/a	
Yukon[17] Non-M&P	4	15	15	49.67

H = Tax holidays are available to certain corporations in the provinces indicated.

* The lower rate applies to active business income of CCPCs up to $400,000. The higher rate applies to active business income of CCPCs from $400,000 to $500,000.

Notes:

1. See the table, **General and M&P Corporate Income Tax Rates**, for the rates that apply to CCPCs on active business income above $500,000.

   The federal small business threshold increased from $400,000 to $500,000 on January 1, 2009. The $500,000 threshold also applies in:
   * New Brunswick, Newfoundland and Labrador, Northwest Territories, Nunavut, Ontario (see footnote 13 below), Prince Edward Island and Saskatchewan;
   * Quebec, after March 19, 2009 (see footnote 15 below);
   * Alberta, after March 31, 2009 (see footnote 4 below);
   * British Columbia, after December 31, 2009 (see footnote 5); and
   * the Yukon, after December 31, 2010 (see footnote 17).

   Manitoba and Nova Scotia have not harmonized with this increase.

2. See footnote 5 to the table, **Federal Corporate Tax Rates**, for:
   * recent changes to the federal small business deduction and threshold; and
   * a description of the federal small business deduction clawback and threshold.

   The clawback also applies for the purposes of the provincial/territorial small business deductions in the territories and all provinces except Ontario. Ontario had a clawback before July 1, 2010, as outlined in footnote 13, below.

3. Rates on investment income are 19.67% higher than the general rates for 2012 (see the table, **General and M&P Corporate Income Tax Rates**), because:
   * CCPC investment income does not benefit from the 13% federal general rate reduction; and
   * the rates on investment income includes a 6⅔% tax that is refundable when the CCPC pays taxable dividends.

   Generally, 26⅔% of a CCPC's aggregate investment income is added to its refundable dividend tax on hand (RDTOH). This amount is refundable at a rate of $1 for every $3 of taxable dividends paid by the CCPC.

CCPC Income Tax Rates — 2012 (continued)

4. Recent Alberta changes are shown in the following table:

	Alberta changes effective after December 31, 2007		
	From	To	Effective
CCPC rate on over-integrated income*	3%	9.7%	January 1, 2009
Threshold up to which CCPC rate applies	$430,000	$460,000	April 1, 2008
	$460,000	$500,000	April 1, 2009

> * Commencing January 1, 2009, an "over-integration tax payable" effectively increases Alberta's tax rate by 6.7% from 3% to 9.7% on income that is eligible for the Alberta CCPC small business deduction (SBD), but exceeds the federal SBD threshold. In general, this 6.7% tax applies only when this income is distributed as eligible dividends. However, because the federal SBD threshold increased from $400,000 to $500,000 on January 1, 2009, this tax in effect no longer applies.

5. Recent British Columbia changes are shown in the following table:

	British Columbia changes effective after December 31, 2007		
	From	To	Effective
CCPC rate	4.5%	3.5%	July 1, 2008
	3.5%	2.5%*	December 1, 2008
Threshold up to which CCPC rate applies	$400,000	$500,000	January 1, 2010

> * British Columbia's 2012 budget maintains the small business rate at 2.5% and rescinds the decrease in the rate to 0% that was scheduled for April 1, 2012.

6. Recent Manitoba changes are shown in the following table:

	Manitoba changes effective after December 31, 2007		
	From	To	Effective
CCPC rate	3%	2%	January 1, 2008
	2%	1%	January 1, 2009
	1%	0%	December 1, 2010

7. Recent and planned New Brunswick changes are shown in the following table:

	New Brunswick changes effective after December 31, 2007		
	From	To	Effective
CCPC rate	5%	4.5%*	January 1, 2012
Threshold up to which CCPC rate applies	$400,000	$500,000	January 1, 2009

> * New Brunswick's 2011 budget announced that the small business tax rate will decline in stages to 2.5% over the next three years.

8. Recent Newfoundland and Labrador changes are shown in the following table:

	Newfoundland and Labrador changes effective after December 31, 2007		
	From	To	Effective
CCPC rate	5%	4%	Taxation years beginning after March 31, 2010
Threshold up to which CCPC rate applies	$400,000	$500,000	January 1, 2009

9. Recent Northwest Territories changes are shown in the following table:

	Northwest Territories changes effective after December 31, 2007		
	From	To	Effective
Threshold up to which CCPC rate applies	$400,000	$500,000	January 1, 2009

10. Recent and planned Nova Scotia changes are shown in the following table:

	Nova Scotia changes effective after December 31, 2007		
	From	To	Effective
CCPC rate	5%	4.5%	January 1, 2011
	4.5%	4%	January 1, 2012
	4%	3.5%	January 1, 2013

CCPC Income Tax Rates — 2012 (continued)

11. Recent Nunavut changes are shown in the following table:

	Nunavut changes effective after December 31, 2007		
	From	To	Effective
Threshold up to which CCPC rate applies	$400,000	$500,000	January 1, 2009

12. Corporations subject to Ontario income tax may also be liable for corporate minimum tax (CMT) based on adjusted book income. The minimum tax is payable only to the extent that it exceeds the regular Ontario income tax liability. For rates and thresholds, see the table, **General and M&P Corporate Income Tax Rates** (note 8).

13. Recent Ontario changes are shown in the following table:

	Ontario changes effective after December 31, 2007		
	From	To	Effective
CCPC rate	5.5%	4.5%	July 1, 2010

Recent changes related to Ontario's CCPC clawback are shown below:

		Ontario CCPC clawback* effective after December 31, 2007		
		Addition to rate (between thresholds) due to clawback		
Lower threshold	Upper threshold	Non-M&P	M&P	Effective
$500,000	$1,500,000	4.25%	3.25%	Before July 1, 2010
n/a	n/a	0%	0%	July 1, 2010

> * Before July 1, 2010, a surtax clawed back the benefit of Ontario's small business deduction when taxable income of associated corporations exceeded $500,000. The benefit was eliminated completely once taxable income, on an associated basis, reached $1,500,000. The addition to the rate, due to the clawback, increased the rate that would otherwise apply.

14. Recent Prince Edward Island changes are shown in the following table:

	Prince Edward Island changes effective after December 31, 2007		
	From	To	Effective
CCPC rate	4.3%	3.2%	April 1, 2008
	3.2%	2.1%	April 1, 2009
	2.1%	1%	April 1, 2010
Threshold up to which CCPC rate applies	$400,000	$500,000	January 1, 2009

15. Recent Quebec changes are shown in the following table:

	Quebec changes effective after December 31, 2007		
	From	To	Effective
Threshold up to which CCPC rate applies	$400,000	$500,000	March 20, 2009

16. Recent Saskatchewan changes are shown in the following table:

	Saskatchewan changes effective after December 31, 2007		
	From	To	Effective
CCPC rate	4.5%	2%	July 1, 2011
Threshold up to which CCPC rate applies	$450,000	$500,000	July 1, 2008

17. Recent Yukon changes are shown in the following table:

	Yukon changes effective after December 31, 2007		
	From	To	Effective
Threshold up to which CCPC rate applies	$400,000	$500,000	January 1, 2011

¶475

Prescribed Interest Rates

The following rates have been set under the floating rate provisions commencing in 1994:

- Deemed interest on employee and shareholder loans and effective July 1, 2010, rate also applies to overpaid taxes for corporate taxpayers
- Rate for overpaid taxes for all taxpayers prior to July 1, 2010 and for non-corporate taxpayers after June 30, 2010
- Late or deficient income tax payments and unremitted withholdings

	Jan. 1 - Mar. 31			Apr. 1 - June 30			July 1 - Sept. 30			Oct. 1 - Dec. 31		
1994	5	7	7	4	6	6	6	8	8	5	7	7
1995	6	8	8	8	10	10	9	11	13	7	9	11
1996	7	9	11	6	8	10	5	7	9	5	7	9
1997	4	6	8	3	5	7	4	6	8	4	6	8
1998	4	6	8	5	7	9	5	7	9	5	7	9
1999	5	7	9	5	7	9	5	7	9	5	7	9
2000	5	7	9	6	8	10	6	8	10	6	8	10
2001	6	8	10	6	8	10	5	7	9	5	7	9
2002	3	5	7	2	4	6	3	5	7	3	5	7
2003	3	5	7	3	5	7	4	6	8	3	5	7
2004	3	5	7	3	5	7	2	4	6	3	5	7
2005	3	5	7	3	5	7	3	5	7	3	5	7
2006	3	5	7	4	6	8	4	6	8	5	7	9
2007	5	7	9	5	7	9	5	7	9	5	7	9
2008	4	6	8	4	6	8	3	5	7	3	5	7
2009	2	4	6	1	3	5	1	3	5	1	3	5
2010	1	3	5	1	3	5	1	3	5	1	3	5
2011	1	3	5	1	3	5	1	3	5	1	3	5
2012	1	3	5	1	3	5	1	3	5	1	3	5

¶477

Automobile Rates and Limits

The following rates and limits are prescribed in sections 7305.1 to 7307 of the Income Tax Regulations. In recent years, the Department of Finance has been adjusting the amounts by News Release issued at the end of the calendar year.

See the definitions of "automobile" and "passenger vehicle" in subsection 248(1) of the *Income Tax Act*

	Jan. 1/01-Dec. 31/02	Jan. 1/03-Dec. 31/04	Jan. 1/05-Dec. 31/05	Jan. 1/06-Dec. 31/07	Jan. 1/08-Dec. 31/11	Jan. 1/12-Dec. 31/12
Operating expense benefit - per kilometre [1]						
Employees	16¢	17¢	20¢	22¢	24¢	26¢
Employees employed principally in selling or leasing automobiles	13¢	14¢	17¢	19¢	21¢	23¢

	Jan. 1/01-Dec. 31/02	Jan. 1/03-Dec. 31/04	Jan. 1/05-Dec. 31/05	Jan. 1/06-Dec. 31/07	Jan. 1/08-Dec. 31/11	Jan. 1/12-Dec. 31/12
Reasonable allowance per kilometre [2]						
Deductible by employer where tax-free allowance paid to employee:						
All Provinces*	41¢/35¢	42¢/36¢	45¢/39¢	50¢/44¢	52¢/46¢	53¢/47¢
Nunavut, Yukon and Northwest Territories*	45¢/39¢	46¢/40¢	49¢/43¢	54¢/48¢	56¢/50¢	57¢/51¢

	Jan. 1/01-Dec. 31/02	Jan. 1/03-Dec. 31/04	Jan. 1/05-Dec. 31/05	Jan. 1/06-Dec. 31/07	Jan. 1/08-Dec. 31/11	Jan. 1/12-Dec. 31/12
Cost of passenger vehicle [3]	$30,000**	$30,000**	$30,000**	$30,000**	$30,000**	$30,000**
Prescribed monthly interest [4]	$300	$300	$300	$300	$300	$300
Monthly lease amount [5]	$800**	$800**	$800**	$800**	$800**	$800**

* First number applies to the first 5,000 kilometres driven in the year. The second number applies to subsequent kilometres driven in the year.
** Applicable federal and provincial sales taxes are added to these figures to calculate the ceiling amount.

[1] Reg. 7305.1; prescribed for s. 6(1)(*k*).
[2] Reg. 7306; prescribed for s. 18(1)(*r*).
[3] Reg. 7307(1); prescribed for ss. 13(2), 13(7)(*g*), 13(7)(*h*)(iii), 20(4), 20(16.1), the description of B in s. 67.3(*d*), and s. 85(1)(*e*.4)(i).
[4] Reg. 7307(2); prescribed for the description of A in s. 67.2.
[5] Reg. 7307(3); prescribed for the description of A in s. 67.3(*c*).

¶480

Foreign Exchange Rates

The rates for the following currencies have been supplied by the Bank of Canada and the Canada Revenue Agency whereby one unit of the foreign currency multiplied by the exchange rate, equals the equivalent amount in Canadian dollars. Please see http://www.bankofcanada.ca/en/exchange_avg_pdf.html for the most up-to-date exchange rates.

Annual Average Exchange Rates

	Exchange Rate	
Country/(Monetary Unit)	**2011**	**2010**
Argentina "floating" (peso)	0.2277	0.2593
Australia (dollar)	1.0206	0.9470
Bahamas (dollar)	0.9891	1.0299
Brazil (new real)	0.5920	0.5853
Burma (Myanmar) (kyat)	0.1835	0.1847
Chile (peso)	0.002047	0.002022
China (renminbi)	0.1531	0.1521
Colombia (peso)	0.000536	0.000543
Communauté Financière Africaine (franc)	0.002099	0.002083
Comptoirs Français du Pacifique (franc)	0.01154	0.01145
Croatia (kuna)	0.1852	0.1875
Czech Republic (koruna)	0.05603	0.05404
Denmark (krone)	0.1848	0.1834
East Caribbean (E.C. dollar)	0.3705	0.3882
European Monetary Union (euro)	1.3767	1.3661
Fiji (dollar)	0.5517	0.5380
Ghana (cedi)	0.6398	0.7190
Guatemala (quetzal)	0.1252	0.1278
Honduras (lempira)	0.05235	0.05451
Hong Kong (dollar)	0.127055	0.132572
Hungary (forint)	0.004945	0.004968
Iceland (krona)	0.008524	0.008445
India (rupee)	0.02126	0.02255
Indonesia (rupiah)	0.000113	0.000113
Israel (shekel)	0.2766	0.2759

Country/(Monetary Unit)	2011	2010
Jamaica (dollar)	0.01156	0.01186
Japan (yen)	0.01242	0.01176
Malaysia (ringgit)	0.3234	0.3201
Mexico (peso)	0.07976	0.08157
Morocco (dirham)	0.1222	0.1224
Netherlands Antilles (guilder)	0.5641	0.5825
New Zealand (dollar)	0.7824	0.7430
Norway (krone)	0.1765	0.1706
Pakistan (rupee)	0.01145	0.01209
Panama (balboa)	0.9891	1.0299
Peru (nuevo sol)	0.3592	0.3646
Philippines (peso)	0.02285	0.02285
Poland (zloty)	0.3350	0.3423
Romania (nouveau leu)	0.3250	0.3247
Russia (rouble)	0.03369	0.03392
Serbia (dinar)	0.01351	0.01329
Singapore (dollar)	0.7868	0.7560
South Africa (rand)	0.1368	0.1409
South Korea (won)	0.000893	0.000891
Sri Lanka (rupee)	0.008950	0.009112
Sweden (krona)	0.1525	0.1432
Switzerland (franc)	1.1187	0.9896
Taiwan (new Taiwan $)	0.03365	0.03269
Thailand (baht)	0.03244	0.03250
Trinidad and Tobago (dollar)	0.1549	0.1623
Tunisia (dinar)	0.7033	0.7202
Turkey (new lira)	0.5910	0.6837
United Arab Emirates (dirham)	0.2693	0.2804
United Kingdom (pound)	1.58607000	1.59177012
United States (dollar)	0.98906920	1.02993904
Venezuela (bolivar)	0.2303	0.2468
Vietnam (dong)	0.000048	0.000054

¶485

Capital Tax Rates and Exemptions for 2012

In addition to federal capital taxes on financial institutions:

- one province (Nova Scotia) levies a general capital tax on corporations (other than financial institutions) that have a permanent establishment there; and

- most provinces levy a capital tax on financial institutions such as trust and loan companies and banks.

The calculation of the tax base may differ from province to province. Alberta, British Columbia, Ontario and the territories impose neither a general or financial institutions capital tax.

The table below sets out capital tax rates for a twelve-month taxation year ending December 31, 2012. See the table under **Financial Institutions** for capital tax rates for financial institutions (other than insurance companies), which follow special rules not applicable to other corporations.

Corporations in General

		Rate	Exemption[1] (for December 31, 2012 year-end)
Federal Large Corporations Tax[2]			
Alberta		No capital tax	
British Columbia			
Manitoba[3]			
New Brunswick[4]			
Newfoundland and Labrador			
Nova Scotia[5]	If taxable capital < $10 million	0.050%	$5 million
	If taxable capital ≥ $10 million	0.025%	Nil
Ontario[6]		No capital tax	
Prince Edward Island			
Quebec[7]			
Saskatchewan[8]			

Notes:

1. Exemptions are generally shared by associated or related corporations.

2. The Large Corporations Tax was eliminated on January 1, 2006. See the table, **Other Federal Corporate Tax Rates for 2012**, above.

3. Recent changes to Manitoba's general capital tax are shown below:

			Manitoba changes effective after December 31, 2007 On taxable capital employed in Manitoba (before Manitoba's $10 million capital tax deduction)			
			≤ $10 million	> $10 million and ≤ $20 million	> $20 million and ≤ $21 million	> $21 million
General capital tax rate**	Taxation years commencing after	January 1, 2007	Nil	0.3%*	2.5%*	0.5%*
		January 1, 2008		0.2%	2.4%	0.4%
		January 1, 2009		0.1%	2.3%	0.3%
		January 1, 2010		Nil	2.2%	0.2%
	After 2010			Nil		

* These rates continue to apply to Crown corporations.

** On July 1, 2008, the general capital tax was eliminated for companies that use more than 50% of their labour and capital in Manitoba in M&P activities.

4. Recent changes to New Brunswick's general rate are shown below:

	New Brunswick changes effective after December 31, 2007		
	From	To	Effective
General capital tax rate	0.2%	0.1%	January 1, 2008
	0.1%	Nil	January 1, 2009

Capital Tax Rates and Exemptions for 2012 (continued)

5. Recent and planned changes to Nova Scotia's general rate are shown below:

Nova Scotia changes effective after December 31, 2007			
		From	To	Effective
General capital tax rate	If taxable capital ≥ $10 million	0.225%	0.2%	July 1, 2008
		0.2%	0.15%	July 1, 2009
		0.15%	0.1%	July 1, 2010
		0.1%	0.05%	July 1, 2011
		0.05%	Nil	July 1, 2012
	If taxable capital < $10 million	0.45%	0.4%	July 1, 2008
		0.4%	0.3%	July 1, 2009
		0.3%	0.2%	July 1, 2010
		0.2%	0.1%	July 1, 2011
		0.1%	Nil	July 1, 2012

6. Recent changes to Ontario's general rate and exemption are shown below:

Ontario changes effective after December 31, 2007			
	From	To	Effective
General capital tax rate*	0.225%	0.15%	January 1, 2010
	0.15%	Nil	July 1, 2010
General capital tax exemption	$12.5 million	$15 million	January 1, 2008

   * Before July 1, 2010, the general capital tax was eliminated or reduced, as follows:

% of salaries and wages related to M&P and resource activities[(i)]		Capital tax changes
	≥ 50%	Eliminated.
	> 20% and < 50%	Reduced proportionately (straight-line).

   (i) Applies to corporations that had employees reporting to a permanent establishment in Ontario on March 25, 2008.

7. Recent Quebec changes are shown below:

Quebec changes effective after December 31, 2007			
	From	To	Effective
General capital tax rate*	0.49%	0.36%	January 1, 2008
	0.36%	0.24%	January 1, 2009
	0.24%	0.12%	January 1, 2010
	0.12%	Nil	January 1, 2011

   * For taxation years ending after March 13, 2008, the general capital tax was eliminated or reduced, as follows:

% of activities attributable to M&P[(i)]		Capital tax changes
	≥ 50%	Eliminated.
	> 20% and < 50%	Reduced proportionately (straight-line).

   (i) Based on M&P assets and labour.

   Quebec's $1,000,000 general capital tax exemption was reduced by $1 for every $3 of the previous year's paid-up capital of the associated group exceeding that year's maximum capital tax exemption. Therefore, before 2011, the exemption was eliminated when the previous year's paid-up capital of the associated group reached $4,000,000.

8. Saskatchewan imposes a capital tax surcharge on large resource corporations. The surcharge rates decreased from July 1, 2006 to July 1, 2008.

   Recent changes to Saskatchewan's general rate are shown below:

Saskatchewan changes effective after December 31, 2007			
		From	To	Effective
General capital tax rate**	Capital (other than new capital)*	0.15%	Nil	July 1, 2008

   * A nil rate applied to new capital acquired after June 30, 2006 (i.e., additions of depreciable property in Saskatchewan) and was implemented by applying a non-refundable tax credit against the corporation's capital tax liability.

   ** The rate changes do not apply to Saskatchewan Crown corporations, for which the rate remains 0.6%. (An additional 0.9% rate applies to telecommunications Crown corporations.)

   Saskatchewan had a $20 million general capital tax exemption. It included a $10 million exemption, which was available to each corporation and an additional exemption (above $10 million), which had to be shared by the associated group. The extent to which the additional exemption was available to a corporation depended on the proportion of salaries and wages paid in Saskatchewan by that corporation in relation to the total salaries and wages paid by the associated group.

Capital Tax Rates and Exemptions for 2012 (continued)

Financial Institutions

The table below sets out capital tax rates for financial institutions (other than insurance companies) and includes banks and trust and loan corporations. For other corporations, see table above.

				Rate	Exemption[1]
				(for December 31, 2012 year-end)	
Federal	Large Corporations Tax (LCT)[2]			No capital tax	
	Part VI Financial Institutions Capital Tax[3]			1.25%	$1 billion
Alberta				No capital tax	
British Columbia[4]					
Manitoba[5]	If taxable paid-up capital < $4 billion				
	If taxable paid-up capital ≥ $4 billion			4%	$10 million
New Brunswick[6]				3.75%	
Newfoundland and Labrador	If paid-up capital ≤ $10 million				$5 million
	If paid-up capital > $10 million				Nil
Nova Scotia	Trust and loan corporations		Head office in N.S.	4%	$30 million
			Other		$500,000
	Banks				
Ontario[7]				No capital tax	
Prince Edward Island				5%	$2 million
Quebec[8] (compensation tax on paid-up capital)				0.25%	Nil
Saskatchewan[9]	If taxable paid-up capital ≤ $1.5 billion				
	If taxable paid-up capital > $1.5 billion	If taxable paid-up capital ≤ $1.5 billion in taxation year ending after October 31, 2008 and before November 1, 2009	On first $1.5 billion of taxable paid-up capital	0.7%	Up to $20 million[10]
			On taxable paid-up capital > $1.5 billion	3.25%	
		Other			

Notes:

1. Associated or related corporations may be required to share the exemption.
2. The Large Corporations Tax was eliminated on January 1, 2006. See the table, **Other Federal Corporate Tax Rates for 2012**.
3. See the table, **Other Federal Corporate Tax Rates for 2012**.
4. Recent changes to British Columbia's capital tax rates are shown below:

		British Columbia changes effective after December 31, 2007			
		Net paid-up capital ≥ $10 million and ≤ $1 billion		Net paid-up capital > $1 billion	
	Effective	B.C. paid-up capital < $10.25 million	B.C. paid-up capital ≥ $10.25 million	Based in and has head office in B.C.	Other
Capital tax rates	Before April 1, 2008	Reduced rates	1%		3%
	April 1, 2008*		0.667%		2%
	April 1, 2009*		0.333%		1%
	April 1, 2010*		Nil **		

  * After March 31, 2008 and before April 1, 2010, British Columbia's rate reductions were implemented by deducting from its financial corporation's capital tax payable:
  - 33⅓% of the capital tax payable for April 1, 2008 to March 31, 2009;
  - 66⅔% of the capital tax payable for April 1, 2009 to March 31, 2010; and
  - 100% of the capital tax payable after March 31, 2010, if the taxation year includes March 31, 2010.

  ** A minimum tax that was to have been imposed commencing April 1, 2010, on financial institutions with paid-up capital of $1 billion or more was repealed.

5. In Manitoba, starting taxation years ending after April 12, 2011, financial institutions with taxable capital under $4 billion are exempt from capital tax.

   Recent changes in Manitoba's capital tax rates are shown below:

	Manitoba changes effective after December 31, 2007		
	From	To	Effective
Capital tax rates	3%	4%	Taxation years ending after April 17, 2012

6. Recent changes in New Brunswick's capital tax rates are shown below:

	New Brunswick changes effective after December 31, 2007		
	From	To	Effective
Capital tax rates	3%	4%	April 1, 2012

Capital Tax Rates and Exemptions for 2012 (continued)

7. Recent changes to Ontario's exemption and rates are shown below:

	Ontario changes effective after December 31, 2007		
	From	To	Effective
Capital tax exemption*	$12.5 million	$15 million	January 1, 2008

    * For taxation years straddling January 1, 2008, the $12.5 million exemption applies for the number of days in the year before January 1, 2008.

		Ontario changes effective after December 31, 2007		
		Adjusted taxable paid-up capital* ≤ $400 million	Adjusted taxable paid-up capital* > $400 million	
	Effective		Deposit-taking	Other
Capital tax rates	Before January 1, 2010	0.45%	0.675%	0.54%
	January 1, 2010	0.3%	0.45%	0.36%
	July 1, 2010	Nil		

    * The adjusted taxable paid-up capital of a financial institution is net of the capital tax exemption.

8. The 0.25% Quebec rate is the 0.25% compensation tax on paid-up capital. The rate applies to financial institutions (other than insurance companies) and includes savings and credit unions. A compensation tax on payroll also applies as shown in the table below:

		Quebec changes effective after December 31, 2007		
		From	To	Effective
Compensation tax on salaries	Banks and loan, trust and security trading companies	2%	3.9%	Taxation years ending after March 30, 2010, and beginning before April 1, 2014
	Savings and credit unions	2.5%	3.8%	
	Other (excluding insurance companies)	1%	1.5%	

Recent changes in Quebec's base rate are shown below:

	Quebec changes effective after December 31, 2007		
	From	To	Effective
Capital tax rates	0.98%	0.72%	January 1, 2008
	0.72%	0.48%	January 1, 2009
	0.48%	0.24%	January 1, 2010
	0.24%	Nil	January 1, 2011

9. The threshold at which Saskatchewan's 3.25% financial institutions capital tax rate applies increased from $1 billion to $1.5 billion for taxation years ending after October 30, 2008.

Retroactive to taxation years ending after October 31, 2009, financial institutions that qualified for the 0.7% capital tax rate in taxation years ending after October 31, 2008, and before November 1, 2009, are subject to a:
- 0.7% capital tax rate on their first $1.5 billion of taxable capital; and
- 3.25% capital tax rate on taxable capital exceeding $1.5 billion.

10. Saskatchewan's $20 million exemption includes a $10 million exemption, which is available to each corporation and an additional exemption (above $10 million), which must be shared by the associated group. The extent to which the additional exemption is available to a corporation will depend on the proportion of salaries and wages paid in Saskatchewan by that corporation in relation to the total salaries and wages paid by the associated group.

¶490

Payroll Tax Rates for 2012

Only those provinces and territories listed in the table below have payroll taxes (by various names).

		Rate	Payroll[1]	Payroll tax
Manitoba[2]	Health and Post-Secondary Education Tax	2.15%	Over $2,500,000	Payroll × 2.15%
		4.3%	$1,250,000 to $2,500,000	(Payroll − $1,250,000) × 4.3%
		0%	$0 to $1,250,000	$0
Newfoundland and Labrador[3]		2%	Over $1,200,000	(Payroll − $1,200,000) × 2%
		0%	$0 to $1,200,000	$0
Northwest Territories[4] **Nunavut[4]**	Payroll Tax	2%	Over $0	Payroll × 2%
Ontario	Employer Health Tax	1.95%	Over $400,000	(Payroll − $400,000) × 1.95%
		0%	$0 to $400,000	$0
Quebec[5]	Health Services Fund	4.26%	Over $5,000,000	Payroll × rate
		Reduced rates	$1,000,000 to $5,000,000	
		2.7%	$0 to $1,000,000	

Notes:

1. Associated employers must aggregate their payroll costs to apply the thresholds.
2. Recent changes to the thresholds at which Manitoba's Health and Post-Secondary Education Tax apply follow:

		Manitoba threshold changes effective after December 31, 2007		
		From	**To**	**Effective**
Rate	2.15%	Over $2,000,000	Over $2,500,000	January 1, 2008
	4.3%	$1,000,000 to $2,000,000	$1,250,000 to $2,500,000	
	0%	$0 to $1,000,000	$0 to $1,250,000	

3. Recent changes to the thresholds at which Newfoundland and Labrador's Health and Post-Secondary Education Tax apply follow:

		Newfoundland and Labrador threshold changes effective after December 31, 2007		
		From	**To**	**Effective**
Rate	2%	Over $700,000	Over $1,000,000	January 1, 2008
	4%	$600,000 to $700,000*	n/a	
	0%	$0 to $600,000	$0 to $1,000,000	
	2%	Over $1,000,000	Over $1,200,000	January 1, 2011
	0%	$0 to $1,000,000	$0 to $1,200,000	

  * If the payroll was between $600,000 and $700,000, the $600,000 exemption was gradually reduced to $500,000 by decreasing the exemption by $1 for every dollar of payroll above the exemption. The result was an effective rate of 4%.

4. In the Northwest Territories and Nunavut, payroll tax is paid by employees. It is not levied on employers, but employers must deduct the tax from remuneration paid to employees.
5. Quebec's Health Services Fund rate is reduced for employers with annual payrolls between $1 million and $5 million, using a formula that reflects both the calendar year and the employer's total payroll.

   Starting 2013, employers can reduce Health Services Fund contributions for employees who are 65 or older.

   Every Quebec employer with a payroll of $1 million or more must:
   • allot at least 1% of payroll to training; or
   • contribute to a provincial fund the difference between that amount and the amount actually spent on training.

   In limited cases, corporations may be exempt from contributing to the Health Services Fund, and refunds may be made. Financial institutions (excluding insurers) and investment holding corporations may also be subject to a compensation tax on payroll (see footnote 8 to the table **Financial Institutions**).

   Employees, employers and the self-employed must contribute to the Quebec Parental Insurance Plan (QPIP), from which maternity, adoption and parental leave benefits will be paid. Individuals may be required to contribute to the Health Services Fund (see **Provincial Health Insurance Premiums**).

¶495

Provincial Health Insurance Premiums

Only British Columbia, Ontario and Quebec have health care premiums that are payable by individuals. Alberta's premiums were eliminated on January 1, 2009.

Alberta Health Care Premiums

		Alberta monthly premium effective after December 31, 2007	
		Single	Couple/Family
Effective	Before January 1, 2009*	$44	$88
	January 1, 2009	Nil	

* In Alberta, seniors were exempt from health care premiums.

British Columbia Medical Services Plan Premiums

		British Columbia monthly premium effective after December 31, 2007		
		Single*	Family*	
			(2 persons)	(> 2 persons)
	Before January 1, 2010	$54	$96	$108
	January 1, 2010	$57	$102	$114
Effective	January 1, 2011	$60.50	$109	$121
	January 1, 2012	$64	$116	$128
	January 1, 2013	$66.50	$120.50	$133

* In British Columbia, assistance is available to low-income earners.

Ontario Health Premiums

Ontario imposes a health care premium on individuals who are residents of Ontario on the last day of the taxation year, depending on taxable income, as shown in the table below.

		Ontario annual premium effective after December 31, 2007 per individual*
	Up to $20,000	Nil
	$20,000 to $25,000	6% of income > $20,000
	$25,000 to $36,000	$300
	$36,000 to $38,500	$300 + 6% of income > $36,000
Taxable	$38,500 to $48,000	$450
income	$48,000 to $48,600	$450 + 25% of income > $48,000
	$48,600 to $72,000	$600
	$72,000 to $72,600	$600 + 25% of income > $72,000
	$72,600 to $200,000	$750
	$200,000 to $200,600	$750 + 25% of income > $200,000
	$200,600 and over	$900

* Trusts are not liable for premiums.

Quebec Health Contribution and Health Services Fund Premiums

Commencing 2010, Quebec imposes a health contribution on individuals 18 years of age or older who are residents of Quebec on the last day of the taxation year. In addition, individuals whose income from certain sources, excluding remuneration, exceeds a certain threshold ($13,660 for 2012) must contribute to the Health Services Fund (see **Payroll Tax Rates** for employer contributions).

			Quebec annual premium effective after December 31, 2007 per individual
Health contribution*	Effective	Before 2010	n/a
		2010	$25
		2011	$100
		After 2011	$200
Health Services Fund**			Up to $1,000

* In Quebec, low-income earners are exempt from health contribution premiums.

** The Health Services Fund contribution gives rise to a tax credit.

¶520

Rates of Withholding Tax under Income Tax Agreements Signed by Canada

Countries	Date	Interest	Dividends — % of Ownership	Regular Dividends	Royalties	Pension and Annuity	From Estate or Trust
Algeria	1999	15%[3]	15%	15%	15%, royalties for use of computer software and patents exempt.	15%[9,14,16]	—
Argentina	1993	12.5%[3]	10%[5]	15%	15% generally 3%, 5%, 10% for specific items	15%[9,14,16]	—
Armenia	2004	10%[3]	5%[5] for investment >US $100,000.	15%	10%	pen. 15%[9,14,16]	15%
Australia	1980[2]	10%	5%[4,6]	15%	10%	15%[10,17]	15% (Can)
Austria	1976[2]	10%[3]	5%[4,6]	15%	10%[8]	[9,11]	15% (Can)
Azerbaijan	2004	10%[3]	10%[4]	15%	5% on computer software, patents, industrial, commercial or scientific experience royalties; 10% on other royalties	—	15%
Bangladesh	1982	15%[3]	15%	15%	10%	15%[9]	—
Barbados	1980	15%[3]	15%	15%	10%[7]	15%[9,14,16]	15% (Can)
Belgium	2002	10%[3]	5%[4]	15%	10%[8]	[9,11]	15%
Brazil	1984	15%[3] 10% Brazil in certain circumstances	15%[4]	rate not specified	15% 25% on trademarks	13 for certain pensions 15 [9] unless over $4,000	—
Bulgaria	1999	10%[3]	10%[4,6]	15%	10%[7]	pen. 15%[9] ann. 10%[9]	15% (Can)
Cameroon	1982	15% (Can) 20% (Cam)	15% (Can) 20% (Cam)	15% (Can) 20% (Cam)	15% (Can) 20% (Cam)	[11]	—
Chile	1998	15%	10%[5]	15%	15%	pen.[13]. ann. 15%[9]	15% (Can)

Countries	Date	Interest	Dividends — % of Ownership	Regular Dividends	Royalties	Pension and Annuity	From Estate or Trust
China	1986	10%[3]	10%[4]	15%	10%	11	—
Colombia	2008[1]	10%[3]	5%[4]	15%	10%	15%[9,14,16]	15% (Can)
Croatia	1997	10%	5%[4,5,6]	15%	10%	pen. 15%[15], ann. 10%[9]	15%
Cyprus	1984	15%[3]	15%	15%	10%[7]	15%[9], 13 for certain pensions [15,16]	15%
Czech Republic	2001	10%[3]	5%[4]	15%	10%	15%[9]	15%
Denmark	1997	10%[3]	5%[5] (if owned by a company) 10% if paid by Cdn. NRO invest. corp.	15%	10%[8]	9,13	15%
Dominican Republic	1976	18%[3]	18%	18%	18%[7]	18%[9,16]	18%
Ecuador	2001	10%[3]	5%[5]	15%	10% on use of industrial, commercial, or scientific equipment; 15% on other	pen. 15%[14,16,15]; ann. 15%[9]	15%
Egypt	1983	15%[3]	15%	15% (20% if paid to an individual resident in Canada)	15%	11	15%
Estonia	1995	10%[3]	5%[5,6]	15%	10%	15%[16], ann. 10%[9]	15%
Finland	2006	10%[3]	5%[4]	15%	10%[8]	pen. 20%[14], ann. 15%[9]	15%
France	1975[2]	10%[3]	5%[4] 10% if paid by Cdn. NRO invest. corp.	15%	10%[8]	pen. 13,14, ann. 9,11	15%
Gabon	2002	10%[3]	15%	15%	10%	pen. 11, ann. 11	—
Germany	2001	10%[3]	5%[4]	15%	10%[8]	pen. 11, ann. 9,11	—
Greece	2009	10%[3]	5%[5]	15%	10%[7]	15%[9,14,15,16]	15%

Countries	Date	Interest	Dividends — % of Ownership	Regular Dividends	Royalties	Pension and Annuity	From Estate or Trust
Guyana	1985	15% (Can)[3], 25% (Guy)[3]	15%	15%	10%	9,11,14	—
Hungary	1992[2]	10%[3]	5%[5] 10% if paid by Cdn. NRO invest. corp.	15%	10%[7]	pen. 15%[14,16], ann. 10%[9]	15%
Iceland	1997	10%[3]	5%[4,6]	15%	10%[8]	pen. 15%[14,16], ann. 15%[9]	15%
India	1996	15%[3]	15%[4]	25%	10% 15% 20%	13	15%
Indonesia	1979[2]	10%[3]	10%[5]	15%	10%	15%[9,14]	—
Ireland	2003	10%[3]	5%[4,6]	15%	10%[8]	pen. 15%[14,16] ann. 15%	15%
Israel	1975	15%[3]	15%	15%	15%[7]	15%[9,14,17]	15%
Italy	2002	10%[3]	5%[4,6]	15%	5%[7] on computer software, patents, industrial, commercial or scientific experience royalties, 10% on other royalties	pen. 15%[14,15,16]	15%
Ivory Coast	1983	15%[3]	15% 18% on certain divs. from Ivory Coast	15% 18% on certain divs. from Ivory Coast	10%	15%	15% (Can)
Jamaica	1978	15%[3]	15% 22.5% (Jam)[4]	15%	10%	pen. 11,14,16, ann. 15%[9]	—
Japan	1986[2]	10%[3]	5%[5]	15%	10%	11	—
Jordan	1999	10%[3]	10%[4,6]	15%	10%	13	—
Kazakhstan	1996	10%[3]	5%[4,6]	15%	10%	pen. 15%[9], 13 for certain pensions	—
Kenya	1983	15%[3]	15%[4]	25%	15%	15%	—
Korea	2006	10%[3]	5%[5]	15%	10%	pen. 15%[9,16] ann. 10%	—
Kuwait	2002	10%[3]	5%[4,5,6]	15%	10%	15%	—

Countries	Date	Interest	Dividends — % of Ownership	Regular Dividends	Royalties	Pension and Annuity	From Estate or Trust
Kyrgyzstan	1998	15%[3]	15%	15%	10%[8]	15% [9,14,16]	15%
Latvia	1995	10%[3]	5%[5,6]	15%	10%	pen. 15% [16], ann. 10% [9]	15%
Lebanon	1998[1]	10%[3]	5%[4,6]	15%	5% on cultural, computer software, industrial, commercial or scientific "know-how" royalties, 10% on other royalties	pen. 15% [9,14]	—
Lithuania	1996	10%[3]	5%[5,6]	15%	10%	pen. 15% [16], ann. 10% [9]	15%
Luxembourg	1999	10%[3]	5%[4] (if owned by a company) 15% 10% if paid by Cdn. NRO invest. corp.	15%	10%[8]	[9,11,14, 13] for certain pensions	15%
Malaysia	1976	15%[3]	15%	15%	15% certain royalties excluded	15% [14,16]	15% (Can)
Malta	1986	15%[3]	15% (Can) not to exceed tax on profits (Malta)	15% (Can) not to exceed tax on profits (Malta)	10%[7]	15% [9,14,16]	15%
Mexico	2006	10%[3]	5%[4]	15%	10%[7]	pen. 15% [9,14,16] ann. 15%	15%
Moldova	2002	10%[3]	5%[5]	15%	10%	15% [14]	15%
Mongolia	2002	10%[3]	5%[4]	15%	5% on cultural, computer software, patent, industrial, commercial or scientific experience royalties, 10% on other royalties	pen. 15% [14,16], ann. 15% [9]	15%
Morocco	1975	15%[3]	15%	15%	10% 5% on cultural royalties	[11]	—
Namibia	2010[1]	10%[3]	5%[5]	15%	10%[7]	pen. [12]	15%
Netherlands	1986[2]	10%[3]	5% [4,5] (if owned by a company) 10% if paid by Cdn. NRO invest. corp.	15%	10%[8]	15%[9]	15% (Can)
New Zealand	1980	15%	15%	15%	15%	15% [15,16]	15% (Can)

Countries	Date	Interest	Dividends — % of Ownership	Regular Dividends	Royalties	Pension and Annuity	From Estate or Trust
New Zealand ..2012[1]	10%[3]	5%[4]	15%	5% on cultural, computer software, industrial, commercial, or scientific info; 10% on other royalties	pen. 15%[14,16], ann. 15%[9]	15% (Can)
Nigeria.......1992	12.5%[3]	12.5%[4]	15%	12.5%	14,11	—
Norway 2002	10%[3]	5%[4,6]	15%	10%[8]	15[9,14]	15%
Oman 2004	10%[3]	5%[4]	15%	10%[8]	pen. 15%[14,16], ann. 15%[9]	15%
Pakistan......1976	15% (Can)[3], 25% (Pak)[3]	15% (Can) 15% (Pak)[5]	15% (Can) 20% (Pak)	15% (Can)[7], 20% (Pak)[7] copyright, trademark equipment, films 15% (Pak) technical know-how	13	15% (Can)
						Canada may withhold 15% on alimony	
Papua New Guinea....1987	10%[3]	15% (Can) 25% (PNG)	15% (Can) 25% (PNG)	10%	15[10,14,16]	—
Peru.........2001	15%	10%[4]	15%	15%	15[9,14]	15%
Philippines...1976	15%[3]	15% (Can) 15% (Phil)[4]	15% (Can) 25% (Phil)	15%	13	—
Poland.......1987	15%[3]	15%	15%	10%[7]	15[9,14,16]	15%
Poland.......2012[1]	10%[3]	5%[4]	15%	5% on cultural, industrial, commercial, or scientific info; 10% on other royalties	pen. 15%[14,16], ann. 15%[9]	15%
Portugal......1999	10%[3]	10%[5,6]	15%	10%	15[9,14,16]	15%
Romania 2004	10%[3]	5%[4]	15%	5% on cultural, software, industrial, commercial, scientific info.	pen. 15%	—
Russia 1995	10%[3]	10%[4]	15%	10%[8]	13	—
Senegal 2001	15% (Can)[3], 20% (Sen)[3], 16% (Sen)[3]	15% (Can) 16% (Sen)	15% (Can) 16% (Sen)	15%	15[9,14]	15%
Serbia ....2012[1]	10%[3]	5%[5]	15%	10%	pen. 15%	15%

Countries	Date	Interest	Dividends — % of Ownership	Regular Dividends	Royalties	Pension and Annuity	From Estate or Trust
Singapore	1976	15%[3]	15% 0% (Sing) depending on domestic law	15% 0% (Sing) depending on domestic law	15%	[13]	15% (Can)
						Canada may withhold 15% on alimony	
Slovak Republic	2001	10%[3]	5%[4]	15%	10%[7]	pen. 15%[14,16] ann. 15%	15%
Slovenia	2000	10%[3]	5% (Can)[4,6], 5% (Slo)[5]	15%	10%	pen. 15%[16] (Can) (Slo)[13] ann. 10%[9]	15%
South Africa	1995	10%[3]	5%[4,6]	15%	10% 6% on cultural, software, industrial, commercial, scientific info.	[11]	15%
Spain	1976	15%[3]	15%	15%	10%[7]	15%[9,14,16]	—
Sri Lanka	1982	15%[3]	15%	15%	10%[7]	15%[9,14,16]	15% (Can)
Sweden	1996	10%[3]	5%[5] 10% if paid by Cdn. NRO invest corp.	15%	10%[8]	9, 14, 11	15% (Can)
Switzerland	1997[2]	10%[3]	5%[4]	15%	10%[8]	15%[9,14]	—
Tanzania	1995	15%[3]	20%[5]	25%	20%	15%[9,14,16] (Can)	—
Thailand	1984	15% (Can) 10% (Thai) if to fin. instit. 25% (Thai) otherwise[3]	15% (Can) 15% (Thai) 20%[5] (Thai)	15% (Can) taxed under laws of Thailand	15% 5% on cultural	[13]	15% (Can)
Trinidad and Tobago	1995	10%[3]	5%[4,6]	15%	10%[7]	pen. 15%[9,14]	—
Tunisia	1982	15%[3]	15%	15%	20%[7] on patents, trademarks, films, videos, industrial, commercial, scientific or harbour equip; 15% on other	[11]	15%
Turkey	2009	15%[3]	15%[4]	20%	10%	15%[9,14,15,16]	—

Countries	Date	Interest	Dividends — % of Ownership	Regular Dividends	Royalties	Pension and Annuity	From Estate or Trust
Ukraine 1996	10%[3]	5%[5,6]	15%	10% computer software exempt	[13]		15%
United Arab Emirates 2002	10%[3]	5%[4] 10% if paid by Cdn. NRO invest. corp.	15%	10%[8]	[11]		15%
United Kingdom 1978[2]	10%[3]	5%[4]	15%	10%[8]	pen.[12], ann. 10%[9]	15% (Can)
U.S.A. ....1980[2]	0%[3,18]	5%[4]	15%	10%[8]	15%[9,14]	15%
Uzbekistan 1999	10%[3]	5%[4]	15%	5% on cultural, computer software, industrial, commercial or scientific "know-how" royalties, 10% on other royalties	[13]	—
Venezuela 2001	10%[3]	10%[5]	15%	5% on cultural, computer software, industrial, commercial or scientific experience royalties, 10% on other royalties	[11,14]	—
Socialist Republic of Vietnam 1997	10%[3]	5% (if 70% controlled by corporate owner) 10% (if 25%–69% controlled by corporate owner)	15%	10%	pen. 15% ann. [9,11]	15%
Zambia 1984	15%[3]	15%	15%	15%	15%[14]	15% (Can)
Zimbabwe 1992	15%[3]	10%[5]	15% (Can) 20% (Zim)	10%	15%[9,14,16]	15% (Can)

Notes:

[1] Not yet ratified.

[2] Revised by subsequent Protocol.

[3] No withholding tax under the treaty on certain types of interest. After 2007, the Canadian *Income Tax Act* exempts interest payments to non-residents from withholding tax, except for certain interest paid or payable to a non-arms length person or participating debt interest. See paragraph 212(1)(*b*).

[4] If recipient owns at least 10% of voting stock or has 10% of voting power of stock on which dividends are paid (see specific treaty).

[5] If recipient owns at least 15% to 25% of capital or voting power of stock on which dividends are paid (see specific treaty for level of ownership specified).

[6] Does not apply to dividends from a non-resident-owned investment corporation resident in Canada.

[7] Cultural royalties are exempt from withholding tax. These include copyright royalties for production or reproduction of literary, dramatic, musical or artistic work. They usually do not include royalties on films or videotapes.

[8] Cultural royalties, computer software, industrial, commercial or scientific "know-how" royalties are exempt.

[9] Alimony and child support taxed only in the country of person receiving the payment.

[10] Alimony and child support taxed only in the paying country.

[11] May be taxed in source country — No treaty rate.

[12] Exempt from tax in source country.

[13] Taxed only in source country.

[14] Certain pensions exempt from tax in both countries.

[15] Tax withheld only if payment over a certain amount.

[16] For pensions, tax withheld is not to exceed the amount that would be payable if the recipient were resident in the source country.

[17] For pensions and annuities, tax withheld is not to exceed the amount that would be payable if the recipient were resident in the source country.

[18] Under the Canada–U.S. Treaty, the Fifth Protocol provides that withholding tax on interest will be completely eliminated for interest paid or credited after December 31, 2009. The maximum rate for withholding on interest paid or credited between January 1, 2008 and December 31, 2008 is 7%, and 4% on interest paid or credited between January 1, 2009 and December 31, 2009.

Chapter I

Introduction to Income Taxation in Canada

Scope of this Chapter 700

Brief History of Income
Taxation in Canada 725

The Constitutional
Background 750

Constitutional Basis of
Federal Income Taxation 755

Canadian System of
Government 760

United States System of
Government Compared 765

Canadian Charter of Rights
and Freedoms 770

Constitutionality of Budget
Resolutions 775

Organization of Legislation
and Interpretive Sources 800

The Income Tax Act 805

Income Tax Application
Rules 810

Income Tax Regulations 815

Forms 820

Judicial Decisions 825

Interpretation Bulletins,
Information Circulars and
Advance Tax Rulings 830

Technical Notes and
Explanations 835

Generally Accepted
Accounting Principles 840

International Tax
Conventions or Treaties 845

Administration and
Enforcement 850

General Administration 855

Secrecy 860

Onus of Proof 865

Appeals 870

Tax Evasion, Tax Avoidance
and Tax Planning 875

Terms and Issues 900

Terms and Issues 905

Income 910

Deductions 915

Exemptions and Credits 920

Accounting Methods 925

Corporations, Partnerships
and Trusts 930

Tax Rates 935

Residence and Source of
Income 940

Discretion 945

Interpretation of Tax
Legislation 950

Construction of Taxing
Statutes 955

Intention of the Legislature
and Literal Interpretation 960

Ambiguity 965

"Object and Spirit Test" —
Form Over Substance 970

Conflict with General
Provisions 975

Ejusdem Generis Rule 980

Precedents 985

Interpretation Act 990

English and French
Versions 995

General Liability for Tax 1000

General Nature of Tax —
Taxable Income 1005

"Person", "Taxpayer",
"Individual" Defined 1010

1

Taxation Year — Fiscal
Period — Change in
Fiscal Period 1015
The Alternative Method 1017
Accrual Rules for Significant
Incremental Corporate
Partners 1018
Residence 1020
Constructive Residence —
Sojourners 1025
Part-Time Residents 1030
Non-Residents in Canada 1035
Non-Residents Employed or
Carrying on Business in
Canada 1040
Carrying On Business
Through Agent 1045

Employees Temporarily
Outside of Canada 1055
"In Canada" Defined 1060
Government Officials and
Members of Canadian
Forces 1065
**Minimum Income —
Individuals 1070**
Tax Liability — Minimum
Income 1075
Residence — Corporations 1080
Residence of Corporations 1085
Partnerships and Trusts 1090
Partnerships 1095
Trusts and Estates 1100

Recent Changes

Appeals to TCC under Informal Procedure

On June 8, 2012, draft legislation was released to improve the caseload of the Tax Court of Canada. These proposals would increase the monetary limits for appeals under the Informal Procedure so that the aggregate limit for all amounts in issue is raised to $25,000 from $12,000 and the limit for a loss determination is raised to $50,000 from $24,000. These increased limits will come into force after Royal Assent to the enacting legislation. See ¶870.

Indexation of 2012 Personal Tax Brackets and Credits

In the 2012 taxation year, the federal income tax rates for individuals remain the same, but a 2.8% indexation factor applies to tax bracket thresholds, personal amounts and other amounts relating to non-refundable credits, as well as the refundable medical expense supplement, Old Age Security repayment threshold, Working Income Tax Benefit, certain board and lodging allowances, and the tradesperson's tools deduction. Because of their particular features, increases to the Canada Child Tax Benefit (including the National Child Benefit Supplement and the Child Disability Benefit) and the Goods and Services Tax Credit will take effect on July 1, 2012, to coincide with the beginning of the program year for payment of these benefits. See ¶920 and ¶935.

[¶700] Scope of this Chapter

The federal and provincial governments of Canada impose a tax on the income of residents of Canada and on the income of non-residents derived from Canadian sources. The purpose of this chapter is to provide an overview of the structure of the income tax legislation in Canada.

Students, practitioners, and lecturers have long recognized that the study of taxation is a most difficult discipline. The CCH CANADIAN MASTER TAX GUIDE is accepted by tax experts as a basic working tool with which the intricacies and complexities of the tax system can be understood.

[¶725] Brief History of Income Taxation in Canada

From Confederation until World War I, the major sources of federal revenue were customs and excise taxes. Income tax was first imposed federally in 1917 as a temporary measure to help finance World War I. The *Income War Tax Act* was a relatively simple document of some 10 pages in length, which was reworded and codified in chapter 52 of the 1948 Statutes of Canada as the *Income Tax Act*, with very few changes in policy. That Act later became chapter 148 of the 1952 Revised Statutes of Canada.

Major reform of income tax legislation in Canada began in 1962 with the Carter Commission, which recommended fundamental changes in tax legislation (e.g., that the government should use a comprehensive tax base including capital gains). Drawing on the Carter recommendations, the government issued a White Paper on Tax Reform in 1969, and public hearings were held culminating in a complete transformation of the tax legislation with S.C. 1970-71-72, c. 63, the legislation that implemented the 1972 tax reform. Section 1 of that Act was a sweeping amendment to the 1952 Act, and repealed and replaced nearly all its contents. That Act also introduced the *Income Tax Application Rules, 1971*. The Bill received Royal Assent in December 1971 to become effective January 1, 1972. Since then, every Budget has introduced amendments to the Act to either "fine tune" it or introduce new tax policies.

On June 18, 1987, the federal government released a White Paper on Tax Reform, which was implemented in two phases. Phase One, implemented in 1988, included changes to the personal and corporate income tax systems and interim changes to the existing federal sales tax. The implementing legislation, Bill C-139, was passed on September 13, 1988. Phase Two replaced the existing federal sales tax with a broad-based multi-stage Goods and Services Tax (GST), effective January 1, 1991.

Tax practitioners should be aware that the "Fifth Supplement of the Revised Statutes of Canada, 1985", proclaimed into force effective March 1, 1994, included new versions of the *Income Tax Act* and *Income Tax Application Rules*. On that date, the 1972 Act, including all amendments that had been made to it over the years, was repealed and replaced by the Fifth Supplement version.

[¶750] The Constitutional Background

[¶755] Constitutional Basis of Federal Income Taxation

The *British North America Act, 1867*, renamed the *Constitution Act, 1867*, granted authority for all taxation in Canada, separating federal and provincial powers to impose income taxes. Subsection 91(3) of the *Constitution Act, 1867*, provides the federal government with unlimited powers of taxation. On the other hand, subsection 92(2) limits provincial powers to direct taxation of income earned in the province and of income of persons resident in the province. At the present time, all the provinces impose personal and corporate income taxes.

Most taxes are collected on behalf of the provinces by the federal government. The exceptions are Quebec, which collects its own personal and corporate income taxes, and Alberta, which collects its own corporate income tax. Ontario previously collected its own corporate income tax, but for taxation years ending after December 31, 2008, Ontario's corporate income tax will be collected by the federal government.

[¶760] Canadian System of Government

In Canada, the cabinet or parliamentary system prevails, with the Governor General, appointed by and responsible to the Queen, acting on the advice of a Cabinet ordinarily composed of majority party members in Parliament. Parliament consists of a Senate and a House of Commons. Bills passed by Parliament are presented to the Governor General for the Queen's assent.

In the 10 provinces, the legislative systems are similar. The Lieutenant Governors are appointed by the Governor General in Council.

[¶765] United States System of Government Compared

The federal system established for Canada resembles the American system in many respects; however, there are distinctions of which American residents must be particularly aware.

The most important difference is that in Canada the provinces exercise delegated powers and the federal government retains all the residue, while in the United States the reverse is true. Thus, section 91 of the *Constitution Act, 1867* extends the federal legislative authority to "all matters not coming within the classes of subjects by this Act assigned exclusively to the legislature of the provinces". Without limiting the generality of the foregoing, exclusive legislative authority is specifically vested in the federal government with respect to the regulation of trade and commerce and the raising of money by any mode or system of taxation.

Section 92 grants exclusive jurisdiction to the provinces with respect to direct taxation within the province in order to assist in the raising of revenue for provincial purposes.

[¶770] Canadian Charter of Rights and Freedoms

On April 17, 1982, the *Constitution Act, 1982* came into force to repatriate the Canadian constitution until then codified as the *British North America Act, 1867*. The *Canadian Charter of Rights and Freedoms* (the Charter) is Part I of the *Constitution Act, 1982* and came into force on April 17, 1982, with the exception of section 15 (equality rights) which came into force April 17, 1985.

The Charter represents a fundamental shift away from the notion of Parliamentary supremacy. Section 52 provides that "any law that is inconsistent with the Constitution is, to the extent of the inconsistency, of no force or effect". Section 24 of the Charter empowers the courts to provide remedies where rights and freedoms guaranteed by the Charter have been infringed or denied.

The legal rights provided under sections 7 to 14 of the Charter apply to offences, searches, seizures, and prosecutions under the *Income Tax Act*. Other Charter provisions (section 15, equality rights; section 2, fundamental freedoms; and section 6, mobility rights) may also provide areas under which particular provisions of the Act may come under scrutiny.

[¶775] Constitutionality of Budget Resolutions

In order to change the tax laws, it is necessary for Parliament to pass amending statutes. These statutes must receive three readings in both the House of Commons and the Senate, and, finally, Royal Assent. However, before an amending tax bill can be introduced into the House of Commons, it is necessary for the House to pass a resolution, referred to as a "Notice of Ways and Means Motion", deeming it expedient to introduce a bill amending the particular Act in question. These are the resolutions which are presented to the House on Budget night by the Minister of Finance.

The origins of this procedure lie in both the constitution and the House Rules. Under section 53 of the *Constitution Act, 1867*, tax bills must originate in the House of Commons. Under section 54, it is unlawful for the House of Commons to adopt or pass any vote, resolution, address, or bill for the appropriation of money or the composition of any tax that has not first been recommended to the House by the Governor General in the session in which the vote, resolution, address, or bill is proposed. This means that it must first be approved by the Government of the day and this approval is never given to a money bill except one introduced by a Minister of the Crown.

It is also required by parliamentary practice and the rules of the House that a money or tax bill be preceded by a resolution considered by a

Committee of the Whole House. In practice, this means that the Budget proposals are introduced into the laws in two stages. There is first a series of resolutions introduced by the Minister of Finance and considered in a Committee of the Whole House. It is only after the resolutions have been adopted that the second stage may be reached of considering and passing the amending Acts which, after Royal Assent, have the effect of law. Although the first stage of adopting the resolutions is purely procedural, all steps have to be completed in order to amend the law.

Tax amendments are normally made retroactive to the date of the Budget in the case of customs and excise changes and to the beginning of a taxation year or the Budget date in the case of income tax. However, in the period between the bringing down of the Budget by the Minister and the giving of the Royal Assent to the amending Acts, the position of the taxpayer may be uncertain. That is why taxes are normally paid and collected during that period on the assumption that the Budget is in force merely as a matter of administrative convenience and not of law. By proceeding this way, depending on the direction of the Budget changes, the taxpayer avoids the necessity of having to pay interest and penalties on back taxes. However, in years where the tax payable is increased, the CRA cannot strictly enforce collection of taxes at the new rates until after the statutory amendments have received Royal Assent.

[¶800] Organization of Legislation and Interpretive Sources

[¶805] The Income Tax Act

To study income taxation, one must become thoroughly familiar with the organization, structure, and coverage of the *Income Tax Act*. When a tax problem arises, knowing where to find the provisions in the Act which are most likely to deal with the problem will save a considerable amount of time in the resolution of the problem. An overview of the Act can best be obtained from an inspection of the Table of Contents to the Act. A detailed sectional list of the Act is provided at the beginning of the CCH Canadian edition of the Act.

[¶810] Income Tax Application Rules

The *Income Tax Application Rules* (ITAR) provide largely for the transition from the pre-1972 Act and its system of taxation to the current Act and its system of taxation, including the taxation of capital gains.

[¶815] Income Tax Regulations

The *Income Tax Regulations* are set out to handle various specific situations and to carry on the general purposes and provisions of the Act.

Unlike the Act itself, these regulations may be passed by Order-in-Council without ratification of Parliament.

[¶820] Forms

Forms issued by the CRA and officially prescribed by the legislation may provide some insights to the interpretation of a provision in the legislation.

[¶825] Judicial Decisions

Although not part of the statute itself, the Canadian court decisions have importance in the interpretation of the Act over the years of income taxation in Canada.

The Supreme Court of Canada, by reason of its nation-wide jurisdiction, constitutes the appellate court for the whole of Canada. It hears appeals from the provincial courts of last resort and from the Federal Court of Appeal.

The middle level of court hearing tax cases is the Federal Court of Appeal, which hears appeals from final judgments of the Federal Court–Trial Division, the Tax Court of Canada, and appeals under certain federal legislation. Appeals in certain circumstances lie to the Supreme Court of Canada. Prior to January 1, 1991, the Federal Court–Trial Division heard proceedings relating to federal income taxation as it was designated to hear, as trials *de novo*, appeals under the *Income Tax Act* from the Tax Court of Canada. This jurisdiction was abolished effective January 1, 1991.

The Tax Court of Canada hears appeals from assessments made by the Minister of National Revenue under the *Income Tax Act*. Prior to the creation of the Tax Court of Canada, initial appeals from assessments could be heard by the Tax Review Board (1970–83), the Tax Appeal Board (1950–70), and the Income Tax Appeal Board (1946–50).

Court decisions, which are almost always based on a particular set of facts, interpret the application of the law to these facts. While the court decisions may be useful as a guide in interpreting the law, each set of facts differs from the previous cases in some degree, and a slight difference in the facts of a given case may materially affect the outcome.

[¶830] Interpretation Bulletins, Information Circulars and Advance Tax Rulings

The CRA releases some explanatory information on its official position in various taxation matters through a series of publications, such as: Information Circulars (ICs), which deal mainly with administrative and procedural matters; Interpretation Bulletins (ITs), which outline the CRA's interpretation of specific sections of the tax law; and Advance Tax Rulings (ATRs), which contain disguised summaries of certain advance income tax rulings given by the CRA and selected for publication.

These publications explain the CRA's "departmental practice" and are not law, although in the case of *Nowegijick v. The Queen*, 83 DTC 5041, Mr. Justice Dickson of the Supreme Court of Canada stated that "administrative policy and interpretation are not determinative, but are entitled to weight and can be an *important factor* in case of doubt about the meaning of legislation".

[¶835] Technical Notes and Explanations

In addition, technical notes are issued by the Department of Finance to explain new legislation. Although the impact of the technical notes on judicial decisions has yet to be determined, they should at least establish the general or broad intention of Parliament in respect of a particular issue.

[¶840] Generally Accepted Accounting Principles

"Generally accepted accounting principles" (GAAP) have been important guides in the interpretation of the Act where the statutory law was silent on a particular point. If there is no specific provision for including or deducting an item in the Act, often the treatment of that item under generally accepted accounting principles will be followed.

However, despite the fact that many provisions in the tax legislation result in treatment of an item similar to its treatment for financial accounting purposes, it must be emphasized that the existence of specific statutory provisions to be used in the computation of income for tax purposes results in an income computation that will vary widely from income for financial accounting purposes. A major cause of this variance is the use of the capital cost allowance system for tax purposes based on a "declining balance" method of capital cost write-off, in lieu of depreciation for financial accounting purposes, which is usually based on a "straight-line" method.

[¶845] International Tax Conventions or Treaties

The *Income Tax Act* must be interpreted in light of International Tax Conventions that Canada has negotiated with other countries in order to reduce the incidence of double taxation (e.g., the *Canada–United States Tax Convention (1980)* and the *Canada–U.K. Income Tax Convention (1978)*).

It is important to note that tax conventions override the provisions of the *Income Tax Act* and, hence, should be the first reference source when examining the tax implications of cross-border transactions.

[¶850] Administration and Enforcement

[¶855] General Administration

The federal income tax laws are administered and enforced by the Canada Revenue Agency (the "CRA").

The central offices of the CRA are located in Ottawa, Ontario. There are eight Taxation Centres, one in each of the provinces of Newfoundland, Prince Edward Island, Manitoba, and British Columbia and two in each of the provinces of Ontario and Quebec. Non-resident returns are processed in the International Taxation Office, a separate location in Ottawa.

Inquiries and requests for forms may be directed to any convenient Tax Service Office. Matters relating to audits and assessments would normally be directed to the Tax Service Office responsible for the taxpayer's area. The CRA assigns Tax Service Offices to taxpayers based on their postal codes.

Direct contact between the taxpayer and the CRA is generally made through one of its Tax Service Offices. Trained assessors and special investigators who conduct desk audits of an individual's return or filed audits of business returns are located in these offices.

The Head Office in Ottawa serves to maintain efficiency and uniformity of tax treatment across Canada by supervising and directing the activities of the Tax Service Offices.

The regional Taxation Centres are maintained to do routine operations and the initial processing of all individual income tax returns.

[¶860] Secrecy

Every employee of the Taxation Division takes a solemn oath on entering the service to maintain complete secrecy with regard to all matters coming before him or her in the course of his or her duties. Violation of the oath would ordinarily mean immediate dismissal for the employee as well as liability to penalties.

[¶865] Onus of Proof

In tax matters, it has been established by the Supreme Court of Canada in *Johnston v. M.N.R.*, [1948] 3 DTC 1182, that the taxpayer always has the burden of proving that the Minister's assessment is incorrect since under our self-assessment system, the taxpayer is assumed to have all the basic data under his or her control. The standard of proof in cases dealing with the *Income Tax Act* need only be that of the "balance of probabilities" used in civil cases rather than the more rigorous standard of "beyond a reasonable doubt" used in criminal proceedings. However, where penalties are assessed, the burden of proof is on the Minister to prove the underlying facts. The standard of proof that the Minister must demonstrate is that of the "balance of probabilities".

[¶870] Appeals

Prior to taking any formal steps in the appeal procedure, the taxpayer may consult with officials responsible for his or her file in the appropriate Tax Services Office. Many differences can be resolved in this less formal manner.

If, however, a difference cannot be resolved in this manner to the taxpayer's satisfaction, a notice of objection may be filed in prescribed form as the first formal step. The notice of objection simply contains a statement of the facts and the reasons for objection, and it must be filed within 90 days from the date on the notice of assessment or one year from the due date of the return, whichever is later. For instance, a taxpayer may file a notice of objection to an assessment of his or her 2012 return, assuming it was due April 30, 2013, up to the later of April 30, 2014, or 90 days from the mailing date of the notice of assessment or reassessment for the 2012 taxation year.

Next, the taxpayer can appeal to the Tax Court of Canada, which conducts its hearings in cities across Canada. The Tax Court of Canada now has exclusive jurisdiction to hear appeals over tax cases. On filing a notice of appeal to the Tax Court, the taxpayer is given the option of an "informal procedure", subject to a limit of $12,000 in tax and penalty (and $24,000 in loss determination) or a "general procedure". A taxpayer may waive amounts in excess of the $12,000/$24,000 limits on amounts in dispute and proceed with the informal procedure for the limited amounts. After Royal Assent to the enacting legislation, the $12,000/$24,000 limits will be increased to $25,000/$50,000.

The only requirement of the informal procedure is that the appeal be submitted in writing. Court rules of evidence are flexible, and thus the taxpayer can represent himself or herself or be represented by an agent other than a lawyer. However, decisions reached through the informal procedure cannot be used as a precedent in subsequent cases and may be appealed only on issues of law, jurisdiction, or gross error.

Where the general procedure is chosen in the Tax Court of Canada, the Court will be bound by strict rules of evidence. The taxpayer can only represent himself or herself or be represented by legal counsel. In the general procedure, the taxpayer can appeal the decision of the Tax Court to the Federal Court of Appeal, and the Tax Court decision can be used as a precedent in other cases. Appeals to the Federal Court of Appeal must be filed within 30 days of the Tax Court judgment or order.

The ultimate court of appeal for tax cases in Canada is the Supreme Court of Canada. At this level, questions of legal interpretation are raised rather than questions of facts alone. Not many cases on tax matters are given leave to appeal to the Supreme Court of Canada.

[¶875] Tax Evasion, Tax Avoidance and Tax Planning

It is important to distinguish the terms "tax evasion", "tax avoidance", and "tax planning".

"Tax evasion" involves knowingly reporting tax that is less than the tax payable under the law with an attempt to deceive by omitting revenue, fraudulently claiming deductions, or failing to use all of the facts of a situation. This is clearly illegal and can be prosecuted as such.

"Tax avoidance" is considered to arise in cases in which the taxpayer has legally circumvented the law, resulting in the reduction or elimination of tax through a scheme or series of transactions which do not truly reflect the facts. While not illegal, the CRA will challenge such tax avoidance by various means available to it.

Finally, "tax planning" involves cases of tax reduction or elimination that are clearly provided for, or not specifically prohibited, in the law in a manner that is genuine and open within the framework of the law.

Despite these attempts at distinguishing the terms, there are undoubtedly judgments that must be made in distinguishing between cases of tax evasion and tax avoidance and between cases of tax avoidance and tax planning.

[¶900] Terms and Issues

[¶905] Terms and Issues

It is difficult to understand any part of income tax law without knowing something of the whole structure. The problem is more complicated than with other legal subjects because income tax is an artificial statutory structure which cannot be grasped by any exercise of pure intuition.

[¶910] Income

The starting point in any analysis of income tax is to determine what is income. It should be noted that there is no definition of the word "income" in the Act. In the absence of a statutory definition, it is customary to refer to judicial decisions which, in turn, may refer to a standard dictionary to establish the ordinary meaning of the word. The *Concise Oxford Dictionary* defines "income" as "periodical (usually annual) receipts from one's business, lands, work, investments, etc.". While income is usually thought of as a monetary receipt or currency, it may take the form of money's worth, that is, something of commercial value such as gold, shares, wheat, etc.

Income versus capital. Receipts can be classified as either income or capital. As long as taxation has existed in Canada, receipts of capital have received more favourable tax consequences than receipts of income. The problem of determining whether a given receipt is one of capital or one of income has been the subject of countless court cases. In subsequent chapters, the major factors used by the courts in their determination will be examined and a number of cases will be used to illustrate these factors. A common analogy used by the courts likens capital to a tree which produces income in the form of fruit. Sale of the tree results in a receipt of capital and capital gains treatment, whereas sale of the fruit results in a receipt of income.

Taxable income. The taxable income of a taxpayer is "income for the year plus or minus the additions and deductions permitted". It should be noted that income for tax purposes has a broader meaning than income for accounting purposes. Income for tax purposes refers not only to the income inclusions but also to the related deductions, which is more akin to net income for accounting purposes. Although income is not defined, once it has been determined that there is income, then this income must be attached to a particular source. For example, income from employment found in Subdivision a of Division B gathers together all of the employment income inclusions as specifically determined in sections 5, 6, and 7 minus all of the permitted deductions found in section 8.

[¶915] Deductions

Deductions are specifically allowed for some items and specifically disallowed for a number of others. Several provisions authorize deductions of expenses and losses incurred in a trade or business or in the production of income.

It will often be convenient to think of income and deduction items separately, but it is important to remember that it is only a convenience. Usually, if an item is included in income it will provide the basis for an offsetting deduction.

The allowance of a deduction will reduce the income tax below what it would otherwise be, and therefore a deduction is sometimes thought of as providing a kind of government subsidy for the deductible expenditure itself. The rate of subsidy will naturally depend on the taxpayer's rate of tax.

[¶920] Exemptions and Credits

In recognition of the fact that some individuals have family responsibilities, personal disabilities, or low income levels that make them less able than other individuals to afford the payment of tax, certain basic credits are allowed against income tax. These are discussed in Chapter VIII.

All persons, except some part-time residents or non-residents, may earn at least $10,822 in 2012 without paying any federal income tax. Provinces vary this number, and for several provinces (like Manitoba, Prince Edward Island, New Brunswick, Nova Scotia, and Newfoundland and Labrador), the basic exemption is lower whereas for some other provinces (like Alberta) the basic exemption is higher.

Each year, tax bracket thresholds, personal tax credits, and most other personal tax amounts are indexed to inflation using the Consumer Price Index data, as reported by Statistics Canada. The indexation factor for these figures is set at 2.8% effective January 1, 2012. However, increases to the Canada Child Tax Benefit (including the National Child Benefit Supplement and the Child Disability Benefit) and the Goods and Services Tax Credit will take effect on July 1, 2012, to coincide with the beginning of the program year for payment of these benefits.

Note, however, that not all income is equal. Only 50% of capital gains are included in income (Chapter V), whereas 125% to 145% of most Canadian source dividends are included in income (although special dividend offset this result). (See ¶8275.)

[¶925] Accounting Methods

The taxation year of an individual (including an estate or an *inter vivos* trust) is the calendar year, and that of a corporation is the fiscal period for which its accounts are ordinarily made up and accepted for income tax purposes. The fiscal period of a taxpayer other than a corporation may not exceed 12 months and that of a corporation may not exceed 53 weeks.

Most individual taxpayers use the "cash method" of accounting, which means that items are reflected when actually or constructively received. In the case of businesses, the "accrual method" of accounting must be used unless the tax legislation provides otherwise. Farmers and fishers may, however, elect to use the cash method. Under the accrual method, income is generally computed for the period during which it has been earned, i.e., at the time that goods are delivered or services are rendered, even though accounts receivable for such goods or services may not have been collected.

These accounting requirements sometimes produce harsh results, either by causing deduction items to fall in non-income or low-rate years or by causing income items to be bunched together in a single year. There are a number of special relief provisions applicable to such situations (for example, the carrying forward of past years' losses and the averaging provisions for farmers and fishers).

[¶930] Corporations, Partnerships and Trusts

The tax treatment of corporations depends upon whether the corporation is classed as a public corporation or a private corporation, the type of income of the corporation, and the type of distribution to shareholders. A corporation that is resident in Canada will be subject to tax upon all of its taxable income derived from sources both inside and outside Canada. The tax may be reduced by various credits, including credits in respect of foreign taxes. A corporation that is not resident in Canada is subject to tax upon its taxable income earned in Canada for a year if it has carried on business in Canada or has disposed of taxable Canadian property.

Partnership income is calculated at the partnership level and then taxed in the hands of the partnership members.

Income received by a trust and payable to a beneficiary is generally included in the beneficiary's income and deductible by the trust. Income received by a trust but not payable to a beneficiary, so that it accumulates in the trust, is taxed in the trust as if the trust were an individual without the benefit of personal exemptions or standard deductions.

[¶935] Tax Rates

In 2012, individual tax rates remain the same and vary from 15% to 29% of taxable income with the rates increasing as income increases (see ¶8005). However, the income levels at which these rates begin to apply are all indexed by 2.8% effective January 1, 2012. This means that, effective January 1, 2012, the following tax rates and income tax brackets apply to individuals:

- 15% for taxable income less than or equal to $42,707;

- 22% for taxable income greater than $42,707 and less than or equal to $85,414;

- 26% for taxable income greater than $85,414 and less than or equal to $132,406; and

- 29% for taxable income greater than $132,406.

In addition, provincial income taxes are imposed, the rate of which varies depending on the province or territory in which an individual resides or carries on business.

All provinces and territories (except Quebec) impose a graduated income tax on taxable income as measured for federal purposes. These provincial taxes are collected on behalf of the provinces by the federal government as part of the federal tax return process.

Residents of Quebec, or persons carrying on business in Quebec, are allowed a 16.5% abatement from the federal tax and must file a separate Quebec income tax return. In Quebec, the income tax payable by individuals on their taxable income is determined by means of a table providing three tax rates that increase gradually with the table's taxable income brackets. In 2012, these rates are: (i) 16% for individuals whose taxable income is equal to or less than $40,100, (ii) 20% for the taxable income bracket over $40,100, without exceeding $80,200, and (iii) 24% for the bracket over $80,200.

¶935

Very roughly speaking, on income in excess of $85,414, combined federal and provincial (or federal and territorial) rates in 2012 range from 35% to 45.71%, depending on the province of residence.

[¶940] Residence and Source of Income

An individual who is a Canadian resident (or deemed to be) is taxed on all of his or her income, regardless of whether the income is from sources inside or outside of Canada. A non-resident individual is taxed only on income from Canadian sources. In many cases, it is of particular importance to determine both the residence of an individual taxpayer and the source of income.

[¶945] Discretion

The CRA has the discretion to waive penalties and interest assessable under the income tax legislation. Discretion in a taxpayer's favour will not be exercised, however, unless a reasonable amount of care has been taken in attempting to comply with the law. If possible, efforts should have been made to avoid or at least minimize the delay in complying or paying. Any delay or omission should be remedied within a reasonable time after a taxpayer becomes aware of the delay or omission.

The CRA's discretion to waive penalties and interest in such cases applies for requests that are for a taxation year ending in the ten previous calendar years. For example, a request made in 2013 will only be accepted for 2003 and subsequent taxation years.

[¶950] Interpretation of Tax Legislation

[¶955] Construction of Taxing Statutes

The development of tax legislation over the years has included the acceptance of rules of interpretation or construction of the income tax legislation. First, every attempt is made to achieve precision in the language of the legislation so that it is clearly understood, thereby providing the taxpayer with some degree of certainty about his or her tax liability. However, the choice of language is not an easy task for the draftsperson (try reading subsection 256(3) as an example of such language!). To quote Lord Stephen in the famous British case of *In re Castioni*, [1891] 1 Q.B. 149 at page 167, on the question of the drafting of legislation:

> It is not enough to attain a degree of precision which a person reading in good faith can understand, but it is necessary to attain if possible a degree of precision which a person reading in bad faith cannot misunderstand. It is all the better if he cannot pretend to misunderstand it.

Under such difficulties, the Courts have developed principles of interpretation which should be particularly noted in construing a taxing statute. These principles are set out in ¶960 *et seq.* below.

[¶960] Intention of the Legislature and Literal Interpretation

In interpreting a taxing statute, inferences about the intention of Parliament are often made. No rule of construction is allowed to defeat the plain intention of the legislation. This has been stated as follows in *A.G. v. Carlton Bank*, [1899] 2 Q.B. 158, at p. 164:

> The duty of the Court is in all cases the same, whether the Act to be construed relates to taxation or to any other subject, namely, to give effect to the intention of the Legislature as that intention is to be gathered from the language employed, having regard to the context in connection with which it is employed, Courts have to give effect to what the Legislature has said.

The Courts assume that what is stated in the Act is what is meant by Parliament. To illustrate this point, reference should be made to the case of *Witthuhn v. M.N.R.*, 57 DTC 174 (TAB), in which a taxpayer was denied a deduction for certain medical expenses because the patient was confined to bed or a special type of rocking chair rather than to "a bed or wheel chair" as required by the Act as it then read (it was amended in 1986).

[¶965] Ambiguity

In more recent years, the adherence to literal construction appears to have softened to some extent. For example, in the case of *Overdyk v. M.N.R.*, 83 DTC 307 (TRB), where the taxpayer used a leg brace to go to work and a chair with castor-like wheels while at work, the same wording was given a much more liberal interpretation on the basis that if the taxpayer had been left completely alone without external aid or assistance, he would have been in bed at all times as a result of paralysis in one leg. In fact, it has been stated in another British case that:

> ... the Court's task is merely one of construction of the words used, although, in the case of ambiguity, that construction will be favoured, which seems to the Court more consonant with fairness in the circumstances ...

Thus, while taxing statutes were to be interpreted according to strict rules of interpretation, in the case of doubt, the construction of the statute is to be resolved in favour of the taxpayer in the case of a charging provision, and in favour of the Crown in the case of an exemption provision.

[¶970] "Object and Spirit Test" — Form Over Substance

The Supreme Court of Canada has suggested in *Stubart Investments Ltd. v. The Queen*, 84 DTC 6305, that the strict interpretation rule is obsolete and should be replaced by the "object and spirit" test. Under such a test, provisions are to be interpreted within their context in the Act on a basis consistent with the object of the Act and the intention of Parliament. This rule seems to have gained acceptance by the Courts recently.

The issue of form versus substance has long posed a problem in the application of the tax legislation to a taxpayer's situation. It was addressed in the often cited British case of *I.R.C. v. Duke of Westminster*, [1936] A.C. 1 (H.L.). In that case, the House of Lords viewed with disfavour the doctrine that in taxation cases, taxpayers or transactions are to be categorized in a particular way so as to fit within the contemplation or spirit of the legislation. The House of Lords said that taxpayers are not to be taxed by inference or by analogy but only by the plain words of the legislation applicable to the facts and circumstances of the individual case. The attitude of the Court in this case was based on the principle that taxpayers are entitled, if they can, to order their affairs so that the tax attaching under the legislation is less than it might otherwise be. The issue of form versus substance was addressed as follows by the House of Lords:

> Every man is entitled if he can to order his affairs so that the tax attaching under the appropriate Acts is less than it would otherwise be. If he succeeds in ordering them so as to secure this result, then, however unappreciative the Commissioners of Inland Revenue or his fellow taxpayers may be of his ingenuity, he cannot be compelled to pay an increased tax. This so-called doctrine of "the substance" seems to me to be nothing more than an attempt to make a man pay notwithstanding that he has so ordered his affairs that the amount of tax sought from him is not legally claimable ...

Thus, the form or legal effect of a transaction must prevail in attempting to determine the tax effects, unless the taxing statute requires that such form be disregarded or unless the form is considered to be a "sham" that misrepresents the true form, based on the facts of the case.

The Courts have even applied what has come to be known as a "repugnancy" or "smell" test in certain situations where substance was at considerable variance with the form of a transaction.

[¶975] Conflict with General Provisions

The Act contains a number of statements of general principle followed by a specific exception or series of exceptions to that rule. An exception or other specific provision of the legislation will override the general provision, but the former must be given a strict interpretation. It was expressed as follows in the British case of *Pretty v. Solly*, [1859] Beav. 606, at page 610:

> Whenever there is a particular enactment and a general enactment in the same statute, and the latter taken in its most comprehensive sense would overrule the former, the particular enactment must be operative and the general enactment must be taken to affect only the other parts of the statute to which it may properly apply.

[¶980] Ejusdem Generis Rule

Another rule has been important in the interpretation of the Act over the years. It is the *ejusdem generis* rule for enumeration of similar items. According to this rule, when a series of specific words in a statute is followed by general words, the general words are confined to the same scope as the specific words. For instance, where subsection 5(1) of the Act refers to "other remuneration" in providing that "a taxpayer's income for a taxation year from an office or employment is the salary, wages and other remuneration, including gratuities, received by the taxpayer in the year", the scope of the meaning of "salary", "wages", and "gratuities" might be used to constrain the meaning of "other remuneration".

[¶985] Precedents

Normally, former decisions are binding, particularly if they were made at a higher jurisdiction level. In the case of *B.B. Fast & Sons Distributors Ltd. v. M.N.R.*, 82 DTC 1017, the Tax Review Board indicated that judgments of Courts of equal or co-ordinate jurisdiction should be followed in the absence of strong reasons to the contrary. However, it has been recognized that too rigid adherence to precedents might lead to injustice in a particular case and also unduly restrict the proper development of the law.

[¶990] Interpretation Act

All words and phrases in the taxing statutes of Canada are governed by the *Interpretation Act*, R.S.C. 1970, c. I-23, which is of general application to all federal statutes. Section 27 deals with the interpretation of time limits specified in a statute. For example, if a deadline falls on a holiday, the deadline is extended to the following day that is not a holiday. Section 32 provides that deviations from a prescribed form which do not affect the substance do not invalidate a form used. Gender is addressed in subsection 33(1) which states that "words importing male persons include female persons and corporations". (Note, however, that the new Fifth Supplement version of the *Income Tax Act* is written in gender-neutral language, as are all new amending bills.)

[¶995] English and French Versions

Section 18 of the *Canadian Charter of Rights and Freedoms* provides that statutes must be printed and published in English and French and both versions are equally authoritative.

[¶1000] General Liability for Tax

[¶1005] General Nature of Tax — Taxable Income

Income tax is imposed upon the taxable income of all persons resident or ordinarily resident in Canada at any time in the taxation year.[1] Such a resident of Canada is taxable upon his entire taxable income derived from sources inside and outside of Canada for each taxation year.

A Native Canadian residing on a reserve and receiving wages from an employer situated on the reserve in respect of work performed off the reserve is not liable for income tax.[2] However, a Native Canadian who resided on a reserve in Quebec but who was employed in the United States was taxable as a resident of Canada on earnings outside the reserve even if the *Indian Act* exempts personal property from tax.[3]

A non-resident is only taxable on his or her taxable income earned in Canada. The taxable income to be reported for this purpose includes income from an office or employment in Canada (including director's fees, employment benefits, and stock options), income from carrying on a business in Canada, taxable capital gains from the disposition of taxable Canadian property, and certain other Canadian source income, such as interest, dividends, rents, pensions, and other passive income. If a non-resident performs services or carries on business both inside and outside Canada, the non-resident will be subject to Canadian tax on the portion of income attributable to the duties performed or the business carried on in Canada, *minus* the applicable proportion of deductions from income. Special rules are provided for a person who is a part-time resident. See ¶14,005 *et seq.*

[¶1010] "Person", "Taxpayer", "Individual" Defined

"Person" includes a corporation, and also the heirs, executors, or other legal representatives of a person.[4] It has been held that a Minister of the Crown is not a "person" within the meaning of the Act.[5] However, it has been held that a province is a "person".[6]

"Taxpayer" includes any person whether or not the person is liable to pay tax. "Individual" means a person other than a corporation.[7] Thus, a person who does not receive any *taxable* income may still fall within certain provisions of the *Income Tax Act*.

[¶1015] Taxation Year — Fiscal Period — Change in Fiscal Period

The fiscal period of a business carried on by an individual, a partnership of which an individual or professional corporation is a member, or a

---

[1] CCH ¶1003, ¶28,340; Sec. 2(1), 250(3).
[2] Nowegijick, 83 DTC 5041.
[3] Snow, 79 DTC 5177.
[4] CCH ¶28,196; Sec. 248(1) "person".
[5] Burnett Estate, 68 DTC 121.
[6] Braithwaite, 70 DTC 6001.
[7] CCH ¶28,139; Sec. 248(1) "individual".

professional corporation which is a member of a partnership, must coincide with the calendar year. An "alternative method" is, however, available if certain conditions are met (see ¶1017).

This calendar year requirement for self-employed professionals and unincorporated businesses does not affect the end date of fiscal periods of other corporations (including professional corporations which are not members of a partnership), which are allowed any fiscal period 53 weeks or less in duration.

The provision of a 53-week year for corporations accommodates corporations which want to end their fiscal period on the same weekday each year, typically for inventory reasons. For example, a retailer might end its fiscal period each year on the Saturday following Christmas. This can result in a taxation year in which there is no fiscal period end. To rectify such a situation, the next following period end is deemed to end on the last day of the particular year. For example, where a corporation has a fiscal period commencing on December 29, 2011, and ending on January 3, 2013, its taxation year is deemed to end on December 31, 2012.[8]

A partnership which has no individuals or professional corporations as members is also relieved from the calendar year end requirement and is allowed any fiscal period that does not exceed 12 months. Similarly, a testamentary trust, a tax-exempt entity, or a registered charity is allowed any fiscal period as long as it does not exceed 12 months.[9] A mutual fund trust may elect to have a December 15 fiscal year end.

As a result of the 2011 Budget, a partnership (no members of which are individuals or professional corporations), which is a member of another partnership, or has a member that is a partnership, must have a year end of December 31, if a corporation has significant interest (at least 10%) in any of the partnerships (see the discussion at ¶1018). This mandatory calendar year end was introduced to eliminate the deferral of tax by a corporation that has a significant interest in a partnership having a fiscal period different from the corporation's tax year and they generally apply to tax years of significant incremental corporate members ending after March 22, 2011.

Subject to the limitations described above, the fiscal period of a person or partnership cannot exceed 12 months. If a taxpayer has once adopted a fiscal period for a business, he or she may not change the fiscal period in subsequent years without the consent of the CRA.[10] Revenue Canada will normally grant its consent for changes which are demonstrably prompted by business considerations, but not for changes motivated primarily by tax considerations.

A reference to a given *taxation year* by the *calendar year* (e.g., "the 2012 taxation year") means the taxation year coinciding with or ending in

---

See page ii for explanation of footnotes.

[8] CCH ¶28,332h; Sec. 249(3).   [10] CCH ¶28,333l; Sec. 249.1(7).
[9] CCH ¶13,578, ¶28,333f; Sec. 104(23), 249.1(1).

¶1015

that calendar year (*viz.* 2012).[11] Thus, the 2012 taxation year of a corporation (other than a professional corporation discussed at ¶1017) whose fiscal period ends on March 31 will be the taxation year commencing April 1, 2011, and ending March 31, 2012. There may be fewer than 12 months in a taxation year. Thus, where the above taxation year is changed from March 31 to June 30, this period of three months will be a taxation year. See ¶4370 concerning taxation years where depreciable property has been disposed of, and ¶4375 concerning recaptures. For taxation year of a bankrupt, see ¶9003 *et seq.* and for the year end of a corporation on a change of control, see ¶15,390.

[¶1017] The Alternative Method

The calendar year requirement for professionals and sole proprietors (see discussion at ¶1015) does not apply where an election has been made to use the "alternative method" of computing income.[12] Under this method, income earned in a fiscal period is included in the taxation (calendar) year in which the fiscal period ends. To such income is added an estimate of the stub period income earned during the remainder of the calendar year (additional business income referred to as ABI).[13] The ABI included in one year is deducted from income the following year, when a further ABI calculation is made in respect of that year.[14] Basically, the alternative method allows an individual to retain an off-calendar year fiscal period for a business, while effectively reporting income from the business on a calendar year.

The alternative method is available only to a business carried on by an individual, alone or as a member of a partnership. In the case of a partnership, the alternative method is available to the individual only if each member of the partnership is an individual and the partnership is not a member of another partnership, throughout the period from the start of the relevant fiscal period to the next calendar year end. The alternative method is not available to a business where, in a prior fiscal period, or throughout the current fiscal period up to and including the end of the current calendar year, the expenditures made in the course of carrying on the business were primarily the costs or capital costs of tax shelter investments.[15]

The election to use the alternative method for a business must be made in the individual's tax return, by the filing date for the taxation year which includes the first day of the first fiscal period of the business beginning after 1994. For a fiscal period beginning in 1995, this means that the election must be made by June 15, 1996. However, if an individual is a member of a partnership of which a testamentary trust is a member, the election must be made by the earlier of the trust's filing date and the individual's filing date, for their respective taxation years which include the first day of the first fiscal period of the business beginning after 1994.

See page ii for explanation of footnotes.

[11] CCH ¶28,330; Sec. 249(1).
[12] CCH ¶28,333i; Sec. 249.1(4).
[13] CCH ¶5786; Sec. 34.1.
[14] CCH ¶5787; Sec. 34.2.
[15] CCH ¶28,333j; Sec. 249.1(5).

In the case of a business carried on through a partnership, an election made by one partner is valid only if is made on behalf of all of the partners and the electing partner has the authority to act for the partnership. In such case, all of the other partners are deemed to have made a valid election. Otherwise, the election is invalid and the partnership will have a calendar year fiscal period. Therefore, all of the partners must report the partnership income in the same manner: under the alternative method or under the calendar year-end rule,

One can revoke the election to use the alternative method for a business.[16] The revocation is effective for a fiscal period beginning in a taxation year if the revocation is made in the individual's tax return which is filed by the filing-due date for that year. Once an election is revoked, the mandatory calendar-year end applies to the business and the alternative method is no longer available.

[¶1018] Accrual Rules for Significant Incremental Corporate Partners

The mandatory calendar year end requirement for partnerships with individuals conducting business as partners (see ¶1015) does not prevent a partnership, all of the members of which are corporations, from selecting a fiscal period different from the taxation year of its corporate partners. For taxation years of a corporation ending after March 22, 2011, a corporate partner is required to accrue additional income in respect of the partnership (other than dividends for which a deduction is available), when:

(1) the corporate partner (other than a professional corporation) is a member of a partnership at the end of the taxation year;

(2) the partnership's last fiscal period that began in the taxation year ends in a subsequent taxation year of the corporate partner; and

(3) the corporate partner in (1) holds a significant interest in the partnership, meaning that the corporation, together with affiliated and related parties, was entitled to more than 10% of the partnership's income (or assets in the case of wind-up) at the end of the last fiscal period of the partnership that ended in the taxation year.[17]

The accrued income (adjusted stub period accrual) will generally be a prorated amount of the partner's income from the partnership for the fiscal period of the partnership ending in the taxation year of the partner (similar to the alternative method of income described at ¶1017). The corporate partner can override the default accrual rule by designating an amount in respect of its Stub Period Accrual.

Some partnerships may want to change their fiscal periods, for example, to align with the taxation year of one or more corporate partners. A

See page ii for explanation of footnotes.
[16] CCH ¶28,333k; Sec. 249.1(6).   [17] CCH ¶5787ag; Sec. 34.2(2).

¶1018

one-time election (a "Single-Tier Alignment Election") will allow a partnership to change its fiscal period if certain conditions are met.[18]

If a partnership has one or more partnerships as members, all of those partnerships will have to adopt a common fiscal period. In general, partnerships that are not required before the March 22, 2011 Budget to have a December 31 fiscal period will be allowed a one-time election (a "Multi-Tier Alignment Election") to choose a common fiscal period.[19]

[¶1020] Residence

There is no definition of "residence" or "resident" in the *Income Tax Act*. However, it is provided that persons who sojourn in Canada for 183 days or more in a year, members of the Canadian Forces, and servants of the Crown (including children whose income does not exceed a limitation amount, i.e., $10,822 for 2012; and individuals who, by virtue of their relationship to them, are exempt from tax in another country under a tax treaty or international agreement) are deemed to be resident in Canada throughout the year (see ¶1065). The 183-day rule applies only if the individuals are not otherwise resident in Canada, and this status may change from year to year without any substantial change in their way of life. For example, a resident of New York state might visit Canada for 200 days in 2012 and 150 days in 2013 in connection with his or her employment as an engineer. While in Canada, the individual lives in various hotels. For 2012, the individual will be considered a Canadian resident and will be taxable in Canada on income from all sources. For 2013, the individual is considered a nonresident of Canada and is taxable in Canada only on income from Canadian sources. This type of individual must be distinguished from one who actually takes up permanent residence in Canada during the year whether or not that individual is present for more than 183 days in that year. An individual who actually takes up residence in Canada (or leaves Canada) during the year will be taxed as a part-time resident.

Also deemed to be resident are persons who performed services at any time in the year in a country other than Canada under a prescribed international development assistance program of the Canadian government and who were resident in Canada at any time in the three months preceding the day on which such services commenced. Persons who were, at any time during the year, members of the overseas Canadian Forces school staff, who filed returns on the basis that they were persons resident in Canada throughout the period during which they were such members, shall also be deemed to have been resident in Canada throughout a taxation year.[20] Each of the international development assistance programs of the Canadian International Development Agency that is financed with funds (other than loan-assistance funds) established by External Affairs Vote 30a, *Appropriation Act*

See page ii for explanation of footnotes.

[18] Sec. 249.1(8); Sec. 249.1(10).
[19] Sec. 249.1(9); Sec 249.1(11).

[20] CCH ¶28,334, ¶28,338 Sec. 250(1), 250(2); Interp. Bul. IT-221R3.

No. 3, 1977–78, as amended, is prescribed as an international development assistance program of the Government of Canada.[21] (See also ¶1065.) A reference to a person resident in Canada includes a person who was, at the relevant time, ordinarily resident in Canada. Consequently, if a person is resident or ordinarily resident in Canada, the person is subject to Canadian tax.[22]

For the residence of corporations, see ¶1085.

The determination of whether a person is resident or not resident in a given country is essentially a question of fact. Residence is quite different from domicile; it is also different from citizenship. Citizenship or nationality is not a condition of liability to Canadian income tax. An individual may be held to be a resident of Canada (even though he or she resides abroad) if:

(a) the individual visits Canada for part of the year as part of his or her regular habit of life; or

(b) the individual keeps a place of abode ready for use and occupation by the individual or the individual's family and does, in fact, visit it for some period.[23]

A degree of permanence and substance must be present to create a residence.[24] However, an individual who left Canada and set up a dwelling establishment abroad was held not to be resident in Canada even though the individual intended to return to Canada.[25] Similarly, an individual was held not to be a resident of Canada when it was shown that the individual severed all relations with the country, even though he left his family here for some time for technical reasons.[26] An intention to live abroad permanently and the putting up for sale of his Canadian home did not affect the taxpayer's status as a Canadian resident.[27]

However, a taxpayer who, with his spouse, was domiciled in California and resident in Quebec, was held subject to Canadian income tax laws, the California laws regarding community of property having no application in this respect.[28] Similarly, a U.S. citizen who was a Canadian resident and who paid U.S. income taxes was held to be subject to Canadian tax laws; the individual should have filed income tax returns in Canada and claimed a foreign tax credit.[29] Despite the fact that his employment was outside Canada, and that his entire income came from that source, a taxpayer was held to be "ordinarily resident" in Canada when it was shown that several facts, none of which was conclusive individually, indicated that the taxpayer did not intend to abandon his Canadian residence.[30] Taxpayers who lived in the

---

See page ii for explanation of footnotes.

[21] CCH ¶28,336; Reg. 3400.

[22] CCH ¶1003, ¶28,340; Sec. 2(1), 250(3).

[23] Thomson, 2 DTC 812, Reeder, 75 DTC 5160, Reed, 89 DTC 34.

[24] Meldrum, 50 DTC 232.

[25] Beament, 52 DTC 1183, McFadyen, 2000 DTC 2473.

[26] Schujahn, 62 DTC 1225.

[27] Reid, 76 DTC 1003.

[28] Bedford, 64 DTC 419.

[29] Mallon, 64 DTC 449.

[30] Smith, W.C. 73 DTC 85.

United States but worked in Canada and for whom Canada was the centre of their working, social, and economic lives were resident in Canada.[31] A taxpayer employed as a sailor occasionally lived with his parents when his ship was in Canada, although he also shared an apartment in Bermuda with a friend. The taxpayer was held to be resident in Canada, because he could not claim his ship as a place of residence, and his failure to maintain a fixed abode did not negate Canadian residency.[32]

If an individual is physically absent from Canada and has no home in Canada but does have one in a foreign country, even if the individual intends to return to Canada, he or she may not be a resident in Canada, although the individual may be *domiciled* here.

Most tax agreements that Canada has entered into with another country provide that the expression "resident in Canada" means a person who is resident in Canada for purposes of Canadian tax and not resident in the other country for purposes of tax. Hence, a person who is resident both in Canada and the other country under their respective tax laws is not resident in Canada for purposes of these tax agreements. Under the *Canada–U.S. Tax Convention*, if an individual is resident in both countries under such domestic law, a series of four "tie-breaker" rules is applied to resolve the issue.[33] (See ¶14,395.) However, before February 24, 1998, Canada's income tax system did not explicitly take these treaty *tie-breaker* rules into account so that individuals could seek the best of both worlds by claiming Canadian residence (in effect claiming dual residence), thus escaping departure tax, and invoking tax-treaty protection on foreign-source income. Effective February 24, 1998, this alternative is no longer available to the extent that a dual resident of Canada and a country with which Canada has a tax treaty is compelled to determine Canadian residence for all Canadian tax purposes under the terms of that treaty.[34] This means that individuals who establish dual residence in a treaty country after February 23, 1998 will be deemed to cease Canadian residence at the time the treaty rules deem them to be resident of the treaty country. This may involve departure tax on ceasing Canadian residence. Individuals who had residence status in a treaty country before February 24, 1998, will not be subject to this rule until they next become resident under a treaty in a treaty country.

[¶1025] Constructive Residence — Sojourners

A temporary visitor may become a resident for reasons outlined at ¶14,010. It should be remembered that it is quite possible to be a resident in more than one country at the same time.

A mere transient visitor to Canada will not be deemed a resident unless the visitor sojourns in the country for a period of 183 or more days in the

See page ii for explanation of footnotes.

[31] Shpak and Shpak, 81 DTC 366.

[32] Reed, 89 DTC 34.

[33] CCH ¶30,226c; Art. IV, *Canada-U.S. Income Tax Convention*.

[34] CCH ¶28,343; Sec. 250(5).

year. Where a person does sojourn in Canada for such a period, the person is then deemed to have been a resident of Canada *throughout* the year.[35]

[¶1030] Part-Time Residents

For a discussion of part-time residents, see ¶14,005 *et seq.*

[¶1035] Non-Residents in Canada

[¶1040] Non-Residents Employed or Carrying on Business in Canada

A non-resident person employed in Canada, carrying on business in Canada, or who disposes of taxable Canadian property at any time in the year, is taxable.[36] A resident of Uruguay who owned two buildings in Montreal and was collecting rents from the tenants, arranging repairs, etc., was held to have carried on a business in Canada.[37] A company operating in Ireland but incorporated in Canada was not taxable on the profits from a purchase and sale of shares in Canada. The transaction did not constitute carrying on business in Canada and the profits were not taxable by virtue of the Canada–Ireland Tax Agreement.[38] A special tax (branch tax) at the rate of 25% is payable by every non-resident corporation carrying on business in Canada on the amount by which their taxable income exceeds certain deductions.[39] See ¶14,275.

"Employed" is defined to mean "performing the duties of an office or employment".[40] See ¶2040 for a discussion of office or employment. Some part of the services of an employee must be performed within the boundaries of Canada. Thus, a full-time officer of a company, who performs all duties in New York, is not taxable in Canada.

"Carrying on business" includes carrying on a profession, calling, trade, manufacture, or undertaking of any kind whatsoever and includes an adventure or concern in the nature of trade (see also ¶3003) but does not include an office or employment.[41] Thus, a non-resident professional person is liable to tax in Canada if he or she exercises a profession in Canada whether or not employed by any person in Canada in such professional capacity. The term carrying on business also extends to those who produce, grow, mine, create, manufacture, fabricate, improve, pack, preserve, or construct anything, either in whole or in part, in Canada, and to those who solicit orders or offer anything for sale in Canada through an agent or servant, whether the contract or transaction is to be carried out in whole or in part in Canada or outside Canada.[42] See ¶3003 *et seq.* and ¶14,060 concerning carrying on business.

See page ii for explanation of footnotes.

[35] CCH ¶28,334; Sec. 250(1).
[36] CCH ¶1250; Sec. 2(3).
[37] Rubinstein, 62 DTC 100.
[38] Tara Exploration and Development Co. Ltd., 72 DTC 6288.

[39] CCH ¶26,900; Sec. 219; Interp. Bul. IT-137R3.
[40] CCH ¶28,097; Sec. 248(1) "employed".
[41] CCH ¶28,024; Sec. 248(1) "business".
[42] CCH ¶28,378; Sec. 253.

A person is carrying on business and taxable if his activity is such as to constitute an adventure or concern in the nature of trade.

"Carrying on business *in* Canada" is not the same as "carrying on business *with* Canada".[43] The former connotes a certain active trading, negotiating, contracting, etc., within the country. It includes the following:

(a) merchants, wholesalers, and dealers who maintain a stock of goods in Canada from which deliveries are made. The goods may be in the merchant's own building or in a public warehouse;

(b) manufacturers who further process or develop goods in Canada, no matter where the goods are eventually sold;

(c) financiers, brokers, investment bankers, etc., who maintain an office in Canada from which an agent or employee effects or could effect transactions;

(d) generally, any non-resident who habitually enters into contracts in Canada either personally or through an agent, under which goods are sold to other persons. The delivery may take place anywhere, as also might the payment, as long as the contract was entered into in Canada and the business was transacted there;

(e) any person who renders services in Canada to any other person resident or carrying on business in Canada; and

(f) any person who disposes of taxable Canadian property other than in an isolated transaction.

[¶1045] Carrying On Business Through Agent

A non-resident person who solicits orders or offers anything for sale in Canada through an agent or servant is deemed to carry on business in Canada. If a non-resident delivers goods to a distributor or jobber or other person resident in Canada, for sale in Canada, the question of whether the non-resident is carrying on business in Canada may depend upon whether the distributor or jobber is an agent of the non-resident person. The question of whether a distributor is an agent of a non-resident or purchases and resells for his or her own account will ultimately depend on the degree of control that the non-resident exercises over the distributor's activities. In considering this question, some of the factors that might be taken into account are: whether the goods are sold in the name of the distributor or in the name of the non-resident; whether the distributor maintains an inventory or places an order with the non-resident only after receiving an order; whether the distributor is entitled to accept orders without authority from the non-resident; whether the distributor is free to fix the price at which the

---

See page ii for explanation of footnotes.

[43] CCH ¶1270; Sec. 2(3).

goods are sold; and whether the price is paid by the customer to the distributor or directly to the non-resident.[44]

In some circumstances a person resident in Canada may be considered an agent for a non-resident for the manufacture or other processing of products. In these circumstances, the non-resident may be held to be carrying on business in Canada by manufacturing or processing goods through an agent.

[¶1055] Employees Temporarily Outside of Canada

Persons hired and employed by a resident employer who is carrying on business in Canada and who have been sent outside Canada temporarily to perform services on behalf of such employer are taxable.[45] Such persons usually will not be taxable in the country to which they are sent.

[¶1060] "In Canada" Defined

Whenever it appears in the Act, the expression "in Canada" is deemed to include (and to have always included) the sea bed and subsoil of the submarine areas adjacent to the coasts of Canada in respect of which grants are issued by the Government of Canada or of a province, of a right, license, or privilege to explore for, drill, or take any minerals, petroleum, natural gas, or any related hydrocarbons. It is also deemed to include the seas and airspace above these submarine areas in respect of such resource exploration.[46]

[¶1065] Government Officials and Members of Canadian Forces

In addition to individuals sojourning in Canada for a total of 183 days in any calendar year (see ¶1020 and ¶1025), any individual (other than a factual resident of Canada) who is included in any one of the categories described below, is deemed to be a resident of Canada, regardless of where that individual lives or performs services. These categories are:

(a) persons who were members of the Canadian Forces at any time in the year;

(b) persons who were officers or servants of Canada or a province, at any time in the year, who received representation allowances or who were factually or deemed resident in Canada immediately prior to their appointment or employment by Canada or the province;

(c) persons who performed services, at any time in the year, outside Canada under an international development assistance program of the Canadian International Development Agency, provided they were

---

See page ii for explanation of footnotes.

[44] CCH ¶28,378; Sec. 253.
[45] CCH ¶1250; Sec. 2(3).
[46] CCH ¶28,382; Sec. 255.

either factually or deemed resident in Canada at any time in the three-month period prior to the day the services commenced;

(d) persons who were, at any time in the year, members of the overseas Canadian Forces school staff who have filed their returns for the year on the basis that they were resident in Canada throughout the period during which they were such members;

(e) persons who were, at any time in the year, a child of, and dependent for support on, an individual described in (a) to (d), and whose income for the year did not exceed an amount of the person's basic personal tax credit for the year (i.e., $10,822 for 2012); and

(f) persons who at any time in the year were, under an agreement or a convention (including a tax treaty) between Canada and another country, entitled to an exemption from an income tax that would otherwise be payable in that other country in respect of income from any source and

(i) the exemption under the agreement or convention applies to all or substantially all of their income from all sources (that is, they are subject to tax in the other country on less than 10% of their income as a result of the exemption), and

(ii) the persons were entitled to the exemption because they were related to, or a member of the family of, an individual (other than a trust) who was resident (including deemed resident) in Canada at the particular time.[47]

An individual who ceases to be described in (a) to (e) at a particular date in the year will be deemed to be resident in Canada only to that date. Thereafter, residence will depend on the tie factors outlined at ¶1020.[48]

Officers and employees of Crown corporations or agencies are advised by the CRA to consult their employers as to their residence status for tax purposes and employers in turn are advised to consult the CRA.[49] An employee of Atomic Energy of Canada Ltd. was a servant of the Crown and taxable as a resident of Canada, despite the fact that the employee was transferred to India.[50]

It should also be noted that under the *Visiting Forces Act*, members of the armed forces of a designated country present in Canada in connection with their duties, as well as accompanying civilian personnel (from some but not all of those countries) are deemed not to be resident in Canada for tax purposes.[51] Similarly, their presence in Canada is deemed not to cause a change in either their residence or domicile for tax purposes. Canada's tax treaties with other countries may also provide special treatment for visiting

---

See page ii for explanation of footnotes.

[47] CCH ¶28,334; Sec. 250(1); Interp. Bul. IT-221R3.   [50] Strachan, 73 DTC 5343.
[48] CCH ¶28,338; Sec. 250(2).
[49] Interp. Bul. IT-106R3.   [51] CCH ¶73,003; *The Visiting Forces Act,* Sec. 22.

forces from that country, whether or not it is designated in the *Visiting Forces Act.*

[¶1070] Minimum Income — Individuals

[¶1075] Tax Liability — Minimum Income

Income tax is only payable if the tax otherwise payable exceeds the person's personal tax credits plus additional amounts for dependants and certain other credits. See Chapter VIII for determination of personal tax credits.

See ¶8005 for current rates of tax.

[¶1080] Residence — Corporations

[¶1085] Residence of Corporations

A corporation is liable to tax under the Act if it is a "resident" of Canada, or if it is "carrying on business" in Canada, or possibly if it merely derives income from services rendered in Canada. A corporation is deemed to be resident in Canada throughout the taxation year if it was incorporated in Canada after April 26, 1965. A corporation incorporated in Canada prior to April 27, 1965 is deemed to be a resident of Canada if it was resident in Canada or carried on business in Canada during any taxation year ending after April 26, 1965. If a corporation was a non-resident corporation before April 27, 1965, its status will remain unchanged as long as its management and control remain outside Canada and it does not carry on business in Canada.

A corporation is also deemed to be a resident in Canada if it was incorporated in Canada before April 9, 1959, and:

(a) on June 18, 1971, was a foreign business corporation that was controlled by a corporation resident in Canada;

(b) during the 10-year period ending on June 18, 1971, carried on business in a country other than Canada, but during this period paid dividends to shareholders resident in Canada upon which the shareholders paid tax to the government of the other country; and

(c) at any time in the taxation year or in any preceding taxation year commencing after 1971, it was resident in Canada or carried on business in Canada.[52]

A corporation, at common law, is deemed to be a resident in the country where its central control and management are situated. Thus, a

---

See page ii for explanation of footnotes.

[52] CCH ¶28,342; Sec. 250(4).

company which was incorporated in Canada but the management and control of which was exercised from London (England), was held not to be resident in Canada.[53] Central management of a corporation may be divided between two countries, i.e., the corporation may have its head office in one country and its main business office in another. In such a case, the corporation is deemed to be resident in both countries. However, it has been held that the country where the legal power to control a corporation exists is the country where the corporation resides, although the corporation directors may be acting entirely on the direction of non-resident shareholders.[54]

An Ontario corporation with its central management and control in the United States was found to be carrying on business in Canada even though it was used by the parent company solely to give the Iraqi government the appearance that they were dealing with a Canadian company.[55]

Under the *Canada–U.S. Tax Convention (1980)*,[56] a corporation created or organized under the laws of any of the United States is not subject to taxation by Canada in respect of its industrial and commercial profits except the profits applicable to a permanent establishment in Canada. This is so regardless of whether the corporation is resident in Canada within the ordinary meaning of that term. See ¶8645 concerning the meaning of the term "permanent establishment".

Under the *Canada–U.K. Income Tax Convention*, a company is resident in the country in which it is resident for tax purposes.[57]

It should be noted that non-resident corporations must file an information return where they claim a treaty exemption from Part I tax on their Canadian-source business income.

[¶1090] Partnerships and Trusts

[¶1095] Partnerships

Partnerships, (other than SIFT partnerships described at ¶13,385), are not taxed as such under the Act; however, the computation of income, with certain exceptions, is made at the partnership level and is made on an accrual basis. Individual partners are assessed on their respective shares of the partnership profits.[58] This will be so even if the partnership is not registered, provided that the existence of a partnership agreement and its actual performance are established by satisfactory evidence.[59] The obligations imposed by the Act cannot be excluded by the partnership agree-

---

See page ii for explanation of footnotes.

[53] Yamaska Steamship Co. Ltd., 61 DTC 716, Unit Construction Ltd. v. Bullock, [1959], 3 W.L.R. 1022.

[54] Sifneos, 68 DTC 522, Zehnder and Co., 70 DTC 6064, Bedford Overseas Freighters Ltd. [No. 2], 70 DTC 6072.

[55] Gurd's Products Company Ltd., 85 DTC 5314.

[56] CCH ¶30,226f; Art. VII, *Canada–U.S. Income Tax Convention.*

[57] CCH ¶30,249; Art. IV, *Canada–U.K. Income Tax Convention.*

[58] CCH ¶12,103; Sec. 96(1).

[59] Shields, 62 DTC 1343.

ment.[60] If a partnership doing business in Canada has a non-resident partner, that non-resident would be taxed on his or her share of partnership profits. This would apply equally even if the non-resident were a limited partner whose name was not published. Syndicates are analogous to partnerships and for taxation purposes are treated in the same way. See ¶7005 *et seq.*

[¶1100] Trusts and Estates

Trusts and estates are considered to be resident in Canada if one of their trustees is a resident of Canada. A trust or estate is taxed as an individual,[61] but it is only taxable when it accumulates income which is not payable in the year to beneficiaries. See ¶7260 *et seq.*

An estate was resident in Canada where the executor was a Canadian Resident, notwithstanding that the beneficiaries were U.S. residents.[62] Under English tax legislation, a trustee resident in England was subject to income tax in respect of estate income even though the deceased was an American citizen resident in the United States and the trust property was in the United States.[63]

Difficult questions may arise where there are several trustees of one trust or estate. If a majority of the trustees are resident in Canada and if control over the trust property is exercised in this country, the trust or estate would appear to be clearly a resident of Canada. If, on the other hand, a majority of the trustees are not resident in Canada and those who are resident in Canada do not exercise any management or control over the trust property, it would appear that the trust might not be considered resident in Canada. This is analogous to the conditions concerning the residence of corporations. (See ¶1085, where it is mentioned that a corporation is said to be resident where its control and management are located. See ¶8645, which discusses the meaning of "permanent establishment".)

---

[60] Coupienne, 69 DTC 300.
[61] CCH ¶13,114; Sec. 104(2); Interp. Bul. IT-447.
[62] Holden, 1 DTC 243.
[63] Kelly v. Roberts, [1935] 2 K.B. 466.

Chapter II

Taxation of Individuals

Computation of Income **2000**

General 2005

Income from a Source or
Sources 2010

When Income Taxable 2020

Items Included in Income 2025

Amounts Not Included in
Income 2030

**Income from Office or
Employment** **2035**

Salary, Wages and Other
Remuneration 2040

Employee or Independent
Contractor 2050

Board, Lodging and Other
Employment Benefits 2055

Administrative Exclusion of
Employment Benefits 2057

Housing Loss
Reimbursements and
Other Employer-Provided
Housing Subsidies 2060

Health and Welfare Trusts
for Employees 2065

Allowances — Personal or
Living Expenses of
Employees 2070

Director's or Other Fees 2075

Allocations, etc. under Profit
Sharing Plan 2080

Automobile Benefits 2085

Employee's Use of Aircraft 2090

Employee Insurance
Benefits 2095

Group Sickness and
Accident Insurance Plans 2100

Salary Deferral
Arrangements 2105

Payments by Employer to
Employee 2110

Restrictive Covenants 2112

Premium for Group Term
Life Insurance 2115

Employment at Special
Work Site or Remote
Location 2120

Interest-Free, Low-Interest
and Forgiven Loans 2130

Employee Stock Option
Plans 2135

Exchanges of Options or
Shares 2140

Other Sources of Income **2145**

Pension Benefits, etc. 2150

U.S. Social Security
Payments 2155

Retiring Allowances 2160

Death Benefits 2165

Eligible Funeral
Arrangements 2168

Employment Insurance
Benefits 2170

Benefits under Government
Assistance Programs 2175

Alimony or Maintenance
Payments 2180

Annuity Payments 2185

Disposition of Income-
Averaging Annuity
Contract 2190

RRSPs, DPSPs, RRIFs, and
Supplementary
Unemployment Benefit
Plans 2195

Home Buyers' Plans 2198

Life Insurance Policies 2200

Award of Legal Costs 2205

Scholarships, Bursaries, etc. 2210

Artists' Grants 2213

Registered Education Savings Plan (RESP) Payments 2215

Home Insulation or Energy Conversion Grants 2220

Registered Retirement Income Fund (RRIF) Payments 2225

Social Assistance Payments 2230

Workers' Compensation 2235

Salary Deferral Arrangements 2240

Retirement Compensation Arrangements (RCAs) 2245

Indirect Payments 2250

Transfer of Rights to Income 2255

Loans to Non-Arm's Length Individuals 2260

Miscellaneous Income Receipts 2280

Income from Personal-Injury Awards 2290

Employment Expenses 2295

General Restriction 2300

Salespersons' Expenses 2305

Travelling Expenses and Meals 2310

Other Expenses and Membership Dues 2315

Automobile and Aircraft Expenses 2320

Legal Expenses 2325

Clergy Residence 2330

Exchange Fund Contributions of Teachers 2335

Certain Railway Company Employees 2340

Persons Employed in Forestry 2345

Transport Employees 2350

Truck Drivers' Meal Expenses 2353

Employment Insurance Premiums 2355

Contributions to Registered Pension Plans (RPPs) 2360

Salary Reimbursement 2370

Top-Up Disability Reimbursements 2373

Forfeited Amounts under a Salary Deferral Arrangement 2375

Overseas Employment 2380

Musical Instruments 2385

Artists' Expenses 2387

Apprentice Mechanics' Tools 2388

Tradespeople's Tool Expenses 2389

Home Office Expenses 2390

GST/HST Rebate on Employment Income Deductions 2391

Other Deductions 2395

Moving Expenses 2400

Child Care Expenses 2405

Disability Support and Attendant Care Expenses 2410

Capital Element of Annuity Payments 2415

Interest on Death Duties 2420

Canada or Quebec Pension Plan Contributions 2425

Quebec Parental Insurance Plan (QPIP) — Self-Employed Premiums 2427

Premiums or Payments under Registered Retirement Savings Plans (RRSPs) or Registered Retirement Income Funds (RRIFs) 2430

Transfer of Superannuation Benefits 2435

Pension Income Splitting 2437

Transfer of Retiring Allowances 2440

Transfer of Refund of Premiums under RRSP/RRIF 2445

Rollover of RRSP, RRIF, or RPP Proceeds to RDSP on Death 2447

Estate Tax and Succession
Duties Applicable to
Certain Property 2450

Overpayments of Pension
or Benefits 2455

Expenses of Objection or
Appeal 2460

Income Averaging Annuity
Contracts 2465

Payments Included in
Income 2470

Northern Area Residents'
Travel Benefit Deduction 2480

Northern Area Residents'
Housing Benefit
Deduction 2485

Canadian Forces Personnel
and Police 2487

**Rules Relating to
Computation of Income 2490**

General Limitation of
Expenses 2495

Amounts in
Part Consideration for
Disposition of Property 2500

Inadequate Considerations 2505

Inadequate Consideration
— Appropriation of
Property to Shareholders 2520

Price Adjustment Clauses 2530

Deemed Proceeds of
Disposition 2535

Inter Vivos Transfer of
Property to Spouse, etc.
or Trust 2540

Inter Vivos Transfer of
Farming and Fishing
Property to Child 2545

Inter Vivos Transfer of
Family Farm or Fishing
Corporations and
Partnerships 2550

Death of a Taxpayer 2555

Periodic Payments — Rights
or Things 2560

Eligible Capital Property of
Deceased Taxpayer 2565

Resource Properties and
Land Inventories of
Deceased Taxpayer 2570

Depreciable and Other
Capital Property of
Deceased Taxpayer 2575

Transfer or Distribution to
Spouse/Common-Law
Partner or Trust 2580

Special Rules Applicable to
Spousal or Partner Trust 2585

Transfer of Farm or Fishing
Property to Child 2590

Transfer of Family Farm or
Fishing Corporation or
Partnership to Child by
Deceased or Spousal or
Partner Trust 2595

Transfer to Parent 2600

Reserves, etc. for the Year
of Death 2605

Attribution Rules for Income 2615

Transfers or Loans to
Spouse/Common-Law
Partner 2620

Spouse/Common-Law
Partner as Employee or
Partner 2625

Transfers and Loans to
Minors 2630

Capital Gains and Losses 2635

Transfers to RRSP, RDSP
and TFSA 2640

Transfer or Loan Not at
Arm's Length 2645

Trusts 2650

Transfers and Loans to
Corporations 2655

Exemptions 2660

Anti-Avoidance Rules 2665

Exception from Attribution
Rules 2667

Security in Satisfaction of
Income Debt 2670

Bond Conversions 2675

Unpaid Amounts —
Transactions Not at
Arm's Length 2680

Unpaid Remuneration 2685

Mortgage Foreclosures and
Conditional Sales
Repossessions 2690

Recent Changes

New Tax on Employer Contributions to Group Sickness and Accident Insurance Plans

As a result of the 2012 Budget, effective March 29, 2012, employer-paid contributions to a group sickness and accident insurance plan for an employee's coverage after 2012 will be taxable to the employee to the extent that such contributions are not in respect of a wage loss replacement benefit payable on a periodic basis. This measure will apply to employer contributions after March 28, 2012 that are attributable to an employee's coverage after 2012, except that such contributions made after March 28, 2012 and before 2013 will be included in the employee's income for 2013. For contributions made after 2012, the income inclusion is required in the same year as the employer contributions are made. See ¶2025, ¶2065, and ¶2100.

Governor General's Salary To Be Taxed

For 2013 and subsequent taxation years, the income tax exemption for the Governor General's salary will end in order to make it subject to income tax in the same manner as the salary of other Canadians. See ¶2030.

2012 Automobile Operating Cost Benefit Rates

The general prescribed rate used to determine the taxable benefit relating to the personal portion of automobile operating expenses paid by employers for 2012 will increase from 24 cents to 26 cents per kilometre. For taxpayers employed principally in selling or leasing automobiles, the prescribed rate will increase from 21 cents to 23 cents per kilometre. This rate is prescribed every year to reflect the costs of operating an automobile. The statutory rates used in the calculation of an automobile "standby charge" remain unchanged. The government made this announcement on December 29, 2011. See ¶2070 and ¶2085.

Restrictive Covenant Rules

Pending draft legislation, reported here last year, would include in income amounts received or receivable under a restrictive covenant granted after October 7, 2003, subject to transitional rules. With the last release on July 10, 2010 of this draft legislation, there are now three exceptions to this income inclusion rule. At the time of writing, this draft legislation has not been enacted yet. See ¶2112.

2012 Automobile Deduction Limits

For 2012, the ceiling on the capital cost of passenger vehicles for CCA purposes remains at $30,000, the limit of deductible leasing costs remains at $800 per month (plus applicable federal and provincial taxes), and the maximum allowable interest deduction for amounts borrowed to purchase an automobile remains at $300 per month. This announcement was made on December 29, 2011. See ¶2320.

2012 Limit for Money Purchase RPPs

In 2012, the limit on total allowable employer-employee contributions to money purchase registered pension plans (RPPs) is increased from $22,970 to $23,820. See ¶2360.

Phase-Out of the Overseas Employment Tax Credit (OETC)

Beginning in 2013 the OETC is gradually phased out over a three-year period so that it becomes completely eliminated after 2015. During the 2013–2015 phase-out period, the percentage applied to qualifying foreign employment income (QFEI) is reduced from 80% to 60% in 2013, 40% in 2014, and 20% in 2015. As a result, the maximum QFEI for those years is reduced from $100,000 to $60,000, $40,000, and

$20,000, respectively. The phase-out for the 2013–2015 taxation years does not apply to an individual's QFEI that is earned in connection with a contract that was committed to in writing before March 29, 2012. Beginning in 2016, the OETC is eliminated in all cases. See ¶2380.

Elimination of the HST and Reinstatement of the PST in British Columbia

On August 26, 2011, the Government of British Columbia announced that it would be reinstating its provincial sales tax (PST) following the referendum on the elimination of the harmonized sales tax (HST) in the province. The 12% HST will be replaced, effective April 1, 2013, by the federal GST and the PST. On February 17, 2012, transitional rules were proposed for the elimination of the HST and the reinstatement of the PST in British Columbia. Under these rules, not enacted yet, the rate for calculating rebates of GST/HST to employees with respect to certain expenses on which the 12% HST rate was payable would be reduced to 6.75% for the 2013 taxation year and 5% beginning with the 2014 taxation year. See ¶2391.

RRSP/RRIF Rollover to Infirm Child

For deaths occurring in 2012, the amount of income above which a physically or mentally infirm dependant is presumed not to be dependent on a parent or grandparent for RRSP rollovers on death is increased to $17,868 as a result of the indexation of the basic personal amount and the disability amount for 2011. See ¶2445.

[¶2000] Computation of Income

[¶2005] General

A taxpayer is required to calculate income from each source separately and total the various amounts to compute "income" for income tax purposes.[1] The taxpayer is to include income from any source inside or outside Canada.

There are four main sources of income:

(1) business;

(2) property;

(3) office; and

(4) employment,

each of which is calculated in accordance with rules from various parts of the *Income Tax Act.*

It is currently provided that, unless a contrary intention is evident, no provision should be interpreted to require an amount to be included or deducted more than once in computing a taxpayer's income.[2] Accordingly, amounts deducted for a statute-barred taxation year and not disallowed may

---

See page ii for explanation of footnotes.

[1] CCH ¶2003; Sec. 3.　　　　[2] CCH ¶28,329y; Sec. 248(28).

not be deducted again for a subsequent year, including any year in which it was actually deductible.

[¶2010] Income from a Source or Sources

A taxpayer is required to include income from all sources. Generally, income or loss is calculated on a source-by-source basis. Each "office",[3] "employment",[4] "business",[5] and "property"[6] is to be treated as a separate source of income.

"Amounts" included in income will encompass "money, rights, or things expressed in terms of the amount of money or the value in terms of money of the right or thing".[7] Barter transactions, being the reciprocal exchange of goods or services without the use of money, are considered to be within the purview of the *Income Tax Act*.[8] However, an employee giving occasional help to a friend or neighbour in exchange for something would not be taxable unless a regular habit was made of providing such service.

[¶2020] When Income Taxable

There are two methods of computing income from a business or property for tax purposes: the "cash" basis and the "accrual" basis.

Under the cash method of accounting, amounts are included in income only when received and expenses are deducted only when paid. Income from an office or employment is always computed on the cash basis.

Under the accrual method of accounting, income is computed for the period during which it has been earned, notwithstanding that it may not have been collected or actually received. When computing income from a business or property, with the exception of farmers, the accrual method rather than the cash method must be used.

[¶2025] Items Included in Income

The following items are expressly required to be included in the income of a taxpayer for a taxation year to the extent set out in the sections cited:

- Alimony or maintenance payments (not including child support payments) (s. 56(1)(*b*), s. 56(1)(*e*));

- Allowances for personal, living, or any other expenses paid to an employee or officer (s. 6(1)(*b*));

- Amounts allocated to an employee under an employees' profit sharing plan (s. 6(1)(*d*), s. 12(1)(*n*));

See page ii for explanation of footnotes.

[3] CCH ¶28,190; Sec. 248(1) "office".
[4] CCH ¶28,094; Sec. 248(1) "employment".
[5] CCH ¶28,024; Sec. 248(1) "business".
[6] CCH ¶28,220; Sec. 248(1) "property".
[7] CCH ¶28,012; Sec. 248(1) "amount".
[8] Interp. Bul. IT-490.

- Amounts deducted by the vendor on a sale of accounts receivable are included in the purchaser's income (s. 22(1));

- Amounts not taxed to a deceased person which are transferred to a beneficiary (s. 70(3));

- Amounts of an income nature payable by a trust or estate to the taxpayer as beneficiary (s. 12(1)(*m*), s. 104(13));

- Amounts of pension income allocated to the taxpayer's spouse or common-law partner after 2006 (s. 56(1)(*a*.2));

- Amounts paid by a trust or estate for upkeep, etc., for property to be maintained for benefit of beneficiary (s. 105(2));

- Amounts paid on income bonds deemed dividends (s. 15(3));

- Amounts paid to another person at the direction of or with the concurrence of the taxpayer (s. 56(2));

- [Amounts receivable for restrictive covenants agreed to after October 7, 2003 (s. 6(3.1))];

- Amounts receivable in the future for property sold or services rendered in course of business in the year (s. 12(1)(*b*));

- Amounts receivable of an income nature by a deceased person (s. 70(2));

- Amounts received by non-life insurance companies, whether mutual or not, from any arrangement to insure (s. 138);

- Amounts received by non-life insurance companies, whether mutual or not, from property vested in them (s. 138);

- Amounts received for services or goods not rendered or delivered in the year, or for returnable containers (s. 12(1)(*a*));

- Annuity payments (s. 56(1)(*d*));

- Appropriations by a corporation for the benefit of shareholders (s. 15(1));

- Automotive industry employees' transitional assistance (s. 56(1)(*a*)(v));

- Bad debts recovered (s. 12(1)(*i*));

- Benefits conferred by non-arm's length transactions (s. 245(2));

- Benefits (except those constituting a distribution or payment of capital) from or under any trust (s. 12(1)(*m*), s. 105(1));

- Benefits or advantages (with certain exceptions) conferred by corporations on shareholders (s. 15(1)(*c*));

¶2025

- Benefits received under a Home Buyers' Plan (s. 56(1)(h.1), s. 146.01);

- Benefits received under registered retirement savings plans (s. 56(1)(h), s. 146(8));

- Benefits under employee benefit plans or trusts (s. 6(1)(g), s. 6(1)(h));

- Benefits under the *Labour Adjustment Benefits Act*, the *Department of Labour Act*, the Plant Workers Adjustment Program, and the Northern Cod Compensation and Adjustment Program (s. 56(1)(a)(vi));

- Benefits received after 2005 under the new Quebec Parental Insurance Plan (s. 56(1)(a)(vii));

- Board, lodging, and other benefits attached to an office or employment (s. 6(1)(a));

- Capital gains — $\frac{1}{2}$ included in income with certain exceptions (s. 3, s. 38);

- Company automobile, value of personal use (s. 6(1)(e), s. 6(2));

- Death benefits (s. 56(1)(a)(iii));

- Deemed dividends from non-tax-paid corporate surpluses, by reason of:

  (a) a distribution or appropriation on the winding-up, discontinuance, or reorganization of business (s. 84(2)),

  (b) redemption, acquisition, or conversion of common shares (s. 84(3)), or

  (c) capitalization of undistributed income by stock dividend, increase in paid-up capital, or otherwise (s. 84(1));

- Deferred profit sharing plan payments (s. 56(1)(i));

- Directors' fees (s. 6(1)(c));

- Dividends, including stock dividends, are grossed up by a factor of 25% with an offsetting tax credit at the rate of $\frac{2}{3}$ of the gross-up amount. In the case of eligible dividends, the gross-up factor is 45% from 2006 until 2010, 44% for 2010, 41% for 2011, and 38% beginning in 2012, with offsetting tax credits of the gross-up amount of $\frac{11}{18}$ until 2010, $\frac{10}{17}$ in 2010, $\frac{13}{23}$ in 2011, and $\frac{6}{11}$ in 2012, (s. 82(1), s. 121);

- Employer-paid contributions to a group sickness and accident insurance plan for an employee's coverage after 2012 to the extent that such contributions are not in respect of a wage loss replacement benefit payable on a periodic basis (s. 6(1)(e.1));

¶2025

- Evidence of indebtedness received in lieu of payment of income debt (s. 76);

- Fair market value of assets sold or distributed to shareholders at a price below such value (s. 69(4), s. 69(5));

- Fees (s. 6(1)(c));

- Fellowships, scholarships, and research grants in excess of the scholarship exemption (s. 56(1)(n), 56(1)(o)); 56(3);

- Gratuities (s. 5(1));

- Income-averaging annuity receipts (s. 56(1)(e), s. 56(1)(f));

- Income from controlled trust deemed settlor's (s. 75(2));

- Income from property transferred or loaned to certain minors attributed to transferor (s. 74.1(2));

- Income from property transferred or loaned to spouse attributed to transferor (s. 74.1(1));

- Income from eligible funeral arrangement (s. 148.1);

- Income of trusts and estates payable to beneficiaries (s. 104(13));

- Insurance payments for damage in depreciable property which are expended in the taxation year and within a reasonable time on repairing the damage (s. 12(1)(f));

- Inducement payments to prospective employees (s. 6(3));

- Insurance premiums (except for group life or medical services) paid by employer for the benefit of employee (s. 6(1)(a));

- Interest deemed received on certain loans to non-residents (s. 17(1));

- Interest on bond transferred with interest until the date of transfer (s. 20(14));

- Interest payments (s. 12(1)(c));

- Interest payments which are blended with capital payments (s. 16);

- Inventory sale proceeds (s. 23, s. 28);

- Loans by corporations to shareholders (s. 15(2));

- Medicare contributions by employer (s. 6(1)(a));

- Non-competition payments to departing employees (s. 6(3));

- Patronage dividends, except those from consumer goods and services (s. 135(7));

- Payments based on the use of or production from property (s. 12(1)(g));

- Payments by corporation to shareholders other than in a *bona fide* transaction (s. 15(1));

- Pension benefits (s. 56(1)(a));

- Periodic payments which are deemed to accrue daily where a person dies (s. 70(1));

- Portion of beneficiaries' share of profits under employees' profit sharing plan (s. 144(7));

- Profit from business (s. 9(1));

- Profit from property (s. 9(1));

- Recaptured depreciation (s. 13(1));

- Remuneration (s. 5(1));

- Reserves deducted in previous year (s. 12(1)(d));

- Reserves of banks which are unreasonably large in the opinion of the Minister of Finance (s. 26(1));

- Resource property sale receipts (s. 59);

- Retirement compensation arrangement payments (s. 12(1)(n.3));

- Retiring allowances (s. 56(1)(a)(ii));

- RRSP payments (s. 56(1)(h));

- Salary (s. 5(1));

- Salary deferral arrangement payments (s. 6(1)(e));

- Securities received in lieu of payment of income debt (s. 76);

- Social assistance payments (s. 56(1)(r), s. 56(1)(u));

- Stock option rights granted to employees, etc. (s. 7(1));

- Superannuation benefits (s. 56(1)(a)(i));

- Supplementary unemployment benefit plan payments (s. 56(1)(g), s. 145(3));

- Top-up disability payment (s. 6(18));

- Transfer of right to income in a non-arm's length transaction (without transfer of property source of income) giving rise to inclusion of remaining income in transferor's hands (s. 56(4));

- Employment insurance benefits (s. 56(1)(a));

¶2025

- Wages (s. 5(1));

- Workers' compensation payments (s. 56(1)(v)).

[¶2030] Amounts Not Included in Income

Certain payments or amounts are not included in computing the income of a taxpayer for a taxation year. The following is a list of exemptions together with references to applicable sections of the *Income Tax Act.*

- Amounts declared to be exempt by legislation of the Parliament of Canada (s. 81(1)(a));

- Amounts received from a mining property or for shares thereof received by a prospector, a prospector's employer, or a financial backer, if not received under an option to purchase or during or after a campaign to sell such shares to the public (s. 81(1)(l));

- Amounts received under War Savings Certificates or similar certificates issued by Newfoundland before April 1, 1949 (s. 81(1)(b));

- Board and lodging of employees at special work sites (s. 5(2), s. 6(6), and s. 6(7));

- Certain payments from employees' profit sharing plans (s. 81(1)(k), s. 144);

- Certain payments under Government or like annuities issued before June 25, 1940 (s. 58);

- Employees at special work sites — value of board and lodging or transportation or allowance therefor, received by construction workers and certain other employees under certain conditions (s. 6(6));

- German compensation payments (s. 81(1)(g));

- Group Disability benefits — Insolvent insurer (s. 6(17));

- Halifax disaster pensions (s. 81(1)(f));

- Income from the office of Governor-General of Canada until the exemption is repealed beginning in 2013 (s. 81(1)(n));

- Non-resident person's income from the operation of ships or aircraft where reciprocal exemption is granted by the country of the person's residence (s. 81(1)(c));

- Patronage dividends in respect of consumer goods and services (s. 135(7));

- Pensions for war services (s. 81(1)(d));

- Portion of benefits under a pension plan which was tax-exempt at any time (s. 57(3));

- Portion of elected M.L.A.'s expense allowance (s. 81(2));

- Portion of elected municipal officer's expense allowance (s. 81(3));

- Private health services plan — benefit of employer's contributions (s. 6(1)(a));

- Provincial indemnities (s. 81(1)(q));

- Public officers' expense allowances up to ½ of salary (s. 81(3)(b));

- RCMP pension or compensation (s. 81(1)(i));

- Refunds of registered education savings plan payments (s. 81(1)(o));

- Scholarships, fellowships, and bursaries received by students enrolled in: (i) post-secondary programs eligible for the education tax credit; and (ii) after 2006, elementary and secondary school programs, subject to certain restrictions for students enrolled after 2009 in part-time programs) (s. 56(3));

- Service pensions paid by foreign allies where reciprocal exemption exists (s. 81(1)(e));

- Stock rights conferred by a corporation on all holders of its common shares (s. 15(1)(c)).

[¶2035] Income from Office or Employment

[¶2040] Salary, Wages and Other Remuneration

A taxpayer's income for a taxation year from an office or employment is the salary, wages, and other remuneration, including gratuities, received by the taxpayer in the year.[9] The taxpayer's loss for a taxation year from an office or employment is the amount of his or her loss, if any, for the taxation year from that source computed by applying the provisions of the Act relating to the computation of income.[10] Salaries and wages are generally taxed in the year in which they are received.

The amounts to be included in employment income extend to the value of benefits from employment, such as board and lodging (¶2055 *et seq.*), amounts received as personal and living expenses (¶2070), directors' fees, the value of the personal use of a company automobile (¶2085), income maintenance payments (¶2095 *et seq.*), certain payments made on behalf of an employee by his or her employer (¶2110), certain group insurance premiums (¶2115), and the amounts received out of a salary deferral arrangement that exceed the amount previously included in income and taxed. This does not include the benefits the employee derives from his or her employer's contributions to or under a registered pension fund or plan,

---

See page ii for explanation of footnotes.
[9] CCH ¶2201; Sec. 5(1).   [10] CCH ¶2202; Sec. 5(2).

group sickness or accident insurance plan, private health services plan, supplementary unemployment benefit plan, deferred profit sharing plan (DPSP), group term life insurance policy, employee benefit plan, or employee trust.

"Office" means the position of an individual entitling him or her to a fixed or ascertainable stipend or remuneration. It includes a judicial office, the office of a Minister of the Crown, the office of a member of the Senate or House of Commons of Canada, a member of a legislative assembly, a member of a legislative or executive council and any other office, the incumbent of which is elected by popular vote or is elected or appointed in a representative capacity, and also includes the position of a corporation director. "Officer" means a person holding such an office.

"Employment" means the position of an individual in the service of some other person, including Her Majesty or a foreign state. "Employee" means a person holding such a position, and includes an officer of a company. "Employer", in relation to an officer, means the person from whom the officer receives his or her remuneration.[11]

"Salary" has been said to possess the following characteristics:

(1) it is remuneration for services rendered;

(2) it is payable under contract (express or implied);

(3) it is computed by reference to time; and

(4) it is payable at certain definite dates or times.

"Wages" are payments made at regular intervals, whether by the day or week or month, for time during which a workman or servant is at an employer's disposal. It includes payment computed on the basis of the amount of work done by an employee.

Despite the reference to the word "legacy" in their uncle's will, the $15,000 the taxpayers received from his estate to perform their duties as executors was taxable as an income from an office or employment.[12] The situation remains the same if, under the terms of a will, a taxpayer is appointed as the liquidator of an estate and given a piece of property in appreciation of his or her services. Considering that the characterization of income is not based on its amount, but rather on its source, it did not matter that the property value ($70,000) may have been in excess of any liquidator's fee.[13] Similarly, where shares of his employer were never distributed to the taxpayer and continued to be held in escrow until his employer's successor ceased operations, the value of the shares was taxable as employment income since they were issued as compensation for past services.[14]

See page ii for explanation of footnotes.

[11] CCH ¶28,091; Sec. 248(1) "employer".
[12] Messier et al., 2008 DTC 4609.
[13] Boisvert, 2011 DTC 1296.
[14] Lockhart, 2008 DTC 3044.

On the other hand, not all remuneration need be classified as wages or salary. A lawyer who was the president of an insurance company and who received from it a sum of money for legal work was held to have received the fees as a lawyer rather than as income from an office or employment.[15] Where one of two shareholders of a company was to receive $\frac{1}{2}$ of the profit from a real estate transaction in exchange for performing the company duties of the other shareholder, her share of the profit was taxable as compensation for services rendered.[16] When a company president received $9\frac{1}{2}$ months' salary in lieu of reasonable notice of his termination, it was determined to be income, not damages for wrongful dismissal, and was taxable as such.[17]

Damages for wrongful dismissal from employment constitute income (see ¶2160). An amount received from an employer in consideration for the release from a contract of employment was income, not a capital indemnity, nor a retirement allowance.[18] If the employee's debt to the employer was cancelled and the cancelled debt was treated as severance pay by the employer, the amount was income to the employee and was a deductible expense of the employer.[19]

"Other remuneration" includes "gratuities" which includes such items as bonuses, tips, and honoraria.

Whether a payment made by an employer to his or her employee is an advance on account of future earnings or a *bona fide* loan is a question of fact. An advance on account of future earnings is properly included in the employee's income for the year in which it is received.[20] Where an employee who is taxed on an advance subsequently, on leaving employment, repays part or all of the outstanding balance, the amount so repaid is ordinarily deductible from income for the year of repayment. When the amount repaid exceeds the advances received in the year, the excess is deductible from the preceding year. Where a loan, as distinguished from an advance, is made to an employee, the amount so received should not be included in income. The employee should include in income for the year those amounts of earnings which are applied against the loan plus any other salary, wages, or commissions that are paid to the employee.

An employee who receives a loan from an employer which is subsequently forgiven will be deemed to have received a benefit from employment which must be included in income.[21] The value of the benefit is calculated as the amount of the loan or obligation forgiven. See also ¶2130 and ¶3117 concerning low-interest loans to employees.

A taxpayer received $389,700 upon termination of employment for cancellation of rights to receive a percentage of company profits during the

---

See page ii for explanation of footnotes.

[15] Biron, 62 DTC 20.
[16] Stenstrom, 63 DTC 479.
[17] Quance, 74 DTC 6210,Bye, 75 DTC 33.
[18] Choquette, 74 DTC 6563.

[19] S. de Waal et al, 75 DTC 127.
[20] Randall, 87 DTC 553.
[21] CCH ¶2689; Sec. 6(15).

¶2040

term of his employment. The payment was determined to be income from employment in satisfaction of an agreement made during his employment.[22]

[¶2050] Employee or Independent Contractor

Income from an office or employment is determined by different rules than those applicable to determining income from a business or property. Differences arise as to the availability of deductions, the time of recognition of income, and the "taxation year". Therefore, it is of importance to a taxpayer to determine whether his or her income or some portion thereof is from an office or employment or from a business or property.

There may be difficult cases where it will be necessary to determine the answer as a matter of fact, having reference to the definitions referred to above and the common law as to whether the income in question is from an office or employment or from business carried on by the taxpayer as an independent contractor. For example, in some circumstances it may be difficult to determine whether a commission agent receives income from an office or employment or from a business carried on by himself or herself. A similar problem frequently arises with entertainers and musicians.[23]

Under the common law dealing with master and servant relationships, the general test to be applied is the nature and degree of control over the person alleged to be the employee. In addition to the control test, there are three other tests which courts have developed to ascertain whether a taxpayer is an employee or an independent contractor. These are:

(a) the integration test;

(b) the economic reality test; and

(c) the specific result test.

Under the integration test, distinction is made between a contract *of* service and a contract *for* service. In the former situation one is employed as part of the business and work is done as an integral part of the business. In the latter situation, the taxpayer's work, although done for the business, is not integrated into it but is only accessory to it, and therefore the taxpayer is an independent contractor. Using this test, part-time lecturers and teachers who do not appear to be under the direct control and supervision of the educational institution have been found to be employees.[24]

Under the economic reality test, the courts have determined that a person who is in business as an independent contractor runs the risk of financing equipment, supplying the help necessary to operate and administer the business, and having to ensure that there are sufficient clients to render the business economically viable. [25]

---

[22] Markin, 96 DTC 6483.

[23] Interp. Bul. IT-525R.

[24] Rosen, 76 DTC 6274;Hecht, 80 DTC 1438.

[25] Hauser, 78 DTC 1532;Alexander, 70 DTC 6006.

With respect to the specific result test, the courts again make a distinction between a contract *of* service and a contract *for* service, the former indicating an employer–employee relationship.

The courts have stressed the importance of examining the facts of the alleged employment relationship in detail rather than trying to establish a mechanistic test or series of tests.[26] In other words, the factors of control, chance of profit, risk of loss, and ownership of equipment do not constitute an exhaustive list, and there is no set formula as to their application. The relative weight of each will depend on the particular facts and circumstances of the case.[27]

[¶2055] Board, Lodging and Other Employment Benefits

There is to be included in the income of a taxpayer for a taxation year from an office or employment the *value* of board, lodging, and other benefits of any kind whatsoever, received or enjoyed by the taxpayer in the year in respect of, in the course of, or by virtue of an office or employment.[28]

Considering that "any kind" of economic advantage arising from a taxpayer's employer which renders his office of greater value to him requires income inclusion, the Tax Court of Canada has upheld Revenue Canada's assessment as a taxable benefit of a Christmas party at which the taxpayer and his guests were put up overnight at the Westin Hotel in Ottawa. The taxpayer was assessed a benefit of $200 for the party and another $100 for room charges.[29] This case attracted so much attention that Revenue Canada had to clarify that it will accept as a non-taxable privilege an employer-provided party if the cost per employee is reasonable in the circumstance. As a guideline, those events costing up to $100 per person will be considered to be non-taxable. Parties costing more than that will generally be considered to be beyond the "privilege" point and may result in taxable benefits.

Amounts included in income as board and lodging or other benefits include:

(a) the value of board and lodging;

(b) rent-free and low-rent housing;

(c) travel benefits;

(d) gifts (including Christmas gifts);

(e) holiday trips;

(f) prizes and incentive awards;

(g) frequent-flyer programs;

See page ii for explanation of footnotes.

[26] Wiebe Door Services Ltd., 87 DTC 5025, Grimard, 2009 DTC 5056, O'Hara, 2009 DTC 1011.

[27] TBT Personnel Services Inc., 2011 UDTC 128, Integranuity Marketing Ltd., 2012 UDTC 1.

[28] CCH ¶2305; Sec. 6(1)(a); Interp. Bul. IT-470R.

[29] Dunlap, 98 DTC 2053.

(h) travelling expenses of employees' spouses or common-law partners;

(i) employee premiums under provincial hospitalization and medical care insurance plans;

(j) tuition fees;

(k) reimbursement for cost of tools;

(l) wage-loss replacement plans;

(m) interest-free and low-interest loans; and

(n) financial counselling and income tax return preparation.

Amounts not included in income are: discounts on merchandise and discount commissions on sales, subsidized meals where employees pay a reasonable amount, uniforms and special clothing, certain subsidized school services in remote areas, transportation to a job, recreational facilities, removal expenses, premiums under private health service plans, employer contribution under provincial hospitalization and medical care plans, transportation passes, certain reimbursed expenses of public office holders, certain employee counselling services, and professional membership fees if the employer is the primary beneficiary.[30]

An exception to the inclusion of employer-paid tuition fees in income will be made where the course was primarily undertaken for the benefit of the employer rather than the employee.

Where an employer provides transportation to and from work, including parking, for employees who are blind or have severe and prolonged mobility impairment, such benefits are not included in income.[31]

The employer's contributions to the *Canada Pension Plan* do not constitute a taxable benefit to the employee. However, should the employer also pay the employee's contribution on the employee's behalf, the amount of the contribution would be considered a taxable benefit.

U.S. social security benefits are included in income for Canadian tax purposes, and payment of social security taxes by an employer is a taxable benefit to the employee.

Where an employer provides financial counselling by outside firms to an employee, and pays the fees, the amount of the fees is a taxable benefit to the employee. The fees are deductible from the employer's income.[32] However, financial counselling services in respect of the re-employment or the retirement of an employee will not result in a taxable benefit to the employee. Similarly, employer-provided counselling services in respect of the mental or physical health of the taxpayer or a person related to the taxpayer

---

See page ii for explanation of footnotes.

[30] Interp. Bul. IT-470R.
[31] CCH ¶2694; Sec. 6(16).

[32] Interp. Bul. IT-470R.

on the re- employment or retirement of the taxpayer will not be included in the employee's income.[33]

In calculating the benefit to be included in income, that cost is determined to be inclusive of the Goods and Services Tax (GST).[34]

The benefit relating to the operation of an employer-provided automobile is a taxable benefit;[35] see ¶2085.

In relation to tuition fees, it was determined that reimbursement of tuition fees for the instruction of the taxpayer's children paid for by the employer should not be included in the taxpayer's income. The reimbursement did not enhance the taxpayer's net worth but merely put him in the same position as if he had not been compelled by the nature of his employment to send his children to a private school.[36]

[¶2057] Administrative Exclusion of Employment Benefits

The following benefits, which would normally be included in an employee's income, are excluded under the CRA's administrative policies released June 11, 2009:

- *Overtime Meals*: Employees being reimbursed for the cost of their meals if they work overtime do not have to include such a reimbursement in their employment income as a tax benefit if they work two or more hours of overtime right before or after their regular work hours, if the value of their meal does not exceed $17, and if the overtime is infrequent or occasional. Overtime less than three times a week is considered infrequent or occasional, but more than twice a week in certain peak periods could also meet the third condition. This policy is effective for 2009.

- *Loyalty Programs*: Employees using a personal credit card for business expenses do not have to include the loyalty points collected in respect of those expenses in their employment income as a tax benefit, provided the points are not converted to cash, and the plan is neither indicative of an alternate form of remuneration nor undertaken for tax avoidance purposes. This policy is effective for 2009.

- *Non-Cash Gifts and Awards*: An employee may receive any number of non-cash gifts and awards from an arm's length employer without having to include them in his or her income provided their annual total value does not exceed $500; any gift or award in excess of this $500 limit would be taxable. The employee may receive a separate non-cash, long-service or anniversary award of up to $500 in addition to the non-cash gifts and awards; any long-service or anniversary award in excess of this $500 limit would be taxable. Immaterial

---

See page ii for explanation of footnotes.

[33] CCH ¶2301; Sec. 6(1)(a).
[34] CCH ¶2630; Sec. 6(7).
[35] CCH ¶2305; Sec. 6(1)(a).
[36] Guay, 97 DTC 5267.

items like coffee mugs or t-shirts with the employer's logo are not taxable and excluded from this calculation. Note that performance-related or cash/near-cash awards are fully taxable and excluded from this calculation. This policy is effective for 2010. Prior to 2010, employees may exclude from their employment income two non-cash gifts costing $500 or less to the employer and two non-cash awards also costing $500 or less to the employer for a total annual exclusion of $1,000. However, there is no special exclusion in respect of long-service or anniversary awards.

- *Surface Transit Passes*: Free or discounted passes provided to employees of bus, streetcar, subway, commuter train, and ferry services for their exclusive use are not taxable to them but those provided to members of their families are considered a tax benefit to be included in their incomes. Passes for municipal employees not working in the transit area are also taxable. This policy is effective in 2010. Prior to 2010, employees are not taxed in respect of passes used by their families.

For more details on these four policies, see *Income Tax Technical News* No. 40 on the CRA's website at www.cra.gc.ca.

[¶2060] Housing Loss Reimbursements and Other Employer-Provided Housing Subsidies

Any amount paid in respect of a housing loss (other than an eligible housing loss) to or on behalf of a taxpayer in respect of, in the course of, or because of an office or employment is deemed to be an employment benefit and is fully included in the taxpayer's income.[37] An eligible housing loss means a loss incurred on the disposition of a house in respect of an eligible relocation.[38] Generally, an "eligible relocation" means a relocation enabling the taxpayer to be employed at a location in Canada or to be a full-time student at a location of a post-secondary institution if: (i) both the taxpayer's old residence and new residence are in Canada, and (ii) the distance between the old residence and the new work location is not less than 40 kilometres greater than the distance between the new residence and the new work location.[39] Generally, only $\frac{1}{2}$ of the amount in excess of $15,000 of employer-paid amounts in respect of eligible housing losses is treated as an employment benefit received by the taxpayer.[40] When the taxpayer's employment was terminated, he moved back to Ottawa and his employer purchased the house that he had built. The purchase price was the cost of construction, but was $91,870 above fair market value. The recouped loss of $91,870 was included in his income. It did not involve an "eligible relocation" to the extent that it resulted from the termination of his employment and did not occur to enable him to carry on business in Ottawa.[41]

See page ii for explanation of footnotes.

[37] CCH ¶2697a; Sec. 6(19).
[38] CCH ¶2697d; Sec. 6(22).
[39] CCH ¶28,080; Sec. 248(1) "eligible relocation".

[40] CCH ¶2697b; Sec. 6(20).

[41] Thomas, 2007 DTC 5151.

An eligible housing loss need not be crystallized to be reimbursed. One may choose any particular time to determine the amount of the taxpayer's housing loss. A housing loss at any particular time in respect of a residence of a taxpayer is calculated as the amount by which the greater of:

(a) the adjusted cost base of the residence at that time to the taxpayer or to another person who does not deal at arm's length with the taxpayer; and

(b) the highest fair market value of the residence within the six-month period that ends at that time

exceeds:

(c) if the residence is disposed of by the taxpayer or the other person before the end of the first taxation year that begins after that time, the lesser of:

(i) the proceeds of disposition of the residence, and

(ii) the fair market value of the residence at that time, and

(d) in any other case, the fair market value of the residence at that time.[42]

In its technical notes, the Department of Finance provided the following example (which we have updated):

Example:

Paul purchases a home in 2006 in his hometown for $400,000 and begins work at a national corporation. In 2008, the land bordering Paul's home is rezoned to permit the development of an industrial park. In January 2012, Paul is offered a promotion on the condition that he relocates to a new community (11,000 kilometres from his hometown) by March 1, 2012. Paul has trouble selling his home because of the heavy industry that now surrounds the property; however, he eventually accepts an offer of $335,000 and completes the sale in August 2012. Paul's eligible housing loss therefore amounts to $65,000. His employer agrees to compensate Paul for any eligible housing loss he incurs on the sale of his property. Because of the size of the loss, the employer pays out the compensation in two payments: $30,000 in September 2012 and $35,000 in February 2013. Paul's taxable benefit in 2012 is $7,500 (one-half of the amount paid in 2012 that is more than $15,000). In 2013, Paul's taxable benefit is $17,500, calculated as follows:

- one half of the total amounts paid in 2012 and 2013 that is more than $15,000 ($1/_2$ × [$65,000 - $15,000] = $25,000);

minus

- the amount included in income in 2012 ($7,500).

For greater certainty, any amount paid or the value of assistance provided by any person in respect of, in the course of, or because of an individual's office or employment in respect of the cost of, the financing of, the use of, or the right to use a residence is a taxable benefit received by the individual.[43] This provision includes virtually any employer-provided subsi-

[42] CCH ¶2697c; Sec. 6(21).   [43] CCH ¶2697e; Sec. 6(23).

dy made to the employee to enable the employee to acquire or to use a residence, including interest subsidies on a mortgage, rent subsidies, payments on account of the purchase price of the home, and mortgage principal reimbursements.

[¶2065] Health and Welfare Trusts for Employees

Health and welfare benefits for employees are sometimes provided through a trust arrangement under which the trustees, usually with equal representation from the employer (or employers' group) and the employees (or their union), receive the contributions from the employer or employers' group to provide such health and welfare benefits as have been agreed to between the employer and the employees (or their union).

If the benefit programs adopted are limited to a group sickness or accident insurance plan, a private health services plan, a group term life insurance policy, or any combination thereof, and the arrangements meet certain conditions, the trust arrangement qualifies as a health and welfare trust.[44]

An employee does not receive or enjoy a benefit at the time the employer makes a contribution to a health and welfare trust. However, effective March 29, 2012, employer-paid contributions to a group sickness and accident insurance plan for an employee's coverage after 2012 will be taxable to the employee to the extent that such contributions are not in respect of a wage loss replacement benefit payable on a periodic basis. See discussion at ¶2100.

[¶2070] Allowances — Personal or Living Expenses of Employees

Personal and living expenses are intended to be borne by the taxpayer. Therefore, where an employee receives an allowance for personal or living expenses, it is included in the taxpayer's income.[45] Personal or living expenses[46] include:

(a) the expenses of properties maintained by any person for the use or benefit of a taxpayer or any person connected with the taxpayer by blood relationship, marriage or common-law partnership, or adoption, but does not include properties maintained in connection with a business carried on for profit or with a reasonable expectation of profit;

(b) expenses, premiums, or other costs of a policy of insurance, annuity or similar contract, if the proceeds of the policy or contract are payable to or for the benefit of the taxpayer or a person connected with the taxpayer by blood relationship, marriage or common-law partnership, or adoption; and

---

See page ii for explanation of footnotes.

[44] Interp. Bul. IT-85R2.
[45] CCH ¶2322; Sec. 6(1)(*b*).
[46] CCH ¶28,199; Sec. 248(1) "personal or living expenses".

(c) expenses of properties maintained by an estate or trust for the benefit of the taxpayer as one of the beneficiaries.

The Act excepts the following from the rule concerning the taxability of amounts received for personal or living expenses:

(a) travelling, personal, or living expense allowances expressly fixed in an Act of the Parliament of Canada or pursuant to the *Inquiries Act* (e.g., expense allowances paid to members of the House of Commons and Senate);

(b) special allowances for absence from Canada given to diplomatic representatives of Canada or members of the armed forces or of the overseas Canadian Forces school staff, or given under an international development assistance program;

(c) travelling and separation allowances paid to members of the armed forces under service regulations;

(d) representation or other special allowances received by an agent-general of a province for the period that he or she was in Ottawa as the agent-general of the province;

(e) travelling expenses received by an employee in connection with the selling of property or negotiating of contracts for the employer;

(f) reasonable allowances for travelling expenses (other than allowances for the use of a motor vehicle) received by an employee for travelling away from the municipality and metropolitan area where the employer's establishment at which the employee ordinarily worked was located, in the performance of the duties of the office or employment;

(g) reasonable allowances for the use of a motor vehicle received by an employee (other than an employee employed in connection with the selling of property or the negotiating of contracts for the employer) from the employer for travelling in the performance of the duties of the office or employment. For 2012, the general rate used to determine the benefit from the personal portion of operating expenses paid by employers in respect of automobiles provided to employees is increased from 24 cents to 26 cents per kilometre. In the case of taxpayers principally employed in the selling or leasing of automobiles, the prescribed rate is increased from 21 cents to 23 cents per kilometre driven for personal use;

(h) reasonable allowances received by ministers or members of the clergy for transportation expenses incidental to their ministerial duties; and

(i) allowances paid by an employer for the education of an employee's child where the employee is required to live in a specific location by

¶2070

reason of his or her employment, and instruction in the official language of the employee is not available in that area. For the exemption to apply, the following must be true:

(i) the allowance must be reasonable,

(ii) the child must not live with the employee in the area where the employee works,

(iii) the child must be in full-time attendance at a school which is in a community not farther from the employee's home than the nearest community having suitable boarding facilities and providing instruction in the appropriate language,

(iv) the language of instruction primarily used in the school must be the official language of Canada which the employee uses, and

(v) such a school must not be available in the location where the employee is required to live.

An emergency service volunteer shall not include the first $1,000 of amounts received in a year from a government, municipality, or public authority for the performance of the volunteer services.[47] The provision applies to persons who volunteer their duties as ambulance technicians, firefighters, or in the search or rescue of individuals or in other emergency situations. Note that the $1,000 exclusion from income does not apply to remuneration received for emergency services carried on by a person in their capacity as an actual employee. In this regard, if requested by the Minister, the payer of the amount must certify that the recipient was at no time in the relevant year employed or otherwise engaged in connection with the services, other than as a volunteer.

Note that reasonable allowances in respect of travelling expenses and motor vehicle expenses will be excluded in computing the income of an individual from an office or employment.[48] Accordingly, allowances that are not reasonable may be included in income and the taxpayer will be entitled to a deduction with respect to those travelling expenses. (For allowances received in connection with the business use of automobiles, see ¶2085.) Where the taxpayer received an automobile allowance that he considered to be unreasonably low, he included the allowance in income and deducted the actual expenses. However, the deduction was denied where the taxpayer failed to show specific evidence as to whether the allowance was intended as a full reimbursement for the use of the automobile.[49]

Travelling allowances are different from reimbursement for out-of-pocket expenses which are proved by vouchers and which do not have to be included in income. For example, a member of an office staff who uses his

---

See page ii for explanation of footnotes.

[47] CCH ¶9982; Sec. 81(4).
[48] CCH ¶2322; Sec. 6(1)(b).

[49] Lemire, 94 DTC 1772.

or her own automobile on an errand for the company and is then reimbursed for this is not required to show the amount of the reimbursement as income. See also ¶2325 and ¶2335.

[¶2075] Director's or Other Fees

Where a director's fee is paid in addition to a salary from the same employer, the fee will be added to the salary for the pay period and the required tax deduction will then be completed in accordance with tax deduction tables.

Where the fee is the only remuneration paid by the employer, and it is estimated that such fees will not exceed the director's personal exemptions, no tax need be deducted at source.

Where the director's fee is the only remuneration paid by the employer, but it is estimated that the fee will exceed the personal exemptions, the tax deductions should be made in accordance with the monthly tax deduction table by converting the fee to its monthly equivalent.

The word "fee" is not defined in the Act. Presumably it will be interpreted in accordance with its ordinary meaning to include fees received by professional persons, musicians, etc.

[¶2080] Allocations, etc. under Profit Sharing Plan

Amounts allocated to an employee in the year by a trustee of an employee's profit sharing plan are included in the employee's income.[50] This includes the allocation of capital gains and losses. See also ¶10,294.

[¶2085] Automobile Benefits

The benefit an employee enjoys as a result of the employer paying operating expenses is required to be included in income.[51] The value of the benefit is an amount equal to the portion of the operating costs paid by the employer that relates to the personal use plus a "reasonable standby charge", plus the equivalent to the GST thereon. In general, this standby charge is 2% per month of the cost of the automobile to the employer, or ⅔ of the lease costs if leased, for the number of days the automobile was available to the employee or to a person related to an employee.[52]

Where an automobile is supplied by an employer (or a person related to the employer)[53] to an employee (or a person related to the employee), there are two methods for computing the operating cost benefit.

(1) The benefit is computed at a prescribed rate of 26 cents (up from 24 cents for 2009–2011) for each kilometre of personal use during the period for which the automobile was made available. The general prescribed

---

See page ii for explanation of footnotes.

[50] CCH ¶2350; Sec. 6(1)(d).   [52] Interp. Bul. IT-63R5.
[51] CCH ¶2301; Sec. 6(1)(a).   [53] CCH ¶2392a, ¶2392b; Sec. 6(1)(k), 6(1)(l).

rate is reduced to 23 cents per kilometre (up from 21 cents for 2009–2011) for taxpayers employed principally in selling or leasing automobiles.

(2) The second method is only available to employees who use the automobile in respect of which the standby charge is incurred primarily (i.e., more than 50%) in the performance of duties of employment. If this test is met, the operating costs benefit may be calculated as simply $\frac{1}{2}$ of the standby charge for the year (see below). To use this method, the employee must notify the employer in writing before the end of the year.

In both cases, the operating costs benefit will be reduced by all amounts repaid by the employee or a relative of the employer within 45 days of the end of the calendar year to which the costs relate. The resulting income inclusion is considered to include the GST component and no further inclusion is required. Any benefit related to parking is not considered to be a benefit in respect of the use (including the operation) of an automobile.[54] See item (g) at ¶2070 for a discussion of reasonable allowances paid by an employer for the use of an automobile by an employee.

The reasonable standby charge[55] is determined by the following formula:

$$\frac{A}{B} \times [2\% \times (C \times D) + \tfrac{2}{3} \times (E - F)]$$

Where:

A is the lesser of:

  (a) total personal-use kilometres driven during the total available days; and

  (b) the value determined for B (see below) during the total available days if the taxpayer is required by the employer to use the automobile for business purposes and the distance travelled is primarily (i.e., more than 50%) for business purposes.

B is 1,667 kilometres × $\frac{[ix](\text{total available days})^*}{30}$

C is the cost to the employer of the automobile.

D is $\frac{[ix]\text{days the employer owns the automobile}^*}{30}$

E is leasing costs payable by the employer.

F is the portion of the leasing costs relating to insurance against loss, damage, or liability resulting from use of the automobile.

---

* after rounding

See page ii for explanation of footnotes.

[54] CCH ¶2392c; Sec. 6(1.1).   [55] CCH ¶2400; Sec. 6(2).

The standby charge may be reduced proportionally for its business use if the automobile is driven for personal reasons for less than 1,667 kilometres per month, or 20,004 kilometres per year, and the driving is done primarily (more than 50%) for business reasons. For example, an employee driving 25,000 kilometres for business purposes and 15,000 kilometres for personal purposes in 2012 will be allowed to include only 75% (15,000 personal kilometres/20,000 kilometres upper limit) of the standby charge in his or her income.

Note that no standby charge is calculated for any period during which the employee leaves the car keys with the employer or for any vehicle excluded from the definition of "automobile". All employees provided with an automobile by their employer should keep good records of their business and personal driving to be able to document the optional calculation of their standby charge.

The application of the optional method of reducing the standby charge would cause a hardship for employees who have a number of automobiles available for their personal use from a pool which their employer owns. In such cases, the employer and employee may agree to use an "average cost automobile" to determine the reasonable standby charge.

An employee who is employed principally in selling or leasing automobiles may either compute the standby charge in the manner provided for other employees, or the amount of the minimum reasonable standby charge may be calculated in the same manner as above, except that the reference to 2% is replaced by 1.5%.[56] The capital cost of the automobile to the employer will be calculated by determining the total cost of all new automobiles acquired by the employer for sale during the year and dividing this by the number of such automobiles. Employees employed principally in leasing automobiles may also use the optional method of calculating the standby charge. Unrestricted use of an employer's automobile by the taxpayer is not a prerequisite to the application of the automobile standby provisions. The standby charges will be included in a taxpayer's income even in situations where the taxpayer has paid what would otherwise be considered a fair price for his or her use of an employer's automobile.[57]

See also ¶4120 regarding capital cost allowance for automobiles.

The following example illustrates the calculation of the operating cost benefit and the standby charge in the case of an employer-leased automobile for 2012:

See page ii for explanation of footnotes.

[56] CCH ¶2420; Sec. 6(2.1).   [57] Adams, 98 DTC 6266, Boucher, 2008 DTC 4475, Martin et al., 2009 DTC 1037.

Facts

    Lease cost — $600 per month including GST, PST, or HST, but excluding insurance

    Operating cost for the year: $6,200; excluding parking costs

    Car available to employee for 12 months of the year

    Reimbursements to employer: Operating costs: NIL;
                         Availability: $500

Calculation of Taxable Benefits:

Total kilometres driven		50,000
Percentage of personal use		30%
Personal kilometres (P)		15,000
(a)	Standby charge benefit	
	Reasonable standby charge:	
	$600 × $^2/_3$ × 12 months × (15,000/20,000)	$ 3,600
	Less: Reimbursement	(500)
	Net benefit	$ 3,100
(b)	Operating cost benefit	
	(i) Using optional method	
	$^1/_2$ standby charge	$ 1,800
	OR	
	(ii) Using general method	
	26¢ × personal kilometre	$ 3,900
	Optimal benefit	$ 1,800
	Less: Reimbursement	Nil
	Net operating benefit	$ 1,800
	Total taxable benefit to be included in employee's income	$ 4,900

    The following example illustrates the calculation of the operating cost benefit and the standby charge for 2012 in the case of an employer-owned automobile:

Facts

    Capital cost of automobile — $32,000 including GST, PST, or HST

    Operating cost for the year: $4,600; excluding parking costs

    Car available to employee for 12 months of the year

    Reimbursements to employer: Operating costs: $120;
                         Availability: $500

Calculation of Taxable Benefits

Total kilometres driven	40,000
Percentage of personal use	25%
Personal-use kilometres (P)	10,000

(a)	Standby charge benefit	
	Reasonable standby charge:	
	12 × $32,000 × 2% × 10,000/20,000	$ 3,840
	Less: Reimbursement	(500)
	Net benefit	$ 3,340
(b)	Operating cost benefit	
(i)	Using optional method	
	$1/2$ of standby charge	$ 1,920
OR		
(ii)	Using general method	
	26¢ × personal kilometres	$ 2,600
	Optimal benefit...	$ 1,920
	Less: Reimbursement...	120
	Net operating benefit	$ 1,800
	Total taxable benefit to be included in employee's income	$ 5,140

[¶2090] Employee's Use of Aircraft

The benefit derived by an employee who is not a shareholder from personal use of an aircraft maintained by his or her employer is included in computing the employee's income from employment. The value of the benefit is the cost to the employee if he or she had chartered a comparable aircraft at the current commercial rate for the time of personal use.

In determining the equivalent charter cost, any flat fee plus all other related costs that would normally be incurred must be included. Generally, the employer may deduct reasonable costs incurred in providing such transportation to the employee.

[¶2095] Employee Insurance Benefits

Payments out of certain employee benefit plans are treated as employment income when received by the employee if the employer has contributed to the plan.[58] The relevant amount must be "payable on a periodic basis" in respect of the employee's loss of any income from an office or employment, and be "pursuant to" a sickness or accident insurance plan, a disability insurance plan, an income maintenance insurance plan, or (after 2009) any of these plans administered by an employee life and health trust (an ELHT).

Where the employee has made contributions to the plan, the amount of the receipts out of the plan included in income are reduced by the amount of the employee's contributions not previously deducted in a prior

---

See page ii for explanation of footnotes.

[58] CCH ¶2370, ¶29,145; Sec. 6(1)(*f*); ITAR 19; Interp. Bul. IT-428.

¶2090

year. A top-up disability payment by an employer or former employer because of the insolvency of an insurer is deemed not to be a contribution under a disability insurance plan.[59] Where the payments are merely reimbursement of, or payment of, medical costs incurred under the terms of the plan, the amount would not be taxable as employment income.

In determining whether a lump-sum settlement payment received in respect of a disputed claim under a disability insurance plan was received "pursuant" to the plan, the Supreme Court of Canada held that the portion of the lump-sum payment representing the taxpayer's future benefits was not made pursuant to the insurance plan, and therefore not included in income because there was no obligation to make such a lump-sum payment under the terms of the plan.[60] However, the portion of the lump-sum payment that was attributable to disability payments in arrears and accruing to the date of the settlement was taxable because it was meant to replace amounts payable pursuant to the plan (the *"surrogatum* principle").

Taking into account the *surrogatum* principle, the Federal Court of Appeal held that the portion of a lump-sum payment that was attributable to disability payments that were in arrears at the time of the settlement was taxable, whereas the portion attributable to future benefits that would have been otherwise paid under the plan was not taxable.[61]

Please note that effective March 29, 2012, employer-paid contributions to a group sickness and accident insurance plan for an employee's coverage after 2012 will be taxable to the employee to the extent that such contributions are not in respect of a wage loss replacement benefit payable on a periodic basis. See discussion at ¶2100.

[¶2100] Group Sickness and Accident Insurance Plans

Wage loss replacement benefits payable on a periodic basis under a group sickness and accident insurance plan to which an employer has contributed are included in an employee's income for tax purposes when those benefits are received (see discussion at ¶2095). However, no amount is included in an employee's income, either when the employer contributions are made or the benefits are received, to the extent that:

- benefits are not payable on a periodic basis; or

- benefits are payable in respect of a sickness or accident when there is no loss of employment income.

To address these two shortcomings, the 2012 Budget would include in income after March 28, 2012, employer-paid contributions to a group sickness and accident insurance plan for an employee's coverage after 2012 to

See page ii for explanation of footnotes.

[59] CCH ¶2696; Sec.6(18).
[60] Tsiaprailis, 2005 DTC 5119.
[61] Siftar, 2005 DTC 5119.

the extent that such contributions are not in respect of a wage loss replacement benefit payable on a periodic basis.[62]

This measure, not yet enacted, will apply to employer contributions after March 28, 2012 that are attributable to an employee's coverage after 2012, except that such contributions made after March 28, 2012 and before 2013 will be included in the employee's income for 2013. For contributions made after 2012, the income inclusion is required in the same year as the employer contributions are made.

[¶2105] Salary Deferral Arrangements

Where a person has deferred receipt of salary or wages to a subsequent year, an amount equal to the deferred amount will be considered to be an employment benefit.[63] The benefit must be included in computing the income of the employee for the year to the extent that the deferred amount has not otherwise been included in income.[64] If there is a right to receive interest or other additional amounts in addition to the deferred salary or wages that accrue during the year under a salary deferral arrangement, the additional amount is deemed to be a deferred amount and must also be included in income.[65]

An exception to these rules is provided with respect to salary deferral arrangements established primarily for the benefit of non-resident employees for services rendered outside Canada.[66]

[¶2110] Payments by Employer to Employee

Certain amounts paid by an employer to an officer or employee will be regarded as remuneration for services.[67] This prevents an officer or employee from excluding such payments from employment income by arranging to receive payment before or after employment. While the provision does not apply to damages for wrongful dismissal that are not paid under a contract, such damages will constitute a retiring allowance and be included in income. A lump sum of money received when an offer of employment was withdrawn was determined not to constitute income from employment.[68]

[¶2112] Restrictive Covenants

In response to two Federal Court of Appeal decisions[69] holding that some of the payments received in respect of restrictive covenants were not taxable, a series of proposed technical amendments, the last of which was released on July 16, 2010, would include such amounts in the recipient's income after April 7, 2003, subject to transitional rules. According to this inclusion rule and subject to many exceptions described below, a taxpayer

---

See page ii for explanation of footnotes.

[62] Sec. 6(1)(e.1).
[63] CCH ¶2680; Sec. 6(11).
[64] CCH ¶2301; Sec. 6(1)(a).
[65] CCH ¶2681; Sec. 6(12).

[66] CCH ¶2682; Sec. 6(13).
[67] CCH ¶2450; Sec. 6(3); Interp. Bul. IT-196R2.
[68] Schwartz, 96 DTC 6103.
[69] Fortino, 2000 DTC 6060, Manrell, 2003 DTC 5225.

must now include in income all amounts received or receivable in a taxation year in respect of a restrictive covenant ("RC") granted by him.[70] This new provision applies to amounts received or receivable by a taxpayer after October 7, 2003 (the first Announcement date), other than to amounts received before 2005, under a grant of a restrictive covenant made in writing on or before October 7, 2003, between the taxpayer and a person with whom the taxpayer deals at arm's length.

The definition of an RC is very broad and will apply to most forms of agreement not to compete. It can take the form of an arrangement between the parties, or an undertaking or a waiver of an advantage or right. It does not have to be enforceable to be subject to the proposed restrictive covenant rules.

There are three exceptions to the proposed general income inclusion rule and they only apply when the grantor of a restrictive covenant deals at arm's length with the person to whom the covenant is granted. These exceptions are:

(1) *Employment income* — The general inclusion rule does not apply if the amount is required to be included in the calculation of the grantor's employment income or would be so required if the amount had been received in the tax year.

(2) *Eligible capital property* — Sometimes an agreement to sell a business and its underlying assets includes a non-competition agreement by the seller (grantor). An amount received under a restrictive covenant that is the proceeds of disposition of eligible capital property (an eligible capital amount) is income under the general rule unless the grantor and buyer jointly elect, in prescribed form with their return of income for the tax year that includes the date of the covenant. In this case, the amount is an eligible capital expenditure to the buyer and an eligible capital amount to the grantor.

(3) *Shares and partnership interests* — In cases where the consideration for certain types of restrictive covenants directly relates to the grantor's disposition of an eligible interest and where five additional requirements are satisfied and the grantor and buyer elect in prescribed form. An eligible interest means capital property of the grantor that is a partnership interest in a partnership that carries on a business, or a share of the capital stock of a corporation that carries on a business. In these cases, part of the amount receivable for the covenant may be treated as part of the proceeds for the disposition of the eligible interest, to the extent that the covenant increases the FMV of the grantor's eligible interest. The remaining part of the amount receivable for the covenant (that is in excess of the part treated as proceeds of disposition of the eligible interest) will be taxable as ordinary income.[71]

See page ii for explanation of footnotes.

[70] Sec. 56.4(2).   [71] Sec. 56.4(3).

Futhermore, the July 16, 2010 revised technical proposals add a new exception to the extent that no consideration is deemed to be received or receivable by an individual who grants a restrictive covenant to an eligible person (an individual related to the vendor who is at least 18 years old) in the course of a sale of shares and no proceeds are received or receivable by the vendor for granting the covenant.[72]

Amounts related to covenants made in the context of an office or employment are generally included in income on a "received basis". In this regard, any amount receivable by an employee (that is not part of a salary deferral arrangement) in respect of an RC granted more than 36 months before the end of a particular year is deemed to have been received by that employee in the taxation year.[73]

At the time of writing, these rules, first announced on October 7, 2003 and revised many times since then, have not been enacted yet.

[¶2115] Premium for Group Term Life Insurance

An employee must include in income premiums paid by his or her employer under a group term life insurance policy of which the employee is insured.[74] The amount to be included is prescribed by regulations. In general terms, premiums paid in respect of the year are included in income in that year, with a special provision which includes the full amount of "lump-sum premiums", even though such premiums relate to periods in future years.

The amount of the taxable benefit is based on the full amount of insurance coverage. The average cost of insurance is determined separately for each group of employees or former employees for whom a separate premium rate is established under the policy. Sales tax in respect of premiums is expressly included as part of the taxable benefit.

[¶2120] Employment at Special Work Site or Remote Location

A taxpayer who is required to live at a special work site or remote location by virtue of his or her office or employment is not required to include in income the value of board, lodging, and transportation, or any allowance paid by the employer in respect thereof, if the following conditions are fulfilled:[75]

(1) The taxpayer must be employed at a special work site or remote location where duties of a temporary nature are performed.

(2) The employee must have a permanent residence at another location to which the employee could not reasonably be expected to return on a daily basis due to the distance between locations.

See page ii for explanation of footnotes.

[72] Sec. 56.4(8.1).
[73] Sec. 6(3.1).

[74] CCH ¶2500; Sec. 6(4).
[75] CCH ¶2600; Sec. 6(6).

(3) If the employee is not at a special work site, he or she must be at a location which is so remote from any established community that the employee would not reasonably be expected to establish and maintain a self-contained domestic establishment at that location.

(4) The board and lodging, the transportation, or the allowances therefore must have been received by the taxpayer in respect of a period of absence of not less than 36 hours from the taxpayer's ordinary place of residence.

(5) The amounts received for transportation, or an allowance for transportation, must be for travelling between:

(a) the employee's principal residence and the special work site; or

(b) the remote location and a location in Canada or a location in the country in which the employee is employed;

for the period during which the taxpayer received board and lodging benefits.

(6) The exemption will apply to the value of transportation, or an allowance therefor, only in respect of a period during which the taxpayer received from the employer board and lodging or a reasonable allowance.

(7) The allowance must not be in excess of a "reasonable amount". It is understood that transportation allowances should not be in excess of what is the fare for any acceptable and normal form of transportation.

A special deduction is available with respect to certain housing and travel benefits for employees living in the north and other prescribed areas.

[¶2130] Interest-Free, Low-Interest and Forgiven Loans

In certain circumstances an individual may have a benefit included in income by virtue of the fact that a person or partnership obtained an interest-free or low-interest loan or other indebtedness by virtue of a previous, current, or intended office or employment of the individual[76] (see ¶3117). In the case of an interest-free loan or below-market loan received by an employee because of or as a consequence of his employment or intended employment, a deemed benefit will normally arise and will be included in employment income to the extent that the prescribed rate of interest is not paid by the employee on the loan.[77] Essentially, the benefit is measured as the difference between the amount of interest for the year that would be payable on the indebtedness if interest thereon was calculated at the prescribed rates (see ¶475) in effect from time to time during the year, and the amount of interest actually paid by the taxpayer in the year or within 30 days after the end of the year. In response to a decision of the Federal Court of

---

[76] CCH ¶9896; Sec. 80.4; Interp. Bul. IT-421R2.   [77] CCH ¶2660; Sec. 6(9).

Appeal[78] that an employer-provided housing loan was received by the employee for the purpose of purchasing the new home and not because of or as a consequence of the employee's employment, a deemed interest benefit provision was added after February 23, 1998. After that date, a loan is deemed to have been received because of or as a consequence of the employee's employment if it is reasonable to conclude that, but for an individual's previous, current, or intended office or employment, the terms of the loan would have been different or the loan would not have been received.[79] Note that the deemed interest benefit on up to $25,000 of the principal amount of a "home relocation loan" is exempt from tax for up to five years (a deduction is allowed to offset the inclusion of such amount). See ¶3120.

[¶2135] Employee Stock Option Plans

As a general rule, when a corporation agrees to sell or issue its shares to an employee, or when a mutual fund trust grants options to an employee to acquire trust units, the employee is taxed in the year in which the employee exercises the option and acquires the shares or units. The taxable benefit is deemed to be the difference between the fair market value of the shares or units when the employee acquired them and the amount paid, or to be paid, for them, including any amount paid for the rights to acquire the shares or units. Also, a benefit can accrue to the employee if his or her rights under the agreement become vested in another person, or if he or she transfers or sells the rights. The amount of the deemed employment benefit is added to the adjusted cost base of the share or unit when it is acquired.[80]

There are two exceptions to the above general rule, both of which defer the recognition of the deemed benefit until the employee disposes of the shares or mutual fund units acquired under the option.[81] These two exceptions apply to (i) options on publicly traded shares and units exercised before 4 p.m. on March 4, 2010; and (ii) options on shares of Canadian-controlled private corporations (CCPCs).

The deferral in respect of publicly traded shares and mutual fund units in (i) above was elective, at the employee's option. This particular deferral is repealed for options exercised after 4:00 p.m. EST on March 4, 2010. For such options, the regular timing rule will apply such that the recognition of the deemed benefit will take place in the year of acquisition of the shares or units.

As a transition, an individual who has elected to have the deferral for publicly traded shares and mutual fund units apply before 4 p.m. on March 4, 2010 may file an election if he or she disposes of the shares or units before 2015. This election will have the effect of replacing the otherwise deemed taxable benefit with a capital gain equal to the lesser of such

[78] Siwik, 97 DTC 5444.
[79] CCH ¶9896a; Sec. 80.4(1.1).
[80] CCH ¶2700; Sec. 7(1); Interp. Bul. IT-113R4.
[81] CCH ¶2702; Sec. 7(1.1).

benefit and the capital loss otherwise incurred on the disposition of the shares or mutual fund units. For the year of disposition, the taxpayer is subject to tax equal to the proceeds of disposition ($^2/_3$ in Quebec).

In many cases, the inclusion in income of the deemed employment benefit will be offset by a 50% deduction. For this 50% deduction to be allowed in respect of shares in CCPCs, the shares must be held for at least two years.[82] In this respect, shares that are identical properties but which are acquired at different times are deemed to have been disposed of in the order in which the taxpayers acquired them for purposes of determining whether the two-year holding period has been satisfied.[83] The effect of the 50% deduction is to tax stock option benefits at the same rate as capital gains.

Where the employee does not acquire the underlying securities, a deemed benefit may also arise in certain circumstances. A deemed benefit will arise if the employee transfers or otherwise disposes of the option, or if the option has been transferred by one or more transactions between persons not dealing at arm's length and a transferee has either acquired securities under the option or has transferred or disposed of the option to a person with whom the transferee was dealing at arm's length. Furthermore, if the employee dies while holding an unexercised option, the employee will be deemed to have received a benefit equal to the amount by which the value of the right immediately after the employee's death exceeds the amount that the employee paid to acquire the right (if any).

Before 4 p.m. on March 4, 2010, the above deemed benefit arising where an employee did not acquire the underlying securities could qualify for the 50% deduction in computing income. However, after 4 p.m. on March 4, 2010, the one-half deduction is not allowed unless the employee or a person not dealing at arm's length with the employee actually acquires the securities, such that employees receiving employer "cash-outs" of options are not eligible for the deduction. An exception where the deduction is still allowed is provided if the employer elects that it and any non-arm's length person will not deduct any amount in respect of a payment made to or for the benefit of the employee for the employee's transfer or disposition of the option (other than a "designated amount", which is generally a payment made to an arm's length person for the purpose of managing the qualifying person's financial risk in respect of the option agreement), the employer provides the employee with evidence in writing of such election, and the employee files such evidence with his or her return of income for the year in which the stock option deduction is claimed.[84]

If a security is acquired by a trustee for an employee either absolutely, conditionally, or contingently, the employee will be deemed to have acquired the security at the time the trustee commenced to hold it for the

---

See page ii for explanation of footnotes.

[82] CCH ¶15,015, ¶15,272; Sec. 110(1)(*d*), 110(1)(*d*.1).

[83] CCH ¶2706; Sec. 7(1.3).

[84] CCH ¶15,311a; Sec. 110(1.1).

employee and to have disposed of the security at the time the trust disposed of the security to a third party.[85]

If a person ceases to be an employee before the transaction is completed, that person is nevertheless treated as an employee until the transaction is completed and will be deemed to have received a benefit as though still an employee.[86] Thus, a former employee can be subject to the deemed benefit rules if the option was granted during the period of employment.

A corporation or mutual fund trust is not allowed to deduct the benefits included in any person's income. In other words, unlike most other forms of remuneration, stock option benefits are not deductible for the employer or issuing entity.[87]

[¶2140] Exchanges of Options or Shares

Special rules provide a tax-deferred "rollover" for certain qualifying exchanges where an employee's option to acquire securities of a particular qualifying person (old option) is exchanged for a different option to acquire securities of a "designated person" (new option).[88] A designated person includes the particular qualifying person, another qualifying person who does not deal at arm's length with the particular qualifying person, a corporation formed on an amalgamation of the particular qualifying person with another corporation, or a qualifying person with which the above-mentioned amalgamated corporation does not deal at arm's length immediately after the exchange. A designated person also includes a mutual fund trust to which the particular qualifying person has transferred property under the mutual trust reorganization rules (see ¶9131).

For exchanges or dispositions after December 19, 2007, and before 2013, a designated person also includes a "SIFT wind-up corporation" in respect of a "SIFT wind-up entity" if the old securities were equity in the SIFT wind-up entity that was a mutual fund trust. Effectively, this means that a qualifying exchange will occur where an old option in respect of old securities in a SIFT trust that is a mutual fund trust (commonly known as an income trust) is exchanged for a new option in respect of new securities in a corporation in the course of the reorganization of the trust into the corporate form.

For the above rollover to apply, the employee must receive no consideration for the old option other than the new option, and the fair market value of the new securities immediately after the exchange in excess of the old option exercise price must not exceed the fair market value of the old securities immediately before the exchange in excess of the new option exercise price. If these conditions are met, the employee is deemed not to have disposed of the old option, the new option is deemed to be the same as

---

See page ii for explanation of footnotes.

[85] CCH ¶2710; Sec. 7(2).

[86] CCH ¶2720; Sec. 7(4).

[87] CCH ¶2715; Sec. 7(3).

[88] CCH ¶2707; Sec. 7(1.4).

the old option, and the issuer of the new option is deemed to be the same person as, and a continuation of, the particular qualifying person. As a result, the exchange will not itself give rise to a deemed taxable benefit.

A similar rollover applies where an employee, typically in the course of a corporate reorganization or upon an amalgamation, disposes of or exchanges a security (old security) that was acquired under an employee stock option agreement in exchange for another security (new security).[89] For this rollover to apply, the employee must receive no consideration for the old securities other than new securities of either the same qualifying person or a non-arm's length qualifying person, a corporation formed on the amalgamation of the qualifying person and another corporation, a qualifying person that does not deal at arm's length with such amalgamated corporation immediately after the exchange, or a mutual fund trust to which the particular qualifying person has transferred property under the mutual trust reorganization rules (see ¶9131).

If the above conditions are met, the employee is deemed not to have disposed of the old securities, the new securities are deemed to be the same as and a continuation of the old securities, and the qualifying person that issued the new securities is deemed to be the same person and a continuation of the qualifying person that issued the old securities. Therefore, the deferral of the employment benefit associated with the old securities will not be affected by the exchange. The employee will not lose eligibility for the one-half deduction simply because of the disposition or exchange. Furthermore, if the share is a CCPC share, the employee will be entitled to the one-half deduction from the benefit associated with the old securities, as long as the total holding period for the old and the new securities is two years or more.

[¶2145] Other Sources of Income

[¶2150] Pension Benefits, etc.

Amounts received by the taxpayer in the year on account of "superannuation or pension benefits" (other than amounts received out of or under an employee benefit plan; see ¶10,474) are included in income. This expression is defined to include any amount received out of or under a superannuation or pension fund or plan, including payments to a beneficiary, or to an employer or former employer, in accordance with the terms of the fund or plan or resulting from amendment to, modification of, or termination of the fund or plan.[90] These superannuation or pension benefits specifically include:

See page ii for explanation of footnotes.

[89] CCH ¶2708; Sec. 7(1.5).

[90] CCH ¶8005, ¶28,275; Sec. 56(1)(a), 248(1) "superannuation or pension benefit"; Interp. Bul. IT-499R.

(a) a pension, supplement, or spouse's allowance under the *Old Age Security Act* and similar payments under provincial law;

(b) benefits received under the *Canada Pension Plan* or similar provincial pension plans; and

(c) benefits received, in certain circumstances, out of a foreign retirement arrangement.

It is immaterial whether the fund or plan was funded by contributions which were deductible for Canadian tax purposes. Any CPP/QPP death benefit received upon the death of an individual will be included in the income of the estate rather than in the income of the deceased individual.

[¶2155] U.S. Social Security Payments

Starting in 2010, taxpayers and their surviving spouses or common-law partners receiving U.S. social security benefits may claim a deduction equal to 35% of those benefits provided they meet the following conditions:

(1) they have been resident in Canada continuously in the period beginning before 1996 and ending in the current taxation year; and

(2) they have received those benefits in each taxation year ending in the period.[91]

To qualify for the 35% deduction, the benefits must be subject to the application of Article XVIII(5) of the *Canada–U.S. Tax Convention*.[92]

[¶2160] Retiring Allowances

Amounts received by a taxpayer in the year as, on account of, in lieu of payment of, or in satisfaction of a "retiring allowance" (other than amounts received out of or under an employee benefit plan; see ¶10,474) are included in income.[93]

"Retiring allowance" means an amount received:

(1) on or after retirement of a taxpayer from an office or employment in recognition of the taxpayer's long service; or

(2) in respect of a loss of office or employment of a taxpayer, whether or not received as, on account or in lieu of payment of, damages or pursuant to an order or judgment of a competent tribunal,

by the taxpayer or, after the taxpayer's death, by a dependant or a relation of the taxpayer or by the legal representative of the taxpayer.[94]

See page ii for explanation of footnotes.

[91] CCH ¶15,295; Sec. 110(1)(h).
[92] Fourth Protocol amending the Canada–U.S. Income Tax Convention, 1984; 30,229cx, Canada–U.S. Income Tax Convention.
[93] CCH ¶8017; Sec. 56(1)(a); Adler, 94 DTC 6605.
[94] CCH ¶28,253; Sec. 248(1) "retiring allowance".

The words " long service" in (1) refer to the total number of years in an employee's career with a particular employer or with affiliated employers. A payment for unused sick leave credits qualifies as a retiring allowance.[95] As to the words "in respect of" in (2), they denote a connection between the loss of employment and and the subsequent receipt.[96] Accordingly, where an individual receives compensation on account of damages as a result of a loss of employment, the amount received will be taxed as a retiring allowance.[97] Since it did not relate to his loss of employment as a university dean but to the loss of the instructor position he had elected to take up in the future, the damage award received by the taxpayer was not taxable as retiring allowance.[98] The same conclusion was reached when an employee demoted by his employer due to the interference of his employer's major customer sued the customer and received a damage award.[99]

In a case where a taxpayer received $152,968 from his employer under a release agreement and, as consideration for the payment, the taxpayer tendered his resignation and terminated his harassment suit against his employer, the Federal Court of Appeal[100] reversed the Tax Court of Canada[101] to hold that only a portion of the payment had to be included in his income as a "retiring allowance". The portion of the payment paid as consideration to the taxpayer to abandon his harassment suit against his employer did not constitute a retiring allowance, and was not required to be included in his income.

To the extent that employment commenced before 1996, payments received as a retiring allowance may be deducted from income up to certain limits if transferred into a registered pension plan or a registered retirement savings plan (RRSP) in the year of receipt or within 60 days thereafter and the proper election is filed.[102] This special rollover into an RRSP or RPP for pre-1996 years of service is discussed at ¶10,357. The rollover is not available for employment commencing after 1995. Legal fees incurred by the taxpayer in the year or in any of the seven preceding taxation years in collecting or establishing a right to collect a retiring allowance are deductible from income.[103]

[¶2165] Death Benefits

Amounts received by a taxpayer in the year as, on account of, in lieu of payment of, or in satisfaction of a death benefit are included in income.[104] A death benefit consists of an amount or amounts received by any person on or after the death of an employee in recognition of service in an office or employment, subject to specified exemptions.[105]

See page ii for explanation of footnotes.

[95] Harel, 77 DTC 5438.
[96] Interp. Bul. IT-337R4.
[97] Tremblay, 2009 DTC 1284.
[98] Schewe, 2010 DTC 1056.
[99] Ahmad, 2002 DTC 2065.
[100] Forest, 2008 DTC 6008.

[101] Forest, 2007 DTC 632.
[102] CCH ¶8495, ¶8500; Sec. 60(j.1), 60(k).
[103] CCH ¶8541; Sec. 60(o.1).
[104] CCH ¶8021; Sec. 56(1)(a)(iii); Interp. Bul. IT-499R.
[105] CCH ¶28,060; Sec. 248(1) "death benefit".

The following points should be noted:

(1) Where the taxpayer is the only person who has received such a payment and is the surviving spouse or common-law partner of the officer or employee, the amount of the death benefit included in income is reduced by $10,000. If the amount actually received as a death benefit in the year is less than this amount, the exemption for the year will be limited to the amount so received.

(2) Where the recipient is not the surviving spouse or common-law partner of the employee, the amount of the exemption is limited to the amount by which $10,000 exceeds all amounts received by the surviving spouse/common-law partner at any time in recognition of the employee's service. The exemption is divided among the non-spouse/common-law partner recipients in proportion to the amounts received by them.

(3) Where the benefit is payable in more than one annual amount, and where such amount does not in the first year equal the amount of the permitted exemption, the difference will be applicable to the following years' payments to the extent that there remains, for each successive year, an unused balance of the amount of the exemption.

The term "death benefit" as used in the *Canada Pension Plan* is not a death benefit for the purpose of the *Income Tax Act*.[106]

Any CPP/QPP death benefit received upon the death of an individual will be included in the income of the estate rather than in the income of the deceased individual.

[¶2168] Eligible Funeral Arrangements

An individual can contribute up to $35,000 to an eligible funeral arrangement that covers both eligible funeral and cemetery care services.[107] Contributions need not be made at once but may be made over time as long as they do not exceed an overall limit of: (i) $35,000 if the arrangement covers both funeral and cemetery services; (ii) $20,000 if it covers only cemetery services; and (iii) $15,000 if it covers only funeral services. Contributions for these services are not deductible, but they accumulate tax-free as long as they are not disbursed. When the money is used to pay for qualifying funeral or cemetery services, it is included in the income of the service provider. If the individual withdraws the funds from the arrangement, any income earned on the individual's contributions is included in the individual's income. If there is more money in the fund than required for funeral and cemetery services, the excess is refunded to the taxpayer's estate as income from property.

The term "eligible funeral arrangement" generally means an arrangement established for the purpose of funding funeral services for one or more

---

See page ii for explanation of footnotes.

[106] Cumming, 76 DTC 6265.   [107] CCH ¶21,651; Sec. 148.1.

individuals by a qualifying person. A qualifying person is a person who is licensed or authorized under the laws of a province to provide funeral or cemetery services for individuals. There must be a custodian of such an arrangement who is a trustee of the trust governed by the arrangement or, where there is no trust, a qualifying person who receives a deposit under the arrangement.

[¶2170] Employment Insurance Benefits

Employment insurance payments to a taxpayer, other than payments relating to the cost of a course or program designed to facilitate re-entry into the labour force, are included in income.[108]

An employee's contributions to the employment insurance fund qualify for a tax credit.[109]

See ¶2455 relative to overpayments, and ¶2095 regarding income maintenance plans.

[¶2175] Benefits under Government Assistance Programs

Prescribed benefits received under government assistance programs are treated as taxable income.[110] For this purpose, the following benefits are prescribed:

(1) benefits under the *Labour Adjustment Benefits Act*;

(2) benefits under programs to provide income assistance payments established pursuant to section 5 of the *Department of Labour Act*;

(3) benefits under the Plant Workers Adjustment Program; and

(4) benefits under the Northern Cod Compensation and Adjustment Program.[111]

Under the *Labour Adjustment Benefits Act*, certain employees in designated industries are entitled to apply to the Labour Adjustment Review Board for labour adjustment benefits. Benefits under section 5 of the *Department of Labour Act* are paid to eligible older workers under the Program for Older Workers Adjustment. The Plant Workers Adjustment Program and the Northern Cod Compensation and Adjustment Program result from agreements made under section 5 of the *Department of Fisheries and Oceans Act* and are designed to compensate east coast fishermen for the decline in the cod fishery.

[¶2180] Alimony or Maintenance Payments

Major legislative changes were made to the provisions dealing with alimony or maintenance payments. Previously, payments made for child and

---

See page ii for explanation of footnotes.

[108] CCH ¶8025; Sec. 56(1)(*a*).
[109] CCH ¶18,441; Sec. 118.7.

[110] CCH ¶8027; Sec. 56(1)(*a*)(vi).
[111] Reg. 5502.

spousal support were included in the recipient's income and were deductible from income for the payor. That system remains in effect for support payments made for the benefit of the recipient (usually a spouse/common-law partner or former common-law spouse/partner). In the case of payments made on account of child support, the payments will not be taxable to the recipient nor deductible to the payor.[112] There is a general presumption that payments are child support unless otherwise identified. The same treatment will apply to amounts paid directly to third parties.

The new rules apply automatically to payments required under agreements or orders made after April 30, 1997. For orders or agreements made before May 1997, the prior provisions apply except where: (1) the payor and recipient file a joint election stating that the current rules are to apply to payments made after a specified date after April 30, 1997; (2) the agreement or order is varied after April 30, 1997 or another order or agreement is made after April 30, 1997 which changes the amount of child support provided in the original order or agreement; and (3) the order or agreement specifies that the current rules will apply to payment after a specified date after April 1997.

Example:

> Evelyn and Jean have a court order made on December 1, 1996 under which Jean is required to pay Evelyn support of $400 for maintenance of their child. On July 1, 1997 the order is varied to increase the payment to $500 per month as of that date. During 1997 Jean makes payment to Evelyn under the order totalling $4000. The results for 1997 are: Payments after 1996 ($4000) are deductible to the extent they exceed payments on or after July 1, 1997, when the new rules apply to this agreement (six months × $500 = $3000). There is perforce no amount deducted in a prior year before 1996 in this example, so $4000 - $3000 = $1000 is deductible by Jean and taxable to Evelyn.

Lump-sum payments made in settlement of any right the spouse had to a periodic allowance are no longer deductible. To establish that the payments are periodic, the CRA will look at the following criteria:

- length of periods at which the payments are made;

- whether payments are for an indefinite period or fixed term;

- amount of payments relative to income and living standards of the payor and recipient; and

- whether the payments purport to release the payor from any further obligation to pay maintenance.

[¶2185] Annuity Payments

Amounts received by a taxpayer as annuity payments are included in income, except for amounts that are otherwise required to be included in income or amounts to which the provisions of the Act respecting interests in

---

See page ii for explanation of footnotes.

[112] CCH ¶8031, ¶8410; Sec. 56(1)(b), 60(b).

a life insurance apply. Annuities are defined to include all amounts payable on a periodic basis, whether payable at intervals longer or shorter than a year and whether payable under a contract, will, trust, or otherwise.[113]

It will be observed that amounts will be included in the recipient's income which are partly or entirely in the nature of capital. However, it is provided[114] that the taxpayer may deduct the capital element of each annuity payment included in computing income, other than superannuation or pension benefits. The method of determining the capital element is discussed in ¶2415.

A lottery prize that was payable by way of an annuity was not taxable.[115]

[¶2190] Disposition of Income-Averaging Annuity Contract

Any amount received by a taxpayer as proceeds of the surrender, cancellation, redemption, sale, or other disposition of an income-averaging annuity contract is to be included in income. Any amount deemed to have been received as proceeds of disposition of such a contract is also to be included in income.[116] See also ¶2465.

[¶2195] RRSPs, DPSPs, RRIFs, and Supplementary Unemployment Benefit Plans

Amounts received by a taxpayer from a trustee under an RRSP, a DPSP, a RRIF, or a supplementary unemployment benefit plan are to be included in income.[117] See Chapter X for a discussion of the tax treatment of these types of plans.

[¶2198] Home Buyers' Plans

Amounts relating to a Home Buyers' Plan may be required to be included in the taxpayer's income for the year. (See ¶10,393.) If the taxpayer did not acquire a home or return the funds to the registered retirement savings plan (RRSP) in accordance with the rules respecting the Home Buyers' Plan, the amounts withdrawn from the RRSP will become taxable in the year in which they were withdrawn.[118]

[¶2200] Life Insurance Policies

Amounts received by a taxpayer upon the disposition of an interest in a life insurance policy are to be included in income. See ¶10,516 *et seq.* for a discussion of life insurance policies.[119]

See page ii for explanation of footnotes.

[113] CCH ¶28,015; Sec. 248(1) "annuity".
[114] CCH ¶8401; Sec. 60(a).
[115] Rumack, 84 DTC 1339.
[116] CCH ¶8039, ¶8040; Sec. 56(1)(e), 56(1)(f).

[117] CCH ¶8041, ¶8043, ¶8045b; Sec. 56(1)(g), 56(1)(h), 56(1)(i).
[118] CCH ¶8045; Sec. 56(1)(h.1).
[119] CCH ¶8047; Sec. 56(1)(j).

[¶2205] Award of Legal Costs

A taxpayer must include in income any amount received as legal costs awarded to the taxpayer by a court on an appeal from an assessment of any tax, interest, or penalties and any reimbursement of costs received under employment insurance or the *Canada Pension Plan* if, with respect to the appeal or decision, an amount is deductible.[120]

It is to be noted that legal costs received must be included in income if the expenses are deductible, even though they were not in fact deducted.

A taxpayer must include in income amounts received as an award or reimbursement of legal expenses paid to collect or establish a right to a retiring allowance or benefit under a pension fund or plan to the extent that those legal expenses are deductible.[121]

[¶2210] Scholarships, Bursaries, etc.

A scholarship, fellowship, bursary, or similar prize, whether in cash or kind (other than a prescribed one) is included in income in the year of receipt to the extent it exceeds the scholarship exemption for the year.[122] The scholarship exemption is the total of three amounts:

(i) the full amount of a scholarship, fellowship or bursary received by a taxpayer, if it was received by a student in connection with the student's enrolment at a designated educational institution in a program which entitles the student to claim the education tax credit for the current taxation year, the immediately preceding taxation year, or the subsequent taxation year; or enrolment at an elementary or secondary school;

(ii) the lesser of the amount of a scholarship, fellowship, bursary, or prize to be used by the recipient in the production of a literary, dramatic, musical, or artistic work and the amount of the taxpayer's expenses (other than expenses for which the taxpayer was reimbursed or are otherwise deductible) incurred to fulfill the conditions of that amount received; and

(iii) the lesser of $500 and the amount by which the scholarship, fellowship, bursary, or prize exceeds the amounts under (i) and (ii) described above.[123]

For 2010 and subsequent taxation years, certain limitations are placed on the exemption described in (i) above.[124] In order for the exemption in (i) to apply, it must be reasonable to conclude that the award is intended to support the taxpayer's enrolment in the program, having regard for all of the

---

See page ii for explanation of footnotes.

[120] CCH ¶8049; Sec. 56(1)(*l*).
[121] CCH ¶8050; Sec. 56(1)(*l*.1).
[122] CCH ¶8053; Sec. 56(1)(n); Interp. Bul. IT-75R4, IT-257R, IT-340R.

[123] CCH ¶8106; Sec. 56(3).
[124] CCH ¶8106a; Sec. 56(3.1).

circumstances, such as the terms and conditions of the award, the duration of the program, and the period for which the support is intended. Based on a short illustration in the Department of Finance explanatory notes, it appears the exemption will be denied where the amount of the award is out of proportion to the program to which it relates. Furthermore, for part-time students, the amount of the award that is eligible for the exemption in (i) cannot exceed the cost of materials or the fee paid to the designated educational institution for the program. This particular limitation for part-time students does not apply to students who are eligible for the disability tax credit or who cannot attend full-time because of a physical or mental impairment.

The scholarship exemption does not apply to amounts received in the course of business or in respect of or in the course of an employment; as a rule, such amounts are fully included in income.

A prescribed prize, not included in income, is any prize that is recognized by the general public and that is awarded for meritorious achievement in the arts, sciences, or service to the public but does not include any amount that can reasonably be regarded as having been received as compensation for services rendered or to be rendered.[125]

Amounts received under the Apprenticeship Incentive Grant program are to be included in income in the year received. Repayments made in the taxation year of amounts included in the year or a previous year may be deducted.[126] The Apprenticeship Incentive Grant program, administered by the Department of Human Resources and Social Development, provides a cash grant of $1,000 to apprentices in each of their first two years of apprenticeship.

Research grants, such as Canada Council grants and similar grants, are taxable in the year they are received, with the costs incurred in the year that relate to the research or similar work being deductible from the amount of the grants.[127] Such deductible expenses would include amounts for equipment, fees, travel, and laboratory charges. A deduction is not allowed for personal and living expenses and for expenses in respect of which the taxpayer is reimbursed. Travel expenses incurred while away from home in the course of carrying on the research or similar work are deductible. Although the deductible research expenses must be incurred in the same year in which the research grant is received, the CRA has recognized that research expenses may be incurred in the year immediately before or immediately after the year in which the grant is received. While these expenses cannot be deducted in the year in which they are incurred, they are considered to be deductible in the year in which the grant is received. However, for any expenses incurred in the year before the grant is received, those expenses incurred before the taxpayer is notified that the grant will be paid are not deductible from that

See page ii for explanation of footnotes.

[125] CCH ¶8055; Reg. 7700.
[126] CCH ¶8053a; Sec. 56(1)(n.1).
[127] CCH ¶8053ab, ¶8550; Sec. 56(1)(o), 60(p).

grant. Research expenses incurred more than one year before or more than one year after the year in which the grant is received are not deductible from that grant.

Amounts received as a refund of scholarships, research grants, etc., are to be included in income. A special deduction is provided where such an amount has been included in income and must be repaid to an arm's length party later in the year.[128]

Awards for employees' children are scholarship income in the children's hands if their primary purpose is to recognize scholastic achievement and they require the recipients to maintain a decent annual academic average (for instance, a minimum 70% grade average).[129] As a result of the above decisions by the Federal Court of Appeal in 2009, on August 12, 2009, the CRA announced changes on its Payroll website for the reporting of taxable benefits by a post-secondary educational institution that offers free tuition to an employee's dependant and by other employers that offer a scholarship program for employees' dependants. In such a case, starting with the 2007 tax year, the FMV of tuition fees or the scholarship award for a family member should not be included in the employee's income; it should be reported as a scholarship on a T4A slip for the family member. If the FMV of tuition fees or a scholarship award for a family member was included in an employee's income for 2007 or 2008, that employee's T4 slip may be amended for those years, and a T4A slip may be issued for the family member.

However, if the primary purpose of an award to an employee is to carry out research for its own sake (for example, to further knowledge in a particular field by discovering new facts or by reinterpreting existing knowledge), the award is considered to be a research grant and is included in income. For instance, amounts that Université Laval paid to certain professors on sabbatical leave constituted "research grants", which were to be included in income.[130]

[¶2213] Artists' Grants

Where an artist receives a project grant (other than a grant received for work completed as part of a business or employment), the grant is included in income to the extent it exceeds the scholarship exemption for the year (see ¶2210).[131] Instead of claiming this exemption, the artist may deduct reasonable expenses incurred to fulfil the conditions of the grant, not exceeding the amount of the grant. It should be noted that this rule only applies to amounts eligible for the exemption, so that if the amounts are received in the course of a business or by virtue of employment, the rule is not applicable.[132] A taxpayer is also required to include in income the value

---

See page ii for explanation of footnotes.

[128] CCH ¶8053b, ¶8555; Sec. 56(1)(p), 60(q).

[129] Okonski, 2008 DTC 2992, DiMaria, 2009 DTC 5019, Bartley et al, 2009 DTC 5019.

[130] Ghali, 2005 DTC 5472.

[131] CCH ¶8053; Sec. 56(1)(n); Interp. Bul. IT-257R.

[132] Interp. Bul. IT-75R4.

of workshops, seminars, training programs, and similar programs provided to any person in the year in respect of the taxpayer's membership in a registered national arts service organization.[133]

[¶2215] Registered Education Savings Plan (RESP) Payments

Amounts received in respect of an RESP are required to be included in computing the taxpayer's income.[134] This includes amounts received by the beneficiary as educational assistance payments and amounts required to be taken into the subscriber's income for the taxation year in which registration of the plan is revoked or membership is terminated. For further details on RESPs, see ¶10,399 *et seq.*

[¶2220] Home Insulation or Energy Conversion Grants

When a grant is received under a prescribed program relating to home insulation or energy conversion, that grant will be included in the income of either the recipient or the recipient's spouse or common-law partner, unless it is included in income under ¶3063, which includes in income such grants received with respect to property used principally for the purpose of gaining or producing income from a business or property.[135] The grant shall be included in the income of the spouse/common-law partner with the higher income. In determining which spouse/common-law partner has the higher income, "income for the year" means income before the amount of the grant is added.

[¶2225] Registered Retirement Income Fund (RRIF) Payments

Certain amounts in respect of a RRIF are required to be included in computing income. These include all benefits received under such a plan and the cost of any non-qualified investment.[136] RRIFs are discussed fully at ¶10,411.

[¶2230] Social Assistance Payments

Social assistance payments made on the basis of a means, needs, or income test must be included in income. The amount is to be included in the income of the spouse/common-law partner with the higher income.[137] Thus, the social assistance payments will not reduce the married status tax credit (see ¶8095). Certain social assistance payments included in income are deductible in computing taxable income (see ¶2470). This inclusion in net income and subsequent deduction is done so that the payments are taken into account in determining the amount of tax credits.

See page ii for explanation of footnotes.

[133] CCH ¶8093; Sec. 56(1)(z.1).
[134] CCH ¶8063, ¶9958e; Sec. 56(1)(q), 81(1)(p).
[135] CCH ¶8070, ¶8072, ¶8073, ¶8075, ¶8176; Sec. 56(1)(s), 56(9); Reg. 224, Reg. 5500, Reg. 5501.
[136] CCH ¶8080, ¶21,428g; Sec. 56(1)(t), 146.3.
[137] CCH ¶8005, ¶8082; Sec. 56(1)(a), 56(1)(u).

It is, however, excluded from non-taxable social assistance income received by an individual for the benefit of a foster person (child or adult) under the individual's care where the individual and the foster person reside together in the individual's principal place of residence.[138] The exemption also applies to amounts (often called "bed reservation fees") paid to individuals to maintain their residence and keep it available for use by a foster person. The payment, which is made on the basis of a means test under a federal or provincial program, is exempt if:

(a) the payment is received directly or indirectly for the benefit of an individual who is not the taxpayer, the taxpayer's spouse or common-law partner, and is not related to the taxpayer or the taxpayer's spouse or common-law partner;

(b) no family allowance payments, when they are in effect, are payable to anyone for the beneficiary (note that no reference is made to the Child Tax Benefit); and

(c) the beneficiary resides in the taxpayer's principal place of residence, or that residence is maintained for use as a residence of the beneficiary throughout the period that the social assistance is paid.

When persons in need of long-term services in the taxpayer's special care homes (the "beneficiaries") did not pay the taxpayer, the province did. The fact that some beneficiaries qualified for a provincial government subsidy did not change their contractual relationship with the taxpayer to provide them with services. The beneficiaries in turn paid the taxpayer for those services regardless of whether they used their own funds or those provided by the province. Hence, the payments from the province were income in the taxpayer's hands and not exempt social assistance payments, as she had contended.[139]

[¶2235] Workers' Compensation

Amounts received in respect of injury, disability, or death received under a Canadian federal or provincial employees' or workers' compensation law must be included in income.[140] Amounts included in income are deductible in computing taxable income (see ¶2470) unless received by the employer or former employer of the person in respect of whose injury, disability, or death the payment was made.

[¶2240] Salary Deferral Arrangements

Amounts received by a taxpayer out of or under a salary deferral arrangement in respect of another person will be included in computing the income of the taxpayer unless:

See page ii for explanation of footnotes.

[138] CCH ¶9925; Sec. 81(1)(h).   [140] CCH ¶8084; Sec. 56(1)(v).
[139] Gallant, 2009 DTC 1102.

(a) the amount was received by or from a trust governed by a salary deferral arrangement; or

(b) the amount has been included in computing the income of the other person in the year or in a preceding year.[141]

Salary deferral arrangements are discussed at ¶2105.

[¶2245] Retirement Compensation Arrangements (RCAs)

A taxpayer is required to include in income any amounts received in the year out of an RCA if such amounts can reasonably be considered to have been received in respect of the taxpayer's office or employment.[142] An income inclusion is also required when amounts are paid out of an RCA to *any person* if the RCA relates to the taxpayer's employment. This provision is designed to avoid income splitting, but is not limited to recipients who do not deal at arm's length with the employee.

A non-employee recipient of an amount from an RCA will be required to include the amount in income only if the employee is not required to do so. An exception is made for a return of contributions or other amounts paid out of an arrangement that are included in the income of the employer. A taxpayer's proceeds from the disposition of an interest in an RCA must be included in income.[143]

[¶2250] Indirect Payments

The payment or transfer to others of property that would be regarded as income if it had been paid or transferred to the taxpayer will be deemed to be income in certain circumstances.[144]

This applies to such payments or transfers made to another person at the direction of, or with the concurrence of, the taxpayer for the taxpayer's benefit or as a benefit which the taxpayer wishes to confer on the other person.

It does not apply where a taxpayer directs that a portion of the taxpayer's *Canada Pension Plan* or a similar provincial plan, including a prescribed provincial plan, be paid to the taxpayer's spouse/common-law partner. Such payments would accordingly be included in the spouse/common-law partner's income. "Property" is defined[145] to mean property of any kind whatsoever, whether real or personal or corporeal or incorporeal, and, without restricting the generality of the foregoing, includes a right of any kind whatsoever, a share or a chose in action.

Note that there are three conditions to be fulfilled before the provision will apply:

See page ii for explanation of footnotes.

[141] CCH ¶8086; Sec. 56(1)(w).
[142] CCH ¶8087; Sec. 56(1)(x).
[143] CCH ¶8090; Sec. 56(1)(y).

[144] CCH ¶8100; Sec. 56(2); Interp. Bul. IT-335R2.

[145] CCH ¶28,220; Sec. 248(1) "property".

(a) the payment or transfer must be at the direction of, or with the concurrence of, the taxpayer;

(b) the payment or transfer must be for the taxpayer's benefit, or as a benefit the taxpayer wished to confer on another; and

(c) the payment or transfer would have been included in the taxpayer's income if it had been paid to the taxpayer.

This provision was held to apply to and to make taxable the directors of a private company which made gifts to relatives of the directors and to its former employees. It was held that not only the directors but all of the shareholders of the company should have shared the tax liability in proportion to their individual holdings.[146] The rules governing attributions of transferred income did not apply to the acts of a director participating in the declaration of a corporate dividend. Accordingly, dividends paid to the spouses of taxpayers who controlled a corporation were not attributed to those taxpayers.[147]

[¶2255] Transfer of Rights to Income

In a non-arm's length transaction, where a taxpayer has at any time transferred or assigned to a person the right to an amount which would otherwise have been income of the taxpayer in a taxation year, such an amount is included in the taxpayer's income.[148] An "amount" means money, rights, or things expressed in terms of the amount of money or the value in terms of money of the right or thing.[149]

Spouses and common-law partners are deemed not to be dealing at arm's length and would be subject to the above provision. A "common-law partner" includes a person of the same or opposite sex who lives with the taxpayer in a conjugal relationship for at least 12 months or who is a parent of a child of whom the taxpayer is also a parent.[150] An election may be made jointly by a taxpayer and a taxpayer's same-sex common-law partner to have the new rule apply in the 1998, 1999, and 2000 taxation years.

An exception to this rule arises where the income is from property and the taxpayer has also transferred or assigned the property and directs that a portion of the taxpayer's *Canada Pension Plan* or similar provincial plan, including a prescribed provincial plan, be paid to the taxpayer's spouse or common-law partner. However, it should be remembered that a comprehensive set of rules exists to prevent a taxpayer from splitting his or her income among family members to reduce the total amount of tax payable.[151] See ¶2620 *et seq.*

See page ii for explanation of footnotes.

[146] Bronfman, 65 DTC 5235.
[147] McClurg, 88 DTC 6047.
[148] CCH ¶8150; Sec. 56(4); Interp. Bul. IT-440R2.
[149] CCH ¶28,012; Sec. 248(1) "amount".

[150] CCH ¶28,047a; Sec. 248(1) "common-law partner".
[151] CCH ¶9516–9565; Sec. 74.1–74.5; Lackie, 79 DTC 5309, Murphy, 80 DTC 6314.

This provision applies to transfers or assignments to any person with whom the transferor was not dealing at arm's length and, presumably, whether or not the taxpayer received any consideration for the transfer or assignment.

[¶2260] Loans to Non-Arm's Length Individuals

Where an individual or a trust in which the individual is beneficially interested has received a loan from or has become indebted to:

(a) another individual (a creditor) with whom the individual was not dealing at arm's length; or

(b) to a trust (a creditor trust) to which a person (an original transferor) with whom the individual was not dealing at arm's length has transferred property,

any income which is earned by the individual from that property (or property acquired from the proceeds of the indebtedness or substituted property) will be taxed in the hands of the creditor if it may reasonably be inferred that one of the main reasons for the loan was to avoid tax by shifting income to the individual.

An exception is available if the loan carries a commercial rate of interest.[152] However, if the so-called "attribution rules"[153] apply to attribute income to the creditor, those rules will displace the operation of the above provisions. In respect of income relating to periods commencing prior to 1991, the above provisions apply only to property transferred by way of loan.

[¶2280] Miscellaneous Income Receipts

Certain other receipts will be treated as taxable income including gambling profits, accumulated vacation and sick-leave credits, payments made to induce a person to leave a present position of employment, a voluntary payment received in consequence of a person's employment or business, and fees received for entering into service contracts.[154]

In the case of hobbies, where no reasonable expectation of profit exists, neither amounts received nor expenses incurred are included in the income computation for tax purposes. Where a hobby consists of collecting personal-use property or listed personal property, dispositions should be accounted for as described in ¶5300.

[¶2290] Income from Personal-Injury Awards

Where an infant has suffered mental or physical injury and has received an award or a settlement in respect of an action for damages, the property awarded or received is usually held in trust for the infant by his or her legal

---

See page ii for explanation of footnotes.

[152] CCH ¶8151–8151b; Sec. 56(4.1)–(4.3).   [154] Interp. Bul. IT-334R2.
[153] CCH ¶9516; Sec. 74.1.

representative or by an officer of a court until the infant attains the age of majority.[155] The income arising from the investment of such property is excluded from tax until the end of the year in which the infant reaches the age of 21. The exclusion applies not only to income arising from the property directly but also from property which has been substituted on one or more occasions for the property received on the award or settlement. Furthermore, the excluded income itself may generate additional income which is also excluded from taxation. These exclusions apply equally where damages are awarded directly to the infant or to some other person for the infant's benefit.

Any taxable capital gains arising from a disposition of property awarded as damages is also exempt from inclusion in income.[156] It would appear, however, that where the purchase price of a "substituted" property which is disposed of for a capital gain is provided in part by the original property and in part by income generated by such original property, only that proportion of the taxable gain that the original property was of the purchase price of the substituted property will be so excluded.

Following the year in which the taxpayer attains the age of 21, the exclusion no longer applies. Consequently, income or taxable capital gains derived from the original or substituted property and received after that time would be taxable. A taxpayer may make an election under which gains accrued up to the day he or she attains the age of 21 will not be taxed on a disposition of the property subsequent to his or her attaining the age of 21. This is effected by allowing the taxpayer to elect, in his or her tax return for the taxation year in which the taxpayer turns 21, to treat the property as having been disposed of and reacquired at its fair market value on the day before the taxpayer turns 21. The election is optional. It is generally only advisable to make the election where the fair market value on the day before the taxpayer turns 21 is greater than the adjusted cost base of the property.

The foregoing provisions will not apply in other situations, such as where the infant receives an award under fatal accidents legislation for the death of a parent.

Notwithstanding the fact that in many provinces the age of majority is 18, the infant taxpayer will continue to benefit from the foregoing income exclusions until the end of the year in which he or she attains the age of 21.

[¶2295] Employment Expenses

[¶2300] General Restriction

Except as specifically provided by the Act, no deductions from employment income are permitted.

See page ii for explanation of footnotes.

[155] CCH ¶9921, ¶9922, ¶9984; Sec. 81(1)(g.1), 81(1)(g.2), 81(5); Interp. Bul. IT-365R2.   [156] Mehta, 85 DTC 219.

[¶2305] Salespersons' Expenses

A deduction for certain expenses incurred in the year for the purpose of earning income from employment is given to a person employed in connection with the selling of property or the negotiation of contracts for an employer.[157] The expenses claimed must be reasonable in amount.[158] The deduction applies only to employee-salespersons, which include buyers and purchasing agents, and not to salespersons carrying on their own businesses. No deduction, however, is allowed an employee-salesperson for capital expenditures, other than for aircraft and automobile expenses or for the use of recreational facilities or club dues which would not be deductible if the employment were a business.

The deduction is available for amounts expended for the purpose of earning income up to an amount not exceeding commissions or other similar amounts fixed by reference to the volume of the sales made or contracts negotiated. In order for this to apply, the salesperson must:

(1) under the contract of employment, be required to pay his or her own expenses;

(2) ordinarily be required to carry on the duties of employment away from the employer's place of business;

(3) be remunerated in whole or in part by commissions or other similar amounts fixed by reference to the volume of the sales made or the contracts negotiated; and

(4) not be in receipt of an allowance for travelling expenses for the taxation year that was excluded from income.

It will be noted that the cost of meals is deductible only where the meals are consumed during a period when the salesperson is away, for 12 hours or more, from the municipality or metropolitan area where the salesperson usually reports for work.[159]

Since they had been incurred for the purpose of earning employment income, a stockbroker was entitled to deduct the legal fees to be represented before the Montreal Exchange disciplinary committee and in criminal proceedings.[160] However, when a commissioned salesman had received from his employer a reimbursement of 25 cents per kilometre for his travelling expenses and had also been reimbursed for his meals and lodging expenses, this reasonable allowance was excluded from income so that no sales expenses deduction was available to the taxpayer.[161] Salespeople who spend only part of their working time elsewhere or have occasional absences from their place of employment are not entitled to the deduction.[162]

See page ii for explanation of footnotes.

[157] CCH ¶3050; Sec. 8(1)(f).

[158] CCH ¶9120, ¶29,480; Sec. 67; ITAR 31.

[159] CCH ¶3300; Sec. 8(4).

[160] Mercille, 2000 DTC 1915.

[161] Lavigne, 94 DTC 1571.

[162] Stromberg [No. 2], 56 DTC 61,Turnbull, 60 DTC 634,Neufeld, 81 DTC 18,Jalbert, 86 DTC 1766.

[¶2310] Travelling Expenses and Meals

Travelling expenses expended in the course of employment are deductible[163] if an officer or employee of a company:

(a) is *ordinarily* required to carry on duties away from an employer's place of business or in different places (occasional trips do not qualify);[164]

(b) is required under the contract of employment to pay travelling expenses incurred in the performance of duties;

(c) was not in receipt of travelling allowances, which are exempt from tax; and

(d) did not claim any deduction for the year for the same expenses by virtue of being a railway or transport employee or a salesperson.

Clearly, it is intended that a taxpayer receiving a tax-free allowance for travel expenses not be able to deduct expenses, nor that persons entitled to deduct expenses as a railway or transport employee or a salesperson be able to deduct their expenses twice.

A taxpayer who receives an inadequate allowance as a salesperson or member of the clergy and otherwise qualifies for a deduction for travelling expenses may have an option to include the inadequate allowance in income on the basis that it is not reasonable and deduct the actual expenses as travelling expenses.

Even where the above conditions are fulfilled, the claim for deduction should be accompanied, as a rule, by vouchers and receipts and the expenses claimed must not be unreasonable. For example, a taxpayer whose expenses nearly equalled his salary was allowed only part of the amount claimed, on the grounds that some of the items were not substantiated by receipts and that some of the expenses were beyond the true requirements of the circumstances and seemed to be more the result of largesse than of reasonable outlay.[165] See also ¶2070 concerning personal or living expenses.

Two school principals were allowed to deduct the expenses of using their own automobiles to attend evening meetings with parents, meetings away from the school, and various other trips. Even though the relevant collective agreements did not expressly require them to travel or pay expenses, these were implied terms of employment.[166] A police officer assigned to the canine division was allowed to deduct the cost of transporting his dog, since failure to provide such transportation would have resulted in a poor work performance record. This was sufficient to make it a duty of employment.[167]

See page ii for explanation of footnotes.

[163] CCH ¶3070; Sec. 8(1)(h).
[164] Stromberg [No. 1], 54 DTC 28.
[165] No. 589, 59 DTC 41.
[166] Moore, 87 DTC 5217,Betz, 87 DTC 5223.
[167] Hoedel, 86 DTC 6535.

The cost of meals consumed while travelling for the employer is deductible only where the meal is consumed during a period when the taxpayer is away, for 12 hours or more, from the municipality or metropolitan area where he or she ordinarily reports for work.[168]

An Ontario Jockey Club employee who resided in Toronto worked at two Toronto racetracks, and for three months of the year at a racetrack in Fort Erie. His meal expenses incurred while working at the latter track were deductible. The municipality where he usually or ordinarily reported for work was Toronto, and he was required to be away from Toronto for more than 12 hours in the course of employment.[169] Occasional absences from the place of employment do not qualify the taxpayer as being "ordinarily required" to carry on duties away from the place of employment.[170]

"Commuting expenses", i.e., expenses resulting from a taxpayer's choice of living in one place while working in another, are not travelling expenses within the meaning of this provision. They are personal and living expenses, the deduction of which is prohibited under the Act.[171] See ¶2070.

[¶2315] Other Expenses and Membership Dues

To the extent an employee is not entitled to be reimbursed, the following types of expenses paid by an employee [or, effective on Royal Assent of the technical amendments Bill, by someone else on the employee's behalf if the amount must be included in the employee's income] may be deducted from employment income:

(1) *Certain professional membership dues.*[172] In order to be deductible by an officer or employee, the professional membership dues must have been necessary to maintain a professional status "recognized by statute". Typical examples of such dues would be fees payable by a lawyer to a provincial Law Society or dues paid by a doctor, engineer, or chartered accountant to a professional association. However, the Federal Court of Appeal has recently held that "recognized by statute" merely means acknowledged by statute, nor regulated by statute. Thus, a member of the Appraisal Institute of Canada (AIC) was entitled to deduct membership fees on the ground that members of the AIC who held a certain designation were considered experienced appraisers entitled to make appraisals recognized by statute.[173] Membership fees payable to an association are not deductible if the taxpayer can maintain professional status without paying them. The membership dues must be payable on an annual basis. An initial fee payable upon admission to a professional society would not be deductible since it is an entrance fee and not an annual payment. If a taxpayer remained a member of the professional organization during the period for which dues were in

[168] CCH ¶3300; Sec. 8(4).
[169] Healy, 79 DTC 5060.
[170] Stromberg [No. 2], 56 DTC 61, Tremblay, 70 DTC 1006.
[171] Cross, 98 DTC 6328, Wilkinson, 66 DTC 344, Lahey, 67 DTC 222.
[172] CCH ¶3080; Sec. 8(1)(i); Interp. Bul. IT-352R2.
[173] Montgomery, 99 DTC 5186.

arrears, the subsequent payment of the arrears qualifies in full for deduction in the year of payment since the dues are still "annual professional membership dues". However, if the taxpayer's membership in the professional organization was terminated, the payment of arrears to gain re-admittance will not qualify for deduction.

A teacher who went on strike had his "annual membership dues" for the teachers' association increased by $50 for the last four months of the year. Even though the increase was directly related to the costs of the strike and was not likely to recur, it was held that the additional dues were deductible.[174]

(2) *Office rent and assistant's or substitute's salary.* These expenses may be deducted if they were required to be paid by an employee or officer under the contract of employment.[175]

(3) *Supplies.* The cost of supplies consumed directly in the performance of the duties of employment or that an officer or employee was required under the contract of employment to supply or pay for may be deductible. A plumber's tools were held not to be supplies consumed directly in the performance of the duties of employment.[176] Similarly, an airline pilot's uniform and accessories which the pilot was required to supply as a term of employment were not "supplies" which were "consumed" within the ordinary meaning of the words.[177] Books used by a schoolteacher are not supplies consumed in the performance of duties.[178] For a discussion of expenses connected with a home office, see ¶3183.

(4) *Trade union and association dues.* Dues payable by an officer or employee to a trade union or association of public servants of which the officer or employee is a member are deductible.[179] Such dues must be annual payments to maintain membership. Certain annual dues paid on behalf of an officer or employee of a trade union or association of public servants of which he or she is not a member may be deductible if such payments must be made pursuant to a collective agreement, are retained by the employer from the remuneration of the employee, and are paid by the employer to the trade union or association. The payments must be made in respect of a "trade union" as defined in section 3 of the *Canada Labour Code* or in any provincial statute providing for the investigation, conciliation, or settlement of industrial disputes or an association of public servants, the primary object of which is to promote the improvement of the members' conditions of employment. Union initiation fees are not annual payments and therefore are not deductible,[180] nor is that portion of union dues directed towards payment of old age and mortuary benefits.[181]

See page ii for explanation of footnotes.

[174] Lucas, 87 DTC 5277.
[175] Daley, 50 DTC 877.
[176] Rajewsky, 63 DTC 593.
[177] Martyn, 64 DTC 461.

[178] Carson, 66 DTC 424.
[179] CCH ¶3080; Sec. 8(1)(i).
[180] Madsen, 70 DTC 1475.
[181] Burke, 76 DTC 6075.

¶2315

(5) *Certain committee dues.* Dues paid to a parity or advisory committee or similar body are deductible, provided that such dues are required under the law of a province.

Any part of the dues mentioned under (1), (4), or (5) above that is levied for a superannuation, annuity, insurance, or similar fund or plan or for a purpose not directly related to the ordinary operating expenses of the organization to which the dues are paid, is not deductible.[182] Dues paid in respect of professional or malpractice insurance that is necessary to maintain a professional status recognized by statute are deductible.[183]

Membership fees in boards of trade, chambers of commerce, manufacturers' associations, credit associations, commercial travellers' associations, engineering, and scientific societies and other similar trade, commercial, or learned associations formed for purposes of advancing the collective interest of any particular branch of a trade or commercial enterprise are deductible by the non-salaried taxpayer. Where a salaried taxpayer is a member of such an organization and the conditions mentioned above under (1) or (4) are not fulfilled, the taxpayer's contribution will be considered to be a personal or living expense and therefore not deductible.

[¶2320] Automobile and Aircraft Expenses

A deduction of motor vehicle expenses is allowed where an employee:

(1) was ordinarily required to carry out the duties of employment away from the employer's place of business or in different places;

(2) was required under the contract of employment to pay motor vehicle expenses connected with employment duties;

(3) was not in receipt of a taxable motor vehicle allowance; and

(4) did not claim a deduction for travelling expenses.[184]

Employees who sell property or negotiate contracts, or those who are ordinarily required to travel and pay their own travelling expenses, are allowed to deduct capital cost allowance and interest on money borrowed to acquire a motor vehicle or an aircraft used in their employment.[185] The motor vehicle must be used (not necessarily exclusively) by the employee in the performance of duties whereas the aircraft must be *required* for use by the employee in the performance of employment duties. The deduction in respect of an aircraft is further limited to an amount that is reasonable in the circumstances having regard both to the cost and availability of other modes of transportation.[186]

See page ii for explanation of footnotes.

[182] CCH ¶3350; Sec. 8(5).
[183] CCH ¶3350; Sec. 8(5)(b).
[184] CCH ¶3077; Sec. 8(1)(h.1).

[185] CCH ¶3090; Sec. 8(1)(j).

[186] CCH ¶3650; Sec. 8(9).

Interest is deductible only where it is paid in the year in respect of money borrowed specifically to acquire the motor vehicle or aircraft. Interest on an unpaid purchase balance would not be deductible. The deductibility of interest that relates to the purchase of a "passenger vehicle"[187] acquired from 2001–2012 is limited to $300 per month.[188] The maximum rate of capital cost allowance deductible on automobiles is 30%, and for aircraft is 25%. See the table of rates at Chapter IV.

However, as this deduction may only be taken for a motor vehicle used to earn income, where the motor vehicle is used partly for business and partly for personal reasons, the allowance should be computed at the 30% rate and then apportioned on a mileage basis or according to the fraction of the year that the motor vehicle is used for business purposes.

For capital cost allowance purposes, in 2001–2011 the capital cost of a passenger vehicle is restricted to $30,000 plus applicable federal and provincial sales taxes on $30,000.[189] Automobile leasing costs are limited in a similar manner. Their deduction is limited to the lesser of the following two amounts:

(1) The first amount is determined by multiplying $800 in 2001–2012, plus applicable federal and provincial sales taxes by the number of 30-day periods ending before the earlier of:

(a) the end of the year; and

(b) the end of the lease during which the vehicle was leased,

and deducting from this amount certain items where applicable: the total of all amounts deducted in preceding taxation years in respect of the actual lease charges for the leased vehicle, together with an implicit amount of interest (calculated at prescribed rates) that could have been earned on any refundable deposits in excess of $1,000, and the sum of all reimbursements receivable during the year in respect of the leased vehicle.

(2) The second amount is an amount which reasonably approximates the amount that would be deductible in the case of a purchase. This limitation is computed by multiplying the total of the actual lease charges incurred or paid by the taxpayer during the year by the quotient obtained when $30,000 (+ GST and PST, or HST, on $30,000) is divided by 85% of the greater of:

(a) $35,294 (+ GST and PST, or HST, on $35,294); and

(b) the manufacturer's suggested list price for vehicles.

---

[187] CCH ¶28,195; Sec. 248(1) "passenger vehicle".   [189] CCH ¶4522; Sec. 13(7)(g).
[188] CCH ¶9130; Sec. 67.2; Reg. 7307(2).

¶2320

This amount would be reduced by any amount of prescribed interest on refundable deposits in excess of $1,000 and all reimbursements receivable in respect of the leased vehicle.[190]

Where capital cost allowance taken on an automobile exceeds the actual depreciation incurred, the excess will be subject to the recapture provisions. Note, however, that an employee who is allowed to claim capital cost allowance on an automobile, and who is thus liable to the recapture provisions, is not allowed to claim a terminal loss on disposal of the automobile. See Chapter IV.

For standby charges where an automobile is made available for an employee's use, see ¶2085.

Employees who are required to use their own aircraft to carry out their jobs may in certain circumstances claim capital cost allowance and interest charges on the aircraft similar to the arrangement for automobiles discussed above. The rate of capital cost allowance deductible on aircraft is 25%.

[¶2325] Legal Expenses

Amounts paid by a taxpayer for legal expenses incurred in collecting salary or wages owed to the taxpayer by the taxpayer's employer or former employer are deductible.[191] In addition, a deduction may be taken for legal expenses incurred by an employer to "establish" a right to salary or wages, as well as collect amounts owing. In either case, the amount of the deduction is reduced by any amount received pursuant to an award for costs made by a court.

The damages claimed by a taxpayer as a result of a flawed competition for a job promotion did not relate to salary or wages "owed", but to an amount in lieu of the salary or wages that she would have earned, had the competition been fair.[192] Similarly, when a taxpayer brought a human rights complaint stating that he was refused a promotion because of his political views, his legal expenses were not deductible since they had not been incurred to establish a right to a salary owed to him by his employer.[193] See also ¶2205 and ¶2460.

[The deduction of legal expenses is expanded (for amounts paid after 2000) to cover expenses to collect or establish a right to any income taxed as employment income, whether from an employer or someone else, such as an insurer providing sickness or accident insurance benefits through an employer. This pending technical amendment, first announced on December 20, 2002, is retained in the revised technical proposals that were released on July 16, 2010. At the time of writing, this legislation has not been enacted yet.]

See page ii for explanation of footnotes.

[190] CCH ¶9132; Sec. 67.3.
[191] CCH ¶3010; Sec. 8(1)(b); Interp. Bul. IT-99R5.
[192] Turner-Lienaux, 97 DTC 5294.
[193] Jazairi, 2001 DTC 5163.

[¶2330] Clergy Residence

Certain members of the clergy or of religious orders, as well as certain regular ministers of religious denominations, are allowed to deduct an amount in respect of their living accommodation. To be eligible for the deduction, the individuals have to be in charge of, or ministering to, a diocese, parish or congregation, or engaged exclusively in full-time administrative service by a religious order or a religious denomination. Because in recent years, the CRA was dubious about recognizing the religious status of a denomination, a number of cases reached the courts. Although the CRA had a few victories on specific facts, like the fact that the Ontario Bible College was not a religious order,[194] it generally lost the war on its interpretation of the issues. To be a member of the clergy, ruled the Tax Court of Canada in many cases, one does not have to be ordained.[195] An interfaith chaplain as well as missionaries qualified for the deduction as long as they were regular ministers of a religious order ministering to a congregation.

The amount of the deduction depends upon whether the living accommodation the individuals occupy is: (a) supplied to them by virtue of their employment, (b) rented by them, or (c) owned by them.[196] Where the living accommodation is supplied by virtue of the employment, the amount of the deduction is equal to the value of the benefit derived from the supply of the living accommodation, to the extent that the value is already included in income. Where the living accommodation is rented by the clergy person, the amount of the deduction is equal to the amount of rent paid, not to exceed the amount of remuneration for the year. Where the living accommodation is owned by the clergy person, the deduction is limited to the least of the following three amounts:

(1) the clergy person's total remuneration from the office or employment;

(2) ⅓ of that total remuneration or $10,000, whichever is greater; and

(3) the fair rental value of the residence (reduced by other amounts deducted in connection with the same residence).

Employees claiming the clergy residence deduction must file with their income tax returns a prescribed form signed by their employers to the effect that the employees meet the requirements concerning their status and function as clergy.[197]

[¶2335] Exchange Fund Contributions of Teachers

A taxpayer may deduct a single amount, not exceeding $250, in respect of all employments as a teacher which were paid by the taxpayer in the year to a fund established by the Canadian Education Association for the benefit

---

See page ii for explanation of footnotes.

[194] McRae, 97 DTC 5124.

[195] Noseworthy, 99 DTC 541, Kraft, 99 DTC 693.

[196] CCH ¶3020; Sec. 8(1)(c); Interp. Bul. IT-141R.

[197] CCH ¶3665; Sec. 8(10).

of teachers from Commonwealth countries present in Canada under a teacher-exchange arrangement.[198]

[¶2340] Certain Railway Company Employees

A special deduction is available for certain railway employees employed away from their ordinary residence or home terminal.[199] A deduction for meals and lodging is permitted to relieving telegraphers, station agents, and railway maintenance workers, as well as to other railway workers who are required by their employment to be away from the ordinary residence where they reside and actually support a spouse/common-law partner or a dependent relative. The deduction is available to the extent that the employee has not been, and is not entitled to be, reimbursed.

[¶2345] Persons Employed in Forestry

In connection with taxpayers employed in forestry operations who are required by their contracts of employment to supply power saws, claims for power saw expenses will be allowed by the CRA on the basis of actual expenses only. Each employee will be required to file with his or her return a statement setting out in detail the actual cost of operating the saw. It is not necessary to file receipts and vouchers for expenses, but they must be retained for examination if required.

[¶2350] Transport Employees

Transport employees, i.e., employees of a person whose principal business is passenger or goods transport (such as railway, bus, and truck transport companies) may deduct from income 50% (see ¶2353 for larger deduction available to long-haul truck drivers after March 18, 2007) of the cost of meals and 100% of the cost of lodging (including the cost of showers) to the extent that they have not been reimbursed and are not entitled to be reimbursed.[200] These costs include any GST and provincial sales tax, or HST, paid on these expenses.

Transport employees may claim these costs if they meet the following four conditions:

(1) they work for an airline, railway, bus, or trucking company, or for any other employer whose main business is transporting goods, passengers, or both;

(2) they travel in vehicles their employer uses to transport goods or passengers;

(3) they regularly have to travel away from the municipality and metropolitan area (if there is one) where their terminal is located; and

---

See page ii for explanation of footnotes.

[198] CCH ¶3030; Sec. 8(1)(d).
[199] CCH ¶3040; Sec. 8(1)(e).

[200] CCH ¶3060, ¶9127; Sec. 8(1)(g), 67.1(1); Inf. Cir. 73-21R9.

(4) they regularly incur meal "and" lodging expenses while away from the municipality and metropolitan area (if there is one) where their home terminal is located. The word "and" in this context is clearly conjunctive so that the deductions for meals were disallowed when the taxpayers' duties did not require them to make disbursements for meals and lodging, as required, but only for meals.[201]

A claim will be allowed only if it is supported by records and, where required, by receipts or vouchers. The extent of the records needed and the requirement to maintain supporting vouchers will vary with the method chosen by the transport employee for calculating the deduction. Two methods are available: the detailed method and the simplified method. The detailed method requires anyone who claims a deduction to maintain a record book with the following information: the date the expense was paid, the time the trip started and ended, the geographical location, the name of the restaurant or hotel where the amount was paid, the type of expense, and the amount paid. The simplified method requires the transport employee to maintain a record of trips actually taken during the taxation year. When following this method, the CRA allows for 2006 and subsequent year tax returns a flat rate of $17 per meal (up to a maximum of $51 per day) without requesting a supporting voucher. The flat rate per meal is subject to the 50% meal deduction limit. The simplified method is also available for transport employees travelling to the United States for employment-related duties. For meal expenses incurred in the United States, they are entitled, under the simplified method, to claim US$17 per meal to a maximum of US$51 per day. These amounts must be converted to the equivalent Canadian dollars at the average exchange rate for the year, as determined by the Bank of Canada. Claims made by transport employees travelling to the United States are also subject to the 50% deduction limit.

An inter-city bus driver was permitted to deduct his meal expenses, but was not entitled to lodging expenses because he only reported for work at one place.[202]

[¶2353] Truck Drivers' Meal Expenses

Meal and beverage expenses of long-haul truck drivers are deductible at a higher rate than the 50% permitted for other transportation employees (see ¶2350).[203] During eligible travel periods, meal and beverage expenses are deductible at 60% after March 18, 2007 and before 2008, 65% in 2008, 70% in 2009, 75% in 2010, and 80% beginning in 2011. The increased deduction is also available to employers who pay or reimburse such costs incurred by long-haul truck drivers that they employ.

A long-haul truck driver is defined as an individual whose principal business or duty of employment is driving a truck or tractor designed for

---

See page ii for explanation of footnotes.

[201] Renko, 2003 DTC 5417.

[202] Moreau, 80 DTC 1075.

[203] CCH ¶9127a; Sec. 67.1(1.1).

hauling freight, and that has a gross vehicle weight rating of more than 11,788 kilograms.[204] The eligible travel period in respect of which the driver may claim a greater deduction is defined as a period of at least 24 continuous hours, during which the driver is away from the municipality (metropolitan area) where his regular place of employment is located (in the case of an employee) or from the municipality (metropolitan area) where his place of residence is located (in the case of an independent worker) to drive a longhaul truck that transports goods at least 160 kilometres away.[205]

[¶2355] Employment Insurance Premiums

Premiums paid under the *Employment Insurance Act* give rise to a tax credit equal to the appropriate percentage (currently 15%) of the employee premiums payable for the year by an employee.[206]

Payments by an employee, as an employer, for employment insurance premiums for assistants or substitutes may be deducted in computing the employee's income where the employee is required by the terms of the contract to hire such an assistant or substitute. This deduction is in addition to the deduction for the actual salaries paid to the assistant or substitute if the employee is required by the terms of the contract to hire such a person.[207]

[¶2360] Contributions to Registered Pension Plans (RPPs)

A taxpayer may deduct, in computing income from an office or employment for a particular year, certain amounts contributed to RPPs.[208] An "RPP" is a pension plan that has been registered by the Minister for the purposes of the Act. There are basically two types of RPPs:

(1) *"Defined benefit" plans.* In these plans, the amount of pension payable to the employee-member is determined by a formula based upon years of service and level of earnings at retirement.

(2) *"Money purchase" plans.* These plans provide that the amount of the employee's pension is determined by the contributions of the employee and the employer and accumulated earnings in the plan.

For defined benefit plans, all required contributions for current or past service in respect of personable service are deductible. For money purchase plans, total allowable employer-employee contributions (which are limited to $13,500 for 1996 through 2002 inclusive, $15,500 for 2003, $16,500 for 2004, $18,000 for 2005; $19,000 for 2006; $20,000 for 2007; $21,000 for 2008; $22,000 for 2009; and $22,450 for 2010) are deductible. As a result of indexation, the statutory set limit for 2010 is increased to $22,970 in 2011

See page ii for explanation of footnotes.

[204] CCH ¶9127df; Sec. 67.1(5) "long-haul truck driver".

[205] CCH ¶9127d; Sec. 67.1(5) "eligible travel period".

[206] CCH ¶18,441; Sec. 118.7.

[207] CCH ¶3114; Sec. 8(1)(l.1).

[208] CCH ¶3120, ¶21,541; Sec. 8(1)(m), 147.2(4).

and $23,820 in 2012. These values are supposed to buy pensions equal to the value of pensions which will be permitted under defined benefit plans.

See ¶10,489 for further discussion of employee contribution limits.

[¶2370] Salary Reimbursement

An employee may deduct amounts paid by the employee (or on the employee's behalf) as reimbursement for amounts paid to the employee for a period when the employee did not perform the duties of office or employment, up to a maximum of the amount paid to the employee during that period which was included in his or her income from office or employment.[209] Thus, if an employee receives his or her regular salary while ill or disabled but is required to repay these amounts to the employer out of the proceeds of an insurance policy, the employee may claim a deduction for the repayment. However, the deduction is available for the year in which the repayment is made, even though the employment income which is being repaid may have been subject to tax in a previous year.

[¶2373] Top-Up Disability Reimbursements

A deduction is provided to an individual who reimburses a top-up disability payment.[210] A top-up disability payment is a payment made to the individual by an employer or former employer to replace periodic disability payments that are not made to the individual because of the insolvency of an insurer, where the individual is required to reimburse the payment to the extent that he or she ultimately receives an amount from an insurer in respect of the disability payment.

[¶2375] Forfeited Amounts under a Salary Deferral Arrangement

A deduction is available where the right to receive benefits under a salary deferral arrangement has been forfeited in the year, provided that the forfeited amount has been included in computing income from employment.[211] The deductible amount is the amount by which the previous income inclusion exceeds the aggregate of:

(a) deferred amounts received in prior years;

(b) deferred amounts receivable in later years; and

(c) any forfeited amounts deducted under this rule in a previous year.

See also ¶2105.

See page ii for explanation of footnotes.

[209] CCH ¶3130; Sec. 8(1)(*n*).   [211] CCH ¶3131; Sec. 8(1)(*o*).
[210] CCH ¶3130aa; Sec. 8(1)(*n*.1).

[¶2380] Overseas Employment

Subject to the phase-out period described below, a tax credit is available to individuals resident in Canada working abroad for six or more consecutive months for a specified employer in connection with resource, construction, installation, agricultural, or engineering projects.[212] The amount of the credit will generally be equal to that portion of the employee's tax otherwise payable in the year that the lesser of:

(a) $80,000; and

(b) 80% of the employee's net overseas income taxable in Canada from that employment,

is of the employee's total income for the year. The effect of this formula is to provide a tax reduction in respect of a maximum of $100,000 of overseas employment income.

Beginning in 2013 the OETC will be gradually phased out over a three-year period so that it becomes completely eliminated after 2015. During the 2013–2015 phase-out period, the percentage applied to QFEI is reduced from 80% to 60% in 2013, 40% in 2014, and 20% in 2015. As a result, the maximum QFEI for those years is reduced from $100,000 to $60,000, $40,000, and $20,000, respectively.

The phase-out for the 2013–2015 taxation years does not apply to an individual's QFEI that is earned in connection with a contract that was committed to in writing before March 29, 2012. For example, if an employer has tendered an irrevocable bid in writing for a project before March 29, 2012, the employer will be considered to have committed in writing to the project irrespective of whether the bid has been accepted before March 29, 2012. In this case, the factor applied to an employee's QFEI in determining the employee's OETC will remain 80% for the 2013–2015 taxation years.

Beginning in 2016, the OETC is eliminated in all cases.

[¶2385] Musical Instruments

A deduction is available for taxpayers who are employed as musicians and who are required, as a condition of their employment, to provide their own musical instruments.[213] Deductible expenditures include costs of maintenance, insurance, and rental during the period or periods of employment. Capital cost allowance may be claimed in addition to these expenses, at a rate of 20% on a declining balance basis. The total amount deductible may not exceed the taxpayer's income from the year from employment as a musician.

In some cases, a Canadian resident individual, otherwise considered an employee of a non-resident employer, would incorporate a Canadian resi-

---

See page ii for explanation of footnotes.

[212] CCH ¶19,320; Sec. 122.3.   [213] CCH ¶3140; Sec. 8(1)(p).

dent company to employ the individual and then contract out the services to the non- resident in order to take advantage of the credit. The credit will be denied in circumstances where the employer and the individual are not dealing at arm's length and the employer does not employ more than five full-time employees in the business.[214]

[¶2387] Artists' Expenses

A deduction is provided for employed artists in respect of actual expenses paid for the purpose of earning employment income from qualifying artistic activities.[215] The deduction is limited to the lesser of:

(a) $1,000; and

(b) 20% of the taxpayer's income as an employee from artistic activity.

The maximum amount deductible will be reduced by amounts deductible as motor vehicle and aircraft costs and in respect of musical instruments.

Any expenses paid in the year to earn employment income from qualifying artistic activities that are not deductible for the year because they exceed the above limit, and that are also not deductible under any other provision of the Act, are carried forward to the immediately subsequent year. In the subsequent year, the expenses carried forward plus any new expenses paid in the year (to earn employment income from qualifying artistic activities) are deductible, subject to its limit as calculated for that year. Again, any undeductible amount would be carried forward.

[¶2388] Apprentice Mechanics' Tools

Eligible apprentice mechanics are allowed to deduct the cost of certain extraordinary expenditures incurred in respect to the cost of "eligible tools" they are required to acquire and use as a condition of their employment as an apprentice mechanic.[216] An eligible tool is defined to mean a tool (including ancillary equipment) that is acquired for use in connection with employment as an apprentice mechanic, that was not used for any purpose before such acquisition, and that is certified by the taxpayer's employer to be required to be provided as a condition of employment as an apprentice mechanic. An electronic communication device or electronic communication equipment acquired on or after May 2, 2006 is not an eligible tool, unless it can be used only for measuring, locating, or calculating. The deduction applies to individuals who are registered in a provincial, territorial, or (after May 2, 2006) federal program leading to a designation as a mechanic to repair automobiles, aircraft, and other self-propelled motorized vehicles.[217]

See page ii for explanation of footnotes.

[214] CCH ¶19,320a; Sec. 122.3(1.1).

[215] CCH ¶3143; Sec. 8(1)(q); Interp. Bul. IT-525R.

[216] CCH ¶3146; Sec. 8(1)(r).

[217] CCH ¶3370; Sec. 8(6).

The amount of the deduction is generally limited to the amount by which the employee's cost of an "eligible tool" acquired in the year exceeds the greater of (i) $500 plus the amount on which the Canada employment credit is calculated ($1,000 subject to annual indexation); and (ii) 5% of the sum of the apprenticeship employment income (net of employment deductions except for this one) and the apprenticeship grants under ¶2210 (net of a deduction for any refund of those grants). As a result of the indexation adjustment, the amount on which the Canada employment credit is calculated increased from $1,065 in 2011 to $1,095 in 2012. The amount of the deduction in the year is limited to the taxpayer's income from all sources for the year, meaning that the deduction cannot lead to a loss.[218]

Any part of the otherwise deductible tool costs that are not deducted in the year in which the tools are acquired may be carried forward and deducted in computing the individual's income from employment in future taxation years. Thus, for example, if the taxpayer is precluded from taking a full deduction in the year in which the tool is acquired owing to the above income limitation, the undeducted amount may be carried forward and deducted in the following year (subject again to the above income limitation). Such carryforward can be utilized in the following year even if the taxpayer is no longer employed as an eligible apprentice mechanic at that time. The carryforward can apply indefinitely.

For all other income tax purposes, the cost to the apprentice mechanic of the tools is reduced by the deductible portion of the cost (including, beginning in 2006, the portion deductible under ¶2389 as tools of tradespersons), regardless of whether that amount was actually deducted in the year.[219] When an eligible tool is disposed of for proceeds in excess of this reduced cost by the taxpayer or a person not dealing at arm's length with the taxpayer, the excess will be fully included in the income of the person making the disposition.[220] If, however, the taxpayer transfers an eligible tool into a partnership or corporation on a rollover basis under ¶7120 or ¶6220, the transfer will not lead to immediate income tax consequences. In such a case, the transferee's capital cost of the tool will be deemed to be the taxpayer's original cost of the tool, and the amount that was deductible under the apprentice mechanic or tradesperson tool provisions will be deemed to have been previously deducted by the transferee as capital cost allowance. Thus, if and when the transferee partnership or corporation sells the tool, the sale may result in recapture and a capital gain if the sale proceeds exceed the original cost of the tool to the taxpayer (the capital cost to the transferee).

Note that the apprentice must have his or her employer confirm, on form T2200, that the tools had to be bought and provided as a condition of employment.

See page ii for explanation of footnotes.

[218] CCH ¶3146; Sec. 8(1)(*r*).
[219] CCH ¶3390; Sec. 8(7).
[220] CCH ¶8047c; Sec. 56(1)(*k*).

[¶2389] Tradespeople's Tool Expenses

A taxpayer employed as a tradesperson may deduct from his or her employment income up to $500 of the cost of eligible tools acquired during the year to the extent that the cost exceeds $1,000 (indexed for 2008 and later years). As a result of indexation, the $1,000 threshold is increased to $1,095 in 2012 (up from $1,065 in 2011).[221]

An "eligible tool" is a tool (including ancillary equipment, such as a tool box) that:

(1) is acquired by the taxpayer for use in the taxpayer's employment as a tradesperson;

(2) has not been used for any purpose before it is acquired by the taxpayer;

(3) is certified by the taxpayer's employer, on form T2200, as being necessary for the taxpayer to provide as a condition of employment; and

(4) is not an electronic communication device (like a cellphone) or electronic data processing equipment (unless the device or equipment can be used only for the purpose of measuring, locating, or calculating).[222]

Where a taxpayer is entitled to deduct in a taxation year an amount on account of the cost of an eligible tool under the above deduction or under the apprentice mechanics' tool deduction (see ¶2388), the tax cost of the tool is reduced accordingly, whether that amount was actually deducted or not.[223] More particularly, the tax cost is the actual cost of a tool prorated by the allowed deduction for the year, divided by the cost of eligible tools acquired during the year. For instance, if a taxpayer acquired eight tools at $100 each and was entitled to deduct $500 for the year, the tax cost of each tool would be reduced by $100 × $500/$800 = $62.50. The tax cost for each tool would therefore be $38.50. The significance of the tax cost is that, if the tools are subsequently sold, the proceeds of disposition in excess of the tax cost must be included in income.[224]

Apprentice vehicle mechanics are eligible to claim the $500 tools tax deduction in addition to the existing apprentice vehicle mechanics' tools deduction under ¶2388.

[¶2390] Home Office Expenses

An amount may be deducted in respect of "work space" in a self-contained domestic establishment in which an employee resides.[225] The work space must be the principal place of employment of the employee or used by the employee exclusively for the purpose of earning income from

---

See page ii for explanation of footnotes.

[221] CCH ¶3150; Sec. 8(1)(s).
[222] CCH ¶3380; Sec. 8(6.1).
[223] CCH ¶3390; Sec. 8(7).

[224] CCH ¶8047c; Sec. 56(1)(k).

[225] CCH ¶3915; Sec. 8(13).

employment. The work space must be used on a regular and continuous basis for meeting customers or other persons in the ordinary course of performing the duties of employment. The amount deductible is limited to the employee's income from the office or employment for the year. An indefinite carryforward of unused expenses is provided in computing the employee's income from the same office or employment.

[¶2391] GST/HST Rebate on Employment Income Deductions

Where an employee incurs expenses which are deductible from employment income and those expenses include GST/PST, the employee can deduct for income tax purposes the full GST/PST included cost.[226] However, employees may also recover $^5/_{105}$ of those GST-inclusive expenditures they deduct for income purposes as a "rebate" of the GST.[227] This is intended to allow employees to recover the 5% GST included in the price of goods and services they have acquired for commercial purposes. Accordingly, an employee may not claim this rebate if he or she is an employee of an employer who is not required to charge GST on its basic services. Employees of GST unregistered employers and "listed financial institutions" are ineligible for the rebate. A "listed financial institution"[228] includes a bank, trust company, trader or broker or seller of financial instruments, credit union, insurer or provider of insurance policies, and lender (finance company). An unregistered employer would generally include employers with less than $30,000 per year taxable sales, health care providers, charities, and all levels of government.

On April 1, 1997, New Brunswick, Newfoundland and Labrador, and Nova Scotia replaced their old provincial sales taxes with a new Harmonized Sales Tax (HST) which is essentially identical to the GST and is administered by the federal government. In New Brunswick and Newfoundland and Labrador, the HST rate is 13% (5% federal GST component, plus 8% provincial sales tax component). Effective July 1, 2010, the Nova Scotia HST rate is increased from 13% to 15% (5% federal part and 10% provincial part), and Ontario and British Columbia harmonized their provincial sales tax with the GST to implement the HST. The British Columbia HST rate is 12% (5% federal part and 7% provincial part) and the Ontario HST rate is 13% (5% federal part and 8% provincial part). The rebate applies to the HST inclusive expenditures an employee may deduct from employment income. Where HST applies, the relevant HST fraction should be substituted for the $^5/_{105}$ GST fraction. This means that $^5/_{105}$ in the above formula becomes $^{13}/_{113}$ for expenses incurred at the 13% HST rate, $^{12}/_{112}$ for those incurred at the 12% HST rate, and $^{15}/_{115}$ for those incurred at the 15% HST rate.

On August 26, 2011, the Government of British Columbia announced that it would be reinstating its PST following the referendum on the elimination of the HST in the province. The 12% HST will be replaced, effective

---

See page ii for explanation of footnotes.

[226] CCH ¶3670; Sec. 8(11).
[227] *Excise Tax Act*, s. 253.
[228] *Excise Tax Act*, s. 149(1)(a).

April 1, 2013, by the federal GST and the PST. On February 17, 2012, transitional rules were proposed for the elimination of the HST and the reinstatetement the PST in British Columbia. Under these rules, not enacted yet, the rate for calculating rebates of GST/HST to employees with respect to certain expenses on which the 12% HST rate was payable would be reduced to 6.75% for the 2013 taxation year and 5% beginning with the 2014 taxation year.

Example: Purchased Automobile

In 2012, Brian purchased a car in a 5% GST province (like Alberta, Prince Edward Island, or Saskatchewan). The car cost $23,000 plus $1,840 PST and $1,150 GST. Accordingly, the basic capital cost is $25,990. Brian also paid $4,000 in operating expenses for the car. The car is used 25% for employment purposes. Brian is entitled to a capital cost allowance (CCA) of $975 (25% × $25,900 × 15% (one-half of the CCA rate for year of acquisition)), plus $1,000 for the operating expenses. Accordingly, Brian can deduct $1,975 on his 2012 return filed in 2013.

Brian's GST rebate for 2012 will be $5/105 × $975 = $46.43 on the capital cost allowance and $5/105 × $1,000 = $47.62 on the $1,000 operating expenses, for a total of $94.05. He should receive this amount as a tax credit on line 457 of the T1 return; to the extent it exceeds tax payable it will be included in Brian's tax refund.

Assuming Brian files for and is allowed his GST rebate for 2012 on his 2012 return filed and assessed in 2013, he will have additional taxable income in 2013 of $47.62, being the rebate on his deductible expense of $1,000. The $47.62 will be reported as income on his T1 return and his remaining undepreciated capital cost (UCC) on the car is reduced by his GST rebate of $36.43 based on his CCA claim. His initial 2013 UCC of $25,990 - $3,899 = $22,091 (before application of the 25% employment use factor) is therefore reduced to $22,044.57. For 2013, Brian will be able to take further deductions for 2013 expenses and for CCA based on adjusted opening UCC of $22,044.57. The UCC will be prorated for business use and will be eligible for 30% depreciation. Rebates based on 2013 operating expenses and CCA claims may also be claimed for 2013, using 2013 cost and CCA values (and at the 2013 GST extraction rate of $5/105).

[¶2395] Other Deductions

[¶2400] Moving Expenses

A taxpayer who moves from one residence in Canada to another residence in Canada is permitted to deduct "moving expenses" if the move is made in connection with the commencement of a business or employment at a particular location in Canada or to attend a university or other post-secondary educational institution.[229]

The new residence must be at least 40 kilometres closer, by the closest accessible route, to the new work location or school than the old residence. Moving expenses may be deducted in the year of the move, or, if they cannot be deducted in that year, they may be deducted in the following year. However, the deduction can only be made from income earned in the new work location, or, in the case of a student, from the amounts of any scholar-

---

[229] CCH ¶8650; Sec. 62(1)–(3); Interp. Bul. IT-178R3.

ships, fellowships, bursaries, prizes, or research grants included in computing income.

Effective for the 2008 and subsequent taxation years, any amounts received under the *Wage Earner Protection Program Act* (WEPP), in respect of a taxpayer's employment at a new work location, are considered to be part of the taxpayer's income when computing the deduction for moving expenses. The WEPP provides a level of compensation for lost employee wages due to employer bankruptcy or insolvency. Amounts received thereunder are intended to place employees in a position similar to the one they would have been in had they been fully compensated by their employer.

The minimum distance is not to be measured in a straight line but by the shortest normal route open to the travelling public.[230] According to this requirement, it does not matter if such route includes the use of an occasionally inconvenient ferry.[231] The taxpayer may deduct only the excess of the amount expended over any reimbursements of the expenses obtained by the taxpayer or paid on the taxpayer's behalf by the employer. The deduction does not apply to expenses incurred by residents in moving into or out of Canada[232] except for moves by persons taking up a full-time attendance as students at universities.

The expression "moving expenses" includes:

(a) travelling costs for the taxpayer and the taxpayer's household;

(b) the cost of transporting and storing household effects;

(c) the cost of food and lodging at the old and new location for up to 15 days;

(d) the cost of cancelling a lease on the former residence;

(e) the costs of selling the former residence, including advertising, notarial or legal fees, real estate commissions, and mortgage prepayment or discharge fees incurred on the sale;

(f) where the taxpayer's former residence is being sold by the taxpayer or the taxpayer's spouse or common-law partner as a result of the move, the cost of legal services incurred in purchasing the new residence, together with any taxes payable on the transfer or registration of title to the new residence, except for GST related to the purchase of the new residence;

(g) mortgage interest, property taxes, insurance premiums, and costs associated with maintaining heat and power on a vacant old residence to a maximum of $5,000; and

---

See page ii for explanation of footnotes.

[230] Giannakopoulos, 95 DTC 5477. [232] Webb, 74 DTC 1237.
[231] Higgins, 96 DTC 1291.

(h) the costs of revising legal documents to reflect the taxpayer's new address, replacing drivers' licences and automobile permits, and obtaining utility connections and disconnections.

All other acquisition costs of the taxpayer's new residence are specifically excluded. The deduction for acquisition costs is apparently not available to a taxpayer who does not sell, or whose spouse or common-law partner does not sell, the former residence or to a taxpayer who, as a result of the move, is acquiring his or her first residence.

Fire damage to a taxpayer's furniture sustained in the course of moving did not constitute a moving expense.[233]

Furthermore, such things as the increased cost of the new accommodation over the old, the installation cost of household items transferred to the new residence, and the cost of replacing or refitting transferred household items did not constitute moving expenses.[234] Moving expenses of a taxpayer moving from Russia to Canada were not deductible.[235]

[¶2405] Child Care Expenses

The Act provides for the deduction of "child care expenses" incurred for services rendered in the year in respect of an "eligible child" of the taxpayer.[236] The maximum yearly deduction is the lesser of:

(a) the amount actually paid for child care;

(b) $7,000 for each eligible child who is less then seven years of age; and $10,000 for each eligible child for whom an impairment tax credit may be claimed;

(c) ⅔ of the taxpayer's earned income.

To qualify, child care expenses must be incurred in order to permit the taxpayer or a supporting person of the child to pursue employment, business, training, or research activities. Child care expenses are only deductible as provided by the Act. In a highly publicized case, the salary paid to a nanny was ruled to be non-deductible as a business expense.[237]

Where there is more than one "supporting person" of a child, generally the deduction of child care expenses must be taken by the supporting person who has the lowest income, regardless of who actually incurred the expenses. In the most straightforward situation involving a wife and husband where child care expenses are incurred to permit both spouses to work, the child care expenses will be deductible by the spouse with the lower income. A taxpayer with no income is deemed to have income of zero.[238] This deeming provision was enacted in 1994, retroactively effective to 1990

See page ii for explanation of footnotes.

[233] Rath, 79 DTC 5140.
[234] Loukine, 98 DTC 1566.
[235] Loukine, 98 DTC 1566.

[236] CCH ¶8700; Sec. 63(1)–(3); Interp. Bul. IT-495R3.
[237] Symes, 94 DTC 6001.
[238] CCH ¶2003; Sec. 3(f).

and subsequent taxation years, after court decisions held that where one spouse had no income at all, the spouse with income could deduct the child care expenses since there was only one income.[239] In certain specific circumstances set out in (3) below, the higher income person is allowed to claim the child care expenses. If both the taxpayer and the supporting person are students, the higher income taxpayer may claim child care expenses as calculated under (3) below. The calculation is based on the number of weeks in the year that the taxpayer is a student. If there is a supporting person, the amount is based on the number of weeks both individuals are students.

(1) *Meaning of "eligible child".* An "eligible child" of a taxpayer means a child of the taxpayer or of the taxpayer's spouse or common-law partner or a child who is dependent on the taxpayer or the taxpayer's spouse or common-law partner and whose income for the year does not exceed the basic personal amount ($10,527 for 2011).[240] The child must be under 16 years old at some time during the year (i.e., be under 17 at the end of the year) or be dependent on the taxpayer or the taxpayer's spouse or common-law partner because of a mental or physical infirmity. Note that being dependent by reason of infirmity is different from the child qualifying for the impairment tax credit. A child is generally considered to be dependent if the taxpayer has contributed to the maintenance of the child.

The definition "eligible child" and the definition "supporting person" refer not only to a "spouse" (including an unmarried opposite-sex spouse who has been cohabiting with the taxpayer in a conjugal relationship for at least one year or is the parent of a child of whom the taxpayer is also a parent), they also refer to an unmarried same-sex partner who meets these requirements.[241] Therefore, an eligible child includes the child of a same-sex or opposite-sex common-law partner who has been cohabiting with the taxpayer for at least one year or is the parent of a child of whom the taxpayer is also a parent. For these purposes, a common-law partnership will be considered to have broken down if the two people have not cohabited for at least 90 days. A child of a taxpayer includes a natural or adopted child of the taxpayer, a child of the taxpayer's spouse or common-law partner, the spouse or common-law partner of the taxpayer's child, and a person who is wholly dependent on the taxpayer for support and of whom the taxpayer has or immediately before the person attained the age of 19 had, in law or in fact, custody and control.[242] It should be noted that a taxpayer need not live with the child for the child to be an eligible child of the taxpayer. However, if the taxpayer does not reside with the child, the costs of the child services will likely cease to qualify as child care expenses.

(2) *Child care expenses.* To qualify as a child care expense, the expense must be for providing child care services in Canada for an eligible child of the taxpayer. Babysitting, day nursery, and attendance at a boarding school

---

[239] Fiset, 88 DTC 1226, McLaren, 88 DTC 1259, Fromstein, 93 DTC 726.

[240] CCH ¶8717; Sec. 63(3) "eligible child".

[241] CCH ¶28,047a; Sec. 248(1) "common-law partner".

[242] CCH ¶28,372; Sec. 252(1).

or camp are specifically mentioned but other services could fall within the general meaning of child care services. However, it is specifically provided that child care expenses do not include medical and hospital care expenses, clothing, transportation and education costs, or board or lodging that is not specifically mentioned. Board and lodging expenses are limited to lodging at a boarding school or camp to a maximum of $175 per week for each child who is under seven years of age or has a severe and prolonged mental, physical or sight impairment, and for whom an impairment tax credit may be claimed, and $100 per week for each other child.[243]

In general, child care expenses of a taxpayer include those incurred personally as well as those incurred by a supporting person of the child for the year. However, if the supporting person of the child was, because of a marriage breakdown of the person's marriage or common-law partnership, living separate and apart from the taxpayer for a period of at least 90 days beginning in the year and was living separate and apart at the end of the year, then only the child care expenses paid by the taxpayer are taken into account when calculating the taxpayer's child care expenses deduction.

Receipts for child care expenses need not be filed with the taxpayer's income tax return but the taxpayer should have receipts and keep them on file in the event that the CRA asks for them. Where the child care services are provided by an individual, the taxpayer must include the individual's Social Insurance Number on Form T778 when the claim is made. This requirement is directed toward assuring that the child care expenses will be reported as income of the individual who performs the services. The absence of receipts is not fatal to a claim for child care expenses.[244]

The child care services must be obtained to enable the taxpayer or a supporting person of the child who resided with the child to earn employment or business income or to carry on research or similar work in respect of which a grant is received. The expenses qualify if the child care services allow the taxpayer to attend a designated educational institution or a secondary school for a period of not less than three consecutive weeks in a program requiring a time commitment of at least 10 hours per week on courses or work. Child care expenses may be claimed by part-time students who attend a designated educational institution or a secondary school for a period of not less than three consecutive weeks in a program requiring a time commitment of at least 12 hours per month. Expenses related to the services of a nanny familiarizing herself with her duties while the taxpayer was on maternity leave were held to be within the "object and spirit" of the provisions but were limited to those attributable to the seven days prior to the taxpayer's return to employment.[245]

See page ii for explanation of footnotes.

[243] CCH ¶8708; Sec. 63(2.3).
[244] Senger-Hammond, 96 DTC 3301, Wells, 98 DTC 3402, Barhmed, 98 DTC 3374.
[245] McCluskie, 94 DTC 1735.

¶2405

Finally, the child care services must be provided by a person resident in Canada. However, expenses will not qualify if the services are provided by the child's father or mother, any supporting person of the child, any person under 18 years of age who is connected — by blood relationship, marriage or common-law partnership, or adoption — with the taxpayer or the taxpayer's spouse or common-law partner, or if they are provided by any person in respect of whom the taxpayer or any supporting person of the child has claimed a dependent tax credit.

(3) *Who may claim deduction.* If there is more than one "supporting person" of an eligible child, the deduction must, except in limited circumstances, be taken by the supporting person with the lowest income.[246] A supporting person means a person who resided with the taxpayer at any time during the year and at any time within 60 days after the end of the year if that person is a parent of the child, the taxpayer's spouse or common-law partner, or if the person claimed a tax credit in respect of the child.[247]

The supporting person with the lowest income will not have to deduct child care expenses if such supporting person is:

(a) in full-time attendance at school (i.e., enrolment in a secondary school or designated program of at least three consecutive weeks' duration, requiring at least 10 hours per week, on courses or work in the program);

(b) is certified by a doctor to be incapable of caring for children by reason of medical or physical infirmity;

(c) is in prison for at least two weeks in the year; or

(d) is living apart from the supporting person with the higher income at the end of the year and for a period of at least 90 days beginning in the year because of the breakdown of their marriage or common-law partnership.

In determining which supporting person has the lower income, the deduction for child care expenses is not taken into consideration, nor are deductions for the repayment of employment insurance benefits, family allowance, and/or old age security benefits. If two supporting persons have identical earned income, they must jointly elect to treat one income as being higher.[248]

Single parents may claim a deduction for child care expenses incurred in order to attend school full-time against all types of income to a maximum of $175 for each child who is under seven years of age or who has a severe and prolonged mental, physical, or sight impairment, and for whom an impairment tax credit may be claimed, and $100 for each other eligible

---

See page ii for explanation of footnotes.

[246] CCH ¶8704; Sec. 63(2).   [248] CCH ¶8706; Sec. 63(2.1).
[247] CCH ¶8718; Sec. 63(3) "supporting person".

child, multiplied by the number of weeks during which the supporting parent is in full-time attendance at school. This also applies if the taxpayer is a qualifying student and is the supporting person with the higher income of the year.

A part-time student attending a course lasting at least three consecutive weeks and involving a minimum of 12 hours of courses per month can claim child care expenses of $175 for each child under the age of seven and $100 for each child aged seven to 16 multiplied by the number of months the parent is enrolled in the educational program.[249] If there is a supporting person with a higher income, the supporting person may claim this amount as a child care expense.

[¶2410] Disability Support and Attendant Care Expenses

The disability supports deduction provides a deduction from income for certain types of expenditures paid in the year by a disabled individual for assistive devices or supports that enable the individual to earn certain kinds of taxable income or to attend high school, college, university, or other designated educational institution.[250] It replaces the attendant care expenses deduction with a broader-based deduction so that disabled persons do not pay tax on benefits received to purchase supports. The effect of the disability supports deduction is that no income tax is payable on income (including government assistance) used to pay disability support expenses, and that this income is not used in determining the value of income-tested benefits.

The disability supports deduction includes expenses for attendant care, which were allowed with the former attendant care expenses deduction, and adds several others listed below. Under the disability supports deduction, the disabled individual need not qualify for the disability tax credit in order to claim amounts (other than part-time attendant care). However, for the items listed below after item (i), a medical practitioner must certify in writing that the individual requires such services. The deduction may only be claimed by the disabled taxpayer who is attending school or working. If the taxpayer has insufficient income to claim the amounts as a deduction, an individual who supports the taxpayer may be able to use them for purposes of the medical expense credit.

The types of expenditures that are deductible under the disability supports deduction are:

(i) The amount paid by a person who has a speech or hearing impairment for sign-language interpretation services or real-time captioning services. The amount must be paid to a person who is in the business of providing such services to be deductible. There is no requirement for this item that a medical practitioner prescribe or

---

See page ii for explanation of footnotes.

[249] CCH ¶8707, ¶8708; Sec. 63(2.2), 63(2.3).   [250] CCH ¶8740; Sec. 64; Interp. Bul. IT-519R2.

¶2410

certify that the sign language interpretation services or real-time captioning services are required by the taxpayer.

(ii) A teletypewriter, a telephone ringing indicator, or similar device (prescribed by a medical practitioner) that enables a deaf or mute person to make or receive telephone calls.

(iii) A device or equipment (prescribed by a medical practitioner) that is designed to be used by a blind person for operating a computer. This includes Braille printers, synthetic speech systems, and large-print on-screen devices.

(iv) An optical scanner or similar device (prescribed by a medical practitioner) designed to be used by a blind person to read print.

(v) An electronic speech synthesizer (prescribed by a medical practitioner) to enable a mute person to communicate using a portable keyboard.

(vi) The cost of note-taking services, paid to a person who is in the business of providing such services, paid by a taxpayer who has a mental or physical impairment and who a medical practitioner has certified requires those services.

(vii) Voice recognition software for a person with a physical impairment for whom a medical practitioner has certified requires that software.

(viii) The cost of tutoring services that are supplementary to the primary education of the taxpayer, for a taxpayer with a learning disability or mental impairment for whom a medical practitioner has certified requires such services. The amount must be paid to a person who is in the business of providing tutoring services and is not related to the taxpayer.

(ix) The cost of talking textbooks for a taxpayer attending secondary school in Canada or a designated educational institution for whom a medical practitioner has certified requires talking textbooks because of a perceptual disability.

(x) The cost of attendant care provided in Canada for a person with a mental or physical infirmity. The amount must be paid to a person other than the taxpayer's spouse or common-law partner and who is at least 18 years of age. In order to deduct amounts paid for a part-time attendant, the taxpayer must be eligible for the disability tax credit, which requires completion of CRA Form T2201. An amount may be deducted for the cost of full-time attendant care, if the taxpayer qualifies for the disability tax credit or if a medical practitioner certifies that the taxpayer requires a full-time attendant because of an infirmity that will require the taxpayer to need assistance with personal needs indefinitely. A taxpayer is entitled to claim

¶2410

the disability tax credit as well as a deduction for attendant care under the disability supports deduction.

For 2005 and later years, the following items were added to the list of expenses eligible for the disability supports deduction:

- Job-coaching services for an individual with a severe and prolonged impairment, the need for which is certified by a medical practitioner. The amount must be paid to persons in the business of providing these services and the eligible expenses do not include job placement or career counselling services.

- Reading services for an individual who is blind or has a severe learning disability. The amount must be paid to persons in the business of providing these services and the need for the service by the individual must be certified by a medical practitioner.

- Deaf-blind intervening services for an individual who is both blind and profoundly deaf. The amount must be paid to persons in the business of providing these services.

- Bliss symbol boards for an individual who has a speech impairment. A medical practitioner must certify that the individual needs such device.

- Braille note-takers for use by an individual who is blind, so that the individual can take notes with the help of a keyboard. A medical practitioner must certify that the individual needs this device.

- Page-turners for an individual with a severe and prolonged impairment that markedly restricts the individual's ability to turn the pages of a book. A medical practitioner must certify that the individual needs this device.

- Devices and software designed to enable an individual who is blind or who has a severe learning disability to read print. A medical practitioner must certify that the individual needs such device and software.

The overall deduction is limited to the lesser of:

(a) the actual amounts paid in the year by the taxpayer for the disability supports listed above, which enable the taxpayer to work, to attend secondary school or a designated educational institution, and for which the taxpayer was not reimbursed; and

(b) the total of:

(i) the taxpayer's earned income as described below; and

(ii) if the taxpayer is a student at a designated educational institution or a secondary school, the least of:

¶2410

- $15,000;

- $375 times the number of weeks in the year that the taxpayer was attending school; and

- the amount by which the taxpayer's net income (line 236 of the T1 return) without claiming the disability supports deduction exceeds the taxpayer's earned income for the year.

For the purposes of (a) above, a reimbursement does not include an amount received as assistance that is included in computing the taxpayer's income and is not deductible from the taxpayer's taxable income, and also does not include prescribed assistance. Currently, no assistance has been prescribed. As discussed in the Committee's report, the disability supports deduction is intended to ensure that an individual is not paying tax on an amount received from a government (such as the Canada Study Grant for Students with Permanent Disabilities or Opportunities Fund) or other sources, such as private insurance companies, which is intended to assist the individual to acquire the needed supports. Prior to the implementation of the disability supports deduction, the CRA treated the amount received by a disabled taxpayer as a government grant for disabled students and included it in income.[251] The disability supports deduction now allows a taxpayer in similar circumstances to deduct the full amount of such a grant that is used by the individual to work or further his or her education.

"Earned income" for the purpose of the above income limitations means net business income, gross employment income, net research grants, taxable portion of scholarships, fellowships, bursaries and similar awards, earnings supplements under a government program to encourage individuals to find or keep employment, and financial assistance (usually related to training programs) under the *Employment Insurance Act* and similar provincial programs which operate under an agreement with the EI Commission.

[¶2415] Capital Element of Annuity Payments

Certain annuity payments are included in the income of the recipient (see ¶2185). However, the taxpayer may deduct the capital element of each annuity payment that was included in income.[252]

The computation of the capital element of a contractual annuity is prescribed by regulation.[253] In general, the capital element of annuity payments received in a year is a proportion of the payments which the consideration or purchase price bears to the aggregate of the payments expected.

See page ii for explanation of footnotes.

[251] Simser, 2005 DTC 5001.
[252] CCH ¶8401; Sec. 60(a).
[253] CCH ¶8402; Reg. 300.

[¶2420] Interest on Death Duties

A taxpayer may deduct annual interest accruing in the taxation year in respect of succession duties, inheritance taxes, or estate taxes.[254] Since this deduction is for interest accruing and not for interest paid, the deduction must be taken in each year. Interest on money borrowed to pay succession duties or estate taxes is, however, not deductible.[255]

[¶2425] Canada or Quebec Pension Plan Contributions

A taxpayer is entitled to a personal tax credit equal to the appropriate percentage (15% for the 2007 and subsequent taxation years) times the total of:

(a) the maximum amount of employee's premiums payable under the *Canada Pension Plan* (CPP) or *Quebec Pension Plan* (QPP) for the year by an employee; and

(b) ½ of the amount of premiums payable by a self-employed individual, in respect of self-employed earnings, under the CPP or QPP for the year.[256]

Self-employed individuals may deduct 50% of CPP/QPP contributions (the portion that represents the employer's share) rather than claiming a personal amount credit at the lowest marginal rate. The remaining 50% of their CPP/QPP contributions that represent the employee's portion continue to qualify for a tax credit, as it does for other taxpayers.[257]

The tax credit and, for self-employed individuals, the 50% deduction for CPP/QPP contributions are in addition to the deductions for contributions made under registered pension plans, deferred profit sharing plans (DPSPs), and registered retirement savings plans (RRSPs) and will not affect the maximum amounts of the contributions that may be deducted under these plans.

Payments by an employee, as an employer, for CPP/QPP contributions for assistants or substitutes may be deducted in computing the employee's income where the employee is required by the terms of the contract to hire such an assistant or substitute. This deduction is in addition to the deduction for the actual salaries paid to the assistant or substitute if the employee is required by the terms of the contract to hire such a person.[258]

[¶2427] Quebec Parental Insurance Plan (QPIP) — Self-Employed Premiums

Effective January 1, 2006, Quebec introduced a parent insurance plan (QPIP) under which eligible workers are entitled to benefits when they take

---

See page ii for explanation of footnotes.

[254] CCH ¶8430; Sec. 60(*d*).

[255] Cutten, 56 DTC 454.

[256] CCH ¶18,441; Sec. 118.7.

[257] CCH ¶8436; Sec. 60(*e*).

[258] CCH ¶3114; Sec. 8(1)(*l.1*).

maternity, paternity, adoption, or parental leave. QPIP is like EI, funded by employer and employee (and self-employment) contributions. Employee contributions are personal amounts eligible for personal tax credits. Employer contributions are deductible from income.[259]

As with CPP/QPP, self-employed workers may pay both employee and employer premiums. The employee portion is eligible for the personal amount credit; any excess is deductible from income tax.[260]

[¶2430] Premiums or Payments under Registered Retirement Savings Plans (RRSPs) or Registered Retirement Income Funds (RRIFs)

An amount paid by a taxpayer as a premium under an RRSP, or to a plan under which the taxpayer's spouse or common-law partner is the annuitant, is deductible within certain limitations.[261] Moreover, consequential to the introduction in the 2009 Budget of a deduction in respect of post-death RRSP and RRIF losses, a loss realised in an RRSP or an RRIF after the death of the annuitant can now be carried back and deducted when computing the annuitant's income in the year of death. The amount that may be carried back is generally calculated as the difference between the amount in respect of the RRSP or RRIF included in the annuitant's income as a result of the annuitant's death and the total of all amounts paid out of the RRSP or RRIF after the death of the annuitant.[262] This measure applies in respect of deceased annuitants' RRSPs or RRIFs where the final distribution from the RRSP or RRIF occurs after 2008. See additional commentary in Chapter X.

[¶2435] Transfer of Superannuation Benefits

A taxpayer may transfer certain income receipts to a registered pension plan (RPP) or to a registered retirement savings plan (RRSP) and deduct the amount so transferred in computing income.[263] The only amounts qualifying for such a rollover are:

(a) amounts payable from pension plans attributable to services rendered by a person and by his or her spouse/common-law partner or former spouse/common-law partner in a period during which such person was not resident in Canada;

(b) a lump-sum payment from a foreign retirement arrangement where the payment is included in income and derives from contributions made to the foreign retirement arrangement by the taxpayer or the taxpayer's spouse/common-law partner or former spouse/common-law partner;[264]

See page ii for explanation of footnotes.

[259] Sec. 8(1)(*l.2*).

[260] Sec. 60(*g*).

[261] CCH ¶8480; Sec. 60(*l*).

[262] CCH ¶21,333f, ¶21,428obf; Sec. 146(8.92), 146.3(6.3).

[263] CCH ¶8490; Sec. 60(*j*).

[264] CCH ¶8559k; Sec. 60.01.

(c) lump-sum amounts received by a testamentary trust from the deceased's registered pension plans or deferred profit sharing plans and distributed to the surviving spouse or common-law partner/beneficiary (see ¶7295 for more details); and

(d) the cost of shares of an employer distributed to a beneficiary under a deferred profit sharing plan of the employer (see ¶10,453 for more details).

The deductions are allowed in addition to the taxpayer's RPP/RRSP limit for the year.

[¶2437] Pension Income Splitting

Canadian residents may now allocate up to one-half of their income that qualifies for the pension income tax credit to their resident spouse (or common-law partner) for income tax purposes.

To engage in pension income splitting, a pensioner (pension recipient), and his or her spouse or common-law partner (pension transferee) must make a joint election each year using Form T1032. This form must be filed with their income tax returns for the year on or before their filing-due date (generally April 30 of the year following the tax year, or June 15 if self-employed).[265] The fact that the election must be made annually accords with the fact that the optimal amount to be allocated may change from year to year — for instance, where one spouse's or common-law partner's pension is indexed for inflation and the other's is not.

The amount allocated is deducted in determining the net income of the person who actually received the pension income,[266] and it is included in computing the net income of the pension transferee.[267]

The following amounts received in the year qualify for pension income splitting:

- For those age 65 or older: annuity payments from an RPP, RRSP, DPSP, and the minimum RRIF payments.

- For those under age 65: annuity payments from an RPP (and certain other payments such as a survivor pension annuity).[268]

The following are not included:

- any pension or supplement under the *Old Age Security Act* or similar provincial plan;

- any benefit under the Canada or *Quebec Pension Plan*;

- a death benefit (as defined in ¶2165); and

See page ii for explanation of footnotes.

[265] CCH ¶8559q; Sec. 60.03(1) "joint election".

[266] CCH ¶8420; Sec. 60(c).

[267] CCH ¶8030; Sec. 56(1)(a.2).

[268] CCH ¶8559p; Sec. 60.03(1) "eligible pension income".

- any payment out of a salary deferral arrangement, a retirement compensation arrangement, an employee benefit plan, an employee trust, or a prescribed provincial plan.

A pensioner may not allocate more than 50% of his or her eligible pension income in a year to his or her spouse or common-law partner; there is no dollar limit. More exactly, the amount elected cannot exceed 50% of the eligible pension income for the year multiplied by the number of months in the pensioner's taxation year in which the pensioner was married to, or was in a common-law partnership with the pension transferee, divided by the number of months in the pensioner's taxation year.[269] With regard to this last specification, in its technical notes, the Department of Finance provided the following example (which we have updated):

Example:

(1) Gisèle and Jean-Guy have been cohabiting in a conjugal relationship since July 1, 2011. Jean-Guy will receive pension income under a Registered Pension Plan (RPP) of $26,400 in 2012. Jean-Guy may split up to 50% of his 2012 RPP income for the six-month period in 2012 during which he was considered to be a common-law partner of Gisèle. That is, Jean-Guy may allocate $6,600 of his $26,400 RPP income to Gisèle for 2012: 0.5A × B/C - [0.5 × ($26,400 × 6 months in common-law partnership/12 months in the year)].

For the purpose of calculating the pension credit (see ¶8110), the pensioner is treated as not having received the portion of his or her pension income and qualified pension income allocated to the pension transferee — the "split-pension amount".[270] This means that when calculating the pension credit the pensioner will be able to claim whichever amount is less: $2,000 or the amount of his or her eligible pension income after excluding amounts allocated to his or her spouse or common-law partner. On the other hand, the pension transferee is treated as having received the split-pension amount. This means that the pension transferee will be able to claim whichever amount is less: $2,000 or the amount of his or her pension income that is eligible for the pension income amount, including the allocated pension income.

[¶2440] Transfer of Retiring Allowances

To the extent that it is based on years of service prior to 1996, a retiring allowance which has been included in income (see ¶2160) may be transferred to a registered pension fund or plan or to a registered retirement savings plan (RRSP) and deducted in computing income, subject to certain limitations.[271] This special rollover is not available for employment commencing after 1995. See ¶10,357.

---

[269] CCH ¶8559v; Sec. 60.03(1) "split-pension amount".

[270] CCH ¶8559w; Sec. 60.03(2).

[271] CCH ¶8495; Sec. 60(j.1).

[¶2445] Transfer of Refund of Premiums under RRSP/RRIF

A deduction is allowed to an individual who receives specified amounts of retirement income and transfers a designated portion of such income to a registered retirement savings plan (RRSP), a registered retirement income fund (RRIF), to acquire a specified annuity, or, subject to transitional rules, after March 3, 2010, to make contributions to a registered disability savings plan (RDSP) of a financially dependent infirm child (for more details, see ¶2447). The effect of this deduction is to allow a tax-free transfer (referred to as a"rollover") of certain amounts which the taxpayer is to receive out of an RRSP or a RRIF.[272] In general, where a surviving spouse or common-law partner receives an amount out of the deceased spouse's or common-law partner's RRSP or RRIF, the amount can be transferred to a life annuity, a term-to-age-90 annuity, or a RRIF. A surviving spouse or common-law partner under the age of 71 may make any of the above transfers and also transfer the amount to an RRSP. A child or grandchild who was financially dependent on the deceased by virtue of physical or mental infirmity may also make these transfers. A minor child or grandchild who was financially dependent on the deceased (i.e., whose income for the year preceding death was less than the basic personal amount) can use the amount to provide an annuity payable to age 18 but not, unless dependent by reason of infirmity, to make any of the other types of transfers.

The amounts available for this tax-free transfer are:

(1) The amount included in the taxpayer's income as a refund of premiums under an RRSP of the taxpayer's spouse or common-law partner.

(2) The amount included in computing the taxpayer's income as a refund of premiums under an RRSP of a person upon whom the taxpayer was dependent by reason of mental or physical infirmity. This tax-free rollover is now extended to lump-sum benefits received out of a registered pension plan (RPP) by a financially dependent infirm child or grandchild as a consequence of the death of a supporting parent or grandparent. In determining eligibility for the rollover, an infirm child or grandchild is presumed to be financially dependent if, for the year preceding the parent or grandparent's death, the income of the child or grandchild did not exceed the basic personal amount plus the disability amount (i.e., $17,868 for deaths in 2012).[273]

(3) The least of the following items:

(a) where the taxpayer is a minor, an amount paid by or on behalf of the taxpayer to acquire an annuity to age 18;

(b) an amount (other than an amount referred to in (2) above or in (4) below) included in the taxpayer's income as a lump-sum payment out of a registered pension plan (RPP), as a refund of premi-

---

See page ii for explanation of footnotes.

[272] CCH ¶8510; Sec. 60(*l*).   [273] CCH ¶21,211g; Sec. 146(1.1).

¶2445

ums under an RRSP, or as a designated benefit from a RRIF arising as a consequence of the death of an individual, where the taxpayer is a child or grandchild of the individual; and

(c) where the minimum amount for the year in respect of the RRIF was not withdrawn prior to the death of the annuitant, the amount in (3)(b) above in respect of income from a RRIF to a child or a grandchild of the annuitant is reduced by the excess of the designated benefits over the eligible amounts.

(4) The total of all eligible amounts (see ¶10,418) of the taxpayer for the year in respect of a RRIF.

(5) The amount included in the taxpayer's income as the result of full or partial commutation of an RRSP.

(6) Where the taxpayer is an annuitant under a RRIF as a result of the death of the taxpayer's spouse or common-law partner, the amount received by the taxpayer under the RRIF which exceeds that portion of the minimum amount under the RRIF that was not received by the deceased in the year.

Note that the payments described in items (5) and (6) above must be made by a direct transfer from the issuer of the RRSP or carrier of the RRIF. The taxpayer must designate in the taxpayer's income tax return for the year the amount that is being claimed as a deduction. Form T2097 is provided for this purpose.

[¶2447] Rollover of RRSP, RRIF, or RPP Proceeds to RDSP on Death

After March 3, 2010, the RRSP rollover rules at ¶2445 are extended to allow a rollover of a deceased individual's RRSP proceeds to the RDSP of the deceased individual's financially dependent infirm child or grandchild.[274] This new rollover also applies to amounts transferred to an RDSP from registered retirement income fund (RRIF) proceeds and certain lump-sum amounts paid from registered pension plans (RPP).

To be eligible, the contribution to an RDSP can only be made after June 30, 2011, and, when the death of the annuitant occurs after 2007 and before 2011, the contribution must be made before 2012. For more information, see ¶10,430, ¶10,492, and the Q&A page that the CRA posted on its Web site in response to the March 2010 Budget.

[¶2450] Estate Tax and Succession Duties Applicable to Certain Property

An individual successor who receives a superannuation, pension, death benefit, or a benefit under an RRSP or deferred profit sharing plan (DPSP), or a benefit that is a payment under an income averaging annuity contract

---

See page ii for explanation of footnotes.
[274] CCH ¶8559le; Sec. 60.02(2).

may deduct a portion of the benefit received by the individual.[275] The deduction is to be computed separately for estate tax and provincial succession duty. Estate tax is only exigible where death occurred before 1972.

The deduction is determined by reference to the tax or duties applicable to the benefit. The amount must be received on or after the death of the predecessor in respect of whom the taxpayer is the successor.

[¶2455] Overpayments of Pension or Benefits

A deduction is allowed for amounts repaid by a taxpayer on account of an overpayment received and included in computing income in respect of an old age pension, a retiring allowance, any benefit under the CPP or similar provincial pension plan, a prescribed benefit under a government assistance program (see below), a benefit under the *Unemployment Insurance Act* or *Employment Insurance Act*, earnings supplements and financial assistance, and, beginning in 2006, a benefit under the new Quebec Parental Insurance Plan.[276]

Prescribed benefits under a government assistance program are those benefits received under the *Labour Adjustment Benefits Act*, under section 5 of the *Department of Labour Act*, as well as under the Plant Workers Adjustment Program (as a result of an agreement under section 5 of the *Department of Fisheries and Oceans Act*), and under the Northern Cod Compensation and Adjustment Program.[277]

[¶2460] Expenses of Objection or Appeal

Taxpayers may deduct amounts paid by them in the year in respect of fees or expenses incurred in preparing, instituting, or prosecuting an objection to or an appeal in relation to an assessment of tax (including provincial income tax), interest, or penalties, a decision of the Canada Employment and Immigration Commission, a board of referees or an umpire under the *Employment Insurance Act* or *Unemployment Insurance Act, 1971*, an assessment of foreign tax credits, and any assessment or a decision under the *Canada Pension Plan* or a similar provincial plan.[278]

Legal expenses paid to collect or establish a right to a retiring allowance or pension benefits are deductible to the extent that they do not exceed the retiring allowance or pension benefit.[279] Any costs recovered by, or reimbursed to, the taxpayer on an appeal in relation to which he or she has received this deduction must be brought into income.[280] See also ¶2205 and ¶2305.

---

[275] CCH ¶8520, ¶8522; Sec. 60(*m*), 60(*m*.1).

[276] CCH ¶8530; Sec. 60(*n*).

[277] Reg. 5502.

[278] CCH ¶8540; Sec. 60(*o*).

[279] CCH ¶8541; Sec. 60(*o*.1).

[280] CCH ¶8049; Sec. 56(1)(*l*).

[¶2465] Income Averaging Annuity Contracts

A taxpayer must include in income any annuity payments received in the taxation year. If a taxpayer disposes of an income averaging annuity contract, the proceeds must be brought into income for the year.[281] If a contract ceases at any time to be an income averaging annuity contract, for a reason other than the disposition thereof, the taxpayer must bring into income the fair market value of the contract at that time.[282] Where an annuitant under such a contract dies, payments made under it thereafter are considered to be made under an income averaging annuity contract. Thus, the provisions respecting the deduction of the capital element of an annuity do not apply.[283]

[¶2470] Payments Included in Income

Certain amounts included in income may be deducted in computing taxable income, such that, in the end result, no tax is paid on those amounts.[284] Because these amounts are in fact included in income and then deducted in computing taxable income, they are relevant in determining the extent to which the recipient can be claimed as a dependant by another taxpayer. The amounts include income exempt under an international tax treaty, workers' compensation payments, and social assistance payments.

A deduction is provided to a taxpayer who is required to include benefits paid out of a retirement compensation arrangement in income.[285] A taxpayer will also be entitled to a deduction in respect of any amounts he or she paid (while a Canadian resident) to acquire an interest in a retirement compensation arrangement. Accordingly, a taxpayer will be able to recover an amount equal to the taxpayer's contributions plus the amount he or she paid to acquire the interest in the retirement compensation arrangement before any benefits will be included in income.

Amounts which are otherwise deductible as employee contributions to pension plans which are retirement compensation arrangements are excluded.

A taxpayer is also permitted a deduction upon the sale of his or her interest in the arrangement and is required to include the proceeds in income.

[¶2480] Northern Area Residents' Travel Benefit Deduction

An employee residing[286] for at least six consecutive months in an area or areas each of which was a "prescribed northern zone" or "prescribed intermediate zone" may claim a deduction in computing taxable income in respect of certain travel benefits for trips made in the year for the purpose of

---

See page ii for explanation of footnotes.

[281] CCH ¶8039; Sec. 56(1)(e), 56(1)(f).
[282] CCH ¶8621; Sec. 61.1(1), 61.1(2).
[283] CCH ¶8401; Sec. 60(a).

[284] CCH ¶15,290; Sec. 110(1)(f).
[285] CCH ¶8559, ¶8559a; Sec. 60(t).
[286] Morecroft, 91 DTC 937.

obtaining medical services not otherwise available in the locality in which the employee resided, or for two or fewer trips for other than medical purposes.[287]

To qualify, the six-month residing period may either begin or end in the taxation year. Where a taxpayer moves from one qualifying area to another, the combined periods of residency in those areas will qualify for the six-month test as long as the periods are not interrupted by residence outside of the qualifying areas. The amount of the deduction depends on the area in which the taxpayer resided. Residency in a "prescribed northern zone" qualifies for the full deduction, while residency in a "prescribed intermediate zone" qualifies for the deduction at a rate of 50%.[288]

These travel benefits are deductible only to the extent that their value is included in income from employment.[289]

The deduction applies with respect to all trips made by the employee or a member of the employee's household for the purpose of obtaining necessary medical services not available locally.

In addition, a deduction may be claimed with respect to travelling expenses incurred in connection with not more than two trips made in a calendar year by the employee and each member of the employee's household. For each trip, the deduction cannot exceed a prescribed amount intended to represent the cost of the return economy air fare to the nearest designated city. For this purpose, the designated city with respect to any area is the closest of Vancouver, Edmonton, Calgary, Saskatoon, Winnipeg, North Bay, Toronto, Ottawa, Montreal, Quebec City, Moncton, Halifax, or St. John's.

[¶2485] Northern Area Residents' Housing Benefit Deduction

In addition to the deduction for travel benefits, individuals who resided in a prescribed area throughout a period of six months commencing or ending in the year may claim a special deduction in respect of housing allowances included in their income, equal to $8.25 ($7.50 for 2007 and earlier) multiplied by the number of days that they resided in the area. For a prescribed intermediate zone, the daily living cost component is reduced by 50%. Where the individual maintained and resided in a self-contained domestic establishment (i.e., a dwelling house, apartment or other similar place of residence in which a person, as a general rule, sleeps and eats) and no other person residing in the same establishment claimed a deduction for that day, the deduction is increased to $16.50 per day ($15.00 for 2007 and earlier).[290]

See page ii for explanation of footnotes.

[287] CCH ¶15,999g, ¶15,999i; Sec. 110.7(1), 110.7(3); Reg. 7303.1.

[288] CCH ¶15,999h; Sec. 110.7(2).

[289] CCH ¶15,999g; Sec. 110.7(1)(a).

[290] CCH ¶15,999g; Sec. 110.7(1)(b).

Thus, where a taxpayer and the taxpayer's spouse or common-law partner reside together in a self-contained domestic establishment in a prescribed area, both could claim the deduction of $8.25 per day ($7.50 before 2008) or either could claim $16.50 per day ($15.00 before 2008), provided that no other person living in the same establishment claimed the deduction for that day.

The maximum deduction that can be claimed is 20% of a taxpayer's income for the year.

The deduction arrived at through the above calculations is further limited if the taxpayer normally resides outside a prescribed area and has been employed at a special remote work site in a prescribed area, the benefits of which have been taxable as employment income and excluded by virtue of the exemption for board and lodging at a remote work site described at ¶2120.[291] The limitation operates to offset, against the remote-area deduction, the amount exempted by the remote work site exemption for the period during which a residence is maintained outside the remote area. The reduction for exempt special work-site benefits excludes exempt benefits received in respect of special work sites that are at least 30 kilometres from the nearest boundary of any urban area with a population of at least 40,000 people. In other words, tax-free benefits received in respect of a special work site that is 30 kilometres or more away from a population centre do not reduce the Northern housing benefit deduction, whereas tax-free benefits in respect of special work sites closer to population centres do reduce the deduction.

[¶2487] Canadian Forces Personnel and Police

A member of the Canadian Forces or a Canadian Police Force serving on a deployed operational mission that is assessed for risk allowance pay at level three or higher (as determined by the Department of National Defence) will be entitled to deduct from taxable income the amount of employment earnings from that mission.[292] Eligible individuals will be entitled to deduct from their taxable income the amount of their related employment earnings from the mission to the extent that those earnings have been included in computing income, up to the maximum rate of pay earned by a non-commissioned member of the Canadian Forces (i.e., approximately $6,000 per month).

See page ii for explanation of footnotes.

[291] CCH ¶15,999ib; Sec. 110.7(4).   [292] CCH ¶15,290; Sec. 110(1)(f).

[¶2490] Rules Relating to Computation of Income

[¶2495] General Limitation of Expenses

The Act prohibits the deduction of any otherwise deductible amount except to the extent that it is reasonable in the circumstances.[293]

In years past, there was a line of cases which suggested that expenses would be unreasonable if they exceeded a certain proportion of revenues. Under this school of thinking, the courts considered unreasonable expenses exceeding ⅔ of earnings[294] and travelling expenses equal to a taxpayer's salary.[295]

Those cases have less and less persuasive force. In the Federal Court of Appeal's view regarding the deduction of rental losses, expenses will not be unreasonable merely because they are disproportionate to revenues if objective criteria are otherwise met.[296] For instance, reasonableness of interest could often be determined by reference to market rates. The Federal Court of Appeal acknowledged, however, that in some instances, the determination of reasonableness by objective criteria will be difficult, and frankly admitted that in dealing with amounts that are excessive or extravagant, a judge will be influenced by professional and business experiences, lifestyle, and pragmatic considerations. These objective criteria were met and management fees were held to be reasonable when they were established every year based on a variety of factors including that proportion of the hotel's annual profits that was reasonably attributable to the taxpayer's management efforts in that particular year.[297]

[¶2500] Amounts in Part Consideration for Disposition of Property

Consideration received or receivable for the disposition of a particular property or the provision of particular services [or for a restrictive covenant agreed to after February 26, 2004] must be allocated reasonably among them and the same allocation shall apply to the purchaser as is reasonable for the vendor.[298] The form or legal effect of the contract or other agreement under which the property is disposed of has no bearing on the deduction of the consideration. The burden is on the taxpayer to show that the allocation of the purchase price should be different from what the Minister has determined it to be. Thus, the taxpayer's appeal from the Minister's assessment that part of the purchase price paid by a taxpayer for a shoe manufacturing business was goodwill was allowed by convincing the Court that the price paid for the business was not over the fair market value of the tangibles.[299]

---

[293] CCH ¶9120, ¶29,480; Sec. 67; ITAR 31.

[294] Ramsay, 54 DTC 261.

[295] No. 589, 59 DTC 41.

[296] Mohammad, 97 DTC 5503.

[297] Nielsen Development Co. et al., 2009 DTC 1219.

[298] CCH ¶9140; Sec. 68.

[299] U.S.M. Canada Ltd., 97 DTC 192.

[¶2505] Inadequate Considerations

Where a taxpayer disposes of anything at a price less than the fair market value to a person with whom the taxpayer is not dealing at arm's length or to a person by way of gift *inter vivos* [or after December 23, 1998, to a trust because of a disposition of a property that does not result in a change in the beneficial ownership of the property], for the purpose of determining the taxpayer's income from the business, the taxpayer is deemed to have received proceeds of disposition equal to that fair market value.[300]

Where the taxpayer has acquired anything from a person with whom the taxpayer is not dealing at arm's length at a price in excess of the fair market value, the taxpayer is deemed to have acquired the property at the fair market value.

Where a taxpayer has acquired property by way of gift, bequest, or inheritance [or, after December 23, 1998, because of a disposition that does not result in a change in the beneficial ownership of the property], the taxpayer is deemed to have acquired it at its fair market value.

In addition, where there is an agreement between persons not dealing at arm's length providing for payments of less than a reasonable amount for the use of or the right to use property, upon the disposition of such property, the proceeds of disposition of the property will be deemed to be the greater of:

(a) the fair market value of the property, without reference to the agreement; and

(b) the proceeds of disposition determined without reference to the deeming provision.[301]

In a very recent decision, the Supreme Court of Canada reinstated the trial judge's findings that parties involved in a sale of seismic data were dealing at arm's length even though the vendor also acted as the purchaser's agent.[302] In the case at issue, no party was in a position to impose its will on others, so that the parties could not be said to be acting in concert without separate interests. Having concluded that the transaction was arm's length and that the price paid was reasonable in the circumstances, the fair market value of the seismic database was, in the end, irrelevant. As a result, the taxpayer was entitled to deduct the purchase cost of the asset ($100,000) as a Canadian exploration expense.

[¶2520] Inadequate Consideration — Appropriation of Property to Shareholders

There are also provisions designed to prevent corporations from distributing property to shareholders for no consideration or for a considera-

---

See page ii for explanation of footnotes.

[300] CCH ¶9141, ¶29,175, ¶29,485; Sec. 69(1); ITAR 20(1.3), 32; Interp. Bul. IT-140R3.   [301] CCH ¶9162; Sec. 69(1.2).

[302] McLarty, 2008 DTC 6354.

tion which is less than the fair market value.[303] Where the property of a corporation is appropriated in any manner whatsoever, and if the sale of the property at its fair market value would have increased the corporation's income for a taxation year, the corporation is deemed to have sold the property during the year at its fair market value.

Where, on the winding-up of a corporation, property of the corporation has been appropriated in any manner whatsoever for the benefit of a shareholder, the corporation is deemed to have sold the property immediately before the winding-up and to have received the fair market value at that time.[304]

Accordingly, a corporation may recognize losses as well as gains upon the disposition of property in computing its income for the year in which the property has been appropriated. The shareholder receiving the property is deemed to have acquired it at a cost equal to the corporation's proceeds of disposal, i.e., the fair market value immediately before the winding-up. Except where there is a loss by a shareholder on the disposition of shares to the corporation on a winding-up, there would be an increase in the adjusted cost base of the property as a result of any income that might be deemed to have been received by the shareholder upon receipt of the property.[305]

[¶2530] Price Adjustment Clauses

Where property is transferred in a non-arm's length transaction, the parties sometimes include a price adjustment clause in the covering agreement whereby they agree that if the CRA's value is different from theirs, they will use the CRA's value in their transaction.[306] The CRA will recognize the agreement in computing the income of all parties, provided the following conditions are met:

(1) The agreement reflects a *bona fide* intention of the parties to transfer the property at fair market value and arrives at that value for the purposes of the agreement by a fair and reasonable method.

(2) Each of the parties to the agreement notifies the CRA by a letter attached to his or her return for the year in which the property was transferred:

(a) that he or she is prepared to have the price in the agreement reviewed by the CRA pursuant to the price adjustment clause;

(b) that he or she will take the necessary steps to settle any resulting excess or shortfall in the price; and

(c) that a copy of the agreement will be filed with the CRA if and when requested.

See page ii for explanation of footnotes.

[303] CCH ¶9175; Sec. 69(4).

[304] CCH ¶9180; Sec. 69(5).

[305] CCH ¶6432, ¶7500, ¶7505, ¶7510; Sec. 40(2), 52(1), 52(1.1), 52(2).

[306] Interp. Bul. IT-169.

(3) The excess or shortfall in price is actually refunded or paid, or a legal liability therefore is adjusted.

Whether the method used by the parties to determine fair market value is fair and reasonable in the CRA's view depends on the circumstances in each case.

[¶2535] Deemed Proceeds of Disposition

There is an anti-avoidance provision designed to prevent transactions which the Department of Finance considers to result in the inappropriate use of tax losses or other tax deductions.[307]

The general rule for non-arm's length transfers of property (i.e., that such transfers must occur at fair market value) is extended to certain transactions which would normally be considered to be arm's length. Where a person or partnership disposes of property as part of a series of transactions for proceeds of disposition of less than fair market value, and it may reasonably be considered that one of the main purposes was to obtain certain tax benefits from an affiliated person,[308] then the vendor is deemed to have disposed of the property at fair market value. This is designed to prevent the vendor from obtaining the benefit of any deduction in computing income, taxable income earned in Canada, tax payable under the Act, or any balance of undeducted outlays, expenses, or other amounts where such tax benefits would be available to an affiliated person on a subsequent disposition of the property (or property substituted therefor). The provision will only apply where the subsequent disposition by the affiliated person is arranged within three years from the disposition of the vendor.

It should be noted that the provision applies notwithstanding any other provision of the Act. Therefore, it does not matter if the transaction is structured to take advantage of one of the rollover provisions of the Act.

[¶2540] Inter Vivos Transfer of Property to Spouse, etc. or Trust

A capital property may be transferred between living persons on a tax-deferred rollover basis to:

(a) the spouse or common-law partner of a taxpayer, including a same-sex partner;

(b) the former spouse or common-law partner of a taxpayer, including a same-sex partner, in settlement of rights arising out of their marriage or common-law partnership;

(c) a spousal or partner trust; or

See page ii for explanation of footnotes.

[307] CCH ¶9199; Sec. 69(11).   [308] CCH ¶28,371a; Sec. 251.1(1).

(d) as described below, an *alter ego* trust or a joint partner trust (for taxpayers 65 and over) or a trust that was created for the exclusive benefit of the individual (for taxpayers under 65).[309]

The tax-free rollover of capital property in (d) is available to trusts created after 1999 by an individual who was:

- at least 65 when the trust was created, if the trust was created for the exclusive benefit of the individual (i.e., an *alter ego* trust) or the joint benefit of the individual and the individual's spouse or common-law partner (i.e., a joint partner trust); or

- under 65 when the trust was created, if the trust was created for the exclusive benefit of the individual.

However, a rollover to these trusts is not permitted if the recipient of the property is a trust that is resident in Canada by virtue of a deeming provision and if one of the main purposes of the transfer is to avoid the application of the 21-year deemed disposition rule.

Unless the taxpayer elects not to have the rollover apply, the realization of accrued gains and losses, including any terminal losses or the recapture of capital cost allowance, is deferred until the recipient spouse or common-law partner, former spouse or common-law partner, or trust disposes or is deemed to have disposed of the property.

The property transferred must be a capital property[310] and both the transferor and recipient must be resident in Canada at the time of the transfer. In the case of depreciable property, the transferor is deemed to have received proceeds equal to the undepreciated capital cost of the property. The recipient is deemed to have acquired the property for the same amount. If the transferor has more than one property in a prescribed class of depreciable property, but is transferring only part of the property in that class, the undepreciated capital cost of that property is transferred in proportion to its fair market value as determined immediately before the time of transfer. Where the transferor's capital cost is more than the recipient's cost as determined in accordance with the above provisions, the capital cost to the recipient of the depreciable property will be deemed to be the same amount that was the capital cost of the property to the transferor. Accordingly, any capital cost allowance already claimed by the transferor is deemed to have been allowed to the recipient in years prior to the transfer. Where non-depreciable property, such as land or personal-use property, is transferred, the transferor is deemed to have received proceeds equal to the adjusted cost base of the property. The recipient is deemed to have acquired the property for the same amount.

While the rollover provisions apply automatically, the transferor may elect, on a property-by-property basis, not to have the rollover apply. In such

---

See page ii for explanation of footnotes.

[309] CCH ¶9400; Sec. 73(1)–(2); Interp. Bul. IT-352R2.   [310] CCH ¶7850b; Sec. 54 "capital property".

cases, the general rule respecting non-arm's length transfers or gifts[311] will apply and the transferor is generally considered to have disposed of the property for proceeds equal to the fair market value of the property at the time of the transfer. There is no official form for the election not to have the rollover provisions apply. The election is normally made by the transferor reporting the full tax consequences of the disposition on his or her return for the year of the transfer.

[¶2545] Inter Vivos Transfer of Farming and Fishing Property to Child

An *inter vivos* rollover is allowed when a taxpayer transfers land, depreciable property, or eligible capital property in respect of a farming or fishing business to the taxpayer's child.[312] The rollover is similar to the rollover available on the death of a taxpayer (see ¶2570).

In order for the rollover to apply to a transfer of property by a taxpayer to the taxpayer's child, the following conditions must be met:

- The property must be land in Canada, depreciable property in Canada of a prescribed class, or eligible capital property in respect of a business carried on in Canada by the transferor, and, before the transfer, the property must have been used principally in a farming business in which the taxpayer or the taxpayer's spouse or common-law partner or any of the taxpayer's children was actively engaged on a regular and continuous basis. For transfers after May 1, 2006, the rollover is extended to such properties used principally in a fishing business in which one of the above persons is actively engaged on a regular basis. Furthermore, for transfers after that date, a property can qualify for the rollover if the taxpayer's parent was actively engaged in the fishing or farming business. The property does not have to be used in the farming or fishing business after the transfer. In the case of property used in the operation of a woodlot, the "actively engaged" and "regular and continuous" requirements prior to the transfer are not necessary; it is sufficient that the relevant person (the taxpayer, spouse, child, or parent) was engaged to the extent required by a prescribed forest management plan. Such a plan is one that provides for the necessary attention to the woodlot's growth, health, quality, and composition.

- The child of the taxpayer who acquires the property must be resident in Canada immediately before the transfer. The word "child" includes a grandchild, a great-grandchild, and a person who, when under the age of 19, was dependent on and in the care or control of the taxpayer.[313] A transfer of farm property to several children in undivided shares can qualify for the rollover.[314] Furthermore, if the taxpayer

---

See page ii for explanation of footnotes.

[311] CCH ¶9141; Sec. 69.

[312] CCH ¶9450, ¶9470; Sec. 73(3), 73(4).

[313] CCH ¶9295, ¶9220; Sec. 70(10) "child", 70(2); Interp. Bul. IT-212R3.

[314] Interp. Bul. IT-268R4.

is the sole owner of the land, a transfer of an interest in the land such that the child becomes a joint tenant or tenant-in-common in the land can qualify for the rollover. The taxpayer need not be resident in Canada.

Property owned by the taxpayer may be deemed to be used in the fishing or farming business if the property is used by a "family fishing corporation", a "family farm corporation", a "family fishing partnership", or a "family farm partnership" in the course of carrying on a fishing or farming business in Canada. The taxpayer, the taxpayer's spouse or common-law partner, the taxpayer's child, or the taxpayer's parent must have an interest in the corporation or partnership which uses the property.[315]

Fishing or farming assets transferred to a child may be transferred back to a parent on the death of a child on a tax-free or partially tax-free basis. See ¶2600.

Where there is an *inter vivos* transfer of depreciable farm property of a prescribed class used in a fishing or farming business to a child, the proceeds of disposition are determined by three rules:

(1) If the consideration given by the child for the depreciable property exceeds the greater of both:

(a) its fair market value, and

(b) its undepreciated capital cost,

the transferor's proceeds of disposition are deemed to be the greater of (a) or (b).

(2) If the consideration given by the child is less than the lesser of (a) and (b), the transferor's proceeds are deemed to be the lesser of (a) and (b).

(3) In any other case, the transferor is deemed to receive proceeds equal to the consideration given by the child.[316]

Accordingly, the transferor's proceeds of disposition can be selected by the parties anywhere between the fair market value and the undepreciated capital cost of the property, and the selection is made by transferring the property for particular consideration. The child is deemed to acquire the depreciable property for the same amount deemed to be the proceeds of disposition received by the parent. If the capital cost to the parent exceeds the amount at which the child is so deemed to acquire the depreciable property, the child's capital cost is the parent's capital cost and any such excess is deemed to have been allowed the child as capital cost allowance in an earlier year.

The general effect of the foregoing is to permit a rollover of the depreciable property and a postponement of recapture or terminal loss. However,

[315] CCH ¶9294; Sec. 70(9.8).   [316] CCH ¶9451; Sec. 73(3.1).

because of the flexibility available in fixing the value at which the depreciable property passes to the child, it would be possible for the parent to realize some recapture on the transfer. If the parent has losses otherwise available in the year, this may be desirable.

Example:

Farmer/Fisherman A owns some farming/fishing machinery and wishes to transfer it to his son, B. The capital cost to A was $25,000 and the undepreciated capital cost is $15,000. The fair market value of the machinery is $18,000. Farmer/Fisherman A also has business losses in the year of $3,000.

If A sells the machinery to B for $18,000 (perhaps taking back a promissory note), it will trigger the following results:

Deemed proceeds to A	$18,000
Recapture to A	3,000
Income of A: recaptured amount	
- business loss =	0
Capital cost to B	25,000
Deemed taken by B as c.c.a.	7,000
($25,000 - $18,000)	
U.C.C. of B	18,000

If B were to sell the machinery for its fair market value, he would suffer no recapture. A incurs the recapture and in the circumstances can use it to advantage.

If the machinery were sold to B for $15,000, A would incur no recapture, but on a sale by B, B would do so. Since A has losses to be used up (and assuming B does not) it appears preferable to sell the machinery for $18,000. A sale for less than $15,000 (A's U.C.C.) will not result in a terminal loss for A because his proceeds of disposition must be at least $15,000.

If the subject matter of the transfer consists of farm or fishing land, the transferor's proceeds of disposition are ascertained by the following rules:

(1) If the consideration exceeds both (a) the fair market value of the land and (b) its adjusted cost base to the transferor, the transferor's proceeds are the greater of (a) and (b).

(2) If the consideration is less than both (a) and (b) above, the transferor's proceeds are the lesser of (a) and (b).

(3) In any other case, the transferor's proceeds are the consideration given by his child.[317]

The child is deemed to acquire the land for the amount of the proceeds of disposition deemed to be received by his parent. As with depreciable farm or fishing property, the parties may arrange the transfer at a price which

---

See page ii for explanation of footnotes.

[317] CCH ¶9451; Sec. 73(3.1).

gives rise to some immediate capital gain, but no capital loss may be realized by the transferor.

If the subject matter of the transfer consists of eligible capital property in respect of a fishing or farming business carried on in Canada by a transferor, the transferor's proceeds of disposition are ascertained by the following rules:

(1) If the consideration exceeds both:

(a) the fair market value, and

(b) $^4/_3$ of the *pro rata* portion of the transferor's cumulative eligible capital in respect of the business, such portion equaling the fair market value of the property divided by the fair market value of all of the eligible capital properties in respect of the business,

the transferor's proceeds are the greater of (a) and (b).

(2) If the consideration is less than both (a) and (b) above, the transferor's proceeds are the lesser of (a) and (b).

(3) In any other case, the transferor's proceeds of disposition are the consideration given by the child.[318]

The child is deemed to have acquired a capital property at a cost equal to the aggregate of:

(1) the transferor's proceeds of disposition (as determined above); and

(2) if the child carries on the business, $^4/_3$ of the total cumulative eligible capital deduction taken by the transferor (see ¶3087) prior to the transfer, to the extent it was not "recaptured" and included in the transferor's income on the transfer.

The child is deemed to have taken a previous deduction equal to $^3/_4$ of the amount determined in (2), above.

Where land, depreciable property, or eligible capital property in respect of a fishing or a farming business has been transferred to a minor child and the child disposes of that property during minority and thereupon realizes a capital gain or loss, the gain or loss is attributed to the parent, if the latter is still living and is then a resident of Canada. The usual rules will apply to attribute ordinary income including recaptured capital cost allowance to the parent while the child is under 18 years of age.[319]

[¶2550] Inter Vivos Transfer of Family Farm or Fishing Corporations and Partnerships

A tax-deferred rollover is allowed for the transfer of shares of the capital stock of a family farm corporation or an interest in a family farm partnership

---

See page ii for explanation of footnotes.

[318] CCH ¶9451; Sec. 73(3.1).   [319] CCH ¶9585; Sec. 75.1.

by a taxpayer to his child. For transfers after May 1, 2006, the rollover treatment is extended to a transfer of shares of the capital stock of a family fishing corporation or an interest in a family fishing partnership.[320] The terms "share of the capital stock of a family farm corporation", "share of the capital stock of a family fishing corporation", "interest in a family fishing partnership", and "interest in a family farming partnership" are defined in the commentary at ¶2595.

The proceeds of disposition in respect of the transfer of shares of a family farm corporation or a family fishing corporation will be determined as follows:

(1) If the consideration given by the child for the share or interest exceeds the greater of:

(a) its fair market value, and

(b) its adjusted cost base immediately before the transfer,

then the proceeds of disposition of the transferor are deemed to be the greater of (a) and (b).

(2) If the consideration given by the child is less than the lesser of:

(a) the fair market value of the share, and

(b) its adjusted cost base,

then the transferor's proceeds are deemed to be the lesser of (a) and (b).

(3) In any other case the transferor is deemed to receive proceeds equal to the consideration given by the child.[321]

Accordingly, the transferor's proceeds of disposition (and the child's acquisition cost) can be anywhere between the fair market value and the adjusted cost base of the share, depending on the consideration given by the child. If the transfer is made as a gift or for actual consideration that is less than the lesser of the adjusted cost base and the fair market value of the share, the proceeds of disposition will be the lesser of these two amounts.

For transfers before May 2, 2006, similar rules applied to the transfer of an interest in a family farm partnership. However, for transfers on or after May 2, 2006, the following rules apply to a transfer of an interest in a family farm partnership or an interest in a family fishing partnership:

(1) The partnership interest is treated, except for the purposes of the deemed acquisition of partnership interests on property rollovers to a sole proprietorship (see ¶7180), as not having been disposed of by the taxpayer, and the child is deemed to have acquired the interest at its cost to the taxpayer.

---

[320] CCH ¶9470; Sec. 73(4).   [321] CCH ¶9470d; Sec. 73(4.1).

(2) In order to place the child in the same tax position as the transferor, each amount required to be added or deducted in computing the transferor's adjusted cost base of the partnership interest is deemed to have been added or deducted in computing the child's adjusted cost base of the interest.

Thus, the rules still provide a tax-deferred rollover for the transfer of the partnership interest. However, unlike the rules that previously applied to family farm partnership interests (and that currently apply to shares in family farm and fishing corporations), it appears that there can be no partial rollover on the transfer, nor can the taxpayer realize a capital loss on the transfer.

Any shares or partnership interest that were transferred to a child on a rollover basis may be transferred back to a parent on the death of the child on a tax-free or partially tax-free basis (see ¶2600).

[¶2555] Death of a Taxpayer

[¶2560] Periodic Payments — Rights or Things

In computing the income of a taxpayer for the taxation year in which the taxpayer died, any amount of interest, rent, royalty, annuity (other than an annuity contract deemed to be disposed of on death), remuneration from an office or employment, or other amounts on a periodic basis that were accruing but were not due at the time of death are brought into income.[322] The amount so accrued to the date of death is to be included in computing income for the year in which the taxpayer died.

Amounts receivable for rights or things, which if disposed of by a taxpayer prior to his or her death would have been included in computing income, are to be included in income at their value at the date of death for the year in which the taxpayer died. The rights or things do not include any capital property or any amount described in the preceding paragraph which is to be included in income.[323] Rights or things do not include:

(a) a life insurance policy, unless it was an annuity contract the cost of which was deductible as having been paid out of a "refund of premiums";

(b) eligible capital property;

(c) land inventory of a business;

(d) a Canadian or foreign resource property or a right, license, or privilege in respect of a natural resource property;

(e) certain annuity contracts; or

See page ii for explanation of footnotes.

[322] CCH ¶9200; Sec. 70(1); Interp. Bul. IT-210R2.   [323] CCH ¶9220; Sec. 70(2); Interp. Bul. IT-212R3.

¶2555

(f) [after 2001, a participating interest in a "foreign investment entity" (a non-resident entity that has investment properties representing at least ¹/₂ of its assets), the annual increase in the fair market value of which the taxpayer was required to include in income during his or her lifetime.][324]

Instead of including the value of rights or things in computing the income of the deceased for the year of his or her death, the legal representative may elect to file a separate return for this portion of the deceased's income. Such a return is a return of the deceased and is a return for the year he or she died, but it is regarded as the return of another person entitled to claim the personal tax credits that the deceased was entitled to for the year of death. This means, in effect, that the personal tax credits may be claimed a second time with respect to income arising from the notional realization of rights or things.

On the separate return, the legal representative may also claim tax credits in respect of pension income, charitable donations, medical expenses, disability, tuition, education, and the transfer of unused credits to a supporting person. However, the total credits claimed in respect of these matters may not exceed the amount which could have been claimed had no separate return been filed.

The separate return is an elective matter and does not happen automatically. The legal representative may elect at any time up to the later of:

(a) one year after death, and

(b) 90 days after the mailing of any notice of assessment for the year of death.

This time limit is designed to allow the representative to ascertain the tax position if an election is not made (by filing a return for the year of death and receiving an assessment, if necessary) and, knowing this, to decide whether making one would be advantageous.

Where, before the time for making an election to file a separate return has expired, a right or thing has been transferred or distributed to beneficiaries, the election is not applicable to that right or thing and an amount received by any beneficiary on the realization or disposition of the right or thing is to be included in computing income for the taxation year in which it was received.[325]

An election made by the legal representative of the deceased taxpayer may be revoked within the same time limits that an election may be made.[326] The notice of revocation is to be signed by the legal representative and filed with the Minister.

See page ii for explanation of footnotes.

[324] CCH ¶9232; Sec. 70(3.1); Interp. Bul. IT-212R3. [326] CCH ¶9235; Sec. 70(4).
[325] CCH ¶9230; Sec. 70(3).

For the election to pay tax over a period of 10 years, see ¶12,240.

[¶2565] Eligible Capital Property of Deceased Taxpayer

Upon death, a taxpayer is deemed to have disposed of his or her eligible capital property (such as goodwill and other intangibles) immediately prior to death for proceeds of disposition equal to $\frac{4}{3}$ of the taxpayer's cumulative eligible capital at that time. Therefore, no amount is included in the income of the deceased as a result of the deemed disposition. Ordinarily the balance of a taxpayer's cumulative eligible capital account may be deducted in computing income when the taxpayer ceases to carry on a business, but this does not apply in the case of death.

The person who acquires the eligible capital property as a consequence of the death of the deceased is deemed to acquire it at a cost equal to the deceased's deemed proceeds. If the person continues to carry on the business, he or she is deemed to have made an eligible capital expenditure of an amount equal to the deemed proceeds. Accordingly, the person may take deductions to the same extent that the deceased could have had he or she lived. Where the acquirer does not continue the business and no longer owns any eligible capital property of any value in respect of the business, he or she is deemed to acquire the deceased's eligible capital property as capital property. The cost to the person is $\frac{4}{3}$ of the cumulative eligible capital of the deceased. If the person disposes of the property, a capital gain or loss may result.

Special provisions apply to prevent an overstatement of the deemed taxable capital gain or the amount to be included in income on the subsequent disposition of the eligible capital property by the person.[327] This does not apply if the person acquiring the eligible capital property is the spouse or common-law partner of the deceased or is a corporation which the deceased controlled and the spouse, common-law partner, or corporation continues the business.[328]

[¶2570] Resource Properties and Land Inventories of Deceased Taxpayer

Various properties, rights, licences, and privileges which are in effect Canadian and foreign natural resource properties are not rights or things for the purpose of certain provisions of the Act.[329] Thus, a deceased is not regarded as realizing their value in computing income in the year of death. Instead, special rules apply.

The basic purpose of the rules is to bring into the income of the deceased, for the year of death, the amount that would have been included if the deceased had disposed of the natural resource properties at their fair

---

See page ii for explanation of footnotes.

[327] CCH ¶9266; Sec. 70(5.1).

[328] CCH ¶9266; Sec. 70(5.1); Interp. Bul. IT-313R2.

[329] CCH ¶9232; Sec. 70(3.1).

market value immediately before death. This is done so that the various elections which might otherwise have been made are not available.

However, it is possible to elect to pay the increased tax over a period of up to 10 years (see ¶12,240). Where the natural resource properties pass to the spouse/common-law partner of the deceased or to a spousal or partner trust, the tax burden inherent in the disposition of the properties may be passed on in whole or in part to the spouse or common-law partner. The spouse or common-law partner or the spousal or partner trust must acquire the resource property as a consequence of the deceased's death. It is necessary that the right to the property vest indefeasibly in the spouse, common-law partner, or trust within 36 months of death. The property may vest at a time later than 36 months after death if the Minister considers the extended period to be reasonable in the circumstances and a written application for an extension is made to the Minister within the 36-month period.[330]

Where the deceased was holding land in the inventory of his or her business at the time of death, the deceased is deemed to have disposed of the land immediately before death and to have received proceeds of disposition equal to the fair market value of the land at that time. Where the land has been transferred or distributed to the spouse/common-law partner of a resident deceased or to a spouse or partner trust as a consequence of death, the proceeds deemed to be received by the deceased are the cost amount of the land inventory at the time of death. The phrase "cost amount" means the amount at which the deceased was carrying the land on his or her books (cost or market value). Thus, the deceased would realize no gain by leaving inventory land to his or her spouse or common-law partner or to a spousal or partner trust. The spouse, common-law partner, or trust would take the land at a cost of this same amount and any eventual gain on disposition would be income of the spouse, common-law partner, or trust. The land must vest indefeasibly in the spouse, common-law partner, or trust within 36 months of death.[331] The vesting period may be extended, subject to the same conditions, noted above, which apply in relation to vesting of resource properties.

[¶2575] Depreciable and Other Capital Property of Deceased Taxpayer

An individual who has died is deemed to have disposed, immediately before death, of each non-depreciable capital property owned immediately before death. The individual is deemed to have received proceeds of disposition for each such property equal to the fair market value at the time of the deemed disposition.[332]

A person who, as a consequence of the taxpayer's death, has acquired non- depreciable capital property of the deceased, is deemed to have acquired it at a cost equal to the amount the deceased is deemed to have

See page ii for explanation of footnotes.

[330] CCH ¶9267; Sec. 70(5.2); Interp. Bul. IT-125R4.
[331] CCH ¶9267; Sec. 70(5.2).

[332] CCH ¶9260; Sec. 70(5); Interp. Bul. IT-140R3, IT-416R3.

received as proceeds of disposition. Accordingly, accrued gains and losses at the time of death must be included in computing the deceased's income for the year of death.

Property owned by farmers and fishers which is being depreciated on a straight-line basis[333] is not depreciable property of a prescribed class and, therefore, the deemed disposition rules described above apply. If using the straight line method, a deceased farmer or fisher is deemed to have disposed of the relevant property for proceeds of disposition equal to its fair market value.

The disposition of a taxpayer's depreciable property will be for proceeds that equal the fair market value of the property immediately before death. Accordingly, the terminal losses, recapture, and capital gains arising from the disposition on death of depreciable capital property will, as for other capital property, be determined on the basis of proceeds of disposition that are equal to fair market value. However, separate rules apply where the amount of a deceased taxpayer's proceeds of disposition are re-determined under the provisions respecting the reduction of a terminal loss in the case of the disposition of a building and land.[334] The amount by which the deceased taxpayer's capital cost of the building exceeds the deceased taxpayer's proceeds of disposition, rather than the cost of the building to the person acquiring it, is deemed to have been deducted by the person acquiring the building as capital cost allowance on the building in computing income for previous taxation years. Finally, the cost to the person of the land is deemed to be the amount that was the deceased taxpayer's proceeds of disposition in respect of the land.

Example:

A taxpayer owns, immediately before death, a building and contiguous land that is used for income earning purposes.

The relevant values are:

	ACB/CC	UCC	FMV	CG	Terminal Loss
Land	$ 20,000	n/a	$ 50,000	$ 30,000	n/a
Building	$100,000	$20,000	nil	—	$20,000

Due to reallocation of the proceeds of disposition between the land and building, the land's proceeds of disposition are reduced by $20,000 (the amount of the deceased taxpayer's terminal loss otherwise determined) and the building's proceeds of disposition are increased by an equivalent amount. Thus the proceeds of disposition of the building will be $20,000 and of the land $30,000, producing a capital gain of $10,000 and a terminal loss of nil, respectively.

See page ii for explanation of footnotes.

[333] CCH ¶5048b, ¶9260; Sec. 70(5); Reg. 1700.   [334] CCH ¶9260; Sec. 70(5)(*d*).

By reason of the application of the proposed amendments, the person acquiring the property will be considered to have acquired the land at a cost of $30,000, rather than $50,000. Moreover, the building will be deemed to have been acquired by that person at a capital cost of $100,000, rather than nil and the person will be treated as having claimed capital cost allowance of $80,000, rather than $100,000, in previous years.

For the election to pay tax over a period of 10 years, see ¶12,240.

[¶2580] Transfer or Distribution to Spouse/Common-Law Partner or Trust

The rules described above in ¶2575 relative to depreciable and other capital property of a deceased taxpayer, including an interest in a partnership, do not apply to property transferred to the taxpayer's spouse or common-law partner or a trust created by the taxpayer for their benefit, commonly referred to as a "spousal or partner trust".[335]

Instead, the deceased is deemed to have disposed of each such property immediately prior to death for special proceeds of disposition. Where a particular property was depreciable property of a prescribed class, the proceeds of disposition are deemed to be that portion of the undepreciated capital cost of all properties in the class that the fair market value of the particular property is of the fair market value of all properties in the class. Where a particular property is not depreciable property of a prescribed class, the proceeds of disposition are the adjusted cost base to the deceased immediately before death. The spouse, common-law partner, or the trust receiving the property takes it at a cost equal to these proceeds of disposition. See also ¶4015.

The result of the foregoing is that the deceased realizes no capital gain, capital loss, recapture, or terminal loss on death. The advantage or liability of this is passed on to the spouse, common-law partner, or trust created for their benefit and figures in computing the spouse's, common-law partner's, or trust's income on ultimate disposition of the properties. However, an election may be made by the legal representatives of the deceased so that the "rollover" provisions do not apply with respect to specified property, and consequently, the rules with respect to depreciable and other capital property will apply.[336] See ¶2555.

With respect to depreciable property of a prescribed class, a deceased taxpayer's proceeds of disposition are equal to the lesser of the "capital cost" and the "cost amount" to the taxpayer of the property immediately before the taxpayer's death.[337]

Special provisions apply for the election respecting a taxpayer's "net income stabilization account" acquired under the *Farm Income Protection Act*.[338]

See page ii for explanation of footnotes.

[335] CCH ¶9270; Sec. 70(6); Interp. Bul. IT-305R4.
[336] CCH ¶9274; Sec. 70(6.2).
[337] CCH ¶9270; Sec. 70(6)(d).
[338] CCH ¶9273, ¶9274; Sec. 70(6.1), 70(6.2).

For the above rules to apply, the deceased and the deceased's spouse or common-law partner must have been resident in Canada immediately before the death of the deceased, and the spouse's or common-law partner's trust must be resident in Canada immediately after the time the property vested indefeasibly in the trust. The property in question must vest indefeasibly in the spouse or common-law partner or the trust created for their benefit within 36 months after death. The vesting period can be extended where the legal representative applies in writing to the Minister within the 36-month period and the Minister considers that an extension is reasonable in the circumstances.

A trust is considered to be created by a taxpayer's will if the trust is created under the terms of the taxpayer's will or by a court order in relation to the taxpayer's estate that provides for support or relief of the taxpayer's dependants pursuant to provincial law.[339]

Where a deceased's spouse received over $100,000 in shares for consideration of cash and in settlement of the estate's liabilities together with the spouse's administrative fees, the rollover provisions did not apply. The shares were not transferred as a consequence of the husband's death but rather to settle the debts of the estate.[340]

[¶2585] Special Rules Applicable to Spousal or Partner Trust

A testator may create a testamentary trust which otherwise meets the requirements for a spousal or partner trust except that debts of the deceased owing at the time of death and various income and death taxes are payable from the trust. Since the payment of such debts and taxes will be a benefit to persons other than the spouse or common-law partner, the trust would not meet the strict requirement that no person other than the spouse/common-law partner may have the benefit of any trust property during the spouse's lifetime. Therefore, rules are provided which enable a trust to qualify as a spousal or partner trust, notwithstanding the fact that certain testamentary debts are payable out of it.[341] The value of trust property qualifying for rollover treatment is reduced by the amount of "non-qualifying debts". A net income stabilization account is not one of the properties that may be listed for the purpose of "purifying" a spousal or partner trust.

The term "testamentary debts" refers to amounts payable as a consequence of death and includes income or profits, taxes of the deceased for the year of death or previous years, and any death taxes payable as a consequence of death. "Non-qualifying debts" means testamentary debts other than death taxes in respect of property or of an interest in the trust. For example, if a child of the deceased receives a legacy, succession duties payable out of the trust on the legacy would be non-qualifying debts.

See page ii for explanation of footnotes.

[339] CCH ¶28,329e; Sec. 248(9.1).
[340] Husel Estate, 94 DTC 1765.
[341] CCH ¶9275; Sec. 70(7), 70(8).

¶2585

[¶2590] Transfer of Farm or Fishing Property to Child

In general, a taxpayer is permitted to pass a family farm or fishing property, including an interest in a family farm or fishing partnership, to his or her children on death without the consequences of a deemed realization (see ¶2555), if the following conditions are met:[342]

(1) The deceased taxpayer owned land in Canada or depreciable property in Canada of a prescribed class.

(2) Before the taxpayer's death, the property in question was used principally in a fishing or farming business in which the taxpayer, the taxpayer's spouse or common-law partner, or a child or a parent of the taxpayer was actively engaged on a regular and continuous basis. A child of a taxpayer includes a grandchild or great-grandchild and a person who, when under the age of 19, was wholly dependent on and in the custody and control of the taxpayer.[343] In the case of property used in the operation of a woodlot, the "actively engaged" and "regular and continuous" requirements are not necessary; it is sufficient that the relevant person (the taxpayer, the taxpayer's spouse or common-law partner, etc.) be engaged "to the extent required by a prescribed forest management plan". A prescribed forest management plan is a plan of the taxpayer that provides for the necessary attention to a woodlot's growth, health, quality, and composition. It should be noted that property owned by a taxpayer which is used by a family farm or fishing corporation or a family farm or fishing partnership is deemed to be used by the taxpayer in the farming or fishing business.[344]

(3) On or after the taxpayer's death, the property in question was transferred or distributed to a child of the taxpayer as a consequence of his or her death.

(4) The particular child was resident in Canada immediately before the taxpayer's death.

(5) Within 36 months of death, the property becomes indefeasibly vested in the child. The vesting period can be extended where the legal representative applies in writing to the Minister within the 36-month period and the Minister considers that a longer period is reasonable in the circumstances.

The rollover to a child from a spousal or partner trust applies if:

(1) the deceased owned land in Canada or depreciable property in Canada of a prescribed class;

(2) the land or property has been placed in an *inter vivos* or testamentary spousal or partner trust;

See page ii for explanation of footnotes.

[342] CCH ¶9283, ¶29,332; Sec. 70(9); ITAR 26(18); Interp. Bul. IT-349R3.

[343] CCH ¶9295; Sec. 70(10) "child".

[344] CCH ¶9294; Sec. 70(9.8).

(3) immediately prior to the spouse's or common-law partner's death, the property in question, or a replacement property on which the taxpayer has made an election under the provisions discussed at ¶5355, was used in the farming or fishing business;

(4) on the death of the spouse or common-law partner and as a consequence of that death, the property was transferred or distributed to a child of the taxpayer and within 36 months of death (or such longer period as allowed by the Minister), the property became indefeasibly vested in the child; and

(5) the child was resident in Canada immediately before the spouse's or common-law partner's death.[345]

If these conditions are met, a rollover is allowed on the death of a spouse or common-law partner unless an election is made to obtain only a partial rollover. The original transfer to the spouse or common-law partner would also be made on a tax-free rollover basis.

For *inter vivos* transfer of farming and fishing property to a child, see ¶2545. The re-transfer of property to a parent on the death of a child is discussed at ¶2600.

[¶2595] Transfer of Family Farm or Fishing Corporation or Partnership to Child by Deceased or Spousal or Partner Trust

A "rollover" treatment is provided for certain transfers of the shares of a family farm corporation or an interest in a family farm partnership by a deceased to a child of the deceased or by a spousal or partner trust established by the deceased to a child of the deceased. Effective to dispositions occurring after May 1, 2006, this rollover treatment applies to such dispositions of shares of a family fishing corporation or an interest in a family fishing partnership. [346] The definition of "child" includes a grandchild, great-grandchild, and a person who, when under the age of 19, was wholly dependent on and in the custody and control of the taxpayer.[347]

In the case of a share of a family farm (or fishing) corporation to which the rollover applies, the taxpayer or spousal or partner trust is deemed to have disposed of the shares or interest in the partnership for proceeds of disposition equal to the adjusted cost base of the shares or interest, and the child is deemed to have acquired the shares or interest at a cost equal to this same amount. Thus, the deceased taxpayer or the spousal or partner trust will not realize any capital gain or loss, or only realize the desired amount of gain or loss, and the child, grandchild, or great grandchild who acquires the shares or interest will realize the remaining accrued gain or loss when he or she disposes of, or is deemed to dispose of, the shares or interest in circumstances which do not qualify for a rollover. Alternatively, instead of accessing the full rollover, the taxpayer's legal representative or the spousal trust, as

See page ii for explanation of footnotes.

[345] CCH ¶9284; Sec. 70(9.1).   [347] CCH ¶9295; Sec. 70(10)"child".
[346] CCH ¶9286, ¶9287a; Sec. 70(9.2), 70(9.3).

the case may be, can make an election to have the shares disposed of at any amount that is between the fair market value of the shares and their adjusted cost base to the taxpayer or trust.

In the case of an interest in a family farm (or fishing) partnership (other than a residual interest in partnership described in the commentary at ¶7190), the interest is treated, except for the purposes of the deemed acquisition of partnership interests on property rollovers to a sole proprietorship (see ¶7180), as not having been disposed of by the taxpayer, and the child is deemed to have acquired the interest at its cost to the taxpayer. Similarly, where the partnership interest is subject to a rollover by a spousal trust, the interest is treated, except for the purposes of the deemed acquisition of partnership interests on property rollovers to a sole proprietorship (see ¶7180), as not having been disposed of by the spousal trust, and the child is deemed to have acquired the interest at its cost to the trust. In order to place the child in the same tax position as the transferor, each amount required to be added or deducted in computing the transferor's adjusted cost base of the partnership interest is deemed to have been added or deducted in computing the child's adjusted cost base of the interest.

Further requirements for the rollover in respect of shares of a family farm (or fishing) corporation or an interest in a family farm (or fishing) partnership require that the child of the deceased who is receiving the shares or interest be resident in Canada immediately before the death of the deceased or the death of the spouse beneficiary of the spouse trust, as the case may be. In addition, the shares or the interest in the partnership must indefeasibly vest in the child, i.e., the entitlement cannot be conditional upon any subsequent event. However, where the child receives the shares or interest directly upon the death of the deceased, it is sufficient that the share or interest vest indefeasibly within 36 months of the death of the deceased and the fact of this vesting can be established within this 36-month period. The vesting period can be extended where the legal representative applies in writing to the Minister within the 36-month period and the Minister considers the extension reasonable in the circumstances.

The terms "share of the capital stock of a family farm corporation" and "share of the capital stock of a family fishing corporation" of an individual at any time are defined[348] as a share of the capital stock of a corporation owned by the individual at that time where, at that time, all or substantially all of the fair market value of the property owned by the corporation was attributable to property that had been used by:

(a) the corporation;

(b) a corporation, a share of the capital stock of which was a share of the capital stock of a family farm or fishing corporation of the

---

See page ii for explanation of footnotes.

[348] CCH ¶9295b, ¶9295ba; Sec. 70(10) "share of the capital stock of a family farm corporation",   70(10) "share of the capital stock of a family fishing corporation".

individual or of a spouse/common-law partner, child, or parent of the individual;

(c) a corporation controlled by a corporation described in (a) or (b);

(d) the individual;

(e) a spouse/common-law partner, child, or parent of the individual; or

(f) a partnership, an interest in which was an interest in a family farm or fishing partnership of the individual or of a spouse/common-law partner, child, or parent of the individual;

principally in the course of carrying on a farming or fishing business in Canada in which the individual or a spouse, common-law partner, child, or parent of the individual was actively engaged on a regular and continuous basis, shares of the capital stock or indebtedness of one or more corporations all, or substantially all, of the fair market value of the property of which was attributable to such property. Note that in the case of property used in the operation of a woodlot, the "actively engaged" and "regular and continuous" requirements are not necessary; it is sufficient that the person (the taxpayer, spouse, etc.) is engaged "to the extent required by a prescribed forest management plan". A prescribed forest management plan is a plan of the taxpayer that provides for the necessary attention to a woodlot's growth, health, quality, and composition.

A share in the capital stock of a corporation will qualify for rollover or partial rollover treatment when distributed by a spousal or partner trust if the corporation is a Canadian corporation as defined in ¶6050 and all the requirements of the definition of a share of the capital stock of a family farm corporation or share of the capital stock of a family fishing corporation are met (except for the requirement that the deceased, spouse/common-law partner of the deceased, or a child of the deceased be engaged in the business of farming on a regular and continuous basis).

Where a share is being transferred to a child as a consequence of the taxpayer's death, the share must qualify under these conditions immediately before the death of the taxpayer. Where a share is being transferred from a spousal or partner trust to a child of the deceased, the share must qualify immediately before the transfer of the share to the spousal or partner trust. On the death of the spouse or common-law partner, less restrictive requirements regarding who is engaged in the business will apply.

The terms "interest in a family farm partnership" and "interest in a family fishing partnership" [349] of an individual at any time are defined as a partnership interest owned by the individual at that time if, at that time, all,

---

See page ii for explanation of footnotes.

[349] CCH ¶9295a, ¶9295ab; Sec. 70(10) "interest in a family farm partnership", 70(10) "interest in a family fishing partnership".

or substantially all, of the fair market value of the property of the partnership was attributable to property that has been used by:

(a) the partnership;

(b) the individual;

(c) a spouse, common-law partner, child, or parent of the individual;

(d) a corporation, a share of the capital stock of which is a share of the capital stock of a family farm or fishing corporation of the individual or of a spouse, common-law partner, child, or parent of the individual; or

(e) a partnership, an interest in which is an interest in a family farm or fishing partnership of the individual or of a spouse, common-law partner, child, or parent of the individual.

principally in the course of carrying on a farming or fishing business in Canada in which the individual, or a spouse, common-law partner, child, or parent of the individual was actively engaged on a regular and continuous basis, shares of the capital stock or indebtedness of one or more corporations all or substantially all of the fair market value of the property of which was attributable to such property and partnership interests or indebtedness of one or more partnerships all, or substantially all, of the fair market value of the property of which was attributable to such property.

For *inter vivos* transfers of family farm and fishing corporations and partnerships, see ¶2550. The re-transfer of property to a parent upon the death of a child is discussed at ¶2600.

[¶2600] Transfer to Parent

If farm or fishing property acquired by a child on a rollover basis as a result of the death of a parent or an *inter vivos* transfer from a parent is transferred to one of his or her parents as a consequence of the child's death, the child's legal representative may elect in the final return to have a full rollover or an elective partial rollover apply to the transfer of the property to the parent in the same manner as those rules normally apply in respect of a transfer of property to a child.[350] Three conditions must be met for the rollover to apply and defer the realization of any accrued gain or loss where a child dies before his or her parents. The first requirement is that the farming or fishing assets be acquired by the child on a tax-free rollover basis as a result of the death of a parent (see ¶2590 and ¶2595) or an *inter vivos* transfer from a parent (¶2545 and ¶2550). The second requirement is that the property be transferred or distributed to a parent as a consequence of the death of a child. Transfers of property "as a consequence of the death" of a child include not only transfers under the terms of the child's will or as a

---

See page ii for explanation of footnotes.

[350] CCH ¶9292; Sec. 70(9.6).

result of the application of the laws of intestate succession, it also includes transfers as a result of a disclaimer, release, or surrender by a person who was a beneficiary under the child's will or intestacy.[351] The final requirement is that the legal representatives of the deceased child elect that this rollover apply in the income tax return filed for the year of death.

A transfer of the assets to a parent using the above rollover will allow the assets to be transferred by the parent on a tax-free basis to surviving children or other lineal descendants of the parent or at least defer recognition of any gain until the death of both parents.

Effective May 1, 2006, this rollover treatment is also available where fishing property has been transferred from a parent to a child and, as a result of the child's death before both parents, the property is transferred back to his or her parents.

[¶2605] Reserves, etc. for the Year of Death

An elective procedure is provided whereby certain reserves may be passed from a deceased taxpayer to the taxpayer's spouse or common-law partner or to a trust created for their benefit, failing which election the reserves may not be claimed by any person.[352]

It is first provided that no deduction may be made in the year of death for any reserves for:

(a) uncollected proceeds of a sale made in the course of business;

(b) unearned commissions of insurance agents and brokers;

(c) realized but unreceived capital gains including replacement property;

(d) uncollected proceeds of sale of a foreign natural resource property; and

(e) uncollected proceeds of sale of a Canadian resource property.

As a result, income normally deferred will be included in the deceased's income in the year of death, whether receivable then or not.

An exception to the foregoing is provided where the right to receive any of the above reserves is transferred on or after the death of the deceased to the spouse or common-law partner or a trust created for their benefit, provided the legal representative of the deceased and the spouse, common-law partner, or the trustee of the spousal or partner trust, have jointly executed an election. The deceased and the deceased's spouse or common-law partner must have been resident in Canada immediately before the deceased's death, and the spousal or partner trust must be resident in Canada immediately after death.

See page ii for explanation of footnotes.

[351] CCH ¶28,329c; Sec. 248(8).   [352] CCH ¶9350; Sec. 72.

Where the deceased would have been entitled to claim a reserve in the year of death under (1), (2), (4), or (5) above, and an election is executed, the reserves are to be deducted in computing income for the year of death. The amount so deducted must be included in computing the income of the spouse/common-law partner or the trust receiving the debt obligation for the spouse/common-law partner's or the trust's first taxation year ending after the death. Depending upon which reserve is relevant, the amount claimed will be deemed to have been included in the income of the spouse/common-law partner or the trust for a previous year as income from the appropriate specified source. Thus, the spouse/common-law partner or trust will be entitled to claim a deduction for any allowable reserve and will take the deferred amounts into income as received. Amounts thus included in income do not qualify for the purposes of the capital gains exemption.

Where the deceased would have been entitled to claim a reserve under (3) above, such a reserve is deemed to have been claimed for the year of death where an election has been properly executed. In computing the income of the spouse/common-law partner or the spousal/partner trust for the first taxation year ending after death or any subsequent year, the reserve is deemed to be the proceeds of disposition received in that year and is deemed to be a gain from the disposition of capital property. A capital gains reserve under the rules in respect of replacement property is also unavailable in computing gains in the year of a taxpayer's death.

[¶2615] Attribution Rules for Income

[¶2620] Transfers or Loans to Spouse/Common-Law Partner

The Act provides rules which apply where an individual loans or transfers property to, or for the benefit of, his or her spouse or common-law partner.[353] These rules are applicable to direct or indirect loans or transfers made by means of a trust or in any other manner whatsoever, and to loans and transfers made to a person who later becomes the transferor's spouse or common-law partner. They also apply not only to property loaned or transferred, but to any property substituted therefor, regardless of how many substitutions are made.

Where property is loaned or transferred in these circumstances, any income or loss derived from that property will be attributed to the transferor, provided that it relates to a period during which the transferor was resident in Canada and during which the transferee was the transferor's spouse or common-law partner. It is to be noted that this applies to income from property and not income from a business. Furthermore, certain loans and transfers are exempted under the provisions discussed at ¶2660.

See page ii for explanation of footnotes.

[353] CCH ¶9516; Sec. 74.1(1); Interp. Bul. IT-511R.

A special provision is made to ensure that the attribution rules apply to a loan that:

(a) is used to repay borrowed money that was used to acquire property; or

(b) was used to reduce an amount payable in respect of that property.[354]

A transaction of this nature will be treated as though the property had been acquired directly with the proceeds of the loan. Where a loan that is otherwise exempt from the attribution rules is used to repay a prior loan to a spouse/common-law partner or minor, the rules will continue to apply to the income from the previously loaned property, or property substituted for it. Where the attribution rules technically do not bring income from loaned property back into the income of the lender, the provisions respecting loans to non-arm's length individuals may still apply to tax the income from loaned money or property in the hands of the lender. See ¶2260.

For joint and several liability for payment of tax in this situation and also where a transfer to a minor is involved, see ¶2645 and ¶12,245.

In a judgment released on January 8, 2009, the Supreme Court of Canada held, in a 4:3 split decision, that a taxpayer's reliance on certain spousal attribution rules to achieve the attribution of his wife's interest deductions to him frustrated the purpose of the attribution rules and was subject to GAAR.[355] In this case, the taxpayer's wife obtained a bank loan to purchase shares of a family corporation from him. He then used the proceeds to buy a new house, took out a mortgage on the house, and used it to pay off the bank loan. The mortgage interest on the substituted loan was deducted from his wife's dividend income and the resulting loss on the shares was attributed to him. Because there was no way the taxpayer could have produced this result other than by transferring the shares to his wife and by taking advantage of their non-arm's length relationship, the majority of the Supreme Court held that the purpose of the attribution rules was frustrated.

[¶2625] Spouse/Common-Law Partner as Employee or Partner

A salary paid to a spouse or common-law partner is included in the spouse's or common-law partner's income, and is a deductible business expense to the payer.

[¶2630] Transfers and Loans to Minors

The rules applicable to loans and transfers of property to, or for the benefit of, an individual who is a minor parallel the rules discussed at

---

See page ii for explanation of footnotes.

[354] CCH ¶9520; Sec. 74.1(3).   [355] Lipson, 2009 DTC 5015.

¶2620.[356] These rules apply to a loan or transfer either directly or indirectly or by means of a trust to a person under 18 years of age.

[¶2635] Capital Gains and Losses

Provision is made for the attribution of taxable capital gains and allowable capital losses arising from the disposition of property transferred to, or for the benefit of, a spouse or common-law partner.[357] This also applies to substituted property, and to loans and transfers made to a person who has since become the spouse or common-law partner of the lender or transferor. Similar rules apply with respect to gains and losses from listed personal property. However, due to the special rules relating to dispositions of listed personal property (see ¶5310), such gains and losses are not aggregated with taxable capital gains and net capital losses otherwise attributed.

Taxable capital gains and allowable capital losses which are attributed to an individual on dispositions of property in a year may be included in computing the individual's lifetime capital gains exemption where applicable.[358]

[¶2640] Transfers to RRSP, RDSP and TFSA

The attribution rules do not apply with respect to any premium paid by a taxpayer to a trust governed by an RRSP under which the taxpayer's spouse or common-law partner is the annuitant.[359] It does not matter whether the premium is deductible by the taxpayer or not. When the spouse or common-law partner receives a distribution from the RRSP, it will (subject to specified conditions) be included in the spouse's or common-law partner's income, not the taxpayer's. See ¶10,360.

Furthermore, for 2008 and subsequent taxation years, the attribution rules do not apply to a transfer made as a contribution to a registered disability savings plan (RDSP). This means that a contribution made to an RDSP, of which the contributor's spouse or minor child is a beneficiary, will not trigger the application of the attribution rules.

Finally, for 2009 and subsequent taxation years, the attribution rules do not apply in respect of a transfer of property to an individual's spouse or common-law partner while the property or substituted property is held in the spouse's or common-law partner's tax-free savings account (TFSA). This exception from the attribution rules applies only to the extent that the property is transferred using the spouse's or common-law partner's available TFSA contribution room at the time of the transfer (in particular, to the extent that the spouse or common-law partner does not have an "excess TFSA amount" at the time of the contribution. See ¶13,513.

---

[356] CCH ¶9518; Sec. 74.1(2).   [358] CCH ¶9524; Sec. 74.2(2).
[357] CCH ¶9522; Sec. 74.2(1); Interp. Bul. IT-510.   [359] CCH ¶9559b; Sec. 74.5(12).

[¶2645] Transfer or Loan Not at Arm's Length

It should be noted that where a transfer or loan has been made either to a spouse or common-law partner, to a minor, or to any other person with whom the transferor did not deal at arm's length, the transferor and the transferee are jointly and severally liable for the payment of certain taxes.[360] These taxes are:

(a) the part of transferor's tax liability which he is obliged to pay by reason of this provision; and

(b) any taxes owing by the transferor under the Act at the time of the transfer or loan but not exceeding the value of the property transferred or loaned.

The recipient of a transfer can himself become a transferor for the purpose of these provisions, if at the time of such transfer he is indebted for tax, either on his own behalf, or jointly with the first transferor.[361] These provisions also apply to make a person who transfers property at less than its fair market value jointly and severally liable for the acquirer's tax and other amounts payable as a result of the deemed disposition.[362]

A payment by the transferee on account of the transferor's tax liability discharges the transferee's joint liability to the extent of the payment.[363] However, a payment by the transferor on account of his or her total tax liability is taken to apply, first, to any income tax liability of the transferor other than the joint and several liability, and second, to the discharge of the joint and several liability. The tax liability of the transferee is reduced only to the extent that the total tax liability of the transferor is reduced below the joint and several liability.

There is an exemption to the joint and several liability rule where property is transferred pursuant to a court order or written separation agreement and at a time when the taxpayer and the taxpayer's spouse or common-law partner were living apart as a result of the breakdown of their marriage or common-law partnership.[364]

A separation agreement must contain provisions about child support, custody, and support payments. A document evidencing a transfer of property to the taxpayer from her spouse only referred to the fact that they were separated. This was not enough to justify a finding that the transfer was made under a "written separation agreement".[365]

[¶2650] Trusts

A mechanism is provided for determining the amount to be attributed where an individual has loaned or transferred property to a trust in which a

---

See page ii for explanation of footnotes.

[360] CCH ¶22,774; Sec. 160(1).
[361] Jurak, 2003 DTC 5145.
[362] CCH ¶22,775; Sec. 160(1.1).

[363] CCH ¶22,778; Sec. 160(3).
[364] CCH ¶22,779; Sec. 160(4).
[365] Carrière, 2006 DTC 3098.

"designated person" is beneficially interested at any time.[366] A "designated person" is defined[367] as:

(a) the individual's spouse or common-law partner;

(b) a person under 18 years of age who does not deal at arm's length with the individual; or

(c) a person under 18 years of age who is the niece or nephew of the individual.

A person is deemed to be beneficially interested if that person has any right whatsoever to receive any income or capital of the trust, whether directly or indirectly through one or more trusts.[368] Where a designated person has a beneficial interest in a trust, a loan or transfer to the trust is deemed to be to, or for the benefit of, that person.[369]

The income of a designated person in a taxation year from the loaned or transferred property is the lesser of:

(a) the income of that person from the trust; and

(b) the proportion of the income earned by the trust from the loaned or transferred property (or property substituted therefor) that the income of that person from the trust is of the aggregate income from the trust of all persons each of which is a designated person in respect of the lender or transferor.

Where the designated person is a spouse or common-law partner, taxable capital gains are subject to attribution in an amount that is the lesser of:

(a) the amount designated by the trust to be a taxable capital gain of the designated person for the year; and

(b) the net taxable capital gains for the year from the disposition by the trust of the loaned or transferred property, or property substituted therefor.

The amount of income attributed in respect of a designated beneficiary will in no case exceed the amount of that person's income from the trust.

[¶2655] Transfers and Loans to Corporations

Attribution rules also apply where an individual loans or transfers property to a subject corporation (other than a small business corporation) either directly or indirectly by means of a trust or any other means whatever.[370] In order for attribution to arise, the following conditions must be met in the relevant period:

---

[366] CCH ¶9526; Sec. 74.3(1).
[367] CCH ¶9549; Sec. 74.5(5).
[368] CCH ¶28,325; Sec. 248(2).

[369] CCH ¶9556; Sec. 74.5(9).

[370] CCH ¶9532; Sec. 74.4(2).

(1) One of the main purposes of the transfer or loan may reasonably be considered to be to reduce the income of the transferor and to benefit directly or indirectly, by any means, a person who is a designated person. "Designated person" is defined[371] as:

(a) the transferor's spouse or common-law partner;

(b) a person under 18 years of age who does not deal at arm's length with the transferor; or

(c) a person under 18 years of age who is the niece or nephew of the transferor.

(2) The designated person must be a specified shareholder of the corporation. "Specified shareholder" in this context means a person who, directly or indirectly, owns 10% or more of the issued shares of any class of the corporation at any time in the year, and includes a person who owns at least 10% of the shares of a related corporation (other than in a related small business corporation); see ¶15,415.[372] Shares owned by a trust are deemed to be owned by the beneficiaries in proportions based on the fair market value of their interests in the trust. Shares owned by a partnership are deemed to be owned by the partners in proportions based on the fair market value of their interests in the partnership.

(3) The individual who transferred or loaned the property must be a resident of Canada during the relevant period.

(4) The corporation must not be a small business corporation.

Where these tests are met, deemed interest is attributed to the person who transferred or loaned the property. In general terms, the amount of the deemed interest is calculated at the prescribed rate of interest times the outstanding amount of the loan or unpaid purchase price of the transferred property. The amount of deemed interest is reduced if there is consideration for the loan or transfer. The percentage interest in the corporation held by the designated person does not give rise to proration of the amount of deemed interest. Accordingly, the amount will be the same whether the designated person owns a minority, majority, or all of the shares of the corporation.

[¶2660] Exemptions

The attribution rules do not apply:

(a) to transfers of property for fair market consideration;

(b) to loans of property that bear a commercial rate of interest; and

---

[371] CCH ¶9549; Sec. 74.5(5).   [372] CCH ¶28,273; Sec. 248(1) "specified shareholder".

(c) in the event that spouses or common-law partners are separated by reason of the breakdown of their marriage or common-law partnership:

(i) to any income or loss relating to the period of separation;

(ii) to any capital gain or loss from disposition of the property during the period of separation, provided that the parties jointly elect that the rules not apply; and

(iii) to property loaned or transferred to a corporation the shareholders of which include the spouse/common-law partner or former spouse/common-law partner, a partnership of which such a person is a member, a trust in which such a person is beneficially interested, or another corporation of which such a person is the sole shareholder.[373]

[¶2665] Anti-Avoidance Rules

Rules are provided to ensure that attribution cannot be avoided through the use of intermediaries to effect a loan or transfer to, or for the benefit of, a "specified person".[374] A "specified person" is defined[375] to mean:

(a) a designated person in respect of the individual (see ¶2655); or

(b) a corporation, other than a small business corporation, of which a designated person in respect of the individual would have been a specified shareholder.

This provision would apply where an individual loans or transfers property to a third party, and that property, or property substituted therefor, is ultimately loaned or transferred to the specified person by the third party or by any other person. It would also apply where an individual loans or transfers property to a third party on the condition that the third party loan or transfer any property to the specified person, and where a loan or transfer is made to a trust in which the specified person is beneficially interested.

A similar provision exists to prevent avoidance of the attribution rules where an individual undertakes to guarantee the repayment of a loan made by any person to a specified person.[376]

No attribution will occur where an artificial transaction or series of artificial transactions is undertaken for the purpose of attributing income of the taxpayer to another lower income-earning person.[377]

See page ii for explanation of footnotes.

[373] CCH ¶9540–9546; Sec. 74.5(1)–(4).
[374] CCH ¶9550; Sec. 74.5(6).
[375] CCH ¶9554; Sec. 74.5(8).

[376] CCH ¶9552; Sec. 74.5(7).

[377] CCH ¶9559; Sec. 74.5(11).

[¶2667] Exception from Attribution Rules

Although the attribution rules reduce the opportunities for income splitting, several tax planning techniques have developed over time to avoid the application of these rules and recent case law has provided support for them, contrary to the CRA's policy intent.[378]

To discourage income splitting with minor children, the 1999 Budget introduced an income-splitting tax for the year 2000 and subsequent taxation years to be levied on certain passive income of individuals under the age of 18 (see the commentary at ¶8080 *et seq.*). To ensure that amounts taxed as split income in the hands of a minor child are not also attributed to a parent (or the transferor), income that is subject to this new tax will not be subject to the attribution rules.[379]

[¶2670] Security in Satisfaction of Income Debt

The value of securities or other rights or certificates or other evidences of indebtedness which are received in satisfaction, in whole or in part, of a debt which was then payable, will be included in the income of the recipient when received.[380] The interest, dividend, or other debt must be such that it would have been included in the income of the recipient if it had been paid. If the security or other right or the certificate or other evidence of indebtedness is received in respect of a debt which is not yet payable, and the security is not itself payable or redeemable before that date, it will be deemed to have been received by the person holding it when the debt became payable.

An exception to the foregoing is where a taxpayer delivers grain to a primary elevator in one taxation year and receives in exchange a cash purchase ticket which entitles the taxpayer to payment, without interest, in a later taxation year.[381]

[¶2675] Bond Conversions

There are provisions in the Act governing the determination of the purchase price of bonds acquired and the sale price of bonds surrendered when a taxpayer acquires bonds in exchange for other bonds of the same debtor.[382] The provisions are of limited application, since they apply only to cases in which:

(a) the bond exchanged contains in its terms of issue a provision conferring upon holders the right to make the exchange;

(b) the amount payable on the acquired bond at maturity is the same as the amount which would have been payable at maturity on the bond exchanged.

See page ii for explanation of footnotes.

[378] Neuman, 98 DTC 6297, Ferrel, 99 DTC 5111.   [381] CCH ¶9640, ¶9641; Sec. 76(4), 76(5).
[379] CCH ¶9563; Sec. 74.5(13).
[380] CCH ¶9600–9630; Sec. 76(1)–(3).   [382] CCH ¶9680; Sec. 77.

¶2667

If the taxpayer carries on a business of dealing in bonds and has recorded in its inventory the bond that was exchanged, the purchase price of the bond acquired and the sale price of the bond exchanged are deemed to be the amount at which the bond was valued in the taxpayer's inventory at the end of the last fiscal period preceding the exchange. In all other cases the purchase price of the bond acquired and the sale price of the bond exchanged are deemed to be the purchase price of the exchanged bond.

The above will normally apply to taxpayers who are carrying on a business of dealing in bonds and will preclude the realization of any profit or loss for tax purposes on an exchange of bonds.

[¶2680] Unpaid Amounts — Transactions Not at Arm's Length

There are provisions in the Act to prevent an accumulation of deductible outlays or expenses in non-arm's length relationships where the accumulated amount is not paid at the end of the second taxation year following the taxation year in which the expense was incurred. There are two alternative treatments:[383]

(a) the amount is added to the taxpayer's income for the next taxation year (that is, the third year after the expense is incurred); or

(b) if the taxpayer and the creditor agree, it is deemed to have been paid by the taxpayer and received by the creditor on the first day of the third taxation year. The creditor is then deemed to have made a loan to the taxpayer of an equal amount.

Where the amount is added to the taxpayer's income under (a) above, no deduction can be claimed if the amount is actually paid in a subsequent taxation year.

Where an agreement is filed after the day the taxpayer is required to file his or her return for the third taxation year following that in which the outlay or expense was incurred, the taxpayer is required to include 25% of the unpaid amount in computing income for the third taxation year.[384]

Where a taxpayer is a corporation and the outlay or expense is unpaid when the corporation is wound up, and such winding-up takes place before the end of the second taxation year following the year of the outlay or expense, the unpaid amount is included in computing the income of the corporation for the taxation year in which it is wound up.

[¶2685] Unpaid Remuneration

An employer may deduct expenses in respect of salary, wages, or other remuneration in the taxation year in which they were incurred only if the amount is paid within 180 days from the end of the taxation year.[385] This

---

See page ii for explanation of footnotes.

[383] CCH ¶9700, ¶9705; Sec. 78(1), 78(2); Interp. Bul. IT-109R2.

[384] CCH ¶9710; Sec. 78(3).

[385] CCH ¶9715; Sec. 78(4).

does not apply to reasonable vacation pay, or to a deferred amount under a salary deferral arrangement.

Where payment is not made within the 180-day period, the employer is allowed to deduct the expense in a subsequent taxation year in which it is actually paid.

[¶2690] Mortgage Foreclosures and Conditional Sales Repossessions

Where a taxpayer as mortgagee forecloses a mortgage, or where a taxpayer repossesses property under a conditional sales contract, the following rules apply:[386]

(1) The debtor treats the property in respect of which the claim occurs as having been disposed of at the principal amount and is entitled to treat any further payments on the claim as a loss from the disposition of that property.

(2) The creditor is not required to take into account any reserve for amounts not due until a year later or for proceeds not due until a later year claimed in computing a capital gain or loss or a capital gains reserve claimed in respect of dispositions of property for which a replacement property had been acquired, for the taxation year immediately preceding the taxation year in question.

(3) The creditor's deemed cost of the property is the cost to the creditor of the claim minus the amount of any reserve claimed in respect of the property; the adjusted cost base of the creditor's claim is deemed to be nil so that there is no capital loss by reason of the acquisition and any subsequent payment in respect of the claim will result in a capital gain; and the creditor is not entitled to any further reserves for doubtful accounts or bad debts and presumably must bring into income any reserve for doubtful accounts which he claimed in the preceding year.

See page ii for explanation of footnotes.
[386] CCH ¶9800; Sec. 79.

Chapter III

Income from Business or Property

Business or Property Income **3000**

Business Income 3003

Property Income 3006

Computation of Profit from a Business 3010

Dividends 3015

Interest 3018

Interest of Certain Taxpayers 3021

Canada Savings Bonds — Interest Deduction 3024

Indexed Debt Obligations 3025

Proceeds of Disposition of Right to Receive Production 3026

Use or Production from Property 3027

Proprietor of a Business 3033

Damages — Business Contracts 3036

Compensation for Loss of Income or Property Used in a Business 3039

Compensation for Damage to Property 3042

Illegal Profits — Betting and Gambling 3045

Sale or Gift of Income-Earning Property 3048

Accrual Income of Corporations, etc. 3051

Investment Tax Credit 3057

Reinsurance Commissions 3060

Home Insulation or Energy Conversion Grants 3063

Scientific Research and Experimental Development (SR&ED) Deductions 3066

Fuel Tax Rebates 3067

Amateur Athletic Trust 3068

Eligible Funeral Arrangements 3069

Other Items of Income 3070

Goodwill and Other Intangibles **3072**

General Treatment 3075

Eligible Capital Expenditures 3078

Non-Eligible Capital Expenditures 3081

Deductions — Cumulative Eligible Capital 3087

Negative Balance in Cumulative Eligible Capital Accounts 3088

Replacement Property 3090

Cessation of Business 3093

Transfer of Goodwill to Canadian Corporation 3096

Deemed Proceeds of Disposition 3099

Benefits Conferred on Shareholders **3105**

Benefits to Shareholders 3108

Shareholder Debt 3111

Loans or Debts to Shareholders Not Included in Income 3114

Deemed Benefit on Employee and Shareholder Loans and Debts 3117

Housing Loans 3120

Where Benefit Conferred Is
Not Money 3126

Rights to Purchase Shares 3129

**Payments of Income and
Capital Combined** **3132**

Blended Payments 3135

Annuity Payments 3141

Loans to Non-Residents **3153**

Interest on Loans 3156

**Deductions from Business
or Property Income** **3159**

General Discussion 3162

General Limitation —
Capital Outlay 3165

Entertainers and Musicians 3171

Repairs and Maintenance
of Capital Equipment 3174

Fines and Penalties 3180

Home Office 3183

Illegal Payments 3184

Legal and Accounting Fees 3186

Losses by Fire or Theft 3189

Organization Expenses 3192

Expenses To Earn Exempt
Income 3195

Annual Value of Property 3198

Payments to Farmers 3201

Metric Conversion Costs 3204

Reserves, Contingent
Accounts, and Sinking
Funds 3207

Payments on Income or
Discounted Bonds 3210

Personal or Living
Expenses 3213

Meaning of "Personal or
Living Expenses" 3216

Restriction on Food,
Beverages and
Entertainment Expenses 3219

Employer Contributions to
Plans for Employee
Benefit 3222

Use of Recreational
Facilities and Club Dues 3225

Salary Deferral
Arrangement 3228

Retirement Compensation
Arrangement (RCA) 3231

Political Contributions 3234

Employee Benefit Plan
Contributions 3237

Personal Service Business
Deduction Limitation 3240

Interest and Property Taxes
on Undeveloped Land 3246

Construction Period Soft
Costs 3249

Prepaid Expenses 3252

Penalties, Bonuses and
Rate Reduction
Payments 3253

Matchable Expenditures 3254

Thin Capitalization Rules **3255**

Deduction of Interest by
Certain Corporations —
Thin Capitalization Rules 3258

**Advertising — Non-
Canadian Newspaper or
Periodical — Foreign
Broadcasting** **3261**

Limitation on Advertising
Expense 3264

Foreign Broadcasting 3267

Certain Other Deductions **3270**

Capital Cost Allowance 3273

Cumulative Eligible Capital
Amount 3276

Interest on Borrowed
Money 3277

Weak Currency Debt 3280

Interest on Policy Loans 3282

Repayment of Loans —
Previously Acquired
Property 3285

Interest Incurred to Acquire
Passenger Vehicle 3291

Loss of Source: Borrowed
Money Used to Earn
Income from Capital
Property 3294

Capitalized Interest 3297

Limitation on Interest on
Borrowed Money 3300

Borrowed Money —
Promise To Pay Larger
Amount 3303

Expenses re Financing 3306

Discounts on Interest-
Bearing Obligations 3312

Share Transfer and Other
Fees 3315

Pension Plan Contributions 3321

Employee Life and Health
Trust Contributions 3322

Leasing Properties 3330

Lease Cancellation
Payments 3333

Landscaping of Grounds 3336

Fees Paid to Investment
Counsel 3339

Expenses of
Representation 3342

Cost of Utility Service
Connections 3345

Western Grain Stabilization
Payments 3348

Disability-Related Building
Modifications 3349

Part XII.6 Tax 3350

Investigation of Site 3351

Uncollectible Portion of
Proceeds of Disposition
of Depreciable Property 3352

Sale of Mortgage Included
in Proceeds of
Disposition 3353

Accrued Bond Interest 3354

Convention Expenses 3355

Exploration and
Development Grants 3356

Annuity Contracts 3357

Private Health Service Plan
(PHSP) Premiums 3358

Miscellaneous Deductions 3359

**Charitable Donations —
Corporations 3360**

Deduction Limit and Capital
Gains Inclusion Rate 3361

Institutions that
May Receive Donations 3362

Meaning of "Gift" 3363

Donations that Cannot Be
Deducted 3364

Registered Charities and
Canadian Amateur
Athletic Organizations 3365

Returns, Records and
Receipts 3366

Contents of Receipts 3367

Crown Gifts 3368

Gifts of Cultural Property to
Institutions 3369

Gifts of Ecologically
Sensitive Land 3370

Granting of Options to
Charities and Other
Qualified Donees 3372

Returned Gifts 3373

Donation of Medicines for
the Developing World 3374

Gifts of Capital Property 3375

Limitation on Deductibility 3376

Restrictions upon
Acquisition of Control 3377

**Losses — Inter-Company
Dividends 3380**

Net Capital Loss 3381

Non-Capital Loss (Business
Loss) 3384

Loss from Business or
Property 3387

Limitation of Loss where
Control or Type of
Business Changes 3390

Other Restrictions on
Losses and Their Use 3393

Losses of Hobby-Farmers
— Restricted Farm Loss 3396

Net Capital Loss in Year of
Death 3399

Amended Return for
Succeeding Year's Loss 3402

Inter-Company Dividends —
Deductibility 3405

Losses in Share
Transactions 3408

Order of Deductions 3411

**Reserves, Bad and Doubtful
Debts 3414**

Amounts Included in
Income and Reserves —
Goods and Services 3417

Amounts Receivable — Sale
of Land 3420

Reserves for Undelivered
Goods 3423

Reserves for Unrendered
Services 3426

Reserve for Guarantees 3429

Indemnities and Warranties 3432

Repayment of Amount
Previously Included in
Income 3438

Policy Reserves Deductible
by Insurance Companies 3441

Reserves for Unexpired
Rent 3444

Reserves for Undischarged
Obligations 3447

Reserves for Amounts
Receivable — Land 3450

Reserve for Debt
Forgiveness 3451

Bad Debts and Reserves
for Doubtful Debts 3453

Conditional Sales
Repossessions 3454

Settlement of Debts 3456

Doubtful Debts and
Reserves 3459

Lending Money on Security
of Mortgages, etc., and
Reserves 3462

Quadrennial Surveys and
Reserves 3465

Other Debts and Reserves 3471

Sale of Inventory **3474**

Inventory Valuation 3477

Rules for Sale of Inventory 3480

Inventory Adjustment 3486

**Sale of Accounts
Receivable** **3489**

Rules for Sale of Accounts
Receivable 3492

Vendor's Deductions 3495

Purchaser's Deductions 3498

Election 3501

Receipt of Consideration for
Accounts Receivable after
Ceasing Business 3504

**Ceasing to Carry on
Business** **3507**

Sale of Business 3510

Realization of Assets by
Liquidation 3513

Appropriation of
Corporation's Property 3516

Cumulative Eligible Capital 3519

Ceasing to Carry on a
Farming Business in
Canada 3522

Resource Industries **3531**

Income of Resource
Industries 3534

Exploration and
Development Expenses
— General 3537

Flow-Through Shares 3540

Depletion Allowance 3543

Deduction for Provincial
Mining Taxes 3546

Professional Business **3549**

Income Calculation 3552

Amounts Receivable 3555

Work-in-Progress, Election 3558

Lawyers' Trust Accounts
and Disbursements 3561

Deductions of Professional
Individuals 3567

**Farming or Fishing
Business** **3570**

Cash Method of Computing
Income 3573

"Farming" Defined 3576

Restricted Farm Loss 3579

Clearing or Levelling Land
and Laying Tile Drainage 3582

Feedlot Operation — When
Considered Farming 3588

Payments upon Destruction
of Livestock 3591

**Prospectors and
Grubstakers** **3594**

Disposition of Interest in
Mining Property 3597

**Scientific Research and
Experimental
Development (SR&ED)** **3600**

General 3601

Current Expenses Incurred
in Canada 3603

Current Expenses Incurred
Outside Canada 3606

Expenditures of a Capital
Nature 3609

Repayments 3612

Investment Tax Credit 3615

Meaning of "Scientific
Research and
Experimental
Development" 3618

Capital Cost Allowance 3624

Prohibited Deductions 3627

Filing of Prescribed Form 3628
Crown Corporations 3636
   Income 3639
Grants and Subsidies 3642
   Government Grants and
      Other Subsidies 3645

Recent Changes

2012 Budget

Extension of Credit for Flow-through Shares

Certain individuals who invest in flow-through shares are also entitled to an additional benefit equal to 15% of certain qualifying expenses incurred in Canada as described in the definition of "flow-through mining expenditure". This mineral exploration tax credit was introduced as part of the 2000 Budget and has been extended for an extra year to flow-through share agreements entered into on or before March 31, 2014. Furthermore, flow-through share funds raised in one calendar year with the benefit of the credit can be spent on eligible exploration up to the end of the next calendar year under the existing "look-back" rule. Accordingly, flow-through share funds raised during the first three months of 2013 can support qualifying expenses until the end of 2014. This was enacted in Bill C-38, which received royal assent on June 29, 2012. See ¶3540.

Retirement Compensation Arrangements ("RCAs")

Changes have been proposed to tighten the tax benefits available for contributions to RCAs in response to some perceived abuses of the rules. Budget Resolutions 6 to 11 proposed that RCAs become subject to "prohibited investment", "advantage", and "stripping" rules. Essentially, where an RCA has a specified beneficiary, the RCA will be subject to an additional "Advantage Tax" equal to the fair market value of any advantage obtained by the specified beneficiary or a non-arm's length person. Furthermore, the RCA will be subject to a "Prohibited Investment Tax" equal to 50% of the fair market value of a prohibited investment acquired or held by the RCA. Lastly, the specified beneficiary of an RCA will be jointly and severally, or solitarily, liable for these taxes. The election available in subsection 207.5(2) to deal with a decline in RCA asset value is also to be restricted. These changes have been proposed in draft legislation released on August 14, 2012. See ¶3231 for further discussion.

Corporate Mineral Exploration and Development Tax Credit

The investment tax credit available in respect of pre-production exploration expenditures will continue to apply at 10% for expenses incurred in 2012, but it will be reduced to 5% for expenses incurred in 2013, and it will be eliminated for expenses incurred after 2013. For the pre-production development expenditures, the 10% credit will continue to apply for expenses incurred before 2014, will be reduced (with some transitional relief) to 7% for expenses incurred in 2014, reduced further to 4% for expenses incurred in 2015, and eliminated thereafter. These changes have been incorporated in draft legislation released on August 14, 2012. See discussions at ¶3537 and ¶3540.

Scientific Research and Experimental Development ("SR&ED")

Significant changes to both rates and eligible expenditures have been proposed to the SR&ED program in the 2012 Budget. SR&ED capital expenditures made after

2013 will no longer be deductible, nor will they form part of the SR&ED pool for investment tax credits. These assets will be subject to the general tax treatment rules for capital expenditures. This new rule will also apply to any payments in respect of the use or the right to use property after 2013 that would, if it were acquired by the taxpayer, be capital property of the taxpayer.

In addition, only a portion of contract payments made to arm's length performers of SR&ED will be eligible for computing qualified expenditures. Only 80% of arm's length contract payments will be eligible for investment tax credit treatment to reflect the elimination of capital expenditures from the SR&ED pool.

These changes have been incorporated in draft legislation released on August 14, 2012. See discussions at ¶3600. A review of the changes to the investment tax credit and refundable investment tax credit rates and rates used in the proxy method can be found in Chapter VIII.

Thin Capitalization

Budget 2012 proposed significant changes to the thin capitalization rules, reflecting the recommendations made by the Advisory Panel on Canada's System of International Taxation in 2008. The debt to equity ratio is proposed to be reduced from the current 2:1 to 1.5:1, effective for taxation years that begin after 2012. Further, the wording will reflect partnerships, such that a Canadian corporate partner will be attributed its proportionate share of any partnership debt, and will be required to include in income any interest on the portion of the allocated partnership debt that exceeds the corporate partner's debt to equity ratio. These changes have been incorporated in draft legislation released on August 14, 2012. See discussions at ¶3255. Further changes reflecting the characterization of disallowed interest for withholding tax purposes can be found in Chapter XIV.

Gifts to Foreign Charities

As a result of Budget Resolution 42, foreign charitable organizations that have received a gift from the government may apply for a 24-month "qualified donee" status if they pursue activities that are:

    (i) related to disaster relief or urgent humanitarian aid, or

    (ii) in the national interest of Canada.

They may apply for such designation on or after June 29, 2012. See ¶3362.

Finance Announcements

2012 Automobile Limits — Leasing and Interest

On December 29, 2011, the Department of Finance released the automobile rates and limits for 2012. The limit on deductible leasing costs remains at $800 per month, plus applicable federal and provincial sales taxes; and the maximum interest deduction for amounts borrowed to purchase an automobile remains at $300 per month. See ¶3291.

[¶3000] Business or Property Income

[¶3003] Business Income

A business is treated under the Act as being a source of income of a somewhat different nature than income from property. Both income from a business and income from a property differ from income from an office or employment.

The income of a business is the profit therefrom for the year.[1] The generally accepted definition is that "profit" means net profit, i.e., the gross income of a business minus the expenditures necessary to earn that income. "Business" is defined as including a profession, calling, trade, manufacture, or undertaking of any kind whatsoever, and includes an adventure or concern in the nature of trade but does not include an office or employment.[2]

In most cases, it will be obvious when a business is carried on, but in some cases it is a complex and difficult question. In the case of self-employment, the self-employed taxpayer is generally considered to be carrying on a business which is a source of income.[3] A person will be considered to be self-employed where engaged to achieve a defined objective and given complete freedom as required to attain the end result. In addition, there must be a reasonable expectation of profit as a result of the activity being performed, as opposed to the furtherance of a hobby or interest. See also ¶5105.

[¶3006] Property Income

"Income from property" is generally regarded as the return on invested capital where little or no time, labour, or attention is expended in producing the return. Income from property would normally include dividends, interest, rents and royalties, a right of any kind, a chose in action, and money. However, such receipts might constitute income from business if sufficient time and effort is expended in earning them. For example, if a taxpayer manages office or apartment buildings, the rents may constitute income from a business.[4] Income from a property does not include a capital gain or a capital loss from a disposition of that property.[5]

The term "property" is to be distinguished from the term "capital property" which means:[6]

(a) depreciable property; and

(b) any property other than depreciable property, the disposition of which would result in a capital gain or loss.

See page ii for explanation of footnotes.

[1] CCH ¶4003; Sec. 9(1); Interp. Bul. IT-102R2, IT-359R2, IT-373R2, IT-404R, IT-454, IT-504R2.

[2] CCH ¶28,024; Sec. 248(1) "business".

[3] Interp. Bul. IT-504R2.

[4] Interp. Bul. IT-434R; Martin, 3 DTC 1199, Ginsberg, 53 DTC 445, No. 196, 54 DTC 468.

[5] CCH ¶4009; Sec. 9(3); Interp. Bul. IT-102R2, IT-479R.

[6] CCH ¶7850b; Sec. 54 "capital property".

A capital gain or loss does not arise upon the disposition of:

(a) property, the sale of which would be taken into account in computing ordinary income such as inventory of a business;

(b) eligible capital property, meaning goodwill and other "nothings";

(c) cultural objects which help preserve the national heritage of Canada in certain circumstances;

(d) Canadian and foreign resource properties;

(e) life insurance policies; and

(f) a timber resource property.[7]

The difference between the tax treatments of income from property and income from business will be important in situations involving: non-residents; capital cost allowance; the small business deduction and manufacturing and processing allowance; loss carryovers when there is a change of control; the foreign tax credit; and travelling expenses.

Income may arise as a return on property where a property is placed by a taxpayer at the use or disposal of another person.

It should be kept in mind that income from a business is earned income, while income from property is normally investment income. It should also be observed that certain provisions of the Act which are applicable in connection with a business do not apply where income from a property is concerned, such as the deduction of travelling expenses incurred in the course of carrying on a business.

Income received as a return on real estate, mineral rights, or chattels is variously described as "rent", "royalty", or "share of profits". In the case of money loaned to another, the payment is usually described as "interest". The income from shares is ordinarily described as "dividends".

A disposition of an interest in land was characterized as income despite the taxpayer's claim that the acquisition was made for the development of a shopping centre. No soil tests were done, no tenants had been secured and no financing arranged.[8]

[¶3010] Computation of Profit from a Business

The Supreme Court of Canada has laid to rest the paramount importance of accounting principles in the computation of profit from a business.[9] While conceding that accounting principles may be a useful tool for determining profit for tax purposes, the Supreme Court of Canada went on to hold that they are only interpretative aids which may assist in the ultimate

---

See page ii for explanation of footnotes.

[7] CCH ¶6050; Sec. 39(1).

[8] Bahr, 96 DTC 1576.

[9] Canderel Limited, 98 DTC 6100, Toronto College Park Limited, 98 DTC 6088, Ikea Limited, 98 DTC 6092.

goal of providing an accurate picture of the taxpayer's income. According to the Supreme Court, the following principles apply to the determination of profit for income tax purposes:

(1) The determination of profit is a question of law.

(2) The profit of a business for a taxation year is to be determined by setting against the revenues from the business for that year the expenses incurred in earning said income.

(3) In seeking to ascertain profit, the goal is to obtain an accurate picture of the taxpayer's profit for the given year.

(4) In ascertaining profit, the taxpayer is free to adopt any method which is not inconsistent with:

(a) the provisions of the *Income Tax Act*;

(b) established case law principles or rules of law; and

(c) well-accepted business principles.

(5) Well-accepted business principles, which include but are not limited to the formal codification found in the Generally Accepted Accounting Principles (GAAP), are not rules of law but interpretative aids. To the extent that they may influence the calculation of income, they will do so only on a case-by-case basis, depending on the facts of the taxpayer's financial situation.

(6) On reassessment, once the taxpayer has shown that he or she has provided an accurate picture of income for the year, which is consistent with the Act, the case law, and well-accepted business principles, the onus shifts to the Minister to show either that the figure provided does not represent an accurate picture, or that another method of computation would provide a more accurate picture.

In the *Canderel* and *Toronto College Park* cases, *supra*, it was held that, regardless of the accounting treatment, for income tax purposes the expenses at issue (tenant inducement payments) were fully deductible in the year in which they were incurred. They did not have to be "matched" against future revenues under the matching principle of accounting, because matching was not shown to provide a more accurate picture of the taxpayer's profit.

[¶3015] Dividends

A dividend paid to a taxpayer by a corporation resident in Canada on a share of its capital stock is required to be included in the taxpayer's income,[10] as is the amount of a dividend paid to a taxpayer by a corporation not resident in Canada on a share of its capital stock, or an amount in

See page ii for explanation of footnotes.

---

[10] CCH ¶4356; Sec. 12(1)(j).

respect of a share owned by the taxpayer of the capital stock of a foreign affiliate.[11] Dividends that a taxpayer received from a foreign corporation, in the form of shares of the corporation's subsidiaries, were held to be "dividends in kind" and had to be included in her income.[12]

[¶3018] Interest

Amounts received or receivable in the year as interest are to be included in income, but only to the extent that such interest has not been included in income for a preceding year. Thus, if interest is included in income in one year on the accrual basis, that same interest will not be included in income in a subsequent year when it becomes receivable or is in fact received.[13]

If a payment of interest is made in the form of property or a right of any kind rather than in money, it would nevertheless be included in income. Any payment which discharges all or part of an interest obligation, whether paid by the principal debtor or by someone else on the principal debtor's behalf, must be included in income. In some cases, interest is, in effect, deemed to have been received (such as in the case of loans to non-residents[14] and accrued interest on certain debt obligations sold between interest-due dates).[15]

When a payment under a contract or other arrangement can reasonably be regarded as being partly a payment of interest or other payment of an income nature and partly a payment of a capital nature, the portion which can reasonably be regarded as interest or as being of an income nature is included in the income of the recipient.[16] See ¶3135.

Where a loan repayable at par is made at a discount, or if a loan is made at a discount or at par but is repayable at a premium, the lender will receive more in repayment than was loaned. Whether the discount or premium (bonus) is interest or a capital receipt will depend on the facts of the case.

For interest on borrowed money, see ¶3277; for situations where securities are sold between interest dates, see ¶3354; and for interest on policy loans, see ¶3282.

[¶3021] Interest of Certain Taxpayers

The general rules discussed above (under which interest is included in income when it is received or receivable, depending upon the method followed by the taxpayer) are varied in the case of certain taxpayers.

Corporations, partnerships, unit trusts, or any trust of which a corporation or partnership is a beneficiary must include in income interest on debt obligations if it was previously not included in income.[17] This accrual rule

---

See page ii for explanation of footnotes.

[11] CCH ¶4358; Sec. 12(1)(k).
[12] Yang, 2011 DTC 1156.
[13] CCH ¶4280; Sec. 12(1)(c); Interp. Bul. IT-396R.
[14] CCH ¶4732; Sec. 17.
[15] CCH ¶5142; Sec. 20(14).
[16] CCH ¶4700; Sec. 16(1).
[17] CCH ¶4380; Sec. 12(3).

¶3018

does not apply to interest on an income bond or debenture, a small business development bond, or a small business bond, as interest on these instruments is deemed to have been received on taxable dividends.[18] In addition, the accrual rules do not apply to interest earned on a Net Income Stabilization Account (NISA), as this interest will be included in computing income.[19]

"Anniversary day" [20] is defined as the end of the day that is one year after the day of issue of the investment contract; every successive such day occurring at one year intervals; and the day on which an investment contract is disposed of. For investment contracts acquired or materially altered after 1989, interest accrued on an investment contract up to each anniversary day of the investment contract must be included in income in the taxation year in which the anniversary falls.[21]

The term "investment contract" is defined to include any debt obligation except one whose investment income is already included in income at least annually.[22] This definition specifically excludes income bonds and debentures, small business development bonds or small business bonds, net income stabilization accounts, salary deferral arrangements, retirement compensation arrangements, employee benefit plans, foreign retirement arrangements, indexed debt obligations, and, after 2008, tax-free savings accounts (TFSAs).

In addition, any premium or discount taken upon a prescribed debt obligation (including one for which no interest is stipulated) is deemed to be interest and included in income regardless of whether the discount or premium would otherwise constitute "interest" as determined by the case law.[23]

[¶3024] Canada Savings Bonds — Interest Deduction

A person who purchases a Canada Savings Bond under a payroll or monthly savings plan is, in effect, borrowing money for that purpose. Thus, interest charged on such loans is a deductible expense. The amount of interest paid may be determined by deducting the face value of the bonds purchased from the total of instalment payments or payroll deductions made.[24]

[¶3025] Indexed Debt Obligations

The term "indexed debt obligation" [25] means a debt obligation that provides for an adjustment to the amount payable which is determined by reference to a change in the purchasing power of money. An example would be a security issued at less than market interest rates but carrying a condi-

---

See page ii for explanation of footnotes.

[18] CCH ¶4680, ¶4681, ¶4698, ¶4699; Sec. 15(3), 15(4), 15.1(1), 15.2(1).
[19] CCH ¶4393b; Sec. 12(10.2).
[20] CCH ¶4393d; Sec. 12(11) "anniversary day".
[21] CCH ¶4380a; Sec. 12(4).

[22] CCH ¶4393e; Sec. 12(11) "investment contract".
[23] CCH ¶4391a, ¶4391b; Sec. 12(9); Reg. 7000(1).
[24] Interp. Bul. IT-396R.
[25] CCH ¶28,136a; Sec. 248(1) "indexed debt obligation".

tion that at maturity the investor will be paid a special amount in addition to interest and principal, to take into account a loss of purchasing power as represented by a change in the Consumer Price Index. Accordingly, an amount, prescribed by regulation, is taken into income by the holder and is deductible by the debtor if the purchasing power of money goes down. Similarly, if the purchasing power of money increases, an amount of interest is deemed to be payable by the holder and is deemed to be received or receivable by the debtor.[26]

Any amount required to be included in the holder's income as a result of a decrease in the purchasing power of money is added to the adjusted cost base of the investment. Similarly, the adjusted cost base of the holder's investment is reduced by the total of two amounts. One, the amount that is deemed to be interest payable by the holder on the investment arising from an increase in the purchasing power of money; and two, an amount that is received or receivable as interest arising from a decrease in the purchasing power of money and which was previously added to the adjusted cost base of the investment. Therefore, the adjusted cost base is increased where an amount is deemed to be received and receivable as interest by the holder when the purchasing power of money decreases. The adjusted cost base is decreased by any amount of this deemed interest that is actually received or receivable and that has been added to the adjusted cost base. It is also decreased by an amount that is deemed to be paid and payable as interest by the holder when the purchasing power of money increases. The above tax treatment of the index adjustment on indexed debt obligations does not apply to an indexed debt obligation that is impaired for part of the year and in respect of which a reserve is allowed.

[¶3026] Proceeds of Disposition of Right to Receive Production

Proceeds of disposition of a right to receive production are to be included in the income of the vendor. The "right to receive production" is included in the provisions relating to "matchable expenditures". The deductibility of an otherwise deductible matchable expenditure incurred in respect of a right to receive production is restricted by prorating the deductibility of the amount of the expenditure over the economic life of the right. See ¶3254 for a full discussion of matchable expenditures.[27]

A vendor's proceeds of disposition was determined to include the amount representing the assumption of a reforestation obligation in the sale of a sawmill.[28] At the time of publication, this case has been granted leave to appeal to the Supreme Court.

See page ii for explanation of footnotes.

[26] CCH ¶4724; Sec. 16(6).   [28] Daishowa, 2011 DTC 5157.
[27] CCH ¶4349, ¶4879d–4879v; Sec. 12(1)(g.1), 18.1.

¶3026

[¶3027] Use or Production from Property

Any payment (except an instalment of the sale price of agricultural land) that is dependent upon the use of or production from property is to be included in income.[29] For example, where a woodlot owner or operator grants a person a continuing right to cut and take timber over a period of time and the consideration that the woodlot owner or operator receives is based on the volume of timber taken, the amount received is taxable.

Property includes not only real and personal property but also intangible property such as patents, franchises, copyrights, rights of action, and other rights of any kind.

Amounts are included in a taxpayer's income only if the amounts were dependent upon use of or production from property. For example, amounts received from the sale of timber as part of a ranch-clearing operation were not dependent on use or production of property and were capital receipts.[30] It will, of course, be a question of fact to be determined in the light of all the circumstances in each case whether amounts received by a taxpayer are dependent upon the use of or production from property.

In some cases, amounts may be included in income because they are dependent upon production from property. These amounts would ordinarily include royalties that are based on production from oil wells, mines, clay deposits, timber limits, or other wasting assets.[31]

Other amounts will be included in income by reason of the fact that they are dependent upon use of property. Royalties received on the sale or licence of a patent or patent right would ordinarily be taxable for this reason since the amount received would depend on production of the patented article, which would in turn depend on the use of property, namely, the patent.[32] For the same reason it would appear that, if a business property is sold in return for payments which depend on the amount of profits from the business, the payments would be dependent on the use of the business property and would accordingly be included in the income of the vendor.[33]

On the other hand, where a contract calls for a fixed price that cannot be varied in any event but the timing of instalments of that fixed price is to vary depending on production or use, the income inclusion does not apply since it is only the timing of payments that is dependent on production or use and not the price itself.

If the amount of payments made under an agreement depends on the use of or production from property but may not exceed a stated maximum amount, the payments will nevertheless be included in the income of the recipient. However, where payments received are expressed to depend upon

---

See page ii for explanation of footnotes.

[29] CCH ¶4342; Sec. 12(1)(g); Interp. Bul. IT-462.

[30] Mel-Bar Ranches Ltd., 89 DTC 5189, Cromwell, 90 DTC 1335.

[31] Bartlett, 72 DTC 6293.

[32] 289018 Ontario Ltd., 87 DTC 38.

[33] Brosseau, 86 DTC 1412.

the use of or production from property but may not be less than a fixed minimum amount, the fixed minimum amount is not included in income since it must be paid in any event.[34] However, in such a case any payments made in excess of the fixed minimum amount will be so included since they will be dependent upon the use of or production from property.

The income inclusion of payments for production or use does not apply to an instalment of the sale price of agricultural land. The exception in respect of agricultural land does not include assets associated with the land, such as buildings, machinery, livestock, and crops. When an agreement based on production or use includes the sale of such assets with the land, a reasonable portion of the production or use payment that relates to such assets is included in computing income. Furthermore, this exception does not apply when mineral and petroleum rights of agricultural land, or land itself in addition to these rights, is either sold or leased and payments made to a vendor or lessor are based on production of a mine, or of an oil or gas well.

[¶3033] Proprietor of a Business

An individual who is a proprietor of a business will include in income for a taxation year all business income for the fiscal period of the business ending in the calendar year, and all other income in the calendar year.[35]

In computing income or loss from a business or property, as well as for situations where an individual's income for a taxation year includes income from a business for a fiscal period which does not coincide with the calendar year, references to "taxation year" or "year" with respect to the business refers to the fiscal period of the business ending in the year.[36] See also ¶3552 *et seq.*

[¶3036] Damages — Business Contracts

Damages are often received for non-performance of business contracts and may be paid as a result of a voluntary agreement, an arbitration, or an action in a court of law. In any case, such damages are intended to place the recipient in the same position as he or she would have been had the contract been performed. Normally, the performance of a business contract will result in income and, accordingly, damages for non-performance will also be income. On the other hand, if a contract is of sufficient importance to constitute part of the company's business structure, compensation paid on its termination will be capital.

The following cases should prove to be of assistance in determining whether a damage award for non-performance of a business contract constitutes business income or a capital receipt:

See page ii for explanation of footnotes.

[34] Porta-Test Systems Ltd, 80 DTC 6046.   [36] CCH ¶4205; Sec. 11(2).
[35] CCH ¶4200; Sec. 11(1).

(1) *Income.* Damages awarded to a taxpayer in connection with a trading matter, such as a breach of contract to purchase goods, constituted an income receipt. Damages obtained for infringement of a trademark were held to be taxable as income on the ground that they were in the nature of a refund of business profits that might have been earned by the recipient.[37] Similarly, a road-building contract was held taxable on compensation received from the Ontario Department of Highways for loss incurred on a construction contract because of a dispute between the Department and a railway and consequent suspension of the work for two years.[38] On similar grounds, a lump-sum received from a lessee to cancel a lease was regarded as a payment in lieu of future rent and was therefore taxable.[39] Where a company received an amount upon the cancellation of a contract for the transportation of supplies and building materials, the amount was determined to have been made to enable the company to absorb the loss as a normal incident; since the payment represented the surrender of future profit, the payment was income in nature.[40]

(2) *Capital receipt.* Where, on dissolution of an agency, $100,000 was paid in full settlement of the claim for damages for loss of rights, the amount was held to be a capital receipt, being regarded as compensation for loss of a capital asset of an enduring nature.[41] Also held to be a capital receipt was the amount received by the taxpayer from the taxpayer's former partners upon termination of the partnership as compensation for the taxpayer's rights in the partnership.[42] When the termination of a mail transportation contract materially crippled the structure of a delivery company's profit making apparatus, compensation paid was capital in nature and not taxable.[43]

[¶3039] Compensation for Loss of Income or Property Used in a Business

When a natural disaster strikes, government assistance may be received in respect of the operation of a business, property held for the purpose of earning income, or a personal loss or expenditure. Generally, payments received by an individual from a government for personal losses and expenses incurred as a result of a disaster, including payments for temporary housing and meals during the disaster, are not included in income for tax purposes. As well, government compensation received for loss or damage to personal-use property does not ordinarily result in any tax consequences. However, assistance received in respect of capital property, whether business-related or personal, is ordinarily netted against the cost of the repairs made to that property, or, if it relates to the replacement of that property, it normally reduces the cost or capital cost of the property so acquired. When

---

See page ii for explanation of footnotes.

[37] Hart, 59 DTC 1134.
[38] Sutherland, 60 DTC 13.
[39] Monart Corp., 67 DTC 5181.
[40] Canadian National Railway Company, 88 DTC 6340.
[41] Parsons-Steiner, 62 DTC 1148.
[42] Blauer, 75 DTC 5075.
[43] Courrier M. H. Inc., 76 DTC 6331.

government assistance is received for damaged inventory (e.g., spoiled milk, destroyed or damaged trees), the amount will be included in income to the extent that the assistance does not reduce the amount of costs incurred related to that damage.[44]

[¶3042] Compensation for Damage to Property

There is to be included in a taxpayer's income certain proceeds of insurance policies which are payable to the taxpayer in respect of damage to depreciable property. For the amount to be included in income, it must be expended on repairing the damage to the property within a reasonable time after the damage has occurred. If this is done, the amount to be included in the taxpayer's income in a particular year will be equal to the amount of the insurance proceeds expended in that year on repairing the damage. Thus, in effect, the amount included in income will offset the amount deducted as an expense in the year for repairing the property.[45]

If the proceeds of an insurance policy or any part thereof in respect of damage to property are not expended on repairing the property within a reasonable time after the damage, the unexpended portion of the insurance proceeds is treated as the proceeds of disposition of depreciable property which would constitute a disposition of property, and may be subject to the provisions respecting recapture of depreciation.[46]

Proceeds received from business interruption insurance have been held to constitute income to the recipient.[47]

[¶3045] Illegal Profits — Betting and Gambling

A taxpayer carrying on a business of an illegal nature (such as book-making, bootlegging, or prostitution) is taxable on the profits therefrom.[48] Normally, betting or gambling for mere pleasure or enjoyment will not constitute business and the profits therefrom will not be taxable.[49] Race track winnings are not taxable unless the taxpayer is engaged in the business of racing horses.[50] Similarly, gambling gains were held not to be taxable even where the bets were high and the gains substantial, as long as the gambling remained a hobby and was not organized and conducted as an enterprise of a commercial character.[51] It is possible that a person whose chief source of income is from such winnings might be considered as "carrying on a business" and hence the winnings would be taxable.

See page ii for explanation of footnotes.

[44] Interp. Bul. IT-273R2.

[45] CCH ¶4340; Sec. 12(1)(f).

[46] CCH ¶4562e; Sec. 13(21) "proceeds of disposition".

[47] Seaforth Plastics Ltd., 79 DTC 5174.

[48] Smith, [1927] A.C. 193, No. 275, 55 DTC 439, Christensen, 84 DTC 6184.

[49] No. 230, 55 DTC 74, No. 469, 57 DTC 541, George, 64 DTC 516.

[50] Fraser, 64 DTC 5224.

[51] Morden, 61 DTC 1266.

[¶3048] Sale or Gift of Income-Earning Property

If income-earning property is sold by a taxpayer who is not in the business of dealing in such property, the sale price received by the taxpayer will normally be a capital gain rather than income. Following such a sale, the income earned on the property will be the income of the purchaser.[52]

In some circumstances, the attribution rules will apply where property is transferred, and the income will be attributed to the transferor rather than the transferee. This may occur in the case of a transfer by a taxpayer to the taxpayer's spouse or common-law partner,[53] or in the case of a transfer by a taxpayer to a person under the age of 18 years.[54] See Chapter II.

[¶3051] Accrual Income of Corporations, etc.

Corporations, partnerships, unit trusts, and trusts with a corporation or partnership as beneficiary must include an income element in respect of certain life insurance policies and annuity contracts on an annual basis.[55]

This accrual rule will not apply to an exempt policy which is defined in the Regulations.[56] The formulae in the Regulations are generally intended to provide exemption for those insurance policies which are primarily for insurance protection.

With respect to annual accrual of income on annuity contracts and life insurance policies acquired after 1989, the amount of the income inclusion is equal to the excess of the accumulating fund over the adjusted cost basis of the interest in the life insurance policy or the annuity contract insured, on the anniversary day. "Anniversary day" is defined as the day that is one year less a day after the issue date. Generally, the accumulating fund in respect of an annuity contract where the issuer is not a life insurer is the greater of the cash surrender value less the amount of any loan to the holder and the excess of the present value of future benefits over the present value of future premiums. In the case of a life insurance policy issued by a life insurer, the accumulating fund represents the reserve that the life insurer may claim in respect of the policy, which is similar to the accumulating fund of an annuity contract. The adjusted cost basis of a life insurance policy or annuity contract is increased for the income inclusion.

[¶3057] Investment Tax Credit

A taxpayer must include the amount of an investment tax credit claimed by the taxpayer (¶8340) to the extent that it has not been applied to reduce the cost of depreciable property, the undepreciated capital cost of the depreciable property, the deduction in respect of scientific research, the adjusted cost base of an interest in a partnership, the adjusted cost base of a capital

---

See page ii for explanation of footnotes.

[52] CCH ¶8150; Sec. 56(4).
[53] CCH ¶9516; Sec. 74.1(1).
[54] CCH ¶9518; Sec. 74.1(2).

[55] CCH ¶4420; Sec. 12.2.

[56] Reg. 304, Reg. 306, Reg. 308.

interest in a trust, or the amount of cumulative Canadian exploration expense.[57]

An income inclusion is required only for taxation years following the year in which the related investment credit is claimed. When a tax credit is carried back to a year preceding the year in which it was earned, the required income inclusion will not have to be made until the year following the year in which the property is acquired or the expenditure is made.

[¶3060] Reinsurance Commissions

Reserves for a reinsurance commission paid by a reinsurer in the property and casualty insurance business are included in income.[58] A corresponding deduction is also provided.[59]

[¶3063] Home Insulation or Energy Conversion Grants

A taxpayer is required to include in income the amount of any grant received under a prescribed program for home insulation or energy conversion in respect of property used principally for the purpose of gaining or producing income from a business or property.[60] Regulations prescribe the Canadian Home Insulation Program and the Canada Oil Substitution Program for the purposes of this provision.[61] Home insulation and energy conversion grants do not reduce the adjusted cost base of property or the capital cost of depreciable property.

[¶3066] Scientific Research and Experimental Development (SR&ED) Deductions

If in any year the deductions applicable in determining the SR&ED allowance exceed the additions applicable, such excess is included in income.[62] This provision permits the recapture of amounts claimed as an SR&ED allowance in one year when a government grant is received in respect of that SR&ED in a later year. It may also apply where the investment tax credit in respect of scientific expenditure is claimed in a year in which there are no current scientific expenditures. SR&ED is further discussed at ¶3600.

[¶3067] Fuel Tax Rebates

As a result of fuel tax rebates paid to transportation companies for aviation and diesel fuels pursuant to the *Excise Tax Act*, portions of the rebate are included in income. Where the fuel is not used for "eligible transportation services", the fuel tax rebate must be repaid and taxpayers claiming the rebate must reduce their loss carryforwards by 10 dollars for each dollar of rebate claimed. Accordingly, the "net" rebate is calculated,

---

See page ii for explanation of footnotes.

[57] CCH ¶4375a; Sec. 12(1)(t).
[58] CCH ¶4375; Sec. 12(1)(s).
[59] CCH ¶5128g; Sec. 20(1)(jj).

[60] CCH ¶5117, ¶8070; Sec. 12(1)(u), 56(1)(s).
[61] CCH ¶8072, ¶8073; Reg. 5500, Reg. 5501.
[62] CCH ¶4376ac; Sec. 12(1)(v); Inf. Cir. 97-1.

and 10 times the amount by which the net rebate exceeds the amount claimed as a fuel tax rebate loss abatement is brought into income.[63]

[¶3068] Amateur Athletic Trust

A taxpayer must, in computing income, include amounts in respect of an amateur athletic trust to ensure that such amounts included in the income of the athlete are treated as income from a business or property. This recognizes that the funds held by an amateur athletic trust are generally derived from such sources.[64]

[¶3069] Eligible Funeral Arrangements

An "eligible funeral arrangement" means an arrangement established to provide funeral or "cemetery services" under which the total of all contributions made for the purpose of funding funeral or cemetery services for each beneficiary does not exceed: (i) $35,000 if the arrangement covers both funeral and cemetery services; (ii) $20,000 if it only covers cemetery services; and (iii) $15,000 if it only covers funeral services.[65] Any amount paid under such arrangements for the provision of funeral, burial, Cremation, or cemetery arrangements is included in the income of the provider of funeral services when such services are rendered. If the individual withdraws the funds from the arrangement, the individual will include any income earned on the contribution as income from property.

[¶3070] Other Items of Income

Inducements and reimbursements received by a taxpayer in the course of doing business must be included in income.[66] Where a taxpayer receives an amount in the course of earning income from a business or property, from a person or partnership (the "payer") who pays it in the course of earning income from a business or property in order to achieve a benefit for the payer or for non-arm's length persons, or in circumstances where it is reasonable to conclude that the payer would not have paid the amount but for the receipt by the payer of amounts from a payer, government, municipality, or other public authority, such amount must be included in the taxpayer's income. Amounts received from a government, municipality, or other public authority are expressly included, as are grants, subsidies, forgivable loans, deductions from tax, allowances, or any other form of inducement. Any reimbursement, contribution, allowance, or assistance in respect of the taxpayer's cost of property or in respect of an expense, is also included in income, again including any grant, subsidy, forgivable loan, deduction from tax, allowance or any other form of assistance. Indirect funding received from not-for-profit entities which in turn have been funded by government or another payer in circumstances in which the funds would

---

See page ii for explanation of footnotes.

[63] CCH ¶4376j; Sec. 12(1)(x.1).

[64] CCH ¶4377ac; Sec. 12(1)(z).

[65] CCH ¶21,654; Sec. 148.1(1) "eligible funeral arrangement".

[66] CCH ¶4376c; Sec. 12(1)(x).

have been caught by the inducement rules had the funds been received directly, also falls within the ambit of these rules.

Certain types of payments are expressly excluded. A taxpayer is not required to include the receipt in income if it is a prescribed amount; it was otherwise included in computing the taxpayer's income for the year or any preceding taxation year; it reduced the cost of the capital property or the amount of an expense except as required; it reduced the cost or capital by an election; or, if it is reasonable to consider the receipt to be in respect of the acquisition by the payer or public authority of an interest in the taxpayer, his business, or property. A "prescribed amount" is defined as including amounts paid to Aboriginal-controlled corporations pursuant to the Native Economic Development Program, and "prescribed assistance" includes provincial assistance relating to prescribed venture capital corporation shares, tax credits relating to prescribed labour-sponsored venture capital corporation shares, and provincial tax credits relating to certain shares of taxable Canadian corporations held in prescribed stock savings plans.

For comment on partnership income, benefits from estates, and amounts returned to an employer under an employees profit sharing plan,[67] see Chapter VII and Chapter X.

[¶3072] Goodwill and Other Intangibles

[¶3075] General Treatment

The cost to acquire certain intangible properties such as goodwill, customer lists, and franchises constitutes intangible capital property. This qualifies as "eligible capital property" and is deductible under a system similar to the capital cost allowance system.[68] Three-quarters of the "eligible capital expenditure" is added to the "cumulative eligible capital" of the taxpayer, and the taxpayer is permitted a deduction from income of up to 7% of cumulative eligible capital at the end of the year.[69]

The provisions relating to goodwill and other intangibles are available only for businesses. No value can be attributed for tax purposes to any goodwill element in an investment in property that is not used in a business.

Where the business of the taxpayer was the sale of franchises to others, the proceeds of those sales were not receipts on account of capital, and accordingly the proceeds could not be "eligible capital amounts".[70]

Goodwill often includes more than the classic elements such as customer lists and established reputation. It can also include a potential tax benefit.[71]

See page ii for explanation of footnotes.

[67] CCH ¶4360, ¶4365, ¶4368, ¶4370a; Sec. 12(1)(*l*), 12(1)(*m*), 12(1)(*n*), 12(1)(*n.1*).

[68] CCH ¶4600, ¶7850e; Sec. 14(1), 54 "eligible capital property".

[69] CCH ¶5051; Sec. 20(1)(*b*).

[70] Samoth Financial Corp. Ltd., 86 DTC 6335.

[71] TransAlta Corporation, 2012 DTC 5041.

On disposition of an eligible capital property, a taxpayer may elect to remove a particular asset from the cumulative eligible capital pool and recognize a capital gain on it in the year as if it were a non-depreciable capital property. (This election might be made if a taxpayer has outstanding capital losses to be used and wants to conserve the remaining cumulative eligible capital pool balance.) The election, which can be used to recognize only gains (not losses), is not available for goodwill or other property for which the original cost cannot be determined (i.e., the eligible capital expenditure in respect of the property), nor can it be used to recognize a capital gain that can be sheltered by the taxpayer's exempt gains balance.[72]

[¶3078] Eligible Capital Expenditures

Where a taxpayer has sold some right or property, it will be necessary to determine whether or not the amount received by the taxpayer was an "eligible capital amount" [73] that reduced the taxpayer's cumulative eligible capital pool and was therefore possibly included in the taxpayer's income. Prior to May 2, 2006, the calculation of an eligible capital amount included $3/4$ of an amount received or receivable as a result of a disposition by a taxpayer in respect of a business carried on by the taxpayer, where the consideration given by the taxpayer was such that, if any payment had been made by the taxpayer for that consideration, the payment would have been an eligible capital expenditure of the taxpayer (the "mirror image test"). Under that test, only expenditures made after 1971 that are on capital account and are made for the purpose of gaining or producing income from a *business* may be eligible capital expenditures.[74] For amounts that become receivable after May 1, 2006, the previous mirror image test is overridden to the extent that the concept of an eligible capital amount is not dependent on the nature of the payment to the payer or the taxpayer/recipient as notional payer. After May 1, 2006, the calculation of an eligible capital amount includes $3/4$ of an amount received or receivable as a result of a disposition by a taxpayer in respect of a business carried on by the taxpayer, other than an amount that:

(i) is included in computing the taxpayer's income, or deducted in computing any balance of undeducted outlays, expenses, or other amounts;

(ii) reduces the cost or capital cost of property or the amount of an outlay or expense; or

(iii) is included in computing any gain or loss of the taxpayer from a disposition of a capital property.

Presumably, this amendment was made in response to the *Toronto Refiners and Smelters* decision.[75] In this case, the city of Toronto expropriated the

---

See page ii for explanation of footnotes.

[72] CCH ¶4601, ¶4601a; Sec. 14(1.01), 14(1.02).
[73] CCH ¶4641; Sec. 14(5) "cumulative eligible capital".
[74] CCH ¶4642a; Sec. 14(5) "eligible capital expenditure"; Interp. Bul. IT-123R6.
[75] Toronto Refiners and Smelters, 2003 DTC 5002.

land and building in which the taxpayer carried on its business. The city paid the taxpayer $12 million, of which $9 million was for damages to compensate for the inability to relocate its business. Since the city did not pay the $9 million for the purposes of earning income from a *business* under the previous mirror image test described above, the Federal Court of Appeal held that it was not an eligible capital expenditure and was therefore a non-taxable capital receipt in the taxpayer's hands.

Where an eligible capital expenditure is made in respect of the acquisition of an eligible capital property from a non-arm's length vendor who has claimed a capital gains exemption in respect of the disposition, the eligible capital expenditure of the purchaser is reduced to reflect the exemption claimed by the vendor.[76] This corresponds with the treatment of non-arm's length transfers of depreciable property. However, the deemed reduction will not apply in cases where the property was acquired by the taxpayer as a consequence of the death of the transferor and is, in other cases, reversed to the extent that the taxpayer has received proceeds of disposition for the property in excess of that deemed eligible capital expenditure in a subsequent arm's length transaction.

[¶3081] Non-Eligible Capital Expenditures

The following items do not qualify as eligible capital expenditures:[77]

(a) amounts which are wholly or partially non-deductible by some other provision of the Act,[78] or capital expenditures the deduction of which is prohibited;[79]

(b) outlays which are incurred for the purpose of gaining or producing exempt income;[80]

(c) cost of tangible property;

(d) cost of intangible property that qualifies as depreciable property (goodwill is not defined to be depreciable property);

(e) property for which any deduction is permitted or would be permitted if business income were sufficient to make the amount entirely deductible;

(f) an interest in or a right to acquire property described in items (c), (d), and (e);

(g) an amount paid or payable to a creditor or on redemption of a debt security;

(h) an amount paid by a corporation to a person as a shareholder; and

---

See page ii for explanation of footnotes.

[76] CCH ¶4632; Sec. 14(3).
[77] CCH ¶4642a; Sec. 14(5) "eligible capital expenditure".
[78] CCH ¶5051; Sec. 20(1)(b).
[79] CCH ¶4800; Sec. 18(1)(b).
[80] CCH ¶28,103; Sec. 248(1) "exempt income".

(i) the cost of an interest in a trust or partnership or of any share or other security or an interest therein.

When shares are acquired, the portion of the purchase price paid for what is often referred to as goodwill is not an eligible capital expenditure.

[¶3087] Deductions — Cumulative Eligible Capital

Although the mechanics of amortizing eligible capital expenditures are identical to those for claiming capital cost allowances on capital assets (including the use of a "pool" system for accumulating costs and proceeds of disposal and the use of a declining balance in calculating deductions), the deductions permitted in respect of a taxpayer's cumulative eligible capital[81] are not capital cost allowances. Where the deductions from the cumulative eligible capital pool exceed the additions at the end of a year, the negative balance is included in income or deemed to be a taxable capital gain, similar to the recapture of capital cost allowance.[82]

A formula is provided[83] for calculating the cumulative eligible capital in respect of a business. This formula may generally be described as being the aggregate of:

(a) $3/4$ of the eligible capital expenditures previously made in respect of the business, and

(b) amounts previously included in income as deemed taxable capital gains under ¶3088 (a $3/2$ variable is effective for taxation years after February 27, 2000, to gross up the amount to be included consequential to the change in inclusion rates),

less the aggregate of:

(c) the total of "eligible capital amounts" which, for amounts receivable after May 1, 2006, equals the total of all amounts, each of which is $3/4$ of the amount by which an amount on account of capital in respect of the business received by the taxpayer or that the taxpayer may become entitled to receive, other than an amount that (i) is included in computing the taxpayer's income or deducted incomputing any balance of undeducted outlays, expenses, or other amounts, (ii) reduces the cost or capital cost of a property or an outlay or expense, or (iii) is included in computing any gain or loss of the taxpayer from a disposition of capital property, exceeds the taxpayer's outlays and expenses made or incurred for the purpose of obtaining the amount and that were not otherwise deductible (for amounts receivable before May 2, 2006, see the text below),

(d) amounts previously deducted[84] in respect of the business, and

---

See page ii for explanation of footnotes.

[81] CCH ¶4641; Sec. 14(5) "cumulative eligible capital".

[82] CCH ¶4600; Sec. 14(1).

[83] CCH ¶4641; Sec. 14(5) "cumulative eligible capital".

[84] CCH ¶5051; Sec. 20(1)(b).

(e) reductions in the cumulative eligible capital required where a debt is forgiven. The reduction is basically equal to $3/4$ of the foreign debt amount remaining after the application of other debt forgiveness rules (see ¶3456).

In general, cumulative eligible capital is somewhat analogous to the undepreciated capital cost of depreciable property. It generally consists of the balance remaining when $3/4$ of a taxpayer's eligible capital expenditures are reduced by $3/4$ of eligible capital amounts (which are net of disposal costs) payable and amounts deducted through the amortization of the balance.

For amounts receivable before May 2, 2006, an "eligible capital amount" was generally $3/4$ of the amount receivable by the taxpayer on a disposition (net of disposition costs) where the nature of the consideration given by the taxpayer was such that, if the taxpayer had made a payment for such consideration, it would have been an eligible capital expenditure of the taxpayer. On the basis of two Federal Court of Appeal decisions,[85] a "mirror image" test was required in making this determination. That is, it was necessary to assume that the circumstances of the hypothetical payment by the taxpayer for the consideration were the same as the circumstances of the actual payment by the purchaser. Thus, the taxpayer was notionally placed in the circumstances of the purchaser to determine whether the notional payment for the consideration would have been an eligible capital expenditure of the taxpayer. Owing to the changes in the definition of "cumulative eligible capital", and hence the meaning of "eligible capital amount" (described above), it appears that the mirror image test does not apply to amounts receivable after May 1, 2006.

It is important to note that cumulative eligible capital exists in respect of a particular business, and the sale of eligible capital property in respect of one business carried on by the taxpayer may result in an inclusion in income or a capital gain, notwithstanding the fact that the taxpayer has cumulative eligible capital in respect of another business.

For limitations on the deduction of losses resulting from a decline in the value of eligible capital property where there has been a change in corporate control, see ¶3390.

[¶3088] Negative Balance in Cumulative Eligible Capital Accounts

A taxpayer is required to include in income from a business for a year the amount by which the negative components of the cumulative eligible capital in respect of that business exceed the positive components in respect of that business as at the end of the taxation year; that is, where the taxpayer's cumulative eligible capital account is negative. This will occur, for

---

See page ii for explanation of footnotes.

[85] Goodwin Johnston (1960) Ltd., 86 DTC 6185,
Toronto Refiners and Smelters, 2003 DTC 5002.

example, where the taxpayer's proceeds of disposition from a sale of its eligible capital property exceeds the cost thereof to the taxpayer.[86]

In the case of an individual, trust, or certain partnerships resident in Canada, the negative amount giving rise to the income inclusion may be comprised of two components: a recapture of amounts previously deducted in respect of the eligible capital property and any additional amount, which is treated like a capital gain. Recapture, when 75% of actual proceeds exceeds the pool balance, continues to be taxable in full (in the 75% mode) but any gain element over and above recapture will be stepped down by 2/3 (2/3 of 75% = the 1/2 capital gains inclusion rate).

The capital gains type of treatment does not extend to corporations, partnerships all the members of which are corporations, or partnerships which are not "Canadian partnerships".[87]

In the case of an individual disposing of eligible capital property in respect of qualified farm property, or, after May 1, 2006, qualified fishing property, the amount included as ordinary income is limited to the aggregate of amounts that are essentially a recapture of previous deductions. Any excess of the negative cumulative eligible capital balance (the excess) is deemed to be a capital gain of the taxpayer, eligible for the enhanced $750,000 ($500,000 for gains realized before March 19, 2007) capital gains exemption available for qualified farm property or qualified fishing property, as the case may be.[88]

[¶3090] Replacement Property

At the taxpayer's option, any income inclusion arising from the disposition of eligible capital property may be deferred. This parallels the deferral of recapture of depreciation on voluntary dispositions of capital property. Any amount otherwise included as an eligible capital amount upon the disposition of eligible capital property in the year the proceeds have become payable (i.e., the initial year) is not to be included for that year if, within one year after the end of the initial year, the taxpayer acquires a replacement property and elects to adopt this treatment in the return for the year the replacement property was acquired.[89]

[To accommodate short taxation years, the period to acquire replacement property and defer the income inclusion resulting from the disposition of an eligible capital property is amended in the revised technical proposals that were released on July 16, 2010. For taxation years ending after December 19, 2001, this time period is extended to the later of the end of the subsequent taxation year and the time that is 12 months after the end of the taxation year in which the property was disposed of.]

See page ii for explanation of footnotes.

[86] CCH ¶4602; Sec. 14(1).

[87] CCH ¶28,305; Sec. 248(1) "Canadian partnership".

[88] CCH ¶4602, ¶4602a; Sec. 14(1.1), 14(1.2).

[89] CCH ¶4643; Sec. 14(6), 14(7).

Where an eligible capital property is disposed of in a particular year, this year becomes the "initial year". The taxpayer is allowed until the end of the following taxation year to acquire a replacement property and, having done so, is entitled to elect to exclude the eligible capital amount from the calculation of cumulative eligible capital for the initial year.

"Replacement property" is eligible capital property acquired for the same or similar use as the use of the former property. As well, the replacement property must be acquired for the purpose of gaining or producing income from the same or similar business as that in which the former property was used. Whether or not a use is the same or similar is a question of fact.

Where the taxpayer was a non-resident at the time he or she acquired the replacement property, the property must be used in a business carried on by the taxpayer in Canada.

[¶3093] Cessation of Business

Where a taxpayer has ceased to carry on a business, the remaining balance of cumulative eligible capital applicable to that business is deductible in the year in which the taxpayer has ceased to carry on business and has disposed of all of the eligible capital property, other than property of no value.[90] A negative balance in the cumulative eligible capital pool will result in an income inclusion. A terminal allowance must be deducted from the taxpayer's income for the first taxation year that ends after the time when the requirements for the rollover were met, unless an election is filed.[91]

This deduction is not permitted where the taxpayer is an individual and the taxpayer's spouse or common-law partner or a corporation controlled directly or indirectly by the taxpayer carries on the business after the taxpayer has ceased to do so. In this situation, the individual who has ceased carrying on business will no longer have cumulative eligible capital in respect of that business. However, the spouse/common-law partner or corporation carrying on the business will take over the balance of cumulative eligible capital. Where all of the eligible capital property, other than property of no value, that was held by the taxpayer in respect of the business is transferred to the taxpayer's spouse/common-law partner or the corporation controlled directly or indirectly by the taxpayer, special provisions apply to prevent the overstatement of the deemed capital gain or eligible capital property by the spouse/common-law partner or corporation.[92]

Where, as a result of the death of a taxpayer and, as a consequence of the taxpayer's death, another person (the beneficiary) acquires a property that was eligible capital property of the taxpayer for the business that was

---

See page ii for explanation of footnotes.

[90] CCH ¶5166; Sec. 24; Interp. Bul. IT-313R2.   [92] CCH ¶5167; Sec. 24(2)(d).

[91] CCH ¶5168; Sec. 25.

carried on by the taxpayer until death, the taxpayer is deemed to have disposed of the property before death.[93] The deemed proceeds of disposition are $^4/_3$ of the proportion of any positive balance in the pool that the fair market value of the property is of the total fair market value of all the eligible capital property of the taxpayer for the business. The eligible capital amount for the property is then determined by multiplying the deemed proceeds by $^3/_4$. If the beneficiary continues to carry on the business, the result is the same as that achieved by the rollover that occurs where the taxpayer's spouse/common-law partner or corporation carries on the business. However, the rollover results in the case of a beneficiary carrying on the business will be calculated on each particular property rather than for the entire eligible capital pool.

Where a taxpayer is an individual and the fiscal period of the taxpayer's business does not coincide with the calendar year, a reference to a "taxation year" or to a "year" in connection with the sale of goodwill and other intangibles, is to be read as a reference to a fiscal period.[94]

In certain circumstances, where the taxpayer was a member of a partnership that has been dissolved, the taxpayer may deduct an amount equal to that former member's portion of the amount that would have been deductible by the partnership had it not ceased to exist.[95]

[¶3096] Transfer of Goodwill to Canadian Corporation

An individual, corporation, trust, or partnership may dispose of certain types of property to a taxable Canadian corporation without immediate tax consequences. The Act provides an elective procedure[96] whereby the disposing party and the corporation file a joint election in which they elect an amount that will be deemed to be the disposing party's proceeds of disposition and the corporation's cost of the property.

Where the election is filed, the amount specified in the election will be deemed to be the proceeds of disposition to the transferor and the cost to the corporation. Therefore, unless the amount specified is nil, a portion of the amount specified for eligible capital property will be taxed to the transferor to the extent that it exceeds the transferor's previous cumulative eligible capital balance and that of the individual and this same portion will be amortizable by the corporation. As a result, in most cases it would appear desirable to specify a nil amount for goodwill, or at least an amount which will not exceed the cumulative eligible capital of the transferor. However, even where the elected amount of nil is chosen, the parties must list the property on Form T2057 and state a nominal amount. If not included on the prescribed form, the CRA will consider it to be disposed of at its fair market value.

---

[93] CCH ¶9266; Sec. 70(5.1).

[94] CCH ¶4636; Sec. 14(4).

[95] CCH ¶5167a; Sec. 24(3).

[96] CCH ¶10,500; Sec. 85; Interp. Bul. IT-291R3; Inf. Cir. 76-19R3.

For a complete discussion of transfers of property to a Canadian corporation, see Chapter VI.

[¶3099] Deemed Proceeds of Disposition

In the case of a deemed disposition of eligible capital property any deemed proceeds of disposition are considered to have become payable at the time the deemed disposition occurs.[97] There are several sections in the Act which deem proceeds of disposition to have been received, such as:

(a) gifts and transfers for inadequate consideration;[98]

(b) transfers to a controlled corporation;[99]

(c) winding-up of a subsidiary;[100]

(d) transfer of property to a partnership;[101]

(e) distribution of property by a partnership;[102] and

(f) distribution of property by a trust.[103]

[¶3105] Benefits Conferred on Shareholders

[¶3108] Benefits to Shareholders

The dollar value of a benefit, which a corporation confers on a shareholder (in the person's capacity as a shareholder) or on a person in contemplation of the person becoming a shareholder, must be brought into the income of the recipient for the year in which it is received.[104] No benefit will have been conferred where the transaction is a *bona fide* business transaction. The test of *bona fide* will be met where the transaction is made on the same terms and conditions as if made by parties dealing at arm's length.

For the purposes of determining the value of a shareholder benefit required to be included in income, the cost to the corporation of the property or services provided to the shareholder is to be calculated inclusive of any tax, including the goods and services tax.[105] The shareholder benefit for use in the winter of a luxurious Florida condominium (costing some $4 million) was calculated on the basis of "equity-rate return", i.e., the amount that would have been earned by the corporation had it invested the $4 million at a reasonable rate of return. On that basis, the taxpayer was required to include in income $445,675 for the year in question. The fair market rental value of the condo was held to be irrelevant.[106]

See page ii for explanation of footnotes.

[97] CCH ¶4630; Sec. 14(2).
[98] CCH ¶9141; Sec. 69.
[99] CCH ¶10,500; Sec. 85.
[100] CCH ¶11,160; Sec. 88.
[101] CCH ¶12,175; Sec. 97.

[102] CCH ¶12,251; Sec. 98.
[103] CCH ¶13,800, ¶13,890; Sec. 107, 107.1.
[104] CCH ¶4650; Sec. 15(1); Interp. Bul. IT-432R2.
[105] CCH ¶4664d; Sec. 15(1.3).
[106] Fingold, 97 DTC 5449.

The word "shareholder" is defined[107] to include a member or other person entitled to receive payment of a dividend.

There is no definition of "benefit" in the Act. The word is capable of the broadest possible interpretation and is broad enough to include payments or distributions specifically made taxable under other provisions. The provision will apply to exchanges of property, to additions or improvements made to a shareholder's building, and the personal use of corporate property by a shareholder. Therefore, amounts received by a shareholder from one corporation used to meet losses of another corporation were shareholder benefits and properly included in income.[108]

The provision does not apply where a corporation makes a payment to a shareholder on the reduction of capital; on the redemption, cancellation, or acquisition of shares of its capital stock; on the winding-up, discontinuance, or reorganization of its business; by payment of a dividend, including a stock dividend; by conferring on all common shareholders a right to buy additional shares; or where an insurance corporation converts contributed surplus related to its insurance business into paid-up capital. For this purpose, a right will not be considered identical if the costs of acquiring the right differs.

It should be noted that the exclusion for stock dividends will not apply where one of the purposes of the payment is to significantly alter the value of the interest in the corporation of any specified shareholder of the corporation.[109] A "specified shareholder" is defined[110] as a taxpayer who owns, directly or indirectly, not less than 10% of the issued shares of any class of the capital stock of the corporation or any other related corporation.

For a discussion of the benefit conferred on a shareholder where a company car is made available for the shareholder's use, see ¶2085.

[¶3111] Shareholder Debt

The Act is designed to prevent the distribution of funds of a corporation for the benefit of its shareholders, free of tax, through loans or other transactions where the shareholder becomes indebted to a corporation. In the simplest case, it will apply to include the amount of the loan in the income of that person for the year in which the loan was made, where a corporation makes a loan directly to one of its shareholders. However, it will also apply to any other indebtedness that may arise between a corporation and its shareholders, such as the unpaid purchase price for goods or services.[111] In order to prevent corporations from accomplishing indirectly what is not permitted to be done directly, this provision will apply where the creditor is the corporation itself, any other related corporation, or a partner-

---

See page ii for explanation of footnotes.

[107] CCH ¶28,269; Sec. 248(1) "shareholder".
[108] Vine Estate, 89 DTC 5528.
[109] CCH ¶4664; Sec. 15(1.1).

[110] CCH ¶28,273; Sec. 248(1) "specified shareholder".
[111] CCH ¶4665; Sec. 15(2); Interp. Bul. IT-119R4.

ship of which a corporation or a related corporation is a member. It will also apply where the debtor is a shareholder, is a person that does not deal at arm's length with a shareholder, or is a person that is indirectly a shareholder through a partnership or a trust.[112] Special provisions apply to loans and debts of individuals who are both employees and shareholders.[113]

The value of the benefit in connection with an obligation issued by a debtor that is settled or extinguished is the "forgiven amount" in respect of the obligation.[114] The forgiven amount[115] is, generally, the lesser of the principal amount of the obligation and the amount for which it was issued minus any amounts paid in satisfaction of principal and other adjustments, reflecting the extent to which the obligation has been recognized for income tax purposes. In addition, for the purposes of determining the shareholder benefit, any amount included in income due to settlement or extinguishment of the obligation is not taken into account, except to the extent included in income as a benefit of employment. The forgiven amount is not reduced to reflect the extent to which the obligation is taken into account to determine the proceeds of disposition of any property, and interest payable on the principal obligation is not taken into account. Finally, the provisions respecting the forgiveness of debt after death are not taken into account.[116]

The income inclusion rule will not apply where the loan is subject to one of the statutory exceptions (see ¶3114) or if the loan is between non-resident persons.

A shareholder who has obtained a loan or other indebtedness which is included in income will be entitled to deduct amounts repaid on the loan or other indebtedness in subsequent years.[117] The deduction may be taken only if it is established, by subsequent events or otherwise, that the repayment was not a part of a series of loans or other transactions and repayments. The amount of the deduction is limited to the amount of the loan or other indebtedness that was not deductible from the income of the recipient for the year in which it was received.

[¶3114] Loans or Debts to Shareholders Not Included in Income

Loans or other indebtedness to shareholders are not included in the shareholder's income in the following circumstances:[118]

(1) where the loan or other indebtedness is made by a company whose ordinary course of business is money-lending and if the loan is made on the same basis as to other borrowers;[119]

(2) where the loan or other indebtedness is made to an employee of the company or to an employee's spouse/common-law partner to assist the

---

[112] CCH ¶4666; Sec. 15(2.1).
[113] CCH ¶4666c; Sec. 15(2.4).
[114] CCH ¶4664ac; Sec. 15(1.2).
[115] CCH ¶9850i; Sec. 80(1) "forgiven amount".

[116] CCH ¶4664b; Sec. 15(1.21).
[117] CCH ¶5081; Sec. 20(1)(*j*).
[118] CCH ¶4665; Sec. 15(2).
[119] CCH ¶4666a; Sec. 15(2.2).

employee or the employee's spouse/common-law partner to acquire a home or a share of a co-operative housing corporation for the purposes of inhabiting a dwelling unit (see also ¶3120);[120]

(3) where the loan or other indebtedness is made to an employee of a corporation (or to an employee of a related corporation) to enable the employee to purchase previously unissued fully paid-up shares of the capital stock of the corporation or the related corporation to be held by the employee for his or her own benefit;[121]

(4) where the loan or other indebtedness is made to an employee of the corporation to enable the employee to purchase an automobile for use in the performance of the employee's duties as officer or employee; and[122]

(5) where the loan is repaid within one year from the end of the lending corporation's taxation year and it is established that the payment was not part of a series of loans and repayments.[123]

In order to qualify as an exception, *bona fide* arrangements for repayment within a reasonable time of such loans or other indebtedness must be made at the time of the making of the loan or when the other indebtedness is incurred. The questions as to (i) what is reasonable time, and (ii) whether the arrangements for repayment are *bona fide* will be questions of fact to be determined according to the circumstances of each case. Note, however, that it is not necessary that repayment be made within a reasonable time, but rather that *bona fide* arrangements for such repayment should be made at the time of the making of the loan or when the indebtedness arose.

With regard to the general exception in (5) above, where the loan is repaid within one year, *bona fide* repayments of shareholder loans which are the result of the declaration of dividends, salaries, or bonuses should not be considered part of a "series of loans or other transactions and repayments".[124]

[¶3117] Deemed Benefit on Employee and Shareholder Loans and Debts

A benefit may be deemed to have been received by an individual or by a corporation carrying on a "personal services business" where a loan has been received or a debt has otherwise been incurred by a person or partnership by virtue of a prior, current, or future office or employment or intended office or employment of the individual, or by virtue of the services performed or to be performed by the personal service corporation (as the case may be).[125]

See page ii for explanation of footnotes.

120 CCH ¶4666b; Sec. 15(2.3).
121 CCH ¶4666c; Sec. 15(2.4).
122 CCH ¶4666d; Sec. 15(2.5).
123 CCH ¶4666e; Sec. 15(2.6).

124 Attis, 92 DTC 1128, Uphill Holdings Ltd. et al, 93 DTC 148.
125 CCH ¶9896, ¶9899; Sec. 80.4, 80.5; Reg. 4300; Interp. Bul. IT-421R2.

Similarly, a benefit may be deemed to have been received by a person or partnership where that person or partnership has received a loan or otherwise incurred a debt by virtue of certain shareholdings in a corporation. This does not apply to a corporation resident in Canada, or a partnership where each member is a corporation resident in Canada.

As a general rule, a deemed benefit would arise in a taxation year in respect of a loan or debt to which either of these provisions is applicable if the amount of interest actually paid by the debtor is less than the amount of interest calculated at the interest rates prescribed under the regulations. See ¶475 for the prescribed interest rates.

The Act may give rise to an interest deduction in cases where a loan is used to gain or produce income. The amount of the deemed benefit that is included in the taxpayer's income is generally the difference between interest at the applicable prescribed rate and the amount of interest actually paid by the debtor.

The Act excludes from the deemed benefit provisions a loan or debt on which the rate of interest is not less than the rate of interest that would have been available in the open market at the time the loan or debt was received or incurred, having regard to all its terms and conditions. However, this exception is not applicable where any interest is paid or payable by a party other than the debtor.

The portion of any loan or debt that has been included in the income of the borrower or debtor is also excluded from the deemed benefit provisions. This will include loans and debts received or incurred by virtue of shareholdings which have been included in the income of the borrower or debtor under ¶3111. Certain reimbursements by the debtor of any interest paid or payable by the employer and persons related thereto will reduce the amount of the benefit.

The following examples illustrate the calculation of the deemed benefit under the first provision dealt with above.

Examples:

> In each of the following cases, it is assumed that a loan was received by an individual from the employer by virtue of the individual's employment and that the amount of the loan outstanding throughout the year in question is $100,000. It is further assumed that the prescribed rate for such year is 10%.
>
> (1) The loan is interest free. The amount of the deemed benefit for the year in question will be $10,000.
>
> (2) The loan bears interest at 6%, which has been paid by the employee not later than 30 days after the end of the year in question. The amount of deemed benefit for the year will be $4,000 ($10,000 less a credit for $6,000).
>
> (3) The loan bears interest at 6% but no interest was paid by the employee prior to the expiration of 30 days after the end of the year in question. The deemed benefit for the year will be $10,000.

¶3117

(4) The loan bears interest at 10%. A person related to the employer has undertaken to pay all of the interest, which has in fact been paid prior to the expiration of 30 days after the end of the year in question. The deemed benefit for the year will be $10,000 plus $10,000 less $10,000, or $10,000.

(5) The loan bears interest at 10%. A person related to the employer has undertaken to pay 75% of such interest. However, such interest has not been paid prior to the expiration of 30 days after the end of the year in question. The remaining $2,500 of interest for the year has been paid by the employee during the year. The deemed benefit would appear to be $10,000 plus $7,500 less $2,500, or $15,000.

[¶3120] Housing Loans

Where a loan or debt qualifies as a "home purchase loan", the method for computing the deemed benefit under the first provision dealt with at ¶3117 is modified.[126] In calculating the deemed benefit on a home purchase loan, the interest for a particular year computed at the prescribed rates applicable to that year shall not exceed the interest for that year computed at the prescribed rate in effect at the time the home purchase loan was received. (See ¶475 for the prescribed interest rates.) Where a home purchase loan has a term of repayment exceeding five years, the balance outstanding on the loan at the end of every five years after the loan was received is deemed to be a new home purchase loan received at such time for the purpose of determining the applicable prescribed rate. In effect, any increase in the prescribed rates during the five-year period following the date on which a home purchase loan was received or was deemed to be a new loan will not have the effect of increasing the amount of the deemed benefit.

The following example illustrates the application of the special rules applicable to home purchase loans.

Example:

Mr. A received on January 1, Year 1 an interest-free home purchase loan from his employer in the amount of $100,000. The total principal amount of this loan is not due until Year 10. If the prescribed rate throughout Year 1 was 6% and the prescribed rate through-out Year 2 was 7%, the amount of the deemed benefit for Year 2 will be $6,000 (6% of $100,000) and not $7,000. Assume further that the prescribed rate throughout Year 6 of the loan is 10% and that the prescribed rate for Year 7 is 12%. The amount of the deemed benefit for Year 7 will be $10,000 (10% of $100,000) because the loan will be deemed to be a new home purchase loan received on January 1, Year 6.

An offsetting deduction is provided from taxable income for the benefit received by an employee in respect of a home relocation loan[127] received as a result of an employment relocation to the extent that the benefit is not more than the benefit that would be received on a $25,000 interest-free loan.

The duration of the deduction is the lesser of:

See page ii for explanation of footnotes.

[126] CCH ¶9896; Sec. 80.4(1). [127] CCH ¶15,305, ¶28,129; Sec. 110(1)(*j*), 248(1) "home relocation loan".

(a) five years; and

(b) the period for which the home relocation loan is outstanding.

A "home relocation loan" is defined as a loan received by an individual or an individual's spouse or common-law partner in circumstances where the individual has commenced employment at a location in Canada (referred to as the "new work location") and by reason thereof has moved from the residence in Canada at which, before the move, the individual ordinarily resided (referred to as the "old residence") to a residence in Canada at which, after the move, the individual ordinarily resided (referred to as the "new residence") if:

(a) the distance between the old residence and the work location is at least 40 kilometres greater than the distance between the new residence and the new work location;

(b) the loan is used to acquire a dwelling for the habitation of the individual that is the new residence;

(c) the loan is received in the circumstances resulting in a deemed benefit; and

(d) the loan is designated by the individual to be a home relocation loan, but in no case shall more than one loan in respect of a particular move, or more than one loan at any particular time, be designated as a home relocation loan by the individual.

A "home purchase loan" is defined[128] to mean that portion of any loan or debt received or incurred by an individual in circumstances resulting in a deemed benefit that is used to acquire, or to repay a loan or debt received or incurred to acquire, a dwelling or a share of the capital stock of a co-operative housing corporation acquired for the sole purpose of acquiring the right to inhabit a dwelling owned by the corporation for the habitation of:

(a) the individual by virtue of whose office or employment the loan or debt is received or incurred;

(b) a specified shareholder of the personal service corporation by virtue of whose services the loan or debt is received or incurred; or

(c) a person related to such person.

The provisions respecting benefits resulting from interest-free or low-interest-bearing loans or other forms of indebtedness also apply in the case where the benefit is conferred on a shareholder by a corporation, any related corporation, or a partnership of which a corporation or a related corporation is a member.

See page ii for explanation of footnotes.

[128] CCH ¶9897; Sec. 80.4(7) "home purchase loan".

¶3120

See ¶2400 concerning moving expenses.

[¶3126] Where Benefit Conferred Is Not Money

Where the benefit is not conferred or granted in cash, the determination of the value of the benefit can be at issue and has been the subject of several court cases. The CRA's position is that the value of the benefit is equal to the fair market value of the benefit, and in a situation where corporate property is made available to the shareholder, it is reasonable to consider the value of the benefit to be a normal rate of return on the greater of cost or fair market value of the property, plus related operating costs. The benefit in both of these cases would be reduced by any amount reimbursed to the company by the shareholder. This position was confirmed in a case where the issue centred around the value of the benefit conferred on the shareholder who had the corporation build a house for his own use. It was determined that the value of the benefit would be the price that the shareholder would have had to pay for the same benefit if he had not been a shareholder of the company; this would be a rent that would produce a reasonable rate of return on the company's investment in the house.[129]

The Federal Court of Appeal applied these principles to measure the value of the benefit conferred in a case where a corporation made available for its controlling shareholders use of a Florida condominium, costing some $4 million. The calculation of the benefit conferred was based on the "equity rate of return", i.e., the amount the corporation could have earned had it invested the $4 million at a reasonable rate of return. For the taxation year at issue, this was estimated to be $445,675.[130] So doing, the Federal Court of Appeal reversed the Canadian Tax Court's decision that the value of the benefit conferred was the fair rental value for the year, some $60,000, reduced by 10% business use and for some operating costs paid by the taxpayer.[131]

The same "cost of capital approach" was held to be the proper measure of the benefits received by two shareholders from their use of corporate properties. While there were days in which the properties were used for business functions, the properties were at the shareholders' disposition on any other occasion, even if they chose not to make use of them. Thus, the proper measure of the benefit is not the cost of renting equivalent accommodation for the period of actual personal use, but is the corporate income foregone by having the corporation's capital tied up in unproductive assets.[132]

With respect to an appropriation of funds or property to a shareholder, such an appropriation may take place where there is no consideration or where the consideration is less than the value of the funds or property appropriated, but in circumstances which do not result in the taxability of

---

See page ii for explanation of footnotes.

[129] Youngman, 90 DTC 6322.
[130] Fingold, 97 DTC 5449.
[131] Fingold, 96 DTC 1305.
[132] Arpeg Holdings Ltd. et al., 2008 DTC 6087.

the shareholder under other sections of the Act. It is not necessary that the funds or property actually be received by the shareholder. It is sufficient if they are appropriated in any way for the shareholder's benefit. Thus, the $100,000 difference between the fair market value of a property and the consideration paid by a corporation to its two shareholders for the assignment to it of their interest in an agreement to acquire that property constituted an appropriation of the corporation's property to its shareholders that was required to be included in their income.[133]

For comment on situations where a corporation makes an automobile available to a shareholder for the shareholder's personal use,[134] see Chapter II.

The *Canadian and British Insurance Companies Act* permits, in certain circumstances, the conversion of a Canadian life insurance company into a mutual company through the purchase of its shares by the company involved, and provides that no amount so paid by a company will be required to be included in the income of the recipient as a benefit to shareholders, nor is it to be regarded as a distribution of profits.[135] With respect to the mutualization of a life insurance corporation incorporated under provincial law, see Chapter X.

[¶3129] Rights to Purchase Shares

If a corporation grants to all its common shareholders the right to purchase additional shares, the amount or value of the rights so conferred is not included in income.[136] Identical rights granted must be granted at the same time to all holders of common shares outstanding. For this purpose, rights will not be considered identical if the cost of acquiring the rights differs. Common shares with different voting rights are considered to be identical properties provided no other differences in their terms and conditions would cause their fair market values to differ materially.[137]

See Chapter II for a discussion of stock options.

[¶3132] Payments of Income and Capital Combined

[¶3135] Blended Payments

Where an asset is sold for a price and payment is not required until some time in the future, the normal course of business is to charge some interest in respect of the amount not yet payable. However, under some circumstances, the price of the asset sold and the arrangement may not reflect the interest and capital element separately. Accordingly, a portion of

[133] Muscillo et al, 96 DTC 1128.
[134] CCH ¶4690; Sec. 15(5).
[135] R.S.C. 1985, c. I-12.
[136] CCH ¶4650; Sec. 15(1).
[137] Interp. Bul. IT-116R3.

an amount paid under a contract or other arrangement will be included in income if part of the payment can reasonably be regarded as a payment of interest or other payment of an income nature.[138] The provision will apply if the income portion of the payment is in the nature of interest. If part of the income portion may reasonably be regarded as interest, that part will be deemed to be "interest on a debt obligation held by the person to whom the amount is paid or payable". By deeming such amounts to be not merely interest but specifically "interest on a debt obligation", the accrual rules[139] will apply. Also included is the part of a blended payment that can be regarded as income other than interest. That amount will be included in the income of the taxpayer for the year in which it was received or became due, except to the extent that the amount is otherwise included in income under any other provision of the Act.

[¶3141] Annuity Payments

The rules relating to a payment of income and capital combined, described in ¶3135, do not apply to an annuity payment or a payment in satisfaction of the rights of a taxpayer under an annuity contract.[140]

Amounts received as annuity payments are included in their entirety in the recipient's income. However, the capital element of certain annuity payments may be deducted.[141] See ¶2415.

[¶3153] Loans to Non-Residents

[¶3156] Interest on Loans

Where a corporation resident in Canada has loaned money to a non-resident person and the loan has remained outstanding for one year or longer, without interest at a reasonable rate having been included in computing the lender's income, interest at a prescribed rate is deemed to have been received by the lender.[142] Where withholding tax has been paid on the loan, the above provisions are not applicable, nor are they applicable if the loan was made to a subsidiary-controlled corporation if it is established that the money was used in the subsidiary corporation's business for the purpose of gaining or producing income.

"Subsidiary-controlled corporation" means a corporation, more than 50% of the issued share capital of which (having full voting rights in all circumstances) belongs to the corporation of which it is a subsidiary.[143]

See page ii for explanation of footnotes.

[138] CCH ¶4700; Sec. 16(1).

[139] CCH ¶4380; Sec. 12(3).

[140] CCH ¶4722, ¶4723; Sec. 16(4); Reg. 301.

[141] CCH ¶8401, ¶8402; Sec. 60(a); Reg. 300.

[142] CCH ¶4732; Sec. 17.

[143] CCH ¶28,273c; Sec. 248(1) "subsidiary controlled corporation".

[¶3159] Deductions from Business or Property Income

[¶3162] General Discussion

Deductible expenses are of two classes:

(a) those expenditures which are of a capital nature, and

(b) those which are current expenses of the taxation year.

Expenditures of a capital nature are capitalized and depreciated year by year. Current expenses are deductible from income of the year of the expenditure, provided they meet the requirement that they have been laid out to produce income from property or a business of the taxpayer. Moreover, to be deductible an expense must be "reasonable in the circumstances".[144]

Note that for an expense to be deductible it must be incurred for the purpose of producing income from property or a business of the taxpayer who claims the deduction. Claims which cannot be brought within this rule will be disallowed.

The onus is on the taxpayer to prove that an expense was laid out to produce income. While there is no legal requirement that vouchers and receipts be kept for all expenses as long as a record is kept of the amount paid, it is nevertheless true that difficulties of proving such payments will be considerably lessened if vouchers and receipts are available.

Where expenses are incurred partly to gain income from property or a business of the taxpayer and partly for another reason (e.g., a personal purpose), only the amount expended in respect of producing the income from property or business is deductible. However, in the case of an expense incurred partly for the purpose of earning income from a business or property and partly for the purpose of earning a capital gain, it appears that the entire expense is deductible.[145]

[¶3165] General Limitation — Capital Outlay

No deduction is permitted for an outlay, loss, or replacement of capital, payment on account of capital, or payment in respect of depreciation, obsolescence, or depletion, except as expressly provided in the Act.[146]

The generally accepted test to ascertain whether an item of expense is capital or otherwise is: Did it bring into being an asset of permanent and enduring advantage and was it a once-and-for-all expenditure? If so, it is a capital expense.

The following decisions may help to clarify the distinction:

See page ii for explanation of footnotes.

[144] CCH ¶9120; Sec. 67.   [146] CCH ¶4800; Sec. 18(1)(b).
[145] Ludco, 2001 DTC 5118.

In order to supply a taxpayer company with steam, another company constructed and maintained ownership of pipelines to the taxpayer's plant. Expenses incurred by the taxpayer in construction of the pipelines were a non-deductible capital outlay.[147]

A payment made to Central Mortgage and Housing Corporation to retain rights to ownership of apartment buildings was a non-deductible capital outlay since the taxpayer received a benefit of enduring advantage.[148]

The purchaser of a law practice who paid 25% of the net profits of the practice for the next four years could not deduct such payments as a business expense, as they were part of the purchase price to acquire a capital asset.[149]

The expense of an insurance agency to buy out a competitor was not deductible, as the acquisition was a capital asset capable of increasing the taxpayer's income.[150]

The cost of buying out a processor competitor was not, in substance, prepayment for its raw materials but rather a capital expenditure; the purpose of the transaction was the elimination of a competitor and the acquisition of its goodwill.[151]

Losses suffered by a Canadian company in financing an American subsidiary,[152] and trading losses suffered by a commission stock salesperson buying and selling on his own account[153] were both held to be capital outlays and, therefore, not deductible.

Payment of administrative costs in connection with the purchase of interest-bearing shares in a credit union was a capital outlay and consequently not deductible.[154] Where a shopping centre made a large payment to the local municipality to improve the access routes to the centre, the expenditure was a deductible expense and not a capital outlay. The money was paid to enhance the popularity of the shopping centre and thereby to gain income.[155]

An amount paid to the former owner of the business in lieu of future commissions was a deductible expense, but an amount paid to a franchisee to terminate the franchise was a capital outlay.[156]

The cost to a mining company of acquiring land for the purposes of maintaining the proper slope of the walls in its open pit asbestos mine was a deductible expense.[157]

See page ii for explanation of footnotes.

[147] Canadian Glassine, 76 DTC 6083.

[148] Val Royal, 76 DTC 6119.

[149] McCray, 76 DTC 6480.

[150] Cumberland Investments Limited, 75 DTC 5309.

[151] Longueuil Meat Exporting Co. Ltd., 76 DTC 6145.

[152] Stewart & Morrison Ltd., 72 DTC 6049.

[153] Swansburg, 72 DTC 1096.

[154] Marchand, 78 DTC 6507.

[155] Oxford Shopping Centres Ltd., 81 DTC 5065.

[156] Bomag (Canada) Limited, 84 DTC 6363.

[157] Johns-Manville Canada Inc., 85 DTC 5373.

Prepayment of 60 years' rent on the acquisition of a leasehold interest was a capital outlay.[158]

Where a taxpayer pursued the business objective of assembling a diversified conglomerate of companies whose shares would be publicly traded, it was found that the expenses of investigating opportunities were capital outlays, but that the expenses of supervising the companies acquired were deductible business expenses.[159]

Note that capital losses are deductible from capital gains (see ¶5005 *et seq.*).

[¶3171] Entertainers and Musicians

The deductibility of expenses incurred by part-time and professional entertainers is determined by their status, i.e., whether they can be described as employees or as freelance, independent business people. Whether a person is an employee or an independent business person is a question of fact to be decided by all the circumstances of the case. Normally, the terms of the contract of service between the entertainer and the party to whom the entertainer's services are offered provide an indication as to the status.

A freelance, independent entertainer is deemed to be carrying on a business and will be permitted to deduct any expenses which would be deductible under ordinary commercial and accounting practices unless the deduction thereof is prohibited by the Act.[160]

[¶3174] Repairs and Maintenance of Capital Equipment

Amounts expended on the repair and maintenance of capital equipment are ordinarily deductible as incurred by a taxpayer in connection with income-earning activities. In some cases, however, where major alterations in capital equipment are made, the expense of making the alterations is a capital expenditure.[161]

The rule applied in distinguishing between capital and income expenditures is that an expenditure is capital if it is made "not only once and for all, but with a view to bringing into existence an asset or advantage for the enduring benefit of a trade".

The *amount* of the expenditure in no way determines whether it is a capital or a current expense. The determining factor is whether or not the expenditure increases the value of an existing capital asset or creates a lasting advantage. If it does either of these things, it is a capital expenditure. Thus, rental expenses for items such as repairs to cracks in the foundation of

---

See page ii for explanation of footnotes.

[158] Moore, 87 DTC 5215.
[159] Firestone, 87 DTC 5237.

[160] CCH ¶4751; Sec. 18(1)(*a*).
[161] CCH ¶4751; Sec. 18(1)(*a*).

a building that was very rundown, replacement of the electric wiring system, and rebuilding of the parking lot were all non-deductible capital outlays.[162]

The following questions are important in determining whether an expenditure in connection with a capital asset is a capital or an income expense:

(1) Does the expenditure result in substantially changing the character of the asset?

(2) Did the expenditure result in the alteration or replacement of a major part of the capital asset rather than a subordinate part?

If both of the above questions are answered in the affirmative, the expenditure will ordinarily be considered to be of a capital nature. Accordingly it will not be deductible in the year in which it is paid or incurred, but will be added to the undepreciated capital cost of property of the class and will be depreciable. Some stress has also been put on the distinction between movable parts of a whole and parts that become immovable through their permanent attachment to a larger unit such as a building, plant, etc.

It is not always proper to focus on the asset itself when determining whether a recurring expense is or is not a current expenditure. It may be necessary to view the amount in question from the point of view of the taxpayer. For example, a taxpayer who acquires a building unsuitable for use may have to paint and repair many items while performing substantial renovation. Under these circumstances, the expenses which would normally be considered to be current expenditures are classified as part of the capital expenditures.

Generally speaking, repairs and alterations made by a tenant to leased premises do not qualify as a current expenditure. Rather, the tenant is required to treat the expense as part of the cost of the "leasehold interest" in Class 13 of Schedule II and deduct the expense over the life of the lease. Certain expenditures in respect of repairs, renovations, or alterations to land or buildings are specifically provided for under the Act. It is important to keep in mind that any expenditure in respect of repairs or alterations must be for the purpose of producing or earning income before it is deductible.

Certain amounts that are payable to a taxpayer under an insurance policy in respect of damage to depreciable property are to be included in the taxpayer's income to the extent that the taxpayer has expended amounts on repairing the damage within a reasonable time after it occurs. Otherwise, proceeds of an insurance policy in respect of damage to or the loss or destruction of depreciable property in cases not covered above will be treated as the proceeds of disposition of depreciable property. Where included in income, the amounts expended on replacing the property will ordinarily be treated as capital expenditures which will not be deductible,

[162] Mbénar, 2011 DTC 1230.

but will constitute capital cost of the property on which capital cost allowances may be claimed.

[¶3180] Fines and Penalties

Current rules

No deduction may be made in respect of any amount that is a fine or penalty (other than a prescribed fine or penalty) imposed after March 22, 2004 under a law of a country or of a political subdivision of a country (including a state, province, or territory) by any person or public body that has authority to impose the fine or penalty.[163] This position does not extend to prescribed fines or penalties. Such prescribed fines and penalties include penalty interest imposed by the *Excise Act*, the *Air Travellers Security Charge Act* and the GST/HST portions of the *Excise Tax Act*. It should be noted that penalties or damages paid under a private contract (e.g., penalties for late performance) are not covered by this rule and they will continue to be deductible if they meet the general deductibility test for business expenses.

Rules prior to March 23, 2004

Prior to the 1999 Supreme Court of Canada decision in the *65302 British Columbia Ltd.* case (see below), fines and penalties incurred in the course of earning income from a business or property were often not deductible. In general terms, the courts reasoned that allowing the deduction of fines and penalties that were meant to be punitive and deterrent in nature would reduce their intended impact and would therefore be contrary to public policy.[164] However, in certain cases, fines or penalties for relatively minor infractions were deductible if they resulted from the day-to-day operation of the taxpayer's business, were impossible or at least impractical to avoid, and were necessary expenses.[165]

Post March 23, 2004

All of the foregoing changed with the Supreme Court's decision in the *65302 British Columbia Ltd.* case.[166] The taxpayer ran a poultry farm and the provincial egg marketing board imposed an over-quota levy that the taxpayer attempted to deduct in computing its income. The Tax Court of Canada allowed the deduction as a business expense,[167] but the Federal Court of Appeal denied the deduction[168] on the basis that there was a strong public policy argument precluding the taxpayer from claiming the over-quota levy as a business expense. The Supreme Court decided that the over-quota levy was incurred as part of the taxpayer's day-to-day operations and so was deductible pursuant to subsection 9(1) and paragraph 18(1)(a) of the *Income Tax Act*. The Court stated that to deny the deduction of fines and penalties

---

See page ii for explanation of footnotes.

[163] CCH ¶9139e; Sec. 67.6.
[164] Amway, 96 DTC 6135.
[165] Day & Ross Ltd., 76 DTC 6433.

[166] 65302 British Columbia Ltd., 99 DTC 5799.
[167] 65302 British Columbia Ltd., 96 DTC 2049.
[168] 65302 British Columbia Ltd., 98 DTC 6002.

on the basis of public policy would cause uncertainty and not be consistent with tax policy goals of neutrality and equity.

This decision established that a fine is deductible if it is incurred for the purpose of gaining or producing income. For purposes of establishing whether a fine or penalty has been incurred for the purpose of gaining or producing income:

- the taxpayer need not have attempted to prevent the act or omission that resulted in the fine or penalty; and

- the taxpayer need only establish that there was an income-earning purpose for the act or omission, regardless of whether that purpose was actually achieved.

As a result of the Supreme Court's decision in the *65302 British Columbia Ltd.* case, the CRA released Interpretation Bulletin IT-104R3 on August 9, 2002 which sets out the following guidelines:

- The characterization of a levy as a "fine" or "penalty" is of no consequence (i.e., does not make it any less deductible), because the income tax system does not distinguish between levies (which are essentially compensatory in nature) and fines and penalties (which are punitive in nature).

- The deduction of a fine or penalty cannot be disallowed solely on the basis that to allow it would be considered contrary to public policy.

- Prohibiting the deductibility of fines and penalties is inconsistent with the practice of allowing the deduction of expenses incurred to earn illegal income.

- In order for a fine or penalty to be deductible in computing income from a business or property, it must be incurred for the purpose of gaining or producing income from that business or property.

- The Act contains no requirement that a fine or penalty must be unavoidable in order for it to be deductible.

- Notwithstanding that a fine or penalty may have been incurred for the purpose of gaining of producing income from a business or property, its deduction may be expressly prohibited under the Act. Examples of such provisions are paragraphs 18(1)(*b*) re a capital outlay; 18(1)(*c*), if incurred to earn tax-exempt income; 18(1)(*h*) re a personal expense; and 18(1)(*t*) re an amount paid or payable under the *Income Tax Act*.[169]

See page ii for explanation of footnotes.

[169] Interp. Bul. IT-104R3.

[¶3183] Home Office

There are restrictions on the deduction of expenses incurred by an individual in respect of a home office. In order to deduct an amount in respect of a "work space" in a self-contained domestic establishment, the work place must be either the principal place of business or used exclusively for the purpose of earning income from business and be used on a regular and continuous basis for meeting clients, customers, or patients in respect of the business.[170]

The amounts deductible are limited to the amount of income from the business for the year, but any excess work space expenses may be carried forward indefinitely. The individual's income from the business is to be computed without reference to the rules for reserve deductions and inclusions arising from changes to the definition of "fiscal period" for years after 1994.[171]

[¶3184] Illegal Payments

There is a prohibition against any deduction in respect of illegal payments made to government officials in Canada, officials engaged in the administration of justice in Canada, persons under a duty as agents or employees, and persons responsible for collecting fares or admission fees.[172]

Deductions for such payments are prohibited where the payment is made to induce, or attempt to induce, the recipient to breach his or her duty and the payment is made for the purpose of doing anything that is an offence under certain provisions of the *Criminal Code*. Deductions are also prohibited where the payment is made in furtherance of a conspiracy to commit an offence under one of the specified provisions, or a conspiracy in Canada to commit a similar offence under the law of another country.

[¶3186] Legal and Accounting Fees

Legal and accounting fees are deductible only to the extent that they are incurred for the purpose of gaining or producing income from a business or property, and they are not outlays of a capital nature.[173] Legal and accounting fees incurred on the acquisition of capital property are normally included as part of the cost of the property. In the case of depreciable property, the claim for capital cost allowance is based on the total capital cost including such fees.

The tendency is to view legal expenses as simply current expenditures unless and until it is proven that the legal expenses were directly connected with a specific capital item.

See page ii for explanation of footnotes.

[170] CCH ¶4878; Sec. 18(12); Interp. Bul. IT-514.   [172] CCH ¶9138; Sec. 67.5.
[171] Sec. 34.1, 34.2.   [173] Interp. Bul. IT-99R5.

All taxpayers, including those persons who report income from sources other than business or property (such as salary or capital gains), may deduct fees or expenses incurred and paid-for advice or assistance in preparing, instituting, or prosecuting an objection or appeal in respect of:

- an assessment of tax, interest, or penalties under the *Income Tax Act* or a similar provincial law,

- a decision of the Canada Employment and Immigration Commission, the Canada Employment and Insurance Commission, or a board of referees or an umpire under the *Unemployment Insurance Act* or the *Employment Insurance Act,*

- an assessment of income tax, interest, or penalties levied by a foreign government or political subdivision thereof, if the tax is eligible for a foreign tax credit, or

- an assessment or decision under the Canada Pension Plan or a similar provincial plan.[174]

A taxpayer may also deduct amounts expended in connection with legal and accounting fees incurred for advice and assistance in making representations after having been informed that the taxpayer's income or tax for a taxation year is to be reviewed, whether or not a formal notice of objection or appeal is subsequently filed. However, any costs awarded or reimbursed to a taxpayer in respect of expenses deducted or deductible must be included in income for the year in which the award was received.[175]

For the deductibility of legal expenses incurred by an employee in collecting salaries and wages owed to the employee, see Chapter II.

[¶3189] Losses by Fire or Theft

Where a business suffers loss by fire or theft, the normal procedure would be to claim such loss as an ordinary expense of doing business. This procedure may be followed in losses by theft, whether the loss is occasioned by an outside thief or by an employee's theft.[176]

If the loss is unusual and large, the CRA would be inclined to question it as a normal, routine cost of doing business. Likewise, if the articles or cash stolen or destroyed belonged to the capital equipment of the business (for example, office equipment, cash raised for capital purposes, etc.) the CRA would treat the replacement expense as a capital loss and therefore would not allow it as a deductible expense of the business.

On the other hand, losses of inventory or cash collected in the day's business (representing proceeds of sales, etc.) would be considered deductible losses incurred in the ordinary course of doing business. Thus, funds

---

See page ii for explanation of footnotes.

174 CCH ¶8540; Sec. 60(*o*); Interp. Bul. IT-99R5.   176 Interp. Bul. IT-185R, IT-256R.
175 CCH ¶8049; Sec. 56(1)(*l*).

embezzled by a taxpayer's officers were deductible since they were wrongfully drawn from the taxpayer's operating line of credit, so that the misappropriations occurred while the funds were being dealt with in the course of the taxpayer's regular activities.[177]

The amount of loss allowable is the net amount after taking into account any insurance recovery or restitution in the year in which the deduction is claimed. This loss also includes the cost to the taxpayer of discharging a liability to a third party (for example, to a customer) created by a theft or defalcation.

The allowable loss will usually be deductible in computing income for the year in which the loss is discovered. Where the application of this rule would create a hardship (as might be the case when the thefts have forced the taxpayer into bankruptcy), the loss may be deducted, at the taxpayer's request, in the year (or years) in which the event causing the loss took place, provided that the year (or years) is not statute-barred.

[¶3192] Organization Expenses

Expenses incurred prior to the commencement of business operations, such as incorporation fees and legal expenses, are capital expenses and are therefore not deductible. Such expenses relate to the capital equipment of the business rather than to the actual earning income after trading has commenced. However, such outlays may be deductible as eligible capital expenditures.[178]

However, organization expenses may be an allowable expense in the case of a business formed for a single venture, as opposed to a continuing business. A single venture can be said to be profitable only if it shows an excess of total receipts over total disbursements. Preliminary expenses might well be included in such total disbursements. Thus, the Supreme Court of Canada held that the preliminary organizational expenses of a corporation, formed for the purpose of developing a prototype model of a sports car and selling it to an established car manufacturer, were deductible as an outlay for gaining income from "an adventure in the nature of trade". The Court noted that, from its inception, the venture was not for the purpose of deriving income from an investment but rather was purely speculative, and if a profit had been obtained, the profit would have been taxed as income. Therefore, the same rule should be applied for a loss.[179]

[¶3195] Expenses To Earn Exempt Income

An expenditure which is made for the purpose of earning exempt income or which is made in connection with property that would produce exempt income is not deductible.[180]

See page ii for explanation of footnotes.

[177] Parkland Operations Ltd., 90 DTC 6676.
[178] CCH ¶4641; Sec. 14(5).

[179] Freud, 68 DTC 5279.
[180] CCH ¶4817; Sec. 18(1)(c).

"Exempt income" is defined[181] as including money or property received or acquired by the taxpayer in such circumstances that it is not included in computing income by reason of some provision in Part I of the Act and, specifically, it does not include a dividend on a share. The Act specifies certain amounts which are not included in computing a taxpayer's income[182] and also specifies persons who are exempt from tax.[183] The Act also provides for deductions from income of certain inter-company dividends.[184] See ¶2290, ¶10,501, and ¶3405 respectively.

[¶3198] Annual Value of Property

The annual value of property owned by the taxpayer and used in the taxpayer's business may not be deducted, but rent for property leased by the taxpayer for use in the taxpayer's business is deductible. Accrued rent may similarly be deducted.[185]

[¶3201] Payments to Farmers

Any amount received by a taxpayer as a stabilization payment or a refund of levy under the *Western Grain Stabilization Act* is to be included in income. This will also apply to any amount received in the year as a payment or as a refund of a premium in respect of the "gross revenue insurance program" under the *Farm Income Protection Act*.[186] See also ¶3348.

[¶3204] Metric Conversion Costs

The cost of converting any measuring instrument or tool to the metric system will be considered a deductible expense, even when an improvement results. Replacement costs will be considered capital expenditures.

[¶3207] Reserves, Contingent Accounts, and Sinking Funds

In computing income, an amount as or on account of a reserve, contingent liability or amount, or a sinking fund may not be deducted except as expressly permitted.[187]

The most common reserves for which deductions are expressly allowed are:

- the reserve for doubtful debts (see ¶3453);

- the reserve for insurers whose ordinary business includes the lending of money in respect of credit risks (see ¶3429);

- the reserve in respect of: (a) undelivered goods, services not rendered, rent, or other amounts paid in advance for the possession or use of

---

See page ii for explanation of footnotes.

[181] CCH ¶28,103; Sec. 248(1) "exempt income".
[182] CCH ¶9901; Sec. 81.
[183] CCH ¶21,723; Sec. 149.
[184] CCH ¶16,301; Sec. 112.

[185] CCH ¶4819; Sec. 18(1)(*d*).
[186] CCH ¶4373; Sec. 12(1)(*p*).
[187] CCH ¶4822; Sec. 18(1)(*e*).

land or chattels, and (b) returnable containers, other than bottles (see ¶3423 *et seq.*);

- the manufacturer's warranty reserve (see ¶3432);

- the reserve in respect of instalment sales (see ¶3450);

- the reserve for quadrennial or other surveys required under the *Canada Shipping Act* (see ¶3465);

- the reserve in computing a taxpayer's gain on the disposition of property (see ¶5160); and

- the reserves in the year of death (see ¶2605).

The amount of reserves deducted in computing income for the year must be included in income in the following year.[188] Thus, a taxpayer must include in his income for the year the amount of the reserve for doubtful accounts that he deducted in the immediately preceding year.

The deduction of a contingent liability or amount is expressly prohibited. A contingent liability is a liability that depends for its existence upon an event that may or may not happen.[189] This definition relies on the well-accepted test set out by the House of Lords in *Winter v. Inland Revenue Commissioners* ((1963) A.C. 235 (H.L.)). Applying this test to a promissory note used to acquire Canadian exploration expenses, the Supreme Court of Canada[190] pointed out that, with a promissory note, there is an inherent risk of non-payment, and that repayment risk is one of the factors used in determining interest rates. In the case at issue, the uncertainty as to profits led to uncertainty as to the quantum that would ultimately be repaid on the note. However, uncertainty as to an amount to be paid does not affect the fact that a liability to pay has been incurred. Though the amount that would be paid may have been based on uncertain events, the liability itself was not uncertain and had been incurred absolutely.

[¶3210] Payments on Income or Discounted Bonds

Normally, a corporation which borrows money by issuing bonds may deduct the interest it pays[191] (see ¶3277). However, payments on income bonds or income debentures are deemed to be dividends rather than interest.[192] Payments by a corporation as interest or otherwise to holders of its income bonds or income debentures may not be deducted from the income of the corporation. Payments in respect of principal where a bond is issued at a discount are deductible where expressly permitted.[193] See ¶3312.

See page ii for explanation of footnotes.

[188] CCH ¶4330; Sec. 12(1)(d).

[189] Wawang Forest Products Limited, 2001 DTC 5212.

[190] McLarty, 2008 DTC 6354.

[191] CCH ¶5061; Sec. 20(1)(c).

[192] CCH ¶4680; Sec. 15(3).

[193] CCH ¶4832; Sec. 18(1)(f).

[¶3213] Personal or Living Expenses

No deduction is permitted for personal and living expenses of a taxpayer except travelling expenses incurred while away from home in the course of carrying on business.[194] In most cases, personal and living expenses would not be deductible in any event because of the provision in the Act that an outlay or expense may not be deducted, except to the extent that it was made or incurred for the purpose of gaining or producing income from the taxpayer's property or business.[195] See ¶3162.

[¶3216] Meaning of "Personal or Living Expenses"

The phrase "personal or living expenses" is defined[196] to include:

(1) the expenses of properties, including mortgage interest,[197] maintained by any person for the use or benefit of the taxpayer or any person connected with the taxpayer by blood relationship, marriage or common-law partnership or adoption, and not maintained in connection with a business carried on for profit or with a reasonable expectation of profit;

(2) the expenses, premiums, or other costs of a policy of insurance, annuity contract, or other like contract if the proceeds of the policy or contract are payable to or for the benefit of the taxpayer or a person connected with the taxpayer by blood relationship, marriage or common-law partnership (see (1) above), or adoption; and

(3) expenses of properties maintained by an estate or trust for the benefit of the taxpayer as one of its beneficiaries.

[¶3219] Restriction on Food, Beverages and Entertainment Expenses

The deduction in respect of food, beverages, and entertainment is limited to 50% of either the amount paid or an amount that is reasonable in the circumstances, whichever is less.[198] This limitation applies for all purposes of the Act except for costs deductible as moving expenses, child care expenses, medical expenses, or adoption expenses. Therefore, the above limit in respect of food, beverages, or entertainment also applies for other purposes, such as when the expenses are included in capitalizing the cost of inventory or if they are included in a taxpayer's research and development expenditures.

See page ii for explanation of footnotes.

[194] CCH ¶4834; Sec. 18(1)(h).

[195] CCH ¶4751; Sec. 18(1)(a).

[196] CCH ¶28,199; Sec. 248(1) "personal or living expenses".

[197] Dorman, 77 DTC 251.

[198] CCH ¶9127; Sec. 67.1; Interp. Bul. IT-518R.

Long-haul truck drivers incurring food and beverage expenses on or after March 19, 2007, during an eligible travel period, may claim a greater percentage of these expenses than the above 50% general limitation (see ¶2353).

Exceptions to the deduction limit are provided in the following circumstances:

(1) Where the amount is paid or payable for food, beverages, or entertainment provided for, or in the expectation of, compensation in the ordinary course of the business of providing food, beverages, or entertainment for compensation from customers. This will exempt businesses such as restaurants, hotels, and airlines in respect of costs incurred in providing food, beverages, or entertainment.

(2) Where the expense relates to a fundraising event, the primary purpose of which is to benefit a registered charity.

(3) Where the expense is an amount for which the taxpayer is compensated and the amount of compensation is reasonable and is specifically identified in writing to the person paying the compensation. For example, where a taxpayer spends an amount in respect of food, beverages, or entertainment for which he or she bills a client and identifies such expense in the accounts submitted to the client, then the taxpayer is entitled to a full deduction in respect of the expense, while the client would be subject to the deduction limit.

(4) Where the amount paid or payable by a employer is included in the income of an employee at a remote work area or would normally be so included but for the special provision where employees at remote work areas cannot be expected to maintain a self-contained domestic establishment. For example, if the amounts spent by an employer on an employee's food, beverages, or entertainment are a taxable benefit in the hands of the employee, then the employer can deduct the entire amount. If the amount paid by the employer is not included in the employee's income for reasons other than the employee not being expected to maintain a self-contained domestic establishment (for example, a reasonable allowance paid to a salesperson while travelling away from home is not included in the salesperson's income), then the deduction limit applies to the employer.

(5) Where the amount is not a taxable employment benefit by virtue of an employment at a special work site (as opposed to a remote work area). The amount must be paid or payable in respect of the taxpayer's duties performed at a work site that is at least 30 kilometres from the nearest point of the boundary of any urban area with a population of at least 40,000 persons. Furthermore, the amount cannot be paid or payable in respect of a conference, convention, seminar, or similar event.

¶3219

(6) Where the amount is incurred to provide food, beverages, or entertainment that is enjoyed by and available to all employees of the taxpayer at a particular place of business. For example, all such costs incurred for a Christmas party or similar event to which all employees at a particular location have access will be exempt. This exception is limited to expenses incurred at six such "special events" held in a calendar year.

(7) In certain circumstances where food and beverages are provided to an employee at a remote construction work camp. There are various requirements that must be met in order for this exception to apply. The duties of the employee must be performed at a site in Canada at which the taxpayer carries on a construction activity or at a work camp that was constructed or installed at or near the site to provide board and lodging to employees while they are engaged in construction at the site. The site must be a special work site, which generally means a work site where (i) the duties performed by the employees were of a temporary nature, (ii) the employee maintained at another location a self-contained domestic establishment as the employee's principal place of residence (A) that was, throughout the period, available for the employee's occupancy and not rented by the employee to any other person, and (B) to which, by reason of distance, the employee could not reasonably be expected to have returned daily from the special work site, and (iii) the period during which the employee was required to be away from their principal place of residence, or to be at the special work site or location, was for not less than 36 hours.

[¶3222] Employer Contributions to Plans for Employee Benefit

Amounts paid by an employer to a trustee under a registered supplementary unemployment benefit plan[199] (¶10,325) or under a profit sharing plan which is an employees' profit sharing plan (¶10,291), a deferred profit sharing plan[200] (¶10,432), a registered pension plan[201] (¶3321), or, after 2009, an employee life and health trust[202] (¶3322), are deductible by the employer to the extent provided in the relevant provisions relating to these plans.[203]

[¶3225] Use of Recreational Facilities and Club Dues

Specifically disallowed under the Act are expenses paid to maintain or use a yacht, camp, lodge, or golf course facility other than in the ordinary course of business, and amounts paid as membership fees or dues (whether initiation fees or otherwise) in any club, the main purpose of which is to provide dining, recreational, or sporting facilities for its members.[204]

See page ii for explanation of footnotes.

[199] CCH ¶21,125; Sec. 145.

[200] CCH ¶21,015, ¶21,541; Sec. 144, 147.2.

[201] CCH ¶5106; Sec. 20(1)(q).

[202] CCH ¶2370; Sec. 20(1)(s).

[203] CCH ¶4843–4846; Sec. 18(1)(*l*)–(*k*).

[204] CCH ¶4848; Sec. 18(1)(*l*); Interp. Bul. IT-148R3; Jaddco Anderson Ltd., 84 DTC 6135.

There is no provision in the Act to include the disallowed expense in the income of any employee on whose behalf the expense has been incurred.

Note that the expenses of a taxpayer in attending not more than two conventions in a year will continue to be allowed as a business deduction if the conventions are held at places reasonably consistent with the territorial scope of the organizations concerned.[205] See ¶3355.

[¶3228] Salary Deferral Arrangement

An employer is allowed to deduct a deferred amount under a salary deferral arrangement in respect of an employee provided that the deferred amount was included as an employment benefit for the employee in the calendar year which ends in the employer's taxation year and the deferred amount relates to services rendered by the employee to the employer.[206] Expenses incurred by an employer for a salary deferral arrangement established primarily for non-resident persons rendering services outside Canada is also deductible. See ¶2105 for a discussion of salary deferral arrangements.

[¶3231] Retirement Compensation Arrangement (RCA)

A taxpayer may deduct contributions made under an RCA where such contributions are made by an employer to the custodian of an RCA in respect of the employer's employees or former employees.[207]

Budget 2012 indicated that the CRA has uncovered "tax motivated arrangements" perceived to be an abuse of the RCA rules. Budget 2012 further stated that "some arrangements involve the deduction of large contributions that are indirectly returned to the contributors through a series of steps ending with the purported RCA having little or no assets but still being able to claim the refundable tax using the impaired asset exception.[208] Other arrangements use insurance products to allocate costs to the arrangement for benefits that arise outside the arrangement".

Accordingly, new rules propose that RCAs will now be subject to "prohibited investment", "advantage", and "stripping" rules, which are very similar to those recently enacted into law in December 2011 applicable to RRSPs and RRIFs.

Through draft legislation released on August 14, 2012, if an RCA has a specified beneficiary, the RCA will be subject to an additional tax equal to the fair market value of any advantage obtained by the specified beneficiary or a non-arm's length person (the "Advantage Tax"). Furthermore, the RCA

See page ii for explanation of footnotes.

[205] CCH ¶5138; Sec. 20(10); Interp. Bul. IT-131R2.   [207] CCH ¶4852ce; Sec. 18(1)(o.2).

[206] CCH ¶4852ca, ¶5128l; Sec. 18(1)(o.1), 20(1)(oo).   [208] The 207.5(2) election.

will be subject to tax equal to 50% of the fair market value of a prohibited investment acquired or held by the RCA (the "Prohibited Investment Tax"). Lastly, and perhaps most importantly, the specified beneficiary of an RCA will be jointly and severally, or solitarily, liable, for the Advantage Tax and Prohibited Investment Tax.

The Prohibited Investment Tax will be payable in respect of investments acquired, or that became prohibited investments, on or after March 29, 2012. The tax will be refundable if the RCA disposes of the prohibited investment by the end of the year following the year in which it was acquired (or any such later time as the Minister considers reasonable). As with the Part XI.07 tax, the CRA will have the power to waive or cancel the tax when it is just and equitable to do so.

The Advantage Tax will be payable in respect of advantages extended, received, or receivable on or after March 29, 2012. However, advantages that relate to property acquired or transactions occurring before March 29, 2012 will not be subject to the Advantage Tax if (i) the advantage is obtained by a specified beneficiary (or a non-arm's length person) and is included in computing the income of the specified beneficiary, or (ii) the advantage is obtained by the RCA and the amount of the advantage is distributed from the RCA and included in the income of a beneficiary or employer of the arrangement — in this instance the advantage will be treated as a normal RCA distribution for the purpose of determining refundable tax.

Furthermore, the election available in subsection 207.5(2) to deal with a decline in RCA asset value is to be restricted. The election will only be available where (i) the decline in value is not reasonably attributable to a prohibited investment or an advantage, or (ii) the Minister of National Revenue is satisfied that it is just and equitable having regard to all the circumstances.

[¶3234] Political Contributions

A taxpayer may not deduct a political contribution in computing income from a business or property.[209] See, however, the discussion of tax credits for political contributions at ¶8545.

[¶3237] Employee Benefit Plan Contributions

A taxpayer may not deduct an amount paid or payable as a contribution to an employee benefit plan in computing income from a business or property.[210] See ¶10,474.

See page ii for explanation of footnotes.

[209] CCH ¶4852b; Sec. 18(1)(n).   [210] CCH ¶4852c, ¶4875; Sec. 18(1)(o), 18(10).

[¶3240] Personal Service Business Deduction Limitation

The Act limits the deductions of expenses by a corporation in computing its income from a "personal service business".[211] All such expenses are disallowed except:

(a) salary, wages, or other remuneration paid to an "incorporated employee";

(b) selling and similar expenses that would have been deductible in computing employment income if the taxpayer had been employed and had been required by a contract of employment to pay them; and

(c) legal expenses incurred in collecting amounts owing for services rendered.

Related amendments dealt with at ¶8435 have the effect of denying the small business deduction to a corporation in respect of income from a personal services business. The provision dealt with here ensures that the use of a personal service corporation does not permit the deduction of an expense which would not have been deductible had the income been earned directly by the incorporated employee.

[¶3246] Interest and Property Taxes on Undeveloped Land

The deduction of interest expense and property taxes incurred in connection with undeveloped land is restricted unless the land can reasonably be considered to be used or held in the carrying on of business (excluding the unincorporated business of selling or developing land) or held primarily for the purpose of gaining or producing income from the land.[212]

The land to which the restrictions apply is essentially vacant land held for investment purposes. It does not apply to a building and the land on which it is situated or adjoining land used in connection with the building. Interest and property taxes on land subject to the restriction can only be deducted to the extent that gross revenues exceed all other expenses.

If the land is regarded as a capital asset, the non-deductible part of interest and property taxes can be added to the cost base of the land in the computation of cost for capital gains purposes.[213] If the land is regarded as inventory, the non-deductible costs can be added to the cost of inventory.[214]

The limitation extends to land held primarily for resale or development and vacant land held by a business but not used in the course of the business. However, corporations whose principal business is the leasing, rental, or sale and development of land therefor are permitted to deduct

---

See page ii for explanation of footnotes.

[211] CCH ¶4852d; Sec. 18(1)(p).

[212] CCH ¶4853, ¶4854; Sec. 18(2), 18(3).

[213] CCH ¶7627; Sec. 53(1)(h).

[214] CCH ¶4144; Sec. 10(1.1).

carrying charges in excess of net income before deducting such carrying charges. The limitation of this deduction is the corporation's "base level deduction" computed as interest at a prescribed rate on a loan of $1,000,000 outstanding throughout the year.

Example 1:

> Allison Chang owns a piece of undeveloped land, which she holds as an investment. She receives no rent from the land and therefore cannot deduct any interest or property taxes.

Example 2:

> Charles Stevens owns two parcels of undeveloped land and had the following transactions in 2011:

	Parcel 1	Parcel 2
Rent received from allowing storage on the land	$1,200	$3,000
Liability insurance premiums paid	200	500
Mortgage interest paid	5,000	1,500
Property taxes paid	1,000	400

> For Parcel 1, Charles will be able to deduct $1,000 of property taxes and interest, since his net rental income before these items is $1,200 – $200, or $1,000. The remaining $5,000 will be added to his adjusted cost base of the property.

> For Parcel 2, Charles may deduct all the interest and property taxes since his net rental income exceeds these items.

[¶3249] Construction Period Soft Costs

In general, no deduction is available for soft costs attributable to the period of construction, renovation, or alteration of a building, except to the extent of the taxpayer's income in the year from renting the building for which they are incurred.[215] Costs over and above rental income must be added to the cost of the building and/or the related land, rather than deducted on a current basis. Soft costs include interest expenses referable to borrowed money used in respect of construction, renovation, or alteration of a building or the ownership of related land.

Reasonable outlays and expenses relating to prescribed disability-related modifications to a taxpayer's building will not be subject to the rule requiring capitalization of construction soft costs.

[¶3252] Prepaid Expenses

A taxpayer must deduct certain prepaid expenses in the period to which they reasonably relate. Thus, the deduction for accounting and tax purposes

---

See page ii for explanation of footnotes.

[215] CCH ¶4856–4856f, ¶5145y; Sec. 18(3.1)–(3.7), 20(29); Interp. Bul. IT-371.

with respect to these expenses should be similar. The payments to which this requirement applies are outlays or expenses (called "prepayments") that can reasonably be regarded as having been made or incurred in a taxation year:

(a) as consideration for services to be rendered after the end of the year;

(b) as, on account of, in lieu of payment of, or in satisfaction of, interest, taxes (other than taxes imposed on insurance premiums, as noted in the commentary below), rent, or royalties in respect of a period after the end of the year; and

(c) as consideration for insurance in respect of a period after the end of the year (with exceptions for reinsurance and paid-up group term life insurance).[216]

Farmers and fishermen who elect to use the cash method are expressly excluded from this deferral rule. Similarly, taxes imposed on insurance premiums and an amount paid in respect of reinsurance by an insurer can be deducted when made. However, only premium taxes imposed on an insurer in respect of a non-cancellable or guaranteed renewable accident and sickness insurance policy or a life insurance policy that is not a group term life insurance policy that provides coverage for a period not exceeding 12 months continue to be deductible on a current basis. Furthermore, payments to certain entities such as approved associations, universities and colleges, and tax-exempt corporations that carry out SR&ED in Canada, are fully deductible by the payer in the year of payment and are not subject to the deferral rule if the SR&ED is related to the payer's business, the payer is entitled to exploit the results of the SR&ED, the payee and payer deal at arm's length, and the SR&ED is not carried out for, or on behalf of, the payer.

Example: Prepaid Expenses

Prepayment of building maintenance for December 2011 and January and February 2012.

Amount of payment	$900

Date of payment — December 1, 2011
Fiscal year end — December 31, 2011

Amount deductible in 2011	$300
Amount deductible in 2012	$600

Presumably this apportionment should be made on a daily accrual basis.

See page ii for explanation of footnotes.

[216] CCH ¶4872; Sec. 18(9); Interp. Bul. IT-417R2.

[¶3253] Penalties, Bonuses and Rate Reduction Payments

An amount paid in the course of earning income from business or property to reduce the interest rate on borrowed funds or on the unpaid purchase price of property will be treated as an interest expense for a future taxation year to the extent that it relates to and does not exceed the value, at the time the fee is paid, of a payment of interest that would have been made by the taxpayer in such future taxation year.[217] This also applies to a bonus or penalty paid in consideration of the early repayment of all or part of the principal amount of a borrowing or an unpaid purchase price for property.

The deduction of interest payable for a year by a corporation, partnership, or trust is limited generally where interest for future years has been paid in advance. The amount of deductible interest in such case is generally limited to interest calculated on the principal amount outstanding less any previously prepaid interest amounts. In other words, the prepaid interest for future years will reduce the principal amount of the debt for the purpose of determining the amount of interest payable in respect of years prior to those future years.

[¶3254] Matchable Expenditures

Restrictions have been imposed on the use of royalty-type arrangements to bring about tax-assisted financing by structuring the arrangements as tax shelters or debt substitutes. Accordingly, the deductibility of otherwise deductible matchable expenditures incurred in respect of a right to receive production will be limited by prorating the amount of the expenditure over the economic life of the right to which it pertains.[218]

A matchable expenditure is deductible in computing a taxpayer's income for a taxation year to the extent it is determined to be the least of the following three amounts:

(1) The first amount is the portion of the matchable expenditure, not exceeding one-fifth, that the number of months in the taxation year after the right to receive production is acquired is to the total number of months, not exceeding 240, of the term of the right to receive production. To this prorated amount is added the amount that would have been deductible in the preceding year but for the second amount. In other words, a carryover may be available where the first amount in the preceding year was not fully deductible in that year because of the second limitation in (2). In determining when a right to production was acquired and how long its term is, a

---

See page ii for explanation of footnotes.

[217] CCH ¶4874a–4874h; Sec. 18(9.1)–(9.8).   [218] CCH ¶4879d–4879v; Sec. 18.1.

matchable expenditure that is made before the day on which the taxpayer acquires the right to receive production is deemed to have been made on that day. Where the taxpayer has the option to renew the term of the right to receive production for one or more terms, the term of the right is deemed to include the renewable terms. Where the term of the right is for an indeterminate period, it is deemed to have a term of 240 months.

(2) The second amount is the total of the income included in the taxation year in respect of the right to receive production, other than any portion deducted in the year as a reserve, plus the amount determined for the preceding taxation year in excess of the amount deductible in that year because of the first limitation in (1). This latter amount means that a carryover is available to the extent the second amount in the preceding year was not fully deductible in the year because of the first limitation in (1).

(3) The third amount is the total of all amounts of the matchable expenditure that would otherwise have been deductible in the year or prior years, in excess of the total amounts in respect of the matchable expenditure for prior years in respect of the right to receive production.[219]

Except in certain circumstances involving non-arm's length transactions, where the entire right is disposed of, or the right expires, the taxpayer is allowed a full "terminal deduction" of the remaining matchable expenditure.[220] This "terminal deduction" does not apply to a disposition of only a portion of a right, so that for partial dispositions it appears that the amount of the taxpayer's deduction continues to be the lesser of the three amounts set out above, until the year in which the taxpayer's remaining right is entirely disposed of.

A right to receive production is defined as a right under which a taxpayer is entitled, either immediately or in the future and either absolutely or contingently, to receive an amount, all or a portion of which is computed by reference to use of property, production, revenue, profit, cash flow, commodity price, cost or value of property, or any other similar criterion, or by reference to dividends paid or payable to shareholders of any class of shares where the amount is in respect of another taxpayer's activity, property, or business. The definition is obviously broad and catches any such amount in respect of another taxpayer's property or business activity. A right to receive production does not include an income interest in a trust, a

---

See page ii for explanation of footnotes.

[219] CCH ¶4879k–4879l; Sec. 18.1(4)–(5).   [220] CCH ¶4879n; Sec. 18.1(7).

¶3254

Canadian resource property, or a foreign resource property. Furthermore, an important exception is made to the matchable expenditure rules to the extent that a matchable expenditure is not subject to the above rules if:

(1) no portion of the expenditure can reasonably be considered to have been paid to another taxpayer, or to a person with whom that taxpayer does not deal at arm's length, to "acquire" the right to receive production from the other taxpayer, *and either:*

(a) the expenditure cannot reasonably be considered to relate to a tax shelter or tax shelter investment, and none of the main purposes for making the expenditure is that the taxpayer or a non-arm's length person obtain a tax benefit; or

(b) the amount included in the taxpayer's income in respect of the right for the taxation year in which the matchable expenditure is made (not including any amount for which a reserve is claimed) exceeds 80% of the amount of the expenditure; or

(2) the expenditure is in respect of a reinsured's share of sales commissions or other expenses incurred in respect of an insurance policy for which all or a portion of a risk has been ceded to the reinsurer and both the reinsurer and the person to whom the reinsurer made the expenditures are insurers, subject to the federal supervision of the Superintendent of Financial Institutions or a similar provincial supervisory authority.

[On September 18, 2001, the government announced that certain tax shelter arrangements have been designed to exploit the 80% revenue threshold exception in 1(b) above and proposed to amend it to avoid these unintended results. Under the proposed rules, if the 80% threshold is met, expenditures are deductible only to the extent of revenues received from the right to receive production. This restriction will apply where the matchable expenditure relates to a tax shelter or a tax shelter investment, or where one of the main purposes of incurring the matchable expenditure is to obtain the reduction, avoidance, or deferral of tax. This pending technical amendment is reprised in the revised technical proposals that were released on July 16, 2010, but is not enacted yet. It will apply to expenditures made after September 17, 2001, subject to transitional rules.]

In its explanatory notes, the Department of Finance provided the following example of how the matchable expenditure rules are meant to apply.

Example: Taxpayer Holds Right Until Expiry

Taxpayer A incurs $1,000 of matchable expenditures that relate to a right to receive production from Taxpayer B's business over a six-year period (i.e., 25% of the annual gross sales from the sale of a particular product).

The $1,000 was expended for the purpose of earning income. Taxpayer A has a reasonable expectation of profit from the right to receive production, and the amount is otherwise deductible. The deductibility of the matchable expenditure is therefore determined as the least of the three amounts discussed in the above commentary.

● Taxpayer A receives the following gross revenue payments from Taxpayer B:

Year 1: $100

Year 2: $200

Year 3: $300

Year 4: $200

Year 5: $100

Year 6: $500

● Taxpayer A's right to receive production expires in year 6 (i.e., the "terminal deduction" [discussed in the above commentary] applies in that year).

Calculation of Taxpayer A's Deduction:

Year 1: Taxpayer A may deduct $100, which is the least of:

(a)   the total of

● the lesser of
$200 (1/5 + $1,000)
$167 ($1,000/6)

● Nil
$167

(b)   the total of

● $100 (receipts included in income)

● Nil
$100

(c) $200 ($200 - Nil) (Assuming a five-year matching period under general principles).

Year 2: Taxpayer A may deduct $200, which is the least of:

(a)   the total of

● the lesser of
$200 (1/5 + $1,000)
$167 ($1,000/6)

● $ 67 (year 1: $167(a) - $100(b))
$234

(b)   the total of

● $200 (receipts included in income)

● Nil
$200

(c) $300 ($400 - $100)

Year 3: Taxpayer A may deduct $201, which is the least of:

(a)   the total of

● the lesser of
$200 (1/5 + $1,000)
$167 ($1,000/6)

● $ 34 (year 2: $234(a) - $200(b))
$201

¶3254

(b)   the total of

- $300 (receipts included in income)

- Nil
$$\overline{\$300}$$

(c) $300 ($600 - $300)

Year 4: Taxpayer A may deduct $167, which is the least of:

(a)   the total of

- the lesser of
$200 (1/5 + $1,000)
$167 ($1,000/6)

- Nil
$$\overline{\$167}$$

(b)   the total of

- $200 (receipts included in income)

- $ 99 (year 3: $300(b) - $201(a))
$$\overline{\$299}$$

(c) $299 ($800 - $501)

Year 5: Taxpayer A may deduct $167, which is the least of:

(a)   the total of

- the lesser of
$200 (1/5 + $1,000)
$167 ($1,000/6)

- Nil
$$\overline{\$167}$$

(b)   the total of

- $100 (receipts included in income)

- $132 (year 4: $299(b) - $167(a))
$$\overline{\$232}$$

(c) $332 ($1,000 - $668)

Year 6: Taxpayer A may deduct $165 because the "terminal deduction" applies. The amount otherwise deductible would have been the least of:

(a)   the total of

- the lesser of
$200 (1/5 + $1,000)
$167 ($1,000/6)

- Nil
$$\overline{\$167}$$

(b)   the total of

- $500 (receipts included in income)

- $ 65 (year 5: $232(b) - $167(a))
$$\overline{\$565}$$

(c) $165 ($1,000 - $835)

[¶3255] Thin Capitalization Rules

[¶3258] Deduction of Interest by Certain Corporations — Thin Capitalization Rules

The thin capitalization rules[221] are directed at preventing non-residents who own significant shareholdings (generally over 25%) in Canadian resident corporations from withdrawing profits in the form of interest payments rather than in the form of dividends paid on the shares of the corporation which must be paid out of earnings accumulated after Canadian tax. Both dividends and interest paid to non-residents are subject to withholding tax under Part XIII, but since interest is deductible in computing the income of the resident corporation subject to Canadian tax, it would clearly be to a non-resident's advantage to finance the operation of a Canadian resident corporation through interest-bearing debt rather than through share capital, which would lead to the establishment of thinly capitalized corporations. It should be noted that this limitation is only applicable where the debtor is a corporation and not another type of entity, such as a partnership.

The thin capitalization rules limit this advantage by imposing a limit on the amount of interest paid to non-residents that may be deducted in computing the income of the Canadian resident corporation. For taxation years beginning after 2000, the interest otherwise deductible that is disallowed as a deduction is determined by the following formula:

$$\text{interest otherwise deductible on outstanding debts to specified non-residents} \times \frac{\text{average outstanding debts to specified non-residents during the year } LESS \text{ 2 times equity of corporation}}{\text{average outstanding debts to specified non-residents during the year}}$$

Proposed changes August 14, 2012

Draft budget legislation released on August 14, 2012 proposed significant changes to the thin capitalization rules, largely to reflect the recommendations made by the Advisory Panel on Canada's System of International Taxation (the "Advisory Panel") in 2008.

For tax years beginning after 2012, the above debt to equity ratio will be reduced from 2:1 to 1.5:1. The Advisory Panel noted that the existing 2:1 ratio is too high compared to actual industry ratios in the Canadian economy, as well as general global standards.

The rules will also be amended to address partnership debt. Pursuant to this proposed amendment, a Canadian corporate partner will be attributed to its proportionate share of any partnership debt, and will be required to include in income any interest on the portion of the allocated partner-

---

See page ii for explanation of footnotes.

[221] CCH ¶4858–4866; Sec. 18(4)–(8); Interp. Bul. IT-59R3.

ship debt that exceeds the corporate partner's debt to equity ratio under subsection 18(4). This proposed change will be effective for taxation years ending after March 29, 2012.

Some technical amendments will also eliminate the risk of double taxation in the context of debts owing to controlled foreign affiliates.

[¶3261] Advertising — Non-Canadian Newspaper or Periodical — Foreign Broadcasting

[¶3264] Limitation on Advertising Expense

Ordinarily, reasonable advertising expenses are deductible as expenses incurred for the purpose of gaining or producing income from a business or property. However, where an advertisement in a newspaper is directed primarily to a market in Canada, the expense of advertising space is only deductible if the newspaper meets certain Canadian ownership criteria. Prior to June 2000, this restriction also applied to advertisements placed in periodicals. However, the Canada–U.S. Agreement of June 3, 1999, implemented an amendment to exclude advertisements in periodicals from its application. Periodicals are now subject to an 80% "original editorial content" rule.[222] A publication that otherwise qualifies will not be disqualified because it has been typeset or printed in the United States.

Advertising in foreign newspapers

Amounts paid to a non-Canadian newspaper for advertising are not deductible in computing income if the advertisement is directed primarily to a market in Canada.

A "Canadian newspaper" is defined as being a newspaper, the *exclusive* right to produce and publish issues of which is held by one or more of:

(1) a Canadian citizen or an association or society of which at least ³/₄ of the members are Canadian citizens;

(2) a partnership of which at least ³/₄ of the income or loss of the partnership from any source is included in the determination of the income of Canadian citizens or eligible corporations who also own at least ³/₄ of the total value of the partnership property;

(3) the Crown in right of Canada or a province, or a Canadian municipality; or

(4) a corporation incorporated in Canada of which the chairperson or other presiding officer and at least ³/₄ of the directors or similar officers are Canadian citizens.

See page ii for explanation of footnotes.

[222] CCH ¶4880e; Sec. 19.

If the corporation has share capital, at least $3/4$ of the voting shares, and shares representing at least $3/4$ of the fair market value of the shares, must be beneficially owned by Canadian citizens or by corporations that are not controlled by citizens or subjects of a foreign country.

Where the exclusive right to produce or publish is held as property of a trust or estate, the newspaper is classified as non-Canadian unless *each* beneficiary is a person, partnership, association, or society described in (1) to (4) above. Furthermore, where one or more persons or partnerships not described in (1) to (4) above have influence that, if exercised, would result in effective control of a newspaper, the newspaper is deemed not to be a Canadian newspaper at that time.

For purposes of the test for Canadian ownership, rules similar to the associated corporations rules determine the number of shares of a corporation ultimately owned by Canadian citizens. For public corporations, a Canadian-control test applies.

A "Canadian issue" of a newspaper is defined as an issue, including a special issue:

    (a) the type of which, other than type for advertisements or features, is set in Canada;

    (b) which, except for comics supplements, is printed in Canada; and

    (c) which is both edited by individuals resident in Canada and published in Canada.

The above restriction regarding Canadian ownership does not apply to ads in a special issue of a non-Canadian newspaper that is published twice a year or less and is devoted to features or news related primarily to Canada.

Advertising in Canadian or foreign periodicals after May 2000

Regardless of the ownership of the periodical, the cost of advertisements in periodicals published after May 2000 will be fully deductible if the periodical contains at least 80% "original editorial content". If the periodical contains less that 80% original editorial content, then 50% of the cost of advertisements will be deductible.[223] Original editorial content means non-advertising content, the author (i.e., a writer, journalist, illustrator, or photographer) of which is a Canadian, or that is created for the Canadian market and has not been published in any other edition of that issue of the periodical published outside Canada.

These rules reflect the Canada–U.S. Agreement of June 3, 1999, regarding periodicals.

See page ii for explanation of footnotes.

[223] CCH ¶4898d; Sec. 19.01(1) "original editorial content".

[¶3267] Foreign Broadcasting

A taxpayer may not deduct the expense of an advertisement directed primarily to a market in Canada if it is broadcast by a "foreign broadcast undertaking".[224]

The expression "foreign broadcast undertaking" is defined to mean:[225]

(1) a network operation located outside Canada or on a ship or aircraft not registered in Canada; the term "network" is defined to include an operation which involves two or more broadcasting undertakings where all or part of the programming and scheduling of any of these undertakings is delegated to a network operator; or

(2) a broadcasting transmitting undertaking located outside Canada or on a ship or aircraft not registered in Canada.

While this is a very broad definition, it is designed primarily to include those undertakings located in the northern United States which broadcast into Canada.

[¶3270] Certain Other Deductions

[¶3273] Capital Cost Allowance

In computing a taxpayer's income for a taxation year from a business or property, there may be deducted such part of the amount of the capital cost to the taxpayer of property as is allowed by regulation.[226] The subject of capital cost allowances is dealt with in Chapter IV.

[¶3276] Cumulative Eligible Capital Amount

A taxpayer may claim as a deduction from income an amount not in excess of 7% of the taxpayer's cumulative eligible capital on hand at the end of the taxation year.[227] See ¶3075 *et seq.* for comment on cumulative eligible capital.

[¶3277] Interest on Borrowed Money

On October 31, 2003, the Minister of Finance released draft legislation and IT-533 in direct response to three Supreme Court of Canada decisions in which the reasonable expectation of profit test was rejected as a general test for determining whether a taxpayer has a source of income, and in which "income" was interpreted to mean gross income. The proposals require that, for taxation years beginning after 2004, a taxpayer's loss from a business or property, including a loss generated by interest expense, be only deductible

See page ii for explanation of footnotes.

[224] CCH ¶4899; Sec. 19.1(1).

[225] CCH ¶4899c; Sec. 19.1(4) "foreign broadcasting undertaking".

[226] CCH ¶4902; Sec. 20(1)(a).

[227] CCH ¶5051; Sec. 20(1)(b).

¶3277

in a year if it is reasonable to expect in that year that the taxpayer will realize a cumulative profit over the period during which the taxpayer may reasonably be expected to carry on the business or hold the property. According to the explanatory notes accompanying the draft legislation, the requirement that the expectation of cumulative profit be reasonable is intended to ensure that the determination is made on an objective basis rather than a subjective basis. These proposals are discussed below under the subheading "Proposed tax regime after 2004". However, during a period of consultation that ended on August 31, 2004, many commentators expressed concerns that a complete denial of losses where no source of income existed could inappropriately deny the deductibility of a wide variety of ordinary commercial expenses. To address those concerns, the Department of Finance announced in the 2005 Budget that it would make further changes to the proposals' structure by developing a more modest legislative initiative. This alternative proposal, not released yet, will be combined with a CRA publication that addresses certain administrative questions relating to deductibility.

Pre-2005 tax regime

Interest is deductible in respect of money borrowed, or payable for property acquired, for the purpose of earning income from a business or property.[228] If the money was borrowed or property acquired for some other purpose, for example for domestic purposes or other personal purposes, the taxpayer is not permitted to deduct the interest. It should also be noted that interest is not deductible if borrowed to acquire property, the income from which would be exempt, or where the property is an interest in a life insurance policy.

The term "borrowed money" has been expanded to include proceeds to a taxpayer from the sale of a post-dated bill drawn by the taxpayer on a bank to which the *Bank Act* or the *Quebec Savings Bank Act* applies. These post-dated bills are commonly referred to as "banker's acceptances".

It does not appear that the lender must be a non-arm's length party so long as a genuine borrower-lender relationship exists, the amount of interest payments are reasonable, and the direct use of the borrowed money is for the purpose of earning income from a business or a property. Where trustees borrowed money to make capital allocations to the beneficiary of a trust rather than liquidate certain capital properties in the trust, which the trustees felt would be commercially inadvisable, the interest paid on the borrowed money was not deductible. It was only the direct use to which a taxpayer put borrowed money that determined whether the interest payment would be deductible.[229] In effect, taxpayers are required to trace the use of the borrowed money to a specific eligible use in order to qualify for a deduction.

See page ii for explanation of footnotes.

[228] CCH ¶5064; Sec. 20(1)(c).   [229] Bronfman Trust, 87 DTC 5059.

The Supreme Court has held that taxpayers are entitled to structure their affairs in order to meet the requirements of interest deductibility under the *Income Tax Act*. Thus, even if the taxpayers' motivation is a reduction of tax, the taxpayers must be taxed based on what they do, not what they could have done. As a result, the economic realities of a transaction cannot be used to recharacterize a *bona fide* legal relationship.[230] Where a partner in a law firm had withdrawn funds from his partnership account, purchased a home, and borrowed money to replace the funds in the partnership account all in the same day, the Supreme Court held that this was an eligible use for the borrowed money and the interest was deductible.[231] Thus, the Supreme Court has concluded that in the absence of a sham or artificial transaction, the economic realities of a transaction cannot be used to recharacterize a taxpayer's *bona fide* legal relationships.

For interest to be deductible, the CRA, historically, has required a taxpayer to show that the business carried on or investment acquired with the borrowed funds gives rise to net income after accounting for the interest expense. However, the Supreme Court has held in the *Ludco* decision that the term "income", as used in the interest expense deduction provision, refers to gross income rather that net income or profit.[232] By virtue of the *Ludco* decision, interest expense incurred on borrowed money used to acquire a capital gains investment will be fully deductible as long as there is a reasonable expectation that some amount of gross property or business income will be generated from the investment.

The significance of the *Ludco* decision will be diminished significantly if draft legislation released on October 31, 2003, which is scheduled to apply to taxation years beginning after 2004, is passed in its current form. The draft legislation proposes to deny a taxpayer's loss from a business or property, including a loss generated by interest expense, unless it is reasonable to expect that the taxpayer will realize a cumulative profit from the business or property. Thus, for example, if a taxpayer borrowed money for the purpose of making a loan at a lower rate of interest or at no interest, the taxpayer would likely not meet the cumulative profit requirement, meaning that the taxpayer's loss from the loan (interest income in excess of interest expense) would be denied. The draft legislation is discussed below.

Proposed tax regime after 2004

Draft legislation announced on October 31, 2003, scheduled to apply to taxation years that begin after 2004, will have a significant effect on the deduction of interest expense in those cases in which the investment made with the borrowing cannot be reasonably expected to generate income in excess of the interest expense on the borrowing. The draft legislation was announced by the Department of Finance in response to the Supreme Court's decision in *Ludco*, discussed earlier in the commentary and the

---

See page ii for explanation of footnotes.

[230] Shell Canada, 99 DTC 5669. [232] Des Enterprises Ludco Lté et al., 2001 DTC 5505.
[231] Singleton, 2001 DTC 5533.

Court's subsequent decisions in the *Stewart* and *Walls* cases, discussed below.

In both of its decisions in *Stewart*[233] and *Walls*,[234] the Supreme Court rejected the application of the reasonable expectation of profit (REOP) to commercial activities without a personal element. The Court held that, where the nature of a taxpayer's activity is clearly commercial, the pursuit of profit is established and there is no need to further analyze the taxpayer's business decisions or its REOP. The Court relegated REOP to a secondary role to be applied only to activities with a personal element. The Court held that REOP is only one of many factors to be considered in the personal element cases, in the determination of whether the activity in question is carried on in a sufficiently commercial manner, and, therefore, whether it constitutes a source of income. In *Stewart*, the Supreme Court also rejected the Crown's argument that the taxpayer's anticipated capital gain on the disposition of its rental properties was irrelevant in the determination of whether the taxpayer had a source of income. In contrast, the Court held that a taxpayer's anticipation of a capital gain could, in the personal element cases, be a factor in the assessment of whether the taxpayer had a source of income.

As a response to the Supreme Court of Canada decisions in *Stewart* and *Walls*, in which REOP was relegated to a secondary role for determining whether a taxpayer has a source of income, and in *Ludco*, in which "income" was interpreted to mean gross income, the Minister of Finance released draft legislation and IT-533[235] on October 31, 2003. The draft legislation is scheduled to apply for taxation years beginning after 2004 and effectively resurrect a net income/REOP requirement for business and property investments.

Under this draft legislation, a taxpayer can have a loss from a source that is a business or property for a taxation year only if, in that year, it is reasonable to expect that the taxpayer will realize a cumulative profit from the business or property during the applicable period described therein. In the case of a business, the period is that in which the taxpayer has carried on and can reasonably be expected to carry on the business. In the case of a property, the period is that in which the taxpayer has held and can reasonably be expected to hold the property.[236]

"Profit", for the purposes of the cumulative profit test, is determined without reference to capital gains or losses.[237] Therefore, anticipated capital gains cannot be taken into account in the cumulative profit determination. However, if an anticipated sale of property would generate income from a business, either because the taxpayer was in the business of selling the property or if the transaction constituted an adventure in the nature of a

---

See page ii for explanation of footnotes.

[233] Stewart, 2002 DTC 6983.
[234] Walls and Buvyer, 2002 DTC 6964.
[235] CCH ¶5064; Interp. Bul. IT-533.

[236] Sec. 3.1(1).

[237] Sec. 3.1(2).

trade, this anticipated income would be included in the cumulative profit determination.

The cumulative profit determination is made on an annual basis. Thus, for example, the determination as to the expectation of cumulative profit could be affirmative in one year, in which case a business or property loss could be claimed in that year, but negative in the next year, in which case a loss could not be claimed in that next year. According to the explanatory notes accompanying the draft legislation, the requirement that the-expectation of cumulative profit be reasonable is intended to ensure that the determination is made on an objective basis rather than a subjective basis.

In the 2004 Budget, the Department of Finance reiterated its position that the intent of the draft legislation is to restore the law and related CRA administrative positions to what they were generally understood to be prior to the Supreme Court decisions in the *Ludco*, *Stewart*, and *Walls* cases; in other words, the draft legislation is meant to effectively restore the REOP doctrine. The Department acknowledged, however, that some commentators had expressed concerns that the draft proposals could have more far-reaching effects, and that it was important to ensure that there was adequate opportunity for taxpayers to comment on the proposals and for the Department to consider those comments. Accordingly, the Department stated that it would accept and consider written submissions on the draft legislation until the end of August 2004. Following this extensive period of public consultation, the government finally announced in the 2005 Budget that it would develop a more modest codification of the REOP doctrine that would respond to the taxpayers' concerns while still achieving the government' objectives. This alternative proposal will be released for comment at the earliest opportunity together with a CRA publication that will answer certain administrative questions relating to deductibility. At press time, this more modest proposal had not yet been released.

[¶3280] Weak Currency Debt

If a currency ("weak currency") is expected to decline in value over some period of time relative to another currency ("final currency"), the interest rate on a borrowing in the weak currency will be greater than the interest rate on a comparable borrowing made in the final currency. If a taxpayer borrows in the weak currency and that currency depreciates as anticipated, the increased interest payments will be offset by a foreign exchange gain that is realized as the loan is repaid (owing to the depreciation of the weak currency). If the increased interest is deductible for income tax purposes as incurred, and the foreign exchange gain is deferred, the borrower is better off after-tax, as compared to a borrowing in the final currency. The benefit is increased if the foreign exchange gain is treated as a capital gain rather than ordinary income. Note that a borrower can essentially ensure this beneficial result, if it hedges its interest payments and principal repayment made in the weak currency (e.g., using foreign exchange forward contracts).

In the *Shell Canada* case, Revenue Canada (now the CRA) challenged the taxpayer's weak currency borrowing (made in N.Z. dollars), and attempted to limit the taxpayer's interest deduction to the market rate that applied to a final currency borrowing (U.S. dollars). The Supreme Court of Canada held in favour of the taxpayer, and allowed the full deduction of interest payable on the borrowing at the weak currency interest rate.[238] Furthermore, the taxpayer's net foreign exchange gain that was realized when the principal of the loan was repaid was treated as a capital gain. The *Shell* case involved taxation years that predated the general anti-avoidance rule (GAAR). Although the government takes the view that GAAR would apply to such weak currency borrowings, it has introduced specific rules to combat such transactions "for greater certainty".

These rules apply to "weak currency debt", which essentially means debt in a non-Canadian currency (weak currency), where the proceeds of indebtedness are converted into funds of another currency (final currency) which are used for the purpose of earning income from a business or property. The amount of the debt must exceed C$500,000, and the interest payable on the weak currency debt must exceed the rate on an equivalent borrowing in the final currency by two percentage points or more.[239]

In general terms, the rules work as follows. The interest paid on the weak currency debt that exceeds the amount of interest that would have been payable on an equivalent debt in the final currency is disallowed as a deduction.[240] If the weak currency interest payments were hedged, the weak currency interest for these purposes is computed net of the hedge gain or loss.[241] The disallowed interest expense then serves to reduce the foreign exchange gain or loss that is realized when the debt is repaid. That foreign exchange gain or loss, including any gain or loss realized on a hedge in respect of the principal amount of the debt, is on ordinary account. The net result will see the weak currency debt essentially being treated, for tax purposes, as a final currency borrowing. Note that in order for the hedge gain or loss to be treated on income account under this rule, the taxpayer must identify the hedge on or before the 30th day after the day the taxpayer enters into the hedge agreement.[242]

These rules apply to taxation years that end after February 27, 2000.

[¶3282] Interest on Policy Loans

A limited deduction is permitted for life insurance premiums on a policy assigned as collateral for a loan, where the assignment is required by the lender, the lender is a restricted financial institution,[243] and the interest payable on the money borrowed is or would be deductible in computing the

---

[238] Shell Canada Ltd., 99 DTC 5669.

[239] CCH ¶5145znc; Sec. 20.3(1) "weak currency debt".

[240] CCH ¶5145znd; Sec. 20.3(2).

[241] CCH ¶5145zne; Sec. 20.3(3).

[242] CCH ¶5145znb; Sec. 20.3(1) "hedge".

[243] CCH ¶28,247a; Sec. 248(1) "restricted financial institution".

taxpayer's income.[244] The amount deductible in respect of eligible premiums for a taxation year may not exceed the lesser of the premiums payable under the policy for the year and the net cost of pure insurance in respect of the policy for the same period. Once the ceiling amount in respect of the life insurance premiums is determined, the amount deductible is that portion of the ceiling amount that may reasonably be considered to relate to the amount owing under the loan for which the insurance policy has been assigned as collateral.

[¶3285] Repayment of Loans — Previously Acquired Property

If money is borrowed to repay previous loans, the repayment is deemed to have been made for the same purpose as the previous loans. The same applies to instances where borrowed money is used to pay for property previously acquired, for property the income from which would not be exempt, or property that is not an interest in a life insurance policy.[245]

[¶3291] Interest Incurred to Acquire Passenger Vehicle

There are restrictions on the amount that is deductible in respect of interest expenses related to the acquisition of a passenger vehicle.[246] Generally, deductible interest is limited to the lesser of:

(a) the actual interest expense, and

(b) $300 per month for automobiles acquired in 2001–2012.

[¶3294] Loss of Source: Borrowed Money Used to Earn Income from Capital Property

Interest on borrowed money will continue to be deductible under circumstances where the source of income has ceased to exist, such as in the decline in value of the property and where a business has ceased to operate.[247] If the property has become worthless, interest on borrowed funds used to acquire the property will continue to be deductible. Where the property has declined in value and has been sold for less than its original cost, the portion of the borrowed funds that can be traced to the sale proceeds is subtracted from the total borrowed funds outstanding to determine the amount eligible for relief. This amount is then deemed to be used for an income-earning purpose and the interest on that amount will continue to be deductible.

Where a taxpayer ceases to carry on a business, borrowed funds used for business purposes before the cessation are deemed to continue to be used in the business. The interest on the borrowed funds continues to be eligible for deduction. The amount of the borrowed funds is reduced to the

See page ii for explanation of footnotes.

[244] CCH ¶5074e; Sec. 20(1)(e.2); Interp. Bul. IT-309R2.

[245] CCH ¶5130; Sec. 20(3).

[246] CCH ¶9130; Sec. 67.2.

[247] CCH ¶5145zb, ¶5145zc; Sec. 20.1(1), 20.1(2).

extent that the funds are traceable to property that was used in the business and which has been disposed of by the taxpayer.

[¶3297] Capitalized Interest

A taxpayer who has acquired depreciable property in a particular taxation year may elect to capitalize any borrowing expenses, including annual financing fees, referable to that property to which the taxpayer would ordinarily be entitled to a deduction for that year.[248]

Where the taxpayer so elects, he or she may not claim a deduction for the year in respect of the borrowing expenses specified in the election. Instead, the expenses otherwise deductible are added to the taxpayer's capital cost of the property. An election will not be allowed, however, where the provisions respecting construction period soft costs (see ¶3249) would require that the interest be added to the capital cost of depreciable property. Where an election is made in respect of the year in which the property is acquired, any borrowing expenses referable to that property for the preceding three years may also be capitalized. For example, if the taxpayer was having a plant constructed over several years, he or she might incur standby fees in the early years which could then be capitalized when the plant became the property of the taxpayer.

The Minister is required to reassess the preceding three years to give effect to an election in respect of them.[249] A taxpayer who incurs exploration or development expenses or acquires a resource property in a particular taxation year is permitted to capitalize his or her applicable borrowing expenses otherwise deductible for that year.[250] To the extent that expenses are capitalized, they are treated as Canadian exploration and development expenses, foreign exploration and development expenses, Canadian exploration expenses, Canadian development expenses, or Canadian oil and gas property expenses, or foreign resources expenses (FRE) in respect of a country, as the case may be, and are deductible.[251]

The above elections apply only to the taxation year in which a depreciable property is acquired, or exploration or development expenses are incurred, or a resource property is acquired, and to the preceding three years. If the taxpayer wishes to capitalize borrowing expenses referable to a later year, the taxpayer must make a separate election.[252] It should be noted that the taxpayer must elect in respect of each successive year after the property is acquired or the exploration or development expenses are incurred in order to be entitled to elect for further years. While an election may be made with respect to all or any portion of the borrowing expenses of the year to which the election relates, an election on a portion only precludes any election in a subsequent year.

See page ii for explanation of footnotes.

[248] CCH ¶5146; Sec. 21.
[249] CCH ¶5150; Sec. 21(5).
[250] CCH ¶5147; Sec. 21(2).

[251] CCH ¶8900–9079, ¶9083; Sec. 66–66.2, 66.4.

[252] CCH ¶5148, ¶5149; Sec. 21(3), 21(4).

A taxpayer may make an election by simply stating so in the return of income for the year.

[¶3300] Limitation on Interest on Borrowed Money

A taxpayer is prohibited from deducting financing charges on funds borrowed or property acquired for the "purpose" of contributing or making payments to certain deferred or partially deferred income plans.[253] If indebtedness is incurred in respect of a property, and the property or a substituted property is then used for the purpose of making such a contribution or payment, the indebtedness is deemed to have been incurred at that time for that purpose. Thus, the limitation on financing charges cannot be circumvented by incurring indebtedness upon the purchase of a property, using the property for one purpose, and subsequently contributing the property (or the proceeds therefrom) to the deferred income plan.

The financing charges that are not deductible are those on funds borrowed or property acquired in order to:

(a) make a payment for an income-averaging annuity contract (with certain exceptions);

(b) pay a premium on an RRSP, (including any contributions which are repayments of amounts withdrawn under the Home Buyers' Plan — see ¶10,393 *et seq.*);

(c) make a contribution to a registered pension plan or deferred profit sharing plan;

(d) purchase an annuity if the purchase price is deductible (see commentary below);

(e) make an employee contribution to a retirement compensation arrangement, where the contribution is deductible;

(f) make a contribution to a net income stabilization account;

(g) make a contribution to an account under a prescribed provincial pension (currently, the *Saskatchewan Pension Plan* is so prescribed);

(h) make a contribution to a registered education savings plan;

(i) make a contribution to a registered disability savings plan; or

(j) make a contribution to a tax-free savings account (TFSA).

The financing charges to which the provision applies are interest, compound interest, other expenses of borrowing money, annual fees such as stand-by and guarantee fees, and discounts on certain obligations.

See page ii for explanation of footnotes.

[253] CCH ¶4876; Sec. 18(11).

The provision will not apply to financing charges relating to an employer's contribution to a registered pension plan or a DPSP on behalf of an employee. These contributions must, however, be otherwise deductible.

Under certain conditions described at ¶2445, a surviving spouse, common-law partner, or dependent child is allowed to purchase an annuity upon receipt of the refund of premiums of an RRSP of the deceased annuitant and avoid paying taxes on such amount. By virtue of item (d) above, the financing charges incurred on money borrowed to make such a payment are not deductible.

[¶3303] Borrowed Money — Promise To Pay Larger Amount

Where a sum of money is borrowed and the borrower promises to repay a larger amount than the amount borrowed, plus interest on that larger amount, interest is deductible on the larger amount.[254] Thus, for example, if a builder borrowed $8,500 to build a house and gave in exchange a $10,000 mortgage on the house with a promise to pay interest at 6% on the face value of the mortgage ($10,000), the builder could deduct such interest in computing income.

If only part of the amount borrowed is used for the purpose of earning income from a business or property, the amount of interest deductible is that proportion of the face value of the loan that the amount used to earn income is of the amount actually borrowed. In the example above, if only $5,000 of the $8,500 borrowed had been used to earn the income, then the interest deductible would be:

$$6\% \text{ of } \frac{\$5,000}{\$8,500} \times \$10,000 = \$352.94$$

[¶3306] Expenses re Financing

Expenses incurred by a unit trust in the course of issuing or selling its units, by a partnership or syndicate in the course of issuing or selling interests therein, and by a corporation in the course of issuing or selling its shares, may be deducted as financing expenses. In addition, expenses incurred by any taxpayer in the course of borrowing money or incurring indebtedness for certain purposes may be deducted.[255] In the absence of this provision, it is questionable whether many expenses incurred in the course of issuing trust units, partnership interests, or corporate shares, or in the course of borrowing, would be deductible. Many such expenses would be considered capital expenses, and at best, might qualify as eligible capital expenditures. In some cases, it could be argued that the expenses were not incurred for the purposes of earning income from a business or property. This provisions ensures that even if this were the case, the expenses will remain deductible.

---

[254] CCH ¶5129; Sec. 20(2).

[255] CCH ¶5073, ¶5074c; Sec. 20(1)(e), 20(1)(e.1); Interp. Bul. IT-341R4.

The deduction is limited in any one year to 20% of the expense incurred, the effect being that expenses incurred in a taxation year are spread out over five years. The 20% limit is reduced *pro rata* for shortened taxation years. However, if the taxpayer repays the debt obligations for which the expenses were incurred in a taxation year, he may deduct the entire balance of such expenses in that year, providing the repayment was not part of a re-financing and was not satisfied by issuance of a further unit, interest, share, or debt obligation. With respect to partnerships, where a partnership ceases to exist, any remaining undeducted expense is allocated proportionately to each ex-partner, and is deductible over the remainder of the five-year period.

The expenses which will be deductible will include the related legal, accounting, and printing costs and a commission, fee, or other amount paid or payable for the services of a salesperson, agent, or dealer in securities, rendered in the course of issuing or selling the units, interests, or shares. The expenses are deductible only by the unit trust, partnership, or corporation whose units, interests, or shares are being issued or sold. Accordingly, if a parent company incurred expenses in connection with the issuance or sale of shares of a subsidiary, the expenses would not be deductible by the parent company. It will be noted that the cost of increasing a company's authorized capital as a preliminary to the issuance of shares is not currently deductible,[256] But, presumably, this would be an "eligible capital expense".[257]

An office building company which had agreed, as a condition of a loan, to pay the lender 1% of its gross rental income for 25 years was allowed to deduct these payments as expenses incurred in the course of borrowing money to earn income.[258]

A participating debt (normally issued by a corporation) is, generally speaking, a hybrid debt obligation in which normal interest expressed as a percentage of principal is supplemented or replaced by payments based on other criteria, such as cash flow or gross or net profits above a certain level.

Prior to the *Sherway Centre* decision (discussed below), Revenue Canada's (now the CRA's) position was that participation payments made on a borrowing were generally not considered interest because they did not accrue on a day-to-day basis, and they were not normally referable to the principal amount of the borrowing. It also took the view that participation payments made as compensation for the use of borrowed money were not deductible. However, its administrative practice was to treat participation payments as interest if the payments were limited to a stated percentage of the principal amount of the borrowing and the limited percentage reflected existing commercial rates of interest.

See page ii for explanation of footnotes.

[256] The Enterprise Foundry, 59 DTC 318.   [258] Yonge-Eglinton Building Ltd., 74 DTC 6180.
[257] CCH ¶4600; Sec. 14.

In the *Sherway Centre* decision, the Federal Court of Appeal held that the participation payments made in that case, which did not come within Revenue Canada's (now the CRA's) strict guidelines, nonetheless constituted interest and were deductible.[259] The Court found that the day-to-day accrual was not a prerequisite to deductibility as interest. Rather, an amount paid as compensation for the use of money for a set period of time, including a participation payment, can be considered interest and can be said to accrue from day to day. Furthermore, because the participation payments in that case were payable only as long as there was principal outstanding on the loan, they were clearly referable to the principal sum. Lastly, the Court held that the participation payments were also deductible as expenses incurred in the course of a borrowing.

An amendment effective after November 30, 1999 reverses the *Sherway* decision to the extent that it denies the deductibility as financing expenses of participation payments and similar "excluded amounts". Participation payments made by a borrower under a debt obligation are typically based on the borrower's profitability or other revenue measure. An excluded amount is broadly defined to include any payment that is contingent or dependent upon the use of or production from property, or any amount that is computed by reference to revenue, profit, cash flow, or similar criterion. As a result, it appears that these amounts are deductible in computing income only if they qualify as interest.

[¶3312] Discounts on Interest-Bearing Obligations

All or a portion of bond discount paid in the year on interest-bearing obligations issued after June 18, 1971 is deductible.[260] The discount is determined as the amount paid in satisfaction of principal (not exceeding the face amount) to the extent it exceeds the amount for which the obligation was issued.

The deduction may be claimed for the whole of the discount of any bond, debenture, bill, note, mortgage, hypothec, or similar obligation issued after June 18, 1971, if:

(a) the obligation was issued for at least 97% of its face value, and

(b) the actual yield does not exceed $4/3$ of the interest rate shown to be payable on the outstanding balance at the time the payment was made.

In any other case, the amount deductible is $1/2$ of the lesser of:

(a) the amount paid, and

See page ii for explanation of footnotes.

[259] Sherway Centre Ltd., 98 DTC 6121.   [260] CCH ¶5075; Sec. 20(1)(f).

¶3312

(b) the amount by which the lesser of the principal amount and the amount paid in the year or in any preceding year exceeds the amount for which the obligation was issued.

The relevant amount is deductible when the amount in satisfaction of principal is paid, and presumably must be prorated when principal payments are made over a period of years.

[¶3315] Share Transfer and Other Fees

Corporate taxpayers are permitted to deduct certain expenses relating to their dealings with their own shareholders.[261] The amounts which are deductible are:

(1) fees payable for services rendered by persons as registrar or transfer agent for shares of the taxpayer's capital stock;

(2) fees payable for services rendered by a person as dividend paying agent;

(3) listing fees payable to stock exchanges; and

(4) expenses incurred in printing and issuing financial reports to shareholders and others entitled thereto.

Expenses incurred to produce information circulars informing shareholders of three takeover bids were not deductible as share transfer expenses and other fees. However, they were allowed as general administrative fees.[262]

[¶3321] Pension Plan Contributions

A deduction is allowed for employer contributions to a registered pension plan made in the year, or within 120 days after the end of the taxation year, provided the contribution is made on behalf of the employer's employees or former employees and the contribution is made in accordance with the plan as registered.[263]

By limiting the amount deductible to the amount permitted under the plan as registered, employer contributions on behalf of a particular member are effectively restricted to the amounts allowed under the terms of the plan, which must comply with the numerous registration requirements.

[¶3322] Employee Life and Health Trust Contributions

After 2009, an employer is allowed to set up an Employee Life and Health Trust ("ELHT") to fund designated employee benefits for the employer's employees, the employees' spouses or common-law partners, and related members of the employees' households. The designated employee benefits will generally be health and insurance benefits. The employer will

---

See page ii for explanation of footnotes.

[261] CCH ¶5077; Sec. 20(1)(g). [263] CCH ¶5106; Sec. 20(1)(q).
[262] Boulangerie St-Augustin Inc., 95 DTC 164.

generally be able to claim a deduction for amounts contributed to the ELHT.[264] The extent to which these deductions are allowed is set out in greater detail at ¶10,320 in Chapter X.

[¶3330] Leasing Properties

In order to restrict the use of leases as a means of after-tax financing, special provisions restrict the capital cost allowances for lessors. However, a joint election may be filed by a lessor and lessee to have the lease treated as a purchase and loan.[265] The loan is then considered to be for an amount equal to the fair market value of the leased property. The lease payments are treated as blended payments of principal and interest and the lessee is entitled to claim capital cost allowance. The lessor's position is unchanged by the election. If the election is not made, the lessee's tax position is unchanged by the leasing property restrictions placed on the lessor.

The election is available for tangible depreciable property (otherwise referred to as "specified leasing property") that is the subject of an arm's length lease for a term of more than one year and which, at the time the lease was entered into, had an aggregate fair market value in excess of $25,000. The rules do not apply to intangible property (such as systems software), or to prescribed property[266] (such as office furniture, computers costing less than $1 million, cars, and tangible property which at the time the lease was entered into had an aggregate fair market value not in excess of $25,000).

As a result of the 2010 Budget, the above-specified leasing property rules are extended after 4:00 p.m. EST March 4, 2010 to property in excess of $1 million that is leased to: a tax-exempt individual, organization, or trust (see Chapter XI); a person who uses the property in the course of carrying on business, the income of which is exempt from Part I tax; a Canadian government; or a non-resident, except where the property is used primarily in the course of carrying on business in Canada that is not a treaty-protected business.

[¶3333] Lease Cancellation Payments

Where the owner of a property is required to pay an amount to a lessee for the cancellation of the lease, the cost of cancelling the lease is treated as a type of prepaid expense, as long as the property continues to be owned by the lessor or by a non-arm's length person.[267] As a result, the costs may be deducted over what would have been the remaining term of the lease, including renewal periods, to a maximum of 40 years. A deduction is provided for the unamortized balance of the costs ($^1/_2$ of the unamortized balance,

---

[264] CCH ¶5116; Sec. 20(1)(s).
[265] CCH ¶4727–4730ab; Sec. 16.1.

[266] CCH ¶4730c; Reg. 8200.
[267] CCH ¶5123; Sec. 20(1)(z).

in the case of capitalized property) if the property is sold.[268] An amount that does not meet these conditions is not deductible.[269]

[¶3336] Landscaping of Grounds

Where a taxpayer pays an amount in the year for the landscaping of grounds around a building or other structure of the taxpayer, such payment is deductible if the building or other structure is used primarily by the taxpayer for the purpose of gaining or producing income therefrom (e.g., rental income), or from a business.[270]

[¶3339] Fees Paid to Investment Counsel

The full amount of fees, other than commissions, paid to an investment counsel for advice as to the advisability of purchasing or selling specific shares or securities is deductible.[271] However, the principal business of such a person must be the advising of others as to the advisability of purchasing or selling specific shares or securities or the provision of services for the management or administration of the shares or securities.

No deduction is available for any fees or services in respect of an **RRSP** or **RRIF** plan. Beginning in 2009, this prohibition also applies to the payment of fees in respect of a tax-free savings account (**TFSA**), of which the taxpayer is the holder.[272]

[¶3342] Expenses of Representation

Amounts paid by a taxpayer for expenses incurred by the taxpayer in making any representation concerning a business carried on by the taxpayer, including any representation made for the purpose of obtaining a licence, permit, franchise, or trademark relating to such business, are deductible in the year in which they are paid.[273]

Under this section and in order to be deductible, the expenses must relate to representations made to:

(1) the government of a country, province, or state, or to a municipal or public body performing a function of government in Canada; or

(2) an agency of a government or of a municipal or public body referred to in (1) above that has authority to make rules, regulations, or by-laws relating to the taxpayer's business.

In lieu of the deduction permitted by this provision, a taxpayer may, if he or she so elects in prescribed manner, make a deduction of $1/10$ of that

---

See page ii for explanation of footnotes.

[268] CCH ¶5123a; Sec. 20(1)(z.1).
[269] CCH ¶4852e; Sec. 18(1)(q).
[270] CCH ¶5124; Sec. 20(1)(aa); Interp. Bul. IT-485.

[271] CCH ¶5125; Sec. 20(1)(bb); Interp. Bul. IT-238R2.
[272] CCH ¶4852kc; Sec. 18(1)(u).
[273] CCH ¶5126; Sec. 20(1)(cc).

amount in computing income for that taxation year and a like deduction in computing income for each of the nine immediately following years.[274]

[¶3345] Cost of Utility Service Connections

In computing income from a business, the taxpayer may deduct amounts paid by him or her for the purpose of making a service connection to the taxpayer's place of business for the supply of electricity, gas, telephone, water, or sewers.[275] Certain conditions must be met in order for a deduction to be claimed under this provision:

(1) The service connection must be for the supply of electricity, gas, telephone service, water, or sewers supplied by the payee.

(2) The supply must be by means of wires, pipes, or conduits.

(3) The service connection must be to the taxpayer's place of business.

(4) The deduction may not be claimed if the amount is paid to a person with whom the taxpayer does not deal at arm's length.

(5) Such an amount will not be deductible in a taxation year unless it is paid in that year, regardless of when liability for it was incurred.

(6) An amount will not be deductible to the extent that it was paid to acquire property of the taxpayer. To that extent, it will normally be subject to capital cost allowances.

(7) An amount will not be deductible under this provision to the extent that it was paid as consideration for goods or services such as gas, water, telephone service, or electricity. To that extent, however, it would normally be deductible, provided the goods and services are purchased for business purposes.

[¶3348] Western Grain Stabilization Payments

A producer of grains (wheat, oats, barley, rye, flaxseed, rapeseed, etc.), in designated areas, who participates in the net proceeds stabilization program under the *Western Grain Stabilization Act*, may deduct amounts paid as a levy in respect of grain sale proceeds.[276] Amounts received as stabilization payments under this program and any refund of levy must be included in income (see ¶3201). The deduction also applies to premiums paid in respect of the "gross revenue insurance program" under the *Farm Income Protection Act* or amounts paid as an administration fee in respect of a "net income stabilization account".

See page ii for explanation of footnotes.

[274] CCH ¶5137, ¶5137a; Sec. 20(9); Reg. 4100.   [276] CCH ¶5128ac; Sec. 20(1)(ff).
[275] CCH ¶5128; Sec. 20(1)(ee).

[¶3349] Disability-Related Building Modifications

A taxpayer may deduct reasonable costs relating to eligible disability-related modifications to the taxpayer's building where the building is used to earn income from a business or property.[277]

The eligible modifications, prescribed by regulation, include the installation of interior and exterior ramps and hand-activated power door openers, the widening of doorways, and modifications to bathrooms for the benefit of individuals who have a severe and prolonged mobility impairment.

In addition, the cost of renovations and alterations made after February 25, 1992 may be deductible by a taxpayer even though the building is not owned by the taxpayer. A deduction from income from a business or property is also allowed for costs relating to eligible devices or equipment acquired primarily to assist individuals having sight or hearing impairment. Eligible devices or equipment include the installation or acquisition of elevator car position indicators, visual fire alarm indicators, telephone devices, listening devices for group meetings, and disability-specific computer software and hardware attachments.

[¶3350] Part XII.6 Tax

Tax paid or payable by a taxpayer under Part XII.6 for a taxation year is deductible in computing the taxpayer's income for the year.[278]

[¶3351] Investigation of Site

A taxpayer may deduct amounts paid in the year for investigating the suitability of a site for a building or other structure planned for the taxpayer's use in connection with a business carried on by the taxpayer.[279] Three conditions must be satisfied:

(1) the expense must be incurred in connection with a site investigation for a building or other structure which the taxpayer plans to erect or construct in the future;

(2) the taxpayer must already be carrying on a business in connection with which the planned building or structure is to be used; and

(3) the amount must be paid in the year in which the deduction is claimed.

In ruling on the deductibility of a large sum of money allegedly expended on investigating the suitability of a site, the Court limited the deduction to a small sum paid for a feasibility study. It stated that payments for the following were not deductible: persuading prospective tenants to rent in the

---

See page ii for explanation of footnotes.

[277] CCH ¶5128n, ¶5128o; Sec. 20(1)(*qq*), 20(1)(*rr*).　　[279] CCH ¶5127; Sec. 20(1)(*dd*).
[278] CCH ¶5128k; Sec. 20(1)(*nn*).

complex, and related negotiations; attempting to have municipal zoning and other regulations changed; obtaining municipal approval for the project; preparation of plans, etc., for the above; attendance of company representatives at meetings related to the above; legal services connected with the above; and public relations counsel designed to create a receptive climate for the project.[280]

[¶3352] Uncollectible Portion of Proceeds of Disposition of Depreciable Property

A taxpayer may claim a deduction if he or she has disposed of depreciable property, other than a timber resource property, and any portion of the proceeds of disposition becomes a bad debt.[281] See ¶3414 *et seq.* for comment on bad debts.

The amount deductible is the lesser of:

(a) the amount of the bad debts; and

(b) the amount by which the capital cost to the taxpayer of the property disposed of exceeds the amount realized on the disposition.

Where an amount is owing for proceeds of disposition of a timber resource property of the taxpayer and it is established to have become a bad debt, the amount owing to the taxpayer is deductible.[282]

For discussion of capital cost allowances and depreciable property, see Chapter IV.

[¶3353] Sale of Mortgage Included in Proceeds of Disposition

A taxpayer may claim a deduction from income for a loss suffered on the sale of an agreement for sale or of a mortgage or hypothec on land that has been taken back as part of the proceeds of disposition of depreciable property (other than a timber resource property) sold in a previous year.[283] The deduction can be claimed only if the sale of the agreement, mortgage, or hypothec and the sale of the depreciable property are both at arm's length. The amount of the deduction will be the lesser of:

(a) the amount by which the principal amount outstanding on the agreement, mortgage, or hypothec at the time of sale exceeds the sale price; and

(b) such excess minus any amount realized by the taxpayer on the disposal of the depreciable property in excess of the capital cost to the taxpayer of the property.

Where a timber resource property has been disposed of to a person with whom the taxpayer was dealing at arm's length, the taxpayer may

---

See page ii for explanation of footnotes.

[280] Queen & Metcalfe Carpark Ltd., 74 DTC 6007.   [282] CCH ¶5131ac; Sec. 20(4.1).
[281] CCH ¶5131; Sec. 20(4).   [283] CCH ¶5132; Sec. 20(5).

deduct any loss suffered on the sale of an agreement for sale or of a mortgage or hypothec on land taken back as part of the proceeds of disposition and sold in a subsequent year in an arm's length transaction. The deduction is available in the subsequent year. The deduction is the amount by which the agreement, etc., exceeds the consideration paid by the purchaser for the agreement.[284]

[¶3354] Accrued Bond Interest

Securities are often sold on the market between interest dates so that at the time of sale some interest has accrued. The price at which the securities are sold ordinarily reflects the fact that interest has accrued at the date of the sale. Where a debt obligation (other than an income bond, an income debenture, a small business development bond, and a small business bond) is transferred between interest dates, the interest which is payable on the interest date next following the transfer will be apportioned between the transferor and the transferee.[285]

The transferor is required to include in income, for the taxation year in which the transfer occurred, the portion of the accrued interest which has not been included in income for a preceding year. If the debt obligation had been acquired by the transferor between interest dates, then the previous holder would have been required to include accrued interest in income. If the transferee includes the total interest received in income, then he or she may deduct the portion accrued prior to the transfer.

An issue of a debt obligation (other than an income bond, an income debenture, small business development bond, and a small business bond) is deemed to be an assignment of a debt obligation if the debt obligation was issued with accrued interest and if it is reasonable to assume that the original lender paid an amount in respect of interest accruing before the issue date (referred to as the "unearned interest amount").[286] See the comment on interest at ¶3021. For comment on interest on borrowed money, see ¶3277.

[¶3355] Convention Expenses

The Act permits a deduction for expenditures incurred by a taxpayer in attending up to two conventions per year in connection with the taxpayer's business or profession.[287]

The deduction may be claimed under this provision only for expenses of attending a convention held by a business or professional organization. It should be noted that expenses are deductible only if paid in the year in which the convention is held and at a location that may reasonably be regarded as consistent with the territorial scope of the organization.

See page ii for explanation of footnotes.

[284] CCH ¶5132c; Sec. 20(5.1).
[285] CCH ¶5142; Sec. 20(14).
[286] CCH ¶5145; Sec. 20(14.1).
[287] CCH ¶5138; Sec. 20(10); Interp. Bul. IT-131R2.

Expenses incurred in attending business or professional conventions held outside the geographical limits of the sponsoring organization's ordinary area of activity are not deductible. The deductibility of conference expenses is limited by the meal and entertainment expense rules below.

Where a fee is paid or payable for an attendance at such event, and entitles the participant to food, beverages, or entertainment (other than incidental beverages and refreshments made available during the course of meetings or receptions, such as coffee, donuts, etc.), and a reasonable portion of the fee has not been allocated or identified by the organizer of such event as pertaining to the food, beverages, or entertainment, $50 for each day of the event shall be deemed to have been paid or payable in respect of the food, beverages, and entertainment. The $50 per day will be subject to the deduction limit described at ¶3219.[288] Where a portion of the convention fee is identified as the charge for food, beverages, or entertainment, the deduction limit described at ¶3219 will generally apply to such portion of the fee, rather than the $50 per day amount described above. Therefore, where such amounts would otherwise exceed $50 per day, it is advantageous to the convention-goer not to have the amount separately identified, so that the deduction limit will apply only to the lower amount of $50 per day.

Example:

    (1) Cathy attended a two-day convention in May 2011 that cost her $600. The organizer did not indicate what part of the $600 fee was for food and entertainment. Her convention expense is $500 ($600 - ($50 × 2)).

    (2) Cathy could also claim a meal and entertainment expense of $50 ($50 × 2 × 50%).

The deduction for convention expenses is available only to a taxpayer who carries on a business or profession. It cannot be claimed in computing income from an office or employment. If an employee is sent to a convention by his or her employer, the employee will normally be reimbursed by the employer for the expense, in which case the cost is an expense of the employer rather than of the employee. In this case the employee would not be required to include the reimbursement in income if it is *bona fide* and paid for the benefit of the employer and not as a benefit to the employee. See also ¶3225.

[¶3356] Exploration and Development Grants

The Act permits a taxpayer to deduct the amount of any assistance or benefit received as a deduction from or reimbursement of a tax other than the goods and services tax or royalty to the extent that:

    (a) the tax or royalty would have been deductible had the deduction or reimbursement not taken place; and

---

[288] CCH ¶9127b; Sec. 67.1(3).

(b) the deduction or reimbursement reduced the taxpayer's cumulative Canadian exploration expense, cumulative Canadian development expense, or cumulative Canadian oil and gas property expense.[289]

[¶3357] Annuity Contracts

The Act permits a deduction with respect to a payment received under an annuity contract where an amount has been included in income for a taxation year with respect to that annuity contract.[290] The amount of the deduction is to be determined by regulation. The amount deducted under this subsection will reduce the cost base of the annuity in a life annuity contract.[291]

[¶3358] Private Health Service Plan (PHSP) Premiums

Individuals whose net income from self-employment for the current or previous year is more than 50% of their total income or whose total income for the current or previous year from all other sources is $10,000 or less are allowed to deduct health and dental premiums made to a private health services plan (PHSP) if they meet the following conditions:

- they are actively engaged in their business on a regular and continuous basis, individually or as a partner;

- the premiums are paid to insure themselves, their spouse/common-law partner or any member of their household;

- all their qualified employees are entitled to PHSP coverage that is at least equivalent to their own coverage. Qualified employees are arm's length full-time employees who have three months' service with the individual's business. Temporary or seasonal workers are not qualified.[292]

The deduction for the individual and household members is limited to the amount that he or she would have to pay for his or her employee with the same number and type of household members, multiplied by the percentage or the employee premium paid for equivalent coverage.

Example:

It costs contractor John $1,000 to insure himself and his spouse. It cost him $800 for equivalent coverage for one of his employees and his spouse. He pays 50% of his employee's premiums. The deduction for John and his spouse is limited to $800 × 50%, which equals $400.

See page ii for explanation of footnotes.

[289] CCH ¶5128h; Sec. 20(1)(kk).

[290] CCH ¶5145f; Sec. 20(19).

[291] CCH ¶21,611; Sec. 148(9).

[292] CCH ¶5145zab–5145zad; Sec. 20.01.

If there is a period in the year when the self-employed individual has no employee or when his or her insurable arm's length employees represent less than 50% of all the insurable persons in his or her business, the deduction is limited to $1,500 for the self-employed individual and each household member over 18 years of age before the beginning of the year, and $750 for each household member not yet 18 at the beginning of the year.

[¶3359] Miscellaneous Deductions

Certain other deductions are permitted in computing income from a business or property and are discussed elsewhere in this book:

- Repayment of a loan or other indebtedness by a shareholder[293] — ¶3111.

- Combined income and capital — ¶3135.

- Reserve and debts[294] — ¶3417.

- Scientific research[295] — ¶3603.

- Patronage dividends[296] — ¶9159.

- Provincial mining taxes[297] — ¶3546.

- Resource allowances deductions until the year 2006[298] — ¶3534 *et seq.*

- Inventory adjustment[299] — ¶3486.

- Over-accrual of income on the disposition of a life insurance policy or an annuity contract[300] — ¶3051.

[¶3360] Charitable Donations — Corporations

[¶3361] Deduction Limit and Capital Gains Inclusion Rate

A corporation will be allowed to claim its charitable donations and any Crown gifts as a deduction, subject to certain limits, as well as the full amount of gifts of cultural property made to specific institutions and gifts of ecologically sensitive land.[301] The limit for charitable donations and Crown gifts is 75% of the corporation's income, plus, for gifts of capital property, (i) 25% of the taxable capital gain arising from the gift and taken into income in the year and (ii) 25% of the lesser of any recapture of capital cost allowance on the property included in the taxpayer's income in the year

---

See page ii for explanation of footnotes.

293 CCH ¶4665, ¶5081; Sec. 15(2), 20(1)(j).

294 CCH ¶5084–5105; Sec. 20(1)(l)–(p).

295 CCH ¶5900; Sec. 37.

296 CCH ¶5117, ¶20,301; Sec. 20(1)(u), 135.

297 CCH ¶5118, ¶5118a; Sec. 20(1)(v); Reg. 3900.

298 CCH ¶5119a, ¶8800, ¶8900, ¶9000, ¶9050; Sec. 20(1)(v.1), 65, 66, 66.1, 66.2.

299 CCH ¶5128f; Sec. 20(1)(ii).

300 CCH ¶5145g; Sec. 20(20).

301 CCH ¶15,750; Sec. 110.1; Interp. Bul. IT-110R3, IT-288R2, IT-297R2.

and the property's capital cost or proceeds of disposition. Cultural gifts to institutions and ecological gifts are not subject to these limits (see ¶3369 and ¶3370).

Corporations making an eligible medical gift (of medicines) after March 18, 2007, may claim a special additional deduction for the lesser of the cost of the medicines and 50% of the excess of the fair market value of the medicines over their cost (see ¶3374).

If the gift is a capital property, the resulting deemed disposition may give rise to a taxable capital gain. However, capital gains realized on gifts of certain capital property to a registered charity or other qualified donee may be eligible for an inclusion rate of zero.[302] This zero inclusion rate applies to capital gains deemed realized on the following gifts of property:

- a share of the capital stock of a mutual fund corporation;

- a unit of a mutual fund trust;

- an interest in a related segregated fund trust;

- a prescribed debt obligation;

- ecologically sensitive land (including a covenant, an easement, or, in the case of land in Quebec, a real servitude) donated to a qualified donee other than a private foundation; and

- a share, debt obligation, or right listed on a designated stock exchange.

For donations of publicly traded securities, this zero inclusion rate is extended to any capital gain realized on the exchange of shares of the capital stock of a corporation for those publicly listed securities donated when:

- at the time they were issued and at the time of disposition, the shares of the capital stock of a corporation included a condition allowing the holder to exchange them for the publicly traded securities;

- the publicly traded securities are the only consideration received on the exchange; and

- the publicly traded securities are donated within 30 days of the exchange.[303]

In cases where the exchanged property is a partnership interest (other than prescribed interests), the capital gain will generally be the lesser of:

- the capital gain otherwise determined; and

See page ii for explanation of footnotes.

[302] CCH ¶6007; Sec. 38(a.1).   [303] CCH ¶6007; Sec. 38(a.2).

- the amount, if any, by which the cost to the donor of the exchanged interests (plus any contributions to partnership capital by the donor) exceeds the ACB of those interests (determined without reference to distributions of partnership profits or capital).

If there is no advantage or benefit to be conferred as a result of the gift, the full amount of the capital gain is eligible for the zero inclusion rate. Otherwise, the zero inclusion rate only applies to that proportion of the gain that the "eligible amount" of the gift (see ¶8135) is of the taxpayer's total proceeds of disposition in respect of the property.

As a result of the 2011 Budget, the capital gains tax exemption on donations of publicly listed shares issued under a flow-through share (FTS) agreement after March 21, 2011 is only available to the extent that cumulative capital gains realized on their deemed dispositions exceed their original cost, determined without regard to the nil cost base otherwise applicable to FTS shares.[304] In effect, to the extent that a taxpayer has incurred costs to acquire shares issued under a FTS agreement after March 21, 2011, the taxpayer is required to pay tax at normal capital gains rates on capital gains realized on their dispositions whether the shares are sold for consideration, or are donated to a qualified donee.

More specifically, if a share of a particular class is issued to a taxpayer under a flow-through share agreement after March 21, 2011, the capital gains exemption on donations of publicly listed shares is available in respect of a subsequent donation by the taxpayer of a share of that class only to the extent that the capital gain on the disposition exceeds the "exemption threshold" at the time of the donation. The exemption threshold of a taxpayer in respect of a flow-through share class of property is generally a pool of the actual cost (without reference to the deemed cost of nil applicable to FTS) to the taxpayer of flow-through shares acquired after the later of March 22, 2011 and the taxpayer's "fresh-start date", less prior capital gains of the taxpayer from the disposition of the shares or identical properties.[305]

The fresh-start date of a taxpayer in respect of a flow-through share class of property is, except in the case of a partnership interest, the day that is the later of March 22, 2011, and the last day, if any, on which the taxpayer disposed of a property that is included in the flow-through share class of property and at the end of which the taxpayer held no such property.[306] In the case of a partnership interest, a taxpayer's fresh-start date at any particular time is the later of August 16, 2011 and the last day, if any, before the particular time on which the taxpayer held an interest in the partnership.

In general, if a taxpayer at any time sells all shares that the taxpayer owns that were either flow-through shares or other shares of the taxpayer of the same class as the flow-through shares, the calculation of the taxpayer's

---

See page ii for explanation of footnotes.

[304] Sec. 40(12).   [306] Sec. 54 "fresh start date".
[305] Sec. 54 "exemption threshold".

¶3361

exemption threshold starts again beginning from the next time that the taxpayer acquires such shares.

As well, the pool of the actual cost of FTSs is reduced to the extent that the taxpayer has realized capital gains, after the fresh-start date, from the disposition of the shares or identical shares. This does not include capitals gains on a transfer of shares or identical shares in a rollover transaction.

[¶3362] Institutions that May Receive Donations

To be deductible, the charitable donation must be made to one or more of the following institutions:

(1) registered charities and Canadian Amateur Athletic organizations;

(2) tax-exempt low-cost housing corporations for the elderly resident in Canada;

(3) Canadian municipalities or, for gifts made after May 8, 2000, a municipal or public body performing a function of government in Canada;

(4) United Nations agencies;

(5) prescribed foreign universities;[307]

(6) certain charitable organizations outside Canada to which the federal government has made a gift during the year or during the preceding year;

(7) the Government of Canada, a province, or a territory;[308] and

(8) a designated foreign organization where the organization has applied for designation on or after June 29, 2012.[309]

Generally, if a corporation has U.S. income, it can claim any gifts to U.S. charities that would be allowed on a U.S. return. It can claim the eligible amount of a U.S. gift up to 75% of the net U.S. income it reports on its Canadian return.

As a result of the 2012 Budget, certain foreign charitable organizations may apply for 24-month "qualified done" status where the foreign charitable organization has received a gift from the Government, and if they pursue activities that are

(i) related to either disaster relief or urgent humanitarian aid, or

(ii) in the national interest of Canada.

If a foreign charity already qualifies as a "qualified donee" under the pre-existing rules, the status will continue until the expiry of their current status. Such organizations may apply for designation on or after June 29, 2012.

See page ii for explanation of footnotes.

[307] Reg. 3503, Sch VIII.
[308] Inf. Cir. 84-3R6.
[309] Sec. 149.1(26)

[¶3363] Meaning of "Gift"

Traditional meaning

The accepted meaning of the term "gift" is that it is something parted with for no consideration. If the donor expects some benefit or enjoyment in return, it is not a true gift.[310]

Charitable contributions made as a form of advertising or to attract business from charities in the community may be regarded as business expenses deductible in full rather than as gifts subject to the 75% limitation (50% in 1996 and 20% for taxation years prior to 1996).

Where a taxpayer buys tickets for a fund-raising event involving an element of return in the form of entertainment, the taxpayer may deduct the amount paid minus the greater of the fair market value of the tickets and a reasonable part of the total cost of the event.[311]

Proposed split gifts rules

The traditional definition of gift disqualifies as a gift a transfer of property for partial consideration, notwithstanding that there is a clear gift element and donative intent, a result with which the government and the courts are not comfortable. Therefore, on December 20, 2002, the Department of Finance proposed amendments to the Act which would permit split gifts. Under these proposals, the last version of which was part of the draft legislation that was released on July 16, 2010, a corporation may make a gift after December 20, 2002 and receive consideration of a lesser value without wholly disqualifying the gift for deduction.[312] If the advantage received as partial consideration for, or in gratitude for the gift does not exceed 80% of the fair market value of the gift, the corporation will be allowed a deduction equal to the fair market value of the gift less the advantage received. If the advantage exceeds 80% of the fair market value of the gift, the gift will not necessarily be disqualified if the corporation can establish that the transfer of property was made with a donative intent.[313]

For more information on the new split gifts rules, see ¶8175.

[¶3364] Donations that Cannot Be Deducted

The following donations cannot be deducted:

(1) Donations to individuals.

(2) Court-ordered transfers of property to charities.

(3) Gifts of services (for example, donated time, labour).

See page ii for explanation of footnotes.

[310] No. 688, 60 DTC 130.
[311] Interp. Bul. IT-110R3.

[312] Sec. 248(30).
[313] Sec. 248(32).

(4) Gifts of promises (for example, gift certificates donated by the issuer, hotel accommodation).

(5) Pledges.

(6) The value of merchandise where its cost has been charged as an expense of a business.

(7) Amounts paid for card parties, bingos, and lotteries, even where such activities may be held for the benefit of charity. It is the CRA's view that participants in lotteries, while perhaps influenced in choosing which lottery they will participate in by the identity of the organizing charity, are primarily motivated by the chance to win the significant prizes that are offered. Therefore, in some cases, while there may be an element of donative intent, the amount of the advantage cannot be reasonably quantified. Accordingly, it continues to be the CRA's view, after the coming into force of the new split gifts rules (after December 20, 2002), that no part of the cost of a lottery ticket is a gift which may be receipted for income tax purposes.

(8) The payment of a basic fee for admission to an event or to a program.

(9) The payment of membership fees that convey the right to attend events, receive literature, receive services, or be eligible for entitlements of any material value that exceeds 80% of the value of the payment.

(10) A donation for which the fair market value of the advantage or consideration provided to the donor exceeds 80% of the value of the donation.

(11) A gift in kind for which the fair market value cannot be determined.

(12) Donations provided in exchange for advertising/sponsorship.

(13) Loans of property.

(14) Use of timeshare.

(15) The lease of premises.

(16) Donations subject to a direction by the corporation that they benefit a particular person or family or a non-qualified donee such as a foreign charity.[314]

[¶3365] Registered Charities and Canadian Amateur Athletic Organizations

In order to obtain a deduction for donations to these organizations, the organization must be devoted to the specified activity and no part of its income can be available for the personal benefit of any proprietor, member,

See page ii for explanation of footnotes.

[314] Interp. Bul. IT-110R3.

or shareholder. In addition, the organization must have registered with the CRA. Where there is any doubt as to whether a charity has registered, and the deductibility of the donation is a prime consideration, it would be advisable to discuss this matter with the organization's officials before contributing.

[¶3366] Returns, Records and Receipts

Registered charities and Canadian amateur athletic organizations are required to keep records and books of accounts. This includes a duplicate of each receipt for a donation received. The records must contain sufficient information to enable the donations to be verified.[315] Each receipt must contain a statement that it is an official receipt[316] for income tax purposes. Donations are deductible only if supported by official receipts.

[¶3367] Contents of Receipts

Each donation receipt issued by a registered charity and Canadian amateur athletic organization should indicate the organization's registration number.[317] It is a requirement for donations to foreign universities that they be receipted by serialized receipts showing the name and address of both the donor and the recipient, the place of issue of the receipt, the amount of the donation, the year in which the donation was received, and a signature authorized by the recipient.

[¶3368] Crown Gifts

Gifts to the Government of Canada, a Canadian province, or a territory are now subject to the same limits as any other charitable donations (see ¶3361). This means the amount deductible by a corporation in respect of Crown gifts is limited to 75% of the corporation's income, plus, for gifts of capital property, (i) 25% of the taxable capital gain arising from the gift and taken into income in the year and (ii) 25% of the lesser of any recapture of capital cost allowance on the property included in the taxpayer's income in the year and the property's capital cost or proceeds of disposition.[318]

If, in any one year, the amount in respect of Crown gifts is not deducted (e.g., the corporation's income is too low to absorb it), the corporation may carry forward the undeducted amount to the next five years. The amount of Crown gifts carried forward from a preceding taxation year must be claimed before claiming any gifts made in the current taxation year.

Heritage Canada Foundation, a registered charity, has been specially authorized to receive gifts in trust for the federal Crown, so gifts to Heritage Canada are now limited to 75% of the corporation's income for the year.

See page ii for explanation of footnotes.

[315] Reg. 3501.

[316] Reg. 3500.

[317] Reg. 3501.

[318] CCH ¶15,754; Sec. 110.1(1)(b); Interp. Bul. IT-297R2.

[¶3369] Gifts of Cultural Property to Institutions

A corporation is allowed a deduction for the fair market value of gifts (other than ecological gifts) of cultural property made to institutions designated under the *Cultural Property Export and Import Act*. The gift must be one that the Canadian Cultural Property Export Review Board has-determined meets all of the criteria in paragraphs 29(3)(*b*) and 29(3)(*c*) of the *Cultural Property Export and Import Act*. The deduction is to be made from income, if any, remaining after claiming deductions for charitable donations (see ¶3361) and gifts to the Crown (see ¶3368). Amounts not deducted in a given taxation year may be carried forward for up to five years.[319]

The fair market value of a gift of cultural property is the fair market value as determined by the Canadian Cultural Property Export Review Board, and such value is deemed to be the fair market value of the cultural property for two years from the date of determination.[320] A taxpayer may appeal the determination of the fair market value to the Tax Court of Canada. A taxpayer may be assessed beyond the normal assessment period for amounts arising from the redetermination of the fair market value of a cultural property.[321]

[¶3370] Gifts of Ecologically Sensitive Land

A corporation may deduct the fair market value of a gift of land that has been certified by the Minister of the Environment (or a person designated by that Minister) to be ecologically sensitive, the conservation and protection of which is important to the preservation of Canada's environmental heritage.[322]

Donations of ecologically sensitive land are not subject to the income limits for charitable gifts described in ¶3361. As well, any unused deduction may be carried forward up to five years. The deduction for a donation of ecologically sensitive land is made after deductions for charitable gifts (¶3361), Crown gifts (¶3368), and cultural gifts (¶3369).

Ecologically sensitive land, including a covenant, easement, or servitude must be certified by the Minister of the Environment or a person designated by the Minister. An Environment Canada Information Circular, "Ecological Gifts", sets out a list of certification authorities for various regions of the country, and outlines the national general criteria for ecologically sensitive land.

Land that qualifies must be under private title; therefore, a corporation cannot donate leased rights of use. If a parcel of land that is donated contains ecologically sensitive land, the entire parcel will be considered to be ecologically sensitive land.

See page ii for explanation of footnotes.

[319] CCH ¶15,756; Sec. 110.1(1)(*c*).
[320] CCH ¶18,365; Sec. 118.1(10).
[321] CCH ¶18,367; Sec. 118.1(11).
[322] CCH ¶15,756a; Sec. 110.1(1)(*d*).

The land must be donated to a registered charity approved by the Minister of the Environment or to one of its provinces or territories, or a "municipality" [or for gifts made after May 8, 2000, a municipal or public body performing a function of government in Canada]. The Minister of the Environment, or a person designated by that minister, has to certify that the land is important to the preservation of Canada's environmental heritage. The Minister will also determine the fair market value (FMV) of the gift.

For a gift of a covenant or an easement, or a real servitude (in Quebec), the FMV of the gift will be the greater of:

(1) the FMV of the gift otherwise determined; and

(2) the amount of the reduction of the land's FMV that resulted from the gift.[323]

Gifts of ecologically sensitive land to public charities were subject to only 50% of the capital gains tax up to May 2, 2006 and have been completely tax-free since then.[324] This special tax treatment does not apply to gifts to private foundations.

[¶3372] Granting of Options to Charities and Other Qualified Donees

If a corporation grants an option to acquire property to a charity (or other qualified donee) after March 21, 2011, no charitable donation deduction will be allowed until such time that the option is exercised so that the property is acquired by the donee. The deduction allowed at that time will be based on the amount by which the fair market value of the property at that particular time exceeds any consideration paid for the property. As a result of proposed split-gift rules (see ¶3363), a deduction will generally not be available if the consideration paid by the donee for the property exceeds 80% of its fair market value at the time of acquisition.

In effect, an option granted by a corporation to a qualified donee after March 21, 2011 is not deductible as a charitable donation unless the option is subsequently exercised (at a particular time) so that the property is disposed of to the qualified donee, and either

(1) 80% of the fair market value of the property at the particular time exceeds the total amount paid by the qualified donee to acquire the option and underlying property; or

(2) the CRA is satisfied that the granting of the option was made with a donative intent.[325]

At the time of exercise of the option, the corporation is deemed to have disposed of the property for proceeds equal to its fair market value. It is also entitled, in the year in which the option is exercised, to a charitable dona-

---

See page ii for explanation of footnotes.

[323] CCH ¶15,770a; Sec. 110.1(5).
[324] CCH ¶6007; Sec. 38(a.2).

[325] Sec. 110.1(10), 110.1(11).

tion deduction equal to that fair market value minus the total amount paid by the qualified donee to acquire the option and the underlying property. This deduction is permitted notwithstanding that the disposition of a property as a result of the exercise of the right of an option holder may not be a gift at law.[326]

If the option to acquire a corporation's property is subsequently disposed of (at a particular time) by a qualified donee, the corporation is deemed to have disposed of another property for proceeds equal to the lesser of the fair market value of any consideration received by the qualified donee for the option and the fair market value of the property that was the subject of the option. The permitted deduction for the taxation year in which the option was disposed of by the qualified donee is then equal to the proceeds of disposition (as calculated above) minus any consideration paid, if any, by the qualified donee to acquire the option.[327]

[¶3373] Returned Gifts

After March 21, 2011, a corporation cannot retain tax assistance in the form of a charitable donation deduction in respect of property transferred to a qualified donee if the property is returned. In such a case, no gift is recognized and if the returned property is identical to the transferred property, the returned property is deemed to be the transferred property. If the returned property is not identical, the corporation is deemed to have disposed of the transferred property at the time of its return for consideration that is the returned property. For returned property in excess of $50, an information return must be filed within 90 days of the return.

These measures address situations where an official donation receipt has been issued by a qualified donee in respect of the transfer of property by a corporation and an identical or substituted property has subsequently been returned to the corporation.[328] In such a case and irrespective of whether the transferred property was a gift, the corporation is deemed not to have disposed of the original property at the time of the transfer nor to have made a gift.[329] If the returned property is identical to the original property, the returned property is deemed to be the original property, such that a future disposition of the returned property will have the same result as if the property had never been disposed of to the qualified donee.[330] If the returned property is only substituted property, the original disposition is not recognized but the corporation is considered to have disposed of the original property for consideration that is the returned property, and at the time that the property is returned to the corporation.[331] If the fair market value of the returned property exceeds $50, the qualified donee who has already issued an official donation receipt at the time of original transfer of property is required to file an information return within 90 days of the

[326] Sec. 110.1(12).
[327] Sec. 110.1(13).
[328] Sec. 110.1(14).

[329] Sec. 110.1(15)(a).
[330] Sec. 110.1(15)(b).
[331] Sec. 110.1(15)(c).

subsequent return of that property or substituted property and send a copy to the corporation.[332] The CRA may reassess the return of income of any person to the extent that the reassessment can reasonably be regarded as relating to a return of property from a qualified donee.[333]

These new provisions apply to transfers of property made after March 21, 2011, except that an information return required that is filed before the day that is 90 days after August 16, 2011 is deemed to have been filed on time.

[¶3374] Donation of Medicines for the Developing World

After March 18, 2007, a corporation giving medicines from its inventory may claim a special additional deduction equal to the lesser of the cost of those medicines and 50% of the excess of their fair market value over their cost.[334] The special deduction is only available if the gift qualifies as an eligible medical gift. Any amount not claimed in the year the gift is made may be carried forward for up to five years. To be considered eligible, the gift must meet the following conditions:

(1) It must be made for charitable activities outside Canada.

(2) Beginning July 1, 2008, it must be donated at least six months prior to the expiration date of the medicine (prior to this change, medicines meeting the requirements of the *Food and Drugs Act* were eligible for this deduction, even if the expiry date of the medicines was imminent). In this regard the six-month period does not modify the World Health Organization Guidelines (the WHO Guidelines) requirement that donated drugs should generally have a shelf-life of 12 months when received by the recipient country.

(3) After October 2, 2007, it must meet the requirements of the *Food and Drugs Act*, and not be a food, cosmetic, medical device, natural health product, or veterinary drug (if made before October 3, 2007, the gift must be medicine).

(4) It must be part of the corporation's inventory.

(5) On or after July 1, 2008, it must be made to a registered charity that, in the opinion of the Minister of International Cooperation (or the Minister responsible for the Canadian International Development Agency (CIDA), if there is no such Minister) meets the conditions prescribed by regulation (gifts made prior to July 1, 2008 must be made to a registered charity that has received a disbursement under an international assistance development program of CIDA).[335]

See page ii for explanation of footnotes.

[332] Sec. 110.1(16).

[333] Sec. 110.1(17).

[334] CCH ¶15,752; Sec. 110.1(1)(a.1).

[335] CCH ¶15,770d, ¶15,770g; Sec. 110.1(8), 110.1(9).

The prescribed conditions a registered charity must meet include the registered charity acting in a manner consistent with the principles and objectives of the WHO Guidelines, having sufficient expertise in delivering medicines, as well as in designing, implementing, and monitoring an international development assistance program (or, if applicable, an international humanitarian assistance program), and delivering the medicine received outside Canada or transferring it to another registered charity that also meets the conditions set out in the regulation. The registered charity is also required to make an application to the Minister for a determination of whether the conditions have been met.[336]

[¶3375] Gifts of Capital Property

Rules are provided for determining the amount of the deduction for donations of capital property.[337] These rules apply to capital property donated as a charitable gift, a Crown gift, or an ecological gift. They also apply, in the case of a non-resident corporation, to a donation of Canadian real property to a prescribed donee. In the latter case, the donee must provide a satisfactory undertaking that it will hold the property for use in the public interest. To date, the only prescribed donee is the Nature Conservancy, a charity established in the United States. The following two additional conditions must be met for these rules to apply:

(a) the fair market value of the property must exceed its adjusted cost base to the corporation at the time of the gift; and

(b) the making of the gift must be proved by filing receipts containing prescribed information with the Minister.

The corporation is entitled to designate an amount not greater than the fair market value and not less than the adjusted cost base of the property as its proceeds of disposition and the amount of its gift. The amount that a corporation will want to designate will depend on its particular situation, since proceeds in excess of the tax basis of the property will result in capital gains and possibly recaptured depreciation. If depreciable property of a prescribed class is involved, these rules will permit the corporation to avoid a capital gain on the property but they will not reduce any recapture that would otherwise arise.

See page ii for explanation of footnotes.

[336] Reg. 3505(1).

[337] CCH ¶15,765; Sec. 110.1(3); Reg. 3504; Interp. Bul. IT-288R2.

Example:

> In 2011, a corporation resident in Canada with yearly income of $750,000 donates a building with a fair market value of $1,000,000 to a charity. The corporation paid $100,000 for the building in 1995 and has taken capital cost allowance of $12,000. The corporation may designate any amount between $100,000 and $1,000,000. The following examines two of the corporation's possible choices:

> > *Case 1:* The corporation designates the lowest possible amount of $100,000. It will have recapture (income) of $12,000 and will have a charitable donation of $100,000. Given the facts set out above, the corporation's taxable income will be $662,000 ($750,000 + $12,000 - $100,000).

> > *Case 2:* The corporation designates the highest possible amount of $1,000,000. It will have a capital gain of $900,000 and recapture of $12,000 and a charitable donation of $1,000,000. Assuming that the corporation will have a taxable capital gain equal to $1/2$ of the capital gain, the corporation will have net income of $1,212,000. Its charitable donations deduction for the year will be limited to 75% of its net income, plus for gifts of capital property, (i) 25% of the taxable capital gain arising from the gift and taken into income in the year and (ii) 25% of the lesser of any recapture of capital cost allowance on the property included in income in the year and the property's capital cost or proceeds of disposition less expenses incurred on the disposition of the property. Thus, in this example, if the corporation makes the donation in 2011 and designates $1,000,000 as proceeds of disposition and the amount of its gift, it will be entitled to deduct the whole amount of $1,000,000 in 2011. The deduction limit is equal to 75% of its income plus 25% of its capital gains and of the lesser of the recapture of the property's capital cost or proceeds of disposition, i.e., $1,024,500 (75% of $1,212,000 + 25% of $450,000 + 25% of $12,000).

[¶3376] Limitation on Deductibility

There are two rules respecting the deductibility of charitable donations and other gifts. First, the amount that has been deducted in a taxation year may not be carried forward to be deducted again in the future. Second, gifts are to be considered deducted in the order that they were made (i.e., deductions are on a "first-in, first-out" basis).[338]

[¶3377] Restrictions upon Acquisition of Control

Following an acquisition of control of a corporation, previously undeducted charitable gifts, Crown gifts, cultural property gifts, and ecological gifts cease to be deductible.[339] This is an anti-avoidance measure aimed at preventing trading in undeducted charitable and like gifts. It also extends to gifts made following an acquisition of control of a corporation if the gift was part of an arrangement that included the acquisition of control. These restrictions apply to gifts made after March 22, 2004.

See page ii for explanation of footnotes.

[338] CCH ¶15,756b; Sec. 110.1(1.1).   [339] CCH ¶15,758; Sec. 110.1(1.2).

[¶3380] Losses — Inter-Company Dividends

[¶3381] Net Capital Loss

Net capital losses for a year may be carried back three years and forward indefinitely to reduce capital gains arising in those years.[340] The term "net capital loss" is defined to mean, in general, the excess of allowable capital losses for the year over taxable capital gains for that year.[341] However, allowable capital losses which qualify as allowable business investment losses (ABILs) are treated as non-capital losses to the extent they are not used in full in the year they are realized. ABILs that have not been used within ten taxation years following the year in which they arise become net capital losses. The extension of the carryforward period of non-capital losses from 10 to 20 taxation years (see ¶3384) will not apply to ABILs; rather, ABILs that have not been used within ten taxation years after the year in which they arise will continue to be included in taxpayers' net capital losses.

The income for a year against which net capital losses may be deducted differs depending on whether the taxpayer is a corporation or an individual:

(1) *Corporations.* A net capital loss of a corporation may be deducted to the extent that the corporation's taxable capital gains exceed its allowable capital losses in the year the deduction is being applied.

(2) *Individuals.* A net capital loss of an individual for one year may be deducted against any excess of taxable capital gains over allowable capital losses in another year.

An adjustment to net capital loss amounts which are carried forward or backward is required where the capital gains inclusion rate differs between the year the loss arose and the year the loss is applied. The purpose of the adjustment is to ensure that the gross capital gain which could have been sheltered in the year that the net capital loss arose will equal the amount of gross capital gain which can be sheltered in the year that the net capital loss is applied. In effect, the benefit of using a net capital loss remains constant regardless of the inclusion rate in existence during the year the loss is applied. This result is accomplished by multiplying the net capital loss claimed by the fraction that is the inclusion rate for the year in which the loss is to be claimed, over the inclusion rate for the year in which the loss arose.[342]

See page ii for explanation of footnotes.

[340] CCH ¶16,004, ¶16,200; Sec. 111(1)(b), 111(8) "net capital loss"; Interp. Bul. IT-232R3.

[341] CCH ¶16,200; Sec. 111(8) "net capital loss".

[342] CCH ¶16,090; Sec. 111(1.1).

Example:

> In 2001, Elizabeth sold two different securities resulting in a taxable capital gain of $300 ($^1/_2$ × $600) and an allowable capital loss of $500 ($^1/_2$ × $1,000). After applying her allowable capital loss against her taxable capital gain, Elizabeth has a net capital loss of $200 ($500 - $300).
>
> While she cannot deduct the $200 from other sources of income in 2001, she can apply the loss against her taxable capital gains in any of the three preceding years, or in any future year.
>
> If Elizabeth carries back this loss to apply against a taxable capital gain of $1,000 in 1999, she will calculate her adjustment factor as follows:
>
> $$\frac{\text{Inclusion rate for year to which loss is applied (75\%)}}{\text{Inclusion rate for originating year (50\%)}} = 150\%$$

To determine the net capital loss she can carry back to 1999, Elizabeth will multiply this adjustment factor by the net capital loss for 2001:

$$150\% \times \$200 = \$300$$

Elizabeth is therefore entitled to apply $300 against her 1999 taxable capital gain.

[¶3384] Non-Capital Loss (Business Loss)

Non-capital losses may be carried back three years and forward 20 years (ten years for losses arising in taxation years ending after March 22, 2004 and before 2006 and seven years for losses arising in taxation years ending before March 23, 2004) and deducted against income from any source.[343] If the taxpayer is a corporation, its non-capital loss will be:[344]

(i) losses for the year from business and property plus allowable business investment losses;

plus

(ii) an amount deducted as a net capital loss carryover from another taxation year;

plus

(iii) taxable dividends received from taxable Canadian corporations or from Canadian resident corporations which it controls (except NROs) to the extent deductible as an inter-corporate dividend;

plus

(iv) any amount deductible in respect of dividends received from a foreign affiliate;

plus

(v) amounts deductible in respect of certain exempt payments;

See page ii for explanation of footnotes.

[343] CCH ¶16,003; Sec. 111(1)(a).   [344] CCH ¶16,200; Sec. 111(8) "non-capital loss".

¶3384

plus

(vi) any amount voluntarily added to taxable income to take full advantage of foreign tax credits;

plus

(vii) the unused part of the amount deductible as Part VI.1 tax by a corporation (2.5 times its Part VI.1 taxes payable in respect of dividends paid on taxable preferred shares);

minus

(viii) income for the year from all sources;

(ix) any farm loss for the year;

(x) all amounts deducted as fuel tax rebate loss abatement; and

(xi) the reductions to the taxpayer's non-capital loss as required under the debt forgiveness rules (see ¶3456).

Where the taxpayer is not a corporation, the non-capital loss for a year is *the aggregate of* the taxpayer's losses from an office, employment, business, or property, the taxpayer's allowable business investment loss for the year, any amount deductible in respect of employee stock options benefits, in respect of grubstaker's shares, in respect of shares received out of a deferred profit sharing plan, in respect of certain social assistance payments, income exempt under treaty, worker's compensation and income from employment with a prescribed international organization or in respect of relocation loans, or with respect to certain financial assistance payments received for tuition for adult basic education, an amount *deducted* as a capital gains deduction, an amount deducted as a net capital loss carryover from another taxation year, and an amount deducted when employee option securities (or proceeds of disposition of such securities) are donated to a qualifying charity *minus* the sum of the taxpayer's income from taxable dividends and foreign affiliate dividends and the taxpayer's farm loss.

A taxpayer is not entitled to carry forward losses that it incurred prior to becoming a resident of Canada. However, losses for the entire year in which a taxpayer becomes a resident are deductible.[345]

[¶3387] Loss from Business or Property

A taxpayer's "loss of business or property" (except in the case of hobby-farming) is defined as the amount of loss for the taxation year from that source computed by applying the rules for computing income from that source.[346]

See page ii for explanation of footnotes.

[345] Oceanspan Carriers Ltd., 87 DTC 5102. [346] CCH ¶4006, ¶16,003; Sec. 9(2), 111(1); Interp. Bul. IT-232R3.

The definition of "loss from business or property" requires that the loss be computed by applying the provisions of the Act respecting the computation of income without consideration of credits permitted for charitable donations, medical expenses, or personal exemptions. Furthermore, in determining the amount of a loss that may be deducted from a taxpayer's income in a particular year, no account will be taken of a credit to which the taxpayer might be entitled in respect of foreign taxes paid.

In the case of bankruptcy, special provisions are made in the Act not permitting the loss to be carried forward after the termination of a bankruptcy. However, a credit in respect of foreign business taxes paid may be carried forward. See ¶8570.

[¶3390] Limitation of Loss where Control or Type of Business Changes

To prevent taxpayers from dealing in corporations having net capital losses or unrealized capital losses, the corporation's taxation year is deemed to have ended immediately before the change of control.[347] Accordingly, any net capital loss for preceding years may not be deducted in computing income for any subsequent year.

The foregoing does not apply where control is acquired of a corporation that is a foreign affiliate of a taxpayer resident in Canada and that did not carry on business in Canada at any time in its last taxation year commencing before that time.[348] Furthermore, a corporation's net capital loss for a taxation year beginning after a change of control may not be carried back to taxation years commencing before the change of control.

In order to prevent trading in corporations having unrealized capital losses, if the adjusted cost base of any non-depreciable capital property at the time control is acquired exceeds its fair market value, the adjusted cost base of that property is thereupon reduced to its fair market value.[349] Depreciable property whose fair market value is less than its undepreciated capital cost will be subject to a similar rule.[350] The amount by which the adjusted cost base is reduced is deemed to be a capital loss for the year ended immediately before the acquisition of control from the disposition of the property.

As a result of amendments applicable generally after April 26, 1995, the rules curtailing the transferability of losses between "affiliated" parties were simplified. In general, the rules continue to deny the losses on transfer but retain the property characteristics in the transferor's hands for continued amortization (if any) or eventual loss treatment. Persons are considered to be affiliated with themselves; control means *de facto* control; an affiliated group means a group of persons each member of which is affiliated with

---

See page ii for explanation of footnotes.

[347] CCH ¶28,333a; Sec. 249(4).   [349] CCH ¶7644; Sec. 53(2)(b.2).
[348] CCH ¶16,140; Sec. 111(4).   [350] CCH ¶16,150; Sec. 111(5.1).

¶3390

every other member; and merged corporations continue their prior affiliations with the new corporation shareholders.

[¶3393] Other Restrictions on Losses and Their Use

Several other specific restrictions are placed on a taxpayer as follows:

(1) A corporation cannot realize a loss by selling property to a parent or any corporation controlled by its parent.[351]

(2) Subject to certain exceptions, no loss can be realized if the taxpayer (whether an individual or corporation) or an "affiliated person" [352] acquires identical property within 30 days before or after a disposition of the original property and still owns the substituted property 30 days after the original disposition. This is known as a "superficial loss".[353] See also ¶5180.

(3) A taxpayer who disposes of an asset to a person with whom the taxpayer was not dealing at arm's length for no proceeds, or for proceeds less than its fair market value, or to any person by *inter vivos* gift, is deemed to have received proceeds equal to its fair market value.[354]

(4) No allowable loss can result from the disposition of a debt or other right to receive an amount, unless the debt or right was acquired for the purpose of gaining or producing income from business or property or as consideration for an arm's length disposition of capital property.[355] See ¶3456.

(5) No allowable loss may be claimed on the disposition of personal-use property (see ¶5315) other than listed personal property (see ¶5300). Losses on listed personal property are allowable only to the extent of gains from such property.[356] However, this provision does not prevent the deduction of a capital loss on the disposition of personal-use property or arm's length debt in certain circumstances.

(6) No deduction is permitted for a loss on an interest in a corporation, partnership, or trust, to the extent that such loss is attributable to a loss of the corporation, partnership, or trust in personal-use property.[357]

(7) The amount of any prescribed assistance received in respect of the acquisition of shares in a prescribed venture capital corporation or a prescribed labour-sponsored venture capital corporation will reduce any loss realized on their disposition.[358]

(8) No allowable capital loss may arise on a disposition of property to a deferred profit sharing plan (DPSP), an employees profit sharing plan, a

---

See page ii for explanation of footnotes.

[351] CCH ¶6459; Sec. 40(3.3).

[352] CCH ¶28,371a–28,371f; Sec. 251.1.

[353] CCH ¶6434, ¶6439, ¶7621–7623, ¶7850; Sec. 40(2)(g), 40(2)(h), 53(1)(f)–(f.2), 54 "superficial loss".

[354] CCH ¶9146; Sec. 69(1)(b).

[355] CCH ¶6434, ¶7852; Sec. 40(2)(g), 54 "proceeds of disposition".

[356] CCH ¶6434, ¶6510; Sec. 40(2)(g), 41(2).

[357] CCH ¶6960; Sec. 46(4).

[358] CCH ¶6439b; Sec. 40(2)(i).

registered retirement income fund, or a registered retirement savings plan (RRSP).[359]

(9) No allowable capital loss may arise on a transfer by a shareholder to a controlled corporation.[360]

(10) No allowable capital loss may arise on the disposition of property to a partnership by a majority interest partner.[361]

(11) The losses of a partnership allocated to a limited partner in the partner's taxation year will be deductible by the partner only to the extent of the partner's at-risk amount as at the end of the fiscal period of the partnership ending in that year.[362]

Applicable generally after April 26, 1995, the rules curtailing the transferability of losses between "affiliated" parties were simplified. In general, the rules continue to deny the losses on transfer but retain the property characteristics in the transferor's hands for continued amortization (if any) or eventual loss treatment. Persons are considered to be affiliated with themselves; control means *de facto* control; an affiliated group means a group of persons each member of which is affiliated with every other member; and merged corporations continue their prior affiliations with the new corporation shareholders.

[¶3396] Losses of Hobby-Farmers — Restricted Farm Loss

The Act restricts a loss deductible in any one year by a taxpayer whose chief source of income for a taxation year is neither farming nor a combination of farming and some other source of income (i.e., "hobby-farmer").[363] In such cases, the loss deductible is the lesser of:

(a) the amount by which the taxpayer's total losses for the year from all farming businesses computed without reference to any amounts expended for scientific research[364] exceeds the total income from all such business; and

(b) $2,500 plus the lesser of:

(i) ½ the amount by which the total farming losses exceeds $2,500, and

(ii) $6,250,

for a maximum deduction of $8,750.

Any loss in excess of the actual amount deducted is a "restricted farm loss". See also ¶3573 for comment on farming business.

See page ii for explanation of footnotes.

[359] CCH ¶6434; Sec. 40(2)(g).

[360] CCH ¶10,580a; Sec. 85(4).

[361] CCH ¶12,191; Sec. 97(3).

[362] CCH ¶12,149ac; Sec. 96(2.1).

[363] CCH ¶5660, ¶7630, ¶16,025; Sec. 31, 53(1)(i), 111(1)(c); Interp. Bul. IT-322R.

[364] CCH ¶5900; Sec. 37; Interp. Bul. IT-232R3.

The carryforward of business loss provisions are extended to "restricted farm losses". Such a loss may be carried back three years or forward 20 years (ten years for losses arising in taxation years ending after March 22, 2004 and before 2006 and seven years for losses arising in taxation years ending before March 23, 2004) and deducted only to the extent of the taxpayer's income from farming.

Where a taxpayer disposes of a farm and has losses which have not been deducted as incurred or as restricted farm losses, they may be applied, within certain limits, to increase the adjusted cost base of the farm property. Any loss so applied is deemed not to be a loss for purposes of the loss carryover provisions.[365] Furthermore, any such loss is not available in later years to reduce income from other farming businesses.[366]

[¶3399] Net Capital Loss in Year of Death

The total net capital losses for all taxation years that can be deducted in the year of death and the immediately preceding year from sources of income other than capital gains will be reduced to the extent of the total of all capital gains exemptions that had been claimed by the deceased individual.

The amount that may be deducted in respect of net capital losses in the year of death and the immediately preceding year must be adjusted to ensure the offset of a capital loss against an equal amount of capital gain as a result of increased inclusion rates. However, for net capital losses deducted against other income, no adjustment need be made. Therefore, the excess of the total amount of unadjusted net capital losses claimed for deduction over the amount of such unadjusted losses that were used to offset the net taxable capital gains for the year will be deductible against other income in the year of death or the preceding year.[367]

[¶3402] Amended Return for Succeeding Year's Loss

A taxpayer who is filing a return for a year in which the taxpayer has taxable income does not know whether he or she will have a loss in the next succeeding year. Consequently, if a taxpayer sustains a loss in such succeeding year, he or she is entitled to amend the return by filing with the Minister a prescribed form on or before the due date for filing the return of income for the taxation year from which the carryback is made.

Where an individual is not required to file a return for the latter taxation year because no tax is payable for such year, the Act requires the prescribed form claiming the carryback to be filed on or before the return-due date which would have been applicable if tax were payable for that year.[368]

See page ii for explanation of footnotes.

[365] CCH ¶7630; Sec. 53(1)(i).
[366] CCH ¶16,180; Sec. 111(6).

[367] CCH ¶16,100; Sec. 111(2).
[368] CCH ¶22,255; Sec. 152(6).

[¶3405] Inter-Company Dividends — Deductibility

In general terms, where a corporation's income has been subject to Canadian tax, after-tax profits will not be taxed again when they are distributed to corporate shareholders by way of dividend. However, there are exceptions to this general rule in certain cases where the dividend is paid on a "term preferred share", where certain defined financial corporations provide a guarantee or security with respect to any share, or where shareholder values are secured.[369]

While a corporation may deduct the amount of a particular dividend in computing taxable income, the effect of so doing is merely to exclude the dividend from tax under Part I. Part IV of the Act may then apply to impose a refundable tax of 25% on the dividend.[370] It should also be noted that the above rules apply only to dividends received by resident corporations. Non-residents are subject to Part XIII tax on dividends paid to them by residents of Canada.[371]

Where a corporation receives a taxable dividend from a corporation resident in Canada, the amount of the dividend is to be included in computing the recipient corporation's income.[372] The amount of the dividend may be deducted in computing the recipient's taxable income[373] if one of two conditions are met:

(1) The taxpayer corporation must be a "taxable Canadian corporation".[374] This means a corporation that is resident in Canada, that was either incorporated in Canada or has been resident here continuously since June 18, 1971, and that is not exempt from Part I tax.

(2) The payor corporation must be resident in Canada and be controlled by the corporation receiving the dividend, but must not be a non-resident owned investment corporation or a corporation exempt from tax under Part I.

It will be noted that the deduction for intercorporate dividends applies only to "taxable dividends". This term is defined generally to mean a dividend that is not payable out of the paying corporation's tax-paid undistributed surplus, 1971 capital surplus, or capital dividend account.[375]

[¶3408] Losses in Share Transactions

Stop-loss rules may reduce the amount of loss that a shareholder incurs on the disposition of a share, generally by the amount of dividends previously received on the share. In general terms, the stop-loss rules do not apply [to a "qualified dividend" defined below after March 21, 2011] where the selling

---

[369] CCH ¶16,345–16,367; Sec. 112(2.1), 112(2.2), 112(2.4).
[370] CCH ¶24,350; Sec. 186.
[371] CCH ¶26,105; Sec. 212(2).
[372] CCH ¶10,003; Sec. 82(1)(a).
[373] CCH ¶16,301; Sec. 112(1).
[374] CCH ¶11,206; Sec. 89(1) "taxable Canadian corporation".
[375] CCH ¶11,209; Sec. 89(1) "taxable dividend".

shareholder owned the share throughout the 365-day period immediately prior to its disposition and the shareholder and non-arm's length persons did not own more than 5% of the issued shares of any class in the corporation at the time the relevant dividends were received.[376] [In order for the above exception to the stop-loss rules to apply after March 21, 2011, a dividend must not only meet the above 365-day ownership test and 5% ownership test, it must also be a "qualified dividend". In simple terms, qualified dividends are dividends received on a share other than those deemed to have been received by a corporation upon a redemption of shares if the dividends are received, whether directly or indirectly through a partnership or trust, from another corporation, unless, at the time the divided is deemed paid and received, the recipient corporation is a private corporation other than a financial institution and the payor is another private corporation.][377] Where both of these conditions are not met, a shareholder's loss on the disposition of a share is generally reduced as follows:

(i) if the shareholder is an individual (other than a trust) and the corporation is a taxable Canadian corporation, the loss is reduced by the amount of all dividends (except a capital gains dividend from a mutual fund corporation) received on the shares;

(ii) if the shareholder is a trust, the loss is reduced to the extent that dividends have been received by the trust on the share or have been allocated to a beneficiary;

(iii) if the shareholder is a partnership, the loss is reduced by the total of any dividend, other than a capital gains dividend from a mutual fund corporation, received by the partnership on the shares (i.e., the reduction of the loss takes place at the partnership level, rather than at the partner level); and

(iv) if the shareholder is a corporation, the loss is reduced by the amount of all non-taxable dividends plus the amount of all taxable dividends to the extent that the amount thereof was deductible in computing the corporation's taxable income or taxable income earned in Canada for any taxation year by reason of the corporation being a non-resident corporation or a life insurer.

[¶3411] Order of Deductions

Where an individual is entitled to deduct amounts in computing taxable income under more than one section of the Act, the Act provides that the order in which these deductions are to be taken is as follows:[378]

See page ii for explanation of footnotes.

[376] CCH ¶16,380–16,432, ¶16,470; Sec. 112(3)–(4.3), 112(7); Interp. Bul. IT-328R3.

[377] Sec. 112(6.1).

[378] CCH ¶16,235; Sec. 111.1.

(1) deductions such as employee stock options and home relocation loans;[379]

(2) deductions for certain lump-sum payments;[380]

(3) deductible losses;[381]

(4) deductions for the capital gains exemption;[382] and

(5) deduction of amounts in respect of northern allowance.[383]

It should be noted that the deductions which cannot be carried over to another taxation year and cannot be shared with any other taxpayer are the first deductions that must be taken.

[¶3414] Reserves, Bad and Doubtful Debts

[¶3417] Amounts Included in Income and Reserves — Goods and Services

Amounts *received* in the taxation year that are not earned in that year because they are subject to the supplying of future services or goods, or the making of refunds, are to be included in computing business income.[384]

Inasmuch as receivables are to be included in a taxpayer's income, the Act makes provision for the deduction of certain reserves.[385] The amount which may be deducted as a reserve must be reasonable. A reserve of $4,500 in respect of deferred profit of $21,000 on property sold and secured by a mortgage was held to be reasonable in the circumstances.[386] Similarly, the total profit content of a mortgage, allowed as a reserve, was held to be the maximum amount allowable as a reserve under the Act.[387]

[¶3420] Amounts Receivable — Sale of Land

Where property is sold, an amount is required to be included in the computation of a taxpayer's income from a business at the time that the amount becomes "receivable by the taxpayer" (unless the taxpayer is permitted to use the "cash basis" of reporting). Since the amount that becomes receivable in respect of property sold is the sale price, the taxable event in respect of the sale of property can be stated as occurring on the date that the sale price becomes receivable to the vendor. The sale price of any property sold is brought into account for income tax purposes when the vendor has an absolute but not necessarily immediate right to be paid. As long as a "condition precedent" remains unsatisfied, a vendor does not have an absolute right to be paid. A condition precedent is an event (beyond the

---

See page ii for explanation of footnotes.

[379] CCH ¶15,015; Sec. 110.
[380] CCH ¶15,877; Sec. 110.2.
[381] CCH ¶16,003; Sec. 111(1).
[382] CCH ¶15,976, ¶15,976a, ¶15,976b; Sec. 110.6.
[383] CCH ¶15,999g; Sec. 110.7(1).

[384] CCH ¶4251, ¶4256, ¶4375; Sec. 12(1)(a), 12(1)(b), 12(1)(s); Interp. Bul. IT-152R3, IT-154R.
[385] CCH ¶5085; Sec. 20(1)(m).
[386] Aden Building Enterprises, 60 DTC 31.
[387] Felgor Investments, 60 DTC 350.

direct control of the vendor) that suspends completion of the contract until the condition is met or waived and that could cancel the contract *ab initio* if it is not met or waived.

Many agreements involving the sale of real property propose a "closing date" for the completion of the sale. This is normally the date that beneficial ownership is intended to pass from the vendor to the purchaser and the time that the vendor is entitled to the sale price, but the facts of a particular situation must support that the expressed intent was in fact carried out. In cases where the "closing date" is to occur "on or before" a specified date, the actual date of closing must be determined by the particular facts such as:

(a) the date funds required to be paid on closing were actually paid;

(b) the date that the title was conveyed;

(c) the date of adjustments of insurance premiums, rentals, mortgage interest, realty taxes, etc.; and

(d) the date of possession by the purchaser.[388]

When the total sale price has been included and part of the sale price or instalments is not due until after the end of the taxation year, the deduction of a reserve for the profit portion of the instalments is permitted. See ¶3450.

For a discussion of real estate transactions, see ¶5110 *et seq.*

[¶3423] Reserves for Undelivered Goods

Where the taxpayer, in computing business income, has included amounts received in the taxation year or a previous taxation year for goods not delivered by the end of the taxation year, the taxpayer may deduct a reasonable amount as a reserve in respect of the goods, since it is reasonably anticipated that they will have to be delivered after the end of the year.[389]

It is common in the construction industry for the owner of property not to pay the full amount owing for particular work until the owner receives a certificate from the architect or engineer that the work has been satisfactorily performed.

It has been held that if obtaining this certificate is a condition precedent to the contractor's receiving payment, the amount is not "receivable" until the certificate is issued.[390] On the other hand, once the certificate is issued, the amount is receivable whether the contractor learns of the issue at once or some time later.

See page ii for explanation of footnotes.

[388] Interp. Bul. IT-170R.

[389] CCH ¶4335, ¶5085; Sec. 12(1)(e), 20(1)(m).

[390] John Colford Contracting Co. Ltd., 62 DTC 1338.

Payment as a result of the certificate may in fact be delayed, but as long as the contractor has a right to payment not dependent on the happening of a condition, the amount is receivable and must be included in income.

Where the goods are articles of food and drink, the amount deducted as a reserve must not exceed the amounts included in income for that year in respect of food or drink to be delivered after the year end.[391]

No deduction under this provision may be claimed by taxpayers who keep their accounts on a cash basis.[392] A chain food store company which gave trading stamps to its customers along with purchased merchandise was found to be entitled to deduct a reasonable amount as a reserve in respect of goods that it reasonably anticipated would have to be delivered upon redemption of the stamps after the end of the year.[393]

[¶3426] Reserves for Unrendered Services

Where the taxpayer has included in business income amounts received in the taxation year or a previous taxation year for services not rendered by the end of the taxation year, the taxpayer may deduct a reasonable amount as a reserve in respect of services that it is reasonably anticipated will have to be rendered after the end of the year.[394]

Where the unrendered service is transportation, this deduction must not exceed the amount included in computing income in respect of transportation to be provided after the end of the year.[395] Thus "ticket reserves" of companies at the end of a taxation year may not exceed the dollar amount of unredeemed tickets issued during the year and credited to that year's income.

No deductions under this provision may be claimed by taxpayers who keep their accounts on a cash basis.[396]

[¶3429] Reserve for Guarantees

A taxpayer is permitted to deduct a reasonable amount as a reserve for certain arm's length credit risks such as guarantees.[397] Where a taxpayer has taken such a reserve in a particular taxation year, an inclusion in income must be made in the following year equal to the amount previously taken as such a reserve.[398] Accordingly, the taxpayer will eventually deduct the amount as a cost of doing business (when paid in settlement of the guarantee or credit risk) or return it into income.

See page ii for explanation of footnotes.

[391] CCH ¶4335, ¶5133; Sec. 12(1)(e), 20(6).
[392] CCH ¶5134; Sec. 20(7).
[393] Dominion Stores Ltd., 66 DTC 5111.
[394] CCH ¶4335, ¶5085; Sec. 12(1)(e), 20(1)(m).

[395] CCH ¶4335, ¶5133; Sec. 12(1)(e), 20(6).
[396] CCH ¶5134; Sec. 20(7).
[397] CCH ¶5084h; Sec. 20(1)(l.1).
[398] CCH ¶4332; Sec. 12(1)(d.1).

[¶3432] Indemnities and Warranties

No deduction is permissible as a reserve in respect of indemnities or warranties (except for extended warranties granted by the taxpayer to an arm's length person relating to property manufactured by the taxpayer).[399] The amount of the reserve is the lesser of:

(a) a reasonable amount in respect of goods or services that it is reasonably anticipated will have to be delivered or rendered after the end of the year under the extended warranty; and

(b) insurance premiums paid or payable to an insurer who carries on business in Canada to insure against the taxpayer's liability under the extended warranty to the extent those premiums relate to a period after the end of the year.

[¶3438] Repayment of Amount Previously Included in Income

A deduction is provided, as opposed to a reserve which is brought back into income later, when a taxpayer repays an amount which was brought into income in respect of future goods or services. This deduction would apply, for example, where a taxpayer received a payment for services or goods to be delivered in the future, but was required to repay all or a portion of this amount because the services or goods were not in fact delivered.[400]

[¶3441] Policy Reserves Deductible by Insurance Companies

An insurance corporation may, in computing its income from its insurance business (other than life insurance) for a taxation year, deduct as policy reserves such amounts as have been prescribed.

[¶3444] Reserves for Unexpired Rent

A taxpayer may deduct a reasonable amount as a reserve in respect of periods for which payment for the possession or use of land or chattels has been received in advance. This amount represents an expenditure that is not properly attributable to the year's business activity.[401]

[¶3447] Reserves for Undischarged Obligations

Provided that the taxpayer has brought into income account amounts received in respect of undischarged obligations, the taxpayer may deduct a reasonable amount as a reserve in respect of repayments reasonably anticipated to be due at the end of the taxation year under an arrangement or understanding that an amount received is repayable in whole or in part on the return or resale to the taxpayer of articles in or by means of which goods,

---

See page ii for explanation of footnotes.

[399] CCH ¶5085a, ¶5134; Sec. 20(1)(m.1), 20(7); Mister Muffler Ltd., 74 DTC 6615, Amesbury Distributors Ltd., 85 DTC 5076.

[400] CCH ¶5085b; Sec. 20(1)(m.2).

[401] CCH ¶5085; Sec. 20(1)(m); Interp. Bul. IT-154R.

such as returnable containers, were delivered to a customer.[402] This reserve does not apply in respect of bottle containers.

[¶3450] Reserves for Amounts Receivable — Land

Where an amount has been included in computing a taxpayer's income in respect of the sale of land and any part of the proceeds is not due until after the end of the taxation year, a deduction is permitted in computing the taxpayer's income of a reasonable amount as a reserve in respect of that part of the amount included in income that can reasonably be regarded as a portion of the profit from the sale.

"Reasonable" in this context is not defined, nor is any method prescribed for the computation of the amount of the reserve. However, two different methods have evolved for the determination of the reserve, depending upon whether or not a mortgage was assumed by the taxpayer on the purchase of the land.

Where the taxpayer assumes a mortgage on the purchase of land and the taxpayer's obligations are taken over by the purchaser, the amount *receivable* is changed, thus affecting the basis of the calculation of the amount of the reserve.[403]

However, where at the end of the year or at any time in the immediately following year a taxpayer was not resident in Canada and did not carry on a business in Canada or was exempt from tax, no reserve is allowed. The purpose of this provision is to prevent a taxpayer from transferring income from a year in which the taxpayer would be taxable to a year in which no tax is payable by virtue of the taxpayer's exempt status or by virtue of being a non-resident not subject to tax. This prohibition would not apply to a Canadian resident taxpayer who subsequently ceased to be a resident of Canada but continued to carry on business in Canada. The claiming of the reserve for a taxation year where the sale occurred more than 36 months before the end of that taxation year is prohibited. Thus, unless taxation years of less than 12 months are involved, a reserve may be claimed in the year of sale and the two subsequent years and the balance, if any, of the amount receivable will be brought into income no later than the third year subsequent to the year of sale. [Furthermore, for sales after December 20, 2002, the reserve will be denied to a taxpayer if the purchaser is a corporation controlled by the taxpayer, or is a partnership of which the taxpayer is a majority interest partner. This amendment, first announced on December 20, 2002, is reprised in the revised technical proposals that were released on July 16, 2010. It is not enacted yet.][404]

A company received debentures for the sale of its land. The debentures were payable in instalments commencing six years later. No reserve could be

---

[402] CCH ¶5085; Sec. 20(1)(*m*); Interp. Bul. IT-154R. [404] CCH ¶5136; Sec. 20(8).
[403] CCH ¶5086, ¶5136; Sec. 20(1)(*n*), 20(8).

¶3450

deducted in respect of the instalments, since the debentures themselves were the price of the land and the instalments were on account of the principal of the debentures, rather than the sale price.[405]

The determination of the amount of the reserve does not necessarily require the application of any precise and inflexible formula, but is to be made on a case-by-case basis.[406]

[¶3451] Reserve for Debt Forgiveness

In general, the "debt forgiveness rules" [407] apply where a debtor's obligation is settled for an amount which is less than the lesser of the principal amount of the obligation and the amount for which it was issued. The rules apply to commercial obligations and general debt obligations incurred in the course of earning business or property income. Where the rules apply, the forgiven amount of the obligation reduces certain tax attributes or tax accounts of the debtor, such as a loss carryforward, resource pool, or the tax cost of property. If, after the application of these rules there is a remaining forgiven amount, $1/2$ of the remainder is included in the debtor's income. In such a case, a reserve may be available.[408] For individuals, other than trusts, a reserve is allowed to the extent the forgiven amount included in income exceeds 20% of the debtor's other income in excess of $40,000. In other words, it ensures that the forgiven amount is included in income in any one year, only to the extent of 20% of the debtor's other income in excess of $40,000. The reserve, for corporations, effectively allows a taxpayer to spread out the debt forgiveness income over five years, including at least 20% each year. The reserve allowed for the year of forgiveness is $4/5$ of the income inclusion. That amount is then added back into income in the next year and in Year Two a reserve up to $3/5$ of the original income inclusion can be claimed. That amount is added back into income in Year 3 and the pattern continues through Year 5, after which no reserve remains. Finally, a deduction is given for certain insolvent corporations, which effectively limits the debt forgiveness income inclusion to twice the fair market value of the corporation's net assets at the end of the year.

[¶3453] Bad Debts and Reserves for Doubtful Debts

A taxpayer may deduct a reasonable amount as a reserve for doubtful debts.[409] Provision is made for that inclusion in income of the amount which the taxpayer deducted as a reserve for doubtful debts in the previous year.[410] When the debt is no longer doubtful but is established to be bad, it may then be deductible.[411] However, if such a debt is subsequently recovered, the amount recovered will ordinarily be included in the taxpayer's income in the year of recovery.

See page ii for explanation of footnotes.

[405] Avril Holdings Ltd., 70 DTC 6366.
[406] The Ennisclare Corporation, 84 DTC 6262.
[407] CCH ¶9850, ¶9867, ¶9868, ¶9869, ¶9870; Sec. 80, 80.01, 80.02, 80.03, 80.04.
[408] CCH ¶8631, ¶8639, ¶8642; Sec. 61.2, 61.3, 61.4.
[409] CCH ¶5084; Sec. 20(1)(l); Interp. Bul. IT-442R.
[410] CCH ¶4330; Sec. 12(1)(d).
[411] CCH ¶5097; Sec. 20(1)(p).

A taxpayer whose business includes the lending of money on the security of mortgages, hypothecs, or agreements of a sale of real property may deduct a reserve under this provision. Where a deduction has been made in respect of inventory that has been reduced below cost, a bad debt deduction may also be made in respect of that same property. In the event of recovery, the excess of the amount deducted as a bad debt over the amount included in income as a bad debt recovery will also be included as income.[412]

It is the taxpayer who is required to establish that a debt has become bad. A bad debt may be designated as such when the creditor, after having considered all factors relevant to it, honestly and reasonably determines that it is uncollectible, notwithstanding the fact that it may subsequently be collected.[413] There is no necessity that a debt be unequivocally irrecoverable and the possibility of recovery in the future is not an absolute bar to a determination of uncollectibility.[414] In some cases, the report of a collection agency may be relied on as evidence that an amount has become uncollectible. In other cases, as for example, where the debtor has become bankrupt, there will be little question as to the time at which the debt became bad. Whether or not lending of money is part of the taxpayer's ordinary course of business will be closely examined; loans made by a lawyer to a corporation she was a minority shareholder of were held not to be part of the taxpayer's ordinary course of business and a reserve for bad debts not deductible.[415] In this respect, it is open to the Tax Court judge, on the evidence before him, to conclude that the taxpayer's ordinary business did not include the lending of money.[416]

See ¶5425 in connection with bad debts and capital gains where the proceeds of disposition exceed the adjusted cost base of the debt. See also ¶3495 and ¶3498 relative to reserves and the sale of accounts receivable.

[¶3454] Conditional Sales Repossessions

Where property is surrendered by a debtor and acquired or reacquired by a creditor as a result of foreclosure or repossession under a conditional sales agreement, the following rules apply.[417] The debtor is deemed to have surrendered the property for proceeds of disposition equal to total unpaid principal and interest at the time of surrender. Where several properties are subject to one debt, the proceeds are allocated on the basis of the fair market value of the properties. Any further payments made by the debtor following surrender are deemed to be losses on the disposition of the property.

The creditor is deemed to acquire or reacquire the property at a cost equal to the cost base of the debt, adjusted in the case of capital property for

---

See page ii for explanation of footnotes.

[412] CCH ¶4458; Sec. 12.4.

[413] Flexi-Coil Ltd., 96 DTC 6350, Anjalie Enterprises Ltd., 95 DTC 216.

[414] Berretti, 86 DTC 1719.

[415] Martin, 2007 DTC 1284.

[416] 725685 Alberta Ltd., 2009 DTC 5117.

[417] CCH ¶9800, ¶9830; Sec. 79, 79.1.

¶3454

non-arm's length transactions, plus other expenses incurred to protect the creditor's interests. In the case of several properties being covered by a single debt, the cost base of the debt is allocated among the properties in proportion to their fair market value. The reserve will reduce the deemed cost of the acquired or reacquired property to the creditor, but must be recognized where the cost base is reduced below zero in order to raise the cost base back to nil.

[¶3456] Settlement of Debts

Where a debt is settled by paying less than the amount owed, or is extinguished without full payment, the following rules will apply.[418] The "forgiven amount" is, generally, the principal amount, reduced by:

(1) any amount paid at the time of settlement in satisfaction of the principal amount;

(2) amounts included in the income of an employee or shareholder on the forgiveness of a debt owed in that capacity and, in the case of a shareholder, loans already included in the shareholder's income;

(3) amounts included in income under the prepaid interest rules;

(4) amounts recognized as deemed capital gains on the repurchase of debt issued by the taxpayer (typically this applies only to bonds, debentures, and similar obligations issued by a corporation and traded in an open market);

(5) any portion of the principal amount related to resource deductions renounced by a corporation to other corporations under specified provisions;

(6) amounts accounted for as debtor's proceeds of disposition under the foreclosure rules (see ¶3454);

(7) amounts accounted for under the debt parking rules;

(8) amounts added to principal amounts representing accrued interest included in the income of an employee or personal service corporation or shareholder as imputed interest;

(9) the entire principal amount where the debtor is bankrupt;

(10) the principal amount of a loan recognized as assistance for income tax purposes or of a loan recognized as assistance from a government, municipality, or public authority reducing the cost base of a depreciable asset;

---

[418] CCH ¶9850, ¶9867, ¶9868, ¶9869, ¶9870; Sec. 80, 80.01, 80.02, 80.03, 80.04.

(11) a loan, issued by the debtor, which has been included back in income under the unpaid amount rules;

(12) principal amounts included in the debtor's income by other provisions of the Act (typically this might be certain trade payables); and

(13) consideration given previously by the debtor to another person for the assumption of the obligation by the other person.

In addition, the "forgiven amount" is also nullified in the event that a debtor is an "active" member of a partnership and the obligation has always been payable to an active member of the partnership.

The forgiven amount may be applied in the following order to reduce:

(1) unapplied non-capital losses of preceding years, excluding allowable business investment losses, starting with the oldest losses;

(2) farm losses of preceding years (oldest first);

(3) restricted farm losses of preceding years (oldest first);

(4) allowable business investment losses of preceding years (oldest first);

(5) net capital losses of preceding years (oldest first);

(6) capital cost of depreciable property;

(7) the undepreciated capital costs of a prescribed class of depreciable property until such balance reaches nil;

(8) cumulative eligible capital;

(9) any resource account balances for successor pools;

(10) adjusted cost base of non-depreciable capital property with certain exceptions, principally for shares and debt where the debtor is a specified shareholder (a 10% shareholder including the related persons' shares), and non-taxable Canadian property of non-residents;

(11) adjusted cost base of shares or debt of unrelated companies in which the taxpayer is a specified shareholder, subject to complex limitations;

(12) the adjusted cost base of shares or debt of related companies, as designated by the taxpayer, subject to complex limitations; and

(13) current year capital losses, including those arising on wind-up of a subsidiary.

In addition, there are debt parking rules to force a deemed forgiveness where arm's length debt is acquired by a related company or specified

¶3456

shareholder at a greater than 20% discount.[419] There are also special rules that apply to non-residents.

[¶3459] Doubtful Debts and Reserves

An annual reasonable reserve for doubtful debts may also be set up, but the amount of the reserve must be included in the next year's income.[420] In that year, there will be a corresponding deduction by reason of a new reserve for doubtful debts. The only debts for which such a reserve is allowed are those which have previously been included in computing the taxpayer's income or those arising in the ordinary course of the taxpayer's business, part of which is lending money. Interest on a loan to a non-resident company could not be claimed as a reserve for doubtful debts when no written document as to payment of interest existed between the two parties, and they were not dealing at arm's length.[421]

There is no provision for the creation of a reserve for doubtful debts where the amount receivable constitutes capital property. The term "doubtful debt" implies a definite financial indebtedness that probably (but not certainly) will not be satisfied by the debtor.[422]

There are several methods of determining a reserve for doubtful debts:

(1) calculating a percentage of the outstanding accounts;

(2) performing an appraisal of each account; and

(3) classifying the outstanding accounts by age and taking a percentage which increases according to the age of the account.

It should be noted that past experience must be taken into account. If this shows exceedingly high recovery, the reserve will be substantially lessened.[423]

See ¶5425 for comment on capital gains and debts receivable that meet the definition of capital property. See also ¶3495 and ¶3498 relative to reserves and the sale of accounts receivable.

[¶3462] Lending Money on Security of Mortgages, etc., and Reserves

Institutions such as banks and insurers are permitted to deduct reserves under the provisions relating to the deduction of reserves for taxpayers whose business includes the lending of money.[424]

A definition of "lending asset" [425] is a bond, debenture, mortgage, note, hypothec, agreement of sale, or any other indebtedness and includes a preferred share owned by a bank that is an alternative or substitute for a

---

See page ii for explanation of footnotes.

[419] CCH ¶9867; Sec. 80.01.
[420] CCH ¶4330, ¶5084; Sec. 12(1)(*d*), 20(1)(*l*).
[421] K. R. Ranches Ltd., 73 DTC 49.
[422] Harlequin Books, 54 DTC 453.

[423] No. 81, 53 DTC 98.
[424] CCH ¶5084; Sec. 20(1)(*l*).
[425] CCH ¶28,153; Sec. 248(1) "lending asset".

loan, but does not include any of the aforementioned listed assets that are part of a trading account of a bank or the inventory of any other taxpayer.

[¶3465] Quadrennial Surveys and Reserves

A taxpayer may deduct a prescribed amount of expenses incurred for quadrennial or other special surveys required under the *Canada Shipping Act*.[426] Income Tax Regulations provide that the prescribed amount which is deductible in a taxation year is an increasing proportion of the estimate of the expenses of the survey. Note, however, that any amount deducted in a year as a reserve for a survey must be added to income in the following year.[427]

[¶3471] Other Debts and Reserves

For a discussion of bad debts in connection with capital gains,[428] see ¶5425; for reserves on death,[429] see ¶2590; for reserves, contingent accounts, or sinking funds,[430] see ¶3207; for situations where proceeds of disposition of depreciable property become a bad debt,[431] see ¶3353.

[¶3474] Sale of Inventory

[¶3477] Inventory Valuation

A taxpayer is required to include his "profit" when computing his income from a business for the year. The determination of profit is a legal one, and is not simply an adoption of accounting profit. The legal determination may require consideration of "well accepted business principles" (which includes accounting principles), to the extent that they are consistent with the provisions of the Act, and established legal principles that provide an accurate picture of the taxpayer's profit.[432] Well-established business principles include inventory accounting methods.[433] And, like other such principles, they are subject to the provisions of the Act. A taxpayer may choose one of two methods in valuing inventory at the end of a taxation year, regardless of which method is most appropriate under generally accepted accounting principles.[434]

Where a taxpayer has inventory in a business that is not an adventure or concern in the nature of trade, a taxpayer may:

(a) value each item (or class of items if specific items are not distinguishable) in the inventory at the lower of its cost or its fair market value; or

---

See page ii for explanation of footnotes.

[426] CCH ¶5094, ¶5095; Sec. 20(1)(*o*); Reg. 3600.

[427] CCH ¶4352; Sec. 12(1)(*h*).

[428] CCH ¶7400; Sec. 50.

[429] CCH ¶9350; Sec. 72.

[430] CCH ¶4822; Sec. 18(1)(*e*).

[431] CCH ¶5131; Sec. 20(4).

[432] Canderel Limited, 98 DTC 6100, Toronto College Park Limited, 98 DTC 6088, Ikea Limited, 98 DTC 6092.

[433] Friesen, 95 DTC 5551.

[434] CCH ¶4100, ¶4104; Sec. 10(1); Reg. 1801.

(b) value the entire inventory at fair market value.

In using the lower of cost or fair market value, cost must be the cost at which the taxpayer acquired the property, and fair market value must be the fair market value of the inventory at the end of the year for which profit is being determined. Accordingly, businesses which have valued their property at the lower of cost and fair market value at the end of Year 1, when fair market value is less than cost, must, if fair market value has increased at the end of Year 2, write up the Year 2 value to the lower of cost and fair market value at the end of Year 2.

Inventory in a business that is an adventure or concern in the nature of trade must be valued at its original acquisition cost to the taxpayer.[435] Accordingly, a taxpayer does not have the option of valuing inventory that is part of an adventure or concern in the nature of trade at the lower of original cost or fair market value (i.e., the LCM method).

Factors that may be relevant to the analysis of whether inventory is part of an adventure or concern in the nature of trade could include the time, attention, and resources accorded to the transactions, the frequency or regularity of similar transactions, the taxpayer's intention and course of conduct with respect to the property, and the nature of the property itself. It should be noted that the distinction between a "business" and "adventure in the nature of trade" is a question of fact.

Special rules apply to the work-in-progress of a professional, advertising or packaging material, and parts and supplies for the purposes of the valuation of inventory in computing income from a business.[436] Work-in-progress and advertising or packaging materials are deemed to be inventory of the taxpayer. However, anything used primarily for the purpose of advertising or packaging property that is included in inventory is deemed not to be property held for sale or lease such that the property would not qualify for the 3% inventory allowance. Injection substances, the cost of which are deductible (¶3372), are deemed to be inventory which has no cost except for the purposes of the deduction from business and property income.

For the purposes of determining the inventory of a business that is a profession, the fair market value of the work-in-progress means the amount that can reasonably be expected to become receivable in respect thereof after the end of the year. Certain professionals (accountants, dentists, lawyers, medical doctors, veterinarians, and chiropractors) may elect to exclude work-in-progress from their incomes (see ¶3558).

For other taxpayers who are not members of these enumerated professions, work-in-progress can be valued at the lower of cost or fair market value (the LCM method). That this method produces a result that is inconsistent with Generally Accepted Accounting Principles (GAAP) is no bar to its

---

[435] CCH ¶4101; Sec. 10(1.01).   [436] CCH ¶4155, ¶4160; Sec. 10(4), 10(5).

application.[437] Considering that there is no basis for reserving the application of the LCM method to certain professions, management consultants were therefore allowed to value their work-in-progress based on the cost, which was lower than the fair market value.[438]

For the purpose of computing income from an artistic endeavour in a taxation year, an individual (other than a trust) may elect that the value of the property described in inventory is nil. This inventory will be valued at nil in computing the individual's income for each subsequent taxation year unless the Minister agrees to allow the individual to revoke the election. An "artistic endeavour" is defined to mean the business of creating paintings, prints, etchings, drawings, sculptures, or similar works of art where such works of art are created by the individual, but does not include a business of reproducing works of art.[439]

The fair market value of inventory that is advertising or packaging material or parts and supplies is deemed to be the replacement cost of the inventory, except for property that is obsolete, damaged, or defective, or that is held for sale or lease or for the purpose of being converted into property for sale or lease.

Supplies on hand, other than depreciable property, are to be included in inventory if they are:

(a) held as stock in trade;

(b) attached to or incorporated in goods being manufactured or processed for sale;

(c) to be consumed in the rendering of services;

(d) spare parts, provided that their total cost or value is material to the company's overall operation; or

(e) any other supplies the cost or value of which is reflected as an asset in the company's balance sheet in accordance with good accounting practice.[440]

Special provisions are made for the inclusion of carrying charges in respect of vacant land held as inventory.[441] See ¶3246.

Where it is not possible to ascertain the cost of specific items in an inventory, valuation must be ascertained by one of the following methods:

(1) average cost;

(2) "fifo" (first in, first out) — i.e., items first purchased are deemed first disposed of; and

---

See page ii for explanation of footnotes.

[437] Friesen, 95 DTC 5551, Canderel, 98 DTC 6100. [440] Interp. Bul. IT-51R2.
[438] CDSL Canada Ltd., 2009 DTC 5030. [441] CCH ¶4144; Sec. 10(1.1).
[439] CCH ¶4177, ¶4178, ¶4179; Sec. 10(6), 10(7), 10(8); Interp. Bul. IT-504R2.

¶3477

(3) "lifo" (last in, first out) — i.e., the last items brought into the inventory are deemed the first ones out.

The Department has recognized the average cost and the fifo methods as appropriate in determining the costs of inventories for income tax purposes, but does not recognize the lifo method for this purpose.

The use of replacement cost in determining "market" may not give a proper result where goods or materials have deteriorated in value by year end to the extent that they cannot be disposed of in the normal way (i.e., those goods or materials that are in such condition that a taxpayer would have to depart from the normal merchandising procedure in order to dispose of them). In such a case, the use of net realizable value (the estimated selling price in the ordinary course of business less reasonably predictable preparation and marketing costs) in determining the market for these goods or materials will be accepted, notwithstanding that the taxpayer may use replacement cost in determining market for the remainder of the inventory.[442]

The valuation of the inventory of a lumber store and yard at 80% of its retail value to provide a reserve against obsolescence was inadmissible; the full value of the inventory was to be taken into account.[443] The value of a stock trader's closing inventory of speculative mining shares was held to be the market value of the shares at the end of the year; they could not be valued on any basis lower than the average cost of the shares.[444] However, where the taxation year of a broker-dealer ended while a no-trading ban was in force on the shares he was distributing, the shares making up his inventory were correctly valued by the Minister at cost, and not at the nil value created by the ban.[445] The cost of a company's stationery supplies on hand at year end, not previously deducted, was an allowable expense and not inventory in the normal sense. The supplies had no market value and were of no use to anyone but the company.[446]

If the property described in the inventory of a taxpayer at the commencement of a taxation year has not been valued as required by the rules set out above, the Minister may direct that it be deemed to have been so valued for the purpose of computing the taxpayer's income for the year.[447] The purpose of this provision is to give the Minister the power to prevent a taxpayer whose closing inventory is adjusted under the above rules from claiming a corresponding adjustment to his or her opening inventory. If the inventory of a taxpayer at the end of a taxation year has not been valued as required under the above rules, the Minister may increase the taxpayer's income on reassessment by revaluing such inventory on an appropriate basis. Under this provision, the Minister may at the same time deem the

---

See page ii for explanation of footnotes.

[442] Interp. Bul. IT-188R, IT-473R.
[443] Funk, 61 DTC 590.
[444] Lawson, 69 DTC 5155.

[445] Goldmack Securities Ltd., 72 DTC 1530.
[446] Kelly, 76 DTC 1090.
[447] CCH ¶4150; Sec. 10(3).

opening inventory to have been correctly valued without adjustment and in so doing bring the whole amount of the income into the year under review.

Inventory at the commencement of a taxation year is to be valued at the same amount as that at which it was valued at the end of the immediately preceding taxation year.[448] This will avoid situations under which amounts might otherwise escape tax or be taxed twice because of a change in the method of valuing inventory. Additionally, a taxpayer must value inventory at the end of a year using the same method of inventory valuation used at the end of preceding year.[449]

If the Minister does not apply the revaluation provisions, the taxpayer may presumably change the method of valuing both the opening and closing inventories for each taxation year in which the inventory was not valued as required.

The "base-stock" method of inventory valuation, by which the value of stock is averaged out at the lowest cost of acquisition during the year, was held to be not acceptable when it was shown that, contrary to the company's claim, the method was not in accordance with generally accepted accounting principles.[450] Where a taxpayer entered into an agreement to purchase lumber but did not take delivery until the following year, the loss resulting from a drop in the market price of lumber was not deductible, because the lumber had not formed a part of the company's inventory in the year for which the loss was claimed.[451]

[¶3480] Rules for Sale of Inventory

Sales of property included in the inventory of a business upon or after disposing of or ceasing to carry on the business or a part of the business are deemed to have been made by the taxpayer in the course of carrying on the business, and thus the proceeds of sale will be included in income.[452]

Accordingly, the consideration for the inventory will be included in income and the cost or book value of the inventory will be deducted in the same way as if it had been sold in the ordinary course of business. The consideration will be included in income for the last year in which business was carried on.

The operation of the sale of inventory provisions extends to property that would have been included in the inventory of a business if the income from the business had not been computed in accordance with the cash method, which is available to farmers.[453]

See page ii for explanation of footnotes.

[448] CCH ¶4145; Sec. 10(2).

[449] CCH ¶4147; Sec. 10(2.1).

[450] Handy and Harman of Canada Ltd., 73 DTC 5401.

[451] Jawl Industries Ltd., 74 DTC 6133.

[452] CCH ¶5161; Sec. 23(1); Interp. Bul. IT-287R2.

[453] CCH ¶5163; Sec. 23(3).

¶3480

[¶3486] Inventory Adjustment

The amount of depreciation included in a taxpayer's inventory at a year end is required to be included in income for that year and will be deductible in the subsequent year. In the reconciliation between income for financial statements and income for tax purposes, a taxpayer adds the amount of depreciation written in its accounts and deducts the amount of capital cost allowance it chooses to claim. Where part of the depreciation for the year has not been charged to the profit and loss account, but has been reflected as part of the inventory cost, the amount of depreciation added back in the reconciliation is correspondingly reduced. This adjustment is offset by the inventory adjustment provision of the Act.[454]

[¶3489] Sale of Accounts Receivable

[¶3492] Rules for Sale of Accounts Receivable

Special rules are provided for cases where accounts receivable are sold in connection with a sale of all or substantially all of the property used in carrying on a business.[455] The rules will apply if:

(1) the vendor has been carrying on a business;

(2) the vendor has sold all or substantially all the property used in carrying on the business (this will not apply if the property is disposed of by way of a gift or bequest or in any other manner than by sale);

(3) the property sold includes all the outstanding debts which were included in the vendor's income for the year of sale or a previous year. If the vendor retains some of the accounts receivable of the business, the section would appear not to be applicable;

(4) the business being carried on was a money lending business and if the property sold includes all the outstanding loans made in the ordinary course of that business (if the vendor retains some of the loans made in the ordinary course of the business, this would appear not to be applicable);

(5) the purchaser proposes to continue the business; and

(6) the vendor and purchaser have jointly executed an election in prescribed Form, then the sale of accounts receivable provisions of the Act are to be applicable subject to the inadequate consideration provisions of the Act (see ¶2505).

Where a lawyer took a young solicitor into partnership, opened a new set of books, and collected most of the previous accounts receivable, an election could not be exercised under this provision, as the lawyer did not

---

See page ii for explanation of footnotes.

[454] CCH ¶4374a, ¶5128f; Sec. 12(1)(r), 20(1)(ii).   [455] CCH ¶5153; Sec. 22; Interp. Bul. IT-188R.

dispose of or cease to carry on a business or part of a business.[456] A similar conclusion was reached when two accountants operating as a partnership took in a third partner.[457]

[¶3495] Vendor's Deductions

Ordinarily, when accounts receivable are sold, the vendor will be required to take into income for that year any reserve for doubtful debts which the vendor had deducted in the preceding year.[458] Similarly, since the accounts receivable have not been included in computing the income of the purchaser, a deduction for bad debts or for a reserve for doubtful debts cannot be made. See ¶3453 and ¶3459.

If the conditions in (1) to (6) of the rules relative to the sale of accounts receivable in ¶3492 above are met, the vendor may deduct any difference between the face value of the debts and what the vendor receives for them, other than bad debts for which the vendor has already made a deduction. In computing income for the year of the sale, the vendor will be required to add to income any reserve for doubtful debts for the previous taxation year.

[¶3498] Purchaser's Deductions

The purchaser must include in income, in the year of purchase, the difference between the price he or she paid for the debts and their face value, but he or she may deal with the accounts receivable as though they had arisen while such purchaser was the owner of the business. This means that the purchaser may establish a reserve for doubtful accounts with respect to purchased accounts that are still outstanding at the end of his or her fiscal period. For these accounts, the purchaser may claim a deduction for a reserve for doubtful debts and may deduct as bad debts any bad debt that the vendor has not previously deducted. If the purchaser should collect a receivable previously deducted by the vendor, it must be included in income. See ¶3453 and ¶3459.

[¶3501] Election

The joint election referred to in (6) of the rules in ¶3492 above, must contain a joint statement of the amount paid for the debts. It is binding upon the parties and against the Minister.

[¶3504] Receipt of Consideration for Accounts Receivable after Ceasing Business

If, upon or after disposing of or ceasing to carry on a business or part of a business, an individual receives consideration for accounts receivable that arose in the course of carrying on the business, the amount will be included

---

See page ii for explanation of footnotes.

[456] Siegal, 63 DTC 516.
[457] Ewens, 69 DTC 722.
[458] Interp. Bul. IT-188R.

in income as if it had been received in the course of carrying on that business.[459]

Normally, this will only be of importance where the cash method of computing income is used, since under the cash method an amount is normally included in income when it is received.

[¶3507] Ceasing to Carry on Business

[¶3510] Sale of Business

The amount received by a vendor upon the sale of all or substantially all the assets of a business will normally be classified as capital rather than income in the vendor's hands, unless the vendor is in the business of purchasing and re-selling businesses.

A recent decision in the *Morguard Corporation* case[460] held that break fees received by a suitor after an unsuccessful takeover bid can be taxable as income, not capital gain.

A business is regarded as a capital asset of the person who operates it and a realization of that business will not constitute trading. Problems may arise, however, in connection with certain types of assets that are sold as part of a business.

A business normally consists of a number of different types of assets, including accounts receivable,[461] inventory[462] and other current assets, land, and depreciable property. The price payable for a business will be payable for all the assets comprised therein and it may or may not be allocated in the sale agreement among the various assets.

Where depreciable assets are included in the assets sold, problems may arise in determining the extent, if any, to which recapture of depreciation is involved. There may also be questions as to the capital cost to the purchaser of the various depreciable assets purchased.

See also Chapter V.

[¶3513] Realization of Assets by Liquidation

The mere realization of assets by a liquidator who is engaged in winding up a company, or by executors or administrators winding up an estate, is not considered a trade or business.[463] On the other hand, a liquidator of a company or the administrator of an estate may continue the trade or business, and in that case any profit realized as a result of such continuation of

---

See page ii for explanation of footnotes.

[459] CCH ¶5179; Sec. 28(5).
[460] Morguard Corporation, 2012 DTC 1099 (T.C.C.).
[461] CCH ¶5153; Sec. 22.

[462] CCH ¶5161; Sec. 23.

[463] Wilson Box Ltd., [1936] 3 All E.R. 728.

the business is taxable in the liquidator's or administrator's hands. See also ¶6375 *et seq.*, concerning the winding-up of a company's affairs.

[¶3516] Appropriation of Corporation's Property

If a corporation's property has been appropriated in any way to or for the benefit of a shareholder on winding up, the corporation is deemed to have disposed of the property at its fair market value and will be able to recognize losses as well as gains on the disposition. There is no increase in the adjusted cost base of the property to the shareholder.[464] See also ¶2505 and ¶6375 *et seq.*

[¶3519] Cumulative Eligible Capital

Where a taxpayer has ceased to carry on a business, the taxpayer is permitted to deduct the balance in the cumulative eligible capital pool of the business in computing income for the taxation year in which the taxpayer ceased to carry on the business and has disposed of all eligible capital property, other than property of no value, that was held by the taxpayer in respect of the ceased business.[465]

However, this deduction cannot be claimed by an individual ceasing to carry on a business where the business is subsequently carried on by the individual's spouse/common-law partner or by a corporation controlled directly or indirectly by the individual in any manner whatever.[466] Under these circumstances, the cumulative eligible capital pool of the individual is transferred to the spouse/common-law partner or to the controlled corporation. See ¶3075 *et seq.* for commentary on cumulative eligible capital, and goodwill and other "nothings".

[¶3522] Ceasing to Carry on a Farming Business in Canada

Under certain conditions, the value of a taxpayer's accounts receivable will be included in calculating the taxpayer's income for a taxation year.[467] These conditions will be met where a taxpayer who carried on a business the income from which was computed in accordance with the cash method is, at the end of the year, both not resident in Canada and not carrying on the business in Canada; for example, where:

(1) a Canadian resident ceases to carry on a Canadian farming business and becomes non-resident;

(2) a Canadian resident ceases to carry on a farming business in another country and becomes non-resident; or

(3) a non-resident ceases to carry on a Canadian farming business.

---

[464] CCH ¶9180; Sec. 69(5).　　　　[466] CCH ¶5167; Sec. 24(2).
[465] CCH ¶5166; Sec. 24(1); Interp. Bul. IT-313R2.　　[467] CCH ¶5178; Sec. 28(4).

This test will apply annually with respect to accounts receivable outstanding during each taxation year, but will only require the inclusion in a taxpayer's income of amounts that were not so included in a preceding year. As noted above, the amount included in a taxpayer's income is based on the *value* of the taxpayer's accounts receivable and, as a result, may be affected by evidence that a particular debt is doubtful or uncollectible.

In addition, under certain conditions, a taxpayer will be treated as having disposed of inventory owned by the taxpayer for proceeds of disposition equal to its fair market value.[468] This will occur at any time when property that is inventory of a taxpayer who carried on a business in accordance with the cash method is not used by the taxpayer in a business carried on in Canada and the taxpayer is not resident in Canada; for example, where:

(1) a Canadian resident carrying on business in Canada becomes non-resident and moves some or all of the inventory of the Canadian business to another country (note that the taxpayer may or may not have ceased to carry on the Canadian business);

(2) a Canadian resident carrying on business in another country becomes non-resident; or

(3) a non-resident carrying on business in Canada moves some or all of the inventory of the Canadian business to another country.[469]

[¶3531] Resource Industries

[¶3534] Income of Resource Industries

Generally speaking, resource income is treated as business income and taxed in the same manner as business income from other sources (see ¶8300).

Historically

The reduction in the general statutory rate of corporate income tax, from 28% to 21% over five years beginning on January 1, 2001 (see ¶8475) did not apply to resource income. However, legislation amending the *Income Tax Act* with respect to the resource sector received Royal Assent on November 7, 2003 and introduced a new tax structure for resource income, beginning January 1, 2003 (see below). The new rules were fully implemented in 2007, and resource income is now subject to the same corporate income tax rate as other corporate income. As well, actual costs of provincial and other Crown royalties and mining taxes are deductible, replacing the current resource allowance.

The rules regarding the taxation of resource income were phased in over a period of five years as follows:

See page ii for explanation of footnotes.

[468] CCH ¶5178b; Sec. 28(4.1).   [469] CCH ¶5167a; Sec. 24(1).

- • a reduction of the federal statutory corporate income tax rate on income earned from resource activities from 28 to 21%, beginning with a 1-percentage-point reduction to 27% in 2003, and declining to 21% in 2007;

- • the elimination of the 25% resource allowance; and

- • a deduction for Crown charges, such as royalties and mining taxes.

The federal corporate income tax rate reductions became effective on January 1 of each year and were prorated for corporations with taxation years that included days in more than one calendar year. The tax rate reductions began with a 1% reduction in 2003 as follows:

	2003	2004	2005	2006	After 2006
Corporate income tax rate	27	26	25	23	21

The previous tax structure required the inclusion in income, or disallowed the deduction from income, of royalties or mining taxes which were receivable by the Crown or payable to the Crown. The new amendments have the effect of removing this inclusion in income, or prohibition on deduction, of Crown royalties and mining taxes over a five-year transitional period in the following percentages, prorated for taxation years that do not match the calendar year:

	2003	2004	2005	2006	After 2006
Percentage of Crown royalties and taxes on resource production required to be included in income, or prohibited from deduction	90	75	65	35	0

The resource allowance, calculated as 25% of adjusted resource profits has been phased out such that a declining percentage of the allowance was deductible in determining income subject to tax. These percentage amounts were effective as of January 1 of each year and were prorated for corporations with taxation years that include days in more than one calendar year. The deductible percentage of the resource allowance matches the amount of Crown royalties and mining taxes that were disallowed as a deduction or included in income, as follows:

	2003	2004	2005	2006	After 2006
Percentage of resource allowance deductible in computing income	90	75	65	35	0

The current structure now results in the same federal corporate income tax rate being imposed on resource income as on other corporate income. It also allows the deduction of actual costs of provincial and other Crown royalties and mining taxes incurred instead of a 25% arbitrary resource allowance.

¶3534

[¶3537] Exploration and Development Expenses — General

Taxpayers are allowed to deduct expenses incurred in exploring and developing mineral deposits to the point of commercial production and their expenses incurred in drilling and exploring for petroleum and natural gas.

In general, taxpayers who incur exploration or development expenses in respect of one deposit may deduct them currently against income from other producing deposits or non-resource sources. However, prepaid amounts for services or rent may not be deductible or recognized on a current basis.[470]

Expenses incurred after 1971 and before May 7, 1974 to explore in Canada for minerals, oil, and natural gas and to develop mineral deposits to the point of commercial production are referred to as "Canadian exploration and development expenses".[471] Similar expenses incurred after May 6, 1974 are segregated into "Canadian exploration expenses" [472] and "Canadian development expenses".[473] A further distinction is made for expenses incurred in taxation years ending after December 11, 1979. Certain expenses that previously qualified as Canadian development expenses became Canadian oil and gas property expenses, which are deductible at a reduced rate.[474] Expenses incurred after 1971 in exploring for or developing deposits outside Canada are described as "foreign exploration and development expenses".[475]

The right of a taxpayer to deduct Canadian exploration and development expenses, Canadian exploration expenses, and Canadian development expenses varies depending upon whether or not the taxpayer is a "principal-business corporation".[476]

Exploration and development expenses may be transferred among corporate taxpayers in certain circumstances. The costs of exploring for and developing a deposit may be shared among corporate investors by means of joint exploration corporations and by the issue of "flow-through shares."

[¶3540] Flow-Through Shares

The term "flow-through shares"[477] is used in general to describe shares of a corporation issued to a person who provides funds to the corporation for exploration or development work or for the acquisition of a resource property under arrangements whereby the tax deductions generated by the work or acquisition are flowed through to the shareholder and deducted in computing the shareholder's income.

See page ii for explanation of footnotes.

[470] CCH ¶8972b; Sec. 66(15).
[471] CCH ¶8972b; Sec. 66(15).
[472] CCH ¶9030; Sec. 66.1(6).
[473] CCH ¶9070; Sec. 66.2(5).
[474] CCH ¶9083; Sec. 66.4.

[475] CCH ¶8982; Sec. 66(15) "foreign exploration and development expenses".
[476] CCH ¶8988; Sec. 66(15) "principal-business corporation".
[477] CCH ¶8981; Sec. 66(15) "flow-through share".

The renunciation provisions for flow-through shares deal separately with Canadian exploration expenses,[478] Canadian development expenses,[479] and Canadian oil and gas property expenses.[480] The person acquiring a flow-through share under an agreement entered into after February 1986 is deemed to have acquired the share at a cost of nil.[481] The increase in a corporation's paid-up capital upon the issue of flow-through shares is, generally, limited to 50% of the expenses renounced.[482] For the mining industry, grass roots exploration expenses incurred by a corporation within 60 days after the end of a calendar year can, in some cases, be deducted by the shareholder in respect of that calendar year.[483] The consideration for the agreement may not include property to be exchanged or transferred in circumstances of the special rollover rules. To implement the renunciation provisions, various filings are required.

There has been a tightening of measures to ensure that flow-through shares are only used to finance more risky expenditures such as exploration and development costs. Canadian oil and gas property expenses and those Canadian development expenses that relate to the cost of mining properties are no longer eligible flow-through share expenditures. In addition, the amount of oil and gas development costs that can be reclassified as Canadian exploration expenses under a flow-through share agreement has been reduced from $2 million to $1 million per year and the reclassification is restricted to issuing corporations with less that $15 million in taxable capital employed in Canada, as defined for the purposes of the Large Corporations Tax. Also, the flow-through share treatment for certain seismic expenses has been denied. Off-the-shelf seismic costs are no longer eligible for flow-through share treatment.

[¶3543] Depletion Allowance

A taxpayer is permitted to deduct in computing income an amount allowed by regulation and generally referred to as "depletion allowance".[484] Deductions in the form of depletion allowance are contemplated for the oil and gas, mining, and forestry industries, but the regulations currently in effect apply mainly to mining and mineral processing. Prior to 1981,depletion allowance was widely available in the oil and gas industry but has been mostly phased-out for that industry and now applies only to certain non-conventional oil recovery projects. There are no regulations providing depletion allowance to the forestry industry.

Deductions must be earned by incurring certain types of expenditures during periods detailed by regulation. The expenditures are directly deductible in computing income under various other provisions of the Act so that depletion allowance is a form of incentive deduction.

See page ii for explanation of footnotes.

478 CCH ¶8966d, ¶8966e; Sec. 66(12.6), 66(12.61).
479 CCH ¶8966f, ¶8966g; Sec. 66(12.62), 66(12.63).
480 CCH ¶8966h, ¶8966i; Sec. 66(12.64), 66(12.65).
481 CCH ¶9082b; Sec. 66.3(3).

482 CCH ¶9082c; Sec. 66.3(4).
483 CCH ¶8966j; Sec. 66(12.66).
484 CCH ¶8800; Sec. 65(1).

Taxpayers of all kinds, whether corporations, individuals, or trusts are entitled to such a deduction for depletion allowance. A trust may claim the deduction in computing its own income, but may not pass the deduction on to its beneficiaries. In the case of a partnership, the deduction for depletion allowance is taken at the partner level and not in computing the income of the partnership.

In general terms, the depletion allowance deduction that may be claimed by a taxpayer in computing income for a taxation year is 25% of the taxpayer's "resource profits" for the year, to a maximum of the taxpayer's "earned depletion base" as at the end of the year. Resource profits consist, in broad terms, of the taxpayer's income from resource-related activities.[485] Earned depletion base is determined as $^1/_3$ of the sum of specified resource-related expenses incurred by the taxpayer.[486]

The Act provides successor and second successor rules which apply to determine the depletion allowance available to a corporation which acquires resource properties from a person having an unused depletion base.[487] Special rules apply in the case of a change of control or loss of tax-exempt status.[488]

[¶3546] Deduction for Provincial Mining Taxes

A taxpayer is allowed to deduct in computing income from a business or property an amount allowed by regulation in respect of taxes on income for the year from mining operations.[489] The deduction is of very narrow application and applies, in general, only to certain industrial mineral mines where the mineral is laid down in bedded deposits. The deduction is only allowed in respect of provincial taxes that are restricted to persons engaged in the mining industry; accordingly, provincial taxes of general application, such as taxes on corporate income, do not give rise to a deduction.

[¶3549] Professional Business

[¶3552] Income Calculation

Income for tax purposes of a taxpayer carrying on the professional practice of an accountant, dentist, lawyer, medical doctor, veterinarian, or chiropractor is calculated according to a modification of the accrual method; use of the cash method has been discontinued.[490]

Any person carrying on one of those professional practices, whether a sole practitioner, partner, or corporation, is required to use the modified accrual method of calculating income.

See page ii for explanation of footnotes.

[485] CCH ¶8815; Reg. 1204.

[486] CCH ¶8820; Reg. 1205.

[487] CCH ¶8809, ¶8810; Reg. 1202(2), Reg. 1202(3).

[488] CCH ¶8808, ¶8810ac; Reg. 1202(1), Reg. 1202(4).

[489] CCH ¶5118, ¶5118a; Sec. 20(1)(v); Reg. 3900.

[490] CCH ¶5750; Sec. 34; Interp. Bul. IT-189R2.

For professional corporations and individuals carrying on a business, fiscal periods for such persons and partnerships with at least one such member must coincide with the calendar year.[491] This eliminates the deferral of income previously allowed such taxpayers. Transitional relief in the form of a 10-year reserve was provided whereby a reserve for business income earned in the fiscal year ending in December 1995 effectively spread that income over 10 years.[492]

An alternative method for calculating business income for individuals and partnerships, all members of which are individuals, is provided where the election is made by June 15, 1996.[493] The alternative method allows a taxpayer to retain an off-calendar fiscal period year end but includes the income earned in the fiscal period on a regular basis. In addition, an estimate of the business income earned in the stub period between the end of the fiscal period and the calendar year, must be included. This stub-period amount is based on the amount of business income earned in the previous fiscal period. The additional amount that was included in a previous taxation year will be subtracted. For taxation years ending after March 22, 2011, the tax deferral on income earned by a corporation through the use of a partnership with a fiscal period that differs from the corporation's taxation year was eliminated by requiring incremental corporate members (corporations holding more than 10% income interest) to accrue additional partnership income for the portion of the partnership's fiscal period that falls within the corporation's tax year (the "stub period accrual"). The stub period accrual is generally a pro-rated amount of the corporation's partnership income for the fiscal period of the partnership ending in the taxation year of the corporation (similar to the alternative method of income for professional corporations and individuals carrying on businesses). A corporate incremental member of a partnership can override these rules by designating an amount in respect of its stub period accrual. For more details, see the CRA's Q&A document entitled "Partnerships–Deferral of Corporate Tax" posted on its website.

[¶3555] Amounts Receivable

A taxpayer who carries on the professional practice of an accountant, dentist, lawyer, medical doctor, veterinarian, or chiropractor is required to include in income amounts received in respect of goods sold or services rendered after the end of the year in the year of receipt.[494] However, the taxpayer may claim a reserve to defer the inclusion in income on any portion of the receipt that will be earned in a later period.[495]

Every amount that becomes receivable in the taxation year with respect to property sold or services rendered in the course of the business must also be included in income.[496] An amount is deemed to become receivable when

---

See page ii for explanation of footnotes.

[491] CCH ¶5786; Sec. 34.1.
[492] CCH ¶5787; Sec. 34.2.
[493] CCH ¶28,333f; Sec. 249.1.

[494] CCH ¶4251; Sec. 12(1)(a).
[495] CCH ¶5085; Sec. 20(1)(m).
[496] CCH ¶4256; Sec. 12(1)(b).

a bill is rendered or when a bill would have been rendered in the absence of undue delay, whichever is earlier.

See ¶3417 *et seq.*, for a discussion of reserves and bad and doubtful debts.

[¶3558] Work-in-Progress, Election

A professional who is an accountant, dentist, lawyer, medical doctor, veterinarian, or chiropractor may elect to exclude from income his or her work-in-progress at the end of the year. If the professional so elects, the election is binding for subsequent years and can only be revoked with the concurrence of the Minister.[497]

Corporate taxpayers can be professionals for the purposes of the work-in-progress deduction from income.[498]

In the absence of an election, the cost of unbilled services would be included in the inventory of the professional business at the end of the taxation year.

[¶3561] Lawyers' Trust Accounts and Disbursements

With the exception of advances that, by specific agreement with the client, a lawyer is entitled to treat as his or her own and retainers which the lawyer is entitled to keep whether or not he or she renders any services or makes any disbursements, the advances received from a client for services to be rendered or disbursements to be made are considered to be trust funds and are not income at the time of receipt.[499]

Disbursements that a lawyer customarily makes in the ordinary course of practice which are not chargeable directly to funds advanced by clients are considered to be the lawyer's own expenses which may or may not be recoverable from the lawyer's clients through regular billings. Consequently, such expenses of a business nature incurred in a taxation year are deductible in computing income for that year, unless the lawyer chooses to defer, for income tax purposes, that part of such expenses that relate to work-in-progress.

[¶3567] Deductions of Professional Individuals

In order that an expense may be deducted in computing income of a professional individual from a business:

(a) it must have been incurred by the individual for the purpose of earning income from the business;[500]

See page ii for explanation of footnotes.

[497] CCH ¶5750; Sec. 34; Interp. Bul. IT-457R.

[498] Publicité Cogem Ltée and Cogem Inc., 82 DTC 1596.

[499] Interp. Bul. IT-129R.

[500] CCH ¶4751; Sec. 18(1)(a).

(b) it must not be a capital expenditure;[501] and

(c) it must have been reasonable in the circumstances.[502]

Subject to these limitations, the following rules are, generally speaking, applicable in determining what amounts may be deducted in computing income from a professional business. In all cases, adequate books and records should be kept to substantiate the amounts claimed.

(1) *Annual fees paid to professional and scientific associations or societies.* These fees are deductible; however, an entrance fee payable on admission to a professional society (e.g., a fee for a call to the bar) may not be deducted.[503] Payment of fees in arrears is deductible if the taxpayer remained a member of the organization despite being in arrears. If the taxpayer's membership was terminated, payment of the overdue fees is in the nature of an entrance fee and is not deductible.

(2) *Rents paid for business premises.* These rents are deductible. In claiming this deduction, the owner's or agent's name and address should be furnished to the CRA.

(3) *Office maintenance expenses and carrying charges on business premises.* These expenses, which include business and property taxes, light, heat, insurance, repairs, depreciation, and mortgage interest, are deductible. Where a deduction of mortgage interest is claimed, the name and address of the mortgagee must be stated on the return. See ¶3183 for a discussion of the deduction of expenses incurred in connection with a home office.

(4) *Salaries paid to employees such as professional assistants or associates, secretaries, bookkeepers, and medical and dental assistants.* These salaries are deductible expenditures. The names and addresses of such employees are to be furnished annually to the CRA. If a salary is paid to the taxpayer's spouse or common-law partner, a deduction is permitted if the salary is reasonable and the amount received by the spouse or common-law partner is included in his/her income.

(5) *Contributions to superannuation or pension funds, profit sharing plans, supplementary unemployment benefit plans, registered retirement savings plans (RRSPs), and deferred profit sharing plans (DPSPs) for employees.* Such contributions are deductible.

(6) *Contributions to CPP/QPP.* As an employer, a taxpayer can deduct the employer portion (50%) of CPP or QPP contributions payable on employees' remuneration. As a self-employed individual, a taxpayer is also permitted to deduct 50% of his or her own CPP/QPP contributions rather than claiming a personal amount credit at the lowest marginal rate. The remaining 50% of

---

See page ii for explanation of footnotes.

[501] CCH ¶4800; Sec. 18(1)(b).
[502] CCH ¶9120; Sec. 67.

[503] CCH ¶3080; Sec. 8(1)(i); Interp. Bul. IT-211R; Daley, 50 DTC 877.

¶3567

his or her CPP/QPP contributions qualify for a tax credit, as they do for other individuals.

(7) *Employment Insurance premiums, Quebec Parental Insurance Plan premiums, and Workers' Compensation amounts.* As an employer, a taxpayer can deduct the employer portion of Employment Insurance premiums, Quebec parental insurance plan premiums, and Workers' Compensation amounts payable on employees' remuneration.

(8) *Fees paid to consultants.* These fees may be deducted.

(9) *Legal and accounting expenses.* If related to the earning of income, these expenses are deductible; if related to capital, they are not deductible.

(10) *Legal expenses incurred in collecting salary owed to the taxpayer.* Such expenses are deductible, if the claim is successful.

(11) *Telephone, postage, and stationery expenditures.* These are deductible.

(12) *Insurance premiums.* These are deductible in two types of cases. One is where the insurance is against a loss of a revenue nature (e.g., malpractice insurance). The other type is where it is regular commercial practice to carry the insurance (e.g., fire insurance on business property).

(13) *The cost of a professional library.* This cost is not deductible but depreciation is allowed on the capital cost of a library. The CRA ordinarily permits the deduction of the cost of professional periodicals and library books purchased individually. *Professional library fees* may be deducted.

(14) *Tuition fees.* Such fees are deductible if paid for full-time attendance at a university leading to a degree, or at a college or other educational institution in Canada in respect of a course lasting 13 consecutive weeks or longer.

(15) *Automobile expenses.* These expenses may be claimed by a professional person who uses his or her own car while away from home in the course of carrying on business. Automobile expenses incurred in driving to and from work are not deductible. If a professional person uses his or her own car partly for business and partly for personal transportation, the proportions of each would have to be proven and the expenditures apportioned. Depreciation may also be deducted. See ¶2320 for a discussion of automobile expenses.

(16) *Expenses of attending conventions of professional bodies.* Expenses of attending up to two conventions a year, in connection with the taxpayer's profession, are deductible subject to certain limitations. See ¶3355.

(17) *Christmas gifts, entertainment expenditures, and the like.* These are deductible, subject to certain limitations, if it can be proven that they were incurred for the purpose of earning income. See ¶3219.

¶3567

(18) *The cost of medical, surgical, and like supplies.* Other than capital expenditures, these costs are deductible in computing the income of a doctor or dentist.

(19) *Capital cost allowance.* This is allowed on the undepreciated cost of capital assets of professional persons as follows:

(a) office furniture and fixtures (Class 8);

(b) library (Class 8);

(c) medical and dental instruments costing less than $500 if acquired after May 1, 2006 or less than $200 if acquired before May 2, 2006 (Class 12);

(d) medical or dental instruments costing $500 or more if acquired after May 1, 2006 or $200 or more if acquired before May 2, 2006 $200 or more (Class 8);

(e) the proportion of the capital cost of an automobile used in earning income (Class 10 or 10.1);

(f) office building or office portion of house (Class 3); and

(g) a leasehold interest (Class 13).

See Chapter IV for the application of the capital cost allowance system to the particular classes.

(20) *A provision for doubtful and bad debts.*

(21) *Sundry expenses.* Such expenses, if not otherwise classified, may be deducted if made for the purpose of earning income.

(22) *Fees paid to an investment counsel.* These fees may be deducted from the income from shares or securities but not from professional income. The fees must be for advice as to the advisability of purchasing or selling specific shares or securities.

(23) *Income taxes.* Such amounts paid to the government of a foreign jurisdiction are not deductible in computing income, although the taxpayer may be entitled to a credit against tax in respect of income taxes paid to a foreign jurisdiction.

In addition to the deductions which might be claimed in computing income from a professional business, certain additional deductions may be claimed in computing taxable income, such as medical expenses, etc.

¶3567

[¶3570] Farming or Fishing Business

[¶3573] Cash Method of Computing Income

The cash method authorized for farmers and fishers consists of two principles:[504]

(1) The first principle requires the taxpayer to include in income all amounts that would be included under the usual accrual method where such amounts are actually received in the year or are deemed by the Act to have been received in the year in the course of carrying on the farming or fishing business. Similarly, the taxpayer is permitted to make deductions on a similar basis. Under the cash method, all amounts deductible under the accrual method which were actually paid in the year or are deemed by the Act to have been paid in the year are deductible.

(2) The second principle in calculating farm income involves two inventory adjustments. The first is a flexible inventory adjustment that is taken out on a voluntary basis whether or not the taxpayer is in a loss position. The second adjustment is a mandatory inventory adjustment that must be taken in loss years. The flexible inventory election is extended to all farm inventory, not just livestock. Any amount included in income in the year by virtue of this election is deducted in the following year. The inventory adjustments do not apply in a year in which a taxpayer has died.

The mandatory inventory adjustment is required in loss years. This adjustment in respect of purchased inventory on hand at the end of the year (including purchased livestock) requires an addition to income equal to the lesser of the amount of the loss and the value of purchased inventory on hand. Any amount required to be included in income by virtue of this adjustment is deducted in the following year.

Where inventory is acquired, in circumstances involving inadequate consideration, by a farmer who computes income in accordance with the cash method of accounting, the acquired inventory is deemed to have been purchased and paid for.[505] The taxpayer is therefore allowed to deduct the fair market value of the inventory and is required to consider such acquired inventory as purchased inventory for the purposes of the mandatory inventory adjustment. The mandatory inventory adjustment generally reduces a farm loss, computed in accordance with the cash method of accounting, by the lesser of the loss and the fair market value of purchased inventory on hand at year end.

Income from farming includes recaptured depreciation and recaptured deductions in respect of eligible capital property. Accordingly, deductions

---

See page ii for explanation of footnotes.

[504] CCH ¶5175–5177; Sec. 28(1)–(3); Interp. Bul.   [505] CCH ¶5175b; Sec. 28(1.1).
IT-373R2, IT-425, IT-433R, IT-526.

will be permitted for eligible capital property and capital cost allowance including terminal losses and write-off of eligible capital property.

Generally, inventory will be valued at the lower of cost or fair market value; however, the taxpayer may elect to value "specified animals" on a diminishing value basis. "Specified animals" includes all horses and any animal registered under the *Livestock Pedigree Act.*

If the cash method is adopted by a taxpayer for computing income from a farming or fishing business for one taxation year, the taxpayer's income from that business will be computed according to the same method for subsequent years, unless the taxpayer adopts some other method with the concurrence of the Minister and upon such terms and conditions as are specified by the Minister.

Payments (other than for inventory) that reduce cash basis income of a farming or fishing business for a year do not include prepaid expenses relating to a taxation year of the business that is two or more taxation years after the year of payment.

A deduction is provided for amounts paid in a previous taxation year where the amounts would be deductible in computing income for the current taxation year from the taxpayer's business of farming or fishing if that income were not computed in accordance with the cash method. To be deductible, the amount is required to have been paid by the taxpayer in a preceding taxation year in the course of carrying on the business of farming or fishing and cannot be deductible in computing the income of the business for any other taxation year.[506]

If two or more persons carry on a farming or fishing business jointly as partners or otherwise, neither of them may elect to have income from the business computed in accordance with the cash method unless each of the others has made a similar election.

The cash method of computing income was found to be appropriate both for a company operating a wildlife preserve[507] and for a company engaged in chicken processing, with respect to two farms which it used to breed and raise chickens.[508]

For situations where a taxpayer whose business was computed on the cash basis ceases to be a resident of Canada or ceases to carry on business, see ¶3522. For capital cost allowances available to farmers and fishers, see ¶4345.

[¶3576] "Farming" Defined

"Farming" is defined as including:

See page ii for explanation of footnotes.

[506] CCH ¶5175; Sec. 28(1)(e.1).
[507] Al Oeming Investments Ltd., 72 DTC 1057.
[508] Crawford Foods Ltd., 79 DTC 517.

¶3576

(1) the tilling of soil;

(2) livestock raising or exhibiting;

(3) maintaining of horses for racing;

(4) raising of poultry;

(5) fur farming;

(6) dairying;

(7) fruit farming; and

(8) the keeping of bees.[509]

Farming does not include the activities of farm employees. The growing of Christmas trees has been considered to be a farming operation.[510] It has also been held that the act of "maintaining horses for racing" need not be physically performed by the person who undertakes that activity. It can be accomplished by paying someone else to furnish the requisite services.[511]

[¶3579] Restricted Farm Loss

Where farming, or a combination of farming and other sources of income, is not the chief source of a taxpayer's income, the deduction permitted for farming losses is limited. In such cases, income may not be less than the taxpayer's income from all sources, minus the lesser of:

(a) the taxpayer's farming loss for the year before making any deduction for scientific research;[512] and

(b) $2,500 plus $1/2$ of the next $12,500 for a maximum deduction of $8,750.[513]

Any loss which is not deductible currently is termed the taxpayer's restricted farm loss. A "restricted farming loss" is reduced by any amount taken into account pursuant to the provisions on debt forgiveness.[514]

Early cases from 1977 to 2002 were decided on the principles outlined by the Supreme Court of Canada in *Moldowan*, which divided farmers into three classes: the hobby farmer who cannot deduct farming losses; (ii) the "sideline business" farmer who is restricted to deducting a maximum of $8,750 of farming losses per year; and (iii) the farmer whose livelihood is farming and is therefore entitled to unlimited deduction of farming losses.[515] The primary test utilized during this period of case law was the reasonable expectation of profit (REOP) test which, if a taxpayer's farming activities satisfied this test, moved the taxpayer at least into the classification of a

---

See page ii for explanation of footnotes.

[509] CCH ¶28,106; Sec. 248(1) "farming".

[510] Dept. of Nat. Rev. Farmer's and Fisherman's Guide.

[511] Juster, 74 DTC 6540.

[512] CCH ¶5900; Sec. 37.

[513] CCH ¶5660; Sec. 31; Interp. Bul. IT-322R.

[514] CCH ¶16,025; Sec. 111(1)(c).

[515] Moldowan, 77 DTC 5213.

sideline farmer conducting a business and entitled him to the deduction of the capped farm loss amount of $8,750, but no more. If the taxpayer could further prove that farming was his or her chief source of income (or that it, in combination with another source, was his or her chief source of income), then all farming losses would be fully deductible.

The practical application of the above principles in the subsequent cases was to determine, firstly, if the taxpayer had a REOP (where the REOP test factors include profit and loss experience, start-up costs, the capability of the venture to show a profit, etc.) and, if so, then secondly, whether farming was the taxpayer's chief source of income (where the factors considered include time spent, capital committed, profitability, etc.).

The second generation of cases (from 2002 until now) resulted from the Supreme Court of Canada's decision in *Stewart*, which rejected the REOP test outlined in *Moldowan* as the test to use in order to determine if a taxpayer operates a business (i.e., a source of income that is taxable and from which losses may be deducted).[516] While *Stewart* was not a farming case of any type, it did replace the *Moldowan* REOP test with a "commercial manner" test that would be utilized in farming cases after 2002 when a determination was required to be made as to whether a farmer was engaged in a business or not (which is a prerequisite to deducting farming losses from other income).

Gunn is the third generation of authority (2006 to present) to the extent that the Federal Court of Appeal in this case built on the principles outlined in *Moldowan* (those principles that have survived) and *Stewart*, which resulted in the development of direct modern tests to be employed to determine if the "combination question" applies to a given set of facts. In *Gunn*, the Federal Court of Appeal developed three questions or factual requirements for which a taxpayer must provide sufficient evidence to a court which, if accepted by the court, will result in the taxpayer being successful in answering the combination question in the affirmative (meaning that the deduction of farming losses will not be restricted).[517] The three requirements to be met in order to be able to deduct all farming losses are:

(1) The taxpayer has invested significant capital in a farming enterprise.

(2) The taxpayer spends virtually all of his or her working time on a combination of farming and the other principal income-earning activity.

(3) The taxpayer's day-to-day activities are a combination of farming and the other income-earning activity, and the time spent on each is significant.

Gunn has been followed or considered in the following cases, all of which were decided in favour of the taxpayer: where a doctor had a large-scale farming operation including horse breeding, organic crops, and cat-

---

See page ii for explanation of footnotes.

[516] Stewart, 2002 DTC 6983.   [517] Gunn, 2006 DTC 6544.

tle;[518] where a dentist husband and lawyer wife operated a horse breeding and emu business;[519] where an engineer operated a cattle, lamb, goat, and turkey farm;[520] where a police officer operated a cattle farm;[521] and most recently, where a lawyer operated a horse breeding and racing business.[522]

This last case, *Craig*, later went on to the Supreme Court in 2012, and in a unanimous decision[523] the Supreme Court did somewhat overturn its own earlier decision in *Moldowan* in the way that case interpreted the combination test, in favour of the lower court approach used in *Gunn*. The combination question should only require an examination of the cumulative effect of the aggregate of capital invested in, time spent in, and income derived from farming and the second source of income, considered in light of the taxpayer's ordinary mode of living and farming history. If these factors show that a taxpayer places significant emphasis on both farming and non-farming sources of income, there is no reason that such a combination should not constitute a chief source of income.

The Act contains provisions for the carryback and carryforward of all or a part of a taxpayer's restricted farm losses.[524] See ¶3396.

[¶3582] Clearing or Levelling Land and Laying Tile Drainage

Amounts paid by a taxpayer in the year for clearing or levelling land, or for laying tile drainage, for the purpose of carrying on a farming business are deductible.[525] The taxpayer must be engaged in the business of farming and, to be deductible, the expenditure must be made for the purpose of carrying on such a business.

[¶3588] Feedlot Operation — When Considered Farming

A "feedlot" is considered to be a confined space where livestock are fed a concentrated diet for the purposes of producing a marketable animal.

Whether or not a feedlot operator is raising livestock and consequently would be considered to be farming is always a question of fact. To be considered to be farming, a feedlot operator must make an appreciable contribution to the growth and maturity of the livestock. In the case of a feedlot operation for cattle, appreciable contribution to the growth and maturity of the livestock would be considered to have been made if the animals are held in the feedlot for an average of at least 60 days or gain an average of at least 90 kilograms in weight. A feedlot operator may own all, some, or none of the livestock on the feedlot and may grow or purchase the feed used in the operation.

See page ii for explanation of footnotes.

[518] Stackhouse, 2007 DTC 620.
[519] Loyens, 2008 DTC 4698.
[520] Johnson, 2009 DTC 1245.
[521] Scharfe, 2010 DTC 1078.

[522] Craig, 2011 DTC 5047.
[523] Craig, 2012 DTC 5115
[524] CCH ¶16,003; Sec. 111.
[525] CCH ¶5650; Sec. 30; Interp. Bul. IT-485.

The following operations are not considered to be making an appreciable contribution to the growth and maturity of the livestock and are not considered to be farming:

(a) acting as agent or broker for the sale of livestock;

(b) buying livestock for resale as soon as a favourable opportunity presents itself; or

(c) assembling and preparing livestock for shipment.

[¶3591] Payments upon Destruction of Livestock

A taxpayer who is in the farming business and who receives compensation in respect of the destruction of livestock pursuant to statutory authority must include such payment in income in the year received, subject to an offsetting deduction for the year up to the amount included in income.[526] Any amount so deducted is deemed to be income from the business for the following year.

A deduction is also provided for a portion of the proceeds of the sale of breeding animals by a taxpayer who carries on the business of farming in a prescribed drought region and whose breeding herd has been reduced by at least 15% in a drought year.[527]

The deferral of income in respect of a farming business as noted above does not apply for a year in which a taxpayer dies or for a year at the end of which the taxpayer is a non-resident unless the taxpayer carried on business throughout the year in Canada.[528] This deferral, however, does not apply to income received or receivable by the taxpayer in the taxation year in which the taxpayer dies or ceases to be a resident of Canada or in any subsequent taxation year.[529]

[¶3594] Prospectors and Grubstakers

[¶3597] Disposition of Interest in Mining Property

Where a prospector or a grubstaker transfers a mining property acquired in specified circumstances to a corporation for shares of the corporation, the transfer is treated as a tax-free rollover. The shares are considered to have no cost to the grubstaker or prospector. At the time of disposition or exchange of the shares, if the shareholder is an individual, an income inclusion of the lesser of:

(a) the fair market value of the shares at the time of acquisition, and

(b) the proceeds received on the sale of the shares,

See page ii for explanation of footnotes.

[526] CCH ¶9895b, ¶9895c; Sec. 80.3(2), 80.3(3). [528] CCH ¶9895f; Sec. 80.3(6).
[527] CCH ¶9895d; Sec. 80.3(4). [529] CCH ¶9895; Sec. 80.3.

will be included in income.[530] A deduction is provided equal to $\frac{1}{2}$ of the amount included in income so that the individual prospector or grubstaker will include $\frac{1}{2}$ of the amount in income. If the shareholder is a corporation or a partnership made up of corporations, a capital gain or income receipt will be realized when the shares are disposed of depending on whether or not the shares are capital property to the shareholder.

A "prospector" means an *individual* who prospects or explores for minerals, or develops a property for minerals, either on his or her own behalf or on behalf of himself or herself and others, or as an employee. The mining property must have been acquired by the prospector as a result of his or her prospecting efforts, either alone or with others. Profits were deemed taxable where a prospector was found not to be an independent prospector nor an employee of a syndicate involved in a mining transaction, but rather was found to be an employee of a related administration company that managed the syndicate.[531]

A "grubstaker" may be an individual or a corporation which advanced money for or paid all or part of the expenses of prospecting, exploring, or developing a property for minerals. The money must have been advanced under an agreement with a prospector made *before* the prospecting, exploration, or development work was carried out, or as an employer of a prospector, and the mining property must have been acquired under the agreement with the prospector or, if the grubstaker is the prospector's employer, through the employee's efforts.

For a discussion of natural resource industries, see ¶3534 *et seq.*

[¶3600] Scientific Research and Experimental Development (SR&ED)

[¶3601] General

A taxpayer carrying on business in Canada may deduct SR&ED capital expenditures incurred in Canada and SR&ED current expenditures incurred in Canada or outside Canada.[532] The deduction for current expenditures incurred in Canada is discussed at ¶3603, outside of Canada at ¶3606, and the deduction for capital expenditures is discussed at ¶3609.

[¶3603] Current Expenses Incurred in Canada

After February 22, 2005, expenditures on SR&ED made in Canada are deemed to include those made by a taxpayer in the course of carrying on business in Canada for the prosecution of SR&ED in the exclusive economic zone (EEZ) of Canada, as defined in the *Oceans Act*, or in the airspace above

---

See page ii for explanation of footnotes.

[530] CCH ¶5800; Sec. 35.
[531] Geophysical Engineering Ltd., 76 DTC 6390.

[532] CCH ¶5900, ¶5902; Sec. 37(1), 37(2); Inf. Cir. 86-4R3.

or the subsoil or seabed below the EEZ.[533] The EEZ consists of the area that is up to 200 nautical miles from the low-water line along the coasts of Canada.

For taxation years ending after February 25, 2008, certain expenditures incurred outside of Canada are treated as having been made in Canada and, therefore, are potentially deductible as current expenditures incurred in Canada.[534] Specifically, the deemed expenditures are permissible salaries and wages paid by the taxpayer to Canadian resident employees in respect of SR&ED carried on outside of Canada that relate to a business of the taxpayer and are solely in support of SR&ED carried on in Canada. The SR&ED activities outside Canada must be directly undertaken by the taxpayer. Permissible salaries and wages are limited to 10% of the total salaries and wages directly attributable to SR&ED carried on in Canada by the taxpayer during the taxation year. (For the first taxation year ending after February 25, 2008, this 10% cap will be prorated based on the number of days in the taxation year after February 25, 2008.) Salaries and wages paid to an employee undertaking SR&ED outside Canada can be treated as expenditures in respect of SR&ED carried on in Canada only if the taxpayer reasonably believes that they are not subject to income or profits taxes imposed by such country because of the presence or activities of the employee in that country.[535] Presumably, the intent of this provision is to limit the taxpayer's deduction to salaries and wages that are fully taxable to the employee in Canada.

The following current expenses incurred *in Canada* are deductible:

(1) amounts expended in the year of scientific research and experimental development related to the taxpayer's business and directly undertaken by or on behalf of the taxpayer;

(2) payments to an approved association which undertakes SR&ED related to the class of business of the taxpayer;

(3) payments to an approved university, college, research institute, or similar institution if they are to be used to carry on SR&ED "related to the class of business" of the taxpayer;

(4) payments to a non-profit corporation for SR&ED that is exempt from tax;

(5) payments to a corporation resident in Canada for SR&ED related to the business of the taxpayer;

(6) payments to an approved organization; and

See page ii for explanation of footnotes.

[533] CCH ¶5901c; Sec. 37(1.3).
[534] CCH ¶5901g, ¶5901k; Sec. 37(1.4), 37(1.5).
[535] CCH ¶5927; Sec. 37(9).

¶3603

(7) payments by corporations to non-profit SR&ED corporations resident in Canada to be used for basic or applied research carried on in Canada.

In respect of point (5) above, contract payments currently made to a non-arm's length performer of the SR&ED are eligible for the investment tax credit, but generally only to the extent of the performer's costs of carrying out the SR&ED — in other words, the credit does not apply to the profit element, if any, in the contract payment made by the payer to the performer.

Draft budget legislation released on August 14, 2012 proposes a similar restriction for contract payments made to an arm's length performer of SR&ED. Using an arbitrary rate, the resolution proposes that 80% of the contract payment will qualify for the investment tax credit. However, the payment for these purposes (prior to calculating the 80% amount) will be reduced to the extent it reflects capital expenses incurred by the performer that are no longer eligible for investment tax credit treatment themselves (i.e., for capital expenses incurred after 2013 — see above).

The amount of wages and salaries eligible for the SR&ED tax incentives is limited in the case of specified employees. The limit is five times the year's maximum pensionable earnings for the purposes of the *Canada Pension Plan.* A specified employee is an employee who does not deal at arm's length with the taxpayer or a specified shareholder. A specified shareholder is one who owns 10% or more of any class of shares.[536]

In order to qualify as a deduction, an SR&ED expenditure must be related to a business of the taxpayer in which the taxpayer was actively engaged at the time the expenditure was made. Where expenditures have been made in a year in respect of a particular business of the taxpayer but not claimed as a deduction, the expenditures may be carried forward and deducted in a subsequent year in computing income from that or any other business carried on in the subsequent year.

For the purposes of the "related-to-business" test, the prosecution of SR&ED will not itself be considered to be a business to which SR&ED is related unless the taxpayer derives all or substantially all of his or her revenue from the prosecution of SR&ED.[537]

SR&ED related to a business actively carried on by a related corporation will be considered an eligible SR&ED expenditure.[538]

Expenditures in respect of the acquisition of a building or a leasehold interest in a building or rental or lease expenses in respect of a building are not deductible as SR&ED expenditures unless the building is a prescribed special purpose building.[539] Computer technology research and develop-

---

See page ii for explanation of footnotes.

[536] CCH ¶5927a–5927e; Sec. 37(9.1)–(9.5).
[537] CCH ¶5926; Sec. 37(8).
[538] CCH ¶5901; Sec. 37(1.1).
[539] CCH ¶5926; Sec. 37(8)(d).

ment expenditures made after February 27, 1995 by financial institutions or registered securities dealers will not qualify as scientific research and development and therefore will not qualify for investment tax credits.

[¶3606] Current Expenses Incurred Outside Canada

Current expenses incurred in respect of SR&ED carried on *outside Canada* are deductible if made:

(a) on SR&ED related to the business and directly undertaken by or on behalf of the taxpayer (except to the extent that such expenses are deemed to have been made in Canada (see ¶3603)); and

(b) by payments to an approved association, university, college, research institute, or other similar institution to be used for SR&ED related to the class of business of the taxpayer.[540]

The provisions discussed above relating to the "related-to-business" test apply in respect of SR&ED carried on outside Canada.

[¶3609] Expenditures of a Capital Nature

Expenditures of a capital nature made in Canada in acquiring property, other than land, may be deducted if the SR&ED is related to the taxpayer's business and is directly undertaken by or on behalf of the taxpayer, and does not exceed the lesser of:

(a) the actual expenditure; and

(b) the undepreciated capital cost of the property acquired as of the end of the taxation year.[541]

It will be noted that an amount deducted for a capital expenditure is deemed to be an amount allowed as a capital cost allowance (see below). The combined effect of these rules is that the total capital expenditure deductions which may be claimed in any year may not exceed the capital cost of the property *minus* the sum of:

(a) the deductions previously claimed; and

(b) proceeds of disposition of the property. The deduction of expenditures of a capital nature applies only in respect of property that would otherwise be a depreciable property and excludes a leasehold interest in land.

It will be noted that, where a taxpayer incurred capital expenditures in respect of which he/she received assistance payments, the payments will reduce the amounts deductible. But the taxpayer is allowed to claim a deduction for any amounts repaid. (See ¶3612).

See page ii for explanation of footnotes.

[540] CCH ¶5902; Sec. 37(2).   [541] CCH ¶5900; Sec. 37(1)(b).

¶3606

Draft budget legislation released on August 14, 2012 proposes to eliminate this full deduction benefit. Capital expenditures made after 2013 will no longer be deductible, nor will they form part of the SR&ED pool for investment tax credits. Furthermore, this new rule (non-deduction, no credit) will apply to any payments in respect of the use or the right to use property after 2013 that would, if it were acquired by the taxpayer, be capital property of the taxpayer.

[¶3612] Repayments

Repayments of grants by a taxpayer who had originally received them under an *Appropriation Act* are deductible.[542] The deduction also applies to any governmental assistance or non-governmental assistance in respect of SR&ED expenditures repaid by the taxpayer. See also grants and subsidies at ¶3645.

[¶3615] Investment Tax Credit

The taxpayer's pool of SR&ED expenditures must be reduced by the amount of a claim for an investment tax credit earned in respect of qualifying SR&ED expenditures.[543] The taxpayer may deduct an investment tax credit in respect of, among other things, SR&ED expenditures of a current nature.[544] The investment tax credit arising in respect of a particular scientific research expenditure might be deducted in a year in which no current expenditures are made.

If the investment tax credit arising in respect of a particular scientific research expenditure is deducted in a year in which no current expenditures are made, then it will be included in income in that year. Furthermore, such amounts are only included in income once.[545] However, a reduction of the SR&ED pool is made only for taxation years following that in which a related investment tax credit is made.

[¶3618] Meaning of "Scientific Research and Experimental Development"

The term "scientific research and experimental development" means a systematic investigation or search carried out in a field of science or technology by means of experiment or analysis.[546] Such work must be aimed at:

(1) basic research (i.e., work undertaken for the advancement of scientific knowledge without a specific practical application in view);

(2) applied research (i.e., work undertaken for the advancement of scientific knowledge with a specific practical application in view);

See page ii for explanation of footnotes.

[542] CCH ¶5900; Sec. 37(1)(c).
[543] CCH ¶5900; Sec. 37(1)(e).
[544] CCH ¶19,825; Sec. 127(5).

[545] CCH ¶5900, ¶19,831a; Sec. 37, 127(10.1).
[546] CCH ¶28,257c; Sec. 248(1) "scientific research and experimental development"; Inf. Cir. 86-4R3.

(3) experimental development (i.e., use of the results of basic or applied research for the purpose of creating or improving materials, devices, products, or processes); and

(4) work undertaken by or on behalf of the taxpayer with respect to engineering, design, operations research, mathematical analysis, computer programming, data collection, testing and psychological research, where that work is commensurate with the needs, and directly in support, of the work described in (1) to (3) that is undertaken *in Canada* by or on behalf of the taxpayer.

The above definition was revised in 1998, applicable to work performed after February 27, 1995, to emphasize that the work described in (4) is limited to work undertaken by or on behalf of the taxpayer in support of work in (1) to (3) that is undertaken in Canada.

"Scientific research and experimental development" does not include the following: market research; sales promotion; quality control or routine testing of materials, devices, products or processes; research in the social sciences or the humanities; prospecting, exploring, or drilling for or producing minerals, petroleum, or natural gas; commercial production of a new or improved material, device, or product or the commercial use of a new or improved process; style changes; or routine data collection.

[¶3624] Capital Cost Allowance

An amount claimed for capital expenditures is deemed for capital cost allowance purposes to be an amount allowed as depreciation and for that purpose, the property acquired by the expenditures on scientific research and experimental development is deemed to be of a separate prescribed class and accordingly subject to recapture. See also Chapter IV.

[¶3627] Prohibited Deductions

Expenditures made to acquire rights in, or arising out of, scientific research (patent rights, trademarks, etc.) are not deductible from income as scientific research expenditures.[547]

[¶3628] Filing of Prescribed Form

An expenditure is expressly denied as a deduction unless the prescribed form is filed in respect of the expenditure within 12 months of the taxpayer's "filing-due date" for the year in which the expenditure is otherwise incurred.[548] Thus, for a corporate taxpayer the form must be filed within 18 months after the year end of the year in which the expenditure is incurred. For an individual, it will have to be filed by April 30 or June 15 (in the case of a self-employed individual) of the second calendar year following the year in which the expenditure was incurred. The prescribed forms are T661 and

---

See page ii for explanation of footnotes.

[547] CCH ¶5906; Sec. 37(4). [548] CCH ¶5929; Sec. 37(11).

T2038. Furthermore, an unpaid expense in the form of unpaid remuneration which cannot be deducted in the year because of ¶2685 must nonetheless be reported in the prescribed form for the year (in which case it becomes deductible in the subsequent year in which it is paid).

Generally speaking, the CRA has the discretion to waive the filing deadline for prescribed forms (see ¶15,006). [Draft technical amendments re-released on July 16, 2010 would remove the CRA's waiver of filing forms T661 and T2038 on time after November 16, 2005. As a result, a taxpayer will not be allowed a deduction or an investment tax credit in relation to an SR&ED expenditure if the claim is not made within 12 months of the taxpayer's filing due date.][549]

If the form is not filed on time, the affected expenditures are deemed not to be on account of or in respect of scientific research and experimental development.[550] In such case, the deductibility of the expenditures will be determined as if they were "regular" expenditures not subject to the scientific research and development provisions. (Capital expenditures may constitute depreciable capital property, and current expenditures would likely be deductible in the year they were incurred under the general computation of profit.)

[¶3636] Crown Corporations

[¶3639] Income

The income from a federal Crown corporation as agent of the Crown and from any property of the Crown administered by the corporation is subject to tax.[551] This does not apply to the *Federal Development Bank Act.*[552] The purpose of the provision is to make the financial statements of these corporations more comparable with those of private corporations and to make it easier to assess the efficiency of their operations.

The ownership of property is attributed to the Crown corporation, thereby ensuring the capital gains and losses realized in respect of Crown property administered by Crown corporations will be included in the income of the Crown corporations.

[¶3642] Grants and Subsidies

[¶3645] Government Grants and Other Subsidies

Government assistance includes federal, provincial, municipal, or other public authority grants, subsidies, forgivable loans, deductions from tax, investment allowances, and any other form of assistance other than an

---

[549] Sec. 220(2.2).
[550] CCH ¶5929a; Sec. 37(12).

[551] CCH ¶5172; Sec. 27.
[552] CCH ¶5174a; 1974-75-76, Chap. 14.

amount authorized to be paid under an *Appropriation Act* on terms and conditions approved by the Treasury Board in respect of scientific research expenditures (e.g., scientific research expenditures authorized under the federal *Enterprise Development Program* (EDP)), or an amount deducted as an allowance in respect of an oil or gas well, mine, or timber limit.

Government assistance given to enable a taxpayer to acquire capital property does not increase the taxpayer's net income. However, in the case of depreciable property,[553] or in the case of other capital property,[554] the capital cost or the cost (as the case may be) of the property is reduced by the amount of the assistance. Assistance repaid, received, or entitled to be received after the disposition of the property, also affects the computation of capital cost. It has been held that all of a government incentive grant had to be deducted from the capital cost of a manufacturing facility even though a portion of the grant was calculated, not on the basis of the costs of construction, but on the number of new jobs created.[555]

See page ii for explanation of footnotes.

[553] CCH ¶4532; Sec. 13(7.1); Interp. Bul. IT-273R2.

[554] CCH ¶7669; Sec. 53(2)(k); Interp. Bul. IT-151R5, IT-257R.

[555] British Columbia Forest Products Limited, 85 DTC 5577.

¶3645

Chapter IV

Capital Cost Allowance

Depreciable Property **4000**

General Rules 4005

Capital Cost of Property 4010

Grants, Subsidies, and
Other Incentives 4012

Townsite Costs, Surface
Constructions, and
Bridges 4014

Proceeds of Disposition for
Depreciable Property
Owned on December 31,
1971 4015

**Capital Cost Allowance
Classes and Rates** **4020**

Classes of Property and
Schedule of Rates 4025

Capital Cost Allowance
Rates for Classes 38 to
40 4030

Classes of Property Not
Included in the
Schedule of Rates 4035

Election re Grouping of
Assets 4037

Transferred and
Misclassified Property 4040

Separate Classes 4045

**Acquisition of Depreciable
Assets and When Capital
Cost Allowance May Be
Claimed** **4050**

Date of Acquisition of
Depreciable Assets 4055

Available-for-Use Rules 4060

Half-Year Rule: Capital Cost
Allowance in Year of
Acquisition 4062

Taxation Year Less Than 12
Months 4065

Death of a Taxpayer 4067

**Official Government
Publications** **4070**

Interpretation Bulletins and
Information Circulars 4075

**Buildings — Leaseholds —
Sale-Leasebacks** **4080**

Buildings and Component
Parts — Capital Cost
Allowance 4085

Leasehold Interests 4090

**Patents, Vehicles, Power-
Operated Movable
Equipment, and Pipelines** **4105**

Patents, Concessions,
Franchises, Licences, etc. 4110

Election — Limited Period
Franchise, Concession, or
Licence 4115

Automobiles, Trucks, and
Aircraft 4120

Trucks 4122

Power-Operated Movable
Machinery (Classes 10,
22, and 38) 4124

Pipelines 4127

**Timber and Industrial
Mineral Mines** **4130**

Timber Limits 4135

Timber Resource Property 4140

Property Acquired to Cut
and Remove Timber 4145

Industrial Mineral Mines,
Sand, and Gravel Pits 4150

**Additional Capital Cost
Allowances** **4155**

Railway Property 4165

Canadian Vessels and
Offshore Drilling Vessels 4170

Mining Assets (Classes 28,
41, and 41.1) 4172

**Accelerated Capital Cost
Allowances** **4180**

Water and Air Pollution
Control Equipment
(Classes 24 and 27) 4190

Manufacturing and
Processing Machinery
and Equipment 4210

Energy-Efficient Equipment
(Classes 43.1 and 43.2) 4215

Temporary Accelerated
CCA for Computer
Hardware and Systems
Software (Class 52) 4220

**Motion Picture Films,
Videotapes, Computer
Software, and Electronic
Equipment** **4270**

Certified Productions 4275

Television Commercial
Message 4280

Videotapes and Laser Disks
for Rental 4281

Computers, Systems
Software, and Ancillary
Data Processing
Equipment 4282

Electronic Office Equipment
and Data Network
Infrastructure Equipment 4283

Rental Properties **4285**

Rental Properties 4290

Leasing Properties **4295**

Leasing Properties 4300

Specified Leasing Property 4305

Election to Treat Lease as
Loan: Lessee's Position 4307

**Property Not Subject to
Capital Cost Allowance** **4335**

Property Not Included 4340

**Farming and Fishing
Assets** **4345**

Methods of Computing
Capital Cost Allowance 4350

Deductions Allowed 4355

Deductions Not Permitted 4360

Fiscal Period 4365

Assets with More Than One
Use 4370

Transfer of Farm and
Fishing Property to Child 4375

**Disposal of Depreciable
Property and Recapture
of Capital Cost
Allowance** **4380**

Recapture 4385

Undepreciated Capital
Cost 4387

Proceeds of Disposition 4388

Taxation Year — Individuals
Carrying On Business 4390

Additions to Class within
Taxation Year 4395

Examples Illustrating
Disposition of Assets
under a Capital Cost
Allowance System 4400

Assets Converted to
Personal or Business
Use 4410

Assets Used Partly for
Personal and Partly for
Business Purposes 4415

Change in Proportionate
Use 4420

Non-Arm's Length Transfer
of Depreciable Property 4425

Deemed Disposition of
Depreciable Property
upon a Change of
Control 4430

Non-Residents and
Recapture 4435

Lease-Option Agreements 4450

Mortgage Included in
Proceeds of Disposition 4455

Exchanges of Property and
Replacement Property 4460

Recapture of
Representation Costs 4465

Terminal Loss **4470**

Terminal Loss on Disposal
of Assets of a Class 4475

Assets Destroyed, Stolen,
Lost, or Obsolete 4480

Allocation of Proceeds
between Land and
Building 4485

Examples of Allocation of
Proceeds between Land
and Building 4490

Dispositions to Affiliated
Persons 4495

Alphabetical Table of Rates 4500

Alphabetical List of Assets
— Capital Cost
Allowance Classes and
Rates 4505

Recent Changes

2012 Capital Cost Limit on Automobiles

The ceiling on the capital cost of passenger vehicles purchased in 2012 will remain at $30,000. The government's decision was announced on December 29, 2011. See ¶4010, ¶4040, and ¶4120.

Energy-Efficient Equipment

Class 43.2 accelerated CCA for clean energy generation equipment. The 2012 Budget announced the extension of the accelerated CCA under Class 43.2 to:

- Waste-fuelled thermal energy equipment used for space and water heating applications.

- Equipment that is part of a district energy system that distributes thermal energy primarily generated by waste-fuelled thermal energy equipment, so as to provide an alternative to equipment that uses only fossil fuels.

- Equipment that uses residue of plants (i.e., straw, corn cobs, leaves) to generate electricity and heat.

These additions will apply to equipment acquired after March 28, 2012 that has not been used or acquired for use before March 29, 2012. Waste-fuel equipment that is not in compliance with environmental laws at the time it first becomes available for use will not benefit from this 50% accelerated CCA rate. See ¶4215.

Deferral of Recapture on Concessions, Franchises, and Licences

Concessions, franchises, and licences will be treated as former business property for purposes of the deferral of recapture of CCA, provided there is a joint election between the transferor and the transferee. These outstanding technical amendments are reprised in the draft legislation that was released on July 16, 2010. See ¶4115 and ¶4460.

Time Limits for Acquiring Replacement Property

To accommodate short taxation years, the specified time limits for acquiring replacement property and defer recapture of CCA are amended in the technical draft legislation that was released on July 16, 2010. See ¶4460.

[¶4000] Depreciable Property

[¶4005] General Rules

The Act provides that in computing a taxpayer's income from a business or property, there may be deducted such part of the capital cost to the taxpayer of property (or such amount in respect of the capital cost to the taxpayer of property) as is allowed by regulation.[1] Capital cost allowance is a permissive deduction. The taxpayer may not deduct more than the maximum permitted by regulation for each class of asset but may in any year deduct an amount equal to or less than the maximum allowed or in fact nothing at all. Under certain circumstances, the CRA will accept a request from a taxpayer to revise capital cost allowance claims for previous years.[2]

The rate of depreciation or capital cost allowance, which is fixed by regulation for each class of assets, is applied to a particular asset on its original cost or its undepreciated capital cost. See ¶4387 for a description of undepreciated capital cost. Capital cost allowance is calculated on a declining balance method for most classes of assets. See ¶4035 for the exceptions to the declining balance method. The amount of the deduction in the first year is generally $1/2$ the prescribed percentage of the cost of the asset. Hence, an asset originally costing $100 and subject to an allowance of 10% will be depreciated $5 in the first year and $9.50 in the second year (i.e., 10% of ($100 – $5)). Similarly, the capital cost allowance in the third year will be 10% of $85.50, and so on. Under this method, a taxpayer does not have to claim the maximum amount of CCA in any given year. For example, a taxpayer who does not have to pay income tax for the year may not want to claim CCA. Claiming CCA reduces the balance of the class by the amount of CCA claimed. As a result, the CCA available for future years will be reduced.

It is important to note that under this system of depreciation, where a taxpayer has a number of assets within a particular class, the assets of that class are grouped as one unit, or pooled, for capital cost allowance purposes. (See "Separate classes" at ¶4045 for some exceptions to this general rule.) The capital cost allowance that may be deducted each year in respect of property of a particular class is, with minor exceptions, a percentage of undepreciated capital cost to the taxpayer of all property in that class as of the end of the taxation year. See ¶4060 concerning the available-for-use rule, which determines the earliest taxation year in which capital cost allowance may be claimed in respect of the acquisition of an asset after 1989.

If a taxpayer disposes of some of the assets of a class before the end of the year, the taxpayer must deduct from the total undepreciated capital cost of the class the proceeds of disposition up to the amount of the original capital cost of the asset disposed of. If an asset which is the sole property in its class is disposed of for proceeds less than its undepreciated capital cost, the balance of the undepreciated capital cost is a terminal loss and can be deducted as an expense of the taxpayer (see ¶4475). On the other hand, if the proceeds of disposition of such an asset exceed its undepreciated capital cost, then under the recapture provisions the excess up to the amount of the original capital cost of the asset will be considered income (see ¶4385 *et*

See page ii for explanation of footnotes.

[1] CCH ¶4902, ¶4952a; Sec. 20(1)(a); Reg. 1105;   [2] Inf. Cir. 84-1.
Interp. Bul. IT-128R, IT-285R2.

¶4005

seq.). Any amount by which the proceeds exceed the original capital cost of the asset is a capital gain (see Chapter V).

"Depreciable property" is defined as property acquired by the taxpayer in respect of which the taxpayer has been allowed (or, if the taxpayer owned the property at the end of the year, would, without taking into account the available-for-use rules, be entitled to) a deduction under the regulations relating to capital cost allowances.[3] The capital cost allowance system is designed to ensure that a taxpayer will be allowed to recover the full capital cost of depreciable property; however, the case law does produce some varied decisions. Where a mining company claimed capital cost allowance on the underground passageways constructed and used in its mining operations, the Supreme Court of Canada disallowed the claim on the grounds that: the cost of constructing the passageways had been met by the value of the ore extracted; there was (because of this fact) no capital cost involved in the construction; and where there is no capital cost, there can be no capital cost allowance.[4] A natural gas company was entitled to add to the undepreciated capital cost of the relevant class of assets its expenditure incurred in relocating pipelines on the request of third parties, regardless of reimbursements in the form of contributions received from those parties. Such contributions were contributions to capital made more for the benefit of these third parties than the gas company.[5]

It is to be noted that in order to be depreciable, an asset must be acquired for the purpose of gaining or producing income. It is not just possession of the asset that determines whether an allowance will be granted.[6] Thus, when, during the five-day period between the wind-up of its subsidiaries and their sale to a related corporation, the depreciable assets acquired by the corporate taxpayer had been used to produce some business income, they were eligible for CCA treatment in its hands.[7] See also ¶4340. For a discussion of the sale of goodwill and other "nothings", see ¶3072 *et seq.*

[¶4010] Capital Cost of Property

Under normal circumstances, capital cost allowance is applied on the undepreciated capital cost of the assets as of the end of the taxation year. This is defined[8] as the capital cost of the asset plus adjustments for recapture and government assistance or inducements repaid after the disposal of a property less adjustments for capital cost allowance claimed in previous years, amounts credited upon the disposition of a property, and investment tax credits and government assistance claimed or received after the disposition of a property. See ¶4387 for a more detailed description of undepreciated capital cost.

See page ii for explanation of footnotes.

[3] CCH ¶4562bc; Sec. 13(21) "depreciable property".
[4] Denison Mines Ltd., 74 DTC 6525.
[5] The Consumers' Gas Company Ltd., 84 DTC 6058, The Consumers' Gas Company Ltd., 87 DTC 5008.
[6] Dowbiggin, 66 DTC 97.
[7] Hickman Motors Ltd., 97 DTC 5363.
[8] CCH ¶4562h; Sec. 13(21) "undepreciated capital cost".

The term "capital cost" is not defined but is the amount actually expended by a taxpayer to acquire a capital asset. Capital cost is the cost of an asset, not its value. It includes all "laid-down" costs such as freight, installation, duties, and goods and services tax and is calculated net of any amounts received such as inducements, grants, or tax credits, including goods and services tax credits or rebates.[9] Contingent liabilities are not considered to be part of the cost of the asset.[10] In a case where the taxpayers received a vendor warranty that gave them a chance to walk away from the purchase of computer software, they were denied their CCA claims on the grounds that they never incurred an absolute obligation to purchase the software. Since the obligation was only contingent, the software cost was nil.[11]

Where a taxpayer owes money and settles the debt for less than its full amount, the gain implicit in the settlement is not recognized but goes to reduce the loss carryovers of the taxpayer, and, if they are insufficient, the capital cost of depreciable property.[12] This reduction applies for capital cost allowance purposes.[13]

If a taxpayer acquires a depreciable property after November 1992, using a trade-in as part of the consideration, the portion of the cost of the depreciable property attributed to the trade-in cannot exceed the fair market value of the property traded in. Note that this rule only imposes an upper limit of fair market value on values assigned to the trade-in. It does not actually substitute fair market value for the assigned or contract value. Accordingly, the rule prevents the cost of depreciable property acquired in whole or in part with a trade-in from being inflated by overstating the trade-in value.[14]

Special rules are provided to determine the capital cost of depreciable property in certain circumstances.[15] For example, a taxpayer who has acquired property for some other purpose and later commences to use it for the purpose of gaining income, is deemed to have acquired it for a specified amount.[16] (See ¶4410 for the definition of "specified amount".) This specified amount is the capital cost of the property for capital cost allowance purposes. Where an asset is regularly used partly for personal and partly for business purposes, the capital cost allowance will be computed on the proportion of the total capital cost of the asset that its use for business is of its overall use.[17] Thus, for example, where a car is used 25% of the time for personal purposes and 75% for business, only $3/4$ of the capital cost allowance computed on its total undepreciated capital cost will be allowed. If the proportion of use changes, the basis of capital cost allowance will change

---

See page ii for explanation of footnotes.

[9] CCH ¶4535, ¶4535a; Sec. 13(7.1), 13(7.2); Interp. Bul. IT-285R2.
[10] Mandel, 80 DTC 6148.
[11] Sherman et al, 2009 DTC 5042.
[12] CCH ¶9854; Sec. 80(5).
[13] CCH ¶4535; Sec. 13(7.1).
[14] CCH ¶4591; Sec. 13(33).
[15] CCH ¶4522; Sec. 13(7).
[16] CCH ¶4522; Sec. 13(7)(b).
[17] CCH ¶4522; Sec. 13(7)(c).

accordingly[18] (see ¶4420). In the case of non-arm's length transfer of depreciable property, special rules determine the capital cost of the asset depending on the circumstances[19] (see ¶4425). Similarly, special rules limit the capital cost of property that has been deemed to have been disposed of and immediately re-acquired when a corporation undergoes a change in control[20] (see ¶4430).

Passenger vehicles are limited to a maximum capital cost of $30,000 in 2001–2012 plus GST/HST, PST, and other provincial levies for the purpose of claiming capital cost allowance[21] (see ¶4120).

Any depreciable property acquired by a corporation or a partnership of which the corporation is a majority interest partner in the 12 months preceding the acquisition of control of the corporation will be deemed not to have been acquired at that time, but rather to have been acquired immediately after the acquisition of control.[22] Accordingly, capital cost allowance will not be available for the taxation year that ends immediately prior to the acquisition of control. This restriction will not apply if the property was used or was acquired for use in a business that was carried on by the corporation 12 months prior to the acquisition of control or if it was owned by the corporation or an affiliated person for the period beginning 12 months prior to the acquisition of control and ending upon the acquisition of the property by the corporation.

If a taxpayer becomes resident in Canada, the taxpayer is deemed to dispose of any property at its fair market value just before becoming a Canadian resident and to reacquire it right after.[23] As a result, the capital cost of depreciable property owned by a taxpayer who becomes a Canadian resident is the fair market value of the property at the time the taxpayer becomes resident in Canada. This will not apply to assets already being used in a business in Canada and already subject to Canadian CCA rules.

[¶4012] Grants, Subsidies, and Other Incentives

Where a taxpayer receives (or is entitled to receive) government assistance in the form of a grant, subsidy, or other incentive from a government or a government agency to buy depreciable property, the amount of the grant, subsidy, or other incentive is subtracted from the property's capital cost.[24] The government assistance may be received from federal or provincial governments, municipalities, or other public bodies performing a governmental function in Canada. It may be in the form of a grant, subsidy, forgivable loan, deduction from tax, investment allowance, or any other form. An input tax credit or rebate for the GST or HST paid on depreciable

---

See page ii for explanation of footnotes.

[18] CCH ¶4522; Sec. 13(7)(*d*).

[19] CCH ¶4522; Sec. 13(7)(*e*).

[20] CCH ¶4522; Sec. 13(7)(*f*).

[21] CCH ¶4522, ¶4523, ¶28,195; Sec. 13(7)(*g*), 13(7)(*h*), 248(1) "passenger vehicle"; Reg. 7307; Interp. Bul. IT-521R, IT-522R.

[22] CCH ¶4582, ¶4583; Sec. 13(24), 13(25).

[23] CCH ¶20,025b; Sec. 128.1(1)(*b*).

[24] CCH ¶4535; Sec. 13(7.1); Interp. Bul. IT-273R2.

property acquired for use in a proportion of at least 90% in the course of business activities is deemed to be government assistance,[25] as is the investment tax credit. The investment tax credit reduces the capital cost of the asset in the year after it is deducted by the taxpayer. For instance, an investment tax credit claimed or received in 2012 will be subtracted from the undepreciated capital cost (UCC) of the class the property belongs to at the start of 2013 and, if there is no property left in the class, the amount is included in income in 2013. Other forms of government assistance reduce the capital cost in the year the taxpayer receives or is entitled to receive them.

Receipts of government or non-government assistance in respect of scientific research and experimental development (SR&ED) expenses are not treated as government assistance.[26] As well, grants received under a prescribed program of the federal government, and which are included in income, are not treated as government assistance. The Canadian Home Insulation Program and the Canada Oil Substitution Program are prescribed programs.[27] Depletion allowance can be earned in some cases by acquiring depreciable property (e.g., mining machinery). Depletion allowance is not, however, regarded as government assistance for purposes of determining the capital cost of the depreciable property.[28] Amounts received by the taxpayer as contributions towards the relocation of its natural gas pipelines from government corporations, as well as the private sector, were not government assistance so did not reduce the taxpayer's capital cost of the pipelines.[29]

Where a taxpayer receives any particular amount as an inducement, contribution, refund, reimbursement, or allowance in respect of the acquisition of an asset or otherwise in the course of earning income (to the extent that the amount has not otherwise been included in income or resulted in an assessment that reflected a reduction in the cost of a property or the amount of an outlay or expense), the amount must be included in income.[30] Alternatively, rather than including the inducement or other such amount relating to the acquisition of a depreciable asset in income, the taxpayer may elect to reduce the capital cost of the asset acquired in the year that the inducement was received or in any of the three immediately preceding years or the following year.[31] The taxpayer must file the election on or before the day that the taxpayer is required to file his or her tax return for the year during which the inducement was received or the following year if the property was acquired in the following year. The elected amount by which the capital cost of the depreciable property can be reduced cannot exceed the least of:

See page ii for explanation of footnotes.

[25] CCH ¶28,329l; Sec. 248(16).

[26] CCH ¶4535, ¶5900; Sec. 13(7.1), 37(1)(d).

[27] CCH ¶8070, ¶8072, ¶8073; Sec. 56(1)(s); Reg. 5500, Reg. 5501.

[28] CCH ¶4535, ¶8800; Sec. 13(7.1), 65.

[29] The Consumers' Gas Co. Ltd., 84 DTC 6058, The Consumers' Gas Company Ltd., 87 DTC 5008.

[30] CCH ¶4376c; Sec. 12(1)(x).

[31] CCH ¶4536; Sec. 13(7.4).

(a) the amount received by the taxpayer;

(b) the capital cost of the property as otherwise determined; and

(c) nil, where the taxpayer has disposed of the property before the year.

An increase in the capital cost of the property is provided in the event that a taxpayer repays all or a portion of the inducement in respect of which the taxpayer previously elected to reduce the capital cost of the property. The addition to the taxpayer's cost can only be made if the taxpayer owns the property at the time of payment. See ¶4387 for treatment of a repayment that occurs after the disposition of the property. See item (13), "*Grants, subsidies, etc.*", and item (21), "*Inducement payments*", at ¶5185 concerning the treatment of subsidies and inducements received by a taxpayer for non-depreciable capital property.

A trust or partnership is required to reduce the capital cost of depreciable property where any form of government assistance or tax credit is received by a taxpayer who is a beneficiary of the trust or a member of the partnership in respect of such property that is held or acquired by the trust or partnership.[32]

[¶4014] Townsite Costs, Surface Constructions, and Bridges

Where a taxpayer is required under the terms of a contract made after March 5, 1996 to make a payment to the Crown or to a municipality in respect of certain townsite costs incurred or to be incurred by the recipient to acquire specified townsite properties in respect of a mine that would, if it had been acquired by the taxpayer, be property included in Class 10(l), the taxpayer is deemed to have acquired the property at a capital cost equal to the portion of the payment that can reasonably be regarded as being in respect of those costs.[33] The time of acquisition of the property by the taxpayer is deemed to be the later of the time the payment is made and the time at which those costs are incurred.

Similarly, where, at any time after March 5, 1996, a taxpayer incurs a cost on account of capital for the building of, for the right to use, or in respect of roads or similar surface constructions, including bridges, and the amount of the costs would otherwise not be included in the capital cost to the taxpayer of depreciable property of a prescribed class, the taxpayer is deemed at that time to have acquired the property at a capital cost equal to the amount of the costs.[34]

Where a taxpayer acquires an intangible property as a consequence of making a payment or incurring a cost described above, the intangible property is treated as part of the depreciable property that is deemed to be acquired.[35] The capital cost of a particular intangible property is equal to a

---

See page ii for explanation of footnotes.

[32] CCH ¶4535a; Sec. 13(7.2).
[33] CCH ¶4537e; Sec. 13(7.5)(a); Reg. 1102(14.2).
[34] CCH ¶4537e; Sec. 13(7.5)(b); Reg. 1102(14.3).
[35] CCH ¶4537e; Sec. 13(7.5)(c).

proration factor multiplied by the lesser of the deemed capital cost of the depreciable property and the fair market value of all intangible properties so acquired. The proration factor for a particular intangible property is its fair market value divided by the fair market value of all the intangible properties so acquired.

Example:

> In order to be able to establish a factory at a particular location, a taxpayer builds a road to the factory at a cost of $10 million. The road is owned by the municipality in which the factory is located, but the municipality provides the taxpayer with exclusive access to two parts of the road indefinitely. The fair market values of these access rights are $200,000 and $300,000. As a consequence of incurring these costs, the taxpayer is deemed to acquire the road (Class 17 property) for $10 million. The access rights are considered to be part of the road. The capital costs of these rights are considered to be $200,000 and $300,000, respectively.

Any property deemed by the above rules to have been acquired at any time by the taxpayer is deemed to have been acquired for the purpose for which the payment was made or the cost was incurred and is deemed to be owned by the taxpayer at any subsequent time that the taxpayer benefits from the use of the property.[36]

The purpose of these deeming provisions is to prevent costs associated with the building of roads and similar projects from being considered as eligible capital expenditures while, at the same time, ensuring that classification of such costs as Canadian exploration expenses, Canadian development expenses, and foreign exploration and development expenses is restricted to the building of temporary access roads to oil and gas wells. The resulting capital cost allowance claimed by a taxpayer in respect of such costs can result in a reduction of the taxpayer's resource allowance, described at ¶3534.

[¶4015] Proceeds of Disposition for Depreciable Property Owned on December 31, 1971

Where the capital cost to a taxpayer of any depreciable property of a prescribed class acquired before 1972 and owned from December 31, 1971, until the time the taxpayer disposes of it is less than the fair market value of the property on Valuation Day, and less than the proceeds of disposition, the following transitional provisions apply.[37]

(1) For the purpose of the provisions relating to capital gains, recapture, and capital cost allowances, the proceeds of disposition are deemed to be the capital cost plus the excess of the actual proceeds over the Valuation Day value.

See page ii for explanation of footnotes.

[36] CCH ¶4537e; Sec. 13(7.5)(d).

[37] CCH ¶29,130, ¶29,155; ITAR 18, 20(1); Interp. Bul. IT-218R.

Example:

Capital cost of a building	$50,000
Valuation Day value	70,000
Ultimate proceeds of sale	80,000

The taxpayer's proceeds of disposition will be deemed to be $60,000: $50,000 + ($80,000 - $70,000). The taxpayer will be subject to full recapture and will have a capital gain of $10,000. If the ultimate proceeds of sale had been $65,000, the taxpayer's proceeds of disposition would be deemed to be $50,000. The taxpayer would be subject to full recapture, but would have no capital gain or loss.

(2) If the property is transferred in one or more non-arm's length transactions, each non-arm's length purchaser, for purposes of calculating capital cost allowance, capital gains, and recapture is deemed to have incurred a capital cost equal to the proceeds the vendor is deemed to have received under rule (1) above. Upon a subsequent disposition, the transferee calculates the proceeds under rule (1) above as if the transferee had owned the property since December 31, 1971. See the example below.

These Income Tax Application Rules transitional provisions are not applicable to a transfer of depreciable property to a spouse, common-law partner, or trust, *inter vivos* or on death, or to a transfer of farm property upon the death of a taxpayer from the taxpayer to the taxpayer's child, grandchild, or great-grandchild. However, upon the subsequent disposition of the property by the spouse, common-law partner, trust, or child, the Income Tax Application Rules will apply.[38] In the case of a taxpayer who acquires depreciable property under other forms of tax-free rollovers after 1971 from a person who owned it at December 31, 1971, the Income Tax Application Rules deem the taxpayer to have acquired the property before 1972 and to have owned it continuously from December 31, 1971, so that the rules may be applicable on a subsequent disposition by the taxpayer.[39]

If property owned on December 31, 1971, is used in farming or fishing and the taxpayer has continuously taken capital cost allowance on the straight-line basis, the taxpayer is not subject to recapture of depreciation on the sale of the property.

The following is an example of the operation of the transitional provisions described in rules (1) and (2) above:[40]

Example:

Assume:

Capital cost to taxpayer A of a depreciable property acquired before 1972	$6,500
Fair market value of the property on Valuation Day	$7,200
Selling price of property in 1973	$7,800

See page ii for explanation of footnotes.

[38] CCH ¶29,160; ITAR 20(1.1).
[39] CCH ¶29,170; ITAR 20(1.2).
[40] CCH ¶29,155; ITAR 20(1).

Results on sale in 1973:

A's deemed proceeds of disposition:

$6,500 + ($7,800 - $7,200) = $7,100

A's capital gain for taxation purposes:

$7,100 - $6,500 = $600

If the purchaser was dealing at arm's length with A, the purchaser's capital cost would be $7,800, but if the purchaser of A's property was A's son B (or any other person not dealing at arm's length with A, other than a spouse or common-law partner), then B's capital cost for capital cost allowance purposes is the deemed proceeds of $7,100.

Assume:

B subsequently disposes of the property for	$9,000

B's deemed proceeds: $6,500 + ($9,000 - $7,200) = $8,300

B's capital gain for tax purposes: $8,300 - $7,100 = $1,200

The overall gain can be broken down into:

Gain accrued to A prior to Valuation Day, not taxable	$ 700
Gain in A's hands	600
Gain in B's hands	1,200

Overall gain:

($9,000 - $6,500)	$2,500

[¶4020] Capital Cost Allowance Classes and Rates

[¶4025] Classes of Property and Schedule of Rates

The capital cost allowance rates applicable to the various classes of assets are listed below:[41]

Class 1 -- 4%	Class 8 -- 20%
Class 2 -- 6%	Class 9 -- 25%
Class 3 -- 5%	Class 10 -- 30%
Class 4 -- 6%	Class 10.1 -- 30%
Class 5 -- 10%	Class 11 -- 35%
Class 6 -- 10%	Class 12 -- 100%
Class 7 -- 15%	Class 16 -- 40%

See page ii for explanation of footnotes.

[41] Reg. 1100(1)(a) for the text of Schedule II of the Income Tax Regulations specifying the coverage of each class of assets, see ¶4955 *et seq.* of CCH's CANADIAN TAX REPORTER.

Class 17 -- 8%	Class 41.1 -- 25%
Class 18 -- 60%	Class 42 -- 12%
Class 22 -- 50%	Class 43 -- 30%
Class 23 -- 100%	Class 43.1 -- 30%
Class 25 -- 100%	Class 43.2 -- 50%
Class 26 -- 5%	Class 44 -- 25%
Class 28 -- 30%	Class 45 -- 45%
Class 30 -- 40%	Class 46 -- 30%
Class 31 -- 5%	Class 47 -- 8%
Class 32 -- 10%	Class 48 -- 15%
Class 33 -- 15%	Class 49 -- 8%
Class 35 -- 7%	Class 50 -- 55%
Class 37 -- 15%	Class 51 -- 6%
Class 41 -- 25%	Class 52 -- 100%

New Class 41.1 (25% rate) was added to implement the phase-out of the accelerated CCA on certain oil sands property acquired after March 18, 2007 (the 2007 Budget date). Paragraph (*a*) of new Class 41.1 includes oil sands property acquired after March 18, 2007 and before 2016 and for which the accelerated CCA is phased out by reducing the amount of the additional allowance by a specific percentage each year for a four-year period beginning in 2011. The percentage allowed as accelerated CCA, in each calendar year during that period, is 90% in 2011, 80% in 2012, 60% in 2013, and 30% in 2014 of the amount otherwise allowable as accelerated CCA. No accelerated CCA is allowed after 2014, and only the regular 25% CCA rate applies after 2014, with no additional allowance. Paragraph (*b*) of new Class 41.1 includes oil sands property acquired after 2015 that, if the property had been acquired before March 19, 2007, would have been included in Class 41. The accelerated CCA for oil sands is maintained for oil sands assets acquired before 2012 that are required for the completion of project phases on which major construction commenced before March 19, 2007.

[¶4030] Capital Cost Allowance Rates for Classes 38 to 40

The rates for Classes 38, 39, and 40 have been phased in as follows:

	Rates			
Class	1988	1989	1990	1991 and beyond
38	40%	35%	30%	30%
39	40%	35%	30%	25%
40	40%	35%	30%	*

* Not applicable after 1990

For taxpayers whose taxation year straddles a calendar year, the rate is prorated based on the number of days in the taxation year in which one rate applies and the days in the taxation year in which the other rate applies. Assets acquired after 1987 and before 1990 which were included in Class 40 had to be transferred to Class 10 for taxation years commencing after 1989.[42] See ¶4210.

[¶4035] Classes of Property Not Included in the Schedule of Rates

Classes 13, 14, and 15 refer to leaseholds, patents, and woods assets, respectively. Capital cost allowance on properties in these Classes is calculated according to a special formula in each case. See ¶4090 (leaseholds), ¶4110 (patents), and ¶4145 (woods assets).

Special allowances also apply to Classes 24 and 27 (water and air pollution control equipment), Class 29 (manufacturing and processing machinery and equipment acquired after March 18, 2007 and before 2014), and Class 34 (energy conservation equipment). See ¶4190, ¶4210, and ¶4215, respectively.

Class 36 refers to property that is deemed to be depreciable property by virtue of the Act. Special rules are provided with respect to property which was leased by a taxpayer and then acquired at a cost of less than fair market value.[43] See ¶4450.

[¶4037] Election re Grouping of Assets

A taxpayer may elect to adopt one general classification for all assets that would otherwise be included in Classes 2 to 10 and Classes 11 and 12 that are acquired for the purpose of gaining or producing income from the same business.[44] The rate allowed in such cases is restricted to 4% (i.e., all the assets will be included in Class 1 of Schedule II). See ¶4025 for the schedule of capital cost allowance rates. Such an election may simplify the taxpayer's computation of capital cost allowance and defer recapture of capital cost allowance that might otherwise be included in income on the sale of some of the assets.

A taxpayer whose chief depreciable properties are in Classes 2, 4, or 17 (i.e., subject to a maximum rate of 6% for Classes 2 and 4, and 8% for Class 17), may elect to include in any of these three classes a property that would otherwise be included in another class and that was acquired by the taxpayer before May 26, 1976, for the purpose of gaining or producing income from the same business as that for which those properties otherwise included in Class 2, 4, or 17 were acquired.[45]

Elections under either provision are to be made by letter attached to the return and addressed to the District Office at which the taxpayer cus-

See page ii for explanation of footnotes.

[42] CCH ¶4950f; Reg. 1103(2e).
[43] CCH ¶4519, ¶5042a; Sec. 13(5.2); Reg. 1101(5g).
[44] CCH ¶4950; Reg. 1103(1).
[45] CCH ¶4950a; Reg. 1103(2).

¶4035

tomarily files returns. The election must be made not later than the last day on which the taxpayer's income tax return is due. It will be effective from the first day of the taxation year in respect of which the election is made and will continue to be effective for all subsequent years.[46] Serious consideration should be given to any step of this nature, however, having regard to the irrevocability of the election and the relatively low rate of depreciation allowed.

A taxpayer may elect to include in Class 37 (amusement parks) all of the taxpayer's property as described in Class 37 but which would not otherwise be included in Class 37 because the property was acquired before February 26, 1982, the date upon which Class 37 became effective.[47]

If a taxpayer disposes of a property of a class in Schedule II, such as Class 29, and acquires a property before the end of the year that is included in a different class, such as Class 39, only because of its date of acquisition, the taxpayer may elect to transfer the property disposed of from the former class to the present class in the year of its disposition.[48] The taxpayer may make this election in order to defer recapture as long as the present class is not a separate prescribed class.[49] A grandfathering provision allows a taxpayer to elect to transfer a property of a class in Schedule II or a part thereof, acquired after May 25, 1976, from the present class to the former class, or the part of the property acquired before May 26, 1976, from the former class to the present class.[50]

[¶4040] Transferred and Misclassified Property

Special rules are provided for determining the undepreciated capital cost of depreciable property that is transferred from one prescribed class to another.[51] In effect, the undepreciated capital cost to the taxpayer of depreciable property of the former class is adjusted such that it becomes the amount it would have been if the transferred property had never been in that class. This result is achieved by the application of the following rules:

(1) The capital cost is deducted from the former class and added to the other class.

(2) The greater of the following amounts is included in computing the depreciation allowed the taxpayer in respect of the other class, and is deducted in respect of the former class:

   (a) the excess, if any, of the capital cost of the transferred property over the undepreciated capital cost of the former class at the time of transfer; and

---

See page ii for explanation of footnotes.

[46] CCH ¶4950j–4950l; Reg. 1103(3)–(5).
[47] CCH ¶4950c; Reg. 1103(2b).
[48] CCH ¶4950e; Reg. 1103(2d).
[49] CCH ¶4940; Reg. 1101(1).
[50] CCH ¶4950d; Reg. 1103(2c).
[51] CCH ¶4514; Sec. 13(5); Interp. Bul. IT-190R2.

(b) the aggregate of all amounts that would have been claimed as capital cost allowance on the transferred properties using the effective rate that had actually been used in claiming CCA on those assets. For example, if a taxpayer claimed CCA of $50 on property with a UCC of $1,000 in a class with a prescribed CCA rate of 20%, the effective rate would be 5%.

Example 1:

F transfers to Class 9 (25%) property having an original capital cost of $10,000 and which has up to now been included by F in Class 8 (20%).

Assume that the property was purchased two years previously and that maximum capital cost allowance for assets in Class 8 has been claimed. Assume also that the total undepreciated capital cost of Class 8 immediately before the transfer was $100,000.

		Effect on	
		Class 8	Class 9
Total undepreciated capital cost immediately before transfer		$100,000	nil
Capital cost of property transferred to Class 9		(10,000)	$10,000
(a) Amount to be added to the capital cost to the taxpayer of the depreciable property of the old class (i.e., Class 8) -- the greater of:			
(i) Capital cost to the taxpayer of the transferred property	$10,000		
Undepreciated capital cost of the old class before the transfer	100,000		
Excess of capital cost of transferred property over undepreciated capital cost of old class	nil		
(ii) The total of the capital cost allowances which have been allowed, using the effective rate in the old class, in respect of the transferred property	$2,800	2,800	
(b) Amount added to the total depreciation allowed to the taxpayer for property of the new class -- greater of (i) or (ii) above			(2,800)
Undepreciated capital cost after transfer		$ 92,800	$ 7,200

Example 2:

F transfers to Class 9 (25%) property having an original capital cost of $150,000 and which has up to now been included by F in Class 8 (20%). Assume that the property was purchased 2 years previously and that maximum capital cost allowance for assets in Class 8 has been claimed. Assume also that the total undepreciated capital cost of Class 8 immediately before the transfer was $50,000.

¶4040

	Effect on	
	Class 8	Class 9
Total undepreciated capital cost immediately before transfer	$50,000	nil
Capital cost of property transferred to class	(150,000)	$150,000
(a) Amount to be added to the capital cost to the taxpayer of the depreciable property of the old class (i.e., Class 8) -- the greater of:		
(i) Capital cost to the taxpayer of the transferred property $150,000		
Undepreciated capital cost of the old class before the transfer 50,000		
Excess of capital cost of transferred property over undepreciated capital cost of old class $100,000		
(ii) The total of the capital cost allowances that have been allowed, using the prescribed rates for Class 8 in respect of the transferred property	$ 42,000	$100,000
(b) Amount added to the total depreciation allowed to the taxpayer for property of the new class -- greater of (i) or (ii) above		(100,000)
Undepreciated capital cost after transfer	nil	$ 50,000

When a taxpayer converts a leasehold interest in an asset into a freehold interest (by, for example, buying a building that had previously been leased), the leasehold interest is deemed to have been disposed of for proceeds equal to the undepreciated capital cost of the leasehold interest. The original capital cost of the leasehold interest is added to the freehold's relevant capital cost allowance class, and the capital cost allowance claimed to date on the leasehold interest is added to the total depreciation allowed with respect to the freehold class. Thus, what otherwise may have been a terminal loss on the leasehold interest is deductible as capital cost allowance on the freehold interest.[52]

If a taxpayer has misclassified depreciable property or not reclassified depreciable property after an amendment to the Regulations, the taxpayer may be reassessed to correct the classification and the capital cost allowance claim. However, if the correction is not done retroactively with a reassessment, the Minister may direct that the property is deemed to have been properly included as property of the old class prior to the commencement of the particular taxation year and to have been transferred to the new class at the commencement of that year.[53] The Minister may make such

---

See page ii for explanation of footnotes.
[52] CCH ¶4515; Sec. 13(5.1).   [53] CCH ¶4520; Sec. 13(6).

direction with respect to any of the taxation years in which he may make an assessment or reassessment. However, the Minister may only make such a direction if the taxpayer has not disposed of the property. According to Interpretation Bulletin IT-190R2, where the taxpayer has already disposed of depreciable property previously misclassified, the proceeds of disposition shall remain as a credit to that class.

It has been held that, where property falls into a more advantageous capital cost allowance class by the process of elimination, this is its proper class.[54]

[¶4045] Separate Classes

Under certain circumstances, properties must be included under separate classes, as described below.

Properties of one class used for more than one purpose

When properties that would otherwise be in the same class are acquired by a taxpayer for more than one income-producing purpose (such as if the properties are acquired for the purpose of producing income from two or more businesses), the properties are split into separate classes.[55] Properties acquired for the purpose of producing income from each business form a separate class and properties acquired for the purpose of producing income from property form another separate class. For example, two brick buildings are acquired for two different purposes, one for use in a manufacturing business and one to be rented out. Both buildings are Class 3 assets, but separate classes must be established. Where the taxpayer is a life insurer, separate classes are established for property used by the life insurer in its non-life insurance business and in its life insurance business.[56]

The establishment of separate classes is important for purposes of the timing of terminal losses and the recapture of capital cost allowances (see ¶4380 and ¶4470). Under the usual pool method, recapture or a terminal loss may be deferred by adding more assets into the class. This option is not available, especially if each asset is to be placed in a separate class (see *Property required to be included in a separate class*, below).

The rate for each separate class is the rate prescribed for the class in which the properties would otherwise be included. In a case in which a hotel business was sold and another business with property in the same classes was acquired, the Minister was allowed to prescribe separate classes for the properties of each business and to recapture capital cost allowance on the property sold.[57]

Where, at the end of 1971, more than one property of a taxpayer who was a member of a partnership is described in the same class and one of the

---

See page ii for explanation of footnotes.

[54] Windsor Raceway Holdings Ltd., 73 DTC 96.
[55] CCH ¶4940; Reg. 1101(1).
[56] CCH ¶4940a; Reg. 1101(1a).
[57] Midwest Hotel Co., 72 DTC 6440.

properties can reasonably be regarded to be the interest of the taxpayer in a depreciable property that is partnership property of the partnership, a separate class is prescribed for the depreciable property.[58] Property described under Part XI of the regulations or in Schedule II is deemed not to include any property that is an interest of a taxpayer in depreciable property that is partnership property of the partnership.[59]

Property required to be included in a separate class

Certain types of property are required by regulation to be included in a separate class and for certain other assets the taxpayer may elect that they be included in a separate class. Assets which are required to be included in a separate class include:

(a) rental property less than $50,000 (¶4290);

(b) rental property over $50,000 and MURBs over $50,000 (¶4290);

(c) passenger vehicles costing over a prescribed threshold (in 2001–2010, $30,000 plus applicable GST/HST, PST, and other provincial levies, see ¶4120);

(d) timber limits and cutting rights (¶4135);

(e) industrial mineral mines (¶4150);

(f) certain railway cars, track, and related property (¶4165);

(g) certain vessels (¶4170);

(h) new or expanded mine properties (¶4172);

(i) leasing property (¶4300);

(j) telecommunication spacecraft;[60]

(k) certified productions acquired after 1987 (¶4275);

(l) specified energy property (¶4215);

(m) specified leasing property (¶4305);

(n) deemed depreciable property in Class 36 (¶4450); and

(o) computer software tax shelter property (¶4282).

Assets which the taxpayer may *elect* to put into a separate class include:

(a) each Class 2 pipeline, including extensions or conversions costing not less than $10,000,000, that was commenced after 1984 and completed after September 1, 1985 (see ¶4127);

See page ii for explanation of footnotes.

[58] CCH ¶4940b; Reg. 1101(1ab).
[59] CCH ¶4944a; Reg. 1102(1a).

[60] CCH ¶4981, ¶5033, ¶5034; Reg. 1101(5a), Class 10, Class 30.

(b) outdoor advertising signs acquired after 1987;[61]

(c) earth-moving equipment acquired after 1987;[62]

(d) exempt property of a principal business corporation for purposes of the specified leasing property rules (¶4305);

(e) rapidly depreciating electronic equipment in Class 8 or Class 10 costing over $1,000 and acquired after April 26, 1993 (see ¶4282 and ¶4283). This equipment includes computer software, photocopiers, fax machines, electronic telephone equipment including related ancillary equipment, and general-purpose electronic data processing equipment and systems software therefor;

(f) manufacturing or processing property included in Class 43 and acquired after February 27, 2000, for a cost of at least $1,000;[63]

(g) transmission pipelines for petroleum, natural gas, or related hydro-carbons, including control and monitoring devices, valves, and other ancillary equipment included in new Class 49 and acquired after February 22, 2005[64] (see ¶4127);

(h) pumping, compression, and any ancillary equipment related to the transmission pipelines for petroleum, natural gas, or related hydro-carbons included in Class 7(j) and acquired after February 22, 2005, or pumping, compression, and any ancillary equipment related to the transmission pipelines for carbon dioxide included in Class 7(k) and acquired after February 25, 2008[65] (see ¶4127); and

(i) after March 18, 2007, non-residential buildings described in Class 1 (4% CCA) for which the taxpayer intends to claim an additional allowance of 6% in the case of buildings used for manufacturing and processing, or 2% in the case of other non-residential buildings (see ¶4085).

The separate class election is made by attaching a letter to the tax return for the taxation year in which the property is acquired.[66] For assets described in (a) to (d) above, the separate class election is effective from the first day of the taxation year in which the election is made and continues for all subsequent taxation years. For the electronic equipment in (e) and the manufacturing and processing equipment in (f), any such property remaining in a separate class five years after the property became available for use, is to be transferred into the regular Class 8 or Class 10 pool.[67] Therefore, the property may be depreciated in a separate class for five years beginning when the first property in the class becomes available for use. Immediately after the

---

See page ii for explanation of footnotes.

[61] CCH ¶4978, ¶5043f; Reg. 1101(5l), Class 8.

[62] CCH ¶5043d, ¶5043f; Reg. 1101(5l), Class 38.

[63] Reg. 1101(5q), Reg. 1101(5s).

[64] Reg. 1101(5v).

[65] Reg. 1101(5u).

[66] CCH ¶4940zb, ¶4940zi; Reg. 1101(5j), Reg. 1101(5q), Reg. 1101(5s), Reg. 1101(5u), Reg. 1101(5v).

[67] CCH ¶4950h; Reg. 1103(2g).

end of the fifth taxation year in which some capital cost allowance could be claimed in the class, the class as a whole merges into Class 8 or 10 as the case may be.

For the assets described in (e) above, it appears that one cannot aggregate the values of class 8 equipment to achieve the $1,000 threshold. With respect to computers, the reference to ancillary data processing equipment seems to make it clear that the regulation allows one separate Class 10 for a computer and all peripheral equipment acquired in the year as long as the aggregate value is at least $1,000. It also appears that one cannot aggregate the assets described in (f), to achieve the $1,000 threshold.

[¶4050] Acquisition of Depreciable Assets and When Capital Cost Allowance May Be Claimed

[¶4055] Date of Acquisition of Depreciable Assets

Capital cost allowance may only be claimed on assets owned by the taxpayer or in which the taxpayer has a leasehold interest at the end of the taxation year. The asset must have been acquired for the purpose of producing income.

For assets acquired after 1989, there are two important dates for the taxpayer to determine. The first is the date of acquisition, which is the date on which the cost is credited to the capital cost allowance class. The second is the date on which the asset is available for use which is the date that determines when capital cost allowance may be claimed. Often these dates will coincide. The acquisition date is important because by crediting an asset to the capital cost allowance class, the taxpayer may defer recapture or a terminal loss in a year even if capital cost allowance may not yet be claimed on that asset.

Where a taxpayer's year end occurs between the date the taxpayer ordered a depreciable asset and the date it was delivered to the taxpayer in usable condition, a question may arise as to whether or not the taxpayer had "acquired" the asset before the end of his or her taxation year.[68] (See ¶4010 for comments on the acquisition of property prior to a change of control.) Generally speaking, a purchaser will be considered to have acquired an asset at the earlier of:

(a) the date on which the purchaser obtains title to it, and

(b) the date on which the taxpayer has all the incidents of title such as possession, use, and risk, even though legal title remains with the vendor as security for the purchase price (such as under a conditional sales contract).

See page ii for explanation of footnotes.

[68] Interp. Bul. IT-285R2.

The purchaser must have a right in the asset itself and not merely rights under a contract to acquire the asset in the future.

Where all that was necessary to sell the property to the taxpayer had been done, and there had been a meeting of the minds between the vendor and the taxpayer as to the sale, the price, and the date, but the registration of certain documents permitting the taxpayers to become the registered owners took place a year later, the taxpayers were entitled to the capital cost allowance as of the year before when there was a meeting of the minds.[69]

Where a building or other structure is being erected by or for a taxpayer on land owned by the taxpayer, he or she is considered to have acquired a building or other structure, at any particular time, to the extent of the construction costs incurred by the taxpayer to that time, including the cost to the taxpayer of materials that have been put in place or progress billings received by the taxpayer to that time.

[¶4060] Available-for-Use Rules

For depreciable property acquired after 1989, the "available-for-use" rules defer the right to deduct capital cost allowance (or to claim investment tax credit or scientific research deduction) on the property until it becomes available for use.[70] Under these rules, generally speaking, capital cost allowance is allowed on an asset at the earlier of the time that it is first used by the taxpayer for the purpose of earning income, or the second taxation year after the date the property was acquired by the taxpayer ("rolling start" rule). As well, a public corporation may depreciate acquisitions (other than buildings) for tax purposes when it depreciates them for book purposes, and a taxpayer may depreciate buildings when they are either complete or "substantially" (usually 90%) in use. These rules replace the former rule that property may be depreciated when acquired on a legal or practical title basis.

In general, the half-year rule (¶4062) will apply when property is finally recognized for capital cost allowance purposes under the available-for-use rules. There is an exception, however, for property recognized only under the two-year deferral rule ("rolling start" rule described below in (1)(b) — assets other than buildings or (2)(c) — buildings). Property recognized by virtue of this rule will not be subject to the half-year rule in the year it becomes eligible for depreciation.

The available-for-use rules are as follows:

(1) Property other than a building is generally considered to become available for use and therefore eligible for capital cost allowance and investment tax credit on the earlier of:[71]

See page ii for explanation of footnotes.

[69] Kimmel et al, 76 DTC 6259.

[70] CCH ¶4584; Sec. 13(26).

[71] CCH ¶4585; Sec. 13(27).

(a) The date the property is first used for the purpose of earning income.

(b) The second tax year after the year the property was acquired (the two-year "rolling start" rule). That is, if the property is acquired in Year 1 (say, 2010) but is not used by the taxpayer in Year 1 or 2 (2010 or 2011), capital cost allowance can be claimed in Year 3 (2012), provided there is no intervening short taxation year.

(c) The time immediately before the property is disposed of.

(d) The time the property (a) is delivered to the taxpayer or to a person or partnership (the "other person") that will use the property for the benefit of the taxpayer, or, where the property is not of a type that is deliverable, is made available to the taxpayer or the other person and, (b) is capable, either alone or with another property in the possession of the taxpayer or the other person at that time, of producing a saleable product or performing a saleable service, including an intermediate product or service that is used or consumed, or to be used or consumed, by the taxpayer or the other person in producing or providing any such product or service (the "intermediate product" rule). This rule would allow capital cost allowance on property delivered or available for delivery if the property (together with other property on hand) has the capability of making a saleable intermediate product even if that product is not sold. For instance, suppose a production plant takes raw wood and makes paper. An intermediate state is the production of wood chips, which could be sold commercially, although the plant does not sell them. If the plant acquires a machine which is necessary to the manufacture of saleable chips and, in fact, has the capacity to make them, it can depreciate the machine even though it has not acquired the additional machinery necessary to make paper from the chips, and does not in fact sell the chips.

(e) In the case of property acquired by the taxpayer for the prevention, reduction, or elimination of air or water pollution created by operations carried on by the taxpayer, or that would be created by such operations, or, if the property has not been acquired, the time at which the property is installed and capable of performing the function for which it was acquired. With the addition of reference to pollution from operations carried on by the taxpayer, this rule contemplates the case where pollution control equipment is used only periodically; for example, when local pollution levels reach a certain point. As long as the equipment is operational, it can be depreciated even though conditions do not yet require its use.

(f) In the case of property acquired by a corporation (a) listed on a designated stock exchange or (b) which has elected to be treated as or has been designated as a public corporation, or is a wholly owned subsidiary of a corporation in (a) or (b), at the end of the first

¶4060

taxation year for which depreciation in respect of the property is first deducted in computing the earnings of the corporation in accordance with generally accepted accounting principles (GAAP) and for the purpose of financial statements of the corporation for the year in which they are presented to its shareholders. In short, a public corporation may depreciate property or a portion thereof for tax purposes in the same year in which it depreciates the property or portion for book purposes on its GAAP financial statements to shareholders.

(g) In the case of property acquired for use in a farming or fishing business, the time at which the property is delivered and capable of operation. Farming or fishing business property may be depreciated when delivered in serviceable condition, even though the season (or some other contingency) may prevent its immediate use.

(h) In the case of certain transportation equipment in respect of which various permits, licences, and certificates may be required, the time at which the permits, licences, and certificates have been acquired.

(i) In the case of spare parts, the time at which the property for which the spare part may be required is available for use.

(j) In the case of certain offshore production facilities, the time at which the concrete gravity base structure deballasts and lifts the topside facilities (such as oil rigs).

(k) Where the property is a replacement property for property which has been involuntarily disposed of but which was acquired before 1990 or had otherwise become available for use, the time at which the replacement property is acquired.

(2) A building is considered to become available for use and therefore eligible for capital cost allowance and investment tax credit on the earlier of:[72]

(a) The time at which all or substantially all of the building (generally taken to mean 90% or more) is used by the taxpayer for its intended business purpose.

(b) In the case of the construction, renovation, or alteration of a building, the date the construction, renovation, or alteration is completed or, if earlier, the date 90% of the building is used for the business purpose for which it was constructed, renovated, or altered.

(c) The second taxation year after the year of acquisition of the building (the "rolling start" rule).

(d) The time immediately before the building is disposed of.

---

[72] CCH ¶4586; Sec. 13(28).

(e) Where the building is a replacement property for property which has been involuntarily disposed of (for example, expropriation) but which was acquired before 1990 or had otherwise become available for use, the time at which the replacement property is acquired.

For purposes of the available-for-use rules only, a renovation, alteration, or addition to a building will be considered to be a separate building.

(3) A special elective rule is provided for property, including buildings other than rental buildings, acquired for use in a long-term project.[73] Under this provision, the general available-for-use rule will be applied to all expenditures incurred in the first two years of the project. However, in the third and subsequent years of the project, application of the available-for-use rule will be limited so that only those expenditures in any such year in excess of certain threshold amounts will be subject to the rule. These threshold amounts are determined with reference to expenditures on property incurred during the earlier years of the project that end at least 358 days before the beginning of the year under consideration.

(4) Rollovers are provided for non-arm's length transfers of property. In these cases and in the case of a butterfly reorganization, as long as the property was available for use by the transferor, it will be considered available for use at the earlier of the time it is acquired by the transferee or, if applicable, at a time prescribed in the Regulations.[74]

(5) An anti-avoidance provision deals with the situation where a taxpayer leases depreciable property from a non-arm's length person before the property would be considered to be available for use if the taxpayer had acquired it.[75] In this case the lease payments that would otherwise be deductible by the taxpayer are deemed to be a leasehold interest Class 13 asset. Capital cost allowance would therefore only be allowed on these lease payments after the property became available for use.

[¶4062] Half-Year Rule: Capital Cost Allowance in Year of Acquisition

In the year in which an asset is acquired or becomes available for use, the claim for capital cost allowance is generally limited to $1/2$ the allowable rate in respect of that asset.[76]

The calculation of the capital cost allowance claim in the year of acquisition of property is best illustrated by an example.

See page ii for explanation of footnotes.

[73] CCH ¶4587; Sec. 13(29).

[74] CCH ¶4588, ¶4589; Sec. 13(30), 13(31); Reg. 1100(2.2).

[75] CCH ¶4590; Sec. 13(32).

[76] CCH ¶4917; Reg. 1100(2); Interp. Bul. IT-285R2.

Example:

Assumptions: Opening undepreciated capital cost for Class 8 assets		$100
Acquisitions during the year		80
Proceeds from disposals during the year		20
Opening undepreciated capital cost		$100
Additions in the year	$80	
Disposals in the year	(20)	
	$60(a)	
50% of (a)		$30
Undepreciated capital cost before capital cost allowance claim		$130(b)
Capital cost allowance: 20% of (b)		(26)
		104
Add: Capital cost deferred (50% of (a))		30
Undepreciated capital cost at end of year		$134

It should be noted that limiting the claim for capital cost allowance in respect of assets acquired during the year to ½ the normal rate is achieved by providing for a notional reduction in the undepreciated capital cost of property in the class equal to ½ the net additions (i.e., cost of additions net of proceeds of disposals). The normal capital cost allowance rates are then applied to this notionally reduced balance. In the event that disposals exceed additions, there is no 50% reduction of this negative amount.

The additions in the calculation of the half-year rule are equal to the capital cost of the property acquired during the year and any assistance or inducement that has been repaid by the taxpayer in the year in respect of property in a class that the taxpayer no longer owns. It is interesting to note that assistance or inducements that are repaid in a subsequent taxation year while the taxpayer still owns the property do not appear to be affected by the half-year rule.

The half-year rule does not apply when the available-for-use rules discussed at ¶4060 deny a CCA claim until the second tax year after the year the property was acquired (the "two-year rolling start rule").

The following assets are excluded from the application of the half-year rule:

(a) Canadian vessels;

¶4062

(b) certified productions acquired after 1987 and before March 1996;

(c) Class 12 assets, *other than* dies, jigs, patterns, moulds or lasts, the cutting or shaping part in a machine, certified feature films acquired before 1988, motion picture films, television commercial messages, computer software, videotapes acquired for rental purposes, and laser disks acquired after December 12, 1995, for rental purposes;

(d) Class 13 assets — leasehold interests;

(e) Class 14 assets — patents, franchises, or licences for a limited period;

(f) Class 15 property acquired for cutting and removing merchantable timber or a timber resource;

(g) Class 23 assets — leasehold interests and buildings relating to Expo '67 and Expo '86;

(h) Classes 24, 27, and 34 assets — pollution control and energy conservation equipment;

(i) Class 29 assets — manufacturing equipment acquired before 1988;

(j) Class 52 assets — new general-purpose electronic data processing equipment and systems software for that equipment ("computer equipment") acquired after January 27, 2009, and before February 2011;

(k) property that is specified leasing property of a corporation the principal business of which throughout the year is renting or leasing property;

(l) leased property that has actually been acquired that had been deemed to have been acquired in a preceding taxation year because of an election to treat the lease as a purchase; and

(m) property that has become available for use in the year under the two-year rolling start rule (see ¶4060).

Despite these exceptions, other regulations provide adjustments which produce results similar to the half-year rule for Canadian vessels[77] (see ¶4170), leasehold interests[78] (see ¶4090), and Classes 24, 27, 29, and 34 (see ¶4190).[79]

There are transitional rules for calculating the capital cost allowance for property acquired after November 12, 1981 (the date the half-year rule was implemented) and before 1983. Under these rules, property is effectively

---

See page ii for explanation of footnotes.

[77] CCH ¶4975; Reg. 1100(1)(v).
[78] CCH ¶4995; Reg. 1100(1)(b).

[79] CCH ¶5031, ¶5032; Reg. 1100(1)(t), Reg. 1100(1)(ta).

permitted the same tax treatment as if it had been acquired prior to the introduction of the half-year rule.[80]

In addition, the half-year rule for property acquisitions will not apply to the following acquisitions (if certain criteria are met):

(a) property acquired by a taxpayer in a type of reorganization such as a "butterfly" transaction designed to de-merge the corporation; or

(b) property acquired from a person with whom the taxpayer does not deal at arm's length. For these purposes, however, persons who do not deal at arm's length excludes persons who are deemed not to deal at arm's length by virtue only of certain rights or option agreements.[81]

In order for the half-year rule not to apply, the vendor must have acquired the property as depreciable property and owned it continuously prior to its transfer to the purchaser. In addition, one of four criteria must also be met:

(1) the vendor acquired the property prior to November 13, 1981;

(2) the vendor acquired the property at least 364 days before the taxation year end of the purchaser;

(3) the transitional rules relating to property acquired before 1983 applied to the vendor in respect of the property;[82] or

(4) the rules relating to a reorganization or non-arm's length transaction applied to the vendor on his or her original acquisition of the property.[83]

Property in Class 24, 27, 29, or 34 that is acquired in a non-arm's length or butterfly transfer will be deemed to have been acquired by the transferee at the beginning of the transferee's first taxation year, starting after the property was acquired by the transferor. This allows a catch-up claim of capital cost allowance by the transferee if the transferor has not claimed the full amount in the preceding years. That is, if the transferor had held a Class 27 asset for three years but claimed no CCA on it and then transferred it to the transferee, the transferee could claim 100% CCA in the year of acquisition (as could the transferor if it had held the property).

[¶4065] Taxation Year Less Than 12 Months

If a taxation year of a business is less than 12 months in duration, the amount of capital cost allowance for depreciable property used in the business must not exceed the proportion of the maximum amount otherwise

---

See page ii for explanation of footnotes.

[80] CCH ¶4918; Reg. 1100(2.1).

[81] CCH ¶28,354, ¶4919; Sec. 251(5); Reg. 1100(2.2).

[82] CCH ¶4918; Reg. 1100(2.1).

[83] CCH ¶4919, ¶4920; Reg. 1100(2.2), Reg. 1100(2.3).

allowable that the number of days in the taxation year is of 365.[84] "Month" means a calendar month.

The proration of capital cost allowance also applies to the amount which would be computed under the half-year rule (see ¶4062) and to additional allowances (see ¶4155 *et seq.*), with some exceptions. The allowances for Class 14 (patents, franchises, etc.), for Class 15 (woods assets) for timber limits and cutting rights, and for industrial mineral mines are not prorated. The allowances respecting patents and franchises will vary in any event according to the length of the taxation year. Allowances respecting timber limits, wood assets, and industrial mineral mines will vary according to the number of units of timber cut or mineral mined in the taxation year. The proration of capital cost allowance for a short taxation year also does not apply to the additional allowance in respect of Canadian film or video productions in Class 10(x), certified productions in Class 10(w), and certain mining equipment in Classes 28, 41, and 41.1. These additional allowances are limited by income which presumably will be reduced in a short taxation year in any event.

Notwithstanding the fact that the taxation year may be less than 12 months in duration, the taxpayer is still entitled to a deduction for a terminal loss on disposition of all assets of a class in the taxation year.

Where income-producing property is acquired by an individual taxpayer and the income is from property and not from business, the taxation year will be a full 12 months, since income from property is reported on a calendar year basis. As decided, the provision of janitorial services, heat, stoves, refrigerators, etc. resulting from ownership of apartment buildings is a function normally performed by a landlord and rentals received for these services are income from property rather than from business. Therefore, there is no proration of capital cost allowance.[85]

When an individual starts a job part-way through the year which entitles the individual, as an employee, to claim capital cost allowance on an automobile or aircraft, as at December 31, the individual will not have to prorate the capital cost allowance based on the length of the taxation year. The automobile is subject to the half-year rule in the year of acquisition.[86]

Where an individual taxpayer's income includes income from a business whose fiscal period does not coincide with the calendar year, capital cost allowance must be computed according to the fiscal year of the business and the allowance which the taxpayer may claim will be the capital cost allowance taken for the business in the fiscal year that ended in the individual taxpayer's taxation year.[87] This means that an asset that is acquired by an individual to be used in the individual's business in the taxation

---

See page ii for explanation of footnotes.

[84] CCH ¶4924; Reg. 1100(3).
[85] Walsh and Micay, 65 DTC 5293.

[86] Interp. Bul. IT-522R.
[87] CCH ¶4951a; Reg. 1104(1).

(calendar) year is eligible for capital cost allowance for the full year (subject to the half-year rule).[88]

Example:

> COO Ltd. incorporated and started business on May 1, 2012. It has a December 31 fiscal year end. During the first year, COO Ltd. purchased a truck for $30,000 for use in its business. The capital cost allowance claim on this truck in 2012 is as follows:

	DPA 30%
	(Class 10)
2012	
Additions	$30,000
Minus: $1/2$ net additions	15,000
	$15,000
CCA claim: 30% × 15,000 × $\frac{245}{365}$	(3,021)
	$11,979
Add: capital cost deferred	15,000
Undepreciated capital cost January 1, 2013	$26,979

[¶4067] Death of a Taxpayer

In the case of a taxpayer's death, all depreciable property is deemed to have been disposed of immediately before death. As a result, if capital cost allowance is claimed on a calendar year basis, capital cost allowance cannot be claimed in the year of death; however, a terminal loss may be available. See ¶2555.

[¶4070] Official Government Publications

[¶4075] Interpretation Bulletins and Information Circulars

The following Interpretation Bulletins and Information Circulars dealing with capital cost allowances have been issued by the CRA. These Bulletins and Circulars are all reproduced in CCH Canadian's CANADIAN TAX REPORTER, Vol. 8.

IT-79R3	Capital cost allowance -- Buildings or other structures
IT-128R	Capital cost allowance -- Depreciable property
IT-147R3	Capital cost allowance -- Accelerated write-off of manufacturing and processing machinery and equipment

---

See page ii for explanation of footnotes.

[88] Harvey, 94 DTC 1910.

IT-190R2   Capital cost allowance -- Transferred and misclassified property

IT-195R4   Rental property -- Capital cost allowance restrictions

IT-220R2   Capital cost allowance -- Proceeds of disposition of depreciable property

IT-259R4   Exchanges of property

IT-267R2   Capital cost allowance -- Vessels

IT-273R2   Government assistance -- General Comments

IT-274R   Rental properties -- Capital cost of $50,000 or more

IT-285R2   Capital cost allowance -- General comments

IT-304R2   Condominiums

IT-306R2   Capital cost allowance -- Contractor's movable equipment

IT-371   Rental property -- Meaning of "principal business"

IT-411R   Meaning of "construction"

IT-418   Capital cost allowance -- Partial dispositions of property

IT-422   Definition of tools

IT-443   Leasing property -- Capital cost allowance restrictions

IT-464R   Capital cost allowance -- Leasehold interests

IT-469R   Capital cost allowance -- Earth-moving equipment

IT-472   Capital cost allowance -- Class 8 property

IT-476R   Capital cost allowance -- Equipment used in petroleum and natural gas activities

IT-477   Capital cost allowance -- Patents, franchises, concessions, and licences -- Consolidated

IT-478R2   Capital cost allowance -- Recapture and terminal loss

IT-481   Timber resource property and timber limits -- Consolidated

IT-482R   Pipelines

IT-485   Cost of clearing or levelling land

IT-491   Former business property

IT-492   Capital cost allowance -- Industrial mineral mines

IT-501   Capital cost allowance -- Logging assets

IT-521R   Motor vehicle expenses claimed by self-employed individuals

IT-522R   Vehicle, travel and sales expenses of employees

IC 84-1   Revision of capital cost allowance claims and other permissive deductions

[¶4080] Buildings — Leaseholds — Sale-Leasebacks

[¶4085] Buildings and Component Parts — Capital Cost Allowance

The term "building" has a broad interpretation, covering any structure with walls and a roof affording protection and shelter. The term "structure" has been defined by the courts to include anything of substantial size that is built up from component parts and intended to remain permanently on a permanent foundation. This definition of structure was considered by the Supreme Court of Canada, which also concluded that the word "structure", when used in the context of "building or other structure", does not mean only a structure in the nature of a building.[89] Bridges or hydro-electric transmission towers, for example, while clearly not buildings, are structures. Any component parts that ordinarily go with the building when it is bought or sold or which relate to the functioning of the building must be included in the building class.[90]

Most buildings are included in Class 1, 3, or 6.[91] Buildings of the construction described in paragraph (*a*) of Class 6 will qualify whenever constructed, if they are used in a farming or fishing business or if they have no footings or base support below ground level. If the building has base support below ground level and is not used in a farming or fishing business, it will be included in Class 6 only if it was acquired before 1979, or if acquired after 1978 and the tests as to the installation of footings prior to 1979, the existence of an agreement to acquire, and/or the commencement of construction (as set out in subparagraphs (*a*)(ix) and (x)) are satisfied. Buildings of the construction described in paragraph (*a*) of Class 6 that are acquired after 1979 and do not meet the tests will fall either within Class 3 or Class 1, depending on the date of acquisition. In this regard, the Tax Court of Canada held that an old hotel which the taxpayer purchased, renovated, and opened for business, ought not to be excluded from Class 6 (and placed in Class 1) simply because a portion thereof was below ground level. The words "has no footings or any other base support below ground level" in Class 6 are intended to describe the manner of construction of the entire building.[92]

Buildings and component parts are included in Classes 1 or 3 only if not included in any other class. The classification of buildings was changed from Class 3 (5%) to Class 1 (4%) to implement the June 18, 1987, tax reform proposals to reduce the CCA rate on buildings acquired after 1987, subject to certain grandfathering provisions. Buildings that are not included in any other class will be included in Class 3 if acquired before 1988, as will buildings acquired before 1990, if acquired pursuant to an obligation in writing entered into by the taxpayer before June 18, 1987, or if under construction by or on behalf of the taxpayer on June 18, 1987. A component part of a building that was under construction on June 18, 1987 will also be included in Class 3 if acquired before 1990.

Buildings that are not included in Class 6 and do not meet the date of acquisition tests for inclusion in Class 3, fall within Class 1. In general, this includes buildings and component parts acquired after 1987 (subject to grandfathering provisions). Additions and alterations to existing buildings

---

See page ii for explanation of footnotes.

[89] British Columbia Forest Products Ltd., 71 DTC 5178.
[90] Interp. Bul. IT-79R3.
[91] CCH ¶4955, ¶4965, ¶4972; Class 1, Class 3, Class 6.
[92] R.E.A.D. Enterprises Ltd., 99 DTC 820.

may be included in any of Class 1, 3, or 6, depending in which class the building itself is included and when the addition or alteration is made.

A building that would otherwise be in Class 3 or Class 6 may be in Class 31 or 32 if it qualifies as a multiple-unit residential building (MURB). (See the commentary at ¶4290.) Additions to these classes were discontinued after June 17, 1987, unless qualifying by virtue of the grandfathering provisions. Certain leasehold interests in properties can also be considered buildings. See ¶4090.

The 2007 Budget and its implementing Order in Council, published May 13, 2009, provide two additional allowances in respect of certain buildings included in Class 1. They provide a 6% additional allowance for non-residential buildings used for manufacturing or processing and a 2% additional allowance for other non-residential buildings.[93] Both additional allowances apply to property acquired after March 18, 2007. To be eligible for these two additional allowances, the taxpayer who acquires a non-residential building must elect to include it in a separate Class 1 in the taxation year in which the building is acquired.[94] This separate class election is not available unless the taxpayer's building satisfies the definition of an "eligible non-residential building". Such a building is defined as a taxpayer's building:

- that is located in Canada;
- that is included in Class 1;
- that has not been used, or acquired for use, by any person (including a partnership) before March 19, 2007; and
- that has been acquired by the taxpayer after March 18, 2007, to be used by the taxpayer, or a lessee of the taxpayer, for a non-residential use.[95]

[¶4090] Leasehold Interests

Class 13 of Schedule II of the Regulations provides for the deduction of such amount as may be claimed by a taxpayer holding a leasehold interest, except an interest in minerals, petroleum, natural gas, other related hydrocarbons or timber, related property, Expo '67 or Expo '86 leasehold interests (Class 23), and that part of a leasehold interest which is included in another class.[96] Property acquired by a taxpayer after December 23, 1991, which (if it had been acquired by a person with whom the taxpayer was not dealing at arm's length at the time it was acquired by the taxpayer) would be a leasehold interest of that non-arm's length person, is included in Class 13 by the taxpayer. Therefore, leasehold improvements can be depreciated by the taxpayer that acquires them even though that taxpayer does not actually hold

---

See page ii for explanation of footnotes.

[93] Reg. 1100(1)(a.1), Reg. 1100(1)(a.2).

[94] Reg. 1101(5b.1).

[95] Reg. 1104(2) "eligible non-residential building".

[96] CCH ¶4994–4996; Reg. 1100(1)(b), Class 13, Sch III; Interp. Bul. IT-464R.

the lease, as long as the person that does hold the lease is not dealing at arm's length with the taxpayer.[97]

A "leasehold interest" is the interest of a tenant in any leased tangible property (a building or other leased property). A tenant who leases property acquires a leasehold interest in that property whether or not any capital cost is incurred in respect of that interest. However, a depreciable property is not considered to have been acquired until a capital cost has been incurred in respect of that property.

The capital cost of a leasehold interest of Class 13 property includes:

(a) the cost to a tenant in respect of improvements or alterations to a leased property that are capital in nature, other than improvements or alterations that are included as a building or structure; and

(b) the cost to a tenant of obtaining or extending a lease or sublease or the amount paid to a landlord to permit the sublease of the property.

The part of the leasehold interest that results from expenditures by the taxpayer (or by a person with whom the taxpayer does not deal at arm's length) on buildings or other structures or alterations thereto which substantially change the nature of the leased property, is not included under this provision, but may be depreciated in the normal way. Such major alterations or improvements are considered to be a "building or other structure" as the phrase is used in other capital cost allowance classes. This exclusion from Class 13 applies also where the major alteration or addition was done by an old lessee and the taxpayer's leasehold interest was acquired after 1975, or in the case of Class 31 or 32 property, after November 18, 1974.[98] For example, where a warehouse and garages were adapted to be used as business college premises, the taxpayer could not depreciate the expense as the cost of a leasehold interest.[99]

A taxpayer who owned a building built on land under an emphyteutic lease was entitled to capital cost allowance only on the basis that the building was property of Class 13 (a leasehold interest) rather than property of Class 3 (proprietary interest), where the lease was not sufficiently clear to separate the ownership of a building from the ownership of the land.[100] However, where a lease confers ownership of a building, the building can be classified as a Class 3 asset.[101]

The yearly deduction in respect of a leasehold interest is the lesser of the prorated portion of the capital cost of such an interest or the undepreciated capital cost of the leasehold interest at the end of the taxation year before claiming any capital cost allowance. The "prorated portion" of the capital cost is the lesser of:

See page ii for explanation of footnotes.

[97] CCH ¶4994, ¶4996; Reg. 1100(1)(b), Class 13, Sch III.

[98] CCH ¶4997, ¶4998, ¶4998a; Reg. 1102(4), Reg. 1102(5), Reg. 1102(5.1).

[99] McTavish Business College, 57 DTC 141.

[100] Rudnikoff, 75 DTC 5008, Dow Holdings Ltd., 76 DTC 1199.

[101] Plan A Leasing Ltd., 76 DTC 6159.

(a) $\frac{1}{5}$ of its cost, and

(b) the amount obtained by dividing the capital cost of the interest by the number of years the lease has to run plus one renewal term (if any) not in excess of 40 years in total.[102]

In the year of acquisition of a leasehold interest, this allowance is restricted to half the normal claim for acquisitions after November 12, 1981. This has a result similar to the half-year rule set out in ¶4062.[103] Each expenditure is amortized in this way; therefore the capital cost allowance for each expenditure is calculated on the basis of the year in which the expenditure was incurred and the lease to which it applies.

The following rules are applicable when calculating the capital cost allowance for a leasehold interest:

(1) Where a capital expenditure is incurred before the leasehold interest is acquired, it will be deemed to have been incurred in the year the leasehold interest is acquired.

(2) Where a tenant has the right to renew the lease for an additional term or terms, the lease is deemed to expire at the end of the term next succeeding the term in which the capital cost was incurred.

(3) If the capital cost of a leasehold interest does not exceed the aggregate of:

(a) allowances deducted in previous years in respect of the leasehold interest, and

(b) the proceeds of disposition (if any) of part or all of that interest,

then the prorated portion is deemed to be nil. The overall amount deductible in a year is limited to the lesser of:

(i) the undepreciated capital cost of all leasehold interests in Class 13, and

(ii) the total of the remaining prorated amounts for each leasehold interest in the class.

Where, at the end of a taxation year, the undepreciated capital cost to the taxpayer of all leasehold interests is nil, the prorated portion of any part of the capital cost as of that time shall, for all subsequent years, be deemed to be nil.

Example:

George has a December 31 year end and has entered into a 20-year building lease on June 1, 2012, and on June 30 spent $5,000 on leasehold improvements. The prorated portion of this expenditure is calculated as follows:

See page ii for explanation of footnotes.

[102] CCH ¶4996; Sch III.   [103] CCH ¶4995; Reg. 1100(1)(b).

¶4090

Expenditure	**$5,000**
Number of months in period from January 1, 2012, to June 1, 2032	245
Number of 12-month periods in above period = 245 divided by 12	20
Prorated portion = $5,000 divided by 20 = ...	$ 250

If this is George's only leasehold, his 2012 claim for capital cost allowance on Class 13 assets will be $125 (due to the half-year rule). In each subsequent year until 2032, he will be allowed a claim of $250, and in the year 2033 the remaining $125, at which time the entire $5,000 will have been deducted from income. Note that because this is straight-line depreciation over the life of the lease, the half-year rule requires an extra year to depreciate the lease fully; a twenty-year lease is actually written off in twenty-one years.

If George spends another $1,000 in 2013 on improvements, he will make a similar calculation. In this case, the expenditure of $1,000 is divided by 19 (the number of 12-month periods remaining in the lease after January 1, 2013) and the prorated portion of the 2013 expenditure is $1,000 divided by 19, i.e., $52.63. The 2013 capital cost allowance claim for Class 13 equals the aggregate of the prorated portions adjusted for the half-year rule on 2013 expenditures. Thus, the 2013 claim would be ($250 + $\frac{1}{2}$ × $52.63) or $276.32. In subsequent years, assuming no additional expenditures, the deduction will be $302.63. In 2033, the claim will be $125 + $26.31, picking up the leftover balances from the half-year rule.

The number of 12-month periods to be used in the above calculations is limited to a maximum of 40. On the other hand, the maximum claim in any year is limited to $\frac{1}{5}$ of the particular cost, so that, for instance, an expenditure with respect to a lease with only two years to run must be deducted over a five-year period, rather than a two-year period.

[¶4105] Patents, Vehicles, Power-Operated Movable Equipment, and Pipelines

[¶4110] Patents, Concessions, Franchises, Licences, etc.

Property which is a patent, franchise, concession, or licence for a limited period in respect of property, is eligible for capital cost allowance under Class 14.[104] Excluded from this Class are:

(1) a franchise, concession, or licence in respect of minerals, petroleum, natural gas, other related hydrocarbons, or timber, and property relating to such products (except a franchise for distributing gas to consumers or a licence to export gas from Canada or from a province) or a right to explore for, drill for, take, or remove such products;

(2) a leasehold interest;

(3) a property included in Class 23 (a leasehold or licence in respect of land granted under an agreement with the Canadian Corporation for the 1967 World Exhibition or the Expo '86 Corporation);

See page ii for explanation of footnotes.

[104] CCH ¶5001, ¶5002; Reg. 1100(1)(c), Class 14; Interp. Bul. IT-477.

(4) a licence to use computer software; and

(5) a patent or a right to use patented information acquired after April 26, 1993, that is included in Class 44. See comments below.

The cost of the right to use a copyright for a limited period of time is considered to be a licence that is depreciable as a Class 14 asset. However, licences to use computer software for commercial exploitation are Class 12 property. The amount claimed for a Class 14 asset may not exceed the aggregate of the amounts for the year obtained by apportioning the capital cost to the taxpayer of each property equally over the life of the property remaining at the time the cost was incurred. This particular class of assets is depreciated on the straight-line method of depreciation rather than on the declining balance system.

The half-year rule (see ¶4062) for the year in which assets are acquired does not apply to Class 14 assets, nor is the capital cost allowance prorated in short taxation years (see ¶4065). For a long time, the CRA took the position that the cost of an asset in Class 14 should be apportioned over the life of the asset on a *per diem* basis. However, in revisions to paragraph 4 of IT-477, issued in final form November 27, 2001, the CRA indicated that it would in the future accept that the capital cost of a Class 14 property may be apportioned on another basis where, based on the legal agreements and other relevant factors, the taxpayer can clearly demonstrate that it is reasonable. For example, where a three-year licence provides that a television program may be broadcast three times in Year 1, and once in each of Years 2 and 3, it would generally be appropriate to allocate $3/5$ of the capital cost to Year 1 and $1/5$ to each of Years 2 and 3.[105]

Where a franchise is for an indefinite period, no capital cost allowance is permitted.[106] (See the commentary on eligible capital expenditures at ¶3075 *et seq.*) An exclusive selling agency is a franchise, and capital cost allowance on its value may be granted if the value can be established.[107] However, a sales management contract purchased by one company, under which it bound itself to procure and finance salespeople for the sale of securities by another company, was held tantamount to a rental of services by one firm from another.[108] An agreement not to compete is not a property, and since it is not a tangible asset, no capital cost allowance is permitted.[109] "Know-how, techniques, skills, and experience" have been held not to be "property" for capital cost allowance purposes.[110]

There is a special formula for capital cost allowance in respect of a Class 14 patent, where the cost of the patent is determined by reference to its use. Under these circumstances the taxpayer may deduct the lesser of:

See page ii for explanation of footnotes.

[105] Interp. Bul. IT-477.

[106] Clark & Co. Ltd., 70 DTC 1524.

[107] John Marks Ltd., 63 DTC 724.

[108] Investors Syndicate of Canada Ltd., 65 DTC 5120.

[109] No. 614, 59 DTC 238.

[110] Rapistan Canada Ltd., 76 DTC 6177.

(a) the capital cost determined by the use of the patent in the year *plus* the normal allowance claimed (see above) on that portion of the capital cost not determined by use, and

(b) the undepreciated cost to the taxpayer as of the end of the taxation year of property of the class, before making any deduction under this provision for that year.[111]

Patents and the right to use patented information for a limited or unlimited period, acquired after April 26, 1993, may be included in Class 44 and depreciated at 25% on the declining balance. Assets in Class 44 are subject to the half-year rule and proration for a short taxation year. A taxpayer can elect not to include a patent in Class 44 but rather to include the patent in Class 14, if it is for a limited time, or as eligible capital property if for an unlimited time.[112] If a patent for a limited period is acquired late in the life of the patent, Class 14 may give a more favourable capital cost allowance claim than Class 44.

Where a patent or the right to use patented information for a limited or an unlimited period is acquired after April 26, 1993, and all or a portion of the capital cost is based on use, there is a special rule for claiming capital cost allowance in Class 44, similar to that for patents in Class 14. The taxpayer can deduct the lesser of:

(a) the total of the capital cost that is determined by use plus 25% of the undepreciated capital cost of the patent not determined by use, and

(b) the undepreciated capital cost as of the end of the taxation year of property of Class 44.[113]

[¶4115] Election — Limited Period Franchise, Concession, or Licence

Under pending technical amendments, the last version of which was released in a draft form on July 16, 2010, concessions, franchises, and licences that are disposed of or terminated after December 20, 2002, will be treated as former business property for purposes of the deferral of recapture of CCA under the rules at ¶4460, provided there is a joint election between the transferor and the transferee.[114] The election applies only to a franchise, concession, or licence for a limited period that is wholly attributable to the carrying on of a business at a fixed place. It may be made where the property is: (i) disposed of directly by the owner (the transferor) to another person (the new owner or transferee), or (ii) terminated by the owner (the transferor) and other person (the transferee) acquires a similar property in respect of the same fixed place of business. Both parties must make the election in their returns of income for their respective taxation years that include the

---

See page ii for explanation of footnotes.

[111] CCH ¶5003; Reg. 1100(9).

[112] CCH ¶4940a, ¶5045, ¶5045b; Reg. 1100(1)(a), Reg. 1103(2h), Class 44.

[113] CCH ¶5045a; Reg. 1100(9.1).

[114] CCH ¶28,123; Sec. 248(1) "former business property".

year of the disposition or termination.[115] It should be noted that if more than one property of a taxpayer is described in the same CCA class, and one or more of the properties is a property in respect of which the taxpayer is a transferee that has made the above election, a separate class is prescribed for each elected property of the taxpayer that would otherwise be included in the same class.[116]

If the election is made, the transferee is deemed to own that property until such time as the transferee owns neither the former property nor a similar property in respect of the same fixed place to which the former property related. If the transferee instead acquires a similar property in respect of the same fixed place (i.e., the life of the former property was terminated), the transferee is deemed to have also acquired the former property and to continue to own it until the transferee no longer owns the similar property.[117] In either case, for the purpose of claiming a CCA, the life of the former property in the hands of the transferee is deemed to be the term remaining at the time the transferor originally acquired the property. For instance, a licence with a 20-year life when it was originally acquired by the transferor, but with 5 years remaining at the time of the transfer, would be considered to have a 20-year life in the hands of the transferee for the purposes of claiming a CCA.

There may be circumstances where, but for this election, a portion of the consideration given by a transferee might reasonably be considered to be an eligible capital amount to the transferor and an eligible capital expenditure to the transferee (see ¶3075 *et seq.*). For instance, a portion of the consideration may reasonably relate to the preferred status that the transferee may receive in obtaining a new property at the end of the term. Where a joint election is made, such an amount will be neither an eligible capital amount to the transferor, nor an eligible capital expenditure to the transferee, but will instead be included in the cost to the transferee and the proceeds of disposition of the transferor. If the transferee has more than one franchise, etc., in the same capital cost allowance class, a separate class is prescribed for each property that the transferee has acquired under a joint election.

Where, subsequent to the acquisition of the property by the transferee, the life of the property expires and a similar property in respect of the same fixed place is not acquired by the transferee, the transferee would normally be entitled to a terminal loss (see ¶4475), and generally that would be the rule under the election. However, no terminal loss may be claimed by the transferee on property acquired under a joint election if:

    (i) within 24 months after the transferee last owned the former property, the transferee or a person not dealing at arm's length with the transferee acquire a similar property in respect of the same fixed place to which the former property applied; *and*

---

[115] Sec. 13(4.2).
[116] Reg. 1101(1ag).

[117] Sec. 13(4.3).

(ii) at the end of the taxation year, the transferee or the non-arm's length person owns the similar property or another similar property in respect to the same fixed place to which the former property applied.[118]

The following two examples were prepared by the Department of Finance and published with the explanatory notes to the revised technical proposals that were released in a draft form on July 16, 2010.

Example 1

Ms. Mubarak is a franchisee with five years remaining of a 20-year agreement. The original cost was $60,000, and the undepreciated capital cost ("UCC") is $15,000. The agreement is transferable, so she agrees to sell the franchise to Mr. Grando at its fair market value of $85,000. Ms. Mubarak will, in the same taxation year, purchase from Ms. Vincent a replacement franchise that has 15 years remaining of a 20-year term, for $100,000.

But for the making of a joint election, Ms. Mubarak would have a capital gain of $25,000 (i.e., $85,000 - $60,000) and a UCC balance of $55,000 (i.e., $15,000 + $100,000 - $60,000) before deducting any capital cost allowance for the year. The adjusted cost base ("ACB") of her replacement franchise would be $100,000. Mr. Grando would have acquired a Class 14 property with an ACB and capital cost of $85,000, depreciable over five years.

If Ms. Mubarak and Mr. Grando make the above joint election, Ms. Mubarak may elect under the rules at ¶5357 and ¶4460 to defer the capital gain, such that the ACB and capital cost of the replacement franchise will be deemed to be $75,000 (i.e., $100,000 less the $25,000 deferred capital gain). Furthermore, Ms. Mubarak's UCC balance for Class 14 will be $30,000 (i.e., an increase equivalent to the $100,000 cost of the replacement franchise less the $85,000 proceeds from the former property), to be amortized over the remaining 15-year term. In this regard, note that the term for amortizing Ms. Mubarak's replacement franchise is unaffected by her and Mr. Grando's joint election in respect of the former property. Mr. Grando, on the other hand, will be required to amortize his $85,000 cost of the former property over 20 years, which was the term of the former property when it was first acquired by Ms. Mubarak.

If Mr. Grando does not enter into a new agreement with the franchisor after the five-year period, he will be eligible for a terminal loss (even if there are other Class 14 assets, because the $85,000 property will be in a "separate class"). However, a terminal loss will not be available if a person dealing non-arm's length with Mr. Grando, at any time before the time that is 24 months after the expiry of the old agreement, enters into a new franchise agreement in respect of the same fixed place.

See page ii for explanation of footnotes.

[118] Sec. 20(16.1)(b).

¶4115

Example 2

Consider again Example 1, but suppose that the replacement franchise, purchased by Ms. Mubarak from Ms. Vincent, is itself the subject of the above joint election by them. Ms. Mubarak is required to amortize her $30,000 UCC (see Example 1) over the original 20-year term of Ms. Vincent, not over its remaining 15 years.

[¶4120] Automobiles, Trucks, and Aircraft

Automobiles or trucks used to earn income from business or property are eligible for capital cost allowance at the rate of 30% of the vehicle's undepreciated capital cost (Class 10 and Class 10.1). An aircraft is a Class 9 asset, written off at 25%.[119] If a taxpayer is required to use his or her own car or aircraft to fulfill the duties of employment, the taxpayer may claim capital cost allowance at the same rates.[120] Only that part of the depreciation incurred in the course of employment or relating to business use is deductible. If, for example, the undepreciated capital cost of the automobile is $4,800 and it is used 75% of the time for purposes of employment, the capital cost allowance will be calculated as: 30% of $4,800 = $1,440; 75% of $1,440 = $1,080.

"Passenger vehicle" is defined as an automobile acquired after June 17, 1987.[121] This generally includes a motor vehicle designed or adapted to carry individuals on highways and streets and which has a seating capacity of not more than the driver and eight passengers. Vehicles that are specifically excluded from the definition of "automobile" are:

(a) an ambulance;

(b) a taxi;

(c) beginning in 2003, a clearly marked emergency-response vehicle that is used in connection with or in the course of an individual's office or employment with a fire department or the police;

(d) a bus;

(e) a hearse;

(f) a vehicle acquired to be sold, rented, or leased in the course of carrying on a business of selling, renting, or leasing motor vehicles;

(g) a van or pick-up truck having a seating capacity for *not more* than the driver and two passengers if it is used primarily (more than 50%) for the transportation of goods and equipment in the course of producing income;

(h) a van or pick-up truck having a seating capacity for *more* than the driver and two passengers if it is used substantially (at least 90%) for

---

See page ii for explanation of footnotes.

[119] CCH ¶4980, ¶4981, ¶4990a; Class 9, Class 10, Class 10.1.

[120] CCH ¶3090, ¶4548; Sec. 8(1)(j), 13(11).

[121] CCH ¶28,020, ¶28,195; Sec. 248(1) "automobile", 248(1) "passenger vehicle".

the transportation of goods, equipment, or passengers in the course of producing income; and

(i) for taxation years beginning after 2002, an extended cab pick-up truck if it is used primarily (more than 50%) for the transportation of goods, equipment, and passengers in the course of producing income at one or more worksites that are at least 30 kilometres from the nearest urban community having a population of at least 40,000 persons.

Passenger vehicles that cost over a prescribed ceiling are included in Class 10.1 instead of Class 10. The prescribed ceiling is $30,000 in 2001–2012 plus GST/HST, PST, or other provincial levies.[122] The capital cost allowance rate for Class 10.1 is 30%, the same as for Class 10. Class 10.1 assets are subject to the half-year rule (¶4062) in the year of acquisition and proration for short taxation years (¶4065) as are the vehicles in Class 10. Capital cost allowance is claimed in the normal way but only on the prescribed ceiling.[123] The ceiling on the cost of passenger vehicles for capital cost allowance purposes is reviewed annually, towards the end of the calendar year, and adjusted on occasion.

Each vehicle in Class 10.1 is put into a separate class; however, these passenger vehicles are not subject to recapture or terminal loss.[124] When a Class 10.1 vehicle is disposed of in a taxation year, the taxpayer may claim a half-year of capital cost allowance on that vehicle. The taxpayer need not acquire another vehicle of any kind in order to claim this capital cost allowance for the year of disposition. Any positive or negative balance in Class 10.1 after the disposition is brought to nil even though no recapture or terminal loss arises.[125]

If a passenger vehicle is acquired from a person with whom the taxpayer does not deal at arm's length, the capital cost to the taxpayer is limited to the least of:

(a) the fair market value of the vehicle;

(b) the cost amount of the vehicle to the person from whom it was acquired; and

(c) the prescribed amount described above.

Therefore, the depreciable limit for passenger vehicles cannot be circumvented through non-arm's length transfers.[126]

Automobiles costing less than the prescribed amount and other motor vehicles that are excluded from the definition of automobile (as noted above) continue to be included in Class 10. These Class 10 vehicles are subject to normal recapture and terminal loss rules.

See page ii for explanation of footnotes.

[122] CCH ¶4990d; Reg. 7307(1).

[123] CCH ¶4522, ¶4954, ¶4990a; Sec. 13(7)(g); Reg. 1100(1)(a)(x.1); Class 10.1; Interp. Bul. IT-521R, IT-522R.

[124] CCH ¶4511g, ¶4990b, ¶5145ba; Sec. 13(2), 20(16.1); Reg. 1101(1af).

[125] CCH ¶4990c; Reg. 1100(2.5).

[126] CCH ¶4522; Sec. 13(7)(h).

¶4120

Automobiles that have been included in Class 10 in error and that should be in Class 10.1 must be transferred to Class 10.1; see ¶4040.

Example:

Suppose a car acquired in 2012 costs $29,000 plus $2,320 (8%) PST (provincial sales tax, either HST or not) plus $1,450 (5%) GST (if the GST or PST tax rate changes during the year, it is the actual sales tax that is included in both actual and threshold cost). The cost is therefore $32,770. This is compared to a threshold of $30,000 plus (in an 8% PST province) $2,400 PST, plus $1,500 GST (at 5%), or $33,900. Since the car costs less than the threshold, it will be capitalized in Class 10 (not 10.1).

If a car acquired in 2012 costs $31,000 plus $2,480 (8%) PST and $1,550 (5%) GST, the most that can be included in Class 10.1 is $30,000 plus GST/HST/PST thereon, so $30,000 plus $2,400 PST (assuming 8%) and $1,500 GST (assuming 5%), or $33,900.

Once the determination is made as to whether Class 10 or Class 10.1 is appropriate, the amount to be included in the class must be determined taking into account GST/HST and any applicable provincial taxes. For Class 10, this is actual cost plus HST or GST and PST. For Class 10.1, it is the threshold amount which includes HST or GST and PST on the specified prescribed dollar amount. Thus, where $30,000 is the threshold amount, the amount to be included in Class 10.1 for a car that costs more than $30,000 is $30,000 + (for 2012, 5% GST ($1,500)) + (if PST/HST is, say, 8%) $2,400 = $33,900. In principle, GST/PST/HST is included in capital cost, but mere entitlement to GST/HST input tax credits reverses the credits out of capital cost again. For employees or partners in partnerships, even if use of the vehicle is more than 90% for commercial purposes, GST/HST input tax credits should arise only in succeeding years so that the entire cost, including tax, is entered in Class 10 or the threshold cost plus tax thereon in Class 10.1 in the year of acquisition and the GST/HST rebate machinery operates in subsequent years to compensate for that inclusion. For the self-employed, if the vehicle is used less than 90% for business purposes, the results are essentially the same; tax (up to the threshold limits) is included in cost and input tax credits are deferred and received piecemeal. However, if the vehicle is used 90% or more for business purposes, it is in effect immediately eligible for GST/HST input tax credits, and any GST/HST entitlement (whether or not received in the year) must not be included in Class 10 or 10.1 capital cost since it will be otherwise recovered. Note that GST input tax credit on an automobile, subject to Class 10.1 restrictions, is itself limited to the amount permitted in Class 10.1, i.e., for 2012, $1,500 ($30,000 × 5%). HST is similarly restricted to the amount allowed for Class 10.1 purposes.

[¶4122] Trucks

Trucks are generally included in Class 10 along with other automotive equipment and are depreciable at 30%. Passenger vans and small trucks may be captured by the passenger vehicle rules discussed in ¶4120 if they qualify as automobiles as defined in the Act.[127] A van that seats more than a driver and eight passengers is not an automobile.

Also specifically excluded from the definition of automobile and therefore included in the normal Class 10 pool are:

(a) a van or a pick-up truck having a seating capacity for not more than a driver and two passengers, if it is used more than 50% of the time for transporting goods or equipment in the course of earning income;

(b) a van or pick-up truck having a seating capacity for more than the driver and two passengers if it is used at least 90% of the time for transporting goods, equipment, or passengers in the course of earning income; and

(c) for taxation years beginning after 2002, an extended cab pick-up truck if it is used more than 50% of the time for transporting goods, equipment or passengers in the course of producing income at one or more worksites that are at least 30 km. from the nearest urban community having a population of at least 40,000 persons.

Note that a trailer eligible for the 30% rate in Class 10 includes a trailer designed to be hauled on both highways and railway tracks.

Large trucks and tractors with a gross vehicle weight rating in excess of 11,788 kg. (26,000 lbs) that are acquired after December 6, 1991, are included in Class 16 (40%). These trucks and tractors must be used by the taxpayer or a person with whom the taxpayer does not deal at arm's length primarily for hauling freight.[128]

[¶4124] Power-Operated Movable Machinery (Classes 10, 22, and 38)

Certain heavy movable machinery, used by the road building and construction industries for excavating and moving earth and rocks and compacting road building materials, and acquired before 1988, is included in Class 22 (50%).[129] This type of equipment, if acquired after 1987, is to be included in Class 38 (30%). See ¶4025 and ¶4030 for transitional rules on the date of acquisition of the assets and capital cost allowance rates for Class 38.[130] The taxpayer may elect to include equipment in Class 38 in a separate class.[131]

In order to come within the provisions of Class 22 or Class 38, most machines must be "designed" either to be moved around as they work, on their own wheels or treads, or to be carried around, as in the case of compressed-air drills used in excavating rock. The use of the word "movable" in the class ensures that non-movable or semi-portable equipment of all kinds will be excluded. In addition, a machine must be power-operated which means it must be driven or handled either by its own motor or by a closely

---

See page ii for explanation of footnotes.

[127] CCH ¶28,020; Sec. 248(1) "automobile".   [130] CCH ¶5043e; Reg. 1100(1)(zd).
[128] CCH ¶5009; Class 16.
[129] CCH ¶5018; Class 22; Interp. Bul. IT-469R.   [131] CCH ¶5043d, ¶5043f; Reg. 1101(5l), Class 38.

related separate source of power such as a tractor, in the case of earth-moving equipment, or by a compressor, in the case of a rock drill. Where equipment could be used for both a Class 22 purpose and another purpose, it falls within the design requirement. It need not be designed *exclusively* for a Class 22 purpose.[132]

Contractor's movable equipment not included in Class 22 or 38 and not designed for use in determining the existence, location, extent, or quality of oil, gas, or minerals, either on land or offshore, is included in Class 10(*h*) (30%). Such equipment in Class 10(*h*) acquired after December 23, 1991, except equipment that was acquired before 1993 pursuant to an agreement in writing entered into before December 24, 1991, or that was under construction on behalf of the taxpayer on December 23, 1991, must be used in the construction business or leased to someone in the construction business.[133]

[¶4127] Pipelines

Prior to February 24, 2005, a pipeline, other than a pipeline that is gas or oil well equipment, is included in Class 1 (4%).[134] A pipeline for oil or natural gas, in respect of which the Minister, in consultation with the Minister of Energy, Mines and Resources, is satisfied that the main source of supply for the pipeline is likely to be exhausted within 15 years from the date on which operation of the pipeline commenced, is specifically excluded from Class 1. Such a pipeline would be a Class 8 asset.[135]

To implement the 2005 Budget, regulations were enacted on June 14, 2006, so that the CCA rate for transmission pipelines (as contrasted with distribution lines) for petroleum, natural gas, or related hydrocarbons be increased from 4% (Class 1 rate) to 8% (Class 49 rate) to better reflect the typical useful life of these assets.[136] Included in Class 49 are control and monitoring devices, valves, and other ancillary equipment (other than pumping and compression equipment, which will go into a 15% class, as discussed below). This increased CCA for Class 49 does not apply to equipment and pipelines for which the Minister, in consultation with the Minister of Energy, Mines and Resources, is satisfied that the main source of supply for the pipeline is likely to be exhausted within 15 years of commencement of operations. Such equipment is generally eligible for a 20% (Class 8) CCA rate. The new CCA rates for transmission pipelines will apply to equipment acquired after February 22, 2005, that has not been used or acquired for use before February 23, 2005.

Distribution pipelines that distribute gas to the ultimate consumers typically have a longer useful life than transmission pipelines. Accordingly, these properties will continue to be included in Class 1, eligible for a 4% CCA rate.

See page ii for explanation of footnotes.

[132] L & R Asphalt Ltd, 89 DTC 266.
[133] CCH ¶4981; Class 10.
[134] CCH ¶4955; Class 1.

[135] Interp. Bul. IT-482R.

[136] Class 49.

The CCA rate for pumping, compression, and any ancillary equipment related to the transmission pipelines for petroleum, natural gas, related hydrocarbons, or carbon dioxide is set at 15%, by including such equipment in existing Class 7. However, this change does not apply to gas or oil well equipment (eligible for a 25% (Class 41) CCA rate) and buildings or other structures. The 15% rate for pumping and compression equipment for petroleum, natural gas, or related hydrocarbons applies to equipment acquired after February 22, 2005, and, in the case of such equipment that pumps or compresses carbon dioxide for the purpose of moving it through a pipeline, it applies to equipment acquired after February 25, 2008.

The useful life of a pipeline can, however, be shortened in cases where production from the associated resource ceases. Accordingly, a separate class election is introduced for transmission pipelines and related pumping and compression equipment. The separate class election, which must be made for the taxation year in which a property is acquired, allows taxpayers to place eligible property in a separate class for CCA purposes. Although the separate class election does not change the CCA rate specified for the class, it does provide that any remaining undepreciated balance in the class after the disposition of the property, can, for the year of disposition, be fully deducted as a terminal loss. This election is generally available for eligible equipment acquired after February 22, 2005.[137]

As a result of the 2007 Budget, a new pipeline, including control and monitoring devices, valves, and other equipment ancillary to the pipeline, used for the distribution (but not the transmission) of natural gas that is acquired after March 18, 2007, is included in new Class 51 which has a CCA rate of 6% on a declining balance basis.[138] Furthermore, a new pipeline used for the transmission of carbon dioxide that is acquired after February 25, 2008, is included in Class 49 (8% rate) whereas any related pumping, compression, or ancillary equipment acquired after that date is included in Class 7 (15% rate).

[¶4130] Timber and Industrial Mineral Mines

[¶4135] Timber Limits

The amount that may be deducted as capital cost allowance in respect of a timber limit other than a timber resource property is calculated under Schedule VI of the *Income Tax Regulations*. This amount is the lesser of:

(a) the undepreciated cost of the timber limit (as of the end of the year and before making any deductions under this provision); and

(b) the aggregate of:

---

[137] Reg. 1101(5u), Reg. 1101(5v).   [138] Class 51.

(i) an amount computed on the basis of a rate per cord, board foot, or cubic metre cut in the year, and

(ii) certain allowances in respect of survey and cruise expenses.[139]

The computation of the rate per cord, board foot, or cubic metre will depend on whether or not the taxpayer has been granted an allowance in respect of the timber limit for a previous taxation year.

Instead of the deductions described above, a taxpayer may elect to claim an amount that is the lesser of:

(a) $100, and

(b) the amount received by the taxpayer in the taxation year from the sale of timber.

Besides survey expenses that are depreciable under the above rules, there may be survey expenses that would be deductible as current expenses of the year. It is essentially a question of fact whether survey expenses are related to capital cost or to current operations.

If two or more limits are owned, each is a separate class of property, and the rate will be determined separately for each.[140]

[¶4140] Timber Resource Property

"Timber resource property" of a taxpayer is a Class 33 asset subject to a 15% rate capital cost allowance on the undepreciated capital cost of the property.

Timber resource property is defined[141] as an "original right" (or an extension, renewal, or substitution of such a right) to cut or remove timber from a limit or area in Canada if the right was acquired by the taxpayer after May 6, 1974. Cutting rights or licences acquired before this date remain depreciable as "timber limits" (see ¶4135 above). Timber resource properties are not required to be included in separate classes.

A disposition of a timber resource property does not give rise to a capital gain. Rather, the full amount by which the proceeds of disposition exceed the undepreciated capital cost of the class will be included in income.[142] See ¶4385.

[¶4145] Property Acquired to Cut and Remove Timber

Deductions may be claimed under Class 15 for logging assets. This class consists of depreciable property acquired for the purposes of cutting and removing merchantable timber from a timber limit and will be of no further

---

139 CCH ¶5046b; Reg. 1100(1)(e), Sch VI; Interp. Bul. IT-481.

140 CCH ¶5046c; Reg. 1101(3).

141 CCH ¶4562f; Sec. 13(21) "timber resource property"; Interp. Bul. IT-481.

142 CCH ¶4562h, ¶6050; Sec. 13(21) "undepreciated capital cost", 39(1).

use to the taxpayer after all merchantable timber the taxpayer is entitled to cut and remove from the limit has been cut and removed from the limit.[143]

The maximum amount which may be claimed is the lesser of:

(a) an amount computed on the basis of a rate per cord, board foot, or cubic metre cut in the taxation year; and

(b) the undepreciated capital cost to the taxpayer of the property of the class as of the end of the taxation year before making a deduction in respect of capital cost allowance for that year.

These assets, at the option of the taxpayer, may be included in Class 10(n) at a 30% rate instead of Class 15. If this option is chosen, all such property must be classified as Class 10. If the taxpayer chooses to include the assets in Class 15, some assets can be placed in another class that is applicable to the asset, excepting, of course, paragraph (n) of Class 10. The half-year rule is not applicable to Class 15 nor is the capital cost allowance prorated in short taxation years.

[¶4150] Industrial Mineral Mines, Sand, and Gravel Pits

The amount that may be claimed in respect of the capital cost of an industrial mineral mine or of a right to remove industrial minerals from such a mine, may not exceed the lesser of:

(a) an amount computed on the basis of a rate per unit of minerals mined in the taxation year, and

(b) the undepreciated capital cost to the taxpayer of the mine or right at the end of the taxation year (before capital cost allowance is deducted).[144]

In lieu of the above deduction, a taxpayer may elect that the deduction for a taxation year shall be the lesser of:

(a) $100, and

(b) the amount received by the taxpayer in the taxation year from the sale of the mineral.[145]

An "industrial mineral mine" includes a peat bog or deposit of peat, but does not include a mineral resource;[146] "mineral" includes peat; and "mining" includes the harvesting of peat. Consequently, gravel or sand pits, building stone quarries, and peat bogs are depreciable under this provision.

---

[143] CCH ¶5004, ¶5005, ¶5006, ¶5007; Reg. 1100(1)(f), Reg. 1102(7), Class 15, Sch IV; Interp. Bul. IT-501.

[144] CCH ¶5047a, ¶5047d; Reg. 1100(1)(g), Sch V.

[145] CCH ¶5047d; Sch V.

[146] CCH ¶5047c; Reg. 1104(3); Interp. Bul. IT-492.

Where a taxpayer has more than one industrial mineral mine or the right to remove minerals from such a mine or both, each mine or right is deemed to be a separate class of property.[147]

For capital cost allowances allowed in connection with mining assets, Classes 10, 28, 41, and 41.1, see ¶4172.

[¶4155] Additional Capital Cost Allowances

[¶4165] Railway Property

Expenditures incurred for the repair, replacement, alteration, or renovation of depreciable railway property of a prescribed class are deemed to result in the taxpayer acquiring depreciable property of that class at a capital cost equal to the amount so expended, if the National Transportation Agency, under its prescribed uniform system of accounting, requires such expenditures to be treated other than as an expense. Such expenditures are not deductible.[148] The expenditure, if incurred before May 26, 1976, is the property enumerated in Class 4, which is depreciable at a rate of 6%. If an expenditure in respect of the repair, replacement, alteration, or renovation is incurred after May 25, 1976, it falls into the class in Schedule II in which the repaired, replaced, altered, or renovated property would be included if it had been acquired at the time the expenditure was incurred.[149]

Railway assets can fall within any of Classes 1, 3, 4, 6, 7, 8, 10, 28, 35, or 41. Railway track and grading that is not part of a railway system or that was acquired after May 25, 1976, as well as railway traffic control or signalling equipment acquired after May 25, 1976, is depreciable at the rate of 4% under Class 1.[150] In respect of railway sidings, a taxpayer is allowed a deduction of 4% of the capital expenditure incurred by the taxpayer in respect of construction of a railway siding to the taxpayer's property or place of business.[151] Marine railways are depreciable under Class 7 at 15%.[152]

Railway cars acquired after May 25, 1976, and before February 28, 2000, qualify as Class 35 property, depreciable at a rate of 7%. A rail suspension device acquired after December 23, 1991, and before February 28, 2000, designed to carry trailers designed to be hauled on both highways and railway tracks, is also a Class 35 asset.[153]

Separate classes are prescribed for railway cars included in Class 35 which are owned by a taxpayer and rented, leased, or used by the taxpayer in Canada, other than those owned by a corporation or a partnership that owns or operates a railway as a common carrier, or a corporation associated with such a corporation. Separate classes are prescribed for:

See page ii for explanation of footnotes.

[147] CCH ¶5047b; Reg. 1101(4).
[148] CCH ¶5875; Sec. 36.
[149] CCH ¶4961aa, ¶4970; Reg. 1102(10), Class 4.
[150] CCH ¶4955; Class 1.
[151] CCH ¶4959; Reg. 1100(8).
[152] CCH ¶4973; Class 7.
[153] CCH ¶5041; Class 35.

(1) railway cars acquired by the taxpayer before February 3, 1990, other than those acquired for rent or lease to another person;

(2) railway cars acquired by the taxpayer after February 2, 1990, and before February 28, 2000, other than those acquired for rent or lease to another person;

(3) railway cars acquired by the taxpayer before April 27, 1989, for rent or lease to another person; and

(4) railway cars acquired by the taxpayer after April 26, 1989, and before February 28, 2000, for rent or lease to another person.

For properties described in (1), a taxpayer is permitted to claim an additional allowance not exceeding 8% of the undepreciated capital cost to the taxpayer of such properties. A reduced 6% additional allowance is available for properties in categories (2) and (4). For properties in category (3) the additional allowance is reduced by $1/3$% each year beginning at $7^2/3$% in 1990 and ending at 6% for 1995 and subsequent years. The half-year rule in the year of acquisition applies when calculating the additional allowance.[154]

A separate class is also prescribed for railway cars and rail suspension devices included in Class 35 that are acquired after December 6, 1991, and before February 28, 2000, by a taxpayer that was at that time a common carrier that owned and operated a railway. The assets in this separate class are eligible for an additional 3% allowance (in addition to the 7% Class 35 rate) on undepreciated capital cost. The additional allowance is subject to the half-year rule in the year of acquisition.[155]

Property that is acquired after February 27, 2000 (other than property acquired before February 26, 2008 (see below) and included in paragraph (*y*) of Class 10), that is a railway car, railway locomotive (other than an automotive railway car), and railway suspension device qualifies for Class 7 depreciation at the 15% rate, rather than the combined 10% or 13% rate (including additional allowances) described above.[156] For leased assets, the lessor is given the option to choose the existing combined 13% CCA rate and not have the specified leasing property rules apply, or choose the new 15% treatment (Class 7) in exchange for accepting the leasing property rules discussed at ¶4305.[157]

Effective for acquisitions after February 25, 2008, railway locomotives (other than automotive railway cars) are eligible for a higher CCA rate of 30% under paragraph (*y*) of Class 10.[158] This increase from the 15% rate under Class 7 to the 30% rate under Class 10 for a railway locomotive first acquired and available for use after February 25, 2008, was proposed in the 2008 Budget and the implementing Order in Council was published on May 13,

See page ii for explanation of footnotes.

[154] CCH ¶5041a, ¶5041b, ¶5041d; Reg. 1100(1)(z), Reg. 1100(1)(z.1a), Reg. 1101(5d).

[155] CCH ¶5041c, ¶5041e; Reg. 1100(1)(z.1b), Reg. 1101(5d.1).

[156] CCH ¶4973; Class 7.

[157] Reg. 1103(2i).

[158] Reg. 1102(19.1), Reg. 1102(19.2).

¶4165

2009. Expenses of a capital nature that are incurred after February 25, 2008, for the refurbishment or reconditioning of a railway locomotive will also be eligible for the 30% CCA rate.

An additional capital cost allowance of 4% can be claimed on railway track and related property included in Class 1 that is acquired after March 31, 1977, and before 1988. This property is placed in a separate class. A railway trestle included in Class 3 that is acquired during the period March 31, 1977, to before 1988 is also placed in a separate class and is eligible for additional capital cost allowance of 3%.[159]

It should also be noted that railway track and related property acquired after March 31, 1977, for the purpose of gaining or producing income from a mine (e.g., a spur line to the mine site) qualifies as Class 10 property where the rate is 30%. In addition, if the track and equipment are acquired before the mine comes into production, it qualifies as Class 28 property (if acquired before 1988) and is eligible for further capital cost allowance in excess of 30%. Such property would be included in Class 41 if acquired after 1987. See ¶4172.[160]

An additional capital cost allowance deduction of 6% on a straight-line basis is allowed for most new railway system assets acquired after April 10, 1978, and before 1988, which are used or situated in Canada and owned by a taxpayer who owns and operates a railway as a common carrier. The deduction is available in the year of acquisition and the succeeding four taxation years on such property as track and grading, traffic control or signalling equipment, bridges, culverts, certain locomotives, certain maintenance and service machinery, and railway cars.[161]

Where the taxpayer is a common carrier that owned and operated a railway at the time the assets were acquired, a separate class (within Class 1, when acquired after December 6, 1991) is to be established for railway property — such as track and grading, including components, railway traffic control or signalling equipment, or a bridge, culvert, subway, or tunnel that is ancillary to railway track and grading. These assets are eligible for an additional allowance of 6% of undepreciated capital costs.[162] All railway trestles, included in Class 3 acquired after December 6, 1991 by a common carrier that owned and operated a railway at that time, are also to be placed in a separate class. These assets are eligible for an additional allowance of 5% of undepreciated capital cost.[163] The additional allowances have raised the capital cost allowance rates on railway cars, track, and other railway equipment acquired after December 6, 1991 to 10%.

See page ii for explanation of footnotes.

[159] CCH ¶4956, ¶4957, ¶4960, ¶4961aa; Reg. 1100(1)(za), Reg. 1100(1)(zb), Reg. 1101(5e), Reg. 1101(5f).

[160] CCH ¶4981, ¶5024, ¶5025, ¶5026; Reg. 1100(1)(w), Reg. 1100(1)(x), Class 10, Class 28.

[161] CCH ¶4958; Reg. 1100(1)(zc).

[162] CCH ¶4956a, ¶4960a; Reg. 1100(1)(za.1), Reg. 1101(5e.1).

[163] CCH ¶4956b, ¶4960b; Reg. 1100(1)(za.2), Reg. 1101(5e.2).

[¶4170] Canadian Vessels and Offshore Drilling Vessels

Vessels and attachments thereto are Class 7 property and are eligible for capital cost allowance at 15%. However, accelerated CCA on a straight-line basis at a maximum rate of 33⅓% of the capital cost of the property is available in respect of each vessel, including attachments thereto, that is constructed and registered in Canada and has not been used for any purpose before being acquired by the taxpayer.[164] Each such Canadian vessel, and attachments thereto, is included in a separate class (subject to the half-year rule in the year of acquisition). For such assets the write-off is over a four-year period with a 16⅔% write-off in Year 1 and Year 4, and a 33⅓% write-off in Years 2 and 3. Capital cost allowance must be prorated for a taxation year of less than 365 days. See ¶4065.[165]

Costs of conversion or major alteration to a vessel in Canada will also qualify for capital cost allowance of 33⅓ on a straight line basis.[166] Qualifying conversion costs form a separate class for each vessel converted or altered.

Offshore drilling vessels acquired before 1988 are included in Class 7 (15%) in a separate class and are eligible for an additional 15% on top of the regular 15% in Class 7.[167] The impact of the additional allowance is, therefore, to increase the effective rate on a Class 7 asset to 30% of the undepreciated capital cost. Both the additional and the regular allowance are subject to the half-year rule (see ¶4062).

Offshore drilling vessels acquired after 1987 are included in Class 41 (25%) rather than in Class 7 and are not eligible for the extra 15% allowance.[168] This shifts the effective depreciation rate down from 30% to 25%. Note, however, that an offshore drilling vessel can be included in a separate class and depreciated at 33⅓% if it meets the criteria of a Canadian vessel described above.

Class 41 (25% CCA rate) plus the separate classes for Canadian vessels and offshore drilling vessels will not be available if the Minister of Industry has agreed to a structured financing facility. In such a case, the maximum CCA rate applicable to the vessel and its attachments will be 15% under Class 7 and no accelerated or additional allowance will be allowed. These pending technical amendments will apply after November 7, 2001.

See page ii for explanation of footnotes.

[164] CCH ¶4973, ¶4975; Reg. 1100(1)(v), Class 7; Interp. Bul. IT-267R2.
[165] CCH ¶4977a; Reg. 1101(2a).
[166] CCH ¶4553, ¶4562ac; Sec. 13(14), 13(21) "conversion".
[167] CCH ¶4976, ¶4977b; Reg. 1100(1)(va), Reg. 1101(2b).
[168] CCH ¶5043p; Class41.

[¶4172] Mining Assets (Classes 28, 41, and 41.1)

All resource extraction assets acquired after 1987, which would previously have been included in Class 28 at 30%, have to be included in Class 41 or 41.1 under which the basic rate of capital cost allowance is 25%.[169]

In addition to the 30% allowance provided in Class 28 or the 25% allowance in Class 41, a taxpayer owning such property and operating the mine may claim an additional allowance in respect of these assets.

The additional allowance is equal to the lesser of:

(a) the remaining undepreciated capital cost of property of the class; and

(b) the taxpayer's income for the year from the mine.

For this purpose, income for the year from the mine should be determined before making any deductions for depletion or exploration and development expenses, or the additional capital cost allowance. The additional allowance is subject to the half-year rule (¶4062) in the year the assets are acquired.

If a taxpayer owns property that qualifies for inclusion in Class 28 or 41 and the properties so owned were acquired for use in more than one qualifying mine, separate classes of property must be established for the fixed assets applicable to each of such mines.[170] The limitation on the additional allowance each year is then calculated separately on the basis of the undepreciated capital cost of each such separate class, and the income and exempt income of each mine.

It should be noted that Class 41 also includes assets acquired after 1987 that relate to resource extraction, other than those mining assets formerly in Class 28. Paragraph (*b*) of Class 41 includes assets that would otherwise be in Class 10 and are designated underground storage costs, mine buildings, oil or gas well equipment, social or townsite assets, railway track, electrical generating equipment, equipment used in resource exploration, and heavy crude oil processing equipment. Drillships and offshore platforms used in exploration or drilling oil or gas wells acquired after 1987 are also Class 41 assets. Equipment for processing foreign ore in Canada is eligible for Class 43 treatment (30%), but the taxpayer may elect Class 41 treatment instead to obtain the additional allowances if the property qualifies for them. See ¶4210 for details of the election.

Some expenditures related to depreciation for mining may be available as development expense rather than as capital cost allowance. Where this is

---

See page ii for explanation of footnotes.

[169] CCH ¶4951e, ¶4951g, ¶4951h, ¶5024, ¶5043p; Reg. 1104(5), Reg. 1104(7), Reg. 1104(8), Class 28, Class 41, Class 41.1.

[170] CCH ¶5025–5028, ¶5043q–5043t; Reg. 1100(1)(w), Reg. 1100(1)(x), Reg. 1100(1)(y), Reg. 1100(1)(ya), Reg. 1101(4a), Reg. 1101(4b), Reg. 1101(4c), Reg. 1101(4d).

true, it will permit not only accelerated write-offs, but syndicated or tax-sheltered financing through flow-though shares (see ¶3540). In its 1996 Budget, the government endeavoured to clarify a number of the rules in this respect. Essentially, the rules were clarified to ensure that townsite roads and similar costs, where the property does not necessarily end up the taxpayer's, are nevertheless depreciable and not eligible capital property. In general, such expenditures in relation to a mine would fall under Class 41. Temporary access roads in the oil and gas mining sectors, however, may qualify instead as Canadian exploration expense or Canadian development expense.

As a consequence of the 2007 Budget, oil sands property acquired after March 18, 2007 is generally included in new Class 41.1. Properties included in paragraph (a) of new Class 41.1 remain eligible for the accelerated CCA until 2010. Beginning in 2011, the accelerated CCA is phased out and the amount of the additional allowance is reduced each year, regardless of whether the constraint is the income from the mine or the amount of the undepreciated capital cost. The percentage allowed as accelerated CCA, in each calendar year, will be 90% in 2011, 80% in 2012, 60% in 2013, and 30% in 2014 of the amount otherwise allowable as accelerated CCA. No accelerated CCA is allowed after 2014, and only the regular 25% CCA rate applies, with no additional allowance. Paragraph (b) of new Class 41.1 includes oil sands property acquired after 2015 that, if the property had been acquired before March 19, 2007, would have been included in Class 41. The accelerated CCA continues to be available in full for assets acquired before 2012 that are part of a project phase on which major construction began before March 19, 2007 (the 2007 Budget date).

[¶4180] Accelerated Capital Cost Allowances

[¶4190] Water and Air Pollution Control Equipment (Classes 24 and 27)

Classes 24 and 27 permit a taxpayer to claim accelerated capital cost allowance in respect of water and air pollution control equipment acquired before 1999.[171]

These assets are eligible for an allowance of 25% in the year of acquisition, 50% the following year, and the balance in Year 3. The accelerated allowance applies on a straight-line basis to the capital cost of the asset and not to the undepreciated capital cost.

The water pollution control equipment in Class 24 and the air pollution control equipment in Class 27 must be new when acquired. The property must be used primarily for the prevention, reduction, or elimination of water or air pollution which is caused by:

See page ii for explanation of footnotes.

[171] CCH ¶5020, ¶5023, ¶5031, ¶5032; Reg. 1100(1)(t), Reg. 1100(1)(ta), Class 24, Class 27.

(1) operations carried on at a site in Canada where the taxpayer has carried on operations prior to 1974;

(2) the operation in Canada of a building or plant, the construction of which commenced, or an agreement in writing for the construction of which was entered into by the taxpayer, prior to 1974; or

(3) the operation of transportation or other movable equipment by the taxpayer in Canada, including any of the inland, coastal, or boundary waters of Canada, from a time prior to 1974.

Class 24 and Class 27 also include property acquired by a taxpayer whose business includes preventing, reducing, or eliminating water or air pollution that is caused primarily by operations referred to in (1) to (3) above that are carried on by other taxpayers. In addition, Classes 24 and 27 include property acquired by a corporation whose principal business is financing the sale price of merchandise or services, lending money, or leasing property or any combination of these activities, if the property is to be leased to a taxpayer to be used in an operation of the kind referred to in these classes in preventing, reducing, or eliminating water or air pollution. Property of this kind will qualify if it is to be leased either to the taxpayer that carries on the operations causing the pollution or to a taxpayer whose business includes preventing, reducing, or eliminating such pollution by other taxpayers under the conditions referred to above.

In order to qualify for the accelerated allowance, the property must, upon application by the taxpayer, be accepted by the Minister of the Environment as property the primary purpose of which is, in the Minister's opinion, the prevention, reduction, or elimination of water or air pollution in the manner described above.

The accelerated capital cost allowance in Classes 24 and 27 applicable to water or air pollution control equipment acquired by a taxpayer for use at a facility continually operated by the taxpayer since before 1974, is also available in situations where a corporation has been amalgamated with, or wound up into, another corporation after 1973.

Classes 24 and 27 are no longer to be available for property acquired after December 31, 1998. Pollution control equipment acquired after 1998 will go into Class 1, 2, 3, 6, 8, 29, 43, 43.1, or 43.2, depending on its description or use.

[¶4210] Manufacturing and Processing Machinery and Equipment

In general, manufacturing and processing equipment (M&P) acquired after February 25, 1992, and before March 19, 2007, is eligible for a CCA declining balance rate of 30% under Class 43, and M&P equipment acquired after March 18, 2007, and before 2014, is eligible for a 50% straight-line (as opposed to a diminishing balance) rate under Class 29, subject to the half-year rule. Taking into account the half-year rule, these Class 29 assets may be written off on average over a three-year period. This results in an effective deduction rate of up to 25% for the first year, 50% for the second year, and the balance for the third year.[172] Class 29 is closed for eligible M&P property acquired after 2013. Such property will instead be eligible for the 30% declining balance rate under Class 43.

Property included in Class 29 or 43 must meet two tests:

(1) it must be used by the taxpayer directly or indirectly in Canada, primarily in the manufacturing or processing of goods for sale or lease; or

(2) it must be leased, in the ordinary course of business in Canada, to a lessee who will use the property primarily in the manufacturing or processing of goods for sale or lease, if the lessor is a corporation whose principal business is:

(a) leasing property,

(b) manufacturing property that it sells or leases,

(c) lending money,

(d) financing the purchase by others of merchandise or services by purchasing conditional sales contracts, chattel mortgages, accounts receivable, or other obligations,

(e) selling or servicing a type of property that it also leases, or

(f) any combination thereof.

Furthermore, the property itself must be property that would otherwise fall into Class 8 (but excluding radio communication equipment and railway rolling stock), an oil or water storage tank, or portable electrical generating equipment that would otherwise fall into Class 9.

Effective for acquisitions after February 27, 2000, a taxpayer may elect to set up a separate Class 43 for one or more items of manufacturing and processing equipment costing more than $1,000 (this election is not available for property swept into the Class 29 straight-line write-off after March 18, 2007, and before 2014).[173] Thus, where the specific equipment is sold at a loss or merely given away, the loss will be fully recognized for tax purposes when incurred, rather than having the proceeds credited to the general Class 43 and so amortized at the 30% declining balance rate forever. The election must be filed in the year of acquisition with the income tax return for that year.[174] Where the property is still on hand at the beginning of the fifth year after it became available for use, it must be merged into the general Class 43 UCC pool immediately after the beginning of that fifth year.[175]

See page ii for explanation of footnotes.

[172] CCH ¶5032, ¶5044aa; Reg. 1102(16.1), Class 29, Class 43.

[173] Reg. 1101(5s).

[174] CCH ¶4940zi; Reg. 1101(5q).

[175] CCH ¶4950h; Reg. 1103(2g).

¶4210

[¶4215] Energy-Efficient Equipment (Classes 43.1 and 43.2)

There are, after February 23, 2005, two fast write-off classes in which energy efficient equipment may fall: Class 43.1 (30%) for assets acquired before February 23, 2005, and Class 43.2 (50%) for assets acquired after February 22, 2005, and before 2020.[176] The eligibility criteria for these two classes are generally the same, except that cogeneration systems that use fossil fuels must meet a higher efficiency standard for Class 43.2 than for Class 43.1. Systems that only meet the lower efficiency standard are eligible for Class 43.1.

Class 43.1 (30% DPA) includes properties that would otherwise be included in Class 1, 2, or 8 acquired after February 21, 1994, or in Class 17 acquired after February 27, 2000. These are electrical generating equipment, equipment that generates both electrical energy and heat energy, and heat recovery equipment, as well as ancillary equipment or additions to such equipment where the equipment is part of an operating system used by the taxpayer or the lessee of the taxpayer for:

(a) generating electrical energy or a combination of electrical and heat energy using only fossil fuel, wood waste, municipal waste, landfill gas, digester gas, or any combination of these fuels; or

(b) subject to other conditions, generating electrical energy using only a combination of natural gas and waste heat from one or more natural gas compression or pumping systems located on a natural gas pipeline.

Energy conservation assets in Class 43.1 also include active solar energy equipment; heat recovery equipment; mini-hydro facilities; fixed-location wind-driven turbines; fixed-location photovoltaic equipment used to generate electricity from solar energy; above-ground geothermal energy equipment used to generate electricity; above-ground equipment used to collect landfill or digester gas; and equipment used to generate heat from the consumption of wood waste, municipal waste, landfill gas, or digester gas if the heat energy produced is used directly in an industrial process.

The Industrial Innovation Group (IIG) - a Group within CanmetENERGY at Natural Resources Canada - is the Technical Authority for Class 43.1 and Class 43.2.

Class 43.2 (50% CCA rate) for property acquired after February 22, 2005, and before 2020 operates by reference to Class 43.1, except that cogeneration systems that use fossil fuels must meet a higher efficiency standard for Class 43.2 than for Class 43.1. For cogeneration equipment to be eligible for inclusion in Class 43.2, it must be part of a high-efficiency cogeneration system that has an annual heat rate from fossil fuel that does not exceed 4,750 BTUs per kilowatt-hour of electricity produced. For

---

See page ii for explanation of footnotes.
[176] CCH ¶5044c; Class 43.1, Class 43.2.

cogeneration equipment to be eligible for inclusion in Class 43.1, it is only required to have a heat rate attributable to fossil fuel of between 4,750 BTU and 6,000 BTU.

Recent budgets have expanded Class 43.1 and Class 43.2 to include space-heating technologies such as active solar and ground-source heat pumps, which can provide low-grade energy particularly suitable for district energy systems (including certain types of heat recovery equipment and distribution equipment of a district energy system acquired after March 4, 2010 and not previously used or acquired for use).

For eligible assets acquired after March 21, 2011, that have not been used or acquired for use before March 22, 2011, the 2011 Budget would include in Class 43.2 equipment that is used by the taxpayer, or by a lessee of the taxpayer, to generate electrical energy in a process in which all or substantially all of the energy input is from waste heat. Eligible equipment would include electrical generating equipment; control, feedwater and condensate systems; and other ancillary equipment, other than: buildings or other structures; heat rejection equipment (such as condensers and cooling water systems); transmission equipment; distribution equipment; and systems that use chlorofluorocarbons (CFCs) or hydrochlorofluorocarbons (HCFCs). Equipment that generates electricity as a second stage in a combined cycle process, using waste heat from a gas turbine, must continue to satisfy the existing energy efficiency thresholds in order to qualify for Class 43.2.

For eligible assets acquired after March 28, 2012, that have not been used or acquired for use before March 29, 2012, the 2012 Budget would include in Class 43.2:

- Waste-fuelled thermal energy equipment used for space and water heating applications.

- Equipment that is part of a district energy system that distributes thermal energy primarily generated by waste-fuelled thermal energy equipment, so as to provide an alternative to equipment that uses only fossil fuels.

- Equipment that uses residue of plants (i.e., straw, corn cobs, leaves) to generate electricity and heat.

Waste-fuel equipment that is not in compliance with environmental laws at the time it first becomes available for use would not be eligible for inclusion in Class 43.2. Non-compliant property must be included in the otherwise applicable class.[177]

If the majority of tangible property in a project is eligible for Class 43.1 or Class 43.2, certain project start-up expenses (e.g., engineering and design

[177] Reg. 1104(17).

¶4215

work and feasibility studies) qualify as Canadian Renewable and Conservation Expenses (CRCE). These expenses can be fully deducted in the year incurred, carried forward indefinitely for use in future years, or transferred to investors using flow-through shares.[178]

[¶4220] Temporary Accelerated CCA for Computer Hardware and Systems Software (Class 52)

For certain computers and systems software acquired on or after January 28, 2009, and before February 2011, the CCA rate is increased to 100% (Class 52) from 55% (Class 50). This 100% CCA rate will not be subject to the half-year rule so that a taxpayer will be allowed to fully deduct the cost of an eligible computer in the first year that the CCA claim is available. Eligible property is general-purpose electronic data processing equipment and systems software for that equipment, including ancillary data processing equipment, but not including property that is principally or is used principally as:

(a) electronic process control or monitor equipment,

(b) electronic communications control equipment,

(c) systems software for equipment referred to in (a) or (b), or

(d) data handling equipment (other than data handling equipment that is ancillary to general-purpose electronic data processing equipment).[179]

Such property will qualify for the 100% CCA rate if it is situated in Canada, it has not been used, or acquired for use, for any purpose whatever before it is acquired by the taxpayer, and it is acquired by the taxpayer

(i) for use in a business carried on by the taxpayer in Canada or for the purpose of earning income from property situated in Canada, or

(ii) for lease by the taxpayer to a lessee for use by the lessee in a business carried on by the lessee in Canada or for the purpose of earning income from property situated in Canada.

The computer tax shelter property rules, which prevent CCA deductions from being used by investors to shelter other sources of income, apply to computer equipment that is eligible for the 55% CCA rate of Class 50 or the 100% CCA rate of temporary Class 52.[180]

See page ii for explanation of footnotes.

[178] Reg. 1219.
[179] Class 52.
[180] CCH ¶4937m; Reg. 1100(20.2).

[¶4270] Motion Picture Films, Videotapes, Computer Software, and Electronic Equipment

[¶4275] Certified Productions

A "certified production" is a film or videotape production certified by the Minister of Communications[181] to meet Canadian content requirements in respect of the work done to create it.[182] Under the tax shelter rules, where a certificate was so issued by the Minister of Communications, the investor's interest in a film or tape would nevertheless not be a certified production if:

(a) the interest was acquired after the day that is the earlier of:

  (i) the day of the first commercial use of the film or tape, and

  (ii) 12 months after the day the principal photography or taping is completed,

(b) the interest was acquired from a non-resident,

(c) the certificate has been revoked by the Minister of Communications because an incorrect statement was made in the furnishing of information for certification, or

(d) the company has not paid at least 5% of the capital cost in cash to the person from whom it acquired the film or tape.

Certified production acquired after 1987 and before March 1996 become Class 10(w) property and are depreciable at 30% declining balance,[183] but are not subject to the half-year rule when acquired.[184] All Class 10(w) property is placed in a separate class.[185] Certified productions also qualify for an additional allowance equal to the lesser of the undepreciated capital cost of the film and income net of expense and basic capital cost allowance for the year from all certified productions.[186] This additional allowance is not prorated for a short taxation year since it is already limited by income earned in the year.

Various certified productions acquired before 1988 qualified for a capital cost allowance of 100% (Class 12) subject after 1982 to the half-year rule in the year of acquisition.[187]

Any film or tape that is not a certified production and is not a commercial message (see ¶4280) or acquired for short-term rental (see ¶4281) is included in Class 10(s) (30%) and is subject to the half-year rule when acquired.[188]

See page ii for explanation of footnotes.

[181] CCH ¶4951b; Reg. 1104(2) "certified production".
[182] CCH ¶4951j; Reg. 1104(10).
[183] CCH ¶4981; Class 10.
[184] CCH ¶4917; Reg. 1100(2).
[185] CCH ¶4938e; Reg. 1101(5k).
[186] CCH ¶4938a; Reg. 1100(1)(l).
[187] CCH ¶4992; Class 12.
[188] CCH ¶4981; Class 10.

In the 1995 federal Budget, the Minister of Finance announced that the entire CCA system for certified productions would be replaced with a system of refundable credits to prescribed corporations carrying on a Canadian film or video production business in Canada. The phase-out of the old system was accomplished with the denial of CCA for certified Canadian productions acquired after March 1996. The Canadian film tax credit (see ¶8685) is available only to these incorporated producers and is not available for flow-out to investors. Each film is now of a separate class. On December 12, 1995, it was announced that the depreciation on these films would be 30%, but an additional allowance is available on remaining capital cost to the extent of income for the year from the production.[189]

[¶4280] Television Commercial Message

A "television commercial message" is defined as being a billboard or commercial message as defined[190] in the Television Broadcasting Regulations, 1987. These Regulations define a "billboard" to mean an announcement at the commencement or end of any program naming the sponsor, if any. The Television Broadcasting Regulations define a "commercial message" to mean any commercial announcement. Films or videotapes that qualify under these definitions are included in Class 12, 100% write-off, but are subject to the half-year rule in the year of acquisition.[191]

Any motion picture film or videotape that is neither eligible for Class 12 nor "a certified production" qualifying for the special treatment described at ¶4275, is depreciable at 30% under Class 10, subject to the half year-rule.[192]

[¶4281] Videotapes and Laser Disks for Rental

A videotape acquired, or a laser disk acquired after December 12, 1995, for the purposes of short-term rental is a Class 12(r) item. For 1995 and later years, these items are exempt from the half-year rule, with the result that they can be written off 100% in the year of acquisition. Short-term rentals are rentals that are not expected to be made to any one person for more than seven days in any 30-day period.[193]

[¶4282] Computers, Systems Software, and Ancillary Data Processing Equipment

Computers, together with systems software and ancillary data processing equipment, can fall within any of Classes 8, 10, 29, 39, 40, 43, 45, 50, and 52. Computer software that is not systems software is included in Class 12, 100% write-off, subject to the half-year rule in the year of acquisition. "Systems software" means a combination of programs, documentation, and

---

See page ii for explanation of footnotes.

[189] Reg. 1100(1)(m).

[190] CCH ¶4951b; Reg. 1104(2) "television commercial message".

[191] CCH ¶4992; Class 12.

[192] CCH ¶4981; Class 10.

[193] CCH ¶4992; Class 12.

data that allows the hardware to function in the use of other computer programs. That is, systems software generally refers to the operating system that enables the computer to run and directs and co-ordinates its different operations, including input and output between keyboard, CRT screen, printer, disk drives, and the other peripherals.[194] Systems software is classified as follows:

(1) Class 8 (20%), if it is acquired before May 26, 1976, or it is acquired after that date and before March 23, 2004, but either is, or is used principally as, electronic process control equipment, electronic communications control equipment, or data handling equipment not ancillary to general-purpose computer equipment;

(2) Class 10(f) (30%), if acquired before March 23, 2004, unless the asset is, or is used principally as, electronic process control equipment, etc. described in (1) as still being in Class 8;

(3) a separate class of Class 10, if acquired after April 26, 1993, and before March 23, 2004, as part of a package costing more than $1,000 on which an election described at ¶4283 has been made;

(4) Class 29, if qualified as manufacturing and processing equipment (see ¶4210) and acquired after May 8, 1972, and before 1988 (or 1990 under grandfathering rules);

(5) Class 39 (see ¶4210), if it is manufacturing or processing equipment acquired after 1987, and before February 26, 1992, which is process control or communications control equipment otherwise classified in Class 8, as described above;

(6) Class 40 (see ¶4210), if it is manufacturing or processing equipment acquired after 1987, and before 1990, which is general systems software otherwise classified in Class 10;

(7) Class 43 (30%), if it is manufacturing or processing equipment acquired after February 25, 1992, which is process control or communications control equipment otherwise classified in Class 8, as described above;

(8) Class 45 (45%), if acquired after March 22, 2004, and before March 19, 2007 (other than property acquired before 2005 in respect of which a taxpayer elects to have the property included in a separate Class 10);

(9) Class 50 (55%), if acquired after March 18, 2007, and not included in temporary Class 52 (see below); and

(10) Class 52 (100%) with no half-year rule, if acquired after January 27, 2009, and before February 2011. See ¶4220.

See page ii for explanation of footnotes.
[194] CCH ¶4951b; Reg. 1104(2) "systems software".

¶4282

Ancillary data processing equipment is not a defined term, but presumably refers to peripheral equipment such as printers, monitors, separate drive units, modems, and perhaps even cables.

Classes 10(*f*), 45, and 52 exclude computer equipment that is principally, or is used principally, as:

- electronic process control or monitor equipment;

- electronic communications control equipment;

- systems software for electronic control or monitor equipment, or electronic communications control equipment; or

- data handling equipment (other than such equipment that is ancillary to general-purpose electronic data processing equipment).[195]

In addition, the specified leasing property rule exemption for computers will be extended to computer equipment included in Class 45 or 50, other than individual items with a capital cost in excess of $1 million.[196]

The government has, since 1994, been pursuing a broad attack on tax shelters. One of the shelters which all its machinery seems unable to stem is investment in a shelter that acquires applications software for future development and is able to depreciate it over two years. In the government's view, a tax shelter is an investment where the tax benefits over the first four years equal or exceed the amount paid. Where tax shelter software is to produce leasing revenue, its depreciation may be limited to income from the project under the rules at ¶4300. On August 6, 1997, the CRA (then Revenue Canada) announced that it would extend those rules so that depreciation of any software (application or system) which meets its test of being a tax shelter investment will be limited to income from the software, even if the income will arise from sales rather than leases. That is, capital cost allowance on "computer software tax shelter property" cannot be used except to reduce the business income from that property to zero.[197] Where a taxpayer owns tax shelter software and other property of the same class, the tax shelter software must be kept in a separate class of the class, thus separating its recapture/terminal loss characteristics from other property in the class.[198]

[¶4283] Electronic Office Equipment and Data Network Infrastructure Equipment

A taxpayer may elect to set up a separate class for one or more properties, each of which has a capital cost of at least $1,000, that is

- computer software, a photocopier, or electronic communication equipment (such as facsimile transmission devices or telephone

---

See page ii for explanation of footnotes.

[195] CCH ¶4981; Class 10, Class 45, Class 52.   [197] CCH ¶4937m; Reg. 1100(20.1), Reg. 1100(20.2).
[196] CCH ¶4937ad; Reg. 1100(1.13).   [198] CCH ¶4940zia; Reg. 1101(5r).

equipment) normally in Class 8 (which will go into a separate Class 8); or

- if acquired before 2005, computer equipment and systems software therefore, including ancillary data equipment (see ¶4282), normally in Class 10(*f*) (and which will go into a separate Class 10). Such equipment, if acquired after March 22, 2004, and before March 19, 2007, will normally go into Class 45 (45% CCA rate). If acquired after March 18, 2007, and before January 28, 2009, it will go into Class 50 (55% CCA rate). If acquired after January 27, 2009, and before February 2011, it will go into Class 52 (100% CCA rate) and, as such, will not be eligible for the separate class election.[199]

The CCA rate for computer equipment and systems software acquired after March 22, 2004, and before March 19, 2007, has increased from 30% (Class 10) to 45%, and will be included in Class 45. The rate for those acquired after March 18, 2007, and before January 28, 2009, has increased from 45% to 55%, and will be included in Class 50. The rate for those acquired by a taxpayer after January 27, 2009, and before February 2011 has increased from 55% to 100%, and will be included in Class 52, with no half-year rule. The separate class election is not available for equipment that qualifies for the 45%, 55%, or 100% rate. However, a taxpayer may elect to have the special election rule apply for equipment acquired before 2005.

The election is made by a letter attached to the taxpayer's tax return in the year the property is acquired. The taxpayer may elect to put one or more such assets into a separate class. Therefore, if five photocopiers each costing over $1,000 are purchased in a year, they can each be put in a separate Class 8 or all five can be put in one separate Class 8 or any combination thereof (such as two in one separate class and three in another). If another photocopier costing over $1,000 is acquired the following year, it cannot be included in one of the separate classes with the photocopiers of the previous year. Of course, an election can be made to include it in its own separate class. If no election is made, the property is added to the general Class 8 or Class 10 pool that otherwise would apply.

The property that is placed in the separate class will be depreciated at the normal Class 8 or Class 10 rate; however, when the property is disposed of, any remaining undepreciated capital cost will be deductible as a terminal loss. Any undepreciated capital cost remaining in each separate class five years after the property became available for use is to be transferred into the regular Class 8 or Class 10 pool.[200]

Data network infrastructure equipment and systems software for the equipment acquired that would otherwise be in Class 8 by default (20% CCA rate) will, if acquired after March 22, 2004, fall into Class 46 and be eligible for a 30% CCA rate. Generally, "data network infrastructure equipment"

---

[199] CCH ¶4940zh; Reg. 1101(5p).   [200] CCH ¶4950h; Reg. 1103(2g).

means network infrastructure equipment that controls, transfers, modulates, or directs data, and that operates in support of telecommunications applications such as e-mail, instant messaging, audio- and video-over-Internet Protocol or Web browsing, Web searching and Web hosting, including data switches, multiplexers, routers, remote access servers, hubs, domain name servers, and modems.

[¶4285] Rental Properties

[¶4290] Rental Properties

The Regulations provide that, in certain circumstances, a taxpayer or partnership may not deduct capital cost allowance in respect of rental property to the full extent otherwise allowed by the rates set out in Schedule II.[201] The purpose of this restriction is to prevent certain taxpayers from using capital cost allowance to produce a loss from rental property which would reduce or "shelter" other income that would otherwise be subject to tax.

Except with respect to certain lease-leaseback agreements,[202] this restriction does not apply to:

(a) a life insurance corporation;

(b) a corporation whose principal business throughout the year was the leasing, rental, development, or sale, or any combination thereof, of real property owned by it; or

(c) a partnership, each member of which was a corporation described in (a) or (b).[203]

"Rental property" is defined as a building or a leasehold interest in real property if the leasehold interest is property of Class 1, 3, 6, or 13 owned by the taxpayer or partnership and which is used in the taxation year principally for the purpose of gaining or producing gross revenue that is rent. The definition excludes a property leased to a lessee who undertakes to use the property to carry on the business of selling or promoting the sale of the taxpayer's goods or services. This would include property leased in connection with a franchise agreement. In addition, for taxation years prior to 1994, rental property does not include a building which is a multiple-unit residential building (MURB) within Class 31 or 32 (see below).[204]

A taxpayer could not deduct losses created by claiming CCA on several condominiums. Although he claimed to have acquired them for the purpose

---

[201] CCH ¶4926; Reg. 1100(11).
[202] CCH ¶4928; Reg. 1100(13).

[203] CCH ¶4926, ¶4927; Reg. 1100(11), Reg. 1100(12); Interp. Bul. IT-195R4, IT-371.
[204] CCH ¶4930, ¶4930a, ¶4930b; Reg. 1100(14), Reg. 1100(14.1), Reg. 1100(14.2).

of reselling them to generate capital gains, they were in fact being used to produce rental income and were therefore "rental properties".[205] On the other hand, when a subsidiary's employees housed in the taxpayer's building had been previously employed by the taxpayer and market rents were not being charged, the taxpayer was held to rent the subsidiary space in its building as space for its own use as opposed to rental use.[206]

The total capital cost allowance deduction in respect of rental properties may not exceed the net rental income of the taxpayer from rental properties (before deducting capital cost allowance).[207] This net rental income is determined by adding together the rental income from properties owned directly (before capital cost allowance) and any share of rental income of a partnership from rental properties and then deducting rental losses from properties owned directly and any share of rental losses of a partnership from rental properties. In the case of a taxpayer who is not involved in a partnership that owns rental property, the incomes and losses (before capital cost allowance) from rental properties must be netted to determine the aggregate capital cost allowance that may be claimed in respect of classes of property that include rental properties. Assuming the taxpayer has net rental income from rental properties, he or she may then deduct capital cost allowance to the extent of such net income even if the deducting of this capital cost allowance will produce a loss with respect to a particular rental property.

The income derived from room rentals at the taxpayer's various hotels and motels (which comprised 80% of the income from each property) was truly rental income rather than income from services since any services provided in return for such rent were essentially of the type included in the price of a room, and all extra services were charged for separately. As a result, the CCA-generated losses could be absorbed by the taxpayer's rental income from his properties for the taxation years in issue.[208]

Capital cost allowance in respect of partnership property is deducted by the partnership in determining the income or loss that is allocated to the partners. Unless all the members of the partnership are life insurance corporations, or corporations whose principal business is the leasing, development, or sale of real property owned by it and who are not part of a lease-leaseback arrangement,[209] the partnership is subject to the general limitations described above. Thus the partnership may deduct capital cost allowance in respect of rental properties only to the extent that its income from rental properties exceeds its losses from rental properties. Capital cost allowance may not be deducted to produce an overall loss to the partnership from rental properties. Where a loss arises before deducting capital cost

---

See page ii for explanation of footnotes.

[205] Sivasubramaniam, 2008 DTC 3886.

[206] Gulf Canada Resources Ltd., 93 DTC 5345.

[207] CCH ¶4926; Reg. 1100(11).

[208] Malenfant, 92 DTC 2081.

[209] CCH ¶4927, ¶4928; Reg. 1100(12), Reg. 1100(13).

¶4290

allowance, the partner's share is then taken into account in determining the net income of the taxpayer from rental properties for the purpose of determining the capital cost allowance that may be claimed by the taxpayer in respect of rental property owned directly by the taxpayer.

If each member of a partnership is a life insurance corporation or a principal business corporation as described above, the partnership will not be subject to the rental property limitations in claiming capital cost allowance, unless the partnership is part of a lease-leaseback arrangement.

While the Regulations restrict the capital cost allowance that may be claimed in respect of rental property, they also establish separate classes of property where properties would otherwise be in the same class by virtue of the descriptions set out in Schedule II.[210] These provisions establish separate classes for each rental property acquired after 1971 at a cost of $50,000 or more and certain leasehold interests in real property. Rental properties acquired prior to 1972 or acquired after 1972 at a cost of less than $50,000 will form a single class for capital cost allowance purposes.

Example:

J owns two rental properties. A summary of J's 2007 rental operation is as follows:

	Building A	Building B
Rent	$24,000	$15,000
Allowable expenses other than CCA	21,000	16,000
Net rental income (loss) before claiming CCA	$ 3,000	$(1,000)

J can claim $2,000 of capital cost allowance for the year. The income of Building A is combined with the loss of Building B to determine the net income for reduction by capital cost allowance.

2007	Building A	Building B
Opening UCC balance	$100,000	$75,000
Less: CCA claim (maximum allowed)		2,000
Capital cost allowance may be claimed on either of the buildings in separate classes even if it increases the rental loss from that particular building. If J plans to sell Building A in 2008, the capital cost allowance claimed on it could be recaptured. J therefore claimed the 2007 capital cost allowance on Building B.	$100,000	$73,000

See page ii for explanation of footnotes.

[210] CCH ¶4940c–4940e, ¶4940z; Reg. 1101(1ac),
Reg. 1101(1ad), Reg. 1101(1ae), Reg. 1101(5h);
Interp. Bul. IT-274R.

Where rental property is acquired by a taxpayer under certain circumstances, it will not be included in a separate class if it was rental property of the previous owner and was not required to be included in a separate class by that owner immediately before the sale or transfer.[211] The circumstances prescribed by the Regulations are:

(1) the acquisition of rental property through a type of corporate reorganization such as a "butterfly" transaction designed to de-merge the corporation;[212] or

(2) the acquisition of rental property from a person with whom the taxpayer is not dealing at arm's length.

For this purpose, persons who do not deal at arm's length do not include those who are deemed not to deal at arm's length by virtue only of certain rights or option agreements.[213]

Except for corporations exempt from the capital cost allowance restriction, rental property (other than property costing $50,000 or more which is in its own separate class) is prescribed to be in a separate class from non-rental properties that would otherwise be included in the same class.[214]

A building qualifies as a MURB if a certificate has been issued by Canada Mortgage and Housing Corporation (CMHC), certifying that:

(a) the installation of footings or other base support of the building was commenced either after November 18, 1974, and before January 1, 1980, or after October 28, 1980, and before January 1, 1982;

(b) plans and specifications show that not less than 80% of the floor space of the building will be used to provide self-contained domestic establishments and related parking, recreation, service, and storage; and that actual experience with the building shows that at least 80% of the floor space is used for the purposes described in (2) above;

(c) in the case of a CMHC certificate issued after October 28, 1980, the certificate has been issued on or before the later of:

(i) December 31, 1981, and

(ii) the day that is 18 months after the day on which the installation of footings or other base support of the building was commenced; and

(d) the construction of the building has proceeded, after 1982, without undue delay, taking into consideration acts of God, labour disputes,

---

See page ii for explanation of footnotes.

[211] CCH ¶4940c, ¶4940d; Reg. 1101(1ac), Reg. 1101(1ad).
[212] CCH ¶7983, ¶7983a; Sec. 55(2), 55(3).
[213] CCH ¶28,354; Sec. 251(5).
[214] CCH ¶4940e; Reg. 1101(1ae).

¶4290

fire, unusual delay by common carriers or suppliers of materials or equipment, and accidents.

A MURB will fall within Class 31 (5%) or Class 32 (10%), depending upon when the installation of footings or other base supports was commenced and the class within which the building would otherwise fall.

A taxpayer who is an individual or a corporation that does not qualify for an exemption from the rental loss restrictions[215] may claim capital cost allowance on MURBs in excess of the taxpayer's net rental income from all rental properties and thus may use this capital cost allowance to produce a loss that will shelter income from other sources. It has been held that a single unit in a condominium can qualify as a MURB.[216]

Each MURB costing $50,000 or more forms a separate class of property.[217] Thus, on a sale of such building, there may be a recapture of capital cost allowance notwithstanding that the taxpayer owns other MURBs. MURBs costing less than $50,000 will form a single class of Class 31 or Class 32 properties.

[¶4295] Leasing Properties

[¶4300] Leasing Properties

The aggregate capital cost allowance in respect of a prescribed class of "leasing property" is limited to the net income for the year from renting, leasing, or earning royalties from leasing properties.[218] This rule is designed to prevent taxpayers from claiming capital cost allowance in order to increase or create a loss on leasing properties, which could be used to shelter other unrelated income.

Leasing property of a taxpayer or partnership is defined[219] as depreciable property of a taxpayer or a partnership acquired after May 25, 1976[220] which is used or is deemed to be used[221] principally for rental purposes *other than* a rental property or a certified feature film referred to in Class 12(n). Regulations set out that rent is considered to be gross revenue derived from the right of a person or partnership, other than the owner of the property, to use or occupy the property and also includes revenue from ancillary services provided to the person or partnership.[222] The definition also excludes properties leased in the ordinary course of selling goods or rendering services under an agreement by which the lessee undertakes to use the property

---

See page ii for explanation of footnotes.

[215] CCH ¶4927; Reg. 1100(12).

[216] Vaillancourt, 91 DTC 5408.

[217] CCH ¶5036; Reg. 1101(5b).

[218] CCH ¶4933; Reg. 1100(15); Interp. Bul. IT-443.

[219] CCH ¶4933b; Reg. 1100(17).

[220] CCH ¶4933c; Reg. 1100(18).

[221] CCH ¶4933ba; Reg. 1100(17.1).

[222] CCH ¶4933bb, ¶4933bc; Reg. 1100(17.2), Reg. 1100(17.3).

to carry on the business of selling or promoting the sale of the taxpayer's (or partnership's) goods or services.

Property acquired from a non-arm's length person or in connection with a divisive corporate reorganization (a "butterfly transaction") will also be exempt in certain circumstances. This would occur if the transferor had acquired the property before May 26, 1976, or if the property was a replacement for property which was exempt from the leasing property rules. Where a property that was not a leasing property is replaced by another property under the replacement property rules (discussed in ¶4460), then the replacement property also will not be a leasing property. A series of replacements continues to be exempt as long as the replacement property rules apply to each replacement.[223]

The depreciable property may be movable or immovable but must be used in the year principally for the purpose of gaining or producing gross revenue that is rent, royalty, or leasing revenue. If the depreciable property is not used for any purpose in the year in which it is acquired and its first use satisfies this principal purpose test, the property is deemed to have satisfied the principal purpose test in the taxation year in which it was acquired.

Corporations (including corporate partnerships) whose principal business is the leasing or rental property other than real property owned by it or the leasing or rental of such property, combined with the sale of property of the same general type and description, are exempt from the leasing property restrictions where their gross revenue in the year from such sources amounts to at least 90% of their gross revenue from all sources.[224]

[¶4305] Specified Leasing Property

The specified leasing property rules[225] discourage the use of leases to transfer capital cost allowance deductions from the user of an asset to the person financing its acquisition.

To neutralize the tax consequences of substituting a lease for a loan, these rules recharacterize the lease to be a loan by the lessor, with the lease payments received being treated as blended payments of interest and principal. The lessor's claim for capital cost allowance on the leased property is then restricted to the lesser of the amount of capital cost allowance that

---

See page ii for explanation of footnotes.

[223] CCH ¶4933c–4933e; Reg. 1100(18), Reg. 1100(19), Reg. 1100(20).

[224] CCH ¶4933a; Reg. 1100(16).

[225] CCH ¶4937a–4937al; Reg. 1100(1.1)–(1.3).

would otherwise be deductible and the amount of lease payments received, less a calculation of notional interest amount for the year. In other words, the specified leasing property rules put lessors in the same position as lenders who receive blended payments of principal (not taxable) and interest (taxable).

The restrictions imposed by these rules apply to all lessors, including principal business corporations[226] that make arm's length leases of specified leasing property for periods of greater than one year. These rules do not affect the lessee's position. See ¶4307.

In general terms, "specified leasing property" is defined as depreciable property, other than exempt property, that is:

(1) used principally to earn rental or leasing revenue;

(2) the subject of an arm's length lease with a specified term of more than one year; and

(3) subject to a lease of property with, at the time the lease was made, an aggregate fair market value in excess of $25,000.

However, the definition specifically excludes include intangible property such as systems software and other software, as well as certified feature films or certified productions.[227]

"Exempt property", which is protected from the specified leasing property rules, is defined as:

(a) general-purpose office furniture and equipment in Class 8 (including cellular phones and pagers) or general-purpose electronic and ancillary data processing equipment in Class 10(f), other than any individual asset having a capital cost in excess of $1 million;

(b) general-purpose electronic data processing equipment and ancillary data processing equipment, included in Classes 45 and 50 (if acquired after March 18, 2007, and not included in temporary Class 52), or 52 (if acquired after January 27, 2009, and before February 2011), other than any individual item of that type of equipment having a capital cost in excess of $1 million;

(c) furniture, appliances, television receivers, radio receivers, telephones, furnaces, hot-water heaters, and other similar properties designed for residential use;

(d) automobiles of all kinds, including ambulances, funeral vehicles, taxis, rental vehicles, vans, pick-up trucks, and trucks or tractors for

---

See page ii for explanation of footnotes.

[226] CCH ¶4933a; Reg. 1100(16).   [227] CCH ¶4937ab; Reg. 1100(1.11).

highway use as well as trailers designed to be hauled by such trucks or tractors;

(e) buildings and component parts (i.e., electrical wiring, plumbing, etc.), other than a building, leased primarily to a person who is exempt from tax and who owned the building, or part thereof, at any time before the commencement of the lease (other than for a period of less than one year or at no time when the building was complete);

(f) vessel mooring space; and

(g) a railway car or a rail suspension device designed to carry trailers that are designed for both highways and railway tracks provided, for acquisitions after February 27, 2000, an election has been made under the rules at ¶4165.[228]

[In response to the 2010 Budget, draft regulations released on August 27, 2010 (but not enacted yet) propose to exclude certain property leased in specific circumstances that is otherwise protected as "exempt property". For leases entered into after 4:00 p.m. EST March 4, 2010, property with a total fair market value in excess of $1 million will be excluded from the above definition of "exempt property" if it is leased to:

(a) a tax-exempt individual, organization, or trust (see Chapter XI);

(b) a person who uses the property in the course of carrying on business, the income of which is exempt from Part I tax;

(c) a Canadian government; or

(d) a non-resident, except where the property is used primarily in the course of carrying on business in Canada that is not a treaty-protected business.

An anti-avoidance rule will apply to prevent the conclusion of two or more leases in order to fall below the above $1 million threshold.]

Note that special purpose office equipment, such as medical and dental equipment, do not qualify as exempt property and, therefore, the specified leasing property restrictions apply to these assets. In addition, a building leased after February 2, 1990, primarily to a tax-exempt person who formerly owned the building, other than for an ownership period of less than one year or only during construction, also does not qualify as exempt property. This latter restriction is intended to curtail the use of sale leaseback transactions of assets that have appreciated in value, involving tax exempt entities.

See page ii for explanation of footnotes.
[228] CCH ¶4937ad; Reg. 1100(1.13).

¶4305

In the case of a building that is not exempt property, the lease term, in order to qualify as specified leasing property, is three years rather than one year.[229]

Each specified leasing property is to be included in a separate class.[230] The capital cost allowance that may be claimed for a specified leasing property is limited to the lesser of:

(i) a cumulative amount of notional principal repayments less the actual amount of the capital cost allowance claimed in previous years; and

(ii) the cumulative amount of maximum capital cost allowance that could have been claimed in the year and prior years less the actual amount claimed in prior years.[231]

If the taxpayer is a principal business corporation, the half-year rule does not apply to the calculation of capital cost allowance under method (ii).[232] The calculation in (i) treats the lease of the specified leasing property as a fully financed sale; that is, as if the lessee had borrowed the full fair market value of the specified leasing property that is subject to the lease, and the actual rental payments were blended amortization payments, that is, payments consisting of both interest and return of principal (like mortgage payments). Interest is computed on a semi-annual compounding basis at a prescribed interest rate of one percentage point higher than the long-term Government of Canada bond rate for the last Wednesday of the month before the immediately preceding month. The prescribed rate for each month is published by the CRA.[233]

A principal business leasing corporation is permitted to elect to have the specified leasing property rules apply to all the property leased by it, including exempt property and property that is subject to a lease where the aggregate fair market value of all the property subject to the lease does not exceed $25,000.[234] A principal business corporation may also elect to group one or more exempt properties of a certain class together as a separate class.[235] Such an election may be advantageous where, for example, there is one exempt property of a particular class as well as other properties of the same class, none of which is an exempt property or a specified leasing property and it is likely that a terminal loss will result when that exempt property is disposed of. The result will not be beneficial if recapture is expected on the disposition of the exempt property since in the absence of the election, the undepreciated capital cost balance of the other assets will protect against recapture.

See page ii for explanation of footnotes.

[229] CCH ¶4937al; Reg. 1100(1.3).

[230] CCH ¶4937b; Reg. 1101(5n).

[231] CCH ¶4937a; Reg. 1100(1.1).

[232] CCH ¶4917; Reg. 1100(2).

[233] CCH ¶4730b; Reg. 4302.

[234] CCH ¶4937ae; Reg. 1100(1.14).

[235] CCH ¶4937c; Reg. 1101(5o).

A series of rules apply when property subject to a lease is sold or altered.[236] If the leased property is replaced with similar property with the same lease payments, the replacement property assumes most of the attributes of the original property except for the amount by which total capital cost allowance that could have been claimed in previous years exceeds the amount that was actually claimed.[237] If no lease payments are received because of a breakdown of the property during a period before the termination of the lease, the lessor will be deemed to have received the lease payments and so will be able to calculate the notional principal repayments for purposes of determining capital cost allowance.[238] If the leased property is altered and, as a result, the rent is increased, the taxpayer is deemed to have leased "additional property" with the same attributes as the original property.[239] Where a lease is renegotiated in a *bona fide* manner and as a result the lease payment is changed, the original lease will be deemed to have ended and a new lease will be deemed to have been entered into at that time.[240]

There are provisions to prevent a taxpayer from avoiding the specified leasing property rules by structuring what would otherwise be a long-term lease into a series of short-term leases. Similarly, anti-avoidance rules prevent a taxpayer from structuring separate leases each in respect of property with a fair market value of less than $25,000 in order to be excluded from the specified leasing property rules.[241]

Example:

An asset is purchased by R Ltd. on February 1 of Year 1 for $30,000. The capital cost allowance rate applicable to this asset is 30% on a declining balance basis. The asset is used in R Ltd's own business until May 1 of Year 1, at which time the property is leased to an arm's length person for a term of five years, with annual lease payments of $3,942. The prescribed interest rate at the commencement of the lease is 10%.

R Ltd. has a taxation year which corresponds with the calendar year. In addition, R Ltd. is a principal business leasing corporation and the property subject to the lease is a specified leasing property at the end of the year.

The following computes the amount of capital cost allowance deductible by R Ltd. for Year 1 and Year 2 taxation years:

Year	Lease Payment	Principal	Interest	CCA*	UCC	Remaining Principal
					$30,000	$30,000
Year 1 ...	$3,942	$ 942	$3,000	$2,067	27,933	29,058
Year 2 ...	3,942	1,036	2,906	1,036	26,897	28,022

* Lesser of:

See page ii for explanation of footnotes.

[236] CCH ¶4937af–4937aj; Reg. 1100(1.15)–(1.19).   [239] CCH ¶4937aj; Reg. 1100(1.19).

[237] CCH ¶4937ah; Reg. 1100(1.17).   [240] CCH ¶4937ak; Reg. 1100(1.2).

[238] CCH ¶4937ai; Reg. 1100(1.18).   [241] CCH ¶4937al; Reg. 1100(1.13).

¶4305

		Year 1	Year 2
(a)(i)	Return of principal for the period in the year when the asset was specified leasing property	$ 942	$1,978
	plus:		
(ii)	CCA for three months (February 1 to April 30) of the year: $30,000 × 30% × 50% × 3/12	1,125	1,125
	less:		
(iii)	CCA previously deducted after the property became a specified leasing property	--	2,067
		$2,067	$ 1,036
and:			
(b)(i)	Total CCA deductible under normal rules but without the half-year rule, since it is a principal business corporation	$9,000	$15,300
	less:		
(ii)	CCA previously deducted	--	2,067
		$9,000	$13,233
	Maximum CCA entitlement (assume deducted in full)		
		$2,067	$ 1,036

The specified leasing property rules will cease to apply to the lessor when the property ceases to be specified leasing property to the lessor at the end of any taxation year. The normal rules concerning recapture and terminal losses will apply when the lessor disposes of the property.

[¶4307] Election to Treat Lease as Loan: Lessee's Position

Unlike the position of the lessor under the specified leasing property rules whereby the lessor is required to treat certain leases as loans, a lessee may elect to have a lease treated as a purchase and a loan.[242] This election must be made by both the lessor and the lessee in the taxation year that the lease is first entered into; however, this election does not affect the lessor's position. For leases entered into after 3:30 p.m. on August 19, 1998, the election cannot be made by the lessee where the lessor is a tax-exempt entity.

The election is available for tangible depreciable property, *other than* prescribed property, that is the subject of an arm's length lease for a term of more than one year. The property must be leased from a person who is resident in Canada or who carries on a business through a permanent establishment in Canada. The property subject to the lease must have a fair market value greater than $25,000. "Prescribed property" includes intangible

---

See page ii for explanation of footnotes.
[242] CCH ¶4727; Sec. 16.1.

property and also property that is exempt property for purposes of the specified leasing property rules as described in ¶4305.[243]

If the election is made, the lessee is deemed to have acquired the property at its fair market value and to have borrowed an equivalent amount from the lessor for the purpose of acquiring the property. The property will be included in the regular class that the asset would be in if it had been purchased. A separate class for each property is not required. The lessee will be able to depreciate the property under normal rules, and subject to the half-year rule. Its leasing payments will be considered to be blended payments of interest and principal, with the interest factor deemed to accrue on principal outstanding, compounded semi-annually not in advance, at a prescribed interest rate. The interest rate will be determined at the time the lease is made or, if an agreement to the lease is made before the commencement of the lease, at the time of the agreement. If the lease is a floating rate lease, interest is the rate prescribed at the beginning of the period for which the calculation is made. Interest will not be the usual prescribed rate, but will be prescribed quarterly.[244]

If the lease expires, is cancelled, or is assigned, or the property is sublet (except in the case of an amalgamation or a wind-up), the lessee is deemed to have disposed of the property for a specified amount. The specified proceeds of disposition are calculated as the amount, if any, by which the aggregate of:

(a) the deemed principal amount of the original deemed loan (i.e., the fair market value of the property at the beginning of the lease), plus

(b) any consideration received or receivable by the lessee for cancelling, Assigning, or subletting,

exceeds the aggregate of:

(c) all deemed principal repayments, and

(d) all amounts paid or payable by the lessee for the cancellation, Assignment, or subletting of the property.

Example:

An asset with a fair market value of $50,000 is leased by X from an arm's length party. The prescribed interest rate at the commencement of the lease is 13%. The annual lease cost to X is $6,800 and the asset is subject to a 30% CCA rate, on a declining basis. The following example illustrates the effect of a joint election with the lessor to treat the lease as a loan.

See page ii for explanation of footnotes.

[243] CCH ¶4730c, ¶4937ad; Reg. 8200, Reg. 1100(1.13).   [244] CCH ¶4730b; Reg. 4302.

¶4307

Year	Lease Payment	Principal Repaid	Interest	Principal Outstanding	UCC	CCA
0	--	--	--	$50,000	$50,000	--
1	$6,800	$300	$ 6,500	49,700	42,500	$ 7,500
2	6,800	339	6,461	49,361	29,750	12,750
3	6,800	383	6,417	48,978	20,825	8,925
4	6,800	433	6,367	48,545	14,578	6,248
5	6,800	489	6,311	48,056	10,204	4,373
6	6,800	553	6,247	47,503	7,143	3,061
7	6,800	625	6,175	46,878	5,000	2,143
8	6,800	706	6,094	46,172	3,500	1,500
9	6,800	798	6,002	45,374	2,450	1,050
10 ...	6,800	901	5,899	44,473	1,715	735
	$68,000	$5,527	$62,473	$44,473	$ 1,715	$48,285

X would be entitled to deduct both the notional interest and the capital cost allowance each year. At the end of the 10-year lease, X will be deemed to have disposed of the asset for the remaining principal amount which is $44,473. If the asset is the only property in the class, X will be subject to recapture of $42,758 ($44,473 (proceeds) – $1,715 (UCC)). If there are other assets still in the class, recapture does not necessarily result, but the balance in the class is reduced by $44,473. The total deduction allowed to X with respect to the asset over the term of the lease is $68,000 ($62,473 (interest) + $48,285 (CCA) – $42,758 (recapture)).

If the lease is transferred to a non-arm's length corporation by amalgamation or wind-up, the new lessee generally assumes the former lessee's position.[245] If the lease is assigned to another taxpayer, the election will flow through to the assignee automatically if the assignee is non-arm's length, or if the lessee and assignee elect in the case of an arm's length transfer.[246] If the original property is replaced by something similar, the election will not be affected unless the terms of the lease change.[247] If the property is altered and the rent increases, the lessee is deemed to have acquired additional property and to have increased the outstanding principal amount of the earlier deemed loan by the fair market value of the additional property.[248] A renegotiation of the lease that changes the rent payable will be treated as a cancellation of the old lease and the entering into of a new lease.[249]

See page ii for explanation of footnotes.

[245] CCH ¶4730; Sec. 16.1(4).

[246] CCH ¶4728, ¶4729; Sec. 16.1(2), 16.1(3).

[247] CCH ¶4730a; Sec. 16.1(5).

[248] CCH ¶4730aa; Sec. 16.1(6).

[249] CCH ¶4730ab; Sec. 16.1(7).

[¶4335] Property Not Subject to Capital Cost Allowance

[¶4340] Property Not Included

The following classes of property are not eligible for a capital cost allowance:[250]

(1) property the cost of which is deductible as an expense in computing the taxpayer's income;

(2) property described in the taxpayer's inventory;

(3) property not acquired by the taxpayer to gain or produce income;

(4) property acquired by an expenditure allowed as a deduction for scientific research and experimental development (SR&ED);[251]

(5) certain antiques; objects of art, such as a print, etching, drawing, painting, sculpture or similar work of art, where the cost to the taxpayer was at least $200; a hand-woven tapestry or carpet, and handmade appliqué costing at least $215 per square metre, unless any of these items were created by a Canadian;

(6) property of farmers and fishers on which an allowance has been claimed and obtained under the alternative Part XVII of the Regulations which permits such taxpayers to claim depreciation on the straight-line basis (see ¶4350 et seq.);

(7) property of a life insurer used by it in, or held by it in the course of, carrying on an insurance business outside Canada;

(8) property that is a yacht, a camp, a lodge, a golf course, or facility or club the main purpose of which is to provide dining, sporting, or recreational facilities unless the property was acquired in the ordinary course of a business of providing the property for hire or reward;[252]

(9) property that is linefill contained in a pipeline;[253] and

(10) where the taxpayer is a non-resident person, property owned outside Canada.[254]

Land is not depreciable. The classes prescribed for depreciation purposes are deemed not to include the land on which the property described in them is situated.[255] Similarly, the prescribed classes are deemed not to include depreciable property of a partnership.[256]

See page ii for explanation of footnotes.

[250] CCH ¶4944; Reg. 1102(1); Interp. Bul. IT-128R.
[251] CCH ¶5900; Sec. 37(1).
[252] CCH ¶4848, ¶4944, ¶4945c; Sec. 18(1)(l); Reg. 1102(1)(f), Reg. 1102(17); Interp. Bul. IT-148R3.
[253] CCH ¶4944; Reg. 1102(1)(k).
[254] CCH ¶4944c; Reg. 1102(3).
[255] CCH ¶4944b; Reg. 1102(2).
[256] CCH ¶4944a; Reg. 1102(1a).

Whether or not a property is required by the taxpayer to gain or produce income will be a question of fact.[257] Where buildings are bought with land and demolished shortly thereafter, no capital cost allowance will be granted on their cost if the main object of the transaction is the purchase of the land.[258] There must be a connection between the use of the asset and the producing of income. Thus, a motel owner was not allowed a deduction for capital cost allowance where the motel was rented at less than its fair rental value and was therefore demonstrably not acquired for the purpose of gaining or producing income.[259] In the purchase of a taxicab company, the amount paid for the licences was non-depreciable since the licences were renewable and constituted an enduring advantage of a capital nature.[260]

If, at his or her own cost, a person constructs an asset on land owned by another person, or otherwise incorporates an asset into property owned by another as an integral part thereof, and does not have a leasehold interest in the asset, capital cost allowance may not be claimed in respect of such property.[261] This will be the case where a road providing access to a taxpayer's plant is built at the taxpayer's expense on land owned by a municipality.

[¶4345] Farming and Fishing Assets

[¶4350] Methods of Computing Capital Cost Allowance

In the past, taxpayers engaged in farming or fishing were allowed to choose between the general method of claiming capital cost allowance in Part XI of the regulations and the straight-line method in Part XVII of the regulations which applies only to depreciable assets used in the business of farming or fishing. Under the Part XI method, assets of a similar type are pooled for capital cost allowance purposes. Any capital cost allowance recovered on the pool is included in income, and a terminal loss on the pool is allowed as a deduction. Under the Part XVII method, each asset is treated separately for capital cost allowance purposes. Recovered capital cost allowance is not taxable and a loss on disposal is not deductible.

With the introduction of capital gains tax in 1972, the Part XVII method is being phased out. Depreciable assets acquired after December 31, 1971 for use in farming and fishing are eligible for capital cost allowance only through the Part XI method of claiming capital cost allowance.

Taxpayers who were entitled to claim straight-line depreciation under Part XVII on property owned at December 31, 1971, may continue to depreciate that property on the same basis in subsequent years. Any capital cost allowance on that property, whether claimed before or after December 31, 1971, is not subject to tax if recovered on disposal of the property,

---

See page ii for explanation of footnotes.

[257] Electrical Industries (Western) Ltd., 90 DTC 1842, Hickman Motors Ltd., 97 DTC 5363.

[258] William Pitt Hotel, 58 DTC 209.

[259] Clapham, 70 DTC 1012.

[260] Metropolitan Taxi Ltd., 68 DTC 5098.

[261] Saskatoon Community Broadcasting Co. Ltd., 58 DTC 491.

provided the taxpayer has not at any time elected to claim depreciation under the Part XI method.[262]

[¶4355] Deductions Allowed

Taxpayers engaged in farming or fishing have, for assets acquired before January 1, 1972, two methods of claiming depreciation. The first is the declining balance system of capital cost allowance used by all other taxpayers, which is outlined in Part XI of the regulations and discussed in all the other paragraphs in this chapter with the rates as outlined in ¶4025 and ¶4030. The second is the straight-line method with the rates outlined in Regulations 1700 to 1704.[263] The straight-line method is only available for assets that were acquired for a farming or fishing business prior to January 1, 1972. A taxpayer who retains the straight-line method is not subject to the recapture (¶4385) or terminal loss (¶4475) provisions on the disposition of these assets. A taxpayer who chooses the declining balance method for the taxpayer's pre-1972 assets may not later revert to the straight-line method. However, taxpayers claiming under the straight-line method may claim independently the additional allowances for grain storage facilities and for certain vessels as well as the additional capital cost allowance under Class 20.[264]

The maximum allowances for farmers and fishers who use the straight-line system are generally ½ the rates allowed to taxpayers on the declining balance system in Part XI. In a taxation year of less than 12 months, the allowance is confined to the proportion of the amount of depreciation that the number of days is of 365. Similarly, the allowances for assets sold during the year are limited to the proportionate allowance based on the number of months during which they were in use during the year. Depreciation of an asset is limited to the amount by which the capital cost exceeds the aggregate of all deductions previously allowed.

For disposition of a farmer's principal residence see Chapter V, and for comment on a farming business see Chapter III.

[¶4360] Deductions Not Permitted

Farmers or fishers may claim capital cost allowance on the straight-line method only on assets acquired before 1972. Part XVII of the regulations, which sets out the straight-line method provides that no depreciation may be claimed in respect of assets already deductible in the computation of income, or in respect of inventory, scientific research expenditures, classes of assets established by the former *Canadian Vessel Construction Assistance Act*, conversion costs of vessels included in a separate prescribed class, assets not used in the business during the year, animals, herbs, trees, shrubs, or similar growing things, or property not acquired by the taxpayer for the purpose of

---

See page ii for explanation of footnotes.

[262] CCH ¶5048f, ¶29,185; ITAR 20(2); Reg. 1704.   [264] CCH ¶5048f; Reg. 1704.
[263] CCH ¶5048b–5048f, ¶29,185; ITAR 20(2); Reg. 1700–1704.

gaining or producing income from farming or fishing. Where the taxpayer is a non-resident, depreciation may not be claimed on property situated outside of Canada.[265]

[¶4365] Fiscal Period

Where the farmer or fisher's income for the taxation year includes income from a business whose fiscal period does not coincide with the calendar year, depreciation on assets used in the business is to be taken on the fiscal year basis.[266]

[¶4370] Assets with More Than One Use

Depreciable assets used by a farmer or fisher partly for business and partly for other uses are subject to depreciation only in the proportion of business use to total use.[267] Thus, if an asset costing $1,000 is used $1/2$ for business and $1/2$ for personal use, the depreciable cost[268] for depreciation purposes is $500. If the taxpayer is entitled to a subsidy or similar grant, the depreciable cost of the property will be reduced by the amount of such grant.[269] See ¶3645 and ¶4012 regarding grants and subsidies. The depreciable cost of pre-1972 property depreciated on the straight-line basis that is transferred in a transaction not at arm's length[270] is the lesser of:

(a) the actual cost to the taxpayer, and

(b) the amount by which the capital cost to the original owner exceeds depreciation taken or which should have been taken under the *Income War Tax Act* (including at least half rates in loss years), or the *Income Tax Act* by the original owner and all intervening owners.

[¶4375] Transfer of Farm and Fishing Property to Child

Regardless of which method of depreciation is used, where farming and fishing property of a prescribed class is transferred or distributed to a farmer's or fisher's child as a consequence of death and the particular child is resident in Canada, no capital gain, capital loss, recapture of capital cost allowance or terminal loss arises in the income of the deceased. The child is deemed to acquire the depreciable property at an amount equal to the lesser of:

(a) the capital cost, and

(b) the cost amount of the depreciable property to the taxpayer immediately before death.

In effect, potential recapture or terminal losses are passed on to the child. However, an election may be made which substitutes alternative rules

---

See page ii for explanation of footnotes.

[265] CCH ¶5048d; Reg. 1702.
[266] CCH ¶5048e; Reg. 1703(1).
[267] CCH ¶5048e; Reg. 1703(4).

[268] CCH ¶5048e; Reg. 1703(2).
[269] CCH ¶5048e; Reg. 1703(5).
[270] CCH ¶5048e; Reg. 1703(6), Reg. 1703(8).

for the provisions that produce an automatic complete rollover. These elections permit selective realization of such gains, losses, recapture, or terminal losses as the circumstances may warrant. For a more extensive treatment of the subject, see ¶2590.'

Similar rollover provisions apply in respect of an *inter vivos* transfer of farm and fishing property to a child. See ¶2545.

In both cases, the depreciable property must have been property of a prescribed class that was used principally in the farming or fishing business by the transferor, the transferor's spouse or common-law partner, or the transferor's child or parent immediately before the transferor's death.[271]

[¶4380] Disposal of Depreciable Property and Recapture of Capital Cost Allowance

[¶4385] Recapture

Under the so-called "recapture" principle,[272] the capital cost allowance deducted over the years by a taxpayer may be wholly or partially brought back into the taxpayer's income in a later year. Where depreciable property is sold, tax on recaptured capital cost allowance is exigible in the year of sale, notwithstanding that the sale may be the subject of continuing litigation.[273] The deduction to which a taxpayer is entitled in respect of his or her capital cost of particular depreciable property cannot in the long run exceed the actual decline in value of the property. For example, if the taxpayer acquires depreciable property at a cost of $10,000 and some years later sells it for $4,000, the maximum deduction allowable in computing income is $6,000. If the capital cost allowance actually claimed was $7,000, the taxpayer would be obliged to include $1,000 in income.

Recapture applies only to capital cost allowance previously claimed, not to a realization of an amount in excess of the original cost of the property. Continuing the above example, if the property was sold for $12,000, all capital cost allowance claimed would be recaptured, but the excess of selling price over original cost (i.e., $2,000) would be treated as a capital gain.

The one exception to this rule is the case where the property in question is a timber resource property. For property of this kind, any gain over original cost is also subject to recapture, and thus full income inclusion instead of capital gains treatment or partial income inclusion.[274]

The converse of the recapture principle is the terminal loss provision described at ¶4475. The purpose of this provision is to recognize a case where the capital cost allowance claimed on a property has been less than

---

See page ii for explanation of footnotes.

[271] CCH ¶9283, ¶9283a, ¶9450, ¶29,160; Sec. 70(9), 70(9.01), 73(3); ITAR 20(1.1); Interp. Bul. IT-268R4, IT-349R3.

[272] CCH ¶4500; Sec. 13(1); Interp. Bul. IT-478R2.

[273] Picadilly Hotels Ltd., 78 DTC 6444.

[274] CCH ¶4506, ¶4562f, ¶4562h; Sec. 13(1), 13(21) "timber resource property", 13(21) "undepreciated capital cost".

its actual decline in value. For example, if property costing $10,000 is sold for $4,000 but only $5,000 of capital cost allowance has been claimed, the other $1,000 may be deductible as a terminal loss.

[¶4387] Undepreciated Capital Cost

The key element in both the capital cost allowance system and the recapture principle is the "undepreciated capital cost" of a class of property at any time. The capital cost allowance which a taxpayer may claim on a class of property for a year is a particular percentage (prescribed by regulation) of the undepreciated capital cost of the class as at year end. If the negative elements of the undepreciated capital cost calculation exceed the positive elements as at year end, the negative balance must be recaptured and included in income for that year. Unlike a terminal loss, recapture may arise if there are assets remaining in the class at year end. It is the balance of the undepreciated capital cost of the class at the end of the taxation year after taking into account all the positive and negative components that will trigger recapture.

The following are the positive and negative components of the computation of undepreciated capital cost.[275]

(1) *Positive components:*

(a) the capital cost of all properties of the class acquired prior to the time of computation (see ¶4012 regarding subsidies);

(b) any recapture or other amount in respect of the class included in income for a previous year; and

(c) assistance or inducements repaid after property has been disposed of.

(2) *Negative components:*

(a) capital cost allowance taken in respect of the class for preceding years;

(b) the amount by which the undepreciated capital cost of the asset must be reduced under the debt forgiveness rules;[276]

(c) where there have been dispositions out of the class, the lesser of the proceeds of disposition of the particular property disposed of (less any cost of disposition) and its original capital cost;

(d) where the previous disposition was a disposition of a timber resource property, the full proceeds of disposition of the timber resource property (less any costs of disposition);

(e) with respect to a new mine brought into production between November 7, 1969 and December 31, 1973, where the taxpayer has

---

See page ii for explanation of footnotes.

[275] CCH ¶4562h; Sec. 13(21) "undepreciated capital cost".

[276] CCH ¶9854; Sec. 80(5).

elected to claim accelerated capital cost allowance on mining assets, the income from the mine excluded from taxation;

(f) investment tax credits claimed in respect of depreciable property after the property is disposed of; and

(g) assistance in respect of depreciable property received after the property was disposed of.

Applying the above-noted rules may result in recapture without a disposition actually taking place at that time.

The recapture provisions do not apply to farmers and fishers who use the straight-line method of depreciation. See ¶4350.

Where a certain amount of the sale price of depreciable property was added to the vendor's income by way of recapture of capital cost allowance, part of it was held deductible as a bad debt when it was shown that it became uncollectible through the bankruptcy of the purchaser.[277] Where a property given as security for a bank loan was required to be sold by the bank, the amount obtained in excess of the undepreciated capital cost was recaptured depreciation, even though the proceeds were not enough to satisfy the loan.[278] Where the recaptured amount exceeds or is equal to the amount of a loss for the same year, the loss will be wiped out and cannot be carried back.[279]

Taxpayers who agreed to close the sale of their apartment building on December 31, 1968, intended to acquire a larger building before the end of the year, but they were unable to acquire such a building until March of the next year. The Minister was held to have properly recaptured capital cost allowance for the building sold and the taxpayers were not permitted to apply the amount recaptured to reduce the undepreciated capital cost of the newly acquired property.[280] Where the building and equipment of a cheese factory had been subsidized by the government, the capital cost of the assets had to be reduced by the amount of the subsidies when the assets were later sold.[281] Recapture of capital cost allowance on disposed depreciable property was held to apply in the year in which all the conditions of the contract regarding the disposition of the property were fulfilled and in which the vendor became entitled to the proceeds of disposition.[282]

[¶4388] Proceeds of Disposition

"Proceeds of disposition" is the sale price or other consideration received by the transferor.[283] The CRA's practice appears to be to treat the sale price as net sale price and to allow the deduction of any commissions, legal fees, and similar expenses of the sale.

Proceeds of disposition also includes:

See page ii for explanation of footnotes.

[277] Roy, 58 DTC 676.
[278] Chenevert, 65 DTC 265.
[279] Rainy Lake Hotel Co. Ltd., 61 DTC 249.
[280] Wolff et al., 71 DTC 239.

[281] Fortier [No. 1], 73 DTC 5181.
[282] Victory Hotels Ltd., 62 DTC 1378.
[283] CCH ¶4562e; Sec. 13(21) "proceeds of disposition"; Interp. Bul. IT-220R2.

(a) compensation for property stolen, damaged, expropriated, etc.;

(b) proceeds of insurance policies payable on the destruction or loss of property;

(c) that part of the proceeds of an insurance policy payable on damage to property which is not spent on repairing the damage within a reasonable time after the damage occurs;

(d) the reduction in a mortgagor's liability to a mortgagee caused by the exercise of a power of sale of property under the terms of the mortgage, plus any proceeds from that sale which are received by the mortgagor; and

(e) any amount included in a taxpayer's proceeds of disposition by virtue of foreclosures and conditional sales repossessions (see ¶3454).

Special rules are provided for determining the time of disposition of capital property that has been stolen, destroyed, or expropriated and the time when the proceeds of disposition are considered to have become receivable.[284] The disposition is deemed to have taken place and the proceeds are deemed to have become receivable on the earliest of five specified days:

(a) the day on which the taxpayer agrees to the *full* compensation for the stolen, destroyed, or expropriated property; if the taxpayer agrees to a certain minimum amount and actually receives that pending final agreement as to the full compensation, it would appear that the taxpayer would not regard the initial amount as proceeds until he or she has agreed upon the full amount;

(b) the day on which the taxpayer's compensation is finally determined by a court or other competent tribunal;

(c) where the taxpayer has not agreed on full compensation and the matter has not been taken before a court or tribunal within two years of the loss, destruction, or expropriation of the property, the day that is two years after the loss, destruction, or expropriation;

(d) if the taxpayer ceases to be resident in Canada or dies and, as a result, is deemed to have disposed of his or her property, the day of such cessation of residence or death; and

(e) where the taxpayer is a corporation, other than a taxable Canadian corporation all of whose shares are owned by a second taxable Canadian corporation, the day the taxpayer is wound up.

Where, under a rental/sale agreement entered into on June 1, 1985, gas cylinders were to be purchased over five years ($^1/_5$ purchased each year, the remaining portion being rented until eventually purchased), it was held that

See page ii for explanation of footnotes.

[284] CCH ¶6704; Sec. 44(2).

the disposition had not occurred on June 1, 1985, but over the course of five years, as set out in the agreement.[285]

See also ¶4475 *et seq.* regarding terminal losses.

[¶4390] Taxation Year — Individuals Carrying On Business

Although ordinarily an individual's taxation year is the calendar year, if an individual taxpayer's income includes income from a business, the fiscal period of which does not coincide with the calendar year, and depreciable property has been disposed of, the taxation year for purposes of capital cost allowance is the fiscal period of the business.[286]

Where a taxpayer, who has ceased to carry on business, disposes of depreciable property which had been acquired to carry on the business and which has not been used for any other purpose, the reference in the recapture and terminal loss provisions to a taxation year is not to be read as a reference to a fiscal period.[287] The effect of this is that any recapture of capital cost allowance or terminal loss shall be included in income in the calendar year in which the disposition occurred. See ¶4065 for a more complete discussion of "taxation year".

[¶4395] Additions to Class within Taxation Year

If the undepreciated capital cost of a class becomes negative at some point during the taxation year (for example, because all or a substantial portion of the assets in the class have been sold for amounts that recover some part of the capital cost allowance previously claimed) recapture can be avoided through the acquisition of further properties of that class before the end of the taxation year. Recapture arises only if the undepreciated capital cost of the class is negative at the year end. If, before the year end, positive elements can be injected through further acquisitions sufficient to offset any negative balance that might have temporarily arisen during the year, the negative balance will not exist at year end and no recapture will arise that year.[288] As described in ¶4055, crediting an asset to the class can avoid recapture even if capital cost allowance cannot be claimed on that asset in the taxation year because of the available-for-use rule.

This will not be possible if the assets are required to be placed in a separate class such as rental property over $50,000 (see ¶4045). See ¶4037 concerning rules that allow assets of certain classes to be included in other classes, especially the general rule that allows property that is in a different class, only because it was acquired before a change in the regulations, to be transferred to the new class. This will postpone recapture on these assets.[289]

See page ii for explanation of footnotes.

[285] Borstad Welding Supplies (1972) Ltd., 93 DTC 5457.
[286] CCH ¶4512; Sec. 13(3).
[287] CCH ¶4538; Sec. 13(8).
[288] CCH ¶4509; Sec. 13(1).
[289] CCH ¶4950e; Reg. 1103(2d).

[¶4400] Examples Illustrating Disposition of Assets under a Capital Cost Allowance System

Example 1:

The following is an illustration of the working of the system of capital cost allowances when the asset disposed of is the only asset of its class.

	Case 1	Case 2	Case 3
Capital cost of property of prescribed class	$5,000	$5,000	$5,000
Capital cost allowance taken	1,500	1,500	1,500
Undepreciated capital cost	$3,500	$3,500	$3,500
Proceeds of disposition	2,500	4,000	6,000
Recapture	--	500	1,500
Terminal loss	1,000	--	--
Capital gain	--	--	1,000

Example 2:

The following illustrates the working of the system of capital cost allowances where the assets disposed of are simply part of the property of a particular class held by the taxpayer:

	Case 1	Case 2	Case 3	Case 4
Total assets of class -- Capital cost	$100,000	$100,000	$100,000	$100,000
Accumulated capital cost allowances	80,000	80,000	80,000	50,000
Undepreciated capital cost of property of class immediately before disposition	20,000	20,000	20,000	50,000
Dispositions of property included in group:				
Capital cost	30,000	30,000	30,000	10,000
Proceeds	15,000	25,000	35,000	25,000
Amount deducted from undepreciated capital cost of property of class*	15,000	25,000	30,000	10,000
Capital gain	nil	nil	5,000	15,000
Amount recaptured	nil	5,000	10,000	nil
Undepreciated capital cost of assets remaining in class	5,000	nil	nil	40,000

* The definition of undepreciated capital cost restricts the deduction to the lesser of (a) proceeds of disposition and (b) capital cost.

[¶4410] Assets Converted to Personal or Business Use

Where a taxpayer acquired a property to gain or produce income and later begins to use the property for some other purpose, the taxpayer is deemed to have disposed of the property at the time of the change and to have reacquired it immediately afterwards at an amount equal to the proceeds of disposition.[290] The proceeds of disposition are deemed to be the fair market value of the property at that time. This means that where the property is a depreciable property, the undepreciated capital cost of the class to which the property belongs will be reduced by the lesser of this fair market value and the cost of the property. Future capital cost allowance for the class will therefore be reduced and recapture may arise. A common example is the case where an individual acquires a house for rental purposes and some time later begins to live in it. On the change in use, the individual would be deemed to dispose of the house at its fair market value. Assuming that the house is the only property in the class, the individual would usually be subject to recapture or be entitled to a terminal loss.

In the reverse situation to that described above, where a taxpayer acquires property for some purpose other than the earning of income and later converts the property to an income earning use, the taxpayer is deemed to have acquired the property for a specified amount that constitutes the capital cost of the property for capital cost allowance purposes.[291] If the fair market value of the property at the time of the change in use is less than the cost of the property to the taxpayer, the specified amount is the fair market value. However, where the cost of the property to the taxpayer is less than its fair market value at the time of the change in use, the specified amount will be the aggregate of the actual cost of the property to the taxpayer and $1/2$ of the excess of the property's fair market value over such cost to the extent that a capital gains deduction was not claimed in relation to such excess. The limitations imposed on the step-up in cost limits capital cost for capital cost allowance purposes to cost plus any capital gain recognized by the taxpayer on the change in use. The taxpayer cannot claim capital cost allowance on the full gain since only a portion (50%) is included in income. Any capital gains deduction claimed by the taxpayer in respect of the disposition also reduces the step-up in cost so that the taxpayer cannot claim capital cost allowance on any capital gain that has not been subject to tax.

Where the change in use of the property involves gaining income in relation to a business, in the case of a non-resident, "business" means a business being carried on by the non-resident in Canada.[292]

Note that as described in ¶5362, where an asset changes from a non-income-earning property to an income-earning property, a taxpayer may elect not to have had a change of use for the property. If the taxpayer so

---

See page ii for explanation of footnotes.

[290] CCH ¶4522; Sec. 13(7)(a). [292] CCH ¶4539; Sec. 13(9).
[291] CCH ¶4522; Sec. 13(7)(b).

elects, then there is no deemed acquisition of an income-earning property and no capital cost allowance will be claimed.

[¶4415] Assets Used Partly for Personal and Partly for Business Purposes

Another recapture provision designed to return to income excess capital cost allowance claimed is the provision respecting assets used for both personal and income-earning purposes.[293] An example of this is a house which is both a doctor's residence and office, or a duplex where the taxpayer rents half and lives in the other half. If the doctor acquires a house with an office for $100,000 and the office part is $\frac{1}{5}$ of the whole house, the taxpayer will be deemed to have paid $20,000 for the business asset. Then, if the whole house is sold for $150,000, the doctor will be deemed to have sold the depreciable business asset, i.e., the office, for $\frac{1}{5}$ of the total selling price, i.e., $30,000.

Where a building is occupied in part by the owner and in part by tenants, capital cost allowance may be taken on the portion leased to tenants and, upon the disposition of the property, the class would be credited in the normal way with the lesser of the percentage of cost or proceeds that relates to the rental portion of the property.

[¶4420] Change in Proportionate Use

If a taxpayer changes the proportion of use made of property to earn income, the capital cost of that property will, in effect, be changed.[294]

An *increase* in the proportion of use to earn income will result in the deemed acquisition of additional depreciable property, and its capital cost will be the same proportion of a specified amount that the increase in the use of earning income is of the entire use for all purposes. The specified amount will be the fair market value of the property at the time of the change in the proportion of use of the capital asset, if that value is less than the cost of the property to a taxpayer. If, however, the fair market value of the property at the time of the change in the proportion of use exceeds the cost of the property to the taxpayer, then the specified amount is determined as the aggregate of:

(a) the actual cost of the property to the taxpayer, and

(b) $\frac{1}{2}$ of the excess of the property's fair market value over such cost to the extent that the capital gains exemption was not claimed in relation to such excess.

See page ii for explanation of footnotes.

[293] CCH ¶4522; Sec. 13(7)(c).   [294] CCH ¶4522; Sec. 13(7)(d).

This rule may be expressed in the following formula:

$$
\text{Capital cost} = \begin{array}{c}\text{Present}\\\text{proportion}\\\text{of property}\\\text{used to}\\\text{earn income}\end{array} - \begin{array}{c}\text{Former}\\\text{proportion}\\\text{of property}\\\text{used to}\\\text{earn income}\end{array} \times \begin{array}{c}\text{Specified}\\\text{amount}\end{array}
$$

This capital cost will be added to the undepreciated capital cost of property of the class and will accordingly increase the amount on which the taxpayer may claim capital cost allowance. Note that applicable after 1992, the capital cost of depreciable property to a taxpayer at the time of the taxpayer's death is to be determined without this adjustment.[295]

Example:

> Assume that a doctor acquired a brick house for the sum of $50,000 in 1997 and used 20% of it for an office and the balance as a residence. Assume also that this is his only asset in that class.

His capital cost of depreciable property of the class will be	$10,000.00
For the taxation years 1997 to 2011 he claims capital cost allowances of	$ 1,200.00
Undepreciated capital cost at the end of the 2011 taxation year	$ 8,800.00
Assume that during the 2012 taxation year the office space is increased from 20% to 35% of the house (an increase of 15% of the entire house) and the fair market value of the house at that time is	$60,000.00
Capital cost of depreciable property deemed to have been acquired will be 15/100 × ($50,000 + 1/2 × ($60,000 - $50,000))	$ 8,250.00
Undepreciated capital cost upon which capital cost allowances may be calculated	$17,050.00

In the above example, the increase in use is in the physical proportion of the property which is used for earning income. Other standards of measurement will apply in other circumstances such as, for example, mileage travelled or the time during the year in which the asset is used to earn income.

A *decrease* in the proportion of use to earn income will result in a deemed disposition of depreciable property. The proceeds of disposition are deemed to be the same proportion of the fair market value of the property at the time of such decrease as the decrease in the use for earning income is of

---

[295] CCH ¶9300; Sec. 70(13).

the entire use for all purposes. This rule may be expressed in the following formula:

Proceeds of disposition	=	Former proportion of property used to earn income	−	Present proportion of property used to earn income	×	Fair market value of entire property

The undepreciated capital cost to the taxpayer of property of the class will be reduced by the lesser of:

(a) the deemed proceeds of disposition, and

(b) the capital cost to the taxpayer.

This will accordingly decrease the amount which the taxpayer may claim as capital cost allowance.[296] If the proceeds of disposition exceed the undepreciated capital cost of property of the class so that the balance of the class is negative at the year end, recapture will arise.[297]

[¶4425] Non-Arm's Length Transfer of Depreciable Property

If depreciable property is acquired in a non-arm's length transaction from an individual resident in Canada, a partnership with at least one partner who is an individual resident in Canada, or a partnership with at least one partner who is another partnership, and the capital cost to the transferee is greater than the capital cost to the transferor, the capital cost to the transferee is deemed to be the sum of the transferor's capital cost plus half of the amount by which the transferor's proceeds of disposition exceeds:

(a) the capital cost of the property to the transferor; plus

(b) (2/1) any capital gains exemption claimed in respect of the excess of the transferor's proceeds of disposition over the transferor's capital cost.[298]

Moreover, if the transferor's capital cost immediately before the transfer is greater than the transferee's capital cost, the transferee's capital cost (not taking into account the above formula) is reduced to the transferor's capital cost and the difference is considerered the CCA that the transferee has claimed. The transferee is thus put in the same position as the transferor in terms of potential recapture.

In the absence of this provision, the transferor's profit on the sale of the property could qualify for the capital gains exemption and the taxpayer would have an increased tax basis for capital cost allowance purposes.

If the depreciable property is acquired in a non-arm's length transaction from a corporation or from an individual who is not resident in Cana-

---

See page ii for explanation of footnotes.

[296] CCH ¶4562h; Sec. 13(21) "undepreciated capital cost".

[297] CCH ¶4500; Sec. 13(1).

[298] CCH ¶4522; Sec. 13(7)(e).

da, or a partnership with no partners who are individuals resident in Canada, or with no partners that are other partnerships, the transferor's capital cost is deemed to be the aggregate of the transferor's capital cost and half of the amount by which the transferor's proceeds of disposition exceeds the capital cost of the property to the transferor.

For the purposes of dealing with non-arm's length purchases of depreciable property, two corporations shall be deemed not to be related to each other simply because they are controlled by the same trustee or executor and it is established that:

(1) the trustee or executor acquired control of the companies as a result of the death of an individual; and

(2) control of the two companies was not acquired as a result of one or more trusts or estates created by the same individual or two or more individuals not dealing with each other at arm's length.[299]

[¶4430] Deemed Disposition of Depreciable Property upon a Change of Control

A corporation may elect a deemed disposition of any capital property immediately before the year end resulting from an acquisition of control and a deemed reacquisition of such property immediately thereafter. The elected proceeds can be anywhere between the adjusted cost base and the fair market value of the property. Any property so elected to have been disposed of is deemed to have been reacquired at a capital cost equal to the amount elected.[300] However, for capital cost allowance purposes, the capital cost of property that is depreciable property, other than a timber resource property, is limited to the aggregate of the capital cost to the corporation at the time of disposition, and half (or other applicable capital gains inclusion rate) of the amount, if any, by which the corporation's proceeds of disposition exceed the capital cost of the property at the time of disposition.[301]

[¶4435] Non-Residents and Recapture

A non-resident who has received rental income from Canadian real estate or timber royalties from timber resource properties or timber limits in Canada is given the option of paying tax on the net income from such sources rather than being subject to the non-resident withholding tax (see ¶14,255).

However, if the non-resident does so and claims a capital cost allowance on the real property, the timber resource property, or the timber limit and later disposes of such property in such circumstances that an amount would be recaptured, the non-resident is required to file a return under the ordinary provisions of the Act and pay tax for the year of disposal on a net

---

See page ii for explanation of footnotes.

299 CCH ¶4535b; Sec. 13(7.3).   301 CCH ¶4522; Sec. 13(7)(f).
300 CCH ¶16,140; Sec. 111(4)(e).

income basis so that he or she will be subject to tax on recaptured depreciation.[302]

Where a taxpayer ceased to be a resident of Canada, the taxpayer was liable for recapture on the capital cost allowance claimed while the taxpayer was a resident, even though the property upon which the capital cost allowance had been claimed was sold after the taxpayer ceased to be a resident of Canada.[303]

[¶4450] Lease-Option Agreements

Rather than purchase a depreciable asset or real property, a taxpayer may lease that property for a number of years and at the termination of the lease, purchase the property as provided by an option contained in the lease.

The determination of whether payments under lease-option or sale-leaseback agreements constitute payments of rent, payments on account of the terms of purchase, or repayment of a loan must be made on the basis of the terms of the agreement and the factual circumstances relevant to both the making and execution of that agreement. The aim is to determine whether or not the object of the transaction at its inception is to transfer the equity in the property to the lessee. If the lessee is required to buy the property during or at the end of the lease, or automatically acquires title after a certain number of rental payments, the transaction would be considered by the CRA to be a sale. Similarly, if the option price is significantly less than the fair market value of the asset at the time it is exercised, it is likely that the lease is actually a sale. Under these circumstances, especially if the costs associated with ownership (i.e., insurance, maintenance, taxes) fall to the lessee, the lessee-purchaser would be entitled as owner to claim capital cost allowance at the appropriate rate for the class in which the asset belongs. The lessor would also account for the transaction as a sale.

If the above-mentioned conditions are not met in the lease agreement, the payments are generally regarded as a current expense of renting property which, if made for the purpose of gaining or producing income, will be deductible to the extent reasonable. The lessor will treat the payments as income from a business or property. If the lessor is in the business of lease-options, the property will be included in his or her inventory, whereas if the lessor has entered into a lease-option agreement on a casual, non-recurring basis, he or she will be entitled, as the owner, to claim capital cost allowance on the property.

Where a company leased expensive machinery from other companies, with options to purchase the equipment for one dollar at the end of the

---

See page ii for explanation of footnotes.
[302] CCH ¶26,630; Sec. 216(5).　　　　[303] Deitcher, 79 DTC 5415.

lease period, the lease arrangements were held to be shams designed to disguise what were really time-payment purchases.[304]

Statutory rules deal with the situation where a taxpayer originally leases property, acquires that property pursuant to an option contained in the lease, and later disposes of that property.[305] These rules apply generally where a taxpayer has acquired property at a cost less than fair market value from a lessor and has previously paid rent for the use of that property which has been deducted in computing his taxable income. These provisions will not apply where the lease was considered to be a sale at the outset. They will apply in cases where the lease is not treated as a sale for income tax purposes but, when the option to purchase is exercised, the fair market value of the property is in excess of the option exercise price. These rules operate to ensure that a portion of amounts paid as rent for the property will be recaptured when the property, or an option thereon, is sold at more than the actual cost of the property or the option.

Under these rules, the taxpayer is deemed, at the time of the exercise of the option, to acquire the property for an amount that is equal to the lesser of:

(a) the fair market value of the property at the time of the exercise of the option (determined without taking into consideration any option on that property), and

(b) the actual cost of the property at the time of the exercise of the option plus all previous payments on account of rent for the use of that property.

For these purposes, rental payments include rental payments made by persons with whom the taxpayer was not dealing at arm's length. However, rental payments made to a person with whom the taxpayer does not deal at arm's length are not included for the purposes of (b). If the taxpayer acquiring the property is a corporation that was not in existence at the time when rental payments were made by another corporation not operating at arm's length, the new corporation will be deemed to have been in existence at the time the rental payments were made and to have been not dealing at arm's length with the other corporation.

To the extent that the actual cost of the property is less than the deemed cost determined as described above, that difference is added to the total of the depreciation previously allowed to the taxpayer with respect to the capital cost allowance class to which the property belongs. Consequently, any proceeds of disposition up to (but not exceeding) the deemed cost of the property will reduce the undepreciated capital cost of the class to which the property belongs, whereas, if these rules did not apply, only proceeds of

---

See page ii for explanation of footnotes.
[304] Chibougamau Lumber Ltée, 73 DTC 134.   [305] CCH ¶4519–4519e; Sec. 13(5.2)–(5.5).

¶4450

disposition up to the actual cost would reduce the undepreciated capital cost of the class.

Where the property leased and then acquired is not depreciable property, but rather is real property, such as land or property which does not constitute depreciable property because it is not acquired to gain or produce income, that property is deemed to be depreciable property of a separate prescribed class, specifically Class 36.[306] To the extent that the deemed cost is greater than the actual cost, recaptured depreciation, rather than a capital gain, could result on the subsequent sale of the real property. The fact that the real property is deemed to be property of a prescribed class does not, however, entitle the taxpayer to claim capital cost allowance on that property.

Where a taxpayer disposes of a capital property that is an option to acquire either depreciable property or real property where the property has been rented by the taxpayer or a non-arm's length party, the difference between the proceeds of disposition of the option and its cost is deemed to be recapture, which is included in income.[307]

Where rental payments were incurred after the taxpayer acquired the depreciable property, such as in a lease-leaseback arrangement, the deductible payments will, within limits, be added to the capital cost of the property and will be considered to be capital cost allowance allowed to the taxpayer before the disposition. The amount which is added to the capital cost of the depreciable property is the lesser of:

(a) the total amount of the deductible outlays or expenses incurred prior to the disposition; and

(b) the fair market value of the depreciable property at the earlier of:

(i) the expiry of the last period in respect of which the deductible outlay or expense was made or incurred, and

(ii) the time of disposition of the property.

An exception is provided in certain circumstances where the depreciable property is disposed of in a non-arm's length transaction.[308]

The purpose of this provision is to ensure that the appropriate amount of recapture is recognized when a depreciable property is disposed of. The rules are intended to operate so that the amounts paid for the use of or right to use a depreciable property will be taken into account in determining any recapture. The provisions are applicable where a taxpayer, or a person with whom a taxpayer was not dealing at arm's length, disposes of a property for which a deduction in respect of an outlay or expense was made or incurred for the use of or right to use the property. The outlay or expense involved is

---

See page ii for explanation of footnotes.

[306] CCH ¶5042, ¶5042a; Reg. 1101(5g), Class 36.   [308] CCH ¶4519d; Sec. 13(5.4).
[307] CCH ¶4519a; Sec. 13(5.3).

generally rent. Lease cancellation payments otherwise deductible are excluded from the amount which may be recaptured.[309]

Example:

S Ltd. entered into an arm's length lease agreement with T Ltd. requiring annual rental payments of $2,000 for land and $8,000 for the building on the land. S Ltd. had the option at the end of the five years of acquiring the land for $5,000 and the building for $5,000. At the time the option is exercised, the fair market value of the land is $30,000 and the building is $20,000. In Year 6 the land and building are sold for $21,000 and $29,000, respectively.

		Land	Building
		$	$
Cost of exercising the option	(A)	$ 5,000	$ 5,000
Deemed cost -- Lesser of:			
(a) fair market value		30,000	20,000
(b) aggregate of all expenditures made on the lease, including cost of the option		15,000	45,000
Lesser value: deemed cost	(B)	15,000	20,000
Depreciation deemed to have been allowed (which is potentially subject to recapture) ((B) - (A))	(C)	10,000	15,000
On sale in Year 6:			
Proceeds		21,000	29,000
Deemed cost	(B)	15,000	20,000
Capital gain		6,000	9,000
Recaptured depreciation	(C)	10,000	15,000*

* If the taxpayer owns more than one building, the recapture of depreciation will not be immediately recognized. Instead the proceeds up to the amount of deemed cost will reduce the undepreciated capital cost of the remaining buildings of the same class. However, the land will form a separate class for these purposes.

[¶4455] Mortgage Included in Proceeds of Disposition

Where an agreement for sale of land or a mortgage on land which was included in the proceeds of disposition of depreciable property (other than a timber resource property) is sold at a loss by a taxpayer, the loss may be deducted by the taxpayer to the extent that it exceeds the capital gain realized on the sale of the depreciable property. Both the sale of the agreement or mortgage and the sale of the depreciable property must have been carried out at arm's length.[310]

[¶4460] Exchanges of Property and Replacement Property

In certain circumstances, a taxpayer may elect to defer adding to income a recapture of capital cost allowance where the depreciable property

See page ii for explanation of footnotes.

[309] CCH ¶4519e; Sec. 13(5.5).   [310] CCH ¶5132; Sec. 20(5).

the taxpayer disposed of is replaced with a similar one within a reasonable period of time.[311]

The election is available in respect of depreciable property, including a timber resource property, where the proceeds arise as a result of certain involuntary dispositions, or in respect of a voluntary disposition of property described as "former business property".[312] A former business property is real property or an interest therein that is capital property used by the taxpayer or a person related to the taxpayer primarily for the purpose of earning business income. Former business property does not include a rental property, land on which the rental property is situated, land adjacent to the rental property such as parking areas, or a leasehold interest in rental property and related land. For dispositions after July 13, 1990, real property rented to a related party qualifies as former business property provided it was used in the related party's business. [Note that the definition of former business property is to be expanded to include a franchise, concession, or licence if it is disposed of or terminated after December 20, 2002, and the transferor and transferee make a joint election. For more details, see ¶4110.]

In order to qualify for this deferral of recapture, a replacement property must be acquired within certain time limits. In the case of an involuntary disposition, the replacement property must be acquired before the later of the end of the second taxation year following the year of disposition and [for dispositions occurring in taxation years ending after December 19, 2000, 24 months after the end of the taxation year of disposition]. In the case of a voluntary disposition of a former business property, the replacement property must be acquired before the later of the end of the first taxation year following the year of disposition and [for dispositions occurring in taxation years ending after December 19, 2001, 12 months after the end of the taxation year of disposition].

The types of proceeds covered by the rollover for an involuntary disposition are compensation for stolen or destroyed property, including proceeds of insurance and compensation for property that is expropriated, and the selling price of property sold to an expropriating authority after notice of expropriation has been given. See ¶4388 for comments on when such proceeds will be deemed to have become receivable.[313]

Where the election is made on either a voluntary or involuntary disposition, the proceeds of disposition may be reduced by the amount that otherwise would be the recapture of capital cost allowance. Consequently, recapture will not be income in the year but instead will reduce the undepreciated capital cost of whichever class of property the replacement property falls into. Where the replacement property is in the same class as the property disposed of, the result is the same as if the replacement proper-

---

See page ii for explanation of footnotes.

[311] CCH ¶4513; Sec. 13(4); Interp. Bul. IT-259R4.   [313] CCH ¶6704; Sec. 44(2).
[312] CCH ¶28,123; Sec. 248(1) "former business property".

ty had been acquired at the same time as the former property had been disposed of. Where the cost of the replacement property is less than the amount of recapture of capital cost allowance otherwise determined, the net difference will remain as recapture. Where the replacement property is acquired after the prescribed time limits, no deferral of recapture income will be allowed in respect of that disposition. The reference to a time of acquisition relates to the time of actual acquisition rather than the time a property is considered available for use.

Example:

Capital cost of former property	$45,000	
Undepreciated capital cost of former property	$35,000	(1)
Proceeds	$40,000	(2)
Recapture otherwise determined ((2) - (1))	$ 5,000	(3)
Cost of replacement property	$42,000	(4)
Restated proceeds -- Proceeds minus lesser of: (i) recapture; and (ii) cost of replacement property ((2) - (3))	$35,000	(5)
Recaptured CCA ((5) - (1))	nil	

The recognition of recapture is deferred by the acquisition of the replacement property. The capital cost of the replacement property is thus deemed to be reduced by proceeds of disposition equal to the reduction in recapture

Cost of replacement property	$42,000
Less: deemed proceeds of disposition (equal to reduction above)	5,000
Undepreciated capital cost of replacement property before CCA ..	$37,000

Where the replacement property is acquired before the compensation for the former property becomes receivable, any amount otherwise included in recapture in the year when the compensation does become receivable is considered to be proceeds of disposition in respect of the class applicable to the replacement property, so that the taxpayer's right to claim future capital cost allowance in respect of the replacement property is reduced but no immediate recapture occurs. If the replacement property is acquired prior to the disposal of the former property, the taxpayer must still own the replacement property when the former property is disposed of in order to make the election.

Where the replacement property is acquired in a year subsequent to the disposition, the taxpayer may often face a dilemma in reporting income for the year of disposition. It would appear necessary to file an amended return for the initial year which would delete the recapture already reported. Where the taxpayer knows that a replacement property will be acquired within the prescribed time limit, the taxpayer may provide acceptable security to the CRA in lieu of payment of taxes.

¶4460

To qualify for this deferral of recapture on property disposed of, voluntarily or involuntarily, there must eventually be a replacement property. In order to qualify as replacement property, it must be depreciable property acquired for the same or a similar use as the use to which the taxpayer or a person related to the taxpayer put the former property, and it must be reasonable to conclude that the property was acquired by the taxpayer to replace the former property. Even though the replacement property must be acquired by the taxpayer, it can still so qualify if it is used for the same or similar use by a person related to the taxpayer.[314] It should be noted that the replacement property need not be property of the same class as the former property. If the property was used by the taxpayer or a person related to the taxpayer for earning business income, the replacement must be acquired for use by the taxpayer or a person related to the taxpayer for earning income from the same or a similar business as that for which the former property was used. It would appear that the related person using the replacement property need not be the same related person as that using the former property.

If the former property was taxable Canadian property (or would have been taxable Canadian property if the taxpayer had been a non-resident throughout the year in which the former property was disposed of and the former property was used in a business carried on by the taxpayer), the replacement property must also be taxable Canadian property (or what would have been taxable Canadian property if the taxpayer were a non-resident throughout the year of acquisition and the replacement property were used in a business carried on by the taxpayer). Essentially, this means that buildings located in Canada or capital property used in carrying on a business in Canada must be replaced with property with such a Canadian location or use. For dispositions occurring in taxation years ending after 1997, if the former property was taxable Canadian property that was not "treaty-protected property", the replacement property must similarly be taxable Canadian property that is not treaty-protected property. Treaty-protected property is essentially property the income or gain from the disposition of which, by the taxpayer at that time, would be exempt from Canadian income tax under a Canadian tax treaty.[315]

A similar election is available with respect to capital gains (see ¶5357). An election under either of these provisions is deemed to be an election under the other.[316]

[¶4465] Recapture of Representation Costs

A taxpayer is permitted to deduct amounts paid in the year for expenses of making certain representations to a governmental authority in respect of certain businesses. Alternatively, a taxpayer may elect to deduct $1/10$ of this

---

See page ii for explanation of footnotes.

[314] CCH ¶4513a; Sec. 13(4.1).

[315] CCH ¶28,312; Sec. 248(1) "treaty-protected property".

[316] CCH ¶6700, ¶6712; Sec. 44(1), 44(4).

amount for the year in question and a like deduction for each of the nine immediately following taxation years.

The election is to be made by filing a letter in duplicate with the Minister, specifying the amount. In the case of a corporation, duplicate certified copies of the resolution of the directors authorizing the election are required.[317] Where an amount has been deducted under either of these provisions, and the payment was made with respect to the capital cost of depreciable property, it is deemed to have been allowed to the taxpayer as capital cost allowance for the year or for the year in which the property was acquired, whichever is later.[318] Therefore a taxpayer is prevented from claiming a deduction for the representation costs and claiming capital cost allowance on the same amount. If the depreciable property is sold at a later date at a price in excess of the undepreciated capital cost (including the cost of representations), the excess will be recaptured.

[¶4470] Terminal Loss

[¶4475] Terminal Loss on Disposal of Assets of a Class

In addition to capital cost allowance, which is a permissive deduction, the Act provides that a taxpayer must deduct the unclaimed balance in a particular capital cost class where the taxpayer owns no assets of that class at the end of the taxation year.[319] The amount to be deducted is the "undepreciated capital cost" of that class at the end of the year, after which the undepreciated capital cost balance of that class is brought to nil.[320] This deduction is commonly referred to as a terminal loss and is mandatory unless the taxpayer acquires additional assets of that class before the end of the year. Any amount that cannot be absorbed by income in the year is carried forward as a non-capital loss. See the example illustrating terminal loss and recapture at ¶4400.

In certain cases, a particular asset will fall into a separate class and, consequently, it will not be possible to postpone recognition of a terminal loss by acquiring a similar asset. This result occurs, for example, with real estate rental property costing at least $50,000 where a separate class is prescribed for each property.[321] As discussed at ¶4120, a terminal loss deduction is denied in respect of a passenger vehicle having a cost in excess of a prescribed amount ($30,000 plus GST/HST, PST, and other provincial levies for 2001–2012). [Moreover, for taxation years ending after December 20, 2002, such a loss is denied in respect of limited period franchises, concessions, or licences under the stop-loss rules described at ¶4115.][322]

See page ii for explanation of footnotes.

[317] CCH ¶5126, ¶5137, ¶5137a; Sec. 20(1)(cc), 20(9); Reg. 4100.

[318] CCH ¶4550; Sec. 13(12).

[319] CCH ¶4902, ¶5145ae, ¶5145ba; Sec. 20(1)(a), 20(16), 20(16.1); Interp. Bul. IT-478R2.

[320] CCH ¶4562h; Sec. 13(21) "undepreciated capital cost".

[321] CCH ¶4940c; Reg. 1101(1ac).

[322] CCH ¶5145ba; Sec. 20(16.1).

¶4470

[¶4480] Assets Destroyed, Stolen, Lost, or Obsolete

Where one or more depreciable assets of a particular class, but not all the assets of the class, are destroyed during the year (e.g., by fire) or are lost, stolen, or scrapped, or simply become obsolete and are hence taken out of production, the terminal loss provisions will not operate since not all of the assets will have been disposed of.

The fact that the lost, destroyed, or obsolete asset is no longer used to produce income does not affect the taxpayer's claim for capital cost allowance. Accordingly, if not all of the assets of the class are affected and there are no insurance proceeds covering the loss, the taxpayer will be entitled to continue taking capital cost allowance on the undepreciated capital cost of the assets of the class including the cost of the lost, destroyed, or obsolete items. Where such assets are covered by insurance, however, a disposition of the assets is deemed to have been made.[323]

If all of the assets of a class are lost or become obsolete in a taxation year in circumstances which result in their effective elimination, and no proceeds of disposition are received on the loss of the last of such assets, there may be a danger that no "disposition" has taken place and that no terminal loss can be claimed. However, the CRA expresses the view that where it is satisfied that a disposition has taken place within the general meaning of the term, proceeds of zero may be used and a disposition accounted for accordingly.[324]

See also ¶4388 concerning insurance payments as proceeds of disposition.

[¶4485] Allocation of Proceeds between Land and Building

The terminal loss that would otherwise be realized on a sale of a building may be reduced where the proceeds of disposition of the building (otherwise determined) are less than the lesser of:

(a) the undepreciated capital cost, and

(b) the capital cost of the building.[325]

Where there is more than one building in the class, the undepreciated capital cost of the class will be decreased by more than the actual proceeds of disposition allocable to the building. This provision will only apply if the taxpayer disposes of a building that is depreciable property and the land on which it is situated or adjacent to it was owned by the taxpayer or a person with whom the taxpayer did not deal at arm's length.

---

[323] CCH ¶4562e; Sec. 13(21) "proceeds of disposition".

[324] CCH ¶28,069; Sec. 248(1) "disposition"; Interp. Bul. IT-460.

[325] CCH ¶4578; Sec. 13(21.1).

In general terms, this provision applies to take the amount by which the undepreciated capital cost of the building exceeds the proceeds of disposition of the building otherwise determined and applies this amount first to reduce the capital gain that would otherwise be realized on the land.

One part of the provision allocates the aggregate proceeds of disposition between land and building when both the building and the land on which it is situated and/or the land immediately contiguous to and necessary for the use of the building are sold in the same year. It is not necessary that the taxpayer who disposes of the building also be the one who disposes of the land. It is sufficient to attract the application of this provision if the land is disposed of in that year by a person who does not deal at arm's length with the taxpayer who disposed of the building. The year referred to is the taxation year of the person who disposes of the building.

Where the parcel of land that is sold is larger than need be for the use of the building, it would appear necessary to treat the parcel as two parcels of land, with this rule applying to determine the proceeds of disposition only of the portion of the land necessary to the use of the building. For these purposes, it will be necessary to allocate the total fair market value of the land and the total adjusted cost base of the land between the portion of the land that is necessary for the use of the building and the portion which is not so necessary.

In the most common circumstances, the proceeds of disposition of the building will be deemed to equal the cost amount of the building. However, if the fair market value of the building immediately before the disposition is greater than the lesser of:

(a) that cost amount, and

(b) the capital cost of building,

then the proceeds of disposition of the building will be deemed to equal that fair market value. The "cost amount" of a building is essentially the undepreciated capital cost of the building.[326]

Circumstances may arise where a building is disposed of but the related land is not disposed of in the same year. As noted above, the land on which the building is situated, or adjacent to it and necessary to its use, must have been owned previously by the taxpayer who disposed of the building or by a non-arm's length party. In these circumstances, the proceeds of disposition of the building are deemed to be the proceeds of disposition of the building otherwise determined plus $\frac{1}{2}$ of the amount by which the greater of:

(a) the cost amount of the building, and

---

[326] CCH ¶28,054; Sec. 248(1) "cost amount".

(b) the fair market value of the building immediately before the disposition

exceeds the proceeds otherwise determined.

In most cases, the proceeds of disposition of the building otherwise determined will be the fair market value of the building when the building is sold. However, where a building is torn down, the proceeds of disposition of the building may be nil while the building may have had a significant fair market value before it was torn down.

The effect of this part of the provision is to allow as a terminal loss only $^1/_2$ of the difference between the fair market value of the building and its undepreciated capital cost. If there are additional assets in the class, the undepreciated capital cost of the class is reduced by not only the actual proceeds of disposition but also by an additional amount of $^1/_2$ of that difference. Effectively, the loss on the disposition of the building is treated as a capital loss and therefore the fluctuating capital gains inclusion rates must be considered to achieve the correct income inclusion or adjustment to the undepreciated capital cost of the class.

[¶4490] Examples of Allocation of Proceeds between Land and Building

It is assumed in each of these examples that the building is the only asset in the class such that the provision operates to reduce what would otherwise be a terminal loss. If there were other buildings in the class, the amount referred to as a terminal loss that is disallowed or denied would instead be a greater than the usual reduction in the undepreciated capital cost of the class, which would have the effect of reducing the amount of capital cost allowance that would otherwise be available in the future. It is also assumed that the land related to the building is owned by the same person who owned the building and that no previous non-arm's length dispositions of the land were made. Furthermore, the capital cost of the building is assumed to be greater than its cost amount. Dispositions are considered to occur at a time when the $^1/_2$ inclusion rate applies.

Example 1: Sale of land and building

Building		Land	
UCC	$30,000	ACB	$100,000
FMV	$20,000	FMV	$150,000

The total proceeds of the land and building are $170,000. But for this deeming provision, a terminal loss of $10,000 would be realized on the building. A capital gain of $50,000 would be realized on the land with $^1/_2$ of that amount ($25,000) being included in income. There would be a net income inclusion of $15,000 after deducting the terminal loss. The deemed proceeds of disposition of the building will be determined as follows:

¶4490

Lesser of: (a) aggregate fair market values $170,000

    less: lesser of:

        ACB land $100,000

        FMV land $150,000   100,000

                                                         $70,000

and

(b) greater of:

        FMV building .... $ 20,000

        UCC building .... $ 30,000 $30,000

The deemed proceeds of disposition of the building are $30,000; therefore, no terminal loss arises. The proceeds of disposition of the land are deemed to be $140,000 ($170,000 - $30,000). A capital gain of $40,000 is realized and $1/2$ of this amount ($20,000) is included in income. The terminal loss is denied and is instead applied to reduce the capital gain on the land.

Example 2: Only building disposed of

Building	
UCC	$70,000
FMV	$20,000

If the taxpayer sold the building alone for $20,000 (combined possibly with a lease of the land), a terminal loss of $50,000 would otherwise result. However, this provision deems the proceeds of disposition to be:

The aggregate of:

(a) proceeds otherwise determined $20,000

and

(b) 1/2 of the greater of:

      -- UCC building $70,000

      -- FMV building $20,000

    less: amount in (a)

    or 1/2 ($70,000 - $20,000)   25,000

                                             $45,000

The proceeds of disposition of the building are deemed to be $45,000; and a terminal loss of $35,000 is realized.

¶4490

[¶4495] Dispositions to Affiliated Persons

The affiliated person rules supplement the concept of non-arm's length transactions (see ¶15,400 *et seq.*).[327] Essentially, these rules deny a terminal loss (or potential terminal loss) on dispositions to affiliated persons (see ¶15,445) until there is a final arm's length disposition or an event occurs in the disposing corporation which triggers recognition of gains and losses. Under the rules, where:

(a) a corporation, trust, or partnership (the transferor) disposes of depreciable property of a prescribed class (other than certain deemed dispositions arising from death, the expiry of an option, change of use of property, etc.),

(b) the tax cost of the property exceeds its proceeds of disposition to the transferor otherwise determined (the tax cost is the lesser of capital cost and the portion of undepreciated capital cost that the fair market value of the property is of the fair market value of all property of the class; and

(c) the transferor or an affiliated person (¶15,445) owns or has a right to acquire the property (other than a security right under a mortgage, sale agreement, or the like) on the 30th day after the transfer,

the transferor is deemed to have disposed of the property for proceeds equal to its tax cost, so any terminal loss or potential terminal loss in the class is denied, and proceeds of disposition equal to the tax cost must be credited to the CCA pool. However, the transferor is also deemed to continue to own a property with a capital cost equal to the loss denied (that is, to the excess of tax cost over proceeds of disposition). When this notional property is disposed of (on a final non-affiliated disposition of the original property), the loss denied will be crystallized in the hands of the transferor. In the meantime, the notional property continues to be available in the particular capital cost allowance class of the original property.

The transferee (which can be the transferor through a series of transactions) acquires the property at its actual or deemed cost (typically fair market value) but is deemed for capital cost allowance and terminal loss purposes to have acquired it at its original cost to the transferor, and to have previously deducted capital cost allowance equal to capital cost in excess of fair market value. This provides for potential recapture to the transferee on final disposition. The effect of this machinery is to divide the remaining undepreciated capital cost (UCC) between the transferee and the transferor.

Example:

Corporation A sells a depreciable property to affiliated person B (perhaps the individual who owns A). The property had a cost of 100, a UCC immediately before disposition of 70, and a fair market value of 50.

See page ii for explanation of footnotes.

[327] CCH ¶4579c; Sec. 13(21.2).

On the transfer, A will be deemed to have received proceeds of disposition of 70, credited to the class. However, A also is deemed to have previously acquired a property of the same class (or, for an interim transaction where an election has been made, a separate prescribed class of the same class) for the loss denied, which is 20 (UCC of 70 minus proceeds of 50). A will be able to depreciate this notional property.

B acquires the property at 50 (under the general non-arm's length rules) but is deemed to have originally acquired the property at 100 and to have already claimed 50 (original cost of 100 minus fair market value of 50) as depreciation. Thus the property will in effect have a UCC of 50 upon which capital cost allowance can be claimed. On a final disposition there is potential for recapture as well as terminal loss.

When there is finally a non-affiliated disposition, actual or deemed, A will be deemed to no longer own the notional property with its remaining UCC of 20 less any further depreciation claimed. Presumably, there are no further deemed proceeds to A, so at that point it may realize a terminal loss if there is no other property in the class (as will certainly be the case if the class is a separate class). If the property has appreciated, B will suffer the recapture; if not, B will also have an appropriate reduction of class UCC, or a terminal loss.

The notional property is deemed to be owned by the transferor until immediately before the earliest of the following triggering events:

(a) a subsequent disposition of the transferred property so that neither the transferor nor an affiliated person of the transferor owns the property, provided that neither owns the property or a right to acquire the property throughout the 30-day period after that subsequent disposition;

(b) a change in use of the transferred property, where it is not used by the transferor or an affiliated person for the purpose of earning income, and is used for another purpose;

(c) upon the transferor becoming a non-resident, or if the transferor is a corporation, upon the corporation becoming or ceasing to be exempt from Part 1 tax;

(d) where the transferor is a corporation, immediately before the acquisition of control of the transferor by a person or group of persons; or

(e) a winding-up of the transferor, except where it is wound up into a parent corporation.

Upon the occurrence of the earliest of these events, the transferor is no longer deemed to own the notional depreciable property. Therefore, if the transferor does not own any other depreciable property in the same class, it can claim a terminal loss, which will normally equal the previously denied terminal loss minus any CCA claimed in the interim in respect of the notional depreciable property. The subsequent owner of the transferred property (the affiliated person owning the property on the 30th day following the disposition of the property by the transferor) inherits the transferor's capital cost of the property, and is deemed to have claimed CCA on the amount of such capital cost in excess of its fair market value at the time of the disposition.

¶4495

If the transferor of the transferred property is a partnership that otherwise ceases to exist before one of the triggering events occurs, the partnership is deemed to continue to exist, and the members of the partnership to continue to be members, until immediately after the triggering event occurs. Therefore, any terminal loss previously denied on the transfer of the property is allowed at the time of the triggering event and is in turn flowed out to the former partners in the regular manner accorded to partnership income and loss.

[¶4500] Alphabetical Table of Rates

[¶4505] Alphabetical List of Assets — Capital Cost Allowance Classes and Rates

The following table sets out the capital cost allowance rates and classes for certain types of assets — listed alphabetically. This table is for use only as a quick reference guide. See Part XI and Schedules II, III, IV, V, and VI of the Income Tax Regulations for detailed rules relating to capital cost allowance.

Item	Rate	Class
Access roads and trails for the protection of standing timber	30%	10
Air conditioning equipment (other than window units) — same rate as building[1]		
Aircraft[16]	25%	9
furniture and fittings	25%	9
hangars[1]	10%	6
Airplane runways[16]	8%	17
Amusement park components (including fences, bridges, canals, stalls, tractors, etc.)	15%	37
land improvements[39]	15%	37
Apparel, used for earning rental income[1,26]	100%	12
Asphalt surface, storage yard[16]	8%	17
Assets, tangible capital[1,2]	20%	8
used primarily in manufacturing or processing[10,15]		29, 39, 40, 43
Automobiles[1]	30%	10
acquired after June 17, 1987 in excess of prescribed amount (Reg. 7307(1))[1,7]	30%	10.1
for lease or rental[22]	40%	16
Automotive equipment[1]	30%	10

Item	Rate	Class
designed for and used in amusement parks	15%	37
Bar code scanners — see Cash registers		
Billboards		
acquired before 1988	35%	11
acquired after 1987 [10]	20%	8
Boats — see Vessels		
Boilers		
heating use — same rate as building		
used primarily in manufacturing or processing [10, 15]		29, 39, 43
Books of lending libraries [26]	100%	12
Breakwaters		
wooden	10%	6
other	5%	3
Bridges [1]	4%	1
Buildings [1]		
addition or alteration — same class as buildings [13]		
amusement park stalls	15%	37
brick, stone, cement, etc., acquired before 1988	5%	3
brick, stone, cement, etc., acquired after 1987	4%	1
component parts — generally same class as building (see individual items)		
farm ensilage storage	20%	8
foundation excavation — same rate as building		
frame, log, stucco on frame, galvanized iron or corrugated metal [25]	10%	6
kiln, tank, vat used in manufacturing or processing	20%	8
manufacturing or processing [43]	4%	1
mining (except refineries and office buildings not at mine)	30%	10
multiple-unit residential [7, 18]		
non-residential [43]	4%	1
portable camp	30%	10
rental property [7]		
storage of fresh fruits and vegetables	20%	8
Buses	30%	10

¶4505

Item	Rate	Class
Cable TV converters and descramblers		
acquired before Mar. 5, 2010	30%	10
acquired after Mar. 4, 2010	40%	30
Cables — telephone, telegraph or data communication		
acquired before Feb. 23, 2005	5%	3
acquired after Feb. 22, 2005	12%	42
fibre optic	12%	42
Calculator	20%	8
Canals [1]	4%	1
Canoes	15%	7
Capital tangible assets [1,2]	20%	8
used primarily in manufacturing or processing [10,15]		29, 39, 40, 43
Cash registers	20%	8
electronic, to record multiple sales taxes acquired after Aug. 8, 1989 and before 1993	100%	12
Catalyst [21]	5%	26
Cattle	nil	—
Chinaware [26]	100%	12
Cold storage structures	20%	8
Computer hardware and systems software		
acquired before Mar. 23, 2004 [30]	30%	10
acquired after Mar. 22, 2004 and before Mar. 19, 2007 [44]	45%	45
acquired after Mar. 18, 2007 [44]	55%	50
acquired after Jan 27, 2009 and before Feb. 2011 [44]	100%	52
Computer software [10,16,24,30]	100%	12
Condominiums — same rate as buildings		
Concessions, for a limited period		14
Contractors' movable equipment, heavy	30%	10
acquired before 1988 [5]	50%	22
acquired after 1987 [5,10]	30%	38
Conversion cost — see Vessels		
Copyrights, for a limited period		14
Costume and accessories for earning rental income [1,26]	100%	12

Item	Rate	Class
Culverts [1, 10]	4%	1
Cutlery [26]	100%	12
Cutting part of a machine [1, 27]	100%	12
Dams [1]	4%	1
Data communication equipment — wire and cable		
acquired before Feb. 23, 2005	5%	3
acquired after Feb. 22, 2005	12%	42
Data communication switching equipment [16]	8%	17
Dental instruments costing less than $500 [29]	100%	12
Deuterium enriched water [21]	5%	26
Dies [1, 27]	100%	12
Digital video disk — See DVD		
Display fixtures (window)	20%	8
Distribution equipment for heat, electrical energy, or water [4]		
acquired before 1988	6%	2
acquired after 1987	4%	1
for water or steam, acquired after Feb. 27, 2000	8%	17
for electrical energy, acquired after Feb. 22, 2005 [34]	8%	47
Docks [1]	5%	3
Drive-in theatre property	30%	10
DVD, for rental [23, 26]	100%	12
Electrical advertising signs [10, 16]	20%	8
Electrical generating and distributing equipment [6, 10]		
acquired before 1988 [4]	6%	2
acquired after 1987	4%	1
acquired after Feb. 27, 2000 for generation [10]	8%	17
acquired after Feb. 22, 2005 for transmission or distribution [34]	8%	47
combustion turbines acquired after Feb. 22, 2005 [34]	15%	48
energy efficient generating equipment [19, 34, 35]	50%, 30%, 50%	34, 43.1, 43.2
portable or maximum load 15 kw	20%	8
Electric wiring — same rate as building		
Electronic communications equipment including fax machines and telephone equipment [10]	20%	8

Item	Rate	Class
Electronic data processing equipment [1, 15, 16, 30]		
used primarily in manufacturing or processing [15]		10, 29, 40
Electronic data processing equipment — data network infrastructure and systems software		
acquired before Mar. 23, 2004 [10]	20%	8
acquired after Mar. 22, 2004	30%	46
Electronic data processing equipment — general purpose and systems software		
acquired before Mar. 23, 2004 [10]	30%	10
acquired after Mar. 22, 2004 and before Mar. 19, 2007 [44]	45%	45
acquired after Mar. 18, 2007 [44]	55%	50
acquired after Jan 27, 2009 and before Feb. 2011 [44]	100%	52
Elevators — same rate as building		
Equipment (see specific types)		
if not specifically mentioned [2]	20%	8
manufacturing or processing [10, 15]		29, 39, 40, 43
Escalators — same rate as building		
Farming and fishing assets [38]		
Fences [1]	10%	6
Fibre optic cable	12%	42
Films, motion pictures [16]	30%	10
Canadian production [7, 36]	30%	10
certified production [36]	100%	12
certified production acquired after 1987 and before March 1996 [7, 36]	30%	10
television commercials	100%	12
Franchises, for a limited period		14
Furniture (not otherwise listed) [15]	20%	8
Gas manufacturing and distributing equipment, plants and pipelines [4, 8]		
acquired before 1988 [10]	6%	2
acquired after 1987	4%	1
distribution pipelines acquired after Mar. 18, 2007 [33]	6%	51
liquefied natural gas facilities acquired after Mar. 18, 2007 [34]	8%	47

Item	Rate	Class
transmission pipelines acquired after Feb. 22, 2005 [10,33]	8%	49
Gas well equipment		
acquired after 1987	25%	41
acquired before 1988	30%	10
Generating equipment and plant of producer or distributor of electrical energy [4,6]		
acquired before 1988	6%	2
acquired after 1987	4%	1
acquired after Feb. 27, 2000	8%	17
energy efficient [34,35]	30%, 50%	43.1, 43.2
wave and tidal energy equipment [34,35]	30%, 50%	43.1, 43.2
Glass tableware [1,26]	100%	12
Grain drying machinery [11]	20%	8
Grain storage facilities — see buildings [11]		
Greenhouses [1]	10%	6
rigid frame with plastic cover	20%	8
Hangars [1]	10%	6
Harness equipment [1]	30%	10
Heat production and recovery equipment [19,34,35]	50%, 30%, 50%	34, 43.1, 43.2
Heating equipment		
distribution plant, acquired before 1988	6%	2
distribution plant, acquired after 1987	4%	1
general — same rate as building		
solar or energy efficient, acquired before Feb. 22, 1994 [19,34]	50%	34
solar or energy efficient, acquired after Feb. 21, 1994 [19,34,35]	30%, 50%	43.1, 43.2
Heavy water [21]	5%	26
Herbs	nil	—
Horses	nil	—
Instruments, dental or medical costing less than $500 [1,26,29]	100%	12
Jetties [16]	5%	3
wood	10%	6
Jigs [1,27]	100%	12
Kitchen utensils costing less than $500 [1,26,29]	100%	12

Item	Rate	Class
Land	nil	—
deemed depreciable[7]	nil	36
Lasts[1,27]	100%	12
Leasehold interest		13
Lending library books[1,26]	100%	12
Licences, for a limited period		14
Lighting fixture — same rate as building		
Linen[1,26]	100%	12
Logging mechanical equipment[3]	30%	10
Machinery and equipment		
additional capital cost allowance on grain elevators[11]	14%	8
not specifically listed[2]	20%	8
used primarily in manufacturing or processing[10,15]		29, 39, 40, 43
Marine railways	15%	7
Medical instruments costing less than $500[1,26,29]	100%	12
Mining equipment	30%	10
Mining equipment, acquired after Feb. 25, 1992 for processing foreign ore in Canada	30%	43
Mining equipment, new or expanded mines[7,14]		
acquired before 1988	30%	28
acquired after 1987	25%	41
oil sands property acquired after March 18, 2007	25%	41.1
Moles[1,16]	5%	3
Motion picture drive-in theatres	30%	10
Motion picture films — see Films		
Moulds[1,27]	100%	12
Multiple-unit residential buildings[7,18]	5%, 10%	31, 32
Office equipment[30]	20%	8
Offshore drilling platforms		
acquired before 1988	30%	10
acquired after 1987	25%	41
Offshore drilling vessels[7,16,17]		
acquired before 1988	15%	7

Item	Rate	Class
acquired after 1987	25%	41
Oil pipelines		
acquired before 1988 [8, 10]	6%	2
acquired after 1987	4%	1
acquired after Feb. 22, 2005 — transmission [33]	8%	49
Oil sands — see Mining equipment, new or expanded mines		
Oil storage tanks [1, 15]	10%	6
used primarily in manufacturing or processing [15]		29, 39, 43
Oil well equipment [1]		
acquired before 1988	30%	10
acquired after 1987 [14]	25%	41
Overburden removal cost, designated [1, 26]	100%	12
Parking area [16]	8%	17
Passenger vehicles — see Automobiles		
Patents [20]		14
	25%	44
Patterns [1, 27]	100%	12
Photocopy machines [10, 15, 30]	20%	8
Pinball machines — see Video games		
Pipelines		
acquired before 1988 [8, 10]	6%	2
acquired after 1987	4%	1
acquired after February 22, 2005 and used for transmission of oil and natural gas [33]	8%	49
acquired after March 18, 2007 for distribution of natural gas [33]	6%	51
acquired after Feb. 25, 2008 for transmission of carbon dioxide	8%	49
Plumbing — same rate as building		
Pollution control equipment [12]		
air, certified, acquired before 1999	50%	27
water, certified, acquired before 1999	50%	24
not specifically listed — Class 1, 2, 6, 8, or 43 depending on type of asset		
Portable construction camp buildings	30%	10

Item	Rate	Class
Portable electrical generating equipment [16]	20%	8
Portable equipment used for temporary rentals	30%	10
Power operated movable equipment [5, 15]		
acquired before 1988	50%	22
acquired after 1987	30%	38
Power plants — see Electrical power plants		
Production equipment of distributor of heat (including structures)		
acquired before 1988 [4]	6%	2
acquired after 1987	4%	1
acquired after Feb. 27, 2000	8%	17
Pumping and compression equipment		
Gas and oil acquired before Feb. 23, 2005	20%	8
Gas and oil acquired after Feb. 22, 2005 [10, 33]	15%	7
Carbon dioxide acquired after Feb. 25, 2008 [33]	15%	7
Radar equipment [16]	20%	8
Radio communication equipment (excluding satellites) [16]	20%	8
Radium	nil	—
Railway car and rail suspension devices [1, 7, 16, 31]		
acquired before Feb. 28, 2000 [31]	7%	35
acquired after Feb. 27, 2000 [31]	15%	7
Railway locomotive (excluding automotive railway car) [16]		
acquired after May 25, 1976 [16, 31]	10%	6
acquired after February 27, 2000 [31]	15%	7
acquired after February 25, 2008 [31]	30%	10
Railway, marine	15%	7
Railway track or grading [1, 7, 31]	4%	1
Railway traffic control or signalling equipment [1, 7, 16, 31]	4%	1
Rapid transit car [40]	20%	8
Refrigeration equipment	20%	8
Renewable energy generation equipment [6, 19, 34, 35]		
acquired after February 21, 1994	30%	43.1
acquired after Feb. 22, 2005 and before 2020 [35]	50%	43.2
Rental property [7]		

Item	Rate	Class
Roads [1,16]	8%	17
acquired in relation to a mine	25%	41
forestry (may be depreciated with timber limit) [3]		
oil and gas mining temporary access [41]		
Roller rink floors	30%	10
Rowboats	15%	7
Satellites [7]		
acquired before 1988	40%	30
acquired after 1987	30%	10
Scanners, bar codes, acquired after Aug. 8, 1989 and before 1993	100%	12
Scows	15%	7
Shaping part of a machine [1,27]	100%	12
Ships, including ships under construction [17]	15%	7
Shrubs	nil	—
Sidewalks [16]	8%	17
Sleighs [1]	30%	10
Solar heating equipment [19]		
acquired before Feb. 22, 1994 [34]	50%	34
acquired after Feb. 21, 1994 [34,35]	30%	43.1
acquired after Feb. 22, 2005 and before 2020 [34,35]	50%	43.2
Spacecraft (telecommunication) [7]		
acquired before 1988	40%	30
acquired after 1987	30%	10
Spare parts for an aircraft [16]	25%	9
Sprinkler systems — same rate as building		
Stable equipment [1]	30%	10
Storage area [16]	8%	17
Storage tanks, oil or water [1]	10%	6
direct manufacturing use [15]		29, 39, 43
Subway or tunnel [1,16]	4%	1
Systems software — general purpose electronic data processing equipment [1,16,44]		
acquired before Mar. 23, 2004 [10]	30%	10

Item	Rate	Class
acquired after Mar. 22, 2004 and before Mar. 19 2007 [44]	45%	45
acquired after Mar. 18, 2007 [44]	55%	50
acquired after Jan 27, 2009 and before Feb. 2011 [44]	100%	52
primary manufacturing purpose, acquired after March 18, 2007 and before January 28, 2009 [15, 44]		10, 29, 40
Tableware, glass [1, 26]	100%	12
Tangible capital assets [1, 2]	20%	8
Tank cars, railway [1, 7, 16]	7%	35
Tanks, oil and water storage [1]	10%	6
used primarily in manufacturing or processing [15]		29, 39, 43
Taxicabs [16]	40%	16
Telecommunication spacecraft [7]		
acquired before 1988	40%	30
acquired after 1987	30%	10
Telegraph and telephone equipment, wires and cables [16]		
acquired before Feb. 23, 2005 [1, 16]	5%	3
new and acquired after Feb. 22, 2005	12%	42
poles and masts [1, 16]	5%	3
fibre optic cable	12%	42
Telephone or telegraph communication non-electronic switching equipment [16]	8%	17
Telephone system (purchased) [30]	20%	8
Television aerial [16]	20%	8
Television commercials	100%	12
Television set-top boxes	40%	30
Cable acquired before March 5, 2010		
Cable acquired after March 4, 2010		
Satellite acquired before March 5, 2010		
Satellite acquired after March 4, 2010		
Timber cutting and removing equipment [3]		10, 15
Timber limits — see Sched. VI of the Income Tax Regulations [3, 7]		
Timber resource property [3]	15%	33
Tools costing less than $500 [1, 26, 29]	100%	12
Tractors [1]	30%	10

Item	Rate	Class
for hauling freight[28]	40%	16
Trailers[1,37]	30%	10
Tramways[4,9]	6%	4
Trees	nil	—
Trestles[1]	5%	3
Trolley bus	30%	10
Trolley bus system[4]	6%	4
Trucks, automotive[1]	30%	10
for hauling freight[28]	40%	16
Tunnel[1,16]	4%	1
Uniforms[1,26]	100%	12
Vessels[7,17]	15%	7
furniture, fittings and spare engines[17]	15%	7
offshore drilling after 1987[32]	25%	41
Video cassettes, video laser disks and DVDs[23,26]	100%	12
Video games (coin operated) acquired after Feb. 15, 1984	40%	16
Video tapes[1,16]	30%	10
television commercial	100%	12
Wagons[1]	30%	10
Water pipelines		
acquired before 1988[10]	6%	2
acquired after 1987	4%	1
Water pollution control equipment — see Pollution control equipment		
Water storage tanks[1]	10%	6
primary manufacturing purpose[15]		
Water distribution plant and equipment[4]		
acquired before 1988	6%	2
acquired after 1987	4%	1
Well equipment, oil or gas (for use above ground)		
acquired after 1987	25%	41
acquired before 1988	30%	10
oil sands property acquired after Mar. 18, 2007	25%	41.1
Wharves[1]	5%	3

¶4505

Item	Rate	Class
wooden [1]	10%	6
Wind energy conversion system [19]		
acquired before Feb. 22, 1994	50%	34
acquired after Feb. 21, 1994 [34,35]	30%	43.1
acquired after Feb. 22, 2005 and before 2020 [34,35]	50%	43.2
Windmills [1,42]	5%	3
Wiring, electric — same rate as building		

Notes:

[1] Unless included in another class of assets subject to a different rate.

[2] Not applicable to land, animals, herbs, trees, shrubs or similar growing things, gas wells, mines, oil wells, radium, rights of way, timber limits, tramway track or certain vessels.

[3] See IT-481 and IT-501 regarding timber limits, timber resource property, and logging assets.

[4] Except property included in Class 10, 13, 14, 26 or 28. For distributors of gas, not including a property acquired to produce or distribute gas normally distributed in portable containers, to process natural gas before its delivery to a gas distribution system and to produce oxygen or nitrogen. See also under Gas manufacturing and distribution equipment, plants and pipelines; and Pipelines.

[5] Power-operated and designed for the purpose of excavating, moving, placing or compacting earth, rock, concrete or asphalt.

[6] Electrical generating equipment may be allocated to one of the following different classes: Class 1, if large and acquired by a producer; Class 2, if acquired before 1988; Class 8, if small; Class 9, if acquired before May 26, 1976 and not owned by a producer; or Class 17, if new and acquired after February 27, 2000 (with certain exclusions). Energy-efficient equipment may be in Class 34, if acquired before February 22, 1994; Class 43.1, if acquired after February 21, 1994; or Class 43.2 if acquired after February 22, 2005 and before 2020, and certain requirements are met (see note 35). Only a detailed reading of the classes can determine the appropriate one; see Schedule II of the Income Tax Regulations. If used in manufacturing or processing, see note 15.

[7] Separate classes may be required for each asset, including: certain rental properties costing $50,000 or more; automobiles in Class 10.1; certain vessels, including Canadian vessels and offshore drilling vessels; and Class 28, 41 or 41.1 property relating to a particular mine or group of mines. See Regulation 1101 for the provisions regarding separate classes.

[8] Unless, in the case of a pipeline for oil or natural gas, the Minister is satisfied that the main source of supply for the business is likely to be exhausted within 15 years; such pipelines, not being specifically listed, fall under the general rate of 20% (Class 8).

[9] Tramway tracks: 100% on cessation of tramcar operation.

[10] Separate class elections may be available for certain assets or groups of assets, including: non-residential buildings in Class 1; certain electronic equipment in Class 8; transmission pipelines in Class 49; and equipment relating to transmission pipelines in Class 7. See Regulation 1101 for the provisions regarding separate classes.

[11] A grain elevator or addition to a grain elevator situated in "Eastern Canada", acquired after April 1, 1972 and before August 1, 1974, is entitled to an additional allowance equal to the lesser of: 22% (Class 3), 20% (Class 6), or 14% (Class 8) of the lesser of $15,000 and the capital cost; or the undepreciated capital cost at the end of the taxation year before the allowance. New grain drying equipment for a farm acquired after July 31, 1968 and before January 1, 1970 or after April 1, 1972 but before August 1, 1974 may be depreciated at the rate equal to the lesser of 14% of the capital cost or $15,000.

[12] Certified pollution control equipment in Class 24 or 27 is depreciated 25/50/25 over three years for additions made before 1999. If not certified, the equipment may be Class 8, 39 or 43 if used primarily in manufacturing, or Class 1, 3 or 6, depending on its nature.

[13] An addition or alteration to a building originally placed in Class 3, 6 or 20, but which would no longer be in that class under current rules, may be added to the old class within certain dollar and transitional rule limitations. See IT-79R3 and Regulation 1102(19).

[14] Qualifying assets are included in a special class for each mine. The full amount of undepreciated capital cost up to the amount of income from a mine may be claimed on property for new or expanded mines. This

additional allowance is being phased out for oil sands property acquired after March 18, 2007. See paragraphs 1100(1)(w) to (ya.1) of the Income Tax Regulations.

[15] Specified property used primarily in manufacturing or processing may be allocated to one of the following classes: Class 29 (25%/50%/25% straight line), if acquired after March 18, 2007 and before 2014; Class 43 (30%), if acquired after February 25, 1992 and before March 19, 2007 or after 2013; and Class 39 if acquired after 1987 and before February 26, 1992. (Class 40 applied for certain property acquired in 1988 or 1989.). See note 44 for general-purpose electronic data processing equipment and system software used primarily in manufacturing or processing (Class 29 if acquired after March 18, 2007 and before January 28, 2009). The description of the specified property varies depending on the date it is acquired and the class. See the descriptions of the classes in Schedule II of the Income Tax Regulations.

[16] Acquired after May 25, 1976. Property of this type acquired before May 26, 1976 may be in a different class. See Schedule II of the Income Tax Regulations.

[17] Accelerated capital cost allowances of 33 1/3% are provided on certain prescribed vessels and conversion costs (generally, Canadian vessels and furniture and fittings attached thereto). See Regulations 1100(1)(va) and 1101(2a).

[18] Multiple-unit residential buildings acquired after June 17, 1987 are Class 1(4%). Such buildings acquired before June 18, 1987 that would otherwise be included in Class 3 or 6 and in respect of which a certificate is issued by the Canada Mortgage and Housing Corporation are Class 31 (5%). Such buildings acquired before 1980 that would otherwise be in Class 6 are Class 32 (10%).

[19] Such property acquired after May 25, 1976 and before February 21, 1994 is Class 34. Such assets acquired after this date are eligible for CCA at 30% in Class 43.1. Certain Class 43.1 assets acquired after February 22, 2005 and before 2020 may be eligible for a CCA rate of 50% in Class 43.2. See Regulation 1102(16.1) that would allow a taxpayer to elect Class 29 treatment for property acquired after March 18, 2007 and before 2014 that would otherwise be in Class 43.1 or Class 43.2 and is used in manufacturing or processing.

[20] Patents for a limited or unlimited period acquired after April 26, 1993 are in Class 44 (25%). Patents for a limited period acquired before April 27, 1993 are in Class 14, written off on a straight-line basis over the the life of the patent, but a taxpayer can elect out of Class 44 into Class 14 for limited period patents acquired after April 26, 1993.

[21] The heavy water must be acquired after May 22, 1979. Prior to May 23, 1979, a catalyst was depreciable at 1%.

[22] Automobiles acquired after November 12, 1981 for lease or rental other than to any one person for more than 30 days in a 12-month period.

[23] Items must be acquired for the purpose of renting to any one person for no more than 7 days in any 30-day period.

[24] Computer software in Class 12 is subject to the half-year rule. Systems software is in Class 10, 29, 45, 50, or 52, depending on the date acquired. See note 44.

[25] Building must be used in farming or fishing business, or be unsupported below the ground, or have been acquired before 1979.

[26] The half-year rule does not apply to this item. It may be written off in full in the first year claimed.

[27] The half-year rule applies to assets of this description acquired after December 31, 1987. Prior acquisitions could be written off at 100% in the first year claimed.

[28] Trucks or tractors acquired after December 6, 1991 that have a gross vehicle weight rating in excess of 11,788 kg.

[29] Tools, kitchen utensils, and medical and dental instruments costing more than the $500 limit are Class 8. The limit was $200 for tools, kitchen utensils, and medical and dental instruments acquired before May 2, 2006. Portable tools acquired to earn short-term rental income are Class 10 (30%).

[30] May be eligible for a separate class. Up to $50,000 of computer expenditures (hardware and software combined) may be eligible for 100% deduction in year of acquisition if acquired by a small or medium-sized business in the period January 1, 1998 to October 31, 1999 to deal with year 2000 problems.

[31] Railway equipment may be subject to additional allowances over and above the class rate. Railway locomotives, railway cars and railway suspension devices acquired after February 27, 2000, (other than property included in paragraph (y) of Class 10) are eligible for Class 7 (15%) rather than a combined rate of 10% or 13% (7% + additional allowance of 3% or 6%) previously available for Class 35 assets. Leased assets are included in Class 7 (15%) only if the lessor elects specified leasing property treatment. Railway locomotives acquired after February 25, 2008 and not used previously by any taxpayer for any purpose are Class 10(y) (30%)

[32] After November 7, 2001, Class 41 for offshore drilling vessels is not available if the Minister of Industry has agreed to a structured financing facility. In such a case, the maximum CCA rate applicable to the vessel and its attachments will be 15% under Class 7 (see Regulation 1101(2c)).

[33] Class 49 applies to new transmission pipelines. Taxpayers may elect in the year the pipelines are acquired, to place them in a separate CCA class. The rate for new natural gas distribution pipelines acquired after March 18, 2007 changed from Class 1 (4%) to Class 51 (6%). Eligible assets will include control and monitoring devices, valves, metering and regulating equipment and other equipment ancillary to a distribution pipeline, but not buildings or other structures. See Class 7 for pumping and compression equipment used to move product along a transmission pipeline.

[34] Specified energy property rules may apply. See Regulations 1100(24) to (29).

[35] Class 43.2 (50%) applies to certain assets in Class 43.1 (30%) if they are acquired after February 22, 2005 and before 2020. Co-generation equipment described in paragraphs (a) to (c) of Class 43.1 will be eligible for Class 43.2 if the equipment has a heat rate attributable to fossil fuel not exceeding 4,750 BTU (Class 43.1 allows up to 6,000 BTU). Paragraph (d) of Class 43.1 sets out various other types of renewable energy assets that are eligible for Class 43.2, including active solar equipment, geothermal equipment, photovoltaic equipment, ground source heat pump systems, wind energy conversion systems, equipment used to collect landfill gas and digester gas, equipment used to generate heat energy from eligible waste fuel, and equipment used to produce and store biogas.

[36] Additional allowance and separate class treatment available in certain circumstances. For 1995 and subsequent taxation years, the accelerated CCA incentive for Canadian-owned film or video productions was replaced by a Canadian Film or Video Production Tax Credit under section 125.4 of the *Income Tax Act*. For taxation years ending after October 1997, other film or video productions may qualify for the Film or Video Production Services Tax Credit in section 125.5 of the *Income Tax Act*.

[37] Includes trailers designed for use on both highways and railway tracks.

[38] A straight-line method may be used for assets acquired before 1972 and used in a farming or fishing business.

[39] This item excludes landscaping costs deductible under paragraph 20(1)(aa) of the Act.

[40] Used for public transportation within a metropolitan area and not part of a railway system.

[41] Temporary access roads in the oil and gas mining sectors may qualify as Canadian exploration or development expenses.

[42] Not to be confused with wind energy conversion systems included in Class 43.1 or 43.2.

[43] Additional allowances are available for buildings in Class 1 acquired after May 18, 2007 (including new buildings which are under construction on March 19, 2007) that are used at least 90% (measured by square footage) for manufacturing or processing in Canada or for other non-residential purposes at the end of the year. The additional allowances are 6% for such a building used for manufacturing or processing and 2% for other non-residential buildings. In each case, the building is required to be placed in a separate class in order to claim the additional allowance.

[44] Class 52 (100%) applies to certain general-purpose electronic data processing equipment and systems software for that equipment, acquired after January 27, 2009 and before February 2011 (i.e., situated in Canada and not previously used). Property that is general-purpose electronic data processing equipment and systems software for that equipment is included in Class 29 if acquired after March 18, 2007 and before January 28, 2009 and used primarily in manufacturing or processing. Property that is general-purpose electronic data processing equipment and systems software for that equipment acquired after March 18, 2007, that is not in Class 29 or Class 52, is Class 50 (55%). Such property acquired after March 22, 2004 and before March 19, 2007 is Class 45 (45%).

Chapter V

Capital Gains and Losses

General **5000**	"Capital Property" Defined 5040
Introduction 5001	Meaning of "Eligible Capital
How Capital Gains and	Property" 5045
Losses Are Taxed 5002	Meaning of "Listed Personal
Lifetime Capital Gains	Property" 5050
Exemption **5005**	Meaning of "Personal-Use
Available Exemption over	Property" 5055
the Years 5008	Meaning of "Depreciable
Election for Property Owned	Property" 5060
on February 22, 1994 5010	Meaning of "Cultural
Special Election for Flow-	Property" 5065
Through Entities 5011	Meaning of "Disposition" 5070
Effect of Election on	Meaning of "Proceeds of
Principal Residence	Disposition" 5075
Exemption 5014	Meaning of "Adjusted Cost
Time for Election 5015	Base" 5080
Exemption for Gains from	Meaning of "Principal
Qualified Farm or Fishing	Residence" 5085
Property 5021	Superficial Losses 5090
Small Business Corporation	Meaning of "Taxable
Shares 5022	Canadian Property" —
Capital Gains Deferral for	Non-Residents 5095
Investment in Small	**Distinguishing between**
Business **5025**	**Business Income and**
Permitted Deferral 5026	**Capital Receipts** **5100**
Qualifying Dispositions 5027	Major Factors Involved 5105
Calculating the Capital	Real Estate Transactions 5110
Gains Deferral 5028	Real Estate — Farm
Capital Gain Deferral and	Transactions 5115
ACB Reduction 5029	**Valuation Day** **5125**
Definitions **5030**	General 5130
Meaning of "Capital Gain" 5031	Valuation Day Value —
Meaning of "Capital Loss" 5032	Median Rule or Tax-Free-
Meaning of "Taxable	Zone Method 5135
Capital Gain" and	**Calculation of Gain or Loss** **5140**
"Allowable Capital Loss" 5033	Taxpayer's Gain or Loss 5145
Meaning of "Business	Partial Dispositions of
Investment Loss" 5034	Property 5150
Meaning of "Property" 5035	

427

**Reserves for Future
Proceeds** **5155**

Reserve for Proceeds Not
Due Until After End of the
Year 5160

Reserve for Gift of Non-
Qualifying Security 5162

**Calculation of Adjusted
Cost Base** **5165**

Cost of Property 5170

Adjusted Cost Base and
Deemed Gain 5175

Additions to Adjusted Cost
Base 5180

Deductions from Adjusted
Cost Base 5185

Adjustments to Cost Base
— Partnership Interest 5190

Adjusted Cost Base — Non-
Arm's Length Transfer of
Pre-1972 Capital
Property 5195

**Limitations on Gains and
Losses** **5200**

Prizes from Lottery
Schemes, Pool System
Betting, and Giveaway
Contests 5205

Losses on Transfers to
Registered Retirement
Savings Plans (RRSPs)
and Other Trusts 5210

Losses of a Corporation on
Dispositions to Affiliated
Persons 5217

Loss When Provincial
Assistance Is Received 5220

**Foreign Currencies, Bonds,
Canadian Securities, Tax
Credits** **5225**

Capital Gains and Losses
in Respect of Foreign
Currencies 5230

CRA Yearly Average
Conversion Rates for U.S.
Dollar and U.K. Pound
Sterling 5233

Capital Gains and Losses
— Purchase of Bonds by
Issuer 5235

Disposition of Canadian
Securities 5240

Principal Residence **5255**

Principal Residence —
Exemption for Gains on
Sale 5260

Meaning of "Principal
Residence" 5265

Election Where Change in
Use of Principal
Residence 5270

Principal Residence
Designation 5275

Disposition of Farmland
Including Principal
Residence 5280

Principal Residence
Transferred to
Spouse/Common-Law
Partner or Spousal Trust 5285

Principal Residence in
Satisfaction of Interest in
a Trust 5290

Personal-Use Property **5295**

"Personal-Use Property"
Defined 5300

Capital Gains on
Disposition of Personal-
Use Property 5305

"Listed Personal Property"
Defined 5310

Gains and Losses on Listed
Personal Property 5315

Set of Items of Personal-
Use Property 5325

Personal-Use Property of
Corporation, Partnership,
or Trust 5330

**Special Types of
Dispositions** **5335**

Dispositions Subject to
Warranty 5340

Repayment of Assistance
— Deemed Capital Loss 5342

Shares Acquired on
Disposition of Assets
Deemed to Be Capital
Property 5345

Deemed Disposition on
Corporation Going Public 5347

Intercorporate Dividend —
Deemed Capital Gain 5350

Divided Real Estate
Interests 5353

Exchanges and Replacement of Property **5355**

Deferral of Capital Gain When Property Is Replaced 5357

Reallocation of Proceeds between Land and Building 5358

Change in Use of Property **5360**

Deemed Disposition on Change in Use 5362

Identical Properties **5365**

Adjusted Cost Base — Identical Properties 5370

Becoming or Ceasing to Be Resident in Canada **5375**

Emigration — Ceasing to Be Resident in Canada 5380

Property Excepted from Deemed Disposition Rule 5385

Optional Deemed Disposition 5390

Post-Departure Loss Carryback Rule 5393

Departure Tax — Corporations 5395

Departure Tax and Trusts 5400

Immigration — Becoming Resident of Canada 5405

Options **5410**

General 5415

Bad Debts, Shares of Bankrupt Corporation **5420**

Bad Debts 5425

Convertible Property **5430**

Convertible Securities 5435

Recent Changes

Jurisprudence

There have been two noteworthy court decisions in the past year, impacting gains and losses:

- *Cassidy v. The Queen*, 2011 DTC 5160 (F.C.A.), was a wonderful taxpayer win on defining excess lands in respect of the principal residence exemption. It puts to rest the conflict in the jurisprudence as to how to apply zoning restrictions that exist for some (but not all) years of ownership when determining the availability of the principal residence exemption for larger acreages. See discussions at ¶5085 and ¶5265.

- The Supreme Court of Canada has granted leave to appeal the Federal Court of Appeal decision in *Daishowa-Marubeni International Ltd. v. The Queen*, 2011 DTC 5157, which upheld in part the decision by the Tax Court of Canada. The case involved the taxpayer's sale of two timber mill businesses, and whether the amount of the purchaser's assumption of the reforestation obligation in respect of the timber rights should be included in the taxpayer's proceeds of disposition of those rights. See ¶5075.

[¶5000] General

[¶5001] Introduction

The taxable portion of a capital gain, known as a "taxable capital gain", is included in the taxpayer's income and taxed at the normal personal or corporate rates. The deductible portion of a capital loss, known as an "allowable capital loss", may be offset against a taxable capital gain,[1] with certain exceptions, such as losses from personal-use assets. Allowable capital losses that are allowable business investment losses (¶5030) may be deducted without limit from income from other sources.

A capital gain is measured by deducting the adjusted cost base and the expenses of sale from the proceeds of disposition.[2] "Proceeds of disposition" means the sale price or any compensation received for property, including insurance proceeds not expended on repairing the damage, compensation for lost or damaged property, expropriation proceeds, etc.[3] See ¶5075.

"Adjusted cost base" means the capital cost of depreciable property, and cost with adjustments for other property[4] (see ¶5080). Special transitional provisions apply when property is owned at the start of the system of taxation of capital gains. A Valuation Day is provided for valuing property as of the start of the system in order to avoid taxing gains that resulted prior to beginning the system. See ¶5130.

Although gains from personal-use property are included in income, losses from such property are allowable only if they are from listed personal property. Listed personal property losses are allowable only as offsets against gains from other listed personal property and not against gains from other types of property.

Gains or losses are taxable or deductible not only upon the sale, gift, or other transfer of property, but also upon a deemed disposition which may occur in a number of instances, such as on the death of an individual taxpayer, the change of residence of a taxpayer from Canada to another country, a change in the use of assets, the expiry of an option, the settlement or cancellation of debt, and a negative adjusted cost base.

For a discussion of capital gains and losses in connection with non-residents, see ¶14,025.

[¶5002] How Capital Gains and Losses Are Taxed

A taxpayer includes in income the excess of all taxable capital gains other than from listed personal property (¶5310) plus the net gain from listed personal property minus allowable capital losses other than listed personal property losses and allowable business investment losses.[5] This excess is not taxable at any special rate or by a special computation, but is merely added in with other income and subjected to the ordinary income tax rates. The only separate treatment for capital gains is the reduced inclusion rate (see ¶5001); therefore, due to differences in marginal tax rates (see ¶8005 and ¶8310) there can be wide variations in the rate at which the gains are actually taxed, depending on the taxpayer's total income.

See page ii for explanation of footnotes.

[1] CCH ¶6007; Sec. 38.   [4] CCH ¶7850; Sec. 54 "adjusted cost base".
[2] CCH ¶6400; Sec. 40(1).
[3] CCH ¶7852; Sec. 54 "proceeds of disposition".   [5] CCH ¶2003; Sec. 3.

If, when applying the formula noted above, the allowable capital losses other than allowable business investment losses exceed the taxable capital gains and net gain from listed personal property, the result is called a net capital loss.[6] Provision is made for the carryover and carryback of losses both by individuals and corporations (see ¶3381).[7] In general, net capital losses of a taxpayer for a taxation year may be carried back three years and forward indefinitely to be deducted against net taxable capital gains.

Prior to 1985, an individual could apply allowable capital losses and net capital losses from other years against taxable capital gains and up to $2,000 per year of other income. This right was withdrawn upon the introduction of the capital gains exemption (see ¶5008). However, an individual is still permitted to deduct any pre-1986 capital loss balance against other income to a maximum of $2,000 per year.[8] The pre-1986 capital loss balance is defined generally to be capital losses realized before May 23, 1985, which have not been applied, less any capital gains exemption claimed in previous years.[9]

Corporations may deduct allowable capital losses incurred in a year against taxable capital gains realized in the year, but any deductible excess cannot be applied against other income. Corporations may carry losses back three years and forward an indefinite number of years, but only against capital gains realized, until the losses are absorbed. A corporation cannot deduct losses incurred in a preceding year if the corporation undergoes a change of control[10] (see ¶3390).

[¶5005] Lifetime Capital Gains Exemption

[¶5008] Available Exemption over the Years

An individual may claim a lifetime $750,000 exemption in respect of capital gains realized on the disposition of qualified farm or fishing property (see ¶5021), or qualified small business corporation shares (see ¶5022). The exemption was extended to qualified fishing property in the 2006 federal Budget.

The lifetime limit was previously $500,000 and was increased to the current $750,000 amount in the 2007 federal Budget, effective for dispositions on or after March 19, 2007. In particular, the $750,000 amount applies to taxation years that begin after March 19, 2007, with a transitional provision[11] allowing the extra $250,000 amount for dispositions occurring on or after March 19, 2007 in an individual's 2007 taxation year.

See page ii for explanation of footnotes.

[6] CCH ¶16,200; Sec. 111(8).
[7] CCH ¶16,003; Sec. 111(1).
[8] CCH ¶16,090; Sec. 111(1.1).

[9] CCH ¶16,200; Sec. 111(8).
[10] CCH ¶16,140; Sec. 111(4).
[11] CCH ¶15,976af; Sec. 110.6(2.3).

Since the capital gains inclusion rate is 50%, the current lifetime exemption for taxable capital gains is $375,000 (i.e., 50% of $750,000). The previous exemption limit was $250,000 (i.e., 50% of $500,000).

When the exemption was enacted in 1985, the $500,000 lifetime exemption was available to shelter *all* capital gains realized by an individual. As part of the 1988 Tax Reform, the capital gains exemption was capped at $100,000 for property other than qualified farm property and qualified small business corporation shares. The current $750,000 lifetime exemption applies only in respect of capital gains realized on dispositions of these latter properties, as well as qualified fishing property. In the 1994 Budget, the $100,000 capital gains exemption that applied to other capital properties was eliminated. The exemption was preserved for gains on such properties that accrued up to February 22, 1994, if an election was made by the taxpayer.[12] In general terms, the election allowed individuals to trigger capital gains on properties owned on February 22, 1994, to the extent of their available $100,000 capital gains exemption.

The 1992 Budget eliminated the $100,000 capital gains exemption in respect of gains realized on dispositions of real property (other than qualified farm property). The capital gains exemption in respect of real property thus applied only to real property that was owned by an individual before March 1992. In such a case, where the individual subsequently disposed of the property (before February 22, 1994), the portion of the capital gain that was eligible for the capital gains exemption was prorated, based on the number of months of ownership prior to March 1992 relative to the total months of ownership. Similarly, the eligible capital gain was prorated if the individual still owned the real property on February 22, 1994, and made the election described at ¶5010.

[¶5010] Election for Property Owned on February 22, 1994

On February 22, 1994, the federal government decided that the $100,000 capital gains exemption (or $75,000 taxable capital gains deduction, offsetting $100,000 of actual gains before being reduced to its taxable component of 75%) would be withdrawn after that date, subject to generous but very complex transitional rules in the form of the final capital gains exemption election.

Capital property acquired at any time before February 23, 1994, and still on hand at the end of February 22, 1994, could be made the subject of a special election to utilize any amount of the $75,000 lifetime taxable capital gains deduction remaining after 1993.[13]

The concept of the final capital gains election was that an individual could elect to be deemed to have disposed of any asset or assets he or she

---

See page ii for explanation of footnotes.

[12] CCH ¶15,999fi; Sec. 110.6(19).

[13] CCH ¶15,999fi, ¶15,999fj; Sec. 110.6(19), 110.6(20).

designated. The individual had to elect a value (subject to strict limitations), and he or she was then deemed to have disposed of the property at that value and reacquired it at that value. The result was that any gain on the deemed disposition at the elected value gave rise to capital gain, and therefore taxable capital gain, which could be offset by the individual's remaining $75,000 lifetime deduction. Since the individual was deemed to have acquired the property at the new elected value, when he or she disposed of it in the future the gain at that time would be measured against the elected amount rather than the original cost and the future gain and future tax could thereby be reduced. Subject to the value limitations, the individual could spread the remaining exemption among several assets or concentrate it on one.

The general concept was varied for flow-through entities such as mutual funds and partnerships, and for eligible capital property. The same deemed disposition rules applied, but these entities were deemed to reacquire the property at its old value and the capital gain recognized went into a separate special notional account for each property for use against future gains from that source.

The election was effective at the end of February 22, 1994, so that any actual dispositions after that date could obtain the benefit of the rule to the extent of its fair market value at that date, which is the upper limit of the elected amount.

Example:

Ms. Damato has 1,000 shares of stock which cost $4,000 and are worth $10,000 on February 22, 1994. She has at least $6,000 of unused exemption ($4,500 of taxable capital gains deduction) to offset the full gain. She elects on the shares at their fair market value of $10,000. She is deemed to have sold them for proceeds of disposition of $10,000, and so a taxable capital gain of $4,500 results. She reports the $4,500 gain, which is added to income but offset in calculating taxable income by her capital gains exemption. She is deemed to have acquired the shares on February 22, 1994, at a cost of $10,000. If she sells them in 1994 or later and their value has not changed, there will be no further gain to report. If their value has increased at the time of actual sale, the gain will be measured from $10,000; if it has decreased, she will have a capital loss.

As discussed below, the elected value cannot be less than the adjusted cost base nor more than the fair market value, and this elected value must permit use of the capital gains exemption and cannot create a gain larger than the amount that can be offset by her available capital gains exemption.

For each property covered by his or her final election, an individual had to select a disposition value which was not less than the adjusted cost base (ACB) of the property at the end of February 22, 1994, nor more than the fair market value of the property on February 22, 1994. An election at less than ACB on any property would render the election invalid for all properties. An election in excess of fair market value was valid but subject to penalties, as described below.

For an election to be valid, the elected value for all properties covered by an election needed to create a capital gain which could be fully offset by an individual's available capital gains exemption (or that of the individual's spouse/common-law partner, if the gain is subject to attribution rules). A loss could not be created with an election. An individual could, however, create a gain for any or all of his or her other capital assets which was less than his or her available exemption, and so spread the exemption among several assets.

If an individual overestimated the fair market value chosen for his or her election by more than 10%, there was a severe and automatic penalty.[14] Any excess over 10% further reduced the new ACB. This penalty resulted in an individual squandering the available exemption by electing too high a value, since the individual would not get even the full value of cost base adjustment he or she was entitled to, and would waste an elected amount which might have been applied to other assets. The purpose was to deter deliberate over-elections.

[¶5011] Special Election for Flow-Through Entities

Flow-through entities are defined to include investment corporations, mortgage investment corporations, mutual fund corporations, mutual fund trusts, partnerships, related segregated fund trusts, and trusts governed by an employees' profit sharing plan, and certain trusts established to hold company shares for employees, to protect security interests, or to govern corporate voting rights.[15] Related segregated fund trusts are essentially investment trusts offered by insurance companies.

Elections made on shares or interests in flow-through entities resulted in a deemed disposition and acquisition, so that the elected value and penalty rules applied. However, the capital gain which arose on deemed disposition was not added to the cost base of the asset, but rather flowed into a special account called the "exempt capital gains balance" (ECGB). The deemed reacquisition occurred at the cost to the elector immediately before the deemed disposition. The ECGB could be applied after February 22, 1994, to shelter any capital gain distributions flowed out to the investor from the flow-through entity, as well as any gain on actual disposition, until the end of the year 2004.[16] The ECGB thus preserved any remaining $100,000 capital gains exemption assigned to it into future years. Each flow-through entity subject to an election had its own related ECGB which was not transferable and had to be tracked until the account was exhausted or expired after 2004. Any remaining ECGB after its application in 2004 had to be added to the ACB of the flow-through entity to the elector, and the ECGB itself wound up.

As originally drafted, the election rules did not provide for the situation in which the value of a flow-through property fell after the election and was disposed of before 2005. In this case, there would be an unused and

---

See page ii for explanation of footnotes.

[14] CCH ¶15,999ff; Sec. 110.6(22).
[15] CCH ¶6399a; Sec. 39.1(1) "flow-through entity".
[16] CCH ¶6399; Sec. 39.1(1) "exempt capital gains balance".

unusable exempt capital gains balance following the disposition. Technical amendments correct this anomaly retroactively to 1994 by adding $^4/_3$ before February 28, 2000, $^3/_2$ after February 27 and before October 18, 2000 and $^2/_1$ after October 17, 2000 of the unusable exempt capital gains balance to the adjusted cost base of the property immediately before the disposition, thus giving recognition to the appropriate capital loss.[17]

Example:

   Paula has shares of a mutual fund that were acquired for $8,000 and were worth $10,000 on February 22, 1994. She elects to apply $2,000 of available $100,000 exemption to these shares, and elects a value of $10,000. She is deemed to dispose of them for $10,000 but to reacquire them at $8,000. The $2,000 capital gain ($1,500 taxable capital gain) is income offset by the exemption. The $2,000 (actually $^4/_3$ of $1,500) goes into the ECGB.

   If Paula receives capital gain allocations from the investment of $600 in 1994, $800 in 1995, and $700 in 1996, the special account would offset the $600 and $800 gains completely in 1994 and 1995, and $600 of the $700 gain in 1996. At that point the $2,000 has been exhausted ($600 + $800 + $600 = $2,000) and the remaining $100 in 1996 and all later gains will be subject to capital gains tax in normal fashion. If Paula should sell the shares along the way, any remaining balance of the $2,000 would offset any actual gain on disposition.

If the election related to an interest in a partnership, special adjustments needed to be made to the partnership ACB immediately before the deemed disposition to measure the capital gain which in turn measured the ECGB.[18] Essentially, the individual member of a partnership had to add to the partnership ACB (as determined in ¶5190 immediately before the deemed disposition at the end of February 22, 1994) the total of:

(a) the pre-February 23, 1994, portion of his or her share of partnership net income for its fiscal period that included February 22, 1994, and

(b) his or her share of partnership net capital gains that arose from disposition before February 23, 1994.

For this purpose, the income of the partnership for that fiscal period was prorated on a daily basis. Where the partnership had net losses for that fiscal period and the prorated portion of the net loss was greater than the partnership's pre-February 23, 1994, net taxable capital gains, the excess was required to be deducted in computing the individual's adjusted cost base immediately before the deemed disposition.

The purpose of the partnership ACB adjustments was to ensure that the income or loss of the partnership for the period up to February 22, 1994, was reflected in the value of the partnership interest on that day. In the absence of the adjustments, there would be no mechanism to separate out the February 22, 1994 date, since the mechanics of partnership ACB calculations only dealt with final gain or loss at the end of the fiscal period,

---

See page ii for explanation of footnotes.

[17] CCH ¶7637f; Sec. 53(1)(r).   [18] CCH ¶15,999fm; Sec. 110.6(23).

not its daily accrual up to February 22, 1994. There are no lasting adjustments to ACB carried forward.

[¶5014] Effect of Election on Principal Residence Exemption

As discussed at ¶5260, an individual can claim a special exemption for his or her principal residence based on the number of years he or she claims it as a principal residence (plus 1) divided by the number of years he or she has owned it. When an individual sells a house he or she has always claimed as a principal residence, his or her gains will be wholly exempt, and it would have been foolish to waste the special $100,000 capital gains exemption on the house, and increase current income. However, an individual who was unable to claim the entire exemption, either because he or she did not occupy the house throughout the period of ownership or because he or she had more than one qualifying residence, was able to integrate the $100,000 capital gains exemption with the principal residence exemption.

If a 1994 capital gains exemption election on a principal residence was made and a principal residence exemption on the same property is then claimed on the same property for 1994 and later years, the principal residence exemption formula on actual disposition of a property after February 22, 1994, is: (i) the actual gain determined without reference to the 1994 election, reduced by (ii) the principal residence exemption as traditionally calculated using the number of years the individual designated the principal residence to be such.[19] That is, (ii) is the number of designated years plus one, divided by the number of years of ownership that end after the property was acquired. From the capital gains reduced for principal residence exemption, the individual may, if a 1994 capital gains election was made in respect of the property, deduct the lesser of:

(a) the notional capital gain resulting from the 1994 election calculated as if: (i) the 1994 and earlier years the individual is now designating were designated in the 1994 election, and (ii) the amount designated in the election were reduced to fair market value, or, if there was a penal grind, fair market value reduced by the grind, and

(b) the reported capital gains that arose from the 1994 election, using the principal residence designations actually made in the 1994 election and ignoring the principal residence designation made in the return on actual disposition.

[¶5015] Time for Election

The special 1994 election generally had to be made by April 30, 1995; however, where the election was made on eligible capital property, the filing deadline was the due date for the taxation year in which the fiscal period of the business that included February 22, 1994 ended.[20]

See page ii for explanation of footnotes.

[19] CCH ¶6490a; Sec. 40(7.1).　　　　　　　　　[20] CCH ¶15,999fn; Sec. 110.6(24).

A personal trust must itself have elected by March 31 of the calendar year following the year in which the taxation year of the trust that included February 22, 1994 ended.

[¶5021] Exemption for Gains from Qualified Farm or Fishing Property

The lifetime capital gains exemption is currently available to an individual who disposes of qualified farm property after 1984 or qualified fishing property after May 1, 2006. The exemption is also available for dispositions of qualified small business corporation shares, as discussed at ¶5022.

As noted in ¶5008, the 2007 Budget increased the lifetime capital gains exemption limit from $500,000 to $750,000 for gains from such properties, effective March 19, 2007.[21]

"Qualified farm property" comprises real property, a share of the capital stock of a family farm corporation, an interest in a family farm partnership, and eligible capital property used in the course of carrying on the business of farming in Canada.[22] Similarly, for dispositions after May 1, 2006, "qualified fishing property" comprises real property, a fishing vessel, a share of the capital stock of a family fishing corporation, an interest in a family fishing partnership, and eligible capital property used in the course of carrying on the business of fishing in Canada.[23] However, in either case, the property must meet several criteria for the owners of the property, the users of the property, and the use of the particular property to qualify.

In order to qualify as qualified farm property or qualified fishing property of an individual at any particular time, the property must be owned at that time by the individual, the spouse or common-law partner of the individual, or a family farm (or fishing) partnership in which the individual or his spouse or common-law partner has an interest. Furthermore, the property must be used principally (the "principally" requirement was added for dispositions after May 1, 2006) in the course of carrying on a farming or fishing business in Canada by the following eligible users:

(i) the individual;

(ii) if the individual is a personal trust, a beneficiary of the trust that is entitled to receive any income or capital of the trust;

(iii) a spouse, common-law partner, child, or parent of the individual referred to in (i) or the beneficiary referred to in (ii);

(iv) a family farm (fishing) corporation, a share of which is owned by any individual referred to in (i) through (iii); or

---

See page ii for explanation of footnotes.

[21] CCH ¶15,976; Sec. 110.6(2).

[22] CCH ¶15,975k; Sec. 110.6(1) "qualified farm property".

[23] CCH ¶15,975kb; Sec. 110.6(1) "qualified fishing property".

(v) a family farm (fishing) partnership, an interest in which is owned by any individual referred to in (i) through (iii).

There are two separate rules for determining whether property is considered to be used in the course of carrying on a farming or fishing business in Canada.

The first is a general rule requiring that the following two-part test be met for the property to qualify as a farming or fishing business in Canada at any particular time.

- First, throughout the 24-month period preceding the particular time (e.g., the time of disposition), the property must have been owned by the individual, the individual's spouse or common-law partner, child, or parent, or by a partnership, an interest in which is a family farm (fishing) partnership interest of the individual or the individual's spouse or common-law partner. If the individual is a personal trust, the property must be so owned by the individual from whom the trust acquired the property or a spouse or common-law partner, child, or parent of the individual, or a personal trust from which the individual or a child or parent of the individual acquired the property.

- Second, during a period of at least two years, during which the property was owned by a qualified owner, the gross revenue of a qualified owner ("operator") from the farming (fishing) business carried on in Canada, in which the property was principally used, exceeded the operator's income from all other sources in the year. In order to satisfy this requirement, the property must have been owned by a qualified owner for a period of at least 24 months throughout which it was used by a family farm or fishing corporation or a family farm or fishing partnership (specifically, a corporation referred to in (iv) above or a partnership referred to in (v) above) in the carrying on of the business of farming or fishing in Canada. Additionally, throughout that period, the individual referred to in (i) above, a beneficiary of a personal trust referred to in (ii) above, or a person referred to in (iii) above, must have been actively engaged on a regular and continuous basis in the farming or fishing business.

In 1965, a taxpayer acquired a 42-acre property which he later subdivided, leaving him with 13.6 acres. When he sold this in 1993, he was entitled to the qualified farm property capital gains deduction, since the property was used principally for farming for a five-year period, from 1966 to 1971.[24]

The second rule determines whether a share of the capital stock of a family farm or fishing corporation owned by an individual at a particular time will qualify as a qualified farm or fishing property. Under this rule, two tests must be met for such a share to qualify:

See page ii for explanation of footnotes.

[24] Sevy, 2004 DTC 3442.

- First, throughout any 24-month period ending before that time, more than 50% of the fair market value of the property owned by the corporation must be attributable to any combination of the following types of property:

  (i) property that has been used principally in the course of a Canadian farming (fishing) business by:

  (a) the corporation,

  (b) the individual,

  (c) if the individual is a personal trust, a beneficiary of the trust,

  (d) a spouse, common-law partner, child, or parent of the individual or beneficiary of the trust,

  (e) a related corporation, a share of which is a share in the capital stock of a family farm (fishing) corporation of an individual referred to in (b) through (d), or

  (f) a partnership, an interest in which was an interest in a family farm (fishing) partnership of an individual referred to in (b) through (d);

  (Individuals described in (b) through (d) must have been actively engaged in the farming or fishing business on a regular and continuous basis.)

  (ii) shares or indebtedness of one or more corporations, all or substantially all (i.e., 90%) of the fair market value of the assets of which are properties referred to in (i), (ii), or (iii); or

  (iii) for dispositions after May 1, 2006, an interest or indebtedness in one or more partnerships, all or substantially all of the fair market value assets of which are properties described in (i), (ii), or (iii).

- Second, at that time, all or substantially all (90% or more) of the fair market value of the property owned by the corporation must be attributable to properties described in (i), (ii), and (iii).[25]

A similar test determines whether a partnership interest will qualify as qualified farm or fishing property of an individual.[26] Therefore, in order for the partnership interest to qualify at a particular time (meaning the time of disposition) throughout any period of at least 24 months before that time, more than 50% of the fair market value of its property must have been attributable to any combination of the properties described in (i) through (iii) above.

See page ii for explanation of footnotes.

[25] CCH ¶15,975m, ¶15,975ma; Sec. 110.6(1) "share of the capital stock of a family farm corporation", 110.6(1) "share of the capital stock of a family fishing corporation".

[26] CCH ¶15,975g, ¶15,975gf; Sec. 110.6(1) "interest in a family farm partnership", 110.6(1) "interest in a family fishing partnership".

Finally, eligible capital property of the farming or fishing business may qualify as qualified farm property or fishing property of an individual. To qualify, the eligible capital property must have been used by the eligible users of qualified farm or fishing property referred to in (i) through (v) above.[27]

[¶5022] Small Business Corporation Shares

Effective for dispositions occurring after March 18, 2007, the lifetime capital gains exemption in respect of gains from the disposition of qualified small business corporation shares equals $750,000 ($375,000 of taxable capital gains).[28] As noted in ¶5008, the previous monetary limit of $500,000 was increased to $750,000 in the 2007 federal Budget.

In order for a share to be a "qualified small business corporation share", the following criteria must be met:[29]

(1) The shares must be shares of a Canadian-controlled small business corporation which, at the time of disposition, uses 90% or more of its assets either directly in an active business carried on in Canada or as a holding company for such a corporation. The 90% measurement is based on the fair market value of all assets at the time of disposition. Since the term deposits it maintained were not an integral aspect of its business operations, a corporation did not meet this 90% measurement and, hence, was not a qualified small business corporation for the purpose of the capital gains exemption.[30]

(2) The shares must be owned by the taxpayer, the taxpayer's spouse/common-law partner, or a partnership related to the taxpayer.

(3) The shares must not have been owned by anyone other than the taxpayer or a related person during the 24 months preceding disposition. This rule seems to suggest that a person can incorporate his or her personal proprietorship and sell it immediately, since the shares will not have been held by an unrelated person. It further appears that shares issued on a rollover to a holding company for common shares will qualify, or at least not be automatically disqualified. On the other hand, newly issued treasury shares are disqualified. The death of the individual does not mitigate the 24-month requirement.

(4) Throughout the 24-month holding period, at least 50% of the assets of the corporation must have been used principally in an active business, or to finance a "connected" active business.[31]

A corporation spent several years trying to develop a river's hydro-electric potential. The fact that they were never able to reach an agreement for the

---

See page ii for explanation of footnotes.

[27] CCH ¶15,975p, ¶15,975s; Sec. 110.6(1.2), 110.6(1.3).

[28] CCH ¶15,976a; Sec. 110.6(2.1).

[29] CCH ¶15,975l; Sec. 110.6(1) "qualified small business corporation share".

[30] Skidmore et al, 2000 DTC 6186.

[31] CCH ¶24,357; Sec. 186(4).

sale of the electricity did not mean that they were not carrying on an active business during the years of preparation. Accordingly, its shares were qualified small business corporation shares for the purpose of the capital gains exemption.[32]

[¶5025] Capital Gains Deferral for Investment in Small Business

[¶5026] Permitted Deferral

Where an individual (other than a trust) disposes of shares of a small business corporation and realizes a capital gain, that gain can be deferred where the individual reinvests the proceeds of disposition into eligible small business corporations. Similar to the exchange of property provisions (see ¶5357), this provision only provides a deferral which is reflected in a reduction of the cost base of the new investment. The adjusted cost base of the new investment is reduced by the capital gain deferred from the initial investment. Accordingly, the gain is deferred until the disposition of the new investment (the "replacement shares"), unless the gain is deferred again on those proceeds.[33]

The shares may be acquired from a related individual due to circumstances such as a death or breakdown of a marriage or common-law partnership. For the purposes of the capital gains deferral, an individual who acquires shares in such circumstances will be considered to have acquired them at the time and under the same circumstances that the related individual originally acquired them.[34] The capital gains deferral is also available to individuals in partnerships involved in pooling their investments. For the purposes of the capital gains deferral, any transaction entered into by an investment manager on behalf of an individual under an eligible pooling arrangement is deemed to be a transaction of the individual and not a transaction of the investment manager.[35] An "eligible pooling arrangement" is an arrangement in writing between an individual and an investment manager that provides for: (i) the transfer of funds or other property by the individual to the investment manager; (ii) the use of funds or proceeds from the sale of the property by the investment manager to purchase eligible small business corporation shares on behalf of the individual within 60 days; and (iii) a monthly reporting to the individual by the investment manager of the securities transactions made on behalf of the individual.[36]

[¶5027] Qualifying Dispositions

An individual can have a capital gain deferral only in respect of a gain arising on a "qualifying disposition" of the individual. A qualifying disposi-

---

See page ii for explanation of footnotes.

[32] Hudon et al., 2001 DTC 5630.
[33] CCH ¶6750m; Sec. 44.1(2).
[34] CCH ¶6750o, ¶6750p; Sec. 44.1(4), 44.1(5).
[35] CCH ¶6750n; Sec. 44.1(3).
[36] CCH ¶6750d; Sec. 44.1(1) "eligible pooling arrangement".

tion of an individual is a disposition of common shares of the capital stock of a corporation owned by the individual, where each such share was a share issued by an "eligible small business corporation" at the time the share was acquired, was a common share of the capital stock of an "active business corporation" throughout the ownership period, and was owned throughout the 185-day period that ended immediately before the disposition.[37]

An eligible small business corporation is a Canadian-controlled private Corporation, all or substantially all of the fair market value of the assets of which are used principally in an active business carried on primarily in Canada by the corporation or an eligible small business corporation related to it. It can also be shares of, and/or debt issued by other related eligible small business corporations or a combination of such assets, shares, or debt.[38] To be an eligible small business corporation share, the total carrying value of the assets of the small business corporation (that is, the amount at which the assets would be valued for the purpose of the corporation's balance sheet if it was prepared in accordance with generally accepted accounting principles used in Canada at that time) and related corporations cannot exceed $50 million immediately before and immediately after the investment.[39] An eligible small business corporation and an eligible active business corporation do not include: a professional corporation; a specified financial institution; a corporation the principal business of which is the leasing, rental, development or sale or any combination thereof, of real property owned by it; and a corporation more than 50% of the value of the property of which (net of debts incurred to acquire the property) is attributable to real property.

While the individual holds the shares, the issuing corporation must be an active business corporation. Generally, this is a taxable Canadian corporation, all or substantially all of the fair market value of the assets of which are used in an active business or are shares of, and/or debt issued by other related active business corporations or a combination of such assets, shares, or debt.[40] The active business is required to be primarily carried on in Canada in the period that began when the individual last acquired the shares and ended when the disposition occurred (the "ownership period") if that period is less than 730 days. In any other case, that active business has to be carried on primarily in Canada for at least 730 days during the ownership period.

[¶5028] Calculating the Capital Gains Deferral

The permitted deferral of the capital gain from the disposition of eligible small business corporation shares is determined by the following formula:

See page ii for explanation of footnotes.

[37] CCH ¶6750i; Sec. 44.1(1) "qualifying disposition".

[38] CCH ¶6750e; Sec. 44.1(1) "eligible small business corporation".

[39] CCH ¶6750f; Sec. 44.1(1) "eligible small business corporation share".

[40] CCH ¶6750a; Sec. 44.1(1) "active business corporation".

$$B \times (D \div E)$$

where

B = the total capital gain from the original sale

E = the proceeds of disposition

D = the lesser of E and the total cost of all replacement shares [41]

To be able to defer the capital gain, the individual must purchase the replacement shares in the form of eligible small business corporation shares (see ¶5027) at any time in the year of disposition of the original investment or within 120 days after the end of that year. A designation of the replacement shares in respect of each qualifying disposition must be made in the income tax return for the year of the qualifying disposition.[42] The late filing of this designation could prevent an individual from claiming the deferral, even though the shares would otherwise qualify as replacement shares. Fairness relief in the form of an extension of the time limit (see ¶15,008) is not available to such a designation. This highlights the importance of making a designation in respect of the replacement shares on a timely basis.

[¶5029] Capital Gain Deferral and ACB Reduction

The capital gain that can be deferred ("permitted deferral") in respect of a qualifying disposition of an eligible small business investment is determined as follows:[43]

$$(G/H) \times I$$

Where:

G = the lesser of H and the total cost of all replacement shares (to a maximum of $2 million before February 19, 2003).

H = the proceeds of disposition; and

I = the capital gain from the original sale;

The capital gain to be reported in the year of disposition will thereby be determined by subtracting the capital gain deferral from the total capital gain realized from the disposition.[44] For example, an individual receives proceeds of $1,000,000 from a qualifying disposition of Sellco shares that have an adjusted cost base of $750,000, resulting in a capital gain of $250,000. The individual then uses 60% ($600,000) of the proceeds to acquire Newco shares that are replacement shares. The individual would be entitled to claim a permitted deferral equal to 60% of the gain, or about $150,000, since he or she has used 60% of the proceeds of disposition to acquire replacement shares. The individual would therefore only realize a capital gain of $100,000 for the year of the disposition.

See page ii for explanation of footnotes.

[41] CCH ¶6750s; Sec. 44.1(1) "permitted deferral".

[42] CCH ¶6750l; Sec. 44.1(1) "replacement share".

[43] CCH ¶6750g; Sec. 44.1(1) "permitted deferral".

[44] CCH ¶6750m; Sec. 44.1(2)(a).

Since February 19, 2003, the formula does not place a limit on the amount of capital gains eligible for the deferral.

Finally, the capital gain deferral must be used to reduce the adjusted cost base of *each* of the eligible replacement shares by the amount determined by the following formula:[45]

Example 1:

$$J \times (K/L)$$

Where:

J = capital gain deferral;

K = the cost of replacement shares (to a maximum of $2 million before February 19, 2003); and

L = the total cost of all the replacement shares (to a maximum of $2 million before February 19, 2003).

The following example from the Department of Finance demonstrates the calculations required for dispositions of small business corporation shares after February 18, 2003 (see Example 1 for dispositions after October 17, 2000 and before February 19, 2003).

Facts

An individual makes a qualifying disposition of shares of corporation A with an adjusted cost base of $3,000,000 for proceeds of disposition of $4,500,000. The individual purchases replacement shares in corporation B with a cost of $2,200,000 and in corporation C with a cost of $2,300,000.

Determinations

The capital gain of the individual otherwise determined is $1,500,000 ($4,500,000 - $3,000,000).

The permitted deferral of the individual in respect of the disposition is determined to be $1,500,000 by the formula (G/H) × I, where ($4,500,000/$4,500,000) × $1,500,000 = $1,500,000.

The capital gain from the disposition after deducting the permitted deferral in respect of the disposition is determined as $1,500,000 - $1,500,000 = nil.

[¶5030] Definitions

[¶5031] Meaning of "Capital Gain"

"Capital gain"[46] means the gain from the disposition of any property other than:

(1) property the sale of which would be taken into account in computing ordinary income, such as inventory or property acquired as part of an adventure in the nature of trade;

See page ii for explanation of footnotes.

[45] CCH ¶6750, ¶6750m; Sec. 44.1(1)"ACB reduction", 44.1(2)(b).   [46] CCH ¶6002, ¶6050; Sec. 39(1); ITAR 26(1).

(2) eligible capital property, which includes business goodwill and other intangibles (see ¶5045);

(3) cultural property disposed of to a designated institution or public authority in Canada (see ¶5065);

(4) Canadian or foreign resource properties;

(5) an insurance policy including a life insurance policy other than a segregated fund policy;[47]

(6) specified debt obligations or mark-to-market properties;

(7) a timber resource property;

(8) a beneficiary's interest in a qualifying environmental trust; and

(9) [for dispositions after 2001, participating interests in foreign investment entities].

The disposition of eligible capital property is taxed on a different basis (see ¶3075 *et seq.*) and Canadian and foreign resource properties are also given special income treatment, providing for current deductions and income treatment of proceeds.[48] Proceeds from the disposition of certain life insurance policies are to be included in income; see ¶2200. "Timber resource property" refers to certain rights or licences to cut or remove timber,[49] and proceeds from the disposition of such property are credited to the undepreciated capital cost (see ¶4385).

A capital gain or a capital loss is a gain or loss determined to the extent of the amount that would not otherwise be included or deducted in computing income, if the provisions relating to capital gains and losses were deleted from the Act. Therefore, a gain is considered a capital gain only to the extent that it would not otherwise be included in ordinary income. Since there are no provisions which clearly differentiate between a capital gain and a gain from an adventure in the nature of trade, which is taxed as business income,[50] taxpayers will still have to refer to the numerous Canadian and foreign court decisions that provide the rules for distinguishing between ordinary income and capital receipts. See ¶5105.

[¶5032] Meaning of "Capital Loss"

"Capital loss" is defined[51] as the loss from the disposition of any property other than:

(1) depreciable property;

(2) eligible capital property, which includes business goodwill and other intangibles (see ¶5045);

See page ii for explanation of footnotes.

[47] CCH ¶20,831; Sec. 138.1(1).
[48] CCH ¶8350; Sec. 59(1).
[49] CCH ¶4562f; Sec. 13(21).

[50] Interp. Bul. IT-459.

[51] CCH ¶6050; Sec. 39(1).

(3) Canadian resource property;

(4) foreign resource property;

(5) specified debt obligations or mark-to market properties;

(6) insurance policies, except for life insurance policies that are segregated fund policies;[52]

(7) an interest of a beneficiary in a qualifying environmental trust; and

(8) [for dispositions after 2001, participating interests in foreign investment entities].

Note that capital property for determining capital loss purposes is not quite the same as for capital gain purposes (see ¶5040). The sale of property in an income transaction, such as the sale of inventory, does not give rise to a capital loss.

Capital losses can be applied against capital gains in the taxation year and can be carried back three years and forward indefinitely to reduce net taxable capital gains of other years (see ¶3381). Capital losses that are business investment losses are applied against all forms of income and not just capital gains[53] (see ¶5034).

[¶5033] Meaning of "Taxable Capital Gain" and "Allowable Capital Loss"

The portion of capital gains and losses that are included in computing the taxpayer's income are referred to as "taxable capital gains" or "allowable capital losses".[54] As a general rule, a taxpayer's taxable capital gain is ½ of his or her capital gain and a taxpayer's allowable capital loss is ½ of his or her capital loss. Allowable capital losses may be offset against taxable capital gains, with certain exceptions, such as losses from personal-use assets. Allowable capital losses that are allowable business investment losses (see definition at ¶5034) may be deducted from income from all sources.

However, capital gains realized on gifts of certain capital property to a registered charity or other qualified donee may be eligible for an inclusion rate of zero.[55] This zero inclusion rate applies to capital gains deemed realized on the following gifts of property:

- a share of the capital stock of a mutual fund corporation;

- a unit of a mutual fund trust;

- an interest in a related segregated fund trust;

- a prescribed debt obligation;

See page ii for explanation of footnotes.
52 CCH ¶20,831; Sec. 138.1(1).
53 CCH ¶2003; Sec. 3.
54 CCH ¶6007; Sec. 38.
55 CCH ¶6007; Sec. 38(a.1), 38(a.2).

- ecologically sensitive land (including a covenant, an easement, or, in the case of land in Quebec, a real servitude) donated to a qualified donee other than a private foundation; and

- a share, debt obligation, or right listed on a designated stock exchange.

For donations of publicly listed shares, the zero inclusion rate has been extended to any capital gain realized on the exchange of unlisted shares of the capital stock of a corporation for those donated publicly listed shares if:

- at the time of their issuance and at the time of their exchange, the unlisted shares of the capital stock of a corporation included a condition allowing the holder to exchange them for the publicly listed share;

- the publicly listed shares are the only consideration received on the exchange; and

- the publicly listed shares are donated within 30 days of the exchange.

In cases where the exchanged securities are partnership interests (other than prescribed interests), the capital gain to be reported is the lesser of:

- the capital gain otherwise determined; and

- the amount, if any, by which the cost to the donor of the exchanged interests (plus any contributions to partnership capital by the donor) exceeds the ACB of those interests (determined without reference to distributions of partnership profits or capital).

If there is no advantage or benefit to be conferred as a result of the gift, the full amount of the capital gain is eligible for the zero inclusion rate. Otherwise, the zero inclusion rate only applies to that proportion of the gain that the "eligible amount" of the gift (see ¶8135) is of the taxpayer's total proceeds of disposition in respect of the property.

As a result of the 2011 Budget, the capital gains tax exemption on donations of publicly listed shares issued under a flow-through share ("FTS") agreement after March 21, 2011 is only available to the extent that cumulative capital gains realized on their deemed dispositions exceed their original cost, determined without regard to the nil cost base otherwise applicable to FTS agreements.[56] In effect, to the extent that a taxpayer has incurred costs to acquire shares issued under an FTS agreement after March 21, 2011 (and in respect of which the taxpayer may be entitled to a deduction), the taxpayer is required to pay tax at normal capital gains rates on capital gains realized on their dispositions whether the shares are sold for consideration, or are donated to a qualified donee.

For the purposes of the Act, a taxpayer is deemed to have a capital gain on a disposition of property if another property that is included in a "flow-through share class of property" is subject to a gifting agreement and the

---

See page ii for explanation of footnotes.

[56] Sec. 38.1.

taxpayer has, at the time of the donation, a positive balance in a pool of the actual cost to the taxpayer of flow-through shares of that class acquired after the later of March 22, 2011 and the taxpayer's "fresh start date".[57]

For more details, refer to the commentary on the definition of "exemption threshold" at ¶3361.

[¶5034] Meaning of "Business Investment Loss"

A "business investment loss" is defined[58] as a loss that is a capital loss realized on a disposition of shares or debt owing by a small business corporation.[59] For business investment loss purposes, a small business corporation includes a corporation that was a small business corporation at any time during the 12 months before the disposition. A capital loss realized by a corporation on the disposition of a debt owing to it by a corporation with which it does not deal at arm's length is not a business investment loss. For business investment loss purposes, the shares or debt must be disposed of to a person with whom the taxpayer deals at arm's length, unless it is the result of a deemed disposition of a debt (when the debt becomes a bad debt) or of a share of a small business corporation that:

(1) has gone bankrupt in the year;

(2) is insolvent, and a winding-up order has been made in the year under the *Winding-up Act*; or

(3) is insolvent at the end of the year and neither the corporation nor a corporation it controls carries on business.[60]

Debt or shares received as consideration for the disposition of personal-use property are not covered by this deemed disposition.

In addition, a business investment loss may be available if a taxpayer has honoured a guarantee of the debt of a corporation.[61] Certain conditions must be met for a taxpayer to be eligible for this treatment:

(a) the amount paid under the guarantee must be paid to an arm's length party; and

(b) the corporation owing the debt must be a small business corporation, both at the time the debt was incurred and at any time during the 12 months prior to the time that an amount first became payable under the guarantee.

If these criteria are met, that part of the amount owing to the taxpayer as a result of the guarantee will be deemed to be a debt owing to the taxpayer by a small business corporation. Consequently, the taxpayer will be eligible to

---

See page ii for explanation of footnotes.

[57] Sec. 40(12).

[58] CCH ¶6050; Sec. 39(1)(c); Interp. Bul. IT-484R2.

[59] CCH ¶28,271a; Sec. 248(1) "small business corporation".

[60] CCH ¶7400; Sec. 50(1).

[61] CCH ¶6398e; Sec. 39(12).

claim a business investment loss even if the corporation has ceased to carry on an active business.

The amount of the business investment loss is the amount of a capital loss otherwise determined, less the amount of the capital gains exemption that the taxpayer has claimed in previous years.[62]

One-half (or the applicable rate prior to October 18, 2000) of a taxpayer's business investment loss for a year is deductible. This deductible portion is referred to as the *allowable business investment loss* or ABIL.[63] An ABIL may be deducted from any other source of income for the year in which it arose.[64] A taxpayer's unused ABIL at the end of a year may be carried back three years and forward ten years as a non-capital loss, and applied against income from all sources in those years. For taxation years ending before March 23, 2004, the carryforward period was seven years.[65] If the ABIL is not utilized within the carryforward period, the unused portion is converted into a net capital loss for further carryforward. As a net capital loss, it may be carried forward indefinitely, but can only be applied against future taxable capital gains.[66] Although a taxpayer can generally carry a non-capital loss arising in taxation years ending after 2005 back three years and forward 20 years, this extension does *not* apply to a non-capital loss resulting from an ABIL. Instead, an ABIL that has not been used within ten tax years will become a net capital loss in the eleventh year.

[¶5035] Meaning of "Property"

"Property" is defined[67] as property of any kind whatever, whether real or personal, corporeal or incorporeal, and includes, but is not limited to:

(1) a right of any kind whatever, a share, or a chose in action;

(2) money, unless a contrary intention is evident;

(3) a timber resource property; and

(4) the work-in-progress of a business that is a profession.

The statutory definition of *property* appears extremely broad at first glance since it includes *property of any kind whatever* and *a right of any kind whatever*. This broad interpretation was retained where a taxpayer's *ownership equity* in a corporation was held to constitute *property* for the purposes of the Act.[68]

However, *a right of any kind whatever* cannot be given a meaning that would extend the reach of the Act beyond what Parliament has conceived. On the basis that the meaning given to the term *property* in the Act must

---

See page ii for explanation of footnotes.

[62] CCH ¶6397, ¶6398; Sec. 39(9), 39(10).

[63] CCH ¶6007; Sec. 38.

[64] CCH ¶2003; Sec. 3.

[65] CCH ¶16,208; Sec. 111(8) "non-capital loss".

[66] CCH ¶16,204; Sec. 111(8) "net capital loss".

[67] CCH ¶28,220; Sec. 248(1) "property".

[68] Kieboom, 92 DTC 6382.

respect the legal traditions of the common law, the Federal Court of Appeal held that a general right to carry on a business, which is a right that belongs to everyone, is not the property of anyone and its disposition cannot give rise to a capital gain.[69]

Prior to the appeal to the Federal Court of Appeal, this more restrictive approach was retained by Justice Lamarre of the Tax Court of Canada in a case where the amount of $2,583,465 a taxpayer received from MFO for giving up his groundfish and snow crab commercial licences for the benefit of a First Nations group was held not to constitute proceeds of disposition of "property", the receipt of which could give rise to a taxable capital gain.[70] However, this decision was overturned later by the Federal Court of Appeal who held that Justice Lamarre had erred in deeming the licences invalid at the time of the transfer because one had expired and one had no attached conditions.[71] The commercial reality in the fishing industry combined with the departmental practice to renew licences from one year to the next prior to the completion of related documentation supported the proprietary nature of the licences the taxpayer had relinquished.

[¶5040] "Capital Property" Defined

"Capital property" is defined[72] as depreciable property and any other property in respect of which a gain or loss on disposition would be a capital gain or loss. Under this definition, the question of whether a property is capital property depends on the definition of capital gain and capital loss.[73] Thus, a capital gain does not arise on the disposition of the following types of property:

(1) property the sale of which would be taken into account in computing ordinary income (such as inventory of a business or property acquired as part of an adventure in the nature of trade);

(2) eligible capital property (such as goodwill and other non-deductible intangibles acquired in connection with a business);

(3) cultural property disposed of to a designated institution or public authority in Canada (see ¶5065);

(4) Canadian and foreign resource properties;

(5) an insurance policy, including a life insurance policy other than a segregated fund policy;

(6) specified debt obligations and mark-to-market properties as defined in ¶9277;

(7) property that is a timber resource property;

---

[69] Manrell, 2003 DTC 5225.

[70] Haché, 2010 DTC 1088.

[71] Haché, 2011 DTC 5089.

[72] CCH ¶7850b; Sec. 54 "capital property".

[73] CCH ¶6050; Sec. 39(1).

(8) a beneficiary's interest in a mining reclamation trust as defined in ¶7497; and

(9) for dispositions after 2001, participating interests in foreign investment entities.

As noted above, capital property for capital loss purposes is not quite the same as for capital gain purposes. Generally, a capital property is any property other than one listed in categories (1) to (9) above. The property exclusions in items (2) to (9) above cover property which would probably be considered capital property except for the specific treatment provided elsewhere in the Act. Anomalies arise in some circumstances due to the fact that shares of a corporation are normally capital property, while the assets of a corporation may to a large extent be non-capital property. Therefore, the income tax consequences will vary widely depending upon whether shares or assets are disposed of.

[¶5045] Meaning of "Eligible Capital Property"

"Eligible capital property" means[74] any property, a part of the consideration payable upon disposition of which would be an eligible capital amount in respect of a business.

An eligible capital amount is $1/2$ of the amount by which proceeds from the disposition of eligible capital property exceed the expenses incurred for purposes of the disposition.[75] Generally, eligible capital property includes goodwill and other intangibles acquired in connection with a business.[76] Transactions involving eligible capital property generally do not give rise to capital gains or losses. However, a portion of the negative balance in the cumulative eligible capital account will be treated as a taxable capital gain that is eligible for the capital gains exemption for individuals. See ¶3075 *et seq.*

[¶5050] Meaning of "Listed Personal Property"

"Listed personal property" means[77] personal-use property that is:

(a) a print, etching, drawing, painting, sculpture, or other similar work of art;

(b) jewellery;

(c) a rare folio, manuscript, or book;

(d) stamps; or

(e) coins.

See page ii for explanation of footnotes.

[74] CCH ¶4600, ¶5051, ¶7850e; Sec. 14(1), 20(1)(*b*), 54 "eligible capital property"; Interp. Bul. IT-386R.

[75] CCH ¶4639, ¶28,073; Sec. 14(5), 248(1) "eligible capital amount".

[76] Interp. Bul. IT-143R3.

[77] CCH ¶7850f; Sec. 54 "listed personal property"; Interp. Bul. IT-146R4.

See ¶5310.

[¶5055] Meaning of "Personal-Use Property"

"Personal-use property" includes:[78]

(a) any property that is used primarily for the personal use or enjoyment of a taxpayer or any person related to the taxpayer;

(b) a debt owing to a taxpayer in respect of the disposition of property that was personal-use property; and

(c) an option to acquire property that would, if acquired, be personal-use property.

Property owned by a trust and used primarily for the personal use or enjoyment of a beneficiary or a person related to the beneficiary is personal-use property. Personal-use property of a partnership includes any partnership property that is used primarily for the personal use or enjoyment of any member of the partnership or persons related to members. Corporations may also have personal-use property (see ¶5300).

[¶5060] Meaning of "Depreciable Property"

Although "depreciable property" is specifically stated to be capital property,[79] it is dealt with somewhat differently from other capital property. Under the capital cost allowance system, a disposition of depreciable property will ordinarily result in the recapture of depreciation, a terminal loss, or an adjustment in the allowances available in future years, all of which are taken into account in computing ordinary income. See Chapter IV.

The adjusted cost base of depreciable property is the capital cost to the taxpayer.[80] The capital cost of depreciable property is not subject to the specific adjustments set out for other capital property (see ¶5170); however, some adjustments will be made, such as in the case of the receipt of government grants (see ¶4012). A capital gain results from the disposition of depreciable property for more than its capital cost; however, no capital loss arises on the disposal of depreciable property.

[¶5065] Meaning of "Cultural Property"

"Cultural property" means an object that the Canadian Cultural Property Export Review Board has determined meets the relevant criteria set out in the *Cultural Property Export and Import Act*, and that has been disposed of to an institution or public authority in Canada that was, at the time of

---

See page ii for explanation of footnotes.

[78] CCH ¶7850g; Sec. 54"personal-use property".

[79] CCH ¶7850b, ¶28,045, ¶28,066; Sec. 54 "capital property", 248(1) "capital property", 248(1) "depreciable property".

[80] CCH ¶7850; Sec. 54 "adjusted cost base".

making the disposition, designated for one of the purposes enumerated in that Act.

No capital gain will result if cultural property is disposed of to a designated institution or authority. A capital loss will be allowed in certain circumstances.[81] The value (as determined by the Review Board) of cultural property that is donated by a corporation may be deducted in computing taxable income.[82] Individuals are eligible for a tax credit in respect of such gifts.[83] Amounts not deductible or creditable in a given taxation year may be carried forward for five years. Gifts made in the year of death are deemed to have been made in the preceding year to the extent that those gifts were not deducted in the year of death, and a gift made by will is treated as a donation made in the year of death.[84] In order for a gift by will not to result in a capital gain, the property must be disposed of within 36 months after the death of the taxpayer. The Minister may approve a longer period if it is considered reasonable in the circumstances.

[¶5070] Meaning of "Disposition"

For purposes of determining capital gains and losses, a "disposition" of any property, except as otherwise provided, includes:[85]

(1) a transaction or event that entitles a taxpayer to the proceeds of disposition of the property;

(2) a transaction or event as a result of which:

    (a) a share, bond, debenture, note, certificate, mortgage, hypothec, agreement of sale, or similar property, or an interest in it, is redeemed in whole or in part, cancelled or [acquired];

    (b) a debt owed to a taxpayer or any other right of a taxpayer to receive an amount is settled or cancelled;

    (c) a share is converted by amalgamation or merger;

    (d) an option to acquire or dispose of property expires; and

    (e) a trust that acts as agent for all the beneficiaries of the trust with respect to all dealings with all of the trust's property (commonly known as a "bare" trust) ceases to act as agent for any beneficiary with respect to any dealing with any of the trust's property;

(3) a transfer of property to a trust, or from a trust to a beneficiary (if there is a change in the beneficial ownership); and;

(4) a payment from a trust to a beneficiary under the trust in respect of the beneficiary's capital interest in the trust, whether in money or in kind,

---

[81] CCH ¶6050; Sec. 39(1)(a); Interp. Bul. IT-407R4.

[82] CCH ¶15,756; Sec. 110.1(1)(c).

[83] CCH ¶18,330, ¶18,336; Sec. 118.1(1), 118.1(3).

[84] CCH ¶18,352, ¶18,354; Sec. 118.1(4), 118.1(5).

[85] CCH ¶28,069; Sec. 248(1) "disposition"; Interp. Bul. IT-133, IT-170R, IT-444R, IT-460.

resulting in a disposition of all or part of the beneficiary's capital interest (unless the number of units owned by the beneficiary is not reduced, the payment is out of the income or capital gains of the trust for the same year in which the payment was made, or the payment is in respect of a non-taxable dividend designated by the trust in respect of the beneficiary).

The "acquisition" of a share, bond, debenture, note, certificate, mortgage, hypothec, agreement of sale or similar property is added to the list of transactions or events which fall within the definition of disposition. Before this addition, such transactions or events were limited to the redemption or cancellation of property. However, excluded from the definition of disposition are specified Canadian amalgamations or foreign mergers where the consideration received by the disposing corporation consists only of the shares of the new corporation. Both of these amendments, first announced on December 20, 2002, are reprised in the revised technical proposals that were released on July 16, 2010, but are not enacted yet. They will apply retroactively after December 23, 1998.

The following are specifically *excluded* from the definition of "disposition":

(1) A transfer of property where neither the transferor nor the transferee is a trust and where there is no change in the beneficial ownership of the property. For example, there will be no disposition where an individual's undivided joint ownership interest in real property is converted to a tenancy-in-common interest in the property.

(2) A transfer of property from one trust to another without any change in the beneficial ownership of the property if the following conditions are met:

>   (a) the transfer is not by a trust resident in Canada to a non-resident trust;
>
>   (b) the transferee does not receive the property in satisfaction of the transferee's right as a beneficiary under the transferor trust;
>
>   (c) the transferee trust held no property, or only property having a nominal value, at any time before the transfer and holds no property other than non-depreciable capital property immediately before the transfer;
>
>   (d) the transferor trust ceases to exist as a result of the transfer or a series of transactions that include the transfer;
>
>   (e) the transferee trust does not elect that the transfer be recorded as a disposition; and
>
>   (f) the transferor trust is one of 10 specified types of trust, the transferee trust is of the same type.

¶5070

(3) A transfer of property for the sole purpose of securing a debt or loan, or a transfer by a creditor for the sole purpose of returning property used as security for a debt or loan.

(4) The issue of a bond, debenture, note, certificate, mortgage, or hypothecary claim.

(5) The issue by a corporation of a share of its capital stock or any other transaction that would otherwise be a disposition by a corporation of a share of its capital stock.

It is to be noted that certain events give rise to "deemed dispositions" of property, even though no transfer actually takes place, or the taxpayer receives no actual gain or incurs no actual loss. Some of the events giving rise to deemed dispositions that can result in capital gains or losses include:

(a) the death of an individual taxpayer (¶2555);

(b) a gift or bequest (¶2505);

(c) a change of residence of a taxpayer from Canada to another country (¶5380);

(d) a change in the use of property (¶5360);

(e) the expiry of an option (¶5415);

(f) the settlement or cancellation of debt (¶5420); and

(g) a negative adjusted cost base (¶5175).

[¶5075] Meaning of "Proceeds of Disposition"

"Proceeds of disposition" is defined[86] to include certain listed amounts and, accordingly, amounts received which are not specifically described may still be found to be proceeds of disposition. The specific amounts which are proceeds of disposition are the following:

(1) the sale price of property that has been sold;[87]

(2) compensation for property that has been:

(a) unlawfully taken;

(b) destroyed, including any insurance proceeds;

(c) taken under statutory authority, including the sale price of property sold to a person by whom notice of an intention to take under statutory authority was given;[88]

(d) injuriously affected; or

See page ii for explanation of footnotes.

[86] CCH ¶7852; Sec. 54 "proceeds of disposition"; Interp. Bul. IT-220R2.

[87] Demers, 86 DTC 6411.

[88] E.R. Fisher Ltd., 86 DTC 6364, Sani Sport Inc., 90 DTC 6230, Shaw, 93 DTC 5121, Langlois, 94 DTC 1597.

(e) damaged, including insurance proceeds for property damage unless the compensation or insurance has, within a reasonable time, been used to repair the damage;

(3) the amount by which a taxpayer's liability to a mortgagee or hypothecary creditor is reduced as the result of the sale of the mortgaged or hypothecated property under a provision of the mortgage or hypothec, plus any amount received by the taxpayer from the proceeds of the sale;

(4) any amount included as a result of the extinguishment of a debt resulting from foreclosure of a mortgage or hypothecary claim or repossession of property sold under a conditional sales contract;[89]

(5) in the case of a share, the amount deemed in certain circumstances not to be a dividend on that share.[90] On a winding-up, a portion of the winding-up dividend not exceeding the pre-1972 capital surplus on hand of the corporation is deemed not to be a dividend.

The following amounts, however, are not included in proceeds of disposition:

(1) any amount which would otherwise be proceeds of disposition of a share to the extent that the amount received is deemed to be a dividend such as in a winding-up distribution or redemption,[91] provided that any portion of that deemed dividend that is deemed not to be a dividend (see (5) above) is not excluded from the proceeds of disposition of a share;

(2) any amount that would otherwise be proceeds of disposition to the extent that such amount is deemed to be a dividend in a non-arm's length sale of shares.[92] There is a deemed dividend when there is a non-arm's length transfer of shares by a resident individual or trust and the consideration received on the transfer exceeds both the paid-up capital and the adjusted cost base of the shares transferred. A dividend is deemed to have been paid to a non-resident when that non-resident transfers shares of one Canadian corporation to another Canadian corporation in exchange for non-share consideration in excess of the paid-up capital of the shares transferred, if both corporations are subject to a certain specified degree of common control.

In *Daisahawa*,[93] an assumption of future costs was determined to constitute part of the proceeds of disposition on the sale of a business. The case involved the taxpayer's sale of two timber mill businesses, each of which included timber rights and a corresponding reforestation obligation. The purchaser's assumption of the reforestation obligation was included in the proceeds of disposition. At the time of writing, this case has been granted leave to appeal to the Supreme Court.

See page ii for explanation of footnotes.

[89] Brill et al, 96 DTC 6572.

[90] CCH ¶11,170; Sec. 88(2)(b).

[91] CCH ¶7983, ¶10,240, ¶10,280; Sec. 55(2), 84(2), 84(3).

[92] CCH ¶10,384, ¶26,270; Sec. 84.1, 212.1.

[93] Daishowa-Marubeni International Ltd. v. The Queen, 2011 DTC 5157.

[¶5080] Meaning of "Adjusted Cost Base"

"Adjusted cost base" (ACB) is defined[94] to mean the capital cost of depreciable property and, for property other than depreciable property, the cost to the taxpayer of the property with specified adjustments. The adjustments may not reduce the adjusted cost base of a property at the time of disposition to less than zero. If the property involved is property that has been reacquired after a previous disposition, adjustments that were required to be made to the property before the reacquisition will not be made to the property after it is reacquired. There is also provision for a deemed gain when amounts to be deducted from the adjusted cost base exceed the cost plus the amounts to be added to the adjusted base. See ¶5175.[95]

"Cost" means the price the taxpayer gave up in order to get the asset and does not include any expense the taxpayer may have incurred in order to put himself or herself in a position to pay that price or to keep the property afterwards.[96]

[¶5085] Meaning of "Principal Residence"

"Principal residence" means a housing unit, including a leasehold interest therein, and also extends to a share of the capital stock of a co-operative housing corporation.[97] In order to qualify as a principal residence, the residence must be ordinarily inhabited in the year by the taxpayer, by the taxpayer's spouse/common-law partner or former spouse/common-law partner, or by a child of the taxpayer.

A taxpayer must designate[98] a residence as his or her principal residence in order to be allowed the exemption from capital gains tax. A spousal trust may claim the principal residence exemption whether the property was transferred to the trust during the lifetime of the transferor or upon the death of the spouse/common-law partner. The spousal trust designates the property as a principal residence for any year that the transferor could have designated the property, so there is no loss of exemption. Personal trusts that are not spousal trusts are also allowed to claim the principal residence exemption. A personal trust is eligible to claim the principal residence exemption if an individual beneficiary of the trust or the spouse/common-law partner, former spouse/common-law partner, or child of the beneficiary ordinarily inhabits the property and the trust makes the principal residence designation.

Only one residence can be claimed as the principal residence in any one year. Since 1982, each "family unit" has been effectively limited to one principal residence.

See page ii for explanation of footnotes.

[94] CCH ¶7850, ¶29,280; Sec. 54 "adjusted cost base"; ITAR 26(5).

[95] CCH ¶6440; Sec. 40(3).

[96] Stirling, 85 DTC 5199, Bodrug Estate, 91 DTC 5621, Jensen, 86 DTC 1505.

[97] CCH ¶7851; Sec. 54 "principal residence"; Interp. Bul. IT-120R6, IT-437R.

[98] CCH ¶7851, ¶7851a, ¶39,268; Sec. 54 "principal residence"; Reg. 2301; Form T2091.

A principal residence includes up to 0.5 hectares (approximately one acre) of surrounding land if the land contributes to the use and enjoyment of the home as a residence. More than 0.5 hectares of surrounding land may also be exempt if the taxpayer establishes that it is necessary for the use and enjoyment of the principal residence. However, the mere fact that land in excess of one acre contributes to the use and enjoyment of the taxpayer's residence does not make it *necessary* to such use and enjoyment.[99] Where a taxpayer sold her home and the 11 acres of land on which it sat, 10 of those acres were not part of her principal residence, as they were not necessary to the taxpayer's use of the house as a residence.[100] However, where the additional land was an integral part of a taxpayer's home and could not be subdivided, the taxpayer was allowed the principal residence exemption on the whole property of almost nine acres.[101] Further, where the zoning changes during ownership such that the property can be subdivided, the determination and the designation of whether a property constitutes a "principal residence" of a taxpayer is made on a year-by-year basis during the period of ownership. It follows that for those years that the zoning restrictions preclude the ability to obtain a severance of excess lands in a particular year when the property is ordinarily inhabited by the taxpayer, the taxpayer is able to designate the excess portion in those years as a principal residence.[102] See ¶5260 *et seq.*

[¶5090] Superficial Losses

No recognition of a loss on the disposition of property is permitted where the loss is a superficial loss.[103] A "superficial loss" is defined as the loss from the disposition of a property where:

(i) during the period that begins 30 days before the disposition and ends 30 days after the disposition, the disposing taxpayer or a person affiliated with the disposing taxpayer acquired or had a right to acquire the same property or an identical property; and

(ii) at the end of the 60-day period, the disposing taxpayer or a person affiliated with the disposing taxpayer owned or had a right to acquire the same property or an identical property.[104]

The property or identical property that is acquired in the 30-day period before or after the disposition is called a "substituted property". The amount of the loss denied is added to the cost base of the substituted property so that, on a future disposition, the loss is increased or the gain is reduced, as the case may be. See item (10) at (¶5180).

There are a number of exceptions to the superficial loss rules. These are:

---

[99] Rudeloff, 84 DTC 1548.
[100] Madsen, 81 DTC 1.
[101] Augart, 93 DTC 5205.

[102] Cassidy, 2011 DTC 5157.
[103] CCH ¶6434; Sec. 40(2)(g).
[104] CCH ¶7855; Sec. 54 "superficial loss".

(a) deemed dispositions on: change of use (¶5362); write-off of value-less shares or debt (¶5425); death; certain occurrences in trusts; emigration (¶5380); certain specified transactions by mutual funds, insurers, financial institutions, and securities dealers; elections by the trustee of an employees' profit sharing plan and change of status of exempt corporations (¶11,609);

(b) a disposition that is the result of the expiration of an option;

(c) a loss on an obligation between related persons already denied under other rules (this involves the debt parking rules on debt for-giveness at ¶3456);

(d) where there is a change of control of the disposing corporation within 30 days after the disposition; and

(e) where there is a change of exempt status of the disposing corpora-tion within 30 days after the disposition (¶11,609).

[¶5095] Meaning of "Taxable Canadian Property" — Non-Residents

The property listed below is taxable Canadian property which will give rise to capital gain or loss upon disposition by a non-resident:[105]

(1) Real property situated in Canada.

(2) All property, including capital property, eligible capital property, and inventory used by a non-resident (other than an insurer) in carrying on business in Canada, except ships and aircraft used principally in internation-al traffic, if the country in which the non-resident resides grants similar relief to Canadian residents. Where such property commences to be used for some other purpose, it is deemed to have been disposed of at fair market value at that time.

(3) Designated insurance property of a non-resident insurer; generally speaking, this is property used in carrying on an insurance business in Canada.

(4) After March 4, 2010, shares of a corporation (other than a mutual fund corporation) that are not listed on a designated stock exchange, an interest in a partnership, or an interest in a trust (other than a mutual fund trust or an income interest in a resident trust), if, at any time during the 60-month period that ends at that time, more than 50% of the fair market value of the share or interest was derived directly or indirectly from one or any combination of

(i) real or immovable property situated in Canada,

See page ii for explanation of footnotes.

[105] CCH ¶1250, ¶17,101, ¶17,300, ¶28,284; Sec. 2(3), 115, 116, 248(1) "taxable Canadian property".

(ii) Canadian resource properties,

(iii) timber resource properties, and

(iv) interests and options in respect of such properties.

[Draft legislation in respect of other 2010 Budget proposals released on August 27, 2010, but retroactive to March 5, 2010, would ensure that in determining whether the fair market value of the share or interest is derived from such properties, one does not take into account any value derived through a corporation, partnership, or trust the shares or interests in which were not themselves taxable Canadian property.]

(5) After March 4, 2010, a share of the capital stock of a corporation that is listed on a designated stock exchange, a share of the capital stock of a mutual fund corporation, or a unit of a mutual fund trust, if at any time during the 60-month period that ends at that time,

(i) 25% or more of the issued shares of any class of the capital stock of the corporation, or 25% or more of the issued units of the trust, were owned by or belonged to the taxpayer and persons with whom the taxpayer did not deal at arm's length, and

(ii) more than 50% of the fair market value of the share or unit was derived directly or indirectly from one or any combination of properties described under items (4)(i) to (iv) above.

(6) An option or interest in any of the above properties.

The above-noted capital gains and capital losses do not include any gain or loss from a disposition of a taxable Canadian property that is a "treaty-protected property".[106] This rule ensures that a non-resident's capital loss from the disposition of a treaty-protected property (meaning that, had the property been sold at a gain, it would not have been subject to tax in Canada by virtue of an income tax treaty) does not offset taxable capital gains of the non-resident from other capital properties whose gains are not treaty-protected.

[¶5100] Distinguishing between Business Income and Capital Receipts

[¶5105] Major Factors Involved

The definitions of capital gain and capital loss in the present Act do not spell out a distinction between a gain or loss that is a capital gain or loss and one that is ordinary business income. It is therefore necessary to look to the ever-evolving body of case law to provide the guidelines in determining

---

See page ii for explanation of footnotes.

[106] CCH ¶28,312; Sec. 248(1) "treaty-protected property".

whether a gain or loss on the disposition of property is on income or capital account. "Business" is defined[107] as including an adventure in the nature of trade. As a result, a transaction undertaken in isolation from a taxpayer's normal occupation may still be taxed as business income rather than as a capital gain.[108] The question of capital receipt versus business income arises frequently in transactions dealing with real estate[109] (see ¶5110) and is decided based on the circumstances of each case.

While it is often difficult to distinguish between a capital gain and business income in particular circumstances, there appear to be certain factors that the Courts have considered in determining whether a taxpayer has realized an investment (capital receipt) or has been carrying on a business (income receipt) when engaging in a particular transaction. The Courts look at the taxpayer's whole course of conduct not only prior to and during the taxation year, but also in the period following it.[110] In examining the taxpayer's whole course of conduct, the following factors are taken into consideration:

(1) intention;

(2) the relation of the transaction or transactions to the taxpayer's regular business;

(3) the nature of the transaction and the type of asset being disposed of;

(4) the number and frequency of similar transactions; and

(5) in the case of corporations, the declared objects of the corporation.

It has been held that in the absence of a specific provision in the Act bringing a receipt into income, a receipt which is on account of capital for accounting purposes will also be a capital receipt for income tax purposes.[111]

(1) *Intention.* In examining the taxpayer's course of conduct, the courts, among the different factors considered in the cases at law in which income versus capital gain is involved, always direct their research to the taxpayer's intention. In substance, it is the only factor. All other factors indeed (relation of transaction to taxpayer's business, number and frequency of similar transactions, the length of the period of ownership, the nature of transactions and assets involved, the corporation's object, etc.) are studied inasmuch as they are significant to the taxpayer's main intention and secondary intention.[112]

See page ii for explanation of footnotes.

[107] CCH ¶28,024; Sec. 248(1) "business"; Interp. Bul. IT-459.

[108] Bakos, 84 DTC 1509, Papley, 84 DTC 1562.

[109] Interp. Bul. IT-218R.

[110] Rosenblat, 55 DTC 1205.

[111] Consumers' Gas Co, 87 DTC 5008.

[112] Vardalos, 83 DTC 354.

An individual taxpayer and a corporation controlled by the taxpayer were held to be trading in shares since their intention was primarily speculative.[113] If an asset is purchased for investment purposes and is later sold out of necessity, then it would appear that the transaction entered into is not an adventure in the nature of trade and the resulting profit would be a capital receipt.[114] A distinction may be drawn between an intention to resell that is definite and one that is vague or indefinite. The former may very well be conclusive evidence that the transaction was entered into in a spirit of enterprise, whereas the latter may be quite consistent with the idea of investment. A taxpayer acquired 15 to 20 horses as a hobby and one which turned out to have potential for racing was later sold at a profit. The Court held that at the time of purchase there was no secondary intention of selling for a profit and the profit was therefore a capital gain.[115]

If property is bought for investment, a profit on its resale might still be considered taxable as income if it was apparent that from the outset there was also a secondary intention to resell at a profit; thus, for example, a taxpayer who bought a timber licence as a hedge against inflation and resold it two years later without working it, was found to have realized an income profit.[116] Similarly, where a company acquired a coal mine which remained unproductive for nine years and then resold it, the profit was held to be income.[117] Again, if the circumstances surrounding the resale indicate that there was a profit-making scheme, the profit would be considered to be income. Thus, where two associates purchased some land for a shopping centre and apartment house project, transferred the land to two of their own private companies in exchange for shares, and subsequently sold their shares, the profit was held to be taxable as income.[118] Similarly, profit from the purchase and sale of several hotels over a nine-year period was income.[119] Where a dredge was sold and later repurchased and resold, the vendor's intention to make a profit was indicated by the vendor's retention of a purchase option on the original sale.[120] Again, where a company used an option arrangement for putting through its real estate transactions, profits made in exercise of the option were taxable as income.[121]

However, an intention at the time of acquisition of an investment to sell it in the event that it does not prove profitable does not necessarily make the subsequent sale of the investment an adventure in the nature of trade, although it might if the expectation of profit on resale was one of the factors inducing the taxpayer to make the purchase.[122] Where a trader in land acquired a number of apartment properties as an investment and sold them at a profit nine months later, the profit was held to be a capital gain when

---

See page ii for explanation of footnotes.

[113] Wolfin et al., 84 DTC 1382.
[114] Bell, 89 DTC 165.
[115] Armstrong, 85 DTC 5396.
[116] Stekl, 59 DTC 1262.
[117] Inland Resources Co. Ltd., 64 DTC 5257.
[118] Fraser, 64 DTC 5224, De Toro, 65 DTC 5194.

[119] The King Edward Hotel (Calgary) Ltd., 90 DTC 6468.
[120] Sensibar Dredging Corp. Ltd., 67 DTC 5212.
[121] Edgeley Farms Ltd., 69 DTC 5228.
[122] Crystal Glass Canada Ltd., 89 DTC 5143, Snell Farms Ltd., 90 DTC 6693.

the taxpayer successfully proved that the apartments had not been acquired for speculative purposes.[123]

The intention of a taxpayer cannot ordinarily be established by a statement of the taxpayer of what the intention was. Such a statement must be supported by other evidence and the intention will be determined after considering the entire course of conduct of the taxpayer.[124]

If the taxpayer's plan for a property is thwarted, for reasons such as the lack of municipal approval, the high realty taxes and cost of servicing the land, illness, or other unexpected problems that occur, the profit will ordinarily be a capital gain.[125] However, the profit from land bought for a specific purpose and sold after a short period, supposedly because the purpose of the purchase could not be attained, was taxable as income. It was established that the reason for the purchase was abandoned even before the supposed impossibility of achieving it became known and that the land was bought only after a visual inspection.[126] There are a number of cases in which taxpayers have been held to be taxable on profits from real estate transactions on the grounds that their intention in entering the undertakings was in fact to make profits and that, without even realizing it and judging by what they actually did, they were carrying on a real estate business or had entered into adventures in the nature of trade.[127] This might be so even though a taxpayer can show that his or her original plan was frustrated; where it is obvious that the taxpayer could or should have known about the obstacles (e.g., zoning), the profit may be taxable as income as being from an adventure in the nature of trade.[128] The surrounding circumstances will of course be examined. When a taxpayer agreed to sell his interest in land upon being told that the city intended to expropriate it if necessary, the profit was a capital gain.[129]

The original intention may undergo a change; for example, an investor may sell because of the opportunity for a quick profit[130] or merely because the completion of the investment scheme is no longer advantageous or feasible.[131] This may be the case where the original investment intention is abandoned because of external factors such as increased costs of construction,[132] financial difficulties encountered,[133] the lack of interest by tenants in commercial premises offered for rent,[134] or when property was reluctantly sold because of threatened competition.[135] Depending on circumstances and other factors, the change of intention may be construed as indicative of a commercial venture with the resulting profits taxable as income, or it may

---

See page ii for explanation of footnotes.

[123] Hiwako Investments Ltd., 78 DTC 6281.

[124] Loyens, 83 DTC 535.

[125] Ratna Arya, 94 DTC 1526, Smith, 87 DTC 595, Jodare Limited et al, 86 DTC 6054, Valleypark Apartments Limited, 81 DTC 245, Acro Developments Co. Ltd, 79 DTC 727.

[126] Rokosh Engineering & Construction Ltd, 74 DTC 6375, Montpetit, 80 DTC 1273, Kornfeld and Balint, 80 DTC 1827, Dalfen, 81 DTC 37.

[127] Lieber, 63 DTC 530, Common Street Holdings, 64 DTC 325.

[128] Greenberg, 61 DTC 696, Sheftel, 65 DTC 5133.

[129] Desrochers Development Corp., 87 DTC 5363.

[130] Tandon, 85 DTC 332.

[131] Green Heron Investments Ltd., 84 DTC 1617, Hanover Management Ltd. et al, 89 DTC 355.

[132] Plains Investments, 64 DTC 146.

[133] Grand Marais Development Co. Ltd, 65 DTC 5286.

[134] No. 467, 57 DTC 537.

[135] Aldershot Shopping Plaza, 65 DTC 5018.

be viewed as being merely consistent with the original purpose of investing, where the realization of the asset would spell a capital receipt. A taxpayer was held to have changed his intention where in 1976 he unilaterally accepted an unsolicited offer for sale of the land he and his other partners had purchased as an investment in 1974. His other partners repudiated his decision and the land was eventually sold in 1980. The taxpayer's profit was taxed as a capital gain, calculated on the basis of the attempted sale in 1976, and as income thereafter. What happened here is that in 1976 the taxpayer's interest in the land changed use from a capital asset to an income-producing asset.[136]

(2) *Relation of transaction to taxpayer's business*. Where a taxpayer uses the skill and knowledge acquired through experience in trading in a certain line of commodities and later makes a profit on the purchase and sale of such commodities, the courts have held that such profit is taxable as income.[137] Thus, the profits in wool futures realized by a wool products manufacturing company were taxable as income,[138] as were the gains earned by a realtor from mortgage deals.[139] This rule may extend to the taxpayer's spouse/common-law partner.[140] Where two taxpayers, at the direction of their investment consultant spouses, made substantial profits from the acquisition and quick resale of speculative mining stock, the profit was held to be income.[141]

The same principle has been applied in the following cases: dealings by an agent for oil companies in oil leases on the agent's own account;[142] transactions in grain futures by a manager of a company trading in grain;[143] bonuses received in respect of a loan made by a company underwriting mining and oil securities;[144] profits of an investment dealer on its own investments;[145] sale of interest in a large construction contract by a construction company;[146] profits on the resale of lots and land by a coal dealer also carrying on the business of a building contractor;[147] and the sale of a newly built apartment house by the builder.[148] Similarly, where a notary who was familiar with the process of dealing in land sold a parcel of land which had been held for 19 years, the profits from the sale were held to be income.[149] A corporate taxpayer in the business of lending money received shares, share options, and mortgage bonds as partial consideration for loans. Gains from the dispositions of the securities were taxable as income because the taxpayer dealt with such securities either as a trader or as a regular part of its business.[150]

See page ii for explanation of footnotes.

[136] Hyman et al., 88 DTC 1352.
[137] Morrison, 1 DTC 113.
[138] M. Granatstein & Son Ltd., 55 DTC 396.
[139] Cerisano, 64 DTC 99.
[140] Wisniewski, 79 DTC 266.
[141] Darch and Wright, 92 DTC 6366.
[142] No. 331, 56 DTC 143, No. 332, 56 DTC 146.
[143] No. 351, 56 DTC 375.

[144] Stuyvesant-North, 58 DTC 1092.
[145] McMahon and Burns, 56 DTC 1092.
[146] General Construction, 59 DTC 1169.
[147] Gibson, 57 DTC 1119.
[148] Janzen, 64 DTC 756.
[149] Tardif, 79 DTC 758.
[150] Roynat Ltd., 81 DTC 5072.

¶5105

The courts have also considered the amount of the taxpayer's time and the amount of attention that the taxpayer gave to a transaction in determining whether or not the profit from the transaction was taxable.[151] Where a professor who, in addition to teaching, wrote and translated textbooks under contracts with the university later sold all rights under the contracts to the university, the professor was held to have received taxable income from an undertaking for profit or a business venture.[152]

Real estate transactions of building contractors, real estate agents, or brokers and taxpayers in similar occupations will usually be taxed as income.[153] Such a taxpayer will have to present a very strong case when claiming a real estate profit to be from an investment.[154]

(3) *Nature of transaction and assets involved.* If an asset which could not normally be used for either investment or personal pleasure, either because of the quantity or nature of the asset, is purchased and resold, it is likely that the profit will be of an income rather than a capital nature, although this is not conclusive. In two English decisions,[155] for example, such large quantities of toilet paper and whiskey were purchased that it was obvious the taxpayer could not possibly use them all for personal consumption. Similarly, the profit on a single purchase was held taxable as income where a large organization had to be set up to dispose of the purchased commodity.[156]

Normally a sale of fixed capital may be said to result in a capital receipt whereas a sale of circulating capital results in an income receipt. A sale of inventory which was not suited for the purpose for which it was bought was held to result in an income receipt.[157] Sale of oil leases by an exploration and development company resulted in taxable income, since leases, concessions, and other rights were part of the company's stock-in-trade.[158] However, where a family and two companies had been jointly and severally trying unsuccessfully to bring in a producing well on their government leases for about 30 years, and were fortuitous in being able to sell the leases just as they were in imminent danger of losing them, the profit was held to be a realization of a capital asset.[159] A sale of a timber limit was held to result in a capital receipt, where the limit was received from provincial authorities in exchange for freehold timber lands to be used for colonization.[160]

The manner of disposition of assets, otherwise considered capital, may be important. Thus, taxable income was held to have resulted from sales of mineral and timber rights pertaining to lands a railway company had been granted in 1899. Even though the lands were of a capital nature when

---

See page ii for explanation of footnotes.

[151] McDonough, 49 DTC 621.

[152] LaRue, 63 DTC 553.

[153] Bachuk, 61 DTC 536, P. E. Perron, Ltée, 62 DTC 1288, Blain, 64 DTC 367, Upstream Holdings, Inc., 69 DTC 5358, Consolidated Building Corp., 65 DTC 5211.

[154] Fabi, 65 DTC 5160, Bélisle, 64 DTC 490.

[155] Rutledge, (1929), 14 T.C. 490, Fraser, (1942), 24 T.C. 498.

[156] Martin v. Lowry, [1927] A.C. 512, Gordon, 51 DTC 230, Honeyman, 55 DTC 1094.

[157] No. 123, 53 DTC 407.

[158] Great West Exploration, 57 DTC 444.

[159] Moose Securities Ltd., 63 DTC 182.

[160] Gagnon, 58 DTC 562.

received, their character was changed by the manner in which they were later dealt with and used.[161]

With respect to mortgages, profits may be also taxable as income in taxpayers' hands if the mortgages have only a short time to run to their maturity, where they have been purchased at a discount, where the interest rate is much lower than the prevailing rate on first-class second mortgages, or the mortgages are substandard first mortgages, and where they are of a risky nature. The Supreme Court of Canada has held that in instances of this type the taxpayer is regarded as being engaged in the highly speculative business of purchasing mortgages (including agreements for sale and lease-option agreements) at a discount and holding them to maturity in order to realize the maximum amount of profit out of the transactions.[162] It would therefore seem that nearly all profits realized from transactions involving the purchase of mortgages at a discount or under a bonus arrangement are taxable as income.[163]

It is the nature of a transaction, not its singleness or isolation, that must be determined by the courts.[164] Where a taxpayer sought to deduct a trading loss on shares which had been retained as an investment and that had ceased to have any value, the loss on the shares was held to be a capital loss on an investment.[165] In two cases with somewhat similar facts, profits from the sale of shares obtained in exchange for mining claims were on account of capital when the taxpayer engaged a prospector to stake claims for the taxpayer alone[166] but were taxable as income where the taxpayer participated in a syndicate.[167] See ¶5240 regarding an election that a taxpayer can make to have certain securities, described as "Canadian securities," treated as capital property for tax purposes.[168]

The former owner of a family business repurchased the shares of the company when it ran into financial difficulties, and acquired with it certain loans owing to shareholders which, at the time, were valued at nil. The former owner turned the business around and collected on the loans. It was held that the gain on the loans was a capital receipt, since gains arising from an entrepreneur's personal efforts were not, for that reason alone, necessarily income.[169]

(4) *Number and frequency of similar transactions.* Another factor in determining whether profit derived from a transaction is a capital gain or income is the frequency with which the taxpayer has engaged in such transactions. Where a member of a firm of cotton brokers averaged some fifty transactions a year on the member's own account in cotton futures, the profits were

See page ii for explanation of footnotes.

[161] The Algoma Central and Hudson Bay Railway Co., 61 DTC 1027.
[162] Hennick, 64 DTC 307, Walfish, 64 DTC 5121, Posluns, 64 DTC 5168, Davidson, 65 DTC 109.
[163] Wood, 69 DTC 5073, Ferguson, 70 DTC 1779.
[164] Farris, 70 DTC 6179.
[165] Trotter, 70 DTC 1104.
[166] Foster, 71 DTC 5207.
[167] Kay, 71 DTC 5085.
[168] CCH ¶6387; Sec. 39(4); Interp. Bul. IT-479R.
[169] Eidinger, 86 DTC 6594.

found to be income,[170] as were those of a taxpayer involved in the purchase and resale of several restaurant businesses over a period of years.[171]

While a large number of transactions is likely to be indicative of an intention of carrying on a business for profit, the isolated transaction doctrine taken by itself provides a poor ground for an appeal since the term "business" includes an adventure or concern in the nature of trade.[172]

Certain decisions of the Courts and the former Tax Review Board make it abundantly clear that the fact that a transaction is an isolated one does not in itself bring the profit into the capital gain category. In one such case, a profit made by a company director in an isolated transaction not related to the director's employment, involving the sale of four second-hand diesel engines was taxed as income.[173] Similarly, profits realized within a year by a lawyer on three unrelated transactions (deals in pipe, salt prospecting rights, and oil and gas) were held to be taxable as income.[174] Profits realized on the syndication of a stallion were held to be income from an adventure in the nature of trade.[175]

(5) *Corporation's objects.* A corporation's objects and powers as set out in its charter create a *prima facie* presumption that acts done within their ambit must also be held to be within the commercial intent of the corporation. This presumption may, however, be rebutted by looking at the corporation's course of conduct and ascertaining what it in fact did during its commercial life rather than what it intended to do as formally stated in its main object clauses. The inclusion in its charter of a power to sell and deal in real estate is not evidence that the corporation was actually engaged in the business of trading in real estate with a view to resale at a profit. What counts is not what the company can do but what it actually does.[176] To borrow the words used by the Supreme Court of Canada, "the question to be decided is not what business or trade the company might have carried on under its memorandum but rather what was in truth the business it did engage in. To determine this it is necessary to examine the facts with care".[177] Thus, even if a corporation's objects were for investment purposes, its records did not characterize it as an investment company and neither did its course of action when it purchased and resold the stock involved, in the very short period of eight weeks, for the fantastic profit of $41,411.43. The purchase could not be considered an investment as the shares paid no dividends. The transaction was purely a calculated and speculative risk, the company being used as a vehicle for making a quick profit. It was an adventure in the nature of trade in the hope of realizing a quick profit.[178]

See page ii for explanation of footnotes.

[170] Cooper v. Stubbs, 2 K.B. 753.

[171] No. 367, 56 DTC 516.

[172] CCH ¶28,024; Sec. 248(1) "business"; Interp. Bul. IT-459.

[173] Chuter, 59 DTC 1118.

[174] Turnbull, 57 DTC 1170.

[175] Anderson, 80 DTC 1501.

[176] Rivermede Developments Limited, 93 DTC 5365.

[177] Sutton Lumber & Trading Ltd., 53 DTC 1158.

[178] Interoceanic Investments Corporation Ltd., 68 DTC 18.

Of course, the fact alone that taxpayers buying property as capital admit that they could be induced to resell it if a sufficiently high price were offered is not sufficient to change a capital acquisition into an adventure in the nature of trade. The secondary intention to resell at a profit does not merely require the thought of resale at a profit but must have an operating motivation in the acquisition at the time of acquisition. That a company has among its objects transactions of a certain type may make it difficult for the company to prove that a particular transaction corresponding to that type was not part of the regular business operations carried on by it.[179]

[¶5110] Real Estate Transactions

One of the subjects with which the courts have had to deal most is the question of the taxability of profits from real estate transactions. The general rules for distinguishing capital receipts from income will be applicable here.[180]

If there is a series of purchases and resales it is probable that any profit may be taxable as income.[181] However, if it can be shown that the changes were merely a step in the taxpayer's investment program, then any profit will be a capital receipt.[182] Also, when a taxpayer sold a property because of a change in financial circumstances or because of the realization of the time and effort involved in being a landlord, the gain in each case was held to be on account of capital.[183] If some extraneous and, from the taxpayer's viewpoint, independent circumstance or event prevents the taxpayer from keeping the property, the transaction is often determined to be a mere realization of an investment and the resulting profit is a capital receipt.

Much will depend, of course, on the other circumstances surrounding the transaction and on the manner of the disposal of the asset. Thus, profit by a real estate company on expropriated property was held to be taxable as income.[184] Through a series of purchases and sales, a taxpayer sought to liquidate hazardous situations in order to save his capital; because the taxpayer acted for investment rather than commercial purposes, the profits were capital receipts.[185]

There is a wide variety of case law on real estate transactions and some of the cases are difficult to reconcile with others.

Capital receipts were held to have resulted from the following transactions:

    (a) resale of land acquired for erection of apartment houses and resold because of new zoning restrictions;[186]

See page ii for explanation of footnotes.

[179] Regal Heights Ltd., 60 DTC 1270, Glacier Realties Limited, 80 DTC 6243, Witten, 91 DTC 5041.
[180] Interp. Bul. IT-218R.
[181] Lane, 64 DTC 5049, Gagnon, 66 DTC 5099, Kinsella, 64 DTC 56.
[182] Quon Yuen, 62 DTC 1204, Hébert, 86 DTC 6543.

[183] Sini, 88 DTC 1454, Martens, 87 DTC 669.
[184] Upstream Holdings Inc., 69 DTC 5358, Schneider et al., 84 DTC 6286.
[185] Nadeau, 70 DTC 1368.
[186] No. 341, 56 DTC 231, Westmount Lumber Co. Ltd., 65 DTC 666.

(b) resale of houses because of the taxpayer's poor health and because of difficulties in collecting rent;[187]

(c) resale of property because the expected revenue was not forthcoming or the venture appeared too risky;[188]

(d) resale of timber limits by a logging company where the offer was too attractive to refuse;[189]

(e) sale of two duplexes in the suburbs after the taxpayer's family refused to move there;[190] and

(f) resale of property purchased for erecting a family residence when it was found unsuitable for the taxpayer's children.[191]

On the other hand, *income receipts* were held to have been received under similar circumstances:

(a) sale of land bought originally for gardening and resold in lots when the gardening project appeared unprofitable;[192]

(b) resale of a farm for mink raising after the permit was refused;[193]

(c) resale of land after plans for a subdivision were abandoned because of township requirements or other similar reasons;[194]

(d) resale of an apartment house because of lack of funds necessary to finish it;[195]

(e) resale of land before expropriation[196] and because of lack of funds required to erect a proposed building;[197]

(f) resale of houses allegedly built by an excavating contractor for the contractor's employees;[198]

(g) resale of a shopping centre shortly after it had been acquired;[199] and

(h) purchase of land for erection of a shopping centre and its resale, *en bloc* or in lots, because the scheme did not appear practical or for similar reasons.[200]

One important exception to the above rules is the case of the sale or subdivision of land owned by an estate or which has been inherited. For the

---

See page ii for explanation of footnotes.

[187] Esar, 52 DTC 248, Cameron, 56 DTC 348, McGuire, 56 DTC 1042.

[188] Baker Estates, 54 DTC 514, Martin & Frères, 55 DTC 363, No. 225, 55 DTC 32, No. 276, 55 DTC 442, Thibeault, 64 DTC 5151.

[189] Hope Hardware & Building Supply Co. Ltd., 67 DTC 5085.

[190] Mullard, 58 DTC 232, Watters, 59 DTC 129.

[191] Heal, 59 DTC 61, No. 592, 59 DTC 82.

[192] Van den Bussche, 58 DTC 334.

[193] Peace, 58 DTC 422.

[194] Day, 58 DTC 1042, Doré, 64 DTC 501.

[195] Dolais Enterprises Ltd., 58 DTC 346, Harmony Investments Ltd., 65 DTC 5009.

[196] No. 539, 58 DTC 439.

[197] Toole, 64 DTC 53, Sura, 67 DTC 5250.

[198] Bower, 59 DTC 1055.

[199] Dow Shoppers' Park Ltd., 61 DTC 524.

[200] Regal Heights Ltd., 60 DTC 1270, A. & H. Management Ltd., 61 DTC 4, Jarry, 64 DTC 5001, Rothenberg, 65 DTC 5001.

most part such transactions will be regarded as the realization of an asset and any gain or loss will be on capital account.[201]

[¶5115] Real Estate — Farm Transactions

Resale of farmland by a taxpayer who either acquired or inherited the farm and lived on it will usually result in a capital gain (not income), especially if the resale was not carried out in a planned and businesslike manner (i.e., if the taxpayer did not advertise, employ agents, etc.).[202] However-er, when a taxpayer purchased a farm and, upon receiving an unsolicited offer, sold it a few months later at a substantial profit, the profit was held to be taxable as income.[203] Similarly, where the taxpayer, a real estate specula-tor, acquired a 90-acre farm intending to use it as a principal residence, and resold it prior to closing the original transaction, the profit realized was held to be income.[204] On the other hand, where the original intention to live on the farm was abandoned due to circumstances beyond the taxpayer's control, the profit was held to be a capital gain.[205] Similarly, where a taxpay-er purchased a farm site to build apartment houses and a shopping centre but was forced by circumstances to temporarily abandon the project, and then sold a small part of the property to an oil company, the profit on the sale of the small portion was held to be a capital gain.[206]

[¶5125] Valuation Day

[¶5130] General

The taxation of capital gains is effective from the commencement of 1972. It is therefore necessary to value capital property held on Valuation Day shortly before the end of 1971. The value of the property on that day is taken into account in computing capital gains and losses realized subse-quently. For publicly-traded shares and securities Valuation Day is Decem-ber 22, 1971, and for all other property, including bonds, it is December 31, 1971.[207]

Since the law is intended to tax only capital gains arising after the start of the new system, taxpayers should value, as of the applicable Valuation Day, each asset that is likely to be subject to a realized or deemed capital gain at some future date. The majority of taxpayers will not be affected by Valuation Day because the types of property owned by most taxpayers (i.e., a home and such personal effects as household goods and automobiles) usu-ally will not be subject to the capital gains provisions. A home is not subject

See page ii for explanation of footnotes.

[201] Interp. Bul. IT-218R.

[202] Skov, 60 DTC 479, Smith, 63 DTC 1121, Dennis, 61 DTC 65, Carlson, 61 DTC 408, Clocl, 61 DTC 477.

[203] Grant, 63 DTC 1159.

[204] Ravida, 78 DTC 1030.

[205] Caponecchia, 79 DTC 5364, Stroh, 80 DTC 1457.

[206] Terroux, 64 DTC 358.

[207] CCH ¶6002, ¶29,255, ¶29,259, ¶29,261; ITAR 24, 26(1); Reg. 4400.

to capital gains tax if the taxpayer used it only as a principal residence and personal effects generally do not give rise to a capital gain when sold.

Taxpayers will be affected by Valuation Day if they own the following types of property:

(a) real estate other than a principal residence, such as land or rental property, a summer cottage, etc.;

(b) works of art, jewellery, rare folios, manuscripts or books, stamps, or coins worth more than $1,000;

(c) other personal property worth more than $1,000 and likely to increase in value;

(d) investments, such as shares and securities;

(e) business property; and

(f) an interest in a partnership.

A taxpayer who holds shares or securities as of January 1, 1972 should consult Schedule VII of the Regulations which lists shares and securities to which the Valuation Day for publicly-traded shares and securities applies.[208]

The Valuation Day of December 31, 1971 for other property will apply to any share or security not listed in the above noted Schedule. Holders of shares or securities not listed therein or for which no value is prescribed should contact the Business Equity Valuation Officers at the CRA, whose duties include the determination of the value of securities for which there is no quoted market.

Since there is no standard formula for establishing the value of shares in private companies, each holding must be valued on its particular merits and professional assistance may be necessary.

In support of valuations of real estate, taxpayers would be wise to retain documents containing the following information:

(a) a brief description of the property, including location, lot and building size, and construction type;

(b) cost and date of a purchase;

(c) cost of any additions or improvements;

(d) property assessment for municipal tax purposes; and

(e) insurance coverage.

For certain types of property, additional information would be useful:

---

[208] Sch VII.

(1) *Farm property* — type of land (arable, bush, or scrub) and type of farming done.

(2) *Residential rental property* — gross annual rental income and net annual income before depreciation.

(3) *Commercial or industrial property* — type of business for which the property is used, gross annual income so derived, and net annual income before depreciation allowance.

In certain instances, even more exotic documentation may be advisable. Where a taxpayer operated a cheese processing plant, the value of bacteria living in the plant had essential economic value in measuring the worth of the premises.[209]

Taxpayers who own listed personal property that is worth more than $1,000, either as a set or as an individual item, should establish a Valuation Day value. Many such items may be valued by consulting dealers' catalogues or the dealers themselves.

In general, business assets should be valued in the same manner as other properties. However, the following items do not require valuation for capital gains purposes:

(a) the trading assets of a business;

(b) depreciable property which is worth less than its original cost; and

(c) goodwill of a business.

[¶5135] Valuation Day Value — Median Rule or Tax-Free-Zone Method

The computation of a gain or loss realized by an *individual* in 1972 or later on assets held at January 1, 1972, is to be measured from a base value that may be determined by one of two methods:[210]

(1) fair market value on Valuation Day; and

(2) the median rule, also known as the tax-free zone method.

Corporations are required to use the median rule (tax-free zone method).

See page ii for explanation of footnotes.

[209] 86103 Ontario Incorporated, 82 DTC 1652.   [210] CCH ¶29,267, ¶29,286, ¶29,286a; ITAR 26(3), 26(7); Reg. 4700; Interp. Bul. IT-65.

¶5135

Under the median rule, three figures are required before the capital gain or loss can be calculated for property owned on December 31, 1971. These are:

(1) the actual cost of acquisition;

(2) the fair market value on Valuation Day; and

(3) the proceeds of sale or disposal.

The median (middle) amount is deemed to be the base from which gains or losses are to be calculated. When any two amounts are the same, that amount is deemed to be the base. The tax-free zone is the area between items (1) and (2). If the proceeds of disposition fall within this area, the proceeds will be the median amount and will be the deemed cost, so that there will be no gain or loss. If at any time the cost is being determined when there has been no disposition, the fair market value at that time is substituted for item (3) above. See ¶4015 for a calculation on the disposition of depreciable property held on December 31, 1971 and disposed of at a later date.

Under the median or tax-free method, the capital gain or loss on any asset sold after December 31, 1971 is calculated as follows:

Amount of Proceeds	*Capital Gain or Loss*
Greater than both the cost and Valuation Day value	▶ Capital gain = proceeds minus the greater of cost or Valuation Day value
Between original cost and Valuation Day value	▶ No taxable gain or allowable loss
Less than either original cost or Valuation Day value	▶ Capital loss = the lower of cost or Valuation Day value minus the proceeds

If an individual has maintained cost records for assets held on January 1, 1972, he or she may elect either the tax-free zone or Valuation Day value method of computing the adjusted cost base of all assets. The choice of methods should be influenced by whether the fair market value of the taxpayer's assets is above or below cost on Valuation Day and by whether the assets rose or fell in value after Valuation Day. If the majority of the taxpayer's assets are worth more at Valuation Day than cost and subsequently decline in value, the taxpayer might select Valuation Day value as a higher base against which to measure any future losses. On the other hand, if most of a taxpayer's assets were depressed below cost at Valuation Day and subsequently rose in value, electing the tax-free zone method would probably be more advantageous.

¶5135

Illustrations of Valuation Options for Property held on January 1, 1972:

Cost	$100	$100	$100	$100
Valuation Day value	80	90	110	120
Tax-free zone	80-100	90-100	100-110	100-120
Proceeds or value on disposal	75	95	115	115
Gain (Loss):*				
— Tax-free zone method	(5)	--	5	--
— V. Day value option	(5)	5	5	(5)

* Note that under the tax-free zone method the gain or loss is measured as the difference between the proceeds on disposal and the closest figure in the tax-free zone (assuming the proceeds are outside the tax-free zone). Under the Valuation Day option, the gain or loss is measured as the difference between the proceeds on disposal and the Valuation Day value.

Once an individual has made an election to use either the Valuation Day value or the tax-free zone method when filing the first return on which he or she reports a disposal of property, the taxpayer must continue to use the method chosen for all other property owned on December 31, 1971. An individual who files the return late will not be allowed to elect to use the Valuation Day value but must use the median rule or tax-free zone method.[211]

An election may be postponed in a year in which the only disposition of capital property in a taxation year was:

(a) personal-use property that is not listed personal property or real property;

(b) listed personal property where there was neither gain nor loss;

(c) the taxpayer's principal residence if the gain after deducting the principal residence exemption was nil;

(d) other personal-use property that was real property where there was neither gain nor loss;

(e) property which the owner acquired from someone not at arm's length[212] (see ¶5195); or

(f) property deemed to be owned by the taxpayer under the Act but not actually owned by the taxpayer.

If a taxpayer makes an election in a year in which it could have been postponed, the CRA will accept a request for the withdrawal of that election.

---

[211] CCH ¶29,286; ITAR 26(7).   [212] CCH ¶29,280; ITAR 26(5).

¶5135

[¶5140] Calculation of Gain or Loss

[¶5145] Taxpayer's Gain or Loss

A capital gain is measured by deducting an asset's adjusted cost base (see ¶5080) and the expenses of sale from the proceeds of disposition.[213] Expenses of sale include such things as legal expenses relating to the sale, agent or broker commissions, and advertising costs.

Example:

> D acquired land at a cost of $20,000 plus $500 in legal fees. The land was later sold for $24,000. D incurred legal fees of $400 and advertising expenses of $200 on the sale. D's gain would be reported as follows:

Proceeds of disposition		$24,000
Less: (a) adjusted cost base	$20,500	
(b) expenses of sale	600	
		21,100
Capital gain		$ 2,900

"Proceeds of disposition" means the sale price or any compensation received for property, including insurance proceeds for loss or destruction of property, compensation for lost or damaged property, expropriation proceeds, etc.[214] See ¶5075.

If the proceeds of disposition are not to be received until after the end of the year, a taxpayer may defer a portion of the capital gain. Any amount claimed as a reserve in one year must be included in computing gains for the following year. See ¶5160.

A loss from the disposition of property is generally the excess of the adjusted cost base and expenses of sale over the proceeds of disposition. One-half of the gain or loss is defined as a taxable capital gain or allowable capital loss.[215] An allowable capital loss can only be used to reduce taxable capital gains unless it is an allowable business investment loss. See ¶5030. The law provides for the carryover of capital losses, back three years and forward indefinitely, to be used against capital gains. See Chapter III.

[¶5150] Partial Dispositions of Property

When only part of a capital property is disposed of, the taxpayer's gain or loss from that part is computed by attributing a reasonable portion of the adjusted cost base of the whole property to the part disposed of.[216] For example, if the adjusted cost base of the whole property were $1,000 and the

---

See page ii for explanation of footnotes.

[213] CCH ¶6400; Sec. 40(1).
[214] CCH ¶7852; Sec. 54 "proceeds of disposition".
[215] CCH ¶6007; Sec. 38.
[216] CCH ¶6650; Sec. 43; Interp. Bul. IT-264R, IT-418.

taxpayer was disposing of $1/2$ of it for $900, the taxpayer's gain on that half would be computed from an adjusted cost base of $500 and would, as a result, be $400. Where there is a disparity in value between different parts of the same property, it will be a question of fact as to what is a reasonable allocation of the adjusted cost base among those parts.

[¶5155] Reserves for Future Proceeds

[¶5160] Reserve for Proceeds Not Due Until After End of the Year

A taxpayer is permitted to defer a portion of the capital gain on the disposition of property if the proceeds are not receivable until after the end of the year.[217] Amounts claimed as reserves in one year must be brought back into the computation of gains in the succeeding year and a new reserve may be calculated. For most dispositions a taxpayer may only claim a reserve equal to the lesser of:

(a) a reasonable amount represented by the proportion of the proceeds not yet due before the end of the taxation year; and

(b) an amount equal to $1/5$ of the gain on the disposition of property multiplied by four minus the number of preceding taxation years ending after the disposition of the property.

Thus, the taxpayer must recognize capital gains at a cumulative rate of at least 20% annually, commencing in the year of disposition. Less restrictive reserve rules are provided for dispositions of family farm or fishing property, shares in the capital stock of family farm or fishing corporations, interests in family farm or fishing partnerships, and shares in small business corporations to children, grandchildren, and great-grandchildren.[218] In this case, the gain must be brought into income at the rate of 10% per annum on a cumulative basis unless the proceeds of disposition are received at a rate in excess of 10% per annum. The 10-year reserve applicable to capital gains realized on a disposition of fishing property to a child, grandchild, or great grandchild apply to dispositions occurring after May 1, 2006. It should be noted that a reserve is not available to a taxpayer who, at the end of the year or at any time in the following year, was not resident in Canada or was exempt from tax. It is also not available if the purchaser is a corporation which is controlled directly or indirectly by the taxpayer, or which controls the taxpayer if the taxpayer is a corporation. Furthermore, after December 20, 2002, the reserve is not available to a taxpayer if the purchaser is a partnership of which the taxpayer is a majority interest partner.[219]

See page ii for explanation of footnotes.

[217] CCH ¶6400; Sec. 40(1).
[218] CCH ¶6401, ¶9295, ¶9295a, ¶9295ab, ¶9295b, ¶9295ba; Sec. 40(1.1), 70(10) "child", 70(10) "interest in a family farm partnership", 70(10) "interest in a family fishing partnership", 70(10)

"share of the capital stock of a family farm corporation", 70(10) "share of the capital stock of a family fishing corporation".
[219] CCH ¶6420; Sec. 40(2)(a).

No reserve can be claimed in respect of a demand promissory note, since it is immediately enforceable and therefore "due" even though no demand has been made.[220]

The law does not provide a method of computing a reserve, but merely provides for a "reasonable amount". A "reasonable" reserve may be calculated as the percentage of the proceeds not yet due for payment, multiplied by the capital gain, subject to the rule that at least $\frac{1}{5}$, or in the case of farming or fishing property or a share of a small business corporation disposed of to a child, $\frac{1}{10}$ of the gain must be recognized each year.

Example 1:

Proceeds of disposition are $200,000, adjusted cost base is $130,000 and expenses of disposition are $20,000. The balance not yet receivable at year end is $120,000.

Reserve: $\frac{\$120,000}{\$200,000}$ x ($200,000 - ($130,000 + $20,000)) = $30,000

Example 2:

Proceeds of disposition are $200,000, adjusted cost base is $130,000, expenses of disposition are $20,000 and the whole $200,000 is not yet due at the year end. Using the above formula:

Reserve: $\frac{\$200,000}{\$200,000}$ x ($200,000 - ($130,000 + $20,000)) = $50,000

In Example 2, the maximum reserve is limited to $40,000 in the first taxation year. A gain of at least $10,000 (20%) must be recognized in the year of disposition and each succeeding taxation year.[221]

For comment on special reserves in connection with the sale of inventory, accounts receivable, etc., see Chapter III.

[¶5162] Reserve for Gift of Non-Qualifying Security

When a taxpayer makes a charitable gift of a "non-qualifying security", the gift is ignored for the purposes of the charitable donations deduction and tax credit, respectively.[222] However, if the donee disposes of the security within five years, the donor will be treated as having made a gift at that later time. The fair market value of the later gift will be considered to be the lesser of: (i) the fair market value or the consideration received by the donee for the disposition (except to the extent that the consideration is another non-qualifying security), and (ii) the fair market value of the original gift. For these purposes, an individual's non-qualifying security is defined as an

See page ii for explanation of footnotes.

[220] Derbecker, 84 DTC 6549, Pineo, 86 DTC 6322.   [222] CCH ¶15,770b, ¶18,367b; Sec. 110.1(6), 118.1(13).
[221] CCH ¶6400; Sec. 40(1)(*a*).

obligation of the individual or a non-arm's length person, a share issued by a corporation with which the individual does not deal at arm's length, or any other security issued by the individual or a non-arm's length person.[223] Specifically excepted from this definition are obligations, shares, and other securities listed on a prescribed stock exchange, and deposits with financial institutions.

A taxpayer is allowed to claim a reserve in respect of any gains realized from the making of the original gift so that the resulting inclusion in income can be shifted to a later year, including, in particular, the year in which the donor ultimately receives recognition for the donation in the form of a deduction or tax credit.[224] The reserve is available only in taxation years ending within 60 months of the making of the gifts. Moreover, the reserve cannot be claimed once the taxpayer receives tax recognition for the gifts, nor if the taxpayer becomes non-resident or tax-exempt.

[For gifts made after December 20, 2002, the reserve is limited to the "eligible amount" of a gift, meaning the fair market value of the property transferred to the donee minus the advantage provided to the donor. This amendment is consequential on the proposed "split" gift rules, first announced on December 20, 2002 and reprised in the revised technical proposals that were released on July 16, 2010.]

[¶5165] Calculation of Adjusted Cost Base

[¶5170] Cost of Property

The adjusted cost base is the base used to determine whether there is a capital gain or loss on the disposition of property. For depreciable property, the adjusted cost base is the capital cost to the taxpayer. For other property, the adjusted cost base is the cost to the taxpayer plus or minus certain adjustments. However, the adjustments may not bring the adjusted cost to a negative base. See ¶5175.[225]

If the property is property that was reacquired by the taxpayer after a previous disposition, adjustments that were required to be made to the property before the reacquisition are not made to the property after it is reacquired.

In most instances, the cost to a taxpayer of capital property is the amount paid to acquire the property. This may not be the case when a property is acquired from a person with whom the taxpayer is not dealing at arm's length. Generally, when property is acquired from a related person or from any other person with whom the taxpayer is not dealing at arm's length for an amount in excess of its fair market value, the taxpayer is deemed to

---

See page ii for explanation of footnotes.

[223] CCH ¶18,367g; Sec. 118.1(18).   [225] CCH ¶7850; Sec. 54 "adjusted cost base".
[224] CCH ¶6400a; Sec. 40(1.01).

have acquired the property for its fair market value. The actual price paid for the property may therefore be irrelevant for purposes of determining the cost to the taxpayer. Similarly, when the property is disposed of in a non-arm's length transaction for less than its fair market value, the taxpayer is deemed to have received proceeds equal to its fair market value.[226] Special rules apply when property is transferred to a spouse/common-law partner or spousal trust (see ¶2595) and when farm property or, after May 1, 2006, fishing property, is transferred to a child (see ¶2600). There are also special rules concerning the transfer of property to a corporation, trust, or partnership (see ¶6210 *et seq.* and ¶7110 *et seq.*). In addition, several provisions of the Act determine what the cost to the taxpayer is in specific circumstances:[227]

(1) When a taxpayer has acquired a property and has been required to include an amount in respect of the value of the property in computing income, the amount included in income is added to the cost of the property so acquired rather than its adjusted cost base. This provision does not apply to property that is an annuity contract, a right as a beneficiary under a trust to enforce payment of an amount by the trust to the taxpayer or property received as a dividend in kind or stock dividend as described in (2) or (3) below. It also does not apply in the situation when an employee acquires shares from the employer corporation at a discount (see item (17) *Share or fund unit taxed as stock option benefit* at ¶5180).[228] Any adjustment to cost will be made only for amounts that have not otherwise been added to the cost or to the adjusted cost base of the property.

(2) A shareholder in receipt of a dividend in kind, other than a stock dividend, is deemed to have acquired the property at a cost equal to its fair market value at the time. The payor corporation is deemed to have disposed of the property for proceeds equal to that fair market value.[229]

(3) A shareholder in receipt of a stock dividend is deemed to have acquired the shares at a cost equal to the aggregate of:

(a) the amount of the stock dividend; and

(b) an amount included in income when one purpose of the stock dividend was to significantly alter the value of the interest of a specified shareholder of the corporation.[230]

The "amount" of a stock dividend paid by a corporation is the amount of the increase in paid-up capital of the corporation which resulted from the payment of the stock dividend. A stock dividend paid to a corporation or to

---

See page ii for explanation of footnotes.

[226] CCH ¶9141, ¶28,344, ¶28,346; Sec. 69(1), 251(1), 251(2).

[227] CCH ¶7500; Sec. 52.

[228] CCH ¶7500; Sec. 52(1).

[229] CCH ¶7510; Sec. 52(2).

[230] CCH ¶4664, ¶7515; Sec. 15(1.1), 52(3); Interp. Bul. IT-88R2.

a mutual fund trust by a non-resident corporation is not a dividend and therefore has a cost of nil.[231]

(4) A taxpayer who has acquired property as a prize in connection with a lottery scheme is deemed to have acquired the property at a cost equal to the fair market value of the property at the time. A taxpayer's gain or loss from the disposition of a chance to win a prize or a right to receive an amount as a prize in connection with a lottery scheme is nil.[232]

(5) If property used by a non-resident in a Canadian branch operation is transferred to a qualified related corporation, certain deductions are allowed with respect to Part XIV tax (branch tax).[233] The cost base of the shares of the qualified related corporation is reduced to equal the paid-up capital of the shares, so that the amount of the branch tax that is deferred under this transfer will not be tax-free.

The cost[234] of the shares of the qualified related corporation that are received as consideration for the property transferred is equal to the lesser of:

(a) the cost of the shares otherwise determined; and

(b) the amount by which the paid-up capital of that class of shares increased by virtue of the shares being issued.

As a result of the application of these provisions, any amount on which the branch tax is deferred will not be represented by either paid-up capital or adjusted cost base. By reducing the cost of the shares to equal their paid-up capital, the branch tax deferral will form part of a taxable gain if the shares are sold, thus ensuring that the amount will not escape Canadian tax in some form.

(6) Where a corporation becomes resident in Canada, the cost base of the shares (excluding shares that are considered taxable Canadian property) to the non-resident shareholder is equal to the fair market value of the shares at that time.[235]

[¶5175] Adjusted Cost Base and Deemed Gain

Having determined the cost of a capital property, the taxpayer must determine the adjusted cost base of the property. The adjusted cost base of depreciable property is the capital cost of the property at that time. For other property, the adjusted cost base is the cost to the taxpayer (actual or deemed according to ¶5170) plus or minus certain adjustments.[236] These are outlined in ¶5190 for capital property that is a partnership interest, and in ¶5180 and ¶5185 for other capital property.

---

[231] CCH ¶7515, ¶28,071; Sec. 52(3), 248(1) "dividend".

[232] CCH ¶6433, ¶7525; Sec. 40(2)(f), 52(4).

[233] CCH ¶26,900; Sec. 219(1)(l).

[234] CCH ¶7540; Sec. 52(7).

[235] CCH ¶7541; Sec. 52(8).

[236] CCH ¶7850; Sec. 54 "adjusted cost base".

If at any time in the year the total of all amounts which are to be subtracted in computing the adjusted cost base exceeds the cost of the property plus all amounts added to the base, the excess is deemed to be a gain from the disposition of the property (unless the property involved is a partnership interest).[237] The resulting capital gain must be reported as such on that year's tax return, but is added to the ACB of the property so that it will reduce any subsequent gain or increase any subsequent loss.[238]

Example:

Taxpayer R owns shares in a company that have a cost of $1,000. Over the years R has received a series of tax-free dividends which the company indicated would reduce the adjusted cost base of the shares. At the end of last year R had received $1,000 of such dividends, so that his adjusted cost was exactly nil. This year R receives another such distribution in the amount of $200. R is required to report a capital gain as follows:

Cost of shares	$1,000
All prior year reductions	$1,000
Closing prior year ACB	Nil
Less: Current year reduction of cost base	200
Capital gain	$ (200)

The $200 would then be added in determining R's adjusted cost base so that for purposes of calculating any subsequent capital gain or loss R's adjusted cost base will be nil. The taxable portion of R's capital gain would be eligible for the capital gains exemption, on the same basis as any other gain.

A capital gain is required to be reported and included in income even though events later in the year may increase the adjusted cost base of the property so that the base would again be a positive amount.

Where the gain is with respect to a share in a foreign affiliate, an election is available which allows a corporation to treat a portion of the gain as a dividend from the foreign affiliate.[239]

The adjusted cost base (ACB) of a property may never (with one exception) be negative. The exception is that the deemed capital gain provision does not apply to an interest in a partnership. Instead, the Act provides for an additional gain at the time of the actual disposition of the partnership interest.[240] However, where the partnership ACB of a "limited partner" (see ¶7070) or "specified member" (¶7097) of a partnership is negative at the end of a particular fiscal period of the partnership, the amount of negative ACB is a deemed capital gain and the ACB itself is reset to nil.[241] The purpose of this exercise is to prevent the passive investor from claiming deductible losses and receiving cash distributions that exceed the amount

---

See page ii for explanation of footnotes.

[237] CCH ¶6440; Sec. 40(3).
[238] CCH ¶7600; Sec. 53(1)(a).
[239] CCH ¶11,400; Sec. 93(1).

[240] CCH ¶12,326; Sec. 100(2).

[241] CCH ¶6445; Sec. 40(3.1).

invested. These rules will allow a partner (other than an *inter vivos* trust) to elect to treat a subsequent positive ACB in the partnership interest at any fiscal year end as a capital loss.[242] The amount so elected cannot exceed previous deemed gains netted against previous losses so elected. The amount of the loss in turn reduces the ACB of the partnership interest. The loss may be carried back to previous years under the regular loss carryback provisions.

For example, assume that the amount in respect of a limited partner's interest in the partnership (generally, the negative amount of the ACB in the partnership) at its fiscal year end of December 31, 2007 is $1,000. The partner realizes a capital gain of $1,000 in his or her taxation year in which the fiscal period ended; assuming the partner is an individual other than a testamentary trust, that taxation year is calendar 2007. The $1,000 is added to the partner's ACB of the partnership interest, which becomes nil. Assume that as of the December 31, 2008 fiscal year end, $2,000 of partnership income was allocated to the partner, for the partner's 2008 taxation year. The partner's ACB of the interest has been increased to $2,000. The taxpayer can elect that $1,000 of that amount is a capital loss for his or her 2008 taxation year, which can be carried back to offset the capital gains in 2007. The ACB of the interest in then reduced by $1,000, to $1,000.

If one of the main reasons that a member of a partnership is not a specified member is to avoid the application of the negative ACB rule, the member will be considered to have been a specified member of the partnership at all times since becoming a member of the partnership.[243]

[¶5180] Additions to Adjusted Cost Base

A taxpayer may make additions to his or her cost base as follows:

(1) *Deemed gain.* An amount which is deemed to have been a gain of the taxpayer from the disposition of property is added in computing its adjusted cost base (see ¶5175 above).

(2) *Deemed dividend.* Dividends deemed to have been received at an earlier time on a share of a corporation resident in Canada are added in computing the adjusted cost base of the share. The shareholders pay tax on this deemed dividend and the amount thus tax-paid is added to the adjusted cost base of their shares. In this way corporate distributions made through an increase in paid-up capital and a subsequent disposition of the shares are taxed as dividends, not as capital gains.[244]

(3) *Contributions of capital.* Contributions of capital to a corporation that are not by way of loan and which are not a gift or a benefit conferred on any person (other than the corporation) related to the contributor, increase the adjusted cost base of the contributor's shares. If the taxpayer owns shares

---

See page ii for explanation of footnotes.

[242] CCH ¶6447; Sec. 40(3.12).   [244] CCH ¶7609, ¶10,200; Sec. 53(1)(b), 84(1).
[243] CCH ¶6448; Sec. 40(3.13).

of different classes, the increase in the adjusted cost base will be allocated among the shares in proportion to the amount by which their value has been increased by the contribution.[245] This provision does not apply where elections have been made under certain rollover provisions with respect to shares of a foreign affiliate or a Canadian corporation.

(4) *Shares of a foreign affiliate.* Where a taxpayer owns a share in a foreign affiliate, all foreign accrual property income of such affiliate is included in the taxpayer's income. These inclusions, less reserves for foreign exchange restrictions and deductions in respect of tax paid by the foreign affiliate, are added in computing the adjusted cost base of the taxpayer's shares of the foreign affiliate.[246]

(5) *Shares of a demutualized insurer.* Where the conversion benefit received by a stakeholder (otherwise than as a taxable conversion benefit) in connection with the demutualization of an insurance company is a share that is, at the time of the payment, capital property to the stakeholder, the amount of the payment is added in computing the adjusted cost base to the stakeholder of the share.[247]

(6) *Capital interest in a trust.* Certain non-resident trusts are deemed to be corporations for the purposes of the foreign affiliate rules. When the trustees do not have any discretion in the distribution of income and capital, any beneficiary whose beneficial interest in the trust has a fair market value of at least 10% of that of all beneficial interests is deemed to control the notional corporation. Thus, foreign accrual property income of the trust may be attributed to the beneficiary. Amounts attributed to the beneficiary and included in income are added in computing the adjusted cost base of the beneficiary's capital interest in the trust.[248] See item (3) *Capital interest in a trust* at ¶5185.

(7) *Unit in a mutual fund trust.* A mutual fund trust may designate an amount in respect of recapture in the trust. This designated amount will be included in computing the unitholder's income and be deductible in computing the trust's income. This amount will also increase the adjusted cost base of the unitholder's interest in the trust.[249]

(8) *Specified shareholder of a corporation.* A taxpayer is denied a deduction with respect to certain "soft costs", such as interest on debt incurred to acquire land or to construct or renovate a building. See ¶3246 and ¶3249. Where a taxpayer is a specified shareholder[250] of a corporation and a deduction has been disallowed with respect to these costs of property of the corporation, they will be added to the adjusted cost base of the share of capital stock held by the specified shareholder. In general, a specified share-

---

See page ii for explanation of footnotes.

[245] CCH ¶7612; Sec. 53(1)(c); Interp. Bul. IT-456R.
[246] CCH ¶7615; Sec. 53(1)(d).
[247] CCH ¶7616, ¶20,834za; Sec. 53(1)(d.01), 139.1(16).
[248] CCH ¶7616a; Sec. 53(1)(d.1).
[249] CCH ¶7617; Sec. 53(1)(d.2).
[250] CCH ¶4853, ¶4856, ¶28,273; Sec. 18(2), 18(3.1), 248(1) "specified shareholder".

holder of a corporation holds, directly or indirectly, at least 10% of the shares of any class of the corporation or any other related corporation.[251]

(9) *Partnership interest.* See item (1) *Income and loss* and item (2) *Additions* at ¶5190.

(10) *Superficial loss.* A "superficial loss" (as described at ¶5090) should be added to the adjusted cost base of the substituted property.[252] If the superficial loss is in respect of shares of a corporation and the loss would be reduced by certain dividends that have been paid on the shares,[253] it is the reduced loss after giving effect to the reduction for the dividends that is added to the adjusted cost base.

(11) *Transfers from affiliated corporations.* Where a taxpayer disposes of capital property to an "affiliated person", as defined in ¶15,445, the superficial loss rules may apply as described at ¶5090. Where a taxpayer receives capital property from an affiliated corporation or partnership, specific rules may apply which will have much the same result of denying finalrecognition of the loss by the transferor until there is a final non-affiliated disposition.[254]

(12) *Denied loss on transfer of shares to corporation.* A denied capital loss under ¶5217 on a disposition by a taxpayer of a share of a corporation to that corporation, is added to the cost base of the taxpayer's shares in the corporation immediately after the disposition.[255]

(13) *Certain obligations issued at a discount.* Where a resident taxpayer purchases certain debt instruments issued by tax-exempt entities at a discount, the amount of the discount is included in the income of the resident taxpayer for the year in which the instrument is purchased and the appropriate tax on this amount thus becomes payable. However, the amount so included in the taxpayer's income increases the taxpayer's adjusted cost base of the debt instrument.[256] Thus, the amount that has been subjected to tax once will not be subject to capital gains tax if the instrument is disposed of.

(14) *Indexed debt obligations.* A taxpayer who acquires and holds an indexed debt obligation that adjusts the amount payable by reference to the purchasing power of money, must take the amount arising from a decline in the purchasing power of money into income as interest received or receivable in that year. As a result, the amount that the taxpayer must take into income is added to the adjusted cost base of the indexed debt obligation in which the taxpayer has invested.[257] See item (15) *Indexed debt obligations* at ¶5185.

See page ii for explanation of footnotes.

[251] CCH ¶7617c, ¶28,273; Sec. 53(1)(d.3), 248(1) "specified shareholder".

[252] CCH ¶7621, ¶7855; Sec. 53(1)(f), 54 "superficial loss"; Interp. Bul. IT-456R.

[253] CCH ¶16,380, ¶16,385, ¶16,390; Sec. 112(3), 112(3.1), 112(3.2).

[254] CCH ¶7622, ¶10,580a; Sec. 53(1)(f.1).

[255] CCH ¶7623; Sec. 53(1)(f.2); Interp. Bul. IT-456R.

[256] CCH ¶7624; Sec. 53(1)(g).

[257] CCH ¶7625, ¶28,136a; Sec. 16(6), 53(1)(g.1), 248(1) "indexed debt obligation".

¶5180

(15) *Land.* The deduction of interest expense and property taxes incurred in connection with undeveloped land (except to the extent of the revenue produced from that land) is prohibited unless the land is used or held in the course of a business carried on in the year. The interest and realty taxes may be added in computing the adjusted cost base of the land.[258] In other words, the cost of maintaining land which is not held in (or in connection with) the income accounts of the taxpayer is required to be capitalized rather than deducted as an income expense. While this provision refers to property which is land, it presumably also includes buildings erected on the land, since by common law these form part of the realty.

(16) *Restricted farm losses.* A taxpayer who operates a farm but whose main source of income is neither farming nor farming and some other source of income is limited in the amount of farming losses that can be deducted from other income (see ¶3396). When land used in the farming business is disposed of, these losses, which are not deductible, may increase the adjusted cost base of the farm property subject to two limitations:

(a) The adjusted cost base may be increased only to the extent of the realty taxes on the farm and the interest expense incurred in the year on money borrowed to purchase the farm property.

(b) A loss for a given year may only increase the adjusted cost base to the extent that the capital gain on disposition of the farm (calculated without applying these provisions) exceeds the additions to the adjusted cost base resulting from losses in earlier years.[259]

It should be noted that where the farm is owned by a partnership, in computing the adjusted cost base of an interest in that partnership, the Act requires that the capital gain on farmland be computed without the increase in adjusted cost base for the restricted farm losses. In calculating the cost of the partnership interest, however, the whole farm loss is allowed in computing the loss of the partnership, instead of the restricted farm loss amount of $8,750 normally allowed for a taxpayer whose chief source of income is neither farming nor farming and some other source of income. See items (d) and (h) in *Income and loss* at ¶5190.

(17) *Share or fund unit taxed as stock option benefit.* When an employee exercises an employee securities option and acquires shares in the capital of the employer's corporation or units in an employer that is a mutual fund trust, the value of securities at the time they are acquired in excess of the option price (and any amount paid to acquire the option) is taxable in the employee's hands as a benefit from employment (see ¶2135). This taxable benefit is added to the adjusted cost base of the securities when they are acquired,[260] even if the inclusion of the benefit in income is deferred to the year in which the securities are sold. Furthermore, the full amount of the

---

See page ii for explanation of footnotes.

[258] CCH ¶7627; Sec. 53(1)(*h*).   [260] CCH ¶7633; Sec. 53(1)(*j*).
[259] CCH ¶7630; Sec. 53(1)(*i*); Interp. Bul. IT-232R3.

benefit is added to the adjusted cost base even if the employee is entitled to the deduction equal to one-half of the benefit. See ¶2135.

Example:

Jennifer is employed by Company C and in 2011 acquired shares of the company at a cost of $1,000 under the company's stock option plan. The fair market value of the shares was $1,200 and the $200 difference was included in her income. She claimed an offsetting deduction of $100. The adjusted cost base of the share to Jennifer is:

Actual cost	$1,000
Excess of fair market value of shares over her cost	$ 200
Adjusted cost base	$1,200

(18) *Expropriation assets.* Where Canadian residents have had shares of a foreign affiliate, property used to carry on business in a foreign country, or property used by a foreign affiliate to carry on such business (either expropriated or subjected to a forced sale) and have received certain foreign debt instruments in return, special rules are provided for the taxation of interest received on those debt instruments. These rules also provide for adjustments to the cost base of the debt instruments, among other things, increasing the adjusted cost base by the amount of any tax paid to the foreign country in respect of interest on the debt instrument.[261] See item (17) *Expropriation assets* at ¶5185.

(19) *Interest in related segregated fund trust.* Where a taxpayer has a life insurance policy in respect of which all or a portion of an insurer's reserves vary in accordance with the fair market value of specified properties, the taxpayer is deemed to have an interest in a related segregated fund trust.[262] Any gain or loss on disposal of such an interest is treated as a gain or loss on capital property, and is not subject to the rules for computing the taxable gain on disposition of a life insurance policy.[263] The cost of acquiring the segregated fund portion of the policy therefore represents the cost of acquiring a capital property, not the cost of the insurance policy. The following amounts are to be added to the cost of an interest in a related segregated fund trust in determining its adjusted cost base:[264]

(a) the income of the trust which is deemed to be payable to the policy-holder and reported as the policyholder's income;

(b) amounts transferred by the insurer from non-segregated to segregated funds;

(c) the amount of any capital gain allocated to the policyholder pursuant to a special election upon withdrawal from the segregated fund; and

---

See page ii for explanation of footnotes.

[261] CCH ¶7636; Sec. 53(1)(k).
[262] CCH ¶20,831; Sec. 138.1.
[263] CCH ¶21,565; Sec. 148.
[264] CCH ¶7637; Sec. 53(1)(l).

¶5180

(d) capital gains of the fund allocated to the policyholder. See item (20) *Interest in related segregated fund trust* at ¶5185.

(20) *Offshore investment fund property.* Where property is an offshore investment fund property there shall be added to the adjusted cost base of the property amounts deemed to be included in income in respect of the property.[265] A similar increase is provided in respect of an investment in offshore investment property by a controlled foreign affiliate.[266]

(21) *Surveying or valuing property.* The reasonable costs of surveying or valuing property for the purposes of its acquisition or disposition will be added to the adjusted cost base of that property provided those costs are not deducted from the taxpayer's income or attributed to any other property.[267]

(22) *Remainder interests in real property.* The holder of a life estate in real property is deemed to have disposed of the life estate just prior to death for proceeds equal to its adjusted cost base. The holder of the remainder interest in the property becomes the owner of the whole property. After the death of the life estate holder, if that individual and the holder of the remainder interest were not dealing at arm's length, the adjusted cost base of the real property is increased by the lesser of the adjusted cost base of the life estate immediately before the death of the holder of the life estate and any amount by which the fair market value of the whole real property exceeds the adjusted cost base of the remainder interest. This increase in adjusted cost base is applicable for calculating the capital gain or loss on the real property.[268]

(23) *Flow-through entity.* Where an election was made on a flow-though entity under the rules at ¶5011 to create a continuing capital gains exemption balance against the annual gains flowed out to the elector, any remaining unused balance after 2004 is wound up and added to the adjusted cost base of the entity to the elector.[269] Similarly, when the property on which the election was made is disposed of before 2005 and a related capital gains exemption balance remains unused, that balance will be added to the adjusted cost base of the property immediately before the disposition.[270] As a general rule, this will allow recognition of a loss accrued since February 22, 1994.

(24) *Demutualization benefits.* Payments made on shares received under the rollover rules in the course of demutualization of life insurance companies, which are transferred to employees are added to the cost base of the shares as described at ¶9274.

[¶5185] Deductions from Adjusted Cost Base

A taxpayer may make deductions from his or her cost base as follows:

See page ii for explanation of footnotes.

[265] CCH ¶7637ac, ¶11,700; Sec. 53(1)(*m*), 94.1.
[266] CCH ¶7637ac, ¶11,725a; Sec. 53(1)(*m*), 95(1).
[267] CCH ¶7637b; Sec. 53(1)(*n*).
[268] CCH ¶6669, ¶7637c; Sec. 43.1(2), 53(1)(*o*).
[269] CCH ¶7637d; Sec. 53(1)(*p*).
[270] CCH ¶7637f; Sec. 53(1)(*r*).

(1) *Shares of a resident corporation.*[271] Where the property in question is a share of the capital stock of a corporation resident in Canada, four deductions may be applicable in computing the adjusted cost base of the shares at any time:

(a) An amount received by the taxpayer as a dividend on the share, other than a taxable dividend, a capital dividend, or a life insurance capital dividend, will reduce the adjusted cost base of the share.

(b) Where the corporation reduced its paid-up capital in respect of the taxpayer's share, the amount received by the taxpayer on the reduction of capital is deducted from the adjusted cost base of the share, except for the portion of the amount that was deemed to be a dividend. A dividend is deemed to have been paid on a reduction of capital in respect of a share to the extent that the amount paid on the reduction of capital exceeds the paid-up capital of the share. If a public corporation reduces the paid-up capital of a class, the full amount is deemed to be a dividend regardless of the paid-up capital of that class. In either case, the deemed dividend need not reduce the adjusted cost base of the share since it will be subject to tax as a taxable dividend.[272]

(c) There is a reduction in the adjusted cost base of a share for an amount which might otherwise be treated as a deemed dividend arising upon a distribution to shareholders on winding-up, discontinuance, or reorganization. Certain shareholders of a public corporation are treated as receiving proceeds of disposition rather than a deemed dividend. If there is a distribution on a winding-up, discontinuance, or reorganization which does not produce a deemed dividend and at the same time does not result in the shareholder disposing of his or her shares, the adjusted cost base of those shares will be reduced by the amount of the distribution less the paid-up capital of the shareholder's shares.[273]

(d) Finally, the adjusted cost base to the individual on the replacement shares qualifying for a capital gains deferral on the disposition of an eligible small business investment must be reduced by the individual "ACB reduction" in respect of such replacement shares. The ACB reduction is discussed at ¶5029.[274]

(2) *Shares of a non-resident corporation.* In general, foreign passive income of a foreign affiliate of the taxpayer is taxed in the taxpayer's hands whether received or not, and the adjusted cost base of the taxpayer's shares of the foreign affiliate is *increased* to reflect this. See item (4) *Shares of*

See page ii for explanation of footnotes.

[271] CCH ¶7639; Sec. 53(2)(a); Interp. Bul. IT-456R.

[272] CCH ¶7639, ¶10,320, ¶10,330; Sec. 53(2)(a), 84(4), 84(4.1).

[273] CCH ¶7639, ¶10,240, ¶10,383; Sec. 53(2)(a), 84(2), 84(8).

[274] CCH ¶6750m, ¶7639; Sec. 44.1(2)(b), 53(2)(a).

a foreign affiliate at ¶5180. On the other hand, when this income is distributed to the taxpayer by way of dividend, it usually bears no tax and the adjusted cost base of the shares is reduced by the amount of the earlier increase. This reduction is carried through for purposes of the capital gains tax provisions. If the foreign affiliate has suffered expropriation or forced sale of foreign assets and received "expropriation assets" in return, a distribution of these assets to the taxpayer by way of dividend in kind or a benefit to the shareholder will be treated as a dividend to the taxpayer from a foreign affiliate. See also item (18) *Expropriation assets* at ¶5180. The taxpayer may deduct the amount of this dividend in computing income but this deduction is required to be subtracted in computing the adjusted cost base of the taxpayer's shares of the foreign affiliate. Where a non-resident corporation reduces its paid-up capital, any amount received by the taxpayer on the transaction reduces the taxpayer's adjusted cost base of his or her shares.[275]

(3) *Capital interest in a trust.* A beneficiary whose beneficial interest in a non-resident trust has a fair market value of at least 10% of that of all beneficial interests is deemed to control a notional non-resident corporation. Amounts deducted from the beneficiary's income in respect of foreign taxes or a reserve for foreign exchange restrictions will also be deductions from the adjusted cost base of the beneficiary's capital interest in the trust.[276] See item (6) *Capital interest in a trust* at ¶5180.

(4) *Capital property of a corporation on change of control.* If the adjusted cost base of non-depreciable capital property of a corporation exceeds its fair market value, the adjusted cost base is reduced to its fair market value when there is a change of control of the corporation.[277]

(5) *Partnership interest.* See item (1) *Income and loss* and item (3) *Deductions* at ¶5190.

(6) *Partial dispositions.* When a taxpayer disposes of property that is capable of partial disposition, the taxpayer computes gains and losses on that part by prorating the adjusted cost base of the whole to the part disposed of (see ¶5150). In computing the adjusted cost base of the part remaining, the taxpayer deducts from the adjusted cost base of the whole property the prorated amount in respect of the part disposed of.[278]

Example:

Robin owns a summer cottage which has an adjusted cost base of $10,000, and which does not qualify as a principal residence. She sells a half-interest in the cottage to her friend Terry for $6,000. The capital gains to be reported by Robin should be $1,000, being the proceeds of disposition of $6,000 less one-half of the adjusted cost base of the cottage, $5,000. The half-interest in the cottage Robin retained would have an adjusted cost base of $5,000 for the purpose of subsequent capital gain or loss calculation.

See page ii for explanation of footnotes.

[275] CCH ¶7642; Sec. 53(2)(b).
[276] CCH ¶7643; Sec. 53(2)(b.1).
[277] CCH ¶7644; Sec. 53(2)(b.2).
[278] CCH ¶7648; Sec. 53(2)(d).

(7) *Exploration and development expenses.* Where a taxpayer incurs a Canadian exploration expense, a Canadian development expense, or a Canadian oil and gas property expense pursuant to an agreement with a corporation where the taxpayer's sole consideration is the receipt of shares of the corporation, the expense so incurred qualifies as a Canadian exploration expense, a Canadian development expense, or a Canadian oil and gas property expense which is deductible by the taxpayer. Where the shares so acquired are capital property and were acquired before August 1976, their adjusted cost base is reduced by such expenses incurred to acquire them. Shares acquired after July 31, 1976 in consideration of such expenses are deemed to be acquired at a cost of nil.[279]

(8) *Payment to joint exploration company.* Where property was received by the taxpayer as consideration for a payment or loan made to a joint exploration corporation in which the taxpayer held shares, to the extent that the joint exploration corporation renounces an agreed portion of its Canadian exploration and development expenses, its Canadian exploration expenses, its Canadian development expenses, or Canadian oil and gas property expenses to the taxpayer, the amount of such renunciation reduces the adjusted cost base to the taxpayer of the property in question.[280] This reduction also applies to any property that was substituted for the property originally received as consideration for the payment or loan.

(9) *Contribution to joint exploration company.* Where a corporation owns shares of a joint exploration corporation, any contribution of capital made by the shareholder that increases the adjusted cost base of its shares (see item (3) *Contributions of capital* at ¶5180) must be deducted in computing that adjusted cost Base, to the extent that the contribution is used as a basis for a renunciation of Canadian exploration and development expenses, Canadian exploration expenses, Canadian development expenses, or Canadian oil and gas property expenses.[281]

(10) *Settlement of debts.* The reduction in adjusted cost base of capital properties owned by the taxpayer when a debt is settled or extinguished for less than the amount owing is also deducted in computing the adjusted cost base of those properties for the purpose of capital gains tax provisions[282] (see ¶3456).

(11) *Payment by trust.* When a taxpayer holds a capital interest in a trust, a distribution of capital reduces the adjusted cost base of the interest unless the amount is proceeds of disposition of the interest or is included in the beneficiary's income.

There are three exceptions to the above reduction in the adjusted cost base of a capital interest in a trust. First, resident trusts may distribute in a year

---

See page ii for explanation of footnotes.

[279] CCH ¶7651, ¶9080; Sec. 53(2)(e), 66.3.

[280] CCH ¶7654, ¶7656, ¶8958; Sec. 53(2)(f), 53(2)(f.2), 66(10.4).

[281] CCH ¶7655; Sec. 53(2)(f.1).

[282] CCH ¶7657, ¶9850; Sec. 53(2)(g), 80(1).

the untaxed portion of capital gains realized in that year to beneficiaries without any reduction to the adjusted cost base of the beneficiaries' capital interests in the trust. Second, a resident trust may flow through to a beneficiary capital dividends received in a year without any reduction to the beneficiary's adjusted cost base of its capital interest in the trust. Third, beginning after 2004, an assessable distribution subject to withholding tax paid by a resident trust to a non-resident beneficiary does not reduce the beneficiary's adjusted cost base of its capital interest in the trust.

The taxpayer must reduce the adjusted cost base of his or her capital interest in a trust by any amount of the trust's investment tax credit that has been allocated to and deducted by the taxpayer in taxation years ending before the time at which the determination of adjusted cost base is being made.

Where a share-purchase tax credit flows through to a beneficiary of a trust, or where a designation that gives rise to a scientific research tax credit flows through to a beneficiary of a trust, the beneficiary is required to reduce the adjusted cost base of his or her capital interest in the trust by the full amount of the share-purchase tax credit or by 50% of the amount considered designated to the beneficiary in respect of the scientific research tax credit.

Where a beneficiary of a trust receives public assistance in respect of the acquisition of depreciable property by the trust, the amount of that public assistance must be applied to reduce the cost of acquisition of the depreciable property to the trust, and the same amount must also be applied to reduce the adjusted cost base of the beneficiary's capital interest in the trust.[283]

The above rules requiring the reduction of the adjusted cost base of a capital interest in a trust do not apply to interests in personal trusts acquired for no consideration, RCA trusts, employee compensation trusts, cemetery care trusts, eligible funeral arrangement trusts, retirement savings trusts, or related segregated fund trusts and other special trusts.[284]

(12) *Non-resident trusts.* Where a taxpayer purchases a capital interest in a non-resident trust or a unit of a unit trust which was not resident in Canada from a non-resident at a time when the property was not taxable Canadian property, and 50% or more of the trust property consisted of certain types of Canadian property, an amount must be deducted in computing the adjusted cost base of the taxpayer's capital interest or unit. This applies if, at the time of the purchase, more than 50% of the trust property consisted of Canadian resource properties, income interests in resident trusts, taxable Canadian properties, and timber resource properties. The amount to be deducted by the purchaser is the purchaser's share of the amount by which the fair market value of all these Canadian properties

---

See page ii for explanation of footnotes.
[283] CCH ¶7660; Sec. 53(2)(h); Interp. Bul. IT-456R.   [284] CCH ¶13,941; Sec. 108(1).

exceeds their cost amounts. Since resource properties have no cost amount, the entire value of such properties would have to be taken into account.[285]

(13) *Grants, subsidies, etc.* Taxpayers who receive, or who are entitled to receive, assistance of various specified kinds to enable them to acquire property are required to deduct the amount of that assistance in computing the adjusted cost base of the property in question.[286]

Assistance that requires such a reduction includes a grant, subsidy, forgivable loan, deduction from tax, investment allowance, or assistance of any other kind. Government assistance in respect of scientific research and experimental development (SR&ED) expenditures does not necessitate a reduction in adjusted cost base, nor does the tax incentive provided in the form of depletion allowances for the natural resource industries. Also, the amount of prescribed assistance received or receivable in respect of the acquisition of shares of the capital stock of a prescribed venture capital corporation or a prescribed labour-sponsored venture capital corporation or shares of the capital stock of a taxable Canadian corporation that are held in a prescribed stock savings plan does not reduce the adjusted cost base of those shares.[287] While such assistance does not reduce the adjusted cost base of the shares, the amount of the capital loss realized on a disposition of those shares may be reduced by the amount of the assistance.[288] See ¶5220. Only assistance from a government, municipality, or other public authority requires a reduction in adjusted cost base; private assistance programs are not covered. Assistance in the form of home insulation or conversion grants included in income does not reduce the adjusted cost base of the property. Investment tax credit amounts deducted with respect to property will reduce the adjusted cost base of that property. An input tax credit of the federal goods and services tax is deemed to be government assistance and therefore also reduces the adjusted cost base of property.[289]

To the extent that the taxpayer repays any of the assistance originally given to the taxpayer, the amount of the repayment will be added back to the adjusted cost base from the time of repayment. If the taxpayer repays any of the assistance after the disposition of the property, the amount of the assistance repaid will be treated as a capital loss of the taxpayer[290] (see ¶5342). See ¶4012 concerning government assistance received by a taxpayer for depreciable property.

(14) *Bonds, debentures, etc.* Interest accrued on a debt obligation up to the time of transfer to another person may, when received by the transferee, be deducted in computing his or her income, since it is included in computing the income of the transferor (see ¶3360).[291] The deduction allowed from income will also be deducted by the transferee in computing the adjusted

---

See page ii for explanation of footnotes.

[285] CCH ¶7663, ¶7666, ¶28,054; Sec. 53(2)(*i*), 53(2)(*j*), 248(1) "cost amount".

[286] CCH ¶7669; Sec. 53(2)(k).

[287] CCH ¶7669, ¶7670–7670e; Sec. 53(2)(k); Reg. 6700–6705.

[288] CCH ¶6439b; Sec. 40(2)(*i*).

[289] CCH ¶28,329l; Sec. 248(16).

[290] CCH ¶6398f; Sec. 39(13).

[291] CCH ¶5142; Sec. 20(14).

cost base of the debt obligation.[292] When taken together, these provisions enable the transferee to pay the transferor the amounts of the accrued interest at the time of transfer and to recoup his or her payments when the interest falls due without adverse income or capital gains tax consequences.

(15) *Indexed debt obligations.* An indexed debt obligation is a debt obligation that adjusts the amount payable by reference to the purchasing power of money. The adjusted cost base of an indexed debt obligation will be reduced by two amounts:

(a) the amount deductible from the taxpayer's income as interest which reflects the decrease in amounts owing to the taxpayer under the obligation as a result of an increase in the purchasing power of money; and

(b) any amount received or receivable arising from a previous decline in the purchasing power of money and which was added to the adjusted cost base of the obligation.

See item (14) *Indexed debt obligations* at ¶5180.[293]

(16) *Deductible cost of property.* Any part of the cost of property, except depreciable property, which was deductible in computing the taxpayer's income in a previous year must be deducted in computing the taxpayer's adjusted cost base of the property.[294] For example, if a taxpayer incurs costs for the investigation of a building site and the land is subsequently acquired, these costs may otherwise be included in the adjusted cost base of the property. However, since site investigation costs are deductible by the taxpayer in the year incurred,[295] this provision prevents them from being included as part of the adjusted cost base of the property. This cost base reduction does not apply to the cost of an "eligible tool" that an apprentice mechanic is entitled to deduct because such deductible amount reduces the cost of the tool for income tax purpose (see ¶2388).

(17) *Expropriation assets.* Where a resident taxpayer has acquired a particular foreign debt instrument defined to be an "expropriation asset",[296] because of the expropriation or forced sale of shares of a foreign affiliate, or property used by the taxpayer to carry on business in a foreign country, special rules for the taxation of interest received on the debt instrument are provided. In effect, the interest is treated as a return of capital. Similar provisions apply when the taxpayer has received the expropriation asset from a foreign affiliate either as a dividend in kind or a benefit conferred on a shareholder. Interest received and excluded from income and any payment on account of principal on the expropriation asset reduce the taxpayer's

---

See page ii for explanation of footnotes.

[292] CCH ¶7672; Sec. 53(2)(*l*).

[293] CCH ¶4724, ¶7673, ¶28,136a; Sec. 16(6), 53(2)(*l*.1), 248(1) "indexed debt obligation".

[294] CCH ¶7675; Sec. 53(2)(*m*).

[295] CCH ¶5127; Sec. 20(1)(*dd*).

[296] CCH ¶9875; Sec. 80.1.

adjusted cost base of the expropriation asset.[297] See also item (2) *Shares of a non-resident corporation* above and item (18) *Expropriation assets* at ¶5180.

(18) *Right to receive partnership property.* A taxpayer who acquires a residual interest in a partnership on the death of the original owner is deemed to have acquired a right to a partnership property rather than an interest in a partnership. The cost of the right is equal to the proceeds of disposition deemed to have been received by the deceased. There is a reduction in this cost of all amounts received in full or partial satisfaction of the right to receive partnership property.[298]

(19) *Debt issued by a corporation.* A reduction in the adjusted cost base of debt received from a purchaser corporation is provided when that debt is issued in consideration for the sale to the purchaser corporation of shares of another corporation and the conditions relating to arm's length dealings, control, and the period of ownership are met. This applies to transfers before May 23, 1985. The adjusted cost base of debt owed to an individual at March 31, 1977, is reduced to the extent that a debt deficiency applied to that debt under the rules applicable at March 31, 1977.[299]

(20) *Interest in related segregated fund trust.* Where a taxpayer has a life insurance policy in respect of which the insurer's reserves vary in amount depending on the fair market value of a specified group of properties, the taxpayer is deemed to have capital property in the form of an interest in a related segregated fund trust. Certain amounts are added to determine the adjusted cost base of that interest. See item (19) *Interest in related segregated trust fund* at ¶5180. The following two amounts are deducted in determining the adjusted cost base of the interest in the related segregated fund trust:[300]

(a) the amount of any capital loss allocated to the taxpayer pursuant to an election upon withdrawal from the segregated fund; and

(b) the amount of any capital loss of the trust allocated to the taxpayer.

(21) *Inducement payments.* A taxpayer is required to include in income an amount received as an inducement or contribution in respect of the cost of a property.[301] However, as an alternative, the taxpayer can elect to reduce the adjusted cost base of the property (other than depreciable property) relating to the inducement instead of including the amount in income.[302] The election is made for an amount received in respect of non-depreciable capital property that is acquired in the year, in the three preceding taxation years, or in the immediately following taxation year. The amount of the reduction of the adjusted cost base is reduced by any amount that the taxpayer repays to the extent that the repayment is made pursuant to a legal

---

See page ii for explanation of footnotes.

[297] CCH ¶7678; Sec. 53(2)(n).

[298] CCH ¶7679, ¶12,306, ¶12,381; Sec. 53(2)(o), 98.2, 100(3)(a).

[299] CCH ¶7680, ¶10,420; Sec. 53(2)(p), 84.2(2).

[300] CCH ¶7680b, ¶20,831; Sec. 53(2)(q), 138.1.

[301] CCH ¶4376c; Sec. 12(1)(x).

[302] CCH ¶7681, ¶7683; Sec. 53(2)(s), 53(2.1).

¶5185

obligation. If the taxpayer repays any of the assistance after the disposition of the property, the amount of the assistance repaid will be treated as a capital loss of the taxpayer[303] (see ¶5342). See ¶4012 concerning inducement payments received by a taxpayer for depreciable property.

(22) *Deceased taxpayer's employee stock option.* If at the time of a taxpayer's death the fair market value of an unexercised employee stock option exceeds its cost, an amount is included in the deceased's income for the year of death. If the value of the option then declines, the legal representative of the deceased taxpayer can elect to treat the decline in value as a loss from employment which can be carried back to the deceased taxpayer's final return for the year of death. This election by the deceased's legal representative applies where the employee stock option is exercised or disposed of (which includes the expiration of the option) within the first taxation year of the estate of the deceased.

The amount of the loss that can be carried back to the year of death is the amount of the benefit from the option that was included in the taxpayer's income for the year of death less the excess of the value of the option just before it was exercised or disposed of, over the cost of the option to the taxpayer. The loss will be reduced by $1/2$ where one-half of the benefit from the stock option had been deducted as permitted in computing taxable income in the year of death. The adjusted cost base of the option will be reduced by the amount of the loss. However, the amount of the loss for purposes of reducing the adjusted cost base will not be reduced by $1/2$ as is the amount of the loss for income purposes, since the estate acquired the option at its fair market value at the time of death.[304]

(23) *Deemed gain on real estate.* Following the elimination of the capital gains exemption, the adjusted cost base of non-qualifying real property is reduced by the ineligible portion of the deemed capital gain as at February 22, 1994.[305] Where a taxpayer elected to have a deemed disposition of non-qualifying real estate (real estate not used in a business), a portion of the gain is not eligible for the capital gains exemption. This is the portion that relates to the gain accrued after February 1992. Since the value of the property after the election is in most cases deemed to be the value of the elected proceeds which includes the whole amount of the gain on the deemed disposition, the non-eligible portion of the gain is subtracted from the adjusted cost base so that it will be realized in a subsequent disposition.

[¶5190] Adjustments to Cost Base — Partnership Interest

A taxpayer who owns a capital property which is an interest in a partnership computes the adjusted cost base by adding to and deducting from the cost amounts described below.

See page ii for explanation of footnotes.

[303] CCH ¶6398f; Sec. 39(13).
[304] CCH ¶2700, ¶7682b, ¶22,919; Sec. 7(1)(e), 53(2)(t), 164(6.1).
[305] CCH ¶7682c; Sec. 53(2)(u).

(1) *Income and loss.* A taxpayer adds to the adjusted cost base of the taxpayer's share in a partnership his or her share of the profits of the partnership for each fiscal period.[306] Partnership losses allocated to the taxpayer reduce the adjusted cost base of the partnership interest.[307] Limited partnership losses are covered under a separate provision (see item (a) of the list contained in item (3) *Deductions* below) and reduce the adjusted cost base only when deducted by the taxpayer. There are special rules for computing partnership income or losses and generally the income or loss of a partnership from each source is determined separately.

Some of the special rules for computing partnership income and losses are as follows:

(a) The whole of any gain on the disposition of an eligible capital property is included in computing the partnership income or loss.

(b) The whole of any capital gain or loss on the disposition by the partnership of a capital property (including the whole gain on a listed personal property) is included in computing the income or loss of the partnership.

(c) If the partnership itself is a member of a partnership, the second-tier partnership income included in the income of the first-tier partnership is disregarded and will not increase the adjusted cost base of the interests of the partners of the first-tier partnership.

(d) In computing the farming income of the partnership, no deduction is taken in respect of the cost of a basic herd of farm animals.

(e) Any capital gain of farmland is computed without the increase in its adjusted cost base otherwise allowed. See item (16) *Restricted farm losses* at ¶5180.

(f) The capital gains and capital losses of the partnership are computed without reference to the provisions relating to artificial reductions in capital gains or artificial increases in capital losses.

(g) The dividend income of the partnership is computed net of the gross-up otherwise added to dividends from taxable Canadian corporations.

(h) The whole of any farm loss is included in computing the loss of the partnership instead of being restricted to only $8,750 where the main source of income is neither farming nor farming and some other source of income.

---

[306] CCH ¶7618; Sec. 53(1)(e).   [307] CCH ¶7645; Sec. 53(2)(c).

¶5190

(i) Any capital loss of the partnership normally not recognized because of a limiting provision in the Act[308] is included in computing the loss of the partnership.

(j) Income from a new mine which was exempt under the 1971 transitional rules is included.

(k) In computing the income or loss of the partnership, the inclusion in income or the disallowance of a deduction with respect to Crown royalties, the resource allowance, and the inventory allowance are not taken into account. Similarly, the disallowance of a deduction for amounts paid under the *Petroleum and Gas Revenue Tax Act* and the income inclusions for incremental resource royalties are not taken into account.

(l) The additions to the income of the partnership, which may occur as a result of transactions in resources or resource properties with governments which do not take place at fair market value are disregarded for the purposes of determining the income or loss of the partnership, which will increase or decrease the adjusted cost base of the partnership interests.

(m) A partner's share of a loss in respect of a share held by the partnership is not reduced by taxable dividends, capital dividends, or life insurance capital dividends.

The share of income or loss from a partnership will not include any partnership income allocated to a non-partner, such as a retired partner, who is deemed to be a member of the partnership.[309] The interest of the deemed partner is not capital property but is dealt with separately as an income right.

(2) *Additions.*[310] A taxpayer makes additions to the adjusted cost base of his or her partnership interest as follows:

(a) *Capital dividends of partnership.* A taxpayer shall add to the adjusted cost base of the taxpayer's partnership interest his or her share of any capital dividend from a corporation in which the partnership holds stock and his or her share of any life insurance capital dividend received by the partnership. Such dividends are nontaxable.

(b) *Life insurance proceeds.* The mortality gain on a life insurance policy (i.e., the proceeds payable on the death of the life insured less the adjusted cost basis of the policy) is not subject to tax. A taxpayer shall add his or her share of any such gain realized by the

---

[308] CCH ¶6420; Sec. 40(2).   [310] CCH ¶7618; Sec. 53(1)(e).
[309] CCH ¶12,140; Sec. 96(1.1).

partnership to the adjusted cost base of the taxpayer's partnership interest.

(c) *Contributions to capital.* If the taxpayer makes a contribution to partnership capital that is not a loan, any portion of that contribution that cannot be regarded as a gift to or benefit conferred on a member of the partnership who is related to the taxpayer shall be added to the adjusted cost base of the taxpayer's partnership interest.

(d) *Rights or things.* The value of any right or thing which, if realized, would be included in income, is included in computing income in the year of death.[311] Where the deceased taxpayer was a member of a partnership, the value of any right or thing relating to the partnership is added to the adjusted cost base of the partnership interest immediately before death and thus will reduce the capital gain or increase the capital loss realized by virtue of the deemed disposition on death. The value of the right or thing which is included in income for the year of death is added to the adjusted cost base of the partnership interest so that the same value will not be both included in income and form part of the capital gain realized on death. This provision does not apply to increase the adjusted cost base of a retired partner's right under agreement to share in the income of the partnership.

(e) *Deemed capital gain on residual partnership interest.* When a partnership is liquidated and ceases to exist, each person who was a partner continues to be a partner until all the partnership property has been distributed. The right to the undistributed property of the partnership is considered to be an interest in the partnership. Similarly, a taxpayer who has ceased to be a member of a partnership but has not received full settlement of his or her partnership interest is regarded as a partner. The taxpayer's interest is referred to as a "residual interest". If the adjusted cost base of either partnership interest becomes "negative", this negative amount is treated as an immediate capital gain. Any such gain is to be added to the adjusted cost base of the taxpayer's interest in the partnership.

(f) *Resource properties.*

(i) The taxpayer's share of the partnership's Canadian development expense or Canadian oil and gas property expense that was deducted from the adjusted cost base of the taxpayer's partnership interest (see item (3)(b) *Resource-related deductions* below) is added to the adjusted cost base of the taxpayer's partnership interest if the taxpayer makes an election to exclude these

---

See page ii for explanation of footnotes.
[311] CCH ¶9220; Sec. 70(2).

¶5190

expenses in determining the taxpayer's Canadian development expense or Canadian oil and gas property expense.[312]

(ii) Proceeds of disposition of Canadian resource properties and recoveries of exploration or development expenses arising in a partnership are taken into account in computing income at the partner level. The amount so taken into account adds to the partner's adjusted cost base of his or her partnership interest. Accordingly, if the taxpayer disposes of this interest before the proceeds of disposition or the recovery have been distributed to the taxpayer, he or she will not realize a capital gain on an amount already included in income.

(iii) The adjusted cost base of a partnership interest (related to a Canadian resource property or exploration or development expenses incurred in Canada) is increased by the amount of the partner's share of any assistance or benefit the partnership received or becomes entitled to receive from a government, municipality, or other public authority. The assistance or benefit referred to includes grants, subsidies, forgivable loans, deductions from royalties, or tax otherwise payable and investment allowances. This addition to the adjusted cost base will be reduced by any repayments of the assistance made pursuant to a legal obligation to repay.

(g) *Property rolled into a partnership.* In certain circumstances,[313] a taxpayer may transfer property to a Canadian partnership on a tax-deferred basis. An amount is added to the taxpayer's adjusted cost base of the partnership interest where the taxpayer's proceeds of disposition exceed the fair market value of the hard consideration or where a majority-interest partner would otherwise realize a capital loss. Similarly, there is provision for a deduction from the taxpayer's adjusted cost base of his or her partnership interest where the fair market value of the hard consideration received exceeds the taxpayer's proceeds of disposition. See item (3)(d) *Property rolled into a partnership* below.

(h) *Denied deductions.* A taxpayer is denied a deduction with respect to certain soft costs such as interest on debt incurred to acquire land or to construct or renovate a building and property taxes on undeveloped land (see ¶3246 and ¶3249).[314] If a taxpayer's share in a partnership's income or loss is 10% or more, such financing costs of property of the partnership that have been denied shall be added to the adjusted cost base of the taxpayer's interest in the partnership.

See page ii for explanation of footnotes.

[312] CCH ¶9070, ¶9084g; Sec. 66.2(5) "Canadian development expense", 66.4(5) "Canadian oil and gas property expense".

[313] CCH ¶12,175; Sec. 97.

[314] CCH ¶4853, ¶4856; Sec. 18(2), 18(3.1).

(i) *Negative partnership ACB of limited partner.* When a limited or passive partner has a negative partnership adjusted cost base included in income under the rules in ¶5175, the income inclusion is added to the partner's partnership ACB to return it to zero.

(j) *Capital gains election.* When an individual is computing the capital gain on his or her partnership interest for purposes of the capital gains election as at February 22, 1994, an amount is added to the adjusted cost base of the individual's partnership interest. The amount to be added is the individual's share of the partnership income earned in the fiscal period that includes February 22, 1994, prorated for the period before February 23, 1994, and his or her share of the partnership's capital gains realized before February 23, 1994.[315]

These additions to the adjusted cost base of a partnership interest prevent amounts which would be received by the taxpayer free of tax had the taxpayer not received them through a partnership and amounts on which he or she has already paid tax as a partner from bearing capital-gains tax when the taxpayer disposes of his or her partnership interest.

(3) *Deductions.*[316] A taxpayer shall make deductions from the adjusted cost base of his or her partnership interest as follows:

(a) *Limited partnership losses.* The adjusted cost base of an interest in a limited partnership is reduced by the amount of any limited partnership loss attributable to that interest, but only to the extent that the taxpayer has deducted the loss in computing income.

(b) *Resource-related deductions.* A partner's share of any Canadian exploration and development expense, foreign exploration and development expense, Canadian exploration expense, Canadian development expense, and Canadian oil and gas property expense incurred in a particular taxation year which is precluded from being deducted at the partnership level reduces the partner's adjusted cost base of his or her partnership interest. Partnership expenses which give rise to these deductions are shared among the partners and may be deducted by them personally at the partner level.[317] In the event that the taxpayer ceases to be a partner in a particular taxation year, the taxpayer's share of the resource-related deductions and expenses incurred in the following year does not reduce the adjusted cost base of his or her partnership interest.

(c) *Charitable donations and political contributions by partnership.* The taxpayer's share of any charitable donations or political contributions made by the partnership and which were deemed to

---

See page ii for explanation of footnotes.
[315] CCH ¶7618, ¶15,999fl; Sec. 53(1)(e), 110.6(22)(a).   [316] CCH ¶7645; Sec. 53(2)(c).   [317] CCH ¶12,103; Sec. 96(1).

¶5190

have been made by the taxpayer is deducted in computing the adjusted cost base of the taxpayer's interest in the partnership. As a result of the split gift rules in pending technical amendments, the reduction in the ACB of the taxpayer's interest in the partnership will be limited to the eligible amount of the gift or contribution made by the partnership after December 20, 2002. The eligible amount is the difference between the fair market value of the property gifted and the amount of the advantage, if any, the donor is entitled to because of the gift.

(d) *Property rolled into a partnership.* The adjusted cost base of a taxpayer's partnership interest is reduced where a taxpayer has transferred property to the partnership on a tax-deferred basis and has received hard consideration for it, the fair market value of which exceeds the fair market value of the property at the time of the disposition.[318] See item (2)(g) of *Additions* above for additions to the adjusted cost base under similar circumstances.

(e) *Distribution of profit or capital.* The taxpayer's share of distributions of partnership profits or capital reduce the adjusted cost base of the taxpayer's partnership interest, *except* where the share in question is an income right.[319] This deduction would also apply where the taxpayer ceases to be a member of the partnership and receives payments on account of the "residual interest".[320] See Item (18) *Right to receive partnership property* at ¶5185 regarding residual interest acquired on the death of a former partner.

(f) *Investment tax credit of partnership.* The taxpayer must reduce the adjusted cost base of his partnership interest by investment tax credits he deducted after they were allocated to him. Note that the reduction in adjusted cost base takes place when the credit is deducted, not when the credit is allocated.[321]

(g) *Share-purchase or scientific research and experimental development (SR&ED) tax credit.* Where a share-purchase tax credit flows through to a partner,[322] or a designation which gives rise to an SR&ED tax credit flows through to a partner,[323] the partner is required to reduce the adjusted cost base of his or her interest in the partnership by his or her share of the share-purchase tax credit or 50% of the partner's share of the amount designated in respect of the SR&ED tax credit.

(h) *Public assistance.* Public assistance (net of repayments) received by a partner in respect of the acquisition of depreciable property by the partnership must be applied to reduce the cost of acquisi-

---

See page ii for explanation of footnotes.

[318] CCH ¶7645, ¶12,177; Sec. 53(2)(c), 97(2).
[319] CCH ¶7645, ¶12,140; Sec. 53(2)(c), 96(1.1).
[320] CCH ¶12,305; Sec. 98.1(2).
[321] CCH ¶19,828; Sec. 127(8), 127(9).
[322] CCH ¶19,927; Sec. 127.2(4).
[323] CCH ¶19,976; Sec. 127.3(4).

tion of that depreciable property.[324] The same amount is also applied to reduce the partner's adjusted cost base of his or her partnership interest.

(i) *Financing expenses.* Expenses of issuing securities or borrowing money is deductible in equal portions over five years. If a partnership ceases to exist, such undeducted expenses will be deductible over the balance of the five-year period in the hands of the partners. The adjusted cost base of an interest in such a partnership that has ceased to exist will be reduced by these remaining financing expenses, which are deductible by the taxpayer.[325]

(j) *Non-recourse debt financing.* Where a limited or passive partner has financed the acquisition of a partnership interest or an investment in the partnership with non-recourse debt, the ACB of the partner's partnership interest (which on its face would include the amount so financed) is reduced by the non-recourse debt, unless the non-recourse debt is already dealt with under the tax-shelter rules at ¶9300.[326]

(k) *Negative partnership ACB of limited partner.* Where a negative partnership adjusted cost-base has been included in a partner's capital gains under the rules at ¶5175, a subsequent increase in ACB may be treated as a capital loss at the election of the partner, offsetting prior gains. Where this election is made, the loss reduces the partner's ACB.[327]

(l) *Capital gains election.* When an individual is computing the capital gain on his or her partnership interest for purposes of the capital gains election as at February 22, 1994, an amount is deducted from the adjusted cost base of the individual's partnership interest. The amount to be deducted is the individual's share of the partnership losses for the fiscal period that includes February 22, 1994, prorated for the period before February 23, 1994.[328]

(m) *10-year reserve for 1995 additional business income.* The cost base of a taxpayer's passive partnership interest is reduced to the extent that the taxpayer claimed a reserve in respect of the interest in computing the taxpayer's "December 31, 1995 income" in respect of the business carried on as a member of a partnership.[329]

See page ii for explanation of footnotes.

[324] CCH ¶4535a; Sec. 13(7.2).
[325] CCH ¶5073; Sec. 20(1)(e)(vi).
[326] CCH ¶6447; Sec. 40(3.12).

[327] CCH ¶6445; Sec. 40(3.1).
[328] CCH ¶15,999fm; Sec. 110.6(23)(b).
[329] CCH ¶5786–5786b; Sec. 34.1.

[¶5195] Adjusted Cost Base — Non-Arm's Length Transfer of Pre-1972 Capital Property

The transitional rules[330] provide special rules to determine the adjusted cost base of capital property (other than depreciable property or an interest in a partnership) that is owned by a taxpayer on June 18, 1971, and is subsequently transferred to another taxpayer.

Where capital property is transferred in a non-arm's length transaction, for the purpose of determining the adjusted cost base to the subsequent owner at any time after 1971, the subsequent owner is deemed to have owned the property on June 18, 1971, and thereafter without interruption. The cost base of the property to the original owner is attributed to the subsequent owner.

Where the property was acquired by its subsequent owner after 1971, the subsequent owner's adjusted cost base is increased by the amount of any capital gain on the property reported by the transferor and must be decreased by the amount of any capital loss reported by the transferor. Any other cost base adjustments as described in ¶5180 and ¶5185 above must also be made.

If the non-arm's length transfer is made after 1971 and the vendor has elected the Valuation Day value (see ¶5130 *et seq.*) in respect of his or her assets, the transitional rules do not apply. The purchaser's cost base value would be the amount the purchaser paid for the asset and therefore the purchaser would calculate any subsequent gain or loss based on this amount.

[¶5200] Limitations on Gains and Losses

[¶5205] Prizes from Lottery Schemes, Pool System Betting, and Giveaway Contests

A taxpayer who acquires capital property as a prize in connection with a lottery scheme is deemed to have acquired the property at a cost equal to its fair market value at the time for purposes of calculating an adjusted cost base.[331] A taxpayer's gain or loss from the disposition of a chance to win a prize or a right to receive an amount as a prize in connection with a lottery scheme is nil.[332] This means that lottery winnings, along with other gains resulting from gambling, prizes, etc., where chance is the determining factor, are not considered capital gains and are not subject to tax. This exemption does not extend to prizes related to employment where services are ren-

---

See page ii for explanation of footnotes.

[330] CCH ¶29,280, ¶29,286; ITAR 26(5), 26(7).   [332] CCH ¶6433; Sec. 40(2)(*f*); Interp. Bul. IT-213R.
[331] CCH ¶7525; Sec. 52(4).

dered in exchange for the award; or to other activities carried on extensively enough to be considered a business.

[¶5210] Losses on Transfers to Registered Retirement Savings Plans (RRSPs) and Other Trusts

A loss from the disposition of property to a deferred profit sharing plan, an employees' profit sharing plan, a registered disability savings plan, a registered retirement income fund, or a tax-free savings account (TFSA), under which the taxpayer is or becomes a beneficiary, is deemed to be nil. Similarly, a loss from the disposition of property to a registered retirement savings plan of which the taxpayer or the taxpayer's spouse or common-law partner is, or becomes within 60 days after the year end, an annuitant, is deemed to be nil.[333]

[¶5217] Losses of a Corporation on Dispositions to Affiliated Persons

A capital loss is denied on dispositions to affiliated persons until there is a final arm's length disposition or an event occurs in the disposing corporation which triggers recognition of gains and losses.

These rules apply where a corporation, trust, or partnership disposes of non-depreciable capital property other than in a transaction described in items (c) to (e) of the superficial loss rules at ¶5090.[334] If, within the period that begins 30 days before the disposition and ends 30 days after the disposition, the transferor or an affiliated person acquires or has the right to acquire the property (or an identical property), the transferor's loss is deferred until the earliest of the following occurs:

(a) there is a subsequent disposition of the property (or identical property) to a person that is neither the transferor nor a person affiliated with the transferor (provided that neither the transferor nor an affiliated person acquires or has the right to acquire the property or an identical property within 30 days of that subsequent disposition);

(b) there is a deemed disposition of the property under the emigration rules (¶5380) or, in the case of a Crown corporation, the change of status rules (¶11,609); and

(c) there is a change of control of the transferor corporation.[335]

Whether two properties are identical can be determined by one of the following deeming rules:

See page ii for explanation of footnotes.

[333] CCH ¶6434; Sec. 40(2)(g).
[334] CCH ¶6459; Sec. 40(3.3).
[335] CCH ¶6459a; Sec. 40(3.4).

- a right to acquire property (other than a right that is only a security for a debt or similar obligation, such as a right to acquire property under a mortgage) that is deemed to be identical to the property;

- a share of a corporation acquired in exchange for another share in a reorganization transaction to which tax rollover provisions apply is deemed to be identical to the other share; and

- for dispositions on or after November 28, 2008, a share in a SIFT wind-up corporation in respect of a SIFT wind-up entity that was acquired before 2013 is deemed to be property that is identical to equity in the SIFT wind-up entity.[336]

In any other case, it is a question of fact whether two properties are identical. For example, shares of the same class in the capital stock of a corporation are generally considered to be identical. The Canada Revenue Agency's view is that properties are identical if they are the same in all material respects and a prospective buyer would not prefer one property over the other.[337]

These deeming rules also exist in certain cases where a corporation is wound up, merged with another corporation, or the shares are otherwise redeemed or purchased for cancellation. Where the transferred property is a share in the capital stock of a corporation that is subsequently wound up into its parent, the share is deemed to be owned by the parent corporation while the parent is affiliated with the transferor.[338] Although as a result of a merger, the shares a taxpayer sold to an affiliated corporation no longer existed 30 days after their disposition, a capital loss was denied due to the application of the above deeming provision.[339]

Similarly, where the transferred property is share in the capital stock of a corporation which is subsequently merged with another corporation, the merged corporation is deemed to own the share while it is affiliated with the transferor. The same continuity rule applies where the transferred property is a share in the capital stock of a corporation that is subsequently redeemed, acquired, or cancelled by the corporation. In such a case, the transferor is deemed to own the share while the corporation is affiliated with the transferor.[340]

A specific stop-loss rule applies to a disposition of shares in the stock of a corporation to that corporation, where the transferor is affiliated with the corporation (see ¶15,445) immediately afterwards. In such a case, any capital loss is denied and added to the transferor's adjusted cost base of any

---

See page ii for explanation of footnotes.

[336] CCH ¶6459b; Sec. 40(3.5)(a)–(b.1).
[337] Interp. Bul. IT-387R2.
[338] CCH ¶6459b; Sec. 40(3.5)(c).

[339] Cascades Inc., 2009 DTC 5139.

[340] CCH ¶6459b; Sec. 40(3.5)(d).

shares it holds in the transferee corporation immediately after the transfer.[341]

[¶5220] Loss When Provincial Assistance Is Received

A loss arising on the disposition of shares of a prescribed venture capital corporation or a prescribed labour-sponsored venture capital corporation or shares of a taxable Canadian corporation that was held in a prescribed stock savings plan will be reduced by any prescribed assistance that is received or receivable by the taxpayer or by a person not dealing at arm's length with the taxpayer.[342] As outlined in the Regulations, prescribed assistance generally refers to assistance provided by a province, often in the form of a tax credit for the acquisition of certain types of stock. This includes Ontario government assistance with respect to shares of a corporation registered under the *Small Business Development Corporations Act*.

This prescribed assistance does not reduce the adjusted cost base of the shares (see item (13) *Grants, subsidies, etc.* at ¶5185); however, where a loss is realized by the taxpayer on the share, the amount of the assistance previously received in respect of the share by the taxpayer or by a person with whom the taxpayer was not dealing at arm's length will be applied to reduce the loss.

Example:

M acquired a share of a prescribed venture capital corporation costing $100 and received assistance with respect to the share of $30. M sold the share to his daughter J for $80, which was the fair market value at the time.

The assistance of $30 reduced M's $20 loss on the sale of the share to nil. If J later sells the share for $55, J's loss of $25 would be reduced by $10 which is the amount of prescribed assistance received by M which had not previously been applied.

[¶5225] Foreign Currencies, Bonds, Canadian Securities, Tax Credits

[¶5230] Capital Gains and Losses in Respect of Foreign Currencies

Individuals are provided a $200 floor in computing capital gains and losses resulting from any fluctuation in the value of foreign currencies in relation to Canadian currencies.[343] Thus, an individual's capital gain or capital loss from the disposition of foreign currency is the net gain or loss reduced by $200. For taxpayers other than individuals, the computation is made without the $200 floor. Profits on foreign exchange transactions may be capital or income depending on the circumstances and the nature of the

---

See page ii for explanation of footnotes.

[341] CCH ¶6459c; Sec. 40(3.6).

[342] CCH ¶6439b, ¶7670–7670e; Sec. 40(2)(*i*); Reg. 6700–6705.

[343] CCH ¶6360; Sec. 39(2); Interp. Bul. IT-95R.

debt. Whether or not losses on foreign exchange transactions will be deductible from income will depend on whether the transaction involved is a capital transaction or one of an income nature.[344] The determination of the nature of a transaction depends on all the circumstances of each case.[345]

[¶5233] CRA Yearly Average Conversion Rates for U.S. Dollar and U.K. Pound Sterling

The following table shows the average yearly conversion rates for the U.S. dollar and the U.K. pound sterling:

Year	U.S. dollar CRA rate	U.K. pound CRA rate
1999	1.48584024	2.40376733
2000	1.48520240	2.24987680
2001	1.54841633	2.22975618
2002	1.57035976	2.35817530
2003	1.40146175	2.28829960
2004	1.30152024	2.38418532
2005	1.21163240	2.20669880
2006	1.13409360	2.08858760
2007	1.07478127	2.14865378
2008	1.06601429	1.96166905
2009	1.14197729	1.78035578
2010	1.02993904	1.59177012
2011	0.98906920	1.58607000

The rates represent the Canadian dollar equivalents of U.S. $1 and U.K. 1 pound, respectively. This means that a taxpayer who receives taxable income in foreign currency will multiply it by the above rates to report it in Canadian dollars. For example, if a taxpayer received 2010 taxable income reported as U.S. $100, he or she must report Canadian income of 100 × 1.02993904 = Cdn. $102.99. If he or she was reporting Canadian dollar receipts to a foreign government, he or she would divide the Canadian dollars by the conversion factor. For example, if a taxpayer has to report Cdn. $100 on a U.S. tax return for 2010, he or she would report Cdn. $100/1.02993904 = U.S. $97.09.

Recent exchange rates for other foreign currencies are included at ¶480

[¶5235] Capital Gains and Losses — Purchase of Bonds by Issuer

A taxpayer purchasing its own bonds, debentures, or other similar obligations in the open market will realize a capital gain if the amount for which the obligation was issued exceeds the purchase price paid for the open

---

See page ii for explanation of footnotes.

[344] Ethicon Sutures Ltd, 85 DTC 5290.   [345] Neonex International Ltd., 78 DTC 6339.

market acquisition. Similarly, a capital loss will result if the purchase price paid for the open market acquisition exceeds the greater of:

(a) the principal amount of the obligation, and

(b) the amount for which the obligation was issued.[346]

For purposes of computing a capital gain or loss, the principal amount of indebtedness of a taxpayer outstanding on January 1, 1972, is defined as the lesser of:

(a) the principal amount of the obligation, and

(b) the fair market value of the obligation on Valuation Day.

This modified definition is necessary to ensure that accrued but unrealized gains and losses at Valuation Day are excluded when computing capital gains or losses as provided above.

[¶5240] Disposition of Canadian Securities

A taxpayer (other than those specifically excluded) may elect to treat certain securities, described as "Canadian securities", as capital property for tax purposes.[347] The election is made in prescribed form, T123, to be filed with the tax return for the year in which the taxpayer disposes of an asset that qualifies as a Canadian security. Once the election is made, all future dispositions of Canadian securities are treated as capital transactions unless at the time of such future disposition the application of the election is denied to the taxpayer due to a change in the taxpayer's status that would disallow the election (i.e., becoming a securities dealer or non-resident, etc.).

The election is available both to individuals and corporations, provided that either is a Canadian resident. However, the election does not apply to a disposition of a Canadian security by a taxpayer (other than a mutual fund corporation or a mutual fund trust) who, at the time of the disposition, is a trader or dealer in securities, a financial institution such as a bank, trust company, credit union, or insurance corporation, or a corporation whose principal business is lending money or factoring commercial paper. A taxpayer may be regarded as a trader in securities on the basis of the frequency or volume of transactions, even though the normal licensing requirements have not been met.[348] Consequently the election may not be available to those taxpayers with the greatest degree of uncertainty as to the tax status of their transactions. It would appear that the election will be available to and may be advantageous to a person who is not a trader or dealer but who has completed a transaction that could be viewed as a venture in the nature of trade. Where the taxpayer has made the election and at a later time becomes a dealer or trader in securities, the election does not apply in respect of

---

See page ii for explanation of footnotes.

[346] CCH ¶6380, ¶6381; Sec. 39(3); ITAR 26(1.1).   [348] Vancouver Art Metal Works Ltd., 93 DTC 5116.
[347] CCH ¶6387–6389; Sec. 39(4), 39(5), 39(6); Interp. Bul. IT-479R.

¶5240

dispositions made while he or she is a dealer or trader. It would appear that if he or she were later to cease to be a dealer or trader, the election would apply again in respect of future dispositions.

Where a partnership owns Canadian securities, each partner is treated as owning the securities and each partner is treated as disposing of such securities when the partnership disposes of them. When the security is disposed of by the partnership, each partner may elect on his or her own behalf to treat the security as capital property. An election by one partner will not result in each member of the partnership being treated as having made the election.[349]

A Canadian security is defined as a share of the capital stock of a corporation resident in Canada, a unit of a mutual fund trust, or a bond, debenture, bill, note, mortgage, hypothecary claim, or similar obligation, issued by a resident of Canada. It should be noted that certain securities that are prescribed by regulation are excluded from the definition of Canadian security.[350]

A taxpayer had elected under the above provisions to treat a Canada Treasury Bill as a capital property so that, upon its redemption, the difference between its face value and the amount paid for it could be treated as a capital gain. Considering that the return on the T-Bill was interest, the taxpayer was denied the benefit of the election.[351]

[¶5255] Principal Residence

[¶5260] Principal Residence — Exemption for Gains on Sale

An individual's gain on the sale of property that was the individual's principal residence at any time since the acquisition date of the property is reduced by that portion of the gain otherwise determined that:

(a) one plus the number of taxation years ending after the acquisition date for which the property was the individual's principal residence and during which the individual was resident in Canada

is of:

(b) the number of taxation years ending after the acquisition date during which the individual owned the property (whether jointly or otherwise).[352]

In other words, where the home was the taxpayer's principal residence throughout the period of ownership (or all but one year), there should be no capital gains arising on the sale of the home. Where the home was a principal residence for some years but not for others, the calculation of the

---

See page ii for explanation of footnotes.

[349] CCH ¶6387a, ¶12,150; Sec. 39(4.1), 96(3).
[350] CCH ¶6389a; Reg. 6200.
[351] Satinder, 95 DTC 5340.
[352] CCH ¶6424; Sec. 40(2)(b).

capital gain is prorated, based on the number of years the home qualified as the taxpayer's principal residence (plus one) versus the total years of ownership.

The acquisition date of property is defined to be the later of December 31, 1971, and the date on which the taxpayer last acquired or reacquired the property. The term "taxation years" in the numerator and the denominator includes a whole or any part of a taxation year.

The addition of one year in (a) above is to take into account the fact that a taxpayer can only designate one principal residence for a taxation year. But for the addition of this one year in the calculation, a complete exemption would not be available where an individual sells one principal residence and buys another in the same year, since the taxpayer would only designate one of the properties as his or her principal residence in that year. In this case, it will not usually matter which one is designated as the principal residence for that year, assuming the individual ordinarily inhabited the former and will ordinarily inhabit the latter throughout the respective periods of ownership. On the other hand, if the taxpayer has reason to believe that he or she may not always inhabit the new home while it is owned, the taxpayer may wish to designate it as the principal residence for the year of the move and preserve the "plus" year to cover a year of later absence.

Example:

On January 1, 2008, John purchased a house in Calgary which he determines to have an adjusted cost base of $100,000. For 2008 through 2011, the house meets all the requirements of a principal residence and in 2011 John sells the house for $120,000.

John's gain on the sale of the house in 2011 will be exempt from tax under the formula, provided he designates the house as having been his principal residence for 2008 through 2011.

Note that it would not be necessary to designate the house as a principal residence for 2008 through 2011 because of the "bonus" year allowed in the formula. If John designates the house as his principal residence for 2008 through 2010 (or for any three of the four years 2008 to 2011 inclusive) the exempt gains would be calculated as:

$$\frac{1 + 3}{4} \times \text{Gain ($20,000)} = \$20,000$$

Where a transfer of property takes place between spouses/common-law partners, the disposition will be deemed to take place at the adjusted cost base of the property to the transferor (unless an election to the contrary is made). The transferee spouse/common-law partner will be deemed to have owned the property during the period that the transferor spouse/common-law partner owned the property and the property will be deemed to be the principal residence of the transferee spouse/common-law partner for

¶5260

those years for which the property was the principal residence of the transferor spouse/common-law partner.[353] See ¶5285.

For dispositions after 1990, all personal trusts, not only spousal trusts, are eligible to claim the principal residence exemption where an individual who is beneficially interested in the trust or the individual's spouse/common-law partner, former spouse/common-law partner, or child ordinarily inhabits the property. A person is beneficially interested in a trust if the person has a right to receive any of the income or capital of the trust either directly from the trust or indirectly through other trusts.[354]

No deduction is allowed for a loss on the disposition of a principal residence, since a residence is personal-use property and losses on personal-use property are allowed only for listed personal property. See ¶5305.

Only one residence per family unit (taxpayer, spouse/common-law partner, and unmarried children under 18) may qualify as a principal residence in any given year. See ¶5275.

[¶5265] Meaning of "Principal Residence"

The "principal residence" of a taxpayer for a taxation year means a housing unit owned by the taxpayer and, where the taxpayer is an individual other than a personal trust, is ordinarily inhabited in the year by the taxpayer, by the taxpayer's spouse/common-law partner or former spouse/common-law partner, or by a child of the taxpayer, or, where the taxpayer is a personal trust, is ordinarily inhabited in the calendar year ending in the year by a specified beneficiary of the trust or the spouse/common-law partner, former spouse/common-law partner, or child of such a beneficiary.[355]

The expression "housing unit" includes a house; an apartment in a duplex, apartment building, or condominium; a cottage; a mobile home; a trailer; and a houseboat. The taxpayer's ownership of the housing unit may be held jointly with some other person or in any other way. However, each family unit (consisting of the mother, father, and unmarried children under 18) may together claim only one principal residence for tax purposes either directly or through a personal trust.

A duplex was originally built to house the taxpayer and the taxpayer's parents. After the death of the parents, their half was rented out, but yielded no income. When the taxpayer sold the property and claimed the principal residence exemption in respect of the entire property, it was held that the taxpayer was only entitled to claim the principal residence exemption in respect of the half of the property occupied by the taxpayer and the taxpayer's family.[356]

See page ii for explanation of footnotes.

[353] CCH ¶6460; Sec. 40(4).
[354] CCH ¶7851, ¶28,200, ¶28,329v; Sec. 54 "principal residence", 248(1) "personal trust", 248(25).
[355] CCH ¶7851; Sec. 54 "principal residence"; Reg. 2301; Interp. Bul. IT-120R6, IT-437R.
[356] Mitosinka, 78 DTC 6432.

A leasehold interest in a housing unit may qualify as a principal residence if the housing unit covered by the leasehold interest is ordinarily inhabited as described above. Where the taxpayer acquires shares of a co-operative housing corporation solely for the purpose of acquiring the right to inhabit a housing unit owned by the corporation, the shares qualify as a principal residence if the usual rules of ordinary inhabitation are met.

The expression "ordinarily inhabited" is not defined in the Act. It will be noted, however, that the housing unit must only be ordinarily inhabited "in" the year, not throughout the year. This means, for example, that if a taxpayer sells one house and buys another in the same year, the taxpayer may be considered to ordinarily inhabit both of them in the year so that either may be the principal residence. Inhabitation on a periodic basis (such as in the case of a vacation property) would appear to constitute ordinary inhabitation even where the total time spent on the property is only a small portion of the year. However, where the taxpayer intended to live in a newly purchased condominium but was transferred to another city before the building was completed, it was found that the taxpayer did not ordinarily inhabit the residence even though the taxpayer had spent 24 hours in the unit in an attempt to satisfy the technical requirements of a principal residence.[357]

Land upon which a housing unit is built and surrounding land which can reasonably be regarded as contributing to the use and enjoyment of the housing unit are included in the principal residence.[358] Where the land area exceeds 0.5 hectares (approximately one acre), the taxpayer must establish that the excess land is necessary for the use and enjoyment of the housing unit; otherwise the excess will not be considered to be part of the principal residence. The CRA's administrative position is to consider the minimum lot sizes imposed by municipal authorities in determining principal residence status. Where a taxpayer purchased a 10-acre parcel of land for a residence (10 acres being the minimum acreage required by municipal zoning for a residence), the subsequent sale by the taxpayer of a 9.3-acre parcel which did not include the housing unit was held to be a sale of the taxpayer's principal residence.[359] Further, where the zoning changes during ownership such that the property can be subdivided, the determination and the designation of whether a property constitutes a "principal residence" of a taxpayer is made on a year-by-year basis during the period of ownership. It follows that for those years that the zoning restrictions preclude the ability to obtain a severance of excess lands in a particular year when the property is ordinarily inhabited by the taxpayer, the taxpayer is able to designate the excess portion in those years as a principal residence.[360] Land is not, however, considered to be part of a principal residence where the residence consists of shares of a co-operative housing corporation.

See page ii for explanation of footnotes.

[357] Ennist, 85 DTC 669.
[358] Fourt, 91 DTC 5631.

[359] Yates, 86 DTC 6296, Augart, 93 DTC 5205.
[360] Cassidy, 2011 DTC 5157.

[¶5270] Election Where Change in Use of Principal Residence

A housing unit, leasehold interest, or share in a co-operative housing corporation may qualify as a principal residence for a year, notwithstanding the fact that it was not ordinarily inhabited by the taxpayer or the taxpayer's family in that year. This would occur where use of a housing unit changes from being a home for its owner or the owner's family to being a rental property.[361] A taxpayer built a home and, when transferred to another province, was forced to rent it out. When the taxpayer returned nine years later to occupy the home, it was held that a deemed disposition of the property had occurred when the use of the property was changed from a rental property to a principal residence and that the taxpayer had been correctly assessed for recaptured capital cost allowance and a capital gain on the disposition.[362] The taxpayer is entitled to elect that, for tax purposes, no change in use is considered to have taken place. Where this election is made for a particular year, the housing unit will qualify as the taxpayer's principal residence for that year.[363] Subject to one exception discussed below, the property may only qualify as a principal residence for four years of the period to which the election applies.

Where the housing unit is not ordinarily inhabited by the taxpayer or the taxpayer's family in the year because the taxpayer or the taxpayer's spouse/common-law partner is required by his or her employer to move to some other locality, the housing unit may continue to be the taxpayer's principal residence indefinitely.[364] If the unit was rented out during the taxpayer's absence, the taxpayer could elect that no change in use has taken place for each year in question, and, as long as the taxpayer's absence is owing to the requirements of the employer, none of these years will be included in the four-year limitation ordinarily imposed on such elections. This applies only if the taxpayer subsequently satisfies one of the following three conditions:

(1) the taxpayer resumes living in the home during the term of the taxpayer's or the taxpayer's spouse/common-law partner's employment with that employer;

(2) if the employment with that employer is terminated, the taxpayer resumes living in the home before the end of the next taxation year; or

(3) the taxpayer dies during the term of the taxpayer's or the taxpayer's spouse/common-law partner's employment with that employer.

It is also a condition that the housing unit in question be at least 40 kilometres farther from the new place of employment than is the taxpayer's subsequent place of residence. It should be noted that for purposes of calculating the principal residence deduction, only those years in which the taxpayer is resident in Canada will be considered.

See page ii for explanation of footnotes.

[361] CCH ¶6820; Sec. 45(2); Interp. Bul. IT-120R6.　[363] CCH ¶7851; Sec. 54"principal residence".
[362] Woods, 78 DTC 1576.　[364] CCH ¶7950; Sec. 54.1.

Similarly, when a property that has been used to earn income becomes the principal residence of a taxpayer, the recognition of any gain or loss on the deemed disposition arising from the change in use can be deferred. The taxpayer elects out of the deemed disposition by means of a letter to the Minister.[365] This election does not defer the recapture of capital cost allowance on the change in use and, in fact, the election will not be allowed if any capital cost allowance has been claimed on the property after 1984 and before the property becomes the principal residence of the taxpayer. By making this election, the taxpayer can also designate the property as a principal residence for up to four years prior to the change in use.

Example:

Ned owns and lives in a home from 2000 to 2008. On January 1, 2008, Ned moves to an apartment and rents the home to another family. In 2011, Ned sells the home without returning to live in it. The home was purchased in 2000 for $85,000. The fair market value on January 1, 2008 was $120,000. Ned sells the home for $130,000.

If Ned files an election in 2008 deeming no change in use to have occurred, there will be no deemed disposition in 2008. The whole gain of $45,000 in 2011 will be exempt from tax, since the home can be designated as Ned's principal residence for the entire period of ownership.

If no election is filed, there would be a deemed disposition on January 1, 2008, resulting in a gain of $35,000 which would be entirely tax-free due to the principal residence exemption. The property would be deemed to be reacquired by Ned at a cost of $120,000. In 2011, Ned would incur a capital gain of $10,000 which would not be eligible for the principal residence exemption, since in 2008 the home changed in use from a principal residence to a rental property.

[¶5275] Principal Residence Designation

In order to qualify as a principal residence for a particular taxation year, a housing unit, leasehold interest, or share must be designated as such by the taxpayer in prescribed form.[366] This designation is to be made in the return filed for the year of disposition or when an option is granted to someone to acquire the property. The prescribed form is T2091. Only one property may be designated as the taxpayer's principal residence for a particular taxation year, either directly or through a personal trust.

The definition of "principal residence" restricts the ability of a taxpayer to designate a property as a principal residence for a particular year. A designation cannot be made by a taxpayer where any other housing unit, leasehold interest, or share has been designated for that particular year:

(a) by a person who was throughout the year the taxpayer's spouse/common-law partner (other than a spouse or common-law partner who was throughout the year living apart from and was separated, pursuant to a judicial separation or written separation agreement, from the taxpayer);

See page ii for explanation of footnotes.

[365] CCH ¶6830, ¶6831; Sec. 45(3), 45(4).

[366] CCH ¶7851, ¶39,268; Sec. 54 "principal residence"; Reg. 2301; Form T2091.

(b) by a person who was the taxpayer's child (other than a child who was during the year a married person or a person who was in a common-law partnership or 18 years of age or over); or

(c) where the taxpayer was not during the year a married person or a person who was in common-law partnership or a person 18 years of age or over, by a person who was the taxpayer's mother or father, or the taxpayer's brother or sister who was not during the year a married person or a person who was in a common-law partnership or a person 18 years of age or over.[367]

A personal trust may make a principal residence designation for a property as long as each individual who, in the calendar year ending in the taxation year, is beneficially interested in the trust and ordinarily inhabits the housing unit, or has a spouse/common-law partner, former spouse/common-law partner, or child that ordinarily inhabits it, is listed in the designation. No other property may be designated as a principal residence for the year by any specified beneficiary of the trust, the beneficiary's spouse/common-law partner (other than a spouse or common-law partner who was throughout the year living apart from and was separated, pursuant to a judicial separation or written separation agreement, from the beneficiary), the beneficiary's child (other than a child who was during the year a married person or a person who was in a common-law partnership or 18 years of age and over), or, where the beneficiary was not a married person or a person who was in common-law partnership or 18 years of age and over, by the beneficiary's mother, father, brother, or sister where that brother or sister was not a married person or person in a common-law partnership or a person 18 years of age or over.[368] If a corporation or partnership other than a registered charity is beneficially interested in the personal trust at any time in the year, the trust is not entitled to make a principal residence designation.

The above restrictions effectively limit each "family unit", either directly or through a trust, to one principal residence for tax purposes. Prior to 1982, each spouse could designate a different property as a principal residence.

A transitional provision[369] will apply where a person owned a dwelling prior to January 1, 1982, which would have qualified as a principal residence before the change. Specifically, the taxpayer's gain on a dwelling disposed of at a later time will be computed on the assumption that the taxpayer disposed of the property on December 31, 1981, for its then fair market value. The capital gain is determined on the basis of the number of years prior to December 31, 1981 during which the taxpayer owned the dwelling and it was designated the principal residence under the rules as they applied prior to January 1, 1982 (i.e., each member of a family could designate a different principal residence). To this amount is added the gain

---

See page ii for explanation of footnotes.

[367] CCH ¶7851; Sec. 54 "principal residence".   [369] CCH ¶6485; Sec. 40(6).
[368] CCH ¶7851; Sec. 54 "principal residence".

computed under the regular rules,[370] assuming the cost of the property was the fair market value at January 1, 1982. Thus, the difference between the actual proceeds of disposition and the value of the property at January 1, 1982, will be recognized unless the taxpayer designates it as a principal residence for one or more years after December 31, 1981, under the new rules (i.e., a family unit may designate only one principal residence per year). From this aggregate is deducted any loss which accrued between the value at December 31, 1981, and the actual disposition. This latter provision takes into account the fact that the property may have increased in value from the date of acquisition to December 31, 1981, but then decreased in value thereafter.

Example:

In 1977, Dudley acquired a cottage for $40,000. It was valued on December 31, 1981, at $90,000. Dudley sold it in 2011 for $125,000. Dudley's wife owned their city house throughout this period. Dudley may designate the cottage as a principal residence to December 31, 1981, without impairing his wife's principal residence claim on the city house. Suppose Dudley wants to do this, because of the greater potential gain on the city house and his ability to claim capital gains exemption on the remaining taxable gains. Accordingly, he designates the period to December 31, 1981 (on form T2091).

Under the ordinary principal residence rule, Dudley's gain would be:

Proceeds of disposition	$125,000
Less: Adjusted cost base	40,000
Capital gain	$ 85,000

Minus principal residence exemption:

$$\frac{1 + \text{years designated (1977 to 1981)}}{\text{Taxation years of ownership}} \times \text{capital gain}$$

$$\frac{1 + 5}{30} \times \$85,000 = \$17,000$$

Capital gain subject to tax: $85,000 - $17,000 = $68,000

Under the special transitional rule, Dudley's capital gain will be limited to:

Step 1: Gain to December 31, 1981

Proceeds of notional disposition (fair market value at Dec. 31, 1981)	$ 90,000
Cost	40,000
Notional gain	$ 50,000

Designate years to 1981 and apply principal residence exemption:

$$\frac{1 + 5}{5} \times \$50,000 = \$50,000 \text{ (cannot exceed gain)}$$

Taxable gain: $50,000 - $50,000 = nil

---

[370] CCH ¶6424; Sec. 40(2)(b).

¶5275

Step 2: Gain after December 31, 1981

Actual proceeds of disposition	$125,000
Fair market value at Jan. 1, 1982	90,000
Notional gain	$ 35,000

Designate any years since 1981 and apply principal residence exemption:

$$\frac{0}{30} \times \$35,000 = nil$$

Notional gain: $35,000 - nil = $35,000

Step 3: Gain under transitional rule

Gain from Step 1 (nil) plus gain from Step 2 ($35,000) equals gain recognized: $35,000.

Notes:

(1) In Step 1, Dudley would not normally designate more years than needed to reduce his gain for the period to nil.

(2) If Dudley elected in 1994 to utilize any or all of his remaining 1994 $100,000 capital gains exemption on the cottage, there will be a further step to reduce the $35,000 gain, as discussed above. Remember that this election could be late-filed, normally up to April 30, 1997. If Dudley had disposed of the property before February 23, 1994, the $35,000 gain under Step 2 would have been eligible for capital gains exemption provided Dudley made the claim on a 1994 return filed no more than a year late.

(3) If the accrued value since January 1, 1982, exceeds the value accrued before that date, the transitional rule calculation will yield a higher value than the ordinary calculation. In this case, the ordinary calculation will prevail. The transitional rule provides a limitation only; it cannot set a higher capital gain than the general rule.

(4) If the value of the property declined between January 1, 1982, and the date of sale, that decrease would be subtracted from the sum of the gains recognized in Steps 1 and 2.

(5) If Dudley's wife had disposed of their city house in, say, 1986 Dudley would want to claim an additional designation on the cottage for that and subsequent years. The alternatives must always be weighed where more than one family member (spouse or child under 18 years of age) owns a principal residence in a year.

(6) Where a partial designation is made on the disposition of a principal residence, form T2091 should be filed. This need not be done if all the years of ownership are being designated.

A taxpayer may have elected to have a deemed disposition on February 22, 1994, on a property which may also be eligible for the principal residence exemption under the rules at ¶5010 in order to utilize any amount of the lifetime capital gains exemption remaining after 1993. Where such an election has been made, a second level of computation is added to the general rule above. Essentially, on an actual disposition after February 22, 1994 of a principal residence on which an election has been made, a taxpayer faces two choices.

¶5275

First, a taxpayer can ignore the principal residence exemption (unless 1994 was designated as a year of principal residence in the 1994 election) and calculate any tax payable on a gain or loss from the revised cost base arising from the 1994 election. If 1994 was designated as a principal residence year in the election, the taxpayer is compelled to use the principal residence rules.

Second, a taxpayer can use the principal residence exemption to supplement the election. A taxpayer who uses the principal residence exemption at all on the elected property will calculate the exemption in three steps:

(1) The taxpayer will begin with the capital gains, ignoring the 1994 election. That is, the taxpayer begins with the proceeds of disposition for the actual sale and subtracts the historical adjusted cost base of the house (the original cost plus any major additions or renovations which are capital).

(2) From this capital gain (if negative, there is no gain or loss for tax purposes) the taxpayer subtracts the principal residence exemption based on the general rules described above (and including the pre-1981 rule). Since the taxpayer may choose how many years to designate at this stage, he or she will control the amount of the exemption in light of the next step.

(3) Finally, the taxpayer deducts the deemed capital gains created by the 1994 election. This is measured as $^4/_3$ of the capital gains deduction claimed as a result of the 1994 election on the property. It should be noted that in Step 2 the taxpayer must designate at least the same principal residence years on actual disposition as designated in the 1994 election.

When disposing of a principal residence on which no 1994 deemed disposition election was made, the taxpayer can ignore all this and go directly to the general rule above.

[¶5280] Disposition of Farmland Including Principal Residence

A farmer who disposes of land that was used in a farming business and that includes property used as a principal residence is allowed an exemption for the gain from that portion used as a principal residence.[371] If the farmer claims this exemption, the farmer then pays tax on any gain arising on the sale of the farmland. Alternatively, the farmer may elect to have his or her gain determined without claiming the principal residence exemption, but instead take a deduction from the gain in respect of the total farmland disposed of equal to the aggregate of:

(a) $1,000, and

See page ii for explanation of footnotes.
[371] CCH ¶6428, ¶6429; Sec. 40(2)(c); Reg. 2300; Interp. Bul. IT-120R6.

(b) $1,000 for each taxation year ending after the acquisition date for which the property was the farmer's principal residence and during which the farmer was resident in Canada.

The acquisition date is defined to be the later of:

(a) December 31, 1971, and

(b) the date on which the taxpayer last acquired or reacquired the property.

[¶5285] Principal Residence Transferred to Spouse/Common-Law Partner or Spousal Trust

The Act provides for the extension of the exemption granted principal residences to property transferred to a spouse/common-law partner or to a spousal trust.[372]

When an individual acquires property from a spouse/common-law partner (living or deceased) or when a trust is set up for the benefit of a spouse/common-law partner, the deemed disposition of property at that time results in the acquisition of the property by the spouse/common-law partner or trust for an amount equal to the adjusted cost base of the property immediately before the disposition.[373] When a taxpayer who has acquired a principal residence in this manner disposes of it, the following two rules apply in computing the gain on the disposition under either the general provisions relating to gain on a principal residence or under the provisions relating to a principal residence located on part of land used in a farming business:

(1) The spouse/common-law partner receiving the residence is placed in the same position as the deceased spouse/common-law partner as regards the period of ownership of the property and the number of years for which the property was the principal residence.

(2) A trust receiving such property will be deemed to have been resident in Canada during each taxation year during which the spouse/common-law partner transferring the property was a resident.

[¶5290] Principal Residence in Satisfaction of Interest in a Trust

If a taxpayer receives property from a trust in satisfaction of all or a part of that person's capital interest in a trust,[374] the property will be acquired at the adjusted cost base of the property to the trust. The taxpayer will be deemed to have owned the property throughout the period that it was owned by the trust and therefore can claim the principal residence exemption if the property was also used as the taxpayer's principal residence throughout the period that the property was owned by the trust.

See page ii for explanation of footnotes.

372 CCH ¶6460; Sec. 40(4). 374 CCH ¶6490, ¶13,820; Sec. 40(7), 107(2).
373 CCH ¶9270, ¶9400; Sec. 70(6), 73(1).

[¶5295] Personal-Use Property

[¶5300] "Personal-Use Property" Defined

"Personal-use property" includes any property owned by a taxpayer that is used primarily for the personal use or enjoyment of the taxpayer and related individuals.[375] It includes property owned by a trust for the personal use or enjoyment of a beneficiary or a person related to the beneficiary and partnership property used primarily for the personal use or enjoyment of a partner or related individuals. A debt owed to the taxpayer on the disposition of personal-use property and an option to acquire personal-use property also constitute personal-use property. Corporations may own personal-use property, such as in the situation where a property is used primarily for the enjoyment of an individual who controls the corporation or who is related to the person who controls the corporation.

Personal-use property includes cars, boats, furniture, cottages, and other similar property.

[¶5305] Capital Gains on Disposition of Personal-Use Property

Although ¹/₂ of capital gains realized on the disposition of personal-use property is taxable, a $1,000 cost floor is provided in determining the amount of gain.[376] Thus, if the proceeds from the disposition of personal-use property are less than $1,000, no gain is recognized. If the proceeds are more than $1,000, a deduction is allowed in computing the gain for the greater of the actual cost or $1,000.

Example:

Susan acquires a boat for $900 and sells it 3 years later for $1,200. There is a capital gain of $200 on the sale.

Proceeds of disposition	$1,200
Adjusted cost base — minimum	1,000
Gain	$ 200

If the boat had been sold for $950 there would be no gain since both proceeds and adjusted cost base would be deemed to be $1,000.

No losses are allowed on the disposition of personal-use property, other than listed personal property (see ¶5310 below), only gains. A capital loss is allowed on the disposition of a debt that arose from the sale of personal-use property where the debt is owing to the taxpayer by a person with whom the taxpayer deals at arm's length. The loss created as a result of the bad debt cannot exceed the gain realized on the original disposition of the personal-use property.[377]

See page ii for explanation of footnotes.

[375] CCH ¶7850g; Sec. 54 "personal-use property".   [377] CCH ¶6434, ¶7405; Sec. 40(2)(g), 50(2); Interp.
[376] CCH ¶6900; Sec. 46(1).   Bul. IT-159R3.

If a taxpayer disposes of part of a personal-use property and retains the remaining portion, the cost floor is that portion of $1,000 that the adjusted cost base of the part disposed of is of the adjusted cost base of the whole.[378] The adjusted cost base of the part disposed of is the portion of the adjusted cost base of the whole property that is reasonably attributable to the part.

The $1,000 deemed cost base for personal-use property will not apply where, as part of an arrangement, plan, or scheme promoted by another person or partnership, the property is acquired for donation to a qualified donee, i.e., a donee eligible to issue a tax credit for a charitable donation.[379]

A taxpayer donated of a collection of insects, with a fair market value ("FMV") of $25,519, to a university. It was arguable that the collection was not "personal-use property", but if it was, each insect was a separate item with a separately listed ACB of $1,000 and a separately listed FMV of less than $1,000. The taxpayer, therefore, realized no capital gain.[380]

[¶5310] "Listed Personal Property" Defined

"Listed personal property" is a special category of personal-use property consisting of:

(a) paintings, etchings, drawings, prints, sculpture, or similar works of art;

(b) jewellery;

(c) a rare folio, manuscript, or book;

(d) stamps; and

(e) coins.

This list is exclusive except for a work of art similar to a painting, etching, drawing, or sculpture and would, therefore, appear to exclude the many other categories of collectors' items such as antique silver and furniture.[381]

[¶5315] Gains and Losses on Listed Personal Property

A "listed personal property loss" means the amount, if any, by which the aggregate of losses for the year from dispositions of listed personal property exceeds the aggregate of the gains for the year from dispositions of listed personal property other than "Canadian cultural property"[382] (see ¶5065).

In computing the net gain for a taxation year from dispositions of listed personal property, the aggregate gains for the year, other than gains from the disposition of Canadian cultural property, are first offset by aggregate losses for the year.[383] If a gain results, any losses from listed personal proper-

---

See page ii for explanation of footnotes.

[378] CCH ¶6920; Sec. 46(2).

[379] CCH ¶6970; Sec. 46(5).

[380] Plamondon, 2011 DTC 1137.

[381] CCH ¶7850f; Sec. 54 "listed personal property"; Interp. Bul. IT-146R4.

[382] CCH ¶6520; Sec. 41(3).

[383] CCH ¶6510; Sec. 41(2).

ty for the seven years immediately preceding and the three years immediately following the taxation year are deducted from the gain, using the earliest year's losses, next earliest, etc. Losses from listed personal property are deductible only to the extent of gains from such property; they may not be used to offset gains from dispositions of other kinds of property and they may not be applied against other income.

There is a $1,000 floor in computing gains or losses on the disposition of listed personal property (other than property acquired after February 27, 2000 as part of an arrangement, plan, or scheme promoted by another person or partnership in circumstances in which it is reasonable to conclude that the property will be the subject of a gift in respect of which a charitable deduction or credit will be claimed).[384] The proceeds of disposition are deemed to be the greater of actual proceeds or $1,000. Similarly the adjusted cost base is deemed to be the greater of the adjusted cost base or $1,000.

Example:

Herb sells a sculpture, which has an adjusted cost base of $1,500, for $750. Herb has a listed personal property loss of $500.

Proceeds of disposition — minimum	$1,000
Adjusted cost base	1,500
Loss	$ 500

If the adjusted cost base was $900, there would be no loss since both proceeds and ACB would be deemed to be $1,000.

One-half (or the applicable rate prior to October 18, 2000) of a taxpayer's net gain from dispositions of listed personal property is referred to as the taxpayer's taxable net gain and is included in income.[385] The inclusion rate of a taxpayer's net gain from dispositions of listed personal property is the same as for capital gains on other property. See ¶5005.

[¶5325] Set of Items of Personal-Use Property

A taxpayer who disposes separately of parts of personal-use property that would ordinarily be disposed of as a set will be deemed to have made a single disposition of the property if all the pieces of property have been acquired by one person or by a group of persons who are not dealing at arm's length.[386] This provision is designed to prevent taxpayers from taking advantage of the $1,000 cost floor provided for personal-use property by selling assets piece by piece in units of less than $1,000 when the assets would ordinarily be sold as a set.

See page ii for explanation of footnotes.

[384] CCH ¶6900, ¶6970; Sec. 46(1), 46(5).   [386] CCH ¶6940; Sec. 46(3).
[385] CCH ¶6500; Sec. 41(1).

[¶5330] Personal-Use Property of Corporation, Partnership, or Trust

If, due to a decrease in the fair market value of personal-use property of a corporation, partnership, or trust, a taxpayer's gain from the disposition of a share of the capital stock of the corporation, an interest in the trust, or an interest in the partnership has become a loss, or if the gain is less than it would have been if the decrease had not occurred, or if a loss is greater than it would have been had the decrease not occurred, the amount of the gain or loss, as the case may be, is deemed to be the amount it would have been but for the decrease in the fair market value.[387] The provision prevents a shareholder, beneficiary, or partner from obtaining an indirect deduction because of a decrease in value of personal-use property (even listed personal property) of a company, trust, or partnership.

[¶5335] Special Types of Dispositions

[¶5340] Dispositions Subject to Warranty

Where a taxpayer has disposed of capital property and the proceeds of disposition (received or receivable) include an amount in consideration of a warranty, covenant, or other conditional or contingent obligation incurred by the taxpayer in respect of the property, that consideration must be included in the taxpayer's proceeds of disposition in the year of sale.[388]

If, in the year of sale or any subsequent year, the taxpayer is required to incur any cost as a result of the warranty, covenant, or other obligation referred to above, that cost will be deemed to be a loss of the taxpayer from the disposition of capital property in the year the cost was incurred. For purposes of the computation of the taxpayer's entitlement to the capital gains exemption, the cost of the warranty claim would also be a factor in the year it is incurred.

Generally, warranties are given in connection with the sale of shares of a closely held company or the sale of a business. Usually, no consideration is expressed to be paid for giving the warranty; the giving of the warranty is often a condition precedent to the making of the agreement of purchase and sale rather than the making of a commitment for a separate consideration. However, any separate consideration given, or expressed to be given, for making a warranty must be included in the proceeds of disposition of the property.

Agreements not to compete

The CRA has historically taken the position that an amount received for a non-competition covenant made in respect of a sale of shares should be treated as an eligible capital amount in asset deals and as a part of the

---

See page ii for explanation of footnotes.

[387] CCH ¶6960; Sec. 46(4). [388] CCH ¶6600; Sec. 42.

proceeds of disposition of the shares in share transactions (see paragraphs 5 and 6 of old IT-330).

In *Fortino*[389] and *Manrell*[390], the Federal Court of Appeal disagreed with the CRA's position as set out in its Interpretation Bulletin. The Court held that where a vendor sells shares of a corporation and the vendor receives a payment for a covenant not to compete with the corporation's business, the payment is not an eligible capital amount since the payment was not received in the course of carrying on a business. Because a non-competition covenant is neither conditional nor contingent, the above tax treatment of property dispositions subject to a warranty does not apply either. Finally, the payment does not result in a capital gain because a non-competition covenant is not "property" as defined in the Act and, as such, the payment cannot be proceeds for the disposition of property. In summary, the receipt of a payment for a non-competition covenant by a vendor of shares is treated as a non-taxable receipt.

In response to these Federal Court of Appeal decisions holding that some of the payments received in respect of restrictive covenants were not taxable, a series of proposed technical amendments, the last of which was released on July 16, 2010, would include such amounts in the recipient's income after April 7, 2003, subject to transitional rules. According to this inclusion rule and subject to many exceptions described below, a taxpayer must now include in income all amounts received or receivable in a taxation year in respect of a restrictive covenant ("RC") granted by him.[391] This new provision applies to amounts received or receivable by a taxpayer after October 7, 2003 (the first announcement date), other than to amounts received before 2005, under a grant of a restrictive covenant made in writing on or before October 7, 2003, between the taxpayer and a person with whom the taxpayer deals at arm's length.

The definition of an RC is very broad and will apply to most forms of agreement not to compete. It can take the form of an arrangement between the parties, or an undertaking or a waiver of an advantage or right. It does not have to be enforceable to be subject to the proposed restrictive covenant rules.[392]

There are three exceptions to the proposed general income inclusion rule, and they only apply when the grantor of a restrictive covenant deals at arm's length with the person to whom the covenant is granted. These exceptions are:

(1) *Employment income* — The general inclusion rule does not apply if the amount is required to be included in the calculation of the grantor's employment income or would be so required if the amount had been received in the tax year.

See page ii for explanation of footnotes.

[389] Fortino, 2000 DTC 6060.
[390] Manrell, 2003 DTC 5225.

[391] Sec. 56.4(2).
[392] Sec. 56.4(1) "restrictive covenant".

(2) *Eligible capital property* — Sometimes an agreement to sell a business and its underlying assets includes a non-competition agreement by the seller (grantor). An amount received under a restrictive covenant that is the proceeds of disposition of eligible capital property (an eligible capital amount) is income under the general rule unless the grantor and buyer jointly elect, in prescribed form with their return of income for the tax year that includes the date of the covenant. In this case, the amount is an eligible capital expenditure to the buyer and an eligible capital amount to the grantor.

(3) *Shares and partnership interests* — Exceptions apply in cases where the consideration for certain types of restrictive covenants directly relates to the grantor's disposition of an eligible interest, and where five additional requirements are satisfied, and the grantor and buyer elect in prescribed form. An eligible interest means capital property of the grantor that is a partnership interest in a partnership that carries on a business, or a share of the capital stock of a corporation that carries on a business. In these cases, part of the amount receivable for the covenant may be treated as part of the proceeds for the disposition of the eligible interest, to the extent that the covenant increases the FMV of the grantor's eligible interest. The remaining part of the amount receivable for the covenant (that is in excess of the part treated as proceeds of disposition of the eligible interest) will be taxable as ordinary income.[393]

Furthermore, the July 16, 2010 revised technical proposals add a new exception to the extent that no consideration is deemed to be received or receivable by an individual who grants an RC to an eligible person (an individual related to the vendor who is at least 18 years old) in the course of a sale of shares and no proceeds are received or receivable by the vendor for granting the covenant.[394]

In the explanatory notes that accompany these proposals, the Department of Finance provided the following example:

Assumed facts:

Terence and Isabelle each own 50 of 100 common shares of X Ltd., which carries on a business. The adjusted cost base to them of their shares is nil. In 2004, they agree to sell their shares of X Ltd. to Y Ltd., a person with whom they deal at arm's length, for $1.8 million plus $200,000 for Terence's covenant not to compete with the business of Y Ltd. and X Ltd. after the sale. The example assumes that Y Ltd. would pay $2 million for the shares with the non-competition covenant and only $1.8 million for the shares without the covenant. As a result of the sale, Terence will receive $1.1 million ($900,000 for his shares plus $200,000 for the non-competition covenant) and Isabelle will receive $900,000 for her shares.

---

[393] Sec. 56.4(3).   [394] Sec. 56.4(8.01).

Application of proposed rules:

To Isabelle:

Because no proceeds were receivable by Isabelle for a restrictive covenant with respect to the business of X Ltd., her $900,000 in proceeds relate solely to the disposition of her shares of X Ltd.

(1) Capital gain = $900,000 ($900,000 proceeds less nil adjusted cost base).

(2) Ordinary income from covenant = Nil.

To Terence:

Because Terence will receive $200,000 for his restrictive covenant, he may add a portion of those proceeds to the $900,000 he is to receive for the sale of his shares of X Ltd. The portion of the $200,000 that can be added to those share proceeds is the amount by which the value of his share interest would increase if the covenant were provided for no consideration (when compared to the value of those shares if no covenant were provided).

(1) Capital gain = $1,000,000 ($1,000,000 of proceeds less nil adjusted cost base).

Where proceeds of disposition are:

- $900,000 in proceeds of disposition for shares of X Ltd. plus
- $100,000 of the covenant's proceeds (which can be added to the proceeds of disposition from the sale of the shares), determined as follows:

Lesser of:

(i) $200,000 (amount receivable)

(ii) $100,000 (value by which Terence's share interest in X Ltd. would increase if covenant were provided for no consideration when compared with a sale in which no covenant is granted), computed as follows:

To the extent

- $1 million (50% of $2 million if covenant for no consideration)

  exceeds

- $900,000 (50% of $1.8 million if no covenant granted).

(2) Ordinary income = $100,000 ($200,000 less $100,000 allocated to proceeds of disposition for the shares).

At the time of writing, these RC rules have not been enacted yet.

¶5340

[¶5342] Repayment of Assistance — Deemed Capital Loss

If a taxpayer receives government assistance, a subsidy, or an inducement payment in respect of non-depreciable capital property, the adjusted cost base of the property is reduced by the amount of the assistance or inducement received. See item (13) *Grants, subsidies, etc.* and item (21) *Inducement payments* at ¶5185. If the taxpayer repays some or all of the assistance received after the property has been disposed of, the amount of the repayment is deemed to be a capital loss in the year of repayment. The amount of the loss would be treated as any other capital loss, which can be applied and carried back and forward according to the ordinary rules applicable to capital losses realized in the year.[395]

[¶5345] Shares Acquired on Disposition of Assets Deemed to Be Capital Property

Where a person disposes of all or substantially all (at least 90%) of the assets of an active business to a corporation and receives shares as consideration, the shares are deemed to be capital property of the person.[396] As a result, shares received by an individual who sold all the assets of his or her business to a newly formed corporation would be capital property and eligible (if all other conditions are satisfied) for the lifetime capital gains exemption for shares of a small business corporation.

[¶5347] Deemed Disposition on Corporation Going Public

Individuals who own shares of a qualified small business corporation that becomes disqualified by going public can utilize the $750,000 ($500,000 before March 19, 2007) capital gains exemption by electing to create a notional disposition and reacquisition of the shares immediately before the time of disqualification. If the election is made, the individual is deemed to have disposed of and reacquired his or her shares immediately before the corporation goes public for proceeds equal to the amount specified in his or her election. The elected proceeds can be any amount from the adjusted cost base up to the fair market value of the shares. Therefore, the individual can decide on the amount of taxable capital gain that will be included in his or her income so that he or she can match that gain to his or her remaining capital gains exemption and/or use up capital losses.[397]

Example:

An individual owns shares of a small business corporation which is about to become a public corporation. The ACB of the shares is $150,000 and the fair market value is $1,800,000. The individual has never claimed a capital gains exemption and the shares would on disposition qualify for the enhanced capital gains exemption in respect of qualified small business corporation shares (see ¶5022). The individual qualifies to make the election since all criteria are met.

See page ii for explanation of footnotes.

[395] CCH ¶6398f; Sec. 39(13). [397] CCH ¶7260; Sec. 48.1(1).
[396] CCH ¶7970; Sec. 54.2.

The individual can specify deemed proceeds anywhere from the ACB of $150,000 to the fair market value of $1,800,000. To utilize the available capital gains exemption, deemed proceeds of $900,000 ($650,000 before March 19, 2007) would be reacquired. If proceeds are specified at an amount less than $900,000 ($650,000 before March 19, 2007), the maximum available capital gains exemption would not be utilized. If proceeds are specified at an amount greater than $900,000 ($650,000 before March 19, 2007), a taxable capital gain will result. In deciding the elected proceeds, other considerations should be addressed, such as the application of the alternative minimum tax.

The election would normally be required by the individual's balance-due date (generally April 30 of the year following the taxation year that the corporation became public).[398] Subject to a penalty, a late-filed election may be filed within two years from the date on which it was due.[399] The penalty charge for a late-filed election is $1/4$ of 1% of the individual's capital gains resulting from the elected disposition for each month, or part thereof, during the period the election is late, to a maximum of $100 per month or part thereof (i.e., maximum penalty is $2,400).[400] If an election is filed late, the estimated penalty tax must be paid when the late-filed election is made.

[¶5350] Intercorporate Dividend — Deemed Capital Gain

The Act contains a set of rules to treat an intercorporate dividend that would normally be tax-free to the recipient (see ¶6030) as proceeds of disposition of shares or as a capital gain.[401] These provisions were enacted to prevent the avoidance of tax on capital gains through the use of devices which resulted in the receipt of a dividend for tax purposes instead of proceeds of disposition. The rule applies where a dividend is received by a corporation as part of a transaction (or series of transactions) that results in a significant change in the ownership of the corporation that paid the dividend if the effect of paying that dividend is to result in a reduction of the capital gain that would have been realized on a disposition of the shares at fair market value before the dividend was paid. In such a case, the dividend is deemed for most purposes not to be a dividend. This deeming rule does not apply to the portion of a dividend that is subject to Part IV tax, provided the tax is not refunded as a consequence of the payment of another intercorporate dividend that is part of the series of transactions or events triggering this avoidance provision. If the shares on which the dividend was received have been disposed of, the amount of the dividend is added to the proceeds of disposition of the shares; otherwise, the amount of the dividend is deemed to be a capital gain realized. There does not appear to be any limitation on the time between the receipt of the dividend and the disposition of the shares.

This provision will only apply where the transaction or event or series of transactions or events resulted in either:

See page ii for explanation of footnotes.

[398] CCH ¶7262; Sec. 48.1(2).
[399] CCH ¶7264; Sec. 48.1(3).

[400] CCH ¶7266; Sec. 48.1(4).
[401] CCH ¶7983–7986; Sec. 55(2)–(5).

(a) a disposition of property to a person with whom the receiving corporation was dealing at arm's length, or

(b) a significant increase in the interest in any corporation of such an arm's length party.

This rule does not apply to specific corporate reorganizations such as a "butterfly transactions" as long as certain conditions are met.[402] It applies, however, to cross-border purchase butterfly transactions.[403]

[¶5353] Divided Real Estate Interests

An owner of real estate may create different interests in the property, and each interest constitutes a separate property. The owner of real property may divide the property into a life estate which is retained by the original owner and the remainder interest which is disposed of to another person. The life estate may be based on the life of the owner or on the life of another individual (an estate *pur autre vie*), but in either case the individual who holds the life estate can occupy and use the property during the lifetime of the individual on whose life the right is based. The remainder interest in the property is the right to full ownership of the whole property after the termination of the life estate.

If a taxpayer who owns real property disposes of the remainder interest while retaining the life estate (for example, by gifting the remainder to children), the taxpayer will be deemed to have disposed of the life estate for proceeds equal to its fair market value at that time and to have reacquired it immediately after at a cost equal to the same fair market value. As a result, the whole capital gain is realized at the time of the carve-out of the file interest, since the taxpayer is actually disposing of the remainder interest and is deemed to dispose of the life interest.[404] This provision does not apply to a transfer of a remainder interest in farm or fishing property left to a child which is otherwise eligible for the tax-deferred rollover (see ¶2545). It also does not apply where the remainder interest is disposed of to any charity or donee described in the definition of "total charitable gifts" or "total Crown gifts".[405] See ¶8150 and ¶8185.

When the life estate is terminated due to the death of the individual on whose life it is based, the holder of the life estate is deemed to have disposed of it just prior to death for proceeds equal to its adjusted cost base. Accordingly, there will be no capital gain or loss to the life interest holder when the interest expires. After the death, if the holder of the life estate and the person holding the remainder interest were not dealing at arm's length, there is an addition to the adjusted cost base of the real property. The amount added to the adjusted cost base is the lesser of:

---

[402] CCH ¶7983a; Sec. 55(3).

[403] CCH ¶7984aa; Sec. 55(3.1).

[404] CCH ¶6668; Sec. 43.1(1).

[405] CCH ¶18,330, ¶18,330a; Sec. 118.1(1) "total charitable gifts", 118.1(1) "total Crown gifts".

(a) the adjusted cost base of the life estate immediately before death, and

(b) the amount, if any, by which the fair market value of the real property, immediately after the death, exceeds the adjusted cost base of the remainder interest immediately before the death.[406]

[¶5355] Exchanges and Replacement of Property

[¶5357] Deferral of Capital Gain When Property Is Replaced

When capital property (other than shares) is disposed of involuntarily or when real property is used in the course of a business and then disposed of, a taxpayer may elect to defer recognition of a capital gain if the former property is replaced within specified time limits with a similar property used in the same or a similar business.[407] A similar election is available under the capital cost allowance provisions[408] (¶4460) in respect of any recapture of capital cost allowance arising from the same disposition. An election under either of these provisions is deemed also to be an election under the other.

Involuntary dispositions. The election is available with respect to capital property (other than shares) where the proceeds arise as a result of certain involuntary dispositions. In order to qualify for the election, a replacement property must be acquired before the end of the second taxation year following the year in which the proceeds of disposition become receivable. [To accommodate short taxation years, the specified time frame to acquire a replacement property and defer tax on capital gains is adjusted in the revised technical proposals that were released on July 16, 2010. In the case of involuntary dispositions occurring in taxation years ending after December 19, 2000, the replacement property must be acquired before the later of the end of the second taxation year following the year of disposition and 24 months after the end of the taxation year of disposition.]

The type of proceeds receivable on involuntary dispositions are: compensation for stolen property, compensation for property destroyed (including insurance proceeds) and compensation for property expropriated (or the sale price of property sold to an expropriating authority after notice of expropriation is given).[409] Special rules are provided for determining the time of disposition of capital property that has been stolen, destroyed, or expropriated and the time when the proceeds of disposition are considered to have become receivable. In general, these rules recognize that on dispositions of this kind the proceeds seldom are received or even determined until some considerable time after the taxpayer ceases to have the use of his or

---

See page ii for explanation of footnotes.

[406] CCH ¶6669; Sec. 43.1(2).

[407] CCH ¶6700–6713; Sec. 44(1)–(5); Interp. Bul. IT-259R4.

[408] CCH ¶4513; Sec. 13(4).

[409] CCH ¶7852; Sec. 54 "proceeds of disposition".

her property. The disposition is deemed to have taken place and the proceeds are deemed to have become receivable on the earliest of five specified days:[410]

(a) the day on which the taxpayer agrees to the *full* compensation for the stolen, destroyed, or expropriated property; if the taxpayer agrees to a certain minimum amount and actually receives that pending final agreement as to the full compensation, it would appear that the taxpayer would not regard the initial amount as proceeds until he or she has agreed upon the full amount;

(b) the day on which the taxpayer's compensation is finally determined by a court or other competent tribunal;

(c) where the taxpayer has not agreed on full compensation and the matter has not been taken before a court or tribunal within two years of the loss, destruction, or expropriation of the property, the day that is two years after the loss, destruction, or expropriation;

(d) if the taxpayer ceases to be resident in Canada or dies and as a result is deemed to have disposed of his or her property, the day of such cessation of residence or death; and

(e) where the taxpayer is a corporation, other than a taxable Canadian corporation all of whose shares are owned by a second taxable Canadian corporation, the day the taxpayer is wound up.

Dispositions of business property. The exchange and replacement provisions also apply to voluntary dispositions of what is described as "former business property". In order for the election to be made in these circumstances, a replacement property must be acquired before the end of the first taxation year following the year in which the proceeds of disposition became receivable. [To accommodate short taxation years, the specified time frame to acquire a replacement property and defer tax on capital gains is adjusted in the revised technical proposals that were released on July 16, 2010. In the case of voluntary dispositions occurring in taxation years ending after December 19, 2001, the replacement property must be acquired before the later of the end of the first taxation year following the year of disposition and 12 months after the end of the taxation year of disposition.]

"Former business property" means real property or an interest therein that is capital property used primarily for the purpose of earning business income,[411] including such property that was owned by one taxpayer but was used in the business of a related taxpayer. [Note that the definition of former business property is to be expanded to include a franchise, concession, or licence with a defined term if it is disposed of or terminated after December 20, 2002, and the transferor and transferee make a joint election. For

---

See page ii for explanation of footnotes.

[410] CCH ¶6704; Sec. 44(2).

[411] CCH ¶28,123; Sec. 248(1) "former business property"; Interp. Bul. IT-491.

more details, see ¶4110.] Former business property does not include a rental property, land related to rental property such as the parking areas, driveway, yard, or garden, or a leasehold interest in rental property and related land. Rental property does not include a property leased by a taxpayer to a related person who then uses the property to earn income other than rent. It also does not include property that is leased under an agreement whereby the lessee will use the property to carry on the business of selling or promoting the sale of the taxpayer's goods or services, i.e., a gasoline service station or franchise restaurant. It would appear that allowing a rollover for a former business property permits a business to change location without creating a capital gain on the sale of its land or recapture of capital cost allowance on the sale of its building.

Replacement property rules. Where an election under the exchange and replacement provisions is made for either an involuntary disposition or a voluntary disposition of a former business property, the rules determine the capital gain and cost to the taxpayer of the property acquired as replacement property. The capital gain for the initial year in which an amount becomes receivable as proceeds of disposition of a former property is the lesser of:

(a) in the case of depreciable property, the proceeds of disposition of the former property less the lesser of:

(i) the proceeds of disposition of the former property computed without reference to the reallocation of proceeds between land and building (see ¶5358); and

(ii) the aggregate of the adjusted cost base of the property plus the expenses incurred to make the disposition;

or, in the case of property other than depreciable property, the gain otherwise determined, being the proceeds of disposition less the aggregate of the adjusted cost base of the property plus the expenses incurred to make the disposition; and

(b) the amount by which the proceeds of disposition of the property exceeds the aggregate of the cost (or in the case of depreciable property, the capital cost) to the taxpayer of the replacement property plus expenses incurred to make the disposition. The cost or capital cost is determined without reference to any reduction of the cost or capital cost of the replacement property by the amount of the gain that would have been realized but for the election.

Any portion of the gain used to acquire a replacement property is thus not regarded as a "gain" and does not give rise to capital gains tax.

¶5357

Example:

Adjusted cost base of former property	$1,000	(1)
Compensation	3,000	(2)
Gain otherwise determined ((2) - (1))	2,000	(3)
Cost of replacement property	2,800	(4)
Minimum gain ((2) - (4))	$ 200	

The taxpayer in this case has made a gain of $2,000 of which the taxpayer has, in effect, used only $1,800 ((4) – (1)) to acquire replacement property. The taxpayer must recognize the remaining $200 gain in the year of disposition. If the cost of the replacement property were equal to or less than the adjusted cost base of the former property (e.g., $1,000), there would be no deferral of capital gain. Where the cost of the replacement property equals or exceeds the proceeds of disposition, the full capital gain would be deferred.

In order to qualify as a replacement property, the property acquired must meet several specific tests.[412] Essentially these are:

(a) it is reasonable to conclude that the property was acquired by the taxpayer to replace the former property;

(b) it must be property acquired by the taxpayer and used by the taxpayer or a related person for the same or similar use as the use to which the taxpayer or a person related to the taxpayer used the former property;

(c) where the property disposed of was used in a business (rather than merely as an income producing property, i.e., rental property) by the taxpayer or a related person, the replacement property must be acquired for use by the taxpayer in the same or a similar business or by a person related to the taxpayer for such a purpose;

(d) where the former property was taxable Canadian property (or would have been taxable Canadian property if the taxpayer had been a non-resident throughout the year in which the former property was disposed of and the former property was used in a business carried on by the taxpayer), the replacement property must also be taxable Canadian property (or what would have been taxable Canadian property if the taxpayer was a non-resident throughout the year of acquisition and the replacement property was used in a business carried on by the taxpayer); and

(e) if the former property was taxable Canadian property which was not "treaty-protected property", the replacement property must similarly be taxable Canadian property which is not treaty-protected property. Treaty-protected property is essentially property the gains (if any)

---

[412] CCH ¶6713, ¶17,101; Sec. 44(5), 115(1).

from which would be exempt from Canadian income tax under a Canadian tax treaty if disposed of at the relevant time.[413]

When a taxpayer makes an election, a capital gain will be realized only to the extent that the cost of the replacement property is less than the proceeds of disposition of the former property. The realization of this gain may be deferred in cases where a portion of the proceeds of disposition is not due until a subsequent year. The taxpayer may claim a reserve in respect of such proceeds that are not due to the taxpayer until after the end of the year as may reasonably be regarded as a portion of the gain. At least $1/5$ of the gain is to be brought into income in the year of disposition and the remaining gain is to be brought into income over the following four years.[414] Less restrictive rules that allow the gain to be brought into income at a cumulative rate of at least 10% per year, rather than 20%, apply in the case of farming, or, after May 1, 2006, fishing assets disposed of to a child, grandchild, or great-grandchild.[415] If the taxpayer becomes a non-resident or exempt from tax, the reserve is denied for that year and the immediately preceding year. Also, the reserve is denied when the person to whom the property was disposed was:

(a) a corporation controlled by the taxpayer;

(b) a corporation that controlled the taxpayer;

(c) a corporation that was controlled by the same person or group of persons who controlled the taxpayer; or

(d) after December 20, 2002 a partnership in which the taxpayer was, immediately after the disposition, a majority interest partner.[416]

Where the taxpayer acquires the replacement property before the proceeds of disposition of the former property are receivable, the taxpayer must own the replacement property at the time the proceeds become receivable if the election is to apply. The capital cost of the replacement property will not be reduced until after the disposition of the former property.

Where the replacement property is acquired in a year subsequent to the disposition, the taxpayer may face a dilemma in reporting income in the year of disposition. When the taxpayer knows that a replacement property has been acquired within the time limits, the taxpayer may presumably file on the basis that a rollover will be available. In any other case it would appear necessary to file an amended return for the year in which the disposition took place to delete the capital gain already reported.

Any gain postponed reduces the taxpayer's cost of the replacement property, or its capital cost where the replacement property is depreciable property.[417] This preserves the potential capital gain that is deferred by

---

[413] CCH ¶28,312; Sec. 248(1) "treaty-protected property".

[414] CCH ¶6700; Sec. 44(1).

[415] CCH ¶6702, ¶9295; Sec. 44(1.1), 70(10) "child".

[416] CCH ¶6723; Sec. 44(7).

[417] CCH ¶6700; Sec. 44(1)(f).

acquiring replacement property and prevents the taxpayer from claiming capital cost allowance on an increased value of replacement property which has not borne the appropriate capital gains tax.

Example:

Capital cost of former property	$2,000	(1)
Compensation	$3,500	(2)
Actual cost of replacement property	$3,000	(3)
Gain otherwise determined ((2) - (1))	$1,500	(4)
Gain recognized ((2) - (3))	$ 500	(5)
Deemed capital cost of replacement property [(3) - ((4) - (5))]	$2,000	(6)
Reduction ((3) - (6))	$1,000	

In this case, the gain which must be recognized is $500, that portion of the $1,500 actual gain which is not reinvested in replacement property. The balance of the gain ($1,000) is postponed. Accordingly, the capital cost of the replacement property is reduced from the $3,000 actual cost to $2,000.

The provisions of the Act with respect to rights or things transferred to beneficiaries on the death of a taxpayer do not apply to compensation on an involuntary disposition that is deemed to be receivable on the taxpayer's death.[418] The value of this right or thing may not be excluded in computing the taxpayer's income for the year of death by distributing it to the beneficiaries as can ordinarily be done with rights and things.

[¶5358] Reallocation of Proceeds between Land and Building

If the property disposed of is a former business property consisting of a building and land (or an interest therein), the taxpayer can elect to change the allocation of the proceeds between land and building for purposes of calculating the gain on the disposition of the former property.[419] If the proceeds of disposition otherwise determined of either the land or building exceed adjusted cost base of the land or buildings, as the case may be, the taxpayer can elect in the year the replacement property is acquired to treat all or a portion of that excess (for example, regarding the land) as being proceeds of disposition of the building. This election permits the taxpayer to adjust the allocation of proceeds between land (or an interest therein) and building, as determined in a reasonable manner, to a different allocation which will result in the recognition of less gain than would otherwise occur. This reallocation of the proceeds could be advantageous in cases where the relationship between the value of the land and building which made up the former property is different from the relationship between the value of the land and building which make up the replacement property.

---

[418] CCH ¶6711; Sec. 44(3).   [419] CCH ¶6720; Sec. 44(6).

Example

D sold a store (land and building) in 2006 and moved to a new location that was purchased in the same year.

	Land	Building
Proceeds of disposition	$80,000	$ 50,000
ACB/capital cost	$30,000	$ 90,000
Replacement cost	$60,000	$ 120,000
Calculation of capital gain		
Lesser of:		
(a) Proceeds of disposition	$80,000	$ 50,000
Less: ACB/capital cost	30,000	90,000
Capital gain otherwise determined	$50,000	nil
(b) Proceeds of disposition	$80,000	$50,000
Less: Cost of replacement property	60,000	120,000
Proceeds not reinvested	$20,000	nil
Capital gain recognized	$20,000	nil

If $20,000 of the proceeds are reallocated from land to building, the calculation would be as follows:

	Land	Building
Calculation of capital gain		
Lesser of:		
(a) Reallocated proceeds	$60,000	$70,000
Less: for building, lesser of original proceeds and ACB for land, ACB	30,000	50,000
Capital gain otherwise determined	$30,000	$20,000
(b) Reallocated proceeds	$60,000	$70,000
Less: cost of replacement property	60,000	120,000
Capital gain	nil	nil

By reallocating the proceeds, the gain on the land is deferred. The cost of the replacement land will be $30,000 ($60,000 – $30,000 deferred gain). The cost of the replacement building will be $100,000 ($120,000 – $20,000 deferred gain). As long as the replacement cost of the building and land is greater than the combined proceeds, a complete rollover of the building and land can be achieved.

[¶5360] Change in Use of Property

[¶5362] Deemed Disposition on Change in Use

If a taxpayer acquires property for some other purpose and later uses it for the purpose of gaining or producing income from the property or from a business, or *vice versa*, the taxpayer is deemed to have disposed of the property for proceeds equal to the fair market value of the property at the time of the change in use and to have reacquired the property immediately thereafter, also at the fair market value.[420]

If the property has been regularly used partly for the purpose of gaining or producing income and partly for another purpose, the taxpayer is deemed to have acquired the property for the other purpose at a cost equal to the ratio of the use for the other purpose to the total use multiplied by the total cost. Thus:

$$\text{Cost of property for other purpose} = \frac{\text{Use for other purpose}}{\text{Total use}} \times \text{Total cost}$$

When the property is disposed of, the proceeds of disposition of that part of the property used for the other purpose will be determined by use of the same ratio.

Similarly, if a taxpayer changes the proportion of use of a property between income earning and another purpose, the taxpayer is deemed to have disposed of the property and to have immediately reacquired it at the cost of the proceeds. The proceeds of disposition are equal to the proportion of the fair market value of the property that the increase or decrease, as the case may be, in the use regularly made for the other purposes is of the whole use. Thus:

$$\text{Proceeds of disposition} = \frac{\text{Increase or decrease in use for other purposes}}{\text{Whole use of property}} \times \text{Fair market value}$$

It should be noted that the CRA does not consider a transfer of property from one income-producing use to another income-producing use by the same taxpayer to be a change in use.[421]

A taxpayer may elect, in the income tax return for the year in which the change in use is made, to be deemed not to have begun to use the property for income-producing purposes. If the election is rescinded in the income tax return in a subsequent year, the taxpayer is deemed to have begun to use the property for income-producing purposes on the first day of that subse-

---

See page ii for explanation of footnotes.

[420] CCH ¶6800; Sec. 45(1).   [421] Interp. Bul. IT-218R.

quent year. This election is applicable for depreciable or non-depreciable property that was used originally not for the purpose of producing income.[422] See ¶5270 for a discussion of this election used for a principal residence.

[¶5365] Identical Properties

[¶5370] Adjusted Cost Base — Identical Properties

If a taxpayer owns one property, or two or more identical properties, each of which was acquired after 1971, and acquires one or more additional properties identical to the previously owned property or properties, the cost of the properties is averaged up or down, as the case may be, in order that each will have the same value for purposes of determining the adjusted cost base upon disposition.[423] This is done by providing that the taxpayer be deemed to have disposed of the previously acquired property immediately before the time the newly acquired property was acquired and to have acquired each of the identical properties at the same time as the newly acquired property and at a cost equal to the total adjusted cost bases divided by the number of properties.

Thus, if in Year 1 a taxpayer acquired three identical properties at $2,000 each and in Year 2 acquired one more property identical to the first three at a price of $4,000, he would be deemed to have acquired all four items in Year 2 at a price of $2,500 each ($10,000 divided by four).

However, for bonds, debentures, bills, notes, or other similar obligations issued by debtors, the averaging is done by dividing:

(a) the aggregate adjusted cost bases of the property owned after the last acquisition,

by

(b) the quotient obtained by dividing the aggregate of the principal amounts of all the properties by the principal amount of the identical property.[424]

This can be expressed as the following fraction:

$$\frac{\text{Aggregate cost bases of properties}}{\text{Aggregate principal amounts/principal amount of identical property}}$$

For example, assume a taxpayer owned four bonds having principal amounts of $10,000 each, which he purchased at a cost of $9,750 each. At a

---

See page ii for explanation of footnotes.

[422] CCH ¶6820; Sec. 45(2).
[423] CCH ¶7100; Sec. 47(1); Interp. Bul. IT-387R2.
[424] CCH ¶7120; Sec. 47(2).

later date he purchased a fifth bond, identical to the others in everything except the principal amount, which was $30,000. The purchase price of this bond was $29,000. Averaging the cost bases of these bonds results in the following averaged adjusted cost bases:

$68,000 is the total adjusted cost base and $70,000 is the total principal amount.

$$\frac{\$68,000}{\$70,000/\$30,000} = \$29,142.84 \qquad \frac{\$68,000}{\$70,000/\$10,000} = \$9,714.29$$

A bond, debenture, bill, note or other similar obligation issued by a debtor is identical to another obligation issued by the debtor if both are identical in respect of all rights, whether in equity or otherwise, either immediately or in the future and either absolutely or contingently, attaching thereto, except as regards the principal amount of the obligation.[425]

[¶5375] Becoming or Ceasing to Be Resident in Canada

[¶5380] Emigration — Ceasing to Be Resident in Canada

A taxpayer (individual, trust, or corporation) who has ceased to be resident in Canada at any particular time, is deemed to have disposed of immediately before that time, each property which the taxpayer owned immediately before becoming a non-resident (with certain exceptions) for proceeds equal to the fair market value of the property at the time of the deemed disposition.[426] The taxpayer is also deemed to have reacquired the property immediately after ceasing to be resident in Canada at a cost equal to the same amount. The taxpayer will therefore realize accrued capital gains or losses and pay all appropriate tax. This is commonly referred to as the departure tax. An individual may elect, on giving adequate security to the Minister, to defer payment of an amount of tax owing as a result of the deemed disposition of a particular property (other than an employee benefit plan right). The security remains in place until the property is disposed of, and no interest is charged. However, to ensure that the departure tax does not result in undue hardship, the first $50,000 of an emigrating individual's taxable income arising from the deemed disposition does not require security (see ¶9012).

[¶5385] Property Excepted from Deemed Disposition Rule

Virtually *all* property held by an emigrating individual at the time of departure is subject to deemed disposition. Under these rules, an individual

---

See page ii for explanation of footnotes.

[425] CCH ¶28,329h; Sec. 248(12).   [426] CCH ¶20,026b–20,026g; Sec. 128.1(4); Interp. Bul. IT-451R.

who emigrates from Canada after October 1, 1996, is treated as having disposed of *all* properties except:[427]

(1) real property situated in Canada, Canadian resource properties, or timber resource properties;

(2) capital property used in, eligible capital property in respect of, or property described in the inventory of a business carried through a permanent establishment in Canada, immediately before departure;

(3) an excluded right or interest of the taxpayer (chiefly RPP, RRSP, RRIF, RESP, and similar employee benefit rights);

(4) if the taxpayer is not a trust and was not during the 10-year period preceding departure resident in Canada for more than 60 months, property owned on moving to Canada, or property inherited while resident; and

(5) taxable Canadian property still held by a returning former resident who elects to unwind the deemed departure tax.

For a more detailed description of these exclusions see ¶9012a.

[¶5390] Optional Deemed Disposition

An individual other than a trust may, upon ceasing to be resident in Canada, elect to recognize a deemed disposition of the property (in (1) and (2) at ¶5385), which would otherwise be excluded from the deemed disposition rule.[428] An emigrating individual might make this choice to recognize a latent loss in the property in order to offset a gain arising from the deemed disposition.

Where a taxpayer has elected to realize a deemed disposition, limits are imposed to ensure that the election cannot be used to realize a loss exceeding any gain realized on the deemed disposition on emigration. In other words, a taxpayer who has taxable capital gains from actual dispositions may not reduce them by allowable capital losses from deemed dispositions. To prevent such a situation, the electing taxpayer's income for the year of departure is deemed to be the greater of:

(a) the income otherwise determined, and

(b) the lesser of:

(i) the income determined without reference to the departure tax on emigration, and

(ii) the income determined without reference to the elective disposition.

See page ii for explanation of footnotes.

[427] CCH ¶20,026c; Sec. 128.1(4)(*b*).   [428] CCH ¶20,026e; Sec. 128.1(4)(*d*).

Conversely, the amount of the taxpayer's non-capital loss, net capital loss, restricted farm loss, and limited partnership loss for the year of departure is deemed to be the lesser of:

(a) the amount otherwise determined, and

(b) the greater of:

(i) the amount determined without reference to the departure tax on emigration, and

(ii) the amount determined without reference to the elective disposition.

The form for making an election must be filed with the Minister not later than the "balance-due day" for the year in which the taxpayer ceased to be a resident of Canada.[429]

[¶5393] Post-Departure Loss Carryback Rule

A special loss carryback rule addresses the situation where a property owned by an emigrant may carry an accrued gain on departure, but decline in value after emigration. This rule allows an individual (other than a trust) to deduct any loss arising from actual disposition of taxable Canadian property after departure from any pre-departure gain arising from the deemed disposition.[430]

However, some post-emigration reductions in the value of a property (particularly a share) will be the result of the extraction of value in another form by the taxpayer. To prevent surplus stripping, stop-loss rules apply for non-resident individuals, adapted from the rules that already apply to corporations.[431] To the extent that an individual has received dividends on a share since the last time the individual acquired the property, the dividends will reduce the individual's loss on the share that would otherwise be available to offset the pre-departure gain from the deemed disposition. Any withholding tax paid on the dividends, meanwhile, will be credited against the departure tax imposed on the gain from the deemed disposition of the share. The post-emigration loss that an individual may carry back is subject to a stop-loss rule for dividends received *since the last time the individual acquired the property*.[432]

It should be noted that this loss carryback does not affect any interest or penalties owing by the individual at the time of making the election, including interest and penalties levied on taxes in respect of the property.

See page ii for explanation of footnotes.

[429] CCH ¶28,020b; Sec. 248(1) "balance-due day".   [431] CCH ¶6459i; Sec. 40(3.7).

[430] CCH ¶20,028e; Sec. 128.1(7).   [432] CCH ¶18,500; Sec. 119.

[¶5395] Departure Tax — Corporations

The Act contains special rules applying where a corporation ceases to be a resident of Canada. See ¶1085 for commentary on factors used to determine whether or not a corporation is resident in Canada. If a corporation that was incorporated in Canada was continued in a foreign jurisdiction after 1992, the corporation will no longer be treated as having been incorporated in Canada and therefore may no longer be resident unless the central management and control remain in Canada.[433]

When a corporation ceases to be resident in Canada, the taxation year of the corporation is deemed to have ended immediately before the time the corporation ceased to be resident and a new one is deemed to have begun at that time.[434] Immediately before the end of the taxation year, the corporation is deemed to have disposed of all of its assets at their fair market value. Thus, all accrued capital gains and capital losses inherent in the value of the assets will be realized and the gain net of losses arising from the deemed disposition will be subject to Canadian tax. The deemed disposition applies to all property of the corporation, with no exceptions. The corporation is also deemed to have reacquired each property at its fair market value for the purposes of any later disposition that could be subject to Canadian tax.

In addition to any tax that may arise as a result of the deemed disposition, the corporation is subject to a special tax when it ceases to be resident in Canada.[435] This additional tax is 25% of the amount by which the deemed proceeds of disposition of all property owned by the corporation immediately before becoming a non-resident exceeds the total of:

(a) the paid-up capital in respect of all the corporation's shares before year end;

(b) the corporation's debts and obligations, other than amounts payable in respect of dividends and amounts payable in respect of the departure tax; and

(c) a further amount where a corporation has paid branch tax or departure tax for a taxation year that began before 1996.

This additional tax may be equated to the branch tax a non-resident corporation would be subject to if it carried on business in Canada and repatriated all its after-tax profits, or the withholding tax a resident corporation would be required to remit if it paid all its after-tax earnings as dividends to non- resident shareholders. Where the corporation becomes resident in a country whose tax treaty with Canada limits the rate of tax Canada may impose on dividends paid by a wholly-owned subsidiary in Canada to its

---

See page ii for explanation of footnotes.

[433] CCH ¶28,343ac; Sec. 250(5.1).

[434] CCH ¶20,026b; Sec. 128.1(4)(a); Interp. Bul. IT-451R.

[435] CCH ¶26,935; Sec. 219.1.

parent in that country, the additional tax for dividends will be limited to that rate.[436]

[¶5400] Departure Tax and Trusts

Trusts which have ceased to be resident in Canada are also subject to a departure tax. A trust is normally considered to be resident in the place where a majority of the trustees reside.[437] It will therefore be common to find changes in the residence of a trust. Where a trust ceases to be resident in Canada, the taxation year of the trust is deemed to have ended just before that time and a new taxation year is deemed to have begun. The deemed disposition of property occurs just before the taxation year ends on ceasing to be resident.[438] Some of the exclusions from the deemed disposition rule available to individuals do not apply to trusts. The exclusion for returning former residents, and for those residing in Canada for five years or less during the ten- year period preceding departure, does not apply to trusts. In all other respects, trusts are subject to the same comprehensive deemed disposition proposals governing individuals (see ¶5385). Essentially, these proposals no longer exclude taxable Canadian property from the ambit of the departure tax, with few exceptions. It follows that upon ceasing residence, virtually all property held by trusts will be subject to deemed disposition. Previously, many of the assets typically held by trusts, such as shares, which were and remained taxable Canadian property as defined in ¶5095, were subject to tax only when actually disposed of.

[¶5405] Immigration — Becoming Resident of Canada

Where a corporation or a trust becomes resident in Canada, the taxation year of the corporation or trust is deemed to have ended immediately before becoming resident and a new taxation year is deemed to have started at the time of becoming resident. A similar provision is contained in the Act for a corporation that was a foreign affiliate immediately before becoming resident in Canada.[439]

Where a corporation, trust, or individual has become a resident of Canada at any time, the taxpayer is deemed to have disposed of immediately before that time each property which the taxpayer owned immediately before becoming resident in Canada for proceeds equal to the fair market value of the property at the time of the deemed disposition. The taxpayer is also deemed to have reacquired the property immediately after becoming resident in Canada at a cost equal to the same amount.[440] The practical effect of this provision is that taxpayers who become resident in Canada will be subject to the capital gains tax provisions in respect of dispositions of property after they take up Canadian residence, in a similar manner to other residents of Canada. Gains and losses will, however, be computed from a

---

See page ii for explanation of footnotes.

[436] CCH ¶26,942; Sec. 219.3.

[437] Thibodeau Family Trust, 78 DTC 6376.

[438] CCH ¶20,026b–20,026g; Sec. 128.1(4).

[439] CCH ¶20,025d; Sec. 128.1(1)(*d*).

[440] CCH ¶20,025c; Sec. 128.1(1)(*c*).

cost base established at the time these taxpayers become resident in Canada. This rule applies for purposes of the Act and not just for purposes of calculating capital gains and losses. Therefore the value of the property at the time of the deemed acquisition will be relevant for capital cost allowance and inventory valuation purposes as well.

The deemed disposition and reacquisition rules apply to all property except:

(1) taxable Canadian property;

(2) inventory of a business carried on in Canada at the time of immigration;

(3) eligible capital property of a business already carried on in Canada at the time of immigration;

(4) stock and mutual fund options subject to the rules in ¶2135; and

(5) excluded rights or interests (chiefly pension and other similar employee benefits), other than an interest in a non-resident testamentary trust that was never acquired for consideration.

These exceptions do not apply to a corporation that becomes a resident of Canada after February 23, 1998. Corporations immigrating to Canada after February 23, 1998, will be treated as having disposed of *all* of their assets, including taxable Canadian property. If an immigrating corporation owns a share of a Canadian corporation (other than a share on which any gain of the immigration corporation is taxable in Canada), a dividend will be deemed to have been paid equal to the excess of the Canadian share's value over its paid-up capital. In this way, the corporation's immigration is treated in the same manner as a sale of the share for fair market value proceeds by the non-resident corporation to a resident company. These amendments are designed to deal with the opportunity for surplus stripping when an immigrating corporation owns shares of a Canadian corporation and the shares of the non-resident corporation are transferred to a Canadian corporation before the corporate immigration.

[¶5410] Options

[¶5415] General

The general rule regarding options is that when an option is granted there is a deemed disposition of property having an adjusted cost base of nil. The adjusted cost base of the option to the grantor immediately before the grant is nil.[441] Accordingly, a capital gain can result to the extent of the amount received in respect of the option, less any expenses incurred. The cost to the person who receives the option is the consideration given, plus

---

See page ii for explanation of footnotes.

[441] CCH ¶7300; Sec. 49(1); Interp. Bul. IT-96R6, IT-403R.

expenses. This applies to most types of options, other than those described in (1), (2), or (3) below. The types of options are:

(1) options to acquire or to dispose of a principal residence;

(2) options granted by a corporation under which the holder may acquire shares of the capital stock or bonds or debentures to be issued by the corporation;

(3) options granted by a trust to acquire units of the trust to be issued by the trust; and

(4) options over other types of property.

The sale or other disposition of an option by the option holder to a third party is a disposition of property from which a capital gain or loss may result. Where an option expires, it is considered to have been disposed of by the holder of the option.[442] A loss will usually result to the extent of the adjusted cost base at the time of expiry. Whether this results in an allowable capital loss depends upon the type of property involved.

When an option is exercised, the original granting of the option is no longer considered to be a disposition of property. Instead, the option price is taken into consideration by the vendor in the disposition of the property to which it relates; while the purchaser includes the cost of the option in computing the cost of the property acquired.[443] If the grantor of the option is the purchaser, the consideration received is to be deducted from the cost of the property acquired, while the vendor will deduct the cost of the option in computing the proceeds of disposition.

Where an option is exercised in a year subsequent to the year in which it was granted and the consideration received by the grantor gave rise to a disposition in the year of the grant, an amended return may be filed for that year.[444] The amended return would exclude the capital gain arising from the consideration received for the option in the year of the grant, and the amount excluded would be used to adjust the cost of acquisition or the proceeds of disposition, as the case may be. The amended return is to be filed on or before the date the grantor is required to file a return for the year in which the option is exercised.

Under an amendment made necessary by the capital gains election rules, the option grantor who is an individual other than a trust may elect, for dispositions of property after February 22, 1994, pursuant to options granted before February 23, 1994, not to include the option price as part of the proceeds of disposition of the property when the option is exercised. In this way the grantor can continue to treat the gain from the granting of the option as a pre-February 23, 1994, gain against which the capital gains exemption could be applied. An amended return for the year in which the option was granted would not be required in these circumstances.

See page ii for explanation of footnotes.

[442] CCH ¶7850c; Sec. 54 "disposition". [444] CCH ¶7315; Sec. 49(4); Interp. Bul. IT-384R.
[443] CCH ¶7310, ¶7311; Sec. 49(3), 49(3.1).

The granting of an option to acquire or dispose of a principal residence is not a disposition and the amount received for the option is not taxable.[445] The option to acquire a principal residence is personal-use property;[446] therefore, the optionee cannot deduct the amount paid as a loss. If the option is exercised, however, the amount paid for the option would form part of the vendor's proceeds of disposition and part of the purchaser's cost.

Where an option is granted by a corporation to acquire capital stock or bonds or debentures to be issued by the corporation, there is no disposition at the time of granting; however, if the option expires, a disposition is deemed to have taken place in the year of expiry.[447] The adjusted cost base to the corporation immediately before the deemed disposition is nil, with the result that the proceeds for granting the option will be treated as a capital gain. The optionee would usually be entitled to a capital loss on the expiration. An option granted by a trust to acquire a unit of a trust that is issued by the trust is treated in the same way. Therefore, there is no disposition at the time such an option is granted; however, if the option to acquire a unit of the trust expires, a disposition is deemed to occur in the year of expiry resulting in a capital gain for the grantor and a capital loss for the optionee.[448]

Where a taxpayer has granted an option and then one or more extensions or renewals to the option, each extension or renewal is deemed to be the granting of an option at the time the extension or renewal is granted. The original option and each extension or renewal are deemed to be the same option and when the option is finally exercised, amended returns can be filed for each of the years of the granting of the original option and any extension or renewal.[449]

For example, assume A grants to B an option to acquire certain property and charges $1,000 for the grant. B does not exercise his option during the permitted time but pays A another $500 to extend or renew the option for a further period. In this case, A would incur a second gain of $500 (assuming the property were not a principal residence or securities to be issued by a corporation). B would be considered not to dispose of his original option on expiration and so could claim no loss. If the option were finally exercised, $1,500 would be added to B's cost and to A's proceeds and A would be entitled to file amended returns for the year when he granted the original option and the year he extended or renewed it.

See page ii for explanation of footnotes.

[445] CCH ¶7300; Sec. 49(1).
[446] CCH ¶7850g; Sec. 54 "personal-use property".
[447] CCH ¶7305; Sec. 49(2); Interp. Bul. IT-96R6.
[448] CCH ¶7306; Sec. 49(2.1).
[449] CCH ¶7317; Sec. 49(5).

¶5415

[¶5420] Bad Debts, Shares of Bankrupt Corporation

[¶5425] Bad Debts

When a debt is established to be a bad debt and the creditor elects to have a deemed disposition of the debt in its return of income for the year, the debt is deemed to have been disposed of at the end of the creditor's taxation year for nil proceeds of disposition, and to have been reacquired immediately after the end of that year at a cost of nil.[450] Thus, the taxpayer would be allowed a capital loss on the debt for the taxation year. The election is mandatory in order to claim the capital loss. Since the taxpayer is deemed to have reacquired the debt at a zero cost, if the debt is later repaid, the taxpayer would have a capital gain on the entire amount repaid. In general, a debt is considered to have become bad where the taxpayer has exhausted all legal means of collecting it or where the debtor has become insolvent and has no means to pay it.

The bad debt provisions also apply in a situation where the capital stock of a corporation has become worthless by virtue of the fact that the corporation has become a bankrupt in the year, within the meaning assigned by the *Bankruptcy and Insolvency Act*, or is subject to a winding-up order under the *Winding-up Act*. In this case, the shareholders would ordinarily have no market for the shares and would be unable to realize their loss by way of disposition. This loss is recognized by deeming that the shares have been disposed of and reacquired at a nil amount. In addition, shares will be deemed to have been disposed of at the end of the year and to be reacquired at a cost of nil if all the following conditions are met:

(1) the corporation is insolvent;

(2) neither the corporation nor a corporation controlled by it carries on business;

(3) the fair market value of the shares is nil;

(4) it is reasonable to expect that the corporation will be dissolved or wound up and will not start to carry on business; and

(5) the taxpayer elects to have the deemed disposition rule apply.

If the taxpayer does meet these conditions and elects to take the capital loss under the deemed disposition rule but within 24 months the corporation or a corporation controlled by it carries on business, there will be a deemed acquisition resulting in a capital gain equal to the previous capital loss realized.[451] If the taxpayer does not elect a deemed disposition, the taxpayer may still be able to claim a capital loss under the bankrupt or winding-up conditions mentioned above. As well, a loss can be claimed on the share if an actual disposition occurs.

See page ii for explanation of footnotes.

[450] CCH ¶7400; Sec. 50(1); Interp. Bul. IT-159R3.   [451] CCH ¶7400, ¶7401; Sec. 50(1), 50(1.1).

The rules noted above do not apply to shares which have been acquired by reason of a disposition of personal-use property. If a debt owed to a taxpayer at the end of a taxation year in relation to the disposition of personal-use property is established to have become a bad debt in the year, the taxpayer is deemed to have disposed of the debt at the end of the year for proceeds equal to the excess of its adjusted cost base over the gain, if any, from the disposition of the personal-use property, the proceeds of which included the debt.[452] The taxpayer is also deemed to have reacquired the debt immediately after the end of the year at a cost equal to the amount of the proceeds determined as stated above. Therefore, capital losses in respect of bad debts may be claimed on the disposition of personal-use property where the debt is owing to the taxpayer by a person with whom the taxpayer deals at arm's length. However, the loss created as a result of the bad debt cannot exceed the gain realized on the original disposition of the personal-use property.

If an amount receivable by a taxpayer in respect of the sale of an eligible capital property becomes uncollectible, the taxpayer may deduct three-quarters of the bad debt. However, to the extent that the taxpayer's previous taxable capital gain in respect of the eligible capital property was sheltered by a capital gains exemption, or the previous income inclusion was sheltered by the taxpayer's "exempt capital gains balance" (see ¶5011), the unrecoverable debt is deemed to be an allocable capital loss, deductible only against capital gains. If a portion of the bad debt is later recovered, it will be treated as a taxable capital gain.[453]

[¶5430] Convertible Property

[¶5435] Convertible Securities

Where the terms of a share, bond, debenture or note of a corporation permit the security to be exchanged for shares of the capital stock of the corporation, the exchange of the security for shares will not be considered to be a disposition of the original security held. Instead, the adjusted cost base of the original security will merely be transferred to the shares of the corporation acquired upon conversion and no capital gain or loss will arise until these shares are eventually disposed of.[454] The right to convert the security need not have been conferred upon the security holder at the time the security was issued, and the exchange is permitted even though the terms and conditions of the shares given up did not permit a right of exchange or conversion. However, the shares received must be received from the corporation issuing the shares and not from another shareholder of the corporation.

Following a conversion, the taxpayer will retain the adjusted cost base which the taxpayer had in respect of the convertible security immediately

---

See page ii for explanation of footnotes.

[452] CCH ¶7405; Sec. 50(2); Interp. Bul. IT-159R3.   [454] CCH ¶7450; Sec. 51(1); Interp. Bul. IT-115R2,
[453] CCH ¶5131b, ¶6398d; Sec. 20(4.2), 39(11).   IT-146R4.

before the conversion. The adjusted cost base is allocated to the various classes of shares received on conversion based on the proportion that the fair market value, immediately after conversion, of all shares of a particular class received on conversion is of the fair market value, immediately after conversion, of all the shares received by the taxpayer on conversion.

Example:

> X owns a convertible debenture acquired for $100 and exchanges it for 5 common shares as allowed in the conversion feature. The common shares have a fair market value of $30 each. X is deemed to have acquired each common share for $20 ($100/5). The gain of $10 per share is deferred.

The paid-up capital of the classes of shares received on the exchange of shares may be reduced. This permits any paid-up capital deficiency of the old shares to flow through to the new shares.[455]

If the result of the exchange is to confer a benefit on a related person because the value of the shares received on the exchange is less than the value of the convertible property, other rules apply that may force the recognition of a capital gain and alter the adjusted cost base of the shares received on conversion.[456] These other rules will apply if all of the three following conditions are met:

(1) the rollover provisions noted above would have otherwise applied to the conversion of the property;

(2) the fair market value of the convertible property before the conversion is greater than the fair market value of the shares received after the conversion; and

(3) the difference in (2) above, which is referred to as the "gift portion", can reasonably considered to be a benefit that the taxpayer desired to have conferred upon a person related to the taxpayer.

In this situation the deemed proceeds of disposition of the convertible property will be equal to the lesser of:

(a) the adjusted cost base of the convertible property immediately before the disposition plus the gift portion; and

(b) the fair market value of the convertible property immediately before the conversion.

If the deemed proceeds of disposition would otherwise result in a capital loss on the conversion, the capital loss is deemed to be nil.

The cost of all shares of a particular class received on the conversion is deemed to be the proportion of the lesser of:

(a) the adjusted cost base of the convertible property immediately before the exchange; and

---

See page ii for explanation of footnotes.
[455] CCH ¶7461; Sec. 51(3).   [456] CCH ¶7460; Sec. 51(2).

(b) the aggregate of the fair market value, immediately after the conversion, of all shares received on the conversion and the amount of any capital loss which is denied as a result of the exchange,

that the fair market value immediately after the conversion of all the shares of the particular class is of the fair market value of all shares received on conversion.

Example:

J holds Class A preference shares of J Limited which are convertible to Class B preference shares. The Class A preference shares have a adjusted cost base of $50,000 and a fair market value of $100,000. The Class A preference shares are converted into Class B preference shares of J Limited which have a fair market value of $60,000 immediately after the conversion. The children of J are the only other shareholders of J Limited. In this situation a benefit is being conferred on a related person and so the rules to force a realization of a capital gain will apply. The gift portion on the conversion would be the excess of the fair market value of the Class A preference shares ($100,000) over the fair market value of the Class B preference shares ($60,000) or $40,000.

The proceeds of disposition of the Class A preference shares are deemed to be the lesser of:

(a) The adjusted cost base of the Class A preference shares	$ 50,000
Plus the gift portion	40,000
	$ 90,000
(b) The fair market value of the Class A preference shares immediately before the conversion	$100,000

Therefore, the proceeds of disposition are $90,000 and a $40,000 capital gain is realized by Mr. J as a result of the conversion. The adjusted cost base of the Class B preference shares received on the conversion will be equal to the lesser of:

(a) The adjusted cost base of the Class A preference shares before the conversion	$ 50,000
(b) The fair market value of the Class B preference shares after the conversion	$ 60,000
Plus any capital loss denied	nil
	$ 60,000

There is no reduction of the adjusted cost base of the Class B preference shares but there is an immediate recognition of a capital gain equal to the gift portion.

The provisions concerning convertible property do not apply for purposes of a rollover by shareholders of eligible property to a taxable Canadian corporation or an exchange of shares by a shareholder in the course of a reorganization of capital.[457]

See page ii for explanation of footnotes.

[457] CCH ¶7462; Sec. 51(4).

Chapter VI

Corporations and Their Shareholders

Corporations Resident in Canada **6000**

Taxation of Corporations 6005

"Public Corporation" Defined 6010

"Private Corporation" Defined 6020

Dividends 6025

Deduction for Inter-Company Dividends 6030

Dividends on Term Preferred Shares 6035

Dividends on Short-Term Preferred Shares 6040

Dividends on Shares Having Protection 6045

Types of Dividends 6050

Dividend Gross-Up and Dividend Tax Credit 6052

Dividends Deemed Received 6055

Dividends Received by Spouse or Common-Law Partner 6060

Corporate Distributions out of Surplus **6070**

Distributions out of Surplus 6075

Tax-Paid Undistributed Surplus or 1971 Capital Surplus Distributions 6080

Cost Base and Adjusted Cost Base of Shares 6095

Capital Dividend Distributions by Private Corporation 6110

Procedure for Making Capital Dividend Election 6115

Capital Dividend Account 6120

Pre-1972 Capital Surplus on Hand 6125

Deemed Dividend Distributions **6140**

Deemed Dividends 6145

Deemed Dividends and Return of Capital 6150

Simultaneous Dividends 6155

Capital Gains and Losses 6160

Stock Dividends 6165

"Paid-Up Capital" Defined 6170

Distribution on Winding-Up, etc. 6185

Redemptions, Acquisitions, or Cancellations 6190

Reduction of Paid-Up Capital 6195

Where Amount Distributed Includes Shares 6200

Deemed Dividend Provisions Not Applicable 6205

Transfer of Property to Corporation — Rollovers **6210**

Rollovers 6215

Transfer of Property to Corporation 6220

Joint Election 6225

Consideration for Disposition 6230

Domestic Share-for-Share Exchange 6275

Foreign Share-for-Share Exchange 6277

Rollover on SIFT Unit-for-Share Exchange 6278

551

**Transfers to Corporation
from Partnership —
Rollovers** **6280**

Transfer of Property to
Corporation from
Partnership 6285

Rollover Where Partnership
Wound Up 6290

**Property Transferred to
Controlled Corporation —
Losses** **6295**

Loss on Certain Properties 6300

Loss on Shares 6302

**Reorganization of Capital —
Rollovers** **6305**

Dispositions of Shares 6310

Cost Basis of Shares and
Other Property 6315

**Foreign Spin-Offs —
Rollovers** **6320**

Tax-Deferred Rollover 6321

Eligible Distributions 6322

Cost Base Adjustments 6323

Inventory 6324

Amalgamations **6325**

Meaning of
"Amalgamation" 6327

Amalgamations — Rollovers **6335**

General 6340

Shareholders of
Predecessor
Corporations 6345

Exchanged Shares 6350

Options To Acquire Shares
of Predecessor
Corporation 6355

Obligations and Debts
Issued by Predecessor
Corporation 6360

Winding Up **6370**

Winding Up a 90%-or-
Greater-Owned Taxable
Canadian Corporation 6375

Winding-Up of Corporation
That Is Not a 90%-
Owned Subsidiary 6380

Deemed Dividends 6385

SIFT Trust Wind-Up Rollover 6390

Winding-Up of an NRO 6395

Recent Changes

2012 Budget

Split Dividend Designation

Budget 2012 amends the legislation to provide that a *portion* of a taxable dividend received by a person after 2005 can be designated as an eligible dividend. In addition, changes will allow for a late designation of an eligible dividend where, in the opinion of the CRA, "the circumstances of a case are such that it would be just and equitable to permit a designation". The late designation must be made within three years after the day it should have been made, being the time that the dividend was paid. These changes received Royal Assent on June 29, 2012 (Bill C-38) and apply only to dividends paid on or after March 29, 2012. See ¶6052.

Foreign Affiliate Dumping

The Budget proposed a new anti-avoidance rule relating to investments by a Canadian corporation in the shares of a foreign corporation generally where (i) following the investment, the foreign corporation is a foreign affiliate of the Canadian corporation; (ii) the Canadian corporation is controlled by another foreign corporation; and (iii) it is reasonable to conclude that the investment was not made primarily for *bona fide* purposes other than to obtain a tax benefit. The proposals target certain transactions that are capable of generating interest deductions in Canada in respect of the acquisition of shares of a foreign affiliate (and that are not otherwise caught under the thin capitalization rules of subsection 18(4)) or that strip cash out of a Canadian corporation without triggering Canadian dividend withholding tax (and that are not otherwise caught under existing section 212.1). This change and related consequential amendments were proposed in draft legislation released on August 14, 2012. See ¶6145.

[¶6000] Corporations Resident in Canada

[¶6005] Taxation of Corporations

A corporation that is resident in Canada is subject to Canadian tax on its taxable income derived from sources both within and without Canada. A corporation which at no time in the taxation year is resident in Canada is subject to this tax if it carries on business in Canada or disposes of taxable Canadian property in the taxation year or a previous year. In this case, the tax is computed on the corporation's taxable income earned in Canada for the year determined under special rules.[1]

A corporation is deemed to be resident in Canada throughout a taxation year if the corporation:

(1) was incorporated in Canada after April 26, 1965; or

(2) was incorporated in Canada between April 9, 1959, and April 26, 1965, and has been resident or has carried on business in Canada since that date.

Corporations not deemed to be resident will be considered residents if their central management and control are located in Canada.[2]

Several special provisions apply to the taxation of private corporations (¶6020) as distinct from public corporations (¶6010). These include:

(a) the small business deduction (¶8425);

(b) refunds of tax when dividends are distributed to the shareholders (¶9027); and

(c) the right of a private corporation to distribute its capital dividend account to its shareholders on a tax-free basis (¶6110).

In some cases, only Canadian-controlled private corporations (¶8435) qualify for special treatment.

For rates of corporate tax, see ¶8300.

For the tax treatment of foreign affiliates, foreign accrual property Income, and non-resident shareholders, see Chapter XIII.

See page ii for explanation of footnotes.

[1] CCH ¶17,101; Sec. 115(1).   [2] CCH ¶28,342; Sec. 250(4).

[¶6010] "Public Corporation" Defined

"Public corporation" is defined[3] as a corporation resident in Canada having a class of its shares listed on a designated stock exchange. The term also includes a resident corporation which has elected or has been designated by the Minister of National Revenue to be a public corporation. A prescribed labour-sponsored venture capital corporation is not a public corporation unless a class of its shares becomes listed on a designated stock exchange.

[¶6020] "Private Corporation" Defined

"Private corporation" is defined[4] to mean a corporation which is resident in Canada, is not a public corporation, and is not controlled by one or more public corporations (other than prescribed venture capital corporations) or prescribed federal Crown corporations or any combination thereof.

For commentary on private corporations, the small business deduction, and manufacturing and processing profits, see Chapter IX.

[¶6025] Dividends

Dividends are either taxable or tax-exempt, and they may or may not affect a taxpayer's adjusted cost base for capital gains purposes.

"Taxable dividend" is defined[5] as a dividend other than a dividend where the paying corporation has made an election to pay the dividend out of its capital dividend account, and a qualifying dividend paid by a public corporation to shareholders of a prescribed class of tax-deferred preferred shares of the corporation.

"Dividend" is defined to include a stock dividend other than a stock dividend paid to a corporation or a mutual fund trust by a non-resident corporation.[6]

[¶6030] Deduction for Inter-Company Dividends

A corporation may deduct in computing taxable income an amount equal to taxable dividends received by it from:

(a) a taxable Canadian corporation; or

(b) any other corporation (except a non–resident-owned investment corporation or a corporation exempt from tax) which is resident in Canada and controlled by it.[7]

See page ii for explanation of footnotes.

[3] CCH ¶11,191, ¶52,396; Sec. 89(1) "public corporation"; Interp. Bul. IT-391R.

[4] CCH ¶11,189, ¶52,396; Sec. 89(1) "private corporation"; Interp. Bul. IT-391R.

[5] CCH ¶11,209; Sec. 89(1) "taxable dividend".

[6] CCH ¶28,072, ¶52,071; Sec. 248(1) "dividend"; Interp. Bul. IT-67R3.

[7] CCH ¶16,301, ¶16,340, ¶16,460; Sec. 112(1), 112(2), 112(6).

For the purposes of this provision, one corporation is controlled by another corporation if more than 50% of its issued shares having full voting rights under all circumstances belong to the other corporation, to persons with whom the other corporation does not deal at arm's length, or to the other corporation and persons with whom the other corporation does not deal at arm's length.[8]

Certain exceptions exist with respect to the above rule permitting the deduction in computing taxable income of taxable dividends received by a corporation. Financial institutions may not deduct dividends received on a term preferred share. Corporations which are not financial institutions may not deduct dividends received on a share if a financial institution provides protection with respect to that share. In some circumstances, an amount received as a dividend may be treated as a capital gain instead of a dividend if the dividend is paid as part of a series of transactions which have the result of reducing the gain that would otherwise arise on the disposition of property. See ¶5150.

A private corporation is required to pay a special refundable tax at the rate of $33\frac{1}{3}$% on taxable dividends distributed to it by corporations with which it is not connected (¶13,135).[9] The rate of $33\frac{1}{3}$% applies to any dividend received from an unconnected payer corporation and will indirectly apply to dividends received from a connected payer corporation to the extent the payer received a dividend refund at the $\frac{1}{3}$ rate.

[¶6035] Dividends on Term Preferred Shares

Dividends on a term preferred share will not qualify for the deduction outlined in ¶6030 (and thus they will be included in income and subject to full rates of tax) if the share is a term preferred share acquired in the ordinary course of business by a specified financial institution.[10]

A "Specified financial institution"[11] is defined to mean a bank, a corporation licensed to offer its services to the public as a trustee, a credit union, an insurance corporation, or a corporation whose principal business is the lending of money to persons with whom it deals at arm's length or the purchasing of debt obligations issued thereby. The term also includes any corporation that is controlled by one or more of these corporations or is associated with one or more of such corporations in a specified financial institution.

Dividends received by a restricted financial institution on shares of a mutual fund corporation or an investment corporation which has elected not to be treated as a restricted financial institution will be considered to

---

See page ii for explanation of footnotes.

[8] CCH ¶16,460; Sec. 112(6).

[9] CCH ¶24,350; Sec. 186(1).

[10] CCH ¶16,345; Sec. 112(2.1).

[11] CCH ¶28,272ag; Sec. 248(1) "specified financial institution".

¶6035

have been received on a term preferred share acquired in the ordinary course of business.[12]

In very general terms, a share will be a "term preferred share" [13] if the holder has the right to require anyone to redeem, acquire, cancel, or reduce the paid-up capital of the share, or if anyone provides a guarantee, security, or covenant with respect to the share. Also, a share may be a term preferred share in cases where one or more specified financial institutions have an absolute or contingent right to control the issuing corporation.

[¶6040] Dividends on Short-Term Preferred Shares

Dividends paid on short-term preferred shares issued after December 15, 1987, are subject to a 66²/₃% special tax.[14]

A share will be a "short-term preferred share"[15] if it is issued after December 15, 1987, and if:

(1) the issuing corporation or a specified person in relation thereto may, under the terms of the share or an agreement respecting same, be required to redeem, acquire, or cancel the share in whole or in part or to reduce its paid-up capital at any time within five years from the date of the issue of the share; or

(2) the share is convertible or exchangeable within five years from the date of its issue, except where it is converted or exchanged only into a share of the issuing corporation or a related corporation, or a right or warrant to acquire such a share, which, if issued, would not be a short-term preferred share.

A prescribed share and a share issued by a corporation in financial difficulty are deemed not to be short-term preferred shares.

[¶6045] Dividends on Shares Having Protection

There is a provision[16] which prohibits the deduction by a corporation of dividends received on shares where the shareholder has the benefit of a "guarantee agreement". While the share to which the provision applies could well be a term preferred share, as defined, it is not necessary that the share be a term preferred share for the provision to operate. This provision applies to all corporations, although an exception is made for shares held by a specified financial institution in certain circumstances.

Another provision[17] prohibits the deduction by a corporation of dividends on what are commonly referred to as "collateralized preferred shares". Generally, the provision will apply where the corporation receiving a divi-

---

See page ii for explanation of footnotes.

[12] CCH ¶16,345; Sec. 112(2.1).

[13] CCH ¶28,305; Sec. 248(1) "term preferred share".

[14] CCH ¶24,556; Sec. 191.1(1).

[15] CCH ¶28,270; Sec. 248(1) "short-term preferred share".

[16] CCH ¶16,360; Sec. 112(2.2).

[17] CCH ¶16,367–16,372; Sec. 112(2.4)–(2.9).

ᶜ dend on shares is provided with security to protect it from any loss it may realize in respect of the shares or where it retains control over the subscription proceeds of such shares. It is limited to those transactions where the intercorporate dividend deduction is used to transfer the benefit of losses or deductions as between corporations. The provision does not apply to dividends received on "exempt shares", as defined in the Act.

[¶6050] Types of Dividends

Dividends may be classified[18] as follows:

(1) *Dividends payable before 1979 out of tax-paid undistributed surplus.* These dividends are tax-exempt and are deducted in computing the adjusted cost base of shares. They may be received from either private or public corporations until December 31, 1978.

(2) *Dividends payable out of 1971 capital surplus.* These dividends are also tax-exempt and are deducted in computing the adjusted cost base of shares. They may be received from either public or private corporations before 1979, and thereafter only upon the winding-up of the corporation.

(3) *Capital dividends.* These dividends may be received from private corporations only and are tax-exempt. The dividends are paid out of the untaxed portion of the net capital gain made by the private corporation after 1971. Capital dividends are not deducted in computing the adjusted cost base of shares.

(4) *Dividends payable after 1978 on tax-deferred preferred shares issued by certain public corporations.* These are tax-exempt and reduce the adjusted cost base of the shares.[19]

(5) *Taxable dividends.* These dividends include all dividends that do not fall within classifications (1) to (4) above and may be received from either public or private corporations, and from either taxable or non-taxable corporations. A dividend tax credit may be claimed with respect to such dividends[20] (¶8275). Taxable dividends are not deducted in computing the adjusted cost base of shares. For dividends paid after 2005, a subset of taxable dividends called "eligible dividends" are subject to an enhanced dividend gross-up and credit mechanism (see ¶6052).

[¶6052] Dividend Gross-Up and Dividend Tax Credit

For dividends paid after 2005, an individual, other than a registered charitable trust, must include in income a gross-up amount equal to 45% until 2010 (see below for reduced gross-up after 2009) of all eligible dividends and 25% of all other taxable dividends received from taxable Canadian corporations. Thus, 145% (until 2010) and 125%, respectively, of the

---

See page ii for explanation of footnotes.

[18] CCH ¶10,019; Sec. 82(1).

[19] CCH ¶10,100, ¶10,193, ¶10,102; Sec. 83(1), 83(6); Reg. 2107.

[20] CCH ¶10,003, ¶19,200; Sec. 82, 121.

taxable dividends received are included in income. All other dividends (described in ¶6050) are not included in the gross-up calculation.[21]

To reflect scheduled reductions in the general corporate tax rate, the 45% gross-up factor is reduced to 44% for 2010, 41% for 2011, and 38% beginning in 2012.

It is worth noting that because an eligible dividend must be a taxable dividend received by a person resident in Canada, capital dividends and capital gains dividends will in no case be eligible dividends. However, deemed dividends, such as those that are described under ¶6145, can be eligible dividends if they otherwise satisfy the requirements set out in the definition of "eligible dividend" and are designated as such by the corporation that is treated as having paid them. Furthermore, after 2006, the taxable dividend deemed to be received by the beneficiary of a SIFT trust as a result of the distribution of the trust's non-portfolio earnings is considered an eligible dividend.[22]

Generally, a dividend is an eligible dividend if the dividend-paying corporation has given the dividend recipient written notice to that effect. The recipient can rely on that notice, and need not know anything about the tax status of the corporation. However, some corporations will have a limited capacity to pay eligible dividends. If their designations exceed that capacity, they are liable to an additional tax under Part III.1 that applies to the excess amount, or, if the corporation can reasonably be considered to have attempted to artificially increase its capacity to pay eligible dividends, to the full amount of the eligible dividend. [23]

As a result of recent legislative changes arising from the 2012 Budget, a *portion* of a taxable dividend received by a person after 2005 can be designated as a "eligible dividend". The ability to designate partial eligible dividends is limited to dividends paid after March 28, 2012.

A late designation of an "eligible dividend" may also be permitted where, in the opinion of the CRA, "the circumstances of a case are such that it would be just and equitable to permit a designation"[24] will allow for. The late designation must be made within three years after the day it should have been made, being the time that the dividend was paid and applies only to dividends paid after March 29, 2012. It is expected that the CRA will release some guidance on what circumstances it will consider "just and equitable" for these purposes.

A corporation's capacity to pay eligible dividends will depend mostly on its status. If a corporation is a Canadian-controlled private corporation (CCPC) or a deposit insurance corporation, it can pay eligible dividends only to the extent of its "general rate income pool" (GRIP), a balance

---

See page ii for explanation of footnotes.

[21] CCH ¶10,003; Sec. 82(1).

[22] CCH ¶11,182a; Sec. 89(1) "eligible dividend".

[23] CCH ¶11,182c, ¶24,345a; Sec. 89(1) "excessive eligible dividend designation", 185.1(1).

[24] Sec. 89(14.1).

¶6052

generally reflecting taxable income that has not benefited from the small business deduction or any of certain other special tax rates.[25] A corporation resident in Canada that is neither a CCPC nor a deposit insurance corporation (a "non-CCPC") can pay eligible dividends in any amount, unless it has a "low rate income pool" (LRIP). The LRIP is generally made up of taxable income that benefited from the small business deduction, either in the hands of the dividend-paying non-CCPC itself (at a time when it was a CCPC) or in the hands of a CCPC that paid an ineligible dividend to the non-CCPC.[26] Many non-CCPCs will never have an LRIP, and thus will be able to designate all of their dividends as eligible dividends. However, if it exists, the LRIP balance must be reduced through the payment of ineligible dividends before a non-CCPC can pay an eligible dividend.

The individual in receipt of taxable dividends is entitled to a dividend tax credit. For dividends paid after 2005 and before 2010, the credit is $^{11}/_{18}$ of the gross-up in respect of eligible dividends (for an effective credit of approximately 19% of the grossed-up dividend) and $^{2}/_{3}$ of the gross-up in respect of all other taxable dividends (for an effective credit of $13^{1}/_{3}\%$ of the grossed-up dividend). See ¶8275.

To reflect scheduled reductions in the general corporate tax rate, the dividend tax credit moves from $^{11}/_{18}$ of the gross-up amount to $^{10}/_{17}$ for 2010, $^{13}/_{23}$ for 2011, and $^{6}/_{11}$ for 2012 and subsequent years.

Carrying charges and other expenses of earning dividend income, such as fees paid to an investment counsel,[27] do not reduce the amount on which the dividend tax credit is calculated.

[¶6055] Dividends Deemed Received

Where a dividend has been received by a person with whom the taxpayer does not deal at arm's length, by the taxpayer's spouse or common-law partner, or by a minor to whom the taxpayer has transferred property, and the amount of the dividend is included in computing the taxpayer's income (by reason of the taxpayer having assigned to such person the right to the dividend or by reason of the attribution rules), for all purposes of the Act, the dividend is deemed to have been received by the taxpayer.[28] Thus, if the taxpayer is an individual, he or she will obtain the dividend tax credit, and if the taxpayer is a corporation resident in Canada, it will obtain a deduction in respect of intercorporate dividends.

[¶6060] Dividends Received by Spouse or Common-Law Partner

A notch provision is provided which permits a taxpayer to elect to have a taxable dividend received by the taxpayer's spouse or common-law partner

---

See page ii for explanation of footnotes.

[25] CCH ¶10,909hb; Sec. 89(1) "general rate income pool".

[26] CCH ¶10,909hc; Sec. 89(1) "low rate income pool".

[27] CCH ¶5125; Sec. 20(1)(bb).

[28] CCH ¶10,040; Sec. 82(2).

from a taxable Canadian corporation included in the taxpayer's income.[29] This election would ordinarily be made where the amount of a taxpayer's tax credit for a dependent spouse or common-law partner is reduced as a result of the taxpayer's spouse's or common-law partner's receipt of dividends, and where no tax is payable by the spouse or common-law partner. Where such an election is made, the grossed-up amount of the dividend received by the spouse/common-law partner is included in the taxpayer's income.

[¶6070] Corporate Distributions out of Surplus

[¶6075] Distributions out of Surplus

Dividends include any distribution out of corporate surplus. A "dividend" includes a stock dividend, other than a stock dividend that is paid to a corporation or to a mutual fund trust by a non-resident corporation. Certain amounts received by a shareholder on the winding-up of a corporation, on a redemption of shares, on a reduction of capital, or on an increase in the paid-up capital are deemed to be received as dividends (see ¶6145).

Distributions made by a private corporation may result in refunds of tax previously paid by the corporation.[30] A corporation is entitled to a dividend refund in respect of taxable dividends paid by it while it is private, whether or not it is private at the year end for which the dividend refund is claimed. A corporation may also incur special taxes arising from distributions of surplus in such a way that shareholders receive capital gains eligible for the capital gains exemption, and from excessive elections.[31] A corporation receiving a taxable dividend may exclude it from taxable income but incur a special tax in respect of portfolio dividends.[32]

[¶6080] Tax-Paid Undistributed Surplus or 1971 Capital Surplus Distributions

Dividends which were payable before 1979 out of a corporation's tax-paid undistributed surplus or 1971 capital surplus were not included in computing the income of its shareholders, and when paid to a non-resident shareholder, were not subject to withholding tax.[33]

[¶6095] Cost Base and Adjusted Cost Base of Shares

The cost base of shares for capital gains purposes is the actual cost of the shares if they were acquired after 1971. If they were owned before the end of 1971, the cost base may be either actual cost or fair market value at V-Day, depending upon the rules applicable to the taxpayer or the election the

---

See page ii for explanation of footnotes.

[29] CCH ¶10,060, ¶52,300; Sec. 82(3); Interp. Bul. IT-295R4.

[30] CCH ¶20,039; Sec. 129.

[31] CCH ¶24,155–24,166, ¶24,300; Sec. 183.1–183.2, 184.

[32] CCH ¶24,350; Sec. 186.

[33] CCH ¶10,100, ¶10,103, ¶29,499, ¶52,150; Sec. 83(1); ITAR 32.1; Reg. 2100; Interp. Bul. IT-146R4.

taxpayer has made (see ¶5135). This cost base may be adjusted by subsequent events and the new amount is called the "adjusted cost base". It is from this amount that the actual capital gain or loss is measured when the share is disposed of. Tax-deferred dividends are deducted in determining the "adjusted cost base" of shares on which such dividends have been paid.[34]

[¶6110] Capital Dividend Distributions by Private Corporation

A private corporation may elect that the full amount of a dividend which it proposes to pay will be a capital dividend. Such a dividend is not included in the income of a resident shareholder and does not reduce the adjusted cost base of the shares.[35]

A capital dividend may not exceed the corporation's capital dividend account immediately before the dividend becomes payable. If the shareholder is a private corporation, the capital dividends would be added to its capital dividend account and thus it may in turn pay out a dividend tax-free to its shareholders upon meeting the necessary conditions. An anti-avoidance rule will apply, subject to certain exceptions, where one of the main purposes of an acquisition of shares is to acquire a right to a capital dividend.[36] A capital dividend paid to a non-resident shareholder is subject to withholding tax.[37]

If a corporation pays out an excess amount as a capital dividend, it must pay a Part III penalty tax equal to three-quarters of the excess.[38] A corporation may also choose to avoid Part III penalty tax by electing to treat the excess dividend as a separate taxable dividend or loan. To do so, however, all of the shareholders entitled to the dividend and whose addresses are known to the corporation must concur in the election, which must be filed not later than 90 days after the Notice of Assessment of Part III tax is mailed.[39] In view of the fact that the capital dividend account may be varied by the CRA on reassessment, it is often advisable to make capital dividend distributions in amounts which are conservative until the amount of the capital dividend account is well-established. A revision of this account could arise from a variety of circumstances, such as differences of opinion as to the adjusted cost base of an asset giving rise to a capital gain or differences of opinion as to whether the particular gain resulted in ordinary income rather than a capital gain.

[¶6115] Procedure for Making Capital Dividend Election

An election[40] to pay a capital dividend is made by filing with the Minister a prescribed form (T2054), together with a certified copy of the

---

See page ii for explanation of footnotes.

[34] CCH ¶7639, ¶7850; Sec. 53(2)(a), 54 "adjusted cost base".

[35] CCH ¶10,150, ¶11,181, ¶52,073; Sec. 83(2), 89(1) "capital dividend account"; Interp. Bul. IT-66R6.

[36] CCH ¶10,167–10,170; Sec. 83(2.1)–(2.4).

[37] CCH ¶26,105; Sec. 212(2).

[38] CCH ¶24,305, ¶52,073; Sec. 184(2); Interp. Bul. IT-66R6.

[39] CCH ¶10,159, ¶24,318, ¶24,319; Sec. 83(2), 184(3), 184(3.1).

[40] CCH ¶10,150, ¶10,153; Sec. 83(2); Reg. 2101.

directors' resolution authorizing the election or a certified copy of the authorization to make the election, as the case may be. These are to be accompanied by schedules showing the computation of the capital dividend account. All relevant documents must be filed in duplicate on or before the earlier of the day on which the dividend became payable and the first day on which any part of the dividend was paid. However, if an election is not made on time, a late and retroactive election can be made.[41] The retroactive election must be accompanied by an estimate of the penalty in respect of a late-filed election and must be authorized by the directors or other persons legally entitled to administer the affairs of the corporation. The penalty for a late-filed election is 1% per annum of the amount of the dividend, to a maximum of $500 per year.[42]

[¶6120] Capital Dividend Account

The term "capital dividend account" is defined[43] to be the aggregate of:

(1) The non-taxable portion of the capital gains realized in the period commencing with the initial taxation year starting after the corporation last became a private corporation and ending immediately prior to the calculation (referred to as the "period"), minus the difference between the capital losses and the allowable capital losses for that period. Capital gains and losses resulting from gifts, other than those that qualify as gifts to qualified donees for which a capital gains exemption is available, are not included in the computation of the capital dividend account. As a consequence of the 2011 Budget, a taxable capital gain is deemed to arise on the charitable donation of a flow-through share class of property after March 21, 2011 if, at the time of the donation, the taxpayer has a positive balance in a pool of the actual cost of flow-through shares of that class (see ¶5033), the tax-exempt portion of a taxpayer's capital gains from the disposition of flow-through shares is not entirely added to the capital dividend account. The amount that would otherwise be added to the capital dividend account is reduced by an amount equal to the taxable portion of the deemed gain.

For these purposes, the portion of a capital gain or loss resulting from the disposition of a property is excluded from the computation of the capital dividend account if the portion can reasonably be regarded as having accrued on the property (or property for which it was substituted) while it was owned by a corporation that was not a private corporation, investment corporation, mortgage investment corporation, or mutual fund corporation (unless the property was "designated property"). Similarly, the portion of any gain or loss on the property (or property for which it was substituted) that accrued while the property was owned by a corporation controlled by non-residents is excluded if the property became a property of a Canadian-controlled private corporation (CCPC), otherwise than by reason of the

---

[41] CCH ¶10,175; Sec. 83(3).
[42] CCH ¶10,177; Sec. 83(4).

[43] CCH ¶11,181; Sec. 89(1) "capital dividend account".

change in residence of one or more of its shareholders. Lastly, the portion of any gain or loss on the property (or property for which it was substituted) that accrued while the property was owned by a tax-exempt corporation is excluded if the property became the property of a taxable private corporation. The foregoing rules are intended to ensure that when a corporation changes status (e.g., from a tax-exempt to a taxable private corporation, or from a corporation controlled by non-residents to a CCPC), only those gains and losses in the value of property that accrue during the period following that change in status will be reflected in the capital dividend account. These rules will also apply, for example, when property is acquired by a taxable private corporation or CCPC on a rollover basis from a corporation that is a tax-exempt corporation or a corporation controlled by non-residents, as the case may be.

The amounts included for capital gains and losses in the calculation of the capital dividend account are not adjusted for changes in the inclusion rate for capital gains and losses. Therefore, if a corporation realized a capital gain of $100,000 in 1998 when the inclusion rate was 75%, non-taxable portion $25,000; and a capital loss of $50,000 in 2001 when the inclusion rate was 50%, allowable portion $25,000; the net addition to the capital dividend account would be nil (i.e., $25,000 minus $25,000).

(2) Capital dividends received in the period from other private corporations.

(3) The non-taxable portion of eligible capital property income inclusion, to the extent those amounts represent pool proceeds in excess of recapture. When proceeds of disposition of eligible capital properties in a year exceed the balance of unamortized costs in the pool at the end of the year, the excess is included in income first as recapture, up to the total of depreciation previously claimed and not recaptured and, if an excess remains, as income included at capital gain rates. See ¶3088. Since the amount included in income as recapture is already stepped down to the 75% in which the cumulative eligible capital account operates and any excess is stepped down further to match capital gains inclusion rates, that part of the income inclusion that does not represent recapture must be multiplied by $2/3$ after October 17, 2000 ($2/3$ of 75% = the 50% non-taxable portion of capital gains) to obtain the non-taxable portion.

(4) The proceeds of life insurance received in the period on the death of the insured less the adjusted cost basis of the policy.

(5) The balance of the corporation's life insurance capital dividend account immediately before May 24, 1985.

(6) The non-taxable portion of capital gains distributed by a trust to the corporation. This amount is actually equal to the lesser of two amounts:

(i) The amount by which the distribution amount of such capital gains exceeds the amount designated as taxable capital gains by the trust in respect of those capital gains; and

(ii) [A × B], where

"A" = (reciprocal of the capital gains inclusion rate for the trust) - 1

"B" = the amount designated as a taxable capital gain by the trust.

(7) The amount of non-taxable dividends distributed by a trust to the corporation (e.g., capital dividends received by the trust from other corporations). This amount will equal the lesser of the amount of the distribution to the corporation and the amount designated by the trust in respect of the corporation for the particular non-taxable dividends.

Minus

(8) Capital dividends which previously became payable by the corporation.

However, when a private corporation controlled by non-residents becomes a CCPC (otherwise than by reason of a change in the residence of one or more of its shareholders), the capital dividend account of the corporation is reduced to nil.[44] Similarly, when a corporation ceases to be exempt from tax under Part I, its capital dividend account is reduced to nil.[45] These rules ensure that the corporation's capital dividend account after the change in status (corporation controlled by non-residents to CCPC; tax-exempt to taxable private corporation, as the case may be), will not reflect any account that accrued prior to the change in status.

A taxpayer implemented an estate freeze and a program for the annual redemption of estate freeze shares for an amount equal to the positive balance of his company's capital dividend account. In 2004, the company redeemed 63 shares at $1,000,283. However, an audit discovered errors in the capital dividend account, resulting in a reduced balance and a tax assessment. The taxpayer's motion to rectify the documents and modify the 2004 redemption to reflect the true intention was granted.[46]

[¶6125] Pre-1972 Capital Surplus on Hand

This amount is a continuation of a corporation's 1971 capital surplus on hand as calculated at December 31, 1978, and subsequently adjusted for dispositions of capital property thereafter. It can only be distributed upon the winding-up of a Canadian corporation, and is received by the shareholders tax-free as a return of capital.[47]

---

[44] CCH ¶11,230; Sec. 89(1.1).   [46] Brochu, 2008 DTC 6096.
[45] CCH ¶11,231; Sec. 89(1.2).   [47] CCH ¶11,176; Sec. 88(2.1).

[¶6140] Deemed Dividend Distributions

[¶6145] Deemed Dividends

A dividend will be deemed to be paid when certain corporate proceedings are taken, namely:

(1) an increase in paid-up capital without a corresponding increase in net assets, but not, however, by means of:

    (a) a stock dividend;

    (b) transactions where the increase in the paid-up capital of a class is at least matched by a decrease in the aggregate paid-up capital of one or more of the other classes of shares of the corporation; and

    (c) capitalizations of contributed surplus by insurance corporations, banks, or other corporations where the contributed surplus arose on a share issue after March 31, 1977, other than one to which certain special provisions apply;[48]

(2) a distribution of property to shareholders on a winding-up, discontinuance, or reorganization of a corporation's business;[49]

(3) a redemption, acquisition, or cancellation of any shares, including redeemable preferred shares;[50] or

(4) a reduction of paid-up capital in any other manner.[51]

These rules are modified where the corporation involved is a public corporation,[52] and where the deemed dividend relates to guaranteed shares or term preferred shares owned directly or indirectly by a specified financial institution.[53] Furthermore, where a mutual insurance corporation converts into a corporation with share capital, its paid-up capital will be determined according to a very specific set of rules.[54] Their purpose is to prevent stakeholders from being deemed to receive dividends because of an increase in stated capital on the issuance of shares as a conversion benefit. Instead, a deemed dividend will arise at the time, if ever, when the shares are redeemed or acquired by the insurance corporation.

The deemed dividends referred to above relate only to distributions by corporations resident in Canada. A distribution by a non-resident corporation on a liquidation, redemption of shares, or reduction of capital stock does not result in a deemed dividend. Distributions of this kind may result in taxable capital gains or losses.

See page ii for explanation of footnotes.

[48] CCH ¶10,200; Sec. 84(1).
[49] CCH ¶10,240; Sec. 84(2).
[50] CCH ¶10,280; Sec. 84(3).
[51] CCH ¶10,320; Sec. 84(4).

[52] CCH ¶11,191; Sec. 89(1) "public corporation".
[53] CCH ¶10,335, ¶10,344; Sec. 84(4.2), 84(4.3).
[54] CCH ¶20,835; Sec. 139.1(5).

Where a dividend is deemed to have been paid at a particular time, it is deemed to have become payable at that time.[55]

More recently, the CRA has commented that a deemed dividend may also occur in a standard "pipeline" scheme, routinely used in estate-planning situations involving the death of a taxpayer. Fortunately, this position was recently overturned[56] and the Tax Court confirmed that "subsection 84(2) must be read more literally in all cases and GAAR applied in cases of abuse". At the time of publication, the Crown has appealed this decision.

[As a result of Budget 2012, a new anti-avoidance rule has been proposed in draft legislation released on August 14, 2012, relating to investments by a Canadian corporation in the shares of a foreign corporation generally where (i) following the investment, the foreign corporation is a foreign affiliate of the Canadian corporation; (ii) the Canadian corporation is controlled by another foreign corporation; and (iii) it is reasonable to conclude that the investment was not made primarily for *bona fide* purposes other than to obtain a tax benefit.

The rule generally targets certain transactions that are capable of generating interest deductions in Canada in respect of the acquisition of shares of a foreign affiliate (and that are not otherwise caught under the thin capitalization rules) or that strip cash out of a Canadian corporation without triggering Canadian dividend withholding tax (and that are not otherwise caught under existing section 212.1).

A corporation resident in Canada (referred to as the "CRIC") will be deemed to have paid a dividend to a non-resident corporation that controls the CRIC (referred to as the "parent") at the time the CRIC makes certain "investments" (which is defined to include the acquisition of shares, debt or options, contributions to capital, and transactions under which an amount becomes owing to the CRIC) in a corporation that is immediately after the investment (or becomes, as a part of a transaction or event, or series of transactions and events, that includes the investment) a foreign affiliate of the CRIC. Investments that can reasonably be considered to have been made primarily for *bona fide* purposes other than to obtain a tax benefit are generally excluded from this rule.

The dividend will generally be based on the fair market value of any property (other than shares of the CRIC) transferred by the CRIC in respect of the investment and will be subject to Canadian dividend withholding tax, subject to a reduction under any applicable tax treaty. There are also proposed adjustments to prevent an increase in the paid-up capital of the class of shares of the CRIC issued in connection with the investment.

This measure will apply to transactions that occur on or after March 29, 2012, other than transactions that occur before 2013 between parties that

---

[55] CCH ¶10,380; Sec. 84(7).   [56] MacDonald, 2012 DTC 1145 (TCC).

deal at arm's length and that are obligated to complete the transaction pursuant to the terms of an agreement in writing between the parties that is entered into before March 29, 2012.]

There are several provisions under which the paid-up capital of a class of shares for corporate purposes is reduced for tax purposes. These reductions are anti-dividend stripping provisions which operate, in general, to prevent an increase of the paid-up capital where shares of one corporation were sold before April 1, 1977, to another corporation in a non-arm's length transaction. See ¶6170 for comment on the calculation of paid-up capital.

[¶6150] Deemed Dividends and Return of Capital

The general principle of income tax law is that shareholders may receive a tax-free return of the paid-up capital of their shares but that any distribution in excess of that amount will be deemed to be paid and received as a dividend.

With the exception of reductions of capital by a public corporation and certain reductions of capital on term preferred shares, payments made to shareholders on a reduction of capital, redemption, or winding-up are treated first as a tax-free return of paid-up capital. A tax-free return of paid-up capital will generally reduce the adjusted cost base of a share.

[¶6155] Simultaneous Dividends

Where a dividend becomes payable at the same time on more than one class of shares of the capital stock of a corporation, the dividend on any one class is deemed to become payable at a different time than the other class or classes of shares.[57] The dividends will be deemed to become payable in the order designated by the corporation. In the event the corporation does not designate any order, the Minister will make the designation. This provision is applicable in connection with dividends out of tax-paid undistributed surplus or 1971 capital surplus, capital dividends,[58] deemed dividends,[59] and dividends of a subsidiary on winding up.[60]

[¶6160] Capital Gains and Losses

Where a corporation is winding up or redeeming any of its shares, a shareholder must consider both whether or not he or she is deemed to receive a dividend and whether or not he or she has a capital gain or loss. Proceeds of disposition[61] do not include any amount which is deemed to be a dividend. Therefore, the proceeds will be the amount received on the winding-up or redemption less the portion of that amount which is deemed to be a dividend.

See page ii for explanation of footnotes.

[57] CCH ¶11,253; Sec. 89(3).
[58] CCH ¶10,100; Sec. 83.
[59] CCH ¶10,200; Sec. 84.
[60] CCH ¶11,160; Sec. 88.
[61] CCH ¶7852; Sec. 54 "proceeds of disposition".

¶6160

A shareholder may have a taxable capital gain if the shareholder's adjusted cost base is less than the proceeds of disposition. Conversely, a shareholder may have a large deemed dividend which will reduce the shareholder's "proceeds of disposition", creating a substantial capital loss. A capital loss is deductible only from capital gains. If the shareholder deals at arm's length with a Canadian-controlled private corporation which is also a small business corporation, the loss may be a business investment loss, $1/2$ of which is deductible against all sources of income. The amount of a taxpayer's business investment loss is subject to reduction where the taxpayer has claimed a capital gains exemption in a previous year. When this occurs, the reduction in the business investment loss is treated as an ordinary capital loss.

[¶6165] Stock Dividends

A dividend includes a stock dividend.[62] A stock dividend[63] includes any dividend (determined without reference to the definition of "dividend") paid by the issuance of shares of any class of the capital stock of the corporation. The dollar amount is added to the stated capital of the class of shares issued as the stock dividend. The "amount" of a stock dividend is generally the dollar amount of the increase in the paid-up capital of the corporation resulting from payment of the dividend. However, if the recipient of the dividend is prohibited from deducting the amount of the dividend by virtue of the restrictions imposed on term preferred shares, the amount of the dividend is the greater of the addition to paid-up capital and the fair market value of the shares issued. The amount of the stock dividend is included in income. An election (see ¶6110) may be made with respect to the amount of a stock dividend.

The shareholder's cost base of a share acquired as a stock dividend is equal to the "amount" of the stock dividend or, where the stock dividend is not a dividend (i.e., one paid to a corporation or to a mutual fund trust by a non-resident corporation), nil. Any gain or loss arising on future disposition will be measured against that cost.[64] The cost of such a share will be increased by any amount included in income where one purpose of the stock dividend was to significantly alter the value of the interest of a specified shareholder of the corporation. The difference between the amount of the stock dividend and the value of the shares received is included in income.

[¶6170] "Paid-Up Capital" Defined

The Act defines "paid-up capital" in respect of an individual share, in respect of a class of shares, and in respect of all the shares of a corporation.[65] The determination of the paid-up capital of an individual share or

---

See page ii for explanation of footnotes.

[62] CCH ¶28,071; Sec. 248(1) "dividend".

[63] CCH ¶28,273b; Sec. 248(1) "stock dividend".

[64] CCH ¶7515; Sec. 52(3).

[65] CCH ¶11,183, ¶52,468; Sec. 89(1) "paid-up capital"; Interp. Bul. IT-463R2.

the paid-up capital of all the shares of a corporation is based on the calculation of the paid-up capital of each class of shares.

The paid-up capital of a share of any class of capital stock of a corporation is determined by dividing the number of shares of that class outstanding at a particular time into the paid-up capital of that class of shares. The paid-up capital of a single share of a particular class is thus the average paid-up capital for the whole class. For example, if 10 common shares were issued to A for $1 each and later 10 more were issued to B for $10 each, the paid-up capital of each of the 20 shares would be $110/20 = $5.50.

The definition of paid-up capital of a class of shares has changed several times since 1971. Where a determination is being made after March 31, 1977, the paid-up capital of the class of shares is computed without reference to the Act, except for certain required adjustments. The amount will therefore be determined under the applicable corporate statute.

Where shares with a par value are issued, the paid-up capital will usually reflect only the stated par value and any additional consideration will be reflected as contributed surplus. Where shares without par value are issued, the paid-up capital will usually reflect the fair market value of the consideration received for the shares.

The paid-up capital in respect of a class of shares will be the paid-up capital as determined for corporate purposes subject to a downward adjustment by two basic groups of provisions. The first group essentially contains measures to prevent dividend stripping by means of increasing the paid-up capital of a corporation through a non-arm's length share exchange or an amalgamation, while the other group is designed to prevent the realization of capital gains which could be available for the capital gains exemption by the redemption or purchase for cancellation of shares issued in certain circumstances.

[¶6185] Distribution on Winding-Up, etc.

Where a corporation resident in Canada distributes funds or property to shareholders on the winding-up, discontinuance, or reorganization of its business, it is deemed to have paid a dividend.[66] The "deemed dividend" in respect of each class of shares is the amount or value of the funds or property distributed, minus the reduction in the paid-up capital in respect of the shares of that class. Where the corporation is wound up, this would ordinarily be the full amount paid up on those shares.

[¶6190] Redemptions, Acquisitions, or Cancellations

A corporation that redeems, acquires, or cancels any of its shares other than by a purchase in the open market will be deemed to have paid a

---

[66] CCH ¶10,240; Sec. 84(2).

dividend of the amount paid in respect of the transaction minus the paid-up capital of the shares involved.[67]

A corporation may redeem or purchase for cancellation an amount of shares equal to its paid-up capital without being deemed to pay a dividend. Such a redemption or purchase could be of either preferred or common shares.

[¶6195] Reduction of Paid-Up Capital

A corporation may be deemed to have paid and its shareholders deemed to have received a dividend when the corporation makes a payment to its shareholders in connection with a reduction of capital by a corporation in respect of a class of shares. The dividend is deemed to have been paid on the class of shares in respect of which the paid-up capital was reduced and the amount of the deemed dividend is the amount paid on the reduction less the amount by which the paid-up capital of that class was reduced. Shareholders of that class are deemed to have received a dividend equal to the portion of the total dividend deemed to have been paid that the number of shares of that class held by them is of the number of shares of that class.[68]

The rules differ when the reduction of capital is carried out by a public corporation. In such a case, the amount paid by the public corporation on the reduction of capital is deemed to have been paid by the public corporation and received by the shareholder as a dividend unless the reduction of capital takes place (1) on a redemption, acquisition, or cancellation of shares, (2) on a winding-up as described in ¶6185, or (3) on an exchange of shares in the course of a reorganization of capital as described in ¶6310.[69] [Pending draft technical amendments released July 16, 2010 will add a fourth exception to the deemed dividend rule for distributions of paid-up capital made after 1996. For distributions after 1996, but before February 27, 2004, the paid-up capital reduction will not generate a deemed dividend provided that the distribution is derived from proceeds realized by the corporation in a transaction out of the ordinary course of the corporation's business. For example, a paid-up capital distribution paid out of proceeds realized on the sale of a business unit of a corporation, where the proceeds were not required for reinvestment, would generally not be considered to be a distribution from amounts realized in the ordinary course of the corporation's business. For distributions occurring after February 26, 2004, the distribution of paid-up capital must still be derived from proceeds realized in a transaction out of the ordinary course of the corporation's business, but these proceeds must also have been realized within 24 months of the distribution and only one distribution may be made. According to the Department of Finance explanatory notes, these 24-month/one distribution

---

See page ii for explanation of footnotes.

[67] CCH ¶10,280; Sec. 84(3). [69] CCH ¶10,330; Sec. 84(4.1).
[68] CCH ¶10,320; Sec. 84(4).

restrictions were added to ensure that the proceeds from an extraordinary transaction are not used to fund a stream of regular or periodic distributions.]

If the share in respect of which paid-up capital is reduced is a "term preferred share" (¶6035) owned directly or indirectly by specified financial institutions, the full amount received is deemed to be a dividend rather than a tax-free return of capital and is consequently taxable under the general term preferred share rules.[70] Similarly, the total amount received by a shareholder corporation on the reduction of the paid-up capital of a guaranteed share will be treated as a dividend.[71]

Generally, certain specified financial institutions cannot deduct dividends on term preferred shares and any other corporations may not deduct dividends received on shares in respect of which a specified financial institution has provided security or protection or dividends received on so-called "collateralized preferred shares".[72]

[¶6200] Where Amount Distributed Includes Shares

Where the amount of property distributed or appropriated on a winding-up, discontinuance, or reorganization of a corporation's business or the amount paid by a corporation on the redemption of shares or on the reduction of capital includes a share of the capital stock of the corporation, special rules apply. The share is to be valued at an amount equal to the paid-up capital in respect of the share and such value is to be included in computing the amount paid by the corporation.[73]

[¶6205] Deemed Dividend Provisions Not Applicable

Where a corporation has issued shares at a discount or has purchased its shares in the open market, the deemed dividend provisions applicable to winding up, etc., and redemption of shares do not apply.[74]

[¶6210] Transfer of Property to Corporation — Rollovers

[¶6215] Rollovers

The general rule under the Act is that a capital gain or loss must be recognized for tax purposes in the year it is realized by the taxpayer. However, in certain circumstances where a taxpayer's economic interests in a capital property remain unchanged, a deferral of any capital gain is permitted until the time of disposal of the property received in exchange. Where such a deferral is permitted, it is commonly called a "rollover".

See page ii for explanation of footnotes.

[70] CCH ¶10,335; Sec. 84(4.2).
[71] CCH ¶10,344; Sec. 84(4.3).
[72] CCH ¶16,345–16,372; Sec. 112(2.1)–(2.9).

[73] CCH ¶10,350; Sec. 84(5).

[74] CCH ¶10,370; Sec. 84(6).

[¶6220] Transfer of Property to Corporation

The Act provides an elective provision under which a taxpayer or a partnership may dispose of eligible property to a taxable Canadian corporation without the immediate income tax consequences that would ordinarily result from the disposition.[75] The general purpose of the provision is to permit a disposition of eligible property to a taxable Canadian corporation on a rollover basis, that is, in a manner whereby the disposing party avoids some or all of the tax which would otherwise arise on disposition and the corporation inherits this as a potential liability. Basic to the operation of this provision is a joint election by the disposing party and the corporation in which they elect an amount that will be deemed to be the disposing party's proceeds of disposition and the corporation's cost of the property.

Generally, eligible property does not include a capital property of a non-resident person that is real property, or an interest or option therein. However, upon meeting certain conditions,[76] a non-resident may transfer real property where the property was used by the non-resident in the course of carrying on a business in Canada.

The rules concerning the dispositions of stock options to a non-arm's length party did not apply where the taxpayer transferred stock options to his own numbered company and then sold the shares of the numbered company to another company using a section 85(1) rollover. The transaction was legal and could not be dismissed as a sham. The "substance over form" test could not ignore the legal existence of the numbered company and the part it played in the series of transactions so that the transaction in which it was involved could not be ignored.[77]

[¶6225] Joint Election

Only eligible property may be the subject of an election.[78] "Eligible property" is:

(1) *Capital property.* An election may be made in respect of any capital property if the person disposing of it is resident in Canada. Where the disposing party is a non-resident, most capital property qualifies for an election. The exceptions are real property, interests in respect of real property, and options in respect of real property owned by a non-resident.

(2) *Real property owned by non-resident insurers.* Non-resident insurers carrying on an insurance business in Canada may take advantage of the election to transfer on a tax-deferred basis a capital property that is real property under two conditions. First, the real property must be designated insurance property for the year. Second, all property (often debt and cer-

---

See page ii for explanation of footnotes.

[75] CCH ¶10,500, ¶10,540a, ¶51,162; Sec. 85(1), 85(2).

[76] CCH ¶10,506, ¶10,507c; Sec. 85(1.2), 85(1.3).

[77] [Bowens, 96 DTC 6128.

[78] CCH ¶10,505; Sec. 85(1.1).

tainly shares) received as consideration for the transfer of the real property must also be designated insurance property for the year.

(3) *Eligible capital property.* A disposition of eligible capital property by a resident or non-resident may be elected upon.

(4) *Inventory.* Where the property disposed of is inventory of the person making the disposition, other than real property, inventory, or mark-to-market property held by a financial institution, an election may be made.

(5) *Canadian resource property.* Canadian natural resource properties and rights and licences in connection with them may be elected upon. The elected amount will become a negative component in calculating the transferor's cumulative Canadian oil and gas property expense and may result in an income inclusion if the transferor has insufficient positive components to that account or their cumulative Canadian development expense account. The transferee will have an addition to its cumulative Canadian oil and gas property expense account.

(6) *Foreign resource property.* For foreign resource properties, the elected amount will be included in the transferor's income. The transferee will have an addition to its foreign exploration and development expense account. However, a foreign resource property, or an interest in a partnership that derives all or part of its value from one or more foreign resource properties, is not eligible property if the transferor and the corporation do not deal at arms' length and it is reasonable to conclude that one of the purposes of the disposition, or a series of transactions or events of which the disposition is a part, is to increase the extent to which any person may claim a foreign tax credit.[79]

(7) *Security or debt obligations.* Property, other than capital property and inventory, which is a security or debt obligation used or held by the taxpayer in an insurance or money lending business is eligible for tax-deferred transfers to a corporation.

(8) *A NISA (net income stabilization account) Fund No. 2.*

[The 2010 Budget proposals to abandon the previous FIE proposals and to retain the existing rules relating to "offshore investment fund property", with an additional 2% being added to the annual interest charge at which foreign investments are deemed to accrue for Canadian tax purposes, remain outstanding in draft form, as released on August 27, 2010. A taxpayer who voluntarily complied in previous years with the proposed rollover restrictions on a participating interest in an FIE will have the option of requesting to have those years reassessed by the CRA. Such a request must be made on or before the day that is 365 days after these rules receive Royal Assent.

See page ii for explanation of footnotes.

[79] CCH ¶10,505a; Sec. 85(1.11).

If the taxpayer does not wish to be reassessed by the CRA, and had *more income* than would have been the case under the existing rules, the taxpayer will be entitled to a deduction for the excess income. Under such an option, the FIEs held by the taxpayer for 2001 to 2008 would be deemed to be the amount of tax required to be remitted, and the taxpayer would be allowed a deduction for the amount, if any, by which the amounts included in income in respect of those investments for those years was in excess of the amount that would otherwise have been included in income in respect of those investments for those years The deduction must be claimed by the taxpayer in computing the taxpayer's income for the first taxation year that ends after the last taxation year of the taxpayer that ends before March 4, 2010.

If a taxpayer voluntarily complied with the FIE proposals in previous years in respect of a participating interest, and included *less in income* than would have been the case under the existing rules, the excess is not required to be included in income. Instead, the taxpayer will be required to deduct an amount in computing the adjusted cost base of those participating interests held after the start of the taxpayer's first taxation year that ends after March 4, 2010. The deduction amount is the amount by which the deductions reported by the taxpayer under the FIE proposals exceed the income inclusions reported by the taxpayer under the FIE proposals.]

When an election is made, the prescribed form (T2057) must be filed no later than the day on which the parties to the election must file their Part I returns for the year in which the transaction took place.[80] When the returns of the parties are due on different days, the election must be filed by the earlier of these days. Once the election is made, the elected amount is fixed and cannot later be amended by the parties.[81]

An election will be considered to have been made when required if it is filed at any time up to three years after it was due and a penalty is paid. The penalty is payable by the taxpayer or the partnership which disposes of the property to which the election relates. The penalty is the lesser of: (i) $1/4$ of 1% per month of any excess of the fair market of the property transferred over the elected amount, and (ii) $100 per month to a maximum of $8,000.

The Act also permits an effective election to be filed beyond the three-year period described above or for any election to be amended, where the Minister considers it just and equitable in the circumstances. When such an extra-late election or amended election is approved by the Minister, the penalty calculated, as described above, must be paid at the time the extra-late or amended election is filed.

Following the taxpayer's divorce, she and her former spouse agreed that shares she held should be rolled over to a holding corporation and then redeemed. Following the redemption, a deemed dividend was included in

---

See page ii for explanation of footnotes.

[80] CCH ¶10,614a; Sec. 85(6)–(9).   [81] [One For Three Ltd, 80 DTC 1244.

¶6225

her income, since the rollover never actually took place. She did not file the election in a timely fashion and there was no evidence that she transferred the shares. Also, the Tax Court did not have jurisdiction to hear a judicial review application regarding the Minister's refusal to accept a late-filed election.[82]

[¶6230] Consideration for Disposition

One of the prerequisites of an election is that the taxpayer who disposes of the property must receive as consideration (or as part of the consideration) some shares in the capital of the corporation which acquires the property. The shares taken as consideration may be of any class. The taxpayer may also receive non-share consideration for the property. There is no specific requirement that the taxpayer making the disposition take back consideration equal to the value of the property the taxpayer is transferring to the corporation.

Where a taxpayer transferred five properties to a taxable Canadian corporation and filed an election that rollover treatment apply but the election failed to mention four of the five properties, the Minister assessed the taxpayer with a capital gain on the one property based on the full elected amount. The Court held that, although the failure to mention the four properties in the election was inadvertent, the rollover did not apply to them. The intention of the taxpayer was not sufficient where full information was not supplied.[83] When a corporation's authorized capital had been amended retroactively to December 28, 1995, the shares issued thereafter for the transfer of an apartment building could form part of an election.[84] To avoid unintended results in a case where the taxpayers had transferred their shares of a corporation to a second corporation and took back as consideration a promissory note rather than shares of the second corporation, a rectification order was granted to substitute shares of the second corporation for its promissory note. [85]

[¶6275] Domestic Share-for-Share Exchange

A taxpayer who holds shares of a taxable Canadian corporation as capital property may dispose of them to a second Canadian corporation in exchange for treasury shares of the Canadian corporation and defer recognition of any accrued capital gain or loss on the original shares until the taxpayer disposes of the newly-acquired shares of the Canadian corporation.[86] This is one of the so-called "rollover" provisions of the Act. However, the rollover is not mandatory. The taxpayer may choose to recognize the gain or loss in the year of disposition.

To obtain a rollover, a vendor need not file a formal election. All that is necessary is that the taxpayer treat the transaction as a rollover in his or her

---

See page ii for explanation of footnotes.

[82] [Vachon, 2007 DTC 321.

[83] [Deconinck, 90 DTC 6617.

[84] [Dale, 97 DTC 5252.

[85] [Juliar et al., 2000 DTC 6589.

[86] CCH ¶10,620; Sec. 85.1(1).

income tax return for the year in which the exchange occurred by not including in income *any* portion of the gain or loss which would otherwise have arisen on the taxpayer's exchanged shares. Therefore, no partial rollover is available.

An example of the application of this rollover would be the acquisition of shares of Company A by Company B in return for treasury shares of Company B being issued to the present owner of the Company A shares. It should be noted that no rollover is provided in situations where a taxpayer disposes of shares of one corporation in return for previously issued shares of another corporation owned by the acquiring party. For example, there is no rollover where a shareholder of Company C disposes of his shares to a shareholder of Company D in exchange for those shares of Company D.

[¶6277] Foreign Share-for-Share Exchange

Where a Canadian taxpayer holds shares in a foreign corporation that are exchanged for shares issued by another foreign corporation to the taxpayer, a tax-deferred rollover is allowed.[87] Under these rules, the shareholder's tax cost of the exchanged foreign shares becomes the tax cost of the newly issued foreign shares with the result that any capital gain is deferred. These rules are similar to those on domestic exchanged shares (see ¶6275), except that they will deny the rollover where the vendor is a foreign affiliate and the exchanged foreign shares are "excluded property", meaning property used to produce income from an active business.[88]

As with the domestic share election, the election is optional but is an all or nothing situation. That is, the taxpayer must either elect on all shares in a particular transaction or none of them.

[The 2010 Budget proposals to abandon the previous FIE proposals and to retain the existing rules relating to "offshore investment fund property", with an additional 2% being added to the annual interest charge at which foreign investments are deemed to accrue for Canadian tax purposes, remain outstanding in draft form, as released on August 27, 2010. A taxpayer who voluntarily complied in previous years with the proposed rollover restrictions on a participating interest in an FIE will have the option of requesting to have those years reassessed by the CRA. Such a request must be made on or before the day that is 365 days after these rules receive Royal Assent.

If the taxpayer does not wish to be reassessed by the CRA, and had *more income* than would have been the case under the existing rules, the taxpayer will be entitled to a deduction for the excess income. Under such an option, the FIEs held by the taxpayer for 2001 to 2008 would be deemed to be the amount of tax required to be remitted, and the taxpayer would be allowed a deduction for the amount, if any, by which the amounts included

---

See page ii for explanation of footnotes.

[87] CCH ¶10,648; Sec. 85.1(5).   [88] CCH ¶10,649a; Sec. 85.1(6).

¶6277

in income in respect of those investments for those years was in excess of the amount that would otherwise have been included in income in respect of those investments for those years The deduction must be claimed by the taxpayer in computing the taxpayer's income for the first taxation year that ends after the last taxation year of the taxpayer that ends before March 4, 2010.

If a taxpayer voluntarily complied with the FIE proposals in previous years in respect of a participating interest, and included *less in income* than would have been the case under the existing rules, the excess is not required to be included in income. Instead, the taxpayer will be required to deduct an amount in computing the adjusted cost base of those participating interests held after the start of the taxpayer's first taxation year that ends after March 4, 2010. The deduction amount is the amount by which the deductions reported by the taxpayer under the FIE proposals exceed the income inclusions reported by the taxpayer under the FIE proposals.]

[¶6278] Rollover on SIFT Unit-for-Share Exchange

For dispositions after July 14, 2008, and before 2013, a taxpayer is allowed to exchange, on a tax-deferred basis, its SIFT units for shares of a corporation that are equal in value to the exchanged units if:

- the exchange occurs during a 60-day period at the end of which the corporation owns all the SIFT units;

- as consideration for its SIFT units, the taxpayer receives only shares of the capital stock of the corporation; and

- all the exchanged shares issued to SIFT unitholders are shares of a single class.[89]

If the exchange qualifies for the rollover, the unitholder is considered to have disposed of his or her units for proceeds equal to the cost amount of the units, and to have acquired the shares of the successor corporation at a cost equal to the same amount. In keeping with the share-for-share exchange rules, the corporation is considered to have acquired the SIFT unit for an amount equal to the lesser of the fair market value of the unit before the disposition and the portion of the SIFT trust's outstanding capital that is attributable to the particular unit. The portion of the SIFT trust's outstanding capital that is attributable to the particular unit is calculated as the difference between the consideration received by the SIFT trust on the issuance of the particular unit and any amounts that have ever become payable (other than as income or capital gains) in respect of the particular unit to a holder of the particular unit.[90] These rollover rules apply to transactions that occur after July 14, 2008, and before 2013. However, they may also apply to transactions that occur after December 19, 2007, and

---

See page ii for explanation of footnotes.

[89] CCH ¶10,649d; Sec. 85.1(7).   [90] CCH ¶10,649m; Sec. 85.1(8).

before July 14, 2008, if the corporation elects in a timely manner to have the rollover rules apply.

[¶6280] Transfers to Corporation from Partnership — Rollovers

[¶6285] Transfer of Property to Corporation from Partnership

A rollover virtually identical to that where property is transferred to a taxable Canadian corporation by a shareholder is provided for where the property in question is owned by a partnership.[91] In place of the rule that real property, an interest in respect of real property, or an option in respect of real property owned by non-residents cannot be elected upon, the Act provides that an election cannot be made in respect of real property, an interest in respect of real property, or an option in respect of real property owned by a partnership that is not a "Canadian partnership" at the time of disposition. The only other difference is that the election must be made by the corporation to which the transfer is made and all members of the partnership. Where the partners are corporations with different fiscal years, the time for filing the election will therefore need to be determined carefully.

[¶6290] Rollover Where Partnership Wound Up

Where a partnership has transferred property to a corporation and availed itself of the rollover provisions, and:

(a) the partnership is wound up within 60 days of the transfer , and

(b) immediately before the winding-up, the only assets of the partnership were money or property received from the corporation,

a rollover is provided for the transfer of the consideration (including shares of the corporation) from the partnership to the partners.[92] This rollover is similar in principle to the other rollover provisions and may be summarized as follows:

(1) The cost to a partner of any property distributed (other than shares of the corporation) is its fair market value.

(2) The partner's cost of any preferred shares will be the adjusted cost base of his or her partnership interest minus the value of the property described in (1). If common shares are also received, the partner's cost of the preferred shares is limited to their fair market value. If preferred shares of the corporation of more than one class are distributed, the above cost is allocated between them in proportion to their fair market value.

See page ii for explanation of footnotes.

[91] CCH ¶10,540a; Sec. 85(2).

[92] CCH ¶10,562, ¶52,383; Sec. 85(3); Interp. Bul. IT-378R.

(3) The partner's cost of any common shares will be the adjusted cost base of his or her partnership interest minus the value of the property described in (1) and minus the fair market value of any preferred shares of the corporation received as determined under (2). If common shares of the corporation of more than one class are received, this cost is allocated among them in proportion to their fair market value.

(4) The partner's proceeds of disposition of his or her partnership interest is the sum of the costs in (1), (2), and (3), plus any money received on winding up the partnership.

(5) Property distributed by the partnership is considered to have been disposed of for its cost amount. The partnership will therefore realize neither a gain nor a loss on this disposition.

(6) For the purposes of determining any amount relating to cumulative eligible capital, eligible capital amount, eligible capital expenditure, or eligible capital property, a member is deemed to carry on the business of the partnership until that member's undivided interest in the eligible capital property is disposed of.[93]

There are other rules applicable to the winding-up of a partnership.[94] However, these rules are not applicable in cases to which the foregoing rollover provisions apply. See also ¶6375 *et seq.*

[¶6295] Property Transferred to Controlled Corporation — Losses

[¶6300] Loss on Certain Properties

Where a corporation or partnership or trust has disposed of eligible capital property or non-disposable capital property, and the transferor or a person "affiliated" with the transferor acquires the transferred property or an identical property (i.e., the "substituted property") during the period that begins 30 days before and ends 30 days after the disposition, and the transferor or an affiliated person owns the substituted property at the end of the period, no loss or deduction may be recognized on the transfer.[95] Such loss or deduction is deferred until the earliest of a specified subsequent disposition of the property, a specified deemed disposition of the property, an acquisition of the corporation's control in the case of a corporation, a winding-up of the transferor, or, in the case of eligible capital property, where the property no longer constitutes eligible capital property. Note that these provisions do not apply to transfers by individuals other than trusts. The denied capital loss is preserved in the hands of the transferor to be deducted as a loss from the transferred property when it is no longer owned

---

[93] CCH ¶12,263; Sec. 98(3)(g).
[94] CCH ¶12,263, ¶12,265; Sec. 98(3), 98(4).

[95] CCH ¶4647e, ¶6459, ¶6459a; Sec. 14(12), 40(3.3), 40(3.4).

by an affiliated person, when it is deemed to be disposed of, or when control of a corporate transferor is acquired. As reported below, an exception is made for a loss incurred on the disposition of a share in the stock of an affiliated corporation to that corporation (say, on a redemption or repurchase of the corporation's stock).

[¶6302] Loss on Shares

A specific stop-loss rule applies to a disposition of shares in the stock of a corporation to that corporation, where the transferor is affiliated with the corporation immediately afterward.[96] This rule may apply, for example, to a redemption, acquisition, or purchase for cancellation of the taxpayer's share by the corporation. In such a case, the taxpayer's capital loss, if any, is deemed to be nil. The amount of the denied loss is added to the cost base of the shares in the corporation owned by the taxpayer immediately after the disposition. If the taxpayer owns no shares in the corporation immediately after the disposition but is nonetheless affiliated with the corporation, the loss is denied, with no relief in the form of increased cost basis.

[¶6305] Reorganization of Capital — Rollovers

[¶6310] Dispositions of Shares

A rollover is provided where, under a reorganization of the capital structure of a corporation, a taxpayer disposes of all the shares of any particular class of the capital stock of the corporation (old shares) and as consideration therefore, property is receivable from the corporation that includes other shares of the capital stock of the corporation (new shares).[97] This applies only where the old shares are capital property of the shareholder.

In connection with the reorganization of the capital structure of a corporation, several points should be noted:

(1) For the provision to apply, a shareholder must actually dispose of his or her shares.

(2) The provision does not apply to the disposition of securities other than shares, such as bonds or other debt securities.

(3) The shares disposed of must constitute capital property of the shareholder.

(4) Where shares are other than capital, such as where they are inventory, the provision does not apply.

(5) The shareholder must dispose of all shares of a particular class of the corporation's capital stock. If, by inadvertence or otherwise, all of the

---

See page ii for explanation of footnotes.

[96] CCH ¶6459c; Sec. 40(3.6).   [97] CCH ¶10,650; Sec. 86(1).

shareholder's shares of a particular class are not disposed of, the rollover will not apply.

This provision applies to non-residents as well as to residents, provided that all the requisite conditions of the Act are met. It is not necessary that the relevant corporation be a Canadian corporation.

[The 2010 Budget proposals to abandon the previous FIE proposals and to retain the existing rules relating to "offshore investment fund property", with an additional 2% being added to the annual interest charge at which foreign investments are deemed to accrue for Canadian tax purposes, remain outstanding in draft form, as released on August 27, 2010. A taxpayer who voluntarily complied in previous years with the proposed rollover restrictions on a participating interest in an FIE will have the option of requesting to have those years reassessed by the CRA. Such a request must be made on or before the day that is 365 days after these rules receive Royal Assent.

If the taxpayer does not wish to be reassessed by the CRA, and had *more income* than would have been the case under the existing rules, the taxpayer will be entitled to a deduction for the excess income. Under such an option, the FIEs held by the taxpayer for 2001 to 2008 would be deemed to be the amount of tax required to be remitted, and the taxpayer would be allowed a deduction for the amount, if any, by which the amounts included in income in respect of those investments for those years was in excess of the amount that would otherwise have been included in income in respect of those investments for those years The deduction must be claimed by the taxpayer in computing the taxpayer's income for the first taxation year that ends after the last taxation year of the taxpayer that ends before March 4, 2010.

If a taxpayer voluntarily complied with the FIE proposals in previous years in respect of a participating interest, and included *less in income* than would have been the case under the existing rules, the excess is not required to be included in income. Instead, the taxpayer will be required to deduct an amount in computing the adjusted cost base of those participating interests held after the start of the taxpayer's first taxation year that ends after March 4, 2010. The deduction amount is the amount by which the deductions reported by the taxpayer under the FIE proposals exceed the income inclusions reported by the taxpayer under the FIE proposals.]

[¶6315] Cost Basis of Shares and Other Property

Where property other than shares is received by the taxpayer as consideration or as part consideration for the old shares disposed of, the cost to the taxpayer of the property is deemed to be its fair market value at the time of disposition.[98] Any excess by which the adjusted cost base of the old shares

---

[98] CCH ¶10,650; Sec. 86(1).

exceeds the fair market value of the non-share property is carried over as the adjusted cost base of the new shares. If there is more than one class of new shares, the excess is apportioned between the classes.

Where no property other than shares is received or receivable by the taxpayer, the adjusted cost base of the old shares immediately before disposition carries over as the adjusted cost base of the new shares. If more than one class of new shares is received by the taxpayer, the adjusted cost base of the old shares is apportioned between the classes of new shares on the basis of their relative fair market value.

In connection with proceeds of disposition, the taxpayer is deemed to have disposed of the old shares for proceeds of disposition equal to the aggregate of the cost of the new shares and any non-share property. Where the fair market value of the non-share property does not exceed the adjusted cost base of the old shares, the deemed proceeds of disposition of the old shares will be equal to the adjusted cost base of the old shares. Thus, no capital gain is realized where the fair market value of the non-share property does not exceed the adjusted cost base of the old shares. If the fair market value exceeds the adjusted cost base of the old shares, the excess is a capital gain. In this case, the new shares will have an adjusted cost base of nil.

Special rules are provided where the taxpayer disposes of shares in a transaction by which the taxpayer confers a benefit on a related person.[99]

[¶6320] Foreign Spin-Offs — Rollovers

[¶6321] Tax-Deferred Rollover

The shares received in an eligible distribution will not be included in the recipient shareholder's income, and will not give rise to any other immediate tax consequences.[100] Effectively, the recognition of any accrued gain in respect of the shares will be deferred until the shares are disposed of. Two types of eligible distributions are contemplated for these purposes — distributions that are not prescribed and distributions that are prescribed. The former are distributions involving corporations resident in the United States, while the latter are distributions involving corporations resident in other countries with which Canada has an income tax treaty. The requirements for each type of distribution and the tax effects to the recipient shareholder are set out below.

[¶6322] Eligible Distributions

As noted in ¶6321, a share received by a taxpayer that qualifies as an "eligible distribution" is not included in the taxpayer's income. An eligible

---

See page ii for explanation of footnotes.

[99] CCH ¶10,651; Sec. 86(2).   [100] CCH ¶10,690; Sec. 86.1(1).

¶6320

distribution includes two types of distributions made by non-resident corporations: distributions that are prescribed and those that are not prescribed.[101]

An eligible distribution that is not prescribed is one in which a taxpayer who owns common shares of a particular U.S. resident corporation ("original shares") receives, in respect of all of the taxpayer's original shares, common shares of another U.S. resident corporation ("spin-off shares") that were owned immediately prior to the distribution by the particular corporation. The taxpayer must receive only spin-off shares on the distribution and thus cannot receive any non-share consideration. At the time of the distribution, the class of the original shares must be widely held and actively traded on a designated stock exchange in the United States. Additionally, the distribution must be non-taxable under the United States *Internal Revenue Code* for shareholders of the particular corporation who are resident in the United States. [The condition that the shares be actively traded on a U.S. stock exchange will be amended effective after 1999 to require that the taxpayer's original shares of the foreign corporation be, at the time of the distribution, widely held, and either actively traded on a designated stock exchange in the United States, or required to be registered under the U.S. *Securities Exchange Act of 1934* with the Securities Exchange Commission (and are so registered).]

An eligible distribution that is prescribed is essentially the same as that just described, except that both corporations involved in the spin-off must be resident in a foreign country (other than the United States) with which Canada has an income tax treaty. The class of the original shares must be widely held and traded on a designated stock exchange in the foreign country, and the shareholders of the particular corporation who are resident in the foreign country must not be subject to tax in that country in respect of the distribution. Additionally, the distribution must satisfy prescribed terms and conditions "as are considered appropriate in the circumstances". At the time of writing, no terms and conditions had been prescribed.

Furthermore, in order for a distribution of shares to qualify as an eligible distribution, the distributing corporation must provide the CRA with information regarding the nature of the original shares, the corporations involved in the distribution, the spin-off shares distributed to the Canadian resident shareholders, the identities of the Canadian resident shareholders, and information establishing that the distribution is not taxable in the United States for U.S. resident shareholders (in the case of a non-prescribed distribution) or in the foreign country for residents of that country (in the case of a prescribed distribution). The information must be provided within six months of the day on which the distribution occurs.

See page ii for explanation of footnotes.

[101] CCH ¶10,693; Sec. 86.1(2).

The recipient shareholder must elect in writing to have the rollover rules apply, and must provide evidence satisfactory to the CRA of certain matters relating to the distribution and to the shareholder. This information includes the number, cost amount and fair market value of the original shares owned by the shareholder immediately before the distribution, and the number, cost amount, and fair market value of the spin-off shares owned immediately after the distribution. The election must be made on the shareholder's return of income for the year in which the distribution occurs. In these cases, where the election is not made in the shareholder's tax return for the year in which the distribution takes place, the shareholder must state the manner in which the distribution was originally reported by the shareholder for tax purposes and the details of any subsequent dispositions of the shareholder's original shares or spin-off shares. This information will enable the CRA to reassess the shareholder's prior tax returns in order to take into account the effects of the tax-deferred distribution.

For distributions received before 2005, if the recipient shareholder of a spin-off share was a taxpayer to which the foreign property rules in former Part XI applied (e.g., an RRSP, DPSP, or RRIF), the taxpayer was not required to file the election. Furthermore, because the taxpayer's cost amount of its original share would have been allocated on a *pro rata* basis to the original share and the spin-off share, the distribution would not have affected the aggregate cost amount of the taxpayer's foreign property for the purposes of former Part XI. In other words, the distribution would not, in itself, put the taxpayer offside of the foreign property rules. The foreign property rules were repealed, effective for months ending after 2004, so that this particular concern is irrelevant for distributions after 2004.

[¶6323] Cost Base Adjustments

Shares received by a taxpayer as an "eligible distribution" are not included in the taxpayer's income. As a result, there will be no immediate tax consequences to a taxpayer receiving shares on an eligible distribution.

However, the taxpayer will be required to adjust the cost amount of each of the taxpayer's original share (the common share in the distributing corporation) and the taxpayer's spin-off share (the share in the other corporation received on the eligible distribution in respect of the original share). Essentially, the taxpayer's cost amount of each original share as it stood immediately before the distribution is allocated on a *pro rata* basis to the original share and the spin-off share, based on their respective fair market values immediately after the distribution. These rules provide for an amount to be both deducted from the cost amount of each original share and set as the cost of the corresponding spin-off share.[102]

The Department of Finance provided the following example in its explanatory notes.

See page ii for explanation of footnotes.

[102] CCH ¶10,696; Sec. 86.1(3).

Example:

John owns one original common share of DC Ltd. (resident in the U.S.), which distributes one spin-off share of SO Ltd. (also resident in the U.S.) on a per share basis to holders of common shares of DC Ltd. The cost amount of John's original share of DC Ltd. is $10 immediately before the distribution and its fair market value immediately after the distribution is $70. The fair market value of the SO Ltd. spin-off share is $30 immediately after the distribution.

The cost amount of John's spin-off share and the reduction to cost of the original share is:

$$A \times (B/C)$$

Where:

A = $10

B = $30

C = $100 ($70 + $30)

Accordingly, the cost amount of John's spin-off share in SO Ltd. is ($10 × (30/100)) = $3, and the $10 cost of the original share is reduced by $3 to $7.

[¶6324] Inventory

Where the original share and spin-off share are inventory of the recipient, the eligible distribution of the spin-off share is deemed not to be an acquisition of property for the purposes of calculating the value of the recipient's inventory.[103] This rule prevents the double-counting of cost that would occur if the cost of the spin-off share were added to the cost of inventory acquired in the year (that is, its cost would have been already reflected in the cost of the original share in the opening inventory for the year). For greater certainty, the value of the spin-off share is to be included in the value of the inventory at the end of the year.[104]

[¶6325] Amalgamations

[¶6327] Meaning of "Amalgamation"

The amalgamation provisions of the Act apply only to an amalgamation of two or more *taxable* Canadian corporations.[105]

The amalgamated corporation is treated for tax purposes as a new corporation with its first taxation year[106] commencing at the time of the amalgamation, and the taxation years of predecessor corporations are deemed to have ended immediately before the amalgamation. Thus, since a corporation formed through an amalgamation is deemed to be a new corporation, the transfer of property by a parent to its subsidiaries, and by them

---

See page ii for explanation of footnotes.

[103] CCH ¶10,699; Sec. 86.1(4)(*a*).
[104] CCH ¶10,699; Sec. 86.1(4)(*b*).

[105] CCH ¶10,750, ¶11,206, ¶52,479; Sec. 87(1), 89(1) "taxable Canadian corporation"; Interp. Bul. IT-474R2.
[106] CCH ¶10,766; Sec. 87(2)(*a*).

to the taxpayer formed by the amalgamation of P Ltd. and another corporation, did not allow the taxpayer to stand in P Ltd.'s shoes in order to deduct the unused exploration expenses of P Ltd.'s predecessor corporation.[107]

Although a taxpayer may intentionally structure an amalgamation to fall offside the section 87 rules, certain resulting continuations of tax balances can apply notwithstanding.[108] In certain provinces the "continuation model" of amalgamation may be broad enough to include certain predecessor tax balances. At the time of publication, leave to appeal to the Supreme Court of Canada has been filed, so this may not be the final word on these issues.

An "amalgamation" is essentially a corporate transaction and each of the applicable provincial *Companies Acts* and the *Canada Business Corporations Act* provide for statutory amalgamations. The definition would cover most statutory amalgamations, but it may be possible to carry out a transaction under the amalgamation provisions of a particular corporate statute without undergoing an amalgamation for income tax purposes.

Amalgamations are normally divided into two main categories. These are the so-called "horizontal" amalgamations which involve the merger of corporations which do not own shares of one another, and "vertical" amalgamations in which a parent corporation and one or more of its subsidiaries merge. The Act is intended to apply to both types of amalgamations, provided that all the conditions discussed below are fulfilled.

The following conditions must be met for an amalgamation:

(1) All property of the predecessor corporations immediately before the amalgamation (except intercorporate debt between, or shares of, the predecessors) must become the property of the new corporation by virtue of the amalgamation.

(2) All liabilities of the predecessor corporations immediately before the amalgamation (except intercorporate debt) must become liabilities of the new corporation by virtue of the amalgamation.

(3) All shareholders who owned shares of the capital stock of the predecessor corporations immediately before the amalgamation must become shareholders of the new corporation by virtue of the amalgamation. Where one predecessor owned shares of another, it is excepted from this rule.

(4) All predecessor corporations must be taxable Canadian corporations.

Where there is a merger of either:

(a) a corporation and one or more of its wholly owned subsidiaries, or

---

[107] [Pan Ocean Oil Ltd., 94 DTC 6412.   [108] Envision Credit Union, 2012 DTC 5055.

(b) two or more corporations which are wholly owned subsidiary corporations of the same corporation,

shares of a predecessor corporation which are not cancelled on the merger are deemed to be shares of the new corporation received by the shareholder on the merger as consideration for the disposition of the shares of the predecessor corporation.[109] By virtue of this provision, certain amalgamations, such as the short form of amalgamation under the *Canada Business Corporations Act*, will qualify as amalgamations for tax purposes even though no new shares of the amalgamated corporations are issued as a result of the amalgamations.

A "subsidiary wholly owned corporation" includes:[110]

(a) a corporation, all the shares of which are owned by the parent; and

(b) a corporation, all the shares of which are owned by one or more subsidiary wholly owned corporations of the parent or by a combination of the parent and one or more subsidiary wholly owned corporations of the parent.

Thus, if Company A owns all the shares of Company B, which in turn owns all the shares of Company C, Company C is a subsidiary wholly owned corporation of A for the purposes of the amalgamation. This will also be true if each of Company A and Company B owned shares of Company C, provided they together owned all the issued shares of Company C.

In deciding whether an amalgamation occurred before or after a particular date, the relevant provincial or federal corporate law will govern. One of the methods which a corporation may select for remitting instalments of tax relates to its instalment base for the immediately preceding taxation year. An amalgamated corporation has no immediately preceding taxation year. However, the instalment bases of predecessor corporations are added together to become the instalment base of the amalgamated corporation for the immediately preceding taxation year.

[¶6335] Amalgamations — Rollovers

[¶6340] General

Amalgamations are usually classified as vertical or horizontal. A vertical amalgamation involves the merger of a parent corporation with its subsidiary and compares in the ultimate result to a winding-up of a subsidiary. A horizontal amalgamation involves the merger of corporations which do not own shares of one another. For tax purposes, a transaction under which one corporation purchases property from another or acquires proper-

---

See page ii for explanation of footnotes.

[109] CCH ¶10,751; Sec. 87(1.1).   [110] CCH ¶10,755; Sec. 87(1.4).

ty on the winding-up of another is not an amalgamation.[111] For tax purposes, the amalgamated corporation is treated as a continuation of the predecessor corporations standing in their place with respect to various assets, liabilities, surpluses, and other tax-oriented accounts. However, unless specifically provided, the amalgamated corporation is a new corporation for most purposes. The result is a form of tax-free rollover allowing the assets and tax-related accounts of the predecessors to pass to the amalgamated corporation without immediate tax.

Taxpayers have attempted to structure an amalgamation as either vertical or horizontal solely for the purpose of preserving or eliminating predecessor tax attributes, but not always with success. In *Copthorne*,[112] the taxpayer unsuccessfully argued that a vertical amalgamation would result in "throwing away" the subsidiary PUC, and that taking reasonable steps to preserve a valuable tax attribute was not abusive. In response, the SCC stated that it is the operation of the GAAR that denies the benefit of this asset, and that it was not "thrown away". The preservation of existing tax attributes is apparently, at least in respect of section 87 amalgamations, potentially abusive, depending on the subsequent use of the preserved tax attribute.

[¶6345] Shareholders of Predecessor Corporations

A shareholder of a predecessor corporation on an amalgamation may be entitled to a tax-free rollover when shares of the predecessor corporation are converted into shares of the new corporation.[113]

A rollover is also provided where shareholders receive shares of a parent company in respect of the surrender of their shares of a predecessor company in circumstances where the amalgamated corporation is a wholly owned subsidiary of the parent company.[114]

The following conditions must be satisfied in order for the rollover provisions of the Act to apply to a particular shareholder:

(1) There must be an amalgamation after May 6, 1974.

(2) The shareholder must own shares of a predecessor corporation immediately before the amalgamation ("old shares").

(3) These shares must be held as capital property.

(4) The only consideration received by the shareholder for the disposition of the shares on amalgamation must be shares of the amalgamated corporation ("new shares") or a parent corporation (see ¶6340). Although the Act provides that the shareholder must receive no consideration other than the new shares, the CRA has stated that it will not deny the rollover

---

See page ii for explanation of footnotes.

[111] CCH ¶10,750; Sec. 87(1). [113] CCH ¶10,940; Sec. 87(4).
[112] 2012 DTC 5007 (SCC). [114] CCH ¶11,040; Sec. 87(9).

merely because the shareholder is required to receive cash or other consideration in lieu of a fraction of a new share of the amalgamated corporation.

(5) The rollover may be limited if the fair market value of the shares received on the amalgamation is less than the fair market value of the shares held before the amalgamation, and it is reasonable to regard a portion of that difference (the "gift portion") as a benefit conferred on a related person. In this case, the deemed proceeds of disposition of the old shares will equal the lesser of:

>   (a) the adjusted cost base of the old shares plus the gift portion; and

>   (b) the fair market value of the old shares before the amalgamation.

If these requirements are met, the shareholder is deemed to dispose of the old shares at their adjusted cost base. Thus, the shareholder receives no capital gain and may not recognize a capital loss. The cost of new shares of each class is a prorated portion of the adjusted cost bases of all old shares. The prorating formula is:

$$\text{the cost of new shares of a particular class} = \text{the adjusted cost bases of all old shares} \times \frac{\text{the fair market value of new shares of the particular class}}{\text{the fair market value of all new shares of all classes}}$$

Where the old shares were taxable Canadian property (TCP), the new shares are also deemed to be TCP. After March 4, 2010, this deemed TCP rule only applies for 60 months after the exchange. As a result, if the new shares are disposed of after the 60-month period has elapsed, the shareholder will no longer be required to comply with the reporting requirements associated with the disposition of TCP.

[¶6350] Exchanged Shares

Special provision is made for continuing the "grandfathered" status of a term preferred share issued by a corporation when that corporation is amalgamated with one or more other corporations to form a new corporation.[115] Also, preferred shares issued on an amalgamation in exchange for substantially similar shares issued by a predecessor are treated as having been issued when they were issued by the predecessor and under the same circumstances.[116]

A new right to acquire a share in exchange for a right as described in the definition of "grandfathered share" to acquire a share of a predecessor corporation will be deemed to be the same right, provided the terms and conditions of the rights and shares are the same or substantially the same.[117]

See page ii for explanation of footnotes.

[115] CCH ¶10,951; Sec. 87(4.1).   [117] CCH ¶10,955; Sec. 87(4.3).

[116] CCH ¶10,952; Sec. 87(4.2).

[¶6355] Options To Acquire Shares of Predecessor Corporation

Where a taxpayer holds an option to acquire shares of a predecessor corporation and receives nothing for it on the amalgamation except an option to acquire shares of the amalgamated corporation, the taxpayer receives a tax-free rollover. The shares need not be similar and the rollover would be available, for example, if an option to acquire preference shares was turned in for an option on common shares.

Similarly, an option to acquire one share of the predecessor could apparently be exchanged for an option on any number of shares of the amalgamated corporation. The option on shares of the predecessor must, however, be capital property to the particular taxpayer. The option-holder is deemed to have disposed of the option at its adjusted cost base. The option-holder thus may not realize either a capital gain or a capital loss.

The cost of the option on shares of the amalgamated corporation is deemed to have a cost amount of the same disposition price. In any case, where the old option was taxable Canadian property, the new option is also taxable Canadian property.[118]

Provision is made for the preservation of the tax-free zone if the old option was held on December 31, 1971.[119]

[¶6360] Obligations and Debts Issued by Predecessor Corporation

Where a taxpayer who held a bond, debenture, mortgage, note, or other obligation of a predecessor immediately before the amalgamation, receives as the only consideration for this property a bond, debenture, mortgage, note, or other obligation of the amalgamated corporation on which the same amount is payable at maturity, the taxpayer is given a rollover.[120] The taxpayer is deemed to dispose of the old property for its adjusted cost base and is deemed to acquire the new property at a cost equal to the same amount. The tax-free zone, if any, is preserved.[121] It will be noted that the old property must be held as capital property.

It does not appear that there need be any similarity between the old and new property except for the price payable on maturity; the old property could be a secured debenture and the new property could be a long-term note; the interest rate can also apparently be varied as can the due date of the obligation.

Where the amalgamated corporation assumes a debt or other obligation of a predecessor corporation which was outstanding at the time of amalgamation and thereby agrees to pay the same amount on maturity, the amalgamated corporation is deemed to have issued the debt at the time

---

See page ii for explanation of footnotes.

[118] CCH ¶10,960; Sec. 87(5). [120] CCH ¶11,000; Sec. 87(6).
[119] CCH ¶10,965; ITAR 26(22). [121] CCH ¶29,339ac; ITAR 26(23).

when the predecessor incurred it.[122] This means, for example, that the amalgamated corporation will be entitled to any deep or shallow discount deductions when it repays the debt.

[¶6370] Winding Up

[¶6375] Winding Up a 90%-or-Greater-Owned Taxable Canadian Corporation

A generally complete set of rules governs the winding-up of a taxable Canadian corporation (referred to as the "subsidiary") where not less than 90% of the issued shares of each class of capital stock of the subsidiary are held by a second taxable Canadian corporation (referred to as the "parent"), and all the remaining shares of the corporation being wound up are owned by persons who deal at arm's length with the parent.

These rules provide, in general, a tax-free rollover to these taxable corporations, although it may be denied where the applicable anti-avoidance rule operates.[123] No tax-free rollover is available to the holder of a minority interest position in the corporation being wound up. The minority interest shareholders will generally receive capital gain or loss treatment on the disposition of their shares based on the value of the property they receive on the winding-up as compared to the adjusted cost base of their shares.

A taxpayer who was a land developer owned a subsidiary with $4 million unrealized loss on land. When the taxpayer wound up the subsidiary and immediately sold the land to trigger the loss, such loss was deductible.[124]

One of the significant provisions of subsection 88(1) is the so-called "bump" rule of paragraph (d), which allows the parent to add certain amounts to the cost of the subsidiary's former capital property distributed to the parent on winding-up (other than depreciable property and other "ineligible property", a lengthy definition of which is found in paragraph (c)). The total bump for all such properties is generally limited to the amount by which the adjusted cost base of the parent's former shares in the subsidiary exceeds the total of the subsidiary's cost amounts of its properties and the money owned immediately before the winding-up (with certain further adjustments, as set out in subparagraphs (d)(i) and (ii)). Among other restrictions, the parent can bump up the cost of a particular capital property only to the extent that the fair market value of the property at the time the parent last acquired control of the subsidiary exceeds the cost amount of the property immediately before the winding-up. Furthermore, the property

---

See page ii for explanation of footnotes.

[122] CCH ¶11,020; Sec. 87(7).

[123] CCH ¶11,160, ¶52,131, ¶52,153; Sec. 88; Interp. Bul. IT-126R2, IT-149R4.

[124] [Mara Properties Ltd., 96 DTC 6309.

must have been owned by the subsidiary at the time the parent last acquired control of the subsidiary and thereafter without interruption, until it was distributed to the parent on the winding-up.

The following factors should be considered on the winding-up:

(1) *Pre-1972 capital surplus on hand.* A subsidiary may not increase or decrease its pre-1972 capital surplus on hand through a deemed realization of its pre-1972 capital gains or losses on winding up. The potential adjustments to pre-1972 capital surplus on hand flow up to the parent and are made only when the parent actually disposes of the assets in question.[125]

(2) *Proceeds of disposition of shares.* The parent is deemed to dispose of its shares of the subsidiary on the winding-up.[126] The proceeds of disposition of the shares is deemed to be the greater of:

(a) the lesser of:

(i) the paid-up capital in respect of the capital stock of the subsidiary's shares owned by the parent immediately before the winding-up, and

(ii) the net asset value of the subsidiary's properties; and

(b) the adjusted cost base of the shares to the parent immediately before the winding-up.

The effect of this formula is to provide that the proceeds of disposition will be at least equal to the adjusted cost base of the shares of the subsidiary to the parent. Thus, the parent may not realize a capital loss on its shares of the subsidiary on winding up, but may in some cases realize a capital gain.

(3) *Proceeds of capital properties.* These consist of depreciable properties and all other properties which, on disposition, would be capable of giving rise to a capital gain or loss as opposed to an income gain or loss.[127] The subsidiary is deemed to dispose of these proprieties at their "cost amount" [128] to it immediately before the winding-up. Generally, the cost amount to the parent of each property of the subsidiary distributed to the parent on the winding-up is reduced by any reduction of the cost amount to the subsidiary of the property as a result of the application of the debt forgiveness rules[129] on the winding-up. The debt forgiveness rules may apply where a debt owing by a subsidiary to its parent is settled or extinguished on a winding-up.

(4) *Trade receivables.* These are deemed to be disposed of by the subsidiary for their cost amount, which is their face amount.[130] The subsidiary may claim an allowance for doubtful debts in the year it transfers its properties to the parent, where the debt obligations of the subsidiary are assumed by

---

See page ii for explanation of footnotes.

[125] CCH ¶11,160; Sec. 88(1)(e.2).
[126] CCH ¶11,160; Sec. 88(1)(b).
[127] CCH ¶7850; Sec. 54 "adjusted cost base".
[128] CCH ¶28,054; Sec. 248(1) "cost amount".
[129] CCH ¶9850–9861d; Sec. 80.
[130] CCH ¶28,054; Sec. 248(1) "cost amount".

the parent.[131] In effect, the parent will be deemed to have taken this allowance in the year preceding the year it acquires the receivables; thus the parent will include the subsidiary's allowance in its own income for the year of distribution.[132]

(5) *Inter-company payables.* If the parent owes money to the subsidiary and this property right is among the properties distributed to the parent on winding up, it would appear that the parent's debt may be cancelled without payment. In such a case, the subsidiary would be deemed to dispose of this debt at its face amount and would usually incur no gain or loss.

(6) *Inventory.* The subsidiary is deemed to dispose of its inventory at its cost amount immediately before the winding-up. The cost amount is the value of the inventory used by the subsidiary for calculating its income.[133] Special rules apply to inventory used by the subsidiary in a farming business if the subsidiary uses the cash method of accounting.

(7) *Eligible capital property.* Eligible capital property is deemed to have been disposed of by the subsidiary for proceeds equal to the cost amount of the eligible capital property to the subsidiary immediately before the winding-up.[134] The cost amount of an eligible capital property is equal to $4/3$ of the cumulative eligible capital in respect of the business at that time.[135]

(8) *Partnership interest.* Where a subsidiary has distributed a partnership interest to a parent on winding up, the subsidiary is deemed not to have disposed of the partnership interest. The parent's cost of the interest in the partnership is the subsidiary's cost amount, and the parent also inherits any "negative" cost base of the subsidiary.[136]

(9) *Cost of non-depreciable capital property to parent.* If the subsidiary has any non-depreciable capital property and distributes it to the parent on winding up, the parent's cost of each such property is the amount deemed to be the proceeds of disposition to the subsidiary, plus an elective amount. The addition of this elected amount is available only in respect of non-depreciable capital property that was owned by the subsidiary at the time the parent last acquired control of the subsidiary, that had been owned by the subsidiary thereafter without interruption, and that was distributed to the parent on the winding-up.

(10) *Reserves.* A subsidiary may claim for the taxation year in which it distributes its property to or has its obligations assumed by a parent any reserve to which it would have been entitled if it had not distributed the property or had its obligations assumed, but had continued to hold it until the year end.[137] No amount is included in income for the year following the year in which its assets were transferred or obligations assumed. The parent

---

See page ii for explanation of footnotes.

[131] CCH ¶11,167; Sec. 88(1)(e.1).
[132] CCH ¶11,168; Sec. 88(1)(e.2).
[133] CCH ¶28,054; Sec. 248(1) "cost amount".
[134] CCH ¶11,160; Sec. 88(1)(a)(iii).

[135] CCH ¶28,054; Sec. 248(1) "cost amount".
[136] CCH ¶11,162; Sec. 88(1)(a), 88(1)(a.2), 88(1)(c), 88(1)(e.2).
[137] CCH ¶11,167; Sec. 88(1)(e.1).

is deemed to have taken the reserve claimed by the subsidiary and so must include the reserve in its own income, subject to any right to a continuing reserve.

(11) *Refundable dividend tax on hand.* A parent corporation that is a private corporation immediately after its subsidiary is wound up will include the subsidiary's RDTOH, less any dividend refund, in its own RDTOH for its first taxation year ending after the winding-up.[138]

(12) *Investment tax credit and employment tax credit.* The Act permits unused investment tax credits[139] and unused employment tax credits[140] of a 90%-owned subsidiary corporation to flow through to the parent on winding up. Any reductions determined in respect of a subsidiary's investment tax credit will also reduce the investment tax credit that flows through to the parent.

(13) *Debts of subsidiary.* The debtholders of a 90%-owned subsidiary are entitled to a tax-free rollover on a winding-up provided they receive similar debt from the parent.[141]

(14) *Charitable gifts.* Any amount of charitable gifts, Crown gifts, or gifts of Canadian cultural property made by the subsidiary in a taxation year ("the gift year") that was not deducted by the subsidiary will be deemed to have been an amount in respect of a gift made by the parent in the gift year that was not deducted by the parent in any taxation year ending on or before the winding-up.[142] If the parent is newly incorporated, it is deemed to have had prior taxation years for these purposes. The parent can then deduct these gifts within the limits provided in the Act. It is proposed [former Bill C-10, draft legislation released July 16, 2010] that if a charitable donation is determined to have been made by a subsidiary corporation after it has ceased to exist, the gift will be treated as if made by the subsidiary's parent company.

(15) *Unused foreign tax credits.* Any unused foreign tax credit of a subsidiary in respect of a country is deemed to become an unused foreign tax credit of the parent for the taxation year of the parent in which the subsidiary's "foreign tax year" ended. The subsidiary's foreign tax year is the subsidiary's taxation year in which the unused foreign tax credit arose. The unused foreign tax credit which flows up to the parent in this manner is reduced to the extent that the subsidiary used that unused foreign tax credit in any taxation year to reduce its tax payable. This rule ensures that the subsidiary's carryforward period for unused foreign tax credits will be maintained in the parent and will not be shortened or lengthened by the wind-up.[143]

(16) *Winding-up of subsidiary insurance corporations.* A parent corporation is treated as a continuation of a subsidiary insurance corporation for

---

See page ii for explanation of footnotes.

[138] CCH ¶11,160; Sec. 88(1)(e.2).
[139] CCH ¶11,160; Sec. 88(1)(e.3).
[140] CCH ¶11,160; Sec. 88(1)(e.4).

[141] CCH ¶11,168; Sec. 88(1)(e.2).
[142] CCH ¶11,169b; Sec. 88(1)(e.6).
[143] CCH ¶11,169ba; Sec. 88(1)(e.7).

¶6375

the purposes of certain tax provisions relating to insurance corporations. Special rules determine the gross investment revenue and gains and losses from property of the subsidiary and parent.[144]

(17) *Non-capital, net capital, restricted farm, farm, and limited partnership losses on winding up.* The losses covered are the non-capital, net capital, restricted farm, farm, and limited partnership losses of the subsidiary that were not deducted by the subsidiary in any year, but which would have been deducted by the subsidiary in computing its taxable income in the first taxation year of the subsidiary starting after the commencement of the winding-up (assuming that the subsidiary had such a subsequent taxation year and had sufficient income in that subsequent year to use these losses).[145]

(18) *Qualified research expenditures of subsidiary.* For the purpose of computing the additional allowance for scientific research of the parent, its base will include any base period of the subsidiary, and the qualified expenditures paid in its base period will include qualified expenditures made by the subsidiary in its taxation years ending in the same calendar years as the parent's base period.[146] Similarly, any receipts in respect of scientific research of the subsidiary will be treated as receipts of the parent in the same period.

(19) *Appropriation of property to shareholders.* The rules relating to the appropriation of corporation property for the benefit of a shareholder provide that the rules relating to a loss from disposition of property to a controlled corporation do not apply to an appropriation of property to shareholders on the winding-up of a corporation.[147]

(20) *Taxable income and business limit of parent.* For certain purposes, the taxable income of the parent and the business limit of the parent for the year in which the assets are received from the subsidiary will be increased by the taxable income and business limit of the subsidiary for the subsidiary's year ending in that taxation year of the parent.[148]

(21) *Resource deductions.* On a winding-up to which the provisions discussed in this paragraph apply, the parent is deemed to be the same corporation for the purposes of the deduction of certain resource expenses. These expenses include Canadian exploration and development expenses, foreign exploration and development expenses, Canadian exploration expenses, Canadian development expenses, and Canadian oil and gas property expenses. Accordingly, such expenses incurred but not deducted by the subsidiary will be deductible by the parent. The deeming provision also applies for the purposes of certain successor rules.[149]

See page ii for explanation of footnotes.

[144] CCH ¶11,160; Sec. 88(1)(*g*).

[145] CCH ¶11,169d; Sec. 88(1.1), 88(1.2).

[146] CCH ¶11,169i; Sec. 88(1.4).

[147] CCH ¶9180; Sec. 69(5).

[148] CCH ¶11,169bb; Sec. 88(1)(e.8).

[149] CCH ¶11,169k; Sec. 88(1.5).

[¶6380] Winding-Up of Corporation That Is Not a 90%-Owned Subsidiary

The rules for winding up a taxable Canadian corporation into its parent taxable Canadian corporation where the parent owns 90% of the issued shares of the subsidiary do not apply where one of the corporations is not a taxable Canadian corporation, or where the corporation being wound up is not owned as to 90% by the parent with all remaining shares owned by persons who deal at arm's length with the parent.[150] When these circumstances exist, the provisions which are applicable are scattered throughout the Act, mostly in provisions of general application.

[¶6385] Deemed Dividends

The following rules apply to the deemed dividends that arise on a winding-up, discontinuance, or reorganization of a business:

(1) The corporation may elect that a separate dividend be payable out of its capital dividend account,[151] or, in the case of an NRO or an investment corporation, out of its capital gains dividend account.[152]

(2) A portion of the winding-up dividend equal to the corporation's pre-1972 capital surplus on hand[153] will be received as a return of capital and will form part of the proceeds of disposition of shares.

(3) The balance of the winding-up dividend will be a taxable dividend subject to gross-up in the case of non-corporate shareholders (see ¶6052). Corporate shareholders may be subject to tax under Part IV. Non-resident shareholders will be subject to withholding tax under Part XIII.[154]

[¶6390] SIFT Trust Wind-Up Rollover

Following a SIFT unit-for-share exchange (see ¶6278 and distribution of the SIFT trust's property, the successor corporation is allowed after July 14, 2008, to wind up the SIFT trust and its subsidiary on a tax-deferred basis.[155] This wind-up will apply if the distributing trust has only a taxable Canadian corporation as its beneficiary and the distribution takes place within 60 days of the first distribution of property, if any, on the wind-up of a second-tier trust.[156] On the wind-up, the SIFT trust will be treated as a taxable Canadian corporation that is not private, the distribution by the trust as the winding-up of the corporation, and the taxpayer's interest as a beneficiary of the trust as shares of the corporation. In addition, the proceeds of disposition of the trust units are deemed to be equal to the adjusted cost base to the taxpayer of the interest in the trust immediately before the distribution, so that no gain is realized on the disposition of the trust units

---

See page ii for explanation of footnotes.

[150] CCH ¶11,175; Sec. 88(2).
[151] CCH ¶10,150; Sec. 83(2).
[152] CCH ¶20,243; Sec. 133(7.1).
[153] CCH ¶11,176; Sec. 88(2.1).

[154] CCH ¶26,105; Sec. 212(2).
[155] CCH ¶11,179ae; Sec. 88.1(2).
[156] CCH ¶11,179ac; Sec. 88.1(1).

on the wind-up. The benefit of this wind-up is that the tax attributes of the SIFT trust's property, such as the tax cost of the properties and unutilized deductions, will flow through to the successor corporation of the distribution.

[¶6395] Winding-Up of an NRO

Where an NRO winds up and in the course of doing so distributes all or substantially all its property to its shareholders, the various special surpluses are distributed by way of the dividend. An NRO may have the same special surpluses as other Canadian corporations except that it has no capital dividend account but may have instead a capital gains dividend account. Where it is desired to elect to have any dividend deemed to arise paid out of the various special surpluses, rules are provided which allow this dividend to be separated in the same way as for other corporations. The only difference is that whereas other corporations may distribute capital dividends under one section of the Act, the NRO distributes capital gains dividends under another provision.[157]

A taxable dividend paid by an NRO to non-residents bears tax at the usual withholding rates. It should be observed, however, that no withholding tax is payable on a capital gains dividend or on payment of its pre-1972 capital surplus on hand.

---

[157] CCH ¶11,175; Sec. 88(2).

Chapter VII

Partnerships and Trusts

General Rules for Computing Partners' Income **7000**

Distinction between Partner and Partnership Income 7005

Investment Clubs 7010

What Constitutes a Partnership 7015

Allocation of Profits to Partners 7020

Allocation of Share of Income to Retiring Partner 7025

Deemed Dividend of SIFT Partnership 7026

Partnership Income **7030**

Partnership Level Income and Loss 7035

Elections by Members of Partnership 7040

Exclusions from Computation at Partnership Level 7045

Fiscal Period of Partnership 7047

Limited Partnerships **7050**

Limited Partners — At-Risk Rules — General Comment 7055

Limitation on Deduction of Partnership Losses 7060

"At-Risk Amount" Defined 7065

Meaning of "Limited Partner" 7070

Meaning of "Exempt Interest" 7075

At-Risk Resource Rules 7085

Transactions in Partnership Interests **7090**

When Dispositions Occur 7095

Negative Partnership ACB of Limited Partner 7097

Non-Recourse Financing 7098

Adjusted Cost Base — Amounts To Be Added 7100

Adjusted Cost Base — Amounts To Be Deducted 7105

Foreign Partnerships 7107

Contribution of Property to Partnership **7110**

Property Transfer to Partnership 7115

Election for Canadian Partnerships 7120

Transfer of Depreciable Property — Recapture 7130

Purchase of Partnership Interest by New Partner — Goodwill 7135

Effect of Election — Example 7137

Disposition of Partnership Property **7140**

Deemed Disposition of Property by Partnership 7145

Partnership Ceasing to Exist 7150

Election on Cessation of Partnership — Rollover 7155

Partner's Deemed Proceeds of Disposition of Partnership Interest 7160

Deemed Cost of Properties Received 7165

Recaptured Depreciation on Termination of Partnership 7170

Continuation of Partnership **7175**

Property Rollovers from
Partnership to Sole
Proprietorship 7180

Amalgamations 7183

Continuation of Former
Partnership — Rollover 7185

Residual Interest in
Partnership 7190

**Fiscal Period of Terminated
Partnership** **7195**

Partnership Fiscal Period 7200

Fiscal Period of Partner 7205

**Disposition of Partnership
Interest** **7210**

Gain on Disposition to
Exempt Person 7215

Gain on Disposition of
Partnership Interest 7220

Loss re Interest in
Partnership 7225

Replacement of Partnership
Capital 7230

Canadian Partnership **7235**

"Canadian Partnership"
Defined 7240

**Income Allocation
Adjustments** **7245**

Adjustments by Minister 7250

**Trusts — Taxation of Trusts
and Beneficiaries** **7255**

General Treatment 7260

Reference to Trust or
Estate 7265

Income of Trusts **7270**

Taxation of Trust Income 7275

Rate of Tax 7280

Additional Tax for SIFT
Trusts 7282

Twenty-One-Year Deemed
Disposition Rule 7285

Date of Deemed
Realization 7290

Deduction by Trust Other
than Employee Trust or
SIFT Trust 7295

Deduction Where Capital
Interest Greater than
Income Interest 7300

Deduction by Employee
Trust 7305

Deduction by SIFT Trust 7307

**Non-Residents — Trusts and
Beneficiaries** **7310**

General Treatment 7315

Withholding Tax 7320

Capital Gains of Non-
Resident 7325

Capital Interest in Resident
Trust Considered
"Taxable Canadian
Property" 7330

Canada–U.S. Tax
Convention 7335

Canada–U.K. Tax
Convention 7337

**Accumulating Income —
Election — Preferred
Beneficiaries** **7340**

Preferred Beneficiary
Election After 1995 7345

Share of Preferred
Beneficiary under a Trust 7355

SIFT Deemed Dividend 7357

Amounts Deemed Not Paid 7360

Property Transfers to
Spouse, Common-Law
Partner, or Minor —
Attribution 7365

**Capital Cost Allowances —
Dividends — Capital
Gains — Principal
Residence Exemption** **7370**

Deduction for Capital Cost
Allowance and Depletion 7375

Flow-Through of Taxable
Dividends to a
Beneficiary 7380

Designation in Respect of
Non-Taxable Dividends 7385

Flow-Through of Taxable
Capital Gains to
Beneficiaries 7390

Non-Resident Trusts (NRTs) 7394

Foreign Investment Entities
(FIEs) 7395

Principal Residence
Exemption 7397

Foreign Tax Credits **7400**

Rules for Allocation of
Foreign Taxes 7405

**Testamentary Trusts and
Minors** **7410**
Taxation Year of Trust 7415
Trust for Minor 7420
Benefits under Trust **7425**
Benefits 7430
Amounts Expended for
Upkeep, etc. 7435
**Income and Capital
Interests** **7440**
Income Interest in Trust 7445
Capital Interest in Trust 7450
Income and Capital
Interests — Capital Gains
or Losses 7455
Distribution in Satisfaction
of Capital Interest — Cost
Amount 7460
Example Illustrating
Disposition of Capital
Interest and Distribution
in Satisfaction Thereof 7465
Distribution of Depreciable
Property 7470

Proceeds of Disposition of
Capital Interest 7475
Proceeds of Disposition of
Eligible Capital Property 7477
Trusts in Favour of Spouse
or Common-Law Partner 7480
Distribution to Non-Resident
Beneficiary 7485
Distribution by SIFT Wind-
Up Entity 7486
Distribution of Property with
an Accrued Loss 7487
Distributions by Employee
Trust or Employee Benefit
Plan 7490
Distributions by Retirement
Compensation
Arrangement 7495
Qualifying Environmental
Trusts 7497
Transfers to Bare Trusts,
Protective Trusts, and
Similar Vehicles 7500

Recent Changes

Partnerships

2012 Budget

Tax Avoidance through Partnerships

Continuing with tightening on the partnership rules begun in the 2011 Budget, this year's budget closes further perceived loopholes. The "section 88 bump" on an amalgamation/wind-up of a subsidiary that is a member of a partnership will not apply to the extent that the accrued gain in respect of the partnership interest is reasonably attributable to the inherent gain on income assets of the partnership for amalgamations that occur, and windings-up that begin, on or after March 29, 2012. This change was released in draft form on August 14, 2012. See ¶7183.

Generally, a taxpayer's taxable capital gain for a year from the disposition of an interest in a partnership to any tax-exempt entity is $1/2$ of the portion of the capital gain that can reasonably be attributed to increases in value of non-depreciable capital property of the partnership, plus the whole of the remaining portion of such capital gain. As a result of draft legislation released on August 14, 2012, this rule will be extended to indirect dispositions of partnership interests to tax-exempt entities, and both direct and indirect dispositions of partnership interests to non-resident purchasers. These measures will apply to dispositions of interests in partnerships that occur on or after March 29, 2012, other than an arm's length disposition made by a taxpayer before 2013 that the taxpayer is obligated to make pursuant to a written agreement entered into by the taxpayer before March 29, 2012. See ¶7215.

Finance

T5013 Partnership Information Return

On the "Partnerships" page of its website, the Canada Revenue Agency has posted various clarifications and modifications concerning the T5013, Partnership Information Return. The website provides information that is not yet reflected in the CRA's T4068, Guide for the Partnership Information Return (T5013 Forms) and the related T5013. Under the topic of Filing Schedule 50, Partnership Ownership and Account Activity, the CRA provided some transition period information (initially released in February 2012 and later revised in July 2012). See ¶7035.

Trusts

Proposed Technical Amendments

Stapled Securities — SIFTs and REITs

In some structures involving stapled securities, a corporation or SIFT (alone or together with a subsidiary) might issue equity and debt instruments — at least one of which is publicly traded — that are stapled together. Draft amendments proposed on July 25, 2012 will (notwithstanding general rules applicable to interest deductibility) deny the deduction of interest that is paid or payable on the debt portion of such a stapled security by the payer for income tax purposes. Similar limitations will apply to REITs. See ¶7307.

Jurisprudence

Trusts — Existence, Residence and Attribution

There were two important decisions involving various trust aspects:

- *St. Michael Trust Corp.*, 2012 DTC 5063 (Supreme Court) — This case has upended the long-standing rule used in the determination of the residence of a trust. The Supreme Court determined that trusts — like corporations — are resident where the central management and control is carried out, and further stated that there is no legal rule in subsection 104(1) that the residence of a trust has to be that of the trustee. See ¶7260.

- *The Queen v. Sommerer*, 2012 DTC 5126 (FCA) — This case clarifies the existence of trusts in the context of non-Canadian entities, and confirms that subsection 75(2) is not engaged by a fair market value sale of property by a beneficiary to the trust. See ¶7275.

[¶7000] General Rules for Computing Partners' Income

[¶7005] Distinction between Partner and Partnership Income

A taxpayer who is a member of a partnership must include in income from all sources the share of income or loss allocated by the partnership. The same tax treatment will apply to any capital gain or loss from the disposition of the taxpayer's interest in the partnership, which generally will be treated as capital property, subject to special rules. A taxpayer may be a general member of the partnership, a limited partner, or a deemed member of the partnership under certain rules dealing with terminated partnerships or withdrawing partners.

Although it is the partners themselves who are taxed, a separate calculation of the partnership income must be done as though it were a separate entity; the income or loss so calculated then flows through to the partners and is taxable in their hands.

[¶7010] Investment Clubs

Members of an investment club may elect to treat the club for tax purposes, essentially as if it were a partnership on a "modified partnership" basis.[1]

[¶7015] What Constitutes a Partnership

The term "partnership" is defined in provincial partnership acts as the relation which subsists between persons carrying on business in common with a view to profit.[2] Under provincial law, a partnership is formed as long as there is a profit-making purpose, even if such purpose is not the predominant purpose of the parties. If a partnership is not a sham and is valid under provincial law, the tax consequences applicable to partnerships will flow. Thus, the fact that a taxpayer had sought the tax benefits as its predominant purpose for the creation of a partnership did not negate the fact that the parties also had the ancillary purpose of sharing profit and there was otherwise a partnership under provincial law into which the taxpayer could roll over its assets under ¶7120.[3] In reaching its decision, the Court set out the three essential elements of a partnership: namely, (i) a business; (ii) carried on in common; (iii) with a view to profit. These essential elements were not established in a case where new Canadian participants never intended to carry on business with a view to profit in respect of a real estate development nor with respect to an interest in an oil and gas property.[4] By contrast, the Court held that such elements did exist in a case where the taxpayers adduced objective evidence indicating the continuity of the business of a partnership (i.e., the continued rental of an apartment building for a profit) and the management effort required to sustain such business.[5]

Family members, in particular, often try to establish a partnership with respect to their various activities in order to split income and share losses. Such arrangements are not prohibited by statute. The tests of the validity of family partnerships will be the facts of joint endeavour and the reasonableness of allocations. By itself, joint interest in work is consistent with marital relationship and does not establish partnership.[6] For a partnership to exist

---

See page ii for explanation of footnotes.

[1] CCH ¶51,129; Inf. Cir. 73-13.
[2] CCH ¶52,096; Interp. Bul. IT-90.
[3] Continental Bank Leasing Corporation, 98 DTC 6505.

[4] Backman, 2001 DTC 5149.
[5] Spire Freezers Ltd, 2001 DTC 5158.
[6] Sedelnick Estate, 86 DTC 1563, Comforth, 82 DTC 6058.

between husband and wife, there must be sharing in capital contributions, risks, and profits.[7]

Although members of partnerships are ordinarily individuals, corporations may also be members. Special rules limit the small business deduction available to corporations on their partnership income.

See ¶7240 for the meaning of the term "Canadian partnership".

[¶7020] Allocation of Profits to Partners

The members of a partnership are taxed as if their prorated share of the gain or loss computed for the partnership from all sources were the income or loss of the partner from those sources. Each partner must, in computing income for the taxation year in which the fiscal period of the partnership ends, include his or her share of the partnership's income or loss from all sources.[8] Note that a partner may be allocated a standby charge benefit on an automobile provided by the partnership.[9] Note also that pursuant to the goods and services tax (GST), a GST unregistered partner of a partnership registered under the GST may be entitled to a GST rebate on the use of the partner's car or plane in the business of the partnership on the same basis as an employee.

Partnership agreements will often divide profits and losses among the partners on a combination formula, incorporating provisions for interest on partners' capital and salaries to partners with the remainder being divided in a particular ratio. No deduction may be claimed for tax purposes (in the partnership's accounts) for partners' salaries or interest on their capital. Such items must be added to the partners' shares of profits and thus must be included in their income from the partnership. Drawings of partners should be ignored in determining partnership profits.

Life insurance premiums paid through the partnership are not deductible in arriving at partnership profits. If the policy proceeds are payable to an individual partner's estate or beneficiaries, the premiums should be added to that partner's share of income. If the policy proceeds are payable to the partnership, the premiums should be divided among the partners, in the profit and loss ratio, and added to their share of income.

However, rent paid to a partner is an expense of the partnership and personal income of the particular partner. It is not an allocation of partnership income.

The limited partners of a limited partnership enjoy limited liability with respect to the partnership operations and, as such, are not permitted

---

See page ii for explanation of footnotes.

[7] Hansen, 86 DTC 1697, Wessell, 85 DTC 206.

[8] CCH ¶4360, ¶12,103, ¶12,149, ¶52,088; Sec. 12(1)(*l*), 96(1), 96(2); Interp. Bul. IT-81R.

[9] CCH ¶4377; Sec. 12(1)(y).

to deduct allocated losses in excess of their liability to fund such losses ("at risk amount"). See ¶7055 *et seq.*

Members of a partnership are permitted to enter into an agreement under which continuing income or losses of the partnership can be allocated to a retired partner or to a retired partner's spouse/common-law partner, estate, heirs, or other persons who have acquired the retired partner's rights under the agreement. The person to whom such income or losses are allocated is treated as a member of the partnership (see ¶7025).

[¶7025] Allocation of Share of Income to Retiring Partner

Where a taxpayer has ceased to be a member of a continuing partnership, the taxpayer will ordinarily not continue to share in partnership profits. However, members of a partnership whose principal activity is carrying on a business in Canada are permitted to enter into an agreement under which continuing income or losses of the partnership can be allocated to a retired partner or to a retired partner's spouse/common-law partner, estate, heirs, or other persons who have acquired the retired partner's rights.[10]

The person to whom such income or loss is allocated is treated for tax purposes as a member of the partnership, so that the amounts allocated will be included in his or her income in the year in which the partnership fiscal year end occurs.

A right under the agreement to a share of the income or loss of the partnership is deemed not to be capital property.[11] Any proceeds of disposition of this right must be included in the taxpayer's income. Any property received in satisfaction of the right is given a cost equal to its fair market value at the time of receipt.

Where the deemed partner dies, his or her right is deemed to be a right or thing.[12] Its fair market value is included in computing the income of the deceased unless the right is transferred to the deceased's beneficiaries. The beneficiary in this case would become the deemed partner and would be taxable on any further allocations of income from the partnership.

Any cost incurred by the deemed partner to acquire the right to an allocation of partnership income is deductible to the extent of the amount of such income allocated to the partner in any year. However, where the right to income expires before full deduction of the cost occurs, there is no provision for the balance to be deducted.

An "income interest" in a partnership is separate and distinct from a "residual interest", which is discussed at ¶7190.

See page ii for explanation of footnotes.

[10] CCH ¶12,140–12,147; Sec. 96(1.1)–(1.6); Interp. Bul. IT-242R.

[11] CCH ¶12,143; Sec. 96(1.4).

[12] CCH ¶9220; Sec. 70(2).

[¶7026] Deemed Dividend of SIFT Partnership

A new tax was enacted under Part IX.1 (see ¶13,385) to level the playing field between public partnerships relative to public corporations. That is, prior to the new tax, public partnerships were not subject to a corporate-type tax at the entity level, such that they could flow through their income to their investors and provide an after-tax advantage relative to the public corporate vehicle. Part IX.1 imposes a tax on the "taxable non-portfolio earnings" of a specified investment flow-through partnership (SIFT partnership) at a rate that approximates the general corporate tax rate. A SIFT partnership means a Canadian resident partnership if, at any time in the taxation year, the partnership holds non-portfolio property and investments in it are listed or traded on a stock exchange or other public market.

If the SIFT partnership is liable to tax for a taxation year under Part IX.1, its Part I income from a source for the year is the income from that source in excess of the taxable non-portfolio earnings applicable to that source. Such excess income, if any, is included in the income of the partners of the partnership. However, the SIFT partnership is deemed to have received a taxable dividend in the taxation year from a taxable Canadian corporation equal to the amount by which the partnership's taxable non-portfolio earnings for the year exceed the partnership's Part IX.1 tax payable for the year.[13] In other words, the partnership's "after-Part IX.1 tax" non-portfolio earnings for the year are treated as a deemed taxable dividend, which flows out to the partners along with other source income of the partnership. The dividend is considered an "eligible dividend", such that individual partners are eligible for the enhanced dividend tax credit. As a result, the tax regime applicable to taxable non-portfolio earnings of a SIFT partnership is similar to that which applies to income earned by a public corporation that is distributed as taxable dividends to its shareholders.

This new tax regime came into force on October 31, 2006, but owing to the application of the definition of "SIFT partnership", the earliest that it can apply is to a SIFT partnership's taxation year ending after 2006. Furthermore, owing to grandfathering rules that apply to partnerships that otherwise would have been considered SIFT partnerships on October 31, 2006 (had the definition been applicable at that date), this regime does not apply to such partnerships until the 2011 taxation year, provided they do not exceed certain "normal growth" guidelines issued by the Department of Finance.

See page ii for explanation of footnotes.

[13] CCH ¶12,140m; Sec. 96(1.11).

[¶7030] Partnership Income

[¶7035] Partnership Level Income and Loss

Partnership level income and loss is computed as if the partnership were a separate person resident in Canada with a taxation year concurrent with the partnership's fiscal period.[14] The fiscal period of a partnership that includes any individuals or professional corporations as partners must end at the end of the calendar year in which it began, unless an alternative election is made, as discussed below at ¶7047. There are exceptions for testamentary trusts and tax-exempt individuals which typically are tax-exempt trusts.

If the partnership earns income or has losses from more than one source, the income or loss from each source must be determined separately. Similarly, taxable capital gains and allowable capital losses must be determined and reflected in the income of the partnership.

A limited partnership's losses are restricted to a partner's at-risk amount, i.e., the cost of the partner's interest in the partnership less amounts owing to the partnership and reductions for any guarantees to the partner.[15] See ¶7055 *et seq.*

When a partnership receives dividends from a taxable Canadian corporation,[16] and there are expenses applicable thereto, the partnership may allocate to each member his or her share of both the gross dividend and the expenses. The effect is that the gross-up of the dividend and the dividend tax credit are calculated on the gross dividend rather than on the net dividend income.

Capital cost allowance is claimed at the partnership level rather than by the partners.[17] The partnership also claims allowance on eligible capital property, that is, goodwill or other nothings, and computes its own capital gains and losses on dispositions of partnership property. When calculating the deemed cost of capital property which it owned on December 31, 1971, a partnership must always use the tax-free zone method; it is not eligible to elect the Valuation Day value method.

The CRA has revised the returns, forms, and schedules that make up the partnership information return for 2011. The changes reflect the new requirements for filing a partnership information return starting for fiscal periods ending in 2011. As set out in T4068, "Guide for the Partnership Information Return", four new forms have been added to the T5013, three previous forms are no longer in use, and several other forms have been changed. The 2011 version of T5013, "Schedule 50" has been completely redesigned from the 2010 version. It is now called "Partner's Ownership and

---

See page ii for explanation of footnotes.

[14] CCH ¶12,103; Sec. 96(1)(b).   [16] CCH ¶10,003; Sec. 82(1).
[15] CCH ¶12,149ac–12,149t; Sec. 96(2.1)–96(2.7).   [17] CCH ¶12,103; Sec. 96(1)(a)–(c).

Account Activity". Schedule 50 requires information on each partner's adjusted cost base ("ACB") of the partnership interest and the at-risk amount ("ARA"). On February 29, 2012, the CRA announced that it recognizes that preparers of the information return may have a difficult time supplying the information required in Schedule 50 and that a transition period is required. The CRA stated the following:

> To ease concerns about providing updated ACB and ARA information, we will accept returns filed by the due date if they contain either the 2010 or 2011 version of schedule 50 with complete information on partner identification and the annual transactions between partners and the partnerships.

> The CRA will not impose penalties on T5013 returns for 2011 fiscal periods as a result of incomplete ACB and ARA information on the schedule 50. We want to assure partnerships and tax preparers that penalties for incomplete returns are not intended to be applied on T5013 returns filed for 2011 fiscal periods that have been completed, to the best knowledge and abilities of the partnerships and preparers, by the filing deadline.

[¶7040] Elections by Members of Partnership

Certain elections may be available for computing income from a partnership activity. Generally, these elections permit the partnership to elect in the same way an individual could elect in similar circumstances.[18] Elections may be made by a partnership when dealing with:

(1) exchanges of property;[19]

(2) sale of certain vessels;[20]

(3) treatment of investments as small business bonds;[21]

(4) representation expenses;[22]

(5) capitalization of interest;[23]

(6) sale of accounts receivable;[24]

(7) optional reduction of basic herd;[25]

(8) work-in-progress of professionals;[26]

(9) option to have a non-calendar year end (see ¶7047);

(10) optional proxy amount calculation for deductions and investment tax credits on scientific research and experimental development expenditures;[27]

See page ii for explanation of footnotes.

[18] CCH ¶12,150; Sec. 96(3); Interp. Bul. IT-413R.

[19] CCH ¶4513, ¶4643, ¶6700, ¶6720; Sec. 13(4), 14(6), 44(1), 44(6).

[20] CCH ¶4554, ¶4555; Sec. 13(15), 13(16).

[21] CCH ¶4699; Sec. 15.2.

[22] CCH ¶5137; Sec. 20(9).

[23] CCH ¶5146–5149; Sec. 21(1)–(4).

[24] CCH ¶5153; Sec. 22.

[25] CCH ¶5182; Sec. 29(1).

[26] CCH ¶5750; Sec. 34.

[27] CCH ¶5926; Sec. 37(8)(a).

(11) bad debts and shares of bankrupt corporations;[28]

(12) optional reduction of the cost of capital properties under the debt forgiveness rules;[29]

(13) transfer of a forgiven amount from a debtor to an eligible transferee under the debt forgiveness rules;[30]

(14) property acquired from a partner by a Canadian partnership;[31]

(15) choosing or revoking a non-calendar year end;[32]

(16) the election to have the foreign spin-off rules apply to an exchange of shares (¶6321) and the related foreign affiliate election;[33]

(17) the elections under the demutualization rules (see ¶9274);

(18) [the elections under the former FIE regime (see below), to treat an affiliate as a controlled foreign affiliate and to use alternative methods of calculating FIE income;] and

(19) the election when disposing of eligible capital property after February 27, 2000, to withdraw the property from the pool of eligible properties and so realize a capital loss on the disposition.[34]

[In its 2010 Budget, the government announced that it would abandon its outstanding proposals to amend the FIE rules, with existing rules remaining in force, subject to a few minor amendments. As a result, the elections under the FIE rules to treat an affiliate as a controlled foreign affiliate and to use alternative methods of calculating FIE income (see item (18) above) would no longer be available after March 4, 2010. Draft legislation to implement these changes was released for consultation on August 27, 2010, but the changes are not yet enacted. A taxpayer who voluntarily complied with the outstanding proposals in previous years will have the option of having those years reassessed. If the taxpayer does not wish to be reassessed for those years, and had more income than would have been the case under the existing rules, the taxpayer will be entitled to a deduction in the current year for the excess income.]

In order to make one of the above elections, all of the partners must agree to it. The election is then made by one or more of the partners who has authority to act for the partnership. If the partnership as a whole does not make these elections, individual partners cannot make them independently in computing partnership income.

The election to treat all Canadian securities as capital property (¶5240), better known as the "guaranteed capital gains election", cannot be

---

[28] CCH ¶7400; Sec. 50(1).

[29] CCH ¶9854, ¶9858, ¶9859, ¶9860; Sec. 80(5), 80(9), 80(10), 80(11).

[30] CCH ¶9870c; Sec. 80.04(4).

[31] CCH ¶12,177; Sec. 97(2).

[32] CCH ¶28,333i, ¶28,333k; Sec. 249.1(4), 249.1(6).

[33] CCH ¶10,690; Sec. 86.1.

[34] CCH ¶4601; Sec. 14(1.01).

made at the partnership level. Accordingly, each partner's gain or loss from the disposition of his or her share of a Canadian security held by a partnership depends on whether the partner has personally elected under the guaranteed capital gain provision.

[¶7045] Exclusions from Computation at Partnership Level

The following items do not enter into the computation of partnership income:

(1) *Resource-related income and deductions.* Income at the partnership level is computed without deductions for depletion allowance (this allowance is repealed after 2006), Canadian and foreign exploration and development expenses, Canadian exploration expenses, Canadian development expenses, foreign resource expenses, or Canadian oil and gas property expenses. Partnership expenses that give rise to these deductions are shared among the partners and may be deducted by them personally at the partner level. A partner's share of such expenses reduces the adjusted cost base of his or her partnership interest.[35]

The proceeds of disposition of resource properties and recoveries of exploration or development expenses are ignored in computing income at the partnership level. Instead, each partner's share of the proceeds of disposition or the recovery of expenses is taken into account as a negative component of his or her own pool of cumulative Canadian exploration expense or cumulative Canadian development expense at the partner level. Similarly, the proceeds of disposition of Canadian oil and gas properties are taken into account on the basis of the share of each partner. The general purpose of these provisions is to permit dispositions and recoveries to be pooled against other resource-related expenses, which, as noted above, are deducted at the partner level.

(2) *Restricted farm loss computations and adjustments to the cost base of farmland.* If the partnership is engaged in farming operations, the income or loss is allocated to the partners. If the principal source of income for a partner for a taxation year is neither farming nor a combination of farming and some other source of income, only a portion of the allocated farm losses is deductible by the partner, according to the restricted farm loss rules in ¶3579.[36]

A partner is required to deduct his or her share of the annual farm loss from his or her adjusted cost base (but not in the computation of the partner's share of the annual income of the partnership) without reference to the farm loss limitations.[37] As a result, the partnership's gain from disposition of the farm land must be computed without reference to the general cost base adjustment for individuals; that is, the non-deductible losses cannot be

See page ii for explanation of footnotes.

[35] CCH ¶12,103; Sec. 96(1).

[36] CCH ¶5660, ¶12,103, ¶12,149; Sec. 31, 96(1), 96(2).

[37] CCH ¶7645; Sec. 53(2)(c).

¶7045

added to the cost of the farm land owned by the partnership. The partner's share of the gain from disposition of the farm land by the partnership is also determined without reference to this addition in computing his or her adjusted cost base.

To compensate the partner for not being able to use this addition in computing his or her adjusted cost base, the partner is permitted a maximum deduction for the portion of a farm loss not deductible because of the chief source of income restrictions,[38] equal to his or her share of the capital gain realized by the partnership on the sale of the farmland.[39] The partner's share of the gain would be included in income.[40]

(3) *Charitable donations.* The tax credit for charitable donations is also made at the partner's level. A partner is deemed to have made a gift equal to his or her share of the eligible amount of the gift (i.e., fair market value of the transferred property minus the advantage conferred in return) made by the partnership in the taxation year in which the taxation year of the partnership ended.[41] For example, assuming a company with a June 30 year end belongs to a partnership with a December 31 year end, a donation by the partnership in its year ending December 31 of Year 1 will be picked up by the corporation in its year ended June 30 of Year 2. These donations would therefore be grouped with other donations paid by the partner and would be eligible for the charitable donations tax credit.

Charitable donations made by the partnership, therefore, flow through to the partner but not by way of his or her share of partnership income, since in calculating the partnership income (as in calculating income generally), no credits are permitted for charitable donations. This treatment of the charitable donations therefore necessitates a separate deduction for charitable donations in calculating the adjusted cost base of the partner's interest in the partnership.[42]

The charitable donations deemed to have been made by the partner are deducted from his or her tax payable in the year in which they were paid in calculating his or her adjusted cost base, even though the partner may not have deducted any, or only a portion thereof, in calculating the tax payable for the year.

(4) *Individual expenses.* No specific provisions cover a number of other expenses that may have been incurred by the partner to earn his or her share of partnership income, such as:

> (a) car expenses not paid by the partnership (the partnership agreement may provide that partners must use their own cars for partnership business without reimbursement by the partnership);

See page ii for explanation of footnotes.

[38] CCH ¶5660; Sec. 31.
[39] CCH ¶12,385; Sec. 101.
[40] CCH ¶12,103; Sec. 96(1).

[41] CCH ¶15,770; Sec. 110.1(4).

[42] CCH ¶7645; Sec. 53(2)(c)(iii).

(b) business promotion;

(c) convention expense and professional dues; and

(d) the cost of using assets owned outside of the partnership.

The CRA's position (as announced in its Income Tax Technical News No. 6) is that partner-level expenses in respect of the partnership business are deductible only on a fiscal-period basis. Presumably, however, carrying charges in respect of the partnership interest are deductible only on a calendar year basis.

(5) *Political contributions.* Each person who is a member of a partnership at the end of its fiscal period is considered to have made a political contribution equal to his or her share of the eligible amount of such contributions (fair market value of transferred property minus the advantage conferred in return) made by the partnership in that period.[43] In this way, the amount which any partner may contribute and deduct in computing his or her own tax is reduced on account of contributions made by the partnership. The partner's share of partnership contributions reduces the partner's adjusted cost base of his or her partnership interest.[44]

[¶7047] Fiscal Period of Partnership

A partnership's fiscal period ends on December 31, unless an alternative election is made, if any of the following are its members:

(1) an individual (other than a testamentary trust or a tax-exempt individual, which typically is a tax-exempt trust);

(2) a professional corporation (that is, a corporation which carries on the professional practice of an accountant, dentist, lawyer, medical doctor, veterinarian, or chiropractor);

(3) beginning December 31, 2011, one or more partnerships for which a "multi-tier alignment election" is not made (as discussed below); or

(4) any other partnership.[45]

There are exceptions. A person or partnership who joins the partnership in a fiscal period, but after December 31, does not put the partnership offside for that fiscal period (but would for the next one). A person or partnership that would not have a share of partnership income or loss for a fiscal period of a partnership, if that fiscal period ended at December 31, is deemed not to be a member of the partnership for that fiscal period. The calendar year-end rule does not apply to the fiscal periods of partnerships not carrying on business in Canada.

See page ii for explanation of footnotes.

[43] CCH ¶19,823; Sec. 127(4.2).   [45] CCH ¶28,333f; Sec. 249.1(1).
[44] CCH ¶7645; Sec. 53(2)(c).

¶7047

Once a non-calendar fiscal period is elected or converted to calendar year basis, no change can be made without the permission of the CRA.

A partnership otherwise compelled to have a calendar year fiscal period may elect to maintain a non-calendar fiscal period provided that: (a) each member of the partnership is an individual (which can include a trust) and (b) the partnership is not a member of another partnership. It follows that a partnership with both corporate and individual members cannot make this election.

The alternative election to have a non-calendar fiscal period cannot be made by a partnership whose primary expenditures are for registered tax shelters.

In general, the election must be made on form T1139 with a timely return filed by the authorized partner by that partner's tax-due date, which will normally be June 15th of the year following the year in which the fiscal period commences. Where a testamentary trust is a partner, the election must be filed by the earliest filing-due date of any member of the partnership for the taxation year that includes the first day of the fiscal period; that is, it must be filed with the first trust return due among the partners, if any, before June 15.

The election must be made by the partnership as a whole and is then binding on the partners, including new partners who may be admitted later. Where the election is made, it compels each of the partners to prepay the tax on the estimated deferred income for the fiscal period that commenced in the year, but did not end in the year due to the election.[46]

The tax deferral that was available under a corporate partnership structure that is not aligned with the corporation's taxation year is now limited by requiring corporate members with a significant interest to accrue additional partnership income for the portion of the partnership's fiscal period that falls within the corporation's tax year.[47] As a result of these measures, some partnerships may wish to change their fiscal periods to align them with the taxation year of their corporate partners. For partnerships in a single-tier structure, a one-time election (a "single-tier alignment election") will enable them to align their fiscal periods if:

- each member of the partnership is, on the particular day, a corporation that is not a professional corporation;

- the partnership is not, on the particular day, a member of another partnership (i.e., it is a single-tier partnership);

- at least one member of the partnership is, on the particular day, a corporation that has a significant interest in the partnership, mean-

---

See page ii for explanation of footnotes.

[46] CCH ¶5786; Sec. 34.1(1). [47] Sec. 34.2.

ing that the corporation, together with affiliated and related parties, was entitled to more than 10% of the partnership's income (or assets in the case of wind-up) at the end of the last fiscal period of the partnership that ended in the taxation year; and

- at least one member with a significant interest in the partnership has a taxation year end that differs from the day on which the fiscal period of the partnership would end if there was not a valid single-tier alignment election.[48]

The deadline to file an election to change the fiscal period of the partnership was the first filing due date of any corporate partner for its first tax year ending after March 22, 2011. The election is not valid unless it is filed in the form of a letter signed by an authorized officer of the partnership and filed with the CRA and no other election is filed that attempts to align the fiscal period of a partnership.[49] If more than one election is filed, and there are two or more different days elected for the alignment of the partnership fiscal period, none of the elections are valid.

The single-tier alignment election described above is not available to multi-tier partnerships to the extent they must elect a common fiscal period (a "multi-tier alignment election") that does not need to correspond to the taxation years of their corporate members.[50] As a result of such an election not being filed, a default fiscal period of December 31 applies beginning December 31, 2011 (see item (3) in the above commentary).

[¶7050] Limited Partnerships

[¶7055] Limited Partners — At-Risk Rules — General Comment

In general terms, the amount of losses which can be deducted by a limited partner for tax purposes is limited to the "at-risk amount", less certain deductions.[51] Any amount which is not deductible in computing the partner's income for the year is deemed to be a "limited partnership loss" which may be deductible in a subsequent year against future income from the partnership.[52]

The amount of the investment tax credit which a limited partner could claim is also limited to the at-risk amount.[53]

A "limited partner" is defined, for the purposes of the provisions dealing with losses[54] and with investment tax credits,[55] to include not only a

---

See page ii for explanation of footnotes.

[48] Sec. 249.1(8).
[49] Sec. 249.1(10).
[50] Sec. 249.1(9).
[51] CCH ¶12,149ac–12,149t; Sec. 96(2.1)–(2.7).

[52] CCH ¶16,070; Sec. 111(1)(e).
[53] CCH ¶19,828–19,828e; Sec. 127(8)–(8.5).
[54] CCH ¶12,103, ¶16,003; Sec. 96, 111.
[55] CCH ¶19,828; Sec. 127(8).

partner of a limited partnership, but also a partner in certain other partnership arrangements.[56]

Certain partnership interests are exempted from the application of the "at-risk" rules by "grandfathering" certain partnerships which were carrying on business prior to February 26, 1986, as well as certain partnerships established pursuant to a prospectus which was filed with a securities commission before February 26, 1986.[57] Anti-avoidance rules are provided relating to artificial transactions.[58]

[¶7060] Limitation on Deduction of Partnership Losses

There is an exception to the general manner in which a taxpayer who is a member of a partnership calculates his or her share of the losses of the partnership from business or property.[59]

For the exception to apply, the taxpayer must be a limited partner of a partnership. "Limited partner" includes partners of certain partnerships which are not limited partnerships. See ¶7070.

The deduction of business losses (other than those from a farming business) or property losses (including non-capital losses) by a limited partner is disallowed to the extent that the amount of the losses exceeds the difference between the taxpayer's at-risk amount (see ¶7065) in respect of the partnership at the end of the fiscal period and the aggregate of the following amounts:

(a) the partner's investment tax credits from the partnership for the year;[60]

(b) the partner's share of losses from a farming business of the partnership for the fiscal period. It should be noted that losses from a farming business carried on by a partnership are not restricted by the at-risk rules (although the farm losses may be restricted under the general rules applicable to farming losses);[61] and

(c) the taxpayer's share of foreign exploration and development expenses,[62] Canadian exploration expenses,[63] Canadian development expenses,[64] and Canadian oil and gas property expenses[65] incurred by the partnership in the fiscal period.

In other words, a limited partner is restricted in deducting his or her share of most business and property losses from a partnership to the extent that such losses exceed the difference between the at-risk amount and the

See page ii for explanation of footnotes.

[56] CCH ¶12,149d; Sec. 96(2.4).
[57] CCH ¶12,149e; Sec. 96(2.5).
[58] CCH ¶12,149f–12,149g; Sec. 96(2.6), 96(2.7).
[59] CCH ¶12,149ac; Sec. 96(2.1).
[60] CCH ¶19,828; Sec. 127(8).

[61] CCH ¶5660; Sec. 31.
[62] CCH ¶8982; Sec. 66(15).
[63] CCH ¶9030; Sec. 66.1(6).
[64] CCH ¶9070; Sec. 66.2(5).
[65] CCH ¶9084g; Sec. 66.4(5).

limited partner's share of the aggregate of investment tax credits, farming losses, and exploration and development expenses of the partnership.

Losses rendered non-deductible are designated as limited partnership losses and as such are eligible for an indefinite carryforward against future income from the partnership which generated the losses. As well, limited partnership losses may be deducted in future years where the taxpayer's at-risk amount in respect of the partnership increases, for example, by way of an increased investment in the partnership. [66]

[¶7065] "At-Risk Amount" Defined

The "at-risk amount" at any particular time is calculated as follows:

(a) the limited partner's adjusted cost base of his or her partnership interest,

plus:

(b) when computed at the end of the partnership's fiscal period, the limited partner's share of the current year's income and of proceeds of disposition of resource property which may be added to the partner's ACB of the partnership interest for the year,

minus:

(c) all amounts owing by the partner (or a person not dealing at arm's length with the partner) to the partnership (or a person not dealing at arm's length with the partnership) and all amounts or benefits to which the partner (or a person not dealing at arm's length with the partner) is entitled, where such amount or benefit is intended to protect the partner from an investment loss.[67]

With the introduction of new negative ACB rules for limited partners (¶7097), certain non-recourse financing of the partners' partnership interest will reduce the cost base of the partner and potentially create income. Where the adjustment is made to partnership ACB, it does not also reduce the at-risk amount under (c) above. Similarly, where the cost of a partnership interest is reduced by a loan to the partnership under the non-recourse financing rules at ¶9300, the at-risk amount is not reduced again.

For the purpose of the reduction of the at-risk amount in respect of amounts owing to the partnership, loans between persons not dealing at arm's length with the partner or the partnership are taken into account.[68] Thus, for example, where a general partner of a partnership has lent money to a limited partner in order to fund that limited partner's contribution to the partnership, the amount of that loan will reduce the limited partner's at-risk amount. Similarly, where an amount or benefit is made available to a

---

[66] CCH ¶16,070; Sec. 111(1)(e). [68] CCH ¶12,149g; Sec. 96(2.7).
[67] CCH ¶12,149b; Sec. 96(2.2).

person with whom the limited partner does not deal at arm's length, a reduction of the limited partner's at-risk amount will be required. A limited partner's at-risk amount is not reduced by protection from a loss on his or her investment that takes the form of:

(1) normal liability insurance protection;

(2) an agreement to purchase the partnership interest at any time at its fair market value at that time; or

(3) a buy-sell agreement relating to the partnership interest that applies in the event of the death of the owner.

Where a limited partner or a non-arm's length person has a right to exchange the partnership interest for some other property, the partner or person is considered to be entitled to an amount or benefit protecting the partner from loss, to the extent of the fair market value of the other property at the time at which the at-risk amount is being computed.

Where a limited partnership interest is acquired by a second or subsequent owner, a special rule provides for the determination of the amount to be used as a limited partner's cost of his or her partnership interest.[69] If the limited partner is not the first person to acquire the interest, the cost of the interest, for the purposes only of the at-risk rules, is the lesser of its actual cost and the adjusted cost base of the taxpayer from whom it was acquired (but not less than zero).

Anti-avoidance provisions prevent artificial increases in the at-risk amount of a limited partner by way of a series of payments or loans and repayments between the partner and the partnership.[70]

[¶7070] Meaning of "Limited Partner"

Only a limited partner is subject to the at-risk rules. The definition of "limited partner" is drafted in such a way as to include not only limited partners of a limited partnership as determined under provincial law, but also certain partners in a general partnership where limited liability is achieved indirectly.[71] For the CRA's views on the meaning of partnership, see Interpretation Bulletin IT-90, "What Is a Partnership?". In general terms, under the partnership legislation of each province, a partnership can be structured as a general partnership in which each partner is jointly and severally liable for the debts of the partnership. Alternatively, a partnership can be structured as a limited partnership in which the limited partners are only liable for the debts of the partnership in an amount not exceeding their unpaid capital committed to the partnership.

Members of a limited liability partnership ("LLP"), structured under the laws of certain provinces that govern many professional partnerships,

---

See page ii for explanation of footnotes.

[69] CCH ¶12,149c; Sec. 96(2.3).   [71] CCH ¶12,149d; Sec. 96(2.4).
[70] CCH ¶12,149f; Sec. 96(2.6).

are excluded from the scope of the limited partnership rules, at least as far as the activities of the LLP are concerned.

The definition of limited partner excludes partners whose interest in the partnership is an exempt interest (see ¶7075). If the partnership interest is not an exempt interest, a partner is deemed to be a limited partner for the purposes of the at-risk rules if, at the time or within three years after that time, one or more of the following conditions are met:

(1) The partner's liability as a partner is limited by law. This provision would generally apply to the limited partners of a limited partnership. For example, under section 8 of the *Limited Partnership Act of Ontario*, a limited partner is not liable for the obligations of the limited partnership except in respect of the value of money and other property the partner contributes or agrees to contribute to the limited partnership, as stated in the declaration.

(2) The partner (or a non-arm's length person) is entitled either immediately or in the future and either contingently or absolutely to receive an amount or obtain a benefit which reduces the "at-risk amount" described at ¶7065 (assuming those benefits did not exclude amounts not included in the at-risk rules in the first place).

(3) One of the reasons for the existence of the partner may reasonably be considered to be to limit the liability of any person in respect of the partnership interest and may not reasonably be considered to be to permit a person who has an interest in the partner to carry on his business (other than an investment business) in the most effective manner. It appears that this provision is meant to include a "shell" corporation (i.e., corporation with no assets) that is a partner in a general partnership. If not for this provision, losses which are incurred by such a shell corporation could be utilized in the future by amalgamating the shell corporation with a profitable corporation or by transferring a profitable business to the shell corporation. However, if it can be shown that the business is being carried on in the most effective manner, the partner will not be considered to be a limited partner.

(4) There is an agreement or other arrangement for the disposition of the partnership interest and one of the main reasons for such agreement or arrangement may reasonably be to avoid the definition of limited partner. It is difficult to imagine such a situation that would not also be caught under (2) above. However, the Department of Finance in the technical explanation to the legislation refers to an agreement to wind up the partnership as being covered by this provision.

[¶7075] Meaning of "Exempt Interest"

The definition of limited partners specifically excludes a partner from being a limited partner if his or her partnership interest is an exempt interest at the relevant time.

¶7075

The at-risk rules apply to a taxpayer who is a limited partner at any time during the taxpayer's taxation year.[72] Accordingly, it is relevant to maintain exempt interest status throughout the partner's taxation year. The fiscal period of the partnership is not relevant for this purpose.

In general, "exempt interest" is defined as at a particular time and means[73] an interest in a partnership that was carrying on business or earning income from the rental or leasing of property on a regular and continuous basis on February 25, 1986 (June 17, 1987, for resource expenses) and continually thereafter until that particular time. Nevertheless, a partnership interest can lose exempt status where, after February 25, 1986 (June 17, 1987, for resource expenses), there has been substantial contribution of capital to the partnership or substantial partnership borrowings. The rules allow three circumstances where such contributions or borrowings will not be considered substantial. These circumstances are:

(1) where the funds are required to fulfill contractual obligations entered into by the partnership before February 26, 1986 (June 18, 1987, for resource expenses);

(2) where the funds are raised pursuant to a prospectus, preliminary prospectus, or registration statement filed with the appropriate securities authority before February 26, 1986 (for resource expenses, pursuant to an "offering memorandum or notice required to be filed before any distribution of securities may commence" filed before June 18, 1987); or

(3) where the use of the funds was for the day-to-day operations or maintenance of the activity as it existed on February 25, 1986 (June 17, 1987, for resource expenses).

Funds will be considered to have been *required* to fulfil a contractual obligation to make an expenditure entered into before February 26, 1986 (June 18, 1987, for resource expenses), if the obligation is unconditional, or, if a condition is applicable after June 11, 1986 (June 17, 1987, for resource expenses), the condition does not relate to any change in the tax consequences of the expenditure. Accordingly, an obligation conditional upon entitlement to transitional relief or grandfather protection would not be considered to have been *required* to have been made.

[¶7085] At-Risk Resource Rules

The at-risk rules for limited partnerships apply to resource expenditures incurred by such partnerships. As a result, the deductibility of resource expenditures allocated to a limited partner is restricted to the amount of investment the partner has at risk.[74] Where the taxpayer's share of expenditures is greater than the at-risk amount, the excess may be carried forward

---

See page ii for explanation of footnotes.

[72] CCH ¶12,149ac; Sec. 96(2.1).   [74] CCH ¶9105; Sec. 66.8.
[73] CCH ¶12,149e; Sec. 96(2.5).

indefinitely and deducted in future years when the taxpayer is at risk for the excess.

[¶7090] Transactions in Partnership Interests

[¶7095] When Dispositions Occur

A taxpayer's interest in a partnership is considered capital property (except for a person who trades in partnership interests as a business). Thus, any sale or deemed disposition will give rise to a capital gain or loss. A partner can acquire an interest in a partnership by merely becoming a member of a partnership and contributing cash or property to it. Alternatively, a partner may purchase an existing interest from one of the partners.

A partner may dispose of an interest in a partnership by transferring all or part of it to another taxpayer or by receiving full payment from the partnership in satisfaction of his or her interest. Where a partnership is dissolved, the partners are deemed to have disposed of their partnership interest, subject to rollover rules discussed at ¶7155.

Generally, for the purposes of calculating capital gains, when the ACB of a capital property is a negative amount, the negative amount is considered to be a capital gain (see Chapter V). However, if the ACB of an interest in a partnership is negative, no capital gains will arise, except in the following circumstances:

(1) If a partner disposes of all or part of his or her interest in a partnership when the ACB of the interest is negative, that partner must report a capital gain equal to the proceeds of disposition plus the negative ACB of his or her interest in the partnership, or the part of the interest that is sold.[75]

(2) Where the partner's residual interest is satisfied in full in the partnership's fiscal year in which he or she withdraws, it is deemed not to have been disposed of until the end of the fiscal period of the partnership. This provision allows time for any adjustments to be made in respect of his or her last fiscal year before the deemed disposition occurs. Where the ACB of the residual interest becomes negative at the fiscal year end of the partnership, the negative amount is deemed to be a capital gain.[76]

(3) Where a partnership ceases to exist but all of the partnership property has not been distributed, each person who was a partner is deemed not to have ceased to be a partner and the right of each such person to share in the partnership property is deemed to be an interest in the partnership. If the ACB of such a partnership interest is a negative amount, the person deemed to own such partnership interest will be deemed to have a capital gain in that year equal to the negative amount.[77]

See page ii for explanation of footnotes.

[75] CCH ¶12,326; Sec. 100(2).   [77] CCH ¶12,251; Sec. 98(1).
[76] CCH ¶12,304; Sec. 98.1(1).

[¶7097] Negative Partnership ACB of Limited Partner

As explained at ¶7095 above, because of its unique characteristics and numerous adjustments (see ¶7100 and ¶7105), the ACB of a partnership is generally exempt from the rule that a negative ACB at the end of the year results in a deemed capital gain. However, after February 21, 1994, where the partnership ACB of a "limited partner" or "specified member" of a partnership is negative at the end of a particular fiscal period of the partnership, the amount of negative ACB is a deemed capital gain and the ACB itself is reset to nil. The purpose of this exercise is to prevent the passive investor from claiming deductible losses and receiving cash distributions that exceed the amount invested. These rules will allow a partner's subsequent positive ACB at the end of a partnership's fiscal period to be claimed (and carried back to offset the gain where timing permits) as a capital loss to the extent of prior deemed gains. The rules do not apply to members of a limited liability partnership (LLP) (see below).[78]

These rules apply only where, at the end of the fiscal period of the partnership, a partner is a limited partner or a specified member of a partnership, and was a specified member at all times since becoming a member. They do not apply where the partner held the partnership interest on February 22, 1994, and the partnership has been carrying on an active business, or earning income from a property owned continuously on and after that date. However, the exception will cease where there is a substantial contribution of capital to or substantial increase in the indebtedness of the partnership. Added capital or debt is permitted to finance an activity carried on by the partnership on February 22, 1994, but not to finance a significant expansion of the activity.

The term "limited partner" has a special extended meaning in the context of the negative partnership ACB rules. A limited partner in this context at a particular time will include a partner if, within three years after the time, the partner acquires a limited liability by operation of partnership law.

A specified member of a partnership is either a limited partner under the definition at ¶7070, or any member of a partnership who is not:

(a) actively engaged in activities of the partnership business other than financing, or

(b) carrying on a similar business outside the partnership as that carried on by the partnership

on a regular, continuous, and substantial basis throughout that part of the period or year during which the business of the partnership is ordinarily carried on and during which the member is a member of the partnership.[79] This definition will generally include any passive partner.

See page ii for explanation of footnotes.

[78] CCH ¶6445–6454; Sec. 40(3.1)–(3.19).   [79] CCH ¶28,272d; Sec. 248(1) "specified member".

Several provinces have introduced legislation to allow professionals to carry on their practice as a limited liability partnership (LLP) if all partners agree, professional standards permit, and professional liability insurance is carried. These rules are not unlike the ordinary provincial limited liability partnership laws to the extent that, under the professional LLP rules, partners remain liable for the general debts and obligations of the partnership. The benefit under the professional LLP rules is that in the case of a claim by a client for negligence, only the assets of the partner providing advice would be available to the claimant, and not the assets of all partners.

Technical amendments, sanctioned June 14, 2001, but retroactive to 1998, provide that the rule taxing negative ACB of a limited partner will not apply where the limited liability arises from a statutory provision providing only the kinds of limitation found in professional LLP statutes. Specifically, a limited partner will not include a partner whose liability is limited by operation of a federal or provincial statute that limits the partner's liability only for debts, obligations, and liabilities of the partnership or any member, arising from negligent acts or omissions that another member or employee, agent, or representative committed in the course of the partnership business.

[¶7098] Non-Recourse Financing

Where the partnership interest of a limited partner or a specified member (as defined in ¶7097) is financed with non-recourse debt, other than a debt entered into pursuant to an agreement in writing entered into by the taxpayer before September 27, 1994, the adjusted cost base as described at ¶7105 is further reduced by the unpaid principal amount of any debt of the partner in respect of which recourse against the partner is limited, either absolutely or contingently, if it can reasonably be considered to have been used to acquire the property.

Non-recourse financing associated with the acquisition of tax shelters which are or should have been registered as such will include the following types of financing:

(a) those where a rate of interest equal to or greater than the prescribed rate of interest in effect at the time the unpaid principal arises or is incurred, is not charged and paid within 60 days after the end of the tax shelter investor's taxation year; and

(b) those where *bona fide* arrangements are not made, at the time the unpaid principal arises or is incurred, for the repayment within a reasonable period not exceeding 10 years of the principal, and any interest thereon, in full.

These new rules are effective after November 30, 1994, subject to elaborate grandfathering provisions, primarily for investments made in certain tax shelters in process in 1994, and in some cases, 1995.

¶7098

[¶7100] Adjusted Cost Base — Amounts To Be Added

Basically, the adjusted cost base of an interest in a partnership is the cost of the interest after adjustments for drawings, earnings, and other transactions which affect the value of the interest in the partnership. The word "cost" has its usual meaning in that it is the value of any payment by the partner, either in cash or other consideration, to acquire his or her partnership interest.

The adjusted cost base is arrived at by adding or subtracting various adjustments to the cost of an interest in a partnership. The following amounts are *added:*

(1) *Income of partnership.* A partner must add to the cost of the partnership interest his or her share of the income of the partnership, excluding, however, income allocated to a retired partner who is deemed to be a member of the partnership (see ¶7190).

In this computation, income is calculated under the normal income tax rules except that:

(a) 100% instead of 50% (or the applicable percentage for the year) of capital gains on the disposal of partnership capital properties are included;

(b) 100% of any hobby farm loss is included in computing the loss of the partnership instead of only $8,750 of this amount;

(c) the actual amount of any income or expense relating to eligible capital property is included, not the percentage added to (or recaptured from) the depreciation pool;

(d) exempt income from a new mine is included;

(e) amounts paid to the federal government pursuant to the *Petroleum and Gas Revenue Tax Act* are deducted;

(f) the "gross-up" of taxable dividends received from taxable Canadian corporations is excluded;[80]

(g) royalties payable or receivable pursuant to a federal statute in respect of resource property or production are excluded;[81]

(h) the deduction for the 3% inventory allowance is excluded;

(i) the deduction for the cost of a basic herd of farm animals is excluded;

(j) deemed fair market values as they apply to the trading of resources with governments are excluded from consideration;

See page ii for explanation of footnotes.

[80] CCH ¶10,003; Sec. 82(1)(b).   [81] CCH ¶4371, ¶4852, ¶5119a; Sec. 12(1)(o), 18(1)(m), 20(1)(v.1).

(k) any capital gain on farmland is computed without the increase in its adjusted cost base otherwise allowed for hobby-farm losses; and

(l) capital gains and losses are computed without reference to any artificial reduction in capital gains as calculated by the CRA.

(2) *Capital dividends of partnership.* The partner adds to the cost of the partnership interest his or her share of any capital dividend from a corporation in which the partnership holds stock and his or her share of any life insurance capital dividend received by the partnership.

(3) *Superficial loss.* Added to the cost of an interest in a Partnership is the amount of any superficial loss relating to a transaction by the partner involving an interest in the partnership (see ¶5090).

(4) *Life insurance proceeds.* The partner's share of the proceeds of any life insurance policy is added to the cost of his or her partnership interest, less the adjusted cost base of the policy immediately before the death of the insured.

(5) *Contributions to capital.* If the partner makes a contribution to partnership capital, any portion of that contribution that cannot be regarded as a benefit conferred on another partner who is related to the partner by blood, marriage, or adoption is added to the adjusted cost base of the partnership interest.

(6) *Rights or things.* The legal representatives of a deceased taxpayer must include in the taxpayer's income for the year of death the value of any right or thing which, if realized or disposed of, would be included in computing income. Any amount so included in respect of the partnership is added to the partner's adjusted cost base of his or her partnership interest.

(7) *Resource properties.* Proceeds of disposition of Canadian resource properties and recoveries of exploration or development expenses arising in a partnership are taken into account in computing income at the partner level. The amount so taken into account adds to the partner's adjusted cost base of his or her partnership interest. Accordingly, if the partner disposes of this interest before the proceeds of disposition or the recovery have been distributed, the partner will not realize a capital gain on an amount already included in computing income.

(8) *Government assistance in respect of resource properties.* The adjusted cost base of a partnership interest is increased to the extent of the partner's share of any government money received in respect of a Canadian resource property or an exploration or development expense incurred in Canada reduced by any repayments of such amounts.

(9) *Deemed capital gain on residual partnership interest.* A partner may have a residual interest in a partnership either because the partner has a right to the undistributed property of a partnership that has ceased to exist, or because the partner has ceased to be a member of a partnership without

¶7100

receiving full settlement of his or her partnership interest. In both cases, if the adjusted cost base of the partnership interest becomes "negative", this negative amount is treated as an immediate capital gain.

(10) *Vacant land and construction soft costs.* For partners with a 10% or more share of income or loss at any particular time, any amount of interest or tax on vacant land or construction soft costs denied to them for years commencing before that time is added to ACB.

(11) *Negative partnership ACB of limited or passive partner.* Where a limited or passive partner has a negative partnership adjusted cost base (ACB) included in income under the rules in ¶7097, the income inclusion is added to the partner's partnership ACB to return it to zero.

(12) *Final capital gains exemption election.* Where an election was made to have a deemed disposition of a partnership interest on February 22, 1994, and there is a final disposition before the exempt capital gains balance expires immediately before 2004, the unused balance is added to the cost base of the partnership interest.

(13) *Property rolled into partnership.* In certain circumstances, a partner is permitted to transfer property to a Canadian partnership on a tax-deferred basis provided that the partner is one of its partners immediately after the transfer.[82] An amount must be added to the partner's adjusted cost base of the partnership interest where the partner's proceeds of disposition exceed the fair market value of the hard consideration received or where a majority interest partner would otherwise realize a capital loss. Similarly, a deduction is provided from a partner's adjusted cost base of his or her partnership interest where the fair market value of the paid consideration received exceeds the partner's proceeds of disposition.

(14) *Recapture of investment tax credit.* Where an amount is added to the partner's tax payable as recapture of an investment tax credit formerly allocated by the partnership to the partner, the amount is in turn added to the partner's adjusted cost base of his interest in the partnership.

(15) *[Gains from the disposition of certified cultural property.* As previously noted in (1), the full amount of a partnership's capital gain from the disposition of property is added to the adjusted cost base (ACB) of the members' interest in the partnership. However, since gains from certified cultural property are excluded from the definition of capital gains, such gains generated within a partnership are not added in computing the members' ACB of their partnership interest. Consequently, the disposition by a partnership of a certified cultural property to a designated institution may result in a capital gain to the partners on the disposition of their interest. In a comfort letter dated January 29, 2004, the Department of Finance announced that it will recommend an amendment so that the exempt gain

---

[82] CCH ¶12,175; Sec. 97(1).

from the disposition of a certified cultural property is included in computing the ACB of a partnership interest, except such property that is related to a tax shelter gifting arrangement. It will recommend that such an amendment apply in respect of dispositions of certified cultural property made after 2003.]

(16) [*Foreign resource property (FRP)*. Where a taxpayer is a member of a partnership, the taxpayer's share of the net proceeds of disposition of an FRP disposed of by the partnership is deemed to be included in the taxpayer's income. However, there is no provision of the Act that permits an addition to the adjusted cost base of the partnership interest held by the taxpayer. In a comfort letter dated July 16, 2004, the Department of Finance recommended that a concurrent amendment be made to ensure that the proceeds of disposition deemed to become receivable by a partner be added to the ACB of that partner's partnership interest. Such an amendment will apply in respect of fiscal periods that begin after 2000.]

(17) [*Non-deductible resource Crown charges*. Where a taxpayer reimburses another person for specified non-deductible resource Crown charges, resource rules provide for the transfer of those charges and the associated resource allowance to the taxpayer, subject to certain adjustments which may deny elements of deduction. Pending technical amendments, first published in 2005 and last contained in the revised technical proposals that were released on July 16, 2007, will allow an addition to the partnership cost base for such non-deductible amounts, for taxation years ending after 2002.]

[¶7105] Adjusted Cost Base — Amounts To Be Deducted

If a taxpayer holds an interest in a partnership, the adjusted cost base of that interest must be reduced by the following amounts:

(1) the partner's share of any loss of the partnership, computed according to the same exceptional rules followed when determining the share of income added to the adjusted cost base (see item (1) at ¶7100). It should be noted that losses *allocated* must be deducted from the adjusted cost base, regardless of whether the loss is utilized by the partner at that time. Limited partnership losses (that is, the excess of losses over at-risk amount) are not subject to this rule, but are deducted from the adjusted cost base only when deducted from the partner's taxable income;

(2) the partner's share of any Canadian exploration and development expenses, Canadian exploration expenses, Canadian development expenses, and Canadian oil and gas property expenses. These amounts, while incurred by the partnership, are not deducted by it in computing its income or loss, but by the individual partner. In the event that the partner ceases to be a partner in a particular taxation year, the partner's share of the resource-related deductions and expenses for that year does not reduce the adjusted cost base of the partner's partnership interest;

(3) the partner's share in the "eligible amount" of (see ¶8175) any charitable donations or political contributions made by the partnership and deductible or creditable, as the case may be;

(4) any amount paid to a partner in respect of the partner's share of profits of the partnership or the partner's investment in the capital of the partnership, except for amounts paid to a former partner in respect of his or her income rights under the partnership;

(5) the amount of any investment tax credit, claimed by the partner, that was allocated by the partnership. In this case, the reduction in adjusted cost base takes place when the credit is deducted, not when the credit is allocated;

(6) the partner's share of a share-purchase tax credit or the amount of the partner's share in any scientific research tax credit that was allocated by the partnership;

(7) any grant, subsidy, or other governmental assistance (net of repayments) received by the partner in connection with the acquisition of the partnership interest;

(8) the partner's share of undeducted financing costs described at ¶3303 and ¶3306 which have ceased to be deductible to the partnership by virtue of its termination;

(9) any amount received by a retired partner or any beneficiary as payment of account of his or her residual interest;

(10) any amount which is required to be deducted because of settlement of a debt by a partner for less than its principal amount;

(11) where there has been a partial disposition of an interest in the partnership, the adjusted cost base at the time of disposition of the part so disposed;

(12) the partner's drawings on account of his or her share of the partnership's income or capital. Any expenses incurred at the partnership level that were not allowed in computing the partnership income and that were personal expenses of a partner represent payments on behalf of that partner and should be treated as drawings on account of income or capital;

(13) where a limited or passive partner has financed the acquisition of a partnership interest or an investment in the partnership with non-recourse debt described at ¶7098, the adjusted cost base of the partner's partnership interest (which on its face would include the amount so financed) is reduced by the non-recourse debt, unless the non-recourse debt is already dealt with under the tax shelter rules at ¶9300;

(14) where a negative partnership adjusted cost base (ACB) has been included in a partner's capital gains under the rules at ¶7097, a subsequent increase in ACB may be treated as a capital loss at the election of the

partner, offsetting prior gains. Where this election is made, the loss reduces the partner's ACB;

(15) only for the purpose of calculating the partnership's adjusted cost base (ACB) in making a final capital gains exemption election to have a deemed disposition of the partnership interest at February 22, 1994, the normal reduction to ACB for current-year losses is prorated for the period of the year before February 23, 1994. This limited-purpose reduction does not permanently affect ACB; it exists only for calculating election values; and

(16) the amount of private health insurance premiums that were deductible in computing the income of an individual carrying on business through a partnership (see ¶3358).

[¶7107] Foreign Partnerships

Where a resident of Canada becomes a member of a partnership which previously had no Canadian resident members (for instance, as a result of an existing member becoming resident in Canada, or of a resident of Canada becoming a new member of the partnership), the (new) Canadian partner is prevented from claiming losses previously realized in the partnership from dispositions of property, and from benefiting from unrealized losses inherent in any partnership property.[83] In such a case, the partnership's capital cost of its depreciable capital property becomes the lesser of the fair market value thereof immediately after the Canadian resident becomes a partner, and the cost otherwise determined. This forms the basis for claiming future capital cost allowance, but subject to adjustments for previous recapture inclusions or depreciation deductions made for Canadian tax purposes. Similarly, the partnership's inventory, non-depreciable capital properties and eligible capital properties are effectively marked down to the lesser of fair market value and the cost otherwise determined. Prior partnership losses from dispositions of property (occurring before there were any Canadian resident partners) are denied for Canadian tax purposes.

Were it not for this provision, partnership properties with unrealized losses (which accrued while no members were resident in Canada) could be sold at a loss and arguably be allocated to the Canadian resident partner for the purposes of computing that partner's income or loss from the partnership for Canadian income tax purposes.

Where there already is a Canadian resident member of the foreign partnership before another Canadian resident becomes a partner, and it may reasonably be considered that one of the main reasons for the first Canadian resident member being a partner is to avoid the future application of the foreign partnership rule upon the second Canadian resident becoming a partner, the first Canadian member will be deemed not to be resident in Canada.[84]

---

[83] CCH ¶12,170; Sec. 96(8).   [84] CCH ¶12,171; Sec. 96(9).

[¶7110] Contribution of Property to Partnership

[¶7115] Property Transfer to Partnership

Property transfers to a partnership from partners or from persons who, immediately after the transfer, are partners, are deemed to have taken place at the fair market value of the property at the time of transfer.[85] Accordingly, on the formation of a partnership or on admittance to an existing partnership, the new partner is deemed to have disposed of the property introduced into the partnership at its fair market value and the partnership is deemed to have acquired the property at that value.

[¶7120] Election for Canadian Partnerships

To avoid the tax on what may in fact be an unrealized gain, partners of a Canadian partnership may jointly elect, in prescribed form and within prescribed time, to have an "agreed amount" deemed to be the proceeds of disposition of the property to the partners and the same amount deemed to be the cost of the property acquired by the partnership. (See ¶7240 for a definition of "Canadian partnership".) This election may be made with respect to transfers of capital property, resource properties, eligible capital property, and inventory.[86]

The following rules apply to the election:[87]

(1) The agreed amount constitutes the proceeds of disposition and the cost of the property transferred, subject to the provisions for adjustments to the agreed amount to ensure that it reflects the transaction's economic substance (see (2) to (7) below).

(2) An excessive agreed amount is automatically reduced to the fair market value of the transferred property, preventing an artificial increase in the transferee's cost base of the property. Correspondingly, an initial agreed amount is increased to the fair market value of the hard consideration received if the initial agreed amount is less than this value.

(3) An agreed amount will be automatically increased to the lesser of:

(a) the property's fair market value, and

(b) its cost amount.

(4) An initial agreed amount is automatically adjusted to the least of:

(a) the undepreciated capital cost (UCC) of all property in the class, or $^4/_3$ of the cumulative eligible capital (CEC) of the business, as the case may be (the gross-up of CEC is required to reflect the fact that only $^3/_4$ of the cost of eligible capital property acquired is

---

See page ii for explanation of footnotes.

[85] CCH ¶12,175; Sec. 97(1).
[86] CCH ¶12,177, ¶52,418; Sec. 97(2); Interp. Bul. IT-413R.
[87] CCH ¶10,500, ¶12,177; Sec. 85(1)(a)–(f), 97(2).

added to the CEC); note that no adjustment to the $^4/_3$ fraction is necessary in or after 2000, since the eligible capital property pool continues to operate in the $^3/_4$ mode;

(b) the cost of the property; and

(c) the fair market value of the property.

(5) When the UCC (or CEC) represents more than one property, the transferor is allowed to determine the order of disposition and failing so, the order can be designated by the Minister. For example, consider two class 8 properties:

	Property A	Property B
Cost of property	$2,000	$5,000
Fair market value	1,000	6,000
Undepreciated capital cost of class	$4,000	

The transferor could designate Property A as the first disposed of (at an agreed amount of $1,000), reducing the undepreciated capital cost of the class to $3,000 so that this amount could be used as the minimum agreed amount for Property B.

(6) The agreed amount may automatically be adjusted where the total value of the consideration received (both hard consideration and partnership interests) is less than the fair market value of the property transferred. The adjustment will only be made if it is reasonable to regard any portion of the shortfall as a gift or benefit that the transferor made or conferred on another member of the partnership and then only to the extent the agreed amount does not reflect the value of the gift or benefit. In this case, the agreed amount will be increased by the gift portion, up to the value of the property transferred.

Example:

Assume Mr. X transfers property with a tax value of $500 and a value of $5,000 to a partnership in which his children are the only members; he takes a partnership interest value at $100 as the only consideration, and elects an agreed amount of $500. This represents a $4,900 benefit or gift, only $500 of which has been reflected in the agreed amount. Theoretically, the amount of the gift increases the agreed amount up to the value of the transferred property. Technically, $4,500 (the difference between the $5,000 value of the property and the greater of the $500 agreed amount and the total consideration of $100) is added to the initial agreed amount.

The result in this example is an adjusted agreed amount (and therefore proceeds of disposition) equal to the fair market value of the transferred property so that there is not a rollover.

(7) The deemed amounts are in turn subject to the rules described in (2) above.

(8) The cost of the property received as consideration will be the lesser of:

(a) the value of the property received, and

(b) a prorated portion of the value of the transferred property. This portion is determined by dividing the value of the particular property received by the value of all property received as hard consideration.

(9) Any excess of the agreed amount over the value of all hard consideration received is added to the transferor's adjusted cost base of his or her partnership interest and the adjusted cost base of a partnership interest is reduced by any excess of the value of hard consideration received over the value of the property transferred.

(10) The partnership interest received as consideration for the disposition is deemed to be property excluded from the deemed disposition rule upon departure, if the transferred property was so excluded.

An election must be made on or before the earliest deadline for filing an income tax return of any member of the partnership.[88] Where only individuals are members of the partnership, the filing deadline will be April 30 of the year following the transaction. However, where corporations having different taxation years are in partnership, the requirement becomes more complicated.

Example:

Corporation A has a March 31 year end, and on February 28 transfers property to a partnership with a January 31 year end. Corporation B is the other partner and has a December 31 year end. An election must be made on or before September 30, which is the deadline for filing Corporation A's return. Where an election is being made in respect of the dissolution of the partnership on February 28, both Corporation A and Corporation B must file their elections by September 30.

A late election will be accepted if made within three years of the deadline and the estimated penalty amount is paid together with the election.[89] An effective election may also be filed beyond the three-year period or amended if the Minister considers it just and equitable in the circumstances.[90] The penalty for a late-filed or amended election is the lesser of:

(a) one-quarter of 1% of the difference between the elected amount and the fair market value of each property for each month or part thereof falling after the deadline, and

(b) $100 per month or part thereof to a maximum of $8,000.[91]

The Minister is required to examine the election or amended election, assess the penalty, and issue a notice of assessment, at which time any balance of penalty becomes payable.[92]

[88] CCH ¶12,155; Sec. 96(4).
[89] CCH ¶12,160; Sec. 96(5).
[90] CCH ¶12,162; Sec. 96(5.1).

[91] CCH ¶12,165; Sec. 96(6).

[92] CCH ¶12,167; Sec. 96(7).

[¶7130] Transfer of Depreciable Property — Recapture

Depreciable property transferred to a partnership at an amount agreed upon by all partners, as reported in a prescribed election form, will carry with it into the partnership the potential recapture of depreciation not recaptured by the transferring partner at that time. Where a partner transfers such property to a partnership for an amount less than his or her capital cost, the partnership will be deemed to have acquired the property at an amount equal to the capital cost of the property to the partner and will be subject to tax on recaptured depreciation realized on a future sale.[93]

Example:

Assume that Mr. T, a partner in an existing partnership, transfers depreciable property in 1972 to the partnership, having a Valuation Day value and a fair market value at the time of transfer of $9,000, for an amount agreed upon by all partners of $10,000 and receives as consideration $8,000. Assume further that the capital cost of this property to Mr. T amounted to $15,000 and his undepreciated capital of this relevant class of assets at the time of transfer was $7,500.

Since the amount agreed upon of $10,000, is in excess of the fair market value of $9,000, it would not be acceptable and the "deemed" amount would be $9,000.

The capital cost of the property to the partnership would be $15,000, and it would be deemed to have been allowed $6,000 as capital cost allowance deductions in computing income for taxation years prior to the year of acquisition. Accordingly, the potential tax liability for $6,000 of depreciation not recaptured by Mr. T (cost $15,000 less $9,000 deemed consideration = $6,000) is passed on to the partnership. Any gain realized by the partnership on the subsequent sale of this depreciable property in excess of $15,000 would be taxable as a capital gain.

The partner transferring the property to the partnership would account for this transaction as follows:

(1) His deemed proceeds (the amount "deemed" agreed by all partners) of $9,000 would be credited to his asset class of property transferred. If the property is the only asset in the class, he would be subject to tax on recaptured depreciation of $1,500 (deemed proceeds of $9,000 less undepreciated capital cost of $7,500).

(2) No capital gain would result as the deemed proceeds of $9,000 are less than the greater of Valuation Day value of $9,000 or cost of $15,000. No capital loss would result, since the property disposed of is depreciable property and, as such, its disposal cannot cause a capital loss.

(3) The partner's adjusted cost base in the partnership would be increased by $1,000, the difference between the deemed proceeds of $9,000 and the consideration received on the transfer of the depreciable property of $8,000.

The partner would not be precluded from selling the depreciable property to the partnership at less than his undepreciated capital loss, subject to the possible application of the stop-loss rules described at ¶4485.

[¶7135] Purchase of Partnership Interest by New Partner — Goodwill

The valuation rules pertaining to the transfer of property to a partnership also apply to property transferred to an existing partnership on admission to the partnership by a new partner who formerly was a partner in another partnership, was a sole proprietor, or was not in business. Where on

---

See page ii for explanation of footnotes.

[93] CCH ¶12,201; Sec. 97(4).

¶7130

admission to partnership the incoming partner does not transfer property to the partnership, but instead, purchases a partnership interest from one or more of the other partners, the new partner will treat the purchase price as the cost of his or her partnership interest. No portion of this cost is deemed to represent an eligible capital expenditure. Therefore, the new partner will not be allowed to depreciate $3/4$ of that part of the outlay that he or she might consider to be applicable to goodwill (at a maximum rate of 7% per annum on a declining balance). The partner's cost of the partnership interest and the adjusted cost base would reflect any goodwill existing within the partnership and, on disposal, would reflect a capital gain or loss.

[¶7137] Effect of Election — Example

The joint election permits property to be transferred to a Canadian partnership on a fully or partially tax deferred basis as desired. Generally, the election is used to fully defer tax by transferring the property at tax values (e.g., adjusted cost base, undepreciated capital cost). In this case, the tax values of the property are allocated to the consideration received (forming its cost base) and the partnership assumes the transferee's tax position in respect of the property. The following example will illustrate the effect of an election.

Example:

Assume the following:

	Original cost	Tax values	Market value	Fair agreed amount
Inventory	$ 300	$ 300	$ 400	$ 300
Building	20,000	12,000	15,000	12,000
Land	10,000	10,000	30,000	10,000

Further assume that the only consideration received was a partnership interest with a value equal to the combined fair market value of the property transferred.

The agreed amount was selected for each property so that the transferee would not realize any income, recapture, or capital gains. The adjusted cost base of the partnership interest will be $22,300 (equal to the total of the agreed amounts, and also the tax values of the transferred property).[94]

The partnership will be deemed to have acquired the property at the agreed amounts and will use these for computing its taxable income in the future. The partnership will be deemed to have the same original cost of $20,000 for the building as the transferor and to have claimed capital cost allowance of $8,000, being the difference between the cost and the agreed amount (i.e., the undepreciated capital cost).[95] The partnership, therefore, inherits the transferor's position regarding future recapture and/or capital gains on the building.

As an alternative, the transferee could have received property other than a partnership interest (such as cash or debt, i.e., "hard consideration") as part of the consideration. The tax-deferred status of the transfer is preserved in this case provided this form of consideration

See page ii for explanation of footnotes.

[94] CCH ¶12,177; Sec. 97(2)(b).   [95] CCH ¶12,201; Sec. 97(4).

does not exceed the agreed amounts. In this example, the transferor could, for instance, receive $22,300 of debt and a partnership interest valued at $23,100 for total consideration equal to the value of the property transferred ($45,400). The adjusted cost base of the partnership interest will be nil since the entire agreed amount is absorbed by the debt consideration.

[¶7140] Disposition of Partnership Property

[¶7145] Deemed Disposition of Property by Partnership

In the absence of any special provision, a transfer of assets from a partnership to a partner is treated as a simple sale and purchase at fair market value regardless, apparently, of the actual consideration.[96]

If all property of the partnership has been distributed to the partners, the partnership is no longer deemed to exist. If the property has been distributed in such a manner that each partner received his or her individual share of the property (such as specific accounts receivable allocated to each partner, inventory distributed in separate lots to each, or marketable securities divided amongst them), the fair market value applies to the property distributed.

[¶7150] Partnership Ceasing to Exist

Under partnership law, a partnership ceases to exist when one or more partners give notice of dissolution or when the business carried on by the partnership ceases. For income tax purposes, however, the partnership will continue to exist until such time as all the partnership property is distributed to those persons entitled by law to receive it. Each such person will be deemed to continue as a partner in the partnership until this distribution has taken place.

There are limited rollover rules for a Canadian partnership (defined at ¶7240) where the partnership is continued by some of the former partners or as a proprietorship by one of the former partners.

Where none of the rollover provisions apply, each property transferred to or taken by a partner is deemed to be disposed of by the partnership at fair market value. Where a new partnership carries on the business of the former partnership, and the rollover provisions are not used, each member of the old partnership is deemed to have disposed of his or her interest in the partnership at its fair market value and to have acquired an interest in the new partnership for the same amount. This deemed disposition would appear to occur when the last of the property of the old partnership is transferred to the new partnership or otherwise disposed of.

Where a member of a discontinued partnership continues to hold a right to receive partnership property, this right continues to be treated as an

See page ii for explanation of footnotes.

[96] CCH ¶12,259; Sec. 98(2).

interest in the partnership and the taxpayer continues to be a partner for income tax purposes.

Note the commentary at ¶7200 in respect of the fiscal period of a partnership which ceases to exist.

[¶7155] Election on Cessation of Partnership — Rollover

If a Canadian partnership has dissolved and all its property has been distributed to persons who were partners immediately before that time in such a manner that immediately after the distribution each such person has an undivided interest in each property distributed, the former partners have the right to elect that fair market values should not apply.[97]

These rules only apply if all the partners so elect and if each asset of the partnership is distributed to the partners prorated in the same proportion as every other asset. The purpose of the election is to permit a tax-free rollover of partnership property to the partners.

[¶7160] Partner's Deemed Proceeds of Disposition of Partnership Interest

If a valid election has been made, special rules apply for determining each partner's proceeds of disposition of his or her partnership interest.[98]

The proceeds (which also represent the cost of the property acquired from the partnership, if the partner realizes a gain on distribution and no depreciable property is involved) are deemed to be the greater of:

(a) the adjusted cost base of the partner's partnership interest immediately before distribution of the property, and

(b) the amount of any money received plus the partner's undivided interest in the property received from the partnership, expressed as a percentage of all the undivided interests in the property so distributed, applied to the "cost amount" to the partnership of each such property, immediately before its distribution.

The aggregate of the partner's share of all "cost amounts" of all properties will have to be calculated in order to determine whether or not it exceeds the adjusted cost base of the partner's interest in the partnership, which could result in a capital gain on distribution of partnership property. While the partner may realize a capital gain on distribution, he or she cannot realize a capital loss, since the proceeds are deemed to be the greater of:

(a) the adjusted cost base, and

(b) the aggregate of the partner's share of the cost amounts received.

See page ii for explanation of footnotes.

[97] CCH ¶12,263; Sec. 98(3).   [98] CCH ¶12,263; Sec. 98(3).

The partner's proceeds of disposition will therefore be deemed to be the adjusted cost base, even though the aggregate of the partner's share of cost amounts is less.

[¶7165] Deemed Cost of Properties Received

The partner's share of the cost amounts is not necessarily his or her "cost" of the property received. If the adjusted cost base of the interest in the partnership exceeds the aggregate of the partner's share of the cost amounts (theoretically resulting in a capital loss at that time, if permitted to recognize it), the partner can designate the excess to apply to non-depreciable capital property.[99] However, the designation of such excess is subject to certain restrictions.[100]

[¶7170] Recaptured Depreciation on Termination of Partnership

In order to preserve the potential tax on recaptured depreciation in respect of depreciable property distributed, the following additional rules are applicable to a former partner:[101]

(1) the capital cost of the former partner's interest in the depreciable property is deemed to be an amount equal to his or her former percentage interest in the partnership multiplied by the total (original) cost of that property to the partnership; and

(2) the excess of this deemed capital cost over the former partner's deemed proceeds is deemed to have been allowed as capital cost allowance deductions against income in earlier years and, accordingly, will remain subject to recapture in his or her hands.

Example:

Depreciable property — capital cost to partnership		$10,000
— total capital cost allowance claimed by partnership		8,000
Undepreciated capital cost (cost amount) to partnership		$ 2,000
Partners' calculated percentage — based on cost	40%	60%
Partners' deemed capital cost (40% and 60% of $10,000)	$ 4,000	$ 6,000
Partners' real costs (40% and 60% of cost amount of $2,000)	800	1,200
Excess — deemed capital cost allowance to partner	$ 3,200	$ 4,800

The two partners would remain subject to a potential recapture totalling $8,000 which is the total depreciation deducted by the partnership.

See page ii for explanation of footnotes.

[99] CCH ¶12,263; Sec. 98(3)(b).   [101] CCH ¶12,263; Sec. 98(3)(e).
[100] CCH ¶12,263; Sec. 98(3)(c).

¶7165

[¶7175] Continuation of Partnership

[¶7180] Property Rollovers from Partnership to Sole Proprietorship

A tax-free rollover is permitted on a partner's share of the property of a Canadian partnership to a sole proprietorship (whether an individual, a trust, or a corporation) where, within three months of the termination of the Canadian partnership, one, but not more than one, of the partners commences to carry on the business of the previous partnership as a sole proprietor, using the partnership property received as proceeds of disposition of his or her partnership interest.[102] As a matter of law, a partnership ceases to exist when one partner acquires the partnership interests of all other partners. The rules for determining the proprietor's cost and proceeds of disposition of partnership property are similar in principle to those applicable on the cessation of a partnership.

In a situation where some partners dispose of their partnership interests to one partner, that one partner is thereby deemed to acquire the partnership interests rather than the property of the partnership. The cost incurred by the acquiring partner is then added to the adjusted cost base of his or her partnership interest in determining the proceeds of disposition of this partnership interest when the partnership ceases to exist.

[¶7183] Amalgamations

When a parent corporation amalgamates with a subsidiary under a vertical amalgamation, or if the subsidiary is wound up into the parent, the "section 88 bump"[103] effectively allows the parent to add certain amounts to the cost of the capital property distributed by the subsidiary to the parent on the vertical amalgamation or winding-up.

The bump does not apply to depreciable property, inventory, or other income assets, since these properties could have accrued gains or profit that, from a policy perspective, should not benefit from a bumped-up cost attributable to non-depreciable capital property (i.e., the parent's shares in the subsidiary).

According to the 2012 Budget papers, corporate partnership structures have been used with increasing frequency to attempt to circumvent the denial of the section 88 bump in respect of a subsidiary's inventory or income assets. The income assets would be held by the subsidiary through a partnership. Upon the acquisition of control of the subsidiary, the parent winds up the subsidiary and then claims the bump for the cost of the partnership interest, even in circumstances where all of the fair market value of the partnership interest is derived from inventory or other income assets.

See page ii for explanation of footnotes.

[102] CCH ¶12,291; Sec. 98(5).   [103] CCH ¶11,164; Sec. 88(1)(d).

August 14, 2012 draft legislation provides that the section 88 bump will not apply to a partnership interest to the extent that the accrued gain in respect of the partnership interest is reasonably attributable to the amount by which the fair market value of income assets of the partnership exceed their cost amount. More particularly, the fair market value of the partnership interest at the time the parent last acquired control of the subsidiary will be reduced to the extent that the accrued gain of the interest at that time was attributable to accrued gains of depreciable property, Canadian or foreign resource property, or inventory or other property (other than capital property or resource property). Since the amount by which the fair market value of the partnership interest exceeds the cost of the interest to the subsidiary will be thus reduced, the amount by which the parent can bump up the cost of the partnership interest will also be reduced.

These measures will apply to amalgamations that occur, and windings-up that begin on or after March 29, 2012. An exception is provided where a taxable Canadian corporation amalgamates with a subsidiary before 2013, or begins to wind up its subsidiary before 2013, generally if the parent acquired control of the subsidiary before March 29, 2012 or was obligated in writing before March 29, 2012 to acquire control of the subsidiary and the parent had the intention as evidenced in writing before Budget Day to amalgamate with or wind up the subsidiary.

[¶7185] Continuation of Former Partnership — Rollover

A full rollover is permitted if a Canadian partnership ceases to exist and all of its property is transferred to another Canadian partnership whose partners were *all partners* in the old partnership. The new partnership is deemed to be a continuation of the old partnership and each partner's interest in the new partnership is deemed to be a continuation of his or her interest in the predecessor partnership.[104]

[¶7190] Residual Interest in Partnership

Where a taxpayer withdraws from a partnership but retains a right to receive property of the partnership in satisfaction of his or her interest, such a right, described as a "residual interest", is deemed to be an interest in the partnership and, as such, is subject to the various additions and deductions to its adjusted cost base.[105]

If the partner's residual interest is satisfied in full in the partnership's fiscal year in which the partner withdraws, it is deemed not to have been disposed of until the end of the fiscal period of the partnership. This provision allows time for any adjustments to be made[106] in respect of the last fiscal year before the deemed disposition occurs.

See page ii for explanation of footnotes.

[104] CCH ¶12,301; Sec. 98(6).   [106] CCH ¶7600; Sec. 53.
[105] CCH ¶12,304; Sec. 98.1.

If the partner withdraws without receiving full payment for his or her interest in the partnership before the fiscal year end, his or her residual interest is deemed to have been disposed of for capital gains purposes where he or she elects to recognize gains in respect to the partnership interest that accrued to the end of February 22, 1994. In any other case, the residual interest is not considered to have been disposed of until full satisfaction occurs, unless, in the meantime, the taxpayer ceases to be a resident of Canada or dies.

Where the adjusted cost base of the partner's residual interest becomes negative at the fiscal year end of the partnership (by virtue of the amounts required to be deducted being greater than the cost of the interest plus the amounts required to be added), the negative amount is deemed to be a capital gain for the partner's taxation year which includes the end of the partnership's fiscal year. There is also a deemed disposition at that time so that a taxpayer may elect to recognize gains in respect of the partnership interest that accrued to the end of February 22, 1994, thereby obtaining the benefit of the capital gains exemption in respect of those gains.

Although the residual interest is deemed to be an interest in a partnership, the former partner is deemed not to be a member, except for the limited purposes of deducting his or her share of partnership donations and political contributions made in the fiscal year in which he or she withdraws, and qualifying for the tax-free rollover[107] in the event that the partnership business is incorporated and the partnership is wound up.

It should be noted, however, that a former partner who holds a residual interest in the partnership may also have a right to receive further partnership income. By virtue of this right, the former partner would be deemed to be a member of a partnership and separate calculations would be necessary in order to maintain a record of both the former partner's residual interest and the former partner's income right from the partnership. (See ¶7025.)

On the dissolution of a partnership, the partnership continues to exist and each member continues to be a partner until all of the partnership property has been distributed. Since a former partner holding a residual interest is deemed not to be a member of the partnership and therefore is not protected, a special rule is introduced to provide continuance of the interest where members of another partnership have agreed to satisfy all or part of the former partner's rights.

A person who acquires a retired partner's residual interest on the death of the retired partner obtains a "right to receive partnership property" and not a residual interest.[108] The cost of this right is equal to the proceeds deemed to have been received by the deceased. As with a residual interest,

---

See page ii for explanation of footnotes.

[107] CCH ¶10,562; Sec. 85(3).

[108] CCH ¶12,306, ¶52,282; Sec. 98.2; Interp. Bul. IT-278R2.

the right to receive partnership property is disposed of when the final payment in respect thereof is received.

Where a partner dies prior to withdrawing from the partnership, a partner's right to receive partnership property is treated as a separate right in the hands of the estate rather than an interest in the partnership, and the holder thereof is not deemed to become a member of the partnership.[109] The adjusted cost base of this right will be its fair market value immediately before death if a deemed disposition occurs, or it will be equal to the adjusted cost base of the interest in the partnership if the partner's interest passes to a spouse/common-law partner or to a post-1971 spouse's or partner's trust.

[¶7195] Fiscal Period of Terminated Partnership

[¶7200] Partnership Fiscal Period

The fiscal period of a terminated partnership is deemed to have ended on the date the partnership ceased to exist, regardless of whether or not all the partnership property has been distributed to the respective partners at that time.[110]

[¶7205] Fiscal Period of Partner

If a partnership's fiscal period is not subject to the "alternative fiscal period rule" (see ¶7047), a partner may elect to have the fiscal period terminate on the date it would have normally ended, had the partnership not ceased to exist.[111] Such an election is valid only if the individual partner is resident in Canada at the time the fiscal period would normally have ended.[112]

[¶7210] Disposition of Partnership Interest

[¶7215] Gain on Disposition to Exempt Person

A special provision ensures that there is no reduction in tax on the disposition of a partnership interest to any persons exempt from tax.[113] The taxpayer's capital gain in this situation is deemed to be the aggregate of:[114]

(a) ½ of the capital gain reasonably attributable to the increase in the value of partnership capital property other than depreciable property, and

(b) the whole of the remaining portion of the capital gain.

See page ii for explanation of footnotes.

[109] CCH ¶12,381; Sec. 100(3).
[110] CCH ¶12,309; Sec. 99(1).
[111] CCH ¶12,311; Sec. 99(2).
[112] CCH ¶12,313; Sec. 99(3).
[113] CCH ¶21,721; Sec. 149.
[114] CCH ¶12,325; Sec. 100(1).

The purpose of this provision is to ensure that a portion of the gain, to the extent that it represents recaptured depreciation that would be fully taxable if the property had been sold instead of the partnership interest, is taxed as ordinary income and not as a capital gain. Where little recapture is involved in this type of sale, it may be advisable to sell the depreciable assets separately and pay the tax on recapture instead of jeopardizing the capital gain applicable to depreciable property, which conceivably could be taxed as ordinary income under this provision.

Draft legislation released on August 14, 2012 will extend this rule to indirect dispositions of partnership interests to tax-exempt entities, and also to direct and indirect dispositions of partnership interests to non-resident purchasers.[115] These measures will apply to dispositions of interests in partnerships that occur on or after March 29, 2012, other than an arm's length disposition made by a taxpayer before 2013 that the taxpayer is obligated to make pursuant to a written agreement entered into by the taxpayer before March 29, 2012.

The proposed change does not apply to the disposition of the partnership interest to a non-resident if the partnership, immediately before and after the sale, is carrying on business in Canada through a permanent establishment, in which all of the assets of the partnership are used. In such cases, as the Budget documents note, "the income assets remain within the Canadian income tax base."

[¶7220] Gain on Disposition of Partnership Interest

The general rule for computing a capital gain is that the gain is the excess of net proceeds of disposition over the adjusted cost base of the property disposed of. The adjusted cost base calculation is set out at ¶7100.

As a general rule for most types of capital property, a negative adjusted cost base will give rise to an immediate capital gain recognition of the negative amount. However, this rule does not apply to a partnership interest. If a negative balance should arise in the adjusted cost base of a partnership interest, the negative balance would not be a capital gain at that time. If the interest is sold while the negative balance still exists, the capital gain otherwise arising would never become taxable to the partner because the adjusted cost base for purposes of calculating the gain or loss on disposal of capital property cannot be less than nil.[116]

The gain or loss on disposal of a partnership interest is therefore adjusted to bring the negative balance into the capital gain or disposal.[117]

See page ii for explanation of footnotes.

[115] Sec. 100(1).

[116] CCH ¶7850; Sec. 54.

[117] CCH ¶12,326; Sec. 100(2).

[¶7225] Loss re Interest in Partnership

The capital loss of a taxpayer from the disposition at any time of an interest in a partnership is deemed to be:

(a) the amount of the loss otherwise determined;

minus:

(b) the aggregate of all amounts each of which is the amount by which the taxpayer's share of the partnership's loss (in respect of a share of the capital stock of a corporation that was property of a particular partnership at that time) would have been reduced[118] if the fiscal period of every partnership that includes that time had ended immediately before that time and the particular partnership had disposed of the share immediately before the end of that fiscal period for proceeds equal to its fair market value at that time.[119]

[¶7230] Replacement of Partnership Capital

There may be circumstances under which a former member of a partnership or an heir of a deceased member is required to pay an amount to the partnership to cover a deficit in the former member's equity account. Such a situation could arise, for instance, where the partnership has a net loss for the partnership's fiscal period in which the taxpayer ceased to be a member. The former member may have been deemed to have realized a capital gain upon disposition of the partnership interest, if the former member had at that time a negative adjusted cost base (see ¶7220). A pending technical amendment deems a taxpayer to have a capital loss from the payment of an amount after the time of disposition of the partnership interest, if that amount would have been a capital contribution to the partnership if the taxpayer had still been a member at the time of the payment.[120] The loss is available to the former member or to an heir who has been deemed to have acquired a right to acquire partnership property.

The Department of Finance provided the following example in its explanatory notes that were released with its revised technical proposals on July 16, 2010:

Example:

Mr. Green was a partner in XYZ Partnership until June 30. The fiscal period end of the partnership was December 31. The adjusted cost base of his partnership interest on January 1 was nil. From January to June 30, he withdrew $16,000 in capital.

Shortly after the fiscal period end, all the partners agreed that Mr. Green's share of the partnership loss for the period was $20,000. During the following year he paid $36,000 owing by him to the partnership in satisfaction of his obligation.

A summary of Mr. Green's adjusted cost base is as follows:

See page ii for explanation of footnotes.

[118] CCH ¶16,385, ¶16,431; Sec. 112(3.1), 112(4.2).   [120] Sec. 100(5).

[119] CCH ¶12,383; Sec. 100(4).

		Adjusted Cost Base
January 1, Year 1:		Nil
January 31, Drawings	$(16,000)	(16,000)
Retirement of Mr. Green, June 30 December 31, Year 1,		
Share of loss for 6 months	(20,000)	(36,000)
March 31 - Repayment of partnership capital	36,000	Nil

Mr. Green is entitled to claim a partnership loss of $20,000 for the taxation year in which he retired (Year 1). He had a $36,000 negative adjusted cost base for his partnership interest as at the time that he left the partnership, giving rise to a deemed capital gain for Year 1 (see ¶7220). However, he will be allowed a $36,000 capital loss for the taxation year in which he repaid the deficit.

At the time of publication these changes have not been enacted.

[¶7235] Canadian Partnership

[¶7240] "Canadian Partnership" Defined

A "Canadian partnership" is defined[121] as a partnership, all of the members of which were, at the relevant time, resident in Canada. The members may themselves be partnerships. However, a person who is deemed to be a member of a partnership solely because a continuing partnership interest is retained is not considered to be a member of a partnership for purposes of the definition. Thus, for example, a retired partner who has not yet withdrawn his or her entire capital from the partnership can take up residence in another country without causing the partnership to be classified as a non-Canadian partnership.

The election provisions for property transfers to partnerships, specifically refer to Canadian partnerships.[122] See ¶7115 *et seq.* It is therefore important to note that, anytime a transfer of assets to a partnership is considered, its status as a Canadian or a non-Canadian partnership must be determined. The existence of even one non-resident partner at the relevant time will result in failure to comply with the definition of a Canadian partnership and consequently will render the partnership ineligible for the election provisions. As a result, all asset transfers would be deemed to take place at fair market value.[123]

---

[121] CCH ¶12,391; Sec. 102(1).　　[123] CCH ¶12,175; Sec. 97(1).
[122] CCH ¶12,177; Sec. 97(2).

[¶7245] Income Allocation Adjustments

[¶7250] Adjustments by Minister

Annual incomes or losses of a partnership are allocated in the profit and loss sharing ratio to the partners. (The "at-risk" rules set out in ¶7055 *et seq.* may limit partners' abilities to deduct their shares of partnership losses.)

The Minister is permitted to adjust the income allocation if he or she considers that it is not reasonable, having regard to all the circumstances, including the proportion in which the members have agreed to share profits and losses of the partnership from other sources or from sources in other places. Where the members of a partnership have allocated profits or losses in specified proportions, the principal reason for which is the reduction or postponement of income tax, or where the members of a partnership who are not dealing at arm's length have allocated profits or losses in unreasonable proportions, the allocation may be challenged by the Minister.[124] The Federal Court reapportioned partnership losses between two partners in a proportion of 70% and 30% in 1979 in order to reflect their workload during that year.[125]

Example:

> Assume A and B share equally in the profits of a partnership. In Year 1, however, A may have a non-capital loss from another source. The partners may agree to allocate for tax purposes a higher proportion of Year 1 income to A but continue to share cash distributions equally. In Year 2, the proportionate allocation might be reversed. In this case, the allocation might be subject to review. In some cases a disproportionate allocation for income tax purposes only might be appropriate in the circumstances. For example, if A were to transfer inventory worth $50,000 to the AB partnership in exchange for a capital account of $50,000, and if A and B elected a transfer price of $30,000 (see ¶7120), the inherent profit of $20,000 would be income, for tax purposes only, to the partnership. If this income were to be allocated equally to A and B, then B might be taxed on income that B had never received. Consequently, the allocation of an additional amount of income to A would seem to be appropriate in the circumstances, and not offensive for income tax purposes.

[¶7255] Trusts — Taxation of Trusts and Beneficiaries

[¶7260] General Treatment

Generally speaking, a trust is taxed as an individual on its income, including taxable capital gains, for each taxation year without benefit of personal tax credits. It may, however, claim a deduction on account of actual charitable donations or Crown gifts.[126]

Tax applies to the income of a Canadian resident trust. For many years, the residence of a trust had always been interpreted to be the residence of its

---

See page ii for explanation of footnotes.

[124] CCH ¶12,395; Sec. 103.
[125] [Graves et al., 90 DTC 6300.

[126] CCH ¶13,114, ¶19,255; Sec. 104(2), 122(1.1).

trustee.[127] However, recent jurisprudence has changed that determination rule entirely. At the Tax Court level (cited as *Garron*, 2009 DTC 1287), it was decided that the trusts were resident in Canada because the central management and control of the trusts were being carried out in Canada. The Federal Court of Appeal upheld the Tax Court decision (2010 DTC 5189), and the same determination was recently upheld by the Supreme Court (*St. Michael Trust Corp.*, 2012 DTC 5063). The Supreme Court stated that there is no legal rule in subsection 104(1) that the residence of a trust has to be that of the trustee. The Court also stated that the similar characteristics between a trust and a corporation, including holding assets to be managed, acquiring and disposing of assets, managing a business, requiring banking arrangements, requiring professional advice, and distributing income, would justify using the central management and control test to determine the residence of a trust as it is used to determine the residence of a corporation. It noted that no reasons were given by the taxpayers as to why different tests should be applied for trusts.

A "trust" includes an *inter vivos* trust and a testamentary trust.[128]

However, the tax rules relating to deemed dispositions of property by a trust;[129] deduction of part of the accumulating income included in a preferred beneficiary's income;[130] election by a trust and a preferred beneficiary;[131] and a preferred beneficiary's share of accumulating income[132] do not apply to a unit trust (including a mutual fund trust) or trusts in which all interests have vested indefeasibly (except an *alter ego* trust, a joint spousal or common-law partner trust, a post-1971 spousal or common-law partner trust, a trust that has elected in its first taxation year ending after 1992 not to have the definition of trust apply, a trust which, before 1999, has made an exempt beneficiary election, and, after December 23, 1998, a trust resident in Canada that has a non-resident beneficiary, unless the total fair market value of the interests of the non-resident beneficiary is 20% or less of the total fair market value of the interests in the trust).[133]

Furthermore, such rules, as well as those respecting benefits under a trust,[134] income interests,[135] disposition of capital interests,[136] and amounts deemed unpaid[137] do not apply to: an amateur athletic trust, a registered pension plan, a foreign retirement arrangement, an employees' profit sharing plan, a registered supplementary unemployment benefit plan, a registered retirement savings plan (RRSP), a deferred profit sharing plan (DPSP), a registered education savings plan (RESP), a registered retirement income fund (RRIF), an employee benefit plan, an employee trust, a related segre-

---

[127] Sec. 104(1).

[128] CCH ¶13,941; Sec. 108(1) "trust".

[129] CCH ¶13,150, ¶13,153; Sec. 104(4), 104(5).

[130] CCH ¶13,343; Sec. 104(12).

[131] CCH ¶13,410, ¶52,399; Sec. 104(14); Interp. Bul. IT-394R2.

[132] CCH ¶13,480; Sec. 104(15).

[133] CCH ¶13,941; Sec. 108(1) "trust".

[134] CCH ¶13,600; Sec. 105.

[135] CCH ¶13,700; Sec. 106.

[136] CCH ¶13,800; Sec. 107.

[137] CCH ¶13,404, ¶13,405; Sec. 104(13.1), 104(13.2).

gated fund trust, a deemed communal organization trust, a registered compensation arrangement trust, a cemetery care trust or an eligible funeral arrangement trust, a health and welfare trust, a registered disability savings plan (beginning in 2008), or a tax-free savings account (TFSA) (beginning in 2009).[138]

A distinction is made between "testamentary trusts" and *inter vivos* trusts". A "unit trust" is an *inter vivos* trust under which the interest of each beneficiary is described by reference to units of a trust and which meets certain other conditions.[139] Unit trusts and trusts governed by registered pension plans, employees' profit sharing plans, RRSPs, registered supplementary unemployment benefit plans, RCAs, RESPs, RRIFs, DPSPs, amateur athlete reserve funds, and eligible funeral and cemetery care arrangements are generally exempt from tax. See also Chapter X.

A person or partnership is deemed to be beneficially interested in a trust where it has any right (immediate, future, absolute, contingent, or subject to the exercise of a discretionary power) as a beneficiary under a trust to receive any income or capital of the particular trust either directly from it or indirectly through one or more other trusts.[140] The term "beneficially interested" deems a person or partnership to be beneficially interested in a particular trust at a particular time where:

(a) the particular person or partnership is not otherwise beneficially interested in the particular trust at the particular time;

(b) because of the terms or conditions of the particular trust or any arrangements, such as an arrangement evidenced by a letter of wishes in respect of the trust, the particular person or partnership might become, because of the exercise of any discretion by anyone, beneficially interested in the particular trust at the particular time or at a later time; and

(c) at or before the particular time either (i) the particular trust has acquired property directly or indirectly in any manner whatever from the particular person or partnership or a "connected person" or (ii) the particular person or partnership or a connected person has given a guarantee on behalf of the particular trust or provided it with any other type of financial assistance.

[¶7265] Reference to Trust or Estate

The terms "trust" and "estate" include a reference to the trustee or the executor, administrator, liquidator of a succession (a concept used in Quebec), heir, or other legal representative who has ownership or control of the trust property.[141] The word "trust" includes an "estate", and this meaning is adopted for all purposes of the Act.

See page ii for explanation of footnotes.

[138] CCH ¶13,941; Sec. 108(1) "trust".
[139] CCH ¶13,960; Sec. 108(2).
[140] CCH ¶28,329v; Sec. 248(25).
[141] CCH ¶13,101; Sec. 104(1).

However, the word "trust" does not include an arrangement under which a trust can reasonably be considered to act as agent for all the beneficiaries under the trust with respect to all dealings with all of the trust's property. In such an arrangement, which is commonly known as a bare trust, the trustee holds legal title to the trust property, but has no authority to do anything with the property without the direction and consent of the beneficiaries. Prior to December 24, 1998, it was the CRA's administrative policy to ignore bare trusts; as of that date, the exception is legislated.

[¶7270] Income of Trusts

[¶7275] Taxation of Trust Income

Generally, income of a trust that is payable to a beneficiary in the year in which it arises is taxable in the hands of the beneficiary rather than the trust, whether or not it was actually paid to the beneficiary in the year.[142]

An exception is the "designated income" of an *inter vivos* trust which is payable to non-resident beneficiaries (see ¶7315 below). A further exception is the business income earned by an employee trust.

Certain types of income — such as dividends, interest, and taxable capital gains — may maintain their character when paid out to beneficiaries for the purpose of determining the tax payable by the beneficiaries (see ¶7380, ¶7385, and ¶7390 below).

Certain fees paid by testamentary trusts in settling the estate, such as probate fees and associated professional fees may be claimed as disposition costs or added to the cost of trust assets for purposes of computing gains and losses on disposition at death.[143]

Income which accumulates in the trust and is not payable to a beneficiary (other than a preferred beneficiary) in the year in which it arises, is taxable in the hands of the trustee.

In the case of trusts in which certain rights are reserved to the settlor, the income from the trust property is deemed to be income of the settlor.[144] However, this attribution rule will not be engaged by a fair market transfer of property by a beneficiary to the trust for consideration.[145]

The taxation year of a trust, other than a trust arising on death, is the same as for individuals (i.e., the calendar year). For the taxation year of a testamentary trust, see ¶7415.

See page ii for explanation of footnotes.

[142] CCH ¶13,400, ¶52,386, ¶52,394; Sec. 104(13); Interp. Bul. IT-342R, IT-381R3.

[143] Estate of the Late Gunnar Brosamler, 2012 DTC 1193 (TCC).

[144] CCH ¶9570; Sec. 75(2).

[145] The Queen v. Sommerer, 2012 DTC 5126 (Federal Court of Appeal).

Where there are multiple trusts and substantially all property has been received from one person and income accrues or will ultimately accrue to the same beneficiary or group or class of beneficiaries, the Minister may designate two or more of the trustees as one individual for income tax purposes.[146] Tax will be determined by applying to the total income of all the trusts the graduated rates applicable to individuals. This prevents a settlor from splitting income so as to reduce tax liability. See Chapter IX.

As a general rule, the income of a trust will be subject to tax on the same basis as that of an individual.

[¶7280] Rate of Tax

Instead of graduated income tax rates, *inter vivos* trusts are generally taxed at the top marginal rate of income tax on their undistributed income, currently 29%. They will also be subject to provincial tax at the relevant rate for the particular province.[147]

An *inter vivos* trust is defined to be a trust other than a testamentary trust (for the definition of a "testamentary trust" see ¶7415).[148] An *inter vivos* trust that is established before June 18, 1971, and resident in Canada on that date is taxed at graduated rates and not the 29% flat rate. However, such a trust will become "tainted", such that it will pay the 29% flat rate, if any of the following occurs:

(1) it was not resident in Canada for some period after June 18, 1971;

(2) it carried on an active business during the relevant taxation year;

(3) it received any property as a gift after June 18, 1971;

(4) it incurred, after June 18, 1971, any debt or other obligation to pay an amount to, or guaranteed by, any person with whom any beneficiary of the trust was not dealing at arm's length; and

(5) it received property after December 17, 1999, as a result of a transfer from another trust that did not result in any change of beneficial ownership of the property.[149]

Although it had not exercised any management role in its limited partnership, a trust was still carrying on its business and, hence, was subject to the 29% flat rate tax considering that, under the partnership law of Manitoba, persons comprising a limited partnership are carrying on its business.[150]

Beginning in 2007, if an *inter vivos* trust is a "SIFT trust" for a taxation year, it may be subject to an additional tax in respect of its "taxable SIFT trust distributions" for the year, which are essentially equal to the before-tax amount of its "non-portfolio earnings" for the year that are distributed to its

---

See page ii for explanation of footnotes.

[146] CCH ¶13,114; Sec. 104(2).

[147] CCH ¶19,250, ¶52,411; Sec. 122(1)(a); Interp. Bul. IT-406R2.

[148] CCH ¶13,925; Sec. 108(1) "inter vivos trust".

[149] CCH ¶19,260; Sec. 122(2).

[150] Robinson et al., 98 DTC 6065.

beneficiaries. This additional tax, along with the regular 29% tax on trusts, is meant to parallel the general corporate tax rate and is discussed below at ¶7282.

[¶7282] Additional Tax for SIFT Trusts

A trust that is a specified investment flow-through trust ("SIFT trust") for a taxation year, is effectively subject to tax at a rate that approximates the general corporate tax rate on the before-tax amount of its non-portfolio earnings in a taxation year that are payable to its beneficiaries in the year. "Non-portfolio earnings" are defined in ¶7307, and include the SIFT trust's net income from businesses it carries on in Canada, its net income from non-portfolio properties other than taxable dividends, and its taxable capital gains in excess of its allowable capital losses from dispositions of non-portfolio properties.

More particularly, a SIFT trust is subject to the above regular tax applicable to *inter vivos* trusts, equal to 29% of the trust's taxable income for the year. This 29% tax is "new" for a SIFT trust, to the extent of the trust's distributed non-portfolio earnings because, as discussed at ¶7307 below, such amounts are no longer deductible in computing the trust's income and are therefore taxable to the trust.

In addition, the SIFT trust may be subject to an additional tax rate in respect of its "taxable SIFT trust distributions" for the year.[151] "Taxable SIFT trust distributions" are defined as the lesser of (a) the trust's taxable income for the year, and (b) an amount determined by a formula that effectively equals the before-tax amount of the trust's non-deductible distributions amount for the year.[152] The trust's non-deductible distributions amount[153] reflects the trust's non-portfolio earnings that are payable to its beneficiaries, but are not deductible by the trust, due to the limitation on the deduction by a SIFT trust of its distributed non-portfolio earnings (see ¶7307).

The additional tax rate comprises the "net corporate income tax rate" in respect of the year, which equals the general corporate rate net of the general rate reduction and the provincial abatement, plus the "provincial tax factor" for the year of 13%, which is meant to represent an average provincial general corporate tax rate, minus the 29% general rate that applies to *inter vivos* trusts. Thus, the additional tax rate is intended to equal the amount by which the combined federal and provincial general corporate tax rate exceeds the 29% federal tax rate that applies to *inter vivos* trusts.

The net result is that the SIFT trust is liable to pay the average combined federal and provincial general corporate tax rate in respect of its taxable SIFT distributions. This tax rate for 2007 is 34%, and owing to

---

See page ii for explanation of footnotes.

[151] CCH ¶19,250; Sec. 122(1)(b).

[152] CCH ¶19,262; Sec. 122(3) "taxable SIFT trust distributions".

[153] CCH ¶19,261; Sec. 122(3) "non-deductible distributions amount".

scheduled decreases in the federal corporate tax rate, will decrease to 28% for the 2012 taxation year.

Beginning in 2009, the "provincial SIFT tax factor" is replaced with the "provincial SIFT tax rate" of the SIFT trust for the relevant taxation year. The definition of the provincial SIFT tax rate states that it will be the prescribed amount determined in respect of the SIFT trust, and the prescribed amount is intended to equal the relevant province's general corporate tax rate for public corporations.[154] SIFT trusts can elect that the new definition apply for the 2007 and/or 2008 taxation years. Although the prescribed amount had not been enacted at the time of writing, the Department of Finance explanatory notes to the provision state: "In general terms, for a SIFT trust or partnership with a permanent establishment in only one province, the prescribed amount will be the decimal fraction representing that province's general corporate income tax rate for public corporations. If that province is Quebec, the decimal fraction will be nil to take into account the SIFT tax imposed by that province. For SIFT trusts or partnerships with permanent establishments in more than one province the prescribed amount will be the decimal fraction amount that is an average of the relevant provincial general corporate income tax rates for public corporations weighted on the basis of the general corporate taxable income allocation formula in Part IV of the Income Tax Regulations (i.e., by reference to wages and salaries and gross revenues attributable to those permanent establishments). The provincial rate for amounts allocated to the province of Quebec will be deemed to be nil in determining this weighted average. If under the allocation formula amounts are not allocated to any province, then [the] prescribed amount will be the decimal fraction 0.10."

This new tax applies as of 2007 to new SIFT trusts, but is deferred until 2011 for SIFT trusts that were publicly traded as of October 31, 2006, provided they do not exceed certain "normal growth" guidelines issued by the Department of Finance.[155]

[¶7285] Twenty-One-Year Deemed Disposition Rule

To prevent individuals from circumventing the deemed disposition provisions applicable on death by settling their property upon trusts of prolonged duration, a trust is deemed to dispose of certain properties periodically. The properties covered by this deemed disposition are capital property (both depreciable and non-depreciable), Canadian and foreign resource properties, and land inventory of the trust.[156] These rules do not apply to "excluded property", meaning a share of the capital stock of a non-resident-owned investment corporation that is not taxable Canadian property.[157]

See page ii for explanation of footnotes.

[154] CCH ¶28,222h; Sec. 248(1) "provincial SIFT tax rate".

[155] CCH ¶19,284; Sec. 122.1(2).

[156] CCH ¶13,150–13,155; Sec. 104(4)–(5.2).

[157] CCH ¶13,919; Sec. 108(1) "excluded property".

Furthermore, after December 23, 1998, the 21-year deemed realization rule will not apply to "exempt property" of a non-resident trust. A property will be exempt property if any income or gain arising on the disposition of the property would not be subject to Canadian tax (because of a tax treaty or simply because the trust is non-resident).[158]

This change ensures that the deemed realization rule will not result in an increase in the tax cost of trust property unless the deemed proceeds of disposition are subject to Canadian tax.

On deemed disposition day, the trust is deemed to have disposed of each property (other than exempt property) that was capital property (other than excluded property and depreciable property) and land inventory for proceeds of disposition equal to its fair market value and to re-acquire each immediately thereafter for the same amount.[159] Any loss so arising will not be a superficial loss.

The trust is also deemed to have disposed of each property (other than exempt property) that was depreciable property of each prescribed class for proceeds equal to fair market value and to have re-acquired it generally at a capital cost equal to the same amount.[160] On the deemed disposition day, the trust may realize capital gains or recapture. No capital loss may be realized on a disposition of depreciable property.

Unless the deemed disposition occurred on the death of the beneficiary spouse who was alive on January 1, 1976 (or May 26, 1976, in the case of an *inter vivos* trust), the first possible date on which the rule applied was January 1, 1993. Deemed dispositions of the trust's assets will occur every 21 years thereafter. However, in the event that a beneficiary spouse died before 1976 (or before May 26, 1976, in the case of *inter vivos* trust), a deemed disposition would occur first on the day of death and subsequent deemed dispositions 21 years after.

Every post-1971 spousal or common-law partner trust that holds an interest in a NISA Fund No. 2 transferred to it by way of a rollover is considered to have been paid the amount, if any, by which the fund's balance at the end of the day on which the spouse/common-law partner dies exceeds the amount included in the deceased spouse's or common-law partner's income.[161] Therefore, if the spouse/common-law partner has not included any of the NISA Fund No. 2 in his or her income, the total balance will be income to the post-1971 spousal or common-law partner trust for the period ending immediately before the spouse's death. However, the trust and the spouse's/common-law partner's legal representative may elect to deem a portion of the NISA Fund No. 2 to be paid to the spouse or common-law partner immediately before death.

See page ii for explanation of footnotes.

[158] CCH ¶13,919; Sec. 108(1) "exempt property". [160] CCH ¶13,153; Sec. 104(5).
[159] CCH ¶13,150; Sec. 104(4). [161] CCH ¶13,154; Sec. 104(5.1).

Special rules are applicable where the trust owns a Canadian resource property or a foreign resource property at the deemed disposition date.[162] The general intent of these rules is to ensure that the deemed disposition of Canadian resource properties whose costs have been added to a tax pool, triggers income to the extent that the fair market value of the properties exceeds the unclaimed balance in the pools. This is accomplished by triggering, for purposes of the income inclusion, a deemed year end on the deemed disposition day.

After December 23, 1998, a non-resident trust is not deemed to dispose of and reacquire property under the 21-year rule unless the proceeds of disposition are taken into account in determining the non-resident trust's Canadian tax position. In addition, for 1999 and later years, the 21-year rule applies to non-resident discretionary trusts deemed resident in Canada.

[¶7290] Date of Deemed Realization

For the purposes of these deemed realization rules, trusts are divided into six basic categories:

(1) *Post-1971 spousal or common-law partner trusts.* Such a trust is one under the terms of which:

(a) the spouse/common-law partner of the taxpayer who created the trust was entitled to receive all of the income arising in the trust during the spouse's or common-law partner's lifetime; and

(b) no person other than the spouse/common-law partner could, before that spouse's/common-law partner's death, receive or have the use of any income or capital of the trust;

and which was created either:

(c) by the will of a taxpayer who died after 1971;

(d) after June 17, 1971, by a taxpayer during his or her lifetime; or

(e) by the will of a taxpayer who died after 1971 to which property was transferred on a rollover basis in circumstances to which the rollover provisions on resource properties and land inventories of a deceased taxpayer or the transfer or distribution to a spouse/common-law partner or post-1971 spousal or common-law partner trust applied, provided that the beneficiary spouse died after December 20, 1991. If the beneficiary spouse/common-law partner died before that date, the deemed disposition would occur 21 years after the later of January 1, 1972, and the date on which the trust was created.

See page ii for explanation of footnotes.

[162] CCH ¶13,155; Sec. 104(5.2).

The time for determining whether a testamentary trust is a qualifying post-1971 spousal or common-law partner trust is the time the trust was created. In the case of a testamentary trust to which the rollover provisions on resource properties and land inventories of a deceased taxpayer or the transfer or distribution to a spouse/common-law partner or post-1971 spousal or common-law partner trust applied, the relevant time is immediately after the transferred property vested indefeasibly in the trust. In the case of an *inter vivos* trust, it will be included in this new class of spousal or common-law partner trusts if it was a spousal or common-law partner trust at any time after 1971.

It is important to note that not all post-1971 spousal or common-law partner trusts, created for the benefit of an individual's spouse or common-law partner, will meet the criteria of this spousal or common-law partner trust category. For example, if the trustees have the power to encroach on capital for the benefit of the settlor's children, the criteria will not be met. The terms of the trust must be carefully reviewed to make this determination. Such trusts not meeting the definition will have a deemed disposition on the later of January 1, 1993, and 21 years after the trust's creation date.

(2) *Alter ego trusts and joint spousal or common-law partner trusts.* For 2000 and subsequent taxation years the first deemed disposition date for:

- an alter ego trust is the day on which the settlor dies; and

- a joint spousal or common-law partner trust is the day on which the last survivor dies.

These rules parallel the rules for spousal trusts. For a trust to be an alter ego trust, it must satisfy the following conditions:

(a) at the time of the trust's creation, the taxpayer creating the trust was alive and had attained 65 years of age;

(b) the trust was created after 1999;

(c) the taxpayer was entitled to receive all of the income of the trust that arose before the taxpayer's death;

(d) no person except the taxpayer could, before the taxpayer's death, receive or otherwise obtain the use of any of the income or capital of the trust; and

(e) the trust did not elect not to be treated as an alter ego trust.[163]

In other words, an alter ego trust is a trust that one establishes for him/herself. The settlor can place all of the assets accumulated during his or her lifetime in the trust but must be the only person entitled to receive all of the income from the trust as well as the

---

See page ii for explanation of footnotes.

[163] CCH ¶28,009c; Sec. 248(1) "alter ego trust".

capital of the trust during his/her lifetime. He or she is permitted to transfer his or her assets to the trust on a rollover basis. The gain on these assets is deferred until the time of the person's death.

The joint spousal or common-law partner trust is similar to both the post-1971 spousal or common-law partner trust and the alter ego trust. With a joint spousal or common-law partner trust, both the settlor and his or her spouse/common-law partner are the beneficiaries of the trust and are entitled to receive the income and the capital during their lifetimes. After death, the trust can specify to whom the assets are to be transferred. Again, the settlor must be at least 65 years old in order to establish a joint spousal or common-law partner trust and receive the rollover treatment.[164]

(3) *Bare trusts.* A bare trust, which acts as agent for all the beneficiaries under the trust in respect of all dealings with all of the trust's property, is not considered a trust for the purposes of the deemed disposition rules nor for most other purposes of the Act.

(4) *Pre-1972 spousal trusts.* For their taxation years ending after February 11, 1991, these trusts will be deemed to dispose of their relevant properties on the later of January 1, 1993, and the day on which the beneficiary spouse dies. Additional deemed dispositions will occur every 21 years thereafter.

A "pre-1972 spousal trust" is defined as a trust created:

(a) by the will of an individual who died before 1972, or

(b) before June 18, 1971, by an individual during his or her lifetime.[165]

Such a trust will qualify as a pre-1972 spousal trust at a particular time if, throughout the period commencing when it was created and ending at the earliest of January 1, 1993, the day of the beneficiary spouse's death, and the time at which the definition is applied, the beneficiary spouse is entitled to receive all the income of the trust that arose before his or her death. A trust will be deemed not to be a pre-1972 spousal trust if a person other than the beneficiary spouse received or otherwise obtained the use of any of the income or capital of the trust before the above-noted period ended.

A trust may qualify as a pre-1972 spousal trust even where there is a condition such that beneficiaries other than the spouse may have access to the income or capital of the trust, e.g., in the event that the beneficiary spouse remarries. In such a case, the trust would cease to be a pre-1972 spousal trust only in the event that the beneficiary spouse actually did remarry.

See page ii for explanation of footnotes.

[164] CCH ¶28,151c; Sec. 248(1) "joint spousal or common-law partner trust".

[165] CCH ¶13,927; Sec. 108(1) "pre-1972 spousal trust".

¶7290

It should be noted that a trust must qualify as a pre-1972 spousal trust on January 1, 1993, in order to obtain the deferral of the deemed disposition until the date of the spouse's death (assuming that the spouse died after January 1, 1993). Not all pre-1972 trusts created for the benefit of an individual's spouse will qualify as a pre-1972 spousal trust. For example, a trust under which the trustees have the power to encroach on capital for the benefit of the settlor's children will not qualify. The terms of the trust document and the trust's transactions for the relevant period must be carefully reviewed to make this determination. If the definition of a pre-1972 spousal trust is not met on January 1, 1993, the deemed disposition rule will apply on January 1, 1993.

(5) *Other trusts.* The deemed disposition rules will first apply to a trust not qualifying as any of an alter ego trust, joint spousal or common-law partner trust, a post-1971 spousal or common-law partner trust, or a pre-1972 spousal trust 21 years after the later of January 1, 1972, and the date on which the trust was created. Additional deemed dispositions will occur every 21 years thereafter.

Furthermore, for deemed disposition days determined after December 17, 1999, two new sets of circumstances will cause a trust to have a deemed disposition day:

(a) *Property distribution financed by a trust liability.* After December 17, 1999, a trust which distributes property that was financed by a liability of the trust (e.g., a loan assumed by the trust) will have a deemed disposition day immediately after the distribution, if one of the purposes of the transaction was to avoid taxes otherwise payable on an individual's death.

(b) *Property transfer in anticipation of emigration.* If, after December 17, 1999, an individual transfers property to a trust on a rollover basis and the transfer was made in anticipation that the individual would subsequently cease to reside in Canada, the trust will have a deemed disposition when the individual emigrates.

An anti-avoidance provision prevents a trust from avoiding the deemed disposition rules by varying its terms. If a trust has varied its terms, for the purpose of the deemed realization rules, the trust is deemed to be the same trust.[166] However, this deeming provision does not apply to pre-1972 spousal trusts. Therefore, for example, if such a pre-1972 spousal trust varies its terms before 1993 so that it does not meet the definition of a pre-1972 spousal trust on January 1, 1993, and does not meet the test in (3) above, the deemed disposition rules will apply on January 1, 1993. As a result, an additional deferral of the deemed disposition rules to the date of the

---

See page ii for explanation of footnotes.

[166] CCH ¶13,993; Sec. 108(6).

spouse's death (assuming that the spouse dies after January 1, 1993) cannot be obtained.

[¶7295] Deduction by Trust Other than Employee Trust or SIFT Trust

In computing its income, a trust (other than an employee trust or SIFT trust) may deduct the following amounts:[167]

(1) In the case of a trust governed by an employee benefit plan, the amount paid in the year to a beneficiary.

(2) In the case of a previously tax-exempt trust governed by an RRSP or RRIF that lost its tax-exempt status due to the death of the last annuitant, the amount actually paid in the year to a beneficiary.

(3) With certain exceptions, an amount not exceeding the amount of income (including taxable capital gains, but not including payments out of the trust's NISA Fund No. 2) that was payable in the year to a beneficiary.

However, a post-1971 spousal or common-law partner trust may not deduct income payable to a beneficiary if that income arose as a result of the deemed disposition of property when the spouse/common-law partner dies[168] or when property is distributed to a capital beneficiary other than the spouse/common-law partner while the spouse/common-law partner is alive.[169] The income arising from such deemed dispositions must be taxed in the post-1971 spousal or common-law partner trust. Similarly, a recent amendment[170] Disallows, after July 19, 1995, a deduction to post-1971 spousal or common-law partner trusts for capital gains and certain other income items arising from dispositions of property in the year in which the spouse/common-law partner died, but before the death of the spouse/common-law partner. This rule ensures that the trust, rather than any beneficiary, will be taxed on these income amounts.

In addition, a post-1971 spousal trust or common-law partner trust (described in ¶7290) cannot deduct amounts payable to anyone other than the spouse/common-law partner if the spouse/common-law partner is alive at the end of the year, unless the trust was created before December 21, 1991 or has been varied before that date to allow for such distributions. These restrictions for post-1971 spousal or common-law partner trusts are extended to alter ego trusts and joint spousal or common-law partner trusts created after 1999. The restrictions for alter ego trusts apply until the settlor's death. The restrictions for joint spousal or common-law partner trusts apply until the later of the settlor's death and that of his or her spouse or common-law partner. For further details on these specified trusts, see the commentary at ¶7290.

See page ii for explanation of footnotes.

[167] CCH ¶13,170; Sec. 104(6).
[168] CCH ¶13,150, ¶13,153; Sec. 104(4), 104(5).
[169] CCH ¶13,870; Sec. 107(4).
[170] CCH ¶13,170; Sec. 104(6)(b)(iii).

Moreover, with respect to the NISA Fund No. 2, a trust cannot deduct income derived from a payment out of it unless the payment is made to a testamentary post-1971 spousal or common-law partner trust while the spouse/common-law partner is alive. A testamentary post-1971 spousal or common-law partner trust holding an interest in a NISA Fund No. 2 which it received on a rollover basis, cannot deduct amounts deemed to be received by it upon the death of the spouse/common-law partner. For 1998 and subsequent taxation years, these restrictions will not apply to a trust deemed to exist because of the special rule for communal organizations (see ¶9285).

As discussed above, a post-1971 spousal or common-law partner trust and, after 1999, an alter ego trust or a joint partner spousal or common-law trust are not allowed to deduct amounts payable in a taxation year to anyone except the relevant beneficiary, if he or she is alive throughout the year. When the relevant beneficiary (spouse, common-law partner or settlor of the trust) dies on a day in the trust's taxation year, the trust is not allowed to deduct income for that year that is payable to any other beneficiary that relates to any disposition by the trust, before the end of that day, of capital property (other than excluded properties), land described in an inventory, Canadian resource property or foreign resource property.

The ability to claim a deduction may be restricted in cases involving non-resident beneficiaries if the trust is not a resident of Canada or where beneficial interest in income of the trust is less than the beneficial interest in the capital (see ¶7305 below).

An amount is payable in the year if it is paid in the year or if the person to whom it was payable had a right to enforce payment in the year.[171] Where trust income has not become payable in the year and the income is held in the Canadian resident trust for an individual who is under 21, the right to which was vested at the end of the year without the exercise of a discretionary power, and the right was not subject to any future condition (other than a condition that the individual survives to an age not exceeding 40), the income will be deemed to be payable to the individual in the year.[172]

(4) Income of the trust required to be used for the upkeep, maintenance, or taxes on property that the trust maintains for a beneficiary.[173]

Testamentary trusts can also deduct superannuation or pension benefits that they receive when they designate these benefits as incalculable in the income of the spouse or common-law partner[174] of the deceased.[175] Benefits received from a foreign retirement arrangement after 1989 are also eligible for this treatment. This enables such spouses or common-law partners themselves to deduct the pension income tax credit (see ¶8110) with

---

See page ii for explanation of footnotes.

[171] CCH ¶13,580, ¶52,291; Sec. 104(24); Interp. Bul. IT-286R2.

[172] CCH ¶13,510; Sec. 104(18).

[173] CCH ¶13,170, ¶13,620; Sec. 104(6), 105(2).

[174] CCH ¶21,211g; Sec. 146(1.1).

[175] CCH ¶13,592; Sec. 104(27)(d).

respect to those benefits, as well as to roll them over without immediate tax consequences to their own registered retirement savings plans (RRSPs) or registered pension plans (RPPs) under certain circumstances. (See ¶10,357.) Similar rules permit testamentary trusts, under similar circumstances, to deduct amounts received by them from RRSPs or deferred profit sharing plans (DPSPs), where the beneficiary designated is the spouse or common-law partner of the deceased.[176]

Where a trust borrowed money in order to make discretionary capital allocations to the beneficiary rather than liquidating capital assets, interest paid on the borrowed money was not deductible from trust income.[177] Substantial legal fees incurred by a testamentary trust in order to enhance its investment income were also held to be non-deductible.[178]

[¶7300] Deduction Where Capital Interest Greater than Income Interest

A trust, other than a personal trust, may make no deduction in respect of income payable to any beneficiary, and all of its income will be subject to tax if it is reasonable to consider that one of the main reasons for the creation of an interest in the trust is to give a beneficiary a percentage interest in the capital of the trust that is greater than the beneficiary's percentage interest in its income.[179]

This prevents the further use of trusts which were structured along the following lines: a trust would be established with two classes of beneficial interest, for example, A units and B units. The A units would be entitled to all the income of the trust and the B units would be entitled to all the capital. The A units would be sold to investors interested in receiving dividend income and the B units would be sold to investors interested in realizing capital gains. The trust would invest in the shares of a single company which had a fixed dividend or an established dividend policy. After a fixed period of time, this trust would be terminated and the shares would be sold or distributed to the B unitholders. This structure permitted investors in different circumstances to each realize a greater after-tax return than if they had purchased the shares directly.

Personal trusts are excepted from this rule but virtually all *inter vivos* "commercial trusts" are covered and in such trusts it will be necessary that all beneficiaries have the same interest in the income and capital of the trust.

Furthermore, if a taxpayer has a right to acquire an interest in or property of a trust and one of the main reasons for acquiring that right was to avoid the application of the above rule, any gain realized on the disposition of this right or trust interest or property is an income gain.[180] But for

---

See page ii for explanation of footnotes.

[176] CCH ¶13,593, ¶21,324; Sec. 104(27.1), 146(8.1).   [179] CCH ¶13,201; Sec. 104(7.1).

[177] [Bronfman Trust, 87 DTC 5059.

[178] [Pappas Estate, 90 DTC 1646.   [180] CCH ¶13,202; Sec. 104(7.2).

¶**7300**

this rule, that gain would be treated as a capital gain, only a portion of which would be included in income.

[¶7305] Deduction by Employee Trust

An employee trust is permitted to make a deduction equal to the amount of its income other than business income.[181] This corresponds to the amount the trustee is required to allocate annually to the beneficiaries in order to qualify as an employee trust and to the amount on which the beneficiary is taxed.[182] As a result, only net business income is taxed in the trust. Since an employee trust will pay tax at a minimum federal rate of 29%,[183] this provision is presumably designed to deter such trusts from carrying on business.

[¶7307] Deduction by SIFT Trust

As a result of the federal government's crackdown on the use of income trusts and public partnerships, first announced on October 31, 2006, an income trust that is a "SIFT trust" (meaning a specified investment flow-through trust), is generally prohibited from deducting its "non-portfolio earnings" for a taxation year that are payable to its beneficiaries in the year.[184] Non-portfolio earnings include the SIFT trust's net income from businesses it carries on in Canada, its net income from non-portfolio properties other than taxable dividends, and its taxable capital gains in excess of allowable capital losses from dispositions of non-portfolio properties.[185]

This restriction on the deduction by SIFT trusts came into force on October 31, 2006, but owing to the application of the definition of "SIFT trust", the earliest it can have practical effect is for a trust's taxation year ending after 2006. Furthermore, owing to grandfathering rules that apply to trusts that otherwise would have been considered SIFT trusts on October 31, 2006 (had the definition been applicable on that date), this regime does not apply to such trusts until the 2011 taxation year, provided they do not exceed certain "normal growth" guidelines issued by the Department of Finance.

Further restrictions have been announced with draft legislation released on July 25, 2012. In some structures involving stapled securities, a corporation or SIFT (alone or together with a subsidiary) might issue equity and debt instruments — at least one of which is publicly traded — that are stapled together. The income tax provisions are proposed to be amended to provide that, notwithstanding the general rules applicable to the deductibility of interest, interest that is paid or payable on the debt portion of such a stapled security will not be deductible in computing the income of the payer

See page ii for explanation of footnotes.

[181] CCH ¶13,170; Sec. 104(6)(a).
[182] CCH ¶2374; Sec. 6(1)(h).
[183] CCH ¶19,250; Sec. 122(1).

[184] CCH ¶13,170; Sec. 104(6)(b)(iv).
[185] CCH ¶19,274; Sec. 122.1(1) "non-portfolio earnings".

for income tax purposes. However, stapling arrangements that involve only shares issued by publicly traded corporations (the distributions on which are treated as dividends for tax purposes) are not intended to be affected by the amendment.[186]

In other structures, a REIT (or a subsidiary of a REIT) might issue a security to its investors in circumstances in which the security similarly can be transferred only together with an interest in another entity, such as a trust or a corporation. Typically, the other entity, directly or through its subsidiaries, carries on a business or holds property that the REIT could not carry on or hold directly without losing its status as a REIT. The income tax provisions are proposed to be amended to provide that, notwithstanding the general rules applicable to the deductibility of amounts, any amount (including, but not limited to rent) that is paid or payable by the other entity (or its subsidiaries) to the REIT (or its subsidiaries, and including "back-to-back" intermediary arrangements) will not be deductible in computing the income of the payer for income tax purposes.

These proposed changes would be applicable for taxation years ending after July 20, 2011.

[¶7310] Non-Residents — Trusts and Beneficiaries

[¶7315] General Treatment

A trust that is not a resident of Canada throughout a taxation year may not deduct any amount that was payable to a "designated beneficiary" that is a non-resident or a non-resident-owned investment corporation. The non-resident beneficiary's share of taxable income earned in Canada by a designated trust will therefore be subject to tax in the hands of the trust under Part I, whereas amounts paid by the non-resident trust to a designated beneficiary will not be subject to Canadian tax. But for this provision, a non-resident trust with designated beneficiaries could earn taxable income in Canada and distribute it to the beneficiaries without incurring any Canadian tax.[187]

A special tax under Part XII.2,[188] generally equal to 36% of the designated income of an *inter vivos* trust, is also imposed, unless the amount of income distributed by the trust to its beneficiaries and deductible as such is less than 64% of the designated income of the trust for the year.[189] See ¶14,135.

Where all the trust beneficiaries are non-residents of Canada, dividends and interest received by the trust from a non-resident-owned investment corporation are deductible by the trust.[190] However, these amounts

---

See page ii for explanation of footnotes.

[186] Sec. 122.1.
[187] CCH ¶13,200; Sec. 104(7).
[188] CCH ¶25,883; Sec. 210.2.

[189] CCH ¶25,885; Sec. 210.2(3).
[190] CCH ¶13,300; Sec. 104(10).

are, for the purposes of liability for non-resident tax, deemed to have been paid to the non-resident person on the last day of the year.[191]

[¶7320] Withholding Tax

A withholding tax is imposed on income of or from a resident trust that is paid or credited to non-residents. The tax is at the rate of 25% in the absence of a treaty that stipulates a lower rate.[192]

[¶7325] Capital Gains of Non-Resident

There is excepted from withholding tax any payment from a trust that is a distribution or payment of capital (see ¶14,135).

Taxable capital gains realized in a trust from the disposition of taxable Canadian property (together with the other items comprised in designated income — see ¶14,135) are taxed in the trust to the extent that they are payable to non-resident beneficiaries. Adjustments are made to the withholding tax to take this into account.

[¶7330] Capital Interest in Resident Trust Considered "Taxable Canadian Property"

A capital interest in a resident trust is "taxable Canadian property".[193] Accordingly, a non-resident capital beneficiary will be taxable on any taxable capital gain realized on the disposition of his or her capital interest in a trust.

[¶7335] Canada–U.S. Tax Convention

The *Canada–U.S. Tax Convention (1980)* provides that, to the extent that income distributed by an estate or trust resident in one Contracting State is deemed under the domestic law of that State to be a separate type of income "arising" within that State, such income distributed to a beneficiary resident in the other Contracting State may be taxed in the State of source at a maximum rate of 15% of the gross amount of such distribution.

Such a distribution will, however, be exempt from tax in the State of source to the extent that the income distributed by the estate or trust was derived by the estate or trust from sources outside that State. Thus, in a case where the law of Canada treats a distribution made by a trust resident in Canada as a separate type of income arising in Canada, Canadian tax is limited to 15% of the gross amount distributed to a U.S. resident beneficiary.[194]

See page ii for explanation of footnotes.

[191] CCH ¶13,330; Sec. 104(11).
[192] CCH ¶29,024; ITAR 10(6).

[193] CCH ¶17,101, ¶28,284; Sec. 115(1)(b), 248(1) "taxable Canadian property".
[194] CCH ¶30,227d; Art. XXII(2), Canada-U.S. Income Tax Convention.

[¶7337] Canada–U.K. Tax Convention

The *Canada–U.K. Tax Convention (1978)* provides that a U.K. resident who receives income from an estate or trust resident in Canada may be taxed at a rate of up to 15%.

Payments from a trust which is connected to a business with a permanent establishment, or to a professional services business with a fixed base in Canada, are not subject to the 15% limit.

If contributions to the trust are deductible under Canadian tax law, the trust is deemed not to be a trust.[195]

[¶7340] Accumulating Income — Election — Preferred Beneficiaries

[¶7345] Preferred Beneficiary Election After 1995

For trusts' taxation years beginning after 1995, a trust and a "preferred beneficiary" under the trust may elect to have a portion of the trust's accumulating income for the trust's taxation year, not exceeding the allocable amount for the preferred beneficiary, included in computing the income of the preferred beneficiary for the beneficiary's taxation year in which the trust's taxation year ended. Such elected amount is excluded from the income of any beneficiary under the trust (not necessarily the beneficiary making the election) for a subsequent taxation year in which it is paid. The allocable amount for a preferred beneficiary for a taxation year generally means the trust's accumulating income for the year. A trust's accumulating income for a taxation year generally means its income for the taxation year calculated before deducting any amount included in computing income of a preferred beneficiary because of a preferred-beneficiary election.

For a trust's taxation year that ends after 1996, a preferred beneficiary under a trust generally means an individual beneficiary who is eligible for a disability tax credit or an adult beneficiary for whom a dependant tax credit can be claimed by another individual because of the beneficiary's mental or physical infirmity.[196]

The preferred beneficiary election must generally be filed within 90 days from the end of the trust's taxation year. Late, amended, or revoked elections can be made in limited circumstances (generally those beyond the control of the trustee and beneficiary) if the Minister so permits and a late-filing penalty is paid. The election requires the filing of these two documents:

See page ii for explanation of footnotes.

[195] CCH ¶30,265; Art. XX, Canada–U.K. Income Tax Convention.

[196] CCH ¶13,343, ¶13,410, ¶13,415, ¶13,420, ¶13,430, ¶13,930, ¶52,379; Sec. 104(12), 104(14), 104(14.01), 104(14.02), 108(1) "preferred beneficiary"; Reg. 2800; Interp. Bul. IT-394R2.

(1) A signed statement by the preferred beneficiary and a trustee designating that part of the accumulating income in respect of which the election is being made. A statement is required for each year in which an election is made.

(2) A statement signed by the trustee showing the computation of the amount of the preferred beneficiary's share in the accumulating income of the trust for the year, along with any other supporting information which might be necessary for this purpose.

With two exceptions, all income of a trust payable in the year to a beneficiary (and amounts not so payable, but on which a preferred beneficiary election has been made for the year) is included in the income of the beneficiary for that year.

The exceptions arise where a trust governed by an employee benefit plan is involved. First, amounts *paid* to a person who has contributed to the plan as an employer are included in that person's income. Second, amounts *payable* to a beneficiary of a trust governed by an employee benefit plan are not included in the beneficiary's income.

If an amount is payable but not paid, it is not included in the beneficiary's income in a later year when it is paid. Once a preferred beneficiary election is made on a particular amount of income, that amount is not included in the income of any beneficiary in a later year when it is actually paid.[197] An amount is not considered to be payable in the year unless the beneficiary was entitled to enforce payment in that year. If, without the exercise or non-exercise of a discretionary power, trust income has unconditionally vested (other than survival to an age not exceeding 40 years) in a beneficiary less than 21 years of age at the end of the year, it will be considered to be payable to such a beneficiary during the year.[198]

[¶7355] Share of Preferred Beneficiary under a Trust

A preferred beneficiary (together with the trust) may make an election with respect to all or a portion of his or her share of the accumulating income of the trust (the "allocable amount").

In the case of a post-1971 spousal or common-law partner trust or a pre-1972 spousal trust, if the beneficiary spouse or common-law partner is still alive at the end of the taxation year of the trust, the beneficiary spouse or common-law partner's allocable amount for the year is all of the accumulating income, and the allocable amount of any other beneficiary is considered to be nil. Even if the spouse/common-law partner is not entitled to receive any portion of the trust's taxable capital gain, the spouse/common-law partner is nevertheless the only person entitled to elect to pay tax on such gains. If the trust continues after the death of the spouse/common-law

---

See page ii for explanation of footnotes.
[197] CCH ¶13,400, ¶13,580; Sec. 104(13), 104(24).   [198] CCH ¶13,510, ¶52,347; Sec. 104(18); Interp. Bul. IT-342R.

partner, the trust will be governed by the other preferred beneficiary provisions for the year of death and after.[199]

For 2000 and subsequent taxation years, the preferred beneficiary election will be available with respect to income allocations from: (i) an alter ego trust, to the settlor, during the settlor's lifetime; and (ii) a joint spousal or common-law partner trust, to the settlor and the settlor's spouse/common-law partner, during the lifetimes of the settlor and the settlor's spouse/common-law partner. Alter ego trusts and joint spousal or common-law partner trusts are defined in ¶7290.

For any other trust, the allocable amount for a preferred beneficiary for a taxation year is:

(a) the accumulating income of the trust for the year, provided the beneficiary has a right of any type to any portion of that income and such right is not entirely contingent on the death of another beneficiary who has a capital interest in the trust and who does not have an income interest in the trust, and

(b) in any other case, nil.

[¶7357] SIFT Deemed Dividend

As discussed at ¶7307, a SIFT trust is prohibited from deducting its non-portfolio earnings for a taxation year that are otherwise payable to its beneficiaries in the year. The amounts so payable, but not deductible, referred to in the aggregate as the trust's "non-deductible distributions amount" for the taxation year, are treated as taxable dividends in the hands of the recipient beneficiaries of the trust.[200] Accordingly, the non-portfolio earnings of the trust that are distributed to its beneficiaries are treated similarly to income earned by a public corporation and distributed to its shareholders as taxable dividends.

More particularly, each beneficiary of a SIFT trust to whom any amount became payable by the trust in the taxation year is deemed to have received a taxable dividend from a taxable Canadian corporation at that time, if the SIFT trust has a non-deductible distributions amount for the taxation year, which, as noted, effectively equals its after-tax non-portfolio earnings for the year that are payable to its beneficiaries in the year.[201] The amount of the deemed dividend for each such beneficiary is determined as the *pro rata* portion of the non-deductible distributions amount of the trust, based on the amount payable to the beneficiary divided by all amounts payable to all beneficiaries in the taxation year.[202] Since this *pro rata* fraction is determined using the amount payable to the beneficiary, and not just the non-portfolio earnings of the trust payable to the beneficiary (if any), it

---

See page ii for explanation of footnotes.

[199] CCH ¶13,480, ¶13,483; Sec. 104(15); Reg. 2800(3), Reg. 2800(4).

[200] CCH ¶13,491; Sec. 104(16).

[201] CCH ¶13,491; Sec. 104(16)(*a*).

[202] CCH ¶13,491; Sec. 104(16)(*b*).

is possible that a particular beneficiary will be deemed to have received a dividend, notwithstanding that the beneficiary did not receive any of the trust's non-portfolio earnings, nor, indeed, any of the trust's income.

The amount of the dividend deemed to have been received by a beneficiary of the SIFT trust is considered an "eligible dividend" (see ¶6052). As such, if the beneficiary is a Canadian resident individual, the beneficiary will be entitled to the enhanced dividend tax credit (see ¶8280). If the beneficiary is a Canadian corporation, it will be eligible for the inter-corporate dividend deduction (see ¶6030). If the beneficiary is non-resident, the deemed dividend is treated as a taxable dividend received from a corporation resident in Canada for the purposes of the Part XIII withholding tax, which may be reduced by an income tax treaty.[203]

This deemed dividend treatment of the distributed non-portfolio earnings of a SIFT trust came into force on October 31, 2006, but owing to the application of the definition of "SIFT trust", the earliest it can have practical effect is for a trust's taxation year ending after 2006. Furthermore, owing to grandfathering rules that apply to trusts that otherwise would have been considered SIFT trusts on October 31, 2006 (had the definition been applicable that date), this treatment does not apply to such trusts until the 2011 taxation year, provided they do not exceed certain "normal growth" guidelines issued by the Department of Finance.

[¶7360] Amounts Deemed Not Paid

A trust can designate all or part of the trust income payable to a beneficiary as not so payable. The designated amount is deemed not to be included in the income of the beneficiary. A trust might make such a designation if it has not deducted from its income the full amount paid or payable to its beneficiaries. The effect of the designation is that the amount designated will not be included in the income of the beneficiary and so will not be subject to double taxation, as the designated amount is included in the income of the trust and so taxed in the trust. A trust which is not resident in Canada throughout a taxation year cannot make a designation.[204]

[¶7365] Property Transfers to Spouse, Common-Law Partner, or Minor — Attribution

Where a taxpayer has transferred property to or for the benefit of the taxpayer's spouse or common-law partner, to a person who has since become the taxpayer's spouse or common-law partner, to a person under 18 years of age with whom the taxpayer does not deal at arm's length, or to the taxpayer's nephew or niece under 18 years of age by means of a trust or

---

[203] CCH ¶13,491; Sec. 104(16)(*d*).   [204] CCH ¶13,400–13,405; Sec. 104(13)–(13.2).

by any other means, the income from the property so received is deemed to be income of the transferor and not of the transferee.[205] See ¶2620 *et seq.*

Discretionary or revocable trusts, where the power to exercise the discretion or revocation lies with the transferor, are taxed such that any income or loss, or capital gain or loss, is considered to be that of the transferor.

Although the above attribution rules reduce the opportunities for income splitting, several tax planning techniques have developed over time. To discourage income splitting with minor children, the 1999 Budget introduced an income-splitting tax (the "kiddie tax") beginning in the year 2000 to be levied on certain income of individuals under 18 years of age at the end of a calendar year. These individuals will be subject to tax at the highest marginal rate (currently 29%) on the following types of income: taxable dividends and shareholder benefits on unlisted shares of any corporation (whether received directly or through a trust or partnership); and income from a partnership or trust if that income is derived from providing goods or services to a business carried on by a relative of the child or in which the relative participates. In order to avoid double taxation, income subject to the income-splitting tax will be deductible in computing the minor's taxable income under Part I. Further, income that is subject to the income-splitting tax will not be eligible for any deductions other than the dividend tax credit and foreign tax credit. Income that will be taxed under this new measure will not be subject to the attribution rules.

Since the introduction of the kiddie tax, new income splitting techniques have developed that use capital gains being realized for the benefit of a minor on a disposition of shares to a relative of the minor. In response, the 2011 Budget extended the kiddie tax to capital gains realized by a minor from a disposition of shares to a minor's relative, if taxable dividends on those shares would have been subject to the kiddie tax. More specifically, twice the amount that would otherwise have been the minor's taxable capital gains from the disposition of shares is deemed to be a taxable dividend received by the minor and becomes subject to the 29% kiddie tax. This budgetary measure was enacted in Bill C-13 which received Royal Assent on December 15, 2011 and applies to capital gains realized by a minor after March 21, 2011. For more details, see ¶8085 in Chapter VIII.

See page ii for explanation of footnotes.

[205] CCH ¶9516–9560a, ¶52,374, ¶52,515, ¶52,516;   IT-511R; Sachs, 80 DTC 6291, Lackie, 79 DTC
Sec. 74.1, 74.5; Interp. Bul. IT-369R, IT-510,   5309.

[¶7370] Capital Cost Allowances — Dividends — Capital Gains — Principal Residence Exemption

[¶7375] Deduction for Capital Cost Allowance and Depletion

If a trust owns depreciable property or a capital resource property, it is entitled to claim the capital cost allowances or depletion.

For taxation years of a trust commencing before January 1, 1988, a trust had the option of allocating these deductions to its beneficiaries rather than making the claim itself. No such allocations to beneficiaries can be made after 1988.[206]

Capital cost allowances are subject to possible recapture upon sale of the property. Recaptured depreciation will be income of the trust and not of the beneficiary, even though it is the beneficiary who has deducted the capital cost allowances.

[¶7380] Flow-Through of Taxable Dividends to a Beneficiary

A trust may attribute to its income beneficiaries the taxable dividends it received from taxable Canadian corporations during the year. The trust does this by designating a reasonable portion of the income payable or accumulating income allocated to a beneficiary as being composed of these dividends. If the trust makes such a designation, the taxable dividend on a share of a taxable Canadian corporation is deemed to be a taxable dividend on that share received in the year by the beneficiary for all purposes of the Act, other than non-resident withholding tax under Part XIII. Where a non-resident beneficiary is involved, non-resident withholding tax will be applicable on the basis that income of a trust is paid or credited and not on the basis that the non-resident beneficiary received a taxable dividend.[207]

Except for the purposes of the dividend gross-up and the stop loss, the amount designated by the trust as a taxable dividend received in the year by a beneficiary will still be treated as having been received by the trust and will be included in the beneficiary's income. However, in most cases, the trust will be allowed a corresponding deduction to offset the resulting income inclusion (see ¶7295). No deductions are allowed for income from *alter ego* trusts, joint spousal or common-law partner trusts, and post-1971 spousal or common-law partner trusts payable to a beneficiary, other than the settlor or the settlor's spouse or common-law partner, as the case may be, during the lifetime of the settlor or spouse or common-law partner.

Where a resident beneficiary, other than a trust which is a registered charity, is deemed to receive part of his trust income as a dividend from a taxable Canadian corporation, the dividend gross-up and the dividend tax

See page ii for explanation of footnotes.

[206] CCH ¶13,400; Sec. 104(13).   [207] CCH ¶13,540, ¶52,529; Sec. 104(19); Interp. Bul. IT-524.

credit apply. If the beneficiary happens to be a corporation, it is normally eligible for the intercorporate dividend deduction (see ¶6030). However, the corporate beneficiary may be subject to the provisions of Part IV or of Part IV.1 of the Act in respect of the dividend it is deemed to have received.

[¶7385] Designation in Respect of Non-Taxable Dividends

A trust may designate a reasonable portion of non-taxable dividends received from a Canadian resident corporation as part of an amount payable to a particular beneficiary. This portion of a dividend is then excluded by the beneficiary in computing income.

This designation is made for the purposes of the adjusted cost base of the beneficiary's interest, the computation of a loss on the disposition by a corporate beneficiary of its interest, the computation for a corporate beneficiary of the loss of the trust arising with respect to the share of capital and non-capital property, and the loss limitation rules where a partnership realizes a capital loss from a disposition of an interest in a trust.[208]

A trust which was not resident throughout a taxation year is not permitted to make such a designation.

[¶7390] Flow-Through of Taxable Capital Gains to Beneficiaries

Under trust law, a capital gain realized by a trust is generally considered to be part of the capital of the trust. For income tax purposes, though, a taxable capital gain realized by a trust is included in computing its income. However, a trust may designate a portion of its net taxable capital gains for a taxation year as a taxable capital gain of a beneficiary of the trust.[209] In essence, the designated portion of the net taxable capital gains of the trust is deemed to be the taxable capital gain of a particular beneficiary. Accordingly, the beneficiary may use allowable capital losses realized in the year or previous years to offset this income. The amount of the net taxable capital gains that may be designated to a particular beneficiary is limited to the portion of the net taxable capital gains as may reasonably be considered, having regard to all circumstances, including the terms and conditions of the trust arrangement, to be part of the amount included in computing the beneficiary's income for the taxation year. For this purpose, the amount of the trust's net taxable capital gains equals the amount (if any) by which the trust's taxable capital gains for the year exceed the total of:

(a) its allowable capital losses for the year, and

(b) the amount of net capital losses of other years that are deducted by it in determining its taxable income for the year.[210]

See page ii for explanation of footnotes.

[208] CCH ¶13,542; Sec. 104(20).   [210] CCH ¶13,552; Sec. 104(21.3).
[209] CCH ¶13,544, ¶52,386; Sec. 104(21); Interp. Bul. IT-381R3.

[For trust taxation years that begin after 2000, allowable business investment losses (ABILs) may be disregarded in the computation of a trust's allowable capital losses. As a result, ABILs will not result in a reduction of taxable capital gains that may be flowed through to beneficiaries under trusts and against which allowable capital losses can be claimed. This technical proposal was released on July 16, 2010 with other proposed draft legislation, but is not yet enacted.]

The designation (made in the trust's Part I return for the year) may be made only if the trust is a mutual fund trust or if the particular beneficiary is resident in Canada. It is not available to trusts that were not resident in Canada throughout the taxation year.

The amount designated does not automatically qualify for the capital gains exemption. The trust must also designate to the beneficiary an amount or amounts in respect of its eligible taxable capital gains, if any, for the year.[211] The term "eligible taxable capital gains" is defined to mean the lesser of:

(a) the trust's "annual gains limit" for the year, which, for taxation years beginning after February 22, 1994, is generally the trust's taxable capital gains, net of losses, from dispositions of qualified farm property and qualified small business corporations in the year, plus, for dispositions after May 1, 2006, the trust's taxable capital gains net of losses from dispositions of qualified fishing property for the year, minus net capital losses from other years that are deducted from such net gains and the trust's allowable business investment losses for the year; and

(b) the amount by which (i) the trust's "cumulative gains limit", which is generally the amount by which the cumulative positive components of the annual gain limit for previous years exceeds its cumulative negative components for previous years and the trust's cumulative net investment loss at the end of the year, exceeds (ii) amounts designated by the trust in previous taxation years. [212]

The amount arrived at through these calculations is deemed, for the purposes of the capital gains exemption, to be a taxable capital gain realized by the beneficiary, and the beneficiary is deemed to have disposed of these three types of capital property.

[¶7394] Non-Resident Trusts (NRTs)

Taxation years beginning before 2007

Undue deferral of tax through the use of non-resident trusts is prevented by deeming such trusts to be resident in Canada for Part I purposes. This

---

[211] CCH ¶13,548; Sec. 104(21.2).

[212] CCH ¶13,918; Sec. 108(1) "eligible taxable capital gains".

rule will apply to trusts which are not resident in Canada if a person resident in Canada was directly or indirectly beneficially interested in the trust and either the trust had directly or indirectly acquired property from a person resident in Canada, or the beneficiary had directly or indirectly acquired the trust interest from a person resident in Canada. It does not apply in respect of a trust governed by a foreign retirement arrangement (essentially a U.S. IRA.).[213]

The manner in which non-resident trusts that meet the above criteria are treated for Canadian tax purposes will depend on whether the trust is a discretionary trust or a non-discretionary trust.

If the non-resident trust is a discretionary trust, it is treated as a Canadian resident who must compute its income based on the total of its Canadian source income and its foreign accrual property income, if any. Each beneficiary is jointly and severally liable to pay the Canadian tax of the trust. However, the liability can be enforced against a particular beneficiary only to the extent that the beneficiary has received a distribution from the trust or proceeds from the sale of an interest in the trust.

If the non-resident trust is a non-discretionary trust, it is treated as a corporation resident in Canada with respect to beneficiaries who have a 10% or more beneficial interest in the trust. Consequently, the foreign accrual property income rules apply to the trust and the beneficiary, requiring the beneficiary to include a portion of the foreign accrual property income of the trust in income.

Taxation years beginning after 2006

Under outstanding proposals regarding the taxation of non-resident trusts after 2006, whenever a Canadian resident who is related to a Canadian beneficiary has made a "contribution" of property to a non-resident trust, the trust is deemed to be resident of Canada and taxable on all of its world income, with each Canadian contributor and related Canadian beneficiary jointly and solidarily liable for tax payable by the trust.

The outstanding proposals would have made the deemed resident trust taxable on all of its income, regardless of who contributed the property upon which the income was earned or the source of the income. After concerns were raised about the complexity of these outstanding proposals and the uncertainty as to how they would apply in a variety of situations, the government decided in its 2010 Budget to simplify the scope of the outstanding proposals and to better target them. For this purpose, the 2010 Budget proposed to divide the non-resident trust into a resident portion and a non-resident portion so that income not arising from the resident portion, other than Canadian-source income, be excluded from the trust's income. In addition, it was proposed that the trust's income be attributed to its resident contributors in

---

[213] CCH ¶11,550; Sec. 94.

proportion to their relative contributions to the trust. The trust would be entitled to a deduction for both the amount of its income that is payable to its beneficiaries in the year and for amounts attributed to resident contributors. As a result, the trust itself would ordinarily pay tax in Canada only on income derived from contributions of certain former resident contributors.

Under these new non-resident trust rules, when income of the trust is not distributed to beneficiaries, the amount of the accumulated income for the relevant taxation year will be deemed to be a contribution by the trust's connected contributors and will form part of the resident portion for the next taxation year. There will be an exception to this deeming rule; accumulated income that arises from property that is part of the non-resident portion will not be subject to the deeming rule if it is kept separate and apart from all the property of the resident portion.

Concern was also raised about the outstanding proposals that they do not fully recognize the foreign taxes paid to another country that also treats the trust as a resident for tax purposes. The 2010 Budget proposed to address this concern by permitting a trust that is deemed to be resident in Canada under these rules to claim a foreign tax credit for income taxes paid to another country that treats the trust as a resident of that country for income tax purposes, irrespective of the statutory limits but up to the Canadian tax rate (which generally limits the foreign tax credit in respect of property income to 15% of the foreign income).

The 2010 budgetary measures regarding non-resident trusts would apply after 2006, subject to an election allowing a trust to be deemed resident for the 2001 and subsequent taxation years. The attribution of trust income to resident contributors would apply only to taxation years that end after March 4, 2010. These budget proposals were found in the 2010 Budget implementing draft legislation that was released on August 27, 2010, but were not picked up by Bill C-47, which received Royal Assent on December 15, 2010 as S.C. 2010, ch. 25.

[¶7395] Foreign Investment Entities (FIEs)

Taxation years beginning before 2007

Whenever it may reasonably be considered that one of the main reasons for an investment in an offshore investment fund is to reduce the tax that would apply if the investment had been made directly in the underlying securities, a minimal annual income is to be reported. In general terms, this amount is determined by multiplying the cost amount of the investment by prescribed interest rates. There is an exception for inherited interests in foreign mutual funds.[214]

See page ii for explanation of footnotes.

[214] CCH ¶11,700; Sec. 94.1.

Taxation years beginning after 2006

Under previous proposals in draft form regarding the taxation of foreign investment entities (FIEs) after 2006, investors would have three alternatives to calculate their investment income from a participating interest in an FIE: (1) the mark-to-market method if their interest has a readily available fair market value; (2) the accrual method (based on their share of entity level income) if the required information is available; and (3) the imputed income method (based on a prescribed rate applied to the designated cost or the interest). However, in its 2010 Budget, the government announced that it would not proceed with its proposed FIE regime and revert to the pre-2007 existing "offshore investment fund property" rules, subject to a certain minor modification. The only change was to increase by 2% the prescribed rate of interest at which foreign investments are deemed to accrue for Canadian tax purposes. These proposals apply after March 4, 2010, and are found in the consultation draft legislation that was released on August 27, 2010, but is not yet enacted. A taxpayer who voluntarily complied with the FIE proposals in previous years will have the option of requesting to have those years reassessed by the CRA. Such a request must be made on or before the day that is 365 days after these rules receive Royal Assent.

If the taxpayer does not wish to be reassessed by the CRA, and had *more income* than would have been the case under the existing "offshore investment fund property" rules, the taxpayer will be entitled to a deduction for the excess income. Under such an option, the foreign investment entities held by the taxpayer for 2001 to 2008 would be deemed to be the amount of tax required to be remitted, and the taxpayer would be allowed a deduction for the amount, if any, by which the amounts included in income in respect of those investments for those years was in excess of the amount that would otherwise have been included in income in respect of those investments for those years The deduction must be claimed by the taxpayer in computing the taxpayer's income for the first taxation year that ends after the last taxation year of the taxpayer that ends before March 4, 2010.

If a taxpayer voluntarily complied with the FIE proposals in previous years in respect of a participating interest, and included *less in income* than would have been the case under the existing "offshore investment fund property" rules, the excess is not required to be included in income. Instead, the taxpayer will be required to deduct an amount in computing the adjusted cost base of those participating interests held after the start of the taxpayer's first taxation year that ends after March 4, 2010. The deduction amount is the amount by which the deductions reported by the taxpayer under the previous FIE proposals exceed the income inclusions reported by the taxpayer under the previous FIE proposals.

¶7395

[¶7397] Principal Residence Exemption

A personal trust may claim the principal residence exemption on a transfer of principal residence to a beneficiary of the trust in satisfaction of all or part of his or her interest in the trust.[215] Where the trust so elects in its return for the year in which the transfer is made, the trust is deemed to have disposed of the property (the principal residence) immediately before the transfer at fair market value and to have re-acquired the property at that same fair market value. If the property qualifies as a principal residence of the trust, the trust should be able to claim the principal residence exemption on any resulting capital gain.

As a result, the beneficiary will generally acquire the property (the trust's principal residence) at fair market value, and any subsequent accretion in value can be sheltered upon a subsequent disposition by the beneficiary, assuming the property becomes the principal residence of the beneficiary. Without this provision, the beneficiary acquiring the property may be put in a position where he or she will be paying tax (on a subsequent disposition by the beneficiary) on the gain which accrued while the property was in the trust, for which no principal residence exemption was previously claimed.

[¶7400] Foreign Tax Credits

[¶7405] Rules for Allocation of Foreign Taxes

Subject to certain limits, a taxpayer who receives income from foreign sources and has paid foreign taxes thereon is entitled to deduct the foreign taxes paid from Canadian tax otherwise payable.[216] This principle also applies to income from trusts where a portion of this income represents foreign income earned by the trust.

The trust is permitted to allocate to its beneficiaries the foreign taxes it has paid.[217] This will permit the beneficiaries to utilize the foreign taxes as credits against their Canadian taxes. However, where the trust has claimed the foreign taxes paid as a deduction in computing its income, the foreign taxes may not also be allocated to its beneficiaries.

The following rules apply for the allocation of foreign tax credits:

(1) If a portion of the income of the trust for a taxation year is from sources in a foreign country, a portion of that income may be deemed to have been income of a beneficiary from sources in the foreign country, assuming that part of the income of the trust is paid or payable to the beneficiary in the year and is included in the beneficiary's income.

See page ii for explanation of footnotes.

[215] CCH ¶13,842; Sec. 107(2.01).

[216] CCH ¶19,700, ¶52,187; Sec. 126; Interp. Bul. IT-395R2.

[217] CCH ¶13,560, ¶13,564, ¶52,205; Sec. 104(22)–(22.4); Interp. Bul. IT-201R2.

(2) In such circumstances, a beneficiary who is deemed to have obtained income from a source in a foreign country will be deemed to have paid a certain proportion of the business income tax or non-business income tax, as the case may be, which was paid by the trust to the government of the foreign country or political subdivision of that country.

(3) Any amount designated by the trust to be income of beneficiaries from a source in the foreign country is deducted in computing the trust's income from that source.

(4) Any amount of business income tax or non-business income tax in respect of a source in a foreign country that is deemed to be paid by a beneficiary because of a designation is to be deducted in computing the business income tax or non-business income tax paid by the trust in respect of that source.

Before applying these rules to the circumstances of a particular trust it will be necessary to ascertain the income of the trust for the taxation year from a source in a foreign country. It will then be necessary to determine the income or profits tax paid to the government of the foreign country on that source. It should be noted, in particular, that only income from sources in the foreign country which qualifies as "income" as determined under the Canadian *Income Tax Act* will be taken into consideration.

[¶7410] Testamentary Trusts and Minors

[¶7415] Taxation Year of Trust

A "testamentary trust" is defined[218] as a trust or estate that arose upon the death of an individual and in consequence of the individual's death; the term does not, however, include any trust that was created by any person other than that individual.

The taxation year of such a trust is the period for which the accounts of the trust are ordinarily made up and accepted for assessment purposes.[219] This period cannot be more than 12 months and its end may be changed only with the consent of the Minister. Note that testamentary trusts are *not* subject to the new calendar-year fiscal rules, applicable to individuals carrying on a business.

A beneficiary of a testamentary trust is taxable for a particular calendar year only on benefits derived from the trust during the taxation year of the trust ending in that calendar year. Thus, benefits received after the end of the taxation year of the testamentary trust, but before the end of the calendar year, are not taxable until the following calendar year.

If the beneficiary of a testamentary trust dies after the end of the taxation year of the trust but before the end of the same calendar year, a separate tax

---

See page ii for explanation of footnotes.

[218] CCH ¶13,940; Sec. 108(1) "testamentary trust".   [219] CCH ¶13,578; Sec. 104(23).

return for the period from the end of the taxation year of the trust until his or her death may be filed as if the beneficiary were another person. For example, if the taxation year of a testamentary trust ends on September 30 of each year and an income beneficiary dies on November 1, 2007, a return separate from his or her income from the trust for the period from October 1, 2006, to November 1, 2007, may be filed.[220] This return is to be filed as if the beneficiary were another person, the period were a taxation year, the other person's only income for the period were the beneficiary's income from the trust for that period, and the person were entitled to personal tax credits and deductions.

To the extent that they are not claimed on another return, the beneficiary may claim medical expenses, charitable donations, and the pension income credit. Where separate returns are filed for a deceased taxpayer, the total credits allowed for medical expenses, charitable donations, and pension income are limited to the total claim available if separate returns were not filed.[221] The personal credits are allowed on each separate return as well as the ordinary return.

A trust arising on death is not required to make tax instalment payments. It must pay the tax as estimated in its return within 90 days of the end of its taxation year.

Under outstanding technical amendments, for taxation years ending after December 20, 2002, a testamentary trust will become an *inter vivos* trust and lose its tax status as a testamentary trust if it incurs a debt or obligation to pay an amount to, or guaranteed by, a beneficiary or any other non-arm's length person or partnership. This rule does not apply to debts or obligations that are: (i) incurred in satisfaction of a beneficiary's right to enforce payment of an amount payable by the trust or to receive any part of the trust's capital; (ii) owed to the beneficiary for services rendered for the trust; or (iii) owed to the beneficiary as a result of a payment on the trust's behalf for which property was transferred to the beneficiary within 12 months of the payment and the payment would have been made had the beneficiary dealt at arm's length with the trust.

[¶7420] Trust for Minor

Income of a trust payable to a beneficiary in the year is taxed to the beneficiary and not the trust.[222]

If the income of a trust is not paid or payable to a beneficiary, but instead is held in trust for an individual who did not reach 21 years of age before the end of the trust year, the income will be considered to have been payable to the individual in the year if:

See page ii for explanation of footnotes.

[220] CCH ¶13,578; Sec. 104(23)(d).

[221] CCH ¶17,019; Sec. 114.2.

[222] CCH ¶13,170; Sec. 104(6).

(a) the right to the income vested at or before the end of the trust year otherwise than because of the exercise of or failure to exercise any discretionary power; and

(b) the right to the income is not subject to any future condition (other than a condition that the individual survive to an age not exceeding 40 years).[223]

[¶7425] Benefits under Trust

[¶7430] Benefits

The value of all benefits (other than capital distributions) to a taxpayer during a taxation year from a trust, contract, arrangement, or power of appointment are to be included in the taxpayer's income for the year,[224] except amounts expended for the maintenance, upkeep, and taxes on the trust property.

[¶7435] Amounts Expended for Upkeep, etc.

If property is required by the trust document to be maintained for a life tenant or beneficiary, the amounts paid to maintain the property, as well as all taxes on the property, are included in computing the income of the life tenant or other beneficiary to the extent reasonable.[225] A common example would be where a person and the person's spouse/common-law partner own the family home in joint tenancy and the person provides in a trust will that upkeep, maintenance, and taxes on the home are to be charged to the income of his or her estate.

The life-tenant is taxed on the portion of expenses for the upkeep of the property that can reasonably be considered to have been expended for his or her benefit, e.g., normal repairs, painting, gardening, annual real estate taxes, etc. Major and long-term expenses (such as landscaping or special assessments for local improvements) would generally not be considered to fall into this category.

[¶7440] Income and Capital Interests

[¶7445] Income Interest in Trust

An "income interest" in a personal trust is a right of a taxpayer as a beneficiary under that trust to (or to receive) all or any part of the income of the trust. The right may be immediate or future, absolute or contingent, and includes a right to enforce payment of an amount by the trust, unless the right was acquired before 2000 and disposed of before March 2000.[226]

See page ii for explanation of footnotes.

[223] CCH ¶13,510; Sec. 104(18).
[224] CCH ¶13,600; Sec. 105(1).

[225] CCH ¶13,620; Sec. 105(2).
[226] CCH ¶13,920; Sec. 108(1) "income interest".

A taxpayer who disposes of an income interest in a trust must include in income for the year the entire proceeds from the disposition, subject to deduction of the cost of the income interest.[227] No capital gain or loss is taken into account.[228]

If the taxpayer has paid anything to acquire the income interest, the taxpayer may deduct the cost not previously deducted, but the deduction in any year is limited to any amounts included in income for the year (i.e., income payable by the trust). This cost may not be set off against other income. Thus, the taxpayer carries forward the cost until it has all been set off against this type of income.

Example:

> Assume that Mina is an income beneficiary of a testamentary trust set up by her late father and that in June 2011 she sold her income interest to her friend Mary for $20,000. Mina must include $20,000 in her investment income for 2011, whereas Mary, who, at the end of December 2011, received $16,000 from the trust as a distribution of income, would not include in her income for 2011 any income received from the trust, since her cost ($20,000) exceeds the income distributed to her ($16,000). Mary can carry forward the remaining $4,000 as a deduction to be applied against future trust income she receives from the trust.

This deduction for cost interest is denied to the extent that the beneficiary is entitled, in calculating taxable income, to the inter-corporate dividends deduction[229] or the deduction for dividends received by a life insurer[230] in respect of the income distributions of the trust.

The beneficiary's proceeds of disposition do not have to be included in income where the trust distributes property in satisfaction of all or part of an income interest. In such a case, the trust is deemed to dispose of the property at fair market value, and the beneficiary to acquire it at that value.[231]

[¶7450] Capital Interest in Trust

Where a personal or prescribed trust distributes property to a capital beneficiary, other than as a SIFT trust wind-up event described at ¶6278 and ¶7486, and there is a resulting disposition of part or all of the beneficiary's capital interest in the trust, the adjusted cost base of such interest immediately before the disposition is deemed to be the greater of:

(a) the adjusted cost base computed in the ordinary manner, and

(b) the "cost amount" of the capital interest.[232]

If the capital interest of a taxpayer in a trust is fully or partially satisfied on the distribution of property by the trust, the "cost amount" of the taxpayer's satisfied interest is the total of any cash and the cost amounts to the trust of other property so distributed. In any other case, the "cost amount" of the

---

See page ii for explanation of footnotes.

[227] CCH ¶13,710; Sec. 106(2)(a).

[228] CCH ¶13,710; Sec. 106(2)(b).

[229] CCH ¶16,301; Sec. 112(1).

[230] CCH ¶20,709; Sec. 138(6).

[231] CCH ¶13,720, ¶52,390; Sec. 106(3); Interp. Bul. IT-385R2.

[232] CCH ¶13,800, ¶13,820; Sec. 107(1), 107(2).

taxpayer's interest in a trust is determined by prorating the amount obtained by subtracting the trust's debts from the total of the trust's cash on hand and cost amounts of trust property. The proration factor for this purpose is the fair market value of all capital interest in the trust.[233]

Where original beneficiaries of a trust have not purchased their capital interest (e.g., the children of the testator who take subject to their parent's life interest), the adjusted cost base, computed in the ordinary manner, will be nil.

A taxpayer who disposes of a capital interest in an *inter vivos* trust not resident in Canada calculates his or her gain in the ordinary manner and is not subject to the special rules set out above. However, the distribution of property by such a trust is a deemed disposition of capital interest to which the above rules apply in computing taxable capital gains.

[¶7455] Income and Capital Interests — Capital Gains or Losses

When a trust transfers property to a beneficiary in satisfaction of an income interest, any capital gains or losses are absorbed by the trust. When a trust distributes property to an income beneficiary other than as a SIFT trust wind-up event described at ¶6278 and ¶7486, the beneficiary takes the assets at their cost to the trust, so that any future capital gains or losses are the beneficiary's and not those of the trust.[234]

This rollover applies only to personal and prescribed trusts. "Personal trusts" [235] are either testamentary trusts or *inter vivos* trusts in which no beneficial interest was acquired for consideration payable to the trust, or a person who has made a contribution to the trust. A "prescribed trust" [236] is a trust that is:

(a) maintained principally for the purpose of holding employer shares;

(b) established exclusively for the purpose of securing a debt; or

(c) established as a voting trust with respect to shares.

With the exception of a tax-deferred transfer of property from one mutual fund to another, on distribution of property by a trust (other than a personal or prescribed trust) to satisfy a beneficiary's capital interest, the trust is deemed to have disposed of the property for proceeds equal to its fair market value and the beneficiary is deemed to have acquired it at the same value.[237] This rollover applies only in circumstances where there is a distribution of property by a trust (other than a distribution as a SIFT trust wind-up event described at ¶6278 and ¶7486), which constitutes a disposition of all or part of the capital interest in a trust. If there is no disposition of a capital interest in a trust, a distribution of trust property to a beneficiary in satisfaction of all or part of the capital interest in a trust will result in the trust being deemed to

---

[233] CCH ¶13,915; Sec. 108(1) "cost amount".   [236] CCH ¶13,825; Reg. 4800.1.

[234] CCH ¶13,820; Sec. 107(2).

[235] CCH ¶13,940; Sec. 108(1) "testamentary trust".   [237] CCH ¶13,845; Sec. 107(2.1).

have disposed of the property for proceeds equal to its fair market value and the beneficiary will be deemed to have acquired the property at a cost equal to the deemed proceeds of the trust. The beneficiary will also be deemed to have disposed of the capital interest in the trust for proceeds of disposition which will be reduced by an amount of any gains realized by the trust because of the disposition and any "eligible offset". Generally speaking, the eligible offset is the proportionate amount of the trust liabilities assumed by the beneficiary as a condition for the distribution of the trust property.[238]

For purposes of computing a taxable capital gain, the adjusted cost base is the cost amount to the taxpayer of the capital interest immediately before disposal. For purposes of computing an allowable capital loss, the adjusted cost base to the taxpayer is the amount determined under the general rules for capital gains and losses. This amount will normally be less than the cost amount of the capital interest.

[¶7460] Distribution in Satisfaction of Capital Interest — Cost Amount

Where capital assets of a personal or prescribed trust are distributed to a beneficiary, either as a discretionary encroachment on capital or under a mandatory provision, there is ordinarily no deemed realization by the trust at fair market value and the trust is deemed to have disposed of the property at its "cost amount".[239] In the ordinary case, the beneficiary is deemed to have acquired it at the trust's cost amount. The "cost amount" of the property, or a part thereof, to the trust would be as follows:[240]

(a) the undepreciated capital cost of depreciable property of a class, allocated in proportion to the capital cost of assets in the class;

(b) the adjusted cost base of capital assets other than depreciable property;

(c) the value, for purposes of computing income, of any inventory;

(d) the cost to the taxpayer for a "mark-to market" property of a financial institution;

(e) $4/3$ of the cumulative eligible capital of eligible capital property;

(f) the amortized cost of accounts receivable or, if they have not been written off prior to that time, their face value (except in the case of a net income stabilization account);

(g) nil for a policy loan of an insurer;

(h) nil for an interest of a beneficiary under a mining reclamation trust; and

---

See page ii for explanation of footnotes.

[238] CCH ¶13,916; Sec. 108(1) "eligible offset".
[239] CCH ¶13,820, ¶29,540; Sec. 107(2)(a); ITAR 36.
[240] CCH ¶28,054; Sec. 248(1) "cost amount".

(i) in any other case, the cost to the taxpayer as determined for the purpose of computing income, less any amount previously deducted in computing income.

There is an exception to the foregoing rule where a post-1971 spousal or common-law partner trust distributes capital property to a person other than the spouse or common-law partner.[241] There is a further exception where a capital distribution of property other than property excluded from the deemed disposition rule at the time of departure is made to a non-resident beneficiary.[242]

[¶7465] Example Illustrating Disposition of Capital Interest and Distribution in Satisfaction Thereof

The following example illustrates the disposition of a capital interest in a personal trust and the distribution in satisfaction thereof:

Example:

Taxpayer A has a vested remainder interest in a personal trust subject to his mother's life interest. His mother is now age 80. The assets in the trust consist of cash of $1,000 and securities which have an adjusted cost base of $5,000 but a fair market value of $20,000. Mr. A sells his remainder interest to Mr. B for $18,000. Two years later, Mr. A's mother dies and the corpus of the trust is distributed to Mr. B.

Mr. A's proceeds of disposition are $18,000. His adjusted cost base is the greater of the adjusted cost base computed in the ordinary manner, i.e., nil, and the "cost amount" of his capital interest. This is calculated under the definition of "cost amount" in ¶7460 as follows:

Assets in trust — Cash	$1,000
Securities at adjusted cost base	5,000
	$6,000

Mr. A's proportion of the assets =

$$\$6,000 \times \frac{\text{f.m.v. of his capital interest}}{\text{f.m.v. of all capital interest}}$$

This equals $6,000 as he had the only capital interest.

Thus, Mr. A has a capital gain of $18,000 − $6,000 = $12,000 on the disposition of his capital interest.

On A's mother's death, the trustees immediately distributed the $1,000 in cash to Mr. B. Mr. B now has an adjusted cost base (computed in the ordinary manner) of $18,000 − $1,000, i.e., $17,000. His cost amount of his capital interest is the amount to the trust of the securities, i.e., $5,000. Several months later the trustees distribute the securities to Mr. B. Mr. B's proceeds of disposition are calculated as follows:[225]

$5,000 + ($17,000 − $5,000) = $17,000

See page ii for explanation of footnotes.

[241] CCH ¶13,870; Sec. 107(4).   [242] CCH ¶13,880; Sec. 107(5).

¶7465

Thus Mr. B realizes neither a capital gain nor a capital loss. However, he has securities worth $20,000 at a cost of only $17,000. On disposition of them he would realize a gain of $3,000. Thus the actual gain of $15,000 is split as $12,000 to Mr. A and $3,000 to Mr. B.

[¶7470] Distribution of Depreciable Property

If the property distributed to the taxpayer was depreciable property, and if the original capital cost to the trust of the property exceeds the cost at which the taxpayer is deemed to have acquired it, then the capital cost to the taxpayer for purposes of recapture, etc., is the original capital cost to the trust.[243] The taxpayer is considered to have claimed as capital cost allowance any excess of the trust's capital cost over the cost at which the taxpayer is deemed to acquire the asset.

Example:

A trust has certain depreciable property, claims capital cost allowance in respect of it and eventually distributes it to the sole capital beneficiary in satisfaction of the beneficiary's capital interest, which was acquired gratuitously.

capital cost to trust	$100,000
undepreciated capital cost	80,000
fair market value	95,000
deemed cost to beneficiary	80,000
deemed capital cost to beneficiary	100,000
deemed allowed to beneficiary as capital cost allowance ($100,000 - $80,000)	20,000
undepreciated capital cost to beneficiary	80,000

The beneficiary then sells the property for its fair market value ($95,000) and realizes recapture of $15,000.

[¶7475] Proceeds of Disposition of Capital Interest

A taxpayer will be deemed to have disposed of the capital interest in the trust for proceeds equal to the cost at which the property distributed is deemed to have been acquired, minus any "eligible offset". Generally speaking, the eligible offset is the proportionate amount of the trust liabilities assumed by the beneficiary as a condition for the distribution of the trust property.[244]

[¶7477] Proceeds of Disposition of Eligible Capital Property

Where eligible capital property is distributed in satisfaction of all or part of the capital interest, the trust is deemed to have received an amount equal to $4/3$ of the cost amount of the property to the trust immediately before that time. The beneficiary is deemed to have acquired the property at $4/3$ of that

---

See page ii for explanation of footnotes.

[243] CCH ¶13,820, ¶29,170; Sec. 107(2)(d); ITAR 20(1.2).   [244] CCH ¶13,820, ¶13,916; Sec. 107(2)(c), 108(1) "eligible offset".

same cost amount, plus adjustments in certain cases. This treatment provides the rollover for eligible capital property, since the trust only includes $3/4$ of the proceeds in the calculation of its cumulative eligible capital (CEC) account.

Additionally, the beneficiary is deemed to have previously deducted $3/4$ of any of the excess of the trust's eligible capital expenditure with respect to the property over the cost at which the beneficiary is deemed to have acquired the asset, so that the beneficiary "steps into the shoes" of the trust with respect to the CEC account.[245]

Example:

A trust distributes eligible capital property to a beneficiary in satisfaction of the beneficiary's capital interest in the trust.

ECE to trust		$100,000
CEC to trust		$ 60,000
Deemed cost to beneficiary	$4/3$ X $60,000 =	$80,000
Deemed ECE to beneficiary		$100,000
Amount deemed to have been pre- viously deducted by beneficiary under sec. 20(1)(b)	$3/4$ X ($100,000 - $80,000) = $3/4$ X $20,000 =	$ 15,000
Deemed CEC to beneficiary	($3/4$ X $100,000) - $15,000 =	$ 60,000

[¶7480] Trusts in Favour of Spouse or Common-Law Partner

Where a post-1971 spousal or common-law partner trust distributes depreciable capital property of a prescribed class, non-depreciable capital property, Canadian or foreign resource property, or land inventory, the trust is deemed to have proceeds of disposition equal to the fair market value of such property.[246] As a result, the post-1971 spousal or common-law partner trust will realize any accrued capital gains or losses and inventory profits or losses in respect of the capital property or inventory. Capital gains, recapture, or terminal losses could arise as a result of the application of this rule to depreciable property of a prescribed class. In addition, the deemed proceeds of disposition for the resource properties could result in an income inclusion. The deemed disposition of property at fair market value will apply to a distribution by *alter ego trusts* and *joint spousal or common-law partner trusts*, where the individual (or, in the case of a joint spousal or common-law partner trust, either the individual or the spouse/common-law partner) is alive on the day of the distribution and the distribution is made to a beneficiary other than the individual (or, in the case of a joint spousal or common-law partner trust, the individual or the spouse/common-law partner).

---

[245] CCH ¶13,820; Sec. 107(2)(f). [246] CCH ¶13,150, ¶13,870; Sec. 104(4), 107(4).

The beneficiary to whom the distribution is made is deemed to have acquired the property at a cost equal to its deemed proceeds of disposition to the post-1971 spousal or common-law partner trust. On any later disposition of capital property or land inventory, this base will be used to compute the beneficiary's capital gain or loss or profit or loss. Likewise, this base will be the beneficiary's original cost for purposes of computing capital cost allowance and the amount of any recaptured capital cost allowance on a subsequent disposition of the depreciable property by the beneficiary.

The beneficiary who has paid nothing for the trust interest is deemed to have acquired property for its cost amount. If such a beneficiary had to assume any debt of the trust as a condition of the distribution of the property, the amount of the debt is subtracted in arriving at the deemed proceeds of disposition of the capital interest.

[¶7485] Distribution to Non-Resident Beneficiary

Distribution of property by a trust to a non-resident beneficiary (other than as a SIFT trust wind-up event described at ¶6278 and ¶7486) is treated as disposition of property by the trust. As a result, the distribution may give rise to a capital gain. However, the trust may elect to include such gain in its income instead of having the beneficiary include the gain.[247] This deemed disposition does not apply to shares of a non-resident-owned investment corporation; real property situated in Canada; Canadian resource property; timber resource property; capital property used in, eligible capital property in respect of, and property described in the inventory of a business carried on in Canada through a permanent establishment in Canada; and certain interests in trusts and deferred income streams.

[¶7486] Distribution by SIFT Wind-Up Entity

On the winding-up of a SIFT trust and redemption of its units after July 14, 2008, a SIFT trust may distribute its shares of a Canadian corporation to its unitholders, on a tax-deferred basis. This rollover will also apply where a SIFT trust holds all of the equity interests in a second-tier trust and the second-tier trust distributes shares of a Canadian corporation to the SIFT trust on the winding-up of the second-tier trust. For this rollover to apply, there must be a distribution of all of the trust's property to its unitholders and the distribution must occur within 60 days of the first distribution of property, if any, on the wind-up of the second-tier trust. The only property that can be distributed to former SIFT unitholders under this rollover is shares of a single class of the capital stock of a taxable Canadian corporation.[248]

The following deemed proceeds of disposition achieve the tax-free rollover. The trust being wound up is deemed to have disposed of the property for proceeds of disposition equal to the adjusted cost base to the trust of the property immediately before the disposition. As to the unitholder, it is deemed

See page ii for explanation of footnotes.
[247] CCH ¶13,845, ¶13,847; Sec. 107(2.1), 107(2.11).   [248] CCH ¶13,860, ¶13,860g; Sec. 107(3), 107(3.1).

to have disposed of its units for proceeds of disposition equal to the cost amount of the unit immediately before the distribution. If the taxpayer is the only beneficiary of the trust, as would happen where the trust is wholly owned by another trust or corporation, and the taxpayer is a "SIFT wind-up entity" or a taxable Canadian corporation, the taxpayer is deemed to have acquired the trust property at a cost equal to the adjusted cost base to the trust immediately before the disposition. In any other case, such as where the beneficial interests in the trust are held by the public, the property is deemed to be acquired at the cost amount to the taxpayer of the taxpayer's interest as a beneficiary of the trust. Furthermore, if the taxpayer's interest as a beneficiary under the trust was taxable Canadian property, the new property received is deemed to continue to be taxable Canadian property of the taxpayer.

Under the above conversion method of a SIFT trust into a corporation, the trust must first transfer its property to a taxable Canadian corporation. If a liability owed by the trust is, as a consequence of the distribution, assumed by the corporation (i.e., the corporation whose shares are being distributed) and the amount payable on maturity by the corporation is the same as that amount payable by the trust, the trust may transfer this liability to the corporation without any income tax consequences. In such a case, the liability is deemed to have been incurred or issued by the corporation and not the trust.

These SIFT conversion rules apply only to the redemption of units or winding-up of a trust that occurs after July 14, 2009, and before 2013.

[¶7487] Distribution of Property with an Accrued Loss

The acquisition of a capital interest in a trust that has property with an accrued loss as a means of transferring losses is discouraged. Where the property is distributed to the beneficiary in satisfaction of that interest, any loss on a subsequent disposition of the property will be denied to the extent that it can be considered to have accrued while owned by the trust and at a time when neither the beneficiary nor a person affiliated with the beneficiary had a capital interest in the trust.[249] Without this anti-avoidance rule, a person or partnership acquiring a capital interest in a trust which has a property with an accrued loss could cause the property to be distributed in satisfaction of such interest at its cost amount to the trust and realize a loss on a subsequent disposition.

[¶7490] Distributions by Employee Trust or Employee Benefit Plan

Special rules[250] apply with respect to the distribution of property by an employee trust or an employee benefit plan to a beneficiary in satisfaction of all or part of the beneficiary's interest in the trust.

In the case of an employee trust, the trust is deemed to have disposed of the property immediately before the distribution for proceeds equal to fair

---

See page ii for explanation of footnotes.

[249] CCH ¶13,882; Sec. 107(6). [250] CCH ¶13,890; Sec. 107.1.

market value. Any gain or loss resulting on the deemed disposition would form part of the amount which the trustee must allocate among the beneficiaries of the trust. The beneficiary is deemed to have acquired the distributed property at a cost equal to its fair market value.

In the case of an employee benefit plan, the trust is deemed to have disposed of the distributed property for proceeds equal to the cost amount of the property to the trust (thus realizing neither a gain nor a loss). The taxpayer is deemed to have acquired the property at a cost equal to the greater of its fair market value at that time and the adjusted cost base of his or her interest in the trust (immediately before that time). It is this fair market value of the property distributed that is the "amount" received by the taxpayer from the plan for the purpose of computing the income inclusion. If the taxpayer would otherwise have a loss on the disposition of his or her interest in the trust, that loss is added to the adjusted cost base of the property received by the beneficiary from the trust.

The taxpayer is deemed to have disposed of his or her interest in the employee trust or employee benefit plan for proceeds equal to its adjusted cost base, thus recognizing no gain or loss on the disposition.

The recognition in an employee trust or employee benefit plan of any gain or loss in respect of property distributed to a beneficiary will apply after 1998 to a health and welfare trust.

Where depreciable property is distributed in satisfaction of the beneficiary's interest, special rules apply where the capital cost of the property to the trust exceeds the deemed cost thereof to the beneficiary. In general, these rules place the beneficiary in the trust's position for claiming capital cost allowance and recognizing recapture or terminal losses. The beneficiary's capital cost is deemed to be the trust's capital cost. The beneficiary is considered to have claimed as capital cost allowance any excess of the trust's capital cost over the cost at which the beneficiary is deemed to acquire the asset. For an example, see ¶7470.

[¶7495] Distributions by Retirement Compensation Arrangement

Special rules apply when a trust governed by a retirement compensation arrangement (RCA) distributes property to a beneficiary in satisfaction of all or part of his or her interest in the trust.[251] They can be summarized as follows:

(1) The trust is treated as having disposed of the property at its fair market value and, as such, may have to recognize a gain or loss on the distribution.

(2) The trust is deemed to have made a distribution to the beneficiary equal to the fair market value of the property. This may trigger an income inclusion as well as a refund of tax to the custodian of the arrangement under

See page ii for explanation of footnotes.

[251] CCH ¶13,892; Sec. 107.2.

Part XI.3. It should be noted that the beneficiary who receives the distribution may not be the taxpayer required to include the amount of the distribution in his or her income.

(3) The beneficiary is treated as having acquired the trust property at a cost equal to its fair market value.

(4) The beneficiary will not realize a capital gain or a loss in respect of a disposition or partial disposition of his or her interest in the trust on the distribution. Instead, he or she is deemed to have disposed of his or her interest in the RCA for proceeds of disposition equal to the adjusted cost base of his or her interest.

(5) Where the property distributed is depreciable property, a special rule will apply where the capital cost to the trust of the property exceeds the fair market value of the property. If this is the case, the beneficiary inherits the capital cost to the trust of the property for the purposes only of calculating any recapture of capital cost allowance, and the beneficiary will, on a disposition of the property at a price greater than the fair market value at the time distributed to him or her, be liable to include in income any recovery of capital cost allowance that was previously claimed by the trust.

[¶7497] Qualifying Environmental Trusts

Special rules permit the deduction of contributions to trusts maintained for the sole purpose of funding the reclamation of a site in Canada that has been used primarily for, or any combination of, the operation of a mine, the extraction of clay, peat, sand, shale or aggregates (including dimension stone and gravel), or the deposit of waste.[252]

Contributions to (or the purchase of a beneficial interest in) a qualifying environmental trust are deductible in the year made (or bought) and taxable in the year withdrawn (or when the beneficial interest is sold).[253] Investment income earned in the trust on the funds on deposit will be taxable both to the trust and the beneficiary (the contributor or purchaser which buys the beneficial interest). The trust itself is taxable under special Part XII.4 at 28%, intended to equal the corporate tax rate, since it is typically an operating corporation that will have the restoration liabilities the trust is intended to fund.[254] The same income taxed in the trust is considered ordinary taxable income of the beneficiary,[255] but the beneficiary will receive a refundable tax credit on its income allocation for the tax paid in the trust.[256] Thus, if the trust earns $1,000, it pays $280 federal tax (similar to the federal corporate rate). The $280 is a refundable credit to the beneficiary who receives from the trust a $1,000 income allocation. If the beneficiary has a net income of nil for the year (or a loss), it receives the $280 tax credit. Provision is made for the trust to flow out

---

See page ii for explanation of footnotes.

[252] CCH ¶28,226b; Sec. 248(1) "qualifying environmental trust".

[253] CCH ¶13,894; Sec. 107.3.

[254] CCH ¶25,950–25,954; Sec. 211.6.

[255] CCH ¶4377b, ¶4377c; Sec. 12(1)(z1), 12(1)(z2).

[256] CCH ¶19,998j; Sec. 127.41(1).

losses as well as income. Income or loss should retain its underlying characteristics.[257]

For taxation years ending after February 18, 1997, mining reclamation trusts were renamed "qualifying environmental trusts" and the rules were extended to similar trust funds for the reclamation of waste disposal sites and quarries for the extraction of aggregates and similar materials.

[¶7500] Transfers to Bare Trusts, Protective Trusts, and Similar Vehicles

Depending on the type of property and the type of trust, various tax consequences will result from the transfers to bare trusts, protective trusts, and similar vehicles where under current rules there is no change of beneficial ownership. These proposed amendments would preserve the CRA's administrative position with respect to bare trusts, which is essentially that such trusts are agents for their beneficiaries. However, where a Canadian resident transfers property to a non-resident bare trust after December 23, 1998, that transfer will be treated as a disposition and the bare trust will be treated as an ordinary trust.

Where bare trusts are not involved, transfers of property which do not result in any change of beneficial ownership are treated as dispositions, subject to explicit rollover rules. Where all or part of a trust interest created under the rollover rules is subsequently disposed of, it is considered to have been disposed of for proceeds of disposition that are not less than an amount based on the fair market value of the net trust assets associated with the interest.[258]

See page ii for explanation of footnotes.

[257] CCH ¶5128p, ¶5128q; Sec. 20(1)(ss), 20(1)(tt).   [258] CCH ¶13,897; Sec. 107.4.

Chapter VIII

Tax Rates, Averaging, and Credits

Individual Rates **8000**

Rates 8005

Quebec Tax Abatement 8020

Aboriginal Government Tax
Abatement 8021

CPP/QPP and UCCB
Benefits for Previous
Years 8022

Lump-Sum Payments 8023

Provincial Tax Rates for
Individuals 8025

Allocation of Tax Collected 8030

Determination of Income
Earned in a Province
(Individuals) 8035

Additional Tax on Income
Not Earned in a Province 8037

Minimum Tax **8060**

Minimum Tax 8065

Calculation of Alternative
Minimum Tax 8070

Exception for Certain
Returns and Trusts 8075

Alternative Minimum Tax
Carryover 8077

Income-Splitting Tax **8080**

Income Splitting with Minor
Children 8081

Split Income Defined 8082

Tax Computation 8083

Exclusions 8084

Taxable Capital Gains 8085

Personal Tax Credits **8090**

Overview 8091

Personal Tax Credits 8095

Age Credit 8100

EI, CPP, and QPP Credits 8105

Pension Income Credit 8110

Canada Employment
Credit 8111

Transit Pass Credit 8112

Child Fitness Tax Credit 8113

Children's Arts Tax Credit 8114

Home Renovation Tax
Credit 8115

First-Time Home Buyers'
Credit (HBTC) 8117

Volunteer Firefighters Tax
Credit 8118

Tuition Credit 8119

Full-Time Education Credit 8120

Part-Time Education Credit 8121

Post-Secondary Textbook
Credit 8122

Credit for Interest on
Student Loan 8123

Carryforward of Tuition,
Textbook, and Education
Tax Credits 8124

Medical Expense Credit 8125

Types of Expenses
Qualifying for Credit 8130

Medical Expenses
Prescribed by Regulation 8135

Mental or Physical
Impairment Credit 8145

Caregiver Tax Credit 8147

Adoption Expense Credit 8148

Charitable Donations
Credit 8150

Proof of Gift 8155

Member of Religious Order 8160

Gifts of Art 8165

Commuters 8170

Meaning of "Gifts" 8175

Donations Not Eligible for
Credit 8180

Crown Gifts 8185

Cultural Gifts 8190

Ecological Gifts 8193

Gifts by Partnership 8195

Gifts of Capital Property 8200

Gifts of Securities 8202

Gifts of Non-Qualified
Securities 8203

Granting of Options to
Charities and Other
Qualified Donees 8204

Returned Gifts 8205

Gifts by Will 8206

Gifts by Direct Designation 8207

Gift in Year of Death 8210

Transfer of Tax Credits 8215

Separate Return in Year of
Death 8220

Non-Resident Individuals —
Availability of Credits 8225

Credits in Year of
Bankruptcy 8227

Indexing of Tax Credits 8230

**Canada Child Tax Benefit
(CCTB) 8235**

National Child Benefit
System 8237

**Working Income Tax Benefit
(WITB) 8240**

Overview 8241

Eligibility 8242

Calculation 8243

Advance Payment 8244

**Overseas Employment Tax
Credit (OETC) 8250**

Tax Credit for Specified
Work Outside Canada 8251

**Refundable Medical
Expense Supplement 8255**

Refundable Medical
Expense Supplement for
Low-Income Earners 8260

**Goods and Services
Tax/Harmonized Sales
Tax (GST/HST) Credit 8265**

GST/HST Tax Credit 8270

Dividend Tax Credit 8275

Dividend Tax Credit 8280

**Labour-Sponsored Funds
Tax Credit 8285**

Labour-Sponsored Funds
Tax Credit 8290

Minimum Holding Period 8294

Corporation Rates 8295

Tax Payable for
Corporations 8300

Federal Corporate Rates 8310

Federal Tax Abatement —
Deduction from
Corporation Tax re
Provincial Taxes 8315

Corporate Surtax 8320

Additional Tax on
Investment Income 8323

Forms for Reporting
Corporate Income 8330

Investment Tax Credit 8335

General Features of the
Investment Tax Credit 8340

Basis for and Effect of
Investment Tax Credit 8341

Investment Tax Credit
Rates 8342

Expenditures which Qualify
for the Investment Tax
Credit 8343

Recapture of Investment
Tax Credit 8344

**Refundable Investment Tax
Credit 8345**

Taxpayers Eligible for
Refundable Investment
Tax Credit 8350

Individuals, Trusts, and
Qualifying Corporations 8355

Qualifying Corporations 8360

Canadian-Controlled Private
Corporations Other than
Qualifying Corporations 8365

Other Taxpayers 8370

Filing of Form T2038 8371

Balance of Investment Tax
Credit 8372

**Part VI (Financial
Institutions) Tax Credit 8375**

Part VI Tax Credit 8380

Rates for Trusts 8385

Tax Payable by Inter Vivos
Trust 8390

Manufacturing and Processing Profits **8395**

Calculation of Credit on Manufacturing and Processing Profits 8400

Formula for Calculation and Definition of Terms 8405

Partnerships 8410

Resource Industries 8415

Small Manufacturers 8420

Small Business Deduction **8425**

Small Business Deduction 8430

Canadian-Controlled Private Corporation 8435

Active Business Income 8440

Specified Investment Business 8445

Personal Services Business 8450

Computation of Small Business Deduction 8455

Partnerships and the Small Business Deduction 8460

Corporation Member of More than One Partnership 8463

Allocation of Small Business Deduction among Associated Corporations and Short Taxation Years 8465

Reduction of Small Business Deduction for Certain Large Corporations 8467

Corporate Tax Rate Reduction **8470**

General Corporate Rate Reduction 8475

Former CCPC Rate Reduction 8480

Resource Rate Reduction 8490

Political Contributions **8535**

Contributions to Registered Parties and Candidates 8537

Foreign Tax Credit **8545**

Foreign Tax Credit 8550

Non-Business Income Tax — Foreign Tax Credit 8555

Limitation on Non-Business Income Tax Credit 8560

Business Income Tax — Foreign Tax Credit 8565

Limitation on Business Income Tax Credit 8570

Short-Term Securities Acquisitions 8572

No Economic Profit 8573

Employees of International Organizations 8575

Portion of Foreign Tax Not Included 8580

Foreign Oil and Gas Levies 8585

"Business Income Tax" Defined 8590

Determination of Territorial Source of Income 8595

Carryforward and Carryback of Foreign Business Tax Credits 8600

"Non-Business Income Tax" Defined 8605

Territorial Source of Income from Property 8610

Example of Calculation of Foreign Tax Credit — Corporations 8620

Provincial Tax Credit **8625**

Provincial Corporation Tax 8630

Taxable Income Earned in a Province by a Corporation 8635

Special Cases 8640

Permanent Establishment 8645

Gross Revenue Reasonably Attributable to a Province 8650

Exclusions from Gross Revenue and Special Rules 8655

Salaries and Wages 8660

Logging Tax Credit **8665**

Logging Tax 8670

Provincial Logging Tax Rates 8675

Canadian Film or Video Production Tax Credit (CFVPTC) **8680**

Tax Credit 8685

Qualified Labour Expenditure 8687

Film or Video Production Services Tax Credit **8700**

Elimination of Film Tax
Shelter 8705
Tax Credit 8710

Qualified Canadian Labour
Expenditure 8715

Recent Changes

2012 Budget

Atlantic Investment Tax Credit

Certain parts of the oil and gas Atlantic Investment Tax Credit are proposed to be phased out over a four-year period for assets acquired on or after March 29, 2012 for use in certain oil and gas and mining activities. The credit in respect of these assets will continue to apply at a rate of 10% for assets acquired before 2014. It will be reduced to a rate of 5% for assets acquired in 2014 and 2015, and it will not be available for such assets acquired after 2015. The Atlantic Investment Tax Credit for electricity generation equipment will be extended for qualified property to include "prescribed energy generation and conservation property" acquired on or after March 29, 2012, if it is used primarily for manufacturing and processing, farming, fishing, and logging. These changes have been incorporated in draft legislation released on August 14, 2012. See discussions at ¶8342.

Scientific Research and Experimental Development ("SR&ED")

Significant changes have been proposed to the SR&ED program in the 2012 Budget. Budget Resolution 20 proposed to reduce the investment tax credit rate for SR&ED qualified expenditures, from its current rate of 20% to 15% for taxation years after 2013, with the rate being prorated for taxation years that straddle January 1, 2014. The refundable investment tax credit, which is currently 40% of the 20% investment tax credit amount, would be reduced accordingly to 40% of the new 15% amount.

The "proxy method" used in computing SR&ED expenditures will also be revised. The current prescribed proxy amount of 65% of salaries and wages is proposed to be reduced to 60% for 2013 and to 55% after 2013, prorated for taxation years that straddle the beginning of the 2012, 2013, or 2014 calendar years.

These changes have been incorporated in draft legislation released on August 14, 2012. See discussions at ¶8343, ¶8355, and in Chapter III.

Mineral Exploration Tax Credit Extended by One Year

The 2012 Budget extends eligibility for the Mineral Exploration Tax Credit by one year to flow-through share agreements entered into before March 31, 2013. Furthermore, flow-through share funds raised in one calendar year with the benefit of the credit can be spent on eligible exploration up to the end of the next calendar year under the existing "look-back" rule. Accordingly, flow-through share funds raised during the first three months of 2013 can support qualifying expenses until the end of 2014. This was enacted in Bill C-38 which received Royal Assent on June 29, 2012. See ¶8343.

Technical Amendments

Personal Services Business Tax Rate

On October 31, 2011, Finance released draft legislation removing a corporation's personal services business income from the corporation's taxable income that is eligible for the "general rate reduction percentage". That is, personal services business income would now be subject to federal corporate tax at the full unreduced rate, being 28% (assuming the availability of the 10% "federal abatement"). See ¶8450.

Finance Announcements

Indexation of 2012 Personal Tax Brackets and Credits

In the 2012 taxation year, the federal income tax rates for individuals remain the same, but a 2.8% indexation factor applies to tax bracket thresholds, personal amounts, and other amounts relating to non-refundable credits, the refundable medical expense supplement, the Old Age Security repayment threshold and the tradesperson's tools deduction. Because of their particular features, this 2.8% indexation takes effect July 1, 2012 for the Canada Child Tax Benefit and the Goods and Services Tax Credit. See ¶8005 and ¶8095 *et seq.*

[¶8000] Individual Rates

[¶8005] Rates

Federal tax rate brackets for individuals are fully indexed,[1] meaning that the tax brackets are reset every year to reflect the full increase in the Consumer Price Index for the 12-month period ending on September 30 of the preceding taxation year. As a result of the 1.4% indexation of the tax bracket, effective January 1, 2011, the tax rate structure is as follows:[2]

Taxable income	Tax
$42,707 or less	15%
In excess of:	
$41,544	$ 6,146 + 22% on next $42,707
$85,414	$15,371 + 26% on next $46,992
$132,406	$27,256 + 29% on remainder

A minimum federal tax has been in effect for taxation years commencing after 1985[3] (see ¶8065), and an income-splitting tax has applied to certain minors' income since 2000 (see ¶8080).

In addition, see ¶13,010 regarding Part I.2 tax, the clawback of old-age security benefits.

All provinces and territories except Quebec (which administers its own provincial personal income taxes) use a tax-on-income system (TONI). These provinces apply their provincial tax rates to a taxpayer's taxable income, using the same taxable income amount as determined for federal tax purposes. See ¶425 preceding Chapter I for provincial and territorial tax rates.

See page ii for explanation of footnotes.

[1] CCH ¶18,201–18,207; Sec. 117.1(1)–(4).   [3] CCH ¶19,999a; Sec. 127.5.
[2] CCH ¶18,015, ¶18,046; Sec. 117(1), 117(2).

[¶8020] Quebec Tax Abatement

There is a deemed 3% payment in respect of tax otherwise payable by individuals who have earned income in a province that provides school allowances which, in effect, means the province of Quebec.[4] In addition, since Quebec has remained outside the tax collection and cost-sharing arrangements for established programs, there is a tax abatement of 13.5% as compensation for Quebec financing its own established programs. The net result is that a Quebec resident is entitled to a 16.5% abatement of basic federal tax on income earned in Quebec. But, where a Quebec resident, who was an inactive partner in a New Jersey bottling company, claimed an abatement on the grounds that the income received was from property and not from business, the claim was disallowed.[5]

Tax otherwise payable means the greater of:

(a) the federal Part I tax payable, but for the foreign tax credit, the credits in respect of investments, political contributions and logging taxes, the share-purchase tax credit, the labour-sponsored funds tax credit, the Part XII.4 tax credit, the split income tax ("kiddie tax"), and, beginning in 2008, the working income tax benefits (WITB) advance payments; and

(b) the alternative minimum tax before any carryforward averaging adjustments.[6]

[¶8021] Aboriginal Government Tax Abatement

The Act provides for a reduction of an individual's Part I income tax liability for a taxation year by the amount of the individual's tax payable for the year to an Aboriginal government, pursuant to a law of that government made in accordance with a tax sharing agreement between that government and the Government of Canada. The reduction in Part I tax is accomplished by deeming the individual to have paid on the last day of a taxation year, on account of the individual's Part I tax payable for the year, the amount of the tax payable to the Aboriginal government.[7]

[¶8022] CPP/QPP and UCCB Benefits for Previous Years

Amounts received by an individual as a CPP/QPP benefit and as a Universal Child Care Benefit (UCCB) are required to be included in income in the year in which they are received. Such benefits, particularly the initial payment, received by the individual in a year often relate to prior years, and, as a result, an individual might pay a higher rate of tax on such benefits, since they are all included in one year. An individual may choose not to include a portion of such benefits in his or her income for the year to the extent that the portion exceeds $300 and relates to one or more preceding taxation years.[8]

See page ii for explanation of footnotes.

[4] CCH ¶18,950, ¶18,965, ¶19,050; Sec. 120(2), 120(4); Reg. 6401.

[5] Hollinger, 73 DTC 5003.

[6] CCH ¶19,050; Sec. 120(4).

[7] CCH ¶18,970; Sec. 120(2.2).

[8] CCH ¶8175; Sec. 56(8).

The individual calculates the additional tax, if any, that would have been payable in the previous years had the benefits been included in income in those years, and adds this amount to the tax otherwise payable in the year of receipt.[9] The amount of tax calculated is payable in the year of receipt; however, by spreading the calculation of the tax over previous years, the total tax liability will likely be lower than if the tax payable is calculated on the whole amount for one year.

[¶8023] Lump-Sum Payments

Sometimes, when individuals receive lump-sum payments, a portion of the amount may relate to prior years. Because income is generally taxable in the year it is received, the tax payable on such lump-sum payments may be significantly higher than it would have been if payment had been received and taxed on an ongoing basis. Relief is provided to individuals (other than trusts) by allowing them to deduct in computing their taxable income for a year the specified portion of a qualifying amount received by the individual in that year.[10]

The individual's tax is reduced by the amount that the tax otherwise payable on the receipts exceeds the sum of tax, plus interest at the prescribed rate, that would have been payable had the lump-sum payment been taxed in the taxation year to which it relates. A notional amount of interest is added to reflect the delay in payment of tax on the retroactive lump-sum payment.[11] The notional amount of interest (which is not considered to be interest for any purpose of the Act) is computed for the period that begins May 1 of the year following the year to which the qualifying lump-sum payment relates, and ceases at the end of the year preceding its receipt.

Lump-sum payments that qualify for the relief are:

(a) support amounts for the maintenance of a child, spouse, or common-law partner;

(b) superannuation or pension benefits, other than non-periodic benefits;

(c) employment insurance benefits and benefits paid under wage-loss replacement plans; and

(d) income received from an office or employment (or because of a termination of an office or employment) under the terms of a court order or judgment, an arbitration award, or in settlement of a lawsuit.

The relief is available only to the principal portion of such payments that relate to a preceding taxation year throughout which the recipient was resident in Canada. The right to receive the amount must have existed in a year prior to the year of receipt and only applies if the total qualifying payments received in a particular year is $3,000 or more.

See page ii for explanation of footnotes.

[9] CCH ¶19,150; Sec. 120.3. [11] CCH ¶19,166; Sec. 120.31(3).
[10] CCH ¶15,877; Sec. 110.2.

[¶8025] Provincial Tax Rates for Individuals

All provinces and territories except Quebec (which administers its own provincial personal income taxes) use a tax on income ("TONI") system whereby provincial taxes are calculated by applying provincial tax rates to taxable income. The TONI provinces use the same taxable income amount as determined for federal tax purposes. The TONI system allows provinces to establish their own income brackets and rates of tax on these brackets, entirely independently from the federal brackets and rates. For a chart of the provincial and territorial tax rate components, see ¶425.

[¶8030] Allocation of Tax Collected

The Minister is authorized to make an allocation of tax collected, where the tax collected includes both federal and provincial taxes, in accordance with the federal–provincial tax collection agreements, notwithstanding that the taxpayer may direct a different allocation or that no such direction was made. The taxpayer is discharged from liability to pay tax only in accordance with such allocation.[12]

[¶8035] Determination of Income Earned in a Province (Individuals)

The Act defines "income earned in a province" as meaning amounts determined under rules prescribed by regulations.[13]

The determination of an individual's income earned in a particular province will depend on whether the individual was resident in the province on the last day of the taxation year, whether or not the individual carried on business with a permanent establishment outside the province, and whether or not the individual was a resident of Canada. The basic principle of the rules set out in the regulations is to attribute to the province in which an individual resided on the last day of the taxation year the individual's income from all sources less his or her business income earned through a permanent establishment outside the province. Income earned through a permanent establishment outside a province is then attributed to a province in which the permanent establishment is located (if it is so located); if it is located in a country other than Canada, income from such an establishment is not attributable to any province and is thus subject to the surtax discussed at ¶8037. The allocation is done on Form T2203.

An individual whose residence has changed from one province to another during the year will be deemed to have earned all income for the year in the latter province. Where an individual was resident in more than one province on the last day of the taxation year, the individual will be deemed to have resided on that day only in the province which may reasonably be regarded as the individual's principal place of residence. If an individual ceases to reside in Canada before the end of the year, the last day of

---

See page ii for explanation of footnotes.

[12] CCH ¶27,330; Sec. 228. [13] CCH ¶19,050, ¶19,060–19,077; Sec. 120(4); Reg. 2600–2607.

residence in a province will be deemed to be the day the individual ceased to be a resident of Canada.

[¶8037] Additional Tax on Income Not Earned in a Province

In order to approximate the combined federal-provincial tax imposed on income earned in a province, the Act imposes a surtax on the income of individuals that is not attributable to a province.[14] Such persons would include resident individuals who carry on business outside Canada through a foreign permanent establishment, or non-resident individuals subject to Part I tax. This surtax applies at a rate of 48% of basic federal tax.

Example:

Antonio lived in Ontario and operated a business with its head office in Ontario and sales offices in Alberta and the U.S. He is married and his net business income was $40,000 and he also received personal investment income of $6,000. His basic federal tax is $5,048. Allocation of income to both of the provinces and the U.S. based on sales and salaries paid were as follows:

	Sales	% x Business Income (1)	Salaries	% x Business Income (2)
Ontario	$200,000	$20,000	$75,000	$24,000
Alberta	150,000	15,000	40,000	12,800
U.S.	50,000	5,000	10,000	3,200
	$400,000	$40,000	$125,000	$40,000

Antonio's business income is allocated to the jurisdictions as follows (allocation is equal to 1/2 of (1) + (2)):

Alberta:	($15,000 + $12,800) × 1/2	$13,900
U.S.:	($ 5,000 + $ 3,200) × 1/2	4,100
		$18,000
Ontario:	$40,000 (net business income) minus $18,000 (net business income allocated to other povinces)	22,000
	Investment income	6,000
	Total income	$46,000

The 48% surtax is calculated as follows:

48% of $\dfrac{\$\,4,100\ (U.S.\ income)}{\$46,000\ (total\ income)}$ x $75,048 **$ 216**

The remaining allocation, $41,900/$46,000, will be subject to provincial tax.

See page ii for explanation of footnotes.

[14] CCH ¶18,900, ¶19,000, ¶19,050, ¶19,060; Sec. 120(1), 120(3), 120(4); Reg. 2600(1).

[¶8060] Minimum Tax

[¶8065] Minimum Tax

Generally speaking, the alternative minimum tax (AMT) requires a revised computation of income ("adjusted taxable income"), which adds back a number of deductions allowed to individuals.[15] The amounts added back are normally in respect of certain so-called "tax-preference" items (for example, income tax deductions related to some tax shelters, capital gains, etc.). Certain deductions are permitted in arriving at AMT payable (for example, the dividend "gross-up" deduction). A basic exemption of $40,000 is allowed in arriving at AMT taxable income. The resulting AMT taxable income is subject to tax at the lowest marginal rate (currently 15%). Only foreign tax credits and the refundable portion of investment tax credits may be claimed against this tax. The taxpayer is required to compare his or her AMT liability with his or her regular tax liability and pay the higher of the two amounts. Provisions are made to allow for a seven-year carryforward of AMT in excess of regular tax which may be recovered to the extent that the regular tax liability is in excess of the AMT liability in a future year.[16]

After the capital gain inclusion rate dropped to 50% and the deductions for stock option benefits and for prospectors' and grubstakers' shares are adjusted accordingly, the effective top marginal basic federal tax rate applicable to such gains and benefits becomes 14.5% (50% of 29%), which is lower than the alternative minimum tax rate (currently 15%).

To ensure that taxpayers who realize capital gains or stock option benefits, but have little other income, are not inappropriately subject to alternative minimum tax after the 2000 drop in the capital gains inclusion rate, the alternative minimum tax inclusion rate for capital gains was reduced from 100% to 80% for 2000 and subsequent taxation years. Similarly, 40% of the stock option deduction claimed in calculating regular income tax on taxable stock option benefits is deductible in calculating taxable income for alternative minimum tax purposes in order to arrive at a net inclusion rate of 80% (100% - (40% × (50% of 100%))). These inclusion rates result in an effective federal alternative minimum tax rate of 12% (80% of 15%) after 2006, and 12.2% (80% of 15.25%) in 2006 for capital gains and qualifying stock option benefits, which is lower than the above effective 14.5% federal regular tax rate.

[¶8070] Calculation of Alternative Minimum Tax

An individual may be required to pay a minimum tax in a taxation year.[17] This obligation will arise when an individual's tax that would otherwise be payable under Part I for the year, but for the tax payable for income not earned in a province (see ¶8037), is less than the amount by which the individual's "minimum amount" determined under (1) below exceeds the

---

See page ii for explanation of footnotes.

[15] CCH ¶19,999a–19,999l; Sec. 127.5–127.55.   [17] CCH ¶19,999a; Sec. 127.5.
[16] CCH ¶19,120; Sec. 120.2.

foreign tax credit determined under (5) below. In turn, the minimum tax payable by the individual is the total of the amount by which the individual's minimum amount exceeds the foreign tax credit determined under (5) below for the year, plus the amount, if any, required to be added to the individual's tax payable for income earned in a province.

Definitions and Rules

The following definitions of terms and descriptions and explanations of rules and general guidelines apply to the calculation of alternative minimum tax.

(1) *Minimum amount.* An individual's *minimum amount* of tax for a taxation year is the appropriate percentage (currently 15%) of the amount by which:

> (a) the individual's *adjusted taxable income* (see item (2) below) exceeds
>
> (b) the individual's *basic exemption* for the year ($40,000 for individuals, testamentary trusts, and pre-1972 *inter vivos* trusts; see item (3) below),

less the *basic minimum tax credit* (see item (4) below) for the year.[18]

(2) *Adjusted taxable income.* The term "adjusted taxable income" is defined for the purpose of the computation of the *minimum amount* described above.[19] An individual's adjusted taxable income for a year means the amount that would be the individual's taxable income for the year under the following conditions and assumptions:

> (a) No deductions are allowed for resource related expenses and for capital cost allowance (CCA) in respect of certified Canadian films and rental/leasing properties, except to the extent that such a deduction does not give rise to a loss or to an increased loss from that source. As a result, losses from these sources, arising otherwise than by virtue of CCA or resource deductions, are not added back in calculating adjusted taxable income. However, the AMT tax base will include losses deducted by limited partners and members of a partnership who have been specified members at all times since becoming members, in respect of their partnership interest, losses deducted in respect of registered investments in tax shelters and associated carrying charges, as well as those related to rental/leasing properties, film properties, and resource related deductions. Furthermore, the deduction from the AMT base for a property to which the CCA restrictions on rental properties or leasing properties apply is restricted in respect of both CCA and carrying charges. The AMT deduction, which may be claimed for CCA and carrying charges, is limited to the aggregate income for the year from rental or leasing property computed without reference to related CCA and carrying charges in excess of aggregate losses for

See page ii for explanation of footnotes.

[18] CCH ¶19,999b; Sec. 127.51.   [19] CCH ¶19,999c; Sec. 127.52(1).

the year. For a limited or specified partner, deductions for financing or carrying charges related to each partnership interest are limited to income from that partnership.

(b) Except in situations where capital gains arise from charitable donations and other gifts for which a charitable donation deduction or tax credit may be claimed, ⁴/₅ of capital gains net of capital losses are included in income and ⁴/₅ of business investment losses are deducted. In situations where capital gains arise from charitable donations, only the reduced amount of any taxable capital gain is included in the base for determining AMT. This means that after May 1, 2006, deemed capital gains from donations of ecologically sensitive lands and publicly listed securities (including those acquired through employee stock options) will not be added to the AMT base, since their inclusion rate is reduced from 25% to zero. After February 25, 2008, the same treatment will apply to gains realized on the exchange of unlisted shares for publicly traded securities that are donated to a qualified donee within 30 days of the exchange.

However, the capital gains exemption[20] is deductible for adjusted taxable income purposes, but only to the extent that it was claimed for regular tax purposes. The result is that the untaxed portion of the gain will, unless arising on charitable donations, always be subject to AMT (after the $40,000 exemption and other adjustments) even if the capital gains exemption is claimed on the taxable portion.

The capital loss rules are the converse of the capital gains rules. Beginning in 2000, 80% of whole capital losses net of whole capital gains for the year are available for carryover (back three years and forward indefinitely) against net capital gains of other years in computing the alternative minimum tax, provided the taxable portion (50%) has been applied to the taxable portion of capital gains (50%) on the ordinary return for that year.

(c) Only the actual amount of taxable dividends received from taxable Canadian corporations (i.e., excluding the gross-up) are included in income. Dividends designated as capital dividends for regular tax purposes are non-taxable for minimum tax purposes.

(d) Only certain deductions are taken into account in calculating adjusted taxable income for minimum tax purposes, including the deduction for vows of perpetual poverty; the capital gains deduction for qualified farm or fishing property; the capital gains deduction for qualified small business corporation shares; the spousal trust deductions; the deduction for residing in a prescribed zone; the deduction of social assistance and certain other benefits; and

---

See page ii for explanation of footnotes.

[20] CCH ¶15,976, ¶15,976b, ¶15,999c; Sec. 110.6(2), 110.6(3), 110.6(12).

¶8070

the deduction for tuition fee assistance received for adult basic education.

Sometimes the deduction of resource-related expenses and CCA on rental/leasing property and Canadian films arises in the form of two sources: business losses (i.e., before CCA and resource deductions); and losses arising from (including) resource deductions or CCA. In such cases, the loss will be required to be split into two components. While both components will continue to be deductible and reduce regular tax payable, only the portion of business, rental, or other losses not relating to these special tax deductions will be deductible in determining adjusted income for the purposes of the minimum tax.

Forty percent of the stock option benefit deduction,[21] the prospector or grubstaker deduction,[22] and the offsetting deduction for gains on shares received as part of a lump-sum settlement on withdrawal from a DPSP[23] may be claimed in calculating adjusted taxable income.

(e) The special transitional rules relating to certain lump-sum payments out of pension plans and other employee compensation plans do not apply for minimum tax purposes.[24]

Partnerships, as such, are not liable to AMT. However, where any partnership income or loss is relevant in computing AMT of a partner, the partner must, in computing taxable income for AMT purposes, claim deductions allocated from the partnership in the same proportion as income or loss allocation.[25]

It should be recognized that no adjustment is made to adjusted taxable income for forward averaging income additions or deductions. However, full forward averaging tax or credits are added or subtracted from the minimum tax.

(3) *Basic exemption.* A $40,000 *basic exemption* is provided in computing taxable income subject to minimum tax for individuals and certain qualifying trusts.[26] Where more than one eligible trust arises as a consequence of contributions to the trust by the same individual, rules are provided to apportion the $40,000 exemption between the trusts.[27]

(4) *Basic minimum tax credit.* The *basic minimum tax credit*[28] for a year is the aggregate of:

(a) personal tax credits;[29]

(b) effective July 1, 2006, the new Canada employment credit;[30]

See page ii for explanation of footnotes.

[21] CCH ¶15,015, ¶15,272; Sec. 110(1)(*d*), 110(1)(*d*.1).

[22] CCH ¶15,274; Sec. 110(1)(*d*.2).

[23] CCH ¶15,276; Sec. 110(1)(*d*.3).

[24] CCH ¶29,585; ITAR 40.

[25] CCH ¶19,999e; Sec. 127.52(3).

[26] CCH ¶19,999g; Sec. 127.53(1).

[27] CCH ¶19,999h–19,999i; Sec. 127.53(2)–(3).

[28] CCH ¶19,999if; Sec. 127.531.

[29] CCH ¶18,250, ¶18,302; Sec. 118(1), 118(2).

[30] CCH ¶18,321; Sec. 118(10).

(c) beginning in 2005, adoption expense tax credits;[31]

(d) effective July 1, 2006, the transit pass tax credit;[32]

(e) beginning in 2007, the child fitness tax credit;[33]

(f) for 2009, the home renovation tax credit;[34]

(g) beginning in 2009, the first-time home buyers' tax credit;[35]

(h) beginning in 2011, the volunteer firefighter tax credit;[36]

(i) beginning in 2011, the children's arts tax credit;[37]

(j) the charitable donation tax credit;[38]

(k) the medical expense tax credit;[39]

(l) the disability tax credit;[40]

(m) the education tax credit;[41]

(n) the EI and CPP contributions tax credit;[42] and

(o) the logging tax credit.[43]

As noted above, an individual's basic minimum tax credit is subtracted from the appropriate percentage (currently 15%) of the amount by which his or her *adjusted taxable income* exceeds his or her *basic exemption* to arrive at the *minimum amount*.

(5) *Tax credits.* An individual subject to the minimum tax may claim a *special foreign tax credit* in an amount equal to or, in certain circumstances, greater than, the credit to which he or she is entitled under the usual rules (see example below).[44] The special foreign tax credit allowed for minimum tax purposes is the greater of:

(a) the foreign tax credit otherwise allowed,[45] and

(b) the lesser of:

(i) "foreign taxes" for the year, and

(ii) the appropriate percentage (currently 15%) of "foreign income" for the year.[46]

For the purposes of this credit, the foreign tax paid by a taxpayer is the aggregate of:

See page ii for explanation of footnotes.

[31] CCH ¶18,323; Sec. 118.01(2).
[32] CCH ¶18,326; Sec. 118.02.
[33] CCH ¶18,329d; Sec. 118.03(2).
[34] CCH ¶18,329mp; Sec. 118.04.
[35] CCH ¶18,329pp; Sec. 118.05.
[36] Sec. 118.06.
[37] Sec. 118.031.
[38] CCH ¶18,330; Sec. 118.1.

[39] CCH ¶18,370; Sec. 118.2.
[40] CCH ¶18,390; Sec. 118.3(1).
[41] CCH ¶18,415, ¶18,426; Sec. 118.5, 118.6.
[42] CCH ¶18,441; Sec. 118.7.
[43] CCH ¶19,810; Sec. 127(1).
[44] CCH ¶19,999k; Sec. 127.54(2).
[45] CCH ¶19,700; Sec. 126.
[46] CCH ¶19,999j; Sec. 127.54(1).

¶8070

(a) the foreign tax which has been paid by the taxpayer in respect of businesses carried on by him or her in foreign countries, and

(b) ²/₃ of the foreign tax paid by the taxpayer in respect of foreign source, non-business income.

The example below illustrates the computation of the special foreign tax credit for 2012.

Example:

Foreign income		$ 200
Foreign non-business taxes		30
Foreign tax credit otherwise allowed		0*
Adjusted taxable income		1,000
"Minimum amount" — $1,000 × 15		$ 150
Less: "Special foreign tax credit"		
Greater of (a) foreign tax credit otherwise allowed		0
(b) lesser of (i) 30 × 2/3 = 20		20
(ii) 15% × 200 = 30		
Minimum tax		$ 130

* Assuming no regular taxes payable.

"Foreign income" is defined to mean the total income from business and from other sources (on which the taxpayer has paid non-business-income taxes) to governments of countries other than Canada.

Certain tax credits will not be affected by the imposition of the minimum tax. These include the refundable portion of the investment tax credit and the Quebec abatement.

However, other tax credits may be rendered ineffective by virtue of the application of the minimum tax. These include the dividend tax credit, overseas employment tax credit, investment tax credit (including exploration credit and scientific research credit), political contribution tax credit, share purchase tax credit, labour-sponsored funds tax credit, and logging tax credit. Essentially, these restricted credits will only be allowed to reduce regular taxes payable (before these credits) to the amount of federal tax calculated on adjusted taxable income for minimum tax purposes, less any minimum tax carryover from prior years.

[¶8075] Exception for Certain Returns and Trusts

The minimum tax is not applicable to the special returns of income filed on behalf of bankrupt or deceased taxpayers, to an individual in the year of death, to a spousal or common-law partner trust for the trust's taxation year that includes the time of the beneficiary spouse's or common-law partner's death, and to a taxation year of a trust throughout which it is a related segregated fund trust, a mutual fund trust, and a prescribed master trust. One of the conditions that a master trust must satisfy to be prescribed is that each of its beneficiaries must be a trust governed by a registered pension plan or a deferred profit sharing plan.[47]

[¶8077] Alternative Minimum Tax Carryover

There is provision for a seven-year carryover for additional taxes that have been paid as a result of the AMT.[48] The carryover of additional taxes is not available to reduce regular taxes payable in respect of separate returns of income filed on behalf of a deceased taxpayer. A trustee in bankruptcy can utilize any minimum tax carryover of the bankrupt individual in the tax return he or she is required to file on behalf of the bankrupt in respect of income arising from the bankrupt's estate or business. The bankrupt individual cannot, however, claim it in the second separate return that he or she must file for the period from the date of bankruptcy to December 31. See ¶9009.[49]

"Additional taxes" are defined generally as the excess of the minimum amount (¶8070) over the total of the taxpayer's regular tax (before any foreign tax deductions, logging tax credits, political contributions tax credits, investment tax credits, share-purchase tax credits, scientific research and experimental development tax credits, or labour-sponsored fund tax credits) and any additional foreign tax credit allowed in a year.[50] The additional tax carried forward will reduce regular tax payable in a following year to the extent that the regular tax liability exceeds the minimum amount calculated for that subsequent year.

Example: AMT Carryforward

	2010		2011		2012	
	Regular tax	AMT	Regular tax	AMT	Regular tax	AMT
Provisional federal tax	200	900	800	700	700	0
Less: AMT carryover from previous years	n/a		100		600	
Basic federal tax	900		700		100	
Unused carryforward	700		600		0	

See page ii for explanation of footnotes.

[47] CCH ¶19,999l; Sec. 127.55; Reg. 5001. [49] CCH ¶19,123; Sec. 120.2(4).

[48] CCH ¶19,120; Sec. 120.2(1). [50] CCH ¶19,122; Sec. 120.2(3).

[¶8080] Income-Splitting Tax

[¶8081] Income Splitting with Minor Children

Although the attributions rules (¶2615 *et seq.*) reduce the opportunities for income splitting, several tax-planning techniques have developed over time to avoid their application.[51]

To discourage income splitting with minor children, the 1999 Budget introduced an income-splitting tax (the "kiddie tax"), beginning in the year 2000, to be levied on certain passive income of individuals under the age of 18 at the end of a calendar year.

[¶8082] Split Income Defined

The types of income to be taxed under this measure are:

(1) taxable dividends (eligible and other than eligible) from ownership of shares of a corporation (other than publicly listed shares and shares of a mutual fund corporation), whether received directly or through a trust or partnership (other than a mutual fund trust);

(2) shareholder benefits (other than from ownership of publicly listed shares) whether conferred directly or through a trust or partnership (other than a mutual fund trust); and

(3) other income received from a partnership or trust (other than a mutual fund trust) where the income is derived by the partnership or trust from the business or providing property or services to, or in support of, a business carried on by:

(a) a person related to the minor at any time in the year;

(b) a corporation of which a person related to the minor holds more than 10% of the corporation's shares (called a "specified shareholder") at any time in the year; or

(c) a corporation of which a person related to the minor holds any number of shares.[52]

[¶8083] Tax Computation

The income-splitting tax is imposed at the rate of 29% of a minor's split income (see ¶8082) for a taxation year.[53] It will be reduced only by any dividend tax credit and foreign tax credit available in respect of amounts included in that split income.[54] However, in order to avoid double taxation, income subject to this tax will be deductible in computing a minor's taxable income under Part I. In addition, income taxed under this measure will not be subject to the attribution rules.

See page ii for explanation of footnotes.

[51] Neuman, 98 DTC 6297, Ferrel, 99 DTC 5111.

[52] CCH ¶19,178; Sec. 120.4(1) "split income".

[53] CCH ¶19,179; Sec. 120.4(2).

[54] CCH ¶19,180; Sec. 120.4(3).

[¶8084] Exclusions

The kiddie tax does not apply if:

- the income is from, or the taxable capital gain (see ¶8085) is from the disposition of, property inherited by the minor from a parent;

- the income is from, or the taxable capital gain (see ¶8085) is from the disposition of, property inherited by the minor from anyone else and, during the year, he or she either is enrolled full-time in a post-secondary institution or qualifies for the disability tax credit;

- the minor was a non-resident at any time during the year; or

- neither of the minor's parents were residents of Canada at any time in the year.[55]

[¶8085] Taxable Capital Gains

Since the introduction of the "kiddie tax", income splitting techniques had developed that used capital gains being realized for the benefit of a minor on a disposition of shares to a relative of the minor. In response, the kiddie tax was extended to a taxable capital gain (other than an excluded taxable capital gain described in ¶8084) from the disposition of shares after March 21, 2011 (other than publicly listed shares and shares of a mutual fund corporation) to a minor's relative, if taxable dividends on those shares would have been subject to the "kiddie tax". More specifically, twice the amount that would otherwise have been the minor's taxable capital gains from the disposition of shares is deemed to be a taxable dividend received by the minor.[56]

As a result, the special 29% tax on split income applies to the deemed taxable dividend. Furthermore, the taxable dividend is not an "eligible dividend", such that the rules relating to eligible dividends (such as the particular rate of dividend tax credit) do not apply. However, these rules do not result in a dividend having been paid by a corporation.

[¶8090] Personal Tax Credits

[¶8091] Overview

Individuals are entitled to claim certain non-refundable tax credits (called "personal tax credits") in calculating taxes payable for a taxation year. These credits reduce the amount of income tax an individual owes. If the total of these credits is more than the income tax the individual would otherwise owe for the year, the individual will not get a refund for the difference.

See page ii for explanation of footnotes.

[55] CCH ¶19,176, ¶19,177; Sec. 120.4(1) "excluded   [56] Sec. 120.4(4), 120.4(5). amount", 120.4(1) "specified individual".

The personal tax credits are expressed as the appropriate percentage (currently 15%) of an aggregate or single dollar value.[57] These dollar values are subject to annual indexation for each taxation year. The indexation factor for a given taxation year is the percentage in the average Consumer Price Index (CPI) for the 12-month period ending on September 30 of the preceding year relative to the average CPI for the 12-month period ending on September 30 of the year earlier. See ¶8230.[58] The personal and other tax credits are to be applied in the following order:[59]

(1) personal tax credits (basic; spouse or common-law partner; eligible dependant, formerly called "equivalent-to-spouse"; and dependants tax credit);

(2) age credit;

(3) EI and CPP credit;

(4) pension income credit;

(5) Canada employment credit;

(6) public transit passes credit;

(7) children's arts credit, available in 2011 and subsequent taxation years;

(8) adoption expense credit;

(9) child fitness credit, available in 2007 and subsequent taxation years;

(10) home renovation credit, available only in 2009;

(11) first-time home buyers' credit, available in 2009 and subsequent taxation years;

(12) volunteer firefighter credit, available in 2011 and subsequent taxation years;

(13) impairment credit;

(14) unused tuition, textbook, and education credit carried forward from previous year;

(15) tuition credit;

(16) education and textbook credits;

(17) transfer of tuition, textbook, and education credits to parents and grandparents;

(18) transfer of spouse's or common-law partner's unused credits;

(19) medical expenses credit;

(20) charitable donations credit;

See page ii for explanation of footnotes.

[57] CCH ¶18,250; Sec. 118(1).
[58] CCH ¶18,201; Sec. 117.1(1).
[59] CCH ¶18,457; Sec. 118.92.

(21) credit for interest paid on student loans; and

(22) dividend tax credit.

[¶8095] Personal Tax Credits

The personal tax credits for the 2012 taxation year are as follows:

(1) *Basic amount.*[60] The basic tax credit in 2012 is $1,623 ($10,822 × 15%).

(2) *Married or common-law.*[61] An individual who at any time in the year is married or in a common-law partnership, supports his or her spouse or common-law partner, and is not living separate and apart from his or her spouse or common-law partner due to a breakdown of their marriage or common-law partnership, is entitled to a basic personal tax credit of $1,623, as well as a credit in respect of a spouse or common-law partner. The dollar value to compute the married or common-law credit is now the same as the basic personal amount ($10,822 × 15% = $1,623 in 2012), and this amount is now reduced by each dollar of income of the individual's spouse or common-law partner for the year.

In the year of a marriage or a breakdown of a marriage or common-law partnership, a taxpayer may claim the married or common-law credit. However, this credit is not available to an individual who supports his or her spouse or common-law partner through support payments in the years following a separation or divorce. In the year of marriage or common-law status, the credit is reduced by the taxpayer's spouse/partner's income for the entire year. If there is a breakdown of the marriage or common-law partnership and the taxpayer and the taxpayer's spouse or common-law partner are living separate and apart at the end of the year, only the spouse's or common-law partner's income while married and not separated is counted for this purpose. In the year of a breakdown of the marriage or common-law partnership, a taxpayer can claim either the spousal credit or spousal support payments (if deductible) in that year, but not both.

Beginning in 2012, caregivers of a dependant spouse or common-law partner with a mental or physical infirmity benefit from a family caregiver tax credit by adding $2,000 to the indexed $10,822 value used in the computation of the spousal or common-law partner tax credit. Only one family caregiver tax credit will be available in respect of each infirm dependant. The $2,000 family caregiver tax credit amount will be indexed to account for inflation for 2013 and subsequent taxation years.

(3) *Eligible dependant (formerly referred to as the "equivalent-to- spouse").* An individual who cannot claim the married or common-law credit may claim this eligible dependant credit for a wholly dependent person if all the following conditions are met at a point in time during the year (the relevant time):

See page ii for explanation of footnotes.

[60] CCH ¶18,250; Sec. 118(1)(c).　　　　[61] CCH ¶18,250; Sec. 118(1)(a).

(a) The individual must not have a spouse or common-law partner, or, if so, can neither have supported, nor lived with, nor have been supported by his or her spouse or common-law partner.

(b) The individual must support a dependant and live with the dependant in a self-contained domestic establishment (the home) that he or she maintains (either alone or jointly with another person).

(c) At the relevant time the supported person must be:

(i) related to the taxpayer by blood, marriage, common-law partnership, or adoption;

(ii) under 18, or mentally or physically infirm, unless the person is a parent or a grandparent;

(iii) resident in Canada, unless the person is a child of the taxpayer; and

(iv) wholly dependent for support on the individual, or on the individual and other person(s) who maintain the home.[62]

The above distinction between wholly dependent persons under the age of 18 and over the age of 18 is not founded on a pertinent personal characteristic enumerated in the Charter and is justified in a free and democratic society.[63]

Even if all of the preceding conditions have been met, a taxpayer cannot claim this credit in respect of a child for whom he or she was required to make support payments. However, in the year of a breakdown of the marriage or common-law partnership, a taxpayer can still claim an eligible dependant tax credit for that child (plus any credit for infirm dependants over the age of 18, the caregiver tax credit, and the disability tax credit transferred from a dependant) as long as the taxpayer does not deduct any support amounts paid to his or her spouse or common-law partner. The taxpayer may choose whichever deduction is more advantageous. If both parents make a child support payment during the taxation year, they are not both denied the claim for the wholly dependent person or child tax credit. Instead, one of them may claim the credits.[64]

Note that a taxpayer who is residing outside Canada may be deemed to be a Canadian resident as described in ¶1025 and ¶1065. In this situation, and where the other conditions are met, the taxpayer may claim the eligible dependant tax credit for a child who is living outside Canada with the taxpayer.[65]

The amount of the credit is $1,623 ($10,822 × 15%) in 2012. The dollar value to compute the eligible dependant credit is now the same as the basic personal amount, and this amount is now reduced by each dollar of income of the individual's eligible dependant for the year.

See page ii for explanation of footnotes.

[62] CCH ¶18,250; Sec. 118(1)(b).
[63] Mercier, 96 DTC 6596.

[64] CCH ¶18,312, ¶18,312c; Sec. 118(5), 118(5.1).
[65] Ruzicka, 95 DTC 365.

The eligible dependant tax credit may not be claimed in respect of more than one dependant. Thus, if a taxpayer supports more than one wholly dependent relative, the taxpayer's personal credits will be the basic credit of $1,623, plus $1,623 for one dependent relative, plus whatever credits may be claimed for other infirm dependent relatives under item (5) below. Where a taxpayer claims a credit for a wholly dependent relative, the taxpayer may not claim an additional credit for that same relative under other provisions of the Act, such as for dependent children, nieces, or nephews, etc. Similarly, a taxpayer may not claim both a spouse or common-law partner credit and an eligible dependant credit in the same year. Only one taxpayer is entitled to the credit, so if two or more persons are supporting the dependant and cannot agree who will get the credit, no credit will be allowed.[66]

A taxpayer must wholly support the relative in a self-contained domestic establishment in which both the taxpayer and the dependant live. "Self-contained domestic establishment" is defined to mean a dwelling, house, apartment, or other similar place of residence in which a person, as a general rule, sleeps and eats.[67]

Example:

E lives with and supports her mother and father in her home. Her mother's income for 2012 was $2,800 and her father's was $7,000. E may claim the eligible dependant tax credit for one parent. If the other parent, say the father, is infirm, E may claim an infirm dependant's tax credit (see (4) below) in respect of her father. The claim would be calculated as follows:

Eligible dependant amount for mother	$10,822	
Less: Mother's income	$2,800	
Net amount		$8,022
Dependant amount for father (see item (5))	$4,402	
Less: Father's income in excess of $6,420 ($7,000 - $6,420)	$ 580	
Net amount		$3,822
Total credit base for parents		$11,844
Tax credit at 15%		$1,777

The eligible dependant credits may be claimed if the required conditions are met *at any time* during the year and not necessarily throughout the year. Thus, if a widowed father lived with and provided the sole support for his daughter, he could claim the eligible dependant credit for his daughter even if she married or began a common-law relationship and moved away during the year. In this case, the daughter's husband or common-law partner would also be able to claim the married or common-law tax credit for his wife or common-law partner since the relevant prohibition is that the *eligible dependant* amount cannot be claimed by two or more taxpayers. In this example, one person is claiming the married or common-law amount and

---

See page ii for explanation of footnotes.

[66] CCH ¶18,310; Sec. 118(4).

[67] CCH ¶28,260; Sec. 248(1) "self-contained domestic establishment".

the other the eligible dependant amount. The daughter's husband's or common-law partner's claim would be reduced by his wife's or partner's income earned by her in the year. The father's amount would also be reduced by his daughter's income earned by her in the year.

(4) *Child Tax Credit.* An individual may claim a non-refundable tax credit for each child under the age of 18 at the end of the year. Before 2011, this credit could be claimed by either parent (but not both) where the child resided with both parents throughout the year. The rule that limits the number of claimants to one per domestic establishment was repealed for 2011 and onward. If the child does not reside with both parents, the credit may be claimed by the parent who is entitled to claim the dependent person credit (or who would be entitled to claim it if the child were the parent's only child). In 2012, the credit is calculated as $2,191 per child and multiplied by the lowest personal tax rate (15%).[68]

Beginning in 2012, caregivers of an eligible child with a mental or physical infirmity benefit from a family caregiver tax credit by adding $2,000 to the indexed $2,191 value used in the computation of the child tax credit. Only one family caregiver tax credit will be available in respect of each infirm dependant. The $2,000 family caregiver tax credit amount will be indexed to account for inflation for 2013 and subsequent taxation years. An individual is eligible for the increased tax credit if the child is likely to be, for a long and continuous period of indefinite duration, dependent on others by reason of mental or physical infirmity for significantly more assistance in attending to the dependant's personal needs and care, when compared to other children of the same age.

(5) *Infirm Dependant over 18.* An individual may claim a dependant tax credit for a person who is 18 years of age or older at the end of the year *and* who is dependent on him or her at any time during the year by reason of mental or physical infirmity. In 2012, the amount on which the credit is calculated is fixed at $4,402, which is reduced by the excess of the dependant's income over $6,420.[69]

Beginning in 2012, caregivers of an infirm dependant over 18 benefit from a family caregiver tax credit by adding $2,000 to the indexed $4,402 value used in the computation of the child tax credit. Only one family caregiver tax credit will be available in respect of each infirm dependant over 18. The $2,000 family caregiver tax credit amount will be indexed to account for inflation for 2013 and subsequent taxation years. The threshold at which the infirm dependant credit begins to be phased out will also be increased, so that the enhanced amount is fully phased out at the same income level as the 2012 enhanced spousal or common-law partner credit.

The following restrictions are placed on the ability to claim an amount for an infirm dependant:

See page ii for explanation of footnotes.

[68] CCH ¶18,250; Sec. 118(1)(b.1).   [69] CCH ¶18,250; Sec. 118(1)(d).

(1) No amount may be claimed in respect of a dependant for whom an eligible dependant tax credit or a deduction for support payments has already been claimed.[70] However, in the year of a breakdown of the marriage or common-law partnership, a taxpayer can still claim a credit for infirm dependants over the age of 18, as long as the taxpayer does not deduct any support amounts paid to his or her spouse or common-law partner. The taxpayer may choose whichever claim is more advantageous.[71]

(2) If two or more supporting individuals are entitled to claim a dependant amount in respect of the same person, they must allocate the available amount between them.[72] If they cannot do so, the Minister can stipulate an apportionment. In any case, the total claim cannot exceed the amount that would be available if there were only one supporting person. For example, where both parents contribute to the support of a 20-year-old child dependent by reason of infirmity, whose income does not exceed $6,420 in 2012, they may divide the $4,402 infirm dependant amount between them in any way provided their separate claims do not exceed $4,402. It does not matter what proportion of the infirm dependant amount each parent claims, as long as the parent has enough tax payable to absorb the full credit.

A dependant is defined as a person who, at any time in the year, is dependent on the individual for support.[73] In addition, such a person must be:

(a) a child or grandchild of the individual or the individual's spouse or common-law partner; or

(b) a parent, grandparent, brother, sister, uncle, aunt, niece, or nephew of the individual or the individual's spouse or common-law partner. In this case, the dependant must be resident in Canada at some point during the year.

The meaning of the term "child" is extended[74] to include:

(a) a person of whom the taxpayer is the natural parent, whether born within or outside marriage;

(b) a person who is wholly dependent on the taxpayer for support and of whom the taxpayer has custody and control or had custody and control immediately before the person attained 19 years of age;

(c) a child of the taxpayer's spouse or common-law partner;

(d) an adopted child; and

(e) a spouse or common-law partner of a child of the taxpayer.

See page ii for explanation of footnotes.

[70] CCH ¶18,310; Sec. 118(4)(c).   [73] CCH ¶18,314; Sec. 118(6).
[71] CCH ¶18,312; Sec. 118(5).
[72] CCH ¶18,310; Sec. 118(4)(e).   [74] CCH ¶28,372; Sec. 252(1).

¶8095

Furthermore, the meaning of *parent* is extended to include a person where the taxpayer is the person's child, or where the taxpayer qualified as a child under (b) above.[75]

[¶8100] Age Credit

An individual who turns 65 before the end of the year 2012 is entitled to a credit of $1,008 ($6,720 × 15%), which is reduced as his or her net income exceeds a certain income level.[76] In 2012, the age amount is reduced by 15% of net income over $33,884, with no minimum, so that the age tax credit disappears entirely at an income level of $78,684.

If a taxpayer's spouse or common-law partner reached the age of 65 by December 31 and did not completely use the age tax credit, the unused portion of his or her credit will be available to the taxpayer as an additional deduction. See ¶8215. This would occur where the taxpayer's spouse or common-law partner does not have sufficient income to utilize the credit. The spouse or common-law partner's age tax credit could, in theory, be reduced by the spouse's or common- law partner's income over $33,884, leaving a reduced amount available for transfer, although it would seem that if the spouse or common-law partner's income is that high, there would not be a transfer in any event. However, the transferred amount cannot be reduced again in the transferee's hands, regardless of his or her income.[77]

If a capital gain is realized in the year by virtue of reacquiring property on default of the purchaser to pay any mortgage or other debt (¶2690), the gain may be excluded from income when calculating the income in excess of $33,884.

[¶8105] EI, CPP, and QPP Credits

In 2012, an individual is entitled to a tax credit of 15% of CPP/QPP contributions and Employment Insurance (EI) premiums paid in the year, not exceeding the maximum premiums allowed for the year.[78] This credit is available for contributions or premiums paid by the individual through employee deductions or on self-employed earnings. Since 50% of a self-employed taxpayer's CPP/QPP contributions (the portion that represents the employer's share) are deductible as a business expense, the credit remains available only with respect to the remaining 50% portion that represents the employee's share. See ¶2425.

[¶8110] Pension Income Credit

In computing tax payable under Part I for a taxation year, an individual may deduct a pension tax credit to a maximum of $300 (for 2012) in respect of certain pension income received in the year. In order to determine what pension income qualifies for the pension tax credit, it is necessary to distin-

---

See page ii for explanation of footnotes.

[75] CCH ¶28,374; Sec. 252(2).
[76] CCH ¶18,302; Sec. 118(2).

[77] CCH ¶18,445; Sec. 118.8.
[78] CCH ¶18,441; Sec. 118.7.

guish between individuals who have reached the age of 65 before the end of the year and those who have not.

If the individual is 65 or over, the pension credit he or she is entitled to claim is determined by multiplying the appropriate percentage (currently 15%) by the lesser of $2,000 and the individual's "pension income" received in the year.[79]

If an individual's taxes have already been reduced to nil and the individual is therefore unable to fully use his or her pension tax credit, the individual may transfer the portion of unused pension credit to his or her spouse or common-law partner.[80] See ¶8215.

"Pension income" received by an individual in a taxation year is defined as the sum of:[81]

(a) payments in respect of a life annuity out of or under a superannuation or registered pension plan (RPP), including RPP bridging benefits;

(b) annuity payments under a registered retirement savings plan (RRSP), including an amended plan, and annuity payments under an annuity purchased with a refund of RRSP premiums;

(c) payments received out of or under a registered retirement income fund (RRIF), including an amended fund;

(d) annuity payments received under a deferred profit sharing plan (DPSP), including a revoked plan;

(e) annuity payments purchased by a DPSP trustee as a payout of the taxpayer's vested interest;

(f) the income element of annuity payments;

(g) amounts included in income in respect of insurance policies or annuity contracts; and

(h) RRIF-type payments received under a money purchase registered pension plan (see ¶10,425.

Certain amounts are not to be included as "pension income" (or "qualified pension income" as described below). These amounts include:

(i) any pension or supplement under the *Old Age Security Act* or similar provincial plan,

(ii) any benefit under the *Canada Pension Plan*, *Quebec Pension Plan*, or *Saskatchewan Pension Plan*,

(iii) a death benefit as defined in ¶2165,

See page ii for explanation of footnotes.

[79] CCH ¶18,304; Sec. 118(3).
[80] CCH ¶18,445; Sec. 118.8.

[81] CCH ¶18,316, ¶18,318c; Sec. 118(7), 118(8.1).

¶8110

(iv) any payment out of a salary deferral arrangement, a retirement compensation arrangement, an employee benefit plan, an employee trust, or a prescribed provincial plan, and

(v) lifetime pensions payable under an unfunded supplemental employee retirement plan, other than lifetime pensions established for federally appointed judges and Lieutenant Governors.[82]

Pension income receipts that would otherwise qualify for the credit are excluded if the payments are exempt income (for example, foreign pension income which is protected by treaty). This prevents a double benefit being obtained for the same payment. A similar exclusion applies to the portion of any receipt that would otherwise qualify as pension income that is specifically deductible under some other provision of the Act. For example, any amount of superannuation benefits, retiring allowances, and RRSP refund of premiums transferred into an RRSP would not qualify as pension income or qualified pension income.

If the individual has not reached the age of 65 before the end of the year, the pension credit he or she is entitled to deduct is determined by multiplying the appropriate percentage (currently 15%) by the lesser of $2,000 and the individual's "qualified pension income" received in the year.[83]

Qualified pension income is a more limited category than pension income.[84] It is restricted to superannuation or pension benefits of the type described in (a) above and to receipts of the type described in (b) to (g) above, provided the latter receipts arise as a result of the death of the taxpayer's spouse or common-law partner.[85]

[¶8111] Canada Employment Credit

An individual with earned office or employment income during the year may claim a Canada employment credit. The credit is non-refundable and calculated at the appropriate percentage (currently 15%) on the lesser of: (i) the total office or employment income, including, beginning in 2008, amounts received under the *Wage Earner Protection Program Act*; and (ii) the indexed value of $1,000 (i.e., $1,095 in 2012, $1,065 in 2011, $1,051 in 2010, and $1,044 in 2009).[86] The purpose of this credit is to recognize various work-related expenses which are incurred by employees but not deductible from their income.

[¶8112] Transit Pass Credit

An individual can claim the cost of monthly public transit passes or passes of longer duration such as an annual pass for travel within Canada on public transit. These passes must permit unlimited travel on local buses,

---

[82] CCH ¶8559c, ¶18,318; Sec. 118(8); Reg. 7800.   [85] CCH ¶28,377; Sec. 252(3).

[83] CCH ¶18,304; Sec. 118(3).

[84] CCH ¶18,316; Sec. 118(7).   [86] CCH ¶18,321; Sec. 118(10).

streetcars, subways, commuter trains or buses, and local ferries.[87] The cost of shorter duration passes can also be claimed if each pass entitles the individual to unlimited travel for an uninterrupted period of at least five days and the individual purchases enough of these passes so that he or she is entitled to unlimited travel for at least 20 days in any 28-day period. The cost of electronic payment cards when used to make at least 32 one-way trips during an uninterrupted period not exceeding 31 days also qualifies for the credit.[88]

To qualify for the credit, public transit passes must be attributable to the use of public transit by the individual, his spouse or common-law partner, and his or her children (or those of his or her spouse or common-law partner) who are under 19 years of age at the end of the year.[89]

The credit is equal to the appropriate percentage (currently 15%) of the eligible amounts paid for the year. Such amounts are reduced by a reimbursement, allowance, or any other form of assistance an individual receives in respect of the cost of an eligible public transit pass or eligible electronic payment card (other than amounts included in computing that individual's income that are not deductible in computing taxable income).[90]

In situations where more than one person is eligible to claim the credit with respect to a particular pass or electronic payment card, the credit must be divided between the eligible individuals, and must not exceed the maximum amount that one individual could deduct. If the individuals cannot agree on how to divide the credit, the Minister may arbitrarily assign amounts to the parties in question.[91]

[¶8113] Child Fitness Tax Credit

An individual is entitled to claim a basic tax credit of up to $500 of eligible fitness expenses paid with respect to each qualifying child registered in a "prescribed program of physical activity".[92] In order to be considered eligible, the child must be under 16 years of age at the beginning of the taxation year.[93]

This age limit is increased to under 18 years of age with respect to children who are also eligible for the disability tax credit. As well, a child who qualifies for the disability tax credit and is under 18 years of age at the beginning of the taxation year is eligible for an additional $500 credit. The additional amount is available to individuals who claim a minimum of $100 of eligible fitness expenses under the general child fitness tax credit.[94]

The general credit is calculated by multiplying the eligible amount by the lowest tax rate for individuals (currently 15%).

Only fees paid by the taxpayer (or his or her spouse or common-law partner) that are related to the cost of registering a child in an eligible

---

See page ii for explanation of footnotes.

[87] CCH ¶18,326b; Sec. 118.02(1) "public commuter transit services".

[88] CCH ¶18,326a; Sec. 118.02(1) "eligible electronic payment card".

[89] CCH ¶18,326d; Sec. 118.02(1) "qualifying relation".

[90] CCH ¶18,326e; Sec. 118.02(2).

[91] CCH ¶18,326f; Sec. 118.02(3).

[92] CCH ¶18,329d; Sec. 118.03(2).

[93] CCH ¶18,329b; Sec. 118.03(1) "qualifying child".

[94] CCH ¶18,329dc; Sec. 118.03(2.1).

program of physical activity can be claimed. Fees paid to a taxpayer's spouse, common-law partner, or any individual under the age of 18 (at the time of payment) are not eligible for the credit. Amounts deductible as child care expenses in the computation of income are also not eligible for this credit.[95] The year in which the tax credit can be claimed is determined by the date that the fees are paid, not when the activity takes place.

In a situation where more than one person is eligible to claim the general and additional child fitness tax credits, the credits must be divided between the eligible individuals, and must not exceed the maximum amount that one individual could deduct. If individuals cannot agree on how to divide the credit, the Minister may arbitrarily assign amounts to the parties in question.[96]

An "eligible fitness expense" is defined as a fee paid to a qualifying entity as a cost for registration or membership in a "prescribed program of physical activity". This includes costs related to the program's administration, instruction, rental of required facilities, and uniforms and equipment that are unavailable to the participant at less than fair market value. Costs associated with accommodation, travel, food, or beverages are excluded from the definition of eligible fitness expense.[97] Organizations providing eligible programs are to determine the portion of the fee that qualifies for the credit.

A "prescribed program of physical activity" is defined as one of the following:

(a) a weekly program of eight or more consecutive weeks, in which all or substantially all of the activities include a significant amount of physical activity;

(b) a program of five or more consecutive days, of which more than 50% of the daily activities include a significant amount of physical activity;

(c) a program of eight or more consecutive weeks offered by a club, association, or similar organization in which participants can select among a number of activities, if more than 50% of the activities offered are activities that include a significant amount of physical activity, or more than 50% of the scheduled time is scheduled for activities that include a significant amount of physical activity; or

(d) a membership in an organization of eight or more consecutive weeks, if more than 50% of all the activities offered include a significant amount of physical activity.[98]

The term "physical activity" is defined as a supervised activity suitable for children that "contributes to cardio-respiratory endurance and to one or

---

See page ii for explanation of footnotes.

[95] CCH ¶18,329a; Sec. 118.03(1) "eligible fitness expense".

[96] CCH ¶18,329e; Sec. 118.03(3).

[97] CCH ¶18,329a; Sec. 118.03(1) "eligible fitness expense".

[98] CCH ¶18,329ed; Reg. 9400(2).

more of muscular strength, muscular endurance, flexibility and balance".[99] Horseback riding is deemed to meet the requirements of this definition.[100] With respect to children who are eligible for the disability tax credit, the term "physical activity" is defined to mean a supervised activity suitable for children "that results in movement and in an observable expenditure of energy in a recreational context". Activities not considered to be eligible for the credit include activities where riding a motorized vehicle is an essential component of the activity and programs offered as part of a school's curriculum.

The following is an example, provided in the Explanatory Notes to Bill C-28, illustrating what constitutes a prescribed program of physical activity:

Example:

Sabrina just joined the Girl Guides of Canada. Her mother paid $100 in registration fees for two hours of activities per week for 10 weeks. The Girl Guides program provides that one hour and 15 minutes of the two hours of activities will be devoted to physical activity. Therefore, the program will be considered a prescribed program of physical activity and Sabrina's mother may claim a child fitness tax credit of $15.00 ($100 × 15%).

In cases where a program is not a prescribed program of physical activity because it does not meet the 50% requirement set out in item (c) above, a taxpayer may claim a portion of the amount paid for the program as an eligible fitness expense.[101] In such cases, the portion a taxpayer may claim is the percentage of activities that are activities that include a significant amount of physical activity, or the percentage of the time that is scheduled for activities that include a significant amount of physical activity.

The following is an example, provided in the Explanatory Notes to Bill C-28, which illustrates the application of the above provision:

Example:

Sabrina's mother pays $200 for the registration of her daughter at a community centre. The portion of the activity offered to children by the centre that qualifies as physical activities for the purpose of the credit is 40 percent. Therefore, only 40 percent of the program will be considered a prescribed program of physical activity and Sabrina's mother may claim a child fitness tax credit of $12.00 ($200 × 40 percent × 15%).

In cases where a membership in an organization does not meet the 50% requirement set out in item (d) above, the portion of the expense that will be eligible for the purposes of the definition of "eligible fitness expense" is the percentage of all of the activities offered to children by the organization that include a significant amount of physical activity, assuming the activity is not part of a school's curriculum.[102]

See page ii for explanation of footnotes.

[99] CCH ¶18,329ed; Reg. 9400(1) physical activity.   [101] CCH ¶18,329ed; Reg. 9400(3).
[100] CCH ¶18,329ed; Reg. 9400(5).   [102] CCH ¶18,329ed; Reg. 9400(4).

¶8113

[¶8114] Children's Arts Tax Credit

Parents may claim a 15% non-refundable tax credit up to $500 in respect of eligible expenses for the enrolment of a child under 16 (under 18 if the child is eligible for the disability tax credit) in an eligible program of artistic, cultural, recreational, or developmental activities.[103] For a child under 18 who is eligible for the disability tax credit, the 15% non-refundable tax credit may be claimed on an additional $500 disability supplement amount, when a minimum of $100 is paid for eligible expenses.[104] Either parent may claim the credit or the credit can be shared if the total amount claimed does not exceed the maximum allowed if only one parent made the claim.[105]

An eligible expense will be a fee paid in the taxation year to a qualifying entity to the extent that the fee is for the registration or membership of a child in an eligible program of artistic, cultural, recreational, or developmental activities. Fees for registration or membership may be paid in respect of expenses for the operation and administration of the program, instruction, renting facilities, equipment used in common, and incidental supplies. Registration or membership fees will not be eligible to the extent that they are paid for the purchase or rental of equipment for exclusive personal use (e.g., musical instruments), travel, meals, and accommodation.[106]

[¶8115] Home Renovation Tax Credit

The home renovation tax credit (HRTC) was a time-limited credit for work performed or goods acquired after January 27, 2009, and before February 1, 2010, in respect of dwellings that are eligible to be an individual's principal residence or that of one or more of other family members. In general, a housing unit is considered eligible to be an individual's principal residence where it is owned by the individual and ordinarily inhabited by the individual, the individual's spouse or common-law partner, or their children. Expenditures incurred pursuant to an agreement that was entered into before January 28, 2009, will not be eligible for the credit.[107]

The credit applied to eligible expenditures of more than $1,000, but not more than $10,000, resulting in a maximum credit of $1,350 ($9,000 × 15%). To be eligible, expenditures incurred in relation to a renovation or alteration to an eligible dwelling (or the land that forms part of the eligible dwelling) must be of an enduring nature and integral to the dwelling, and includes the cost of labour and professional services, building materials, fixtures, rentals, and permits. For instance, the following expenditures will not be eligible for the HRTC:

- the cost of routine repairs and maintenance normally performed on an annual or more frequent basis;

See page ii for explanation of footnotes.

[103] Sec. 118.031(1) "qualifying child", 118.031(2).   [106] Sec. 118.031(1) "eligible expense".
[104] Sec. 118.031(3).
[105] Sec. 118.031(4).   [107] CCH ¶18,329mp; Sec. 118.04.

- expenditures that are not integral to the dwelling, and other indirect expenditures that retain a value independent of the renovation;

- expenditures for appliances and audio-visual electronics; and

- financing costs.

The HRTC (including in respect of expenditures made in January 2010) could only be claimed in an individual's 2009 tax return.

[¶8117] First-Time Home Buyers' Credit (HBTC)

The HBTC is a non-refundable tax credit for certain home buyers who acquire a qualifying home after January 27, 2009 (i.e., closing after this date).[108] Individuals will qualify for the HBTC if:

- they acquire a qualifying home; and

- neither the individual nor the individual's spouse or common-law partner owned and lived in another home in the year of purchase or any of the four preceding years.

If the house is bought by a person with a disability or for a related person with a disability, the individual does not have to be a first-time home buyer. However, the home must be acquired to enable the person with a disability to live in a more accessible dwelling or in an environment better suited to the personal needs and care of that person.

A qualifying home is a housing unit located in Canada. This includes single-family homes, semi-detached homes, townhouses, mobile homes, condominium units, and apartments in duplexes, triplexes, fourplexes, or apartment buildings. It also includes a share of the capital stock of a cooperative housing corporation, where the holder of the share is entitled to possession of a housing unit located in Canada. However, a share that only provides the holder with a right to tenancy in the housing unit does not qualify. As well, the individual or the related person with a disability must intend to occupy the home as a principal place of residence no later than one year after buying it.

The HBTC is calculated by multiplying the lowest personal income tax rate for the year (currently 15%) by $5,000. For 2012, the credit is $750.

[¶8118] Volunteer Firefighters Tax Credit

Volunteer firefighters may claim a 15% non-refundable tax credit [available for 2011 and onward], based on an amount of $3,000, if they have performed at least 200 hours of eligible volunteer firefighting services for one or more fire departments.[109] Eligible firefighting services are services provided to a fire department as a volunteer firefighter, which consist primarily of responding to and being on call for firefighting and related emergency calls, attending meetings held by the fire department, and participating in

---

[108] CCH ¶18,329pp; Sec. 118.05.   [109] Sec. 118.06(2).

required training related to the prevention or suppression of fires. Volunteer services performed for a particular fire department are not eligible if the firefighter also provides non-volunteer firefighting services to that department.[110]

An individual who claims this credit will not be allowed to claim the current tax exemption up to $1,000 for honoraria paid by a government, municipality, or other public body in respect of volunteer firefighting services.

[¶8119] Tuition Credit

A student who is enrolled full-time or part-time at an educational institution may deduct a tax credit of the appropriate percentage (currently 15%) of eligible tuition fees where such fees are greater than $100.[111]

"Eligible tuition fees" are those paid to a post-secondary educational institution in Canada or (for individuals aged 16 and over at the end of the year), an institution certified by Human Resources and Social Development Canada as being an institution that develops or improves skills in an occupation. Also eligible for the credit are tuition fees paid to: (i) a university outside Canada if the student is in full-time attendance for courses of at least three (13 before 2011) consecutive weeks' duration and leading to a degree; and (ii) an educational institution in the U.S. for post-secondary level courses if the student lived in Canada near the border throughout the year and commuted to the school.

An individual may also claim as tuition fees certain ancillary fees and charges paid in respect of the individual's enrolment at a post-secondary institution, if the payment of these fees or charges is made to the institution and is required from all of the institution's full-time students or part-time students, depending on whether the individual is enrolled on a full-time or part-time basis.[112] However, mandatory fees or charges will not qualify for the tuition tax credit to the extent that they are levied in relation to a student association, property to be acquired by students, services not ordinarily provided at post-secondary institutions in Canada, or tax-exempt financial assistance to students. In addition, mandatory charges paid for the construction, renovation, or maintenance of a facility generally will not qualify for the credit, except to the extent that the facility is owned by the institution and is used to provide post-secondary level courses or services that, if charges were required to be paid by all of the institution's students for such services, would be eligible for the tuition tax credit.

Where ancillary fees paid in respect of an individual's enrolment at a post-secondary educational institution would qualify for the credit, but for the fact that the payment of those fees is not required from all of the institution's full-time or part-time students, as the case may be, an amount

---

See page ii for explanation of footnotes.

[110] Sec. 118.06(1).

[111] CCH ¶18,415; Sec. 118.5(1).

[112] CCH ¶18,421; Sec. 118.5(3).

not exceeding $250 in respect of the fees may be included in computing the individual's tuition fee credit.

The list of eligible tuition fees also includes fees paid to an institution, association, or ministry for an examination required to obtain a professional status or to be licensed or certified to practice a trade or profession in Canada [effective 2011 and onward]. The total of tuition and examination fees paid to an institution, association, or ministry for a year must exceed $100 to be eligible.

A student will not be allowed a tax credit for tuition fees if such tuition fees are paid by the student's employer and not included in the student's income or were part of an allowance received by the student's parent from the parent's employer and not included in the parent's income. Similarly, tuition fees paid under a federal or provincial job training program, for which the individual is entitled to be reimbursed, are eligible for the credit only if the reimbursement is included in the individual's income. Fees paid on behalf of an individual or reimbursed to an individual under a federal program designed to assist athletes are not eligible for the credit unless such payment or reimbursement is included in computing income.

A student may transfer the unused portion of the tuition credit to a spouse or common-law partner, parent, or grandparent, or carry it forward for their own future use (see ¶8123). A student may also transfer part of the unused portion of the credit and carry forward the remainder. The amount that can be transferred is limited to the amount the student designates in writing. In 2012, the amount that can be so designated is limited to the lesser of the total tuition, textbook, and education tax credits combined and $750 (transfer limit of $5,000 × 15%).[113]

[¶8120] Full-Time Education Credit

An individual may also deduct from taxes payable a credit of 15% of $400 a month in 2012 (i.e., $60 a month) for each month in the year that the individual was enrolled as a full-time student at a designated educational institution and enrolled in a qualifying educational program. This includes full-time post-secondary students enrolled in distance education programs or correspondence courses.[114] There is no full-time enrolment requirement for students who are disabled.[115] In order for the student to qualify for the education tax credit with part-time enrolment, the student must be eligible for the impairment credit (¶8145), or a medical doctor, optometrist, audiologist, occupational therapist, psychologist, speech language pathologist, or physiotherapist must certify [in writing] that the individual cannot be enrolled on a full-time basis because of the impairment. No credit will be allowed for any student unless the student's enrolment is proven by filing a prescribed form of certificate issued by the educational institution.[116]

---

[113] CCH ¶18,437–18,438, ¶18,445, ¶18,447, ¶18,451; Sec. 118.61, 118.8, 118.81, 118.9.
[114] CCH ¶18,428; Sec. 118.6(2); Interp. Bul. IT-515R2.
[115] CCH ¶18,429; Sec. 118.6(3).
[116] CCH ¶39,297; Form T2202.

A designated educational institution, for purposes of the education credit, is generally the same as described in ¶8119 for the tuition credit. A qualifying educational program is one that requires at least 10 hours per week of work and is at least three consecutive weeks in duration. The program must be at a post-secondary school level except in the case of courses to improve occupational skills certified by Human Resources and Social Development Canada. For 2010 and subsequent years, an educational program at a post-secondary level consisting principally of research will not be eligible for the education tax credit, unless that program leads to a college or CEGEP diploma, or a bachelor, master, or doctoral degree (or an equivalent degree).

Fees paid on behalf of a student who is enrolled in a certified vocational job training course will not qualify for the education tax credit unless the student has reached the age of 16 before the end of the year.

Generally, students cannot claim the education tax credit for a program for which they received a benefit, a grant, an allowance, or a reimbursement of their tuition fees. However, students can claim the credit even if they received salary or wages from a job that is related to their program of study, certain other kinds of payments, such as scholarships and student loans, or if they received and included in their income any financial assistance provided under the *Employment Insurance Act* (Part II) or the *Department of Human Resources and Skills Development Act*. As with the tuition and textbook credit, the unused portion of the education credit may be transferred to a spouse or common- law partner, parent, or grandparent or carried forward for future use by the student. A student may also transfer part of the unused portion of the credit and carry forward the remainder. The amount that can be transferred is limited to the amount that the student designates in writing. In 2012, the amount which can be so designated is limited to the lesser of the total tuition, textbook, and education tax credits combined and $750 (transfer limit of $5,000 × 15%).

[¶8121] Part-Time Education Credit

Part-time students are eligible for a partial credit equal to the appropriate percentage (currently 15%) of $120 a month.[117] To be eligible, students must be enrolled in an educational program lasting at least three consecutive weeks and involving a minimum of 12 hours of courses per month. A specified educational program is essentially a qualifying educational program (described at ¶8120), except that the 10-hour-per-week course requirement is replaced by a 12-hour-per-month course requirement. The unused portion of the part-time credit may be transferred to a supporting person or carried forward for future use (see ¶8124).

---

[117] CCH ¶18,427a, ¶18,428; Sec. 118.6(1) "specified educational program", 118.6(2).

[¶8122] Post-Secondary Textbook Credit

Students may claim a tax credit in respect of textbooks for each month for which they qualify for the education tax credit. The credit is non-refundable, and for full-time students is calculated as the appropriate percentage (currently 15%) × $65 × the number of months during the year in which the student was entitled to claim the education credit as a full-time student. For part-time students, the credit is the appropriate percentage × $20 × the number of months during the year in which the student was entitled to claim the education credit as a part-time student.[118] Disabled students will qualify for the full textbook amount of $65 per month, even if they are not enrolled on a full-time basis.[119]

[¶8123] Credit for Interest on Student Loan

A personal tax credit is allowed for interest paid in a year or in any of the previous five years on a loan made under the *Canada Student Loans Act* or a similar provincial statute.[120] This credit is not transferable. Only the student to whom the loan was made or who legally owes interest can claim the credit. However, to qualify, the interest may be paid by the student or a person related to the student.

Financial institutions and Human Resources and Social Development Canada (or provincial government departments or agencies administering these loans) will provide taxpayers with statements indicating eligible interest payments. The credit applies to interest only, not repayment of principal. It does not apply to interest accrued but not paid or to any forgiven interest.

[¶8124] Carryforward of Tuition, Textbook, and Education Tax Credits

The combined tuition, textbook, and education credits that the student cannot claim in a year (because his or her income is too low) will automatically carry forward for future use by the student, unless the student has designated the unused portion to a spouse/common-law partner, parent, or grandparent. The student must use these carryforwards immediately in future years as sufficient income arises to absorb them. It is a first-in first-out system in which old credits must be used before new ones, and any new credits so blocked are added to the carryforward.

Technically, the amount that may be carried forward to future taxation years is determined by first, adding to the student's unused tuition, textbook, and education tax credits at the end of the previous year, the portion of the student's tuition, textbook, and education credits for the current year that is not needed to eliminate the student's tax payable for the current year. This total is then reduced by the amount of the tuition, textbook, and education tax credits carryforward that is deductible for the year.[121] The amount of the carryforward that is deductible for the year is equal to the lesser of the previous year's carryforward and the tax that

---

See page ii for explanation of footnotes.

[118] CCH ¶18,428d; Sec. 118.6(2.1).   [120] CCH ¶18,439; Sec. 118.62.
[119] CCH ¶18,429; Sec. 118.6(3).   [121] CCH ¶18,437; Sec. 118.61(1).

would be payable for the year by the student if no tuition, textbook, and education tax credits were allowed.[122] Finally, this total is further reduced by the tuition, textbook, and education tax credits transferred for the year by the student to the student's spouse/common-law partner, parent, or grandparent.

[¶8125] Medical Expense Credit

The medical expense tax credit for 2012 is calculated as 15% of qualifying medical expenses that are in excess of the lesser of:

(a) $2,109; and

(b) 3% of the individual's net income.[123]

The expenses giving rise to the tax credit may be for the taxpayer, a spouse, a common-law partner, a child under 18, or other dependent relatives.[124] (as defined at ¶8095).

Before 2011, the medical expenses an individual could claim for another dependent relative (i.e., a dependant other than a spouse/common-law partner, or child under 18) could not exceed $10,000. The 2011 Budget removed this $10,000 limit so that eligible expenses for this other group of dependent relatives are only subject to the above minimum expense threshold, i.e., the lesser of 3% of the individual's net income and $2,109 in 2012.

The medical expenses must be paid either by the taxpayer or by the taxpayer's legal representative within any 12-month period ending in the year of claim. Where the individual has died in the tax year, the expenses must be paid within any 24-month period that includes the date of death. Receipts must be filed with the taxpayer's return to support the claim for a medical expense credit.

The Act lists certain items which are included as medical expenses for purposes of calculating the credit.[125] So that the Act will not become unwieldy by additions to the list, it is provided that certain devices and equipment, when prescribed by a medical doctor or practitioner, and as prescribed by Regulation, will be considered medical expenses. There is no restriction that eligible medical expenses be paid for treatment in Canada. Premiums paid to a private health services plan are eligible medical expenses.[126]

After March 4, 2010, expenses incurred for purely cosmetic purposes (including related services and other expenses such as travel) are not eligible for the medical expense tax credit.[127] This exclusion of purely cosmetic procedures generally includes surgical and non-surgical procedures purely aimed at enhancing one's appearance, such as liposuction, hair replacement procedures, botulinum toxin injections, and teeth whitening. A cosmetic

---

See page ii for explanation of footnotes.

[122] CCH ¶18,438; Sec. 118.61(2).

[123] CCH ¶18,370; Sec. 118.2; Interp. Bul. IT-519R2.

[124] CCH ¶18,314, ¶18,372; Sec. 118(6), 118.2(2).

[125] CCH ¶18,372, ¶18,374; Sec. 118.2(2); Reg. 5700.

[126] CCH ¶18,372; Sec. 118.2(2)(q); Interp. Bul. IT-339R2.

[127] CCH ¶18,372f; Sec. 118.2(2.1).

procedure, including those identified above, will continue to qualify for the credit if it is required for medical or reconstructive purposes, such as surgery to ameliorate a deformity arising from, or directly related to, a congenital abnormality, a personal injury resulting from an accident or trauma, or a disfiguring disease.

An individual is allowed to claim as a medical expense an amount that is included in the taxpayer's income from employment in respect of a medical expense that is paid or provided by the taxpayer's employer. Medical expenses — for which the taxpayer, the taxpayer's legal representative, or the patient (if the patient is not the taxpayer) has been or is entitled to be reimbursed — do not qualify for the credit unless the reimbursement is included in income. In order for the expense to be eligible for the medical expense tax credit, any reimbursement must be included in income and not be deductible in computing taxable income.[128]

[¶8130] Types of Expenses Qualifying for Credit

To qualify as eligible medical expenses for purposes of computing the credit (see ¶8125), the Act provides that payments are to be made on behalf of the taxpayer, the taxpayer's spouse/common-law partner, or the taxpayer's dependant as follows:[129]

(1) *Payments for medical practitioners, hospitals, etc.* Payments are eligible if made to a medical practitioner (as defined below), dentist, pharmacist, nurse, optometrist, or to a public or licensed private hospital in respect of medical or dental services provided to the taxpayer, the taxpayer's spouse/common-law partner, or any dependant. "Medical practitioner" encompasses not only a medical doctor but also the following medical professionals as long as they are authorized to practice according to the laws of the jurisdiction where the expenses are incurred: an osteopath; a chiropractor; a naturopath; a therapeutist (or therapist); a physiotherapist; a chiropodist (or podiatrist); a Christian Science practitioner; a psychoanalyst who is a member of the Canadian Institute of Psychoanalysis or a member of the Quebec Association of Jungian Psychoanalysts; a psychologist; a qualified speech-language pathologist or audiologist such as, for example, a person who is certified as such by The Canadian Association of Speech-Language Pathologists and Audiologists (CASLPA) or a provincial affiliate of that organization; an occupational therapist who is a member of the Canadian Association of Occupational Therapists; an acupuncturist; a dietitian; a dental hygienist; and, beginning in 2005, a physiotherapist.

(2) *Payments for a full-time attendant or care in a nursing home.* Such payments are made as remuneration for one full-time attendant, other than the taxpayer's spouse/common-law partner or a person under 18 years of age; or as payment for the full-time care in a nursing home for an individual who has "one or more severe and prolonged impairments in physical or mental functions". An impairment is prolonged if it has lasted, or is expected

---

See page ii for explanation of footnotes.

[128] CCH ¶18,382; Sec. 118.2(3).   [129] CCH ¶18,372; Sec. 118.2(2); Interp. Bul. IT-519R2.

¶8130

to last, for a continuous period of at least 12 months. An impairment is severe if the individual is markedly restricted in performing one basic activity of daily living or would be so restricted were it not for extensive therapy (i.e., averaging at least 14 hours per week) in order to sustain a vital function. An individual whose ability to perform one basic activity of daily living and is not "markedly restricted" will still qualify if the individual's ability to perform more than one basic activity of daily living is significantly restricted, and the cumulative effect of those multiple restrictions is equivalent to a marked restriction in one basic activity of daily living. In other words, an individual may have multiple restrictions, none of which is in itself a marked restriction in performing one basic activity of daily living and still qualify for the credit if the cumulative effect of those multiple restrictions is tantamount to the individual's ability to perform a basic activity of daily living being markedly restricted. The marked restrictions must be present together, all or substantially all of the time.

The Tax Court defined remuneration paid to "one full-time attendant" as the total remuneration paid to any number of attendants in the relevant period provided the total remuneration so claimed only covered the services of one attendant at any given time.[130] The basic activities of daily living are speaking, hearing, walking, elimination (bowel or bladder functions), feeding (which does not include preparing food due to dietary restrictions, or obtaining food), dressing (which does not include obtaining clothing), and "mental functions necessary for everyday life". The expression "mental functions necessary for every day life", includes memory, problem solving, goal setting and judgment (taken together), and adaptive functioning. General activities such as working, housekeeping, or a social or recreational activity are not considered to be basic activities of daily living (see ¶8145).[131] If a taxpayer is so impaired and does not take into account any amount paid to a full-time attendant or to a nursing home in computing his or her medical expense credit, the taxpayer may be entitled to a disability tax credit under the rules discussed at ¶8145. Accordingly, in these circumstances, a taxpayer may have an option to make a claim under this provision including items (4) and (5) below or under the rules set out at ¶8145. A medical doctor, an optometrist for a sight impairment, an audiologist for a hearing impairment, an occupational therapist for a mobility impairment, a psychologist for an impairment with respect to mental functions necessary for everyday life, a speech language pathologist for a speech impairment, or a physiotherapist for an impairment with respect to an individual's ability in walking, must certify the extent of the impairment on a prescribed form.[132]

(3) *Payments for part-time attendant care.* Payments made as remuneration for attendant care up to a maximum of $10,000 ($20,000 in the year of death) may qualify as eligible medical expenses. The attendant must be 18 years of age or over and must not be the individual's spouse/common-law partner. The taxpayer must file receipts showing the Social Insurance

---

See page ii for explanation of footnotes.

[130] Wakelyn, 71 DTC 35.
[131] CCH ¶18,405; Sec. 118.4(1).
[132] CCH ¶39,296; Form T2201.

Number of the attendant, if the receipt is issued by an individual. Unlike for expenses noted in items (2), (4), and (5), the medical expense credit under this provision may be claimed in conjunction with the credit for mental or physical impairment, described at ¶8145. After suffering severe disabilities from a car accident, the taxpayer had to hire a cleaning company to do the housecleaning tasks that she could no longer do. These costs constituted "remuneration for attendant care" and qualified for a medical expense tax credit.[133]

(4) *Payments for an attendant in one's home.* Such payments are made as remuneration for a full-time attendant for an individual (the "cared-for person") in a self-contained domestic establishment where such person lives. The cared-for person must be certified [in writing] by a qualified medical practitioner as likely to be dependent upon others for a long period of indefinite duration by reason of mental or physical infirmity. Note that this provision refers to "infirmity" which, unlike "impairment", is not a defined term in the Act. The CRA's view is that a person is infirm if the person is incapable of being gainfully employed for a considerable period of time due to the infirmity.[134] The attendant cannot be the individual's spouse or common-law partner or a person under the age of 18. Each receipt filed with the Minister to prove payment to the attendant must contain the Social Insurance Number of the person who issued the receipt.

(5) *Training courses.* Reasonable expenses incurred to train an individual to care for a relative having a mental or physical infirmity may qualify as eligible medical expenses. To qualify, the relative must live with the individual or must be dependent on the individual for support. It is the CRA's view that a person is infirm if the person is incapable of being gainfully employed for a considerable period of time due to the infirmity.

(6) *Payments to a nursing home for full-time care.* These are payments made to a nursing home for the full-time care of an individual who is, and will, as far as can be foreseen, continue to be, dependent on other people for personal needs and care because of impaired mental capacity. A qualified medical practitioner must have certified [in writing] that this is the case.

(7) *Payments to schools and institutions.* Such payments are made to a school, institution, or other place that is equipped to provide care and training to persons who are physically or mentally handicapped, for the care, or the care and training, of an individual. The individual's condition and special requirements must be certified [in writing] by an appropriately qualified person.

(8) *Payments for transportation by ambulance.* These are payments made for transportation by ambulance to or from a public or licensed private hospital for the patient.

(9) *Payments to a commercial service for transportation to obtain medical services.* Payments made to a commercial service providing transportation

---

[133] Zaffino, 2007 DTC 1178.   [134] Interp. Bul. IT-513R.

¶8130

to obtain medical services for a patient and for one attendant may qualify, provided that the distance exceeds 40 kilometres and the medical services could not be obtained locally. A medical practitioner must certify [in writing] that the patient is incapable of travelling alone in order for the transportation costs of the attendant to qualify. Where a person engaged in the business of providing transportation services is not readily available, the taxpayer may deduct a reasonable amount in respect of the operation of a vehicle used for the above purpose, such amount being deemed to have been paid to a person engaged in the business of providing transportation services.[135] The CRA interprets "vehicle" to mean any type of conveyance by which a person can be transported by land or water, or through the air, including a vehicle owned by a taxpayer or a member of the taxpayer's family.[136]

(10) *Payments for travelling expenses to obtain medical services.* Such payments are made for reasonable travelling expenses incurred in respect of a patient and, if the patient is certified [in writing] as being incapable of travelling alone, one individual who is the patient's attendant, to obtain medical services not available locally in a place that is not less than 80 kilometres from the locality where the patient was dwelling. Where those travelling expenses are paid for or are provided by an employer and are included in the taxpayer's income from office or employment, the taxpayer is deemed to have paid the expenses. Thus the taxpayer-employee will be entitled to claim the medical expense credit in respect of those expenses.[137]

(11) *Payments for artificial limbs, medical equipment, etc.* These are payments made for or in respect of an artificial limb, an iron lung, rocking bed for poliomyelitis victims, a spinal brace, crutches, a brace for a limb, iliostomy or colostomy pad, truss for hernia, artificial eye, laryngeal speaking aid or an aid for hearing, a wheelchair, an artificial kidney machine [and phototherapy equipment for the treatment of psoriasis or other skin disorders, or an oxygen concentrator] for the patient.

(12) *Payments for items related to incontinence.* Such payments are for or in respect of all products such as diapers, disposable briefs, catheters, catheter trays, tubing or other products required by the patient for incontinence caused by illness, injury, or affliction.

(13) *Payments for vision care.* Such payments are made for eyeglasses or other devices for the treatment, or correction of a defect of vision, for the patient, as prescribed by a medical practitioner or an optometrist qualified to practice under the laws of the place where the expenses were incurred.

(14) *Payments for certain medical requirements.* These are payments for an oxygen tent and oxygen administering equipment, or for insulin, oxygen, liver extract injectable for pernicious anemia, or vitamin B12 for pernicious anemia for use by the patient, as prescribed by a medical practitioner.

See page ii for explanation of footnotes.

[135] CCH ¶18,384; Sec. 118.2(4).   [137] CCH ¶18,382; Sec. 118.2(3).
[136] Interp. Bul. IT-519R2.

(15) *Payments for trained animals.* Such payments are for an animal which has been trained to guide or assist a blind or profoundly deaf person, or an animal specially trained to assist an individual who has a severe and prolonged impairment that markedly restricts the use of the individual's arms or legs or has severe autism or severe epilepsy. Such expenses include:

    (a) the cost of the animal, provided that it is purchased from a person or organization, one of whose main purposes is training such animals;

    (b) the costs involved in caring for the animal, including food and veterinary bills;

    (c) travelling costs of the patient to and from a special training facility; and

    (d) board and lodging for the patient, if required to live away from home because the patient is attending, on a full-time basis, a school that trains persons with physical disabilities in handling such animals.

(16) *Payments for arranging transplants.* These are payments for expenses incurred to arrange a bone marrow or organ transplant. These expenses include legal fees and insurance premiums, as well as the travelling expenses and room and board (other than the expenses outlined in items (8) and (9) above) for the donor and the patient and an accompanying person for each.

(17) *Payments for renovations or alterations to one's home.* Such payments are made for reasonable expenses relating to renovations or alterations to the dwelling of the patient who lacks normal physical development or who has a severe and prolonged mobility impairment (e.g., confined to a wheelchair) to enable the patient to gain access to, or to be mobile or functional within the dwelling, provided that such expenses would not typically be expected to increase the value of the dwelling and would not typically be incurred by a person with a normal physical development or without a severe and prolonged mobility impairment.

(18) *Payments for rehabilitative therapy.* Such expenses include training in lip reading and sign language incurred to adjust for the individual's hearing or speech loss.

(19) *Payments for sign-language interpretation services or real-time captioning services.* Fees for sign language interpretation services and, for 2003 and subsequent taxation years, fees for real-time captioning services provided to an individual who has a speech or hearing impairment may qualify, if the fees are paid to a person engaged in the business of providing such services.

(20) *Payments for note-taking services.* The cost of note-taking services used by individuals with mental or physical impairments and paid to per-

¶8130

sons engaged in the business of providing such services may qualify, if the need for these services is certified in writing by a medical practitioner.

(21) *Payments for the cost of voice recognition software.* Payments for the cost of voice recognition software used by individuals with a physical impairment may qualify, if the need for the software is certified in writing by a medical practitioner.

(22) *Payments for reading services.* Payments for reading services used by individuals who are blind or who have a severe learning disability and made to persons engaged in the business of providing such services may qualify, if the need for these services is certified in writing by a medical practitioner.

(23) *Payments for deaf-blind intervening services.* Payments for deaf-blind intervening services used by individuals who are both blind and profoundly deaf may qualify, if the payments are made to persons engaged in the business of providing such services.

(24) *Payments for drugs purchased under Health Canada's Special Access Program and medical marijuana.* Payments for drugs purchased under Health Canada's Special Access Program and medical marijuana may qualify. To be an eligible expense, medical marijuana will have to be purchased from either Health Canada or a designated grower, by an individual authorized to use the drug for medical purposes under Health Canada's Medical Marijuana Access Regulations or an exemption under section 56 of the *Controlled Drug and Substances Act.* With the exception of the cost of seeds purchased from Health Canada, expenses incurred by authorized users to grow their own marijuana will not be eligible.

(25) *Payments for moving expenses.* Such payments are made for reasonable moving expenses (up to a maximum of $2,000) of an individual who lacks normal physical development or has a severe and prolonged mobility impairment to move to a dwelling that is more accessible by the individual or in which the individual is more mobile or functional.

(26) *Payments for alteration to driveway.* Such payments represent the reasonable costs of alterations to the driveway of the principal place of residence of an individual who has a severe and prolonged mobility impairment to facilitate the individual's access to a bus.

(27) *Payments for a van.* Such payments are the lesser of $5,000 and 20% of the cost of a van that, at the time of acquisition or within six months thereafter, has been adapted for the transportation of the patient who requires the use of a wheelchair.

(28) *Payments for other medical equipment.* These are payments made for any other device or equipment not described above of a prescribed kind, for use by the patient as prescribed by a medical practitioner (to the extent that the amount so paid does not exceed the amount, if any, prescribed in respect of the device or equipment).

¶8130

(29) *Payments for drugs, medications, etc.* These are payments made for any drugs, medications, or other preparations or substances (other than those described in (13) above) prescribed by a medical practitioner or dentist, provided it is recorded by a pharmacist. Under this provision, an individual will be able to claim all prescribed items provided they are used in the diagnosis or prevention of a disease, disorder, abnormal physical state, or the symptoms thereof, or in restoring, correcting, or modifying an organic function. As a result of recent court decisions that have interpreted this provision to include the costs of vitamins, supplements, and drugs that could otherwise be purchased without a prescription,[138] drugs, medications, and other substances and preparations that can lawfully be acquired for use by a patient without a prescription by a medical practitioner or dentist are ineligible for this credit. However, drugs, medications, or other substances or preparations that are prescribed by regulation will qualify for this credit, although a medical prescription is not required in some cases (e.g., insulin). Such drugs or substances are prescribed for this purpose if they:

(a) are used in diagnosing, treating, or preventing a disease, disorder, or abnormal physical state, or its symptoms, or in restoring, correcting, or modifying an organic function;

(b) are prescribed by a medical practitioner; and

(c) may, in the province in which they are acquired, be lawfully acquired for use by the patient only with the *intervention* of a medical practitioner in the province in which it is acquired.[139]

(30) *Payments for diagnostic procedures.* These are payments for laboratory, radiological, or other diagnostic procedures or services, together with necessary interpretation, as prescribed by a medical practitioner or dentist where these tests or services aid in maintaining the health, preventing disease or assisting in the diagnosis or treatment of the patient.

(31) *Payments for dentures.* Payments for making or repairing dentures may be eligible, provided that the person providing the services is authorized by the laws of the province to carry on this business. Payments for impressions, bite registrations, and insertions in respect of the making, producing, constructing, and finishing of dentures will also qualify.

(32) *Payments in relation to private health services plan.* Included are payments made as a premium or consideration to a private health services plan in respect of the taxpayer, the taxpayer's spouse or common-law partner, or any member of the household with whom the taxpayer is connected by blood relationship, marriage, common-law partnership, or adoption.[140] An individual may claim premiums paid on behalf of another individual, despite the fact that such individual would not be classified as a dependant for the purpose of the dependant tax credit. Premiums paid to government medical and hospital care plans are not eligible medical expenses.

See page ii for explanation of footnotes.

[138] Breger, 2007 DTC 1156.
[139] Reg. 5701.

[140] Interp. Bul. IT-339R2.

¶8130

(33) *Remuneration for the care and education of disabled persons.* These are payments made in respect of the remuneration for: (i) the care and supervision of persons with severe and prolonged disabilities living in a group home; (ii) therapy for persons with severe and prolonged disabilities; and (iii) tutoring for persons with learning disabilities or other mental impairments.

(34) *Payments for gluten-free products.* The incremental cost of acquiring gluten-free food products as compared to comparable non-gluten-free food products for individuals with celiac disease who require a gluten-free diet may qualify. In order to be eligible as medical expenses, a medical practitioner must certify in writing that the patient is a person who, because of celiac disease, requires a gluten-free diet. Comparable gluten-free food products are food products produced as a substitute for food products that typically contain a gluten-laden agent as a principal component and are generally targeted at persons requiring a gluten-free diet. In that sense, products such as rice, corn or buckwheat-based breads constitute eligible products. However, products that do not have gluten as a principal component, such as dairy products or fruits, are not eligible for this purpose.

[¶8135] Medical Expenses Prescribed by Regulation

The following devices and equipment, when prescribed by a medical practitioner, have been prescribed by Regulation[141] for the purposes of the medical expense tax credit:

(1) wigs made to order for individuals who have suffered abnormal hair loss owing to disease, medical treatment, or accident;

(2) needles and syringes designed to be used for the purpose of giving injections;

(3) any device or equipment, including replacement parts, designed exclusively for use by an individual who is suffering from a chronic respiratory ailment or a severe chronic immune system disregulation to assist the individual in breathing (but not including air conditioners, humidifiers, dehumidifiers, heat pumps, or heat or air exchangers);

(4) an air or water filter or purifier to be used by an individual suffering from a severe chronic respiratory ailment or a severe chronic immune system disregulation;

(5) an electric or sealed combustion furnace which replaces a furnace of a different type, where the replacement was necessary for an individual suffering from a severe chronic respiratory ailment or a severe chronic immune system disregulation;

(6) 50% of the cost of an air conditioner prescribed by a medical practitioner for an individual with a severe chronic ailment, disease or disorder, to a limit of $1,000;

See page ii for explanation of footnotes.

[141] CCH ¶18,374; Reg. 5700; Interp. Bul. IT-519R2.

(7) any device or equipment designed to pace or monitor the heart of an individual who suffers from heart disease;

(8) orthopaedic shoes or boots and inserts for shoes and boots made to order for an individual in accordance with a prescription to overcome a physical disability of the individual;

(9) any power-operated guided chair installation for an individual that is designated to be used solely in a stairway;

(10) any mechanical device or equipment designed to be used to assist an individual to enter or leave a bathtub or shower or to get on or off a toilet;

(11) any hospital bed and attachments;

(12) any device that is designed to assist an individual with a mobility impairment in walking;

(13) any external breast prosthesis that is required because of a mastectomy;

(14) any teletypewriter or similar device (including telephone ringing indicator) that enables an individual who is deaf or mute to make and receive telephone calls;

(15) any optical scanner or similar device designed to enable an individual who is blind to read print;

(16) any power-operated lift designed exclusively for use by or for an individual with a disability, to allow the individual access to different levels of a building, to gain access to a vehicle, or to place the individual's wheelchair in a vehicle;

(17) a device designed exclusively to enable an individual with a mobility impairment to operate a vehicle;

(18) a device or equipment used in the operation of a computer, including a synthetic speech system, Braille printer, and large print-on-screen device, designed exclusively to be used by an individual who is blind;

(19) an electronic speech synthesizer that enables an individual who is mute to communicate by use of a portable keyboard;

(20) a device to decode special television signals to permit the vocal portion of the signal to be visually displayed;

(21) a visual or vibratory signalling device, such as a visual fire alarm indicator, for an individual with a hearing impairment;

(22) a device designed to be attached to infants diagnosed as being prone to sudden infant death syndrome in order to sound an alarm if the infant ceases to breathe;

¶8135

(23) an infusion pump and disposable peripherals used in the treatment of diabetes or a device designed to enable an individual with diabetes to measure his or her blood sugar level;

(24) electronic or computerized environmental control systems for use by an individual with a severe mobility restriction;

(25) extremity pumps or elastic support hose to reduce swelling caused by lymphedema;

(26) electronic bone healing devices for non-fusion complications;

(27) talking textbooks prescribed by a medical practitioner for use by an individual with a perceptual disability, in connection with the individual's enrolment at a Canadian educational institution.

(28) altered auditory feedback devices for the treatment of a speech disorder;

(29) electrotherapy devices for the treatment of a medical condition or a severe mobility impairment;

(30) standing devices for standing therapy in the treatment of a severe mobility impairment; and

(31) pressure pulse therapy devices for the treatment of a balance disorder.

An air conditioner had been designed to assist a disabled individual in walking, within the meaning of (12) above, and its cost was therefore deductible as a medical expense when it had been developed in a medical context in order to lower body temperature and thereby assist in the restoration of mobility.[142]

[¶8145] Mental or Physical Impairment Credit

In 2012, an individual who has one or more severe and prolonged impairments in physical or mental functions is entitled to a basic tax credit of $1,623 ($10,822 × 15%). To that basic personal amount is added a supplemental credit of $660 ($4,402 × 15%) for a disabled person who was under 18 at the end of 2012. Such a supplement is reduced by child care and attendant care expenses in excess of $2,578.[143] This credit may be claimed by a taxpayer if the following three conditions are met:

(1) The taxpayer suffers from a severe and prolonged impairment in physical or mental functions certified in prescribed form by a medical doctor, an optometrist, an audiologist, an occupational therapist, a psychologist, a speech language pathologist, or a physiotherapist, as an impairment that significantly restricts one basic activity of daily living or would restrict it were it not for extensive therapy (i.e., averaging at least 14 hours per week) in order to sustain a vital function. An individual may have multiple restric-

---

See page ii for explanation of footnotes.

[142] Brown, 95 DTC 5126.   [143] CCH ¶18,390; Sec. 118.3; Interp. Bul. IT-519R2.

tions, none of which is in itself a significant restriction in performing one basic activity of daily living, and still qualify for the credit if the cumulative effect of those multiple restrictions is tantamount to the individual's ability to perform a basic activity of daily living being significantly restricted. The significant restrictions must be present together, all or substantially all of the time.

(2) The taxpayer has filed the certificate described in (1) with the Minister of National Revenue.

(3) The taxpayer, in calculating a credit in respect of medical expenses, did not include remuneration paid to a full-time attendant or payments for care in a nursing home, otherwise than for attendant care as described in item (3) at ¶8130. If the medical expense credit is claimed under item (2), (4), or (5) at ¶8130, regarding attendant or nursing home care, the individual is not also entitled to claim the disability tax credit. In this case, the taxpayer may claim either the medical expense credit for the attendant or nursing-home care, or the disability credit.

One or a multitude of impairments will qualify for this credit if their severity meets the criteria described in (1) and they are expected to last for at least 12 months. As such, blindness (even with the use of corrective lenses and medication) qualifies as a severe and prolonged impairment, the effect of which is to significantly restrict at least one basic activity of daily living and qualify for the credit. The basic activities of daily living are speaking, hearing, walking, elimination (bowel or bladder functions), feeding (which does not include preparing food due to dietary restrictions, or obtaining food), dressing (which does not include obtaining clothing), and "mental functions necessary for everyday life". The expression "mental functions necessary for every day life", includes memory, problem solving, goal setting and judgment (taken together), and adaptive functioning.[144]

"Feeding oneself" and "dressing oneself" are distinct basic living activities under the eligibility criteria for the disability tax credit. Therefore, an individual does not need to have an impairment of both the ability to feed oneself and dress oneself in order to satisfy the eligibility criteria. The credit may be claimed if the individual's mental or physical impairment markedly restricts the individual's ability to feed or dress oneself (and not necessarily both). However, "feeding oneself" does not include any of the activities of identifying, finding, shopping for or otherwise procuring food, or the activity of preparing food to the extent that the time associated with that activity would not have been necessary in the absence of a dietary restriction or regime. In other words, feeding oneself does not include the additional time and effort of preparing food owing to a dietary restriction. Note, however, that the incremental cost of gluten-free food for individuals with celiac disease now qualifies for the medical expense tax credit. (See item (34) at ¶8130.) Individuals who are markedly restricted in their ability to prepare food because of a physical impairment (such as arthritis), as opposed to a

---

[144] CCH ¶18,405; Sec. 118.4(1).

dietary restriction or regime, continue to be eligible for the credit. As to the phrase "dressing oneself", it excludes identifying, finding, shopping for, or otherwise procuring clothing.

A taxpayer who is entitled to the disability credit may deduct unreimbursed amounts paid to purchase supports, including attendant care, that are necessary to earn certain kinds of taxable income, or to attend high school, college, university, or any other designated educational institution.[145] The expenses cannot include any amount for which the individual or anyone else claimed a medical expense tax credit, and they are reduced by any reimbursement or any other form of assistance the individual is entitled to receive in respect of the qualifying expenses, unless those amounts are taxable income to the individual not offset by deductions. This deduction for disability support and attendant care expenses is discussed at ¶2410.

Under certain circumstances, where a taxpayer supports a disabled child under the age of 18 or has claimed a dependant credit in respect of a dependant suffering from one or more severe and prolonged impairments in physical or mental functions (see ¶8095), the taxpayer may deduct, in computing tax payable, an amount in respect of an eligible dependant ($1,623 in 2012), less the child and attendant care expenses in excess of $2,578 in 2012.[146] Any unused impairment tax credits can be transferred to the parent, where the parent supports more than one disabled child. The impairment tax credit may be transferred to the supporting individual, as long as the spouse/common-law partner of the disabled person is not claiming any non-refundable tax credits in respect of the disabled person. In order to claim the credit, the following conditions must be met:

(a) the dependant was resident in Canada at any time in the year;

(b) the taxpayer claimed (or could have claimed, if the dependant had no income for the year and had been 18 years of age or older) an eligible dependant or dependant tax credit where that person was the taxpayer's child or grandchild, parent, or grandparent;

(c) the dependant would otherwise qualify for the disability credit; and

(d) no amount in respect of remuneration for an attendant, or care in a nursing home, other than for an attendant as described in item (3) of ¶8130, was claimed as a medical expense for the year by the taxpayer or any other person.

If more than one taxpayer is entitled to claim this credit in respect of a dependant, the total claim cannot exceed the maximum allowed for that dependant. The Minister may determine the allocation if the taxpayers cannot agree.[147]

See page ii for explanation of footnotes.

[145] CCH ¶8740; Sec. 64.
[146] CCH ¶18,392; Sec. 118.3(2).
[147] CCH ¶18,393; Sec. 118.3(3).

[¶8147] Caregiver Tax Credit

A personal tax credit is offered to individuals who provide in-home care for parents or grandparents who are 65 years of age or older.[148] The tax credit also applies if in-home care is provided to the individual's child, grandchild, parent, grandparent, sibling, aunt, uncle, niece, or nephew, or if the person is an adult who is dependent on the individual by reason of mental or physical infirmity. It is the CRA's view that a person is infirm if the person is incapable of being gainfully employed for a considerable period of time due to the infirmity.

The credit is based on a caregiver amount of $4,402 in 2012, which is reduced dollar for dollar by the dependant's income over $15,033. The maximum credit therefore available is $660 (15% of $4,402) in 2012. No credit will be available in 2012 if the dependant's net income exceeds $19,435 ($15,033 + $4,402) or if an eligible dependant tax credit or dependant tax credit has been claimed in respect of the dependant by any person. These figures will be adjusted to reflect the full increases in the Consumer Price Index.

For 2012 and onward, individuals who provide in-home care for parents or grandparents who are at least 65 years of age and dependent on them by reason of physical or mental disability benefit from a family caregiver tax credit by adding $2,000 to the indexed $4,402 value used in the computation of the caregiver tax credit. Only one family caregiver tax credit will be available in respect of each infirm adult relative. The $2,000 family caregiver tax credit amount will be indexed to account for inflation for 2013 and subsequent taxation years.

[¶8148] Adoption Expense Credit

The adoption expense credit is a non-refundable credit equal to the appropriate percentage (currently 15%) of eligible adoption expenses incurred during the adoption period, up to a maximum of $11,440 in 2012.[149] The eligible adoption expenses are reduced by reimbursements and other forms of assistance that the individual is or was entitled to receive in respect of the eligible adoption expenses (other than an amount that is included in computing the individual's income and that is not deductible in computing the individual's taxable income). Parents may each claim a portion of the tax credit up to the maximum amount per adopted child.[150]

Eligible adoption expenses include:

- Fees paid to an adoption agency licensed by a provincial or territorial government.

- Court, legal, and administrative expenses related to an adoption order in respect of the child.

See page ii for explanation of footnotes.

[148] CCH ¶18,250; Sec. 118(1)(c.1), 118(1)(e).   [150] CCH ¶18,323; Sec. 118.01(3).
[149] CCH ¶18,323; Sec. 118.01(2).

- Reasonable travel and living expenses for the child and the adoptive parents.

- Document translation fees.

- Mandatory fees paid to a foreign institution.

- Any other reasonable expenses required by a provincial or territorial government or an adoption agency licensed by a provincial or territorial government.[151]

The above expenses must be incurred during the period (referred to as the "adoption period") that begins at the earlier of the time the child's adoption file is opened with the provincial or territorial ministry responsible for adoption or a licensed adoption agency, and the time, if any, that an application related to an adoption is made to a Canadian court, and ends at the later of the time the adoption is finalized and the time the adopted child begins to live with the adoptive parent.[152] As such, the cumulative eligible adoption expenses incurred during the adoption period will qualify for the one-time credit.

To be eligible for the credit, a parent must submit proof of an adoption in the form of a Canadian or foreign adoption order, or otherwise demonstrate that all of the legal requirements of the jurisdiction in which the parent resides have been met in completing the adoption. Parents will be able to claim the credit once in respect of an adoption and in one taxation year only — the year in which the adoption period ends.

[¶8150] Charitable Donations Credit

A credit, rather than a deduction, is given for charitable donations by individuals. Most donations are subject to a limitation that total donations are not eligible for the credit in the current year to the extent they exceed 75% of net income (no income limit in the year of death and the preceding year). Unused donations can be carried forward for up to five years.

The donation credit is unusual in that it is calculated at two rates: the appropriate percentage (currently 15%) of the first $200 of donations plus 29% of donations over $200.[153] The credit claim for charitable donations is optional. It follows that donations may be accumulated within the five-year carryforward period and claimed when they aggregate more than $200, and thereby avoid the low rate of credit where gifts in a particular year are less than $200.

The maximum amount that an individual may claim for charitable gifts is set out in the definition of "total gifts".[154]

The limit for donations is equal to 75% of the individual's net income for the year (100% of net income in the year of death and the immediately

---

See page ii for explanation of footnotes.

[151] CCH ¶18,323; Sec. 118.01(1) "eligible adoption expense".

[152] CCH ¶18,323; Sec. 118.01(1) "adoption period".

[153] CCH ¶18,336; Sec. 118.1(3).

[154] CCH ¶18,330d; Sec. 118.1(1) "total gifts".

preceding year) *plus*, for gifts of capital property, (i) 25% of the taxable capital gain arising from the gift and taken into income in the year, and (ii) the lesser of any recapture of capital cost allowance on the property included in the taxpayer's income in the year and the property's capital cost or fair market value.

To be claimed as a tax credit, the gift must be made to one of the following institutions:[155]

(1) registered charities;

(2) registered Canadian amateur athletic associations;

(3) registered national arts service organizations;

(4) Canadian tax-exempt housing corporations that only provide low-cost housing for seniors;

(5) Canadian municipalities;

(6) under proposed changes [released July 16, 2010], for gifts made after May 8, 2000, municipal or public bodies performing a function of government in Canada;

(7) the United Nations or its agencies;

(8) universities outside Canada prescribed to be universities whose student bodies ordinarily include Canadians;[156]

(9) charitable organizations outside Canada to which the Government of Canada has made a gift during the donor's tax year, or in the 12 months just before that period;[157] and

(10) the Government of Canada, a province, or a territory.

See ¶8185 and ¶8190 for gifts to governments and qualified cultural gifts.

The maximum must be calculated on total income received, even where, as a partner in a law firm, an individual was permitted to report a reduced amount because he had two fiscal periods in the same taxation year.[158] A charitable donation was made, entitling the taxpayers to a tax credit, in a situation where they loaned money to a registered charity and subsequently forgave some of the loans.[159]

[¶8155] Proof of Gift

A receipt containing prescribed information must be filed with the Minister in order for a gift to be included in computing a tax credit for an individual or to be deductible by a corporation.[160]

See page ii for explanation of footnotes.

[155] CCH ¶18,330; Sec. 118.1(1) "total charitable gifts"; Interp. Bul. IT-110R3, IT-244R3.
[156] Reg. 3503, Sch VIII.
[157] CCH ¶51,234; Inf. Cir. 84-3R6.
[158] Goodman, 75 DTC 5022.
[159] Interp. Bul. IT-244R3; Benquesus et al., 2006 DTC 2747.
[160] CCH ¶18,334; Sec. 118.1(2); Interp. Bul. IT-110R3.

[¶8160] Member of Religious Order

A member of a religious order who has taken a vow of perpetual poverty may deduct an amount equal to his or her earned income and an amount equal to the superannuation and pension benefits received in the year if these amounts were paid to the order.[161] Where this deduction is claimed in a taxation year, the individual cannot also claim a charitable donations tax credit in respect of this year.

The deduction does not apply where a person, whether or not the person has taken a vow of perpetual poverty, who arranges for the salary to which he or she may be entitled for teaching or other services to be paid to a religious institution in return for board, lodging, and a small living allowance. In this case, the person is entitled to a credit as a charitable donation (subject to the net income limitation described in ¶8150) of the difference between the salary paid to the person by the institution and the value of the board, lodging, and living allowance. The members of a religion-based farming community, the operations and profits of which belonged to the trustees of the community, who devoted their time and efforts to the operations without wages or reward except the subsistence they received from the trustees, were taxable only on the value of such subsistence.[162]

[¶8165] Gifts of Art

Where an artist donates artwork that was created by him or her and held as inventory to a charitable organization or to The Queen in right of Canada or to a province (i.e., a Crown gift, see ¶8185), the artist or his or her legal representative may designate an amount not greater than the gift's fair market value and not less than its cost amount that will be considered to be the artist's proceeds of disposition for the purpose of calculating the artist's income. Upon such a designation, the amount designated is also deemed to be the fair market value of the gift for the purpose of calculating the tax credit for a charitable donation allowed under ¶8150.[163] [For gifts made after December 20, 2002, if the gift confers an advantage to the artist that is greater than the gift's cost amount, the amount designated may not be less than the amount of the advantage. As a result, the artist will have business income from the disposition to the extent that the amount of the advantage in respect of the gift (or some other amount designated, if greater) exceeds the cost amount to the artist of the artwork.]

If an artist donates artwork that is certified as a cultural gift from the inventory of artwork created by him or her, the artist is treated as having received proceeds of disposition equal to the cost amount of the artwork (nil if so designated by the artist), but the fair market value of the artwork is not affected.[164] This means that the artist is entitled to a credit for the donation based on the fair market value of the artwork established by the Canadian Cultural Property Export Review Board, but that the artist recog-

---

See page ii for explanation of footnotes.

[161] CCH ¶15,314; Sec. 110(2); Interp. Bul. IT-86R.   [163] CCH ¶18,358; Sec. 118.1(7); Interp. Bul. IT-504R2.
[162] Wipf et al, 76 DTC 6059.   [164] CCH ¶4177; Sec. 10(6).

nizes neither a profit nor a loss on the disposition of the artwork in computing business income.[165] [For gifts made after December 20, 2002, if the gift confers an advantage to the artist that is greater than its cost amount, the artist is treated as having received proceeds of disposition equal to the amount of the advantage. As a result, the artist will have business income from the disposition if the amount of the advantage in respect of the gift exceeds the cost amount to the artist or the artwork.]

[¶8170] Commuters

Taxpayers who live near the United States border and commute to a principal place of employment or business in the United States will be entitled to a credit for charitable gifts that would be allowed as a deduction in the United States.[166]

[¶8175] Meaning of "Gifts"

Traditional meaning

The accepted meaning of the word "gift" is that it is something parted with for no consideration. If the donor expects some benefit or enjoyment in return, it is not a true gift. For instance, donations to religious schools attended by the taxpayer's children or gifts to sporting organizations in which the taxpayer's children were actively involved were held to involve a consideration or benefit for the taxpayer, consisting of the education and training of his child, and so were not true gifts, and not eligible for deduction or credit.[167] If payments made to charitable organizations can be shown to have been made to bring in or maintain trade which would otherwise have gone elsewhere, such payments may be deducted in full as business promotion and advertising expenses, without being subject to the net income limitation described in ¶8150. A gift made for such purposes is not a gift and is not subject to the maximum limit for charitable donations. On the other hand, gifts made to avoid criticism, which might arise if donations were made to some deserving causes but refused for others, are not deductible as business expenses and, consequently, are subject to the maximum limit for donations.[168]

It should be noted that, administratively, the CRA has made an exception to the general rule for certain payments, including purchases of tickets for entertainment or dinners at greater than fair market value.[169] Thus, the difference between the purchase price of a ticket to attend a "dinner, ball, concert or show" and the fair market value of the food, entertainment etc., available to a ticket purchaser is considered to be a gift by the CRA. This exception to the general rule is not extended to anything that is not a dinner, ball, concert, show, or a like event. A "like event" is an event which

---

See page ii for explanation of footnotes.

[165] CCH ¶18,330b, ¶18,358, ¶18,359; Sec. 118.1(1) "total cultural gifts", 118.1(7), 118.1(7.1).

[166] CCH ¶18,364; Sec. 118.1(9).

[167] CCH ¶51,152; Inf. Cir. 75-23; McBurney, 85 DTC 5433, Burns, 90 DTC 6335.

[168] Olympia Floor & Wall Tile (Que.) Ltd., 70 DTC 6085.

[169] Interp. Bul. IT-110R3.

provides services and consumable goods, the equivalent of which are readily available in the marketplace and which by their very nature are necessarily purchased with the intention that they be used on a specific date in the near future by the ticket purchaser (and guests) and which, if not used, have no resale value. An auction, for example, is not a "like event". A dinner coupled with an auction is not considered a "like event" unless people are invited to bid and can bid at the auction without paying the admission fee for the dinner. As well, the CRA has administratively permitted charitable receipts to be issued when the benefit has a nominal value.

The definition of gift utilized by the CRA is generally accepted under the common law. (Although there have been certain decisions made under the common law where it has been found that a transfer of property to a charity was made partly in consideration for services and partly as a gift.)[170] However, under section 1806 of the *Civil Code of Quebec*, a transfer of property can be "split" between a purchase or sale portion and a gift portion.[171] This has given rise to the possibility that a transaction which would be characterized as a gift in Quebec would not be characterized as a gift in the rest of Canada.

Proposed split gift rules

In response to requests from many charities, the Department of Finance has proposed [in draft legislation released on July 16, 2010, and as yet not passed] amendments to the Act effective December 20, 2002, which would permit "split" gifts throughout Canada. After December 20, 2002, a transfer of property will not necessarily be disqualified from being a gift, where the transferor is provided with some advantage. If the amount of the advantage the transferor is entitled to does not exceed 80% of the value of the property transferred, a donation tax credit will be allowed for the fair market value of the gift less the advantage (otherwise called the "eligible amount of a gift").[172]

The amount of an advantage in respect of a gift or contribution is, in general, the total value of all property, services, compensation, or other benefits to which the donor of a property is entitled as partial consideration for, or in gratitude for, the gift or contribution.[173] Under the proposed amendments, for gifts made after February 18, 2003, the advantage also includes any limited-recourse debt in respect of the gift at the time it was made.

The advantage may be contingent or receivable in the future, either to the donor or to a person not dealing at arm's length with the donor. It is not necessary that the advantage be receivable from the donee. However, a tax credit or deduction resulting from a charitable donation is not considered a benefit. The Department of Finance provides the following example in its explanatory notes.

---

[170] Woolner, 2000 DTC 1956.
[171] Aspinall, 70 DTC 1669.
[172] Sec. 248(30), 248(32).
[173] Sec. 248(31).

Example:

Mr. Short transfers land and a building with a fair market value of $300,000 to a registered charity. The charity assumes liability for an outstanding $100,000 mortgage on the property. The assumption of the mortgage by the charity does not necessarily disqualify the transfer from being a gift for the purposes of the Act. If the value of the mortgage is equal to the outstanding amount (e.g., the interest rate and terms and conditions are representative of current market conditions), the eligible amount of the gift, in respect of which Mr. Short may be entitled to a tax credit is $200,000.

If the amount of an advantage in respect of a transfer of property exceeds 80% of the fair market value of the transferred property, the transfer will not necessarily be disqualified from being a gift if the transferor can establish to the satisfaction of the Minister that the transfer was made with the intention to make a gift.

Example:

In the above example, if the amount of the mortgage outstanding had been greater than $240,000, Mr. Short (or the charity on Mr. Short's behalf) could apply to the Minister of National Revenue for a determination as to whether the transfer was made with the intention to make a gift.

Official receipts issued by a registered organization after December 20, 2002 must contain, in addition to the information already prescribed, the eligible amount of the gift and the amount of the advantage, if any, in respect of the gift. According to the proposed guidelines on "split receipting" issued by the CRA on December 24, 2002, any advantage received or obtained by the donor or a person not dealing at arm's length with the donor must be clearly identified and its value ascertainable. If its value cannot be reasonably ascertained, no charitable tax credit will be allowed. In this regard, the donee will be required to identify the advantage and the amount thereof on any receipt provided to the donor. In respect of valuations, the donee should consider obtaining a qualified independent valuation of the amount of the advantage.

[¶8180] Donations Not Eligible for Credit

The following donations are not eligible for the credit:

(1) Donations to individuals.

(2) Court ordered transfers of property to charities.

(3) Gifts of services (for example, donated time, labour).

(4) Gifts of promises (for example, gift certificates donated by the issuer, hotel accommodation).

(5) Pledges.

(6) Donations of merchandise where the cost has been charged as a business expense.

(7) Amounts paid for card parties, bingos, and lotteries, even where such activities may be held for the benefit of a charity. It is the CRA's view that participants in lotteries, bingos, etc., while perhaps influenced in choos-

ing which lottery they will participate in by the identity of the organizing charity, are primarily motivated by the chance to win the significant prizes that are offered. Therefore, in some cases, while there may be an element of donative intent, the amount of the advantage cannot be reasonably quantified. Accordingly, it continues to be the CRA's view, after December 20, 2002, that no part of the cost of a lottery ticket, bingo, etc., is a gift which may be receipted for income tax purposes.

(8) The payment of a basic fee for admission to an event or to a program.

(9) The payment of membership fees that convey the right to attend events, receive literature, receive services, or be eligible for entitlements of any material value that exceeds 80% of the value of the payment.

(10) A donation for which the fair market value of the advantage or consideration provided to the donor exceeds 80% of the value of the donation.

(11) A gift in kind for which the fair market value cannot be determined.

(12) Donations provided in exchange for advertising/sponsorship.

(13) Loans of property.

(14) Use of timeshare.

(15) The lease of premises.

(16) Donations subject to a direction by the donor that they benefit a particular person or family or be in turn donated to a non-qualified donee such as a foreign charity. Donations can be directed to a particular program operated by the charity, provided there is no benefit for the donor or persons not at arm's length with the donor.

(17) Items obtained at charity auctions on the basis that the bid determines the value of the various items put up for auction. However, where the value of an item is clearly otherwise ascertainable (e.g., there is a retail price for the item) and made known to all bidders in advance, an eligible amount would be present where the amount bid is in excess of the posted value. Where donative intent can be established, which may be the case here, and the posted value of the item does not exceed 80% of the accepted bid, a tax receipt may be issued for the eligible amount.

(18) While a particular event may be a charity fundraiser and all or a portion of the proceeds designated in favour of a charity, there will need to be clear evidence that the ticket price is in excess of the usual and current ticket price to allow a finding that there is an eligible amount. Where the amount of the advantage (including the usual and current ticket price) is 80% or less of the actual ticket price, a tax receipt may be issued for the difference. If there is no reasonably comparable event, then no portion of the ticket price can be viewed as an eligible amount.

¶8180

(19) Whether or not there is an eligible amount associated with the payment of membership fees or other amount to a registered charity of which an individual is a member will be determined on the basis of whether the membership fee or other amount exceeds the amount of the advantage. If the amount of the advantage is 80% or less of the payment to the charity, a tax receipt may be issued for the eligible amount. Prior to December 21, 2002, the rule was that the payment of membership fees that convey the right to attend events, receive literature, receive services, or be eligible for entitlements of any material value did not qualify as a gift. The right to vote at meetings and to receive reports of the charity's activities (unless such reports were otherwise available for a fee) were not considered to be of any material value.

(20) In general, donations where any kind of return or personal benefit of more than nominal value is expected do not qualify if made before December 21, 2002, and only the value in excess of the benefit qualifies after December 20, 2002. Thus, except as noted in (18) and (19), payments for goods and services are not eligible for the charitable donations tax credit (before December 21, 2002) or are eligible for a reduced credit (after December 20, 2002) where the individual pays more than what the items received are worth. However if the items received in exchange for a donation are of nominal value, the donation will not be disqualified or reduced. A benefit is considered to be of nominal value where its fair market value does not exceed the lesser of $75 ($50 before December 21, 2002), or 10% of the amount of the gift.

(21) In general, for gifts made after December 20, 2002, any advantage received by the donor must be clearly identified and its value ascertainable. If its value cannot be reasonably ascertained, no credit is allowed.

(22) Effective April 26, 1999, the CRA revised its position that the loan of a property to a registered charity could result in a gift, and now considers that the loan of property (including money) is not a gift. However, a charity may pay rent or interest on a loan of property and later accept the return of all or a portion of the payment as a gift, provided it is returned voluntarily. The donor would have to account for the taxable income that would be realized, offset by the charitable donation tax credit.[174]

[¶8185] Crown Gifts

Gifts to the Government of Canada, a province, or a territory are treated the same way as gifts to eligible charitable organizations and subject to the 75% net income limit discussed at ¶8150.[175]

[¶8190] Cultural Gifts

The value of gifts of cultural property [minus, after December 20, 2002, the advantage, if any, conferred to the donor in respect of the gift] made to institutions designated under the *Cultural Property Export and Import Act* are

---

See page ii for explanation of footnotes.

[174] Interp. Bul. IT-110R3, IT-297R2. [175] CCH ¶18,330a; Sec. 118.1(1) "total Crown gifts".

eligible donations for the purpose of computing a credit, where a receipt containing prescribed information is filed with the Minister.[176] A taxpayer who donates such a certified cultural property realizes no taxable capital gain on the disposition. The value of the donation taken into account for purposes of the tax credit is not limited to a percentage of the donor's income as is the case for gifts discussed at ¶8150. Amounts not used in a given taxation year will be carried over to the five subsequent years. See also ¶13,545 for the application of Part XI.2 tax. The Canadian Cultural Property Export Review Board has the responsibility of determining the fair market value of a cultural gift. Such a determination will be deemed to be the fair market value of the property for a period of two years from the determination date.[177]

The Federal Court of Appeal struck down a transaction in which a taxpayer purchased a collection of cultural property with the intention of donating it to a Canadian museum and did donate it, receiving from the museum a much higher valuation than the actual purchase price.[178]

If a gift meets the criteria of two or more categories of total cultural gifts, total Crown gifts, and total charitable gifts, it will first be considered a cultural gift, then a Crown gift, and lastly a charitable gift.[179]

For the treatment of gifts of cultural property by bequest, see ¶8206.

[¶8193] Ecological Gifts

Gifts of ecologically sensitive land may, in certain circumstances, be eligible for the charitable donation tax credit for their full fair market value, without regard to the normal 75% net income limitation discussed at ¶8150. To qualify for the exemption from the limitation, such gifts must:

(a) be made either to Canada, a province or territory of Canada, a Canadian municipality (or under proposed changes [released July 16, 2010], for gifts made after May 8, 2000, a municipal or public body performing a function of government in Canada), or to a registered charity acknowledged by the Minister of the Environment to be both a charity, the primary purpose of which is the conservation and protection of Canada's environmental heritage, and one which is a suitable recipient of the gift, and

(b) be gifts of land, including a servitude for the use and benefit of the dominant land, a covenant, or easement, certified by the Minister of the Environment to be ecologically sensitive land important to the preservation of Canada's environmental heritage, the fair market value of which is certified by the Minister.[180]

See page ii for explanation of footnotes.

[176] CCH ¶18,330b; Sec. 118.1(1) "total cultural gifts"; Interp. Bul. IT-407R4.

[177] CCH ¶18,365; Sec. 118.1(10).

[178] Friedberg, 92 DTC 6031.

[179] CCH ¶18,330d; Sec. 118.1(1) "total gifts".

[180] CCH ¶18,330c; Sec. 118.1(1) "total ecological gifts".

¶8193

In addition, if the ecological gift is a capital property and the gift is made to a qualified donee, the deemed taxable capital gain is zero for gifts after May 1, 2006 (previously, an inclusion rate of $1/4$ applied).[181]

If a gift is made in compliance with these rules, a charitable donation credit may be claimed for the full fair market value of the property [minus, after December 20, 2002, the advantage, if any, conferred to the donor in respect of the gift], including the fair market value of a restrictive covenant, easement, or servitude for the use and benefit of the dominant land. To the extent that an individual chooses not to take the entire deduction in the year the gift is made, any undeducted portion may be carried forward and deducted to the extent chosen in any of the following five years.

Since the fair market value of the gift of a servitude, covenant, or easement may be difficult to establish, a new rule was added, with retroactive effect to such gifts made after February 27, 1995, providing that the fair market value of such gifts is equal to the greater of the fair market value otherwise determined and the amount by which the fair market value of the land is reduced as a result of the gift.[182] This rule ensures that the fair market value of a gift of a servitude, covenant, or easement cannot be less than the resulting decrease in value of the dominant land. Such fixed value is also subject to the election discussed at ¶8200 to designate both the value of the gift and the proceeds of disposition at any value between adjusted cost base and fair market value of the gift.

A penalty tax is imposed if a charity or municipality (or under proposed changes [released July 16, 2010], a public body performing a function of government in Canada) that receives a donation of ecologically sensitive land subsequently disposes of it or changes its use without approval from Environment Canada.[183] The penalty tax is 50% of the fair market value of the property at the time of the unauthorized disposition or change in use.

As mentioned in (b) above, for gifts of ecologically sensitive land made after February 27, 2000, the donor must also obtain from the Minister of the Environment not only a certificate regarding the qualified nature of the property, but a valuation as well. A taxpayer who intends to dispose of ecologically sensitive land to a qualified donee can obtain a prospective valuation from the Minister and can, within 90 days, ask for a redetermination.[184] However, the Minister can also make a redetermination on his own initiative at any time. The Minister's valuation may be appealed to the Tax Court of Canada, but only after an irrevocable gift has been made. Only the donor has this right of appeal; the CRA does not have authority to appeal a valuation by the Minister. The fair market value, as determined or redetermined by the Minister, applies for all purposes of the Act for two years.[185]

See page ii for explanation of footnotes.

[181] CCH ¶6007; Sec. 38(a.2).

[182] CCH ¶18,367ac; Sec. 118.1(12).

[183] CCH ¶25,751; Sec. 207.31.

[184] CCH ¶18,366b, ¶18,366d; Sec. 118.1(10.2), 118.1(10.4).

[185] CCH ¶18,366a; Sec. 118.1(10.1).

¶8193

[¶8195] Gifts by Partnership

Where a gift is made by a partnership, each member of the partnership is deemed, at the end of the taxation year of the partnership, to have given his or her proportionate share of any gift donated by the partnership during that year.[186] [After December 20, 2002, each member will be deemed to have given his or her proportionate share of the "eligible amount" of the gift donated by the partnership, i.e., the fair market value of the gift less the advantage conferred to the partnership in respect of the gift.]

[¶8200] Gifts of Capital Property

Where a taxpayer has made a gift of capital property to a charitable organization (listed in ¶8150) or to the Crown (¶8185) or under the ecology rules (¶8193), the taxpayer or the taxpayer's legal representative may, within certain limitations, designate any amount between the adjusted cost base of the property and its fair market value, the amount so designated being deemed to be the proceeds of disposition and the amount of the gift made by the taxpayer.

The amount so designated is deemed to be both the individual's proceeds of disposition of the property and the fair market value of the gift, but the amount so designated may not exceed the fair market value of the property otherwise determined and may not be less than the greater of:

(a) in the case of a gift made after December 20, 2002, the amount of the advantage, if any, in respect of the gift, and

(b) the adjusted cost base of the property or, if the property is depreciable property of a prescribed class, the undepreciated capital cost of that class at the end of the individual's taxation year (determined without reference to proceeds of disposition designated in respect of the property.

Three conditions must be met before such a designation is permitted:

(1) the property must be capital property;

(2) the fair market value of the property must exceed its adjusted cost base (ACB) to the taxpayer at the time of the gift or testamentary disposition; and

(3) receipts containing prescribed information must be filed with the Minister.

This election is also available to non-resident taxpayers donating real property situated in Canada to a prescribed non-resident charity (i.e., the Nature Conservancy in the United States).[187] In addition to meeting the criteria set out in (2) and (3) above, the non-resident taxpayer must obtain an undertaking that the real property will be held for use in the public interest. The

---

See page ii for explanation of footnotes.

[186] CCH ¶18,362; Sec. 118.1(8).   [187] Reg. 3501.

designation is to be made at the time of filing the taxpayer's return for the year in which the gift or testamentary disposition was made.[188]

If depreciable property of a prescribed class is involved, the above election will permit the individual to avoid a capital gain on the property, but it will not reduce or avoid any recapture. This problem was solved when the limit on gifts of capital property was fixed at 75% of net income plus 25% of taxable capital gains, plus 25% of recapture of any capital cost allowance arising on the gift.[189] The amount of recapture eligible for this 25% claim is equal to the lesser of (i) recapture of that property class included in income, and (ii) the total of amounts for each gift equal to the lesser of its proceeds of disposition (minus related expenses) and its capital cost to the taxpayer.

Example:

Mr. Adams transfers a rental property with a fair market value of $200,000 to a registered charity, in exchange for proceeds of disposition of $95,000. The original cost to Mr. Adams when he purchased the property in 1992 was $65,000. The rental property is the only depreciable property in its class, with an undepreciated capital cost balance before the transfer of $45,000.

Assuming that the transfer qualifies as a gift, Mr. Adams may designate any amount between $95,000 and $200,000 as the proceeds of disposition for the gift. Mr. Adams could have designated an amount as low as $45,000, if he had received a lesser amount in actual proceeds from the charity. Mr. Adams decides to designate $150,000 as its proceeds of disposition. The taxable gain to Mr. Adams on the transfer can therefore be allocated as follows:

Designated proceeds		$150,000
Adjusted cost base (original cost)	65,000	65,000
Capital Gain		85,000
Taxable Capital Gain		42,500
Undepreciated Capital Cost	45,000	
Recaptured depreciation		20,000
Total Income Inclusion		$ 62,500

The eligible amount of the gift is calculated as follows:

Designated proceeds	$150,000
Amount of advantage (consideration)	95,000
Eligible amount of the gift	55,000
	$300,000

See page ii for explanation of footnotes.

[188] CCH ¶18,356; Sec. 118.1(6); Interp. Bul. IT-288R2,   [189] CCH ¶18,330d; Sec. 118.1(1) "total gifts".
IT-297R2.

¶8200

[¶8202] Gifts of Securities

Publicly listed securities

The inclusion rate for capital gains realized on gifts of publicly traded securities to qualified donees is zero. In other words, such gains are not included in income.[190] The securities that qualify for this treatment include shares, debt obligations, and rights listed on a designated stock exchange, units of mutual fund trusts and shares in mutual fund corporations, and prescribed debt obligations. This capital gains exemption is now extended to gifts made to private foundations. Donations of publicly listed securities that were acquired through employee stock options are also eligible for a special deduction that has the effect of taxing the employment benefit at a 0% inclusion rate. A transfer of property will not necessarily be disqualified from being a gift where the transferor is provided with some advantage. Such a transfer will qualify as a gift if the amount of the advantage does not exceed 80% of the value of the property transferred. To concord with this, the special inclusion rate for capital gains arising from gifts to qualified donees of certain securities is only applicable to the portion of the gain that relates to the value of the property transferred minus the advantage.][191] The securities, including shares, bonds, bills, warrants, and futures, must be listed on a designated stock exchange, Canadian or foreign.

Securities acquired through an employee stock option plan

When an employee acquires a publicly listed security under an option granted by the employer and donates the security to a qualified donee (including a private foundation) within 30 days after its acquisition, the employee may be eligible for a special deduction, the general effect of which is to exempt the associated employment benefit (see ¶2135) from tax. The donation must take place in the same year in which the security is acquired. Excluded from this beneficial treatment are donations to a non-qualifying private foundation — in general terms, one that has not complied with certain time-specific limits on its corporate holdings. For additional details regarding the excess corporate holdings rules for private foundations, refer to the commentary at ¶11,643.

As discussed at ¶2135, employee stock or mutual fund options normally involve an employment benefit either when the options are exercised or when the shares or units are sold. That benefit is then reduced by an offsetting deduction of ½ (hereafter called the "regular deduction"), so that it is, in effect, taxed at capital gains rates rather than employment income rates.[192] In addition to this regular ½ deduction, a taxpayer who donates his or her employee option securities within the above time limits is allowed a special deduction of ½ of the amount of the benefit included in income.[193] Effectively, this means that the taxpayer includes none of the resulting stock option benefit in income in the year in which the security is acquired. In order to qualify for this special deduction, the security must be a share listed on a

---

See page ii for explanation of footnotes.

[190] CCH ¶6007; Sec. 38(a.1).
[191] Sec. 38.1.

[192] CCH ¶15,015; Sec. 110(1)(d).
[193] CCH ¶15,200; Sec. 110(1)(d.01).

designated stock exchange or a unit in a mutual fund trust. Additionally, the taxpayer must meet the requirements for the regular deduction in respect of the security. These requirements are discussed at ¶2135. If the value of the security is less at the time of donation than at the time it was acquired, the ¹/₂ deduction will be based on the amount of the benefit that would have been included in income if the security had been acquired at that lesser amount.

[¶8203] Gifts of Non-Qualified Securities

Gifts of a "non-qualifying security" (NQS), other than an excepted gift (see below), are ignored for purposes of all the charitable donation rules; that is to say, no tax credit is permitted at the time the gift is made.[194] However, if the recipient of the gift (the qualified donee) disposes of the NQS within five years for consideration that is not the NQS of *any* person or the security ceases to be an NQS of the individual within five years, the individual is deemed to have made a gift at that later time and the fair market value (FMV) of the gift is deemed to be the lesser of:

(1) the FMV of any consideration, other than an NQS of any person [before March 22, 2011 of *any* individual] received by the donee on the disposition or, in the case of the security ceasing to be a NQS, its FMV at that later time; and

(2) the amount of the actual gift.

In short, a gift of an NQS will be recognized upon subsequent disposition by the recipient and that subsequent disposition will fix the maximum (but not the minimum) value of the charitable donation. The above deferral will also apply, if, as a result of a series of transactions, a particular person holds the donor's NQS and the qualified donee acquires, directly or indirectly, a NQS of the donor or of the particular person (effective March 2011).[195]

If, in the course of a disposition of a beneficial interest in a trust that is a non-qualifying security of an individual, the donee receives as consideration only other non-qualifying securities of the individual, the gift is considered to be a gift of those other non-qualifying securities, rather than a gift of the interest in the trust. As such, the individual donor will not be allowed to claim the charitable donations tax credit (originally denied when the gift was made of the interest in the trust) until those other non-qualifying securities are disposed of by the donee.[196]

A non-qualifying security of an individual means an obligation of the individual or the individual's estate (or of a non-arm's length person or partnership to the individual or estate); a share of a corporation with which the individual or estate does not deal at arm's length; a beneficial interest in a trust that is affiliated with the individual or estate or which holds a non-qualifying security; or any other security issued by the individual or estate or non-arm's length person or partnership. Specifically excluded from the

---

See page ii for explanation of footnotes.

[194] CCH ¶18,367b; Sec. 118.1(13).   [196] CCH ¶18,367cd; Sec. 118.1(14.1).
[195] Sec. 118.1(13.1), 118.1(13.2), 118.1(13.3).

definition are obligations, shares, and other securities listed on a designated stock exchange and obligations of a financial institution to repay deposits with the institution. If the individual is a trust, a non-qualifying security includes a share of a corporation with which a person affiliated with the trust (see ¶15,483) does not deal at arm's length. A non-qualifying security of an individual at any time includes a beneficial interest of the individual or the estate in a trust that immediately after that time is affiliated with the individual or the estate, or in a trust that immediately after that time holds a non-qualifying security of the individual or estate, or held, at or before that time, a share of a corporation as described above that is, after that time, held by the donee.[197]

A non-qualified security will not be subject to the above restrictions if the gift is an excepted gift. A gift will be so excepted if all the following conditions are met:

(a) the security is a share;

(b) the donee is not a private foundation;

(c) the taxpayer deals at arm's length with the donee; and

(d) where the donee is a charitable organization or a public foundation, the taxpayer deals at arm's length with each director trustee, officer, and like official of the donee.[198]

Where an individual makes an NQS gift and dies before the donee disposes of the NQS, or the NQS status is eliminated within the five-year period, the individual's gift is considered to have been made in the year of death rather than the later time, so the appropriate gains and tax credit can be recognized on terminal returns.[199]

There are also complex provisions to deny charitable donation treatment to a taxpayer who, through a series of loan-back or other arrangements with a charity, contrives a charitable donations tax credit without having to forego the use of the donated funds or property or without the donee disposing of non-qualifying securities.[200] These provisions apply in two cases:

(i) where a donee holds a non-qualifying security of an individual within five years after the individual makes a gift to the donee, and the individual acquired the security no earlier than five years before the gift was made; or

(ii) where an individual or a non-arm's length person uses property of the donee, pursuant to an agreement made no earlier than five years before the making of the gift, and the property was not used in the course of carrying on the donee's charitable activities.

See page ii for explanation of footnotes.

[197] CCH ¶18,367g; Sec. 118.1(18).
[198] CCH ¶18,367h; Sec. 118.1(19).
[199] CCH ¶18,367d; Sec. 118.1(15).
[200] CCH ¶18,367e; Sec. 118.1(16).

In the first case, the fair market value of the gift is reduced by the consideration given by the donee to acquire the non-qualifying security. In the second case, the fair market value of the gift is reduced by the fair market value of the property so used.

[¶8204] Granting of Options to Charities and Other Qualified Donees

If an individual grants an option to acquire property to a charity (or other qualified donee) [after March 21, 2011], no charitable donations tax credit is allowed until such time that the option is exercised so that the property is acquired by the donee. The credit allowed to the individual at that late time is based on the amount by which the fair market value of the property at that time exceeds any consideration paid by the donee for the option and the property. As a result of proposed split-gift rules (see ¶8175), a credit will generally not be available to the individual if the total amount paid by the qualified donee for the property and the option exceeds 80% of the fair market value of the property at the time of acquisition by the donee.

In effect, an option granted by an individual to a qualified donee after March 21, 2011 is not eligible for a charitable donations tax credit unless the option is subsequently exercised (at a particular time) so that the property is disposed of to the qualified donee, and either

(1) 80% of the fair market value of the property at the particular time exceeds the total amount paid by the qualified donee to acquire the option and underlying property; or

(2) the CRA is satisfied that the granting of the option was made with a donative intent.[201]

At the time of exercise of the option, the individual is deemed to have disposed of the property for proceeds equal to its fair market value. In the year in which the option is exercised, the individual is also entitled to a donation tax credit equal to that fair market value minus the total amount paid by the qualified donee to acquire the option and the underlying property. This credit is permitted notwithstanding that the disposition of a property as a result of the exercise of the right of an option holder may not be a gift at law.[202]

If the option to acquire an individual's property is subsequently disposed of (at a particular time) by a qualified donee, the individual is deemed to have disposed of another property at the time of disposition for proceeds equal to the lesser of the fair market value of any consideration (other than a non-qualifying security of any person) received by the qualified donee for the option and the fair market value of the property that was the subject of the option. The permitted deduction for the taxation year in which the option was disposed of by the qualified donee is then equal to the proceeds

---

See page ii for explanation of footnotes.

[201] Sec. 118.1(21), 118.1(22).   [202] Sec. 118.1(23).

of disposition (as calculated above) minus any consideration paid, if any, by the qualified donee to acquire the option.[203]

[¶8205] Returned Gifts

An individual cannot retain tax assistance in the form of a charitable donations tax credit in respect of property transferred to a qualified donee if the qualified donee returns the property or substituted property to the individual [after March 21, 2011]. In such a case, no gift is recognized and if the returned property is identical to the transferred property, the returned property is deemed to be the transferred property. If the returned property is not identical, the individual is deemed to have disposed of the transferred property at the time of its return for consideration that is the returned property. For returned property in excess of $50, an information return must be filed within 90 days of the return.

These measures address situations where a property was transferred by an individual by a qualified donation, yet a charitable donations receipt was issued to the individual, and the property is later returned to the individual or another property is returned as compensation for or in substitution for the original property.[204] In such a case and irrespective of whether the transfer of the original property by the individual to the qualified donee was a gift, the individual is deemed not to have disposed of the original property at the time of the transfer nor to have made a gift.[205] If the original property or substituted property is returned, the returned property is deemed to be the original property, such that a future disposition of the returned property will have the same result as if the property had never been disposed of to the qualified donee.[206] If the returned property is in compensation or substitution for the original property, the original disposition is not recognized but the individual is deemed to have disposed of the original property for consideration that is the returned property, and at the time that the property is returned to the individual.[207] If the fair market value of the returned property exceeds $50, the qualified donee who has already issued an official donation receipt at the time of original transfer of property is required to file an information return within 90 days of the subsequent return of that property or substituted property and send a copy to the individual.[208] The CRA may reassess the return of income of any person to the extent that the reassessment can reasonably be regarded as relating to a return of property from a qualified donee.[209]

[¶8206] Gifts by Will

If a charitable gift is made in an individual's will, the gift is deemed to have been made by the individual immediately before the individual died.[210] Accordingly, the donation can be claimed on the terminal year return, even though the transfer is made by the deceased's representatives, rather than

[203] Sec. 118.1(24).
[204] Sec. 118.1(25).
[205] Sec. 118.1(26)(a).
[206] Sec. 118.1(26)(b).

[207] Sec. 118.1(26)(c).
[208] Sec. 118.1(27).
[209] Sec. 118.1(28).
[210] CCH ¶18,354; Sec. 118.1(5).

the deceased, and might not be made until a subsequent taxation year. Gifts in the year of death and the preceding year, including bequests or legacies, are deductible up to 100% of net income in the year of death or the immediately preceding year.[211]

If the gift is not made under the deceased's will, it will most likely be viewed as having been made by the deceased's estate, meaning that the charitable credit will be available to the estate, rather than the deceased.

According to the CRA, a gift is made under an individual's will if the amount that the charity (or other eligible recipient) is entitled to receive can be determined by reference to the will at the time of death. If the amount cannot be so determined, it likely will not be considered as having been made under the will. Thus, for example, if the will refers to a fixed amount of cash or a specified property to be donated to a specified charity, the gift will be considered as having been made under the will and it will qualify for the tax credit for the deceased. On the other hand, if the executors of the deceased's estate have full discretion to choose charities and to determine how much each charity will receive out of the estate, the donations will not be considered as having been made under the will.

[¶8207] Gifts by Direct Designation

Under certain conditions described below, direct designations of the proceeds of a deceased individual's life insurance policy, RRSP, RRIF, or, beginning in 2009, tax-free savings account (TFSA) in favour of a charity will qualify for the donation tax credit.[212] The transfer to the charity from the insurer, RRSP, RRIF, or, beginning in 2009, a TFSA, must be a transfer of money or a transfer by means of a negotiable instrument (i.e., transfer of shares or other property would not qualify), and the transfer to the charity must be made solely because of the charity's interest as a beneficiary under the plan. In addition, the taxpayer must be the RRSP or RRIF annuitant or, beginning in 2009, the TFSA holder, immediately before his or her death.

In the case of a life insurance policy, the taxpayer must have had, immediately before death, a right of consent to a change of beneficiary and the charity must not be the policyholder or an assignee of the taxpayer's interest under the policy.

In each case, the transfer to the charity from the insurer, RRSP, RRIF, or a TFSA, must be made within the 36-month period after death (or such longer period as approved by the Minister).

If all these requirements are met, the gift to the charity under the above policy, plan, fund, or other arrangement will be considered to have been made immediately before the individual's death and the value of the gift is deemed to be the fair market value, at the time of the individual's death, of the right to the transfer (determined without reference to any risk

---

See page ii for explanation of footnotes.

[211] CCH ¶18,352; Sec. 118.1(4).   [212] CCH ¶18,354a–18,354c; Sec. 118.1(5.1)–(5.3).

of default with regard to the obligations of the insurer or the issuer of the plan).

[¶8210] Gift in Year of Death

Where a gift is made in the year of a taxpayer's death and the full amount of the gift is not deducted under ¶8150, ¶8185, or ¶8190, the undeducted portion is deemed to be a gift made in the previous taxation year.[213] A gift may not be deductible in full in the year of death because it exceeds the net income test in ¶8150 or because a gift otherwise deductible under ¶8185 or ¶8190 exceeds the income for the year. The legal representatives of the deceased taxpayer will be able to file an amended return for that previous taxation year claiming a deduction to the extent possible for the excess portion of the gift and obtain a refund of tax previously paid in respect of that previous year.

[¶8215] Transfer of Tax Credits

The unused portion of an individual's impairment credit for the year is transferable to the individual's spouse/common-law partner, supporting parent, grandparent, child, grandchild, the person who is entitled to an eligible dependant tax credit in respect of the individual or the person who is the brother, sister, aunt, uncle, nephew, or niece of the individual or of the individual's spouse or common-law partner. A supporting person may deduct the unused portion of an impairment credit only if the spouse or common-law partner of the person with a disability is not claiming the impairment tax credit nor any other non-refundable tax credits in respect of the person with a disability.[214] The unused portion of an individual's age and pension income credits are transferable to the individual's spouse or common-law partner, and the tuition, textbook, and education tax credits, up to a maximum of $750 in 2012 of credits or $5,000 of eligible fees and amounts are transferable to the individual's spouse or common-law partner or supporting parent or grandparent to the extent the student has designated them for transfer in writing to the spouse, common-law partner, parent, or grandparent.[215]

[¶8220] Separate Return in Year of Death

Where separate returns are filed for a deceased taxpayer with respect to "rights and things" receivable on death, a testamentary trust return, or a return on the death of a partner or proprietor[216] in the same period ending in the calendar year that the regular return for the taxpayer is filed, the combined credits deductible cannot exceed those that would have been available if only one return were filed for the year.[217] The combined credits that cannot exceed those available if separate returns were not filed are those deductible in respect of charitable donations, eligible adoption

---

See page ii for explanation of footnotes.

213 CCH ¶18,352; Sec. 118.1(4).
214 CCH ¶18,392; Sec. 118.3(2).
215 CCH ¶18,445, ¶18,451; Sec. 118.8, 118.9.

216 CCH ¶9220, ¶13,578, ¶22,031; Sec. 70(2), 104(23), 150(4).
217 CCH ¶18,459; Sec. 118.93; Interp. Bul. IT-326R3.

expenses, transit pass credit, child fitness credit, pension income, Canada employment credit, medical expenses, disability, and tuition, education and textbook credits (including tuition, education and textbook amounts transferred to parents and grandparents).

[¶8225] Non-Resident Individuals — Availability of Credits

An individual who is not a resident of Canada at any time in the year is not entitled to deduct most of the tax credits available to individuals for purposes of computing Part I tax, unless substantially all (generally considered to be 90% or more) of the taxpayer's income for the year is included as taxable income earned in Canada. The credits specifically disallowed if the "substantially all" test is not met are the personal credits, adoption credit, transit pass credit, child fitness credit, home renovation credit, first-time home buyers' credit, medical credit, impairment credit for dependants and partial dependants, education credit, textbook credit, transfer of unused credits from a spouse or common-law partner, or transfers of unused tuition, textbook, and education credits to a parent or grandparent.[218]

If a non-resident is employed or is carrying on business in Canada or has capital gains from taxable Canadian property, certain credits may be claimed even if the "substantially all" test is not met. These credits are for charitable donations, Crown gifts and cultural gifts, the impairment credit for the taxpayer only, the tuition credit, the tuition carryforward credit, the credit for student loan interest, and the CPP and EI credits.

If an individual is resident in Canada for part of the year and not resident for the other part, the individual will be entitled to the non-refundable tax credits only for the period throughout which the individual was resident in Canada.[219] Amounts such as the personal credits (other than the pension credit), impairment credits, unused credits transferred from a spouse or common-law partner, and unused tuition, textbook, and education credits transferred from a child or grandchild must be prorated based on the number of days resident in Canada. Other credits (such as for charitable gifts, medical expenses, tuition, textbook, CPP and EI, and, for 2006 and subsequent taxation years, transit pass credits) will be allowed based on the actual expenditures incurred while the taxpayer was a resident, limited of course by the maximum that would be allowed if the taxpayer had been resident for the whole year.

[¶8227] Credits in Year of Bankruptcy

Where the taxpayer becomes bankrupt in the year, two returns are required for the year, one for the pre-bankruptcy period and one for the post-bankruptcy period. Non-refundable tax credits in respect of the pre- and post-bankruptcy periods will generally be calculated on a *pro rata* basis, except for certain credits that are based on expenditures or the receipt of certain types of income during the period. Thus, the personal tax credits

---

[218] CCH ¶18,461; Sec. 118.94.   [219] CCH ¶18,455; Sec. 118.91.

(other than the pension credit), the age tax credit, the disability tax credit, and the transfers of unused credits will be subject to proration based on the number of days in the period for which the return is filed. On the other hand, the pension credit, the Canadian employment credit, the adoption credit, the transit pass credit, the child fitness credit, the home renovation tax credit, the first-time home buyers' tax credit, the charitable donations tax credit, the medical tax credit, and the tuition, textbook and education and student loan interest tax credits will be based on the related amounts in respect of each period. In all cases, the total of the amounts claimed in respect of each of these credits for both the pre- and post-bankruptcy periods cannot be greater than the amount that could be claimed in respect of the calendar year had the individual not become bankrupt.[220] These rules are discussed in greater detail at ¶9009.

[¶8230] Indexing of Tax Credits

Personal amounts eligible for tax credits, including the income limits above which an individual must reduce personal amounts he or she may claim for a dependant, are indexed every year.[221] The indexation factor for a given taxation year is the percentage in the average Consumer Price Index (CPI) for the twelve-month period ending on September 30 of the preceding year relative to the average CPI for the 12- month period ending on September 30 of the year earlier. This average CPI determines annual adjustments which are rounded to the nearest dollar.

[¶8235] Canada Child Tax Benefit (CCTB)

[¶8237] National Child Benefit System

The child tax benefit was introduced in the 1992 Budget. Beginning in January 1993, it replaced the family allowance, the personal tax credit for a minor dependant, and the refundable child tax credit with a single non-taxable monthly payment made to the custodial parent (referred to as an "eligible individual") of a child (referred to as a "qualified dependant").[222] Effective July 1, 1998, this program was replaced by an enriched and simplified program, the Canada Child Tax Benefit (CCTB). The CCTB actually comprises three components and is paid in monthly instalments. The first component is the basic benefit; the second is the national child benefit supplement; and the third is the child disability benefit. The three components of the benefits are described in the commentary below.

An "eligible individual" in respect of a qualified dependant is a person who:

(a) resides with the qualified dependant;

(b) is the parent of the qualified dependant who:

---

[220] CCH ¶18,463; Sec. 118.95.   [222] CCH ¶19,348a–19,348x; Sec. 122.6–122.64.
[221] CCH ¶18,201; Sec. 117.1(1).

(i) is the parent who has the primary responsibility for the dependant's care and upbringing and, after June 2011, is not a shared-custody parent; or

(ii) after June 2011, is a shared-custody parent in respect of the qualified dependant (see definition below);

(c) is resident in Canada;

(d) is not an officer or servant or a family member of such, of the government of a country other than Canada whose duties require the individual to live in Canada; and

(e) is, or whose cohabiting spouse or common-law partner is:

(i) a Canadian citizen,

(ii) a permanent resident,

(iii) a visitor in Canada or the holder of a permit in Canada, who was resident in Canada throughout the preceding 18-month period, or

(iv) a refugee as determined by the Convention Refugee Determination Division of the Immigration and Refugee Board.[223]

Each eligible parent in a shared custody situation is entitled to half of the child benefit for that child every month that they qualify as shared custody parents [effective June 2011]. To qualify as a shared custody parent of a qualified dependant at a particular time, an individual must be one of the two parents of a qualified dependant who:

(a) are not at the time cohabiting spouses or common-law partners of each other;

(b) reside with the qualified dependant on an equal or near equal basis, and

(c) primarily fulfil the responsibility for the care and upbringing of the qualified dependant when residing with the qualified dependants, as determined by prescribed factors.[224]

A qualified dependant is a person under 18 years of age, but does not include a person in respect of whom either a spouse or common-law partner tax credit has been claimed for the base taxation year or a special allowance is payable under the *Children's Special Allowances Act*.[225]

The amount of child tax benefit payable each month is based on family net income and child care expenses for the base taxation year. The base taxation year for payments from January to June is the second preceding taxation year, and for August to December payments it is the preceding taxation year.[226] Therefore, in 2012, the child tax benefit payable for the

---

[223] CCH ¶19,348ae; Sec. 122.6 "eligible individual".
[224] CCH ¶19,348zc; Sec. 122.6 "shared-custody parent"; Reg. 6302.
[225] CCH ¶19,348ag; Sec. 122.6 "qualified dependant".
[226] CCH ¶19,348ac; Sec. 122.6 "base taxation year".

¶8237

months of January through June will be based on 2010 income. Entitlement for the months of July through December will be based on 2011 income.

The income measurement that is used in calculating the child tax benefit is family net income, which is essentially the net income figure on the tax return of the eligible individual and his or her cohabiting spouse or common-law partner. If the eligible individual or spouse/common-law partner were non- residents of Canada for part or all of the year, family net income includes their world income for any part of the year they were not residents of Canada.[227]

The three components of the benefit are described below.[228]

Basic benefit:

For the period from July 2012 to June 2013, the basic benefit equals:

(1) $117.08 per month for each of the first two qualified dependants plus $125.24 per month for each of the third and subsequent dependants, reduced by 25% of all child care expenses claimed for all qualified dependants in the base taxation year (2011); minus:

(2) 4% (2% for one-child families) of family net income for the base taxation year (2011) over $42,707.

National child benefit supplement:

For the period from July 2012 to June 2013, the national child benefit supplement equals:

(1) for a one-child family, $181.41 per month, reduced by 12.2% of the amount of family net income for the base taxation year (2011) that is more than $24,863;

(2) for a two-child family, $181.41 per month for the first child, plus $160.50 per month for the second child, reduced by 23% of the amount of family net income for the base taxation year (2011) that is more than $24,863; and

(3) for a three-or-more child family, $181.41 per month for the first child, $160.50 per month for the second child, plus $152.66 per month for each additional child, reduced by 33.3% of the amount of family net income for the base taxation year (2011) that is more than $24,863.

Child disability benefit:

The third component of the child tax benefit is the child disability benefit (CDB), which is paid for each qualified dependant who meets the eligibility criteria for the disability tax credit (see ¶8145). For the period from July 2012 to June 2013, the maximum CDB equals $214.58 per month or ($2,575 per year) for each child who qualifies for the disability tax credit. The annual amount is reduced by 4% (2% for one-child families) of family

---

See page ii for explanation of footnotes.

[227] CCH ¶19,348d; Sec. 122.61(3).   [228] CCH ¶19,348b; Sec. 122.61(1).

net income for the base taxation year (2011) in excess of a base amount which rises with the number of children (including those not disabled). For families with one child, the base amount is $42,707; two children, $42,702; three children, $42,686; four children, $48,187; five children, $53,689; and so on, in increments of approximately $5,501 (subject to rounding). For instance, a single mother with a net family income of $100,000 and one child eligible for the disability tax credit will receive $1,429.04 in CDB benefits for the 2012-2013 benefit year, i.e., $2,575 - 2% × ($100,000 - $42,702).

The dollar amounts noted above are adjusted annually to reflect the full increase in the average Consumer Price Index in the 12-month period ending September 30 of the preceding year.[229] The child tax benefit cannot be attached, assigned, or garnished, nor can it be discounted or retained.[230] Where an overpayment of a child tax benefit has been made, the taxpayer is not charged interest on the debt and the CRA will not pay interest to a taxpayer on any payment of a child tax benefit.[231]

Where an eligible individual becomes bankrupt, his or her entitlement to the child tax benefit and the supplement in subsequent calendar years will be calculated based on income from both the pre- and post-bankruptcy periods. If the individual's spouse/common-law partner becomes bankrupt, the spouse's/common-law partner's income from both periods will also be taken into consideration.[232]

A person who is entitled to receive the child tax benefit in a particular month must file the required notice with the Minister of National Revenue before the end of the eleventh month following the particular month. This period may be extended by the Minister.[233]

If, in a particular month, an individual ceases to be an eligible individual, other than by reason of the qualified dependant becoming 18 years of age, the person must notify the Minister of National Revenue before the end of the following month.

Upon a change of marital status by reason of death, separation, marriage, or common-law partnership after June 2011, an individual who receives the Canada Child Tax Benefit must notify the Minister of National Revenue of the change before the end of the first calendar month following the change. If the change in marital status results in a family income change, revised entitlements will be effective for each month following the month of marital status change.[234]

The Minister of Finance may enter into an agreement with a province to modify the basic amount of the child tax benefit with respect to persons resident in that province. The amount may be modified only on the basis of the number or age (or both) of qualified dependants and cannot be less

---

[229] CCH ¶19,348f; Sec. 122.61(5).

[230] CCH ¶19,348e; Sec. 122.61(4).

[231] CCH ¶22,783; Sec. 160.1(1).

[232] CCH ¶19,348da; Sec. 122.61(3.1).

[233] CCH ¶19,348i–19,348l; Sec. 122.62(1)–(4).

[234] CCH ¶19,348m–19,348o; Sec. 122.62(5)–122.62(7).

than 85% of the amount that would otherwise have been paid.[235] As they did with family allowance payments, the provinces of Alberta and Quebec have elected to modify; Alberta, on the basis of age, and Quebec on the basis of age and family size.

[¶8240] Working Income Tax Benefit (WITB)

[¶8241] Overview

Low-income individuals earning employment or business income during a year may claim a refundable tax credit called the Working Income Tax Benefit (WITB). The WITB is made up of two components: a basic amount (Basic WITB) available to any taxpayer and an additional amount (WITB Supplement) available only to a taxpayer who is eligible to claim the disability tax credit. Since the main purpose of the credit is to assist low-income individuals and families, the Basic WITB and the WITB Supplement are reduced if the adjusted net income of those individuals or families is in excess of certain thresholds. Any taxpayer expecting a WITB may apply to the Minister of National Revenue for an advance payment of up to one-half of the estimated credit.

[¶8242] Eligibility

To qualify for the WITB for a particular taxation year, an individual must meet the following conditions:

(1) The individual is not:

(a) an employee of a foreign country, or servant or family member of such employee in the year,

(b) a full-time student at a designated educational institution (see ¶8120) for more than 13 weeks during the year unless he or she also has a qualified dependant during the year, or

(c) an individual confined to a prison for a period of at least 90 days during the year.

(2) The individual resides in Canada throughout the year and meets one of the following conditions at year end:

(a) is 19 or older,

(b) is a cohabiting spouse or common-law partner, or

(c) is the parent of a child with whom the individual resides.

(3) The individual has earned enough working income during the year in respect of which he/she claims the credit.[236]

See page ii for explanation of footnotes.

[235] CCH ¶19,348r; Sec. 122.63. [236] CCH ¶19,349q; Sec. 122.7(1) "eligible individual".

An individual working income would include the following items: employment income; research grants, fellowships, scholarships, bursaries, or prizes included in income; amounts received under the *Wage Earner Protection Program Act*; business income provided it is not earned by the individual as a specified member of a partnership; $1,000 exempt portion of an emergency volunteer allowance; and income otherwise taxable but exempted by a tax treaty.[237]

To qualify for the WITB for a particular taxation year, the individual must have at least $3,000 of working income. If he or she has an eligible spouse, they may both combine their working income to determine if they qualify for the credit. To qualify for the WITB Supplement, the individual must have at least $1,150 of working income and qualify for the disability tax credit. The above rates and limits may vary by province or territory.

[¶8243] Calculation

For 2012, the Single WITB of an individual with no eligible dependant is equal to 25% of the individual's working income over $3,000 up to a $970 maximum credit and reduced by 15% of his or her adjusted net income over $11,011. The credit is eliminated for individuals with an adjusted net income over $17,477.[238]

For 2012, the Family WITB of a couple or a single parent with an eligible dependant is equal to 25% of the working income of the individual (and the individual's eligible spouse if there is one) over $3,000 up to a $1,762 maximum credit and reduced by 15% of the adjusted net income of the individual (and the individual's eligible spouse if there is one) over $15,205. The credit is therefore eliminated for a couple or a single parent with an adjusted net income over $26,951. The higher Family WITB is available only to an eligible individual who has either an eligible spouse or an eligible dependant in the year in respect of which the credit is claimed.

For 2012, the WITB Supplement of a disabled individual with no dependants is equal to 25% of his or her working income over $1,150 up to a $485 maximum credit and is reduced by 7.5% of his or her adjusted net income over certain limits if he or she has an eligible spouse entitled to claim the disability tax credit, and 15% of his or her adjusted net income over certain limits if he or she does not have a disabled spouse. The adjusted net income limit is $17,478 in the case of a single individual with no dependants and $26,950 in the case of a couple or a single individual with at least one dependant.[239]

All of the above rates and limits may vary by province or territory.

---

[237] CCH ¶19,349u; Sec. 122.7(1) "working income".   [239] CCH ¶19,349w; Sec. 122.7(3).
[238] CCH ¶19,349v; Sec. 122.7(2).

[¶8244] Advance Payment

Individuals entitled to receive a WITB may apply for an advance payment of up to 50% of the estimated WITB for the year, based on estimated earned income and net family income.[240] Application for prepayment must be made annually, in prescribed form, and submitted no later than September 1st of the taxation year.

A recipient of a prepayment must file an income tax return for the taxation year in which a prepayment is received.[241] Further, if a prepayment has been made for a taxation year, no repayment will be made for a subsequent taxation year until the income tax return for the earlier year is filed.

Once approved, the prepayments are made in equal instalments and according to the same schedule as the GST credit (see ¶8270). Any WITB in excess of the prepayments will first be applied to reduce tax payable. Any remaining amount will be included in the income tax refund for the year. If the prepayment exceeds the total WITB for the year, the overpayment must be included in tax payable for the year.

[¶8250] Overseas Employment Tax Credit (OETC)

[¶8251] Tax Credit for Specified Work Outside Canada

In certain circumstances, an individual's employer may enter into a contract to perform services outside Canada, either in another country or on a project in international waters, for an extended period of time. If, for Canadian income tax purposes, the individual who performs these services as an employee is considered to be a resident of Canada, the individual will be taxed in Canada on employment income, notwithstanding the fact that the individual is performing the services outside Canada and that the individual may also be taxable in a foreign jurisdiction. The application of Canadian tax rules was considered to have discouraged Canadian employers from using Canadian residents to perform certain foreign contracts. The overseas employment tax credit eases this burden.[242]

In general terms, the credit is available to individuals resident in Canada working abroad for six or more consecutive months for a "specified employer" (see (3) below) in connection with resource, construction, installation, agricultural, or engineering projects. Income from employment under a prescribed international development assistance program will not qualify for the overseas employment tax credit (OETC).[243] However, when the taxpayer's employer entered into a contract with an international organization for the purpose of establishing dairy farms in Malawi, the taxpayer was entitled to deduct an overseas employment tax credit on the basis that

---

See page ii for explanation of footnotes.

[240] CCH ¶19,349zb; Sec. 122.7(7).

[241] CCH ¶18,049; Sec. 117(2.1).

[242] CCH ¶19,320, ¶39,185l; Sec. 122.3(1); Interp. Bul. IT-497R4; Form T626.

[243] CCH ¶28,336; Reg. 3400.

the lack of a predominant profit motive did not prevent his employer from carrying on a "business" within the meaning of the Act.[244]

The amount of the credit is generally equal to that portion of the amount that would otherwise be the employee's Canadian tax payable for the year that the lesser of $80,000 and 80% of the employee's net overseas income taxable in Canada is of the employee's net income for the year. The effect of this formula is to provide a tax reduction in respect of a maximum of $100,000 of overseas employment income. For example, if a Canadian employee is overseas throughout a year and earns $90,000 of qualifying income, the employee's overseas employment tax credit would equal the amount of the employee's tax otherwise payable on $72,000 (i.e., 80% of $90,000). If the employee had earned $120,000 of qualifying income, the credit would be the amount of tax otherwise payable on $80,000, since, in this case, 80% of $120,000 (i.e., $96,000) exceeds the $80,000 limit. The $80,000 amount represents an annual limitation and is therefore prorated where the employee is abroad for less than a full year.

The credit is denied where the employee interposes a small Canadian service corporation, partnership, or individual employer between itself and a foreign or otherwise unqualified employer to attempt to obtain the credit. Specifically, no credit may be claimed from employment income where all the following conditions are met:

(1) the employer carries on a business of providing services, but does not employ more than five full-time employees in the business throughout the year;

(2) the employee does not deal at arm's length with the employer, is a specified shareholder of the employer (generally meaning he or she owns at least 10% of the shares of any class in the corporate employer or a related corporation), or, if the employer is a partnership, the employee does not deal at arm's length with or is a specified shareholder of a member of the partnership; and

(3) but for the existence of the employer, the individual would reasonably be regarded as an employer of an individual, corporation, or partnership that is not a qualified employer for purposes of the overseas employment tax credit (see (c) and (d) below).[245]

In a recent case, the taxpayer was an employee of PCCI, a company which he and his wife owned. He worked in Europe on Nortel projects acquired by PCCI through a British placement agency. Without the existence of PCCI, he would not have been regarded as an employee of either Nortel or the placement agency, since neither he nor PCCI had a contract with Nortel, and the relationship with the agency was that of an independent contractor. Therefore, the exclusionary provision in (3) did not apply, and he was entitled to OETCs.[246]

See page ii for explanation of footnotes.

[244] Timmins, 99 DTC 5494.
[245] CCH ¶19,320a; Sec. 122.3(1.1).
[246] Perrin, 2007 DTC 555.

[Proposed technical amendments (released July 16, 2010) will also deny the overseas employment tax credit where, at any time in the "qualifying period" (see below) in the employee's taxation year, the employee's services are provided to a corporation, partnership, or trust with which the employer does not deal at arm's length and less than 10% of the fair market value of the capital stock of the corporation or of all interests in the partnership or trust are held by persons resident in Canada. This anti-avoidance rule will apply to taxation years that begin after Royal Assent.]

To qualify for the overseas employment tax credit, an individual must:

(a) be a resident of Canada at some time in the particular taxation year;

(b) perform all or substantially all the duties of office or employment outside Canada for a period of more than six consecutive months that commenced in the year or a previous year (referred to as the "qualifying period");

(c) be employed throughout that period by a person (i.e., an individual, corporation, or political entity) resident in Canada or by a partnership of which Canadian residents, including Canadian-controlled corporations, own more than 10%, or by a foreign affiliate of a person resident in Canada;[247]

(d) perform those duties throughout the period for the purpose of obtaining a contract for his or her employer or in connection with a contract by such employer. The contract must relate to one of the following qualified activities:

    (i) the exploration for or exploitation of petroleum, natural gas, or other similar resources;

    (ii) a construction, installation, agricultural, or engineering project; or

    (iii) such activities as may be prescribed (at the time of writing, activities performed under contract with the United Nations are prescribed).[248]

The Federal Court of Appeal decided that the "all or substantially all" test in (b) requires that, throughout the qualifying period (in this case, the full year), all or substantially all of the taxpayer's work must be done outside of Canada. It did not require, as the Crown had argued, that the taxpayer has to be employed continuously outside of Canada for six months.[249]

If all of the above criteria are met, the individual may deduct an amount from the individual's tax payable for the year based on the following formula:

See page ii for explanation of footnotes.

[247] CCH ¶19,321; Sec. 122.3(2) "specified employer".

[248] Reg. 6000.

[249] Rooke, 2002 DTC 7442.

$$T \times \frac{\text{lesser of: (a) } \$80{,}000 \times n/365; \text{ or (b) } 80\% \text{ of } E}{I}$$

Where:

T = Tax otherwise payable. Tax otherwise payable is computed as the amount of tax payable under Part I after deducting credits listed in ¶8095 to ¶8215, but before making any addition or deduction in respect of the surtax on income not earned in a province, the reduction in respect of income earned in the Province of Quebec, any deductions for minimum tax carryover, the tax on a minor child's "split income", an individual's dividend tax credit, the foreign tax credits, the logging tax credit, the political donations tax credit, the investment tax credit, the employment tax credit, the share-purchase tax credit, the scientific research and experimental development tax credit, or the labour-sponsored funds tax credit.[250]

n = The number of days in the year during which the individual was working in the foreign country and was a resident in Canada.[251]

I = Where the individual is resident throughout the year, "I" equals his or her income for the year plus any portion of accumulated averaging amount included in taxable income. From this is deducted the capital gains deduction claimed in the year, net capital losses claimed in the year, and any amount deductible in respect of income exempt under a treaty, prospector's and grubstaker's shares, employer's shares, and home relocation loans. If the individual is a part year resident to which the part-time residents provisions apply, "I" will only include income for the periods in the year during which the individual was resident in Canada, and the individual's taxable income earned in Canada for the period during the year in which the individual was not resident in Canada less any of the applicable deductions listed above. The taxable income earned in Canada will be calculated before certain deductions.[252]

E = Income for the year from employment reasonably attributable to qualifying foreign duties performed during the period defined as "n" above. Income from any other employment during that period is excluded.

Example:

John was employed on an engineering project in Saudi Arabia. He has left his family (spouse and two children) in Ontario and continues to be a Canadian resident. His term of overseas employment is for a period of one year. He received $15,000 for employment prior to March 1 and $100,000 ($10,000 per month) from March to December inclusive. His net income is $115,000, of which his net overseas income is $100,000. (Note that net income might well include other items, such as bank interest which have been ignored here.)

Federal tax otherwise payable (tax on $115,000, net of $3,955 personal amount credits	$20,423

Numerator: lesser of:

(a) $67,068 ($80,000 × $\frac{306 \text{ days}}{365}$)

(b) $80,000 ($100,000 × 80%)

Credit: $67,068 × $\frac{\$20{,}423}{\$115{,}000}$	$11,911

See page ii for explanation of footnotes.

[250] CCH 19,322; Sec. 122.3(2), tax otherwise payable under this Part for the year.

[251] CCH 19,320; Sec. 122.3(1)(c).

[252] CCH 19,320; Sec. 115(1)(d)-(f), 122.3(1)(e)

¶8251

Federal tax:

Otherwise payable	$20,423
Credit	11,911
Net	$8,512

[¶8255] Refundable Medical Expense Supplement

[¶8260] Refundable Medical Expense Supplement for Low-Income Earners

A refundable medical expense tax credit exists for low-income working individuals with higher than average medical expenses.

This refundable tax credit may be claimed by an individual who is resident in Canada throughout the year, is 18 years of age or older at the end of the year, and has income in excess of a minimum threshold ($3,268 in 2012) from an office, employment or from businesses carried on by the individual (either alone or as an active partner), or from the "WEPP" program (under the *Wage Earner Protection Program Act*).[253] Income for this test does not include wage loss replacement insurance benefits. A business loss for this purpose is treated as being nil so it will not reduce the income from other sources for purposes of meeting the minimum income test. Effective for the 2008 and subsequent taxation years, the WEPP provides a level of compensation for lost employee wages due to employer bankruptcy or insolvency.

In 2012, the credit is equal to the lesser of $1,119 and 25% of the total of allowable medical expenses claimed under the disability supports deduction (see ¶8145) and the medical expense tax credit.[254] To target assistance to those with low incomes, the credit is reduced by 5% of family net income minus any Universal Child Care Benefit in excess of a fully indexed threshold of $24,783 in 2012. Individuals can claim this credit for the same medical expenses that they claimed under the medical expense tax credit or the disability supports deduction.

[¶8265] Goods and Services Tax/Harmonized Sales Tax (GST/HST) Credit

[¶8270] GST/HST Tax Credit

The GST/HST credit helps individuals and families with low and modest incomes offset all or part of the GST or HST that they will pay.[255]

The GST/HST credit is novel in its form of payment. Unlike other tax credits, it cannot be used to reduce current tax payable. Rather, the credit is calculated on the basis of tax payable for a year and then paid in quarterly

---

See page ii for explanation of footnotes.

253 CCH ¶19,347d; Sec. 122.51(1) "eligible individual".   255 CCH ¶19,334; Sec. 122.5.
254 CCH ¶19,347e; Sec. 122.51(2).

instalments over the succeeding year, commencing about July. For example, if an individual has a GST credit calculated on his or her income tax return (generally filed by April), he or she cannot use the credit to reduce that year's taxes but must rather accept payment of one-quarter of the credit in July and October of the same year and January and April of the following year. It follows that no further accounting for the credit is necessary on subsequent returns. Improperly paid credits are recovered under normal reassessment procedures for the year the credit was claimed. Both an individual and a qualified relation are jointly and severally liable to repay any excess credit claimed.[256]

Although the taxpayer cannot use the credit to offset tax owing, the CRA can apply the credit to unpaid amounts as it becomes payable to the taxpayer. The result is that a taxpayer whose tax for a year is exactly offset by the GST/HST credit will be liable for interest on tax unpaid for periods for which the credit is not yet payable.

For payments commencing July 1, 2012, the GST credit is equal to the total of:

(a) $260 for an "eligible individual";

(b) $260 for a "qualified relation" of the individual (such as a spouse or common-law partner) or for a person under 19 in respect of whom the individual claims an eligible dependant tax credit (see ¶8095); and

(c) $137 for each other person under 19 years of age who is dependent on the individual or the individual's spouse or common-law partner; and

(d) if the individual is single without dependants, the lesser of $133 and 2% of the individual's income for the taxation year in excess of $8,439.

From this total is then subtracted 5% of the amount by which the individual's "adjusted net income" exceeds $33,884. An individual's adjusted net income is the total of the incomes for the year of the individual and the individual's "qualified relation", as defined below.[257] The Universal Child Care Benefit or a capital gain resulting from the application of the debt forgiveness rules are excluded from such income. Starting in 2008, also excluded from the adjusted income are payments received out of a registered disability savings plan.

A qualified relation is defined as the individual's spouse or common-law partner who, at the beginning of the specified month, is cohabiting with the individual within the meaning assigned by the child tax benefit rules. These rules define a cohabiting spouse or common-law partner as the individual's spouse or common-law partner who at that time has not been

---

See page ii for explanation of footnotes.

[256] CCH ¶22,783a; Sec. 160.1(1.1).　　　[257] CCH ¶19,334; Sec. 122.5(1) "adjusted income".

¶8270

living separate and apart from the individual for 90 days or more.[258] The definition of a "qualified relation" is now based on the applicable relationships at the beginning of each quarter, and more particularly, at the beginning of a "specified month" for a taxation year. A specified month for a taxation year is defined as July and October of the year following the taxation year, and January and April of the second year following the taxation year.[259]

A person is not considered to be an eligible individual, a qualified relation or a qualified dependant in relation to a specified month if that person dies before the month, is confined to prison for a period of at least 90 days that includes the first day of the month, is an officer or servant (or a family member or servant of such a person) of a foreign country who is exempt from Part I tax, or is a non-resident person at the beginning of the month (other than a non-resident person who is a cohabiting spouse or common-law partner of a person who is deemed to be resident in Canada throughout the taxation year that includes the first day of the specified month, and who was resident in Canada at any time before the specified month).[260]

Where an individual has a qualified relation in respect of a specified month, only one of them may claim the credit for the month. (The person claiming the credit may, however, claim an amount in respect of the qualified relation.) If both such individuals attempt to claim the credit, the Minister will designate which person is the eligible individual in relation to the specified month.[261] Furthermore, only one individual may claim a person as a qualified dependant in relation to a specified month. In particular, two or more individuals who would otherwise be eligible to claim the person as a qualified dependant must agree as to who will claim the person as a qualified dependant for the month. If the individuals fail to make such an agreement, the person will be the qualified dependant of the individual who is entitled to the Canada Child Tax Benefit (CCTB) in respect of the person. If no CCTB is paid in respect of the person, the Minister will designate which individual may include the person as a qualified dependant.[262]

Each eligible parent in a shared custody situation is entitled to half of the child benefit for that child every month that they qualify as shared custody parents [effective June 2011]. To qualify as a shared custody parent of a qualified dependant at a particular time, an individual must be one of the two parents of a qualified dependant who:

(a) are not at the time cohabiting spouses or common-law partners of each other;

(b) reside with the qualified dependant on an equal or near equal basis, and

---

See page ii for explanation of footnotes.

[258] CCH ¶19,334c, ¶19,348ad; Sec. 122.5(1) "qualified relation", 122.6 "cohabiting spouse or common-law partner".

[259] CCH ¶19,340; Sec. 122.5(4).

[260] CCH ¶19,336; Sec. 122.5(2).

[261] CCH ¶19,342; Sec. 122.5(5).

[262] CCH ¶19,344; Sec. 122.5(6).

(c) primarily fulfill the responsibility for the care and upbringing of the qualified dependant when residing with the qualified dependants, as determined by prescribed factors.[263]

Where an individual becomes bankrupt, his or her entitlement to the GST/HST credit in subsequent calendar years is calculated based on income from both the pre- and post-bankruptcy periods. Where a spouse or common-law partner becomes bankrupt, the spouse's/common-law partner's income from both periods will also be taken into consideration.[264]

[¶8275] Dividend Tax Credit

[¶8280] Dividend Tax Credit

To determine the amount of the dividend to be brought into a shareholder's income, a "gross-up amount" is added to the actual dividend received by the shareholder. For eligible dividends received after 2005 and before 2010, the gross-up is 45%, reduced to 44% for 2010, 41% for 2011, and 38% thereafter. The gross-up for non-eligible dividends is 25%. Before 2006, the gross-up was 25% for all taxable dividends received.[265] However, the individual is entitled to claim a credit against federal tax. The dividend tax credit for eligible dividends equals $^{11}/_{18}$ of the gross-up for eligible dividends received after 2005 and before 2010, $^{10}/_{17}$ for those received in 2010, $^{13}/_{23}$ in 2011, and $^{6}/_{11}$ thereafter. The dividend tax credit for non-eligible dividends is $^{2}/_{3}$ of the gross-up. Before 2006, the credit was equal to $^{2}/_{3}$ of the 25% gross-up for all taxable dividends received.[266]

As a general rule, dividends paid out of income that has been taxed at the high corporate tax rate will be considered eligible dividends and dividends paid out of income that has been eligible for the small business deduction will not be considered eligible dividends. For more details on the definition of "eligible dividend" and the designation to be made by a corporation paying them, see ¶6050.

Dividends which fall under these rules include not only ordinary dividends, but also deemed dividends.

The dividend tax credit is non-refundable and there is no carryover provision, so that if an individual has insufficient income to use the whole amount of the credit in a particular year, the unused part of the dividend tax credit is lost. Under certain circumstances a taxpayer can elect to have all of the taxable dividends received by his or her spouse/common-law partner from taxable Canadian corporations (including eligible dividends received after 2005) included in the taxpayer's income. This may be done where the amount of a taxpayer's marital tax credit is reduced as a result of the receipt of the dividends by a spouse or common-law partner, and where no tax is

---

[263] CCH ¶19,348zc; Sec. 122.6"shared-custody parent".

[264] CCH ¶19,345; Sec. 122.5(7).

[265] CCH ¶10,003; Sec. 82(1).

[266] CCH ¶19,200; Sec. 121; Interp. Bul. IT-67R3.

payable by the spouse or common-law partner. Where such an election is made, the taxpayer would include in income the grossed-up amount of the dividends received by the spouse/common-law partner and be eligible for the dividend tax credit on the grossed-up amount.[267]

[¶8285] Labour-Sponsored Funds Tax Credit

[¶8290] Labour-Sponsored Funds Tax Credit

For shares of a labour-sponsored venture capital corporation (LSVCC) purchased in 1998 and subsequent taxation years, a federal tax credit of up to 15% of the first $5,000 of their cost is available to an individual (other than a trust), for a maximum credit of $750 per year.[268] The shares may be acquired directly by the individual claiming the credit, or by an RRSP under which either the individual or the individual's spouse is the annuitant, if it can reasonably be considered that the individual's contributions have been used to acquire the shares. The credit claimed in a year is reduced to the extent that shares purchased during the first 60 days of the year are utilized to claim a credit in the preceding taxation year.

The tax credit available relates to the net cost for an original acquisition of an approved share. "Net cost" means the consideration paid for the share, less any assistance (other than federal and provincial tax credits on the share).[269] "Approved share" means a share in the capital stock of a prescribed labour-sponsored venture capital corporation.[270] A prescribed LSVCC is a corporation registered under Part X.3, or a provincially registered corporation.[271] An "original acquisition" means the first acquisition of the share by an individual who is the first registered holder, other than a broker or dealer in securities, or the first transaction whereby such individual irrevocably subscribes and pays for the share.[272]

No credit is allowed unless the required information return issued by the registered LSVCC is filed with the individual's tax return for the year. Moreover, no credit is allowed where the LSVCC share was acquired after the individual's death, say by the individual's estate or by the RRSP of the individual's spouse or common-law partner. Finally, no credit is allowed for the year if the share has been redeemed or disposed of, and the Minister has refunded Part XII.5 penalty tax (see ¶13,665). Generally speaking, under Part XII.5, the Minister may refund an amount previously paid by reason of an early redemption of LSVCC shares, where such amount exceeds the previously claimed LSVCC credit.

See page ii for explanation of footnotes.

[267] CCH ¶10,060; Sec. 82(3); Interp. Bul. IT-295R4.

[268] CCH ¶19,998h–19,998i; Sec. 127.4(5)–(6).

[269] CCH ¶19,998b; Sec. 127.4(1) "net cost".

[270] CCH ¶19,998; Sec. 127.4(1) "approved share".

[271] Reg. 6701.

[272] CCH ¶19,998ba; Sec. 127.4(1) "original acquisition".

[¶8294] Minimum Holding Period

LSVCC shares are effectively subject to a minimum holding period, in that redemptions made during that period result in the required repayment of any previously claimed credit. For shares purchased after March 5, 1996, the holding period for LSVCC shares was increased to eight years (up from the previous five years) and there is no overall reduction for persons 65 years or older, persons retiring, or those ceasing to be resident in Canada. This eight-year holding period is part of the registration requirements for LSVCCs discussed at ¶13,486. Part XII.5 imposes a penalty for redemptions or cancellation occurring before the eight-year period expires. Part XII.5 penalty tax is basically equal to the tax credit that would have been available when the share was acquired (see ¶13,655).[273]

[¶8295] Corporation Rates

[¶8300] Tax Payable for Corporations

The tax rate for corporations on income from general business is 38%.[274] However, a corporation's tax rate is reduced by the following:

- A deduction of 10% of the corporation's taxable income earned in the year in a province (provincial tax abatement).

- A general corporate rate reduction on fully taxed corporate income (i.e., income that is not reduced by other tax deductions) of 8.5% for any portion of the taxation year that falls in 2008, 9% for any portion in 2009, 10% for 2010, 11.5% for 2011, and 13% for 2012 and later calendar years.

- A rate reduction (to a combined federal rate of 11% for 2012) on the amount of active business income of a small business corporation that does not exceed its business limit for the year, i.e., $400,000 after 2006 and before 2009, and $500,000 effective January 1, 2009 (small business deduction).

- A reduction of the tax on a corporation's manufacturing and processing profits (manufacturing and processing credit).

- A reduction from tax for foreign taxes paid on income from countries outside of Canada (foreign tax credit).

- A logging tax credit for logging taxes paid to a province.

- A political contribution tax credit.

- A tax credit for certain kinds of property purchased for use in certain parts of the country and for investments in scientific research and experimental development (investment tax credit).

See page ii for explanation of footnotes.

[273] Reg. 6706.
[274] CCH ¶19,350; Sec. 123(1).

Other tax credits relating to specific taxation years or types of taxpayers include the unused Part VI tax credit, the unused Part I.3 tax credit, the special tax credit available to credit unions, and the Unemployment Insurance premium tax credit. As well, until January 1, 2008, a corporate surtax of 4% of federal income tax payable is imposed on corporations other than non-resident-owned investment corporations.[275] See ¶8320.

Finally, from January 1, 2004 until January 1, 2006, a federal capital tax was imposed on taxable capital employed in Canada in excess of $50 million. The threshold for application of the tax was $10 million until January 1, 2004, when the tax began to be phased out.[276] See ¶13,030.

[¶8310] Federal Corporate Rates

Please see paragraph ¶460 for the federal corporate tax rates for 2005–2012.

[¶8315] Federal Tax Abatement — Deduction from Corporation Tax re Provincial Taxes

Corporations may deduct from their tax otherwise payable an amount equal to 10% of the corporation's taxable income earned in a province.[277] While this deduction is intended to compensate corporations for provincial taxes payable by them, it is taken independently of any taxes actually payable by the corporation to any province. For a complete discussion of the provincial tax credit, see ¶8630 *et seq.* Federal Crown corporations prescribed by regulation are not entitled to claim a credit for provincial taxes, and taxable income of a corporation that is exempt from tax because of an Act of Parliament is also not eligible for the abatement.[278]

[¶8320] Corporate Surtax

The corporate surtax has been repealed for all corporations effective January 1, 2008. There is a prorating requirement for years that straddle that date. Until then, a 4% federal surtax was applied to Part I tax otherwise payable after the 10% abatement for income earned in a province, but before credits such as the small business deduction and credits for foreign taxes paid (see below).[279] A corporation that was throughout the year a non-resident investment corporation was excluded from this surtax.

The amount of the surtax imposed until January 1, 2008 is equal to 4% of the tax otherwise payable under Part I by the corporation for the year determined without reference to: the additional $6^2/_3\%$ on investment income (¶8323); the corporate tax reductions (¶8475); the small business deduction (¶8430); the manufacturing and processing deduction (¶8400); the Part VI tax credit (¶8380); the Canadian film or video production tax credit (¶8685); the film or video production services tax credit (¶8710); the foreign tax

---

See page ii for explanation of footnotes.

[275] CCH ¶19,390a; Sec. 123.2.
[276] CCH ¶24,059; Sec. 181.1.
[277] CCH ¶19,400; Sec. 124(1).

[278] CCH ¶19,520, ¶19,521; Sec. 124(3); Reg. 7100.

[279] CCH ¶19,390a; Sec. 123.2.

credit (¶8550); the political contribution tax credit (¶8537); the investment tax credit (¶8340); the recapture provisions applicable to the investment tax credit (¶8344); and the tax credit for credit unions (¶9207).

As well, a special calculation backed out from the amount subject to surtax payable by mutual fund and investment corporations the amount of their capital gains refund (up to current Part I tax payable) for the current year (¶9063 and ¶9099). In effect, the surtax was not meant to apply to capital gains which were taxed and paid by the investment or mutual fund corporation.

[¶8323] Additional Tax on Investment Income

An additional amount of tax under Part I is imposed on the investment income of a Canadian-controlled private corporation (CCPC).[280] A corporation that is a CCPC throughout a taxation year adds to its tax otherwise payable under Part I for that year an amount equal to $6^2/_3\%$ of the lesser of two amounts. The first amount is the corporation's aggregate investment income for the year. The second amount is the corporation's taxable income for the year less any amount in respect of which the corporation claimed the small business deduction. This additional tax is reflected in a CCPC's refundable dividend tax on hand discussed at ¶9027; accordingly, it is refundable to the corporation when it pays a taxable dividend.

[¶8330] Forms for Reporting Corporate Income

The basic form to be used by the corporation in its return is Form T2, "Corporation Income Tax Return".[281] With this form, the CRA supplies its "T2 Corporation Income Tax Guide" to explain how Form T2 is to be completed. The basic T2 is typically supplemented by a number of additional schedules. The CRA provides forms for only some of the schedules; the taxpayer is responsible for preparing the others.

[¶8335] Investment Tax Credit

[¶8340] General Features of the Investment Tax Credit

Investment tax credits are fully deductible by corporations and individuals against federal tax otherwise payable under Part I. However, for individuals, investment tax credits in any one year cannot exceed the amount, if any, by which tax otherwise payable under Part I exceeds that individual's "minimum amount", as calculated under the alternative minimum tax (see ¶8070).[282]

The investment tax credit at the end of the year is a pool that includes certain amounts carried over from other years. For investment tax credits earned in the 1998 and subsequent taxation years, the credits may be

See page ii for explanation of footnotes.

[280] CCH ¶19,396; Sec. 123.3. [282] CCH ¶19,825; Sec. 127(5).
[281] CCH ¶39,075, ¶39,095; Form T2.

¶8323

carried forward 20 years; previously, the carryforward period was 10 years. Credits may be carried back 3 years.[283] There are restrictions on the amount and type of expenditures giving rise to credits that can be allocated to limited partners. Special rules are provided for investment tax credits earned by co-operative corporations, trusts, and partnerships.[284]

The investment tax credit of a taxpayer at the end of a taxation year is a pool of amounts which includes:

- the specified percentage of the capital cost of certain types of qualified property and expenditures acquired or made in the year;

- any investment tax credit amounts allocated to the taxpayer by a testamentary trust or a partnership; and

- any amounts carried forward or back from other taxation years.[285]

An increased investment tax credit is provided in some instances in respect of a taxpayer which was a Canadian-controlled private corporation throughout the taxation year.[286] Repayments of government assistance, non-government assistance, or a contract payment made by the taxpayer that resulted in a reduction of the investment tax credit, will earn an investment tax credit which is added to the pool at the same percentage that applied to the cost of property or the amount of the expenditure.

The balance in the credit pool is reduced by credits claimed in preceding years. In addition, a corporation's investment tax credit is reduced by the amount used to offset its liability for Part VII tax under the share- purchase tax credit system (see ¶13,265). Similarly, a corporation's qualified expenditures in respect of scientific research and experimental development are reduced by the amount specified by the corporation to obtain a refund of Part VIII tax (see ¶13,315). The rates at which qualified property acquisitions and qualified expenditures earn investment tax credits in a particular year are discussed below. The definition of "specified percentage" [287] sets out the rates applicable in various circumstances. An investment tax credit claim reduces the undepreciated capital cost balance of depreciable assets in the year following that in which the credit is claimed.[288]

All claims for investment tax credits must be filed on a prescribed form (i.e., claimed on Form T2038(IND) for individuals or Schedule 31 for corporations) on or before the date that is one year after the filing-due date for the particular year in which the expense was made or incurred. [289]

A corporation's investment tax credit is reduced where there is a change of control. A corporation is deemed to have a year end immediately before a change in its control.[290] The formula for calculating the reduction of the

---

See page ii for explanation of footnotes.

[283] CCH ¶19,829k, ¶19,829x, ¶19,829y; Sec. 127(9) "investment tax credit", 127(9.01), 127(9.02).

[284] CCH ¶19,826–19,828a; Sec. 127(6)–127(8.1).

[285] CCH ¶19,829k; Sec. 127(9) "investment tax credit".

[286] CCH ¶19,831a; Sec. 127(10.1).

[287] CCH ¶19,829u; Sec. 127(9) "specified percentage".

[288] CCH ¶4562h; Sec. 13(21) "undepreciated capital cost".

[289] CCH ¶19,829k; Sec. 127(9) "investment tax credit".

[290] CCH ¶28,333a; Sec. 249(4).

¶8340

corporation's investment tax credit in respect of property acquired and expenditures made *prior* to the acquisition of control is provided.[291] Investment tax credits earned prior to the change of control may be:

(a) refunded to the taxpayer (see ¶8350);

(b) applied to reduce any Part VII tax liability related to flow-through shares (see ¶13,265); and

(c) applied against any Part I tax liability arising on profits from that business or a similar business.

Investment tax credits limited on a change of control may be re-established as a result of tax arising in respect of income generated by the same or a similar business as that in which the credit was earned. Such income cannot be taken into account in a year if it has been offset by a loss carryover from those businesses from another year.

A similar formula for calculating the investment tax credits earned *after* the acquisition of control is provided.[292] Investment tax credits earned subsequent to the change in control may be:

(a) refunded to the taxpayer (see ¶8350);

(b) applied to reduce any Part VII tax liability related to flow-through shares (see ¶13,265); and

(c) carried back and applied against any Part I tax liability arising on profits from the business or a similar business.

Income generated by the same or similar business cannot be taken into account for investment tax credit purposes in a year if it has been offset by a loss carryover for those businesses from another year.

[¶8341] Basis for and Effect of Investment Tax Credit

The investment tax credit is calculated as a percentage of the capital cost of certain property, the amount of qualified expenditures in respect of SR&ED, qualified Canadian exploration expenditures, flow-through mining expenditures, pre-production mining expenditures, eligible child care space expenditures, or apprenticeship expenditures. Investment tax credits will be generated only when the income from the business to which the property or expenditure relates is subject to tax. Property is not considered to be acquired nor expenditures made for purposes of claiming the investment tax credit until the property has become "available for use" for capital cost allowance purposes.[293] This available-for-use rule applies to the deduction and refundability of the investment tax credit, but not to the eligibility or the rate. For purposes of determining the eligibility for the credit or its rate, the relevant date is the date of acquisition. The rules outlining when a

---

See page ii for explanation of footnotes.

[291] CCH ¶19,830; Sec. 127(9.1).
[292] CCH ¶19,830a; Sec. 127(9.2).

[293] CCH ¶4585, ¶4586, ¶19,832b; Sec. 13(27), 13(28), 127(11.2).

property is acquired and when it is available for use are found at ¶4055 and ¶4060.

The capital cost of a property, or the amounts of qualified expenditures in respect of SR&ED, qualified Canadian exploration expenditures, flow-through mining expenditures, pre-production mining expenditures, eligible child care space expenditures, or apprenticeship expenditures are reduced by the amount of any government or non-government assistance, or contract payments in respect of SR&ED that the taxpayer (or a non-arm's length person or partnership) receives, is entitled to receive, or can reasonably be expected to receive in respect of such cost or expenditures. However, with respect to the amount of the taxpayer's qualified Canadian exploration expenditure, any amount received or receivable under the federal *Petroleum Incentives Program Act* or the *Petroleum Incentives Program Act* of Alberta, will not reduce the amount qualifying for the investment tax credit.[294]

If a taxpayer subsequently repays any government assistance, non-government assistance, or contract payments that formerly reduced the taxpayer's investment tax credit, as described above, the credit is earned at the rate which was applicable to the expenditure or property. Thus, where the repayment relates to an amount in respect of first term shared-use equipment or second term shared-use equipment, $1/4$ of the amount will qualify for an SR&ED investment tax credit.[295] For this purpose, the expenditure eligible for the investment tax credit is limited to the cost to the non-arm's length party of providing the goods and services.[296] An amount of assistance is deemed to have been repaid by the taxpayer if the amount of assistance has not been received by the taxpayer and is not recoverable (i.e., if entitlement has expired).[297]

Where a taxpayer pays another person to carry out scientific research and experimental development activities ("contract payment"), he or she can claim the investment tax credit on the expenditure. [As a result of draft changes released on August 14, 2012, it is proposed that only 80% of contract payments will be eligible. See ¶3600]. The person receiving the payment would deduct it from the scientific research and experimental development expenditures that are eligible for the investment tax credit. The definition of "contract payment" applies to activities that can reasonably be considered to have been performed by or on behalf of another person. A payment from the Canadian Commercial Corporation, which often acts as a conduit when Canadian businesses are dealing with foreign governments, is excluded from the definition of "contract payment".[298]

The investment tax credit on SR&ED expenditures, in the case of non-arm's length contract payments, stays with the performer, unless transferred by joint election of the non-arm's length payor and the payee (performer).

See page ii for explanation of footnotes.

[294] CCH ¶19,832a, ¶19,832me–19,832mj; Sec. 127(11.1), 127(17)–127(22).
[295] CCH ¶19,832e; Sec. 127(11.5).
[296] CCH ¶19,832f–19,832i; Sec. 127(11.6)–127(11.8).
[297] CCH ¶19,831h; Sec. 127(10.8).
[298] CCH ¶19,829f, ¶19,832v; Sec. 127(9) "contract payment"; Reg. 4606.

Where there is no transfer there is no investment tax credit adjustment to the payor's expenditure pool. To the extent of a transfer, the payor's pool is reduced by transferred credits. The election must be made by the return-due date of the payor and cannot exceed the least of: (a) the amount specified therein, (b) the amount of the performer's SR&ED investment tax credit pool, and (c) qualifying SR&ED payments of the payor for the research actually paid within 180 days of the performer's year end. Moreover, the payment must be for qualified SR&ED expenditures of the performer paid by the performer within 180 days of its year end or amounts effectively transferred to the performer from another non-arm's length taxpayer that are attributable to the same SR&ED. A qualified expenditure is considered paid if the associated expenditure is paid. For example, a qualified expenditure for mixed-use equipment is considered paid if the full cost is paid. The rate of refund on transferred credits will be governed by the character of the expenditure incurred by the performer. When credits are transferred under this election, associated repayments of assistance track the credits.[299]

The capital cost of depreciable property is deemed to be reduced by certain kinds of assistance from a government, municipality, or other public authority by way of a grant, subsidy, forgivable loan, deduction from tax, investment allowance, or otherwise.[300] The investment tax credit is a type of assistance which will reduce the capital cost of the qualified depreciable property, if the taxpayer still owns the property. In the event that the property has been disposed of, the undepreciated capital cost of the class will be reduced, resulting in recapture or reduced capital cost allowance claims.[301] However, the capital cost on which the investment tax credit is calculated does not reflect any reduction. The amount qualified in respect of the SR&ED expenditure, qualified Canadian exploration expenditure, flow-through mining expenditure, pre-production mining expenditure, eligible child care space expenditure, or apprenticeship expenditure made by a taxpayer is the actual amount of the expenditure less the amount of any government assistance, non-government assistance, or contract payment with respect to SR&ED, which, at the time of filing the tax return, the taxpayer has received, is entitled to receive, or can reasonably be expected to receive. The amount of the investment tax credit deduction is to be deducted from the adjusted cost base of capital property for purposes of computing a capital gain or loss.[302]

The CRA's administrative position for many years (supported by case law) has been that provincial tax credits received by a taxpayer under provincial super-allowance programs are not considered government assistance. Consequently, these credits did not reduce the amount of investment tax credit that a taxpayer could claim for federal income tax purposes. For taxation years ending after February 2000, the deductions available in respect of SR&ED expenses are reduced by an amount equal to the provin-

---

See page ii for explanation of footnotes.

[299] CCH ¶19,832ma–19,832mh; Sec. 127(13)–127(20).

[300] CCH ¶4535; Sec. 13(7.1).

[301] CCH ¶4562h; Sec. 13(21) "undepreciated capital cost".

[302] CCH ¶7645, ¶7660, ¶7669; Sec. 53(2)(c), 53(2)(h), 53(2)(k).

¶8341

cial income tax credits claimed by the taxpayer.[303] As a result, a taxpayer should no longer be able to claim deductions in excess of the actual SR&ED costs incurred.

[¶8342] Investment Tax Credit Rates

The investment tax credit is earned in respect of a number of different expenditures. The most recent additions to the credit include that for a taxpayer's "child care space amount", which equals 25% of the "eligible child care space expenditure" incurred on or after March 19, 2007 on the creation of a new child care space, to a maximum credit of $10,000 per child care space. See the commentary in item (1) at ¶8343. Another recent addition is the credit available in respect of a taxpayer's "apprenticeship expenditure" for a taxation year, which equals the lesser of $2,000 and 10% of the eligible salary and wages payable by the taxpayer to an "eligible apprentice" in respect of the eligible apprentice's employment in the taxation year and on or after May 2, 2006. See the commentary in item (2) at ¶8343. In terms of the other expenditures that qualify (or previously qualified) for the investment tax credit, the applicable rate of the credit often depends on when the relevant property was acquired or the qualified expenditure was made, where it was to be used or incurred, the type of property involved, and the type of taxpayer. The regions and effective dates of the applicable rates are summarized in the following table:

Area and acquisition dates	Qualified property	Flow-through mining expenditure	Qualified scientific research expenditures Non-CCPC	Qualified scientific research expenditures CCPC[1]	Qualified transportation and construction[2] equipment
October 17, 2000 and thereafter					
General rate all locations in Canada	Nil	15%	20%	35%	Nil
Atlantic provinces and Gaspé[7]	10%	15%	20%	35%	Nil
Prescribed offshore areas (East Coast)	10%	15%	20%	35%	Nil
Calendar 1995 to October 16, 2000					
General rate all locations in Canada	Nil	N/A	20%	35%	Nil
Atlantic provinces and Gaspé[3]	10%	N/A	20%	35%	Nil

See page ii for explanation of footnotes.

[303] CCH ¶5900, ¶19,829va; Sec. 37(1)(d.1), 127(9) "super-allowance benefit amount".

| Area and acquisition dates | Qualified property | Flow-through mining expenditure | Qualified scientific research expenditures | | Qualified transportation and construction[2] equipment |
			Non-CCPC	CCPC[1]	
Prescribed offshore areas (East Coast)	10%	N/A	20%	35%	Nil
Calendar years 1989 through 1994					
Atlantic provinces and Gaspé[3]	15%	N/A	30%	35%	Nil
Prescribed offshore areas (East Coast)	15%	N/A	20%	35%	Nil
Other locations in Canada (general rate)	Nil	N/A	20%	35%	Nil
Anywhere in Canada, for qualified small businesses after Dec. 2, 1992 and before 1994	10%	N/A	N/A	35%	10%
Special designated areas[4]	30%	N/A	N/A	N/A	N/A
Cape Breton approved projects (to Dec. 31, 1992)[5]	45%	N/A	N/A	N/A	N/A
Canadian exploration expenses (to Dec. 31, 1990)	25%	N/A	N/A	N/A	N/A
Calendar 1988					
Atlantic provinces and Gaspé[3]	20%	N/A	30%	35%	3%
Prescribed offshore areas (East Coast)	20%	N/A	20%	35%	3%
Other locations in Canada (general rate)	3%	N/A	20%	35%	3%
Special designated areas[4]	40%	N/A	N/A	N/A	N/A
Cape Breton approved projects[5]	60%	N/A	N/A	N/A	N/A
Canadian exploration expenses	25%	N/A	N/A	N/A	N/A
Calendar 1987					
Atlantic provinces and Gaspé[3]	20%	N/A	30%	35%	5%
Prescribed offshore areas (East Coast)	20%	N/A	20%	35%	5%

Area and acquisition dates	Qualified property	Flow-through mining expenditure	Qualified scientific research expenditures		Qualified transportation and construction[2] equipment
			Non-CCPC	CCPC[1]	
Special designated areas[4]	40%	N/A	N/A	N/A	N/A
Cape Breton approved projects[5]	60%	N/A	N/A	N/A	N/A
Canadian exploration expenses	25%	N/A	N/A	N/A	N/A
Other locations in Canada (general rate)	5%	N/A	20%	35%	5%
May 24, 1985 to December 31, 1986, inclusive					
Atlantic provinces and Gaspé[3]	20%	N/A	30%	35%	7%
Prescribed offshore areas (East Coast) (after Feb. 25, 1986)	20%	N/A	20%	35%	7%
Designated regions[6] . .	10%	N/A	20%	35%	7%
Special designated areas[4]	50%	N/A	N/A	N/A	N/A
Cape Breton approved projects[5]	60%	N/A	N/A	N/A	N/A
Canadian exploration expenses (after Nov. 30, 1985)	25%	N/A	N/A	N/A	N/A
Other locations in Canada (general rate)	7%	N/A	20%	35%	7%
Taxation years including November 1, 1983 to calendar May 23, 1985					
Atlantic provinces and Gaspé[3]	20%	N/A	30%	35%	7%
Designated regions[6] . .	10%	N/A	20%	35%	7%
Special designated areas[4]	50%	N/A	N/A	N/A	N/A
Other locations in Canada	7%	N/A	20%	35%	7%
November 17, 1978 to April 19, 1983					
Atlantic provinces and Gaspé[3]	20%	N/A	20%	25%	7%
Designated regions[6] . .	10%	N/A	10%	25%	7%

Area and acquisition dates	Qualified property	Flow-through mining expenditure	Qualified scientific research expenditures		Qualified transportation and construction[2] equipment
			Non-CCPC	CCPC[1]	
Other locations in Canada	7%	N/A	10%	25%	7%
Special designated areas[4]	50%	N/A	N/A	N/A	N/A
April 1, 1977 to November 16, 1978					
Atlantic provinces and Gaspé[3]	10%	N/A	10%	10%	N/A
Designated regions[6] . .	7.5%	N/A	7.5%	7.5%	N/A
Other locations in Canada	5%	N/A	5%	5%	N/A
June 24, 1975 to March 31, 1977					
Atlantic provinces and Gaspé[3]	5%	N/A	N/A	N/A	N/A
Designated regions[6] . .	5%	N/A	N/A	N/A	N/A
Other locations in Canada	5%	N/A	N/A	N/A	N/A

[1] CCPC and scientific research - The 35% rate is available in respect of an amount up to but not exceeding the "expenditure limit"of a Canadian-controlled private corporation (CCPC). For taxation years ending on or after February 26, 2008, the expenditure limit is a maximum of $3 million, but is phased out if the taxable income of the corporation and any associated corporations for the preceding taxation year exceeds the small business limit of $400,000; for the 2010 and subsequent taxation years, the phase-out occurs if such taxable income for the preceding taxation year exceeds the (increased) small business limit of $500,000. The expenditure limit is also reduced if the taxable capital employed in Canada of the corporation (plus that of associated corporations) for the preceding taxation year exceeds $10 million. For 2007 and subsequent taxation years, except a 2007 or 2008 taxation year that immediately follows a taxation year that ended before 2007, the 35% rate is available to Canadian-controlled private corporations which, together with any corporations associated with them, have an aggregate taxable income not exceeding $600,000 in the year preceding the year in which the expenditures are made. However, the $2 million of expenditure limit eligible for this rate is reduced by $10 for every dollar of (associated group) taxable income for the preceding year in excess of $400,000. For taxation years that end after 2002, other than taxation years that immediately follow taxation years that end before 2003, the 35% rate is available to Canadian-controlled private corporations which, together with any corporations associated with them, have an aggregate taxable income not exceeding $500,000 in the year preceding the year in which the expenditures are made. However, the $2 million of expenditure limit for this rate is reduced by $10 for every dollar of (group) taxable income for the preceding year in excess of $300,000.

Where expenditures exceed the amount available for 35% credit, the company may designate which expenditures it chooses to have qualify; undesignated expenditures should qualify for the general scientific research rate applicable to the region.

[2] Construction equipment qualifies only if acquired after April 19, 1983.

[3] Gaspé Peninsula is defined as the portion of the Gaspé region of the Province of Quebec that extends to the western border of Kamouraska County and includes the Magdalen Islands.

¶8342

[4] A special investment tax credit rate of 50% was allowed on the capital cost of new investments (certified property) made in selected prescribed incentive regions after October 28, 1980 and before 1987. Effective January 1, 1987, the rate was reduced to 40% and then to 30% for property acquired after 1988. The credit is discontinued for acquisitions after December 31, 1994, except for property: (a) acquired pursuant to a written agreement entered into before February 22, 1994, (b) that was under construction by or on behalf of the taxpayer before February 22, 1994, or (c) that is machinery or equipment that will be a fixed and integral part of property under construction by or on behalf of the taxpayer before February 22, 1994. The special credit applied to investments in new plant and equipment to be used in facilities as defined under the *Regional Development Incentives Act*

[5] Approved Cape Breton projects are projects involving a minimum acquisition of $25,000 of depreciable property approved by the Minister of Regional Industrial Expansion. Application must be made before July 1, 1988.

[6] Designated region incentives were withdrawn for property acquired after 1985. A designated region was a region of Canada other than the Province of Newfoundland, Prince Edward Island, Nova Scotia, New Brunswick, or the Gaspé Peninsula, that was designated as such under the *Regional Development Incentives Act* If a location becomes a prescribed designated location during the year, the higher rate applies only to acquisitions and expenditures made after that date. Maps showing prescribed regions may be found in Appendix B of Information Circular IC 78-4R3.

[7] Certain parts of the oil and gas Atlantic Investment Tax Credit are proposed to be phased out over a four-year period for assets acquired on or after March 29, 2012 for use in certain oil and gas and mining activities. The credit in respect of these assets will continue to apply at a rate of 10% for assets acquired before 2014. It will be reduced to a rate of 5% for assets acquired in 2014 and 2015, and it will not be available for such assets acquired after 2015. The Atlantic Investment Tax Credit for electricity generation equipment will be extended for qualified property to include prescribed energy generation and conservation property acquired on or after March 29, 2012, if it is used primarily for manufacturing and processing, farming, fishing, and logging. These changes have been incorporated in draft legislation released on August 14, 2012, but not yet enacted.

[¶8343] Expenditures which Qualify for the Investment Tax Credit

The only current expenditures which now qualify for the investment tax credit are as follows:

(1) *Child care spaces.* The 2007 federal Budget expanded the investment tax credit to include a taxpayer's eligible expenditures incurred on or after March 19, 2007 in respect of the creation of a child care space. The amount added to the credit is 25% of the taxpayer's "eligible child care space expenditure", to a maximum amount of $10,000 per child care space.[304] Thus, up to $40,000 of eligible child care space expenditure per child care space created qualifies for the credit at a rate of 25%. Unused credits can be carried back three years and forward 20 years, as is currently the case with other investment tax credits. The child care space amount credit is available to a taxpayer only if the provision of the child care space is ancillary to one or more businesses of the taxpayer carried on in Canada that do not otherwise include the provision of child care spaces. In other words, the credit does not apply to child care businesses such as those carried on by daycare centres for children.

Eligible child care space expenditures will include the cost of eligible depreciable property and the amount of specified child care start-up costs acquired or incurred solely for the purpose of the creation of the new child care spaces in a licensed child care facility operated for the benefit of the children of the taxpayer's employees, or of a combination of children of the taxpayer's employees and other children. Eligible depreciable property will include the cost or incremental cost of the building or portion of the

---

See page ii for explanation of footnotes.

[304] CCH ¶19,829ec; Sec. 127(9) "child care space amount".

building in which the child care facility is located, as well as the cost of furniture, appliances, computer equipment, audio-visual equipment, playground structures, and playground equipment.[305] The specified start-up costs will include initial start-up costs such as landscaping costs for the children's playground, architect's fees, costs of initial regulatory inspections, initial licensing fees, building permit costs, and costs to acquire children's educational material.[306]

However, eligible expenditures will not include specified property. Specified property will include motor vehicles and property that is, or is located in or is attached to, a residence of the employer, of an employee of the employer, of a person who holds an interest in the employer, or of any person related to the employer.[307] The credit will not be available for any of the ongoing or operating expenses of the child care facility such as supplies, wages, salaries, utilities, etc.

The credit will be fully or partially recaptured if, at any time within the five calendar years after the creation of the new child care space, the new child care space ceases to be available, or property that was an eligible expenditure is sold or leased to another person or is converted to another use.[308] The amount to be recaptured (i.e., added to tax payable) will be 25% of the lesser of:

- the amount that can reasonably be considered to be a taxpayer's child care space amount, and

- the proceeds of disposition of the eligible property, or, if the eligible property is disposed of to a related party, the fair market value of the property at the time of the disposition.[309]

(2) *Apprenticeship job creation.* The 2006 Budget introduced an investment tax credit for employers who pay salary or wages to apprentices in eligible trades after May 1, 2006. The credit is equal to 10% of such salary or wages up to a maximum of $2,000 per year per apprentice.[310] To add an amount in respect of the salary and wages paid to an apprentice in computing an employer's investment tax credit, the following requirements must be met:

(a) the employer must carry on a business in the taxation year;

(b) the apprentice must be an individual who is working in a prescribed trade (which includes one of the 45 trades currently included in the Red Seal trades or a trade that is prescribed in the regulations by the Minister of Finance working with the Minister of Human Resources and Social Development);

---

[305] CCH ¶19,829fb; Sec. 127(9) "eligible child care space expenditure".

[306] CCH ¶19,829tc; Sec. 127(9) "specified child care start-up expenditure".

[307] CCH ¶19,829u; Sec. 127(9) "specified property".

[308] CCH ¶19,840d, ¶19,840f; Sec. 127(27.1), 127(27.11).

[309] CCH ¶19,840h; Sec. 127(27.12).

[310] CCH ¶19,828h; Sec. 127(9) "apprenticeship expenditure".

(c) the apprentice must be working in the first two years of their provincially-registered apprenticeship contract;

(d) the salary and wages must be payable to an eligible apprentice, and do not include other remuneration such as profits, bonuses, benefits, or employee stock options;

(e) such salary and wages must be in respect of the eligible apprentice's employment in Canada; and

(f) such salary and wages must be payable in the taxation year and during the first 24 months of apprenticeship.[311]

In order to avoid duplication of the credit, particular restrictive rules will apply where an apprentice is employed by the taxpayer and a related person (or partnership) in a year.[312]

(3) *Pre-production mining expenditures.* An investment tax credit for qualifying mineral exploration expenses was introduced in 2003. It applies at a rate of 10% beginning in 2005. The credit is available only to corporations that directly incur eligible expenses, and is not transferable under a flow-through share agreement, allocable by a trust or partnership, or refundable. The credit applies to a "pre-production mining expenditure", which, generally speaking, is a grassroots exploration and pre-production development expenditure in Canada for qualifying minerals.[313]

These expenses must be incurred before a new mine in the mineral resource comes into production in reasonable commercial quantities. Qualifying minerals are diamonds, base or precious metals, and industrial minerals that become base or precious metals through refining. The taxable Canadian corporation which claims an investment tax credit in respect of a pre-production mining expenditure must actually incur the expense, in order for the expense to qualify as a pre-production mining expenditure. Specifically, an expense which has been renounced to the taxable Canadian corporation under a flow-through share agreement does not qualify as a pre-production mining expenditure. Pre-production mining expenditures that are not claimed in the year they arise can be carried back three years and forward 20 years for the purposes of the investment tax credit. The 20-year carryforward period applies to credits earned in the 1998 and subsequent taxation years; previously, the carryforward period was 10 years.

(4) *Flow-through mining expenditures.* The current investment tax credit rate in respect of flow-through mining expenditures is 15%. A flow-through mining expenditure is an expense incurred after October 17, 2000 and before April 2014 by a corporation conducting grassroots mining exploration activity from or above the surface of the earth for the purpose of determining the existence or location of a mineral resource. The credit period has been extended several times; most recently, the 2012 federal Budget extended the

---

See page ii for explanation of footnotes.

[311] CCH ¶19,829fa, ¶19,829fc; Sec. 127(9) "eligible apprentice", 127(9) "eligible salary and wages".

[312] CCH ¶19,832d; Sec. 127(11.4).

[313] CCH ¶19,829ma; Sec. 127(9) "pre-production mining expenditure".

credit period by one year to include expenses incurred before April 2014. Flow-through mining expenditures that are not claimed in the year they arise can be carried back three years and forward 20 years for the purposes of the investment tax credit. The 20-year carryforward period applies to credits earned in the 1998 and subsequent taxation years; previously, the carryforward period was 10 years.

(5) *Scientific research and experimental development.* "Qualified expenditures for scientific research and experimental development" is defined to mean those expenditures used in a systematic investigation or search carried out in a field of science or technology by means of an experiment or analysis. It does not include such activities as market research or sales promotion, quality control or testing, research in the social sciences or humanities, style changes, data collection, commercial production derived from development, or exploring for minerals, oil, or gas.[314]

A taxpayer may elect to establish a prescribed proxy amount for purposes of the investment tax credit claim, instead of doing an item by item apportioning of certain expenditures. The prescribed proxy amount is 65% of the total salaries of employees directly engaged in scientific research and experimental development in Canada. In computing this total of eligible salaries, salaries of specified employees (i.e., 10% or more interest) are limited to the lesser of five times the Year's Maximum Pensionable Earnings (YMPE) under the CPP and 75% of their salaries.[315] This method is intended to be easier for diversified businesses to administer. [As a result of 2012 Budget measures, it is proposed that the prescribed proxy amount be reduced to 60% for 2013 and to 55% after 2013, prorated for taxation years that straddle the beginning of the 2012, 2013, or 2014 calendar years. These measures were released in draft legislation issued on August 14, 2012.]

In addition, "qualified expenditure" includes expenditures on first-term shared-use equipment and second-term shared-use equipment acquired after December 2, 1992. First-term shared-use equipment is defined as depreciable property used by the taxpayer from the time of acquisition to the end of the first taxation year ending at least 12 months after the time of acquisition, primarily (more than 50%) for the pursuance of scientific research and experimental development in Canada.[316] When the equipment is acquired (becomes available for use) part-way through the year, it will not qualify as first-term shared-use equipment until the end of its next taxation year. Expenditures for general-purpose office equipment or furniture and prescribed depreciable property are excluded from the definition of first-term shared-use equipment. Prescribed depreciable property includes a building, a leasehold interest in a building, a property, including a part thereof, used initially for scientific research but that would be used during its operation time during its expected useful life or that would be consumed primarily in activities other than scientific research and experimental development.

See page ii for explanation of footnotes.

[314] CCH ¶5900, ¶19,832n; Sec. 37(1); Reg. 2902.
[315] Reg. 2900(4), Reg. 2900(7), Reg. 2900(8).
[316] CCH ¶19,829h; Sec. 127(9) "first term shared-use equipment".

¶8343

"Second-term shared-use equipment" is similar to first-term shared-use equipment except that it must be used by the taxpayer from the time of acquisition to the end of the first taxation year ending at least 24 months after the time of acquisition, primarily (more than 50%) for the pursuance of scientific research and experimental development in Canada. Property cannot be second-term shared-use equipment unless it has previously been first-term shared-use equipment. In the case of first- and second-term shared-use equipment, the property is acquired when it becomes available for use. See ¶4060. One-quarter of the capital cost of such property is treated as a qualified expenditure eligible for the investment tax credit in the first taxation year ending after the first 12-month period and one-quarter in the taxation year ending after the second 12-month period.[317]

Only the use of a prescribed form (T661) can entitle a taxpayer to claim investment tax credits for SR&ED. The form must be filed by the time the return for the year following the year of expenditure is due or would be due if tax were payable for that year. That is, expenditures must be identified on a Form T661 filed no later than 18 months after the end of the taxation year in which the expenditures were incurred (assuming no short taxation years). Furthermore, an expenditure which remains unpaid at the end of the year will be required to be reported in the year in which it is actually incurred in order to qualify as an eligible expenditure for the taxation year in which it is paid.[318] Where a taxpayer misclassifies an expenditure which is subsequently reclassified as an SR&ED expenditure as the result of a Revenue Canada-initiated assessment, the expenditure will qualify.[319]

As previously discussed at ¶8341, SR&ED investment tax credits in respect of payments to non-arm's length parties for goods and services are restricted to the extent that the expenditures eligible for the investment tax credit are limited to the cost to the non-arm's length party of providing the goods and services. In order to increase its information-gathering efforts in the SR&ED area, the T661 form requires taxpayers contracting out SR&ED to provide further information, such as the name of the performer, the amount of the contract expenditures, and the performer's GST registration number, if the contract expenditures for the year in respect of the particular performer exceed $30,000.

The definition of "qualified expenditure" requires all current SR&ED expenditures to be paid within 180 days of the year end in order to be eligible for investment tax credits. Otherwise, the amounts will be deemed to have been incurred for tax credit purposes in the year they are actually paid.[320]

Generally speaking, the current investment tax credit rate in respect of a *qualified expenditure* (defined as an expenditure in respect of scientific research and experimental development) made after 1994 is 20%. [As a result of 2012 Budget measures, it is proposed that the investment tax credit be

---

See page ii for explanation of footnotes.

[317] CCH ¶19,832a; Sec. 127(11.1); Reg. 2900(11).

[318] CCH ¶19,829p; Sec. 127(9) "qualified expenditure".

[319] CCH ¶19,832d; Sec. 127(11.4).

[320] CCH ¶19,832mn; Sec. 127(26).

reduced from its current rate of 20% to 15% for taxation years after 2013, with the rate being prorated for taxation years that straddle January 1, 2014. The refundable investment tax credit, which is currently 40% of the 20% investment tax credit amount, would be reduced accordingly to 40% of the new 15% amount. These measures were released in draft legislation issued on August 14, 2012.]

The rate for qualified expenditures made prior to 1995 is 30% for scientific research and experimental development that is carried out in the Maritimes and 20% in any other area in Canada. [As a result of 2012 Budget measures, it is proposed that the investment tax credit be reduced from its current rate of 20% to 15% for taxation years after 2013, with the rate being prorated for taxation years that straddle January 1, 2014. The refundable investment tax credit, which is currently 40% of the 20% investment tax credit amount, would be reduced accordingly to 40% of the new 15% amount. These measures were released in draft legislation issued on August 14, 2012.] Where the expenditure is made after 1994 but is pursuant to a written agreement entered into by the taxpayer before February 22, 1994 for scientific research and experimental development carried out in the Maritimes, the 30% rate will apply to that expenditure.

In order to provide a 35% investment tax credit to smaller corporations, an additional credit is provided on qualifying expenditures available to certain corporations in certain circumstances. The additional credit of 15% plus the 20% credit available to all corporations [As a result of 2012 Budget measures, it is proposed that the investment tax credit be reduced from its current rate of 20% to 15% for taxation years after 2013, with the rate being prorated for taxation years that straddle January 1, 2014. The refundable investment tax credit, which is currently 40% of the 20% investment tax credit amount, would be reduced accordingly to 40% of the new 15% amount. These measures were released in draft legislation issued on August 14, 2012.] on qualifying expenditures provides the 35% credit for smaller corporations.[321] Where a corporation that would have been entitled to a credit at the 35% rate repays assistance that had previously reduced the investment tax credit, the credit will be reinstated at the full 35% rate.[322] Expired assistance, where the taxpayer ceases to be entitled to the assistance, is treated as repaid assistance.[323]

The quantum of additional credit arising in any year is limited by the "expenditure limit". This limit sets a maximum annual amount of qualifying expenditures upon which the additional credit may be claimed. The expenditure limit has been increased several times in recent years, most recently in the 2008 federal Budget. It is determined by a formula, described below.[324]

For a taxation year ending after February 25, 2008, the expenditure limit has been increased to $3 million per year (up from $2 million), for a maximum investment tax credit of $1.05 million (i.e., 35% of $3 million).

See page ii for explanation of footnotes.

[321] CCH ¶19,831a; Sec. 127(10.1).   [323] CCH ¶19,831h; Sec. 127(10.8).
[322] CCH ¶19,831g; Sec. 127(10.7).   [324] CCH ¶19,831b; Sec. 127(10.2).

However, the expenditure limit is phased out if the taxable income of the corporation and its associated corporations for the preceding taxation year exceeded $400,000, at a rate of $10 for each $1 of taxable income, such that the expenditure limit is phased out entirely at the taxable income amount of $700,000. Beginning with the 2010 taxation year, the $400,000 amount is replaced by the amount of $500,000 in respect of the preceding year, since the small business limit is increased to $500,000 effective for the 2009 year, meaning that the phase-out starts when the taxable income for the preceding year exceeds $500,000 and is complete when such taxable income equals or exceeds $800,000. Furthermore, the expenditure limit is phased out if the taxable capital employed in Canada of the corporation and its associated corporations for the preceding year exceeded $10 million, at a rate of $3 for every $40 of taxable capital, such that the expenditure limit is phased out completely at a taxable capital amount of $50 million.

The previous expenditure limit, generally applicable beginning with the 2007 taxation year, had a maximum amount of $2 million. The expenditure limit was phased out at a rate of $10 for each $1 of taxable income over $400,000 in the preceding taxation year, such that it was phased out entirely at a taxable income amount of $600,000. The expenditure limit was also phased out at a rate of $2 for every $5 of taxable capital employed in Canada in excess of $10 million, such that it was fully phased out at a taxable capital amount of $15 million.

For a taxation year straddling February 26, 2008, the current expenditure limit is prorated, based on the number of days in the year on or after February 26, 2008. The expenditure limit relating to the portion of the taxation year before February 26, 2008 will be based on the previous expenditure limit.

The explanatory notes to Bill C-50 provide the following example where two associated corporations have a taxation year straddling the February 26, 2008 date:

Example:

A Co and B Co are CCPCs and have taxation years ending on November 30. For the 2007 taxation year, each corporation had $200,000 in taxable income and $10 million of taxable capital employed in Canada. In the 2008 taxation year, each corporation spent $2 million on SR&ED carried on in Canada. For the 2008 taxation year, A Co and B Co are associated with each other and have agreed to share equally all benefits available to them under the Act

For the 2008 taxation year, their expenditure limit — under the old formula — is $0, because their combined taxable capital employed in Canada exceeds $15 million. Neither A Co nor B Co can, therefore, claim the 15% enhanced ITCs.

The corporations' combined expenditure limit for 2008 — under the new formula — would be $2.25 million. This is not the amount they can actually use as their expenditure limit, however, because of the pro-rating described below.

The corporations' expenditure limit under the old formula is $0 and the expenditure limit under the new formula is $2.25 million. Because the corporations' 2008 taxation year includes February 26, 2008, any increase in the expenditure limit for that taxation year is prorated based on the number of days that are in that year and that are after February 25, 2008:

$$\$2.25 \text{ million} \times 279/366 = \$1,715,164$$

A Co and B Co have agreed to equally share the expenditure limit of $1,715,164, thereby entitling each corporation to claim the 15% enhanced ITCs on $857,582.

Previously, for taxation years after 2003, the phase-out began at $300,000 of taxable income of the corporation and associated corporations, and generally for taxation years commencing in and after 1994 and up to and including 2003, the phase-out began at $200,000 of taxable income. The taxable capital of the corporation and associated corporations also served to phase out the expenditure limit, which was previously limited to the "business limit" of the corporation and associated corporations, and which would be phased out when the taxable capital amount exceeded $10 million.

In the case of corporations associated at any time in the year, the annual expenditure limit must be shared by all of the CCPCs in the associated group. The corporations can file a prescribed form allocating the limit amongst themselves.[325] If they fail to file the prescribed form within 30 days after written notification that the form is required, the Minister can allocate the expenditure limit to each of the associated corporations.[326]

For taxation years ending after March 22, 2004, the enhanced investment tax credit is not limited simply because of a majority interest in share capital owned by a group of common investors. Because the enhanced investment tax credit must be shared by an associated group and may be reduced or eliminated based on the taxable income and capital of that associated group, certain CCPCs controlled by a group of common investors will not be considered associated, for purposes of determining the enhanced investment tax credit, if the following three conditions are met:

- the corporation is associated with the other corporation, but would not be associated were it not for the extended definition of "group of persons" (see ¶15,500);

- the corporation issued shares to one or more persons who were also issued shares by the other corporation; and

- at least one shareholder of the corporation is not a shareholder of the other corporation or *vice versa*.[327]

This relieving provision can only apply if the Minister is satisfied that the CCPCs seeking relief are not controlled in law or in fact by the same person or group of persons, and were not structured to gain access to multiple expenditure limits.[328]

Special rules are provided where a CCPC has more than one taxation year ending in the same calendar year and is associated with another CCPC in two or more of those years. In that case the amount allocated in the first

---

See page ii for explanation of footnotes.

[325] CCH ¶19,831c; Sec. 127(10.3). [327] CCH ¶19,831bc; Sec. 127(10.22).
[326] CCH ¶19,831d; Sec. 127(10.4). [328] CCH ¶19,831be; Sec. 127(10.23).

¶8343

year must also be the amount allocated in every other taxation year ending in the calendar year.

In the case of a short taxation year, the expenditure limit is prorated by the number of days in the taxation year over 365. This prorating applies both to associated and unassociated corporations.[329]

(6) *Qualified property*. The rate for "qualified property" (defined below as prescribed buildings or machinery and equipment) acquired for use in the Maritimes or a prescribed offshore region after 1994 is 10%. For qualified property acquired after 1988 and before 1995, the rate is 15%. Such property that is acquired under a written agreement entered into by the taxpayer before February 22, 1994 or was under construction before February 22, 1994 will continue to be eligible for the 15% rate.

Maritimes refers to Nova Scotia, New Brunswick, Prince Edward Island, Newfoundland and Labrador, and the Gaspé Peninsula. "Prescribed offshore region" is defined to be the submarine areas of the waters above the submarine area around these provinces and area mentioned above and extending 200 nautical miles out from the coast.[330] Other than the credit for qualified small-business property (see (2) below) acquired after December 2, 1992 and before 1994, there is no longer any investment tax credit for qualified property used elsewhere in Canada.

"Qualified property" is defined as prescribed buildings or machinery and equipment acquired by the taxpayer after June 23, 1975. It should be noted that additions made after June 23, 1975 to buildings, construction of which commenced on or before that date, will normally qualify. To qualify, the property must be depreciable property, prescribed by regulation,[331] acquired after June 23, 1975 and must not have been used for any purpose prior to being acquired by the taxpayer. It will not include a certified property or an approved project property.[332] The property must be a prescribed building or prescribed machinery and equipment.[333]

A prescribed building includes a building or grain elevator erected on land owned or leased by the taxpayer, which is included in Classes 1, 3, 6, 20, 24, and 27 or paragraph (*c*), (*d*), or (*e*) of Class 8, or paragraph (*g*) of Class 10, if it were not for Class 28 or 41.

The definition of "prescribed machinery and equipment" is extremely broad and will include most capital expenditures falling into Classes 8, 9, 10, 15, 21, 22, 24, 27, 28, 29, 34, 39, 40, and 43, as well as electrical generating equipment falling in Class 1 or 2, and ships falling in Class 7. Notable exclusions from the definition include automobiles and trucks designed for highway use, except logging trucks acquired after March 31, 1977 weighing in excess of 16,000 pounds, and railway rolling stock.

See page ii for explanation of footnotes.

[329] CCH ¶19,831f; Sec. 127(10.6).
[330] CCH ¶19,832y; Reg. 4609.
[331] CCH ¶19,832p; Reg. 4600.

[332] CCH ¶19,829q, ¶19,832r, ¶19,832t; Sec. 127(9) "qualified property"; Reg. 4602, Reg. 4604.
[333] CCH ¶19,832p; Reg. 4600.

To qualify for the credit, the prescribed building, machinery, or equipment must be used primarily in one of a broad range of qualified activities, including manufacturing and processing of goods for sale or lease, resource-related activity, farming, fishing, logging, the storing of grain, processing industrial minerals, Canadian field processing (after 1996), the harvesting of peat, or producing or processing electrical energy or steam in the Maritime region where the property was acquired after 1991. There is no minimum-use period, nor any provision for recapture of the credit in the event there is a change to a non-qualifying use or the asset is sold.

The credit may also be claimed by a lessor acquiring and leasing prescribed property to a lessee who uses it primarily for any of the purposes described above (except the producing of energy or steam), provided that the first lessee begins to use the property after June 23, 1975. The tax credit is available to all lessors in respect of the acquisition of the prescribed building. However, for a lessor to obtain the credit in respect of the acquisition of machinery or equipment, the property must be leased in the ordinary course of business by a lessor which is a *corporation* whose principal business consists of:

(a) leasing property;

(b) manufacturing property that it sells or leases;

(c) lending money;

(d) purchasing conditional sales contracts, accounts receivable, or other obligations representing part or all of the sale price of merchandise or services; or

(e) selling or servicing a type of property which the corporation also leases.

The definition of "qualified property" was amended in 1994 for 1985 and subsequent taxation years with respect to fishing vessels that are leased by an individual taxpayer (other than a trust) to a corporation controlled by the individual for use in a fishing business in connection with one or more commercial fishing licences issued by the government of Canada to the individual. Such a vessel, including the furniture, fittings, and equipment attached to it, is a qualified property and is eligible for the investment tax credit.

In addition, the above uses of qualified property do not include any of the following activities:[334]

(a) storing (other than the storing of grain, shipping, selling and leasing of finished goods);

(b) purchasing of raw materials;

(c) administration, including clerical and personnel activities;

See page ii for explanation of footnotes.

[334] CCH ¶19,832; Sec. 127(11).

¶8343

(d) purchase and resale operations;

(e) data processing; and

(f) providing facilities for employees, including cafeterias, clinics, and recreational facilities.

[¶8344] Recapture of Investment Tax Credit

Investment tax credits on property acquired in the current taxation year or any of the 20 preceding years (10 preceding years for property acquired before 1998), the cost of which was a qualified expenditure incurred in respect of scientific research and experimental development, are recaptured if the property, or property which incorporated it, is converted to commercial use, or is disposed of without having previously been converted to commercial use.[335]

If the property is disposed of to an arm's length person, the recapture is limited to the proceeds of disposition of the property multiplied by the rate that originally applied in computing the investment tax credit in respect of the expenditure. If the property is disposed of to a non-arm's length person or is converted to commercial use, the recapture is limited to the fair market value of the property at the time of disposition or conversion multiplied by the ITC rate that originally applied in computing the investment tax credit in respect of the expenditure. The rate that originally applied in computing the ITC would normally be 20%, or 35% in the case of certain expenditures incurred by Canadian-controlled private corporations. [As a result of 2012 Budget measures, it is proposed that the investment tax credit be reduced from its current rate of 20% to 15% for taxation years after 2013, with the rate being prorated for taxation years that straddle January 1, 2014. The refundable investment tax credit, which is currently 40% of the 20% investment tax credit amount, would be reduced accordingly to 40% of the new 15% amount. These measures were released in draft legislation issued on August 14, 2012.] (See the chart at ¶8342 for the investment tax credit rates that apply to qualified scientific research and experimental development expenditures.)

Investment tax credits in respect of property used for SR&ED are recaptured where the property is sold or converted to commercial use. It is a question of fact whether a property has been converted to commercial use. When determining if shared-use equipment was converted to commercial use, it is the CRA's position that a conversion will only occur when the usage of the equipment for SR&ED becomes incidental. For this purpose, there will only be recapture of the ITC in respect of shared-use equipment when the property has been all or substantially all converted to commercial use.

[335] CCH ¶19,840–19,848; Sec. 127(27)–(35).

[Pending technical amendments would amend the ITC recapture rules applicable to dispositions and conversions of shared-use equipment that occur after December 20, 2002. Once enacted, these amendments will reflect that, since only a portion of the cost of the property that is shared-use equipment (25% or 50%) is a qualified expenditure, then only this percentage of the proceeds of disposition or the fair market value will be included in the recapture calculation, and not the full amount. Furthermore, recapture of the credit will apply where the cost (or a portion of the cost) of the property would have been a qualified expenditure, but for the application of the 180-day-unpaid-amount rule (see ¶8343). The revised technical proposals that were released on July 16, 2010 reprise these amendments that are not enacted yet.]

A similar recapture of the credit is required if a child care space or other amount that qualified for the child care space amount credit is of, ceases to be available, or is converted to another use, within 60 months of the creation of the child care space.[336] See ¶8343.

[¶8345] Refundable Investment Tax Credit

[¶8350] Taxpayers Eligible for Refundable Investment Tax Credit

An additional incentive with respect to investment tax credits earned for qualifying assets or qualifying expenditures is provided for taxpayers who are individuals, qualifying corporations, trusts (each beneficiary of which is an individual), or qualifying corporations and Canadian-controlled private corporations other than qualifying corporations and excluded corporations.[337] The investment tax credit earned or a portion thereof may, at the option of the taxpayer, be paid in cash to the taxpayer as a tax refund. The percentage not so refunded will be available to be used in the ordinary manner. The earning of investment tax credits thus becomes of much more interest to taxpayers who are not currently taxable and who cannot use the credit to obtain a refund of tax paid in earlier years. The investment tax credits earned in this period can provide a positive cash flow to the taxpayer instead of being accumulated until such time as the taxpayer is in a position to pay tax.

As noted previously, however, investment tax credits which qualify for the tax refund have been significantly reduced. They are now basically earned only on qualified property and certified property in the Maritimes and qualified expenditures in respect of scientific research and experimental development throughout Canada.

Depending upon the status of the taxpayer and the nature of the expenditure which entitled the taxpayer to an investment tax credit, the rate

---

See page ii for explanation of footnotes.

[336] CCH ¶19,840d, ¶19,843; Sec. 127(27.1),   [337] CCH ¶19,900; Sec. 127.1(1).
127(30).

of the refundable investment tax credit varies from 100% to 0% of the taxpayer's investment tax credit.

For purposes of calculating the refundable investment tax credit, the following chart depicts the general categories and rates:

Type of taxpayer	Rate
Taxpayers filing special returns and non-taxable persons	0%
Individuals, trusts and qualifying corporations which are excluded corporations	40%
Qualifying corporations which are not excluded corporations	100%
Canadian-controlled private corporations other than a qualifying corporation or an excluded corporation	100%

The refund of the refundable investment tax credit may not be claimed in conjunction with the special returns permitted with respect to rights or things on death, the separate return permitted when the beneficiary of a testamentary trust dies between the end of the year of the trust and the end of the calendar year, and the separate return permitted when a partner or a proprietor dies between the end of a fiscal period and the end of the calendar year. A trustee in bankruptcy can claim a refundable investment tax credit of the bankrupt individual in the tax return he or she is required to file on behalf of the bankrupt in respect of income arising from the bankrupt's estate or business. The bankrupt individual cannot, however, claim it in the second separate return that he or she must file for the period from the date of bankruptcy to December 31. See ¶9009.

Persons exempt from tax are not entitled to a refund in respect of refundable investment tax credit.

[¶8355] Individuals, Trusts, and Qualifying Corporations

The definition of "refundable investment tax credit" provides for a refundable amount of 40% of the investment tax credits earned in the taxation year [As a result of 2012 Budget measures, it is proposed that the investment tax credit be reduced from its current rate of 20% to 15% for taxation years after 2013, with the rate being prorated for taxation years that straddle January 1, 2014. The refundable investment tax credit, which is currently 40% of the 20% investment tax credit amount, would be reduced accordingly to 40% of the new 15% amount. These measures were released in draft legislation issued on August 14, 2012.] by an individual, a trust (each beneficiary of which is an individual, other than another trust), or a qualifying corporation.[338] The refundable amount is based on the total investment tax credits earned during the year in respect of property, other than a

---

See page ii for explanation of footnotes.

[338] CCH ¶19,902b; Sec. 127.1(2) "refundable investment tax credit".

qualified small-business property, and qualified expenditures in respect of scientific research and experimental development. The refundable amount is reduced to the extent that investment tax credits are applied to reduce the taxpayer's tax liability for the year.

The investment tax credit for a year to which the refundable percentage is applied is reduced to the extent that the investment tax credit in respect of the property acquired or expenditures made may be reasonably considered to be deducted for the year or a preceding year. The investment tax credit of a trust for a year to which the percentage is applied is also reduced by the portion of the investment tax credit that the trust designates in favour of its beneficiaries as may reasonably be considered to be an investment tax credit earned as a result of acquisitions or expenditures made in the relevant period.

[¶8360] Qualifying Corporations

As previously discussed at ¶8355, a qualifying corporation is eligible for the refundable credit of 40% of the applicable investment tax credit. Furthermore, a qualifying corporation can claim the fully refundable 35% enhanced tax credit in respect of SR&ED qualified expenditures of a current nature, as described in more detail in the commentary below [As a result of 2012 Budget measures, it is proposed that the investment tax credit be reduced from its current rate of 20% to 15% for taxation years after 2013, with the rate being prorated for taxation years that straddle January 1, 2014. The refundable investment tax credit, which is currently 40% of the 20% investment tax credit amount, would be reduced accordingly to 40% of the new 15% amount. These measures were released in draft legislation issued on August 14, 2012.].

A "qualifying corporation" for a particular taxation year ending in a calendar year is defined as a corporation that is a Canadian-controlled private corporation (CCPC) in the particular taxation year, the taxable income of which for its immediately preceding taxation year does not exceed the "qualifying income limit" of the corporation for the particular year.[339] If the corporation is associated in the particular taxation year with one or more other corporations, the taxable income of each associated corporation for its last taxation year that ended in the preceding calendar year is combined with the corporation's taxable income in its immediately preceding taxation year for the purposes of the qualifying income limit threshold.

Subject to the transitional provisions noted below, for 2010 and subsequent taxation years, the maximum "qualifying income limit" of a corporation for a particular taxation year is $500,000.[340] However, the qualifying income limit is reduced if the corporation's taxable capital employed in Canada for its preceding taxation year, along with the taxable capital of its

---

See page ii for explanation of footnotes.

[339] CCH ¶19,902b; Sec. 127.1(2)"qualifying corporation".

[340] CCH ¶19,902ac; Sec. 127.1(2) "qualifying income limit".

¶8360

associated corporations for their taxation years ending in the calendar year that ended before the conclusion of the particular taxation year, exceeds $10 million. The qualifying income limit is reduced at a rate of $12,500 per $1 million of taxable capital in excess of the $10 million threshold, such that the qualifying income limit is reduced to nil if such taxable capital equals $50 million or more. For taxation years beginning after February 26, 2008, and ending before 2010, the maximum qualifying income limit is $400,000, and for 2010 taxation years that begin before 2010, the maximum amount is prorated between the $400,000 and $500,000 amounts, based on the number of days in the taxation year before 2010 and after 2009, respectively.

For taxation years ending before February 26, 2008, a qualifying corporation for a particular taxation year is a CCPC, the taxable income of which for its preceding taxation year together with the taxable incomes of all associated corporations for their preceding taxation years does not exceed the total of the "business limits" (see ¶8430) of the corporation and the associated corporations for the preceding years. As noted above, the current definition of qualifying corporation refers to the concept of the corporation's qualifying income limit rather than its business limit. Therefore, for taxation years straddling the February 26, 2008 date, the taxable income threshold is based on the former business limit and the current qualifying income limit, prorated based on the number of days before that date and after that date, respectively.

A corporation's taxable income for the preceding taxation year, for the above purposes, does not take into account the "specified future tax consequences" for that preceding taxation year.[341] As defined, the phrase "specified future tax consequences" includes the consequence of loss carrybacks from subsequent years, reversals of income inclusions where an option is exercised in a subsequent year, plus the consequence of a reduction of Canadian exploration expenses and Canadian development expenses previously purported to be renounced by a corporation, generally where the purported renunciation took place within 90 days after the end of a calendar year so that the effective date of the renunciation was the last day of the calendar year.

As noted, a qualifying corporation is entitled to the 40% refundable investment tax credit described above in ¶8355.

However, a qualifying corporation, other than an excluded corporation (see below), may be entitled to a 100% refund on investment tax credits earned in respect of current qualified expenditures rather than the 40% refund. The 100% refund applies to the 35% investment tax credit for qualified expenditures in respect of scientific research and experimental development carried on in Canada, other than capital expenditures. The 40% refund applies to capital expenditures for scientific research and experi-

---

See page ii for explanation of footnotes.

[341] CCH ¶28,272ba; Sec. 248(1) "specified future tax consequence".

mental development which qualify for the 35% investment tax credit. To the extent that the investment tax credit is applied to reduce the taxpayer's tax liability for the year or, in the case of a cooperative corporation, allocated to its members, the amount is not refundable.

The 35% investment tax credit, which, as noted, is fully (100%) refundable, applies to a maximum "expenditure limit" of $3 million of qualified expenditures of a current nature in respect of SR&ED for taxation years ending after February 25, 2008 (previously, the expenditure limit was $2 million). However, the expenditure limit for a taxation year is phased out if the taxable income of the corporation and its associated corporations for the preceding taxation year exceeds $400,000, at a rate of $10 for each $1 of taxable income, such that the expenditure limit is phased out entirely at the taxable income amount of $700,000 (beginning with the 2010 taxation year, the $400,000 amount is replaced by a $500,000 amount in respect of the preceding year, meaning that the phase-out starts when the taxable income for the preceding year exceeds $500,000 and is complete when such taxable income equals or exceeds $800,000). Furthermore, the expenditure limit is reduced if the taxable capital employed in Canada of the corporation and its associated corporations for the preceding year exceeds $10 million, at a rate of $3 for every $40 of taxable capital, such that the expenditure limit is phased out completely at a taxable capital amount of $50 million.[342] (The previous expenditure limit, generally applicable beginning with the 2007 taxation year, had a maximum amount of $2 million. The expenditure limit was phased out at a rate of $10 for each $1 of taxable income over $400,000 in the preceding taxation year, such that it was phased out entirely at a taxable income amount of $600,000. The expenditure limit was also phased out at a rate of $2 for every $5 of taxable capital employed in Canada in excess of $10 million, such that it was fully phased out at a taxable capital amount of $15 million.)

The fully refundable 35% credit does not apply to an "excluded corporation", which is defined as a corporation controlled directly or indirectly, in any manner whatsoever, by one or more persons exempt from tax under Part I, Her Majesty in right of a province, a Canadian municipality or any other public authority, or any combination of such persons.[343] An excluded corporation is also a corporation that is related to any such person.

The portion of the investment tax credit which is not refundable may be applied to reduce the taxpayer's tax liability for the current, preceding three, or following 20 taxation years. The 20-year carryforward period applies to credits earned in the 1998 and subsequent taxation years; previously, the carryforward period was 10 years.

When the current expenditure qualifies for both the 40% refund and the 100% refund, the latter will apply.

See page ii for explanation of footnotes.

[342] CCH ¶19,831a, ¶19,831b; Sec. 127(10.1), 127(10.2). [343] CCH ¶19,902; Sec. 127.1(2) "excluded corporation".

¶8360

[¶8365] Canadian-Controlled Private Corporations Other than Qualifying Corporations

A CCPC that is not a qualifying corporation because its taxable income exceeds its qualifying income limit (or business limit) for the preceding year can nonetheless qualify for the refundable 35% investment tax credit in respect of SR&ED qualified expenditures (40% of the credit for capital expenditures, 100% of the credit for expenditures of a current nature).[344] In such case, the amount of the refundable investment credit will be reduced as the expenditure limit for the year is reduced in the manner described at ¶8360. For example, if a CCPC incurred $3 million of qualified expenditures of a current nature in 2010, and its taxable income in 2009 was $650,000 ($150,000 over the $500,000 qualifying income limit), it would be entitled to a 100% refund of the 35% credit earned in respect of $1.5 million of expenditures.[345] The remaining (20%) investment credit in respect of the other $1.5 million of expenditures would not be refundable.

[¶8370] Other Taxpayers

Taxpayers other than individuals, qualifying corporations, and trusts (each beneficiary of which is an individual or a qualifying corporation) may also qualify for a refund of investment tax credits, but only with respect to qualified acquisitions and expenditures made before 1988, or in the case of qualified Canadian exploration expenditures, those made in taxation years commencing before 1988. The rate of refund will vary between 20% and 40% depending on the nature of expenditure made or property acquired.

[¶8371] Filing of Form T2038

The refundable investment tax credit is claimed by filing the prescribed form (T2038). The form is filed either with the tax return for the year or at a later date amending a return previously filed. Upon filing the prescribed form, the taxpayer is deemed to have paid on account of tax for the year to which the return relates an amount equal to his refundable investment tax credit for the year. It does not appear to be possible to request this treatment for only a portion of the refundable investment tax credit for the year. The payment of tax is deemed to have taken place on the date the return is filed if the prescribed form is included with the return or on the date the prescribed form amending a previous return is filed. In cases where the taxpayer is not otherwise subject to tax, this deemed payment of tax will put the taxpayer in the position of having made an overpayment of tax which will be refunded, together with interest.

See page ii for explanation of footnotes.

[344] CCH ¶19,903; Sec. 127.1(2.01).

[345] CCH ¶19,831a, ¶19,831b; Sec. 127(10.1), 127(10.2).

[¶8372] Balance of Investment Tax Credit

When the refundable investment tax credit is treated as a deemed payment of tax, that amount reduces the investment tax credit otherwise available to be deducted. The remaining investment tax credit earned in a year, if any, remains available to be deducted.[346]

[¶8375] Part VI (Financial Institutions) Tax Credit

[¶8380] Part VI Tax Credit

Large financial institutions are subject to a tax under Part VI of the Act on capital over $1 billion employed in Canada (threshold increased from $200 million effective July 1, 2006). Life insurance corporations are subject to Part VI tax as well.[347] See ¶13,210.[348] Unused Part VI tax credits may be carried back three years and forward seven years.

Part I tax is creditable against Part VI tax[349] to allow corporations to avoid reducing the foreign tax credit available in other countries for Canadian income tax paid.

The term "unused Part VI tax credit" for a taxation year is defined as a corporation's Part VI tax for the year before it is reduced by the Part I tax credit, minus the difference between the corporation's Part I tax (including surtax) for the year and the lesser of its Canadian surtax credit and its Part I.3 tax before any reduction for the surtax credit. Therefore, Part I tax that was already credited under Part I.3 will not also reduce the amount of Part VI tax that may be eligible for carryover to other years. As a rule, the definition of unused Part VI tax credit is determined without including the additional Part VI tax payable by life insurance corporations.

Unused Part VI tax credits must be utilized in the order they arose. An unused Part VI tax credit for a taxation year applied in another taxation year may not be claimed again in a subsequent year.[350]

[¶8385] Rates for Trusts

[¶8390] Tax Payable by Inter Vivos Trust

In general, trusts are taxed at the rates prescribed for individuals but are not allowed personal tax credits. However, if a trust is an *inter vivos* trust, including a mutual fund trust, its income is taxed at the flat rate of 29%.[351] A trust other than a related segregated fund trust or a mutual fund trust is

---

See page ii for explanation of footnotes.

[346] CCH ¶19,904; Sec. 127.1(3).

[347] CCH ¶24,470, ¶24,480; Sec. 190(1), 190.1.

[348] CCH ¶19,690, ¶39,187a; Sec. 125.2; Form T921.

[349] CCH ¶24,482a; Sec. 190.1(3).

[350] CCH ¶19,691; Sec. 125.2(2).

[351] CCH ¶19,250, ¶19,255; Sec. 122(1)(a), 122(1.1); Interp. Bul. IT-406R2.

subject to the alternative minimum tax.[352] The trust is also subject to provincial tax at the relevant rate for the particular province.

If all of the following conditions are met, an *inter vivos* trust other than a mutual fund trust is taxed at the ordinary marginal rates for individuals instead of at 29%:[353]

(1) the *inter vivos* trust was established before June 18, 1971 and was resident in Canada on that date and without interruption until the end of the taxation year;

(2) it did not carry on an active business in the year;

(3) it did not receive property by way of gift after June 18, 1971;

(4) it did not incur, after June 18, 1971, any debt or other obligation to pay an amount to, or guaranteed by, any person with whom any beneficiary of the trust was not dealing at arm's length; and

(5) it did not receive property after December 17, 1999, as a result of a transfer from another trust that did not result in any change of beneficial ownership of the property.

If an *inter vivos* trust is a "SIFT trust" for a taxation year, it may be subject to an additional tax in respect of its "taxable SIFT trust distributions", which are essentially equal to the before-tax amount of the SIFT trust's "non-portfolio earnings" distributed to beneficiaries. This additional tax, along with the regular 29% tax on trusts, is meant to parallel the general corporate tax rate and is discussed at ¶7282.

[¶8395] Manufacturing and Processing Profits

[¶8400] Calculation of Credit on Manufacturing and Processing Profits

Corporations are taxed at a reduced rate on their Canadian manufacturing and processing profits. The Canadian manufacturing and processing profits credit is not available in respect of income that is eligible for the small business deduction. The rate set for the manufacturing and processing tax credit has fluctuated over the years. The rate has been 7% since 1994, but, beginning in 2008, increased to be equal to the "general rate reduction percentage" (see ¶8475). This means that the rate is 8.5% for 2008, 9% for 2009, 10% for 2010, 11.5% for 2011, and 13% for 2012 and subsequent taxation years, subject to proration for non-calendar years.[354]

Currently, the manufacturing and processing tax credit (on income not subject to the small business deduction) is the "general rate reduction percentage" for the year multiplied by the lesser of:

See page ii for explanation of footnotes.

[352] CCH ¶19,999a; Sec. 127.5.
[353] CCH ¶19,260; Sec. 122(2).

[354] CCH ¶19,635; Sec. 125.1(1); Interp. Bul. IT-145R.

(a) the amount by which Canadian manufacturing and processing profits exceed income subject to the small business credit; and

(b) the amount by which taxable income exceeds the aggregate of:

(i) income subject to the small business credit;

(ii) $^{10}/_4$ of the amount of the foreign tax credit on business income deducted for the year (see ¶8565). (For 2001 and subsequent taxation years, the amount is determined excluding the effect of the special CCPC rate reduction (discussed at ¶8475)); and

(iii) where the corporation was a Canadian-controlled private corporation throughout the year, its "aggregate investment income" for the year as defined in ¶9027.

The manufacturing and processing profits deduction is now available to corporations that generate electrical energy for sale or produce steam for sale.[355]

Manufacturing or processing does not include the following activities:[356]

(a) farming or fishing;

(b) logging;

(c) construction;

(d) operating an oil or gas well or extracting petroleum or natural gas from a natural accumulation of petroleum or natural gas;

(e) extracting minerals from a mineral resource;

(f) processing ore (other than iron ore or tar sands ore) from a mineral resource located in Canada to any stage not beyond the prime metal stage or its equivalent;

(g) processing iron ore from a mineral resource located in Canada to any stage not beyond the pellet stage or its equivalent;

(h) processing tar sands ore from a mineral resource located in Canada to any stage not beyond the crude oil stage or its equivalent;

(i) producing industrial minerals;

(j) producing or processing electrical energy or steam for sale;

(k) processing natural gas as part of a business of selling or distributing gas in the course of operating a public utility;

---

[355] CCH ¶19,637; Sec. 125.1(2).   [356] CCH ¶19,641; Sec. 125.1(3) "manufacturing or processing"; Interp. Bul. IT-411R.

¶8400

(l) processing heavy crude oil recovered from a natural reservoir in Canada to a stage that is not beyond the crude oil stage or its equivalent;

(m) Canadian field processing (defined in ¶4210); or

(n) manufacturing and processing where less than 10% of the gross revenue from active business carried on in Canada is from the selling or leasing of goods manufactured or processed in Canada, and from manufacturing and processing in Canada of goods for sale or lease by others (including the taxpayer's share of any such revenues earned by a partnership).

A taxpayer's assembly of kits containing automobile and truck parts for export to offshore vehicle manufacturers constituted "processing".[357] The taxpayer was held to be engaged in manufacturing, since it manufactured the parts it needed to repair hydraulic components. It was unrealistic to split its activities into a true manufacturing component (i.e., the manufacture of parts specified by a customer) and a repair component.[358] The corporate taxpayer's business consisted primarily of applying rubber covers to roll cores for pulp and paper industry mills. The business was held to be "manufacturing and processing" its goods "for sale". It was replacing the rubber covers (considered to be specially manufactured products) and selling them to the customer.[359] In addition to providing services related to the drilling of oil and gas wells, the taxpayer provided a related specialized product. The profits received from the processing of the specialized product could be treated as manufacturing or processing profits.[360]

On the other hand, the production of asphalt for use in the taxpayer's paving contracts, which were essentially contacts for work and materials, did not entitle the taxpayer to claim an M&P tax credit.[361] The dispensing of prescription tablets or capsules does not constitute "processing". The drugs were already in dosage form when received from the manufacturer, and were not changed or made more marketable in being dispensed.[362] The installation of mufflers on automobiles does not constitute creating new goods for sale.[363] The processing and developing of X-ray films of patients for diagnostic purposes by radiologists was found to constitute a business of providing a service and not of providing goods for sale.[364]

For the capital cost allowance available for manufacturing and processing machinery and equipment, see ¶4210.

See page ii for explanation of footnotes.

[357] TDS Group Limited, 2005 DTC 786.

[358] Coopers & Lybrand, 92 DTC 6452.

[359] Stowe-Woodward Inc., 92 DTC 6149.

[360] Halliburton Services Ltd., 90 DTC 6320.

[361] Will-Kare Paving & Contracting Ltd., 2000 DTC 6467, Nova Construction Company Limited, 85 DTC 5594.

[362] Harvey C. Smith Drugs Ltd., 92 DTC 6349.

[363] Tenneco Canada Inc., 91 DTC 5207.

[364] Dixie X-Ray Associates Ltd., 88 DTC 6076, Reg Rad Tech Ltd., 91 DTC 5518.

[¶8405] Formula for Calculation and Definition of Terms

The formula for the calculation of "Canadian manufacturing and processing profits" is prescribed by regulation.[365] The formula, which does not apply to corporations which qualify for the small manufacturers' rule (see ¶8420), is as follows:

$$MP = ABI \times \frac{MC + ML}{C + L}$$

Where:

    MP = Canadian manufacturing and processing profits
    ABI = Adjusted business income
    MC = Cost of manufacturing and processing capital
     C = Cost of capital
    ML = Cost of manufacturing and processing labour
     L = Cost of labour

The above terms are defined as follows:[366]

(1) *Adjusted business income* (ABI) for companies with no resource income is income minus losses from active business carried on in Canada. The meanings of "active business" and "income from an active business" are discussed at ¶8440.

(2) *Cost of capital* (C) is 10% of the "gross cost" of depreciable property owned by the taxpayer plus the total rental cost of such property rented by the taxpayer.

(3) *Gross cost of depreciable property* means the actual capital cost without adjustments for grants and subsidies, deemed 15% addition to cost, capitalized interest, forgiveness of debts, or the deemed disposition of capital property resulting from the acquisition of control:[367] that is, the amount that would normally be the actual out-of-pocket cost. The gross cost is in respect of property that has become available for use. The gross cost of depreciable property and the rental cost for companies that do not have resource income do not include the cost of property used in an active business carried on outside Canada or to earn investment income.

(4) *Cost of labour* (L) is the total of:

(a) salaries and wages paid or payable to employees of the corporation for services performed during the year; and

(b) amounts paid to non-employees for management or administration of the corporation, scientific research, and services that would normally be performed by an employee.

The cost of labour does not include amounts which are included in the "cost of capital" for the year or amounts which are related to an active business

---

See page ii for explanation of footnotes.

[365] CCH ¶19,653; Reg. 5200.
[366] CCH ¶19,657; Reg. 5202.
[367] CCH ¶19,657; Reg. 5202 gross cost.

¶8405

carried on by the corporation outside Canada. For the purposes of calculating cost of labour, salaries and wages include salaries, wages, and commissions but *not* any other type of remuneration such as pension benefits, retiring allowances, directors' fees, employee benefits, and stock option benefits.

The taxpayers' "cost of labour" was increased to include their proportionate share of the "cost of labour" of a related corporation to which they had paid management fees. The result was a reduction in the MPP tax credits claimed by the taxpayers.[368]

(5) *Cost of manufacturing and processing capital* (MC) is $^{100}/_{85}$ times the portion of the cost of capital that relates to assets used directly in qualified activities. This amount may not exceed the cost of capital.

(6) *Cost of manufacturing and processing labour* (ML) is $^{100}/_{75}$ times the portion of the cost of labour that relates to employees or outsiders directly engaged in qualified activities. This amount may not exceed the cost of labour.

(7) *Qualified activities,* as used in the definitions in (5) and (6) above, means the activities performed in Canada *directly* in connection with manufacturing and processing of goods for sale or lease. It *includes* the following activities if they are performed in Canada in connection with manufacturing and processing of goods for sale or lease:

(a) engineering design of products and production facilities;

(b) receiving and storing of raw materials;

(c) producing, assembling, and handling of goods in process;

(d) inspecting and packaging of finished goods;

(e) line supervision;

(f) production support activities including security, cleaning, heating, and factory maintenance;

(g) quality and production control;

(h) repair of production facilities;

(i) pollution control; and

(j) scientific research and experimental development.[369]

None of the activities specifically excluded from the definition of "manufacturing and processing" (see ¶8400) are qualified activities. The following items are also specifically *excluded* from the definition of qualified activities:

See page ii for explanation of footnotes.

[368] Quali-T-Tube ULC Inc. et al, 2005 DTC 1161.   [369] Reg. 2900.

¶8405

(a) storing, shipping, selling, and leasing of finished goods;

(b) purchasing of raw materials;

(c) administration, including clerical and personnel activities;

(d) purchase and resale operations;

(e) data processing; and

(f) providing facilities for employees (including cafeterias, clinics, and recreational facilities).

Example:

Assume the following facts for C Limited. C Limited is not a Canadian-controlled private corporation.

Active business income — Canadian	$100,000
Investment income — Canadian	$50,000
Taxable income	$120,000
Fixed assets — manufacturing assets	$201,000*
— finished goods warehouse	300,000
	$501,000
Salaries and wages — production labour	$150,000
— plant cleaning	20,000
— office and finished goods warehouse	20,000
— directors' fees	10,000
fringe benefits	25,000
	$225,000
Rental — production machinery	$10,000
Fees paid to company that handles raw material purchasing — purchasing fee	$10,000
Fees paid to firm for accounting services	5,000
	$15,000

* Includes $1,000 deemed cost under 4210, being 15% of the capital cost of property qualifying under that provision.

The Canadian and processing profits would be calculated as follows:

Adjusted business income (ABI)			$100,000
Cost of capital (C) — manufacturing assets		$201,000	
less deemed capital cost		1,000	
		$200,000	
— warehouse		300,000	
		$500,000	
10% × $500,000		$ 50,000	
rental — production machinery		10,000	$ 60,000

¶8405

Cost of labour (L)

— production labour	$150,000	
— plant cleaning	20,000	
— office and finished goods warehouse staff	20,000	
— purchasing fees	10,000	
— accounting fees	5,000	$205,000

Cost of manufacturing processing capital (MC)

10% of manufacturing assets	$ 20,000
rental — production machinery	10,000
	$ 30,000

$$\frac{100}{85} \times 30,000 = \qquad \$ 35,294$$

Cost of manufacturing and processing labour (ML)

— production labour	$150,000
— plant cleaning	20,000
	$170,000

$$\frac{100}{75} \times 170,000 = 226,666^* \qquad \$205,000$$

* Cannot exceed cost of labour (L) of $205,000.

Canadian manufacturing and processing profits

$$= ABI \times \frac{MC + ML}{C + L}$$

$$= \$100,000 \times \frac{\$35,294 + \$205,000}{\$60,000 + \$205,000}$$

$$= \$90,677$$

Amount eligible for manufacturing and processing credit:

Lesser of:

(i) Canadian manufacturing and processing profit		$90,677
(ii) Taxable income	$120,000	
Less: investment income	50,000	70,000
Amount eligible		$70,000

Manufacturing and processing credit:

$$8.5\% \times \$70,000 \qquad = \$ \ 5,950$$

[¶8410] Partnerships

Corporations which are members of a partnership must include in the definition of the factors used in determining manufacturing and processing profits (see ¶8405), i.e., "cost of capital", "cost of labour", "cost of manufacturing and processing capital" and "cost of manufacturing and processing labour" their share of partnership assets and labour.[370] The corporation's share of the part-

See page ii for explanation of footnotes.

[370] CCH ¶19,661; Reg. 5204.

nership's Canadian active business income or loss is included in the "adjusted business income" (ABI). The factors used in the formula are to be increased or decreased based on the proportion that the corporation's share of the partnership's income or loss for the year is of the partnership's income or loss for the partnership's year coinciding with or ending in the corporation's taxation year. This proportion is referred to as "the ratio".

Cost of capital (C) (gross cost and rental cost otherwise determined) is increased by the ratio times the amounts in respect of those partnership assets which would be included if all the assets of the partnership were owned by the corporation.

Cost of labour (L) (the total of salaries, wages, and other amounts) is increased by the ratio times the salaries, wages, and other similar amounts incurred or paid by the partnership which would be included under the usual formula if incurred or paid by the corporation.

Cost of manufacturing and processing capital (MC) is increased by $^{100}/_{85}$ of the ratio times that portion of the cost of capital of the corporation for that year which reflects the extent to which each property included was used directly in qualified activities of the partnership. The total may not exceed the cost of capital referred to above.

Cost of manufacturing and processing labour (ML) is increased by $^{100}/_{75}$ of the ratio times that portion of the cost of labour which reflects the extent to which the salaries and wages were paid or payable by the partnership to persons for the portion of their time in which they were directly engaged in qualified activities, and which reflects the extent to which amounts included in the cost of labour were paid or payable to non-employees for the performance of functions directly related to qualified activities. The total may not exceed the cost of labour referred to above.

[¶8415] Resource Industries

Where a corporation has resource activities, the definitions of the amounts used for the calculation of manufacturing and processing profits at ¶8405 are also modified.[371] The changes to the definitions effectively remove the resource portion of the business (income, capital, and labour) from the amounts to be used in the equation. With the provision to include the processing of foreign ore for purposes of calculating the M&P credit, the corporation's income from the processing of foreign ore is excluded from its net resource income.[372]

[¶8420] Small Manufacturers

A special rule applies to those small manufacturers that meet certain prescribed tests.[373] Their Canadian manufacturing and processing profits will

---

See page ii for explanation of footnotes.

[371] CCH ¶19,659; Reg. 5203.
[372] CCH ¶19,657; Reg. 5202 specified percentage.
[373] CCH ¶19,655; Reg. 5201.

¶8415

equal the "adjusted business income" (¶8405). In order to qualify as a small manufacturer, the following conditions must be met:

(1) The activities of the corporation during the year must be *primarily* manufacturing or processing in Canada of goods for sale or lease. For a discussion of the meaning of "primarily" (generally more than 50%), see Interpretation Bulletin IT-145R and Interpretation Bulletin IT-147R3. The determination of a corporation's primary activity is presumably a question of fact.

(2) Active business income less active business losses of the corporation plus active business income of associated corporations (¶15,450) must not exceed $200,000.

(3) The company must not carry on any active business outside Canada in the year.

(4) The company must not carry on any activities specifically excluded from "manufacturing and processing" (see ¶8400). As detailed in ¶8400, the credit for manufacturers qualifying for the small-business deduction is eliminated for the portion of taxation years ending after June 30, 1988. However, small manufacturers which are not Canadian-controlled private corporations may continue to use this rule to calculate the M&P credit.

(5) The company must not be engaged in the processing of foreign tar sands and ore.

[¶8425] Small Business Deduction

[¶8430] Small Business Deduction

Beginning in 2008, a corporation which is a Canadian-controlled private corporation (CCPC) throughout a taxation year may deduct from its tax otherwise payable 17% of its active business income earned in Canada, not exceeding its "business limit" for the year (and subject to certain other limitations). Prior to 2008, the deductible percentage was 16%. The percentage rate is prorated if the corporation's taxation year overlaps a calendar year end with different rates.[374]

Beginning with the 2009 taxation year, the business limit of a CCPC is generally $500,000. For a 2009 taxation year beginning before 2009, the business limit is prorated based on the number of days prior to 2009 (using the former $400,000 business limit) and the number of days after 2008 (using the current $500,000 limit). The business limit must be shared if the CCPC is associated with one or more CCPCs in the year.

The business limit has been increased several times in recent years. Before 2003, the "business limit" of a CCPC was $200,000. The 2003 Budget increased the $200,000 business limit over four years to $300,000 by January 1, 2006. The

See page ii for explanation of footnotes.

[374] CCH ¶19,550; Sec. 125(1).

2004 Budget accelerated the increase to $300,000 by one year, increasing the limit from $250,000 to $300,000 on January 1, 2005. The 2006 Budget further increased the limit to $400,000, beginning in the 2007 taxation year (prorated for taxation years straddling the end of the 2007 calendar year).[375]

Given the basic federal corporate tax rate of 38%, the above deduction, which is commonly referred to as the "small business deduction", reduces the effective rate of federal tax on such active business income to 11% after the 10% federal abatement for provincial taxes (see ¶8315).

Income from a "specified investment business" (see ¶8445) does not give rise to any small business deduction. Rather, such income is subject to ordinary rates of tax and a portion of this tax is refundable to the corporation when dividends are paid by the corporation. Income from a "personal services business" (see ¶8450) is also subject to ordinary rates of tax, but no portion of such tax is refundable.

While the small business deduction is calculated as 17% of active business income for 2008 and subsequent years (increased from 16% prior to 2008), there are several limitations that apply in this regard. The main limitation, as noted earlier, is the business limit of the corporation. Another limitation provides that associated corporations must share the business limit. Lastly, the small business deduction is phased out for a so-called "large corporation", generally meaning a corporation subject to the Part I.3 capital tax in its preceding taxation year, or that would have been subject to the Part I.3 tax had that tax not been repealed (it was repealed as of the 2006 taxation year). In general terms, the deduction is restricted on a straight-line basis for such corporations with taxable capital in excess of $10 million, with the deduction eliminated entirely where the taxable capital reaches $15 million.

[¶8435] Canadian-Controlled Private Corporation

A "Canadian-controlled private corporation" (CCPC) means a private Canadian corporation other than:

(a) a corporation that is controlled, directly or indirectly in any manner whatsoever, by one or more non-resident persons, by one or more public corporations (other than a prescribed venture capital corporation), by one or more corporations with a class of shares listed on designated stock exchanges or by any combination thereof;

(b) a corporation that would be controlled by a person directly or indirectly, etc., as described in (a), if all of the shares of the corporation owned by non- resident persons, public corporations (other than prescribed venture capital corporations), and corporations with a class of shares listed on designated stock exchanges were owned by that person; or

---

See page ii for explanation of footnotes.
[375] CCH ¶19,553; Sec. 125(2).

(c) a corporation that has a class of shares listed on a designated stock exchange.[376]

Generally speaking, control is considered to be established when more than 50% of the voting shares of a corporation are directly or indirectly owned by an individual, a corporation, or a related group. To determine CCPC status, a corporation is considered controlled where the potential controller has any direct or indirect influence that, if exercised, would result in control in fact of the corporation. An exception is provided where the corporation and controller deal at arm's length and the controller's influence is derived from an agreement regarding the conduct of the business, e.g., a franchise, distribution, or management agreement, etc. This test will apply to previously existing arrangements. For more details, see ¶15,540.

A person who has a right to acquire shares of a corporation or to control the voting rights of shares, or a right to cause a corporation to redeem, cancel, or acquire its shares owned by other shareholders, is deemed to be in the same position in relation to the control of a corporation as if the person owned the shares for the purpose of determining whether or not the corporation is a CCPC.[377] It should be noted that this deeming provision does not apply if such right is not exercisable until the death, bankruptcy, or permanent disability of a named individual. Therefore, for example, if a non-resident person or a public corporation has an option to acquire the shares of a corporation, the optioned shares must be taken into account in determining control for the purposes of ascertaining whether a corporation is a CCPC (unless the exercise of the option is contingent on the death of an individual or the bankruptcy or permanent disability of an individual).

For 2006 and subsequent taxation years, a corporation that would otherwise be a CCPC can elect to be treated as not being a CCPC for the purposes of the small business deduction and the rules generally concerning the tax treatment of "eligible dividends" (see ¶6052).[378] This election would permit a corporation that would otherwise qualify as a CCPC to forego the small business deduction in exchange for the ability to pay unlimited eligible dividends subject only to the restrictions described in the definition of "low rate income pool" (LRIP) at ¶6052.

[¶8440] Active Business Income

A corporation which is a Canadian-controlled private corporation *throughout* the year may claim a deduction from the tax otherwise payable equal to 17% (16% prior to January 1, 2008) of its income from an active business carried on in Canada. The deduction is subject to the limitations described in ¶8455 *et seq.* The limitations relate primarily to the amount of income in respect of which the deduction is available in a given taxation year,

---

See page ii for explanation of footnotes.

[376] CCH ¶19,559a; Sec. 125(7) "Canadian-controlled private corporation"; Reg. 3200, Reg. 3201; Interp. Bul. IT-458R2.

[377] CCH ¶28,354; Sec. 251(5).

[378] CCH ¶11,269; Sec. 89(11).

the amount of income earned through a partnership, and the sharing of the small business deduction by associated corporations.

The term "active business" is defined[379] to mean any business carried on by the corporation excluding a specified investment business (see ¶8445) and a personal service business (see ¶8450). The term "active business carried on by a corporation"[380] uses the same definition, but also includes an adventure or concern in the nature of trade.

An expanded definition of "income of the corporation for the year from an active business" is also provided.[381] Under this definition, income from an active business includes "income pertaining to or incidental to that business". While the wording of this phrase is not very specific, it would appear that it is intended to include such types of income as income from the investment of surplus cash, rental of excess space, recaptured capital cost allowance, and interest on accounts receivable. As well, amounts paid by one corporation to an associated corporation which are deductible by the payor in calculating the payor's active business income and which would otherwise be income of the recipient from property, are deemed to be income of the recipient from an active business.[382] Accordingly, if Corporation A carries on an active business and pays rent to Corporation B, which is associated with Corporation A, such rental income will be active business income for Corporation B. The definition of "income of a corporation for the year from an active business" specifically excludes from "active business income" income that is deemed to be income from property.[383] The income from a "specified investment business" is deemed to be income from property. The definition of "income of the corporation for the year from an active business" also includes amounts received from a corporation's Net Income Stabilization Account (NISA) Fund No. 2.[384]

Where a taxpayer derived its income from farming and from royalties from three producing oil wells on its farm property, the royalties were held to be incidental to its active business of farming and thus qualified as active business income.[385] However, a taxpayer could include in income pertaining to its fur-selling business only part of the income from its term deposits, which amount was based on the amount estimated to be required by the company to meet its contingent liabilities, maintain its financial stability, and enable it to extend lines of credit to its customers.[386] The amount needed could be based on the minimum balance held in short-term investments by a taxpayer in any given year.[387] If the balance of investments fell to zero in the year, then the company needed all of the funds in the business, and any income earned on short-term investments during the year was active business income.

---

[379] CCH ¶28,004; Sec. 248(1) "active business"; Interp. Bul. IT-73R6.

[380] CCH ¶19,559; Sec. 125(7) "active business carried on by a corporation".

[381] CCH ¶19,559b; Sec. 125(7) "income of the corporation for the year from an active business".

[382] CCH ¶20,060b; Sec. 129(6).

[383] CCH ¶20,058; Sec. 129(4.1).

[384] CCH ¶4393b; Sec. 12(10.2).

[385] Alamar Farms Ltd, 93 DTC 121.

[386] Irving Garber Sales Canada Limited, 92 DTC 6498.

[387] Cornwall Gravel Company, 94 DTC 1709.

[¶8445] Specified Investment Business

Income from a specified investment business does not give rise to the small business deduction, but, rather, a portion of the tax paid on this income may be refunded[388] when taxable dividends are paid (see ¶9027). Income from a specified investment business is deemed to be income from property.[389] A "specified investment business" carried on by a corporation is defined[390] as a business (other than a business carried on by a credit union or a business of leasing property other than real property), the "principal purpose" of which is to derive income from property, including interest, dividends, rents, or royalties, but does not include a business where:

(a) the corporation employs in the business *throughout* the year more than five full-time employees; or

(b) any other corporation associated with the corporation provides it with managerial, administrative, financial, maintenance, or other similar services to the corporation in the year and the corporation could reasonably be expected to require more than five full-time employees if those services had not been provided.

In short, the income from a business which exists primarily to earn income from property is treated as property income unless the business has achieved a certain minimum size. This prevents small Canadian-controlled private corporations from obtaining the preferable active small business rates, but entitles them to refundable tax treatment on the payment of dividends.

Case law had indicated that the "more than five full-time employees" requirement in item (a) entails at least six full-time employees.[391] According to this interpretation by the Federal Court–Trial Division in 1994, if a corporation that earns its income principally from property employs only five full-time employees and one or more part-time employee, the corporation would not meet the requirement. However, in 2001, the Federal Court of Appeal questioned this finding in an *obiter dictum* and stated that five full-time employees plus one part-time employee could meet the requirement.[392] The CRA continues to take the position that the corporation must employ at least six full-time employees to meet the requirement; see paragraph 15 of Interpretation Bulletin IT-73R6. However, in a recent decision,[393] the Tax Court concluded that the term "more than five employees" was satisfied by five full-time employees and one part-time employee.

In terms of the requirement that the corporation employ more than five full-time employees in the business "throughout the year", the CRA now takes the view that this requires the corporation to employ more than five full-time employees throughout the period in which the corporation carries

[388] CCH ¶20,039; Sec. 129.
[389] CCH ¶20,058; Sec. 129(4.1).
[390] CCH ¶19,559d; Sec. 125(7) "specified investment business"; Interp. Bul. IT-73R6.
[391] Hughes & Co. Holdings Limited, 94 DTC 6511.
[392] Lerric Investments Corp., 2001 DTC 5169.
[393] 489599 B.C. Ltd., 2008 DTC 4107.

on the business in the year, and not necessarily the entire year; see CRA Document No. 2002-0144935, dated June 18, 2002.

Where a corporation (co-owner in eight apartment projects) employed two full-time employees and shared the expenses of 15 others, it was considered a specified investment business and denied a small business deduction.[394] According to the Federal Court of Appeal, the definition of "specified investment business" conceives of a single corporation employing more than five full-time employees. There are no words in the provision that imply that a proportional or sharing approach of the same employee by different employers is contemplated. As a result of that decision, IT-73R5 was cancelled and replaced by IT-73R6, dated June 3, 2002. Paragraph 17 of IT-73R6 now states: "If a corporation carries on a business as a member of a joint venture, employees working for the joint venture are the employees of its members collectively, but not of any of them individually. In other words, such employees, if full-time, cannot be counted as the full-time employees of the corporation, either in whole or in proportion to its interest in the joint venture".[395]

The term "principal purpose" of a business is not defined in the Act. The factors set out in Interpretation Bulletin IT-371 relating to a "principal business" may be considered relevant in determining what criteria will be applied.[396] Also, in cases where more than one business is carried on, it may be difficult to determine which employees are full-time in respect of which business.

The leasing of real property may be a specified investment business but the leasing of other types of property will not. However, if real property is leased it is still necessary that the principal purpose of the business is to earn income from property in order for the business to be a specified investment business.

The determination of a specified investment business is based on the nature of a corporation's income, not on its activities. Thus, a money-lending corporation with less than six full-time employees throughout the year may be conducting an active business in the ordinary meaning of the expression. However, since its income consists of interest, a form of property income, its purpose may be seen to be the earning of property income and to be a specified investment business.

[¶8450] Personal Services Business

A "personal services business" is excluded from the definition of "active business" and, therefore, income from such a business is not eligible for the small business deduction.

---

[394] Lerric Investments Corp, 2001 DTC 5169.   [396] Interp. Bul. IT-371.
[395] Interp. Bul. IT-73R6.

A personal services business consists of providing the services of an "incorporated employee" to an entity of which the incorporated employee would otherwise reasonably be regarded as an officer or employee.[397] Accordingly, it will be necessary to determine whether the corporation is providing the services of an employee or an independent contractor. The critical issue is whether there is a contract *of* services (an employee) or a contract *for* services (an independent contractor). Paragraph 3 of Interpretation Bulletin IT-525R[398] states that "a contract of service generally exists if the person for whom the services are performed has the right to control the amount, the nature, and the management of the work to be done and the manner of doing it. A contract for services exists when a person is engaged to achieve a defined objective and is given all the freedom required to attain the desired result."

To have a personal services business, the incorporated employee or a person related to the incorporated employee must be a "specified shareholder" of the corporation providing the services. Specified shareholder is defined[399] as a person who owns directly or indirectly 10% or more of the issued shares of any class of the corporation at any time in the year and includes a person who owns at least 10% of the shares of a "related corporation". Shares owned by someone who does not deal at arm's length with a person are deemed to be owned by the latter person. Similarly, shares owned by a trust are deemed to be owned by the beneficiaries in proportions based on the fair market value of their interests in the trust. In cases where different beneficiaries have interests in the income and capital of a trust, it may be difficult to determine the relative fair market value of their interests. As well, shares owned by a partnership are deemed to be owned by the partners in proportions based on the fair market value of their interests in the partnership. In addition, an individual is deemed to be a specified shareholder of a corporation carrying on a personal services business if the individual performs services for the corporation and the individual, or a person or partnership not dealing at arm's length with the individual, may under some arrangement become entitled to at least 10% of the assets or shares of the corporation.

However, a corporation will not be regarded as carrying on a personal services business in a taxation year if *throughout* the year it employs "more than five full-time employees" or if the amount paid to the corporation for the services rendered is received by it from an associated corporation. Accordingly, if an individual wishes to provide services to a corporation which the individual controls through a corporate entity, the corporate entity would not be carrying on a personal services business because the two corporations would be associated.

---

[397] CCH ¶19,559c; Sec. 125(7) "personal services business"; Interp. Bul. IT-73R6.

[398] Interp. Bul. IT-525R.

[399] CCH ¶28,273; Sec. 248(1) "specified shareholder".

The case law is inconsistent on whether the requirement of "more than five employees" is satisfied by five full-time employees plus one part-time employee. A recent case concluded that it is.[400] However, in a previous case, it was decided that "more than five full- time employees" means at least six full-time employees.[401]

In addition to a personal services business being excluded from the definition of an "active business", the Act also contains a provision to limit deductions in computing the income from such a business.[402] All such deductions are disallowed except:

(a) salary, wages, or other remuneration paid to an incorporated employee;

(b) selling and similar expenses that would have been deductible in computing employment income if the individual had expended them; and

(c) legal expenses incurred in collecting amounts owing for services rendered.

Income from a personal services business is not eligible for either a small business deduction or a refund of tax on the basis of taxable dividends paid. It is therefore taxed at the highest corporate rate. However, more recently, with historic corporate tax rate reductions and the reduced rate on eligible dividends, it has become advantageous for certain taxpayers to work as incorporated employees. In response, draft legislation released on October 31, 2011 proposes to eliminate this advantage by removing entitlement to the general rate reduction for income earned by a personal services business. Assuming entitlement to the 10% federal abatement, this would increase the tax rate to 28%.

[¶8455] Computation of Small Business Deduction

The amount of the small business deduction is 17% (16% prior to January 1, 2008) of the least of the following three amounts:[403]

(1) The aggregate of:

(a) the corporation's income from an active business carried on by it directly in Canada (other than that income earned through a partnership of which it is a member); and

(b) its specified partnership income;

minus:

See page ii for explanation of footnotes.

[400] 489599 B.C. Ltd., 2008 DTC 4107.

[401] Hughes & Co. Holdings Limited, 94 DTC 6511.

[402] CCH ¶4852d; Sec. 18(1)(p).

[403] CCH ¶19,550; Sec. 125(1).

(c) the losses of the corporation from an active business carried on by it directly in Canada (other than the loss incurred through a partnership of which it is a member); and

(d) its specified partnership loss.

If the corporation did not have any interest in a partnership, the amount will be the corporation's income for the year from active businesses carried on in Canada less losses from such businesses. If the corporation is a member of one or more partnerships which carried on an active business, special rules exist to ensure that limitations apply to the aggregate income and losses of the corporation earned from partnerships. See ¶8460.

(2) The corporation's taxable income for the year minus the aggregate of:

(i) $^{10}/_3$ [this factor will be amended to $^{100}/_{28}$ for fiscal years ending after October 31, 2011 to adjust for the elimination of the surtax] of the amount that would be deductible as a foreign non-business income tax credit (see ¶8555) if that credit was determined without the refundable tax on the CCPC's investment income (see ¶8323) and without reference to the corporate tax reduction (see ¶8475);

(ii) three times (pending technical amendments released July 16, 2010 would change the $^{10}/_4$ factor to three after 2002) the amount that would be deductible as a foreign business income tax credit (see ¶8565) if that credit was determined without reference to the corporate tax reduction (see ¶8475); and

(iii) any of the corporation's taxable income which is exempt from Part I tax.

The purpose of this limitation is to ensure that the small business deduction is calculated only on that portion of taxable income which would otherwise be subject to full taxation in Canada (before deducting the provincial and other domestic tax credits). The amounts deducted from taxable income in (i) and (ii) represent the theoretical gross foreign income on which no Canadian tax was paid because of the foreign tax credit claimed at a notional rate (30% for investment income and 33.3% for business income).

(3) The business limit of the corporation for the year, which is defined as $500,000 beginning in 2009, and $400,000 for 2007 and 2008. For taxation years straddling a calendar year end, the previous limit applies for the number of days in the year on or before that date. The business limit may be reduced if the CCPC is associated with another CCPC, and it is reduced in respect of short taxation years as well as for a CCPC that is subject to the

large corporation capital tax (as described in ¶8467), or that would have been subject to the capital tax had that tax not been repealed.[404]

The three limitations are formulated to ensure that the base for the small business deduction does not exceed any of the following:

(a) active business income from business carried on in Canada net of all losses;

(b) the amount of business income which would otherwise be fully taxed in Canada, before deducting provincial and other tax credits; and

(c) the corporation's business limit.

[¶8460] Partnerships and the Small Business Deduction

The income or loss of a partnership from a particular source is included in the income of each partner to the extent of its share of such income or loss.[405] For each taxation year, the partner includes in its income its share of partnership income or loss for fiscal periods of the partnership ending in the taxation year of the partner. All or a portion of a corporation's share of the active business income or loss earned by a partnership of which the corporation is a member is taken into account for the purposes of determining the amount upon which the small business deduction is calculated by reference to the terms "specified partnership income" and "specified partnership loss". All or a portion of such income or loss from the partnership will be added to or subtracted from the active business income of the corporate partner for the purposes of determining the amount in respect of which the corporation may claim a small business deduction.

The rules described below are designed to ensure that only a maximum aggregate amount of $500,000 (reduced for taxation years prior to 2009 — see ¶8455) of active business income earned by a partnership or, in some cases, by a group of partnerships in a year, is taken into account in determining the total small business deduction available to all of the partners in respect of the partnership income. But for these rules, the fact that a number of corporations carried on business in partnership instead of having that business carried on by a corporation in which they were shareholders could result in a much greater small business deduction. In addition, there are provisions designed to prevent the use of numerous partnerships with substantially the same membership to avoid the intent of the rules.

It should be noted that the rules discussed below only apply to corporations which are members of partnerships. In certain situations, it may be advantageous to structure business affairs so that the relationship will not be characterized as a partnership.

See page ii for explanation of footnotes.

[404] CCH ¶19,553; Sec. 125(2).   [405] CCH ¶12,103; Sec. 96(1).

¶8460

The "specified partnership income" of a corporation is generally defined to mean the lesser of (a) the corporation's share of a partnership's income from active businesses carried on in Canada less amounts deducted by the corporation in respect of that income, and (b) that proportion of $500,000 that is the corporation's share of partnership income from an active business carried on in Canada.[406] For partnership fiscal periods ending before 2009 and after 2006, the monetary limit was $400,000 rather than $500,000. For partnership fiscal periods ending before 2007, the $400,000 figure is reduced to $300,000. The limitation in (b) above would apply only if the partnership's income from an active business in Canada was greater than $500,000 (or the reduced figure for fiscal periods ending before 2009 as described above). For example, if in 2012, a partnership was composed of three equal corporate partners and the partnership's income from an active business carried on in Canada was $150,000, each corporate partner would include $50,000 as specified partnership income of the corporation for the year, for the purpose of calculating the small business deduction (i.e., $1/3$ of $150,000). If such income was in excess of $500,000 (the figure that applies for the 2012 year), the amount that would be included as specified partnership income by each partner would be $1/3$ of $500,000 or $166,667, and any excess would not be subject to the small business deduction.

In the event that the partnership's fiscal period is less than 365 days, the definition requires that the $500,000 amount be prorated on a daily basis at $1,370 per day ($500,000 divided by 365); for fiscal periods ending before 2009, the prorated amount is based on the reduced figure as described above. This proration is similar to the proration of the business limit required when a corporation has a short fiscal period (see ¶8465). Therefore, in the example in the preceding paragraph (involving the 2012 year), if the partnership's fiscal year was 300 days, the maximum claim by each partner would be $50,000 if the income of the partnership was $150,000 (the lesser of (a) $1/3 \times \$150,000$ and (b) $1/3 \times \$1,370 \times 300$) and would be $137,000 if the income of the partnership was in excess of $411,000 ($1,370 \times 300$).

The formula for determining the specified partnership income of a corporation also provides that, in the event the corporation has a loss in the year from an active business carried on in Canada by it or by a partnership of which it was a member, as well as income from the year from an active business carried on by it in Canada as a member of a partnership, the losses are to be offset first against the business income of the partnership that is not eligible for the small business deduction. This provision would only apply if the corporation had suffered losses from an active business and it had earned active business income through a partnership which would not otherwise qualify as "specified partnership income". The formula provides

---

[406] CCH ¶19,559e; Sec. 125(7) "specified partnership income".

for an addition to the specified partnership income of the corporation of the lesser of:

(a) its losses; and

(b) the difference between its share of partnership income and its share of $1,370 (reduced for fiscal periods ending before 2009, as discussed above) of partnership income per day.

"Specified partnership loss" is defined[407] as the corporation's share of losses of a partnership of which it is a member from active businesses carried on in Canada. The amount of the specified partnership loss is a deduction for the purpose of calculating the amount of income eligible for the small business deduction. As noted above, such loss is not "double counted" because the definition of specified partnership income permits its addition in certain situations in the calculation of specified partnership income.

The calculation of specified partnership income and specified partnership loss and the impact these have on the calculation of the small business deduction is illustrated in the example below.

Example:

Assume a corporation's only assets in its 2012 taxation year are a 50% interest in each of Partnerships A and B and these partnerships have income from active businesses carried on in Canada of $500,000 and $200,000, respectively, and the corporation deducts $150,000 in respect of expenditures made as a member of Partnership B. Further, assume that the corporation is not associated with any other corporations, and that its net income for the year is equal to the aggregate of its share of the active business income of Partnerships A and B less amounts deducted in respect of expenditures made by it as a member of Partnership B.

SPECIFIED PARTNERSHIP INCOME

(1) Partnership A — the lesser of:

(a) Corporation's share of Partnership A income (i.e., $500,000 × 50%)	$250,000	
(b) Corporation's prorated business limit (i.e., $250,000/$500,000 × $500,000)	250,000	
Lesser of (a) and (b) is		$250,000

(2) Partnership B — the lesser of:

(c) Specified partnership loss (see below)	50,000	
(d) Amount, if any, by which amount determined in (a) (i.e., $250,000) exceeds amount determined in (b) (i.e., $250,000):		
$250,000 - $250,000 =	NIL	
Lesser of (c) and (d) is		NIL
Total specified partnership income		$250,000

See page ii for explanation of footnotes.

[407] CCH ¶19,559f; Sec. 125(7) "specified partnership loss".

¶8460

SPECIFIED PARTNERSHIP LOSS

(1) Partnership B — the amount by which

Amount deducted by the corporation in respect of		
(a) Partnership B		$150,000
exceeds		
(b) Corporation's share of Partnership B income		
$200,000 × 50%)		100,000
Specified partnership loss		$ 50,000

In this example, the small business deduction available to the corporation would be $17,000 calculated as 17% of the least of:

(a) The amount by which specified partnership income (i.e., $250,000) exceeds specified partnership loss (i.e., $50,000)		$200,000
(b) Corporation's taxable income (assuming no deductions for foreign business or non-business income tax)		
Partnership A (500,000 × 50%)	$250,000	
Partnership B (200,000 × 50%)	100,000	
Amount deducted by corporation in respect of Partnership B	(150,000)	$200,000
(c) Corporation's business limit for the year		$200,000

[¶8463] Corporation Member of More than One Partnership

The use of more than one partnership for the purpose of increasing a corporation's entitlement to the small business deduction is prevented if a corporation is a member of the partnership, and in the year the corporation or an associated corporation is a member of another partnership, it may be reasonable to conclude that one of the main reasons for their separate existence is to reduce the taxes which would otherwise be payable by increasing the amount of the small business deduction.[408] Because the definition of specified partnership income requires corporate partners to pro-rate the active business income of a partnership if the partnership earns in excess of $500,000 for fiscal periods ending after 2008 (for previous taxation years, the $500,000 figure is reduced; see ¶8455), corporations could, but for this provision, enter into numerous partnerships and effectively increase their specified partnership income beyond the $500,000 amount (or the reduced figure that applies to fiscal periods ending before 2009).

If one of the main reasons for the creation of more than one partnerships is to increase the amount of the small business deduction of any corporation, the specified partnership income of the corporation for the year shall be computed on the basis that only the greatest amount of active business income from any single partnership is to be included in calculating the specified partnership income and the active business income of all the other partnerships is deemed to be nil. Accordingly, only the corporation's

---

See page ii for explanation of footnotes.

[408] CCH ¶19,558; Sec. 125(6).

share of active business income from one of such partnerships, or a portion thereof is entitled to the small business deduction. It is unclear what occurs if the corporation's income from two or more of such partnerships are equal. It should also be noted that the provision applies in a manner different from that which applies to associated corporations.

Example:

> Corporation A and Corporation B are associated corporations in the 2011 year ($500,000 business limit) and no other corporation is associated with them. Corporation A earns $50,000 of active business income from businesses in Canada and Corporation B earns $100,000 of such income. Each corporation would be entitled to the small business deduction because in the aggregate the associated corporations have not earned more than $500,000 of active business income. However, if Corporation C is a member of two partnerships one of which earns $50,000 and one of which earns $100,000 of such income and the above anti-avoidance rules apply, Corporation C would only be entitled to the small business deduction in respect of the partnership from which it received the greatest specified partnership income.

In the above example, it may have been possible to stack the partnerships to improve the results. However, another anti-avoidance provision was added to prevent corporations from setting up tiers of partnerships to maximize the amount of income eligible for the small business deduction. If a corporation is a member of a partnership which in turn is a member of another partnership, the corporation is deemed to be a member of the second tier partnership. In determining the specified partnership income of the corporation, the corporation's share of income of each partnership of which it is a member (deemed or direct) is to be considered.[409]

The income of a partnership will not qualify for the small business deduction if the partnership is controlled directly or indirectly by any combination of non-resident persons or public corporations.[410] A partnership is deemed to be controlled by one or more persons if their share of the partnership income from any source is greater than 50%.[411]

[¶8465] Allocation of Small Business Deduction among Associated Corporations and Short Taxation Years

Where two or more Canadian-controlled private corporations are associated with one another in a taxation year, the annual business limit must be allocated among them. The associated corporations may file an agreement (T2, Schedule 23, *Agreement Among Associated Canadian-Controlled Private Corporations to Allocate the Business Limit*) annually making this allocation.[412] Thus, for example, if a corporation's allocated percentage was 50% and its business limit for the year was $500,000 (e.g. a taxation year coinciding with the 2010 calendar year), the corporation's allocated amount would equal $250,000.

---

[409] CCH ¶19,558a; Sec. 125(6.1).

[410] CCH ¶19,558b; Sec. 125(6.2).

[411] CCH ¶19,558c; Sec. 125(6.3).

[412] CCH ¶19,555, ¶28,384; Sec. 125(3), 256(1); Interp. Bul. IT-64R4.

¶8465

If the associated corporations have failed to file such an agreement within 30 days after notice in writing by the Minister requiring such an agreement, the Minister will make the allocation.[413] The maximum amount the Minister can allocate among a group of associated corporations is the least business limit of all the associated corporations in the group, calculated as if the corporations were not associated with any other corporation during the taxation year.

Special rules are provided for determining the business limits of a corporation with a short taxation year or with two or more taxation years ending in a calendar year.[414] First, the business limit of a corporation is proportionately reduced if the corporation's taxation year is less than 51 weeks. In such case, the business limit equals the business limit otherwise determined multiplied by the number of days in the taxation year and divided by 365. This reduction is similar to that required for partnerships (¶8460).

The second rule applies only if a Canadian-controlled private corporation (the "first corporation") has more than one taxation year ending in a calendar year and it is associated in two or more of those taxation years with another Canadian-controlled private corporation that has a taxation year ending in that calendar year. In such event, the business limit for the first corporation for each taxation year in which it is associated with the other corporation ending in that calendar year is, subject to the proration rule, an amount equal to the lesser of (i) the business limit allocated to it for its first such taxation year and (ii) the business limit allocated to it for each subsequent taxation year in the calendar year.

Example:

Corporation A has active business income of $175,000 for its taxation year ending December 31, 2011 (365-day taxation year, business limit was $500,000). Corporation B, which is associated with Corporation A, has active business income of $175,000 for its taxation year ending January 31, 2011 (365-day taxation year) and a further $250,000 of such income for its taxation year ending December 31, 2011 (334-day taxation year, business limit was $500,000). No other corporations are associated with Corporation A and Corporation B. Because Corporation B has two year ends in 2011 and is associated with Corporation A in each year, the above rule would apply. Accordingly, Corporations A and B would elect that the business limit for Corporation A would be $175,000 and the balance of $325,000 would be allocated to Corporation B's first taxation year ending in 2011. Because Corporation A's first taxation year and Corporation B's first taxation year are not less than 51 weeks, each would be entitled to the full small business deduction. However, the business limit for Corporation B's second taxation year would be 334/365 × $325,000 (or $297,397). Therefore, $350,000 - $297,397 (or $52,603) of Corporation B's income during its second taxation year would not qualify for the small business deduction. In this case the amount under (i) of the rule would be the same as the amount under (ii): $325,000.

See page ii for explanation of footnotes.

[413] CCH ¶19,556; Sec. 125(4). [414] CCH ¶19,557; Sec. 125(5).

[¶8467] Reduction of Small Business Deduction for Certain Large Corporations

The small business deduction is phased out for a corporation in a taxation year where it or an associated corporation was subject to the Part I.3 large corporations capital tax in the preceding taxation year, or would have been subject to the Part I.3 tax but for its repeal (see below).[415] In particular, the business limit for a corporation for a particular taxation year ending in a calendar year is reduced by the amount of its business limit otherwise determined for the particular year (amount "A") multiplied by a fraction that has a numerator equaling the corporation's Part I.3 tax payable in the preceding taxation year, plus, where it is associated with another corporation in the particular year, the other corporation's Part I.3 tax payable for its taxation year ending in the preceding calendar year (amount "B"), and a denominator of $11,250. Note that for these purposes, the corporation's (or the associated corporation's) Part I.3 tax payable is calculated without the regular *pro rata* calculation for short taxation years and without the credit for surtax payable.

Prior to 2004, the Part I.3 capital tax was payable by a corporation at a rate of 0.225% on its taxable capital employed in Canada in excess of $10 million (see the commentary at ¶13,030 *et seq.* for more details). Therefore, where a corporation's taxable capital employed in Canada in one year exceeds $10 million, its small business deduction is reduced for the next taxation year. It becomes apparent that where the taxable capital reaches $15 million in one year, the small business deduction for the next taxation year is eliminated entirely (that is, 0.225% of $5 million equals $11,250, so that the fraction described above becomes 1).

The Part I.3 capital tax was repealed, effective for 2006 and subsequent years. However, for the purposes of computing the reduction of the corporation's small business limit, the 0.225% rate and $10 million capital deduction will continue to apply (see ¶13,031). In other words, even though the Part I.3 tax itself is repealed, the 0.225% tax rate and the $10 million capital deduction will continue to apply for the foregoing purpose. Thus, if a corporation has taxable capital of $15 million in a taxation year, its small business deduction in the next taxation year will be eliminated (see above) even if the corporation is no longer subject to the Part I.3 capital tax.

Proposed technical amendments [released July 16, 2010] would amend the above formula such that amount "B" therein would refer to 0.225% of the corporation's (plus any associated corporation's) taxable capital employed in Canada in excess of $10 million for the preceding taxation year. The formula would continue to phase out the small business limit on a straight-line basis when the taxable capital exceeded $10 million, and it would be eliminated completely when the taxable capital equalled $15 mil-

---

See page ii for explanation of footnotes.
[415] CCH ¶19,557a; Sec. 125(5.1).

lion or more. These amendments were part of the revised draft technical amendments that were released on July 16, 2010, but they are still outstanding in draft form. They will be effective for taxation years beginning after December 20, 2002. If a corporation's taxation year falls after 2008 ($500,000 small business limit), the phase-out would occur at a rate of $1 per $10 of taxable capital over the $10 million amount, and as noted, would eliminate the small business limit if the taxable capital equalled $15 million, i.e., $\frac{1}{10}$ of $5 million ($15 million - $10 million) equals $500,000.

[¶8470] Corporate Tax Rate Reduction

[¶8475] General Corporate Rate Reduction

The general federal corporate tax rate net of the provincial abatement is 28% (see ¶8300). However, in recent years, the federal government has moved to reduce the general corporate tax rate further, ostensibly as a competitive tax measure to keep Canada's corporate tax rates in line with or even lower than those in other countries (most notably, the United States). As a result, a further general deduction from tax has been provided.[416] Under this general deduction from tax, the corporate rate of tax on "full rate taxable income" (generally, income that is not reduced by other tax deductions) is reduced by the "general rate reduction percentage".[417] This general rate reduction percentage equals 8.5% for calendar year 2008, 9% for calendar year 2009, 10% for calendar year 2010, 11.5% for calendar year 2011, and 13% thereafter.[418] Therefore, the general rate reduction will serve to reduce the general federal corporate tax rate to 15% by the 2012 calendar year (i.e., 28% minus 13%).

If a corporation's taxation year straddles a calendar year, the tax rate is calculated on a *pro rata* basis. The general rate reduction is applicable to all corporations except investment corporations, mortgage investment corporations, mutual fund corporations, and non-resident owned investment corporations (NROs).

[¶8480] Former CCPC Rate Reduction

Until 2005, the tax on a CCPC's active business income in excess of its business limit and up to a maximum of $300,000 is reduced by 7%, from 28% to 21%.[419] This rate reduction applied to CCPCs after the 2000 calendar year. However, owing to the fact that the general 7% rate reduction in ¶8475 applies after 2003, this special CCPC rate reduction was repealed as of the 2005 taxation year (it remained in effect for 2004, so that it could apply to CCPCs with a taxation year straddling the 2003 calendar year end).

See page ii for explanation of footnotes.

[416] CCH ¶19,398a; Sec. 123.4(2).
[417] CCH ¶19,397o; Sec. 123.4(1) "full rate taxable income".
[418] CCH ¶19,398; Sec. 123.4(1) "general rate reduction percentage".
[419] CCH ¶19,398b; Sec. 123.4(3).

Prior to its repeal in 2005, this special CCPC rate reduction was computed in the form of a 7% tax credit, the computation of which involved a three-stage process.

(1) The corporation determined the least of the following items:

(a) ³/₂ of the corporation's business limit as determined under ¶8465; however, for the 2003 and 2004 taxation years, the fraction was 300,000/225,000 and 300,000/250,000, respectively (and prorated for taxation years straddling a calendar year end), to account for the corresponding increases in the small business limit in those years;

(b) the amount that would be the corporation's active business income under ¶8440 if the amounts in the description of M in the definition "specified partnership income" were read as $300,000 and $822;

(c) taxable income as measured for small business deduction purposes minus aggregate investment income.

(2) From the least of these amounts, the corporation subtracted the total of the following:

(a) the taxable income of the corporation that was subject to other reduced tax rates,

(b) $100/16$ times the small business deduction claimed by the corporation.

(3) The remainder was multiplied by the corporation's CCPC rate reduction percentage for the year to give the special CCPC tax reduction for the year.[420] The CCPC rate reduction percentage was essentially 7%, computed *pro rata* when the corporation's taxation year straddled December 31, 2000.

[¶8490] Resource Rate Reduction

Generally speaking, resource income is treated as business income and taxed in the same manner as business income from other sources (see ¶8300). However, the 2000 Budget provided that the general corporate income tax rate reduction from 28% to 21% over five years beginning on January 1, 2001 (see ¶8475) would not apply to income eligible for the resource allowance. Subsequently, as a result of discussions between the government and the resource industries, the 2003 Budget gradually reduced the corporate tax rate on resource income from 28% to 21% over five years beginning on January 1, 2003. The corporate tax rate reductions in respect of resource income is effective on January 1 of each year and is prorated for

---

See page ii for explanation of footnotes.

[420] CCH ¶19,397m; Sec. 123.4(1) "CCPC rate reduction percentage".

corporations with taxation years that include days in more than one calendar year. The tax rate reduction begins with a 1% reduction in 2003 as follows:

	2003	2004	2005	2006	After 2006
Corporate income tax rate	27%	26%	25%	23%	21%

For taxation years that begin after 2006, resource income is treated as full rate taxable income and is subject to the general rate reduction rules.

[¶8535] Political Contributions

[¶8537] Contributions to Registered Parties and Candidates

A taxpayer may deduct up to certain limits from its Part I tax otherwise payable a monetary contribution made in the year to a registered party or a candidate in a federal election or by-election.[421] A taxpayer seeking to claim this credit (the deduction from tax payable) must file a receipt with the Minister that is signed by an agent authorized under the *Canada Elections Act* to accept the contribution.

The tax credit is limited to:

(a) 75% of the first $400 contributed;

(b) 50% of the next $350 contributed; and

(c) $33^{1}/_{3}$% of the next $525 contributed.

The maximum credit allowed in one taxation year is therefore $650, and it is reached where the taxpayer has contributed $1,275. Where the total contributions in a taxation year exceed $1,275, no amount may be claimed in respect of this excess and the taxpayer may not carry the excess to a subsequent taxation year.

[As with the policies governing charitable donations (see ¶8175), pending technical amendments released on July 16, 2010 provide that for political contributions after December 20, 2002, the tax credit will be based on the fair market value of the monetary contribution less any advantage received or to be received by the donor for making it (the "eligible amount"). The advantage is generally the total value of any property, service, compensation, use or any other benefit that an individual is entitled to as partial consideration for, or in gratitude for, the monetary contribution.]

See page ii for explanation of footnotes.

[421] CCH ¶19,820–19,823c, ¶51,144; Sec. 127(3)–(4.2); Reg. 2000–2002; Inf. Cir. 75-2R8.

Example:

	Case A	Case B	Case C
Part I tax otherwise payable	$5,000	$800	$ 0
Credit	(650)	(650)	(650)
Part I tax payable	$4,350	$150	$ 0

Prior to 2007, each person who was a member of a partnership at the end of its fiscal period was considered to have made a political contribution equal to his or her share of such contributions made by the partnership in that period. This provision was repealed for contributions made after 2006. Since the partnership itself is not a taxpayer, it follows that there is no longer a tax credit for anyone for political contributions made by partnerships.

No deduction may be made in respect of a contribution to a registered party or association or an officially nominated candidate, unless the contribution is proven by filing a receipt signed by a registered agent of the party or by the official agent of the candidate. Receipts may only be issued for a "monetary contribution" and may only be issued to the person who made the contribution.[422] All monetary contributions must be in cash or in the form of a negotiable instrument (such as a cheque) issued by the contributor.

No credit will be available for contributions in respect of which the taxpayer has received or is entitled to receive any financial benefit (other than a prescribed financial benefit or a credit) from a government or other political authority. Thus, a contribution that qualifies for a grant, subsidy, or other provincial credit will not qualify for the credit.

The amount contributed is to be deposited on a timely basis in a bank, trust company, or credit union. This provision does not apply, however, to the official agent of a candidate in certain rural electoral districts specified in Schedule III to the *Canada Elections Act.* A contribution made by the official agent of a candidate or by a registered agent of a party (acting in that capacity) to another such agent does not qualify as a monetary contribution. Thus, a taxpayer may not contribute to one official agent and receive a receipt, then obtain a second receipt for the same amount by reason of the first official agent passing the contribution on to a second such agent.

The person required to sign receipts must file with the Minister an information return in a prescribed form. That person must also maintain adequate records and books of account at a designated place that will enable the contributions to be verified.[423]

[¶8545] Foreign Tax Credit

[¶8550] Foreign Tax Credit

A taxpayer who was resident in Canada at any time in a taxation year is subject to tax on his or her world income.[424] In order to avoid double

---

[422] CCH ¶19,821, ¶19,822a; Sec. 127(3.1), 127(4.1).   [424] CCH ¶1003; Sec. 2.
[423] CCH ¶27,400; Sec. 230.1.

taxation on income earned from foreign sources, provision is made for the deduction from the tax otherwise payable under Part I of the Act of an amount computed with reference to the taxes paid on foreign source income to the government or political subdivision of a foreign country.[425] The deduction is computed separately with respect to "non-business-income tax" paid to a foreign government and to "business-income tax" paid to such a government.

Part of the foreign tax paid in respect of income from property may be deductible in computing income rather than subject to credit treatment. See ¶8555 and ¶8605.

[¶8555] Non-Business Income Tax — Foreign Tax Credit

The taxpayer may deduct from tax any non-business income tax paid for the year to a government of a foreign country[426] not exceeding the proportion of the tax for the year otherwise payable under Part I (see ¶8560) that:

(a) the aggregate of the taxpayer's incomes for the year from sources in each foreign country (excluding any portion thereof that was deductible under a tax convention,[427] any portion of an individual's foreign employment income which qualifies for the overseas employment tax credit and which the taxpayer actually deducted,[428] or any portion in respect of which an amount was deducted under the lifetime capital gains exemption,[429] or "tax-exempt income", i.e., income which is not subject to tax in the foreign country because of a treaty exemption)[430] on the assumption that no businesses were carried on by the taxpayer and that, if a corporation, the taxpayer had no income from shares of a foreign affiliate, or if an individual, no deduction was permitted in respect of dividends from a foreign affiliate,

is of:

(b) the taxpayer's income for the year including, in the case of a minor child, the child's "split income" determined under ¶8082, plus any previously forward-averaged amounts included in taxable income for the year, minus

(i) deducted net capital losses;[431]

(ii) capital gains deducted under the lifetime capital gains exemption;[432]

(iii) certain intercorporate dividends deductible by corporations;[433]

See page ii for explanation of footnotes.

[425] CCH ¶19,700, ¶19,702, ¶19,750, ¶19,770; Sec. 126(1), 126(2), 126(7) "business-income tax", 126(7) "non-business-income tax"; Interp. Bul. IT-270R3.

[426] CCH ¶19,700; Sec. 126(1); Interp. Bul. IT-270R3, IT-395R2.

[427] CCH ¶15,290; Sec. 110(1)(f).

[428] CCH ¶19,320; Sec. 122.3.

[429] CCH ¶15,976b; Sec. 110.6.

[430] CCH ¶19,794; Sec. 126(9).

[431] CCH ¶16,003; Sec. 111(1).

[432] CCH ¶15,976b; Sec. 110.6.

[433] CCH ¶16,301; Sec. 112.

(iv) certain foreign affiliate dividends deductible by corporations;[434]

(v) an amount deductible in respect of an employee stock option plan;[435]

(vi) any amount deductible in respect of prospectors' and grubstakers' shares and shares received from a deferred profit sharing plan;[436]

(vii) amounts deductible in respect of a home relocation loan;[437] and

(viii) amounts deductible in respect of social assistance payments, workers' compensation payments, amounts exempt from tax in Canada by virtue of a tax convention with another country, and income from employment with a prescribed international organization such as the United Nations.[438]

To this net figure a taxpayer that is a corporation may add an amount to taxable income that will increase the foreign tax credit claim.[439] Such an amount added will increase the corporation's non-capital loss to be carried over to other taxation years.

This calculation is done for the non-business tax paid in each foreign country.

Under proposed legislation (former Bill C-10), for taxation years beginning after 2006, the foreign tax credit does not apply to non-business income tax paid in respect of a participating interest in a foreign investment entity (FIE) in respect of which the taxpayer has elected FIE accrual treatment. The revised technical proposals that were released on July 16, 2010 reprise these amendments that were not enacted when Parliament was dissolved on September 7, 2008.

Where the taxpayer is an individual who was resident in Canada for only part of the year[440] (see ¶14,005), the taxpayer's income is apportioned. The above fraction is then modified so that only income for the period or periods in the year during which the taxpayer was resident in Canada is included in the amounts in (a) and (b) and the denominator described in (b) above will also include the individual's taxable income earned in Canada while the individual was not resident.[441] Taxable income earned in Canada for the period during which the individual was not resident in Canada, for the purpose of calculating the non-business foreign tax credit, will be determined before deductions for certain items such as an employee stock option plan, prospectors' and grubstakers' shares, social assistance and workers' compensation payments, income earned from employment with a pre-

---

See page ii for explanation of footnotes.

[434] CCH ¶16,500; Sec. 113.

[435] CCH ¶15,015, ¶15,272; Sec. 110(1)(d), 110(1)(d.1).

[436] CCH ¶15,274, ¶15,276; Sec. 110(1)(d.2), 110(1)(d.3).

[437] CCH ¶15,305; Sec. 110(1)(j).

[438] CCH ¶15,290; Sec. 110(1)(f).

[439] CCH ¶15,970; Sec. 110.5.

[440] CCH ¶17,003; Sec. 114.

[441] CCH ¶17,003, ¶19,700; Sec. 114, 126(1).

scribed international organization, income exempt by treaty, and loss carryovers.[442]

An individual is allowed, at the individual's option, to claim a foreign non-business tax credit in respect of certain foreign taxes[443] rather than the overseas employment tax credit.[444] A taxpayer may choose to use foreign non-business income tax credits as opposed to the overseas employment tax credit in the situation where the overseas employment tax credit would be rendered ineffective by virtue of the application of the alternative minimum tax.[445] As a result, "non-business income tax", defined at ¶8605, excludes any foreign tax that may be reasonably regarded as attributable to employment income eligible for the overseas employment tax credits only when the taxpayer has made a claim for the overseas employment tax credit.

An individual who emigrates from Canada is deemed to have disposed of and reacquired all the individual's property at its fair market value, with very few exceptions. The deemed disposition will give rise to Canadian tax if there was an accrued gain or profit on the property at the time of emigration, and the cost of the property will be stepped up accordingly to fair market value for Canadian tax purposes. The individual may also be subject to tax in a foreign jurisdiction if the property is subsequently disposed of at a profit or gain when the individual is no longer resident in Canada. If the foreign jurisdiction computes the gain using the individual's original cost of the property, the pre-emigration portion of the gain may be subject to the foreign tax even though it was subject to Canadian tax under the deemed disposition rule.

To avoid double taxation where a non-resident individual disposes of property in these circumstances, a credit is allowed to the individual to offset the Canadian tax that was payable in the year of emigration as a result of the deemed disposition of the property. The credit equals the portion of the foreign tax paid on the actual disposition of the property by the former resident individual that can reasonably be regarded as being paid in respect of the portion of the profit or gain that accrued up to the time of the individual's emigration from Canada.[446]

A similar rule applies when a non-resident individual disposes of a property that was previously subject to the deemed disposition at fair market value rule under ¶7455 when it was distributed to the individual from a Canadian resident trust. In such case, a credit is available to the Canadian trust to offset the Canadian tax that was payable in the year of the distribution of the property as a result of the deemed disposition rule. The credit is equal to the individual's foreign tax paid on the disposition of the property, as can reasonably be regarded as being paid in respect of the gain that accrued up to the time of the distribution of the property from the trust,

---

See page ii for explanation of footnotes.

[442] CCH ¶17,101; Sec. 115(1)(d)–(f).
[443] CCH ¶19,700; Sec. 126(1)(b).
[444] CCH ¶19,320; Sec. 122.3(1).

[445] CCH ¶19,999a; Sec. 127.5.

[446] CCH ¶19,721; Sec. 126(2.21).

¶8555

and from the later of: (1) the time that the trust became resident in Canada, (2) the time that the individual became a beneficiary under the trust, and (3) the time that the trust acquired the property.[447]

For the purposes of computing the credit available to a former resident, the foreign tax paid on the disposition of the property by the non-resident individual is to be reduced by any credit or reduction in tax that is available under the foreign law, or under a tax treaty, against the Canadian tax paid or payable on the actual disposition or any previous disposition of the property.[448]

The credit applies if the foreign tax is paid to a country that has an income tax treaty with Canada and in which the individual is resident at the time of the disposition of the property. However, if the property is real property situated in another country and the foreign tax is paid to that country, the credit is allowed regardless of whether that country or the individual's country of residence is a treaty country.

At the Canadian Tax Foundation's annual conference in September 2003, the CRA reviewed the treatment of social security taxes as income or profits taxes for the purposes of the foreign tax credit and announced that, as a rule, social security taxes paid to a foreign government will no longer be accepted as non- business income taxes for the purposes of the foreign tax credit. The CRA's position, summarized in Income Tax Technical News No. 31, dated June 23, 2004, is based on the case law dealing with what constitutes a tax for purposes of the definition of "non-business income tax". This case law supports the contention that a tax is characterized as a compulsory payment, enforceable by law, and levied for a public purpose.[449] Since a payer of social security derives specific economic benefits from his contributions, the amount cannot be said to be levied for a public purpose. For this reason, social security contributions generally do not qualify as income or profits taxes because they are not really taxes at all, within the judicially accepted meaning of that term. As a result, the CRA's technical interpretations regarding the tax treatment of social security contributions in France and Germany as foreign tax credits are considered obsolete and unreliable. Taxes paid under the United States *Federal Insurance Contributions Act* ("FICA taxes") are an exception to this policy because of provisions in the Canada–United States Income Tax Convention. This change is effective for the 2004 and subsequent taxation years.

As an alternative to the foreign tax credit, the Act provides for the deduction from income of foreign non-business income tax paid to a government of a country other than Canada. This deduction is available only for foreign taxes paid in respect of income from a business or property and must be deducted from the source of income to which the tax relates.[450] Ordinarily, a taxpayer would prefer to claim a foreign tax credit rather than a

---

See page ii for explanation of footnotes.

[447] CCH ¶19,721a; Sec. 126(2.22).
[448] CCH ¶19,721b; Sec. 126(2.23).

[449] Yates, 2001 DTC 761, Lawson, 1931 S.C.R. 357.
[450] CCH ¶5140; Sec. 20(12).

deduction. However, there are a number of circumstances where a taxpayer's ability to claim a foreign tax credit is limited. In such cases, a deduction may be preferable. Either an individual or a corporation can deduct in computing income, foreign tax paid for the year to the extent that the amount was not deductible under the provisions described below at ¶8605. Any amount thus deducted is not eligible for foreign tax credit relief. Consequently, a taxpayer would first determine his or her eligibility for foreign tax credit relief, and then apply any unused balance of foreign tax paid as a deduction. Non-business income tax paid on dividends from a foreign affiliate does not qualify for this deduction.

[¶8560] Limitation on Non-Business Income Tax Credit

For the purpose of calculating the limitation on a non-business income tax credit, the phrase "tax for the year otherwise payable under this Part" means[451] the amount by which:

(a) the tax payable under Part I, before making any addition or reduction in respect of forward-averaged income or for the special tax on CPP/QPP retroactive disability payments and the additional $6^2/_3\%$ tax on the investment income of CCPCs, and before making any deductions for:

(i) individual's dividend tax credit;

(ii) overseas employment tax credit;

(iii) corporate small business deduction;

(iv) manufacturing and processing deduction;

(v) foreign tax credits;

(vi) logging tax credit;

(vii) political donations;

(viii) investment tax credit;

(ix) share-purchase tax credits;

(x) scientific research and experimental development tax credits;

(xi) labour-sponsored funds tax credits; or

(xii) credits for beneficiaries of qualifying environmental trusts,

exceeds:

See page ii for explanation of footnotes.

[451] CCH ¶19,789e; Sec. 126(7) "tax for the year otherwise payable under this Part".

(b) the amount of the Quebec tax abatement and the Aboriginal government tax abatement deemed to have been paid on account of tax (see ¶8020 and ¶8021).

[¶8565] Business Income Tax — Foreign Tax Credit

A taxpayer who carries on business in a foreign country is permitted to deduct from his or her Part I tax otherwise payable, a portion of the "business income tax" paid by the taxpayer for the year in respect of the business carried on by him or her in that country, plus the taxpayer's "unused foreign tax credit" in respect of that country for the year.[452] See ¶8600 for a discussion of the carryforward and carryback provisions. The deduction is limited to the lesser of the following two amounts:

(1) The proportion of the "tax for the year otherwise payable under this Part" that:

(a) the taxpayer's income for the year from business carried on by the taxpayer in that country, other than any portion that was deductible under a tax convention[453] and "tax-exempt income", i.e., income not subject to tax in the foreign country because of a treaty exemption,[454] is of:

(b) the aggregate of the taxpayer's income for the year and any previously forward-averaged amounts included in taxable income for the year, minus:

(i) capital gains deducted under the lifetime capital gains exemption for individuals;[455]

(ii) net capital losses;[456]

(iii) an amount deductible in respect of an employee stock option plan;[457]

(iv) any amount deductible in respect of prospectors' and grubstakers' shares and shares received from a deferred profit sharing plan;[458]

(v) amounts deductible in respect of a home relocation loan;[459]

(vi) amounts deductible in respect of tuition fee assistance received for adult basic education;[460]

(vii) amounts deductible in respect of social assistance payments, workers' compensation payments, amounts exempt from tax in

---

See page ii for explanation of footnotes.

[452] CCH ¶19,702, ¶19,703; Sec. 126(2), 126(2.1).
[453] CCH ¶15,290; Sec. 110(1)(f).
[454] CCH ¶19,794; Sec. 126(9).
[455] CCH ¶15,975a–15,979; Sec. 110.6.
[456] CCH ¶16,003; Sec. 111(1).
[457] CCH ¶15,015, ¶15,272; Sec. 110(1)(d), 110(1)(d.1).
[458] CCH ¶15,274, ¶15,276; Sec. 110(1)(d.2), 110(1)(d.3).
[459] CCH ¶15,305; Sec. 110(1)(j).
[460] CCH ¶15,293; Sec. 110(1)(g).

Canada by virtue of a tax convention with another country, and income from employment with a prescribed international organization such as the United Nations;[461]

(viii) taxable dividends that are deductible, received by a corporation from a corporation resident in Canada;[462] and

(ix) dividends that are deductible, received from a foreign affiliate.[463]

To this figure a taxpayer that is a corporation may add an amount to taxable income that will increase the foreign tax credit claim.[464] An individual will also add, if applicable, that proportion of the 48% surtax on income not earned in a province that the individual's income as described above in (a) is of the individual's income as described above in (b) that is not earned in a province.[465]

(2) The amount by which the "tax for the year otherwise payable under this Part", exceeds the deduction for the non-business income tax credit, thereby allowing non-business income taxes to be deducted first (see ¶8555).

Where the taxpayer is an individual who was resident in Canada only part of the year[466] (see ¶14,005), the taxpayer's income is apportioned. The above fraction in (1) is then modified so that only income for the period or periods in the year during which the taxpayer was resident in Canada is included in the amounts in (a) and (b) and the denominator described in (b) above will include the individual's taxable income earned in Canada while the individual was not resident in Canada.[467] Taxable income earned in Canada will be determined before deductions for certain items such as an employee stock option plan, prospectors' and grubstakers' shares, social assistance and workers' compensation payments, income earned from employment with a prescribed international organization, and income exempt by treaty and loss carryovers.[468]

The calculation of the amount of foreign business tax credit that can be claimed is done for the business tax paid in each foreign country in which the taxpayer does business.

[¶8570] Limitation on Business Income Tax Credit

For the purpose of calculating the limitation on the business income tax credit in ¶8565, the phrase "tax for the year otherwise payable under this Part" means the tax for the taxation year otherwise payable under Part I before making:

See page ii for explanation of footnotes.

461 CCH ¶15,290; Sec. 110(1)(f).
462 CCH ¶16,301; Sec. 112.
463 CCH ¶16,500; Sec. 113.
464 CCH ¶15,970; Sec. 110.5.

465 CCH ¶18,900; Sec. 120(1).
466 CCH ¶17,003; Sec. 114.
467 CCH ¶17,003, ¶19,703; Sec. 114, 126(2.1).
468 CCH ¶17,101; Sec. 115(1)(d)–(f).

(a) any addition for income not earned in a province or for tax on CPP/QPP disability benefits received in one year that relate to preceding years;

(b) any addition for the additional 6²/₃% tax on investment income of CCPCs; or

(c) any deduction for the following:

(i) dividend tax credit;

(ii) overseas employment tax credit;

(iii) the corporate tax credits in respect of provincial income;

(iv) the corporate small-business and manufacturing and processing deductions;

(v) the foreign tax credit;

(vi) the logging tax credit;

(vii) the political donation credit;

(viii) the investment tax credit;

(ix) the share-purchase tax credit;

(x) the scientific research and experimental development tax credit;

(xi) the labour-sponsored funds tax credit; or

(xii) the credit for beneficiaries of qualifying environmental trusts.[469]

Non-business income taxes are to be deducted first and business income taxes second, thereby preserving any foreign business tax carryover.

[¶8572] Short-Term Securities Acquisitions

When shares or debt acquired after February 23, 1998 are held for one year or less, the amount of creditable foreign tax available to a Canadian taxpayer is limited to a notional rate (30% for business income tax, 40% for non-business income tax) of the taxpayer's gross profit from the transaction. This would include the net gain or loss from holding the security together with the amount of distributions on the security.[470]

The above restriction does not apply to capital property, debt issued to the taxpayer having a term of less than one year and held to maturity, or securities which would be subject to the restrictions in ¶8573.[471] This rule only applies to foreign withholding taxes on dividends and interest which would otherwise be included in business or non-business tax for foreign tax credit purposes. In general terms, the amount of foreign withholding tax

---

See page ii for explanation of footnotes.

[469] CCH ¶19,789e; Sec. 126(7) "tax for the year otherwise payable under this Part".

[470] CCH ¶19,732; Sec. 126(4.2).

[471] CCH ¶19,733; Sec. 126(4.3).

eligible to be recognized for FTC purposes will be limited to 40% or 30% (depending on whether the foreign tax constitutes business or non-business income tax) of the taxpayer's gross profit from the share or debt. Gross profit from the security will include both the dividend and interest income payment while the security is owned and any gains or loss on resale.

[¶8573] No Economic Profit

Where property is acquired after February 23, 1998 and it is reasonable to expect that the "economic profit" on the property would be insubstantial relative to the amount of foreign tax that is expected to be payable in respect of the property and "related transactions", no amount may be included in business or non-business income tax for purposes of calculating foreign tax credits.[472]

Any credit denied under this anti-avoidance rule may be available as a deduction from income, but only to the extent of income for the year attributable to the property or related transactions.[473] An "economic profit" is defined to be computed on the basis that the only permitted expenses were:

(a) interest and related financing expenses;

(b) Canadian and foreign taxes; and

(c) other directly attributable outlays and expenses relating to the acquisition, holding, or disposition of the property.[474]

Economic profit is calculated for the period of continuous ownership of the property from acquisition to disposition, but includes income attributable to the property for that period and income in respect of related transactions. "Related transactions" are defined as transactions entered into by the taxpayer as part of the arrangement under which the property was owned.[475]

Example:

Mr. X has a bond of a United States corporation with an underlying value of 10,000, on which a regular interest payment of $500 is about to be paid. The interest is subject to withholding tax in the United States of 10%. Therefore, Mr. X will receive $450, net of $50 of withholding tax. Assume that Mr. X is not able to use a foreign tax credit.

Mr. X sells the bond to Mr. Y, just prior to the interest payment date for $10,450. Mr. Y also receives the $500 interest payment on which $50 has been withheld. Assume that Mr. Y has a federal tax rate of 30%.

A few months later, Mr. Y sells the bond on the market for $10,000, plus accrued interest of $100.

See page ii for explanation of footnotes.

[472] CCH ¶19,731; Sec. 126(4.1).

[473] CCH ¶5140d; Sec. 20(12.1).

[474] CCH ¶19,760; Sec. 126(7) "economic profit".

[475] CCH ¶19,789d; Sec. 126(7) "related transactions".

The economic profit to Mr. Y is as follows:

Proceeds	$10,100
Interest	500
Less: Acquisition cost	(10,450)
Gross profit	150
Less: Foreign tax withheld	(50)
Economic profit (loss) before Canadian tax	$100

The foreign tax credit available to Mr. Y is limited to the following amount:

Gross profit X federal tax rate = 150 X 30% = 45

[¶8575] Employees of International Organizations

A tax credit is granted to employees of certain specified international organizations.[476] The Asian Development Bank is an organization whose employees qualify for tax credit under these rules. Different rules apply to employees of the United Nations and its affiliated agencies and to employees of the International Air Transport Association and the Société internationale de télécommunications aeronautiques.[477] They are entitled to a full tax deduction for their employment income from such organizations rather than a tax credit.

For a person who is entitled to the tax credit, the actual credit that may be claimed is the proportion of Canadian income taxes otherwise payable under Part I that the income from employment with such an organization is of the total income for the year including any previously forward-averaged amounts, less any amount deducted as a capital gains exemption or net capital loss carried over, an amount deductible in respect of an employee stock option, prospectors' and grubstakers' shares, deferred profit sharing plans, home relocation loans, social assistance and workers' compensation payments, amounts exempt from tax in Canada by virtue of a tax convention with another country, and income from employment with a prescribed international organization. Where the taxpayer is an individual who is resident in Canada for only part of the year, the taxpayer's income is apportioned. The income for the period or periods in the year during which the taxpayer is resident in Canada is taken into account in the numerator and denominator of the fraction and the denominator will also include the individual's taxable income earned in Canada while not a resident.

The amount of the credit may not exceed that proportion of the amount paid by the individual to the organization as a levy that:

(a) the individual's income for the year from employment with the organization

---

See page ii for explanation of footnotes.

[476] CCH ¶19,725; Sec. 126(3).   [477] Reg. 8900.

¶8575

is of:

(b) the amount of the individual's income for the year from employment with the organization if no part was exempt from income tax by an Act of Parliament.

The levy refers to an amount that the international organization levies in lieu of income tax.

[¶8580] Portion of Foreign Tax Not Included

An income or profits tax paid to the government of a foreign country or to any political subdivision of that country by a resident of Canada does not include any tax imposed by such foreign country that would not have been imposed if the person were not entitled to a foreign tax credit for Canadian tax purposes, or to a deduction for purposes of computing the taxable amount of passive foreign income for Canadian tax purposes.[478] The apparent purpose of this provision is to discourage "tax haven" countries from imposing a tax on Canadian residents in order to allow them to obtain a Canadian foreign tax credit and then perhaps refunding the tax.

[¶8585] Foreign Oil and Gas Levies

Where a Canadian resident taxpayer carries on a foreign oil and gas business in a taxing country (i.e., a foreign country that imposes an income or profits tax on such a business), the taxpayer is deemed to have paid income or profits taxes to the government of the taxing country equal to the lesser of (a) the amount by which 40% of the taxpayer's income from the business in the taxing country in the year exceeds the income and profits taxes actually paid to such government in respect of the business, and (b) the taxpayer's "production tax amount".[479]

The production tax amount in respect of a taxpayer's foreign oil and gas business in a taxing country means the total of all amounts that meet certain requirements. For instance, the amount must become receivable by the government of the country because of an obligation that was not a commercial obligation of the taxpayer in respect of the business and be paid to the government or an agent or instrumentality of the government.[480]

For purposes of determining a taxpayer's available foreign tax credits, the production tax amount is effectively deemed to be foreign income or profits tax subject to a ceiling of 40% of the taxpayer's income in respect of the oil and gas business. As a result, certain amounts paid by a Canadian resident taxpayer to a foreign government in connection with a foreign oil and gas business that would ordinarily not qualify for foreign tax credits are afforded special status that provides the taxpayer an opportunity to significantly reduce its Canadian tax burden in respect of such amounts.

See page ii for explanation of footnotes.

[478] CCH ¶19,730; Sec. 126(4).
[479] CCH ¶19,735; Sec. 126(5).

[480] CCH ¶19,789aa; Sec. 126(7) "production tax amount".

[¶8590] "Business Income Tax" Defined

"Business income tax" is defined[481] for purposes of the foreign tax credit as such portion of any income or profits tax paid by the taxpayer to the government of any country other than Canada or to the government of a state, province, or other political subdivision of any such country as may reasonably be regarded as tax in respect of the income of the taxpayer from any business carried on by the taxpayer in that country, but does not include a tax, or the portion of a tax, that may reasonably be regarded as relating to an amount that any other person or partnership has received or is entitled to receive from that government. Thus, an income or profits tax paid to a state or city in the United States would qualify. However, the portion of a tax that is refundable to any person or partnership from the taxing government is excluded from the definition of a business income tax. In addition, a business income tax does not include any foreign tax relating to an amount that was deductible by the taxpayer in computing Canadian tax by virtue of a tax treaty. Furthermore, treaty-protected foreign income is excluded from foreign income in determining the ratio of income from that country to all income. Treaty-protected foreign income will continue to enter into the formula, however, if it is subject to an income or profits tax to which the treaty does not apply.

Not only will income taxes paid to the foreign country in which the business is carried on qualify for the tax credit, but also taxes paid to other foreign countries will qualify, provided such taxes may reasonably be regarded as being payable in respect of income from the business in question. For example, a Canadian corporation's U.K. branch engaged in the business of lending or leasing may have customers in France and be required to pay French withholding taxes, as well as U.K. income tax. The French withholding taxes will be included in the U.K. branch's business income tax paid in respect of its U.K. business and will qualify for the Canadian foreign tax credit. There is no similar treatment of the foreign tax credit for non-business income tax.

Where a taxpayer's business or non-business income for a taxation year is from sources in more than one foreign country, the rules are to be read as providing separate deductions in respect of each such foreign country.[482]

[¶8595] Determination of Territorial Source of Income

A business of a taxpayer is considered a separate source of income.[483] The term "business" is defined[484] to include a profession, calling, trade, manufacture, or undertaking of any kind whatsoever including, in certain circumstances, an adventure or concern in the nature of trade. However, the term does not include an office or employment.

See page ii for explanation of footnotes.

[481] CCH ¶19,750; Sec. 126(7) "business-income tax".

[482] CCH ¶19,741; Sec. 126(6).

[483] CCH ¶2003; Sec. 3; Interp. Bul. IT-270R3.

[484] CCH ¶28,024; Sec. 248(1) "business".

¶8590

In many cases in which income is derived from a business, there will be little difficulty in determining the location of the source of the income. However, where the business properties or operations are found in two or more countries, difficult questions may arise in determining the territorial source of income. In some circumstances, it may be necessary to apportion the business income between the countries in question.

With respect to employment income, Canadian income tax is imposed on a non-resident who is employed in Canada in respect of income which is reasonably attributable to the duties performed in Canada.[485] In view of these provisions, it would appear to be reasonable (in the absence of a tax treaty provision to the contrary) to consider for purposes of the non-business foreign tax credit that income from an employment is derived from sources in the country in which the actual services are rendered. It is conceivable, however, that in some circumstances it might be held that the source of income from an employment is the country in which the contract of employment was entered into or the country in which the employer from whom the income is received is resident.

[¶8600] Carryforward and Carryback of Foreign Business Tax Credits

Foreign income or profits taxes on business income from a foreign country that are not claimed as credits against Canadian income tax in the particular year ("unused foreign tax credits") may be carried back and applied in the three preceding years and carried forward and applied in the ten succeeding years.[486]

The current system requires that the amount available for carryforward or carryback be determined separately in respect of each foreign country. Thus, any unused foreign tax credit in respect of a particular country will only be creditable against Canadian tax in the three previous years or the ten succeeding years to the extent that the taxpayer has income from business in that particular country which is subject to foreign tax.

It should be noted that, in order to have a valid carryback claim, the prescribed form must be filed at the time for filing the tax return for the year in which the unused credit arose.[487] Failure to file the prescribed form within the proper time frame will result in the unused credit only being available for the for the ten-year carryforward period.

The unused foreign tax credit is computed on a country-by-country basis. It is calculated as the amount of foreign business income tax paid for the year that was not deductible as a foreign business tax credit in the year. This excess could arise for instance in a case where the taxpayer's overall taxable income was low and the corresponding tax liability was less than the

---

See page ii for explanation of footnotes.

[485] CCH ¶1250, ¶17,101; Sec. 2(3), 115.

[486] CCH ¶19,702, ¶19,722, ¶19,792; Sec. 126(2), 126(2.3), 126(7) "unused foreign tax credit"; Interp. Bul. IT-520.

[487] CCH ¶22,255; Sec. 152(6).

foreign taxes paid or where the effective rate of foreign tax on the foreign income was higher than the rate the taxpayer pays on his or her total income for Canadian tax purposes.

The first credit claimed is in respect of the tax paid for the current year for the particular country. Any additional claim for the year is then considered to come out of the prior or subsequent years' unused foreign tax credit pool.

The pool of unused foreign tax credits is reduced in a specific order. The pool of unused credits for each country is reduced by applying the earliest arising credits first. For instance, in utilizing an unused foreign tax credit in 2011, any 2009 unused foreign tax credits must be deducted before any 2010 or 2012 unused foreign tax credits.

Unused foreign tax credits claimed in one year cannot be claimed again in another year. This provision is necessary because the definition of "unused foreign tax credits" does not in itself provide for a reduction of the balance for amounts claimed.[488]

It should be noted that an individual taxpayer is entitled to utilize the unused foreign tax credits against income tax payable under Part I.

[¶8605] "Non-Business Income Tax" Defined

The term "non-business income tax", for the purposes of foreign tax credits, is defined[489] as the total of non-business income or profits tax paid to a foreign country or to a political subdivision of that country for the year, minus any part of this tax that is deductible or deducted, as described below.[490] Non-business income tax paid to a foreign country does not include:

- tax that can be reasonably attributed to an amount that relates to employment income from that country for which the taxpayer has claimed the overseas employment tax credit;

- any tax that relates to capital gains from that country for which the taxpayer or taxpayer's spouse or common-law partner has claimed the capital gains deduction;

- any tax reasonably attributable to an amount that was taxable in the foreign country because the taxpayer was a citizen of that country, and that relates to income from a source within Canada;

- the portion of any tax that the foreign country is refunding to any other person or partnership;

See page ii for explanation of footnotes.

[488] CCH ¶19,722; Sec. 126(2.3).
[489] CCH ¶19,770; Sec. 126(7) "non-business-income tax".

[490] CCH ¶5139, ¶5140; Sec. 20(11), 20(12); Interp. Bul. IT-506.

- any foreign tax relating to interest received or receivable in respect of an eligible loan of an international banking centre;

- a foreign tax relating to an amount that was deductible by the taxpayer under a tax treaty.

Any amount of tax paid to a foreign government in excess of the amount the taxpayer had to pay according to a tax treaty is considered a voluntary contribution and does not qualify as foreign taxes paid.

A trust can designate foreign trust income to be included in a beneficiary's income causing the beneficiary to qualify for a foreign tax credit on any foreign tax paid by the trust in respect of this income. The business and non-business tax of the trust for the year is deemed to be reduced by the amount in respect of which a designation is made on behalf of the beneficiary. The amount of business income tax that is reduced because of this cannot be reclassified as non-business income tax.[491]

Income or profits taxes paid by an individual on income from property other than real property to a government of a foreign country in excess of 15% of the income from that property may be deducted in computing income.[492] Accordingly, foreign income or profits taxes paid to a government of a foreign country in excess of 15% of the foreign income will not be available to an individual for a foreign tax credit but rather may be deducted in computing income. Foreign tax up to 15% of the amount of such income would be deductible as a foreign tax credit from tax otherwise payable. Foreign income or profits tax on income from real property are excluded from the application of this provision and the full amount of tax paid qualifies for the foreign tax credit. As well, taxpayers who are not individuals will qualify for the foreign tax credit treatment. Non-business income taxes paid to a government of a country other than Canada or to the government of a state, province, or other political subdivision of such a country by an individual or a corporation are deductible from income except to the extent that such tax may reasonably be regarded as having been paid by a corporation in respect of income from a share in a foreign affiliate of the corporation.[493] This deduction is available only with respect to foreign taxes paid in respect of income from a business or property. To the extent that such taxes are in fact deducted from income, they do not also qualify as non-business income taxes for purposes of the foreign tax credit.

An individual's foreign employment income which qualifies for the overseas employment tax credit[494] and which the individual actually made a claim in respect thereof is effectively free from Canadian tax. Such amounts are not included in foreign source income for purposes of the foreign tax credit.[495] As a result, individuals have the option to claim either the overseas employment tax credit (which cannot be used to reduce the minimum tax) or the foreign tax credit in respect of foreign taxes.

See page ii for explanation of footnotes.

[491] CCH ¶13,563; Sec. 104(22.3).

[492] CCH ¶5139; Sec. 20(11).

[493] CCH ¶5140; Sec. 20(12).
[494] CCH ¶19,320; Sec. 122.3(1).
[495] CCH ¶19,700; Sec. 126(1)(b).

Furthermore, treaty-protected foreign income will be excluded from foreign income in determining the ratio of income from that country to all income. Treaty-protected foreign income will continue to enter into the formula, however, if it is subject to an income or profits tax to which the treaty does not apply.

Non-business income tax does not include a tax, or portion of a tax, that may reasonably be regarded as relating to an amount that any person or partnership has or will receive from the taxing government. This would occur, for example, in countries where taxes are withheld but then are refunded to the taxpayer. The refundable portion of this tax is not non-business income tax of the Canadian lender for tax credit purposes. These taxes will be deductible, however, by virtue of another provision of the Act as described above.[496]

The definition of "non-business income tax" excludes any capital gains in respect of which an exemption has been claimed. The individual will be deemed to have claimed the exemption in a year in respect of those taxable capital gains specified by the individual in the tax return for the year. If the taxpayer does not specify the order, the Minister may do so.[497]

It should be noted that there is no provision to carry forward or carry back non-business foreign tax credits.

Example:

Hillary's non-business income from a foreign country was $400 on which Hillary paid $125 in taxes. Hillary's net income including the foreign non-business income after being adjusted for the foreign taxes paid in excess of 15% (as calculated below) was $11,270.

Hillary's federal tax, after relevant deductions to arrive at taxable income, was $415.

Gross foreign non-business income	$400
Less: taxes paid in excess of 15%	65
Amount to be included in income	$335
Non-business income tax paid	$125
Less: amount allowed as a deduction in computing foreign non-business income	65
Amount available for foreign tax credit	$ 60
Foreign tax credit is lesser of:	
(a) $60; and	

(b) $\dfrac{\$335 \text{ (Foreign non-business income)}}{\$11,270 \text{ (Net income)}} \times \$415 = \$12$

Allowable foreign tax credit	$ 12

See page ii for explanation of footnotes.
[496] CCH ¶5140; Sec. 20(12); Interp. Bul. IT-506.   [497] CCH ¶19,736; Sec. 126(5.1).

¶8605

The excess foreign tax credit on non-business income of $48 ($60 - $12) may not be carried forward but may be claimed as a reduction of the provincial tax payable or as a deduction in arriving at net income as described above.

[¶8610] Territorial Source of Income from Property

The principal types of income from property are rents, dividends, interest, and royalties.

Under the Act, the source of income from property is the property itself. Accordingly, it would appear that rentals from real property, and royalties from such things as mining or petroleum rights, would be held to be from a source in the country in which the property was located. It is not quite so easy to determine the source of interest income. However, Canada imposes a withholding tax on the interest paid or credited by a resident of Canada to a non-resident. In view of this provision and on general principles, there seems to be strong support for the position that interest is derived from sources in the country in which the debtor is resident.

Where a taxpayer in Canada makes a loan to a non-resident borrower who resides in a foreign country in which the lender has no permanent establishment, ordinarily the interest paid by the debtor will be recognized nevertheless for the purposes of the foreign tax deduction as being from a source in that country. One exception under certain conditions is in connection with a loan to a wholly-owned subsidiary where an election is applied to deem the interest payments not to have been made by the non-resident.[498] In these circumstances, the interest received by the Canadian lender is deemed to be from sources in Canada.

Where a taxpayer in Canada receives a dividend on shares of a non-resident corporation which is a resident of a foreign country, the dividend paid ordinarily will be recognized as being from a source in that country. However, where a company incorporated in a foreign jurisdiction is resident in Canada, the payment of dividends by that corporation to non-residents of that foreign country (including Canadian residents) may require the payment of a withholding tax to the foreign jurisdiction. In these circumstances the withheld tax is usually an income tax, but the dividend paid to a Canadian resident is generally not considered income from sources in that foreign jurisdiction but as income from Canada.[499]

There is not complete unanimity about the territorial source of dividends but in general, it may be said that where dividends are received by residents of Canada from a corporation which is resident in another country, they should be treated for foreign tax credit purposes as being income

---

See page ii for explanation of footnotes.

[498] CCH ¶26,750; Sec. 218. [499] Interp. Bul. IT-270R3.

from a source in that country. This is borne out in several of the treaties between Canada and other countries.

[¶8620] Example of Calculation of Foreign Tax Credit — Corporations

The following is an illustration of the calculation of the foreign tax credit for corporations:

Example:

Taxpayer Ltd. maintains a branch operation in the United States from which it earns $20,000 business income during the year. On this income $8,640 tax is paid to the government of the United States and $2,000 tax is paid to New York State and New York City. In addition, there is $1,000 United States business-income tax available for carryover from the immediately preceding tax year.

Taxpayer Ltd. also receives a dividend of $1,000 from its U.K. foreign affiliate; $150 (15%) withholding tax is paid to the government of the U.K. This dividend is non-taxable for Canadian tax purposes. Taxpayer Ltd. also receives dividend income of $2,000 from a U.K. non-affiliate from which $300 (15%) is withheld. Canadian source business income is $100,000. The combined federal and provincial tax rate is 50%.

Calculation of Canadian Tax:

Non-business Income:			
Dividend from U.K. affiliate	$ 1,000		
Deduction	$ (1,000)		
Dividend income — U.K.	$ 2,000	$ 2,000	
Business income:			
Canadian		$100,000	
United States		20,000	$120,000
Taxable income			$122,000
Federal and Provincial tax — 50% . .			$ 61,000
Foreign tax credit (calculated below)			10,300
Net Canadian tax payable			$ 50,700

Non-Business Income Foreign Tax Credit — U.K.

Non-business income tax paid to U.K. ($150 + $300)		$ 450
Less: portion applicable to non-taxable dividend from affiliate		(150)
Available for credit		$ 300
Non-business income — U.K.	$ 2,000	
Income for year	$122,000	
Federal and Provincial tax	$ 61,000	
Limitation: $(\frac{\$2,000}{\$122,000} \times \$61,000)$ (Assuming a provincial tax credit)		$ 1,000
Non-business income foreign tax credit — U.K.		$ 300

Business Income Foreign Tax Credit — United States

Business-income tax paid to the United States ($8,640 + $2,000 + unused foreign tax credit of $1,000)		$ 11,640*
Business income — U.S	$ 20,000	
Income for year	$122,000	
Canadian and Provincial tax	$ 61,000	
Limitation: $(\frac{\$20,000}{\$122,000} \times \$61,000)$	$ 10,000	
Business-income foreign tax credit (lesser of $11,640 and $10,000)		$ 10,000
Total Foreign Tax Credit		$ 10,300

* $1,640 ($1,000 + $8,640 + $2,000 − $10,000) unused foreign tax credit available for carryforward and carryback. $640 ($8,640 + $2,000 − $10,000) can be carried forward ten years and back three years from the current taxation year. $1,000 can be carried forward for the next nine years from the current taxation year. A carryback is not available for the $1,000 as the filing for a carryback must be made in the year in which the unused foreign tax credit arises.

[¶8625] Provincial Tax Credit

[¶8630] Provincial Corporation Tax

All Canadian provinces and territories impose tax on corporate income. To compensate corporations for provincial taxes payable by them, a federal tax abatement is provided.[500] Thus, corporations are permitted to deduct from the tax otherwise payable by them an amount equal to 10% of the corporation's taxable income earned in the year in a province. The deduction is taken independently of any taxes actually payable by the corporation to a province. Note that this provision does not provide complete relief where a province has a rate higher than that provided in the Act.

The phrase "taxable income earned in the year in a province" is defined to mean the amount determined under rules prescribed by regulations. See ¶8635 below. The phrase "tax otherwise payable" is not given a special definition and therefore must be taken to mean all amounts of tax and special tax imposed under various provisions and all permissible deductions. The term "province" includes the Newfoundland and Nova Scotia offshore area.[501]

The rates of corporation income tax levied by the provinces are shown at ¶465. Except in the cases of Quebec and Alberta, these taxes are collected by the federal government. Ontario's harmonized tax system takes effect for an Ontario-resident corporation's taxation year ending after December 31,

---

See page ii for explanation of footnotes.

[500] CCH ¶19,400; Sec. 124(1).   [501] CCH ¶19,525; Sec. 124(4) "province".

2008. Under the harmonized system, the CRA will administer and collect Ontario's corporate income tax, capital tax, corporate minimum tax, and the special additional tax paid by life insurers, resulting in a single corporate tax return beginning in 2009.

[¶8635] Taxable Income Earned in a Province by a Corporation

The phrase "taxable income earned in the year in a province" is defined by regulation as being the aggregate of the taxable income of the corporation earned in the year in each of the provinces (including the Northwest Territories, the Yukon Territory and the Nunavut Territory).[502]

The computation of the amount of taxable income of a corporation earned in a year in a particular province requires the application of a formula, and certain items have to be considered before applying this formula. In certain special cases the computation will depend on the type of corporation concerned. The general allocation rules for determining the amount of taxable income earned in the year in a province are as follows:

(1) If a corporation has a permanent establishment in one province and no permanent establishment outside the province, its income earned in the year is attributable to that permanent establishment.[503]

(2) If a corporation has no permanent establishment in a particular province, no part of its taxable income for the year is deemed to be earned therein.[504]

(3) Where a corporation has a permanent establishment inside and outside the province, taxable income will be apportioned between the provinces by a formula based on the gross revenue and salaries and wages paid to employees of that permanent establishment.[505] The amount of its taxable income earned in the year in the province is deemed to be:

(a) in any case other than a case specified in (b) or (c) below, one-half of the aggregate of:

(i) that proportion of its taxable income for the year that the gross revenue for the year reasonably attributable to the permanent establishment in the province is of its total gross revenue for the year, and

(ii) that proportion of its taxable income for the year that the aggregate of the salaries and wages paid in the year by the corporation to employees of the permanent establishment in the province is of the aggregate of all salaries and wages paid in the year by the corporation;

See page ii for explanation of footnotes.

[502] CCH ¶19,400a, ¶19,401; Reg. 400(1), Reg. 401.   [504] CCH ¶19,402; Reg. 402(2).
[503] CCH ¶19,402; Reg. 402(1).   [505] CCH ¶19,402; Reg. 402(3).

(b) in any case where the gross revenue for the year of the corporation is nil, that proportion of its taxable income for the year that the aggregate of the salaries and wages paid in the year by the corporation to employees of the permanent establishment in the province is of the aggregate of all salaries and wages paid in the year by the corporation; and

(c) in any case where the aggregate of the salaries and wages paid in the year by the corporation is nil, that proportion of its taxable income for the year that the gross revenue for the year reasonably attributable to the permanent establishment in the province is of its total gross revenue for the year.

For corporations not resident in Canada, "total gross revenue" of a corporation does not include revenue reasonably attributable to a permanent establishment outside Canada.[506]

Example:

Assume that a corporation with permanent establishments in the provinces of Manitoba, Ontario, and Quebec, and in the United States, has taxable income of $250,000.

Assume also that the corporation's gross revenue and salaries and wages are attributable to its permanent establishments under the provisions of Regulation 402 as follows:

	Gross revenue	Salaries and wages
Manitoba	$ 600,000	$ 100,000
Ontario	1,800,000	400,000
Quebec	2,000,000	450,000
United States	300,000	50,000
	$4,700,000	$1,000,000
Dividends — not attributable under Reg. 402(5)	100,000	—
	$4,800,000	$1,000,000

The proportion of taxable income attributable to each province under Regulation 402 would be computed as follows:

(1) Manitoba:

$$\frac{1}{2} \text{ of } \left(\frac{600,000}{4,700,000} + \frac{100,000}{1,000,000} \times \$250,000 \right) \quad \ldots \ldots \ldots \ldots \quad \$ \quad 28,457$$

(2) Ontario:

$$\frac{1}{2} \text{ of } \left(\frac{1,800,000}{4,700,000} + \frac{400,000}{1,000,000} \times \$250,000 \right) \quad \ldots \ldots \ldots \ldots \quad 97,872$$

See page ii for explanation of footnotes.

[506] CCH ¶19,415; Reg. 413(2).

(3) Quebec:

$$\frac{1}{2} \text{ of } \left(\frac{2,000,000}{4,700,000} + \frac{450,000}{1,000,000} \times \$250,000 \right) \dots \dots \dots \quad 109,442$$

Total taxable income Canadian provinces . . . . **$ 235,771**

> The amount deductible from the corporation's tax otherwise payable would be computed as follows:

10% of $235,771 . . . . **$23,577.10**

[¶8640] Special Cases

Special provisions are contained in the regulations which provide for the computation of taxable income earned in a province by the following types of corporations: insurance corporations, chartered banks, trust and loan corporations, railway corporations, airline corporations, grain elevator operators, bus and truck transportation operators, pipeline operators, and ship operators. There are also special provisions for divided businesses and non-resident corporations.[507]

[¶8645] Permanent Establishment

The term "permanent establishment" [508] means a fixed place of business of the corporation and includes offices, branches, mines, oil wells, farms, timber lands, factories, workshops, and warehouses. Where the corporation does not have any fixed place of business, its permanent establishment is the principal place in which the corporation's business is conducted. If a corporation carries on business through an employee or agent who is:

(a) established in a particular place, and

(b) who has general authority to contract for the employer or principal, or who has a stock or merchandise owned by the employer or principal from which the employee or agent regularly fills orders which he or she receives,

the corporation is deemed to have a permanent establishment in that place. However, the fact that a corporation has business dealings through a commission agent, broker, or other independent agent, or maintains an office solely for the purchase of merchandise, does not in itself mean that the corporation has a permanent establishment.

The use of substantial machinery or equipment in a particular place at any time in a taxation year constitutes a permanent establishment in that place as does the ownership of land in a province by a corporation that otherwise has a permanent establishment in Canada. An insurance corporation is deemed to have a permanent establishment in each province and country in which the corporation is registered or licensed to do business. Where a corporation has a subsidiary-controlled corporation or a subsidia-

---

See page ii for explanation of footnotes.

[507] CCH ¶19,405–19,417; Reg. 403–415.   [508] CCH ¶19,400a; Reg. 400(2); Interp. Bul. IT-177R2.

ry-controlled corporation engaged in trade or business which is situated in a place, this fact of itself does not mean that the corporation is operating a permanent establishment in that place.[509] A sales representative office in a branch limited to repairs and sale of accessories cannot be considered a "permanent establishment" if the representative has neither general authority to contract for the firm nor a stock of merchandise from which to fill orders.[510] However, where the sales agency maintains inventory and is authorized to make quotations without reference to head office, a permanent establishment does exist.[511] See also ¶1085 concerning the residence of corporations.

[¶8650] Gross Revenue Reasonably Attributable to a Province

The regulations contain the following rules for establishing the gross revenue reasonably attributable to a permanent establishment in a particular province or country other than Canada. If the rules are not applicable to any particular type of revenue, it will be a question of fact as to which permanent establishment the revenue is reasonably attributable.[512]

(1) Where the destination of a shipment of merchandise to a customer to whom the merchandise is sold is in the particular province or country, the gross revenue derived therefrom will be attributable to the permanent establishment in the province or country.

(2) Except as provided in (3) below, where the destination of a shipment of merchandise to a customer to whom the merchandise is sold is in a province or country in which the taxpayer has no permanent establishment, if the person negotiating the sale may reasonably be regarded as being attached to the permanent establishment in the particular province or country, the gross revenue derived therefrom will be attributable to that permanent establishment.

(3) Where the destination of a shipment of merchandise to a customer to whom the merchandise is sold is in a country other than Canada in which the taxpayer has no permanent establishment:

    (a) if the merchandise was produced or manufactured, or produced and manufactured, entirely in the particular province by the taxpayer, the gross revenue derived therefrom will be attributable to the permanent establishment in the province; or

    (b) if the merchandise was produced or manufactured, partly in the province and partly in another place by the taxpayer, the gross revenue derived therefrom attributable to the permanent establishment in the province will be that proportion that the salaries and wages paid in the year to employees of the permanent establishment in the province where the merchandise was produced or

See page ii for explanation of footnotes.

[509] Enterprise Foundry (N.B.) Ltd., 64 DTC 660.
[510] Ronson Art Metal Works, 56 DTC 440.
[511] Chicago Blowers (Canada) Ltd., 66 DTC 471.
[512] CCH ¶19,402; Reg. 402(4).

manufactured (or partly produced and manufactured) is of the aggregate of the salaries and wages paid in the year to employees of the permanent establishment where the merchandise was produced or manufactured (or partly produced and manufactured).

(4) Where a customer to whom merchandise is sold instructs that shipment be made to some other person and the customer's office with which the sale was negotiated is located in the particular province or country, the gross revenue derived therefrom will be attributable to the permanent establishment in the province or country.

(5) Except as provided in (6) below, where a customer to whom merchandise is sold instructs that shipment be made to some other person and the customer's office with which the sale was negotiated is located in a province or country other than Canada in which the taxpayer has no permanent establishment, if the person negotiating the sale may reasonably be regarded as being attached to the permanent establishment in the particular province or country, the gross revenue derived therefrom will be attributable to that permanent establishment.

(6) Where a customer to whom merchandise is sold instructs that shipment be made to some other person and the customer's office with which the sale was negotiated is located in a country other than Canada in which the taxpayer has no permanent establishment:

(a) if the merchandise was produced or manufactured, or produced and manufactured, entirely in the particular province by the taxpayer, the gross revenue derived therefrom will be attributable to the permanent establishment in the province; or

(b) if the merchandise was produced or manufactured, or produced and manufactured, partly in the particular province and partly in another place by the taxpayer, the gross revenue derived therefrom attributable to the permanent establishment in the province will be that proportion that the salaries and wages paid in the year to employees of the permanent establishment in the province where the merchandise was produced or manufactured (or partly produced and manufactured) is of the aggregate of the salaries and wages paid in the year to employees of the permanent establishment where the merchandise was produced or manufactured (or partly produced and manufactured).

(7) Where gross revenue is derived from services rendered in the particular province or country, the gross revenue will be attributable to the permanent establishment in the province or country.

(8) Where gross revenue is derived from services rendered in a province or country other than Canada in which the taxpayer has no permanent establishment if the person negotiating the contract may reasonably be regarded as being attached to the permanent establishment of the taxpayer

¶8650

in the particular province or country, the gross revenue will be attributable to that permanent establishment.

(9) Where standing timber or the right to cut standing timber is sold and the timber limit on which the timber is standing is in the particular province or country, the gross revenue from such sale will be attributable to the permanent establishment of the taxpayer in the province or country.

(10) Gross revenue which arises from leasing land owned by the taxpayer in a province and which is included in computing its income will be attributable to the permanent establishment, if any, of the taxpayer in the province where the land is situated.

The rules in (1) and (4) above do not apply and the rules in (3) and (6) are revised, in a situation where the destination of a shipment of merchandise to a customer is a country other than Canada, the corporation has a permanent establishment in that other country, and the corporation is not subject to income tax in that other country either because of the tax rules in that country or because of a treaty between Canada and the other country.[513]

[¶8655] Exclusions from Gross Revenue and Special Rules

Gross revenue does not include interest on bonds, debentures or mortgages, dividends on shares of capital stock, or rentals or royalties from property that is not used in connection with the principal business operations of the corporation.[514]

Special rules for establishing gross revenue are provided in cases where a corporation operates in partnership with other persons and for corporations that are not resident in Canada. Where a corporation conducts part of its operations in partnership with one or more other persons, its gross revenue for the year is to include only that proportion of the total gross revenue of the partnership that its share of income or loss from such a partnership is of the total loss or income of the partnership.[515]

[¶8660] Salaries and Wages

When computing the taxable income earned in a province, the corporation has to take into account the aggregate of all salaries and wages paid by it in the year to the employees of each permanent establishment and the aggregate of all salaries and wages paid by it in the year to its employees. Certain fees for services which would normally be performed by employees of the corporation are deemed to be salary. However, a commission paid to a person who is not an employee of a corporation will not be considered a fee.[516] Amounts paid to officers or agents who are not employees of the corporation will not be taken into account.

See page ii for explanation of footnotes.

[513] CCH ¶19,402; Reg. 402(4.1).

[514] CCH ¶19,402; Reg. 402(5).

[515] CCH ¶19,402; Reg. 402(6).

[516] CCH ¶19,402; Reg. 402(7), Reg. 402(8).

It should be noted that there will be taken into account salaries and wages *paid in the year* and not salaries or wages accruing or becoming payable in the year. In practice, however, the Department does not normally object to a taxpayer's taking into account salaries and wages that have accrued during the year. Where a corporation is not resident in Canada, salaries and wages paid to employees of a permanent establishment outside Canada are not taken into account in computing the taxable income earned in the province.[517]

[¶8665] Logging Tax Credit

[¶8670] Logging Tax

A taxpayer is allowed to deduct from his or her tax otherwise payable for a year an amount in respect of provincial logging taxes paid on logging operations in a province.[518] Subject to the overall limitation discussed below, the amount of the deduction is the lesser of:

(a) $2/3$ of any logging tax paid by a taxpayer to a province in respect of income for the year from logging operations in the province; and

(b) $6^2/_3\%$ of the income of the taxpayer for the year from logging operations in the province described in (a).

Under this formula, when the rate of provincial tax exceeds 10% of the income derived from logging operations, the maximum credit will be computed under (b). Quebec presently imposes tax at the rate of 10% and British Columbia imposes it at the lesser of 10% or 150% of the logging tax credit as if the 10% tax was paid. In Quebec, therefore, (a) and (b) give the same result: $2/3$ of 10% is $6^2/_3\%$.

The total deduction in respect of all provinces may not exceed $6^2/_3\%$ of the taxpayer's taxable income (or, where the taxpayer is a non-resident, the taxable income earned in the year in Canada). The taxpayer's taxable income for purposes of the overall restriction on the logging tax credit is to be computed before deductions for alimony and maintenance payments, registered retirement savings plan (RRSP) or registered retirement income fund (RRIF) premiums, contributions to certain provincial pension plans, moving expenses, child care expenses, and attendant care expenses.

The term "logging tax" means a tax imposed by a province that is declared by regulation to be a tax of general application on income from logging operations[519] (see ¶8675). Regulations also provide a definition of "income from logging operations" as well as the formula for computing the deduction.[520]

See page ii for explanation of footnotes.

[517] CCH ¶19,415; Reg. 413(1).
[518] CCH ¶19,810; Sec. 127(1).
[519] CCH ¶19,812; Sec. 127(2).
[520] CCH ¶19,814; Reg. 700(1), Reg. 700(2).

[¶8675] Provincial Logging Tax Rates

The province of British Columbia has a *Logging Tax Act*. In Quebec the logging tax is imposed under Part VII of the *Taxation Act*.[521] The tax in British Columbia is the lesser of 10% of income derived from logging operations in the province or 150% of the federal logging tax credit that would be allowable as if the 10% tax was paid. In Quebec there is no tax on the first $10,000, but if the income is in excess of that figure, the province computes the 10% tax from the first dollar.

Quebec grants a deduction from provincial income tax to all taxpayers of one-third of the logging tax paid.

British Columbia provides a logging tax credit of one-third of the logging tax payable to the province in the year.

[¶8680] Canadian Film or Video Production Tax Credit (CFVPTC)

[¶8685] Tax Credit

As discussed at ¶4275, the system of subsidizing Canadian film productions through authorized tax shelter deductions for accelerated capital cost allowance was replaced for 1995 and later taxation years with the fully refundable Canadian film or video production tax credit (CFVPTC).

The Canadian film or video production tax credit is only available to a prescribed taxable Canadian corporation the activities of which in the year are primarily the carrying on through a permanent establishment in Canada of a business that is a Canadian film or video production business.[522] For this purpose, a "prescribed taxable Canadian corporation" means a taxable Canadian corporation that is Canadian, other than: (i) a corporation controlled directly or indirectly by one or more persons all or part of whose taxable income is exempt from Part I tax, or (ii) a prescribed labour-sponsored venture capital corporation.[523] A corporation in the business of producing films or videos, therefore, must do this through a permanent establishment in Canada as its primary activity in order to qualify for the credit. If the corporation carries on other activities in Canada or carries on production activities outside Canada, it may not qualify for the credit depending on the extent of these other activities. The CRA generally presumes the term "primarily" to mean more than 50%. See ¶8645 for a description of what constitutes a permanent establishment.

The credit is 25% of the "qualified labour expenditure" of each certified production of the corporation on which principal filming or taping com-

---

See page ii for explanation of footnotes.

[521] CCH ¶19,814; Reg. 700(3).
[522] CCH ¶19,697f; Sec. 125.4(1) "qualified corporation".
[523] Reg. 1106(2).

menced before the end of the year. As discussed later in ¶8687, "qualified labour expenditure" cannot exceed 60% [based on draft technical amendments released on July 16, 2010 but not yet enacted. The legislated percentage is currently 48%] of the cost of the production so that the credit is limited to 15% (i.e., 25% of 60%) of the total cost of production, net of assistance. The credit is fully refundable to the extent it exceeds tax payable.[524] Certification is obtained from the Minister of Canadian Heritage.[525]

A corporation may assign its Canadian film tax credit.[526] This may be helpful to a corporation in obtaining financing for a production. It should be noted that the Minister is not bound by the assignment and he is not required to pay the assignee the assigned amount or assume any liability to the assignee.[527]

The credit is not available on a film or video production where an investor or a partnership in which an investor has an interest, may claim a deduction for any taxation year in respect of the production.[528] After November 14, 2003, the holding of an interest in a film or video production by a person other than the production corporation will no longer disqualify the production from eligibility for a tax credit, unless the production, or a person or partnership holding an interest in the production, is a tax shelter. However, it remains a requirement that the production corporation have ownership of copyright. For taxation years ending before November 15, 2003, "investor" is defined as a person, other than a prescribed person, who is not actively engaged on a regular, continuous, and substantial basis in a business carried on through a permanent establishment in Canada that is primarily Canadian film or video production.[529] A "prescribed person" is:

(a) a corporation holding a CRTC television broadcasting license;

(b) a non-profit organization financing a Canadian film or video production;

(c) a Canadian government film agency (such as Telefilm or one of the provincial agencies); and

(d) a non-resident person who does not carry on a business in Canada and whose interest in the production is acquired to comply with certificate requirements of a treaty co-production twinning arrangement.[530]

Therefore, a prescribed person, such as a Canadian broadcaster, may purchase an interest in a production without jeopardizing the production's eligibility for the production tax credit. However, if an investor, other than a prescribed person, acquires an interest in the production, the production is

---

See page ii for explanation of footnotes.

[524] CCH ¶19,697j; Sec. 125.4(3).
[525] CCH ¶19,697c; Sec. 125.4(1) "Canadian film or video production certificate".
[526] CCH ¶27,041; Sec. 220(6).
[527] CCH ¶27,041a; Sec. 220(7).
[528] CCH ¶19,697k; Sec. 125.4(4).
[529] CCH ¶19,697d; Sec. 125.4(1) "investor".
[530] Reg. 1106(7).

disqualified if the investor *may* claim a deduction in *any* taxation year. Not only does this ensure that tax shelters used for production costs will make the production ineligible for the credit, but just the possibility of an investor claiming regular capital-cost allowance at some year in the future also puts the production offside for the credit.

A certificate from the Minister of Canadian Heritage may be revoked where an omission or incorrect statement is made for the purpose of obtaining the certificate or if the production is not a Canadian film or video production. If the certificate is revoked, it is deemed to have never been issued.[531] As a result, any tax credit received prior to the revocation would have to be repaid.

[¶8687] Qualified Labour Expenditure

The notion of qualified labour expenditure is at the heart of this system since it represents the portion of a qualified corporation's labour expenditure upon which the corporation can claim a 25% tax credit in respect of a Canadian film or video production.[532] Two principles govern these technical rules.

First, "qualified labour expenditure" cannot exceed 60% of the cost of production so that the credit is limited to 15% of the total cost of production, net of assistance. The word "assistance" as it applies to the CFVPTC includes a grant, subsidy, forgivable loan, deduction from tax or allowance received either as an inducement or as a reimbursement or allowance and includes government (Canadian or foreign) or private assistance. any investment by a government entity is treated in the same manner as government assistance. Government assistance does not include the CFVPTC, so that this credit will not reduce the cost of the production for claiming the credit. It does include provincial credits such as the Quebec film tax credit or the Ontario film investment program rebates, as well as assistance from agencies such as Telefilm.[533] The CFVPTC is, however, considered to be government assistance for other purposes so that it reduces the cost of the production for capital cost allowance purposes.[534]

Second, the system provides for the transfer of labour expenditures from a parent corporation to a wholly owned subsidiary by having the subsidiary reimburse the parent for the labour expenditure incurred and paid by the parent within 60 days of the subsidiary's year end. If the parent and the subsidiary have different year ends, the qualification of the expenditure must be determined for the parent's year. Therefore, if the parent has a December 31, 2006 tax year end, amounts incurred between January 1 and December 31, 2006 that are paid for by March 1, 2007, will be eligible to be included in the 2006 labour expenditure amount. If the subsidiary has a

---

See page ii for explanation of footnotes.

[531] CCH ¶19,697m; Sec. 125.4(6).

[532] CCH ¶19,697g; Sec. 125.4(1) "qualified labour expenditure".

[533] CCH ¶19,697a; Sec. 125.4(1) "assistance".

[534] CCH ¶19,697l; Sec. 125.4(5).

June 30, 2007 tax year end and reimburses the parent within 60 days after June 30, 2007, the 2006 labour expenditure of the parent can be picked up by the subsidiary in the calculation of its labour expenditure for its June 30, 2007 tax year end. Labour expenditures incurred by the parent for its December 31, 2006 tax year end would be picked up in the subsidiary's June 30, 2007 tax year end.

[¶8700] Film or Video Production Services Tax Credit

[¶8705] Elimination of Film Tax Shelter

Tax shelters for foreign film production services were virtually eliminated after October 1997 when the matchable expenditure rules applied to limit the deduction for investment to no more than 20% of the investment (see ¶3254). To correspond with the elimination of the tax shelter, a new tax credit was implemented: the new Film or Video Production Services Tax Credit. The new credit complements the Canadian Film or Video Production Tax Credit and allows a greater range of productions (usually foreign-owned) to qualify for assistance. It is not a tax-shelter mechanism to the extent that the timing of deductions effectively matches the timing of revenue recognized.

[¶8710] Tax Credit

This refundable tax credit is available at a rate of 16% of qualified Canadian labour expenditures incurred by an eligible production corporation for the production of an accredited film or video production.[535] A producer is not allowed to claim both the credit for Canadian content productions discussed at ¶8685 and this new credit in respect of the same production.[536]

An accredited production is a film or video production the cost of which is in excess of $1 million; or, in the case of a production that is part of a television series, that has more than one episode, or is a pilot for such a series, is in excess of $100,000 for a production shorter than 30 minutes or in excess of $200,000 for any other production.[537] Upon application from the owner of the copyright, the Minister of Canadian Heritage will certify those proposed productions that meet these requirements.

[¶8715] Qualified Canadian Labour Expenditure

"Qualified Canadian labour expenditure" is the portion of an eligible production corporation's Canadian labour expenditures upon which it can claim the 16% investment tax credit in respect of an accredited production

---

See page ii for explanation of footnotes.

[535] CCH ¶19,698n; Sec. 125.5(3).
[536] CCH ¶19,698o; Sec. 125.5(4).

[537] CCH ¶19,698g; Sec. 125.5(1) "accredited production".

¶8700

(explained above at ¶8710). Qualified Canadian labour expenditure means the amount by which the total Canadian labour expenditures of the corporation for the year or a preceding taxation year exceeds the total of:

(a) any assistance for its Canadian labour expenditures that, by the time its tax return for the year is filed, the corporation or any other person or partnership has received, is entitled to receive, or can reasonably expect to receive. This is assistance that has not been repaid and that does not reduce the cost of the production;

(b) the qualified Canadian labour expenditures of the corporation for a preceding year before the end of which the principal filming or taping of the production began; and

(c) any amount for which the corporation is reimbursed by a wholly-owned subsidiary in an agreement to transfer the Canadian labour expenditure to the subsidiary.[538]

"Canadian labour expenditure" describes the underlying expenditures of a corporation that will be eligible for the credit. In the case of a corporation not eligible for the credit, the Canadian labour expenditure is deemed to be nil. In the case of a corporation that is an eligible production corporation for a taxation year, its Canadian labour expenditure in respect of an accredited production is the total of the three following amounts:

(1) the total salary or wages directly attributable to the production that are incurred by the eligible production corporation, in the taxation year of the corporation and paid by it in the year (or within 60 days after the end of the year) in respect of certain stages of the production, i.e., from the end of the final script stage to the end of the post-production stage;

(2) the amounts paid by the eligible production corporation under contract for service, i.e., as non-salaried remuneration, that:

(a) is directly attributable to the accredited production;

(b) is paid in a taxation year (or within 60 days after the end of the year) by the eligible production corporation;

(c) is paid to a person or partnership that is carrying on a business in Canada through a permanent establishment; and

(d) relates to services rendered in Canada to the eligible production corporation and in the year, for the stage of production mentioned in (1); and

(3) the reimbursement by a subsidiary to its parent corporation for Canadian labour expenditures incurred by the parent in a particular year (or within 60 days after the end of the year) in respect of the corporation's production if the expenditures were incurred by the eligible corporation for

---

See page ii for explanation of footnotes.

[538] CCH ¶19,698k; Sec. 125.5(1) "qualified Canadian labour expenditure".

the same purpose as it was by the parent and were paid at the same time and to the same person or partnership as it was by the parent.[539]

"Eligible production corporation" means a corporation that, in the year, carries on through a permanent establishment in Canada a business that is primarily (more than 50%) a film or video production business, or production service business.[540] Specifically excluded are prescribed labour-sponsored venture capital corporations, tax-exempt corporations and corporations controlled by one or more tax-exempt persons. The corporation must either own the copyright in the film or have contracted directly with the owner of the copyright.

---

[539] CCH ¶19,698i, ¶19,698m; Sec. 125.5(1) "Canadian labour expenditure", 125.5(2).

[540] CCH ¶19,698j; Sec. 125.5(1) "eligible production corporation".

Chapter IX

Special Cases

Bankruptcy **9000**

Provisions Applicable to
Both Individuals and
Corporations 9003

Provisions Applicable to
Corporations 9006

Provisions Applicable to
Individuals 9009

Change in Residence **9010**

Implications of Immigration 9011

Paid-Up Capital of
Corporation upon
Immigration 9012

Implications of Emigration 9012a

Returning Former
Residents 9012b

Cross-Border Mergers 9013

Private Corporations **9014**

Attributes of Private
Corporation 9015

"Private Corporation"
Defined 9018

Investment Income 9021

Special Tax on Portfolio
Dividends 9024

Refund of Taxes on other
Investment Income —
Refundable Dividend Tax
on Hand 9027

Anti-Avoidance Rule 9030

Bankrupt Corporations 9033

Procedure for Dividend
Refund 9036

"Aggregate Investment
Income" and "Foreign
Investment Income"
Defined 9039

Investment Income from
Associated Companies 9042

Example of Dividend
Refund 9043

Investment Corporations **9045**

General Characteristics 9048

Qualification as an
Investment Corporation 9051

Income of Investment
Corporation 9054

"Taxed Capital Gains"
Defined 9057

Capital Gains Dividends 9060

Capital Gains Refund 9063

**Mortgage Investment
Corporations** **9066**

General Characteristics 9069

Qualification as a Mortgage
Investment Corporation 9072

Income of Mortgage
Investment Corporation 9075

Capital Gains Dividend
Election 9078

Mutual Fund Corporations **9081**

Types 9084

Qualification as a Mutual
Fund Corporation 9087

Labour-Sponsored Venture
Capital Corporations 9089

Capital Gains Dividends 9090

Late-Filed Elections for
Capital Gains Dividends 9093

Redemption of Shares 9096

Capital Gains Refund 9099

Dividend Refund to Mutual
Fund Corporations 9102

"TCP Gains Distribution" To
Non-Resident
Shareholder 9103

Capital Gains Tax on
Mutual Fund
Corporations 9105

Tax Instalments 9108

Mutual Fund Trusts 9111

Concepts 9114

Mutual Fund Trust
Requirements 9117

Capital Gains Refund 9120

"TCP Gains Distribution" to
Non-Resident Beneficiary 9121

Application of Trust
Provisions 9123

Rate of Tax and Tax
Instalments 9126

Designation by Mutual Fund
Trust 9129

Taxation Year of Mutual
Fund Trust 9130

Mutual Funds — Qualifying
Exchange 9131

**Non-Resident Owned
Investment Corporations
(NROs) 9132**

"Non-Resident Owned
Investment Corporation"
Defined 9135

Computation of Income 9138

Special Tax Rate 9141

Capital Gains 9144

Capital Gains Dividends —
Election 9147

Late-Filed Elections for
Capital Gains Dividend 9150

NRO Deemed Not To Be a
Canadian or Private
Corporation 9156

Patronage Dividends 9159

Deduction for Patronage
Dividends 9161

Limitation Where Non-
Member Customers 9164

What Constitutes a
Payment 9165

What Constitutes an
Allocation in Proportion to
Patronage 9168

Withholding on Payments of
Patronage Dividends 9177

Patronage Dividends
Included in Income 9180

Patronage Dividends from
Agricultural Cooperatives 9181

Co-Operative Corporations 9183

"Co-Operative Corporation"
Defined 9186

**Credit Unions — Savings
and Credit Unions 9189**

"Credit Union" Defined 9195

Credit Union Deemed Not
To Be a Private
Corporation 9198

Allocations in Proportion to
Borrowing 9204

Additional Deduction 9207

Payments in Respect of
Shares 9209

Member's Income 9210

Allocation of Taxable
Dividends and Capital
Gains 9213

**Deposit Insurance
Corporations 9216**

Meaning of Deposit
Insurance Corporation 9219

Insurance Corporations 9222

Insurance Business 9225

"Life Insurer" and "Life
Insurance Business"
Defined 9228

Insurer's Income or Loss 9231

Deductions Allowed in
Computing Life Insurer's
Income 9234

Deductions for Policy
Reserves 9237

Inclusions for Real Property 9240

Deduction for Dividends
from Taxable
Corporations 9243

Foreign Tax Credits 9246

Deductions Not Allowed 9249

Amounts Included in
Computing Income 9252

Income from Participating
Life Insurance Business 9255

Identical Properties 9260

Branch Accounting 9265

Transfer of an Insurance
Business 9268

Transfer of Insurance
Business by Non-
Resident Insurer 9270

**Mutualization of Provincial
Life Insurance
Corporations** **9271**

Conversion of Provincial Life
Insurance Corporation
into Mutual Corporation 9272

**Demutualization of
Insurance Corporations** **9273**

Demutualization Benefits 9274

Financial Institutions **9275**

Specified Debt Obligations
and Mark-to-Market
Property 9277

Communal Organizations **9279**

Taxation of Communal
Organizations 9282

Election in Respect of
Taxable Income 9283

Election in Respect of Gifts 9285

Tax Shelter Financing **9290**

Cost of Tax Shelter
Investments 9295

Non-Recourse Debt 9300

At-Risk Adjustment 9305

Charitable Donation Tax
Shelter Arrangements 9307

Recent Changes

2012 Budget

Life Insurance Policy Exemption Test

The Budget has proposed that the 15% tax payable by a life insurer on its taxable Canadian life investment income be recalibrated to neutralize the impact of associated proposed changes to the investment income tax base and definition of "exempt policy". The government is still in consultation on these changes and draft legislation has not yet been released. See ¶9231.

Technical Amendments

Tax-Deferred Rollover of Insurance Business

[Editorial comment — Last year's issue did deal with October 31, 2011 technical amendments, but this is one that I felt should have been mentioned and added. As it was not, I have added it here since it was released close to the end of last year.]

Draft technical amendments released on October 31, 2011 propose to broaden the availability of a tax-deferred rollover of an insurance business (from parent to subsidiary) to include a transfer of an insurance business between sister corporations in the same corporate group. See ¶9268.

[¶9000] Bankruptcy

[¶9003] Provisions Applicable to Both Individuals and Corporations

When a taxpayer declares bankruptcy, a trustee takes over the administration of the bankrupt's property. From a tax point of view, however, the trustee in bankruptcy is administering the bankrupt's affairs as his or her agent, and the bankrupt's estate is not treated as a trust or estate.[1]

The bankrupt's income and taxable income for any year commencing with the year of bankruptcy are to be calculated as if the bankrupt's property did not pass to and vest in the trustee in bankruptcy, but remained vested in the bankrupt. Thus, a taxpayer was only liable for taxes on business income arising after the date of bankruptcy and his tax liability for the pre-bankruptcy period was a claim provable in bankruptcy.[2] Any dealing in the bankrupt's estate or any act performed in the carrying on of the business of the bankrupt by the trustee is deemed to have been done in his or her capacity as an agent of the bankrupt, so that any trustee's income from such dealing or carrying on is income of the bankrupt and not of the trustee. Where a taxpayer's trustee in bankruptcy refused to appeal the Minister's assessment, the taxpayer was allowed to proceed in the appeal on his own behalf.[3]

When an absolute order of discharge is granted, any losses previously sustained by the bankrupt (whether or not during bankruptcy) are not deductible in computing the former bankrupt's income for any year, commencing with the year of the order.

A taxpayer corporation was granted an order discharging it from bankruptcy. Two months later the Minister reassessed the taxpayer for years prior to the discharge, and disallowed certain deductions. The tax debt claimed by the Minister was held to be a "provable claim" under the former *Bankruptcy Act* from which the taxpayer was freed by the discharge order.[4]

[¶9006] Provisions Applicable to Corporations

A new taxation year of a corporation is deemed to commence on the day of the bankruptcy and the taxation year within which the bankruptcy occurred is deemed to end on the day prior to the bankruptcy.

Where a taxation year of a corporation ends during the period in which the corporation is a bankrupt, and the corporation fails to pay its tax payable, the corporation and the trustee in bankruptcy are jointly and severally liable to pay. However, the trustee is only liable to the extent of the bankrupt's property in his or her possession, and payment by either the corporation or the trustee discharges the liability.

In any taxation year ending in the period of bankruptcy, the corporation is deemed not to be associated with any other corporation.[5]

See page ii for explanation of footnotes.

[1] CCH ¶20,003, ¶20,004; Sec. 128(1), 128(2).   [4] Beauchesne, 77 DTC 5308.

[2] Stillidis, 99 DTC 341.

[3] Leith, 70 DTC 1144.   [5] CCH ¶20,003; Sec. 128(1).

[¶9009] Provisions Applicable to Individuals

Where an individual declares bankruptcy in the taxation year, his or her income (or loss) may be divided among three separate tax returns.

First, an individual is deemed to have a year end the day before the declaration of bankruptcy and must file a return covering that period (as if it were a whole year) by April 30 of the following year, reporting all income and loss and all normal deductions for the period covered.[6] Personal amount credits must be apportioned between this return and the third return described below. The personal amount credits claimed on this return will be prorated by days in the taxation year before the bankruptcy over days in the calendar year, and a similar calculation for days commencing with the day of bankruptcy will apply to determine credits under the third return below. In no case can any particular credit allocated between returns be greater than the amount that could be claimed if there was a single return filed for the year.

Second, the trustee must, before the end of March of the following year, file a tax return covering the trustee's dealings with the bankrupt's property and business during the bankruptcy period in the year and pay any tax payable. This return is filed as if:

(a) in computing taxable income, the individual was not entitled to any deduction, other than loss carryovers and deductions in respect of employee stock options, prospectors' shares, deferred profit sharing plan shares received in lump-sum settlements, and capital gains from the disposition of qualified farm and fishing property or qualified small business corporation shares that are eligible for the lifetime capital gains exemption; and

(b) in computing tax payable, the individual was not entitled to deduct various personal tax credits (except charitable donation tax credits for gifts made before the bankruptcy) and investment tax credits arising from expenditures incurred or properties acquired after the date of absolute discharge.[7]

Third, the individual must file a separate second return for the year, covering the period from the date of bankruptcy to December 31 (whether or not a discharge is granted).[8] This return also treats the portion of the year it covers as if it were a whole year and it must be filed by April 30 of the following year. It covers any income or other transactions not included in the trustee's return, such as employment income for the period. Loss carryovers of any kind cannot be claimed on this return as these are only available to the trustee. Personal amount credits must be apportioned between this return and the first return, above. The deductions and credits

---

See page ii for explanation of footnotes.

[6] CCH ¶20,004; Sec. 128(2)(d).   [8] CCH ¶20,004; Sec. 128(2)(f).

[7] CCH ¶20,004; Sec. 128(2)(e).

which may be claimed on the trustee's return above may not be claimed on the individual's second return even if the trustee did not claim them.

Special rules govern RRSP contributions for bankruptcies. Under these rules, notwithstanding the general division of the year into two taxation years, the two taxation years will be treated as one year for the purposes of determining all the amounts required to calculate present and future RRSP deduction eligibility, such as earned income, RRSP deduction limit, unused RRSP deduction room, and so on. The RRSP deduction is then computed on the taxpayer's first return, using the aggregate earnings, etc. from the two returns, for contributions made to his or her own plan or a spousal plan during the period covered by the return or 60 days thereafter. The taxpayer's deductions on the second return will be for contributions made in the period of that return or 60 days thereafter, and his or her RRSP deduction limit will be reduced by amounts deducted on the first return.

When a taxpayer makes a withdrawal from an RRSP under the Home Buyers' Plan prior to bankruptcy, an income inclusion may arise if annual repayments are not made to the RRSP (see ¶10,395d). The bankruptcy rules require that these inclusions be made in the second return and not the first return for the year of bankruptcy.

Income from both returns of the individual for the year of bankruptcy (first and third returns above) will be included in calculating income for the purpose of determining the GST/HST credit and the child tax benefit.

When an individual receives discharge from bankruptcy, there will be two returns, assuming the discharge follows the calendar year of declaration of bankruptcy. The trustee will file a return for the period during which the trustee administers the bankrupt's affairs and the individual will file an ordinary return for the year, excluding any transactions dealt with by the trustee in the trustee's return.

An individual who is discharged absolutely from bankruptcy may not carry forward any tax losses of any kind which arose in any year prior to the year in which the absolute discharge is granted and apply them in the year of discharge or any later year.[9] A number of other carryforwards are limited for taxation years ending after an absolute discharge from bankruptcy. These are:

(a) minimum tax carryovers may not be deducted from the alternative minimum tax arising from taxation years ending before the absolute discharge;

(b) charitable donation tax credits may not be claimed for gifts made in taxation years ending before the absolute discharge;

See page ii for explanation of footnotes.
[9] CCH ¶20,004; Sec. 128(2)(g).

¶9009

(c) investment tax credits for expenditures incurred or properties acquired in taxation years ending before the absolute discharge may not be claimed; and

(d) carryforwards of unused tuition and education tax credits from taxation years ending before the absolute discharge may not be claimed.

If, for any reason, the trustee deals with any of an individual's affairs after an order of conditional discharge, the general rules covering a trustee's return will operate as if the individual were bankrupt in that year.[10]

[¶9010] Change in Residence

[¶9011] Implications of Immigration

When a taxpayer establishes residence in Canada, the provisions of the Act attempt to put the taxpayer in a position such that gains or losses accrued prior to establishing residence, which are not taxable to a non-resident, are not taxable in Canada.

The first event that is triggered by a taxpayer's immigration is the deemed year end of an immigrating corporation or trust. The taxation year of an immigrating corporation or trust is deemed to have ended immediately before the taxpayer becomes resident in Canada, and a new year is deemed to have commenced at the time at which residence is adopted.[11]

Second, Canadian tax rules deem a taxpayer who establishes Canadian residence to have disposed of and immediately re-acquired each property owned (with certain exceptions discussed below for individuals) at proceeds equal to fair market value immediately before the time of arrival.[12] Accordingly, gains or losses accrued prior to becoming a Canadian resident are irrelevant to Canadian tax liability when the property is later disposed of. The immigrant will calculate eventual capital gain or loss based on fair market value at the date of immigration.

Certain types of property owned by individuals are excluded from the deemed disposition rule. The main exception is taxable Canadian property owned at the time of immigration. Accordingly, when an individual immigrates to Canada, the cost of the individual's taxable Canadian property will remain the original cost and it will not be stepped up to the fair market value of the property. Therefore, if the individual subsequently disposes of the property and realizes a gain, both the pre-immigration portion and the post-immigration portion of the gain will be taxable in Canada. After March 4, 2010, taxable Canadian property of a taxpayer at any particular time is defined as:

See page ii for explanation of footnotes.

[10] CCH ¶20,004; Sec. 128(2)(h).
[11] CCH ¶20,025a; Sec. 128.1(1)(a).

[12] CCH ¶20,025b, ¶20,025c; Sec. 128.1(1)(b), 128.1(1)(c).

(1) real property situated in Canada;

(2) property used or held by the taxpayer in carrying on a business in Canada, including eligible capital property, or the inventory of such a business (other than property used in a life insurance business and property that are ships and aircraft used principally in international traffic and personal or movable property pertaining to their operation provided the country in which the taxpayer is resident grants substantially similar relief to persons resident in Canada);

(3) designated insurance property of an insurer;

(4) shares of the capital stock of a corporation not listed on a designated stock exchange, an interest in a partnership, or an interest in a trust, which derive more than 50% of their fair market value in the preceding 60 months from real or immovable property situated in Canada, Canadian resource properties, timber resource properties, or an interest or option in any of the aforementioned properties (this does not include a share of a mutual fund corporation, a unit of a mutual fund trust, or an income interest in a trust resident in Canada, see (5) below);

(5) shares of the capital stock of a corporation that are listed on a designated stock exchange, a share of the capital stock of a mutual fund corporation, or a unit of a mutual fund trust, if in the preceding 60 months, 25% or more of the shares or units were owned by the taxpayer, a party (or parties) with whom the taxpayer did not deal at arm's length, or a combination thereof, and more than 50% of the fair market value of the share or unit was derived directly or indirectly from real or immovable property situated in Canada, Canadian resource properties, timber resource properties, or an interest or option in any of the aforementioned properties;

(6) an interest, option, or right in civil law to a property described in paragraphs (1) to (5);

(7) Canadian resource property and timber resource property;

(8) an income interest in a Canadian resident trust;

(9) a right to a share of the income or loss under an agreement to allocate a share of the income or loss of a partnership to a retiring partner; and

(10) a life insurance policy in Canada.[13]

This definition presents significant changes from the previous definition. The previous definition for unlisted shares held that all unlisted shares of a Canadian corporation were generally taxable Canadian property and that unlisted shares of a non-resident corporation were taxable Canadian

---

See page ii for explanation of footnotes.

[13] CCH ¶28,284; Sec. 248(1) "taxable Canadian property".

¶9011

property if the 50% test was met in fair market value derived from real property situated in Canada, Canadian resource properties, timber resource properties, or an interest or option in any of the aforementioned properties. The definition for taxable Canadian property is the same for unlisted shares of both a Canadian and non-resident corporation, which is closer to the previous definition for unlisted shares of a non-resident corporation. For shares of a listed corporation, previously they were deemed to be taxable Canadian property if only the 25% share ownership test was met. Now, there is the 50% property test requirement to be met as well.

As noted above, when an immigrated individual disposes of taxable Canadian property that was owned by the individual before the individual became resident in Canada, both the pre-immigration portion and the post-immigration portion of the gain will be taxable in Canada. This will occur even if the pre-immigration gain would have been treaty-exempt from tax in Canada, had the property been sold while the individual was non-resident. Accordingly, prior to immigration, an individual might consider selling any taxable Canadian property, if the capital gain on the property would be treaty-exempt from Canadian tax at that time.

In addition to the exception for taxable Canadian property, the deemed disposition rule does not apply to an individual's "excluded rights or interests". Excluded rights and interests include rights under various types of pension plans and deferred income plans, including registered pension plans, registered retirement savings plans, registered retirement income funds, and foreign retirement arrangements. Excluded rights and interests also include rights to benefits under foreign social security arrangements, employee stock options, and interests in life insurance policies (other than segregated fund policies). For a complete list of excluded rights and interests, see ¶9012.

[¶9012] Paid-Up Capital of Corporation upon Immigration

A corporation's paid-up capital will be proportionately increased or reduced, at the time it becomes resident in Canada, so that the total paid-up capital will be the amount by which the fair market value of the corporation's property exceeds its liabilities.

To ensure that an immigrating corporation's paid-up capital does not exceed the difference between the cost of its assets (as determined for Canadian tax purposes) and its outstanding liabilities, a *pro rata* deduction must be made from the paid-up capital in respect of any particular class of a corporation's shares.[14] The deduction is computed as a proportion of the difference between two amounts:

(1) The first amount is the total of:

See page ii for explanation of footnotes.

[14] CCH ¶20,026; Sec. 128.1(2).

(a) the corporation's total paid-up capital as otherwise determined on all the shares of the corporation;

(b) all the corporation's liabilities; and

(c) any Part XIV investment allowance claimed by the corporation for its last taxation year.

(2) The second amount is computed as the total of:

(a) the cost to the corporation of the property subject to the deemed disposition upon immigration (see ¶9011);

(b) the cost amount of the corporation's other properties;

(c) the total of the corporation's "resource pools"; and

(d) the paid-up capital of all shares held by the immigrant in Canadian resident corporations connected with the immigrant within the meaning of ¶13,150.

Any reduction in paid-up capital is restored to the extent that the reduction has been recognized as a deemed dividend on the shares in question.[15]

[¶9012a] Implications of Emigration

A taxpayer ceasing to be resident in Canada is deemed to have disposed of each property owned by the taxpayer at its fair market value, with some exceptions for individuals, which are discussed below. In general terms, the deemed disposition ensures that an emigrating taxpayer does not avoid paying Canadian tax on unrealized appreciation in the value of property that accrued while the taxpayer was resident in Canada.

Prior to October 2, 1996, it was possible for an individual to emigrate from Canada and avoid the deemed disposition rule for many types of taxable Canadian property, then subsequently claim treaty protection and avoid paying Canadian tax when the property was sold. This prompted the government to make sweeping changes regarding taxpayer migration. Consequently, for changes of residence occurring after October 1, 1996, taxable Canadian property is no longer exempt, as a general rule, from the deemed disposition rule. However, some forms of taxable Canadian property owned by individuals are still excluded — generally speaking, those forms of taxable Canadian property whose gains are not potentially treaty-protected from tax in Canada. The properties owned by individuals that are exempt from the deemed disposition rule can be summarized as follows:

(a) real property situated in Canada, a Canadian resource property, or a timber resource property;

See page ii for explanation of footnotes.
[15] CCH ¶20,026a; Sec. 128.1(3).

¶9012a

(b) capital property used in, eligible capital property in respect of, or property described in the inventory of, a business carried on by the individual through a permanent establishment (see ¶8645) in Canada immediately before departure;

(c) "excluded rights or interests" as described below;

(d) where the individual is not a trust and was resident in Canada for 60 months or less during the 120-month period ending at the time of emigration, property owned by the individual when the individual last became resident in Canada, or property inherited during the period of Canadian residency, and where the individual is not a trust and was resident in Canada for 60 months or less during the 120-month period ending at the time of emigration, property owned by the individual when the individual last became resident in Canada, or property inherited during the period of Canadian residency; and

(e) in those cases where the individual returns to reside in Canada, property in respect of which the individual makes an election to "unwind" the deemed disposition (see the commentary at ¶9012b).[16]

"Excluded rights or interests" (see (c) above) include an individual's rights under most pension and deferred income plans, including registered pension plans, retirement compensation arrangements, registered retirement savings plans, registered retirement income funds, registered education savings plans, registered disability saving plans, tax-free savings accounts, foreign retirement arrangements, and, after 2009, employee life and health trusts. Excluded rights or interests also include rights to receive payments under annuity contracts or income-averaging annuity contracts, rights to receive benefits under the CPP/QPP/OAS/SPP, and rights to benefits under foreign social security arrangements. Employee stock options and interests in life insurance policies (other than segregated fund policies) are also excluded rights and interests.[17]

Individuals ceasing to be resident in Canada can elect to post security with the CRA for the purpose of deferring the payment of the tax that results from the deemed disposition rule. The election must normally be made and the security provided by the individual on or before the balance-due day for the year in which emigration takes place. In such case, the payment of the tax can be deferred until the underlying properties are actually sold. Furthermore, interest is not charged on the deferred amount of tax. Security is not required for the first $50,000 of taxable income that arises from the deemed disposition. Since one-half of capital gains are included in taxable income, security will thus not be required in respect of the first $100,000 of capital gains resulting from the deemed disposition

---

[16] CCH ¶20,026c; Sec. 128.1(4)(b).   [17] CCH ¶20,028k; Sec. 128.1(10) "excluded right or interest".

rule. In cases of undue hardship, the Minister is authorized to accept a lesser or different security.[18]

An individual, other than a trust, may choose to treat properties described in (a) or (b) above that would otherwise be exempt from the deemed disposition rule as having been disposed of.[19] For example, an immigrant might consider this election if he wants to realize a latent loss on such property in order to offset a gain arising from the deemed disposition. Any property on which the election is made is deemed to be disposed of at fair market value, but the losses recognized on such deemed disposition cannot exceed the increase in income arising from other deemed dispositions.

If taxable Canadian property that was subject to the deemed disposition rule decreases in value after the individual ceases to reside in Canada, and is subsequently sold at a loss, the loss may be carried back to offset the capital gain that resulted from the deemed disposition rule uponemigration. Note that this carryback does not apply to losses incurred on property other than taxable Canadian property.[20]

[¶9012b] Returning Former Residents

Individuals, other than trusts, who emigrate from Canada and subsequently return to Canada, may elect to "unwind" the deemed disposition of taxable Canadian property that occurred in the emigration year or reduce the deemed proceeds of disposition of non-taxable Canadian property, if the property is still owned by them at the time of return.[21]

Two elections can be made, one in respect of taxable Canadian property that was subject to the deemed disposition, and the other in respect of certain property other than taxable Canadian property that was subject to the deemed disposition. These elections must be made by the individual's filing-due date for the taxation year in which the individual returns to reside in Canada. Furthermore, the Minister has discretion under the "fairness package" to allow late-filed elections.

If the election is made in respect of taxable Canadian property that was subject to the deemed disposition upon the individual's emigration, the deemed disposition does not apply to the taxable Canadian property. Furthermore, the property is not subject to a deemed disposition upon the return to Canada, so that, subject to an adjustment described below, there will be no gain or loss in the emigration year in respect of the property, and the adjusted cost base of the property will remain the same as it was prior to the individual's emigration from Canada.

An adjustment may be required if the taxable Canadian property were shares in a Canadian resident corporation (or an interest in a trust or

---

See page ii for explanation of footnotes.

[18] CCH ¶27,036aa–27,036k; Sec. 220(4.5)–(4.71).   [20] CCH ¶20,028f; Sec. 128.1(8).
[19] CCH ¶20,026e; Sec. 128.1(4)(d).   [21] CCH ¶20,028d; Sec. 128.1(6).

partnership that owned such shares), the individual received taxable dividends on or in respect of the shares during the period of non-residence, and the property had a post-emigration accrued loss at the time of the return to Canada (that is, the fair market value of the shares or trust or partnership interest at that time was less than the fair market value at the time of emigration). This accrued loss would otherwise be reduced by a "notional loss reduction", i.e., the amount of taxable dividends received on or in respect of the shares by the individual during the period of non-residence (not exceeding the post-emigration accrued loss on the property).[22] If the election is made, the individual is deemed to have disposed of the property upon emigration at its adjusted cost base immediately before that time plus the notional loss reduction, so that the notional loss reduction is effectively taxed as a capital gain arising at the time of emigration. An individual may, however, elect that all or part of the notional loss reduction not be added to the deemed proceeds of disposition upon emigration, which will have the effect of reducing the capital gain at the time of emigration by the elected amount. The elected amount is effectively limited to the adjusted cost base of the property immediately before the emigration. The elected amount will then reduce the adjusted cost base of the property (so that it will be ultimately recognized as a gain when the property is sold).

If the election is made in respect of non-taxable Canadian property that was subject to the deemed disposition upon the individual's emigration, it will allow the individual to reduce the deemed proceeds of disposition of the property upon the emigration by an elected amount, and to reduce, by the same amount, the cost of the property upon the individual's return to Canada. The elected amount is limited to the lesser of the gain on the property that accrued up to the time of emigration and the fair market value of the property at the time of the individual's return to Canada. The effect of the election is to defer the pre-emigration accrued gain on the property in whole or in part until the property is actually sold.

Similar elections are available where an individual who is a beneficiary under a Canadian resident trust emigrates from Canada, receives a distribution of property from the trust while non-resident, and subsequently returns to reside in Canada while still owning the property. The provision allows the beneficiary and the trust to jointly elect to unwind or amend the tax consequences that resulted from the trust's distribution of the property to the individual. Here again, two elections can be made, one in respect of taxable Canadian property, and the other in respect of certain property other than taxable Canadian property.[23]

[¶9013] Cross-Border Mergers

Some corporate law systems allow the reorganization of corporations resident in different jurisdictions to form a single corporation. The tax

---

See page ii for explanation of footnotes.

[22] CCH ¶6459i; Sec. 40(3.7).   [23] CCH ¶20,028e; Sec. 128.1(7).

consequences of such reorganization may be uncertain, since the new corporation may be treated as a continuation of both a predecessor corporation resident in Canada, and a non-resident predecessor corporation. To clarify this situation, all predecessor corporations are treated as having had (or adopted) the same residence status as the amalgamated corporation. Thus, where a corporation formed by any reorganization in respect of two or more predecessors is resident in Canada, any predecessor that was not, before the reorganization itself resident in Canada, is deemed to have become resident here immediately before the reorganization.[24] Similarly, a Canadian-resident predecessor is deemed to have become non-resident immediately before its reorganization into a new non-resident corporation.[25] However, these rules do not apply to reorganizations occurring solely as a result of the acquisition by one corporation of another corporation's property, whether by way of purchase or on a winding-up of that other corporation.[26]

[¶9014] Private Corporations

[¶9015] Attributes of Private Corporation

The distinction between public and private corporations is important in view of their different tax treatment. Corporations that are private corporations at the time dividends are paid are subject to a 33^1/$_3$% refundable tax on portfolio dividend income.[27] Private corporations are also subject to a potentially lower tax rate on other investment income and, if they are Canadian-controlled private corporations, they may be eligible for the small business deduction. See Chapter VIII.

[¶9018] "Private Corporation" Defined

"Private corporation"[28] means a corporation resident in Canada (regardless of where it was incorporated) that is not a public corporation or is not controlled directly or indirectly by one or more public corporations (other than prescribed venture capital corporations),[29] by prescribed federal Crown corporations,[30] or by a combination of public and Crown corporations.

"Public corporation" includes a corporation resident in Canada having a class of its shares listed on a designated stock exchange in Canada.[31] (See ¶6010.) It also includes a resident corporation that complies with certain conditions relating to the number of shareholders, dispersal of ownership of shares, public trading in shares, and size of the corporation, provided the

---

See page ii for explanation of footnotes.

[24] CCH ¶20,029a; Sec. 128.2(1).
[25] CCH ¶20,029b; Sec. 128.2(2).
[26] CCH ¶20,029c; Sec. 128.2(3).
[27] CCH ¶20,039; Sec. 129(1).

[28] CCH ¶11,189; Sec. 89(1) "private corporation".
[29] CCH ¶7670; Reg. 6700.
[30] CCH ¶19,521; Reg. 7100.
[31] CCH ¶11,191; Sec. 89(1) "public corporation".

corporation has either elected to be a public corporation or the Minister has designated it as such.

A "Canadian-controlled private corporation" [32] (CCPC) is a private corporation that was incorporated in Canada (or has been resident in Canada from June 18, 1971) other than one which is controlled directly or indirectly by non-residents, public corporations (other than prescribed venture capital corporations), or a combination thereof.

A private corporation which has a refundable dividend tax on hand (see ¶9027) will receive a refund of taxes paid (or reduction of taxes payable) when the corporation pays a taxable dividend to its shareholders. A corporation which has been public at some point during the year can obtain a dividend refund on dividends paid while the corporation was private.

Although only CCPCs generate refundable dividend tax on hand on the payment of Part I tax on investment income, all private corporations, whether Canadian-controlled or not, can generate refundable dividend tax on hand based on Part IV tax liability on dividends.

[¶9021] Investment Income

Investment income of a private corporation can be generally divided into two classes:

(1) portfolio dividends; and

(2) other investment income, including taxable capital gains, income from property, and income from a "specified investment business".

An exception to this is the exclusion of amounts received from a related Corporation, if the amount paid was deductible by that corporation in computing its income from an active business.[33]

Portfolio dividends are those dividends received by a private corporation which are subject to tax under Part IV and the full amount of this tax may be refunded to the private corporation as a result of the payment of taxable dividends. Apart from the tax under Part IV, dividends between Canadian corporations generally flow free of tax. The refundable tax imposed by Part IV is designed to prevent an undue deferral of tax when portfolio dividends are received by a private corporation rather than directly by an individual shareholder. However, if the shareholder's marginal rate of tax on dividends is more than $33\frac{1}{3}\%$, the fact that the dividends are received by a private corporation will result in some deferral of tax as compared to a direct receipt of such dividends by the shareholder.

Income from specified investment business, taxable capital gains, and income from property (other than portfolio dividends) will be subject to full corporate tax rates, but a percentage of this type of income tax may be

See page ii for explanation of footnotes.

[32] CCH ¶19,559a; Sec. 125(7) "Canadian-controlled private corporation".   [33] CCH ¶20,071; Sec. 129(6).

credited to the refundable dividend tax on hand of the corporation, and this amount may be refunded to the private corporation when sufficient taxable dividends are paid. A percentage of Canadian and foreign investment income is credited to the refundable dividend tax on hand account only if the corporation is a Canadian-controlled private corporation throughout the year.

[¶9024] Special Tax on Portfolio Dividends

A 33$\frac{1}{3}$% tax is imposed on certain dividends received at a time when the shareholders are private corporations or other corporations controlled directly or indirectly by, or for the benefit of, the shareholder or a group of related shareholders.[34] A corporation that was bankrupt at any time in the year or that was a prescribed venture capital corporation, a prescribed labour-sponsored venture capital corporation, a prescribed investment contract corporation, an insurance corporation, a bank, a trust company, or a non-resident-owned investment corporation, throughout the year, is exempt from the tax. The full amount of the tax may be added to the refundable dividend tax on hand of the corporation and may be refunded when sufficient taxable dividends are paid by the corporation.

[¶9027] Refund of Taxes on other Investment Income — Refundable Dividend Tax on Hand

A corporation is entitled to a dividend refund, in respect of taxable dividends paid by it at a time when it was a private corporation, equal to the lesser of:

(a) $\frac{1}{3}$ of taxable dividends paid by it in the year; and

(b) its refundable dividend tax on hand at the end of the year.[35]

To compute its refundable dividend tax on hand at the end of a taxation year, a corporation must first total these three amounts:

(1) where it was a Canadian-controlled private corporation throughout the year, the *least* of:

(a) 26$\frac{2}{3}$% of its aggregate investment income for the year minus the amount, if any, by which its foreign tax credit exceeds 9$\frac{1}{3}$% of its foreign investment income for the year,

(b) 26$\frac{2}{3}$% of the amount, if any, by which its taxable income for the year exceeds the aggregate of:

(i) the amount eligible for the small business deduction for the year,

(ii) $\frac{25}{9}$ [under proposed amendments, $\frac{100}{35}$ for taxation years beginning after October 31, 2011] of its foreign non-business income deductible as a foreign tax credit; and

---

See page ii for explanation of footnotes.

[34] CCH ¶24,350; Sec. 186.

[35] CCH ¶20,039, ¶20,043, ¶20,060c, ¶52,247; Sec. 129(1), 129(3), 129(7); Interp. Bul. IT-243R4.

(iii) under proposed technical amendments, three times after 2002 and before 2010, 3.5714 times for calendar year 2010, 3.7735 times for calendar year 2011 and 4 times after calendar year 2011 its foreign business income deductible as a foreign tax credit,[36] and

(c) its tax payable under Part I for the year excluding its corporate surtax;

(2) the total of its taxes payable under Part IV for the year; and

(3) where it was a private corporation at the end of its preceding taxation year, the corporation's refundable dividend tax on hand at the end of that preceding year.

Under proposed technical amendments (released July 16, 2010), after 2009, the factor used for a corporation's foreign business income deductible as a foreign tax credit will take into account the "general rate reduction percentage" (10% in calendar year 2010, 11.5% in calendar year 2011, and 13% after calendar year 2011) that applies to a corporation's taxation year (see ¶8475). For instance, if a corporation's taxation year corresponds to the 2010 calendar year, its relevant factor will be determined by the formula: 1/(.38 - .10), or 3.5714. If it corresponds to the 2011 calendar year, the formula will be: 1/(.38 - .11.5) or 3.7735 and after the 2011 calendar year, it will be: 1/(.38 - .13) or 4. For a corporation's taxation year that straddles two calendar years, the general rate reduction percentage must be prorated. This amendment was made in the course of the review of provisions that assume a specific underlying corporate income tax rate in the context of the reductions in the general federal corporate income tax rate. The review of other such provisions continues and any other amendment will be announced upon completion of that review.

From this total, the corporation then deducts its dividend refund for its preceding taxation year. The remainder, if any, is the corporation's refundable divided tax on hand ("RDTOH").

Where a tax return reporting Part IV tax payable is not filed within the required three-year limit, the Minister is not entitled to reduce the taxpayer's RDTOH balance in the following taxation year by the amount of the statute-barred dividend tax refund.[37]

[¶9030] Anti-Avoidance Rule

An anti-avoidance rule will stop certain transactions under which a dividend refund was generated without any tax being paid at the shareholder level. This could happen, for instance, if the recipient of the dividend had accumulated tax losses. This kind of abuse will be countered by deeming a dividend not to be a taxable dividend, and therefore denying the dividend refund to the dividend-paying corporation if the dividend was paid in a

---

See page ii for explanation of footnotes.

[36] Sec. 95(1) "relevant factor".   [37] *Tawa Developments Inc.*, 2011 DTC 1324 (T.C.C.).

transaction (or series of transactions), one of the main purposes of which was to obtain the dividend refund.[38]

[¶9033] Bankrupt Corporations

No dividend refund may be obtained in respect of a taxable dividend paid to a controlling shareholder if that controlling shareholder was, at any time in the taxation year of the corporation paying the dividend, a bankrupt.[39]

[¶9036] Procedure for Dividend Refund

When a corporation files its return for a taxation year, within three years after the end of that year, the Minister may refund to the corporation as a dividend refund, the lesser of:

(a) $1/3$ of taxable dividends paid by the corporation in the taxation year, at a time when the corporation was a private corporation, and

(b) the corporation's refundable dividend tax on hand as at the end of the year.[40]

The Minister may make the refund without any application for refund having been made by the corporation. If an automatic refund is not made, the Minister must make a refund if the corporation makes an application for it within prescribed reassessment periods. See ¶11,648.

Instead of making a dividend refund, the Minister may apply the refundable amount to the corporation's other tax liabilities. The Minister must notify the corporation that this has been done. In most cases, the dividend refund earned through the payment of taxable dividends will be used to offset taxes otherwise payable by the corporation as shown in its return for the year.

[¶9039] "Aggregate Investment Income" and "Foreign Investment Income" Defined

A corporation's aggregate investment income for a taxation year is defined as the amount by which the total of the first three items outlined below exceeds the fourth (the result cannot be negative).[41]

(1) The "eligible portion" of its taxable capital gains less the "eligible portion" of its allowable capital losses for the year, less the corporation's net capital losses carried over from other years and deducted in the year. This amount cannot be negative.

(2) The corporation's income from property for the year with certain specific exceptions (see below).

See page ii for explanation of footnotes.

[38] CCH ¶20,040a; Sec. 129(1.2).

[39] CCH ¶20,040; Sec. 129(1.1).

[40] CCH ¶20,039, ¶20,041; Sec. 129(1), 129(2).

[41] CCH ¶20,056; Sec. 129(4) "aggregate investment income".

(3) The corporation's income for the year from a "specified investment business" carried on by it in Canada (not including any income from a source outside of Canada).

minus:

(4) The current year's losses from property and losses for the year from a specified investment business carried on in Canada.

As noted above, in calculating a corporation's aggregate investment income for a year, one only includes the eligible portion of its taxable capital gains for the year, net of the eligible portion of its allowable capital losses for the year. The "eligible portion" is defined as that portion of the taxable capital gains and allowable capital losses realized on property that cannot reasonably have been considered to have accrued while that property was owned by a corporation other than a Canadian-controlled private corporation, an investment corporation, a mortgage investment corporation, or a mutual fund corporation.[42]

The rules regarding the eligible portion of a corporation's taxable capital gains and losses do not apply to "designated property". Therefore, the full amount of taxable capital gains and allowable capital losses on dispositions of designated property are taken into account. "Designated property" is defined to mean property owned by a corporation which changed its status to become a Canadian-controlled private corporation before November 13, 1981 and which was acquired before November 13, 1981 (or pursuant to a pre-November 13, 1981 agreement), or property acquired in replacement for such property as a result of one of the events of involuntary disposition.[43]

As previously noted, income from a source that is property will constitute aggregate investment income except that the following items are not included: (i) exempt income, (ii) income from a Net Income Stabilization Account (NISA), (iii) dividends which are deductible in computing taxable income, and (iv) amounts of income and benefits of a beneficiary of a trust that are deemed to be property income.

The income or loss from a "specified investment business" carried on in Canada is specifically included in the computation of aggregate investment income. A specified investment business of a corporation is defined at ¶8445. It is a business (other than the business of leasing property other than real property or the business of a credit union) the principal purpose of which is to derive income from property unless (i) the corporation employs in the business throughout the year more than five full-time employees or (ii) in the course of carrying on an active business, any other corporation associated with it provides managerial, administrative, financial, maintenance, or other similar services to it in the year and the corporation could reasonably be expected to require more than five full-time employees if those services had not been provided.

See page ii for explanation of footnotes.

[42] CCH ¶20,057a; Sec. 129(4) "eligible portion". [43] CCH ¶11,181c; Sec. 89(1) "designated property".

The income or loss from sources that are property does not include income or loss from any property that is incident to or pertains to an active business carried on by a corporation, or that is used or held principally for the purpose of gaining or producing income from an active business carried on by it. Rather, the income or loss from such property will be considered income or loss from the active business.[44] Thus, where a taxpayer's U.S. dollar deposits in the Philippines were committed to the carrying on of its business there, the interest earned on them was held not to constitute foreign investment income.[45]

"Foreign investment income" is essentially a corporation's "aggregate investment income" from sources outside Canada.[46] However, it is computed without regard to any deduction for net capital losses carried over from other taxation years.

[¶9042] Investment Income from Associated Companies

When income from a source that is a property is paid or payable by an associated company and deducted by the payor in computing its active business income, it is deemed to be active business income in the hands of the recipient corporation.[47] Expenses incurred in connection with this income are deemed to have been incurred by the recipient corporation for the purpose of gaining or producing the income.

For these deeming provisions to apply, the following conditions must be met:

(1) The two corporations must be associated at any time in the relevant taxation year of the recipient. See ¶15,450.

(2) The amount in question was or may be deductible in computing the Canadian active business income of the associated payor corporation in any taxation year.

(3) The amount must be otherwise includible in the property income of the recipient.

This income is not subject to the dividend refund (see ¶9027) but qualifies for the small business deduction. While the types of income caught by the rule include interest, rents, royalties, etc., it would appear that direct reimbursement of salaries and other expenses paid by a corporation on behalf of an associated corporation will not give rise to its application.

[¶9043] Example of Dividend Refund

The following example illustrates the manner in which refundable dividend tax on hand (RDTOH) is accumulated and refunded. It is assumed that the corporation is a Canadian-controlled private corporation throughout that time.

See page ii for explanation of footnotes.

[44] CCH ¶20,057ab; Sec. 129(4) "income or loss".

[45] Ensite Ltd., 86 DTC 6521.

[46] CCH ¶20,057aa; Sec. 129(4) "foreign investment income".

[47] CCH ¶20,071; Sec. 129(6).

Example:

Portfolio dividends	$10,000	
Taxable capital gains	5,000	
Interest	5,000	
Aggregate investment income	$20,000	
Taxable income		$10,000
Part I tax		4,000
Part IV tax		3,333
Taxable dividends paid in year	$18,000	
RDTOH balance at end of preceding year	8,000	
Dividend refund claimed in preceding year	7,000	

RDTOH balance at end of current year:

(1) Least of: (i) 26 $^2/_3$% of aggregate investment income
= 26 $^2/_3$% of $20,000
= $5,333
(ii) 26 $^2/_3$% of taxable income
= 26 $^2/_3$% of $10,000
= $2,667
(iii) Part I tax = $4,000

plus

(2) Part IV tax payable = $3,333

plus

(3) RDTOH balance at end of preceding year = $8,000

minus

(4) RDTOH refund claimed for preceding year = $7,000

Total RDTOH =

$2,667 + $3,333 + $8,000 - $7,000 = $7,000

Refund for the year:

Lesser of (1) $^1/_3$ of $18,000 = $6,000

and

(2) RDTOH at year end = $7,000

The corporation will receive a dividend refund of $6,000.

[¶9045] Investment Corporations

[¶9048] General Characteristics

A corporation may qualify as an investment corporation whether or not it also qualifies as a mutual fund corporation. Similarly, a corporation may qualify as a mutual fund corporation whether or not it also qualifies as an investment corporation. An investment corporation which also qualifies as a mutual fund corporation will be subject to the same income tax treatment (see ¶9081 *et seq.*) except that:

    (a) it is not required to pay the special tax on dividends which is imposed on the mutual fund and which is refundable only on the payment of dividends, and

    (b) its tax on other investment income (other than dividends and capital gains) is reduced by 20% (subject to transitional adjustment).

An investment corporation may be either an open-end or a closed-end corporation, whereas a mutual fund corporation must be an open-end corporation. The distinction between open-end and closed-end corporations lies in the shareholder redemption privilege. An open-end mutual fund corporation is required to provide to shareholders the privilege of share redemption. A closed-end investment corporation or a closed-end mutual fund does not.

[¶9051] Qualification as an Investment Corporation

To qualify as an investment corporation in any year, the corporation must meet the following conditions:[48]

    (1) It must be a Canadian public corporation throughout the year.

    (2) At least 80% of its property throughout the year must consist of shares, bonds, marketable securities, or cash.

    (3) Not less than 95% of its income must be derived from shares, bonds, or marketable securities, or from dispositions of such investments.

    (4) Not less than 85% of its gross revenue for the year must be from sources in Canada. "Gross revenue" means the aggregate of all amounts received or receivable in a year otherwise than as capital.

    (5) Not more than 25% of its gross revenue may be from interest.

    (6) Not more than 10% of its property may consist, *at any time* in the year, of shares, bonds, or securities of any one corporation or debtor, other than Canadian federal, provincial, or municipal government securities.

    (7) No shareholder may own more than 25% of the issued capital stock *at any time* in the year. A person is considered to own not only any shares he or she personally owns but also any shares owned by related persons and a proportionate number of shares held by trusts or partnerships. In this context, the definition of "related persons" is narrowed so that an individual shareholder is considered to be related only to his or her spouse/common-law partner, minor children and grandchildren and corporations controlled by them, the shareholder, or a related group. As a result of this narrow definition, an individual shareholder will not have attributed to him or her shares held by his or her siblings, adult children, or in-laws, for the purpose of the 25% share acquisition limit.

See page ii for explanation of footnotes.

[48] CCH ¶20,079; Sec. 130(3).

¶9051

(8) Not less than 85% of certain income must be distributed to the shareholders before the end of the year. All dividends payable after December 11, 1979, except capital gains dividends, qualify as a distribution to shareholders. This income is the aggregate of:

(a) 66²/₃% of taxable income less taxed capital gains; and

(b) the amount by which intercompany dividends or dividends received from foreign affiliates that are deductible[49] exceed the company's non-capital loss for the year (assuming that the net taxable capital gains for the year are nil);

minus:

(c) any dividends or interest received in the form of shares, bonds, or other securities that are not sold before the end of the year.

Thus, an investment corporation is only obliged to effectively distribute a percentage of the investment income it receives or converts to cash in the year, net of its operating expenses.

For the purpose of meeting the 10% limitation in (6) above, an investment corporation may elect to exclude its investments in wholly owned Canadian subsidiaries and to include the property of those subsidiaries with its own.[50]

[¶9054] Income of Investment Corporation

A corporation that qualifies as an investment corporation is entitled to deduct from its tax otherwise payable an amount equal to 20% of the amount of its taxable income, minus the amount of any taxed capital gains.[51] An investment corporation, being a public corporation, is not subject to tax on dividends received from taxable Canadian corporations or from foreign affiliates. Other investment income, such as interest and non-deductible portfolio dividend income, is subject to an effective tax rate of approximately 20%.

[¶9057] "Taxed Capital Gains" Defined

For the purposes of investment corporations, mutual fund corporations, and mutual fund trusts, the term "taxed capital gains" means the amount of taxable gains for the year from dispositions of property, minus the aggregate of allowable capital losses from dispositions of property and the amount of deductible net capital losses.[52]

[¶9060] Capital Gains Dividends

An investment corporation is entitled to the same benefits as are available to open-end mutual fund corporations with respect to capital gains dividends (see ¶9090).[53] It may distribute its capital gains by electing to pay a special capital gains dividend.[54] This distribution is specifically

---

See page ii for explanation of footnotes.

[49] CCH ¶16,301, ¶16,500; Sec. 112, 113.
[50] CCH ¶20,080; Sec. 130(4).
[51] CCH ¶20,075; Sec. 130(1).

[52] CCH ¶20,079; Sec. 130(3).
[53] CCH ¶20,077; Sec. 130(2).
[54] CCH ¶20,101; Sec. 131(1).

excluded from the deemed dividend provisions.[55] The amount upon which the election may be made is limited to the amount of the capital gains dividend account. The election must be made with respect to the full amount of the dividend payment. If an excessive election is made, a penalty tax of three-quarters of the excess is payable by the corporation.[56]

A capital gains dividend received by a shareholder out of the capital gains dividend account is treated by the shareholder as a capital gain and not as a dividend. The "capital gains dividend account" at any point of time is defined as the amount by which the corporation's capital gains from dispositions after 1971 for all taxation years starting at least 60 days before that particular time, while it was an investment corporation, exceeds the aggregate of:

(a) capital losses from dispositions of property after 1971 for all taxation years starting at least 60 days before that particular time, while it was an investment corporation,

(b) capital gains dividends that became payable before that time and more than 60 days after the end of the last taxation year that ended more than 60 days before that time, and

(c) $^{100}/_{14}$ times the amount of capital gains refunds for previous taxation years ending more than 60 days before that time, during which it was an investment corporation.[57]

In simpler terms, a corporation may pay a capital gains dividend within 60 days after its year end (end of Year 1) to the extent of its net capital gains to that year end (Year 1). Capital gains realized after the year end (in Year 2) may only be distributed as capital gains dividends more than 60 days after the year end (i.e., more than 60 days after the start of Year 2). After the capital gain is distributed as a capital gains dividend, the corporation gets a capital gains refund and the capital gains dividend account is reduced accordingly.

[¶9063] Capital Gains Refund

The Minister may make a capital gains refund without the necessity of an application by an investment corporation.[58] The capital gains refund is an amount equal to the lesser of:

(a) 14% of the total of all capital gains dividends paid by the investment corporation in the period beginning 60 days after the start of the year and ending 60 days after the year end plus the investment corporation's capital gains redemptions for the year; and

(b) the corporation's refundable capital gains tax on hand at the end of the year.

See page ii for explanation of footnotes.

[55] CCH ¶20,119; Sec. 131(4).

[56] CCH ¶24,305; Sec. 184(2).

[57] CCH ¶20,135; Sec. 131(6) "capital gains dividend account".

[58] CCH ¶20,077; Sec. 130(2).

"Refundable capital gains tax on hand" means[59] the least of the following three amounts for the year and any previous years throughout which it was an investment corporation: (i) 28% of its taxable income, (ii) 28% of its taxed capital gains, and (iii) the tax payable under Part I for each of the years (not including the corporate surtax). From this amount is deducted the total of the investment corporation's capital gains refunds for any previous years when it qualified as an investment corporation.

Instead of making an automatic capital gains refund to the investment corporation, the Minister may apply the amount to other tax liabilities of the corporation. The Minister must pay interest on capital gains refunds at the prescribed rate.

[¶9066] Mortgage Investment Corporations

[¶9069] General Characteristics

Loan companies that wish to invest in real estate or leaseholds in Canada for the production of income, either alone or jointly with another corporation incorporated in Canada or any person administering a trust governed by a registered pension plan or deferred profit sharing plan, may be designated as mortgage investment companies if they meet strict borrowing and investing requirements. In turn, these corporations are entitled to special tax treatment similar to investment corporations. A mortgage investment corporation is deemed to be a public corporation.[60]

[¶9072] Qualification as a Mortgage Investment Corporation

From a tax point of view, a corporation is a "mortgage investment corporation" if it complies with the following conditions throughout a taxation year:[61]

(1) The corporation was a Canadian corporation.

(2) Its only undertaking was the investing of funds of the corporation and it did not manage or develop any real property.

(3) The corporation did not invest in mortgages or property outside Canada, loans to non-residents of Canada other than on Canadian property, shares of corporations not resident in Canada, or real property or leasehold interests outside Canada.

(4) The number of shareholders was not less than twenty, with no one shareholder holding more than 25% of the shares of any class. A corporation will meet this requirement throughout its first taxation year if it met it on the last day of that year.[62] A person is considered to own not only shares which that person owns personally, but also (1) any shares owned by persons to whom that person is related, and (2) a proportionate number of any shares held by a trust or partnership of which that person is a beneficiary or

---

See page ii for explanation of footnotes.

[59] CCH ¶20,140; Sec. 131(6) "refundable capital gains tax on hand".
[60] CCH ¶20,096; Sec. 130.1(5).
[61] CCH ¶20,097; Sec. 130.1(6).
[62] CCH ¶20,099; Sec. 130.1(8).

member. In this context, the definition of "related persons" is narrowed so that an individual shareholder is considered to be related only to his or her spouse/common-law partner, minor children and grandchildren and corporations controlled by them, the shareholder, or a related group. As a result of this narrow definition, an individual shareholder will not have attributed to him or her shares held by his or her siblings, adult children, or in-laws.

(5) Preferred shareholders participated equally with common shareholders.

(6) Fifty per cent of the cost of the corporation's property (assets) was invested in residential mortgages, hypothecs, deposits insured by the Canada Deposit Insurance Corporation (or Quebec DIC), or in a credit union or held in cash.

(7) The cost of real property held did not exceed 25% of the cost of total assets.

(8) The corporation did not exceed, generally speaking, a 3-to-1 debt-equity ratio, or, if more than two-thirds of the corporation's property is invested in residential mortgages, hypothecs, or CDIC or QDIC deposits, a 5-to-1 ratio.

[¶9075] Income of Mortgage Investment Corporation

A corporation that qualifies as a mortgage investment corporation throughout the year is entitled to deduct from its income all ordinary dividends paid to its shareholders during the year or within 90 days after the end of the year so long as they were not deducted in the preceding year, and one-half of capital gains dividends paid within the period beginning 91 days after the first of the year and ending 90 days after the year end.[63]

Regular dividends received by shareholders from a mortgage investment corporation will be treated as bond interest received by those shareholders and not as dividends from other Canadian corporations.[64]

[¶9078] Capital Gains Dividend Election

A mortgage investment corporation may elect to distribute its capital gains by electing to pay a special capital gains dividend.[65] Note that capital gains dividends must be elected and paid in the period beginning 91 days after the start of the year and ending 90 days after the year end, in respect of capital gains realized by the mortgage investment corporation in the year. Otherwise, the opportunity to distribute the Mortgage Investment Corporation's capital gains as capital gains dividends is lost.

Dividends paid after February 22, 1994 and relating to taxation years ending prior to February 28, 2000

As a result of the repeal of the $100,000 capital gains exemption, for dividends paid after February 22, 1994 and before February 28, 2000, ⁴/₃ of

See page ii for explanation of footnotes.

[63] CCH ¶20,092; Sec. 130.1(1).   [65] CCH ¶20,095; Sec. 130.1(4).
[64] CCH ¶20,093; Sec. 130.1(2).

the mortgage investment corporation's taxed capital gains (i.e., net capital gains for the year) are treated as capital gains from the disposition of property to the recipient. Such capital gains are no longer available for the capital gains exemption. However, they may be offset by the recipient's "exempt capital gains balance" as defined in ¶5011. In general terms, the exempt capital gains balance will represent the capital gains in respect of the taxpayer's shares in the mortgage investment corporation that accrued up to February 22, 1994, when the taxpayer made the special capital gains election.

Taxation years of a mortgage investment corporation after February 27, 2000

Due to the reduction in the capital gains inclusion rate from $^3/_4$ to $^1/_2$, twice (instead of four-thirds) the mortgage investment corporation's taxed capital gains are treated as capital gains from the disposition of property to the recipients. This change is applicable to taxation years that end after February 27, 2000; however for a taxation year of a mortgage investment corporation that includes either February 28, 2000 or October 17, 2000 or begins after February 28, 2000 and ends before October 17, 2000, the reference to "twice" should be replaced by a reference to the reciprocal fraction of the capital gains inclusion rate that applies to the corporation for the year.

If the capital gains dividend election was not filed as required, a late-filed election can be filed, provided the required penalty is paid.[66] This penalty is the same as that which applies to late-filed elections by mutual fund corporations (see ¶9093).

[¶9081] Mutual Fund Corporations

[¶9084] Types

A typical mutual fund may be either an open-end or closed-end fund and, if the qualifying conditions are met (see ¶9087), either one may be an investment corporation. Only an open-end mutual fund may qualify as a mutual fund corporation. The distinction between open-end and closed-end corporations lies in the shareholder share redemption privilege. This privilege applies only to an open-end corporation.

If a closed-end mutual fund qualifies as an investment corporation, it will be taxed as such. Otherwise, the corporation and its shareholders will be taxed as if the corporation were an ordinary corporation under the various rules for public and private corporations.

All prescribed labour-sponsored venture capital corporations (LSVCC) qualify as mutual fund corporations. However, special limitations apply to their mutual fund treatment (see ¶9089).[67]

See page ii for explanation of footnotes.

[66] CCH ¶20,095a; Sec. 130.1(4.1).   [67] Reg. 6701.

[¶9087] Qualification as a Mutual Fund Corporation

To qualify as a mutual fund corporation, a corporation must be either a prescribed labour-sponsored venture capital corporation or the following conditions must be met:[68]

(1) It must be a Canadian public corporation.

(2) Its only undertakings must be the investing of its own funds (other than real property or a leasehold interest in it), the acquiring, holding, maintaining, improving, leasing, or managing of any real property (or a leasehold interest therein) that is capital property of the corporation, or any combination of such activities.

(3) 95% of the issued shares of the corporation, based on their fair market value, must have conditions attached which require the corporation to accept, at the demand of the holder, the surrender of the shares at prices determined and payable in accordance with the conditions.

Corporations that would otherwise qualify as mutual fund corporations do not so qualify if they are established or maintained primarily for the benefit of non-residents of Canada.[69] The purpose of this rule is to restrict the use of mutual funds as intermediaries through which non-residents can invest in real property in Canada and other taxable Canadian property (TCP) without recognizing taxable gains on the disposition of their shares in the mutual funds. An exception to this rule provides that where all or substantially all of the property of the mutual fund consists of property other than TCP (e.g., if no more than 10% of the fund's property is TCP), the mutual fund may continue to be a mutual fund corporation even where it was established or maintained primarily for the benefit of non-residents. In the computation of the 10% threshold, Canadian resource properties and timber resource properties are included after March 22, 2004. However, any mutual fund that exceeds the 10% threshold on March 23, 2004 will have until January 1, 2007 to comply with this rule.

[¶9089] Labour-Sponsored Venture Capital Corporations

There are several overriding provisions concerning the treatment of prescribed labour-sponsored venture capital corporations as mutual fund corporations. Taxable capital gains, allowable capital losses, and net capital losses are excluded from the determination of the refundable dividend tax on hand of a prescribed labour-sponsored venture capital corporation that is a private corporation. Such a corporation is also precluded from declaring a capital dividend.[70]

[¶9090] Capital Gains Dividends

A mutual fund corporation may distribute its capital gains by electing to pay a special capital gains dividend. The dividend so paid is treated as a capital gain to the shareholder who receives it. The prescribed form for this

---

See page ii for explanation of footnotes.
[68] CCH ¶20,147; Sec. 131(8).   [70] CCH ¶20,155; Sec. 131(11).
[69] CCH ¶20,147a; Sec. 131(8.1).

election is form T2055. This distribution is specifically excluded from the deemed dividend provisions.[71] The election must be made with respect to the full amount of the dividend. If an excessive election is made, that is, the elected amount exceeds the amount eligible for the capital gains treatment, a penalty tax of $3/4$ of the excess is payable by the corporation.[72]

The election must be filed on or before the earlier of the date the dividend becomes payable and the date any part of the dividend is paid. However, see ¶9093 with respect to late-filed elections.

With the repeal of the $100,000 capital gains exemption, all capital gains realized by a mutual fund corporation simply form part of the capital dividend account (see below). If the corporation makes the election, the dividends paid out to its shareholders are treated as capital gains to the shareholders and are no longer eligible for the capital gains exemption. However, those capital gains may be offset to the extent of the individual's "exempt capital gains balance" as defined in ¶5011. In general terms, a taxpayer's "exempt capital gains balance" is comprised of accrued gains in respect of the shares in the corporation to February 22, 1994, where the taxpayer elected to realize such accrued gains in order to take advantage of the $100,000 capital gains exemption. See ¶5011 for more details.

A mutual fund corporation's "capital gains dividend account" is computed at a particular point in time and the particular time will be when a capital gains dividend is payable by the corporation.[73] The account includes all capital gains of the corporation for all taxation years starting at least 60 days before the particular time. In other words, where the particular time is within the first 60 days of the taxation year, the capital gains dividend account will not include capital gains realized in those first 60 days, but will include capital gains realized in prior years.

In calculating the corporation's capital gains dividend account at a particular time, the sum of prior capital gains is reduced by previous allowable capital losses from taxation years which began at least 60 days before that time. For the period from 1992 up to February 22, 1994, there is a reduction of capital losses from property other than non-qualifying real property in the relevant period, and a further reduction for the amount of capital losses from the disposition of non-qualifying real property held prior to March 1992, again for the relevant period. The loss is prorated in a manner similar to the manner in which taxable capital gains from such properties are prorated.

Next, the capital gains dividend account is reduced by the amount of capital gains dividends which became payable before that time and more than 60 days after the end of the last taxation year that ended more than 60 days before that time. The account is reduced by $100/14$ times the amount of capital gains refunds for taxation years ending more than 60 days before that time.

See page ii for explanation of footnotes.

[71] CCH ¶20,101, ¶20,103, ¶20,119, ¶29,499; Sec. 131(1), 131(4); ITAR 32.1; Reg. 2104.
[72] CCH ¶24,305; Sec. 184(2).

[73] CCH ¶20,135; Sec. 131(6) "capital gains dividend account".

¶9090

In simpler terms, a corporation may pay a capital gains dividend within 60 days after its year end (end of Year 1) to the extent of its net capital gains to that year end (Year 1). Capital gains realized after the year end (in Year 2) may only be distributed as capital gains dividends more than 60 days after the year end (i.e., more than 60 days after the start of Year 2). After the capital gain is distributed as a capital gains dividend, the corporation gets a capital gains refund and the capital gains dividend account is reduced accordingly.

[¶9093] Late-Filed Elections for Capital Gains Dividends

A late-filed election is deemed to have been made within the time limits,[74] provided the mutual fund corporation fulfills all three of the following conditions:

(1) the late-filed election is made in the prescribed manner and prescribed form;

(2) the mutual fund corporation makes an estimate of the penalty tax in respect of the late-filed election and pays the penalty tax at the time the election is made; and

(3) before the time the election is made, the directors or other persons legally entitled to administer the affairs of the corporation authorize the filing of the late-filed election.[75]

This penalty tax for the purposes of item (2) above is calculated as 1% per annum of the amount of the dividend for each month or part of a month between the date the election should have been made and the date the election is in fact made, with the maximum penalty being $500 per year.[76]

The Minister must issue a notice of assessment for the amount of the penalty tax after a late-filed election has been made.[77] On assessment, the mutual fund corporation must remit any penalty tax assessed in excess of amounts already paid.

Where a dividend has become payable by a mutual fund corporation, the Minister may request that the mutual fund corporation file a late-filed capital gains dividend election. If the mutual fund corporation does not file the election within 90 days, the dividend is effectively confirmed as an ordinary taxable dividend and the mutual fund corporation may not subsequently make a late-filed election in respect of the dividend.[78]

[¶9096] Redemption of Shares

A mutual fund corporation may distribute capital gains to its shareholders through a redemption of its shares.[79] This distribution is specifically excluded from the deemed dividend provisions. The redemption of shares is

---

See page ii for explanation of footnotes.

[74] CCH ¶20,101; Sec. 131(1).
[75] CCH ¶20,102; Sec. 131(1.1).
[76] CCH ¶20,102b; Sec. 131(1.3).

[77] CCH ¶20,102c; Sec. 131(1.4).
[78] CCH ¶20,102a; Sec. 131(1.2).
[79] CCH ¶20,101, ¶20,119; Sec. 131(1), 131(4).

treated as a capital transaction giving rise to a capital gain in the shareholder's hands.

Capital gains redemptions entitle a mutual fund corporation to a refund out of the refundable capital gains tax on hand. "Capital gains redemption" means that proportion of the aggregate of:

(a) $100/14$ times the corporation's refundable capital gains tax on hand at the end of the year; and

(b) the excess of the fair market value of its issued shares and debt owing by the corporation;

over:

(c) cost amounts of property, including cash;

that:

(d) the amounts paid in the year on the redemptions of shares

is of:

(e) the fair market value at the end of the year of its issued shares plus amounts paid on share redemptions.[80]

[¶9099] Capital Gains Refund

The Minister may make a capital gains refund without any application therefor having been made by a mutual fund corporation. The capital gains refund is the lesser of:

(a) 14% of the aggregate of all capital gains dividends paid by the corporation in the period commencing 60 days after the commencement of the year and ending 60 days after the end of the year and its capital gains redemptions for the year; and

(b) the corporation's refundable capital gains tax on hand at the end of the year.[81]

"Refundable capital gains tax on hand" [82] is the amount for the current and any previous year throughout which it was a mutual fund corporation which is the least of:

(a) 28% of its taxable income for each of those years;

(b) 28% of its taxed capital gains for each of those years; and

(c) the tax payable under Part I for each of those years, excluding the corporate surtax;

minus:

(d) the aggregate of the capital gains refunds for those previous years when it qualified as a mutual fund corporation.

See page ii for explanation of footnotes.

[80] CCH ¶20,136; Sec. 131(6) "capital gains redemptions".
[81] CCH ¶20,113; Sec. 131(2).
[82] CCH ¶20,140; Sec. 131(6) "refundable capital gains tax on hand".

Instead of making an automatic capital gains refund to the mutual fund corporation, the Minister may apply the amount to other tax liabilities of the corporation.[83] The Minister must pay interest on capital gains refunds at the prescribed rate.[84]

If the appropriate capital gains refund for a year is not received with the notice of original assessment, the mutual fund corporation may apply for such a refund at any time within four years from the date of the original assessment. This period is extended to seven years if the refund arises as a result of a carryback from a subsequent year, such as a loss carryback or investment tax credit carryback.

[¶9102] Dividend Refund to Mutual Fund Corporations

Every corporation that was a mutual fund corporation throughout a taxation year will be treated as a private corporation for the purposes of the dividend refund and the refundable dividend tax on hand (see ¶9027).[85] The refundable dividend tax on hand is available to a mutual fund corporation if it has paid Part IV tax in earlier years before becoming an investment corporation. Part IV tax for a given year is not payable by a mutual fund corporation that was an investment corporation (other than a subject corporation) at any time in the year.

Dividends received will therefore be subject to Part IV tax of $33^{1}/_{3}\%$ and dividends paid will generate a refund of this tax. To compute its refundable dividend tax on hand at the end of a taxation year, a mutual fund corporation simply totals two amounts:

(1) its taxes payable under Part IV for the year, and

(2) if it was a private corporation at the end of its preceding taxation year, its refundable dividend tax on hand at the end of the preceding year.

From this total, the mutual fund corporation then deducts its dividend refund for its preceding taxation year. The remainder, if any, is the corporation's refundable dividend tax on hand.

The above dividend refund does not apply to a prescribed labour-sponsored venture capital corporation since such a corporation is exempt from Part IV tax.

[¶9103] "TCP Gains Distribution" To Non-Resident Shareholder

If a mutual fund corporation makes a capital gains dividend election (see ¶9090) in respect of a dividend, each shareholder to whom the dividend is paid is deemed to have received a "TCP gains distribution" equal to the lesser of the amount of the dividend and the shareholder's *"pro rata* portion" at that time of the corporation's "TCP gains balance".[86] The corporation's TCP gains balance at any time is computed by taking the total of its capital gains from the disposition of TCP after March 22, 2004 and before that time and the TCP gains distributions received from other mutual fund

---

See page ii for explanation of footnotes.

[83] CCH ¶20,114; Sec. 131(3).
[84] CCH ¶20,115, ¶20,117; Sec. 131(3.1), 131(3.2).
[85] CCH ¶20,123; Sec. 131(5).
[86] CCH ¶20,123c; Sec. 131(5.1).

corporations and trusts (generally meaning amounts received from other mutual funds out of their TCP gains balances) before that time. The corporation's losses from dispositions of TCP after March 22, 2004 and any amounts previously distributed to its shareholders as TCP gains distributions are deducted in computing the TCP gains balance.[87] The shareholder's *pro rata* portion of the corporation's TCP gains balance equals the TCP gains balance multiplied by the fraction equal to the amount of the dividend received by the shareholder divided by the total amount of the dividend.[88]

Because the TCP gains distribution equals the lesser of the dividend received by the shareholder and the shareholder's *pro rata* portion of the corporation's TCP gains balance, if the dividend received exceeds such *pro rata* portion, the excess will not be a TCP gains distribution, and instead will continue to be a capital gains dividend (assuming the capital gains dividend election was made).

If the recipient shareholder is a non-resident person or a partnership that is not a Canadian partnership, the portion of a capital gains dividend that is a TCP gains distribution is deemed not to be a capital gains dividend, except for the purpose of computing the mutual fund corporation's capital gains dividend account. Instead, the TCP gains distribution is deemed to be a taxable dividend subject to the 25% non-resident withholding tax. The mutual fund corporation will be required to withhold such tax on the payment of the deemed taxable dividend. The rate of tax will often be reduced by treaty, as is often the case with other taxable dividends paid to treaty-resident shareholders.

If the recipient shareholder is a resident, the TCP gains distribution is of no practical consequence, as it continues to be a capital gains dividend. However, as noted above, if the recipient is a mutual fund corporation or mutual fund trust, any TCP gains distribution that it receives is added to its TCP gains balance.

These rules apply after March 22, 2004 to a dividend paid by a mutual fund corporation only if more than 5% of the dividend is received by or on behalf of shareholders that are non-residents or partnerships that are not Canadian partnerships.[89]

[¶9105] Capital Gains Tax on Mutual Fund Corporations

A mutual fund corporation that does not qualify as an investment corporation is subject to the tax on capital gains,[90] which is at the normal corporate rate of 28% (after deducting a provincial tax credit) of the taxable portion of the gain, or an effective rate of approximately 14% ($1/2$ of capital gains are included as taxable capital gains). When the fund distributes the gain to its shareholders, it receives a "capital gains refund" equal to 14% of the gain distributed.

See page ii for explanation of footnotes.

[87] CCH ¶20,141; Sec. 131(6) "TCP gains balance".
[88] CCH ¶20,139; Sec. 131(6) "pro rata portion".
[89] CCH ¶20,123g; Sec. 131(5.2).
[90] CCH ¶20,143; Sec. 131(7).

[¶9108] Tax Instalments

The monthly tax instalments of a mutual fund corporation may be reduced by $1/12$ of the aggregate of the corporation's capital gains refund and the amount of the corporation's dividend refund for the year.[91]

[¶9111] Mutual Fund Trusts

[¶9114] Concepts

The concepts of a mutual fund trust and a mutual fund corporation are relatively new in Canadian tax law. Inasmuch as there are mutual funds that conduct their operations as open-end trusts, the concept of a mutual fund trust has become recognized for tax purposes.

[¶9117] Mutual Fund Trust Requirements

A trust is a "mutual fund trust" at any time if it meets the following conditions at that time:[92]

(1) it was a unit trust resident in Canada;

(2) its only undertakings were the investing of its funds in property (other than real property or an interest therein), the acquiring, holding, maintaining, improving, leasing, or managing of any real property (or an interest therein) that is capital property of the trust, or any combination of such activities; and

(3) it complied with conditions[93] relating to the number of its unitholders, dispersal of ownership of its units, and public trading of the units.

A new trust that becomes a mutual fund trust at any time before the 91st day after the taxation year in which it was created is deemed to have been a mutual fund trust from the day that it was created, if the trust so elects in its return for the year.[94] This provision, in effect, permits the creation of a trust and the subsequent filing of a prospectus. Once the prospectus is filed, distribution to the public is complete, and the above three conditions are met, the trust is deemed to have been a mutual fund trust since the time of its creation.

A "unit trust" is an *inter vivos* trust where the interest of each beneficiary under the trust is described by reference to the units of the trust.[95] A trust is a unit trust if at least 95% of its issued units have conditions attached which provide for a unit holder's right of unit redemption, similar to that of a mutual fund corporation with respect to its shares, at prices determined and payable in accordance with the conditions attached to the units.

Alternatively, a trust is considered a unit trust if the following conditions are met:

See page ii for explanation of footnotes.

[91] CCH ¶22,704; Sec. 157(3).
[92] CCH ¶20,168i; Sec. 132(6).
[93] CCH ¶20,168m–20,168o; Reg. 4801–4803.
[94] CCH ¶20,168j; Sec. 132(6.1).
[95] CCH ¶13,960; Sec. 108(2).

¶9108

(1) It is resident in Canada.

(2) Its only undertaking is the investing of its funds in property (other than real property or an interest in real property), the acquiring, holding, maintaining, improving, leasing, or managing of any real property, or interest in real property, that is capital property of the trust, or any combination of such activities.

(3) Not less than 80% of its property throughout the year consists of shares, share warrants, bonds, debentures, mortgages, hypothecary claims, marketable securities or cash, notes or similar obligations, real property located in Canada and interests in such property, or of rights to or interests in any rental or royalty from an oil or gas well, or from a mineral resource situated in Canada. Note that where the fund otherwise meets this 80% requirement, but it would not meet the requirement if one ignored its real property located in Canada or interests in real property, the units of the trust must be listed on a designated stock exchange at any time in the year or in the following taxation year. This latter requirement generally applies to real estate investment trusts (REITs), meaning the REITs must be publicly traded on designated exchanges to qualify as unit trusts.

(4) Not less than 95% of its income for the year is from investments described in (3) above or from dispositions of such investments.

(5) Not more than 10% of its property may consist, at any time in the year, of shares, bonds, or securities of any one corporation or debtor, other than Canadian federal, provincial, or municipal government securities.

(6) All holdings of and transactions in any of its units must comply with prescribed conditions relating to the number of unitholders, dispersal of ownership of units, and public trading of units.

A trust is deemed not to be a mutual fund trust if at any particular time it can reasonably be considered as having been established or maintained primarily for the benefit of non-residents of Canada.[96] The purpose of this rule is to prevent non-residents from avoiding Canadian tax by using a mutual fund trust to invest indirectly in taxable Canadian property (TCP). However, such a trust may qualify as a mutual fund trust at the particular time (assuming it otherwise meets the criteria) under either of two circumstances:

(a) if, at that time, all or substantially all of the trust's property consisted of property other than TCP; or

(b) if it did not issue any units after February 20, 1990 to a person who, after reasonable inquiry, it had reason to believe was not resident in Canada.

[¶9120] Capital Gains Refund

Without any application having been made by a mutual fund trust, the Minister may make a capital gains refund where a mutual fund has distribut-

---

[96] CCH ¶20,168l; Sec. 132(7); Reg. 4801.

ed its capital gains to its unitholders through a redemption of units.[97] The redemption of units is treated as a capital transaction giving rise to a capital gain in the unit holders' hands. The capital gains refund is an amount equal to the lesser of:

   (a) 14.5% of all the trust's capital gains redemptions for the year; and

   (b) the trust's refundable capital gains tax on hand at the end of the year.

   If the appropriate capital gains refund for a year is not received with the notice of original assessment, the mutual fund trust may apply for such a refund at any time within four years from the date of the original assessment. This period is extended to seven years if the refund arises as a result of a carryback from a subsequent year such as a loss carryback or investment tax credit carryback.

   Instead of making an automatic capital gains refund to a mutual fund trust, the Minister may apply the refund to its other tax liabilities.[98] In either case, the Minister must notify the trust.

   Interest must be paid or applied on the capital gains refund at prescribed rates.[99] For taxation years ending after June 2003, the interest is calculated for the period beginning on the day that is 30 days after the later of 90 days after the end of the trust's year and the day the return for the year was filed, and ending on the day the refund is paid or applied. For taxation years ending before July 2003, the interest is calculated for the period beginning on the day that is 45 days after the later of 90 days after the end of the trust's year and the day the return for the year was filed, and ending on the day the refund is paid or applied.

   If it is subsequently determined that the capital gains refund initially paid or applied to the trust was in excess of that which should have been paid or applied, the interest shall be recalculated and the difference repaid to the Minister, together with interest on that difference calculated from the date the original interest was paid or applied to the date such repayment is made.[100]

   The "capital gains redemptions" of a mutual fund trust are a proportion of the aggregate of:

   (a) $^{100}/_{14.5}$ of the trust's refundable capital gains tax on hand at the end of the year; and

   (b) the excess of the fair market value of its issued units and the debt owing by the trust at the end of the year over the cost amount of all its properties, including any money of the trust on hand at that time.[101]

See page ii for explanation of footnotes.

[97] CCH ¶20,165; Sec. 132(1).
[98] CCH ¶20,167; Sec. 132(2).
[99] CCH ¶20,167a; Sec. 132(2.1); Reg. 4301.

[100] CCH ¶20,167b; Sec. 132(2.2).

[101] CCH ¶20,168a, ¶20,168f; Sec. 132(4), 132(5).

¶9120

The proportion applied to the aggregate is the total of the amounts paid in the year on the redemption of units to the total of those amounts plus the fair market value of all the issued units at the end of the year.

Example:

Assume the following for the 2011 taxation year:

Refundable capital gains tax on hand at the end of the year	$ 20,000
Amount paid in the year on the redemption of units	30,000
Fair market value of issued units at the end of the year	100,000
Debt outstanding at the end of the year	50,000
Cost amount of properties and money at the end of the year	140,000

The capital gains redemptions for the year will be:

$$\frac{30,000}{(30,000 + 100,000)} \times ((\frac{100}{14.5} \times 20,000) + (100,000 + 50,000 - 140,000)) =$$

$$\frac{30,000}{130,000} \times 147,931 = \$34,138$$

The capital gains refund for the year will be the lesser of:

14.5% of 34,138 = $4,950

or $20,000

= $4,950

[¶9121] "TCP Gains Distribution" to Non-Resident Beneficiary

If a mutual fund trust makes a designation under which taxable capital gains are flowed through to its beneficiaries (see ¶7390), each beneficiary in respect of which the designation is made is deemed to have received as a "TCP gains distribution" the lesser of: (i) twice the amount so designated, and (ii) the beneficiary's *pro rata* portion of the trust's "TCP gains balance" for the taxation year.[102] The "TCP gains balance" of a mutual fund trust for a particular taxation year is defined as the total of its capital gains from dispositions of TCP after March 22, 2004 and at or before the end of the taxation year, plus any TCP gains distributions received from other mutual fund trusts (generally meaning amounts received from other mutual fund trusts out of their TCP gains balance) at or before the end of the taxation year. Deducted from the trust's TCP gains balance for the taxation year are the trust's capital losses from dispositions of TCP after March 22, 2004 and at or before the end of the taxation year, plus any amounts distributed to its beneficiaries as TCP gains distributions in previous taxation years.[103]

The beneficiary's *pro rata* portion of the trust's TCP gains balance for a taxation year equals the trust's TCP gains balance for the year multiplied by the fraction equal to the amount designated to the beneficiary for the year divided by the total of all amounts designated for the year.[104]

If the above designation is made in respect of a non-resident beneficiary or of a partnership that is not a Canadian partnership, the amount so designated is deemed to be a taxable capital gain of the beneficiary only to the extent that it exceeds the amount of the TCP gains distribution. In addition, ½ of the TCP gains distribution will be included in the benefici-

See page ii for explanation of footnotes.

[102] CCH ¶20,168g; Sec. 132(5.1). [104] CCH ¶20,168b; Sec. 132(4) "pro rata portion".

[103] CCH ¶20,168d; Sec. 132(4) "TCP gains balance".

ary's income and therefore subject to the 25% non-resident withholding tax. As with other trust income so distributed, the 25% withholding tax may be reduced by tax treaty or convention (typically to 15%, as is the case with the *Canada–U.S. Income Tax Convention*).

A resident beneficiary in respect of which a designation is made will not be affected by the above characterization: the amount designated will remain a taxable capital gain to the beneficiary from the disposition of a capital property. If the beneficiary is another mutual fund trust or a mutual fund corporation, the amount of the TCP gains distribution must be added to its own TCP gains balance.

These rules apply to an amount designated by a mutual fund trust for a taxation year only if more than 5% of all such amounts designated in the year are in respect of beneficiaries that are non-residents or partnerships that are not Canadian partnerships.[105]

[¶9123] Application of Trust Provisions

A mutual fund trust can distribute capital dividends to its unit holders free of tax. However, it is prevented from making a tax-free distribution of dividends which it has received and which have been paid out of a corporation's tax-paid undistributed surplus or 1971 capital surplus.[106] Such dividends would therefore normally be retained by the trust and distributed only on the redemption of its units.

[¶9126] Rate of Tax and Tax Instalments

The rate of tax payable by a mutual fund trust on both income and capital gains retained by the trust is 29%.[107] When a provincial tax rate of 50% and the federal surtax which is applicable to mutual fund trusts are included, the combined federal and provincial tax on a mutual fund trust is approximately 45%.

The quarterly tax instalments payable by a mutual fund trust may be reduced by one-quarter of the trust's capital gains refund for the year.[108]

[¶9129] Designation by Mutual Fund Trust

A tax mechanism addresses problems relating to the fact that a mutual fund trust must recognize recapture, and no mechanism existed before 1988 to assign the recapture to the beneficiaries who received the benefit of previous claims of capital cost allowance. A mutual fund trust can now designate an amount in respect of a unit owned by a taxpayer.[109] This designated amount is deductible from trust income and included in the taxpayer's income in the year in which the year of the trust ends. Any amount included in the taxpayer's income is added to the adjusted cost base of the trust unit. The amount that may be designated is limited to the aggregate of:

See page ii for explanation of footnotes.

[105] CCH ¶20,168h; Sec. 132(5.2).   [108] CCH ¶22,685; Sec. 156(2).
[106] CCH ¶20,189; Sec. 132(3).
[107] CCH ¶19,250; Sec. 122(1).   [109] CCH ¶20,209; Sec. 132.1.

¶9123

(a) the excess of capital cost allowance designated to taxpayers before 1988 over designated capital cost allowance amounts for the year and previous years other than the amount designated for the year in respect of a particular unit; and

(b) the excess of adjusted cost base reductions in previous years over reductions for the year and previous years other than the amount designated for the year in respect of the particular unit.

A trust cannot use these designated amounts to create a loss. Amounts that are not deductible due to this limitation may be carried forward to the following year. The deduction is also denied where the beneficiary of the unit is tax exempt.

Example:

> A and B each own one unit in a mutual fund trust at the end of 2009. Each unit has an adjusted cost base (ACB) of $200. In 2010, the trust flowed through $50 in rental income to each unit holder and sufficient capital cost allowance (CCA) was allocated to shelter this income. In 2011, the trust earns $40 a unit and takes CCA sufficient to shelter this income. The trust distributes the cash received to each unit holder.

> On January 2, 2012, the trust sells the property and experiences recapture of $90 a unit. In 2012, the trust may designate a total amount of $50 and $40 to each unit holder. This results in no recapture being taxed in the hands of the trust. The $90 is added to the ACB of the unit and therefore no capital gain or loss occurs on the surrender of the unit. As a result, each unit holder is in the same position as he or she would be in if he or she owned the interest in real property personally.

[¶9130] Taxation Year of Mutual Fund Trust

Qualifying trusts may elect to have a December 15 year end for tax purposes rather than a December 31 year end.[110] This election allows them to calculate their income and distributions on a more administratively workable basis and reduce the risk of errors. In order to qualify for this election, the trust must be a mutual fund trust on the 74th day of the following calendar year, i.e., on the 90th day following the December 15 year end.

The income of an electing trust for a particular taxation year that ends on December 15 of a calendar year is adjusted to take into account the trust's interest in each partnership with a fiscal period that ends in the last 16 days of that calendar year and in each other trust that has a taxation year ending in the same 16 days. In these circumstances, each amount paid, or made payable, by an electing trust until the end of the calendar year is deemed to have been paid or payable to its unitholders at the end of the particular year ending December 15.

In addition, any mutual fund trust, as well as any electing trust with a December 15 year end, may choose an amount designated by it for a taxation year to be added in when computing its income for the year. To the extent that it is allocated to unitholders as income in the trust's tax return for the year and is in respect of amounts paid or payable in the year to

---

See page ii for explanation of footnotes.

[110] CCH ¶20,213a; Sec. 132.11(1).

unitholders, this additional income may be flowed through to unitholders who will be allowed to treat it as ordinary income distribution. The trust will generally be allowed to deduct the amount of those overdistributions in computing its income for the following year. This new mechanism will allow a mutual fund trust to maximize its capital gains refunds.

[¶9131] Mutual Funds — Qualifying Exchange

Reorganizations of certain mutual funds are allowed to take place on a tax-deferred basis. In general terms, investors in one mutual fund (the transferor fund) can exchange their interests in the transferor fund for units in another fund (transferee fund) on a tax-deferred basis, in an exchange where all or substantially all of the property of the transferor fund is transferred to the transferee fund. The transfer of property from the transferor to the transferee also takes place on a tax-deferred basis.[111]

These tax-deferred "rollovers" are allowed if the reorganization is a "qualifying exchange". A qualifying exchange is defined as a transfer of all or substantially all of the property of a mutual fund corporation, other than a SIFT wind-up corporation, after December 19, 2007, or mutual fund trust (the "transferor" fund) to a mutual fund trust (the "transferee" fund), where all or substantially all of the shares or units in the transferor are disposed of to the transferor within 60 days after the transfer in exchange for units of the transferee (and no other consideration is received other than pursuant to the exercise of a statutory right of dissent).[112] After December 19, 2007, a mutual fund corporation that is a SIFT wind-up corporation may not be part of a qualifying exchange giving rise to the above tax-deferred rollover between mutual funds (as reported in Chapter 6, SIFT entities have their stand-alone regime for conversion to corporations after July 14, 2008). This rollover is elective, so that it applies only if the transferor and transferee jointly file a prescribed election form within six months after the transfer of property. The CRA has historically taken the position that "all or substantially all" generally means 90% or more. In this case, however, it is not clear whether this determination is made on a fair market value basis or cost or other basis. These rollover provisions can be summarized as follows:

(1) *Deemed year end.* Both the transferor and transferee have deemed year ends at the acquisition time, with their next taxation years beginning immediately after that time. However, for the purposes of the Part 1.3 capital tax only, the transferor's year is deemed to end immediately before the transfer time, so that its capital tax liability for the year reflects its assets and liabilities before the transfer.

(2) *Rollover of transferred property in qualifying exchange.* The proceeds of disposition to the transferor and the cost to the transferee of each transferred property are generally equal to an amount elected by the parties in their joint election in respect of the qualifying exchange. The elected amount in respect of the property cannot be less than the cost amount of the property to the transferor (or less than the lesser of its capital cost and

---

See page ii for explanation of footnotes.

[111] CCH ¶20,214; Sec. 132.2(1).   [112] CCH ¶20,215; Sec. 132.2(2) "qualifying exchange".

cost amount, in the case of depreciable property) and the elected amount is also effectively restricted from being less than the fair market value of any consideration (other than units in the transferee) received by the transferor for the transfer of the property. Note, however, that if the property's fair market value is less than its cost amount, or less than the lesser of its cost amount and capital cost in the case of depreciable property (i.e. it has an accrued loss), the loss must be realized, because the property is deemed to be disposed of at fair market value.

(3) *Property not transferred in a qualifying exchange.* Property held by either the transferor or transferee fund, which was not transferred in the qualifying exchange, must be written down, so that accrued capital losses and terminal losses are realized where applicable. More particularly, property other than depreciable property of a prescribed class is deemed to have been disposed of immediately before the acquisition time (in other words, in between the transfer time and the acquisition time) at the lesser of (1) the property's fair market value, and (2) the greater of the property's cost amount (or in the case of depreciable property, the lesser of its cost amount and capital cost), and an amount designated by the fund. Effectively, this means that accrued losses must be realized in the taxation year that ends at the acquisition time, while any accrued gains can be realized if so designated by the fund. A similar rule applies to a "latent" terminal loss in respect of depreciable property of a class held by the fund immediately before the acquisition time; the terminal loss must be realized in the fund's taxation year ending at the acquisition time.

(4) *Property taken back by transferor fund.* The cost of property received by the transferor in the qualifying exchange, other than units in the transferee fund, is deemed to be its fair market value. Units in the transferee fund received by the transferor are deemed to have a cost of nil, and if, within 60 days, those units are disposed of by the transferor to (former) investors in the transferor in exchange for their shares or units in the transferor, the disposition takes place on a tax-free rollover basis.

(5) *Rollover for investors in transferor fund.* If the investors in the transferor fund dispose of their shares or units in that fund in exchange for units in the transferee fund within 60 days of the transfer time, the exchange takes place on a tax-deferred rollover basis. Any "exempt capital gains balance" of an investor in respect of the transferor fund (see ¶5011) is flowed through to the transferee fund, so that it remains available to shelter future capital gains realized by the investor in respect of his or her units in the transferee fund.

(6) *Other consequences of a qualifying exchange.* Once the qualifying exchange is complete, the transferor fund is deemed to be neither a mutual fund corporation nor trust, as the case may be, effective for taxation years beginning after the transfer time. Effectively, this means that the transferor fund loses its mutual fund status for the taxation year beginning at the acquisition time.[113]

See page ii for explanation of footnotes.

[113] CCH ¶20,214; Sec. 132.2(1).

A special rule provides that a share or unit in the transferor which otherwise would be a "qualified investment" for certain deferred income plans (but for the qualifying exchange) retains its status as a qualified investment, until the earlier of the 60 days after the transfer time and the day it is exchanged for a unit in the transferee fund. This means that the merger of two mutual fund trusts or a mutual fund trust and a mutual fund corporation will not cause shares or units of the transferor fund to cease to be qualified investments for trusts governed by registered retirement savings plans, registered retirement income funds, deferred profit sharing plans, registered education saving plans, registered disability savings plans, and, beginning in 2009, tax-free savings accounts. Another special rule provides that the transferor's "refundable capital gains tax on hand" (RCGTOH) at the end of its taxation year that includes the transfer time (in almost all cases, meaning the taxation year ending at the acquisition time), minus any capital gains refund it claims for the year, is flowed through and added to the transferee fund's RCGTOH account for its taxation years beginning after the transfer time.

Furthermore, both a transferor fund and transferee fund in a qualifying exchange are prohibited from carrying forward any non-capital loss, net capital loss, restricted farm loss, farm loss, or limited partnership loss from a year beginning before the transfer to a taxation year beginning after the transfer time.

[¶9132] Non-Resident Owned Investment Corporations (NROs)

[¶9135] "Non-Resident Owned Investment Corporation" Defined

To qualify as an NRO, the shares and funded debt of the company must be 100% owned by non-residents or other NROs.

An "NRO investment corporation" means[114] a corporation incorporated in Canada that, throughout the period beginning on the day of its incorporation and ending on the last day of the taxation year in which it ceased to be such a corporation, complied with the following conditions:

(1) All of its issued shares and bonds, debentures and other funded indebtedness were owned:

    (a) beneficially by non-resident persons other than any foreign affiliate of a resident taxpayer;

    (b) by trustees for the benefit of non-resident persons or their unborn issue; or

    (c) by one or more NRO investment corporations meeting the requirements of (a) and (b) above.

---

[114] CCH ¶20,263; Sec. 133(8) "non-resident-owned investment corporation".

(2) Its income for each taxation year ending in the period was derived from:

    (a) ownership of or trading in bonds, shares, debentures, mortgages, hypothecary claims, bills, notes, etc., and interest thereon;

    (b) lending money with or without security;

    (c) rents, hire of chattels, charter-party fees or remunerations, annuities, royalties, interest, or dividends;

    (d) estates or trusts; or

    (e) disposition of capital property.

(3) Not more than 10% of its gross revenue for each taxation year ending in the period was derived from rents, hire of chattels, charter-party fees, or remunerations.

(4) Its principal business in each taxation year ending in the period was not:

    (a) the making of loans; or

    (b) trading or dealing in bonds, shares, debentures, mortgages, hypothecary claims, bills, notes, etc., or any interest therein.

(5) It has on or before the earlier of February 28, 2000 and the day that is 90 days after the commencement of its first taxation year, elected in prescribed manner to be taxed as an NRO investment corporation.[115]

(6) It has not, before the end of the last taxation year in the period, revoked the election referred to in (5).

In the case of an amalgamation, each of the predecessor corporations must have been an NRO immediately before the amalgamation.

As noted in (5), a corporation must elect to be an NRO on or before the earlier of February 27, 2000 and the day that is 90 days after the commencement of its first taxation year beginning after 1971. The significance of the February 27, 2000 date is that the federal government announced on this date that NROs were being phased out, for income tax purposes, over a three-year period. In this regard, the NRO definition now provides that a corporation is not an NRO in any taxation year that ends after the earlier of (i) the first time after February 27, 2000 that the corporation effects an "increase in capital", and (ii) the corporation's last taxation year that begins before 2003. An increase in capital is defined as any transaction under which the corporation issues debt or shares that increase the total of the corporation's liabilities and the fair market value of all of its shares to an amount that is substantially greater than the total on February 27, 2000.[116] A transitional rule allows a corporation to take advantage of the dividend refund mechanism applicable to NROs in the first taxation year in which it is no longer an NRO.

---

[115] CCH ¶20,231–20,233; Reg. 500–502.   [116] CCH ¶20,262; Sec. 133(8) "increase in capital".

[¶9138] Computation of Income

In computing the income of an NRO investment corporation, no deduction is allowed for:[117]

(a) interest on bonds, debentures, securities, or other indebtedness; and

(b) depletion allowances.

The income and taxable income of an NRO investment corporation is computed by:

(1) including taxable capital gains and allowable capital losses from dispositions of taxable Canadian property;

(2) including twice ($3/2$ for taxation years that include days after February 27 and before October 18, 2000 and $4/3$ for taxation years ending before February 28, 2000) the amount of the taxable capital gains and allowable capital losses, i.e., the full amount of the gain or loss which is taxed at a 25% rate; and

(3) including the full amount of capital dividends received from a private corporation.

In computing taxable income, the only deductions allowed are:[118]

(a) interest received from other NRO investment corporations;

(b) foreign taxes paid on foreign source income; and

(c) net capital losses on taxable Canadian property which may be carried forward or back.

Although, as noted in (b) above, an NRO investment corporation is allowed a deduction for foreign taxes paid on foreign source income, NRO investment corporations are not allowed a tax credit for taxes paid to either foreign governments or to Canadian provincial governments.[119]

[¶9141] Special Tax Rate

The special rate of tax applicable to NRO investment corporations is 25%.[120] Except with respect to capital gains, this tax is refundable when the surplus is distributed to non-residents; the applicable rate of withholding tax then applies.

[¶9144] Capital Gains

An NRO will be subject to a 25% non-refundable tax[121] on the full amount of capital gains realized on taxable Canadian property. See ¶5095. Capital gains on other capital property are not taxed. In order to provide a mechanism for distributing net capital gains on specified Canadian property tax free to shareholders, a surplus account has been created, i.e., the capital

---

[117] CCH ¶20,217; Sec. 133(1).

[118] CCH ¶20,219; Sec. 133(2).

[119] CCH ¶20,223; Sec. 133(4).

[120] CCH ¶20,221; Sec. 133(3).

[121] CCH ¶20,257, ¶20,269; Sec. 133(8) "allowable refund", 133(9) "allowable refundable tax on hand".

gains dividend account,[122] which is the aggregate (in respect of the period January 1, 1972, to the end of any immediately preceding taxation year) of:

(a) capital gains from dispositions of Canadian property[123] or shares of another NRO; and

(b) capital gains dividends from other NROs (but not capital dividends from ordinary private corporations);

minus:

(c) capital losses from dispositions of Canadian property or shares of another NRO;

(d) 25% of the excess of capital gains over capital losses on taxable Canadian property; and

(e) all capital gains dividends previously paid.

Canadian property means any other property that is not foreign property. The rules for capital gains on Canadian property are similar to those for capital gains of private corporations.

Capital gains realized by an NRO on taxable Canadian property that is also Canadian property will be effectively taxed at a rate of 25% on the full amount thereof and may be distributed without any further tax. Also, by means of the capital gains dividend account, capital gains on other Canadian property realized by an NRO may be distributed without any tax.

[¶9147] Capital Gains Dividends — Election

A dividend paid by an NRO is deemed to be a capital gains dividend to the extent that it does not exceed the capital gains dividend account.[124]

If an NRO so elects:[125]

(1) the dividend will be deemed a capital gains dividend, with the result that it will not be subject to withholding tax, and it will not be considered to be a taxable dividend for the purpose of earning a refund of NRO tax;[126] and

(2) the dividend will not be included in the income of another NRO that receives the amount.

The election is to be filed on or before the day on which the dividend becomes payable or is paid. However, see ¶9150 regarding late-filed elections.

Where a dividend becomes payable simultaneously on more than one class of shares of an NRO, it may be desirable to elect[127] to pay the dividend on one or more classes out of the NRO's capital gains dividend account. The dividend is then deemed to be paid on each class to become payable at

---

See page ii for explanation of footnotes.

[122] CCH ¶20,261; Sec. 133(8) "capital gains dividend account".

[123] CCH ¶20,259; Sec. 133(8) "Canadian property".

[124] CCH ¶20,243; Sec. 133(7.1).

[125] CCH ¶20,231, ¶20,243, ¶20,243a; Sec. 133(7.1); Reg. 500, Reg. 501, Reg. 502, Reg. 2105.

[126] CCH ¶20,239; Sec. 133(6).

[127] CCH ¶20,243; Sec. 133(7.1).

different times for purposes of an election. The NRO may designate the order in which the dividends are to become payable on the different classes. However, that designation must be made on or before the day that the election is required to be filed. In any other case, the Minister designates the order of payment.[128]

[¶9150] Late-Filed Elections for Capital Gains Dividend

A late-filed election for a capital gains dividend by an NRO is deemed to have been made within the time limits[129] if all three of the following conditions are met:

(1) the late-filed election is made in the prescribed manner and prescribed form;

(2) the NRO makes an estimate of the penalty tax in respect of the late-filed election and pays the penalty tax at the time the election is made; and

(3) before the time the election is made, the directors or other persons legally entitled to administer the affairs of the corporation authorize the filing of the late-filed election.[130]

The penalty tax which must be remitted along with a late-filed election is calculated as 1% per annum on the amount of the dividend for each month or part of a month from the date the election should have been made to the date the election was made with a maximum of $500 per annum.[131]

The Minister is required to issue a Notice of Assessment for the amount of the penalty tax after a late-filed election has been made. On assessment, the NRO must remit any penalty tax assessed in excess of amounts already paid.[132]

Where a dividend has become payable by an NRO, the Minister may request that a late-filed capital gains dividend election be made. The Minister may make this request at any time but the request must either be served personally or by registered mail. After receipt of this request, if the NRO wishes to make a capital gains dividend election in respect of the dividend, it must file the appropriate election within 90 days after the Minister has served the request. If the NRO does not file the election within 90 days, the dividend is effectively confirmed as an ordinary taxable dividend and the NRO may not subsequently make a late-filed election in respect of the dividend.[133]

[¶9156] NRO Deemed Not To Be a Canadian or Private Corporation

An NRO is deemed not to be a Canadian corporation, taxable Canadian corporation, or private corporation[134] except for purposes of:

(a) computing the NRO's pre-1972 capital surplus on hand, capital dividend Account, and its capital gains dividend account resulting

---

See page ii for explanation of footnotes.

[128] CCH ¶20,244; Sec. 133(7.2).
[129] CCH ¶20,243; Sec. 133(7.1).
[130] CCH ¶20,245; Sec. 133(7.3).
[131] CCH ¶20,102b; Sec. 131(1.3).

[132] CCH ¶20,102c; Sec. 131(1.4).
[133] CCH ¶20,102a; Sec. 131(1.2).
[134] CCH ¶20,289; Sec. 134.

from the deemed disposition of the NRO's property at fair market value in the course of a winding-up of the NRO;

(b) amalgamations;

(c) the exemption from branch tax; and

(d) certain non-arm's length transfers of shares of a Canadian corporation by a non-resident.

[¶9159] Patronage Dividends

[¶9161] Deduction for Patronage Dividends

A taxpayer is allowed a deduction for certain payments made in respect of allocations in proportion to patronage.[135] This deduction will apply primarily to co-operatives, although it is not limited to such organizations. The deduction of patronage payments will be claimed only in the case of a company whose method of operation results in income being derived by it from its transactions with its customers or on their behalf.

The deduction for payments allocated in proportion to patronage is allowed for payments made within the taxation year or payments made within 12 months thereafter to the taxpayer's customers of the year. In addition, a taxpayer may deduct payments made in a previous year, the deduction of which for a prior year was not permitted. Thus, if the deduction of any payment is prohibited in one year, the payment may be carried forward and deducted in a subsequent year.

For payments made after March 22, 2004, the above deduction does not apply to any payment made by a taxpayer (other than a co-operative or a credit union) to a customer with whom the taxpayer does not deal at arm's length.[136] For instance, a patronage dividend paid after March 22, 2004 by a wholly-owned Canadian subsidiary to its U.S. parent company will not give rise to a tax deduction.

[¶9164] Limitation Where Non-Member Customers

The deduction for patronage dividends may be reduced in certain circumstances.[137] If the taxpayer has not made allocations in proportion to patronage to all his or her customers (members and non-members) at the same rates, except to allow for differences in types of goods, products or services, or for grades or qualities thereof, the deduction is limited to the lesser of:

(1) the amount as ascertained under ¶9161; and

(2) the total of:

(a) that part of the taxpayer's income for the year attributable to business done with members; and

---

See page ii for explanation of footnotes.

135 CCH ¶20,301; Sec. 135(1).   137 CCH ¶20,313; Sec. 135(2).
136 CCH ¶20,301c; Sec. 135(1.1).

(b) the allocations in proportion to patronage made to non-member customers in the year.

In effect, this results in the disallowance of allocations made to members to the extent they are made out of profits arising from business with non-members. Any non-deductible excess dividends paid to members may be carried forward and deducted in the subsequent year with the maximum deduction in any year being limited to income from business done with members.[138]

Example:

> Assuming that a co-operative during a year sells to its customers $2,000,000 of goods ($600,000 to members), has $150,000 of income before the deduction, and that patronage dividends are paid during the year (or 12 months thereafter) to customers at the rates of 10% for members and 5% for non-members, the deduction will be limited to the lesser of:
>
> (a) the patronage dividends paid to:
>
> | | |
> |---|---:|
> | non-members — 5% of $1,400,000 | $ 70,000 |
> | members — 10% of $600,000 | 60,000 |
> | | $130,000 |
>
> and
>
> (b) the aggregate of:
>
> (i) the income attributable to business done with members
>
> $$\frac{\$600,000}{\$2,000,000} \times \$150,000 \qquad \$ 45,000$$
>
> and
>
> | | |
> |---|---:|
> | (ii) patronage dividends allocated to non-members | 70,000 |
> | | $115,000 |
>
> which in this case is (b) — $115,000.

[¶9165] What Constitutes a Payment

The customer must be entitled to payment of an amount when it is credited to him or her if it is to qualify for deduction for patronage dividends. "Payment" includes:[139]

(1) the issue of a certificate of indebtedness, or shares of the taxpayer or of the parent corporation of the taxpayer, if the taxpayer or the parent corporation has within the year or within 12 months thereafter redeemed similar certificates or shares that were previously issued in an equal amount;

(2) a set-off of the amount against the liability of a member of the taxpayer pursuant to a by-law of the taxpayer, statutory authority, or the request of the member; or

(3) a payment or transfer that the member would be required to include in income as an indirect payment (see ¶2250).

See page ii for explanation of footnotes.

[138] CCH ¶20,314; Sec. 135(2.1).   [139] CCH ¶20,339; Sec. 135(4) "payment".

[¶9168] What Constitutes an Allocation in Proportion to Patronage

An allocation in proportion to patronage for a taxation year is an amount that meets all the following requirements:[140]

(1) it must be credited to a customer of that taxation year within the year or within 12 months thereafter;

(2) it must be credited on terms that the customer is entitled to or will receive payment thereof;

(3) it must be computed at a rate that is applied in relation to the quantity, quality, or value of goods or products acquired, marketed, handled, dealt in, or sold, from or to the customer or on his or her behalf; or in relation to the quantity, quality, or value of services rendered to the customer or on his her behalf; the transaction may be carried out by the taxpayer either as a principal dealing with the customer or as an agent acting on behalf of the customer or otherwise;

(4) the rate mentioned in (3) must be at the same rate either for all customers of the year, or for all member customers of the year, although the rate may vary for different classes, grades, or qualities of goods, products, or services; and

(5) the prospect that amounts would be so credited must have been held forth by the taxpayer to his or her member customers or non-member customers as the case may be.[141]

[¶9177] Withholding on Payments of Patronage Dividends

Where a payment pursuant to an allocation in proportion to patronage is made, the taxpayer is required to withhold 15% of all patronage dividends in excess of $100[142] paid in the year to each customer who was resident in Canada and not an exempt "person".[143] Amounts withheld are to be remitted to the Receiver General and credited to the customer's tax liability.

After 2005, this withholding obligation does not apply to payment pursuant to an allocation in proportion to patronage that is made by an agricultural cooperative corporation through the issuance of a tax deferred cooperative share (see ¶9181). Instead, a 15% withholding obligation arises if the share is redeemed, acquired, or cancelled by the agricultural cooperative corporation.[144]

[¶9180] Patronage Dividends Included in Income

As a general rule (see exception below for dividends in the form of tax-deferred cooperative shares), the amount of payments made in respect of an allocation are included in the income of the recipient when they are received, unless allocated in respect of consumer goods or services. Such payments are not to be reported as dividends and are not eligible for the

---

See page ii for explanation of footnotes.

[140] CCH ¶20,327; Sec. 135(4) "allocation in proportion to patronage".

[141] CCH ¶20,345; Sec. 135(5).

[142] CCH ¶20,321; Sec. 135(3).

[143] CCH ¶21,721; Sec. 149.

[144] CCH ¶20,371, ¶20,372; Sec. 135.1(6), 135.1(7).

dividend tax credit. Furthermore, the amount of any certificates of indebtedness or shares that are distributed to the customer pursuant to such an allocation must be included in the customer's income in the year of receipt, but not in the year when the indebtedness is discharged or the shares redeemed.[145]

Notwithstanding this general rule, for 2006 through 2015 inclusive, members of an agricultural cooperative who receive patronage dividends in the form of tax-deferred cooperative shares are not taxable until disposition or deemed disposition of those shares. This exception is discussed at ¶9181.

Payments in respect of an allocation for consumer goods or services are not required to be included in the income of the recipient. The term "consumer goods or services"[146] means goods or services, the cost of which was not deductible by the taxpayer in computing income from a business or property.

Sales of goods or products to a marketing board by a member of the taxpayer are deemed to be sales to the taxpayer[147] if:

(1) the marketing board has sold or delivered the same quantity of goods or products to the taxpayer; and

(2) the taxpayer has credited the member with an amount based on the quantity of goods or products of that class, grade, and quality acquired from the marketing board.

[¶9181] Patronage Dividends from Agricultural Cooperatives

For 2006 through 2015, eligible members of agricultural cooperative corporations may defer the inclusion in income of all or a portion of any patronage dividend they receive as a "tax-deferred cooperative share". This deferral lasts until the disposition or deemed disposition of the share.[148] Essentially, eligible members of agricultural cooperative corporations may elect to include in income all or a portion of their receipt of tax-deferred cooperative shares in the year they are issued, and assuming the shares are not disposed of in the year they are issued, the amount so elected is added to the taxpayer's "tax paid balance" at the end of the year and is carried forward to the next year.[149] This amount is deductible from the proceeds of disposition of a future disposition (or deemed disposition) of the shares that are required to be included in income. If the eligible member disposes of the tax-deferred cooperative share in the year in which it was issued, the amount elected is subtracted from the proceeds of disposition that are required to be included in income in that year.

To be eligible for this deferral, agricultural cooperative corporations must be resident in Canada, their principal business activity must be carried out in Canada and be either farming or the provision of goods or services required for farming. The other test to be met is that at least 75% of their

---

[145] CCH ¶20,371, ¶20,372; Sec. 135.1(6), 135.1(7).

[146] CCH ¶20,329; Sec. 135(4) "consumer goods or services".

[147] CCH ¶20,360; Sec. 135(4) "consumer goods or services".

[148] CCH ¶20,367; Sec. 135.1(2).

[149] CCH ¶20,366; Sec. 135.1(1) "tax paid balance".

members must be agricultural cooperative corporations or have as their principal business a farming business.[150] Members of the cooperative corporation must generally meet the same criteria in order to qualify for the deferral.[151]

In order to qualify as a tax-deferred cooperative share, the share must be issued after 2005 and before 2016, and must not, except in the case of death, disability, or ceasing to be a member, be redeemable or retractable within five years of issuance.[152] Furthermore, if the share is pledged as collateral security or the paid-up capital of the share is reduced (other than by way of a redemption) a disposition of the share will be deemed to have occurred.[153]

Despite the deferral accorded to eligible members receiving tax deferred cooperative shares as patronage payments, the deduction for the agricultural cooperative corporation issuing the shares is not deferred and is allowed in the year in which the shares are issued (see ¶9161). However, such deduction is limited to 85% of the corporation's income for the taxation year attributable to business done with its members (calculated without reference to the dividend).[154]

The issuance of a tax deferred cooperative share as a patronage payment is excluded from the withholding obligation otherwise imposed on patronage payments (see ¶9177).[155] However, if the share is redeemed, acquired, or cancelled by the agricultural cooperative corporation or any person or partnership not dealing at arm's length with the cooperative corporation, withholding of 15% of the amount payable on the redemption, acquisition, or cancellation is required.[156]

[¶9183] Co-Operative Corporations

[¶9186] "Co-Operative Corporation" Defined

A "co-operative corporation" is a corporation that was incorporated [or, after June 2005, continued] under a federal or provincial law providing for the establishment of such corporations. The purposes of a co-operative corporation must be:

(1) marketing (including processing) of natural products belonging to its members or customers or acquired from them;

(2) purchasing of supplies, equipment, or household necessities for its members or customers or to be sold to them; or

(3) performing services for its members or customers.[157]

---

[150] CCH ¶20,366; Sec. 135.1(1) "agricultural cooperative corporation".

[151] CCH ¶20,366; Sec. 135.1(1) "eligible member".

[152] CCH ¶20,366; Sec. 135.1(1) "tax deferred cooperative share".

[153] CCH ¶20,369; Sec. 135.1(4).

[154] CCH ¶20,368; Sec. 135.1(3).

[155] CCH ¶20,371; Sec. 135.1(6).

[156] CCH ¶20,372; Sec. 135.1(7).

[157] CCH ¶20,407, ¶20,409; Sec. 136(1), 136(2).

The following conditions must also be met by a co-operative corporation:

(1) the statute under which it was incorporated, its charter or articles of association, its by-laws, or its contracts with its members or its members and customers, must hold forth the prospect that patronage dividends will be paid;

(2) none of the members, except other co-operative corporations, may have more than one vote in the conduct of the co-operative's affairs; and

(3) at least 90% of the co-operative's members must be individuals, other co-operative corporations, or corporations or partnerships that carry on the business of farming and at least 90% of its shares must be held by such persons or partnerships.

[Pending technical amendments would amend the condition in (3) to accommodate cases where the shares of a co-operative are held not only by the members themselves, but also by their registered plans (RRSPs, RRIFs, RESPs or, after 2008, TFSAs). If shares are held by a trust that is governed by such a plan, provided a member of the co-operative is the plan's subscriber or annuitant, as the case may be, those shares will be counted in the same way as if they were held by a member personally. These amendments would apply to the 1998 and subsequent taxation years.]

A co-operative corporation is deemed not to be a private corporation except for certain limited purposes. If the co-operative corporation otherwise qualifies as a private corporation, it will be entitled to the small business deduction [and, under pending technical amendments, to the special rate reduction for CCPCs] and to the tax credit for a corporation's Canadian manufacturing and processing profits. A co-operative corporation that otherwise qualifies as a private corporation will also be entitled to issue a small business development bond and continue to be treated as a private corporation for the purposes of determining the amount of investment tax credit in respect of its qualifying scientific research expenditures, the amount of investment tax credit which is refundable and for the purposes of determining the normal reassessment period and the timing of tax payments. It will also retain its status as a private corporation for the purpose of the definition of "mark-to-market property" governing financial institutions (see ¶9277). Lastly, a taxpayer's capital losses on disposition of shares or debt of co-operative corporations which otherwise satisfy the definition of "small business corporation"[158] will qualify as business investment losses.

See page ii for explanation of footnotes.

[158] CCH ¶28,271a; Sec. 248(1) "small business corporation".

¶9186

[¶9189] Credit Unions — Savings and Credit Unions

[¶9195] "Credit Union" Defined

A "credit union" means[159] a corporation, association, or federation incorporated or organized as a credit union or a co-operative credit society that derives all of its revenues from:

(1) loans to, or cashing cheques for, members;

(2) debt obligations or securities of or guaranteed by the federal or provincial governments, a Canadian municipality, or their agents;

(3) debt obligations or securities of a municipal or public body, or their agencies, performing a function of government in Canada;

(4) debt obligations of or deposits with, or guaranteed by, a corporation, commission, or association not less than 90% of the shares or capital of which is owned by the federal or provincial governments, or by a Canadian municipality;

(5) loans to or deposits with another credit union or a co-operative credit society of which it is a member;

(6) debt obligations of or deposits with, or guaranteed by, a Canadian bank or trust company;

(7) charges, fees, and dues levied against members or members of members; or

(8) a prescribed revenue source.

A credit union may alternatively qualify if all of the members of the credit union are corporations, associations, or federations that:

(1) were incorporated as credit unions or co-operative credit societies, all of which derived all or substantially all their revenues from sources described in the preceding paragraph, or all of whose members were credit unions, co-operatives, or a combination thereof;

(2) were incorporated, organized, or registered under or governed by federal or provincial laws relating to co-operatives;

(3) were incorporated or organized for charitable purposes; or

(4) were corporations, associations, or federations, no part of the income of which was payable to, or otherwise available for the personal benefit of any member or shareholder.

A corporation, association, or federation will qualify as a credit union if it would qualify as a credit union under one of the above four tests if membership and full voting rights in it were held by members (other than individuals) of credit union members thereof.

See page ii for explanation of footnotes.

[159] CCH ¶20,543; Sec. 137(6) "credit union".

A member of a credit union is a person who is recorded as a member on the records of the credit union and is entitled to participate in and use the services of the credit union [or, under pending technical amendments, an RRSP, RRIF, or RESP if the plan's annuitant or subscriber is such a person].[160]

[¶9198] Credit Union Deemed Not To Be a Private Corporation

A credit union that is a corporation is deemed not to be a private corporation except for purposes of the small business deduction, the related exemption from the corporate surtax, the investment tax credit, the refundable investment tax credit, and the timing of tax payments.[161] In addition, a taxpayer's capital losses on disposition of shares or debt of credit unions which are Canadian-controlled private corporations that otherwise satisfy the definition of "small business corporation",[162] will qualify as business investment losses.[163] Accordingly, the tax provisions that apply only to private corporations will not apply to incorporated credit unions or savings and credit unions.

[¶9204] Allocations in Proportion to Borrowing

A credit union may deduct a "bonus interest payment" and all payments made pursuant to allocations in proportion to borrowing that are paid to its members within the year or within twelve months thereafter.[164] This deduction may be made to the extent that the payments were not deductible in the immediately preceding taxation year.

The expression "bonus interest payment" means an amount credited to a member on terms that the member will receive, or will be entitled to receive, payment of such amount.[165] The amount credited must be computed at the rate that is related to:

(a) the amount of interest payable to the member on money standing to his or her credit with the credit union; or

(b) the amount of money standing to the member's credit, and the same rate must be applied to all members of the same class in relation to their interest payable or money.

Allocation in proportion to borrowing means an amount that is credited to a member on terms that the member will receive, or will be entitled to receive, payment of such amount.[166] The amount credited is to be computed at a rate that is related to:

(a) the amount of interest payable by the member on money he or she has borrowed from the credit union; or

(b) the amount of money the member has borrowed.

See page ii for explanation of footnotes.

[160] CCH ¶20,547; Sec. 137(6) "member".

[161] CCH ¶20,549; Sec. 137(7).

[162] CCH ¶28,271a; Sec. 248(1) "small business corporation".

[163] CCH ¶6050; Sec. 39(1)(c).

[164] CCH ¶20,511; Sec. 137(2).

[165] CCH ¶20,542; Sec. 137(6) "bonus interest payment".

[166] CCH ¶20,541; Sec. 137(6) "allocation in proportion to borrowing".

The amount must be credited to the member within the year or within 12 months thereafter, and must be credited at the same rate with respect to the amount of interest or money as is similarly credited to all other members of the credit union of the same class. For this purpose a class includes all members for whom the rates of interest payable in relation to the money borrowed are the same.

[¶9207] Additional Deduction

A credit union that would otherwise be a private corporation is deemed not to be a private corporation except for certain tax purposes, including the small business deduction (see ¶8430) and the special corporate reduction for Canadian-controlled private corporations (see ¶8475 and ¶8480).[167] Thus, a credit union may be eligible for the small business deduction with respect to its income from active business. In addition to this deduction, a credit union which is a corporation may deduct from the tax otherwise payable an amount equal to 17% of the lesser of:

(a) the amount of the corporation's taxable income less the least of the amounts relative to the small business deduction in respect of the corporation for the taxation year; and

(b) the amount, if any, by which ⁴⁄₃ of the corporation's maximum cumulative reserve at the end of the year exceeds the corporation's preferred-rate amount at the end of the preceding year less the least of the amounts relative to the small business deduction in respect of the corporation for the year.[168]

A credit union's maximum cumulative reserve[169] is, in general terms, an amount equal to 5% of the total of debts owing by the credit union to its members (including deposits) and the amount of any share of any member.

The preferred-rate amount of a corporation[170] represents, in general terms, the income of the corporation that has been eligible for the small business deduction.

[¶9209] Payments in Respect of Shares

Where a credit union makes a distribution to its members on their shares not listed on a designated stock exchange, this distribution is treated as a payment and receipt of interest and is deemed not to be a dividend. A distribution of the paid-up capital on a share by way of a reduction of capital or a redemption, acquisition, or cancellation of the share is, however, neither interest nor a dividend; it is merely a return of capital and as such is not taxable to the recipient. Any distribution treated as interest must be included in the recipient's income.[171]

See page ii for explanation of footnotes.

[167] CCH ¶20,549; Sec. 137(7).
[168] CCH ¶20,517; Sec. 137(3).
[169] CCH ¶20,545; Sec. 137(6) "maximum cumulative reserve".

[170] CCH ¶20,534; Sec. 137(4.3).
[171] CCH ¶20,529, ¶20,531; Sec. 137(4.1), 137(4.2).

[¶9210] Member's Income

If a taxpayer receives a payment from a credit union in respect of an allocation in proportion to borrowing, the amount is to be included in the taxpayer's income if the borrowed money was used by the taxpayer for the purpose of earning income from a business or property.[172] However, this does not apply if the borrowed money was used to acquire property the income from which would be exempt, or to acquire a life insurance policy.

[¶9213] Allocation of Taxable Dividends and Capital Gains

A central credit union (referred to as the payer) may, within 120 days after the end of its taxation year, elect in prescribed form to allocate to members that are credit unions the portion of:

(a) taxable dividends received by the payer from a taxable Canadian corporation in the year; and

(b) the payer's taxable capital gains in excess of the allowable capital losses from dispositions of property in the year that are reasonably attributable to the member credit union.

Where a payor allocates such taxable dividends and net taxable capital gains to member credit unions, the amount of taxable dividends which would otherwise be deductible in computing taxable income[173] will be reduced by the amount that was allocated to member credit unions. The taxable capital gains in excess of the allowable capital losses that are allocated to member credit unions must be included in computing the income of the payor. The credit union member to whom the above two amounts are allocated may deduct them in computing its taxable income for the taxation year that includes the last day of the taxation year of the payor in respect of which the amounts were so allocated. In addition, to accommodate credit unions whose corporate structure involves more than two tiers of credit unions, member credit unions may flow through dividends and capital gains which have been allocated to them from a central credit union to their own members that are also credit unions.[174]

These provisions provide a tax planning opportunity for a central credit union and its member credit unions. If the central credit union does not elect, an amount that is paid or payable by a credit union to a member in respect of his or her shares is deemed to be an interest expense to the payor and interest income to the recipient. If the central credit union earns taxable dividends or realizes net taxable capital gains in the year, they can only be transferred to the member credit union as interest.[175] The central credit union may have no income or incur losses for tax purposes and the member credit union may be in a taxable position. The effect of an election to allocate the taxable dividends and net taxable capital gains to member credit unions increases the income of the central credit union and allows the member credit union a deduction for that amount. When the amounts

---

See page ii for explanation of footnotes.

[172] CCH ¶20,535; Sec. 137(5).
[173] CCH ¶16,301; Sec. 112.

[174] CCH ¶20,537–20,538; Sec. 137(5.1)–(5.2).
[175] CCH ¶20,529; Sec. 137(4.1).

¶9210

allocated are actually paid by the central credit union, the payment and receipt will be a tax-free transaction.

[¶9216] Deposit Insurance Corporations

[¶9219] Meaning of Deposit Insurance Corporation

A deposit insurance corporation is a corporation incorporated in Canada primarily to provide or administer a stabilization, liquidity, or mutual aid fund to credit unions and to assist in the payment of any losses suffered by members of unions in liquidation.[176] The deposit insurance corporation must be a Canadian corporation throughout the taxation year and the cost amount for the corporation of its investment property throughout the taxation year must be at least 50% of the cost amount of all its property (excluding debt obligations issued by a member institution when it was in financial difficulty), or the corporation must be incorporated under the *Canada Deposit Insurance Corporation Act.*

A deposit insurance corporation is deemed not to be a credit union and is deemed not to be a private corporation.

A member institution means a corporation whose liabilities in respect of deposits are insured by the particular deposit insurance corporation, or a credit union that is qualified for assistance from the particular deposit insurance corporation.

The tax payable by a deposit insurance corporation is an amount equal to 21% of its taxable income for the year. This rate was reduced from 22%, effective January 1, 2008, as a result of the one percentage point increase in the small business deduction rate (see ¶8430 and ¶8455).

The corporation's income is to be computed under Part I. There is to be included in computing the corporation's income the aggregate of profits or gains made in the year on the disposition of bonds, debentures, etc., owned by it; the amount by which the principal amount of a bond, debenture, etc., at the time it was acquired exceeds the cost of acquiring it as was included by the corporation in computing its profit for the year; and any amount deducted as a reserve for the immediately preceding year.

The amount of any premiums or assessments received or receivable by the corporation from its member institutions in a taxation year is not included in computing its income. The amount of the premiums or assessments is deductible in computing the member's income. [To accommodate situations where two or more DICs may share responsibilities toward a group of members, pending technical amendments will also exclude from a DIC's income any amount it receives from another DIC, to the extent the amount can reasonably be considered to have been paid out of premiums or assessments received or receivable by the other DIC from its member institutions. As a result, such premiums or assessments will no longer be deducti-

---

See page ii for explanation of footnotes.
[176] CCH ¶20,571–20,586; Sec. 137.1(1)–(11).

ble in computing the member institutions' income. These amendments apply to the 1998 and subsequent taxation years.]

A deposit insurance corporation may deduct the total of its losses sustained in the year on bonds, debentures, etc., disposed of by it in the year. It may also deduct the amount by which the cost to the corporation of acquiring a bond, debenture, etc., exceeds the principal amount of the bond, debenture, etc., at the time it was acquired as was deducted by the corporation in computing its profit for the year. Also deductible are investment reserves, and expenses incurred in collecting premiums or assessments, in performing its duties as curator of a bank or as liquidator or receiver of a member institution, and for making inspections.

[¶9222] Insurance Corporations

[¶9225] Insurance Business

Any corporation which enters into insurance contracts or any arrangements or relationships to insure other persons against loss, damage, or expense of any kind in a taxation year is deemed to carry on an insurance business for profit in that taxation year. A corporation is also deemed to carry on an insurance business where it undertakes to make payments on the death of any person, on the happening of an event or contingency dependent on human life, for a term dependent on human life, or at a fixed or determinable future time. These deeming provisions are applicable to any such corporation regardless of the form or legal effect of the contracts, arrangements, or relationships into which it enters.[177]

A life insurer resident in Canada is deemed to be a public corporation.[178] Taxable dividends received from taxable Canadian corporations, other than dividends on term preferred shares that are acquired in the ordinary course of the life insurer's business, may be fully deducted in computing taxable income.[179]

A non-life insurance corporation will be a private corporation except for the purpose of the refundable tax treatment on investment income and Part IV tax on taxable dividends; the rules which treat an inter-corporate dividend as proceeds of disposition or capital gains; and the rules preventing it from having a capital dividend account and making tax-free distributions therefrom. However, the company will be a private corporation for the purpose of the small business deduction, for the entitlement of its shareholders to an allowable business investment loss, and the special treatment of stock option plans for its employees, provided the other relevant conditions are met. It could also be subject to the corporate distributions tax on dividends.

A life insurer that is resident in Canada is subject to Canadian tax only on the portion of its business income which arises in Canada.[180] Such an insurer is not required to include in income taxable capital gains and allowable capital losses on dispositions that are not "designated insurance proper-

See page ii for explanation of footnotes.

[177] CCH ¶20,619; Sec. 138(1).
[178] CCH ¶20,845; Sec. 141.
[179] CCH ¶20,709; Sec. 138(6).
[180] CCH ¶20,625; Sec. 138(2).

¶9222

ty" where the property is used or held in the course of carrying on an insurance business.[181] The segregated funds of a life insurance corporation are deemed to be held in a trust, and the income and capital gains and capital losses in the segregated funds are allocated to policyholders in a manner similar to that accorded to the beneficiaries of a trust and are excluded in the computation of the income of the life insurance corporation.[182]

Certain insurance companies are exempt from tax. A mutual insurance corporation which receives premiums wholly from the insurance of churches, schools, or other charitable organizations is exempt.[183] An insurer who is not engaged in any business other than insurance and whose gross premium income is at least 50% from insurance of farm property, property used in fishing, or residences of farmers or fishers is also exempt.[184] See ¶11,570.

However, it is to be noted that the above exemptions do not apply with respect to the taxable income of a benevolent or fraternal benefit society or order, derived from carrying on a life insurance business and that, in the case of such societies or orders, the taxable income from carrying on a life insurance business is to be computed on the assumption that there was no income or loss from any other source.[185] See ¶11,564.

For a discussion of life insurance policies, see ¶10,516.

[¶9228] "Life Insurer" and "Life Insurance Business" Defined

"Life insurance business" is defined as including an annuities business and the business of issuing contracts, all or any part of the insurer's reserves which vary in amount depending upon the fair market value of a specified group of assets carried on by the life insurance corporation or the life insurer. "Life insurance corporation" or "life insurer" means a corporation that carries on a life insurance business that is not a business described above, whether or not the life insurance corporation or the life insurer also carries on this type of business.[186]

[¶9231] Insurer's Income or Loss

Income from carrying on an insurance business (except for a resident insurer that does not carry on a life insurance business) means the amount of an insurer's income for the year from carrying on its insurance business in Canada and its loss sustained in a taxation year computed under the provisions of the Act relative to the computation of income from an insurance business of the class carried on by it.[187] [Pending technical amendments ensure that, beginning in 2000, only gross investment revenue and capital gains/losses from property that is "designated insurance property" are included in the computation of an insurer's income.]

---

[181] CCH ¶20,804; Sec. 138(12) "designated insurance property".

[182] CCH ¶20,831, ¶20,831g; Sec. 138.1; Reg. 6100.

[183] CCH ¶21,791; Sec. 149(1)(m).

[184] CCH ¶21,805; Sec. 149(1)(t).

[185] CCH ¶21,817; Sec. 149(3).

[186] CCH ¶28,157, ¶28,159ac; Sec. 248(1) "life insurance corporation", 248(1) "life insurer".

[187] CCH ¶20,625; Sec. 138(2).

Where a life insurance company carries on some non-life insurance business, its income will be determined as for general insurers. Insurance companies must include investment income in taxable income. Taxable "life investment income" is taxed at a rate of 15%.[188] Companies are to report their policy reserves for an insurance business other than life insurance on the 80% basis.[189] In addition, non-resident insurers are allowed a deduction for head office expenses provided they are reasonable and can properly be attributed to an insurance business carried on in Canada.

[¶9234] Deductions Allowed in Computing Life Insurer's Income

Certain deductions are permitted in computing a life insurer's income from carrying on its life insurance business in Canada. An amount in respect of a policy reserve for life insurance policies of a particular class, amounts payable or allocated to policyholders, and policy loans may be deducted.[190]

A life insurer is allowed a deduction in respect of unpaid claims reserves and policy dividends paid, payable, or accrued for policyholders and in respect of experience rating refunds.[191] A deduction is also allowed for policy loans.[192]

[¶9237] Deductions for Policy Reserves

In computing a life insurer's income for a taxation year from carrying on its life insurance business in Canada, policy reserves are allowed as a deduction, provided they do not exceed a prescribed maximum.[193]

With respect to deposit administration policies, the total of the insurer's liabilities as of the end of the taxation year to policyholders of such policies may be deducted.

For group term insurance policies that provide coverage for a period not exceeding twelve months, the reserve is determined by apportioning the net premium over the policy period. For this purpose, "net premium" is defined as the premium paid, less acquisition costs of 5%.

For ordinary life policies, the preliminary term method rather than the net level premium method is allowed. The interest and mortality assumptions for calculating the reserves are those used in setting the premiums in the case of non-participating policies, and those used in establishing the cash surrender value for participating policies.[194]

An additional reserve is permitted in respect of qualified annuities, in the amount calculated by assuming a reduction in the rate of interest of one-half per cent. Qualified annuities include annuities:

See page ii for explanation of footnotes.

[188] Budget 2012 proposes some changes to the life investment income tax base; however, the government is still in consultation on this matter.

[189] CCH ¶5134, ¶5135, ¶20,636; Sec. 20(7)(c); Reg. 1400, Reg. 1404.

[190] CCH ¶20,631; Sec. 138(3).

[191] CCH ¶20,631; Sec. 138(3)(a).

[192] CCH ¶20,631; Sec. 138(3)(e).

[193] CCH ¶20,631, ¶20,632–20,636; Sec. 138(3); Reg. 1401–1404.

[194] CCH ¶20,632–20,636; Reg. 1401–1404.

(a) under which periodic payments have commenced, or will commence within one year of date of issue,

(b) with no cash surrender value, and periodic payments commencing not later than age 71, or

(c) issued under a registered retirement savings plan, registered pension plan, or deferred profit sharing plan, providing the interest rate is guaranteed for at least ten years and there is no participation in profits.

As part of the 1996 Insurance Tax Reform, the Department of Finance released draft tax reserve regulations on October 7, 1996, culminating in final regulations in SOR/2000-413, dated November 30, 2000.[195] Under these rules, tax policy reserves for post-1995 life insurance policies are the lesser of the life insurer's reported reserves and its policy liabilities. The reported reserve is the amount included in the insurer's annual report, while its policy liability is the positive or negative amount of the insurer's liability in respect of the policy as determined in accordance with accepted actuarial practice. Both reserves are determined without reference to income or capital taxes. Tax reserves for group term policies and experience rating refunds or claims fluctuations remain the same as for pre-1996 policies.

[¶9240] Inclusions for Real Property

A life insurer must include a prescribed amount in computing its income in respect of the cost or capital cost of land, building under development, or an interest therein.[196] Such amount is to be added to the cost or capital cost, as the case may be, of the land or building under development. For these purposes, the construction, alteration, or renovation is considered to be completed at the earlier of the actual completion date or the date substantially all of the building is used for its intended purpose.[197] Anti-avoidance rules prevent an insurer from transferring property to a non-arm's length designated corporation, individual, or partnership in order to avoid the income inclusion. In the event of such non-arm's length transfer, the prescribed amount will be included in the insurer's income and added to its cost of the shares or interest in the properties so transferred. However, an election made jointly by the insurer and the transferee permits instead the prescribed amount to be added to the cost of the property to the transferee. The election, however, may not be filed after the due date for filing a tax return by any party to the transfer.[198]

[¶9243] Deduction for Dividends from Taxable Corporations

In computing its taxable income, a life insurer may deduct from its income the aggregate of taxable dividends received from taxable Canadian corporations, other than dividends on certain term preferred shares, with the additional requirement that such taxable dividends be included in computing the insurer's income.[199] This deduction applies to dividends received

See page ii for explanation of footnotes.

[195] CCH ¶20,636–20,639; Reg. 1404–1407.
[196] CCH ¶20,702, ¶20,767; Sec. 138(4.4); Reg. 2410.
[197] CCH ¶20,702b; Sec. 138(4.6).
[198] CCH ¶20,702a; Sec. 138(4.5).
[199] CCH ¶20,709; Sec. 138(6).

by the life insurer in respect of both its life insurance business and its non-life insurance business. However, it does not apply to dividends received on shares held in segregated funds, which are deemed to be held in a separate segregated fund trust. See ¶10,525.

[¶9246] Foreign Tax Credits

Life insurers resident in Canada are denied the foreign tax credit in respect of foreign income or profits taxes that relate to their insurance businesses inside or outside Canada. However, income or profits taxes that relate to any other foreign source income do qualify for a foreign tax credit.[200]

[¶9249] Deductions Not Allowed

In computing its income from its life insurance business in Canada, an insurer cannot deduct a reserve for doubtful debts in respect of a premium or other consideration for a life insurance policy in Canada.[201] Presumably a life insurer can still claim a reserve for doubtful accounts in respect of other debts such as rents receivable or salespeople's advances.

In the case of a non-resident insurer or a life insurer resident in Canada that carries on any insurance business outside Canada, the deduction of interest expense is limited. An interest deduction can only be claimed in respect of designated insurance property [or property for which designated insurance property for the year was substituted property] and only in respect of the portion of the year during which such property was held by the insurer in respect of the business. Interest expense can also be claimed by such an insurer in respect of deposits received or other amounts held by the insurer that arose in connection with life insurance policies in Canada or with policies insuring Canadian risks. These limitations on the deductibility of interest expense do not apply to resident life insurers that only carry on an insurance business in Canada.

[¶9252] Amounts Included in Computing Income

Policy reserves, unpaid claim reserves, and policy dividend reserves which were claimed as a deduction in the preceding taxation year are brought back into the income of the current year.[202]

A life insurer must include in taxable income the net negative policy reserves as determined for all its post-1995 life insurance policies.[203] Generally, negative policy reserves only arise when the present value of a life insurer's future premiums exceeds the present value of future estimated benefits and expenses in respect of its life insurance policies. Net negative policy reserves result when the total sum of all the tax reserves (net of policy loans) for post-1995 life policies plus the tax reserves for non-cancellable or guaranteed renewable accident and sickness policies is a negative value. Where a life insurer is so required to include an amount in taxable income

---

See page ii for explanation of footnotes.

[200] CCH ¶20,721; Sec. 138(8).
[201] CCH ¶20,703; Sec. 138(5).

[202] CCH ¶20,694; Sec. 138(4).
[203] CCH ¶20,636; Reg. 1404(2).

for the preceding taxation year, it may claim a deduction for this same amount in the following taxation year.

[¶9255] Income from Participating Life Insurance Business

A deduction is allowed to the insurer for policy dividends paid to its participating policyholders out of its non-segregated property. The deduction is limited to the insurer's accumulated income from its participating life insurance business in Canada, less amounts deducted for prior years.[204] A life insurer is permitted to deduct a reserve for policy dividends that have accrued under participating life insurance policies to or for the benefit of the policyholders. In determining the portion of policy dividends that accrue in the year, policy dividends in respect of a policy accrue in equal daily amounts between anniversary dates of the policy. This provides a better matching of the income and expenses of life insurers since the deduction for policy dividends, which may be either a distribution of income or a cost of funds, is claimable as the income being distributed to policyholders is earned, or as the expense is incurred.[205]

[¶9260] Identical Properties

Generally, the adjusted cost base of identical properties acquired by the same taxpayer is determined on an average cost basis.[206] This determination is inappropriate for taxpayers in the life insurance industry since many of their investments are held for a variety of purposes and capital gains or losses arising on their disposition must be separated.[207] For this reason, separate categories of capital property to which the identical property general rules would apply have been established. The general rules now apply separately to each of the following categories of investments:

(1) property of the life insurance corporation which is not included in a segregated fund and is used or held by the corporation in the year in the course of carrying on its life insurance business in Canada; and

(2) property of the life insurance corporation not included in a segregated fund which is held by it or used in the year in the course of carrying on an insurance business other than a life insurance business.

The distinction in (1) and (2) above is necessary because in some circumstances a corporation may be carrying on both a life and non-life business, in which case certain rules would apply to a computation of income from its life insurance business and the general rules would apply to the computation of its income from its non-life business.

[¶9265] Branch Accounting

Where a life insurer operates inside and outside Canada, there are specific tax rules to determine the amount of gross investment revenue to be

---

See page ii for explanation of footnotes.

[204] CCH ¶20,631, ¶20,641, ¶20,763; Sec. 138(3); Reg. 2402, Reg. 2409(3).

[205] CCH ¶20,619; Sec. 138(1)(b)(iv).

[206] CCH ¶7100; Sec. 47.

[207] CCH ¶20,793; Sec. 138(11.1).

included in income of the Canadian insurance business.[208] These rules involve, generally, the computation of a "Canadian Investment Fund" [209] (CIF) for the year, i.e., the total value of investments which are considered to be used in the Canadian business in the year. Once this total fund is struck, then assets are identified in a certain manner to account for the fund, and it is the actual revenue from those assets which is included in Canadian business income. The CIF for the year is the average of the opening and closing CIF. An insurer is required to include in income for a taxation year a minimum amount of net investment revenue from its Canadian business.

For a resident life insurer, the CIF is calculated by prorating worldwide assets to Canada in the proportion which Canadian liabilities bear to total liabilities. In effect, this attributes to Canada a *pro rata* part of the worldwide surplus, regardless of the actual operating results in and out of Canada. For a non-resident life insurer, the CIF is based on Canadian liabilities plus surplus arising from Canadian operations. However, the surplus so included cannot be less than a minimum "attributed" surplus. This attributed surplus is based on a *pro rata* allocation of worldwide surplus (if the insurer chooses to report on that basis), or 10% of liabilities.

Once the CIF for the year has been determined, there are certain rules concerning the types of property and the order in which they may be included in accounting for the CIF. Land, depreciables, and mortgages and hypothecary claims in Canada must be included. Beyond that category, the choice is up to the taxpayer, although there is a limit on the extent to which Canadian shares may be included. For a resident life insurer, the proportion of branch assets represented by Canadian equities cannot exceed the overall proportion of equity to total assets for the company as a whole. For a non-resident life insurer, the limit is based on the overall equity proportion (if the insurer has computed his or her CIF in that fashion) or 8% of CIF for the year. The choice of bonds to make up the balance of the CIF is up to the taxpayer. If the investment property designated by the insurer for the year is insufficient to cover the CIF for the year, the Minister has the power to designate additional investment property. Property which has been designated in a particular taxation year forms part of the designated properties in the following year.

The bases for valuing assets to be included in the CIF are specified in the tax regulations. For example, land is included at cost, depreciable property at undepreciated capital cost, bonds at book value as determined for the relevant authority, and shares at cost. For property which is held for less than a year, or for which the value changes during the year, there are specific rules to determine the equivalent value for the year to be matched against the CIF for the year.

---

[208] CCH ¶20,727, ¶20,747, ¶20,763; Sec. 138(9);   [209] CCH ¶20,828a; Sec. 138(14).
Reg. 2400, Reg. 2401, Reg. 2404, Reg. 2405,
Reg. 2406, Reg. 2409.

¶9265

[¶9268] Transfer of an Insurance Business

An insurance business carried on in Canada by a resident insurer can be transferred to a wholly owned Canadian subsidiary on a tax-deferred or "rollover" basis. The provision does not apply to an insurance business carried on outside Canada.[210] Four conditions must be met:

1. The transferor must cease to carry on "all or substantially all" of an insurance business in Canada.

2. The transferor must transfer all or substantially all of the property used in the insurance business to the transferee who commences to carry on that insurance business within 60 days. Consideration for the transfer must include shares of the transferee.

3. The transferee must assume or reinsure all or substantially all of the obligations of the transferor within 60 days of the transfer.

4. The transferee and the transferor must elect in prescribed form.

Draft technical amendments released on October 31, 2011 propose to expand availability of this rollover to transfers of an insurance business between sister corporations in a related group that do not have a vertical parent-subsidiary relationship.

[¶9270] Transfer of Insurance Business by Non-Resident Insurer

A non-resident insurer may transfer, on a tax-deferred basis, an insurance business carried on in Canada to a qualified Canadian corporation. The insurer must transfer all or substantially all of the property owned by it at that time and that was designated insurance property in respect of the insurance business it ceases to carry on in Canada in that year to a qualified related corporation (the "transferee") that began immediately after that time to carry on that insurance business in Canada and for consideration that includes shares of the transferee.[211]

[¶9271] Mutualization of Provincial Life Insurance Corporations

[¶9272] Conversion of Provincial Life Insurance Corporation into Mutual Corporation

There are income tax consequences from the mutualization of a provincial life insurance corporation.[212] If, pursuant to a mutualization program, such a corporation pays an amount for the shares it purchases, the shareholders are not required to include in income the amount received for their shares under the provisions relating to:

See page ii for explanation of footnotes.

[210] CCH ¶20,796w.
[211] CCH ¶20,796e; Sec. 138(11.5).
[212] CCH ¶20,833; Sec. 139.

(a) payments, appropriations, or benefits to shareholders; or[213]

(b) corporate distributions to shareholders as deemed dividends;[214]

[¶9273] Demutualization of Insurance Corporations

[¶9274] Demutualization Benefits

Demutualization is the conversion of a mutual insurance company into an insurance company with share capital. Policyholders of the mutual company become shareholders of the stock company. Newly enacted legislation sets out a demutualization regime for all federally incorporated mutual insurance companies.[215] These rules treat policyholders as if they were shareholders participating in the reorganization of the share capital of the corporation. In particular, they enable them to receive shares in exchange of their mutual ownership rights, with no tax consequences until they dispose of them.

Cash payments and other non-share benefits will be treated as taxable corporate dividends from a Canadian corporation and will be eligible for the gross-up and dividend tax credit discussed at ¶8280.

Where an employer holds a policy for the benefit of employees, the rules contemplate that the employer can flow out the benefits received to the individuals, who will in turn receive them under these rules as exchanged shares or dividends, as the case may be, and not as employment income. Although this rule contemplates an employer/employee relationship, it is broad enough to cover any situation in which a policyholder transfers demutualization receipts to an individual who has rights or benefits under the policy and had borne part of the cost of the policy.

Where the policyholder is an employer holding a group-employee-paid policy on behalf of employees, which typically provides disability or other benefits which are tax free to the employees so long as the employer has not contributed to premiums, the demutualization rules contemplate that the employer can apply demutualization benefits it receives toward benefit enhancements under such policies without tainting the policy, so that benefits remain tax free.

[¶9275] Financial Institutions

[¶9277] Specified Debt Obligations and Mark-to-Market Property

A comprehensive set of rules determines the tax treatment of shares and debt obligations held by financial institutions.[216]

The rules regarding specified debt obligations (that are not mark-to-market property) require that a portion of the gain or loss on disposition (the "current amount") be included or deducted in computing income in the

---

See page ii for explanation of footnotes.

[213] CCH ¶4650; Sec. 15. [215] CCH ¶20,835–20,837; Sec. 139.1.
[214] CCH ¶10,200; Sec. 84. [216] CCH ¶20,860–20,900fd; Sec. 142.2–142.6.

year of the disposition. The balance is amortized and included or deducted in computing income over the remaining term of the obligation to maturity. The rules relating to mark-to-market property require that: (i) gains or losses on disposition be on income account; and (ii) mark-to-market property be "marked to market" at the year end. The mark-to-market requirement is achieved through a deemed disposition at fair market value (and immediate deemed reacquisition at the same amount). Thus, every year, any accrued gain or loss on mark-to-market property is realized and is included or deducted in computing the income of the financial institution.

Generally, a specified debt obligation is an interest in most types of indebtedness, other than those specifically excluded. A mark-to-market property is, generally, (i) a share; (ii) a specified debt obligation of a financial institution that is not an investment dealer if the obligation is also a "fair value property" of the financial institution; (iii) a specified debt obligation held by an investment dealer; and (iv) a "tracking property" (i.e., property that is carried at fair value in the financial statements) if the obligation is also a "fair value property" of the financial institution. "Fair value property" is defined generally as any property that is or, it is reasonable to expect, would be valued on the taxpayer's balance sheet at its fair value, as determined in accordance with generally accepted accounting principles. However, this definition will not apply where (a) the property is valued at fair value solely because the fair value was less than the taxpayer's cost in the property; or (b) if the property is a specified debt obligation because of a default of the debtor.

Even if a property falls under one of the above four broad categories of mark-to-market property, it must be determined whether such property qualifies as an "excluded property" and is, therefore, outside the ambit of the mark-to-market property rules. "Excluded property" generally means property of the taxpayer that is either:

- a share of a corporation in which the taxpayer holds a " significant interest"; a financial institution will have a significant interest in a corporation if the financial institution is related to the corporation at that time or if the financial institution holds shares which represent at least 10% of the votes and at least 10% of the value of all the shares of the corporation;

- a prescribed payment card corporation share of the taxpayer (particular credit card companies the shares of which qualify for this purpose);

- a prescribed securities exchange investment of the taxpayer, provided the taxpayer is an investment dealer (particular shares qualify for this purpose);

- a share of a corporation, control of which is subsequently acquired by the taxpayer or persons related to the taxpayer within the 24-month period following the end of the year, provided the taxpayer elects in the appropriate manner; or

- a prescribed property, which includes shares of a qualified small business corporation; shares that are lending assets of the taxpayer (i.e., a preferred share issued in substitution for a loan to the issuer); certain collateralized bonds; certain distress preferred shares; and certain shares held by a credit union.[217]

[¶9279] Communal Organizations

[¶9282] Taxation of Communal Organizations

A congregation (commonly known as a "communal organization") is treated as an *inter vivos* trust and all the income and property of the corporation, and such corporations or trusts as it effectively manages or controls, are treated as being the income and property of the *inter vivos* trust. The congregation may either pay tax on the income itself or allocate the income among the families which make up the congregation so that the adult members of the congregation pay tax on their allocated shares.[218]

"Congregation" is defined as a community, society, or body of individuals, whether or not incorporated, that adheres to and operates according to the practices and beliefs of a religious organization of which it is a constituent part. A religious organization is defined to mean an organization other than a registered charity that adheres to beliefs, evidenced by the religious and philosophical tenets of the organization, and these must include a belief in the existence of a supreme being. The effect of the definition of a religious organization is that a group of people living and working together on a communal basis for personal or ideological reasons would not be covered, unless they are a constituent part of a religious organization with the above-mentioned religious beliefs. The congregation must carry on a business or have the effective management or control of one or more corporations, trusts, or other persons, collectively referred to as "business agencies". One of the purposes of the business agencies must be the support of the congregation's members or the members of any other congregation. All the members of the congregation, none of whom are permitted by the congregation to own property personally, must live and work together and devote their working lives to the activities of the congregation.

In the above circumstances, the following rules apply:

(a) The property of the congregation and the property of its "business agencies" are deemed to be the property of an *inter vivos* trust as at December 31, 1976.

(b) If the congregation is incorporated, the trustee is the corporation; if unincorporated, the trustee is the group charged with management of the congregation.

See page ii for explanation of footnotes.

[217] Reg. 9001, Reg. 9002.

[218] CCH ¶20,920–20,938, ¶51,185; Sec. 143(1)–(5); Inf. Cir. 78-5R3.

(c) The congregation and its business agencies are deemed to act as the agents of the trust and the beneficiaries of the trust are the members of the congregation.

(d) Tax is to be paid by the *inter vivos* trust deemed to exist with respect to the communal organization on its taxable income for each taxation year.

(e) No deduction is permitted for salaries or other benefits paid to members.

(f) If the congregation is incorporated, the rules in (a) and (c) do not preclude the corporation from issuing "small business development bonds" (see ¶3651). However, if the corporation is not an "eligible small business corporation" or fails to use proceeds from the issue of a bond in the financing of an active business, a trust deemed to exist will be required to report additional amounts of income.

Returns are to be filed within 90 days from the year end. The taxation year for an *inter vivos* trust is the calendar year. It should be noted that the 21-year deemed disposition rules discussed in ¶7285 do not apply, nor do the provisions applicable to preferred beneficiary election apply to the *inter vivos* trust.

[¶9283] Election in Respect of Taxable Income

A congregation may elect that its taxable income be allocated among the families of the congregation. Amounts so allocated are deemed to have been paid to the beneficiaries of the *inter vivos* trust and are deductible by the trust. The amounts allocated to each family that is in the congregation are deemed to have been paid and received by one adult member of the family, who is specified in the election. This amount is deductible in computing the income of the trust and is included in the income of the adult member. All other members are deemed to be dependants of the specified person and the specified person is deemed to have supported each of the other family members. The specified person can then take the personal tax credits.

In a communal organization, 80% of the community's income is allocated to the members as follows: one designated spouse/common-law partner in each family is allocated one full share of income; each non-designated spouse/common-law partner is allocated half a share; and each single member is allocated one full share of income. The remaining 20% of the organization's income is divided among all members, whether they are single, married, or in common-law partnerships, as decided by the organization.

[¶9285] Election in Respect of Gifts

A communal organization may elect to have its total charitable, Crown, cultural, and ecological gifts made in a year flowed through to its participating members who have been allocated income for the year. This election allows such a participating member to take into account a percentage share of such gifts in computing his or her tax credit for charitable donations.[219] [As a result of the new "split" gift rules that are proposed after December 20, 2002 and revived in draft legislation released on July 16, 2010, a transfer of property will not necessarily be disqualified from being a gift where the transferor is provided with some advantage (see ¶8175). This means that if the communal organization is entitled to some advantage in respect of the gift, the flow-through election in respect of the gift will be limited to its fair market value less the advantage (the "eligible amount of a gift")].

[¶9290] Tax Shelter Financing

[¶9295] Cost of Tax Shelter Investments

The cost or expense of a person's or partnership's interest in a tax shelter is reduced by the unpaid principal of any associate financing for which recourse is limited, either immediately or in the future and either absolutely or contingently. Tax shelter expenditures are also reduced by any amounts or benefits which might reduce the impact of any loss arising from the expenditure.[220]

[¶9300] Non-Recourse Debt

To limit tax deductions to money which has actually been put up in cash or borrowed on legitimate, indeed stringent, commercial terms, the amount of a tax shelter expenditure, i.e., the cost or capital cost of a taxpayer's tax shelter investments, is reduced by the aggregate of all limited-recourse amounts in respect of an expenditure.[221] In this context, a "limited-recourse amount" means the unpaid principal amount of any indebtedness for which recourse is limited, either immediately or in the future and either absolutely or contingently.[222] It refers to such amount of the taxpayer and of a taxpayer not dealing at arm's length with the taxpayer, where the particular limited-recourse amount can reasonably be considered to relate to the expenditure. This reduction occurs at the time the expenditure was acquired, made, or incurred, including where the limited-recourse amount arises after the acquisition, making, or incurring of the expenditure.

Any unpaid principal of any debt is deemed to be a limited-recourse amount unless:

(a) *bona fide* arrangements exist, for repayment of all principal and interest within a reasonable period not exceeding 10 years;

(b) interest is payable at least annually at the prescribed rate in effect, either at the time the debt arose or from time to time during the term of the debt; and

(c) the amounts in (a) and (b) are in fact paid no later than 60 days after the end of the taxation year of the debtor.[223]

---

[219] CCH ¶20,925a; Sec. 143(3.1).
[220] CCH ¶20,971; Sec. 143.2(6).
[221] CCH ¶20,971; Sec. 143.2(6)(b)(i).

[222] CCH ¶20,966c; Sec. 143.2(1) "limited-recourse amount".
[223] CCH ¶20,972; Sec. 143.2(7).

[¶9305] At-Risk Adjustment

One of the mechanisms which used to make tax shelters attractive was that, in some cases, the taxpayer would put up in cash only a fraction of the supposed cost of the investment, signing notes for the balance to be paid off from investment profits or income guarantees. Effective April 26, 1995, any amount or benefit which reduces the impact of any loss arising from a tax shelter expenditure will restrict the recognition of the expenditure. The cost or capital cost of a tax shelter expenditure will, in effect, be reduced to the extent of the taxpayer's at-risk adjustment in respect of the expenditure.[224]

The "at-risk adjustment" means any amount or benefit that the taxpayer or another non-arm's length taxpayer is or may be entitled to receive whether by way of reimbursement, compensation, revenue guarantee, proceeds of disposition, loan, or any other form of indebtedness granted to protect the expenditure from loss.[225] Specifically excluded from a taxpayer's at-risk adjustment are amounts or benefits arising under normal liability insurance protection or as a consequence of the taxpayer's death.[226]

[¶9307] Charitable Donation Tax Shelter Arrangements

As a result of the 2003 Budget, any limited-recourse debt incurred by a donor after February 18, 2003 is treated as an advantage that will reduce the amount of a charitable donation that is eligible for a tax credit or deduction. For additional details regarding the amount of an advantage, see the commentary at ¶8175.

For the purpose of these split gift rules, a limited-recourse debt refers not only to the unpaid principal amount of any indebtedness for which recourse is limited, but also to any indebtedness (limited-recourse or not) that relates to the gift and for which there is a guarantee, security, or similar indemnity or covenant in respect of the debt.[227] For example, if a donor enters into a contract of insurance whereby all or part of a debt will be paid upon the occurrence of either a certain or contingent event, the debt is a limited-recourse debt in respect of a gift if it is in any way related to the gift.

Such indebtedness is also a limited-recourse debt if it is owed by a person dealing at non-arm's length with the taxpayer or by a person who holds an interest in the taxpayer. This extended definition of "limited-recourse debt" will apply in respect of expenditures, gifts, or monetary contributions made after February 18, 2003.

---

[224] CCH ¶20,971; Sec. 143.2(6)(b)(ii).   [226] CCH ¶20,968; Sec. 143.2(3).
[225] CCH ¶20,967; Sec. 143.2(2).   [227] Sec. 143.2(6.1).

Chapter X

Deferred and Special Income Arrangements

Amateur Athletes' Reserve Funds 10,000

Amateur Athlete Trust 10,005

Amounts Distributed Taxable 10,010

Termination of Trust 10,015

Death of a Beneficiary 10,020

Employees Profit Sharing Plans 10,288

Main Features of Employees Profit Sharing Plan 10,291

Trust Not Subject to Tax 10,294

Contingent or Absolute Allocations — Capital Gain or Loss Allocations 10,297

Deductibility of Contributions 10,300

Deductibility of Beneficiary's Receipts 10,303

Dividends — Allocation of Credit 10,306

Foreign Tax Deduction 10,309

Employees Who Leave Plan and Forfeit Amounts 10,312

Payments Out of Profit 10,315

Taxation Year of Trust 10,316

Employee Life and Health Trust 10,317

Introduction 10,318

Qualification as an ELHT 10,319

Employer Contributions 10,320

Employee Contributions 10,321

Taxation of Trust 10,322

Treatment of Benefit in Employees' Hands 10,323

Registered Supplementary Unemployment Benefit Plans 10,325

"Supplementary Unemployment Benefit Plan" Defined 10,326

Tax Advantages of Registration 10,327

Registration 10,330

Registered Retirement Savings Plans 10,333

Characteristics 10,336

Retirement Savings Plans 10,339

Retirement Income 10,342

Conditions for Acceptance of Plan for Registration 10,345

Taxability of Trust 10,348

Deductibility of Premiums 10,350

RRSP Dollar Limit 10,351

Pension Adjustment (PA) 10,352

RRSP Deduction Limit 10,353

Total Pension Adjustment Reversal (Total PAR) 10,354

Net Past Service Pension Adjustment (Net PSPA) 10,355

Unused RRSP Deduction Room 10,356

Rollovers to an RRSP 10,357

Deductible Contribution to Spousal or Common-Law Partner Plan 10,360

Amounts To Be Included in Income in Respect of a Spousal or Common-Law Partner Plan 10,363

Refund of Premiums on Death of Annuitant 10,366

935

Post-Death Increase in
RRSP Value 10,367

Post-Death Reduction in
RRSP Value 10,368

Refund of Non-Deductible
Premiums — Penalties on
Excess 10,369

Meaning of "Earned
Income" 10,372

Disposition of Non-Qualified
Investment 10,375

Meaning of "Qualified
Investment" 10,378

Foreign Investments 10,381

Property Used as Security
— Disposition of Property 10,384

Benefits Taxable 10,387

Deregistration if Terms of
Plan Amended 10,389

Premiums Paid in Taxation
Year — Benefits when
Plan Is Not Registered at
End of Year 10,391

Transfers from Prescribed
Provincial Pension Plans 10,392

Home Buyers' Plan **10,393**

Characteristics 10,393a

Limitations on Ordinary
RRSP Contributions 10,393b

Qualifying Withdrawals for a
Qualifying Home 10,395

Acquisition of Property
Deadline 10,395a

Return of Withdrawals Not
Used to Acquire
Qualifying Home 10,395b

Repayments of Withdrawals
Used to Acquire
Qualifying Home 10,395c

Where Individual Becomes
a Non-Resident 10,395d

Where Individual Dies 10,395e

Filing of Prescribed Form 10,395f

**Lifelong Learning Plan
(LLP)** **10,396**

Eligibility 10,396a

Repayment Period 10,396b

Ceasing Residence in
Canada 10,396c

**Registered Education
Savings Plans** **10,398**

General 10,399

Canada Education Savings
Grant and Canada
Learning Bond 10,400

Registration Date 10,401

Trust Income 10,402

Tax-Free Savings Accounts ... **10,403**

Characteristics 10,404

Eligibility 10,405

Taxability of Trust 10,406

**Registered Retirement
Income Funds** **10,408**

Registered Retirement
Income Funds in
General 10,411

Meaning of "Retirement
Income Fund" 10,414

Transitional Rules for RRIF
Annuitants Turning 70 or
71 in 2007 10,415

Benefits Taxable 10,417

Effect of Death of
Planholder 10,418

Treatment of RRIF
Withdrawals Where RRIF
Created from Spousal or
Common-Law Partner
Plan 10,419

Registration of Fund 10,420

Change in Fund after
Registration 10,421

Transfers 10,422

Taxability of Trust — Non-
Qualified Investments 10,423

**Registered Disability
Savings Plan (RDSP)** **10,424**

Characteristics 10,425

Registration Requirements 10,426

Specified Disability Savings
Plan 10,427

Canada Disability Savings
Grant and Canada
Disability Savings Bond 10,428

Provincial Payments 10,428a

Non-Compliant Plan 10,429

Rollover to RDSP on Death 10,430

**Deferred Profit Sharing
Plans** **10,431**

Principal Features of
Deferred Profit Sharing
Plans 10,432

Conditions for Registration 10,435

Acceptance of Employees
Profit Sharing Plan as
Deferred Profit Sharing
Plan 10,438

Contribution Limits 10,441

Taxability of Trust 10,444

Deductibility of Employer
Contributions 10,447

Amounts Received Taxable 10,453

Appropriation of Trust
Property by Employer 10,456

Revocation of Registration 10,459

Revoked Plans 10,462

Inadequate Consideration
on Purchase from or Sale
to a Trust 10,465

Transfers out of Deferred
Profit Sharing Plan 10,468

Registered Pension Plans 10,471

Registration Requirements 10,474

Phased Retirement 10,475

Pension Adjustment Limits 10,477

Past Service Benefits 10,480

Revocation of Registration 10,483

Employer Contributions 10,486

Employee Contributions 10,489

Letters of Credit 10,490

Transfers 10,492

Withdrawal of Excessive
Transfers to RRSPs and
RRIFs 10,493

RPP Annuity Contracts 10,494

Individual Pension Plans 10,495

**Pooled Registered Pension
Plans 10,496**

Introduction of New Rules 10,497

Employee Benefit Plans 10,500

Deferred Employment
Compensation 10,501

Employee Trusts 10,502

Employee Benefit Plans 10,504

**Salary Deferral
Arrangements 10,507**

Receipt of Benefits from
Salary Deferral
Arrangements 10,510

Life Insurance Policies 10,513

Proceeds of Life Insurance
Policy 10,516

Proceeds of Disposition
and Adjusted Cost Basis 10,519

Income from Disposition 10,522

Interest, Dividends and
Capital Gains from a
Segregated Fund 10,525

**Eligible Funeral
Arrangements (EFAs) 10,530**

Tax Exemption 10,535

Distribution out of an EFA 10,540

Recent Changes

2012 Budget

Employees Profit Sharing Plans (EPSPs)

To address concerns over certain potential abuses of the EPSP rules, a special tax was proposed in Budget 2012. The special tax is payable by a "specified employee" (defined in subsection 248(1) of the *Income Tax Act* and generally includes an employee who has a significant equity interest in the employer or does not deal at arm's length with the employer) on an "excess EPSP amount". Generally, an excess EPSP amount will be the portion of the employer's EPSP contribution (allocated by the trustee to a specified employee) that exceeds 20% of the specified employee's salary for the year. These changes were released in draft form on August 14, 2012. See ¶10,303.

Registered Disability Savings Plans (RDSPs)

The 2012 Budget proposed several changes to the rules governing RDSPs. First, a temporary measure was introduced to allow certain family members to become the plan holder of an RDSP for adult individuals who lack the mental capacity to enter into a contract themselves. Second, a proportional repayment rule replaces the 10-year repayment rule where a withdrawal is made from an RDSP (the 10-year repayment rule remains for all other events such as RDSP termination or deregistration or where the beneficiary dies or ceases to be Disability Tax Credit-eligible). This measure was passed in Bill C-38 on June 29, 2012 and applies from the date of Royal Assent until the end of 2016. See ¶10,425.

Proportional Repayment Rule — RDSPs

There is currently a 10-year repayment rule where withdrawals are made from an RDSP and Canada Disability Savings Grants or Bonds had been paid into the RDSP within the last 10 years. The Budget proposed a proportional repayment rule to replace the current repayment rule. The proportional repayment rule will require that, for each $1 withdrawn from the RDSP, $3 of any CDSGs or CDSBs paid into the plan in the 10-year period preceding the withdrawal be repaid, up to a maximum of the assistance holdback amount. This measure will apply to withdrawals made from an RDSP after 2013. See ¶10,428.

Primarily Government-Assisted Plans

Specific rules limit the maximum amount that may be withdrawn annually from an RDSP where Canada Disability Savings Grants or Bonds paid into the RDSP exceed private contributions. Where this occurs, the RDSP is known as a "primarily government-assisted plan" (PGAP). Budget 2012 increased the maximum annual limit for withdrawals from a PGAP and added a new minimum annual withdrawal requirement beginning in the calendar year in which the beneficiary turns 60 years of age. The maximum and minimum withdrawal measures will apply after 2013. These changes were released in draft form on August 14, 2012. See ¶10,425 and ¶10,428.

Rollover of RESP Investment Income

Budget 2012 introduced a tax-free rollover of investment income earned in a Registered Education Savings Plan (RESP) to an RDSP if both plans have a common beneficiary. The RESP investment income can be rolled over to an RDSP on a tax-free basis, similar to a contribution to an RRSP of an accumulated income payment. Canada Education Savings Grants and Canada Learning Bonds in the RESP will have a requirement to be repaid by the end of February of the year following the year in which the rollover is made. This measure was released in draft form on August 14, 2012 and applies to rollovers made after 2013. See ¶10,398 and ¶10,425.

Termination of an RDSP following Cessation of Eligibility for the DTC

An RDSP is only available to an individual who qualifies for the DTC. Where a beneficiary's condition improves to the point that the beneficiary no longer qualifies for the DTC for the full taxation year, the RDSP must be terminated by the end of the following year. Budget 2012 changes allow an RDSP plan holder to make an election to extend the period for which an RDSP remains open (upon becoming DTC-ineligible) by four years. This measure was released in draft form on August 14, 2012 and applies to elections made after 2013. See ¶10,425.

Technical Amendments

Pooled Registered Pension Plans (PRPPs)

On December 14, 2011, the Department of Finance released draft income tax legislation, regulations, and explanatory notes regarding pooled registered pension plans PRPPs for comment. These will be new measures that will set the stage for the provinces to introduce complementary legislation allowing for the implementation of PRPPs. The current rules for RPPs and RRSPs are to be amended to accommodate PRPPs. See ¶10,497.

Administrative Announcements

2012 Money Purchase Limits

The CRA has released the money purchase limit for 2012, which corresponds to the RRSP limit for 2013. For 2011 and 2012, the money purchase limit is $22,970 and $23,820, respectively. As a result, the RRSP limit for 2012 and 2013 is $22,970 and $23,820, respectively. See ¶10,351.

RRSP/RRIF Rollover to Infirm Child

For deaths occurring in 2012, the amount of income above which a physically or mentally infirm dependant is presumed not to be dependent on a parent or grand-parent for RRSP or RRIF rollovers on death is $17,868, based on the basic personal amount and the disability amount for 2011. For deaths occurring in 2013, the threshold will be $18,368. See ¶10,366.

[¶10,000] Amateur Athletes' Reserve Funds

[¶10,005] Amateur Athlete Trust

Where an individual who is an amateur athlete enters into an arrangement to deposit specified types of income into a qualifying account administered by an eligible national sports organization or other third party issuer, an *inter vivos* trust, termed an "amateur athlete trust", is deemed to be created for the benefit of that individual. Amounts deposited into or earned in the trust account are deemed to be income of the trust and not of the individual, and no tax is payable by the trust on its taxable income. The individual athlete is taxed only on amounts distributed from the trust during the taxation year.[1]

This tax deferral applies where a national sport organization that is a registered Canadian amateur athletic association receives eligible income amounts for the benefit of an individual under an arrangement made according to the rules of an international sport federation which require such amounts to be held, controlled, and administered by the organization in order to preserve the individual's status as an amateur athlete to compete in sanctioned sporting events. However, beginning in 2008, an individual athlete may also enter into a "qualifying arrangement" with a third-party issuer (financial institution, credit union, or insurance company) for speci-fied types of income to be deposited into an eligible account controlled and administered by the issuer for the exclusive benefit of the individual. To qualify as an amateur athlete trust, no amount other than qualifying per-formance income or interest or other income attributable to property of the trust account may be deposited into the account.

See page ii for explanation of footnotes.

[1] CCH ¶20,951; Sec. 143.1(1).

[¶10,010] Amounts Distributed Taxable

Any amounts distributed to the beneficiary under an amateur athlete trust are to be included in computing the beneficiary's income. Amounts distributed by the trust include all payments by the national sport organization under the arrangement to or for the benefit of the athlete.[2] Such amounts will be included in the individual's income.[3]

The trust becomes subject to Part XII.2 tax when it distributes an amount to a non-resident beneficiary. The tax is 36% of $^{100}/_{64}$ of that amount.[4]

[¶10,015] Termination of Trust

Where an individual has not competed in an international sporting event as a Canadian national team member for eight years, the amounts held by the amateur athlete trust at the end of the year are deemed to be distributed to the individual athlete at that time.[5] Where the athlete is a non-resident at the time, the amount of such deemed distribution is reduced to 64% of the fair market value at that time of the property of the trust. The eight-year period commences with the later of the last year in which the athlete so competed and the year in which the trust was created. A trust will cease to exist at the time the deemed distribution comes into operation.

[¶10,020] Death of a Beneficiary

On the death of the beneficiary under the trust, all amounts remaining in the trust are deemed to have been distributed to the beneficiary immediately before death, and as a consequence will be included in the beneficiary's income for the year of death.[6] Where the athlete is a non-resident at that time, the amount of such deemed distribution is reduced to 64% of the fair market value at that time of the property of the trust. A trust will cease to exist at the time the deemed distribution comes into operation. Furthermore, in determining the income of a corporation for its first taxation year ending after the time of change of its tax status, the corporation will be treated as having claimed or deducted, in the year immediately before that time, the maximum amount which it is entitled to claim or deduct as a reserve. Such reserves are therefore included in the corporation's income for the year in which it ceases or commences to be exempt from Part I tax so that a corporation will not be able to accumulate or "bank" them in years in which it is tax-exempt.

See page ii for explanation of footnotes.

[2] CCH ¶20,951, ¶20,952; Sec. 143.1(1), 143.1(2).   [5] CCH ¶20,953; Sec. 143.1(3).

[3] CCH ¶4377ac; Sec. 12(1)(z).

[4] CCH ¶25,883a; Sec. 210.2(1.1).   [6] CCH ¶20,954; Sec. 143.1(4).

¶10,010

[¶10,288] Employees Profit Sharing Plans

[¶10,291] Main Features of Employees Profit Sharing Plan

An employees profit sharing plan is an arrangement under which an employer pays a portion of the profits from its business to a trustee to be held and invested for the benefit of its employees who are members of the plan.[7] The principal distinction between an employees profit sharing plan and a deferred profit sharing plan (DPSP) (see ¶10,432) is that under the former, the members pay tax each year on the contributions and trust income allocated to them, whereas under the latter they pay tax only as these amounts are actually received from the trust. In either case, the employer's contributions are deductible in the year they are made (subject to upper limits in the case of a DPSP). Unlike DPSPs, employees profit sharing plans do not need to be registered with the Minister of National Revenue.

The following are the main features of an employees profit sharing plan:[8]

(1) The plan must involve a sharing arrangement with employees either of the employer or of a corporation with whom the employer does not deal at arm's length, in connection with profits derived from the employer's business or from the business of the employer and a corporation with which the employer does not deal at arm's length. The amounts payable by the employer must be computed by reference to profits.[9]

(2) The payments made by the employer must be made to a trustee in trust for the benefit of employees of the employer or of a corporation with which it does not deal at arm's length. It is not stated that all employees must benefit.

(3) It is permissible, but not necessary, that the employees who may benefit from the employer's contributions under such a plan themselves contribute to the plan.

(4) There must be an allocation by the trustee on an ongoing annual basis, either contingently or absolutely, to individual employees of:

    (a) all amounts received from the employer or from a corporation with which the employer does not deal at arm's length;

    (b) all the profits from the trust property;

    (c) all the capital gains and losses sustained by the trust after 1971; and

---

See page ii for explanation of footnotes.

[7] Inf. Cir. 77-1R5.

[8] CCH ¶21,015; Sec. 144(1) "employees profit sharing plan"; Interp. Bul. IT-280R.

[9] CCH ¶21,067; Sec. 144(10).

(d) all amounts previously allocated to and included in the income of a beneficiary who, under the terms of the plan, forfeited his right thereto because he left his employment.

[¶10,294] Trust Not Subject to Tax

The trust governed by an employees profit sharing plan is not subject to tax on its taxable income for a taxation year if the trust was governed by the employees profit sharing plan throughout the year.[10]

[¶10,297] Contingent or Absolute Allocations — Capital Gain or Loss Allocations

An employee is taxable on amounts allocated contingently or absolutely to him or her by the trustee under the plan, including capital gains and losses.[11] The amounts allocated consist of the portions of the contributions to the plan made by the employer and any corporation with which the employer is not dealing at arm's length, and portions of the profit from the trust property, including capital gains and losses. However, an employee is not taxable on amounts allocated from his or her own contributions.

Capital gains less capital losses are allocated proportionately to employees as if they had been realized by the employees and accordingly are taxable to an employee as a capital gain or capital loss in the year of allocation. However, an employee profit sharing plan is a "flow-through entity" for purposes of the capital gains exemption election discussed at ¶5011. Accordingly, if an election is made under those rules, capital gains allocated by the plan will be eligible for an offsetting deduction to the extent of the "unused portion of a beneficiary's exempt capital gains balance" (see ¶10,303) created by the election in respect of the plan.

At any time before 1976, a trustee of a trust governed by an employees profit sharing plan could make an election by which each asset of the trust owned on December 31, 1971 was deemed to have been disposed of on that date for proceeds equal to the fair market value and to have been re-acquired by the trust on January 1, 1972 at an amount equal to fair market value.[12] This allowed the trustee to allocate capital gains or losses accrued up to January 1, 1972 among the beneficiaries whether or not the gains or losses were realized by the trust. The trustee was required to make the allocation before 1976.

For a trust that made the election before 1976 and for a trust that came into existence after December 31, 1971, an election must be filed each time the trust wishes to have realized accrued capital gains or losses. Such elections can only be made after 1973.[13] That property elected upon will be deemed to be disposed of by the trust on any day the trustee designates for

---

See page ii for explanation of footnotes.

[10] CCH ¶21,021; Sec. 144(2).

[11] CCH ¶21,027, ¶21,029; Sec. 144(3), 144(4); Interp. Bul. IT-379R.

[12] CCH ¶21,030; Sec. 144(4.1).

[13] CCH ¶21,031, ¶21,031a; Sec. 144(4.2); Reg. 1500.

proceeds of disposition equal to any amount the trustee selects between its fair market value and its adjusted cost base to the trust at the time of this further election. On the making of such an election, the trust will be deemed to have re-acquired the property at an amount equal to those proceeds of disposition.

The purpose of the elections is to permit the orderly allocation of capital gains or losses to the employees and allow the trustee to deal more freely with the property of the trust, without incurring substantial capital gains or losses in any one year. A capital loss is not treated as a superficial loss.

[¶10,300] Deductibility of Contributions

An employer's contributions made during a taxation year or within 120 days thereafter are treated as a deductible expense of the employer, except to the extent that they are deductible in the preceding year.[14]

An employee's contribution to an employees profit sharing plan is not deductible by the employee. An employee is taxable on his or her employment income, including any part of such income contributed to an employees profit sharing plan.[15]

An amount paid by an employer to a trustee in trust for employees of the employer or of a corporation with whom the employer does not deal at arm's length under an employees profit sharing plan is deductible to the extent provided under the plan's provisions.[16] However, an amount paid by an employer to a trustee under a profit sharing plan that is not an employees profit sharing plan, a deferred profit sharing plan, or a registered pension fund or plan, is not deductible.[17]

An employer is taxable on any amounts received under an employees profit sharing plan established for the benefit of the employer's employees or for those of a corporation with whom it does not deal at arm's length.[18] Normally, however, an employer does not receive any such payments.

[¶10,303] Deductibility of Beneficiary's Receipts

An employee is not taxable on amounts received as a beneficiary under an employees profit sharing plan.[19] However, this applies only where the amount received by the employee is attributable to one or more of the following sources. The amounts attributable to such sources will have borne tax at an earlier time or will be of such a nature that no tax is payable at any time. The amounts referred to are:[20]

(a) payments made by the employee to the trustee;

See page ii for explanation of footnotes.

[14] CCH ¶21,035; Sec. 144(5).
[15] CCH ¶2201; Sec. 5.
[16] CCH ¶5120; Sec. 20(1)(w).
[17] CCH ¶4846; Sec. 18(1)(k).

[18] CCH ¶4368; Sec. 12(1)(n).
[19] CCH ¶21,041; Sec. 144(6).
[20] CCH ¶21,043; Sec. 144(7).

¶10,303

(b) amounts required to be included in computing the income of the employee for the immediate or a previous taxation year;

(c) capital gains made by the trust prior to 1972;

(d) capital gains made by the trust for a taxation year ending after 1971 to the extent allocated by the trust to the beneficiary;

(e) a gain after 1971 from the disposition of capital property to the extent it is not a capital gain under (d);

(f) the portion of any increase in value of property transferred to the employee that would have been considered to be a capital gain made by the trust if the property had been sold on December 31, 1971, at its fair market value; or

(g) a dividend received from a taxable Canadian corporation and allocated by the trust to the beneficiary.

In determining the above receipts, the amounts are reduced by such portion of all capital losses of the trust for taxation years ending after 1971 as has been allocated by the trust to the beneficiary and has not already been applied to reduce the amount of the receipts.

Where the beneficiary receives an amount from the trust in a form other than cash, a rollover is effected to the employee.[21] The trust is deemed to dispose of the property for its "cost amount". The cost to the beneficiary is:

$$\text{Cost} = \begin{array}{c}\text{portion of amount received by}\\\text{beneficiary that would be non-taxable}\\\text{if received in cash}\end{array} \times \frac{\text{cost amount of the property to the trust}}{\begin{array}{c}\text{cost amount to the trust of all}\\\text{property transferred to the beneficiary}\\\text{(except money)}\end{array}}$$

This same portion is deemed to be the amount received for the purposes of the deductibility of the beneficiary's receipts. For example, if the trust were to distribute a share on which there was an accrued but unrealized capital gain, the gain would not be taxed on distribution to the beneficiary, but would be taxed when the share was disposed of by the beneficiary.

An additional amount may be available to be included in the cost of property received from the trust in satisfaction of all or a portion of the beneficiary's interest, in order that the beneficiary be able to make full use of an exempt capital gains balance in respect of the trust. The total amount available to be included in the cost of properties received in satisfaction of all or a portion of the beneficiary's interests is the "unused portion of a beneficiary's exempt capital gains balance" in respect of a trust governed by an employees profit sharing plan. This amount[22] equals the amount that would have been the exempt capital gains balance in respect of the trust for the beneficiary's taxation year minus any increase to the adjusted cost base

---

See page ii for explanation of footnotes.

[21] CCH ¶21,045; Sec. 144(7.1).

[22] CCH ¶21,016; Sec. 144(1) "unused portion of a beneficiary's exempt capital gains balance".

¶10,303

of an interest or a part of an interest of the beneficiary in the trust that was disposed of (other than in a disposition that is part of a transaction in which property was received from the trust in satisfaction of all or a portion of the beneficiary's interests in it). The unused portion of a beneficiary's exempt capital gains balance can be used to bump the adjusted cost base of property, other than money, received from an employee profit sharing plan.

Proposed Special Tax on Excess EPSP Amount

There has been concern that EPSPs have increasingly been used as a vehicle for business owners to direct business profits to members of their families to reduce or defer payment of income tax on these profits. There were also concerns that EPSPs have been used in certain situations to eliminate employee withholding requirements as well as EI and CPP payments. To address concerns over certain potential abuses of the EPSP rules, a special tax was proposed in Budget 2012 [draft legislation released August 14, 2012]. The special tax is payable by a specified employee (an employee that has a significant equity interest in the employer or does not deal at arm's length with the employer) on an "excess EPSP amount".[23] Generally an "excess EPSP amount" will be the portion of the employer's EPSP contribution (allocated by the trustee to a specified employee) that exceeds 20% of the specified employee's salary for the year.

The proposed special tax will contain two components and will apply to the total of all excess EPSP amounts received by the specified employee for the year. The first component will be equal to 29% (the top federal marginal tax rate). The second component will be equal to the top marginal tax rate of the employee's province of residence (0% in Quebec). A new deduction will be introduced to ensure that an excess EPSP amount is not subject to regular income tax in addition to the special tax. A specified employee will not be able to claim any other deductions in respect of an excess EPSP amount.

The Minister of National Revenue will be able to waive or cancel the application of these new rules where the Minister considers it just and equitable to do so. In these circumstances, the regular rules regarding EPSPs will apply.

Once passed, this measure would apply to EPSP contributions made by an employer on or after Budget Day. However, in the case of contributions to an EPSP pursuant to a legal agreement entered into before Budget Day, this measure will only apply to contributions made as of 2013.

[¶10,306] Dividends — Allocation of Credit

If the income of a trust includes taxable dividends from a taxable Canadian corporation, employees are entitled to a dividend tax credit in

---

[23] Sec. 207.8.

respect of the portion of the dividends allocated to them by the trustee.[24] However, the amount of the taxable dividends allocated to the employees is included in the employees' incomes as though they had received it directly from the corporation.

[¶10,309] Foreign Tax Deduction

The law provides for the allocation, by a trustee, of non-business income received from sources in a foreign country to beneficiaries of an employees profit sharing plan.[25] The beneficiary is entitled to a foreign tax credit for amounts paid as taxes to the government of the foreign country, state, province, or other political subdivision of the country.[26] See also ¶8550.

[¶10,312] Employees Who Leave Plan and Forfeit Amounts

An employee who leaves the employees profit sharing plan and forfeits payments may deduct from *employment* income amounts forfeited in the year employment ceases that were included in income in that year or an earlier year. Very specific rules determine the amount which may be deducted.[27]

Where an employee ceases to be an employees profit sharing plan beneficiary during the year (and does not rejoin the plan during the year), he or she may deduct from employment income the total of all amounts included in computing income for the year and preceding years *except* that the following adjustments must be made to the current and prior year income inclusions:

(a) where dividends from taxable Canadian corporations have been allocated to the employee, the "gross-up" is ignored and only the actual amount of the dividend is included; in addition, 25% of such dividends must also be deducted from current and prior year income allocations;

(b) capital gains or loss allocations are not included in the amount deductible; and

(c) amounts actually received or receivable (as opposed to taxable allocations) are not included in the amount deductible.

When an employee rejoins a plan in the year of forfeiture, no deduction is permitted. Where an employee rejoins a plan in a year subsequent to the year of forfeiture, any carryforward amounts on hand cease to be available for deduction.

See page ii for explanation of footnotes.

[24] CCH ¶21,043, ¶21,049; Sec. 144(7), 144(8). [26] CCH ¶19,700; Sec. 126(1); Interp. Bul. IT-270R3.
[25] CCH ¶21,055; Sec. 144(8.1). [27] CCH ¶21,061; Sec. 144(9).

¶10,309

The forfeiture deduction does not necessarily come into play when an individual dies; rather, if forfeiture occurs after death, the estate or heir would be entitled to the deduction.

[¶10,315] Payments Out of Profit

A plan may provide that the employer will pay into it either a fixed proportion of profits or a proportion which varies according to the scale of the profits. If the plan provides for payment out of profits, but the payment is not computed with reference to profits, the employer may elect that the payments be computed by reference to profits.[28]

A scheme which was little more than a promise to establish a plan was held not to qualify, especially when it was shown that in the year in question shares in the profits were received also by persons who were not employees.[29]

[¶10,316] Taxation Year of Trust

Where an employees profit sharing plan is accepted for registration as a deferred profit sharing plan, the taxation year of the trust administering the plan is deemed to end immediately before the plan was deemed to have been registered.[30] The trustee of the profit sharing plan is required to make an allocation to employees of amounts received for them for the current year up to the date of registration of the deferred profit sharing plan.

[¶10,317] Employee Life and Health Trust

[¶10,318] Introduction

The employee life and health trust (ELHT) is a tax vehicle that allows employers to pre-fund employee and retiree health and welfare benefits and receive a tax deduction for their contributions, if any, that relate to designated employee benefit payments in a given future taxation year. "Designated employee benefits" generally means benefits under a group sickness or accident insurance plan, a group term life insurance policy, or a private health services plan.[31] The ELHT legislation is applicable to trusts established after 2009.

[¶10,319] Qualification as an ELHT

In order for a trust to qualify as an ELHT for a taxation year, it must meet all the following conditions *throughout* that year:

(a) The trust's objects are limited to the provision of designated employee benefits. In this regard, all activities that are reasonably

---

See page ii for explanation of footnotes.

[28] CCH ¶21,067; Sec. 144(10); Interp. Bul. IT-280R.

[29] No. 615, 59 DTC 244.

[30] CCH ¶21,075; Sec. 144(11).

[31] CCH ¶21,080c; Sec. 144.1(1) "designated employee benefit".

related to providing designated employee benefits, such as managing investments, administering payments, and similar supporting activities, will be considered to be activities that further the trust's object of providing designated employee benefits.

(b) On the wind-up of the trust, its remaining funds are only distributed to the remaining beneficiaries other than the key employees (or an individual related to a key employee), another ELHT, or, after the death of the last beneficiary, the Government of Canada or a province. A key employee is either a "specified employee" (i.e., a specified shareholder of the employer or a person who does not deal at arm's length with the employer), or is a high income employee whose earnings for two of the last five years exceeded five times the year's maximum pensionable earnings (YMPE) for CPP purposes. For CPP purposes, the YMPE is $46,300 in 2009, $47,200 in 2010, $48,300 in 2011, and $50,100 in 2012.

(c) The trust is resident in Canada.

(d) Each beneficiary of the trust is an employee of a participating employer, an employee's spouse or common-law partner, a member of the employee's household who is connected to the employee by blood relationship, marriage or adoption, another employee life and health trust or the government Canada, a province or a territory. For this purpose, "employee" includes both current and former employees as well as individuals for whom an employer has assumed the responsibility of providing benefits as a result of a business acquisition.

(e) The trust contains at least one class of beneficiaries which class represents at least 25% of all of the beneficiaries of the trust. In addition, at least 75% of the members of the class must be non-key employees of the employer.

(f) The rights of key employees, as defined in (b), who are beneficiaries under the trust are not more advantageous than those of the class of beneficiaries described above in (e).

(g) The trust does not provide any rights to an employer (or to a person not dealing at arm's length with the employer). Certain exceptions are provided. One exception is for the provision of designated employee benefits to a person not dealing at arm's length with the employer. For example, this exception would permit the controlling shareholder of an employer who is also an employee of the employer, or her spouse, to receive designated employee benefits under the trust. Another exception allows for the existence of covenants and warranties in favour of participating employers to enable them to require the maintenance of ELHT status. The third exception accommodates "prescribed payments", i.e., payments made under health care trusts established for retired auto workers who are former employees of GM of Canada Ltd. or Chrysler Canada Inc. or of related entities.

(h) The trust does not make a loan to, or an investment in, a participating employer or a person not dealing at arm's length with a participating employer.

(i) Employer representatives do not constitute a majority of trustees or otherwise control the trust.[32]

Because these conditions must be met *throughout* the year, a trust which fails to satisfy one of these conditions at any time during the year will lose its ELHT status for that taxation year.

[¶10,320] Employer Contributions

No deduction is permitted in a taxation year for the portion of an employer contribution to the trust made in the taxation year which relates to anything other than designated employee benefits being provided in that year.[33] Instead, the portion of the pre-funding, if any, that relates to designated employee benefit payments in a given future taxation year is deducted in that future year. As a result of these rules, employer contributions to the trust in excess of the amount that is actuarially determined to be necessary to fund the contemplated benefits being provided over the life of the trust will not be deductible in any year.

To the extent that an obligation to the trust is satisfied with the issuance and contribution to the trust of a promissory note (or similar evidence of indebtedness) of the employer or a related party, payments in respect of any portion of the principal amount evidenced by the promissory note, or interest thereon, are deemed to be payments in satisfaction of the employer's liability to the trust, and not payments of principal or interest.[34] From the employer's perspective these payments will, provided they are made in order to fund the payment of designated employee benefits and subject to normal tax rules, generally be deductible in the later of the year to which the portion relates and the year in which the payment to the trust is made.[35]

[¶10,321] Employee Contributions

Employee contributions are permitted (but not required) and are given the same tax treatment they would receive if they were made for a particular benefit rather than through an ELHT. For example, an employee's contributions that are used to pay premiums to a private health services plan will be

---

See page ii for explanation of footnotes.

[32] CCH ¶21,080d, ¶21,080e, ¶21,081; Sec. 144.1(1) "employee", 144.1(1) "key employee", 144.1(2); Reg. 9500.

[33] CCH ¶2370, ¶21,083; Sec. 20(1)(s), 144.1(4).

[34] CCH ¶21,087; Sec. 144.1(8).

[35] CCH ¶21,087; Sec. 144.1(8).

eligible for the medical expense tax credit.[36] Similarly, employee contributions to a wage loss replacement plan that is administered by the employee life and health trust will reduce the taxable portion of any wage loss replacement received from the trust.

[¶10,322] Taxation of Trust

In the computation of its net income for a year, an ELHT is entitled to deduct all amounts payable by it in the year as designated employee benefits.[37] Where the amount of designated employee benefits payable in a year exceeds the trust's income for that year, the excess is treated as a type of loss, with special rules allowing it to be deductible against income in any of the three preceding or three following taxation years, provided that the trust retained its status as an employee life and health trust for the year.[38]

Where benefits are administered on behalf of employees of more than one employer, an election may be made for the trust to be treated as a separate trust.[39]

[¶10,323] Treatment of Benefit in Employees' Hands

Of the designated employee benefits (generally health and insurance benefits), some are currently taxable in the hands of employees on receipt (i.e., benefits under a wage loss replacement plan or coverage under a group term life insurance policy), while others are generally tax exempt when received directly by employees (i.e., medical or dental benefit). Either taxable or tax-exempt benefits, or a combination of the two, could be provided through an employee life and health trust, but their tax treatment in the hands of employees would not change due to the existence of the trust.

For example, private health services benefits would generally be tax exempt in the hands of the employees, while disability insurance payments would generally be taxable. No benefit would be considered to be received or enjoyed by an employee because of an employer contribution to the trust, except to the extent that the trust provides group term life insurance coverage. The value of group term life insurance coverage is currently a taxable employment benefit during each year of coverage, while life insurance proceeds received on death are generally tax exempt. This tax treatment would be preserved when similar benefits are provided through the trust.

Payments made on the wind-up of the trust, otherwise than for the provision of designated employee benefits, will be taxable to the recipient.

To the extent that a particular benefit is taxable to the employee, the benefit paid from the trust will be required to be reported as an employment benefit and not as a trust distribution.

See page ii for explanation of footnotes.

[36] CCH ¶21,089; Sec. 144.1(10).
[37] CCH ¶21,090; Sec. 144.1(11).
[38] CCH ¶16,192; Sec. 111(7.4).
[39] CCH ¶21,091; Sec. 144.1(12).

[¶10,325] Registered Supplementary Unemployment Benefit Plans

[¶10,326] "Supplementary Unemployment Benefit Plan" Defined

A "supplementary unemployment benefit plan" is an arrangement under which payments are made by an employer to a trustee exclusively for the payment of periodic amounts to employees or former employees who are, or may be, laid off for any temporary or indefinite period. Such a plan does not include any arrangement in the nature of a superannuation or pension fund or plan (whether or not registered) or an employees profit sharing plan.[40]

[¶10,327] Tax Advantages of Registration

Only registered supplementary unemployment benefit plans can derive the following tax advantages:

(1) The trust governed by a registered plan is not taxable on its income.

(2) The employer may deduct payments made to the trustee during a taxation year or within 30 days thereafter, to the extent not previously deducted.

(3) An employee or former employee is taxable on any amount received from the trustee during the year.

(4) An employer must include in income any amounts received in the year from the trustee of the plan as a result of an amendment or modification of the plan, or as a result of the termination or winding-up of the plan.

(5) An amount paid by a taxpayer to a trustee of the plan is deductible.[41]

(6) A trust under the plan is exempt from tax.[42]

[¶10,330] Registration

A registered supplementary benefit plan is a plan which has been accepted by the Minister for registration in respect of the plan's operations and constitution.[43] Applications for registration should be made by letter directed to the Registered Plans Directorate of the Canada Revenue Agency.

The minimum requirements for registration are that:

(1) the employer's contributions must be made to a trust with a fiscal period ending on December 31;

See page ii for explanation of footnotes.

[40] CCH ¶21,125; Sec. 145.
[41] CCH ¶5121; Sec. 20(1)(x).

[42] CCH ¶21,799; Sec. 149(1)(q).
[43] Inf. Cir. 72-5R2.

¶10,330

(2) the plan must not be a superannuation or pension plan or an employees profit sharing plan;

(3) the funds of the trust must be used exclusively for the benefit of employees or former employees who are laid off for an indefinite period for reasons other than sickness or accident and who are not retired;

(4) most employees should be those covered by unemployment insurance (e.g., a plan covering executives and senior personnel will not be acceptable); and

(5) the amounts and timing of employer contributions should be laid down in the plan and the amounts should be reasonable.

[¶10,333] Registered Retirement Savings Plans

[¶10,336] Characteristics

An individual taxpayer may establish a "retirement savings plan"[44] which, upon registration with the Minister of National Revenue, becomes a "registered retirement savings plan" (RRSP).[45] Together with (or as an alternative to) the registered pension plan (RPP) which employers often offer their employees as an employment benefit (see ¶10,471 *et seq.*), the RRSP allows individual taxpayers to deduct from taxable income limited amounts contributed to the plan.[46] These amounts are invested primarily in Canadian securities, which may earn interest, dividends, or capital gains, depending on the plan chosen by the taxpayer. These earnings accumulate in the plan free of current tax, so that they grow more rapidly than would the same investments made by the taxpayer directly.[47] When the accumulated premiums and accrued earnings are eventually paid out, they are included in income at that time unless they are "excluded withdrawals" received pursuant to the Home Buyers' Plan described in ¶10,395a *et seq.*[48] When money is withdrawn from the plan, either for current needs or for retirement income, the taxpayer will only include in income for the particular year the amount received in that year. In that respect, an RRSP is a government-sanctioned tax shelter or tax deferral mechanism.

A taxpayer may deduct premiums paid to a plan of which the taxpayer's spouse/common-law partner is the annuitant, provided that the total deduction in respect of the taxpayer's own RRSP and the taxpayer's spousal or common-law partner plan RRSP does not exceed the amount deductible in respect of the taxpayer.[49]

Upon the maturity of an RRSP, the taxpayer may choose among:

See page ii for explanation of footnotes.

[44] CCH ¶21,211d; Sec. 146(1) "retirement savings plan".

[45] CCH ¶21,211b, ¶21,229; Sec. 146(1) "registered retirement savings plan", 146(2).

[46] CCH ¶21,249; Sec. 146(5).

[47] CCH ¶21,243; Sec. 146(4).

[48] CCH ¶21,323, ¶21,323k; Sec. 146(8), 146(8.01).

[49] CCH ¶21,262; Sec. 146(5.1).

(1) receiving the full value of the property in the plan (and paying tax thereon);

(2) receiving the forms of annuities which qualify as "retirement income" (as defined in ¶10,342) and paying tax on the annuity payments when received; or

(3) using the property in the plan to establish a registered retirement income fund (RRIF).

When an annuitant dies, either before or after the maturity of a plan, the value of the remaining annuity payments in the case of a matured plan and the amount to which the deceased is entitled in the case of an unmatured plan will be included in the income of the deceased for the year of death unless these amounts pass to, or for the benefit of, the annuitant's spouse/common-law partner or certain dependent children or grandchildren.[50] For further commentary on the manner in which such payments are taxed, see ¶10,366.

It should be observed that all amounts received from an RRSP are included in computing income. No distinction is made between that portion of the return that represents premiums paid and that portion that represents earnings on those premiums. Nor is the nature of the earnings taken into account. For example, the earnings may be interest income, dividends, or capital gains, which may be taxed on a different basis or to a different extent if earned directly. No special tax treatment is given to earnings from an RRSP. All accumulated earnings of whatever nature are fully taxable when received by the annuitant.

An annuitant may transfer some or all of the funds standing to his or her credit in a plan to another plan, to a registered pension plan, or to a registered retirement income fund.[51] For example, an individual with $40,000 of combined premiums and earnings thereon in Plan A could transfer this amount or part of it to Plan B. Any amount actually paid to the annuitant out of Plan A and thus not transferred would be included in the individual's income in the year it was received.

All registered plans must provide for the refund of all or a portion of premiums in excess of the amounts deductible as premiums paid to plans for a taxpayer or his or her spouse/common-law partner. Excess premiums paid over the maximum deductible amount per year attract tax under Part X.1 at the rate of 1% per month. See ¶13,455 *et seq.*

Many RRSPs are accompanied by a trust under which the premiums and earnings are held. If the trust acquires non-qualified investments,[52] the annuitant of the plan must include the value of such investment in computing income for the year of acquisition. The annuitant is allowed a deduction

---

See page ii for explanation of footnotes.

[50] CCH ¶21,331; Sec. 146(8.8).
[51] CCH ¶21,363; Sec. 146(16).

[52] CCH ¶21,207; Sec. 146(1) "non-qualified investment".

when such investments are disposed of.[53] In addition, the trust itself may be subject to tax in respect of non-qualified investments under Part XI.I (see ¶13,525 *et seq.*) and in respect of excess holdings of foreign property under Part XI.

[¶10,339] Retirement Savings Plans

"Retirement savings plan" (RSP) means certain types of contracts or arrangements under which an individual or an individual's spouse/common-law partner pays certain periodic or other amounts as consideration for payment under the contract or arrangement of retirement income commencing at maturity.[54] Arrangements may be made between an individual and a corporation licensed or authorized under federal or provincial law to carry on the business of offering to the public its services as trustee; payment may also be made to a corporation licensed under federal or provincial law to issue investment contracts, or to a member or eligible member of the Canadian Payments Association or a credit union. A contract may also be entered into with an organization licensed to carry on an annuities business.

Before an RSP will qualify for a deduction of premiums or contributions, it must be accepted by the Minister for registration.[55] No deduction will be allowed for amounts paid into an "unregistered plan".[56]

[¶10,342] Retirement Income

"Retirement income" means[57] one of two forms of annuity commencing at maturity or a combination of these forms:

(1) The first form is for the life of the annuitant or for the annuitant's lifetime and afterward until the death of the annuitant's spouse/common-law partner. This annuity may have a guaranteed term which may not exceed in years the number obtained when the age of the annuitant in full years at the maturity of the plan is subtracted from 90, or when the annuitant's spouse/common-law partner is younger and the annuitant so elects, the number obtained when the age of the spouse/common-law partner at that time is subtracted from 90.

(2) The second form of annuity is one for a term of years during the life of the annuitant or during the joint lives of the annuitant and the annuitant's spouse/common-law partner. The term of years may not exceed the number obtained when the age of the annuitant in whole years at the maturity of the plan is subtracted from 90, or, where the spouse/common-law partner is younger and the annuitant so elects, the age of the spouse/common-law partner is subtracted from 90.

See page ii for explanation of footnotes.

[53] CCH ¶21,265; Sec. 146(6).

[54] CCH ¶21,211d; Sec. 146(1) "retirement savings plan".

[55] CCH ¶21,211b; Sec. 146(1) "registered retirement savings plan".

[56] No. 643, 59 DTC 451.

[57] CCH ¶21,211c; Sec. 146(1) "retirement income".

An annuity for life or joint lives must be payable in equal annual (or more frequent) periodic amounts throughout the lifetime of the annuitant.[58] In the case of a joint life annuity, the payments after the annuitant's death may be equal to or less than (but may not exceed) those payable during the annuitant's lifetime.[59] A joint life annuity may also provide for a reduction in payment after the spouse/common-law partner's death, provided that payments thereafter are in equal annual or other periodic amounts payable throughout the remainder of the annuitant's life. In cases where partial commutation takes place, payments thereafter must continue to be in equal annual or more frequent periodic amounts.[60]

The plan may provide for an annuity that is integrated with the pension payable under the *Old Age Security Act*; i.e., an annuity that is reduced if and when a pension becomes payable to the annuitant under the *Old Age Security Act*. The amount of the reduction may not, however, exceed the Old Age Security pension that actually becomes payable to the annuitant.[61]

The annuity may also be a variable annuity.[62] It may also be an annuity which increases or decreases from the initial rate upon which it was issued on the basis of changes in generally available Canadian market interest rates.[63]

The annuity may be adjusted annually to reflect in whole or in part increases in the Consumer Price Index, or may increase at a specified rate per annum so long as that rate does not exceed 4% per annum.[64]

The annuity may be increased annually to reflect the excess of the rate of return on a pool of investment assets which could be purchased by the public and which are specified in the annuity contract, over the rate of return specified in the RRSP.[65]

Note that although a plan may provide for "retirement income" in the form of an annuity as described above, it need not do so. Whether it does or not, as an alternative to an annuity, a plan annuitant may (provided his plan permits it) transfer his RRSP funds directly to a registered retirement income fund. Under the same rule, funds may be transferred to other RRSPs which appear to offer more favourable annuities. As well, a taxpayer who is not required to "mature" his plan by virtue of reaching 71 years of age in the year (age limit was 69 after 1996 and before 2007) may nevertheless withdraw funds from the plan, thus creating an "income" subject to tax. Thus the alternatives available to provide "retirement income" in a colloquial sense are considerably broader than might be indicated by the technical definition used in the context of the required terms of a plan.

See page ii for explanation of footnotes.

[58] CCH ¶21,229; Sec. 146(2)(b.1).

[59] CCH ¶21,229; Sec. 146(2)(b.2).

[60] CCH ¶21,235; Sec. 146(3)(b)(i).

[61] CCH ¶21,235; Sec. 146(3)(b)(ii).

[62] CCH ¶21,235; Sec. 146(3)(b)(iii).

[63] CCH ¶21,235; Sec. 146(3)(b)(ii).

[64] CCH ¶21,235; Sec. 146(3)(b)(iv).

[65] CCH ¶21,235; Sec. 146(3)(b)(v).

[¶10,345] Conditions for Acceptance of Plan for Registration

The requirements for the registration of a plan are as follows:[66]

(1) The plan cannot provide for maturity after the end of the year in which the annuitant turns 71 years of age (age 69 after 1996 and before 2007).

(2) The plan must not provide for the payment of any premium after maturity.

(3) The plan must not provide for the payment of any benefit before maturity except a refund of premiums or a payment to the annuitant.

(4) The plan, where it involves a depositary, must provide that the depositary has no right of offset as regards the property held under the plan in connection with any debt or obligation owing to the depositary and the property held under the plan cannot be pledged, assigned, or in any way alienated as a security for a loan or for any purpose other than that of providing for the annuitant, commencing at maturity, a retirement income. A plan issued by a depositary means a plan issued by a credit union or by an organization that is eligible to become a member of the Canadian Payments Association (in general terms, such organizations include banks, trust companies, credit union centrals, and loan companies).

(5) The plan cannot provide for the payment of benefits after maturity except by way of:

(a) retirement income (see ¶10,342);

(b) full or partial commutation to the annuitant; or

(c) full commutation when a person other than the annuitant becomes entitled to annuity payments under the plan.

(6) Retirement income must be in the form of equal annual or more frequent periodic payments unless commutation occurs. If commutation is partial, payments thereafter must continue to be equal, periodic, and annual or more frequent. There are, however, several exceptions to this rule.[67] These include changes in annuity payments upon the death of a spouse/common-law partner, changes to reflect pension payments under the *Old Age Security Act*, indexing of payments to the Consumer Price Index (maximum 4% per year), and adjusting payments in accordance with changes in interest rates or the value of or return on a specific group of assets. Further details are set out below.

(7) When the annuity under the plan is for joint lives, yearly payments after the death of the first annuitant cannot increase above the level applicable in a year before the death of the first annuitant.

See page ii for explanation of footnotes.

[66] CCH ¶21,229, ¶21,235; Sec. 146(2), 146(3); Inf.   [67] CCH ¶21,235; Sec. 146(3)(b).
Cir. 72-22R9.

¶10,345

(8) The plan must contain a specific prohibition against assignment of retirement income in whole or in part.

(9) The plan may be adjoined to a contract or other arrangement that is not a retirement savings plan, such as a policy of life insurance.

(10) The plan must comply with regulations.

(11) Before March 23, 2011 (see below), the plan must not provide that any advantage which is conditional in any way on the existence of the plan be extended to the annuitant of the plan or a person who does not deal at arm's length with the annuitant other than:

(a) a "benefit" or an amount received by a person from an RRSP that is deemed to be included in the income of a deceased annuitant, or an amount received in a year after the year of the death of the last annuitant under the plan;

(b) an advantage arising from the payment or allocation of an amount to the plan by the issuer; for example, from the registration as an RRSP of the savings component of a life insurance policy;

(c) an advantage from life insurance in effect on December 31, 1981; or

(d) an advantage derived from the provision of administrative or investment services in respect of the RRSP.

For transactions occurring after March 22, 2011, the special Part XI.01 taxes on TFSA advantages applies to RRSPs, subject to certain enhancements. This means that the 100% tax on TFSA advantages will be extended to RRSPs. As a result of the extended application of the TFSA advantage rules to RRSPs, the above condition in (11) is repealed after March 22, 2011. For further information on Part XI.01 tax on RRSP advantages, see ¶13,518.

Most of the organizations licensed to carry on an annuities business in Canada, as well as most banks, trust companies, and corporations licensed to issue investment contracts, have developed plans and forms that qualify under the Act. Therefore it is normally a simple matter to have a retirement savings plan accepted by the Minister for registration.

[¶10,348] Taxability of Trust

In general a trust governed by a registered retirement savings plan is not subject to tax.[68] This means, in effect, that annual earnings accumulate on a tax deferred basis and bear tax only when eventually paid out (usually in the form of annuity payments) to the annuitant.

In four circumstances, however, the trust may be taxable.

See page ii for explanation of footnotes.

[68] CCH ¶21,243; Sec. 146(4).

(1) If the trust borrows money in the year or has on hand at the commencement of the year monies borrowed after June 18, 1971, it is fully taxable that year.

(2) If the trust carries on a business in the year, it is taxable on the income attributable to that business, but not on other income. However, business income attributable to qualified investments (for example, business income allocated to units in a limited partnership held by the RRSP), or attributable to the disposition of qualified investments for RRSPs, is not taxable.

(3) Tax is payable for each year beginning with the second year following the year of death of the last annuitant. Previously, tax was payable for each year the RRSP existed following the death.

(4) The trust is taxable on its income from "non-qualified investments".[69]

It should also be noted that if the trust acquires a non-qualified investment (before March 23, 2011) or permits any trust property to be used as security for a loan, the annuitant becomes subject to tax (see ¶10,375 and ¶10,384). Before March 23, 2011, the trust itself may be subject to tax under Part XI.1 on property that was a qualified investment when acquired but has since ceased to qualify and has been retained (see ¶13,525). In light of the extended application of Part XI.01 penalty tax of 50% to non-qualified RRSP investments, the Part XI.1 penalty tax on non-qualified RRSP investments will no longer apply to such investments acquired after March 22, 2011. An RRSP trust may also be subject to tax under Part X.1 in respect of contributions in excess of permitted amounts (see ¶13,450).

[¶10,350] Deductibility of Premiums

The tax-assisted retirement savings system is based on a comprehensive annual limit of 18% of earned income. This uniform limit of 18% of earnings applies to employer-sponsored registered pension plans (RPPs), deferred profit sharing plans (DPSPs), and registered retirement savings plans (RRSPs). That is, annual aggregate contributions to these savings vehicles will generally be limited to 18% of the taxpayer's earned income (based on the previous year's income) up to a maximum dollar amount.

The maximum deductible contribution to a taxpayer's RRSP (or to a spousal or common-law partner plan RRSP) in any one year is the lesser of:

(a) amounts contributed to an RRSP as premiums in the year or within 60 days after year end which have not been deducted in prior years, other than premiums which qualify as rollover amounts discussed at ¶10,357, and subject to certain adjustments discussed below; and

(b) the taxpayer's "RRSP deduction limit" for that particular year (discussed in detail below). The RRSP deduction limit reflects 18% of the

See page ii for explanation of footnotes.
[69] CCH ¶21,336; Sec. 146(10.1).

¶10,350

taxpayer's earned income for the immediately preceding year, to a maximum of the RRSP dollar limit for that particular year, minus the taxpayer's "pension adjustment" (PA) in respect of an employer for the preceding taxation year.

It should be noted that the CRA may extend the deadline for making RRSP contributions. In such a case, RRSP contributions made after the first 60 days of a taxation year will be treated as if made at the beginning of the year.[70] It will exercise this discretion in response to a hardship that affects a community or group of individuals. For example, this rule was used to respond to the January 1998 ice storm, which affected many communities in Eastern Canada.

For taxpayers who do not use their RRSP deduction limit in any one year, unused RRSP deduction room can be carried forward to be used in a subsequent year. Unused RRSP contributions may be carried forward indefinitely.

In addition, the RRSP deduction limit will be reduced by a taxpayer's net past service pension adjustment for the year (for service benefits provided in respect of service after 1989) and increased by the taxpayer's total pension adjustment reversal for the year (for taxation years after 1997).

Certain premiums will not be deductible. These include premiums which are already deductible as prescribed premiums.[71] Prescribed premiums are generally re-contributions of amounts previously withdrawn by a taxpayer from an RRSP to create room for past service benefits under a defined benefit RPP.[72] Additionally, premiums which have been deducted to reflect previously undeducted premiums paid to an RRSP[73] are not deductible again.

[¶10,351] RRSP Dollar Limit

A taxpayer's RRSP dollar limit is defined as being the money purchase limit (see ¶10,477) for the immediately preceding calendar year for years other than 1996.[74] The 2005 Budget increased the RRSP contribution limit to $19,000 for 2007, $20,000 for 2008, $21,000 for 2009, $22,000 for 2010, and $22,000 indexed to the growth in the average industrial wage for 2011 and following years. As a result of indexation, the limit increases to $22,450 for 2011, $22,970 for 2012, and $23,820 for 2013. In summary, the RRSP dollar limits are as follows:

1991	$11,500
1992	$12,500
1993	$12,500
1994	$13,500
1995	$14,500
1996 to 2002	$13,500

See page ii for explanation of footnotes.

[70] CCH ¶21,364f; Sec. 146(22).
[71] CCH ¶21,295; Sec. 146(6.1).
[72] Reg. 8307(7).
[73] CCH ¶21,325; Sec. 146(8.2).
[74] CCH ¶21,211; Sec. 146(1) "RRSP dollar limit".

2003	$14,500
2004	$15,500
2005	$16,500
2006	$18,000
2007	$19,000
2008	$20,000
2009	$21,000
2010	$22,000
2011	$22,450
2012	$22,970
2013	$23,820

Note that since the contribution limit will be the lesser of the RRSP dollar limit for the current year and 18% of earned income for the immediately preceding year, there is, for years in which the RRSP dollar limit changes, a one-year time lag between the earned income limit and the RRSP dollar limit. That is, the 2012 contribution limit will be the lesser of $22,970 or 18% of 2011 earned income, so that the $22,970 RRSP dollar limit for 2012 is reached at $127,611 of 2011 earned income. As well, an individual must have $132,333 of earned income in 2012 in order to reach the RRSP dollar limit of $23,820 in 2013.

[¶10,352] Pension Adjustment (PA)

A taxpayer's PA is meant to reflect the amounts of benefits accruing to a taxpayer under employer-sponsored RPPs and DPSPs of which the taxpayer is a member. For DPSPs, the PA is basically the amount of employer contributions to the DPSP. For money purchase RPPs, the PA reflects the sum of the employee and employer contributions to that plan. For defined benefit RPPs, the PA reflects the amount of benefits accruing to the taxpayer in that year, according to the defined benefit formula in the plan. Basically, the PA for defined benefit RPPs (other than multi-employer RPPs or specified multi-employer RPPs) is equal to nine times the benefit entitlement minus $600, so that a 2% of earnings per year benefit plan (thus the PA being nine times 2% of earnings minus $600) will use up most of the taxpayer's RRSP deduction limit. In this way, deductible contributions to RRSPs are directly limited by benefits accruing to the taxpayer under employer-sponsored retirement saving vehicles. For details on the calculations of the PAs, see the commentary at ¶10,477.

The RPP rules provide for the reporting of PAs by all employers who sponsor RPPs or DPSPs. The CRA informs taxpayers of their RRSP deduction limit for a taxation year in their Notice of Assessment for the prior taxation year. This Notice of Assessment is sent to taxpayers each year once their tax return for the previous year has been filed. The taxpayer's RRSP deduction limit is based on his or her earnings and PAs from the prior year, so the CRA has all this information by the time the Notice of Assessment is prepared. For example, a taxpayer's RRSP deduction limit in 2012 depends on his or her PA and earnings for 2011. His or her employer must report his or her 2011 PA by the end of February 2012 on the taxpayer's T4. In turn, the CRA will include the RRSP deduction limit for 2012, which is based on

2011 earnings and PA, in the taxpayer's Notice of Assessment for 2011, which is usually delivered to the taxpayer within six to eight weeks after the receipt of his or her income tax return.

[¶10,353] RRSP Deduction Limit

As discussed at ¶10,350, the maximum deductible contribution to a taxpayer's RRSP or spousal or common-law partner plan RRSP in any one year is limited to the taxpayer's RRSP deduction limit. The "RRSP deduction limit" [75] is calculated by taking the lesser of the RRSP dollar limit for the year and 18% of the taxpayer's earned income for the immediately preceding year less the taxpayer's PA for the immediately preceding year or other prescribed amount. Added to the RRSP deduction limit is the taxpayer's "unused RRSP deduction room" at the end of the immediately preceding taxation year, which includes unused RRSP deduction limits from previous years and the taxpayer's total pension adjustment reversal (PAR) for the year. Subtracted from the taxpayer's RRSP deduction limit for the year is his or her net past service pension adjustment (net PSPA) for the year, which is basically equal to the benefits granted by his or her employer to an RPP in the year in respect of service of prior years (see ¶10,355 for more details).

[¶10,354] Total Pension Adjustment Reversal (Total PAR)

As discussed at ¶10,350, a taxpayer's RRSP deduction limit for a year is increased by the taxpayer's total PAR for the year. A taxpayer's total PAR for a year is the total of all pension adjustment reversals (PARs) determined in connection with the individual's termination in a year from a DPSP or from an RPP.[76]

In general, under a defined benefit RPP, the PAR is the amount that will restore RRSP deduction room to an individual who receives a termination benefit which is less than the taxpayer's total pension adjustments and past service pension adjustments. A PAR under a DPSP or a money purchase RPP is the amount included in the taxpayer's pension credits but to which the individual ceases to have any rights at termination. A taxpayer will only have a PAR under a DPSP or a money purchase RPP when they are not fully vested on termination.

[¶10,355] Net Past Service Pension Adjustment (Net PSPA)

As discussed at ¶10,350, a taxpayer's RRSP deduction for a year is reduced by the taxpayer's net PSPA[77] for the year. A taxpayer's net PSPA is equal to the taxpayer's accumulated PSPA minus certain prescribed PSPA withdrawals. Generally, a taxpayer's accumulated PSPA for a year reflects improvements to RPP benefits granted by his or her employer in that year with respect to past service benefits (but only with respect to service after 1989), reduced by certain PSPA transfers from other RRSPs, DPSPs, and RPPs, as described further in the following paragraph. Such past service

---

See page ii for explanation of footnotes.

[75] CCH ¶21,210; Sec. 146(1) "RRSP deduction limit".
[76] CCH ¶28,309; Sec. 248(1)"total pension adjustment reversal"; Reg. 8304.1.
[77] CCH ¶21,206; Sec. 146(1) "net past service pension adjustment".

benefits might be provided, for example, as an upgrade in benefit plans for previous years, or as benefits for previous years in which the employee was not a member of the RPP. Generally speaking, and with certain exceptions, past service benefits are allowed to the extent of $8,000, plus the taxpayer's unused RRSP deduction room (that is, amounts of the taxpayer's RRSP deduction limits for previous years not used), plus any qualifying transfers from other plans and qualifying withdrawals from RRSPs.

The first step in determining the taxpayer's net PSPA is to determine the accumulated PSPA. Generally, the taxpayer's accumulated PSPA is the sum of all increases in pension credits associated with the benefit improvements in the year reduced by certain prescribed PSPA transfers for the year (i.e., this amount is the sum of the taxpayer's "provisional PSPAs").[78] These prescribed PSPA transfers or "qualifying transfers"[79] are transfers from RRSPs, DPSPs, or money purchase accounts of RPPs to fund all or a portion of the past service benefits being granted. To obtain the taxpayer's net PSPA, the taxpayer's accumulated PSPA is reduced by prescribed PSPA withdrawals. "Prescribed PSPA withdrawals"[80] are basically equal to amounts withdrawn from the taxpayer's RRSP to make room for past service benefits, as reflected in the taxpayer's accumulated PSPA. In effect, the taxpayer exchanges previous RRSP contributions for defined benefit RPP contributions.

Therefore, the net effect of PSPAs on the RRSP deduction limit in any one year can be summarized as follows: Assuming that there are no PSPA transfers or withdrawals, where an employer contributes to the employee's defined benefit RPP in the year in respect of past service, that amount (which generally can be up to the taxpayer's unused RRSP deduction room plus $8,000) is deducted from the RRSP deduction limit for that year. PSPA transfers made in the year are not subtracted from the RRSP deduction limit because they, in effect, represent amounts that were contributed to other plans in previous years and therefore their deductibility has already been accounted for in those previous years. There is simply a transfer of tax-sheltered income. Analogously, PSPA withdrawals in the year are not subtracted from the RRSP deduction limit because they merely represent the amounts that the taxpayer is withdrawing from his or her RRSP in order to make the additional room for past service benefits as reflected in his or her PSPA.

Past service pension adjustments (PSPAs) arising from improved pension plans (exempt PSPAs as opposed to certifiable PSPAs) do not reduce RRSP contribution room until the year following the past service event.[81] This ensures that exempt PSPAs do not affect the deductibility of RRSP contributions that were made before the occurrence of a past service event on the expectation that the contributions would be deductible.

---

[78] Reg. 8303(3).

[79] Reg. 8303(6).

[80] Reg. 8307(6).

[81] Reg. 8303(2).

¶10,355

[¶10,356] Unused RRSP Deduction Room

As discussed at ¶10,350, a taxpayer's "RRSP deduction limit" for a year includes the taxpayer's unused RRSP deduction room at the end of the preceding year.

Generally speaking, the taxpayer's "unused RRSP deduction room" [82] at the end of any taxation year is equal to the amount of the taxpayer's RRSP deduction limit for that year that the taxpayer did not use. That is, it is equal to the taxpayer's RRSP deduction limit for that year minus premiums paid to his or her RRSP and deducted in that year (or premiums paid to his or her spouse/common-law partner's RRSP and deducted in that year), and amounts contributed to the *Saskatchewan Pension Plan* and deducted in that year. Additionally, the unused RRSP deduction room for the year includes the unused RRSP deduction room from the preceding taxation year, thus providing the carryforward of the unused RRSP deduction room.[83]

Unused RRSP contributions can be carried forward indefinitely without limit.

RRSP Contribution Limits — Summary

Year	% Income Limit ("Earned Income")	Maximum Dollar Limit Non-RPP/DPSP Members	RPP/DPSP Members
1991	18% of prior year's	$11,500	(same dollar amount but
1992	18% of prior year's	$12,500	reduced by the PA from pri-
1993	18% of prior year's	$12,500	or year and net PSPA for
1994	18% of prior year's	$13,500	that year and, after 1997, it
1995	18% of prior year's	$14,500	is increased by the PAR for
1996 to 2002	18% of prior year's	$13,500	the year)
2003	18% of prior year's	$14,500	
2004	18% of prior year's	$15,500	
2005	18% of prior year's	$16,500	
2006	18% of prior year's	$18,000	
2007	18% of prior year's	$19,000	
2008	18% of prior year's	$20,000	
2009	18% of prior year's	$21,000	
2010	18% of prior year's	$22,000	
2011	18% of prior year's	$22,450	
2012	18% of prior year's	$22,970	
2013	18% of prior year's	$23,820	

Note: Unused contribution limit in any year can be carried forward indefinitely.

Example 1 — Calculation of a taxpayer's 2012 RRSP deduction limit (with PSPA)

Facts:

2011 contributions to taxpayer's RRSP and deducted	$ 5,000
Earned income: 2010	$60,000
2011	$70,000

See page ii for explanation of footnotes.

[82] CCH ¶21,211f; Sec. 146(1) "unused RRSP deduction room". [83] CCH ¶21,211f; Sec. 146(1) "unused RRSP deduction room".

Pension adjustment (PAs) under defined benefit RPP (1% of earned income)

2010	$ 4,800
2011	$ 5,700

2011 — Net PSPA: Taxpayer's employer contributes past service benefits to RPP (for service in 2008 and 2009)....................................... $ 2,000

Calculations:

(1) Unused RRSP deduction room at the end of 2011

= *lesser of*

(a) $10,800 (18% × $60,000)

and

(b) $22,450

minus $4,800 (PA for 2010) = $6,000

minus $5,000 (RRSP premiums paid and deducted in 2011) = $1,000

(2) 2012 RRSP deduction limit

= $1,000 (unused RRSP deduction room at end of 2011)

plus the lesser of

(a) $12,600 (18% × $70,000)

and

(b) $22,970

minus $5,700 (PA for 2011)

minus $2,000 (net PSPA for 2012) = $5,900

Therefore, in 2012, the taxpayer can contribute and deduct up to $5,900 to his/her RRSP.

Because a taxpayer's RRSP deduction limit in a particular year is based on the preceding year's PA, he or she may be precluded from contributing to his or her RRSP in the particular year even where in that year he or she has not accrued benefits under an RPP or DPSP (for instance, if the taxpayer accepts new employment not offering an RPP or DPSP benefit). Certainly, this seems like an inequitable result which in large part can be remedied by a "pension adjustment reversal" (PAR). In general terms, the PAR will equal the individual's total pension credits since 1990 (forming the individual's reported PAs) in excess of the amount of the termination benefit received when the individual ceased to be a member of the RPP or DPSP. PARs will be added to the individual's RRSP deduction room for the year of termination.

Example of calculation of a taxpayer's 2012 RRSP deduction limit (with PAR):

Facts:

The taxpayer became a member of a defined contribution RPP on January 1, 2010. The taxpayer's employer matched the taxpayer's contribution of 5% of earned income to the RPP. The taxpayer's employment was terminated, such that the taxpayer only contributed to the RPP for the period prior to July 1, 2011, and the taxpayer was not vested of any employer contributions in the RPP. The taxpayer did not find employment after being terminated.

¶10,356

2011 contributions to taxpayer's RRSP and deducted .... $ 4,000
Earned income: 2010 .... $60,000
2011 .... $30,000
Pension adjustments (PAs) under defined contribution RPP
2010 .... $ 6,000
2011 .... $ 3,000
Pension adjustment reversals (PARs) under defined contribution RPP
2011 .... $ 4,500

Calculations:

(1) Unused RRSP deduction room at the end of 2011 = *lesser of*

(a) $10,800 (18% × $60,000)

and

(b) $22,450

minus $6,000 (PA for 2010)

minus $4,000 (RRSP premiums paid and deducted in 2011)

plus $4,500 (total PAR for 2011) = $5,300

(2) 2012 RRSP deduction limit

= $5,300 (unused RRSP deduction room at the end of 2011) *plus the lesser of*

(a) $5,400 (18% × $30,000)

and

(b) $22,970

minus $3,000 (PA for 2011) = $7,700

Therefore, in 2012, the taxpayer could contribute and deduct up to $7,700 to his/her RRSP.

[¶10,357] Rollovers to an RRSP

A taxpayer may transfer certain income receipts to an RRSP and deduct the amount so transferred in computing income.[84] The income receipts that are eligible to be transferred to an RRSP under this rollover provision are:

(1) superannuation or pension benefits payable out of an unregistered pension plan and attributable to services rendered by a person and a person's spouse/common-law partner or former spouse/common-law partner in a period during which such person was not resident in Canada;

(2) a lump-sum payment from a foreign retirement arrangement where the payment is included in income and derives from contributions made to the foreign retirement arrangement by the taxpayer or the taxpayer's spouse/common-law partner or former spouse/common-law partner;

---

[84] CCH ¶8490; Sec. 60(*j*).

(3) lump-sum amounts received by a testamentary trust from the deceased's registered pension plans or DPSPs and distributed to the surviving spouse/common-law partner who is designated as beneficiary; and

(4) the cost of shares of an employer distributed to a beneficiary under a deferred profit sharing plan of the employer.

The transfers of RPP and DPSP contributions are dealt with under the direct transfer provisions discussed at ¶10,492 (for transfers from RPPs) and ¶10,453 (for transfers from DPSPs).

The amount to be deducted under these rollover provisions must be "designated" on Schedule 7 of the income tax return for the year in which the deduction is claimed.

A taxpayer who transfers an amount to an RRSP under these provisions may also contribute to an RRSP in respect of his or her current year's earned income. That is, the deduction under the rollover provisions is allowed in addition to the taxpayer's RRSP deduction limit for the year.

Cash payments in the nature of a retiring allowance a taxpayer receives on leaving employment, either in recognition of long service or as damages for loss of office will also qualify for the special rollover treatment, to the extent the employment originally commenced before January 1, 1996.[85] The amount of a retiring allowance which can be so transferred tax-free to an RRSP cannot exceed the lesser of:

(1) the amount received; and

(2) the sum of:

(a) $3,500 times the number of years before 1989 during which the taxpayer was employed by the employer or a person related to the employer. This $3,500 limit is reduced to $1,500 in respect of the number of years before 1989 during which the taxpayer was employed by the employer or a person related to the employer and for which employer contributions under either an RPP or DPSP of the employer or a person related to the employer may reasonably be considered to have vested in the taxpayer at the time of payment of the retiring allowance;

(b) $2,000 per year for each year of service after 1988 and before 1996, regardless of RPP or DPSP considerations; and

(c) nil for year of service after 1995.

The retiring allowance/termination payment rollover is effectively phased out by rule (c) above. The rollover will not be available for employment commencing after 1995. It will continue to be available for earlier employment to the extent of years of service prior to 1996.

---

[85] CCH ¶8495; Sec. 60(j.1).

¶10,357

Note that awards of legal fees may be included in income (but not as a retiring allowance) and actual legal fees may be deducted from awards to the extent the awards have not been contributed to an RRSP (see ¶2205 and ¶2325).

Finally, rollover provisions can be used when an RRSP's annuitant dies. In such a case, any lump sum paid to the annuitant's spouse/common-law partner (and included in the spouse's or common-law partner's income) can be paid as a premium into an RRSP of which the spouse/common-law partner is the annuitant and deducted in computing the spouse/common-law partner's income to the extent that it is designated.[86] To the extent that such a payment is not designated, it will constitute an RRSP premium. The same rollover provisions apply where the amount is paid to the deceased person's estate to be distributed to his or her spouse or common-law partner.

[¶10,360] Deductible Contribution to Spousal or Common-Law Partner Plan

A taxpayer who is married or in a common-law partnership may pay a premium to a registered retirement savings plan of which his spouse or common-law partner is the annuitant and (within the limits discussed below) deduct such payment in computing his or her own income.[87] This does not in any way increase the amount of the taxpayer's annual deductible contributions; it does, however, allow contributions to accumulate in plans for the benefit of two persons so that the amounts eventually paid out will be divided and often taxed at lower marginal rates than would be so if only one person received all of the return. In effect, this is a form of income splitting. However, premiums paid to a spousal or common-law partner plan may be included in the income of the taxpayer if these premiums are withdrawn by the spouse/common-law partner within two years of the year in respect of which the contribution was made. See also ¶10,363.

An individual's total contributions to both his or her plan and a spousal or common-law partner plan are restricted to the individual's own contribution limit. Therefore, a contribution made by an individual to a spousal or common-law partner plan RRSP does not affect the spouse's or common-law partner's personal RRSP contribution limit for the year.

Amounts deductible under a spousal or common-law partner plan also exclude premiums in respect of which the taxpayer or the taxpayer's spouse or common-law partner has received payments tax-free out of an RRSP as they are in respect of previously contributed but undeducted premiums.[88]

The so-called attribution rules do not apply in respect of premiums paid to a spousal or common-law partner plan. As a result, income paid out of the spousal or common-law partner plan is not attributed to the taxpayer

---

See page ii for explanation of footnotes.

[86] CCH ¶8510; Sec. 60(l). [88] CCH ¶21,325; Sec. 146(8.2).
[87] CCH ¶21,262; Sec. 146(5.1); Interp. Bul. IT-307R4.

although the contributions which gave rise to that income may have been made in whole or in part by the taxpayer. See also ¶10,363.

A taxpayer may set up a spousal or common-law partner plan for the benefit of a common-law partner, including a same-sex partner after 2000, who has lived with the taxpayer in a conjugal relationship for at least 12 months or is the parent of a child of whom the taxpayer is also a parent.

There are two main tax advantages to spousal or common-law partner plans. Firstly, a taxpayer and his or her spouse/common-law partner will be able to split income at retirement, and so reduce the overall tax burden based on marginal tax rates. Secondly, if a taxpayer can no longer contribute to an RRSP because of his or her age (¶10,345), but still has earned income or contribution room available and has a younger spouse/common-law partner who is still eligible to have a plan, he or she can continue making RRSP contributions.

Example:

> Mr. and Mrs. Smith are now approaching retirement. During most years of their marriage, Mr. Smith had substantial earned income while Mrs. Smith had little or no earned income. Mr. Smith has always saved through an RRSP and expects that it will provide $40,000 per year to supplement his OAS/CPP and other income. In addition, Mr. Smith will personally have about $10,000 of other income (perhaps OAS/CPP). Total income will therefore be about $50,000 per year.

> If Mr. Smith has made spousal RRSP contributions throughout the marriage so that each spouse now has equal RRSPs, he will be taxed on $30,000 per year and Mrs. Smith on $20,000. The total tax for the two of them will be about $6,400. If Mr. Smith had contributed only to his own RRSP, he would be taxed on the entire $50,000 and pay about $9,900 in tax. Accordingly, there is an annual tax saving of about $3,500 on retirement income resulting from the use of spousal RRSPs.

> Note that a large measure of the tax savings arises because income would be taxed in a higher bracket if it were taxed to one spouse only. If the total income for Mr. and Mrs. Smith together after retirement were less than $42,707 for 2012 (as indexed from year to year, i.e. if their combined income for the years after retirement does not exceed the lowest rate bracket in those years), the tax savings arising from a spousal RRSP would be less significant. However, there would still be savings in most cases arising from multiple access to the pension income credit and other basic personal amount credits.

> For 2007 and subsequent taxation years, a similar income-splitting benefit can be achieved (even without a spousal RRSP) through the pension-splitting provisions described at 2437.

The legal representative of a deceased taxpayer may make contributions to a spousal or common-law partner plan for the spouse/common-law partner of the deceased. That is, any amounts which the deceased could have contributed at the time of death to his or her own plan or spousal plan over and above amounts already contributed at the time of death can be contributed to a spousal or common-law partner plan. The contributions by the legal representative may be made up to 60 days following the end of the calendar year in which the deceased died.

¶10,360

A deductible payment to a spousal or common-law partner plan may also be made for a year where the contributor dies in the stub period of 60 days following the year end. In this case, a deductible spousal or common-law partner plan contribution can be made within the 60-day stub period and deducted for the year preceding death. Such a contribution would still not include ordinary earnings for the year preceding death, but earnings of the year preceding a stub period death could be contributed and deducted in the year of death. It is also possible in the case of a stub period death to ignore the stub period and make a year of death spousal plan contribution under the general rule. For example, suppose X dies in January 2012. X's legal representative can make a spousal or common-law partner plan contribution for X's spouse/common-law partner by March 1, 2012, based on X's 2010 earned income and carryforwards (X's 2011 contribution limit). This will be deductible in 2011. A further contribution based on remaining 2012 contribution limits (generated by 2011 earned income) can be deducted for 2012.

[¶10,363] Amounts To Be Included in Income in Respect of a Spousal or Common-Law Partner Plan

In certain circumstances, amounts which would otherwise be included in a spouse/common-law partner's income as a result of payments out of the spousal or common-law partner plan, will be included in the income of the contributing taxpayer if the taxpayer has made contributions to any spousal or common-law partner plan RRSP within a specified time period.[89] This rule does not apply to amounts received while the taxpayer and the taxpayer's spouse or common-law partner are living separate and apart due to a breakdown of their marriage or common-law partnership. The amount included in the taxpayer's income rather than the spouse's or common-law partner's income will be the lesser of:

(a) the fair market value of all the property of the plan which would otherwise be included in the spouse's or common-law partner's income on the collapse of the plan;[90] and

(b) the total contributions made by the taxpayer to the plan for that year or either of the two preceding years.

Thus (subject to the exceptions below), in situations where contributions have been made to a spousal or common-law partner plan, the spouse/common-law partner will have to wait until the third taxation year following the year in respect of which the last of such contributions were made to avoid the inclusion of amounts in the contributor's income. This will be true even if the spouse/common-law partner has made contributions to the plan on his or her own account in addition to those made by the taxpayer.

See page ii for explanation of footnotes.

[89] CCH ¶21,326; Sec. 146(8.3).   [90] CCH ¶21,347; Sec. 146(12).

A plan will be a "spousal or common-law partner plan" in respect of a taxpayer if the taxpayer has paid premiums to the RRSP, or the RRSP has received a payment or transfer from another RRSP or RRIF that was itself a spousal or common-law partner plan with respect to a taxpayer.[91]

Where a taxpayer has made more than one deductible contribution to a spousal RRSP and amounts are included in the taxpayer's income under the above rules, the inclusion in income is deemed to relate to the contributions in the order in which they were made.[92] Where an amount has been included in a taxpayer's income, no further inclusion in income is to be made with respect to that particular contribution or part of it.[93]

The above rules do not apply:

(a) to the year in which the taxpayer dies;

(b) where either the taxpayer or the taxpayer's spouse/common-law partner is not resident in Canada at the particular time;

(c) to amounts paid out of a plan which was revised or amended prior to May 26, 1976;

(d) where the annuitant claims a deduction in respect of the transfer to an RRSP.[94] However, if that deduction is claimed on the basis of the purchase of an annuity, the terms of the annuity must provide that it cannot be commuted within three years and in fact it must not be commuted within that period; and

(e) in respect of amounts deemed to have been received by a taxpayer out of an RRSP immediately prior to death.

Furthermore, they will not apply if the taxpayer and the taxpayer's spouse or common-law partner are separated and living apart due to a breakdown of their marriage or common-law partnership. Note that this test is just a factual one and does not require a formal separation agreement as in the case of a transfer of funds.

Example:

Assume that the following contributions have been made by both a taxpayer and the taxpayer's spouse or common-law partner to a spousal or common-law partner plan and deducted for the years shown:

	2009	2010	2011	2012
Taxpayer	$1,000	$3,000	nil	nil
Spouse/partner	$2,000	$1,000	$1,000	$1,000

See page ii for explanation of footnotes.

[91] CCH ¶21,211da; Sec. 146(1) "spousal or common-law partner plan".

[92] CCH ¶21,328; Sec. 146(8.5).

[93] CCH ¶21,329; Sec. 146(8.6).

[94] CCH ¶21,329c; Sec. 146(8.7).

Situation 1

If the spouse or common-law partner were to withdraw $2,000 from the RRSP in 2010, this amount would be included in the income of the taxpayer, notwithstanding the fact that the spouse or common-law partner could be considered to have been withdrawing his or her own contributions from the plan. If the spouse or common-law partner went on to withdraw a further $3,000 from the plan in 2011, only $2,000 would be included in the taxpayer's income.

Situation 2

If the spouse or common-law partner were to withdraw $4,000 from the RRSP in 2012, only $3,000 would be included in the taxpayer's income since this is the total of deductible contributions made by the taxpayer in the year or either of the two preceding taxation years.

Situation 3

Assuming that no further deductible contributions are made by the taxpayer, the spouse or common-law partner may withdraw any amount from the RRSP in the 2013 and subsequent taxation years without any income inclusion in the taxpayer's income.

[¶10,366] Refund of Premiums on Death of Annuitant

When an annuitant dies, the income tax consequences will depend upon whether the amounts payable out of or under the deceased's RRSP pass to the deceased's heirs under the terms of the plan itself or whether the amounts are payable to the deceased's legal representative. Also the identity of the beneficiary will be important. Generally, the full value of property held under an RRSP will be included in the income of the deceased for the year of death even if the amounts are paid out of the plan to another person, unless the recipient is the spouse/common-law partner of the deceased or, subject to certain conditions, a dependent child or grandchild of the deceased.[95]

If the plan had matured prior to the annuitant's death and the remaining annuity payments under the plan are payable directly to the spouse or common-law partner, these payments will be included in the income of the spouse or common-law partner, who becomes the annuitant, or who can elect with the estate to become the annuitant (see below).

If the spouse or common-law partner is not the beneficiary under the plan, the annuity payments which pass at the death of the annuitant to a beneficiary other than the spouse or common-law partner must be commuted.[96] The value of these payments will be included in the income of the deceased for the year of death (but not included in the income of the beneficiary)[97] unless the amounts are paid to dependent children or grandchildren and qualify as, or are deemed to qualify as, a "refund of premiums" (see below).

See page ii for explanation of footnotes.

[95] Interp. Bul. IT-500R.
[96] CCH ¶21,229; Sec. 146(2)(c.2).
[97] CCH ¶21,331; Sec. 146(8.8).

If the annuitant dies before the maturity of the plan, it is common that the accumulated value of the plan is paid out in a lump sum to his or her estate or other beneficiary provided for in the plan. Again, subject to the following, the annuitant will be subject to tax on this amount in the year of death unless the amount passes directly to the spouse or common-law partner or a dependent child or grandchild and qualifies as a refund of premiums.

If an amount is paid out of or under an RRSP to the estate of the annuitant and not directly to a beneficiary, the amount will be included in the income of the annuitant for the year of death unless one of the elections described below is available and is used. These elections permit amounts paid to the estate to be treated as if they had been paid directly to a beneficiary such that they will not be included in the income of the deceased.

For RRSPs wound up after 2008 following the death of the annuitant, losses incurred on the RRSP investments following that death may be carried back and deducted from the annuitant's RRSP income.[98] The deduction is the amount by which the total of amounts included in the annuitant's income, plus taxable amounts received from the RRSP from the date of death to the date the RRSP is wound up, plus "tax-paid amounts" that exceed amounts distributed from the RRSP during the same period. Tax-paid amounts are certain amounts paid from an RRSP after the RRSP's tax-exempt period (i.e., after December 31 of the year following the year of the annuitant's death). The RRSP must be wound up by the end of the year following the year of death and must not hold non-qualified investments during the post-death period, in order for the deduction to be available without special permission by the Minister of National Revenue. For more details, see ¶10,368.

If the payment arising on the death of the annuitant prior to the maturity of the plan is made to the spouse or common-law partner or to a dependent child or grandchild and qualifies as a refund of premiums, the amount of the payment will be included in the recipient's income. Otherwise, it will be included in the income of the deceased for the year of death.[99] Where it is the spouse or common-law partner who receives these amounts, he or she is given the alternative of transferring the amount received to another RRSP, a RRIF, or certain forms of annuity, and may deduct the amount so transferred.[100]

"Refund of premiums" is defined[101] as any amount paid out of or under an RRSP (other than a "tax-paid amount", as defined in ¶10,367) to the spouse or common-law partner of an annuitant as a consequence of the annuitant's death prior to the plan's maturity, or amounts paid out of or

[98] CCH ¶21,333f; Sec. 146(8.92).

[99] CCH ¶21,331; Sec. 146(8.8).

[100] CCH ¶8510; Sec. 60(l).

[101] CCH ¶21,211a; Sec. 146(1) "refund of premiums".

¶10,366

under an RRSP after the annuitant's death to a dependent child or grandchild (whether the death occurred before or after the maturity of the plan), subject to the following two limitations:

(1) At the time the annuitant died, the child or grandchild must have been financially dependent on the annuitant.

(2) It is assumed, unless the contrary is established, a child or grandchild is not financially dependent on the annuitant at the time of the annuitant's death if the income of the child or grandchild for the taxation year preceding the year of the annuitant's death exceeded the basic personal amount described in ¶8095 for the preceding year ($10,527 for 2011, which therefore applies for deaths occurring in 2012). For deaths occurring after 2002, if the child or grandchild was dependent by reason of mental or physical infirmity, the income threshold for these purposes is equal to the basic personal amount plus the disability amount for the preceding year ($17,868 for deaths in 2012 based on the basic personal amount plus the disability amount for 2011; $18,368 for deaths in 2013).[102]

A financially dependent non-infirm child or grandchild can make a tax-deferred transfer of a refund of premiums to an annuity to age 18. The amount received will then be taxed as the annuity payments are received. The annuity must be acquired within 60 days of the end of the year of receipt of the refund of premiums. A child or grandchild, who, regardless of age, was dependent on the deceased parent or grandparent by reason of physical or mental infirmity can make a tax-deferred transfer of a refund of premiums to an RRSP, RRIF, eligible annuity, or annuity to age 18. The transfer must be made or the annuity purchased within 60 days of year end. [Under pending legislation released July 16, 2010 and to be effective after 2000, a refund of premiums paid in favour of a person who is physically or mentally infirm (whether a spouse or dependent child or grandchild) may also be transferred to a life annuity or a term-to-age 90 annuity of which the annuitant is a "lifetime benefit trust". A lifetime benefit trust is a trust under which the taxpayer is the sole person beneficially interested in amounts payable under the annuity (determined without regard to any right of a person to receive an amount from the trust only on or after the death of the beneficiary). The rule that the rollover recipient can name a trust which can have other beneficiaries after the recipient's death would ensure that provision could be made for any residual amounts remaining after death. For 2005 and later years, an annuity may only name a trust for a beneficiary who is mentally infirm. From 2001 to 2005, the beneficiary may be mentally or physically infirm at the time of acquisition.][103]

Amounts paid out of the deceased's RRSP to the deceased's financially dependent children or grandchildren qualify as a refund of premiums,

---

See page ii for explanation of footnotes.

[102] CCH ¶21,211g; Sec. 146(1.1).   [103] Sec. 60.011.

regardless of whether the deceased had a surviving spouse (similar rules apply to amounts paid out of the deceased's RRIF).

If an amount paid to the estate would have qualified as a refund of premiums if paid directly to a beneficiary, the legal representative of the estate and the beneficiary can file a joint election (using Form T2019) such that all or a portion of that amount is deemed to be received by the beneficiary as a refund of premiums.[104] A refund of premiums may be transferred to another RRSP, to a RRIF, or used to acquire certain forms of annuity under the rollover provisions. The amount covered by an election (or received directly by child beneficiaries of the RRSP) which qualifies as a refund of premiums will be deducted from the amount included in the income of the deceased.[105] That is, these amounts will be taxable in the hands of the spouse or common-law partner or dependent children, as the case may be, and not the estate, and may (but need not) be rolled over by them into another tax deferral plan. The election will be of interest in cases where the taxpayer dies before the maturity of a plan and his or her spouse or common-law partner is a beneficiary of his or her estate or where the taxpayer has no spouse or common-law partner and the beneficiaries of the estate are dependent children as described above. It does not appear that the amount designated in the election must actually be paid to the beneficiary.

After March 3, 2010, a refund of premium under an RRSP may on the annuitant's death be rolled over to the registered disability savings plan (RDSP) of a financially dependent infirm child or grandchild (see income test above) to the extent there is room under the $200,000 RDSP contribution limit. The contribution from the rollover cannot be made before July 1, 2011. Transitional rules provide access to the rollover where death occurred after 2007 and before 2011. See ¶10,430.

An election is possible where a taxpayer has died after the maturity of a plan and the estate receives the remaining amounts owing under the plan.[106] Where such amounts are held by the legal representative for the benefit of the Spouse or common-law partner, the legal representative and the spouse or common-law partner may file a joint election such that the spouse or common-law partner is deemed to have become the annuitant under the plan and amounts paid to the estate will be deemed to be received by the spouse or common-law partner as a benefit under the plan. Accordingly, the spouse or common-law partner will include the payments in income in the same manner as if the remaining payments under the plan had been payable to the spouse or common-law partner under the terms of the plan. It is not necessary that the amounts received by the estate in fact be paid to the spouse or common-law partner. The effect of the election will be that payments out of or under the RRSP after the death of the taxpayer will be

---

[104] CCH ¶21,324; Sec. 146(8.1).   [106] CCH ¶21,333; Sec. 146(8.91).
[105] CCH ¶21,332; Sec. 146(8.9).

¶10,366

included in the spouse or common-law partner's income and not in the income of the deceased.

[¶10,367] Post-Death Increase in RRSP Value

There are relieving rules that alter the calculation of amounts to be included in the income of the deceased. The representatives of the deceased may elect to treat less than the full amount as eligible for refund of premiums treatment as taxable to the qualified beneficiary rather than the deceased where this gives a better result.

As well, the effect of growth of RRSP assets after the death of the annuitant is minimized by allowing amounts accrued in the plan after death to be taxed to (and in the case of a spouse or common-law partner or infirm child rolled over by) the survivors rather than the deceased. Under these rules, the amount eligible for refund of premiums treatment is the value of the plan at death plus a specified fraction of post-death growth. For this purpose, the total growth in RRSP assets after the death of an RRSP annuitant is considered to be the amount, if positive, equal to:

(a) the total payments (referred to as the "relevant payments") out of or under the RRSP after the annuitant's death and before the later of the end of the first calendar year commencing after the death and the time immediately after the distribution of all refunds of premiums;

plus:

(b) the fair market value of property of the RRSP at the later of the two times described in (a) (called the "residual value" and usually nil);

minus:

(c) the fair market value of all the property of the RRSP at the time of the annuitant's death.

The specified fraction of that growth, eligible for refund of premiums treatment, is the total of such refunds divided by the sum of relevant payments in (a) plus the residual value in (b).

Rules ensure that where the RRSP funds are distributed to both qualifying and non-qualifying beneficiaries, any post-death accumulations in the RRSP cannot be sheltered from tax in the hand of the deceased to the extent they represented distributions to non-qualified beneficiaries. The rules on post-death accumulations are harmonized with the rules under which RRSP trusts become taxable beginning with the year following the year of death. In particular, the rules provide that distributions of RRSP funds of a deceased taxpayer representing post-death accumulations will bear some measure of taxation in the year-of-death return of the deceased even when all distributions are made to a surviving spouse or common-law partner or other qualified beneficiaries.

Where the RRSP is divided between a surviving spouse or common-law partner and another beneficiary, the offset of the value included in the deceased's year of death return is fixed as the percentage of total distribution paid out to refund of premiums beneficiaries. The refund of premiums beneficiary takes all receipts (including post-death growth in the trust) except those arising after January 1st following the year of death as a refund of premiums. Other beneficiaries receive taxable amounts. To the extent the estate elects to be taxable on post-death growth, the recipient will not be taxable.

The refund of premiums excludes the "tax-paid amount".[107] This amount represents the surviving Spouse or common-law partner's share of the increase in value of the plan from January 1 of the year following the year of death. This amount is taxed either in the RRSP trust (since that becomes taxable in the year following death) or in the hands of the recipient beneficiary if paid to the beneficiary in the year. In either case, the amount does not qualify for refund of premium treatment.

[¶10,368] Post-Death Reduction in RRSP Value

For RRSPs wound up as a result of the annuitant's death after 2008, losses incurred on the RRSP investments after death may be carried back and deducted against the year of death income inclusion discussed at ¶10,366.[108] The allowed deduction is the difference between the following two variables (A - B) where:

- A is the amount included in the annuitant's income in the year of death, plus taxable amounts received from the RRSP from the date of death to the date the RRSP is wound up, plus "tax-paid amounts" (see below); and

- B is the total of all amounts paid out of the RRSP (otherwise called "RRSP distributions") after the annuitant's death.

"Tax-paid amounts" are certain amounts paid from an RRSP after the RRSP's tax exempt period (i.e., after December 31 of the year following the year of the annuitant's death).

The following example is based on the Department of Finance's Explanatory Notes accompanying the 2009 Budget implementing Bill C-10 (now S.C. 2009, c. 2):

> *Example:*
>
> An RRSP annuitant dies in June 2008. The fair market value of his RRSP assets is $100,000. In November 2009, the annuitant's estate distributes $80,000 to two beneficiaries of the annuitant and the executor winds up the RRSP. As discussed at ¶10,366), an amount of $100,000 must be included in the annuitant's income for 2008. Under new subsection 146(8.92), the legal representative of the annuitant can claim a deduction of $20,000 against the deceased annuitant's 2008 income (i.e., $100,000 - $80,000).

See page ii for explanation of footnotes.

[107] CCH ¶21,211ea; Sec. 146(1) "tax-paid amount".   [108] CCH ¶21,333f; Sec. 146(8.92).

The deduction is only available if the following two conditions are met:

(1) the RRSP is wound up by the end of the year following the year of death, and

(2) the RRSP does not hold non-qualified investments during the post-death period.[109]

If either of those conditions is not met, the deceased annuitant's legal representative can submit a request in writing to the Minister of National Revenue that the offsetting deduction be allowed. The Minister may allow some or all of the deduction, subject to possible additional conditions to be met, as appropriate.

[¶10,369] Refund of Non-Deductible Premiums — Penalties on Excess

Every RRSP must provide for the refund of all or a portion of the premiums paid and gifts made to the plan in a year in excess of amounts deductible by the payor in computing income for that year or the previous year.[110] Amounts so refunded would be included in computing the recipient's income in the year of receipt,[111] although the contribution itself would not have produced any deduction. Amounts refunded in these circumstances may be deducted by the recipient in computing income.[112] Form T3012 issued by the CRA is to be filed for the purposes of the deduction. So long as an excessive contribution remains unrefunded, there will be a special tax payable under Part X.1 (discussed at ¶13,455 *et seq.*).[113]

It should be noted that the deduction is available only if the refund of the excess amount is received in the year the excessive premiums were paid, the year in which the notice of assessment for the excess contribution year is sent, or in the year following either of those years. Since the taxpayer earns no deduction for excess premiums paid to a plan it is to his or her advantage to take them out as a refund within the time limits and thereby receive the deduction. If the taxpayer leaves the relevant amount in the plan, it will be included in income on eventual distribution as part of his or her annuity; the taxpayer will in effect have paid a non-deductible premium to the plan that attracts tax on its return as a benefit. As well, a continuing Part X.1 tax will be incurred.

Where the taxpayer over-contributes to a spousal or common-law partner plan, the refund may be made to the taxpayer or the spouse or common-law partner.

Under Part X.1, a 1% monthly tax is imposed on a taxpayer's cumulative excess amount in respect of RRSPs.[114] The cumulative excess amount is, generally, equal to the amount by which the taxpayer's paid but undeducted RRSP premiums exceed the taxpayer's RRSP deduction limit plus $2,000 (there is no $2,000 cushion for persons under 18 years of age). See ¶13,455.

The deduction of undeducted RRSP premiums paid back to a taxpayer does not apply to "prescribed withdrawals" which are designated "qualifying

---

See page ii for explanation of footnotes.

[109] CCH ¶21,333h; Sec. 146(8.93).
[110] CCH ¶21,229; Sec. 146(2)(c.1).
[111] CCH ¶21,323; Sec. 146(8).
[112] CCH ¶21,325; Sec. 146(8.2).
[113] CCH ¶25,545c; Sec. 204.1(2).
[114] CCH ¶25,545; Sec. 204.1.

withdrawals" withdrawn from a taxpayer's RRSP in order to make room for the certification of past service benefits under a defined benefit pension plan. Past service benefits cannot be certified by the Minister unless there is sufficient room (represented by amounts such as the taxpayer's unused RRSP deduction room, qualifying withdrawals, and qualifying transfers) available for the past service benefits. If the withdrawn amounts are designated for the purposes of certification, they are excluded from deduction; if they are not so designated, they may qualify for the deduction to the extent they represent previously undeducted premiums.

Amounts of undeducted RRSP premiums paid back to a taxpayer and deducted are deemed not to be premiums paid to an RRSP and therefore cannot be deducted again where a taxpayer subsequently learns that he or she had sufficient room to make the deduction with respect to those premiums paid.[115] This ensures that such amounts cannot be deducted twice.

[¶10,372] Meaning of "Earned Income"

A taxpayer's "earned income" includes:[116]

(1) Income from office or employment, without reference to deduction of employee contributions to a registered pension plan (RPP), the residence deduction for members of the clergy, and employee contributions to a retirement compensation arrangement.

(2) Royalties in respect of a work or invention, authored or invented by the taxpayer.

(3) Rental income from real property.

(4) Income from carrying on business as a proprietor or active partner.

(5) Support payments taxable in the hands of a spouse or common-law partner, former spouse or common-law partner (these can include amounts previously paid and deducted by a taxpayer and eventually refunded to the taxpayer under a court order).

(6) Amounts received under a supplementary unemployment benefit plan.

(7) Net research grants.

(8) For 2008 and subsequent taxation years, amounts received under the *Wage Earner Protection Program Act*.

(9) CPP/QPP disability pensions received in the year, regardless of whether the amounts relate to another year and are included in income of another year.

---

[115] CCH ¶21,325e; Sec. 146(8.21).   [116] CCH ¶21,203; Sec. 146(1) "earned income".

(10) Non-residents will include employment or business income only to the extent that the employment or business is in Canada, and only to the extent that such income is not exempt by treaty.

From the aggregate of the amounts described above there are to be deducted the following amounts:

(1) Losses from carrying on a business as proprietor or active partner; for non-residents the loss is calculated only if the business is carried on in Canada.

(2) Losses from rental of real property.

(3) Support payments made by the taxpayer to his former spouse or common-law partner (for 1991 and later years, these can include amounts previously received by the taxpayer and taxable to the taxpayer and eventually repaid by the taxpayer under a court order).

(4) The portion of business income from a disposition of eligible capital property in excess of recaptured tax deduction, i.e., the gain element of such disposition is excluded from earned income.

[¶10,375] Disposition of Non-Qualified Investment

In light of the extended application of Part XI.01 penalty tax of 50% to non-qualified RRSP investments, the following income inclusion and deduction regime for RRSP non-qualified investments no longer apply to such investments acquired after March 22, 2011. For further information on Part XI.01 tax on RRSP non-qualified and prohibited investments, see ¶13,518.

When a non-qualified investment is acquired by a registered retirement savings trust before March 23, 2011, the fair market value of that investment at the time it was acquired is included in the income of the annuitant.[117] On the other hand, when the trust disposes of the non-qualified investment before March 23, 2011, the annuitant is entitled to a deduction equal to the lesser of the proceeds of disposition or the amount originally included in income. It will be observed, therefore, that if a loss is incurred on the investment, the amount included in income will exceed the eventual deduction.

A non-qualified investment, before March 23, 2011, is any property acquired by a trust that is not a qualified investment.[118]

[¶10,378] Meaning of "Qualified Investment"

A "qualified investment" includes:[119]

See page ii for explanation of footnotes.

[117] CCH ¶21,265; Sec. 146(6).

[118] CCH ¶21,207; Sec. 146(1) "non-qualified investment".

[119] CCH ¶21,209, ¶21,341, ¶25,540; Sec. 146(1) "qualified investment", 146(11); Reg. 4900; Interp. Bul. IT-320R3.

(1) Cash and amounts on deposit with a bank, trust company, or credit union (money, the fair market value of which exceeds its stated value as legal tender, or money that is held for its numismatic value is non-qualified). However, after February 22, 2005, regulations allow investment-grade gold and silver bullion coins and bars, and certificates on such investments, as qualified investments. Investment-grade gold must have a purity of at least 99.5%, while investment-grade silver must have a purity of at least 99.9%. Legal tender bullion coins will qualify if they are produced by the Royal Canadian Mint and all or substantially all of their fair market value is attributable to their precious metal content. Bullion bars will qualify if they are produced by a metal refinery accredited by the London Bullion Market Association, as evidenced by a hallmark identifying the refiner, purity, and weight. Certificates will qualify if they are issued by a federally or provincially regulated financial institution, and represent a claim on precious metal holdings of the issuing institution. For all such investments (i.e., coins, bars, and certificates) the investment must be acquired either from the producer of the investment or from a regulated financial institution.

(2) Effective March 18, 2007, any securities, other than futures contracts or other derivative instruments in respect of which the holder's risk of loss may exceed the holder's cost, that are listed on a prescribed Canadian or foreign stock exchange. Before March 18, 2007, shares listed on prescribed stock exchanges and debts of companies whose shares were so listed qualified. Effective December 14, 2007, the list of prescribed stock exchanges is replaced with a list of designated stock exchanges, the difference being that the Minister of Finance can change the list without bothering with the formality of promulgating regulations. All formerly prescribed stock exchanges, Canadian and foreign, will become designated stock exchanges.

(3) Debt obligations issued by a corporation, mutual fund trust, or limited partnership, the shares or units of which are listed on a prescribed stock exchange in Canada (after December 14, 2007, see (2) above), by a corporation whose shares are listed on a prescribed stock exchange outside Canada (after December 14, 2007, see (2) above), or by an authorized foreign bank and payable at a branch in Canada of that bank.

(4) After March 18, 2007, all debt obligations that have an investment grade rating and that are part of a minimum $25 million issuance.

(5) Units of a Canadian mutual fund trust. Canadian Real Estate Investment Trust (REIT), and income trusts which are structured as mutual fund trusts qualify under this rule.

(6) Shares or debt (bonds, debentures, notes, or similar obligations) of a Canadian public corporation (other than a mortgage investment corporation; see (18) below).

(7) Debt obligations of a Canadian corporation if (i) payment obligations are guaranteed by, or (ii) the corporation is controlled by another

¶10,378

corporation or mutual fund trust listed on a prescribed Canadian stock exchange. Debt obligations of other corporations may also qualify if they meet certain restrictive conditions as to the amount and distribution of their debt.

(8) Bonds, debentures, notes, mortgages, hypothecary claims, or similar obligations of or guaranteed by Canada, of a province or municipality in Canada or of their agents, or of an educational institution or hospital if repayment is guaranteed by a province. As well, Saskatchewan Community Bonds and Manitoba Rural Development Bonds acquired after June 1991 together with Ontario and New Brunswick Community Development bonds acquired after August 1993 will be eligible RRSP investments.

(9) Guaranteed investment certificates of a Canadian trust company.

(10) Debt obligations and shares of certain co-operatives or credit unions.

(11) A mortgage secured by Canadian real estate if the mortgagor and the RRSP annuitant are not dealing at arm's length. Alternatively, a taxpayer can use RRSP funds to provide the mortgage on his or her own real estate provided the mortgage is administered by an approved lender under the *National Housing Act*, is insured, has normal commercial interest rates and other terms, and in general is administered on an arm's-length basis. After February 27, 2004, a mortgage qualifies only if the amount of the mortgage obligation (together with the amount of any other indebtedness in respect of the property that is of equal or superior rank) does not exceed the fair market value of the property, except as a result of a decline in the fair market value of the real property after issuance of the mortgage obligation.

(12) An investment contract issued by an approved corporation that provides for the payment of a fixed or determinable amount at maturity.

(13) An annuity for purposes of the plan, if purchased from a "licensed annuities provider", i.e., a person licensed or otherwise authorized under the laws of Canada or a province to carry on an annuities business in Canada.[120]

(14) accumulation annuities, including segregated income funds, provided that the annuity contract satisfies two conditions:

> (a) the RRSP trust must be the only person that has the right to receive any annuity payments under the contract (unless the trust disposes of the annuity); and
>
> (b) the annuity contract must give the holder of the contract an ongoing right to surrender the contract for an amount that, ignoring reasonable sales and administrative charges, approximates the

---

See page ii for explanation of footnotes.

[120] CCH ¶28,153c; Sec. 248(1) "licensed annuities provider".

amount that could be required to fund the future periodic payments under the contract.

(15) Life insurance policies if they meet the following conditions:

(a) The RRSP trust must be the only person entitled to benefits under the policy. This means that the trust must own the policy, although the life insured will obviously be a beneficiary of the plan.

(b) Beginning in 2007, the cash surrender value of the policy must reach the maximum benefit payable under the policy at some time prior to the end of the year in which the insured person turns 71 years of age. Accumulated dividends are excluded both from the computation of cash surrender value and from the calculation of maximum benefit. This rule effectively excludes term insurance as a qualified investment. From 1997 through 2006, the requirement relating to the cash surrender value of the policy had to be satisfied by the end of the year in which the insured person turned 69 years of age.

(c) The premiums payable under the policy in any one year cannot exceed twelve times what the monthly payment in the first year would have been, if the first year's premium had been payable monthly. This means that the annual premiums must be level, subject only to fluctuations for payment on a semi-annual, quarterly, or monthly basis.

(16) Rights or warrants giving the owner a right to acquire (exclusively) a qualified investment. It is no longer necessary that the warrant or right itself be traded on an exchange. However, there must be a right to actually acquire the underlying qualified investment. For property acquired after February 27, 2004, the issuer of the warrant or right is required, on an ongoing basis, to deal at arm's length with the annuitant. In addition, the underlying property must be a share or unit of the issuer or a person or partnership that, at the time of issuance, does not deal at arm's length with the issuer.

(17) Shares or similar interest in a credit union.

(18) A share of the capital stock of a mortgage investment corporation that does not hold as part of its property at any time during the calendar year any indebtedness of an annuitant under the plan or of any person with whom the annuitant does not deal at arm's length.

(19) A debt obligation issued or guaranteed by the International Bank for Reconstruction and Development, the International Finance Corporation, the Inter-American Development Bank, the Asian Development Bank, the Caribbean Development Bank, the European Bank for Reconstruction and Development, or the African Development Bank. This rule is repealed,

in favour of the more general investment grade debt rule in (4) above, applicable to property acquired after March 12, 2009.

(20) A royalty unit acquired after July 16, 1992, that is listed on a prescribed stock exchange in Canada and the value of which is derived solely from Canadian resource properties (but this rule is repealed after March 18, 2007, in favour of the more general rule for securities under (2) above).

(21) An interest in a trust or a share of the capital stock of a corporation that was a registered investment for the plan trust during the current or immediately preceding year.

(22) A qualifying "small business investment limited partnership", as long as the return on the investment is not related to services provided by the plan annuitant.

(23) A qualifying "small services investment trust", providing the return on investment is not related to services provided by the annuitant.

(24) Shares of a prescribed Canadian-controlled venture capital corporation which is not a financial institution, as long as the annuitant is not a connected shareholder. Connected shareholders are essentially individuals and their families whose collective interest (personal and through RRSPs) in any class of shares of a particular corporation reaches 10%. Shares in excess of this collective limit are ineligible investments.

(25) Shares of a Canadian corporation carrying on a qualifying active business primarily in Canada, as long as the corporation is not controlled by non-residents and the annuitant is not a designated shareholder.

(26) Shares of Canadian corporations 90% engaged directly or indirectly in active businesses. Canadian corporations which meet the investment criteria that 90% or more of assets are invested directly in an active business and/or in 10% holdings in companies so engaged, will be qualified investments. There are limitations to prevent "connected shareholders" from using RRSPs to make these investments.

(27) Shares in certain production, marketing, or purchasing corporations, as long as they are not held by "connected shareholders".

(28) Limited partnership units listed on a prescribed Canadian stock exchange (after December 14, 2007, see (2) above).

(29) Shares in Canadian corporations registered under section 11 of the Nova Scotia *Equity Tax Credit Act* or section 39 of the NWT *Risk Capital Investment Tax Credit Act.*

(30) Debt of a Canadian corporation represented by a banker's acceptance, provided the corporation deals at arm's length with the annuitant.

¶10,378

(31) Debt issued by arm's length Canadian corporations exempt from Canadian income tax as not-for-profit entities provided the debt is issued as part of a debt issue of at least $25 million.

(32) Commercial mortgage-backed securities which, when acquired, have an investment grade rating and are part of an issue of $25 million or more and meet specified criteria with respect to the mortgage backing.

(33) American Depositary Receipts (ADR), provided that the underlying security which the ADR represents is listed on a designated stock exchange.

[¶10,381] Foreign Investments

Effective January 1, 2005, the Part XI penalty tax is repealed, thus eliminating the foreign property limit on investments held by RRSPs and other deferred income plans (see ¶13,497). As a result, RRSPs and other deferred income plans may now invest in any kind of qualified investment without regard to whether it is foreign property. However, the qualified investment requirement (including the Part XI.1 tax on non-qualified investments) remains in force.

[¶10,384] Property Used as Security — Disposition of Property

If an RRSP trust uses or permits to be used any of the trust property as security for a loan, the fair market value of the property is to be included in the annuitant's income.[121] When the loan for which the trust property was given as security ceases to exist, the annuitant may deduct the amount previously included in income minus any loss sustained by the trust as a consequence of using such property as security for a loan.

Where a trust disposes of property for a consideration less than its fair market value or acquires property for a consideration that is greater than its fair market value, the difference between the fair market value and the consideration is to be included in the beneficiary's income.[122]

[¶10,387] Benefits Taxable

All amounts received by a taxpayer as a benefit under an RRSP must be included in income in the year received, other than amounts included in the taxpayer's income because an RRSP is revised, amended, or a new plan substituted for it so that the revised, amended, or substituted plan is no longer acceptable for registration or other than "excluded withdrawals" received by a taxpayer pursuant to the Home Buyers' Plan, described in ¶10,393 *et seq.*[123] Normally, the person receiving the benefits will be the annuitant (i.e., the taxpayer who has paid the premiums). However, in the case of an annuity for the joint lives of the annuitant and the annuitant's

---

See page ii for explanation of footnotes.

[121] CCH ¶21,317, ¶21,335; Sec. 146(7), 146(10).   [123] CCH ¶21,323, ¶21,323k; Sec. 146(8), 146(8.01).
[122] CCH ¶21,334; Sec. 146(9).

¶10,381

spouse or common-law partner, the benefit payments will be taxable in the hands of the surviving annuitant. An annuity which passes to a beneficiary other than the annuitant's spouse or common-law partner as a result of the annuitant's death after the plan has matured must be commuted and the payments will be included in the income of the deceased for the year of death unless the amounts pass to dependent children or grandchildren and qualify as a refund of premiums. An annuity which passes to a spouse or common-law partner after death and after the plan's maturity need not be commuted but is to be included in the spouse's or common-law partner's income.

The annuitant under a plan may decide to terminate (or, as it is sometimes put, to "collapse") his or her plan before maturity. The payment of any amount to the annuitant prior to maturity will require an amendment to the plan, and, by virtue of this amendment, the fair market value of the property of the plan will be included in income. Amounts received at that time are included in income in the year of receipt. Notwithstanding the taxpayer's failure to deduct premiums in prior years, the entire amount withdrawn by a taxpayer was found to be properly included in his income.[124] Where the annuitant wishes to transfer the funds in one plan to another plan, this may be done without tax.[125]

The term "benefit" is defined to specifically include any amount paid under the plan in accordance with the terms of the plan, or resulting from an amendment to or modification of the plan, or resulting from the termination of the plan.[126]

A benefit includes any amount received under a retirement savings plan other than:

(a) the amount received by a person other than the annuitant that can be reasonably regarded as part of the amount included in the annuitant's income for the year of death;[127]

(b) a premium;

(c) an amount in respect of the income of the trust governing the plan for a taxation year following the year of death of the annuitant; and

(d) an amount received from a depositary RRSP that relates to an interest or another amount that was credited or accrued after the end of the first calendar year commencing after the death of the annuitant if such interest or other amount has otherwise been included in computing income.

See page ii for explanation of footnotes.

[124] Carroll, 84 DTC 1614.

[125] CCH ¶21,363; Sec. 146(16).

[126] CCH ¶21,202; Sec. 146(1) "benefit".

[127] CCH ¶21,331, ¶21,332; Sec. 146(8.8), 146(8.9).

[¶10,389] Deregistration if Terms of Plan Amended

Generally, if the terms of an RRSP are changed after registration so that in its new form the plan would not qualify for registration, the plan ceases to be an RRSP and any further payment of premiums will not be deductible.[128] The fair market value of all property held in an RRSP trust at the time the plan becomes an "amended plan" will be included in the annuitant's income.

However, for various reasons, an annuitant may wish to transfer some or all of the funds in his or her plan to another plan, or to a registered pension plan, or to a registered retirement income fund. This can be done without tax consequences to the annuitant.[129] It should be noted, however, that the funds must be paid by the trustee of the existing plan directly to the trustee of the new plan or the fund carrier; the annuitant may not, at any time, have the use of the funds.

From 1997 through 2006, RRSPs were required to mature by the end of the year in which the annuitant turned 69 years of age. Prior to 1997, RRSPs could mature up to the end of the year in which the annuitant turned 71 years of age. Rules were introduced to deal with RRSPs registered before 1997 and not amended to reflect this earlier maturity deadline (age 69). If such plans did not mature by the end of the year in which the annuitant turned 69, they became amended plans and effectively were deregistered immediately after that year. However, in the 2007 Budget, the previous (71 years of age) maturity deadline was reinstated, such that after 2006, an RRSP can mature up to the end of the year in which the annuitant turns 71 years of age. The reinstatement of the pre-1997 maturity deadline (age 71) makes obsolete after 2006 the deregistration of pre-1997 plans that were not amended to reflect the earlier maturity deadline (age 69).

Transfers can be made without tax consequences from an annuitant's plan to an annuitant's spousal or common-law partner plan RRSP on or after the breakdown of their marriage or common-law partnership, if made pursuant to an order of a competent tribunal or a written agreement dividing property in settlement of rights arising out of the marriage or common-law partnership.

A trust governed by an RRSP is exempt from tax only if the trust is governed by the plan throughout that part of the year during which the trust exists (see ¶10,348). Accordingly, unless the trust terminates at the same time that the plan ceases to qualify as an RRSP, the trust will be taxable on all income earned in the particular year.

See page ii for explanation of footnotes.
[128] CCH ¶21,347, ¶21,349; Sec. 146(12), 146(13).   [129] CCH ¶21,363; Sec. 146(16).

¶10,389

[¶10,391] Premiums Paid in Taxation Year — Benefits when Plan Is Not Registered at End of Year

Premiums paid under a retirement savings plan that has not qualified as a registered plan at the time the premium was paid, but was so qualified at the end of the taxation year, are deductible as a premium paid under an RRSP.[130]

An amount received as a benefit under an RRSP that was not a registered plan at the end of the year is deemed not to be a benefit received under such a plan.[131]

[¶10,392] Transfers from Prescribed Provincial Pension Plans

Lump-sum amounts from the *Saskatchewan Pension Plan* may be transferred directly from such a plan on behalf of an individual to RRSPs or RRIFs under which the individual is the annuitant.[132] Such amounts may also be transferred to RRSPs or RRIFs under which the individual's spouse or common-law partner or former spouse or common-law partner is the annuitant, if the two individuals are living separate and apart and the payment or transfer is made under a judicial order or a written agreement relating to a division of property between the two individuals on the breakdown of their marriage or common-law partnership. Such amounts may also be transferred to acquire an annuity for the benefit of the individual or the individual's spouse or common-law partner or former spouse/common-law partner.

The transferred amount is not included in an individual's income and no deduction in computing the individual's income may be made with respect to the transferred amount.

The above does not apply, however, if the amount transferred was transferred as a result of a third person's death (i.e., not the individual on whose behalf the amount is transferred, or that individual's spouse or common-law partner or former spouse or common-law partner).

[¶10,393] Home Buyers' Plan

[¶10,393a] Characteristics

When first introduced, the Home Buyers' Plan allowed individuals to withdraw up to $20,000 from RRSPs tax-free to purchase a home in Canada. They are allowed a period of up to 15 years to repay the withdrawn funds.

The Plan was introduced as a temporary measure scheduled to end on March 1, 1994 and was not initially limited to first-time buyers. However,

---

See page ii for explanation of footnotes.

[130] CCH ¶21,361; Sec. 146(14).   [132] CCH ¶21,364e; Sec. 146(21).
[131] CCH ¶21,362; Sec. 146(15).

the 1994 Budget made the Plan permanent after March 1, 1994 but limited it to "first-time buyers", i.e., individuals and their spouses/common-law partners who did not own a home which they lived in as their principal residence in any of the five calendar years preceding withdrawal. The following commentary discusses the rules applicable after March 1, 1994.

The Home Buyers' Plan now allows an individual to borrow up to $25,000 ($20,000 before January 28, 2009) of money previously contributed to an RRSP to acquire a home in Canada to be used as the individual's principal residence. Each individual can withdraw up to $25,000 ($20,000 before January 28, 2009) from any combination of plans of which he or she is the annuitant, so that a married couple, for example, could withdraw up to $25,000 ($20,000 before January 28, 2009) each if they each have that much in their own RRSPs for the purchase of a jointly owned house. Common-law partners can similarly do this and any group of related or unrelated individuals, provided they can agree on the intricacies of collective home ownership. If one spouse/common-law partner's plan is a spousal or common-law partner plan RRSP to which all contributions have been made by the other spouse/common-law partner, withdrawals under the Home Buyers' Plan can be made from the spousal or common-law partner plan by the annuitant spouse/common-law partner and will not be included in the contributing spouse/common-law partner's income, unless for some reason they prove to be unqualified and would otherwise be included in the annuitant's spouse/common-law partner's income.[133]

The money withdrawn under the Home Buyers' Plan is, in effect, an interest-free loan from the individual's RRSP. It must be repaid in annual instalments over a 15-year period, commencing with the second year following the withdrawal.[134] As with ordinary RRSP contributions, individuals are in fact given 60 days following the year end to make a repayment. Thus, if an individual withdraws funds under the Home Buyers' Plan in 2009, he or she must commence repayments by March 1, 2012.

Once an individual has repaid all the funds withdrawn for a prior home purchase, he or she may use the Plan again, commencing with the year following the final repayment. This does not, however, waive the five-year rule below.

Although the Plan was essentially intended for first time home buyers, the government has recognized that such a rule would be unfair in a variety of situations. It has therefore chosen a five-year period of non-ownership as the test to ensure that current or recent homeowners cannot use the Home Buyers' Plan. However, the five-year rule will be waived where a person who

---

See page ii for explanation of footnotes.

[133] CCH ¶21,365ib, ¶21,372; Sec. 146.01(1) "regular eligible amount", 146.01(2).   [134] CCH ¶21,374, ¶21,375; Sec. 146.01(3), 146.01(4).

¶10,393a

qualifies for the disability credit (or a related individual) buys a home which is more accessible for, or better suited to, the care of the disabled person.[135]

[¶10,393b] Limitations on Ordinary RRSP Contributions

If an individual withdraws RRSP funds under the Home Buyers' Plan, he or she will not be allowed to deduct any ordinary RRSP contributions made less than 90 days before the withdrawal to the extent that the contribution is greater than his or her RRSP balance after the withdrawal.[136]

Example:

> Jennifer has $20,000 in her RRSP at the beginning of 2012 and $10,000 in cash. She is entitled to put another $10,000 into her RRSP before March 1, 2012 and in fact uses the cash to pay this amount as an RRSP contribution on February 15, 2012. She now has $30,000 in her RRSP. On March 31, her RRSP is credited with a further $750 earnings in respect of preceding years. On May 1, 2012 (i.e., less than 90 days after the contribution payment on February 15) she withdraws $25,000 under the Home Buyers' Plan, leaving a balance of $5,750. Her RRSP balance immediately after the withdrawal will be $5,750 and her contribution within the 90-day period was $10,000, a difference of $4,250. This amount will be disallowed as an RRSP deduction. In effect, Jennifer has been allowed to withdraw the $20,000 that was on hand originally, plus all earnings in the plan (whether on old or new money), but she has not been allowed to contribute funds within the 90-day period and both deduct them and withdraw them.

> Jennifer could withdraw $20,750 without penalty. She could also withdraw the $20,750 on May 1 and, if she had not acquired her home within the 30 days preceding the 90th day after February 15 (i.e., she had not acquired her home within 30 days preceding May 16), she could now withdraw the remaining $4,250 and use it to further pay down her home cost. The 30-day rule is one of the limitations on Home Buyers' Plan withdrawals (see Rule (3) at 10,395).

> The same rules will apply to funds Jennifer's spouse or common-law partner withdraws from a spousal or common-law partner plan.[137] If Jennifer contributes funds to her spouse or common-law partner plan and her spouse or common-law partner withdraws the funds under the Home Buyers' Plan within 90 days of her contribution, Jennifer will not be allowed to deduct the RRSP contribution to the extent that the contribution is greater than her spouse's or common-law partner's RRSP balance after the withdrawal.

The denial of a deduction for an RRSP contribution applies only to "ordinary" contributions. That is, it does not apply to contributions made and deducted under the rollover rules which permit special RRSP contributions for retirement allowances, termination payments, refunds of premiums received on the death of a spouse/common-law partner, or, in some cases, a parent, and direct transfer of funds between RRSPs or from other pension plans to RRSPs.

[¶10,395] Qualifying Withdrawals for a Qualifying Home

Each individual may withdraw funds under the Home Buyers' Plan from one or more RRSPs of which the individual is the annuitant, so long as

---

See page ii for explanation of footnotes.

[135] CCH ¶21,365ja, ¶21,365jb; Sec. 146.01(1) "specified disabled person", 146.01(1) "supplemental eligible amount".

[136] CCH ¶21,249; Sec. 146(5).

[137] CCH ¶21,262; Sec. 146(5.1)

the total of funds withdrawn does not exceed $25,000 ($20,000 before January 28, 2009).[138] The funds need not be withdrawn at precisely the same time, but all withdrawals must be received in the same calendar year, and further limitations will be imposed by the 30-day rule in (3) below. A general exception to the rule that all funds must be withdrawn in the same calendar year permits a withdrawal of funds requested in Year 1 but not received until January of Year 2 to be considered a Year 1 withdrawal, where an individual has already made a qualifying Year 1 withdrawal.

All of the following rules must be met in respect of each withdrawal by an individual from an RRSP to ensure that it qualifies under the Home Buyers' Plan:

(1) All the funds withdrawn must actually be received in the same calendar year, subject to the exception discussed above.

(2) The funds must be withdrawn by completing Form T1036; this form requires an applicant to set out the location of a qualifying home which the applicant has begun, or intends to begin not later than one year after acquisition, to use as a principal place of residence. [Rather than reporting HBP withdrawals on a quarterly basis by filing the relevant T1036, RRSP issuers will instead be required to report such withdrawals on an annual basis using the T4RSP. This pending draft technical amendment (July 16, 2010) will apply to the 2002 and subsequent taxation years.]

(3) Neither the individual nor his or her spouse/common-law partner may have acquired the qualifying home more than 30 days before receiving the RRSP withdrawal amount.

(4) The individual must have entered into a written agreement for the acquisition of the qualifying home or with respect to its construction before he or she applies to withdraw the RRSP funds.

(5) The individual must not have had an owner-occupied home in the period that began at the beginning of the fourth preceding calendar year that ended before the date of the RRSP withdrawal and ended on the 31st day before the withdrawal.

(6) The individual's current spouse or common-law partner may not have had an owner-occupied home during the period in (5) above that was inhabited by the individual during the marriage or common-law partnership.

(7) The individual must be resident in Canada when he or she receives the funds.

See page ii for explanation of footnotes.

[138] CCH ¶21,365ib; Sec. 146.01(1) "regular eligible amount".

¶10,395

(8) The individual must remain resident in Canada from the time he or she receives the funds out of the RRSP until he or she actually acquires the qualifying home.

(9) The total of the amount withdrawn and all funds withdrawn under the Home Buyers' Plan before receiving a particular withdrawal must not exceed $25,000 ($20,000 before January 28, 2009).

(10) The individual's "HBP balance" at the beginning of the withdrawal year must be nil. The individual's "HBP balance" is the total of qualifying amounts withdrawn on a prior use of the plan minus designated repayments and minus amounts included in the individual's income upon failure to make scheduled repayments and amounts included in income upon becoming a non-resident of Canada.[139]

(11) The individual must in fact use the funds within time limits discussed at ¶10,395a.

If all the above rules are not met, the amount withdrawn from an RRSP will be added to an individual's income for the year it was withdrawn.[140]

A "qualifying home" is a housing unit located in Canada. It also includes a share of the capital stock of a cooperative housing corporation, where the holder of the share is entitled to possession of a housing unit located in Canada.[141] An individual must also intend at the time of withdrawal of the RRSP funds to use the home as a "principal place of residence" within one year of its actual acquisition.

[¶10,395a] Acquisition of Property Deadline

The Home Buyers' Plan rules require that the qualifying home specified in a withdrawal of RRSP funds, or a replacement property, be acquired before October 1 of the year following the year the individual first receives funds out of an RRSP under the Home Buyers' Plan (the "completion date").[142] Thus, if the funds from an RRSP under the Home Buyers' Plan are received in 2011, the qualifying home must be acquired before the completion date of October 1, 2012. If the funds are withdrawn for the first time anytime in 2012, the completion date is October 1, 2013.

If the qualifying home originally specified is not acquired, for example because an intended transaction failed to close, the withdrawn funds can be kept in hand while looking for a replacement property, but the replacement property must be acquired on or before the completion date which originally applied.

An individual is considered to have acquired a qualifying home if it was jointly acquired with one or more other persons.[143]

See page ii for explanation of footnotes.

[139] CCH ¶21,365ea; Sec. 146.01(1) "HBP balance".   [142] CCH ¶21,365b; Sec. 146.01(1) "completion date".
[140] CCH ¶21,323; Sec. 146(8).
[141] CCH ¶21,365h; Sec. 146.01(1) "qualifying home".   [143] CCH ¶21,372; Sec. 146.01(2)(a).

¶10,395a

Where an individual agrees to purchase a condominium unit, the individual is treated as having acquired the unit on the date the individual is entitled to immediate vacant possession of the unit.[144]

If an individual has withdrawn an amount from an RRSP pursuant to the Home Buyers' Plan in respect of a qualifying home but has not acquired the qualifying home or replacement property before the completion date, he or she will be deemed to have acquired the home before that date in two sets of circumstances:[145]

(1) First, the individual will be considered to have met the original completion date deadline if the individual:

(a) is obliged under the terms of an agreement in writing in effect on the original completion date to acquire the qualifying home or replacement property on or after that day;

(b) ultimately acquires such property by the day that is one calendar year following the original completion date; and

(c) was resident in Canada throughout the period commencing on the original completion date and ending on the day the property was acquired.

(2) Second, the individual will be considered to have met the original completion date deadline if he or she has made payments totalling all amounts withdrawn under the Home Buyers' Plan to an arm's-length person or company and the payments:

(a) were all made in the period beginning with his or her first withdrawal under the Home Buyers' Plan and ending before the completion date;

(b) were all made to persons (or companies) with whom the individual was dealing at arm's length; and

(c) were made in respect of the construction of the original qualifying home or a replacement property.

[¶10,395b] Return of Withdrawals Not Used to Acquire Qualifying Home

If an individual fails to acquire a qualifying home (or replacement property) before the applicable completion date and the extension rules discussed at ¶10,395a do not apply, the amounts withdrawn must be returned to the RRSPs with the same issuers from whom the funds were withdrawn.[146] This return of withdrawals must be made no later than December 31 following the completion date. Thus, if funds are taken out in

---

See page ii for explanation of footnotes.
[144] CCH ¶21,372; Sec. 146.01(2)(b).   [146] CCH ¶21,374; Sec. 146.01(3).
[145] CCH ¶21,372; Sec. 146.01(2)(c).

¶10,395b

2011 so that the completion date is October 1, 2012, and the individual failed to acquire a qualifying home before that date, he or she has until December 31, 2012, to return the funds to his or her RRSP.

If an individual fails to acquire the home set out on the original withdrawal form, he or she is not required to delay the return of funds to the Plan. The individual can return them at any time before December 31 of the year following withdrawal. If the funds are returned under this mechanism, the Home Buyers' Plan is considered not to have been used.

If an individual did not return the funds because he or she expected to qualify for an extension described at ¶10,395a, but failed to qualify solely because he or she did not eventually acquire the home by the extended deadline, the individual can return the funds to the RRSP before January 1 following the extended date. Thus, if an individual made a 2011 withdrawal, had an original completion date of October 1, 2012, and qualified for an extended completion date of October 1, 2013, but still failed to complete the transaction by that date, he or she could return the funds by December 31, 2013.

If the individual has not acquired the home nor returned the funds within the time limits, he or she will become taxable on the amounts withdrawn in the year they were withdrawn, as if they had been ordinary taxable withdrawals from an RRSP.

[¶10,395c] Repayments of Withdrawals Used to Acquire Qualifying Home

If an individual acquires a qualifying home within the required time limit, he or she must repay the money withdrawn over a 15-year period, with the first payment being made no later than 60 days after the end of the second year following the first withdrawal. Thus, if an individual withdrew funds under the plan in 2011, the repayment schedule does not start before 2013 but the individual has until March 1, 2014, to make the first repayment.[147]

The repayment required to avoid an income inclusion for any subsequent taxation year is a fraction of the individual's "balance" under the Home Buyers' Plan at the beginning of the year. This balance, at the beginning of a particular year, is equal to the total of all eligible amounts received by the individual minus the sum of repayments made before that time and shortfalls included in the individual's income for previous years.

[¶10,395d] Where Individual Becomes a Non-Resident

If an individual withdraws funds from an RRSP under the Home Buyers' Plan and becomes a non-resident after acquiring a qualifying Canadian home, the individual must repay the entire withdrawal (less any repayments

---

See page ii for explanation of footnotes.
[147] CCH ¶21,375; Sec. 146.01(4).

already made as discussed at ¶10,395b) or income inclusion he or she may have had under the rules discussed at ¶10,395c within 60 days of becoming a non-resident.[148] To the extent that such an individual does not make the repayment within 60 days, the unrepaid balance will be included in the individual's income for the period of the year in which he or she was still a resident of Canada.

[¶10,395e] Where Individual Dies

If an individual has withdrawn funds from an RRSP under the Home Buyers' Plan and properly acquired a qualifying home before death and dies with an outstanding balance of repayment instalments owing to the RRSP, the outstanding balance is included in his or her income for the year of death.[149] However, the surviving spouse or common-law partner of the deceased individual may, with his or her legal representatives, elect to avoid such income inclusion if the spouse is resident in Canada immediately before the individual's death. If this election is made in the deceased's terminal return, the surviving spouse or common-law partner in effect assumes the position of the deceased by being treated as having received an eligible amount, at the time of the deceased's death, equal to the excess. This amount is added to any balance of eligible amounts received by the surviving spouse/common-law partner that have not been previously repaid to RRSPs.[150]

The election only applies to a spouse/common-law partner on the death of an individual where:

(a) the surviving spouse/common-law partner (or the deceased) had not previously received an eligible amount under the Home Buyers' Plan; or

(b) the period for repayments under the Home Buyers' Plan of any eligible amounts received by the surviving spouse/common-law partner coincides with the corresponding period for the deceased.

Furthermore, for the purposes of determining the surviving spouse's or common-law partner's own eligibility under the Home Buyers' Plan, such a spouse or common-law partner is considered to have received eligible amounts at such times as they were received by the deceased. As a consequence, a surviving spouse/common-law partner who makes the election on the death of his or her spouse/common-law partner will generally be precluded from subsequently participating in the Home Buyers' Plan after such death.

See page ii for explanation of footnotes.

[148] CCH ¶21,380; Sec. 146.01(5).   [150] CCH ¶21,381c; Sec. 146.01(7).
[149] CCH ¶21,381; Sec. 146.01(6).

¶10,395e

[¶10,395f] Filing of Prescribed Form

A prescribed form submitted to an issuer of an RRSP in connection with the Home Buyers' Plan must be filed with the CRA no later than 15 days after the calendar quarter in which it was submitted to the issuer.[151]

[¶10,396] Lifelong Learning Plan (LLP)

[¶10,396a] Eligibility

RRSP annuitants may make tax-free withdrawals from their RRSP (other than a locked-in RRSP) to finance full-time training or education for themselves or their spouses/common-law partners. Withdrawals may not exceed $10,000 in a year. More than one withdrawal may be made in any given year from any number of specific RRSP accounts, provided that the annual limit is not exceeded. Withdrawals under this plan are permitted for a withdrawal period of up to four calendar years, provided that the total amount withdrawn does not exceed $20,000.[152] However, the withdrawal period for a participant in the plan must end before the start of a year for which repayment by the participant is required in accordance with the rules described at ¶10,396b.

RRSP funds may be withdrawn under the plan where the recipient, or the recipient's spouse or common-law partner, is enrolled, or committed to enroll, as a full-time student in a qualifying educational program of at least three months' duration at an eligible educational institution.[153] However, a disabled student may qualify as a student under the plan whether or not studying on a full-time basis.[154] Where RRSP funds are withdrawn before the enrolment of the recipient or the recipient's spouse or common-law partner, the enrolment must occur in the year of the RRSP withdrawal or before March of the following year.

Special rules apply where RRSP funds are withdrawn under the plan and the student does not finish the qualifying educational program. Under these circumstances, an RRSP withdrawal in respect of a program is still considered to have been received under the plan if any of the following three conditions is met:

(a) the student withdraws from the program more than two months after the year of the RRSP withdrawal;

(b) less than 75% of the student's tuition is refundable as a consequence of leaving a program; or

(c) the student enrolls in another qualifying educational program before April of the year following the year of the RRSP withdrawal.

See page ii for explanation of footnotes.

[151] CCH ¶21,382a; Sec. 146.01(8).

[152] CCH ¶21,382m; Sec. 146.02(1) "eligible amount".

[153] CCH ¶21,382t; Sec. 146.02(1) "qualifying educational program".

[154] CCH ¶21,382p; Sec. 146.02(1) "full-time student".

In all other cases, the RRSP withdrawal will be included in the recipient's income unless the recipient repays the RRSP withdrawal and files an approved form with the CRA.[155] Where this procedure is followed, the RRSP withdrawal is not included in computing income and the recipient is treated as having not participated in the plan.

Under the LLP, RRSP annuitants are permitted to withdraw funds in respect of the education of themselves or their spouses/common-law partners, but they cannot have a positive LLP balance in respect of the education of more than one individual. This restriction limits administrative complexity associated with the calculation of repayments required under the Plan. Nonetheless, both spouses/common-law partners could withdraw funds from their RRSPs in respect of the same spouse/common-law partner.

[¶10,396b] Repayment Period

RRSP withdrawals under the LLP are repayable to the withdrawing individual's RRSPs in equal instalments over a 10-year period, beginning no later than 60 days following the fifth year after the year in which the individual first received the funds.[156] However, repayment will be required to start earlier if the student fails to qualify for a full-time education tax credit for at least three months in two consecutive years that end before that fifth year. Where this failure occurs, repayment is required to start within 60 days following the second of those years. In short, a full-time student is expected to spend nine months a year in school, counting the month in which the program commences and the month in which it ends. As under the Home Buyers' Plan, any amount not repaid for a year by the recipient as required will be included in computing the recipient's income for the year, reducing the amount that must be repaid in subsequent years.[157]

Example:

> Susan withdraws an eligible amount of $5,000 from her RRSP in September 2008 and uses the funds for a full-time 12-month course running from September 2008 to August 2009 that she completes. In January 2012, she makes a designated repayment of $300 for the year 2011. Because it is an eligible amount, the $5,000 withdrawal is not included in Susan's income for the 2008 taxation year. The required repayment for the year 2011 is $500 ($5,000/10). As only $300 is repaid for that year, the shortfall of $200 is included in computing Susan's income for that year. The "repayment period" starts at the beginning of the year 2011 because Susan was not entitled to an education credit for at least three months during the years 2010 and 2011.

[¶10,396c] Ceasing Residence in Canada

Recipients of RRSP withdrawals must be resident in Canada.[158] If a recipient subsequently emigrates from Canada, the recipient's outstanding balance under the plan will generally be included in the recipient's income

See page ii for explanation of footnotes.

[155] CCH ¶21,382o, ¶21,382v; Sec. 146.02(1) "excluded withdrawal", 146.02(2).

[156] CCH ¶21,382u, ¶21,382w; Sec. 146.02(1) "repayment period", 146.02(3).

[157] CCH ¶21,382u, ¶21,382x; Sec. 146.02(1) "repayment period", 146.02(4).

[158] CCH ¶21,382m; Sec. 146.02(1) "eligible amount".

to the extent that the recipient does not repay the balance within 60 days from the time of emigration.[159] This is consistent with a similar rule under the Home Buyers' Plan.

Example:

> Brian withdraws two eligible amounts of $6,000 from his RRSP in September 2007 and September 2008, respectively, and uses the funds for an educational program to be completed in April 2009. In 2011 (the first year of Brian's repayment period), he makes the required repayment of $1,200 to his RRSP (i.e., $12,000/10). In December 2011, Brian ceases to be resident in Canada. In January 2012, he makes a further repayment of $1,000. He files his income tax return for 2011 in March 2012. Brian is required to include $9,800 ($12,000 - $1,200 - $1,000) in computing his income for the period in the 2011 taxation year during which he was resident in Canada. If he had repaid the outstanding balance of $9,800 before filing in March 2012, this income inclusion would have been avoided.

Rules on the death of a participant under the plan parallel those under the Home Buyers' Plan. (See ¶10,395e.)[160]

[¶10,398] Registered Education Savings Plans

[¶10,399] General

A subscriber to a registered education savings plan (RESP) is not required to include in income the income generated by his or her contributions. However, the RESP contributions are not deductible in computing the subscriber's income, so the contributions are made out of after-tax dollars.

An "education savings plan" means a contract entered into between the subscriber and a person or organization referred to as a "promoter" under which, in consideration for amounts paid under the contract by the subscriber, the promoter agrees to make educational assistance payments to a designated beneficiary to further the latter's education at the post-secondary school level.[161]

A "trust" for the purposes of an education savings plan includes any person who irrevocably holds property or money pursuant to an education savings plan for the purpose of providing:

(a) educational assistance payments;

(b) scholarships or other amounts to persons other than the beneficiary to assist them in furthering their post-secondary school education;

(c) refunds of payments made by the subscriber;

See page ii for explanation of footnotes.

[159] CCH ¶21,382y; Sec. 146.02(5).

[160] CCH ¶21,382z, ¶21,382za; Sec. 146.02(6), 146.02(7).

[161] CCH ¶21,383; Sec. 146.1; Inf. Cir. 93-3R1.

(d) payments to designated educational institutions; or

(e) payments to another trust holding funds or property for any of the above described purposes.

The plan must be accepted for registration by the Minister and the registration is conditional on the fulfillment by the promoter of certain requirements. As a condition for registration, the plan must be wound up by the end of the 35th year following the year in which it is set up, and contributions may be made only for the first 31 years after the year in which the plan is set up. Beginning in 2008, the maximum duration of an RESP was extended from 25 to 35 years, and the maximum contribution period was extended from 21 to 31 years. In the case of an RESP where the beneficiary qualifies for the disability tax credit (called a "specified plan"), the maximum contribution period is extended from 31 years to 35 years, and the termination date is extended from the 35th to the 40th anniversary of the opening of the plan. Beginning in 2008, the maximum duration of a specified plan is extended from 30 to 40 years, and the maximum contribution period is extended from 25 to 35 years.

Neither the subscriber nor the trust is taxable with respect to the income earned by the trust for a taxation year throughout which the trust was governed by a registered education savings plan. As the income is distributed to the beneficiary in the form of educational assistance payments, the beneficiary includes it in his or her income.

In the event that the Minister revokes registration of the plan, the trust loses its special status and becomes subject to tax on its income in the manner of all *inter vivos* trusts. Any distributions from the revoked plan made as educational assistance payments or accumulated income payments are also included in the recipient's income.

Starting in 2007, there is no annual limit for contributions to RESPs. For each beneficiary, the lifetime limit on the amounts that can be contributed to RESPs is $50,000. Contributions made before 2007 were subject to an annual contribution limit of $4,000 per beneficiary and to a lifetime limit of $42,000. Excess contributions attract a penalty tax of 1% per month.[162]

Refunds of RESP earnings may be made to a contributor where none of the intended beneficiaries is pursuing post-secondary education by age 21 and the plan has been running for at least 10 years. The Minister may waive the "10-year" and "age 21" conditions where a beneficiary is mentally impaired.[163] Refunds of accumulated income payments will be included in the contributor's income. However, the contributor will be allowed to transfer such RESP withdrawals to his or her own RRSP or spousal or common-law partner plan RRSP on a tax-deferred basis, to the extent of RRSP deduction room available for the year of transfer (and subject to a lifetime

---

See page ii for explanation of footnotes.

[162] CCH ¶21,385; Sec. 146.1(2).   [163] CCH ¶21,385b; Sec. 146.1(2.2).

¶10,399

total of $50,000). However, plan earnings received by the contributor which cannot, or are not contributed to an RRSP, are subject to a special tax of 20% in addition to regular tax payable.

Budget 2012 proposed a tax-free transfer ("rollover") of investment income earned in a Registered Education Savings Plan (RESP) to an RDSP if both plans have a common beneficiary. As proposed, the RESP investment income can be rolled over to an RDSP on a tax-free basis, similar to a contribution to an RRSP of an accumulated income payment.[164] Canada Education Savings Grants and Canada Learning Bonds in the RESP will have a requirement to be repaid by the end of February of the year following the year in which the rollover is made. This measure was introduced in draft legislation on August 14, 2012 and would apply to rollovers made after 2013.

For a payment to qualify as an educational assistance payment (EAP), at the time it is made, the individual must be enrolled either full-time or part-time in a qualifying educational program at a post-secondary educational institution (either in attendance at the institution or enrolled in distance education courses). Also, for plans entered into after 1998, the amount payable to an individual before the individual has completed 13 consecutive weeks in a qualifying educational program is limited to $5,000. Beginning in 2007, a payment may also qualify as an EAP if, at the time it is made, the individual is at least 16 and is enrolled as a student in a specified educational program. A specified educational program means a program at a post-secondary school level that is not less than three consecutive weeks in duration and that requires each student taking the program to spend not less than 12 hours per month on courses in the program. The total amount of EAPs made to the individual under the RESP (and other RESPs from the same promoter) in the preceding 13-week period cannot exceed $2,500.

However, beginning in 2008, a six-month grace period is allowed for receiving an EAP. More specifically, an RESP may provide for the payment of an EAP to an individual for up to six months after the individual ceased to be enrolled as a student in a qualifying educational program or a specified educational program, as the case may be. This additional flexibility will apply only where the payment would have qualified under the normal rules for EAPs, if it had been made immediately before the individual's enrolment ceased.[165] Thus, for example, an individual who had received a $2,000 EAP while enrolled in a 10-week specified educational program would be entitled to receive up to $500 of additional EAPs during the six-month period following the end of the program (that is, without having to enroll in another program). An EAP that is made within this grace period is treated as having been made immediately before the cessation of enrolment for the purposes of applying the EAP limits.[166]

See page ii for explanation of footnotes.

[164] Sec. 146.1(1.1) and (1.2).

[165] CCH ¶21,385e; Sec. 146.1(2.21).

[166] CCH ¶21,385h; Sec. 146.1(2.22).

In a family plan, the beneficiary must not have reached 21 years of age when he or she is named as beneficiary and contributions are made in the plan for his or her benefit. In the case of a transfer from one family plan to another, if the beneficiary is 21 years of age or older, the beneficiary must have been a beneficiary under the old plan.

[Under pending technical amendments effective January 1, 2004, an education savings plan will not permit an individual to be designated as a beneficiary under the plan and not allow a contribution for a beneficiary under the plan, unless the individual's SIN has been provided to the promoter of the plan and the individual is resident in Canada. The residency requirement does not apply when the designation is made in conjunction with a transfer of property from another RESP under which the individual was a beneficiary immediately before the transfer. However, subject to two exceptions (described below), the individual's SIN has to be provided to the promoter in order for the individual to be designated as a beneficiary under the transferee RESP.

The first exception to the SIN condition allows an education savings plan that was entered into before 1999 to not require that an individual's SIN be provided in respect of a contribution to the plan. Such contributions, however, continue to be ineligible for the Canada Education Savings Grant and Canada Learning Bond (see ¶10,400). It should be noted that this exception is only relevant for contributions made for existing beneficiaries under such plans. An individual without a SIN is prevented from being designated as a new beneficiary under such a plan.[167]

Under the second exception, an education savings plan may permit a non-resident individual who does not have a SIN to be designated as a beneficiary under the plan, provided that the designation is being made in conjunction with a transfer of property into the plan from another RESP under which the individual was a beneficiary immediately before the transfer.

As well as amending their RESP specimen plan(s) to comply with the proposed changes for new contracts, RESP issuers may also need to amend existing contracts so that they may maintain their registered status and eligibility for the Canada Education Savings Grant. The CRA will require that the amendments be submitted a year from the date of Royal Assent. However, the plans must be administered as if they were amended as of January 1, 2004.]

[¶10,400] Canada Education Savings Grant and Canada Learning Bond

The Government of Canada provides grants of up to 20% of annual contributions made to RESPs for beneficiaries up to and including age 17,

---

See page ii for explanation of footnotes.
[167] Sec. 146.1(2.3).

¶10,400]

to a maximum grant of $500 ($400 before 2007) per year per beneficiary. Starting in 2005, the CES grant was increased to 40% of the first $500 of annual contributions (up to an extra $100 grant) for families with adjusted incomes (used for the purposes of the child tax benefit) equal to or less than $35,000 (indexed annually for inflation); for families with adjusted incomes between $35,000 and $70,000 (indexed annually), the CES grant was increased to 30% of the first $500 of annual contributions (up to an extra $50 grant). The lifetime limit for CES grants that can be paid into an RESP in respect of an individual beneficiary is $7,200. The CES grants made to an RESP do not reduce the annual and lifetime RESP dollar contribution limits.

When the CESGs are paid out of the plan to the beneficiary-student, they are considered educational assistance payments and included in the beneficiary's income.[168] The CESG cannot be withdrawn by the subscriber under the plan. If the beneficiary does not pursue higher education, the RESP is revoked, or if RESP funds are withdrawn for non-educational purposes, the CESG normally must be repaid to the government.

In addition to the CESG, the government initiated the Canada Learning Bond (CLB) in 2004. Generally speaking, the CLB is an initial $500 supplement made in respect of a child if the child's family is entitled to the National Child Benefit (NCB) supplement, and an additional $100 annual supplement for each year up to and including the year in which the child turns 15 years of age in which the family is entitled to the NCB supplement. The CLB is paid into an RESP in which the child is a beneficiary. The CLB does not affect the RESP or the CES grant contribution limits.

Beginning in 2007, the RESP provisions were amended to ensure that similar amounts paid to an RESP under a designated provincial program, such as the education saving incentive program introduced by Quebec in its 2007 Budget, are not considered contributions to the RESP and, therefore, do not affect the RESP contribution limits. Before 2009, only amounts paid under a "designated provincial plan" (DPP) were excluded from the definition of "contribution". Beginning in 2009, amounts paid into an RESP under any program that is similar to a designated provincial program and that is funded by a province will not be considered to be a contribution under the plan.[169] However, payments made by a public primary caregiver, including a children's aid or child welfare agency, will continue to be treated as private contributions.

Furthermore, effective for 2007 and subsequent taxation years, the definition of DPP is amended to include a program that is established under a provincial law that has a purpose consistent with the *Canada Education Savings Act* to encourage the financing of children's post-secondary educa-

---

[168] CCH ¶21,395; Sec. 146.1(7). [169] CCH ¶21,383ab; Sec. 146.1(1) "contribution".

tion through their RESP. Prior to 2007, only a prescribed program identified by regulation on a case-by-case basis could qualify as a DPP.

[¶10,401] Registration Date

The taxation year of all *inter vivos* trusts including trusts established under and governed by a registered education savings plan is the calendar year. The deemed date of registration of an education savings plan is the first day of January regardless of the day and month when the plan was actually accepted for registration. Therefore, if this occurs in mid-year, no tax is payable either by the trust or by the subscriber on income earned by the trust for the year.

A deemed year of registration is also provided where an education savings plan is initially incapable of registration solely because its promoter does not have registerable plans with 150 other subscribers as required. If such a plan is eventually registered, it is deemed to have been registered on the later of:

(a) the first day of the year in which it met all registration requirements other than the mandatory minimum number of other subscribers; and

(b) the first day of the year preceding the year in which the plan was accepted for registration.

This, in effect, gives a promoter up to two full years to obtain 150 subscribers.

[¶10,402] Trust Income

No tax is payable by the trust on its taxable income for any taxation year throughout which it was governed by a registered education savings plan. Since the deemed date of registration of the plans is January 1 of the relevant year, the trust is exempt from tax for the entire year no matter what month of the year the plan was accepted for registration. For any taxation year during which an education savings plan is not registered, the trust governed by the plan is deemed to be an *inter vivos* trust subject to tax on its income. The taxable income of an *inter vivos* trust is taxed at a rate of 29%. The appropriate provincial tax is, of course, added to this tax.

The income of a trust governed by a registered education savings plan is subject to tax as income of the beneficiary or former beneficiary when an educational assistance payment is paid to the beneficiary or on the beneficiary's behalf. Also, amounts that are paid to or for the benefit of a beneficiary or former beneficiary will be included in income to the extent that the amount may reasonably be regarded as a distribution of property transferred from the trust, or of property substituted therefor, or of income from such property.

¶10,401

[¶10,403] Tax-Free Savings Accounts

[¶10,404] Characteristics

The concept of the tax-free savings account (TFSA) was introduced in the 2008 federal Budget, effective beginning in 2009. The TFSA allows individuals to earn investment income, including interest, dividends, and capital gains, on a tax-free basis. Contributions to the TFSA are not deductible, although the income in the account is not subject to Part I tax, either while in the account or upon withdrawal. However, the TFSA may be subject to Part I tax if it acquires a "non-qualified investment" or carries on a business.

The annual contribution limit for a TFSA begins at $5,000 for 2009, and will be increased annually to inflation and rounded to the nearest $500. Unused TFSA room can be carried forward indefinitely. Withdrawals from the account will free up more TFSA room. For more details, see the definition of "excess TFSA amount" in ¶13,513.

Excess contributions to a TFSA are subject to a penalty tax of 1% per month (see ¶13,513). Other potential penalties apply if a non-resident contributes to the TFSA, the TFSA acquires a non-qualified investment, or the TFSA confers an advantage on the holder or a person not at arm's length with the holder (see ¶13,513 through ¶13,516).

One of the relative advantages of a TFSA (especially compared to an RRSP or RRIF) is that withdrawals from the TFSA will not be included in income for the purpose of determining eligibility for various income-based credits and benefits, including the age credit and OAS benefits. In other words, unlike withdrawals from an RRSP or RRIF, which can reduce the individual's age credit or serve to claw back the individual's OAS benefits, withdrawals from the TFSA will have no effect on such credits or benefits. Furthermore, unlike an RRSP, there is no time limit at which the TFSA must be wound up or converted into another investment vehicle. Thus, the TFSA can be used to fund pre-retirement years or post-retirement years, and there are no limits on withdrawals or the use of the withdrawn funds.

[¶10,405] Eligibility

A TFSA is a "qualifying arrangement" if the issuer of the arrangement makes an election in prescribed form before March of the year following the year in which the arrangement is entered into.[170] A qualifying arrangement is an arrangement that meets the following requirements:

(1) it is made between the issuer and an individual who is at least 18 years of age;

See page ii for explanation of footnotes.

[170] CCH ¶21,418; Sec. 146.2(5).

(2) it is an arrangement that is either in trust with the issuer as trustee, an annuity contract with a licensed annuities provider, or a deposit with a financial institution (e.g., a bank) that is or is eligible to be a member of the Canadian Payments Association or a credit union;

(3) the arrangement provides for contributions to be made to the issuer in consideration of, or to be used, invested, or otherwise applied for the purpose of, making distributions to the holder of the arrangement;

(4) the issuer and the individual agree that the issuer will file the above-noted election with the Minister of National Revenue to register the arrangement as a TFSA; and

(5) at all times, beginning with the time that the arrangement is entered into, it complies with certain conditions.[171]

The conditions that must be complied with for an arrangement to meet the above definition of "qualifying arrangement" are as follows:

(a) the arrangement must require that it be maintained for the exclusive benefit of the holder. However, this requirement does not preclude the arrangement from providing a payment to a person on or after the death of the holder;

(b) the arrangement must prohibit, while there is a holder of the arrangement, anyone that is neither the holder nor the issuer of the arrangement from having rights under the arrangement relating to the amount and timing of distributions and the investing of funds;

(c) the arrangement must prohibit anyone other than the holder from making contributions under the arrangement. However, this requirement does not prevent the holder's spouse from transferring property to the holder for the purpose of making the contributions, and the attribution rules will generally not apply in such case. Furthermore, as indicated in the explanatory notes to the provision, it does not preclude contributions from being made on behalf of the holder under an agency agreement, such as contributions made under an employer-sponsored group arrangement;

(d) the arrangement must permit distributions to be made to reduce the amount of penalty tax otherwise payable by the holder on excessive contributions (see ¶13,513) and contributions made while non-resident (see ¶13,514);

(e) the arrangement must provide that, at the direction of the holder, the issuer shall transfer all or any part of the property held in connection with the arrangement (or an amount equal to its value) to another TFSA of the holder;

See page ii for explanation of footnotes.

[171] CCH ¶21,413; Sec. 146.2(1) "qualifying arrangement".

¶10,405

(f) if the arrangement is an arrangement in trust, it must prohibit the trust from borrowing money or other property for the purposes of the arrangement; and

(g) the arrangement must comply with prescribed conditions. However, at the time of writing none was prescribed.[172]

However, none of the conditions in (a), (b) and (e) will apply to prevent a TFSA holder from using his or her interest in the TFSA as security for a loan or other indebtedness if:

(i) the terms and conditions of the indebtedness are those that persons dealing at arm's length with each other would have entered into; and

(ii) it can reasonably be concluded that none of the main purposes for that use is to enable a person (other than the holder) or a partnership to benefit from the TFSA's exemption from tax under Part I.[173]

An arrangement ceases to be a TFSA immediately before the earliest of the death of the last holder, the arrangement ceasing to be a qualifying arrangement, or the arrangement not being administered in accordance with the above conditions.[174] Upon the death of the individual who entered into the TFSA (that is, the original holder), the individual's spouse or common-law partner, referred to as the "survivor", becomes the holder of the TFSA, if he or she acquires all of the individual's rights under the TFSA. As such, the tax-free status of the TFSA can continue until the death of the survivor. In any other case, since the arrangement will cease to be a TFSA immediately before the death of the holder, any income earned in the TFSA after that time will be subject to tax.

[¶10,406] Taxability of Trust

Part I tax is not payable by a trust governed by a TFSA on its taxable income for a taxation year.[175] However, if the trust holds a non-qualified investment or carries on a business in the year, it will be subject to Part I tax on the income from the investment or business, and if it disposes of the investment, the entire capital gain or loss is included in the trust's income for these purposes. The types of property that are qualified investment for TFSA trusts correspond for the most part to those that are prescribed for RRSP trusts. See ¶10,378.

[172] CCH ¶21,415; Sec. 146.2(2).   [174] CCH ¶21,418; Sec. 146.2(5).

[173] CCH ¶21,416, ¶21,417; Sec. 146.2(3), 146.2(4).   [175] CCH ¶21,418a; Sec. 146.2(6).

[¶10,408] Registered Retirement Income Funds

[¶10,411] Registered Retirement Income Funds in General

A registered retirement income fund (RRIF) permits taxpayers to spread the receipt of amounts accumulated in their RRSPs over the years between the establishment of the fund and their death. A RRIF can be established at any time but a minimum amount must be withdrawn every year following the year of its establishment. This minimum amount is, for years prior to the year in which the annuitant reaches 71 years of age, the opening balance of the RRIF at the beginning of the calendar year, divided by 90 minus the annuitant's age at the beginning of the year. Once an annuitant has reached 71, the minimum amount is determined by a fixed percentage set out in government regulations described at ¶10,414. Payments out of or under a RRIF are subject to tax when received. The RRIF is an alternative to using the amounts in a matured RRSP to purchase an annuity. The detailed provisions applying to RRIFs are described below, but may be summarized as follows:

(1) A registered retirement income fund may be established with amounts transferred from an RRSP, another RRIF, a registered pension plan (RPP), or a prescribed provincial pension plan.[176] Included are amounts received from the RRSP of another person as a refund of premiums (see ¶10,366) from the registered pension plan, RRSP, or RRIF of a spouse or common-law partner on the breakdown of a marriage or common-law partnership (and from the RPP, upon the death of the spouse or common-law partner), and from the *Saskatchewan Pension Plan.*

(2) The plan must be established before any relevant RRSP reaches maturity. Thereafter, the funds of the matured plan would have to be used to purchase an annuity and would not be available for transfer to the plan.

(3) The fund itself consists of an arrangement between the *annuitant* and an authorized financial institution providing for payments to the annuitant, and where the annuitant so elects, to his or her spouse/common-law partner after death, of a portion of the property held by the carrier in respect of the fund.[177] The definition of "annuitant" was amended so that, in addition to the taxpayer, it may include the taxpayer's spouse or common-law partner after his or her death, and may include the spouse/common-law partner of the survivor. The survivor becomes the annuitant if the carrier has undertaken to make payments to the survivor in accordance with the election of the taxpayer or the consent of the taxpayer's legal representative. The spouse/common-law partner of the survivor becomes the annuitant if the carrier has undertaken to make payments to that spouse/common-law partner in accordance with the consent of the survivor's legal representative. Whoever becomes the "annuitant" pays tax on the annual payments. The

---

See page ii for explanation of footnotes.
[176] CCH ¶21,428h; Sec. 146.3(2)(e.1).   [177] CCH ¶21,428g; Sec. 146.3(1) "annuitant".

annual payments must be no less than the "minimum amount", but can be greater than this amount. See ¶10,414.

(4) If the taxpayer dies and the spouse/common-law partner does not become the annuitant, the carrier must distribute the property held in connection with the fund. This distribution may be governed by the arrangement or the taxpayer's will. If the property passes to someone other than certain children or grandchildren of the deceased, the value of the benefits will be included in the income of the deceased for the year of death and the beneficiary will receive the full value of property in the fund at the time of death free of tax.

(5) A trust governed by a RRIF is exempt from tax until after the death of the last annuitant, unless:

(a) it has borrowed money, or has received unauthorized gifts or income from the carrying on of a business (other than business income from, or from the disposition of, a qualified investment);[178]

(b) it has acquired non-qualified investments;[179]

(c) it has acquired excess foreign property, *et seq.*; or

(d) it participates in certain resource property transactions that create special tax penalties under Part XII or Part XII.1.

(6) The annuitant will be subject to tax:

(a) on amounts received out of the fund;[180]

(b) if the trust acquires non-qualified investments before March 23, 2011 or uses its property as security for a loan;[181] or

(c) if the trust buys or sells property at other than fair market value.[182]

(7) Tax must be withheld from payments out of or under a RRIF if made to a resident[183] or to a non-resident.[184]

[In light of the extended application of Part XI.01 penalty tax of 50% to non-qualified RRSP investments, the above tax in (6) on non-qualified RRSP investments no longer apply to such investments acquired after March 22, 2011. For further information on Part XI.01 tax on RRSP non-qualified and prohibited investments, see ¶13,518.]

See page ii for explanation of footnotes.

[178] CCH ¶21,428l; Sec. 146.3(3).

[179] CCH ¶21,428r; Sec. 146.3(9).

[180] CCH ¶21,428n; Sec. 146.3(5).

[181] CCH ¶21,428p; Sec. 146.3(7).

[182] CCH ¶21,428m; Sec. 146.3(4).

[183] CCH ¶22,300; Sec. 153(1)(*l*).

[184] CCH ¶26,103; Sec. 212(1)(q).

[¶10,414] Meaning of "Retirement Income Fund"

A "retirement income fund" (RIF) is defined as a certain arrangement between a carrier and an annuitant.[185] The arrangement may be one under which certain property and the income therefrom are held in trust for the annuitant or an arrangement under which the carrier retains beneficial ownership of the property but agrees to make payments to the annuitant based on the value of the property transferred to it. A carrier is:

(a) a person licensed to carry on an annuities business;

(b) a corporation authorized to offer its services to the public as a trustee;

(c) a corporation approved to issue investment contracts; or

(d) a person referred to as a depositary.

Thus, banks, credit unions, insurance companies, and trust companies will qualify as carriers that are entitled to issue RRIFs.

Under the definition of a retirement income fund, the arrangement between the annuitant and the carrier must provide that, in consideration for the transfer of property to the carrier, the carrier undertakes to make payments to the annuitant, and, if the annuitant so elects, to the spouse or common-law partner of the annuitant. The plan must provide for annual payments beginning no later than the year after the year the plan is established of no less than the "minimum amount". (See ¶10,415 for transitional rules regarding the "minimum amount" for annuitants turning 70 or 71 years of age in 2007.) Up until 1992, the "minimum amount" [186] was calculated by dividing the value of the RRIF at the beginning of the year by the difference between 90 and the age of the annuitant (or the annuitant's spouse if the annuitant so elects) at that time. The election with respect to the use of the age of the younger spouse was available for years prior to 1992, even if the spouse was not a beneficiary under the RRIF.

Significant changes were made to the calculation of the minimum amount effective for the 1992 and subsequent taxation years. This amount is expressed as a prescribed percentage of the fund assets that must be paid out in a year depending on the age of the annuitant.[187] Payments may be made until the latest of the death of the first annuitant, the surviving spouse/common-law partner (the "survivor"), or the spouse/common-law partner of the survivor. Minimum amounts only are prescribed; the plan may provide for greater annual payments. However, in some circumstances, provincial legislation may prescribe a maximum allowed annual payment.

See page ii for explanation of footnotes.

[185] CCH ¶21,428gg; Sec. 146.3(1) "retirement income fund"; Inf. Cir. 78-18R6.

[186] CCH ¶21,428gc; Sec. 146.3(1) "minimum amount".

[187] Reg. 7308.

¶10,414

For tax year 2008 only, the required minimum withdrawal amount for RRIFs is reduced to 75% of the minimum withdrawal amount otherwise calculated. This 25% reduction in the minimum amount does not apply for: (1) withholding tax exemption on RRIF withdrawals up to the minimum amount, (2) non-resident withholding taxes, and (3) spousal attribution rules described in ¶10,419.

Two schedules of payments are prescribed; the schedule for "qualifying" RRIFs and the schedule for RRIFs other than qualifying RRIFs. Generally speaking, the new schedule of minimum withdrawals for qualifying RRIFs mirrors the old schedule for minimum withdrawals, prior to the annuitant reaching age 78. At age 78, the new schedule for qualifying RRIFs requires the same withdrawals as the old schedule. After age 78, withdrawals under the new schedule for qualifying RRIFs are lower than those required under the old schedule. The minimum withdrawal rates for the new schedule for qualifying RRIFs increase annually until reaching a withdrawal requirement of 20% of the assets in the fund at age 94 (and over). Under the old schedule, the minimum withdrawal rates increased to 20% at age 85 and continued to increase to 100%, or full withdrawal of the assets, by age 90. The new schedule for RRIFs other than qualifying RRIFs is identical to the new schedule for qualifying RRIFs except at the ages 71 to 77. At these ages, larger minimum withdrawals are required for RRIFs other than qualifying RRIFs.

There are two types of RRIFs considered qualifying RRIFs: (i) RRIFs entered into prior to 1993, where the carrier has not accepted any property for the fund after 1992 and at or before the time a determination is required, and (ii) other RRIFs, where the carrier has not accepted property on the same basis as above except for property transferred from another qualifying RRIF.

Note that the tax treatment previously available to a spouse or common-law spouse was extended after 2000 to a "common-law partner", i.e., a person, regardless of sex, who is cohabiting with the taxpayer in a conjugal relationship and has so cohabited for a continuous period of at least one year or is a parent of a child of whom the taxpayer is also a parent.[188]

Notwithstanding the required yearly minimum payment as described above, the amount of any payment cannot exceed the value of the property held in connection with the arrangement immediately before the time of payment. This would operate in later years where losses have been incurred or accrued with respect to the property held in connection with the arrangement between the beginning of the year and the time of a payment in respect of that year, or where the annuitant has chosen annual payments which exceed the minimum amount.

See page ii for explanation of footnotes.

[188] CCH ¶28,047a; Sec. 248(1) "common-law partner".

To avoid the difficulty of determining the fair market value of a locked-in annuity each year and make it practical for a minimum amount to be calculated and distributed where a locked-in annuity is held by a RRIF trust, the minimum amount for the year under a RRIF will be the total of:

(1) the prescribed fraction for the year multiplied by the total fair market value of properties (other than locked-in annuities) held in connection with the fund at the beginning of the year; and

(2) the total of all amounts, each of which is either a periodic payment received by the trust in the year under a locked-in annuity or an estimate of a periodic payment the trust would have received under a locked-in annuity, held at the start of the year if it had not disposed of the right to the payment during the year.

As a result, if a RRIF trust holds only locked-in annuities at the beginning of a year, the minimum amount for the year under the RRIF will never exceed the annuity payments received by the trust in that year.

[¶10,415] Transitional Rules for RRIF Annuitants Turning 70 or 71 in 2007

In the 2007 Budget, the government extended the maturity deadline for RRSPs to the end of the year in which the annuitant of the RRSP turns 71 years of age, effective after 2006. Since the previous deadline was the end of the year in which the annuitant turned 69 years of age, individuals who turned 69 in 2005 or 2006 may have converted their RRSPs into RRIFs. As a transitional measure, a RRIF annuitant who is 71 years of age or younger at the end of 2007 will be able to reconvert the RRIF to an RRSP, as long as the re-established RRSP is converted to a RRIF before the end of the taxation year in which the individual turns 71 years of age. In addition, the minimum RRIF withdrawal requirement will be waived in 2007 for those turning 70 or 71 in 2007, and in 2008 for those turning 71 in 2008.

[¶10,417] Benefits Taxable

Subject to the exceptions involving the death of the last annuitant under a RRIF and where contributions have been made to a spousal or common-law partner plan RRSP, amounts received by a taxpayer in a year out of or under a RRIF are included in computing income.[189] Amounts received out of or under a RRIF which are included in income qualify as pension income for the purposes of the pension income tax credit.[190]

A RRIF trust is not exempt from tax for taxation years beginning with the year following the year of death of the last annuitant. Amounts received by a taxpayer in respect of the income of the trust for a taxation year during which the trust was not exempt from tax will not be included in the income of the taxpayer when received.

See page ii for explanation of footnotes.

[189] CCH ¶21,428n; Sec. 146.3(5).   [190] CCH ¶18,304; Sec. 118(3).

[¶10,418] Effect of Death of Planholder

If a planholder dies and the property in the plan passes to a person other than his or her spouse/common-law partner or a qualified child or grandchild, the fair market value of the property in the plan immediately before his or her death must be included in the planholder's income.[191] The person receiving the property will only be taxed on any increase in value after the date of death of the planholder.

Very often a RRIF planholder names his or her spouse or common-law partner as a successor annuitant; in such a case, the RRIF payments will continue to be made to the surviving spouse/common-law partner and the amounts paid after the date of death are taxed to the surviving spouse or common-law partner.[192]

If the planholder dies and no election has been made, and the RRIF property passes to the estate for the benefit of a surviving spouse/common-law partner, the spouse/common-law partner and estate may jointly elect for the spouse or common-law partner to become a successor annuitant.[193]

If the planholder dies and some or all of the RRIF property passes to the spouse or common-law partner, and no election has been made before or after the death to treat the surviving spouse or common-law partner as a successor annuitant, the lump-sum payment to the spouse/common-law partner is called a "designated benefit" and is taxed to the surviving spouse or common-law partner rather than included in the final return of the deceased. However, the surviving spouse/common-law partner may transfer part of a designated benefit (an "eligible amount") to an RRSP, RRIF, or annuity issuer.[194] An eligible amount is the amount of the RRIF passing to the spouse/common-law partner reduced by that proportion that any unpaid minimum RRIF amount for the year of death is of the total RRIF amount paid to the spouse/common-law partner.

If the recipient is the child or the grandchild of the deceased who was financially dependent on the deceased, amounts received by the child or grandchild will be included in the income of the recipient as a designated benefit. Such amounts qualify as a designated benefit regardless of whether the deceased had a surviving spouse or common-law partner.[195] These amounts, which are called "designated benefits", are treated exactly as if they were paid under the "refund of premium" rules for an RRSP. This means that they can be rolled over into another RRSP, RRIF, or eligible annuity. See ¶10,366.

See page ii for explanation of footnotes.

[191] CCH ¶21,428o; Sec. 146.3(6).

[192] CCH ¶21,428n; Sec. 146.3(5).

[193] CCH ¶21,428g; Sec. 146.3(1) "annuitant".

[194] CCH ¶8510, ¶21,428ob; Sec. 60(*l*), 146.3(6.11).

[195] CCH ¶21,428oa, ¶21,428o; Sec. 146.3(6.1), 146.3(6.2).

After March 3, 2010, an eligible amount (otherwise called a "designated benefit") from a RRIF may on the annuitant's death be rolled over to the registered disability savings plan (RDSP) of a financially dependent infirm child or grandchild (see income test at ¶10,366) to the extent there is room under the $200,000 RDSP contribution limit. The contribution from the rollover cannot be made before July 2011. Transitional rules provide access to the rollover where death occurred after 2007 and before 2011. See ¶10,430.

As with RRSP "refund of premiums" rules, it is open to the legal representative of the deceased to forgo any amount of the deduction available to the deceased for amounts treated as designated benefits. To the extent the designated benefit is thus taxed in the hands of the deceased, it is not taxed to the recipient. Also, as with the RRSP refund of premiums rules at ¶10,367, the rules are amended to minimize the effect of the growth of RRSP assets after the death of the annuitant by allowing amounts accrued in the plan after death to be taxed to (and in the case of a spouse/common-law partner or infirm child, rolled over by) the survivors rather than the deceased. The amounts of post-death growth in asset values are calculated under rules identical to those for RRSPs at ¶10,367.

Furthermore, effective for RRIFs wound up after 2008 following the death of the last annuitant, the losses incurred on the RRIF investments following that death may be carried back and deducted from the year-of-death RRIF income inclusion.[196] The allowed deduction is the difference between variable A and variable B. Variable A is the amount included in the deceased annuitant's income, plus taxable amounts received from the RRIF from the date of death to the date the RRIF is wound up, plus tax-paid amounts. Tax-paid amounts are certain amounts paid from a RRIF after the RRIF's tax-exempt period (i.e., after December 31 of the year following the year of the last annuitant's death). Variable B is the total of all amounts distributed from the RRIF after the last annuitant's death. The deduction is only available if the two conditions are met:

(1) the RRIF is wound up by the end of the year following the year of death of the last annuitant, and

(2) the RRIF does not hold non-qualified investments during the post-death period.[197]

If either of those conditions is not met, the last deceased annuitant's legal representative can submit a request in writing to the Minister of National Revenue that the deduction be allowed. The Minister may allow some or all of the deduction, subject to possible additional conditions to be met, as appropriate.

---

[196] CCH ¶21,428obf; Sec. 146.3(6.3).   [197] CCH ¶21,428obh; Sec. 146.3(6.4).

¶10,418

[¶10,419] Treatment of RRIF Withdrawals Where RRIF Created from Spousal or Common-Law Partner Plan

Rules are provided[198] to deal with the situation where a taxpayer makes a deductible contribution to the taxpayer's spousal or common-law partner plan and the spouse/common-law partner transfers the property in that plan to a RRIF. Included in the taxpayer's income will be the amount paid to the spouse or common-law partner under the RRIF which is in excess of the "minimum amount" for the year, but only to the extent the taxpayer made deductible contributions to the particular RRSP in the year or the two previous taxation years.

Where there is an inclusion in the income of the taxpayer for a year, that amount will reduce the amount of deductible contributions considered to have been made to the spousal or common-law partner plan in the order in which such contributions were made when it comes time to calculate the amount to be included in the taxpayer's income in a subsequent year. This avoids double taxation for the taxpayer. For the meaning of the term minimum amount, see ¶10,414. The reference to this amount in the calculation means that an income inclusion to the taxpayer will arise only if the spouse elects, when establishing the RRIF, to accelerate the payments to be received under the fund.

This treatment of RRIF withdrawals will not apply in the following circumstances:

(a) the parties are living separate and apart because of the breakdown of their marriage or common-law partnership;

(b) during the year the taxpayer died;

(c) if the taxpayer or the spouse/common-law partner is non-resident at the time;

(d) where there is a matching deduction for a transfer to an RRSP, a RRIF, or purchase of an annuity, except that if an annuity is purchased, it must not be commutable or in fact commuted for three years; or

(e) where the spouse/common-law partner dies and there is an income inclusion with respect to his or her RRIF.

[¶10,420] Registration of Fund

A retirement income fund must be accepted by the Minister of National Revenue for registration, and must be registered under the Social Insurance Number of the first annuitant.[199] To be accepted for registration, the following conditions must be met:

See page ii for explanation of footnotes.
[198] CCH ¶21,428na–21,428ne; Sec. 146.3(5.1)–(5.5).   [199] CCH ¶21,428h; Sec. 146.3(2).

¶10,420

(1) the carrier must be required to make the prescribed payments and no others;

(2) payments out of the fund cannot be assigned;

(3) the fund, where it involves a depositary, must provide that the depositary has no right of offset as regards the property held under the fund in connection with any debt or obligation owing to the depositary and the property held under the fund cannot be pledged, assigned, or in any way alienated as security for a loan or for any purpose other than that of the making by the carrier to the annuitant those payments described in ¶10,417;

(4) the carrier must, on the death of an annuitant, distribute the property held in connection with the arrangement or an amount equal to that value at the time of death except where the terms of the arrangement or the provisions of the will of the deceased make the spouse or common-law partner of the deceased the annuitant under the fund;

(5) the carrier must be required to transfer, in prescribed form and manner at the direction of the annuitant to another RRIF carrier or to a money purchase RPP, all of the property held in connection with the arrangement or an amount equal to its value at the time of the direction, together with all information necessary for the continuance of the fund and the transferor carrier must retain sufficient property to pay the minimum amount under the arrangement for the year);

(6) the carrier must be permitted to accept as consideration for the arrangement only:

(a) property transferred from an RRSP under which the individual is the annuitant;

(b) property transferred from another RRIF under which the individual is the annuitant;

(c) an amount received by the individual as a refund of premiums under the RRSP of another person;

(d) property transferred from an RRSP or a RRIF of a spouse or common-law partner on the breakdown of the marriage or common-law partnership;

(e) a registered pension plan under which the individual is a member;

(f) a registered pension plan, where the monies are transferred as a consequence of either death or the breakdown of a marriage or common-law partnership;

(g) a prescribed provincial pension plan; and

(h) after March 20, 2003, a deferred profit sharing plan.

¶10,420

(7) before March 23, 2011, the fund must provide that no benefit or loan which is conditional in any way on the existence of the fund may be extended to the annuitant or to any person who does not deal at arm's length with the annuitant other than:

(a) a benefit included in the annuitant's income;

(b) the payments after the death of the annuitant; or

(c) a benefit resulting from the provision of administrative or investment services in respect of the fund.[200]

For transactions occurring after March 22, 2011, the special Part XI.01 taxes on TFSA advantages applies to RRIFs, subject to certain enhancements. This means that the 100% tax on TFSA advantages is extended to RRIF benefits and loans. As a result of the extended application of the TFSA advantage rules to RRIFs, the above condition in (7) is repealed after March 22, 2011. For further information on Part XI.01 tax on RRSP advantages, see ¶13,518.

[¶10,421] Change in Fund after Registration

If the terms of the plan are changed after registration or a new fund is substituted so that the new form of plan (or the substituted plan) would not qualify for registration, the plan ceases to be a RRIF.[201] A substitution is deemed to have taken place for these purposes where rights or obligations under a plan are released in exchange for other rights or obligations or where prohibited loans are extended or continued.[202]

The annuitant is required to include in income the fair market value of all property held in connection with the fund determined immediately before the revision or substitution.[203]

[¶10,422] Transfers

A "direct" transfer of property from an annuitant's RRIF to the RRSP or RRIF of his/her current or former spouse or common-law partner under a court order or separation agreement after the breakdown of their marriage or common-law partnership will not result in any income inclusion or tax deduction for the annuitant.[204]

Similarly, a transfer of RRIF property on a rollover basis is allowed if: (1) the property is transferred at the direction of the annuitant; (2) the transfer is made "directly" to an RPP under which the annuitant was already a member or to a prescribed RPP; and (3) the property is allocated to the annuitant under a "money purchase provision".[205]

See page ii for explanation of footnotes.

[200] CCH ¶21,428h; Sec. 146.3(2)(e.1).
[201] CCH ¶21,428t; Sec. 146.3(11).
[202] CCH ¶21,428u, ¶21,428v; Sec. 146.3(12), 146.3(13).

[203] CCH ¶21,428t; Sec. 146.3(11)(b).
[204] CCH ¶21,428w; Sec. 146.3(14).
[205] CCH ¶21,428wa; Sec. 146.3(14.1).

Finally, a direct transfer of an annuitant's RRIF property to another RRIF in the name of the same annuitant will not result in any income inclusion or tax deduction for the annuitant.[206]

Money purchase RPPs are now allowed to make RRIF-type payments to their members, instead of being restricted to the purchase of a life annuity or the transfer to an RRSP or a RRIF. The above-mentioned direct transfer rules will allow former members of a money purchase RPP who have moved their RPP funds to an RRSP or RRIF, to transfer them back tax-free to their RPP.

[¶10,423] Taxability of Trust — Non-Qualified Investments

In light of the extended application of Part XI.01 penalty tax of 50% to non-qualified RRIF investments, the following regime for RRIF non-qualified investments no longer apply to such investments acquired after March 22, 2011. For further information on Part XI.01 tax on RRSP non-qualified and prohibited investments, see ¶13,518.

A trust governed by a RRIF is exempt from tax until after the death of the last annuitant when it becomes taxable, unless:

(a) it has borrowed money, or has received unauthorized gifts or income from the carrying on of a business (other than business income from, or from the disposition of, a qualified investment); or

(b) before March 23, 2011 (see above commentary) it has acquired non-qualified investments.[207]

It should be noted that, if the trust acquires a non-qualified investment before March 23, 2011 or permits any of its property to be used as security for a loan, the annuitant becomes subject to tax.

If the trust disposes of property at less than, or acquires property at more than, the fair market value of that property, the annuitant will be subject to tax. If property is acquired at a cost greater than its fair market value or disposed of for less than its fair market value, two times the difference between the fair market value and the consideration given or received, as the case may be, is included in the income of the annuitant at the time.

If the trust uses or permits its property to be used as security for a loan, the fair market value of the property at that time is included in the annuitant's income. When the loan ceases to be outstanding, a deduction is available to the annuitant. The deduction is the amount previously included in income minus any loss suffered by the trust for having used the property.

See page ii for explanation of footnotes.

[206] CCH ¶21,428wb; Sec. 146.3(14.2).

[207] CCH ¶21,428l, ¶21,428m, ¶21,428n, ¶21,428p, ¶21,428q, ¶21,428s; Sec. 146.3(3), 146.3(4), 146.3(5), 146.3(7), 146.3(8), 146.3(10).

When a trust acquires a non-qualified investment before March 23, 2011, the fair market value of the investment at the time it was acquired is included in the income of the person who is the annuitant at the time of acquisition. When the investment is disposed of, the lesser of the proceeds of disposition and the amount previously included in income as a result of the acquisition of that property may be deducted by the person who is the annuitant at the time of disposition. In addition to the tax on the annuitant, a tax is imposed on the trust in respect of the non-qualified investment.[208] In computing this income, the full amount of capital gains and capital losses are used. "Qualified investment" is defined to mean the following property:[209]

(1) Money that is legal tender (other than money the fair market value of which exceeds its stated value as legal tender or money that is held for its numismatic value) and certain deposits of such money standing to the credit of the trust (as described below). However, after February 23, 2005, regulations allow, as qualified investments, investment-grade gold and silver bullion coins and bars, and certificates on such investments. Investment-grade gold must have a purity of at least 99.5%, while investment-grade silver must have a purity of at least 99.9%. Legal tender bullion coins will qualify if they are produced by the Royal Canadian Mint and all or substantially all of their fair market value is attributable to their precious metal content. Bullion bars will qualify if they are produced by a metal refinery accredited by the London Bullion Market Association, as evidenced by a hallmark identifying the refiner, purity, and weight. Certificates will qualify if they are issued by a federally or provincially regulated financial institution and represent a claim on precious metal holdings of the issuing institution. For all such investments (i.e., coins, bars, and certificates) the investment must be acquired either from the producer of the investment or from a regulated financial institution.

(2) Effective March 18, 2007, any securities or other derivative instruments in respect of which the holder's risk of loss may exceed the holder's cost, or shares listed on a prescribed Canadian or foreign stock exchange. Before March 18, 2007, shares listed on prescribed stock exchanges and debts of companies whose shares were so listed, qualified. Effective December 14, 2007, the list of prescribed stock exchanges is replaced with a list of designated stock exchanges, the difference being that the Minister of Finance can change the list without bothering with the formality of promulgating regulations. All formerly prescribed stock exchanges, Canadian and foreign, will become designated stock exchanges.

(3) Debt obligations issued by a corporation, mutual fund trust, or limited partnership, the shares or units of which are listed on a prescribed stock exchange in Canada (after December 14, 2007, see (2) above), by a

---

See page ii for explanation of footnotes.

[208] CCH ¶21,428p, ¶21,428r; Sec. 146.3(7), 146.3(9).   [209] CCH ¶21,428ge; Sec. 146.3(1) "qualified investment".

corporation whose shares are listed on a prescribed stock exchange outside Canada (after December 14, 2007, see (2) above), or by an authorized foreign bank and payable at a branch in Canada of that bank.

(4) After March 18, 2007, all debt obligations that have an investment grade rating and that are part of a minimum $25 million issuance.

(5) Guaranteed investment certificates issued by a Canadian incorporated trust company.

(6) Certain investment contracts (annuities) issued by corporations approved by the Canadian government.

(7) Certain types of accumulation annuities and segregated fund policies if the RRIF trust is the only person (other than the insurer who issued the contract) entitled to future rights or benefits under the contract, and the timing and amount of the RRIF trust's entitlements affected by the personal circumstances of any individual, other than the length of the life of the individual who was the RRIF annuitant immediately after the contract was acquired.

(8) Such other investments as may be prescribed by regulation. The investments prescribed by regulation are the same as those prescribed for RRSPs. For a detailed list, see ¶10,378.[210]

[¶10,424] Registered Disability Savings Plan (RDSP)

[¶10,425] Characteristics

The concept of the registered disability savings plan (RDSP) was introduced in the 2007 federal Budget, with the stated purpose of helping parents and others save for the long-term financial security of a child with a severe disability. An RDSP can invest and earn income tax free for the purpose of making future payments to the beneficiary.

The RDSP was introduced along with the Canada disability savings grant (CDSG) program, under which the federal government will provide matching grants to an RDSP, depending on net family income, and the Canada disability savings bond (CDSB) program, under which the government will contribute bonds to an RDSP for low- and modest-income level beneficiaries and families. The CDSG and CDSB programs are governed by the *Canada Disability Savings Act*, whereas the RDSP program is governed by the *Income Tax Act*. These programs are applicable beginning in 2008.

An RDSP may be set up for the benefit of a beneficiary who is eligible for the disability tax credit (DTC) and resident in Canada. The RDSP can be

---

[210] CCH ¶25,540; Reg. 4900.

set up regardless of the age of the beneficiary, although contributions to the plan are allowed only to the end of the year in which the beneficiary turns 59 years of age. Contributions are prohibited at any time if the beneficiary is not eligible for the DTC in the year that includes that time, the beneficiary is not resident in Canada at the time, or the beneficiary has died before that time. There is a $200,000 lifetime limit of contributions per beneficiary.[211] (The foregoing conditions, along with others, are discussed in ¶10,426.)

Contributions to an RDSP are not deductible, although the investment income earned on the contributions and the CDSGs and CDSBs are not subject to Part I tax while in the plan. However, an RDSP will be subject to Part I tax in a taxation year if it borrows money in the year or did not repay previously borrowed money before the year, or if it carries on a business or acquires a property that is not a "qualifying investment" in the year. Furthermore, an RDSP may be subject to a penalty tax under Part XI if it acquires a property that is not a qualifying investment or if it disposes of or acquires property for consideration that is less or greater than its fair market value, respectively. See ¶10,427.

The payment of "disability assistance payments" out of an RDSP must begin by or before the end of the year in which the beneficiary turns 60 years of age. The payments are subject to a maximum annual limit depending on the age of the beneficiary and the fair market value of the plan's assets (there is no maximum in certain cases where the beneficiary is terminally ill). [Specific rules limit the maximum amount that may be withdrawn annually from an RDSP where Canada Disability Savings Grants or Bonds paid into the RDSP exceed private contributions. Where this occurs, the RDSP is known as a "primarily government-assisted plan" (PGAP). Budget 2012 increased the maximum annual limit for withdrawals from a PGAP and added a new minimum annual withdrawal requirements beginning in the calendar year in which the beneficiary turns 60 years of age. The maximum and minimum withdrawal measures will apply after 2013. These changes were released in draft on August 14, 2012. See also ¶10,428.] Each disability assistance payment is included in the beneficiary's income (or, where the beneficiary has died, in the beneficiary's estate income), generally to the extent that it exceeds the "non-taxable portion" of the payment. Effectively, this means that contributions to the plan are not included in income when paid out of the plan, whereas CDSGs, CDSBs, and the investment income earned in the plan are included in the income of the beneficiary when paid out of the plan.[212]

An RDSP must be terminated by the end of the year following the earlier of the year in which the beneficiary dies and the year in which the beneficiary ceases to be entitled to the DTC. [Pending changes released in draft on August 14, 2012, the period for which an RDSP remains open when

---

[211] CCH ¶21,429d; Sec. 146.4(1)"contribution".   [212] CCH ¶21,429zj, ¶21,429zk; Sec. 146.4(6), 146.4(7).

a beneficiary becomes DTC-ineligible, can be extended by filing an election. An RDSP plan holder will be able to make an election in prescribed form and submit it to the RDSP issuer along with written certification from a medical doctor that the beneficiary will be eligible for the DTC again in the near future. The election must be made on or before December 31 of the year following the first full calendar year that the beneficiary is DTC-ineligible. The election will generally be valid for four years following the first full calendar year of DTC-ineligibility. The RDSP must be terminated by the end of the first year following the end of the election. This measure will generally apply to elections made after 2013.][213]

As a result of the 2011 Budget, the concept of a "specified disability savings plan" (SDSP) was introduced to allow an RDSP beneficiary with a life expectancy of five years or less to make annual RDSP withdrawals of up to $10,000 in taxable plan savings, as well as a prorated amount of plan contributions, without triggering the repayment of CDSGs and CDSBs paid into the plan in the preceding 10 years.

Under the current RDSP rules, the plan holder of an RDSP must be either the beneficiary or a legal representative (where the beneficiary lacks the legal capacity to enter into a contract). However, there may be difficulties in establishing an RDSP where the potential beneficiary's capacity to enter into a contract is in doubt. Matters of capacity and legal representation are subject to provincial and territorial laws, and determining capacity and appointing a legal guardian can potentially be a lengthy process.

Budget 2012 introduced a temporary measure to allow certain family members to become the plan holder of an RDSP for adult individuals unable to enter into a contract. Where an RDSP issuer has doubts regarding an individual's ability to enter into a contract, the spouse, common-law partner, or parent of the individual will be considered a "qualifying family member". This person will be able to establish the RDSP for the individual. If an RDSP issuer subsequently no longer doubts the individual's legal capacity, or the individual is determined to be legally capable to enter into a contract by an authorized public agency or tribunal, the individual may replace the qualifying family member as the plan holder.[214]

If the RDSP has been established by a qualifying family member and a legal representative (i.e., a guardian or other person legally authorized to act on the individual's behalf) is appointed, the legal representative will replace the qualifying family member as the plan holder. This measure will not apply where the RDSP has already been established by the individual or where the individual already has a legal representative.

This measure was passed in Bill C-38 on June 29, 2012 and applies from the date of Royal Assent until the end of 2016.

---

[213] Sec. 146.4(4), 146.4(4.1), 146.4(4.2).   [214] Sec. 146.4(1) and 146.4(1.5).

¶10,425

RESP Rollovers

Budget 2012 proposed a tax-free transfer ("rollover") of investment income earned in a Registered Education Savings Plan (RESP) to an RDSP if both plans have a common beneficiary. To qualify for the rollover, the beneficiary must meet the existing age and residency requirements with respect to RDSP contributions. In addition, one of the following conditions must be fulfilled:

- the beneficiary has a severe and prolonged mental impairment that can reasonably be expected to prevent the beneficiary from pursuing a post-secondary education;

- the RESP has existed for at least 10 years and the beneficiary is at least 21 years of age and is not pursuing a post-secondary education; or

- the RESP has existed for at least 35 years.

Currently, the above conditions would allow for the beneficiary to receive an "accumulated income payment" from an RESP. Accumulated income payments are essentially the investment income earned in the RESP that are not educational assistance payments (as the beneficiary is not attending a post-secondary institution). An accumulated income payment will generally be included in the RESP subscriber's income and is further subject to a Part X.5 penalty tax of 20%. An RESP subscriber can reduce the accumulated income payment by contributing a portion of it to an RRSP subject to certain conditions. This allows the rollover amount not to be subject to income tax or the 20% penalty tax.

Under the Budget 2012 proposal, the RESP investment income can be rolled over to an RDSP on a tax-free basis, similar to a contribution to an RRSP of an accumulated income payment.[215] Canada Education Savings Grants and Canada Learning Bonds in the RESP will have a requirement to be repaid by the end of February of the year following the year in which the rollover is made.

The amount of RESP investment income rolled over to an RDSP may not exceed the beneficiary's available RDSP contribution room, and the amount rolled over will reduce the available RDSP contribution room. The rollover amount will be considered a private contribution for the purposes of determining whether an RDSP is a PGAP but will not attract CDSGs. The rollover amount is to be included in the taxable portion of any RDSP withdrawals.

This measure was introduced in draft legislation on August 14, 2012 and would apply to rollovers made after 2013.

See page ii for explanation of footnotes.

[215] Sec. 146.1(1.1) and 146.1(1.2).

[¶10,426] Registration Requirements

In order to be registered as an RDSP, a disability savings plan must meet the following conditions:

(a) The plan must stipulate that it will be operated exclusively for the benefit of the beneficiary under the plan, that the designation of the beneficiary is irrevocable, and that no right of the beneficiary to receive payments from the plan is capable of surrender or assignment.

(b) The plan can allow an entity to acquire rights as a successor or assignee of a holder of the plan, only if the entity is the beneficiary, the beneficiary's estate, a holder of the plan at the time the rights are acquired, a qualifying person in relation to the beneficiary at the time the rights are acquired, or a legal parent of the beneficiary who was previously a holder of the plan. The person acquiring such rights as a successor or assignee is then considered a holder of the plan.

(c) The plan must provide that an entity (other than a legal parent of the beneficiary) ceases to be a holder of the plan if the entity ceases to be a qualifying person in relation to the beneficiary. Thus, for example, if a beneficiary reaches the age of majority and has legal competence to enter into contracts, a guardian or public agency that was formerly a holder of the plan will cease to be a holder.

(d) The plan must provide that there be a holder of the plan at all times, and the plan can provide that the beneficiary or his or her estate automatically acquire rights as an assignee or successor, in order to ensure compliance with this requirement.

(e) The plan must provide that an entity becoming a holder after the plan is entered into is prohibited from exercising rights as a holder (except to the extent otherwise permitted by either the Minister of National Revenue or the specified minister) until the issuer has been advised of the entity having become a holder and has been provided with the entity's Social Insurance Number or business number, as the case may be.

(f) The plan must prohibit contributions in a year if the beneficiary is not a DTC-eligible individual in respect of the year or at any time after the beneficiary dies.

(g) The plan must prohibit contributions after the year in which the beneficiary turns 59 years of age or if the beneficiary is not resident in Canada. The plan must limit lifetime contributions to the plan and other RDSPs of the beneficiary to $200,000.

(h) The plan must prohibit contributions by anyone other than a holder of the plan, except with the written consent of a holder. Otherwise, there are no restrictions on who may contribute to the plan.

(i) The plan must provide that no payments may be made from the plan other than disability assistance payments, which are defined as any payments made to the beneficiary or the beneficiary's estate; a qualifying transfer to another RDSP of the beneficiary; and repayments under the *Canada Disability Savings Act* (generally, repayments of CDSG and CDSB amounts will be required under that Act if they were made within the 10 years before the beneficiary ceased to be eligible for the dividend tax credit or the death of the beneficiary) or under a designated provincial program.

(j) The plan must prohibit a disability assistance payment being made if the payment would cause the value of the plan's assets to fall below the "assistance holdback amount" in relation to the plan. The assistance holdback amount is defined under the *Canada Disability Savings Act* to include CDSG and CDSB amounts that were paid into the plan in the 10 preceding years.[216] This prohibition is meant to ensure that the plan has sufficient assets to satisfy any repayment obligations under the *Canada Disability Savings Act*, as outlined above in paragraph (i).

(k) The plan must provide that "lifetime disability assistance payments" begin to be made no later than the end of the year in which the beneficiary turns 60 years of age, or, if the plan is established in or after that year (i.e., it is set up to receive funds transferred from another RDSP in respect of the beneficiary), no later than the end of the year in which it is established. Lifetime disability assistance payments must, once they begin to be made, be payable at least annually until the earlier of the death of the beneficiary and the day that the plan is terminated.[217] The maximum amount of lifetime disability assistance payments that may be paid in any particular year is described in paragraph (l), below.

(l) The plan must provide that the maximum amount of lifetime disability assistance payments in a particular calendar year is equal to the amount determined under the formula: $A/(B + 3 - C) + D$. Amount A is the fair market value of the plan's property at the beginning of the year, excluding a so-called locked-in annuity (generally, an annuity that makes at least annual periodic payments for the benefit of the beneficiary for the life of the beneficiary). Amount B is the greater of 80 and the beneficiary's age at the beginning of the year. Variable C is the beneficiary's age at the beginning of the year. Accordingly, once the beneficiary turns 80 years of age, the maximum limit for any year will be one-third of the value of the plan's property at the beginning of the year, before taking into account amount D. Amount D is the total amount of periodic payments that

See page ii for explanation of footnotes.
[216] CCH ¶21,429b; Sec. 146.4(1) "assistance holdback amount".   [217] CCH ¶21,429n; Sec. 146.4(1) "lifetime disability assistance payments".

¶10,426

are paid to the trust in the year under a locked-in annuity as described above, and, if the trust disposes of the right to any such payment in the year, a reasonable estimate of the payment that the trust would have received, but for the disposition. Note that these maximums do not apply in a "specified year", which is the year in which the beneficiary has been certified as terminally ill and not likely to survive more than five years, and each of the following five years.[218]

(m) The plan must stipulate whether disability assistance payments other than lifetime disability assistance payments are allowed under the plan. Such payments would include periodic or non-periodic amounts paid from the plan prior to the year in which the beneficiary turned 60 years of age, or any other payment that did not occur at least annually, to the earlier of the death of the beneficiary or the termination of the plan.

(n) The plan must provide that if, at the beginning of a particular year, the total of previous CDSG and CDSB amounts paid into all RDSPs of the beneficiary exceeds the total of all previous contributions paid into such plans, the disability assistance payments for the particular year are to be subject to further thresholds. In general terms, these thresholds provide that if the beneficiary turned 59 years of age before the particular year, the disability assistance payments for the year must equal the maximum amount determined under paragraph (l) described above. If the year is a specified year (see above), the minimum amount payable is the amount determined under paragraph (l), and there is no maximum for the year. If the beneficiary was at least 27 years of age but under 59 before the particular year, the beneficiary must be allowed to direct that disability assistance payments be made in the year, subject to the paragraph (l) maximum and the constraints in paragraphs (i) and (j) described above. Again, if the year is a specified year, the paragraph (l) maximum amount does not apply.

(o) The plan must allow a transfer of property to another RDSP of the beneficiary, at the direction of the holders of the plan.

(p) The plan must provide for its termination by the end of the year following the earlier of the year in which the beneficiary dies and the year throughout which the beneficiary has no severe and prolonged impairments that would otherwise qualify the beneficiary for the disability tax credit. Any amounts remaining in the plan, after the repayment of CDSG grants or CDSB bonds, and after the repayment under a designated provincial program, if any, must be paid to the beneficiary or the beneficiary's estate.[219]

---

[218] CCH ¶21,429x; Sec. 146.4(1) "specified year".   [219] CCH ¶21,429zd; Sec. 146.4(4).

¶10,426

[¶10,427] Specified Disability Savings Plan

Beginning in 2011, a new tax vehicle was introduced, called the "specified disability savings plan" (SDSP), which allows RDSP beneficiaries with a shortened life expectancy to make withdrawals without triggering the repayment of CDSGs and CDSBs paid into an RDSP in the preceding 10 years (the "assistance holdback amount").

The following conditions must be met by an RDSP to qualify as an SDSP:

(1) a medical doctor certifies that the beneficiary of an RDSP is unlikely to survive more than five years;

(2) the holder of the RDSP elects that the plan be treated as an SDSP and provides the election and medical certification to the RDSP issuer; and

(3) the RDSP issuer notifies the Minister of Human Resources and Skills Development.[220]

Withdrawals made at any time following an election will not trigger the repayment of CDSGs and CDSBs provided that the total of the taxable portions of the withdrawals does not exceed $10,000 annually. (A transitional provision raises this threshold from $10,000 to $20,000 if the required medical certification in (1) is obtained before 2012.)[221] If withdrawals of taxable amounts exceed the annual $10,000 limit, the normal 10-year repayment rule will apply, to the extent that grants and bonds and other assets remain in the plan to satisfy that requirement.

Once an election has been made for an RDSP to qualify as an SDSP, the following rules will apply:

(a) No further contribution to the RDSP is allowed, except that a rollover of a deceased individual's RRSP or RRIF proceeds to the RDSP of a financially dependent infirm child or grandchild is still permitted.

(b) No new CDSGs or CDSBs will be paid into the plan. Upon the the beneficiary's death, any CDSGs and CDSBs remaining in the RDSP and that were received within the preceding 10 years must be repaid.

(c) No CDSG or CDSB entitlements will be carried forward in respect of years under election, other than for the year in which the election is made.

(d) The minimum withdrawal requirements that ordinarily apply in the year in which a beneficiary attains 60 years of age will apply to the SDSP starting in the year following the election, regardless of the age of the beneficiary.

See page ii for explanation of footnotes.

[220] CCH ¶21,429y; Sec. 146.4(1.1).   [221] CCH ¶21,429ya; Sec. 146.4(1.2).

[¶10,428] Canada Disability Savings Grant and Canada Disability Savings Bond

The government will contribute, in the form of CDSGs, funds equivalent to 100% to 300% of RDSP contributions, up to a maximum of $3,500, depending on the net income of the beneficiary's family. Income thresholds are updated each year based on the rate of inflation. For families with net income equal to or less than $85,414 in 2012, the government will provide: (i) $3 for every $1 on the first $500 of contributions; and (ii) $2 for every $1 on the next $1,000 of contributions. For families with net income over $85,414 in 2012, it will provide $1 for every $1 on the first $1,000 of contributions.

In order to better support low- and modest-income families, children in care, and adults without family support, the government will also contribute up to $1,000 annually in Canada Disability Savings Bonds (CDSB), depending on the net income of the beneficiary's family. Income thresholds are updated each year based on the rate of inflation. CDSBs will not be dependent on contributions. The maximum annual amount of $1,000 will be paid to an RDSP where family net income does not exceed $24,863 in 2012. The CDSB will be decreased gradually for those with family net income between $24,863 and $42,707 in 2012. A maximum lifetime amount of $20,000 of CDSBs and $70,000 of CDSGs may be paid in respect of the beneficiary.

Starting in 2011, families of children with disabilities may carry forward unused grant and bond entitlement to future years. The carryforward period can only start after 2007 and is for a period of 10 years.

Under the current RDSP rules, any CDSGs or CDSBs paid into an RDSP in the preceding 10 years must be repaid to the federal government where: (i) any amount is withdrawn from the RDSP; (ii) the RDSP is terminated or deregistered; or (iii) the RDSP beneficiary dies or ceases to be eligible for the DTC. This is known as the "10-year repayment rule".

RDSP issuers must set aside an "assistance holdback amount" to guarantee that potential obligations under this rule will be met. The assistance holdback amount will equal the total CDSGs and CDSBs paid into the RDSP for the last 10 years less any CDSGs and CDSBs already repaid for the same period. Where one of the above events occurs, the required repayment is the amount of the assistance holdback amount immediately before the event occurs.

[Budget 2012 introduced a proportional repayment rule to replace the 10-year repayment rule where a withdrawal is made from an RDSP. (The 10-year repayment rule remains for all other events such as RDSP termination or deregistration or where the beneficiary dies or ceases to be DTC-eligible.) The proportional repayment rule requires that, for each $1 withdrawn from the RDSP, $3 of any CDSGs or CDSBs paid into the plan in the 10-year period preceding the withdrawal be repaid, up to a maximum of the

¶10,428

assistance holdback amount. Repayments will be attributed to CDSGs and CDSBs that make up the assistance holdback amount in the order in which they were paid into the RDSP, starting with the oldest amounts. This measure would apply to withdrawals made from an RDSP after 2013.]

When the CDSG and CDSB amounts are paid out of the plan as "disability assistance payments", they are included in the income of the recipient beneficiary or estate. [Specific rules limit the maximum amount that may be withdrawn annually from an RDSP where CDSGs or CDSBs paid into the RDSP exceed private contributions. Where this occurs, the RDSP is known as a PGAP. Budget 2012 increased the maximum annual limit for withdrawals from a PGAP and added a new minimum annual withdrawal requirement beginning in the calendar year in which the beneficiary turns 60 years of age. The maximum and minimum withdrawal measures will apply after 2013. These changes were released in draft on August 14, 2012.] If the beneficiary dies or ceases to be eligible for the disability tax credit, the plan may be required to repay CDSG and CDSB amounts paid into the plan in the 10 preceding years. Since the CDSG and CDSB amounts are payable until the year in which the beneficiary turns 49 years of age, the repayment requirement should not be an issue if the beneficiary remains disabled and lives beyond the age of 59.

[¶10,428a] Provincial Payments

Before 2009, only prescribed payments identified by regulation on a case-by-case basis were excluded from the definition of "contribution". Beginning in 2009, any payments made under a designated provincial program (DPP) or under another program funded by a province and with a purpose similar to a DPP are excluded from the definition of "contribution".[222] A designated provincial program means a program established under a provincial law and with a purpose consistent with the *Canada Disability Savings Act* to support savings in an RDSP.[223] Payments made by government agencies authorized to act on behalf of an RDSP beneficiary, like children's aid organizations and public guardians, continue to be treated as contributions.

[¶10,429] Non-Compliant Plan

If, at any particular time, an RDSP ceases to comply with the registration requirements in ¶10,426 or a condition or obligation imposed under the *Canada Disability Savings Act* that, in the specified minister's opinion, makes the plan non-compliant because of the failure, the plan ceases to be an RDSP, as of the particular time. In such a case, a disability assistance payment is deemed to have been made at the time that is immediately before the particular time to the beneficiary (or the beneficiary's estate if the

---

See page ii for explanation of footnotes.
[222] CCH ¶21,429d; Sec. 146.4(1) "contribution".   [223] CCH ¶21,429e; Sec. 146.4(1) "designated provincial program".

beneficiary is not alive).[224] The amount of the deemed payment is equal to the amount by which the fair market value of the property of the plan at the particular time exceeds the plan's "assistance holdback amount" (this latter amount will normally have to be repaid under the *Canada Disability Savings Act*). The amount of the deemed payment, in excess of the non-taxable portion of the payment, will be included in the beneficiary's income.

If the plan made a disability assistance payment that brought the value of the plan's assets below its assistance holdback amount, an additional payment (in addition to any deemed payment described above) is deemed to have been made at the relevant time to the beneficiary or estate. The additional amount is, in effect, the portion of the assistance holdback amount that was paid out, causing the value of the plan's assets to dip below the assistance holdback amount. Furthermore, the non-taxable portion of this additional payment is deemed to be nil, which means that the entire additional amount will be included in the income of the beneficiary or estate. However, assuming that this amount is then repaid to the government (e.g., under the *Canada Disability Savings Act*), an offsetting deduction is allowed.[225]

[¶10,430] Rollover to RDSP on Death

Before the 2010 Budget, when an individual dies, amounts paid out of the deceased's RRSP as a refund of premiums can be rolled over on a tax deferred basis to the RRSP of a child or grandchild who was financially dependent on the deceased individual (see ¶10,366). Similar rules exist for the refund of premiums from a RRIF (see ¶10,418) and certain lump-sum amounts paid from RPPs on death (see ¶10,492).

For deaths occurring after March 3, 2010, the 2010 Budget extended these rules to allow these proceeds to be rolled over to an RDSP subject to certain conditions. The beneficiary of the RDSP must be, at the time of the deceased's death, a financially dependent child or grandchild of the deceased by reason of physical or mental infirmity (financially dependent infirm child).[226] This means that the beneficiary must be entitled to a deduction under the current tax deferral rules had the proceeds been transferred to his/her RRSP as a "refund of premiums" (see ¶10,366).

The mechanism for providing the rollover is a deduction of proceeds contributed to an RDSP (called a "specified DPSP payment"), which offsets the RRSP, RRIF or RPP income inclusion that occurred as a consequence of the death of the annuitant or plan member.[227] The contribution from the rollover must comply with existing RDSP contribution rules, cannot be made before July 1, 2011, and cannot exceed the amount of the proceeds that were included in computing the beneficiary's income. Unlike other RDSP contributions, for which no tax deduction is available, the amount of

---

See page ii for explanation of footnotes.

[224] CCH ¶21,429zp; Sec. 146.4(10).
[225] CCH ¶8490; Sec. 60(*l*).

[226] CCH ¶85,591a; Sec. 60.02(1) "eligible individual".
[227] CCH ¶85,591e; Sec. 60.02(2).

¶10,430

a "specified DPSP payment" will be included in the recipient's income on withdrawal from the RDSP.

Where the death of an individual occurs after 2007 and before 2011, transitional rules will allow for a contribution to be made to the RDSP of a financially dependent infirm child of the deceased individual that would provide a result that is generally equivalent to the above measures (subject to similar conditions).[228] Where death occurs after 2007 and before 2011, the contribution from the rollover must be made after June 2011, but before 2012.

[¶10,431] Deferred Profit Sharing Plans

[¶10,432] Principal Features of Deferred Profit Sharing Plans

A "deferred profit sharing plan" (DPSP) is an arrangement under which an employer contributes a portion of the annual profits from his or her business (or those from a corporation with which the employer does not deal at arm's length) to a trustee who holds and invests the contribution for the benefit of those employees who are members of the plan.[229] The employer's contributions are deductible, within certain limits, in computing income for the year in respect of which the contributions are made, provided that they have been made in accordance with the terms of the plan as registered. (See ¶10,447.) The employee-beneficiary is not taxed on the contributions made on his or her behalf or the earnings thereon until he or she actually receives an amount from the plan. It should be noted that the benefit that an employee derives from his or her employer's contribution to a DPSP is specifically excepted from the usual rule that benefits enjoyed in a year in respect of an office or employment are included in computing income for that year. Hence, a tax deferral opportunity is available to the employee.

Amounts vested in a beneficiary must become payable no later than the end of the year in which the beneficiary turns 71 years of age (age 69 after 1996 and before 2007). Upon maturity, the beneficiary has the option of receiving the vested amounts directly, having them paid in instalments for up to 10 years, or using the vested amount to purchase an annuity with a guaranteed term not exceeding 15 years.

Prior to 1991, a profit sharing plan could also provide for employee contributions on either a mandatory or voluntary basis. Beginning in 1991, employee contributions are no longer permitted.

No tax is payable by the trust on the annual profit from investing and reinvesting the contributions made to the plan. In some cases, however, the

---

See page ii for explanation of footnotes.

[228] CCH ¶8559lg, ¶8559lh; Sec. 60.02(4), 60.02(5).   [229] CCH ¶21,429; Sec. 147(1) "deferred profit sharing plan"; Inf. Cir. 77-1R5.

trust may be taxable on non-qualifying investments or on foreign property held in the trust.

A DPSP consists of two basic elements. The first is the plan itself, which must be accepted for registration by the Minister of National Revenue before contributions are deductible for tax purposes. The second element is the trust established to hold the employer's contributions, and through which these contributions are invested for the benefit of plan members.

Membership in a deferred profit sharing plan may restrict the amount an employee may contribute to an RRSP. For additional information on this point, see ¶10,350 *et seq.*

[¶10,435] Conditions for Registration

In order to be accepted for registration, the plan must conform to the following conditions:[230]

(1) Employer's contributions must be allocated to specific beneficiaries in the year in which they are received.

(2) All contributions must either be made by the employer in accordance with the terms of the plan as registered, or must be amounts transferred on a tax-free basis from another deferred profit sharing plan or other registered plan.

(3) No loan may be made to an employee or other beneficiary.

(4) No part of the trust's funds may be invested in:

    (a) notes, bonds, debentures, bankers' acceptances, or similar obligations of an employer making payments under the plan or of a corporation with which it does not deal at arm's length; or

    (b) the shares of a corporation, at least 50% of the property of which consists of the property described in (a).

(5) No right or interest of an employee who is a beneficiary under the plan is capable, either in whole or in part, of surrender or assignment. [Under proposed technical amendments released July 16, 2010 (to take effect after March 20, 2003), this condition is amended to apply to all persons who have a right under the plan, not just employee beneficiaries. The proposed amendment will also permit the plan to allow the assignment of benefits under a court order or written agreement due to the breakdown of a marriage or common-law partnership, an assignment by a deceased individual's legal representative on distribution of the individual's estate and a surrender of benefits in order to avoid revocation of the plan. Plans may be administered as if the law has been passed. Once the law is passed, the plans will have to be amended accordingly.]

See page ii for explanation of footnotes.

[230] CCH ¶21,439; Sec. 147(2).

¶10,435

(6) Two different types of trustee are permitted; the trustee may be a Canadian trust company or the trustees may be at least three individuals resident in Canada. In the latter case, at least one trustee must be independent of the employer and not a shareholder.

(7) All income received, capital gains made, and capital losses sustained by the trust are to be allocated to beneficiaries under the plan within 90 days after the end of the trust year, unless they have been allocated in previous years.

(8) All amounts allocated or reallocated to a beneficiary must vest irrevocably in that beneficiary no later than the latter of either the time of allocation or reallocation, or the day on which the beneficiary completes a period of 24 consecutive months as a beneficiary under the plan, or under any other DPSP for which the plan can reasonably be considered to have been substituted.

(9) Each forfeited amount and earnings that can be reasonably attributed to the forfeited amount must be paid to participating employers or be reallocated to beneficiaries on or before December 31 of the year immediately following the calendar year in which the amount is forfeited, or such later time that the Minister permits it in writing.[231]

(10) The trustee must inform, in writing, all new beneficiaries of their rights under the plan.

(11) All amounts vested in each employee who is a beneficiary must become payable to the employee or, in the event of the employee's death, to a beneficiary designated by the employee or to the employee's estate, not later than the end of the year in which the employee attains 71 years of age (age 69 after 1996 and before 2007) and 90 days after the earliest of:

(a) the death of the employee;

(b) the day on which the employee ceases to be employed by a participating employer;

(c) the termination or winding-up of the plan.

The vested amount need not be paid in a lump sum. The plan may provide for the employee to elect one of two alternative methods of payment. One such method is equal instalments payable not less frequently than annually over a period of up to 10 years from the date the whole amount becomes payable. The other is that the employee may direct the trustees to purchase an annuity to commence no later than the end of the year in which the beneficiary turns 71 years of age (age 69 after 1996 and before 2007). This annuity may have a guaranteed term not exceeding 15 years (a DPSP

See page ii for explanation of footnotes.
[231] CCH ¶21,439aa; Sec. 147(2.2).

may also permit members to withdraw all or a portion of their vested interest in the plan while continuing in employment).

(12) No benefits or loans which are in any way conditional upon the existence of the plan can be extended to a beneficiary or to a person with whom the beneficiary was not dealing at arm's length.[232]

(13) The plan must require that none of the following can become a beneficiary:

(a) a person related to the employer;

(b) a specified shareholder of the employer or a corporation related to the employer or a person related to such specified shareholder;

(c) where the employer is a partnership, a person related to a member of the partnership; or

(d) where the employer is a trust, a person who is a beneficiary under the trust or is related to a beneficiary under the trust.[233]

In addition, there is a further requirement that the terms of the plan must be established such that the contribution limits will be met each year.[234]

[¶10,438] Acceptance of Employees Profit Sharing Plan as Deferred Profit Sharing Plan

If a profit sharing plan is accepted for registration, it is deemed to have become registered on the date on which the application for registration was made or at a later date specified in the application for the commencement of the plan.[235]

The Minister will not accept a plan for registration unless the trustee has allocated all capital gains and losses to the employees and other beneficiaries before making the application.[236] The trustee may request the Minister to determine the amounts that will be deemed to be such capital gains or losses.[237]

The plan is not an employees profit sharing plan while it is a deferred profit sharing plan.[238]

[¶10,441] Contribution Limits

All deferred profit sharing plans must comply with contribution limits.[239] If any of these limits are not met, the Minister may revoke the registration of the plan.[240]

See page ii for explanation of footnotes.

[232] CCH ¶21,439; Sec. 147(2).
[233] CCH ¶21,439; Sec. 147(2)(k2).
[234] CCH ¶21,439a; Sec. 147(2.1).
[235] CCH ¶21,449; Sec. 147(5).
[236] CCH ¶21,445, ¶21,447; Sec. 147(3), 147(4).

[237] CCH ¶21,501; Sec. 147(17).
[238] CCH ¶21,451; Sec. 147(6).
[239] CCH ¶21,450; Sec. 147(5.1).
[240] CCH ¶21,491; Sec. 147(14).

Three separate limits must all be met for a particular year. The first limit requires that the aggregate of the individual's "pension credit" for the year, as a result of the individual's membership in a DPSP, not exceed ½ of the "money purchase limit" for the year and 18% of the individual's "compensation" for the year.

The individual's pension credit for a calendar year in respect of a deferred profit sharing plan is the total of:

(a) all contributions made in the year to the plan by the employer in respect of the individual; and

(b) forfeited amounts under the plan in the year, including earnings thereon, that are reallocated in the year to the individual, unless they are paid out of the plan to the individual in the year.[241]

[For the 2002 and subsequent calendar years, excess DPSP employer contributions will be ignored for the purposes of determining an individual DPSP pension credit, provided the excess is refunded to the plan in the year or before the end of February of the following year. This December 20, 2002 draft technical amendment to the Regulations will provide relief where contributions made early in the year give rise to excess contributions when the employee goes on leave without pay or terminates employment later in the year.]

As described at ¶10,477, the 1996 Budget froze the money purchase limit at $13,500 from 1996 through the year 2002. The 2003 Budget then increased it to $15,500 for 2003, $16,500 for 2004, and $18,000 for 2005. As a result of the 2005 Budget, the limit was increased to $19,000 for 2006, $20,000 for 2007, $21,000 for 2008, and $22,000 for 2009, and, as a result of indexation after 2009, the limit is increased to $22,450 for 2010, $22,970 for 2011, and $23,820 for 2012.[242] For 1996 to 2012, the DPSP limit of one-half of the money purchase limit is:

1996 to 2002	$ 6,750
2003	$ 7,750
2004	$ 8,250
2005	$ 9,000
2006	$ 9,500
2007	$10,000
2008	$10,500
2009	$11,000
2010	$11,225
2011	$11,485
2012	$11,910
after 2012	indexed amount

See page ii for explanation of footnotes.

[241] Reg. 8301(2).　　　　　　　　　　　　[242] CCH ¶21,521f; Sec. 147.1(1) "money purchase limit".

¶10,441

"Compensation" generally means the amount required to be included in the individual's income.[243] It will therefore include all taxable benefits included in the individual's income for the year and exclude any deductible employment expenses. Compensation excludes a notional amount of remuneration that relates to a period when an individual is disabled or on an approved leave of absence, or for some other reason remuneration is otherwise reduced. By definition, compensation also excludes all amounts in respect of the individual's employment that relate to any period during which the individual was not resident in Canada and an amount was not attributable to the performance of duties of employment in Canada, unless the Minister accepts the amount to be included.

A special definition of compensation applies for the year in which an employee terminates employment.[244] In this circumstance, the employee's compensation can be based on the compensation for the immediately preceding year, if it is more than the compensation for the year of termination. By allowing the contributions limits to be based on the employee's compensation for the preceding year, excess contributions arising in the year of termination of employment do not result in adverse tax consequences. Beginning in 2003, this mechanism was repealed and replaced by a broader relief mechanism that applies not only to excess contributions arising from termination of employment but also to excess contributions arising from unpaid leave of absence. The revised mechanism, which applies to 2002 and subsequent taxation years, provides relief by allowing overcontributions to be ignored for purposes of the DPSP contributions limits, provided the excess is refunded to the plan in the year or before the end of February of the following year. For excess contributions arising from termination of employment occurring in 2002, employers will be entitled to use the old mechanism or the new refund mechanism.

The second overall limit applies to the individual's membership in all DPSPs of the employer or of an employer which does not deal at arm's length with the employer. The aggregate of all of the individual's pension credits under all DPSPs of the employer and of those employers that do not deal at arm's length with the employer cannot exceed $1/2$ of the "money purchase limit" for the year.

The third overall limit applies to the individual's "pension adjustment" for the year under all registered plans of the employer. This would have application, for example, where the individual is a member of the employer's registered pension plan in addition to the DPSP. The limit provides that the individual's pension adjustment for the year in respect of the employer and all employers that do not deal at arm's length with the employer cannot exceed the lesser of the money purchase limit for the year and 18% of the aggregate of the individual's compensation for the year from the employer or any other employer that does not deal at arm's length with the employer.

See page ii for explanation of footnotes.

[243] CCH ¶21,521c; Sec. 147.1(1) "compensation".   [244] CCH ¶21,450a; Sec. 147(5.11).

¶10,441

An individual's pension adjustment is basically the total of the individual's pension credits with respect to his or her membership in all DPSPs of a related employer group and membership in all registered pension plans of a related group.[245] For registered pension plans, the determination of the pension credit will depend on whether the plan is a money purchase (defined contribution) plan or a defined benefit plan. By including this third limit, it will be necessary for employers to coordinate the contributions made to all registered plans on behalf of their employees each year to ensure that the employee's overall pension adjustment for the year in respect of the employer does not exceed the specified limits. In addition, it will ensure that where an individual is employed by various members of a related group of companies in a particular year, the employee's aggregate pension adjustment for that year does not exceed the specified limits.

[¶10,444] Taxability of Trust

No Part I tax is payable by a trust on taxable income for a period during which the trust was governed by a deferred profit sharing plan.[246] The trustee must, however, file an annual return (Form T3D) together with financial statements.

A trust governed by a DPSP may be required to pay tax under other Parts of the Act. These are as follows:

(1) Part X (see ¶13,395) imposes a tax on non-qualified investment acquired by the trust.

(2) Part X.1 (see ¶13,455) imposes a tax on the trust where gifts are made to it after May 25, 1976 or where the trust accepts and retains contributions from a member of the plan in excess of $5,500 per year.

(3) Part X.2 (see ¶13,480) imposes a tax on registered investments in certain circumstances.

(4) Part X.I imposes a tax on foreign property.

(5) Part XI.1 (see ¶13,525) imposes a tax where property that was a qualified investment when it was acquired later ceases to be qualified, but the trust retains it.

Returns are required under each of these Parts but they consist of portions of the basic T3D return mentioned above.

[¶10,447] Deductibility of Employer Contributions

Contributions made by an employer to a trustee of a deferred profit sharing plan may be deducted in computing the income of the employer for a taxation year provided the following conditions are met:[247]

See page ii for explanation of footnotes.

[245] Reg. 8301(1).
[246] CCH ¶21,457; Sec. 147(7).
[247] CCH ¶21,463; Sec. 147(8).

(1) the contribution is made in the taxation year or within 120 days after the end of the taxation year;

(2) the contribution is made for the benefit of the employer's employees who are beneficiaries under the plan;

(3) the contribution is made in accordance with the terms of the plan as registered. In order for a plan to be registered as a deferred profit sharing plan, *inter alia*, its terms must ensure that the contribution limits described in ¶10,441 will be met each year; and

(4) the contribution was not deducted in the preceding taxation year.

Where the requirements respecting contribution limits are not satisfied for a particular calendar year, then the particular employer is not entitled to any deduction except to the extent expressly permitted by the Minister of National Revenue.[248] This rule prevents a deduction of employer deferred profit sharing plan contributions where the contributions are in fact made in accordance with the terms of the plan, but those terms are not adequate to ensure that the limits will be respected.

An amount contributed within the first 120 days in one taxation year may only be deducted in computing income for that year to the extent that it is not deducted in respect of the preceding year.

[¶10,453] Amounts Received Taxable

As a general rule, when the member of a deferred profit sharing plan (or his or her estate or beneficiary, in the case of his or her death) receives a distribution from the plan, the amount so received is included in income in the year of receipt.[249] This reflects the fact that as the employer made contributions and as income was earned in the trust no amount was taxable to the employee-member. There are, however, several exceptions to this general rule:

(1) The trust may distribute part of the member's entitlement in the form of shares of the employer company or a related company. When this is done, the member may elect to exclude from income in the year of distribution an amount representing the accrued but unrealized increase of the value of the shares over their cost amount.[250] When the shares are actually sold, or when the taxpayer ceases to be resident in Canada, the unrealized gain (the difference between the fair market value of the shares at the time of acquisition by the beneficiary over the cost amount of the shares) will be included in income.[251] A deduction of one-half of the amount so included is available,[252] so that the excess is being included in income at the capital gains inclusion rate.

See page ii for explanation of footnotes.

[248] CCH ¶21,469; Sec. 147(9).
[249] CCH ¶21,475; Sec. 147(10).
[250] CCH ¶21,476, ¶21,477; Sec. 147(10.1), 147(10.2).
[251] CCH ¶21,477b; Sec. 147(10.4).
[252] CCH ¶15,276; Sec. 110(1)(d.3).

¶10,453

(2) Where the plan was once an employees profit sharing plan, amounts that have previously been included in income that represent the taxpayer's contributions to the employees profit sharing plan, or that represent pre-1972 capital gains of the plan, are not included in income.[253]

(3) If the member has made contributions to the deferred profit sharing plan (permitted only before 1991), such contributions are not included in income.[254]

(4) Where the member so elects, the trustee may, instead of paying the member's entitlement to him or her, pay it over to a "licensed annuities provider" (e.g., an insurer) as the purchase price for an annuity.[255] The amount so used is not included in the member's income for the year; rather, the annuity payments are included in income as they are received. The guaranteed term of the purchased annuity, if any, cannot exceed 15 years.[256]

(5) The amount distributed can be transferred directly (without tax consequences) to an RRSP, a registered pension plan, or another deferred profit sharing plan for the individual's benefit.[257] [After March 20, 2003, the direct transfer ("rollover") rules are amended to allow:

(a) a transfer to be made from a DPSP to a RRIF;

(b) a transfer to be made on behalf of a former spouse or common-law partner of a deceased employee; and

(c) a transfer to be made on behalf of a spouse (or common-law partner) or former spouse (or common-law partner) of an employee or former employee, where the transfer relates to the division of property mandated under an order of a competent tribunal or by virtue of a written agreement and arising on the breakdown of their marriage or partnership.]

It should be noted that amounts received from a deferred profit sharing plan and included in the recipient's income lose their character as capital gains, dividends or interest as they pass through the trust and out to the recipient. While income of various kinds might have been taxed on a different basis or to a different extent if earned directly by a member of the plan, no special treatment is given to this income when it is distributed by the trust to the member. For example, if a member realized a capital gain of $100, only $1/2$ of this would be taxable; where a trust governed by a deferred profit sharing plan realizes such a gain and eventually distributes the $100 to the member, he or she includes the full $100 in income. Within limits, the election described in (1) above permits a flow-through of the character of unrealized capital gains.

---

[253] CCH ¶21,478; Sec. 147(11).
[254] CCH ¶21,479; Sec. 147(12).
[255] CCH ¶21,430a; Sec. 147(1) "licensed annuities provider".

[256] CCH ¶21,439; Sec. 147(2)(k).
[257] CCH ¶21,505; Sec. 147(19).

[¶10,456] Appropriation of Trust Property by Employer

If any funds or property of the trust are appropriated in any manner for the benefit of an employer making payments under the plan or to a non-arm's length corporation, the amount or value of such funds or property is to be included in computing the income of the recipient in the year of appropriation.[258] There are two exceptions to this rule:

(1) where a payment is made for treasury shares (subject to the restrictions noted below); and

(2) where the amount was repaid to the trust within one year from the end of the taxation year in which the appropriation was made and it is established by subsequent events or otherwise that the repayment was not made as part of a series of appropriations and repayments.

When a trust governed by a deferred profit sharing plan intends to purchase shares (especially those of an employer corporation), the following restrictions apply. The trust may not invest in shares of a corporation if 50% or more of the corporation's property consists of debt obligations,[259] and the shares must be qualified investments. Shares are qualified investments if they are listed in a stock exchange in Canada, or if they are shares of a public corporation. Furthermore, shares of an employer are a qualified investment if they are freely transferable and meet certain earnings and dividends tests.[260]

[¶10,459] Revocation of Registration

The Minister may revoke the registration of deferred profit sharing plans[261] where any of the following situations arises:

(1) the existing plan has been revised or amended in such a way that, following the revisions or amendments, the plan no longer complies with the requirements for a deferred profit sharing plan;

(2) a provision of the plan is not complied with;

(3) a benefit or loan is extended or continues to be extended as a consequence of the existence of the plan, which would be prohibited if the plan were required to be submitted for registration;

(4) an amount is transferred to another registered plan otherwise than by a direct transfer, or where the amount is deductible under various rollovers relating to inter-plan transfers;[262]

(5) the plan does not comply with registration requirements;

See page ii for explanation of footnotes.

[258] CCH ¶21,485; Sec. 147(13).
[259] CCH ¶21,439; Sec. 147(2)(d).
[260] CCH ¶25,534g; Sec. 204 "qualified investment".
[261] CCH ¶21,491; Sec. 147(14).
[262] CCH ¶8490, ¶8498, ¶8500; Sec. 60(j), 60(j.2).

(6) there has been a failure to comply with rules respecting loans or benefits to beneficiaries, or the rules prohibiting certain classes of persons from becoming beneficiaries;[263]

(7) requirements relating to contributions limits are not complied with; or

(8) there has been a failure to file an information return as required.[264]

Revocation may be made as of the day the cause for revocation arose or on any subsequent day.

[¶10,462] Revoked Plans

Special rules apply for the treatment of a revoked plan, as follows:[265]

(1) The revoked plan cannot be re-registered for at least one year after revocation.

(2) The trust governed by the plan will be subject to Part I tax on income for the taxation year where, *at any time in the year*, the plan was a revoked plan.

(3) The employer cannot deduct contributions made when the plan is a revoked plan.

(4) Beneficiaries continue to be taxable on distributions to the same extent that they would have been had the plan remained registered.

(5) The plan is deemed not to qualify as an employees profit sharing or a retirement compensation arrangement.

[¶10,465] Inadequate Consideration on Purchase from or Sale to a Trust

Where property of the trust governed by a deferred profit sharing plan is disposed of to a taxpayer for a price which is less than the fair market value at the time of the transaction, or where the trust acquires property from a taxpayer at a price in excess of its fair market value at the time of the transaction, the difference between the fair market value and the sale or purchase price, as the case may be, will be deemed to be a benefit received by the taxpayer at the time of the disposal or acquisition;[266] i.e., as if the taxpayer were a beneficiary under the deferred profit sharing plan.

Similarly, where the plan is a "revoked plan" at the time of the transaction, the above-mentioned difference is included in the taxpayer's income at the time of the disposal or acquisition.[267] In addition, the amount is taxable

---

See page ii for explanation of footnotes.

263 CCH ¶21,439; Sec. 147(2)(k), 147(2)(k.1), 147(2)(k.2).

264 CCH ¶21,439; Sec. 147(2)(k.1).

265 CCH ¶21,497; Sec. 147(15).

266 CCH ¶21,503; Sec. 147(18).

267 CCH ¶21,475, ¶21,497; Sec. 147(10), 147(15).

at a rate of 50% to be paid by the trust governed by the deferred profit sharing plan.[268]

[¶10,468] Transfers out of Deferred Profit Sharing Plan

After 1988, only direct transfers of lump-sum payments under a deferred profit sharing plan will qualify for transfer to a registered pension plan or another deferred profit sharing plan for the benefit of the beneficiary under the deferred profit sharing plan, or to a registered retirement savings plan under which the beneficiary of the deferred profit sharing plan is the annuitant. Failure to comply with these rules may result in the revocation of the plan.

[¶10,471] Registered Pension Plans

[¶10,474] Registration Requirements

A "registered pension plan" (RPP) means a pension plan that has been registered by the Minister for tax purposes, whose registration has not been revoked.[269] It should be noted that registration of a pension plan is not compulsory, but is required to obtain the maximum tax benefits. These include the deductibility of employer contributions in respect of individual employee-members of the plan within prescribed limits, the deductibility of employee contributions within prescribed limits, the exclusion from income of the benefit derived from the employer's contribution to the plan made on the employee-member's behalf, and the non-taxability of annual investment earnings under the plan.

There are two different types of RPPs: "defined benefit" and "money purchase" (defined contribution):

(1) *Defined benefit plans* guarantee a predetermined amount of retirement income based on a flat amount per year of service or a percentage of the employee's earnings over a defined period. The defined benefit RPPs are funded by actuarially determined contributions by the employee and/or employer.[270]

(2) *Money purchase plans* provide whatever pension income the contributed funds in the plan can purchase through the acquisition of an annuity. No predetermined amount of pension income is guaranteed under these plans. Benefits will depend upon the actual contributions, the investment return of the plan, and annuity rates at the date of purchase.[271] Beginning in 2004, money purchase RPPs are allowed to provide retirement benefits by way of RRIF-type payments (referred to as "variable benefits") to their

---

See page ii for explanation of footnotes.

[268] CCH ¶25,450; Sec. 201.

[269] CCH ¶28,235; Sec. 248(1) "registered pension plan".

[270] CCH ¶21,521d; Sec. 147.1(1) "defined benefit provision".

[271] CCH ¶21,521g; Sec. 147.1(1) "money purchase provision".

members instead of being restricted to the purchase of a life annuity from a licensed annuities provider.[272] The amount of variable benefits payable each year from the member's account must not be less than a minimum amount. The minimum amount is determined on the basis of the balance in the member's account at the beginning of each year and the attained age of either the member or the member's spouse or common-law partner.[273] These rules are similar to the minimum withdrawal rules that apply to RRIFs (see ¶10,414). An RPP becomes a revocable plan at the beginning of a calendar year if the total amount of variable benefits paid from a member's account in the year is less than the minimum amount for the account for the year.[274]

The registration requirements for both types of plans[275] are as follows:

(1) An application must be made by the plan administrator in prescribed manner and forwarded by registered mail.

(2) The plan must comply with the following prescribed conditions:[276]

  (a) the primary purpose of the plan must be to provide periodic payments to individual members after retirement and until death in respect of their service as employees;

  (b) the plan must not provide for any benefits other than benefits required by federal or provincial legislation governing pension plans, or various types of benefits prescribed by regulation;[277]

  (c) the plan must require the retirement benefits to commence no later than the end of the calendar year in which the member attains 71 years of age (age 69 after 1996 and before 2007), and such benefits must be paid no less frequently than annually. However, in the case of a defined benefit plan, the benefits can commence at a later time that is acceptable to the Minister if the total amount of benefits payable does not exceed the amount of benefits that would be payable if the benefits began at the end of the year in which the member turns 71 (age 69 after 1996 and before 2007). Furthermore, in the case of a money purchase plan (generally, a plan that replicates the payout allowed by a RRIF), the payments out of the plan can commence in the year in which the member turns 72 years of age;[278]

  (d) no rights of a person under the plan may be assigned or given as security, except as a result of the breakdown of the marriage/common-law partnership or the death of the person;

See page ii for explanation of footnotes.

[272] Reg. 8506(1)(e.1).
[273] Reg. 8506(5)–(6).
[274] Reg. 8506(4).
[275] CCH ¶21,523; Sec. 147.1(2).

[276] Reg. 8501.
[277] Reg. 8503.
[278] Reg. 8502(e).

(e) the amounts determined for an individual member's pension adjustment and past service pension adjustment must be appropriate having regard to the requirements of the regulations;[279]

(f) the plan must meet regulatory requirements respecting defined benefit provisions[280] under which an employee's current service contributions are restricted to the lesser of:

(i) 9% of the employee's compensation for the year from a participating employer, and

(ii) $1,000 plus 70% of the employee's pension adjustment for the year,

and past service payments by a member are allowed up to an amount that is reasonably necessary to fund past service benefits;

(g) the plan must meet regulatory requirements respecting money purchase provisions[281] under which the employer contributions are to be set at a minimum level acceptable to the Minister (1% for a stand-alone money purchase plan);

(h) there must be no reason, based on the plan documents, to expect that the plan will become a revocable plan or that conditions regarding past service benefits will not be complied with; and

(i) there must be no reason to expect that the plan will become a revocable plan due to the fact that, contrary to regulations, it allows employees to convert a salary or a retiring allowance to an employer-funded past service contribution or that it does not meet pension adjustment limits.

Certain other conditions apply only to defined benefit provisions of a plan. The more important conditions include:

(a) Restriction on employee contributions (see (f) above).

(b) Restriction on the maximum lifetime retirement pension benefits that may be provided to a member. The restriction at the time the pension commences is defined to be the lesser of: (i) 2% of average best earnings times the number of years of service; and (ii) the defined benefit limit for the year of commencement.[282] The defined benefit RPP limit is $1,833 for 2004, $2,000 for 2005, $2,111 for 2006, $2,222 for 2007, $2,333 for 2008, $2,444 for 2009, $2,494.44 for 2010, $2,552.22 for 2011, $2,646.67 for 2012, and indexed to average wage growth thereafter.

(c) Restrictions on the benefits that may be accrued in respect of persons "connected with an employer". A "person connected with an

---

See page ii for explanation of footnotes.

[279] Reg. 8300.
[280] Reg. 8503(4)(a), Reg. 8503(4)(c).
[281] Reg. 8506(2)(a).
[282] Reg. 8504(1).

employer" means a person who owns not less that 10% of the issued shares of any class (may be voting or non-voting) of the capital stock of the employer or of any corporation related to the employer, is related to the employer, or is a "specified shareholder" of the employer (person carrying on a personal services business).[283]

(d) The maximum normal term of retirement benefit shall be a 66²/₃% last survivor annuity with a 5-year guarantee or for a single person, a single life annuity guaranteed 15 years.

(e) The maximum benefit for years of pre-1990 pensionable past service credited after 1989 shall be restricted to $1,150 per year.

(f) A member's pension entitlement can be indexed to inflation subject to certain limits both before and after the time the pension commences.[284]

The effective date of registration is January 1 of the calendar year in which the application was filed, unless the plan actually commenced at a later date in the calendar year, in which case the effective date will be the date of commencement.[285]

Whenever an amendment is to be made to the plan, the details of the amendment must be provided to the Minister by way of an application in prescribed manner by the plan administrator.[286] The Minister may impose any reasonable additional conditions with respect to registered pension plans as may be considered necessary.[287]

[¶10,475] Phased Retirement

Beginning in 2008, employers are allowed to offer qualifying employees up to 60% of their accrued defined benefit pension while they continue to accrue additional benefits under the plan.[288] The 60% limit is based on the amount of pension benefits (including bridging benefits) that would be paid from the plan if the employee were fully retired. There is no requirement that the partial pension be based on a reduction in work time or that there be a corresponding reduction in salary. As a result, qualifying employees will be able to receive up to 60% of their accrued pension benefits while continuing to work, part-time or full-time, as well as continuing to accrue benefits for that work.

Employers may also offer stand-alone bridge benefits to qualifying employees while they continue to be employed by a participating employer. When the employee ceases employment, the employer may continue paying stand-alone bridge benefits, if payment of the lifetime retirement benefits has started. Unlike bridge benefits, which are retirement benefits that are

---

See page ii for explanation of footnotes.

[283] CCH ¶28,273; Sec. 248(1) "specified shareholder"; Reg. 8500(3).

[284] Reg. 8504(1)(b), Reg. 8504(5)(b), Reg. 8504(6).

[285] CCH ¶21,523; Sec. 147.1(2)(b).

[286] CCH ¶21,525; Sec. 147.1(4).

[287] CCH ¶21,525a; Sec. 147.1(5).

[288] Reg. 8503(16)–(25).

payable for a predetermined period and generally after payment of the lifetime retirement benefits has started, stand-alone bridge benefits are payable, subject to certain conditions, even when payment of lifetime retirement benefits has not started.

Current rules that enable benefits to accrue for periods of absence or reduced pay do not apply to employees who receive phased retirement benefits and continue to accrue further benefits under the plan.

To qualify for phased retirement benefits, employees must be:

- at least 60 years of age; or
- at least 55 years of age and eligible for a pension that is not reduced because of their age, pensionable service, or a combination of both their age and pensionable service.

Phased retirement benefits are not permitted under a designated plan, or to an employee who was at any time connected with a participating employer.

There are no restrictions on when, or how often, an employee's accrued pension amount can be recalculated to take into account the employee's additional pensionable service and increased annualized earnings (if any) during a period of simultaneous benefit accrual and pension payment. Employers are not prevented from limiting participation to specific employees under the plan terms.

Since this tax measure is not mandatory, it is up to employers to decide whether to amend the defined benefit pension plan to provide this benefit to all or some of their employees.

[¶10,477] Pension Adjustment Limits

Compliance with the rules respecting pension adjustment limits[289] ensures that contributions made to, and the benefits accrued under, employer-sponsored registered plans do not exceed the overall limits for tax-assisted retirement savings.

For any particular taxation year, the pension adjustment of an individual, which is basically the aggregate of the pension credits of an individual in respect of an employer) may not exceed the lesser of the "money purchase limit" for the year and 18% of the member's compensation for the year. The money purchase limit was $13,500 for 1996 to 2002, $15,500 for 2003, $16,500 for 2004, $18,000 for 2005, $19,000 for 2006, $20,000 for 2007, $21,000 for 2008, and $22,000 for 2009. As a result of indexation to the average wage increases after 2009, the limit is increased to $22,450 for 2010, $22,970 for 2011, and $23,820 for 2012.[290]

See page ii for explanation of footnotes.

[289] CCH ¶21,528; Sec. 147.1(8).   [290] CCH ¶21,521f; Sec. 147.1(1) "money purchase limit".

A member's "compensation" [291] for the year includes all income from employment including taxable benefits included in income for the year, less any deductible employment expenses. Compensation also includes certain prescribed amounts, and excludes all amounts relating to a period during which the individual was not resident in Canada and not attributable to the performance of duties of employment in Canada, unless the Minister accepts the amount to be included.

The purpose of the pension credit is to measure the benefit that has accrued to the individual in the year as a result of his or her membership in the plan. For a deferred profit sharing plan of an employer, the individual's pension credit for a calendar year is basically the aggregate of the contributions made by the employer in respect of the individual and the forfeited amounts allocated to the individual in the year, including related earnings.

For a money purchase provision of a registered pension plan (RPP), the individual's pension credit in respect of an employer for a calendar year is basically equal to the aggregate of:

(a) the contributions made to the plan by the employer in respect of the individual;

(b) contributions made by the individual (other than amounts transferred directly from another RPP, a registered retirement savings plan (RRSP), or a deferred profit sharing plan (DPSP)); and

(c) amounts allocated to the individual in the year that are attributable to forfeited amounts, to surplus under the money purchase provision, or to surplus transferred from a defined benefit provision [or, for 1999 and subsequent taxation years, to surplus transferred to the money purchase provision from another money purchase provision].

Forfeited amounts (and earnings thereon) and surpluses allocated will not, however, be included in the calculation where the amount was included in determining the individual's pension credit in respect of any other employer who participates in the plan, where the amount had been paid to the individual in the year. Forfeited amounts transferred directly to another RPP, RRSP, or deferred profit sharing plan in the year allocated are deemed not to be paid to the individual.[292] In this way, they will be included in the calculation of the individual's pension credit in the year of allocation.

For purposes of calculating the individual's pension credit for a calendar year in respect of the plan, contributions made by the employer to the plan in respect of an individual after the end of the calendar year and before the last day of February in the year following that relate to services provided by the individual in the calendar year will be considered to have been made in the calendar year.

See page ii for explanation of footnotes.

[291] CCH ¶21,521c; Sec. 147.1(1) "compensation".   [292] Reg. 8301(4).

Under a defined benefit plan, the calculation of the pension credit in respect of an employer is more complicated and is based on a formula designed to calculate the amount of benefits accruing to the individual based on the defined benefit amount in the plan. This formula is generally nine times the "benefit entitlement", less $600.[293]

The individual's benefit entitlement under a defined benefit provision of a registered pension plan in respect of an employer for a calendar year is defined to mean that portion of the individual's benefit accrual for the year that can reasonably be attributed to the individual's employment with the employer. In other words, it measures the amount of retirement benefits that accrued in respect of the individual's employment in the year.[294] The "benefit accrual" of an individual in respect of a calendar year is the individual's "normalized pension" as defined below.

Where the benefits under the defined benefit provision of the pension plan are offset by benefits under a deferred profit sharing plan or a money purchase provision of the plan, the amount may be reduced by $1/9$ of the individual's pension credit for the year in respect of the deferred profit sharing plan or money purchase provision.

An employee's benefit entitlement under a defined benefit RPP is limited to the greater of: (1) $1,722.22 for the 1996 to 2003 pension credit years, $1,833 for 2004, $2,000 for 2005, $2,111 for 2006, $2,222 for 2007, $2,333 for 2008, $2,444 for 2009, $2,494.44 for 2010, $2,552.22 for 2011, $2,646.67 for 2012, and indexed to average wage growth thereafter; and (2) $1/9$ of the money purchase limit for the year. Because these increases in the defined benefit limit after 2003 are caused by increases in the money purchase limit announced in the 2003 and 2005 Budgets, they are excluded in determining an individual's past service pension adjustments (PSPAs). This will ensure that no PSPA will be required to be reported for members whose benefits are increased simply as a result of the increases to the defined benefit limit.

The "normalized pension" [295] of an individual means the amount of lifetime benefits that would be payable to the individual immediately after the end of the year if certain assumptions are made. These include:

(a) the individual had attained age 65;

(b) immediate vesting of benefits under the defined benefit provisions;

(c) no reduction for early retirement;

(d) the individual's remuneration in other years was the same as for the current year;

---

[293] Reg. 8301(6).
[294] Reg. 8302(2).
[295] Reg. 8302(3).

¶10,477

(e) no reduction to lifetime retirement benefits when a plan member is receiving public disability benefits, workers' compensation, and accident, sickness, or disability insurance benefits; and

(f) no adjustment to lifetime retirement benefits payable to a member while the member is receiving remuneration from a participating employer.

The pension adjustment of the member, in respect of all employers who do not deal at arm's length with the employer, cannot exceed the money purchase limit for the year. This ensures that overall limits cannot be circumvented on the transfer of an employee from one employer to another employer in a related group. The limits also apply to multi-employer plans.[296]

[¶10,480] Past Service Benefits

Restrictions apply to the amount of past service benefits that may be provided in respect of periods after 1989.[297] In order for the rules relating to past service benefits to apply, a "past service event" must occur. A past service event is any transaction, event, or circumstance after 1989 that results in a retirement benefit being provided in respect of a period before the time of the transaction, event, or circumstance, or where the method of determining retirement benefits provided under a defined benefit provision of the plan is amended before the time of the transaction, event, or circumstance.[298] Examples of a past service event are a retroactive increase of benefits and the crediting of pensionable service with another registered pension plan from a previous employer.

Before a past service benefit may be paid to a member of a pension plan after 1989, certain conditions must be met. Where the individual member is alive at the time of the past service event, the Minister must certify that prescribed conditions are met. The only prescribed condition for certification is that the member has sufficient unused RRSP deduction room to accommodate the past service benefits.[299] Specifically, the "past service pension adjustment" (PSPA) associated with the past service event cannot exceed:

(a) the total of:

(i) $8,000;

(ii) the member's "unused RRSP deduction room" at the end of the year immediately preceding the calendar year of the past service event;

(iii) the member's qualifying withdrawals for purposes of the certification, as of the calendar year;

[296] CCH ¶21,529; Sec. 147.1(9). [298] Reg. 8300(1) past service event.
[297] CCH ¶21,530; Sec. 147.1(10). [299] Reg. 8307(2).

(iv) the member's PSPA withdrawals for the calendar year; plus

(v) for calendar years after 1997, the Pension Adjustment Reversal (PAR) in the calendar year for the member's termination from DPSP or RPP in the particular year;

minus

(b) the aggregate of all amounts, each of which is the accumulated PSPA of the member for the year with respect to the employer.

Where the individual's RRSP deduction room is deficient by more than $8,000, the individual will be allowed in certain situations to make a special withdrawal from his RRSP to create sufficient room. The amount withdrawn must be designated as such for purposes of obtaining the certification and this is done by filing a prescribed form with the Minister. Certain conditions must be met before the withdrawal will qualify.[300]

The past service benefit is measured by the provisional past service pension adjustment which basically represents the difference between the pension adjustment otherwise calculated for the member in respect of the plan and what the pension adjustment would have been if the improved benefits had been provided at the earlier time. As the pension adjustment reduces the individual's RRSP contribution limit for a particular year, the individual must have sufficient unused RRSP contribution room in respect of those years to which the past service benefit relates in order for the past service benefit to be paid. If the individual contributes an amount in excess of his unused RRSP contribution room, he or she could be subject to penalty tax.

It should be noted that, for years prior to 1996, an $8,000 margin was provided to each individual over eighteen whereby excess RRSP contributions can be made before the penalty tax applies. This corresponds to the $8,000 inclusion in (a)(i) above. Therefore, in the simplest case prior to 1996, a past service benefit could be paid to the extent the past service pension adjustment did not exceed the individual's unused RRSP contribution room (which could be restored by special RRSP withdrawals referred to above) by more than $8,000.

The calculation of cumulative excess amounts in respect of RRSPs was amended for 1996 and subsequent taxation years. The formula no longer provides an $8,000 margin, but provides only a $2,000 margin to each individual over eighteen, whereby excess RRSP contributions can be made before penalty tax applies. In addition, the formula no longer deducts PSPAs from the amount for the year. Therefore a PSPA will not cause RRSP contributions to become subject to the penalty tax in the year in which the PSPA arises. However, PSPA will reduce the unused RRSP deduction room that is carried forward and so will be taken into account for penalty tax

See page ii for explanation of footnotes.
[300] Reg. 8307(4).

¶10,480

purposes in subsequent years. Refer to the detailed discussion of tax on cumulative excess amounts in respect of RRSP contributions after 1990 at ¶13,455.

[¶10,483] Revocation of Registration

The conditions under which the registration of a pension plan may be revoked[301] include the failure:

(a) to comply with the prescribed conditions of registration;

(b) of the administrators of the plan to administer the plan in accordance with its terms as registered;

(c) to meet the conditions specified in the Act and the regulations which result in the plan becoming a revocable plan (see ¶10,474);

(d) to comply with a condition imposed by the Minister of National Revenue;

(e) to pay past service benefits or make past service contributions contrary to prescribed conditions;

(f) of the administrator to satisfy the requirements and obligations of his or her position;

(g) of the plan administrator or participating employer to file an information return relating to the plan or a member of the plan as and when required by regulation;

(h) of the plan administrator to file an actuarial report relating to the plan as and when required by regulation; and

(i) to receive approval for the registration of a plan under the applicable federal or provincial pension benefits legislation or where registration under the same is subsequently revoked.

Where any of these conditions applies, the Minister may revoke the pension plan. The first step of revocation is to send a "notice of intent" to the plan administrator by registered mail. The notice will contain a proposed date of such revocation.

[¶10,486] Employer Contributions

To be deductible, an employer's contribution to an RPP must be made in the year to which the deduction is to apply or within 120 days after the end of that taxation year.[302] Contributions made in the 120-day period which are in excess of the deduction limit for the preceding year may be deductible in the year in which they are made if the deduction limit for the year is not exceeded.

See page ii for explanation of footnotes.

[301] CCH ¶21,531; Sec. 147.1(11).   [302] CCH ¶21,541; Sec. 147.2(1).

In addition to the timing requirement of the contribution, the contribution must also meet other requirements which will depend on whether the contribution is being made under a money purchase or defined benefit provision of the plan, or under a specified multi-employer plan.

(1) *Money purchase provision.* In the case of money purchase provisions, the amount of the employer's contribution is effectively limited by the pension adjustment limits discussed at ¶10,477. The employer's contribution must be made in accordance with the plan as registered.

(2) *Defined benefit provision.* In order for an employer's contribution under a defined benefit provision of a registered pension plan to be deductible, three conditions must be met:

(a) it must be an "eligible contribution".[303] An "eligible contribution" includes a contribution prescribed by Regulation[304] or a contribution recommended by an actuary and approved by the Minister;

(b) the contribution must be made to fund benefits to employees and former employees of the employer in respect of the period before the taxation year; and

(c) the contribution must comply with requirements relating to the funding of past service benefits (see ¶10,474).

(3) *Specified multi-employer plans.* For contributions made to a "specified multi-employer" plan, the contribution made must be in accordance with the plan as registered and in respect of periods before the end of the taxation year. This includes compliance with pension adjustment limits with respect to plan members. For a specified multi-employer plan, the pension credit in respect of a member under a defined benefit provision of the plan is determined on a similar basis as a money purchase provision, in that the pension credit is calculated as the aggregate of contributions made by the employee and by the employer rather than based on the defined benefit formula.

A specified multi-employer plan is a plan that is established pursuant to a collective bargaining agreement, under which the employers deal at arm's length, contributions to the plan are based on a negotiated formula, and the board of trustees who have ultimate control over the pension plan are not controlled by any of the employers.[305]

[¶10,489] Employee Contributions

An employee's contributions[306] to a plan may represent contributions made after 1990 for current service and for past service in respect of years after 1989, contributions for past service before 1990 while the employee was not a contributor to the plan, and contributions for past service while

---

See page ii for explanation of footnotes.

303 CCH ¶21,542; Sec. 147.2(2).
304 Reg. 8514.
305 Reg. 8510.
306 CCH ¶21,544a; Sec. 147.2(4).

the employee was a contributor to the plan. Subject to the specific limits, a taxpayer may make a deductible contribution under any or all of the above.

Employee contributions in respect of service after 1989 or prescribed eligible contributions are deductible to the extent they are in accordance with the plan as registered. Note that this rule applies for all service after 1989 regardless of whether it is for current service or for past service, whether the contribution is optional or voluntary, or whether the contribution is made under a defined benefit or money purchase provision of the plan. For the purpose of this rule, prescribed eligible contributions refer to certain employee contributions that are made under a defined benefit provision pursuant to an arrangement under which members of the plan make contributions towards an unfunded liability under the plan.[307]

The employee's contributions must be made in the year in respect of which the deduction is deemed. Amounts paid after the year cannot be deducted for that year. By limiting the deduction to the amount permitted under the plan as registered, the amount an employee may contribute will be subject to the various registration requirements. These registration requirements will have the general effect of limiting contributions by:

(a) limiting the amount of employee contributions in respect of defined benefits. A member's current service contribution may not exceed the lesser of 9% of the member's compensation and $1,000 plus 70% of the member's pension adjustment in respect of the employer for the year;

(b) limiting the pension adjustment of each member; and

(c) limiting the benefits that can be paid.

For years of past service in which the employee was not a contributor to the plan, the deductible contribution is limited to the least of:

(a) the amount of contributions (other than an additional voluntary contribution) made in the year or a preceding year before 1990, minus deductions previously claimed;

(b) $3,500; and

(c) $3,500 for each year of service before 1990, minus deductions previously claimed.

"Additional voluntary contributions" is defined[308] to mean contributions made by the employee under a money purchase provision of a registered pension plan on an optional basis and that will be used to provide money purchase benefits. After 1986, additional past service contributions are no longer allowed and their deductibility is denied. Disallowed contribu-

---

See page ii for explanation of footnotes.

[307] Reg. 8501(6.1), Reg. 8501(6.2). [308] CCH ¶28,005; Sec. 248(1) "additional voluntary contribution".

tions could be returned to the contributor before 1991 without tax but will be taxed if returned after that date.[309]

For contributions made in respect of years of service before 1990 where the employee was a contributor to the plan, the maximum deduction that may be claimed is limited to the lesser of:

(a) the amount of the contributions made by the individual in the year or a previous year in respect of years of service prior to 1990 (other than additional voluntary contributions, prescribed contributions or the aggregate of contributions eligible for deduction in respect of service before 1990 while not a contributor) less the amounts deducted in respect of those contributions in previous years; and

(b) the amount by which $3,500 exceeds the aggregate of deductions claimed in respect of service after 1989 or before 1990 while not a contributor.

Where a taxpayer dies after 1992, past services contributions which he or she was unable to deduct prior to death, because of the above $3,500 annual limits, can generally be deducted on death, whether or not he or she was a contributor in past years.[310] In both cases, for the purposes of determining the amounts that can be deducted with respect to past service contributions in the year in which a taxpayer dies and for the preceding year, the $3,500 annual limits are disregarded.

[¶10,490] Letters of Credit

For defined benefit plans, the *Pension Benefits Standards Act, 1985* and the Pension Benefits Standards Regulations, 1985, require solvency deficits to be funded over five years. However, in the 2006 federal Budget, the government proposed temporary measures to provide solvency funding relief in response to "difficult circumstances". Specifically, the solvency funding payment was extended to 10 years with letters of credit; that is, employers were permitted to extend the period for making solvency funding payments to 10 years when the difference between the 5-year and 10-year level of payments was secured by a letter of credit. In the event of default, the financial institution issuing the letter of credit would pay the amount to the plan.

The use of letters of credit in this manner and any payment by the issuer of the letter of credit to the plan will not give rise to adverse tax consequences. In particular, an amount paid to a registered pension plan by the issuer of a letter of credit issued in connection with an employer's funding obligations under a defined benefit provision of the plan is deemed to be an eligible contribution made to the plan by the employer.[311] This deeming rule ensures that the employer can deduct the amount of the

---

See page ii for explanation of footnotes.

[309] Vivian, 95 DTC 291, Vivian, 95 DTC 664.   [311] CCH ¶21,545f; Sec. 147.2(7).
[310] CCH ¶21,545a; Sec. 147.2(6).

¶10,490

payment, and that the payment is an eligible contribution to the plan (see ¶10,486).

[¶10,492] Transfers

Where lump-sum amounts are transferred from RPPs to other RPPs or RRSPs or RRIFs, the transfers take place on a tax-free basis. The amounts must be transferred directly from one plan to another, and only the transfers of lump-sum amounts are allowed.[312]

Where an amount is transferred in accordance with these rules, that amount is deemed not to be included in any taxpayer's income, and no deduction can be made in respect of the transfer to the transferee plan. Thus, the transferred amount "rolls over" from the transferor plan to the transferee plan, and is allowed in addition to the usual contribution limits for RPPs and RRSPs. Where an amount is transferred between registered plans on behalf of a taxpayer and the transfer does not comply with the rules, then the excess portion that is not transferred in accordance with the rules is deemed to have been paid to the taxpayer (and therefore included in the taxpayer's income), and the taxpayer is deemed to have paid the amount as a contribution to the transferee RPP or RRSP. In the case of a transferee RRIF, the taxpayer is deemed to have paid the amount as a contribution to an RRSP. In such cases, the transferred amounts to the new plans are subject to the usual RPP and RRSP contribution limits, i.e., the taxpayer's "RRSP deduction limit" is decreased correspondingly, and if the amounts so transferred exceed the taxpayer's RRSP deduction limit, Part X.1 tax may be payable on such excess. Some relief for excess transfers may be offered (see the discussion below under "Withdrawal of excessive transfers to RRSPs and RRIFs" at ¶10,493).

These rules permit the following direct transfers:

(a) the transfer of lump-sum amounts from one money purchase RPP to another money purchase RPP, to an RRSP, or to a RRIF;

(b) the transfer of lump-sum amounts from a money purchase RPP to a defined benefit RPP;

(c) the transfer of lump-sum amounts from one defined benefit RPP to another defined benefit RPP;

(d) the transfer of lump-sum amounts from a defined benefit RPP to either a money purchase RPP, to an RRSP, or to a RRIF;

(e) the transfer of actuarial surplus from a defined benefit RPP to a money purchase RPP;

(f) the transfer of actuarial surplus from a money purchase RPP to another money purchase RPP, when the second plan replaces the

See page ii for explanation of footnotes.
[312] CCH ¶21,551; Sec. 147.3; Interp. Bul. IT-528.

benefits of all or a significant number of the member of the first plan; and

(g) the transfer of a lump-sum amount from an RPP to another RPP, an RRSP, or a RRIF for the benefit of the spouse or a former spouse of a plan member, where the spouse or common-law partner or former spouse or common-law partner is entitled to the amount pursuant to a court order or written agreement relating to a division of property on breakdown of the marriage or common-law partnership.

Finally, lump sum proceeds received by an individual on a plan member's death after March 3, 2010 can be rolled over into the RDSP of a financially dependent infirm child or grandchild if the contribution from the rollover:

• complies with existing RDSP contribution rules and the $200,000 RDSP contribution limit;

• is not made before July 2011; and

• does not exceed the amount of the proceeds previously included in the individual's income.

For deaths occurring after 2007 and before 2011, transitional rules will allow for a contribution to be made to the RDSP of a financially dependent infirm child of the deceased plan member that would provide a result that is generally equivalent to the above measures. For more details, see ¶10,430.

[¶10,493] Withdrawal of Excessive Transfers to RRSPs and RRIFs

Relief from double taxation is granted where amounts are transferred from an RPP to an RRSP or RRIF in excess of the amounts permissible.[313] An individual on whose behalf an excess transfer has been made to an RRSP or RRIF, and who withdraws the excess or another amount from an RRSP or RRIF, may claim a deduction in respect of the withdrawn amount to offset the income inclusion resulting from the withdrawal. The deduction is equal to the lesser of the following two amounts:

(1) the total amount of withdrawals included in the taxpayer's income for the taxation year from RRSPs and RRIFs,

minus the total of:

(a) "prescribed withdrawals" (i.e., amounts withdrawn by an individual from an RRSP that result in the individual being able to acquire past service benefits for 1990 and later years);

(b) deductions claimed in a taxation year for a "refund of premiums" from an RRSP, a RRIF, or the purchase of an annuity;[314] and

---

See page ii for explanation of footnotes.
[313] CCH ¶21,555a; Sec. 147.3(13.1).   [314] CCH ¶8510; Sec. 60(*l*).

¶10,493

(c) deductions claimed in the taxation year for the withdrawal of excess RRSP premiums; and[315]

(2) the total of all amounts for the current and all preceding taxation years, each of which is an "excess transfer" (as described below) from an RPP to an RRSP or a RRIF,

minus the sum of:

(a) the deductions claimed for the withdrawal of excessive transfers to RRSPs and RRIFs for preceding taxation years; and

(b) the deduction claimed for RRSP contributions in respect of the deemed RRSP premiums arising as a result of excess transfers.

An "excess transfer" is an amount in respect of a transfer from an RPP to an RRSP or a RRIF that is deemed to be a premium paid to an RRSP (see the discussion above).

[¶10,494] RPP Annuity Contracts

Individuals may acquire ownership of annuity contracts in satisfaction of their entitlement to benefits under an RPP on a tax-deferred basis.[316] This might occur, for example, where a plan discharges its benefit obligations with respect to an individual either by transferring ownership of an existing annuity contract held in connection with the plan to the individual or by purchasing an annuity contract under which the individual is both the annuitant and the owner. Under these circumstances, the individual is deemed not to have received an amount from the RPP as a result of acquiring the annuity, and any amounts received under the contract are deemed to be amounts received under the RPP. As a consequence, there is no immediate taxation on acquisition of the annuity and any payments under the contract are included in the recipient's income in the year in which they are received. In order for this mechanism to apply, the following conditions must be met:

(1) the rights provided for under the annuity contract are not materially different from those provided for under the RPP;

(2) the annuity contract does not provide for any further premiums to be paid after it is acquired by the individual; and

(3) at the time of acquisition of an RPP annuity contract, the registration of the plan is not revocable. However, the Minister of National Revenue has the authority to ignore the fact that the registration of the plan is revocable, and it is expected that he would do so where there is no connection between the cause of the plan being revocable and the benefits being provided by way of the annuity.

See page ii for explanation of footnotes.

[315] CCH ¶21,325; Sec. 146(8.2).   [316] CCH ¶21,557; Sec. 147.4(1).

These deeming rules do not apply where an individual acquires an interest in an annuity contract by way of a transfer to an RRSP or RRIF. In such cases, the rules governing inter-plan transfers at ¶10,492 apply.

Where an individual acquires ownership of an annuity contract under an RPP otherwise than in accordance with these rules, the individual is considered to have received a payment in kind from the RPP and is required to include the value of the contract in income. The following is an example of an RPP annuity acquisition that does not satisfy the conditions for the deeming rules to apply.

Example:

> On retirement, Catherine, a member of a defined benefit RPP, is entitled to an indexed pension of $20,000 a year. Catherine's RPP gives her the option of either transferring the value of her benefits to a locked-in RRSP or acquiring from a life insurance company an indexed annuity of $20,000 a year. Catherine elects the annuity option, but foregoes the indexing in exchange for additional lifetime annuity payments of $5,000 a year (an option that was not provided for under her RPP). The deeming rules do not protect the acquisition of the annuity contract since it provides for rights that are materially different from those provided under the RPP.

If the rights provided for under the annuity contract are materially altered as a result of an amendment to the contract, the individual with an interest in the contract immediately before the amendment is deemed to have received an amount from a pension plan equal to the fair market value of that interest and is required to include this amount in income.[317] This rule does not apply to an amendment that:

(a) defers the commencement of the annuity to no later than the end of the year in which the annuitant turns 71 (age 69 after 1996 and before 2007); or

(b) enhances benefits under an annuity contract in connection with the demutualization of an insurance corporation that is considered to have been a party to the annuity contract.

As long as the rights provided for under a replacement annuity contract are not materially different from those provided for under the original contract, the replacement contract is considered to be the same contract as the original contract.[318] As a result, any annuity payments received under the replacement contract will be treated as superannuation or pension benefits.

[¶10,495] Individual Pension Plans

IPPs are defined benefit RPPs set up for as few as one member. In some instances, taxpayers have set them up to transfer the commuted value of

---

See page ii for explanation of footnotes.

[317] CCH ¶21,558; Sec. 147.4(2).   [318] CCH ¶21,559; Sec. 147.4(3).

¶10,495

their pension and create a large pension surplus that does not require withdrawals under the existing tax rules applicable to RPPs, thus allowing an IPP member to defer tax for a longer period than is generally possible for other RPP members or RRSP annuitants. To correct this inequity, 2011 budgetary changes now require minimum withdrawals from IPPs, similar to the rules for RRIFs. The requirement for these RRIF-like withdrawals apply to the 2012 and subsequent taxation years. For those IPP members who reached 71 years of age in 2011 or earlier, the required withdrawals will start in 2012. For those IPP members who attain 71 years of age after 2011, the required withdrawals will start in the year in which they attain 71 years of age.

An IPP member's ability to have past service recognized under an IPP may have also created an unfair tax advantage to the extent that the amount required to fund past service in an IPP could be much greater than the amount required to reduce RRSP assets or accumulated RRSP contribution room. For that reason, changes introduced in the 2011 Budget now require that the cost of past service under an IPP must first be satisfied by transfers from all existing RRSP assets or from a reduction of accumulated RRSP contribution room before new past service contributions are permitted. The requirement for past service contributions applies to contributions made after March 22, 2011.

For the purpose of these rules, an IPP means a defined benefit RPP with three or fewer members, if at least one member is related to the participating employer. A defined benefit RPP will also fall within the ambit of these rules if at least 50% of the total PAs of plan members in a year belong to individuals who are connected to the employer or who are highly compensated employees (called a "designated plan") and there are reasons to believe that the rights of one or more members under the plan exist primarily to avoid the application of these rules.

[¶10,496] Pooled Registered Pension Plans

[¶10,497] Introduction of New Rules

On November 17, 2011, the Minister of Finance tabled Bill C-25, *Pooled Registered Pension Plans Act*. This Bill sets up the framework to create and administer PRPPs. This type of plan is a new vehicle which will allow individuals to participate in a defined contribution pension plan.

Then on December 14, 2011, the Department of Finance released draft income tax legislation, regulations, and explanatory notes regarding PRPPs for comment. These will be new measures that will set the stage for the provinces to introduce complementary legislation allowing for the implementation of PRPPs. Generally, the current rules for RPPs and RRSPs are to be amended to accommodate PRPPs.

As noted in the Backgrounder accompanying the draft legislation, the key elements of the proposed PRPP tax rules are summarized below:

- An eligible PRPP administrator will be defined as a corporation resident in Canada that is licensed to administer a PRPP under the PRPP legislation of Canada or the similar legislation of a province.

- There will be no employer-employee relationship required for participation in a PRPP. This will permit employees whose employer has no involvement with a plan, as well as self-employed individuals, to participate in a PRPP.

- Contributions to a PRPP made by employers, employees, and self-employed individuals will generally be deductible for tax purposes. All PRPP contributions for a year made by and on behalf of a PRPP member will be limited to the member's available RRSP contribution limit for the year.

- To help prevent situations where large employer contributions might create overcontributions for a PRPP member in relation to the member's RRSP limit, annual employer contributions to a PRPP in respect of an employee will be limited to a maximum of the RRSP dollar limit for the year, unless the employee directs the employer to contribute more than this amount.

- Employers will be permitted to make direct contributions to a PRPP in respect of an employee, which will be excluded from salaried compensation (like employer contributions to an RPP). Immediate vesting of employer PRPP contributions will be required. There will be no requirement for an employer to make a minimum contribution to a PRPP. Since PRPP contributions will be made under a member's available RRSP limit, there will be no requirement for an employer to report pension adjustments in respect of employer and employee contributions, as is required in respect of employer and employee contributions to an RPP.

- There will be no "qualified investment" rules for PRPPs. Instead, some general rules will apply to ensure that investments are reasonably diversified and do not present risks of self-dealing. For large PRPPs, the administrator will be required to avoid intentionally acquiring investments in which a member has a significant interest. They will also be required to take reasonable precautions to avoid concentrating more than 10% of plan assets in a particular business (or non-arm's length group of businesses). Since there are no legislated restrictions on the size of a PRPP, small PRPPs (generally those with fewer than 10 unrelated employers participating) will be required to comply with those two rules, and to avoid holding investments in participating employers in connection with the PRPP.

¶10,497

- The existing transfer rules for defined contribution RPPs (governing transfers between RPPs and between an RPP, an RRSP, a RRIF, and certain other registered plans), with some exceptions, will generally apply to a PRPP.

- Pension payment or decumulation options will be limited to those currently available to defined contribution RPPs (that is, the purchase of a life annuity for the member, the transfer of the member's PRPP account funds to an RRSP or RRIF, or the payment of variable benefits (RRIF-type payments) from the member's PRPP account).

- A deceased PRPP member's spouse or common-law partner will be permitted to become a successor PRPP member, taking over ownership of the deceased member's PRPP account funds and making ongoing decisions in respect of those funds as a member of the plan. Alternatively, a surviving spouse or common-law partner will be permitted to transfer the funds to his or her own RRSP, RRIF, PRPP account, or RPP account, or to use the funds to acquire a qualifying annuity. These latter options (plus the option of transferring the funds to a Registered Disability Savings Plan (RDSP) to the extent RDSP contribution room is available) will also be permitted for an infirm financially dependent child or grandchild of the deceased member.

[¶10,500] Employee Benefit Plans

[¶10,501] Deferred Employment Compensation

The Act contains rules directed toward employment compensation arrangements under which a payment is made by an employer to someone other than an employee for the purpose of providing benefits to the employee in the future. Without these rules, a payment could, in certain circumstances, be made to a trustee for the benefit of an employee, and the employer could obtain an immediate deduction for the payment, but, the employee would not be required to include that amount in income until the amount was actually received.

The rules are directed toward ensuring that the employer does not obtain a deduction for income tax purposes as a result of such a payment until an equivalent amount is included in the employee's income. These rules do not apply to plans specifically provided for in the Act such as RPPs, sickness and accident plans, deferred profit sharing plans, employee profit sharing plans, and vacation pay trusts.

[¶10,502] Employee Trusts

"Employee trust" is defined[319] to mean an arrangement under which payments are made to a trustee to provide benefits to employees or former employees if:

(1) the benefits payable do not depend on the position, performance, or compensation of the employee;

(2) the trustee has each year allocated to employees the full amount received from the employer plus any income earned by the trust; and

(3) the trustee has elected to qualify the trust as an employee trust.

Employer contributions to an employee trust will be deductible by the employer in the year made. As a result of the allocations made by the trustee, each employee will include in income the amount allocated to him or her in the year.[320] The trust itself will not be subject to tax.[321] The employee need not actually receive any portion of the amount allocated to him or her for a particular year. When amounts allocated to an employee in one year are in fact paid in a later year, the employee will not pay tax in that later year on the amounts actually paid.

[¶10,504] Employee Benefit Plans

"Employee benefit plan" is defined to mean an arrangement under which contributions are made by an employer to a custodian and under which payments are to be made for the benefit of employees or former employees.[322] Specifically excluded from the definition of an employee benefit plan are those plans described in ¶10,501. An employer may not deduct a contribution made to an employee benefit plan.[323] Rather, when contributions made by the employer to the plan are actually distributed by the plan to employees or to the heirs or legal representatives of employees or former employees, the employer may claim a deduction at that time.[324] The employee includes in income amounts actually received from the employee benefit plan.[325]

[¶10,507] Salary Deferral Arrangements

[¶10,510] Receipt of Benefits from Salary Deferral Arrangements

Salary deferral arrangement rules[326] effectively prevent the tax-free deferral of compensation. When an amount is deferred, the employee is deemed to receive a benefit by virtue of his or her employment and the

---

See page ii for explanation of footnotes.

[319] CCH ¶28,086; Sec. 248(1) "employee trust"; Interp. Bul. IT-502.
[320] CCH ¶2374; Sec. 6(1)(h).
[321] CCH ¶13,170; Sec. 104(6).
[322] CCH ¶28,085; Sec. 248(1) "employee benefit plan"; Interp. Bul. IT-502.

[323] CCH ¶4852bb; Sec. 18(1)(o).
[324] CCH ¶5726; Sec. 32.1.
[325] CCH ¶2372, ¶2670; Sec. 6(1)(g), 6(10).
[326] CCH ¶2680–2682; Sec. 6(11)–(13); Interp. Bul. IT-529.

value of the benefit (the amount deferred) is included in computing income from employment for the year. The employer is permitted a corresponding deduction for the deferred amount provided the amount is included in the employee's income. This achieves a matching of income and expense. See Chapter II.

[¶10,513] Life Insurance Policies

[¶10,516] Proceeds of Life Insurance Policy

Complex rules govern the computation of income to be reported by a taxpayer on the disposition of an interest in a life insurance policy, other than a life insurance policy which is effected as a RRIF. This income is measured at any particular time by the excess of proceeds received by the policyholder over the cost up to that time. Income accruing on certain life insurance policies and on annuity contracts must also be reported.

A policyholder must include in income, in respect of a disposition of certain life insurance policies, the amount by which the proceeds of disposition of an interest in that policy exceeds the adjusted cost basis of the interest to the policyholder.[327] A life insurance policy includes an annuity contract and a segregated fund contract. However, policies issued pursuant to an RRSP, an income averaging annuity contract, or a DPSP, and an annuity contract purchased with the proceeds of an RRSP received as a refund of premiums by a surviving spouse or common-law partner over 69 years of age or by a child that was dependent by virtue of physical or mental infirmity are specifically excluded from the income inclusion. The disposition of a term certain annuity contract is subject to the same rules.

A tax-free rollover is available on the transfer of an interest in a life insurance policy (other than annuity contract) in certain circumstances. A tax-free rollover can be obtained only if the policy insures the life of the transferee, a child of the transferee, or a child of the policyholder. An interest in a life insurance policy (other than an annuity contract) is deemed to be disposed of for proceeds to its adjusted cost basis if it is transferred to the policyholder.[328]

The transfer of a life insurance policy or an annuity contract to a spouse/common-law partner or former spouse/common-law partner may be made on the same tax basis as the transfer of capital property. An *inter vivos* transfer of a life insurance policy (including an annuity contract) will result in a disposition for proceeds equal to the adjusted cost basis of the policy, unless the transferor elects otherwise in the year of transfer.[329] Effective January 1, 2001, the tax treatment available to a "spouse" or "common-law spouse" is extended to all couples, regardless of sex, who have lived

See page ii for explanation of footnotes.

[327] CCH ¶21,571; Sec. 148.
[328] CCH ¶21,604; Sec. 148(8).
[329] CCH ¶21,605; Sec. 148(8.1).

together in a conjugal relationship for a continuous period of at least one year or, failing that, who are both parents of the same child.[330] Rollover treatment is also provided with respect to dispositions to a spouse/common-law partner as a consequence of death, unless an election is made in the tax return of the deceased spouse or common-law partner for the year of death.[331]

Lump-sum proceeds on death under a life annuity and non-life annuities are now covered under the general rules concerning disposition of life insurance policies on death. See ¶10,519. The Act also sets out certain additional circumstances in which a life insurance policy or annuity is deemed to have been disposed of.[332]

[¶10,519] Proceeds of Disposition and Adjusted Cost Basis

The terms "disposition", "proceeds of disposition", and "adjusted cost basis" are very specifically defined. "Disposition" is defined to include a surrender, a dissolution of interest on maturity, a disposition of interest by operation of law, a policy loan made after March 31, 1978, and lump-sum proceeds from a life annuity contract entered into after November 10, 1978 and before November 13, 1981.[333]

Where the insured, under an exempt life insurance policy, has a total and permanent disability, the exercise of a right to convert the policy into an annuity contract will not constitute a disposition of the policy.

The term "proceeds of disposition" [334] includes the deemed proceeds and is also specifically defined to mean the amount of any policy loan made after March 31, 1978, limited to the balance of cash surrender value. Upon surrender or maturity of the policy, any remaining excess of the cash surrender value (excluding the segregated fund portion) over the amount of an unpaid policy loan or premiums is treated as proceeds. However, applicable to transactions after December 20, 1991, where any amount in respect of a policy surrender or policy loan is automatically applied to pay a premium under the policy, such amount is not included in the proceeds of disposition. Interest paid or credited by life insurance companies to policyholders on accumulated policy dividends is taxable in the hands of the policyholder as is interest credited in respect of prepaid premiums, proceeds on deposit, delayed payment of claims, and other amounts held on behalf of policyholders.

The "adjusted cost basis" of an interest in a policy means the amount, if any, by which the aggregate of:[335]

(a) previous costs of acquisition;

See page ii for explanation of footnotes.

[330] CCH ¶28,047a; Sec. 248(1) "common-law partner".

[331] CCH ¶21,606; Sec. 148(8.2).

[332] CCH ¶21,567; Sec. 148(2).

[333] CCH ¶21,615; Sec. 148(9) "disposition"; Interp. Bul. IT-430R3.

[334] CCH ¶21,620a; Sec. 148(9) "proceeds of the disposition".

[335] CCH ¶21,611; Sec. 148(9) "adjusted cost basis".

¶10,519

(b) premiums previously paid (including interest paid on policy loans, except to the extent such interest was deductible, and any non-refundable premium, but excluding costs that relate to accidental death and disability benefits and to certain additional risks);

(c) amounts previously reported as income in respect of a disposition of an interest in the policy (other than any segregated fund portion);

(d) amounts included in income in respect of an interest in the policy;

(e) previous repayments of policy loans to the extent included in loans payable on proceeds of disposition, except to the extent deductible;

(f) any excess of the cash surrender value of the policy at its first anniversary date after March 31, 1977 over the adjusted cost basis as at that date, computed under the former definition of adjusted cost basis and without reference to the special provision which applied to policies held at October 22, 1968;

(g) the portion of an annuity payment to a non-resident that was subject to withholding tax;

(h) amounts previously included in the taxable income earned in Canada in the case of a non-resident; and

(i) the mortality gain, as determined by regulation, in respect of a life annuity contract that is subject to the income accrual rules or, in respect of a life insurance policy (other than an annuity contract), that is subject to the rollover provisions in respect of the transfer of an interest in a life insurance policy to the spouse or common-law partner on the death of the policyholder;

exceeds the aggregate of:

(j) previous proceeds of disposition (including deemed proceeds in respect of a transfer by the insurer from non-segregated to segregated funds);

(k) amounts deducted in respect of an interest in the policy;

(l) the amount of any policy loan payable at March 31, 1978;

(m) previous deductions in respect of the capital element of annuity payments;

(n) the net cost of pure insurance at the end of each calendar year of a life insurance policy acquired after December 1, 1982 that is not an annuity contract;

(o) annuity payments made after 1982 in respect of annuity contracts which are subject to the income accrual rules; and

¶10,519

(p) the mortality loss, as determined by regulation in respect of life annuity contracts acquired before December 2, 1982, where annuity payments did not start before that date.[336]

[¶10,522] Income from Disposition

An income inclusion may arise where a portion of a life insurance policy is acquired or an annuity contract is disposed of. This rule does not apply to a deemed disposition arising as a result of an entitlement to a policy dividend or to a policy loan.

The adjusted cost basis for that part of the policy or annuity that is disposed of is the proportion of the adjusted cost basis of the entire policy that the proceeds of disposition are of the accumulating fund before the disposition.[337]

Where an insurance policy is acquired after December 1, 1982, its conversion into an annuity triggers a disposition with proceeds equivalent to cash surrender value.[338]

[¶10,525] Interest, Dividends and Capital Gains from a Segregated Fund

The segregated fund of an insurer means all or any part of the insurer's reserves which vary in amount depending upon the fair market value of a specified group of assets. The Act provides for a flow-through of taxable dividends, interest, capital gains, and foreign tax in respect of amounts allocated to a policyholder from a segregated fund, in the same manner as a trust.[339]

A dividend tax credit is provided for, which permits a deduction to be made by an individual of $13^1/_3$% of the total grossed-up amount of taxable dividends received.[340] See ¶8275. The Act also provides for a foreign tax deduction for taxes paid to the government of a country other than Canada.[341]

[¶10,530] Eligible Funeral Arrangements (EFAs)

[¶10,535] Tax Exemption

Income on prepaid funeral or cemetery expenses under an eligible funeral arrangement is allowed to accrue on a tax-free basis. "Eligible funeral arrangement" means an arrangement established with any person licensed or authorized under provincial law to provide funeral or cemetery services[342] under which the total of all contributions made for the purpose

---

See page ii for explanation of footnotes.

[336] CCH ¶21,567, ¶21,611; Sec. 148(2), 148(9).
[337] CCH ¶21,580; Sec. 148(4).
[338] CCH ¶21,593; Sec. 148(6).
[339] CCH ¶21,593; Sec. 148(6).

[340] CCH ¶10,003, ¶19,200; Sec. 82(1), 121.
[341] CCH ¶19,700; Sec. 126.
[342] CCH ¶21,654; Sec. 148.1(1) "eligible funeral arrangement".

of funding funeral or cemetery services for each individual beneficiary does not exceed:

(a) $15,000 for an arrangement that covers only funeral services;

(b) $20,000 for an arrangement that covers only cemetery services; and

(c) $35,000 for an arrangement that covers both funeral and cemetery services.[343]

The funeral director or cemetery operator may establish a formal trust to hold prepayment of funeral or cemetery expenses, or may simply hold them as custodian.[344] The funeral director or cemetery operator need not be the trustee or custodian. In either case, contributions to the plan by the beneficiary are not deductible. However, funds in the plan may earn income (typically interest). The income will not be taxed while the plan is in force.[345]

[¶10,540] Distribution out of an EFA

When the funds in an EFA are used to pay for the funeral or cemetery services of an individual, the money that is paid out to the funeral or cemetery provider is included in that person's income at that time as business income. If there is more money in the fund than is required for these services, the excess will be refunded to the individual's estate. Similarly, if the arrangement is cancelled, there will be a distribution to the taxpayer. If there is any payment out of the plan for anything other than the provision of funeral or cemetery services, there will be an income inclusion to the recipient.[346] The amount that the recipient must include in income on a refund from an EFA is the lesser of the amount received and a second amount determined by the formula: A + B - C where:

A is the balance in the EFA immediately before the refund;

B is the total of all payments from the fund immediately before that time for funeral or cemetery services for the individual; and

C is the total of the relevant contributions to the individual's EFA before that time.

For the purpose of the description of C, an amount is defined to be a "relevant contribution" in respect of a particular EFA account if:

- the amount was contributed to the particular EFA account otherwise than by way of transfer from another EFA account, or

- the amount was contributed to another EFA account (otherwise than by way of transfer) and subsequently transferred (either from the

---

See page ii for explanation of footnotes.

[343] CCH ¶21,652, ¶21,655; Sec. 148.1(1) "cemetery services", 148.1(1) "funeral or cemetery services".

[344] CCH ¶21,653; Sec. 148.1(1) "custodian".

[345] CCH ¶21,659; Sec. 148.1(2).

[346] CCH ¶21,660; Sec. 148.1(3).

original or a subsequent EFA account) to the particular EFA account.[347]

This means that the inclusion in the income of the taxpayer is equal to the lesser of the amount received and an amount which generally represents the income accumulated in the EFA account. If the amount received by the taxpayer is greater than the amount included in the taxpayer's income, the excess generally represents a non-taxable refund of relevant contributions (represented by the variable C in the formula).

[With effect from December 20, 2002, the description of C will be amended by pending technical amendments (released July 16, 2010) so that its value is reduced, in effect, by any relevant contributions previously transferred from the EFA account to another EFA account. This ensures that the amount of the transferred relevant contribution (which can be distributed from the recipient EFA account tax-free) cannot also be used to support a subsequent tax-free withdrawal from the transferor EFA account. In addition, for transfers made after December 20, 2002, the amount transferred from one EFA account to another EFA account of the same or another person is deemed to be a distribution from the transferor account and a contribution made (otherwise than by way of transfer) under the recipient account. Consequently, the transferred amount will be included in computing the income of the deemed recipient (to the extent it does not exceed the income accumulated in the transferor account) and its earnings portion will not be taxed again when it is distributed from the recipient account.]

As cemetery care trusts are irrevocable under provincial law, any growth in those trusts need not be considered for purposes of the income inclusion to the taxpayer, so that any transactions with or balances under such a trust are ignored for the purpose of the above calculation.

Example:

> The EFA of an individual had a balance of $9,300. The individual had contributed $8,000 and after the payment of funeral services of $8,500, the individual's estate received $800. The formula would include $800 in the income of the estate calculated as follows:
>
> The lesser of:
>
> > (a) amount received ($800); and
>
> > (b) the total of:
>
> > > (i) the balance in the fund before the refund ($800)

See page ii for explanation of footnotes.

[347] CCH ¶21,658; Sec. 148.1(1) "relevant contribution".

plus

(ii) all payments from the EFA for funeral services or cemetery services ($8,500)

less

(iii) all contributions to the EFA ($8,000).

(b) is therefore equal to: $800 + $8,500 - $8,000 = $1,300

This formula ensures that the taxpayer will include in income only that portion of the investment income that is not used to pay for funeral or cemetery services. If the funeral services in the above example had cost $7,000, the estate would have received a refund of $2,300, of which $1,300 would have been taxable.

Income calculated under these rules is considered to be income from property.[348]

---

[348] CCH ¶4377e; Sec. 12(1)(z.4).

Chapter XI

Tax Exemptions

Tax-Exempt Individuals **11,000**
Foreign Government
Employees, Families and
Servants 11,010
Tax-Exempt Organizations ... **11,050**
Municipal Authorities 11,100
Municipal, Provincial, or
Federal Corporations 11,200
Agricultural Organizations,
Boards of Trade, and
Chambers of Commerce 11,300
Registered Charity 11,400
Association of Universities
and Colleges of Canada 11,500
Low-Cost Housing
Corporations for the
Aged 11,552
Labour Organizations 11,564
Non-Profit Organizations 11,565
Mutual Insurance
Corporations 11,566
Limited Dividend Housing
Company 11,567
Pension Corporation 11,568
Small Business Investment
Corporation 11,569
Farmers' and Fishers'
Insurers 11,570
Non-Profit Corporation for
Scientific Research and
Experimental
Development **11,574**
Tax Exemption 11,575
Deductions and Election 11,576
Gifts as Income 11,577
Information Returns 11,578
Acquisition of Control 11,579
Tax-Exempt Trusts **11,580**
Types of Tax-Exempt Trusts ... 11,580a

Pension Trust 11,581
Master Trust 11,582
Trust Governed by Eligible
Funeral Arrangement 11,583
Cemetery Care Trust 11,584
Registered Education
Savings Plans 11,585
Amateur Athlete Trusts 11,586
Trusts Providing
Compensation 11,587
Registered Retirement
Income Funds 11,588
Vacation-With-Pay Trusts 11,589
Qualifying Environmental
Trusts 11,590
Social Environmental Trusts 11,595
Special Rules **11,597**
Capital Gains Not Included
in Income of Certain
Exempt Groups 11,598
Investment Income of
Certain Clubs 11,600
Apportionment Rule for
Exemption Purposes 11,603
Acquisition or Loss of Tax-
Exempt Status 11,609
Charities **11,612**
Registered Charity 11,615
Charitable Organizations in
General 11,618
National Arts Service
Organization 11,620
Income of Registered
Charities 11,621
Charitable Organizations —
Related Business 11,624
Charitable Organizations —
Political Activities 11,625

Charitable Organizations —
Disbursements to Other
Charities and
Accumulation of Property 11,627

Charitable Organizations —
Disbursement
Requirements 11,628

Charitable Organizations —
Revocation of
Registration 11,630

Charitable Organizations —
Revocation Tax 11,631

Charitable Organizations —
Intermediate Sanctions 11,632

Charitable Foundations in
General 11,633

Charitable Foundations —
Revocation of
Registration 11,636

Charitable Foundations —
Disbursement Quotas 11,639

Charitable Foundations —
Political Activities 11,640

Private Foundations —
Excess Corporate
Holdings Regime 11,643

Accumulation of Property 11,645

Registered Charity —
Returns 11,648

Recent Changes

Foreign Charitable Organizations as Qualified Donees

The ability of foreign charitable organizations that are the recipient of a gift from Her Majesty in right of Canada to obtain "qualified donee" status is restricted in the 2012 Budget to only such organizations that carry on activities in at least one of the following areas: disaster relief, urgent humanitarian aid, or activities in the national interest of Canada. These rules will come into effect on January 1, 2013. If granted, the qualified donee status will be valid for a 24-month period that includes the time at which Her Majesty in right of Canada has made the gift to the foreign organization. Foreign charitable organizations that have received qualified donee status before 2013 will continue to be qualified donees until the expiration of their qualifying period. See ¶11,618.

Charities' Political Activities

Effective January 1, 2013, a charity that funds a qualified donee for the purpose of enabling it to pursue political activities will be required to count that donation against its own allowable limits for political activities. Failure to comply with this new requirement may trigger intermediate sanctions, such as monetary penalties or a one-year suspension of receipting privileges, as well as revocation of registration. These 2012 Budget proposals were implemented by Bill C-38, the *Jobs, Growth and Long-term Prosperity Act*, which received Royal Assent on June 29, 2012. See ¶11,625, ¶11,633, and ¶11,640.

Corporations Owned by Public Bodies Performing Governmental Functions

In its 2012 Budget, the government announced its intention to proceed with the previously announced tax exemption for any corporation, commission, or association, at least 90% of the capital of which was owned by a public body performing a governmental function in Canada. The CRA took the initiative of applying this tax exemption retroactively to May 8, 2000. See ¶11,200.

[¶11,000] Tax-Exempt Individuals

[¶11,010] Foreign Government Employees, Families and Servants

Officers and servants of governments of countries other than Canada whose duties require them to reside in Canada are not taxable in Canada if:

(a) immediately before assuming such duties they resided outside Canada;

(b) that country grants similar privileges to Canadian officers or servants of the same class;

(c) they were not at any time engaged in a business or employment in Canada other than their government position; and

(d) they were not, during the period, Canadian citizens.[1]

Family members residing with the persons described above or servants employed by them will also be exempt from Canadian tax if:

(a) the foreign country grants similar privileges to family members and servants of Canadian officials abroad who are of the same class;

(b) in the case of family members, they were not at any time lawfully admitted to Canada for permanent residence;

(c) in the case of servants, immediately before their duties as servants of the persons described above, they resided outside Canada;

(d) they have not, at any time in the period, engaged in business or been otherwise employed in Canada; and

(e) they were not, during the period, Canadian citizens.

It should be noted that only officers or servants of the government of a country qualify. An employee of a state, province, territory, or other political subdivision of a country would not be exempt from tax under the above rule.

[¶11,050] Tax-Exempt Organizations

[¶11,100] Municipal Authorities

No tax is payable by a municipality in Canada or a municipal or public body performing a function of government in Canada.[2] This includes school district bodies, rural and unorganized district bodies, as well as incorporated municipalities.

[¶11,200] Municipal, Provincial, or Federal Corporations

Any corporation, commission, or association or wholly owned subsidiary of such a corporation, commission, or association, at least 90% of the

---

[1] CCH ¶21,723, ¶21,725; Sec. 149(1)(a), 149(1)(b).   [2] CCH ¶21,731; Sec. 149(1)(c).

capital of which is owned by a Canadian municipality, a provincial government, or the federal government is exempt from tax.[3]

The exemption does not apply where a person other than the federal government, a province, or a municipality has the right to acquire shares or capital of the corporation, commission, or association.[4] Where a land trading company sold its shares to a municipality that wanted the company's land inventory, and later sold the inventory to the city, the company's profit on the sale of the land was exempt.[5]

To prevent a situation where effective control could be in the hands of another entity or combination of entities, the tax exemption is granted to:

(a) a corporation, commission, or association if 100% of its shares (except directors' qualifying shares) or capital are owned by a provincial government or the federal government;[6]

(b) a corporation, commission, or association if 90% of its shares (except directors' qualifying shares) or capital are owned by a provincial government or the federal government;[7]

(c) a wholly owned corporation subsidiary to a corporation, commission, or association all of the shares (except directors' qualifying shares) or capital of which are owned by a provincial government or the federal government, as well as any wholly owned corporation that is a subsidiary to such a wholly owned subsidiary;[8]

(d) a corporation, commission, or association if not less than 90% of its shares (except directors' qualifying shares) or capital are owned by a provincial government or the federal government, a corporation, commission, or association that is tax-exempt under (a), a wholly owned corporation subsidiary to such corporation, commission, or association, or one or more municipalities in combination with any such entity;[9]

(e) a corporation all the shares (except directors' qualifying shares) or capital of which are owned by a corporation, commission, or association or by one that is, itself, exempt under (a) to (d);[10]

(f) a corporation, commission, or association not less than 90% of the capital of which is owned by one or more Canadian municipalities [after May 8, 2000, a shareholder under this test also includes any public body performing a function of government in Canada if the income of the corporation, commission, or association from activities carried on outside the geographical boundaries of the municipalities [or public bodies performing a function of government] does

---

[3] CCH ¶21,733; Sec. 149(1)(d).
[4] CCH ¶21,810d; Sec. 149(1.1).
[5] [Enterprises Chelsea Ltée., 70 DTC 6379.
[6] CCH ¶21,733; Sec. 149(1)(d).
[7] CCH ¶21,733a; Sec. 149(1)(d.1).
[8] CCH ¶21,733b; Sec. 149(1)(d.2).
[9] CCH ¶21,733c; Sec. 149(1)(d.3).
[10] CCH ¶21,733d; Sec. 149(1)(d.4).

¶11,200

not exceed 10% of its total income for the relevant period, subject to certain geographical limitations;[11] or

(g) a wholly owned subsidiary of a corporation, commission, or association referred to in (f).[12]

In computing the entity's income earned outside the geographical boundaries of the municipality [or any public body performing a function of government] that owns the corporation, commission, or association described in (f) and (g), one does not include income from activities carried on pursuant to an agreement in writing with the federal government, a provincial government, or a municipality [municipal or public body]. For this purpose, the Tax Court of Canada held that a bylaw enacted under the Saskatchewan's *Northern Municipalities Act* was an agreement in writing with the Saskatchewan government that entitled a municipal corporation to a tax exemption on the income earned outside its geographical boundaries.[13] Furthermore, the income from activities carried on in a province by an entity, as a producer of electrical energy or natural gas or as a distributor of electrical energy, heat, natural gas, or water is not included in the determination, where those activities are regulated under the laws of the province.[14]

Ninety per cent of the capital of a corporation referred to in (f) that has issued share capital is considered to be owned by one or more municipalities [or public bodies performing a function of government after May 8, 2000] only if the municipalities [or public bodies performing a function of government after May 8, 2000] are entitled to at least 90% of the votes associated with the shares of the corporation.[15] For taxation years ending after December 20, 2002, this anti-avoidance provision is reinforced to the extent that it deems a corporation referred to in (f) to lose its tax-exempt status if, at any time during the period it has issued shares, it becomes controlled directly or indirectly in any manner whatever by a private sector taxpayer.

The 100% and, in some cases, 90% capital ownership test referred to above can be met through combined ownership. For example, where the federal government and a provincial government each owns 50% of the shares of a corporation, the taxable income of the corporation will be exempt by virtue of item (a).

The proposed amendment that would extend the ownership test in (f) to any public body performing a function of government in Canada after May 8, 2000 puts an end to the incertitude that resulted from conflicting case law as to whether an Indian band may be considered a municipality.[16] As a result of this amendment, a corporation, commission, or association not less than 90% of the capital of which is owned by a band earning 90% or

---

See page ii for explanation of footnotes.

[11] CCH ¶21,733e; Sec. 149(1)(*d*.5).

[12] CCH ¶21,733f; Sec. 149(1)(*d*.6).

[13] Sakitawak Development Corporation, 2009 DTC 1025.

[14] CCH ¶21,810e; Sec. 149(1.2).

[15] CCH ¶21,810f; Sec. 149(1.3).

[16] Otineka Development Corporation Limited, 94 DTC 1234, Tawich Development Corporation, 2001 DTC 5144.

¶**11,200**

more of its income on a reserve would be exempt from income tax if it qualifies as a "public body performing a function of government in Canada".

Given the intent of the Department of Finance to make these amendments retroactive to May 9, 2000, it is the CRA's administrative position that any entity that would, under the proposed legislation, be considered to be a public body performing a function of government may now qualify for the tax exemption.

[¶11,300] Agricultural Organizations, Boards of Trade, and Chambers of Commerce

The taxable income of an agricultural organization, a board of trade, or a chamber of commerce is exempt from tax if no part of its income is payable to or otherwise available for the personal benefit of any proprietor, member, or shareholder.[17] In computing the part, if any, of any income of the exempt organization that is payable to, or otherwise available for the personal benefit of any person, the amount of income is to be determined by excluding the amount of any taxable capital gains.[18]

An agricultural organization, board of trade, or chamber of commerce that is exempt from tax is required to file an information return if the organization has received dividends, interest, rentals, or royalties in excess of $10,000 in a fiscal period, or if the total assets of the organization exceed $200,000 at the end of the immediately preceding fiscal period.[19] Once an organization has been required to file an information return in respect of a fiscal period, it will be required to file returns for all subsequent periods. The information return is to be filed within six months of the end of the fiscal period.

[¶11,400] Registered Charity

A registered charity is exempt from Part I tax.[20] In general terms, a "registered charity" is a charitable organization or a charitable foundation that has been registered with the Minister. For commentary on registered charities, see ¶11,615.

[¶11,500] Association of Universities and Colleges of Canada

The income of the Association of Universities and Colleges of Canada is exempt from tax.[21]

[¶11,552] Low-Cost Housing Corporations for the Aged

A corporation constituted exclusively to provide low-cost housing for the aged is exempt from tax.[22] In order to be eligible for the exemption,

---

See page ii for explanation of footnotes.

[17] CCH ¶21,735; Sec. 149(1)(e). [20] CCH ¶21,737; Sec. 149(1)(f).
[18] CCH ¶21,811; Sec. 149(2). [21] CCH ¶21,771; Sec. 149(1)(h.1).
[19] CCH ¶21,868; Sec. 149(12). [22] CCH ¶21,773, ¶21,811; Sec. 149(1)(i), 149(2).

¶11,300

no part of the corporation's income may be payable to or otherwise available for the benefit of any proprietor, member, or shareholder. In computing the part, if any, of any income that is payable to or otherwise available for the personal benefit of any person, the amount of income is to be determined by excluding the amount of any taxable capital gains.

[¶11,564] Labour Organizations

Labour unions, lodges, fraternal organizations, and benevolent orders or societies are exempt from Part I tax. However, benevolent or fraternal organizations do not benefit from the exemption in respect of taxable income derived from carrying on a life insurance business. Thus, where the assets in the life insurance fund created by a fraternal benefit society had exceeded what was necessary for the purpose of its life insurance business, only the investment income earned on the necessary amounts was taxable.[23] Taxable income from carrying on a life insurance business includes income derived from the sale of property used or held in the course of carrying on that business. Such taxable income is to be computed as though the organization had no income or loss from any other source.[24]

[¶11,565] Non-Profit Organizations

Non-profit clubs, societies, or associations that are not registered charities (see ¶11,615) are exempt if:

(1) they are organized and operated exclusively for such community endeavours as service clubs, rotary clubs, lodges, golf clubs, tennis clubs, fishing clubs, etc.; and

(2) no part of the income of the association is payable to or otherwise available for the personal benefit of any proprietor, member, or shareholder, unless the proprietor, member, or shareholder was a club, society, or association, the primary purpose of which was the promotion of amateur athletics in Canada. In determining income for the purposes of this requirement, the amount of income is to be determined by excluding the amount of any taxable capital gains or any allowable capital losses.[25]

This exemption covers community endeavours, service clubs, etc. For example, a partnership selling beer in a community and distributing all profits for charitable, educational, etc., purposes was held tax-exempt.[26] It should be noted, however, that the charter of the club or organization, as well as the provisions of the Act under which it was organized, should be carefully examined. Thus, the taxpayer's letters patent, general by-law, and its profit and loss results supported its claim that it was a non-profit organization exempt from tax. The taxpayer's high level of commercial activity and large stabilization reserve did not prove that the taxpayer was being operated

---

See page ii for explanation of footnotes.

[23] ACTRA Fraternal Benefit Society, 97 DTC 5243.

[24] CCH ¶21,787, ¶21,817, ¶21,823; Sec. 149(1)(k), 149(3), 149(4).

[25] CCH ¶21,789, ¶21,811; Sec. 149(1)(l), 149(2); Interp. Bul. IT-496R.

[26] Bégin, 62 DTC 1099.

for profit.[27] However, a taxpayer's argument that the interest earned on its short-term deposits and on a small bond were tax-exempt as part of its operating income as a non-profit organization was untenable, considering that its golf and other recreational operations did not constitute a business or a source of income and its investment activities were not part of a separate business.[28] An association, whose primary purpose was to promote amateur sport, did not qualify as a registered Canadian amateur athletic association, since it only operated on a provincial level. It was not a charitable organization because its objective did not constitute a charitable purpose or activity.[29]

A tax-exempt non-profit organization (NPO) is required to file an information return (Form T1044) if:

(a) the total of all amounts received or receivable in the fiscal period by the NPO for taxable dividends, interest, rentals, or royalties is more than $10,000;

(b) the total assets of the association (determined in accordance with generally accepted accounting principles) at the end of its immediately preceding fiscal period exceeded $200,000; or

(c) the association had to file an NPO information return for a preceding fiscal period.[30]

An NPO information return must be filed within six months after the end of the association's fiscal period.

[¶11,566] Mutual Insurance Corporations

A mutual insurance corporation that receives its premiums wholly from the insurance of churches, schools, or charitable organizations is exempt from tax.[31]

[¶11,567] Limited Dividend Housing Company

A limited dividend housing company envisaged in the *National Housing Act*, all or substantially all of the business of which is the construction, holding, or management of low-rental housing projects, is exempt from tax.[32]

[¶11,568] Pension Corporation

A corporation incorporated and operated solely for the administration of a registered pension plan and for no other purpose than acting as trustee and administrator of a trust governed by a retirement compensation arrangement providing for benefits supplementary to those provided under

---

See page ii for explanation of footnotes.

[27] The Canadian Bar Insurance Association, 99 DTC 653.

[28] Elm Ridge Country Club Inc., 98 DTC 6672.

[29] A.Y.S.A. Amateur Youth Soccer Association, 2007 DTC 5527.

[30] CCH ¶21,868; Sec. 149(12).

[31] CCH ¶21,791; Sec. 149(1)(m).

[32] CCH ¶21,793; Sec. 149(1)(n).

the registered pension plan, is exempt from tax if it has been accepted as a funding medium for registration purposes.[33]

Also exempt are corporations that were incorporated before November 17, 1978 solely in connection with, or for the administration of, a registered pension fund or plan, or that at all times since the later of November 16, 1978 and the date on which it was incorporated met certain tests as to the purpose of incorporation or the activities carried on by the corporation. All the shares of the corporation and all rights to acquire shares of the corporation must be owned by one or more registered pension funds or plans, by one or more trusts or segregated fund trusts, all the beneficiaries of which are registered pension funds or plans, or by one or more prescribed persons. In the case of a corporation without share capital, all the property of the corporation must be held exclusively for the benefit of one or more registered pension funds or plans.[34]

A corporation will not lose its tax-exempt status solely because of an investment in an interest of a partnership that limits its activities to acquiring, holding, maintaining, improving, leasing, or managing capital property that is real property or an interest in real property owned by the partnership.

[¶11,569] Small Business Investment Corporation

A small business investment corporation, basically described as a corporation investing pension funds in small businesses, is exempt from tax under Part I.[35] In general terms, for each $1 a pension fund invests in a prescribed small business investment corporation, the pension fund may acquire an additional $3 of "foreign property" without incurring tax under former Part XI. Part XI was repealed for months that end after 2004, thus eliminating the "foreign property" rules.

[¶11,570] Farmers' and Fishers' Insurers

A non-life insurer who earns more than 20% of its gross premium income (net of reinsurance ceded) from the insurance of property used in farming or fishing or residences of farmers or fishers ("farm risks") is exempt from tax on a portion of its taxable income.[36]

For the insurer to be entitled to this exemption, two conditions must be met. First, the insurer must not engage in any business other than the business of insurance throughout the period. Second, in the opinion of the Minister (on the advice of the Superintendent of Financial Institutions, or the provincial Superintendent of Insurance if the insurer is provincially regulated), at least 20% of the gross premium income (net of reinsurance) earned in the period by the insurer and other insurers that are specified shareholders of the insurer or are related to the insurer, is in respect of farm

---

See page ii for explanation of footnotes.

[33] CCH ¶21,795e; Sec. 149(1)(o.1).
[34] CCH ¶21,796a; Sec. 149(1)(o.2).

[35] CCH ¶21,796b; Sec. 149(1)(o.3).
[36] CCH ¶21,805; Sec. 149(1)(t).

risks. In the case of a mutual fund corporation, the gross premium income (net of reinsurance) earned in the period by the insurer and all other insurers that are part of a group that controls directly or indirectly in any manner whatever, or is controlled directly or indirectly in any manner whatever by the insurer, is included in the computation of the 20% threshold. An insurer prescribed by regulation[37] is not required to include the gross premiums earned (net of reinsurance ceded) by other related insurers for purposes of meeting the second condition.

If an insurer and its related insurers (including specified shareholders) earn more than 20% of gross premium income (net of reinsurance ceded) from farm risks, their exempt taxable income is the proportion of gross premium income (net of reinsurance ceded) earned from insuring farm risks to the total gross premium income (net of reinsurance ceded) earned in the year.[38] However, to the extent that the insurer and its related insurers earn between 20% and 25% of gross premium income (net of reinsurance ceded) from farm risks, the tax exemption is limited to only one-half of the associated taxable income.

Notwithstanding the above formula, all of the insurer's (and certain related insurer's) taxable income for a taxation year is tax exempt where more than 90% of the gross premium income (net of reinsurance ceded) earned in the year is from farm risks.[39] In determining the taxable income of an insurer for a particular taxation year, an insurer is not allowed to accumulate or "bank" certain discretionary tax deductions in years in which it is exempt from tax on all or part of its taxable income.[40]

[¶11,574] Non-Profit Corporation for Scientific Research and Experimental Development

[¶11,575] Tax Exemption

A non-profit corporation for scientific research and experimental development is exempt from taxation if it meets the following conditions:[41]

(1) The corporation must be constituted exclusively for carrying on or promoting scientific research and experimental development.

(2) No part of the corporation's income may be payable to or otherwise available for the personal benefit of any proprietor, member, or shareholder.

(3) The corporation must not have acquired control of any other corporation. A corporation is controlled by another corporation for these purposes if more than 50% of its issued share capital (having full voting

See page ii for explanation of footnotes.

[37] Reg. 4802(2).
[38] CCH ¶21,824; Sec. 149(4.1).
[39] CCH ¶21,825; Sec. 149(4.2).

[40] CCH ¶21,826; Sec. 149(4.3).

[41] CCH ¶21,775, ¶21,859; Sec. 149(1)(j), 149(8).

rights under all circumstances) belongs to the other corporation or to the other corporation and persons with whom the other corporation does not deal at arm's length. However, a corporation is deemed for such purpose *not* to have acquired control of a corporation if it has not purchased or otherwise acquired for consideration any of the shares in the capital stock of that corporation.

(4) The corporation must not carry on any business during the period for which exemption is claimed.

(5) The corporation must, in each period for which it claims exemption, have expended amounts in Canada each of which is (a) an expenditure on scientific research and experimental development directly undertaken by it or on its behalf; or (b) a payment to an approved association, university, college, research institution, or other similar institution to be used for scientific research and experimental development, the aggregate of which is not less than 90% of the corporation's gross revenue for the period minus any penalties and interest payable for failing to file an information return.

[¶11,576] Deductions and Election

The aggregate of the amounts expended on scientific research and experimental development in the manner described above must not be less than 90% of the corporation's gross revenue for the period minus any penalties and interest payable for failing to file an information return (see ¶11,578). However, in computing gross revenue for a taxation year, a corporation may deduct an amount not exceeding its gross revenue for the taxation year, but must include any amount deducted for the preceding taxation year.[42]

The net result of these provisions is to permit a corporation to accumulate and keep on hand as a reserve an amount equal to its gross revenue for the preceding year. In addition, the corporation may accumulate an amount each year in respect of the 10% of its income for the period which it is not required to distribute. Since the corporation must expend the relevant amount in the period, it will be necessary for it to make the expenditure on the basis of an estimate of its gross revenue for the period.

[¶11,577] Gifts as Income

There must be included in computing the income of a non-profit corporation for scientific research and experimental development and in determining its gross revenue, all gifts received by it and all amounts contributed to it that are used for scientific research and experimental development. Thus, the value of such gifts or contributions must be taken into account in determining the amount that the corporation must distribute during the period in order to qualify for exemption.[43]

See page ii for explanation of footnotes.

[42] CCH ¶21,865; Sec. 149(9). [43] CCH ¶21,859; Sec. 149(8).

In computing the part, if any, of any income of a non-profit scientific research and experimental development corporation that is payable to, or otherwise available for, the personal benefit of any person, the amount of income is to be determined by excluding the amount of any capital gains.[44]

[¶11,578] Information Returns

A non-profit scientific research and experimental development corporation must file a prescribed form containing prescribed information by its income tax return filing-due date for the year.[45] The filing-due date for a corporation is six months from the end of its taxation year. Failure to file will attract a penalty equal to the greater of 2% of the corporation's taxable income for the year and $500 for each month (up to 12) that the form is late.[46]

[¶11,579] Acquisition of Control

For the purposes of the exemption from taxation for a non-profit scientific research and experimental development corporation, a corporation is considered to be controlled by another if more than 50% of its issued capital with voting rights belongs to another corporation or to the other corporation and persons with whom it does not deal at arm's length. However, a corporation is deemed not to have acquired control if it has not purchased any of the shares of the other corporation.[47]

The corporation's income must include all gifts that it received and all amounts contributed to the corporation for scientific research and experimental development.

[¶11,580] Tax-Exempt Trusts

[¶11,580a] Types of Tax-Exempt Trusts

The following trusts are exempt from income tax under Part I:[48] trusts under profit sharing plans, registered supplementary unemployment benefit plans, retirement compensation arrangements (RCAs), registered education savings plans (RESPs), registered retirement savings plans (RRSPs), registered retirement income funds (RRIFs), deferred profit sharing plans (DPSPs), registered disability savings plans (RDSP), tax-free retirement savings accounts (TFSA), eligible funeral and cemetery care arrangements, amateur athlete trusts, and qualifying environmental trusts.

See page ii for explanation of footnotes.

[44] CCH ¶21,811; Sec. 149(2).
[45] CCH ¶21,844; Sec. 149(7).
[46] CCH ¶21,845; Sec. 149(7.1).
[47] CCH ¶21,859; Sec. 149(8).

[48] CCH ¶21,797–21,804a, ¶21,806, ¶21,806m, ¶21,806q, ¶21,807, ¶21,810, ¶21,810c; Sec. 149(1)(p)–(s.2), 149(1)(u), 149(1)(u.1), 149(1)(u.2), 149(1)(v), 149(1)(x), 149(1)(z).

It should be noted, however, that Parts XI.01 and XI.1 impose a penalty tax in respect of non-qualified investments held by RRSPs, DPSPs, RRIFs, RESPs, RDSPs, and TFSAs.

[¶11,581] Pension Trust

A trust governed by a registered pension fund or plan is exempt from tax.[49]

[¶11,582] Master Trust

A trust whose only undertaking is the investing of funds from a registered pension plan or a deferred profit sharing plan is exempt from Part I tax if it elects to be a "master trust" in its return of income for its first taxation year. In the absence of such election, the trust income must actually be distributed each year to the beneficiaries to avoid having Part I tax payable by the trust even though all of the beneficiaries of the trust are tax exempt.[50]

A trust is a master trust if, since its creation: it was resident in Canada; its sole undertaking was the investing of funds; it has borrowed no money except for a term of 90 days or less; it has never accepted deposits; and each beneficiary is a registered pension plan or a deferred profit sharing plan.[51]

[¶11,583] Trust Governed by Eligible Funeral Arrangement

A trust governed by an "eligible funeral arrangement" (EFA) is exempt from tax.[52] Such arrangements are established for the purpose of pre-funding an individual's funeral or cemetery services. Up to a limit of $15,000 for funeral services, $20,000 for cemetery services and $35,000 for a combination of funeral and cemetery services, the contributions to such a trust accumulate tax-free until they are distributed for funeral services, cemetery services, or as a distribution to the taxpayer or the taxpayer's estate. See ¶10,530.

[¶11,584] Cemetery Care Trust

The income earned by a trust established for the care and maintenance of a cemetery (sometimes known as "perpetual care funds") is exempt from taxation.[53] However, under the definition of EFA (see ¶11,583), contributions to such trusts are relevant for the purposes of determining whether an arrangement with a cemetery operator is considered to be an EFA. If an arrangement with a cemetery operator is not an EFA, any income earned under a pre-needs cemetery contract that is part of such an arrangement would be subject to taxation. Thus, if an arrangement does not qualify or ceases to qualify as an EFA, income that accumulates under the arrangement could be included, for example, in the income of a contributor or a

---

See page ii for explanation of footnotes.

[49] CCH ¶21,795; Sec. 149(1)(o).
[50] CCH ¶21,796c; Sec. 149(1)(o.4).
[51] CCH ¶21,796d; Reg. 4802(1.1).

[52] CCH ¶21,803e; Sec. 149(1)(s.1).

[53] CCH ¶21,804a; Sec. 149(1)(s.2).

trust governed by the arrangement, depending on the facts of the case. However, income earned in a cemetery care trust is still exempt from Part I tax, even if the arrangement (under which contributions are made to the cemetery care trust) is not an EFA.[54]

[¶11,585] Registered Education Savings Plans

A trust governed by a registered education savings plan is exempt from Part I tax.[55] However, Part XI.1 penalty tax is imposed on the fair market value of all property held by the trust that is not a "qualified investment". See ¶13,525.

[¶11,586] Amateur Athlete Trusts

Amateur athlete trusts are exempt from Part I tax.[56] The rules governing the taxation of these trusts are discussed at ¶10,005 *et seq.*

[¶11,587] Trusts Providing Compensation

A mutual insurance corporation that receives its premiums wholly from the insurance of churches, schools, or charitable organizations, is exempt from tax.[57]

A trust established to compensate persons for claims against the owner of a business who cannot or will not pay compensation himself or herself is exempt from tax.[58] An example of such a trust would be a trust established to provide compensation to travellers who have paid for their trips in advance but had them cancelled because of the bankruptcy of the travel agent involved.

[¶11,588] Registered Retirement Income Funds

A trust governed by a registered retirement income fund is exempt from Part I tax.[59] Such trust is, however, subject to Part XI.1 penalty tax on non-qualified investments.

[¶11,589] Vacation-With-Pay Trusts

A trust established pursuant to the terms of a collective bargaining agreement for the sole purpose of providing for the payment of employees' holiday pay is exempt from tax, as long as the property of the trust (after payment of reasonable expenses) is available after 1980, or paid after December 11, 1979, only to employees (or their heirs) and to labour organizations described in ¶11,564.[60]

See page ii for explanation of footnotes.

[54] [Interp. Bul. IT-531.
[55] CCH ¶21,806; Sec. 149(1)(u).
[56] CCH ¶21,807; Sec. 149(1)(v).
[57] CCH ¶21,791; Sec. 149(1)(m).

[58] CCH ¶21,808; Sec. 149(1)(w).
[59] CCH ¶21,810; Sec. 149(1)(x).
[60] CCH ¶21,810b; Sec. 149(1)(y).

[¶11,590] Qualifying Environmental Trusts

A qualifying environmental trust (see ¶7497) is exempt from tax under Part I but must pay a special tax under Part XII.4 equal to 28% of its income under Part I (see ¶13,645).[61] The 2011 Budget provides that the Part XII.4 rate of tax to the trust will, starting in 2012, be reduced from the former general corporate tax rate of 28% to the general corporate tax rate for the relevant year.

[¶11,595] Social Environmental Trusts

A trust set up to fund a requirement imposed by the *Environmental Quality Act* (EQA) of Quebec or the federal *Nuclear Fuel Waste Act* (NFWA) is tax exempt.[62] Section 56 of the EQA requires certain residual materials elimination facilities to provide financial guarantees by way of establishment of a social trust to cover certain costs after the closure of the facility, whereas subsection 9(1) of the NFWA requires specified entities to contribute moneys to a trust fund for the management of nuclear fuel waste. These exemptions only apply where no persons are beneficially interested in the trust, other than the Crown, a municipality, or a Crown-owned nuclear energy corporation. This pending technical amendment, re-released in a draft form on July 16, 2010, ensures that the tax consequences to such a trust are the same as if the municipality or Crown-owned nuclear energy corporation accumulated the funds internally, rather than in a trust.

[¶11,597] Special Rules

[¶11,598] Capital Gains Not Included in Income of Certain Exempt Groups

In computing the income of certain organizations where part of such income is payable to, or otherwise made available for, personal benefit of any person, income is to be computed without inclusion of taxable capital gains or allowable capital losses.[63] This provision applies to certain organizations such as non-profit corporations for scientific research and experimental development and non-profit organizations.

[¶11,600] Investment Income of Certain Clubs

A club, association, or society described as an exempt non-profit organization, whether or not incorporated, whose main purpose is to provide dining, recreational, or sporting facilities for its members, is subject to certain special rules.[64] Such an organization, commonly known as a "club", is deemed to be subject to an *inter vivos* trust throughout the period in which

---

See page ii for explanation of footnotes.

[61] CCH ¶21,810c; Sec. 149(1)(z).
[62] Sec. 149(1)(z.1)-(z.2).

[63] CCH ¶21,811; Sec. 149(2).
[64] CCH ¶21,829; Sec. 149(5); Interp. Bul. IT-83R3.

it is a non-profit organization. An *"inter vivos* trust" is defined as a trust other than a testamentary trust.

If the club is a corporation, its property is deemed to be the property of the trust and the corporation is deemed to be the trustee having control of the trust property. If the club is not a corporation, the officers of the club are deemed to be the trustees.

The trust is subject to tax on its taxable income, the income and taxable income of the trust being computed on the assumption that it had no income or losses other than income or losses from property and taxable capital gains and allowable capital losses from dispositions of property. Property as used in this sense does not include gains or losses in connection with property used exclusively and directly to provide dining, recreational, or sporting facilities for the club's members, which remain exempt.

In computing the taxable income of the trust, a deduction of $2,000 in addition to other permissible deductions is allowed. However, deductions may not be claimed for taxable dividends received from a corporation resident in Canada, or dividends received from a foreign affiliate.

The provisions relating to trusts and their beneficiaries do not apply to the *inter vivos* trust of a non-profit club, with certain exceptions, i.e., a reference to a trust is a reference to the trustee having ownership or control of the trust property and a trust is to be taxed as an individual.[65]

[¶11,603] Apportionment Rule for Exemption Purposes

When it is necessary to apportion income for purposes of determining what is exempt and what is not, taxable income for the period will be deemed to be the proportion of the taxable income for the taxation year that the number of days in the period is of the number of days in the taxation year.[66]

[¶11,609] Acquisition or Loss of Tax-Exempt Status

When a corporation becomes or ceases to be exempt from Part I tax, it is deemed to have a taxation year ending at the time the exemption ceases and a new taxation year beginning at the time of the change of status. In keeping with this "fresh start" principle, a corporation may, after the change of tax status, establish a new fiscal period.[67] Furthermore, in determining the income of a corporation for its first taxation year ending after the change of its tax status, the corporation will be treated as having claimed or deducted, in the year immediately before that time, the maximum amount which it was

---

See page ii for explanation of footnotes.

[65] CCH ¶13,101, ¶13,114; Sec. 104(1), 104(2).   [67] CCH ¶21,866; Sec. 149(10).
[66] CCH ¶21,843; Sec. 149(6).

entitled to claim or deduct as a reserve.[68] Such reserves are therefore included in determining the corporation's income for the year in which it ceases or commences to be exempt from Part I tax so that a corporation will not be able to accumulate or "bank" them in years in which it is tax exempt.

The corporation is deemed to have disposed of all its property, for proceeds equal to its fair market value, at the time immediately before it becomes or ceases to be exempt from tax, and to have reacquired the property at the time the change of status took place. This means the reacquisition takes place in the new taxation year immediately thereafter. Thus, all gains and losses accrued in respect of the corporation's property will be realized for income tax purposes in the taxation year that ends immediately before the time the tax-exempt status begins or ceases. The deemed reacquisition at fair market value means the corporation will start the period during which it has a new status with a new cost base of the property. In particular, gains or losses in the value of the property which occurred while the corporation was exempt from tax will not increase or reduce taxable income for the period during which the corporation is taxable.

Canadian and foreign resource properties are covered by the deemed disposition and reacquisition rules when a corporation becomes or ceases to be exempt from tax. Accordingly, positive balances in the relevant resource accounts leading to income inclusions will arise in the year ending before the change in status, except to the extent the corporation has unutilized credits in those accounts. No credit arises in these accounts for the deemed reacquisition at fair market value because the deemed reacquisition takes place after the end of the year in which the deemed disposition takes place.

In keeping with a clear separation between a corporation's tax history before its status changes and its treatment afterwards, a corporation is not allowed to claim after the change any SR&ED deduction and credit, resource property deduction, loss carryover, foreign tax credit, and investment tax credit it may have accumulated before the change, and *vice versa*. A corporation that becomes or ceases to be exempt from tax is to be treated for these purposes as a new corporation, the first taxation year of which began with its change in status.

The corporation must deduct, in its taxation year ending immediately before the change in tax status, any latent loss in respect of its cumulative eligible capital (CEC). Specifically, this means the amount by which the corporation's CEC in respect of a business exceeds three-quarters of the fair market value of the eligible capital property of the business plus the CEC amount otherwise deducted in that last year.

See page ii for explanation of footnotes.

[68] CCH ¶5051–5145za, ¶20,619–20,828a, ¶20,839–20,840; Sec. 20, 138, 140.

[¶11,612] Charities

[¶11,615] Registered Charity

The term "registered charity" includes both charitable organizations and charitable foundations.[69] Charitable foundations may be either private foundations or public foundations. The Minister may designate registered charities as charitable organizations, private foundations, or public foundations and change such designations. The Minister may make such designations or redesignations upon his own initiative or upon application by a registered charity. Different rules apply to charitable organizations, private foundations, and public foundations.

For a discussion of charitable donations, see ¶8150.

[¶11,618] Charitable Organizations in General

A registered charity may qualify for registration as a "charitable organization" if:

(a) it devotes all of its resources to charitable activities carried on by itself;

(b) no part of its income is payable or otherwise available for the personal benefit of any of its proprietors, members, shareholders, trustees, or settlors;

(c) more than 50% of its directors/trustees deal with each other and with each of the other directors/trustees at arm's length; and

(d) not more than 50% of the funds that the charity has received have come from one person or organization, or from a group of people or organizations that do not deal with each other at arm's length. However, some organizations are excepted, so that large gifts from them do not affect the charity's designation. The excepted organizations are:

- the federal government,

- a provincial government,

- a municipality,

- another registered charity that is not a "private foundation", or

- a club, society, or association that the Act treats as a non-profit organization.[70]

See page ii for explanation of footnotes.

[69] CCH ¶28,232; Sec. 248(1) "registered charity".   [70] CCH ¶21,921; Sec. 149.1(1) "charitable organization".

¶11,612

A charitable organization may carry on a business which is related to its charitable activities or it may make donations within limits to "qualified donees".[71] This expression is defined to include any of the following:

(a) a registered charity (including a registered national arts service organization);

(b) a registered Canadian amateur athletic association;

(c) a listed housing corporation resident in Canada constituted exclusively to provide low-cost housing for the aged;

(d) a listed Canadian municipality;

(e) a listed municipal or public body performing a function of government in Canada;

(f) a listed university outside Canada that is prescribed to be a university, the student body of which ordinarily includes students from Canada;

(g) a listed charitable organization outside Canada to which Her Majesty in right of Canada has made a gift if, beginning January 1, 2013, it carries on its charitable activities in the following areas:

- disaster relief,

- urgent humanitarian aid, or

- activities in the national interest of Canada;

(h) Her Majesty in right of Canada or a province; and

(i) the United Nations and its agencies.[72]

As mentioned in (g), the ability of foreign charitable organizations that are the recipient of a gift from Her Majesty in right of Canada to obtain "qualified donee" status is restricted in the 2012 Budget to only such organizations that carry on activities that are related to: disaster relief, urgent humanitarian aid, or activities in the national interest of Canada. These rules come into effect on January 1, 2013. If granted, the qualified donee status will be valid for a 24-month period that includes the time at which Her Majesty in right of Canada has made the gift to the foreign organization. Foreign charitable organizations that have received qualified donee status before these limitations come into force will continue to be qualified donees until the expiration of their qualifying period.

A community legal clinic was held not to be a charitable organization when it participated in activities of a political nature in addition to its charitable activities.[73] However, a non-profit organization the objects of

---

See page ii for explanation of footnotes.

[71] CCH ¶21,936; Sec. 149.1(6).
[72] CCH ¶21,936; Sec. 149.1(1) "qualified donee".

[73] Scarborough Community Legal Services, 85 DTC 5102.

which were to produce radio and television programs of relevance to Native people, to train Native people as communications workers, and to publish a newspaper dealing with matters of Native interest was found to be a charitable organization; its activities were beneficial to the community and helped promote cohesion amongst Native people.[74] Likewise, a non-profit organization offering free access to the Internet, was granted charity status on the basis that free exchange of information among members of society has long been recognized as a public good.[75]

A charitable organization that has been registered with the Minister is exempt from Part I tax.[76] It may become subject to tax under another Part if its registration as a charity is revoked or if it participates in certain property transfers.[77] It may also be subject to penalties generally if it undertakes prohibited activities or investments or if it does not comply with its information reporting and receipting obligations.[78] See ¶13,207.

[¶11,620] National Arts Service Organization

Where an organization has applied in prescribed form, the Minister of National Revenue may register such an organization as a charitable organization for tax purposes if it has been designated by the Minister of Canadian Heritage as a national arts service organization, its exclusive purpose is the promotion of arts in Canada on a nation-wide basis, it is resident in Canada and was formed or created in Canada, and it complies with the following two conditions:

(1) The organization must be an organization which:

(a) is a non-profit organization exempt from tax;

(b) represents the community of artists from one or more of the following sectors of activity in the arts, in an official language of Canada: theatre, opera, music, dance, painting, sculpture, drawing, crafts, design, photography, the literary arts, film, sound recording and other audio-visual arts, and such other sectors as the Minister of Canadian Heritage may recognize;

(c) has no part of its income payable to, or otherwise available for, the personal benefits of any proprietor, member, shareholder, trustee, or settlor of the organization, unless the payment is for services rendered or is a scholarship, fellowship, or bursary included in income (see ¶2210);

(d) has more than 50% of the directors, trustees, officers, and like officials dealing with each other and the other directors, trustees, officers, or officials at arm's length; and

---

[74] Native Communications Society of B.C., 86 DTC 6353.
[75] Vancouver Regional FreeNet Association, 96 DTC 6440.
[76] CCH ¶21,737; Sec. 149(1)(f).
[77] CCH ¶24,400; Sec. 188.
[78] CCH ¶24,425; Sec. 188.1.

¶11,620

(e) has had no more than 50% of its property at any time contributed by one person or members of a group of persons not dealing with each other at arm's length (excluding the federal government, a provincial government, a municipality, or a registered charity that is not a private foundation or any club, society, or association described in ¶11,565).

(2) The activities of the organization must be confined to one or more of:

(a) promoting one or more art forms;

(b) conducting research into one or more art forms;

(c) sponsoring art exhibitions or performances;

(d) representing the interests of the arts community before legal or governing bodies;

(e) conducting workshops, seminars, training programs, and similar development programs relating to the arts for members of the organization where such activity results in members including the value of the program in income;

(f) educating the public about the sector represented by the organization;

(g) organizing and sponsoring conventions, conferences, competitions, and special events relating to the sector represented by the organization;

(h) conducting art studies and surveys of interest to members of the organization relating to the sector represented by the organization;

(i) being an information resource by maintaining resource libraries and databases relating to the sector represented by the organization; and

(j) paying scholarships, fellowships, or bursaries which must be included in the recipient's income and which relate to the sector represented by the organization.

The operations of the organization will be subject to the overriding provisions relating to registered charities, i.e., the extent of its political activities will be limited to activities that are ancillary and incidental to the activities of the organization.[79]

The Minister of Canadian Heritage may revoke the designation of an organization as a national arts service organization if an incorrect statement was made in the furnishing of information for the purpose of

See page ii for explanation of footnotes.
[79] CCH ¶21,936d; Sec. 149.1(6.4).

obtaining the designation, or the organization has amended its objects after its last designation was made. In the case of such a revocation, the organization is deemed to have ceased to comply with the tax requirements for registration so that the Minister of National Revenue may revoke its registration as a charitable organization.[80]

[¶11,621] Income of Registered Charities

A charitable organization may disburse up to 50% of its income for a year to qualified donees or may disburse its income to an associated charity.

Income of a charity[81] includes gifts received in the year, including gifts from another charity, *unless*:

(a) the gift is a "specified gift" from a registered charity;[82]

(b) the gift was not made out of the donor charity's income;

(c) the gift is capital received as a bequest or inheritance;

(d) the donor has required the property given or property substituted therefor to be held for at least 10 years; or

(e) the gift is from a donor who is not a charity and the donor has not been allowed a deduction for the gift (in the case of a corporation) or a tax credit (in the case of an individual) or is not subject to tax under Part I in the year the gift is made.

Where a charitable foundation is a trust, income is not reduced by distributions to the beneficiaries as it is for other trusts.

[¶11,624] Charitable Organizations — Related Business

A charitable organization is considered to be devoting its resources to its charitable activities to the extent that it carries on a related business. While the expression "related business" is not specifically defined, it includes a business that is unrelated to the objects of the organization if substantially all those employed in the business are volunteers.[83] A corporation established as a fundraising vehicle for various registered charities solicited goods that were sold by a separate company, the corporation receiving a minimum guaranteed amount; all monies were used for charitable purposes. The court held that the business aspect of the corporation's activities were merely incidental to its charitable objects.[84]

On March 31, 2003, the CRA released Charities Policy Statement No. CPS-019, "What is a Related Business?". It sets out the CRA's policy for determining whether a charity is carrying on a related business or an unre-

---

See page ii for explanation of footnotes.

[80] CCH ¶21,936e; Sec. 149.1(6.5).

[81] CCH ¶21,942; Sec. 149.1(12).

[82] CCH ¶21,930; Sec. 149.1(1) "specified gift".

[83] CCH ¶21,921; Sec. 149.1(1) "charitable organization".

[84] Alberta Institute for Mental Retardation, 87 DTC 5306.

lated business for purposes of acquiring or maintaining registered charity status. The Policy Statement describes two kinds of related businesses:

(1) businesses that are run substantially (i.e., 90%) by volunteers; and

(2) businesses that are linked to a charity's purpose and are subordinate to that purpose.

With respect to (2), a business will be considered linked to a charity's purpose if it fits within one of the following categories:

(a) *A usual and necessary concomitant of charitable programs.* Examples include: a hospital's parking lots, cafeterias, and gift shops for the use of patients, visitors, and staff; gift shops and food outlets in art galleries or museums for the use of visitors; and book stores, student residences, and dining halls at universities for the use of students and faculty.

(b) *An offshoot of a charitable program.* The charity carries out its charitable programs, not in order to create the asset, but to achieve its charitable purpose. The asset is simply a by-product of the charity's programs.

(c) *A use of excess capacity.* This type of business activity involves using a charity's assets and staff, which are currently needed to conduct a charitable program, to gain income during periods when they are not being used to their full capacity within the charitable program.

(d) *The sale of items that promote the charity or its objects.* Examples include pens, credit cards, and cookies clearly displaying the charity's name or logo, and T-shirts or posters depicting the work of the charity.

[¶11,625] Charitable Organizations — Political Activities

A charitable organization may engage in non-partisan political activities as long as it devotes substantially all of its resources to charitable activities.[85] The CRA usually considers "substantially all" to mean 90% or more. Therefore, as a general rule, the CRA considers a charity that devotes no more than 10% of its total resources a year to political activities to be operating within the "substantially all" provision. However, in a Policy statement (CPS-022), released on September 2, 2003, the CRA recognizes that this may have a negative impact on smaller charities. To alleviate this hardship, it will exercise its discretion and not revoke the registration of smaller charities for the excessive use of their resources on political activities as long as they meet the following administrative guidelines:

See page ii for explanation of footnotes.

[85] CCH ¶21,931a, ¶21,936b; Sec. 149.1(1.1), 149.1(6.2).

- Registered charities with less than $50,000 annual income in the previous year can devote up to 20% of their resources to political activities in the current year.

- Registered charities whose annual income in the previous year was between $50,000 and $100,000 can devote up to 15% of their resources to political activities in the current year.

- Registered charities whose annual income in the previous year was between $100,000 and $200,000 can devote up to 12% of their resources to political activities in the current year.

The political activities to which a registered charity devotes the required percentage of its resources must be ancillary and incidental to its charitable activities. A political activity is considered partisan if it involves direct or indirect support of, or opposition to, a political party or candidate for public office. When a political party or candidate for public office supports a policy that is also supported by a charity, the charity is not prevented from promoting this policy. However, a charity in this situation must not directly or indirectly support the political party or candidate for public office. This means that a charity may make the public aware of its position on an issue provided:

(a) it does not explicitly connect its views to any political party or candidate for public office;

(b) the issue is connected to its purposes;

(c) its views are based on a well-reasoned position;

(d) public awareness campaigns do not become the charity's primary activity.

A charity may provide information to its supporters or the public on how all the Members of Parliament or the legislature of a province, territory, or municipal council voted on an issue connected with the charity's purpose. However, a charity must not single out the voting pattern on an issue of any one elected representative or political party.

Effective January 1, 2013, a charitable organization that funds a qualified donee for the purpose of enabling it to pursue political activities will be required to count that donation against its own allowable limits for political activities. Failure to comply with this new requirement may trigger intermediate sanctions, such as monetary penalties or a one-year suspension of receipting privileges, as well as revocation of registration.[86] See ¶13,207.

See page ii for explanation of footnotes.

[86] CCH ¶24,425; Sec. 188.1.

¶11,625

[¶11,627] Charitable Organizations — Disbursements to Other Charities and Accumulation of Property

A charitable organization is considered to be devoting its resources to its own charitable activities to the extent that, within limits, it disburses its income to other charities. The organization may disburse up to 50% of its income for a year to "qualified donees".[87] This expression, in general, refers to institutions which, upon receipt of a gift from a taxpayer, may issue a receipt which permits the taxpayer to deduct the amount given in computing taxable income. For more details, see ¶11,618. Thus, for example, if a charitable organization donates up to 50% of its income to other registered charities, the amount so donated will be considered to have been devoted to the donating charitable organization's own charitable activities. It should be noted that the recipient charities may have to include the amount received in their incomes.

A charitable organization which disburses income to a registered charity associated with it will be considered to have devoted that income to its own charitable activities. A registered charity will be considered to be associated with a charitable organization if it is so designated.[88] Registered charities who want designation as associated charities must complete Form T3011. The CRA will approve a designation as associated charities if it is satisfied that he charitable aim or activity of each of the registered charities is substantially the same. If the charities' aims or activities are different, they can still become associated in order to undertake a joint project. In the latter case, they should explain on the application how the project will operate and what each of the registered charities will do to achieve the common goal. A charitable foundation that is granted associated status with another registered charity cannot be redesignated as a charitable organization solely on the basis of such associated status.

A charitable organization may pay amounts other than income to a qualified donee (see ¶11,618) and thereby be considered to have devoted resources to its own charitable activities.[89] For example, a charitable organization could donate part of the gifts received by it in the year or part of its own capital to a registered charity.

A charitable organization may accumulate property for a particular purpose with the written consent of the Minister. Property so accumulated and any income thereon are deemed to have been expended on the organization's charitable activities in the taxation year in which they were so accumulated and not to have been expended in any other year.[90] With the repeal of the charitable expenditure (80%) rule in the 2010 Budget (see ¶11,628), this rule is amended for taxation years ending after March 3, 2010 in order to give the Minister the discretion to exclude property accumulated

---

See page ii for explanation of footnotes.

[87] CCH ¶21,936; Sec. 149.1(6).
[88] CCH ¶21,937; Sec. 149.1(7); Inf. Cir. 77-6.
[89] CCH ¶21,940; Sec. 149.1(10).
[90] CCH ¶21,938; Sec. 149.1(8).

for a particular purpose from the capital accumulation (3.5%) rule calculation.

[¶11,628] Charitable Organizations — Disbursement Requirements

Registered charities designated as charitable organizations are subject to certain rules that require them to spend each year a minimum amount on their own charitable activities or on gifts to qualified donees as defined in ¶11,618 (for example, other registered charities). These are called the disbursement quota rules, and they are discussed in more detail at ¶11,639. For charitable organizations, the disbursement quota rule can be summarized as follows:

- For taxation years ending after March 3, 2010, the disbursement quota rule for a charitable organization only applies if the average value of a charitable organization's property not used directly in charitable activities or administration during the 24 months before the beginning of the fiscal period exceeds $100,000. If the $100,000 threshold is reached, the charity's disbursement quota is calculated as 3.5% of the average value of that property.

- For taxation years beginning after March 22, 2004 and ending before March 4, 2010, the rule is more complex to the extent that the charitable organization must make expenditures on charitable activities carried on by it in the year, or on gifts to qualified donees (see ¶11,618), equal to the aggregate of:

  (a) 80% of the previous year's tax-receipted donations plus other amounts relating to enduring property and transfers between charities (in other words, a "charitable expenditure rule"); and

  (b) 3.5% of all assets not currently used in charitable programs or administration, if these assets exceed $25,000 (in other words, a "capital accumulation rule"). Before 2009, this 3.5% disbursement quota rule only applied to those charities that were "foundations", but as of 2009, it applies to all charities, including all charitable organizations. The calculation of the 3.5% disbursement quota is based on the average value of property owned by the charity at any time in the 24 months before the beginning of the fiscal period, which was not used directly in charitable activities or administration. If the total of the charity's assets not used in charitable programs does not exceed $25,000, it will not have a 3.5% disbursement quota and it will not have to calculate the 3.5% disbursement quota.[91]

See page ii for explanation of footnotes.

[91] CCH ¶21,924; Sec. 149.1(1) "disbursement quota".

¶11,628

[¶11,630] Charitable Organizations — Revocation of Registration

The registration of a charitable organization may be revoked if it ceases to comply with the requirements for registration or breaches any of its obligations to report or maintain proper records.[92] In addition, registration may be revoked if:

(1) The organization carries on a business not related to its charitable activities. As to the right of a charitable organization to carry on a related business (see ¶11,618) above.

(2) The organization fails to expend, in a particular taxation year, on charitable activities carried on by it and by way of gifts to qualified donees (see ¶11,618), amounts the total of which is at least equal to the organization disbursement quota for that year. The disbursement quota requirement for charitable organizations is described at ¶11,628.

(3) The organization makes a gift in a taxation year other than one made in the course of charitable activities carried on by it or to a qualified donee. This rule removes a previously available argument that once a charity had met its disbursement quota it was free to make distributions to foreign charities, which would not qualify as registered charities.

(4) The organization obtained its registration on the basis of false or deliberately misleading information. The Minister will also be able to assess the revocation tax at the same time as the proposed deregistration notice to avoid the dissipation of assets and, provided judicial authorization is obtained, to begin immediate collection of that tax. This expedited revocation power applies to proposed deregistration notices issued after June 13, 2005.[93]

A charitable organization may receive other funds, such as business revenue, which are not subject to any distribution requirement.

The Minister may also revoke the registration of:

(a) a registered charity if it makes a gift to another registered charity and it can reasonably be considered that one of the main purposes of making the gift was to unduly delay the expenditure of amounts on charitable activities;

(b) the recipient charity referred to in (a) if it can reasonably be considered that it acted in concert with the donor;

(c) any registered charity if a false statement was made in circumstances amounting to culpable conduct in the furnishing of information for the purpose of obtaining registration of that charity; and

(d) a registered charity, if, for taxation years ending after March 3, 2010:

See page ii for explanation of footnotes.
[92] CCH ¶23,220; Sec. 168(1).   [93] CCH ¶21,932; Sec. 149.1(2).

(i) it has in a taxation year received a gift of property (other than a "designated gift") from another registered charity with which it does not deal at arm's length; and

(ii) it has expended before the end of the next taxation year, in addition to its disbursement quota for each of those taxation years, an amount that is less than the fair market value of such property on charitable activities carried on by it or by way of gifts made to qualified donees with which it deals at arm's length.[94]

The rule in (d) essentially provides that when a registered charity receives a gift of property from a non-arm's length charity, it will need to spend an amount equal to the fair market value of the property on its own charitable activities or transfer the amount by way of gift to arm's length qualified donees within the current or subsequent taxation year or else its registration may be revoked. However, for taxation years ending after March 3, 2010, if the donor charity designates all or a portion of the gift of property in its information return for the year as a "designated gift", the designated portion will not be subject to the immediate disbursement requirement in the hands of the recipient charity.[95]

The CRA is now allowed to refuse or revoke registration of a charitable organization or to suspend its ability to issue receipts, if a director, trustee, officer, or any individual who controls or manages the operation of the organization has been found guilty of a "relevant criminal offence" which has not been pardoned or a "relevant offence" in the last five years.[96] A "relevant criminal offence" is a criminal offence relating to financial dishonesty, including tax evasion, theft, and fraud, or any other offence pertaining to the operation of the charity.[97] A "relevant offence" is any other offence relating to financial dishonesty, including one under charitable fundraising legislation, consumer protection, or securities legislation.[98] However, in a Release dated June 7, 2011, the Charities Directorate of the CRA pointed out that, in more limited cases, the offence might not involve financial dishonesty, but is nonetheless relevant to the operation of the charity or association (e.g., an offence which if repeated by the individual could inflict harm on the organization or its beneficiaries).

A registered charity which expends a "disbursement excess" may apply such excess to satisfy its minimum disbursement requirements in the immediately preceding taxation year and five or fewer of its immediately subsequent taxation years.[99] Disbursement excess means the amount, if any, by which the aggregate of amounts expended in the year by the charity in charitable activities carried on by it or by way of gifts to qualified donees exceeds the minimum disbursement requirement.[100] For example, if a regis-

---

[94] CCH ¶21,934a; Sec. 149.1(4.1).
[95] CCH ¶21,923a; Sec. 149.1(1) "designated gift".
[96] Sec. 149.1(1) "ineligible individual".
[97] Sec. 149.1(1) "relevant criminal offence".
[98] Sec. 149.1(1) "relevant offence".
[99] CCH ¶21,950; Sec. 149.1(20).
[100] CCH ¶21,951; Sec. 149.1(21).

tered charity expended $100,000 in a year when its minimum disbursement requirement was $75,000, the registered charity may apply the $25,000 excess to its immediately preceding taxation year if it failed to meet its minimum disbursement requirement in order to eliminate such shortfall, or the excess may be carried forward and applied in any of the five subsequent taxation years as a credit which goes toward satisfying its minimum disbursement requirements in those years.

A charity that was registered to promote education and provide relief of poverty and sickness in a foreign country had its registration revoked when it did not comply with the Act.[101] The specific infractions included: a $20,000 grant to a museum that was reported as a scholarship; failure to issue a T4 slip for salary paid to an employee; donation receipts that could not be reconciled with the T3010 return and financial statements; and a brochure produced by the agent that mentioned specific Canadian donors for projects claimed as the charity's projects. The latter practice suggested that the individual donor or the agent, and not the charity, was in control of where and how funds were disbursed and how contributions were recognized. The decision to revoke the charity's registration was upheld on the ground that a registered charity cannot act as a conduit for funds to be funnelled overseas and needs to show that it has direction and control over its activities, including the use of its funds by an agent.

[¶11,631] Charitable Organizations — Revocation Tax

A revoked charity loses its tax-exempt status and its privilege to issue tax receipts. It must also transfer its assets within one year from its revocation to one or more registered charities. For notices of revocation issued after December 31, 2004, the ability of a revoked charity to divest assets within one year no longer applies if the CRA obtains authorization from a judge to commence collection proceedings before that time. Any property remaining one year after revocation must be transferred to the Crown. This requirement is often referred to as the revocation tax.

The 2004 Budget restricted the eligible transfers on revocation to "eligible donees". Eligible donees only include registered charities that are in compliance with the Act, are not the subject of a certificate under the *Charities Registration (Security Information) Act,* and more than 50% of the directors or trustees of which deal at arm's length with each director or trustee of the charity whose registration is revoked. Other qualified donees such as municipalities, foreign universities, and United Nations agencies will no longer be eligible for transfers on revocation. The intent is to keep the money invested within the charitable sector in Canada and applied to charitable purposes that are analogous to those for which the funds were

---

See page ii for explanation of footnotes.

[101] The Canadian Committee for the Tel Aviv Foundation, 2002 DTC 6843.

originally raised. This measure applies to notices of intended revocation issued after June 13, 2005.

[¶11,632] Charitable Organizations — Intermediate Sanctions

Before the 2004 Budget revisions to the regulatory regime for charities, the only sanction available to the CRA in response to non-compliant charities was the revocation of its status as a registered charity. Because of its harshness, revocation was seldom imposed for minor infractions and lesser forms of non-compliance could go unchecked. The revised regulatory regime implements more effective sanctions that are more appropriate than revocation for relatively minor forms of non-compliance. This sanction regime applies in respect of taxation years beginning after March 22, 2004.

For specific incidents of non-compliance, these sanctions include:

- tax at rates of up to 100% on gross revenues from prohibited business activities, e.g., a private foundation carrying on any business, a public foundation or charitable organization carrying on an unrelated business, or a foundation acquiring control of a corporation;

- suspension of tax-receipting privileges for one year and having to notify supporters of the suspension if donated funds are used for non-charitable purposes, or if adequate books and records are not maintained, or other verification and enforcement requirements are not met;

- monetary penalties for late filing or failure to file, or issuing incomplete receipts;

- tax of 105–110% of the amount of undue personal benefits or restricted gifts;

- tax at 125% of amounts receipted where there was no gift or where the receipt contains false information; in addition, if the amounts so receipted exceed $20,000, the suspension of receipting privileges;

- tax at 10% of amounts transferred among registered charities to delay the disbursement quota requirements.

If the tax and penalties payable exceed $1,000, the sanctioned charity may transfer an equivalent amount to another registered charity instead of paying the amounts to the CRA, provided the recipient is an "eligible donee". This condition will be met if the charity in compliance with the Act is not the subject of a certificate under the *Charities Registration (Security Information) Act*, and more than 50% of its directors or trustees deal at arm's length with each director or trustee of the sanctioned charity. A sanctioned charity has the right to appeal the sanctions to the CRA administratively and to the Tax Court.

¶11,632

[¶11,633] Charitable Foundations in General

To qualify for registration as a "charitable foundation", a corporation or a trust must be constituted and operated exclusively for charitable purposes and no part of its income may be payable or otherwise available to any of its proprietors, members, shareholders, trustees, or settlors.[102] Political activities are not considered to be charitable. However, a charitable foundation may engage in non-partisan political activities that are ancillary and necessary to its charitable purposes. See ¶11,640.

Charitable foundations are divided into "public foundations" and "private foundations".[103] A charitable foundation is considered to be a public foundation if:

(1) the foundation has been registered or designated as a private foundation or charitable organization and more than 50% of the directors, trustees, officers, or like officials deal with each other and each of the other directors, trustees, officers, or officials at arm's length, and not more than 50% of the capital contributed or paid to the foundation comes from one person or members of a group of persons who do not deal with each other at arm's length (excluding the federal government, a provincial government, a municipality, another registered charity that is not a private foundation, or any club, society, or association described in ¶11,565); or

(2) in any other case, more than 50% of its trustees and directors deal with each other at arm's length and not more than 75% of its capital was derived from the donations of a single person or a group of persons not dealing at arm's length with one another.

[Generally applicable after 1999, the 50% contribution test to be met by a "public foundation" in order to maintain its status will be replaced by a control test. As a result, a foundation will not be redesignated as a private foundation solely because it received more than 50% of its capital from one person or group of non-arm's length persons. However, such a person or group is not permitted to control the charity in any way, nor may the person or the members of the group represent more than 50% of the directors, trustees, officers, and similar officials of the foundation. Failure to satisfy the control test will result in a charity being designated as a private foundation. The Charities Directorate is now applying the control test in its review of applications for registration and redesignation. Applications for redesignation can be made retroactively for taxation years that begin after 1999. However, the proposed legislation contains a limited 90-day time frame within which a registered charity can apply for redesignation for a prior taxation year. As such, registered charities have up to 90 days after the July 16, 2010 version of the proposed technical amendments is enacted to apply for retroactive redesignation. Applications received after that date will

---

See page ii for explanation of footnotes.

[102] CCH ¶21,920; Sec. 149.1(1) "charitable foundation".

[103] CCH ¶21,925, ¶21,926; Sec. 149.1(1) "private foundation", 149.1(1) "public foundation".

still fall under these new rules, but the redesignation will only become effective for future taxation years.]

Charitable foundations that do not qualify as public foundations are classed as private foundations. However, a private foundation may apply to the Minister to be designated as a public foundation.[104]

A public foundation may carry on a related business, whereas a private foundation may not carry on any business at all. A public foundation may not acquire control of any corporation. However, a public foundation will be deemed not to have acquired control of a corporation as long as it has not purchased or otherwise acquired for consideration more than 5% of the issued shares of any class of the corporation.

Before March 19, 2007, the registration of a private foundation could be revoked if it acquired control of any corporation. However, for taxation years beginning after March 18, 2007, a private foundation is instead subject to the excess corporate holdings regime described at ¶11,643. More specifically, the Minister may revoke the registration of a private foundation that has not, in respect of its shareholdings of a corporation, reduced its divestment obligation percentage for a taxation year (if any) to zero by the end of that year.[105]

With certain exceptions (see ¶11,636), a charitable foundation may not incur any debts. Both private and public foundations are required to expend particular portions of the funds available to them each year.

Where a charitable foundation does not comply with the rules applicable to it, the Minister may revoke its registration.[106] A charitable foundation that has been registered with the Minister as a registered charity is exempt from tax. It is also entitled to issue receipts to taxpayers who make gifts to it so that those taxpayers will be entitled to claim a charitable donations tax credit or, in the case of a corporation, to deduct the amount of the gift from income.[107]

[¶11,636] Charitable Foundations — Revocation of Registration

The Minister may revoke the registration of a private foundation which carries on any business.[108] Public foundations, however, may carry on a related business. The Minister may revoke the registration of a public foundation if it carries on a business that is not a related business.[109] A "related business" includes a business which is unrelated to the objects of the foundation if substantially all those employed in the business are unpaid volunteers.[110]

See page ii for explanation of footnotes.

[104] CCH ¶21,943; Sec. 149.1(13).

[105] CCH ¶21,934; Sec. 149.1(4)(c).

[106] CCH ¶23,220; Sec. 168(2).

[107] CCH ¶15,750; Sec. 110.1(1)(a).

[108] CCH ¶21,934; Sec. 149.1(4)(a).

[109] CCH ¶21,933; Sec. 149.1(3).

[110] CCH ¶21,929; Sec. 149.1(1) "related business".

¶11,636

The Minister may revoke the registration of a public or private founda-tion if it acquires control of a corporation. A corporation will be considered to be controlled by a charitable foundation if more than 50% of its issued share capital having full voting rights under all circumstances belongs to the foundation or to it and persons with whom it does not deal at arm's length. These provisions do not prevent a charitable foundation from acquiring control of a corporation by a gift of its shares. If the foundation has not purchased or otherwise acquired for consideration more than 5% of the issued shares of any class of the shares of the corporation, it is deemed not to have acquired control of the corporation.[111] For example, a donor could give 51% of the voting shares of a corporation to a foundation and the foundation could retain the shares without risk of its registration being revoked. However, if a foundation purchased a 10% share interest in a corporation as an investment and later a donor gifted a further 41% share interest to the foundation, the exemption provisions would not have been satisfied because the foundation would have acquired more than 5% of its shares by purchase. In these circumstances the Minister could revoke the foundation's registration.

A charitable foundation may not incur any debts except for current operating expenses or debts incurred in connection with the purchase or sale of its investments, or in the course of administering its charitable activities.[112] The Minister may revoke the registration of a public or private foundation that breaches this rule.

[Pending technical amendments that were re-released in a draft form on July 16, 2010, add the making of gifts to non-qualified donees as a ground for revoking the registered status of public foundations and private foundations. Under the existing legislation, provided a foundation satisfied its disbursement quota requirements to give certain amounts to qualified donees (primarily Canadian registered charities), gifts could be made to foreign charities that still met the foundation's obligation to be operated exclusively for charitable purposes. Because a foreign charity cannot become a registered charity, such gifts will no longer be permitted after December 20, 2002 unless the foreign charity is otherwise a qualified donee.]

[¶11,639] Charitable Foundations — Disbursement Quotas

Public foundations and private foundations must expend certain amounts each year on their own charitable activities or by way of donations to "qualified donees", which are essentially other Canadian registered chari-ties.[113] Failure to comply with these requirements may result in revocation of the charitable foundation's registration. The "disbursement quota" is the amount to be expended in a year.

See page ii for explanation of footnotes.

[111] CCH ¶21,942; Sec. 149.1(12).

[112] CCH ¶21,933, ¶21,934; Sec. 149.1(3), 149.1(4)(d).

[113] CCH ¶21,933, ¶21,934; Sec. 149.1(3), 149.1(4).

Taxation years ending before March 4, 2010

The disbursement quota for a charitable foundation for a taxation year beginning after March 22, 2004 and ending before March 4, 2010 is determined by the following formula:

$$A + A.1 + B + B.1$$

where

- A is 80% of the aggregate amount of gifts received by the foundation in the immediately preceding taxation year for which receipts were issued, other than gifts of "enduring property" (i.e., gifts by way of bequest or inheritance, a "10-year gift", gifts made to a registered charity as a result of a designation of the charity as the direct beneficiary of the individual's RRSP, RRIF, or life insurance policy) or gifts received from registered charities;

- A.1 is the sum of:

  (a) 80% of the amount of enduring property expended in the year, other than enduring property that was received by the charity as a specified gift, or a bequest or inheritance received by the charity in a taxation year that included any time before 1994; and

  (b) 100% of the fair market value, when transferred, of enduring property (other than enduring property that was received by the charity as a specified gift) transferred by the charity in the taxation year by way of a gift to a qualified donee.

  This amount is then reduced by the amount, if any, claimed by the charity, that may not exceed the lesser of:

  (c) 3.5% of the amount determined under D (discussed below, generally 3.5% of the market value of its investment assets); and

  (d) the capital gains pool of the charity for the taxation year.

  The result of this calculation is that a registered charity may meet its 3.5% disbursement quota out of realized capital gains on enduring property without the expenditure of those gains giving rise to the special 80% or 100%, as the case may be, disbursement quota on expenditures of enduring property.

- B, in the case of a charitable organization or public foundation, is 80% (100% for a private foundation) of the aggregate amount of gifts received in the immediately preceding taxation year from registered charities other than specified gifts or gifts of enduring property.[114] A specified gift is treated as a "nothing" in that it is deemed to be neither an amount expended nor an amount received;[115] a gift of an

See page ii for explanation of footnotes.
[114] CCH ¶21,924a; Sec. 149.1(1) "enduring property".   [115] CCH ¶21,931a; Sec. 149.1(1.1).

enduring property is, in general terms, a gift intended by the donor to form part of the capital endowment of the recipient charity.

- B.1 is determined by the formula

$$C \times 0.035 \ [D - (E + F)] \ / \ 365$$

where

C is the number of days in the taxation year.

D is 3.5% of the value, as prescribed by regulation, of property (except for certain prescribed property) owned by a registered charity in the immediately preceding 24 months (that was not used directly in charitable activities or administration) if that value is greater than $25,000.

E is the total of the amount determined for paragraph (b) of the description of A.1, and $^5/_4$ of the total of the amounts determined for A and paragraph (a) of the description of A.1, for the year in respect of the charity.

F is equal to

(a) for a private foundation, the amount of B for the year for a private foundation; or

(b) for a public foundation, $^5/_4$ of the amount of B for the year for a public foundation.

Basically, this measure ensures that at least 3.5% of the value of investment assets (other than those already included in the calculation of the disbursement quota under A, A.1, or B) is disbursed each year.[116]

The Minister is allowed to authorize a change to the valuation methods adopted by the foundation that will result in values different from those prescribed.[117] Part XXXVII of the Regulations provides for the manner in which the value of investment property held during the previous 24 months is to be determined. In general terms, this is to be the average value of such investments determined as at the end of a number of equal consecutive periods adding up to 24 months. The number of periods can, at the election of the foundation, range from two to eight. Certain rules are prescribed for determining the value of specific investment assets.[118] The effect of this deduction is to eliminate from the pool of investment assets on hand at the beginning of the taxation year all of the gifts received in the previous taxation year which must be expended, at least to the extent of 80%, on charitable activities or gifts to qualified donees. After such mandatory expenditures are made, it is assumed that the balance, or a portion thereof,

See page ii for explanation of footnotes.

[116] CCH ¶21,924; Sec. 149.1(1) "disbursement quota".

[117] CCH ¶21,931b; Sec. 149.1(1.2).

[118] CCH ¶21,954; Reg. 3702.

will be expended on administrative costs. However, any amounts not so expended will form part of the pool of investment assets in the following year.

The disbursement quota provisions ensure that 80% of the receipted donations, with certain important exceptions described above, and 80% of gifts from registered charities (100% in the case of gifts received by private foundations), again subject to exceptions, must be disbursed. In addition, in general terms, 3.5% of the average value of investment assets over the previous 24 months must be expended in the current taxation year on direct charitable activities or gifts to qualified donees. The intended result is that investment assets must generate income of at least 3.5% annually, which must be disbursed. Where the required level of income is not generated by the investment assets, other funds must be found (e.g., encroachment of capital) for the foundation to meet its disbursement quota.

Taxation years ending after March 3, 2010

The 2010 Budget reform significantly amended the disbursement quota rules. As a result, the above formula is replaced with a simpler formula that establishes the annual disbursement quota for a public or private foundation as 3.5% of the average value of its property in excess of $25,000 that was not used directly in charitable activities or administration during the 24 months before the beginning of its fiscal period.[119]

The average value of property is based on a specified number of periods (decided by the charity) over a 24-month span. The 24-month span can be divided into two to eight equal, consecutive periods. The number of periods is usually chosen when the charity files its first information return. Once chosen, the charity must get the CRA's written permission to change it. For example, if a charity calculates the value of its property only once a year, it will use two 12-month periods to calculate an average value. If it values its property every six months, then it will use four six-month periods to calculate an average value. To establish the average value of property for the purpose of calculating the disbursement quota, the charity determines the value of property that is not used directly in charitable activities or administration at the end of each period; it then adds all the values together and divides the total by the number of periods. For more details, see the CRA's *Disbursement quota calculation* Web page.

The CRA has a certain amount of discretion to permit a charity to accumulate property without violating the disbursement quota in certain circumstances.[120] For example, the CRA has noted that such permission may be granted where the temporary accumulation is necessary to make a major expenditure, such as buying a building or a costly piece of equipment which cannot be financed out of the charity's current revenue. A request to accu-

---

See page ii for explanation of footnotes.

[119] CCH ¶21,924; Sec. 149.1(1) "disbursement quota".   [120] CCH ¶21,938; Sec. 149.1(8).

mulate property must identify, among other things, (i) the specific purpose to which the funds will be used; (ii) the amount required; and (iii) the length of time needed to accumulate the funds (minimum of three years and maximum of 10 years). Any property accumulated by the charity after the receipt of, and in accordance with, such Ministerial approval (including any income earned in respect of the accumulated property) is generally excluded from the computation of the charity's capital accumulation requirement for the disbursement quota.

[¶11,640] Charitable Foundations — Political Activities

A charitable foundation is required to operate exclusively for "charitable purposes" by virtue of its definition (see ¶11,633). However, a charitable foundation is allowed to devote part of its resources to political activities provided that:

(1) it devotes substantially all (i.e., 90% or more) of its resources to charitable activities, not including the part of those resources devoted to political activities; and

(2) the political activities that fall within the 10% allowable limit in (1) are:

(a) ancillary and incidental to its charitable purposes, and

(b) do not include the direct or indirect support of, or opposition to, any political party or candidate.[121]

Effective January 1, 2013, a charitable foundation that funds a qualified donee for the purpose of enabling it to pursue political activities will be required to count that donation against its own allowable limits for political activities. Failure to comply with this new requirement may trigger intermediate sanctions, such as monetary penalties or a one-year suspension of receipting privileges, as well as revocation of registration.[122] See ¶13,207.

[¶11,643] Private Foundations — Excess Corporate Holdings Regime

After March 18, 2007, donations of publicly listed securities to private foundations no longer attracted capital gains tax on the deemed disposition (see ¶5033). At the same time that the government extended this exemption to private foundations, it introduced the "excess business holdings" regime to limit potential opportunity for persons connected with a private foundation to use their own and the foundation's shareholdings for their own benefit.

Generally speaking, under the excess holdings regime, a private foundation can hold up to 2% of any class of shares of a corporation without consequence (called the "safe harbour" threshold). If the combined share-

---

See page ii for explanation of footnotes.

[121] CCH ¶21,936a; Sec. 149.1(6.1).   [122] CCH ¶24,425; Sec. 188.1.

holdings of the foundation and any relevant, non-arm's length person) exceeds 20% of the shares of any class, the foundation is required to divest itself of enough shares such that it meets the 2% safe harbour threshold for its own shares and does not exceed, in combination with the non-arm's length person, the 20% limit. The time frame for a divestiture will depend upon the circumstances that resulted in the 20% threshold being exceeded, with a maximum time frame of five years, although transitional rules allow foundations to divest, over a period of five to 20 years, excess business holdings that were present on March 18, 2007.[123]

However, a private foundation does not have to divest itself of exempt shares. The term "exempt shares" is defined to generally include three different categories of shares.[124]

The first category of exempt shares are shares that were acquired by the foundation by way of a gift that was subject to a trust or direction that the shares are to be held for a certain time which is after the end of the current fiscal period. The shares are deemed to be exempt only if they were acquired:

(a) before March 19, 2007;

(b) on or after March 19, 2007, and before March 19, 2012, under the terms of a will executed before March 19, 2007, and not amended on or after that date (and there is no other will executed or amended on or after March 19, 2007); or

(c) on or after March 19, 2007, under the terms of a testamentary or *inter vivos* trust created before March 19, 2007, and not amended on or after March 19, 2007.

The second category of exempt shares are shares of a corporation that are not listed on a designated stock exchange and that were last acquired by the foundation before March 19, 2007. However, such shares will not be exempt if the unlisted corporation directly or indirectly holds shares of the public corporation (referred to as the "equity percentage"). In making this determination, the shareholdings in the public corporation by all corporations that are controlled directly or indirectly in any manner whatever by the foundation and/or relevant persons must be considered. Moreover, in determining a corporation's equity percentage, rights to acquire shares or to control the voting rights in respect of shares will be considered to represent the ownership of shares.[125] Moreover, shares of the above category will not be exempt if the foundation, alone or together with any controlled corporation referred to above, holds no more than 2% of all issued and outstanding shares of that class of the public corporation.

See page ii for explanation of footnotes.

[123] CCH ¶21,977d, ¶21,977r; Sec. 149.2(1), 149.2(8).   [125] CCH ¶21,977g; Sec. 149.2(2.1).
[124] CCH ¶21,924afb; Sec. 149.1(1) "exempt shares".

The third category of exempt shares are "substituted shares", which are defined as shares acquired by the private foundation in exchange for exempt shares as a result of:

- an exchange of shares for certain convertible property (see ¶5435);

- a share-for-share exchange (see ¶6275);

- an exchange in the course of a reorganization of capital (see ¶6315); or

- an amalgamation (see ¶6327).[126]

If a share ceases to be an exempt share, the change in status does not affect the foundation's divestment obligation in prior years. However, the share will be treated as if it had not been exempt on March 18, 2007, and will therefore be subject to the transitional rules (summarized above) for taxation years after the time that the share ceased to be exempt.

The CRA explains the new excess corporate holdings regime in Guide T2082, *Excess Corporate Holdings Regime for Private Foundations*, last updated May 17, 2010. This document is available at www.cra-arc.gc.ca/E/pub/tg/t2082/README.html.

[¶11,645] Accumulation of Property

Instead of expending its donations and income each year, a charity may wish to accumulate amounts to carry out a major project. It may do so with the consent of the Minister and the amount so accumulated in a particular year in accordance with any terms or conditions imposed by the Minister will be deemed to have been expended on its own charitable activities in that year and not to have been expended in any other year.[127] Thus, the charity will not be subject to revocation of its registration for not having actually expended the required amount in that year.

The amount so accumulated, when actually expended in a future year, will be deemed *not* to have been expended in that future year. This ensures that the foundation cannot meet its disbursement quota in a future year by simply expending amounts which were previously allowed to be accumulated.

With the repeal of the charitable expenditure (80%) rule in the 2010 Budget, this rule is amended for taxation years ending after March 3, 2010 in order to give the Minister the discretion to exclude property accumulated for a particular purpose from the capital accumulation (3.5%) rule calculation.

If the charity fails to use the property for the approved particular purpose within the time period specified by the Minister, the property is

---

See page ii for explanation of footnotes.

126 CCH ¶21,930b; Sec. 149.1(1) "substituted shares". 127 CCH ¶21,938; Sec. 149.1(8).

treated as income of the charity and the "eligible amount" of a gift for which it issued a tax receipt.[128] This affects the calculation of the disbursement quota of the charity, with the result that the amount of the property must be actually disbursed in the year following default.

[¶11,648] Registered Charity — Returns

Every registered charity is required to file both an information return and a public information return within six months after the end of each taxation year.[129] Notwithstanding the usual rule that returns are to be held by the CRA as confidential, the Minister has discretion to disclose to the public appropriate information and may make publicly available an annual listing of registered charities.[130]

---

[128] CCH ¶21,939; Sec. 149.1(9). [130] CCH ¶21,945; Sec. 149.1(15).
[129] CCH ¶21,944; Sec. 149.1(14).

¶11,648

Chapter XII

Returns, Assessments, Payments, and Appeals

Returns **12,000**	Amounts Excluded from
Filing of Returns 12,005	Assessments 12,085
Electronic Filing of Returns	Reassessments for
(EFILE/NETFILE/TELEFILE) 12,006	Deductions Carried Back
Corporations 12,010	to Previous Years 12,090
Mandatory Internet Filing for	"Net Worth" Assessment 12,100
Corporations' Income Tax	**Payment of Tax** **12,105**
Returns 12,011	Withholding of Tax 12,110
Mandatory Electronic Filing	Remittance of Deductions 12,115
for Tax Preparers 12,012	Amounts To Be Withheld at
Tax Returns for Deceased	Source 12,120
Taxpayers 12,015	Machine Computation of
Trusts and Estates 12,020	Deductions 12,125
Individuals 12,025	Withholding Tables 12,130
Designated Persons 12,030	Provincial Tax Rates 12,135
Time for Filing Returns 12,035	Where Withholding Not
Voluntary Disclosure	Required 12,140
Program 12,040	Variation in Deduction 12,145
Demand for Returns 12,045	TD1 Form 12,150
Information Returns 12,050	Penalty for Failure To
Estimate of Tax 12,055	Withhold Tax 12,155
Tax Rulings 12,060	Tax Transfer Payment 12,160
Assessments **12,065**	Bonuses or Retroactive Pay
Basic Procedure for	Increases 12,165
Assessments 12,070	Lump-Sum Payments 12,170
Determination of Loss for a	Payments to Non-
Year and Determination	Residents 12,175
Pursuant to GAAR 12,071	Payment of Balance of Tax 12,180
Determination of Eligibility	Unclaimed Dividends,
for Disability Tax Credit	Interest and Proceeds 12,185
(DTC) 12,072	Instalment Payments by
Assessments of	Farmers and Fishers 12,190
Partnerships 12,073	Instalment Payments by
Incorrect or Incomplete	Other Individuals 12,200
Assessment 12,075	Instalment Payments by
Time Allowed for	Mutual Fund Trusts 12,205
Assessments 12,080	

Regular Instalment
Payments by
Corporations 12,210

Instalment Payments by
Small CCPCs 12,211

Example of Corporate
Instalment Base
Calculation 12,212

New Corporations 12,215

Instalment Payments by
SIFT Trusts 12,220

Reduction of Instalment
Payments 12,225

Payment of Remainder of
Tax 12,230

Persons Acting for Others 12,235

Elections — Instalment
Payments — Departure
Tax — Death of a
Taxpayer — Deemed
Disposition by Trust 12,240

Joint Tax Liability Re Non-
Arm's Length Transfer of
Property 12,245

Joint Tax Liability Re Split
Income Tax 12,246

Joint Tax Liability Re Split
Pension Income Tax 12,247

Interest 12,250

Interest on Underpayments,
Including Instalment
Payments of Tax 12,255

Interest Offset Method for
Late and Deficient Tax
Instalment Payments 12,260

Limitation of Interest on
Corporation Instalment
Payments 12,265

Offsetting of Interest on
Corporate Tax
Overpayments and
Underpayments 12,267

Amounts Deemed to be
Paid as Instalments —
Non-Residents 12,270

Canadian Wheat Board
Participation Certificate 12,280

Income from Blocked
Currency Countries 12,285

Foreign Tax Adjustment 12,290

Flow-Through Share
Renunciations 12,292

Effect of Loss Carryback 12,295

Interest on Late Payment of
Penalties 12,300

Penalties 12,305

Failure to File Return When
Required 12,310

Failure of Trustee, etc., To
File Returns 12,315

Failure To Provide
Information 12,320

Penalties in Respect of
Foreign-Based
Information Returns 12,325

Penalties for Failure To
Report Income 12,330

Third-Party Civil Penalties 12,333

Penalty for Late or Deficient
Instalments 12,335

Small Penalty Amounts 12,337

Refunds 12,340

Refunds of Overpayments 12,345

Assignment of Tax Refunds 12,346

Refunds of Taxes in
Dispute 12,347

Excess Refunds 12,350

Interest on Overpayments 12,355

Effect of Carryback of Loss,
etc. 12,360

Reduction of Tax Where
Disposition of Property by
Legal Representative of
Deceased Taxpayer 12,365

Reduction of Tax Where
Realization of Deceased
Employees' Options 12,366

Appeals 12,370

Amended Procedure 12,375

Objections to Assessments 12,380

Extensions of Time to
Object to Assessments
or to Appeal 12,383

**Appeals to the Tax Court of
Canada 12,385**

Informal Procedure 12,390

General Procedure 12,395

Special References
Governed by General
Procedure 12,400

Disposition of Appeals 12,405

Appeals to the Federal Court–Trial Division **12,415**

Original and Appellate Jurisdiction 12,420

Appeals to the Federal Court of Appeal **12,425**

General Appellate Jurisdiction in Income Tax Matters 12,430

Special Appellate Jurisdiction 12,435

Disposition of Appeals 12,440

Appeals to the Supreme Court of Canada **12,445**

Jurisdiction in Income Tax Matters 12,450

Recent Changes

Service of CRA's Demands for Returns

Service in person or by registered mail is no longer required when the CRA issues a demand for a tax return. Effective June 29, 2012, it is sufficient for the demand to be "sent" by the CRA. As a result of this amendment made by the *Jobs, Growth and Long-term Prosperity Act* (Bill C-38), the CRA may now send a demand via online notice or regular mail. See ¶12,045.

Mandatory Electronic Filing of Tax Returns for Commercial Tax Preparers

Beginning in 2013, commercial tax preparers are required to file electronically any returns they prepare for individuals (T1 returns) or corporations (T2 returns), except that in each year they may file up to 10 T1s and T2s in a non-electronic format. This electronic filing requirement applies to tax returns for 2012 and subsequent taxation years that are filed after 2012. Failure of a tax preparer to file a return in the electronic format will trigger a penalty of $25 in the case of a T1 and $100 in the case of a T2. See ¶12,011.

Partnership Waivers of Time Limit for CRA's Determination

As a result of the 2012 Budget, and effective June 29, 2012, a single designated partner of a partnership may extend, on behalf of the partnership, the time that the CRA has to make a determination in respect of the partnership. Before the Budget implementing Bill C-38 was assented to on June 29, 2012, the CRA had to obtain a waiver from all the members of the partnership. See ¶12,073.

Monthly Instalments Required for SIFT Trusts

For taxation years beginning after July 20, 2012, SIFT trusts will be subject to the same monthly instalment rules that apply to public corporations. They were previously subject to the quarterly instalment rules that apply to individuals. This new regime for SIFT trusts was announced on July 20, 2012, and implementing draft legislation was released on July 25, 2012. See ¶12,220.

Canadian Wheat Board Participation Certificate

With the passage of the *Marketing Freedom for Grain Farmers Act* and the reorganization of the Canadian Wheat Board, the interest waiver for persons who receive payments under participation certificates from the Canadian Wheat Board is no longer necessary and is repealed by Bill C-38, effective on June 29, 2012 (Royal Assent date). See ¶12,280.

Appeals to the Tax Court of Canada (TCC)

On June 8, 2012, draft legislation was released to improve the case load of the TCC. These proposals would:

> • increase the monetary limits for appeals under the Informal Procedure so that the aggregate limit for all amounts in issue is raised to $25,000 from $12,000, and the limit for a loss determination is raised to $50,000 from $24,000; and
>
> • permit the TCC to hear a question affecting a group of two or more taxpayers that arises out of substantially similar transactions and make the decision binding across the group.
>
> They will come into force after Royal Assent to the enacting legislation. See ¶12,375, ¶12,390, and ¶12,400.

[¶12,000] Returns

[¶12,005] Filing of Returns

Income tax returns must be filed by:

(1) corporations;

(2) legal representatives of deceased taxpayers;

(3) trusts or estates;

(4) individuals liable to pay tax or, as the case may be, their guardians, curators, tutors, committees, or other legal representatives; and

(5) any person required to do so, in writing, by the Minister.[1]

[¶12,006] Electronic Filing of Returns (EFILE/NETFILE/TELEFILE)

The CRA offers three electronic tax-filing methods that individual taxpayers can use to file their current personal income tax and benefit return: EFILE, NETFILE, and TELEFILE. TELEFILE uses telephone technology, where NETFILE uses the Internet to transmit income tax information from the individual's home to the CRA. EFILE uses computer technology and the services of a third party, called an EFILE service provider. This service provider prepares the tax return using special tax calculation software and then transmits the income tax information to the CRA. While the term "electronic filing" can be used to describe these three methods, each is referred to specifically by its given name.

EFILE

EFILE is a system of filing returns directly by computer transmission, with no paper return required.[2] The EFILE system is designed for use by tax return preparation services, and not for use by individual filers, although some EFILE preparation services may be willing to accept and submit a return prepared by an individual on suitable computer software. Professional users of the system must register with the CRA and comply with its

---

See page ii for explanation of footnotes.

[1] CCH ¶22,003; Sec. 150(1).   [2] CCH ¶22,096; Sec. 150.1.

specifications as to timing, computer software, transmission procedures, and the like.[3]

For individuals who have their returns prepared for them, this offers the option of using a preparer who participates in the EFILE program. Such participants are authorized to publicize the fact that they are "authorized by the CRA for the year to electronically file (EFILE) eligible returns". The EFILE return preparer must have the taxpayer sign Form T183, authorizing electronic filing. The advantages of EFILE should be in speed of assessment and refund since the process bypasses the CRA's manual input of data from the return into its computer. This may save days or even weeks of processing time. There may be offsetting disadvantages for individuals who prefer to deal with the CRA themselves and use a paper return common to the CRA and the taxpayer.

Taxpayers who use an EFILE service should expect to review the return as prepared by the preparer and to take responsibility for it. Taxpayers who use an EFILE service and therefore sign Form T183 should note that it authorizes the preparer to make adjustments in the refund or balance owing up to $300 without referring back to the taxpayer.

Returns that are properly filed on a timely basis by EFILE registrants will be accepted as timely by the CRA.

There are certain returns which the EFILE system is not equipped to accept. These include returns involving non-resident status, bankruptcy status, and income tax payable in more than one province. Filers in these (and perhaps a few other) situations must file paper returns. The CRA estimates that 95% of personal returns should be eligible for EFILE.

NETFILE

Until recently, individual taxpayers could only send their tax returns electronically by paying a fee to an EFILE preparer-transmitter. The CRA has developed the NETFILE service to allow individual taxpayers who have access to the Internet to send their returns electronically. NETFILE cannot be used to send an amended tax return, a tax return for any year before the 2002 tax year, or a tax return for another person. Furthermore, it is not available if a taxpayer is in bankruptcy, a non-resident of Canada, or has income from a business with a permanent establishment outside his or her province or territory of residence.

Internet-filed tax returns must be prepared using one of the commercial tax preparation software packages that the CRA has certified to meet its system requirements.

See page ii for explanation of footnotes.

[3] Inf. Cir. 97-2R11.

TELEFILE

TELEFILE is an interactive computer program that allows eligible individuals to electronically file their tax return for free using a touch-tone telephone. All they need to use the service is a touch-tone telephone, their social insurance number (SIN), their personalized access code, and their completed return.

TELEFILE is a service designed for individuals with simple or basic returns. The system accepts the most common types of income tax information such as employment income, pension income, interest income, registered pension plan contributions, and charitable donations. More complex tax information, such as self-employment income, capital gains and rental income are not accepted by the system because they would take more telephone time and could require documentation. It should be noted that first-time filers are not eligible to use TELEFILE. The TELEFILE service is available to taxpayers who have received a T1 Special, T1S-A, or T1S-C (wage earners, students, seniors, and credit and benefit filers) income tax package. The TELEFILE service is also available to taxpayers who receive the tax package for computer software users and who would otherwise receive the T1 Special, T1S-A, or T1S-C package.

[¶12,010] Corporations

A corporation is required to file a return on Form T2 within six months of the end of each taxation year (defined as the corporation's fiscal period) if:

(1) at any time in the year,

    (a) it is resident in Canada,

    (b) it carries on business in Canada, unless, effective January 1, 2001, the corporation's only revenue was derived from the carrying on of a business of providing acting services in Canada and tax was paid on that income,

    (c) it has a taxable capital gain (after 2008, otherwise than from an "excluded disposition" as defined below), or

    (d) it disposes of a taxable Canadian property (after 2008, otherwise than from an "excluded disposition" as defined below), or

(2) tax under Part I is payable by the corporation, or would be payable but for a tax treaty (after 2008, otherwise than from the disposition of "treaty-protected property" as defined at ¶14,080.[4]

With respect to the exception in (1)(b) regarding non-resident actors' corporations, effective January 1, 2001, a 23% withholding tax applies to payments to non-resident film and video actors and their corporations, with an option to have the actor and corporation pay regular Part I tax on the net earnings instead (see ¶12,110). If Part I taxation is not chosen, the non-

---

See page ii for explanation of footnotes.

[4] CCH ¶22,003; Sec. 150(1)(a).

resident corporation carrying on business in Canada is not required to file a Part I return.

For dispositions of property after 2008, a non-resident corporation will no longer be required to file an income tax return for a year if they solely had a taxable capital gain in the year or disposed of taxable Canadian property in the year, where the gain or disposition is in respect of an excluded disposition. A disposition of property at any time in a taxation year is an excluded disposition if the taxpayer is a non-resident corporation, no Part I tax is payable for the taxation year, and each taxable Canadian property disposed of is either excluded property (as defined at ¶14,045) or property in respect of the disposition of which the CRA has issued a clearance certificate. To qualify for an "excluded disposition", it is also required that the non-resident corporation owe no amount under the Act for any previous taxation year, other than an amount for which it has posted adequate security.[5]

Furthermore, beginning in 2009, a corporation will no longer be required to file a "treaty-based return" described in (2) where this requirement arises solely because of a disposition of taxable Canadian property that is treaty-protected property, as defined at ¶14,080.

A corporation is required to file a return for any year for which tax under Part I is payable by the corporation, or would be payable but for a tax treaty.

[¶12,011] Mandatory Internet Filing for Corporations' Income Tax Returns

For taxation years ending after 2009, all corporations who have gross revenues in excess of $1 million will be required to Internet file their T2 return (using CRA approved commercial software) with the exception of: insurance corporations, non-resident corporations, corporations reporting in functional currency, and tax-exempt corporations described at ¶11,050 *et seq.*[6] The fact that some corporations will not be required to Internet file does not affect the general requirement that corporations must file a T2 Corporation Income Tax Return.

Corporations required to file electronically will be subject to a penalty if they file a paper return. The penalty will be implemented gradually for taxation years ending after 2010. If a paper T2 return is filed and processed, and it is determined that the return should have been Internet filed, a penalty will be assessed as follows:

- $250 for the 2011 taxation year;
- $500 for the 2012 taxation year; and
- $1,000 for 2013 and subsequent taxation years.[7]

There will not be any penalty for the taxation years ending in 2010.

See page ii for explanation of footnotes.

[5] CCH ¶22,033; Sec. 150(5).
[6] CCH ¶22,097d; Sec. 150.1(2.1).
[7] CCH ¶22,860n; Sec. 162(7.2).

[¶12,012] Mandatory Electronic Filing for Tax Preparers

Bill C-38, the *Jobs, Growth and Long-term Prosperity Act*, assented to June 29, 2012, introduces a requirement for commercial tax preparers to file income tax returns electronically. For these purposes, a person or partnership is a "tax preparer" for a calendar year if, in the year, they accept consideration to prepare more than 10 income returns for corporations (T2) or more than 10 income returns for individuals (T1 returns), other than trusts.[8] An employee who prepares returns of income in the course of performing his or her employment duties is not a tax preparer. For tax returns to be filed after 2012 (respecting the 2012 and subsequent taxation years), these commercial tax preparers must file electronically any T1 and T2 tax returns they prepare for consideration, except that in each year they may file up to 10 T1s and T2s in a non-electronic format.[9] Exceptions to the mandatory electronic filing also apply in the following situations:

- The CRA may deny a tax preparer the authority to file electronically for the year because the tax preparer does qualify as a "tax preparer". This exception would apply if a tax preparer's application for the authority to file electronically has been denied or if the authority has been revoked for the year.

- Tax returns for insurance corporations, non-resident corporations, and corporations reporting in functional currency are not subject to the electronic filing requirement.

- The CRA may specify that it does not accept certain types of returns in an electronic format.[10]

Failure of a tax preparer to file a return in the electronic format will trigger a penalty of $25 in the case of a T1 and $100 in the case of a T2.[11]

[¶12,015] Tax Returns for Deceased Taxpayers

If a return for the year of death was not filed by the deceased, then the executor, administrator, or other person having control of the deceased's property must file a return known as a "final return".[12] In other words, the executor will file a return for the income of the deceased from January 1 of the year of death to the date of death. This final return must be filed by the later of six months after the date of death and the normal filing date for the deceased (normally April 30th of the year following death, but June 15th if the deceased or a cohabiting spouse or common-law partner of the deceased had business income for the year of death).

---

[8] Sec. 150.1(2.2).   [11] Sec. 162(7.3).
[9] Sec. 150.1(2.3).
[10] Sec. 150.1(2.4).   [12] CCH ¶22,003; Sec. 150(1)(*b*).

If the deceased had failed to file a return for an earlier year, the legal representative must file this overdue return as quickly as possible to avoid continuing interest on unpaid amounts. However, returns for a taxation year where death occurred in the period commencing November 1st and ending either April 30th, or if the deceased would have qualified for the extension for the self-employed and their cohabiting spouses or common-law partners, June 15th, are due on the later of six months after the date of death and the April 30th or June 15th date otherwise applicable. If the deceased had filed a return for the year (as might have happened if death occurred in, say, the following April) the legal representative still has up to six months from the date of death to refile as of right.

Example:

Assuming that X dies on March 15, 2013, and did not file tax returns for 2011 and 2012, there is no extension in the filing requirement for 2011; the return was due April 30, 2012, and interest and penalty will continue to run on any shortfall of tax paid. The 2012 return deadline (and any payment date for any balance owing) is deferred to September 15, 2013 (six months after the date of death). The terminal return for 2013 for the period January 1 to March 15, 2013 would not be due until April 30, 2014 (June 15, 2014 if X or X's cohabiting spouse or common-law partner had self-employment income for 2013, although payment would still be due by April 30, 2014).

The legal representative may also elect to file separate returns in the following circumstances:

(1) Where a taxpayer had rights or things at the time of death, the value of which would be included in income for the year of death, the representative of the deceased may elect to file a separate return for the value of the rights or things owned by the deceased at the time of death.[13] This return must be filed by the later of one year from the date of death, or 90 days after the assessment date of the ordinary return for the year of death.

(2) If a taxpayer died after the close of the fiscal period of his/her proprietorship or partnership business and before the end of the calendar year in which that fiscal period of the business closed (and had income in that period from the business), the legal representative may elect to file, by the later of six months after death or June 15th of the year following death, a separate T1 return which includes the business income of the stub period. If the deceased taxpayer was carrying forward a transitional reserve as a result of switching to a calendar year period at the end of 1995, the legal representative may elect to claim a reserve in the ordinary year of death return and recognize the income (with no further reserve) on this separate return, even though there is no stub period. If this election is made, the separate return is mandatory. As well, where the taxpayer is operating on the non-calendar year "alternative method" described in ¶3552, and died in the year after the close of the normal fiscal period of the business causing a second fiscal period to end at the date of death, a separate return may be filed within

See page ii for explanation of footnotes.

[13] CCH ¶9220; Sec. 70(2).

these time limits for the income from the business pertaining to the period from the close of the fiscal year to the time of death. If the election is made, a prescribed addition to income under the alternative method must be added to the year of death return, but is then deducted on the separate return.[14]

(3) Where a taxpayer died after the fiscal year end of a testamentary trust from which he or she has income, the income received by the taxpayer for the period between the fiscal year end of the testamentary trust and the date of death may be included in a separate return.

Where separate returns are filed for each of the following credits and deductions, the aggregate credits or deductions claimed for that item in the terminal return and the separate returns described under (1) to (3) above cannot exceed the aggregate that could be claimed with respect to the deceased taxpayer if separate returns were not filed. The credits and deductions involved are:

(1) the adoption expenses credit;

(2) the education, textbook, and tuition fees credits, including credits transferred from a child or grandchild, but not credits transferred from a spouse or common-law partner;

(3) the disability credit, including credits transferred from a dependant, but not credits transferred from a spouse or common-law partner;

(4) the interest paid on certain student loans;

(5) the medical expenses credit, which can be split between the final return and any optional returns. However, the total expenses must be reduced by a threshold which is the lesser of $2,109 for the 2012 taxation year and 3% of the total net income reported on all returns;

(6) the charitable donations credit, but donations for which credit is claimed on each return cannot be more than the net income reported on that return;

(7) cultural, ecological, and Crown gifts;

(8) the public transit passes amount;

(9) the children's fitness amount;

(10) the home renovation expenses; and

(11) the homebuyers' amount.

Example:

Assuming that X dies on March 15, 2012, his total medical expenses for the year of death are $9,000, his executor decides to file a rights or things return in addition to the final

See page ii for explanation of footnotes.

[14] CCH ¶22,031; Sec. 150(4).

¶12,015

return, the total of his net income on the two returns is $40,000 ($30,000 reported on the final return and $10,000 reported on the rights or things return). The executor decides to claim $^2/_3$ of the medical expenses ($6,000) on the final return and $^1/_3$ ($3,000) on the rights or things return. In this example, the medical expense reduction is $1,200 ($40,000 × 3%) and must be split between the two returns in the same proportion as the medical expenses, i.e., $800 ($^2/_3$ of $1,200) on the final return and $400 ($^1/_3$ of $1,200) on the right or things return. The medical expenses amounts qualifying for credit conversion at the rate of 15% are therefore $5,200 ($6,000 - $800) on the final return and $2,600 ($3,000 - $400) on the right or things return.

The following deductions and credits can be claimed only on the return on which the related income is reported:

(1) the pension income credit;

(2) the deductions for employees' stock options, prospectors' shares, and deferred profit sharing plan (DPSP) distributions;

(3) the deduction for employee home relocation loans;

(4) vow of perpetual poverty deduction;

(5) Canada Pension Plan (CPP) or Quebec Pension Plan (QPP) credit;

(6) Employment Insurance credit; and

(7) the offsetting deduction for workers' compensation, social assistance payments, and treaty exempt income if those items are included in income.

The credits and deductions above must be allocated among the various returns that can be filed for the year of death, and cannot exceed the credit or deduction that would be claimed on a single return.[15]

In addition to filing returns of the deceased's income, the executor is also required to file a return for income of the estate arising after the date of death.

For greater detail, see CRA publication T4011, "Preparing Returns for Deceased Persons".

[¶12,020] Trusts and Estates

Returns for trusts and estates must be filed within 90 days from the end of the taxation year.[16] The taxation year of a trust arising on death is its fiscal period. A trust arising otherwise than on death is treated as an individual and its taxation year is therefore the calendar year. Trustees in bankruptcy and certain other trustees and agents administering or dealing with the property of any person who has not filed a return are required to file a return of that person's income.

---

[15] CCH ¶17,019; Sec. 114.2; Interp. Bul. IT-326R3.   [16] CCH ¶22,003, ¶22,028; Sec. 150(1)(c), 150(3); Inf. Cir. 78-14R4.

If the trust is one which was created on the death of another person, the income of the deceased beneficiary for this second period (from the end of the trust's last fiscal period to the date of death of the beneficiary) may be excluded from income reported in the final return of the deceased beneficiary and may be included as the only item of income in a separate return.[17] The separate return is prepared in the same manner as outlined in ¶12,015. This provision is applicable only where the trust has a non-calendar year. If the trust did not arise on the death of another person, the income for the second period must be included in the regular return and no separate return is permitted with respect to this income.

[¶12,025] Individuals

As a general rule, returns must be filed by or on behalf of individuals liable to pay tax by April 30 of the year following the taxation year.[18] The taxation year of an individual not carrying on a business is the calendar year and all individuals carrying on a business must have a December 31 year end or pay tax as though they did, as discussed at ¶15,390.

Because individuals carrying on business are no longer able to defer tax by choosing a non-calendar year end, they are given an extension to file their tax returns. Individuals carrying on a business are given until June 15th of the following year to file their return although tax owing by them for the preceding year must be paid by April 30. Their spouses or common-law partners are also granted the June 15th extended deadline unless, at December 31 of the taxation year, they are living separate and apart from them by reason of a breakdown of the marriage or common-law partnership and for a period of at least 90 days. The June 15 deadline does not apply if the individual's expenditures made in the course of carrying on the business were primarily for the cost or capital cost of a tax shelter.

Example:

> Joe and Edna Parsons are both regularly employed. Edna also runs a small business from a stand in the flea market on Saturdays. Some years the business makes money and some years it loses a bit. Edna always reports the income and deducts the losses, as the case may be. For 2012, there was a loss. Joe and Edna are nevertheless both entitled to delay filing their returns until June 15, 2013, although their tax must be paid in full by April 30, 2013.

An individual is not required to file a return in a taxation year unless

(1) tax is payable by the individual for the year;

(2) the individual is resident any time in the year and has a taxable capital gain or disposes of capital property in the year;

(3) the individual is non-resident throughout the year and has a taxable capital gain or disposes of a taxable Canadian property in the year (unless,

---

See page ii for explanation of footnotes.
[17] CCH ¶13,578; Sec. 104(23)(*d*).   [18] CCH ¶22,003; Sec. 150(1)(*d*).

¶12,025

after 2008, the gain or disposition is in respect of an "excluded disposition" described below); or

(4) the individual has an RRSP Home Buyers' Plan (HBP) or Lifelong Learning Plan (LLP) balance outstanding.[19]

For dispositions of property after 2008, non-resident individuals described in (3) above will no longer be required to file income tax returns for a year solely because they had a taxable capital gain or disposed of taxable Canadian property in the year, where the gain or disposition is in respect of an "excluded disposition". A disposition of property, at any time in a taxation year, is an excluded disposition if the taxpayer is a non-resident individual, no Part I tax is payable for the taxation year, and each taxable Canadian property disposed of is either excluded property (as defined at ¶14,045) or property in respect of the disposition of which the CRA has issued a clearance certificate. To qualify for an excluded disposition, it is also required that non-resident individuals owe no amount of tax for any previous taxation year, other than an amount for which they have posted adequate security.[20]

An individual who files a return not showing his or her Social Insurance Number is deemed not to have filed a complete return[21] and is subject to a penalty of $100.[22]

In addition to the penalties for failure to file and late filing discussed at ¶12,310 *et seq.*, failure by individuals to file a timely return may result in a denial of their claim for a forward averaging credit, or of their right to carry back losses incurred in the year. Failure to report a capital gain in their return may deny them a later claim for capital gains exemption on that gain, and failure to file a return claiming capital gains exemption within one year of the due date for a return may also deny their claim for the exemption.

Although the deduction of loss carrybacks from 1998 eliminated any taxes owing for 1996 and 1997, a taxpayer was still liable for late filing penalties and interest on the tax that would have been payable (but for the loss carryback) up to the date on which the returns were filed.[23]

[¶12,030] Designated Persons

The Minister may, by notice in writing, require that a person file a return where no return has been filed in the case of a corporation, a deceased person, or an individual. The notice must specify a reasonable time in which the return is to be filed.[24]

See page ii for explanation of footnotes.

[19] CCH ¶22,004a; Sec. 150(1.1).

[20] CCH ¶22,033; Sec. 150(5).

[21] CCH ¶27,640; Sec. 237.

[22] CCH ¶22,858; Sec. 162(5).

[23] Yang, 2004 DTC 2579.

[24] CCH ¶22,003; Sec. 150(1)(e).

[¶12,035] Time for Filing Returns

The Minister may extend the time for filing a return.[25] If the return is filed by this extended deadline, no penalty for late filing is assessed. However, if the return is filed after the extended deadline, the penalty will apply based on the original filing deadline. If no extension is granted, a late filed return will make the taxpayer liable to a penalty.[26]

The taxpayer's return was e-filed by her accountant on April 29, but a non-acceptance notice was sent to the accountant's computer. When the accountant became aware that the return had not been accepted, he re-filed it on May 26. Until then, he believed that the original return had been e-filed in a timely manner. The taxpayer and her accountant acted with sufficient due diligence to justify deleting late filing penalties.[27]

[¶12,040] Voluntary Disclosure Program

The CRA's Voluntary Disclosures Program (VDP) encourages taxpayers to come forward and correct deficiencies to comply with their legal obligations.[28] Taxpayers can make disclosures to correct inaccurate or incomplete information, or to disclose information they never previously reported. For example, taxpayers may not have met their tax obligations if they claimed ineligible expenses or failed to remit source deductions. Taxpayers who make a valid voluntary disclosure will have to pay the taxes and duties owing, plus interest. In this situation, the CRA can provide relief from monetary penalties and prosecution that would otherwise be imposed. Relief is determined on a case-by-case basis, providing the disclosure is voluntary, complete, and involves a monetary penalty and information one year or more overdue.

[¶12,045] Demand for Returns

Any person, including a corporation, may be required, on receipt of a demand sent by the Minister, to file a return within a reasonable time. Effective June 29, 2012, the servicing in person or by registered mail is no longer required when the Minister issues a demand for a tax return; it is sufficient for the Minister to send the demand via online notice or regular mail. The recipient of such a demand must comply with it, regardless of his or her tax liability and regardless of a previous return having been filed.[29] Failure to do so is an offence liable to a penalty. However, failure to file within the time period specified in a demand is a strict liability offence rather than one of absolute liability. Thus, a taxpayer who placed the matter in his accountant's hands before expiry of the time limit was not liable when the accountant failed to file a return within the time allowed.[30]

See page ii for explanation of footnotes.

[25] CCH ¶27,014; Sec. 220(3).
[26] CCH ¶22,846, ¶27,660; Sec. 162, 238.
[27] Bateman, 2007 DTC 156.

[28] Inf. Cir. 00-1R2.
[29] CCH ¶22,025; Sec. 150(2).
[30] Merkle, 80 DTC 6027.

The Minister, by the same means, may also demand additional information, including a supplementary return.[31] However, the demand for information cannot be used to conduct a "fishing expedition".[32]

[¶12,050] Information Returns

The following persons are required by regulation[33] to file returns without notice or demand each year on or before the last day of February in respect of the preceding calendar year, unless otherwise specifically provided.

(1) *Withholding.* Any person who has made payments or allocations from which tax is required to be withheld[34] must make a return in prescribed form. This includes payments on account of scholarships, bursaries, research grants, adult training allowances, and similar types of payments; value of board or lodgings; allocations under an employee trust; amounts paid in respect of interest on employee or shareholder loans; and amounts paid under a sickness, disability, or accident insurance plan or income maintenance plan to which the employer has made a contribution, and automobile benefits included in income (Form T4-T4A Summary or Supplementary, as applicable).

(2) *Investment income.* A return must be made by persons making certain investment-type payments (dividends, interest, etc.) to residents of Canada, and by persons who receive such payments as nominees or agents for a person resident in Canada (Form T5).

(3) *Payments to non-residents.* The return (Forms NR4 and NR4A) must show payments of dividends, interest, rents, royalties, or any determinable income, including payments of pension benefits, received annually or periodically from Canadian sources and be filed on or before March 31st.

(4) *Estates and trusts.* Persons acting in a fiduciary capacity must, within 90 days from the end of the taxation year, file returns of income they receive or over which they have control (Form T3).

(5) *Ownership certificates.* When bearer instruments representing payment of interest are negotiated by or on behalf of a Canadian resident, an ownership certificate must be delivered to the debtor or encashing agent and filed with the Minister on or before the 15th of the month following the negotiation (Form NR601).

(6) *Income-averaging annuity contracts.* Persons making payments to Canadian residents on the disposition of an income-averaging annuity contract must file an information return (Form T4A).

See page ii for explanation of footnotes.

[31] CCH ¶27,437; Sec. 231.2(1)(a).
[32] James Richardson and Sons Limited, 84 DTC 6325.
[33] CCH ¶22,035–22,086; Reg. 200–238.
[34] CCH ¶22,300; Sec. 153(1).

(7) *Accrued bond interest.* Payments in respect of accrued interest on a security other than an income bond or income debenture must be reported and the return filed on or before the 15th day of the month following the payment (Form T600 or T600B).

(8) *Employees' profit sharing plans.* Trustees of profit sharing plans must file an information return (Form T4PS).

(9) *Discontinuance of business.* Persons discontinuing business must file a return within 30 days of the day of discontinuance for the calendar year or portion thereof prior to the discontinuance.

(10) *Deceased persons.* Legal representatives must file a return within 90 days of the date of death.

(11) *Withholding tax.* A person who is required to withhold tax must make a return upon demand by the Minister.

(12) *Electric, gas, or steam corporations.* Such corporations must make returns within six months from the end of the taxation year.

(13) *Retirement savings plans.* All benefits paid under these plans must be reported (Form T4RSP).

(14) *Registered retirement income funds (RRIFs).* Payments out of a RRIF must be reported (Form T3GR).

(15) *Registered amateur athletic associations.* A return is to be filed for each fiscal period of the association within three months from the end of the fiscal period (Form T2052).

(16) *Disposition of interest in annuities and life insurance policies.* Amounts required to be included in income in respect of the disposition of an interest in a life insurance policy must be reported by the issuer of the policy where the issuer is a party to, or has been notified in writing of, the disposition (Form T5).

(17) *Patronage dividends.* Persons making payments to residents of Canada pursuant to an allocation in proportion to patronage must file an information return (Form T2SCH16).

(18) *Cash bonuses paid on Canada Savings Bonds.* Redemption agents paying cash bonuses (as opposed to any payments agreed to be paid under the terms of the bond at time of issue) must furnish the recipient with a return and must file a return with the Minister on or before the 15th day of the month following the month of payment (Forms T600C and T652).

(19) *Qualified investments.* A corporation claiming that a share of its capital stock is a qualified investment or a trustee who claims that an interest as a beneficiary under a trust is a qualified investment is required to furnish a return in prescribed form within 90 days after the end of the taxation year to which it refers (Form T3F).

¶12,050

(20) *Tax-free savings accounts (TFSAs)*. A TFSA information return must be filed by the issuer.

(21) *Canadian Home Insulation Program and Canadian Oil Substitution Program*. Where an amount has been paid to a person under the Canadian Home Insulation Program and the Canadian Oil Substitution Program, the payor must file a return.

(22) *Certified films and video tapes*. When the principal photography or taping of a film or tape has been completed, a return must be provided to any person who owns an interest in the film or tape.

(23) *Scientific research tax credits*. Corporations designating an amount in respect of scientific research tax credits, traders or dealers in securities, banks, credit unions, and trust companies involved with scientific research tax credits are required to file a return.

(24) *Share-purchase tax credits*. Corporations designating an amount in respect of share-purchase tax credits, traders or dealers in securities, banks, credit unions, and trust companies involved with share-purchase tax credits are required to file a return.

(25) *Resource flow-through shares*. Corporations renouncing expenses pursuant to a flow-through share arrangement are required to make an information return in respect of the renounced expenses. Under such arrangements, the renounced expenses are deemed to have been incurred by the holder of the share and the holder becomes entitled to the tax benefits in respect of the renounced expenses.

(26) *Partnerships*. Every member of a partnership that carries on business in Canada or that is a Canadian partnership must make an information return in prescribed form. An information return made by any member of the partnership is deemed to have been made by each member. An information return must also be filed by any person who holds an interest in a partnership as nominee or agent for another person. The Minister may exempt the members of any partnership or class of partnerships from these requirements. Information Circular 89-5R, paragraph 11 indicates that partnerships with five or fewer members will not be required to file the annual information return. A filing date of March 31st applies for partnerships where all the members are individuals. Where all the members of a partnership are corporations, the filing-due date for the information return is within five months after the end of the fiscal period. For partnerships that have both individuals and corporations as members, the filing date is the earlier of those two dates (Regulation 229(5)). Form T5011 is to be used when applying for a partnership identification number.

(27) *Security transactions*. Every trader or dealer in securities who purchases a security as principal or sells a security as agent must make an information return in prescribed form. A return must also be filed whenever a person redeems, acquires, or cancels any of that person's securities (sub-

ject to exceptions for certain transactions); makes a payment in respect of a sale of any precious metals in the form of certificates, bullion, or coins; or is a nominee or agent carrying out certain transactions in his or her own name.

(28) *Tax shelters.* Information returns must be filed in respect of the acquisition of an interest in a tax shelter. The prescribed form is Form T5003.

(29) *Workers' compensation benefits.* Every person who pays an amount in respect of workers' compensation benefits is required to file an information return.

(30) *Social assistance payments.* Every person who makes social assistance payments is required to file an information return unless the payment is in respect of medical expenses, child care expenses, funeral expenses, legal expenses, job training or counselling, is part of a series of payments the total of which does not exceed $500, or is not part of a series of payments.

(31) *Farm support payments.* Every government, municipality or municipal or other public body or producer organization or association that makes a payment of an amount that is a farm support payment (other than an amount paid out of a net income stabilization account) to a person or partnership is required to file an information return.

(32) *Treaty exemption to non-resident corporations.* Non-resident corporations are required to file an information return where they claim a treaty tax exemption.

(33) *Construction contract payments.* Construction businesses are required to record payments they make to subcontractors who provide construction services, and to report these payments to the CRA within six months of the end of their reporting period. Goods-only payments do not have to be reported. Mixed service and goods payments have to be reported if there is a service component of $500 or more.

In most cases, two copies of these returns must be sent to the taxpayer whose income the return concerns, at the taxpayer's last known address, or delivered to the taxpayer in person, on or before the date the return is required to be filed.

[¶12,055] Estimate of Tax

Every person who is required to file a return is required to make an estimate of the tax payable.[35] An incorrect estimate may result in unpaid tax and a consequential demand for interest. Furthermore, a taxpayer who fails to complete the information contained in a prescribed form is subject to a

---

[35] CCH ¶22,134; Sec. 151.

penalty of $100. The Minister may waive all or part of this penalty in the case of an individual.[36]

[¶12,060] Tax Rulings

There may be uncertainty as to the tax consequences of certain proposed business transactions. Upon request, the CRA will give advance tax rulings to taxpayers.[37] Rulings of general interest are published by the CRA in a series of "Tax Rulings".

[¶12,065] Assessments

[¶12,070] Basic Procedure for Assessments

The Minister is required to examine, with all due dispatch, *each* return and to assess tax for the taxation year, plus interest and penalties, if any.[38] Thus, although a taxpayer had not resided in Canada in 1992 and 1993, the Minister was still required to examine the returns she had filed for those years.[39]

The Minister is also required to determine the amount of refund, if any, that may be available to the taxpayer for the year out of specified refundable tax accounts. It should be noted that the Federal Court of Appeal recently held that, although the minister's assessment of a taxpayer's returns had not been made "with all due dispatch", the taxpayer's tax liability was not affected by the fact that no assessment had been made.[40]

The requirement that the Minister examine the taxpayer's return and determine the amount of any refund or tax owing and the requirement that the Minister send a notice of assessment do not apply to determinations of disability tax credit eligibility (see ¶12,072), loss determinations, and determinations pursuant to the General Anti-Avoidance Rule (see ¶12,071).[41]

While an assessment has been held to include a "nil" assessment,[42] it has also been held that a taxpayer has no right of appeal against a nil assessment, since no tax is payable.[43] The lack of jurisdiction of the Tax Court of Canada to hear an appeal from a nil assessment was held to apply even when the question at issue relates to the CRA's determination of an individual's disability tax credit (DTC) eligibility and, as a consequence, the individual's entitlement to be named as a beneficiary under a registered disability savings plan.[44] However, see ¶12,072 for the new procedure of determination of disability tax credit eligibility.

"Assessment" is defined to include a reassessment.[45]

See page ii for explanation of footnotes.

[36] CCH ¶22,858; Sec. 162(5).
[37] Inf. Cir. 70-6R5.
[38] CCH ¶22,180, ¶22,190; Sec. 152(1), 152(2).
[39] Schatten, 96 DTC 6102.
[40] Ginsberg, 96 DTC 6372.

[41] CCH ¶22,182; Sec. 152(1.2).
[42] Anjulin Farms Ltd., 61 DTC 1182.
[43] Newfoundland Minerals Ltd., 69 DTC 5432.
[44] Tozzi, 2010 DTC 1374.
[45] CCH ¶28,018; Sec. 248(1) "assessment".

Despite a taxpayer's claim of having been subjected to undue duress, the taxpayer, who had waived his right of appeal and signed both an agreement and documents accepting several reassessments in order to avoid prosecution for tax evasion, was held to be liable for his actions, and the appeal was dismissed.[46]

[¶12,071] Determination of Loss for a Year and Determination Pursuant to GAAR

A taxpayer may, at his or her option, request that the Minister determine the amount of the taxpayer's non-capital, net capital, restricted farm, farm, or limited partnership loss for a year if the Minister ascertains that the amount of the taxpayer's loss is different from the amount (if any) reported by the taxpayer in his return of income for the year.[47] It should be noted that it is only the taxpayer that can initiate the determination, but it is not clear how the taxpayer is to know that the Minister has ascertained the amount of the loss to be different from that reported in the taxpayer's return of income. Once the taxpayer requests the determination to be made, the Minister is required to make the determination with all due dispatch and send a notice of the determination to the person by whom the return was filed.

When the taxpayer is aware that the Minister disagrees with the calculation of the loss as reported, the taxpayer has two alternatives. He or she may request that the Minister determine the amount of the loss immediately pursuant to the above procedure, or he or she may decide that it is preferable to raise the matter in the taxation year in which he or she claims the loss against other income.

It should be noted that there does not appear to be any maximum time period within which the taxpayer must exercise his or her right to request a determination. However, once a determination is made, the time limitations governing objections and appeals in respect of assessments also apply to the determination.

The Minister may also determine an amount as a consequence of applying the general anti-avoidance rule (GAAR) (see ¶15,307).[48] Pursuant to GAAR, where a transaction is an avoidance transaction, the tax consequences are to be determined as is reasonable in the circumstances to deny a tax benefit, "tax consequences" meaning the amount of income, taxable income, taxable income earned in Canada, tax or other amount payable by, or refundable to, the taxpayer, or any other amount relevant to computing such amounts. Therefore, amounts that can be determined pursuant to GAAR include amounts such as the adjusted cost base of a property, the paid-up capital of a share, or the undepreciated capital cost of a class of property.

See page ii for explanation of footnotes.

[46] Smerchanski, 76 DTC 6247.

[47] CCH ¶22,181; Sec. 152(1.1); Interp. Bul. IT-512.

[48] CCH ¶22,181a; Sec. 152(1.11).

¶12,071

Where the Minister determines such amounts, he has two alternatives. He may determine the amount immediately pursuant to the above procedure, or he may decide that it is preferable to assess the taxpayer later in a subsequent taxation year in which the taxpayer makes a claim with respect to such an amount.

Pursuant to GAAR, where the Minister has issued an assessment or made a determination in respect of a taxpayer, any other person can request a further determination with respect to that same transaction. In such case, the Minister *must* make such a determination under the above procedure. Where the Minister makes such a determination pursuant to GAAR, he must send to the taxpayer, with all due dispatch, a notice of determination stating the amount determined.

The determination of the loss or determination pursuant to GAAR by the Minister is final and binding on both the taxpayer and the Minister for the purposes of calculating the taxpayer's income, taxable income, tax or other amount payable, or amount refundable, in any year subject to the taxpayer's right to object and appeal the determination.[49] For example, once a determination is made and the appeal procedure is either exhausted or not invoked, the taxpayer cannot object to the computation of income in a subsequent taxation year where the income tax payable is affected by a "determined" loss.

[¶12,072] Determination of Eligibility for Disability Tax Credit (DTC)

To resolve the problems associated with the lack of jurisdiction of the Tax Court of Canada in respect of "nil" assessments, an individual is now allowed to make a request from the Minister for a determination of DTC eligibility.[50] Thus, a nil assessment will not preclude the individual from appealing a negative determination by the Minister in respect of DTC eligibility as was the case in *Tozzi* (see ¶12,070).

Before these amendments, an individual had to wait for a notice of assessment to file an objection relating to DTC and was precluded from objecting to a nil assessment. The time limit for filing an objection to the CRA's determination of DTC eligibility will be either 90 days after the sending of the CRA's notice of determination or one year after the due date for the tax year in question, whichever is later.

This new relief for DTC eligibility determination is applicable after the 2009 taxation year in respect of forms filed for the DTC with the Minister after June 26, 2011. However, for forms filed for the DTC with the Minister after the 2007 taxation year and before June 26, 2011, and where the Minister has issued a notice that no tax is payable, then the Minister is deemed to have issued a notice of determination on the latter of the date of June 26, 2011 or the actual day the notice of no tax payable was issued. The

---

See page ii for explanation of footnotes.

[49] CCH ¶22,183; Sec. 152(1.3). [50] CCH ¶22,185a; Sec. 152(1.01).

determination may be objected to within 180 days of the date of the deemed notice.

DTC eligibility can affect claims for other amounts than RDSP eligibility (the question at issue in *Tozzi*). Eligibility for the DTC affects the amount claimed for child care expenses, claims for part-time attendant care for the disability supports deduction, and claims for the education tax credit. DTC eligibility can also affect disability support not to be included in income, the definition of a "preferred beneficiary" under a trust, and special rules in relation to the Home Buyer's Plan and to registered education savings plans.

[¶12,073] Assessments of Partnerships

The Minister may assess partnership returns and issue a determination of a partnership's income or loss as a whole, the consequences of which will be binding on the partners even if they are not personally served with the notice.[51] The Minister's determination must be issued within three years after the later of (i) the day on which an information return in respect of the partnership for the fiscal period is required to be filed (see ¶12,050), and (ii) the day on which such a return is actually filed. If no return is due because the partnership is excused from filing, the Minister has three years from the later of the date the return would have been due, had the partnership not been excused, and the actual date of filing.

The three-year time limit for making a determination is extended if the members of the partnership waive it. As a result of the 2012 Budget, effective June 29, 2012, a single member of a partnership may waive, on its behalf, the three-year time limit. To be so empowered, such member must be designated in the partnership return for the fiscal period or otherwise authorized to act in such a capacity.[52] Before the 2012 Budget implementing Bill C-38 was assented to June 29, 2012, the waiver had to be made by all the members of the partnership.

When a determination is made, the Minister is required to send a notice of the determination to the partnership and to each person who was, during the applicable fiscal year, a member of the partnership.[53] It should be noted, however, that a determination is not invalid simply because one or more members of the partnership do not receive a notice of the determination.[54]

Subject to the right of objection and appeal of the partnership's designated member, the determination is binding on the Minister and all members of the partnership.[55] Only one member of a partnership can object to a determination made by the Minister. Such person can be either (i) the member of the partnership designated in the annual partnership return, or (ii) a member of the partnership expressly authorized by the partnership to

---

See page ii for explanation of footnotes.

[51] CCH ¶22,186; Sec. 152(1.4).
[52] Sec. 152(1.9).
[53] CCH ¶22,187; Sec. 152(1.5).
[54] CCH ¶22,187f; Sec. 152(1.6).
[55] CCH ¶22,188; Sec. 152(1.7).

¶12,073

so act.[56] The Minister will then have one year after the expiration of the designated member's right to object or appeal to assess the tax liability of, or to determine any amount deemed to have been paid or to have been an overpayment by, any member of the partnership and any other affected taxpayer. Such assessment or determination can only be made to the extent that it is necessary to give effect to the determination or redetermination that was previously made at the partnership level or to a decision of a court relating thereto.

In the event that, following a partnership determination, a purported partner is found not to have been a partner or the partnership not to have existed, the CRA has a year from that finding to reassess the non-partner in respect of the same issues, notwithstanding the usual statutory limitations on assessment periods.[57]

[¶12,075] Incorrect or Incomplete Assessment

Liability for tax is not affected by an incorrect or incomplete assessment or by the fact that no assessment has been made.[58] Nor is it affected by the fact that CRA officials may have given the taxpayer incorrect advice, or advice the results of which are unacceptable to the CRA. Subject to being varied or vacated on an objection or appeal, or being voluntarily reassessed by the Minister, an assessment is deemed to be valid and binding notwithstanding any error, defect, or omission. In a case where the Minister had relied on sections of the Act that had been repealed, the taxpayer's notice of objection and appeal were dismissed since the critical question was not the section of the Act under which the Minister's assessment was based, but whether or not tax was owing by the taxpayer.[59]

[¶12,080] Time Allowed for Assessments

The Minister may make an original assessment, reassessment, or additional assessment for taxes, interest, or penalties at any time.[60] However, the Minister may assess, reassess, or make additional assessments, as a general rule, only within the "normal reassessment period" for the taxpayer with respect to the year in question.

As a general rule, reassessments may be made by the Minister only within three years (four years for mutual fund trusts and corporations other than Canadian-controlled private corporations (CCPCs)) after the earlier of the day of sending of a notice of original assessment and the day of sending of a notification that no tax is payable.[61] Effective December 15, 2010, the Minister is allowed to send notices and other communications electronically, which previously would have been sent by mail.[62] In certain circum-

---

See page ii for explanation of footnotes.

[56] CCH ¶23,021fa; Sec. 165(1.15).
[57] CCH ¶22,188f; Sec. 152(1.8).
[58] CCH ¶22,210, ¶22,280; Sec. 152(3), 152(8).
[59] Riendeau, 91 DTC 5416.

[60] CCH ¶22,220; Sec. 152(4).
[61] CCH ¶22,216; Sec. 152(3.1).
[62] CCH ¶27,844a; Sec. 244(14.1).

stances, where a reassessment of a taxpayer is required as a result of a deduction claim in respect of losses, gifts, tax credits, or other deductions carried back from subsequent taxation years of the taxpayer or another taxpayer, the reassessment period is extended by three years to six years (seven years for mutual fund trusts and corporations other than CCPCs), for the purpose of taking into account the effects of the deduction claimed.[63] For example, if a taxpayer incurred a loss in 2012, which could be carried back to 2009, his or her 2009 return can be reassessed at any time within six years from its original assessment date.

In addition, this six-year extended reassessment period applies to reassessments made with respect to: transactions between a taxpayer and a non-arm's length non-resident person; certain reallocations of revenues or expenses or national transactions of a non-resident taxpayer that carries on business in Canada; additional payments or reimbursements of tax to or by a foreign country, which result in a change in Canadian tax consequences; reductions in amounts renounced in respect of a flow-through share; and donations of non-qualifying securities, where the donor has died or where there has been a loanback arrangement. This extended reassessment period may also be further lengthened where a taxpayer files a waiver within the three-year period following the normal reassessment period.

Where a reassessment of provincial tax is issued that results in a change in the allocation of a taxpayer's income earned in a province, a corresponding reassessment may be issued under the federal Act up to one year after the later of 90 days following the date of sending of the notice of reassessment of provincial tax or the day on which the Minister is notified of the provincial reassessment. This provision was added, effective March 12, 2009, consequential to the new federal–Ontario corporate tax collection agreement. The change in the allocation of a taxpayer's income earned in a province would be determined in accordance with the rules in Part IV of the Regulations.

Either the CRA or the taxpayer can require a reassessment of a statute-barred year, notwithstanding the above time limitations, if the tax balances for that particular year are altered by a "settlement" of balances for another year.[64] A settlement may arise from an assessment (where issues have been in dispute with the CRA and an agreement is reached) or from a court decision. A "balance" means[65] income, taxable income, taxable income earned in Canada, loss, or any tax or other amount payable or refundable or deemed paid or overpaid. The reassessment of the statute-barred year must be made by the CRA or demanded by the taxpayer within one year after all rights of objection and appeal have expired for the year for which the settlement was reached. Revisions to the statute-barred year can only be made to the extent

---

See page ii for explanation of footnotes.

[63] CCH ¶22,220; Sec. 152(4).
[64] CCH ¶22,222a; Sec. 152(4.3).
[65] CCH ¶22,222b; Sec. 152(4.4).

that the changes can reasonably be considered to relate to the changed balances for the settlement year.

This rule might work for or against the taxpayer. Either side, however, may not go back to years preceding the settlement date. Only changes to years subsequent to the settlement will be permitted. For instance, if a taxpayer has an adjustment in a Year 1 assessment that would produce a beneficial result in Year 2, the taxpayer can demand a change to Year 2 even though statute-barred. On the other hand, if the Year 1 adjustment could give the CRA a benefit in Year 0 which is statute-barred, they could not go back and reassess to make that change.

In a successful Tax Court appeal, the taxpayer established its entitlement to a small business deduction for 1995–1997. The Minister later denied its small business deduction claim for 1998 and 1999, but the taxpayer failed to file timely notices of objection. The taxpayer's application for an order of *mandamus* compelling the Minister to reassess for 1998 and 1999 was dismissed, since the Tax Court decision did not have a consequential effect on any balance for those years, as required.[66]

In January 2009, the Tax Court of Canada dealt with the issue of whether, in appealing an assessment in which gains on index futures contracts realized by the taxpayer in its 2002 taxation year were on income account, the taxpayer could claim that losses on dispositions in similar transactions in 1998 (a statute-barred year) were also on income account and could be carried forward to offset the gains in 2002.[67] The Tax Court of Canada (per Chief Justice Gerald Rip) ruled in favour of the taxpayer on the basis that the Minister was only asked to correct an assessing error made for that year, in order to arrive at a correct non-capital loss carryover for 2002.

In any event, the right to reassess *at any time* remains with the Minister if:

(a) the taxpayer has made any misrepresentation that is attributable to neglect, carelessness, or wilful default or has committed any fraud; or

(b) the taxpayer has filed a waiver with the Minister within three years of the date of sending of the original notice of assessment or of the notice of no tax payable; and

(c) the reassessment can reasonably be regarded as relating to the matters described in (a) and (b), because of which the Minister is able to reassess beyond the normal reassessment period.[68]

Once filed, a valid waiver may be revoked upon six months' notice to the Minister, after which no further assessment can be made under it (with the exceptions of fraud and misrepresentation).[69]

See page ii for explanation of footnotes.

[66] LJP Sales Agency Inc., 2007 DTC 5262.   [68] CCH ¶22,220, ¶22,220a; Sec. 152(4), 152(4.01).
[67] Leola Purdy, Sons Ltd., 2009 DTC 1042.   [69] CCH ¶22,221; Sec. 152(4.1).

¶12,080

The Minister may also reassess individuals or testamentary trusts at their request, in order to give effect to a reduction in tax originally assessed or to a late refund request for any of the 10 preceding taxation years.[70] That is, for 2012, the CRA will consider requests in respect of 2002 and later taxation years. It appears that the intention under this rule is that the CRA will give effect to written requests for such adjustments where it is satisfied that the request for adjustment would have been processed if it had been made within the normal reassessment period. Guidelines describing the circumstances in which such requests may be granted and the manner in which the applications should be made are outlined in Information Circular 07-1. After 2006, those circumstances also cover the payment of working income tax benefits (WITB) and WITB disability supplements.

The day of sending of a notice of assessment or determination is presumed to be the date appearing on such notice or determination.[71] The presumption is therefore rebuttable. The onus is on the Minister to establish that assessments are mailed or sent electronically in a timely manner to the proper mailing or electronic address of the taxpayer.

In order for a notice to have been properly "sent", it does not necessarily have to have been received by the taxpayer. However, where, due to a postal strike, the CRA's employees attempted to personally serve the taxpayer, but were unable to locate the taxpayer, the notice had not left the possession of the CRA and had therefore not been "sent".[72]

Where the Minister makes reassessments outside the three-year limit alleging fraud or misrepresentation, and if the taxpayer appeals, the burden of proof is on the Minister. If the Minister provides proof, the onus of showing the assessment to be incorrect in any way shifts to the taxpayer. After reading a newspaper article alleging that the taxpayer had been charged with fraud, the Minister conducted an audit, resulting in a reassessment. In light of the taxpayer's misrepresentation and grossly negligent conduct, the Minister was justified in reassessing beyond the normal reassessment period and imposing penalties. The taxpayer's Charter arguments were untenable.[73]

The fact that misrepresentation must be the result of neglect, carelessness, or wilful default appears to mean that "innocent" misrepresentation, i.e., false statements made in the honest belief that they are true, is not a reason for breaking the time limit. This was not the case when a taxpayer's 1981 return, prepared by his accountant, reported his share of a capital gain as $71,392, rather than $711,392. Considering that the taxpayer's perfunctory perusal of the return did not amount to reasonable care, the Minister could reassess him in 1989.[74] Similarly, when a taxpayer, who had been given shares by a venture capitalist, declared a cost acquisition in excess of nil, the

See page ii for explanation of footnotes.

[70] CCH ¶22,222; Sec. 152(4.2).
[71] CCH ¶27,844; Sec. 244(14).
[72] Flanagan, 87 DTC 5390.
[73] Deep, 2008 DTC 6016.
[74] Nesbitt, 96 DTC 6588.

Federal Court of Appeal considered that his misrepresentation was sufficiently substantial to be attributable to "neglect, carelessness, or wilful default".[75]

The fact that a reassessment is under appeal does not prevent the Minister from making a second reassessment. The second reassessment displaces the first and makes it a nullity, thus the basis for the appeal ceases to exist.[76] However, the Federal Court of Appeal held that a reassessment was not really a reassessment so as to annul and replace an earlier reassessment, but rather was an additional assessment. Being an additional assessment, the taxpayer remained liable on the original assessments.[77]

Finally, the law does not require a taxpayer to report profits in the way that best pleases the minister. Where the taxpayer's explanation that the sale of his residence was prompted by his mother giving him a riverfront property on which to build a residence was reasonable and reporting the resulting profit as an exempt profit from the sale of his principal residence was also reasonable, the Minister failed to show that his reassessment beyond the normal reassessment period was justified.[78]

[¶12,085] Amounts Excluded from Assessments

Where a taxpayer is reassessed beyond the three-year (or six-year) limitation period, the reassessment cannot include in income any amount that was not included in income for the purpose of an assessment, reassessment or additional assessment made before the end of the period.[79]

In computing the income of the year being reassessed, the Minister can, however, include an amount (revenue or expense) that relates to the subject matter of the notice of objection, such as:

(a) personal exemptions where a disallowance of alimony payments is the subject matter; and

(b) capital cost allowance where a disallowance of repairs is the subject matter.[80]

If the taxpayer filed a waiver within the three-year limit, there may not be included in any reassessment any amount that the taxpayer can establish as not being reasonably related to a matter specified in the waiver.

[¶12,090] Reassessments for Deductions Carried Back to Previous Years

If a taxpayer wants to carry back deductions and credits of all descriptions (non-capital losses, net capital losses, donation tax credits, unused

---

See page ii for explanation of footnotes.

[75] Angus, 98 DTC 6661.

[76] Walkem, 71 DTC 5288.

[77] Lambert, 76 DTC 6373.

[78] Cameron, 2011 DTC 1166.

[79] CCH ¶22,247, ¶29,838; Sec. 152(5); ITAR 62(1); Inf. Cir. 75-7R3.

[80] CCH ¶23,030; Sec. 165(3).

foreign tax credits, etc.), he or she must have filed within the prescribed time limit the return of income for the year in which the deduction or credit arises.[81]

The carryback request is made by filing with this return a T1A form amending the return of income for the taxation year from which the carryback is made. If no tax was payable in the latter taxation year so that the taxpayer was not required to file a return for such year, the carryback request must be filed on or before the return due date which would have been applicable if tax were payable for that year. In failing to file an amended return claiming a non-capital loss within this time limitation period, a taxpayer was precluded from moving a loss incurred by him in 1978 forward for deduction against his income for 1982.[82]

Upon the filing of the carryback request, the Minister will reassess the tax for the taxation year to which the deduction is carried back to take into account the deduction claimed and will reassess the tax for any subsequent taxation year affected by this carryback request.

[¶12,100] "Net Worth" Assessment

If a taxpayer's records are inadequate to properly determine the taxpayer's tax liability, the Minister may issue a "net worth" assessment.[83] The net worth assessment is arrived at by:

(a) determining the taxpayer's assets and liabilities (i.e., net worth) at the end of the taxation year and at the end of the last previous year for which tax could be determined; and

(b) assuming that the taxpayer's income for the intervening period was equal to the increase in his or her net worth in the period plus the estimated amount spent for personal and living expenses.

It has been well established that the onus of proving these assessments wrong is on the taxpayer,[84] who may attack them, for instance, by proving that:

(a) the increase in the net worth arose from non-taxable receipts, such as inheritances[85] or gambling;[86]

(b) the net worth at the beginning of the period was undervalued[87] or the assets at the end overvalued;[88]

(c) liabilities at the end were omitted or undervalued;[89]

(d) money was held in trust for others;[90] or

---

[81] CCH ¶22,255; Sec. 152(6).
[82] Dauphinais, 94 DTC 1153.
[83] CCH ¶22,260; Sec. 152(7).
[84] Dezura, 3 DTC 1101.
[85] Markakis, 86 DTC 1237.

[86] Luprypa, 97 DTC 1416.
[87] Garvey Estate, 58 DTC 263.
[88] Pothitos, 58 DTC 549.
[89] Markakis, 86 DTC 1237.
[90] Gentile, 88 DTC 6130.

(e) income losses were greater than assessed.[91]

Satisfactory evidence must be produced; a mere statement is not enough.[92] Cogent evidence is required to disprove a net worth assessment.[93]

[¶12,105] Payment of Tax

[¶12,110] Withholding of Tax

Every person who makes certain payments must withhold from them a prescribed amount of tax on account of the payee and remit it to the Receiver General.[94] Employers are required to withhold income taxes, CPP contributions, and employment insurance (EI) premiums from their employee's pay and remit those amounts, along with the employer's portion of EI and CPP, to the Receiver General. Most employers are required to remit withholding amounts on a monthly basis, while large employers must remit more frequently. Amounts deducted or withheld on a monthly basis must be remitted on or before the 15th day of the following month.[95] However, those with average monthly withholding amounts between $15,000 and $50,000 remit bi-monthly, and those with withholding amounts greater than $50,000 must remit within three days of the pay period.[96] The frequency of remittances to be made by very small employers is reduced by allowing those with average monthly withholding amounts of less than $3,000 (prior to 2008, the monetary threshold was $1,000) for either of the two preceding calendar years and perfect compliance history for the preceding 12 months to remit only on a quarterly basis. In this context, perfect compliance history means that the employer has remitted its taxes payable and filed all the required returns on time, under both the *Income Tax Act* and Part IX (GST/HST portion) of the *Excise Tax Act*, during the preceding 12 months.[97] Quarterly remittance periods end on March 31, June 30, September 30, and December 31, and the remittances are due by the 15th of the month following the end of the quarters.

The payments from which tax must be withheld are:

(1) salary, wages, or other remuneration (other than amounts paid to non-resident actors that are subject to the 23% tax withholding);

(2) a superannuation or pension benefit;

(3) a retiring allowance;

(4) a death benefit;

See page ii for explanation of footnotes.

[91] Laurion, 54 DTC 152.
[92] Rose, 2003 DTC 5077.
[93] Naguib, 2004 DTC 6082.
[94] CCH ¶22,300, ¶22,326; Sec. 153(1); Reg. 101.

[95] CCH ¶22,340; Reg. 108(1).
[96] CCH ¶22,340; Reg. 108(1.1), Reg. 108(1.11).
[97] CCH ¶22,340; Reg. 108(1.12).

(5) a benefit under the *Unemployment Insurance Act* or the *Employment Insurance Act*;

(6) supplementary unemployment plan benefits;

(7) annuities and payments in full or partial commutation of annuities;

(8) fees, commissions, or other amounts for services rendered;

(9) payments from deferred profit sharing plans (DPSPs) or revoked DPSPs;

(10) payments from a registered retirement savings plan (RRSP);

(11) payments on surrender, cancellation, or redemption of an income-averaging annuity contract;

(12) payments out of a registered retirement income fund (RRIF);

(13) prescribed benefits under government assistance programs (i.e., benefits under the *Labour Adjustment Benefits Act* and income assistance payments under the *Department of Labour Act*, the Plant Workers Adjustment Program, and the Northern Cod Compensation and Adjustment Program);

(14) amounts paid to any person who has elected in prescribed form in respect of such amounts (for example, a fisher could elect to have amounts withheld out of the proceeds of the sale of fish);

(15) services to be performed by non-residents;

(16) payments relating to retirement compensation arrangements;

(17) employment earnings supplements received as social assistance under projects sponsored by the federal government; and

(18) payments under registered education savings plans.

The prescribed amount may be reduced where the taxpayer can establish undue hardship; a taxpayer may also apply to increase the amount to be withheld.

Where a claim for payment of taxes withheld from employees' wages was filed by the Minister against one of two related companies undergoing bankruptcy, and the claim was disallowed by the trustee on the ground that the wages in question were paid by the company which was not their employer, it was held that the taxes were still payable, since taxes are required to be withheld by all persons paying wages, not merely employers.[98] However, where a taxpayer company, in managing the affairs of another company, paid that other company's employees by means of cheques drawn on the other company's bank account, the taxpayer, being simply an agent,

---

See page ii for explanation of footnotes.

[98] G. & G. Equipment Ltd., 74 DTC 6407.

¶12,110

was not obligated to make payroll deductions or remittances.[99] Similarly, where receiver-managers under a debenture merely guaranteed or provided funds to honour payroll cheques distributed by the defaulting companies to their employees prior to the receiver-managers' appointment, there was no obligation on the receiver-managers to make payroll deductions or remittances.[100]

Where the employer retains from any remuneration paid to an employee an amount that is:

(a) a contribution under the *Canada Pension Plan* or the *Quebec Pension Plan*;

(b) a premium under the *Unemployment Insurance Act* or the *Employment Insurance Act*; or

(c) a contribution under a registered pension plan,

only the balance remaining after deducting such amounts is considered to be the amount of remuneration paid for purposes of the withholding of tax by an employer.[101] Once an amount is deducted or withheld, it is deemed to have been paid to the employee so that the employee cannot claim that his or her income for tax purposes is his or her net income after tax.[102]

Any person, including a partnership, who has any influence, whether direct or indirect, over the property or affairs of another person, and who authorizes or causes certain payments to be made by the other person that are subject to deductions at source, is deemed to have made the payment and is jointly and severally liable with the other person for all amounts payable for failure to deduct at source.[103] Joint and several liability is not limited to trustees and other persons acting in a similar fiduciary capacity. It also extends to persons such as receivers, secured creditors, monitors, and their agents.

[¶12,115] Remittance of Deductions

Amounts which have been deducted or withheld under ¶12,110 may be paid at a financial institution or tax centre, or a cheque or money order may be mailed directly to the CRA in Ottawa. The remittance must be accompanied by Form PD7A.[104] Where an employer ceases to carry on business, any amounts deducted or withheld that have not been paid to the Receiver General must be remitted within seven days of the day when the employer ceased to carry on business.[105]

Prescribed persons (in general, large employers)[106] are required to remit amounts withheld to the account of the Receiver General at a "designated

---

See page ii for explanation of footnotes.

[99] Canadian Pacific Hotels Limited, 79 DTC 274.
[100] Fowlis and Peat Marwick Ltd., 79 DTC 369.
[101] CCH ¶22,324; Reg. 100(1)–(3).
[102] CCH ¶22,400; Sec. 153(3).

[103] CCH ¶27,267–27,267b; Sec. 227(5)–(5.2).
[104] CCH ¶22,340; Reg. 108(3).
[105] CCH ¶22,340; Reg. 108(2).
[106] Reg. 110.

financial institution". This term is defined as a bank, a trust company, or a deposit-taking mortgage lending company. A foreign bank that is subject to the restrictions in subsection 524(2) of the *Bank Act*, generally meaning a foreign bank that operates only as a so-called lending branch, is excluded from the definition.[107] This requirement to remit amounts withheld to a designated financial institution is to ensure that the payments are immediately credited to the Government of Canada. A failure to so remit could result in penalties to the large employer described at ¶12,155. This was the situation in a case[108] where the Tax Court of Canada ordered the CRA to reconsider its decision to impose penalties on a large employer that had made its remittance directly to the Tax Services Office on the due date. In response to this unintended effect of the mandatory financial institution remittance requirement, the Act was amended to deem a remittance to be in compliance with the requirement that it be remitted to a designated financial institution if it is received directly by the CRA at least one full day before the due date. This exception to the mandatory financial institution remittance requirement applies to remittances by prescribed persons that are first due on or after February 26, 2008 (the 2008 Budget day).[109]

[¶12,120] Amounts To Be Withheld at Source

The amount to be deducted or withheld is determined in the prescribed withholding tax tables.[110] It is determined with reference to the establishment of the employer where the employee reports for work, and, accordingly, will vary depending upon the province in which the establishment is located.

A person who is not required to report for work at any establishment of an employer is deemed to report for work at the establishment from which the remuneration is paid. However, in the case of remuneration other than salary or wages, a person is deemed to report for work at the establishment of the employer in the province of residence and, for that purpose, an employer who has no establishment in that province will be deemed to have one.[111]

[¶12,125] Machine Computation of Deductions

A booklet providing for machine computation of tax, Canada Pension Plan contributions, and employment insurance premiums is published by the CRA and is available from local District Taxation Offices.

[¶12,130] Withholding Tables

The amounts to be withheld in the prescribed tax withholding tables take into account the rates of federal and provincial tax, reductions of basic

---

See page ii for explanation of footnotes.

[107] CCH ¶22,610; Sec. 153(6).
[108] Pontiac Buick Cadillac Ltd., 2007 DTC 5014.
[109] CCH ¶22,386ab; Sec. 153(1.4).

[110] CCH ¶22,328; Reg. 102(1), Reg. 102(2), Sch I.

[111] CCH ¶22,324; Reg. 100(4).

federal tax, the employment expense deduction, as well as a slightly reduced withholding to allow for other deductions or credits to which an employee may be entitled upon filing an income tax return.

[¶12,135] Provincial Tax Rates

Except for Quebec, the provincial tax rates are expressed as a percentage of the basic federal tax. In Quebec, the rate is imposed on taxable income as computed under the province's own income tax legislation.

The federal government collects the tax on behalf of the provinces and remits it to them, except for Quebec, which collects its own tax.

For provincial tax rates for individuals, see ¶8025.

[¶12,140] Where Withholding Not Required

If an employee certifies on Form TD1 that the total earnings received and receivable during the calendar year from all sources will not exceed the personal amount value of personal tax credits claimed, no tax need be withheld.[112] No tax need be withheld on account of a person who was neither employed nor resident in Canada at any time in the taxation year, except in the case of an employee who receives remuneration while on leave of absence, unless that employee is liable to pay tax in a foreign country or is paid for business carried on in the foreign country by a foreign affiliate.[113]

[¶12,145] Variation in Deduction

Where an employer pays remuneration to an employee in a taxation year:

(a) for a period not covered by the withholding tables; or

(b) for a pay period in an amount that is greater than any provided for in the tables,

the amount to be deducted or withheld by the employer is calculated by applying to the payment amount the proportion of tax that can reasonably be expected to be payable on the employee's total remuneration for the year to the employee's total remuneration for the year.[114]

A taxpayer may apply to have the amount of tax to be withheld reduced where the taxpayer can establish that amounts required to be withheld would cause undue hardship.[115] For example, a taxpayer earning a salary will have an amount withheld from each payment received. However, if the taxpayer becomes obliged to pay a substantial portion of the remainder of each payment as an alimony or maintenance payment, he or she may be able to establish that the amount of tax otherwise required to be deducted

---

See page ii for explanation of footnotes.

[112] CCH ¶22,332; Reg. 104(1). [114] CCH ¶22,336; Reg. 106.
[113] CCH ¶17,150, ¶22,332; Sec. 115(2); Reg. 104(2). [115] CCH ¶22,386; Sec. 153(1.1).

from his or her salary is excessive and results in a cash shortage to the taxpayer, causing him or her undue hardship. Beginning in 2007, a joint election made or expected to be made in regard to pension income splitting (see ¶12,247) is not to be considered a basis on which the Minister may determine a lesser amount.[116]

A taxpayer may also make a request to increase the amount to be withheld.[117] This could prove to be beneficial in equalizing tax liability where a taxpayer has income from more than one source.

[¶12,150] TD1 Form

A TD1 form, which is an employee's tax deduction return, is to be filed with the employer when employment commences, and a new return filed within seven days of the date on which a change occurs in the personal tax credits of the employee.[118]

[¶12,155] Penalty for Failure To Withhold Tax

A penalty is imposed upon any person who has failed to deduct or withhold tax on account of a taxpayer.

If the withholding was required with respect to salary, wages, or remuneration paid to an employee, or certain similar types of payment, the penalty will be 10% of the amount that should have been deducted or withheld upon first occurrence, and 20% of the amount not deducted or withheld upon a second or further occurrence.

The second occurrence penalty applies where another penalty has been assessed against the same person in the same calendar year. However, the second occurrence penalty does not come into play unless the failure to deduct or withhold was made knowingly or under circumstances amounting to gross negligence. The 10% or 20% penalties also apply to amounts that should have been deducted or withheld from certain payments to nonresidents.

If the withholding was required with respect to any other kind of payment, the penalty is the entire amount that should have been deducted or withheld.

In all cases, interest will be charged on the unpaid tax from the day the amount was required to be withheld or deducted.[119] Interest will cease at the time of payment, unless it is in respect of withholdings on account of a Canadian resident, in which case it will cease on April 30 following the year during which default occurred or the date of payment, whichever occurs first.[120] Where a person fails to deduct or withhold tax from certain payments to a non-resident, the non-resident person will be jointly and severally liable with that person to pay the interest.

See page ii for explanation of footnotes.

[116] CCH ¶22,386aa; Sec. 153(1.3).
[117] CCH ¶22,386a; Sec. 153(1.2).
[118] CCH ¶27,254, ¶22,338; Sec. 227(2); Reg. 107.

[119] CCH ¶27,278, ¶27,279, ¶27,284; Sec. 227(8), 227(8.1), 227(8.3), 227(8.4); Reg. 4300.
[120] CCH ¶27,281; Sec. 227(8.3).

A penalty is also imposed for not remitting to the Receiver General the amount of tax that has been deducted or withheld. For remittances due on or after February 26, 2008, the penalty for late remittances is dependent upon the number of days the payment is overdue:

- one to three days late — 3%;
- four to five days late — 5%;
- six to seven days late — 7%; and
- more than seven days late — 10%.

For remittances due before February 26, 2008, the penalty is fixed at 10%. As well, there is a further penalty for second or subsequent occurrences of failure to remit or pay an amount during the same year. In such a case, the penalty will be 20% of the amount that should have been remitted or paid, if the same person has already been assessed a penalty for a failure to remit or pay in the same calendar year and the failure to remit was made knowingly or under circumstances amounting to gross negligence. The penalty applies only to the amount by which the total of the required remittance (including source deductions, Canada Pension Plan contributions, and Employment Insurance premiums) exceeds $500. This limitation does not apply where the delay or deficiency is wilful.[121] See also Chapter XIV.

[¶12,160] Tax Transfer Payment

The Minister may, on behalf of the federal government, enter into an agreement with a province to provide for tax transfer payments from one government to the other with respect to income tax deducted or withheld at source.[122] A rate of 45% has been prescribed for these tax transfer payments.

To avoid the possibility of double taxation where employees live in one province and work in another province, a province will allow a resident a credit against income tax payable to it, of an amount equal to the tax deducted on account of provincial income tax in another province. Where the amount withheld is in excess of the tax payable to the province of residence, the taxpayer is entitled to a refund of the excess.

The appropriate tax transfer payments are deemed to have been received by the taxpayer and by the Receiver General.

[¶12,165] Bonuses or Retroactive Pay Increases

Where an employer makes a payment to an employee in respect of a bonus or a retroactive pay increase, and the employee's total remuneration, *including the bonus or increase*, does not exceed $5,000, the amount to be withheld is 10% in any province or territory, and 15% outside Canada or in Canada beyond the limits of any province or territory.[123]

See page ii for explanation of footnotes.

[121] CCH ¶27,282, ¶27,283a, ¶27,283b, ¶27,283c; Sec. 227(9), 227(9.2), 227(9.3), 227(9.4).   [122] CCH ¶22,622, ¶22,627; Sec. 154(1); Reg. 3300.   [123] CCH ¶22,330; Reg. 103(1).

Where the total exceeds $5,000, the amount to be withheld is established on the basis of an "assumed rate of pay per year", ascertained by dividing the bonus by the number of pay periods in the year and by adding the result to the amount of regular pay per pay period. From the tax which would be withheld under the tables from this total, the amount to be withheld from the regular pay is deducted and the resulting difference is multiplied by the number of pay periods; the resulting figure is the amount to be withheld from the bonus.

Example:

Diana earns a salary of $400 per week. In September, she was given a bonus of $300. Her province of employment is British Columbia. The claim code that applies to her TD1 and TD1BC forms is "1".

Step 1: Divide the bonus by the number of pay periods in the year ($300 ÷ 52 = $5.77).

Step 2: Add the $5.77 to the current pay rate of $400. As a result, the adjusted pay rate for the year is $405.77 per week

Step 3: In the T4032, Payroll Deductions Tables, see Part D, "Federal tax deductions", and Part E, "Provincial tax deductions". Refer to the "Weekly (52 pay periods)" table to find the increased weekly tax that should be deducted on the additional $5.77 per week.

Calculate as follows:
• Federal and provincial tax to deduct on $405.77 per week.
• Minus the federal and provincial tax to deduct on $400 per week.

The result is the tax to be deducted on the additional $5.77 per week.

Step 4: Multiply the additional tax on $5.77 per week by 52 (the number of pay periods in the year) in order to obtain the amount of income tax to deduct from the bonus of $300.

The amount to be withheld from a payment in respect of a retroactive increase is computed in a similar manner, taking into account, however, only the past period to which the increase applies.

Example:

In this example, Diana's pay increased from $440 to $460 per week. The increase was retroactive to 12 weeks, which gives her a total retroactive payment of $240 (12 × $20). Her province of employment is Nova Scotia. The claim code that applies to her TD1 and TD1NS forms is "6."

Step 1: In the T4032, Payroll Deductions Tables, refer to Part D, "Federal tax deductions", and Part E, "Provincial tax deductions". Refer to the "Weekly (52 pay periods a year)" table to find the increase in the weekly tax that should be deducted because of the increased pay rate.

Calculate as follows:
• Federal and provincial tax to deduct on $460 per week.
• Minus federal and provincial tax to deduct on $440 per week.

The result is the tax to be deducted on the additional $20 per week.

Step 2: Multiply the additional tax on $20 per week by the number of weeks to which the retroactive pay increase applies. This amount represents the tax to be deducted on the retroactive payment

¶12,165

[¶12,170] Lump-Sum Payments

Lump-sum payments made to Canadian residents on retirement, as compensation for loss of office, in recognition of long service and not out of or under a superannuation fund or plan, or as a retiring allowance are subject to withholding tax at the rate of 10% (5% in Quebec) if the payment does not exceed $5,000, 20% (10% in Quebec) if the payment exceeds $5,000 but does not exceed $15,000, and 30% (15% in Quebec) if the payment exceeds $15,000.[124] The same rates apply to a lump-sum payment from an income-averaging annuity contract, a registered retirement savings plan (RRSP), or an amended RRSP.

In the case of a lump-sum payment made by an employer as a death benefit, the same basis of withholding applies, except that a death benefit paid to a spouse or common-law partner is the lump sum paid reduced by the lesser of $10,000 and the salary paid to the deceased during the last 365 days of employment.[125]

If the lump-sum payment represents pension income or qualified pension income of the employee (see ¶8105), the total amount upon which the withholding tax is calculated is reduced by the lesser of $1,000 and the amount of the payment.[126]

No tax need be withheld from a lump-sum payment if the total earnings received and receivable during the calendar year (including the lump-sum payment) do not exceed the personal tax credits claimed. However, this does not apply to lump-sum payments made to non-residents.

[¶12,175] Payments to Non-Residents

Non-residents of Canada who are *engaged in regular and continuous employment* are subject to tax deductions on the same basis as residents. Payments for services rendered in Canada by a non-resident in *other than regular and continuous employment* are subject to a tax deduction of 15%.[127] This requirement to withhold tax applies regardless of any tax treaty between Canada and the recipient's country.

A 23% withholding tax applies under Part XIII to payments to non-resident film and video actors and their corporations, with an option to have the actor and corporation pay regular Part I tax on the net earnings instead. If Part I taxation is not chosen, the non-resident corporation carrying on business in Canada is not required to withhold Part I tax on amounts paid to non-resident actors who are employed in Canada.

Tax is required to be withheld at the prescribed rate for non-residents in receipt of taxable Part XIII type income from Canada. The non-resident tax is withheld at source by the resident payor (including a tenant, mortgagor, or debtor) from the gross amount paid or credited with respect to

---

See page ii for explanation of footnotes.

[124] CCH ¶22,330; Reg. 103.
[125] CCH ¶22,300, ¶28,060; Sec. 153(1), 248(1) "death benefit".
[126] Reg. 103(5).
[127] CCH ¶22,334; Reg. 105; Inf. Cir. 75-6R2, 76-12R6.

management or administration fees or charges, interest, rent, royalties and similar payments, alimony, dividends, motion picture or video tape payments, superannuation and pension benefits, payments under an RRSP, a deferred profit sharing plan, a registered supplementary unemployment benefit plan, and retiring allowances or benefits. All such payments to non-resident persons and the amount of tax withheld is required to be reported on Form T4A-NR Supplementary and Form T4/T4A Summary.

Non-resident withholding tax does not apply to that portion of any superannuation or pension benefit paid to a non-resident person that can reasonably be considered attributable to services rendered by that person in a taxation year when that person was neither resident in Canada at any time or employed (other than occasionally employed) in Canada. Non-resident withholding tax also does not apply on certain amounts[128] that if the non-resident were resident in Canada would not be taxable, such as:

(a) social assistance from a registered Canadian charitable organization or from federal or provincial authorities;

(b) exempted superannuation or pension benefits; and

(c) income exempt under the Indian Act and war pensions, and amounts transferred from pension plans to RRSPs.

Under the tax agreements which Canada has concluded with other countries in order to prevent double taxation, a resident of the other country is exempt from Canadian tax on his or her remuneration for personal services performed in Canada if certain conditions are fulfilled. Thus, under Article XV of the *Canada–U.S. Income Tax Convention*, a U.S. resident receiving employment income for services performed in Canada (the source country) will be exempt from tax in Canada if either of the following two conditions is met: (1) the remuneration for the employment performed in Canada does not exceed $10,000 (in Canadian funds) in the calendar year, or (2) the employee is not present in Canada for more than 183 days in the calendar year and the remuneration is not borne by an employer who is a Canadian resident or by a permanent establishment of the employer in the source country. The term "borne by" means allowable as a deduction in computing taxable income. However, the U.S. resident's pay is subject to tax deductions at source. Analogous provisions are contained in most of the other treaties. Notwithstanding any exemptions applicable under the treaties, the CRA's view is that tax must be withheld at the source from any payments of remuneration made to a non-resident. If any overpayment of tax is thus created, the tax will be refunded to the non-resident upon his or her filing a return of income for the year.

---

[128] CCH ¶26,083; Sec. 212(1)(h).

It should be noted that where non-residents receive any payments from which tax has to be withheld at source, the deduction must be made even if the non-resident's exemptions exceed the amount of the payment. Where the withholding results in overpayment of tax, the tax will be refunded upon the non-resident filing a return of income for the year in question.

There is no withholding requirement for salary, wages, or other remuneration paid in respect of activities performed by certain non-residents, such as non-resident athletes and their coaches and support staff, in connection with the 2010 Olympic Games or 2010 Paralympic Games.

[¶12,180] Payment of Balance of Tax

All individuals (outside Quebec) are now required to make quarterly instalments if the difference between the total tax liability (federal and provincial) in the current year and in one of the two preceding years exceeds the amount of tax withheld at source by $3,000 (before 2008, the monetary threshold was $2,000). See ¶12,200. For Quebec residents, the threshold amount is $1,800 ($1,200 before 2008) to recognize that it does not include provincial tax, and the net tax owing is limited to federal tax and surtax. On or before the balance-due date for each taxation year, these individuals must pay for that year the amount by which their tax payable exceeds the total of all amounts deducted or withheld from remuneration or other payments and all other amounts paid by quarterly instalments.[129] Generally this balance-due date is April 30 of the following year; however, where an individual has died during the year, the balance-due date is the later of April 30 of the following year, and six months after the date of death.

[¶12,185] Unclaimed Dividends, Interest and Proceeds

Remittance of tax is imposed upon dividends, interest, and proceeds of disposition received by brokers and security dealers on behalf of unknown shareholders.[130] The due date for remitting tax on unclaimed amounts is no later than 60 days after the year end following the year in which the amounts are received. In the case of dividends, the amount to be remitted is $33^{1}/_{3}\%$ of the dividends. In the case of interest and proceeds of disposition, it is 50% of the interest and proceeds. Any outlays and expenses incurred for the purpose of disposing of the property may be deducted from the proceeds of disposition in computing the 50% tax. Amounts so remitted are deemed to have been received by the person beneficially entitled to receive the dividends, interest, or proceeds, and to have been deducted from the amount otherwise payable to that person.

---

[129] CCH ¶22,698; Sec. 156.1(4).

[130] CCH ¶22,578–22,584; Sec. 153(4), 153(5); Reg. 108(4); Inf. Cir. 71-9R.

Example:

Assume the following facts with respect to a broker having a taxation year of 12 months ending on December 31 of each year:

Total of unclaimed dividends received prior to December 31, 2011	$25,000
Less dividends claimed in the taxation year 2011	1,000
	$24,000
Dividends received in 2012 taxation year but unclaimed at the end of the year	7,000
Balance of unclaimed dividends at December 31, 2012	$31,000
Amount subject to tax for 2012 taxation year	$24,000
Withholding tax of 33 1/3% thereon	$8,000

Assume further that in October 2012 an individual resident of Canada claimed as beneficial owner a dividend from a Canadian company of $1,000 which had been received by the broker in February 2011. The broker would pay the owner $667, being the dividend minus the 33 1/3% tax deducted at source. If the beneficial owner reported income on a cash basis, the dividend of $1,000 would be included in income for 2011 since it was received by the broker on behalf of the owner in that year. The owner might file an amendment income tax return for 2011 showing the following details:

Total income tax before dividend tax credit		$12,600
Deduct dividend tax credit on Canadian dividends (including the $1,000 dividend referred to above)		1,600
Tax payable for 2011		$11,000
Less: Tax deducted at source	$ 8,750	
Tax paid in April 2012, on filing first return	2,000	
Tax withheld by broker	333	11,083
Amount of refund claimed		$ 83

[¶12,190] Instalment Payments by Farmers and Fishers

Payment due dates differ somewhat for farmers and fishers, as compared with other individuals, since they must pay their tax in two instalments.[131]

The first instalment to be paid on or before December 31 of the taxation year is two-thirds of:

(a) the estimated tax for the year, calculated by applying the appropriate tax rates for the year to the estimated taxable income for the year; or

(b) the actual taxes payable for the preceding year.

See page ii for explanation of footnotes.

[131] CCH ¶22,652; Sec. 155.

If the "net tax owing" for the taxation year or either of the two preceding years is less than the instalment threshold of $3,000 ($1,800 for residents of Quebec), no December payment need be made and only the payment on or before April 30 of the next year is required.[132] Before 2008, the instalment threshold for self-employed individuals whose chief source of income is from farming or fishing was $1,200 for residents of Quebec, and $2,000 for any other individual.

The net tax owing is essentially the taxpayer's total tax liability, including the provincial tax liability (for provinces other than Quebec) and any tax payable to an Aboriginal government, less taxes withheld at source and tax credits to which the taxpayer is entitled. The net tax owing is determined before taking into account "specified future tax consequences" (for example, the consequences of carrying back losses and other amounts from subsequent taxation years). For residents of Quebec, the 3% Quebec tax abatement deemed to have been paid on account of tax is also deducted. Thus, for example, if a farmer resident in Ontario at the end of 2011 has federal and provincial tax owing of $3,000 or less in either 2009 or 2010, or expects to have such tax owing of less than $3,000 in 2011, no instalment is required in December 2011. If the exemption is based on estimated tax for the current year and the estimate proves wrong, interest will run on the entire amount that should have been paid from January 1 until final payment.

With the second instalment to be made on or before April 30 of the next year, the balance of tax actually payable for the year must be paid.

As an alternative to paying an instalment as outlined above, a fisher may elect to have taxes withheld from the catch proceeds. The prescribed rate of withholding is 20%.[133]

[¶12,200] Instalment Payments by Other Individuals

All other individuals are not required to make quarterly instalment payments for a taxation year if their "net tax owing" for the current taxation year or each of the two preceding taxation years is less than the instalment threshold of $3,000 ($1,800 for Quebec residents). Before 2008, the instalment threshold for individuals was $1,200 for residents of Quebec, and $2,000 for any other individual.[134] The net tax owing is essentially the taxpayer's total tax liability, including the provincial tax liability (for provinces other than Quebec) and any tax payable to an Aboriginal government, less taxes withheld at source and tax credits to which the taxpayer is entitled. The net tax owing is determined before taking into account "specified future tax consequences" (for example, the consequences of carrying back losses and other amounts from subsequent taxation years). For residents of Quebec, the 3% Quebec tax abatement deemed to have been paid on account of tax is also deducted.[135] Once a taxpayer's instalment

---

See page ii for explanation of footnotes.

[132] CCH ¶22,695, ¶22,695a; Sec. 156.1(1) "instalment threshold", 156.1(1) "net tax owing".

[133] CCH ¶22,335; Reg. 105.1.

[134] CCH ¶22,695; Sec. 156.1(1) "instalment threshold".

[135] CCH ¶22,695a; Sec. 156.1(1) "net tax owing".

liability is determined under this test, the instalment payments are calculated under one of the following three options:

- no-calculation option (CRA instalment reminders);

- prior year option; or

- current year option.

No-calculation option (CRA instalment reminders)

The no-calculation option amounts are provided on the instalment reminders that the CRA will automatically send if the taxpayer had an instalment liability for any of the two previous taxation years. If this option is chosen and the payments shown on the CRA instalment reminders are made by their due dates, the CRA will not charge instalment interest or a penalty, even if the total of the payments is less than the total amount of tax the taxpayer owes for the year. Under this option, the CRA will calculate a taxpayer's 2011 instalment payments as follows:

- The taxpayer's instalments for March 15 and June 15, 2011 will be based on the taxpayer's tax return for 2009 and each instalment will equal one-quarter of the taxpayer's net tax owing and any CPP contributions payable.

- For the September 15 and December 15, 2011 instalments, the CRA subtracts the total amount of the March and June 2011 instalment reminders from the taxpayer's 2010 net tax owing and any CPP contributions payable. It then divides the remaining amount equally for the September 15 and December 15, 2011 instalments.

Prior year option

Under this option, the taxpayer calculates the instalment payments based on the prior year net tax owing and any CPP contributions payable. Then, on each instalment due date, the taxpayer pays one-quarter of the calculated amount. If the taxpayer uses the prior year option and makes the payments in full by their due dates, the CRA will not charge instalment interest or a penalty, even if the total of the payments is less than the total amount of tax the taxpayer owes for the year. However, if the instalment payments the taxpayer makes in a taxation year under the prior year option are late or less than the prior year's total instalment amount due, the CRA may charge instalment interest (and possibly a penalty).

Current year option

Under this option, the taxpayer calculates the instalment payments based on the estimated current year net tax owing and any CPP contributions payable. Then, on each instalment due date, the taxpayer pays one-quarter of the calculated amount. If the taxpayer uses the current year option and makes the payments in full by their due dates, the CRA will not charge instalment interest or a penalty unless the amounts the taxpayer estimated when calculating the total instalment amount due were too low.

¶12,200

For instance, when, as a result of unexpected sources of income during the last quarter of 1995 the taxpayer underestimated his total income figure for 1995, he was charged interest on his deficient instalment payments.[136]

[¶12,205] Instalment Payments by Mutual Fund Trusts

The quarterly instalments payable by a mutual fund trust may be reduced by one-quarter of the trust's capital gains refund for the year.[137]

[¶12,210] Regular Instalment Payments by Corporations

Corporations must make instalment payments of their tax at the end of each month. For small CCPCs, the frequency of the remittance may be reduced from monthly to quarterly for taxation years that begin after 2007 if certain conditions, described at ¶12,211, are met.[138] The balance of the taxes is payable on the last day of the second month following the end of the taxation year, or, for corporations eligible for the small business deduction and certain credit unions and corporations making patronage allocations, on the last day of the third month following the year end. Corporate instalments will only be considered to have been received on time if received by the due date, i.e., postmarks will not suffice.[139]

The 12 monthly instalment payments may be determined in one of three ways:

(1) Each instalment may be $1/12$ of the corporation's estimated taxes under Parts I, I.3, VI, VI.1, and XIII.1 for the year.[140]

(2) Each instalment may be $1/12$ of the corporation's first instalment base.

(3) The first two instalments may be $1/12$ of the corporation's second instalment base and the next 10 instalments may be $1/10$ of the corporation's first instalment base after deducting the first two payments.

Although the third method above appears more complex, it has the advantage of allowing two months after the year end for the accumulation of information needed to determine the prior years' instalment base, and complements the date for remittance of the final balance (see below). For these reasons it is commonly used. There is nothing to prevent a corporation changing from one method to another at any time and it is common to utilize, say, the third method, if estimated income is higher than the instalment base, and then shift to the first method if it becomes apparent in the year that estimated taxable income will fall below the instalment base. However, use of the first method on unrealistic estimated income may incur non-deductible interest charges on underpayments at the prescribed rate of interest, which is established on a quarterly basis. See ¶12,255.

See page ii for explanation of footnotes.

[136] Newland, 97 DTC 1391.
[137] CCH ¶22,685; Sec. 156(2).
[138] CCH ¶22,700; Sec. 157(1).

[139] CCH ¶28,329b; Sec. 248(7).
[140] CCH ¶19,388, ¶19,396–19,398d; Sec. 123.1, 123.3–123.4.

The "first instalment base" of a corporation for a particular taxation year is defined to be the tax payable by the corporation under Parts I, I.3, VI, VI.1, and XIII.1 before taking into account any future tax consequences (i.e., carryback of losses, tax credits, etc. or adjustments of flow-through share renunciations) for the immediately preceding taxation year.[141] If that immediately preceding taxation year was less than 365 days in length, the instalment base is increased to the full year equivalent by multiplying the taxes for that immediately preceding year by 365 and dividing by the number of days in the taxation year. However, if the relevant taxation year had less than 183 days, the first instalment base is the greater of the amount arrived at by applying the foregoing rules to that immediately preceding taxation year and the amount arrived at by applying those rules to the most recently preceding taxation year which had more than 182 days.

The "second instalment base" is defined to be the amount determined under the rules for determining the first instalment base applied to the second preceding taxation year. The above rule relating to short taxation years also applies in determining the second instalment base.

Where the corporation involved was formed on an amalgamation of two or more corporations, the first or second instalment base of the amalgamated corporation will be the aggregate of the instalment bases of the predecessor corporations for taxation years ending prior to or on the amalgamation. There cannot be a negative instalment base: the fact that one predecessor was in a loss position will not reduce the instalment base carryover from another predecessor which was taxable.

Special rules apply to the winding-up of a subsidiary into a parent corporation and to the transfer of all or substantially all of a corporation's assets to a corporation not dealing at arm's length. Basically, in both cases, the first or second instalment base of the subsidiary or transferor corporation will be added to the first or second instalment base of the parent or transferee corporation.

If the corporation's tax payable under Parts I, VI, VI.1, and XIII.1 for the year or its first instalment base for the year is $3,000 or less, the corporation is not required to make the above monthly instalment payments. For taxation years beginning before 2008, the monetary threshold is $1,000 rather than $3,000.[142] Instead, the corporation will be required to pay its full tax by the end of the second or third month after the end of its taxation year, depending on its eligibility for the small business deduction.

[¶12,211] Instalment Payments by Small CCPCs

For taxation years beginning after 2007, a small CCPC is allowed to make quarterly instalments instead of monthly instalments if it meets the following requirements:

See page ii for explanation of footnotes.

[141] CCH ¶22,705, ¶22,706, ¶28,272ba; Sec. 157(4), 248(1) "specified future tax consequence"; Reg. 5301. [142] CCH ¶22,703; Sec. 157(2.1).

- The corporation's taxable income, or the total of its taxable income and the taxable income of any associated corporations, does not exceed the small business limit (see below) for the year or the preceding taxation year;

- The corporation deducted an amount of the small business deduction in computing its tax payable for the taxation year or for the preceding taxation year;

- The corporation's taxable capital employed in Canada, or the total of its taxable capital employed in Canada and that of any associated corporations, does not exceed $10 million in the year or in the preceding taxation year; and

- Throughout the 12 months ending at the last instalment payment date, the corporation made all tax remittances and filings under the *Income Tax Act* and Part IX (the goods and services tax/harmonized sales tax (GST/HST) portion) of the *Excise Tax Act* on a timely basis.[143]

For 2009 and subsequent taxation years, the small business limit is increased from $400,000 to $500,000. If the 2009 taxation year straddles the end of the 2008 calendar year, a corporation's small business limit for the year is prorated for the number of days in the taxation year before 2009 and after 2008, while the limit for the taxation year immediately before that year remains at $400,000.

A corporation that so qualifies as a small-CCPC may determine its four quarterly instalments in one of three ways, at the option of the corporation:

(1) Each instalment may be $1/4$ of the corporation's estimated Part I and Part VI.1 taxes for the current taxation year;

(2) Each instalment may be $1/4$ of the tax payable for the previous taxation year (the first instalment base);

(3) The first instalment may be $1/4$ of the tax payable for the second preceding year (the second instalment base), and the next three instalments may be $1/3$ of the amount, if any, by which the tax payable for the previous taxation year (the first instalment base) exceeds the first instalment payment.

If a corporation ceases to be a small CCPC at a particular time in a taxation year, it is required to make monthly instalments for the rest of the year. The monthly instalments for the rest of the year can be either:

(a) the corporation's estimated taxes for the year under Parts I, VI, VI.1, and XIII.1, minus the previous quarterly instalments payable in the year, divided by the number of months remaining in the year after the particular time; or

---

[143] CCH ¶22,721e; Sec. 157(1.2).

(b) the corporation's first instalment base for the taxation year less the previous quarterly instalments payable in the year, plus its estimated taxes for the year under Parts VI and XIII.1, divided by the number of months remaining in the year after the particular time.[144]

[¶12,212] Example of Corporate Instalment Base Calculation

The following example illustrates the computation of the instalment base for a corporation:

Assume the following fact situations (Cases A, B and C):

Taxation year	Part I Taxes payable	Number of days in taxation year		
		Case A	Case B	Case C
Current Yr. - 3	$9,000	365	365	292
Current Yr. - 2	$1,000	365	365	146
Current Yr. - 1	$4,200	365	146	146

The first instalment base and second instalment base in each of Cases A, B, and C are as follows:

First instalment base   Second instalment base

Case A

$$\$4,200 \times \frac{365}{365} = \$4,200 \text{ (I)}$$ $$\$1,000 \times \frac{365}{365} = \$1,000 \text{ (II)}$$

Case B

Greater of:

$$\text{(a) } \$4,200 \times \frac{365}{146} = \$10,500 \text{ (I)}$$ $$\$1,000 \times \frac{365}{365} = \$1,000 \text{ (II)}$$

or

$$\text{(b) } \$1,000 \times \frac{365}{365} = \$1,000$$

Case C

Greater of: Greater of:

$$\text{(a) } \$4,200 \times \frac{365}{146} = \$10,500$$ $$\text{(a) } \$1,000 \times \frac{365}{146} = \$2,500$$

or   or

$$\text{(b) } \$9,000 \times \frac{365}{292} = \$11,250 \text{ (I)}$$ $$\text{(b) } \$9,000 \times \frac{365}{292} = \$11,250 \text{ (II)}$$

See page ii for explanation of footnotes.

[144] CCH ¶22,701i; Sec. 157(1.5).

¶12,212

[¶12,215] New Corporations

Since a new corporation has no preceding taxation year, the tax estimated on that basis would be nil. Therefore, no instalment payments of tax will be required until after the first fiscal year of the corporation has been completed.

[¶12,220] Instalment Payments by SIFT Trusts

For taxation years beginning after July 20, 2012, SIFT trusts will be subject to the same monthly instalment rules that apply to public corporations and will no longer benefit from the more lenient quarterly instalment regime that applies to individuals.[145] See ¶12,210 for the instalment regime applicable to public corporations and ¶12,200 for the one applicable to individuals. This new regime for SIFT trusts was announced on July 20, 2012, and implementing draft legislation was released on July 25, 2012.

[¶12,225] Reduction of Instalment Payments

The following corporations may reduce by certain amounts each of the required instalments calculated under the formula at ¶12,210:[146]

(1) *Private or non-private corporations* — by $^1/_{12}$ of the corporation's dividend refund for the year.

(2) *Mutual fund corporations* — by $^1/_{12}$ of the aggregate of the corporation's capital gains refund and the amount of the corporation's dividend refund for the year.

(3) *Non-resident-owned investment corporations* — by $^1/_{12}$ of the corporation's allowable refund.

(4) Finally, a corporation is allowed to reduce its monthly instalment by $^1/_{12}$ of the following amounts:

   (a) any refundable Canadian film or video production tax credit to which it is entitled under ¶8685;

   (b) any mining reclamation trust tax credit that is refundable for the year under ¶7497;

   (c) any film and video production services tax credit (as determined in ¶8710); and

   (d) any refundable investment tax credit for the year (as determined in ¶8350).

See page ii for explanation of footnotes.
[145] Sec. 157(2).   [146] CCH ¶22,704; Sec. 157(3).

[¶12,230] Payment of Remainder of Tax

Any amounts assessed which remain unpaid when a notice of assessment is sent are payable forthwith.[147] Payment is to be made to the Receiver General.

[¶12,235] Persons Acting for Others

For all purposes of the Act, the legal representative of a taxpayer is made the taxpayer's agent and he or she is jointly and severally liable with the taxpayer to:

(a) pay any amount payable by the taxpayer to the extent that the legal representative is in possession or control of the property of the taxpayer or the taxpayer's estate; and

(b) perform any obligation or duty imposed under the Act on the taxpayer to the extent that the obligation of duty can be reasonably considered to relate to the legal representative's responsibilities as a representative (i.e., the scope of liability will vary depending on the duties normally undertaken by the legal representative).[148]

Actions or proceedings by the Minister against the taxpayer can be taken in the name of the legal representative acting in that capacity and they will have the same effect as if they were taken against the taxpayer. In summary, the legal representative is deemed to be the agent of the taxpayer for all tax purposes, including assessments, objection, appeals, collection, administration, and enforcement, provided such duties are in the legal representative's capacity as a legal representative.

Persons acting in a representative or fiduciary capacity (legal representatives) are required to obtain a clearance certificate before distributing property under their control.[149] This certificate is a certificate of the Minister certifying that certain amounts have been paid or that the Minister has accepted security for payment. The certificate is to cover all amounts of tax, penalties, or interest for which the taxpayer is liable for the taxation year of the distribution, or any prior taxation year, and which remains unpaid. The legal representative is or can be expected to become liable in his or her capacity as the legal representative as long as he or she possesses or controls the taxpayer's property, or property held for the taxpayer's benefit.

The legal representative who distributes property under his or her control without obtaining a clearance certificate is personally liable for the payment of amounts which should have been certified as having been paid, but such liability is limited to the value of the property distributed. As noted above, only amounts for which the legal representative is or can be expected to become liable in a representative capacity must be certified as having been paid. The Minister has the right to assess the legal representative in

---

See page ii for explanation of footnotes.

[147] CCH ¶22,725; Sec. 158. [149] CCH ¶22,747; Sec. 159(2).
[148] CCH ¶22,740, ¶28,152a; Sec. 159(1), 248(1) "legal representative"; Inf. Cir. 82-6R9.

¶12,230

respect of the legal representative's liability [and after December 20, 2002, the legal representative so assessed is subject to interest on the assessment without any limit on the amount of interest for which the representative may be liable].[150]

If a legal representative appropriates property of the taxpayer that is in the possession or control of that legal representative, the appropriation will be deemed to be a distribution.[151] The legal representative will therefore be required to obtain a clearance certificate prior to the appropriation if personal liability is to be avoided. This ensures that the requirement to obtain a clearance certificate is not defeated when assets are allocated to a related person in the course of a voluntary winding-up.

Where the liquidators of a deceased taxpayer's estate deposited some of the proceeds of two insurance policies on his life in the estate's bank account, the Minister could not assess them for distributing the proceeds without obtaining a certificate of discharge since they did not form part of the estate's assets, and there was no reason to have deposited any part of them in the estate's bank account.[152]

[¶12,240] Elections — Instalment Payments — Departure Tax — Death of a Taxpayer — Deemed Disposition by Trust

A taxpayer whose income is unusually large in any given year because of certain deemed realizations may elect to pay tax over a period of up to 10 years.[153] The taxpayer, must, however, furnish security acceptable to the Minister for the payment of the tax which is so deferred. This election is available in four sets of circumstances:

(1) where the individual has died and the value of certain rights and things have been included in his or her income in the year of death[154] (see ¶2560);

(2) where the individual has died and, as a result, is deemed to have disposed of capital properties or resource properties[155] (see ¶2555);

(3) where the individual carried on a professional business and had to include in income for the year of death the previous year's reserves for 1971 receivables;[156] or

(4) where a trust is deemed to have disposed of and reacquired capital properties, resource properties, and land inventories every 21 years.[157]

The amount of tax on which a taxpayer may elect is restricted to the extra tax arising from one of the above circumstances. For trusts, only the tax resulting from the deemed disposition rule for non-depreciable capital

---

See page ii for explanation of footnotes.

[150] CCH ¶22,748; Sec. 159(3).
[151] CCH ¶22,752a; Sec. 159(3.1).
[152] Nguyen et al, 2010 DTC 1397.
[153] CCH ¶22,753–22,761, ¶22,764, ¶7202, ¶22,754; Sec. 159(4)–(7); Reg. 1001, Reg. 1300, Reg. 1301.

[154] CCH ¶9220; Sec. 70(2).
[155] CCH ¶9260; Sec. 70(5).
[156] CCH ¶22,764, ¶29,235; ITAR 23(3); Reg. 1001.
[157] CCH ¶13,150; Sec. 104(4).

property and land inventory can be deferred by making this election. All other tax arising in the year must be paid in the usual manner. For instance, the election will not apply to tax arising in a trust as a result of a deemed disposition of depreciable property and resource property.

At the time of making an election, the taxpayer must choose the number of equal instalments of tax he or she wishes to make. The first of these is payable when tax for the year would normally be payable and the others on the next consecutive anniversaries of that date. Thus the deferred tax may be spread over 10 taxation years. As a condition of this election, the taxpayer must agree to pay interest at a prescribed rate with each instalment on the amount of that instalment. The interest is computed from the time the tax would normally have become payable to the time of making the particular instalment payment.

At the time of making the election, the taxpayer must furnish security acceptable to the Minister for the payment of the deferred tax. This security may be in the form of a charge on the taxpayer's property, a charge on the property of some other person, a guarantee from some other person, or any other acceptable form.

In the case of a deceased taxpayer, the election is to be made by his or her legal representative. Where the legal representative has elected to report the income arising from the notional realization of rights and things in a separate return, the tax payable in the year of death is considered to be the total tax payable under the two returns. Thus it is clear that two elections may be made. See also ¶5390.

Under the taxpayer migration rules, an individual who ceases to be a Canadian resident may choose to post security in lieu of paying departure tax on the gain realized on the deemed disposition of property held at departure.[158] Election and security will be considered timely made and furnished if effected before the taxpayer's balance-due date for the emigration year. The Minister has discretion to extend this deadline.[159]

The concept is that the security remains in place until the property is actually disposed of so that there will be proceeds to pay the tax, or until the individual returns to Canada and unwinds the tax.

Security will be deemed to have been posted on the lesser of:

(1) the tax payable at top marginal rates on $50,000 of taxable capital gains; and

(2) the greatest amount of tax for which the Minister is required to accept security for any particular taxation year of the individual.[160]

The effect of this provision is to excuse individual emigrants (other than trusts) from the requirement to provide security on the first $50,000 of taxable capital gains arising from the deemed-disposition on departure. In

---

See page ii for explanation of footnotes.

[158] CCH ¶27,036aa, ¶20,026c; Sec. 220(4.5), 128.1(4)(b).

[159] CCH ¶27,036e; Sec. 220(4.54).

[160] CCH ¶27,036b; Sec. 220(4.51).

¶12,240

cases of undue hardship, the Minister is authorized to accept a lesser or different security.[161]

[¶12,245] Joint Tax Liability Re Non-Arm's Length Transfer of Property

Where property has been transferred to the taxpayer's spouse or common-law partner, to a person who has since become the taxpayer's spouse or common-law partner, to a person under 18 years of age, or to any other person with whom the taxpayer did not deal at arm's length, the transferor and transferee are jointly and severally liable for certain taxes for which the transferor would otherwise be solely liable. The Minister may assess the transferee for such a liability [and after December 20, 2002, the transferee so assessed is subject to interest on the assessment without any limit on the amount of interest for which the transferee may be liable].[162]

Exempted from this joint and several liability are transfers made pursuant to a decree, order, or judgment of a competent tribunal or pursuant to a written separation agreement if, at the time of transfer, the taxpayer and the taxpayer's spouse or common-law partner were living apart as a result of the breakdown of their marriage or common-law partnership.[163]

Where the taxpayer's husband made mortgage interest, property tax, and other similar payments in respect of the matrimonial home directly to third parties through corporations of which he was a major shareholder, such payments were made in satisfaction of the husband's legal obligation to support his wife and children and, therefore, they did not constitute a "transfer" for the purpose of the application of the joint liability provision.[164] In another case, where the taxpayer's spouse deposited amounts from his RRSP into a joint bank account with her, it was held that the property in the deposits never vested in the taxpayer in her personal capacity, but only in her capacity as her spouse's agent. Therefore, there had not been a "transfer" of property to justify a joint liability assessment.[165]

[¶12,246] Joint Tax Liability Re Split Income Tax

A parent of a minor child is, in certain circumstances, jointly and severally liable for the tax payable on the child's split income (see ¶8080 *et seq.*). The minor child's split income on which tax is imposed includes taxable dividends received on shares of a corporation (other than those listed on a prescribed stock exchange or of a mutual fund corporation), and the child's share of income from a trust or partnership that is derived from the provision of goods or services [property or services after December 20, 2002] to a business carried on by a person related to the child, a corporation in which a person related to the child is a specified shareholder, or a professional corporation in which a person related to the child is a shareholder.

See page ii for explanation of footnotes.

[161] CCH ¶27,036j, ¶27,036k; Sec. 220(4.7), 220(4.71).

[162] CCH ¶9516, ¶9570, ¶22,774; Sec. 74.1, 75, 160(1).

[163] CCH ¶22,779; Sec. 160(4).

[164] Ferracuti, 99 DTC 194.

[165] Leblanc, 99 DTC 410.

The parent of the minor child is jointly and severally liable to pay the tax on the child's split income in a year if, during the year, the parent was a specified shareholder of a corporation or a shareholder of a professional corporation, dividends of which were directly or indirectly included in the child's split income for the year; or if the parent carried on a business that purchased goods or services [property or services after December 20, 2002], or was a specified shareholder of a corporation or a shareholder of a professional corporation that purchased goods or services from a business the income of which was included directly or indirectly in the child's split income for the year.[166] A "specified shareholder" of a corporation means, in general terms, a person who owns, directly or indirectly, 10% or more of the class of any shares in the corporation.[167] For these purposes, the person is deemed to own any shares owned by a non-arm's length person. Thus, for example, a parent will be a specified shareholder of a corporation, and potentially subject to joint and several liability for split income tax, if the parent's child owns 10% or more of a class of shares in the corporation, even if the parent owns no shares in the corporation.

[¶12,247] Joint Tax Liability Re Split Pension Income Tax

Beginning with their 2007 income tax returns, Canadian residents will be able to allocate up to one-half of their income that qualifies for the pension income tax credit to their resident spouse or common-law partner. To engage in this pension income splitting, a pensioner and his or her spouse or common-law partner must make a joint election with their income tax returns on or before their filing-due date. Where such an election is made, a pensioner and pension transferee are jointly liable for the portion of the tax payable by the pension transferee that results from the inclusion of the split pension amount in the income of the pension transferee.[168]

[¶12,250] Interest

[¶12,255] Interest on Underpayments, Including Instalment Payments of Tax

Deficient payments of tax under Parts I, I.3, VI, and VI.1 are subject to interest at a rate which is set quarterly based on the average interest rate on 90-day treasury bills during the first month of the preceding quarter, plus, for payments outstanding on or after July 1, 1995, an additional 4%.[169] A table of interest rates by quarter to the end of last year is found in the information material at ¶475, immediately preceding Chapter I. Interest, whether owed to or by the taxpayer, is compounded on a daily basis.[170] Thus, actual interest is slightly higher than stated interest. For example, 10% interest on $100 compounded daily for one year would be $10.51 (simple

---

See page ii for explanation of footnotes.

[166] CCH ¶22,776; Sec. 160(1.2).

[167] CCH ¶28,273; Sec. 248(1) "specified shareholder".

[168] CCH ¶22,776c; Sec. 160(1.3).

[169] CCH ¶22,800, ¶22,904; Sec. 161(1); Reg. 4301.

[170] CCH ¶28,329g; Sec. 248(11).

interest, i.e., not compounded, is $10). The interest at 10% on $100 compounded daily over five years is $64.86, compared to $50 simple interest. Compounding applies to most interest accrued on and after January 1, 1987.[171]

Interest is calculated on the amount by which the taxpayer's total liability under Parts I, I.3, VI, and VI.1 for a taxation year exceeds the total of all amounts paid on account of such taxes and applied as at that time against the taxpayer's tax liability under these Parts for the year. But, where the underpayment of tax was the result of a reassessment error on the part of the Minister, the taxpayer was not required to pay interest.[172] However, where the error in the taxpayer's return was due to the wrong advice the taxpayer received from a tax official, the taxpayer was still liable for interest.[173]

A person who is required to make instalment payments of tax but fails to do so is similarly required to pay interest at the prescribed rate on the unpaid amount from the day on which payment should have been made until the date of payment or to the beginning of the period in respect of which the taxpayer was required to pay interest on tax outstanding after the balance-due day, whichever is earlier.[174]

For the purpose of determining the deficiency of instalments to which the prescribed interest rate is applied, individuals will be deemed to have been liable to pay instalments based on the least of:

(1) the tax payable for the year before taking into consideration the specified future tax consequences, such as carryback of losses, tax credits, etc.;

(2) their instalment base for the immediately preceding taxation year;

(3) for individuals other than farmers and fishers who elect to make their first two quarterly instalments on the basis of tax payable for the second preceding year, the amount so determined; or

(4) the amount stated in the Tax Instalment Reminder notice sent by the CRA.[175]

Where a taxpayer has paid all amounts (other than interest and penalty) in full and there is interest or penalty of $25 or less outstanding, the CRA has discretion to waive the interest or penalty.[176]

[¶12,260] Interest Offset Method for Late and Deficient Tax Instalment Payments

An individual who has forgotten to make an instalment payment when it was due can cure the defect by an early payment of a subsequent instalment (allowing for quarterly interest changes) or by an overpayment of the

---

See page ii for explanation of footnotes.

[171] CCH ¶4732; Sec. 17(1).
[172] Lowry, 73 DTC 163.
[173] Barron, 75 DTC 221.
[174] CCH ¶22,802; Sec. 161(2).

[175] CCH ¶22,815, ¶22,815a, ¶28,272ba; Sec. 161(4), 161(4.01), 248(1) "specified future tax consequence".
[176] CCH ¶22,845m; Sec. 161.3.

deficient instalment calculated to accrue sufficient interest on a daily basis (compounded daily) for the period of deficiency. For individuals, the minimum instalment required to be paid on each due date is the amount that brings the total instalments to date equal to the lowest total amount required to be paid by the individual by that date.[177] This interest offset only operates to reduce potential interest liability on instalment payments for the taxation year as a whole; it cannot create an obligation on the government to pay interest on excess instalments. For instance, 2011 instalment interest for the period commencing January 1, 2011 and ending April 30, 2012 cannot exceed:

(a) total interest for a particular deficient instalment period calculated as if no instalment had been paid

minus

(b) interest that would be paid by the government on a refund of instalments for 2011 made in the period if there were no tax owing for 2011 and no April 30, 2012 final payment, and the refund were calculated on instalments from the later of January 1, 2011 or the day the overpayment arose.

Under these rules, instalment interest is calculated by first computing a debit interest charge from the due date of each instalment to the date the final instalment is due (the "balance-due date"). A credit offset ("offset interest") is allowed on each instalment payment at the instalment interest rate from the payment date to the balance-due date. Interest will be chargeable only to the extent that the debit instalment interest charge exceeds the offset interest.

For the purposes of the contra-interest rule, the rate to be used in calculating the interest offset on the overpayment will be the same as the one used for calculating interest on taxes in arrears (see ¶12,255).

[¶12,265] Limitation of Interest on Corporation Instalment Payments

For the purpose of determining interest payable on deficient instalment payments by a corporation, the corporation is considered to have been liable to pay instalments on the basis of the least of:

(1) the total of the taxes payable for the year under Parts I, I.3, VI, and VI.1, without taking into consideration the specified future tax consequences, such as carryback of tax credits and losses and adjustments to flow-through share renunciations;

(2) its first instalment base for the year; and

(3) a combination of its first and second instalment base for the year,

reduced in each case by the amount for dividend refunds, capital gains refunds, or allowance refunds applicable to private corporations, mutual

---

[177] CCH ¶22,805; Sec. 161(2.2).

fund corporations, or non-resident owned investment corporations (see ¶12,225).[178]

[¶12,267] Offsetting of Interest on Corporate Tax Overpayments and Underpayments

A corporation may offset income tax refund amounts on which refund interest is accruing in the corporation's favour against concurrent income tax arrears amounts in respect of which arrears interest is accruing against the corporation. This rule effectively enables a corporation to avoid paying non-deductible arrears interest for a period for which refund interest is being calculated in the corporation's favour in respect of an equal but opposite underlying balance. By offsetting the underlying tax and refund amounts owed, both types of interest are eliminated for the period for which the interest-carrying balances overlap. Since refund interest is taxable, while arrears interest is both non-deductible and calculated at a higher rate than refund interest, the corporation is better off eliminating the two interest amounts.

For any period of time for which interest is calculated both on an amount owed by a corporation in respect of an underpayment of income tax and on an amount owed by the CRA to the corporation in respect of an overpayment of income tax, the corporation may request that the two amounts be offset for interest calculation purposes.[179] Eligible amounts include tax (other than instalments), interest accrued prior to the period of overlapping balances, and penalties. Interest will only be payable on the net balance owing, with the rate of interest depending on whether there is a net overpayment or underpayment.

The offset will be achieved by reallocating the refund amount (as of the time from which refund interest was calculated) as if it were a payment against the arrears amount.[180] As a result, no refund interest accrues after the effective date with respect to the portion of the overpayment amount reallocated, and no arrears interest accrues after that date with respect to the portion of the accumulated underpayment amount offset by the reallocation. Thus, all interest on the offsetting balances is eliminated for the offset period.

If the refund has already been paid, the reallocation will be conditional on repayment by the taxpayer of the refund and refund interest received.[181] Arrears interest will be charged for the period of time that the corporation had the use of these funds.

The corporation is required to apply in writing for an interest offset between any two taxation years within 90 days of sending of the first notice of assessment giving rise to any portion of the corporation's overpayment or

[178] CCH ¶22,816, ¶28,272ba; Sec. 161(4.1), 248(1)"specified future tax consequence".
[179] CCH ¶22,845f; Sec. 161.1(2).
[180] CCH ¶22,845h; Sec. 161.1(4).
[181] CCH ¶22,845i; Sec. 161.1(5).

underpayment amount, as the case may be, to which the application relates.[182]

Example:

> Assume that the first notice of assessment for a corporation's 2011 taxation year is issued on September 1, 2012, and indicates tax payable of $10,000. If $8,000 had already been paid prior to that day, the assessment would give rise to an underpayment amount of $2,000 (ignoring interest) owed since the corporation's balance-due date. As a result of a subsequent audit, a notice of reassessment is issued on February 1, 2013, indicating a revised tax payable amount of $13,000. Since no further payments have been made, the underpayment amount is thus increased to $5,000, again owed since the corporation's balance-due date for 2011. If the corporation relies on this date of reassessment as a trigger date for the 90-day period within which to apply for offsetting, it would only be such in respect of the incremental tax assessed of $3,000. That is, only the incremental $3,000 portion of the underpayment amount would be eligible for offsetting if the underpayment reassessment date were the basis for the binding time limit. An attempted offset in respect of the full $5,000 would not be valid, since the reassessment was not the first assessment giving rise to a portion ($2,000) of the amount sought to be offset, in respect of which the 90-day period will have ended on November 30, 2012.

If the taxpayer has filed an objection or appeal, the deadline will be extended to the date 90 days after the date of the notice of confirmation or 90 days after the date of the final court decision, as the case may be. The request for offsetting must specify the amounts, dates, and taxation years of the reallocation requested.

If a reallocation results in the creation of a new refund, the corporation will not be entitled to have the new refund reallocated under this rule unless that request is contained in the request for the original reallocation.[183] This prevents a reallocation request from becoming the first in a series of consecutive consequential reallocations.

The Minister may reassess interest and penalties payable by a corporation in order to take into account a reallocation under the interest offset provisions.[184] Since the time limit for requesting a reallocation is the latest of a number of dates including the first notice of assessment of the taxation year to which an underpayment or overpayment amount relates, it is possible that one of the taxation years will have become statute-barred under the normal rules by the time the reallocation is requested. This provision specifies that the Minister shall assess or reassess interest and penalties as necessary in order to take into account a reallocation, notwithstanding the expiry of the normal reassessment period.

[¶12,270] Amounts Deemed to be Paid as Instalments — Non-Residents

The tax payable by either the vendor or the purchaser on disposition by non-residents of certain taxable Canadian property (see ¶14,040) is deemed to be an instalment of tax with interest accruing from the date the amount

See page ii for explanation of footnotes.

[182] CCH ¶22,845g; Sec. 161.1(3). [184] CCH ¶22,845k; Sec. 161.1(7).
[183] CCH ¶22,845j; Sec. 161.1(6).

¶12,270

becomes due.[185] In the case of the purchaser, the due date is the 30th day following the month in which the disposition took place. In the case of the vendor, the relevant date is the day upon which an amount was remitted or acceptable security was furnished to satisfy the potential tax liability computed with reference to the estimated proceeds of disposition. Interest on any deficiency runs from that date.

[¶12,280] Canadian Wheat Board Participation Certificate

Until June 29, 2012, an interest waiver is provided to persons who receive payments under participation certificates from the Canadian Wheat Board to the extent that no interest in respect of the amount of increase in tax payable by reason of such payments is to be exigible until 30 days after the payment is made.[186] With the passage of the *Marketing Freedom for Grain Farmers Act* and the reorganization of the Canadian Wheat Board, the above interest waiver is repealed as of June 29, 2012.

[¶12,285] Income from Blocked Currency Countries

Even though a taxpayer may be prohibited from repatriating income from certain countries because of foreign exchange restrictions, cash basis taxpayers must include income received in the foreign country by an agent. Accrual basis taxpayers must include in their income all sales made, regardless of how or when payment is to be made. If the payment of tax on such income will impose extreme hardship, the Minister has the discretion to postpone payment of the tax for a period to be determined by the Minister.[187] No interest is payable on the postponed tax during the period of postponement.

[¶12,290] Foreign Tax Adjustment

No interest is payable by a taxpayer on any additional tax liability for the first 90 days following the date the taxpayer is first notified of a foreign tax adjustment.[188] The 90-day period is to allow for the taxpayer to recompute the effect of the foreign tax adjustment on his or her Canadian tax position or notify the CRA, and to make any payment which is required.

[¶12,292] Flow-Through Share Renunciations

Flow-through shares are discussed in ¶3540. They are essentially tax shelters through which investors can participate in (receive a flowout of) resource expenditures with the hope of eventual profit. The flow-through share rules permit companies to flow out expenditures as Year 1 deductions although the expenditures will not actually be incurred until Year 2. It follows that the expenditures may not in fact be incurred, and the system

---

See page ii for explanation of footnotes.

[185] CCH ¶22,840; Sec. 161(8).
[186] CCH ¶22,820; Sec. 161(5).

[187] CCH ¶22,825; Sec. 161(6).
[188] CCH ¶22,827; Sec. 161(6.1).

will deal with this by forcing revision of amounts previously flowed out. In such a case, the investor will have a retroactive tax burden imposed.

While the burden of a lower deduction will fall on the investor, the concomitant costs of retroactive interest, both in general and for inadequate instalments, will in effect be borne by a special tax on the issuing company (see ¶13,675). The investor who is issued a notice reducing a prior flow-through share allocation of Canadian exploration expenses and Canadian development expenses is given a grace period until April 30th of the calendar year following the year in which the flow-through deduction was originally claimed to ante up the difference without having to pay interest.[189]

[¶12,295] Effect of Loss Carryback

Certain deductions and exclusions to which a taxpayer may be entitled for a taxation year (earlier year) as a consequence of circumstances occurring in a subsequent taxation year will not affect any interest due on unpaid taxes or unpaid instalments of taxes or the penalty for late or deficient tax instalments for the former year, until the day that is 30 days after the latest of:

(a) the first day following that subsequent taxation year;

(b) the day the taxpayer's or his or her legal representative's return for that subsequent taxation year was filed;

(c) where an amended return or prescribed form amending the return or form for the earlier year is filed, the day that return or form was filed; and

(d) where a written request was made which resulted in the Minister reassessing the taxpayer's tax for the year to take into account the deduction or exclusion, the day on which the request was made.

Up until the accrual date, the interest and the penalty are calculated as if there had been no reduction in the taxpayer's tax liability as a result of any such deduction or exclusion claim arising in a subsequent year. The tax payable includes taxes incurred under Parts I, I.3, VI, and VI.1. The effect is that interest and penalties on unpaid instalments and unpaid taxes are payable without consideration of the deduction or exclusion claim up to the latest of the specified days. From the latest of these days onward, interest and penalties are payable only on the unpaid tax (if any) calculated after taking the deduction or exclusion claims into consideration.

The deduction and exclusion claims to which this applies are:[190]

(1) the deduction of listed personal property losses for a taxation year in computing the net gains from dispositions of listed personal property for the three taxation years immediately preceding such year;

See page ii for explanation of footnotes.

[189] CCH ¶22,828; Sec. 161(6.2).　　　　[190] CCH ¶22,836; Sec. 161(7).

(2) the exclusion from income of proceeds received in a taxation year for the granting of an option where such option is exercised in a subsequent taxation year;

(3) the deduction of the charitable donation tax credit;

(4) the deduction of non-capital, net capital, restricted farm, farm, and limited partnership losses for a taxation year in computing taxable income for the three immediately preceding taxation years;

(5) the deduction of net capital losses for the year in which an individual has died, in computing taxable income for the immediately preceding year;

(6) the deduction of unused foreign tax credits in respect of foreign tax paid in a taxation year in respect of a business in computing the tax otherwise payable for the three immediately preceding taxation years;

(7) the deduction, claimed in the deceased's tax return for the year of death, of capital losses or terminal losses realized within the first taxation year of the estate in respect of which the taxpayer's legal representative has elected;

(8) the deduction of investment tax credits in respect of property acquired or an expenditure made in the taxation year in computing the tax otherwise payable in the three immediately preceding taxation years;

(9) the deduction of unused Part VI tax credits for a taxation year in computing the tax otherwise payable in the three immediately preceding taxation years;

(10) the deduction of unused Part I.3 tax credits (in respect of large corporation tax) for a taxation year in computing the tax otherwise payable in the three immediately preceding taxation years;

(11) repayments of fuel tax rebates;

(12) the deduction from Part I.3 tax of any unused surtax credit from a subsequent year;

(13) the deduction from Part VI tax of any unused Part I tax credit from a subsequent year;

(14) the deduction on a taxpayer's death of RPP contributions in respect of pre-1990 service;

(15) the deduction allowed to former residents in respect of the disposition of a taxable Canadian property in a subsequent year (this provision, discussed at ¶5393, provides a special tax credit in certain cases where the "stop-loss" rule applies to an individual who ceased to be resident in Canada);

(16) the deductions allowed to former residents which provide (i) limited credits against an individual's Canadian tax that arises in the year of the individual's departure from Canada for post-departure foreign taxes, and (ii) similar limited credits against a trust's Canadian tax that arose in the year of a distribution by the trust to a non-resident beneficiary, for the beneficiary's subsequent foreign taxes, respectively; and

(17) the deductions allowed to returning former residents when they return to reside in Canada in a subsequent year; these provisions, discussed at ¶5393, generally "unwind" the previous application of the deemed-disposition rules that applied upon emigration.

[¶12,300] Interest on Late Payment of Penalties

Interest at the prescribed rate will be charged on late payments of penalties.[191]

Penalties assessed for failure to file a return or other document, filing an incomplete return or other document, or filing a return or other document containing false statements will bear interest from the due date for filing or making the return of income, information return, return, ownership certificate, or other document in respect of which the penalty is payable.

Interest charged on the penalty for late or deficient tax instalments will be computed from the date that the balance of tax is due until the date of payment.

Interest charged on the penalty for failure to comply with the reporting requirements in respect of tax shelters will run from the day on which the taxpayer became liable to the penalty to the day of payment.

Interest on other penalties will be charged from the day of sending of the notice of original assessment of the penalty.

[¶12,305] Penalties

[¶12,310] Failure to File Return When Required

An individual who fails to file an annual return of income when required is liable to a penalty equal to the aggregate of:

(1) 5% of the tax unpaid when the return was due; and

(2) 1% of such unpaid tax times the number of months the return is not filed, to a maximum of 12%.[192]

Thus, the maximum penalty is 17% of the tax unpaid.

See page ii for explanation of footnotes.

[191] CCH ¶22,843; Sec. 161(11).   [192] CCH ¶22,846; Sec. 162(1).

A second occurrence penalty provides a penalty of 10% of the unpaid amount plus 2% per month of default, to a maximum of 20 months if a penalty under the first occurrence rule was assessed for failure to file a return for any of the three preceding taxation years.[193] The second occurrence penalty is imposed only if the taxpayer has failed to file for the year and a formal demand for filing has been issued by the Minister.

The above penalties for failure to file a return will not be reduced for carrybacks to the year for which the return was not filed on a timely basis.

An individual who fails to file a required return may also be convicted of an offence, and, on summary conviction, is liable to an additional fine of not less than $1,000 nor more than $25,000, and up to 12 months' imprisonment.[194]

The Minister is allowed to waive or cancel all or any part of a penalty or interest otherwise payable under the Act by a taxpayer or a partnership. This discretion was originally introduced as part of the 1991 "Fairness Package" applicable in respect of the 1985 and subsequent taxation years. Since 2004, an application for such relief must be made within 10 years of the end of the taxation year to which the interest or penalty relates.[195] (See ¶15,006).

Intentional failure to file a return within the required time limit is not a wilful attempt to evade payment of tax and no further penalty will be imposed.[196]

[¶12,315] Failure of Trustee, etc., To File Returns

Where a trustee or person who acts in a similar representative capacity is required to file a return, failure to file brings a penalty of $10 for each day of default to a maximum of $50.[197]

[¶12,320] Failure To Provide Information

An individual who fails to complete the required information on a return is liable to a penalty of $100 for every failure.[198] However, if the information could only be obtained from a third party and was not obtained despite reasonable effort, this penalty is excused. Specific penalties are also provided for failure to file returns of information in respect of Social Insurance Numbers, returns in respect of partnerships, and reporting of non-arm's length transactions between non-residents and a corporation resident in Canada.[199]

See page ii for explanation of footnotes.

[193] CCH ¶22,851; Sec. 162(2).

[194] CCH ¶27,660, ¶27,668; Sec. 238(1), 238(3).

[195] CCH ¶27,015; Sec. 220(3.1).

[196] Pongratz, 82 DTC 6200.

[197] CCH ¶22,851; Sec. 162(3); ITAR 62(3).

[198] CCH ¶22,858; Sec. 162(5).

[199] CCH ¶22,859–22,863; Sec. 162(6)–(10).

¶12,320

[¶12,325] Penalties in Respect of Foreign-Based Information Returns

Penalties are imposed for the failure to file foreign-based information returns and for false statements and omissions in those returns. The foreign reporting requirements may be summarized as follows:

(1) In general terms, corporations resident in Canada or carrying on business in Canada must file an information return within six months of the end of the taxation year in respect of each non-resident person with whom the corporation did not deal at arm's length.[200]

(2) A return is required of a person who has transferred or loaned any property to a non-resident trust in certain circumstances, or to a controlled foreign affiliate of the trust, including transfers by a partnership of which the person is a member, or by a person whose controlled foreign affiliate has transferred or loaned property to a non-resident trust or to a controlled foreign affiliate of the trust. This return is required to be filed by the normal tax-filing deadline for the filer.[201]

(3) Persons or partnerships that own specified foreign property, the total cost of which exceeds $100,000, are required to file an information return.[202] This return must be filed by the normal tax filing deadline, except that partnership filers must file this return by the deadline for partnership returns (see ¶12,050).

(4) Reporting is generally required of a person resident in Canada or a partnership of which a corporation or trust is a foreign affiliate.[203] This return must be filed within 15 months after the end of the taxation year or fiscal period for the reporting entity.

If the taxpayer is liable to a penalty for the failure to file any of these returns, knowingly or under circumstances amounting to gross negligence, the penalties vary depending on whether or not a demand has been made by the CRA for its filing. If a demand has not been made, the penalty is $500 per month up to 24 months, starting with the month in which the return was required to be filed. Otherwise, the penalty is $1,000 per month up to 24 months.[204]

If the failure to file is not done knowingly or under circumstances amounting to gross negligence, the taxpayer is liable for a penalty only once a demand has been made, and only if the taxpayer fails to comply with it knowingly or under circumstances amounting to gross negligence.[205] In such a case, the penalty is $1,000 per month up to 24 months, starting with the month in which the demand was served.

See page ii for explanation of footnotes.

[200] CCH ¶27,576; Sec. 233.1.

[201] CCH ¶27,576a–27,576g; Sec. 233.2.

[202] CCH ¶27,576h–27,576l; Sec. 233.3.

[203] CCH ¶27,576m–27,576p; Sec. 233.4.

[204] CCH ¶22,863; Sec. 162(10)(a).

[205] CCH ¶22,863; Sec. 162(10)(b).

In all cases, the penalty is reduced by the general penalty to which the person or partnership is liable in respect of the information return (see ¶12,320).

If the failure to file returns described in (2) to (4) lasts more than 24 months, additional penalties are imposed as follows:[206]

(a) for returns described in (2), the additional penalty is 5% of the fair market value of the property transferred or loaned to the non-resident trust or foreign affiliate;

(b) for returns described in (3), it is 5% of the greatest of all amounts, each of which is the total cost of the person's or partnership's specified foreign property at any time in the year; and

(c) for returns described in (4), it is 5% of the greatest of all amounts, each of which is the total cost amount to the person or partnership (the filer) of shares or debt issued by the foreign affiliate and owned by the filer at any time in the year.

With respect to the additional penalty in (c) above, any shares or debt owned by a controlled foreign affiliate of the filer are deemed to be owned by the filer, and the cost amount of such shares or debt to the filer is deemed to be equal to 20% of their cost amount to the controlled foreign affiliate.[207]

Penalties for false statements or omissions in foreign-based-information returns are as follows:

(a) for returns described in (1), the penalty is $24,000;[208]

(b) for any other foreign-based information returns, it is the greater of $24,000 and 5% of:

(i) for returns described in (2), the fair market value of the property transferred or loaned to the non-resident trust or foreign affiliate that gave rise to the filer's obligation to file the return;

(ii) for returns described in (3), the greatest of all amounts, each of which is the total cost of the filer's specified foreign property at any time in the year;

(iii) for returns described in (4), the greatest of all amounts, each of which is the total cost amount to the filer of its shares or debt issued by the foreign affiliate in the year and that gave rise to the obligation to file; and

(iv) for returns required of persons resident in Canada and certain partnerships that receive distributions from or who are indebted to

[206] CCH ¶22,863a; Sec. 162(10.1).   [208] CCH ¶22,871d; Sec. 163(2.4).
[207] CCH ¶22,863b; Sec. 162(10.2).

foreign trusts in which they are beneficially interested, all amounts in respect of the return, each of which is the fair market value of a property that is distributed to the filer in the year from a non-resident trust, plus the greatest unpaid principal amount of each debt that is owing to the trust by the filer in the year.

For the purposes of determining the amount of the penalty for false statements and omissions, any shares or debt owned by a controlled foreign affiliate of the filer are deemed to be owned by the filer, and the cost amount of such shares or debt to the filer is deemed to be equal to 20% of their cost amount to the controlled foreign affiliate.[209]

[¶12,330] Penalties for Failure To Report Income

Penalties are assessed as follows:

(1) Failure to report an amount required to be included in income will result in an automatic penalty of 10% of the amount not reported where there has been a previous failure to report an amount in a return of any of the three preceding taxation years.[210] The only exception is where a more severe penalty is imposed under (2) in respect of the same amount.

(2) For "knowingly" or "under circumstances amounting to gross negligence" participating in or acquiescing in the making of a false statement or omission in a return, form, certificate, statement, or answer filed or made for the purposes of the Act, including the volunteering of false information for such purposes, a penalty of the greater of:

(a) $100; and

(b) 50% of the tax evaded because of the false statement or omission

will apply.[211]

Penalties for income omission will not be reduced where specified carrybacks reduce tax liability as it appeared at the time of the failure to report income.[212]

A penalty is also imposed where a taxpayer makes a false statement or omission in a renunciation of resource expenses. The penalty is equal to 25% of the amount by which the expenses the taxpayer has purported to renounce exceed the expenses the taxpayer was entitled to renounce as of the effective date of the renunciation.[213] In addition to such penalty, a 25% penalty is levied where a taxpayer makes, participates in, assents to, or acquiesces in the making of a false statement or omission in a form required to be filed for the allocation of assistance in respect of resource expenses in certain circumstances.[214]

See page ii for explanation of footnotes.

[209] CCH ¶22,871e; Sec. 163(2.5).

[210] CCH ¶22,866; Sec. 163(1).

[211] CCH ¶22,869; Sec. 163(2).

[212] CCH ¶22,874; Sec. 163(4).

[213] CCH ¶22,871; Sec. 163(2.2).

[214] CCH ¶22,871c; Sec. 163(2.3).

¶12,330

Penalties are also imposed on a taxpayer who makes a false statement or omission in a renunciation of resource expenses under the one year look-back rule in ¶12,292 or late files the document required.[215] The penalty is equal to 25% of the excess renounced, determined with reference only to what the person knew or ought to have known as of the end of the year of the renunciation.

The onus of proving the elements of knowledge or gross negligence is on the Minister and the taxpayer can require that the Minister establish the fact showing knowledge or gross negligence.[216] The Crown will have to prove that the taxpayer was wilfully or grossly negligent; the taxpayer will not have to prove that he or she was not. However, if the taxpayer disputes the assessment upon which the penalties were based, the onus remains on the taxpayer to prove that the assessment is wrong.[217]

It has been held that taxpayers who hired accountants to prepare their returns were still responsible for their accuracy.[218] It has also been held that the gross negligence of an accountant was not attributable to the taxpayer,[219] except where the taxpayer left everything to the discretion of the accountant,[220] and that a very understandable error made by an accountant likewise did not justify penalizing the taxpayer.[221] Carelessness in keeping records has been found to amount to gross negligence,[222] as has the failure to report sums so large that they could not possibly have been overlooked.[223] Failure to report certain income items, overstatement of expense items, failure to maintain an adequate bookkeeping system, and failure to follow the advice of an accountant were held to constitute gross negligence.[224]

In addition to these administrative penalties for evasion, the government can file criminal charges leading to a fine of 50% to 200% of the tax sought to be evaded and imprisonment for up to five years. See ¶15,270.

[¶12,333] Third-Party Civil Penalties

Third-party civil penalties, first announced in the February 1999 Budget, were enacted by Bill C-25 which received Royal Assent on June 29, 2000. These penalties apply to statements made after June 29, 2000. Prior to that date, Canadian tax law included both criminal and civil penalties that might apply to misrepresentations of tax matters, but only the criminal penalty provisions applied to a third party who participated in tax evasion in respect of another person's taxes.

See page ii for explanation of footnotes.

[215] CCH ¶22,871a, ¶22,871b; Sec. 163(2.21), 163(2.22).

[216] CCH ¶22,872; Sec. 163(3); ITAR 62(3).

[217] Taylor, 84 DTC 6459.

[218] Fortin, 68 DTC 461;Bany, 70 DTC 1728.

[219] Udell, 70 DTC 6019; Kornfeld, 72 DTC 1451; Columbia Enterprises Ltd., 81 DTC 5133; Joris, 81 DTC 470.

[220] Columbia Enterprises Ltd., 83 DTC 5247.

[221] Weeks, 72 DTC 6001.

[222] Cowan, 69 DTC 553.

[223] Warren, 58 DTC 17, Frenette, 58 DTC 579, Morin, 88 DTC 1596.

[224] Barbeau, 80 DTC 1181; Monarch Metal Co. Ltd. and Bereskin, 82 DTC 1398; Labelle, 83 DTC 599; Nadeau, 84 DTC 1180; Stirton, 88 DTC 1205.

Third-party civil penalties were first considered by the CRA (then Revenue Canada) in 1992 in the context of perceived overvaluations of tax shelter properties and business plans that were never intended to be carried out. Promoters of abusive tax shelters were also targeted in the 1996 Auditor General's Report and the House of Commons Standing Committee on Public Accounts that in February 1997 instructed Revenue Canada and the Department of Finance to take prompt steps to introduce third-party civil penalties. In 1997, the matter was referred to the Technical Committee on Business Taxation (the "Mintz Committee"). The Mintz Committee recommended that the tax law be revised to provide civil penalties against those who knowingly, or in circumstances amounting to gross negligence, made false statements or omissions in respect of another person's tax matters.

The February 1999 Budget proposed civil penalties that would, in general, apply to persons who knowingly, or in circumstances amounting to gross negligence, made false statements in tax planning arrangements, or who counselled or assisted in the filing of false tax returns. As a result of numerous representations, the Department of Finance abandoned the gross negligence test and introduced the "culpable conduct" definition and the good faith reliance defence in the initial draft legislation that was released on September 10, 1999. Further representations to the Department of Finance resulted in additional amendments that were contained in a December 7, 1999 Notice of Ways and Means Motion, enacted by Bill C-25 on June 29, 2000.

Culpable conduct test

"Culpable conduct" is relevant for the application of the civil third-party penalties in that, where the third party does not have knowledge that a statement is a false statement, the third party will be subject to penalties only if the third party should have known that the statement was a false statement but for circumstances amounting to culpable conduct. Culpable conduct is defined as conduct, whether an act or a failure to act, that (a) is tantamount to intentional conduct; (b) shows an indifference as to whether the Act is complied with; or (c) shows a wilful, reckless, or wanton disregard of the law.[225] The "culpable conduct" definition is based upon the following dicta of Mr. Justice Strayer in *Venne*, a leading case on gross negligence:

> With respect to the possibility of gross negligence, I have with some difficulty come to the conclusion that this has not been established either. "Gross negligence" must be taken to involve greater neglect than simply a failure to use reasonable care. It must involve a high degree of negligence tantamount to intentional acting, an indifference as to whether the law is complied with or not. I do not find that high degree of negligence in connection with the misstatements of business income.[226]

The case law which has interpreted and applied the *Venne* definition of gross negligence should be of assistance in defining the circumstances in

See page ii for explanation of footnotes.

[225] CCH ¶22,886a; Sec. 163.2(1) "culpable conduct".   [226] Venne, 84 DTC 6247.

¶12,333

which the new penalty provisions could apply. In applying the *Venne* definition, the Tax Court of Canada addresses the issue of whether there has been an "indifference as to whether the law is compiled with or not" and applies a test of wilful blindness.[227] The CRA has confirmed that this is the test they will be applying. In discussing the difference between the "wilful, the reckless, the wanton" standard for gross negligence laid down by the Ontario Court of Appeal in *Harper v. Prescott (Municipality)*, [1939] O.W.N. 492, and the standard of "indifference as to whether the law is complied with or not" stipulated by Strayer J in *Venne*, the Tax Court of Canada concludes that there is "little, if any, difference" between these two definitions.[228]

Penalty for misrepresentations in tax-planning arrangements

The first situation where a third-party penalty is imposed is where a person makes or furnishes, or participates in the making of, or causes another person to make or furnish a statement that the person knows or would reasonably be expected to have known, but for circumstances amounting to culpable conduct, is a false statement that may be used by another person for tax purposes. The amount of the penalty for a "planning activity" or a "valuation activity" is the greater of $1,000 and the person's "gross entitlements" from the activity. For any other activity, the penalty is $1,000.[229] Gross entitlements generally means all amounts to which the third-party planner or valuator, or a non-arm's length person, is entitled in respect of the planning or valuation activities.[230]

Penalty for participating in a misrepresentation

The second type of penalty applies where a person makes (or participates in the making of) a statement to, by, or on behalf of another person that the person knows, or would reasonably be expected to know, but for circumstances amounting to culpable conduct, is a false statement that may be used by, or on behalf of another person for the purpose of the Act. Subject to there being a minimum penalty of $1,000, the amount of the penalty in this case is the lesser of the penalty to which the other person whose taxes could be reduced by the statement might be liable under the gross negligence penalty provision at ¶12,330 (generally 50% of the federal taxes in issue) and the total of $100,000 and the person's "gross compensation" at the time the penalty is assessed.[231] "Gross compensation" is defined to mean generally all amounts to which the third-party adviser, or a non-arm's length person, is entitled in respect of the false statement.[232]

Reliance in good faith

An adviser will not be considered to act in circumstances amounting to culpable conduct solely because the person relies in good faith on informa

---

See page ii for explanation of footnotes.

[227] Colangelo, 98 DTC 1607.

[228] Malleck, 98 DTC 1019.

[229] CCH ¶22,886m–22,886n; Sec. 163.2(2)–(3).

[230] CCH ¶22,886f; Sec. 163.2(1) "gross entitlements".

[231] CCH ¶22,886o–22,886p; Sec. 163.2(4)–(5).

[232] CCH ¶22,886e; Sec. 163.2(1) "gross compensation".

tion provided to the adviser by or on behalf of the other person or, because of such reliance, the adviser fails to verify, investigate, or correct the information.[233] The September 1999 draft legislation provided that the good faith defence would not apply in respect of "planning" or "valuation" activities. In response to submissions made by several professional bodies and others, the Department of Finance in the December 7, 1999 Notice of Ways and Means Motion removed this exception from the good faith defence. The compromise for this concession from the Department of Finance was that the good faith exception does not apply to a statement the adviser makes (or participates in, assents to or acquiesces in the making of) in the course of an "excluded activity", which is defined as:

- promoting or selling (whether as principal or agent or directly or indirectly) an arrangement where it can reasonably be considered that the arrangement concerns a flow-through share or a tax shelter or is an arrangement where one of the main purposes of participation is to obtain a tax benefit; or

- accepting (whether as principal or agent or directly or indirectly) consideration in respect of the promotion or sale of such an arrangement.[234]

False statements in respect of a particular arrangement

Two or more false statements made or furnished by a person in the course of one or more planning activities or in the course of a valuation activity in respect of a single arrangement constitutes one false statement for the purpose of applying the penalty for misrepresentations in tax planning arrangements, but not for the purposes of applying the penalty for participating in a misrepresentation.[235] Although not stated in the Technical Notes, based on informal discussions with the Agency, the penalties for participating in a misrepresentation were carved out of this provision to ensure that those individuals who make a profession of counselling taxpayers to take filing positions in their tax returns that are without merit, will be assessed for each separate false statement made in a return.

Clerical services

A person providing clerical (other than bookkeeping services) or secretarial services will not be considered a third-party participant for purposes of these penalties.[236]

Valuations

A statement as to the value of a property or a service (the "stated value") made by a person who opined as to the value of a property or service or by a person in the course of an excluded activity is deemed to be a

---

See page ii for explanation of footnotes.

[233] CCH ¶22,886q; Sec. 163.2(6).

[234] CCH ¶22,886c, ¶22,886r; Sec. 163.2(1) "excluded activity", 163.2(7).

[235] CCH ¶22,886s; Sec. 163.2(8).

[236] CCH ¶22,886t; Sec. 163.2(9).

statement that the person would reasonably be expected to know, but for circumstances amounting to culpable conduct, is a false statement if the stated value falls outside a prescribed percentage of error (to be established by regulation after consultation on the appropriate percentages).[237] An inference can be drawn from this that valuations within the prescribed percentage will not be sufficiently unreasonable as to be considered recognizably false. The CRA has stated, however, that in its view, this deeming provision does not provide a safe harbour for individuals providing valuations in the above-described circumstances. According to the CRA, if the stated value of a property or service is inside of the prescribed percentage, it will bear the onus of proof. Where, however, the CRA establishes that the stated value of a property or service is outside the prescribed percentage, the person will be held to a reverse onus of proof to the extent that the person must establish that the stated value was reasonable in the circumstances, the statement was made in good faith, and, where applicable, was not based on one or more assumptions that the person knew or would reasonably be expected to know, but for circumstances amounting to culpable conduct, were unreasonable or misleading in the circumstances.[238]

Maximum penalty

The February 1999 Budget proposals and the wording of the quantum of the penalties suggest that the first type of penalty applies to planning and valuation activities and the second type applies to compliance activities. Nevertheless, the wording of the two penalty provisions provide for a substantial overlap. In circumstances where a person may be liable to a penalty under both penalty provisions, only the more financially onerous penalty will have application.[239]

Employees

One of the initial criticisms of the initial draft legislation was that it subjected employees to the third-party civil penalties, although employees might be under significant compulsion to file tax returns or participate in planning in order to maintain their employment. As a result of submissions made to the Department of Finance, a provision was added so that, in general, employees would be exempted from the civil penalty provisions.[240] This does not extend to a "specified employee", i.e., an employee of a corporation who holds, directly or indirectly, 10% or more of the shares of any class of the corporation, or who does not deal at arm's length with the corporation. It also does not extend to an employee engaged in an excluded activity.

Administration and consultation process

The CRA has stated that all proposed assessments under the civil third-party penalties will first be referred to a Head Office Review Committee for

See page ii for explanation of footnotes.

[237] CCH ¶22,886u; Sec. 163.2(10).
[238] CCH ¶22,886v; Sec. 163.2(11).
[239] CCH ¶22,889; Sec. 163.2(14).
[240] CCH ¶22,889l; Sec. 163.2(15).

consideration before a penalty is assessed. It is currently anticipated that practitioners will only be able to make written representations before such Committee.

On September 18, 2001, the CRA released the final version of Information Circular 01-1 that sets out the CRA's guidelines for the third-party civil penalties. In this Circular, the CRA enunciated the following eight application principles that it stated will be the gauge against which behaviour will be considered:

(1) The legislation is intended to apply mainly to arrangements and plans that contain false statements, often without the knowledge of the client. They are marketed typically as tax shelters and tax shelter-like arrangements that may be defective because of overvaluations of property, excessive or inflated costs, or lack of actual or intended business activity.

(2) Tax-planning arrangements that comply with the law are not affected by these penalties. The legislation is intended to apply to those advisers, tax return preparers, and promoters who make (or participate in the making of) false statements knowingly or in circumstances amounting to culpable conduct. Such behaviour goes beyond the bounds of the law in search of a result that under-reports tax payable or overstates a refund or rebate claim.

(3) The legislation is intended to apply to those tax return preparers and advisers who counsel and assist others in making false statements when they file their returns. It also applies to advisers and tax return preparers who are wilfully blind to "obvious" errors when preparing, filing, or assisting a taxpayer in filing a return.

(4) The legislation is not meant to impede regular day-to-day business activities and conventional tax planning involving the application of the law to issues such as estate freezes, rollovers, reorganizations, amalgamations, and owner-manager remuneration. These activities will not be impeded as long as they do not contain a false statement made knowingly or with culpable conduct.

(5) The legislation is not intended to apply to honest mistakes, oversights, and errors in judgment. Evidence concerning a person's conduct will be gathered to determine whether the error was made honestly (with good faith) or dishonestly (with bad faith, or with a wilful, reckless, or wanton disregard of the law).

(6) The legislation is not intended to apply to differences of interpretation where a reasonable argument (an argument that is not obviously wrong) exists as to the application of the law. The case law will often indicate whether such an uncertainty exists.

Similarly the penalty would not be applied to honest differences of opinion on such issues as:

● capital expenditures versus repairs;

¶12,333

- capital gains versus income; and

- personal versus business expense determination.

(7) The legislation is not intended to create additional audit or verification work for accountants and lawyers who conduct their affairs in accordance with their professional standards. Advisers and tax return preparers are entitled to rely in good faith on information provided to them by a client, or another person acting on the client's behalf, that is not obviously incorrect, misleading, or contradictory to other information. However, this reliance in good faith does not apply to a person who is also selling or promoting tax shelters or tax-shelter like arrangements, since this is defined as an "excluded activity".

(8) These penalties are not intended to apply to activities that are administratively acceptable to the CRA as the correct application of the law. Examples include paying a bonus to the principal shareholder-manager or other key employees to reduce small business income to the small business deduction limit.

[¶12,335] Penalty for Late or Deficient Instalments

A penalty is imposed for late or deficient tax instalments, in addition to the interest payable under ¶12,255.[241] This penalty is 50% of the interest payable on instalment shortfalls for the year (offset by contrainterest if applicable) *minus* the greater of:

(a) $1,000; and

(b) 25% of the interest the taxpayer would have had to pay for instalment shortfalls if he or she had made no instalment payments at all in the year.

Thus, this penalty can only apply where the interest on instalment shortfalls reaches a threshold of $1,000 after the application of the contrainterest calculation. In general, this implies an instalment requirement of at least $10,000 for the year.

Although the Minister's delay in assessing the taxpayer's 1990 return until December 27, 1991 (because of employee strike action and computer failures) had the effect of increasing the amounts of interest and penalty on the taxpayer's deficient tax instalments, such amounts could not be reduced by the Tax Court of Canada.[242]

[¶12,337] Small Penalty Amounts

The Minister may cancel small interest and penalty amounts owing if the taxpayer pays the principal amount of tax owing for the taxation year

---

See page ii for explanation of footnotes.
[241] CCH ¶22,883; Sec. 163.1.   [242] Flaska, 93 DTC 1254.

and the total amounts of interest and penalty payable for the year is not more than $25.[243]

[¶12,340] Refunds

[¶12,345] Refunds of Overpayments

Where an assessment shows that tax has been overpaid, a refund payment will in most cases be made with the notice of assessment for the year with no further application being necessary.[244] The CRA may, instead of refunding the amount, apply it against any other tax liability of the taxpayer or the taxpayer can request that this be done.[245] Effective April 1, 2007, the payment of a refund or offset of a credit will be withheld until all tax returns required to be filed by a taxpayer under all federal tax statutes have been filed. The federal tax statutes requiring the filing of a return are the *Income Tax Act*, the *Air Travellers Security Charge Act*, the *Excise Act, 2001* and the *Excise Tax Act*.[246]

If the refund is not made at the time the notice of assessment is sent, the taxpayer may make a written application to the Minister within the taxpayer's normal reassessment period, which is three years after the date of sending of the notice of reassessment in the case of an individual, including a trust other than a mutual fund trust, and Canadian-controlled private corporations, and four years for other taxpayers and mutual fund trusts (see ¶12,080).[247]

In order to obtain this refund as of right, the taxpayer must file the related tax return within three years from the end of the tax year, i.e., by December 31st of the third year following the year for which refund is sought. Thus, to obtain a refund for 2012, a taxpayer has to file a return by December 31, 2015. Subject to the discretion described below, refunds due for 2009 or earlier years are now lost if a return has not been filed, although, of course, a taxpayer's liability for unpaid tax continues until a return is filed and the return has become statute-barred, as discussed at ¶12,080.

However, legislation introduced as part of the "Fairness Package" allows the Minister to give refunds to taxpayers who are individuals (other than trusts) and testamentary trusts where the taxpayer's return is filed three years after the end of the taxation year for which refund is sought. This late filed return must be filed within 10 years of the relevant taxation year.[248]

Likewise, late refunds of overpayments may be made, at the discretion of the Minister where:

---

[243] CCH ¶22,845m; Sec. 161.3.
[244] CCH ¶22,891; Sec. 164(1).
[245] CCH ¶22,894; Sec. 164(2).
[246] CCH ¶22,894a; Sec. 164(2.01).
[247] CCH ¶22,222; Sec. 152(4.2).
[248] CCH ¶22,893ba; Sec. 164(1.5).

- a reassessment or redetermination is made, at the request of an individual (other than a trust) or a testamentary trust, beyond the three-year normal reassessment period and relevant adjustments are made that result in a refund or reduction of tax payable (the request must be made within 10 years of the relevant taxation year); and

- after March 4, 2010, a non-resident becomes entitled to a refund by reason of the assessment of another person for failure to withhold and remit an amount on account of the non-resident's tax liability and the non-resident claims the refund by filing a tax return no more than two years after the date of that assessment.

Where a taxpayer has succeeded on the disposition of an appeal, the Minister must make a refund, regardless of any time period.[249]

[Pending technical amendments will allow the CRA to refund excessive instalment amounts paid on account of a taxpayer's tax liability.[250] In order for such a refund to be made, all of the following conditions must be met:

- the taxpayer must have paid one or more instalments of tax under Part I or, where the taxpayer is a corporation, Parts I.3, VI, VI.1, or XIII of the Act;

- it must be reasonable to conclude that the total amount of the instalments the taxpayer has paid exceeds the total amount of taxes payable by the taxpayer under those Parts for the year;

- the Minister must be satisfied that the payment of the instalments has caused or will cause the taxpayer undue hardship; and

- the Minister must agree to make the refund.[251]

The last condition emphasizes that the refund is completely at the Minister's discretion. Similarly, the amount of any instalment refund is to be decided by the Minister — the Minister may refund all or any part of an excessive instalment. For the purpose of computing interest and penalties, a taxpayer that receives an instalment refund is treated as not having paid the instalment to that extent.][252]

[¶12,346] Assignment of Tax Refunds

Notwithstanding any other provision of a federal or provincial law, a corporation may assign any amount "payable" to it under the federal *Income Tax Act*.[253] However, unlike other assignments, such assignments do not in any way affect the rights or obligations of the Crown.[254] The Minister is not required to pay an assignee the assigned amount, the assignment does not create any liability of Her Majesty to the assignee, and the rights of the

See page ii for explanation of footnotes.

[249] CCH ¶22,905; Sec. 164(4.1).
[250] Sec. 164(1.51).
[251] Sec. 164(1.52).

[252] Sec. 164(1.53).
[253] CCH ¶27,041; Sec. 220(6).
[254] CCH ¶27,041a; Sec. 220(7).

assignee are subject to all equitable and statutory rights of set-off in favour of Her Majesty. In other words, the CRA's right to apply the refund to any tax debts owing by the corporation will take precedence over any right of the assignee.

[¶12,347] Refunds of Taxes in Dispute

To obtain a refund of amounts paid which are in dispute, the taxpayer must have filed an objection to an assessment and 120 days must have elapsed without there being a confirmation or variation of the assessment or a reassessment. Alternatively, the taxpayer must have appealed an assessment to the Tax Court of Canada. Accordingly, where a confirmation or variation is issued within 120 days of the notice of objection, the right to a refund does not arise until an appeal is filed with the Tax Court of Canada.

To obtain a refund of amounts paid while an appeal is outstanding, the taxpayer is required to make an application in writing to the Minister for the refund. Upon such an application being made, the Minister is required to make the refund "with all due dispatch".

The Minister is not required to refund amounts assessed which are not in controversy. Accordingly, where an assessment involves several issues and not all issues are the subject of the appeal, a refund may only be obtained of amounts paid which relate to the issues under appeal. However, large corporations cannot obtain a full refund of the amount under dispute. Large corporations are entitled to obtain as a refund only one-half of the amounts which relate to issues under appeal.

Furthermore, the Minister is not required to refund amounts where there are reasonable grounds for believing that, if the amounts were not retained, their collection would be jeopardized.[255]

The Tax Court of Canada may impose a penalty when there are no reasonable grounds for all or part of an appeal and one of the main purposes for instituting or maintaining an appeal was to defer payment of amounts owing.[256]

[¶12,350] Excess Refunds

Provision is made for recovery of a refund of tax paid to a taxpayer or applied to a liability of a taxpayer where the refund or application is greater than the amount to which the taxpayer was properly entitled.[257]

The excess refund is deemed to be an amount that became payable by the taxpayer on the day on which the amount was refunded. The taxpayer is required to pay interest at the prescribed rate on the excess refund from the date upon which it became an amount payable until the date of payment.[258]

See page ii for explanation of footnotes.

[255] CCH ¶22,892–22,893bb; Sec. 164(1.1)–(1.6).
[256] CCH ¶23,885; Sec. 179.1.
[257] CCH ¶22,783; Sec. 160.1.
[258] CCH ¶22,783; Sec. 160.1(1).

The interest is compounded daily.[259] However, no interest is payable on the portion of the refund that relates to a repayment of the goods and services tax (GST) credit or the child tax credit.

[¶12,355] Interest on Overpayments

Up to July 1, 2010, interest rates on overpayments of taxes by *all* taxpayers are determined quarterly, based on an average three-month yield of government treasury bills, rounded up to the nearest percentage point, bumped up by 2%. Effective July 1, 2010, the prescribed interest rates applicable to overpayments of taxes by *corporate* taxpayers will be based on the same three-month average yield, but without the 2% bump-up. This means that, effective July 1, 2010, the prescribed interest rate used to calculate tax refunds payable by the government will be 2% lower for corporate taxpayers than for individual taxpayers (including trusts).

A table of prescribed interest rates by quarter is found in the information material at ¶475. The interest constitutes income subject to tax when received.

The government will pay a taxpayer interest on tax overpayments from the date that is the latest of:

(a) where the taxpayer is an individual, the day that is 30 days after the "balance-due day" for the year, i.e., April 30th of the year following the taxation year, regardless of whether the return is due April 30th as is generally the case, or June 15th, as is the case for self-employed individuals and their spouses or common-law partners;

(b) where the taxpayer is a corporation, 120 days after the end of the year;

(c) where the taxpayer is a corporation, the day that is 30 days after the day on which its tax return was filed unless the return was filed on or before its filing-due date;

(d) where the taxpayer is an individual, the date that is 30 days after the day on which the individual's tax return was filed; and

(e) the day the overpayment arose.[260]

The combined effect of (a) and (d) above would be that an individual's refund interest would begin, for example, 30 days after May 10th when the individual's return of income is required to be filed by June 15th but is filed on May 10th.

In the case of a repayment of tax in controversy, special provisions will apply. Interest paid on refunds will be compounded daily.[261]

See page ii for explanation of footnotes.

[259] CCH ¶28,329g; Sec. 248(11).
[260] CCH ¶22,899, ¶22,904, ¶28,020b; Sec. 164(3), 248(1) "balance-due day"; Reg. 4301.
[261] CCH ¶28,329g; Sec. 248(11).

Where it is subsequently determined that the actual overpayment of a taxpayer for a taxation year was less than an overpayment for such year in respect of which interest was paid to, or applied to a liability of, the taxpayer, recovery may be made of any such interest in excess of the amount to which the taxpayer was properly entitled. The excess interest is deemed to be an amount that became payable by the taxpayer at the time of the subsequent determination and the taxpayer is required to pay interest thereon at the prescribed rate from the time when it became an amount payable until the date of payment.[262] Similarly, interest paid or credited to a taxpayer on a refund of taxes in controversy becomes repayable, together with interest thereon, to the extent that it is determined that the tax refunded was properly payable.[263]

[¶12,360] Effect of Carryback of Loss, etc.

Any portion of an overpayment of tax or a refund of tax, interest, or penalty in dispute for a taxation year that arose as a result of the carryback of certain losses, gifts, or tax credits, or the exclusion of option proceeds resulting from the subsequent exercise of the options will be deemed to have arisen in the later of four possible dates (discussed below). The taxpayer will only be entitled to interest on this portion of any overpayment or refund from the day on which it is deemed to have arisen until the day on which it is refunded or otherwise applied. Interest on any remaining portion of the overpayment is to be calculated in the ordinary manner for interest on overpayments of tax.[264]

These provisions apply to any portion of an overpayment or refund resulting from:

(1) the repayment of fuel tax rebates claimed under the *Excise Tax Act*;

(2) the deduction of listed personal property losses for a taxation year in computing the net gains from dispositions of listed personal property for the three taxation years immediately preceding such year;[265]

(3) the exclusion from income of proceeds received in a taxation year for the granting of an option where such option is exercised in a subsequent taxation year;[266]

(4) the deduction, permitted in the year immediately preceding the year in which an individual has died, of certain amounts in respect of gifts made by the individual in the year of death;[267]

(5) the deduction of non-capital, net capital, restricted farm, and farm losses for a taxation year in computing taxable income for the three immediately preceding taxation years;[268]

See page ii for explanation of footnotes.

[262] CCH ¶22,900; Sec. 164(3.1).
[263] CCH ¶22,902; Sec. 164(4).
[264] CCH ¶22,910, ¶22,920; Sec. 164(5), 164(7).
[265] CCH ¶6500; Sec. 41.
[266] CCH ¶7315; Sec. 49(4).
[267] CCH ¶18,352; Sec. 118.1(4).
[268] CCH ¶16,003; Sec. 111(1).

¶12,360

(6) the deduction permitted for net capital losses for the year in which an individual has died, in computing taxable income for the immediately preceding year;[269]

(7) the deduction for unused foreign tax credits in respect of foreign taxes paid in respect of a business which are carried back from any of the three subsequent taxation years;[270]

(8) the deduction for investment tax credits in respect of property acquired or an expenditure made which are carried back from any of the three subsequent taxation years;[271]

(9) the deduction for unused Part VI tax credits carried back from any of the three subsequent taxation years;

(10) the deduction, claimed in the deceased's tax return for the year of death, of capital losses or terminal losses realized within the first taxation year of the estate in respect of which the taxpayer's legal representative has elected;[272]

(11) the deduction for an unused Part I.3 tax credit in respect of large corporations tax carried back from any of the three subsequent taxation years;

(12) the deduction against the large corporations tax in respect of an "unused surtax credit" carried back from any of the three subsequent taxation years;[273]

(13) the deduction against Part VI tax in respect of an "unused Part I tax credit" carried back from any of the three subsequent taxation years;[274]

(14) the deduction on a taxpayer's death after 1992 of RPP contributions in respect of pre-1990 service;[275]

(15) the deduction allowed to former residents in respect of the disposition of a taxable Canadian property in a subsequent year (this provision, discussed at ¶5393, provides a special tax credit in certain cases where the "stop-loss" rule applies to an individual who ceased to be resident in Canada);[276]

(16) the deductions allowed to former residents which provide: (i) limited credits against an individual's Canadian tax that arises in the year of the individual's departure from Canada for post-departure foreign taxes; and (ii) similar limited credits against a trust's Canadian tax that arose in the year of a distribution by the trust to a non-resident beneficiary, for the beneficiary's subsequent foreign taxes, respectively; and[277]

See page ii for explanation of footnotes.

[269] CCH ¶16,100; Sec. 111(2).
[270] CCH ¶19,700; Sec. 126.
[271] CCH ¶19,825; Sec. 127(5).
[272] CCH ¶22,915; Sec. 164(6).
[273] CCH ¶24,062; Sec. 181.1(4).

[274] CCH ¶24,482a; Sec. 190.1(3).
[275] CCH ¶21,544a; Sec. 147.2(4).
[276] CCH ¶18,500; Sec. 119.
[277] CCH ¶19,721; Sec. 126(2.21).

(17) the deductions allowed to returning former residents when they return to reside in Canada in a subsequent year; these provisions, discussed at ¶5393, generally "unwind" the previous application of the deemed disposition rules that applied upon emigration.[278]

Where the overpayment or refund arises as described above, the calculation of interest payable to the taxpayer commences 30 days after the latest of:

(a) the first day of the taxation year following the taxation year in which the amount to be carried back arose;

(b) the day of the filing of the taxpayer's or his or her legal representative's return for the taxation year in which the amount to be carried back arose;

(c) the day of filing of the amended return or prescribed form amending the return for the year in which the deduction or credit is to be claimed; and

(d) if the Minister reassessed at the taxpayer's request, the day upon which the taxpayer's request was made.

It should be noted that a taxpayer must file a return of income for a year in which a deduction or exclusion claim arises in order to be entitled to interest on any taxes refunded to him or her for any preceding taxation year in which such deduction or exclusion claim is applied.

[¶12,365] Reduction of Tax Where Disposition of Property by Legal Representative of Deceased Taxpayer

A deceased taxpayer's legal representative may elect to treat certain capital losses or terminal losses of the estate for its first taxation year as capital losses or terminal losses of the deceased taxpayer for the year of death.[279] An estate, arising on the death of a taxpayer, is allowed to reduce the income tax that would otherwise be payable by it in its first taxation year by the amount of the tax reduction that the deceased would have enjoyed if capital losses of the estate in excess of its capital gains or any terminal loss on depreciable property realized by the estate during its first taxation year had been realized by the deceased in the year of death. The notional tax reduction will be applied against the tax liability of the estate and in fact may give rise to a refund where the estate has no income.

The legal representative of an estate may elect to treat all or any part of the aggregate capital losses in excess of the aggregate capital gains realized in the first taxation year of the estate as though the elected amount of these net losses had been losses of the deceased in the year of death. Such an election will not, however, have the effect of reducing the deceased taxpay-

---

See page ii for explanation of footnotes.

[278] CCH ¶20,028d; Sec. 128.1(6).   [279] CCH ¶22,915, ¶22,916; Sec. 164(6); Reg. 1000.

¶12,365

er's capital loss on a share by the tax-free dividends received by the estate. An election may also be made to treat all or any part of deductions under the capital cost allowance provisions and under the terminal loss provisions on assets disposed of in the first taxation year, as if the elected part of these deductions were deductible by the deceased in the year of death.[280] This latter election is restricted in that the elected amount cannot exceed the amount that would have been the aggregate of the non-capital loss and the farm loss of the estate for its first taxation year in the absence of the election.

Any capital loss which the legal representative elects to apply to the income of the deceased is deemed not to be a loss of the estate for purposes of computing its income or its net capital loss for its first taxation year. The deduction under the capital cost allowance provisions or for a terminal loss that is applied against the income of the deceased is deemed not to be included in computing any loss of the estate for purposes of computing the income of the estate for its first taxation year.

For example, if a capital asset which originally cost $40,000 had a fair market value of $50,000 at the date of death, the deceased would be deemed to have realized the asset for $50,000 and the estate would acquire the asset at a deemed cost of $50,000. If for some reason the property realized only $45,000 on disposition a few months later, the resulting allowable capital loss to the estate would not be deductible if the estate had no capital gains. This provision permits the estate to elect to have all or any part of the capital loss applied as if it were a loss of the deceased in the year of death.

An election is made by the legal representative by filing with the Minister the following:

(1) a letter specifying the part of the one or more capital losses from the disposition of property and the part of the amount of deductions as terminal losses in respect of which the election is made;

(2) a schedule of the capital losses and capital gains, where applicable;

(3) a schedule of the undepreciated capital costs, where applicable;

(4) a statement of the non-capital loss of the estate for its first taxation year; and

(5) a statement of the farm loss of the estate for its first taxation year.[281]

The above documents must be filed by the later of:

(a) the last day the legal representative is required or has elected to file a return for the year in which the taxpayer died; and

(b) the day the return for the first taxation year of the deceased's estate is required.

See page ii for explanation of footnotes.

[280] CCH ¶22,917; Sec. 164(6).   [281] CCH ¶22,916; Reg. 1000.

The CRA is authorized (but not required) to accept late-filed elections (see ¶15,008).

In addition to the election, the legal representative must file an amended return for the deceased taxpayer for the year of death. The amended tax return must be filed at or before the time prescribed for filing the elections. As a result, capital losses and terminal losses in respect of which an election has been made will be reported in the deceased taxpayer's return and will affect the computations required for the purpose of computing the deceased taxpayer's capital gains exemption. Amounts in respect of which an election has been made are only deductible by the deceased taxpayer for the year of death.

[¶12,366] Reduction of Tax Where Realization of Deceased Employees' Options

Where an employee dies while holding unexercised options to acquire shares in an employer corporation or units in an employer mutual fund trust, the employee is deemed to have received a benefit equal to the amount by which the value of the right immediately after the employee's death exceeds the amount the employee paid to acquire the right. The benefit is taxed as employment income in the year of death.[282]

If the value of the option decreases after the date of death, the above benefit will be overstated in comparison to the actual benefit realized. In effect, there will be a loss. Relief is provided when the option is either exercised or disposed of by the deceased's legal representative, or expires within the first taxation year of the deceased's estate.[283]

In these circumstances, an election can be made such that any loss determined under this provision can be carried back to the deceased's final return.

The amount of the loss that the legal representative may elect to carry back to the deceased's final return is equal to the amount of the benefit the deceased is deemed to have received less the amount by which the value of the option immediately before it was exercised or disposed of exceeds the amount paid by the deceased for the option. In addition, if a deduction was claimed in the final tax return in respect of the stock option benefit, only half of the above-noted loss can be carried back since the deceased was only taxed on half of the benefit.

Any amount deducted in respect of the employee stock option for the taxation year in which the taxpayer died is ignored in computing the adjusted cost base of the option to the estate, since the estate acquired the option at its fair market value at the time of death.

To give effect to the loss claimed as a result of the election, the legal representative must amend the deceased's final return and make the election by the later of the filing-due date for the deceased's final return and the filing-due date for the estate's first taxation year.[284]

See page ii for explanation of footnotes.

[282] CCH ¶2700; Sec. 7(1)(e).
[283] CCH ¶22,919; Sec. 164(6.1).

[284] CCH ¶22,919; Reg. 1000.1.

¶12,366

Example:

An individual died in June 2012 holding an unexercised option to acquire shares of XYZ Company under an employee stock option plan. The details are as follows:

	$
Value of option at death	10,000
Price paid to acquire the option	(1,000)
Deemed employment benefit	9,000
Deduction claimed (1/2 × $9,000)	(4,500)
Net amount included in final income tax return ($9,000 - $4,500)	4,500

The deceased's legal representative disposed of the option on January 10, 2013 and received proceeds of $8,000. An election will be made which will result in a deemed loss from employment calculated as follows:

	$	
Deemed employment benefit	9,000	(A)
minus the total of:		
value of the option on January 10, 2013 net of the cost to acquire option ($8,000 - $1,000)	7,000	(B)
(A - B) × 1/2	1,000	
	8,000	
Deemed loss from employment	1,000	

In effect, there was a $2,000 loss in value, half of which is recognized because only half was taxed.

Therefore, the net amount taxed in the deceased's final return is equal to $3,500 (i.e., the amount included in the original return of $4,500 minus the employment loss of $1,000). This is in effect equal to the net inclusion that would have been required if the option was valued at $8,000 at the time of death, calculated as follows:

	$
Value of option at death	8,000
Price paid to acquire the option	(1,000)
Deemed employment benefit	7,000
Deduction claimed (1/2 × $7,000)	(3,500)
Net inclusion regarding stock option benefit	3,500

[¶12,370] Appeals

[¶12,375] Amended Procedure

S.C. 1988, c. 61 substantially amended the provisions of the *Income Tax Act*, the *Tax Court of Canada Act*, and the *Federal Courts Act* relating to all proceedings involving appeals under the *Income Tax Act* from notices of assessment and reassessment.

The purpose of these amendments, which became applicable on proclamation, January 1, 1991, was to eliminate the Federal Court–Trial Division as a court of original or appellate jurisdiction in income tax matters, and to give the Tax Court of Canada exclusive original jurisdiction over such matters.

A second purpose of these amendments was to permit appellate proceedings before the Tax Court of Canada to retain their informal character only in those situations where:

(a) the aggregate of all amounts in issue does not exceed $12,000;

(b) the amount of the loss determined by the Minister does not exceed $24,000; or

(c) the only subject matter of the appeal is an amount of interest.

Draft legislation released on June 8, 2012 proposes to increase the monetary limits for appeals under the Informal Procedure so that the aggregate limit for all amounts in issue is raised to $25,000 from $12,000, and the limit for a loss determination is raised to $50,000 from $24,000. These new monetary limits will come into force after Royal Assent to the enacting legislation.

This procedure, which is referred to as the "informal procedure", only applies when the taxpayer so elects. All other proceedings before the Tax Court are governed by the "general procedure", which is a code of procedural rules not dissimilar to the *Rules of Civil Procedure* common to most superior courts of first instance.

Rules governing both the informal and the general procedures were formally promulgated by the rules committee of the Court on September 7, 1990, and became effective on January 1, 1991.

[¶12,380] Objections to Assessments

Under the current procedure, all objections to assessments continue to be initiated by serving, generally within 90 days of the date on which the notice of assessment was sent, a notice of objection in duplicate in prescribed form, setting out the reasons for the objection together with all relevant facts. However, individuals (other than trusts) and testamentary trusts are afforded a longer period for service of notices of objection to the extent that they must serve such notices within one year after their filing-due date for the year, or within 90 days after the day of sending of the notice of assessment, whichever is later. Thus, for example, a taxpayer can file a notice of objection to an assessment of his or her 2011 return, assuming it was due April 30, 2012, up to the later of April 30, 2013, or 90 days from the mailing or, effective December 15, 2010, the electronic sending by the CRA of the notice of assessment (or reassessment) for taxation year 2011.[285]

See page ii for explanation of footnotes.
[285] CCH ¶23,021a, ¶28,108b; Sec. 165(1), 248(1) "filing-due date".

Note that the additional period of up to one year following the return due date only applies to ordinary income tax, surtax, and clawback taxes on Old Age Security payments. Special taxes such as the penalties on excess contributions to an RRSP are not eligible for this additional time period and objections must be filed within 90 days. Similarly, the additional period is only available to individuals and testamentary trusts, and not to corporations and other trusts.

Objections need not be sent by registered mail; it will be sufficient if the notice of objection is addressed to the Chief of Appeals in a District Office or Taxation Centre of the CRA and delivered or mailed to that office or centre.[286] However, the Minister may accept a notice of objection not served in accordance with these rules.[287]

On receipt of a notice of objection, the Minister is required "with all due dispatch" to reconsider the assessment, vacate, confirm, or vary it, and notify the taxpayer in writing of the action taken.[288] If, however, the Minister fails to do so, and fails to notify the taxpayer of the result within 90 days following service of the notice of objection, the taxpayer may at that point appeal to the Tax Court of Canada or await the Minister's response, following which the taxpayer will have 90 days to appeal to the Tax Court of Canada.[289] Failure by the Minister to act "with all due dispatch" upon receipt of a notice of objection by a taxpayer does not have the effect of vacating the Minister's assessment, and the taxpayer's only recourse is to appeal to the Tax Court of Canada.[290]

Once a notice of objection has been served, the Minister is free to reassess or make additional assessments without being subject to the limitations imposed on normal reassessments (see ¶12,080) as to, respectively, the time within which to reassess and the scope of such reassessments.[291] If the Minister does so, the taxpayer may, without serving a notice of objection, appeal to the Tax Court of Canada or, if an appeal is already in progress, it can be amended by joining thereto an appeal against the reassessment or additional assessments.[292] This direct appeal and joinder process is extended to situations where the reassessment or additional assessment relates to other amounts such as interest or penalties.

[¶12,383] Extensions of Time to Object to Assessments or to Appeal

The period for filing the appeal to the Tax Court of Canada can be extended upon application to the Tax Court of Canada within one year after the expiration of such time limit,[293] provided that the Tax Court of Canada is satisfied that the application was brought in a timely manner, that there are reasonable grounds for objecting to the assessment, and that the appeal would have been launched on time had circumstances reasonably permitted.[294] In that respect, extension of time for filing an objection was allowed where the application was mailed in time but received late; and where an

---

See page ii for explanation of footnotes.

[286] CCH ¶23,021h; Sec. 165(2).
[287] CCH ¶23,050; Sec. 165(6).
[288] CCH ¶23,030; Sec. 165(3).
[289] CCH ¶23,250; Sec. 169(1)(a), 169(1)(b).
[290] Bolton, 96 DTC 6413, James, 96 DTC 6416.

[291] CCH ¶23,044; Sec. 165(5).
[292] CCH ¶23,070; Sec. 165(7).
[293] CCH ¶23,150; Sec. 167(1).
[294] CCH ¶23,180; Sec. 167(5).

RCMP officer had been constrained from exercising a choice by an RCMP directive.[295] However, where the Minister had sent a letter advising the taxpayer to apply "no later than one year from the 90-day limit" and efforts were being made to settle, no extension was allowed.[296] Reasons for failing to file on time must accompany all applications for extension,[297] and all such applications are governed by the informal procedure (see ¶12,390).

The code of procedure applicable to extensions of time for objecting to assessments involves a two-tier application process. The first involves an application to the Minister (within one year from the expiration of the deadline for objecting), and the second, an application to the Tax Court of Canada (within 90 days following the Minister's decision) in the event that the Minister decides to dismiss the initial application. The requirements for obtaining the extension (from the Minister or from the Tax Court of Canada) will also change. The applicant taxpayer must set out the reasons for failing to meet the deadline and for objecting to the relevant assessment. No application will be granted unless the taxpayer demonstrates that he or she was unable to act or instruct someone else to act for him or her within the required time frame, or that he or she had a *bona fide* intention to act. Finally, the applicant must show that it would be just and equitable to grant the extension. Both the Minister and the Tax Court of Canada in this two-tier process are to be bound by the same set of criteria in reaching their decisions.[298]

[¶12,385] Appeals to the Tax Court of Canada

[¶12,390] Informal Procedure

The informal procedure is governed by a series of provisions contained in the *Tax Court of Canada Act*, R.S.C. 1985, c. T-2 (as amended), as amplified by the *Tax Court of Canada Rules* (Informal Procedure), promulgated effective January 1, 1991. Pursuant to these provisions and Rules, the taxpayer is permitted to elect, in the notice of appeal to the Tax Court or at any subsequent time up to 20 days (or such lesser time as the Court may, upon motion, allow) before the start of the hearing, to be governed by the "informal procedure". This election can only be made when:

(a) the amount of federal tax and penalties in issue for one taxation year does not exceed $12,000 (to be increased to $25,000 upon Royal Assent to implementing draft legislation released on June 8, 2012);

(b) the amount of the losses determined by the Minister does not exceed $24,000 (to be increased to $50,000 upon Royal Assent to implementing draft legislation released on June 8, 2012); or

(c) the only subject matter of the appeal is an amount of interest.

In the absence of such an election, the taxpayer's appeal will automatically be governed by the "general procedure" (see ¶12,395).

See page ii for explanation of footnotes.

[295] Batey, 86 DTC 1294, Charpentier, 86 DTC 1768.   [297] CCH ¶23,151; Sec. 167(2).
[296] Pennington, 87 DTC 5107.   [298] CCH ¶23,110; Sec. 166.1.

Appeals using the informal procedure are to be made in writing setting out, in general terms, the reasons for the appeal and the relevant facts, without any requirement for any special form of pleadings. The appeal may, however, be brought in the form (Schedule 4) set out in the Rules of the Court governing the informal procedure, and is to be instituted by filing in, or mailing to, an office of the Registry of the Court (in Montreal, Toronto, or Vancouver) the original written appeal.

In addition, all appeals governed by the informal procedure are to be dealt with by the Court as informally and expeditiously as the circumstances and considerations of fairness permit. Thus, where, during the course of a hearing conducted under the informal procedure, the taxpayer's agent was not permitted to testify by the Tax Court of Canada, its decision was set aside on the ground that lay counsel is not an officer of the court whose credibility could be put in issue by giving evidence. Preventing the taxpayer's agent from testifying was contrary to the direction for the conduct of informal hearings.[299]

Taxpayers using the informal procedure will be entitled to appear before the Tax Court of Canada in person, or to be represented by an agent or by counsel, and may be entitled to costs in the discretion of the Court where the judgment reduces the aggregate of the amounts in issue by more than one-half. Judgments rendered in appeals involving the informal procedure, however, have no precedential value.

Unless the Tax Court of Canada otherwise directs, or unless the taxpayer otherwise consents, the Minister is given 60 days under the informal procedure to file a reply (by mail or otherwise) to the taxpayer's notice of appeal. The Minister's failure to do so results in the taxpayer's allegations of fact contained in the notice of appeal being presumed to be true. Unless the Minister and the taxpayer otherwise consent, or unless the matter in issue is before the Tax Court of Canada or any other court in Canada in another case, the Tax Court must fix a date for the hearing of the appeal no later than 180 days following the filing of the Minister's reply and must, in the absence of "exceptional circumstances", render judgment no later than 90 days after the conclusion of the hearing. "Exceptional circumstances" are deemed to include failure by either party to submit any written material required by the Tax Court of Canada. If the taxpayer fails to appear on the date set for the hearing, the Tax Court of Canada must dismiss the appeal unless it feels that the circumstances justify an adjournment; and an appeal by the taxpayer from such dismissal and for an order fixing a new date for the hearing of the appeal can only be made to the Tax Court of Canada within 180 days of the mailing of the order of dismissal.

[¶12,395] General Procedure

The general procedure is governed by a series of provisions contained in the *Tax Court of Canada Act*, R.S.C. 1985, c. T-2 (as amended), as amplified by the *Tax Court of Canada Rules* (General Procedure), promulgated effective January 1, 1991. Pursuant to these provisions and Rules, appeals

---

See page ii for explanation of footnotes.

[299] Muszka, 94 DTC 6076.

not governed by the informal procedure (see ¶12,390) are governed by the general procedure, although taxpayers otherwise governed by the general procedure may, by abandoning that portion of their appeal which exceeds the monetary limits to which the informal procedure applies, elect to be governed by the latter.

Appeals under the general procedure are instituted by filing in the Court registry the original and two copies of the notice of appeal in prescribed form (Form 21(1)(a)) and by paying the filing fee set out in the *General Procedure Rules.* An officer of the Court then serves the notice of appeal on the Crown via the office of the Deputy Attorney General of Canada, and a certificate evidencing such service is then delivered or forwarded by registered mail to the taxpayer (or counsel) by an officer of the Registry of the Court.

Individual taxpayers using the general procedure must either represent themselves or be represented by counsel, and corporate taxpayers must be represented by counsel.

Under the general procedure, the Court has full discretionary power over the payment of costs by all parties involved, including the Crown. The Court is also given ample discretion where necessary, in the interests of justice, to dispense with compliance with any Rule and to grant relief from non-compliance. In addition, oral discoveries are not permitted in appeals where the aggregate of all amounts involved does not exceed $25,000 or where the amount of any loss determined by the Minister does not exceed $50,000 unless all parties consent thereto, unless the Court feels that such discoveries are virtually indispensable, or unless any party requesting such discoveries agrees to pay the costs in accordance with the tariff set out in the Rules. The Rules also provide a special procedure governing examination for discovery by written questions.

[¶12,400] Special References Governed by General Procedure

Where the Minister and the taxpayer agree in writing that a question of law, fact, or mixed law and fact arising under the *Income Tax Act* in respect of any assessment should be determined by the Tax Court of Canada, or where the Minister alone is of the opinion that any such question arising out of one and the "same" transaction or occurrence is common to assessments in respect of two or more taxpayers, the Tax Court of Canada alone has jurisdiction to make these determinations.[300] In addition, the general procedure applies thereto, except by leave of the Court upon the application of the Attorney General of Canada, in which case resort may be had to the informal procedure.

Draft legislation released on June 8, 2012 proposes to allow the Minister to apply to the Tax Court of Canada for a determination if, in the Minister's opinion, the question at issue is common to assessments in respect of two or more taxpayers and is a question of law, fact, or mixed law and fact arising out of *substantially similar* transactions or occurrences.

See page ii for explanation of footnotes.

[300] CCH ¶23,500, ¶23,550; Sec. 173, 174.

These amendments will come into force after Royal Assent to the enacting legislation.

[¶12,405] Disposition of Appeals

The Tax Court of Canada may dispose of an appeal by:

(a) dismissing it;

(b) allowing it and vacating or varying the assessment; or

(c) referring the assessment back to the Minister for reconsideration and reassessment.[301]

No assessment, however, may be vacated or varied on appeal by reason only of any irregularity, informality, omission, or error on the part of any person in the observation of any directory provision of the *Income Tax Act*.[302] On the other hand, where the Court determines that there were no reasonable grounds for the appeal, and that one of the main purposes for instituting it was to defer the payment of tax, it may, in addition to awarding costs, order the taxpayer to pay to the Receiver General an amount not exceeding 10% of the amount that was in controversy.

The above provision can apply with respect to any part of an appeal, as well as to the entire proceeding. One reported case involving an extreme abuse of the appellate process by a practicing solicitor has resulted in such a finding.[303]

[¶12,415] Appeals to the Federal Court–Trial Division

[¶12,420] Original and Appellate Jurisdiction

As previously mentioned, under the amended appellate procedure (see ¶12,375) the Federal Court–Trial Division no longer has original or appellate jurisdiction to hear appeals involving income tax matters. Appeals from judgments of proceedings instituted on or after January 1, 1991 before the Tax Court lie to the Federal Court of Appeal rather than the Federal Court–Trial Division as was previously the case. Appeals from decisions of proceedings instituted before the Tax Court prior to 1991 continue to lie to the Federal Court–Trial Division.

[¶12,425] Appeals to the Federal Court of Appeal

[¶12,430] General Appellate Jurisdiction in Income Tax Matters

Under the *Federal Courts Act*, R.S.C. 1985, c. F-7 (as amended), an appeal lies as of right from any final judgment of the Tax Court of Canada which was handed down under the general procedure. Under the *Tax Court of Canada Act*, however, no appeal lies from any judgment of the Tax Court

---

See page ii for explanation of footnotes.

301 CCH ¶23,350; Sec. 171.
302 CCH ¶23,100; Sec. 166.
303 Raynier, 90 DTC 1387.

of Canada handed down under the informal procedure, other than by way of a judicial review under the *Federal Courts Act.* Such reviews, however, are limited to situations in which the Tax Court of Canada has acted beyond its jurisdiction, has failed to observe a principle of natural justice or procedural fairness, has erred in law, has based its decision on an erroneous finding of fact made in a perverse or capricious manner, or has acted by reason of fraud or perjured evidence.

[¶12,435] Special Appellate Jurisdiction

If the Minister refuses to accept for registration any charitable organization, any Canadian amateur athletic association, any retirement savings plan, any education savings plan, any pension plan, or any retirement income fund, or if the Minister sends notice of intent to revoke the registration of any charitable organization, Canadian amateur athletic association or education savings plan, an appeal lies as of right to the Federal Court of Appeal within 30 days from the date of such action, with provision for the extension of the deadline by the Court.[304] Such an appeal is to be heard and determined in a summary way,[305] and may, upon the application of the taxpayer, be heard *in camera* if the Court is satisfied that the circumstances so warrant.[306] In addition, the Minister is deemed to have refused any of the above applications for registration, if he or she has not responded within 180 days.[307]

[¶12,440] Disposition of Appeals

The Federal Court of Appeal may dismiss the appeal, give the decision that should have been given, or refer the matter back for determination in accordance with such directions as it considers to be appropriate.

[¶12,445] Appeals to the Supreme Court of Canada

[¶12,450] Jurisdiction in Income Tax Matters

An appeal to the Supreme Court of Canada lies with leave of the Federal Court of Appeal from any of its judgments concerning an income tax matter where, in its opinion, the question involved in the appeal is one that ought to be submitted to the Supreme Court. Where, however, the Supreme Court is of the opinion that any question involved is, by reason of its public importance, one that ought to be decided by the Supreme Court, such an appeal lies without leave of the Federal Court of Appeal, but with leave of the Supreme Court itself.

See page ii for explanation of footnotes.

[304] CCH ¶23,402, ¶23,900; Sec. 172(3), 180. [306] CCH ¶23,880; Sec. 179.
[305] CCH ¶23,940; Sec. 180(3). [307] CCH ¶23,460; Sec. 172(4).

Chapter XIII

Special Transactions Taxes

Special Transactions 13,000

Special Transactions Taxes
in General 13,005

**Clawback Tax on Old Age
Security Benefits
(Part I.2) 13,010**

Clawback Tax on Old Age
Security Benefits 13,015

Clawback Tax and Treaty-
Exempt Income 13,016

Tax Returns and
Administrative Provisions 13,020

**Tax on Large Corporations
(Part I.3) 13,025**

Large Corporations Tax
(LCT) 13,030

Deduction from Large
Corporation Tax 13,031

Taxable Capital of
Corporations 13,035

Capital Deduction 13,040

Tax Returns and Payments 13,045

**Tobacco Manufacturers'
Surtax (Part II) 13,047**

Surtax 13,048

Return 13,049

**Tax on Corporate
Distributions (Part II.1) 13,050**

Tax on Corporate
Distributions 13,055

Application of Tax 13,060

Stock Dividends 13,065

Purchase of Shares 13,070

Indirect Payments 13,075

The Purpose Test 13,080

Information Return, Interest,
Assessment, Payment,
etc. 13,090

**Additional Tax on Excessive
Elections (Part III) 13,095**

Excessive Election by
Private Corporation 13,100

Mortgage Investment
Corporation — Excessive
Capital Dividend Election 13,110

Mutual Fund Corporation —
Excessive Capital
Dividend Election 13,115

Election to Treat Excess as
Separate Dividend 13,120

Joint and Several Liability
from Excessive Elections 13,122

Tax, Interest, Penalties,
Returns, Assessments,
etc. 13,123

**Additional Tax on Excessive
Eligible Dividend
Designations (Part III.1) 13,125**

Liability for Tax 13,127

Return 13,128

**Tax on Taxable Dividend
Received by Private
Corporation (Part IV) 13,130**

Special Refundable Tax —
Private Corporations 13,135

Special Refundable Tax —
Subject Corporations 13,140

Amount Subject to Tax 13,145

Connected Corporations 13,150

Application of Non-Capital
Losses and Farm
Losses 13,155

Exceptions 13,160

Information Return, Interest,
Assessment, Payment,
etc. 13,165

**Taxes on Dividends on
Certain Preferred Shares
Received by Corporations
(Part IV.1)** **13,170**

Tax on Dividends Received
on Taxable Preferred
Shares 13,175

Tax on Dividends on
Taxable RFI Shares 13,180

**Tax in Respect of Qualified
Donees (Part V)** **13,185**

Revocation of Charity's
Registration 13,190

Charitable Foundation's
Transfer of Property 13,195

Private Foundation's Non-
Qualified Investments 13,200

Returns, Interest, etc. 13,205

Intermediate Taxes and
Penalties on Registered
Charities and RCAAAs 13,207

**Tax on Capital of Financial
Institutions (Part VI)** **13,210**

Special Tax on Capital of
Financial Institutions 13,215

Deduction 13,217

Taxable Capital Employed
in Canada 13,220

Capital of a Financial
Institution 13,225

Investment in a Related
Financial Institution 13,230

Capital Deduction 13,235

Returns and Tax
Instalments 13,240

**Tax on Corporations Paying
Dividends on Taxable
Preferred Shares
(Part VI.1)** **13,245**

Tax on Taxable Dividends 13,250

Excluded Dividends 13,255

**Refundable Tax on
Corporations Issuing
Qualifying Shares
(Part VII) and Refundable
Tax on Corporations Re
SR&ED Tax Credit
(Part VIII)** **13,260**

**Tax on Deduction Under
Section 66.5 (Part IX)** **13,370**

Tax in Respect of
Cumulative Offset
Account 13,375

Returns and Instalments 13,377

Administrative Provisions 13,379

**Tax on SIFT Partnerships
(Part IX.1)** **13,380**

Liability for Tax 13,385

Meaning of "Taxable Non-
Portfolio Earnings" 13,387

Return 13,389

**Tax on Deferred Profit
Sharing Plans (DPSPs)
and Revoked DPSPs
(Part X)** **13,390**

Special Taxes Payable by
DPSPs 13,395

Tax on Non-Qualified
Investments and on
Property Used as
Security 13,400

"Qualified Investments" and
"Non-Qualified
Investments" Defined 13,405

Refund of Tax on
Disposition of Non-
Qualified Investment 13,410

Tax Where Consideration Is
Inadequate 13,430

Returns and Payment of
Estimated Tax 13,440

Assessment, Objections,
Appeals, etc. 13,445

**Tax in Respect of Over-
Contributions to Deferred
Income Plans (Part X.1)** **13,450**

Special Taxes on Excess
Contributions to
Registered Retirement
Savings Plan (RRSP) or
Deferred Profits Sharing
Plan (DPSP) 13,455

Tax on Excess
Contributions to
Registered Retirement
Savings Plan (RRSP) 13,465

Group RRSP and Over-
Contributions Involving
Past Service Pension
Adjustments (PSPAs) 13,466

Tax on Excess
Contributions to Deferred
Profit Sharing Plans
(DPSPs) 13,470

Waiver of Tax 13,471

Administrative Provisions
Respecting Tax under
Part X.1 13,472

**Tax in Respect of
Registered Investments
(Part X.2) 13,475**

Special Tax When
Corporation or Trust
Which Is Registered
Investment Does Not
Maintain Qualified
Investments 13,476

**Labour-Sponsored Venture
Capital Corporations
(LSVCCs) (Part X.3) 13,480**

Labour-Sponsored Venture
Capital Funds 13,485

Investment Requirements
for Federally or
Provincially Registered
LSVCCs 13,486

Revocation of a Federally
Registered LSVCC 13,487

Penalty Tax Where Venture
Capital Business
Discontinued 13,488

Returns and Payment of
Tax 13,489

**Tax in Respect of
Overpayments to
Registered Education
Savings Plans (RESPs)
(Part X.4) 13,490**

Tax Payable by
Subscribers 13,491

Special Rules 13,492

**Tax on Income Payments
from Registered
Education Savings Plans
(RESPs) (Part X.5) 13,493**

Application of Tax 13,494

**Former Foreign Property
Tax on Trusts Governed
by Deferred Income Plans
(Repealed Part XI) 13,496**

Foreign Property Limit
Eliminated 13,497

**Taxes in Respect of RRIFs,
RRSPs, and TFSAs
(Part XI.01) 13,500**

Overview 13,510

Tax Payable on TFSA
Excess Contributions 13,513

Tax Payable on Non-
Resident Contributions 13,514

Tax Payable on Prohibited
or Non-Qualified
Investments 13,515

Tax Payable in Respect of
Advantage 13,516

Return and Payment of Tax 13,517

Taxes in Respect of RRSPs
and RRIFs 13,518

**Tax in Respect of Certain
Property Held by Trusts
Governed by Deferred
Income Plans (Part XI.1)   ... 13,520**

Tax in Respect of Non-
Qualified Investments 13,525

Tax in Respect of
Acquisition of Shares by
Tax Exempt Persons 13,530

Payment of Tax — Liability
of Trustee 13,535

**Tax in Respect of
Dispositions of Certain
Properties (Part XI.2) 13,540**

Disposition of Certain
Properties 13,545

**Tax in Respect of
Retirement Compensation
Arrangements (RCAs)
(Part XI.3) 13,550**

Overview 13,555

Refundable Tax Obligation 13,560

Calculation of "Refundable
Tax" 13,565

Special Election 13,566

Refundable Tax Mechanism
— Example 13,567

Special Rules 13,570

Prescribed Plan or
Arrangement 13,571

Transfers 13,573

Tax on Prohibited
Investments and
Advantages 13,575

Returns and Payment of
Tax 13,576
**Tax on Excessive Employer
Contributions to EPSPs
(Part XI.4)** **13,577**
Overview 13,578
Tax on Excess EPSP
Amount 13,579
**Tax in Respect of Certain
Payments Made by
Exempt Taxpayers
(Part XII)** **13,580**
Tax with Respect to
Resource Payments
Made by Tax-Exempt
Persons 13,585
Payment of Tax 13,590
**Tax on Carved-Out Income
(Part XII.1)** **13,595**
Tax on Carved-Out Income 13,600
**Tax on Designated Income
of Certain Trusts
(Part XII.2)** **13,605**
Tax on Designated Income 13,610
Application of Part XII.2 Tax 13,615
Designated Beneficiary 13,620

Part XII.2 Tax Returns 13,625
**Tax on Investment Income
of Life Insurers
(Part XII.3)** **13,630**
Tax on Investment Income
of Life Insurers 13,635
**Tax on Qualifying
Environmental Trusts
(Part XII.4)** **13,640**
Tax on Qualifying
Environmental Trusts 13,645
**Recovery of Labour-
Sponsored Funds Tax
Credit (Part XII.5)** **13,650**
Special Tax for Recovery of
LSVCC Tax Credit 13,655
Where Part XII.5 Tax Not
Payable 13,657
Redemption of Quebec
LSVCC Shares Held
Within an RRSP 13,658
Withholding and
Remittance 13,660
Refund of Clawback 13,665
**Tax on Flow-Through
Shares (Part XII.6)** **13,670**
Tax Imposed 13,675

Recent Changes

Income Threshold for OAS Clawback Indexed for 2012

As a result of the 2.8% indexation factor for 2012, the income threshold for OAS clawback increases from $67,668 in 2011 to $69,562 in 2012. See ¶13,005 and ¶13,015.

Suspension of Charity's Tax-Receipting Privileges

As a result of the 2012 Budget, effective June 29, 2012, tax-receipting privileges may be suspended for one year if a registered charity devotes its resources to political activities in excess of its allowable limit. A charity's power to issue tax receipts will also attract an intermediate sanction in the form of a suspension of its tax-receipting privilege if it fails to provide complete and accurate information in relation to any aspect of its annual return. In such a case, the suspension will remain in effect until such time as the charity provides the required information. Registered Canadian amateur athletic associations (RCAAAs) could be subject to the same sanctions as registered charities for exceeding the limit on political activities or for failing to provide required information. See ¶13,207.

Part IX.1 Tax on Specified Investment Flow-Through (SIFT) Partnerships

Part IX.1 tax applies to publicly traded SIFT partnerships and special rules can apply to treat an otherwise privately held partnership as a SIFT, unless the partnership is an "excluded subsidiary entity", defined as an entity none of the equity of which is publicly traded or held by any person or partnership other than certain qualifying interest holders. So far, only real estate investment trusts (REITs), taxable Canadian corporations, SIFTs, and other excluded subsidiary entities are listed as qualifying interest holders. Finance Canada released draft legislation on July 25, 2012 to expand the list of qualifying interest holders to include persons or partnerships that do not have, in connection with the holding of a security of the entity, property the value of which is determined, all or in part, by reference to a security that is listed or traded on a stock exchange or other public market. This measure, first announced on July 20, 2011 and reported here last year, is deemed to have come into force on October 31, 2006 (subject to a special election). See ¶13,385.

New Part XI.3 tax on RCA Advantages and Prohibited Investments

As a result of the 2012 Budget, effective March 29, 2012, RCAs will be subject to certain penalty taxes under Part XI.3 that are very similar to those applicable under Part XI in respect of RRSP advantages and prohibited investments. As a result, after March 28, 2012, the custodian of an RCA will be required to pay a Part XI.3 tax equal to:

- the fair market value of any advantage obtained by a specified beneficiary of the RCA or a person who does not deal at arm's length with the specified beneficiary; and

- 50% of the fair market value of any prohibited investment acquired or held by the RCA.

An RCA's specified beneficiary refers to an individual who has an interest or right in the RCA and who has a significant interest (at least 10%) in an employer sponsoring the plan. See ¶13,575.

New Part XI.4 tax on Excessive Employer Contributions to EPSPs

To discourage excessive employer contributions to employee profit sharing plans (EPSPs), a special tax under new Part XI.4 was introduced after March 28, 2012. This tax will apply when the employer contribution allocated in respect of a specified employee exceeds an "excess EPSP amount". In general terms, an "excess EPSP amount" is the portion of the employer's EPSP contribution, allocated to a specified employee, that exceeds 20% of the specified employee's salary for the year. Specified employees are employees who have a significant equity interest (at least 10%) in their employer or who do not deal at arm's length with their employer. The special tax is made up of two components: the top federal marginal tax rate of 29% and the top marginal tax rate of the employee's province of residence (0% in Quebec). See ¶13,577

[¶13,000] Special Transactions

[¶13,005] Special Transactions Taxes in General

Parts I.2 to XII.4 set out rules for a number of particular cases, most of which involve specialized transactions by corporations with resultant tax consequences.

Part I.2 tax results in the repayment of old age security benefits included in computing the taxpayer's income, to the extent that the taxpayer's income is in excess of an indexed threshold ($69,562 for 2012; $67,668 for

2011; $66,733 for 2010; $66,335 for 2009; $64,718 for 2008; $63,511 for 2007; $62,144 for 2006; $60,806 for 2005; $59,790 for 2004; $57,879 for 2003; $56,968 for 2002; $55,309 for 2001; $53,960 for 2000; and $53,215 for 1992–1999).

Up until January 1, 2006, Part I.3 imposed a capital tax on a corporation whose taxable capital employed in Canada at the end of a taxation year exceeded its capital deduction for the year. The capital deduction was $10 million up to and including 2003, and $50 million in 2004 and 2005. The capital tax rate was 0.225% up to the end of 2003, 0.2% for 2004, and 0.175% for 2005. Beginning in 2006, no capital tax is payable. Legislation had already been enacted to eliminate the Part I.3 capital tax after a four-year phase-out period beginning January 1, 2004 and ending January 1, 2008. This phase-out was accelerated in the 2006 Budget to the extent that the capital tax was eliminated as of January 1, 2006 (two years earlier than originally scheduled). For corporations that do not have a December 31 year end, the 2005 capital tax rate of 0.175% applied on a *pro rata* basis.

Part II provides for a surtax equal to 50% of a corporation's Part I tax on tobacco manufacturing profits for the year.

Part II.1 is an anti-avoidance tax that applies where a corporation effects a distribution of corporate surplus that would otherwise be taxable, directly or indirectly, to its shareholders in the form of proceeds of disposition that result in an exempt capital gain in the hands of individual shareholders. This tax is intended to approximate the shareholder tax that would have been paid had the distribution been received as a dividend.

Part III relates to the additional tax imposed where a corporation elects to pay a dividend out of its tax-paid undistributed surplus or its 1971 capital surplus on hand that is in excess of the amounts available from these sources.

Part III.1 relates to the additional tax imposed where a corporation has made an excessive eligible dividend designation in respect of eligible dividends paid by it after 2005. If a dividend has been designated as an eligible dividend, an enhanced gross-up and dividend tax credit (DTC) are generally available. The higher gross-up factor is 45% from 2006 until 2010, 44% for 2010, 41% for 2011, and 38% for 2012. The enhanced DTC rate is $^{11}/_{18}$ of the gross-up amount from 2006 until 2010, $^{10}/_{17}$ for 2010, $^{13}/_{23}$ for 2011, and $^{6}/_{11}$ beginning in 2012. The designation by itself makes a taxable dividend an eligible dividend in the hands of the recipient. However, an excessive eligible dividend designation by the corporation paying the dividend attracts an additional tax to the corporation under Part III.1.

Part IV levies a refundable tax imposed on certain taxable dividends received by private corporations or closely held corporations.

Part IV.1 and Part VI.1 taxes are special taxes which apply to dividends paid and received on taxable preferred shares or taxable restricted financial institution (RFI) shares.

Part V provides for special taxes and sanctions that may be imposed on qualified donees.

Part VI imposes an annual tax on a financial institution's capital employed in Canada in excess of its capital deduction for a taxation year. For taxation years ending on or after July 1, 2006, the tax rate is 1.25% and the capital deduction is $1 billion, such that the tax equals 1.25% of taxable capital employed in Canada in excess of $1 billion. For taxation years that ended before July 1, 2006, the Part VI tax was levied at an effective rate of 1% on taxable capital employed in Canada between $200 million and $300 million, and at a rate of 1.25% on taxable capital employed in Canada in excess of $300 million.

Part VII and Part VIII impose a refundable tax on a corporation creating a share-purchase tax credit or a scientific research and experimental development (SR&ED) tax credit.

Part IX imposes a 30% tax on the amount deducted by a corporation for Canadian exploration expenses and Canadian development expenses that had previously been applied to offset Petroleum and Gas Revenue Tax.

Effective October 31, 2006, Part IX.1 imposes a tax on the taxable non-portfolio earnings of a specified investment flow-through partnership (a "SIFT partnership"). Up to 2009, the rate of SIFT tax is made up of two components: (i) the federal general corporate tax rate, and (ii) the "provincial SIFT tax factor", meaning 13% or the *average provincial* general corporate tax rate. Beginning in 2009, the second component is replaced by the "provincial SIFT tax rate", meaning the general provincial corporate income tax rate of *each province* in which a SIFT has a permanent establishment.

Part X concerns taxes imposed on non-qualified investments and forfeitures of trusts governed by deferred profit sharing plans; Part X.1 relates to the penalty tax in respect of overcontributions to deferred income plans (DPSPs); Part X.2 tax is imposed on "registered investments" of pooled fund trusts and investment corporations; Part X.3 deals with various taxes imposed on labour-sponsored venture capital corporations (LSVCCs) that fail to meet their federal or provincial investment requirements; Part X.4 imposes a special tax on overcontributions to registered education savings plans (RESPs); and Part X.5 sets out a special 20% tax on any distribution from an RESP that is not an educational assistance payment or a refund of payments.

Part XI.01 imposes penalty taxes where an individual has an excess TFSA amount, a non-resident contributes to a TFSA, a TFSA acquires a non-qualified investment or prohibited investment, and a TFSA confers an advantage on the holder of the TFSA or a person not dealing at arm's length with the holder. As a result of the 2011 federal Budget, Part XI.01 penalty tax has been extended to RRSPs and RRIFs, applicable to transactions occurring, income earned, capital gains accruing, and investments acquired after March 22, 2011.

Part XI.1 imposes a special tax whenever RESPs or DPSPs retain property that is not a qualified investment or, in some cases, retain excessive amounts of certain qualified investments.

Part XI.2 tax applies to dispositions of cultural property by public authorities or institutions and to dispositions of ecologically sensitive land by charities and Canadian municipalities. Part XI.3 tax applies to retirement compensation arrangements (RCAs).

Part XII imposes a tax on non-exempt persons in respect of certain royalties and related payments; Part XII.1 imposes a special tax at the rate of 50% on carved-out income; Part XII.2 imposes a special tax on the designated income of certain trusts that are resident in Canada with respect to distributions to non-residents and other designated beneficiaries; and Part XII.3 imposes a tax on the accumulated investment income of life insurance companies.

Part XII.4 imposes a special tax on the income of a qualifying environmental trust. Prior to 2012, the tax rate was 28%, the general federal corporate tax rate before the general corporate rate reduction. For 2012 and subsequent years, the rate will equal the general federal corporate income tax rate after that reduction. The rate is currently 15%.

Part XII.5 provides for a special tax that is designed to recover the federal LSVCC tax credit when shares are redeemed prior to the expiry of the minimum holding period, i.e., eight years for shares first issued after March 5, 1996 and five years for shares first issued before March 6, 1996.

Part XII.6 levies a tax which compensates the fisc for the acceleration of the deduction resulting from the application of the one-year look-back rule for flow-through shares.

[¶13,010] Clawback Tax on Old Age Security Benefits (Part I.2)

[¶13,015] Clawback Tax on Old Age Security Benefits

A "clawback" tax is imposed on federal Old Age Security (OAS) benefits included in the income of a taxpayer. The concept is that, to the extent the taxpayer's net income including these benefits exceeds $50,000, or such amount after indexation ($69,562 in 2012; $67,668 in 2011; $66,733 in 2010; $66,335 for 2009; $64,718 for 2008; $63,511 for 2007; $62,144 for 2006; $60,806 for 2005; $59,790 for 2004; $57,879 for 2003; $56,968 for 2002; $55,309 for 2001; $53,960 for 2000 and $53,215 for 1992–1999), the benefits are subject to a 15% tax which will, ultimately, recover the entire payment if income is high enough. It follows that at the $69,562 threshold for 2012, 100% of OAS is clawed back at a net income level of the threshold plus (OAS ÷ 15%). As both the threshold and OAS are indexed every three months, this is a moving target; for 2012, it should be $112,966, assuming a maximum OAS benefit of $544.98 a month (the maximum benefit payable from July 1 to September 30, 2012). Note that it is the taxpayer receiving the OAS and including it in income that is liable for the special tax.

The amount of the Part I.2 clawback tax is the lesser of:

(a) the total of all payments included in income as pension, supplement, or spouse's or common-law partner's allowance under the *Old Age Security Act* ("OAS benefits") minus any deduction allowed for repayment of excess receipts by the taxpayer; and

(b) 15% of the taxpayer's "adjusted income" in excess of a threshold amount which is subject to indexation ($69,562 in 2012; $67,668 in 2011; $66,733 for 2010; $66,335 for 2009; $63,511 for 2007; $62,144 for 2006; $60,806 for 2005; $59,790 for 2004; $57,879 for 2003; $56,968 for 2002; $55,309 for 2001; $53,960 for 2000; $53,215 for 1992–1999).

Where the taxpayer is a non-resident, the Part I.2 tax is reduced to take into account any Part XIII tax payable on the OAS benefits. Thus, if Part XIII tax of 25% was payable on the OAS benefits, the Part I.2 tax would be reduced to 75% of the amount determined above.[1]

A taxpayer's "adjusted income" in (b) above means the amount that would be the taxpayer's Part I income for the year if no amount were deductible for the clawback tax or included in respect of a capital gain realized on mortgage foreclosures or conditional sales repossessions.[2] In addition, the Universal Child Care Benefit (UCCB) that became payable, effective July 2006, to all families for each child under the age of six years ($100 per month) will not reduce Old Age Security benefits.

There is a special withholding tax levied on OAS benefits paid in respect of the taxpayer's clawback tax liability. Where net income in the base taxation year exceeds the current year clawback threshold ($69,562 in 2012), OAS payments will be subject to withholding on the potential clawback. For the first six months of a calendar year, the base taxation year is the second preceding calendar year, and for the last six months of the year, the base taxation year is the immediately preceding calendar year. In effect, then, the clawback tax is withheld from the current year's OAS payments based on the taxpayer's adjusted income in each of the two preceding years. When the taxpayer files his or her return for the (current) year, there will be a refund,

---

See page ii for explanation of footnotes.
[1] CCH ¶24,042; Sec. 180.2(2).   [2] CCH ¶24,041; Sec. 180.2(1) "adjusted income".

or tax owing, based on the difference between the current year's clawback tax liability and the amount withheld from the current year's OAS benefits.

In order to receive payment of OAS benefits, non-residents are also required to file a return of worldwide income to be used in determining the amount of the OAS benefit. If no return has been filed for a relevant base year and the taxpayer was a non-resident at any time in that year, the government may withhold the entire OAS payment (less any Part XIII non-resident tax currently being withheld).[3]

[¶13,016] Clawback Tax and Treaty-Exempt Income

The CRA has indicated that the provisions of Part I.2 in general apply to non-residents only to the extent they do not conflict with a tax treaty. In other words, with respect to non-residents, the general rule that provisions contained in tax treaties supersede any conflicting provisions that may be contained in domestic legislation, such as the *Income Tax Act*, is not displaced by the clawback tax withholding system as it applies to non-residents.

Several Canadian tax treaties limit the amount of tax that Canada can impose on OAS payments made to residents of the other treaty country, and these rules override the 100% withholding requirement. Thirty-six countries now protect their residents from the OAS clawback tax, although not necessarily from ordinary withholding tax. Those countries include, among others, Australia, Germany, Italy, Ireland, Israel, Mexico, Poland, Portugal, Spain, the United Kingdom, and the United States. Non-resident seniors living in these 36 tax-treaty countries do not have to file an Old Age Security Return of Income (OASRI) or pay recovery or clawback unless they move before July 1 of any given year to a non-treaty-protected country. The 36 tax-treaty countries are listed by the CRA at: http://www.cra-arc.gc.ca/tx/nnrsdnts/ndvdls/snrs_sr-eng.html#c. In addition, senior non-residents do not have to file an OASRI or pay recovery tax if they are a resident of Brazil and are Brazilian nationals, or the Philippines, and their Canadian pensions total $5,000 or less.

[¶13,020] Tax Returns and Administrative Provisions

Every person liable to pay tax under Part I.2 must file a return by April 30th of the following year and pay the tax on or before the "balance-due day" for the year (see definition at ¶5390).[4] For an individual who is resident in Canada, the filing required will form part of the regular return of income for the year. In the case of a non-resident, the Minister will accept, in lieu of a return, a form containing relevant tax data for the year.[5] Most of the administrative provisions of Part I are applicable to Part I.2,[6] including the provision allowing the Minister to provide for the withholding of a lesser

---

[3] CCH ¶24,043, ¶24,044; Sec. 180.2(3), 180.2(4).
[4] CCH ¶24,045; Sec. 180.2(5).
[5] CCH ¶24,041b; Sec. 180.2(1) "return of income".
[6] CCH ¶24,046; Sec. 180.2(6).

¶13,016

amount than otherwise required on the ground of undue hardship.[7] Individuals for whom the withholding of amounts from OAS benefit payments would result in undue hardship (for example, because of a significant decrease in income between the base taxation year on which the withholding is calculated and the income for the year of receipt) may apply to the Minister for relief.

[¶13,025] Tax on Large Corporations (Part I.3)

[¶13,030] Large Corporations Tax (LCT)

Up to calendar year 2006, Part I.3 imposed a capital tax on a corporation whose taxable capital employed in Canada at the end of a taxation year exceeded its "capital deduction".[8] The capital deduction was $10 million up to and including 2003 and was increased during the phase-out period to $50 million in 2004 and 2005. The capital tax rate was 0.225% up to the end of 2003 and was reduced during the phase-out period to 0.2% for 2004 and 0.175% for 2005. Beginning in calendar year 2006, no capital tax is payable. For corporations that do not have a December 31 year end, the 2005 capital tax rate of 0.175% is applied on a *pro rata* basis. The reduced rates and the increased capital deduction in effect during the 2004-2005 phase-out period did not apply for the purpose of determining a corporation's ability to carry back unused surtax credits to reduce its federal capital tax liability, if any, for the three previous tax years. See ¶13,031. The large corporations tax was prorated for corporations on the basis of the number of days in a corporation's taxation year.[9] It was payable in monthly instalments following the same pattern as corporate instalments of income tax under Part I.

Exempt from the large corporation tax were non-resident-owned investment corporations, bankrupt corporations, deposit insurance corporations, tax-exempt corporations, corporations that were neither resident in Canada nor carrying on business from a permanent establishment in Canada at any time in the year, and co-operative corporations whose principal business was the marketing or processing of natural products of their members or customers.[10]

As indicated above, where a corporation was bankrupt at the end of its taxation year, it was exempt from Part I.3 tax with respect to that particular taxation year. However, in such a case, a taxation year of the corporation was deemed to have ended on the day immediately before the day on which the corporation became a bankrupt so that the corporation was not a bankrupt as of the end of that deemed taxation year. The corporation would therefore be liable for Part I.3 tax with respect to that deemed taxation year.[11]

---

[7] CCH ¶22,386; Sec. 153(1.1).
[8] CCH ¶24,059; Sec. 181.1(1).
[9] CCH ¶24,060; Sec. 181.1(2).

[10] CCH ¶24,061; Sec. 181.1(3).

[11] Interp. Bul. IT-532.

[¶13,031] Deduction from Large Corporation Tax

In computing its large corporation tax for a taxation year up to calendar year 2006, a corporation could deduct an amount equal to the total of its Canadian surtax payable for the year and its unused surtax credits.[12]

Unused surtax credits may be carried forward seven years and carried back three years, and they must be claimed in the order in which they arose. Although the ability to carry forward unused surtax credits is irrelevant with the elimination of the capital tax on January 1, 2006, corporations will continue to be able to apply these credits, including any arising in the 2006 and subsequent taxation years, against the federal capital tax liability, if any, for the three previous tax years. These excess credits are computed by reference to a notional Part I.3 tax liability, based on the 0.225% capital tax rate and the $10 million capital deduction applicable immediately prior to the phasing-out of the tax that began in 2004.[13] For the purposes of the deduction from Part I.3 tax otherwise payable, the "unused surtax credit" of a corporation (other than a financial institution) for a taxation year means the amount, if any, by which its Canadian surtax payable for the year exceeds the aggregate of its large corporation tax for the year (before the deduction) and any pre-1992 Part I.3 tax credits offset against Part I tax for the year.[14] For financial institutions, "unused surtax credits" are the lesser of the amount calculated for non-financial institutions and the amount, if any, by which Part I tax for the year exceeds the aggregate of Parts I.3 and VI tax before the deduction.

The carryforward (up to calendar year 2006) or carryback of unused surtax credits is restricted where control of a corporation has been acquired by a person or by a group of persons.[15] Unused surtax credits arising in a taxation year before an acquisition of control are only deductible by the corporation in a subsequent year if the corporation carries on the same business for profit or with a reasonable expectation of profit throughout the subsequent year. The portion of any unused surtax credits that can be carried back (or carried forward up to calendar year 2006) upon an acquisition of control is based on the income from the continued business in the taxation year the surtax credits arose, and not the income for the year in which the surtax credits are applied. Therefore, the unused surtax credits for a particular year arising before an acquisition of control could be deducted in a taxation year after the acquisition of control to the extent that the proportion of the corporation's income from the continued business or a similar business in the year the credit arose is of that corporation's total taxable income for that same year.

---

[12] CCH ¶24,062; Sec. 181.1(4).
[13] CCH ¶24,059b, ¶24,083a, ¶24,086a; Sec. 181.1(1.2), 181.5(1.1), 181.5(4.1).
[14] CCH ¶24,064a; Sec. 181.1(6) "unused surtax credit".
[15] CCH ¶24,064b; Sec. 181.1(7).

[¶13,035] Taxable Capital of Corporations

For a corporation other than a financial institution resident in Canada, taxable capital employed in Canada was generally computed as follows:[16]

Share capital		$xxx
Add: Contributed surplus	$xxx	
Retained earnings and other surpluses	xxx	
Reserve funds (except amounts deducted under Part I)	xxx	
Deferred unrealized foreign exchange gains at the end of the year	xxx	
Loans, advances, and indebtedness represented by bonds, debentures, bankers' acceptances and similar securities as well as other forms of indebtedness outstanding for more than 365 days, and dividends declared but not paid by the year end	xxx	xxx
Capital		$xxx
Less: allowance for investments in other corporations		xxx
Taxable capital		$xxx
Percentage of capital employed in Canada		X x%
Taxable capital employed in Canada		$xxx

A corporation was allowed to deduct the above investment allowance for certain debts owed to it by a partnership, all the members of which were corporations as well. The allowance was denied, however, where a debt was owed by a partnership to one of its members or where any of the members of the partnership were Part I.3 tax-exempt financial institutions or corporations (other than non-resident corporations that at no time in the year carried on business in Canada through a permanent establishment).

If a trust was used as a conduit for loaning money from a corporation to another related corporation (other than a financial institution), the loan was, for the purposes of determining the first corporation's investment allowance, considered to have been made directly from the lending corporation to the borrowing corporation.[17]

There are specific rules provided to determine the taxable capital of financial institutions,[18] which include banks, credit unions, mortgage investment corporations, insurance companies, and loan or trust companies and prescribed corporations.[19] For this purpose a prescribed corporation means

---

[16] CCH ¶24,066–24,069; Sec. 181.2(2)–(5).

[17] CCH ¶24,070; Sec. 181.2(6).

[18] CCH ¶24,075; Sec. 181.3.

[19] CCH ¶24,051, ¶24,097b; Sec. 181(1) "financial institution"; Reg. 8604.

a corporation all or substantially all of the assets of which are shares or indebtedness of financial institutions related to the corporation.

A corporation may be prescribed as a financial institution for the purposes of Part I.3 without necessarily being treated as a financial institution for other purposes of the Act, such as the "mark-to-market" rules in Part I and the limitations with respect to term preferred shares. Such prescribed corporations are treated as financial institutions for the purposes of Part I, and as restricted financial institutions and specified financial institutions for all purposes of the Act.

Because Canadian banks are subject to capital tax largely on regulatory capital under Canadian rules, and foreign banks are not, a special capital tax wave was introduced for foreign banks that operate full-service branches in Canada. The capital of a foreign bank that has a Canadian branch is, for LCT purposes, 10% of the "risk-weighted assets" of the Canadian branch, which will be determined based on the risk-weighted asset guidelines of the Superintendent of Financial Institutions.

Where working capital was provided to a taxpayer by advances from a sister corporation against work to be done, these advances were included in the taxpayer's capital as advances, regardless of the reserve claimed by the taxpayer in the computation of income.[20] Similarly, amounts owing to a bank by a bus dealer under conditional sales contracts were included in its capital to the extent that they were "represented by bonds, debentures ... mortgages ... or similar obligations".[21]

The taxpayer, who provided payroll services, required its clients to provide it with adequate funds in advance from which to pay the clients' salaries and deductions. The taxpayer held these funds in a separate Client Funds Obligations account. Funds in this account were not "advances" and were not required to be included in the taxpayer's taxable capital.[22]

[¶13,040] Capital Deduction

A corporation was allowed a capital deduction in computing the amount subject to Part I.3 tax. The capital deduction was $10 million up to and including calendar year 2003 ($50 million during the two-year phase-out period beginning January 1, 2004) unless the corporation was related to any other corporation during the taxation year.[23] Related corporations could share the capital deduction by filing an agreement in prescribed form.[24] Alternatively, the Minister could allocate the capital deduction amount if the related corporations failed to file the agreement within 30 days of receiving a request from the Minister to do so.[25] If neither of the

---

See page ii for explanation of footnotes.

[20] Oerlikon Aerospatiale Inc., 99 DTC 5318.
[21] Autobus Thomas Inc., 2001 DTC 5665.
[22] ADP Canada Co., 2009 DTC 5091.

[23] CCH ¶24,083; Sec. 181.5(1).
[24] CCH ¶24,084; Sec. 181.5(2).
[25] CCH ¶24,085; Sec. 181.5(3).

¶13,040

corporations nor the Minister allocated the capital deduction amount, the capital deduction for each related corporation was nil.

For purposes of the capital deduction calculation, two corporations that would be related only because of the control of a corporation by the Crown or of a right to acquire control of a corporation were not treated as being related.[26] However, if one of the main purposes in acquiring such a right was to avoid the capital deduction limitation for related corporations, the two corporations were treated as if the right acquired to avoid the limitation were an immediate and absolute right and as if the taxpayer had exercised it.

For the purposes of the capital deduction calculation, a Canadian-controlled private corporation (CCPC) and another corporation which were otherwise related for the purposes of the Act were deemed *not* to be related unless they were associated according to the rules discussed at ¶15,450 *et seq.*[27] Thus, for example, where two related persons each of which controls a corporation but there is no cross-ownership, or there is cross-ownership of less than 25% of any one of the corporations, the corporations will be otherwise related but may not be associated and therefore may be deemed not to be related. If so, the two corporations would not have to share the capital deduction.

[¶13,045] Tax Returns and Payments

A corporation liable to pay large corporation tax must file a return containing an estimate of its tax payable within six months after the end of its taxation year.[28] Such a return must be filed where a corporation, but for the deduction under ¶13,031, would have been liable to pay tax under Part I.3. Corporations with a Part I.3 tax liability are required to make monthly instalment payments. Whereas corporations were previously required to remit separate instalments in respect of Part I and Part I.3 tax to the CRA, now all instalments (i.e., Parts I, I.3, VI, and VI.1) may be made to a single account, thereby allowing for the offset of under and over instalments. The administrative provisions of Part I.3 are integrated with Part I. Thus, the rules relating to interest, instalments, remainder of tax payable, assessment, penalties, objections, and appeals apply equally to Parts I, I.3, VI, and VI.1.[29]

A penalty will be imposed for a late-filed return in respect of Part I.3 tax. It is assessed, on a monthly basis, at the rate of one-quarter of 1% of the amount of Part I.3 tax payable for the year.[30] The penalty is computed before any amount is deducted under ¶13,031. It will continue to accrue for each complete month that the return remains outstanding, up to a maximum of 40 months, after the later of:

See page ii for explanation of footnotes.

[26] CCH ¶24,088; Sec. 181.5(6).
[27] CCH ¶24,089; Sec. 181.5(7).
[28] CCH ¶24,115; Sec. 181.6.

[29] CCH ¶24,116; Sec. 181.7(1).

[30] CCH ¶27,593; Sec. 235.

(a) the day on which the return was required to be filed; and

(b) December 17, 1991.

This penalty is in addition to the penalty imposed under ¶12,310 which is calculated by reference to Part I tax payable.

[¶13,047] Tobacco Manufacturers' Surtax (Part II)

[¶13,048] Surtax

Initially, the tobacco manufacturers' surtax was intended to run for a three-year period from February 9, 1994, to February 8, 1997, inclusive. In 1997, it was extended for three more years and in 2000, it became permanent.

The surtax is 50% of a corporation's Part I tax on tobacco manufacturing profits for the year.[31] "Part I tax on tobacco manufacturing profits" is defined as 21% of the company's Canadian manufacturing and processing profits, generally as determined for the manufacturing and processing tax credit (see ¶8400), prorated by the company's tobacco manufacturing capital and labour divided by the total manufacturing capital and labour.[32] Tobacco manufacturing is any activity, other than an "exempt activity", relating to the manufacturing or processing in Canada of tobacco or tobacco products into any form that is, or would after any further activity becomes, suitable for smoking. An "exempt activity" is farming, or processing leaf tobacco if:

(i) that processing is done by, and is the principal business of, the particular corporation;

(ii) the particular corporation does not manufacture any tobacco product; and

(iii) the particular corporation is not related to any other corporation that carries on tobacco manufacturing.[33]

[¶13,049] Return

The surtax is to be calculated on a separate form although the filing, payment, and instalment dates are the same as for the corporation's T2 return for Part I tax.[34]

The final payment is due on or before the corporation's balance-due day for the year, which is the last day of the second or third month after the end of the corporation's taxation year, depending on the type of corporation. The administrative and enforcement provisions pertaining to Part I returns are also applicable to the Part II tax.

See page ii for explanation of footnotes.

[31] CCH ¶24,140; Sec. 182(1).
[32] CCH ¶24,141; Sec. 182(2) "Part I tax on tobacco manufacturing profits".

[33] CCH ¶24,140d, ¶24,142; Sec. 182(2) "exempt activity", 182(2) "tobacco manufacturing".
[34] CCH ¶24,150–24,152; Sec. 183.

[¶13,050] Tax on Corporate Distributions (Part II.1)

[¶13,055] Tax on Corporate Distributions

Part II.1 is an anti-avoidance provision that is intended to apply where amounts are distributed by a corporation to individuals as proceeds of disposition of the corporation's shares, rather than as taxable dividends.[35]

As an example, consider the situation where a public company issues a stock dividend to its shareholders and then repurchases some or all of the stock dividend shares as part of the same series of transactions. If one of the main purposes of this series of transactions can reasonably be considered to have been to enable shareholders of the public company who are individuals, to realize, either directly or indirectly, a distribution of the public company's corporate surplus, the public company will be subject to Part II.1 tax.

Part II.1 tax applies to transactions involving public corporations or other corporations (other than mutual fund corporations) resident in Canada having a class of shares outstanding that are purchased and sold in the manner in which such shares normally are purchased and sold by any member of the public in the open market.[36] Where Part II.1 applies, a special tax is paid by the corporation that approximates the shareholder tax that would have been paid had the distribution been received as a dividend.

Where Part II.1 is applicable in respect of an event that occurred in a taxation year, the tax is to be paid by the corporation on or before its balance-due day for its taxation year that includes that time. A corporation's balance-due day is at the end of the second month following the end of its taxation year or, for small business corporations, at the end of the third month following the end of its taxation year.[37]

[¶13,060] Application of Tax

The Part II.1 tax will only apply where it may reasonably be considered, having regard to all the circumstances, that proceeds of disposition have been paid by a corporation, or a person with whom the corporation does not deal at arm's length, as a substitute for dividends that would otherwise have been paid in the "normal course" by the corporation (i.e., dividends arising in special or unusual circumstances, such as a corporate reorganization, would be excluded from Part II.1 tax). This is an objective test and some of the circumstances to consider could include the corporation's past dividend policy and the amount of dividends paid in the current year. Part II.1 tax might apply where a corporation acquires shares for an amount that reflects a future dividend payment.

See page ii for explanation of footnotes.

[35] CCH ¶24,156; Sec. 183.1(2).
[36] CCH ¶24,155; Sec. 183.1(1).
[37] CCH ¶28,020b; Sec. 248(1) "balance-due day".

If Part II.1 tax is applicable, 45% of the amount or portion of the amount paid as proceeds of disposition of property that can reasonably be considered to be a substitute for dividends is payable as a special tax.[38]

[¶13,065] Stock Dividends

If a share is issued by a corporation as a stock dividend at less than its fair market value and that share (or any other share) was purchased, directly or indirectly, by the corporation or a non-arm's length person for more than its paid-up capital, Part II.1 tax will apply.[39]

The excess of the purchase price over the paid-up capital of the share purchased will be treated as a substitute for dividends that would otherwise have been paid in the normal course by the corporation.

For Part II.1 tax to apply in these circumstances, the payment of the stock dividend and the repurchase of the shares must be established to be part of the same transaction or series of transactions.

[¶13,070] Purchase of Shares

If a corporation or any non-arm's length person purchase shares, directly or indirectly, and a dividend has been declared but not paid at the time of purchase, special rules apply.[40] The amount that may reasonably be considered to be the consideration for the dividend will be deemed to have been paid as a substitute for dividends that would otherwise have been paid in the normal course by the corporation (notwithstanding that the dividend may be paid afterwards) and Part II.1 tax will apply to that amount.

[¶13,075] Indirect Payments

In the event that a person receives a payment from a corporation or a non-arm's length person in consideration for paying an amount to any other person as proceeds of disposition of any property, the corporation will be deemed to have paid the amount indirectly to the other person.[41] For example, if a company pays an amount to Mr. X (assume that he deals at arm's length) on condition that he purchase a property from Mr. Y, a shareholder of the company, the amount will be considered to have been paid indirectly by the corporation to Mr. Y.

[¶13,080] The Purpose Test

Part II.1 tax will not apply where it can be established that no transaction or series of transactions was done to enable shareholders who are individuals or non-resident persons to receive an amount as proceeds of

---

See page ii for explanation of footnotes.

[38] CCH ¶24,156; Sec. 183.1(2). [40] CCH ¶24,158; Sec. 183.1(4).
[39] CCH ¶24,157; Sec. 183.1(3). [41] CCH ¶24,159; Sec. 183.1(5).

¶13,065

disposition of property instead of as a dividend on shares listed on a stock exchange or traded in the open market.[42]

This exception will override the test in ¶13,060 even where, on an objective basis, the proceeds of disposition are received as a substitute for dividends. For example, the exception would apply where none of the shareholders is an individual or where the shares are not listed or traded. It might also apply where a corporation has declared a dividend and purchases its shares in the open market purely for business reasons.

[¶13,090] Information Return, Interest, Assessment, Payment, etc.

A corporation liable to pay Part II.1 tax must file a return (Form T2141) on or before the day the corporation is required to file its Part I tax return for the year.[43] Part I's general provisions pertaining to assessment, payment, interest, penalties, refunds, objections, and appeals are made applicable to Part II.1.[44] There is no requirement to pay instalments in respect of Part II.1 tax.

[¶13,095] Additional Tax on Excessive Elections (Part III)

[¶13,100] Excessive Election by Private Corporation

In certain circumstances a private corporation may elect to distribute as a capital dividend a portion of its net capital gains and certain tax-free receipts. Such a distribution will not be included in the incomes of the shareholders.

In the event that the amount that a private corporation has elected to be treated as a capital dividend exceeds the amount available to be paid as such a dividend, a penalty tax equal to 75% of the excess is imposed. [Pending technical amendments reduce this rate to 60% for the 2000 and subsequent taxation years.][45]

If the private corporation obtains the consent of its shareholders, it can avoid this special tax by treating the excess amount as a separate taxable dividend. See ¶13,120.

[¶13,110] Mortgage Investment Corporation — Excessive Capital Dividend Election

The purpose of a mortgage investment corporation is to act as a conduit for passing interest income earned on residential mortgage loans to its shareholders. A mortgage investment corporation may designate dividends

---

See page ii for explanation of footnotes.

[42] CCH ¶24,160; Sec. 183.1(6).
[43] CCH ¶24,165; Sec. 183.2(1).

[44] CCH ¶24,166; Sec. 183.2(2).
[45] CCH ¶24,305; Sec. 184(2).

paid within a prescribed period as capital gains dividends.[46] Capital gains dividends so designated are received by shareholders as a capital gain and not as a regular dividend.

In the event that the amount that a mortgage investment corporation has elected to be treated as a capital gains dividend exceeds the amount available to be paid as such a dividend, a penalty tax equal to 75% of the excess is imposed. [Pending technical amendments reduce this rate to 60% for the 2000 and subsequent taxation years.][47] This tax is levied on the corporation, not on the shareholder who receives the elected dividend as a capital gains dividend. However, with its shareholders' consent, a mortgage investment corporation may avoid this special tax by treating the excess amount as a separate taxable dividend (see ¶13,120).

[¶13,115] Mutual Fund Corporation — Excessive Capital Dividend Election

A mutual fund corporation is established to permit a shareholder in a mutual fund to receive the income and capital gains of the fund without imposition of taxation at the corporation as well as the shareholder level. Accordingly, the taxes payable by such corporations are largely refundable when distributions are made to shareholders, and capital gains may be distributed to shareholders out of a capital gains dividend account without being deemed dividends.

In the event that the amount that a mutual fund corporation has elected to be paid as a capital gains dividend exceeds the amount available to be paid as such a dividend, a penalty tax equal to 75% of the excess is imposed. [Pending technical amendments reduce this rate to 60% for the 2000 and subsequent taxation years.][48] However, with its shareholders' consent, a mutual fund corporation may avoid this special tax by treating the excess amount as a separate taxable dividend (see ¶13,120).

[¶13,120] Election to Treat Excess as Separate Dividend

A corporation may use an elective procedure to avoid the penalty tax on excessive elections if the payment of a dividend (and the earlier election made in respect of that dividend) would result in penalty tax.[49] In general terms, the effect of the election is to divide the earlier dividend upon which the excessive election was made into three separate dividends:

(1) The first separate dividend is in the amount that the corporation could have paid and elected upon without incurring an excessive election tax.

---

[46] CCH ¶20,095; Sec. 130.1(4).
[47] CCH ¶24,305; Sec. 184(2).
[48] CCH ¶24,315; Sec. 184(2).
[49] CCH ¶24,323, ¶24,325; Sec. 184(3); Reg. 2106.

(2) The second separate dividend is such amount that the corporation may claim for the purposes of making an election such that this second separate dividend be paid out of another surplus account.

(3) The third separate dividend is the remainder of the original dividend and it is deemed to have been a taxable dividend.

The election must be made in the prescribed manner not later than 90 days after the sending of the notice of assessment in respect of the penalty tax. For example, a corporation may compute the balance in its capital dividend account based on the assumption that a particular transaction resulted in a capital gain rather than business income. On this basis, the corporation elected to distribute a capital dividend. Later, on reassessment, it is determined that the gain on the transaction was business income and an amount must be removed from the capital dividend account. This could make the dividend paid exceed the reassessed balance in the capital dividend account. The election will allow the corporation to avoid the penalty tax by separating the dividend paid into a part that does not exceed the balance in the capital dividend account and a part than can be considered as a taxable dividend.

The election is not valid unless:

(1) it is made with the concurrence of all the shareholders who received or were entitled to receive the dividend and whose addresses were known to the corporation; and

(2) it is made within 30 months of the day on which the dividend became payable or all of the shareholders who received or were entitled to receive any part of the dividend in question concurred with the election.

Note that all the shareholders who received or were entitled to receive a portion of the dividend must concur even though they may not be shareholders at the time the election is made.

The election must be made by filing with the Minister in duplicate:[50]

(1) a letter signed on behalf of the corporation stating that the corporation elects in respect of a particular dividend;

(2) a certified copy of a resolution by the directors or the authorization of the other persons legally entitled to administer the affairs of the corporation authorizing the election to be made;

(3) a certified copy of the declaration by the directors or other persons legally entitled to administer the affairs of the corporation that the election is made with the concurrence of all shareholders who received or were entitled to receive all or any portion of the dividend and whose addresses were known to the corporation;

See page ii for explanation of footnotes.

[50] CCH ¶24,323; Reg. 2106.

(4) a schedule showing:

(a) the date of the assessment of tax under Part III,

(b) the amount and date of the dividend, and

(c) the manner in which the amount of the particular dividend is to be divided up as a result of the election; and

(5) any retroactive election in respect of a part of the particular dividend.

[¶13,122] Joint and Several Liability from Excessive Elections

Every person who receives a dividend in respect of which an election to pay a special tax-free dividend has been made will be jointly and severally liable with the corporation to pay the proportion of the Part III tax that the amount of the dividend received by the person is of the full amount of the dividend.[51]

Where a corporation and another person have become jointly and severally liable to pay part or all of the corporation's Part III tax, a payment by the other person on account of the liability will, to the extent of the payment, discharge his or her joint liability. However, a payment by the corporation on account of its liability will discharge the other person's liability only to the extent of that proportion of the payment (in excess of any other liability of the corporation) that the amount of the dividend received by the other person is of the total amount of the dividend.[52]

[¶13,123] Tax, Interest, Penalties, Returns, Assessments, etc.

The Minister issues an assessment after examining with all due dispatch an election to pay a special tax-free dividend. Where the Minister has assessed penalty taxes for excessive elections, the corporation is required to pay the tax and penalties due under the assessment "forthwith", a term which presumably means immediately upon receipt of the notice of assessment. Interest at a prescribed rate per annum on unpaid tax and penalties will accrue from the day of the election. The general provisions of Part I relating to assessments, penalties, refunds, objections, and appeals are made applicable.[53]

---

[51] CCH ¶24,337; Sec. 185(4).
[52] CCH ¶24,342; Sec. 185(6).
[53] CCH ¶22,904, ¶24,330; Sec. 185; Reg. 4300.

[¶13,125] Additional Tax on Excessive Eligible Dividend Designations (Part III.1)

[¶13,127] Liability for Tax

Part III.1 relates to the additional tax imposed where a corporation has made an excessive eligible dividend designation in respect of eligible dividends paid by it after 2005. If a dividend has been designated as an eligible dividend, an enhanced gross-up and dividend tax credit (DTC) are generally available. The higher gross-up factor is 45% from 2006 until 2010, 44% for 2010, 41% for 2011, and 38% for 2012. The enhanced DTC rate is $^{11}/_{18}$ of the gross-up amount from 2006 until 2010, $^{10}/_{17}$ for 2010, $^{13}/_{23}$ for 2011, and $^{6}/_{11}$ beginning in 2012. There is no corresponding additional tax or penalty imposed on a recipient of eligible dividends. Rather, since the corporation bears the onus of properly designating dividends as being eligible dividends, only the corporation bears the liability in the event that an excessive designation is made. However, the corporation may have the ability in certain circumstances to elect to treat the amount of the excessive designation as an ordinary dividend as opposed to an eligible dividend, which will directly affect the tax consequences to the dividend recipient.

The amount of tax imposed on a corporation under Part III.1 depends primarily on whether the excessive designation was inadvertent (in which case the tax is equal to 20%), or whether it resulted from an attempt to artificially manipulate a corporation's "general rate income pool" (GRIP) or "low rate income pool" (LRIP) (in which case the tax is equal to 30%).

The tax is equal to 20% of the excessive designation if:

(1) the excessive designation arises because a CCPC or a deposit insurance corporation (DIC) in a taxation year designated an amount as an eligible dividend that exceeds its GRIP at the end of the year;

(2) a corporation that is neither a CCPC nor a DIC pays an eligible dividend at a time when it has a positive balance in its LRIP.[54]

In either of these cases where Part III.1 tax is imposed at the 20% rate, the dividend paying corporation can elect to treat all or part of the excessive designation amount as a separate, ordinary dividend and not as an eligible dividend.[55] If such an election is made, Part III.1 will not apply and the shareholders will be considered to have received an ordinary dividend, to the extent of the elected amount. This election is similar to that offered under existing Part III of the Act (see the commentary at ¶13,120) in respect of excessive capital dividends and capital gains dividends.

The tax is equal to 30% of the excessive designation if the excessive designation resulted from an attempt to artificially manipulate a corpora-

---

See page ii for explanation of footnotes.

[54] CCH ¶24,345a; Sec. 185.1(1)(a).   [55] CCH ¶24,345b–24,345d; Sec. 185.1(2)–(4).

tion's GRIP or LRIP.[56] In such a case, there is no mechanism provided to allow the corporation to elect to unwind the effect of its excessive designation, even if the shareholders of the corporation would otherwise concur with such an election.

[¶13,128] Return

Every corporation resident in Canada that pays a taxable dividend (other than a capital gains dividend) in a taxation year must file a return (in prescribed form) for the year under Part III.1, including an estimate of the corporation's tax payable under the Part for the year.[57] The return must be filed no later than the corporation's balance-due day for the taxation year in which the dividend to which the excessive designation relates was paid.

[¶13,130] Tax on Taxable Dividend Received by Private Corporation (Part IV)

[¶13,135] Special Refundable Tax — Private Corporations

Subject to certain exceptions (see ¶13,160), private corporations and subject corporations described below are subject to Part IV tax of 33⅓% on assessable dividends.[58]

A dividend is "assessable", i.e., subject to Part IV tax, if it is received by a private corporation or subject corporation, during the period when it was a private or subject corporation, as:

(a) a taxable dividend from a taxable Canadian corporation which is not connected with the corporation (see definition of connected corporations at ¶13,150);

(b) a taxable dividend from a taxable Canadian corporation which is connected with the recipient corporation to the extent that the payor corporation received a dividend refund as a result of the payment of the dividend; or

(c) a dividend from a foreign affiliate, other than a connected foreign affiliate, to the extent of that portion of the dividend which is deductible (except for the deduction for withholding taxes paid by the Canadian corporation in respect of dividends received from taxable surplus of a foreign affiliate).[59]

The Part IV tax is added to the refundable dividend tax on hand and is refunded to the corporation when it, in turn, pays taxable dividends to its shareholders. For the calculation of refundable dividend tax on hand of a "subject corporation", see ¶13,140.

See page ii for explanation of footnotes.

[56] CCH ¶24,345a; Sec. 185.1(1)(b).
[57] CCH ¶24,346a; Sec. 185.2(1).

[58] CCH ¶24,350; Sec. 186(1); Interp. Bul. IT-269R4.
[59] CCH ¶24,356; Sec. 186(3) "assessable dividend".

¶13,128

A "private corporation" means a corporation resident in Canada which is not a public corporation and is not controlled by one or more public corporations.[60] A "subject corporation" is any corporation resident in Canada, other than a private corporation, which is controlled (whether by reason of a beneficial interest in a trust or otherwise) by or for the benefit of an individual (other than a trust) or a related group of individuals (other than trusts).[61] The inclusion of subject corporations under Part IV ensures that the tax cannot be circumvented by a personal or family corporation simply listing a class of its shares on a designated stock exchange.

Part IV tax used to apply to a corporation that was a private corporation or a subject corporation at any time in the taxation year. However, beginning in 1993, a corporation is subject to Part IV tax only if it is a private or subject corporation at the time it receives such dividends.

For taxation years beginning after June 2003, Part IV tax is payable on the corporation's balance-due day for the taxation year. A corporation's balance-due day is at the end of the second month following the end of its taxation year or, for small business corporations, at the end of the third month following the end of its taxation year.[62] There is no requirement for instalment payments of the Part IV tax. An annual return is required to be filed within six months of the corporation's year end.

[¶13,140] Special Refundable Tax — Subject Corporations

As the refundable dividend tax on hand account only applies to private corporations, there is a mechanism through which a "subject corporation" may also obtain a dividend refund.[63] This mechanism deems a subject corporation to be a private corporation, whose refundable dividend tax on hand consists of the total of its Part IV taxes payable for the year plus, if it was a subject corporation at the end of its preceding taxation year, its refundable dividend tax on hand at the end of that preceding year, minus its dividend refund for its preceding taxation year.

Investment income (other than dividends) which is included in the refundable dividend tax on hand of a private corporation is not included in the refundable dividend tax on hand of a subject corporation.

Where a subject corporation is amalgamated with, or wound-up into, either a subject corporation or a private corporation, the refundable dividend tax on hand will flow through to the amalgamated or parent corporation.

See page ii for explanation of footnotes.

[60] CCH ¶11,189; Sec. 89(1) "private corporation".   [62] CCH ¶28,020b; Sec. 248(1) "balance-due day".
[61] CCH ¶24,356b; Sec. 186(3) "subject corporation".   [63] CCH ¶24,358; Sec. 186(5).

[¶13,145] Amount Subject to Tax

A corporation that was a private or a subject corporation at any time in a taxation year is required to pay tax equal to the amount by which the total of:

(a) ⅓ of all "assessable dividends" (see ¶13,135) received in the year from a corporation, other than from a corporation connected with it;

and

(b) an amount with respect to assessable dividends received from a connected corporation equal to the proportion of the dividend refund obtained by the payer for the year that the amount of the dividend received by the corporation is of the total of taxable dividends paid by the payer that year;

exceeds ⅓ of the total of:

(c) the portion of non-capital losses or farm losses for the year as the corporation decides to claim; and

(d) such portion as the corporation may claim of its non-capital losses for each of the 20 preceding years and the following three years and such portion as it may claim of its farm losses for each of the 20 preceding years and the following three years.[64]

Where both Part IV and Part IV.1 taxes apply with respect to the same dividend, the Part IV tax will be reduced by 10% of the amount otherwise payable (30% for dividends from connected corporations).[65]

[¶13,150] Connected Corporations

A payer corporation is connected with a recipient corporation at any time that the recipient "controlled" the payer. Two corporations will also be connected at any time that the recipient owns shares representing more than 10% of the votes and value of the payer.[66]

For the purpose of Part IV (other than the definition of subject corporation), control exists where more than 50% of the issued shares having full voting rights under all circumstances belong to the recipient, to persons with whom the recipient does not deal at arm's length, or to the recipient and persons with whom the recipient does not deal at arm's length.[67] For these purposes, control that may be seen to exist by virtue of rights to acquire shares is ignored. For the payer to be connected with the recipient, control must exist at the time the dividend is received. It will be a question

---

See page ii for explanation of footnotes.

[64] CCH ¶24,350; Sec. 186(1).
[65] CCH ¶24,351; Sec. 186(1.1).
[66] CCH ¶24,357; Sec. 186(4).
[67] CCH ¶24,355; Sec. 186(2).

¶13,145

of fact whether two persons deal at arm's length, but related persons are deemed not to deal at arm's length.

In a controversial case, the Tax Court of Canada found that this expanded definition of "control" cannot be used to determine whether two corporations are connected.[68] This decision was eventually reversed in 2002 by the Federal Court of Appeal.[69] As a "hedge" against the possibility of an adverse decision by the Federal Court of Appeal, the federal government enacted in 2001 a new provision to ensure that, unless a contrary intention is evident, one must take into account the extended meaning of "control" to determine the meaning of "connected".[70]

A payer corporation will also be connected with a recipient corporation at any time that both of the following conditions are met:

(1) the recipient owns more than 10% of the issued shares (having full voting rights in all circumstances) of the payer; and

(2) the fair market value of all the shares (voting as well as preference, non-voting, or special shares) owned by the recipient is more than 10% of the fair market value of all the issued shares of the payer.

[¶13,155] Application of Non-Capital Losses and Farm Losses

A corporation may apply $^1/_3$ of any available non-capital losses or farm losses to reduce its Part IV tax.[71] The losses so applied will not be available to reduce Part I taxable income. The taxpayer has an option. The non-capital losses or farm losses may be deducted for the purpose of computing the Part IV tax. Alternatively, such losses may be deducted in the year or carried over to another year and deducted in computing Part I tax. The same options exist with respect to non-capital losses or farm losses that are carried forward or backward from another year.

Since Part IV tax is refundable, it is usually preferable to claim non-capital losses and farm losses against Part I income. Generally, it is advantageous to deduct these losses in computing Part IV tax only under the following circumstances:

- the non-capital or farm losses are about to expire;

- there is little or no prospect that the losses will be used in the foreseeable future in computing the corporation's Part I tax liability; or

- it is unlikely that taxable dividends will be paid and the Part IV tax refunded in the foreseeable future.

See page ii for explanation of footnotes.

[68] Olsen, 2000 DTC 2121.
[69] Olsen, 2002 DTC 6770.
[70] CCH ¶24,359a; Sec. 186(7).
[71] CCH ¶24,350; Sec. 186(1).

Part IV tax applies to the gross dividends received, minus $1/3$ of non-capital and farm losses available for deduction. No other deductions are permitted. Thus, if substantial carrying charges are incurred to obtain the dividend income, a tax in excess of the available income might well be imposed. If profits were unavailable for dividend payments, then a refund of the tax could not be obtained. In this situation, unless it is anticipated that the company will have Part I income against which to claim its losses, it might be advantageous to apply the losses to reduce the Part IV tax base. This is illustrated below:

Example:

Assume that a corporation with $50,000 of capital borrows a further $50,000 at 10% interest to acquire $100,000 of portfolio investment which yields dividends at the rate of 6%:

Dividend income	$6,000
Interest expense	$5,000
Profit	$1,000
Part IV tax on dividends ($1/3$ of dividends)	$2,000
Cash deficit	$1,000

The company's inability to declare dividends in this situation would prevent it from recovering the refundable tax on dividends.

The Part IV tax could be minimized by the application of the non-capital loss, as follows:

Non-capital loss:	
Income for year	$1,000
Less dividend deduction	$6,000
Non-capital loss	($5,000)
Part IV tax for the year:	
$1/3$ of dividends received	$2,000
Less non-capital loss	($1,667)
Part IV tax on dividends	$ 333
Cash position:	
Dividend income	$6,000
Interest expense	($5,000)
Dividend	$1,000
Part IV taxation dividends.	($ 333)
Net cash available for dividends	$ 667

¶13,155

In this situation, where it is not anticipated that the company will have Part I taxable income against which the losses may be claimed, it is advantageous to apply the losses to reduce the Part IV tax. The application of the non-capital loss in this manner would disqualify it from being applied to reduce income of future years. If the corporation expected income from other sources in the future, then a choice would have to be made whether to use the non-capital loss to reduce Part IV tax, which might later prove to be refundable, or to use the loss carryforward later to reduce Part I tax on other income.

[¶13,160] Exceptions

The following corporations are exempted from Part IV tax:

(a) a corporation that was bankrupt at any time in the year; and

(b) a corporation that was *throughout* the year:

    (i) a prescribed labour-sponsored venture capital corporation,

    (ii) a prescribed investment contract corporation (i.e., a corporation approved to issue RRSP contracts),

    (iii) an insurance corporation,

    (iv) a corporation authorized to carry on in Canada the business of offering to the public its services as a trustee,

    (v) a bank, or

    (vi) a non-resident-owned investment corporation; and

(c) a registered securities dealer, that was throughout the year a member or a participating organization of a designated stock exchange.[72]

A "prescribed investment contract corporation" is a corporation approved to issue RRSP investment contracts providing for the payment to or to the credit of the holder thereof of a fixed or determinable amount at maturity, of any periodic or other amount as a contribution under any such contract between the individual and that corporation.[73] A "prescribed labour-sponsored venture capital corporation" means a corporation established or registered under specified provincial labour-sponsored venture capital legislation in Quebec, Saskatchewan, British Columbia, Ontario, and Manitoba.[74]

Furthermore, certain dividends received by a corporation that was a prescribed venture capital corporation *throughout* the year are deemed not to be taxable dividends such that no Part IV tax will be payable in respect of such dividends.[75] For these purposes, venture capital corporations are those

---

See page ii for explanation of footnotes.

[72] CCH ¶24,371; Sec. 186.1.
[73] CCH ¶21,202; Sec. 146(1) "benefit"; Reg. 6703.
[74] CCH ¶7670; Reg. 6701.
[75] CCH ¶24,372; Sec. 186.2.

established or registered under special legislation of the provinces of Quebec, Ontario, Manitoba, Saskatchewan, Alberta, British Columbia, Newfoundland and Labrador, and the Northwest Territories.[76] The dividends received by such corporations will be exempted from Part IV tax if, at the time the shares were acquired, they were either a qualified investment, an eligible investment, or an investment in an eligible business, as the case may be, under the provincial legislation applicable to the shareholder.[77] In other words, the exemption from Part IV tax is, in the case of prescribed venture capital corporations, restricted to dividends on shares which met the investment requirements of the applicable provincial legislation when they were acquired. Dividends on other shares will not be exempt from Part IV tax even if the recipient retains its registration or status under the provincial legislation.

[¶13,165] Information Return, Interest, Assessment, Payment, etc.

Every corporation liable to pay Part IV tax must file a return for the year in a prescribed form within six months from the end of the corporation's taxation year. Interest at a prescribed rate *per annum* is charged for late payment of the tax. General provisions pertaining to assessment, payment, refunds, penalties, objections and appeals, etc. are applicable.[78]

[¶13,170] Taxes on Dividends on Certain Preferred Shares Received by Corporations (Part IV.1)

[¶13,175] Tax on Dividends Received on Taxable Preferred Shares

A tax of 10% is imposed on dividends received by a corporation on a taxable preferred share.[79] An election is provided whereby a corporation can pay 40% tax and then pay dividends to corporate shareholders free of Part IV.1 tax.[80] Part IV.1 tax is payable by a corporation on or before its balance-due day for the taxation year. A corporation's balance-due day is at the end of the second month following the end of its taxation year or, for small business corporations, at the end of the third month following the end of its taxation year.[81]

Part IV.1 tax does not apply to certain excepted dividends.[82] The exceptions generally include:

(a) dividends on shares of a foreign affiliate except where they are received by a specified financial institution on shares acquired in the ordinary course of business;

See page ii for explanation of footnotes.

[76] CCH ¶7670; Reg. 6700.
[77] CCH ¶24,372a; Reg. 6704.
[78] CCH ¶24,375, ¶22,903; Sec. 187; Reg. 4300.
[79] CCH ¶24,392, ¶24,393e; Sec. 187.2.
[80] CCH ¶24,573; Sec. 191.2.
[81] CCH ¶28,020b; Sec. 248(1) "balance-due day".
[82] CCH ¶24,393; Sec. 187.1.

(b) a dividend on a share of a corporation in which a substantial interest was held at the time the dividend was paid;

(c) a dividend received by a private corporation;

(d) a dividend received by a financial intermediary;

(e) a dividend on a short-term preferred share; and

(f) a dividend received on a share of a mutual fund corporation.

[¶13,180] Tax on Dividends on Taxable RFI Shares

Part IV.1 tax is also levied on dividends received by a restricted financial institution (RFI) in respect of taxable RFI shares.[83] The tax is equal to 10% of the dividend and is payable on dividends received by RFIs which includes banks, trust companies, credit unions, insurance corporations, and corporations in the business of lending money.[84] The Part IV.1 tax does not apply to excepted dividends (see ¶13,175). A "taxable RFI share" is generally defined as a share issued before June 18, 1987 where, under the terms or conditions of the share, the entitlement to dividends or liquidation proceeds is fixed, limited, or established to be not less than a minimum amount.

If, in a taxation year beginning after June 2003, a restricted financial institution receives a dividend on a taxable RFI share, the RFI must pay the special 10% tax on the divided on or before its balance-due day for the taxation year. A corporation's balance-due day is at the end of the second month following the end of its taxation year or, for small business corporations, at the end of the third month following the end of its taxation year.[85]

[¶13,185] Tax in Respect of Qualified Donees (Part V)

[¶13,190] Revocation of Charity's Registration

A charity whose registration has been revoked must, on or before the day that is one year after the day that the revocation is effective ("payment day"), pay a tax equal to the total of the fair market value of its assets on the day that is 120 days before the day that notice of the Minister's intention to revoke its registration is mailed ("valuation day"), plus the amount of receipted donations or inter-charity gifts received in the period beginning on the valuation day and ending immediately before the payment day ("winding-up period").

The amount of this tax is reduced by the value of assets transferred to registered charities, amounts expended on charitable activities, and

---

See page ii for explanation of footnotes.

[83] CCH ¶24,395; Sec. 187.3.

[84] CCH ¶28,247a; Sec. 248(1) "restricted financial institution".

[85] CCH ¶28,020b; Sec. 248(1) "balance-due day".

amounts used to pay outstanding debts, and reasonable expenses in the winding-up period.[86]

If a person, other than a qualified donee, receives an amount from a charity after the valuation day, other than an amount which is received in the course of the charity carrying on its activities, paying its just debts which were outstanding, and its reasonable expenses in the winding-up period, or making a payment or distribution in exchange for full consideration paid, such a person is jointly and severally liable with the charity for any tax payable to the extent of any amount so received.[87]

[¶13,195] Charitable Foundation's Transfer of Property

A transfer of property tax is imposed when a charitable foundation transfers, directly or indirectly, before the end of a taxation year, property owned by it having "net value" greater than 50% of the "net asset amount" of the foundation immediately before the transaction or series of transactions, to one or more charitable organizations, and it may reasonably be considered that the main purpose of the transfer is to effect a reduction in the foundation's disbursement quota. The amount of tax payable by the foundation is equal to 25% of the net value of such property determined as of the date of its transfer less any tax payable for a preceding taxation year in respect of the transaction or series of transactions.

If the recipient organization may reasonably be considered to have acted in concert with the charitable foundation for the purpose of reducing the disbursement quota of the foundation, the organization is jointly and severally liable with the foundation for the tax imposed on the foundation to the extent of the net value of the property.[88]

The transfer of property tax does not apply to a transfer that is a gift [after March 3, 2010, a transaction and not merely "a gift"] the purpose of which was to unduly delay the expenditure of amounts on charitable activities.[89] This exemption is because, under the intermediate sanction regime at ¶13,207, a tax is imposed on 110% of the amount of such gifts.

[¶13,200] Private Foundation's Non-Qualified Investments

A tax is imposed if interest paid within 30 days after the end of the taxation year on a debt owing that was on a non-qualified investment of a registered charity that is a private foundation is less than the amount of interest that would be payable on the debt calculated using prescribed rates.

Non-qualified investments include most non-arm's length investments involving a debt, a share, or a right to acquire a share held by a private foundation that is issued by a person not dealing at arm's length with that

---

See page ii for explanation of footnotes.

[86] CCH ¶24,400; Sec. 188(1).

[87] CCH ¶24,402; Sec. 188(2).

[88] CCH ¶21,924, ¶24,404, ¶24,408; Sec. 149.1(1) "disbursement quota", 188(3), 188(5).

[89] CCH ¶24,405; Sec. 188(3.1).

private foundation. Excluded in determining the tax payable are shares listed on a designated stock exchange, qualifying common or participating shares, and debts or shares of a limited dividend housing company or a corporation whose sole purpose is to hold property to be used by a registered charity in its charitable activities or administration.[90]

When debt owed to a private foundation is a non-qualified investment of the foundation, other than employee loans, a tax is imposed on the borrower equal to the amount, if any, by which the amount of interest that would have been payable on the debt in a taxation year, based on rates prescribed from time to time during such year, exceeds the interest actually paid on such debt during such taxation year or within 30 days thereafter. Interest is to be computed at the lesser of the following rates of interest:

(a) rates prescribed from time to time during the taxation year;

(b) the rate that would have been payable in an arm's length transaction if the foundation had been in the business of lending money; and

(c) where the debt was incurred before April 22, 1982, a rate per annum equal to 6% plus 2% for each calendar year after 1982 and before the relevant taxation year.[91]

Non-qualified investments held by a private foundation which are shares or rights to acquire shares are deemed to be debt owing by the corporation to the foundation. The amount of the deemed debt is equal to the cost amount to the foundation of the share or right. The debt is deemed to be outstanding throughout the period during a taxation year that the share or right was held by the foundation. Dividends paid on such shares during such period are deemed to be interest paid on the debt. The prescribed rates to be used for purposes of determining any tax payable on such deemed debt as a non-qualified investment are $2/3$ of such prescribed rates as are in effect from time to time during the year.[92] A share or right acquired in exchange for another share or right in a transaction is deemed to be the same share or right as the one for which it was substituted.[93]

[¶13,205] Returns, Interest, etc.

Except in the case of charities that are liable to pay a revocation tax, persons subject to Part V tax must file a return, without notice or demand, and pay their tax, if any, at the time their Part I return is due.[94] In the case of charities whose registration is revoked, an information return is required to be filed and tax to be paid by the last day that is one year after the day the revocation is effective.[95]

See page ii for explanation of footnotes.

[90] CCH ¶21,924b, ¶21,925, ¶24,440; Sec. 149.1(1) "non-qualified investment", 149.1(1) "private foundation", 189.

[91] CCH ¶24,442; Sec. 189(2).

[92] CCH ¶24,443, ¶24,445; Sec. 189(3), 189(4).

[93] CCH ¶24,447; Sec. 189(5).

[94] CCH ¶24,449; Sec. 189(6).

[95] CCH ¶24,400; Sec. 188(1).

Interest at a prescribed rate per annum is payable on any amount of unpaid tax owing under Part V from the day on or before which the payment was due to the date of payment.[96] The general administrative provisions of Part I apply to Part V.[97]

[¶13,207] Intermediate Taxes and Penalties on Registered Charities and RCAAAs

Until the 2004 Budget, the only sanction available to the Minister in response to non-compliant registered charities was the revocation of a registered charity's registration — a complex and lengthy procedure that would often be disproportionate to the conduct at issue. For taxation years that begin after March 22, 2004, the Minister is given discretion to levy lesser penalties (called "intermediate sanctions") for specific incidents of non-compliance by a registered charity. While it is generally thought that these intermediate sanctions will be applied in lieu of the revocation of a registered charity's registration, there is no statutory prohibition against applying both sanctions.[98]

As of January 1, 2012, Registered Canadian amateur athletic associations (RCAAAs) are also subject to certain intermediate sanctions.

The charts below describe infractions and the possible penalties and suspensions that may result from them. They were prepared by the CRA's charities division as part of its policies and guidance products.

Penalties and suspensions for registered charities

Infraction	Penalty/Suspension for first infraction	Penalty/Suspension for repeat infractions
Failing to file an annual information return (Form T3010) on time	$500 penalty (Assessed at time of application for re-registration)	$500 penalty (Assessed at time of application for re-registration)
Issuing receipts with incomplete information	5% penalty on the eligible amount stated on the receipt	10% penalty on the eligible amount stated on the receipt
Failing to keep proper books and records	Suspension of tax-receipting privileges	Suspension of tax-receipting privileges
Charitable organization or public foundation carrying on an unrelated business	5% penalty on gross unrelated business revenue earned in a fiscal period	100% penalty on gross unrelated business revenue earned in a fiscal period, and suspension of tax-receipting privileges

---

See page ii for explanation of footnotes.

[96] CCH ¶24,451; Sec. 189(7); Reg. 4300.   [98] CCH ¶24,425–25,432c; Sec. 188.1–188.2.
[97] CCH ¶24,452; Sec. 189(8).

¶13,207

Infraction	Penalty/Suspension for first infraction	Penalty/Suspension for repeat infractions
Private foundation carrying on any business	5% penalty on gross business revenue earned in a fiscal period	100% penalty on gross business revenue earned in a fiscal period and suspension of tax-receipting privileges
Foundation acquiring control of a corporation	5% penalty on dividends paid to the charity by the corporation	100% penalty on dividends paid to the charity by the corporation
Undue benefit provided by a charity to any person (for example, a charity makes a cash gift to the director's son)	105% penalty on the amount of undue benefit	110% penalty on the amount of undue benefit and suspension of tax-receipting privileges
Generally making a gift to an entity other than a qualified donee	105% penalty on the amount of the gift	110% penalty on the amount of the gift
Issuing receipts if there is no gift or if the receipt contains false information (where the penalties in total do not exceed $25,000)	125% penalty on the eligible amount stated on the receipt	125% penalty on the eligible amount stated on the receipt
Issuing receipts if there is no gift or if the receipt contains false information (where the penalties in total exceed $25,000)	Suspension of tax-receipting privileges and 125% penalty on the eligible amount stated on the receipt	Suspension of tax-receipting privileges and 125% penalty on the eligible amount stated on the receipt
Entering into a transaction including making a gift to another registered charity in order to delay expenditures on charitable activities	The charities involved are liable to a 110% penalty on the fair market value of the expenditure avoided or delayed	The charities involved are liable to a 110% penalty of the fair market value of the expenditure avoided or delayed
Private foundation failing to divest itself of a percentage of its shares at the end of its fiscal period, in respect of a class of shares	5% of the result of multiplying the divestment obligation percentage of the private foundation for the fiscal period, by the fair market value of all issued and outstanding shares in that class, except where there is a repeat infraction or another penalty for failure to disclose, as indicated below, that applies for the fiscal period	10% of the result of multiplying the divestment obligation percentage of the private foundation for the fiscal period by the fair market value of all issued and outstanding shares in that class at the end of the fiscal period

Infraction	Penalty/Suspension for first infraction	Penalty/Suspension for repeat infractions
Private foundation failing to disclose a material transaction in a class of shares at the end of its fiscal period, where disclosure is required	10% of the result of multiplying the divestment obligation percentage of the private foundation in that class of shares, by the fair market value of all issued and outstanding shares in that class for the fiscal period	N/A
Private foundation failing to disclose a material interest held at the end of its fiscal period, by a relevant person, in a class of shares where disclosure is required	10% of the result of multiplying the divestment obligation percentage of the private foundation in that class of shares, by the fair market value of all issued and outstanding shares in that class for the fiscal period	N/A
Private foundation failing to disclose its total corporate holdings percentage at the end of its fiscal period in a class of shares where disclosure is required	10% of the result of multiplying the divestment obligation percentage of the private foundation in that class of shares by the fair market value of all issued and outstanding shares in that class for the fiscal period	N/A
Accepting gifts or transfers of property on behalf of a suspended qualified donee	Suspension of tax-receipting privileges	Suspension of tax-receipting privileges
Gifts other than designated gifts, received from a non-arm's length charity that are not spent by the recipient charity on its own charitable activities, or transferred to an arm's length qualified donee in the current or following tax year. This amount is in addition to a charity's disbursement quota requirement	The recipient charity is liable to a penalty of 110% of the amount not expended	The recipient charity is liable to a penalty of 110% of the amount not expended

Penalties and suspensions for RCAAAs

Infraction	Penalty/Suspension for first infraction	Penalty/Suspension for repeat infractions
Failing to file an annual information return (Form T2052) on time	$500 penalty (Assessed at time of application for re-registration)	$500 penalty (Assessed at time of application for re-registration)
Issuing receipts with incomplete information	5% penalty on the eligible amount stated on the receipt	10% penalty on the eligible amount stated on the receipt
Failing to keep proper books and records	Suspension of tax-receipting privileges	Suspension of tax-receipting privileges
Carrying on an unrelated business	5% penalty on gross unrelated business revenue earned in a fiscal period	100% penalty on gross unrelated business revenue earned in a fiscal period, and suspension of tax-receipting privileges
Undue benefit provided by an RCAAA to any person (for example, an RCAAA makes a cash gift to the director's son)	105% penalty on the amount of undue benefit	110% penalty on the amount of undue benefit and suspension of tax-receipting privileges
Issuing receipts if there is no gift or if the receipt contains false information (where the penalties in total do not exceed $25,000)	125% penalty on the eligible amount stated on the receipt	125% penalty on the eligible amount stated on the receipt
Issuing receipts if there is no gift or if the receipt contains false information (where the penalties in total exceed $25,000)	Suspension of tax-receipting privileges and 125% penalty on the eligible amount stated on the receipt	Suspension of tax-receipting privileges and 125% penalty on the eligible amount stated on the receipt
Accepting gifts or transfers of property on behalf of a suspended qualified donee	Suspension of tax-receipting privileges	Suspension of tax-receipting privileges

Note: As a result of the 2012 Budget, effective June 29, 2012, tax-receipting privileges may be suspended for one year if a registered charity or an RCA devotes its resources to political activities in excess of its allowable limit. A charity's or RCA's power to issue tax receipts will also attract a suspension of its tax-receipting privilege if it fails to provide complete and accurate information in relation to any aspect of its annual return. In such a case, the suspension will remain in effect until such time as the charity provides the required information.

If the tax and penalties payable exceed $1,000, the sanctioned charity or RCA may transfer an equivalent amount to a qualified donee instead of paying the amounts to the CRA, provided the recipient is in compliance with the Act, is not the subject of a certificate under the *Charities Registration (Security Information) Act,* and more than 50% of its directors or trustees deal at arm's length with each director or trustee of the sanctioned charity or RCA.

¶13,207

A sanctioned charity or RCA has the right to appeal the sanctions to the CRA administratively and to the Tax Court.

[¶13,210] Tax on Capital of Financial Institutions (Part VI)

[¶13,215] Special Tax on Capital of Financial Institutions

Part VI requires that a financial institution, whose taxable capital employed in Canada exceeds its capital deduction for a taxation year, pay an annual capital tax. For taxation years ending on or after July 1, 2006, the tax rate is 1.25% and the capital deduction is $1 billion, such that the tax equals 1.25% of taxable capital employed in Canada in excess of $1 billion. The capital deduction must be shared and allocated amongst related financial institutions. For taxation years that ended before July 1, 2006, the Part VI tax was levied at an effective rate of 1% on taxable capital employed in Canada between $200 million and $300 million and at a rate of 1.25% on taxable capital employed in Canada in excess of $300 million. For taxation years straddling the July 1, 2006 date, the tax is prorated accordingly.[99]

The term "financial institution" means a bank, trust company, loan or mortgage company, a life insurance company carrying on business in Canada, or a corporation where all or substantially all (generally 90% or more) of its assets are shares or debts of related companies of the type described above.[100]

The term "long-term debt" means subordinated indebtedness evidenced by obligations issued for a term of at least five years.[101] The term "subordinated indebtedness" has the meaning assigned by section 2 of the *Bank Act*, and for insurers it has the meaning assigned by section 2 of the *Insurance Companies Act*. The definitions refer to an instrument that by its terms provides that it will, in the event of insolvency or winding-up of the company, be subordinate in right of payment to all liabilities, including, as applicable, deposit-holder and policy liabilities, except any other liability which by its terms is subordinate or equal to such instrument.

The carrying value of a corporation's assets or any other amount in respect of a corporation's capital, taxable capital, or taxable capital employed in Canada for a taxation year is determined by reference to its non-consolidated financial statements, and the equity method of accounting should not be used.[102]

A corporation may be liable to Part VI tax for a taxation year if it was a financial institution at any time during that year.

[¶13,217] Deduction

A corporation may, in computing its Part VI tax, deduct an amount equal to the total of its Part I tax liability for the year and such amount as it chooses of its unused Part I tax credits and unused surtax credits for the

---

[99] CCH ¶24,470–24,534; Sec. 190–190.22.
[100] CCH ¶24,470; Sec. 190(1) "financial institution".
[101] CCH ¶24,470a; Sec. 190(1) "long-term debt".
[102] CCH ¶24,472; Sec. 190(2).

seven preceding and three following taxation years.[103] The "unused Part I tax credit" is defined as the amount by which its tax payable under Part I for the year exceeds the total Part VI tax payable for the year (before the above deduction from Part VI tax) and Canadian surtax payable for the year.[104] Unused Part I tax credits must be utilized in the order in which they arose; that is, on a first-in, first-out basis.[105]

The carryforward or carryback of unused Part I tax credits and unused surtax credits is restricted where control of a corporation has been acquired by a person or by a group of persons.[106] A corporation's unused Part I tax credits and unused surtax credits for a particular taxation year that ends before an acquisition of its control may be deducted in a taxation year ending after that time if the corporation carries on the same business for profit or with a reasonable expectation of profit throughout the subsequent year, and only to the extent of that proportion of its Part I tax payable for the earlier year that its income from the business or a similar business for the earlier year is of its total taxable income for that year. Similarly, a corporation's unused surtax and Part I tax credits arising in a taxation year after an acquisition of control cannot be applied before the change, unless, in that previous year, the corporation carried on the same business for profit or with a reasonable expectation of profit, and only to the extent of that proportion of its Part I tax payable for the subsequent year that its income from the business or a similar business for the subsequent year is of its total taxable income for that year.

[¶13,220] Taxable Capital Employed in Canada

"Taxable capital employed in Canada" for a financial institution other than a life insurance corporation is that proportion of a corporation's taxable capital for a taxation year that its Canadian assets at the end of the year are of its total assets at the end of the year.[107] The taxable capital of a corporation for a taxation year is its capital for the year minus its investments in related financial institutions.[108] See ¶13,225.

The taxable capital employed in Canada of a life insurance corporation resident in Canada will be the total of:

(a) the portion of the total of its taxable capital and the equity and long-term debt of its foreign subsidiaries for the year that its Canadian reserve liabilities as at the end of the year are of its total reserve liabilities, including reserve liabilities of its foreign subsidiaries; and

(b) the amount by which its reserves relating to its Canadian operations exceed the total of:

---

[103] CCH ¶24,482a; Sec. 190.1(3).

[104] CCH ¶24,482c; Sec. 190.1(5) "unused Part I tax credit".

[105] CCH ¶24,482b; Sec. 190.1(4).

[106] CCH ¶24,483a; Sec. 190.1(6).

[107] CCH ¶24,490; Sec. 190.11.

[108] CCH ¶24,492; Sec. 190.12.

     (i) the reserves that were deductible or deducted in computing its income for the year, and

     (ii) any amount outstanding in respect of a policy loan made by the corporation, to the extent that it was deducted in computing the reserves deductible for purposes of reserve calculations.[109]

With respect to paragraph b) above, deferred income taxes are not considered "reserves" and, therefore, are not to be considered as part of a taxpayer's "taxable capital employed in Canada" for the purpose of Part VI.[110]

In the case of a non-resident life insurer, its taxable capital employed in Canada will be its taxable capital for the year.[111]

[¶13,225] Capital of a Financial Institution

The capital of a financial institution other than a life insurance corporation for a taxation year is the sum of its outstanding long-term debt, its capital stock, retained earnings, contributed surplus and any other surpluses, plus its provisions or reserves not deducted from income, minus any deferred tax debit balance or deficit of the corporation at the end of the year.[112] For these purposes, where a financial institution's particular tax reserve exceeds its matching book reserve, a negative amount should not be included in the calculation. Rather, the value of the book reserve should be reduced to zero.[113]

With the inclusion of authorized foreign banks in the definition of "bank", authorized foreign banks are now financial institutions subject to the Part VI tax. A special rule causes the capital of authorized foreign banks to equal the amount that a Schedule II bank would have if it maintained a risk-weighted asset-to-capital ratio of 10:1. More particularly, the capital of a Canadian branch of a foreign bank is equal to the sum of i) 10% of the branch's risk-weighted assets, as determined under the Office of the Superintendent of Financial Institution's (OSFI) risk-weighting guidelines, and (ii) 100% of certain other amounts (such as goodwill recorded on the bank's balance sheet), in respect of the branch business that would be deducted in computing capital for purposes of OSFI's Capital Adequacy Guidelines if the bank were a Schedule II bank.[114]

The capital of a resident life insurance corporation for a taxation year is the amount by which the total of:

     (a) its long-term debt, and

     (b) its capital stock, retained earnings, contributed surplus, and any other surpluses,

---

See page ii for explanation of footnotes.

[109] CCH ¶24,490; Sec. 190.11(b).
[110] London Life Insurance Company, 2000 DTC 1774.
[111] CCH ¶24,490; Sec. 190.11(c).

[112] CCH ¶24,494; Sec. 190.13.
[113] National Trust Co., 96 DTC 6234.
[114] CCH ¶24,494; Sec. 190.13(d).

exceeds the total of:

(c) its deferred tax debit balance, and

(d) the amount of any deficit deducted in computing its shareholders' equity.[115]

The capital of a non-resident life insurance corporation for a taxation year is the total of:

(a) the greater of:

(i) its surplus funds derived from operations, computed as if no tax were payable under Parts I.3 or VI for the year, in excess of amounts on which branch tax has been paid or would have been paid but for an insurer's election, and

(ii) its attributed surplus;

(b) any other surpluses and any long-term debt that relate to its Canadian insurance business; and

(c) the amount by which its reserves relating to its Canadian operations exceeds:

(i) the portion of those reserves that was either deductible or deducted in computing its income for the year, and

(ii) any amount outstanding in respect of a policy loan made by the corporation to the extent that it was deducted in computing the amount deductible for purposes of reserve calculations.[116]

[¶13,230] Investment in a Related Financial Institution

In computing its taxable capital, a corporation is allowed a deduction for its investments in related financial institutions in order to avoid double taxation.[117] For these purposes, two corporations that would be related only because of the control of a corporation by the Crown or of a right to acquire control of a corporation will not be treated as being related. However, if one of the main purposes of the acquisition of the right was to avoid any limitation on the amount of a corporation's capital deduction, the two corporations will be treated as if the right acquired to avoid the limitation were an immediate and absolute right and as if the taxpayer had exercised it.[118]

The amount of the deduction is the aggregate of the carrying values at the end of the year of shares and long-term debt of related financial institutions owned by the corporation and the amount of surplus of the related

---

See page ii for explanation of footnotes.

[115] CCH ¶24,494; Sec. 190.13(b).   [117] CCH ¶24,496; Sec. 190.14.
[116] CCH ¶24,494; Sec. 190.13(c).   [118] CCH ¶24,504; Sec. 190.15(6).

financial institutions contributed by the corporation (not reflected in the carrying value of the shares or long-term debt).

[¶13,235] Capital Deduction

A corporation is allowed a "capital deduction" in computing the amount subject to Part VI tax. For taxation years ending on or after July 1, 2006, the capital deduction is $1 billion, unless the corporation was related to a financial institution at the end of the year (in which case the $1 billion is shared). For prior taxation years, the capital deduction equaled the aggregate of $200 million and the lesser of $20 million and $1/5$ of the corporation's taxable capital employed in Canada in excess of $200 million for the year, unless the corporation was related to one or more financial institutions at the end of the year. For taxation years that straddle the July 1, 2006 date, the capital deduction is effectively computed on a *pro rata* basis.[119]

Related financial institutions may share the capital deduction by filing an agreement in prescribed form (Form T2045) with the Minister.[120] The Minister may allocate the capital deduction if the related financial institutions fail to do so within 30 days of receiving a request to file the agreement in prescribed form.[121] If neither the related financial institutions nor the Minister allocate the allowable capital deduction, no capital deduction is available to the members of the related group.[122]

[¶13,240] Returns and Tax Instalments

A corporation that would be liable to pay any Part VI tax for a year must file a return containing an estimate of its Part VI tax payable on the prescribed form (Form T2044) by the same day the corporation is required to file its return of income under Part I, i.e., six months after the year end.[123]

The administrative provisions of Part VI were integrated with Part I.[124] Thus, the rules pertaining to interest, instalments, remainder of tax payable, assessment, penalties, objections, and appeals apply equally to Part VI. The integration of the administrative provisions, in particular the instalment requirements, are part of the government's efforts to assist companies in their attempts to improve the cash-flow flexibility of their businesses. That is, where before, corporations were required to remit separate instalments to the CRA in respect of Part I and Part VI tax, all instalments may now be made to a single account, thereby allowing the offsets of under and over instalments.

See page ii for explanation of footnotes.

[119] CCH ¶24,498; Sec. 190.15(1).

[120] CCH ¶24,500; Sec. 190.15(2).

[121] CCH ¶24,501; Sec. 190.15(3).

[122] CCH ¶24,502; Sec. 190.15(4).

[123] CCH ¶24,530; Sec. 190.2.

[124] CCH ¶24,532; Sec. 190.21.

[¶13,245] Tax on Corporations Paying Dividends on Taxable Preferred Shares (Part VI.1)

[¶13,250] Tax on Taxable Dividends

Part VI.1 imposes a tax of 50% (66²/₃% before 2003) on the payer of dividends on short-term preferred shares and a tax of either 25% or 40% on the payer of dividends on taxable preferred shares other than short-term preferred shares.[125] The rate on short-term preferred shares is meant to produce an amount of tax equal to the amount of income tax that would have been collected had a corporate shareholder sought the same after-tax return in the form of interest. The former 66²/₃% rate was based on an assumed tax of 40% on interest income. As part of a series of amendments reflecting recent and planned reductions in income tax rates, the rate of tax on short-term preferred shares was reduced to 50% of the dividend amount for 2003 and subsequent taxation years. This provides the desired result on the basis of an assumed tax of 33.3% on interest income.

The tax does not apply to excluded dividends (see ¶13,255). In addition, the tax is only levied to the extent that the total of non-excluded dividends on taxable preferred shares exceeds a $500,000 dividend allowance.[126] The dividend allowance is reduced by the amount of non-excluded taxable dividends in excess of $1 million paid by the corporation in the previous calendar year on all preferred shares.

If the payer corporation is associated with one or more other taxable Canadian corporations, the dividend allowance must be allocated among the members of the associated group.[127] In general, "short-term preferred shares" are shares which are retractable or which could be required to be redeemed within five years of issue.[128] The very broadly worded definition of "taxable preferred share" will include most preferred or non-common shares issued after June 18, 1987.[129]

The rate of Part VI tax on dividends paid on taxable preferred shares (other than short-term preferred shares) is 25% unless the shares are of a class for which an election has been made to have the 40% rate apply.[130] This election may be made so that recipients of the dividends are not subject to Part VI.1 tax.

Part VI.1 together with the 10% Part IV.1 tax payable by certain recipients of dividends on taxable preferred shares and the various provisions denying deductibility of dividends received on certain preferred shares, constitutes a complex system designed to prevent the use of preferred shares as a means of raising after-tax financing. Part VI.1 is intended to ensure that

---

See page II for explanation of footnotes.

[125] CCH ¶24,556; Sec. 191.1(1).

[126] CCH ¶24,557; Sec. 191.1(2).

[127] CCH ¶24,558, ¶24,559, ¶24,560; Sec. 191.1(3), 191.1(4), 191.1(5).

[128] CCH ¶28,270; Sec. 248(1) "short-term preferred share".

[129] CCH ¶28,300; Sec. 248(1) "taxable preferred share".

[130] CCH ¶24,573; Sec. 191.2.

preferred share dividends are paid out of corporate surplus which has been taxed at a rate of at least 33.3% (44.44% before 2003).

The tax levied under Part VI.1 can be recovered via a deduction mechanism provided for under Part I. This deduction is equal to three times ($^9/_4$ times before 2003) the corporation's Part VI.1 tax liability for the year.[131] The deduction approximates the income that would have generated an amount of income tax equal to the Part VI.1 tax. The multiple of three is based on a presumed combined federal-provincial corporate income tax rate of about 33.3%. The previous $^9/_4$ multiple was based on a presumed rate of about 44.44%. The value of the deduction will, of course, be greater than the actual Part VI.1 tax liability if the corporation's combined federal-provincial tax rate is higher than 33.3%. Conversely, the value of the deduction will be lower than the Part VI.1 tax if the combined rate is less than 33.3%.

Tax liability under Part VI.1 may be transferred among taxable Canadian corporations related throughout the transferor's year (and the transferee's year ending in that year) by filing a joint election on Form T2, Schedule 45.[132] This schedule must be filed by the ordinary due date for the tax return of the transferor corporation, or within 90 days of a notice of assessment under either Part I or Part VI.1 of the transferor for the year, or of the transferee for its taxation year ending in the year the transferor incurred the Part VI.1 tax liability. The transfer rule provides relief where the transferor has insufficient ordinary Part I tax liability to utilize the offsetting deduction discussed above.

Corporations may use the transfer rules where one of them comes into or goes out of existence during the year so long as they are related throughout the period of existence.

The transfer of Part VI.1 tax liability is not available to corporations which are related only by virtue of being controlled by the federal or provincial government.

[¶13,255] Excluded Dividends

Part VI.1 tax does not apply to excluded dividends[133] or to dividends which are deemed to be excluded dividends.[134] Excluded dividends are:

(a) dividends paid to a shareholder holding a "substantial interest" in the payer corporation;

(b) dividends paid by a "financial intermediary corporation" or a "private holding corporation";

(c) dividends paid in certain circumstances by a corporation which would have been a financial intermediary corporation but for certain

---

See page ii for explanation of footnotes.

[131] CCH ¶15,310; Sec. 110(1)(k).
[132] CCH ¶24,583; Sec. 191.3.
[133] CCH ¶24,562; Sec. 191(1) "excluded dividend".
[134] CCH ¶24,554; Sec. 191(4).

exceptions in the definition of that term (referred to as a "quasi-financial intermediary corporation");

(d) dividends paid by a mortgage investment corporation; or

(e) capital gains dividends.

In general, a shareholder will have a "substantial interest" in a corporation if either of the following set of conditions is met:

(1) he or she is related to the corporation;

(2) he or she owns shares of the corporation which carry at least 25% of the total votes which could be cast under all circumstances at an annual meeting *and* which represent at least 25% of the fair market value of all the issued shares of the corporation *and* he or she owns either:

> (a) shares, other than some preferred shares, representing at least 25% of the fair market value of all such shares, or

> (b) at least 25% of the issued shares of every class of outstanding shares of the corporation.[135]

For instance, assume that Mr. Black owns 100% of the preferred shares and 5% of the common shares of Black Co. Ltd., that his uncle Mr. Red owns 20% of the common shares, and the other issued and outstanding common shares are held by unrelated third parties. In the event that Black Co. Ltd. pays dividends of $550,000 in respect of its preferred shares, Part VI.1 tax will be payable since Mr. Black does not have a substantial interest in Black Co. Ltd. In addition, Mr. Black and Mr. Red are not related (see ¶15,405 *et seq.*), therefore, Mr. Black is not deemed to own the shares of Black Co. Ltd. owned by Mr. Red. The Part VI.1 tax will be payable on $50,000 of dividends (see ¶13,250 above concerning the dividend allowance).

[¶13,260] Refundable Tax on Corporations Issuing Qualifying Shares (Part VII) and Refundable Tax on Corporations Re SR&ED Tax Credit (Part VIII)

The refundable tax in Part VII on corporations issuing qualifying shares applied generally to a tax on amounts that could be designated for tax credits on an issue of shares after June 1983 and before 1987.[136] The refundable tax in Part VIII on corporations in respect of scientific research and experimental development (SR&ED) tax credits applied generally to SR&ED credits that could be designated on shares for a certain period between 1983 and 1985.[137] Taxes under Part VII and Part VIII are no longer in effect, but the provisions may be relevant for purposes of computing the

---

See page ii for explanation of footnotes.

[135] CCH ¶24,552, ¶24,553; Sec. 191(2), 191(3).
[136] CCH ¶24,600–24,660, ¶24,670–24,708; Sec. 192, 193.
[137] CCH ¶24,750–24,795, ¶24,800–24,838; Sec. 194, 195.

paid-up capital of a class of shares on which such a designation was made during the applicable period.[138]

[¶13,370] Tax on Deduction Under Section 66.5 (Part IX)

[¶13,375] Tax in Respect of Cumulative Offset Account

Part IX levies a tax of 30% of the amount a corporation deducts in computing Part I income on the basis of its cumulative offset account.

Corporations can designate percentages of their prescribed Canadian exploration and development expenses incurred in the year, subject to certain criteria.[139] The amounts designated are added to the cumulative offset account. Under the *Petroleum and Gas Revenue Tax Act*, 30% of the designated amounts for the year can be applied against tax otherwise payable on production revenue for that year.

Amounts added to the cumulative offset account may be deducted in computing income for a subsequent year when no designation is made. However, Part IX imposes a tax of 30% of the amount deducted. This special Part IX tax is imposed to equal the Petroleum and Gas Revenue tax saved through the designation.

[¶13,377] Returns and Instalments

A corporation liable to pay Part IX tax for a year must file a Part IX return on or before the date on which it must file its Part I return for that year.[140] That date will generally be six months after the end of the taxation year. Monthly instalments are required, with the balance payable on or before the corporation's balance-due day for the year.[141] A corporation's "balance-due day" is at the end of the second month following the end of its taxation year or, for small business corporations, at the end of the third month following the end of its taxation year.[142] Before July 2003, the Part IX tax was to be paid by the corporation on or before the end of the second month following the end of the year.

[¶13,379] Administrative Provisions

The Part I administrative provisions that relate to assessments, appeals, penalties, refunds, and interest apply to Part IX.[143]

See page ii for explanation of footnotes.

[138] CCH ¶24,633, ¶24,768; Sec. 192(4.1), 194(4.1).
[139] CCH ¶9090 et seq.; Sec. 66.5(1).
[140] CCH ¶24,861; Sec. 196(2).
[141] CCH ¶24,862; Sec. 196(3).
[142] CCH ¶28,020b; Sec. 248(1) "balance-due day".
[143] CCH ¶24,863; Sec. 196(4).

¶13,370

[¶13,380] Tax on SIFT Partnerships (Part IX.1)

[¶13,385] Liability for Tax

On October 31, 2006, the Department of Finance announced new tax regimes that apply to publicly traded income trusts and public partnerships. In respect of the latter, the new tax is found in Part IX.1, which imposes a tax on the "taxable non-portfolio earnings" (as defined below) of a SIFT partnership or specified investment flow-through partnership. A SIFT partnership means a Canadian resident partnership that, at any time in the taxation year, holds non-portfolio property and for which investments in the partnership are listed or traded on a stock exchange or other public market.[144] Specifically excluded from the definition of "SIFT partnership" is an "excluded subsidiary entity". An "excluded subsidiary entity" is an entity none of the equity of which is at any time in the taxation year (a) listed or traded on a stock exchange or other public market; nor (b) held by any person or partnership other than a real estate investment trust (REIT), a taxable Canadian corporation, a SIFT trust, a SIFT partnership, or another excluded subsidiary entity for the taxation year.[145] [Draft legislation released on July 25, 2012 proposes to amend the definition of "excluded subsidiary entity" to expand the range of qualifying interest holders in such an entity. Under this proposal, the list of qualifying interested holders would not be limited to REITs, taxable Canadian corporations, SIFTs, and other excluded subsidiary entities, it would also would include a person or partnership that does not have any security or right, in the entity, that is, or includes a right to acquire, directly or indirectly either

(i) any security of any entity that is listed or traded on a stock exchange or other public market; or

(ii) any property the amount, or fair market value, of which is determined primarily by reference to any security that is listed or traded on a stock exchange or other public market.

This proposal, first announced on July 20, 2011, is deemed to have come into force on October 31, 2006 (subject to a special election to have this change apply only to taxation years beginning after July 20, 2011).]

The SIFT tax is made up of two components. The first component is equal to the federal general corporate rate (see ¶8300), net of the general rate reduction (see ¶8475), and the provincial abatement (see ¶8315). Up to 2009, the second component is the "provincial SIFT tax factor", meaning the decimal fraction 0.13, which represents an average provincial general corporate tax rate.[146]

See page ii for explanation of footnotes.

[144] CCH ¶24,877; Sec. 197(1) "SIFT partnership".   [146] CCH ¶24,879; Sec. 197(2).
[145] CCH ¶19,272d; Sec. 122.1(1) "excluded subsidiary entity".

Beginning in 2009 (or earlier, subject to the election described below), the second component of the SIFT tax is replaced by the "provincial SIFT tax rate", meaning the general provincial corporate income tax rate of *each province* in which a SIFT has a permanent establishment.[147] This new formula ensures that the SIFT tax rate is the same as the federal–provincial tax rate for large public corporations with the same activities as the SIFT partnership. Technically, the provincial SIFT tax rate is a prescribed amount, expressed as a decimal fraction, determined in respect of the SIFT partnership for the taxation year. If the SIFT partnership has a permanent establishment in only one province, the prescribed amount is the decimal fraction representing that province's general corporate income tax rate for public corporations with the same activities as the SIFT partnership. If that province is Quebec, the decimal fraction is nil, to take into account the SIFT tax imposed by that province. If the SIFT partnership has permanent establishments in more than one province, the prescribed amount is the decimal fraction amount that is an average of the relevant provincial general corporate income tax rates for public corporations with the same activities, weighted on the basis of the general corporate taxable income allocation formula (i.e., by reference to wages and salaries and gross revenues attributable to those permanent establishments). If, under the allocation formula, amounts are not allocated to any province, then the prescribed amount is 10%. This new formula applies for the 2009 and subsequent taxation years. It also applies for a SIFT's 2007 taxation year if the SIFT partnership elects in its return under Part XI.1 for 2007 to have the new provincial SIFT tax rate component apply starting in that year, or for a SIFT's 2008 taxation year, if the SIFT so elects in its return for 2008.

The Part IX.1 tax is imposed at the partnership level. The amount of the partnership's taxable non-portfolio earnings, net of the Part IX.1 tax, is deemed to be a taxable dividend received by the partnership, and is flowed out to the partners under the regular partnership rules.[148] As a result, a SIFT partnership and its partners are taxed, in respect of the partnership's taxable non-portfolio earnings, in a manner that replicates the taxation of a public corporation and its shareholders on income that is distributed as taxable dividends.

Part IX.1 came into force on October 31, 2006. However, owing to the application of the definition of SIFT partnership, the earliest the Part IX.1 tax can apply is to a partnership's taxation year ending after 2006. Furthermore, owing to grandfathering rules that apply to partnerships that otherwise would have been considered SIFT partnerships on October 31, 2006 (had the definition been applicable on that date), the Part IX.1 tax cannot apply to such partnerships until the 2011 taxation year, provided they do not exceed certain "normal growth" guidelines issued by the Department of Finance.

See page ii for explanation of footnotes.

[147] CCH ¶24,879, ¶28,222h; Sec. 197(2), 248(1)   [148] CCH ¶12,140m; Sec. 96(1.11).
"provincial SIFT tax rate".

¶13,385

[¶13,387] Meaning of "Taxable Non-Portfolio Earnings"

A SIFT partnership's "taxable non-portfolio earnings" for a taxation year are defined as the lesser of the SIFT partnership's income otherwise determined (as if it were a taxpayer) and its "non-portfolio earnings".[149] Non-portfolio earnings of a SIFT partnership for a taxation year mean the total of:

(1) the SIFT partnership's income from a business it carries on in Canada and its income from a non-portfolio property in the year other than taxable dividends, net of losses from any business it carries on in Canada and from its non-portfolio property in the year; and

(2) its taxable capital gains in excess of allowable capital losses from its dispositions of "non-portfolio property" in the year.[150]

A SIFT partnership's non-portfolio property is a property of any of the following three types.[151]

The first type comprises certain securities that either:

- have a total fair market value that is greater than 10% of the equity value of the subject entity; or

- make up, together with any securities that the partnership holds of entities affiliated with the subject entity, more than 50% of the equity value of the partnership.

The second type of non-portfolio property is a "Canadian real, immovable, or resource property".[152] A property that meets this definition will be a non-portfolio property of the partnership only if the total fair market value of all of the Canadian real, immovable, or resource properties held by the partnership is greater than 50% of its equity value. It should be noted that for this purpose there is no difference among the various kinds of Canadian real, immovable, or resource properties. For example, assume that a SIFT partnership that has an equity value of $1 billion holds Canadian resource properties that have a total fair market value of $350 million and real properties situated in Canada that have a total fair market value of $175 million. All of those Canadian resource properties and real properties are non-portfolio properties of the SIFT partnership, since their total fair market value ($525 million) exceeds 50% of its equity value.

The third type of non-portfolio property is property that the partnership (or a non-arm's length partnership) uses in the course of carrying on a business in Canada.

See page ii for explanation of footnotes.

[149] CCH ¶24,878; Sec. 197(1) "taxable non-portfolio earnings".

[150] CCH ¶24,878; Sec. 197(1) "taxable non-portfolio earnings".

[151] CCH ¶19,275; Sec. 122.1(1) "non-portfolio property".

[152] CCH ¶28,033; Sec. 248(1) "Canadian real, immovable or resource property".

[¶13,389] Return

Where Part IX.1 tax is payable by a SIFT partnership in a taxation year, every member of the partnership shall file a return in prescribed form containing an estimate of the Part IX.1 tax payable for the year.[153] However, if a member of the partnership who has authority to act for the partnership files the return, each other member is deemed to have filed the return such that only the first such return needs to be filed.[154] The return is required to be filed and the Part IX.1 tax is required to be paid on or before the day on which the partnership information return is required to be filed.[155]

[¶13,390] Tax on Deferred Profit Sharing Plans (DPSPs) and Revoked DPSPs (Part X)

[¶13,395] Special Taxes Payable by DPSPs

Although a trust governed by a DPSP is not subject to Part I tax on its income, Part X provides for two special taxes to be payable in particular circumstances:

(1) The first of these taxes is imposed where the trust acquires a "non-qualified investment" or uses trust property as security for a loan.[156] The rate of tax is a full 100% of the fair market value of the non-qualified investment or the property used as security. This tax may, however, be refunded if the trust disposes of the investment or ceases to use the trust property as security. See ¶13,400 *et seq.*

> While Part X applies only to DPSPs, other deferred income plans are also subject to similar rules respecting non-qualified investments. A tax is imposed on the annuitant of a registered retirement savings plan (RRSP) which acquires non-qualified investments.

> Under Part XI.1 (¶13,525), a trust governed by an RRSP, a DPSP, a RRIF, or an RESP, must pay a tax on property that was a qualified investment when acquired but later becomes non-qualified and that continues to be held by the trust. The investments that are qualified for each of these three types of plans are listed at ¶13,405.

(2) The second tax imposed by Part X is peculiar to DPSPs and has no counterpart in RRSPs.[157]

> In situations where a DPSP disposes of property at less than fair market value or where it acquires property for more than fair market value, the trust governed by the plan must pay a 50% tax on the difference between the consideration given or received, as the case

---

See page ii for explanation of footnotes.

[153] CCH ¶24,881; Sec. 197(4).   [156] CCH ¶25,300; Sec. 198(1).
[154] CCH ¶24,882; Sec. 197(5).
[155] CCH ¶24,884; Sec. 197(7).   [157] CCH ¶25,450; Sec. 201.

may be, and the fair market value of the property at that time. See ¶13,430.

[¶13,400] Tax on Non-Qualified Investments and on Property Used as Security

A trust governed by a DPSP is subject to a tax equal to the fair market value of a non-qualified investment at the time it was acquired by the trust. Such a trust is also subject to a tax equal to the fair market value of any trust property used as security for a loan at the time that it commenced to be so used. This also applies to a revoked plan. The trustee must remit the tax within 10 days after the non-qualified investment is acquired or trust property is used to secure a loan. A trustee who fails to do so is personally liable for the tax but may recover it from the trust.

[¶13,405] "Qualified Investments" and "Non-Qualified Investments" Defined

"Non-qualified investment" means property that is not a qualified investment. "Qualified investments"[158] include the following:

(1) Money that is legal tender in Canada (other than money whose fair market value exceeds its nominal value) and certain deposits of such money standing to the credit of the trust, i.e., deposits under the *Canada Deposit Insurance Act*, deposits with a Canadian branch of a bank listed in Schedule I or II of the *Bank Act*, or deposits with an authorized foreign bank.

(2) Bonds, debentures, notes, mortgages, or similar obligations issued or guaranteed by the Government of Canada or issued by a province, municipality, Crown corporation, or, if guaranteed or secured by a province, an educational institution or a hospital.

(3) Bonds, debentures, notes, or similar obligations of a corporation whose shares are listed on a designated stock exchange in Canada, other than those of an employer who makes payments to the trust for the benefit of beneficiaries under the plan, or of a corporation with whom the employer does not deal at arm's length (after March 18, 2007, such obligations are now qualified investments under paragraph (5)).

(4) Effective March 19, 2007, debt obligations that have, or had at the time of acquisition by the trust, an investment grade rating with a prescribed credit rating agency, or a debt obligation that was acquired in exchange for a debt obligation that had such a rating when acquired by the trust if the exchange was part of a proposal or arrangement under the *Bankruptcy and Insolvency Act* or the *Companies' Creditors Arrangement Act*. In either case, the debt obligation must be part of a minimum $25 million debt issuance, or, in the case of debt obligations that are issued on a continuous basis under a debt issuance program, the issuer has issued

---

See page ii for explanation of footnotes.

[158] CCH ¶25,534g; Sec. 204 "qualified investment".

outstanding debt obligations under the program of at least $25 million. The prescribed rating agencies are A. M. Best Company, Inc.; Dominion Bond Rating Service, Ltd.; Fitch, Inc.; Moody's Investors Service Inc.; the Standard and Poor's Division of the McGraw-Hill Companies, Inc.[159]

(5) Effective March 19, 2007, all securities listed on designated stock exchanges (other than futures contracts and similar derivative instruments, where the holder's loss may exceed the holder's cost).

(6) Shares listed on a designated stock exchange in Canada or outside Canada (after March 18, 2007, such shares are now qualified investments under paragraph (5)).

(7) Equity shares of a corporation which made payments to the trustees of the plan for the benefit of employees before the date of the acquisition of the shares, provided that there is no restriction on the transferability of such shares and provided also that the dividend payment history relating to such shares complies with certain requirements.

(8) Guaranteed investment certificates issued by a Canadian trust company.

(9) Debt obligations issued by a corporation whose shares are listed on a designated stock exchange outside of Canada (after March 18, 2007, such obligations are now qualified investments under paragraph (4)).

(10) Units of a mutual fund trust, including units of a Canadian Real Estate Investment Trust (REIT) listed on a prescribed Canadian stock exchange.

(11) A right or warrant to acquire immediately, or in the future, property all of which is a qualified investment.

(12) A mortgage secured by real property situated in Canada.

(13) An investment contract issued by an approved company that provides for the payment of a fixed or determinable amount at maturity.

(14) Life insurance policies, if the plan is the only beneficiary under the policy, the cash surrender value of the policy is not less than the face value of the policy by the time the insured attains 71 years of age, and the annual premiums under the policy do not increase after the first year of the policy (before 2007, the requirement relating to the cash surrender value of a policy had to be satisfied by the insured person's 69th birthday).[160]

(15) Royalty units listed on a designated stock exchange in Canada and the value of which is derived solely from Canadian resource properties (after March 18, 2007, such units are now qualified investments under paragraph (5)).

See page ii for explanation of footnotes.

[159] CCH ¶25,533f, ¶25,540; Sec. 204 "debt obligation"; Reg. 4900(2).

[160] CCH ¶25,380–25,390; Sec. 198(6)–(8).

¶13,405

(16) A qualifying small business investment partnership, as long as the return of the investment is not related to services provided by the plan annuitant.

(17) A debt obligation issued or guaranteed by the International Bank for Reconstruction and Development, the International Finance Corporation, the Inter-American Development Bank, the Asian Development Bank, the Caribbean Development Bank, or the European Bank for Reconstruction and Development.

(18) Limited partnership units listed on a prescribed Canadian stock exchange (after March 18, 2007, such units are now qualified investments under paragraph (5)).

(19) Such other investments as prescribed by regulation.[161]

The following are some of the more common non-qualified investments:

- gold and silver bars and other precious metals, although, after February 22, 2005 investment-grade gold with a purity of 99.5% and investment-grade silver with a purity of at least 99.9% will be qualified;

- commodity futures;

- listed personal property such as works of art and antiques;

- shares of private corporations, where the individual and his or her immediate family hold more than 10% of any class of shares;

- gems and other precious stones; and

- real estate.

A trust governed by a registered retirement savings plan (RRSP), a deferred profit sharing plan (DPSP), a registered retirement income fund (RRIF), or a registered education savings plan (RESP) that holds property that is not a qualified investment is subject to a 1% tax of the fair market value of all such property.[162] See ¶13,525.

[¶13,410] Refund of Tax on Disposition of Non-Qualified Investment

Where a trust governed by a DPSP disposes of a property which, when acquired, was a non-qualified investment, the trust may apply for a refund of the lesser of the Part X tax paid when the investment was originally acquired and the proceeds of disposition of the non-qualified investment. Thus, if the trust incurs a loss on the transaction, the amount on which tax is payable will exceed the amount of the refund.[163]

See page ii for explanation of footnotes.

[161] CCH ¶25,540; Reg. 4900.　　　　[163] CCH ¶25,350, ¶25,360; Sec. 198(4), 198(5).
[162] CCH ¶25,725; Sec. 207.1.

Where a loan for which trust property has been used as security ceases to be extant, the trust is entitled to a refund of the Part X tax originally paid on using the trust property as security, less any loss on the transaction. This loss does not include any interest that the trust might have paid in respect of the loan and does not include any loss attributable to a decline in value of the property used as security. For example, a trust governed by a deferred profit sharing plan borrows $10,000 at interest of 9% per annum and pledges shares of X Ltd. worth $15,000 as security. Part X tax will be payable in the amount of $15,000. At the end of one year the trust repays the loan plus $900 interest and recovers the shares which are now worth only $12,000. In this case the trust has not incurred a loss on the loan transaction and will be eligible for a full refund of $15,000.

Refunds of Part X tax must be applied for, as they do not follow automatically. The form of application is a part of the annual TD3 return to be filed by every trust governed by a deferred profit sharing plan.

If a trust governed by a DPSP distributes a non-qualified investment to a beneficiary, the trust is deemed to have disposed of the investment for proceeds of disposition equal to its fair market value at the time of disposition. Thus the trust would be entitled to a refund.[164]

[¶13,430] Tax Where Consideration Is Inadequate

In situations where a DPSP disposes of property at less than fair market value or where it acquires property for more than fair market value, the trust governed by the DPSP must pay a 50% tax on the difference between the consideration given or received, as the case may be, and the fair market value of the property at that time. The amount is payable by the trust governing the DPSP and is due within 90 days of the end of the year.[165]

[¶13,440] Returns and Payment of Estimated Tax

The trustees of a DPSP or a revoked DPSP must remit the tax payable within 10 days of the day on which the investment is acquired or the property is used as collateral. A trustee who fails to remit as required becomes personally liable to pay the tax but may recover from the trust any tax so paid.[166]

Every trust governed by a DPSP or a revoked DPSP must file a return on Form TD3 on or before March 31st of each year. The return must contain:

(1) an estimate of the amount of tax payable under Part X; and

(2) an estimate of the amount of any tax refund due under Part X.

See page ii for explanation of footnotes.

[164] CCH ¶25,430; Sec. 200.
[165] CCH ¶25,500; Sec. 202(1).
[166] CCH ¶25,310, ¶25,320, ¶25,360, ¶25,500; Sec. 198(2), 198(3), 198(5), 202.

The net amount of estimated tax payable must be remitted with the return; or, if the estimate under (1) and (2) indicates that the trust is eligible for a refund, an application for the refund must be made at that time.

[¶13,445] Assessment, Objections, Appeals, etc.

General provisions of Part I pertaining to returns, assessment, penalties, refunds, objections, appeals, etc. are applicable to Part X (see ¶11,603 *et seq.*). Interest for failure or delay in payment of the tax in respect of acquisitions of non-qualified investments is calculated at a prescribed rate per annum. This interest is in addition to Part I interest and is payable from the earlier of:

(a) the day on which the tax became due to the day of payment; and

(b) the expiration of the time for filing an income tax return.

Interest ceases to accrue on the refundable portion of the tax as of the date the non-qualified property is disposed of.[167]

[¶13,450] Tax in Respect of Over-Contributions to Deferred Income Plans (Part X.1)

[¶13,455] Special Taxes on Excess Contributions to Registered Retirement Savings Plan (RRSP) or Deferred Profits Sharing Plan (DPSP)

An individual who makes an excess contribution to an RRSP and a spouse's or common-law partner's RRSP must pay a penalty tax of 1% per month until the "excess" for the year is removed from the plan.[168]

In determining whether there is an excess, the individual includes all amounts contributed to the plan (other than specified transfers) and all gifts made to it, other than gifts made by the individual's spouse or common-law partner. Over-contributions of premiums in the 60-day grace period after the end of the year usually are not considered to be part of the "excess", since the individual can claim them in the year or the following year.

In order to avoid the 1% per month penalty, the excess amount may be withdrawn from the plan, but it will be included in the individual's income in the year of receipt.[169] This income can be reduced by an offsetting deduction if it is withdrawn in the year in which the excess was contributed or in the following year.[170] The withdrawal of contributions on a tax-free basis is allowed only where the taxpayer is not deliberately making excess contributions.

See page ii for explanation of footnotes.

[167] CCH ¶22,904, ¶25,500, ¶25,530, ¶25,531; Sec. 202, 202(5), 202(6); Reg. 4301.

[168] CCH ¶25,545; Sec. 204.1.

[169] CCH ¶21,323; Sec. 146(8).

[170] CCH ¶21,325; Sec. 146(8.2).

If the excess is not withdrawn in those particular years, but is instead left in the plan, then the individual will include in income this excess contribution when it is eventually withdrawn and there will be no offsetting deduction, resulting in double taxation. It is not advisable, therefore, to leave an excess contribution in an RRSP, as benefits of tax-free compounding in the plan are unlikely to offset the combination of the 1% per month penalty and the double taxation on withdrawal.

The 1% penalty tax under Part X.1 is also imposed on a trust governed by a DPSP if it accepts any contributions from any one member (see ¶13,470).

An individual subject to tax in respect of RRSP contributions or a trust governed by a DPSP which is subject to tax under Part X.1 must file a return and pay the relevant tax within 90 days after the year end.[171]

[¶13,465] Tax on Excess Contributions to Registered Retirement Savings Plan (RRSP)

Part VI imposes a monthly tax on an individual who at the end of any particular month has a "cumulative excess amount in respect of RRSPs". Generally speaking, an individual's "cumulative excess amount" at any time in a year is the amount by which all undeducted premiums paid by the individual to RRSPs exceeds the RRSP deduction room available to the individual, including carryforward and current year amounts, plus the individual's total pension adjustment reversal (PAR), plus a margin of $2,000 if the individual is not a minor. The monthly tax is 1% of such excess.[172] For a discussion of PARs, see ¶10,354.

The threshold amount for an excess contribution is $2,000 (see ¶13,466 below).[173] This means that an individual may contribute up to $2,000 in excess of his or her deductible contribution limit without incurring a penalty. In a family context, both spouses may contribute an additional $2,000, so that in total $4,000 may be sheltered without penalty. People under the age of 18 in the previous year may not make this additional contribution. Individuals who contribute to both their own RRSP and a spousal RRSP may not make an additional contribution of more than $2,000 in total.

Generally speaking, the amount of an individual's undeducted RRSP premiums at any time in a year is the amount of all premiums paid by the individual to his or her RRSP or to his or her spouse's or common-law partner's RRSPs (other than amounts rolled over under certain transfer provisions) that have not been deducted in years previous to that time, minus amounts withdrawn by the individual in the year from RRSPs or registered retirement income funds (RRIFs) and included in the individual's income for the year.[174] It should be noted that certain RRSP contributions that are

---

See page ii for explanation of footnotes.

[171] CCH ¶25,548; Sec. 204.3.
[172] CCH ¶25,545d; Sec. 204.1(2.1).
[173] CCH ¶25,546cb; Sec. 204.2(1.1).
[174] CCH ¶25,546cc; Sec. 204.2(1.2).

withdrawn as eligible amounts under the Home Buyers' Plan are excluded from the individual's undeducted RRSP premiums.

The Tax Court found that the CRA's assessments of Part VI tax on the taxpayer's RRSP excess contributions could not be vacated because of the unfair result created by the uneven application among taxpayers of the CRA's policy to tax post-doctoral grants. The tax imposed on excess RRSP contributions applied whether there was taxable income or not.[175]

[¶13,466] Group RRSP and Over-Contributions Involving Past Service Pension Adjustments (PSPAs)

The government has addressed two situations in which inadvertent overcontributions are likely to cause penalties, and provided relief to taxpayers by deferring their inclusion in computing the amount liable to penalty tax until the year after they arise.

The first situation involves taxpayers who are part of a group who receive RRSP contributions for services rendered.[176] The most common example will be employees whose employers have no pension plan but make contributions based on salary to each employee's RRSP. There need not be an actual employer/employee relationship, but the RRSP contribution in question must be a contribution on behalf of an individual of an amount to which the individual is entitled for services rendered. The RRSP must be part of a "group RRSP plan", that is, an arrangement under which at least two individuals have contributions made on their behalf directly to their RRSPs for services rendered to the contributor.[177] As well, the contributions must be mandatory. Contributions will not be eligible if the individual has a right under the arrangement to prevent the contribution at any time after entering the plan and within 12 months prior to the payment.

If qualifying RRSP contributions are paid on a taxpayer's behalf under a plan described above, the contributions are deemed to be paid in the year following the actual year of contribution for purposes of computing penalty tax.[178] The purpose of this deeming provision is to ensure that where an individual takes employment which carries mandatory RRSP contributions as remuneration, the individual is not put offside even if he or she carries into the new employment no RRSP room to shelter contributions which commence immediately. For example, someone entering the workforce for the first time and receiving mandatory contributions as part of standard remuneration would have no opening RRSP room so that, if contributions exceeded $2,000 in the year, the person would, if not for this protection, be subject to penalties.

The second concession the government makes to inadvertent over-contributions involves past service pension adjustments (PSPAs). PSPAs will

---

See page ii for explanation of footnotes.

[175] Lans, 2011 DTC 1102.
[176] CCH ¶25,546ce; Sec. 204.2(1.31).
[177] CCH ¶25,546cf; Sec. 204.2(1.32).
[178] CCH ¶25,546cd; Sec. 204.2(1.3).

¶13,466

not be taken into account for penalty tax purposes until the year following the year they are reported.[179]

[¶13,470] Tax on Excess Contributions to Deferred Profit Sharing Plans (DPSPs)

A monthly tax is imposed on a trust governed by a DPSP if, at the end of any particular month, the trust has an excess amount.[180] The tax is calculated as 1% of this excess amount at the month end.

The "excess amount" of a trust governed by a DPSP at any time is the sum of:[181]

(a) all contributions made by a beneficiary other than transfers between plans; and

(b) gifts made to the trust; contributions from an employer would apparently not be regarded as gifts since they would be made pursuant to the legal obligation assumed by the employer when the plan was established.

No employee contributions to DPSPs are allowed (other than direct transfers from other plans), the penalty being, of course, the Part X.1 tax, as well as possible revocation of the plan.

[¶13,471] Waiver of Tax

The Minister may waive any Part X.1 tax payable for a month where the taxpayer establishes to the Minister's satisfaction that the excessive contributions to his or his spouse's or common-law partner's RRSP arose as a result of reasonable error or that reasonable steps are being taken to eliminate the excess.[182]

[¶13,472] Administrative Provisions Respecting Tax under Part X.1

An individual who is liable to pay tax in respect of excess contributions to registered retirement savings plans (RRSPs) and a trust governed by a deferred profit sharing plan (DPSP) which is liable for tax on the excess amount must file a return in prescribed form within 90 days after the end of each year.[183] The tax payable for each month of the year is to be computed and paid at that time. The various administrative and assessing provisions of Part I apply to Part X.1 returns.

See page ii for explanation of footnotes.

[179] CCH ¶25,546cb; Sec. 204.2(1.1).   [182] CCH ¶25,546b; Sec. 204.1(4).
[180] CCH ¶25,546; Sec. 204.1(3).
[181] CCH ¶25,547c; Sec. 204.2(4).   [183] CCH ¶25,548; Sec. 204.3(1).

[¶13,475] Tax in Respect of Registered Investments (Part X.2)

[¶13,476] Special Tax When Corporation or Trust Which Is Registered Investment Does Not Maintain Qualified Investments

If a trust governed by an RRSP, RRIF, DPSP, or an RESP acquires an investment which is not a "qualified investment", the beneficiary of the trust and/or the trust itself may incur an income tax liability. See ¶10,375, ¶10,426, and ¶13,395, respectively.

The regulations[184] provide that an interest in a trust or the shares of a corporation which has been accepted for registration as a registered investment will be a qualified investment for such a trust. To be registered as a registered investment,[185] the trust or corporation must hold investments which substantially meet the qualified investment requirements at the time the registration is obtained. If at a later time the trust or corporation which is a registered investment holds property which it is not permitted to hold or holds certain types of property in excess of the permitted amounts of such property, the trust or corporation which is a registered investment will be subject to a special tax.[186] This tax is imposed at the rate of 1% per month of the fair market value at the time of its acquisition of each such property and 1% of the amount by which the cost of certain property exceeds the permitted holdings of such property.[187]

[¶13,480] Labour-Sponsored Venture Capital Corporations (LSVCCs) (Part X.3)

[¶13,485] Labour-Sponsored Venture Capital Funds

Labour-Sponsored Venture Capital Funds are venture capital funds established and registered under specific federal or provincial legislation and managed by labour unions or employee groups.

Where an investor in such a fund makes an irrevocable commitment within 60 days of year end to acquire LSVCC shares, the investor is entitled to a federal tax credit. The credit is limited to 15% of the net cost of shares, up to a maximum credit of $750, reached on a $5,000 annual investment.

If shares are redeemed within eight years, the holder is liable to pay the maximum credit which would have been available on their original acquisition.

See page ii for explanation of footnotes.

[184] CCH ¶25,540; Reg. 4900.

[185] CCH ¶25,549, ¶25,549b; Sec. 204.4; Reg. 4901.

[186] CCH ¶25,549–25,549u; Sec. 204.4–204.7.

[187] CCH ¶25,549m, ¶25,549n; Sec. 204.6(2), 204.6(3).

To be registered under Part X.3, an LSVCC must file an application in prescribed form and be incorporated by an eligible labour body whose articles of corporation comply with the following:[188]

(1) A registered LSVCC is restricted to assisting the development of qualifying small and medium-size businesses, and creating, maintaining, and protecting jobs.

(2) The authorized capital of a registered LSVCC is restricted to two classes of shares, subject to the Minister of Finance's approval of additional classes. They are Class A shares, which are essentially common shares with restricted transfer/redemption rights, and Class B shares, which are non-dividend paying and non-participating on liquidation (beyond the amount paid to the LSVCC for the share). The Class A shares may only be issued to individuals (other than trusts), RRSP trusts, and, beginning in 2009, TFSA trusts. These are the shares which entitle the original purchaser or the RRSP or TFSA contributor to a tax credit. The Class B shares can only be issued and held by eligible labour bodies, including labour bodies other than the body which caused the LSVCC to be incorporated. The Class A shares are redeemable and transferable by the original purchaser only in certain limited circumstances.

(3) At least 50% of the directors of a registered LSVCC must be appointed by the eligible labour bodies that hold the Class B shares.

(4) Shareholders, directors, or corporate officers may only be provided with fees or remuneration if the payment has first been approved by a director's resolution.

(5) The holder must hold the shares for at least eight years (for shares acquired before March 6, 1996, the minimum holding period is generally five years, reduced to two years if the holder reached age 65, retired, or became a non-resident).

(6) Investment restrictions with regard to eligible business entities must be complied with.[189]

[¶13,486] Investment Requirements for Federally or Provincially Registered LSVCCs

Various taxes and penalties are imposed under Part X.3 when a federally or provincially registered LSVCC fails to meet the investment requirements imposed by federal or provincial laws, as the case may be.

A 20% one-time tax is levied on a federally registered LSVCC where, at any time in its "start-up period" (i.e, two years), it fails to invest at least 80% of the consideration received by it from the sale of Class A shares in eligible investments and reserves.[190] The tax is calculated as 20% of the deficiency, which is calculated as 80% of the consideration received for Class A shares

---

[188] CCH ¶25,550c, ¶25,551; Sec. 204.8(1) "eligible labour body", 204.81(1).

[189] CCH ¶25,551; Sec. 204.81(1)(c).

[190] CCH ¶25,550l; Sec. 204.8(1) "start-up period".

(less any return of capital) less the cost of eligible investments and reserves.[191]

A tax is also levied on a federally registered LSVCC where, at any time after its start-up period, meaning two years, 60% of the lesser of (a) its shareholders' equity at the end of the preceding taxation year, and (b) its shareholders' equity at the end of the particular taxation year, exceeds the aggregate of (y) the total cost of its eligible investments at that time, and (z) 60% of any refunded taxes or penalties paid by the corporation that did not result in a reduction in shareholders' equity at the end of any preceding taxation year. The excess is referred to as the corporation's "investment shortfall".[192] If the total cost invested in eligible investments at any time in the month is less than the average of the total cost of eligible investments held at the beginning of the particular year and at the end of the year, the average is used in determining the investment shortfall. To encourage LSVCCs to focus more on their investments in small businesses, investments in businesses that have $10 million or less in assets are counted $1^{1}/_{2}$ times towards the federal business investment requirement. As an incentive to invest in very small businesses, every $1 invested in an eligible business with no more than $2.5 million in assets counts as $2 with respect to the LSVCC's federal business investment requirement.

For the purposes of computing a corporation's investment shortfall, its shareholder's equity is calculated without taking into account unrealized gains or losses on eligible investments. The LSVCC's shareholders' equity at the end of a year cannot be reduced by taking into account redemptions of its Class A shares that are expected to occur after the end of the year (with a transitional rule for years ending in 1999 through 2002 where 20%, 40%, 60%, and 80%, respectively, of the expected redemptions occurring after the year are not to be taken into account). This rule does not apply to redemptions made within 60 days after the end of the year where either Part XII.5 tax became payable as a consequence of the redemption or Part XII.5 tax would not have become payable if the redemption had occurred at the end of the year.[193] If there is an investment shortfall at any time in the month, the LSVCC is required to pay a tax in respect of the month equal to the greatest such shortfall in the month, multiplied by $1/_{60}$ of the prescribed rate of interest in effect for the month.[194]

If share attributes of the capital stock of an LSVCC (including a revoked LSVCC) are changed in a manner which is inconsistent with the registration requirements, such a reorganization will have the following tax impact on the LSVCC and its shareholders:

- the subsequent acquisition of any share of the capital stock of the LSVCC will not give rise to any entitlement to the LSVCC tax credit;

---

[191] CCH ¶25,552; Sec. 204.82(1).

[192] CCH ¶25,553a; Sec. 204.82(2.1).

[193] CCH ¶25,553b; Sec. 204.82(2.2).

[194] CCH ¶25,553; Sec. 204.82(2).

- the LSVCC will become subject to a new penalty that will approximate a recovery of the federal LSVCC tax credit for outstanding Class shares;

- the LSVCC's subsequent monthly deficiency will be nil, i.e., there will no longer be penalties levied for the LSVCC failing to meet the federal business requirements; and

- LSVCC investors will not be liable for recovery of the LSVCC tax credit under Part XII.5 (see ¶13,655) on subsequent dispositions of shares issued by the LSVCC.

Where a federally registered LSVCC pays the monthly shortfall tax for 12 consecutive months, an additional tax is imposed[195] as well as a penalty of an amount equivalent to the tax (representing a recovery of federal LSVCC tax credits).[196]

Part X.3 tax is imposed on LSVCCs that are not federally registered, equal to the amount of tax payable to a provincial government as a consequence of failure to acquire sufficient properties (i.e., small business properties) of a character described by provincial law.[197] This tax will not apply to any amount payable under or as a consequence of a prescribed provision of the provincial law. Section 25.1 of the Ontario *Community Small Business Investment Funds Act* is prescribed for this purpose.[198]

The CRA must refund 100% of the tax payable by a federally registered LSVCC and 80% of the penalty payable by it where, throughout any subsequent 12-month period, it has maintained the required level of eligible investments.[199] The CRA will also refund the Part X.3 tax levied on provincially registered LSVCCs to the extent that corresponding amounts have been refunded by the provincial government.[200]

[¶13,487] Revocation of a Federally Registered LSVCC

The Part X.3 registration of an LSVCC may be revoked if:

(1) the corporation fails to comply with its articles of corporation;

(2) the corporation fails to file timely information returns;

(3) the corporation's financial statements do not conform to GAAP;

(4) the corporation fails to have its shares independently valued as at year end, within six months of its year end;

(5) the corporation has not paid the Part X.3 tax or penalties or has had additional tax payable (see ¶13,489) for three or more years;

See page ii for explanation of footnotes.

[195] CCH ¶25,554; Sec. 204.82(3).
[196] CCH ¶25,555; Sec. 204.82(4).
[197] CCH ¶25,555a; Sec. 204.82(5).

[198] [Reg. 6707.
[199] CCH ¶25,556; Sec. 204.83(1).
[200] CCH ¶25,556a; Sec. 204.83(2).

(6) the corporation fails to maintain eligible reserves equal to the cost amount (i.e., 25% of the debt obligation subject to the guarantee) of any guarantee;

(7) an unreasonably large fee or commission in respect of the sale of its shares was paid; or

(8) the 60% investment requirement in eligible business entities is not met in 18 or more months in any 36-month period.[201]

An LSVCC's registration may be revoked if it fails to comply with the above rules. Revocation does not, by itself, affect a former LSVCC's obligations to invest in eligible businesses, nor does it provide any relief for investors from recovery of the LSVCC credit if they redeem their shares before the minimum holding period has passed.

LSVCCs may also voluntarily deregister and, as a consequence, be treated for tax purposes in the same manner as revoked corporations.[202] An LSVCC may voluntarily deregister by providing the Minister with a certified copy of a director's resolution indicating the LSVCC is seeking to have its LSVCC registration withdrawn.

[¶13,488] Penalty Tax Where Venture Capital Business Discontinued

A penalty tax is also levied on federally registered LSVCCs or revoked corporations that have discontinued their venture capital business.[203] The formula for determining this tax is based on a percentage of the consideration received by the LSVCC for Class A shares issued and the number of years that the Class A shares were outstanding. Generally speaking, a corporation discontinues its venture capital business at the time it ceases to comply with the registration requirements at ¶13,485, at the time it begins to wind up, immediately before its amalgamation or merger with another, and at the time it becomes a revoked corporation (see ¶13,487).[204] The effect of these provisions is to recover a portion of the federal tax credits provided to shareholders of the LSVCC.

The penalty taxes triggered by investment shortfalls or the redemption of Class A shares (see ¶13,486) do not apply where the LSVCC has discontinued its venture capital business, thus avoiding double tax in such circumstances.

Finally, Class A shares of an LSVCC that has discontinued its venture capital business will not be "approved shares" for the purposes of a holder claiming federal tax credits in respect of the acquisition of such shares (see ¶8290).

See page ii for explanation of footnotes.

[201] CCH ¶25,551e; Sec. 204.81(6).

[202] CCH ¶25,551ga–25,551gb; Sec. 204.81(8.1)–(8.2).

[203] CCH ¶25,557c; Sec. 204.841.

[204] CCH ¶25,550m; Sec. 204.8(2).

[¶13,489] Returns and Payment of Tax

Every federally registered LSVCC and every revoked corporation must file a return under Part X.3 and must estimate the amount of tax and penalties payable, if any. The tax and penalty is payable within 90 days after the end of the taxation year in which the liability arose.[205] A Part X.3 return must also be filed for each taxation year in which Part X.3 tax becomes payable by a provincially registered LSVCC.[206] A provincially registered LSVCC must pay this new tax within 90 days after the end of the taxation year in which its tax liability arose.

Various administrative provisions of Part I are incorporated into the structure of Part X.3 with such modifications as are necessary.[207]

[¶13,490] Tax in Respect of Overpayments to Registered Education Savings Plans (RESPs) (Part X.4)

[¶13,491] Tax Payable by Subscribers

Part X.4 imposes a monthly tax on subscribers in respect of over-contributions made to RESPs. This tax is equal to 1% of the amount by which the total of the "subscriber's gross cumulative excess" at the end of the month in respect of a particular beneficiary exceeds the total of such an excess that has been withdrawn from the RESP before the end of the month.[208] The subscriber's gross cumulative excess is the total of the "subscriber's share of the excess amount" in respect of the beneficiary, meaning his or her *pro rata* share of the excess amount in respect of the beneficiary.[209] The *pro rata* share is based on the proportion that the contributions made to all RESPs by the subscriber in respect of the particular beneficiary is of all contributions made to RESPs in respect of the beneficiary.

Until 2007, an excess amount for a year, at any time, in respect of an individual, is the amount by which the total of all payments made in the year to an RESP exceeds the lesser of:

(a) the RESP annual limit for the year, which is $4,000 for 1997 through 2006, $2,000 for 1996, and $1,500 for 1990 through 1995; and

(b) the amount, if any, by which $42,000 ($31,500 for 1990 through 1995) exceeds the total of all payments made to RESPs in respect of a beneficiary for all preceding years.

The limit in paragraph (a) above effectively meant that no more than $4,000 could be contributed to an RESP per year per beneficiary. The limit in

---

See page ii for explanation of footnotes.

[205] CCH ¶25,559; Sec. 204.86(1).

[206] CCH ¶25,559; Sec. 204.86(2).

[207] CCH ¶25,560; Sec. 204.87.

[208] CCH ¶25,567; Sec. 204.91(1).

[209] CCH ¶25,563aa, ¶25,563ab; Sec. 204.9(1) "subscriber's gross cumulative excess", 204.9(1) "subscriber's share of the excess amount".

paragraph (b) meant that a contribution in any one year could not push total lifetime contributions over the $42,000 lifetime limit per beneficiary ($31,500 for 1990 through 1995).

Beginning in 2007, the excess amount in respect of a beneficiary effectively means the amount by which the total of all contributions made in the year to an RESP in respect of the beneficiary, plus contributions made before the year, exceeds the lifetime limit of $50,000.[210] In other words, after 2006, there is no longer an annual contribution limit, although there remains a lifetime contribution limit per beneficiary, which has been increased from $42,000 to $50,000. Contributions that go over the $50,000 lifetime limit are subject to the Part X.4 tax.

Where the named beneficiary under a plan is changed, the contributions for the former beneficiary are considered to have been made for the new beneficiary. This rule prevents the multiplication of contribution limits which could otherwise occur by having a number of plans for different named beneficiaries and changing the beneficiary designation just prior to terminating the plans.[211] However, there is an exception to the rule where the new beneficiary is under 21 years of age and is a sibling of the former beneficiary. In such a case, the contributions previously made in respect of the former beneficiary are not counted in determining the excess amount in regard to the new beneficiary. Additionally, this exception will apply where the beneficiaries are under 21 years old and connected to the subscriber by a blood relationship or adoption.

If property is transferred between RESPs, the transfer of property will not itself be considered a payment for purposes of determining whether there is an excess amount in the RESP at the end of a month.[212] However, prior contributions made to the transferor plan are deemed to have been made in respect of the beneficiary under the transferee plan, so that those contributions are counted in determining the excess amount in respect of the beneficiary. There are two exceptions to this rule. It does not apply where:

(1) there is a common beneficiary under the transferor and the transferee plan;

(2) a beneficiary under the transferor plan has a brother or sister who is a beneficiary under the transferee plan; and

(a) the transferee plan allows more than one beneficiary under the plan at any one time, or

(b) in any other case, the beneficiary under the transferee plan had not attained 21 years of age when the plan was opened.

---

[210] CCH ¶25,563, ¶25,563a; Sec. 204.9(1) "excess amount", 204.9(1) "RESP lifetime limit".

[211] CCH ¶25,566; Sec. 204.9(4).

[212] CCH ¶25,566a; Sec. 204.9(5).

In any other case, transfers can result in an excess contribution. Before 2011, the exception in (2) applies when a beneficiary under the transferor plan has a brother or sister (under 21 years of age before the transfer is made) who is a beneficiary under the transferee plan.

The CRA provides the following example in a Q&A document posted on its website and pertains to this particular 2011 Budget measure:

Example:

RESPs were opened for Monique, Suzie, John, and Randy, who are siblings:

Name	Current Age	Age When the RESP Was Opened
Monique	15	1
Suzie	18	3
John	22	5
Randy	23	21

Before 2011, property can only be transferred between Monique's and Suzie's RESPs and from the RESPs of John and Randy to their sisters without adverse consequences as both John and Randy are over two years of age.

For transfers after 2010, property can also be transferred between John's and his sisters' RESPs with no adverse consequences, as these RESPs were established when the beneficiaries were less than 21 years of age. Since Randy's RESP was established after he turned 21 years of age, the second permitted transfer in (2) above does not apply to transfers to his RESP; however, transfers from his RESP to his brother's and sisters' RESPs can be made without adverse consequences, because in each case, the RESP of the receiving beneficiary was established before they turned 21 years of age.

A return estimating the Part X.4 tax payable must be filed within 90 days after the end of the year. The tax is due upon filing of the return.[213] The administrative provisions of Part I are applicable to Part X.4 with such modifications as are necessary.[214]

[¶13,492] Special Rules

The CRA is allowed to waive Part X.4 tax where it is just and equitable to do so, having regard to all the circumstances, including, for instance, whether the tax arose as a consequence of reasonable error.[215]

A mechanism also ensures that a subscriber's spouse or common-law partner or former spouse or common-law partner is liable for Part X.4 tax in the event that he or she acquired the subscriber's right under the RESP

See page ii for explanation of footnotes.

[213] CCH ¶25,567d; Sec. 204.92.   [215] CCH ¶25,567a; Sec. 204.91(2).
[214] CCH ¶25,567e; Sec. 204.93.

¶13,492

because of a division of property on the breakdown of their marriage or common-law partnership. Under this mechanism, for the purpose of determining Part X.4 tax for months that are after the acquisition of such rights, all previous contributions made by the former subscriber are deemed to have been made by the subscriber's spouse or common-law partner or former spouse or common-law partner. Therefore, the former subscriber will no longer be liable for the penalty tax that arises after that time.[216]

Finally, for the purpose of determining Part X.4 tax, where a subscriber has died, the subscriber's estate is deemed to be the same person as, and a continuation of, the subscriber for each month after death.[217] This means that upon a subscriber's death, the estate will remain subject to the penalty tax provisions; in effect, it will step into the shoes of the subscriber.

[¶13,493] Tax on Income Payments from Registered Education Savings Plans (RESPs) (Part X.5)

[¶13,494] Application of Tax

An RESP may make a distribution of accumulated income to a subscriber if all intended beneficiaries are not pursuing higher education by age 21, and the plan has been running for at least 10 years. Subject to a lifetime limit of $50,000, the subscriber is allowed to transfer RESP income to an RRSP, without penalty, if he or she is able to claim an RRSP deduction for the year of the transfer equal to at least the amount of the transferred RESP income. To the extent that RESP income is not fully offset by the subscriber's RRSP deduction, a special 20% tax is imposed in addition to regular taxes for the receipt of the RESP income.[218] The 20% surtax applies to "accumulated income payments" to be included in the income of the plan subscriber, for essentially any distribution that is not: (i) a payment to a beneficiary to assist in post-secondary education, (ii) a refund of contribution made to the plan, (iii) a payment to a designated institution, or (iv) a transfer to another plan.[219]

Example:

> Mr. Smith contributed $42,000 to an RESP for his children. None of the children in fact undertook any post-secondary education in the 25 years before the plan was to be wound-up. By then its value was $182,000, which was returned to Mr. Smith in year X. In year X, Mr. Smith had RRSP contribution room of $13,500 based on prior-year income and $36,500 based on carryforwards of unused contribution room. He in fact contributed $50,000 to an RRSP for himself or his spouse in year X.

See page ii for explanation of footnotes.

[216] CCH ¶25,567b; Sec. 204.91(3).

[217] CCH ¶25,567c; Sec. 204.91(4).

[218] CCH ¶25,572; Sec. 204.94(2).

[219] CCH ¶21,383a, ¶25,571; Sec. 146.1(1) "accumulated income payment", 204.94(1).

¶13,494

Mr. Smith will have to include in his income $140,000 ($182,000 - $42,000). This will be offset by the $50,000 RRSP contribution, (which, of course, cannot offset tax from ordinary income in year X).

Mr. Smith will also be subject to the 20% special tax on $140,000, but the $140,000 will be offset by the lesser of:

(a) the lesser of the income inclusion for RESPs and his total RRSP contributions in the year; and

(b) $50,000 minus all amounts previously claimed as reduction of RESP special tax in prior years.

Mr. Smith's special tax would therefore be equal to 20% of ($140,000 minus the lesser of $50,000 and $50,000), or 20% of $90,000.

If withdrawals commence before the 25th year of the plan and Mr. Smith is not usually in the top marginal rate bracket, he may be able to minimize ordinary tax by withdrawing only enough to use available RRSP room, and making future withdrawals as new room becomes available. He cannot, however, reduce the special 20% tax once the $50,000 lifetime limit is reached.

It should be noted that the return of RESP income creates no additional RRSP contribution room. Essentially, it provides cash to fund any RRSP contribution, to the extent of any *otherwise* unused contribution room. RRSP contributions in the year of taxable RESP receipts, whether made from the RESP income or otherwise, can reduce the special surtax on such income to the extent of a lifetime aggregate of $50,000.

A person liable for Part X.5 tax is required to file a return on or before the person's tax return filing-due date for the year.[220] Unpaid Part X.5 tax for the year must be remitted to the CRA by that date. Administrative rules in Part I apply for the purposes of Part X.5.[221]

[¶13,496] Former Foreign Property Tax on Trusts Governed by Deferred Income Plans (Repealed Part XI)

[¶13,497] Foreign Property Limit Eliminated

The Part XI penalty tax on foreign property was eliminated for months ending after 2004. Prior to 2005, the former Part XI tax applied to foreign property in excess of 30% held by a trust governed by a registered retirement savings plan (RRSP), a deferred profit sharing plan (DPSP), a registered retirement income fund (RRIF), a registered pension plan (subject to certain exceptions), a corporation established in connection with a registered pension fund or plan, and a "master trust" that makes an election. These deferred income plans are now permitted to invest in any kind of qualified investment without regard to whether it is foreign property. The permit-

---

See page ii for explanation of footnotes.

[220] CCH ¶25,573; Sec. 204.94(3).   [221] CCH ¶25,574; Sec. 204.94(4).

¶13,496

ted/qualified investment requirements applicable to these plans (including penalties) remain in force (see Part XI.1).

[¶13,500] Taxes in Respect of RRIFs, RRSPs, and TFSAs (Part XI.01)

[¶13,510] Overview

The concept of the tax-free savings account (TFSA) was introduced in the 2008 federal Budget, effective beginning in 2009. The TFSA allows individuals to earn investment income, including interest, dividends, and capital gains, on a tax-free basis. Although contributions to the TFSA are not deductible, the income earned in the TFSA is not subject to Part 1 tax either while in the account or generally when distributed to the holder of the account. However, the TFSA may be subject to Part I tax if it acquires a "non-qualified investment" or carries on a business. See ¶10,406.

The regular annual contribution limit for a TFSA (TFSA dollar limit) began at $5,000 for 2009, and will be increased annually to inflation and rounded to the nearest $500. Unused TFSA room can be carried forward indefinitely. Furthermore, distributions from the account add to the TFSA contribution room in the year after the distribution.

Part XI.01 of the Act imposes anti-avoidance taxes in respect of TFSAs. The taxes apply where an individual over-contributes to a TFSA and therefore has an "excess TFSA amount" (see ¶13,513), a non-resident contributes to a TFSA (see ¶13,514), a TFSA acquires a "non-qualified investment" or "prohibited investment" (see ¶13,515), or a TFSA extends an "advantage" on the holder of the TFSA or a person not dealing at arm's length with the holder (see ¶13,516).

As a result of changes announced in the 2011 federal Budget, parts of the Part XI.01 penalty tax have been extended to annuitants of registered retirement savings plans (RRSPs) and registered retirement income funds (RRIFs) that acquire a prohibited investment or non-qualified investment, or where an existing property of the plan or fund becomes a prohibited or non-qualified investment. Additionally, the Part XI.01 tax on advantages is extended to annuitants of RRSPs and RRIFs. These amendments generally apply to transactions occurring, income earned, capital gains accruing, and investments acquired after March 22, 2011. See ¶13,518.

[¶13,513] Tax Payable on TFSA Excess Contributions

The concept of the tax-free savings account (TFSA) was introduced in the 2008 federal Budget, effective beginning in 2009. The TFSA allows Canadian resident individuals to earn investment income, including interest, dividends, and capital gains, on a tax-free basis. Contributions to the TFSA are not deductible, but the income in the account is not subject to Part I tax, either while in the account or upon withdrawal. The annual contribution limit for a TFSA begins at $5,000 for 2009, and will be increased annually with inflation. Unused TFSA room can be carried forward indefinitely. Withdrawals from the account will free up more TFSA room. New Part XI.01 imposes a special tax on excess TFSA contributions. If, at any time in a calendar month, an individual has an excess TFSA amount, Part XI.01 imposes a tax on the individual, in respect of that month, equal to 1% of the individual's highest "excess TFSA amount" in that month.[222]

An individual's excess TFSA amount, at a particular time in a particular calendar year, is defined as the total of all TFSA contributions made by the individual in the year and at or before the particular time, other than exempt contributions and contributions made by way of a qualifying transfer.[223] For this purpose, an exempt contribution is, generally speaking, a contribution made in connection with a payment received by the individual, as a consequence of the death of the individual's spouse or common-law partner, from an arrangement that ceased to be a TFSA because of that death. An amount is contributed to a TFSA by way of a qualifying transfer if the amount is transferred from another TFSA of the individual or is transferred in connection with a breakdown of the individual's marriage or common-law partnership.[224] From this total of all TFSA contributions made by the individual in the year and at or before the particular time are deducted the following amounts:

- the amount of contribution room that was available to the individual for the year *minus* the TFSA contributions made by the individual in the year (referred to as the individual's "unused TFSA contribution room");

- the total amount of distributions (meaning withdrawals) made under TFSAs of the individual in the year preceding the particular year;

- the TFSA dollar limit for the particular year ($5,000 in 2009, and to be indexed for inflation in future years); and

- the total amount of distributions (meaning withdrawals) made in the year and at or before the time under TFSAs of the individual — other than withdrawals that exceed the excess TFSA amount that would otherwise be determined at that time.

It should be noted that excess contributions are not determined separately for each TFSA, but rather cumulatively for all of the TFSAs to which the individual has contributed. The Minister may waive all or part of any tax on excess TFSA contributions if the Minister is satisfied that the excess arose because of reasonable error and the individual arranges, without delay, for the excess to be withdrawn.[225]

See page ii for explanation of footnotes.

[222] CCH ¶25,687; Sec. 207.02.

[223] CCH ¶25,673; Sec. 207.01(1) "excess TFSA amount".

[224] CCH ¶25,681; Sec. 207.01(2).

[225] CCH ¶25,711; Sec. 207.06(1).

A joint statement from Finance Canada and the CRA, dated June 25, 2010, announced that the penalty tax on excess contributions to TFSAs may be waived for 2009 (the first year of the program) where a genuine misunderstanding of the TFSA contribution rules occurred. For instance, individuals who used their TFSA as a regular banking account in 2009, making deposits and withdrawals on a frequent basis, or who have transferred funds between TFSAs at different institutions, but whose net contributions never exceeded the 2009 limit of $5,000, may not be required to pay the tax on excess contributions for this year.

According to this statement, 70,000 Canadians exposed to penalty tax on TFSA excess contributions in 2009 received a letter from the CRA asking them to provide further information or explanations in respect of their excess contributions before June 30, 2010 (deadline extended to August 3, 2010). If no additional information or explanation is provided by the August 3 deadline, the CRA will issue a notice of assessment. Only at that time should taxpayers use the request for relief form or a formal notice of objection.

[¶13,514] Tax Payable on Non-Resident Contributions

Part XI.01 imposes a special tax on an individual who makes a TFSA contribution while non-resident. The tax is equal to 1% of the contribution. It is imposed on a monthly basis until such time as the total of all distributions (i.e., withdrawals) subsequently made under TFSAs of the individual, and designated by the individual in connection with the contribution, is at least equal to the amount of the contribution or, if earlier, the individual becomes resident in Canada. This tax applies regardless of whether the individual has TFSA contribution room.[226] The Minister may waive all or part of any tax payable on a non-resident contribution if the Minister is satisfied that the liability for such tax arose because of reasonable error and the individual arranges, without delay, for an amount equivalent to the non-resident contribution to be withdrawn.[227]

[¶13,515] Tax Payable on Prohibited or Non-Qualified Investments

Part XI.01 imposes a tax on the holder of a TFSA when a TFSA trust acquires a non-qualified investment or prohibited investment, or when property held by a TFSA trust becomes a non-qualified investment or prohibited investment.[228] The tax is equal to 50% of the fair market value of the property, with the fair market value to be determined at the time it was acquired or became a non-qualified investment or prohibited investment, as the case may be.[229] The holder is entitled to a refund of any tax payable on prohibited or non-qualified investments if the TFSA trust disposes of the property before the end of the calendar year following the calendar year in

---

See page ii for explanation of footnotes.

[226] CCH ¶25,689; Sec. 207.03.
[227] CCH ¶25,711; Sec. 207.06(1).
[228] CCH ¶25,691; Sec. 207.04(1).
[229] CCH ¶25,692; Sec. 207.04(2).

which the tax arose (or at such later time as permitted by the Minister of National Revenue). However, no refund is available if it is reasonable to expect that the holder knew or ought to have known at the time the property was acquired by the TFSA trust that the property was, or would become, a non-qualified investment or prohibited investment.[230] The list of investments that a TFSA trust may hold, without any Part XI.01 adverse tax consequence, is similar to the list of investments that qualify for RRSP trusts.[231] For more details, see ¶10,378. Also added to that list are the following prescribed investments that are not prohibited investments for the trust:

- a share of the capital stock of a special small business corporation;

- a share of the capital stock of prescribed venture capital corporations; and

- a qualifying share in respect of a specified cooperative corporation and the TFSA.[232]

A "prohibited investment" is the other type of property in respect of which tax is determined under Part XI.01. Specifically, a TFSA is prohibited from holding investment in any entities with which the account holder does not deal at arm's length, including an entity of which the account holder is a "specified shareholder" or in which the account holder has a "significant interest".[233] Generally, a person is a specified shareholder of a corporation if the person, together with related parties, owns or is deemed to own 10% or more of the shares of any class of the capital stock of the corporation.[234] In the case of a partnership or trust, an individual is considered to have a significant interest if the individual, together with non-arm's length parties, holds interests in the partnership or trust that have a fair market value equal to 10% or more of the fair market value of all the interests in the partnership or trust.[235]

Prior to October 17, 2009, Part XI.01 imposed an additional tax on a TFSA holder in respect of any income earned on prohibited investments and capital gains realized on the disposition of such investments. The tax was imposed in each year that the TFSA held a prohibited investment, and was equal to 150% of the amount of Part I tax that would be payable by the TFSA trust if it had no income or losses other than from its prohibited investments and no capital gains or capital losses other than from the disposition of its prohibited investments. After October 16, 2009, income (including a capital gain) that is reasonably attributable to a prohibited investment in a TFSA is considered an "advantage" and therefore subject to the penalty tax, described below at ¶13,516.

See page ii for explanation of footnotes.

[230] CCH ¶25,694; Sec. 207.04(4).

[231] CCH ¶25,676; Sec. 207.01(1) "qualified investment".

[232] Reg. 4900(14).

[233] CCH ¶25,675; Sec. 207.01(1) "prohibited investment".

[234] CCH ¶28,273; Sec. 248(1) "specified shareholder".

[235] CCH ¶25,683; Sec. 207.01(4).

¶13,515

The Minister may waive all or part of any tax imposed in respect of non-qualified TFSA investments where it is just and equitable to do so, having regard for all factors (including whether the tax arose because of a reasonable error and the extent to which the same transaction also gave rise to tax under another provision of Part XI.01).[236]

[¶13,516] Tax Payable in Respect of Advantage

Part XI.01 imposes a penalty tax in a calendar year if a TFSA extends an "advantage" (as defined below) on the holder or a person not dealing at arm's length with the holder.[237] The tax equals the fair market value of the benefit, or, in the case of a loan or indebtedness, the amount of the loan or indebtedness.[238] In other words, the tax is 100% of the advantage. The holder of the TFSA is liable to pay the tax, although if the advantage is extended by the issuer of the TFSA or a person not at arm's length with the issuer, it is the issuer, and not the holder, that is liable to pay the tax.[239]

An "advantage" in relation to a TFSA is any supplementary benefit, loan, or indebtedness that is, in any way, dependent on the existence of the TFSA.[240] It also includes a prescribed benefit. Exceptions are provided for administrative or investment services provided in connection with a TFSA and for loans and debt that are on arm's length terms. An advantage could include, for example, trips, merchandise, interest-free loans, and TFSA investments that do not reflect commercial terms. It is intended that prescribed benefits include benefits derived from transactions designed to artificially shift taxable income away from the holder and into the shelter of a TFSA or to circumvent the TFSA contribution limits.

Effective after October 16, 2009, the definition of "advantage" is expanded so as to include any benefit that is an increase in the fair market value of the property of the TFSA that may reasonably be attributed to a "swap transaction", or to "specified non-qualified investment income" that has not been distributed under the TFSA within 90 days of receipt by the holder of the TFSA of a notice issued by the Minister.

A "swap transaction" generally referred to a transfer of property (other than cash) between accounts (for example, an RRSP) and another registered account) that are generally not treated as a withdrawal and recontribution, but instead as a straightforward purchase and sale.[241] As to the expression "specified non-qualified investment income", it basically means second and subsequent generation income earned on non-qualified investment income or on income from a business carried on by a TFSA.[242]

---

[236] CCH ¶25,712; Sec. 207.06(2).

[237] CCH ¶25,701; Sec. 207.05(1).

[238] CCH ¶25,702; Sec. 207.05(2).

[239] CCH ¶25,703; Sec. 207.05(3).

[240] CCH ¶25,671; Sec. 207.01(1) "advantage".

[241] CCH ¶ 25,678c; Sec. 207.01(1) "swap transaction".

[242] CCH ¶25,678b; Sec. 207.01(1) "specified non-qualified investment income".

Applicable after October 16, 2009, the CRA may notify the holder of the TFSA to remove specified non-qualified investment income from the TFSA within 90 days of the notice.[243] If it is not removed within 90 days of receipt of the notice, it will be considered an "advantage" in respect of the TFSA and subject to the tax on advantages. If it is removed from the TFSA, it is included in the holder's Part 1 income.[244]

Also effective after October 16, 2009, the definition of "advantage" is amended to include a benefit that is income (including a capital gain) that is reasonably attributable, directly or indirectly, to a "deliberate overcontribution", or income from a "prohibited investment" (see definition at ¶13,515). A "deliberate overcontribution" of an individual means a contribution made by the individual that results in, or increases, an excess TFSA amount, unless it is reasonable to conclude that the individual did not know (nor ought to have known) that the contribution could result in liability for a penalty, tax, or similar adverse tax consequences.

The CRA may waive all or part of any tax imposed on supplementary advantages extended in connection with a TFSA where it is just and equitable to do so, having regard for all factors (including whether the tax arose because of a reasonable error and the extent to which the same transaction also gave rise to tax under another provision of Part XI.01).[245] However, effective after October 16, 2009, the CRA shall not waive or cancel the penalty tax imposed on supplementary advantages extended by a TFSA tax unless one or more distributions are made without delay under a TFSA of which the individual is the holder, the total amount of which is not less than the amount of the tax liability that is waived or cancelled.[246] The distributions are taxed to the holder as Part 1 income.[247]

Applicable after October 16, 2009, where a contribution to a TFSA results in the tax on advantages and either the tax on excess TFSA amounts (see ¶13,513) or the tax on non-resident contributions (see ¶13,514), the tax on advantages tax is reduced by the tax payable on excess TFSA amounts or on advantages, as the case may be.

[¶13,517] Return and Payment of Tax

A person liable for Part XI.01 tax for all or part of a calendar year must file a return for the year, and pay any tax owing (net of the person's allowable refund for the year) within 90 days after the end of the year.[248] The "allowable refund" of a person for a calendar year is the total amount refundable to the person for the year as a result of the disposition of a non-qualified investment or prohibited investment.[249] For more details on the refund of any tax payable on prohibited or non-qualified investments, see

---

See page ii for explanation of footnotes.

[243] CCH ¶25,712b; Sec. 207.06(4).
[244] CCH ¶25,714; Sec. 207.061(c).
[245] CCH ¶25,712; Sec. 207.06(2).
[246] CCH ¶25,712a; Sec. 207.06(3).

[247] CCH ¶25,714; Sec. 207.061(b).
[248] CCH ¶25,715; Sec. 207.07(1).
[249] CCH ¶25,672; Sec. 207.01(1) "allowable refund".

¶13,515. The Minister must refund a person's allowable refund for a calendar year, to the extent that it has not been applied against the person's tax payable for the year.[250] Certain provisions of Part I relating to returns, assessments, payments, and appeals apply for the purposes of Part XI.01, with any required modifications.[251]

[¶13,518] Taxes in Respect of RRSPs and RRIFs

Effective for transactions occurring, income earned, capital gains accruing, and investments acquired after March 22, 2011, the above penalty taxes under Part XI.01 that apply to TFSAs in respect of "advantages", "prohibited investments", and "non-qualified investments" are extended to RRSPs and RRIFs.

The TFSA advantage concept (see ¶13,516) will apply to Part XI.01 tax on RRSP or RRIF advantages. However, added to the list of advantages for RRSPs and RRIFs is a reduction in the value of an RRSP/RRIF without a corresponding income inclusion (an "RRSP strip"). More particularly, an RRSP strip refers to a transaction (other than a withdrawal under the Home Buyer's Plan or the Lifelong Learning Plan) one of the main purposes of which is to enable RRSP or RRIF annuitants to access their RRSP or RRIF funds without including the appropriate amount in income.[252] As is the case for TFSA advantages, RRSP and RRIF advantages will be subject to a tax that is generally equal to their fair market value, representing a 100% tax.

The 50% tax on prohibited investments and non-qualified investments held in a TFSA (see ¶13,515) will also apply to RRSPs and RRIFs. However, the 50% tax on the fair market value of a prohibited investment will not apply to a prohibited investment that was acquired or held by an RRSP/RRIF before March 22, 2011, provided that it is disposed of before 2013.

Investment income earned by a TFSA, RRSP, or RRIF on a non-qualified investment remains subject to Part 1 tax. However, any income earned on that income (second generation income) that remains in the plan ("specified non-qualified investment income") can become subject to the 100% advantage tax if it is not removed within 90 days after receipt of a notice from the CRA directing its removal.

These amendments generally apply to transactions occurring, income earned, capital gains accruing, and investments acquired, after March 22, 2011, subject to certain transitional rules. For example, the advantage rules relating to "swap transactions" do not apply to RRSPs and RRIFs, in respect of transfers that accommodate the removal of prohibited investments or investments that would result in an advantage, where the transaction is completed before 2013. In any other case, a swap transaction in relation to

See page ii for explanation of footnotes.

[250] CCH ¶25,716; Sec. 207.07(2).
[251] CCH ¶25,717; Sec. 207.07(3).

[252] Sec. 207.01(1) "RRSP strip".

an RRSP or RRIF is not an advantage if the transaction is completed before July 2011. It should be noted that the extended application of Part XI.01 tax to RRSP or RRIF advantages may apply to certain amounts received after March 22, 2011 by RRSPs and RRIFs which have an interest in income trusts that are not publicly traded. These new rules could also apply to income earned before March 22, 2011 in respect of services and possibly other sources of income if the payments for such services and income sources were received after March 22, 2011.

[¶13,520] Tax in Respect of Certain Property Held by Trusts Governed by Deferred Income Plans (Part XI.1)

[¶13,525] Tax in Respect of Non-Qualified Investments

A special tax is imposed whenever trusts governed by RRSPs, deferred profit sharing plans (DPSPs), RRIFs, and RESPs retain property that is not a qualified investment or, in some cases, retain excessive amounts of certain qualified investments.[253] The purpose of this tax is to discourage the retention of property which qualified as an investment of the trust when it was acquired, but has since ceased to be a qualified investment.

The Part XI.1 tax payable by a trust governed by an RRSP or a RRIF was repealed, effective for an investment acquired after March 22, 2011 and any investment acquired before March 23, 2011 that first becomes a non-qualified investment after March 22, 2011. The repeal is consequential on the application of the 50% tax under Part XI.01 on prohibited investments and non-qualified investments held in an RRSP or RRIF (see ¶13,518).

The tax does not apply to property held by the trust where the fair market value of the property was included in computing the income of the beneficiary in respect of an annuitant under an RRSP or RRIF,[254] or where the cost of the property has resulted in tax to the DPSP trust.[255] Generally, this means that the Part XI.1 tax applies to RRSPs, DPSPs, and RRIFs that hold property that is not currently a qualified investment, but was a qualified investment at the time it was acquired.

Part XI.1 tax is imposed on property of an RRSP that is neither a qualified investment[256] nor a life insurance policy that would normally be a non-qualified investment (described below). Tax is also imposed on property of a DPSP that is not a qualified investment[257] or not a life insurance policy under which the trust is the only beneficiary, and premiums are payable at a fixed annual level such that the cash surrender value of the policy, excluding any dividend accumulations, equals or exceeds the face value of the policy

See page ii for explanation of footnotes.

[253] CCH ¶25,725–25,728b; Sec. 207.1(1)–(5).
[254] CCH ¶21,335, ¶21,428p; Sec. 146(10), 146.3(7).
[255] CCH ¶25,300; Sec. 198(1).
[256] CCH ¶21,213a; Sec. 146(1) "qualified investment".
[257] CCH ¶25,534g; Sec. 204 "qualified investment".

by the time of the insured's 71st birthday. Before 2007, the requirement relating to the cash surrender value of a policy had to be satisfied by the insured person's 69th birthday.[258] For RRIFs and RESPs, Part XI.1 tax is imposed on property of the trust that is not a qualified investment at the end of any month.[259] The tax as it applies to RESPs differs from the tax imposed on RRSPs, DPSPs, and RRIFs, in that it applies to all property held by an RESP that is not a qualified investment. (As noted, for the other plans, the Part XI.1 tax generally only applies to property that was qualified at the time it was acquired, but later became non-qualified.)

The amount of the tax payable under Part XI.1 is 1% of the fair market value (at the time it was acquired) of property that is a non-qualified investment held by the trust at each month end.[260]

[¶13,530] Tax in Respect of Acquisition of Shares by Tax Exempt Persons

With the repeal of Part XI, the penalty tax on tax-exempt taxpayers and registered plans that enter into an agreement to purchase shares of a corporation in the future from a person other than the corporation at a price which may differ from the fair market value of these shares when they are in fact acquired (see ¶13,497) is now moved to Part XI.1.[261]

The taxpayer to whom Part XI.1 tax applies is subject to tax in respect of each month during which it is a party to such an agreement, equal to the amount of dividends paid during each month that the exempt taxpayer is a party to the agreement minus the amount of dividends that are received by the exempt taxpayer. This tax does not apply with respect to the acquisition of options listed on a designated stock exchange or options granted by the corporation itself. This provision is directed toward preventing exempt taxpayers and registered plans from investing in options or similar agreements other than through the acquisition of publicly traded options or acquiring options on the shares of a corporation from that corporation. But for such a provision, the exempt taxpayer or registered plan could indirectly invest in shares which it might not be entitled to invest in directly by acquiring options on those shares but not the shares themselves. This tax is also directed toward preventing exempt taxpayers and registered plans from temporarily transferring shares to persons, particularly corporations, that are able to receive dividends on those shares on a tax-favoured basis.

[¶13,535] Payment of Tax — Liability of Trustee

Every taxpayer to whom Part XI.1 applies is required to file a return in prescribed form within 90 days from the end of each taxation year, whether tax has been incurred or not. On the return, the taxpayer must estimate the

---

See page ii for explanation of footnotes.

[258] CCH ¶25,380; Sec. 146(1) "qualified investment".

[259] CCH ¶21,428g, ¶25,728; Sec. 146.3(1) "qualified investment", 207.1(3).

[260] CCH ¶25,725, ¶25,727, ¶25,728; Sec. 207.1(1), 207.1(2), 207.1(3).

[261] CCH ¶25,728b; Sec. 207.1(5).

amount of tax payable in respect of each month of the year.[262] The trustee is personally liable for the amount of tax payable and is entitled to recover from the taxpayer such amounts as the trustee has paid.[263] Various administrative provisions of Part I are applicable to the Part XI.1 tax.[264]

[¶13,540] Tax in Respect of Dispositions of Certain Properties (Part XI.2)

[¶13,545] Disposition of Certain Properties

Part XI.2 imposes a tax on any institution or public authority that disposes of a cultural object within five years of its acquisition to anyone other than another designated institution or public authority in Canada. The tax is 30% of the fair market value of the object at the time of the disposition.[265]

Part XI.2 also imposes a tax on charities and Canadian municipalities where they dispose of or change the use of land donated to them as an ecologically sensitive land without the approval of the Minister of the Environment. The tax is equal to 50% of the fair market value of the land at the time of the non-approved disposition or change in use.[266]

The fair market value is that amount that would be determined at that time for a donor for the purposes of the tax deduction for a corporate taxpayer or the tax credit for an individual taxpayer. Environment Canada's Information Circular No. 2 sets out examples of changes in land use that would likely be acceptable and unacceptable.

The institution, public authority, charity, or municipality liable to pay Part XI.2 tax for a year must, within 90 days from the end of that year, file a return in prescribed form (Form T913) in which the amount of Part XI.2 tax payable is estimated and pay this amount to the Receiver General.[267] The provisions of Part I regarding returns, assessments, payments, and penalties are applicable to Part XI.2 with necessary modifications.

[¶13,550] Tax in Respect of Retirement Compensation Arrangements (RCAs) (Part XI.3)

[¶13,555] Overview

The rules relating to RCAs were introduced in October 1986 to ensure consistent tax treatment across all employers for pension arrangements that exceed the maximum pension benefit permitted under the RPP contribution limits. Generally, an RCA is defined as an arrangement under which pay-

See page ii for explanation of footnotes.

262 CCH ¶25,729; Sec. 207.2(1).
263 CCH ¶25,731; Sec. 207.2(2).
264 CCH ¶25,733; Sec. 207.2(3).

265 CCH ¶25,750; Sec. 207.3.
266 CCH ¶25,751; Sec. 207.31.
267 CCH ¶25,755; Sec. 207.4.

¶13,540

ments are made by an employer to a custodian in connection with benefits that are to be received by an employee on or after retirement.

Although an RCA trust is not subject to Part I tax, it is subject to the 50% refundable tax calculated under Part XI.3 on RCA contributions, as well as on income and gains earned and realized by an RCA.

Effective March 29, 2012, RCAs will be subject to a prohibited investment and advantage taxes under Part XI.3, very similar to those recently enacted into law in December 2011 and applicable to RRSPs and RRIFs under Part XI.01 (see ¶13,518).

[¶13,560] Refundable Tax Obligation

Contributions made to an RCA are subject to a special 50% refundable tax.[268] This tax must be withheld by the contributor and remitted to the Receiver General. The refundable tax applies to the income of the plan as well. It is refundable at the rate of $1 for each $2 paid to a beneficiary. This 50% rate is intended to equate roughly to the top corporate and personal tax rates such that it removes any tax deferral since the employee obtains a deduction, but there is no immediate income inclusion to the employee.

The refundable tax obligation is placed directly upon the custodian of an RCA in respect of each taxation year of an RCA trust. The custodian is the person to whom contributions are made under the plan.

The tax owing is calculated as the excess of the "refundable tax" [269] of the arrangement at the end of the year over the refundable tax of the arrangement at the end of the preceding taxation year. If the refundable tax at the end of the year is less than the refundable tax of the previous year the custodian will be entitled to a refund of the difference.[270]

[¶13,565] Calculation of "Refundable Tax"

The refundable tax of an RCA is calculated at the end of a taxation year as the sum of:

(a) one-half of all contributions to the RCA for the year and previous years,

(b) one-half of the net income (without any dividend gross-up) of the RCA for the year and previous years, and

(c) one-half of capital gains net of capital losses for the year and preceding years,

minus:

See page ii for explanation of footnotes.

[268] CCH ¶25,781; Sec. 207.7(1).   [270] CCH ¶25,783; Sec. 207.7(2).
[269] CCH ¶25,782; Sec. 207.5(1).

(d) one-half of all benefits paid out of the RCA in the year and in previous years, including a return of contributions.[271]

Where the benefits referred to in (d) are part of a series of contributions to and distributions from an RCA, they will not reduce refundable tax.

[¶13,566] Special Election

An RCA can make election in its Part XI.3 tax return so that the refundable tax at the end of the year is deemed to be the total of:

(a) the RCA's cash at the end of the year;

(b) in respect of any debt obligation held by the RCA, the greater of the principal amount and the fair market value thereof; and

(c) the fair market value of any shares listed on a designated stock exchange and held by the RCA at the end of the year.

The election can be made if the RCA property consists *only* of cash, debt obligations, shares listed on a designated stock exchange, or any combination thereof. The election will generally be advantageous where the RCA has been terminated and has no assets or where it has accrued but unrealized investment losses.

After March 28, 2012, the above election is only available if: (i) the decline in value of the above property is not reasonably attributable to a prohibited investment or an advantage, or (ii) the Minister is satisfied that it is just and equitable to accept the election having regard to all the circumstances (including the extent to which tax has been paid under any other Part).

[¶13,567] Refundable Tax Mechanism — Example

The following example illustrates the functioning of the refundable tax System:

(1) In 2010, an RCA is established with the contribution of $400,000:

- The contributor withholds $200,000 in tax and remits it to the Receiver General.

- The net amount received by the custodian is $200,000.

(2) The RCA trust earns $20,000 in 2010:

- The refundable tax at the end of 2010 is 1/2 ($400,000 + $20,000) = $210,000.

- The custodian must pay $10,000 as the contributor has already withheld $200,000 of the contribution.

(3) In 2011, the RCA trust earns $20,000 and a benefit of $30,000 is paid to a beneficiary:

---

[271] CCH ¶25,782; Sec. 207.5(1) "refundable tax".

- The refundable tax at the end of 2011 is 1/2 ($400,000 (total contributions) + $40,000 (total income)) - 1/2 ($30,000 (distributions)) = $205,000.

- The RCA will be entitled to a refund of tax in the amount by which the refundable tax at the end of 2010 ($210,000) exceeds the refundable tax at the end of 2011 ($205,000) or $5,000.

(4) In 2012, all the assets of the RCA trust are paid to beneficiaries ($205,000):

- If the custodian makes the special election, the RCA's refundable tax at the end of the year will be nil and a refund of $205,000 will be paid to the custodian (amount by which 2011 refundable tax exceeds 2012 refundable tax).

- If the custodian did not make the election, the RCA's refundable tax would be 1/2 ($400,000 (total contributions) + $40,000 (total income)) - 1/2 distributions ($235,000) = $102,500 and the tax refund would only be $102,500. The distribution of that refund would itself generate a refund and so on until the full refund was obtained.

[¶13,570] Special Rules

Certain life insurance policies fall into the ambit of the RCA rules,[272] as do personal service corporations.[273] A plan established for the purpose of deferring the wages of a professional athlete is excluded from the definition of an RCA provided certain conditions are met.

Plans or arrangements (other than athletes' plans) maintained primarily for the benefit of non-residents in respect of services rendered outside Canada are not considered RCAs.[274] However, special rules apply to Canadian residents who are members of such foreign plans to prevent them from using non-resident plans to avoid the RCA rules. If a "resident's contribution" is made to a foreign plan (other than an athlete's plan) maintained primarily for the benefit of non-residents in respect of services rendered outside Canada, the plan will be considered to be an RCA and that contribution, and any investment derived therefrom, will be subject to the refundable RCA tax.[275]

A contribution is a "resident's contribution" to the extent that:

(a) it is made in respect of services rendered by a Canadian resident employee, where those services are rendered primarily in Canada or primarily in connection with a business carried on by the employer in Canada; and

(b) it is not a prescribed contribution.[276]

In general terms, contributions to a foreign plan are prescribed where they are made in respect of the employees of an employer who has elected to report pension adjustments in connection with the participation of the employees in the foreign plan and certain other conditions are met.[277]

See page ii for explanation of footnotes.

[272] CCH ¶25,786; Sec. 207.6(2).
[273] CCH ¶25,787; Sec. 207.6(3).
[274] CCH ¶28,248; Sec. 248(1) "retirement compensation arrangement".
[275] CCH ¶25,789; Sec. 207.6(5).
[276] CCH ¶25,776a; Sec. 207.6(5.1).
[277] [Reg. 6804.

Contributions made in respect of an employee who has been resident in Canada for less than five of the preceding six years are excluded if the employee was a member of the foreign plan before becoming a Canadian resident.

It should be noted that residents' contributions may include, in addition to contributions made by an employer in respect of its employees, contributions made by anyone else (including the employees) in respect of those employees. For example, contributions made to a foreign plan by a foreign parent corporation in respect of employees of its Canadian subsidiary may be residents' contributions.

[¶13,571] Prescribed Plan or Arrangement

Typically, a plan or arrangement must be pre-funded in order for it to be an RCA. However, certain unfunded provincial or federal government retirement plans or arrangements may become prescribed and thus become subject to the RCA rules.[278]

To become prescribed, the following must occur:

(1) the government responsible for the plan or arrangement must apply to have it prescribed;

(2) the plan or arrangement must not be a registered pension plan;

(3) the government must maintain a single account for the plan or arrangement in its government accounts; and

(4) this account must reasonably be expected to approximate or exceed the actuarial liabilities of the plan or arrangement at all times.

Any amount credited to the government account for a prescribed plan or arrangement, except for any refundable tax due to the account, will be deemed to be a contribution to the account and subject to the refundable tax. The custodian of a prescribed plan or arrangement is the Queen in the right of the government sponsoring the plan or arrangement. Thus the sponsoring government will be responsible for submitting the refundable tax.

The balance in the government account established for a prescribed plan or arrangement is considered to be cash.

[¶13,573] Transfers

Lump-sum amounts may be transferred directly from one RCA to another RCA on a tax-neutral basis.[279] This means that there is no inclusion required, or deduction permitted in computing Part I income. The trans-

---

See page ii for explanation of footnotes.

[278] CCH ¶25,776b; Sec. 207.6(6).　　　　[279] CCH ¶25,776c; Sec. 207.6(7).

ferred amount will not be subject to withholding when it is paid out of the transferor plan or when it is paid into the transferee plan.

For the purposes of Part XI.3 tax, an amount so transferred is considered to be a distribution from the transferor plan and a contribution to the transferee plan with the result that the tax liability is transferred from the transferor plan to the transferee plan.

This rollover is not available where the transferee plan has a non-resident custodian or is a foreign plan deemed to be an RCA in respect of Canadian residents participating in the plan (see ¶13,570).

[¶13,575] Tax on Prohibited Investments and Advantages

Beginning March 29, 2012, new anti-avoidance rules in Part XI.3 will prevent the use of schemes that seek to take advantage of the features of the RCA rules to obtain unintended tax benefits. These rules are very similar to those applicable to RRSPs and RRIFs in Part XI.01.

As a result of these new anti-avoidance rules in Part XI.3, the custodian of an RCA will be required to pay a tax equal to:

- 50% of the fair market value of a prohibited investment acquired or held by the RCA; and

- the fair market value of any advantage obtained by a specified beneficiary of the RCA or a person who does not deal at arm's length with the specified beneficiary.

An RCA's specified beneficiary refers to an individual who has an interest or right in the RCA and who has a significant interest (at least 10%) in an employer sponsoring the plan. A specified beneficiary of an RCA that participates in acquiring or holding a prohibited investment, or in extending an advantage, in respect of the RCA, will be jointly liable, to the extent of their participation, for the tax in respect of the prohibited investment or the tax in respect of the advantage.

The tax on prohibited investments will be refundable if the RCA disposes of the prohibited investment by the end of the year following the year in which it was acquired (or any such later time as the Minister considers reasonable) unless any of the persons liable for the tax knew or ought to have known that the investment was a prohibited investment.

[¶13,576] Returns and Payment of Tax

The custodian must file a return in respect of the RCA trust and pay any refundable tax owing within 90 days of the end of the year.[280] Various administrative provisions of Part I apply to the tax imposed under Part XI.3.

See page ii for explanation of footnotes.

[280] CCH ¶25,781; Sec. 207.7(3).

[¶13,577] Tax on Excessive Employer Contributions to EPSPs (Part XI.4)

[¶13,578] Overview

An employees profit sharing plan (EPSP) is an arrangement that allows an employer to share business profits with all or a designated group of employees. Under an EPSP, amounts are paid to a trustee to be held and invested for the benefit of the employees who are beneficiaries under the plan. Each year, the trustee is required to allocate to such beneficiaries all employer contributions, profits from trust property, capital gains and losses, and certain amounts in respect of forfeitures. These allocated amounts, with certain exceptions, are included in computing the taxable income of the beneficiaries for the year in which they are allocated and are not subject to tax when actually received by the beneficiaries. There were concerns that EPSPs were used more and more by some business owners to direct profits to their families in such a way as to reduce or defer the payment of tax. To address these concerns and discourage excessive employer contributions to "specified employees", the 2012 Budget introduced a new penalty tax under Part XI.4.

[¶13,579] Tax on Excess EPSP Amount

After March 28, 2009, whenever employer contributions allocated to specified employees exceed a certain threshold (the "excess EPSP amount"), such employees are required to pay tax on the excess amount. Specified employees are employees who have a significant equity interest (at least 10%) in their employer or who do not deal at arm's length with their employer.

In general terms, the excess EPSP amount is the portion of employer contributions to an EPSP that are allocated for the year to specified employees that exceeds 20% of the specified employee's total income for the year (excluding EPSP allocations, stock option benefits, and deductions in computing income from an office or employment).

The special tax is made up of two components. The first component is equal to 29% (the top federal marginal tax rate). The second component is equal to the top marginal tax rate of the employee's province of residence (or 0% in Quebec).

For more details, see the Q&A document on EPSPs that the CRA has posted on its website at: http://www.cra-arc.gc.ca/gncy/bdgt/2012/qa05-eng.html#_Toc320859884.

¶13,577

[¶13,580] Tax in Respect of Certain Payments Made by Exempt Taxpayers (Part XII)

[¶13,585] Tax with Respect to Resource Payments Made by Tax-Exempt Persons

Part XII imposes a tax on persons who are exempt from tax under Part I and who are thus not penalized by the provisions of Part I which adversely affect taxable entities who make certain payments or otherwise benefit governments with respect to resource revenues or properties.[281]

Under these provisions of Part I, various payments made to the Crown or benefits accorded to the Crown with respect to resource properties are not deductible, or otherwise are not taken into account for federal income tax purposes. These provisions result in a significant increase in the after-tax cost of such payments or benefits to a taxable entity.

Part XII was introduced to deter the use of methods of avoiding the effect of these provisions of Part I.[282] It will impose a tax if a person exempt from Part I tax (other than a prescribed person) has paid or distributed or is liable to pay or distribute to another person an amount with respect to any revenue, production, or income reasonably attributable to production from a Canadian resource property of that tax-exempt person.

The tax payable by such a tax-exempt person is $33^{1}/_{3}\%$ of the amount of payments or transfers made to a provincial government that are in the nature of royalties or profit sharing payments, if the otherwise exempt person is also required to make payments to other persons with respect to revenue or production from that property.

Example:

Pension Plan A has income for the taxation year from the production of oil (after deducting production costs) of $5 million out of which it pays $1.5 million of non-deductible Crown royalties. Out of the remaining $3.5 million it pays a royalty to Company B, a taxable entity, of $2 million. The liability of Pension Plan A to tax under Part XII is as follows:

The lesser of:

(i) 33 1/3% of $1,500,000 = $500,000

and

(ii) 33 1/3% of:

$1,500,000 × $2,000,000/($5,000,000 - $1,500,000)

or

33 1/3% of $857,142 = $285,714

See page ii for explanation of footnotes.
[281] CCH ¶4371, ¶4852, ¶9187, ¶9188; Sec.   [282] CCH ¶25,800; Sec. 208.
12(1)(o), 18(1)(m), 69(6), 69(7).

[¶13,590] Payment of Tax

Every person liable to pay tax under Part XII must file a return and pay the tax on or before the person's balance-due day for the year.[283] A corporation's balance-due day is at the end of the second month following the end of its taxation year or, for small business corporations, at the end of the third month following the end of its taxation year.[284] Various administrative provisions of Part I are applicable to Part XII.

[¶13,595] Tax on Carved-Out Income (Part XII.1)

[¶13,600] Tax on Carved-Out Income

Carved-out income is subject to a special Part XII.1 tax of 45%.[285] In general, "carved-out income" is income from a Canadian resource property in circumstances where the taxpayer's income from the property is predetermined to be a maximum amount or is expected to cease or be reduced substantially within a 10-year period. Such property is referred to as a "carved-out property".

To avoid double taxation of the same income, a taxpayer may deduct, in computing income under Part I, an amount equal to the carved-out income subject to Part XII.1 tax.[286]

Part XII.1 tax is in the nature of a penalty tax. The purpose is to totally eliminate what were considered to be excessive tax avoidance transactions involving resource industries, primarily the oil and gas industry. A taxpayer with profitable operations used to be able to minimize the payment of tax by transferring a temporary interest in producing properties to another taxpayer that had accumulated losses or was tax-exempt (such as a pension fund). Such arrangements were usually for a set period of time with the property being effectively transferred back to the original owner at the end of the arrangement. The objective was to transfer resource income from the profitable taxpayer, where it was subject to tax, to an entity that was tax-exempt or that could shelter the income by offsetting it against accumulated losses. Incidental benefits relating to non-deductible royalties and the increase in available tax credits could also arise. The economics were that the purchaser of the carved-out property would receive production revenue somewhat in excess of the cost of the property, that excess being a fee for the use of the purchaser's tax deductions or tax-exempt status.

Part XII.1 now isolates the income earned on carved-out properties and subjects it to tax. The carved-out income is taxable in the hands of the recipient under Part XII.1, regardless of the fact that the recipient may have deductions available or may be exempt from Part I tax.

See page ii for explanation of footnotes.

[283] CCH ¶25,814; Sec. 208(2).
[284] CCH ¶28,020b; Sec. 248(1) "balance-due day".
[285] CCH ¶25,840–25,850; Sec. 209.
[286] CCH ¶8971f; Sec. 66(14.6).

While the wording of Part XII.1 is broad enough to cover transactions in both the oil and gas industry and the mining industry, the exceptions contained in regulations[287] effectively limit the tax to the oil and gas industry.

[¶13,605] Tax on Designated Income of Certain Trusts (Part XII.2)

[¶13,610] Tax on Designated Income

Part XII.2 tax is designed to prevent a non-resident avoiding tax through the use of a trust to earn income from a business carried on in Canada or from a disposition of taxable Canadian property.

Part XII.2 tax is generally equal to 36% of the designated income of the trust payable to any beneficiary, resident, or non-resident.[288] A proportionate tax credit is available for resident beneficiaries (other than designated beneficiaries) and non-resident beneficiaries who are taxable under Part I.

Where the income distributed by the trust to its beneficiaries is less than 64% of the designated income, then the Part XII.2 tax is 36% of a pre-tax amount determined by grossing up income distributions deducted by the trust. A *pro rata* portion of Part XII.2 tax payable by a trust may be refunded to its taxable resident beneficiaries who are not designated beneficiaries.[289] A Canadian partnership which is a beneficiary of a trust may flow out the Part XII.2 credit to its partners.[290]

[¶13,615] Application of Part XII.2 Tax

Part XII.2 tax will not apply to:

(a) testamentary trusts;

(b) mutual fund trusts;

(c) non-resident trusts;

(d) trusts such as pension fund trusts or registered charities exempt from Part I tax;

(e) most registered trusts;

(f) segregated funds in respect of life insurance policies; and

(g) health and welfare trusts.[291]

See page ii for explanation of footnotes.

[287] CCH ¶25,852; Reg. 7600.
[288] CCH ¶25,903; Sec. 210.2(1).
[289] CCH ¶25,905; Sec. 210.2(3).

[290] CCH ¶25,886; Sec. 210.2(4).

[291] CCH ¶25,902; Sec. 210.1, 210(2).

[¶13,620] Designated Beneficiary

For the purposes of Part XII.2 tax, a "designated beneficiary" includes a non-resident person, a non-resident-owned investment corporation, and certain specified trusts. As well, a designated beneficiary includes an exempt person acquiring an interest in the trust unless the interest was owned continuously by an exempt person since the later of:

(a) October 1, 1987; and

(b) the date of the creation of the trust.[292]

[¶13,625] Part XII.2 Tax Returns

A trust is required to file a Part XII.2 return and pay any Part XII.2 tax owing within 90 days from the end of the taxation year of a trust.[293] A trustee of the trust will be personally liable to pay any portion of tax owing but is entitled to be reimbursed.

The administrative procedures of Part I apply to Part XII.2 tax.[294]

[¶13,630] Tax on Investment Income of Life Insurers (Part XII.3)

[¶13,635] Tax on Investment Income of Life Insurers

Part XII.3 levies a special tax on the accumulated investment income of life insurance companies. The tax payable is 15% of a life insurer's taxable Canadian investment income for the year.[295] An insurer's "taxable Canadian life investment income" is the excess of Canadian life investment income for the year over the aggregate of the insurer's unused Canadian life investment losses from the 20 preceding taxation years which may be carried forward for this purpose. Only losses arising in taxation years which commence after 1989 are eligible for carryforward. A special formula is provided for the determination of a life insurer's Canadian life investment income for a taxation year.[296]

Every life insurer must pay its Part XII.3 tax in monthly instalments, rather than in quarterly instalments, and pay the remainder of tax on or before its balance-due day for the year, i.e., on or before the end of the second month following the end of its taxation year.[297] These monthly instalments must be equal to $\frac{1}{12}$ of the lesser of:

(a) the estimated amount of annualized Part XII.3 tax payable by the insurer for the year; and

---

See page ii for explanation of footnotes.

[292] CCH ¶25,901; Sec. 210.
[293] CCH ¶25,907; Sec. 210.2(5).
[294] CCH ¶25,907; Sec. 210.2(7).

[295] CCH ¶25,926; Sec. 211.1.
[296] CCH ¶25,928; Sec. 211.1(3).
[297] CCH ¶25,930, ¶25,931; Sec. 211.3, 211.4.

(b) the annualized tax payable by the insurer for the preceding year.

If the insurer's taxation year is at least 51 weeks, the annualized tax is equal to its Part XII.3 tax for the year. If the taxation year is less than 51 weeks, the annualized tax is calculated by multiplying its Part XII.3 tax for the year by the ratio of 365 to the number of days in the year (excluding February 29th). When determining the instalments for the first taxation year of a life insurer formed by amalgamation, wind-up or rollover, the Part XII.3 tax payable by all predecessor corporations for their last taxation year will be used.

General administrative provisions under Part I relating to returns, assessments, penalties, refunds, objections, appeals, etc. are applicable to Part XII.3, including the provision relating to interest and penalty on any late or deficient payment of tax and instalments.[298] However, for the purpose of determining any interest or penalty on the monthly instalments required to be paid, a life insurer is deemed to have been liable to pay monthly instalments based on the lesser of its annualized tax for the year and its annualized tax for the previous year.[299] This differs from the instalment requirement, in that the actual tax for the current year is used in place of the taxpayer's estimate of the tax.

[¶13,640] Tax on Qualifying Environmental Trusts (Part XII.4)

[¶13,645] Tax on Qualifying Environmental Trusts

Part XII.4 imposes a special tax on the income of a qualifying environmental trust. Prior to 2012, the tax rate was 28%, the general federal corporate tax rate before the general corporate rate reduction. For 2012 and subsequent years, the rate will equal the general federal corporate income tax rate after that reduction. The rate is currently 15%.[300] Under Part XII.4, a trust's income is determined without regard to many of the normal trust taxation rules.[301] A trust liable under Part XII.4 for a taxation year must file a Part XII.4 tax return (Form T3M) and pay the Part XII.4 tax due within 90 days after the trust's taxation year.[302] The entire amount of the Part XII.4 tax liability is due at the same time.[303]

Provisions with respect to assessments, objections, appeals, and other procedural and administrative matters for the purposes of the tax under Part I will also apply for the purposes of the Part XII.4 tax.[304]

See page ii for explanation of footnotes.

[298] CCH ¶25,932; Sec. 211.5(1).
[299] CCH ¶25,933; Sec. 211.5(2).
[300] CCH ¶25,950; Sec. 211.6(1).
[301] CCH ¶25,951; Sec. 211.6(2).

[302] CCH ¶25,952; Sec. 211.6(3).
[303] CCH ¶25,953; Sec. 211.6(4).
[304] CCH ¶25,954; Sec. 211.6(5).

[¶13,650] Recovery of Labour-Sponsored Funds Tax Credit (Part XII.5)

[¶13,655] Special Tax for Recovery of LSVCC Tax Credit

Part XII.5 tax is payable by a shareholder whose share of a registered LSVCC is, before the discontinuation of its venture capital business, redeemed, acquired, or cancelled prior to the expiry of a minimum period (see below).[305] For shares issued before March 6, 1996, there is no recovery of the tax credit for a share redeemed more than five years after the day on which the share was issued. For shares issued after March 5, 1996, the recovery applies where a share is redeemed less than eight years after the day on which it was issued. [To accommodate taxpayers wishing to acquire new LSVCC shares in the first 60 days of a year with the proceeds from the redemption of LSVCC shares, the redemption requirements are amended so that a share redeemed in February or on March 1st is treated as having been redeemed 30 days later. For example, existing LSVCC shares issued on March 1, 1995 and redeemed on February 29, 2000 would be exempt from a recovery of the federal LSVCC tax credit that was associated with the original acquisition of the shares. This amendment, first announced by Finance Canada in News Release 2000-009, dated February 7, 2000, is part of the revised technical amendments that were released in a draft form on July 10, 2010. It applies to redemptions, acquisitions, cancellations, and dispositions that occur after November 15, 1995.]

The Part XII.5 tax is also payable on redemptions or dispositions of shares in non-federally registered LSVCCs (i.e., those that are prescribed[306] and are registered in a province but not registered at the federal level), where an amount is required to be remitted to the applicable province as a consequence of the redemption or disposition.

In the case of a federally registered LSVCC or a "revoked" LSVCC (one whose federal registration has been revoked), the Part XII.5 tax in respect of the share is equal to the "labour-sponsored funds tax credit" in respect of the share.[307] Basically, this means 20% of the net cost of the share if it was issued before March 6, 1996, and 15% of its net cost if it was issued on or after March 6, 1996. The tax is limited to the proceeds of disposition of the share upon redemption, net of any provincial LSVCC tax credit recovery. After February 16, 1999, there is no redemption, acquisition, or cancellation of shares by a predecessor corporation on the amalgamation or merger of a predecessor corporation to form a corporate entity that is deemed to be a registered labour-sponsored venture capital corporation. In these circumstances, there is no recovery under Part XII.5 of the federal tax credit with respect to the shares of the predecessor corporation.[308]

See page ii for explanation of footnotes.

[305] CCH ¶25,954h; Sec. 211.8(1).

[306] CCH ¶7670a; Reg. 6701.

[307] CCH ¶25,954c; Sec. 211.7(1) "labour-sponsored funds tax credit".

[308] CCH ¶25,954ga; Sec. 211.7(2).

¶13,650

In the case of an LSVCC that is not federally registered (i.e., one that is only registered provincially and is prescribed), the tax equals the amount, if any, that is required to be repaid to a provincial government as a consequence of the redemption or disposition, multiplied by the quotient obtained when the (federal) labour-sponsored fund tax credit in respect of the share (see ¶8290) is divided by the provincial LSVCC credit available on the acquisition of the share. For example, if the amount required to be remitted to the province on the redemption or disposition equals the provincial credit available on the acquisition of the share, the Part XII.5 tax simply equals the labour-sponsored fund tax credit (15% of the net cost, or 20% if the share was issued before March 6, 1996).

[¶13,657] Where Part XII.5 Tax Not Payable

The Part XII.5 tax is not payable in respect of a redemption or disposition of a share in a federally registered LSVCC occurring eight years or more after the day it was issued. Additionally, the tax is not payable in respect of the share if:

(a) the disposition was a redemption of shares on which no credit was claimed as witnessed by the fact that the redemption request was accompanied by the original (unused) tax credit form issued by the LSVCC;

(b) the disposition was a redemption of shares permitted because an individual became disabled and permanently unfit for work or terminally ill;

(c) the disposition was a redemption of shares on which no credit was issued because it was purchased by someone intrinsically not entitled to the credit (e.g., a non-RRSP trust or RRSP trust for someone other than the purchaser or purchaser's spouse or common-law partner);

(d) the share was issued before March 6, 1996, and the disposition was more than five years after issue, or the disposition occurred more than two years after issue pursuant to the articles of the LSVCC, because an individual attained 65 years of age, retired or ceased to be resident in Canada; or

(e) where the redemption takes place before 1998, the corporation is directed to withhold and remit the previously claimed federal credit under the old clawback rules.

In the case of a disposition of a share in a non-federally registered LSVCC (a prescribed LSVCC that is provincially registered), Part XII.5 tax is not payable if no amount is required to be remitted to the applicable province as a consequence of the redemption or disposition of the share. Most provinces have holding period rules similar to those applicable to a federally registered LSVCC. Therefore, for example, if the provincial holding period requirement is met so that the previously claimed provincial credit is not required to be recovered by the province, the federal Part XII.5 tax is not payable.

[¶13,658] Redemption of Quebec LSVCC Shares Held Within an RRSP

The Home Buyers' Plan (HBP) and the Lifelong Learning Plan (LLP) allow a qualifying individual to withdraw RRSP funds on a tax-free basis to purchase a home or to pay for education. HBP withdrawals are repayable over a 15-year period, while LLP withdrawals are repayable over a 10-year period. To the extent that a scheduled repayment for a year is not made, it is added in computing the participant's income for the year. See ¶10,393 and ¶10,396 *et seq.*

The province of Quebec permits a temporary redemption of shares to finance a home purchase or educational studies, under rules similar to the federal RRSP Home Buyer's Plan (HBP) or Lifelong Learning Plan (LLP). Under existing law, the federal credit will not be recovered in these circumstances. Individuals making such withdrawals are expected to acquire replacement shares in annual amounts determined under the existing HBP and LLP repayment schedules, i.e., over a 15-year period for an HBP and a 10-year period for an LLP. These replacement purchases are not eligible for the Quebec LSVCC credit. Where an individual fails to acquire LSVCC replacement shares, a special Quebec tax of 15% of the shortfall is imposed on the individual to recover the LSVCC credit that Quebec provided on the purchase of the redeemed shares.

The federal government will parallel this treatment for Quebec redemptions: that is, there is no penalty on the redemption so long as there is no Quebec penalty, there is no additional LSVCC credit on replacement share acquisitions, and, where Quebec levies the 15% penalty on replacement shortfalls, the federal government will levy its own 15% penalty in addition. The federal announcement was clear that these special rules should apply only to Quebec LSVCC share redemptions. Similar changes are not contemplated for federally registered LSVCCs or LSVCCs registered in other provinces.

[¶13,660] Withholding and Remittance

The person or partnership that redeems, acquires, or cancels the LSVCC share (normally, the LSVCC itself), is liable to withhold the Part XII.5 tax from the proceeds and remit the tax to the Receiver General within 30 days along with a statement in prescribed form.[309] If the person or partnership fails to withhold such amount, it is liable to pay the tax that should have been withheld on behalf of the shareholder, and is entitled to recover that amount from the shareholder.[310]

---

[309] CCH ¶25,954i; Sec. 211.8(2). [310] CCH ¶25,954j; Sec. 211.8(3).

¶13,658

[¶13,665] Refund of Clawback

The Part XII.5 tax is essentially a recovery of an individual's previously claimed LSVCC credit (see ¶8290), but the tax applies even if the individual did not claim the full credit when the share was issued. If the full credit was not claimed, the individual may request a refund in a written application filed with the Minister no later than two years after the end of the calendar year in which the share redemption occurred. A refund is also available where an amount was remitted in respect of a redeemed share of a registered LSVCC before 1998 where the amount exceeds the credit previously claimed. The amount that the Minister, in his discretion, may refund cannot exceed the lesser of the amount of Part XII.5 so paid and 15% of the net cost of the share on the original acquisition.[311] The following example illustrates the exercise of Minister's discretion in this regard:

Example:

An individual acquires $5,000 of LSVCC shares in April 2011. The individual's tax otherwise payable for the 2011 taxation year is $450 and the individual therefore claims a $450 deduction as an LSVCC tax credit for 2011. The $450 amount represents the credit on a $3,000 investment, leaving $2,000 worth of shares on which, in effect, no credit can be claimed. Subsequently, one half of the shares are redeemed for $2,800 in July 2012, but the LSVCC withholds $375 ($2,500 × 15%) under Part XII.5 as a recovery of the LSVCC tax credit. In these circumstances, it would be reasonable to view the individual as having acquired $2,000 of "extra" LSVCC shares (i.e., acquisitions on which no credit was effectively claimed) that are subsequently redeemed. As a consequence, it is generally expected that the Minister would permit a recovery of Part XII.5 tax of up to $300 ($2,000 × 15%).

[¶13,670] Tax on Flow-Through Shares (Part XII.6)

[¶13,675] Tax Imposed

In a flow-through share issue (see ¶3540), qualifying Canadian exploration expenses (CEE) and Canadian development expenses (CDE) incurred in a calendar year can be renounced by oil and gas and mining companies in favour of the investor, who is then entitled to deduct them as if they had been incurred at the end of the preceding calendar year. This rule is referred to as the "one-year look-back rule". Part XII.6 levies a tax on flow-through share issuers, which compensates the fisc for the acceleration of certain CEE and CDE deductions under the one-year look-back rule. Part XII.6 tax is deductible by them in computing income.[312] To compensate for the extra costs associated with retroactive adjustments necessitated by excessive renunciations, Part XII.6 also levies an extra charge in the event that flow-through share funds have not been spent by the end of the calendar year of the issuer's renunciation.

Where because of the application of the one-year look-back rule, an oil and gas or mining corporation purports to renounce qualifying CEE and

---

[311] CCH ¶25,954k; Sec. 211.9; Reg. 6706.   [312] CCH ¶4852k, ¶5128k; Sec. 18(1)(*t*), 20(1)(*nn*).

CDE, it must pay Part XII.6 tax in respect of each month (other than January) in the year of the renunciation. The tax per month is generally equal to the balance of funds at the end of the month in respect of the renunciation that have not been spent on qualifying CEE or CDE, multiplied by an interest rate.[313] The interest rate is equal to $1/12$ of the annual interest rate prescribed for the purposes of determining refund interest (see ¶12,355). However, if funds remain unspent at the end of the year of the renunciation, there is an extra charge levied for December equal to $1/10$ of the unspent balance at the end of that month.

To provide relief for renunciations in respect of CEE or CDE expenses incurred in a province levying a parallel provincial tax, Part XII.6 tax is structured so that it is then equal to one-half of the amount otherwise determined.

A corporation's Part XII.6 tax for a calendar year is calculated on a special return that, together with the tax, is due by the end of February of the following calendar year.[314] The administrative provisions of Part I apply to Part XII.6, with necessary modifications.[315]

---

[313] CCH ¶25,956a; Sec. 211.91(1). [315] CCH ¶25,956c; Sec. 211.91(3).
[314] CCH ¶25,956b; Sec. 211.91(2).

¶13,675

Chapter XIV

Non-Residents, International Income, and Tax Agreements

Part-Time Residents **14,000**

Taxable Income of Part-
Time Residents 14,005

Part-Time Residents and
Sojourners 14,010

Deductions from Income of
Part-Time Individual
Residents To Arrive at
Taxable Income 14,015

Non-Residents **14,020**

Taxable Income Earned in
Canada 14,025

Effect of Tax Agreements 14,030

Capital Gains and
Allowable Capital Losses
— "Taxable Canadian
Property" 14,035

Non-Resident Funds with
Canadian Service
Providers 14,037

Tax Collection Procedure in
respect of Dispositions
by Non- Residents of
Certain Property 14,040

Excluded Property 14,045

Non-Resident Employees
Formerly Residing in
Canada 14,060

Signing Bonuses and
Amounts Payable under
Agreement for Services 14,065

Non-Resident Students,
Researchers and
Employees 14,070

Goods Purchased in One
Country and Sold in
Another 14,075

Applicable Deductions from
Non-Residents' Income 14,080

Credits Restrictions 14,081

**Withholding Tax on Income
from Canada of Non-
Resident Persons** **14,085**

General Non-Resident
Withholding Tax 14,090

Failure to Deduct, Withhold
or Remit — Penalties and
Interest 14,095

Management Fees 14,100

Interest 14,105

Exemption from Withholding
Tax for Arm's Length
Payments of Interest after
2007 14,110

Exemption from Withholding
Tax for Arm's Length (and
Non-Arm's Length)
Payments of Interest
before 2008 14,111

Withholding Tax for Non-
Arm's Length Payments
of Interest after 2007 14,112

Interest — Certificates of
Exemption before 2008 14,115

Dispositions of Certain
Property by Non-
Residents 14,120

Effect of Tax Agreements
on Capital Gains 14,125

Withholding Tax Not
Applicable to Interest on
Certain Loans 14,130

Estate or Trust Income 14,135

Rents, Royalties, or Similar
Payments 14,140

Timber Royalties 14,145

Patronage Dividends 14,155

Pension Benefits and Other
Similar Payments 14,160

Home Insulation or Energy
Conversion Grants 14,165

Pensions and Deferred
Income Plan Benefits 14,168

Amateur Athlete Trusts 14,169

Eligible Funeral
Arrangement 14,170

Employee Life and Health
Trusts 14,171

Tax on Dividends 14,172

Deemed Payments 14,175

Motion Picture Films 14,180

Non-Resident Actors 14,183

Transfers of Certain
Property and Income
Rights, etc. 14,190

Withholding Tax Where
Payor or Payee Is a
Partnership 14,195

Withholding Tax Where
Non-Resident Operates in
Canada 14,197

Non-Arm's Length Sale of
Shares by Non-Resident 14,200

Income and Capital
Combined 14,205

Securities 14,210

Temporary Use of Rolling
Stock 14,215

Transfer of Obligations 14,220

Guarantee Fees and Loans 14,225

Deduction and Payment of
Tax 14,230

Exception to Deduction and
Payment Rules 14,235

Liability for Tax 14,240

Insurers and Others 14,245

Rent and Other Payments 14,250

Election re Rents and
Timber Royalties 14,255

Alternative Method of Tax
Payment re Rents and
Timber Royalties 14,260

Election to File Part I Tax
Returns re Canadian
Pension Benefits 14,265

**Additional Tax on Non-
Resident Corporations** **14,270**

Branch Tax 14,275

Non-Resident Insurers 14,300

Tax Agreements **14,305**

Tax Agreements in General 14,310

**Highlights of the
Canada–U.S. Tax
Convention (1980)** **14,380**

Business Profits 14,385

Income from Real Property 14,390

Residence 14,395

Permanent Establishment 14,400

Related Persons 14,405

Ships, Aircraft and Motor
Vehicles 14,410

Government Service 14,415

Pensions and Annuities 14,420

Registered Retirement
Savings Plans (RRSPs) 14,425

Dependent Personal
Services 14,435

Artists and Athletes 14,440

Withholding of Taxes in
Respect of Personal
Services 14,445

Gains 14,450

Remittances to Students,
Apprentices and
Business Trainees 14,455

Income of Religious,
Scientific, Literary,
Educational or
Charitable Organizations 14,465

Dividends and Interest 14,470

Diplomatic Agents and
Consular Officers 14,475

Royalties 14,480

Mutual Agreement
Procedure 14,485

Elimination of Double
Taxation 14,490

Non-Discrimination 14,495

Exchange of Information 14,500

Entry into Force 14,505

**Highlights of the
Canada–U.K. Income Tax
Convention (1978)** **14,510**

Industrial and Commercial Profits — Permanent Establishment 14,520

Associated Enterprises 14,525

Ship, Aircraft or Container Use, Maintenance, or Rental Profits 14,530

Royalties 14,535

Capital Gains 14,540

Income from Immovable Property 14,545

Pensions and Annuities 14,550

Dividends and Interest 14,555

Income from Employment 14,560

Miscellaneous Income 14,565

Elimination of Double Taxation 14,570

Recent Changes

2012 Budget

Thin Capitalization Amendments

The Budget introduced significant changes to Canada's "thin capitalization" rules. One significant change would recharacterize denied interest (due to exceeding the maximum debt-equity ratio) as a deemed dividend, subject to Part XIII withholding tax. These proposed changes were included in draft legislation released on August 14, 2012. See ¶14,172. Remaining thin capitalization changes are discussed in Chapter III.

Technical Amendments

Withholding and Non-Resident Trust Beneficiaries

On July 25, 2012, the Department of Finance released draft income tax legislation addressing the issue of withholding tax on amounts that are payable from a Canadian resident trust to a non-resident beneficiary but which are actually paid after the trust ceases to be a Canadian resident. The amendment provides that the amount will be deemed to have been paid at the earliest of the day it was paid or credited. See ¶14,135.

Treaty Updates

Columbia

Canada signed a new Income Tax Convention with Columbia on June 12, 2012 that is now in force. See ¶14,310.

Administrative Announcements

Updated IC 72-17R6

Important updates were made to Information Circular IC 72-17R6 "Procedures concerning the disposition of taxable Canadian property by non-residents of Canada — Section 116". See ¶14,040.

[¶14,000] Part-Time Residents

[¶14,005] Taxable Income of Part-Time Residents

The method of calculating taxable income for an individual who is resident in Canada during part of the year currently involves a two-stage computation (the residence period and the non-residence period). First, for the part of the year the individual was resident in Canada, he or she must report his or her worldwide income from all sources. Then, for the part of the year the individual was not resident in Canada, he or she must add only the following sources of income:

- income from employment in Canada or from a business carried on in Canada;

- taxable capital gains from disposition of taxable Canadian property; and

- the taxable part of scholarships, fellowships, bursaries, and research grants received from Canadian sources.[1]

From this income, the part-year resident first deducts loss carryovers against the whole income for the year. In arriving at taxable income, the part- year resident is then allowed to deduct the following amounts, to the extent these relate to amounts that have been included in the above computation of income for the year:

(1) the non-taxable portion (currently ¹/₂) of employee stock option and prospector's and grubstaker's share benefits (see ¶3597);

(2) social assistance payments (see ¶2230);

(3) amounts exempt from Canadian tax under a tax treaty; and

(4) income from employment with the U.N. and its affiliates, the International Air Transport Association, the International Society of Aeronautical Telecommunications, and the World Anti-Doping Agency.[2]

Finally, any other deduction permitted in computing taxable income is allowed to the extent that it can reasonably be considered to be applicable to the resident period or, if all or substantially all of the individual's income (generally interpreted as 90% or more) for the non-resident period is included in income subject to tax in Canada.[3]

Subject to certain limitations, personal tax credits will be allowed for the residence period and the non-residence period (see ¶14,015).

---

[1] CCH ¶17,003; Sec. 114(a).   [3] CCH ¶17,003; Sec. 114(c).
[2] CCH ¶17,003; Sec. 114(b).

¶14,000

[¶14,010] Part-Time Residents and Sojourners

An individual who is not resident in Canada, within the ordinary meaning of that term, but who "sojourns" in Canada for a period of, or periods aggregating, 183 days or more in a taxation year is deemed to be resident in Canada throughout the year.[4]

A student who left Canada in the fall to attend a U.S. university was entitled to full personal exemptions for the year, as the student had been in Canada for more than 183 days and so was deemed to be resident throughout the year.[5] Therefore, the ordinary provisions regarding part-time residents did not apply.

[¶14,015] Deductions from Income of Part-Time Individual Residents To Arrive at Taxable Income

Part-time residents are allowed to claim personal tax credits from their tax payable. However, the calculation of those credits is subject to the following rules.[6]

Where an individual is resident in Canada for only part of the year, the individual is allowed to deduct tax credits that are available to a non-resident for the period in the year that the individual is not resident in Canada and is allowed to deduct tax credits for the period in which the individual is resident in Canada. The rules for the deduction of the non-refundable personal tax credits are divided into a rule for the period in the year in which the part-year resident is not resident in Canada and a rule for the period in the year in which the part-year resident is resident in Canada. Therefore, if an individual is a part-year resident and is employed or carries on business in Canada during some part of the period of non-residency in the year, the individual is taxed as a non-resident on the employment or business income earned in Canada in that period and is entitled to deduct tax credits available to a non-resident against that income.

An individual who is resident in Canada for part of the year is entitled to at least the same non-refundable tax credits that are available to an individual in similar circumstances who is non-resident throughout the year. The credits for personal amounts that are wholly available (i.e., not prorated) for the period of non-residency, to the extent that they are related to that period, are the charitable donation credit, the impairment credit for the individual only and not for a dependant, the tuition credit for the individual only, the tuition carryforward credit, the CPP, QPP, and EI credits, and the credit for interest on student loans. Note that these amounts must qualify under the Canadian rules. All other non-refundable tax credits may be deducted if all or substantially all of the individual's world income for the

---

See page ii for explanation of footnotes.

[4] CCH ¶28,334; Sec. 250(1).　　　　　　[6] CCH ¶17,003, ¶18,455; Sec. 114, 118.91.
[5] Truchon, 70 DTC 1277.

calendar year is included, no matter how long the period of non-residence. "All or substantially all" is taken to mean at least 90%.

For the period of residence, certain personal amounts may be deducted on the basis of proration by using the number of days resident in the year divided by the number of days in the calendar year. The amounts in question are personal amounts other than the pension amount; the impairment credit for self or a dependant; unused credits transferred from a spouse or common-law partner; and unused tuition, education, and textbook amounts transferred from a child or grandchild. All other applicable non-refundable tax credits may be claimed in whole without proration if they are related to the period of residence.

In addition, an individual who is resident in Canada for part of a year may not deduct a greater amount for non-refundable tax credits than that which is available to an individual who is resident in Canada throughout the year. This prevents the double counting of amounts in the two periods during the year.

The following is a brief summary of the above provisions as they apply to part-year residents (on the assumption that all or substantially all of worldwide income during the period of non-residency is not included in taxable income earned in Canada for that period):

(a) *Personal amounts other than pension amounts.* The eligible amounts are prorated based on the number of days resident in Canada and the appropriate percentage (currently 15%) is applied to the prorated amount.

(b) *Pension amount.* The pension income credit is available without proration for amounts received while resident in Canada.

(c) *Charitable gifts.* The usual rules apply to claims for this credit. Gifts made while a resident and as a non-resident will be considered if the conditions of the credit are met.

(d) *Medical expenses.* Those expenses paid while the individual is a resident of Canada will qualify for the credit without proration.

(e) *Physical or mental impairment.* The total amount that may otherwise be claimed is prorated for the number of days resident in Canada. The non-resident taxpayer may claim the impairment credit for himself or herself but not for a dependant for the period of non-residency.

(f) *Tuition.* Otherwise qualifying fees for courses may be claimed as a credit by a non-resident and, where applicable, for the period when the individual is resident.

(g) *Education and textbook amounts and student loan interest.* The education and textbook amounts are available without proration only for the period during which the student is resident in Canada. The

¶14,015

student loan interest credit can be claimed in respect of both the residency and non-residency periods.

(h) *CPP/QPP contributions and EI premiums.* Otherwise qualifying personal amounts paid while resident in Canada will qualify for the credit without proration. Where applicable, a non-resident individual may also claim a credit for these amounts.

(i) *Transfer of spouse's or common-law partner's unused credits.* A spouse's or common-law partner's unused credits can be transferred under the normal rules prorated for the number of days the transferee is resident in Canada.

(j) *Transfer of tuition, textbook, and education credits to parents and grandparents.* Similar to (i) above.

(k) *Canada employment credit, adoption credit, transit pass credit, and child fitness credit.* All those credits may be claimed without proration provided they relate to the taxpayer's period of residence.

Where the individual is claiming a personal amount which includes an income threshold (for example, the infirm dependant over 18), proration of the threshold is required. Note that the relevant period for determining the dependant's income appears to be the period in which the taxpayer, not the dependant, is resident.

A taxpayer who moved to the United States in the middle of the year was held to be entitled to the full personal tax credit for that year on the basis that she earned no income in the United States during the rest of the year so that "all or substantially all" of her income had been included in her Canadian taxable income for that year.[7]

[¶14,020] Non-Residents

[¶14,025] Taxable Income Earned in Canada

Non-residents who were employed in Canada, carried on business in Canada, or disposed of taxable Canadian property, either in a particular taxation year or in a previous year, are required to pay tax on their "taxable income earned in Canada" for the year.[8] The income to be reported for this purpose includes income from an office or employment in Canada (including director's fees and employment benefits), income from carrying on a business in Canada, taxable capital gains from the disposition of taxable Canadian property, and certain other Canadian source income. A non-resident individual also includes income from the duties of an office or employment carried on outside Canada if, at the particular time, the individual was resident in Canada.

See page ii for explanation of footnotes.

[7] Langlois, 92 DTC 1329. [8] CCH ¶17,101; Sec. 115(1); Interp. Bul. IT-420R3.

Employment and business expenses allowed to residents are generally available to non-residents to the extent they relate to income earned in Canada or income from carrying on a business in Canada. Where the non-resident's employment duties are performed or business is carried on both inside and outside Canada, a reasonable basis for allocation of the related income is necessary since only the Canadian source income is taxable under Part I. Also, a distinction must be made between the non-resident's income from carrying on business in Canada and income from property in Canada, since the latter is generally taxable under Part XIII rather than Part I.

For purposes of determining taxable capital gains, some examples of property included in "taxable Canadian property" are real estate in Canada, all property used in carrying on business in Canada, and shares of a corporation resident in Canada (other than a mutual fund corporation), which do not belong to a class of shares listed on a designated Canadian or foreign stock exchange.

Other Canadian source income to be reported includes capital cost allowance recapture and royalty income from a Canadian resource property.

The income of a non-resident is the income determined as if the following assumptions were made:

(1) The non-resident had no income other than:

(a) income from offices and employment performed in Canada and the income from the duties of an office or employment if the duties were performed outside of Canada at a time when the individual was resident in Canada;

(b) income from businesses carried on by the individual in Canada;

(c) taxable capital gains from dispositions of "taxable Canadian property" (other than from dispositions of treaty-protected property);

(d) income consisting of a negative balance of cumulative Canadian development expense less any portion thereof included in computing income from a business carried on in Canada;

(e) income in the form of recapture of capital cost allowance to the extent not included in computing income from a business. This would include, for example, recapture on disposition of a rental property;

(f) for 2008 and subsequent taxation years, the amount received under the *Wage Earner Protection Program Act* ("WEPP") and included in computing the recipient's income;

(g) the amount, if any, claimed as reserve in respect of debt forgiveness income in the preceding year;

¶14,025

(h) where the non-resident carried on a resource business in Canada in the year, income arising in respect of Canadian resource properties to the extent such amounts are not already included under paragraphs (b) or (d) above;

(i) the proceeds of disposition of an income interest in a trust (required to be included in income) less the amount of the deduction which is available to resident taxpayers;

(j) the proceeds of disposal of a right to share in the income or loss of a partnership less the unrecovered cost of such right ordinarily deductible by residents;

(k) the amount to be included in respect of the disposition of certain life insurance policies and certain life annuity contracts in Canada.[9] The latter is defined[10] to mean a life insurance policy issued upon the life of a person resident in Canada at the time the policy was issued; and

(l) certain scholarships, bursaries, research grants, signing bonuses, and compensation for employment to be performed in Canada, and remuneration from an office or employment paid after ceasing to be resident in Canada.

(2) The non-resident's only taxable capital gains and allowable capital losses were from dispositions of taxable Canadian properties or interests therein. The non-resident does not include capital gains or capital losses from dispositions of taxable Canadian property that is "treaty-protected property". This ensures that a non-resident's capital loss from the disposition of a treaty-protected property (meaning that, had the property been sold at a gain, it would not have been subject to tax in Canada by virtue of an income tax treaty) cannot offset the non-resident's taxable capital gains that are not treaty-protected.

(3) The non-resident's only losses (normally described as being from employment, business, or property or allowable business investment losses (ABILs)) were from a business carried on by him or her in Canada, from an office or employment performed in Canada, and ABILs arising from property, any gain on which would be taxable in Canada to the non-resident. A non-resident's losses do not include losses from businesses that are "treaty-protected businesses". This rule prohibits a non-resident from using losses from a business whose income would not be subject to tax under Part I by virtue of an income tax treaty, to offset income from a business whose income is not treaty-protected and thus taxable in Canada.

The taxpayer was employed in Canada, became disabled, and then became resident in Israel. Wage loss replacement payments received from her employer's disability insurance carrier were not income from duties

---

See page ii for explanation of footnotes.
[9] CCH ¶21,565, ¶21,566; Sec. 148(1), 148(1.1).   [10] CCH ¶20,809; Sec. 138(12).

performed in Canada. They were disability insurance benefits, and, hence, did not fall within the taxing provisions of item (1)(a).[11]

It should be observed that non-residents are subject to tax if they were employed or carried on business in Canada or disposed of taxable Canadian property in the year *or in a previous year*. This means, among other things, that if a taxpayer ceases to be resident in Canada and in the following year had income on the assumptions noted above, this income is subject to Part I tax. For example, if a person ceased to be resident in Canada in late 2012, and received in 2013 remuneration for employment performed while he or she was previously resident in Canada, that remuneration will be subject to Part I tax in 2013 and a return must be filed for that year. Similarly, if a person ceases to be resident in Canada in 2012, and in 2013 disposes of a business asset for an amount exceeding the undepreciated capital cost thereof, he or she will be subject to recapture in 2013.

[¶14,030] Effect of Tax Agreements

As with part-time residents, provisions relating to non-residents must be read subject to the tax agreements which Canada has with other countries. The provisions of the tax agreements govern in the case of conflict. See ¶14,310 for more information on the tax agreements.

[¶14,035] Capital Gains and Allowable Capital Losses — "Taxable Canadian Property"

The rule that a portion of capital gains are taxable as income and a portion of capital losses are deductible,[12] applies to non-residents on the disposal of "taxable Canadian property", other than treaty-protected property.[13] For this purpose, after March 4, 2010, taxable Canadian property of a taxpayer at any particular time is defined as:[14]

(1) real property situated in Canada;

(2) property used or held in, eligible capital property in respect of, or inventory of a business carried on (other than property used in a life insurance business and property that are ships and aircraft used principally in international traffic and personal or movable property pertaining to their operation provided the country in which the taxpayer is resident grants substantially similar relief to persons resident in Canada);

(3) all property (not just capital property) of a non-resident insurer that is "designated insurance property", i.e., property used by any insurer (other than a Canadian resident insurer not in the life insurance business) in carrying on an insurance business in Canada;

See page ii for explanation of footnotes.

[11] Blauer, 2008 DTC 2409.

[12] CCH ¶6007; Sec. 38.

[13] CCH ¶17,101; Sec. 115(1)(b).

[14] CCH ¶28,284; Sec. 248(1) "taxable Canadian property".

(4) shares of the capital stock of a corporation not listed on a designated stock exchange, an interest in a partnership, or an interest in a trust, which derive more than 50% of their fair market value in the preceding 60 months from real or immovable property situated in Canada, Canadian resource properties, timber resource properties, or an interest or option in any of the aforementioned properties (this does not include a share of a mutual fund corporation, a unit of a mutual fund trust, or an income interest in a trust resident in Canada, see (5) below);

(5) shares of the capital stock of a corporation that is listed on a designated stock exchange, a share of the capital stock of a mutual fund corporation, or a unit of a mutual fund trust if in the preceding 60 months, 25% of the shares or units were owned by the taxpayer or a party (or parties) with whom the taxpayer did not deal with at arm's length and more than 50% of the fair market value of the share or unit was derived directly or indirectly from real or immovable property situated in Canada, Canadian resource properties, timber resource properties, or an interest or option in any of the aforementioned properties;

(6) an interest, option, or right in civil law to a property described in paragraphs (1) to (5);

(7) Canadian resource property and timber resource property;

(8) an income interest in a Canadian resident trust;

(9) a right to a share of the income or loss under an agreement to allocate a share of the income or loss of a partnership to a retiring partner; and

(10) a life insurance policy in Canada.

This definition for taxable Canadian property, applicable after March 4, 2010, presents significant changes from the previous one. The previous definition for unlisted shares held that all unlisted shares of a Canadian corporation were generally taxable Canadian property and that unlisted shares of a non-resident corporation were taxable Canadian property if the 50% test was met in fair market value derived from real property situated in Canada, Canadian resource properties, timber resource properties, or an interest or option in any of the aforementioned properties. Now the definition for taxable Canadian property is the same for unlisted shares of both a Canadian and non-resident corporation, which is closer to the previous definition for unlisted shares of a non-resident corporation. For shares of a listed corporation, previously they were deemed to be taxable Canadian property if only the 25% share ownership test was met. Now, there is the 50% property test requirement to be met as well.

Taxable capital gains and allowable capital losses from the disposal of taxable Canadian property are to be combined with the non-resident's

Canadian employment and business income and taxed at individual or corporate rates, as the case may be (after allowable deductions).

The transfer by a non-resident of taxable Canadian property by death, gift, or mortgage foreclosure involves a disposition or deemed disposition by the non-resident of such taxable Canadian property, and can give rise to taxable gains subject to tax.[15]

Where a non-resident taxpayer has disposed of taxable Canadian property, but is not subject to immediate tax in respect of such disposition by the jurisdiction in which the taxpayer resides, Canada will (in order to avoid the double taxation resulting from the failure of the foreign tax credit mechanism to provide relief in the situation) grant the taxpayer the same deferred status in respect of that disposition, where Canada has an enabling tax treaty with that jurisdiction. Tax will then normally be imposed by Canada in the taxation year in which the disposition is subjected to tax by the jurisdiction in which the taxpayer resides.[16] Canada has such an enabling treaty (in force) with the United States, and similar enabling provisions are included in its treaties with France and with the Netherlands.

For a general discussion of capital gains and losses, see Chapter V.

[¶14,037] Non-Resident Funds with Canadian Service Providers

If certain conditions are met, foreign investment funds will not be considered to be carrying on business in Canada merely by engaging Canadian advisors to provide investment management, advisory, or administrative functions.[17] This so-called "safe harbour rule" is intended to put Canadian service providers on an equal footing with service providers in the United States and the United Kingdom. Foreign funds will not be subject to domestic taxation in specific circumstances in either of those jurisdictions.

This rule will apply if a qualified non-resident is provided with designated investment services by a Canadian service provider. A "Canadian service provider" is a corporation resident in Canada, a trust resident in Canada, or a Canadian partnership.[18] Furthermore, if the non-resident is an individual (other than a trust), the non- resident must not be affiliated with the Canadian service provider. In the case of a non-resident corporation or trust, the clarifying rule will apply only if:

- the non-resident did not promote or sell investments to persons that the non-resident knew or should have known were Canadian investors;

See page ii for explanation of footnotes.

[15] CCH ¶17,101; Sec. 69, 70(5), 115.

[16] CCH ¶17,191; Sec. 115.1; Art. XIII, Para. 8, Canada-U.S. Income Tax Convention..

[17] CCH ¶17,280a; Sec. 115.2(2).

[18] CCH ¶17,210; Sec. 115.2(1) "Canadian service provider".

- the non-resident did not make a filing under Canadian or provincial securities legislation to distribute its interests to Canadian residents; and

- where the non-resident was in existence more than one year, not more than 25% of the fair market value of its investments were owned by persons and partnerships that were affiliated with the Canadian service provider.

It should be noted that the failure to meet the above conditions does not necessarily imply that a business is being carried on in Canada by the non- resident investment fund. The determination in such case will be based on general principles and other statutory rules relating to the "carrying on" of a business in Canada.

The definition of "designated investment services" [19] details the types of services that may be provided by a Canadian advisor to fall within the scope of the safe harbour rule. Generally, this term means one or more of the following services:

(a) investment management and advice with respect to "qualifying investments" (see below);

(b) purchasing and selling qualifying investments and exercising rights incidental to the ownership of such investments;

(c) investment administration services; and

(d) in the case of services provided to a corporation, trust, or partnership that solely invests its funds in qualified investments, marketing investments in the corporation, trust, or partnership to non-resident investors.

The definition of "qualified investment" for the above purposes means the following six types of property:[20]

- shares and interests in partnerships, trusts, entities, funds, and organizations; note, however, that shares and interests that derive the majority of their value from real property in Canada, Canadian resource property, or timber resource property are excluded unless the share or interest is listed on a designated stock exchange and the qualified non-resident fund does not own 25% or more of the shares of any class of the company or 25% or more of the total value of interests in the partnership, trust, entity, fund, or organization.

- indebtedness;

- annuities;

See page ii for explanation of footnotes.

[19] CCH ¶17,220; Sec. 115.2(1) "designated investment services".

[20] CCH ¶17,270; Sec. 115.2(1) "qualified investment".

- commodities or commodities futures;

- currency; and

- options, interests, rights, and forward and future agreements related to properties listed above, and agreements under which obligations are derived from interest rates, the price of property described above, payments made in respect of such properties, or from certain indices reflecting a composite measure of such rates, prices, etc.

[¶14,040] Tax Collection Procedure in respect of Dispositions by Non-Residents of Certain Property

To encourage non-residents disposing of taxable Canadian property to pay the tax exigible on such dispositions, the Act provides a system whereby an amount in respect of the tax must be remitted by the non-resident vendor in advance of the disposition, or remitted by the purchaser on the vendor's behalf after the disposition. Under the first alternative, a "certificate limit" is applied for in advance of the disposition. Under the second alternative, the disposition is made first and reported to the Minister after the fact. Which of the two alternatives is employed in given circumstances will be decided by the parties, depending upon the facts of their particular transaction. One of the most common considerations will obviously be the time necessary to obtain a certificate prior to the disposition. Notification must be provided to the Minister, in any event, of a disposition of taxable Canadian property by a non-resident, either before disposition or within 10 days of disposition.[21] However more recently, non-resident beneficiaries of a Canadian "estate" were not required to provide notice to the Canada Revenue Agency on the disposition of their capital interests in the estate on the basis that an estate is not a "trust" for purposes of the *Income Tax Act.*[22]

Under the first alternative (certificate prior to disposition), non-residents proposing to dispose of taxable Canadian property (other than property in respect of which a clearance certificate is obtained and "excluded property") will send a notice to the Minister prior to the disposition. The notice is represented by Form T2062. In this form, the non-resident will, among other things, specify the adjusted cost base of the taxable Canadian property being disposed of at the time of sending the notice, and will specify the estimated amount of his proceeds of disposition or the fair market value of the property at the time of the proposed disposition, if the disposition is by way of gift or is between non-arm's length parties. Then, upon payment by the non-resident to the Minister of an amount equal to 25% of the anticipated gain, a certificate in Form T2064 will be issued to the non-resident vendor and the purchaser, specifying the amount of the estimated proceeds of disposition (the "certificate limit"). The amount so paid to the Minister is applied against the non-resident's tax as ultimately assessed. In lieu of the above payment, the Minister may permit the non-resident vendor

See page ii for explanation of footnotes.

[21] Sec. 116.   [22] Lipson v. The Queen, 2012 DTC 1064 (TCC).

¶14,040

to furnish acceptable security.[23] Note, however, that the furnishing of such security is not tantamount to the payment of any tax which may ultimately be assessed. Accordingly, interest and penalties in respect of any late filing of any returns, or in respect of any deficiency between the amount of security furnished and the tax as ultimately assessed, will be exigible.[24]

The second alternative (no certificate prior to disposition) is substantially similar to the first, except that it requires the non-resident person to provide notice in Form T2062 within the 10-day period following the disposition, and to pay the same amount (calculated using the same percentages of the anticipated gain), in return for the issuance of the certificate. Here, again, the Minister may accept suitable security in lieu of payment.[25]

If the certificate is not obtained under either method, the purchaser must, within 30 days after the end of the month in which he or she acquired the property, pay to the Minister a tax equal to 25% of the cost (i.e., the purchase price) of the property. If the actual proceeds of disposition exceed the certificate limit (in cases where the certificate has been obtained), the purchaser must, within the same limitation period, pay the Minister a tax equal to the lesser of:

(a) 25% of the cost to the purchaser of the property; and

(b) 25% of the excess of the proceeds of disposition over the certificate limit.

The purchaser's payment, in either case, is applied against the tax owing by the non-resident in respect of the disposition, and is recoverable by the purchaser from the non-resident. The purchaser will not be required to remit 25% of the purchase price to the Receiver General if, after reasonable inquiry, the purchaser had no reason to believe that the non-resident person was not resident in Canada, or, after 2008, the purchaser came to the conclusion that the vendor was resident in a particular tax-treaty country and certain conditions described below were met.[26]

Beginning in 2009, a purchaser acquiring treaty-protected property from a non-resident vendor will not be required to withhold 25% of the purchase price and remit it to the Receiver General if:

- the purchaser concludes, after reasonable inquiry, that the vendor is resident in a treaty jurisdiction;

- the property would be treaty-protected property of the non-resident person if the non-resident person were resident in the treaty jurisdiction; and

---

See page ii for explanation of footnotes.

[23] CCH ¶17,300–17,345; Sec. 116(1)–(5).

[24] Corporation AAA S.A, 92 DTC 1805.

[25] CCH ¶17,300–17,345; Sec. 116(1)–(5).

[26] CCH ¶17,300–17,345; Sec. 116(1)–(5).

- the purchaser provides notice of the acquisition within 30 days after the acquisition date.[27]

The system does not apply to "excluded property" (see ¶14,045). A non-resident who disposes or proposes to dispose of a property (other than capital property) that is real property situated in Canada [or, after December 23, 1998, eligible capital property that is taxable Canadian property], a timber resource property, a depreciable property that is a taxable Canadian property, or any interest or option therein, may report the details of the transaction to the Minister, either "before or after the fact", but without time limitations, and to procure the issuance of a certificate, similar to the ones mentioned above, upon payment to the Minister of such amount as is acceptable to him or her.[28] Acceptable security may be furnished in lieu of such payment. The purchaser is then required (within the 30-day limitation period mentioned) to pay a tax equal to 50% of any excess of the purchase price over the certificate limit; if no certificate exists, the payment becomes, in effect, 50% of the purchase price itself.[29] All payments by the purchaser are recoverable from the non-resident vendor, but no payment is required if the purchaser can show that, after reasonable enquiry, there was no reason to believe that the non-resident vendor was not resident in Canada or, after 2008, there was every reason to believe that he was resident in a particular tax-treaty country, and the above conditions were met.

Non-residents disposing of Canadian resource properties, certain life insurance policies, and taxable Canadian property (depreciable or non-depreciable, other than "excluded property") by way of gift *inter vivos* or in any non-arm's length transaction involving a consideration less than fair market value, are affected by the same rules (with the same two alternatives) as the ones mentioned above, in respect of non-depreciable property. Purchasers from them are similarly affected.[30] The difference is that, in these situations, fair market value rather than actual proceeds of disposition is the figure which must be reported to the Minister; and this is also the figure in respect of which the purchaser's various liabilities are determined. Properties transferred or distributed as a consequence of a non-resident's death, however, are exempted from these special rules.[31]

Useful guidance on the procedures to follow in reporting dispositions of taxable Canadian property, and reducing the required withholding can be found in Information Circular IC 72-17R6 "Procedures concerning the disposition of taxable Canadian property by non-residents of Canada — Section 116". This circular was updated in September 2011.

See page ii for explanation of footnotes.

[27] CCH ¶17,346–17,347; Sec. 116(5.01)–(5.02).
[28] CCH ¶17,361; Sec. 116(5.2).
[29] CCH ¶17,362; Sec. 116(5.3).
[30] CCH ¶17,352; Sec. 116(5.1).
[31] CCH ¶17,352; Sec. 116(5.1).

¶14,040

[¶14,045] Excluded Property

The various tax collection procedures in ¶14,040 do not apply where the property is excluded property. "Excluded property" is defined as:

(1) property that is a taxable Canadian property solely because a provision of the Act deems it to be a taxable Canadian property;

(2) property that is inventory in a business carried on in Canada, other than real property, Canadian resource property, or a timber resource property;

(3) a share of a corporation listed on a recognized Canadian or foreign stock exchange;

(4) after July 14, 2008, a specified investment flow-through (SIFT) wind-up entity equity listed on a recognized stock exchange;

(5) a unit of a mutual fund trust;

(6) most types of debt instruments;

(7) property of licensed non-resident insurers that carry on business in Canada;

(8) property of an authorized foreign bank that is used or held in the course of the bank's Canadian banking business [pending technical amendments (released July 16, 2010) would exclude all of the property of an authorized foreign bank that carries on a Canadian banking business];

(9) an option in respect of property referred to above;

(10) an interest in any property referred to above; and

(11) beginning in 2009, a property that is a treaty-exempt property of the vendor, at the time of disposition.[32]

With respect to (10), a property is a "treaty-exempt property" of a non-resident vendor if it is a "treaty-protected property" and, where the purchaser and the non-resident vendor are related at that time, the purchaser provides notice of the acquisition within 30 days after the acquisition date.[33] "Treaty-protected property" is defined as property, any income or gain from the disposition of which would be exempt from tax under Part I, because of a tax treaty with another country.[34]

It is important to note that the significance of excluded property is that the enforcement rules in ¶14,040 do not apply on its disposition. Most of these properties are, however, taxable Canadian properties and the non-resident is subject to the tax imposed on their disposition. The reason for exempting certain dispositions from the enforcement rules in ¶14,040

See page ii for explanation of footnotes.

[32] CCH ¶17,365; Sec. 116(6).
[33] CCH ¶17,365d; Sec. 116(6.1).

[34] CCH ¶28,312; Sec. 248(1) "treaty-protected property".

appears to be in some cases commercial expediency and in others the fact that compliance by the non-resident is otherwise ensured.

The CRA has also stated that the enforcement rules in ¶14,040 do not apply in respect of dispositions arising on death, foreclosures of property, and amalgamations.[35]

[¶14,060] Non-Resident Employees Formerly Residing in Canada

A non-resident is deemed to be employed in Canada for a taxation year if, in any previous year, he or she ceased to be resident in Canada and, in the taxation year, received salary, wages, and other remuneration in respect of an office or employment, directly or indirectly, from a person resident in Canada.[36] This deeming provision does not apply unless the individual is entitled to an exemption from an income tax otherwise payable in another country in respect of the salary, wages, or other remuneration, because of the application of an agreement or convention between Canada and one or more other countries. In other words, amounts paid by Canadian employers to former residents will be subject to tax in Canada only where such amounts are exempt from tax in the foreign country as a result of a tax treaty between such foreign country and Canada.

A non-resident person who receives employment income in a non-resident taxation year for work performed outside of Canada in a previous year while he or she was resident in Canada may be subject to Canadian tax on this employment income if it is paid directly or indirectly by an entity in Canada. Such income will be subject to tax unless:

(1) it is subject to income tax imposed by a country other than Canada; or

(2) it is paid in connection with the selling of property, the negotiating of contracts, or the rendering of services for and in the ordinary course of business of the Canadian payor or another business or entity with whom the payor does not deal at arm's length.[37]

[¶14,065] Signing Bonuses and Amounts Payable under Agreement for Services

A non-resident must include in taxable income earned in Canada "signing bonus" or other amounts received under a contract which can reasonably be considered to have been received in whole or in part for entering into an agreement to perform any services in Canada or as remuneration or compensation in whole or in part for employment or services to be performed in Canada, if the amount is deductible for Canadian purposes by the payer.

See page ii for explanation of footnotes.

[35] Inf. Cir. 72-17R6.   [37] CCH ¶17,150; Sec. 115(2)(e)(i).
[36] CCH ¶17,150; Sec. 115(2)(c).

¶14,060

The full amount of such payments is to be included in income even though only a portion of the employment or services will be performed in Canada. This provision is directed primarily at non-resident athletes who come to Canada to play for Canadian teams, and is intended to ensure that all compensation received from the Canadian team is included in the non-resident's taxable income earned in Canada, regardless of when it is paid or the form of the arrangement for payment. Thus, the full amount of such payments will be included in taxable income earned in Canada.

If the amount of the payment had instead been paid as part of a regular remuneration package, the recipient may have included only a portion in taxable income earned in Canada based on the extent to which the recipient carried out his or her employment in Canada.[38]

[¶14,070] Non-Resident Students, Researchers and Employees

Certain non-resident students, researchers under a grant, and persons who have ceased to be resident in Canada are deemed to be employed in Canada.[39] Such persons are taxable in Canada on research grants and like payments received from a source in Canada. Beginning in 2006, amounts received from scholarships, fellowships, bursaries, and prizes are not taxable. However, beginning in 2010, post-secondary programs consisting mainly of research are eligible for the scholarship exemption only if they lead to a college or CEGEP diploma, or a bachelor, masters, or doctoral (or equivalent) degree. As a result, post-doctoral fellowships are now taxable.

Non-resident students who receive amounts out of a registered education savings plan must include this amount in income for Canadian tax purposes.[40]

Non-residents can deduct moving expenses if they move to study courses as full-time students. However, they can only deduct these expenses from the taxable portion of their scholarships, fellowships, bursaries, certain prizes, and research grants.[41] They cannot deduct moving expenses if their only income at the new location is scholarship, fellowship, or bursary income that is entirely exempt from tax.

[¶14,075] Goods Purchased in One Country and Sold in Another

If nothing is done in one country by an enterprise except to purchase goods and deliver those goods to another country where they are sold under contracts completed in the country of sale, it would appear that no part of the profit of the enterprise would be attributed to the country in which the goods are purchased, and that the entire profit will be attributed to the country in which the goods are sold. If the goods are sold in more than one country, presumably the profits will be attributed to the various countries in

---

See page ii for explanation of footnotes.

[38] CCH ¶17,150; Sec. 115(2)(c.1).

[39] CCH ¶17,150; Sec. 115(2).

[40] CCH ¶17,150; Sec. 115(2).

[41] CCH ¶8650, ¶17,150; Sec. 62, 115(2)(f).

which the goods are sold, in the same proportion the gross sales in each country bear to the total gross sales of the enterprise.[42]

[¶14,080] Applicable Deductions from Non-Residents' Income

Non-residents, both corporate and individual, are limited to a very specific set of deductions from income in computing their taxable income earned in Canada.[43]

Individual non-residents are permitted deductions in respect of:

(a) qualifying employee stock-option benefits;

(b) for 2000 and subsequent taxation years, charitable donations of employee option securities to a qualifying donee (see ¶8202) to the extent that the securities option benefit to which the deduction relates is included in computing the non-resident's Part I income;

(c) certain shares received by them as prospectors and grubstakers upon their disposition of certain mining claims;

(d) Canadian workers' compensation and social assistance payments; and

(e) applicable loss carryovers.

Each of these deductions is intended to offset, at least in part, the effects of the inclusions of their counterpart amounts in the incomes of the non-residents affected.[44]

Corporate non-residents are permitted deductions in respect of:

(a) gifts made to registered charities (not exceeding 50% of their net income as determined under the assumptions set out in ¶14,025);

(b) gifts to the Crown in the right of Canada and the provinces;

(c) certain gifts of cultural property meeting the criteria in the *Cultural Property Export & Import Act*; and

(d) gifts of land certified to be ecologically sensitive land.[45]

Non-residents, both corporate and individual, are also permitted to deduct those non-capital losses, net capital losses, and restricted farm losses which may reasonably be considered applicable to employment performed in Canada, a business carried on in Canada, or the disposition of property, if any profit or gain realized on that property would have been included in taxable income earned in Canada.[46] However, such losses from property

---

[42] CCH ¶17,101; Sec. 115(1).
[43] CCH ¶17,101; Sec. 115(1).
[44] CCH ¶15,015, ¶15,200, ¶15,272, ¶15,274, ¶15,290, ¶17,101; Sec. 110(1)(d), 110(1)(d.01), 110(1)(d.1), 110(1)(d.2), 110(1)(f), 115(1)(d).

[45] CCH ¶15,750, ¶17,101; Sec. 110.1(1), 115(1)(d).
[46] CCH ¶16,003, ¶17,101; Sec. 111, 115(1)(e).

disposition may be deducted only if the property disposed of is not treaty-protected property. "Treaty-protected property," is property, any income or gain from the disposition of which by the non-resident would be exempt from Canadian tax because of a Canadian tax treaty between Canada and the non- resident's country of residence.[47] These changes ensure that a non-resident's losses from sources that are treaty protected (i.e., where any gain or income from such sources would not be not taxable in Canada by virtue of an income tax treaty) cannot be carried back or forward to offset Canadian source income that is subject to Canadian tax.

Where all or substantially all of the non-resident's income for the year (considered by the CRA to be 90%) is income used in computing taxable income earned in Canada for the year, the non-resident is also entitled to such other deductions from income permitted for the purpose of computing taxable income as may reasonably be considered wholly applicable.[48] This limits the availability of deductions other than those specified above to non-residents who derive all or substantially all of their income from Canadian sources.

[¶14,081] Credits Restrictions

Non-resident individuals may not claim certain tax credits unless all or substantially all of their income (meaning 90%) for the year is included in their taxable income earned in Canada. If the latter is true, they may claim the same credits that resident individuals may claim in the year.[49]

The credits specifically disallowed if the "substantially all" test is not met are the personal credits, adoption credit, transit pass credit, child fitness credit (after 2006), medical credit, impairment credit for dependants and partial dependants, education credit, textbook credit, transfers of unused credits from a spouse or common-law partner, or transfers of unused tuition, education, and textbook credits to a parent or grandparent.

If a non-resident is employed or is carrying on business in Canada or has capital gains from taxable Canadian property, certain credits may be claimed even if the substantially all rule is not met. These are credits for charitable donations, Crown gifts and cultural gifts, the disability credit for the taxpayer only, the tuition credit for the taxpayer only, the credit for student loan interest, and the CPP/QPP and Employment Insurance credits.

---

[47] CCH ¶28,312; Sec. 248(1) "treaty-protected property".

[48] CCH ¶17,101; Sec. 115(1)(f).

[49] CCH ¶18,461; Sec. 118.94.

[¶14,085] Withholding Tax on Income from Canada of Non-Resident Persons

[¶14,090] General Non-Resident Withholding Tax

Withholding tax applies to every amount that a person resident in Canada pays or credits, or is deemed to pay or credit, to a non-resident person as, on account of, in lieu of payment of, or in satisfaction of certain specific items enumerated in the Act.[50] In the absence of a special election by the non-resident, no deductions are permitted from the amounts required to be withheld,[51] and penalties are provided for failure to withhold when required to do so. (See ¶14,095 and ¶14,255 *et seq.*) The statutory withholding rate is 25%, but is often reduced under bilateral tax treaties to 15%.[52] The withholding tax rate on interest on certain provincial bonds, however, is only 5%.[53]

The tax base includes:

(1) certain dividends, interest, management fees, estate or trust income, rents, royalties, patronage dividends, and alimony;

(2) certain pension benefits, retiring allowances, supplementary unemployment benefit plan payments, registered retirement savings plan (RRSP) payments, registered retirement income fund (RRIF) payments, deferred profit sharing plan (DPSP) payments, income averaging annuity contract payments, registered education savings plan (RESP) payments, registered disability savings plan (RDSP) payments, other annuity payments, payments out of a retirement compensation arrangement (RCA) whether or not the payor custodian is resident, payments on account of the purchase price of an interest in an RCA, payments under an eligible funeral arrangement, and, after 2009, payments out of an employee life and health trust; and

(3) certain amounts that would be subject to Part I tax had the non-resident recipient been resident. See ¶14,175.

[¶14,095] Failure to Deduct, Withhold or Remit — Penalties and Interest

Failure to withhold renders the payor personally liable for the amount not so withheld plus a penalty of 10%.[54] If the failure to withhold was made knowingly, or under circumstances amounting to gross negligence, the penalty is increased to 20% of the amount that should have been withheld.[55] Interest at the prescribed rate will also begin to accrue (on the amount not withheld, but not on the penalty) from the 15th day of the month immediately following the month in which the amount should have been deducted

---

See page ii for explanation of footnotes.

[50] CCH ¶26,010; Sec. 212(1); Inf. Cir. 77-16R4.
[51] CCH ¶26,010; Sec. 212(1); Inf. Cir. 77-16R4.
[52] CCH ¶26,015, ¶29,024; Sec. 212(1); ITAR 10(6); Inf. Cir. 76-12R6.

[53] CCH ¶26,010, ¶26,160–26,180, ¶29,022; Sec. 212(1), 212(6)–(8).
[54] CCH ¶26,400; ¶27,278; Sec. 214(1), 227(8)(a).
[55] CCH ¶27,278; Sec. 227(8)(b).

or withheld.[56] The non-resident will be jointly and severally liable with the payor for this interest.[57] In addition, a penalty may be imposed for failure to remit to the Receiver General amounts actually withheld. For remittances due on or after February 26, 2008, the penalty for late remittances is dependent upon the number of days the payment is overdue:

- one to three days late — 3%;

- four to five days late — 5%;

- six to seven days late — 7%; and

- more than 7 days late — 10%.[58]

For remittances due before February 26, 2008, the penalty is fixed at 10%. As well, there is a further penalty for second or subsequent occurrences to remit or pay an amount during the same year. In such a case, the penalty will be 20% of the amount that should have been remitted or paid, if the same person has already been assessed a penalty for a failure to remit or pay in the same calendar year, and the failure to remit was made knowingly or under circumstances amounting to gross negligence.[59]

A resident is required to withhold and remit taxes on payments made to a non-resident, even if the non-resident pays Part I tax by virtue of an election to file Part I tax returns. Interest on unremitted withholding taxes is assessed against the payor, while the non-resident recipient is jointly and severally liable for the interest.[60]

[¶14,100] Management Fees

A withholding tax is imposed upon management or administration fees or charges paid or credited by a resident of Canada to a non-resident.[61] The Act does not contain a definition of a management or administration fee or charge but it does provide that, for the purpose of withholding tax, a management or administration fee or charge does not include an amount paid or credited to a non-resident for:

(a) a service rendered by a non-resident with whom the payor deals at arm's length and who rendered the service in the ordinary course of his or her business; or

(b) a specific expense incurred by the non-resident for the performance of a service that was for the benefit of the payor.

In either event, the amount paid or credited must be reasonable in the circumstances.[62]

See page ii for explanation of footnotes.

[56] CCH ¶27,281; Sec. 227(8.3).
[57] CCH ¶27,279; Sec. 227(8.1).
[58] CCH ¶27,282; Sec. 227(9)(a).
[59] CCH ¶27,282; Sec. 227(9)(b).

[60] [Pechet, 2008 DTC 3381.
[61] CCH ¶26,010; Sec. 212(1)(a); Interp. Bul. IT-468R.
[62] CCH ¶26,130; Sec. 212(4); Inf. Cir. 77-16R4.

The Tax Court of Canada has held that certain fees paid by a wholly-owned resident subsidiary to its non-resident parent, allegedly for certain accounting and administration services rendered by the latter, were "management and administration" fees subject to withholding tax. The Court also concluded that the nature and purpose of the major portion of the amounts so paid was not explained clearly enough. Accordingly such major portion was not, in the Court's opinion, a "specific expense" qualifying for exemption from the withholding tax.[63]

[¶14,105] Interest

Interest paid or credited by a Canadian resident payer to a non-resident recipient not dealing at arm's length with the payer is subject to the 25% withholding tax, unless the interest is in respect of certain debt obligations such as Canadian government bonds (otherwise called "fully exempt interest"). For more details, see ¶14,112.[64]

As it currently reads, this provision exempts from Part XIII withholding tax payments of interest made to arm's length non-residents. This arm's length test was held to be met when the interest portion of a Canadian payer's outstanding loan to a non-arm's length non-resident was sold to an arm's length Belgian bank, the principal amount of the debt remaining with the non-arm's length non-resident. According to the Court of Appeal, the general anti-avoidance rule (GAAR) did not come into effect for the sole reason that the Belgian Bank acquired the right to be paid the interest on the loan but not the principal amount of the debt.[65]

To counteract the effects of this decision, the Minister of Finance released draft legislation on March 16, 2011 (not as yet passed) that will subject to Part XIII tax interest paid to any non-resident (whether arm's length or not), if the principal amount of the debt is owed to a non-resident with whom the Canadian payer does not deal at arm's length. Once enacted, this proposal will apply to agreements or arrangements entered into on or after March 16, 2011.

Most Canadian income tax treaties reduce the withholding rate to 15% or lower and, as noted below, the Canada–U.S. Treaty will be amended to eliminate withholding on interest payments made between residents of those countries.

The Fifth Protocol to the treaty, signed on September 21, 2007, but formally ratified on December 15, 2008, will exempt from withholding tax any interest paid between unrelated persons as of January 1, 2008. For interest paid between related persons, the withholding tax rate will be reduced from the previous 10% treaty rate to 7% in 2008, 4% in 2009 and nil after 2009 (since the non-arm's length rate of 7% for these types of pay-

---

See page ii for explanation of footnotes.

[63] Agricultural and Industrial Corporation et al, 91 DTC 1286.

[64] CCH ¶26,057; Sec. 212(1)(b).
[65] Lehigh Cement Ltd., 2010 DTC 5081.

ments will apply for all of 2008, a taxpayer that has paid the 10% rate pursuant to the previous treaty provisions will be entitled to a refund of 3%).

The Fifth Protocol came into force on December 15, 2008. Generally speaking, the Protocol will apply to taxes withheld at source on February 1, 2009, and in respect of other taxes for taxation years beginning after December 31, 2008. However, different effective dates apply to specific measures.

[¶14,110] Exemption from Withholding Tax for Arm's Length Payments of Interest after 2007

As discussed in ¶14,105, effective after 2007, the withholding tax does not apply to payments of interest from a Canadian resident person to an arm's length non-resident person, except in the case of a payment of participating debt interest. The phrase "participating debt interest" is defined as interest, all or part of which is computed by reference to revenue, profits, cash flow, commodity prices, or any similar criterion, or by reference to dividend payments made to shareholders of any corporation.[66] However, expressly excluded from the definition are interest payments on a debt obligation secured by real property outside of Canada (unless the interest is deductible in computing income from a business in Canada or a property other than foreign real property) to a prescribed international organization or agency, or under certain securities lending arrangements.[67] These excluded amounts of interest will not be subject to withholding tax. Furthermore, participating debt interest does not include interest on a prescribed obligation (currently prescribed as an indexed debt obligation that provides "participating" interest only to the extent of a change in the purchasing power of money).[68] Any other payment of participating debt interest will be subject to withholding tax.

[¶14,111] Exemption from Withholding Tax for Arm's Length (and Non-Arm's Length) Payments of Interest before 2008

For amounts paid or credited before 2008, there were various exceptions from withholding tax for arm's length (and non-arm's length) payments of interest.[69] These former exceptions are:

(1) interest payable on bonds of, or guaranteed by, the Government of Canada;

(2) interest payable by a prescribed financial institution on an "eligible deposit" recorded in the books of account of an international banking centre;

See page ii for explanation of footnotes.

[66] CCH ¶26,110e; Sec. 212(3) "participating debt interest".

[67] CCH ¶26,110; Sec. 212(3) "fully exempt interest".

[68] CCH ¶26,059; Reg. 806.2.

[69] CCH ¶26,057, ¶26,059; Sec. 212(1)(b); Reg. 806; Inf. Cir. 77-16R4.

¶14,111

(3) interest on bonds, debentures, notes, mortgages,[70] hypothecary claims or similar obligations which are:

(a) of or guaranteed by the Government of Canada;

(b) of the government of a province or agent thereof;

(c) of a municipality in Canada or a municipal or public body performing a function of government in Canada;

(d) of a corporation, commission, or association not less than 90% of the shares or capital of which is owned by The Queen in right of a province or by a Canadian municipality or a wholly-owned subsidiary of such a corporation, commission, or association; and

(e) of an educational institution or hospital where repayment of the principal amount thereof and payment of the interest thereon is to be made, or is guaranteed, assured, or otherwise specifically provided for or secured by the government of a province;

(4) interest payable in a foreign currency on obligations which:

(a) are entered into under an agreement in writing made on or before December 20, 1960 under which the creditor was obliged to advance a specified amount at or by a specified time at a specified rate of interest or at a rate to be determined as provided in the agreement;

(b) are bonds, debentures, etc., arranged for with a dealer in securities on or before December 20, 1960, which arrangement can be established by written evidence given or made on or before that date;

(c) are entered into in the course of carrying on a business in a country other than Canada and the interest is deductible in computing the income of the payor under Part I from a business carried on by the taxpayer in the particular country (or would have been deductible but for limitations in the Act); or

(d) arise on the purchase of property and the purchaser assumed an obligation of the vendor which was secured on the property; this exception is applicable only if the purchaser has undertaken to pay the same amount of principal on assuming the obligation at the same date and with the same interest as the vendor of the property had undertaken to pay;

(5) interest payable to an arm's length person on an obligation entered into in the course of carrying on a life insurance business in a country other than Canada;

See page ii for explanation of footnotes.

[70] Interp. Bul. IT-155R3.

¶14,111

(6) interest payable by a resident corporation to an arm's length person on an obligation, if the corporation is not obliged to pay more than 25% of the principal amount within five years of the date of issue, except in the event of a default under the terms of the obligation or of any agreement relating thereto, or if the terms of the agreement become unlawful or are changed by legislative or judicial action, or if a right is exercised pursuant to the agreement to convert the indebtedness into or exchange it for a prescribed security.

> Interest paid on a corporate debt obligation, however, will not be disqualified from this exemption merely because the borrower may be required to make an early repayment of the debt as a consequence of the death of the lender;[71]

(7) interest payable on any bond, debenture, or similar obligation to a person to whom a certificate of exemption has been issued (e.g., non-taxable trusts, foundations, etc.,) provided that the payor and the payee deal at arm's length (see ¶14,115);

(8) interest payable on a mortgage, hypothecary claim hypothec, or similar obligation with respect to real property (or an interest therein) situated outside Canada, except to the extent that such interest is deductible from income;[72] and

(9) interest payable to a prescribed international organization or agency.[73]

Interest on an obligation insured by the Canada Deposit Insurance Corporation is deemed not to be interest with respect to an obligation guaranteed by the Government of Canada. Such interest payments are therefore subject to non-resident withholding tax.[74]

[¶14,112] Withholding Tax for Non-Arm's Length Payments of Interest after 2007

Although the withholding tax does not apply to arm's length payments of interest after 2007 (other than "participating debt interest"; see ¶14,110), it continues to apply to interest paid or credited by a Canadian resident to a non-arm's length non-resident, subject to substantially the same exceptions that applied prior to 2008. The excepted interest payments are now defined as "fully exempt interest".[75]

The first type of fully exempt interest is interest paid or payable on bonds, debentures, notes, mortgages, hypothecary claims, or similar obligations:

See page ii for explanation of footnotes.

[71] CCH ¶26,057; Sec. 212(1)(b).
[72] Interp. Bul. IT-361R3.
[73] CCH ¶26,057; Sec. 212(1)(b).

[74] CCH ¶26,260; Sec. 212(15).

[75] CCH ¶26,110; Sec. 212(3) "fully exempt interest".

(i) of or guaranteed by the Government of Canada (but not including those insured by the Canada Deposit Insurance Corporation),

(ii) of the government of a province,

(iii) of an agent of a province,

(iv) of a municipality in Canada or a municipal or public body performing a function of government in Canada,

(v) of a corporation, commission, or association not less than 90% of the shares or capital of which is owned by Her Majesty in right of a province, or by a Canadian municipality, or by a wholly-owned subsidiary of such an entity, or

(vi) of an educational institution or a hospital where repayment of the principal and payment of the interest is to be made, guaranteed, assured, or secured by a provincial government.

The second type of fully exempt interest is that which is paid or payable on a mortgage, hypothecary claim, or similar obligation secured by real property or an interest in real property situated outside Canada, and interest paid or payable under an agreement of sale respecting real property situated outside Canada. However, specifically excluded from this type of fully exempt interest is interest that is deductible by the payor in computing its income from a business carried on in Canada or a property other than real or immovable property situated outside of Canada; such interest will therefore be subject to withholding. For example, if the debt obligation is secured by foreign real estate, but the loan proceeds are used for the purpose of earning income from a property or business in Canada, withholding tax will apply, if the recipient/creditor is non-arm's length to the payor/debtor.

The third type of fully exempt interest is interest paid or payable to a prescribed international organization or agency. The Bank for International Settlements and the European Bank for Reconstruction and Development are expected to be prescribed for these purposes.

The last type of fully exempt interest is an amount paid or credited under a securities lending agreement that is deemed to be interest paid by the borrower under the agreement to the lender under the agreement. Under a typical securities lending arrangement, the borrower provides collateral (cash or securities) to the lender as security for the loaned securities, in the event of default by the borrower. In general terms, the deemed interest referred to above is the amount paid by the borrower to the lender as compensation for interest in respect of the loaned security, where the borrower has provided the lender with collateral of money or securities (generally, debt obligations of governments or government bodies or agencies); the fair market value of the collateral is equal to at least 95% of the fair market value of the loaned security; and the borrower is entitled to the benefits of all or substantially all of the income or gain derived from the collateral. The

¶14,112

securities lending arrangement must be entered into by the borrower in the course of carrying on a business outside of Canada, and the security must be either shares of a corporation listed on a stock exchange or debt obligations of governments or government bodies or agencies.

[¶14,115] Interest — Certificates of Exemption before 2008

Before 2008, no tax needs to be withheld on interest payable to an arm's length person who holds a valid certificate of exemption, as described below.[76] With the general exemption of all interest paid by persons in Canada to arm's length non-residents, these certificates are no longer necessary after 2007. This commentary discusses the application of the certificate of exemption prior to January 2008.

The above certificate of exemption could be issued to certain non-resident persons who satisfied the Minister that an income tax was imposed under the laws of the country of residence and that those laws exempted the non-resident from the payment of income tax to the government of that country.[77] Such a certificate of exemption could be issued to: (a) a person who was or would have been, if resident in Canada, exempt from tax; (b) a trust or corporation established or incorporated principally in connection with, or the principal purpose of which was to administer or provide benefits under, one or more superannuation, pension, or retirement funds or plans or any funds or plans established to provide employee benefits; or (c) a trust, corporation, or other organization constituted and operated exclusively for charitable purposes, no part of the income of which was payable to, or was otherwise available for, the personal benefit of any proprietor, member, shareholder, trustee, or settlor of that trust, corporation, or other organization.

[¶14,120] Dispositions of Certain Property by Non-Residents

Non-residents disposing of taxable Canadian property, Canadian resource properties, and certain other kinds of property are liable for tax on any resulting gains. Purchasers of such properties from non-residents can become liable for such tax as well if they do not either withhold and remit the tax from the purchase price, or insist that the tax be prepaid by the non-resident, who will be issued with a certificate evidencing such prepayment. It should be noted that, beginning in 2009, this withholding requirement is eased for dispositions by non-residents of "treaty-protected property". See ¶14,040.[78]

[¶14,125] Effect of Tax Agreements on Capital Gains

The taxation of a non-resident on capital gains is contrary to the provisions of most of Canada's international tax agreements, the majority of

---

See page ii for explanation of footnotes.

[76] CCH ¶26,057; Sec. 212(1)(b); Inf. Cir. 77-16R4.   [78] Inf. Cir. 72-17R6.
[77] CCH ¶26,250; Sec. 212(14).

which exempt capital gains (other than from real estate) from taxation in Canada if the non-resident has no permanent establishment in Canada. The agreements vary from country to country and should be examined at the relevant time.

[¶14,130] Withholding Tax Not Applicable to Interest on Certain Loans

Withholding tax does not apply to certain interest payments made by a loan company resident in Canada to its non-resident parent company.[79] Such interest is exempt from withholding tax only if the following conditions exist:

(1) The non-resident corporation (referred to as the "parent corporation") is indebted to a Canadian resident (corporate or otherwise) or a non-resident insurance corporation carrying on business in Canada.

(2) Interest on the indebtedness is required to be paid in Canadian currency.

(3) The parent corporation has loaned all or part of the money so obtained at the same rate of interest to its wholly-owned subsidiary corporation resident in Canada and either:

(a) the subsidiary's principal business is the making of loans; or

(b) the subsidiary's principal business is not the making of loans but it has re-loaned the money to its wholly owned subsidiary corporation which is resident in Canada and whose principal business is the making of the loans.

(4) An election is made in prescribed form by the creditor and the parent corporation.

[¶14,135] Estate or Trust Income

Any amount paid or credited by a trust or estate to a non-resident beneficiary is subject to withholding tax as income of the estate or trust unless it was a distribution or payment of capital.[80] This is so regardless of the source from which the estate or trust derived the income.

However, no withholding tax will be payable in the following two circumstances:

(1) If the income can reasonably be regarded as having been derived from dividends or interest received by the trustee from a non-resident-owned investment corporation, or as amounts received in satisfaction of a royalty or in respect of a copyright on the production or reproduction of any literary, dramatic, musical, or artistic work, provided such income in either case would have been non-taxable if it had been received directly by the

---

See page ii for explanation of footnotes.

[79] CCH ¶26,750; Sec. 218(1).

[80] CCH ¶26,073, ¶26,220; Sec. 212(1)(c), 212(11); Interp. Bul. IT-465R.

non-resident person instead of the trustee.[81] The exemption also applies with respect to all interest allocated to a non-resident beneficiary that is received by a mutual fund trust maintained primarily for the benefit of non-resident beneficiaries, provided no Part XIII tax would have been payable with respect to the interest if it had been paid directly to the non-resident beneficiary. Finally, a fourth type of trust income is added to the list of exemptions. In recognition of the regulatory requirement for "reinsurance trusts", dividends or interest earned by such trusts that would not have borne Canadian tax if the non-resident had earned them directly, may be distributed to the non-resident free of Part XIII tax. A reinsurance trust is a Canadian trust created by a non-resident reinsurer at the request of the Superintendent of Financial Institutions.

(2) Where all the beneficiaries of a trust established before 1949 reside during a taxation year in one country other than Canada and all amounts included in computing the income of the trust for the taxation year were received from persons resident in that same country.[82]

Certain *inter vivos* trusts distributing "designated income" to "designated beneficiaries" must pay a special 36% refundable tax under Part XII.2 of the Act on such designated income.[83] The *pro rata* share of this tax, allocable to each of the trust's taxable resident beneficiaries who are not designated beneficiaries, is then refunded to them; and no part of any designated beneficiaries' share of such designated income actually distributed to them is subject to the Part XIII withholding tax. The purpose of this scheme is to ensure that the designated beneficiaries' share of the designated income is taxed at the resident *inter vivos* trust's marginal rates, rather than at the lower Part XIII 25% withholding rates (which are lowered even further in many instances by tax treaties). The tax under Part XII.2 is extended to amateur athlete trusts, in circumstances where amounts are distributed by such trusts to non-resident beneficiaries.[84]

"Designated income" is defined to include taxable capital gains from the disposition of taxable Canadian property, as well as income from real property in Canada, businesses carried on in Canada, timber resource properties, and Canadian resource properties.[85]

"Designated beneficiaries" is defined to include, among others, non-resident persons, NRO investment corporations, partnerships with non-resident partners, and *inter vivos* trusts resident in Canada with non-resident beneficiaries.[86]

The Part XII.2 tax is not payable by certain trusts, including testamentary trusts and mutual fund trusts; non-resident trusts; trusts which enjoy a tax-exempt status, such as pension fund trusts, trusts governed by registered

---

See page ii for explanation of footnotes.

[81] CCH ¶26,190; Sec. 212(9).
[82] CCH ¶26,210; Sec. 212(10).
[83] CCH ¶25,883; Sec. 210.2.

[84] CCH ¶25,883a; Sec. 210.2(1.1).
[85] CCH ¶25,884; Sec. 210.2(2).
[86] CCH ¶25,881; Sec. 210.

retirement savings plans (RRSPs), deferred profit sharing plans (DPSPs), registered retirement income funds (RRIFs), and retirement compensation arrangements (RCAs); and master trusts.[87]

On July 25, 2012, the Department of Finance released draft income tax legislation addressing the issue of withholding tax on amounts that are payable from a Canadian resident trust to a non-resident beneficiary but which are actually paid after the trust ceases to be a Canadian resident. Amendments ensure that in circumstances in which an income amount becomes payable by a Canadian resident trust and the trust later becomes non-resident but before the income amount is actually paid or credited, the income amount is deemed to be paid at the earliest of the day it was paid or credited.[88] This amendment is deemed to have come into force on the announcement date.

[¶14,140] Rents, Royalties, or Similar Payments

Withholding tax is imposed on rents, royalties, or similar payments paid or credited by a resident of Canada to a non-resident for the use of property in Canada. The tax is payable on the gross amounts paid or credited without deduction of any expenses.[89]

The withholding tax applies to payments made or credited to a non-resident if the payments are made for any of the following purposes:

(1) for the use of, or for the right to use, in Canada any property, invention, trade name, patent, trademark, design or model, plan, secret formula, process, or other thing whatsoever;

(2) for information concerning industrial, commercial, or scientific experience where the total amount payable as consideration is calculated by reference to its use or benefit, to production or sales of goods or services, or to profits;

(3) for services of an industrial, commercial, or scientific character performed by a non-resident where the total amount payable is calculated by reference to the use or benefit, to production or sales of goods or services, or to profits resultant from such services. This does not apply to a payment for services in connection with the sale of property or the negotiation of a contract;

(4) a payment made under an agreement between a resident and a non-resident where the non-resident agrees not to use or not to permit another person to use any of the property referred to in (1) above or any information referred to in (2) above; and

(5) a payment that is dependent on the use or production of property in Canada, whether or not it is an instalment payment on the sale price of

---

See page ii for explanation of footnotes.

[87] CCH ¶25,882; Sec. 210.1.
[88] Sec. 214(3).

[89] CCH ¶26,075; Sec. 212(1)(d); Interp. Bul. IT-303, IT-494.

¶14,140

the property. This does not apply to an instalment payment on the sale price of agricultural land.

The following types of payments are exempt:

(a) a payment as a royalty or similar payment with respect to a copyright for the production or reproduction of any literary, dramatic, musical, or artistic work;

(b) a payment for the use by a railway company, or by a person whose principal business is that of a common carrier, of railway rolling stock if the payment is made for the use of that property for a period or periods not expected to exceed a total of 90 days in any 12-month period (see also ¶14,215);

(c) a payment made under a *bona fide* cost-sharing arrangement under which the person making the payment shares, on a reasonable basis, with one or more non-resident persons, the research and development expenses in exchange for an interest in any property or thing of value which may result from the arrangement;

(d) a payment in lieu of rent for the use of or the right to use any corporeal property outside Canada;

(e) a payment for services in connection with the sale of property or the negotiation of a contract;

(f) a payment as an instalment on the sale price of agricultural land, whether or not the payment is dependent on use or production;

(g) a payment on an arm's length basis if such payment is deductible by the payor in computing income under Part I from a business carried on by the payor in a country other than Canada; and

(h) a payment on an arm's length basis for the use of property that is an aircraft, furniture, fittings, equipment attached thereto as well as spare parts for such property and, after July 2003, air navigation equipment utilized in the provision of services under the *Civil Air Navigation Services Commercialization Act* or computer software that is necessary to the operation of that equipment that is used by the payor for no other purpose.[90]

Where a non-resident receives rent for real property situated in Canada, the non-resident may elect to file a return and pay tax under Part I on the rents received as though the taxpayer were a resident of Canada. This election is also available to a non-resident member of a partnership which receives such income.[91] See ¶14,255 and ¶14,260. The phrase "in lieu of

---

[90] CCH ¶26,075; Sec. 212(1)(*d*)(xi).   [91] CCH ¶26,600; Sec. 216; Interp. Bul. IT-393R2.

rent", in item (d) above, includes compensation for the anticipatory breach of a rental agreement.[92]

Whether or not the payment in question is a rent will depend on circumstances; thus amounts paid by a taxpayer pursuant to a "Capital Lease Purchase Agreement" were not, in substance, payments of rent but rather payments for the purchase of capital property.[93]

[¶14,145] Timber Royalties

Withholding tax applies on timber royalties in respect of a timber resource property or a timber limit in Canada paid or credited by a resident of Canada to a non-resident person.[94] The Act provides that the term "timber royalty" includes any consideration for a right to cut or take timber from a timber resource property or a timber limit in Canada to the extent that the consideration is dependent upon the amount of timber cut or taken. The tax is payable on the gross amount of the royalties paid without any deduction for expenses incurred to earn such royalties.

As with withholding tax on rental payments, the recipient of timber royalties has the alternative of electing to pay tax as if he or she were a resident, on a net income basis. See ¶14,255 and ¶14,260.

Where a non-resident person pays or credits certain specified amounts to another non-resident person, he or she is deemed to be resident in Canada and the payments will be subject to withholding tax.

[¶14,155] Patronage Dividends

An amount is subject to withholding tax if:

(a) it is a payment made pursuant to an allocation in proportion to patronage in connection with a cooperative or other body paying patronage dividends; or

(b) it would have been included in the income of the non-resident if he or she were resident in Canada.[95]

[¶14,160] Pension Benefits and Other Similar Payments

Superannuation or pension benefits paid to non-residents are generally subject to withholding tax under Part XIII of the Act, unless such payments are attributable to services rendered by the recipient while not resident or employed in Canada.[96] Exceptions, however, include payments to non-residents under provincial and federal workers' compensation legislation and social assistance legislation, as well as other payments to non-residents that are statutorily exempt under the Act or under other related legislation.[97]

See page ii for explanation of footnotes.

[92] Transocean Offshore Limited, 2005 DTC 5201.
[93] Viceroy Rubber and Plastics Limited, 93 DTC 347.
[94] CCH ¶26,077; Sec. 212(1)(e).

[95] CCH ¶26,081; Sec. 212(1)(g).
[96] CCH ¶26,083 et seq.; Sec. 212(1)(h).
[97] CCH ¶26,083 et seq.; Sec. 212(1)(h).

Also subject to withholding tax under the Act are amounts paid to non-residents as "retiring allowances" (see ¶2160), "death benefits" (see ¶2165); retirement compensation arrangement (RCA) payments, and payments from supplementary unemployment benefit plans; registered retirement savings plans (RRSPs); deferred profit sharing plans (DPSPs); IAACs; annuity payments that would, if received by a resident of Canada, be taxable in Canada (other than an amount paid or credited under an annuity issued in the course of carrying on a life insurance business outside of Canada); beginning in 2009, TFSA received from the date of death of the holder to the end of the year following the year of death or the date the trust ceases to exist; if earlier, to the extent they exceed the fair market value of the TFSA immediately before the death of the holder; registered home ownership savings plans (RHOSPs); registered retirement income funds (RRIFs); registered education savings plans (RESPs); and registered disability savings plans (RDSPs).[98] Provisions exist, however, to ensure that direct transfer payments among non-residents' RPPs, RRSPs, DPSPs, and RRIFs, as well as amounts received by non-residents from certain of these plans and rolled over by them into certain other of these same plans, escape non-resident withholding tax.[99] The object is to ensure that non-residents are given the same tax-free treatment as that received by residents with respect to such direct transfers and rollovers.

Non-residents in receipt of most of the various types of pension and other similar payments mentioned above may elect to avoid the Part XIII non-resident withholding tax otherwise applicable thereto by treating them as part of their other Canadian source income and by taking such Part I type deductions and personal tax credits as may reasonably be considered to be wholly applicable under the circumstances.[100] This election, however, is not available with respect to payments to non-residents from RHOSPs, IAACs, RESPs, or RDSPs. See ¶14,265.

[¶14,165] Home Insulation or Energy Conversion Grants

Grants paid to non-residents of Canada under a prescribed program of the government of Canada relating to home insulation or energy conversion are subject to withholding tax.[101]

[¶14,168] Pensions and Deferred Income Plan Benefits

A non-resident to whom a resident of Canada pays or credits a superannuation or pension benefit is required to pay Part XIII tax thereon at the rate of 25%.[102] A person who was a member of a registered pension fund or plan and retires to a foreign country would, for example, be required to pay Part XIII tax on his/her pension receipt. Where part of his/her receipt is attributable to services rendered by him/her in taxation years during which

---

See page ii for explanation of footnotes.

[98] CCH ¶26,083 et seq.; Sec. 212(1)(h)–(r.1).
[99] CCH ¶26,083 et seq.; Sec. 212(1)(h)–(r).
[100] CCH ¶26,700; Sec. 217.
[101] CCH ¶26,104ac; Sec. 212(1)(s).
[102] CCH ¶26,083; Sec. 212(1)(h).

he/she was not resident in Canada at any time and throughout which he/she was not employed in Canada or only occasionally employed in Canada, that part is exempt from Part XIII tax. Whether employment in Canada qualifies as occasional employment will be a question of degree depending on the number of instances of employment and their duration. It should be noted that most of the treaties which Canada has with foreign countries exempt pension payments from Canadian tax.

Receipts under the *Old Age Security Act* (or similar receipts under a provincial law), and under the *Canada Pension Plan* and *Quebec Pension Plan* are subject to Part XIII tax, subject to whatever protection a particular tax treaty may provide. These receipts are also subject to 100% withholding for OAS clawback tax, as discussed at ¶13,015.

Worker's compensation, receipts from an employees' profit sharing plan, certain social assistance payments, income derived from property acquired as a personal injury award, and other receipts are excluded from Part XIII tax to the extent that they would not be included in income if the recipient were resident in Canada.

A payment of a pension benefit will be exempt from Part XIII tax if it is transferred directly to a registered pension plan or to the taxpayer's RRSP or RRIF, pursuant to an authorization in prescribed form and pursuant to the direct transfer provisions, on the assumption that the non-resident is resident in Canada.

Also exempt from the withholding tax are superannuation or pension benefits which would be transferable to a registered pension plan (RPP) or an RRSP, if the non-resident were a resident of Canada.

A non-resident is not subject to Part XIII tax on payments of certain worker's compensation and social assistance payments which could constitute superannuation or pension benefits if he or his spouse or common-law partner would have been able to deduct those payments had they been resident in Canada.[103]

[¶14,169] Amateur Athlete Trusts

Tax is payable on certain amounts received by or on behalf of individuals who are amateur athletes. Withholding tax will apply to any amount paid by an amateur athlete trust to a non-resident beneficiary that would have been included in the beneficiary's income for a year if Part I of the *Income Tax Act* were applicable.[104]

[¶14,170] Eligible Funeral Arrangement

An amount that is distributed to a taxpayer from an eligible funeral arrangement, other than as payment for funeral or cemetery services, is

---

See page ii for explanation of footnotes.

[103] CCH ¶26,083; Sec. 212(1)(*h*).   [104] CCH ¶26,104c; Sec. 212(1)(*u*).

included in the taxpayer's income (see ¶10,540). The amount referred to is the residual of income earned by the contributions while in the plan that may be paid out to the taxpayer's estate after the funeral or cemetery services have been covered, or paid out to a taxpayer on the cancellation of such an arrangement. If such an amount is received by a non-resident, the payment is subject to withholding tax.[105]

[¶14,171] Employee Life and Health Trusts

Payments out of an employee life and health trust (ELHT) made to non-residents after 2009 are subject to withholding tax, except to the extent that they are payments of designated employee benefits.[106] The designated employee benefits will generally be health and insurance benefits. For more details on ELHTs, see ¶10,317 in Chapter 10.

[¶14,172] Tax on Dividends

Withholding taxes are payable on taxable dividends paid or deemed to have been paid, and on capital dividends paid or deemed to have been paid by a private corporation (being dividends out of one-half of a private corporation's accumulated capital gains and certain other amounts which are distributable tax-free to Canadian shareholders).[107]

A taxable dividend does not include a qualifying dividend paid by a public corporation to shareholders of a prescribed class of tax-deferred preferred shares.[108]

What might otherwise have been a means of distributing capital dividends to a non-resident shareholder free of withholding tax by interposing an *inter vivos* trust may be precluded by a provision which has the effect of providing that, although a capital dividend received by a trust would not be income of the trust for tax purposes, a distribution of such an amount to the beneficiary of the trust is deemed to have been paid as income of the trust.[109] Where a non-resident who was lessee of a resident's railway operation received dividends, those dividends were held attributable to the carrying on of business by the non-resident in Canada.[110] Where a Canadian corporation purchased shares of other Canadian corporations from non-residents, the amounts paid for the shares were deemed to be dividends, and withholding tax was payable.[111]

Capital gains dividends paid by a mortgage investment corporation, a mutual fund corporation, or by a non-resident-owned investment corporation are specifically excluded from withholding tax.[112]

See page ii for explanation of footnotes.

[105] CCH ¶26,104d; Sec. 212(1)(v).

[106] Sec. 212(1)(w).

[107] CCH ¶26,105; Sec. 212(2).

[108] CCH ¶11,209; Sec. 89(1) "taxable dividend".

[109] CCH ¶26,220; Sec. 212(11).

[110] Canada Southern Railway Company, 86 DTC 6097.

[111] Placements Serco Ltée, 87 DTC 5425.

[112] CCH ¶26,105; Sec. 212(2)(a).

Dividends (other than capital gains dividends) paid by a non-resident-owned investment corporation to a non-resident are now subject to withholding tax.

A Canadian corporation was wholly owned by a Dutch holding company, which was in turn owned by Swedish and U.K. corporations. It paid dividends to the Dutch company and withheld 5% tax under the Canada–Netherlands Treaty. The Canadian dividends were not beneficially owned by the Dutch company's shareholders, which would require 25% Canadian withholding tax, since the Dutch company enjoyed all the attributes of ownership and was not a conduit for its shareholders.[113]

The Budget introduced significant changes to Canada's "thin capitalization" rules. One significant change would recharacterize denied interest (due to exceeding the maximum debt-equity ratio) as a deemed dividend, subject to Part XIII withholding tax. This is a significant departure from the existing rules. Under the existing rules, the only real downside to exceeding the maximum debt-equity ratio was reduced interest deductibility. However, all interest (whether or not deductible) was still considered to be interest for purposes of Part XIII and could be paid to certain non-resident creditors without the imposition of Canadian withholding tax. This permitted the extraction of funds from Canada free of withholding tax, a planning tool which some may have utilized to avoid dividend withholding tax. The Canadian government has now introduced measures to ensure that any non-deductible interest paid to a "specified lender" does not escape Canadian withholding tax.[114] The new rule applies to interest paid or credited to a non-resident person by a corporation resident in Canada in a taxation year of the corporation, to the extent that an amount in respect of the interest is not deductible to the corporation because of the application of the thin capitalization rules. The rules also include an annual deemed payment provision to avoid the deferral of the withholding tax liability.

These proposed changes were included in draft legislation released on August 14, 2012.

[¶14,175] Deemed Payments

Various amounts that would be subject to Part I tax if the recipient were a resident of Canada are subject to the non-resident withholding tax. These amounts are:

(1) the deemed income or deemed dividend arising on loans to shareholders or appropriations to or for the benefit of a shareholder, payments on income bonds, or the use by a shareholder of a corporation's automobile;

(2) the deemed income on payments or transfers of an income nature made at the direction of, or with the concurrence of, the taxpayer;

See page ii for explanation of footnotes.

[113] Prévost Car Inc., 2009 DTC 5053.   [114] Secs. 214(16) and (17).

(3) the deemed proceeds where an income-averaging annuity contract ceases to qualify as such;

(4) an amount receivable in respect of the disposition of an interest in a retirement compensation arrangement;

(5) the amount paid to the estate of the deceased out of an RRSP plan which is treated as a refund of premiums received by a beneficiary by virtue of the election described at ¶10,366;

(6) the fair market value of property held by a registered retirement savings plan which is deemed to have been received as a benefit under the plan by a deceased annuitant (see ¶10,366);

(7) the amount paid to the estate of a deceased annuitant under a registered retirement savings plan which is included in the income of his or her spouse or common-law partner (see ¶10,366);

(8) the amount included in the income of an annuitant under a registered retirement savings plan because the plan acquired or disposed of property at other than fair market value;

(9) the fair market value to a registered retirement savings plan of a non-qualified investment;

(10) payments out of a DPSP, less certain deductions;

(11) the amount or value of funds or property appropriated to the benefit of an employer included in the employer's income;

(12) payments out of a revoked DPSP;

(13) taxable dividends (other than capital gains dividends) paid by a mortgage investment corporation which are treated as interest;

(14) income of a trust payable in the year to a beneficiary which would be included in a resident beneficiary's income;

(15) the amount designated by a mutual fund trust in respect of a particular unit of the trust owned by a taxpayer, to the extent that the amount would, if Part I was applicable, be included in the non-resident's income;

(16) the fair market value of property held in a plan, fund, or trust at the date of death of the beneficiary if the plan, fund, or trust was a registered home ownership savings plan (RHOSP) on December 31, 1985;

(17) amounts that would have been included in the income of a non-resident in respect of a registered retirement income fund if the individual had been a resident; these amounts arise upon the death of the last annuitant under the fund, when an amount is received as a designated benefit by the legal representative of the last annuitant of the fund, when non-quali-

fied investments are acquired, and when a fund is changed so it no longer meets the requirements for registration;

(18) the portion of the fair market value of property of a trust governed by a registered education savings plan which is included in the income of the subscriber before 1998 when the Minister revokes the registration of the plan;

(19) amounts distributed by an amateur athlete trust that would, if Part I were applicable, be included in the non-resident's income; and

(20) amounts paid out of a taxpayer's net income stabilization account (NISA) Fund No. 2.[115]

Although there were unpaid interest-free loans owing to the taxpayer from its non-resident parent, the taxpayer's balance sheet provided evidence of an intention and an agreement between the parties to net their intercorporate liabilities. In the absence of any net amount owing, no deemed dividend existed on which to impose Part XIII tax.[116]

[¶14,180] Motion Picture Films

Withholding tax of 25% (or a bilateral treaty rate) applies on amounts paid or credited to non-residents as rental income or royalties for the use of a motion picture film or a film or videotape for use in connection with television, where such films have been or are to be used or reproduced in Canada. The withholding tax will be applicable only if the person paying or crediting the amount is resident in Canada. It will not apply if the film or video tape is used in connection with, and as part of, a news program produced in Canada.

As presently worded, this provision can be read as applying even if the payment in question is not for Canadian use or reproduction, but relates instead to employment of the film or video in some other country. Pending technical amendments [released July 16, 2010] would therefore impose tax only to the extent that the amount of the payment relates to the use or reproduction of the product in Canada. This amendment would apply to the 2000 and subsequent taxation years.[117]

Generally this provision is interpreted strictly and is considered to be applicable to any transaction that is not an outright sale of film or videotape and to include all the rights (such as copyright, ownership of copies, etc.).[118] Where any limitation is imposed in the transaction (in terms of time, territory or other conditions), the payment or payments would be subject to tax.

See page ii for explanation of footnotes.

[115] CCH ¶26,420; Sec. 214(3).
[116] Magicuts Inc., 2001 DTC 5665.
[117] CCH ¶26,150; Sec. 212(5).
[118] Vauban Productions, 79 DTC 5186.

[¶14,183] Non-Resident Actors

Withholding tax at the rate of 23% applies to the gross amount paid, credited or provided as a benefit to a non- resident actor (or related corporation) in respect of acting services provided in Canada with no deductions permitted.[119] Whether or not the recipient chooses to have acting services payments taxed under Part I (an option described more fully below), any person, including a non-resident, who makes an acting services payment, must withhold and remit to the Receiver General 23% of the payment.[120]

Non-resident actors have the following choice:

- they can have 23% of their gross acting income withheld and not have to file a return; or

- they can have 23% of their gross acting income withheld, file an elective Part I return, and pay tax at marginal rates on their net income instead of 23% on the gross amount. If the non-resident tax withheld by the payor is more than the amount of tax payable calculated on the return, the excess will be refunded.[121]

Where the 23% withholding should cause undue hardship, the Minister may agree that the payor of an acting services payment may withhold a lesser amount.

This 23% withholding applies to non-resident actors in film or video production, such as feature films, movies of the week, television series, documentaries, video productions, and commercials. It applies only to acting income earned by non-resident actors providing services in Canada. If a non- resident person earns other income in Canada (for services as a producer or director, for example), this income will continue to be subject to withholding at the rate of 15% and the person will be required to file a tax return.

[¶14,190] Transfers of Certain Property and Income Rights, etc.

Where any taxpayer resident in Canada transfers property to a spouse or a common-law partner or to a minor, the income therefrom (or for property substituted therefor) is deemed to be the taxpayer's as the transferor. Where the transferee is a non-resident, however, no withholding tax is imposed on this income that is attributed back to the transferor.[122]

Similarly, where a resident taxpayer transfers rights to income in a non-arm's length transaction, such income is deemed to be the taxpayer's and not that of the transferee unless the property generating the income is also transferred. Again, however, where the transferee is a non-resident, no withholding tax is imposed on the income so transferred.[123]

See page ii for explanation of footnotes.

[119] CCH ¶26,153; Sec. 212(5.1).
[120] CCH ¶26,530; Sec. 215(1).
[121] CCH ¶26,280; Sec. 216.1.

[122] CCH ¶9570, ¶26,230; Sec. 75, 212(12).

[123] CCH ¶8150, ¶26,230; Sec. 56(4), 212(12).

The same ratio applies to low interest non-arm's length loans by resident taxpayers; one of the purposes of this is to reduce the taxpayer's income from the property loaned. In these situations the income from the property loaned is taxed in the hands of the resident taxpayer. Where the borrower is non-resident, no withholding tax applies in respect of such income.[124]

[¶14,195] Withholding Tax Where Payor or Payee Is a Partnership

Where a partnership pays or credits an amount to a non-resident person, the partnership is obligated to withhold any applicable Part XIII tax in respect of the amount to the extent that the amount is deductible in computing the partnership's income from a Canadian source. In addition, where a person resident in Canada pays an amount to a partnership that is not a Canadian partnership by virtue of the fact that all of its members are not resident in Canada, the partnership is deemed to be a non-resident person for the purposes of Part XIII. Accordingly, the Canadian resident payor of the amount will be obligated to withhold any applicable Part XIII tax in respect of the amount paid to the partnership.[125]

A partnership is also deemed to be a non-resident person if it pays, credits, or provides an amount for the provision of acting services in Canada to a non-resident actor, or to a corporation related to the non-resident actor.

Where a taxpayer held a note from a non-resident partnership which it converted into another form of indebtedness, the conversion did not constitute a payment or credit that would be subject to Part XIII withholding tax since the original note did not give rise to a credit, payment, or loan and one instrument was simply substituted for another.[126]

[¶14,197] Withholding Tax Where Non-Resident Operates in Canada

Where a non-resident carries on business, manufactures or processes goods, operates an oil or gas well in Canada, or extracts minerals from a mineral resource in Canada and pays or credits amounts to another non-resident person that are deductible in computing the payor's Canadian-source income, the non-resident is deemed to be a resident person for withholding tax purposes.[127] This rule extends Part XIII tax to apply in particular circumstances, i.e., for the most part, the payment by a non-resident of royalties and similar amounts in respect of a Canadian income source. The principle that underlies this rule is that if a non-resident has Canadian-source business or resource income, and can deduct in computing that income (strictly speaking, in computing "taxable income earned in Canada") a payment to another non-resident, that payment ought to be treated for purposes of Part XIII tax as though it had been made by a person resident in Canada. This is accomplished by treating the first non-resident (i.e., the one making the payment) as a person resident in Canada

---

See page ii for explanation of footnotes.

[124] CCH ¶8151, ¶26,230; Sec. 56(4.1), 212(12).
[125] CCH ¶26,243; Sec. 212(13.1).
[126] Gillette Canada Inc., 2003 DTC 5078.
[127] CCH ¶26,245; Sec. 212(13.2).

for those purposes. This rule does not affect the application of the generally comparable rule at ¶14,250, which imposes Part XIII tax on rents and other amounts paid to non-residents.

In its current form, the above rule applies only if the non-resident making the payment carries on business principally in Canada, manufactures or processes goods in Canada, or carries out any of various resource activities here. Since it does not explicitly link that business or activity to the deductibility of the payment, this rule can be read as applying whether or not the payment is made in relation to the particular business or activity. For amounts paid under obligations entered into after December 20, 2002, pending technical amendments [released July 16, 2010] would amend this rule so that it applies only in respect of any portion of a payment made by one non-resident person to another that is deductible in computing the first non-resident's taxable income earned in Canada from any source. The only exceptions are payments that are deductible in respect of treaty-protected businesses or treaty-protected properties.

[¶14,200] Non-Arm's Length Sale of Shares by Non-Resident

The Act contains an anti-dividend stripping provision directed at non-residents of Canada and at NRO investment corporations who hold controlling interests in Canadian corporations.[128] It is intended to prevent a non-resident or NRO investment corporation from withdrawing from Canada, on a tax-free basis, any amounts in excess of the paid-up capital of the shares of the Canadian corporation after these have been disposed of to another Canadian corporation in a non-arm's length transaction.

In general terms, the provision operates to deem a dividend to have been paid by the purchaser corporation to the non-resident or to the NRO investment corporation to the extent that the non-share consideration given on the transfer exceeds the paid-up capital of the transferred shares. This deemed dividend will be subject to withholding tax or to penalties for failure to withhold.[129]

Anti-avoidance rules exist to discourage the extraction of corporate surplus to non-residents in the context of the demutualization of a life insurance corporation. Specifically, these rules deem any non-resident who sells shares of a Canadian corporation to a purchaser that is a Canadian, or establishes a Canadian partnership or corporation to purchase the shares, to receive taxable dividends, rather than capital gains which are normally exempt from Canadian tax pursuant to Canada's tax treaties. They apply if the disposition is part of an expected series of transactions or events that includes the issue of a share of a Canadian resident insurance corporation on the demutualization of that corporation.[130]

---

128 CCH ¶26,270–26,275; Sec. 212.1(1)–(4).   130 CCH ¶26,298–26,299; Sec. 212.2(1)–(2).
129 CCH ¶26,105; Sec. 212(2); Placements Serco
   Ltée, 84 DTC 6098.

[¶14,205] Income and Capital Combined

Payments are sometimes made to non-residents which are really payments of amounts of both an income nature (e.g., combined interest) and amounts of a capital nature. If a non-resident receives such a blended payment, he or she is subject to withholding tax on that portion of the payment which can reasonably be regarded as interest or of an income nature.[131]

[¶14,210] Securities

Where a person has received a security, right, or other evidence of indebtedness in payment or satisfaction of an income debt, the value of the security or right received will be included in income at the time it is received, if the income debt is payable at that time.[132] If such an amount is paid by a Canadian resident to a non-resident, it will be subject to withholding tax.[133]

[¶14,215] Temporary Use of Rolling Stock

The exemption from non-resident withholding tax with respect to payments for the temporary use of railway rolling stock is inapplicable, unless the country in which the non-resident resides grants substantially similar tax relief.[134]

The exemption applies to payments for use of railway rolling stock for periods not exceeding a total of 90 days in any 12-month period.

[¶14,220] Transfer of Obligations

Part I of the Act includes in a resident transferor's income accrued interest (up to the date of transfer) in respect of most types of debt obligations transferred by the transferor. A corresponding deduction is permitted to the transferee in respect of the same accrued amount (see ¶3360).[135]

Part XIII of the Act contains similar provisions intended to impose non-resident withholding tax on accrued interest up to the date of transfer in respect of transfers of debt obligations by non-resident transferors to resident transferees, in circumstances where the comparable Part I tax would have applied had the transferor been resident.[136] The Part XIII non-resident withholding tax is imposed by deeming the accrued interest involved to be a payment of interest by the resident transferee to the non-resident transferor. The withholding tax applies to debt obligations issued by residents of Canada other than:

(a) obligations issued by the Government of Canada, a province, or a municipality;

See page ii for explanation of footnotes.

[131] CCH ¶26,410; Sec. 214(2).
[132] CCH ¶9600; Sec. 76.
[133] CCH ¶26,430, ¶26,440; Sec. 214(4), 214(5).

[134] CCH ¶26,265; Sec. 212(16).
[135] CCH ¶5142; Sec. 20(14).
[136] CCH ¶26,450–26,525; Sec. 214(6)–(14).

(b) certain obligations providing for the payment of interest in a currency other than Canadian;

(c) those obligations prescribed to be a public issue security; and

(d) obligations in respect of which the issuer is not obliged to pay more than 25% of the principal amount within five years of the date of issue except in the event of default.[137]

This list of exempted debt obligations includes all those transferred on which interest is exempt from non-resident withholding tax under ¶14,110.

[¶14,225] Guarantee Fees and Loans

Where a non-resident has entered into an agreement under which he or she guarantees the repayment, in whole or in part, of the principal amount of a bond, debenture, note, etc., of a person resident in Canada, any amount paid or credited as consideration for the guarantee is deemed to be a payment of interest on the obligation.[138]

Where a non-resident person has entered into an agreement under which he or she agrees to lend money, or to make money available, to a person resident in Canada, any amount paid or credited as consideration for agreeing to lend the money, or to make the money available, is deemed to be a payment of interest, provided that the non-resident is taxable in respect of the interest paid on the principal obligation.

[¶14,230] Deduction and Payment of Tax

Where a person pays or credits, or is deemed to have paid or credited, an amount to a non-resident person on which tax is payable, he or she is required to deduct the tax at the appropriate rate before paying the non-resident.[139] The payor must remit the tax to the Receiver General together with a statement in prescribed form. Where these payments are made by an agent or other person on behalf of the debtor, this person too is required to deduct tax and to remit the tax deducted, with a statement, to the Receiver General.[140]

Where an amount on which tax is payable is paid or credited to an agent or other person for, or on behalf of, the person entitled to payment without the tax having been withheld or deducted, the agent must deduct or withhold the amount of the tax and remit the amount with a statement to the Receiver General.[141]

---

[137] CCH ¶26,450; Sec. 214(6)(a), 214(6)(b).
[138] CCH ¶26,527; Sec. 214(15).
[139] CCH ¶26,530; Sec. 215(1).
[140] CCH ¶26,540; Sec. 215(2).
[141] CCH ¶26,550; Sec. 215(3).

[¶14,235] Exception to Deduction and Payment Rules

The Governor in Council may make regulations with respect to any non-resident person (or class of persons) carrying on business in Canada to provide that the situations described in ¶14,230 are not applicable to amounts paid or credited to the taxpayer. The taxpayer would then be required to file an annual return on a prescribed form and pay the withholding tax within the time limited in the regulations.[142] See ¶14,245.

The Governor in Council is also authorized to make regulations reducing the amount of withholding tax[143] in respect of non-residents to whom amounts are paid or credited in respect of pension benefits, retiring allowances, supplementary unemployment benefits, deferred profit sharing plan (DPSP) payments, as well as payments under registered retirement savings plans (RRSPs), or registered retirement income funds (RRIFs).

[¶14,240] Liability for Tax

Where a person has failed to deduct or withhold any amount of withholding tax, he or she becomes personally liable for the amount of the tax.[144] However, the taxpayer is entitled to recover that amount from the non-resident, either by deducting such amount from any future amount paid or credited to the non-resident or "otherwise". The Canadian resident may, of course, find it difficult to recover the amount if the non-resident has no assets in Canada. Failure to deduct or withhold tax or to remit tax withheld may also be subject to a penalty.[145]

[¶14,245] Insurers and Others

The obligation to withhold tax on amounts paid or credited to non-residents does not apply in the case of amounts paid or credited to:

(1) non-resident insurers registered to carry on business in Canada under the *Insurance Companies Act*; or

(2) non-residents carrying on a business in Canada (but only in respect of those amounts reasonably attributable to such business or where the Minister has so permitted); this exception does not, however, apply to registered non-resident insurers.[146]

[¶14,250] Rent and Other Payments

Where a non-resident person pays or credits rent to another non-resident person for the use in Canada of property, that person is deemed to be resident in Canada.[147] Therefore, rent paid or credited to a non-resident for the use in Canada of property (other than rolling stock) is subject to withholding tax regardless of whether it is paid or credited by a resident or

---

See page ii for explanation of footnotes.

[142] CCH ¶26,560; Sec. 215(4).
[143] CCH ¶26,570, ¶26,572; Sec. 215(5); Reg. 809.
[144] CCH ¶26,580; Sec. 215(6).
[145] CCH ¶27,278–27,282; Sec. 227(8), 227(9).
[146] CCH ¶26,581–26,586; Reg. 800–805.
[147] CCH ¶26,240; Sec. 212(13).

non-resident of Canada. This is also the case where payment is made or an amount is credited by one non-resident to another as:

(1) a timber royalty in respect of a timber resource property or a timber limit in Canada;

(2) a payment of a superannuation or pension benefit under a registered pension plan or a distribution to one or more persons out of or under a retirement compensation arrangement;

(3) a payment of a retiring allowance or a death benefit to the extent that the payment is deductible from the payor's income earned in Canada;

(4) payments under a supplementary unemployment benefit plan, a registered retirement savings plan (RRSP), a deferred profit sharing plan (DPSP), or a registered retirement income fund (RRIF);

(5) interest on a mortgage, hypothecary claim, or other indebtedness entered into, issued, or modified, after March 31, 1977, and secured by real property located in Canada, or an interest therein, to the extent that the amount so paid or credited is deductible in computing the non-resident person's taxable income earned in Canada or the amount on which the non-resident person is liable to pay Part I tax; or

(6) amounts paid or credited after October 7, 2003 by a non-resident for a restrictive covenant that is included in the taxpayer's income (see ¶5340) if the amount affects, or is intended to affect, in any way whatsoever: (i) the acquisition or provision of property or services in Canada, (ii) the acquisition or provision of property or services outside Canada by a person resident in Canada, or (iii) the acquisition or provision outside of Canada of a taxable Canadian property.

[¶14,255] Election re Rents and Timber Royalties

A non-resident, or a partnership of which the non-resident was a member, who receives rent from real property or timber royalties may elect to be taxed on a net income basis.[148] The Canadian resident payor or agent must still withhold and remit the non-resident tax on the gross rents or royalties, but the tax return subsequently filed by the non-resident can result in some or all of the tax so remitted being refunded. The election is made by filing a return of income under Part I of the Act, within two years from the end of the taxation year in which rent or timber royalty is paid.

There is also an election available whereby the agent receiving the rents or royalties may withhold and remit tax on the net amount available from those rents or royalties. This may be done where the non-resident has filed an undertaking with the Minister in prescribed form to file a return of income under Part I within six months of the end of the relevant taxation

---

See page ii for explanation of footnotes.

[148] CCH ¶26,600, ¶26,608; Sec. 216(1), 216(3); Interp. Bul. IT-393R2.

year. The agent may then withhold and remit the tax at the applicable rate on "any amount available" out of the rents or royalties received for remittance to the non-resident. For this purpose non-cash items such as capital cost allowance are not deductible.[149]

If an election is made, the non-resident will be subject to tax as if it were a Canadian resident and the interest in real property, timber resource property, or timber limits in Canada, including the non-resident's share of the income of a partnership of which it was a member from such real property, timber resource property, or timber limit, were the only source of income. The taxpayer will be entitled to deduct from "gross income" the deductions permitted for the purpose of determining "income", but will not be entitled to any deductions from "income" for the purpose of determining "taxable income". Thus, the taxpayer will be able to deduct those expenses related to the Canadian property such as capital cost allowances but will not be entitled to any tax credits in respect of married or single status or dependants, or in respect of charitable donations, medical expenses, or losses carried back or forward.[150] If the taxpayer does take an allowance in respect of capital cost, he or she will be required to file another return for any future year in which all or any part of the taxpayer's interest in the real property, timber resource property, or timber limit is disposed of under circumstances where the taxpayer would be taxable on recaptured depreciation. If a loss from rents or timber royalties is reported, the taxpayer may not set off such loss against income for the same taxation year reported on any other return required under Part I. However, a taxpayer may set off a loss for the year from one section 216 property against the income for the year from another section 216 property. The loss may not be deducted in other years, since it does not qualify as a non-capital loss.

If the person making the election has paid excess non-resident withholding tax, it will be refunded by the Receiver General.

[¶14,260] Alternative Method of Tax Payment re Rents and Timber Royalties

A non-resident may elect within two years from the end of the taxation year to file a return of income in respect of real property rentals or timber royalties instead of paying the withholding tax. However, if a non-resident files an undertaking in prescribed form to file a return of such income within six months from the end of the taxation year, his or her agent may elect not to deduct and remit withholding tax on the gross rents or royalties.[151] If the non-resident makes such an election, he or she will be required to deduct and remit to the Receiver General the withholding tax on the net rents or timber royalties available for remittance to the non-resident.

See page ii for explanation of footnotes.

[149] CCH ¶26,620; Sec. 216(4).
[150] CCH ¶26,600; Sec. 216(1)(d).

[151] CCH ¶26,600, ¶26,608; Sec. 216(1), 216(3); Interp. Bul. IT-393R2.

It should be noted that if a tenant or timber operator pays rent or royalties directly to the non-resident owner and is not appointed as the owner's agent, this provision does not apply.

[¶14,265] Election to File Part I Tax Returns re Canadian Pension Benefits

A non-resident may elect to pay tax under Part I rather than Part XIII withholding tax on certain pension and other payments from Canadian sources.[152] As a result, such payments are included in the individual's taxable income earned in Canada.[153] If the non-resident was a part-time Canadian resident, the payments would be added in computing the individual's taxable income.[154] This helps to ensure that a non-resident who receives such payments is not put in a less favourable position than if he or she was a resident in Canada and could take certain deductions or tax credits that would reduce the tax payable under Part I. The types of payments which qualify for this election include

(a) pension and superannuation benefits including benefits under the *Old Age Security Act*, *Canada Pension Plan*, and *Quebec Pension Plan*;

(b) a death benefit;

(c) a benefit under the *Employment Insurance Act* other than a payment relating to a course designated to enable the taxpayer to re-enter the labour force;

(d) a benefit that is transitional assistance to persons employed in the automotive industry;

(e) a prescribed benefit under a government assistance program;

(f) an amount received under a retirement compensation arrangement;

(g) retiring allowances;

(h) supplementary unemployment plan benefits;

(i) RRSP benefits;

(j) DPSP payments; and

(k) RRIF payments.

This election must be made in a return of income filed within 6 months after the non-resident's taxation year. Once the election is filed, the non-resident is not subject to Part XIII withholding tax in respect of the non-resident's Canadian benefits received in the year. Instead, the Canadian benefits are taxed under Part I along with other Canadian source income (taxable income earned in Canada).

See page ii for explanation of footnotes.

[152] CCH ¶26,700; Sec. 217.
[153] CCH ¶17,101; Sec. 115(1)(a).
[154] CCH ¶17,003; Sec. 114.

[¶14,270] Additional Tax on Non-Resident Corporations

[¶14,275] Branch Tax

The Act[155] imposes what is commonly referred to as the "branch tax". Under this provision, all non-resident corporations are required to pay a tax of 25% on their Canadian source taxable income less deductions for (i) federal and provincial taxes, net taxable capital gains realized on taxable Canadian property not held for Canadian business purposes; and (ii) investment in property in Canada.

[¶14,300] Non-Resident Insurers

Non-resident insurers are required to pay branch tax calculated on a special basis.[156]

The term "insurer" is defined as a corporation which carries on an insurance business.

An insurer other than a resident insurer not carrying on a life insurance business segregates certain of its property as being used in its Canadian business and pays tax on the income earned therefrom. Basic to these calculations is the insurer's "Canadian investment fund". (See ¶9039.) Generally speaking, the larger the Canadian investment fund, the greater would be the investment income of the corporation subject to Canadian corporate tax.

[¶14,305] Tax Agreements

[¶14,310] Tax Agreements in General

Canada has income tax conventions or agreements (commonly referred to as tax treaties) with many countries. These tax treaties are designed to avoid double taxation for those who would otherwise have to pay tax in two countries on the same income. Generally, tax treaties determine how much each country can tax income such as wages, salaries, pensions, and interest. A non-resident who receives Canadian-source employment income or Canadian self-employment business income that is exempt from tax in Canada because of a tax treaty can ask his or her Canadian employer or payer not to withhold tax. However, before the Canadian employer or payer can stop withholding tax, the non-resident needs a waiver letter from the CRA.

See page ii for explanation of footnotes.

[155] CCH ¶26,900; Sec. 219; Interp. Bul. IT-137R3.   [156] CCH ¶26,909, ¶26,913, ¶26,918; Sec. 219(4), 219(5.1), 219(7); Reg. 2403.

¶14,270

Canada has tax treaties in force with the following countries:

Algeria	Latvia
Argentina	Luxembourg
Armenia	Malaysia
Australia	Malta
Austria	Mexico
Azerbaijan	Moldova
Bangladesh	Mongolia
Barbados	Morocco
Belgium	Netherlands
Brazil	New Zealand
Bulgaria	Nigeria
Cameroon	Norway
Chile	Oman
China (PRC)	Pakistan
Columbia	Papua New Guinea
Croatia	Peru
Cyprus	Philippines
Czech Republic	Poland
Denmark	Portugal
Dominican Republic	Romania
Ecuador	Russia
Egypt	Senegal
Estonia	Singapore
Finland	Slovak Republic
France	Slovenia
Gabon	South Africa
Germany	Spain
Greece	Sri Lanka
Guyana	Sweden
Hungary	Switzerland
Iceland	Tanzania
India	Thailand
Indonesia	Trinidad and Tobago
Ireland	Tunisia
Israel	Turkey
Italy	Ukraine
Ivory Coast	United Arab Emirates
Jamaica	United Kingdom
Japan	United States
Jordan	Uzbekistan
Kazakhstan	Venezuela
Kenya	Vietnam
Korea (Republic of)	Zambia
Kuwait	Zimbabwe
Kyrgyzstan	

¶14,310

Currently, new agreements have been signed with Lebanon, Namibia, and Serbia but are not yet in force.

The most comprehensive of the tax agreements are the *Canada–United States Tax Convention* (¶14,385 *et seq.*) and the *Canada–United Kingdom Tax Agreement* (¶14,520 *et seq.*).

The purpose of most tax agreements is twofold: to avoid double taxation and to prevent tax evasion.

(1) *Double taxation.* The problem of double taxation arises from the fact that each country has its own taxation system and its own bases for imposing tax. Thus, the same item of income could be liable to tax in each country.

The most important method of relieving the burden of double taxation is through the exemption of income at its source. Accordingly, under most tax agreements, one country exempts the industrial and commercial profits of enterprises of the other country which do not have a permanent establishment in the taxing country. The income an enterprise of one country derives from the operation of ships or aircraft registered in that country is exempt from taxation in the other country, as are profits from trucking operations between the countries. Royalties from written and artistic works, other than motion picture films, derived from the taxing country and payable to a resident or corporation of the other country, which does not have a permanent establishment in the taxing country, are exempt in the taxing country. Pensions and life annuities derived from the taxing country and payable to a resident of the other country are exempt in the taxing country. There are similar exemptions with respect to directors' fees, undistributed corporate surpluses, certain types of capital gains, and religious, scientific, or charitable organizations.

(2) *Tax evasion.* The problem of tax evasion arises because of the general rule of law that one country does not take cognizance of the revenue laws of another country. The tax agreements permit the exchange of information between the administrative authorities of both countries in order that the authorities may be made aware of the manner in which taxes are being legally avoided so that measures may be adopted and safeguards established for the effective collection of taxes already imposed. This exchange of information includes periodic annual returns, as well as specific information regarding any taxpayer which has been acquired under authority of taxation laws.

Each tax agreement entered into is subsequently accompanied by an implementing Canadian statute which provides that the agreement in question is to have the force of law. The implementing Acts each provide that in the event of any inconsistency between the tax agreement and the Canadian income tax law, the provisions of the tax agreement will, to the extent of the inconsistency, prevail.

¶14,310

Taxpayers suffering from double taxation are permitted to request consideration of their problems in light of the tax agreement provisions.[157] A taxpayer successfully appealed an assessment on the grounds that there was obviously an inconsistency between the *Income Tax Act* and the *Canada–United Kingdom Tax Agreement*. Tax on eligible dividends was held exigible at the rate prescribed in the Treaty.[158]

[¶14,380] Highlights of the Canada–U.S. Tax Convention (1980)

Note: This Convention was signed at Washington on September 26, 1980 and has been amended by five Protocols. The commentary below on the provisions of the Convention is based extensively on the Revised Technical Explanation of the Convention issued by the United States Treasury Department on April 26, 1984 and endorsed August 16, 1984 by the Canadian Department of Finance.

[¶14,385] Business Profits

The "business profits" of an enterprise of one country are taxable in the other country only to the extent that the profits are attributable to a permanent establishment[159] in the other country through which the enterprise carries on, or has carried on, business.[160] Business profits of a permanent establishment are determined as if the permanent establishment were a separate entity which dealt at arm's length with the non-resident.

Deductions are allowed in computing taxable business profits for expenses, wherever incurred, if incurred for purposes of that permanent establishment. These may include a reasonable allocation of executive and general administrative expenses, interest, research and development, and other expenses incurred for purposes of the enterprise as a whole. No business profits are to be attributed to the permanent establishment of a resident of either country by reason of the use of the permanent establishment for purchasing goods or merchandise or merely providing executive, managerial, or administrative facilities or services for the resident. If business profits include management fees (other than excessive amounts), such fees are taxable by the payor's country only in the unlikely event that the recipient has a permanent establishment there.

Separate Convention provisions are applicable to dividends, interest, royalties, and gains derived in one country from the alienation of property owned by a resident of the other country. See ¶14,450, ¶14,470, and ¶14,480.

See page ii for explanation of footnotes.

[157] Inf. Cir. 71-17R5.
[158] Fletcher, 77 DTC 185.

[159] CCH ¶30,226d; Art. V, *Canada–U.S. Income Tax Convention*.
[160] CCH ¶30,226f; Art. VII, *Canada–U.S. Income Tax Convention*.

[¶14,390] Income from Real Property

Income from real property, including income from any natural resources as well as income from agriculture and forestry, may be taxed in the country where the real property is located.[161]

Real property includes the right to use real property and the rights to explore for or to exploit mineral deposits, sources, and other natural resources. Income from real property also includes royalties and other payments in respect of the exploitation of natural resources and gains on the sale, exchange, or other dispositions of any royalty rights or the underlining real property itself. It does not apparently include income in the form of rights to explore for or exploit natural resources which are received as compensation for services. The term "real property" also includes options for similar rights with respect to real property, but excludes ships and aircraft from the definition. Gains on the sale, exchange, or other disposition of real property may also be taxed by the country where the property is located.[162]

[¶14,395] Residence

A person, either an individual or an entity such as a corporation or partnership, is considered to be a resident of a country if, under the laws of that country, the person is subject to taxation by that country because it is that person's country of domicile, residence, place of management, place of incorporation, citizenship, or by reason of other criteria of a similar nature.[163] An estate or trust is considered to be a resident of a country only to the extent that the income it derives is subject to that country's tax, either in its hands or in the hands of its beneficiaries.

In the case of a dual resident individual, a series of "tie-breaker" rules are applicable and the individual will be deemed to be a resident of the country:

(1) in which the person has a permanent home;

(2) that is the centre of the person's vital interests;

(3) where the person habitually resides; and

(4) in which the person has citizenship.

A corporation that is a dual resident under the general rule of Article IV, and which is created under the laws of either country, is treated as a resident of the country in which it was first created. Canada treats a corporation as a resident if it is managed and controlled in Canada. Thus, for example, a U.S.-incorporated company with its management in Canada

---

See page ii for explanation of footnotes.

[161] CCH ¶30,226e; Art. VI, Canada–U.S. Income Tax Convention.

[162] CCH ¶30,226l; Art. XIII, Canada–U.S. Income Tax Convention.

[163] CCH ¶30,226c; Art. IV, Canada–U.S. Income Tax Convention.

would be resident in Canada under Canadian law; however, under the Convention, it would be resident only in the United States.

An individual performing services of a governmental nature for either country will be treated as a resident of that country if the individual is subject to tax by that country as a resident. Such an individual's spouse and dependent children are also residents of the country that employs him or her, provided they too are subject to tax by that country as residents.

[¶14,400] Permanent Establishment

The term "permanent establishment" is defined as a fixed place of business through which a resident of one country engages in business in the other country.[164] It includes:

(a) a place of management;

(b) a branch;

(c) an office;

(d) a factory;

(e) a workshop;

(f) a mine, quarry, or other place of extraction of natural resources; and

(g) a building site or construction or assembly project which exists for more than 12 months.

The use of an installation, drilling rig, or ship in Canada or the United States to explore for or exploit natural resources is also a permanent establishment if its use in either country is for more than three months in any 12-month period.

If a resident of the country maintains an agent in the other country who has, and regularly exercises, the authority to enter into contracts in that other country in the name of the resident, the resident agent will be deemed to constitute a permanent establishment in the other country with respect to the activities the agent undertakes. This rule does not apply where the contracting authority is limited to those activities such as storage, display, or delivery of merchandise which are excluded from the definition of "permanent establishment". In addition, the agency rule does not apply if the agent is a broker, general commission agent, or other agent of independent status acting in the ordinary course of its business.

Where a fixed place of business is used solely for storing, displaying, or delivering merchandise belonging to the resident; the maintaining of a stock

---

See page ii for explanation of footnotes.

[164] CCH ¶30,226d; Art. V, *Canada–U.S. Income Tax Convention.*

of goods belonging to the resident for storage, display, or delivery; or the maintaining of a stock of goods for processing by another person, that place of business does not constitute a permanent establishment. Also exempted from permanent establishment status are activities such as the maintenance of a fixed place of business for the purchase of goods or merchandise, the collection of information, advertising, or scientific research, or for any other preparatory or auxiliary activities for the resident.

The Fifth Protocol to the *Canada–U.S. Tax Convention* (signed and ratified by both countries, and in force December 15, 2008) includes a change to the permanent establishment "PE" article that deems an enterprise of a contracting state that otherwise does not have a PE in the other state to have a PE in that state, if it provides services in the other state and the services are:

(a) performed in the other state by an individual who is present in the other state for a period of 183 days or more in any 12-month period; and

(b) during that period, more than 50% of the gross active business revenues of the enterprise consists of income derived from the services performed; *or*

(c) the services are provided in the other state for an aggregate of 183 days or more in any 12-month period with respect to the same or connected project for customers who either:

    (i) are residents of the other state; or

    (ii) maintain a PE in the other state, and the services are provided in respect of that PE.

The deemed PE changes do not apply when the PE determination is for a building site or construction or installation project described in item (g) above. For those activities, the 12-month threshold is preserved.

These rules that broaden the definition of permanent establishment to include certain cross-border services came into force for the third taxation year ending after December 15, 2008, and any activity before January 1, 2010 (days of presence, services rendered or gross active business revenues) is to be ignored in making the PE determination.

[¶14,405] Related Persons

Where related persons (for example, parent and subsidiary companies and companies under common control) have not conducted transactions between themselves as if they were operating at arm's length, income (or loss) and tax calculations may be adjusted to reflect profit which normally

¶14,405

would have been made in the absence of any non-arm's length arrangements.[165]

A person is deemed to be related to another person if either participates directly or indirectly in the management or control of the other or if a third party or parties participate directly or indirectly in the management or control of both persons.

[¶14,410] Ships, Aircraft and Motor Vehicles

Profits derived by a resident of one country from the operation of ships or aircraft in "international traffic" are exempt from tax in the other country even when such profits are attributable to a "permanent establishment". Gains derived from the alienation of ships, aircraft, or containers used principally in international traffic are also exempt from taxation in the other country. Profits derived by a resident of one state from a voyage of a ship, where the principal purpose of the voyage is to transport passengers or property between points in the other state, are taxable in that other state, whether or not the resident maintains a permanent establishment there.

Profits derived from the operation of motor vehicles (cars, buses, and trucks) or a railway as a common or contract carrier for the transportation of passengers or property between particular locales are exempt from taxation in the other state, notwithstanding the existence of a permanent establishment there. Profits derived by a resident of one country from the use, maintenance, or rental of railway rolling stock, motor vehicles, trailers, or containers used in the other country for a period not expected to exceed 183 days in the aggregate in any 12-month period are exempt from tax in that other state, except where such profits are attributable to a permanent establishment.[166]

[¶14,415] Government Service

Citizens of one country are exempt from taxation by the other country on remuneration (other than pensions) paid by that country, or any political subdivision or local authority thereof, for services rendered in discharge of government functions in that other country. This exemption does not apply to remuneration for services rendered in respect of any trade or business carried on by the government, political subdivision, or local authority in the other country. The provisions applicable to Independent Personal Services (¶14,565), Dependent Personal Services (¶14,435), or Artists and Athletes (¶14,440), as the case may be, apply.[167]

See page ii for explanation of footnotes.

[165] CCH ¶30,226h; Art. IX, *Canada–U.S. Income Tax Convention.*

[166] CCH ¶30,226g; Art. VIII, *Canada—U.S. Income Tax Convention.*

[167] CCH ¶30,227a; Art. XIX, *Canada–U.S. Income Tax Convention.*

[¶14,420] Pensions and Annuities

Pensions and annuities arising in one country and paid to a resident of the other country are taxable in the country of residence. However, the country of residence is required to exempt from taxation the amount of any such pension that would be excluded from taxable income in the country if the recipient were a resident of that source country.

Pensions and annuities are also subject to tax in the source country. This tax on pension payments is not to exceed 15% of the gross amount of the payment. The tax imposed on annuity payments to residents of the other country is not to exceed 15% of the amount of the payment that would be taxable in the source country if the recipient were a resident thereof.[168] Benefits paid under the U.S. or Canadian social security legislation (OAS, CPP, QPP) to a resident of the other country, or, in the case of Canada, benefits to a U.S. citizen, are taxable exclusively in the paying country. Accordingly, the source country will be able to withhold tax at its full withholding rate (i.e., 25% in Canada). This came into effect January 1996.

The Fourth Protocol to the Canada–U.S. Tax Treaty provides that, retroactively to January 1, 1996, Canadians who receive U.S. social security benefits will pay Canadian tax instead of the flat, non-refundable U.S. withholding tax. The Protocol also exempts from tax in Canada, 15% of any U.S. benefit paid to Canadian residents. Under the Protocol, the United States will not tax its residents who receive Canadian benefits that are tax-free in Canada.

For U.S. social security benefits received in 2010 and subsequent years, Canadian residents and their surviving spouses or common-law partners may deduct from Canadian tax an extra 35% of the benefits in addition to the existing 15% deduction allowed in accordance with the current Canada–U.S. tax treaty.[169] They will be allowed this extra 35% deduction if they meet the following conditions: (1) they have been resident in Canada continuously in the period beginning before 1996 and ending in the current taxation year; and (2) they have received those benefits in each taxation year ending in the period. To qualify for the 35% deduction, the benefits must be subject to the application of Article XVIII(5) of the *Canada–U.S. Tax Convention*.

[¶14,425] Registered Retirement Savings Plans (RRSPs)

A U.S. citizen resident in Canada who forms an RRSP is denied the deduction of contributions for U.S. tax purposes and in most cases is taxable on the RRSP's investment income. Double taxation may therefore exist when Canada later taxes the same amount on payment out of the RRSP. The treaty permits the U.S. citizen to elect to defer U.S. tax on the investment

---

See page ii for explanation of footnotes.

[168] CCH ¶30,227; Art. XVIII, *Canada–U.S. Income Tax Convention.*   [169] CCH ¶15,295; Sec. 110(1)(h).

¶14,420

income and capital gains.[170] The election only applies in respect of income reasonably attributable to contributions made while a Canadian resident.[171]

[¶14,435] Dependent Personal Services

A resident of one country who receives employment income for services performed in the other (source) country is exempt from tax in the source country, if either of the following two conditions are met:

(1) The remuneration for employment performed in the source country does not exceed $10,000 in the calendar year.

(2) The employee is not present in the source country for more than 183 days in the calendar year and the employee's remuneration is not borne by an employer who is a resident of the source country or by a permanent establishment of the employer in the source country.

Employees of international transport companies who work "regularly" on ships, aircraft, motor vehicles, and trains will not be taxed in the source country provided the employer and employee are resident in the other country.[172]

[¶14,440] Artists and Athletes

Income of an entertainer or athlete is taxable in the source country in all cases where the amount of gross receipts, including expenses reimbursed or borne on the individual's behalf, exceeds $15,000 in the currency of the source country for the calendar year concerned. Where such income accrues to another person (for example, a corporation), that income may be taxed in the country where the activities are performed. These provisions do not apply to the income of an athlete or a team, particularly in a league with regularly scheduled games in both countries.[173]

[¶14,445] Withholding of Taxes in Respect of Personal Services

Either country may impose a withholding tax at source on remuneration paid to a resident of the other country performing personal services in the source country. The withholding is limited on the first $5,000 paid for personal services during the year by each payor to 10% of the payment. This provision in no way affects the individual's ultimate tax liability with respect to the source country.[174]

See page ii for explanation of footnotes.

[170] CCH ¶30,227k; Art. XXIX(5), *Canada-U.S. Income Tax Convention.*

[171] CCH ¶30,227l; Art. XXX(2)(b), *Canada-U.S. Income Tax Convention.*

[172] CCH ¶30,226n; Art. XV, *Canada–U.S. Income Tax Convention.*

[173] CCH ¶30,226o; Art. XVI, *Canada–U.S. Income Tax Convention.*

[174] CCH ¶30,226p; Art. XVII, *Canada–U.S. Income Tax Convention.*

[¶14,450] Gains

Generally, gains derived in one country from the alienation of property owned by a resident of the other country, will be taxed only in the alienator's country of residence. However, gains derived by a resident of one country from the alienation of *real property* situated in the other country may be subject to tax in the country where the real property is situated. In addition, if a resident of one country has (or had) a permanent establishment in the other country, that other country (or source country) may tax gains from the alienation of personal property realized by the non-resident which constituted business property, if the gains are attributable to the permanent establishment.

Another provision allows the imposition of tax on gains from the alienation of property realized by individuals resident in the other state who were previously resident in the source state, if certain conditions are met.[175]

[¶14,455] Remittances to Students, Apprentices and Business Trainees

Individuals who are residents of one state and who become full-time students, apprentices, or business trainees in the other state are generally exempt from tax in this other state on payments from abroad used for their maintenance, education, or training.[176]

[¶14,465] Income of Religious, Scientific, Literary, Educational or Charitable Organizations

Income derived by a religious, scientific, literary, educational, or charitable organization is exempt from tax in one country if it is resident in the other country to the extent that such income is exempt from tax in that other country. Canadian private foundations are also exempt from the 4% excise tax imposed on their gross U.S. source investment income, provided they are not substantially funded by U.S. citizens or residents.[177]

[¶14,470] Dividends and Interest

Dividends paid by a company resident in one country to a resident of the other may be taxed in that other country. In addition, each may tax dividends paid by a resident company; the rate of tax, however, is limited if the beneficial owner of the dividend is a resident of the other country. For example, Canada can impose a 10% tax on gross dividends paid to a U.S. parent corporation by its Canadian subsidiary. Likewise, Canada can impose a 15% tax on gross dividends paid to a U.S. investor by a Canadian company. However, dividends paid in respect of holdings which form part of the assets of a permanent establishment in Canada or which are otherwise

---

See page ii for explanation of footnotes.

[175] CCH ¶30,226I; Art. XIII, *Canada–U.S. Income Tax Convention.*

[176] CCH ¶30,227b; Art. XX, *Canada–U.S. Income Tax Convention.*

[177] CCH ¶30,227c; Art. XXI, *Canada–U.S. Income Tax Convention.*

attributable to that permanent establishment will be taxed in Canada as either business income or income from independent personal services. The withholding tax on direct dividends paid to a corporate shareholder with a substantial interest is 5%. The branch profits tax is also 5%.

Canada's branch tax on U.S. corporations is also limited to 10% of the amount of the earnings (as defined) which have not been subjected to branch tax in previous taxation years. The United States does not provide a branch tax *per se*, but the Convention provides that the United States may tax dividends paid by a Canadian resident company, if at least 50% of the Canadian company's gross income from all sources, for the three-year period preceding the taxation year of the company in which the dividend is declared, was included in business profits attributable to permanent establishments that the Canadian company had in the United States.[178]

Interest arising in one country and beneficially owned by a resident of the other country may be taxed only in that other country.[179] However, during the period of January 1, 2008, to December 31, 2009, interest paid between related persons (other than tax-exempt interest) may also be taxed in the country in which it arises and according to the law of that country, but the tax so charged may not exceed the following percentage of the gross amount of that interest:

(1) if the interest is paid or credited during calendar year 2008, 7%; and

(2) if the interest is paid or credited during calendar year 2009, 4%.

Since the non-arm's length rate of 7% applies for all of 2008, a taxpayer that has paid the 10% rate pursuant to the previous treaty provisions will be entitled to a refund of 3%.

Notwithstanding the above provisions, a new 15% withholding rate should apply to the payment of contingent/participating interest effective February 1, 2009. These types of interest payments were subject to 10% withholding for all of 2008 under the previous treaty provisions, as there was no separate rule that carved them out for special treatment. Accordingly, the specific coming into force rules in the Fifth Protocol that deal with non-arm's length interest paid during calendar years 2008 and 2009 also apply to payments of contingent/participating interest. Arguably, the non-arm's length rate of 7% applied to these types of interest payments for all of 2008, and a taxpayer that has paid the 10% rate pursuant to the previous treaty provisions is therefore entitled to a refund of 3%. As well, for the month of January 2009, the non-arm's length rate of 4% should apply to such payments.

See also ¶14,505.

---

[178] CCH ¶30,226i; Art. X, *Canada–U.S. Income Tax Convention.*

[179] CCH ¶30,226j; Art. XI, *Canada–U.S. Income Tax Convention.*

[¶14,475] Diplomatic Agents and Consular Officers

This Article provides that the Convention shall not affect the fiscal privileges of diplomatic agents or consular officers that are conferred on them under international law or under special international agreements.[180]

[¶14,480] Royalties

"Royalties" are payments of any kind received as consideration for the use of, or the right to use, any copyright of literacy, artistic, or scientific work, patents, trademarks, designs, models, plans, secret formulae or processes, or any tangible personal property. In general terms, royalties (other than "cultural royalties") that arise in one state and are paid to a resident of the other state may be taxed by both countries. However, the withholding tax imposed in the source country may not exceed 10% of the gross royalty. No withholding tax may be imposed on "cultural royalties", which generally includes copyright royalties and other like payments for the production or reproduction of any literary, dramatic, musical, or artistic work.

The 10% limitation on tax in the country of source and the exemption in the state of source for certain "cultural royalties" do not apply if the beneficial owner of the royalties carries on business in the state of source through a permanent establishment or fixed base and the right or property in respect of which the royalties are paid is effectively connected with such permanent establishment or fixed base.[181] Pursuant to the Third Protocol, withholding tax will be eliminated on royalties for the use of, or the right to use, computer software or any patent or information concerning industrial, commercial, or scientific experience. The withholding tax on other royalties will remain at 10%.

[¶14,485] Mutual Agreement Procedure

The Convention contains the standard mutual agreement provisions authorizing the competent authorities of Canada and the United States to consult to attempt to alleviate individual cases of double taxation or cases of taxation not in accordance with the Convention.[182]

[¶14,490] Elimination of Double Taxation

The Convention provides for reciprocal credits and exemptions to avoid the imposition of double taxation on income that is taxable by both Canada and the United States, including separate rules for relief of double taxation by the United States and Canada. In addition, it provides special rules for U.S. citizens resident in Canada.[183]

See page ii for explanation of footnotes.

[180] CCH ¶30,227j; Art. XXVIII, Canada–U.S. Income Tax Convention.

[181] CCH ¶30,226k; Art. XII, Canada–U.S. Income Tax Convention.

[182] CCH ¶30,227h; Art. XXVI, Canada–U.S. Income Tax Convention.

[183] CCH ¶30,227f; Art. XXIV, Canada–U.S. Income Tax Convention.

¶14,475

[¶14,495] Non-Discrimination

The Convention also contains provisions to protect persons of one country from discrimination by the other country with respect to all taxes of every kind imposed at the national level. A number of specific non-discrimination rules, some of which are limited in scope, are provided.[184]

[¶14,500] Exchange of Information

The Convention provides for the exchange of information necessary to carry out the provisions of the Convention for the prevention of fraud or for the administration of statutory provisions concerning taxes to which the Convention applies. The exchange of information rules apply to any taxes imposed by Canada on estates and gifts, to taxes Canada imposes under the *Income Tax Act*, and to all taxes the United States imposes under the *Internal Revenue Code*.[185]

[¶14,505] Entry into Force

The Convention has effect with respect to source country taxation of dividends, interest, royalties, pensions, annuities, alimony, and child support for amounts paid or credited on or after October 1, 1984. For other taxes, the Convention takes effect for the first taxable year beginning on or after January 1, 1985. Special effective dates are provided for U.S. foreign tax credit computations with respect to taxes paid or accrued to Canada. It also provides that the principles providing for the sourcing of certain dividend, interest, and royalty income to eliminate double taxation of U.S. citizens residing in Canada have effect for taxation years beginning on or after January 1, 1976. The source rules applicable to Article XXIV (Elimination of Double Taxation) have effect for taxation years beginning on or after January 1, 1981.

This Article also provides that the provisions of the 1942 Convention that are more favourable than the provisions of the 1980 Convention remain in effect for the period through the first taxable year beginning on or after January 1, 1985.

It also provides that the estate tax treaty between Canada and the United States has effect for estates or persons who die prior to January 1, 1985, but is terminated with respect to persons who die on or after that date.[186]

See page ii for explanation of footnotes.

[184] CCH ¶30,227g; Art. XXV, *Canada–U.S. Income Tax Convention.*

[185] CCH ¶30,227l; Art. XXVII, *Canada–U.S. Income Tax Convention.*

[186] CCH ¶30,227l; Art. XXX, *Canada–U.S. Income Tax Convention.*

[¶14,510] Highlights of the Canada–U.K. Income Tax Convention (1978)

Note: Proclaimed in force as of December 18, 1980 by the *Canada–United Kingdom Income Tax Convention Act, 1980*, S.C. 1980-81-82-83, c. 44. Three Protocols have subsequently been signed on April 15, 1980, October 16, 1985, and May 7, 2003.

[¶14,520] Industrial and Commercial Profits — Permanent Establishment

The industrial or commercial profits of a U.K. enterprise are not subject to Canadian tax unless the enterprise carries on or has carried on business in Canada through a permanent establishment in Canada. The tax is on that part of the business attributable to Canada.

Profits of a Canadian enterprise are not subject to U.K. tax unless the enterprise carries on business in the United Kingdom through a permanent establishment in the United Kingdom.[187]

The term "permanent establishment" means a fixed place of business in which the business of an enterprise is wholly or partly carried on and specifically includes:

(a) a place of management;

(b) a branch;

(c) an office;

(d) a factory;

(e) a workshop;

(f) a mine, quarry, or other place of extraction of natural resources; and

(g) a building site or construction or assembly project which exists for more than 12 months.

The term "permanent establishment" is deemed not to include:

(a) the use of facilities solely for the purpose of storage, display, or delivery of goods or merchandise belonging to the enterprise;

(b) the maintenance of a stock of goods or merchandise belonging to the enterprise solely for the purpose of storage, display, or delivery;

(c) the maintenance of a stock of goods or merchandise belonging to the enterprise solely for the purpose of processing by another enterprise;

See page ii for explanation of footnotes.

[187] CCH ¶30,252; Art. VII, *Canada–U.K. Income Tax Convention.*

(d) the maintenance of a fixed place of business solely for the purpose of purchasing goods or merchandise or for collecting information for the enterprise; and

(e) the maintenance of a fixed place of business solely for the purpose of advertising, for the supply of information, for scientific research, or for similar activities which have a preparatory or auxiliary character, for the enterprise.[188]

A person acting in one of the countries on behalf of an enterprise of the other country (other than an agent with an independent status) is deemed to constitute a permanent establishment in the first-mentioned country if he has, and habitually exercises in the first-mentioned country, an authority to conclude contracts in the name of the enterprise, unless his or her activities are limited to the purchase of goods or merchandise for the enterprise.

An enterprise of one of the countries is not deemed to have a permanent establishment in the other country merely because it carries on business in that other country through a broker, general commission agent, or any other agent with an independent status, where such persons are acting in the ordinary course of their business.

The fact that a company which is a resident of one of the countries controls or is controlled by a company which is a resident of the other country, or which carries on business in that other country (whether through a permanent establishment or otherwise), does not of itself render either company a permanent establishment of the other.

[¶14,525] Associated Enterprises

Rules are imposed regarding the allocation of profits between associated corporations in the two countries if the profits have been allocated differently between the corporations. Adjustments by the two countries are to be made accordingly to avoid double taxation where the allocation is revised.[189]

[¶14,530] Ship, Aircraft or Container Use, Maintenance, or Rental Profits

The country of residence of an enterprise deriving profits from the operation of shipping or air transport, or the use, maintenance, or rental of containers in international traffic has the exclusive right to tax these profits. This general rule does not apply to profits from the coasting trade: regardless of the residence of the enterprise, the country in which the coasting trade is carried on may tax such profits. These rules also apply to profits

---

[188] CCH ¶30,250; Art. V, *Canada–U.K. Income Tax Convention.*   [189] CCH ¶30,253; Art. VIII, *Canada–U.K. Income Tax Convention.*

derived from participation of an enterprise of this kind in an international pooling agreement.[190]

[¶14,535] Royalties

The term "Royalties" is defined as the payment of any kind received:

(a) for the use of (or the right to use) any copyright, patent, trade mark, design, model, plan, secret formula, or process;

(b) for the use of (or the right to use) industrial, commercial, or scientific equipment;

(c) for information concerning industrial, commercial, or scientific experience; and

(d) in respect of motion picture films and works on film or videotape for use in connection with television.[191]

The Convention gives the country of residence of the recipient a right to tax royalties arising in the country of source. The country of source may also tax royalties, but where the recipient is the beneficial owner, the rate must not exceed 10%. Copyright royalties in respect of production or reproduction of any literary, dramatic, musical, or artistic work (but not including royalties in respect of motion picture films and works on film or videotape for use in connection with television), payments for the use of or right to use a patent or information regarding industrial, commercial, or scientific experience (but not including a payment in connection with a franchise or rental agreement), and payments for the use of or the right to use computer software are exempt from withholding in the country of source. The foregoing does not apply if the recipient of the royalties, being a resident of either country, has a permanent establishment therein and the right to a property giving rise to the royalties is effectively connected with a trade or business carried on through that permanent establishment.

Royalties are deemed to arise in one country when the payor is the state itself, a political subdivision, a local authority, or a resident of that state. Where the royalties have a clear economic link with a permanent establishment of the payor situated in the other state, the state where the permanent establishment is located becomes the state of source.

When, owing to a special relationship between the payor and the recipient, or between both of them and another person, the amount of royalties paid exceeds the amount which would have been agreed upon in the absence of such relationship, the provisions of the Convention apply only to the last mentioned amount.

See page ii for explanation of footnotes.

[190] CCH ¶30,253; Art. VIII, *Canada–U.K. Income Tax Convention.*   [191] CCH ¶30,257; Art. XII, *Canada–U.K. Income Tax Convention.*

¶14,535

[¶14,540] Capital Gains

Gains from the disposition of certain shares deriving the greater part of their value from immovable property situated in one of the countries and gains from the disposition of an interest in a partnership or trust, the assets of which consist principally of immovable property situated in one if the countries, are taxed in that country. This does not apply where the vendor owns less than 10% of the shares or has less than a 10% interest in the partnership or trust and immovable property does not include property other than rental property in which the business of the company, partnership, or trust is carried on.

Gains, other than those described above, are to be taxable only in the country where the vendor is resident. In general, an individual who becomes a resident of the United Kingdom will be subject to capital gains tax only on gains to property accruing after the date of arrival.[192]

[¶14,545] Income from Immovable Property

Income from immovable property and profits from the alienation of immovable property may be taxed in the country in which such property is situated. "Immovable property" is defined in accordance with the laws of the country where it is situated, but in any case it includes livestock and equipment of agricultural and forestry enterprises and rights to payments as consideration for the working of mineral deposit sources and other natural resources.[193]

[¶14,550] Pensions and Annuities

Periodic pension payments are taxable only in the country of residence of the recipient. Pension payments include those under superannuation, pension, retirement, and disability plans and under the social security legislation of either of the countries. Annuities may be taxed in the country of residence but may also be subject to a withholding tax of 10% in the country of source.

The term "annuity" does not include payments of any kind under an income-averaging annuity contract".

The Convention also provides that alimony and similar payments (e.g., maintenance payments in respect of children of the marriage) are taxable solely by the country of residence of the recipient. The provision is subject to the recipient's being the beneficial owner of the payment.[194]

See page ii for explanation of footnotes.

[192] CCH ¶30,258; Art. XIII, *Canada–U.K. Income Tax Convention.*

[193] CCH ¶30,251; Art. VI, *Canada–U.K. Income Tax Convention.*

[194] CCH ¶30,262; Art. XVII, *Canada–U.K. Income Tax Convention.*

[¶14,555] Dividends and Interest

Both countries agree generally not to impose tax in excess of 15% on dividends paid by companies resident in one country to residents of the other country. The withholding tax is reduced to 5% if the beneficial owner of the dividend is a company which owns at least 10% of the voting power of the company paying the dividends.

Both countries have the right to tax interest arising in one country and paid to a resident of the other, but, where the recipient is the beneficial owner, the rate of tax imposed by the country of origin of the interest must not exceed 10%. The definition of "interest" includes a general formula and specific examples.[195]

[¶14,560] Income from Employment

Salaries, wages, and similar remuneration, including directors' fees, derived by a resident of one country in respect of employment are subject to tax only in that country, unless the employment is exercised in the other country, in which case such remuneration as is derived from that other country may be taxed there. In any event, remuneration derived by a resident of one country in respect of an employment exercised in the other country is taxable only in the first-mentioned country if:

(a) the recipient is present in the other country for less than 183 days;

(b) the remuneration is paid by an employer who is not a resident of the other country; and

(c) the remuneration is not deducted from the profits of a permanent establishment which the employer has in the other country.

Remuneration in respect of employment exercised aboard a ship or aircraft in international traffic may be taxed in the country where the effective management of the enterprise operating the ship or aircraft is situated.[196]

[¶14,565] Miscellaneous Income

The following is a list of taxation rules relating to various sources of income:

(1) *Independent personal services.* Income from professional services or other independent activities of similar character are taxable in the country where the recipient resides, unless the recipient has a fixed base regularly available in the other country for the purpose of performing his or her

---

See page ii for explanation of footnotes.

[195] CCH ¶30,256; Art. XI, *Canada–U.K. Income Tax Convention*; Art. III, *Canada–U.K. Income Tax Convention.* [196] CCH ¶30,260; Art. XV, *Canada–U.K. Income Tax Convention.*

¶14,555

activities. In such case, that part of the income which is attributable to that base may be taxed in the other country.[197]

(2) *Artists and athletes.* Income of public entertainers, such as theatre, motion picture, radio or television artists, musicians, and athletes may be taxed in the country where they perform, subject to certain exemptions: where the visit of the entertainer is supported wholly or substantially by public funds, to non-profit organizations whose income is not available for the personal benefit of its owners or members, and to entertainers in respect of services they render to such non-profit organizations.[198]

(3) *Students.* Payments made from one country for the maintenance, education, or training of students or business apprentices are not subject to tax in the country where the student is present if:

(a) the student's presence there is solely for the purpose of education or training; and

(b) the student's normal residence is in the other country.[199]

(4) *Alimony.* Alimony or other maintenance payments are exempt from tax in the country from which they are paid.[200]

(5) *Governmental services.* The general rule is that the government making the payment has the sole right to tax, but there is an exception for remuneration to nationals or permanent residents of one who perform services there for the other country in which case only the country of residence has the right to tax. There is also an exception for services rendered in connection with a business carried on by a government of either country, in which case the article does not apply.[201]

[¶14,570] Elimination of Double Taxation

Double taxation of income arising in one country and received by a resident of the other is to be avoided by having the country of residence give a credit against its tax in respect of tax levied in the other country.[202]

Any Canadian taxpayers having an objection to their tax treatment may request competent authority assistance through the Canada Revenue Agency.[203]

See page ii for explanation of footnotes.

[197] CCH ¶30,259; Art. XIV, *Canada–U.K. Income Tax Convention.*

[198] CCH ¶30,261; Art. XVI, *Canada–U.K. Income Tax Convention.*

[199] CCH ¶30,264; Art. XIX, *Canada–U.K. Income Tax Convention.*

[200] CCH ¶30,262; Art. XVII, *Canada–U.K. Income Tax Convention.*

[201] CCH ¶30,263; Art. XVIII, *Canada–U.K. Income Tax Convention.*

[202] CCH ¶30,266; Art. XXI, *Canada–U.K. Income Tax Convention.*

[203] CCH ¶30,268; Art. XXIII, *Canada–U.K. Income Tax Convention.*

Chapter XV

Administration, Enforcement, and Interpretation

Administration **15,000**

Duties of Minister of
National Revenue 15,005

Minister's Discretion to
Waive Penalty, Interest
and Filing of Documents 15,006

Re-Appropriation of
Amounts 15,007

Late, Amended or Revoked
Elections 15,008

Regulations 15,010

Collection of Tax **15,015**

Debt to the Crown 15,020

Collection Restrictions 15,025

Application of Interest 15,027

**Judgments, Garnishment,
Seizure** **15,030**

Certificate Judgments 15,035

Garnishment 15,040

Moneys Seized by Police 15,045

Acquisition of Debtor's
Property 15,050

Seizure of Chattels 15,055

Collection of Tax from
Taxpayer Leaving
Canada 15,060

Taxes Withheld **15,065**

Withholding — Deemed
Trust 15,070

Excess Withheld under
Parts XIII and XII.5 15,075

Penalty for Failure To
Withhold or Remit Tax 15,080

Payments by Trustees, etc. 15,083

Liability of Directors 15,085

Assessment 15,090

Joint and Several Liability re
Contributions to RCA 15,092

Application of Withholding
Provisions to Crown 15,095

Minister's Receipt
Discharges Debtor 15,100

Special Taxes and Exempt
Corporations 15,105

Partnerships and Provincial
or Municipal
Corporations 15,110

**Books, Records,
Investigations** **15,115**

Keeping of Records 15,120

Investigations 15,125

Requirement To Provide
Information and
Documents 15,130

Non-Arm's Length
Transactions with Non-
Residents 15,131

Transfers and Loans to
Foreign Trusts 15,132

Foreign Property Reporting 15,133

Foreign Affiliate Reporting 15,134

Search Warrants 15,135

Inquiries 15,140

Copies and Compliance 15,145

Access to Foreign
Information 15,150

Compliance Order 15,153

Solicitor-Client Privilege **15,155**

Privilege 15,160

Defence 15,165

Seizure of Documents 15,170

Production of Documents 15,175

Types of Documents to
which Privilege Attaches 15,180

Collection Agreements 15,185

Tax Collection Agreements
with Provinces 15,190

Ownership Certificates 15,195

Obligation to Complete
Ownership Certificates 15,200

Penalty 15,205

Signing Officers 15,210

Authorized Person 15,215

**Social Insurance Number
(SIN) 15,220**

Application for Assignment
of SIN 15,225

Tax Shelters 15,230

Identification Number
Required 15,235

Meaning of "Promoter" and
"Tax Shelter" 15,240

Failure To Comply 15,245

Information Returns 15,246

Enforcement 15,247

**Information Reporting for
Tax Avoidance
Transactions 15,250**

Background 15,251

Persons Subject to the
Reporting Rules 15,252

Reportable Transaction 15,253

Information Return 15,254

Penalty for Failure to
Report 15,255

Due Diligence Defence 15,256

Offences 15,260

Failure To File Returns, etc. 15,265

Penalties for Evasion of Tax 15,270

Communication of
Information 15,275

Liability of Company
Officers, etc. 15,280

Minimum Penalties Not To
Be Decreased 15,285

Taxable Obligation —
Identification of Interest
Coupon 15,290

Procedure and Evidence 15,295

Information or Complaints 15,300

Online Notices 15,301

Tax Avoidance 15,305

General Anti-Avoidance
Rule (GAAR) 15,307

Benefit Conferred on a
Person 15,308

Transfer Pricing 15,310

Transfer Pricing Adjustment 15,311

Contemporaneous
Documentation 15,312

Penalty 15,315

Interpretation 15,320

Meaning of "Tax Payable" 15,325

Property Subject to Certain
Quebec Institutions and
Arrangements 15,330

Interest in Real Property 15,335

Proportional Holdings in
Trust Property 15,340

Substituted Property 15,345

Series of Shares 15,350

Receipt of Things Mailed 15,355

Occurrences as a
Consequence of Death 15,360

Series of Transactions or
Events 15,365

Compound Interest 15,370

Identical Properties 15,375

Interests in Trust and
Partnerships 15,380

Related Corporations 15,385

Partition of Property 15,386

Partition of Property upon
Dissolution of Matrimonial
Regime 15,387

Accounting Methods 15,389

References to "Taxation
Year" and "Fiscal Period" 15,390

Taxation Year of a
Business 15,392

Fiscal Period for
Partnerships with
Significant Corporate
Members 15,393

Extended Meaning of
"Resident" 15,395

Meaning of "Arm's Length" 15,400

Related Persons — Persons
Related by Blood
Relationship, etc. 15,405

Related Persons —
Individuals Related to
Corporations 15,410

Related Persons —
Corporations Related to
Each Other 15,415

Control by Related Group 15,420

Union Employer 15,423

Extended Meaning of
"Carrying on Business" —
Non-Residents 15,425

Investments in Limited
Partnerships 15,427

Contract under Pension
Plan 15,430

Meaning of "Canada" 15,435

Negative Amounts 15,440

Affiliated Persons 15,445

General Rules 15,450

Individuals and
Corporations 15,455

Two Corporations 15,460

Partnerships 15,465

A Corporation and a
Partnership 15,470

A Partnership and a
Majority-Interest Partner 15,475

Two Partnerships 15,480

A Trust and a Majority
Interest Beneficiary 15,482

Two Trusts 15,483

Associated Corporations 15,485

Corporations Associated
with Each Other 15,490

Meaning of "Specified
Class" 15,495

Control of a Corporation 15,500

Parent Deemed to Own
Shares 15,505

Options and Rights 15,510

Person Related to Himself
or Herself 15,515

Fair Market Value 15,520

Anti-Avoidance 15,525

Corporations Deemed Not
To Be Associated or
Controlled 15,530

Corporations Deemed Not
To Be Associated —
Control by Trustee or
Executor 15,535

Control in Fact 15,540

Control Deemed Not To
Have Been Acquired 15,545

Simultaneous Control
Rules 15,547

Deemed Exercise of Right 15,550

Date of Acquisition of
Control 15,555

**Functional Currency Tax
Reporting 15,560**

Canadian Currency
Requirement 15,565

Functional Currency
Reporting Requirements 15,570

Functional Currency
General Rules 15,575

Functional Currency Year —
Establishing Functional
Currency Amounts 15,580

Transitional Rules 15,585

─ **Recent Changes** ─────────────────────

2012 Budget

Tax Shelters

Continuing with restrictions made to the tax shelter rules in previous budgets, this year the existing penalty for selling an interest in a tax shelter before the issuance of the tax shelter identification number is issued has been increased, and a new penalty applies to promoters who do not properly file information returns. Lastly, a tax shelter identification number will now only be valid for the calendar year identified in the application. These changes came into effect through Bill C-38 and take effect on the date of Royal Assent, June 29, 2012. See ¶15,230.

Transfer Pricing Secondary Adjustments

Resolution 28 proposed to clarify the Minister's authority to make "secondary adjustments". As proposed, a secondary adjustment will generally result in a dividend being deemed to have been paid by a corporation that has been the subject of a primary adjustment. The Minister will have discretionary power to reduce the amount of the deemed dividend. The amendments will also legislate the CRA's administrative repatriation policy (TPM-02). This measure will apply to transactions (including transactions that are part of a series of transactions) that occur after March 29, 2012. The amendments have been included in draft legislation released on August 14, 2012. See ¶15,310.

[¶15,000] Administration

[¶15,005] Duties of Minister of National Revenue

While the Minister of Finance formulates tax policy, the Minister of National Revenue controls, regulates, manages, and supervises the income tax system. The Commissioner of Revenue may exercise all the powers and perform the duties of the Minister. The appointment of such officers, clerks, and employees as are necessary for the administration and enforcement of the tax system is also authorized.[1]

The Minister may extend the time for filing returns and may accept security from a taxpayer in arrears.[2] The security may be discharged by the Minister by a document in writing. Upon the taxpayer's written request, the Minister must surrender security to the extent that it exceeds the amount then payable.

The Minister must accept security for payment of tax and interest from a member institution of a deposit insurance corporation where the tax arises because of the inclusion in income of assistance received from a deposit insurance corporation.[3] The Minister will determine the adequacy of the security provided and will require further security if the security furnished is no longer adequate.[4] A member institution of a deposit insurance corporation may also post security where the income inclusion in question arises in a preceding taxation year. Tax officers may be designated by the Minister to administer oaths and receive affidavits, etc., for purposes of administration.

[¶15,006] Minister's Discretion to Waive Penalty, Interest and Filing of Documents

For requests filed on or after January 1, 2005, the Minister may waive penalties and interest for any tax year that ended within 10 years before the calendar year in which the taxpayer's request is filed. Due to this limitation,

---

See page ii for explanation of footnotes.

[1] CCH ¶27,003, ¶27,010; Sec. 220(1), 220(2).   [3] CCH ¶27,035; Sec. 220(4.3).
[2] CCH ¶27,014, ¶27,031; Sec. 220(3), 220(4).   [4] CCH ¶27,036; Sec. 220(4.4).

a taxpayer has 10 years from the end of the calendar year in which the tax year at issue ended to make a request to the CRA for relief. For requests filed before 2005, the Minister's discretion could be exercised for any tax year that ended after 1984. The Minister's discretion to waive interest or penalties will generally be exercised where the non-compliance was due to extraordinary circumstances beyond the taxpayer's control.

Application must be made in writing, giving the reasons justifying the waiver. Examples of situations where the Minister would consider exercising discretion include natural disasters such as floods or fires, strikes, serious illnesses or accidents, or erroneous information received from the CRA. The taxpayer must have taken reasonable care in attempting to comply with the requirements and efforts should have been made to avoid, or at least minimize, the delay in complying or paying the amounts due. Discretion will not be exercised where the non-compliance arose as a result of the neglect or lack of awareness on the part of the taxpayer.[5] Guidelines to the exercise of the Minister's discretion are set out in Information Circular 07-1, "Taxpayer Relief Provisions".[6] While the courts will not review the CRA's discretionary decisions as such, they will review cases to ensure that the CRA follows certain basic principles of administrative fairness, which at a minimum include the taxpayer's right to be informed of the principles governing the application of discretion and to make representations to the decision makers in light of those principles. However, the Federal Court of Appeal has implied that a ministerial discretion can be set aside only if it is so flagrantly egregious as to constitute bad faith; it its not sufficient that it found Revenue Canada/CRA's decision uncongenial.[7]

Generally speaking, the Minister may also waive any requirement to file a prescribed form, receipt, or other document, or to provide prescribed information. Even though the Minister may waive such a requirement, the document or information must be provided if the Minister subsequently requests it.[8] [After November 16, 2005, the Minister's discretion to waive the 12-month filing deadline to claim SR&ED tax incentives is removed.[9] As a result, a person who takes more than the 12 months allowed to file Forms T661 and T2038 after the filing-due date for the taxation year in which the expenditures are made will not be able to deduct them or claim an investment tax credit for them.]

[¶15,007] Re-Appropriation of Amounts

In certain situations, a taxpayer may wish to have amounts that were paid on one tax account transferred to another tax account, as where the taxpayer has overpaid one account and underpaid on another. The various tax accounts are described below. In the absence of the following provisions, this situation would give rise to interest being charged on the deficiency

See page ii for explanation of footnotes.

[5] CCH ¶27,015; Sec. 220(3.1).   [8] CCH ¶27,013; Sec. 220(2.1).
[6] Inf. Cir. 07-1.
[7] Barron, 97 DTC 5121.   [9] Sec. 220(2.2).

despite the fact that an amount that would eliminate the shortfall had been paid on another account. These provisions confer to the Minister explicit authority, on the taxpayer's application, to accept transfers of payments from one account to another. Any amount so transferred is treated as though it had never been paid on account of the first account, and had initially been a payment made in respect of the second account.[10]

The tax "accounts" are in respect of amounts payable under the *Income Tax Act*, the *Employment Insurance Act*, the *Unemployment Insurance Act*, the *Canada Pension Plan*, and a provincial income tax act. Furthermore, for applications made on or after April 1, 2007, transfers may be made in respect of amounts paid under the *Income Tax Act* to amounts payable (the taxpayer's tax debt) under the *Excise Tax Act* (GST and non-GST), the *Excise Act, 2001*, or the *Air Travellers Security Charge Act*, with the reallocation taking effect from the date the overpayment was made under the first Act. This change in the law was initiated by the 2006 federal Budget as part of the standardized accounting measures.

[¶15,008] Late, Amended or Revoked Elections

The Minister has the discretionary authority to extend the statutory time for filing certain elections or to permit certain elections to be amended or revoked. Beginning in 2005, a taxpayer has 10 years from the end of the calendar year in which the tax year at issue ended to make a request to the CRA for relief. Before 2005, the CRA could accept a request for any taxation year ending after 1984. The penalties and interest can be waived retroactively where these elections or revocations are permitted.[11]

The taxpayer or partnership must demonstrate that the failure to elect on time was inadvertent or that the election would have been made on time had the taxpayer or partnership been aware of the election or that the election was not filed on time because of circumstances beyond the control of the taxpayer or partnership.

An amendment to or a revocation of an election may be granted where the taxpayer can demonstrate that the original election would cause an unintended tax result. However, the application would be rejected where it is reasonable to conclude that such action would constitute retroactive tax planning. Furthermore, where there are no adequate records to verify the request and it is reasonable to conclude that the request was being made because the taxpayer was careless, the request will be denied.

The CRA discusses the circumstances in which it is prepared to consider a revised, revoked, or late-filed election in Information Circular 07-1.[12] In general, it will accept such election where there are unintended consequences (for example, a *bona fide* valuation must be revised); where there is

---

See page ii for explanation of footnotes.

[10] CCH ¶27,086; Sec. 221.2.

[11] CCH ¶27,018; Sec. 220(3.2); Reg. 600.

[12] Inf. Cir. 07-1.

a suitable reason beyond the control of the taxpayer (such as fire, flood, strike, illness, death in the family); where the taxpayer acted on incorrect information provided by the CRA; where a purely mechanical error was made in setting out an elected amount in a previous election; where subsequent accounting indicates all parties intended the election to be made; or where the taxpayer was unaware of the election, despite reasonable efforts to comply with the law. The CRA is not prepared to accept late-filed elections where the intention is to accomplish retroactive tax planning; where adequate records do not exist; or where the original failure was negligent or careless oversight.

Application must be made in writing with an explanation as to why the late or amended election should be accepted or why the revocation of the election should be allowed. The elections which may be late-filed or revoked are:

- capitalization of the cost of borrowed money;

- election to defer recapture or capital gain where capital property replaced;

- election to transfer depreciable property among classes;

- election for property to pass to spouse or common-law partner on death at fair market value;

- proceeds of disposition of certain farm property transferred on death;

- election to claim certain reserves where property passes to spouse or common-law partner on death;

- transfers between spouses/common-law partners elected to occur at fair market value;

- preferred beneficiary election;

- election to have dividends included in spouse/common-law partner's income;

- election to reduce capital cost of depreciable property on which inducement payments have been received instead of including the inducement in income;

- election to ignore change of use to income-earning purpose;

- election to ignore change of use from income-earning purpose to principal residence;

- election to deem property to be taxable Canadian property on emigration (under 1992 rules);

¶15,008

- election to deem property not to be taxable Canadian property on emigration (under 1992 rules);

- election to draw down accumulated averaging amounts subject to averaging election before 1988;

- election by representative of a deceased taxpayer to deem losses of estate to be those of the taxpayer;

- election to have a deemed disposition of bad debt or share;

- election to deem property to be taxable Canadian property on emigration (under rules for 1993 and later years);

- election to deem property not to be taxable Canadian property or continuing inventory on emigration (under rules for 1993 and later years);

- election to reduce adjusted cost base of capital property on which inducement payments have been received, instead of including the inducement in income;

- election to transfer RRSP Home Buyer's Plan repayment liability from the deceased taxpayer to the surviving spouse/common-law partner;

- the election by a returning former resident to unwind departure tax;[13]

- the election by an emigrating individual to reduce departure tax on subsequent actual sale of property taxed at a lower amount than used in calculating departure tax;[14]

- the election by a holder of a foreign affiliate with respect to assets received by foreign affiliate on expropriation and received in turn by the holder as dividend or benefit;

- the election by a trust to defer 21-year deemed disposition;

- the election by a corporation under debt-parking rules on wind-up of a subsidiary;

- the election to have a deemed disposition of worthless shares or bad debt (see ¶5415);

- the election by a communal organization to be treated as a trust (see ¶9283);

- the election to obtain rollover treatment under foreign spin-off rules (see ¶6321);

See page ii for explanation of footnotes.

[13] CCH ¶20,028d; Sec. 128.1(6).   [14] CCH ¶20,028e; Sec. 128.1(7).

- the long-term project election to accelerate availability for use of property for CCA purposes (see ¶4060);

- the election by estate to recognize loss on stock options held at death (see ¶2135);

- the election to reduce capital cost of property in place of income inclusion for government assistance (see ¶4012);

- the employee's election to defer tax on stock options or mutual fund units of publicly-traded corporations (see ¶2135);

- the election by a trust to opt out of rollover rules in respect of distributions of capital interest;

- the election to transfer reserves related to future undertakings assumed by new party; and

- beginning with the 2007 taxation year, the election to split pension income between spouses or common-law partners.

A late election or an amended election will be deemed to have been made at the time the election should have originally been made and, in the case of an amended or revoked election, the original election is deemed never to have been made.[15]

Late, amended, or revoked elections (other than late, amended, or revoked elections to split pension income between spouses or common-law partners) are subject to a penalty of $100 for each complete month from the due date of the election to the date that the application was made, subject to a maximum of $8,000.[16] The Minister will examine each election, amended election, and revoked election with all due dispatch, assess any penalty payable and send a notice of assessment to the taxpayer.[17] However, the taxpayer would be entitled to apply for relief from this penalty (see ¶15,006).

[¶15,010] Regulations

The general power to make Regulations is given to the Governor in Council. These Regulations may prescribe, determine, or regulate the purposes of the Act relating to evidence, assessment of tax, persons acquiring bearer instruments, information returns, garnishment of government employee salaries, retention by way of deduction or set-off of tax-indebtedness, and determination of classes of dependants or non-residents.[18] These Regulations are discussed under the subjects to which they relate.

All Regulations are required to be published in the *Canada Gazette* in order to become effective. If no effective date is given in the Regulation, it

---

See page ii for explanation of footnotes.

[15] CCH ¶27,019; Sec. 220(3.3).

[16] CCH ¶27,021; Sec. 220(3.5).

[17] CCH ¶27,022; Sec. 220(3.6).

[18] CCH ¶27,050, ¶27,175, ¶27,570; Sec. 221(1), 224.1, 233.

becomes effective on the date of publication. A regulation may have retroactive effect only where:

(a) it provides relief to taxpayers;

(b) it corrects an ambiguity or deficiency;

(c) it is consequential upon an amendment to the Act which was applicable prior to publication; and

(d) it gives effect to a Budget proposal or other public announcement.[19]

[¶15,015] Collection of Tax

[¶15,020] Debt to the Crown

All taxes, interest, penalties, costs, and other amounts payable are debts due the Crown. These debts are recoverable in the Federal Court of Canada or any other court of competent jurisdiction or in any other manner provided under the Act.[20] The words "and other amounts payable" have the effect of enabling the Minister to sue for unpaid instalments of tax.

Where a person is indebted to The Queen under the Act or under a provincial Act of a province that has entered into a collection agreement, the Minister may require the retention by way of deduction or set-off of any amount that may be or may become payable to such person by The Queen in right of Canada. The amount to be deducted or set-off is such amount as the Minister may specify. Thus, the recovery of federal or provincial taxes, interest, or penalties owing by a federal civil servant by deduction or set-off from his or her salary is permitted. Similarly, if a person performed services for the Crown, amounts owing by that person could be satisfied by deduction or set-off from amounts owing to that person under the contract with the Crown.[21]

A court order charging certain registered retirement savings plans (RRSPs) with payment of support arrears did not take precedence over Crown priority in respect of arrears of income tax. Further, Crown priority over claims of equal rank does not violate equality rights guaranteed under the *Canadian Charter of Rights and Freedoms*. The Crown is not an "individual" for the purposes of the Charter provision governing equality rights.[22]

[¶15,025] Collection Restrictions

Except for taxes and penalties assessed against registered charities, the CRA may not generally commence formal collection proceedings until 90 days after the date of a taxpayer's assessment or reassessment.[23] For regis-

---

See page ii for explanation of footnotes.

[19] CCH ¶27,080; Sec. 221(2).
[20] CCH ¶27,090; Sec. 222.
[21] CCH ¶27,175; Sec. 224.1.

[22] Wright, 88 DTC 6041.

[23] CCH ¶27,207; Sec. 225.1(1).

tered charities, the collection-commencement day is the day that is one year after the day of the mailing of a notice of assessment for penalties, and, in the case of the Part V revocation tax, the day that is one year after the mailing of the notice of intention to revoke registered status. Exceptions to this 90-day collection restriction permit immediate collection where:

(a) reassessments have been issued pursuant to the CRA's discretion to waive the usual three-year limit at a taxpayer's request to give effect to a reduction in tax originally assessed or to a late refund request (see ¶12,345);

(b) reassessments have been issued to give effect to the CRA's discretion to waive interest and penalties (see ¶15,006); and

(c) reassessments have been issued under an agreement with the taxpayer to settle issues where a judicial appeal is pending.

Furthermore, effective April 1, 2007, the 90-day collection restriction does not apply to the Minister's right to collect amounts by deduction or set-off against amounts payable by the Crown to the taxpayer. This means that the Minister will be allowed to commence collection of an amount owing by way of deduction or set-off on the day on which the relevant notice of assessment is mailed [or sent electronically under new legislation].

If a taxpayer files a timely notice of objection, collection procedures will be suspended until 90 days after the objection has been dealt with by formal confirmation or variation from the CRA.[24] Once the CRA has dealt with an objection by formal confirmation or variation, if the taxpayer further appeals within the next 90 days to the Tax Court of Canada, the CRA must further defer collection until the Tax Court has decided.[25]

When appeals are held in abeyance due to a "test" case, the limitations on the Minister's right to use collection procedures are varied.[26] In these circumstances, the CRA may begin to use collection procedures for the purpose of collecting amounts assessed, determined in a manner consistent with the decision of the court in the test case at any time after it has notified the taxpayer in writing that the decision of the relevant court in the test case has been given.

These restrictions to the Minister's power to collect amounts owing do not apply to amounts payable under Part VIII (scientific research and experimental development tax credit), non-resident tax, interest or penalties payable for failure to remit source deductions or non-resident tax, areassessment with the taxpayer's consent, or a reassessment after the waiver of penalty and/or interest.[27]

See page ii for explanation of footnotes.

[24] CCH ¶27,207c; Sec. 225.1(2).

[25] CCH ¶27,208, ¶27,209; Sec. 225.1(3), 225.1(4).

[26] CCH ¶27,210; Sec. 225.1(5).

[27] CCH ¶27,211; Sec. 225.1(6); Inf. Cir. 98-1R3.

The normal collection procedures are overridden by a provision that allows the CRA to collect half of the amount assessed against a large corporation at any time during the first 90 days after the amount is assessed, regardless of whether an objection or appeal has been filed. After this 90-day period, if there is no objection or appeal, the CRA can collect the outstanding balance. After the 90-day period, where an objection or appeal is filed, the CRA can collect up to half of the amount under dispute and any balance not in dispute.[28] A corporation will be a "large corporation" if the large corporation's tax under Part I.3 is payable by it, or if at the end of a particular year it is related to a corporation that is a large corporation (see ¶13,025). This definition continues to apply as if the large corporation tax had not been eliminated as of January 1, 2006 and as if the capital deduction were still $10 million.

In order to be relieved from the above collection restrictions while an objection is pursued or litigated, the Minister must satisfy a judge or local judge of a superior court of a province or a Federal Court judge that there are reasonable grounds to believe that the collection of an assessed amount would be jeopardized by a delay in collection.[29] This judicial authorization may be granted even where no notice of assessment has been sent to the taxpayer, provided that the judge hearing the application is satisfied that the receipt by the taxpayer of the notice of assessment would further jeopardize collection. The Minister is required to serve a copy of the authorization on the taxpayer within 72 hours of the granting of the authorization, unless a judge orders otherwise. A taxpayer may, within 30 days and upon six clear days' notice to the Deputy Attorney General of Canada, apply to a judge of the court that granted the authorization for review of that authorization.

[¶15,027] Application of Interest

When an amendment to the *Income Tax Act* or a related provision has retroactive effect (i.e., it applies from a date before the amendment is enacted), the provisions of the Act concerning interest are, unless intention to the contrary, deemed to have come into force at the commencement of the taxation year in which the amendment became effective. This has the effect of requiring a taxpayer to pay interest on tax that becomes due as the result of an amendment, as if the amendment had been in force prior to enactment. Similarly, the CRA is required to pay interest on any overpayment that may result from such an amendment.[30]

See page ii for explanation of footnotes.

[28] CCH ¶27,211a, ¶27,211b; Sec. 225.1(7), 225.1(8).   [30] CCH ¶27,085; Sec. 221.1.
[29] CCH ¶27,214; Sec. 225.2.

[¶15,030] Judgments, Garnishment, Seizure

[¶15,035] Certificate Judgments

An amount owing and unpaid under the Act or a related Act may be certified by the Minister as an amount payable by the "debtor", and, on registration of the certificate in the Federal Court, it will have the effect of a judgment of that Court for payment of the amount specified plus interest.[31] The interest that is applicable is the rate provided for under the statute under which the amount certified is payable (for example, the *Income Tax Act* or the *Canada Pension Plan*) rather than the interest as provided under the *Federal Courts Act*.

Where the Minister mails a notice of assessment, that part of the amount assessed then remaining unpaid is payable forthwith.[32]

Though the certificate, when registered, has the effect of a judgment, it is not a judgment. It does not extinguish the taxpayer's right to contest any assessment. The taxpayer can apply to a court to prevent disposition of any of the assets seized and to have the grounds relied upon by the Minister for his or her action examined. A reassessment for the same taxation year does not affect the obligation to pay the amount of the original assessment.[33]

For the purposes of collection proceedings, however, the certificate shall be considered to be a judgment of the court. Thus, provincial enforcement of judgment and land registry legislation applies to the certificate and can be used to effectively bind land owned by a tax debtor. A sheriff shall not sell any property of the tax debtor to enforce the certificate without the consent of the Minister.

It is adequate for a certificate to set out one total amount as the amount owing by the debtor without setting out the separate amounts (such as federal tax, provincial tax, or employment insurance premiums) making up that total amount.[34] Several recent cases have held notices of assessment to be invalid where the assessments showed total liability under various statutes but failed to show the particular liability under the *Income Tax Act*. The Court held that the taxpayer was entitled to be informed in the assessment of the particular amount which had been assessed under the *Income Tax Act* alone.[35]

An owner of property which was seized to satisfy outstanding taxes owing by the former owner was precluded from claiming against the Crown for wrongful seizure where the current owner allowed the former owner to continue to treat the assets as his own.[36]

See page ii for explanation of footnotes.

[31] CCH ¶27,130; Sec. 223(3).
[32] CCH ¶22,725, ¶27,110; Sec. 158, 223.
[33] Lambert, 76 DTC 6373.

[34] CCH ¶27,110; Sec. 223.
[35] Leung, 91 DTC 1020, Wallace, 91 DTC 1134.
[36] 384238 Ontario Ltd. et al, 84 DTC 6101.

[¶15,040] Garnishment

The Minister may collect amounts owing under the Act by a taxpayer (the "tax debtor") by requiring that any other person who the Minister knows or suspects is or will be liable to make a payment to the tax debtor, pay the amount otherwise payable to the tax debtor in whole or in part to the Receiver General on account of the tax debtor's liability. The garnishment rules apply to any payments that the Minister knows or suspects will be paid to the tax debtor within one year. Note that the time frame is only 90 days with respect to funds that are to be loaned or advanced to the tax debtor.[37]

Where a person is liable to the tax debtor for continuing and periodic payments such as interest, rent, remuneration, a dividend, an annuity or other periodic payment, the garnishment applies to present and future payments to the extent stipulated by the Minister until the tax liability of the tax debtor is satisfied.[38]

The garnishment rules also apply to amounts to be paid, loaned, or advanced by the federal or provincial governments.[39]

The payment to the Receiver General must be made forthwith with respect to any amount that is immediately payable to the tax debtor. In any other case the payment to the Receiver General must be made as and when the amount is otherwise payable to the tax debtor. Where a person makes a payment to the Receiver General pursuant to such a notice, that person's liability to the tax debtor is discharged to the extent of that payment.[40] However, a notified person who fails to make the payments will be liable to pay to the Crown the amount required by the notice. This liability arises even if the person does not make a payment to the tax debtor.[41]

Where the persons affected are carrying on business under a name or style other than their own names or are persons carrying on business in partnership, notification of the Minister's requirement may be addressed to the name under which the business is carried on or to the partnership name. In the case of personal service, it is sufficient if the notification is left with an adult person employed at the place of business of the addressee or partnership.[42]

The Minister's third-party demand is simply a statutory non-judicial instrument of garnishment which does not create an equitable charge, and it therefore cannot have priority over charges such as an assignment of book debts or a demand debenture.[43] However, where the assessment arose as a result of the tax debtor's failure to withhold employee remittances or payments to non-residents, the third-party demand will have priority even as

[37] CCH ¶27,150–27,153; Sec. 224(1)–(1.2).
[38] CCH ¶27,158; Sec. 224(3).
[39] CCH ¶27,153f; Sec. 224(1.4).
[40] CCH ¶27,154; Sec. 224(2).

[41] CCH ¶27,162; Sec. 224(4).
[42] CCH ¶27,166–27,170; Sec. 224(5)–(6).
[43] Royal Bank of Canada, 86 DTC 6390, Zurich Insurance Co., 84 DTC 6232.

¶15,040

against secured creditors.[44] In this context, a "secured creditor" does not include any person who owns property absolutely. Since a general assignment of book debts does not confer absolute ownership, it is collateral security and falls within the definition of "security interest".[45]

An enhanced garnishment authority is provided with respect to the collection of unremitted source deductions, such as tax withheld from remuneration paid to employees and non-resident withholding tax. The Crown has a garnishment remedy that is effective in certain situations, even where the tax debtor has given security over its assets to a secured creditor. Accordingly, the CRA may garnish a taxpayer's accounts receivable notwithstanding that they have already been validly assigned to a lender who has a valid security which is properly registered. An enhanced garnishment letter transfers property in the garnished funds to The Queen, and the funds must be paid to the Minister in priority over any secured creditor.[46]

The money that is the subject of an enhanced garnishment becomes the property of The Queen only to the extent of the tax debtor's liability for unremitted source deductions as assessed by the Minister.

[¶15,045] Moneys Seized by Police

The Minister may collect amounts owing under the Act or under a provincial Act of a province that has entered into a collection agreement from any person who the Minister knows or suspects is holding moneys that were seized by a police officer in the course of administering or enforcing the criminal law of Canada from the tax debtor and that are restorable to the tax debtor. All the provinces except Quebec have a tax collection agreement with the federal government for personal taxes and all the provinces except Alberta and Quebec have a tax collection agreement for corporate taxes.

The Minister may require the police to turn over the moneys otherwise restorable to the tax debtor in whole or in part to the Receiver General on account of the tax debtor's liability under the Act or the provincial Act. The Minister must give the notification to the police in writing.

The receipt of the Minister for moneys turned over is good and sufficient discharge of the requirement to restore the moneys to the tax debtor to the extent of the amounts so turned over.[47]

[¶15,050] Acquisition of Debtor's Property

For the purpose of collecting debts owed by a person to The Queen under the Act or under a provincial Act of a province that has entered into a collection agreement, the Minister may purchase or otherwise acquire any

---

See page ii for explanation of footnotes.

[44] CCH ¶27,172a; Sec. 224(1.2), 224(1.3).

[45] Province of Alberta Treasury Branches et al, 96 DTC 6245.

[46] CCH ¶27,172a; Sec. 224(1.2).

[47] CCH ¶27,185–27,186; Sec. 224.3(1)–(2).

interest in such person's property that the Minister is given a right to acquire in legal proceedings or under a court order or that is offered for sale or redemption. Any interest so acquired may be disposed of in a reasonable manner. Thus, the Minister may participate in foreclosure and other similar proceedings for tax collection purposes.[48]

[¶15,055] Seizure of Chattels

The Minister may, on 30 days' notice, direct that the goods and chattels of a defaulting taxpayer be seized. After being kept for 10 days at the owner's expense and after advertisement in a newspaper of the pending sale (except in the case of perishable goods), the goods and chattels may be sold at public auction. Any surplus resulting from the sale is to be paid or returned to the taxpayer. The usual exemptions of personal goods, tools, etc., up to the amounts allowed under the law of the province where the taxpayer lives or carries on business are permitted.[49]

The Minister seized an immoveable property occupied by a tax debtor. Although the tax debtor's brother produced documents showing that he owned the property, he was merely holding it as a nominee for the tax debtor and his opposition to the seizure was dismissed.[50]

[¶15,060] Collection of Tax from Taxpayer Leaving Canada

Where the Minister suspects that a taxpayer has left or is about to leave Canada, the Minister may, before the day otherwise fixed for payment, by notice served personally or by registered letter to the taxpayer, demand payment of all taxes, interest, and penalties for which the taxpayer is liable or would be liable if the time for payment had arrived and that amount must be paid forthwith, notwithstanding other provisions of the Act.[51]

The provisions respecting seizure of chattels apply in these circumstances also, but in this case the Minister need not wait 30 days.

[¶15,065] Taxes Withheld

[¶15,070] Withholding — Deemed Trust

No court action may be taken against a person for withholding or deducting any sum of money in compliance or even intended compliance with the Act.[52] Thus, a creditor will not be entitled to bring an action against his or her debtor in respect of tax which the debtor has withheld from a payment made to the creditor, provided that the debtor has, in so doing, complied with the Act. If a debtor deducts an amount which he or she is not

---

See page ii for explanation of footnotes.

[48] CCH ¶27,180; Sec. 224.2.

[49] CCH ¶27,190; Sec. 225.

[50] Gauthier et al., 2006 DTC 6371.

[51] CCH ¶27,231; Sec. 226.

[52] CCH ¶27,250; Sec. 227(1).

¶15,055

required to deduct under the Act but does so intending to comply with the Act, no action may be taken by his or her creditor for making the deduction.

Any agreements not to withhold tax which is required by the Act to be withheld are void.[53] Where a clause in an agreement is void because it provides that the payer shall not deduct income tax from the payments to be made, the clause may be severable from the remainder of the agreement and, accordingly, the remainder of the agreement may be valid.[54]

Every employee whose employer is required to deduct income tax from source is required to file a TD1 form with that employer.[55] This form shows the employee's marital status and number of dependants, so that the employer may compute his or her personal tax credits for tax-withholding purposes. An employee who fails to file this form will have tax withheld at the rates applicable for single persons without dependants and will be subject to a penalty.[56]

A person who deducts or withholds an amount under the Act (e.g., a source deduction from salary or wages) is deemed to hold the amount in trust for the Crown, separate and apart from the person's own property, including property subject to a security interest held by a secured creditor. Tax deducted and withheld by a person (debtor) that is not remitted to the Crown as required is held in trust for the Crown, notwithstanding that the amount has been co-mingled with the assets of the debtor or is subject to a security interest held by a secured creditor, or that the debtor may be in receivership, bankruptcy, liquidation, or has made an assignment.[57] Where an amount deducted or withheld and deemed to be held in trust for the Crown is not paid to the Crown as required, property of the debtor, equal in value to the amount so deducted or withheld, is deemed to be held in trust for the Crown, separate and apart from the debtor's own property from the time of withholding or deduction. This rule also applies to property held by any secured creditor of the debtor that would, but for the creditor's security interest therein, be property of the debtor (again, to the extent of the value of the amount withheld or deducted). The property deemed to be held in trust (both the debtor's property and that held by a secured creditor as described above) is further deemed to form no part of the debtor's estate or property from the time of deduction or withholding, even it is not in fact kept separate and apart from the person's own property and whether or not the property is subject to a security interest. Lastly, the property deemed to be held in trust is beneficially owned by the Crown, notwithstanding any security interest therein or in the proceeds thereof, and the proceeds of such property are to be paid to the Receiver General in priority to all such security interests.

---

[53] CCH ¶27,294; Sec. 227(12).

[54] Talbot-Lehman v. Ryall, 3 DTC 1151.

[55] CCH ¶27,254; Sec. 227(2); Reg. 107.

[56] CCH ¶27,258; Sec. 227(3).

[57] CCH ¶27,262–27,263; Sec. 227(4)–(4.1).

The extension of the deemed trust rules to property subject to a security interest was made in response to a decision by the Supreme Court of Canada. In that decision, the Court held that the previous deemed trust rules did not give priority to the Crown over certain assignments of inventory and that clearer language was required to assign absolute priority to the Crown.[58] The extension of the deemed trust rules purports to remedy that result by giving absolute priority to the Crown over the debtor's property, including secured property, equal to the value of the amount deducted or withheld and not remitted. This means, for example, that where a debtor grants a security interest in property, such as inventory or trade receivables assigned as collateral under a general security agreement or a *Bank Act* security, the deemed trust in favour of the Crown for unremitted source deductions will apply to the inventory or receivables. Note, however, that the deemed trust provisions do not apply to that part of a mortgage securing the performance of an obligation of the debtor that encumbers land or a building, where the mortgage is registered before the deemed trust arises.[59] Effective June 14, 2001, the deemed trust for unremitted source deductions is binding on the Crown, so that it will always take priority over any other security interest in favour of the Crown. An exception to the priority of the Crown's deemed trust is made for a mortgage in land or a building registered before a deemed trust arises.[60]

[¶15,075] Excess Withheld under Parts XIII and XII.5

If an amount has been deducted or withheld under Part XIII (tax on income from Canada of non-residents) or Part XII.5 (recovery of labour-sponsored funds tax credit) and has been paid to the Receiver General by the person withholding it, the taxpayer on whose behalf the amount was paid will be entitled to a refund to the extent that the amount so paid exceeds his or her tax liability. This may occur, for instance, where the tax payable by the non-resident taxpayer was limited or reduced under an income tax treaty. In order to obtain such a refund, the non-resident must apply in writing to the Minister within two years from the end of the calendar year in which the tax was paid to the Receiver General by the person withholding it.[61] Upon receipt of such an application, the Minister will refund any such amount that the taxpayer was not liable to pay, unless he or she is otherwise liable or about to become liable for some other obligation to the Crown. In the case of such liability, the Minister may apply the amount to which the taxpayer is entitled to that liability, rather than make a refund.

A non-resident may apply for a refund of Part XIII tax in the event of repayment of a shareholder loan which was previously subject to withhold-

---

[58] Royal Bank of Canada, 97 DTC 5089.

[59] CCH ¶27,263a; Sec. 227(4.2); Reg. 2201.

[60] CCH ¶27,263b; Sec. 227(4.3); Reg. 2201.

[61] CCH ¶27,270; Sec. 227(6).

ing tax. The application must be made within two years from the end of the calendar year in which the loan repayment is made.[62]

Where, on application for a refund, the Minister is not satisfied that the person is entitled to the applicable refund, the Minister must assess (determine) the tax payable under Parts XIII and XII.5 (the amount of any refund).[63] The taxpayer may then appeal the assessment or determination under the regular appeal provisions applicable under Part I. However, the right to receive a refund of the disputed tax while the appeal is outstanding is denied in these cases.

[¶15,080] Penalty for Failure To Withhold or Remit Tax

Any person required to deduct or withhold taxes from payments such as salary, wages, or remuneration paid to an employee, or certain other similar types of payment or benefit, or from certain payments to non-residents, who fails to do so is liable to pay a penalty of 10% of the amount that should have been deducted or withheld. A second or further occurrence of a failure to deduct or withhold will carry a penalty of 20% of the amount that should have been deducted or withheld, if another penalty of the same kind had been previously assessed against the same person during the same calendar year, and the failure to deduct or withhold was made knowingly or under circumstances amounting to gross negligence.[64]

In addition, a person who has failed to deduct or withhold tax from a payment to a non-resident is liable on behalf of that non-resident for the entire amount of tax that should have been withheld. In a similar fashion, a person who is obliged to deduct or withhold an amount of tax with respect to the payment of a patronage dividend or a person who is obliged to deduct or withhold an amount of tax with respect to a payment to a non-resident is liable for the entire amount of tax that should have been deducted or withheld. However, in each such case, that person is entitled to recover the entire amount from the non-resident, either by deducting such amount from any amount paid or credited to the non-resident or otherwise. Also, in each such case, the person will be liable to pay interest at the prescribed rate in respect of the unpaid tax.

A penalty is also imposed upon a person who has deducted or withheld tax, but has failed to remit it to the Receiver General. For remittances due on or after February 26, 2008, the penalty for late remittances is dependent upon the number of days the payment is overdue:

- one to three days late — 3%;
- four to five days late — 5%;
- six to seven days late — 7%; and
- more than 7 days late — 10%.

See page ii for explanation of footnotes.

[62] CCH ¶27,271; Sec. 227(6.1).

[63] CCH ¶27,274, ¶27,275; Sec. 227(7), 227(7.1).
[64] CCH ¶27,278–27,281a; Sec. 227(8)–(8.4).

For remittances due before February 26, 2008, the penalty is fixed at 10%. As well, there is a further penalty for second or subsequent occurrences to remit or pay an amount during the same year. In such a case, the penalty will be 20% of the amount that should have been remitted or paid, if the same person has already been assessed a penalty for a failure to remit or pay in the same calendar year, and the failure to remit was made knowingly or under circumstances amounting to gross negligence. The penalty applies only to the amount by which the total of the required remittance (including source deductions, Canada Pension Plan contributions, and Employment Insurance premiums) exceeds $500. This limitation does not apply where the delay or deficiency is wilful.[65] Where there are two or more offices or establishments of the payor, each establishment will be deemed to be a separate person for the purpose of applying the 20% penalties.[66]

Where a receiver and manager under a debenture distributed payroll funds supplied by the debenture holder to the employees of the company in receivership, it was liable for 10% of the amount that it failed to deduct from the payroll.[67]

[¶15,083] Payments by Trustees, etc.

The payer's liability under ¶15,080 is extended to "specified persons", such as trustees, liquidators, receivers, assignees, etc., who have direct or indirect influence over the disbursements, property, business, or estate of the payer. If these persons authorize or cause payments to be made by or on behalf of the payer without source deductions, they are jointly and severally liable with the payer for any amount payable because of the failure to deduct and/or remit the applicable source deductions. In effect, a specified person is responsible for ensuring the proper deduction and remittance of taxes made on the payment subject to source deduction. For the purposes of these new rules, both a debtor and a specified person can include a partnership.[68]

[¶15,085] Liability of Directors

If a corporation has failed to deduct, withhold, remit, or pay tax as required, its directors are jointly and severally liable to pay the amount owed. Because the liability is joint and several, each director is liable for the full amount of the liability. However, as noted below, a director may be entitled to claim contribution from a fellow director.

The obligations of a corporation to deduct, withhold, remit, and pay amounts for which a director may be liable are:

---

[65] CCH ¶27,282–27,283c; Sec. 227(9)–(9.4). [67] Coopers & Lybrand Limited, 80 DTC 6281.

[66] CCH ¶27,283d; Sec. 227(9.5). [68] CCH ¶27,267–27,267b; Sec. 227(5)–(5.2).

(1) its obligation to deduct, withhold, and remit, in respect of patronage dividends;

(2) after 2005, its obligation to withhold 15% from the amount otherwise payable on the redemption, acquisition, or cancellation of a tax deferred cooperative share issued by an agricultural cooperative corporation;

(3) its obligation to deduct, withhold, and remit in respect of salary, wages, pension benefits, retiring allowances, and payments out of deferred profit sharing plans (DPSPs), registered retirement savings plans (RRSPs), registered retirement income funds (RRIFs), and income averaging annuity contracts;

(4) the obligation to remit by brokers and security dealers in respect of dividends received on behalf of beneficial owners of shares who are unknown;

(5) its obligation to deduct, withhold, and remit in respect of the payment or crediting of interest, dividends, rents, royalties, management fees, pension benefits, retiring allowances, and DPSP payments, RRSP payments, and RRIF payments to non-residents; and

(6) its obligation to pay a refundable tax under Part VII or VIII in respect of share-purchase or scientific research and experimental development tax credits it designates.

It should be noted that directors of non-resident corporations may be subject to the liability imposed by the Canadian *Income Tax Act*. For example, a non-resident corporation which pays a salary to a person employed in Canada, or pays rent to a non-resident for the use of property in Canada, must withhold tax. If such a non-resident corporation fails to withhold, deduct or remit, its directors may be liable under the Canadian *Income Tax Act*.

A director is only liable if:

(1) a certificate for the amount of the corporation's liability has been registered in the Federal Court and an execution has been returned partially or wholly unsatisfied; or

(2) the corporation has commenced liquidation or dissolution proceedings or has been dissolved, and a claim for the tax liability has been proved within six months after the earlier of the commencement of dissolution proceedings and dissolution; or

(3) an assignment or receiving order has been made under the *Bankruptcy and Insolvency Act* and a claim for the tax liability has been proved within six months thereafter.

¶15,085

The amount recoverable from a director in case (1) above is only the amount remaining unsatisfied after execution.[69] It should be noted that a judgment against a corporation could be registered after the assessment has been issued, even if a notice of objection has been filed.

A director is not liable if proceedings have been commenced more than two years after ceasing to be a director, or if the director exercised the degree of care, diligence, and skill that a reasonably prudent person would have exercised in comparable circumstances.[70]

The director of a corporation was held not to have been responsible for unremitted source deductions where the director's reasonable efforts to ensure remittance were frustrated by the deceit of a co-director. No liability should arise where non-remittance is due to the fraud or deceit of another, which the director did not authorize.[71] There have been many cases in the last several years that have dealt with the issue of a director's liability for unremitted deductions. Personal liability has been imposed upon the director, unless the director can show that the he or she "exercised the degree of care, diligence, and skill to prevent the failure that a reasonably prudent person would have exercised in comparable circumstances".[72] In this regard, inside directors (i.e., those involved in a corporation's day to day management) are likely to have the most difficulty in establishing a due diligence defence. Conversely, to demonstrate due diligence, outside directors are not required to establish and monitor a trust account to pay unremitted source deductions. They are, however, required to take some action when becoming aware of facts possibly leading to the conclusion that there could be a potential problem with remissions. The extent of the director's business knowledge and experience should also be considered.[73]

If a director pays an amount in respect of a corporation's failure to deduct, withhold, remit, and pay tax, this debt against the corporation may be proved in dissolution, liquidation, or bankruptcy proceedings. In such a case, the director is given the same preference as the Crown would have been entitled to, if the amount owed by the corporation had remained unpaid.[74]

A director who has satisfied a claim is entitled to contribution from his or her fellow directors who were liable for the claim.[75]

[¶15,090] Assessment

An assessment may be issued by the Minister to:

(a) any person for any amount payable by that person that has not been withheld or deducted as a non-resident tax;

See page ii for explanation of footnotes.

[69] CCH ¶27,319; Sec. 227.1(5).
[70] CCH ¶27,317, ¶27,318; Sec. 227.1(3), 227.1(4).
[71] Edmondson, 88 DTC 1542.
[72] CCH ¶27,317; Sec. 227.1(3).
[73] Soper, 97 DTC 5407.
[74] CCH ¶27,320; Sec. 227.1(6).
[75] CCH ¶27,315–27,328a; Sec. 227.1(1)–(7); Inf. Cir. 89-2R2.

(b) any person for any penalty or liability for failure to withhold tax or remit tax withheld;

(c) any person for failure to comply with requirements in garnishment proceedings;

(d) any person or partnership for failure to comply with the reporting requirements in respect of tax shelters; and

(e) a corporation's directors for the amount of tax that the corporation was required to deduct, withhold, or remit, together with interest and penalties.[76]

The Minister may also assess any person resident in Canada for any amount payable under Part XII.5 (recovery of labour-sponsored funds tax credit).[77]

Upon the Minister's sending a notice of assessment to the person or partnership involved, the appeal procedures become applicable.[78]

[¶15,092] Joint and Several Liability re Contributions to RCA

A person who has failed to withhold tax from a contribution to a retirement compensation arrangement (RCA) is liable to a penalty and is required to pay interest on the tax that was not withheld. In addition, the person is liable to pay the Crown an amount equal to the contribution. A person who withholds tax from an RCA contribution, but does not remit the tax, is liable to a penalty, is required to pay interest on the amount withheld, and is required to pay as tax the amount withheld. See ¶15,080.

Where the person who has failed to withhold or remit is a non-resident and the contribution to an RCA was made on behalf of employees or former employees of an employer with whom the non-resident does not deal at arm's length, the employer is jointly and severally liable with the non-resident to pay any amounts of penalty, interest, and other amounts described above.[79] This rule would apply, for example, where a foreign parent corporation makes contributions to a foreign pension plan in respect of the Canadian resident employees of its Canadian subsidiary and the rules described in ¶13,570 apply to deem the contributions to be paid to an RCA. If the foreign parent fails to withhold RCA tax from the contributions, the Canadian subsidiary will be jointly liable for any interest, penalties, and other amounts payable by the foreign parent in respect of the failure.

[¶15,095] Application of Withholding Provisions to Crown

Provisions requiring a person to deduct or withhold an amount in respect of taxes from amounts payable to a taxpayer are applicable to the Government of Canada, a province, or territory.[80]

---

[76] CCH ¶27,286; Sec. 227(10).
[77] CCH ¶27,286a; Sec. 227(10.01).
[78] CCH ¶27,287; Sec. 227(10.1).

[79] CCH ¶27,288; Sec. 227(10.2).

[80] CCH ¶27,290; Sec. 227(11).

[¶15,100] Minister's Receipt Discharges Debtor

A person who withholds or deducts tax as required and obtains a receipt from the Minister on remitting tax to the Receiver General will be under no further liability to the person from whom the tax is deducted.[81] A receipt of the Minister can be produced in court and will constitute a valid defence against any action by the creditor for the amount withheld.

[¶15,105] Special Taxes and Exempt Corporations

The payment of special taxes under Parts IV, IV.1, VI, and VI.1 is not applicable to non-profit corporations which are exempt from tax.[82] For special taxes under Parts IV, IV.1, VI, and VI.1, see Chapter XII; for exempt corporations, see Chapter X.

[¶15,110] Partnerships and Provincial or Municipal Corporations

Certain payments made by a partnership are deemed to be made by a resident of Canada and amounts paid to a partnership which is not composed entirely of residents of Canada are deemed to be paid to a non-resident. The collection provisions apply to any tax that has been deducted or withheld from such payments.[83] A corporation that would, but for a provision of an *Appropriation Act*, be exempt from tax because it is a corporation 100% or, in some instances, 90%, of the shares of which (according to the ownership test described at ¶11,200) are owned by the Government of Canada, a province, or a territory or by one or more municipalities in Canada [or other governmental public bodies] is deemed not to be a private corporation for the purposes of Part IV.[84]

[¶15,115] Books, Records, Investigations

[¶15,120] Keeping of Records

Every person carrying on a business, every person required to pay or collect taxes, a registered charity or a registered Canadian amateur athletic association, as well as a registered agent of a registered political party, is required to keep adequate books and records.

The records (including inventory documentation) must be sufficient to determine the income taxes payable or other amounts to be deducted, withheld or collected and, in the case of registered charities, Canadian amateur athletic associations, or political parties, to verify the deductible donations received by them and determine whether there are grounds to revoke the charity's or association's status. In Information Circular 78-10R5, the CRA requires that books and records be supported by "source documents". Source documents include such items as sales invoices, purchase

---

See page ii for explanation of footnotes.

[81] CCH ¶27,298; Sec. 227(13).
[82] CCH ¶27,302; Sec. 227(14).
[83] CCH ¶26,243, ¶27,305; Sec. 212(13.1), 227(15).
[84] CCH ¶27,310; Sec. 227(16).

invoices, cash register receipts, formal contracts, credit card receipts, delivery slips, deposit slips, work orders, dockets, cheques, bank statements, tax returns, and general correspondence whether written or in any other form.[85] If a person has failed to keep adequate records, the Minister may require and specify the records to be kept.

Unless a different period applies, records and books together with accounts and vouchers necessary to verify them must generally be kept until the expiration of six years from the end of the last taxation year to which they relate. Shorter periods are provided for the books and records of corporations which have been dissolved, businesses which have ceased, registered charities and registered Canadian amateur athletic associations whose registration has been revoked, and for trusts and deceased taxpayers. When a corporation is dissolved, books and records must be retained for two years from the date of dissolution. When a person, other than a corporation, ceases carrying on business, books and records must be retained for six years following the end of the taxation year in which business ceased. Registered charities and registered amateur athletic associations whose registrations are revoked are to retain books and records for two years after revocation. The books and records of a trust or deceased taxpayer in respect of which a distribution clearance certificate is issued must be retained up to the date of issuance of the certificate.

A person who keeps records in an electronic format will be required to retain them in that format for the above retention period unless such a person is exempted from this requirement under such terms and conditions as are acceptable to the Minister.[86]

Where a return for a taxation year has not been filed on its due date, books and records relating to that taxation year are to be retained for six years from the day of filing of that return. In the case of objections or appeals, related books and records must be kept until all further rights of appeal have expired.

In any event, the Minister may require a person to retain books and records after the expiration of the required period and may also give written permission to dispose of them before.[87]

The books and records of a practicing lawyer, whether a member of a partnership or not, must contain all accounting records, including supporting vouchers and cheques.[88]

The provisions relating to the keeping of books and records regarding political contributions are outlined at ¶8545.

---

[85] CCH ¶27,370–27,372; Sec. 230(1)–(2); Inf. Cir. 78-10R5.

[86] CCH ¶27,379–27,379a; Sec. 230(4.1)–(4.2).

[87] CCH ¶27,376–27,388; Sec. 230(3)–(8); Reg. 5800.

[88] CCH ¶27,374; Sec. 230(2.1).

[¶15,125] Investigations

An authorized person may:

(1) inspect, audit, or examine books, records, and documents of the taxpayer and any document of *any other person* that may relate to the information that is or should be in the books or records of the taxpayer;

(2) examine the taxpayer's inventory and anything else which may assist in determining the accuracy of that inventory;

(3) enter business premises or any premises where books or records are kept or should be kept. If the premises are a dwelling-house, the warrant provisions described below must be followed; and

(4) require the owner, manager, and any other person on the premises to give all *reasonable* assistance and answer all *proper* questions relating to the administration and enforcement of the Act.

Clearly this right of the authorized person to demand assistance and to ask questions is subject to limitation, but there are no general guidelines as to what is "reasonable" or "proper". It is suggested that assistance may be unreasonable if the cost and effort involved far outweigh the significance of the specific matter being investigated. The propriety of a question will likely depend upon the possible relevance of the answer to matters being investigated and, in some cases, the nature of the matter being investigated.[89]

If the premises to be entered to conduct an audit or examination is a dwelling-house, The CRA must obtain the occupant's consent to enter, unless the Minister has obtained a judicial warrant.[90] The definition of "dwelling-house" includes any part of a building that is kept or occupied as a permanent or temporary residence and a mobile unit that is in fact used as a residence.[91] A warrant to enter a dwelling-house may be obtained by the Minister, without notice to the taxpayer, only if entry into the dwelling-house is necessary for a purpose relating to the administration or enforcement of the Act. In response to the decision of the Supreme Court of Canada in *Baron*[92] (see ¶15,135), which held that the absence of juridical discretion violates the Charter, a judge hearing an application for the issuance of a warrant is given the discretion not to issue the warrant, even where reasonable grounds to issue it exist. Where a judge is not satisfied that actual entry is necessary, he or she may order the occupant of the dwelling-house to give access to the relevant document or property kept or to be kept in the dwelling-house.

The definition of "judge" confers jurisdiction on both provincial superior courts and the Federal Court. The term "documents" is given a broad definition and includes books and records. The audit and examination

---

See page ii for explanation of footnotes.

[89] CCH ¶27,428; Sec. 231.1(1); Inf. Cir. 71-14R3.　　[91] CCH ¶27,420b; Sec. 231 "dwelling-house".
[90] CCH ¶27,429, ¶27,430; Sec. 231.1(2), 231.1(3).　　[92] Baron, 93 DTC 5018.

powers may be exercised by any "authorized person" which is generally any person authorized by the Minister.[93]

[¶15,130] Requirement To Provide Information and Documents

The Minister may require any person to provide any information or document for any purpose related to the administration or enforcement of the Act, including the collection of income tax, interest, and penalty payable by any person. The Minister's demand is to be served personally or by registered or certified mail. The demand may require that any information, additional information, a return of income, a supplemental return, or any document be provided. The demand must provide for a reasonable time within which such information or document is to be provided.[94] It has been held that a demand to produce "without delay" does not satisfy this requirement[95] nor does a motion for further production of documents on the eve of a trial.[96]

If the Minister seeks to impose on a person a demand for information or for a document relating to unnamed third parties, prior judicial authorization is required.[97] The application for this judicial authorization will be made without notice to the taxpayer and the authorization may be granted, subject to such conditions as the judge considers appropriate. In order to grant it, the judge must be satisfied by information on oath that:

(a) the unnamed third party or group of unnamed persons is ascertainable; and

(b) the requirement is made to verify compliance with the Act.[98]

Upon receiving a demand to provide information or documents relating to an unnamed person or group of persons, the third party has the right to apply within 15 days for review of the judicial authorization obtained.[99]

Every person must, on written demand from the Minister and served personally or otherwise, file within such reasonable time as may be stipulated in the demand the information return specified in the demand, including the foreign property information return described at ¶15,133.[100]

It was held that the Minister did not require judicial authorization prior to requesting the donor information in the course of auditing a charitable foundation. The CRA's request for the donor information was legitimately made in the course of investigating the validity of the foundation's status as a registered charity, and the reassessment of the donors was a logical consequence of the determination that the foundation was not operating a valid charitable program.[101] Similarly, the corporate taxpayers were ordered

---

See page ii for explanation of footnotes.

[93] CCH ¶27,420c; Sec. 231 "judge".
[94] CCH ¶27,437; Sec. 231.2(1).
[95] Joseph et al., 85 DTC 5391.
[96] Special Risks Holding, 84 DTC 6215.
[97] CCH ¶27,438; Sec. 231.2(2).

[98] CCH ¶27,439; Sec. 231.2(3).
[99] CCH ¶27,441, ¶27,442; Sec. 231.2(5), 231.2(6).
[100] CCH ¶27,570, ¶27,570a; Sec. 233(1), 233(2).
[101] Redeemer Foundation, 2008 DTC 6474.

to produce the documents and information requested by the Minister. The Minister required the information to verify compliance with the Act by the taxpayers' designated Canadian customer base.[102]

[¶15,131] Non-Arm's Length Transactions with Non-Residents

Every corporation resident in Canada and every non-resident corporation which carried on business in Canada at any time in a taxation year must file an information return (Form T106) for the year, containing prescribed information regarding transactions with non-resident, non-arm's length persons. The information returns must be filed by the corporation's filing-due date for the year (i.e., six months after the end of the year), and a separate return must be filed for each non-resident, non-arm's length person with whom the corporation had transactions during the year.[103]

This filing requirement also extends to partnerships and individuals, including trusts. Any Canadian resident or non-resident carrying on business in Canada (a "filer") is required to file an information return in respect of any year in which it engaged in a non-arm's length transaction with a non-resident person or partnership.[104] The return must be filed by the reporting person's filing-due date for the year or, in the case of a reporting partnership, by the due date for filing a partnership information return.

This filing requirement is offset by a $1 million *de minimis* exception, which excuses a filer from filing if the total fair market value of the property and services involved in the non-arm's length transaction with a particular non-resident does not exceed $1 million.[105] A separate return must be filed for each non-resident person or partnership where the $1 million threshold is met. Although the $1 million filing exemption should eliminate the filing requirement for most individuals, being excused from filing does not excuse the individual from the contemporaneous documentation requirements described at ¶15,312.

[¶15,132] Transfers and Loans to Foreign Trusts

A Canadian resident individual, trust, or corporation who has transferred or loaned any property to a "specified foreign trust" is required to file an information return by the due date set for its income tax return if a "non-arm's length indicator" is present.[106] However, no reporting under this rule is required with respect to: (i) foreign pension or retirement fund trusts which are exempt under local income tax law and are either primarily for the benefit of non-residents or are governed by an employee's profit sharing plan; (ii) foreign retirement arrangements (i.e., U.S. IRAs); or (iii) widely-held foreign mutual funds (150 or more investors of $500 or more), although investing in foreign mutual funds may require Form T1135 reporting as

---

See page ii for explanation of footnotes.

[102] eBay, 2008 DTC 6728.

[103] CCH ¶27,576; Sec. 233.1.

[104] CCH ¶27,576–27,576af; Sec. 233.1(1)–(3).

[105] CCH ¶27,576ag; Sec. 233.1(4).

[106] CCH ¶27,576f; Sec. 233.2(4).

discussed at ¶15,133. However, none of these exemptions applies if the entity becomes a beneficiary of a trust as part of a transaction designed to defeat the reporting requirement.[107]

Subject to those exemptions, specified foreign trusts are non-resident trusts whose beneficiaries fall under the definition of specified beneficiaries.[108] Generally speaking, a "specified beneficiary" is defined as any person beneficially interested in a trust who is not a mutual fund corporation, a non-resident-owned investment corporation, an amateur athlete trust, a segregated fund trust, a religious organization, a retirement compensation arrangement, a funeral arrangement trust and certain sub-trusts of those trusts, as well as registered investment trusts such as RRSPs and similar deferred income plans.[109] This term also includes a corporation or trust with which a person resident in Canada does not deal at arm's length or a controlled foreign affiliate of a Canadian resident.

The reporting requirements cannot be avoided by naming only non-resident beneficiaries, since, where the trust terms allow the naming of additional beneficiaries who could be Canadian residents at the time they are named, a specified beneficiary is deemed to exist. This rule was extended so that where the trust terms permit *any* person other than those specified above as being excluded as specified beneficiaries (i.e., mutual funds, etc.) to become beneficially interested upon any exercise of discretion by anyone, the trust is a specified foreign trust.

A "non-arm's length indicator" must be present in all cases to trigger a reporting requirement. In general terms, a non-arm's length indicator is a transaction which involves a transfer of property by a person who is also a specified beneficiary of the trust or a person related to a specified beneficiary, or which involves a transfer where the consideration given to the transferor for the property is less than the fair market value of the property, or such consideration includes indebtedness with a low rate of interest or shares of a related party; similarly, a loan on favourable terms is generally a non-arm's length indicator. In addition, any transfer or loan which was made as part of a series of transactions to avoid this filing requirement would be a non-arm's length indicator.[110] The filing requirement also operates where a Canadian resident (subject to the exceptions above) loans or transfers property to a corporation that at the time of transfer would have been a controlled foreign affiliate (CFA) of a specified foreign trust had the trust been resident in Canada.

Because the information concerning specified foreign trusts may in some cases be beyond the powers of the filer to obtain, a due diligence exception was added, whereby a person or partnership will be exempted

---

See page ii for explanation of footnotes.

[107] CCH ¶27,576a; Sec. 233.2(1) "exempt trust".

[108] CCH ¶27,576c; Sec. 233.2(1) "specified foreign trust".

[109] CCH ¶27,576b; Sec. 233.2(1) "specified beneficiary".

[110] CCH ¶27,576d; Sec. 233.2(2).

from the application of penalties for omission on the reporting form (Form T1141) in the following circumstances:

(a) there is reasonable disclosure in the return of the unavailability of the information;

(b) the taxpayer has, prior to the filing date, exercised due diligence in attempting to obtain the required information;

(c) it was reasonable to expect at the time of each transaction entered into that gives rise to a filing requirement, that sufficient information would be available to comply with the filing requirement; and

(d) if the information subsequently becomes available to the filer, it is filed no more than 90 days after it becomes available.[111]

[For taxation years beginning after 2006, a non-resident trust (other than an exempt foreign trust) will be subject to tax for a taxation year as a trust resident in Canada, if a contribution was made to the trust by a person who is resident in Canada at the end of the year (other than a recent immigrant to Canada). This approach will apply for the purpose of the foreign property reporting requirements with the result that reporting under the above provisions will generally be required for a taxation year whenever a "contribution" has been made by a person resident in Canada to a non-resident trust at or before the end of the year.[112] Generally speaking, a contribution is considered to be made to a trust where a particular property is transferred or loaned directly to a trust by a person or partnership and such transfer or loan is not an "arm's length transfer". These proposals regarding the taxation of non-resident trusts and foreign investment entities were part of Bill C-10, which died on the Order Paper of the Senate when Parliament was dissolved before the election.]

[¶15,133] Foreign Property Reporting

Canadian resident individuals, corporations, and trusts who own "specified foreign property" worth more than $100,000 on an aggregate basis at any time in the year are required to disclose certain information about the property to the CRA (the $100,000 threshold is per person, not per family).[113] A partnership that is more than 10% Canadian-owned in terms of its entitlement to income must also file an information return.[114] Note that the requirement to file Form T1135 is independent of the T1 filing requirement. That is, Canadian residents with sufficient foreign assets must file Form T1135 regardless of whether they are required to file a tax return.

See page ii for explanation of footnotes.

[111] CCH ¶27,576q; Sec. 233.5.
[112] CCH ¶27,576f; Sec. 233.2(4).

[113] CCH ¶27,576h, ¶27,576l; Sec. 233.3(1) "reporting entity", 233.3(3).
[114] CCH ¶27,576i; Sec. 233.3(1) "specified Canadian entity".

¶15,133

"Specified foreign property" is broadly defined, but is subject to an overriding exception for personal-use property and foreign business property. It includes:

(a) deposits of intangible property situated, deposited or held outside Canada; for example, foreign bank accounts or shares of Canadian companies deposited with a foreign stock broker;

(b) tangible property located outside Canada;

(c) any interest in or right to a non-resident entity (e.g., shares in a foreign company) other than a foreign affiliate subject to a reporting mechanism of its own;

(d) debts owned by non-resident persons (e.g., bonds issued by foreign entities or simply loans to non-residents);

(e) interests in partnerships, unless 90% or more of their income or loss for the fiscal period ending in the taxpayer's taxation year would be attributable to non-residents;

(f) interest in non-resident trusts, except: trusts not acquired for consideration by the reporting person or a related person; trusts which are foreign affiliates of the reporting person (and so subject to a reporting mechanism of their own); and trust which are foreign pension funds or foreign retirement arrangements;

(g) any interest or right, immediately or in the future, absolute or contingent, in specified foreign property; and

(h) any property which by its terms is convertible to or exchangeable for specified foreign property.[115]

In addition to the primary overriding exceptions for personal-use property and foreign business property, further overrides exclude an interest in a foreign trust unless the Canadian resident or a person related acquired the interest for consideration. An interest in a foreign trust which is an exempt trust for purposes of ¶15,132 need not be reported, except in the case of foreign mutual fund investments, which must be reported on Form T1135. A partnership interest does not need to be reported if the partnership itself is required to file Form T1135 for the year. Finally, shares or debts of foreign affiliates which are subject to the reporting requirements of ¶15,134 are not subject to Form T1135 reporting.

---

[115] CCH ¶27,576j; Sec. 233.3(1) "specified foreign property".

The following examples illustrate the application of the reporting mechanism:

Examples:

A taxpayer owns a condominium in Florida with a cost amount of $120,000. If the condominium is personal-use property (used by the taxpayer or a related person primarily for personal use and enjoyment), it does not have to be reported on Form T1135. If the property is rented out with a reasonable expectation of profit, Form T1135 has to be filed.

A husband and wife have a joint foreign bank account and joint ownership of other foreign property. The total cost of the foreign property owned jointly is $180,000. The proportionate ownership of the foreign property will be based on the amount contributed by each person. If the contribution by either person is more than $100,000, that person must file Form T1135.

A warehouse in England with a cost amount of $900,000 is owned by a Canadian corporation and used to store its products for distribution. The corporation does not have to report this on Form T1135 because the warehouse is used exclusively for storing inventory used in the corporation's business. Foreign property that is used or held exclusively in an active business is not specified foreign property and therefore does not have to be reported.

An individual is exempted from the reporting requirement in the year he or she becomes a resident of Canada and certain corporations and trusts are generally exempt. The exempt trusts and corporations would be the same as the ones discussed in ¶15,132, i.e., mutual fund corporations, non-resident owned investment corporations, registered investments, etc.

[For taxation years beginning after 2006, a non-resident trust, other than an exempt foreign trust, will be subject to tax for a taxation year as a trust resident in Canada if a contribution (i.e., a non-arm's length transfer or loan of property) was made to the trust by a person who is resident in Canada at the end of the year, other than a recent immigrant to Canada. This new approach will apply for the purpose of the foreign property-reporting requirements with the result that the deemed-resident trust will be required to file information returns on foreign property holdings in excess of $100,000. These proposals regarding the taxation of non-resident trusts and foreign investment entities were part of Bill C-10, which died on the Order Paper of the Senate when Parliament was dissolved before the election.]

[¶15,134] Foreign Affiliate Reporting

A Canadian entity must file an information return in respect of each of its foreign affiliates during the year, within fifteen months after the end of the reporting entity's taxation year.[116]

For these purposes, a "reporting entity" is defined to mean a taxpayer, resident in Canada, of which a non-resident corporation is a foreign affiliate at any time in the year. It also includes a taxpayer resident in Canada, of which a non-resident trust is deemed to be a foreign affiliate in the year.

See page ii for explanation of footnotes.

[116] CCH ¶27,576p; Sec. 233.4(4).

¶15,134

Generally, a "foreign affiliate" is defined as a non-resident corporation, where a Canadian resident taxpayer's equity percentage is 1% or more, and the equity percentage of the taxpayer and persons related to the taxpayer is 10% or more. However, in order to ensure that the same information be reported by only one Canadian corporation in a related group, a non-resident corporation is only a foreign affiliate of the lowest-tier corporation in a group of Canadian corporations under common control. The one exception in the definition of a reporting entity is a taxpayer all of whose income is exempt from tax under Part I.[117]

A partnership is a reporting entity where one or more non-resident partners are entitled to less than 90% of the income or loss of the partnership and the partnership has a corporate or trust foreign affiliate at any time in the year. Again, if a foreign affiliate is owned directly by a partnership through a Canadian corporation or group of corporations, only the lowest-tier corporation reports for the foreign affiliate.

In determining whether a tiered partnership is a reporting entity, a partner in the top partnership is deemed to be a partner in any underlying partnership and to receive income or loss of the underlying partnership.[118] Thus, if a Canadian resident owns an interest in a partnership, which in turn owns an interest in another partnership, the Canadian resident is deemed to receive the amount of income or loss to which the Canadian resident is directly or indirectly entitled through the partnership tiers.

It should be noted that there are two foreign affiliate information returns. Form T1134-A relates to foreign affiliates that are not controlled foreign affiliates and Form T1134-B is a more detailed return relating to controlled foreign affiliates. It should also be noted that although the Act does not exempt reporting in respect of any foreign affiliates, each of the forms states that the taxpayer does not have to file the return for a foreign affiliate which is "dormant" or "inactive" for the affiliate's tax year ending in the taxpayer's year. A dormant or "inactive foreign affiliate" is defined in each of the forms as an affiliate that had gross receipts (including proceeds from the disposition of property) of less than C$10,000 in the year and at no time in the year had assets with a fair market value of more than C$100,000.

Because the information concerning foreign affiliates may, in some cases, be beyond the powers of the reporting entity to obtain, a due diligence exception was added whereby such entity will be exempted from the application of penalties for omission on the reporting Form T-1134 if the due diligence test described at ¶15,132 is met.

[For taxation years beginning after 2006, a non-resident trust, other than an exempt foreign trust, will be subject to tax for a taxation year as a

---

See page ii for explanation of footnotes.

[117] CCH ¶27,576m–27,576n; Sec. 233.4(1)–233.4(2).   [118] CCH ¶27,576o; Sec. 233.4(3).

trust resident in Canada if a contribution (i.e., a non-arm's length transfer or loan of property) was made to the trust by a person who is resident in Canada at the end of the year, other than a recent immigrant to Canada. This new approach will apply for the purpose of the foreign property reporting requirements, with the result that the deemed resident trust will be required to file information returns on foreign affiliates. These proposals regarding the taxation of non-resident trusts and foreign investment entities were part of Bill C-10, which died on the Order Paper of the Senate when Parliament was dissolved before the election.]

[¶15,135] Search Warrants

The Minister has to obtain a search warrant prior to seizing any document or thing by applying, without notice to the taxpayer, for judicial authorization that any person named in the warrant enter and search any building, receptacle, or place for any document or thing that may afford evidence as to the commission of an offence under the Act, and seize and bring the document or thing before the court or make report to it in order to obtain a retention order.[119] The term "documents" is given a very broad meaning; it includes money, a security, and a "record", i.e. letters, telegrams, vouchers, invoices, accounts, and statements (financial or otherwise), and any other thing containing information, whether in writing or in any other form.[120]

In response to the Supreme Court of Canada decision in *Baron*,[121] which ruled that the use of the word "shall", in the provisions dealing with search warrants, removed "the residual discretion of the issuing judge to refuse to issue a search warrant in the proper circumstances" and, therefore, violated the *Canadian Charter of Rights and Freedoms*. These provisions were amended as of June 15, 1994 to clarify that a judge hearing an application for the issuance of a warrant has the discretion not to issue the warrant, even where reasonable grounds to issue it exist. Thus, the judge "may" issue the warrant if satisfied that there are reasonable grounds to believe that:

(a) an offence under the Act has been committed;

(b) a document or thing that may afford evidence of the commission of the offence is likely to be found; and

(c) the building, receptacle, or place specified in the application is likely to contain such a document or thing.[122]

The warrant is required to identify the offence in respect of which it is issued, the identity of the person who is alleged to have committed the offence, and the particular place to be searched. In addition, the warrant

---

See page ii for explanation of footnotes.

[119] CCH ¶27,450; Sec. 231.3(1).

[120] CCH ¶27,420a, ¶28,227c; Sec. 231 "document", 248(1) "record".

[121] Baron, 93 DTC 5018.

[122] CCH ¶27,452; Sec. 231.3(3).

must be reasonably specific as to what document or thing is to be searched for and seized.

The person executing the warrant may seize, in addition to that which is authorized by the warrant to be searched for and seized, any other document or thing which the person believes on reasonable grounds affords evidence of an offence under the Act. Such additional document or thing seized may be in respect of an offence other than that named in the warrant.[123]

The person executing the warrant is required to bring any document or thing seized before the issuing judge or to make a report to that judge as soon as practicable. If that judge is unable to act, the matter may be brought before another judge of the same court. Once the matter is brought before a judge, the judge may, of his or her own motion or on application by an interested party, order the document or thing seized be returned to the person from whom it was seized or the person legally entitled to it if, according to the judge, it was not seized in accordance with the warrant or the additional powers provided or it will not be necessary for an investigation or criminal proceeding. An interested party must give three clear days notice to the Deputy Attorney General of Canada. Except in the case of a court order or a Minister's waiver, anything seized must be retained by the Minister.[124] It has been held that the appropriate remedy for a seizure of documents which is in violation of a taxpayer's Charter rights is, at the very least, an order for the immediate return of the property illegally seized.[125]

The person from whom a document or thing is seized is entitled to inspect the document or thing at reasonable times, subject to reasonable conditions, and to obtain one copy of the document at the Minister's expense.[126]

The Supreme Court of Canada has ruled that documents from a stolen safe that were photocopied by police and provided to the CRA were inadmissible in tax proceedings, since they were obtained through unreasonable search, contrary to section 8 of the Charter, and their admission would bring the administration of justice into disrepute.[127] The *Law* decision is important because it illustrates the willingness of the courts to ensure that tax investigations comply with Charter requirements and to provide an appropriate remedy when those requirements are not observed.

[¶15,140] Inquiries

The right is conferred on the Minister to conduct an inquiry in respect of anything related to the administration or enforcement of the Act.[128] To conduct that inquiry, the Minister may appoint any person. The inquiry will

---

See page ii for explanation of footnotes.

[123] CCH ¶27,454; Sec. 231.3(5).
[124] CCH ¶27,455; Sec. 231.3(6).
[125] Lagiorgia, 87 DTC 5245.

[126] CCH ¶27,457; Sec. 231.3(8).
[127] Law et al., 2002 DTC 6789.
[128] CCH ¶27,462; Sec. 231.4.

be made by that person before another person appointed by the Tax Court of Canada as a hearing officer. The hearing officer is given all the powers of inquiry of a commissioner under the *Inquiries Act*. They include the power to summon witnesses and require them to give evidence under oath, the power to require the production of documents, and the right to retain counsel or other experts to aid in the inquiry.

If the inquiry is investigating the affairs of any particular person, that person is entitled to be present and to be represented by counsel unless the hearing officer orders otherwise. Such an exclusionary order may be made only on the ground that the presence of the person or counsel would be prejudicial to the effective conduct of the inquiry. Such an order may be made on application by the Minister or a person giving evidence and may be made in respect of the whole or any part of the inquiry.[129] Any person who gives evidence in an inquiry is entitled to be represented by counsel and to receive a transcript of the evidence given.

[¶15,145] Copies and Compliance

Where a document is seized, inspected, audited, examined, or provided, the person seizing, inspecting, auditing, examining, or receiving it may make one or more copies of it or an electronic printout of it. In addition, any document purporting to be certified by the Minister (or a person authorized by the Minister) to be a copy or, as the case may be, an electronic printout is evidence of the nature and content of the original document and has the same probative value as the original document would have, if it had been proven in the ordinary way.[130]

No person shall hinder, molest, interfere with, or prevent or attempt to prevent a tax official from conducting an authorized investigation, search, seizure etc., and every person shall, unless unable to do so, do everything required to be done.[131] Failure to comply may result in severe penalties, which include a fine of not less than $1,000 and not exceeding $25,000 and, in addition to the fine, imprisonment for a term not exceeding 12 months.[132] Effective June 14, 2001, the penalty applicable to persons who hinder tax officials in the performance of certain administrative functions is extended to persons hindering them in the performance of a collection function and to attempts to hinder.

[¶15,150] Access to Foreign Information

A person resident in Canada or a non-resident person carrying on business in Canada must provide, when required by notice of the Minister, any "foreign-based information or document", defined as being any information or any document available or located outside Canada that may be relevant to the administration or enforcement of the Act, including the

---

See page ii for explanation of footnotes.

[129] CCH ¶27,467; Sec. 231.4(6).
[130] CCH ¶27,473; Sec. 231.5(1).
[131] CCH ¶27,477; Sec. 231.5(2).
[132] CCH ¶27,660; Sec. 238(1).

collection of income tax, interest, and penalty payable by any person.[133] The notice must contain a reasonable time for compliance of at least 90 days, a description of the information or document being sought, and the consequences of a failure to comply.[134]

A person served with such a notice may, within 90 days, apply to a judge for a review of the requirement to provide the foreign-based information or documents.[135] The judge may confirm or vary the requirement or set it aside if it is unreasonable.[136]

Failure to provide substantially all information or documents required may result in a prohibition on the introduction into evidence of such information or documents in a civil proceeding.[137] It may also result in the prohibition of the introduction of *any* information or documents covered by that notice. This ensures that a person is prevented from selectively providing certain information or documents which may be advantageous, while refusing to provide other information or documents which may be disadvantageous. If, for example, a person provides 10 out of 20 documents required, that person may be prohibited from introducing into evidence any of the 20 documents required, including the 10 documents that were provided to the Minister.

[¶15,153] Compliance Order

Instead of proceeding by way of summary conviction (see ¶15,265) where a person refuses to provide the access, assistance, information, or document sought in the course of an audit, the Minister may proceed by way of summary application.[138] The judge hearing the application will have the discretion to allow the order or to attach such conditions to the order as he/she considers appropriate.[139] A person who refuses to comply with the judge's order may be found in contempt of court and will be subject to the processes and punishments of the court that issued the order.[140] The order may be appealed to the court to which appeals from the court making the order normally lie.[141] In such a case, however, the execution of the order is not suspended unless it is so ordered by the appeal court.

[¶15,155] Solicitor-Client Privilege

[¶15,160] Privilege

The term "solicitor-client privilege" [142] means the right of a person to refuse to disclose an oral or documentary communication on the ground that it was passed in a professional lawyer-client confidence. An accounting

---

[133] CCH ¶27,481, ¶27,482; Sec. 231.6(1), 231.6(2).

[134] CCH ¶27,483; Sec. 231.6(3).

[135] CCH ¶27,484; Sec. 231.6(4).

[136] CCH ¶27,485; Sec. 231.6(5).

[137] CCH ¶27,488; Sec. 231.6(8).

[138] CCH ¶27,492; Sec. 231.7(1).

[139] CCH ¶27,494; Sec. 231.7(3).

[140] CCH ¶27,495; Sec. 231.7(4).

[141] CCH ¶27,496; Sec. 231.7(5).

[142] CCH ¶27,512; Sec. 232(1) "solicitor-client privilege".

record of a lawyer, including any supporting voucher or cheque, is deemed not to be such a communication.

A lawyer may refuse to disclose information to, or to produce documents relating to the affairs of a client for, the taxation authorities. To be so privileged, the communications must be of a professional nature. Thus, communications to a solicitor in a matter on which the solicitor's advice is not sought are not privileged. The privilege does not extend to any communications made for the purpose of committing a fraud or a crime. The privilege belongs to the client, who can waive it.

[¶15,165] Defence

Where a lawyer is prosecuted for failure to give information or produce a document, it is a valid defence for the lawyer to establish that he or she had reasonable grounds to believe that the client had a solicitor-client privilege with respect to the relevant information or document, and that such privilege had been claimed on behalf of a named client to the Minister or some person duly authorized to act for the Minister.[143] The lawyer must give the client's last known address so that the Minister may get in touch with the client to see if he or she wants to waive the privilege.

[¶15,170] Seizure of Documents

Where an officer is about to seize a document in a lawyer's possession and the lawyer claims, in the course of an on-site inspection or following a written request, a solicitor-client privilege on behalf of a named client, the officer is (without inspecting, examining, or making copies of the document) to seize the document and any other documents in respect of which the privilege is claimed on behalf of the same client and to place them in a package. The package is then placed, after being sealed and identified, in the custody of the sheriff of the district or county where the seizure was made or in the hands of a custodian agreed upon in writing by the officer and the lawyer.[144]

Documents may only be seized and placed into custody where a warrant authorizing seizure has been obtained.

An officer who is about to inspect or examine rather than seize documents in the course of an on-site inspection or following a requirement in writing cannot inspect or examine them if the solicitor-client privilege is claimed. Again the document is to be placed in a sealed package, identified by initials, numbering or otherwise. However, the package or document does not have to be delivered into the hands of a sheriff or other custodian. Rather, the lawyer is required to retain and preserve the package or document and produce it to be dealt with according to a judge's order.[145] This

---

See page ii for explanation of footnotes.

[143] CCH ¶27,515; Sec. 232(2).   [145] CCH ¶27,519; Sec. 232(3.1).
[144] CCH ¶27,518; Sec. 232(3).

procedure does not apply when the lawyer deals with the documents immediately upon receipt of the Requirement to Produce.[146]

No officer may inspect, examine, or seize a document in a lawyer's possession without giving that lawyer a reasonable opportunity to claim the privilege.[147] A lawyer claiming solicitor-client privilege must communicate to the Minister the last known address of the client on whose behalf the privilege is claimed, so that the Minister may endeavour to advise the client of the claim of privilege and to find out if the client is willing to waive the privilege, if it is practicable so to do before the right to privilege is decided.[148] After the documents are placed in custody, the lawyer may be granted a court order authorizing him or her to examine or make a copy of the documents in the presence of the custodian or judge.[149] The documents are then to be repackaged and resealed without alteration or damage.

[¶15,175] Production of Documents

Where a document has been seized and placed in custody, or is being retained, the client or the lawyer may apply to a judge for an order to determine whether the claim of privilege is justified and to require the custodian to produce the document to the judge at the hearing.[150] The application is to be heard *in camera*, and the judge may inspect the document, ensuring that it is repackaged and resealed.[151] If the judge finds that there is a privilege in connection with the document, he or she will order that it be returned to the lawyer. If, on the other hand, the judge decides that there is no privilege, the document will be delivered to the appropriate official. This application must be disposed of without costs to either party.[152]

If the judge of the application cannot act or continue to act for any reason, other applications may be made to another judge.[153] Where a question arises as to the course to be followed in connection with anything done or to be done and the Act does not give any direction, a judge may give directions which, in his or her opinion, are most likely to afford solicitor-client privilege for proper purposes.[154] Documents deposited with a custodian cannot be delivered to any person except in accordance with a judge's order or consent of the parties.[155] The documents may, however, be delivered to the custodian's own officer or servant for the purpose of safeguarding them.

[¶15,180] Types of Documents to which Privilege Attaches

An illustration of the types of documents in which the solicitor-client privilege attaches was provided by rulings made by the Manitoba Court of

---

[146] Cappell, 92 DTC 6591.
[147] CCH ¶27,554; Sec. 232(12).
[148] CCH ¶27,562; Sec. 232(14).
[149] CCH ¶27,558; Sec. 232(13).
[150] CCH ¶27,524; Sec. 232(4).

[151] CCH ¶27,526; Sec. 232(5).
[152] CCH ¶27,542; Sec. 232(9).
[153] CCH ¶27,538; Sec. 232(8).
[154] CCH ¶27,546; Sec. 232(10).
[155] CCH ¶27,550; Sec. 232(11).

Queen's Bench.[156] The following were the main documents seized by the Minister at a solicitor's office and the rulings by the Court:

(1) *Correspondence between the solicitor and another firm of solicitors pertaining to the purchase of shares and to a dispute between the vendor of the shares and the purchasers.* The solicitor-client privilege applied. The correspondence was in respect of obtaining and giving of counsel's opinion.

(2) *Bill of costs received by the solicitor from another firm of solicitors.* The privilege did not apply. The document was a voucher and as such it was part of the solicitor's accounting records.

(3) *Correspondence between the solicitor's client company and another firm of solicitors (this firm was eventually replaced as counsel by the solicitor) in respect of termination and holiday pay and union contracts.* The privilege applied. "A communication or document once privileged is always privileged." The protection was not lost on change of solicitors.

(4) *Letter from a client to the solicitor, only part of which contained privileged matters.* Where there is intermingling of privileged and non-privileged material, the whole of the document is privileged. However, with present copying facilities it should be easy to block out the privileged part and provide the Minister with a copy of the non-privileged part. This was so ordered by the Court.

(5) *Letter to the solicitor from other solicitors relating to corporate reorganization; copy of the letter was sent to the comptroller of a client company.* The privilege applied. The sending of the copy to a responsible officer was not a communication to a third party, which would void the privilege.

(6) *Unexecuted agreement.* Since the agreement was not signed, the inference was that the solicitor's advice was not taken. The document was in the same category as a draft opinion and was privileged.

(7) *Memoranda from accountants pertaining to a proposed corporate reorganization.* It had to be concluded from the evidence that these documents were prepared at the request of the solicitor's clients for submission for the solicitor's advice. They were privileged. However, a letter from the auditors to the client of the solicitor which volunteered some additional suggestions on the reorganization was not a privileged document.

(8) *Correspondence between a firm of solicitors and a trust company, Written, allegedly, on behalf of the solicitor's client, pertaining to an offer to be made to minority shareholders.* The documents were not privileged.

(9) *Check list for closing the sale.* The privilege applied. A document prepared by the solicitor for guidance was privileged.

See page ii for explanation of footnotes.

[156] Sokolov, 68 DTC 5266, Playfair Developments Ltd., 85 DTC 5155.

¶15,180

Solicitor-client privilege also extends to communications between the Minister and the lawyers for the Department of Justice.

[¶15,185] Collection Agreements

[¶15,190] Tax Collection Agreements with Provinces

Under the *Federal–Provincial Fiscal Arrangements* and the *Federal Post-Secondary Education and Health Contributions Act, 1977,* the Minister of Finance may make agreements with individual provinces respecting the collection of provincial personal and corporate taxes by the federal authorities. Such agreements have been concluded with all provinces except Quebec, in respect of its own personal and corporate income taxes, and Alberta, in respect of its own corporate income tax. Ontario previously collected its own corporate income tax, but for taxation years ending after December 31, 2008, Ontario's corporate income tax will be collected by the federal government.

The Minister is authorized to allocate the tax collected in accordance with such agreements and to disregard any directions made by a taxpayer as to allocation of tax or the fact that no such direction was made. The taxpayer is discharged from liability to pay tax only in accordance with such allocation.[157]

[¶15,195] Ownership Certificates

[¶15,200] Obligation to Complete Ownership Certificates

Banks and other encashing agents in Canada are obliged to obtain ownership certificates from the payee before cashing or negotiating:

(a) bearer coupons or warrants representing either interest or dividends payable by any debtor;

(b) cheques representing dividends or interest payable by a non-resident debtor on behalf of a resident of Canada; and

(c) bearer coupons and warrants negotiated by or on behalf of non-residents subject to tax on such coupons or warrants.

The ownership certificates are to be delivered to the debtor or encashing agent at the time of negotiation and the debtor or cashing agent must forward the certificate to the Minister on or before the 15th day of the month immediately following the month in which the coupon, warrant, or cheque was negotiated.[158]

See page ii for explanation of footnotes.

[157] CCH ¶27,330; Sec. 228.   [158] CCH ¶27,580, ¶27,586; Sec. 234; Reg. 207.

[¶15,205] Penalty

A penalty of $50 for each failure may be imposed on the cashing agent for failing to secure and file ownership certificates and the same penalty is applicable to the payee who fails to make out the certificate, and also where the payee fails to deliver the certificate.[159]

[¶15,210] Signing Officers

[¶15,215] Authorized Person

Returns, certificates, or other documents prepared by a corporation must be signed by the president, secretary, or treasurer of the corporation or by any other officer or person duly authorized by the Board of Directors or other governing body of the corporation.[160] Thus, the corporation is made responsible for incorrect information reported on any return, and is subject to a fine. For the liability of company officers, etc., see ¶15,280.

[¶15,220] Social Insurance Number (SIN)

[¶15,225] Application for Assignment of SIN

Every individual (other than a trust) who was resident or employed in Canada at any time in a taxation year and who files an income tax return under Part I must apply to the Minister of Human Resources Development for a SIN, unless that individual already has or has made an application for such a number. The individual's SIN must be supplied for all information and reporting purposes established by regulation.[161]

The application must be made on a prescribed form to the local office of the Canada Employment Insurance Commission not later than February 1, by a taxpayer who is filing a return for the preceding year, or within 15 days after being requested to do so by a person required to complete an information return.

A person required to make an information return requiring an individual's SIN must make a reasonable effort to obtain the number and to not knowingly use, communicate, or allow to be communicated, otherwise than as required, the number without the individual's written consent.[162]

A penalty of $100 for each failure is imposed on every individual who has failed to provide a SIN on a return of income, unless the individual had applied for the assignment of the SIN and had not received it at the time the return was filed. Where an individual fails to provide a SIN on request by another person who requires that number for an information return, that

---

See page ii for explanation of footnotes.

[159] CCH ¶22,857; Sec. 162(4).

[160] CCH ¶27,630; Sec. 236.

[161] CCH ¶27,640; Sec. 237(1); Reg. 3800; Inf. Cir. 82-2R2.

[162] CCH ¶27,644, ¶27,687; Sec. 237(2), 239(2.3).

individual is liable to a penalty of $100, unless, within 15 days of that request, the individual has applied for a SIN and has provided the SIN to that other person within 15 days of its receipt.[163] See also ¶15,270.

[¶15,230] Tax Shelters

[¶15,235] Identification Number Required

A promoter of a tax shelter must apply to the Minister for a shelter identification number.[164] The Minister will issue an identification number for a tax shelter upon receipt of an application, providing prescribed information and an undertaking that books and records for the tax shelter be kept in a place in Canada that is satisfactory to the Minister.[165] Effective June 29, 2012, a tax shelter identification number will only be valid for the calendar year identified in the application.[166] The prescribed information includes the name and address of the promoter, the location of the books and records of the tax shelter, the price per unit, and the number of such units offered for sale. All relevant documents with respect to the tax shelter, such as sales brochures, prospectuses, or offering memoranda are to be attached to the application. As mentioned, the application must be accompanied by an undertaking by a person proposing to sell interests in the tax shelter to keep the books and records of the tax shelter in a satisfactory place. The CRA considers that a satisfactory place would be that person's formal place of business in Canada.

Every promoter of a tax shelter is to make reasonable efforts to ensure that all investors in the tax shelter are provided with the identification number, and must explain on every statement that the issuance of the number does not in any way confirm approval by the Minister of the tax shelter. The tax shelter identification number must be prominently displayed on the right-hand corner of any statement of earnings, as well as on copies of the information return.[167]

[¶15,240] Meaning of "Promoter" and "Tax Shelter"

A "promoter" is any person who, whether as a principal, agent, or adviser, sells, issues, or promotes the sale, issuance, or acquisition of a tax shelter or accepts consideration for it. This definition will apply to all persons responsible for the sale of a tax shelter, as well as to the issuer itself. Typically, brokers, sales agents, and advisers, like lawyers and accountants, will be included. There will usually be more than one promoter for the same tax shelter.[168]

---

[163] CCH ¶22,858, ¶22,859; Sec. 162(5), 162(6).
[164] CCH ¶27,652; Sec. 237.1(2); Inf. Cir. 89-4.
[165] CCH ¶27,653; Sec. 237.1(3); Inf. Cir. 89-4.
[166] Sec. 237(4).
[167] CCH ¶27,655; Sec. 237.1(5).
[168] CCH ¶27,651; Sec. 237.1(1) "promoter".

A "tax shelter" is defined as any "gifting arrangement" (described below) or any property (including any right to income) which can reasonably be expected (based on statements or representations made or proposed to be made in connection therewith) to provide the investor, within the first four years, with an aggregate of losses, credits, and other deductible amounts or reduction in tax, equal to or in excess of the cost of the investment, as reduced by certain prescribed benefits. Further, since February 18, 2003, any gifting arrangement involving limited-recourse amounts (see the commentary at ¶9300) incurred by the investor in connection with creditable or deductible gifts to registered charities or other qualified donees are deemed to be tax shelters.[169] Some of the most popular tax shelters in recent years have been investments in films, multi-unit residential buildings (MURBs), resource investments, scientific research and development, offshore investment funds, nursing homes, motels, hotels, restaurants, mutual fund fees, and Cape Breton tax credits.

A gifting arrangement is defined to include any arrangement which, if entered into, would involve a person making a gift of property acquired as part of the arrangement to a qualified donee.[170] Generally, qualified donees are registered charities and other tax-exempt entities, gifts to which are creditable or deductible. In addition, as described above, a gifting arrangement includes any arrangement involving an investor incurring limited-recourse amounts in respect of property to be gifted to a qualified donee. This latter type of gifting arrangement is also deemed to be a tax shelter, without regard to the four-year net economic cost test otherwise applicable.

According to the CRA, the definition of what constitutes a tax shelter depends entirely on the reasonable inferences to be drawn from the statements or representations made with respect to that property. Such representations include both written and oral statements, such as those contained in sales brochures or advertisements, or any statements made in public or at private sales meetings. Prior to February 18, 2003, it appeared to be that, unless there was a "representation" in the strict legal sense (i.e., an enforceable premise, either at common law or by statute, such as might be found in sale of goods or securities law), there was no tax shelter. However, the economic test portion of the definition was amended to refer to amounts represented or *stated* to be deductible or creditable.

A tax shelter is property, except that a tax shelter does not include property that is a flow-through share, nor does it include prescribed property, i.e., a registered pension fund or plan, an RRSP, a DPSP, a RRIF, a registered education savings plan, or a share of a prescribed venture capital corporation or a prescribed labour-sponsored venture capital corporation, or a share of a taxable Canadian corporation that was held in a prescribed stock savings plan.

See page ii for explanation of footnotes.

[169] CCH ¶27,651a; Sec. 237.1(1) "tax shelter".   [170] CCH ¶27,650; Sec. 237.1(1) "gifting arrangement".

¶15,240

As discussed above, to determine whether or not a property is a tax shelter, it is necessary to determine the aggregate of all amounts, each of which is the amount of any "prescribed benefit". A prescribed benefit in relation to a tax shelter is any amount that may reasonably be expected, having regard to statements or representations made in respect of that shelter, to be received or enjoyed directly or indirectly by an investor, or by a person with whom that investor does not deal at arm's length, and the receipt or enjoyment thereof would have the effect of reducing the impact of any loss that the investor may sustain by virtue of acquiring, holding, or disposing of his investment.[171] For example, such benefits include revenue guarantees, contingent liabilities, limited recourse debt, and rights of exchange or conversion.[172]

[¶15,245] Failure To Comply

An identification number for a tax shelter must be obtained before a person, either acting as a principal or an agent, sells or issues it or accepts consideration for it.[173] Preliminary arrangements are not prohibited as long as no actual sales take place before the identification number is issued. A promoter who files false or misleading information in an application for an identification number and any person who, whether acting as a principal or an agent, sells, issues, or accepts consideration for a tax shelter before an identification number is issued is liable to a penalty. This penalty was increased as a result of the 2012 Budget and is computed as 25% of the greater of:

(i) the total consideration received or receivable for the tax shelter, before the correct information is filed or the identification number is issued, as the case may be, and

(ii) the total of all amounts each of which is an amount stated or represented to be the value of property that the person could donate to a qualified donee, if the tax shelter is a gifting arrangement and if the consideration is received or receivable by the promoter before the tax shelter identification number is issued.[174]

Prior to June 29, 2012, the penalty was computed as the greater of:

(a) $500; and

(b) 25% of the total consideration received or receivable for the tax shelter, before the correct information is filed or the identification number is issued, as the case may be.[175]

Late applications for a tax shelter identification number will be denied until the late filing penalty is paid in full. Investors in a tax shelter in respect

---

See page ii for explanation of footnotes.

[171] CCH ¶27,659; Reg. 231(6).
[172] CCH ¶27,659; Reg. 231(6).
[173] CCH ¶27,654; Sec. 237.1(4).
[174] Sec. 237.1(7.4)
[175] CCH ¶27,657d; Sec. 237.1(7.4).

of which a tax shelter identification number has not been issued may not deduct amounts in respect of that tax shelter. This rule will ensure that investors identify their tax shelter deductions and credits to valid tax shelters with an identification number.[176]

Any person who willfully provides an incorrect tax shelter identification number to another person is guilty of a criminal offence and liable to pay a fine of not less than 100% and not more than 200% of the cost to the other person of his or her interest in the shelter and/or imprisonment for up to two years.[177]

[¶15,246] Information Returns

Promoters are required to file with the Minister by the end of February of the year following the acquisition of a tax shelter an annual information return in respect of the tax shelter. This information return is in addition to and separate from the information that must be submitted upon application for an identification number. The obligation exists for each calendar year in which a promoter accepted consideration for the tax shelter or acted as a principal or agent in respect of a tax shelter. If more than one promoter is obliged to file an annual information return in respect of the same tax shelter, a report by one promoter discharges the other promoters' obligations. Where a promoter's business or activity is discontinued during the year, the return must be filed within 30 days of discontinuance.[178]

A new penalty has been introduced, effective June 29, 2012 for promoters who fail to properly file an information return. The penalty equals 25% of the *greater* of

(a) the total consideration received by the promoter from the particular person who is the subject of the request for information by the CRA, and

(b) if the tax shelter is a gifting arrangement, the total of all amounts stated or represented to be the value of property that the particular person could donate to a qualified donee.[179]

Prior to this change, promoters who failed to make an information return as required were liable to the standard penalty equal to the greater of $100 and $25 per day that the failure continues, to a maximum of $2,500.

[¶15,247] Enforcement

Where an application for a tax shelter has been made, the provisions dealing with audits, inspections, and powers of enforcement[180] apply for the purpose of permitting the Minister to verify or ascertain any information in

---

See page ii for explanation of footnotes.

[176] CCH ¶27,656; Sec. 237.1(6).   [179] Sec. 237.1(7.5).
[177] CCH ¶27,686; Sec. 239(2.1).
[178] CCH ¶27,657–27,657d; Sec. 237.1(7)–(7.4).   [180] CCH ¶27,420–27,457; Sec. 231–231.3.

respect of the tax shelter. They apply even where a return of income has not been filed by any taxpayer for the taxation year of the taxpayer in which an amount is claimed as a deduction in respect of the tax shelter.[181]

[¶15,250] Information Reporting for Tax Avoidance Transactions

[¶15,251] Background

The 2010 Budget proposed a reporting regime for tax avoidance transactions that bear certain of the hallmarks of aggressive tax planning. On May 7, 2010, the Minister of Finance sought public input on proposals to require information reporting of tax avoidance transactions. The submissions received raised various issues, many of which sought clarification regarding the criteria upon which the reporting is based. On August 27, 2010, draft legislation was released to address the issues raised, particularly when the proposed regime is considered as a whole. These 2010 Budget proposals, contained in the August 27, 2010 draft legislation, were not picked up in Bill C-47 (S.C. 2010, c. 25) which implemented most of the remaining 2010 Budget proposals. Their implementation is therefore still pending.

Under these proposals, a transaction would be a reportable transaction if it is an avoidance transaction or a series of transactions that includes an avoidance transaction, and, at any time, it bears two of the hallmarks provided in the definition "reportable transaction". These hallmarks often indicate a greater likelihood that the underlying transactions are ones that could be challenged under the current anti-avoidance rules. This new regime will apply in respect of avoidance transactions that are entered into after 2010, as well as to avoidance transactions that are part of a series of transactions that commenced before 2011 and is completed after 2010.

[¶15,252] Persons Subject to the Reporting Rules

Under these proposals, an information return would be required to be filed by any person for whom a tax benefit could result from an avoidance transaction or series, any person who enters into an avoidance transaction for the benefit of a taxpayer the particular person as well as any advisor or promoter who is entitled to a fee as described in the hallmarks with respect to that transaction. These hallmarks are described below under "Reportable Transaction" at ¶15,253.[182]

Whether a person would be considered to have entered into an avoidance transaction for the benefit of another person would be based on the facts and circumstances of each case. A person could be considered as having entered into an avoidance transaction for the benefit of another

See page ii for explanation of footnotes.

[181] CCH ¶27,658; Sec. 237.1(8).   [182] Sec. 237.3(2).

person where it would be reasonable to consider that the person has undertaken the transaction or has arranged the transaction in order for the transaction to result in a tax benefit for the other person. The particular person for whom the tax benefit could result from the avoidance transaction may be unknown when the person enters into an avoidance transaction. For example, a corporation that undertakes a transaction or series of transactions to increase the paid-up capital of a class of shares of its capital stock might be considered to have undertaken the transaction or series for the benefit of its current or future shareholders, depending on the circumstances.

A person who is an advisor or promoter, and any person with whom an advisor or promoter does not deal at arm's length, also may be subject to a reporting requirement if such a person is entitled to a fee in the following circumstances:

- The person is entitled to a fee that is to any extent based on the amount of a tax benefit from an avoidance transaction or a series of transactions that includes the avoidance transaction.

- The person is entitled to a fee that is to any extent contingent upon the obtaining of, or the failure to obtain, a tax benefit from an avoidance transaction or a series of transactions that includes the avoidance transaction.

- The person is entitled to a fee that is to any extent attributable to the number of persons who enter into an avoidance transaction or series, or a similar avoidance transaction or series, or who have been provided access to advice or an opinion given by the advisor or promoter regarding the tax consequences from the avoidance transaction or series (or similar avoidance transaction or series).

- The person is entitled to a fee in respect of "contractual protection" for a person for whom a tax benefit could result from the avoidance transaction or series of transactions that include the avoidance transaction.[183]

A "contractual protection" means any form of insurance (other than standard professional liability insurance), indemnity, or compensation that:

- protects against a failure of the transaction to result in any portion of the tax benefit being sought from the transaction;

- pays for or reimburses any expenses to be incurred in respect of a tax benefit arising from a transaction; or

- is intended to guarantee a return of, or in respect of, the cost of any property acquired by the taxpayer in the course of the transaction.[184]

[183] Sec. 237.3(1) "fee".   [184] Sec. 237.3(1) "contractual protection".

If more than one person is required to file an information return in respect of a reportable transaction, the filing of a complete disclosure by one of the parties will satisfy the obligation of each party.[185]

[¶15,253] Reportable Transaction

Under these proposals, a reportable transaction is a transaction that is classified as an "avoidance transaction" under the General Anti-Avoidance Rule (GAAR) or a transaction that is part of a series of transactions that includes an avoidance transaction if, at any time, two of the following three hallmarks come into existence in respect of the transaction or series:

(1) A promoter or tax advisor in respect of the transaction is entitled to fees that are to any extent:

(a) attributable to the amount of the tax benefit from the transaction;

(b) contingent upon the obtaining of a tax benefit from the transaction; or

(c) attributable to the number of taxpayers who participate in the transaction or who have been provided access to advice given by the promoter or advisor regarding the tax consequences from the transaction.

(2) A promoter or tax advisor in respect of the transaction requires "confidential protection" with respect to the transaction. In this respect, a "confidential protection" means any limitation on disclosure to any other person, including the CRA, that is placed by a promoter or tax advisor on the taxpayer, or on a person who entered into the transaction for the benefit of the taxpayer, in respect of the details or structure of the avoidance transaction that give rise to any tax benefit.[186]

(3) The taxpayer or the person who entered into the transaction for the benefit of the taxpayer obtains "contractual protection" (see definition at ¶15,252 in respect of the transaction (otherwise than as a result of a fee described in the first hallmark).[187]

Therefore, a transaction that is not an avoidance transaction, and a transaction in a series of transactions that does not include an avoidance transaction, will not be a reportable transaction, regardless of whether any of the hallmarks exist in respect of the transaction or series.

A reportable transaction will include all the transactions in a series of transactions if at least one of the transactions in that series is an avoidance transaction. Reporting will be required for the taxation year in which a tax benefit arises.[188]

See page ii for explanation of footnotes.

[185] Sec. 237.3(4).
[186] Sec. 237.3(1) "confidential protection".
[187] Sec. 237.3(1) "reportable transaction".
[188] Sec. 237.3(3).

If a reportable transaction is also a tax shelter or a flow-through share arrangement, only the reporting requirement for tax shelters or flow-through shares will apply.[189]

[¶15,254] Information Return

The information return with respect to a reportable transaction must be filed on or before June 30 of the calendar year following the calendar year in which the transaction first became a reportable transaction.[190] A transaction first becomes a reportable transaction to a person when the transaction is an avoidance transaction or is part of a series of transactions that includes an avoidance transaction and at least two of the three hallmarks described under "Reportable Transaction" at ¶15,253 are applicable in respect of the avoidance transaction or series. These hallmarks may come into existence before or after the avoidance transaction has been entered into or the end of the series of transactions. Accordingly, the time for filing an information return for an advisor or a promoter may arise after the avoidance transaction or the end of a series of transactions.

For example, if a series of transactions is implemented over two calendar years, but a particular advisor provided assistance or advice only in the second year and only in respect of transactions that occur in the second year, the transactions will have first become reportable transactions in respect of that advisor only in that second year.

For a person to have the possibility to obtain a tax benefit from a reportable transaction, or a series of transactions that includes a reportable transaction, a full and accurate information return in respect of the reportable transaction and of each reportable transaction that is part of such a series that includes the transaction must be filed.[191] This means that a person may obtain a tax benefit from the reportable transaction only if that person's reporting obligation has been satisfied because another person has filed an information return that fully discloses the reportable transaction, or each reportable transaction that is part of a series of transactions, from which the tax benefit can result.[192] Any tax benefit so denied for failure to comply with the new reporting regime may be restored by the Minister once the late-filing penalty and interest thereon is fully paid. In determining whether a person may obtain the tax benefit that was first denied under the new reporting regime, the Minister may consider whether the General Anti-Avoidance Rule (GAAR) otherwise applies to the reportable transaction.

The filing of an information return in respect of a reportable transaction is for administrative purposes only and cannot be considered as an admission by a person that the GAAR applies to the transaction, or that the transaction is an avoidance transaction for the purpose of the GAAR.[193]

See page ii for explanation of footnotes.

[189] Sec. 237.3(14)–(16).
[190] Sec. 237.3(5).
[191] Sec. 237.3(6).

[192] Sec. 237.3(3), 237.3(4).

[193] Sec. 237.3(12).

Conversely, the fact that reporting of a particular transaction may not be required under the new reporting regime should not be taken to suggest that the GAAR does not apply to the transaction.

[¶15,255] Penalty for Failure to Report

If an information return in respect of a reportable transaction does not provide full and accurate disclosure of the transaction or is not filed on time, each person who is required to file is liable to pay a penalty, notwithstanding any agreement between the parties as to who is to file the return.[194] In such circumstances, the penalty payable is the total of all amounts each of which is a fee in respect of the transaction, described in a hallmark, to which a promoter or tax advisor is or would be entitled to receive. If more than one person is liable to a penalty for failure to file, each of them is jointly and severally liable to pay the penalty.[195]

In addition to a late-filing penalty on persons who have failed to satisfy their reporting obligations, the Minister may also redetermine the tax consequences of any person for whom a tax benefit can result from the undisclosed reportable transaction. Such a redetermination could be made as if the GAAR was deemed to apply.[196]

[¶15,256] Due Diligence Defence

The proposed reporting regime provides a due diligence defence for persons who could be subject to these new reporting requirements.[197] To avail themselves of this defence, persons are required to make reasonable efforts to determine whether a transaction is a reportable transaction and whether they are subject to an information reporting requirement in respect of the reportable transaction. If a transaction is a reportable transaction and the person is subject to an information reporting requirement, then the person must determine whether the reporting requirement has been satisfied in all respects by another person. If not, then the person must identify all the information to be provided in respect of the reportable transaction. If, after making reasonable efforts, a particular person determines that no reporting requirement exists, or that another person has satisfied the reporting requirement to which the particular person is subject, the Minister may consider the particular person to have met the due diligence defence test. Whether a person has made such efforts would have to be determined according to the facts and circumstances of each case.

See page ii for explanation of footnotes.

[194] Sec. 237.3(8).

[195] Sec. 237.3(9).

[196] Sec. 237.3(6).

[197] Sec. 237.3(11).

[¶15,260] Offences

[¶15,265] Failure To File Returns, etc.

Every person who:

(a) has failed to file a return as required;

(b) is a non-resident person and has failed to send the appropriate notice to the Minister upon the disposition of taxable Canadian property;[198]

(c) has failed to comply with the receipt and deposit requirements relating to political contributions;[199]

(d) has failed to withhold tax from salary, wages, or other remuneration;[200]

(e) fails to keep books and records;[201]

(f) violates certain provisions regarding registered pension plans;[202]

(g) violates the provisions respecting inspections, searches, and seizures of documents; or[203]

(h) does not comply with a compliance order (see below),

is guilty of an offence and, in addition to any other penalty, is liable on summary conviction to a fine of between $1,000 and $25,000 and/or imprisonment for up to 12 months.[204]

Upon conviction of such an offence, the court may make any order it considers appropriate to enforce compliance.[205] This enables the court to impose further sanctions where non-compliance continues after conviction.

A person who is convicted will not be liable for the penalties for late filing of a return[206] (¶15,270) or for contravention of the withholding provisions[207] (¶15,070), unless those penalties were assessed or demanded before the information or complaint giving rise to the conviction was laid or made.[208] An employer was convicted for failing to remit withholding taxes by a specified date, with the offence commencing from the expiry of the specified date.[209]

A taxpayer may be subject to multiple convictions for each failure to comply with multiple demands for the same information. Each demand creates fresh time periods within which the taxpayer is required to comply and fresh offences for failure to comply with those periods.[210]

See page ii for explanation of footnotes.

198 CCH ¶17,320; Sec. 116(3).
199 CCH ¶19,821, ¶19,821e; Sec. 127(3.1), 127(3.2).
200 CCH ¶22,300; Sec. 153(1).
201 CCH ¶27,370, ¶27,400; Sec. 230, 230.1.
202 CCH ¶21,527, ¶21,538; Sec. 147.1(7), 147.1(18).
203 CCH ¶27,428, ¶27,500; Sec. 231.1, 232.
204 CCH ¶27,660; Sec. 238(1).

205 CCH ¶27,664; Sec. 238(2).
206 CCH ¶22,846; Sec. 162.
207 CCH ¶27,250; Sec. 227.
208 CCH ¶27,668; Sec. 238(3).
209 Sakellis, 70 DTC 6202.
210 Grimwood, 88 DTC 6001.

[¶15,270] Penalties for Evasion of Tax

A person who attempts to evade payment of tax by making, participating in, assenting to, or acquiescing in the making of false statements in any return, or who alters, secretes, or disposes of books or records, or who makes false entries or omissions in books of account, or who conspires to do any of these acts, or in any other manner attempts to evade payment of tax is guilty of an offence and is liable, in addition to any other penalties, on summary conviction to a fine of not less than 50% and not more than double the amount sought to be evaded, or to both fine and imprisonment for a term not exceeding two years.[211] An offence is also created for making false statements, altering documents, etc. for the purpose of obtaining or increasing a tax refund or credit. Such wilful contravention by a person who has no tax payable will, on summary conviction, attract a fine of not less than 50% and not more than twice the refund or credit sought to be obtained, or to both fine and imprisonment for a term not exceeding two years.[212]

In calculating the amount of tax sought to be evaded, no deduction was made for taxes paid to a foreign government on the unreported income after the charge was laid.[213] A taxpayer who certifies as to full disclosure on the T1 return when he or she knows that relevant facts have been omitted is guilty of wilful evasion.[214] So is a taxpayer who understates income even if he or she knew the regular audit would uncover the unreported income. The fact that the taxpayer did not sign the return was no defence to the charge of evasion.[215] Negligence did not constitute wilful tax evasion when a taxpayer did not have the required knowledge of wrongfulness; evidence established that the taxpayer's knowledge of bookkeeping and income tax procedure was nil.[216]

A charge for an offence involving wilful contravention for the purpose of evading tax payable or obtaining tax refund/credit may be prosecuted by indictment, in which case an accused may be liable to a larger fine or a longer term of imprisonment. If convicted, an accused will be liable to a fine of not less than 100%, and not more than 200%, of the tax sought to be evaded or refund/credit sought to be obtained, and to imprisonment for a term of up to five years.[217]

It is an offence for a person to wilfully provide to another person an incorrect identification number for a tax shelter and, in addition to any penalty otherwise provided, that person is liable on summary conviction to a fine at least equal to, and up to double, the cost to the other person of his or her interest in the shelter and/or imprisonment for up to two years.[218]

Every official or authorized person who knowingly violates the non-disclosure rules pertaining to information received for the purposes of the

---

See page ii for explanation of footnotes.

[211] CCH ¶27,680; Sec. 239(1).
[212] CCH ¶27,681; Sec. 239(1.1).
[213] Collins, 85 DTC 5174.
[214] Campbell, 60 DTC 1039.

[215] Kidd, 74 DTC 6574.
[216] Metke, 76 DTC 6313.
[217] CCH ¶27,684; Sec. 239(2).
[218] CCH ¶27,651, ¶27,686; Sec. 237.1, 239(2.1).

Act, the *Canada Pension Plan*, the *Unemployment Insurance Act* or the *Employment Insurance Act*, except as authorized, is guilty of an offence and is liable on summary conviction to a fine not exceeding $5,000 and/or imprisonment for up to 12 months.[219] See also ¶15,275.

Communication of taxpayer information may be provided by an official to any person for the purpose of administering or enforcing the Act, e.g., in order to locate tax debtors or to determine if an amount that could be garnished is owing to a tax debtor, or for the purpose of supervision, evaluation, or discipline of a federal civil servant. Safeguards are in place to prevent misuse or unauthorized disclosure of information.[220]

Every person to whom an individual's Social Insurance Number or a taxpayer's or partnership's business number has been provided who knowingly uses or communicates it for other purposes is guilty of an offence and is liable on summary conviction to a fine of up to $5,000 and/or imprisonment for up to 12 months.[221] This prohibition also extends to the officers, employees, and agents of the person who was provided with the number. Use or communication of the number that is required or authorized by law or that occurs in the course of a person's duties in connection with the administration or enforcement of the Act is permitted.

A person who has been convicted of wilful contravention for the purpose of evading tax or obtaining a tax refund or credit cannot be penalized for false statements or omissions (see ¶12,330) or third-party misrepresentations (see ¶12,333), unless that penalty was assessed before the information or complaint giving rise to the conviction was made.[222]

In dealing with tax evasion, care should be taken not to confuse "evasion" with "avoidance". It has been pointed out that there is an important distinction to be drawn between these two words.[223]

Where a prosecution has been instituted and an appeal made by the taxpayer, and substantially the same facts are in issue in both proceedings, the Minister may file a stay of proceedings with the Tax Court of Canada until final determination of the outcome of the prosecution.[224]

The right not to be punished twice for the same offence does not apply so as to bar criminal proceedings for tax evasion following the imposition of a civil penalty by the Minister.[225]

[¶15,275] Communication of Information

An official or, after March 11, 2009, another representative of a government entity, is prohibited from knowingly providing, or knowingly allowing

---

See page ii for explanation of footnotes.

[219] CCH ¶27,686ac, ¶27,720, ¶27,742; Sec. 239(2.2), 241(1), 241(4).

[220] CCH ¶27,742, ¶27,745; Sec. 241(4), 241(4.1).

[221] CCH ¶27,644, ¶27,687; Sec. 237(2), 239(2.3).

[222] CCH ¶27,688; Sec. 239(3).

[223] Regehr, 68 DTC 5078.

[224] CCH ¶27,692; Sec. 239(4).

[225] Sharma, 87 DTC 5424.

the provision of, to any person, any taxpayer information.[226] An official or other representative of a government entity who contravenes this provision is guilty of an offence (see ¶15,270). For these purposes, "taxpayer information" does not include information that does not reveal the identity of the taxpayer to whom it relates.[227]

There are exceptions to this prohibition against disclosure to the extent that an official or other representative of a government entity may:[228]

(1) provide to any person taxpayer information that can be regarded as necessary for the purposes of the administration or enforcement of the *Income Tax Act*, the *Canada Pension Plan*, the *Unemployment Insurance Act* or the *Employment Insurance Act*, solely for that purpose;

(2) provide to any person taxpayer information that can reasonably be regarded as necessary to determine any tax, interest, penalty, or other amount that is or may become payable by the person, or any refund or tax credit to which the person is or may become entitled, or any other amount that is relevant for the purposes of that determination;

(3) provide a person who seeks certification in respect of past service benefits which are to be paid out of a registered pension plan, the certification or refuse to make the certification;

(4) provide taxpayer information to federal and provincial policy makers, certain provincial officials, officials in federal pension and income support programs, and officials administering certain sections of the *Cultural Property Export and Import Act* under certain federal and provincial fiscal agreements;

(5) provide taxpayer information to an official for the purposes of setting off sums of money owed by Her Majesty in Right of Canada against debts owed to Her Majesty in Right of Canada, as well as those owed for taxes to Her majesty in Right of a province, thereby allowing taxpayer information to be provided for set-offs against any provincial debt;

(6) provide and permit access to an inspection of taxpayer information in specific instances of permitted disclosure under federal legislation;

(7) provide taxpayer information solely for the purposes of subsections (23) to (25) of the *Financial Administration Act*;

(8) compile information if it does not betray the identity of a taxpayer (i.e., tax statistics on classes of taxpayers);

(9) disclose taxpayer information in the course of supervising, disciplining, or evaluating the performance of a person presently or formerly employed or engaged by the federal government in the administration and

---

See page ii for explanation of footnotes.

[226] CCH ¶27,720; Sec. 241(1).

[227] CCH ¶27,775; Sec. 241(10) "taxpayer information".

[228] CCH ¶27,742; Sec. 241(4).

enforcement of the *Income Tax Act*, the *Canada Pension Plan*, the *Unemployment Insurance Act*, or the *Employment Insurance Act*;

(10) provide access to records of taxpayer information to the National Archivist for the purposes of evaluation, destruction, authorization, and transfer to the National Archives;

(11) release taxpayer information or information derived from taxpayer information to a taxpayer;

(12) provide taxpayer information to an official or designated person for the purpose of adjusting social assistance benefits that are based on a means or income test (for example, information relating to a taxpayer's income may be provided to a municipal employee to establish entitlement to municipal social assistance payments, and information relating to the income supplement amount under the Canada Child Tax Benefit may be provided to provincial authorities in connection with amounts payable as a benefit for a child under a provincial law);

(13) provide and permit access to and inspection of taxpayer information to a person otherwise legally entitled to it under an Act of Parliament;

(14) effective March 12, 2009, and subject to certain restrictions described below, share the following BN-related information with a representative of a government entity: the number itself, the name (including trade name) of the holder, and the contact information, corporate information and registration information related to the holder (before March 12, 2009, such an official is allowed to release only the BN, name, address, telephone number, and fax number of the holder to another official of a federal of provincial department or agency, for the purpose of the administration or enforcement of an Act of Parliament or a provincial law);

(15) provide information to any person, solely for the purposes of the administration or enforcement of a law of a province that provides for workers' compensation benefits;

(16) provide relevant taxpayer information to the police for the purpose of investigating whether the acts of a person against an official of the CRA, or against a member of the official's family, constitute an offence under the *Criminal Code*;

(17) share with statistical agency officials taxpayer information in respect of incorporated and unincorporated businesses for the 1997 and subsequent taxation years. Only business-related information can be shared. Thus, for unincorporated businesses, information on the business owner which is unrelated to business activities cannot be shared; or

(18) effective December 14, 2007, provide taxpayer information to an official of the government of a province, solely for the use in the management or administration of a program relating to earnings supplementation or income support.

¶15,275

Certain restrictions are imposed on the information sharing and public disclosure of BN-related information in paragraph (14) above.[229] An official may not disclose information related to a program, activity of service provided by a government entity if the BN is not used as an identifier in the program, activity, or service. The Minister may make public the BN and name or trade name of the BN holder but only if it is made in connection with a program, activity, or service provided by the Minister. A representative of a government entity may make public the BN and name or trade name of the BN holder in respect of a program, activity, or service provided by the government entity, as long as the BN is used only as an identifier for the program, activity, or service. The BN-related information is normally publicly available from the provincial corporate registries and may not be shared if it is in respect of an *excluded individual* defined as an individual holding a BN for withholding tax purposes or some other non-business purposes (e.g., an individual employing a gardener or a nanny).[230]

The above exceptions apply not only to the tax officials but also to "authorized persons", i.e., persons engaged or employed (or formerly engaged) by the Crown to assist in administering the *Income Tax Act*, the *Canada Pension Plan*, the *Unemployment Insurance Act*, or the *Employment Insurance Act*.[231]

It should be noted that Tax Conventions or Tax Agreements with numerous countries permit the Canadian government to pass on to foreign governments information regarding income from Canada of foreign nationals.

Where an order or direction is made in connection with legal proceedings which requires an official or authorized person to give evidence or produce documents, the order or direction may be appealed by the Minister or the person against whom the order or direction is made to a provincial court of appeal or the Federal Court of Appeal, as the case may be. An appeal stays operation of the order until judgment is rendered.[232]

Release of the addresses of taxpayers was not permitted in a case where it was alleged in divorce proceedings that one of the taxpayers had kidnapped the children of the marriage and was in contempt of certain custody orders.[233]

[¶15,280] Liability of Company Officers, etc.

Where a corporation is guilty of an offence, an officer, director, or agent of the corporation who directed, authorized, etc., the offence is guilty of the offence and liable on conviction to the penalty, whether or not the

---

See page ii for explanation of footnotes.

[229] CCH ¶27,761, ¶27,761f, ¶27,761i; Sec. 241(9.2), 241(9.3), 241(9.4).

[230] CCH ¶27,769d; Sec. 241(10) "excluded individual".

[231] CCH ¶27,720, ¶27,764; Sec. 241(1), 241(10) "authorized person".

[232] CCH ¶27,752–27,758; Sec. 241(6)–(8).

[233] Glover, 82 DTC 6035.

corporation has been prosecuted or convicted.[234] The corporation itself may be penalized for the same offence.

[¶15,285] Minimum Penalties Not To Be Decreased

The courts have no power to suspend sentence or to decrease the minimum penalty provided for an offence.[235]

[¶15,290] Taxable Obligation — Identification of Interest Coupon

Any person issuing a taxable or non-taxable obligation bearing a separate or detachable coupon is required to identify the coupon by inserting on the face of the obligation the letters "AX" in the case of a taxable obligation, and the letter "F" in the case of a non-taxable obligation. Failure to comply with this requirement is punishable by a fine not exceeding $500.[236]

[¶15,295] Procedure and Evidence

[¶15,300] Information or Complaints

An information or complaint may be laid by an officer of the CRA, by a member of the RCMP, or by any person authorized by the Minister. It may relate to more than one offence and may be heard, tried, or determined by any court, judge, or justice, if the accused is resident, carrying on business, or is found, apprehended, or in custody within the territorial jurisdiction.[237]

An information or complaint under the *Criminal Code* relating to summary convictions for tax matters may be laid within eight years from the day the matter arose.[238]

A sworn affidavit of an officer of the CRA stating that a request for information, notice, or demand was served personally on a named day on the person to whom it was directed will be received as *prima facie* evidence of personal service of the request, notice, or demand.[239] Where a taxpayer's spouse picked up a registered letter addressed to the taxpayer which requested the taxpayer to file a T4 information return, and the spouse neglected to see that the letter was given to the taxpayer, the taxpayer was held liable for failure to file the return on the ground that the spouse was the taxpayer's agent for the purpose of receiving mail.[240]

Documents over the name in writing of an official authorized to execute them will be deemed to have been validly executed, unless questioned by the Minister or some other person acting for the Minister or on behalf of the Crown.[241]

See page ii for explanation of footnotes.

[234] CCH ¶27,780; Sec. 242.
[235] CCH ¶27,790; Sec. 243.
[236] CCH ¶27,710, ¶27,716; Sec. 240; Reg. 807.
[237] CCH ¶27,800–27,807; Sec. 244(1)–(3).

[238] CCH ¶27,808; Sec. 244(4).
[239] CCH ¶27,816; Sec. 244(6).
[240] Samis, 63 DTC 1269.
[241] CCH ¶27,840; Sec. 244(13).

The date shown on any notice, notification, notice of assessment, or determination by the Minister is presumed to be the date of mailing or the date it is sent electronically.[242] Because this is a presumption only, evidence may be brought to show that the date of the notice or notification was not the same as the date of mailing.[243] Where any notice of an assessment or notice of determination has been sent by the Minister as required, the assessment or determination shall be deemed to have been made on the day of the mailing or the day of the electronic transmission of the notice of the assessment or determination.[244]

Every form purporting to be a form prescribed or authorized by the Minister shall be deemed to be a form prescribed by order of the Minister, unless called into question by the Minister or some person acting for the Minister or The Queen.[245]

Every member of a partnership is to be treated as having been named in any notice or document which contains a reference to the firm name of the partnership. All notices or documents sent to a partnership at the last known address or place of business of the partnership, or at the last known address of any member (whose liability is not limited in the case of a limited partnership), are deemed to have been provided to each member of the partnership.[246]

In any prosecution of an offence, the production of a required return, certificate, statement, or answer purporting to be made, signed, filed, or delivered by or on behalf of the taxpayer is *prima facie* evidence that it is what it purports to be.[247] This obviates the necessity of proving that a return was signed by or on behalf of the taxpayer, unless the taxpayer questions it and puts forward acceptable evidence to the contrary.

In appeals to the Tax Court of Canada or the Federal Court of Appeal, the production of documents purporting to have been filed or made by or on behalf of the taxpayer will be taken as *prima facie* evidence that such documents were so filed or made.[248] For information returns filed electronically, a document purporting to be a printout of the information on a taxpayer will be received by the Minister as *prima facie* proof that the return had been filed at the time the printout was received.[249]

In any prosecution of an offence, the sworn affidavit of an officer of the CRA in charge of certain records setting out that an examination of the records shows that a return, statement, answer, or certificate required to be made has not in fact been made, is to be accepted as *prima facie* evidence of the statements made in the affidavit.[250] Although a trial judge is required to

---

See page ii for explanation of footnotes.

[242] CCH ¶27,844; Sec. 244(14).
[243] Hughes, 87 DTC 635.
[244] CCH ¶27,848; Sec. 244(15).
[245] CCH ¶27,852; Sec. 244(16).
[246] CCH ¶27,861; Sec. 244(20).

[247] CCH ¶27,856; Sec. 244(17).
[248] CCH ¶27,858; Sec. 244(18).
[249] CCH ¶27,862, ¶27,863; Sec. 244(21), 244(22).
[250] CCH ¶27,820; Sec. 244(7).

receive affidavit evidence as *prima facie* evidence, he or she still has discretion to call the deponents involved for cross-examination.[251]

[¶15,301] Online Notices

Effective December 15, 2010, the CRA is allowed to issue electronic notices, such as notices of assessment, that previously had to be mailed (by ordinary, as opposed to registered mail).[252]

For security reasons, these online notices will be made available on the CRA's existing secure online facilities: My Account (for individuals), My Business Account and Represent a Client (for representatives of individuals and businesses). They will be presumed to be sent by the CRA and received by a taxpayer on the date that an electronic message informing the taxpayer that a notice is available on the CRA's secure online facilities is sent to the electronic address most recently provided by the taxpayer. The CRA can only send notices electronically if the taxpayer has authorized it to communicate in this manner. The authorization for online notices is voluntary and, once given, can be revoked.

Notices that are specifically required to be served personally or by registered or certified mail are not eligible for electronic transmission. The government's intention is to provide this electronic service in respect of notices of assessment and reassessment of tax under Part I and notices of determination and redetermination in respect of the GST/HST credit and the Canada Child Tax Benefit and related provincial programs.

[¶15,305] Tax Avoidance

[¶15,307] General Anti-Avoidance Rule (GAAR)

Where a transaction is an avoidance transaction, the tax consequences to the taxpayer are to be determined as is reasonable in the circumstances to deny the tax benefit that would result, directly or indirectly, from that transaction or from a series of transactions that includes that transaction.[253] A "transaction" is defined to include an arrangement or event.[254] A tax benefit is defined to mean a reduction, avoidance, or deferral of tax or other amount payable under the Act or an increase in a refund of tax or other amount under the Act.[255] The tax benefit does not have to be enjoyed by the party entering into the impugned transactions.[256] The phrase "tax consequences" means the amount of income, taxable income, or taxable income earned in Canada, tax or other amount payable by, or refundable to the person under the Act, or any other amount that is relevant for the purposes of computing that amount.[257] This definition is obviously very broad, and

---

See page ii for explanation of footnotes.

[251] Cholodniuk, 92 DTC 6168.
[252] CCH ¶27,844a; Sec. 244(14.1).
[253] CCH ¶27,871; Sec. 245(2); Inf. Cir. 88-2.
[254] CCH ¶27,870b; Sec. 245(1) "transaction".
[255] CCH ¶27,870; Sec. 245(1) "tax benefit".
[256] OSFC Holdings Ltd., 2001 DTC 5471.
[257] CCH ¶27,870a; Sec. 245(1) "tax consequences".

provides the CRA with considerable flexibility in deciding how to counter the effect of the transaction.

An "avoidance transaction" means any transaction (or transaction that is part of a series of transactions) that would result in a tax benefit, unless the transaction may reasonably be considered to have been undertaken or arranged primarily for *bona fide* purposes other than to obtain the tax benefit.[258] This definition, as enacted in 1988, does not contain a stringent business purpose test, in that it does not purport to disallow transactions which, in themselves, have no business purpose, but which nevertheless have a valid family or other purpose. For example, a transaction implementing an estate freeze would probably not survive a business purpose test. Instead of containing a business purpose test, the definition provides that a transaction is acceptable if it is undertaken primarily for *bona fide* reasons, other than to obtain a tax benefit.

Because tax-planning transactions generally result in tax benefits and thus could be characterized as avoidance transactions, where a transaction is entered into for both a *bona fide* purpose and for the purpose of obtaining a tax benefit, the primary purpose of the transaction will need to be determined. This will involve weighting the tax and non-tax purposes of the transaction. A transaction will not be caught where tax considerations are a significant, but not the main, purpose for carrying out a transaction. The reference in the definition to a "series of transactions" is intended to adopt the "step transaction" approach taken by the judiciary in England,[259] i.e., each step in series of transactions must be carried out primarily for *bona fide* non-tax purposes.

For greater certainty, the GAAR does not apply to any transaction where it may reasonably be considered that the transaction would not result in a misuse of the provisions of the Act or an abuse having regard to the provisions of the Act read as a whole.[260] In a judgment released on January 8, 2009, the Supreme Court of Canada in a 4:3 split decision held that a consideration of the entire series of transactions is appropriate in determining whether a particular transaction in the series results in an abuse or misuse.[261] In the case at bar, Mrs. Lipson obtained a bank loan to purchase shares in a corporation from Mr. Lipson on a rollover basis. Mr. Lipson then used the proceeds to buy a new house, took out a mortgage on the house, and used it to pay off his wife's bank loan. The mortgage interest on the substituted loan was deducted from Mrs. Lipson's dividend income and, owing to the subsequent application of the attribution rules, the resulting loss on the shares (i.e., the interest expense on the mortgage loan in excess of the dividends received on the shares) was reported by Mr. Lipson. Bearing in mind that the entire series of transactions should be considered in order to determine whether the individual transactions within the series abuse one or more provisions of the Act, the

---

See page ii for explanation of footnotes.

[258] CCH ¶27,872; Sec. 245(3).
[259] W.T. Ramsay Ltd., [1982] A.C. 300 (H.L.).
[260] CCH ¶27,873; Sec. 245(4).
[261] Lipson, 2009 DTC 5015.

majority of the Supreme Court felt that the rollover and the subsequent application of the attribution rule enabled Mr. Lipson to obtain the result contemplated in the design of the entire series of transactions, namely, the shifting of the interest expense deduction and the resulting loss from his wife to himself. The Court held that using the attribution rules in such a manner frustrated the purpose of the rules, which is to prevent spouses from reducing tax by transferring property between themselves. The specific anti-avoidance rule, namely, the attribution rule, was itself being used to facilitate abusive tax avoidance.

In response to the decision of the Tax Court in *Rousseau-Houle* that the GAAR does not apply to the Income Tax Regulations,[262] the 2004 Budget retroactively amended the GAAR to extend its application to the Income Tax Regulations, the Income Tax Application Rules ("ITARs"), and, perhaps more significantly, to Canada's international treaty obligations. This Budget amendment applies retroactively to transactions entered into after September 12, 1988, i.e., the date of the introduction of the GAAR.

This test incorporates the "object and spirit" approach followed by the Supreme Court of Canada,[263] and draws on the "abuse of rights" doctrine which applies in some jurisdictions to defeat schemes intended to abuse the tax legislation. It recognizes that a number of provisions of the Act either contemplate or encourage transactions that may seem to be primarily tax-motivated. Tax benefits that result from these transactions will not be denied as long as they are carried out within the object and spirit of the Act read as a whole. However, where a taxpayer carries out transactions primarily in order to obtain, through the application of specific provisions of the Act, a tax benefit that is not intended by such provisions and by the Act read as a whole, the GAAR will apply, even where the strict words of the relevant provisions may support the tax result sought by the taxpayer. A 1991 Federal Court of Appeal case held that in order for the GAAR to apply, a transaction or operation must have the effect of unduly or artificially reducing the income — the artificiality of the transaction does not determine the issue.[264]

In determining the tax consequences to a person, as is reasonable in the circumstances in order to deny a tax benefit that would result from an avoidance transaction, the Minister may, among other things, allow or disallow in whole or in part any deduction in computing income, taxable income earned in Canada, or tax payable or any part thereof, allocate to any person any such deduction, any income, or other amount or part thereof, recharacterize the nature of any payment or other amount, and ignore the tax results that would otherwise result.[265]

The determination as to tax consequences made by the Minister may involve adjustments to amounts such as the adjusted cost base of property

---

See page ii for explanation of footnotes.

[262] Rousseau-Houle, 2001 DTC 250.
[263] Stubart, 84 DTC 6305.
[264] Irving Oil Limited, 91 DTC 5106.
[265] CCH ¶27,874; Sec. 245(5).

¶15,307

or the paid-up capital of a share. These adjustments may not affect the amount of income, taxable income, or taxable income earned in Canada, or the tax or other amount payable by, or amount refundable to, a person until a number of years after the avoidance transaction. Therefore, in many cases these adjustments cannot be made through an immediate assessment or reassessment. That is why the Minister is allowed to determine these adjustments without an assessment or reassessment.[266] The Minister may also wait until an assessment or reassessment is possible. Where the Minister determines adjustments without assessing or reassessing the taxpayer, a notice of that determination must be sent to the taxpayer with all due dispatch.[267]

Where the Minister has issued an assessment or made a determination in respect of a taxpayer's avoidance transaction, any other taxpayer may request a further assessment or determination with respect to the same transaction. Such a request must be made in writing within 180 days from the original date of the notice of assessment or determination. Thus, for example, if the Minister assesses X on an amount that was paid to Y, Y could request that this amount be removed from his or her income.[268] Where a request is made, the Minister must consider it with all due dispatch and make an assessment or a determination with respect to the person making the request.[269] The Minister must do so even if the time limitation for reassessment has expired. Upon such an assessment or determination being made, the person who made the request will accordingly be entitled to file a notice of objection and, in due course, to appeal the Minister's assessment or determination.[270]

[¶15,308] Benefit Conferred on a Person

When a person confers a benefit on a taxpayer, the amount of the benefit must be included in the taxpayer's income, provided that it is not otherwise included in the taxpayer's income and would have been included if it were a payment made directly to the taxpayer. Where the taxpayer is a non-resident, non-resident withholding tax may be applicable and any relevant treaty exemption will be available. No benefit, however, will be regarded as having been conferred if the transaction was:

(a) at arm's length;

(b) *bona fide*;

(c) not pursuant to or part of any other transaction; and

(d) not to effect payment or partial payment of any existing or future obligation.

See page ii for explanation of footnotes.

[266] CCH ¶22,181a; Sec. 152(1.11).

[267] CCH ¶22,181c; Sec. 152(1.12).

[268] CCH ¶22,181a, ¶27,875; Sec. 152(1.11), 245(6).

[269] CCH ¶27,877; Sec. 245(8).

[270] CCH ¶22,181a; Sec. 152(1.11).

A transaction will not be excepted unless all four of these conditions are met.[271]

The taxpayer corporation purchased its supply of aluminum from a Canadian company indirectly through a Bermuda corporation that was part of the same corporate structure as that of the taxpayer. Suppliers' discounts were paid to the Bermuda company. This arrangement resulted in an artificial reduction of the taxpayer's income and a benefit being conferred on the Bermuda company by the taxpayer.[272]

The Federal Court of Appeal also held that the issuance of shares to the taxpayer's spouse and children by a corporation controlled by the taxpayer resulted in the conferring of a benefit by the taxpayer. By issuing the shares to the children, the value of the taxpayer's shares of the corporation was diminished, and the amount of the decrease was in effect given to the children.[273]

[¶15,310] Transfer Pricing

[¶15,311] Transfer Pricing Adjustment

All cross-border transactions (not merely reportable) with non-arm's length parties must be priced on an arm's length basis and the CRA has the authority to tax transactions on a reconstructed arm's length basis where arm's length criteria are not met.[274] As well, if the transactions would not be entered into at all by arm's length parties and it appears that the taxpayer or partnership cannot show a primary *bona fide* purpose beyond tax advantage, the CRA can, for tax purposes, restructure the transaction to reflect its nature as if the participants had been dealing with each other at arm's length. These downward adjustments are commonly referred to as "primary adjustments".

Surprisingly, there is little jurisprudence on transfer pricing matters, and at the time of publication *GlaxoSmithKline*[275] has been granted leave to appeal to the Supreme Court on a transfer pricing matter that highlights the difficulty in ensuring the correct amount of tax is levied on these types of transactions.

However, a primary adjustment does not change the fact that, in the case of a downward adjustment, the Canadian resident will have paid an excessive amount to the non-resident. For example, if the amount actually paid by a Canadian resident for goods or services is $100, but the Minister has made a primary adjustment reducing the amount to $80 for tax purposes, the non-resident has nevertheless received the full $100 payment,

---

See page ii for explanation of footnotes.

[271] CCH ¶27,891, ¶27,892; Sec. 246(1), 246(2).

[272] Indalex Ltd, 88 DTC 6053.

[273] Kieboom, 92 DTC 6382.

[274] CCH ¶27,962, ¶27,981; Sec. 247(2); Inf. Cir. 87-2R.

[275] 2010 DTC 5124 (FCA).

¶15,310

which includes a $20 excessive amount. The issue then becomes how to characterize this excessive payment for Canadian tax purposes.

In practice, the Minister has taken the position that these excessive payments are benefits and are recharacterized as dividends subject to Canadian withholding tax.[276] These administrative adjustments are commonly referred to as "secondary adjustments". However, there is no specific statutory provision in the transfer pricing rules addressing such secondary adjustments.

Budget 2012 proposed to clarify the Minister's authority to make secondary adjustments. A secondary adjustment will result in a dividend being deemed to have been paid by a Canadian corporation that has been the subject of a primary adjustment. The dividend will be deemed to have been paid to each non-arm's length non-resident participant in the relevant transaction or series of transactions in proportion to the amount of the primary adjustment that relates to the non-resident. This dividend treatment will apply regardless of whether the non-resident is a shareholder of the Canadian corporation.

The Minister will have discretionary power to reduce the amount of the deemed dividend where the non-resident dividend recipient has repaid a portion of the deemed dividend to the Canadian corporation. The resolution also legislates the CRA's administrative repatriation policy, presently set out in Transfer Pricing Memorandum TPM-02 dated March 27, 2003. The non-resident must first obtain the concurrence of the Minister before any such payment is made.

This measure has been introduced in draft legislation released on August 14, 2012 and will apply to transactions (including transactions that are part of a series of transactions) that occur after March 29, 2012.

[¶15,312] Contemporaneous Documentation

Any transaction in property, goods, and services with non-arm's length non-residents must be documented as to the arm's length nature of the price at the time of the transaction, with potentially severe penalties (see ¶15,315) if the CRA later adjusts the price resulting in increased taxes where the contemporaneous documentation is not on hand.[277]

Records or documents must be made or obtained by the taxpayer's due date for filing an income tax return (a partnership information return).[278] They must provide a complete and accurate description, in all material respects, of the following items:

(1) The property or services to which the transaction relates.

See page ii for explanation of footnotes.

[276] Sec. 214(3)(a); General Electric Capital Canada Inc., 2010 DTC 1007 (T.C.C.), affd 2011 DTC 5011 (FCA)

[277] CCH ¶27,964; Sec. 247(4).

[278] CCH ¶27,952; Sec. 247(1) "documentation-due date".

(2) The terms and conditions of the transaction and their relationship, if any, to the terms and conditions of each other transaction entered into between the persons or partnerships involved in the transaction. For example, in a round-trip transaction (i.e., a transaction whereby a parent company manufactures components that are assembled into a finished product by a foreign subsidiary, and the finished product is sold to the parent for distribution), taxpayers must document how the terms and conditions of each of the transfers relate to each other.

(3) The identity of the persons or partnerships involved in the transaction, and their relationship at the time the transaction was entered into.

(4) The functions performed, the property used or contributed, and the risks assumed by the persons or partnerships involved in the transaction.

(5) The data and methods considered and the analysis performed to determine the transfer prices or the allocations of profits or losses or contributions to costs, as the case may be, for the transaction. This includes:

    (a) a description of the comparable transactions considered and of those used in applying the pricing method;

    (b) an assessment of the degree of comparability of such transactions with the taxpayer's transactions;

    (c) a description of any adjustments made to enhance the degree of comparability; and

    (d) if the taxpayer considers more than one method, the analysis performed using each of those methods, as well as the analysis that led to the selection of the chosen method.

(6) The assumptions, strategies, and policies, if any, that influenced the determination of the transfer prices or the allocations of profits or losses or contributions to costs, as the case may be, for the transaction. This includes all the factors that materially affect the determination of the transfer prices, such as market penetration strategies or any economic assumptions that were relied on to determine the transfer prices.

The documentation required must be provided to the CRA within three months of service, made personally or by registered or certified mail, of a written request. In IC-87-2R, the CRA reminds taxpayers that the above list of documents is not intended to be an exhaustive list of the documents necessary to substantiate that: (i) a taxpayer's transfer pricing is in accordance with the arm's length principle; or (ii) a taxpayer has made reasonable efforts to determine arm's length transfer prices or allocations. The documentation required depends on the facts and circumstances of theparticular transaction. In other words, there is no one set of documents that, if made

¶15,312

or obtained, would constitute a "safe harbour" from the application of the penalty in ¶15,315.[279]

[¶15,315] Penalty

Unless the transfer pricing adjustment relates to a qualifying cost contribution arrangement, or the taxpayer made reasonable efforts to determine an arm's length transfer price, a penalty is imposed on a taxpayer's net transfer price capital or income adjustment.[280] A qualifying cost contribution arrangement means an arrangement under which reasonable efforts are made by the participants to establish a basis for contributing to, and to contribute on that basis to, the cost of producing, developing, or acquiring any property, or acquiring or performing any services, in proportion to the benefits which each participant is reasonably expected to derive from the property or services as a result of the arrangement.[281] For these purposes, a participant who cannot produce on demand contemporaneous documents to support the transfer pricing methodology (see ¶15,312) is deemed not to have made reasonable efforts to establish the correct transfer price.

The penalty is computed as follows:

(1) A determination is made of the total of the taxpayer's transfer pricing capital and income adjustments for the year.

(2) From such total are subtracted any transfer pricing capital or income adjustment and any set-off adjustment that can reasonably be considered to relate to a qualifying contribution arrangement or to transfer prices that in fact turned out to be incorrect but nevertheless were a result of reasonable efforts to establish an arm's length amount.

(3) The balance remaining is compared to the lesser of 10% of the taxpayer's gross revenue for the year (before any transfer pricing adjustment and other adjustments for inadequate consideration and tax avoidance transactions) and $5,000,000. If the amount is greater than the lesser of these two amounts, the penalty is 10% of that amount. Otherwise, there is no penalty.

Any increase in a taxpayer's gross revenue (assuming it is less than $5,000,000) to reduce the amount of the penalty is strictly prohibited.[282]

The penalty applies to the taxpayer's transfer pricing capital and income adjustment, and not to any income tax imposed as a result of such adjustment. Therefore, a taxpayer who has discretionary deductions to offset any income inclusion resulting from a transfer pricing adjustment may still be subject to a penalty.

See page ii for explanation of footnotes.

[279] CCH ¶27,981a; Inf. Cir. 87-2R.

[280] CCH ¶27,963; Sec. 247(3).

[281] CCH ¶27,953; Sec. 247(1) "qualifying cost contribution arrangement".

[282] CCH ¶27,969; Sec. 247(9).

[¶15,320] Interpretation

[¶15,325] Meaning of "Tax Payable"

A reference to "tax payable" by a taxpayer means the tax payable by the taxpayer as fixed by assessment or reassessment, subject to variations on objection or appeal.[283]

[¶15,330] Property Subject to Certain Quebec Institutions and Arrangements

With respect to institutions or arrangements governed by the laws of Quebec, a usufruct, right of use or habitation, or substitution is deemed to be a trust for the purposes of the Act. If the usufruct, right of use or habitation, or substitution was created by will, it is deemed to be a trust created by will. The property subject to the usufruct, right of use or habitation, or substitution is deemed to be transferred into the trust. In the case of an institution created by will, the property is deemed to be transferred to the trust upon the death of the testator. The property subject to a usufruct, right of use or habitation, or substitution is deemed to be held in trust for the purposes of the Act.[284] However, there is an exception to the application of this rule, which deems property that is subject to the right of usufruct or the right of use under Quebec law to have been transferred to a trust.[285] This exception applies in the case of the transfer of bare ownership of land (which occurs where a landowner gives away land while retaining a usufruct or right of use for his or her lifetime) by way of gift to a registered charity, after July 18, 2005, that is eligible for the charitable donations tax credit. Prior to July 19, 2005, such dispositions were deemed to have been transferred to a trust, thus disposing of property as a whole. As a result of the introduction of this exception after July 18, 2005, the dismemberment will entail a disposition only of the bare ownership of an immovable for an amount equal to its fair market value. For capital property, the adjusted cost base of the property will be divided *pro rata* between the bare ownership and the usufruct or right of use. The usufruct or right of use will be considered to have been disposed of only when it is actually disposed of or deemed to be disposed of (e.g., upon death).

An arrangement, other than a partnership, qualifying arrangement (described below), or a trust will be deemed to be a trust, and the property subject to the arrangement will be deemed to be held in trust, if the arrangement is established by written contract before October 31, 2003, is governed by the laws of Quebec, specifies that it is considered to be a trust for the purposes of the Act, and creates rights and obligations substantially similar to rights and obligations under a trust.[286] This determinative rule is meant to address arrangements that were established prior to the replace-

---

See page ii for explanation of footnotes.

[283] CCH ¶28,325; Sec. 248(2).

[284] CCH ¶28,327; Sec. 248(3)(a).

[285] CCH ¶28,327c; Sec. 248(3.1).

[286] CCH ¶28,327; Sec. 248(3)(b).

ment of the *Civil Code of Lower Canada* (CCLC) with the *Civil Code of Quebec* (CCQ). Under the CCLC, certain commercial arrangements that were created for investment purposes were not considered to be trusts under the CCLC since they were not constituted by gift or legacy. While under the CCQ, which replaced the CCLC in 1994, it generally became possible for such arrangements to be established as valid trusts in Quebec. The status of arrangements established prior to the CCLC's replacement continued to rely on the deeming provisions for their trust status under the Act.

With respect to taxation years that begin after October 30, 2003, qualifying arrangements (including those established before the introduction of the CCQ) are deemed to be trusts for the purposes of the Act.[287] Property contributed to such an arrangement by an annuitant, a holder, or a subscriber of the arrangement is deemed to have been transferred to the trust, and the property subject to the rights and obligations under the arrangement is deemed to be held in trust.

An arrangement will be considered a "qualifying arrangement" if it meets the following conditions:

- it is authorized or licensed by federal or provincial law to carry on services in Canada as a trustee to the public;
- it is established by written contract governed by Quebec law;
- it is presented as a declaration of trust or specifies that it shall be considered a trust for the purposes of the Act; and
- it indicates/demonstrates that the corporation will take steps to make the arrangement a Registered Disability Savings Plan (RDSP), Registered Education Savings Plan (RESP), Registered Retirement Income Fund (RRIF), Registered Retirement Savings Plan (RRSP), or Tax-Free Savings Account (TFSA).[288]

[¶15,335] Interest in Real Property

"Interest in real property" includes a leasehold interest but does not include an interest as security only derived by virtue a mortgage, hypothec, agreement for sale, or similar obligation.[289]

[¶15,340] Proportional Holdings in Trust Property

An election is provided to reduce the inclusion in income or tax arising as a result of the acquisition of (or the holding of) a non-qualified investment by a registered retirement savings plan (RRSP), a deferred profit sharing plan (DPSP), a registered retirement income fund (RRIF), a registered pension plan (RPP), a registered education savings plan (RESP), a registered disability savings plan (RDSP), a tax-free savings account (TFSA),

---

See page ii for explanation of footnotes.

287 CCH ¶28,327; Sec. 248(3)(c).
288 CCH ¶28,327e; Sec. 248(3.2).

289 CCH ¶28,328; Sec. 248(4).

or other registered investments, hereafter called "deferred income plans".[290] Prior to 2005, this election also applied in respect of the holding of foreign property by trusts governed by deferred income plans and certain "qualified corporations".

The election is only available with respect to an interest in the property held by a "qualified trust" that was not a qualified investment for the deferred income plan. Thus, the election is available with respect to an interest in a qualified trust if that trust does not satisfy the tests as to the investments which must be maintained if the trust itself is to be a qualified investment. The election will permit the deferred income plan to acquire or to continue to hold an interest in such a trust which does not constitute a qualifying investment and to have the inclusion in income or tax determined on the basis of its proportionate interest in the properties held by the trust.

In order to qualify for the election, the trust must meet the following requirements:

    (a) it is not a registered investment or a small business investment trust;

    (b) it has as its trustee or trustees only a federally or provincially licensed or authorized trust company;

    (c) under the terms of the trust the interests of beneficiaries are divided into identical units; and

    (d) it has never before that time borrowed money or accepted deposits.[291]

Certain short-term borrowing (for a term of 90 days or less) that is not part of a sequence of loans (comparable to the short term borrowing permitted for "master trusts") is excepted, effective for borrowings after 1990.

The election must be made by the trust in prescribed form and can be effective retroactively for as long as 15 months. The election is effective until revoked by the trust.[292] Within 30 days after making the election, the electing trust must notify affected investors, i.e., those investors who were holding a unit of the electing entity before the election and during which the election is applicable, that the election was made. Furthermore, the electing trust must notify each person who acquires a unit after the election was made, at the time of acquisition. Any of such individuals may request in writing, information about how the election will affect them for tax purposes, and the electing trust must provide the information within 30 days after receipt of the request.[293]

The effect of the election is that the deferred income plan is deemed not to acquire, hold, or dispose of an interest in the trust but rather is

---

See page ii for explanation of footnotes.

[290] CCH ¶28,500; Sec. 259(1).

[291] CCH ¶28,513; Sec. 259(5) "qualified trust".

[292] CCH ¶28,510; Sec. 259(3).

[293] CCH ¶28,511; Sec. 259(4).

¶15,340

deemed to acquire, hold, or dispose of, as the case may be, that portion of each property of the trust that its units in the trust are to all outstanding units. The "portion" of any particular property that the deferred income plan is deemed to acquire, hold, or dispose of, depends on the number of units in the trust acquired, held, or disposed of. Each unit relates to a "specified portion" of the property, depending on how many units in the trust are outstanding. The cost amount to the plan, in respect of each unit held, of any property flowing through from the trust is considered to be the specified portion of the cost amount to the trust of such property. In respect of each unit of the trust acquired or held by the deferred income plan, such plan is deemed to acquire or hold the specified portion of the relevant property of the trust on the later of the date on which the trust acquires the property and the date the deferred income plan acquires the unit in the trust. Likewise the deferred income plan is deemed to dispose of the specified portion of the relevant property at the earlier of the date the trust disposes of the property and the date the deferred income plan disposes of a unit in the trust. Proceeds of disposition are the specified portion of the proceeds realized by the trust, or, if the plan sells a unit in the trust, the specified portion of the fair market value of the property at the time the unit is sold.[294]

Whenever a deferred income plan is deemed to have acquired a specified portion of certain property through the application of an election and subsequently is deemed to have disposed of it, the underlying property shall be deemed to have retained its nature in respect of the deferred income plan. For example, if the property was a non-qualified investment at the time it was deemed to be acquired, the deemed disposition of it shall be considered to be the disposition of non-qualified investment. This permits the deferred income plan to take advantage of certain tax benefits on the disposition of a non-qualified investments.

[¶15,345] Substituted Property

Where one property is disposed of or exchanged and a second property is acquired in substitution for the original property, and that second property is disposed of and a third property is acquired in substitution for the second property, the third property is deemed to have been substituted for the original property.[295]

This deeming rule will apply to a fourth property acquired in substitution for the third property and so on, such that no matter how many substitutions are made, the property owned at any particular time is deemed to have been substituted for the original property.

Similarly, any share received as a stock dividend on another share of a corporation is deemed to be property substituted for such other share.

See page ii for explanation of footnotes.

[294] CCH ¶28,500; Sec. 259(1). [295] CCH ¶28,329; Sec. 248(5).

[¶15,350] Series of Shares

Where a corporation has issued shares in one or more series, a reference to a "class" refers to a "series of the class", with such modifications as the circumstances require.[296] As a matter of corporate law, shares having different attributes may be created as separate classes or as different series of the same class. If a corporation wishes to issue a number of different types of preference shares which will differ in aspects such as the issue price per share and the applicable dividend rate but which will otherwise be identical in terms of their other attributes such as voting rights, their right to share on the dissolution of the corporation, and their ranking as compared to other shares in the capital stock of the corporation, it is very common to have a single class of preference shares created by the articles of incorporation which leave to the directors of the corporation, the right to issue the shares of that class in series; each series having the special attributes determined by the directors.

For income tax purposes, each such series will in effect be treated as a separate class, notwithstanding the fact that it is not a separate class of shares for corporate law purposes. This way, the paid-up capital of each series will be accounted for separately and without regard to amounts paid-up on other series or redemptions made of shares of another series.

[¶15,355] Receipt of Things Mailed

Only items sent by first class mail or its equivalent are deemed received when sent. However, with respect to:

(a) the remittance of amounts deducted or withheld by any person; and

(b) the payment of any amount owing by a corporation,

such remittances and payments are deemed to have been paid when actually received by the Receiver General.[297]

[¶15,360] Occurrences as a Consequence of Death

An expanded definition of "transfers of property as a consequence of the death of a taxpayer" is provided. This expanded definition is relevant for the definition of "testamentary trust" and for the intergenerational rollovers of farm property and shares of a small business corporation, where the transfer was made as a consequence of the death of a taxpayer. It ensures that rollovers will be available where consideration was paid by the beneficiary of an estate in satisfaction of the terms of a testamentary instrument. It also ensures that provisions applicable to transfers or dispositions made as a consequence of death will also apply to those made as a consequence of a disclaimer, release, or surrender by a person who was a beneficiary under

---

See page ii for explanation of footnotes.

[296] CCH ¶28,329ac; Sec. 248(6).   [297] CCH ¶28,329b; Sec. 248(7).

¶15,350

the taxpayer's will or intestacy. These latter types of transfers are considered to be transfers made as a consequence of death.

The release or surrender by the beneficiary will not be considered to be a disposition of the property by the beneficiary. A "release or surrender" must not be made in favour of any particular person or persons, and it must be made within three years of the taxpayer's death or such longer period as the Minister, on written application, considers reasonable.[298]

[¶15,365] Series of Transactions or Events

In any reference to a "series of transactions or events", the series is deemed to include any related transactions or events completed in contemplation of these series.[299] References to a series of transactions or events are common with regard to anti-avoidance provisions where, in general terms, an attempt is made to forbid a taxpayer from achieving through a series of transactions a result which could not be achieved directly. Thus, the anti-avoidance rules purport to prevent the transmutation of capital gain into intercorporate tax-free dividend or of personal dividends into exempt capital gains through a series of transactions or events.

[¶15,370] Compound Interest

Interest paid on refunds and charged on unpaid taxes, interest, and penalties is to be compounded daily. In addition, if under any provision interest would not have been computed past a particular day, interest must be computed and compounded daily on the unpaid interest from that day until the day it is paid. Thus, any compound interest on unpaid interest must be paid or credited as would have been required had the interest continued to be computed in accordance with the provision under which the unpaid amount arose.[300]

[¶15,375] Identical Properties

A bond, debenture, bill, note, or similar debt obligation is identical to another such obligation if the rights attaching to those obligations are the same. The principal amount need not be the same. This rule applies for all purposes of the Act.[301]

[¶15,380] Interests in Trust and Partnerships

A person having a direct or indirect interest in a trust or partnership is deemed to be a beneficiary of the trust or a member of the partnership for the purposes of certain provisions.[302]

See page ii for explanation of footnotes.

[298] CCH ¶28,329c, ¶28,329d; Sec. 248(8), 248(9).   [301] CCH ¶28,329h; Sec. 248(12).
[299] CCH ¶28,329f; Sec. 248(10).
[300] CCH ¶28,329g; Sec. 248(11).   [302] CCH ¶28,329i; Sec. 248(13).

[¶15,385] Related Corporations

For the purposes of the definition of "specified financial institution", corporations not otherwise related to each other will be deemed to be related to each other and to all other corporations to which these particular corporations are related, if the main reason for the separate existence of these corporations can reasonably be interpreted as being to avoid the following situations:

(1) a specified financial institution being prevented from deducting taxable dividends on most term preferred shares in computing taxable income;

(2) the intercorporate dividend deduction being denied for dividends on certain shares that are guaranteed by a specified financial institution; and

(3) the deduction permitted to life insurers in respect of taxable dividends from taxable Canadian corporation not applying to the dividends described in (2).[303]

[¶15,386] Partition of Property

Where a co-owner, having an undivided interest or share in a property, receives, upon the partition of that property, title to a separate divided piece of property whose value equals the value of the co-owner's previous interest, such co-owner has neither disposed of nor acquired any property. However, where the value of the separate piece of property (if any) received upon partition is less than the value of the co-owner's previous undivided interest, the co-owner is deemed to have disposed of the part of his or her interest in the property attributable to such shortfall in value. Where the value of the property received (if any) upon partition is greater than the value of the co-owner's previous interest, he or she is deemed to have acquired an interest in the property attributable to such excess.[304]

Example:

A piece of land worth $100,000 is owned by two tenants-in-common, A and B, each having an equal (50%) undivided interest. Upon partition of the land, A and B each receive half of the land, each half being worth $50,000. Under this provision, neither A nor B have disposed of nor acquired any property, and each person's new interest in his or her half of the land is deemed to be a continuation of his or her previous undivided (half) interest in the whole land.

However, if upon the partition A receives 60% (based on value) of the land and B receives 40% (of the value) of the land, B is deemed to have disposed of, and A is deemed to acquire, a 10% interest in the land (representing the difference in the value of the land which each of A and B receives and that of their interests immediately upon the partition). If A pays B $10,000 because of the unequal partition, B's proceeds of disposition and A's acquisition cost of the 10% interest will be $10,000.

See page ii for explanation of footnotes.

[303] CCH ¶16,345, ¶16,360, ¶20,709, ¶28,329j; Sec. 112(2.1), 112(2.2), 138(6), 248(14).   [304] CCH ¶28,329p, ¶28,329q; Sec. 248(20), 248(21).

¶15,385

[¶15,387] Partition of Property upon Dissolution of Matrimonial Regime

Partition of property usually refers to a situation in which property subject to joint ownership is divided. The dissolution of a matrimonial regime involving joint ownership will trigger such a partition.

Where one spouse or common-law partner brings a property into the matrimonial regime and does not subsequently dispose of it, such spouse or common-law partner is deemed to continue to own the property (regardless of the ownership of the property according to any matrimonial laws). Otherwise, the property is deemed to be owned by the spouse or common-law partner who "had the administration of that property".[305]

Where one spouse or common-law partner obtains property upon the dissolution of the matrimonial regime that was previously owned by the other spouse or common-law partner pursuant to the above deeming rule, that other spouse or common-law partner is deemed to have transferred the property to the first-mentioned spouse or common-law partner immediately before the dissolution of the matrimonial regime.[306]

The above partition rules do not apply to partitions occurring on the death of a spouse/common-law partner.[307] Rather, property which transfers to the estate of the deceased spouse/common-law partner is deemed to transfer immediately before death, so that it transfers under the spousal rollover rules (¶2595). If property transfers to the surviving spouse/common-law partner, there is a deemed transfer at death so the property transfers under normal death rules (¶2560).

[¶15,389] Accounting Methods

For greater certainty, neither the equity nor the consolidated method of accounting is to be used in determining any amount under the Act, unless specifically required.[308] All corporations must compute their income and tax payable and file their returns on a non-consolidated basis.

[¶15,390] References to "Taxation Year" and "Fiscal Period"

In the case of an individual, the taxation year is the calendar year.[309] Similarly, an individual carrying on a business must have a calendar year fiscal period unless he or she chooses to use the non-calendar year "alternative method" to compute business income (see ¶15,392).

In the case of a corporation, the taxation year will be the corporation's fiscal period, which is defined as the period not exceeding 53 weeks for which the accounts of the taxpayer's business have been ordinarily made up and accepted for purposes of income tax assessment.[310] The corporation's

---

See page ii for explanation of footnotes.

[305] CCH ¶28,329r; Sec. 248(22).
[306] CCH ¶28,329s; Sec. 248(23).
[307] CCH ¶28,329sa; Sec. 248(23.1).

[308] CCH ¶28,329u; Sec. 248(24).
[309] CCH ¶28,330; Sec. 249(1).
[310] CCH ¶28,333f; Sec. 249.1(1).

fiscal period may not be changed without the concurrence of the Minister.[311] The provision of a 53-week year for corporations accommodates corporations that want to end their fiscal period on the same weekday each year, typically for inventory reasons. For example, a retailer might end its fiscal period each year on the Saturday following Christmas. This can result in a taxation year in which there is no fiscal period end. To rectify such a situation, the next following period end is deemed to end on the last day of the particular year. For example, where a corporation has a fiscal period commencing on December 29, 2010, and ending on January 3, 2012, its taxation year is deemed to end on December 31, 2011.[312]

In the case of a partnership, its fiscal period must end on December 31, unless an alternative election is made, if any of the following are its members:

(1) an individual (other than a testamentary trust or a tax-exempt individual, which typically is a tax-exempt trust);

(2) a professional corporation (that is, a corporation which carries on the professional practice of an accountant, dentist, lawyer, medical doctor, veterinarian, or chiropractor);

(3) [beginning December 31, 2011, one or more partnerships for which a "multi-tier alignment election" is not made (as discussed at ¶15,393)]; or

(4) any other partnership.[313]

Where the Act refers to the taxation year of a taxpayer by reference to a calendar year, the reference is to the taxation year or years coinciding with or ending in that year. For example, if a corporation has a fiscal period of 12 months ending on April 30 of each year, its 2011 taxation year will be its fiscal period commencing on May 1, 2010 and ending on April 30, 2011.

The taxation year of a corporation is deemed to end immediately before the control of the corporation is acquired. This deemed year end is not of great consequence in itself. However, it is a critical component in numerous anti-avoidance provisions directed at restricting or eliminating the use of losses, deductions, and credits after a change in control has taken place.[314] This deemed year end does not apply to acquisitions of control of a corporation that is a foreign affiliate of a taxpayer resident in Canada where the affiliate has not carried on a business in Canada in the year of acquisition of control.

[¶15,392] Taxation Year of a Business

Generally, sole proprietorships, professional corporations that are partners of a partnership, and partnerships (in which at least one partner of the partnership is an individual, professional corporation, or another affected

---

See page ii for explanation of footnotes.

[311] CCH ¶28,333l; Sec. 249.1(7).　　　　[313] CCH ¶28,333f; Sec. 249.1(1).
[312] CCH ¶28,332h; Sec. 249(3).　　　　[314] CCH ¶28,333a; Sec. 249(4).

partnership) must report their business income from a business carried on in Canada on a calendar-year basis.[315] The government will, however, permit an alternative method of ending the tax deferral implicit in a non-calendar fiscal period. Under this method, the business may continue to have (or a new business may choose) any fiscal period for commercial purposes, but will have to prepay tax on notional income for the remainder of the calendar year.[316]

This alternative method, which allows the business to have a fiscal period that does not end on December 31, applies to individuals and partnerships in which all the partners are individuals. An individual who is a partner of a partnership that includes a professional corporation as a partner cannot use the alternative method. Also, partnerships that are partners of other partnerships cannot use the alternative method. An eligible individual who wants to use the alternative method must file an election with the individual's tax return.

Once made, the election continues until it is revoked. An election to revoke and change the fiscal period end to December 31 of the year in which the revocation is filed can be made at any time. However, once an election to revoke is filed to change the fiscal period end to December 31, an individual cannot change it back.[317]

Where the election is made, a special income inclusion must be made to approximate the stub period income for the fiscal period which commenced in the year but did not end in the year due to the election. The inclusion is based on income for the fiscal period that did end in the year. The inclusion is not required for the taxation year in which an individual dies, ceases to carry on the business, or becomes bankrupt.

The special income inclusion, or "additional business income" (ABI), is income for all fiscal periods of the business which did end in the year (but not including deemed taxable capital gains from disposition of eligible capital property included in income but deducted against it under the capital gains exemption rules) prorated by the number of days that the individual carried on business in the fiscal period that commenced but did not end in the year and the number of days the individual carried on the business in fiscal periods that did end in the year. ABI added to the income of an individual in Year 1 is deducted in Year 2 when a new computation of ABI is required.

Example:

Lisa commenced a business on February 1, 2010. She elected to have a January 31, 2011 year end. The business earned $140,000 in that fiscal period. If Lisa makes no election to include income in 2010, she will have no tax on 2010 business income, but will have to report 2011 income of $140,000 plus $128,110 under the ABI rules above. All the ABI income will be taxed at top marginal rates (subject to some variations by province). Howev-

---

See page ii for explanation of footnotes.

[315] CCH ¶28,333f; Sec. 249.1(1).　　　[317] CCH ¶28,333k; Sec. 249.1(6).
[316] CCH ¶28,333i; Sec. 249.1(4).

er, Lisa may elect to report 2010 income of $140,000 × $^{334}/_{365}$ = $128,110. The income will be reported a year early, but (assuming no other 2010 income) will be taxed at lower rates and with a full set of personal amount credits. In 2011, Lisa will report $140,000 of income plus $128,110 minus $128,110 reported in 2008. After the first year of the business, ABI calculations based on income of the fiscal period ending in the year become mandatory until the business elects to move to a calendar-year basis.

It should be noted that this system assumes that Lisa can make a reasonable guess about the 2011 fiscal period when she files her 2010 return. As a business person, she has until June 15, 2011 to file that return, but only until April 30, 2011 to make an estimated tax payment. The election must be made by the filing-due date for the individual's return for the taxation (calendar) year that includes the first day of the fiscal period (2010 in the above example).

Where an individual commences a new business, it must either have a calendar fiscal period or elect to have a non-calendar year, in which case it must compute additional business income in accordance with the alternative election rules above.

[¶15,393] Fiscal Period for Partnerships with Significant Corporate Members

The tax deferral that was available under a corporate partnership structure that is not aligned with the corporation's taxation year is limited by requiring corporate members with a significant interest to accrue additional partnership income for the portion of the partnership's fiscal period that falls within the corporation's tax year.[318] As a result of these measures some partnerships may wish to change their fiscal periods to align them with the taxation year of their corporate partners. For partnerships in a single-tier structure, a one-time election (a "single-tier alignment election") will enable them to align their fiscal periods if:

- each member of the partnership is, on the particular day, a corporation that is not a professional corporation;

- the partnership is not, on the particular day, a member of another partnership (i.e., it is a single-tier partnership);

- at least one member of the partnership is, on the particular day, a corporation that has a significant interest in the partnership, meaning that the corporation, together with affiliated and related parties, was entitled to more than 10% of the partnership's income (or assets in the case of wind-up) at the end of the last fiscal period of the partnership that ended in the taxation year; and

- at least one member with a significant interest in the partnership has a taxation year end that differs from the day on which the fiscal

---

See page ii for explanation of footnotes.
[318] Sec. 34.2.

period of the partnership would end if there was not a valid single-tier alignment election.[319]

The deadline to file an election to change the fiscal period of the partnership is the first filing due date of any corporate partner for its first tax year ending after March 22, 2011. The election is not valid unless it is filed in the form of a letter signed by an authorized officer of the partnership and filed with the CRA and no other election is filed that attempts to align the fiscal period of a partnership.[320] If more than one election is filed, and there are two or more different days elected for the alignment of the partnership fiscal period, none of the elections are valid.

The single-tier alignment election described above is not available to multi-tier partnerships to the extent they must elect a common fiscal period (a "multi-tier alignment election") that does not need to correspond to the taxation years of their corporate members.[321] As a result of such an election not being filed, the default fiscal period of December 31 will apply (discussed at ¶15,390).

These new rules generally apply to taxation years of a corporation that end after March 22, 2011, where the corporation is a member of a partnership.

[¶15,395] Extended Meaning of "Resident"

For a discussion of the meaning of "residence" for both individuals and corporations,[322] see Chapter I.

[¶15,400] Meaning of "Arm's Length"

Related persons are deemed not to deal at arm's length.[323] This presumption is not rebuttable. It is a question of fact whether or not unrelated persons deal with each other at a particular time at arm's length.

A taxpayer and a personal trust (other than a trust governed by a deferred income plan) are deemed not to deal with each other at arm's length if the taxpayer or any person not dealing at arm's length with the taxpayer, is beneficially interested in the trust. For this purpose, a person is "beneficially interested in a trust" if the person has a right to receive any of the income or capital of the trust either directly from the trust or indirectly through other trusts.[324]

See page ii for explanation of footnotes.

[319] Sec. 249.1(8).

[320] Sec. 249.1(10).

[321] Sec. 249.1(9).

[322] CCH ¶28,334; Sec. 250(1).

[323] CCH ¶28,344; Sec. 251(1); Interp. Bul. IT-419R2.

[324] CCH ¶28,329v; Sec. 248(25).

[¶15,405] Related Persons — Persons Related by Blood Relationship, etc.

Persons are connected by blood relationship if one is the child or other descendant of the other, or if one is the brother or sister of the other.[325] The meaning of the word "child" is extended for purposes of the Act to include an illegitimate child, a daughter-in-law or son-in-law, an adopted child, a stepchild, and any person who is or was immediately before the age of 19, wholly dependent and under the custody and control of the putative parent.[326] "Brother" includes a brother-in-law and "sister" includes a sister-in-law.[327]

Persons are connected by marriage if one is married to the other or to a person who is connected by blood relationship to the other. Persons are connected by common-law partnership if one is in a common-law partnership with the other or with a person who is connected by blood relationship to the other. Persons are considered to be common-law partners if they have been cohabiting in a conjugal relationship for at least 12 continuous months, or are the parents of a child by birth or adoption.[328] In addition, two persons immediately become common-law partners if they previously lived together in a conjugal relationship for at least 12 continuous months and have resumed living together in such a relationship. [Under proposed changes, this condition will no longer exist. The effect of this proposed change is that a person will be the common-law partner of another person only after their current conjugal relationship has lasted at least 12 continuous months. The term "12 continuous months" in this definition includes any period that the partners were separated for less than 90 days because of a breakdown in their relationship. This proposed change, first announced on December 20, 2002 but not enacted on the dissolution of Parliament on September 7, 2008, was re-released in a draft form on July 16, 2010. It will apply to 2001 and later years.]

Persons are connected by adoption if one has been adopted as the child of the other or as the child of a person who is connected to the other by blood relationship, otherwise than as a brother or sister. This is the case if the adoption was carried out legally or if it was not carried out legally but had taken place in fact. The result is that an adopted child is connected by adoption to the same persons as those to whom he would be connected if he were a natural child. However, it is not clear whether two adopted children sharing a common parent would be related to each other. The Act is ambiguous on this point and the matter would appear to await judicial interpretation.

A "parent" includes a person whose child is among those specified above, or who had previously supported a person wholly dependent upon

---

See page ii for explanation of footnotes.

[325] CCH ¶28,356; Sec. 251(6).

[326] CCH ¶28,372; Sec. 252(1).

[327] CCH ¶28,374; Sec. 252(2).

[328] CCH ¶28,047a; Sec. 248(1) "common-law partner".

him or her for support and who had the control and custody of that person or who had such control and custody immediately before that person attained the age of 19 years. It also includes a mother-in-law and father-in-law.

The expressions "grandparent", "brother", and "sister" include grandmother-in-law and grandfather-in-law, brother-in-law, and sister-in-law, respectively.[329]

A reference to a "spouse" and "former spouse" of a particular individual is deemed to include another individual who is party to a voidable or void marriage with the particular individual.[330]

[¶15,410] Related Persons — Individuals Related to Corporations

An individual and a corporation are related if:

(1) the individual controls the corporation;

(2) the individual is a member of a related group that controls it; or

(3) the individual is related to an individual described in (1) or (2).

For example, if an individual is related to Corporation A, which is related to Corporation B by virtue of (1) or (2), the individual will be related to Corporation B.[331]

[¶15,415] Related Persons — Corporations Related to Each Other

Two corporations are related to each other[332] if:

(1) one is controlled by the other ;

(2) one corporation is a member of a related group that controls the other;

(3) one corporation is related to a corporation described in (1) or (2) above and is related to an individual described in ¶15,410 above;

(4) one of the corporations is related to a second corporation, which in turn is related to a third corporation under (1) or (2) above; in this case, the first corporation will be related to the third;

(5) both corporations are controlled by the same persons or group of persons;

(6) the corporations are each controlled by one person, and these two persons are related;

See page ii for explanation of footnotes.

[329] CCH ¶28,346, ¶28,356, ¶28,374; Sec. 251(2), 251(6), 252(2).

[330] CCH ¶28,377; Sec. 252(3).

[331] CCH ¶28,346; Sec. 251(2).

[332] CCH ¶28,346, ¶28,348, ¶28,349, ¶28,349a; Sec. 251(2), 251(3), 251(3.1), 251(3.2).

(7) one corporation is controlled by one person and the other corporation is controlled by a related group, and the person is related to any member of the related group;

(8) one corporation is controlled by one person and the other corporation is controlled by an unrelated group, and the person is related to every member of the unrelated group;

(9) one corporation is controlled by a related group and the other corporation is controlled by an unrelated group, and any member of the related group is related to each member of the unrelated group;

(10) both corporations are controlled by unrelated groups, and each member of one unrelated group is related to at least one member of the other unrelated group;

(11) both corporations are related to a third corporation under the rules described in (1) to (10) above;

(12) one corporation is a new corporation formed by an amalgamation or merger and the other corporation is one of its predecessor corporations immediately before the amalgamation or merger, if the shareholders of the new corporation are such that, if the new corporation had been in existence before the amalgamation or merger (and had those same shareholders), the new corporation would have been related to that predecessor corporation under the rules described in (1) to (11) above; or

(13) one corporation is a new corporation formed as a result of the amalgamation or merger of two or more corporations each of which was related to each other immediately before the amalgamation or merger.

[¶15,420] Control by Related Group

A "related group" is defined as a group of persons each member of which is related to every other member of the group.[333]

For the purposes of related persons and arm's length transactions,[334] and for the purposes of the meaning of "Canadian-controlled private corporation" with respect to the small business deduction,[335] a related group is deemed to control a corporation if it is in fact able to control it, although it is part of a larger group by which the corporation is controlled.

If, at any time, a person has a right to acquire shares in a corporation, to control votes, to cause a corporation to redeem, acquire, or cancel any shares owned by other shareholders under a contract in equity or otherwise, either contingently or absolutely, and either presently or in the future, the person having such a right is deemed to have the same position in relation

---

See page ii for explanation of footnotes.

[333] CCH ¶28,350, ¶28,352, ¶28,354; Sec. 251(4) "related group", 251(4) "unrelated group", 251(5).

[334] CCH ¶28,346; Sec. 251(2).

[335] CCH ¶19,559a; Sec. 125(7) "Canadian-controlled private corporation".

to the control of the corporation as if he or she owned the shares, or as if the shares were redeemed, acquired, or cancelled by the corporation, unless the right was not exercisable at that time until the death, bankruptcy, or permanent disability of an individual.[336]

After April 26, 1995, two rights were added to those listed above:

(1) A person who has, at any time, a right to (or to acquire or control) voting rights in respect of a corporation's shares will be considered to be able to exercise those voting rights at that time.

(2) A person who has, at any time, a right to cause the reduction of other shareholders' voting rights will be treated as though those voting rights were so reduced at that time.

A person owning shares in two or more corporations is deemed to be related to himself or herself as a shareholder of each of the corporations.[337]

[¶15,423] Union Employer

A union and its locals and branches are considered to be a single employer for the following purposes:

(1) computing, reporting, and applying pension adjustments (PAs) and past service pension adjustments (PSAs). It will ensure, for example, that an individual who is employed by both a national union organization and a local of the union is not, as a result, entitled to pension benefits under a registered pension plan in excess of those permitted to an individual with a single employer;

(2) determining whether a pension plan is a multi-employer plan (MEP) or a specified multi-employer plan (SMEP). It will ensure that a plan is not considered to have more than one participating employer simply because a union and its various locals participate in the plan;

(3) determining which contributions made to a foreign pension plan are subject to the retirement compensation arrangement (RCA) tax; and

(4) withholding RCA tax from contributions to an RCA or remitting tax that was withheld.[338]

[¶15,425] Extended Meaning of "Carrying on Business" — Non-Residents

A non-resident person who produces, grows, mines, creates, manufactures, fabricates, improves, packs, preserves, or constructs, in whole or part, anything in Canada, whether or not for export, is deemed to have been carrying on business in Canada in the year.

See page ii for explanation of footnotes.

[336] CCH ¶28,354; Sec. 251(5).
[337] CCH ¶28,386a; Sec. 256(1.5).

[338] CCH ¶28,377b; Sec. 252.1.

Similarly, a person who solicits orders or offers anything for sale in Canada through an agent or servant, whether or not the contract is to be performed wholly or partly inside or outside of Canada, is deemed to have been carrying on business in Canada.

Examples:

(1) A sale of goods by a non-resident to a Canadian is not carrying on business in Canada if there is no agent or employee in Canada.

(2) The mere purchase of goods in Canada is not carrying on business in Canada unless further work is done in Canada on the goods.

(3) The sale of machinery in Canada and the giving of subsequent advice and installation or the supervision by employees in Canada is not, in itself, carrying on business in Canada.

A person will be deemed to be carrying on a business in Canada where that person disposes of a Canadian resource property (except where an amount in respect of it has been included), a timber resource property or an interest in it, or any non-capital real property situated in Canada. For example, a non-resident who sells Canadian real estate which is non-capital property is deemed to be carrying on business in Canada for the year.[339]

[¶15,427] Investments in Limited Partnerships

In light of the Federal Court of Appeal decision in *Robinson*, a unit trust holding limited partnership units could be considered to be carrying on the business of the limited partnership.[340] Such a conclusion would mean the unit trust was involved in an undertaking other than investing its funds and, therefore, would cease to qualify for the tax treatment afforded a unit trust under the Act. There are similar restrictions in the Act for mutual funds, mortgage investment corporations, and private holding corporations.

To respond to the above decision, a new interpretative provision was introduced to clarify that ownership of an interest in a limited partnership does not cause certain specialized investment vehicles to violate a common restriction that requires the only undertaking of such vehicles to be the investing of their funds.[341] This amendment ensures that these specialized investment vehicles may invest in limited partnerships without jeopardizing their tax status.

[¶15,430] Contract under Pension Plan

Where a document has been issued or a contract entered into before July 31, 1997, purporting to create, establish, extinguish, or be in substitution for a taxpayer's right to an amount under a superannuation or pension fund or plan, the amount deemed paid out of the fund or plan for tax purposes is computed as follows.

See page ii for explanation of footnotes.

[339] CCH ¶28,378; Sec. 253.
[340] Robinson (Trustee of), 98 DTC 6065.
[341] CCH ¶28,379a; Sec. 253.1.

¶15,427

If the rights provided for in the document or contract are rights provided for by the superannuation or pension plan, or are rights to a payment out of the superannuation or pension fund, and the taxpayer acquired an interest under the document or in the contract before July 31, 1997, any payment under the document or contract is deemed to be a payment out of or under the fund or plan which must be included in the recipient's income when it is received. In these circumstances, no amount is included in the taxpayer's income by reason of the issuance of the document or the entering into the contract. However, if the rights created or established by the document or contract are not rights provided for by the pension fund, an amount equal to the value of the rights created or established by the document or contract is deemed to have been received by the taxpayer out of the fund or plan when the document was issued or the contract entered into.[342]

[¶15,435] Meaning of "Canada"

The term "Canada" includes the seabed and subsoil of the submarine areas adjacent to the coasts of Canada in respect of which grants are issued by the federal or provincial governments of a right, licence, or privilege to explore for, drill, or take any minerals, petroleum, natural gas, or related hydrocarbons, and the seas and airspace above such submarine areas.[343]

[¶15,440] Negative Amounts

Unless otherwise provided, where an amount or a number is to be determined or calculated by or in accordance with an algebraic formula, any resulting negative amount is deemed to be nil.[344] It is not clear whether this rule applies to the older formulae which are expressed in words rather than symbols.

In a case decided before this provision became applicable, the phrase "threshold amount ... minus expenses" in a regulation providing drilling incentives was found to be used in its mathematical sense rather than its ordinary and grammatical sense and, therefore, could result in a negative amount.[345] On the other hand, it was held that "taxable income", as defined, could not be negative, since the word "minus" in the definition was used in its ordinary and grammatical sense and, therefore, a forward averaging calculation could not be made on the assumption that taxable income was negative.[346]

See page ii for explanation of footnotes.

[342] CCH ¶28,380; Sec. 254.

[343] CCH ¶28,382; Sec. 255.

[344] CCH ¶28,424; Sec. 257.

[345] Canterra Energy Limited, 87 DTC 5019.

[346] Capling Estate, 87 DTC 344.

[¶15,445] Affiliated Persons

[¶15,450] General Rules

Effective on and after April 27, 1995, rules were introduced to supplement the concept of non-arm's length transactions (¶15,400 *et seq.*). These affiliated-person rules replace older rules governing dispositions to controlling corporations, majority interest partners, and similar transactions, but they encompass a broader and different range of transactions. They deal with the losses inherent in affiliated-party transfers of depreciable property,[347] capital property,[348] and eligible capital property[349] ("stop loss rules").

A "person" under these rules includes not only an individual and a corporation, as is commonly the case, but a partnership as well.[350] Persons are automatically affiliated with themselves.

"Controlled directly or indirectly in any manner whatever" means *de facto* control.[351] According to this test, a person controls a corporation not only if it holds a majority of shares, but if it has any direct or indirect influence, that, if exercised, would result in control in fact of the corporation.

An "affiliated group" means a group of persons each member of which is affiliated with every other member.[352]

Retroactive to April 26, 1995, merged corporations continue their prior affiliations as those affiliations would have been if the new corporation had previously existed with the new corporation shareholders.[353]

[¶15,455] Individuals and Corporations

An individual is affiliated with itself and with a spouse/common-law partner.[354]

A corporation is affiliated with:

(a) a person by whom the corporation is controlled;

(b) each member of an affiliated group by which the corporation is controlled; and

(c) a spouse/common-law partner of a person described in (a) or (b).[355]

Example:

F, an individual, controls one corporation ("F Ltd.") alone, and controls a second corporation ("FG Ltd.") as a member of a group that consists of F and G, another individual. F is a spouse of a third individual, M, but not of G.

See page ii for explanation of footnotes.

[347] CCH ¶4579c; Sec. 13(21.2).
[348] CCH ¶6459a, ¶6459c; Sec. 40(3.4), 40(3.6).
[349] CCH ¶4647e; Sec. 14(12).
[350] CCH ¶28,371f; Sec. 251.1(4).
[351] CCH ¶28,371d; Sec. 251.1(3) "controlled".

[352] CCH ¶28,371c; Sec. 251.1(3) "affiliated group of persons".
[353] CCH ¶28,371b; Sec. 251.1(2).
[354] CCH ¶28,371a; Sec. 251.1(1)(a).
[355] CCH ¶28,371a; Sec. 251.1(1)(b).

¶15,445

F and M are affiliated persons. F Ltd. is affiliated with F and with M. Since F and G are not affiliated with one another (and are thus not an affiliated group), FG Ltd. is not affiliated with either F or G.

[¶15,460] Two Corporations

In addition to being affiliated by virtue of the rules above, which would be the case where one corporation controls another, two corporations are affiliated if:

(a) each corporation is controlled by a person, and the person by whom one is controlled is affiliated with the person by whom the other is controlled;

(b) one corporation is controlled by a person, the other is controlled by a group of persons, and each member of that group is affiliated with that person; and

(c) each corporation is controlled by a group of persons, and each member of each group is affiliated with at least one member of the other group.[356]

Example:

A Ltd., B Ltd., C Ltd., and D Ltd. are corporations. A Ltd. is controlled by K, an individual. B Ltd. is controlled by Q, K's spouse. C Ltd. is controlled by a group made up of K and Q, and D Ltd. is controlled by a group made up of B Ltd. and C Ltd.

Since K and Q are affiliated, A Ltd. and B Ltd. are affiliated. A Ltd. and C Ltd. are affiliated, as are B Ltd. and C Ltd.. D Ltd. is affiliated with B Ltd. and C Ltd., the members of an affiliated group that controls D Ltd.. Are A Ltd. and D Ltd. affiliated? B Ltd. and C Ltd. are each affiliated with K, because K and Q form the affiliated group that controls both companies. Therefore, A Ltd. and D Ltd. are affiliated.

[¶15,465] Partnerships

Essential to the affiliated-person rules for partnerships is the concept of a majority-interest partner. A majority-interest partner of a particular partnership is defined to be a person or partnership ("the taxpayer"):

(a) whose share of the particular partnership's income from all sources for the last fiscal period of the particular partnership that ended before that time (or, if the particular partnership's fiscal period includes that time, for that period), would have exceeded $1/2$ of the particular partnership's income from all sources for that period if the taxpayer had held throughout that period each interest in the partnership that the taxpayer or a person affiliated with the taxpayer held at that time, or

(b) whose share, if any, together with the shares of every person with whom the taxpayer is affiliated, of the total amount that would be paid to all members of the particular partnership (otherwise than as

See page ii for explanation of footnotes.

[356] CCH ¶28,371a; Sec. 251.1(1)(c).

a share of any income of the partnership) if it were wound up at that time, exceeds $1/2$ of that amount.[357]

In addition to the concept of a majority-interest partner, the affiliated-person rules provide a definition of a "majority-interest group of partners". A majority-interest group of partners of a partnership means a group of persons each of whom has an interest in the partnership such that:

(a) if one person held the interests of all members of the group, that person would be a majority-interest partner, and

(b) if any member of the group were not a member, the test described in (a) would not be met.[358]

Example:

Five partners each holds a 20% interest in a partnership. In this case, any group of three partners is a majority-interest group of partners of the partnership. A group of fewer than three will not represent interests that would, if they were held by one person, make that person a majority-interest partner, and thus will not meet criterion (a). A group of more than three will not meet criterion (b) since even if one member's interest were ignored, the interest of the remaining group members would, if held by one person, make that person a majority-interest partner.

[¶15,470] A Corporation and a Partnership

A corporation and a partnership are affiliated if the corporation is controlled by a particular group of persons, each member of which is affiliated with at least one member of a majority-interest group of partners of the partnership, and each member of that majority-interest group is affiliated with at least one member of the particular group.[359]

[¶15,475] A Partnership and a Majority-Interest Partner

A partnership and a majority-interest partner are affiliated persons.[360] In determining whether a person is a majority-interest partner of a partnership, the definition of "majority-interest partner" (see ¶15,465) looks not only to that person's interest, if any, in the partnership, but also to the interest of all persons affiliated with that person. In effect, then, any person affiliated with a person who holds a majority-interest in a partnership is also a majority-interest partner, and thus is affiliated with the partnership.

[¶15,480] Two Partnerships

Two partnerships are affiliated if:

(a) the same person is a majority-interest partner of both partnerships;

See page ii for explanation of footnotes.

[357] CCH ¶28,160a; Sec. 248(1) "majority interest partner".
[358] CCH ¶28,371e; Sec. 251.1(3) "majority-interest group of partners".
[359] CCH ¶28,371a; Sec. 251.1(1)(*d*).
[360] CCH ¶28,371a; Sec. 251.1(1)(*e*).

(b) a majority-interest partner of one partnership is affiliated with each member of a majority-interest group of partners of the other partnership; or

(c) each member of a majority-interest group of partners of each partnership is affiliated with at least one member of a majority-interest group of partners of the other partnership.[361]

The possibility that a partnership may have more than one majority-interest group of partners means that the interest of all partners and of all persons affiliated with a partner must be carefully considered in order to establish whether two partnerships or a partnership and a corporation are affiliated.

[¶15,482] A Trust and a Majority Interest Beneficiary

A person is affiliated with a trust after March 22, 2004 if the person is, or is affiliated with, a "majority-interest beneficiary".[362] A majority interest beneficiary is defined as a person whose beneficial interest in the income or capital of the trust, together with the beneficial interests of other affiliated persons, is greater than half of the fair market value of all beneficial interests in the income or capital of the trust at that time.[363] In its explanatory notes of the Budget proposals, the Department of Finance gives the following two examples:

Example 1:

Situation: Philip has no interest as a beneficiary in either the income or capital of Trust A, but his wife, Muriel, with whom he is affiliated, has an interest in the income of Trust A, the fair market value of which is more than half of the fair market value of all the interests as a beneficiary in the income of Trust A.

Result: Philip, as well as Muriel, is a majority interest beneficiary of Trust A because he is affiliated with a person who has an interest in the income of Trust A, the fair market value of which is more than half of the fair market value of all the interests as a beneficiary in the income of Trust A.

Example 2:

Situation: Jacqueline is one of ten persons, each of whom would receive as a beneficiary up to 100% of either the income or capital of Trust B, if a discretionary power were fully exercised in their favour.

Result: Jacqueline, along with the other nine persons, is a majority interest beneficiary of Trust B, since the fair market value of Jacqueline's interest, as well as the interest of each of the other nine persons, as a beneficiary in either the income or the capital of the trust, would be deemed to be 100% of the fair market value of all the interests in the income or capital, as the case may be, in Trust B.

In the case of a discretionary trust, these rules apply as between a person and a trust as if any discretion of any person in respect of the trust

---

See page ii for explanation of footnotes.

[361] CCH ¶28,371a; Sec. 251.1(1)(f).

[362] CCH ¶28,371a; Sec. 251.1(1)(g).

[363] CCH ¶28,371da; Sec. 251.1(3) "majority-interest beneficiary".

had been exercised (or not exercised, as the case may be) in determining the rights of the person.

[¶15,483] Two Trusts

Two trusts are affiliated with each other after March 22, 2004 if a "contributor" to one trust is affiliated with a "contributor" to the other trust and:

(a) a majority interest beneficiary of one of the trusts is (or is affiliated with) a majority interest beneficiary of the other trust;

(b) a majority interest beneficiary of one of the trusts is affiliated with each member of a majority interest group of beneficiaries of the other trust; or

(c) each member of a majority interest group of beneficiaries of each trust is affiliated with at least one member of a majority interest group of beneficiaries of the other trust.[364]

A "contributor" is a person who has made a loan or a transfer of property, whether directly or indirectly in any manner whatsoever, for the benefit of the trust.[365] However, a person who has contributed property or transferred funds to the trust on an arm's length basis, or for adequate consideration, will not be a contributor to the trust, if, immediately after the transfer, the person is not a majority interest beneficiary of the trust.

A group of persons is a "majority interest group of beneficiaries" of a trust at any time if two conditions are met:

(i) each member of the group is a beneficiary under the trust at that time, such that if one member held all the interests as a beneficiary of the members of the group that person would be a majority interest beneficiary of the trust; and

(ii) if any member of the group were not a member of the group, the requirement in (i) would not be met.[366]

In its Explanatory Notes of the Budget proposals, the Department of Finance gives the following example:

Example:

Situation: Any of Gail, Richard, and Debra would receive as a beneficiary up to 100% of the income and capital of Trust C if a discretionary power were fully exercised in their favour.

Result: Gail, Richard, and Debra would not constitute a majority interest group of beneficiaries, given that each would be a majority interest beneficiary of Trust C, and thus in no case could the second condition of the "majority interest group of beneficiaries" definition be met.

See page ii for explanation of footnotes.

[364] CCH ¶28,371a; Sec. 251.1(1)(h).
[365] CCH ¶28,371cc; Sec. 251.1(3) "contributor".
[366] CCH ¶28,371dc; Sec. 251.1(3) "majority-interest group of beneficiaries".

¶15,483

In the case of a discretionary trust, a person's beneficial interest in a trust will be disregarded in determining whether such a person deals at arm's length with the trust if, in the absence of such interest, the person would be considered to be at arm's length with the trust.

[¶15,485] Associated Corporations

[¶15,490] Corporations Associated with Each Other

Corporations are associated with one another in a taxation year if any of the following circumstances exist at any time in that year:[367]

(1) one of the corporations controls the other;

(2) both corporations are controlled by the same person, which may be an individual, an estate, or a corporation;

(3) both corporations are controlled by the same group of people;

(4) each corporation is controlled by one person and the person controlling one of the corporations is related to the person controlling the other, provided one of the related controlling persons owns at least 25% of the issued shares of any class, other than a "specified class", of the capital stock of each corporation;

Example:

> If A controls Company X and her brother B controls Company Y and owns at least 25% of a class (not a specified class) of the issued shares of Company X, Company X and Company Y will be associated. However, if A owns less than 25% of any class of the issued shares of Company X, the two companies will not be associated under this rule.

(5) one corporation is controlled by one person who is related to each member of a group of persons which controls the other corporation, provided that the person owns not less than 25% of the issued shares of any class of the capital stock of the other corporation (other than shares of a specified class);

Example:

> If Company X is controlled by A, and Company Y is controlled by a combination of A's spouse (B), A's father (C), and Company D (which is controlled by B), Company X and Company Y will be associated, provided not less than 25% of the issued shares of any class of Company Y (other than shares of a specified class) are owned by A. If A does not own 25% of the issued shares of Company Y, the two companies will not be associated under this rule.

(6) each of the corporations is controlled by a related group and each of the members of one related group is related to all the members of the other, provided one or more persons who are members of both related groups

---

See page ii for explanation of footnotes.

[367] CCH ¶28,384; Sec. 256(1).

own, in total, not less than 25% of the issued shares of any class of the capital stock of each corporation (other than shares of a specified class);

Example:

> If A, A's spouse (B), and Company C (which is controlled by A), together control Company X, and the children of A and B (D, E, and F) together control Company Y, then Company X and Company Y will be associated, provided one or more of the members of the above-mentioned related groups owns at least 25% of any class of the issued shares of each corporation (other than shares of a specified class).

(7) both corporations are associated with the same Canadian-controlled private corporation under any of the above rules (unless a special election is made).[368]

Example

> If Company X is associated with Company Z under one rule, and Company Y is associated with Company Z under another rule, Company X and Company Y will be associated, provided Company Z is a Canadian-controlled private corporation. Even if Company Z is a Canadian-controlled private corporation, it can make a special election not to be associated with either of the other two corporations, in which case its business limit will be deemed to be nil.

[¶15,495] Meaning of "Specified Class"

Shares of a specified class are excluded from the cross-ownership calculations. A class of shares will be a specified class if the articles of incorporation or any agreement in respect of the shares contain the following provisions:

(1) the shares are neither convertible nor exchangeable;

(2) the shares are non-voting;

(3) dividends payable on the shares are a fixed amount or are calculated as a fixed percentage of an amount equal to the fair market value of the consideration for which the shares were issued;

(4) the annual dividend rate, calculated as a fixed percentage of the fair market value of the consideration for which the shares were issued, does not exceed the prescribed rate; and

(5) the amount that a holder of the shares is entitled to receive on their redemption, cancellation, or acquisition by the corporation or a non-arm's length person does not exceed the fair market value of the consideration for which the shares were issued plus any unpaid dividends.[369]

See page ii for explanation of footnotes.

[368] CCH ¶28,387; Sec. 256(2). [369] CCH ¶28,384a; Sec. 256(1.1).

¶15,495

[¶15,500] Control of a Corporation

There are special rules for the purposes of determining whether a corporation will be considered to be controlled for purposes of the associated-corporation rules,[370] as follows:

(1) In determining whether a corporation is controlled by a group of persons, "a group", in respect of that corporation, means any two or more persons, each of whom owns shares of the capital stock of the corporation.

(2) A corporation can be considered to be controlled by a person or particular group of persons, notwithstanding that the corporation is also controlled by another person or group of persons (i.e., a corporation can be controlled at the same time by several persons or groups of persons).

(3) A corporation will be deemed to be controlled by a person or a group of persons at any time where shares of the corporation having a fair market value of more than 50% of the fair market value of all the issued and outstanding shares, or common shares having a fair market value of more than 50% of the fair market value of all the issued and outstanding common shares are owned at that time by the person or group of persons (as the case may be).

(4) A shareholder of a corporation that holds shares of another corporation is treated as owning such of those shares as is proportionate to the value of the shareholder's holdings in the holding corporation.

(5) A member of a partnership that holds shares of a corporation is treated as owning such of those shares as is proportionate to the member's income interest in the partnership. Where both the income and loss of the partnership in a fiscal period are nil, so that a member's income interest is not determinable, this proportion is to be determined as if the partnership had income of $1,000,000 in that period.

(6) Generally, shares of a corporation held by a trust are treated as being owned by its beneficiaries. In the case of a testamentary trust, under which some of the beneficiaries are entitled to all of the income of the trust prior to the death of one or all of them and no other person is entitled to any capital of the trust before that time, the shares are deemed to be owned by such beneficiaries before that time. In the case of a discretionary trust, all discretionary beneficiaries are deemed to own the shares. In any other case, each beneficiary is deemed to own a proportion of the shares based on the fair market value of the beneficiary's interest in the trust. Further, where a trust is one referred to in a certain provision of the Act,[371] such as a "reversionary trust", the person from whom the trust property was received is also deemed to own the shares. The result of the application of these provisions may be that more than one person can be deemed to own the

---

See page ii for explanation of footnotes.

[370] CCH ¶28,385; Sec. 256(1.2).   [371] CCH ¶9570; Sec. 75(2).

same shares at the same time. In addition, the shares will also be held by the trustees of the trust.

(7) In determining the fair market value of a share of the capital stock of a corporation, all issued and outstanding shares of the capital stock of a corporation shall be deemed to be non-voting.

[¶15,505] Parent Deemed to Own Shares

Shares of a corporation owned by a minor child are deemed to be owned by each parent of the child. However, this attribution rule will not apply if it may reasonably be considered that the child manages the business and affairs of the corporation and does so without a significant degree of influence by the parent. Young entrepreneurs, for instance, would be accommodated by this exception.[372]

[¶15,510] Options and Rights

With respect to rights to acquire shares (e.g., options) or rights to cause a corporation to redeem shares of other shareholders, the holder of such rights is deemed to be in the same position as if the rights were exercised.[373]

[¶15,515] Person Related to Himself or Herself

A person is deemed to be related to himself or herself in his or her capacity as shareholder of two or more corporations.[374]

[¶15,520] Fair Market Value

Shares which are "financial difficulty shares" and shares of a "specified class" are to be disregarded for purposes of making the fair market valuations. An amount equal to the greater of the paid-up capital of such shares and their redemption value will be treated as a liability of the corporation.[375]

[¶15,525] Anti-Avoidance

Two or more corporations will be deemed to be associated if it may reasonably be considered that one of the main reasons for their separate existence is to reduce the taxes which would otherwise be payable or to increase the refundable investment tax credit.[376] Where a pattern existed in incorporating a new company as soon as the existing company or companies came close to the low-rate basis for taxation purposes and other evidence pointed in the same direction, the companies were deemed to be associated; the main reason for the separate existence of each company was obviously to reduce the amount of tax payable.[377]

See page ii for explanation of footnotes.

[372] CCH ¶28,385a; Sec. 256(1.3).

[373] CCH ¶28,386; Sec. 256(1.4).

[374] CCH ¶28,386a; Sec. 256(1.5).

[375] CCH ¶28,386b; Sec. 256(1.6).

[376] CCH ¶28,387a; Sec. 256(2.1).

[377] Express Cable Television Ltd., 82 DTC 1431, Alpha Forming Corp. Ltd. et al, 83 DTC 5021.

¶15,505

The same general principle would seem to be applicable in connection with the small business deduction. Where tax reduction is one of the main reasons for separate existence, companies may be deemed to be associated, but where it is not, they are not deemed to be associated.[378]

[¶15,530] Corporations Deemed Not To Be Associated or Controlled

Two corporations which would normally be considered associated will be deemed not to be associated in certain cases.[379] These exceptions to associated corporation rules may be applicable to two corporations only where one controls the other or where both are controlled by the same person. In these circumstances, the two corporations in question will be deemed not to be associated if the following conditions are established to the satisfaction of the Minister:

(1) if, at the time of such control, an enforceable agreement or arrangement is in effect under which it is reasonable to expect that a condition or event will take place upon which the controlled corporation will cease to be controlled by the controller and will become controlled by a person or group of persons all of whom deal with the controller at arm's length; and

(2) if the sole purpose of the control was the safeguarding of the rights or interests of the controller in respect of an outstanding indebtedness by the controller or in respect of the redemption by the controlled corporation or the purchase by the persons referred to in (1) above of shares of the controlled corporation owned by the controller.[380]

Example:

(1) If a lender has taken title to the controlling shares of a corporation as security for a loan, the corporation whose shares are so held would probably be deemed not to be associated with the lender or with any other corporation controlled by the lender.

(2) If the controlling shares of a corporation have been sold by one person in an arm's length transaction under an agreement for sale and the vendor has retained title to the shares as security for payment of the purchase price, the corporation whose shares have been sold would probably cease to be associated with the vendor or with any other corporation controlled by the vendor.

(3) If a person controls a corporation through holding preference shares with voting rights but has entered into an agreement with the corporation for the redemption of those preference shares upon which redemption control would be lost, the controlled corporation would probably not be associated with the person holding the preference shares (if it is a corporation) or any other corporation controlled by it or the preference shares holder.

[¶15,535] Corporations Deemed Not To Be Associated — Control by Trustee or Executor

If two or more corporations are controlled by the same trustee or Executor, they may be associated corporations. In addition, the trustee or

---

[378] Veltri and Son Ltd. et al., 91 DTC 862.   [380] CCH ¶28,394; Sec. 256(6).
[379] CCH ¶28,388; Sec. 256(3).

executor, if it is a corporation, will be associated with each of the corporations. However, if it is established to the satisfaction of the Minister that:

(a) the trustee or executor did not acquire control of the corporations as a result of the creation of one or more trusts or estates by an individual or by individuals not dealing with each other at arm's length; and

(b) the control of the corporations was acquired only on the death of the individual creating the trust or estate,

then the two corporations are deemed not to be associated with each other.[381]

A trust company will ordinarily control a number of corporations in connection with various trusts or estates which it is administering. The purpose of this deeming provision is to prevent these corporations from being associated under the circumstances provided for therein.

Corporations which would otherwise be associated because one is controlled by the other as a trustee under a trust are deemed not to be associated at any time in the year, unless a settlor of the trust controls or is a member of a related group that controls the corporation that is the trustee.[382]

[¶15,540] Control in Fact

As a first approximation to the interpretation of the concept of "control", the common-law definition of legal, or *de jure*, control can be applied. "Legal control" means ownership of more than 50% of the voting shares. However, the concept of control is extended for certain purposes from the *de jure* meaning to control *de facto*, i.e., control in fact. For the purposes of the Act, a corporation will be considered to be "controlled", directly or indirectly in any manner whatsoever, by another corporation, person, or group of persons (the "controller") where the controller has any direct or indirect influence that, if exercised, would result in *control in fact* of the corporation. The control-in-fact test will not apply in arm's length situations where the controller's influence derives only from an agreement, the main purpose of which is to govern the relationship between the controller and the corporation regarding the manner in which a business carried on by the corporation is conducted. This exemption will apply where the influence is derived from a franchise, licence, lease, distribution, supply, management, or similar agreement.[383]

An example of *control in fact* would be where a person held 49% of the voting control of a corporation and the balance was widely dispersed among many employees of the corporation or held by persons who could

[381] CCH ¶28,390; Sec. 256(4).   [383] CCH ¶28,393; Sec. 256(5.1).
[382] CCH ¶28,392; Sec. 256(5).

reasonably be considered to act in respect of the corporation in accordance with that person's wishes. Whether a person can be said to be in actual control of a corporation, notwithstanding that person does not legally control more than 50% of its voting shares, will depend in each case on all of the circumstances.

[¶15,545] Control Deemed Not To Have Been Acquired

A change of control is deemed either to have taken place, or not to have taken place, when certain share acquisitions are made and upon certain amalgamations and share-for-share exchanges.[384] These deeming provisions apply for the purposes of the following:

(1) the provision requiring that at the end of a corporation's last taxation year before a change of control, property described in an inventory of a business that is an adventure or concern in the nature of trade, be valued at the lower of its original cost and its fair market value at the end of that year;[385]

(2) the loss-deferral rule on the transfer, by a corporation, trust, or partnership, of a depreciable property whose tax cost is greater than the amount that would otherwise be the transferor's proceeds from the transfer;[386]

(3) the provision which deems depreciable property acquired by a corporation in the 12-month period preceding an acquisition of control that was not used in a business carried on by that corporation before that period not to have been acquired until after the acquisition of control;[387]

(4) the loss-deferral rule on the transfer, by a corporation, trust, or partnership, of eligible capital property;[388]

(5) the provision deferring certain losses incurred by money lenders and adventurers in trade;[389]

(6) the terminal deduction for a matchable expenditure in respect of a disposed of or expired right to receive production before the acquisition of control of a corporation;[390]

(7) the provision imposing limitations on the deduction of expenditures on scientific research and experimental development made before an acquisition of control;[391]

(8) the loss-deferral rule on the transfer by a corporation, trust, or partnership of non-depreciable capital property;[392]

See page ii for explanation of footnotes.

[384] CCH ¶28,412; Sec. 256(7).
[385] CCH ¶4183; Sec. 10(10).
[386] CCH ¶4579c; Sec. 13(21.2).
[387] CCH ¶4582; Sec. 13(24).
[388] CCH ¶4647e; Sec. 14(12).

[389] CCH ¶4879b; Sec. 18(15).
[390] CCH ¶4879q; Sec. 18.1(10).
[391] CCH ¶ 5900–5989; Sec. 37.
[392] CCH ¶6459a; Sec. 40(3.4).

(9) the definition of "superficial loss" as it applies to the transfer of property by a person affiliated with the transferee;[393]

(10) the provisions which limit the deduction of certain resource-related exploration and development expenses if control of a corporation has been acquired;[394]

(11) the application of the debt forgiveness rules to losses incurred by a debtor corporation prior to the acquisition of control;[395]

(12) the conditions that must be present for a non-resident to roll over real estate to a Canadian corporation. One of these is that control of the corporation was not acquired by anyone;[396]

(13) the provision which allows a new corporation formed by an amalgamation to carry forward non-capital and net capital losses incurred by a predecessor corporation, subject to certain restrictions as to changes in control;[397]

(14) the provisions which allow a parent company to carry forward non-capital and net capital losses incurred by a subsidiary after the winding-up of a wholly owned subsidiary, subject to certain restrictions as to changes in control of the subsidiary or the parent;[398]

(15) the limitations to the deduction of charitable gifts following an acquisition of control;[399]

(16) the numerous restrictions on the deduction of non-capital and net capital losses, cumulative eligible capital, capital cost allowance, and doubtful debt reserves after an acquisition of control;[400]

(17) the restrictions to the ability of a corporation to carry forward investment tax credits on a change of control; and[401]

(18) the deemed year end where change of control occurs.[402]

The acquisition of a particular corporation's shares will not, in certain circumstances, by itself result in an acquisition of the control of that or any other corporation. Those circumstances include:

(a) the acquisition of shares by any person from a related person;

(b) the acquisition of shares, from any person, by a person related to the particular corporation;

(c) the acquisition of shares by an estate;

See page ii for explanation of footnotes.

[393] CCH ¶7855; Sec. 54 "superficial loss".

[394] CCH ¶8960, ¶8964d, ¶8964e, ¶9092, ¶9099, ¶9099f; Sec. 66(11), 66(11.4), 66(11.5), 66.5(3), 66.7(10), 66.7(11).

[395] CCH ¶9850, ¶9870c; Sec. 80, 80.04(4).

[396] CCH ¶10,506; Sec. 85(1.2).

[397] CCH ¶10,910; Sec. 87(2.1).

[398] CCH ¶11,169d, ¶11,169e; Sec. 88(1.1), 88(1.2).

[399] CCH ¶15,758; Sec. 110.1(1.2).

[400] CCH ¶16,003–16,233; Sec. 111.

[401] CCH ¶19,810–19,849; Sec. 127.

[402] CCH ¶28,333a; Sec. 249(4).

¶15,545

(d) the acquisition of shares by any person from the estate of a related person;

(e) [the acquisition of shares of a particular corporation after 1999 where, immediately after their acquisition, the acquiring corporation owns all of the shares of the particular corporation and their fair market value comprises 95% or more of the fair market value of all of the acquiring corporation's assets]; and

(f) [for acquisitions of shares after 2000, the acquisition of shares in the course of a spin-off distribution in which no portion of the dividend is treated as a capital gain by an anti-avoidance rule because of the exception regarding butterfly reorganizations].

Furthermore, a redemption or cancellation of shares, or a change in the rights or conditions attaching to shares of a corporation at any time (or of a corporation that controls it) does not result in an acquisition of control of the corporation where each person and each group of persons that controls the corporation immediately after that time was related to the corporation immediately before that time (or, immediately before the death of a person, where the shares were held by that person's estate at the time of redemption, cancellation, or change).

A change of control of a predecessor corporation is deemed to have taken place immediately before an amalgamation if, immediately after the amalgamation, the new corporation is controlled by a person or a group of persons that did not control the predecessor corporation prior to the amalgamation. This would arise, for example, where, upon the amalgamation of a corporation with another corporation, the majority of the shares of the amalgamated corporation were issued to the shareholders of the other predecessor corporation. However, if the person or group of persons who controls the new corporation would not have been considered to have acquired control of a predecessor corporation if that person or group of persons had acquired all the shares of the predecessor corporation, then the amalgamation will not be considered to constitute an acquisition of control of the predecessor corporation.

Control of a predecessor corporation and of each corporation controlled by it before the amalgamation is also deemed to have been acquired unless:

(a) the predecessor corporation was related, immediately before the amalgamation, to each predecessor corporation, or

(b) if one person had hypothetically acquired all the shares of the new corporation received by shareholders of the predecessor corporation (or another predecessor controlling it) on the amalgamation in consideration for their shares of the predecessor corporation (or other predecessor), that person would have acquired control of the new corporation, or

(c) control of every predecessor would otherwise be deemed to have been acquired, in an amalgamation of two corporations and their controlled subsidiaries, as it would, for example, if two corporations of equal value amalgamated, with the shareholders of each taking back half the shares of the new corporation.

No acquisition of control of a corporation is considered to have occurred solely because of a share-for-share exchange, where the person or group of persons controlling the corporation before the exchange still controls it after the exchange. Similarly an exchange of shares of a particular corporation for shares of another corporation will not give rise to a deemed acquisition of control when the other corporation is not controlled by a person or group of persons immediately after the exchange and the fair market value of the shares of the particular corporation is not less than 95% of the fair market value of the assets of the other corporation.

[For shares acquired after 1999, an acquisition of control of a particular corporation is deemed not to occur when, before the acquisition, the acquiring corporation owns shares of the particular corporation indirectly through a subsidiary-controlled corporation and, as part of a plan or arrangement that includes the acquisition, the acquiring corporation and the subsidiary-controlled corporation are amalgamated. This deeming rule applies if, immediately after the disposition, the acquiring corporation is not controlled by a person or group of persons and the fair market value of the shares of the particular corporation is not less than 95% of the fair market value of all of the assets of the acquiring corporation.]

Finally, after July 14, 2008, control of a corporation will not occur when its shares are distributed by a SIFT trust to its unit holders during the course of a reorganization in corporate form of a SIFT wind-up entity. As discussed in Chapter 6, a SIFT trust can convert into a corporation by distributing all of its property, which must consist solely of shares of a taxable Canadian corporation, to its unit holders, on a tax-deferred basis, on the winding-up of the SIFT trust and the redemption of the SIFT units. If control of the underlying corporation is determined to be with the trustees of the distributing trust, such a distribution could result in the acquisition of control of the corporation by the trustees of the particular trust. However, if certain conditions are met, the distribution itself will not result in the acquisition of control of the corporation. The conditions to be met are that:

- the corporation be controlled by the trustees of the distributing trust immediately before the distribution;

- the particular trust be the only beneficiary under the distributing trust;

- the particular trust be a SIFT wind-up entity or a trust the only beneficiary of which is another trust that is a SIFT wind-up entity; and

- the particular trust would otherwise have acquired control of the corporation on the SIFT trust wind-up event.

Currently, an acquisition of control is deemed to occur on a reverse takeover of a public corporation when shares of the public corporation are exchanged for shares of another corporation (the acquiring corporation). The 2010 Budget proposed to extend this deemed acquisition rule in the case of a reverse takeover of a public corporation so that it also applies to impose restrictions on the use of losses where units of a SIFT trust or partnership are exchanged for shares of a corporation.

It also proposed to amend the acquisition of control rules to ensure that they do not inappropriately restrict the use of losses where a SIFT trust, the sole beneficiary of which is a corporation, is wound up and distributes the shares of a corporation it holds. As a result, where a SIFT trust, the sole beneficiary of which is a corporation, owns shares of another corporation, the wind-up of the trust will not cause an acquisition of control of the other corporation and restrict the subsequent use of that corporation's losses.

The Department of Finance provided the following example in the explanatory notes it released with the budget implementing proposals on August 27, 2010:

Example:

> Trust A, a SIFT trust, owns 100% of the shares of Aco, which in turn owns 100% of the shares of Cco. Bco is a corporation none of the shareholders of which is Trust A or person affiliated with Trust A. On July 1, 2010, Bco acquires from Trust A's unit holders all of the outstanding units of Trust A. As consideration for the trust units acquired, Bco issues to Trust A's unit holders shares of its capital stock carrying 51% of the votes of Bco. Trust A undergoes, on July 2, 2010, a SIFT trust wind-up event, and distributes its shares of Aco to Bco. The proposed amendments will apply to deem there to be no acquisition of control of either Aco or Cco on the distribution.

These proposals were part of the draft legislation that was released on August 27, 2010 but they were not picked up in Bill C-47 (S.C. 2010, c. 25) which received Royal Assent on December 15, 2010. They are scheduled to apply to transactions undertaken after 4:00 p.m. EST on March 4, 2010, subject to certain grandfathering rules.

[¶15,547] Simultaneous Control Rules

Prior to the Federal Court of Appeal decision in *Parthenon*, the CRA took the view that more than one person or group of persons in a multi-tiered corporate structure could exert *de jure* (legal) control over a lower-tier corporation in the corporate chain. For example, under this view, if Holdco II owned all of the shares of Holdco I, which in turn owned all of the shares of Opco, Holdco II and Holdco I would have simultaneous *de jure* control over Opco for the purposes of the Act. However, in the *Parthenon* decision, the Court held that *de jure* control in such circumstances means ultimate control.[403] Applying this approach to the above example, Holdco II would have *de jure* control over Opco, but Holdco I would not. Based on

---

See page ii for explanation of footnotes.

[403] Parthenon Investments Ltd., 97 DTC 5343.

judicial decisions prior to *Parthenon*, it is not entirely clear which of these positions is correct under the common law.

To effectively override the *Parthenon* finding, a statutory interpretative rule now ensures that the notion of *de facto* control flows through a corporate chain. In particular, if a lower-tier corporation (Subsidiary) would be controlled by another corporation (Parent) if one ignored the persons who controlled Parent, Subsidiary is deemed to be controlled by Parent and the person or group of persons that controls Parent.[404] If Subsidiary would be controlled by a "first-tier" group of persons if one ignored the persons who controlled any corporations in the first-tier group, then Subsidiary is deemed to be controlled by the first-tier group, and every group of persons that is comprised of, in respect of each member of the first-tier group, each member of the group or the person or group of persons that controls each member.[405]

In the Explanatory Notes provided by the Department of Finance, the following example is provided:

> X owns 100% of the voting shares of Xco, and Y and Z each owns 50% of the voting shares of YZco. Xco and YZco each owns 50% of the voting shares of XYZco. In this example, XYZco is considered to be simultaneously controlled by: (i) the first-tier group comprised of Xco and YZco, (ii) the higher-tier group comprised of X, Y and Z, (iii) the higher-tier comprised of Xco, Y and Z, and (iv) the higher-tier group comprised of X and YZco.

These rules apply to the *de facto* control rules described in ¶15,540.[406] As a result, there can be simultaneous *de facto* control of a corporation in a multi-tiered corporate structure.

[¶15,550] Deemed Exercise of Right

A taxpayer who acquires a right to acquire shares or to affect their voting rights is deemed to be in the same position in relation to the control of the corporation as if the right were immediate and absolute and had been exercised at that time, if one of the main reasons for the acquisition is to avoid any limitation on the deductibility of net capital, non-capital or farm losses, eligible capital expenditures, capital cost allowance, doubtful debts, business inventory, resource expenditures, SR&ED expenditures, investment tax credits, unused Part I.3 surtax credits, financial institutions' unused Part I tax credits, and the application of the "affiliated persons" rules to certain transfers.[407] For the purposes of this deemed exercise of right, a corporation without share capital is treated as having a single class of shares, and each participant in the corporation is treated as having an appropriate number of those shares, having regard to the total number of participants and the nature of their participation.[408]

See page ii for explanation of footnotes.

[404] CCH ¶28,395; Sec. 256(6.1)(*a*).   [407] CCH ¶28,418; Sec. 256(8).
[405] CCH ¶28,395; Sec. 256(6.1)(*b*).
[406] CCH ¶28,396; Sec. 256(6.2).   [408] CCH ¶28,420a; Sec. 256(8.1).

[¶15,555] Date of Acquisition of Control

The "change of control" rules are generally triggered at the time control is acquired. When change of control is acquired at any time on a particular day, it is deemed to have been acquired at the commencement of that day.

A corporation can elect in its tax return for the year ending immediately before the acquisition of control not to have this deemed date of acquisition of control apply. This deeming provision permits a corporation to disregard the actual time of day a transaction resulting in a change of control closes and have its deemed fiscal year end as at the end of the immediately preceding day.

On the other hand, a corporation can elect in its return that this provision not apply. Such an election could be useful where transactions such as dividend distributions are to be carried out on the same day as, and immediately prior to, the acquisition of control and it is desirable that they be treated as taking place in the taxation year ending immediately before the acquisition of control.[409]

[¶15,560] Functional Currency Tax Reporting

[¶15,565] Canadian Currency Requirement

As a general rule, a taxpayer must determine its Canadian tax results using the Canadian dollar. If a particular amount, determined in the currency (a "foreign currency") of a country other than Canada, is relevant in determining the taxpayer's Canadian tax results, that foreign currency amount must be converted to a Canadian currency amount. The conversion is done using the relevant spot rate for the day on which the particular amount arose (e.g., the day an asset was acquired and the day a liability was incurred).[410] However, certain taxpayers resident in Canada may elect, in some circumstances (see ¶15,570 below), to determine their Canadian tax results for a taxation year using their "functional currency" for that year. This election is available for taxation years beginning on or after December 14, 2007.

[¶15,570] Functional Currency Reporting Requirements

Certain corporate taxpayers resident in Canada elect to determine their Canadian tax results for a taxation year using their "functional currency" for that year. The election is available for taxation years beginning on or after December 14, 2007.[411]

The conditions that must be met for a corporation to determine its Canadian tax results using its functional currency for a taxation year can be summarized as follows:

See page ii for explanation of footnotes.

[409] CCH ¶28,421; Sec. 256(9).
[410] CCH ¶28,567; Sec. 261(2).
[411] CCH ¶28,568; Sec. 261(3).

(a) the taxpayer is, throughout the year, a corporation resident in Canada (other than an investment corporation, a mortgage investment corporation, or a mutual fund corporation);

(b) the taxpayer elects to have foreign currency tax reporting apply in respect of the year and the election was filed on or before the day that is six months before the end of the year;

(c) the taxpayer establishes that it has a functional currency for the year;

(d) the taxpayer has not filed another election under paragraph (b) described above. Thus, once having elected one elected functional currency in respect of a taxation year, the taxpayer cannot make another election; and

(e) the taxpayer has not revoked an election such that the revocation applies to the taxation year.

A taxpayer may revoke an election previously made for a taxation year.[412] The revocation must be made in prescribed form and it applies to every taxation year that begins on or after the day that is six months after the day on which the revocation is filed. The revocation cannot be made in the taxpayer's first functional currency year, meaning that the taxpayer cannot opt out of the functional currency regime until after its first two functional currency years. Once the revocation applies, every subsequent year after the last functional currency year is a reversionary year that may place the taxpayer back in the functional currency regime upon a winding-up of the taxpayer into its parent corporation or upon its amalgamation with another corporation.

[¶15,575] Functional Currency General Rules

When the taxpayer satisfies the requirements of ¶15,570 for a taxation year, the general rules will apply to the taxpayer for that year (a functional currency year). Those rules are designed to substitute the elected functional currency of the taxpayer for the year for the Canadian dollar as the calculating currency. The rules can be summarized as follows:

(1) The taxpayer's Canadian tax results for the taxation year are to be determined using its elected functional currency for that year.

(2) The Canadian dollar amounts set out in the Act (such as the Canadian dollar limits for expenditures and deductions) are to be converted to the taxpayer's elected functional currency for the year using the relevant spot rate on the first day of the year.

(3) Generally, if a particular amount (a second currency amount) that is determined in a currency (a second currency) other than the taxpayer's elected functional currency for the year is relevant in determining the taxpayer's Canadian tax results, that second currency amount must be convert-

---

[412] CCH ¶28,568b; Sec. 261(4).

ed to the taxpayer's elected functional currency using the relevant spot rate on the day that the second currency amount arose.[413]

[¶15,580] Functional Currency Year — Establishing Functional Currency Amounts

Rules are set out for establishing, in respect of the taxpayer, the amounts of certain tax attributes for its functional currency years, determined in its elected functional currency.[414] Essentially, Canadian dollar amounts of the taxpayer's pre-functional currency year tax attributes are converted to amounts determined in the taxpayer's elected functional currency using the relevant spot rate for the last day of the taxpayer's last Canadian currency year; that is, the year ending immediately before the taxpayer's first functional currency year. The effect of these rules is to incorporate or imbed into the cost or adjusted cost base of assets or the amount of expenditure pools or other tax attributes, the foreign exchange gains or losses that accrued to the end of the taxpayer's last Canadian currency year. The foreign exchange gains and losses will then be reflected in the taxpayer's Canadian tax results when those tax attributes become relevant in determining those Canadian tax results in a functional currency year.

[¶15,585] Transitional Rules

A taxpayer's foreign exchange income or loss, or capital gain or loss in respect of a pre-transition debt issued by the taxpayer before the end of the taxpayer's last Canadian currency year is deemed to be the foreign exchange income or loss, or capital gain or loss that would have been determined in Canadian dollars if the taxpayer had settled the entire principal amount of the obligation immediately before the end of its last Canadian currency year.[415] That Canadian dollar amount of the income or loss, or capital gain or loss, is then converted to the taxpayer's elected functional currency using the relevant spot rate for the last day of the taxpayer's last Canadian currency year. The functional currency amount of the income or loss, or capital gain or loss, is recognized as the debt is repaid. The recognition occurs on a *pro rata* basis, based on the amount of the repayment (expressed in the debt currency) relative to the principal amount of the debt at the beginning of the taxpayer's first functional year (also expressed in the debt currency).

Note that if the repayment of the pre-transition debt occurs in a reversionary year (a taxation year that begins after the taxpayer's last functional currency year), the accrued income, gain, or loss amount as determined above is further converted into Canadian currency using the relevant spot rate for the last day of the taxpayer's last functional currency year.

The following example illustrates the operation of the above transitional rules:

See page ii for explanation of footnotes.
[413] CCH ¶28,570; Sec. 261(5).   [415] CCH ¶28,575; Sec. 261(10).
[414] CCH ¶28,572, ¶28,573; Sec. 261(7), 261(8).

¶15,585

Canco transacts predominantly in U.S. dollars, which is also its functional currency. Canco qualifies for, and makes, an election to determine its Canadian tax results using the U.S. dollar for its 2008 and subsequent taxation years.

In 2007, Canco issued a debt for US$500 million and used the borrowed funds to acquire a capital asset for US$500 million. Canco sold the capital asset in 2008 for US$600 million, immediately using the proceeds of sale to repay the debt in full.

For the purpose of this example, assume the following exchange rates:

- at the time the debt was issued and the asset was acquired, the exchange rate was C$1 : US$0.80;

- as of December 31, 2007, the relevant spot rate was C$1 : US$0.95.

In Canco's first functional currency year (2008), the U.S. dollar adjusted cost base of the capital asset is determined (see ¶15,580) as:

$$\frac{US\$500 \text{ million}}{0.80} \times 0.95 = US\$593.75 \text{ million}$$

The accrued and unrealized foreign exchange loss of US$93.75 million is embedded in the adjusted cost base of the capital asset.

When the asset is sold, the capital gain, calculated in U.S. dollars, is computed as follows:

	US$ millions
Sale proceeds	$600.00
Less: Cost base	$593.75
Capital gain	$ 6.25

On transition, the accrued and unrealized foreign exchange gain or loss in respect of the debt is similarly calculated using the relevant spot rate applicable at December 31, 2007. In the example, this unrealized foreign exchange gain is in Canadian dollars as:

$$\frac{US\$500 \text{ million}}{0.80} - \frac{US\$500 \text{ million}}{.95} = C\$98.68 \text{ million}$$

The unrealized foreign exchange gain is then converted to U.S. dollars using the relevant spot rate of C$1:US$0.95, such that it equals US$93.75 million. Of this unrealized foreign exchange gain, 50% will be included in Canco's taxable income in 2008, the year the debt is repaid.

In this simple example, the unrealized foreign exchange gain that accrued in respect of the debt exactly offsets the unrealized foreign exchange loss that accrued in respect of the capital asset. That is, the foreign exchange loss embedded in the cost of the asset (US$93.75 million) equals the foreign exchange gain calculated in respect of the debt (US$93.75 million).

¶15,585

Chapter XVI

*Miscellaneous Taxes**

GST/HST **16,080**
Value-Added Tax 16,085
Registration 16,095
Small Supplier 16,100
Voluntary Registration 16,105
Commercial Activity 16,110
Supply 16,120
Supply in Canada 16,125
Consideration 16,135
When Tax Is Due 16,140
Pricing and Promotional
  Adjustments 16,145
Bad Debts 16,150
Election for Nil
  Consideration 16,155
Election for Exempt
  Supplies 16,160
Sale of a Business 16,165
Supplies of Taxable Real
  Property 16,170
Indian Bands 16,175
Provincial Governments 16,177
Zero-Rated Supplies and
  Exempt Supplies 16,180
Collection of Tax on
  Imports 16,185
Flow-Through of GST Paid
  by Non-Resident 16,190
Self-Assessment of Tax on
  Imported Taxable
  Supplies 16,195
Harmonized Sales Tax **16,200**
Overview of Harmonization 16,201

Supply in a Participating
  Province 16,202
Transitional Rules 16,203
Selected Listed Financial
  Institutions 16,205
Imports into a Participating
  Province 16,207
Property Brought into a
  Participating Province 16,210
British Columbia De-
  harmonization 16,213
Input Tax Credits **16,215**
Commercial Use 16,220
Capital Property — Financial
  Institutions 16,225
Capital Property — Public
  Service Bodies 16,230
Capital Property — Others 16,235
Capital Property —
  Passenger Vehicles and
  Aircraft 16,240
Documentary
  Requirements 16,245
Time Limits 16,250
Restrictions — Meals and
  Entertainment 16,255
Restrictions — Personal
  Use 16,260
Restrictions — Capital or
  Lease Costs of
  Passenger Vehicles 16,265
Employee Reimbursements
  and Allowances 16,275
Special Situations **16,280**
Rebates 16,285

---

* This chapter was originally written by Ryan, a consulting firm that specializes in helping clients to recover overpaid sales taxes, and to cope with ongoing sales tax compliance and administration. Ryan's Canadian branch office is located in Brampton, Ontario. Sheila Wisner, CA, completed the update for this edition. She is an adviser, writer, and trainer in the areas of GST/HST/PST, and in her 20 years of experience she has focused on advising clients, mainly in the financial sector. She now writes for the CCH suite of GST products.

Agents 16,290
Auctioneers 16,295
Taxable Benefits 16,300
Financial Institutions 16,305
Public Sector Bodies 16,310
Drop Shipments 16,315
Direct Sellers 16,320
Buying Groups 16,330
Forfeitures 16,335
Seizures and Claim
  Settlements by Insurers 16,340
Amalgamations and Wind-
  Ups 16,345
Partnerships 16,350
Joint Ventures 16,355

Trusts 16,360
Filing Requirements **16,365**
Reporting Periods 16,370
Simplified Method 16,375
Quick Method 16,380
Interest and Penalties 16,385
Other Sales Taxes **16,390**
Quebec Sales Tax 16,392
British Columbia New and
  Improved PST 16,393
Other Provinces 16,395
First Nations Taxes 16,397
Insurance Companies **16,420**
Excise Tax on Premiums 16,425

Recent Changes

Following the 2011 British Columbia provincial referendum, the government announced its intention to return to a PST regime, to be effective on April 1, 2013. Quebec announced on September 30, 2011 that the province will harmonize its PST with the GST, effective January 1, 2013. The 2012 Prince Edward Island Budget included the government's announcement of harmonization to be effective April 1, 2013.

[¶16,080] GST/HST

[¶16,085] Value-Added Tax

The Goods and Services Tax (GST) is a broad-based consumption tax applicable to most goods and services supplied in Canada. GST was first implemented in 1991, amending the *Excise Tax Act* (ETA), and replacing the former federal manufacturer's sales tax (FST). The inequity caused by the FST made Canadian manufactured goods uncompetitive and prompted a move to a value-added system similar to those in effect elsewhere in the world. Of the various systems studied, the New Zealand model was the one used as a basis for the GST. Unlike the former FST, which was a single-incidence tax, the advantage of a value-added tax is that it applies to a much broader range of goods and services, with few exemptions. The legislative provisions for GST can be found in Part IX of, and Schedules V to X to, the ETA.

In simple terms, the GST is a multi-stage sales tax designed to tax the value of final consumption of goods or services. This is achieved by requiring the tax to be collected on the supply value at each stage in the chain of production and distribution of goods or services.

Tax is collected in several ways. GST is required to be collected by registered businesses on all taxable supplies made in Canada (under Division II of Part IX of the ETA). In addition, the CRA collects tax at the border on goods imported into Canada including, in the case of imports for domestic consumption, the provincial component of HST on goods imported by a resident of a participating province. Tax must also be self-assessed by importers of "imported taxable supplies", including, mainly, services and intangibles, where the supplies are not entirely for commercial use (Division IV of the ETA).

In general, all goods and services sold in Canada are taxable, zero-rated, or exempt supplies. The term supply refers to the provision of goods or services. Taxable supplies are taxed at 5% or the appropriate HST rate and zero-rated supplies are taxed at 0%. Technically, both categories of supplies are "taxable" supplies under the legislation. The supply of taxable and/or zero-rated supplies is defined as a "commercial activity". Excluded from the definition of "commercial activity" is an exempt supply.

A business is entitled to claim an input tax credit ("ITC") for tax paid on the purchase or importation of goods or services to the extent the "inputs" are for use in a commercial activity. In contrast, the making of exempt supplies does not yield input tax credits for GST/HST paid on the purchase of inputs. Through this collection and credit mechanism, which applies at each stage in the trade cycle, tax is imposed and recovered until the point of final consumption, at which no further credit is available. In this way, the consumer bears the full burden of the tax (an exception applies in respect of businesses involved in exempt activities that, due to limited ITC claims, have a bottom line GST/HST cost). The total amount of the tax collected by a business on sales in a given period, less the input tax credits claimed in that period, is remitted to the government. If, in any given period, the input tax credits exceed the tax collected on sales, the business will be entitled to a net refund.

As an expansion of the GST, Harmonized Sales Tax (HST) has been adopted by several provinces (the "participating" provinces), replacing former provincial sales tax (PST) systems in these jurisdictions. The result is GST at a higher rate in participating provinces (see ¶16,200). Throughout this chapter, the federal goods and services tax, whether at the 5% rate or higher harmonized rate, is referred to as GST/HST.

The remaining non-participating provinces currently do not have value-added tax structures, but instead maintain their own retail sales tax systems (with the exception of Alberta, which does not levy a provincial sales tax) (see ¶16,390). Quebec adopted a value-added tax in 1992, which is broadly similar to the GST/HST.

The federal government also administers a First Nations Tax for Indian bands that choose to levy such a tax. This tax applies when a band council,

¶16,085

or other governing body, of a First Nation passes its own law imposing a first nations tax. Further details are provided at ¶16,397.

The following are the GST/HST rates to be in effect in 2013:

GST / HST rates in Canada — 2013
Effective January 1, 2013 to March 1, 2013

GST / HST rates in Canada — 2013
Effective April 1, 2013

Provinces:	GST	HST		Provinces:	GST	HST
British Columbia		12%		British Columbia	5%	
Alberta	5%			Alberta	5%	
Saskatchewan	5%			Saskatchewan	5%	
Manitoba	5%			Manitoba	5%	
Ontario		13%		Ontario		13%
Quebec		14.975%		Quebec		14.975%
New Brunswick		13%		New Brunswick		13%
Nova Scotia		15%		Nova Scotia		15%
PEI	5%			PEI		14%
Nfld & Lab		13%		Nfld & Lab		13%
Territories:				Territories:		
Yukon	5%			Yukon	5%	
Nunavut	5%			Nunavut	5%	
NWT	5%			NWT	5%	

[¶16,095] Registration

Under Division II of the ETA, a registrant is required to collect GST/HST from the recipient of a taxable supply made in Canada, other than a zero-rated supply, on the consideration paid for the supply. Suppliers collect GST/HST as agents of the Crown. Tax is applied at either the 5% GST rate or the applicable HST rate.

Generally, every "person" making a taxable supply in Canada, in the course of carrying on a commercial activity in Canada, is required to register for purposes of GST/HST, unless:

(1) that person is a small supplier (making taxable supplies under a threshold amount) (see ¶16,100);

¶16,095

(2) the only commercial activity carried on by the person is the making of supplies of real property by way of sale otherwise than in the course of a business; or

(3) the person is a non-resident person who does not carry on business in Canada.

Registration for GST also automatically requires the collection of HST, if applicable, and, FNGST, where applicable.

A supplier who conducts a commercial activity through a Canadian permanent establishment is required to register (with exceptions as noted). Many non-residents are also required to register, dependent largely upon whether the non-resident is "carrying on business in Canada".

CRA Policy Statement P-051R2, entitled "Carrying on Business in Canada" lists a number of factors that would be used to determine whether a supplier is carrying on business in Canada. These factors include:

- where agents or employees of the non-resident are located;

- where delivery is made;

- where payment is made;

- where purchases are made or assets acquired;

- where transactions are solicited;

- where assets or inventory are located;

- where business contracts are made;

- where a bank account is;

- where a branch or office is;

- where the non-resident's name and business are listed in a directory;

- where the service is performed; and

- where goods are manufactured or produced.

As to how the factors are applied, the CRA notes that the importance of a particular factor in a certain case will depend on the facts and on the nature of the business activity at issue. The Policy Statement also includes numerous examples. A detailed explanation and critique of the Policy Statement and carrying on business in Canada can be found in Steven K. D'Arcy's book, *Non-Residents, Cross-Border Transactions and the GST* (Toronto: CCH Canadian Limited, 2005).

The determination of whether a supplier is carrying on business in Canada becomes even more complex in relation to e-commerce transactions, such as Internet sales or supplies of electronic products or services.

¶16,095

Once registered, a supplier assumes certain statutory responsibilities, including collection, reporting, remittance, and record-keeping requirements. In addition, a registrant may be entitled to claim input tax credits, refunds, or rebates.

A special rule permits a newly registered supplier to claim an input tax credit for GST/HST paid on certain prepaid inputs to be sold or consumed after the time of registration, such as prepaid rents, royalties, and similar payments attributable to periods after the time of registration.

"Persons" subject to the registration requirement include individuals, estates, trusts and trustees, corporations, partnerships, and partners. Non-resident persons who do not have a permanent establishment in Canada are generally required to post security if they register for GST/HST.

Registration is always required, regardless of sales volumes, by taxi businesses and non-resident performers, as well as certain listed and selected listed financial institutions.

[¶16,100] Small Supplier

Generally, a small supplier is a supplier with taxable worldwide supplies, including those of an associated corporation (excluding sales of capital property, financial services, or goodwill), not exceeding $30,000 annually. In the case of a public service body, the threshold is $50,000.

An additional small supplier rule applies to deem charities and public institutions to be small suppliers if gross revenues for either of the two immediately preceding fiscal years does not exceed $250,000.

Notwithstanding the small supplier rule, all taxi operators are required to be registered. In addition, both residents and non-residents selling books and periodical subscriptions in Canada are deemed to be carrying on business in Canada, and are required to be registered. Further, non-residents that enter Canada to sell admissions to a place of amusement, a seminar, an activity, or an event are required to be registered in advance of making any such supply, and cannot be considered small suppliers regardless of volume of sales.

While a small supplier is not required to register, a supplier is entitled to voluntarily register. A small supplier may choose to voluntarily register if recipients of its supplies are able to claim input tax credits, to enable the supplier to claim input tax credits, while not harming the bottom-line cost to customers. When a small supplier chooses to register, it ceases to be a small supplier under the legislation, and is then required to collect and remit tax on all taxable supplies.

¶16,100

[¶16,105] Voluntary Registration

For certain suppliers carrying on commercial activities in Canada, voluntary registration may be desirable if registration is not required. This is often the choice to take advantage of ITC claims.

Voluntary registration is permitted by a person which is not otherwise required to be registered and satisfies one of the following:

(1) is engaged in a commercial activity in Canada;

(2) is a non-resident who regularly solicits orders for delivery in Canada, or who has entered into an agreement to supply services or intangible personal property in Canada;

(3) is a resident listed financial institution;

(4) is a resident holding company where at least 90% of the property of the subsidiary is held for consumption, use, or supply in commercial activities;

(5) is registering for purposes of eligibility as a party to a section 167 election for the sale of assets of a business; or

(6) is registering to become a "temporary member" for purposes of eligibility as a party to a section 156 election.

There are also voluntary registration rules for certain financial institutions.

In addition to gaining the ability to claim input tax credits, however, a business that voluntarily registers for GST/HST also becomes subject to all the statutory responsibilities of registrants, including the collection of tax on all taxable supplies and regular reporting and remittance requirements.

[¶16,110] Commercial Activity

The concept of "commercial activity" is critical to the GST/HST registration requirement and entitlement to input tax credits. It also influences many other aspects of the legislation. In its broadest sense, this term includes any business, or any adventure or concern in the nature of trade, except to the extent that it involves making exempt supplies. Also excepted are activities carried on without reasonable expectation of profit by an individual, a partnership of individuals, or a personal trust.

"Business" includes a profession, calling, trade, manufacture, or undertaking of any kind, whether or not engaged in for profit, and any activity engaged in on a regular or continuous basis that involves the supply of property by way of lease, licence, or similar arrangement, but does not include an office or employment.

A person is deemed to have acquired, imported, consumed, or used property or services for use in commercial activities to the extent that such property or services were acquired for the purpose of making taxable supplies, for consideration other than nominal consideration. Where taxable property or services are supplied for nominal or no consideration for the purpose of promotion of other supplies, the free property or service will effectively be regarded as acquired for commercial activities if the supplies being promoted are taxable supplies.

In the case of capital property, the use of the property at time of acquisition, importation, or appropriation determines whether and to what extent the goods are for use in a commercial activity. If that use subsequently changes, rules are in place for the recapture of input tax credits claimed at time of original acquisition or additional ITCs.

Generally, the sale of taxable personal property previously used in the course of commercial activities will be considered a taxable supply. Any sale of personal property previously used exclusively in the course of exempt activities will be an exempt supply. "Exclusively" is defined for bodies other than financial institutions as meaning "all or substantially all", which the CRA interprets as meaning 90%. (In several court cases, however, courts have stated that a percentage less than 90% may still satisfy the "all or substantially all" criterion.) For financial institutions, "exclusively" means 100%.

Anything done (other than making a supply) in connection with the acquisition, establishment, disposition or termination of a commercial activity is regarded as being done in the course of a commercial activity. As a result of this special deeming rule, a new business may be able to register early to maximize the recovery of GST/HST paid on start-up purchases.

[¶16,120] Supply

GST/HST is imposed on supplies of taxable goods and services. The definition of "supply" is broad. A supply includes the provision of any property or service in any manner, including sale, transfer, barter, exchange, licence, rental, lease, gift, or disposition. An agreement to make a supply is considered to be the supply of the underlying property or service, and the subsequent actual supply of the property or service is deemed not to be a separate supply.

Where a property or a service is supplied together with another property or service for a single consideration, the total supply will be deemed to be one supply where the other property or service could be regarded as only incidental to the first supply. Where tangible personal property of a particular class is supplied in its usual covering or container, the covering or container is deemed to form part of the property supplied.

The transfer of a security interest to secure the payment of a debt or performance of an obligation, and the re-transfer of that obligation after payment or performance, is not considered to be a supply. Special rules apply to the transfer of mineral exploration rights, which are generally not supplies unless made to consumers directly or indirectly through non-registrants.

A supply by way of lease, licence, or similar arrangement, of the use or the right to use real or tangible personal property is deemed to be the supply of the underlying property itself.

Special rules exist for some types of mixed supplies. In the case of a supply of residential real property and other real property, the properties are each considered a separate supply. In the case of a mixed supply of financial services and non-financial services for one consideration, the total package will be considered a supply of financial services where it is the usual practice to supply these services as a package, and more than 50% of the consideration relates to the supply of financial services. Lastly, where a person acquires, as a condition of membership, a share or debt security of an organization other than a co-op or credit union, the supply of the security is deemed to be a supply of a membership and not a supply of a financial service.

[¶16,125] Supply in Canada

The charging provision of Division II applies only to supplies made in Canada (other Divisions apply to imports). The following supplies are deemed to be made in Canada in the following circumstances:

- the sale of tangible personal property, if the goods are delivered or made available in Canada;
- the supply of tangible personal property otherwise than by way of sale (e.g., by lease), if possession or use of the property is first given or made available in Canada; (the CRA currently considers that if such property is subsequently moved out of Canada, GST could still apply);
- a supply of intangible personal property, if the property may be used in whole or in part in Canada or if the property relates to real or tangible personal property, or a service to be performed in Canada;
- a supply of real property, or of a service in relation to real property, if the property is situated in Canada;
- the supply of a service, if the service is performed in whole or in part in Canada; and
- a prescribed service (there are currently no such prescriptions by regulation).

Rules are modified somewhat when the supply is made by a non-resident. Supplies made by non-residents are deemed to be made outside Canada unless:

- the supply is made in the course of a business carried on in Canada;

- the non-resident is registered for GST/HST; or

- the supply is an admission charged by the non-resident.

Where goods are imported into Canada and have not yet been released from Canada Customs before they are delivered or made available to the purchaser, the sale is deemed to be made outside Canada and is not subject to GST/HST. GST/HST is payable when the goods are released. Books, newspapers, and other periodicals mailed or couriered by a GST-registered non-resident to a recipient at a Canadian address are deemed supplied in Canada.

[¶16,135] Consideration

Generally, the value of consideration on which tax is charged will be the value of money tendered, or the fair market value of goods or services tendered in exchange for the supply. If there is an unreasonable allocation of consideration between two or more supplies, the consideration may be reallocated on a reasonable basis. The value of consideration will include all taxes, fees, and duties with the exception of provincial sales taxes and land transfer taxes. Generally, non-arm's length transactions such as those between related parties, where the recipient is not able to claim full input tax credits, are deemed to take place at fair market value.

Foreign currency: Where consideration is payable in foreign currency, it must be converted to Canadian dollars at the rate in effect on the day the tax is payable. By administrative policy, there are two alternatives available to determine this rate: the rate in effect on the day the currency is acquired; and the average rate of exchange in effect for the month. This applies to the conversion of amounts both of GST/HST collected and input tax credits.

Cash discounts: Unless expressly deducted from consideration on the face of an invoice at the time of billing, discounts granted after the fact for early payment of an invoice, or penalties charged for late payment, do not change the original value of consideration subject to tax. Tax on the full consideration must be collected and remitted. Similarly, charges and penalties for the late return of rolling stock are deemed not to be consideration.

Gift certificates: The issuance of a gift certificate is deemed not to be a supply, and there are no tax consequences at the time of purchase of a gift certificate. When applied to the purchase of goods or services, the certificate is regarded as money, and thereby consideration for the supply at that time.

Coupons: The treatment of a coupon differs depending on whether the coupon is redeemable.

If the coupon is a redeemable coupon for a fixed dollar amount and is exchanged at the retail level for a supply of taxable goods or services, then the retailer calculates tax on the full selling price before applying the coupon. The purchaser, if a registrant, may take an input tax credit for only the "tax fraction" of the consideration net of the coupon value. On redemption, the issuer of the coupon claims an input tax credit equal to the tax fraction of the coupon value, provided the tax has not already been adjusted expressly by debit or credit note.

If the coupon is not a redeemable coupon, the registrant that accepts the coupon in exchange for taxable goods or services has two options. The coupon may be treated as reducing the consideration, in which case, tax will be collected on the net selling price. Alternatively, the registrant may treat the coupon as a redeemable coupon, collecting tax on the full selling price before applying the coupon, and may claim an ITC for the tax fraction of the value of the coupon. Again, the purchaser, if a registrant, may claim an ITC only for the tax fraction of the consideration net of the coupon value.

Barters: Generally barters are treated as two supplies, rather than consideration in kind paid for one supply. However, where property of a particular class or kind is exchanged for property of the same class or kind between two registrants, and each property is acquired as inventory for use exclusively in commercial activities, the value of the consideration is considered in each case to be nil. As a result, GST/HST is not collected on either supply. A series of rules exists regarding the creation and operation of "barter exchange networks".

Trade-ins: Where a registrant accepts from a non-registered customer used goods otherwise subject to tax as full or partial consideration for a supply, the supplier is required to collect GST/HST on the net amount. Where registered customers trade in goods against the purchase of other goods, the trade-in is treated as a supply on which GST/HST is collectible.

Other rules: Special rules apply to determine the allocation of consideration to the taxable and zero-rated elements of such things as tour packages and feedlot operations. Payments made by a union to an employer to compensate the employer for the absence of an employee are deemed not to be consideration for a supply. Special rules also apply to pay telephones, coin-operated devices, and to the rounding of the numerical value of calculated tax.

[¶16,140] When Tax Is Due

As a general rule, tax is payable on the earlier of the day the consideration is paid, and the day the consideration is due. Assuming no undue delay in billing, consideration is regarded as due on the earlier of the day the invoice is issued or dated, or the day the recipient is required to pay consideration under a written agreement. In the case of leases, licences, and similar arrangements, consideration is due on the day it is due under the agreement in writing, irrespective of the date on an invoice.

¶16,140

If consideration is paid in partial payments, for example on progress payments, tax is due on the value of each partial payment at the earlier of the day it is paid and the day it is due. Where a supply of tangible personal or real property is completed and all or any part of the consideration has neither been paid nor become due on or before the last day of the calendar month following the month in which the supply is complete, GST/HST calculated on the outstanding value becomes payable. The supply is treated as having been completed when:

(1) ownership or possession of tangible personal property is transferred to a recipient;

(2) on a consignment sale, sale-or-return or similar arrangement, the recipient acquires ownership or makes a third party sale of the property; or

(3) substantial completion of real property or marine vessel construction, renovation, alteration or repair;

This provision does not apply to the continuous supply of utilities, where the supplier invoices the recipient on a regular or periodic basis. If the tax is payable but not ascertainable on that day, tax is due only on that part which is ascertainable, and the remainder is due when the consideration is finally ascertainable.

If possession of a residential condominium unit is transferred before the condominium complex is registered, tax is due on the earlier of the day ownership of the unit is transferred to the recipient and the day that is 60 days after the complex is registered. In the case of other taxable real property, tax is due on the earlier of the day possession or ownership is transferred.

If a recipient of a taxable supply retains a holdback under a statute or pursuant to an agreement in writing for the construction, renovation, alteration, or repair to real property or a marine vessel, tax on the holdback is due on the earlier of the day it is paid and the day it becomes payable.

In the case where any combination of a service, personal property or real property is supplied for one consideration, for purposes of applying the timing rules above, the supply will be deemed to be a supply of the element that has the greatest value of the supplies made. If this cannot be determined, the supply will be deemed to be a supply of real property if any part of the supply is real property, and a supply of a service in any other case. These special rules are for purposes of the timing of when tax is payable and do not apply in respect of other provisions.

Deposits, except for those related to usual coverings or containers, are not regarded as consideration unless and until applied as consideration for a supply. If the deposit is forfeited, and the deposit was paid in respect of what would have been a taxable supply, the vendor is required to remit the a "tax

¶16,140

fraction" of the deposit. The prospective purchaser may take an input tax credit of a similar amount in respect of the aborted purchase.

[¶16,145] Pricing and Promotional Adjustments

Promotional allowances: Resolving the question of whether or not a volume discount or rebate, freight allowance, warehousing allowance, or other promotional allowance constitutes a price adjustment or a separate supply subject to GST/HST has always been difficult. As a result, specific rules have been enacted with respect to promotional allowances. These rules apply where a vendor pays amounts or provides a discount to a distributor or customer in return for the promotion of goods.

Where the vendor allows a discount (credit) against the price of goods or services supplied to the registrant and tax has already been collected, the credit is treated as a reduction in the consideration for the goods or services. In this event, if the vendor seeks to adjust tax, a debit or credit note must be issued in accordance with the pricing adjustment rules. If tax has not yet been collected in respect of the goods or services, the credit is automatically netted against the consideration for the supply and GST/HST is collected on the net amount.

If no credit or discount against the supply of goods or services is issued by the vendor, the payment of the allowance is treated as a rebate (see the rules discussed below).

Returns and pricing adjustments: Where tax has been charged or collected in excess of the amount of tax that should have been charged, the vendor may adjust, refund, or credit the excess amount within two years of the day tax was originally charged or collected. Where for any reason the consideration for a supply on which tax was collected is subsequently reduced, the vendor may adjust, refund, or credit the excess tax within four years of the reporting period in which the consideration is reduced.

However, where any such adjustment is made, a debit or credit note expressly addressing the tax adjustment must be exchanged between the parties. The note must contain all of the prescribed ITC documentary requirements, such that the recipient is aware of the remittance obligations, and the vendor can support a reversal of tax collected.

Rebates: Where:

(1) a registrant pays a rebate to a purchaser of taxable goods or services either from the registrant or a third party, such as a dealer,

(2) tax in respect of the purchase price of the goods has not been expressly adjusted by way of credit note or debit note, and

(3) the rebate is accompanied by a written indication that the rebate includes an amount on account of tax,

¶16,145

the registrant may claim an input tax credit equal to the applicable tax fraction of the amount of the rebate, and the purchaser, if a registrant, must remit a like amount.

Patronage dividends: The treatment of patronage dividends paid by cooperatives to their members is often difficult due to the mix of taxable and zero-rated supplies on which the dividend is calculated. The cooperative may therefore elect to ignore the tax effect of a patronage dividend altogether, or may choose one of two alternatives.

For cooperatives that have sophisticated systems, the cooperative may treat the payment of each dividend as an individual price and tax adjustment to each member recipient. Alternatively, the payment of the dividend may be regarded as a price and tax adjustment in accordance with a formula. The formula essentially determines the required tax adjustment built into each dividend by prorating the aggregate dividend between the cooperative's taxable supplies (other than sales of capital property) and its zero-rated supplies.

[¶16,150] Bad Debts

Where a registrant writes off an account receivable in respect of an arm's length supply on which the registrant collected and remitted tax, an adjustment may be made to net tax to recover the tax portion not collected.

Several conditions apply. First, both tax and consideration must be written off; if tax was not collected or collected in advance and only consideration was written off, no adjustment is available. Second, the amount must actually be written off the accounts; merely setting up a reserve is not enough. Last, the amount must actually constitute a bad debt. In this context, the registrant must have taken all legal means at its disposal to recover the debt, and the adjustment must not be merely a pricing adjustment to resolve quality disputes, returns, or deductions for promotional allowances. To adjust tax in respect of these latter items, the credit/debit note requirements of the pricing adjustment rules must be observed. The registrant has up to four years from the end of the period in which the write-off occurred to claim the GST/HST relief.

In the event of a recovery of a bad debt, any previous adjustment to net tax to recover GST/HST on the original write-off must be reversed.

[¶16,155] Election for Nil Consideration

Members of a closely related group may elect that transfers of goods or services between them be made for nil consideration if the supply is for consumption, use or supply exclusively in commercial activities (other than transfers of real property). Originally available only to Canadian resident corporate registrants, the election is now available to groups that include Canadian partnerships.

¶16,150

The rules for determination of whether or not two partnerships, two corporations, or a partnership and a corporation are closely related are complex. However, "closely related" generally requires at least 90% direct or indirect ownership of the value and number of the voting stock of a corporation or at least 90% entitlement to both the partnership income and any assets to be distributed on the wind up of the partnership.

[¶16,160] Election for Exempt Supplies

A member of a closely related group, of which a listed financial institution is a member, may elect with another member of the same group to have supplies of services and supplies by lease or licence between them deemed to be exempt financial services. Electing corporations are deemed to be financial institutions for the term of the election. Credit unions and mutual insurance group members are all deemed to have made such elections within their respective groups, and in the case of credit unions, the election extends to transfers of tangible personal property.

The making of such an election may affect the extent of commercial activity of an electing party and thereby limit ITCs and possibly trigger the change of use rules.

[¶16,165] Sale of a Business

Where both parties elect, the sale of a business may take place without the collection of GST/HST. Along with other qualifying conditions, the acquiring party must obtain ownership, possession, or use of all or substantially all of the assets required to carry on a business. The election does not extend to any supply of a service, a supply by lease, licence, or similar arrangement, or to a taxable supply of real property to a non-registrant. In addition, consideration paid for goodwill, where conditions are satisfied, is not subject to tax, even where an election is not filed.

The election may be filed in respect of assets used in non-commercial activities as well as commercial activities, and the supplier may also be a non-registrant such as a small supplier. The election has the effect of deeming the recipient to have acquired capital property which would otherwise have been subject to tax, exclusively for use in commercial activities, and to have acquired capital property which would not have been subject to tax exclusively for non-commercial activities. If the extent of actual use by the recipient differs from the deemed use (for example, a financial institution acquires capital personal property for use in exempt activities), the change of use rules will apply. See the discussion below, at ¶16,225 to ¶16,235.

A similar election applies to relieve the transfer of business assets of a deceased individual to a beneficiary who is also a registered individual.

[¶16,170] Supplies of Taxable Real Property

The rules of who collects the tax on a taxable supply are reversed in the case of a sale of taxable real property (excluding used residential real property and most real property supplied by public service bodies). A supplier of taxable real property is not required to collect GST/HST where either the supplier is a non-resident of Canada, or the recipient is a registrant (and the supply is not a supply of a residential complex made to an individual). Rather, the recipient is required to self-assess the tax and where the property is for use in commercial activities, may claim an input tax credit in proportion to the percentage of commercial use.

[¶16,175] Indian Bands

Under the *Excise Tax Act*, registrants are required to collect GST/HST on all supplies made in Canada (other than exempt supplies and zero-rated supplies).

Any suspension of the application of the ETA to specific recipients is limited. Status Indians, Indian bands, and unincorporated band-empowered entities may generally purchase goods without payment of GST on a reserve or where the goods are delivered to a reserve. These general rules are nicely described in GST/HST Technical Information Bulletin B-039. The *Excise Tax Act* with respect to purchases made by Indians and Indian bands is in keeping with section 87 of the *Indian Act*, which provides that purchases of property by Indians are relieved from direct taxation. The GST does not apply to:

- on-reserve purchases of goods;

- off-reserve purchases shipped to the reserve;

- services purchased on-reserve where the benefit of the service will be realized on-reserve; and

- services purchased by a First Nations band or a band-empowered entity, for band management or in connection with real property located on-reserve.

Detailed rules apply in respect of such concepts as "band-empowered entity" and "band management activities", along with other detailed issues and conditions.

Until June 30, 2010, First Nations in Ontario enjoyed PST point-of-sale exemptions for purchases both on- and off-reserve. With Ontario's HST implementation on July 1, 2010 came the question of the ongoing applications of the federal and provincial components of the HST. Technical Bulletin B-039, "GST/HST Administrative Policy — Application of the GST/HST to Indians", was amended in July 2010 to add a disclaimer at the beginning of the document stating that the bulletin continues to apply to HST in the same manner as it did for GST, but referring to the Ontario point-of-sale relief for the provincial component of the tax, effective September 1, 2010.

For suppliers to status Indian purchasers, CRA Info Sheet GI-106, "Ontario First Nations Point-of-Sale Relief — Reporting Requirements for GST/HST Registrant Suppliers", provides guidance on how the supplier should report HST on the point-of-sale qualifying purchases. Suppliers should note that this point-of-sale rebate needs to be separately disclosed, unlike the other point-of-sale rebates which accompanied Harmonization 2010.

It is worth noting that some First Nation bands have signed agreements which provide that the relief under the *Indian Act* is no longer applicable. (See GST/HST Notice 143, "Application of GST/HST to Yukon First Nations and Yukon Indians".)

Providers of goods and services to First Nations people and lands are also directed to the following guidance:

- Technical Information Bulletin-102 — First Nations Goods and Services Tax — Place of Supply

- CRA Notice No. 264 — Sales Made to Indians and Documentary Evidence — Temporary Confirmation of Registration Document

- GST-HST Information Sheet GI-127 — Documentary Evidence when Making Tax-Relieved Sales to Indians and Indian Bands over the Telephone, Internet or Other Electronic Means

- GST/HST Notice No. 241 — Whether an Application for the First Nations Self-Government Refund May Include the FNGST

- GST-HST Information Sheets:

  - GI-114 — Application of GST/HST to Indian Individuals

  - GI-115 — Application of GST/HST to Indian Bands and Band-empowered Entities

  - GI-116 — Information for Businesses Located on a Reserve

  - GI-117 — Information for Off-reserve Businesses that Sell Goods or Provide Services to Indians, Indian Bands, or Band-empowered Entities

- GST/HST Policy Statement P-246 — Remote stores and other off-reserve stores with significant sales to Indians, Indian bands and band-empowered entities

- Headquarters Ruling and Interpretation letters:

  - 11872-16 — First Nations — Members who are Not Citizens

  - 11950-1 — Sale of leasehold interest in First Nations reserve land

– 11872-13 — Rebate for an Indian band transporting members to medical appointments

The application of GST/HST to First Nations should not be confused with other taxes levied on First Nations. The CRA's publications in respect of the application of GST/HST to First Nations include warnings that the information does not apply to the FNT. Further details on first nations taxes are provided at ¶16,397.

[¶16,177] Provincial Governments

Reciprocal taxation agreements between certain provinces and the Government of Canada regarding the payment of federal and provincial taxes and other fees expired when the GST came into effect. These agreements to pay each other's taxes were required because under the *Constitution Act*, one level of government could not tax another level of government.

The federal government cannot, as a matter of constitutional law, tax a provincial government. Nevertheless, under the *Excise Tax Act*, the provincial government is required to collect and remit tax on those supplies made in the course of a commercial activity. Since not obligated to pay federal taxes, provincial entities and agencies which are listed as part of the provincial entity, will not pay the GST/HST on their own purchases.

Each provincial government is registered as one entity. Since there are many provincial Crown corporations, boards, commissions and agencies in a province, lists have been released to identify those that will be included in each of the provincial entities.

Provincial governments within the HST-participating provinces will, however, pay GST/HST on their purchases. Prince Edward Island and Nunavut have also struck agreements with the federal government for their agencies to pay the GST on purchases. Of course, this applies in Prince Edward Island until the date of harmonization, April 1, 2013, at which point the full HST in Prince Edward Island will apply to purchases by provincial governments.

Provincial entities in the remaining provinces may use exemption certificates to not pay GST/HST on their purchases. These certificates, which are to be provided by the provincial entity when it purchases taxable supplies, provide evidence needed by the supplier to not collect GST on those supplies. The provincial entities, of course, will not be entitled to any input tax credits, as they will not have paid any GST/HST. Suppliers, however, will be able to claim input tax credits on expenses incurred by them in making those supplies. GST/HST Memoranda Series Chapter 18.2 "Provincial Governments" indicates that a document containing the following information will be acceptable as an exemption certificate:

¶16,177

This is to certify that the property and/or services ordered/purchased hereby are being purchased by

Name of Provincial/Territorial Government Department or Institution

are not subject to the GST/HST.

Signature of Authorized Official

The certificates can be used only for purchases made in the name of the province. They may not be used for purchases by employees in their own name, even while on travel in the course of official provincial business. In these cases, the employee will be considered the final consumer, and, even if the province reimburses the employee for any business-related purchases, no special relief will be available.

The following chart shows the provinces which pay the GST/HST, effective January 1, 2013, and also effective April 1, 2013.

PROVINCE/TERRITORY	PAY GST/HST as of January 1, 2013	PAY GST/HST as of April 1, 2013
British Columbia	yes	**no**
Alberta		
Saskatchewan		
Manitoba		
Ontario	yes	yes
Quebec	**yes**	**yes**
New Brunswick	yes	yes
Nova Scotia	yes	yes
Prince Edward Island	yes	yes
Newfoundland and Labrador	yes	yes
Northwest Territories		
Nunavut	yes	yes
Yukon		

[¶16,180] Zero-Rated Supplies and Exempt Supplies

Zero-rated goods or services are taxable supplies that are subject to a 0% rate of tax. Therefore, a vendor that sells zero-rated goods or services is not required to charge GST/HST to customers, but is entitled to ITCs for GST/HST paid on purchases consumed in the course of making the supplies. Hence, GST/HST is completely removed from the cost of zero-rated supplies. Zero-rated supplies are listed in Schedule VI to the *Excise Tax Act*, which is divided into the following Parts:

- prescription drugs and biologicals (Part I);

- medical and assistive devices (Part II);

- basic groceries (Part III);

- agriculture and fishing (Part IV);

- exports (Part V);

- travel services (Part VI);

- transportation services (Part VII);

- international organizations and officials (Part VIII);

- financial services (Part IX); and

- collection of customs duties (Part X).

Tax-exempt goods or services are not subject to tax and the vendor is not entitled to ITCs for GST/HST paid on purchases consumed in the course of making the exempt supply. Accordingly, the vendor bears the full amount of tax on all taxable inputs used or incorporated into the product or service. Exempt supplies are listed in Schedule V to the *Excise Tax Act*, which is divided into the following Parts:

- real property (Part I);

- health care services (Part II);

- educational services (Part III);

- child care and personal services (Part IV);

- legal aid services (Part V);

- supplies by charities (Part V.1);

- public sector bodies (Part VI);

- financial services (Part VII); and

- ferry, road and bridge tolls (Part VIII).

The Parts in both Schedules are very detailed and should be consulted for more information. The CRA GST/HST Memoranda Series also has a number of documents summarizing the tax treatment of various goods and services.

[¶16,185] Collection of Tax on Imports

In general terms, any person importing goods into Canada as the importer of record will be assessed at the border by the CRA for GST on the value of the goods for customs.

¶16,185

Tax paid on imported goods may be claimed as an ITC in the same way and to the same extent that tax paid under Division II may be claimed as an ITC.

Some of the more common exceptions to the application of GST/HST on imports include zero-rated goods, goods imported by mail or courier with a value of $20 or less, and the importation of replacement parts at no charge to fulfill a warranty obligation on tangible personal property.

Rebates of tax paid on importation are available for GST/HST paid with qualifying conditions satisfied on returned consignment goods and for damaged goods. The rebates must be applied for within two years of the day the tax was paid.

[¶16,190] Flow-Through of GST Paid by Non-Resident

Where a non-registered non-resident vendor has paid GST at the border, the tax will not be recoverable as an ITC. Instead, the tax will usually be passed on to the Canadian recipient as part of the import costs billed by the supplier. A flow-through provision entitles a Canadian recipient that is a registrant engaged in commercial activities to claim an ITC for the GST effectively reimbursed to the non-resident who originally paid the tax, provided adequate proof of payment of the tax is maintained by the recipient. This usually means obtaining a copy of the non-resident importer's B3 customs document.

[¶16,195] Self-Assessment of Tax on Imported Taxable Supplies

The general rules of Division IV require that every recipient of an imported taxable supply self-assess GST on the value of the supply, unless acquired exclusively for consumption, use, or supply in the course of commercial activities. Certain residents of a participating province will be required to assess the provincial component of HST on the value of services and intangibles imported. This is addressed in further detail at ¶16,207 and ¶16,210.

"Imported taxable supply" is defined to include a list of supplies, with the main category being supplies of services or intangible property acquired for use, either partially or fully, in exempt activities.

Imported services and intangibles of financial institutions tie the self-assessment obligation more closely to the deductibility of an outlay or expense for income tax purposes. The general imported services rules continue to apply to other industry sectors and, in some cases, to financial institutions.

[¶16,200] Harmonized Sales Tax

[¶16,201] Overview of Harmonization

When implemented in 1991, the federal GST was levied in addition to pre-existing provincial retail sales taxes in all provinces except Alberta. The federal government's ultimate goal has always been to combine the federal GST with the provincial sales taxes across Canada, so that businesses and consumers would face only a single sales tax. For business and industry, compliance requirements would be significantly simplified with only one tax to collect and one taxation authority to deal with. For various reasons, however, complete harmonization across Canada may be years away, and currently most businesses operating in Canada must still consider both federal and provincial sales tax, as well as several harmonized tax regimes.

As a first step toward full harmonization, the federal government reached an agreement with Newfoundland and Labrador, Nova Scotia, and New Brunswick to harmonize their provincial retail sales taxes with the GST in 1997, with the result that a Harmonized Sales Tax (HST) was implemented in these "participating provinces", comprising both a federal and provincial tax component combined into one tax rate. Hence, before July 1, 2010, the rates across Canada were 5% in the non-participating provinces and 13% in the participating provinces. Effective July 1, 2010, the 13% HST rate also applied to Ontario. British Columbia's HST rate was introduced at 12%, and the rate was increased in the province of Nova Scotia, to 15%.

Following the 2011 British Columbia provincial referendum, the government announced its intention to return to a PST regime, to be effective on April 1, 2013. Quebec announced on September 30, 2011 that the province will harmonize its PST with the GST, effective January 1, 2013. The 2012 Prince Edward Island Budget included the government's announcement of harmonization to be effective April 1, 2013.

The fundamentals of collection of the GST and ITCs remain the same, albeit at a higher tax rate in a harmonized tax regime. In the same manner as GST, HST is levied on the supply of most goods and services made in a participating province. The HST base is the same as the GST base, so goods and services that are exempt or zero-rated for GST purposes are also exempt or zero-rated for HST purposes. Registrants for GST purposes are automatically registered for HST, with the GST account number becoming the GST/HST account number. Both taxes are reported on the same return, and a single amount of net tax is reported. In general, registrants deal only with the federal tax authority, the CRA.

The HST, which by legislation is really the GST at a higher rate, is imposed through a subsection of the main charging provision, which imposes the provincial component of HST for supplies made in a participating province. The identification of the participating provinces and prescribed rates of the provincial components are provided in Schedule VIII of the ETA "Participating Provinces and Applicable Tax Rates".

Concepts of a harmonized sales tax are found throughout the legislation. Certainly, levying the same tax but at different rates, all in one country, requires some detailed place of supply rules. In the absence of such rules, since the federal component of GST applies to a supply "made in Canada", it could not be determined if the GST rate or HST rate would apply. The HST has very specific place of supply rules that determine whether a supply of goods or services is made in a "participating" or a "non-participating" province, and consequently whether that supply is subject to HST. The place of supply rules were changed significantly in 2010, with an effective date of July 1, 2010, to apply to all participating provinces from that point onward. It is important to note that the "made in Canada" rules cannot simply be applied on a provincial level. The provincial place of supply rules are specific and unique. However, a supply must first be made in Canada before it is necessary to consult the provincial place of supply rules.

Although only a form of GST, the HST also includes some complicated aspects not found with the GST. Certain point-of-sale rebates are available with respect to the provincial component of HST, which differ among the provinces, and result largely from political pressure to maintain a low tax cost on many purchases not previously subject to the repealed provincial sales tax. Other measures, such as restricted ITCs, for the provincial component may also apply. Financial institutions have special reporting requirements and a special tax adjustment if the definition of "selected listed financial institution" is satisfied (see ¶16,205). Public sector bodies in participating provinces face different rebate rates for the provincial component of HST, compared to the federal rates and the rates provided by other participating provinces (see ¶16,280).

Unique transitional rules were in effect for each of Harmonization 1997 and Harmonization 2010. Canadians have become accustomed to transitional rules over the years, given the several GST rate changes. However, it is important to note that the rate change transitional rules are not the same as the HST transitional rules. Special HST transitional rules apply to the categories of personal property, real property, tangible property, and services, including guidance around prepayments, pre-existing contracts, straddling transactions, and late payments. Close attention to the detailed rules is warranted (see ¶16,203).

Within the HST system itself, many complexities arise from the fact that HST has been implemented in only some of the provinces, and so the system must deal with the flow of goods and services across jurisdictions of harmonized and non-harmonized provinces. This is further complicated by the fact that the harmonized provinces do not all levy the same HST rate. For example, various provisions in the ETA require a calculation based on a tax fraction, which will differ depending upon whether a province is harmonized and the applicable HST rate. Examples of aspects of the legislation that use such tax fractions, along with where they are discussed in this chapter are:

- Coupons — ¶16,135

- Deposits — ¶16,140

- Volume Rebates — ¶16,145

- Selected Listed Financial Institutions — ¶16,205

- Passenger Vehicles and Aircraft — ¶16,240

- Employee Reimbursements and Allowances — ¶16,275

- Taxable Benefits — ¶16,300

- Forfeitures — ¶16,335

- Simplified Accounting Method — ¶16,375

[¶16,202] Supply in a Participating Province

Once it is determined that a supply has been made in Canada, it is then necessary to determine whether or not the supply has been made in a participating province for the purpose of collecting HST, as opposed to GST, on the supply. For this purpose, a separate set of complicated "place of supply" rules operate, which differ from the rules used to determine if a supply is made in Canada.

These rules are contained in Schedule IX to the *Excise Tax Act* and regulations. Part IX of Schedule IX is entitled "Deemed Supplies and Pre-scribed Supplies". Section 3 of this part refers to prescribed supplies. The pre-existing *Place of Supply Regulations* were repealed and replaced with the *New Harmonized Value-Added Tax System Regulations* in 2010. The legislative "trail" to be followed in interpreting the provincial place of supply rules can be confusing. Section 144.1 defines supply in a province and directs the reader to the Schedule IX place of supply rules enacted in 1997. These rules remain in place today, and are still effective for supplies made prior to May 2010 or to supplies not covered in the *New Value Added Tax System Regulations*. An unwary researcher could arrive at the rules found in Sched-ule IX and stop there. However, section 3 of Part IX of Schedule IX provides that any regulation prescribing the place of a supply supercedes those rules set out in Schedule IX. Accordingly, the rules set out in the *New Harmonized Value Added Tax System Regulations* introduced with effect from May 1, 2010 (and that replace the previous *Place of Supply (GST/HST) Regulations*) take priority over Schedule IX, where applicable. Much of the place of supply rules are found in these regulations, and, in general terms, provide that a supply will be deemed made in a particular province if:

¶16,202

- in the case of the sale of tangible personal property, the supplier delivers the property or makes it available in that province; in addition to the direct shipment of goods, this includes the case where the supplier transfers possession of the property to a common carrier retained by the supplier on behalf of the recipient to ship the property to that province;

- in the case of a rental for a period of three months or less, the goods are delivered or made available in that province;

- in the case of leased property other than a motor vehicle, the goods are ordinarily located in that province at the time of supply;

- in the case of a lease of a motor vehicle, the vehicle is required to be registered in that province at the time of supply;

- in the case of real property, the property is situated in that province; if the property is situated partly in one province and partly in another, two separate supplies are considered to be made of each part;

- in the case of a service, the general rule first looks to the location of the recipient to whom the Canadian element of the service is provided. This is based on the address of the recipient which is the most closely connected to the supply. This could be the home or business address, or another address obtained in the normal course of business. If the address is in a participating province, then the applicable HST rate applies. If the address is in a non-participating province, only GST applies; and

- in the case of the supply of intangible property connected to the supply of real or tangible personal property, the place of supply of the intangible personal property is the location where the related property is situated. All other forms of intangible personal property, which do not relate to property, fall under the general place of supply rules for intangible personal property. This includes, as an example, most forms of software rights. This general rule is tied to the right inherent in the intangible and the location of use of the right, if it were used wherever the use is not restricted.

In the case of leases, each lease interval, or payment period, is considered a separate supply for purposes of applying the place of supply rules. Similarly, supplies of continuous services are divided into separate supplies for each billing period.

Freight transportation services are considered supplied in the province of destination. The place of supply of passenger transportation services is based on the point of origin of the transportation specified on the ticket, if the termination point and all stopovers are in Canada.

Repair and maintenance services performed on tangible personal property, including the supply of any repair parts, are regarded as supplied in the

¶16,202

province in which the goods are physically delivered to the recipient after the service is performed.

Internet access services are considered supplied in the province where the end user is located. Telecommunication services that involve the supply of facilities are considered supplied in the province where the facilities are ordinarily located; otherwise, basic telecommunication services are supplied in the province identified by the "two-out-of-three" rule. A particular rule applies to the supply of a telecommunications channel, which sites the supply of the service based on the relative distance of the transmission via the channel in each province crossed by the transmission.

[¶16,203] Transitional Rules

The harmonization transitional rules in Division X of the ETA apply to transactions that straddle a province's harmonization implementation date. The discussion to follow describes the transitional rules in respect of Harmonization 2010, but it is important to note that the key dates are unique to each province's harmonization and in some cases, the detailed rules may also be changed. At date of writing, the transitional rules have not been provided in respect of the harmonizations planned for years beyond 2010.

Key Dates: The critical dates for Harmonization 2010 were:

- transitional release date;

- specified pre-implementation date;

- implementation date; and

- housing grand-parenting date.

These dates are used in the application of transitional rules, and together are designed to ensure there is no leakage of the appropriate tax base. For example, transitional rules in respect of prepayments are in place to ensure that tax is not avoided by long-term prepayments once harmonization is announced. The rules differ according to category as tangible personal property, intangible personal property, real property, or services. In general terms, prepayments and some agreements made before the transitional release date will not be subject to newly harmonized HST in the province. Between this date and the pre-implementation date (which is typically two months before implementation), suppliers will not be required to collect HST from customers. However, in this period, certain business customers may be required to self-assess the provincial component of the tax in respect of prepayments for supplies to be provided after implementation. Between the pre-implementation date and the implementation date, suppliers will need to collect the HST on prepayments from all customers.

Tangible personal property: The general rule for tangible personal property (TPP) is based on the transfer of ownership or possession of the TPP. If one occurs before the implementation date, HST will not apply; if both

¶16,203

occur after implementation, HST will apply. Also, the transitional rule respecting imports into Canada is based entirely on the date of delivery; if after implementation, HST will apply. In most cases, when a province is harmonizing, there will be a pre-existing provincial sales tax (which applied to tangible property) being repealed. Transitional rules are necessary to address the phase-out or wind-down of the PST tax regime. The rules complement the HST transitional rules, such that when the PST ceases to apply to a taxable item, the HST will apply to the supply. The rules are intended to ensure that there is not a situation where both taxes will apply.

Services: The applicable HST rate applies to services performed and payments due on or after implementation date. This general rule ties the application of the HST rate to the date when "all of the consideration for the supply becomes due or is paid", which is typically the billing date of individual invoices. The HST rate is applied to each individual supply unless the override rule applies to a particular supply. This rule overrides the general rule by providing that, even if the billing takes place on or after implementation, the higher HST rate is not applicable if 90% of the invoice relates to services performed before implementation. It is important to emphasize that this rule is not to be considered first or in isolation; it is only to be considered in respect of those supplies for which the general rule would result in the application of the HST rate. Special rules apply in respect of prepayments. Where prepayments for services take place before the transitional release date HST will not apply regardless of when the services are performed. For services to be performed on or after implementation, with prepayment between announcement and the specified pre-implementation date, HST may apply to prepayments from certain "business" customers, but only the GST applies to prepayments from an individual (i.e., a consumer). Transitional tax payable during this period is to be self-assessed by certain businesses subject to the self-assessment rules. For prepayments due during the two-month period between the specified pre-implementation date and implementation, the portion of the prepayment relating to services performed after implementation will be subject to HST collectible by the supplier. Special transitional rules apply to unique services such as funeral/cemetery services, and passenger and freight transportation services.

Intangible Personal Property: The general rule for intangible personal property is based on when consideration is due; if before implementation date, only the GST applies; and if after implementation, the HST will apply. The timing of transfer of the intangible property is not relevant to this transitional rule. Special rules apply in respect of memberships, admissions, and passenger transportation passes.

Real Property: Where either ownership or possession of real property transfers before implementation, HST will not apply. Hence, only one form of transfer need take place before implementation to avoid the full HST rate. If both ownership and possession transfer after implementation, HST will apply.

¶16,203

Residential Real Property: Additional special rules apply in respect of the sale or rental of residential property, including the provincial component new housing rebate. The rebate is intended to ensure that new homes will not be subject to higher tax compared to the PST previously embedded in the price of a new home. Hence, the transitional rules must also address the transition to the rebate mechanism.

[¶16,205] Selected Listed Financial Institutions

The GST issues applicable to financial institutions are discussed at ¶16,305. With the introduction of HST, more goods and services in participating provinces became taxable at the combined HST rate. In order to prevent an exodus from participating provinces of office locations of financial institutions, which cannot claim ITCs for GST paid in respect of exempt activities, the ETA provides for such institutions to account for a tax assessment calculated by formula. The formula applies to "Selected Listed Financial Institutions", national financial institutions that are required to allocate taxable income to at least one participating province and at least one non-participating province for income tax purposes for the current and prior taxation years.

Applied in respect of each participating province, this formula, in general terms, first grosses up unrecovered GST paid in a fiscal year, for example, by a factor of $^8/_5$ for a participating province with a provincial component rate of 8%. This uses the unrecovered federal tax at the federal rate to approximate a proportionate provincial tax cost at the provincial rate. Next, the formula applies the percentage allocation to the participating province that is used in allocating taxable income to that province for income tax purposes. This result is then compared to the total of the provincial component of HST actually paid on purchases in the year. If the calculated value is greater, the excess must be remitted; if less, the difference is refundable. Since the additional tax assessment replaces an HST cost, the rules requiring the self-assessment of the provincial component of HST with respect to imports discussed in ¶16,185, ¶16,195, ¶16,207, and ¶16,210 are not applicable to these institutions.

The GST/HST rules governing selected listed financial institutions are extremely complex. Those interested in this issue should consult the CCH Canadian GST Reporter Commentary, the *Excise Tax Act*, the Selected Listed Financial Institutions Attribution Method (GST/HST) Regulations, government documents, and articles on topic for more details. Also, to further complicate the rules, significant changes were passed into law on July 12, 2010. Also in 2010 and 2012, due to Harmonization 2010 and changes to the GST rules for pension plans, special rules were implemented to deem certain investment plans to be SLFIs. Extremely complicated rules now exist in many respects for this sector.

¶16,205

[¶16,207] Imports into a Participating Province

The CRA will collect the provincial component of HST where the goods are not "commercial" goods and the recipient importer is resident in a participating province. Commercial goods are goods that are for sale or for any other commercial, industrial, occupational, institutional, or similar use. In general terms, goods for personal and non-business use are considered non-commercial goods and thereby subject to the provincial component of HST upon importation. The term "commercial", as used in respect of HST for importation purposes, is not to be confused with the "commercial activity" fundamental GST/HST concept, which refers to all taxable and zero-rated activities. It is uncertain why the same term was adopted to apply to two different concepts in the same body of legislation.

The additional provincial component is not required to be self-assessed where already appropriately collected on a taxable supply by a GST registrant, or assessed (or exempted from assessment) by the CRA on importation from outside Canada. Self-assessment is also not required in respect of zero-rated goods, free replacement parts supplied under warranty, goods that have already been taxed without eligibility for rebate, certain temporary imports, and settlers' or inherited effects.

Imported commercial goods are not subject to the provincial component under Division III at the Canadian border. Imports into Canada from unregistered non-residents may be subject to self-assessment of the provincial component of HST.

A resident of a participating province must self-assess the provincial component of the HST on the proportion of the consideration related to consumption, use, or supply in a participating province of an intangible or service acquired primarily for consumption in the participating provinces.

The exceptions to this rule include property or services acquired exclusively for use in commercial activities, zero-rated supplies, a supply performed on property that is removed from a participating province after the service is performed, litigation services rendered outside the participating province, transportation services, and telecommunication services.

Before July 1, 2010, the rules at that time required that self-assessment take place, only if the imported services were used primarily (more than 50%) in the participating provinces. Hence, with only three participating provinces, the imported services of many companies did not fall within the HST provincial component self-assessment requirements. Since July 1, 2010, the threshold test to be captured within the rules has been lowered to a 10% test. Hence, as of that date, if greater than 10% of the imported service is for use in participating provinces (the total of all), then the rule applies with respect to the provincial component of the tax. As noted, self-assessment on services is not required where the services are for use exclusively in commercial activities.

[¶16,210] Property Brought into a Participating Province

Self-assessment of the provincial component of HST is required for tangible personal property from elsewhere in Canada brought into a participating province in circumstances where a full ITC would not be available. Rules are also in place to adjust the provincial component when goods are transferred between participating provinces with differing HST rates.

[¶16,213] British Columbia De-harmonization

It was announced on August 26, 2011 that British Columbia will return to a GST/PST regime, and effectively de-harmonize by moving away from the HST, which was implemented in that province just 14 months earlier, on July 1, 2010. More than 1.6 million people mailed in their referendum ballots from June to August 2011, which represents about 52% of the voting population. Just under 55% of them voted to extinguish the HST. The provincial and federal governments have agreed to a payment plan for the return of funding received from the federal government when the HST was adopted in 2010.

On February 17, 2012, the federal and B.C. governments announced the first set of transition rules that will apply to sales of new residential housing, leading up to the transition period. The CRA issued GST/HST Notice 270, *Elimination of the HST in British Columbia in 2013 — Questions and Answers*, which discusses many of the common questions expected to arise from the transitional rules. The first draft legislation was released on May 14, 2012. The draft presents a more organized structure to the PST legislation and simplified administration. Many rules remain subject to exceptions in the regulations, which at date of writing, have not been provided. Draft legislation of transitional rules, at date of writing, have also not been released.

Since the announcement of B.C. harmonization in 2009, the province has issued HST notices, many of which are duplicated by the CRA, if applicable. The notices up to HST Notice No. 11 address the HST and harmonization issues. The notices from HST Notice No. 12 onward address the return to PST.

For more information about the transition from the HST and the re-implementation of PST, please see the following documents:

- Bill 45, *Income Tax Amendment Act, 2012*;
- British Columbia News Release, "Government action gives B.C. families and seniors a break" (issued May 3, 2012);
- Bill 54, *Provincial Sales Tax Act*;
- British Columbia News Release and Backgrounder, "Legislation delivers on promise to return to PST" (issued May 14, 2012);

- Bill 56, *New Housing Transition Tax and Rebate Act*;

- British Columbia News Release, "Transition rules for new homes provide certainty" (issued May 28, 2012); and

- 2012 British Columbia Budget Dispatch.

See also later in this chapter at ¶16,393 "British Columbia New and Improved PST".

Transitional HST Measures

New Housing Rebate — Under the harmonized system, the new housing rebate is provided under sections 254 through 254.21 of the ETA. For British Columbia, other than the federal component rebate, the rules provide a 71.43% rebate of the provincial component, to a maximum rebate of $26,250 (i.e., a price of $525,000). The enhancement for British Columbia, in place from April 1, 2012 to April 1, 2013, results in an increase to the cap for the rebate of the provincial component while the HST is still in effect in that province. The rebate will continue to be calculated at 71.43% of the provincial component paid, but to a maximum rebate of $42,500 (i.e., a new home value of $850,000). This new rebate will be available where HST becomes payable between April 1, 2012 and April 1, 2013. This compares favourably to the federal component rebate, which caps at a new home value of $350,000 with a clawback to $450,000.

The administration of the rebate remains the same, with one exception. If the builder chooses to credit only the pre-April 2012 rebate amount, the purchaser may apply for the balance from the CRA. As always, however, the purchaser has the option of not crediting any portion of the rebate to the builder and instead filing a rebate claim with the CRA for the full amount.

Guidance on the enhanced rebates is found in:

- B.C.'s HST Notice No. 12 — Enhanced New Housing Rebates and Transitional Rules for the Re-implementation of the British Columbia Provincial Sales Tax; and

- CRA's Notice No. 272 — Proposed Enhancements to the British Columbia New Housing Rebates and New Residential Rental Property Rebates.

New Housing Grant — Before the de-harmonization date of April 1, 2013, an additional incentive is provided for the purchase of a recreational or second residence, such as a cottage. Since the GST/HST new housing rebates apply only to new homes purchased for use as the primary residence, this is a completely new grant available for the purchase of a non-primary residence. The details of the grant are provided in British Columbia's "HST Notice No. 13 — Guide to the Grant for New Secondary or Recreational Housing". The following summarizes the key aspects:

¶16,213

- Available for HST payable in British Columbia between April 1, 2012 and April 1, 2013;

- For the purchase of a non-primary residence;

- The purchaser or related occupants must be the first occupants of the home, or in the case of a substantial renovation, the first occupants after the renovation;

- Mirrors the provincial component HST rebate, hence, calculated at 71.43% to a maximum rebate of $42,500 (i.e., a secondary home value of $850,000);

- Mirrors the provincial component HST rebate in that it applies to new or substantially renovated homes of all the same types (condos, land, mobile homes, etc.);

- Must be sold to an individual (as opposed to a co-op);

- Excludes properties to be used to any extent for commercial use, such as a property used for vacation rentals; and

- The home must be located in "qualifying areas" in British Columbia, which is outside the Capital Region District and the Greater Vancouver Regional District.

The purchaser does not need to be a resident of British Columbia to qualify for the grant. Rebates claims must be filed within six months of the earlier of transfer of ownership or possession, and prior to October 1, 2013. The rebate application is made to the B.C. Ministry of Finance, not the CRA.

Transitional Rules — De-harmonization

They may be referred to as transitional rules, or the migration back to a PST. The details are found in the Department of Finance February 17, 2012 news release. The transitional rules in respect of the purchase of residential real property are always the most complicated. These rules are addressed first, followed by the general transitional rules.

Residential Real Property — Tax will apply on the sale of residential real property on the earlier of transfer of ownership or possession. If this date is before April 1, 2013, the HST will apply, and if on or after this date, the GST and PST (if applicable) will apply. In the case of a residential condominium unit that has not yet been registered as a condominium, tax becomes payable at the earliest of:

- Transfer of ownership; or

- 60 days after the date of registration.

Transitional Tax Adjustment — With the transition from HST to PST, there will be homes sold on or after April 1, 2013, which were built in the interim period, for which PST is not paid on the cost of the building, nor collected on the sale of the new home. A Transitional Tax Adjustment (TTA) is an amount payable to British Columbia, to replace the lost PST revenues which British Columbia does not receive on the sale of this new home. The TTA is calculated as 2% of the total consideration, and is payable by the purchaser on the same day the GST on the sale of the home becomes payable. The TTA is to be collected by the builder and then remitted to the CRA. The TTA applies if:

- HST (i.e., the provincial component) does not apply to the sale of the home (i.e., effective April 1, 2013);

- Construction is 90% or more complete before April 1, 2013; and

- Ownership and possession transfer before April 1, 2015.

The TTA does not apply to:

- Unaffixed mobile and floating homes sold after April 1, 2013 (because PST will apply to unaffixed homes effective April 1, 2013);

- Owner-built homes (because construction costs are subject to PST as of April 1, 2013); and

- Grandparented homes (agreement before November 18, 2009), since they were subject to the 2010 HST transitional rules.

The TTA does apply to mobiles homes affixed to land which are sold (as affixed) on or after April 1, 2013.

Builder Transitional Rebate — Where the 2% TTA has been charged on the sale of a home which was transferred on or after April 1, 2013, meaning that the home was at least 10% complete before April 1, 2013, it is likely that the builder will pay some PST on the costs of construction necessary to complete the home after April 1. As such, if the PST is paid by the builder and the TTA by the purchaser, double taxation would result. To avoid this, the builder is entitled to a credit, to the extent of the work necessary to complete the home after April 1, 2013. Of course, this rebate does not apply to sales of homes on which the TTA did not apply, such as unaffixed mobile/floating homes and owner-built homes. The builder is required to certify that PST was paid, and keep receipts. This rebate mirrors the 2010 transitional tax adjustment which applied to builders in the 2010 transition to HST.

Builder Disclosure Requirements — A builder in British Columbia is required to make certain disclosures in respect of any sales agreement entered into both before and after February 17, 2012, which involve a sale of residential property transferred on or after April 1, 2013 (i.e., where the TTA applies). This is similar to the disclosure requirements during the transition to Harmonization 2010, with one exception. These 2013 disclosure requirements provide for a penalty in the case of non-compliance. There is a penalty of 1% of the home price (to a maximum of $10,000) for failing to provide disclosure, along with a gross negligence penalty of 4% to a maximum of $40,000 if the builder knowingly makes false statements or does not fully or accurately disclose the required information. The information is to be provided on a specified form. The statement of adjustment is required if the property is more than 10% complete on April 1, 2013.

Sale Agreement Requirements — The contracted price in residential real property agreements signed after February 17, 2012 must not be inclusive of the B.C. transition tax. The builder must disclose in the agreement of purchase and sale that the contracted price is exclusive of any B.C. transition tax and the associated B.C. transition rebate that may apply. The builder must also disclose whether the contracted price is inclusive or exclusive of the 7 per cent provincial component of the HST and the B.C. new housing rebate, if applicable. The builder must also include the following statement in the agreement of purchase and sale (or in a similar document):

> If ownership *and* possession of a newly constructed or substantially renovated home transfer on or after April 1, 2013:
>
> • the 7 per cent provincial component of the HST and the B.C. new housing rebate for primary residences will generally no longer apply;
>
> • a B.C. transition tax of 2 per cent may become payable; and
>
> • the builder may become eligible for an associated B.C. transition rebate.

General Transitional Rules

The transitional rules to return to the PST in British Columbia are similar to the 2010 harmonization transitional rules. In respect of both tangible personal property and services, tax applies based on the earlier of the payment of consideration or when consideration becomes payable. The complication often is in respect of understanding when "payable" is triggered. As defined in the ETA, tax is payable at the earliest of:

• issuance of invoice;

• date of invoice;

• the day an invoice would normally be issued; or

• the day the recipient is required to pay pursuant to a written agreement.

Special rules apply in respect of leases, such that tax becomes due on the date stipulated in the lease agreement. If this date is before April 1, 2013, the HST will apply, and if on or after this date, the GST and PST (if applicable) will apply. In respect of real property, tax will apply on the sale of real property on the earlier of transfer of ownership or possession. If this date is before April 1, 2013, the HST will apply, and if on or after this date, the GST and PST (if applicable) will apply.

¶16,213

Specific transitional rules apply in respect of the following:

- Performance bonds;
- Financial institutions;
- Pension plans;
- Taxable benefits, vehicles, and employee/partner rebates;
- Subsidized housing; and
- Public service bodies.

Imports — For goods brought into the province on or after April 1, 2013, and services invoiced on or after that date, HST will not apply. Goods imported into Canada on or after April 1, 2013, where the customs accounting is done after that date, are not subject to HST. Other imported taxable services are not subject to HST where consideration for the supply is payable on or after April 1, 2013.

Simplified Accounting — The simplified methods of accounting will also result in new ratios to be used during 2013, according to the reporting periods indicated in the following chart:

Method	Ending before April 2013	Beginning after March 2013	Straddling April 1 — consideration due or paid before April 2013	Straddling April 1 — consideration due or paid after March 2013
Quick Method				
— goods in B.C.	4.1%	1.8%	4.1%	1.8%
— services in B.C.	8.2%	3.6%	8.2%	3.6%
Simplified ITC	12/112	5/105	12/112	5/105

[¶16,215] Input Tax Credits

[¶16,220] Commercial Use

In general terms, registrants are entitled to claim an input tax credit for GST/HST paid or payable on the acquisition or importation of taxable property or services to the extent acquired for consumption, use, or supply in the course of commercial activities. GST/HST paid for an improvement to capital property will attract the same proportion of input tax credit that the use of the capital property itself would yield. If property or a service is acquired both for the purpose of improving capital property and for some other purpose, two separate supplies are regarded as taking place and the tax paid is prorated between the two supplies.

For persons other than financial institutions, a full ITC is available in the case of a service or non-capital property where commercial use or consumption is 90% or more. A proportional ITC is available where commercial use or consumption is between 10% and 90%. No input tax credit is available where commercial use or consumption is 10% or less. For financial institutions, the availability of ITCs is directly proportional to the extent of commercial use or consumption.

[¶16,225] Capital Property — Financial Institutions

Financial institutions ("FIs") may claim ITCs for GST/HST paid in respect of capital property and improvements in direct proportion to the extent of commercial use. Except in the case of capital personal property with a cost of $50,000 or less, if the degree of commercial use subsequently changes by more than 10 percentage points, ITCs are increased or recaptured as the case may be through a deemed acquisition or disposition of that part of the property.

The sale of used capital personal property is typically a taxable supply. However, the supply of capital personal property used by a FI exclusively in exempt activities prior to sale is an exempt supply. In the case of a taxable sale of capital personal property with a cost over $50,000 and real property, an ITC is available to recover GST/HST paid on acquisition but previously unrecovered. The purpose of this credit is to prevent the cascading of tax on tax. Passenger vehicles have unique rules, which are discussed at ¶16,240.

[¶16,230] Capital Property — Public Service Bodies

Public service bodies ("PSBs") such as municipalities, non-profit organizations, hospitals, charities, and universities, are subject to the primary use test on all capital property acquisitions to determine ITC entitlement. Where because of a change in use, commercial or non-commercial use crosses the 50% threshold, ITCs may be claimed or will be recaptured through a deemed acquisition or disposition, as appropriate.

In the case of real property, an election is available which permits the PSB to claim ITCs on a basis directly proportional to the extent of commercial use. Where this is the case, subsequent changes in use of 10% or more require adjustment of ITCs.

In the case of a sale of capital personal property of a PSB, if the property was used less than primarily in commercial activities prior to sale, the sale is exempt; otherwise, the sale is taxable. In the event of a taxable sale of real property, an ITC is available to recover any GST/HST paid on acquisition of the property that was not recovered previously.

[¶16,235] Capital Property — Others

Persons other than financial institutions and public service bodies may claim a full ITC where the primary use of capital property is in a commercial activity, except in the case of real property. In the case of real property, a full ITC is available where commercial use or consumption is 90% or more. A proportional ITC is available where commercial use or consumption is between 10% and 90%. No ITC is available where commercial use or consumption is 10% or less.

These registrants are required to account for changes of use in the case of real property where the extent of commercial use changes by 10% or more, and in the case of other property, where commercial use or non-commercial use crosses the 50% threshold.

The sale of capital personal property previously used less than primarily in commercial activities is an exempt supply. In the case of the sale of taxable real property, an ITC is available to recover any GST/HST paid on acquisition and not previously recovered.

[¶16,240] Capital Property — Passenger Vehicles and Aircraft

In the case of individuals and partnerships, no ITC is allowed for GST/HST paid on the acquisition of a passenger vehicle or aircraft where the commercial use is 10% or less. Where the degree of commercial use is between 10% and 90%, however, ITCs are available. The ITC is calculated by applying a tax fraction (based on the amount of tax paid on the vehicle or aircraft) to the amount of capital cost allowance claimed for income tax purposes.

Where the degree of commercial use exceeds 90%, ITCs are available. However, ITCs for passenger vehicles are subject to the same restriction as that applicable under the *Income Tax Act*. The ITC for GST/HST paid on acquisition of a passenger vehicle is capped at an amount calculated on a prescribed maximum value.

In the event of a change in use, no accounting for previously claimed ITCs is required unless the degree of commercial use drops below 90%. In the event of sale, unless the aircraft or vehicle was used exclusively in commercial activities, the sale is deemed an exempt supply. If it was used in a commercial activity, the sale is taxable, but an ITC is available to recover any tax previously unrecovered including an amount not recovered due to the capital cost ceiling.

For registrants other than individuals and partnerships, the eligibility for ITCs is based on the primary use test, and any recapture or establishment of ITCs due to a change in commercial use is also measured by reference to the 50% threshold. The capital cost ceiling also applies to other registrants, as does the ITC available on sale of a passenger vehicle to recover previously unrecovered tax.

Registrants may elect in respect of vehicles or aircraft (used other than primarily in commercial activities), to forgo ITCs in respect of the lease or acquisition costs and associated operating costs. If such an election is made, the aircraft or passenger vehicle will be regarded as used in exempt activities. On a subsequent sale of the asset, no GST/HST need be collected and no ITC will be available.

[¶16,245] Documentary Requirements

In order to substantiate that GST/HST has been paid, and therefore support an ITC claim, recipients must obtain certain documentation. The supporting documentation can be in the form of invoices, cash register receipts, formal written contracts, credit card receipts, or any document validly issued or signed by a registered vendor, or its intermediary, in respect of a purchase on which GST/HST is paid or payable. The information required for each invoice depends on the value of the purchase. For purchases over $30, registrants are required to obtain, among other things, the GST registration number of the supplier and the amount of tax paid on the invoice, or a statement to the effect that the price is tax-included at either the GST or HST rate.

The CRA maintains a Web-based Registry that can be used to verify a supplier's GST/HST registration number. Businesses are encouraged to use this Registry to confirm the registration status of new or large suppliers, in order to support valid ITC claims. The Registry can be accessed at http://www.cra-arc.gc.ca/gsthstregistry/.

The retention period for supporting records for GST/HST purposes is the same as under the *Income Tax Act* — six years.

[¶16,250] Time Limits

For persons other than certain specified persons, ITCs must be claimed in the return for the period that ends within four years of the period that the tax was payable. A specified person is a listed financial institution or an organization with $6 million in taxable and zero-rated supplies for each of the current and prior fiscal years (unless that organization is a charity or at least 90% of the organization's supplies are taxable or zero-rated supplies). For these specified persons, ITCs must be claimed in the return for the period that ends within two years of the year that the tax was payable.

For those entities that are entitled to claim rebates in respect of GST/HST for which no ITC is allowed, the time period for claims for rebates remains at four years.

[¶16,255] Restrictions — Meals and Entertainment

Where the deduction in computing business income for meals and entertainment expenses is limited to 50% under subsection 67.1(1) of the *Income Tax Act*, the *Excise Tax Act* similarly limits the ITCs available to 50% of the GST paid on such expenses. See ¶3219 for further details of the income tax restriction.

¶16,245

For income tax purposes, this restriction is decreased for meal expenses incurred by certain long-haul truck drivers. Corresponding decreases were also implemented for the restriction on GST input tax credits. The restriction on ITCs for qualifying meal and entertainment expenses of eligible long-haul truck drivers is decreased according to the following schedule: 40% for expenses incurred after March 19, 2007, 35% for 2008, 30% for 2009, 25% for 2010, and 20% for years after 2010.

[¶16,260] Restrictions — Personal Use

Outright prohibitions on claiming ITCs are extended to GST/HST paid on the following items:

- membership in a club the main purpose of which is to provide dining, recreational or sporting facilities (*cf.* paragraph 18(1)(*l*) of the *Income Tax Act*);

- home office expenses, unless the office is the principal place of business of the registrant, or the work space is used on a regular and continuous basis for meeting clients, customers or patients (*cf.* subsection 18(12) of the *Income Tax Act*, ¶3183);

- property or services acquired for the exclusive personal use, consumption or enjoyment of a past, present or future officer or employee (or a person related to such a person), unless there would be no taxable benefit if the person was not required to pay for the property or services, or the person paid fair market value for the property or services (*cf.* paragraphs 18(1)(*a*), (*h*) of the *Income Tax Act*);

- a supply made by lease, licence or similar arrangement primarily for the personal consumption, use or enjoyment of an individual who is a registrant, an individual member, officer or employee of a registered partnership, an individual who is shareholder of a registered corporation or an individual beneficiary of a registered trust, including in all the above cases, individuals related to such individuals, unless in any such case the individual pays fair market value for the supply; and

- any acquisition where the consumption or use of property or services is unreasonable in the circumstances of the registrant's commercial activities or the consideration is unreasonable (*cf.* section 67 of the *Income Tax Act*).

[¶16,265] Restrictions — Capital or Lease Costs of Passenger Vehicles

The *Income Tax Act* limits the capital cost allowance in respect of a passenger vehicle to an amount calculated on a prescribed maximum acquisition cost, and limits the deduction for the lease cost of a passenger vehicle to a prescribed monthly amount. Input tax credits for GST/HST paid on the acquisition or lease cost of a passenger vehicle are subject to the same limits (see paragraph 13(7)(g) and section 67.3 of the *Income Tax Act*).

Table of Capital Cost/Lease Cost Threshold Amounts

The following limitation amounts have been prescribed for automobiles leased or acquired and for kilometres incurred in the periods indicated:

Effective date	Cost limit	Monthly MSLP limit (cost/.85)	Lease limit	Daily interest limit
Jan. 1, 2000	$27,000 + taxes*	($27,000 + taxes*)/.85	$700 + taxes*	$8.33
Jan. 1, 2001 through 2012	$30,000 + taxes*	($30,000 + taxes*)/.85	$800 + taxes*	$10.00

* taxes = GST/HST/PST/QST

[¶16,275] Employee Reimbursements and Allowances

When a GST registrant employer or partnership, or a registered charity for income tax purposes, pays an allowance to an employee, member, or volunteer, as repayment for a taxable expense incurred by the employee, the registrant (i.e., Employer) may claim an ITC to recover the GST/HST paid by the employee. The ITC is calculated by applying a "tax fraction" to the amount of the allowance, based on the GST/HST rate. To claim an ITC, the allowance must be considered deductible for income tax purposes and be reasonable in amount.

A similar rule permits the payer to claim ITCs for GST/HST paid in respect of expenses which are reimbursed to the employee, partner, or volunteer. While claims in respect of actual GST/HST paid are subject to documentary requirements, a simplified factor may be applied to expenses if applied consistently to a category of expense for an entire fiscal year. The use of the factor does not waive the requirement to restrict ITCs for GST paid on meals and entertainment expenses to 50% of the otherwise allowable amount.

The following table shows the rates effective January 1, 2013:

PROVINCE / TERRITORY	Employee Allowance	Employee Reimbursement
British Columbia[1]	12/112	11/111
Alberta	5/105	4/104
Saskatchewan	5/105	4/104
Manitoba	5/105	4/104
Ontario	13/113	12/112

PROVINCE / TERRITORY	Employee Allowance	Employee Reimbursement
Quebec[2]	?	?
New Brunswick	13/113	12/112
Nova Scotia	15/115	14/114
Prince Edward Island[3]	5/105	4/104
Newfoundland and Labrador	13/113	12/112
Northwest Territories	5/105	4/104
Nunavut	5/105	4/104
Yukon	5/105	4/104

[1] B.C. ratios will change effective April 1, 2013. At date of writing, the prescribed ratios have not been released, and would be expected to return to the GST ratios, 5/105 for allowances and 4/104 for reimbursements.

[2] At date of writing, the prescribed ratios have not been released for Quebec's HST.

[3] P.E.I. ratios will change effective April 1, 2013. At date of writing, the prescribed ratios have not been released, and would be expected to follow the same mathematical patterns as those in other provinces, which would result in 14/114 for allowances and 13/113 for reimbursements, based on the planned HST rate of 14%.

[¶16,280] Special Situations

[¶16,285] Rebates

In some situations, the ETA provides relief in the form of tax rebates where an ITC is not available. In these cases, tax is considered properly paid at the time the supply is made, rebates are granted to specific taxpayers, or in particular circumstances, or for tax paid on particular supplies. The following is a brief, and very general, listing of some rebates currently provided under the ETA. The specific rebate provisions of the ETA, and related government documents, should be consulted for details of eligibility, application, and additional information.

Exports — commercial goods: A rebate is available for GST paid on goods purchased for use primarily outside Canada (by a non-resident who is not a consumer of the goods) which are exported within 60 days after delivery to the non-resident.

Exports — charities: A rebate is available for GST paid on property or services exported by a charity.

Exports — participating province: A rebate is available for the provincial component of HST paid on goods exported from a participating province to a non-participating province within 30 days. Rules are also in place to adjust the provincial component when goods are transferred between participating provinces with differing HST rates.

Exports — participating province: A rebate is available for the provincial component of HST paid on services and intangibles acquired for use primarily outside a participating province, to the extent acquired for use outside the participating province.

Imports — non-participating province: A rebate is available for the provincial component of HST assessed by the CRA at the Canadian border on the importation of goods, where the goods are not for use in a participating province.

HST Rebates: Special rebates apply in respect of the provincial component of HST paid on specified motor vehicles. Other point-of-sale rebates apply uniquely in certain participating provinces.

Tour packages — short-term accommodation: A rebate of GST/HST paid is available on the short-term accommodation portion of a tour package purchased by a non-resident.

Foreign Conventions: A rebate is available for GST/HST paid on leases of real property by a non-resident for purposes of staging a convention or trade show, or paid on supplies of certain goods and services by sponsors of foreign conventions.

Installation services: A rebate is available for GST/HST paid by an unregistered non-resident on services acquired to install tangible personal property in real property.

Employees and partners: A rebate is available for GST/HST paid by employees and partners on expenses that would be deductible by them in computing income from an office or employment under the *Income Tax Act.*

New housing rebate: A rebate is available for a portion of the GST/HST paid in the construction or substantial renovation of a new home, for initial use by an individual as a primary place of residence, up to a specified maximum amount of GST/HST paid.

Residential rental property rebate: A rebate of a portion of the GST/HST paid on the purchase, construction, or substantial renovation of long-term rental accommodation, up to a specified maximum rebate amount.

Non-registrant sale of real property: A rebate is available for GST/HST paid on the acquisition of real property, which was not recovered as an ITC

Legal aid services: A rebate is available for GST/HST paid on legal services acquired by the administrator of a legal aid plan.

Modifications to vehicles — disabled persons: A rebate is available for GST/HST paid on modifications to vehicles to ease wheelchair access or provide for auxiliary driving controls for the disabled.

Public service bodies and charities: GST paid by public service bodies is rebatable at specific rates (where not claimable as an ITC). There is no requirement to be registered for GST/HST purposes to claim rebates. Rebates apply in respect of the federal component of GST/HST and the provincial components of HST as follows:

¶16,285

Federal and Provincial – PSB Rebates – effective January 1, 2013

	PSB	BC	Quebec*	NB	NS	Nfld & L	Federal
Municipalities	75%	78%	0%	57.14%	57.14%	0%	100%
Univ & Colleges	75%	78%	47%	0%	67%	0%	67%
School Boards	87%	93%	47%	0%	68%	0%	68%
Hospitals	58%	87%	51.50%	0%	83%	0%	83%
FO & External suppl.	58%	87%	51.50%	0%	0%	0%	83%
Charities & Q N-P	57%	82%	50%	50%	50%	50%	50%

Federal and Provincial — PSB Rebates — Effective April 1, 2013

PSB	BC	ON	Quebec*	NB	NS	PEI**	Nfld & L	Federal
Municipalities	n/a	78%	0%	57.14%	57.14%		0%	100%
Univ & Colleges	n/a	78%	47%	0%	67%		0%	67%
School Boards	n/a	93%	47%	0%	68%		0%	68%
Hospitals	n/a	87%	51.50%	0%	83%		0%	83%
FO & External suppl.	n/a	87%	51.50%	0%	0%		0%	83%
Charities & Q N-P	n/a	82%	50%	50%	50%		50%	50%

* This assumes Quebec will adopt the same provincial component rates used for the QST.

** At date of writing, the P.E.I. provincial component rebate rates are not yet available.

Printed books: A rebate is available for GST paid by PSBs on the acquisition of books, audio recordings of "talking" books, and printed versions of the scriptures.

Management services: A rebate is available for the provincial component of HST paid on management services by an investment plan in respect of the proportion of investors resident outside a participating province.

Tax paid in error: A rebate is available for GST/HST paid or remitted in error.

Certain international organizations, and diplomats and their families, may obtain a rebate of GST paid on the purchase of personal property where reciprocal relief is provided to Canadian missions and consulates in another country. However, they must pay tax at time of purchase.

[¶16,290] Agents

What an agent does within the scope of the agency on behalf of the agent's principal is as though done by the principal itself. The agent will collect GST/HST on its fees or commissions charged to the principal, and the principal collects and remits tax on its taxable supplies made through the agent. For administrative ease, the agent and principal may jointly elect to have the agent remit the tax on its return, although both remain jointly and severally liable for remittance of the tax.

Where the principal is not required to collect tax on the supply of tangible personal property (e.g., is a non-registrant), the agent is considered to have made the taxable supply to the recipient, and collects and remits the tax. In addition, in this case, the agent does not collect tax on its commissions charged to the principal. If the principal is a registrant, but is nonetheless not required to collect tax on the supply, the principal and agent may jointly elect to have the principal collect and remit tax on the supply. The commissions charged by the agent will be subject to GST/HST for which the principal may claim an input tax credit.

[¶16,295] Auctioneers

The general rule is that where an auctioneer makes a supply by auction of tangible personal property on behalf of a principal, the auctioneer is regarded as having made a taxable supply, and must collect and remit GST on the supply. The auctioneer is not regarded as making a supply of its services to the principal and therefore does not collect GST/HST on its commissions.

The auctioneer and principal may elect out of these rules in respect of sales of flowers and plants, horses, motor vehicles, natural resource equipment, construction equipment or production equipment sold on behalf of the principal on any given auction day. If so, the sales are regarded as taxable supplies made by the principal, and the auctioneer will collect GST/HST on supplies of its services to the principal.

[¶16,300] Taxable Benefits

Although salary and wages paid to employees are not subject to GST, "employee benefits" compensating employees through non-monetary means may be subject to GST/HST. Mirroring the *Income Tax Act* for benefits to employees or shareholders, registrants supplying goods or services to employees or shareholders, or to persons related to them, are obliged to account for GST/HST on the supplies if:

- the benefits are taxable for income tax purposes; and

- the nature of the benefit is a "taxable supply" for GST purposes.

For example, personal use of an employer's owned or leased automobile would be taxable for GST/HST purposes, but the provision of free housing would not because the latter benefit is exempt for GST/HST purposes.

If a business provides benefits to employees and/or shareholders, or to persons related to them, that are taxable for income tax purposes, it will have to ensure that the GST/HST components, where applicable, are included in the benefits to be reported to the employees and/or shareholders. Businesses would be well advised to determine their GST/HST employee benefit reporting requirements well ahead of the filing deadline (the end of February).

Businesses must account for GST/HST on the total taxable benefit amount, including GST and PST. However, businesses have the opportunity to simplify the area of employee and shareholder benefits by making an election to essentially forgo ITCs on the operating expenses, such as gasoline and repairs, of a passenger vehicle or aircraft. In exchange, the business will not remit GST/HST on the taxable benefit associated with the vehicle or aircraft. GST/HST must, however, still be included as an employee or shareholder benefit.

For GST purposes, the employer is required to remit GST in respect of the value of any benefit taxed under paragraphs 6(1)(a) (general benefits, but excluding taxable allowances), (e) (standby charge for automobiles), and (k) and (l) (automobile operating costs) of the *Income Tax Act*. The employer remittance is calculated as the amount of the benefit multiplied by a prescribed factor. The factors differ according to the type of rebate and also, the province of employment. The following charts provide the rates effective as of January 1, 2013. The tax must be remitted with the return covering the last day of February following the year end.

Province/Territory (effective January 1, 2013)	Non-Auto Taxable Benefit	Auto Standby Taxable Benefit	Auto Operating Cost Benefit
British Columbia[1]	5.75%	5.75%	3.5%
Alberta	4/104	4/104	3%
Saskatchewan	4/104	4/104	3%
Manitoba	4/104	4/104	3%
Ontario	12/112	12/112	9%
Quebec[2]	4/104	4/104	3%
New Brunswick	12/112	12/112	9%
Nova Scotia	14/114	14/114	11%
Prince Edward Island[3]	4/104	4/104	3%
Newfoundland and Labrador	12/112	12/112	9%
Northwest Territories	4/104	4/104	3%
Nunavut	4/104	4/104	3%
Yukon	4/104	4/104	3%

[1] The B.C. rates are blended for 2013, in anticipation of the de-harmonization on April 1, 2013.

[2] At date of writing, the prescribed ratios have not been released for Quebec's HST.

[3] P.E.I. ratios will change effective April 1, 2013. At date of writing, the prescribed ratios have not been released.

No remittance will be required where no input tax credit could have been claimed by the employer. Examples of this situation might include:

- where the provision of the benefit would be an exempt or zero-rated supply;

¶16,300

- where the personal use restrictions apply to the acquisition of the benefit by the employer (see ¶16,260);

- where the asset was acquired less than primarily for use in commercial activity; and

- where an election to forgo input tax credits is in place (see ¶16,240).

[¶16,305] Financial Institutions

Financial services are included in the list of exempt supplies. Most financial institutions carry on a mix of commercial and exempt activities. There are several categories of financial institutions to which unique rules apply, largely due to the mix of supplies and the complicated definition of "financial service". Among the most difficult aspects is restricted ITC eligibility of an FI. Until recently, the legislation provided minimal guidance on how a financial institution is to quantify GST paid to the extent of use in commercial activities, for the purpose of claiming ITCs. Elaborate cost accounting systems were implemented by banks, insurers, and all sectors of FIs requiring extensive defence of the "fair and reasonable" criterion upon supporting the methods to CRA auditors. Taxpayers had the opportunity to choose a system tailored to the business and defend it, leading to no standardization among registrants and complicated auditing standards for the CRA. On July 12, 2010, legislation which was originally proposed in January 2007, was passed, providing input tax credit allocation methods for financial institutions and rules for supplies made between foreign and domestic branches of financial institutions. Also included in the changes were amendments to the definition of financial service, an extension of the time period for financial institutions to file annual GST/HST returns, significant amendments to the input tax credit claims of pension plans, and the requirement to file an annual information schedule for financial institutions.

[¶16,310] Public Sector Bodies

Charities, non-profit organizations, and governments (defined in subsection 123(1) of the *Excise Tax Act* as "public sector bodies") play a significant and distinct role in Canadian society, and the GST/HST legislation governing their treatment has special provisions which reflect this. The public sector can undertake a wide variety of activities, some of which compete with private businesses. However, given the diversity of this group, there are several exemptions for supplies made by this sector.

The unique aspects of the rules for public sector bodies may be for the purpose of simplification and tax relief for this sector, but the result of the rules in many cases is the triggering of complications in other aspects of the legislation, such as the property change-of-use rules, small supplier thresholds, and input tax credit allocations.

With the many different types of bodies in the public sector, there are rules which apply to some sectors and not others, or apply in different fashions to the various sectors. The exempting schedules for public sector bodies provide that many supplies by this sector are exempt when provided by a member of this sector. There are specific carve-outs in place to then ensure that other supplies are taxable. Also, given the usual low operating budgets of bodies in this sector, attempts have been made in the legislation to minimize the administrative burden to the sector through such things as simplified accounting methods. The legislation, in order to be fair and not burden this sector, provides a rebate mechanism to relieve some of the tax incurred on purchases (see ¶16,285).

Part V.1 of Schedule V to the *Excise Tax Act* sets out the exempting provisions that apply only to charities, while Part VI of Schedule V sets out the exempting provisions that apply to other types of public sector bodies (excluding charities). Detailed commentary on this sector is provided in the CCH Canadian GST Reporter.

[¶16,315] Drop Shipments

It is the intent of the legislation that all goods delivered in Canada for consumption, use, or supply be subject to GST on their fair market value. As a result, rules are in place to prevent avoidance of tax by routing the supply of goods through an unregistered, non-resident supplier. If an unregistered non-resident acquires goods from a Canadian supplier for delivery directly to the consignee of the non-resident in Canada, tax must be collected by the supplier on the fair market value — typically, the non-resident's selling price. The ETA recognizes, however, that in this situation, prior to the supply to the ultimate consumer, input tax credits will be available to successive purchasers engaged in commercial activities to recover GST/HST collected by suppliers.

In addition to the flow-through provisions discussed at ¶16,190, relief from the supplier having to collect the tax at the outset is also available through a system of drop shipment certificates which imposes the liability to pay tax on the Canadian consignee of the goods. Where the registered recipient of drop-shipped goods provides such a certificate to the registered supplier, the supplier is relieved from the obligation to collect tax on the supply of the goods.

Where a registered recipient of property drop-shipped in these circumstances is acquiring property otherwise than exclusively for consumption, use or supply in the course of commercial activities, the recipient is regarded as having received an "imported taxable supply". The recipient will therefore be required to self-assess tax under Division IV (see ¶16,195), but may be eligible for an input tax credit in accordance with the normal rules.

GST/HST Memoranda Series Chapter 3.3.1, "Drop Shipments" provides further information and contains numerous examples. For a detailed discussion of the drop shipment rules, see Steven K. D'Arcy, *Non-Residents,*

Cross-Border Transactions, and the GST (Toronto: CCH Canadian Limited, 2005).

[¶16,320] Direct Sellers

Direct sellers (e.g., AVON®, Pampered Chef®) distribute their products to purchasers through independent sales contractors rather than through retail outlets. Various forms of distribution channels exist in the direct selling business. The ETA addresses the supply relationships under the following two business models:

(1) Supply by direct seller to contractor, and then a resupply from the contractor to the customer; and

(2) Supply by the seller (Network Seller) to the final consumer, using the services of a commissioned sales representative (section 178).

An alternate GST/HST collection method allows "direct sellers", which use the first model to apply to the CRA to account for GST/HST collected on sales of their exclusive products at the level of the direct seller or its distributor, rather than have the independent sales contractor collect and remit GST/HST. In this case, the distributor or direct seller remits GST/HST based on the ultimate retail selling price charged by the independent sales contractor.

The second business model used in direct selling, referred to as the "network selling" model, uses a Special GST/HST Accounting Method ("SAM"). Similar to the direct seller rules, with the use of a SAM, the sale by the network seller to the final customer would be subject to the normal rules, and the supplies of the representative's sales services, payments of commission, and certain supplies of sales aids would be effectively ignored. This will have the effect of simplifying the GST/HST accounting for the network seller and essentially eliminating the obligations of the sales representative.

[¶16,330] Buying Groups

Where a member of a buying group orders goods, the central "buyer" ordinarily deals directly with the member for purposes of delivery and invoicing of the goods ordered. In the absence of special relief, the basic rules for GST/HST would require the buyer for the group to invoice individual members for the goods, collecting GST/HST on the sale if taxable. The buyer frequently does not have the information necessary to perform this task since, typically, the only reason for the existence of the buying group is to obtain volume discounts and rebates at rates applicable to higher plateaus reached through aggregation of individual members' volumes.

A person that makes at least 90% of its supplies by way of "pass-through" supplies to members may be designated as a buyer for these purposes. Where the designation is in effect, and the original supplier of the product delivers to and is paid by the member directly, the pass-through sale by the buyer is ignored for GST/HST purposes. The sale by the product supplier to the buyer is regarded as a supply from the supplier direct to the member. The buyer and the member, however, are jointly and severally liable for the payment of GST/HST on the supply.

[¶16,335] Forfeitures

In the case of forfeitures or the extinguishing of debt, remittance of a deemed tax content may be required.

In the event of a breach or cancellation of an agreement for the making of a taxable, other than zero-rated, supply, any amount paid or forfeited to a registrant, otherwise than as consideration, is considered a tax-included amount. The registrant must remit tax calculated at the applicable "tax fraction" of the payment, and the payor, if a registrant, may claim an input tax credit of the same amount (tax fraction of 5/105, or the applicable HST rate fraction).

[¶16,340] Seizures and Claim Settlements by Insurers

Where a creditor seizes or repossesses property, other than property leased by it to the debtor, the debtor is deemed to have made a supply to the creditor for no consideration. If the creditor makes a subsequent taxable supply of the property to dispose of it, the supply is deemed made in the course of commercial activity, and GST/HST paid on costs of disposal is eligible for an input tax credit.

In the event that personal property was seized from a person not required to charge GST/HST (e.g., an unregistered individual), a notional input tax credit is available to the creditor at time of disposition in Canada to remove GST/HST embedded in the cost of the property. In the case where real property is seized from a debtor, a notional input tax credit, or rebate in the case of a non-registrant, to recover the embedded tax is available to the debtor.

Special rules apply where the creditor uses the property prior to sale, and also where the debtor subsequently redeems the property.

Parallel rules apply to insurers who acquire property in the course of settling an insurance claim.

[¶16,345] Amalgamations and Wind-Ups

In the event of an amalgamation of two or more corporations, the new corporation is regarded as a separate person from each of the predecessors. However, for the purpose of applying the provisions of Part IX of the *Excise Tax Act* to acquisitions or importations by a predecessor, bad debt claims, and recoveries, the threshold amounts used to determine GST/HST filing frequencies, and for various prescribed purposes, the new corporation is deemed to be a continuation of each predecessor. Transfers of property to the new corporation by the predecessors as a result of the amalgamation are deemed not to be supplies.

These provisions also apply to the wind-up of a subsidiary into its parent where the subsidiary is owned 90% by the parent.

[¶16,350] Partnerships

Generally, anything done by a partner as a member of the partnership is deemed done by the partnership. However, rules are provided to permit the partner to acquire or import goods on the partner's own account rather than on account of the partnership.

Supplies made by a partner to the partnership outside the partnership's activities are deemed made for consideration equal to the amount paid or other form of consideration such as an increase in the partner's unit interest in the partnership. Supplies of partnership property to a partner are deemed made at the fair market value of the partners' interests in the property at time of transfer.

[¶16,355] Joint Ventures

A joint venture is not regarded as an entity capable of separate GST/HST registration as a person. Generally, each registered participant in the venture will account separately for GST/HST collected or paid in respect of activities of the venture.

However, an election may be made by participants in certain joint ventures to designate the operator as the person responsible to account for GST on sales and purchases made in the course of venture activities. GST/HST does not then apply to revenues subsequently distributed to participants by the operator, or to expense reimbursements made by the participants to the operator. All participants and the operator remain jointly and severally liable for the tax.

The election is available mainly to mining and real estate ventures. The Regulations should be consulted for details on the very specific list of prescribed entities eligible to make the election.

[¶16,360] Trusts

Trustees are jointly and severally liable with the trust for all obligations under the *Excise Tax Act* to the extent of the money and property under their control. For this purpose, anything done by the trustee is regarded as done by the trust, and generally trustee fees charged to the trust are subject to GST/HST. The settlement of property by a settlor on an *inter vivos* trust is regarded as a taxable supply, as is the distribution of property to a benefici-ary. In both cases, consideration is deemed equal to the proceeds applicable for income tax purposes.

¶16,350

[¶16,365] Filing Requirements

[¶16,370] Reporting Periods

Registrants are required to file periodic returns, along with remittances of tax. Assigned reporting periods may be monthly, quarterly, or annual, determined (with certain exceptions) on the basis of the registrant's sales levels, defined to include annual taxable sales made in Canada by the registrant and any associated person, excluding sales of financial services, capital real property, and zero-rated supplies.

Registrants with taxable annual sales of less than $1,500,000 are required to file annual returns. Where a registrant's taxable sales are between $1.5 million and $6 million, quarterly returns are required. If a registrant's annual sales are over $6 million, returns are required to be filed monthly.

Elections are available where a qualifying registrant wishes to file on a more frequent basis than quarterly or annually. In addition, special filing rules exist for certain types of registrants. Non-registrants are assigned a calendar month as a reporting period. Charities and financial institutions are assigned annual reporting periods.

Quarterly instalments of tax are required for annual filers, unless net tax is below the instalment base threshold. Where a registrant's instalment base is less than $3,000, instalments required are deemed to be nil, with all tax to be remitted with the annual return. The instalment base for a registrant that files annually is the lesser of net GST/HST for the filing period, and the net GST/HST for the immediately preceding 12-month period. If instalments are based on an estimate of the net tax for the period, penalty and interest applies if the instalments are deficient.

Returns are due within one month following a monthly or quarterly reporting period, and within three months after year end for annual filers. Certain annual filers have due dates of six months after the year end. This includes certain financial institutions and unincorporated proprietor-based businesses.

Certain registrants are required to file GST/HST returns electronically. This includes registrants which fall within the definition of "large businesses" as defined in subsection 236.01(1) of the ETA, for purposes of the restricted ITC rules, and certain builders. All other registrants have the option of filing electronically, but are still permitted to file paper returns.

[¶16,375] Simplified Method

Registrants with less than $500,000 in annual sales and $2 million in taxable purchases for the previous fiscal year are able to claim input tax credits using a simplified calculation, applying a "tax fraction" to their taxable, other than zero-rated, purchases. The tax fraction is $5/105$ or the fraction using the applicable HST rate. Non-profit organizations and public service bodies other than charities may also use this method by applying the appropriate rebate factor to the calculated tax on purchases, provided it is reasonable to expect that taxable purchases in the current year will not exceed $2 million. In all cases, purchases related to exempt activities must be excluded from the calculation.

[¶16,380] Quick Method

A quick (or "streamlined") method of calculating net tax owing is available to small businesses, non-profit organizations, health care facility operators, and public service bodies other than charities. Using this method, GST/HST is collected on taxable sales in the normal manner. However, the remittance is calculated at prescribed rates that are applied to taxable sales, other than zero-rated sales and sales of capital real and capital personal property. GST/HST collected in respect of sales of the latter must be remitted in full. The resulting amount is remitted and actual input tax credits on general expenses are foregone. The organization is, however, eligible to claim ITCs for GST paid on capital purchases of real and personal property.

Basically, the streamlined methods permit the business or public service body the option of remitting an amount of tax that is a percentage (known as the "remittance rate") of its gross sales. Different remittance rates apply in various situations. The appropriate rate is determined with reference to certain items, including whether mainly goods or services are supplied, whether the business's permanent establishment is in a participating or non-participating province, and whether the supplies in question have been made in a participating or non-participating province.

The advantage of simplified methods is that the registrant need not keep track of tax collected on supplies made and GST/HST paid on inputs. There are a number of eligibility requirements governing the use of these methods; there are also certain exclusions. The Streamlined Accounting (GST/HST) Regulations should be consulted for further information. Since the rates differ among the harmonized provinces, the prescribed rates for streamlined accounting also differ.

The streamlined accounting method for charities under section 225.1 of the ETA allows certain categories of charities to remit net tax based on 60% of the GST/HST collected, as a less complicated method than calculating actual input tax credits. A charity may elect to not use this streamlined method and instead remit net tax based on actual tax collected and paid. This streamlined method for charities appears to not require any special consideration of the location of the supply in a participating or non-participating province. Hence, whether GST or HST is collected, the 60% ratio will apply. The method does not apply to purchases or sales of real property and capital personal property, as well as taxable benefits and certain other supplies. With such supplies, the actual GST/HST collectible is to be remitted, and actual ITCs on such purchases may be claimed.

¶16,380

[¶16,385] Interest and Penalties

Interest is payable on overdue amounts, overpayments, and refunds. Penalties apply under various scenarios including failure-to-file.

[¶16,390] Other Sales Taxes

[¶16,392] Quebec Sales Tax

The QST rate of 9.5% applies to the GST-included price of all taxable goods and services. Quebec announced on September 30, 2011 that the province will harmonize its provincial sales tax with the GST, effective January 1, 2013.

Quebec will continue to administer the QST and the GST/HST in the province, and the QST will continue to be legislated by Quebec. However, the CRA will collect and administer the GST/HST and QST in respect of certain categories of financial institutions. The tax treatment of financial services in Quebec will be harmonized with that of the GST. It will be this sector which experiences the most significant change resulting from Quebec harmonization. Since the implementation of the VAT style of QST in 1992, providers of financial services have enjoyed the tax credit benefits resulting from zero-rating of their services. The compensatory tax on financial institutions, which was implemented in 1992 to offset this revenue loss, will be eliminated but only effective March 2014.

The improved QST will be calculated on the sale price, effective January 1, 2013, instead of the GST-included price which it is currently based on. However, the provincial rate will increase effective that date, to 9.975%, which is an increase of $5/100$ths of the 9.5% rate. This has the same mathematical effect as including the GST in the tax base.

Quebec commits to replicate under the QST legislation any change that Canada makes under the GST legislation. The change will generally apply on the same date as the corresponding GST change but, in any event, no later than 60 days from the coming-into-force date for the GST change. Quebec will adopt the GST administrative, structural and definitional parameters for municipal rebates, as of January 1, 2014.

Canada and Quebec agree to pay GST/HST and QST on government purchases, as of April 1, 2013, to simplify compliance for businesses.

[¶16,393] British Columbia New and Improved PST

British Columbia will reinstate the PST, at the same rate as the pre-harmonization rate of 7%. The rate will apply to tangible personal property (TPP), taxable services, and mobile homes. Taxable services will include hotel accommodations, with a tax rate of 8%. A new section will be added for "related services", which will tax any service that is "in relation to" TPP (with the exception of legally related services). There will be a 10% tax on liquor, and 12% on the private sales of vehicles, boats, and aircraft.

Exemptions from the PST will include food and restaurant meals, manufacturing inputs and prototypes, manufacturing equipment, TPP resupplied by lease, and copies of movies or broadcasts.

As with the repealed PST, small sellers with annual revenues less than $10,000 will not be required to register.

On May 14, 2012, the Government of British Columbia introduced legislation to reimplement provincial sales tax (PST). Bill 54, the *Provincial Sales Tax Act* (PSTA), received Royal Assent on May 31. Bill 54, at nearly 200 pages in length, dwarfs the *Social Service Tax Act* (SSTA) that governed the previous social service tax (SST) regime. Many, if not all, of the government's announcements relating to the reinstated PST have been incorporated into Bill 54. As of April 1, 2013, consumers will only pay PST on goods and services that were subject to SST before the HST was implemented on July 1, 2010.

Originally, PST was introduced into British Columbia in the 1940s. Over the years, the law underwent frequent changes, and this resulted in an overly complex system that was poorly suited to the 21st century. With Bill 54, the Government of British Columbia hopes to neatly consolidate those past changes, along with modern updates, into one statute. New measures to improve the administration of PST include:

- online access for businesses, including the ability to register, update accounts, and make payments (business registration will begin January 2, 2013);

- the due date for remittances and returns will be moved to the last day of the month to match the GST remittance date;

- businesses can register for PST with their federal business number;

- retailers will be allowed to refund tax to customers in a broader range of circumstances;

- businesses that collect and remit tax will again receive commission of up to $198 per reporting period; and

- the hotel room tax will be incorporated into the PSTA, eliminating the need for separate registration, remittances, or returns.

[¶16,395] Other Provinces

Of the remaining provinces, Manitoba and Saskatchewan continue to levy a provincial retail sales tax.

The tax base and application rules under the remaining retail sales tax systems are very different from the federal GST/HST system, and different among the provinces, resulting in additional compliance complexities for business. Businesses operating in these "non-participating" provinces must continue to ensure compliance with both federal GST and the separate application of provincial sales tax. Below is a table setting out the GST/HST and sales tax rates for each province.

GST/HST and PST Rates Across Canada

Province/Territory	GST/HST rate — Jan. 1, 2013	PST rate — Jan. 1, 2013
British Columbia[1]	12%	note 1
Alberta	5%	
Saskatchewan	5%	5%
Manitoba	5%	7%
Ontario	13%	
Quebec	14.975%	
New Brunswick	13%	
Nova Scotia	15%	
Prince Edward Island[2]	5%	10%
Newfoundland & Labrador	13%	
Northwest Territories	5%	
Nunavut	5%	
Yukon	5%	

[1] B.C. ratios will change effective April 1, 2013. At that date, British Columbia will return to a 5% GST and a 7% PST.

[2] On April 11, 2013 with harmonization in Prince Edward Island, the PST will be repealed, and a new HST rate of 14% will apply instead of the 5% GST rate.

In each of the retail sales tax provinces, the tax is designed to be a tax of single incidence, levied on the consumer of taxable products and services. Sales tax predominantly attaches in each province to the sale, lease or rental of tangible personal property, although most of the provinces also levy tax on several taxable services. Examples of taxable services common to each province include accommodations, telecommunications, and various labour services, but other taxable services vary from province to province. In addition to the general retail sales tax rate, each province may impose special taxes on certain types of taxable goods or services.

Exemptions from retail sales tax are numerous and vary widely from province to province. Common examples of exempt goods include food-stuffs (other than snack foods), medical supplies (including optical and dental supplies), books and publications, fuels, and exports. A variety of exemptions are also available for prescribed classes of purchasers such as

¶16,395

manufacturers, farmers, fishermen, foreign diplomats, and status Indians. Various rebates of provincial sales tax are also available.

Each province maintains a system of registering vendors to collect the tax on taxable sales of goods delivered to, or services performed in, their respective jurisdictions. Sales tax is administered by the provincial finance ministry in each retail sales tax province.

[¶16,397] First Nations Taxes

First Nations Tax ("FNT") and First Nations Goods and Services Tax ("FNGST") are imposed by First Nations that have entered into an agreement with the Government of Canada to impose such a tax. FNT is limited in application to alcoholic beverages, fuel, and tobacco products. The FNGST is a broad-based tax which applies instead of the GST or federal part of the HST on all taxable goods and services.

The location of application of the taxes is quite straightforward: all purchasers, including First Nations people, are required to pay the First Nations tax if they acquire taxable goods and services on First Nations' lands where an FNT or FNGST applies. In a participating province, where a First Nations tax applies, it is the federal part of the HST (5%) that is replaced either by the FNT or FNGST. There are currently no federally administered First Nations taxes that replace the provincial part of the HST. Therefore, if an Indian, Indian band, or band-empowered entity were to acquire taxable goods or services on reserve lands where a First Nations tax applies, the supply would be subject only to the FNT or the FNGST at the rate of 5%.

More information on the FNT and FNGST, along with the list of participating first nations, is found at http://www.cra-arc.gc.ca/tx/bsnss/tpcs/gst-tps/frstntns. GST/HST Notice 254, "Collecting First Nations Taxes in a Participating Province", provides that these special taxes apply in the same manner in both participating and non-participating provinces. Further details are provided in Guide RC 4072, "First Nations Tax (FNT)" and Guide RC 4365, "First Nations Goods and Services Tax (FNGST)".

[¶16,420] Insurance Companies

[¶16,425] Excise Tax on Premiums

A tax of 10% is imposed by Part I of the *Excise Tax Act* on the net premiums payable by any person resident in Canada by whom or on whose behalf any insurance contract against a risk ordinarily within Canada is entered into or renewed with certain insurers. The tax applies to contracts with the following insurers:

(1) any insurer not incorporated under the laws of Canada or of any province or not formed in Canada;

(2) any exchange having its chief place of business outside Canada or having a principal attorney-in-fact whose chief place of business is outside Canada, if, in both (1) and (2), the insurer, at the time the contract is entered into or renewed, is not authorized under the laws of Canada, or of any province to transact the business of insurance; or

(3) any insurer that, at the time the contract is entered into or renewed, is authorized under the laws of Canada or of any province to transact the business of insurance, if the contract is entered into or renewed through a broker or agent outside Canada.

"Net premiums" is defined as meaning the gross premiums paid or payable under a contract of insurance, less dividends received or receivable in respect of the contract and less premiums returned on cancellation of the contract. "Insurer" is defined as meaning any corporation incorporated for the purpose of carrying on the business of insurance, any association of persons formed upon the plan known as "Lloyd's" whereby each associate underwriter becomes liable for a stated, limited or proportionate part of the whole amount insured under a contract of insurance and any exchange. "Exchange" means a group of persons formed for the purpose of exchanging reciprocal contracts of indemnity or inter-insurance with each other through the same attorney.

The tax is not exigible on premiums in respect of contracts of reinsurance or of any insurance contracts of life, personal accident, sickness or marine risk, or nuclear risk insurance not available within Canada. The exemption from excise tax on insurance premiums has been extended to include any other contract of insurance to the extent that such insurance is not available within Canada.

Every person liable to pay the 10% net premium tax must pay the tax to the Minister of Finance on or before April 30 in each year, for premiums paid or payable by such person during the immediately preceding calendar year. A return in writing with respect to each contract of insurance entered into or renewed by such person or on such a person's behalf must be made by the same date stating the name of the insurer, the amount of the insurance, and the net premiums paid or payable during the immediately preceding calendar year. The penalty for failure to pay the tax is the sum of:

(a) 1% of the amount of unpaid tax at April 30 of the year that tax is payable; plus

(b) one quarter of the amount determined under paragraph (a) multiplied by the number of months (up to 12) that the tax is overdue.

¶16,425

Brokers or agents effecting insurance with any insurer not incorporated under the laws of Canada or not formed in Canada, insurers, brokers, or agents outside Canada must make a return to the Minister of Finance on or before March 15, showing the name and address of the person in Canada by whom, with whom or on whose behalf the contract was entered into or renewed, the net premiums paid or payable during the immediately preceding calendar year, and the name and address of the broker or agent outside Canada through whom the contract was entered or renewed. Penalties also exist for non-compliance by brokers and insurance companies required to file returns. Every such person failing to file a return is liable to a penalty of $10 for each day of default or $50, whichever is less.

Chapter XVII

Tax Planning

Tax Planning **17,010**
  The Nature of Tax Planning 17,015
Income Splitting **17,035**
  Roadblocks to Income
    Splitting 17,038
  Income Taxed to Trust 17,040
  Loans 17,042
  Testamentary Trusts 17,044
  Gifts or Loans from Non-
    Residents 17,046
  Capital Gains for Minors 17,047
  Income on Income 17,048
  Business Income 17,050
  Fair Market Value Sale 17,052
  RESP 17,054
  Capital Loss 17,056
  Spousal RRSP 17,058
  Reasonable Salary to
    Spouse or Child 17,060
  Canada Pension Plan
    Splitting 17,070
  Pension Income Splitting 17,075
Tax Planning the Will **17,080**
  Introduction 17,085
  The Importance of the
    Spouse as Beneficiary 17,090
  The Principal Residence
    Exemption 17,095
  Bequests of Farm or
    Fishing Property 17,100
  Flow-Through Shares 17,105
  Life Insurance 17,110
  Low-Bracket Beneficiaries 17,115
  The Estate Split 17,120
  RRSPs and RRIFs 17,125
  RESPs 17,130
  Debt Forgiveness 17,135

Association Rules 17,140
Corporations and
  Partnerships 17,145
Charities 17,150
Spouse Trusts 17,155
Rights or Things 17,160
Probate Tax 17,165
Alter Ego and Joint Partner
  Trusts **17,167**
  The Nature of Alter Ego and
    Joint Partner Trusts 17,168
  Advantages 17,169
  Disadvantages 17,170
Joint Tenancy **17,171**
  Potential Complications 17,172
Registered Retirement
  Savings Plans **17,180**
  The Advantages of an
    RRSP 17,185
  Spousal RRSPs 17,190
  RRSPs and the
    Salary/Dividend Mix 17,195
  High Tax/Low Tax
    Investments 17,200
  Contribute Early 17,205
  Contribution of Qualified
    Investments — Tax-Free
    Cash 17,210
  Contributions after Death 17,220
  Catch-Up Contributions 17,225
  Deferred Contributions 17,235
  Last-Chance Contribution 17,240
  Building in Contribution
    Room for Family
    Members 17,245
  "Locked-In" RRSPs 17,250
Tax-Free Savings Accounts ... **17,260**
  Overview 17,262

TFSAs vs. RRSPs 17,265
Capital Gains and Losses 17,300
General Rules and
Reduced Taxation 17,305
$750,000 Exemption 17,315
Capital Gains Deferral for
Investments in Small
Business 17,320
Cumulative Net Investment
Losses (CNILs) 17,325
Capital Loss Timing and
the $750,000 Exemption 17,330
Principal Residence
Exemption 17,335
Capital Gains Reserves 17,340
Electing Capital Gains
Treatment 17,345
Options 17,350
Capital Gains Realizations 17,355
Foreign Currency 17,360
Tax-Free Dividends 17,365
Capital Losses 17,366
Allowable Business
Investment Losses 17,370
Self-Employment 17,380
Independent Contractor or
Employee? 17,385
Proprietorship or
Incorporation? 17,390
**Lower Corporate Tax Rates
& Eligible Dividends 17,400**
Introduction 17,405
Some Planning Points 17,415
**Remuneration of
Owner–Managers of
Private Corporations 17,420**
The Principles of Integration 17,425
Eligible Dividends and
Reduced Corporate Tax
Rates 17,427
Distribution Strategies
Where Small Business
Deduction Available 17,430
Situations Where Dividends
Are Advantageous 17,435
Situations Where Salary Is
Advantageous 17,440
The RRSP/TFSA Factor 17,442

Distribution Strategies
Where Small Business
Deduction Not Available 17,445
Whether or Not To "Bonus
Out" Corporate Profits 17,450
**International
Considerations 17,550**
Leaving/Entering Canada 17,555
Residence 17,560
Deemed Disposition on
Departure 17,565
Ten Reasons Why Not to
Become a U.S. Green
Card Holder or U.S.
Citizen 17,567
Before Leaving Canada 17,570
Before Entering Canada 17,585
U.S. Estate Tax 17,590
"Snowbirds" — Deemed
Residence in the U.S. 17,593
Canada–U.S. Taxation of
Social Security Benefits 17,595
**Other Planning
Considerations 17,600**
Alternative Minimum Tax 17,605
Professional Corporations 17,620
Technical Interpretation on
Professional
Corporations 17,630
**Year-End and New Year Tax
Planning Strategies 17,642**
Year-End Tax Strategies for
Everyone 17,643
Pay These before the New
Year 17,644
The CRA's Prescribed Rate ... 17,644a
Family Trusts 17,644b
Gifts-in-Kind 17,645
Mutual Fund Year Ends 17,645a
Escape Foreign Reporting ... 17,645b
Lower Tax Instalments 17,645c
Increase Business
Expenses 17,646
Watch Deadlines 17,647
Off-Calendar Years 17,647a
Defer Tax on Interest 17,648
RESP Contributions 17,648a
Source Deductions 17,648b
Pay Interest on Employee
Loans 17,648c

Employee Auto Benefits 17,649
Real Estate Tax Losses 17,650
Bad Take-Back Mortgages 17,651
Income Splitting 17,651a
Tax Loss Selling 17,652
Transfers to Children 17,652a
Mutual Fund Losses 17,653
Settlement Date 17,654
Currency Fluctuations 17,655
Labour-Sponsored Venture
  Capital Corporations 17,656
Business Income **17,660**
Advantages of
  Incorporation 17,662
Tax Deferral 17,664
Accounts Payable 17,665
Accounts Receivable 17,670
Reserves for Proceeds not
  Receivable 17,675
Inventory 17,675a
Timing of Fixed Asset
  Acquisitions 17,676
Meals and Entertainment
  Expenses 17,680
Business Use of Home
  Expenses 17,685
Capital Cost Allowance 17,690
Federal and Provincial R&D
  Incentives 17,700
R&D Filing Deadline 17,710
Deferring Gains 17,720
Depreciable Assets in
  Inventory 17,725
Forgiven Indebtedness 17,730

Self-Employed Individuals 17,740
Interest Expense **17,750**
Deductibility of Interest 17,755
Loss of Source of Income 17,765
Capitalization of Interest 17,770
Thin Capitalization 17,775
Shifting of Income 17,780
Exemption from
  Withholding 17,785
Business Losses **17,800**
Losses from Business or
  Property 17,801
Flexibility of Use 17,805
Loss Year Considerations 17,810
Goods and Services Tax;
  Harmonized Sales Tax **17,850**
It's Not That Simple! 17,855
HST Planning 17,857
Input Tax Credits (ITCs) 17,860
Maximizing Recoveries with
  ITC Restrictions 17,863
Employee/Partner GST/HST
  Rebates 17,865
Cash Flow Planning 17,867
Reorganizations 17,870
Contract Wording 17,875
Transactions with Non-
  Residents 17,880
Acting on Behalf of Non-
  Residents 17,885
E-Commerce Transactions 17,887
Deemed Financial Institution
  Status 17,890
Not the Final Word 17,900

[¶17,010] Tax Planning

[¶17,015] The Nature of Tax Planning

Effective tax planning is primarily an ingredient of good financial planning. Although there are a few opportunities to save tax when you come to prepare your return (for example, by claiming capital gains exemption or reserves, or choosing carefully the amount of loss carryover to apply, or which spouse should claim medical expenses and for what 12-month period), most tax planning requires advance thought.

¶17,015

The completion of one's personal tax return may present a good opportunity for that thought. Typically, you will have to gather for your return thorough information on your income and its sources, which is a necessary starting point for financial planning. As well, your return will show you how much you are paying in income tax, and, dividing your total tax payable by net income will show you how much tax you are paying on every dollar of earnings. If that doesn't motivate you to active tax planning, probably nothing will.

This chapter discusses a series of tax planning opportunities available to individuals in general, professionals, and businesses. Many of these opportunities are formally sanctioned by the CRA authorities; a few arise out of ordinary commercial opportunities which happen to carry appealing tax treatment. Many tax planning opportunities deal with savings, but not necessarily on a grand scale.

Some tax planning opportunities, such as the incorporation of a business or investment in commercial tax shelters, assume you can save significant amounts of income to invest, and generally should not be undertaken without professional advice. There are, however, also tax planning strategies available to the ordinary taxpayer who is trying to put aside a bit of money to buy a house, provide for a child's education, or provide for eventual retirement or even the proverbial "rainy day". You can accomplish significant financial and tax planning objectives yourself by utilizing government-sanctioned investments such as RRSP contributions, RESP contributions, TFSA contributions, separate savings accounts for Child Tax Benefits paid by government, etc.

[¶17,035] Income Splitting

[¶17,038] Roadblocks to Income Splitting

Attribution Rules

Although the income attribution rules have been repeatedly revised with a view to curtailing income splitting, planning continues to be available. The income attribution rules will apply where property is given or loaned (other than by commercial loan) to a trust formed for the benefit of a spouse or a person under 18 who does not deal with the individual at arm's length or is a niece or nephew of the individual and the trust derives income from property (including business income from a limited partnership). If the beneficiary is a spouse, the attribution rules would extend to capital gains. The attribution rules cease in the year in which a child attains the age of 18 (unless the funds are loaned on a low- or no-interest basis and income from property is generated) or, in the case of a spouse, on divorce or separation. In both cases the attribution rules cease when the transferor dies or ceases to be resident in Canada.

¶17,035

The attribution rules are discussed at length at ¶2615 *et seq.*

General Anti-Avoidance Rule (GAAR)

GAAR gives the CRA broad powers to nullify the benefits of tax-motivated transactions. Hopefully, this provision would not be applied to transactions that take advantage of specific exceptions or special rules contained in the *Income Tax Act* (e.g., capital gains splitting or the swap rule).

When GAAR was introduced, it was stated that where an income splitting manoeuvre involves the transfer of assets to a family member, and it is apparent that the family member was never really supposed to benefit from the transfer, GAAR might apply — for example, when a gift is made to an adult child who sells the property and simply gives the proceeds back to his or her parents. The CRA later published an Information Circular on GAAR but did not repeat this warning in the Circular.

GAAR should be considered any time tax planning that might be construed as being "aggressive" is on the table. GAAR is discussed at ¶15,307.

The "Kiddie Tax"

The tax on split income restricts income splitting with minors; see ¶8085.

[¶17,040] Income Taxed to Trust

If an individual transfers property to a trust formed for the benefit of a spouse or person who is under 18 and does not deal at arm's length with the individual or is the niece or nephew of the individual, only the income relating to the transferred or loaned property or substituted property will be attributed to the transferor. Attribution will occur only to the extent that the trust income is taxable to a spouse or person under 18. In other words, there will be no attribution if the income is taxable to the trust or to the other beneficiaries. Income accumulated in and taxable to the trust will not be attributed. The reporting of income by the trust will not be a viable alternative for an *inter vivos* trust that is taxable at the top personal marginal rate, except perhaps where the trust is resident in a province with a lower marginal tax rate than the province in which the beneficiaries reside.

One possibility for a discretionary trust having both adult and minor children is to pay all of the income to beneficiaries, other than a spouse or minor child, and to provide for payments out of capital to be made to the minor children where equalization is desired. It should be noted that if a corporation paying dividends to a trust is not a small business corporation and there is a trust for minor children that does not contain an age-18 restriction, the corporate attribution rules may apply if there was a transfer of property. The age-18 restriction would require that no payments of income or capital be made to a child who is under the age of 18. If a discretionary trust has both minor and adult children as beneficiaries, then all trust income can be paid to the adult beneficiaries. This would also avoid the kiddie tax. If a trust is a discretionary trust and all of the income is paid to beneficiaries who are adult children, there will be no attribution. Depending upon the manner in which the trust is settled, the accumulating income may be allocated by means of a trustee resolution and promissory note between the discretionary beneficiaries. Any income allocated to a minor child would be subject to attribution. Any income earned by the trust and not paid or payable to the beneficiaries will be taxable at the trust rate. As the trustee may wish to maintain an even hand among the beneficiaries, equalization can be achieved either by making tax-free capital distributions to the minor children (equal to the after-tax receipt of the adult children) in partial satisfaction of their interest (either while they're still minors if the corporate attribution rules would not apply or when the children are 18) or, alternatively, by making additional income allocations to such children on their attaining the age of majority.

[¶17,042] Loans

Subsection 56(4.1) was enacted to attribute income from property acquired by an individual or a trust with borrowed funds where the loan was from a non-arm's length party and one of the main reasons for the loan was to reduce or avoid tax by causing income from property to be included in the income of the other individual. Subsection 56(4.1) does not apply to loans to or a share investment in a corporation. If the shareholders are adult children, the corporate attribution rule will not apply. A parent could form a holding company and invest by way of a loan or preference shares. The common shares would be issued for nominal consideration to adult children or to a trust for their benefit. The corporation may invest in preference shares of a publicly traded corporation yielding accumulative dividends. The holding company would be subject only to refundable Part IV tax. Assuming all dividends received are paid to the shareholders as dividends, the holding company will not pay any tax. Each child not having any other source of income could receive approximately $50,000 per year of eligible dividends free of tax.

Subsection 56(4.1) would not apply to the following plan, which may afford parents protection similar to a loan. The attribution rules do not apply to gifts to adult children or to trusts for adult children. Parents may wish to settle a discretionary trust to finance university education or other expenses of their adult children. The trust vehicle would have the advantage of affording the parents, in their capacity as trustees, the ability to control the investment and distribution of funds. A parent could settle a trust in favour of his or her children as income beneficiaries, with a power of encroachment in favour of the spouse as a capital beneficiary. The parent could be a trustee. The income would be used to pay the education and other expenses of the children. The parent could effectively take back the capital by distributing it to his or her spouse on a tax-deferred basis as a capital distribution. The attribution rules would apply only to income, not to capital distributions by the trust to the spouse.

[¶17,044] Testamentary Trusts

As the attribution rules cease to apply on the death of the transferor, it is possible to use testamentary trusts in a will to enable beneficiaries to split their income after the death of a testator. Each testamentary trust is entitled to benefit from graduated tax rates. See further ¶17,120.

[¶17,046] Gifts or Loans from Non-Residents

The attribution rules do not apply to loans or transfers of property by non-residents. If there are relatives who reside outside of Canada, funds may be given or loaned to a Canadian minor or to a Canadian trust, without the attribution rules applying. It is essential that the funds emanate from the non-resident and not be part of a back-to-back transaction.

[¶17,047] Capital Gains for Minors

A parent or a grandparent may make an interest-free loan or a gift to an *inter vivos* trust for minor children or grandchildren where the investment is going to give rise to capital gains.

If a trust has been formed for minor children or grandchildren, the funds may be invested to yield primarily capital gains, which would be exempt from income attribution. It is only income from property earned by the trust and payable to a minor beneficiary or to a spouse that is subject to attribution. For example, an investment may be made in the shares of a public company that does not yield dividends or in a mutual fund where non-capital gains dividends are nominal. The attribution rules would apply only to dividends taxable in the hands of the minor beneficiaries. Alternatively, the trust may invest in collectibles (e.g., art, stamps, coins) or commodities to generate capital gains exempt from attribution.

[¶17,048] Income on Income

Because the income attribution rules do not apply to income on income, funds may be loaned to trusts for a spouse or minor children. For the first year, income from property earned by the trust and allocated to the beneficiaries would be subject to attribution. The loan may be repaid and the accumulated income reinvested by the family member or the trust. Any income earned on the reinvestment of the first year's income would not be attributed. The income attribution rules do not apply to income on income. Assume that in Year 1, a loan of $100,000 is made interest free to a spouse or to a trust for a minor child. The borrower then invests the funds at 6%. The interest of $6,000 is attributed to the lender, who must pay tax thereon. In Year 2, the loan is repaid and the $6,000 is invested at 6% by the spouse or trust. The spouse or trust will be taxable on $360 of interest income. It will not be subject to attribution.

[¶17,050] Business Income

Business income (other than that earned by a limited partnership) derived by a spouse, minor, or a trust for a spouse or minor would not be subject to attribution. The kiddie tax may apply if the business income is derived by a trust that provides services to a corporation where there is a related person as a specified shareholder, or to a professional partnership, or to a professional corporation. Subsection 108(5) provides that the treatment of trust income as income from property shall not apply for purposes of the attribution rules. For example, a CFO of a private company in which the CFO does not own any shares can consider having an *inter vivos* trust for the benefit of minor children and a spouse provide his or her services. The agreement must be carefully structured to ensure that the trust is an independent contractor. There are no personal service business rules applicable to a trust. The *Ferrel* case, 97 DTC 1565 (T.C.C.), lends support to the idea that subsection 56(2) should not apply to the consulting income. GST would have to be charged on the fees. The kiddie tax would not be applicable if the CFO owns no shares in the company to which the services are provided.

[¶17,052] Fair Market Value Sale

In *Evans v. The Queen*, 2005 DTC 1762 (T.C.C.), a dentist caused a professional corporation to pay a stock dividend of 487 non-voting class B preference shares to himself. He then sold the class B preference shares to a limited partnership of his wife (as general partner) and his children (as limited partners) in consideration for a promissory note of $487,000 with interest at a reasonable rate. The dentist claimed the capital gains exemption on the disposition. The limited partnership received actual and deemed dividends from redemptions on the class B shares which were taxable in the hands of his wife and children and used to repay the promissory note. The CRA attempted to re-characterize the payments received by the dentist as dividends, using the general anti-avoidance rule. The Court held that the transactions were not abusive and did not defeat the object in spirit of the Act. This is an example of where a fair market value sale of property to a spouse and children was successful.

[¶17,054] RESP

A registered education savings plan (RESP) may be formed for the benefit of a child. While the contributions are non-deductible, funds accumulate in the RESP on a tax-free basis until the child attends post-secondary education. The child will then be taxable on that portion of the RESP payments representing accumulated income. See further, ¶17,130 below.

[¶17,056] Capital Loss

It is possible to trigger a capital loss by transferring shares to a child or a trust for children. Similarly, a terminal loss — for example, on a rental property that has decreased in value — may be realized by a sale to a child or to a trust for a child.

Planning may be possible with a spouse. Assume that a spouse has an accrued capital loss but no capital gains. The other spouse has a capital gain that will be realized in the year. The first spouse sells the stock, realizing a capital loss, and the second spouse purchases it and after 30 days sells it. The effect of the superficial loss rules would be to effectively shift the capital loss to the second spouse (subparagraph 40(2)(g)(i) and paragraph 53(1)(f)) so that it may be applied against the capital gain (see Technical Interpretation 2001-0106905).

[¶17,058] Spousal RRSP

A taxpayer may make a contribution to an RRSP or to a spousal RRSP based on earned income. A contribution to a spousal RRSP is specifically excluded from the attribution rules (paragraph 74.5(12)(a)). However, the income attribution rules will apply if the spouse withdraws funds from the spousal RRSP within three years (the year of contribution plus two years) (subsection 146(8.3)). This may be distinguished from providing funds to a spouse in order that the spouse may contribute to his or her own RRSP based on his or her own earned income. In that case, the attribution rules may apply when the funds are subsequently withdrawn from the RRSP.

[¶17,060] Reasonable Salary to Spouse or Child

It is possible to pay a reasonable salary to a spouse or to a minor child without attribution. Consideration should be given to having the lower-income family member save the full amount of the salary that is earned, rather than have the funds used to pay household expenses. This will allow savings to be accumulated in the hands of the lower-income family members without a transfer of funds and, therefore, without attribution of the income earned on the investment of the funds.

[¶17,070] Canada Pension Plan Splitting

The *Canada Pension Plan* (CPP) contains rules which allow spouses or common-law partners who are living together (not separated or divorced) to assign retirement pensions to each other. With assignment, each spouse can receive a portion of the other's CPP pension. The amount depends on how long you lived together and on your contributory periods. For example, if you have lived together for 20% of both your contributory periods, you keep 80% of your pension and the remaining 20% is divided equally between you and your spouse. It appears that where both spouses are receiving CPP pensions (or one CPP and one QPP pension), the pension sharing must apply to both. Pension sharing commences the month following approval of an application by either spouse to Human Resources and Social Development Canada, and can be terminated by joint application or on certain contingencies such as divorce or death.

The attribution rules specifically provide that an income assigned under these rules (or comparable Quebec Pension Plan rules) is not attributable back to the assignor. It follows that in the right set of circumstances (for example, where one spouse is receiving a pension and the other is not) assignment may result in favourable income splitting.

[¶17,075] Pension Income Splitting

Married couples and common-law partners who are Canadian residents who receive income qualifying for the pension income tax credit would be permitted to allocate to their resident spouse (or common-law partner) up to one-half of that income. In this regard, it may be noted that it has been possible to split Canada Pension Plan payments between spouses since 1978 and the *Income Tax Act* has provided for spousal RRSPs since 1985. However, hitherto, splitting of other types of pension income, including RRSPs, RRIFs, and employer-sponsored registered pension plans was not permitted. When such a policy initiative is undertaken, it is natural to ask who will benefit and who will not? Obviously, pension income splitting will be of no assistance to seniors who are single or senior couples with equal income. Further, pension income splitting will be more or less irrelevant for the poor (i.e., those with little pension income to split) and the very rich. Pension income splitting will be most fruitful to older middle class couples where one spouse accumulated significant pension income and the other was not employed in the workforce.

It should be noted that, because the income allocated retains its character as pension income in the hands of the transferee, subject to limitations re the transferee's age, it will be eligible for the pension credit provided for in subsection 118(3). Remember that, for each individual, there is a $2,000 maximum to this tax credit. Other credits that may be affected by a change in income levels resulting from pension splitting include the spouse credit provided in subsection 118(1) and the age credit provided for in subsection 118(2). Likewise, splitting pension income may allow a pensioner access to Old Age Security Benefits that would otherwise be subject to the "clawback" tax imposed by section 180.2. On the other hand, benefits and tax credits calculated based on the total of the net incomes of both spouses or common-law partners — such as the Goods and Services Tax/Harmonized Sales Tax credit, Canada Child Tax Benefit, and related provincial or territorial benefits — will not be affected by pension splitting.

[¶17,080] Tax Planning the Will

[¶17,085] Introduction

It is generally recognized that everyone should make a will; it is, however, not always recognized that doing so can often be the occasion for some fruitful tax planning.

[¶17,090] The Importance of the Spouse as Beneficiary

To the extent that assets have appreciated in value — that is, so that there is untaxed capital gains — these assets should generally be left to the spouse, or a qualifying spouse trust. That way, the property "rolls over" to the spouse (or spouse trust) without immediate tax. Otherwise, the assets will usually be treated as if they had been liquidated at current market values (an exception arises where qualifying farm property passes to children, grandchildren, and so on).

To obtain tax deferral benefits on transfers to a spouse or common-law partner trust, the property transferred or distributed must indefeasibly vest in the trust within 36 months of the death of the person and the trust must be resident in Canada immediately after the vesting. A trust will be considered a valid spouse or common-law partner trust if it is created by the deceased's will, or by court order. The longer the lapse of time between the death of the transferor-spouse and the death of the beneficiary-spouse, the greater the tax advantage to be derived — whether the transfer is made directly to the surviving spouse, or to a spousal trust, the deemed disposition will be deferred until the death of the surviving spouse.

Obvious candidates for the rollover include real estate, shares of a corporation, investments that have gone up in value, and so on. Accordingly, to defer "death tax", shares of a family business are usually left to a spouse, or more likely, a spouse trust. However, there can be tax exposure even if the asset has not actually appreciated in value. An example of this would be a rental or other property on which depreciation claims have been made. Also, many older tax-shelter investments, even if virtually worthless, may attract tax if they are in what is known as a "negative cost base" position; generally, where the personal cost of an investment is less than the overall tax losses claimed and cash or other distributions from the partnership. If so, these too should be left to the spouse.

Don't forget that a second home is no longer covered by the principal residence exemption, so that if this is not left to a spouse, there could be capital gains tax on its appreciation as well.

If qualifying small business corporation shares (or farm or fishing property) eligible for the enhanced capital gains exemption — of up to $750,000 — are held, a number of options will be available. If the exemption is available, the individual will generally want to use it up by the time he or she passes away. This can be done even if the shares are left to a spouse, because of a special rule that allows an individual to "elect into" a capital gain on a property-by-property basis (e.g., one or more shares of a corporation). Also, the surviving spouse is potentially eligible for his or her own capital gains exemption. If it is expected that, after death, there will be future appreciation in the shares that will more than eat-up the surviving spouse's capital gains exemption, it may be a good idea to leave at least some shares to children (or grandchildren), if it is intended that they remain within the family. This could be done before death through an estate freeze reorganization, to meet the family's financial needs.

[¶17,095] The Principal Residence Exemption

Consideration should be given to leaving a residence to a beneficiary who will be eligible to claim the principal residence exemption on it. Remember, married couples, together with unmarried children under the age of 18, are generally entitled to only one principal residence exemption among them. However, the principal residence exemption might be maximized, for example, by leaving the residence to an adult child who does not already have a principal residence.

[¶17,100] Bequests of Farm or Fishing Property

Special rules apply to farm or fishing property passing to a beneficiary who is a child, grandchild, or great-grandchild of a deceased person. See ¶4375.

[¶17,105] Flow-Through Shares

Flow-through shares are a financing vehicle used in the oil and gas and mining industries and are issued by companies that need cash but do not need tax deductions. Instead, the investors in these issues receive the tax deductions. The investors can use the deductions to offset against other income. Because investors receive tax deductions, the shares acquired are deemed to have a cost base of nil. In the event of death, there is no provision in the Act to pass unused deductions on to the deceased's estate or beneficiaries. At the time of death, the shares are deemed to be sold for fair market value unless they are bequeathed to the spouse or common-law partner.

[¶17,110] Life Insurance

Generally, pursuant to subsection 148, upon the disposition of a life insurance policy, the excess of the cash surrender value over the adjusted cost base will be treated as income in the hands of the owner of the policy. However, subsection 148(9) specifically excludes from the definition of "disposition" a termination of a policy resulting from the death of the insured. Accordingly, the proceeds of a life insurance policy payable on the death of the insured will not produce taxable income to either the deceased or a beneficiary. The designation of a life insurance beneficiary may be made in

¶17,095

the will or in a document outside the will. Even where the designation is made in the will, it can be drafted such that the proceeds will not form part of the estate (which means savings on probate tax and protection from creditors of the estate).

[¶17,115] Low-Bracket Beneficiaries

Consideration should be given to leaving income-earning assets to beneficiaries who are in low tax brackets, such as grandchildren, a low-income child (or his or her spouse), and so on. This is because income from bequests to high-income individuals will, of course, be added to their other taxable income, thus resulting in a significant tax exposure.

[¶17,120] The Estate Split

An estate is treated as a separate taxpayer; therefore, it can take advantage of low-tax brackets, just like an individual. This means that, in effect, beneficiaries can "income split" with the estate. This opportunity has been made even more effective, due to a rule that an estate can choose to pay tax on income even though it is actually payable or distributed to beneficiaries.

To take advantage of this rule, it is recommended that the will make it clear that the estate can continue for a number of years at least. For example, if the will simply leaves assets to beneficiaries "outright", some estate planning experts question whether this favourable tax break can continue longer than one year after death (after which the beneficiaries are normally entitled to a distribution of the property from the estate).

In fact, the estate-split concept can be taken a giant step further by establishing several different "trusts" in a will. Each of these trusts can potentially be taxed separately so that the income-splitting advantages just mentioned can be multiplied. One word of warning, though: the CRA has the power to "lump" the trusts together where they ultimately accrue to the same beneficiary or "group or class" of beneficiaries. However, there are few reported cases where the CRA has successfully taken this position. For example, an owner–manager's will might leave the shares of his or her corporation in a spouse trust, followed by the creation of multiple testamentary trusts for children/grandchildren, to gain low tax rates on dividends paid on the shares. However, consideration should be given to whether *post-mortem* planning procedures would be advisable after the death of the surviving spouse, and if so, the impact on the plan.

The following are some scenarios where the "estate split" may be realized; naturally, the degree to which an estate may split advantageously will depend on its size.

Spousal Trusts

Spousal trusts are effective estate planning tools for reasons that extend beyond tax planning. However, they may also be advantageous from a tax planning perspective. Rather than leaving all assets to a spouse, a portion of the assets may be bequeathed to a trust for his or her benefit. Income earned by the trust may accumulate and be reported by the trust on a separate tax return at graduated rates. This may be advantageous where the income would otherwise be taxable to the spouse at top marginal rates. After its fiscal year end, accumulated income becomes capital and could be distributed as a tax-free capital distribution.

Trusts for Children

Rather than bequeath the entire estate to a spouse and/or a trust for his or her benefit, part of the estate may be bequeathed to a separate trust for the benefit of the children. Assuming that the children are young and that the surviving spouse would have to discharge the expenses out of after-tax dollars, this may be an attractive alternative. The trust would also benefit from graduated tax rates on accumulating income not subject to the preferred beneficiary election. If the testator is concerned that the parent may require the funds, provision may be made for the parent to be a capital beneficiary and to receive the remaining trust property on the child reaching a certain age (e.g., age 25). This would enable the parent to use the income (and capital, if necessary) to finance a child's education and to have the balance of the capital available to assist the parent.

A Trust for Each Child

Rather than bequeath the entire residue of the estate to adult children, a portion may be bequeathed to separate trusts for the benefit of each adult child, so as to enable part of the estate income to be reported on separate trust returns at graduated tax rates rather than being taxable at the top marginal rates of the children.

Trusts for Grandchildren

Rather than bequeath the entire residue of the estate (after the death of the parents) to children, part of the estate may be bequeathed to separate trusts for grandchildren. Each trust would benefit from marginal tax rates and would be able to deduct income paid or payable to the grandchild or allocated to him or her by means of the preferred beneficiary election. Such a trust would enable the parents to use no or low tax dollars to pay for the children's annual expenses and to save up for their university education or to assist them in buying a home or a business. This would be preferable to bequeathing the assets to a child who would be taxable at the top marginal rate and would then use after-tax dollars to pay for his or her children's expenses. If equalization is of concern (the parent wants to treat each child equally), the will could provide for an add-back of the assets bequeathed to grandchildren trusts. Each child would be entitled to an equal share of the grossed-up estate and would be considered to have already received the assets bequeathed to trusts for his or her children.

¶17,120

[¶17,125] RRSPs and RRIFs

Subsection 146(8.8) provides that, immediately before death, the annuitant of an RRSP is deemed to have received as income a sum equal to the fair market value of all of the property of the RRSP. The general rule is that all of this income is taxed as a benefit in the terminal tax return of the deceased pursuant to subsection 146(8) (RRIFs are accorded a similar treatment under subsection 143.6(6)). The first major exception to the general rule is where the annuitant designates his or her spouse as the beneficiary of the RRSP.

Generally, a spouse (or common-law partner) should be designated as beneficiary of an RRSP (or RRIF). Otherwise, the entire balance or value may be included as taxable income in the decedent's final (terminal period) return. However, before the spouse (or common-law partner) is designated as the beneficiary, consider the following questions:

- Does the spouse already have sufficient registered investments?

- Is the spouse the higher income earner?

- Is it probable that the estate would have reduced income, capital losses, or a loss carryforward to report in the year of death?

In certain circumstances, it may be appropriate to make the spouse the beneficiary to only a portion of the RRSPs or RRIFs.

Naming a spouse or other specified individual (rather than one's estate) will serve to exclude the RRSP (or RRIF) proceeds from one's estate for probate purposes. This has a number of advantages, including saving on probate taxes, which are not insignificant in British Columbia and Ontario. Of course, it is possible that his or her spouse will pass away before the testator or that the latter is divorced, unmarried, or otherwise without a spouse or common-law partner. In which case, there is another tax-reducing opportunity: if a child or grandchild who is "financially dependent" is designated, special rules tax the RRSP inheritance in the hands of the child or grandchild — who will probably be in a lower tax bracket than the decedent — instead of being added to the decedent's income in the year that he or she passes away.

It is presumed in the first instance that a child/grandchild was not financially dependent if his or her income in the year preceding the death exceeded a specified amount. That presumption can be rebutted by factual evidence. The specified amount at which the presumption against dependence comes into play is the basic personal amount for the year preceding death, which amount is indexed for inflation. Thus, for a death in 2012, the child is presumed not to have been dependent on the deceased where the child's 2011 income did not exceed the 2011 basic personal amount of $10,527.

Where the child/grandchild was dependent by reason of mental or physical infirmity on a supporting parent/grandparent who died, the preceding year's basic personal amount used as a benchmark in the presumption of dependency is supplemented by the preceding year's disability amount (both as indexed). Thus, where the death occurred in 2012 and the child/grandchild was dependent by reason of mental or physical infirmity, the child/grandchild looks back to a 2011 amount of $10,527 + $7,341 = $17,868.

Under subsection 146(5.1), a contribution can be made on behalf of the deceased taxpayer to a spousal RRSP within 60 days of the calendar year of death.

[¶17,130] RESPs

Given the incentives, parents should be encouraged to establish a registered education savings plan ("RESP") for their children. Where the children are minors, it will be especially important to address the issue of any RESPs of which the testator is the subscriber in the will.

In a technical interpretation (Document No. 2005-0118891E5, August 3, 2005) the CRA was asked to comment on a situation involving an individual who, under the terms of his will, left all his movable and immovable properties to his two-year old son. The terms of the will also provided that, following the settlement of his estate, a RESP, under which he was the subscriber and his son was the beneficiary, would be transferred to a testamentary trust created for his son's benefit. The CRA was asked if the testamentary trust would qualify as a "subscriber" under the definition of this term in subsection 146.1(1) of the Act. The CRA confirmed that, since a trust was deemed by subsection 104(2) of the Act to be an individual in respect of the trust property, it could qualify as an RESP subscriber under paragraph (*c*) of subsection 146.1(1), provided the trust acquired the individual's right in the RESP after his death or contributed into the plan in respect of the beneficiary.

[¶17,135] Debt Forgiveness

If the individual forgives the debt while alive, there will be adverse tax consequences to the debtor if a debt was investment or business-related (that is, the interest was potentially deductible to the debtor). However, paragraph 80(2)(*a*) provides an exception to debt settlement, if by way of "bequest or inheritance". Therefore, if a person is financially indebted to an individual and he or she wishes to forgive the debt, it is best to do this in the will. The concept behind this exception is that the testator could have left the debtor a bequest which would have enabled the debtor to repay the debt; so this provision "short forms" this requirement.

¶17,130

[¶17,140] Association Rules

When leaving the shares of a corporation to beneficiaries, consider carefully the impact of the "association rules", if the beneficiary and/or family members are also shareholders in an incorporated business. Unless care is taken, the result may be that, after death, the corporation may have to share its entitlement to the "small business deduction" (the low rate of tax for business corporations) and certain other tax benefits with that of the beneficiary's corporation.

Alternatives may be to leave the shares to grandchildren, or a son- or daughter-in-law (although the family law aspects of such a course of action must also be taken into account).

[¶17,145] Corporations and Partnerships

If shares of a corporation, or an interest in a partnership, whose value has appreciated, are held, and these assets are to be left to someone other than a spouse, it should be remembered that, in many cases, it will be advisable to undertake some rather complex tax manoeuvres within the first year of the estate; otherwise, there could be "double tax" exposure when the underlying corporation/partnership assets are sold off.

Unfortunately, many executors are not aware of these manoeuvres until it is too late — as stated, the deadline may be one year after the individual passes away. In this situation, it should be ensured that executors are advised to seek professional tax advice. This should generally be done whenever shares or partnership interests are left to someone other than a spouse, and have appreciated in value (a similar situation may arise when the surviving spouse who is the beneficiary under a spouse trust passes away). In addition, the will should give executors and trustees authority to make the various tax elections and designations that are required.

[¶17,150] Charities

A charitable gift made by will is deemed made by the deceased immediately before death and therefore gives rise to charitable donation tax credit in the year of death. If an RRSP or RRIF names the estate of the deceased as beneficiary, the value of the RRSP, etc., is included in income of the deceased immediately before death, and if the proceeds are then donated to charity under the will, there is a correct offset of income by charitable donation credit. However, if the RRSP or RRIF names the charity as beneficiary, there is no donation credit for the estate and the estate and charity are jointly liable for the tax liability. The death benefit under a life insurance policy is subject to the same inconsistency where a charity is the named beneficiary. A donation credit is permitted to the deceased in the year of death where a charity is named as the beneficiary of an RRSP, RRIF, TFSA, or life insurance policy (provided the policy was issued to a Canadian resident).

The effective inclusion rate for donations of listed public securities and shares of private corporations to charitable organizations and public foundations has been reduced from 25% to 0%. The same applies where the publicly traded securities or shares were acquired with employee stock options. Donations of ecologically-sensitive lands to a conservation charity also benefit from the 0% capital gains inclusion rate.

[¶17,155] Spouse Trusts

A spouse trust can be a very effective succession and estate planning vehicle. It combines the tax-deferral advantages of leaving assets to a spouse, with the ability to protect family interests. Where a successful business is involved, it is more usual to use a spouse trust rather than leaving the shares and other assets outright to the surviving spouse, in order to preclude the possibility of the surviving spouse changing the terms of his or her will, e.g., in the event of a remarriage. In addition, the appointment of suitable trustees may protect against mismanagement of the business or distributions which could jeopardize financially the viability of the ongoing business. Specifically, this could provide protection from the surviving spouse exercising retraction rights attaching to freeze shares, e.g., where an elderly surviving spouse has remarried and is under the influence of a spendthrift spouse.

Spouse trusts may be used for *inter vivos* (lifetime) gifts or testamentary bequests. In order to qualify for rollover treatment, the trust must provide that:

- The spouse is entitled to receive all of the income of the trust that arises before the spouse's death; and

- No person except the spouse may, before the spouse's death, receive or otherwise obtain the use of any of the income or capital of the trust (in addition, the capital property transferred or distributed to the spouse or spouse trust must vest indefeasibly in the spouse trust within 36 months of the taxpayer's death or, upon written application to the Minister within that period, within such longer period as the Minister considers reasonable in the circumstances. Further, the deceased must have been a Canadian resident).

Several comments can be made in respect of these requirements:

(1) As noted above, the spouse must be entitled to obtain all of the income of the trust during his or her lifetime. However, if the trust holds shares of a corporation, subject to fiduciary-type considerations, it is possible to effectively control the amount of income received by the trust and, consequently, the amount to which the spouse is entitled. Specifically, where a corporation is held by a trust, the dividends paid on the shares may be regulated by the directors of the corporation (in such circumstances, it may be prudent to ensure that control of the corporation is not held by the trustees themselves; otherwise, the spouse might assert that distributions

should have been made by the corporation as a consequence of the duties of the trustees).

(2) The requirement that no other person can receive or obtain the use of capital does not mean that the spouse is entitled to receive the capital. In other words, as long as no one else may receive or obtain the use of the capital, the trust will not be disqualified as a spouse trust.

(3) In respect of the use of capital requirement, careful drafting is required in order to ensure that this requirement is not violated. For example, a loan to a relative might be interpreted as allowing someone other than the spouse to obtain the use of capital. Provisions in a trust that allow this could throw the trust offside. Although CRA Document No. 9627345, November 14, 1996, and paragraph 16 of IT-305R4 indicate that a loan to a non-spouse on commercial terms (e.g., commercial interest rates) would not taint a spouse trust, Document No. 2003-0019235, July 17, 2003, indicates that where the trust *permits* funds to be loaned (or any other form of assistance to be provided) to anyone other than the spouse for inadequate consideration, this would disqualify the trust, *whether or not such a loan was actually made.* The latter document appears to indicate that the will in question authorized the trustee to lend funds or provide any other financial assistance to any beneficiary with or without consideration.

A Technical Interpretation (Document No. 2006-0185551C6, September 11, 2006) also raised the question of whether the rollover to a spouse trust would be available if the trustee is required to pay life insurance premiums. The CRA's negative answer was based on the argument that a duty to fund a life insurance policy out of trust capital or income would be one under which another person may obtain the use of the trust capital or income.

It appears that the concept of being able to "obtain the use" is potentially very broad. However, paragraph 15 of Interpretation Bulletin IT-305R4 indicates that the doctrine of constructive receipt applies. Consequently, the payment according to the will of, or the provision in the will for the payment of, any income of the trust to a person other than the spouse, on the condition that it be used solely for the benefit of the spouse, does not disqualify an otherwise qualifying spouse trust (notwithstanding the CRA's administrative policy as stated above, even if a loan is on commercial terms, query whether the debtor is nevertheless obtaining the use of the capital). As the "no use" requirement must presumably be met under the terms of the trust, appropriate language should be inserted in the document.

In *Balaz v. Balaz et al.*, 2009 CanLII 17973 (ON S.C.), a rectification order was obtained in order to knock out certain boilerplate within a will, the objective being to create a qualifying spousal trust. This included boilerplate that allowed loans and the use of real estate held by the spousal trust on non-commercial terms. The order also vitiated a standard corporate boilerplate provision allowing the trustees to incorporate and transfer assets of the estate into a corporation on such terms as they consider advisable.

Therefore, it appears to be advisable to examine closely the powers given to trustees in a spouse trust in order to make sure (for example) that the "boilerplate" does not trip over the "no use" requirement, e.g., by providing for a power to lend on any terms they see fit. If there are changes to the CRA policy in respect to spouse trusts from time to time, it would necessitate an amendment to the document — if possible. Another approach would be to provide that trustees must adhere to the policies of the CRA in respect of the "no use" and other requirements in respect of qualifying spouse trust status, as delineated from time to time.

(4) The meaning of "income" and "capital" as mentioned above pertains to trust/estate law. As mentioned previously, in a typical succession plan, freeze shares will be an important (perhaps the primary) asset in a spouse trust. While dividends on the freeze shares are treated as income, and therefore must be distributed to the spouse, a redemption is treated as a return of capital, even though the redemption may trigger a deemed dividend. Therefore, it is not a requirement of a spouse trust that the proceeds of a redemption be distributed to the spouse. It should also be noted that, per subsection 108(3), capital dividends from private corporations are excluded from income for these purposes (as are capital gains dividends from mutual fund corporations); this subsection also applies to alter ego and joint partner trusts.

(5) Question 14 of the 2008 APFF Round Table[1] may suggest that a spouse trust should contain a non-assignability clause. The question itself related to a self-benefit trust; however, the requirements (that the individual is entitled to receive all the income that arises before the individual's death and no person except the individual may, before the individual's death receive or otherwise obtain the use of any of the income or capital of the trust) are similar to the requirements of a spouse trust. The CRA indicated that, without a non-assignability clause, "an individual, residing in Quebec, has the possibility of transferring his rights in the income and capital of the trust pursuant to the Civil Code of Quebec, without being prevented from doing so by a provision of the trust indenture", so as to contravene the conditions in subparagraph 73(1.01)(c)(ii). As can be seen, the question is specifically referenced to Quebec laws, where Article 1285 of the Civil Code of Quebec specifically provides for assignability. Based on informal discussions, it appears that, at time of writing at least, the CRA has not considered the applicability of the foregoing views outside of Quebec and to trusts other than self-benefit trusts. However, consideration should nonetheless be given to including a non-assignability clause.

See page ii for explanation of footnotes.

[1] 2008-0285071C6, October 10, 2008.

¶17,155

One problem arises where the trust provides for the payment of debt that does not exclusively relate to the surviving spouse. This may taint the spouse trust and therefore destroy the tax deferral that is potentially available. Note, however, that subsection 70(7) and related provisions allow a tainted spouse trust to be purified, in respect of particular testamentary debts: certain debts that would otherwise taint the trust because someone other than the spouse is entitled to the trust's capital may be satisfied by specified assets, with the remaining assets qualifying for rollover treatment. For these purposes, eligible testamentary debt means any debt owing by the deceased taxpayer immediately before death and any amount payable in consequence of the taxpayer's death (other than any amount payable to any person as a beneficiary of the taxpayer's estate). Typical eligible testamentary debts include funeral expenses and income taxes payable for the terminal year and prior years.

In general terms, the provision deems properties to pass to the trust at fair market value to the extent of the value of testamentary debts that are non-qualifying debts (generally, the deceased's testamentary debts other than estate or succession taxes, or debts secured by a mortgage). All other properties passing to the spousal trust will remain subject to rollover treatment.

In particular, subsection 70(7) permits the personal representative to designate one or more properties (including any money) to which subsection 70(6) does not apply, with the result that such properties are deemed to have been disposed of for proceeds equal to their fair market value at the time of the deceased's death. Property which is not so designated is eligible for the tax-free rollover to a qualifying spouse trust. The properties so designated (or listed) must have an aggregate fair market value at least equal to the non-qualifying debts to be paid out of the trust property.

Although these special rules may effectively "untaint" a spouse trust, care should be taken in this area. For example, per paragraph 19 of Interpretation Bulletin IT-449, some debts may taint the trust in a manner that cannot be remedied by subsection 70(7), for example, a contingent liability to make good any deficiency that may arise in another trust created under the same will. One solution is to draft the will so as to allow the executors to split assets into two trusts — one which qualifies as a spouse trust and another which does not. Appreciated and other assets that would otherwise result in a tax liability would go to the spouse trust. Liabilities, bequests to other parties, and so on can be paid out of a second trust.

While spouse trusts are a preferred succession planning provision, care should be taken. Under Ontario family law at least, an equalization right is available, notwithstanding the terms of the will.

With respect to the capital gains exemption, subsection 110.6(12) potentially allows a spouse trust to claim the surviving spouse's unused capital gains exemption in respect of the deemed disposition when the surviving spouse passes away (per subsection 104(4), the deemed disposition on the death of the surviving spouse occurs at the end of the day on which the spouse dies, so as to be taxable in the spouse trust. Paragraph 110.6(14)(c) may treat a personal trust as being related to a beneficiary for the purpose of the two-year hold requirement in respect of qualifying small business corporation shares; however the requirements in this situation may be somewhat stringent).

Spouse trusts can give rise to some distinct *post-mortem* tax planning issues. A spouse trust should build-in a "lagged distribution" of assets after the death of the surviving spouse. In addition, special provisions may be included to facilitate a paragraph 88(1)(d) "bump". At the time of writing, the stop-loss rules in subsection 40(3.6) continue to apply to spouse trusts so that the affiliation rules continue to be an issue.

[¶17,160] Rights or Things

By virtue of subsection 70(2), where a deceased at the time of death has "rights or things" which, if they had been realized or disposed of during the taxpayer's lifetime, would have been included in computing income, the value of such rights or things must be included in the final return of the deceased. Although the phrase "rights or things" is not defined in the Act, examples may include work-in-progress of a sole-practice professional, dividends that have been declared but not paid, unused vacation leave credits, unmatured bond bonus coupons, and so on. However, in Document No. 2008-0300791E5, March 20, 2009, the CRA indicated that a dividend that has been paid by an uncashed cheque that is negotiable on the date of death is not a right or thing.

The CRA has indicated that a bonus payable to an owner–manager of the corporation qualifies as a "right or thing", provided that it was declared before death. Where, however, the employer has a contractual obligation to pay a bonus annually or on some other periodic basis, but the bonus for the period has not been declared as at the date of death, the amount is considered to be a periodic payment of remuneration taxable under subsection 70(1).

In simple terms, rights or things can be thought of as amounts to which the taxpayer became entitled before the taxpayer's death and which, if collected or otherwise realized, would have formed part of the deceased's income. "Normal" accounts receivable from the business or property of the deceased are not considered rights or things; however, they are included in the deceased's income in the terminal year either in the computation of profit from the business or property under section 9, or by virtue of paragraph 12(1)(b).

Where there is doubt whether the nature of income is a periodic payment subject to subsection 70(1) or a right or thing under subsection 70(2), it is the CRA's policy to generally resolve the issue in favour of the taxpayer (see IT-210R, paragraph 2). As a general rule, it is preferable to have the amounts considered rights or things because the amounts can be taxable to the deceased's beneficiaries (and not the deceased) in the circumstances described below.

Subsection 70(3) provides that where rights or things of a deceased taxpayer are distributed or transferred to beneficiaries within one year or within 90 days of the mailing of the notice of assessment in respect of the final return, whichever is later, the value of such rights or things may be excluded from the deceased's final return. Instead, the value of such rights or things may be included in computing the beneficiaries' income at the time those rights or things are realized (given the tax burden involved, the personal representative should not make the subsection 70(3) election without the beneficiary's consent; the personal representative should also verify that he or she has the power under the will to make the election).

There are two principal advantages in using subsection 70(3). Firstly, the rate of tax payable on rights or things may be lower if they are transferred to the beneficiaries of an estate; that is, the total income may be spread over several beneficiaries resulting in a lower rate of tax. Secondly, the tax burden attached to the rights or things can be deferred until they are "realized" by the beneficiary. A dividend is "realized" when it is received by the beneficiary. Unpaid salary, vacation pay, commissions, etc., are realized when the beneficiary receives a cheque from the deceased's employer.

If the rights or things are not transferred to a beneficiary as described above, the rights or things can be included in a separate return under subsection 70(2). The separate return includes only the value of the rights or things and assumes that the taxpayer was another person. In other words, income splitting is allowed to the extent of the value of the rights or things because they are not included in the regular terminal return with the deceased's other income. This is beneficial because the marginal tax rate which will apply to the rights or things will normally be lower than the tax rate applicable to the other income in the regular terminal return. Additionally, most personal tax credits may be claimed in the separate return, including the basic personal credit, the married person's credit, the dependent person credit and the age credit, notwithstanding that the full amount of such credits can also be used in the regular terminal return.

Note that, because it is the "value" of the right or thing that is included in income, certain expenses may be deducted by the personal representative. For instance, the personal representative may be entitled to deduct, from the interest received on a bond, interest paid on a loan taken out by the deceased to buy the bond.

To file the separate return, the deceased's personal representative must elect to do so by the later of (1) one year after the day of death, and (2) 90 days of the mailing of the notice of assessment for the terminal year. As noted, the separate return is not applicable where the rights or things

¶17,160

were transferred to the deceased's beneficiaries in the circumstances outlined above.

The rights or things election can be revoked in writing by the personal representative within the time allowed for the filing of the election as noted above (subsection 70(4)).

[¶17,165] Probate Tax

No discussion of tax planning the will would be complete without a brief mention of probate tax (or, as it is referred to in Ontario, "estate administration tax"). In essence, probate planning is aimed at reducing the value of the estate that passes to the personal representative — probate tax is proportional to the value of the estate, so the lower the value of the estate, the lower the probate tax that will be payable. Reducing the value of the estate can be achieved through the use of multiple wills and a variety of will substitutes. These strategies cannot be reviewed here. It will suffice to note that many of the more popular probate planning techniques (such as transferring assets to an alter ego trust or into joint tenancy with the intended beneficiary) present significant potential pitfalls, not the least of which is that they can hinder effective tax planning. For example:

- if the bulk of a testator's assets pass outside his or her estate to the intended beneficiaries, this will mean foregoing the use of one or more testamentary trusts to engage in *post-mortem* income splitting;

- unless the transferee lives there, transferring a principal residence into joint tenancy will mean the loss of half the principal residence exemption from the date of the transfer; and

- transferring assets to an alter ego or joint partner trust raises a host of tax issues, such as the fact that such trusts are taxed at the flat rate applicable to *inter vivos* trusts rather than the marginal rates applicable to individuals and testamentary trusts, and that any capital gains or losses realized on the deemed disposition of assets held in these trusts will be segregated from gains or losses taxable to the deceased in the year of death.

Aside from potential income tax pitfalls, common probate planning techniques may entail increased legal and accounting fees, exposure to creditors, and complicating the administration of the estate. Proceed with caution.

[¶17,167] Alter Ego and Joint Partner Trusts

[¶17,168] The Nature of Alter Ego and Joint Partner Trusts

Traditionally, Canadians have used a will to distribute assets owned at death. However, a number of problems can arise when assets pass under a will. Probate taxes (which are highest in Ontario and British Columbia where they are, respectively, 1.5% and 1.4% of the gross estate) are one high-profile issue. Other disadvantages include variation claims by dependants, and lack of privacy and creditor protection. To avoid these and other disadvantages, many planners have been using will substitutes in order to transfer assets.

It has always been possible to use an *inter vivos* trust as a will substitute. However, a gift of assets to a non-spousal trust that names other persons as beneficiaries usually results in a disposition of those assets at fair market value for income tax purposes. This can result in the payment of significant income tax at the time of the transfer. However, fairly recent tax changes introduced the concepts of an alter ego trust and a joint spousal trust (now referred to as "joint partner trusts" to take into account the inclusion of same-sex couples). Both concepts apply to trusts established after 1999. The key change is to allow a rollover of assets into a qualifying trust. If the trust meets the alter ego conditions, the taxpayer is automatically subject to a rollover and the trust is subject to a deemed disposition on that individual's death (Note: The deemed disposition under paragraph 104(4)(*a*) occurs at the end of the day on which the settlor dies, such that subsection 75(2) does not apply to such gain or loss). If this result is not desired, the trust must elect under subparagraph 104(4)(*a*)(ii.1) for its first tax year, not to have the rollover apply. It should be noted, however, that apart from specific changes pertaining to alter ego and joint partner trusts, the normal rules of the Act apply to these trusts. Practitioners are still in the process of analyzing how these rules apply to particular scenarios. Some of the issues that have been identified are discussed below; however, the list is by no means exhaustive. Some practitioners are coming to the view that these trusts may not be as useful as originally thought, especially if other methods of planning are available (e.g., multiple wills).

Each of these trusts is a modified form of the pre-existing spouse trust. The spouse trust rules allow an individual to transfer assets to a trust on a tax-deferred basis provided that the spouse, prior to his or her death,

(a) is entitled to receive all the income of the trust; and

(b) is the only person able to receive the income or capital of the trust during his or her lifetime.

Alter ego trusts refer to trusts created by those who are least 65 years of age, for their own benefit. A joint partner trust, which requires the same age threshold, refers to trusts established for the joint benefit of a taxpayer and his or her spouse. Under the provisions, which apply starting in 2000, it is possible to transfer assets to these trusts without a current tax liability. These trusts could replace a will since, like a will, they can specify who gets what after a taxpayer passes away.

¶17,168

For both types of trusts, the taxpayer (or the taxpayer in combination with his or her spouse, in the case of a joint partner trust) must be entitled to receive all the income of the trust prior to death. Also, no person can obtain the use of any income or capital of the trust before the taxpayer's death (or that of the taxpayer and the surviving spouse, in the case of a joint partner trust). Because an *inter vivos* trust rather than a will is involved, alter ego and joint partner trusts can be used to avoid probate fees. In fact, they avoid the probate process itself, which involves public disclosure of a deceased's assets and, sometimes more to the point — who gets them.

As stated previously, alter ego and joint partner trusts contemplate that the trust will have contingent beneficiaries who will be able to receive income and capital of the trust after the death of the individual or the surviving spouse (as the case may be). The assets in the trust would then effectively bypass probate, provided that the trust qualifies as a true *inter vivos* trust (if the concern is to avoid wills variation legislation, one may have to be careful about the types of rights retained by the individual. In at least one province, an *inter vivos* trust can become subject to wills variation legislation as a result of reversionary rights enjoyed by the deceased before death).

In the succession planning context, an alter ego or joint partner trust may offer potential advantages, including adding flexibility to the standard estate freeze. In a typical estate freeze, the principal of the corporation exchanges his or her common shares for retractable shares with a fixed value equal to the value of the corporation. A family trust then subscribes for new common shares at a nominal value, since all the value of the corporation resides in the retractable shares owned by the principal. The principal's retractable shares typically have a significant value and a significant inherent capital gain. In order to avoid triggering the inherent capital gain, the principal usually retains personal ownership of the retractable shares, which exposes those shares to probate. Under the legislation, it is possible for the principal to gift the retractable shares to a joint partner trust (as well as an alter ego trust) without triggering immediate tax on the capital gain. All trust income would be available for use by the principal and the principal's spouse during their respective lifetimes. During the lifetime of the principal, that income would generally be taxed in the hands of the principal under the normal income attribution rules. On the death of the survivor of the principal and the spouse, the assets in the trust would be held for new beneficiaries named in the trust deed (presumably, the children), effectively bypassing probate.

In addition, using Ontario as an example, it may be possible to draft the joint partner trust so as to obtain a degree of protection both against spousal claims in the event of a separation, and to protect against the spouse's right to an equalization in *lieu* of taking under the will. Since the freeze shares can often account for most of the value in an estate, the latter right can have a serious effect on a succession plan. As well, the principal can have a degree of creditor protection (see further discussion below).

[¶17,169] Advantages

In Ontario in particular, an alternative approach to probate planning involves multiple wills. The following are some advantages of alter ego/joint partner trusts *vis-à-vis* a will:

- **Marital Property Protection.** In Ontario at least, unless a domestic contract is in place, a spouse may opt for an equalization of net family property if a "valuation date" occurs during lifetime, as well as in *lieu* of what is left to the spouse in a will. However, an individual may choose to dispose of property by gifts *inter vivos*, including to a joint partner (or alter ego) trust. Two possible challenges include improvident depletion under the FLA, (R.S.O. 1990, c. F-3) and a challenge under fraudulent conveyance legislation based on *Stone v. Stone*, (1999) 46 O.R. (3d) 31, aff'd (2001) 55 O.R. (3d) 491, where, under Ontario's *Fraudulent Conveyance Act*, the spouse was held to be a "creditor or other". While commentators have noted these possibilities, it should be remembered that, if the alternative is to "do nothing", the right to an equalization is clear. Practically speaking, a long length of time of the transfer to a trust prior to death may be helpful, as is having a good rationale for the transfer.

Arguably at least, the transfer of property to a joint partner trust might have the effect of eliminating a spouse's equalization rights under the FLA, without the undesired tax consequences. Suppose that an individual, Bill, were to remarry. Bill transfers his investment portfolio to a joint partner trust under which both he and his new spouse have life interests and Bill's children are entitled to the capital after the later to die of Bill and his spouse. The trustees may also have the power to encroach on capital in favour of Bill and his spouse. Suppose further that Bill predeceases his spouse and, under his will, he leaves his spouse with a life interest in his estate. At the valuation date (i.e., the date before the date of Bill's death), Bill would no longer own the investment portfolio; all he would have is an income interest in the joint partner trust. His spouse would have an identical income interest in the same trust (if the transfer were to an alter ego trust, Bill would have an interest in the trust, but this would not be the case for his spouse. Therefore, the transfer is subject to equalization, presumably based on the value (for FLA purposes) of Bill's interest in the trust). Arguably, these equal interests should effectively neutralize each other in the context of determining the equalization payment to which his spouse would be entitled. In effect, the joint partner trust should not only eliminate any need to pay Ontario probate taxes at the time of Bill's death, it may also arguably eliminate his spouse's right to an equalization payment *vis-à-vis* the investment portfolio.

Careful consideration must be given to the terms of the trust in order to avoid any argument that the trust was established in bad faith (the apparent equality of income interests will militate against arguments that there has been an improvident depletion. As discussed, *Stone v. Stone* may also be relevant). For example, arm's-length trustees should be appointed, both spouses should be given an equal income interest, and the power of encroachment in favour of both spouses should be the same. If the income interests are fully discretionary, with the only proviso being that all income must be distributed to the income beneficiaries, a court may not necessarily value the interests of an individual and his or her spouse equally. There may also be certain inherent problems relating to the appointment of trustees for these types of trusts. Usually, the settlor (i.e., the taxpayer who would be transferring the property to the trust) would want to be a trustee, with the power to distribute whenever he or she wanted. However, paragraph (*b*) of the definition of "property" (in subsection 4(1) of the FLA) stipulates that, for the purposes of net family property, property includes therein "property disposed of by a spouse but over which the spouse has, alone or in conjunction with another person, a power to revoke the disposition or a power to consume or dispose of the property". However, if a third party was appointed as a trustee, the settlor may have a difficult time asking for the property to be returned to him or her, as the trustee would have a fiduciary duty to the residual beneficiaries.

- **Asset Protection.** An alter ego or joint partner trust may offer a degree of creditor protection. An estate is subject to the claims of creditors of the decedent. While the transfer of assets to an alter ego or joint partner trust can be set aside, the creditor must take affirmative action; if structured carefully, creditor protection during lifetime may be possible.

It has been observed that the creditor protection of an alter ego or joint partner trust may be limited: the initial transfer into the trust could be challenged under fraudulent conveyance legislation or set aside under the *Bankruptcy and Insolvency Act*. In addition, a bankruptcy trustee could oppose the settlor's discharge, unless the trustees distribute capital to the settlor. While this is true, it should also be remembered that, if the assets to be protected have appreciated in value (or otherwise have a deferred tax exposure), conventional creditor protection techniques involving a transfer of assets require that there be a rollover to the transferee, lest the deferred tax be triggered by virtue of the transfer. Thus, other than a transfer to a spouse, which may not be desirable (or possible), the alternatives to transferring assets to an alter ego or joint partner trust are limited (one alternative could be to transfer assets to a self-benefit trust; however, this may be even more problematic).

¶17,169

It is suggested that (at least the majority of) the trustees of an alter ego or joint partner trust be persons other than the settlor. For one thing, courts would obviously be skeptical of situations where the settlor is also a trustee; in addition, a trustee in bankruptcy can have the settlor removed under the *Bankruptcy and Insolvency Act* and replaced with a more "desirable" person. In addition, capital distributions should be discretionary; obviously, the trust should not be revocable by the settlor.

- **Provincial Tax Planning.** Although careful planning is required, It may be possible to obtain the benefit of lower provincial tax rates on the property in the trust. This is discussed further at ¶17,170 under the heading "Reversionary Trust Rules/Interprovincial Planning".

- **Confidentiality.** Probating a will is a public process. The applicable legislation requires that the probate application list all the assets of the deceased and the total value of those assets. This list is available to any member of the public who cares to pay the nominal fee required in order to obtain a copy of the documents. Of course, there may also be advantages from the non-public disclosure of particular beneficiaries.

- **Dependants' Relief Protection.** Under provincial legislation, various classes of dependants can ask the court to rewrite the will if the dependant is not satisfied with the provisions of the will. These statutes may allow a surviving spouse and surviving children to challenge the will based on the criteria outlined by the Supreme Court of Canada in the *Tataryn* ([1994] 2 S.C.R. 807) decision. In essence, the court is asked to judge whether the deceased fulfilled his or her moral obligation to the person in question (independent of need).

In some provinces, including British Columbia and Nova Scotia, dependants' relief legislation is limited to the assets in the estate; accordingly, an alter ego or joint partner trust can be effective in dealing with these concerns. However, section 72 of Ontario's *Succession Law Reform Act* deems certain assets to be part of the estate; paragraph 72(1)(*e*) includes "any disposition of property made by the deceased in trust or otherwise, to the extent that the deceased at the date of his or her death retained, either alone or in conjunction with another person or persons by the express provisions of the disposing instrument, a power to revoke such disposition, or a power to consume, invoke or dispose of the principal thereof, but the provisions of this clause do not affect the right of any income beneficiary to the income accrued and undistributed at the date of the death of the deceased".

At the very least, this provision greatly weakens the ability to use alter ego and joint partner trusts to avoid dependants' relief in Ontario; a

¶17,169

1554CANADIAN MASTER TAX GUIDE

power of the settlor to revoke or encroach on capital would certainly be problematic.

- **Alternative of Power of Attorney.** Alter ego and joint partner trusts may have advantages over a power of attorney. The use of such trusts offers several advantages with respect to incapacity planning over powers of attorney. First, the terms of the trust may be tailored to the specific needs of the client by providing for specific powers and restrictions. Second, there is greater certainty with respect to the standard of care owed where a trust is used. Third, a trust allows for the general recognition by third parties of the trustees' authority to deal with trust assets across different jurisdictions, which obviates the necessity of multiple powers of attorney in circumstances where an individual has assets in several jurisdictions.

- **Administrative Advantages.** Alter ego and joint partner trusts may provide advantages from centralization of property and continuity of management. Where an individual's property is situate in multiple jurisdictions and the property forms part of an individual's estate passing by wills in each jurisdiction, multiple concurrent proceedings with respect to the vesting of such property in estate trustees can be both time consuming and costly. By transferring property into an alter ego trust or joint partner trust, complexity, loss of time and cost may be avoided. Through the use of a trust, the ownership of property is centralized in one jurisdiction under the control of the trustees whose authority to deal with the assets will not need to be subsequently ratified by a court of any jurisdiction. In addition, on the death of the settlor, or, in the case of a joint partner trust, the death of the last to die of the settlor and his or her spouse or common law partner, the trustees will not need to delay the administration of the trust as they will not need to seek and obtain probate. Thus, the management of trust property will continue seamlessly despite the death of the settlor or his or her spouse or common law partner.

[¶17,170] Disadvantages

Alter ego and joint partner trusts can also have some drawbacks (an alter ego or joint partner trust will not circumvent the deemed disposition on death rules: an alter ego trust is deemed to dispose of its assets on the death of the individual who established it; likewise, a joint partner trust is deemed to dispose of its assets on the death of the last surviving spouse). As time goes by, the list of technical issues has increased, as practitioners delve into the intricacies of these vehicles:

- **Amending Formulae.** Amending a trust may become problematic if the variation is such as to have the effect of resettling the trust. Some practitioners are concerned that this could be problematic even if the trust itself provides an amending formula. If this is indeed an issue, then this would interfere with the flexibility of alter ego and

¶17,170

joint partner trusts, since an individual would usually desire the freedom to amend the trust — just like a will. Note that, in the absence of an amending formula, it would be necessary to amend the trust pursuant to variation of trust legislation; it may be necessary for the Official Guardian (Children's Lawyer) to become involved.

- **Capital Gains Exemption.** Spouse and other testamentary trusts have access to the capital gains exemption by virtue of subsection 110.6(12), but alter ego and joint partner trusts do not.

- **Registration Formalities.** It is quite likely that assets should be re-registered to reflect the alter ego or joint partner trust as the owner. However, query whether there is a continuing requirement for such registration. This may also pose a problem if, for example, an individual simply opens a new bank account and then purports to transfer the bank account to the trust. This would seem to necessarily require the re-registration of the bank account in the name of trust; otherwise, the bank may well insist on a probated will in respect of the bank account. Similar issues will arise if an alter ego or joint partner trust is desired for creditor protection: failure to register assets in the name of the trustee may leave assets with greater vulnerability to creditor claims.

- **Reversionary Trust Rules/Interprovincial Planning.** If a taxpayer wants to be a capital beneficiary of the trust, absent careful planning, any potential interprovincial tax planning opportunity is likely unavailable (i.e., shifting assets to a taxpayer — i.e., the trust — resident in a lower tax rate province such that income and gains will be taxed in that taxpayer's hands). The reason for the foregoing is that, for the most part, the taxation of alter ego and joint partner trusts is governed by the normal tax rules pertaining to trusts. In the above case, the property would normally be held by the trust on condition that it may revert to the transferor; thus subsection 75(2) would apply. In order for subsection 75(2) not to apply, the trust should be irrevocable and under no circumstances (other than by operation of law on the failure of the trust) should it be possible for the property to revert to the settlor. This is a suboptimal feature which should be considered carefully.

Besides this, other constraints of subsection 75(2) would have to be met. Of course, it would also be necessary to establish that the trust is resident in the province, which would presumably entail the appointment of local trustees and meeting other requirements in this respect. In addition, provincial anti-avoidance rules should be considered (Quebec has introduced an anti-avoidance legislation). (Note that although a requirement of an alter ego/joint partner trust is that the settlor/spouse must be entitled to all of the income, elections can be made under subsections 104(13.1) and (13.2) to tax the

¶17,170

income at the trust level.) If, however, the trust were resident in a low-tax province, in addition to benefits relating to ongoing income, tax may be reduced in respect of deemed dispositions on death. Even though subsection 75(2) may apply to an alter ego or joint partner trust, it is the CRA's position that a T3 return must be filed, including Schedule 9 (allocations) and T3 slips. This requirement was indicated by the CRA in a Technical Interpretation released July 11, 2002, Document No. 2001-0114045.

- **Effect of Subsection 75(2) to the Individual.** In most cases, income earned by an alter ego or joint partner trust will be taxable to the settlor rather than the trust itself pursuant to subsection 75(2). This provision is very generally worded, requiring only that income or loss from the property (or substituted property), and taxable capital gains or allowable capital losses from the disposition of property (or substituted property) is taxable to the settlor. However, this provision, in itself, provides little guidance to the intricacies of tax issues that may arise. In Technical Interpretation No. 2006-0216491E5, July 11, 2007, the CRA was asked how Regulation 1100(11), which restricts CCA to net rental income of the taxpayer, would apply where both the settlor and the alter ego trust earn rental income — i.e., would the settlor be able to aggregate the alter ego trust's net rental income with his or her own? The CRA indicated that the CCA limitation for computing the trust's income to be attributed to the individual is computed separately from the CCA limitation on property owned by the individual directly (Regulation 1100(15) would apply in a similar manner). Implicit in this interpretation is that the alter ego trust is a separate taxpayer, whose income is attributed to the settlor pursuant to subsection 75(2). If this is the case, query, for example, whether provisions such as restricted farm loss (section 31) would apply separately to the alter ego trust.

  Similarly, in Question 6 of the Round Table at the 2007 STEP national conference, the CRA indicated that, where a trust pays foreign tax on foreign source income which is attributed to an individual (the "transferor") by virtue of subsections 75(2), 56(4.1), 74.1(1) or 74.1(2), the transferor cannot claim the foreign tax credit because there is no mechanism to allow the tax paid by the trust as having been paid by the transferor; however, a deduction under subsections 20(11) and (12) may apply.

- **Trustee Issues.** Where it is desirable to have third-party trustees (e.g., where there are creditor considerations, as described previously), the settlor may lose effective control of the assets. This could especially be the case if the trustees are concerned with their fiduciary duties to other beneficiaries of the trust. For example, if the trustees are given the power to make discretionary distributions of capital to the settlor, they may be concerned that making such distributions could

put them in jeopardy of proceedings against them by other beneficiaries. While the settlor may provide an indemnity, query whether
his or her assets will be sufficient, especially if the capital distributions are made to meet personal and living expenses. Unless the
settlor can revoke the trust, similar considerations could apply if the
settlor desires that the trustees "unwind" the arrangement, e.g., by
distributing the assets of the trust and transferring them to new alter
ego/joint partner trust with different beneficiaries.

- **Loss of Low Tax Brackets.** Unlike an estate, these trusts will not be
  eligible for graduated tax rates after death: it appears that both types
  of trusts would have to pay tax at high rates, unless the income is
  distributed to beneficiaries. This precludes the possibility of a will
  planning manoeuvre known as estate splitting — i.e., using low tax
  rates available to an estate to reduce taxes. What is interesting about
  this is that these trusts reduce provincial probate fees while increasing federal income tax.

- **Charitable Donations.** A charitable donation made in one's will can
  be applied against the tax exposure due to deemed dispositions on
  death. In addition, the donation limit for the year of death is
  increased from 75% to 100% of income and qualifies for a carryback. The donation limit for the preceding year is also 100%. Assuming that an alter ego or joint partner trust contains a power of
  encroachment, the ability to use a charitable tax credit against the
  deemed realization on death is available only if the gift is made to
  the charity in the taxation year in which death occurs. The transfer of
  property in satisfaction of a charity's income interest cannot be
  deducted against income arising from the deemed realization of
  capital gains of the trust under subsection 104(4) (unlike the special
  treatment available for a donation made in a will, the charitable tax
  credit in an alter ego or joint partner trust cannot be carried back —
  it can only be carried forward; because of the basic requirements of
  alter ego/joint partner trusts, donations cannot be made prior to
  death of the settlor/surviving spouse). Further, depending on the
  drafting of the trust, issues may arise as to whether the transfer to the
  charity is voluntary or is a distribution in satisfaction of the charity's
  capital interest in the trust — governed by subsection 107(2) rather
  than treated as a charitable donation. It has been stated that, in view
  of these issues, charitable gifts should be made by will rather than in
  an alter ego or joint partner trust; however, this is not advantageous if
  an objective of the donation is to shelter the deemed disposition on
  death of assets placed in these trusts (if an alter ego or joint partner
  trust does not contain a power of encroachment, it might qualify as a
  charitable remainder trust; however, the lack of a power of encroachment may not be acceptable; in addition, the taxation of a charitable
  remainder trust differs from a normal *post-mortem* gift in that the

charitable donation is current and is subject to a present-value calculation).

- **Acquisition of Control Issues — Transfer to Alter Ego or Joint Partner Trust.** When control of a corporation is acquired by a trust, control will be considered to have been acquired by the trustees of the trust. If control is transferred to or from an estate, special rules in paragraph 256(7)(*a*) which specifically apply to estates may exempt the provisions that are triggered by an acquisition of control (loss streaming, deemed year end, etc.). These rules do not apply to alter ego or joint partner trusts; therefore, the transfer of control to such a trust could trigger such provisions. However, other exceptions in that paragraph pertaining to related person status, may apply, e.g., where the trustee of an alter ego or joint partner trust is related to the transferor of a control block of shares. It therefore appears that these particular exceptions must be met when control of a corporation is transferred to an alter ego or joint partner trust.

- **Acquisition of Control Issues — Change of Trustees.** A change of trustees could result in an acquisition of control of a corporation if control is held by the trust, particularly if the new trustee is unrelated to the previous trustee (where there is a change of trustees, it is not clear that the saving provision in subsection 267(7) pertaining to related persons applies). If so, loss streaming rules would apply, there would be a deemed year end, and so on. This could be particularly problematic with respect to alter ego and joint partner trusts, where the original trustee is the settlor and/or spouse: when the original trustees pass away, the appointment of an unrelated trustee would appear to be problematic (the current administrative largesse with respect to testamentary trusts is obviously not applicable).

- **Property Transfer Tax.** Depending on the province, there may be an issue as to whether land/property transfer tax may apply if real estate is transferred to an alter ego or joint partner trust. Such transfer tax may be based on the value of consideration and thus, the issue may arise if there is a mortgage on the property which is being assumed by the alter ego or joint partner trust.

- **Emigration.** An interest in alter ego or joint partner trust is normally excluded from the deemed disposition rules on becoming a non-resident by virtue of being an excluded right or interest pursuant to subparagraph 128.1(4)(*b*)(iii) and paragraph (*j*) of the definition of "excluded right or interest" in subsection 128.1(10). However, paragraph 104(4)(*a*.3) provides for a deemed disposition by the trust where it is reasonable to conclude that property was transferred to such a trust in anticipation of the taxpayer subsequently ceasing to be resident in Canada.

¶17,170

- **Post-Mortem Planning.** In respect of *post-mortem* tax planning procedures, an alter ego or joint partner trust is similar to a spouse trust: rather than the mechanism of subsection 164(6) applying (i.e., a "one year carryback" from the estate to the decedent), the mechanism for triggering a *post-mortem* capital loss in such a trust relates to a single entity (i.e., the trust itself) and is the normal three-year carryback. In view of this, it is suggested that the trust should be drafted to allow for the possibility of the trust continuing after the death of the settlor so as to enable such a carryback.

  In addition, *post-mortem* procedures themselves may differ. At time of writing, the subsection 40(3.61) exemption to the stop-loss rules has not been amended to deal with these trusts. Therefore, the affiliation rules are relevant and considerations in respect to spouse trusts may apply. Furthermore, unless special provisions are made in the trust, the use of the paragraph 88(1)(*d*) bump may be greatly restricted: paragraph 88(1)(*d*.3) does not apply to deem control to have been acquired from an arm's-length individual on the death of the beneficiary under an alter ego or joint partner trust. Instead, in determining the ACB of shares of a corporation held by these trusts, one must look to when control was last acquired from an arm's length person; this could be a very modest amount (if any).

- **Stop-Loss Grandfathering.** Shares transferred to an alter ego or joint partner trust will no longer qualify for grandfathering from the stop loss rules in section 112 pertaining the capital dividend account (i.e., relating to qualifying pre-April 27, 1995 arrangements).

- **Principal Residence Exemption.** The principal residence exemption can be claimed by a trust, including an alter ego or joint partner trust. However, if such a designation is made, there are restrictions on beneficiaries and related persons claiming separate exemptions, which should be reviewed carefully. Each beneficiary who "ordinarily inhabits" the home, or has a spouse, former spouse, or child who so uses it, will be a "specified beneficiary". If the exemption is claimed by the trust, a specified beneficiary will not be able to claim a second exemption (paragraph (*f*) of the definition of "principal residence" in section 54 provides that a property designated as a principal residence by a trust for a year under paragraph (*c*.1) of that definition will be deemed to have been designated as a principal residence for each specified beneficiary of the trust for the calendar year ending in that year).

  Also restricted from claiming a separate exemption are a specified beneficiary's spouse (unless legally separated) or single child under 18. Further, it seems that if a specified beneficiary has not attained the age of 18 and is single, a second principal residence exemption will not be available to the beneficiary's parents, i.e., if the exemption is claimed by the trust.

- **Association Rules — Deemed Ownership by Surviving Spouse.** The ownership of shares by the surviving spouse might be advantageous in respect of the association rules. In this respect, it should be noted that there is a special rule which applies in the case of a testamentary spouse trust whereby the surviving spouse is deemed to own the shares in the trust, provided that the spouse's share of income or capital depends on the exercise (or failure to exercise) of any discretionary power. However, this rule does not appear to apply to an alter ego or joint partner trust.

- **Debt Forgiveness.** For the purpose of the debt forgiveness rules, a settlement of indebtedness will not occur if by way of "bequest or inheritance". It is not clear whether debt forgiveness in an alter ego or joint partner trust will qualify for this exception.

- **Rights or Things.** An alter ego or joint partner trust will not be eligible for the special treatment relating to "rights or things" in subsection 70(2) *et seq.* Although some qualifying items are germane only to individuals (e.g., unpaid bonuses, unused vacation leave credits), others could be applicable to such trusts, e.g., unpaid dividends or unmatured bond bonus coupons.

- **GST.** The transfer of property from a decedent to an estate is not a supply, and therefore GST does not apply. However, section 268 of the *Excise Tax Act* provides that, where property is settled by a person on an *inter vivos* trust, for GST purposes, the transfer is treated as a supply of the property by the person to the trust, and that the consideration for the sale is equal to the amount determined for income tax purposes to be the proceeds of disposition of the property. Since there will typically be a rollover into an alter ego or joint partner trust, this would appear to be based on the cost amount of the property to the transferor. Of course, the transfer may well be an exempt supply, such as the transfer of shares or other financial instruments, or certain used residential complexes.

- **U.S. Issues.** Certain double-tax issues may result if such trusts are used as an estate planning tool for a Canadian resident who is also a U.S. citizen. In addition, there are a number of traps for U.S. *situs* assets. For example, it does not appear that the foreign tax credit for U.S. estate taxes (allowed to the extent of the Canadian federal taxes arising on U.S. source income in the year of death) per paragraph 6 of Article XXIXB of the Canada–U.S. Treaty will be available. Therefore U.S. property on which estate tax may be exigible should not be transferred to such trusts.

- **Two Pots of Assets?** Either deliberately or otherwise, it is possible that the settlor will have personal assets/income. If so, there could be added complexities. For example, the settlor may have terminal period losses, and the trust may have gains resultant from the deemed disposition. It is also possible that there could be similar issues prior to death; however, normally income and loss would be attributed to the settlor pursuant to subsection 75(2).

- **Other Tax Disadvantages.** An alter ego or joint partner trust must select a calendar year end; this is not the case with a testamentary trust. These trusts must make quarterly tax installments; again, this is not the case with a testamentary trust. Unlike a testamentary trust, an alter ego or joint partner trust is not entitled to the $40,000 alternative minimum tax exemption.

- **Accounting, Legal, and Trustee Fees.** An alter ego or joint partner trust will entail keeping accounting records for the trust. As stated above, the CRA's position is that annual T3 tax returns are required even if all of the income is taxable to the settlor pursuant to subsection 75(2). There will also be trustee fees if a professional trustee is used. There will be legal fees in establishing the trust which will vary with the degree of customization required. As can be seen by the foregoing discussion, alter ego and joint partner trusts can raise some intricate and difficult issues, especially when marital concerns, creditor protection, *post-mortem* planning, charitable donations and the like are in play. It is suggested that these issues would be commonplace in the milieu of succession planning for the successful business.

- **The X Factor.** For some clients, there exists a very real possibility that the relationship between the settlor and the alter ego/joint partner trust may become muddled because the client does not respect nor understand the significance of creating and maintaining the trust. As mentioned earlier, a client may forget to register new assets. If it is not clear that the assets are held by the alter ego/joint partner trust, will they end up in the estate of the individual, rather than the trust? If so, should a will nonetheless be prepared, e.g., as a fail-safe mechanism to guard against an intestacy? Worse still, could the assets end up being governed by a will which the individual thought was replaced by the trust — e.g., with the "wrong beneficiaries"? As noted previously, the CRA's position is that, even if subsection 75(2) applies to the trust, T3 returns must be filed annually and the CRA has indicated that penalties will apply if this is not done. This might not become apparent until income is to be reported by the trust, e.g., on death. Will probate fees be replaced by tax penalties?

In Ontario, at least, in view of the fact that the *Granovsky* case specifically sanctions the use of multiple wills, the above-mentioned technical deficiencies, along with problems with respect to avoiding dependants' relief

¶17,170

legislation, have made alter ego and joint partner trusts something of a rarity (in other provinces, e.g., British Columbia, these will substitutes may be more popular). However, they may be used where there is a specific advantage over wills. It is also submitted that they may be helpful in the succession planning process because of protection against family law claims. However, the drafter will have to become familiar with a myriad of tax pitfalls and traps.

[¶17,171] Joint Tenancy

[¶17,172] Potential Complications

An individual may transfer property into joint tenancy with another for a variety of reasons, one common one being avoiding probate. Such a transfer avoids probate fees due to the fact that the asset never goes into the taxpayer's estate, but passes automatically (outside the estate) to the surviving joint tenant, by virtue of the right of survivorship inherent in a joint tenancy. However, the apparent simplicity of joint tenancy is subject to a number of potential complications:

- **Estate Splitting.** If an income-earning asset is put in joint tenancy, the ability to take advantage of the transferor's estate to pay taxes at low rates will be lost. Example: A large bank account in joint tenancy would pass to the surviving joint tenant rather than to the transferor's estate where the income could have been taxed at a lower bracket. This is due to the fact that an estate is taxed like an individual — with low tax brackets applying. Creating a joint tenancy means the asset will pass directly to the surviving joint tenant, who may be in a much higher bracket. Accordingly, there is a missed opportunity in this scenario. A well-crafted will can preserve the benefits of low estate tax brackets for years — by creating one or more trusts within the umbrella of the will itself. Within a relatively short time, the lost tax saving will exceed the probate fee reduction.

- **Legal Issues.** Since a joint interest in the asset will now belong to the transferee, a number of legal issues will arise. For example, the asset could be subject to creditor or marital claims against the transferee.

- **Land Transfer Tax.** In Ontario at least, an interest in real estate transferred between generations will attract land transfer tax, if it is subject to a mortgage.

- **Principal Residence Exemption.** If a home is put in joint tenancy, it may no longer qualify for the full principal residence exemption since the joint tenants will now own part of the home. Typically, the principal residence exemption will not be available to the joint tenants because they do not live in the home, or they need the exemption for homes owned by them or their family. Therefore, future appreciation after the transfer may become taxable when the home is sold.

- **Deemed Sale.** When the joint tenant is someone other than a spouse, there will be a deemed sale of a portion of the asset at its current value (e.g., if two children become joint tenants with a parent, two-thirds of the asset will be considered to be sold). This may well be a problem if the asset has appreciated in value. For example, if a second home is put in joint tenancy with a child, it may be necessary to use up part of the principal residence exemption to shelter the gain or pay capital gains tax on the transfer.

Some of the foregoing issues may be affected by the *Pecore* case (*Michael Pecore v. Paula Pecore and Shawn Pecore* (2007 S.C.C. 17)) decided by the Supreme Court of Canada. The case held that the presumption of resulting trust (i.e., the presumption that there is no gift intended), rather than the presumption of advancement (i.e., the presumption that there is a gift intended) applies to gratuitous transfers from a parent to an adult child, while the presumption of advancement applies to the transfer to a minor (the majority opinion indicated that the foregoing applies whether the transfer is from the mother or father of the child). Further, and more importantly, if a gift is intended, it can be a gift *inter vivos* of the property at the time the joint tenancy is created (i.e., the transfer of beneficial ownership), or a gift only of the right of survivorship. In other words, it appears that the right of survivorship can be separated from the beneficial ownership of the joint property during the transferor's lifetime. The right of survivorship can arise when the joint account is opened and is therefore *inter vivos* in nature, even though the beneficial interest of the transferee arises only on death. Somewhat surprisingly to many practitioners, the case indicates that there is no deemed disposition of the right of survivorship at the time of the transfer (the majority indicated that "where the transferor's intention is to gift the right of survivorship to the transferee but retain beneficial ownership of the assets during his or her lifetime, there would appear to be no disposition at the moment of the setting up of the joint account: see s. 73 of the *Income Tax Act …*").

Thus, there was no current gift of the joint interest in the account because of the presumption of resulting trust. However, this presumption was overcome with respect to the gift of the right of survivorship, under the circumstances (in a companion case, *Madsen* (*Madsen Estate v. Saylor*, 2007 S.C.C. 18) the evidence was insufficient to rebut the presumption of resulting trust, in respect of both a current gift and the right of survivorship).

Of course, the applicability of the foregoing result depends on the facts. In *Pecore*, the Court found the evidence was consistent with the father having intended to gift a right of survivorship when the accounts were established. In other words, the presumption of resulting trust was overcome with respect to the gift of the right of survivorship (query the effect of

Pecore on the property law concepts underlying joint tenancies, particularly the requirement of the "four unities" (interest, title, possession, time)).

It is, of course, important to be clear about whether the beneficial interest in the joint account is being granted, and also to be clear about whether the right of survivorship is being granted. Based on *Pecore*, it is possible to grant the latter without granting the former. Given the Court's holding that the presumption of resulting trust applies to a gift from a parent to an adult child, the court will presume that no gift was intended unless the presumption can be overcome. In other words, a joint account between parent and adult child with a right of survivorship does not pass any beneficial interest to the funds in the account either currently or on death, unless it can be established that there was an intention to do so.

Of course, the good news about *Pecore* is that the result is a probate planning dream: a (seemingly) simple structure whereby probate fees can be eliminated through the right of survivorship, but without altering property rights during lifetime. But especially where joint tenancies with adult children are in question (formerly, at least, a common although often misguided financial planning manoeuvre), the effects of the case could often be quite problematic.

[¶17,180] Registered Retirement Savings Plans

[¶17,185] The Advantages of an RRSP

RRSPs offer very important tax advantages:

- Contributions made to an RRSP are tax deductible within certain contribution limits. Because of this, contributions will shelter other sources of taxable income.

- Investment earnings are not taxed while they accumulate in the RRSP. For most investments, the earnings are subject to tax as they are earned or realized. But there is no "tax drain" in an RRSP. All of the earnings will be put to work for the annuitant in the plan.

When funds are taken out of the plan, however, they are taxable. This is an important point to note. Because all funds received from the plan are potentially taxable, the real effect of an RRSP is that tax is deferred until then. In the meantime, however, the two tax advantages combine to enhance the accumulation of capital compared to funds invested in conventional investments. However, tax benefits for particular forms of investments, such as capital gains rates and the dividend tax credit, will generally be lost in an RRSP.

There could also be another form of tax savings in that, by the time an individual is taxed on RRSP payments, he or she may have retired and may therefore be in a lower tax bracket.

¶17,180

Eventually, the RRSP will mature (this can be no later than the end of the year in which the annuitant turns 71, increased from 69 pursuant to the 2007 Budget). At the maturity date, the annuitant should select a maturity option. This will determine how the annuitant will receive retirement income, which must begin when the plan matures to avoid taxation on the full amount in the RRSP. There are two basic types of maturity options: annuities and registered retirement income funds (RRIFs), both of which provide for minimum annual payouts. Most RRSPs, however, allow the annuitant to obtain funds from the plan prior to maturity, if necessary.

On death, an individual is treated as if all RRSPs have collapsed; therefore the annuitant would be taxed based on the fair market value of the plan at the time. This tax may be deferred if the spouse/common-law partner or a financially dependent child or grandchild becomes entitled to receive payments from the RRSP.

In addition to the above and the comments that follow, the RRSP rules are discussed in detail at ¶10,336 *et seq.*

[¶17,190] Spousal RRSPs

A spousal RRSP is a plan where one spouse/common-law partner makes the contributions, but the other spouse/common-law partner "owns" the plan. Contributing to a spousal RRSP allows the contributor-spouse/common-law partner to obtain a deduction from his (or her) taxable income, whereas funds received out of the plan will usually be included in the spouse/common-law partner's income. Accordingly, if it is likely that the spouse/common-law partner will have a lower marginal tax rate when funds are received by the plan, a spousal RRSP will be advantageous. If a retiring allowance has been received, it is not possible to make an additional contribution to a spousal RRSP — the contribution must be made to the annuitant's own RRSP.

Another advantage of a spousal RRSP is that the maturity deadline is based on that age of the spouse/common-law partner. Thus, if an individual is too old to contribute to his or her own RRSP, if may be possible to continue to contribute to a spouse/common-law partner's RRSP, i.e., if the spouse/common-law partner is still eligible to contribute (contributions are not allowed after the end of the year in which the annuitant reaches age 71). It should also be remembered that this may be an alternative to a last chance contribution when an annuitant reaches age 71.

Because the RRSP is owned by the spouse/common-law partner, rather than the contributor, there is a possibility of creditor protection, i.e., if the contributor-spouse/common-law partner might be subject to adverse claims in the future. Of course, there is the possibility that the contributions could be set aside, for example, under applicable fraudulent conveyance legislation. However, depending on the circumstances, this risk could be mitigated if the contributor has historically established a consistent pattern of spousal

¶17,190

RRSP contributions which are motivated by the tax advantages described above (a life insurance company plan should also be considered under such circumstances, in view of specific legislation which affords a significant degree of protection against creditors; however these considerations should be balanced against the financial and other attributes of the plan).

The family law implications of contributing to a spousal RRSP should also be considered. In Ontario, at least, in the absence of a domestic contract, it would appear that the contribution to a spousal RRSP would normally make little difference, since contributing to one's own RRSP would simply increase the amount of net family property subject to equalization in the event of a marriage breakdown.

Withdrawals from a spousal RRSP are generally subject to a "three-year rule". If a taxpayer's spouse/common-law partner receives funds from an RRSP to which the taxpayer has made a contribution, the contributor-spouse/common-law partner must include an amount in income equivalent to any tax deductible contributions to all spousal RRSPs, for the year of withdrawal as well as the two previous years (see subsection 146(8.3)). The amount included in income will, of course, be limited to the withdrawal made by the spouse/common-law partner, if this is less than the contributions made within the three-year period. The three-year rule will operate to bring into income contributions made to other spousal RRSPs within the three-year period — and not solely to the particular plan that is collapsed. The three-year rule applies to commuted or lump-sum payments in respect of maturity options — i.e., annuities and RRIFs. However, regular maturity option payments (e.g., mandatory minimum RRIF payouts) are not subject to the three-year rule.

Obviously, the three-year rule may allow a degree of income splitting by staggering contributions between personal and spousal RRSPs; after contributing to a spousal RRSP, the individual could then contribute to his or her own RRSP for the three-year period, after which he or she could then be able to withdraw from the spousal RRSP (i.e., after the three-year period).

If the contributor's spouse/common-law partner is eligible to make an RRSP contribution (i.e., she or he has earned income, etc.), contributions may be made by the spouse/common-law partner, in addition to the spousal RRSP contributions. In such situations, it may be prudent for the contributor's spouse/common-law partner to set up a separate plan, so that withdrawals can be made from the untainted plan, without regard to the three-year rule.

[¶17,195] RRSPs and the Salary/Dividend Mix

An RRSP deduction is available to the extent of 18% of earned income, thus resulting in an effective personal tax reduction of the same percentage. Based on the $22,970 maximum annual contribution for 2012, the "18% personal tax reduction" will effectively be available in respect of

2011 earned income of up to $127,611. Of course, dividends do not qualify as earned income. Thus, this level can be a significant factor in respect of the salary/dividend mix received from a closely-held corporation, i.e., for relatively sizable levels of distributions.

[¶17,200] High Tax/Low Tax Investments

It has been said that high-tax investments should be held in an annuitant's RRSP and low-tax investments outside the plan. But which investments are high-tax? Traditionally, these have been interest-bearing investments. Stocks and equity funds, on the other hand, may qualify for capital gains treatment (50% of a capital gain is tax-free), as well as the dividend tax credit if Canadian (including the enhanced credit for eligible dividends). These benefits are lost if such investments are held in an RRSP, since all types of investment income earned within an RRSP are treated in the same manner. Retirement and other amounts received from a plan are fully taxable.

Can equities be high tax? A case in point arises if an investor is contemplating a shorter-term capital gain, the taxable portion of which is likely to be in excess of returns on fixed income investments. The equity investment could, in effect, become high-tax, since the tax has to be paid for the year the investment is sold, while the gain could be tax-deferred in an RRSP. Thus, owning shorter-term-hold equities in an RRSP could defer capital gains tax — giving the annuitant the opportunity to take profits and reinvest on a tax-deferred basis. This may more than make up for the tax benefits obtained by holding such investments outside the RRSP.

Accordingly, it may make sense to hold part of a high-appreciation equity position — the portion that may be liquidated in the shorter term — within an RRSP (Note: transferring existing investments into an RRSP triggers a deemed capital gain, if they have appreciated in value). On the other hand, if an equity is a long term hold, the outside-the-RRSP strategy may still apply, although the tax benefits are more limited than they used to be. Finally, it makes little sense to reject low-tax investments in an RRSP merely because the tax benefits are lost — in view of the fact that they are now fairly modest.

[¶17,205] Contribute Early

If possible, RRSP contributions should be made early in the year. Earnings will accumulate on a tax-deferred basis sooner. In addition, an early contribution may enable an employee to apply for a reduction of source deductions under subsection 153(1.1) of the *Income Tax Act* — i.e., in view of reduced tax resultant from the contribution. Technically speaking, the reduction in source deductions is granted when regular withholding would cause "undue hardship". However, over the years, virtually all Canadian tax offices have relaxed their procedures so that most people in this situation may be eligible for a reduction in withholding. The CRA has indicated that all deductions in calculating taxable income as well as non-refundable tax credits will be considered favourably in respect to granting a reduction in source deductions.

[¶17,210] Contribution of Qualified Investments — Tax-Free Cash

If an individual owns qualified RRSP investments, it is possible to transfer these to an RRSP and obtain cash or other RRSP assets of an equivalent value. There will, however, be a deemed sale at fair market value on the transfer. Capital gains in respect of transferred assets will be taxable to the transferor; capital losses to an RRSP are disallowed. It may be possible, however, to trigger a (non-disallowed) capital loss by transferring to a child or parent with the "intermediate transferee" then transferring the assets to the RRSP (subject to the possible application of general anti-avoidance provisions).

[¶17,220] Contributions after Death

While no contributions can be made to a deceased individual's RRSPs, the deceased's legal representatives can make contribution to the surviving spouse/common-law partner's RRSP either in the year of death or during the first sixty days following the end of that year. These contributions can be claimed on the deceased individual's return, up to the deceased's RRSP deduction limit for the year of death.

[¶17,225] Catch-Up Contributions

If an individual has not made the maximum possible RRSP contributions, he or she is entitled to make an additional contribution over and above the normal limit for the year. Unused RRSP contribution limits can be carried forward indefinitely to future years. Of course, one of the biggest barriers could be finding the means to make a catch-up contribution. Possible sources for a catch-up contribution include the following.

Inheritances

Or perhaps an advance on an inheritance. Note that if an individual receives an advance on an inheritance as a gift rather than a loan, and he or she is married when this occurs, it should be ensured that (where possible) the advance is documented so that the gift, and subsequent income earned on it, are not subject to a spousal claim in the event of marital difficulties.

Contributions in kind

For example, if investments are currently held outside of an RRSP which nevertheless qualify as an RRSP investment, these can be transferred into the plan, so their current value will qualify as an additional contribution. However, any appreciation at the point of transfer will be taxed as a capital gain; if there is a capital loss, it will be disallowed (clause 40(2)(g)(iv)(B)).

¶17,210

An RRSP mortgage

Another option could be for the annuitant to have his or her RRSP make a loan secured by a mortgage on the annuitant's home (or other Canadian real estate). This can be permissible if the mortgage loan from the RRSP is insured and the annuitant pays his or her RRSP interest at market rates in effect when the RRSP loan is made. A number of financial institutions offer pre-packaged plans which allow individuals to take advantage of this strategy. As discussed previously, this strategy can be used for other things besides making a catch-up contribution — such as simply paying down an existing mortgage.

Borrowing

This will be effective if the annuitant can pay down his or her loan in the "not-too-distant future".

Profits from non-RRSP investments

By contributing the proceeds to his or her RRSP, the annuitant could not only shelter the gain itself, but if only $\frac{1}{2}$ of the gain is taxable because capital gains status applies, there will be additional deductions available to shelter regular income.

Bear in mind that, the higher the marginal tax rate, the more effective an RRSP catch-up contribution will be. Accordingly, a low-income year may not be a good time to make a catch-up contribution. If an annuitant's annual income is such that he or she is not too far into a particular tax bracket, it may be beneficial to make a series of RRSP contributions which take the individual down to the bottom of the bracket (another alternative could be to make a lump-sum contribution but defer the actual deduction until a year when a higher marginal tax rate applies).

[¶17,235] Deferred Contributions

It is possible to contribute to an RRSP on a current basis, but not make the actual deduction claim until a later year. In spite of the fact that the deduction would be deferred, this could be advantageous if it anticipated that the individual may be subject to a higher marginal tax rate in a future year. Notwithstanding the fact that the deduction in respect of the contribution itself would be deferred, the earnings on the contribution would, nevertheless, continue to accumulate on a tax-deferred basis.

[¶17,240] Last-Chance Contribution

Notwithstanding that an RRSP contribution cannot be made after the year in which the annuitant turns 71, if the individual has "earned income" in the final year in which an RRSP contribution can be made, it may be possible to make the next year's contribution late in the final year, incur a (modest) penalty tax as a result of the temporary over-contribution, and

¶17,240

carry-forward the deduction to the next year. An alternative strategy could be to contribute to a spousal RRSP, if the individual's spouse/common-law partner is still eligible to make contributions.

[¶17,245] Building in Contribution Room for Family Members

If a business is carried on, a prudent strategy could be to pay salary to children. This can be deductible as long as the amounts in question are not unreasonably large, in view of the business-related services performed. If a child has no other income, it is possible to receive up to at least $10,320 (in 2009) without paying tax, because the child can shelter this income by claiming the basic personal tax credit.

The salary the child receives should qualify as "earned income" so that he or she will be entitled to make an RRSP contribution based on 18% of the salary. These amounts can form additional RRSP contribution room, which can be carried forward to future years, when the child is subject to a higher tax rate.

[¶17,250] "Locked-In" RRSPs

Upon leaving the employment of an employer, an individual may wish to transfer his or her vested benefits under the employer's registered pension plan to the individual's RRSP. In such case, under provincial and federal pension laws, the transfer must generally be made to a "locked-in" RRSP, which is more restrictive than a regular RRSP. Funds cannot be received out of a locked-in RRSP before retirement. On retirement, the funds must be used to purchase a life annuity (a RRIF is not an option). Restrictions regarding conversions of "locked-in" RRSPs vary from province to province and can be affected by current legislation.

[¶17,260] Tax-Free Savings Accounts

[¶17,262] Overview

Beginning in 2009, everyone resident in Canada who is 18 years of age or over accumulates $5,000 of TFSA savings room each year. In the course of 2009, a number of technical amendments were made pertaining to TFSAs.

[¶17,265] TFSAs vs. RRSPs

Since it is somewhat unusual for individuals to have sufficient financial resources to make a full contribution to both an RRSP and TFSA, questions arise as to which plan is preferable.

An RRSP is a tax-deferred investment vehicle. It offers deductibility for contributions, tax-free accumulation, and withdrawals/retirement benefits which are fully included in income. On the termination of an RRSP, earnings accumulated in the plan are effectively taxable since all amounts

¶17,245

received from the RRSP are taxable — this will also recapture the initial deductions for contributions. A TFSA, on the other hand, is a tax-free ("tax-paid") investment vehicle: contributions are made in after-tax dollars; like an RRSP, earnings accumulate tax-free; but unlike an RRSP, there is no tax on withdrawal. The financial comparison between these features appears to be similar to the choice between contributing to an RRSP and paying down a mortgage. Provided that a taxpayer remains in the same marginal tax rate before and after retirement, and the interest paid on the mortgage is the same as the return made by the RRSP, the choice between investing in an RRSP and paying down a mortgage appears to be financially neutral. This is also the case as between contributing to an RRSP *versus* TFSA. Since the same investments can be made by each type of plan, the change in marginal tax rates after retirement might superficially appear to favour an RRSP; however, the reduction of tax rates after retirement may be illusory.

While an RRSP has mandatory maturity at the end of the year the annuitant turns 71 whereby taxable payouts must commence, there is currently no mandatory maturity for a TFSA, nor is there an age where an individual can no longer contribute. It therefore appears possible for an individual to extend the benefits of tax-free status indefinitely. Also, the ability to make a tax-free withdrawal from a TFSA which reinstates contribution room presents a potential advantage over RRSP withdrawals, since in the latter case, such withdrawals are taxable. For example, a TFSA could be used as a vehicle to accumulate funds in order to pay down a mortgage, in respect of which contribution room would be reinstated when withdrawals are made.

The following chart[2] shows a comparison between RRSP and TFSA features:

	RRSP	**TFSA**
Additional contribution room per year	Based on 18% of previous year's earned income, less pension adjustment, up to maximum limit for year	$5,000
Carryforward of unused contribution room	Until the year the annuitant turns 71	For life
"Earned income" requirement for contributions	Yes	No

See page ii for explanation of footnotes.

[2] Adapted from the RBC website www.royalbank.com.

	RRSP	**TFSA**
Age limit on contributions	Until the end year the individual turns 71	None
Are contributions tax deductible?	Yes	No
Accumulation of earnings	Tax-deferred until withdrawn	Never taxed
Restrictions on withdrawals	None, but with the exception of Home Buyer's or Lifelong Learning Plan withdrawals, they are taxable	None
How do withdrawals affect contribution room	No effect	Added to contribution room in the following year
Effect on government benefits	Withdrawals are taxable and could therefore effect income-tested government benefits and tax credits	No effect on income-tested benefits and tax credits
Overcontribution penalty	1% per month — but $2,000 excess contribution cushion	1% per month
Does plan "mature"?	Yes — must convert to a maturity option (RRIF or annuity) by the end of the year the individual turns 71 or pay tax on the amount in the plan	No

[¶17,300] Capital Gains and Losses

[¶17,305] General Rules and Reduced Taxation

Investments, such as the purchase of stocks, bonds, real estate, and business interests, typically yield some form of income taxed at general rates.

¶17,300

Dividends are something of an exception, being taxed at special rates. If the investment itself is sold, it will typically yield a capital gain, and the capital gain will be taxed at somewhat favourable rates in that only 50% of it will be considered income (although 100% will go into the Alternative Minimum Tax base, creating the potential for this to apply). In addition, the capital gain may be eligible for the reserves. Capital gains arising from investments in qualifying small business shares and farming and fishing property may be eligible for a $750,000 lifetime capital gains exemption (discussed below); these investments are not publicly traded, but must be made directly in qualifying businesses.

Capital losses have corresponding disadvantages; for example, they are deductible only from capital gains and not from ordinary income.

From a practical point of view, of course, capital gains are inherently speculative. If you buy a bond you know what the return will be. You don't know whether the price of a particular capital property will go up or down in the future.

[¶17,315] $750,000 Exemption

Effective March 19, 2007, the $500,000 lifetime capital gains exemption available in regard to qualified small business shares and farming and fishing property was increased to $750,000.

Small Business Corporation Shares

The capital gains exemption on the disposition of shares of a qualified small business corporation is $750,000. To be eligible for this $750,000 exemption, the shares disposed of must qualify as small business corporation shares at the date of disposition. The rules governing eligibility for the $750,000 exemption are extremely complex (whether it be qualified farm property, small business corporation shares, or fishing property), and generally speaking, professional tax advice is necessary before the disposition to ensure that any particular small business corporation shares or farm assets qualify. See ¶5022.

To maximize the use of the enhanced $750,000 exemption, taxpayers should consider the following:

- Those contemplating the sale of an unincorporated business should consider rolling all, or substantially all, the assets into a newly-incorporated small business corporation in exchange for shares. The exemption will be available on a subsequent disposition of those shares even before the expiry of the 24-month holding period.

- Shareholders of a Canadian-controlled small business corporation that holds passive investment assets (such as cash or investments) with a fair market value of more than 10% at the time of disposition, or a fair market value of more than 50% at any time in the two years preceding the disposition, will be ineligible for the $750,000 exemption. However, it may be possible to move such non-active business assets out of the corporation to make it qualify, provided this is done early enough and is not undertaken in contemplation of a specific sale.

• Taxpayers who hope or expect to realize more than their $750,000 capital gains entitlement during their lifetimes may wish to transfer some shares of a small business corporation to their spouses and/or children, to allow them to take advantage of the $750,000 enhanced exemption. Such transfers can be made by a sale at fair market value or by a reorganization of the capital of the corporation.

• Shareholders of a Canadian-controlled small business corporation that intends to expand significantly into another country or acquire significant non-active business assets would become ineligible for the $750,000 exemption. However, it may be possible to crystallize the exemption by transferring some shares of the corporation to the shareholder's spouse, children, and/or a new corporation before the corporation ceases to qualify. Furthermore, if a Canadian-controlled small business corporation intends to issue shares to the public, it may be possible for the individual shareholders of the company to make a special election to crystallize their $750,000 enhanced exemption before going public. Taxpayers who wish to crystallize their $750,000 enhanced exemptions should be aware that the Alternative Minimum Tax may create an unintended tax liability or prepayment (see ¶17,605).

Farm Property Exemption

Gains on the disposition of "qualified farm property" are also eligible for the $750,000 capital gains exemption. Qualified farm property includes real property used by the taxpayer or members of the taxpayer's family in the course of carrying on the business of farming in Canada. Shares of a family farm corporation and interests in family farm partnerships or trusts may also constitute qualified farm property. Eligible capital property, such as farm quotas may also qualify. Property acquired after June 17, 1987 must have been owned throughout the 24 months preceding its disposition and the gross revenue from the farming business must, in at least two years during the period of ownership, have exceeded the individual's income from all other sources. Where the farm is owned by a corporation or partnership, the gross revenue test is inapplicable. However, the shareholder or partner must have been actively engaged in the farming business on a regular and continuous basis during the 24-month period.

Farm property acquired before June 18, 1987 is exempt from the gross revenue test and will qualify if it is used to "carry on the business of farming" in the year of disposition or for at least five years during the period of ownership. Therefore, individuals who contemplate the disposition of

¶17,315

property acquired before June 18, 1987 should ensure that the property is used to carry on farming in the year of disposition if they are otherwise unable to meet the five-year test. "Hobby farms" are apparently not excluded in this instance. See further at ¶5021.

Qualified Fishing Property

The $750,000 lifetime capital gains exemption available for farm property and small business shares is now allowed in respect of capital gains arising on a disposition of qualified fishing property after May 1, 2006. For the purpose of this new measure, qualified fishing property includes real property, fishing vessels, and eligible capital property used principally in a fishing business carried on in Canada in which the individual, or the individual's spouse/common-law partner, parent, child, or grandchild, was actively engaged on a regular and continuous basis. It also includes shares of the capital stock of family fishing corporations and interests in family fishing partnerships of the individual. See 5023.

[¶17,320] Capital Gains Deferral for Investments in Small Business

This provision was introduced in the February 2000 Budget as a policy measure to stimulate small business investments. It offers a deferral of capital gains tax with respect to a gain from the disposition of the shares of certain active business corporations by an individual (other than a trust) where such individual reinvests the proceeds of disposition into eligible small business investments. When originally introduced, the deferral was restricted by $2,000,000 investment and disposition limits; however, these were repealed pursuant to the 2003 Budget. In contrast to the $750,000 lifetime capital gains exemption, this provision only provides a deferral which is reflected in a reduction of the cost base of the new investment. In this sense, it adopts an approach similar to that underlying the exchange of property provisions discussed at ¶5355 *et seq.* The deferral is discussed at ¶5025 *et seq.*

[¶17,325] Cumulative Net Investment Losses (CNILs)

CNILs reduce the capital gains exemption otherwise available.

Net investment losses are calculated on a cumulative basis since 1988 and consist of the aggregate of investment expenses less the aggregate of investment income. Investment expenses include the cumulative total of:

- deductions (including interest and carrying charges) with respect to property that yields interest, dividend, rent, or other property income;

- losses from, or carrying charges in respect of, a limited partnership (or any other partnership or co-ownership arrangement where the individual is not actively engaged in the business);

¶17,325

- one-half of the deductions attributed to resource flow-through shares other than the Mineral Exploration Depletion Allowance (including exploration and other resource expenses of a partnership or co-ownership arrangement where the individual is not actively engaged in the business);

- losses from property and losses from the leasing of real property owned by the individual or a partnership;

- net capital losses of prior years that are deducted by the individual in the year against taxable capital gains that were not eligible for the capital gains exemption.

Investment income contains the cumulative total of income from such sources, including net taxable capital gains that are not eligible for the exemption (as mentioned above). In this regard, the taxable amount of Canadian dividends (125%/145% of most Canadian source dividends, see ¶6050 *et seq.*) is used as the offsetting amount.

To maximize use of the $750,000 enhanced capital gains exemption, individuals should consider the following ways of minimizing their CNIL:

- Consider deferring the payment of interest to a subsequent year.

- Sole proprietors and active members of a partnership may consider taking distributions from the business or partnership to finance the purchase of investments and replacing the funds with borrowed money, the interest on which would not be included in CNIL.

- Shareholders should consider charging interest on shareholder loans to corporations to offset investment losses.

- Shareholder-managers should draw dividends rather than salary (where the effect is otherwise neutral) to offset investment losses.

It should be noted that the cumulative net investment loss rules are concerned only with the calculation of the capital gains exemption. They do not affect the tax deductibility of interest and carrying charges.

For capital gains realized after October 17, 2000, individuals (but not trusts) can roll over capital gains on the disposition of eligible small business investments where the individual invests the proceeds of disposition in other eligible small business investments. Originally, the deferral was available with respect to capital gains on up to $2 million of eligible small business investments in any particular corporation or related group. To encourage greater access to risk capital, the $2 million limit on the original investment and on reinvestment has been eliminated, effective for dispositions that occur after February 28, 2003.

To qualify as an eligible small business investment, the following criteria must be met: the investment must be in ordinary common shares issued by the company to the investor; the investment must be in a corporation

¶17,325

that is an eligible small business corporation at the time the shares are issued, and while the investor holds the shares, the corporation must be an eligible active business corporation. As well, the total carrying value of the corporation's assets (including related companies) must not exceed $50 million immediately before and after the investment is made.

The cost base of the new investment is reduced by the capital gain deferred with respect to the initial investment. Originally, if the cost of the original investment exceeded $2 million, the deferral was prorated, with only a portion of the shares qualifying. This restriction was eliminated in the 2003 federal Budget, effective for dispositions occurring after February 18, 2003.

The eligible small business investment must be held for at least six months from the time of acquisition before a gain can be deferred, and there are rules regarding when the replacement eligible investment must be acquired.

[¶17,330] Capital Loss Timing and the $750,000 Exemption

A problem may arise whenever the $750,000 exemption for qualifying small business shares or qualifying fishing or farm property is claimed in a year where there are offsetting losses. Where, as is often the case, there is only one such property and the gain is offset by a loss, neither the exemption nor the loss carryover will in practice be available again. A loss carryover from the current to another year is lost because the current year loss is automatically used first against the current year gain. The exemption is lost because there is no other qualified property against which to claim it. Contrast the case in which the gain and loss occur in different years. The gain can then be sheltered by the exemption and the loss carried forward (or back) against other gains, qualifying or otherwise. Of course, it is always open to the taxpayer to build up another business eligible for the $750,000 exemption. Where this is impractical, however, it is imperative to try to plan for separate years of disposition. The same problem could arise with qualified real estate gains offset by other losses, but of course this problem was eliminated with the $100,000 exemption.

Note that this problem does not arise with loss carryovers, since their application is optional.

[¶17,335] Principal Residence Exemption

A special unlimited exemption is provided where a capital gain is realized on the disposition of property that qualifies as a principal residence. While this mainly affects principal residences located in Canada, a residence located outside Canada may also qualify as a principal residence. The technicalities of the principal residence exemption are discussed at ¶5255 *et seq.* The following are some suggestions for maximizing the exemption:

¶17,335

- Make certain that all principal residence and change of use elections are filed on a timely basis regardless of the CRA's administrative position. Administrative concessions are not binding on the CRA and there are reported cases where the CRA has attempted to disallow the principal residence exemption because designations or elections were not filed.

- If you have both a house and a cottage in joint ownership with your spouse, and have held both since before 1982, you may be able to rearrange ownership to benefit from the double principal residence exemption that was available for the period before 1982. Note, however, that where property value increases have occurred primarily after 1981, this tactic is not much use.

- The "one plus" rule should be used to maximize the amount of exempt gain in any situation where two or more properties could potentially qualify as the taxpayer's principal residence in any particular year. For example, where a taxpayer owns both a home and cottage and the home has the larger gain, it may still be advantageous to designate the cottage for one year. This will provide two years of exempt gain on the cottage (one designated year and one free year) and the full exemption could still be available on the home because it also qualifies for a free additional year (which will make up for the year of designation of the cottage). It may even be advisable for the owner of a rental property to ordinarily inhabit the property for part or all of one year so that two years of exempt gains can be obtained.

- If you have more than one home (typically a house and a cottage) and you sell one of them, you should consider whether claiming the principal residence exemption on the property sold will be better than saving the allowance years for use on the other.

- If the family already owns a principal residence (for example, the family home) and is acquiring a second residential property (for example, a cottage), consideration should be given to taking title to the cottage in the name of a trust for the exclusive benefit of family children who are minors. If the trust sells the property, the capital gain that accrues during the period of ownership by the trust will not be attributed back to the trust settlor and instead can be paid out to the children. This will achieve an income splitting effect. Alternatively, the property can be rolled out to the children by the trust on a tax-deferred basis. The ownership of the cottage by the trust or subsequent distribution to the children will not impair the ability of the spouses to claim the principal residence exemption on the family home if no attempt is made to designate the cottage as the family's principal residence in any year during which one of the trust beneficiaries is a minor.

¶17,335

- Where one spouse holds an interest in the principal residence but has little or no income and the other spouse has both a relatively high income and income-producing assets (such as stocks or bonds), the spouses should consider having the high income spouse swap income-producing assets for part or all of the low income spouse's interest in the principal residence. If properly structured, this swap will avoid the attribution rules and the investment income can be taxed in the lower income spouse's hands at a lower tax rate without attribution.

- If you acquire a spouse or common-law partner and you each have a property which qualifies as a principal residence, you should note that the full exemption on one property or the other must begin to erode after the year of marriage. You should review whether any change in the status of these properties, such as the transfer of a cottage to adult children, is warranted by the change.

- Where a property that qualified as a principal residence of the tax-payer is being transferred to a spousal trust, it may be advantageous to elect out of the rollover if the property is not going to be sold by the trust or transferred to the spousal beneficiary. If the principal residence exemption is employed to shelter the gain arising on the transfer to the trust, a tax-free bump in the cost base of the property will benefit the capital beneficiary who ultimately receives the home.

- The deductibility of interest expense depends on the use to which the particular funds are put. That is, if you borrow to buy your own home, the interest is not deductible, whereas if you borrow to buy shares, or an income property, the interest expense is deductible. If you buy a mixed property, such as a house of your own which has a rental apartment in it, the interest will be partially deductible. Typically the deductible portion will be allocated on the basis of square footage allocated to rental use over total square footage.

- If you have substantial investments outside an RRSP which you can sell with minimal capital gain or with capital gain substantially offset by the lifetime capital gain exemption, you can sell the investments to increase your down payment. If you wish, you can then borrow again (on a mortgage or otherwise) to repurchase your investments. The interest on the money borrowed for this purpose will, in general, be deductible, assuming the investments have any potential to show long-run income in excess of borrowing costs. Remember that capital losses on investments sold will not be recognized if the investments are repurchased within 30 days of sale.

- If you are moving out of your home and planning to rent it out, or if you have acquired a rental property which you are intending to occupy eventually, you can elect to treat the rental property as your

¶17,335

principal residence even for the period (of up to four years) during which it is rented out.

- If your parents have sufficient money to lend you enough to buy a house or make a substantial down payment, this is of course a considerable benefit. You do not have to make interest payments to them. If they require the income flow from the money they lend you, you can make periodic (e.g., monthly) repayments of capital. This will not be deductible to you but will not be taxable to them. Their capital is of course being significantly diminished, although their current income flow may remain the same. In effect, they are living off capital and making you a gift of the interest they are forgoing on their capital. Since they are no longer earning income on that capital, the CRA is not getting a share. Another way of looking at it is that they are providing you with your inheritance piecemeal before they die. If their capital is otherwise substantial enough to provide for their remaining years, this may be a tax beneficial use of funds within the family unit.

- If you own two residences, you might consider transferring one of them to an adult child. The child will be able to designate the property (e.g., a summer cottage) as his or her principal residence when he or she sells it. Of course, at the time of the gift, you will realize any appreciation in the value of the property since you purchased it. Note that while you might consider this manoeuvre purely for tax purposes, the property will, nonetheless, legally belong to your child.

Finally, although this suggestion does not pertain to the exemption *per se*, if you have two houses (e.g., a house and cottage), keep a cost record of major home renovation projects so that the costs can be added to your cost base and reduce the gain on the eventual sale of the property not covered by the exemption.

[¶17,340] Capital Gains Reserves

It may be possible to defer the recognition of capital gains arising on the sale of property by taking back a note representing a portion of the purchase price. The income tax legislation permits a taxpayer to claim a reasonable reserve for proceeds not due until after the end of the year, provided that a portion of the gain (at least one-fifth of the gain times the number of taxation years since the disposition) has been included in income. In other words, at least one-fifth of the gain must, on a cumulative basis, be included in the year of sale and in each of the subsequent four taxation years. It is not necessary to claim the maximum reserve in each year and, therefore, a taxpayer has some flexibility when determining the amount of gain subject to tax. This reserve is not available where the purchaser is a corporation controlled by the vendor. Under a proposed amendment, the reserve would also not be available where the purchaser is a partnership in which the vendor is a majority interest partner.

If the property is a family farm property, shares of a "family farm corporation", an interest in a "family farm partnership", or shares of a "small business corporation" that are disposed of to the taxpayer's child who is resident in Canada, the maximum reserve is computed as above except that it will be taxed over a maximum of 10 years rather than five. This 10-year reserve is extended to similar dispositions of fishing property that occur after May 1, 2006.

There is an advantage to claiming a capital gains reserve on a gain otherwise eligible for the enhanced capital gains exemption only if the claim avoids application of the Alternative Minimum Tax. Where such reserves (of either the five or 10-year variety) are claimed, they will survive the death of the testator if the notes are transferred to the testator's spouse or a qualified spousal trust.

[¶17,345] Electing Capital Gains Treatment

Taxpayers (other than traders or dealers in securities and financial institutions) may elect to have gains and losses from the disposition of Canadian securities treated as capital gains or losses. Once made, the election cannot be revoked.

Such an election may be beneficial to taxpayers whose trading activities are sufficiently extensive or of such a nature that resulting gains may be considered to be business income.

Taxpayers who trade in commodities may treat resulting gains or losses as being on either capital or income account. The method chosen, however, must be followed consistently. If commodity transactions are reported as capital gains or losses, related interest and carrying charges are not deductible for tax purposes.

[¶17,350] Options

In certain circumstances, investors may find it advantageous to use the options market to postpone realization of capital gains or to accelerate the deduction of capital losses. For example, consider an investor who has a significant unrealized capital gain in a security for which there is an options market. The investor does not wish to sell the security for tax reasons. The investor may postpone the realization and protect the value of the security by purchasing a put option that matures in the following year.

[¶17,355] Capital Gains Realizations

An actual disposition is required in most cases for capital gains or losses to be recognized for tax purposes. Individuals can rollover the capital gains realized on the disposition of an eligible small business investment (see

¶17,330). In the case of individuals, dispositions are deemed to occur on death or when the individual ceases to be a resident of Canada (see ¶17,565). In the case of corporations, dispositions can be elected to occur when a corporation is declared bankrupt.

If marketable securities are being sold through a stock exchange, keep in mind that disposition for tax purposes occurs on the settlement date (usually three days after the trade date). Thus, the last trading date for the year may fall shortly before Christmas.

[¶17,360] Foreign Currency

Gains or losses arising from an individual's transactions in a foreign currency should be reported as capital gains or losses where the transactions have no relation to the individual's business operations. Such foreign currency gains or losses are recognized only when they are realized. For example, the exchange of U.S. dollars into Canadian dollars could give rise to a gain or loss. However, individuals are required to recognize foreign exchange gains and losses in excess of $200 only. Recognition of an individual's foreign exchange capital gains or losses can be deferred by delaying the conversion of a foreign currency into Canadian funds.

[¶17,365] Tax-Free Dividends

A private corporation may pay a tax-free dividend (except to non-resident individuals) from its Capital Dividend Account. This account consists of the company's non-taxable portion of both net capital gains and net proceeds from the sale of eligible capital property, as well as proceeds under a life insurance policy, less capital dividends paid. An election must be filed by the corporation on or before the date the dividend becomes payable or when any part of the dividend is paid, whichever is earlier. Penalties will apply if the election is filed late. Penalties will also apply if the amount of the capital dividend is calculated incorrectly.

Since the calculation of the Capital Dividend Account is made immediately before payment of the dividend, realization of capital losses, which would reduce the account, should be deferred until after the dividend is paid.

A shareholder is not required to adjust the cost base of his or her shares upon receipt of a capital dividend. Such dividends are particularly attractive if preferred shares in a portfolio investment company are owned by a high bracket taxpayer and the common shares are owned by members of the taxpayer's family. Tax-free capital dividends could be paid on the preferred shares and the remaining shareholders could continue to receive the traditional taxable dividends.

In many situations, it may be advisable to keep the Capital Dividend Account as low as possible to lower the value of the company's equity in the event of the death of a shareholder. The amounts so distributed may be

¶17,360

loaned back to the company if required for working capital purposes, or they can be distributed by means of a dividend in preferred shares.

[¶17,366] Capital Losses

Capital losses realized prior to the end of the year may be used to offset capital gains earned in the year. Furthermore, any excess may be carried back to offset capital gains in the previous three years. The remaining loss, if any, may be carried forward indefinitely and applied against future capital gains.

A capital loss will be denied if identical securities or property are purchased by the taxpayer or persons "affiliated" with the taxpayer, which would include the taxpayer's spouse, or a corporation directly or indirectly controlled by the taxpayer, within 30 days, either before or after the sale. In such a case, however, the non-deductible loss may be added to the adjusted cost base of the property in the hands of the new owner.

If a corporation was declared bankrupt during the year, was wound up pursuant to a winding-up order under the *Winding-Up Act*, or ceased to carry on its business and was insolvent at the end of the year, and if it can be shown that the fair market value of the shares is nil and it is reasonable to expect that the corporation will be dissolved or wound up and will not commence to carry on any further business, the taxpayer may make an election to deem the shares to have been disposed of during the year to claim a capital loss. See ¶5145 *et seq.*

[¶17,370] Allowable Business Investment Losses

Capital losses that arise on certain dispositions of shares or debt in small business corporations are business investment losses. One-half of such losses are allowable business investment losses (ABILs). ABILs are more valuable in tax terms than ordinary allowable capital losses because ABILs can be deducted against all sources of income. ABILs can be carried back three years and forward seven years to offset all sources of income in those years. If the ABIL is not utilized by the seventh subsequent year, it becomes a regular net capital loss that can be used to offset taxable capital gains in future years beyond the seventh year.

In general terms, in order the claim an ABIL, a taxpayer must have realized a capital loss on a disposition of a share or debt in a corporation that, at any time in the twelve months preceding the disposition, was a "small business corporation". A small business corporation is generally a Canadian-controlled private corporation, where "all or substantially all" of the corporation's assets are used principally in an active business carried primarily in Canada (it should be appreciated that the corporation need not actually be "small"). The CRA takes the position that "all or substantially all" means 90% or more of the fair market value of the corporation's assets.

The corporation's assets that qualify for these purposes include shares or debt that the corporation owns in other small business corporations.

An ABIL can arise either on an actual sale, or on a deemed disposition of the share or debt. An actual sale must be made to an arm's length person in order to qualify for ABIL treatment. A deemed disposition of a debt for nil proceeds qualifies for ABIL treatment if the debt is established to be a "bad debt", generally meaning that it has become uncollectible. In the case of a share, a deemed disposition for nil proceeds occurs at the end of a taxation year, if

- the corporation became bankrupt in the year;

- the corporation is insolvent and is being "wound up"; or

- the corporation is insolvent, it no longer carries on a business, the share has a fair market value of nil, and it is expected that the corporation will be wound up or dissolved.

The taxpayer must elect that the deemed disposition take place at the end of the year in question. The election is made in the income tax return filed by the taxpayer for that year.

A taxpayer's ABIL is reduced by any capital gains exemption claimed by the taxpayer in previous years (subsection 39(9)). As a corollary to that rule, if an investor claims an ABIL, the investor must realize an equal amount of taxable capital gains before he or she can subsequently utilize the capital gains exemption (the exemption is discussed below).

See further at ¶5034.

[¶17,380] Self-Employment

[¶17,385] Independent Contractor or Employee?

Of all major groups of taxpayers, it is likely that employees face the harshest tax rules. Tax deductions and deferral opportunities are few and far between; and there can be onerous tax traps awaiting those who attempt to "self-incorporate".

However, the tax rules relating to employees may not apply to what is legally referred to as an "independent contractor". Basically, the concept involves entering into a special arrangement with a would-be employer: instead of simply putting the individual's services at the employer's disposal and under its detailed control, the individual is retained as a "consultant" for specified tasks and assignments.

The potential benefits include the following:

- A wide range of business-related deductions are opened up, including home-office, promotion, entertainment, capital cost allowance on equipment, and so on.

- Although it is possible for an employee to deduct amounts paid to an "assistant", practically speaking, it may be easier to income-split with family members in an independent-contractor situation; e.g., by paying (reasonable) fees/salaries to family members.

- It may also be possible to incorporate and claim the low rate of tax for "active business income" — under 20% in most provinces.

The documentation of the self-employment arrangement and how it is "portrayed" can be critical in determining whether or not an individual will qualify as an independent contractor. For example, instead of being an ordinary employee, a public relations specialist could be retained by the company on a special assignment to enhance the company's relations with the community. Similarly, an accountant could be retained to develop a system of internal control.

The leading case to determine whether an individual is an employee or an independent contractor continues to be the decision of the Federal Court of Appeal in *Wiebe Door Services Ltd. v. M.N.R.* (87 DTC 5025). The *Wiebe Door* case does not prescribe a specific test or list of factors which will indicate an employer/employee relationship as opposed to one of hirer/independent contractor. Instead, it is clear that it is the entire relationship between the parties that must be examined.

Checklist of Relevant Factors

The case law demonstrates that there is no one factor which is determinative of a relationship of employer/employee or of hirer/independent contractor. Instead, the entire nature of the relationship between the parties must be examined. The case law does, however, provide some guidance as to the factors on which the courts will place weight in making that determination.

The following factors would tend to indicate a relationship of an independent contractor:

- a contract indicating a hirer/independent contractor relationship;

- no exclusivity of employment, i.e., the worker may provide services to more than one business;

- remuneration is by reference to sales or billings of the independent contractor — a percentage amount;

- submission of an invoice by worker to the hirer for payment or services rendered;

- worker charges GST;

¶17,385

- no payment to worker if no services performed;

- payment by worker of expenses incurred by the worker in the performance of his or her work such as paying rent for the use of office space and equipment;

- ownership of tools and equipment by the worker;

- lack of restrictions on the hours of work and vacation time;

- no vacation pay or bonuses;

- worker is not required to report to the hirer's premises;

- worker is not required to perform the services personally; he or she may subcontract to a third party;

- hirer does not supervise worker's activities;

- contract for limited period of time or specific project;

- the imposition of a corporation between the worker and the hirer: the contract is between the hirer and a corporation, and the worker is an employee or independent contractor of the corporation; and

- the parties consider their relationship to be that of hirer/independent contractor.

The following factors would tend to indicate an employer/employee relationship:

- worker works exclusively for a particular hirer;

- payment of expenses by hirer;

- payment of a salary or hourly wage as opposed to a percentage of sales;

- payment of worker without reference to worker's performance;

- control and supervision of worker's duties by hirer;

- hirer sets working hours;

- hirer provides worker with all tools and equipment;

- worker is not required to pay any expenses in relation to the work done/services performed;

- provision of a pension or retirement savings plan;

- provision of group benefits to worker including life insurance coverage, extended health and dental benefits and long-term disability;

- payment of a bonus to worker based on performance of the employer's business;

¶17,385

- vacation pay;
- requirement to report to hirer's premises on a regular basis;
- GST is not charged by worker;
- services performed on an indefinite basis;
- service must be performed personally; and
- no written contract between the parties indicating hirer/independent contractor relationship.

[¶17,390] Proprietorship or Incorporation?

An individual may conduct his or her business as either a corporation or proprietorship (another alternative is a partnership). The following are some of the income tax considerations which may affect your decision as to whether your business should be incorporated:

(1) Anticipated earnings

(2) Tax deferrals and savings

(3) Scientific research incentives

(4) Provincial incentives

(5) Income splitting and estate planning.

Anticipated Earnings

A new business often incurs losses in its early years because it has start up costs and low revenues while it is getting established. Losses for tax purposes may be increased further by deducting maximum capital cost allowances. If the business is incorporated and you incur losses, the losses will be incurred by the company and not deductible against your other sources of income. Therefore, if you anticipate losses in your start up years *and* you have sufficient income from other sources, you may wish to defer incorporation until your business is profitable. Once the business has attained a certain level of profit, incorporation may offer certain tax savings and deferrals which are discussed below.

Tax Deferrals and Savings

There are potential tax deferral and savings opportunities in earning active business income through a Canadian-controlled private corporation.

Most Canadian-controlled private corporations with net assets of $10 million or less have an effective corporate tax rate on their active business income up to $500,000 (increased from $400,000 effective January 1, 2009), whether from services, manufacturing, or other activities other than passive investment, of between 13% and 19%, depending on the province in which the income is earned. The increase in the "business limit" to

$500,000 is effective for the 2009 and subsequent taxation years, except that the "business limit" will be pro-rated for taxation years that begin before 2009 and end in 2009 or 2010.

In many provinces, the effective corporate rate on certain kinds of income (manufacturing and processing income) or in certain limited situations (new business) may be considerably lower; in some cases (in the early years of a new business) as low as 11%.

(Note that the income of a personal service business does not qualify for the reduced corporate rates. Essentially this represents the incorporation of what would normally be employment income. The rules relating to this type of business are discussed at ¶8450. Also, corporations which only earn investment income and have five or less employees do not qualify for the above reduced corporate tax rates.)

The additional cash made available through the lower corporate tax rate can either be reinvested in the corporate business, used for investment purposes in the corporation, or distributed as a dividend to the shareholders. To the extent income is distributed to shareholders immediately, no advantage is achieved by incorporation, since the dividend gross-up and credit mechanism will result in approximately the same tax to the individual shareholder as if the income had been earned directly through an unincorporated proprietorship. In this sense, the corporate rate provides a deferral rather than a true tax saving (this would not be true if, by virtue of provincial rules, corporate income is taxed at appreciably less than 23%; in this case, an absolute tax saving can be realized through incorporation). In all cases, a careful analysis must be made in each situation to determine the proper structuring of an owner–manager's earnings (dividend and/or salary) for each particular year.

It was customary in many cases, prior to 2006, to bonus down income in excess of that eligible for low rates to owner–managers, since it would otherwise be subject to an element of double taxation (counting both corporate and personal tax) when paid as dividend. Under the two-tier dividend tax credit system in effect for 2006 and later years, it is possible that income taxed at high rates can be paid out subject to the higher dividend tax credit, which should, at least in theory, eliminate a future double taxation penalty on retaining earnings in the corporation. It follows that, depending on corporate income levels and provincial dividend tax credit rates, it may be beneficial to leave high-rate income in the corporation for dividend treatment rather than bonus it out. No general rule is apparent, but each situation traditionally met with bonuses in the past requires re-examination in the light of the new rules.

Whether corporate earnings should be reinvested in the business or distributed to the shareholders as a dividend should, of course, be a business decision. Further, the timing of the dividend payment to the shareholders should be carefully integrated with the shareholder's personal tax situation to assure the overall tax is minimized.

The tax deferral achieved through incorporation can be rendered a permanent saving if the business is eventually sold at arm's length and it is a "small business corporation". In general, capital gain of up to $750,000 can be received free of tax by an individual shareholder disposing of shares of a "small business corporation"; this is by itself an additional reason for incorporation. Note, however, that investments made by the corporation other than those directly related to its "active" business can, if they exceed 10% of the assets of the corporation, disqualify the corporation from the $750,000 exemption. It is sometimes possible to rearrange the affairs of a potential small business corporation prior to its sale to ensure that only the active business assets remain to be sold; however, this could involve its own tax costs, and it is usually desirable to arrange these matters as early as possible rather than having to attempt them just prior to sale under whatever rules may pertain at that time.

In addition to the $750,000 permanent tax savings available on the sale of small business shares, there can be substantial deferrals of additional capital gains on the sale of shares of corporations which started out as shares of small businesses they are reinvested in new small businesses.

Among the benefits of incorporation is the annual income deferral which may be achieved through the use of bonuses. Remuneration in the form of bonuses accrued in the taxation year of a corporation will normally be deductible to the corporation provided they are *bona fide* obligations and are paid out at some time in the following 180 days. As the individual will be taxed only when he or she receives the bonus, a one-year deferral may be achieved.

Scientific Research Incentives

If your business is incorporated and has certain activities that may be considered research and development activities, various tax incentives are available to it which would not be available to an unincorporated business.

For example, the investment tax credit for qualifying Canadian-controlled private corporations incurring scientific research expenditures is 35%, whereas an individual could not claim credit above 20% for the same expenditure.

In addition to a possible higher rate of credit, scientific research tax credits earned in a corporation may be refunded in cash to the corporation at a higher rate than to individuals. Individuals can obtain a cash refund of 40% of scientific research credits generated in the year in excess of tax. A Canadian-controlled private corporation whose income (together with the income of associated corporations) did not exceed $500,000 in the preceding year can claim a 100% cash refund of investment tax credits earned at a rate of 35% in respect of up to $3 million of scientific research expenditures

¶17,390

made in the taxation year (this will not apply to expenditures on depreciable property). Consequently, annual refunds of up to $1.05 million will be available to small corporations engaging in scientific research. As income exceeds $500,000, the $3 million of eligible expenditure is decreased, ceasing at income of $800,000. Furthermore, the qualifying income limit is reduced if the corporation's taxable capital employed in Canada for its preceding taxation year, along with the taxable capital of its associated corporations for their taxation years ending in the calendar year that ended before the end of the particular taxation year, exceeds $10 million. The 100% refund remains available, however, on whatever amount of R&D expenditure remains eligible for the high rate. The values of $800,000, $3 million, and $1.05 million may be less in 2009 and earlier taxation years, as they were readjusted effective February 26, 2008.

Provincial Incentives

Provinces may vary the $500,000 limit below which the federal government offers low corporate rates, although all provinces offer a low provincial corporate tax rate on some amount. In addition to the low rates, provinces may offer additional incentives to corporations. For example, several provinces offer tax credits to corporations investing in new machinery and equipment. Several provinces provide incentives to individuals and corporations willing to invest in incorporated small businesses in the province, thereby making it easier for the incorporated business to raise capital for start-up or expansion. In short, there may be additional tax or tax-driven benefits to incorporation in any particular province.

Income Splitting and Estate Planning

A reasonable amount of remuneration paid to a spouse or child of the taxpayer for performing employment duties in a proprietorship is deductible for tax purposes to the proprietor. However, incorporation offers other income splitting and estate planning opportunities. For example, if you and your spouse each have wholly-owned corporations, and your corporation has retained earnings from a business which are loaned to your spouse's corporation interest free, investment income on the loaned funds can be paid and taxed to your spouse. Many tax advisers feel that such a loan will not be subject to the "attribution rules", although the matter is perhaps not beyond doubt. Certainly, in the absence of the corporations, attribution rules would apply.

Where a start-up business (one with little current asset or other value) is being incorporated, it is often possible to provide for income splitting by having a spouse purchase shares with the spouse's own money. If the business succeeds, the income can be divided with the spouse through dividends, giving (if the spouse has little other income) a second use of marginal tax rates and personal amount credits. Pursuant to the "Kiddie Tax", dividends allocated to children in this fashion will be taxed at top marginal rates, eliminating any income splitting benefits. Nevertheless, having chil-

¶17,390

dren acquire shares of the incorporated business can permit future growth in the value of the business to be passed on to the next generation in part or in full (depending upon the number and nature of the shares allocated), which can carry the benefits of deferring the costs of taxation on death, spreading the tax costs of any future sale, and perhaps multiplying the $750,000 capital gains exemption. If savings are intended to fund the higher education of minor children, it may be possible to dam up the savings in the corporation, or in holding corporations for the children, and pay them out as dividends to the child shareholders piecemeal when they reach the age of 18, during the years in which their higher education must be paid for.

As presently structured, the special tax on children's dividends will not operate once the child reaches 18. Caution is in order, in that excess funds maintained in the corporation may jeopardize the $750,000 capital gains exemption, although it is conceivable that proper structuring (such as separate holding companies to hold the children's savings until they are 18) can alleviate this problem. Where the splitting of current income with minor children is not part of the exercise, it may not be necessary to have the child use its own money to acquire the shares; shares acquired with a gift or *bona fide* loan will suffice. Note, however, that the 2011 federal Budget added to the concept of split income by providing that capital gains realized by a minor from a disposition of non-publicly listed shares of a corporation to a non-arm's length person will be treated as taxable dividends that are not eligible dividends, and therefore subject to the tax on split income. Using the child's own money prevents application of the regular attribution rules; so as long as no current property income arises in a year before the child reaches 18, attribution is not a problem.

In these situations, it is common for interests for children, especially minor children, to be held by trusts for them. For arrangements in place before 2000, this permitted income to be accrued for them at their tax rates while their parents retained control of the funds (so long as they are used for the children's benefit) so they could be used for specific purposes, usually higher education. Where splitting current year income is not the objective, a trust should still facilitate the parents' control of the children's shares (in the event of sale, for example), and incidentally of the underlying business.

If your family is not in place when your business is first incorporated, essentially the same income splitting and growth transfer objectives can be achieved later through an "estate freeze". This is a series of transactions to rearrange your asset holdings so that future increases in their value will accrue to the benefit of your heirs and thus postpone or reduce taxation on your death. This technique can more readily be applied to an incorporated business than to a proprietorship or partnership interest.

You should know that where incorporation is used to achieve income splitting between spouses by putting shares and then dividends into the hands of a spouse, the CRA may examine such transactions closely with a

¶17,390

view to finding flaws in the plan and taxing the dividends of a spouse not active in the business to the active shareholder. However, the CRA has had no success in challenging plans which are even moderately well constructed.

Summary

The above tax considerations should be reviewed in light of other valid business and personal factors. You should seek professional tax advice where the incorporation of a business is being considered, or where any of the tax planning steps outlined above are contemplated. As a rough measure of thumb, if you have (or are starting) your own unincorporated business and you can make full contributions to an RRSP and still have income in excess of your current needs, you should seriously consider incorporation. On the other hand, if you require more or less all your income for your personal expenses, it is unlikely incorporation will be beneficial.

[¶17,400] Lower Corporate Tax Rates & Eligible Dividends

[¶17,405] Introduction

The taxation of corporations and their owner–managers has been significantly affected by the reduction of corporation tax rates (see ¶8470) that has occurred in recent years, along with legislation relating to eligible dividends (see ¶6052).

The overall effect of these changes has been to foster "integration" in respect of high-rate business income, so that the combined corporate and personal tax rate would be fairly close to the tax rate that would apply if the income had been earned directly by an individual in the top tax bracket (a degree of double-taxation is referred to as "underintegration" and combined personal/corporate tax at less than personal rates, "overintegration").

While the eligible dividend regime is directed largely toward public corporations, eligible dividends will generally include dividends paid after 2005 by Canadian-controlled private corporations ("CCPCs"), to the extent that their income (other than investment income) is subject to tax at the general corporate income tax rate. Also eligible are non-CCPCs that are resident in Canada. Thus the rules will also be of interest to private corporations, particularly those with "high-rate" business income (i.e., income which is not eligible for the small business deduction).

The lowering of corporate tax rates, coupled with the eligible dividend regime, has some fairly significant results. Notably, if they have not already done so, owner–managers should reconsider the practice of bonusing-out income in excess of the small business limit (as of January 1, 2009, $500,000 per associated group of corporations). In general, it can be said that, at worst, the ultimate burden when profits are taxed in the corporation and paid to the shareholder as taxable dividends may be only modestly higher than the top personal rate applicable to bonuses; in the meantime, there may be a significant element of deferral resultant from corporate tax rates which are lower than top personal rates.[3] In addition, the rules may lead many corporations, such as those involved in real estate rental businesses, to consider restructuring so that income is taxed based on corporate tax rates applicable to business income, rather than as investment businesses, which are subject to higher corporate tax rates, coupled with the RDTOH system (restructuring would be possible where the more-than-five-full-time-employee test can be met). The reason is that, under the eligible dividend regime, there would be a significant reduction of corporate tax rates, while the loss of RDTOH may have little or no material adverse effect if eligible dividends can ultimately be paid instead.

The following is a comparison of the eligible dividend calculation at the federal level from 2012. As can be seen, in 2012 there is very little difference in federal tax between eligible and ineligible dividends, leading one to wonder whether the eligible dividend regime, with all of its complexities, will eventually be scrapped — e.g., when the lower corporate tax rate regime is phased-in in 2012. However, when provincial taxes are factored in, the discrepancy between eligible and ineligible dividends may be greater.

Federal Tax: Eligible vs. Ineligible Dividends

	Ineligible	Eligible 2008	Eligible 2009	Eligible 2010	Eligible 2011	Eligible 2012+
Dividend	100	100	100	100	100	100
Gross-up*	25	45	45	44	41	38
Total	125	145	145	144	141	138
Federal tax at 29	36.25	42.05	42.05	41.76	40.89	40.02
Dividend Tax Credit**	16.67	27.50	27.50	25.88	23.17	20.73
Net Federal Tax	**19.58**	**14.55**	**14.55**	**15.88**	**17.72**	**19.29**

* For ineligible dividends, 25% of the actual dividend; for eligible dividends, 45% of the actual dividend in 2008 and 2009, 44% in 2010, 21% in 2011 and 38% in 2012 and beyond.

** For ineligible dividends, 2/3 of the 25% gross-up; for eligible dividends, 11/18 of the 45% gross-up in 2008 and 6/11 of the 38% gross-up in 2012.

As mentioned previously, the provincial taxation of eligible dividends varies from province to province.

See page ii for explanation of footnotes.

[3] In addition, if the corporation subsequently incurs tax losses, carrybacks (with the normal three-year period) should be more tax effective, since corpo- rate losses cannot shelter income bonuses out to the owner-manager.

[¶17,415] Some Planning Points

Eligible dividends, combined with lower corporate tax rates, may have an important impact on the decision as to whether to bonus or retain earnings at the corporate level; in addition, where possible, the regime may encourage the conversion from specified investment business income, particularly where the corporation can meet the more-than-five-full-time-employee test.

The following are some additional planning points:

RDTOH and Eligible Dividends

It is possible for a dividend to result in a dividend refund and be an eligible dividend at the same time. For a CCPC, the latter will occur if a dividend-paying corporation has GRIP balances. This could be the case, for example, if a CCPC ("Holdco") holds the shares of both an investment corporation ("Investco"), i.e., one that generates refundable dividend tax on hand ("RDTOH"), and a corporation which generates GRIP, e.g., from high-rate business income ("Opco"). Investco could pay dividends which would result in a dividend refund to it and Part IV tax/RDTOH increase to Holdco. If Opco pays eligible dividends, Holdco will have both RDTOH and GRIP so that "dual status" can be achieved (this could be particularly advantageous in an estate freeze structure). It should be noted that if Holdco pays a "dual status" dividend, it would deplete both its RDTOH and GRIP, leaving surplus which if paid out as a dividend, may not be eligible for special status on either account, unless Holdco's RDTOH/GRIP were replenished. The following is the descending order of preference of dividends:

- eligible dividends that trigger a dividend refund (i.e., a refund of RDTOH);

- ineligible dividends that trigger a dividend refund;

- eligible dividends that do not trigger a dividend refund;

- ineligible dividends that do not trigger a dividend refund.

Part IV Tax — Portfolio Dividends

The eligible dividend rules were designed to avoid becoming overly-complex. As a result, the rules do not deal with such things as having a lower Part IV tax rate for eligible dividends. As a result, a holding company which receives eligible dividends must pay refundable Part IV tax at the rate of $33^{1}/_{3}$%, which would exceed the tax on eligible dividends to an individual shareholder (at the time of writing). Accordingly, the holding company should, in turn, pay eligible dividends to its individual shareholders.

Safe Income Strips

If a corporation has taxed retained earnings ("safe income"), it is advantageous to pay to distribute this as a tax-free dividend to a holding company prior to sale of the company's shares. This will reduce capital gains tax to the holding company. Previously, the disadvantage would be that, if these safe income dividends were distributed to individual shareholders, the tax rate would be higher than the capital gain. However, if the safe income qualifies as an eligible dividend, this disadvantage may decrease.

Asset Sales

Declining corporate tax rates and eligible dividend status may alter the preferences in respect of whether assets or shares are sold. The sale of shares generates capital gains tax rates (about 25% at the corporate level and about 23% at the individual level, in Ontario). If there is a corporate-level sale of goodwill or other eligible capital property, the tax rate will be one-half of normal business rates, which is considerably less than the applicable capital gains rates (in 2010, the applicable rate is 15.5% in Ontario; this is scheduled to reduce to 12.5% in 2014). Like a capital gain, one-half of the gain in respect of the eligible dividend can be paid as a tax-free capital dividend. The taxable portion will typically generate GRIP and therefore can be paid out as eligible dividends. Until this is done — i.e., the profits are retained at the corporate level — taxes can be deferred, since they are based on one-half of the business rates. To the extent there is integration on eligible dividends, there will be no increase in the ultimate combined personal/corporate tax, relative to capital gains which generate refundable tax balances.

Post-Mortem Planning

The ability to pay eligible dividends may alter *post-mortem* estate planning strategies. Consider the following:

If access to corporate-level cash and other assets is desired, prior to the eligible dividend regime, the most tax-efficient method would generally be the "pipeline" strategy, whereby the terminal period capital gain would bump the ACB of the shares of the decedent's corporation, so that the increased cost base could be used to access corporate-level assets (for example, the shares of the deceased's corporation could be transferred into a Holdco in exchange for a note equal to the increased cost base; tax-free intercorporate dividends could be paid to the Holdco, which could pay down the note, again without tax). If, however, eligible dividends are taxed more favourably than capital gains, it may make more sense to effect a subsection 164(6)-type procedure, whereby a *post-mortem* deemed dividend/capital loss is created and the latter is applied to the terminal period gain.

For example, where there is non-grandfathered corporate-owned life insurance, death taxes can be minimized by the so-called "50% solution", which involves the repurchase of the decedent's corporation's shares held by the estate for a 50% capital dividend/50% taxable dividend (the stop-loss rules in subsection 112(3.2) may, in effect, force taxable dividends of magnitude equal to capital dividends; otherwise part or all of the loss will be denied). Prior to the eligible dividend rules, the "50%" solution was, in reality, more like a "one-third solution", because of the relatively high tax rate attaching to non-eligible dividends. However, the tax rate on taxable dividends may be reduced to the extent that eligible dividends can be paid.

Other Effects of Eligible Dividends

Eligible dividends may increase exposure to minimum tax; as well, they may increase the OAS "clawback". However, this will diminished in future years as the gross-up for eligible dividends will decline somewhat. Capital gains crystallizations (i.e., purposely triggering an exempt capital gain to increase the cost base in a corporation's shares) or purification procedures (i.e., to ensure that the shares of the company continually qualify for the capital gains exemption) may become more important, especially in view of lower corporate tax rates, since the retention of profits at the corporate level — rather than the payment of bonuses to owner–manager — may mean that, without these procedures, that the exemption may be jeopardized in the future, as the corporation's assets may no longer be devoted to qualifying active business use, due to the build up of assets not needed in the business.

Estate freezes will become more important, because the increased retention of income at the corporate level value due to lower corporate tax rates may well increase eventual exposure to death tax.

[¶17,420] Remuneration of Owner–Managers of Private Corporations

[¶17,425] The Principles of Integration

A basic issue relating to the remuneration of owner–managers is whether it is optimal that remuneration be effected via salary-type distributions, which essentially transfer taxable income from the corporate to the individual level, or via the payment of taxable dividends, which leave taxable income within the corporation but result in a second level of taxation at the individual level (subject, of course, to the gross-up and credit treatment that applies to dividends from taxable Canadian corporations).

The Canadian taxation system is now designed, at least in theory, to result in overall equality with respect to combined personal-corporate-taxation of either salary or dividends where a private corporation earns business (or investment) income, whether such income qualifies for the small business deduction at the corporate level or is taxed at general corporate rates applicable to business income. In other words, the overall personal and corporate tax rate on earnings distributed in the form of dividends will be equivalent to the tax rate which would apply had the income been distributed as salary (or earned directly by an unincorporated individual). This equality is referred to as "integration".

For income qualifying for the small business deduction, integration will arise where the combined federal and provincial corporate tax rate is 20%. In this case, income would be distributed via ordinary (ineligible) dividends. For income taxed at the general business rate, integration is ultimately designed to arise at a federal corporate tax rate of about 15% (so that combined federal/provincial rates may be in the 25% range) — a rate that will apply once federal tax changes are fully phased-in. In this case, distributions would normally be made by "eligible dividends". If taxation at the corporate level drops below these levels, there will be a general bias in favour of dividend payments, referred to as "overintegration". Conversely, there will be a bias in favour of salary payments — "underintegration" — if the corporate tax rate exceeds these rates. As will be seen later, however, there are a number of practical distortions to these theoretical niceties.

The reduction of federal corporate general business tax rates, fully phased-in as of 2012, coupled with the ability to pay eligible dividends (effective for dividends paid after 2005) which enhances the dividend gross-up and credit mechanisms combine to integrate corporate and individual shareholder taxes. Prior to these changes, the gross-up and credit mechanisms provided for integration only at rates of corporate tax where the small business deduction applied; income earned by a corporation that was taxable at full rates was underintegrated, resulting in a degree of double taxation when the income was distributed as a dividend to individual shareholders.

[¶17,427] Eligible Dividends and Reduced Corporate Tax Rates

The intent behind the federal reduction in corporate tax rates, along with the eligible dividend rules is to provide integration in respect of income taxed at the general corporate business rate; however, the extent to which under-integration is reduced/eliminated will depend whether the provinces enact similar eligible dividend legislation. The federal dividend gross-up of 38%, and the dividend tax credit of $6/11$ of the (38%) gross-up applies to eligible dividends from taxable Canadian corporations that are resident in Canada. Because of the reduction of corporate tax rates, the taxation of such dividends has been set so that it will not differ dramatically from ineligible dividends, once the changes are fully phased in. CCPCs are able to pay eligible dividends to the extent that their income (other than investment income) is subject to the general rate in 2012.

[¶17,430] Distribution Strategies Where Small Business Deduction Available

In situations where the full federal small business deduction is available, there will be integration or, in some cases, over-integration (due to the factors discussed below). Where the small business deduction is applicable, the following statements may generally be made as to distribution strategies.

¶17,430

(1) Where an owner–manager has virtually no personal taxable income, the combined personal-corporate tax rate will be reduced by paying at least some salary from the corporation, even if distributions are not required by the owner–manager. Generally, such distributions should be made until the personal tax credits and deductions are fully utilized.

In addition, relatively small distributions over and above this level may attract little or no increased overall tax (assuming, of course, that the recipient otherwise has low taxable income). If so, it may be advisable to distribute such funds from the corporation so that the distributions of corporate assets will be "tax-paid".

(2) Once this level is achieved, it is usually not advantageous from a tax standpoint to distribute funds from the corporation unless corporate earnings are in excess of the annual small business limit ($500,000 per corporation or associated group of corporations, starting January 1, 2009), since there will be an overall tax increase as a result of the distribution. Accordingly, maximum tax deferral will be achieved by distributing only what is necessary to defray personal and living expenses.

Note that it is generally not necessary to distribute corporate funds to the personal level in order to make investments — even if they are unrelated to the corporation's ongoing business activities; in fact, this practice may result in significant acceleration of tax liability. If creditor protection is desired, such that retained earnings will not be subject to creditor claims, consideration should be given to transferring the operating company into a holding company, distributing funds as dividends to the holding company, and either making investments at the holding company level or lending the funds back to the operating company on a secured basis.

(3) When the corporation's profit exceeds its annual business limit ($500,000 per corporation or associated group of corporations) it may still be advantageous to retain the profits at the corporate level, since personal tax rates usually exceed the general business rate applicable to the corporation. In other words, the distribution of profits either as salary/bonus or eligible dividends will increase the overall tax. (Obviously, if the general corporate tax rate exceeds the personal tax rate, e.g., where the individual is not yet in the top tax bracket, distributions in the form of salary/bonuses will result in overall tax saving. Bonusing down to the small business limit may nevertheless still be advantageous, in particular if the retention of profits at the corporate level would result in under-integration when the profits are eventually distributed as dividends. However, because of the federal reduction in corporate tax rates phased in as of 2012, as well as the eligible dividend regime, the degree of under-integration will be reduced or eliminated, depending upon the province. Of course, the payment of either bonuses/salaries or eligible dividends will mean that funds are available for personal use by an owner–manager when required. If the excess funds are lent to the company, thus forming a "credit balance" *vis-à-vis* the own-

¶17,430

er–manager, the funds can, of course, be withdrawn in the future on a "tax-paid" basis. In addition, if the excess over the annual business limit is distributed via a deferred-payment bonus, it may be possible to achieve an immediate corporate tax reduction, while deferring tax on the bonus. (Where bonuses are accrued, there is now a 179-day limitation period on the deferral, pursuant to subsection 78(4).) Where the personal tax rate exceeds the corporate rate, these advantages should be balanced against the loss of deferral.

Note: The advisability of bonusing down to the small business limit, as mentioned above, will diminish as a result of the eligible dividend regime.

In many instances, the above factors will be overridden by the fact that the owner–manager will require funds for personal and living expenses, yet the corporation's earnings will be below the limits at which the small business deduction will no longer be available. Under these circumstances, should salary or dividends be distributed, in view of the previous comments relating to integration?

The following paragraph discusses factors which favour either salaries or dividends.

[¶17,435] Situations Where Dividends Are Advantageous

Notwithstanding the theoretical comments respecting integration, in practice, there are usually distortions as to integration, usually resulting in a modest bias in favour of dividends. However, this bias should be balanced against other factors militating in favour of salary, especially the ability to enlarge RRSP contributions. The following factors may create a bias in favour of dividends:

(1) Where income qualifies for the small business deduction, the assumed corporate tax rate where integration arises is 20%. However, in most provinces, the corporate tax rate is less than this amount, especially due to provincial small business rate reductions. Accordingly, over-integration will tend to arise.

(2) Where income qualifies for the small business deduction, the assumed corporate tax rate where integration arises is 20%. However, in most provinces, the corporate tax rate is less than this amount, especially due to provincial small business rate reductions. Accordingly, over-integration will tend to arise. There may be other corporate tax incentives that effectively reduce the corporate tax rate. These include investment tax credits, accelerated capital cost allowances, R & D, and other incentives. To the extent that these deductions and credits reduce the effective rate of corporate tax below the notional 20% (or so) level, and would be lost if salary were paid, there will be an over-integration effect when the after-tax income of the corporation is distributed via dividends.

(3) Dividends may trigger refundable tax to the corporation and thus reduce overall corporate tax rates. In many instances, corporate tax rates on investment income will exceed the levels that would provide enough cash to generate a full dividend refund when investment profits are paid out as dividends. This situation results in a build-up of refundable tax balances which may be "liberated" when dividends are paid out of active business profits.

(4) Personal cash flow may be temporarily increased by the fact that dividends are not subject to withholding tax (depending, of course, on the individual's installment base).

(5) In Ontario, salary will be subject to the Ontario Employee Health Tax, whereas dividends will not. The tax is levied at a rate of 1.95% of gross salary, wages, and other remuneration. The tax applies to aggregate remuneration in excess of $400,000 per associated group of corporations.

(6) Dividends will reduce a taxpayer's CNIL account and may therefore enhance his or her ability to obtain the capital gains exemption.

(7) Distributions as dividends will still leave the corporation in a position to carryback future non-capital losses, i.e., if incurred within three taxation years after the particular year. Similarly, leaving income in the corporation may increase the ability to use non-refundable ITCs.

(8) To the extent that the corporation can pay eligible dividends, the personal tax rate will decrease. For a CCPC, this depends on the extent to which the corporation has a General Rate Income Pool (GRIP).

(9) Retaining income in the corporation may reduce its exposure to Ontario corporate minimum tax.

(10) An individual may be denied the capital gains exemption if a significant portion of the gain may be attributable to the fact that the corporation failed to pay dividends on non-prescribed shares (generally shares other than common shares), per subsections 110.6(8) and (9). Thus, the payment of dividends may reduce this risk. Having said this, it is unclear whether these provisions are commonly invoked by the CRA.

As a result of some of these factors, the combined personal-corporate tax rate on dividends may be lower than the personal tax rate applicable to salary distributions. In other words, over-integration may apply. Moreover, even where there is under-integration, the payment of dividends may still be advantageous where lower-bracket shareholders can be introduced and income splitting objectives achieved. This may occur in situations where the payment of salary to such low-bracket taxpayers is not justified.

¶17,435

[¶17,440] Situations Where Salary Is Advantageous

Although the above-mentioned factors tend to favour dividend distributions, there are others which favour salary, rather than dividend distributions. These include:

(1) Where the corporate tax rate exceeds 20%, there will be a tendency toward under-integration, militating in favour of salary-type distributions. Low provincial personal rates will also tend to give rise to under-integration.

(2) The payment of additional amounts of salary enables larger RRSP contributions to be made. This will not be the case with dividends.

(3) Tax can be deferred by the accrued bonus mechanism. Subject to the 179-day time constraints, the corporation can obtain a current tax deduction while taxation to the owner–manager is deferred until funds are actually received. In addition, the payment of salary will reduce corporate taxes, and therefore the corporation's installment payments, for the current and two following taxation years. On the other hand, dividend distributions will not reduce the corporation's income and therefore its installments, and will increase the owner–manager's installment base.

(4) Insurance and other benefits may be tied to salary.

(5) Canada Pension Plan contributions may be made if salary is paid.

(6) Salary will expand the opportunity to create "defined benefit" pension plans for owner–managers. The contribution limits will be based, in part, on the salary of owner–manager, whereas remuneration by a dividend would not increase contribution limits.

(7) Salary distributions may be preferable where the Alternative Minimum Tax (AMT) exceeds the regular tax; with regard to the AMT, see ¶17,605.

(8) Because there is no gross-up on salary (as opposed to dividends), the payment of salary may be less likely to trigger the OAS clawback.

(9) The payment of salary, as opposed to dividends, may increase the child care expense deduction, as deductions are dependent on earned income, which does not include dividends.

[¶17,442] The RRSP/TFSA Factor

Historically, at least, the potential advantages of overintegration achieved by dividend distributions have often been perceived to be outweighed by the tax advantages obtained when the owner–manager is able to make maximum RRSP contributions. Salary-type distributions enable the owner–manager to increase RRSP contributions, since this qualifies as "earned income" — this is not the case with dividends.

An RRSP enables an owner–manager to inject capital into a tax-sheltered vehicle, thus resulting in tax deferral on investment earnings.

In addition to an RRSP, ongoing investment income may also be sheltered — on a permanent rather than tax-deferred basis — in a TFSA. Starting in 2009, owner–managers and other individuals 18 years of age and older acquire $5,000 of TFSA contribution room each year. Unused contribution room will be carried forward to future years. The owner–manager's spouse and adult children will similarly acquire TFSA contribution room.

Traditionally, it has been perceived that there should be sufficient salary/bonuses distributed to owner–managers to enable the maximum RRSP contribution. As mentioned above, however, when dividends are distributed rather than salary, there is (at time of writing) a degree of over-integration. In Ontario, for example, the effective tax rate on dividends at the highest marginal rate is about 3.1% lower than the applicable tax rate on salary, ignoring Employer Health Tax (EHT). Besides the EHT, dividends also avoid payroll taxes on salaries, notably CPP premiums which are often perceived by owner–managers to be an additional expense. A report issued by CIBC Private Wealth Management[4] suggests that the strategy of paying sufficient salaries to enable maximum RRSP contributions should be reconsidered, and contends that it will be more advantageous to remunerate via dividends and therefore pass up the RRSP contribution. In addition to the overall tax reduction for dividends, tax benefits such as the tax-free portion of capital gains and the dividend tax credit will be lost if investments are made through an RRSP. In addition, because of low corporate tax rates when the small business deduction is available, distributions should generally not be made unless required to defray personal expenses. Since TFSAs have tax advantages that generally parallel those of RRSPs (even though TFSAs are tax-paid investment vehicles whereas RRSPs are tax-deferred investment vehicles), similar comments would presumably apply with respect to distributions to fund TFSA contributions. It would also appear that similar considerations apply to defined benefit plans (i.e., IPPs).

[¶17,445] Distribution Strategies Where Small Business Deduction Not Available

Where the small business deduction is not available — notably, where active business income exceeds the annual small business limit — there was formerly a significant element of under-integration if the profits were distributed as dividends, so that when distributions are desired, they would generally be in the form of salary, rather than dividend payments. This process is known as "bonusing down to the small business limit". In other words, owner–managers have often been advised to pass up the deferral resultant from the fact that the general corporate business rate may be less

See page ii for explanation of footnotes.
[4] *Rethinking RRSPs for Business Owners: Why Taking a Salary May not Make Sense*, Jamie Golombek, October 19, 2010.

¶17,445

than the top personal rate, because of the eventual double tax effects resultant from retaining income at the corporate level, when earnings of the corporation are distributed as dividends. Even with decreasing corporate tax rates that occurred early in the decade — and therefore an increasing element of deferral by retaining profits at the corporate level — this strategy was persistent. However, this strategy has been greatly affected by the dividend reduction of corporate tax rates along with the eligible dividend rules.

The eligible dividend rules are designed to result in integration when income subject to general business corporate rates are paid as dividends, thereby dramatically reducing the downside of deferring tax by retaining income at the corporate level. Whether or not there will be full integration depends on whether (and the extent to which) the provinces match the federal rules. Most provinces have followed the federal rules, although some of the provinces are phasing in their eligible dividend regimes. In general, however, the spectre of underintegration when funds are retained at the corporate level rather than being distributed as bonuses will be much less acute: while there may still be an element of underintegration, depending mainly on provincial taxation, this will be lessened. With the spectre of double tax being reduced when eligible dividends can be paid, the focus should shift to obtaining the advantages of retaining profit at the corporate level: until such time as the eligible dividends are paid, there may be a significant element of deferral, to the extent that personal tax rates exceed corporate rates (unfortunately, one notable exception to the foregoing relates to the Ontario clawback of the small business deduction, which applies for corporate income levels between $500,000 and about $1.1 million. Because corporate tax rates increase by close to 5% in this range, the clawback will result in a significant degree of underintegration).

To the extent that funds are not distributed by bonuses but are retained in the corporation, the value of the corporation will, of course, increase due to the build-up of corporate surplus. But if eligible dividends can be paid to reduce this surplus — and there is therefore reduced underintegration — the dilemma between the advantage of deferral by retention of income at the corporate level and disadvantage of eventual double tax as a result of a distribution (or other taxable event such as a sale or a deemed disposition of the corporation's shares on death) will be greatly reduced, again favouring retention of at the corporate level.

The eligible dividend rules also level the playing field between the taxation of eligible dividends and capital gains. While the precise level of tax will depend on provincial tax rates, and in particular the extent to which a province matches the federal eligible dividend rates, the taxation of these types of income should be close in most provinces. Thus, the manner of realization of the corporate surplus — whether by eligible dividends or capital gains (on a share sale or by virtue of death tax exposure) — should matter less. Of course, this is only the case to the extent that eligible

¶17,445

dividends can be generated. If they cannot, realization of surplus via capital gains will generally be preferable.

[¶17,450] Whether or Not To "Bonus Out" Corporate Profits

The following are some considerations that may lead to the decision of whether or not to "bonus out" high-corporate-rate income:

(1) A significant advantage of retaining profits at the corporate level is the deferral of tax that would otherwise occur if funds are distributed either as eligible dividends or bonuses.

(2) While such deferral may be desirable, it may of course be the case that funds derived from profits in excess of the small business deduction limit are needed from the corporation for personal and living expenses. If so, it is advisable to determine whether tax rates are lower when profits are distributed via salary/bonus or dividends. This will depend on the province.

> *Note:* if profits in excess of the small business deduction are to be invested, it is not necessary to distribute them to individual share-holders. In this case, the additional tax usually resultant from sala-ry/bonuses or dividends (eligible or otherwise) is both costly and unnecessary. If it is desirable to insulate such assets from the risks of the business generating the profits, it is possible to do this by paying tax free dividends to a holding company.

(3) If the corporate tax rate applicable to the earnings exceeds the individual's marginal tax rate applicable to the salary distribution (e.g., the individual is not otherwise in the top bracket), it will be optimal to distribute the funds via salary-type payments in any event.

(4) If the corporation suffers financial reversals in the future, and income is retained in the corporation rather than being "bonused out", it will be possible to carry back the future tax losses — i.e., within the normal three-year carryback period. Distributing the profits as a bonus will, of course, jeopardize this course of action.

(5) The rate at which SR&ED investment tax credits are available depends on a corporation's taxable income. Accordingly, reducing corporate income to the small business limit may increase the ITC rate from 20% to 35%.

(6) To the extent that the Ontario clawback applies, the deferral will be reduced and the underintegration increased. This will occur where corporate profits exceed the small business limit ($500,000) until the clawback ceiling income (in excess of $1.1 million) is reached. In this zone, the decision as to whether to retain profits at the corporate level in order to take advantage of the deferral between corporate and personal rates will be a much closer call and may well militate in favour of bonusing down to the small business limit. The advisability of doing so will be a function of how

long the earnings can be retained at the corporate level. However, as profit increases over the clawback ceiling, this will be less of a factor.

Note: The tax deferral available from leaving profits in the corporation may enable the corporation to earn enough additional income to make up for the eventual increased tax exposure due to underintegration. The required time period will depend on factors that include the difference between personal and corporate rates, anticipated after-tax return (including the tax treatment of accumulating income), and the tax costs of distributing the accumulated income.

In theory, the issue centers on the time period within which the after-tax surplus in the corporation will accumulate to an after-tax amount (realized in the individual shareholder's hands) sufficient to match the future value of after-tax income distributed via a bonus. In this regard, it should be noted that income accumulated at the corporate level will eventually have to be distributed. However, the tax cost of distribution of the income generated may be diminished if the income qualifies for refundable tax treatment. In addition, since top corporate rates are somewhat lower than top personal rates, the income will accumulate at a slightly higher after-tax rate than personal income.

Obviously, this calculation can become quite complex and will vary in accordance with circumstances. Generally, because the eligible dividend regime will reduce the overall personal-corporate tax rate to near to the personal rate applicable if the profits were simply bonused out, the time period to make up for the underintegration, where applicable, will be relatively short; however, the effect of the Ontario clawback will considerably lengthen the time.

[¶17,550] International Considerations

[¶17,555] Leaving/Entering Canada

An individual who leaves Canada to work or retire abroad can sometimes suffer unexpected and adverse tax consequences. A few of the more common and significant tax implications are noted below. An individual's decision to leave Canada can become more complex than was foreseen. Professional advice should be sought prior to departure. Similarly, individuals who come to Canada from another country should examine the tax situations governing the two countries very carefully, well before taking up residence. Professional advice should be obtained from both countries.

[¶17,560] Residence

The most significant problem to be addressed by an individual moving between countries is the determination of residence. Because Canada taxes its residents on their world income, the determination of residence is important for Canadian tax purposes. Although the determination of residency is a question of fact, it can be defined generally as a continuing relationship between an individual and a place.

Some factors considered relevant when determining whether an individual remains a resident of Canada for tax purposes while abroad are:

- the individual's motives and intentions on leaving Canada;

- the length of stay abroad;

- the availability of a dwelling place in Canada;

- the location of the individual's dependants;

- the extent of the individual's continued personal and business connections in Canada;

- the permanence of the individual's accommodations outside Canada; and

- the sources of any employment or business income.

An individual is deemed to be a resident of Canada if that individual visited Canada temporarily for a period or periods totalling 183 days or more in the year. However, where the individual is also resident in a country with which Canada has a tax treaty, the treaty generally will provide rules to prevent dual residency.

[¶17,565] Deemed Disposition on Departure

Generally, an individual who ceases to be a resident of Canada for tax purposes is deemed to have disposed of all of his or her property at fair market value. Any capital gains that result are subject to tax in the year of departure.

All emigrants (including trusts) basically are subject to Canadian tax on any gains that have accrued up to the time of departure. Certain types of future benefits are exempt from the deemed dispositions rules, such as pension plans, including RRSPs and employee profit sharing plans. People leaving Canada calculate Canadian tax as though they had disposed of all their property other than Canadian real estate and a limited group of other assets, such as capital property used in a business carried on in Canada by the taxpayer through a permanent establishment in Canada. The taxpayer can either pay the tax immediately or provide the CRA with security and pay the tax over a period of time. The CRA will not charge interest where adequate security has been provided for the tax balance due.

Previously, a person could lessen the impact of the departure tax by making an election to deem his or her property to be taxable Canadian property. The disposition of such property was not subject to Canadian income tax until the property was actually disposed of sometime in the future. Moreover, if no election was made, foreign tax credits could be mismatched, as Canadian tax was paid in the year of departure while foreign income taxes might have been payable on the gain realized on the future sale of the property.

Emigration from Canada and the departure tax are discussed at ¶5375 *et seq.*

[¶17,567] Ten Reasons Why Not to Become a U.S. Green Card Holder or U.S. Citizen

The following are (tax) reasons why Canadians emigrating to the United States may find it preferable to get a work visa as opposed to a green card or U.S. citizenship.[5]

(1) *A requirement to always file a U.S. 1040 tax return regardless of where you reside and subject to some minor relief (the foreign earned income exemption of approximately $90,000) to pay U.S. tax on worldwide income computed under U.S. rules effectively resulting in U.S. taxpayers living in Canada paying tax at the higher of the two rates on all income and not being able to benefit from tax incentives in the other country.* For example, a U.S. citizen resident in Canada can't benefit on the U.S. tax return from the deduction for an RRSP contribution or the 100% deduction for Canadian exploration expenses. Although Canada has a principal residence exemption, the gain over $250,000 on a sale of a house is taxable in the United States.

(2) *U.S. gift tax which may restrict estate freezing, asset protection and gifting to spouses and children.* The traditional Canadian corporate estate freeze will attract gift tax in the United States. There is a US$13,000 permitted annual gift to each child and US$134,000 to a non-U.S. citizen spouse. It is difficult to do elementary asset protection such as having the family home in the name of the non-U.S. citizen. There is a requirement to also report gifts of US$100,000 or more received from non-residents.

(3) U.S. estate tax and gift tax of up to 35% for estates over US$5 million which may impair or preclude the transfer of wealth to the next generation.

(4) *Annual reporting requirements for settlors and beneficiaries of foreign trusts.* Penalties for not reporting may be 35% of properties transferred to a trust, 35% of distributions from a trust, and 5% a month for gifts from non-U.S. persons. Reporting is also required of foreign grantor trusts.

(5) *Controlled Foreign Corporation (CFC) rules which require paying tax on subpart F (passive) income regardless of whether distributed.* This could apply to a U.S. citizen resident in Canada who forms a Canadian holding company to own investments.

See page ii for explanation of footnotes.

[5] From Jack Bernstein, "Why Not to Become a U.S. Green Card Holder or U.S. Citizen", Tax Profile, October 2011.

(6) *Passive Foreign Investment company (PFIC) rules which require taxation of undistributed passive income and gains in foreign (non-U.S.) companies not controlled by U.S. shareholders.* A PFIC is a foreign corporation having passive income of at least 75% of its gross income and more than 50% of the assets generate passive income. Recent amendments require annual reporting of PFICs, regardless of whether distributions are made. There is a $10,000 penalty for not filing.

(7) *Foreign Bank Account Reporting (FBAR) which results in onerous penalties for non-compliance (e.g., if wilful forfeiture of 50% of the account balance computed annually and possible criminal sanctions).* The penalty for multiple years of non-reporting may exceed the cash in the account. Also, it requires annual reporting of financial interests in or signing authority over bank accounts, securities accounts, or other financial accounts in foreign countries.

(8) *Disclosure requirements for specified foreign financial assets having an aggregate value over $50,000.* It is part of the tax return. This will require reporting of depository accounts, financial accounts, stocks, and securities issued by a non-U.S. person and an interest in a foreign entity. The minimum penalty is $10,000 for not complying. This is separate from the FBAR rules. There is an additional penalty of 40% of undisclosed or undervalued foreign financial assets.

(9) *Expatriation rules (departure tax) which apply if you decide to renounce your green card or U.S. citizenship and some U.S. reporting which is required for 10 years after expatriation if assets in excess of $2 million and annual taxes exceed a threshold.* Recipients of gifts from individuals who have expatriated in the 10 years after expatriation may be subject to gift or estate tax.

(10) *Increased difficulties for a U.S. citizen in opening foreign bank accounts and investment accounts as a result of FACTA (Foreign Account Tax Compliance Rules) which come into effect in 2014.* FACTA can result in 30% withholding for payments made to a financial institution, and a foreign financial institution (FFI), which doesn't enter into a disclosure agreement with the IRS. The agreement requires that the FFI identify U.S. accounts and annually report them to the IRS. The banks will have to inquire not only about citizenship but also the place of birth of the account holder. Many foreign banks are refusing to deal with U.S. citizens.

(11) *Punitive voluntary disclosure rules, which are not permanent, with a fixed penalty as well as taxes and interest.*

[¶17,570] Before Leaving Canada

General Checklist

- Ensure date of non-residency is supported by facts.

- When earning Canadian rental income as a non-resident, make appropriate elections to reduce withholding tax.

- Consider electing no change in use for a former Canadian residence you rent while away to avoid taxation of capital gains when reinhabiting the home upon your return.

- When disposing of taxable Canadian property (land, buildings and other certain properties located in Canada), as a non-resident, obtain the necessary clearance certificates.

- Avoid selling Canadian home while resident in a foreign country to preclude foreign taxation of the capital gain (note that certain tax treaties contain provisions which may override this general rule).

- Consider deemed disposition rules and elections when ceasing residence.

- Review investment portfolio prior to leaving with a view to minimizing departure tax.

- If departure tax liability is high, consider the possibility of moving the date of termination of residence to take advantage of lower graduated rates.

- Short-term residents of Canada may be exempt from deemed disposition rules with respect to property they owned prior to attaining residence or inherited during Canadian residence.

- Maximize RRSP contributions.

- Review the methods of withdrawing funds from an RRSP as a non-resident. Lump-sum withdrawals will be subject to 25% withholding tax. An election to file a Canadian tax return is available and may result in a lower tax liability; however, the ability to reduce taxes using this election has been severely restricted.

- Review taxation of Canadian-related employment receipts as all such amounts are taxable in Canada regardless of when or where received.

- Plan to give up residence at a date which allows you to split your income between the countries to take advantage of lower marginal tax rates. Remember that personal deductions will be prorated.

- Ensure a final Canadian tax return is filed so that any Canadian taxes owing to/from the government can be settled.

- Review all health and pension plans, to determine advisability of continued participation.

- Review principles of taxation of capital property in the foreign jurisdiction. If tax is assessed on original cost, then consideration should be given to realizing accrued gains before departure.

¶17,570

- Review shareholdings of any controlled private corporations, as a private corporation which is non-resident-controlled at any time in the year will be taxed at a higher rate than one which is controlled by Canadian residents throughout the year.

- Consider impact of any relevant income tax convention.

- Canada continues to tax gains on stock options, granted while a resident of Canada, subsequent to ceasing residence.

- Consider availability of the overseas employment tax credit and foreign tax credit if Canadian residence will not cease on departure.

- Ensure form T1161 has been filed, if required, to report property owned at the date of departure.

Moving to the U.S.: Additional Checklist

- Foreign business days while a U.S. resident will generate foreign source income to improve ability to utilize foreign tax credit.

- The Canada–U.S. tax treaty provides for an exemption from U.S. tax for a Canadian resident in respect of certain employment income earned in the U.S.

- The Canada–U.S. tax treaty permits a U.S. citizen who is subject to the Canadian deemed disposition rules to elect to have such gain recognized for U.S. tax purposes. This election is advantageous in the situation where the Canadian departure taxes arising upon such a deemed disposition would not otherwise be available to reduce U.S. taxes payable on the gain when such property is eventually sold. Canada and the U.S. have agreed in principle to extend this to all individuals subject to deemed disposition.

- The *Canada–U.S. Income Tax Convention* provides for a step-up in the U.S. tax basis of a principal residence located in Canada, when a Canadian resident who is not a U.S. citizen ceases Canadian residence upon establishing U.S. residency. However, the convention does not provide relief for the U.S. tax which may be exigible on the foreign exchange gain that is realized upon retirement of a non-U.S.-denominated mortgage.

- Consider the advisability of obtaining an exemption from U.S. Social Security Tax (FICA), if covered by the *Canada–U.S. Social Security Agreement*.

- Consider deferring U.S. income tax on income earned within an RRSP.

- Consider the Canadian taxation of capital gains after ceasing residency under the *Canada–U.S. Income Tax Convention*.

- Consider planning for U.S. estate and gift taxes.

¶17,570

- Consider election to file a U.S. resident tax return when not deemed a U.S. resident in the first year in the U.S.

- Consider exercising stock options prior to establishing U.S. residency.

- Review beneficial ownership or rights in foreign trusts and foreign corporations.

[¶17,585] Before Entering Canada

Depending on the particular circumstances of the individual, the taxation system in the country the individual is leaving, and the existence of a tax treaty with Canada, a wide range of taxation matters should be considered before the individual moves to Canada.

Individuals resident in Canada are normally taxed on employment income upon receipt. As a result, income earned prior to entering Canada but received after establishing Canadian residency will generally be taxable in Canada. Depending on the taxation of such income in the foreign country of residence and the tax rates of that jurisdiction, an individual may wish to arrange to receive such income prior to entering Canada. An individual immigrating to Canada who holds stock options obtained through employment should consider exercising these options prior to becoming resident. If the options are exercised after entering Canada, the amount of the benefit derived from the option will be taxed as employment income in the year of exercise, subject to a possible 25% to 50% deduction.

Before entering Canada, the following tax planning points might be considered:

- The income from certain investments, such as interest on U.S. municipal bonds, which is tax-free in the United States, will be subject to Canadian tax. Thus, it may be desirable to sell the investment before entering Canada.

- Re-evaluate investments that may or may not provide tax shelter in the country of departure to determine how such investments will be treated for Canadian tax purposes. If such investments do not prove to be tax effective for Canadian purposes, it may be better to dispose of them before coming to Canada.

- Consideration might be given to disposing of investments that have accrued losses before Canadian residency commences, to prevent the erosion of their tax cost resulting from the application of the deemed acquisition rules.

- In certain cases, holding investments through a foreign trust established before Canadian residency begins can provide an exemption from Canadian tax on the income earned by such investments for up to five years.

- Canada does not permit spouses or common-law partners to file joint returns. Clear segregation of investment funds between spouses or common-law partners should be established to ensure no attribution of income to the spouse or common-law partner with the higher income. Certain income splitting techniques may be undertaken with one's spouse or common-law partner or children prior to Canadian residency to reduce the amount of tax payable on such income.

- Tax implications on the sale or lease of a principal residence in the country of departure must be considered from the point of view of gain deferral or exemption, reinvestment requirements and their timing, and reporting of the sale or the ongoing lease of property for Canadian and foreign tax purposes.

- Leaving investments (including interest-earning bank deposits) in the home country might provide lower effective tax costs to income earned in Canada due to relieving provisions in Canada's tax treaties (e.g., Article XXIV of the Canada–U.S. tax treaty).

It is not uncommon for employers to provide a tax reimbursement program in conjunction with an overseas assignment. This usually consists of a plan to ensure that the employee is not worse off as a result of accepting the overseas assignment. There are many variations in such plans.

On entering Canada, an individual may import personal and household effects free of duty and taxes, provided they were owned, used and possessed prior to immigrating. Personal effects may also include motor vehicles for personal use. In addition to customs requirements, other agencies may also have further import requirements. Certain items may be restricted, controlled or prohibited entry and it would be wise to verify entry requirements well in advance of arrival. However, note that if personal goods, including motor vehicles, are sold or otherwise disposed of within 12 months after importation, the goods will be subject to full duty and GST.

There are many other matters that should be attended to prior to moving to Canada, including:

- insurance coverage (health, personal, and property);

- motor vehicle license requirements, including the issuing of a Canadian license;

- notification to banking and financial institutions, and arrangement for continuation of payments;

- children's educational matters;

- care and transport of domestic pets and Canadian quarantine rules; and

- consultation with a lawyer, particularly with respect to the validity of a current will on relocation to Canada. If no will exists, consider

¶17,585

whether Canadian intestacy rules may apply should the individual die while resident in Canada.

Since the United States requires its citizens to file U.S. tax returns when residing abroad, U.S. citizens have special considerations on becoming resident in Canada. They must comply not only with Canadian tax requirements, but also with U.S. federal and possibly state taxes as well. While the two systems are not markedly different, there are many areas where they do not mesh, and situations can arise where timing differences produce unexpected results. Consequently, U.S. citizens coming to Canada should seek professional advice in most situations. The following outlines a few of the more common problems:

- **Principal Residence:** When an individual is transferred from the United States to Canada, the individual may acquire or rent a home in Canada. The individual's U.S. residence may be either rented or sold.

  If the U.S. residence is not sold, for Canadian purposes, the individual will be deemed to have reacquired the U.S. residence at its fair market value on establishing residency. Any gain from a subsequent sale during the individual's Canadian stay may be subject to Canadian tax unless the residence qualifies for exemption under the Canadian principal residence rules.

  Where the U.S. residence is rented during the stay in Canada, the income received will be taxed in Canada. Deductions for expenses may be allowed and any loss may be offset against the individual's other income. Where a home is purchased in Canada and occupied by the taxpayer throughout the period of residency as a principal residence, any gain from the subsequent disposition while resident in Canada, or in the first year after the year residency is terminated, will be exempt from Canadian tax. U.S. tax will be a consideration on such a disposition where a citizen or resident of the U.S. disposes of the Canadian home.

- **Individual Retirement Account:** The U.S. *Income Tax Act* limits the availability of Individual Retirement Accounts (IRAs) for making tax deductible contributions. For Canadian taxation purposes, an IRA will be seen as a non-resident trust. Canadian income tax acts may allow an individual to transfer amounts from an IRA to a Canadian Registered Retirement Savings Plan on a tax-free basis. Taxpayers who have IRA accounts should seek professional advice before making such a transfer. All other receipts from an IRA may be taxable in Canada during residency.

- **Canadian Pension Plans:** Canadian income tax acts allow tax deductible contributions to certain pension plans registered in Canada. In addition, a Canadian resident may make certain deductible contributions to an individual Registered Retirement Savings Plan. Withdrawals from the pension plans and Registered Retirement Savings Plans are subject to regular Canadian tax. Although such contributions are not deductible for U.S. purposes, it may be advantageous for a U.S. citizen resident in Canada to make contributions to a Registered Pension Plan or a Registered Retirement Savings Plan to save Canadian personal taxes (in some circumstances, membership in a U.S. pension plan may limit deductibility of Canadian Registered Retirement Savings Plan contributions). Provided that funds are not withdrawn from these plans prior to the individual's return to the U.S., the Canadian tax liability on withdrawal will be limited to 25% withholding tax. As the capital contributions to the plans are not deductible for U.S. purposes, such contributions would not be taxable in the U.S. on withdrawal. Accordingly, the effective rate of tax on the amount of contributions may be reduced to 25%, or perhaps even to 15% if the withdrawals qualify as periodic pension payments rather than a lump-sum withdrawal.

- **RRSPs:** In the past, an individual, after leaving Canada, had the ability to withdraw small amounts from his or her Registered Retirement Savings Plan on a tax-free basis. This is no longer possible where the individual has other sources of income. However, where the contributions have been made to a spousal plan and the spouse or common-law partner has no other income, it may still be possible to withdraw funds on a tax-free basis.

- **U.S. Taxation of RRSPs:** In general, under the Internal Revenue Code, income and gains within an RRSP would be subject to current U.S. taxation in the hands of a U.S. citizen or resident who has created the RRSP. The Canada–U.S. Tax Treaty provides an election (Article XVIII(7)), pursuant to which a citizen or resident of the United States who is a beneficiary of an RRSP may elect to defer U.S. tax on the income within the RRSP until such time as there is a distribution from the plan. Even though U.S. tax may be deferred, there may be U.S. filing requirements that must be met with regard to RRSPs (because for U.S. purposes, they are foreign trusts). Professional tax advice should be sought.

- **Stock Options:** An individual holding an employee stock option should consider exercising the option prior to moving from the United States to Canada. In certain cases, the exercise of the option will not be a taxable event for U.S. purposes; the option benefit is taxed only when the stock is sold. Furthermore, if the option is exercised before moving to Canada, the market value (rather than the exercise price) will become the cost base of the stock for Canadian purposes. If the option is not exercised until after the individual has taken up residence in Canada, the difference between the option price and the market value of the stock at the time of exercise (subject to a

¶17,585

possible 25% to 50% deduction of that difference as described in ¶2135) may be taxed in Canada as employment income in the year of exercise.

- **Alimony:** Alimony and child support payments made by a resident of Canada to a resident of the United States are not subject to Canadian withholding tax.

- **Social Security:** Social security contributions are generally due in the country where one works. However, where an employee is sent to work temporarily in the other country, the *Canada–U.S. Social Security Agreement* provides for contributions to continue in the home country only. Application should be made for a certificate of continuing coverage under the home country system, although this will not usually be granted if the assignment is expected to be for more than five years. In addition, if contributions have been made in both the U.S. and Canada, the agreement provides for contributions to both systems to be taken into account to meet eligibility requirements for social security benefits. It should be noted that the Canada–U.S. Tax Treaty recognizes U.S. social security taxes as a creditable tax for purposes of the Canadian foreign tax credit.

- **Holding Companies:** It has been a common practice for individuals resident in Canada with substantial investments to hold them through a corporation. U.S. citizens in this situation should seek professional advice.

- **Tax-Shelter Investments:** A U.S. citizen resident in Canada should exercise caution when investing in Canadian and U.S. tax-sheltered investments. A tax-sheltered investment generally provides the investor with substantial income tax write-offs or credits. While a thorough review of such investments is well beyond the scope of this checklist, it suffices to say that Canadian investments are usually ineffective in reducing U.S. income tax. However, a U.S. tax-sheltered investment may provide an effective tax shelter in Canada. Before this can be determined, an examination of the "at risk rules", the "matchable expenditure" rules, capital cost limitation rules, and foreign currency translation rules, must be undertaken in respect of each investment.

[¶17,590] U.S. Estate Tax

U.S. Estate Tax Repealed for 2010, but Restored for 2011 and 2012

Contrary to generally held expectations, Congress allowed the federal estate tax to expire on January 1, 2010 — with the result that no U.S. estate tax is payable in regard to deaths occurring in 2010 because U.S. estate tax was repealed for 2010. But, pursuant to a "sunset" provision in the *2001 Tax Act*, which gradually increased the exemption amount and decreased the top

¶17,590

estate tax rate, the repeal was only to last a year. The estate tax was then set to come back into effect on January 1, 2011 with a top rate of 55% and a maximum exemption of only $1 million. The estate tax has, in fact, come back into effect starting January 1, 2011. However, *The Tax Relief, Unemployment Insurance Reauthorization, and Job Creation Act of 2010* (the "Act"), signed into law on December 17, 2010, increases the U.S. estate tax exemption to $5 million for 2011 and 2012. It also decreases the maximum estate tax rate to 35% for 2011 and 2012. The estate of an individual who died in 2010 can choose whether to apply the 2010 or 2011 federal estate tax law. The 2010 option carries no federal estate tax; however, the ability to get a stepped-up cost basis for the estate's assets is limited.

The Act means that a married U.S. couple can now jointly protect up to $10 million of assets from the federal estate tax. The Act also makes it easier for U.S. couples to fully utilize their exemption amounts. Hitherto, if the first spouse to die had not set up a qualifying trust, he or she effectively wasted part or all of the estate tax exemption, thereby effectively raising the tax due on the later death of the second spouse. Now, the exemption is transferable between U.S. spouses; if the first spouse does not use up his or her exemption, the balance can be used by the surviving spouse on his or her later death. This new portability rule is only in effect for decedents dying after January 1, 2011 and before January 1, 2013.

The Act affects Canadians subject to U.S. estate tax on U.S. situs assets, because the U.S. estate tax exemption for a Canadian under the Canada–U.S. treaty's 1995 Protocol is based on the exemption afforded a U.S. citizen or resident. Under the Protocol, a Canadian citizen and resident is entitled to a prorated U.S. estate tax exemption calculated by multiplying the applicable U.S. citizen's estate tax credit by the proportion that the value of the decedent's U.S. situs assets is of the value of the decedent's worldwide assets.

$$\text{exemption amount} \quad \times \quad \frac{\text{value of U.S. situs assets}}{\text{value of worldwide assets}}$$

Accordingly, so long as no portion of the exemption was applied toward gift tax, no estate tax will be payable where the deceased's estate is valued at not more than $5 million.

For the purposes of the above calculation, a person's worldwide estate includes virtually everything: retirement plans, life insurance proceeds, many types of trust interests, a principal residence, and other assets that might not be subject to Canadian income tax or included in the deceased's probate estate under provincial statutes. Further, where the prorated credit is claimed, ownership of all such assets must be reported to the U.S. authorities.

The Protocol also provides a marital credit equal to the prorated credit that may also be available if a Canadian citizen dies owning U.S. situs assets and leaves them to his or her spouse in a manner that would qualify for the U.S. marital deduction from estate tax if the survivor was a U.S. citizen.

¶17,590

The changes brought by the latest statute are effective only for 2011 and 2012. Unless further legislation is enacted, the top U.S. estate tax rate will return to 55% and the exemption will fall US$1 million after December 31, 2012. The future of the U.S. estate tax is uncertain; however, it is likely to survive in some form. Accordingly, Canadians owning substantial U.S. situs assets should still plan to minimize U.S. estate tax exposure.

The following list (which is far from exhaustive) sets out some planning suggestions:

U.S. Estate Planning Checklist

- Rent, rather than buy, a U.S. vacation property and rent, rather than buy, items of personal property — such as boats, automobiles, artwork, etc., — which are to be used at a U.S. vacation property; otherwise, such assets will be U.S. situs assets.

- Purchase of real property by children. Strings can be attached through the use of a long-term lease or a trust arrangement. However, it's cheaper if the children can simply be trusted.

- Purchase by younger spouse. If it is likely that one spouse will survive the other, have that spouse purchase the vacation property or other residence. Often, after the first spouse has died, the surviving spouse will not wish to retain the property and can sell without estate taxes ever being an issue.

- Control residency (or even citizenship) pursuant to the maximum tax advantage.

- Life insurance can be used to create a body of wealth that will not be subject to estate tax and which, therefore, will be available to pay taxes that do arise on death and/or to pass on to a subsequent generation (life insurance on a non-resident alien decedent's life is excluded from his or her U.S. taxable estate, even if the life insurance policy is issued by a U.S. company).

- Sell U.S. stock portfolio and invest in other countries or invest in U.S. securities indirectly through a Canadian mutual fund.

- Sale/leaseback arrangements may serve to avoid U.S. estate tax. Under such a scheme, the Canadian owner would sell his or her U.S. real property and lease it back for a specified term with an option to renew. Tax arising on the disposition of appreciated property could be deferred by arranging to have the purchase price paid in installments.

- The U.S. gift tax does not apply to intangible property, whereas the estate tax does. Therefore, a gift of intangible property during the lifetime of a non-resident will reduce his or her gross estate for U.S. estate tax purposes.

¶17,590

- In regard to U.S. real property and tangible personal property, take full advantage of the exclusions allowed (e.g., the annual $11,000 per donee exclusion and the $100,000 annual marital exclusion). There is no limit to transfers which can be made to a U.S. citizen spouse.

- Divide non-U.S. property between family members, or establish trusts for their benefit, *before* taking up residence in the United States (this may give rise to Canadian tax liability if the assets have appreciated in value). Freezing the value of certain assets may remove future appreciation from the ambit of the U.S. estate/gift tax system — gift tax will not apply if the freeze is completed before the individual takes up U.S. residence.

- Reduce the size of one's worldwide estate. The availability of the unified credit under the Treaty depends in part on the size of the decedent's non-U.S. estate (the credit being prorated by a fraction, the numerator of which is the value of the decedent's U.S. situs assets and the denominator of which is the value of his or her worldwide estate). Rolling Canadian assets over to a spouse prior to death, for example, will increase the amount of the unified credit which will be available to cover the decedent's U.S. property.

- Hold property as tenants in common rather than jointly; however, where the surviving spouse is a U.S. citizen, joint tenancy is preferable.

- A power of appointment gives the holder of the power (usually the trustee of a trust) the right to appoint or give away property, usually the property held by the trust. The power may be limited by the trust document. A special power of appointment (one that a power holder cannot exercise in favour of himself, meaning that the power holder can't get the property out of the trust and into his or her own hands free and clear) is often teamed up with a marital deduction transfer to obtain tax savings. Within the context of cutting estate taxes, this strategy usually goes like this: A spouse is given a special power of appointment over some property placed in a trust, and the power is exercisable during her lifetime, or by will. The spouse also receives a right to use the same property for life. Even if the spouse exercises the power by will, the trust property will not be taxed in her federal gross estate because she can't appoint it to herself.

- Finance of real property acquisitions through a non-recourse mortgage.

- Trusts — Generally speaking, a trustee of a trust may be given broad powers to benefit the beneficiaries of the trust. If the trust is irrevocable, and the grantor retains no significant control over it, the trust property can be removed from the grantor's gross estate. Furthermore, the beneficiary can be given big lifetime benefits under the trust without having the trust principal included in that beneficiary's gross estate.

[¶17,593] "Snowbirds" — Deemed Residence in the U.S.

"Snowbirds" who spend a substantial amount of time in the United States on an annual basis should be careful not to inadvertently become residents of the U.S. for income tax purposes. Where this does occur, relief from double taxation is available, but it requires the filing of the appropriate forms in a timely manner with the IRS.

The Substantial Presence Test

An "alien" will be considered a U.S. resident for tax purposes if he or she meets the substantial presence test for the calendar year. To meet this test, an alien must be physically present in the United States on at least:

(1) 31 days during the current year, and

(2) 183 days during the 3-year period that includes the current year and the two years immediately before that, counting:

(a) all the days present in the United States for the current year, plus

(b) $\frac{1}{3}$ of the days present in the first year before the current year, plus

(c) $\frac{1}{6}$ of the days present in the second year before the current year.

Or, to present this in a formula:

Current year:	days present × 1 =
First preceding year:	days present × $\frac{1}{3}$ =
Second preceding year:	days present × $\frac{1}{6}$ = _____

An individual is considered "present in the United States" if he or she is physically present within the United States at any time during the day. (There are, however, certain exceptions made: e.g., for certain students or trainees.) Regardless of what part of a given day an alien actually was in the United States, for the purposes of the 183-day requirement, each day present in the United States counts as one full day (which is then multiplied by the appropriate fraction).

[¶17,595] Canada–U.S. Taxation of Social Security Benefits

Under the Canada–U.S. Tax Treaty, the country where the recipient of social security benefits is a resident has the exclusive right to tax social security benefits. For a Canadian resident receiving U.S. social security benefits, this means that the U.S. does not apply withholding tax and the U.S. social security benefits are taxable in Canada. However, Canada includes in taxable income only 85% of the benefits received during the taxation year. The remaining 15% of U.S. social security is tax exempt. For a

¶17,595

U.S. resident receiving Canadian social security benefits, this means that Canada does not withhold tax and the Canadian social security benefits will be taxable in the U.S., as they would have been taxed under the U.S. *Social Security Act.*

[¶17,600] Other Planning Considerations

[¶17,605] Alternative Minimum Tax

The Alternative Minimum Tax (AMT) is a minimum tax that is aimed at investors whose income is sheltered by "tax preferences" given to certain types of investments. The tax preferences are listed in the commentary below, and as can be seen, include such items as losses from tax shelters and limited partnerships, and the untaxed portion of capital gains. The AMT is an alternative tax to an individual's regular income tax. The individual must pay the higher of the two, but not both. The AMT is obviously a concern where you have significant income that is sheltered by the tax preferences. For example, if the majority of your regular income for the year is sheltered by losses incurred in a limited partnership investment or tax shelter investment, you may be subject to AMT even if your regular tax liability is otherwise nil.

Individuals with significant amounts of "preference" deductions and credits should attempt to compute the AMT before making tax shelter investments or triggering capital gains. The "preference" deductions and credits for AMT purposes are:

- Capital gains: 80% of realized capital gains and gains allocated from a trust.
- Tax shelter deductions: to the extent that losses are created by deductions for Canadian Exploration Expenses, Canadian Development Expenses, Canadian Oil and Gas Property Expenses, or capital cost allowances on film properties.
- 40% of the employee stock option deduction (resulting in a net inclusion rate of 80% of the stock option benefit).
- Prospectors' and grubstakers' deduction.
- Employee relocation housing loan deduction.
- Pension income tax credit.
- Credits transferred from spouse or other dependants.
- Non-capital losses — the portion of prior years' non-capital losses attributable to preference deductions.

It is also important to note that "preference" tax shelter deductions include all partnership losses incurred by limited or passive partners, all losses deducted in respect of investments identified or required to be identified under the tax shelter identification rules, and all carrying charges relating to the acquisition of partnership interests (other than where the individual is actively engaged in the partnership business, which does not own film or rental/leasing property) and deductible amounts in respect of rental/leasing property, film property, and resource investments. Furthermore, where an individual has an interest in a partnership, the individual is deemed to have claimed a *pro rata* portion of the partnership's deductible amounts.

The AMT is discussed at greater length at ¶8065 *et seq.*

[¶17,620] Professional Corporations

Changes to provincial legislation pertaining to professionals now allows most Canadian professionals the tax benefits of incorporation. However, because of shareholder requirements and other restrictions, the full range of tax benefits normally available on incorporation may not be available. By way of example, the following commentary focuses on the recent changes in Ontario.

Fairly recently, the *Ontario Business Corporations Act* (OBCA) was amended to permit most professionals to incorporate, subject to amendments to be implemented to specific regulations and by-laws for affected professions. This recent development has led to discussion by professionals of the benefits of incorporating, and, specifically, which professionals. From a non-tax perspective, incorporation does not shield an individual from professional malpractice liability; but other business dealings can be protected from personal liability, e.g., trade payables, liability on a lease, and non-guaranteed bank loans. Because applicable Ontario legislation/regulations usually require the professional to be the sole shareholder of a professional corporation, personal liability in respect of malpractice should be considered carefully: the main benefits of incorporation stem from the retention of assets at the corporate level, thus leaving them open to exposure in this respect. On the other hand, practically speaking, an unincorporated professional may be able to take steps to sequester assets in other family members.

From a tax perspective, there are two major tax advantages traditionally associated with incorporation: the ability to obtain low corporate tax rates, and the preservation of these tax benefits by being able to distribute the earnings in the form of dividends to low-bracket family members. However, due to the fact that the new rules as set out in the OBCA require the professional to be the shareholder, "income splitting" benefits are generally not available.

Yet, taking into account federal and provincial small business tax incentives, a qualifying Ontario company will be eligible for a tax rate of less than 16% on the first $500,000 (effective January 1, 2009) of active business income, the rates will drop further towards the end of the decade. However, to the extent that it is necessary to distribute earnings to defray personal and living expenses, the tax benefits will be largely unwound. To the extent that the earnings are reinvested, however, the benefits of the low tax rate can continue to apply.

For sole practitioners, these tax considerations should be straight forward. But for members of larger practices, planning becomes more complicated due to two other roadblocks to incorporation:

- "Personal Services Business" Rules: these rules generally provide that if, disregarding the corporation, an individual is "legally" an employee of the firm, the small business deduction (and similar provincial tax breaks) will not be available, thus losing most of the tax benefits. In addition, there are severe restrictions on deductions, designed to put the company in a similar position to that of an unincorporated employee. Under the technical proposals released by the Department of Finance on October 31, 2011, for corporations with taxation years commencing after this date, personal services business income will no longer qualify for the general business rate reduction under section 123.4 of the Act (13% when fully phased in). This will reduce the degree of tax deferral when income is earned in a corporation; there will also be a significant degree of underintegration (that is, a tax cost when income is earned by a corporation and distributed as dividends to the individual, as compared with the individual earning the income directly).

- Corporate Partnerships: a second set of rules forces corporate partnerships to share the small business deduction (in addition, a professional corporation which is a partner must have a calendar year end). Although it is possible for a number of corporations to purport to form a "joint venture" to carry on a professional practice rather than a partnership, this could be risky: the CRA may well be successful in reclassifying the joint venture as a partnership — which could also result in potential double tax liability to the extent that earnings were left in the corporation in anticipation of the small business deduction.

However, new structures have emerged to give potential partners in larger firms tax benefits of incorporation.

Specifically, it may be possible to incorporate the firm itself, and then allow professionals to form their own corporations, which would bill the practice for services rendered. A series of CRA income tax rulings have given some comfort on this type of structure, ruling that the personal services business and corporate partnership rules (as well as the General Anti-Avoidance Rule) will not apply in such situations (however, one issue that should be reviewed in respect of such structures is whether the reorganization in question could result in loss of limited liability partnership status).

More recent rulings appear to support professional incorporation where the partnership itself is not incorporated, and a partner forms a corporation to receive some or all of his or her would-be partnership

¶17,620

income (applicable professional regulations should also be reviewed).[6] There have been a large number of tax rulings in this area.

[¶17,630] Technical Interpretation on Professional Corporations

The CRA issued a Technical Interpretation on both of the foregoing structures (Document No. 2009-0315011E5, May 27, 2009). With respect to its acceptance of the structures, the CRA stated:

> In some cases, professionals that carry on business as partnerships may provide their professional services to the partnership as employees of their PC, which in turn are independent contractors to the partnership. The professionals, in the capacity as partners, would continue to provide nonprofessional services (i.e., promotional, administrative and other services) to the partnership. Under an alternative reorganization structure, the assets of the partnership may be acquired by a newly formed central corporation ("Newco"). Similarly, the professionals may provide their professional services as employees of the PC, which in turn are independent contractors to Newco.

> The CRA accepts that professionals can provide services through a PC and may access the small business deduction ("SBD"). We would not challenge the transactions simply because that result is obtained, however, it is important that the parties genuinely create and maintain the structure that meets the requirements of the *Income Tax Act*.

In respect of the last paragraph, the CRA cited the personal services business, corporate partnership rules (discussed above) and further indicated that the association rules might also be an issue. In particular, it cited subsection 256(2.1), whereby two or more corporations may be deemed to be associated where it may reasonably be considered that one of the main reasons for the separate existence of those corporations in a taxation year is to reduce the amount of taxes that would otherwise be payable. (However, based on reported cases, it does not appear that this provision has been used frequently by the CRA in recent years.)

The CRA indicated that it would look to whether the arrangement is conducted on an arm's length basis in which the fees and services would be of a kind and amount that would be agreed to between a partnership or Newco and a professional who is not a partner or an employee. In other words, consideration is given to whether the professional corporations and the professionals are providing services as independent contractors and the

---

See page ii for explanation of footnotes.

[6] Clause 3.2(2)5 limits the business of a professional corporation to the practice of the profession. Formerly, it provided that the restriction shall not be construed to prevent the corporation from carrying on activities related or ancillary to the practice of the profession, including the temporary investments of surplus funds earned by the corporation. It was pointed out that if a professional corporation accumulated enough earnings that investment activities were to constitute a separate "business", this could nonetheless be problematic (although it would be fairly easy to avoid such difficulties, for example, by forming a second non-professional corporation and advancing excess funds to it, as a loan or share capital). In any event, the provision was recently changed to delete the word "temporary", thus obviating the issue.

reasons that may exist for providing the services through the professional corporations.

The CRA listed the following as examples of some factors and conditions it would expect before providing an advance income tax ruling:

- There are no restrictions (oral or otherwise) on the professional corporation's or the professional's right to compete with the partnership, Newco or other professional corporations.

- Fees are based on the value of professional services rendered. For example, there would be no inclusion of fringe benefits, vacation, sabbatical or large fixed fees (i.e., guaranteed amounts).

- Fees earned and paid to the particular professional corporation are not based on the success of collecting the revenue billed to the clients of the partnership or Newco in respect of the professional services provided by the professional corporation.

- The professional is responsible for his or her own administrative services, library, and supplies. In this respect, the CRA indicated "if the partnership or Newco were to provide such items to the professional, it would expect to be recompensed".

The first requirement is somewhat curious. In the legal profession at least, if a professional partnership were to retain a "senior lateral", it would be unusual to allow the individual to compete with the firm. As to the responsibility for administrative expenses, the CRA's view — that if the partnership or Newco were to provide such items to the professional, it would expect to be recompensed — appears to differ from the practice of many firms (larger-sized, at least). The following is an excerpt from a recent ruling:[7]

> The Contracting Company shall be responsible for all expenses required to maintain the professional standards required by the Partnership and all fees and expenses necessary to perform the Professional Services, including, without limitation, professional membership fees, professional malpractice and other insurance, continuing education and training, transportation, communication, business entertainment connected to the business of the Contracting Company, travel expenses including automobile, accommodations and meals. The Contracting Company agrees that, to the extent that such expenses are paid by the Partnership, it shall reimburse the Partnership.

More generally, disregarding the consequences of the restriction on shareholders, an Ontario professional corporation will be taxed as any other corporation. The following are some other tax considerations.

See page ii for explanation of footnotes.
[7] 2009-0343391R3 , paragraph 26.

¶17,630

Disadvantages

- The income limits on which the low tax rates apply must be shared with "associated corporations." In general, this will be problematic if a professional who wholly owns his or her corporation also holds more than 25% of the shares of a corporation controlled by one or more related persons (ignoring certain deeming rules).

- The key issue in respect of a professional corporation may be the ability to retain income at the corporate level — i.e., that is not necessary to defray personal living expenses. To the extent that other individuals are not allowed to be shareholders, the distribution of earnings either as salary or dividends will unwind the main advantages of incorporation. Further, where it is advisable to distribute funds as a salary, rather than dividends, payroll taxes should be considered. In Ontario, for example, EHT potentially applies. However, there is a $400,000 exemption in respect of EHT; which may cover salary distributions to the professional. Where others are allowed as shareholders, the distribution of corporate earnings as dividends to low-bracket shareholders may reduce tax rates, through income splitting advantages. However, this may prove to be illusory: in the case of a spouse as a shareholder, he or she may already be on salary to the corporation, so that the availability of low tax brackets will be restricted. For minor children, the "kiddie tax" may apply. Accordingly, it may be the case that income splitting advantages are primarily available to children in university and perhaps low-income parents. In the former case, at least, these benefits may be transitory, thus necessitating the use of family trusts or similar structures, if allowed.

- As discussed above, the personal services business rules generally apply if, disregarding the corporation, an individual is legally an employee of the firm. If the application of these rules is a risk with a professional corporation, new rules will significantly increase adverse tax results if the rules do apply: under the technical proposals released by the Department of Finance on October 31, 2011, for corporations with taxation years commencing after this date, personal services business income will no longer qualify for the general business rate reduction under section 123.4 of the Act (13% when fully phased in). This will reduce the degree of tax deferral when income is earned in a corporation; there will also be a significant degree of underintegration (that is, there will be a tax cost when income is earned by a corporation and distributed as dividends to the individual, as compared with the individual earning the income directly).

Advantages

- A non-calendar year end may be chosen. In addition, there will be no tax instalments in the first year of incorporation.

¶17,630

- An element of deferral may be gained if a bonus is accrued.

- The sale of shares of a professional corporation may potentially qualify for the ($750,000) lifetime capital gains exemption; however, the usual tests must be met, including status as a "small business corporation" which generally requires that all or substantially all of the fair market value of the corporation's assets be used principally in an active business carried on primarily in Canada. Assets such as shareholder advances, excess cash or other non-temporary investments may be problematic.

- Like any business, an Ontario professional corporation is entitled to deduct the usual business-related expenses, such as attendance at two conventions per year, and so on. However, these types of deductions are generally available whether or not the professional self-incorporates. One notable exception (in theory, anyway) is that the office- in-the-home restrictions in subsection 18(12) apply only to individuals.

As discussed above, some firms have set up management structures — i.e., separate corporations and/or partnerships to provide management services to the firm. Generally, the idea is that these would be owned by low-bracket family members of the partners (or trusts for them), so that the income from these management activities can be distributed on a tax-efficient basis. Of course, the so-called "kiddie tax" has greatly restricted these tax breaks; however, many structures have been reorganized in an attempt to cope with these rules. Generally, the new professional corporations can be integrated with these structures, so that they can continue.

[¶17,642] Year-End and New Year Tax Planning Strategies

[¶17,643] Year-End Tax Strategies for Everyone

Year-end tax planning usually involves the deferral of tax by either accelerating tax deductions or deferring income until after the end of the taxation year. However, it may also involve taking steps to arrange one's financial affairs so as to alleviate onerous compliance requirements or timely payments to fall within various favourable tax provisions or escape those which are unfavourable (e.g., the attribution rules).

[¶17,644] Pay These before the New Year

Here is a list of expenses that one should consider paying by December 31:

- Safekeeping fees for investments and investment counsel fees.

- Union dues and professional fees.

¶17,642

- Child care and support payments.

- Charitable donations.

- Moving expenses.

- Fees and expenses incurred in objecting to or appealing an assessment of taxes, penalties or interest under the *Income Tax Act* or any provincial income tax act, a decision of the Canada Employment and Immigration Commission, Canada Employment and Insurance Commission, a board of referees or an umpire under the *Unemployment Insurance Act, 1971* or the *Employment Insurance Act* and an assessment or a decision under the *Canada Pension Plan* or a provincial plan.

- Expenditures which qualify as medical expenses for the purposes of the medical expense tax credit.

- Repayment of a policy loan where that policy loan has been included in income as the proceeds of disposition of a life insurance policy. The deduction in respect of a repayment is limited to the amount by which the total income inclusion exceeds amounts deductible in previous years in respect of repayments;

- Legal expenses incurred by an employee in collecting salary or wages from an employer or former employer.

- Tuition fees paid in respect of the taxation year.

- Interest charges.

[¶17,644a] The CRA's Prescribed Rate

Consider the timing of interest-subsidized housing loans from an employer or income-splitting loans to family members in low tax brackets. The tax benefits for both of these are based on how low the CRA sets its "prescribed interest rates" which are adjusted quarterly, based on previous-quarter Treasury Bill rates. Accordingly, if interest rates for the previous quarter have dropped, it may make sense to hold off on these loans and *vice versa*, if interest rates have increased.

[¶17,644b] Family Trusts

If an individual has a family trust and would like to ensure that the beneficiaries are taxed on the income, in most cases it is now necessary that the income be either *paid* or *payable* by the end of the calendar year. If actual payments are not made, then promissory notes or other evidence that there is a legal obligation to pay should be in place. The "preferred-beneficiary election" method is no longer available, unless a beneficiary is mentally or physically handicapped.

[¶17,645] Gifts-in-Kind

Charitable donations qualify for a credit if made by year end. One overlooked opportunity is to donate smaller items that are no longer needed, i.e., so-called gifts-in-kind. These are eligible for a donation receipt based on their value to the charity. Many charities will give favourable values to encourage donations, especially where the items can be used in classrooms or administration (e.g., faxes, computer equipment), fund-raising auctions (e.g., wine, artwork), etc.

[¶17,645a] Mutual Fund Year Ends

A little-publicized change to tax rules allow mutual funds legally structured as trusts to move their year end forward to as early as December 15. While the main reason for this change relates to internal bookkeeping matters, this shift can affect year-end tax planning strategies.

Mutual funds "distribute" underlying capital gains and other income just prior to year end so that unit holders (other than RRSPs or other exempt holders) pay tax on the distributions. But "buying in" just before the distribution date usually carries a hidden tax penalty. Basically, tax will be paid on someone else's gain (the gains prior to the year-end distribution date are already factored into the cost of the fund, so part of one's purchase price effectively becomes taxable).

If the fund moves its year end forward to December 18, for example, an individual will escape this tax trap if he or she buys after this date — even if one has bought in the current calendar year.

Another advantage that has been cited is that, if the mutual fund makes capital gains distributions, the accelerated year end will give an individual time to trigger tax losses by the end of the year. Strategies involve selling losing stocks, or switching a losing fund to another fund, e.g., within the same mutual fund "family". A better strategy may involve transferring ownership to children. This allows a taxpayer to effectively keep the investment in the family and avoids brokerage fees. However, this does not work with a spouse/common-law partner (since the "superficial loss rules" would, in that case, deny the loss where the same or similar property is reacquired within 30 days).

Although these strategies are indeed possible, it is helpful to find out exactly how much the capital gains distribution will be. If one intends to sell off low-value stock (or other investments with accrued losses), one must bear in mind that most stock market sales must take place more than three business days before the end of the year. It is not clear whether mutual funds that have opted for the accelerated year ends have any plans to bring this data directly to investors' attention. Although a heads-up broker might phone an individual with the information, a more prudent course of action is to contact one's broker or the mutual fund office.

Not all mutual funds intend to take advantage of the accelerated year end. The exact date may vary from fund to fund.

[¶17,645b] Escape Foreign Reporting

If an individual has foreign property, the total cost of which is more than $100,000 the foreign reporting requirements apply if the cost of the holdings exceed $100,000 at any time in the tax year. It may be possible to be under the limit by transferring property to family members. A family of four could hold up to $400,000 of foreign property without having to file a report with the CRA.

If a transfer is made to someone other than a spouse/common-law partner, the general rule is that there is a deemed sale based on market values at the time of the transfer. Accordingly, there could be capital gains tax if the transferred property has appreciated in value (There could also be recaptured depreciation if rental or other depreciable property is transferred, but the flip side is that a tax loss may be available if the property has declined in value.) There may be other things to consider as well, such as potential marital or creditor claims.

Remember that personal-use foreign assets are exempt from the foreign reporting requirements, as are assets used in an active business personally carried on by an individual.

[¶17,645c] Lower Tax Instalments

If an individual is an instalment basis taxpayer whose income has gone down in the last couple of years, the possibility of reducing instalments should be considered.

The CRA's instalment calculations are based partly on an individual's income tax position two years ago and partly on last year's position. Instead of using the CRA's method, an individual is entitled to base his or her instalments on last year's tax position. An individual can even base his or her instalments on the current year's estimated tax position, if lower; but should be careful, as penalties may apply if one underestimates his or her taxes and the instalments turn out to be lower than the other two options required.

[¶17,646] Increase Business Expenses

Deductions for most normal business expenses are based on whether the expense has been incurred by year end, rather than whether the item has actually been paid for (e.g., office supplies, auto and other repairs, etc.,). Exceptions include compound interest charges — regular ("simple") business interest can be expensed when *payable* (by normal method), site investigation and utility service connection charges, and disability-related equipment and building modifications.

Consider accelerating purchases of equipment and other *capital* expenditures before year end. Examples include auto and equipment purchases (half of the normal depreciation can be claimed in the current year and the full depreciation rate in the next year) and so on. Although most businesses claim ongoing expenses as they "accrue" rather than when they are actually paid, a number of deductions can't be claimed unless they are actually paid, including disability-related equipment and modifications to buildings, site investigation and utility service connection charges, and compound interest charges.

[¶17,647] Watch Deadlines

A number of tax deadlines apply to businesses. In some cases, severe penalties may apply if these are missed. One hidden trap is that if a company has amalgamated with another, there is a deemed year end (normally the day before the amalgamation).

Here are a few deadlines to watch out for:

- **Bonuses.** To be deductible in the current year, bonuses must be paid within 179 days after the company's year end.

- **R&D claims.** These must be made within a year of the tax-return due date. There is no specific rule which allows late filing.

- **Shareholder loans.** If a shareholder loan was made in the company's previous taxation year, ensure that it is repaid before the end of the company's current taxation year to avoid income inclusion for the full amount of the loan. If the loan cannot be repaid in cash, consider transferring other assets to the company in repayment of the loan, i.e., with a value equivalent to the amount of the loan that is being reduced. The best way to do this is to transfer business assets, e.g., office equipment, computers, and so on. One should bear in mind that capital gains or other tax exposure on these transfers are possibilities.

[¶17,647a] Off-Calendar Years

Professionals are allowed to retain an off-calendar year for their firms under the so-called "alternative method" of tax accounting per subsection 249.1(4). This election is made on a business-by-business basis, so that an individual can choose to use the alternative method for one business, but not for another business (the other business would then be subject to the calendar year-end rules). The basic concept behind the alternative method is that one *estimates* the firm's income that would occur if it were on a calendar year basis by basing it on the previous year's income.

Where the alternative method applies, the individual includes income from the business in the calendar year in which the fiscal period of the business ends, as was the case under the regular rules. Additionally, the individual must also include "additional business income" in the calendar year under section 34.1, which is an estimate of the "stub period" income for the remainder of the calendar year (i.e., from the start of the fiscal period which begins in the calendar year to December 31 of the year). The additional business income included in one year is in turn deducted from income in the next calendar year (in which a further additional business income amount is included) and the pattern continues in each subsequent calendar year. This mechanism was introduced to allow individuals to maintain their off-calendar year fiscal periods while effectively reporting business income on a calendar year basis.

[¶17,648] Defer Tax on Interest

The *Income Tax Act* allows a deferral of tax on an interest-bearing investment for one year after its purchase, unless the interest is paid or credited to a taxpayer's account in the meantime. Accordingly, for investments on which interest payments are deferred (e.g., payments that occur once or twice a year), it may make sense to make the purchase early in the new year, rather than late in the current year, since this means that at least a portion of the interest payments will be "kicked over" to the next year.

[¶17,648a] RESP Contributions

Making an RESP contribution before year end makes sense, even though the annual contribution limit was eliminated by the 2007 federal Budget, for the annual contribution continues to determine the amount of the annual CESG grant, normally based on 20% of calendar-year contributions, to a maximum of $500 per beneficiary, to a lifetime limit of $7,200.

[¶17,648b] Source Deductions

An unlikely source of cash could be the source deductions withheld on salary income. Many people regularly get tax refunds because of deductions such as support payments, carrying charges on investments, and so on. Such an individual should apply for a reduction of source deductions A taxpayer is entitled to apply for a reduction of source deductions if he or she has legitimate deductions or tax credits that are not considered when his or her employer calculates the source deductions. The reduction in source deductions is granted when regular withholding would cause "undue hardship", although this requirement is not difficult to meet as the CRA has relaxed their procedures. The CRA has indicated that all deductions in calculating taxable income as well as non-refundable tax credits will be considered favourably when it comes to granting a reduction in source deductions.

[¶17,648c] Pay Interest on Employee Loans

If an employee receives a low-interest or interest-free loan from his or her employer (or past or future employer), the employee is considered to have received a benefit from employment. The benefit is set at the CRA's current prescribed rate of interest minus any interest actually paid during the year or within 30 days of the year's end. If such a loan is outstanding, and if the loan proceeds were not used for an income-producing purpose such as making investments, one should bear in mind that interest should be paid on the loan for the current year by January 30th of the next year to reduce or eliminate any taxable benefit.

[¶17,649] Employee Auto Benefits

If an employer provides an employee with an automobile and also reimburses any operating costs during the year, an operating cost benefit of 26¢ per kilometre (in 2012) of personal use will be included in the employee's taxable income. If the employment-related use is more than 50%, one may be able to use an alternative method of calculating operating cost benefit as one-half of the "standby charge" the taxable benefit of which is, essentially, either 2% of the car's original cost for each month it was available to the employee (i.e., 24% per year) or two-thirds of the lease costs. The alternative benefit calculation will generally be advantageous if the car's original cost is relatively low and the personal kilometres are relatively high (even though they must still be less than 50% of the total use). To use this alternative calculation, the employer must be notified in writing by December 31 that the employee intends to do so.

[¶17,650] Real Estate Tax Losses

If one owns a real estate investment that has declined in value, one should consider taking action by year end. More often than not, it should be possible for most individuals to convert bad real estate investments into a tax loss.

[¶17,651] Bad Take-Back Mortgages

Where an individual has sold real estate investment at the peak and took back a large mortgage on the sale, it is likely that capital gains status will have been claimed, along with a large tax deferral, which is available whenever a take-back is involved. However, a problem arises when the mortgagor is about to default or has already done so. The capital gain must be recognized at a minimum of 20% per year, even if the mortgagor has defaulted. Therefore, an individual may be paying tax on money that will never be received.

In these circumstances, it may be possible to claim an offsetting tax loss based on the take-back mortgage qualifying as a "bad debt." But the CRA takes the position that claiming a bad debt write-off on a bad take-back mortgage is an all or nothing proposition: the whole amount of the remaining debt must be uncollectible. Worse still, the CRA's policy is that a person must have exhausted all legal means of collecting the debt, or the debtor has become insolvent and has no means of paying the debt.

¶17,649

For some unlucky investors, the mortgage may indeed be completely bad so the tax loss will be fine. However, if there is still some equity left in the property, it will be necessary to consider other strategies. One possibility is to reacquire the property before year end. Technically, this will stop the clock on any current year capital gains tax that must be paid as a result of the take-back.

Another solution could be to trigger a sale of a take-back mortgage at a loss, e.g., by selling the mortgage at fair market value or giving it to a family member (other than a spouse/common-law partner) as the superficial loss rules will operate to deny a loss. One problem with this is that one will lose one's remaining tax reserves on the original sale. If the loss is big enough, one may still come out ahead.

There are a number of other possibilities as well. However, one should bear in mind that if a person is claiming a tax reserve on the take-back mortgage, he or she should seek professional advice prior to the end of the year. As some of the tax strategies available may take a fair amount of time (including possible negotiations with the purchaser of the property), one should not hesitate to seek professional advice sooner rather than later.

[¶17,651a] Income Splitting

The following are some income splitting strategies which may be relevant at year end:

- If an individual owns a business, the spouse/common-law partner or other family members may be paid reasonable salaries for legitimate services. This salary will provide a base for the employee to make RRSP and CPP contributions.

- The higher wage-earning spouse/common-law partner should pay all household expenses, permitting the lower wage earner to invest his or her income. The income earned on the investments will be taxed on the lower earner's tax return at a lower tax rate.

- Retired couples can split CPP benefits upon reaching age 60. Consider splitting CPP if one spouse/common-law partner has a significantly lower income to produce tax savings.

- If there is a family trust and one wants to ensure that the beneficiaries are taxed on the income, in most cases it is generally necessary that the income be either paid or payable by the end of the calendar year. The "preferred beneficiary election" method (which allows income to be taxed in the hands of beneficiaries without making it "paid or payable") remains available only if the beneficiary is mentally or physically handicapped.

- One can split income with low-bracket family members by making a loan to them (e.g., a spouse/common-law partner or a child under the age of 18), provided that the CRA's "prescribed rate" is charged on the loan (the rate is adjusted quarterly). Interest must be paid within 30 days after the end of each year, otherwise, the "attribution rules" may apply with the result that the income is taxed in the taxpayer's hands. It will be necessary that this is documented, e.g., by a cheque and deposit.

Occasionally one might want to purposely trigger the attribution rules. For example, if the investment is generating losses, the attribution rules may allow a person to claim them on their return. In this case, a strategy may be to *purposely* miss the interest-payment deadline. However, if this is done even once, the "prescribed rate loan" exemption will no longer apply to investments made from the loan.

[¶17,652] Tax Loss Selling

"Tax loss selling" means the sale of investments which are in loss positions prior to year end to obtain a capital loss. In many cases, these losses could result in a valuable tax break.

How It Works

If there are capital gains in the last three years which were not fully sheltered by the capital gains exemption, it probably makes sense to sell off losing investments before year end. This is because capital losses can be claimed against capital gains as far back as three years, or for the current or a future year.

On the other hand, if an individual did *not* have to pay tax on capital gains (e.g., the capital gains were fully covered by the capital gains exemption, or there were no gains to begin with), there is likely no reason to take a tax loss before year end. This is because capital losses can only be deducted against capital gains.

Besides selling on the market, another way to "trigger" a capital loss is by giving or selling the investment at current market value to children or parents (unfortunately this cannot be done with a spouse/common-law partner). It is recommended that the transfer agent should be notified of the change. One should also have a written agreement to document the transfer.

The following are three simple guidelines relating to tax loss selling:

Rule #1: When not to take a tax loss

If there are no taxable capital gains in the last three years, there is no reason to resort to tax-loss selling since capital losses can only be claimed against capital gains. Accordingly, if there are no gains to begin with, there is most likely no reason to take action.

¶17,652

One should also consider the following:

- Consideration might be given to realigning one's investment portfolio by "taking profits". If paying capital gains tax on those profits is a deterrent, sheltering them by tax loss selling may be a prudent strategy.

- One should ensure that there are no "surprise gains" in the year, for example, if a mutual fund (held outside of an RRSP) were to sell some of its portfolio with a capital gain. If an individual has potential tax losses, he or she might want to contact a mutual funds manager to see if there will be some capital gain.

- Losses from investments in "private" corporations devoted to Canadian business *may* qualify as "allowable business losses," so that tax losses can be deducted against all sources of income, not just capital gains. While capital losses can only be used to reduce capital gains, 66²/₃% of an ABIL can be used to reduce any source of income. Therefore, if an individual is a shareholder or creditor of a financially unstable private corporation, he or she should consider selling the shares or debt to an unrelated person to realize an ABIL. In many cases, Canadian "over-the-counter-traded" shares may qualify. Furthermore, to create an ABIL in the current year, an actual transfer of property to a third party must occur before December 31 of the current year.

Rule #2: When to take a tax gain

If one intends to sell off an investment for a capital gain around year end, one may want to defer the gain to the next year, because capital gains tax may be postponed for a year.

Note: One does not have to actually wait until the new year to do this, as long as one sells after the year end *settlement deadline* (this is normally three days after the trade date in Canadian markets). One exception to this strategy is if an individual expects to move into a higher tax bracket in the new year.

Rule #3: When to take a tax loss

If an individual takes a tax loss before year end, it can be "carried back" to cover off capital gains on which he or she has had to pay tax: current-year losses offset current gains, if any. If there is an excess loss and there was a capital gain in an earlier year that can go back as far as three years, one can file a carryback and apply for a tax refund (under Form T1A). Although taking current losses against current gains is mandatory, the carryback is not. Although one would normally want to apply for it, this is not always the case. One example is if an individual was in a lower tax bracket than expected in 2009, and he or she expects to have capital gains sometime after 2014. Although, capital losses can be carried forward indefinitely, i.e., to be applied against future capital gains, the further in to the future the capital gain is, the lower the "present value" of the capital loss carryforward. Therefore, if capital gains are a long way off, it might be better to apply for a carryback and get the benefit of a current tax refund even if one was in a relatively low tax bracket during the carryback period.

Also, if the validity of the current capital loss claim is unsure, applying for the carryback may subject it to more scrutiny than if it were simply left on the return to be carried forward.

Notes:

Before one goes to the trouble of taking a capital loss, consideration should be given to requesting a printout of the "tax carryforward balances" from the CRA. This may show an old capital loss balance from an earlier year which was forgotten about and could be available to shelter the capital gains.

If one is selling on the market to take a loss, and one buys back an identical investment within 30 days before or after the sale, the capital loss will be denied under the "superficial loss" rules. One should either wait until after the 30-day period or have another family member (other than a spouse/common-law partner) buy back the investment.

[¶17,652a] Transfers to Children

One way to trigger a tax loss is to transfer ownership of loss investments to a child (by a gift or sale at market value). This can be done without brokerage fees. Better still, if the investment stays in the family and it goes back up in value, the capital gain will probably be taxable to the child because the attribution rules in respect of capital gains only applies to a spouse/common-law partner. With the basic personal credits available to each taxpayer, a child, or grandchild with no other income can make some $20,764 a year in capital gains, tax-free. Even if a child runs out of a tax shelter, his or her tax rate on capital gains may only be about half of the top-bracket rate (however, a parent's loss cannot be used to shelter the *child's* gain). In the case of minors, one should bear in mind that the strategy applies *only* to capital gains. If dividends or interest are paid after the flip, the general rule is that the parent must pay tax on this income until the year in which the child turns 18. It is recommended that the investment be transferred to a separate account for the child and that one should have documentation to evidence the transfer — especially if the broker insists that the transfer be made to a so-called "in-trust account", which is required to be registered in the name of an adult rather than the transferee-child. The "paper" should document that there has been a transfer of ownership either by way of gift or sale.

¶17,652a

[¶17,653] Mutual Fund Losses

If a mutual fund has declined in value, one way to trigger a tax loss is to convert to another fund within the family, e.g., from a Canadian equity to a U.S. equity or money market fund (as always, tax losses cannot be claimed if the investment is in an RRSP). However, some funds, such as the C.I. Sector Funds, the AIM Canada Fund, and the Synergy Canadian Fund have been structured so that when this conversion takes place, there is no gain or loss recognized for tax purposes (of course, the idea behind this type of structure is to defer capital gains). One should bear this in mind before making the conversion.

[¶17,654] Settlement Date

For open-market trades, the date of the tax loss is the settlement date, not when an individual instructs the broker to sell. On Canadian stock exchanges, this is three business days after the trade date.

[¶17,655] Currency Fluctuations

Needless to say, some of the most likely candidates for loss selling include foreign investments. When assessing whether a person is in a loss position, one should bear in mind that capital gains are calculated in Canadian dollars. Accordingly, currency fluctuations can be a key consideration. If the Canadian dollar has appreciated against the currency there will tend to be losses.

Subsection 39(2) provides that foreign exchange gains and losses on capital account shall be netted in computing overall capital gain or loss, and that individuals can ignore the first $200 of the resulting net gain or loss on capital account. The purpose of the $200 exclusion is presumably to eliminate the technical requirement to account for nuisance amounts, such as the exchange vacationers might incur on redeeming unused foreign denominated travellers' cheques.

[¶17,656] Labour-Sponsored Venture Capital Corporations

LSVCCs are discussed at ¶13,480. Here, it may be noted that investments made in the first sixty days of a year are eligible for credit in either the preceding year or the current year. That is, credit on investments made in the first 60 days of 2012 may be claimed on either 2011 or 2012 returns. For the federal government and most provinces, the credits in excess of tax for the year do not carry over, so there is some advantage to investing in the first sixty days of the year to have the flexibility to apply the credit in either of two years.

[¶17,660] Business Income

[¶17,662] Advantages of Incorporation

There are, of course, a large number of advantages to the small business person in carrying on business through a corporate vehicle. Most of these can be divided into the following categories:

- Tax deferral when business profits are retained within the corporation.

- Tax savings, even after funds are distributed from the corporation to the individual.

- Advantages gained by having the business in a separate entity from that of the taxpayer.

- The ability to gain special tax incentives available only to corporations.

[¶17,664] Tax Deferral

Generally, corporate tax rates applying to business earnings are lower — often dramatically lower — than rates applying to top-bracket individuals. Thus, to the extent of this differential, tax on business earnings may be deferred, at least until distributed to individual shareholders — when such distributions are normally subject to additional tax as dividends.

There are two major factors that result in tax deferral:

(1) A federal small business deduction is available in respect of qualifying active business activities. This is a 7% reduction of corporate tax rates applicable to business income (in 2010, the reduction will decrease until 2012 — see chart below). There is an annual small business limit to which the small business limit applies equal to $500,000 per corporation or associated group of corporations (commencing in 2009). Additional provincial tax incentives (which vary from province to province) may also be available. In most provinces, these incentives reduce corporate tax rates on qualifying income well below 20%.

(2) Currently, with the exception of investment-type income earned by Canadian-controlled private corporations, corporate tax rates applicable to business income are typically lower than top marginal rates applicable to individuals (the differential varies from province to province). [To the extent that the income does not qualify for the small business deduction, an additional corporate-tax-rate reduction of up to 7% is available for qualifying manufacturing and processing activities (the amount of the reduction is usually determined by a formula based on percentages of qualifying manufacturing or processing capital and labour — see section 125.1 and associated regulations). However, the manufacturing and processing deduction reduces the rate reduction applicable to business income. Accordingly, the

manufacturing and processing tax credit no longer reduces federal corporate tax rates.] However, manufacturing and processing activities may affect provincial corporate tax rates. However, even investment-type income earned by Canadian-controlled private corporations may be lower (depending on the province) than the top marginal rates applicable to individuals, albeit only marginally.

The following chart illustrates the federal corporate income tax rates from 2008 to 2012 and beyond:

Federal Corporate Rates

	2008	2009	2010	2011	2012+
Federal tax net of abatement - %	28	28	28	28	28
Rate reduction for business income - %	8.5	9	10	11.5	13
Federal business rate (1 - 2) - %	19.5	19	18	16.5	15
Additional tax on investment income - %	15.17	15.67	16.67	18.17	19.67
Federal tax on investment income (3 + 4) - %	34.67	34.67	34.67	34.67	34.67
Small Business Deduction - %	17	17	17	17	17
Small Business Rate (1 - 6) - %	11	11	11	11	11
Advantage of small business rate over general business rate (3 - 7) - %	8.5	8	7	5.5	4

Ontario Corporate Tax Rates — Investment/Business/Small Business Income

	2008	2009	2010	2011	2012	2013	2014
Investment Income	48.67	48.67	47.67	46.42	45.92	45.17	44.67
Business Income	33.5	33	31	28.25	26.25	25.5	25
Small Business Rate	16.5*	16.5	16	15.5	15.5	15.5	15.5

* Rate of 16.5% applies only to the first $400,000.

Provincial corporate tax is added to these rates. For example, the Ontario small business rate is currently 4.5% (as of July 1, 2010) and the normal corporate rate is 12% (as of July 1, 2010). The Ontario small business rate has been reduced to 4.5%, and the corporate rate will be reduced to 10% by 2014 (as of July 1, 2013). The deferrals from incorporation can be measured against the top Ontario marginal rate of 46.41% (this ignores EHT); non-eligible dividends are taxed at a rate of approximately 32.57%. It should be noted that there is currently overintegration in Ontario with respect to income earned for which the small business deduction applies. Income subject to the small business rate and subsequently distributed as a non-eligible dividend in the same year will attract an overall tax rate of 43.36%, and starting in 2011, this tax rate is reduced to 43.02% (compared to the top marginal rate of 46.41%, ignoring EHT). Accordingly it is advantageous to earn income in a corporation even if the money is needed individually in that same year.

[¶17,665] Accounts Payable

Taxpayers can deduct most business expenses for tax purposes, even if they remain unpaid at year end. However, certain expenses, including convention expenses, site investigation fees, utilities service connections, representation fees, landscaping, investment counsel fees, charitable donations and political contributions, remain non-deductible until they are actually paid.

To deduct contributions to a Deferred Profit Sharing Plan or to a Registered Pension Plan in the current year, employers must make these payments within 120 days of year end. Similarly, salaries, wages, pension benefits and retiring allowances owing at year end are deductible in the current year if paid within 179 days of year end. Otherwise, the deduction is unavailable until the amount is actually paid. To the extent some provinces have announced that personal tax rates will continue to decline in the coming years, it may make sense for corporations to accrue bonuses in one year and pay them within the first six months of the following year, so that owner–managers can take tax advantage of the lower personal rates.

If you owe an amount (other than salary and wages) to a non-arm's length party at the end of the year, you may claim a deduction in the current period provided that amount is paid within two years of that year end. If it is not paid within that time, it is added back to income in the third succeeding year. To avoid this income inclusion, an election may be filed with the tax return for the third year to deem the amounts as being paid. A late-filed election will result in a penalty equal to 25% of the unpaid amount.

[¶17,670] Accounts Receivable

In the calculation of business income for tax purposes, deductions are allowed for both bad debts and doubtful trade accounts receivable. Ideally, the deduction for doubtful accounts should be based on specifically identified non-collectable accounts.

A business may claim a lower allowance for tax purposes than that recorded for accounting purposes, thereby increasing taxable income to offset losses that would otherwise expire. The allowance for doubtful trade accounts receivable claimed in one year must be added to income in the next, with a new claim to be computed then.

You may claim a refund of Goods and Services Tax (GST) charged on amounts written off as bad debts. The refund should be claimed on the GST return within four years of the period in which the debts are written off.

[¶17,675] Reserves for Proceeds not Receivable

A reserve will be permitted where capital assets are sold and the full proceeds not received by year end. However, the reserve must be the lesser of the amount calculated under the general formula for each asset for a given year and 20% of the capital gain in the year of the disposition, 40% of the gain in the following year, and so on. That is, the gain must be recognized in increments of 20% over five years. Note that there may be a lower than 20% recognition in a particular year if more than 20% of the gain was included in a previous year, such as the year of disposition. In each year both the general calculation and the 20% recognition rule must be compared. An exception to the five-year recognition rule is provided where an individual transfers certain farm property, shares of a family farm corporation, an interest in a family farm partnership, or shares in a small business corporation to his children. In these cases, a reserve can be claimed over a maximum ten-year period.

In light of the above, in structuring the sale of appreciated assets, be sure you will have sufficient funds to pay the taxes required; if proceeds are deferred over a long period, the tax may be due before the proceeds are received.

The rules also provide for a (maximum) three-year instalment reserve for dispositions of property that give rise to ordinary income. The reserve will apply to dispositions of land where an amount is due after the end of the year, and to dispositions of other property where an amount is due more than 2 years after the date of sale. The reserve which may be claimed in each of the three years will be that *pro rata* portion of the profit which relates to the proceeds not due by the year end.

[¶17,675a] Inventory

There are extensive rules dealing with the valuation of inventory for income tax purposes. Generally, each item included in inventory must be valued at the lower of cost or fair market value, though provisions do exist permitting a taxpayer to value all inventory at fair market value. The CRA generally accepts any valuation method available under generally accepted accounting principles (GAAP). Once chosen, the method of valuing inventory must be used consistently from year-to-year unless permission is obtained from the Minister to change. The CRA has successfully challenged situations where the valuation method used for financial statement purposes differs from the method used for income tax purposes.

While alternative methods of valuing inventories are permissible, whatever method is used, the taxpayer is required to maintain records of the quantities and nature of the items included to support the valuation arrived at.

[¶17,676] Timing of Fixed Asset Acquisitions

Although only one-half of the normal annual capital cost allowance may be claimed in the year that the asset is acquired, it may nevertheless be advantageous to acquire depreciable assets before the year end rather than in the early months of the next year. Whatever capital cost allowance is available will thereby be accelerated one year. Proration of the allowance is only necessary where the taxation year of the business is less than 12 months. Although "available-for-use" rules require the delay of claims for capital cost allowance in certain cases, it remains true that there will often be a benefit where acquisition can be accelerated to an earlier taxation year. Under the new rules, depreciation for tax purposes cannot be claimed until property is actually put into use to earn income, although there are a number of technical exceptions permitting earlier claims. These considerations, of course, must be evaluated in the context of the business' overall financial position.

If you have depreciable property acquired in 2011 which was not eligible for depreciation in 2011 or 2012 under the "available-for-use" rule, it should be eligible for depreciation in 2012, whether or not it has been put in use; moreover, 2011 acquisitions, which are deemed to be put in use under this "rolling start" rule, are not subject to the half-year rule. Where 2009 property is both put in use and deemed put in use in 2013, the deeming rule should prevail; that is, the half-year rule does not apply and full rate CCA can be claimed on that property for the year.

In light of the above, ensure that business assets to be acquired in the near future are acquired and put in use before business year end. And, when accounting for 2012 acquisitions for tax purposes, do not forget to include prior year acquisitions which were not counted at the time due to the "available-for-use" rules, but are now qualified for tax depreciation. Where these properties have been held at the end of the two prior years without claiming tax depreciation, they may be claimed without regard to the half-year rule. Property put in use in prior years but not claimed for tax depreciation purposes is not now subject to the half-year rule.

[¶17,680] Meals and Entertainment Expenses

Only 50% of the cost of business meals and entertainment expenses is deductible. A broad spectrum of expenses is caught by this limitation, which applies to both corporations and individuals. A similar restriction applies for purposes of the Goods and Services Tax (GST). Therefore, only 50% of the GST paid on business meals and entertainment expenses may be recovered as an input tax credit.

¶17,676

Certain expenses are not affected by the 50% limitation, including those incurred for the general benefit of all employees at each work location, those reported as a taxable benefit to the employees, those related to an event benefiting a registered charity, expenses billed to others, or those incurred in the ordinary operations of restaurants, bars, and hotels. As well, the cost of meals provided to employees at a work camp established specifically for the purpose of providing meals and accommodation to employees working at a construction project are fully deductible.

If the cost of meals and beverages (other than coffee breaks) provided at conventions, conferences or seminars is not disclosed on the receipt for the meeting, the cost of the food and beverages provided is deemed to be $50 per day.

No portion of expenses, such as membership fees or dues to dining, recreational, or sporting facilities, are deductible for tax purposes. The CRA has reversed its position on deductions for golf course meal expenses undertaken in connection with a game of golf. Providing there is a business purpose, golf course meal expenses are subject to the normal 50% limitation.

Special rules apply to meals consumed by long-haul truck drivers during eligible travel period; see ¶3219.

[¶17,685] Business Use of Home Expenses

Self-employed individuals who have a home office or work space that is their principal place of business are able to deduct certain related expenses in the computation of business income. This is possible only if the home office or work space is either:

- the principal place of business; or

- a secondary place of business that is used exclusively to earn business income on a regular and continuous basis for meeting clients, customers, or patients.

Home workplace expenses cannot be used to create a loss from self-employment that could be applied against the individual's other sources of income. However, any business expenses disallowed because of this home workplace restriction can be carried forward indefinitely and used in a later year to shelter income from that same business.

Home workplace expenses include normal, ongoing home expenses. Only a reasonable portion of such expenses (usually based on the portion of the floor area of the home used for the work space) can be claimed as home workplace expenses. These would include, for example, the business portion of the following:

- mortgage interest (but not the principal portion of any mortgage payments) if the home is owned;

- rent, if the home is rented;
- property taxes;
- electricity, heat, water; and
- insurance on the home.

Only specific long distance phone calls incurred on a residential phone may be claimed as a business expense. However, the full monthly rental cost of a separate business line can be deducted as a business expense.

The full cost of insurance on office equipment or a business-use extension to your home policy can be claimed as a business expense.

Claiming capital cost allowance (CCA) on the home work space portion of your principal residence will allow the CRA to disallow any future principal residence exemption in respect of that portion of your home. However, the cost of improvements to a principal residence to accommodate a business workplace can be depreciated (via CCA) in determining income from self-employment.

[¶17,690] Capital Cost Allowance

A taxpayer is entitled to claim CCA on business assets acquired during the fiscal year. An investment tax credit may also be available in limited cases in respect of such assets.

Taxpayers are deemed to "acquire" property for CCA purposes when there is an unconditional contract for the acquisition of specific assets that are in a deliverable state. Specific rules prohibit CCA claims on property until they are "available-for-use". Assets owned for at least two years are deemed to be available-for-use.

The use of inter-class transfers allows a taxpayer to avoid the inclusion of recapture in income or, alternatively, to defer the recognition of a terminal loss. A taxpayer may transfer property from one CCA class to another CCA class, provided that the only difference between the classes is the specified acquisition date contained in the class description (such as Classes 29 and 39). The transfer of a Class 10 automobile to new Class 10.1 to avoid recapture is not allowed. Class 10.1, created for new automobiles, limits the amount available for CCA as "luxury" vehicles. For automobiles purchased in 2012, the CCA limit for Class 10.1 is $30,000 plus GST/HST and PST. For example, a taxpayer may elect to transfer all assets in Classes 2 to 12 (such as buildings, machinery, automotive equipment, etc.,) to Class 1 (4%), thus avoiding a recapture in any of those classes. Obviously, the tax cost associated with the reduced ability to claim CCA as a result of the transfer of assets from a high-rate class to a low-rate class must be compared to the cost of the potential recapture.

¶17,690

Capital cost allowance is a permissive deduction and so the maximum amount need not be claimed. Not claiming capital cost allowance could facilitate the use of non-capital losses carried forward from prior years or the utilization of investment tax credits that might otherwise expire.

Capital cost allowance is an area particularly susceptible to change. See ¶4025 for the current capital cost allowance rates applicable to various classes of assets; see ¶4505 for an alphabetical table of current capital cost allowance rates.

[¶17,700] Federal and Provincial R&D Incentives

A corporation undertaking activities that may be considered research and development activities has various tax incentives available to it, which would not be available to an unincorporated business.

For example, the investment tax credit for qualifying Canadian-controlled private corporations incurring scientific research expenditures is 35%, whereas an individual could not claim a credit above 20% for the same expenditure.

In addition to a possible higher rate of credit, scientific research tax credits earned in a corporation may be refunded in cash to the corporation at a higher rate than to individuals. Individuals can obtain a cash refund of 40% of scientific research credits generated in the year in excess of tax. A Canadian-controlled private corporation whose income (together with the income of associated corporations) did not exceed $500,000 in the preceding year, can claim a 100% cash refund of investment tax credits earned at a rate of 35% in respect of up to $3 million of scientific research expenditures made in the taxation year (this will not apply to expenditures on depreciable property). Consequently, annual refunds of up to $1.05 million will be available to small corporations engaging in scientific research. As income exceeds $300,000, the eligible $3 million of eligible expenditure is decreased, ceasing at income of $700,000. The 100% refund remains available, however, on whatever amount of R&D expenditure remains eligible for the high rate.

The associated corporation rules have been somewhat relaxed to allow access to the full credit for small businesses with common investors, provided certain conditions are met.

[¶17,710] R&D Filing Deadline

Taxpayers must identify SR&ED expenditures and file a prescribed form no later than 12 months after the tax return due date for the year in which the SR&ED expenditure is incurred to claim the related investment tax credits (special rules apply for businesses carried on as a proprietorship or partnership). Though the taxpayer may have to follow complex procedures and do extensive paperwork in the process of identifying qualifying

SR&ED expenditures, the reward in the form of tax savings and/or refunds can be substantial.

See further at ¶3628.

[¶17,720] Deferring Gains

The taxation of capital gains and the recapture of depreciation (CCA) may be postponed with respect to both voluntary and involuntary dispositions of certain business assets, if a qualifying replacement property is acquired within a prescribed time period and the appropriate election is filed. Where a capital property has been expropriated, lost, destroyed, or stolen (an involuntary disposition), a replacement property must be acquired within two taxation years of the deemed disposition. With respect to voluntary dispositions, a replacement property must be acquired within one taxation year. Only property used primarily in earning business income will qualify for the replacement property rules.

In all cases, the replacement property must be acquired for the same or a similar purpose and must be used in the same or a similar business. Additional rules restrict the benefit to replacement property located in Canada where the former property was located in Canada.

[¶17,725] Depreciable Assets in Inventory

A business involved in both selling and leasing depreciable assets may have such assets included in its inventory. When valuing such inventory, a write-down, equivalent to the capital cost allowance that could have been claimed if the assets were capital property, may be permitted.

Complex rules have been adopted to restrict the capital cost allowance deductible by a lessor in respect of specified leasing property owned at the end of the taxation year. "Specified leasing property" is defined as depreciable property used primarily to earn rent or leasing revenue and which is the subject of a lease for a term of more than one year. Certain types of property, such as automobiles, light trucks and trailers, buildings, home furnishings and appliances, and most types of office furniture, office equipment and computers, are exempt from the leasing property rules. These rules do not apply to non-arm's length leases or to the leasing of property with a fair market value of $25,000 or less.

[¶17,730] Forgiven Indebtedness

Where a creditor forgives a debt, the debtor is required to reduce its tax losses and the tax base of the property forgiven by the debt. As well, in most cases the debtor must include all or a portion of any excess forgiven amount in its income. See ¶3451.

¶17,720

[¶17,740] Self-Employed Individuals

Self-employed individuals can deduct one-half of CPP/QPP contributions payable on self-employed earnings. This deduction essentially represents the employer's portion of the CPP/QPP premium.

In computing their income from a business, self-employed individuals and those carrying on business through a partnership can deduct premiums paid for private health services plans in respect of the individual and family members (including same-sex partners) living with the individual. To qualify for this deduction, the premiums must be payable in respect of the year and the individual must be actively engaged in the business. As well, equivalent coverage must be offered to arm's length employees of the individual. There are monetary limits to the amount of the deduction.

[¶17,750] Interest Expense

[¶17,755] Deductibility of Interest

Tax planning in respect of potentially non-deductible interest or other financing charges is a critical part of investment decision-making. In this section, we review some strategies that can allow a taxpayer to maximize (on a "filing basis", at least) interest deductions.

Until recently, leading cases supported even relatively aggressive strategies in respect of interest deductions, including various transactions that could be effected to convert would-be non-deductible interest (i.e., involving personal expenditures) to deductible interest. See the Supreme Court of Canada decisions in *Shell Canada* (1999 DTC 5669), *Singleton* (2001 DTC 5533), and *Ludco* (2001 DTC 5505). On October 31, 2003, the Department of Finance announced draft legislation to reverse the Supreme Court's decisions and impose a statutory requirement that losses from business or property are only deductible in a year if it is reasonable to expect in that year that the taxpayer will realize a cumulative profit over the period during which the taxpayer may reasonably be expected to carry on the business or hold the property. Profit will not include capital gain or loss. In short, the reasonable expectation of profit test is to be legislated back into existence. The proposals have attracted a great deal of criticism. While the Department of Finance has not come forward with details of revisions, it has indicated on a number of occasions that the provisions would be more limited than originally announced.

Also to note, the General Anti-Avoidance Rule ("GAAR") was not a factor in these cases. In *Lipson v. The Queen*, 2009 DTC 5015, the Supreme Court of Canada examined the relationship between interest deductibility manoeuvres and GAAR. While the taxpayer lost the case, the decision appears to support the contention that GAAR should generally not apply when taxpayers arrange their borrowings to minimize their tax liability.

However, *Lipson* may put a number of standard interest deductibility strategies into jeopardy.[8]

[¶17,765] Loss of Source of Income

Where money is borrowed to acquire property that will generate income subject to tax, or where money is borrowed to earn income from a business, the interest paid is generally deductible. However, the courts have established that interest (or a part of it) is no longer deductible if the income-earning property or business is disposed of at a loss or becomes worthless. To alleviate this situation, legislation was enacted to allow interest in such circumstances to continue to be deductible. Unfortunately, the rules are quite complex. Taxpayers who have outstanding borrowings where the related source of income no longer exists should ensure that they take full advantage of these rules.

[¶17,770] Capitalization of Interest

Though there are certain limited exceptions related to money borrowed for various real estate projects, taxpayers are required to capitalize interest (along with certain soft costs) that accrues during the period of construction, renovation, or alteration of a building.

A taxpayer may also elect to capitalize interest on money that was borrowed in the year to acquire depreciable assets, or that was borrowed for the exploration, development, or acquisition of resource properties. The election may also be made with respect to interest incurred in the preceding three years on funds that are expended in the current year to acquire such assets. A taxpayer may wish to make this election if the deduction of interest results in tax losses that may expire. A taxpayer does not have to elect on all interest paid; rather, he or she may capitalize interest with respect to specific assets.

[¶17,775] Thin Capitalization

A limit is imposed on the amount of interest on debt payable by a corporation to certain non-residents. In general terms, if the greatest amount of debt outstanding at any time in the year to non-residents owning 25% or more of any class of shares of the company exceeds three times "equity", a prorated portion of interest paid or payable to such non-residents will be disallowed as a deduction. The thin capital debt-to-equity ratio is two-to-one. As well, the government announced it is considering extending the rules to certain partnerships and trusts as well as to Canadian branches of foreign companies.

---

[8] For a detailed discussion, see ¶25,735 of CCH's *Canada Income Tax Guide.*

For this purpose, "equity" is defined as the aggregate of retained earnings (excluding the earnings of other corporations), and any surplus contributed by the non-resident as at the commencement of the year, and the greater of the legal paid-up capital related to the shareholdings at the commencement or the end of the year. The debt-to-equity ratio is calculated on an average monthly basis and restricted debts include not only back-to-back loan arrangements, but also debts guaranteed by a specified non-resident.

[¶17,780] Shifting of Income

If one corporation within a Canadian corporate group is in a loss position and another is in a taxable position, it may be possible to utilize the losses of the one corporation against the income of the other.

One way of achieving this is to have the loss company borrow funds externally that it would loan to the profitable company at a reasonable rate of interest. The profitable company would then use the funds to acquire shares of the loss company, which would repay the external borrowings and have a source of income (interest from the profitable company) to offset its losses.

Other methods of shifting income are available, but care should be taken to ensure the transactions will not be subject to the numerous anti-avoidance rules. Consultation with your professional adviser is suggested.

[¶17,785] Exemption from Withholding

There is no withholding tax on interest paid to arm's length non-residents if the lender cannot require payment of more than 25% of the principal amount of the debt within five years of the date of issue. It may be possible to refinance existing debt to meet this exemption, and thereby perhaps reduce the cost of borrowing. Other exemptions from withholding may also be available in specific situations. Professional advice is recommended where complex financings are involved.

[¶17,800] Business Losses

[¶17,801] Losses from Business or Property

Generally, if expenses exceed revenues, the resulting business loss may be deducted from any other income for the year the loss occurred.

Legislative proposals originally proposed for 2005 and later years would deny a loss for any year in which the business is not considered to have a reasonable expectation of profit. This proposal appears to have been discarded in favour of more limited restrictions on the deduction of interest expenses. For most businesses this should not be an issue.

[¶17,805] Flexibility of Use

While one generally wants to deduct business losses as soon as possible, it should be noted that the deduction of business losses is optional, not mandatory. This may be of particular interest to small business corporations that might want to utilize losses against income that exceeds amounts eligible for taxation at lower rates ($500,000 effective January 1, 2009) of active business income which is taxed at the lowest rate, or to individuals who expect to have income that will be taxed at a higher rate in subsequent years.

Non-capital losses may be carried back three years and forward:

- 20 years for losses arising in and after the 2006 taxation year,
- 10 years for losses arising in taxation years ending after March 22, 2004, and before 2006,
- seven years for losses arising in taxation years ending before March 23, 2004.

[¶17,810] Loss Year Considerations

If it appears that a loss may not be utilized within the applicable carryforward period, the amount of a business loss may be reduced by deferring certain expenses (discussed below) until subsequent years.

Capital cost allowance (CCA) provides a degree of flexibility in determining the amount of a business loss because it is not a mandatory expense of any given year but can be deferred and claimed in any future year without any time limitation. Thus, if a business loss is suffered in a particular year and there is an income year prior to the expiry of the loss due to the limitation periods discussed above, the taxpayer should consider revising the current year return by reducing the amount of CCA claimed, thus increasing income and the ability to apply a loss carryforward. This will absorb the loss carryforward for that year and preserve the capital cost allowance until some future year. It is usually preferable to defer CCA on the highest rate classes first, since the depreciation can be used most rapidly when needed.

In addition to CCA, there are numerous expenses which are available as a deduction from income on either a current or deferred basis for tax purposes. Examples of these expenses are:

(a) Interest incurred to acquire fixed assets (if certain elections are made);

(b) Cumulative eligible capital deductions;

(c) Reserves for: doubtful debts, goods and services, and capital gains; and

(d) Certain scientific research expenditures.

¶17,805

Note that the CRA will only accept revisions to optional claims after the 90-day period following a notice of assessment if the tax payable for the year in issue does not change. Typically, this presents no problem where there is an overall loss for the year. However, where there is a business loss but a positive total income subject to tax, decisions on the projected rate of loss utilization and the concomitant use of optional claims must be made on a current basis.

Other Considerations

- Keep detailed records of the year of origin of a loss and the subsequent utilization of that loss as carryback or carryforward, so that you can always be certain what carryforward period applies to a particular loss.

- Do not claim optional deductions in loss years unless the loss can be recovered quickly against other years. Where less than full capital cost allowance is to be claimed, always claim in respect of low rate classes first.

- Remember that the half-year rule only applies to limit depreciation in the year a property is acquired; if you have deferred a CCA claim in the year of acquisition, you can claim the full CCA amount in any subsequent year.

- Remember to claim your business loss carryforwards against all sources of income. Do not, however, claim amounts which will eliminate the use of your personal amount credits or other credits, such as political contribution credit, which have no carryover. Depending on your loss situation, you may want to use losses only against income above the (for 2011) $41,544 level. This option is only available for carryovers, not for losses incurred in the current year, which must be fully applied to bring current taxable income to zero.

- When carrying over losses against other years, take account of changing tax rates. The rate on lowest bracket income was 15.25% for 2006, and is scheduled to be 15% for 2007 and later years. Accordingly, a 2009 loss carried back to 2006 against low bracket income will reduce income taxed at 15.25%, while carried back to 2007, it will reduce income taxed at 15%. If carried forward, the 2009 loss will reduce income taxed at 15%, at least until rates change again. Changing provincial components must also be considered. The differences are likely to be small, but should not be overlooked.

¶17,810

[¶17,850] Goods and Services Tax; Harmonized Sales Tax

[¶17,855] It's Not That Simple!

Although the GST/HST appears to be a simple tax at first glance, there are many areas that present continuing difficulties. It is essential that every business monitor its GST/HST position, since penalties may be enforced as a response to failure to submit a return, failure to pay the tax due, or making false statements and allowing omissions in returns. The GST/HST presents a challenge for income tax professionals, since it necessitates a different way of looking at a tax regime. The GST/HST regime is based on a flow-through system and the value added at each step of the production and distribution chain. Hence, with such a multi-level system, the interaction of businesses in collecting and paying the tax needs to be tracked, and this requires paper trails and dependencies on the transactions among businesses. This is a departure conceptually from traditional income tax thinking, where the end result of sales and purchases transactions, i.e., income and expenses, are measured.

[¶17,857] HST Planning

HST

The Harmonized Sales Tax (HST) is simply the GST at a higher rate, implemented in the provinces of New Brunswick, Newfoundland and Labrador, and Nova Scotia in 1997, and British Columbia and Ontario in 2010.

Following the 2011 British Columbia provincial referendum, the government announced its intention to return to a PST regime, to be effective on April 1, 2013. Quebec announced on September 30, 2011 that the province will harmonize its provincial sales tax with the GST, effective January 1, 2013. The 2012 Prince Edward Island Budget included the government's announcement of harmonization to be effective April 1, 2013.

Since the rules are fundamentally the same as the GST rules, all the planning issues discussed in this chapter apply equally to an HST regime. Additional planning is warranted due to the existence of both participating and non-participating provinces creating provincial tax borders. Also, as a province transitions from PST to an HST regime, special consideration should be given to the transition and any planning opportunities to save costs or minimize risk. With a mix of both participating and non-participating provinces, national suppliers need to consider GST, HST, and PST when considering many issues, such as pricing. If tax-inclusive pricing is an option, the higher buried HST in respect of sales in a participating province should be considered. Once registered for GST, a taxpayer is also registered for HST, so to minimize risk, all national businesses should be aware of the compliance requirements, such as the collection of a higher rate of tax.

As a province moves from a retail sales tax structure to an HST structure, the repeal of one and introduction of the other will provide opportunities. Purchases subject to GST, which were not subject to PST, such as many services, will have a higher tax charge to the business or consumer. Hence, where possible, customers may want to stock up on such purchases, or prepay in the case of services to be provided after implementation of an HST. There are, of course, transitional rules to consider which may prevent such planning, particularly in respect of supplies to be provided after implementation of an HST. However, where an opportunity does exist, for example in the case of real property and other PST-exempt goods, a purchaser will consider the cash flow cost of an earlier outlay of cash to take advantage of the pre-implementation savings. Vendors of such consumer goods may wish to take advantage of the market demand before implementation, but will then need to consider the loss of sales after implementation. Similarly, but with the opposite result, many purchasers of business supplies subject to PST may wish to defer the purchase until after implementation of HST, to take advantage of input tax credits, whereas the PST would have been non-recoverable. In this case, vendors will need to consider the loss in sales before implementation and the increased demand after implementation. Vendors may wish to take advantage of the market forces to offer sales or reduced price pre-payment options, for delivery after implementation. Vendors need to consider their customer market to make pricing decisions. For example, where customers of a particular industry sector expect PST savings to be passed along, there will be market pressure for the vendor to reduce prices. Alternatively, this pressure will not exist in cases where the removal of PST is replaced with the recoverable HST.

Capital acquisition plans will need to be reconsidered, both for any possible cash flow increase with the higher HST rate, as well as a possible increase in non-recoverable tax. Where fixed asset systems are established to capitalize the cost including tax paid on the purchase of assets, this system will need to be adjusted so that only the actual cost is capitalized once the provincial component of HST becomes a recoverable payment.

The following additional planning points also warrant consideration:

(1) Where point of sale rebates are implemented with a new HST regime, customers may wish to defer purchases until the rebates are in effect;

(2) In planning for HST implementation, legal departments need to consider where tax-inclusive pricing structures exist. Where possible, renegotiation will be desired by the vendor, but possibly not by the purchaser;

(3) Budgeting for the new tax cost or cash flow cost will also be necessary. In respect of public sector bodies, for example, the rebates of the provincial components will need to be considered and factored into funding requirements;

¶17,857

(4) Many business sectors, such as telecommunications and technology, will benefit from not paying a non-recoverable PST on many inputs. Customers, both individual and commercial, should consider and negotiate how suppliers' reduced costs will be passed along to customers; and

(5) The ongoing cash flow cost should be factored into financing and capital requirements of businesses with high sales and purchase volumes.

[¶17,860] Input Tax Credits (ITCs)

GST/HST incurred by a registered business on costs can be recovered through ITC claims, for purchases related to taxable goods or services provided by the business. At first glance, determining whether an input tax credit may be claimed may appear simple; unfortunately, complexities often arise in certain situations, such as where the businesses makes both taxable and exempt supplies or where assets are used partly for business and partly for personal purposes. A discussion of ITCs is provided in Chapter 16, at ¶16,215 through ¶16,275.

Input tax credits need to be supported with prescribed information. Eligibility for the ITC is not enough to actually secure it. Many assessments have resulted where the registrant may have been eligible for an ITC, but where the documentary requirements were not upheld. Hence, a thorough review of the various rules and administrative policies in this area is advised, to ensure that ITCs are not over-claimed or under-claimed, and that the proper supporting documentation is obtained. As fundamental and simple as it may sound, planning for the capture of all the necessary information, and obtaining the supporting documents, may be as valuable as the implementation of sophisticated tax planning strategies.

Generally, the time period in which a "specified person" may claim an ITC is limited to two years. "Specified persons" include listed financial institutions and businesses with revenues (including those of associated businesses) from taxable supplies made in Canada, exceeding $6 million in each of the current and preceding fiscal years. Other entities have a four-year window in which to recover ITCs. The planning of the timing of claims and making sure a thorough review takes place before ITCs fall off the table have proven to be solid tax saving strategies in many businesses.

[¶17,863] Maximizing Recoveries with ITC Restrictions

The goal of any tax planning is usually one of three key objectives: maximize revenues; minimize expenses through saving tax costs; and minimize the risk of assessment. One way to minimize costs is to claim all input tax credits available. Entities with less-than-full recovery of ITCs, such as financial institutions, public sector bodies, and other entities with acombination of commercial and exempt supplies, need to closely monitor their measurement of the "extent" of use in commercial activities, both to optimize the ITC claims and to ensure compliance with the rules which

¶17,860

govern this measurement. Since the extent of ITC claims depends largely on the mix of commercial and exempt activities, it is necessary that such an entity, a financial institution for example, closely consider whether an item is taxable or exempt. In many respects, where the legislation is grey, such as with the "arranging for" provisions, the financial institution should complete a careful analysis of the rules, not only to ensure that collection requirements are complied with, but also to identify commercial activities and thereby optimize ITCs.

Entities with mixed supplies need to consider their promotional or free supply activities. Often, planning to ensure that free supply activities can be associated with commercial activities will increase ITCs. Without deliberate consideration of this, a free supply may be viewed by the CRA as supporting only the exempt activities. Other inputs and costs of the business should be reviewed to identify how such inputs contribute to the business. An example is advertising costs. For example, where a public sector body advertises exempt activities, the advertisement may also be viewed as supporting related taxable activities if considered at the time of development of the advertising material.

Where mixed activities exist in a corporate group, there may be an opportunity to maximize ITC recoveries by planning the mix of activities of each member of the group. For example, if one entity houses all the commercial activities, another entity may be used to house the staff and charge a taxable fee to the commercial entity. The separate management company could house the exempt activities and increase the ITC recovery base of the exempt activity through a taxable charge to the related commercial entity. Many other considerations such as third party charges are necessary, but clearly, planning around the activities of a corporate group can lead to some GST/HST advantages.

Even entities involved exclusively in commercial activities need to ensure they address certain transactions or issues where ITCs can be restricted. ITC restrictions, such as those implemented with Harmonization 2010, need to be monitored. The bad debt relief provisions become ineffective where receivables have been sold without recourse. Hence, the issue of the lost GST/HST relief should be considered in planning for such financing tools. Other areas of ITC restrictions to be closely monitored by commercial entities include vehicle purchases, employee reimbursements and allowances, and personal-use inputs.

[¶17,865] Employee/Partner GST/HST Rebates

In certain instances, employees or individual partners may purchase goods or services that will be used in carrying out the activities of the business, but as an individual purchaser, would not normally be entitled to claim an ITC for tax paid. Accordingly, employees of GST/HST registrants (other than listed financial institutions) and individuals who are members of a partnership that is a GST/HST registrant, can claim refunds of

GST/HST paid on their income tax deductible, unreimbursed employment/partnership expenses. Claims must be made on form GST 370 which is to be submitted with the individual's income tax return. In the case of expenses incurred by a member of a partnership for the account of the partnership, no rebate is available but the partnership may be able to claim an ITC.

[¶17,867] Cash Flow Planning

With significant volumes of collection and payment of GST/HST, particularly in harmonized provinces at a higher rate of tax, the cash flow cost of the tax needs to be considered. Where a GST/HST registrant is assigned an annual or quarterly reporting period, but is usually in a net refund position (such as an exporter), an election for more frequent filing of GST/HST returns should be considered. Also, monthly filers may choose an accounting month filing system instead of calendar. The year end may also be chosen as different from the taxation year end in certain circumstances.

With related entities, if one entity is usually in a net payable position and the other is in a net receivable position, an offset election, with ministerial approval, may be available. The cash flow costs of GST/HST should also be considered with significant purchases and specifically with such things as lease versus buy decisions.

[¶17,870] Reorganizations

Business reorganizations are generally undertaken for a variety of reasons, which may or may not include tax considerations. Reorganizations may involve the sale or purchase of assets or shares or changes in an entity's function within a corporate group. The legal structures involved can include corporations, partnerships, limited partnerships and joint ventures. Generally, such reorganizations have taken income taxes into account and in some cases, producing beneficial or favourable income tax results may be the primary purpose of reorganizing. Since GST/HST is frequently fully recoverable, it may receive minimal or no consideration. However, unless the GST/HST consequences are considered and reviewed, the overall results could very well be less than favourable. Accordingly, a detailed review of the GST/HST consequences of any proposed reorganization is essential.

The immediate as well as any future GST/HST consequences of proposed reorganizations should be considered. Immediate considerations include the valuation and classification of all transactions resulting from the reorganization. Elections that may eliminate, minimize or defer tax should be utilized. The reporting periods of the entities involved and the timing of transactions among entities should also be considered in order to minimize any negative impact on cash flow. The application of GST/HST to future transactions occurring among the entities may be and often is affected by changes in share holdings, control and association relationships among the entities and therefore the long term impact of such changes should not be overlooked.

The recovery of GST/HST payable in respect of reorganization expenses by way of input tax credits must be reviewed and available claims should be filed. In addition, the more routine administrative requirements such as registration, deregistration, the filing or updating of elections and the selection of reporting periods often trap tax practitioners and these should not be overlooked.

When planning a reorganization, the structure of any new entities will greatly influence the GST/HST result. Unique rules apply to partnerships, joint ventures, and related parties. The rules with respect to mergers and acquisitions and wind-ups should also be reviewed. These are addressed at ¶16,345 through ¶16,360.

[¶17,875] Contract Wording

The GST/HST regime, in many respects, often looks at form over substance in the analysis of a transaction. Hence, the legal wording of contracts and other documents are often significant determinants in a GST/HST audit or tax court defence. In many cases where the GST/HST consequences of the wording of a contract are not considered, what should be a straight-forward interpretation of the GST/HST consequences can become misleading from the contractual wording. This is often true in consideration of such issues as single versus multiple supplies, and tax-inclusive pricing. It is always advisable, for example, to compare the contractual wording to the criteria under the single versus multiple supply guidelines.

Although the standard rule is that a price is tax-extra (i.e., not inclusive of tax), where a contract is silent on GST/HST, there have been many situations where this is not necessarily clear. Hence, intentionally noting whether a price is tax-extra or tax-inclusive may eliminate problems later. Also, suppliers and customers will often negotiate tax-inclusive pricing when contracts are under negotiation. This, in effect, moves any tax payment cost to the vendor and away from the purchaser. When there is an impending increase in a GST/HST rate, the higher rate may create a cost higher than the profit margin, and hence tax-inclusive pricing would result in a poor business decision. Legal departments and tax departments once again have many reasons to compare notes.

[¶17,880] Transactions with Non-Residents

Where goods are sold for export to non-residents, it is essential that the supplier hold satisfactory evidence of the exportation of goods in order to support entitlement to zero-rating. Zero-rating is available for both direct exports and for some goods delivered in Canada for subsequent export by the purchaser. Further conditions must be met before indirect exports can

¶17,880

be zero-rated. If the necessary documentation is not held, the CRA can assess GST/HST plus penalties and interest on the value of the goods.

In the case of services "exported" to non-residents, there are detailed provisions for zero-rating. Care should be exercised in this area, since a service supplied to a non-resident does not necessarily qualify for zero-rating. Services supplied to non-residents will be taxable, for example, if they relate to real property or tangible property located in Canada.

As with services, supplies of certain intangibles are excepted from zero-rating, including for example, supplies that relate to real property or tangible personal property located in Canada, supplies that relate to services made in Canada, supplies of intangible personal property that may only be used in Canada and supplies of specified telecommunications facilities.

[¶17,885] Acting on Behalf of Non-Residents

Agents which deliver goods in Canada on behalf of a non-resident supplier should be cautious. A special "self-supply rule" makes the agent liable for the full amount of GST/HST on the goods in instances where the non-resident vendor is not registered for GST/HST purposes and the goods are delivered to the customer in Canada, unless the customer issues a special "drop shipment certificate" containing prescribed information and undertakings. For example, the agent of a non-resident who receives $1,000 in payment for delivery of a $100,000 item could incur a $5,000 GST liability, unless a proper drop shipment certificate is issued by the non-resident's Canadian customer. Those acting for non-residents should review their operating methods to ensure that they do not inadvertently create a GST/HST liability. The rules regarding drop-shipments under the *Excise Tax Act* are detailed and complex. A brief discussion is provided at ¶16,315.

[¶17,887] E-Commerce Transactions

One of the most complex areas in GST/HST today is that of electronic commerce. The application of GST/HST to e-commerce activities, such as sales conducted over the Internet or supplies of software and related services, can add additional complexities in applying even basic GST/HST rules. For example, e-commerce transactions may present special considerations in the determination of whether a non-resident supplier is carrying on business in Canada or operating through a "permanent establishment" in Canada. E-Commerce transactions create difficulties in applying place of supply rules, and characterizing the nature of a supply or of bundled supplies.

The application of GST/HST to e-commerce activities is an area of ongoing change, as policy considerations and administrative practices evolve. The Canada Revenue Agency has issued administrative documents providing guidance on the application of GST/HST to e-commerce activities.

¶17,885

[¶17,890] Deemed Financial Institution Status

A corporation with sufficient "financial" revenue can unexpectedly find itself within the definition of "financial institution" for GST/HST purposes. A registrant can be a "financial institution", either by specific inclusion as a "listed financial institution", or as a result of a test of dividends, interest and other financial income compared to overall total income (i.e., a "*de minimis* financial institution"). A registrant may be deemed to be a *de minimis* financial institution if financial revenues exceed $10 million and 10% of total income, or if income from credit and loan-related activities exceeds $1 million, in the preceding year.

Businesses deemed to be financial institutions are subject to a variety of special rules; the most significant of which is limited ability to claim input tax credits. Examples of other complex rules are the treatment of capital property, the special self-assessment rules, and special reporting requirements.

Registrants receiving financial service revenue which are not "listed financial institutions" should therefore monitor annual revenues. Planning should be considered before year-end where it is possible to recognize income in the subsequent year or in a related company, to bring the revenue totals below *de minimis* thresholds.

[¶17,900] Not the Final Word

Because the GST/HST is a tax of such broad range, it is not possible to comment on all planning points. There are very specific concessions for certain industries and for certain types of goods and services. Registrants should ensure that they take advantage of all available concessions and elections, and that their compliance procedures will not give cause for concern in the event of a CRA audit.

Paragraph

A

Accelerated capital cost allowance
. air and water pollution control
  equipment .... ¶4190
. computer hardware and software ...... ¶4220
. energy conservation equipment .... ¶4215
. manufacturing and processing
  equipment .... ¶4210

Accident insurance plan
. benefits, employee's income .... ¶2095

Accounting methods
. cash and accrual .... ¶2020
. determination of profit .... ¶3010
. foreign investment entities .... ¶7395
. general .... ¶925

Accounts
. contingent
. . deduction .... ¶3207
. payable .... ¶17,665
. receivable
. . consideration, when discontinuing
      business .... ¶3504
. . deductible amounts .... ¶17,670
. . joint election .... ¶3501
. . partnership, election re sale .... ¶7040
. . sale .... ¶3492
. . vendor's deductions .... ¶3495

Accrual rules
. annuity payments, application to .... ¶2185
. corporate partners .... ¶1018

Acquisitions
. half-year rule .... ¶4062
. shares, deemed .... ¶15,550

Active business
. adjusted income, defined .... ¶8405
. defined .... ¶8440
. income from .... ¶8440
. manufacturing and processing .... ¶8405

Paragraph

Adjusted cost base
. additions .... ¶5180
. capital interest in a trust .... ¶7450
. convertible property .... ¶5435
. deductions .... ¶5185
. deemed gain .... ¶5175
. defined .... ¶5080
. depreciable property .... ¶5060
. determination of .... ¶5175
. identical properties .... ¶5370; ¶9260
. limited partnership
. . negative .... ¶7097
. . non-recourse financing .... ¶7098
. negative
. . limited partner defined .... ¶7097
. partnership interest .... ¶5190
. . additions .... ¶7100
. . deductions .... ¶7105
. . negative .... ¶7095
. partnership property on
    dissolution .... ¶7165
. property transferred, non-arm's length
. . transitional rules .... ¶5195
. shares .... ¶6095

Administration and enforcement
. appeals .... ¶870
. communication of information .... ¶15,275
. federal income tax laws .... ¶855
. Minister's duty .... ¶15,005
. onus of proof .... ¶865
. secrecy .... ¶860
. tax evasion, avoidance, planning .... ¶875

Adoption
. expenses giving rise to credit .... ¶8148
. relationship, defined .... ¶15,405

Advance Tax Rulings
. general .... ¶830

Advances
. loan vs. .... ¶2040
. taxability .... ¶2040

Paragraph

Advertising
. foreign broadcasting ....¶3267
. non-Canadian publication ....¶3264

Affidavits
. proof of matters under Act ....¶15,300

Affiliated persons
. amalgamation of corporations ....¶6345
. basic rule ....¶15,450
. corporation and partnership ....¶15,470
. corporations ....¶15,455
. individuals ....¶15,455
. losses on dispositions ....¶5217;
....¶6300
. partnerships ....¶15,465
. two corporations ....¶15,460
. two trusts ....¶15,483

Age credit ....¶8100

Agents
. carrying on business in Canada ....¶1045
. GST/HST ....¶16,290
. selling livestock, not farmers ....¶3588

Agreements
. provincial tax collection ....¶15,190

Agricultural organizations
. exemption from tax ....¶11,300

Aircraft
. capital cost allowance ....¶4120
. corporations, thinly capitalized,
....interest ....¶3258
. costs and interest ....¶2320
. employee's use of employer's ....¶2090
. input tax credits ....¶16,240

Alimony and maintenance payments
. inclusion in income ....¶2180
. payments to third parties ....¶2180
. retroactive lump sums ....¶8023

Allocation
. dividends and capital gains, credit
....unions ....¶9213

Allowances
. GST/HST input tax credits ....¶16,275

Alter ego trusts
. advantages ....¶17,169
. disadvantages ....¶17,170
. nature of ....¶17,168

Alternative Minimum Tax
. planning considerations ....¶17,605

Paragraph

Amalgamation
. corporations
. . change in fiscal year ....¶1015
. . definition ....¶6325
. . obligations issued by
....predecessor ....¶6360
. GST/HST ....¶16,345
. NRO corporations ....¶9156
. tax-free rollovers, shares ....¶6340–6350

Amateur athlete trust
. amounts distributed ....¶10,010
. death of beneficiary ....¶10,020
. exempt status ....¶11,586
. non-resident withholding tax ....¶14,169
. termination ....¶10,015

Amateur athletic trust fund payments
. business income ....¶3068

Amended returns
. voluntary disclosures ....¶12,040

Amortized cost
. defined ....¶3462
. insurance
. . Canada security ....¶9234

Amounts receivable
. defined ....¶3555
. . reserves ....¶3417

Animals
. trained to assist people with disabilities
. . deductible expenses ....¶8130

Anniversary date
. definition ....¶3018

Annuities
. accrual rules, application of ....¶2185
. *Canada–U.K. Tax Convention* ....¶14,550
. *Canada–U.S. Tax Convention* ....¶14,420
. capital element deductible from
....income ....¶2415
. information returns ....¶12,050
. payments
. . deductible from income ....¶3357
. . included in income ....¶2185
. . of income and capital
....combined ....¶3141
. registered pension plans ....¶10,493
. retroactive lump sum payments ....¶8023

Anti-avoidance
. Part II.1 tax ....¶13,055

Appeals
. amended procedure ....¶12,375

Paragraph

Appeals — continued
. expenses, deductible from
   income .... ¶2460
. expenses reimbursed, income .... ¶2205
. extensions .... ¶12,383
. Federal Court of Canada .... ¶12,430;
   ¶12,435
. . disposition .... ¶12,440
. general .... ¶870
. informal .... ¶870
. new procedure .... ¶12,375
. objections .... ¶12,380
. Supreme Court of Canada .... ¶12,450
. Tax Court of Canada
. . disposition .... ¶12,405
. . general procedure .... ¶12,395
. . improvement of caseload .... ¶12,375;
   ¶12,390; ¶12,400
. . informal procedure .... ¶870; ¶12,390
. . special references .... ¶12,400

Apportionment
. rule for exemptions .... ¶11,603

Appropriation
. property to shareholders .... ¶3516
. . inadequate considerations .... ¶2520
. transfer of payments .... ¶15,007

Armed forces
. members, deemed residents .... ¶1065

Arm's length transactions
. defined .... ¶15,400
. lease cancellation payments .... ¶3333
. property transferred, not at
. . inadequate considerations .... ¶2505

Arm's-length transactions
. mortgage sold at a loss .... ¶4455

Art
. gifts .... ¶8165

Artists
. expenses .... ¶2387
. grants .... ¶2213

Assessments
. basic procedure .... ¶12,070
. disability tax credit eligibility .... ¶12,072
. exclusions from .... ¶12,085
. incomplete, incorrect .... ¶12,075
. loss carryback .... ¶12,090
. losses .... ¶12,071
. net worth method .... ¶12,100
. notice available on line .... ¶15,301
. objections to .... ¶12,380
. partnerships .... ¶12,073

Paragraph

Assessments — continued
. power of Minister .... ¶15,090
. time allowed .... ¶12,080

Asset sales
. eligible dividends .... ¶17,415

Assets
. business
. . change in proportionate use .... ¶4420
. . converted to personal use .... ¶4410
. depreciable
. . available-for-use rule .... ¶4060
. . date of acquisition .... ¶4055
. . destroyed or lost, capital cost
   allowance .... ¶4480
. . partly .... ¶4415
. disposition
. . capital cost allowance system .... ¶4400
. . non-arm's length transaction .... ¶3393
. . proceeds .... ¶4388
. distribution, cost amount to trust .... ¶7460
. farming and fishing
. . partly depreciable .... ¶4370
. manufacturing and processing .... ¶8405
. profits on sale of business .... ¶3513
. realization, by trust .... ¶7285
. Valuation Day .... ¶5130

Assignment
. tax refunds .... ¶12,346

Assistance
. capital loss on repayment .... ¶5342
. limit on losses .... ¶5220
. reduction in adjusted cost base .... ¶5185

Associated corporations .... ¶15,490
. anti-avoidance rule .... ¶15,525
. change of control .... ¶15,545
. control, meaning of .... ¶15,500
. options and rights .... ¶15,510
. parent deemed to own shares .... ¶15,505
. person related to himself .... ¶15,515
. shares, fair market value .... ¶15,520
. small business deduction .... ¶8465
. trustee or executor controlling .... ¶15,535
. two or more under same
   control .... ¶15,535

**Association of Universities and Colleges
of Canada**
. tax exemption .... ¶11,500

Association rules
. impact on wills .... ¶17,140

At-risk
. amount

Paragraph

At-risk
. amount — continued
. . limited partnership ....¶7065

Attorney General
. election to prosecute ....¶15,270

Attribution rules ....¶17,038
. anti-avoidance ....¶2665
. business income ....¶17,050
. capital gains and losses ....¶2635
. corporations ....¶2655
. exception re split income ....¶2667
. exemptions ....¶2660
. gifts from non-residents ....¶17,046
. income from property
. . minors ....¶2630
. . spouse ....¶2620
. income on income ....¶17,048
. non-application
. . spouse as employee or partner ......¶2625
. registered disability savings plans
   (RDSPs) ....¶2640
. registered retirement savings plans
   (RRSPs) rules ....¶2640
. salary to spouse or child ....¶17,060
. spousal RRSP ....¶17,058
. tax-free savings accounts (TFSAs) .....¶2640
. trust income ....¶2650; ¶7365

Auctioneers
. GST/HST ....¶16,295

Automobile expenses
. leasing ....¶2320
. partnerships ....¶7045
. passenger vehicles ....¶2320
. professionals' ....¶3567
. salespeople, purchasing
   agents, etc. ....¶2320

Automobiles
. capital cost allowance ....¶4120
. costs, deductible ....¶2320
. employee's personal use of ....¶2085
. interest on acquisition ....¶3291
. shareholder's use, deemed
   payment ....¶14,175
. standby charges ....¶2085

Available-for-use rule
. depreciable assets ....¶4060

Awards
. personal injury ....¶2290

                B

Paragraph

Bad debts
. GST/HST ....¶16,150

Bankruptcy
. change in fiscal period ....¶1015
. disposition of shares ....¶5425
. dividend refund ....¶9033
. tax credits ....¶8227
. tax returns ....¶9003
. . corporations ....¶9006
. . individuals ....¶9009

Banks
. defined ....¶3021
. exemption from tax ....¶13,135;
                         ¶13,155
. ownership certificates, obligation to
   complete ....¶15,200
. receipt of taxes ....¶15,020; ¶15,100

Barter
. source of income ....¶2010

Basic herd
. destruction of livestock ....¶3591

Beneficiaries
. employees profit sharing plans
. . forfeiture deduction ....¶10,312
. . receipts deductible ....¶10,303
. majority interest
. . affiliation to trust ....¶15,482
. preferred
. . definition ....¶7345
. . trust payments as income ....¶7345
. property acquired from trust,
   capital cost ....¶7465
. trusts
. . acquisition of property ....¶7465
. . capital gains flow-through ....¶7390
. . deductions ....¶7375
. . income ....¶7275; ¶7430
. . non taxable dividends flow-
    through ....¶7385
. . principal residence exemption ....¶7397
. . taxable dividends flow-through ....¶7380

Benefits
. conferred at arm's length ....¶15,400
. conferred directly or indirectly ....¶15,308
. employees
. . deemed ....¶3117
. shareholders ....¶3108–3123
. . deemed ....¶3117
. . deemed income ....¶3108
. . deemed on loans and debts ....¶3117
. . loans ....¶3111

Paragraph

Benefits
. shareholders — continued
. . non-monetary .... ¶3126
. . rights to purchase shares .... ¶3129

Benevolent societies
. tax exemption .... ¶11,564

Blocked currency
. income .... ¶12,285

Blood relationship
. defined .... ¶15,405

Board and lodging
. included in income .... ¶2055
. special work site employees .... ¶2120

Boards of trade
. exemption from tax .... ¶11,300

Bonds
. accrual interest, apportionment .... ¶3354
. amortized cost .... ¶3462
. conversion .... ¶2675
. . adjusted cost base .... ¶5435
. discounted .... ¶3210
. . deductibility .... ¶3306; ¶3312
. identical
. . adjusted cost base .... ¶5370
. income .... ¶3210
. . interest accrual rules .... ¶3021
. interest
. . information returns .... ¶12,050
. purchase of by issuer .... ¶5235

Bonus
. "bonus down" .... ¶17,445
. "bonus out" .... ¶17,450
. income of individual .... ¶2040

Books
. library .... ¶3567

Books and records
. auditing .... ¶15,125
. failure to keep liability .... ¶15,265
. indexed security investment
      plans .... ¶15,120
. inspection .... ¶15,275
. lawyer's .... ¶15,120
. liability to keep .... ¶15,120
. retention until permission for
      disposal .... ¶15,120
. seizure .... ¶15,125
. transfer pricing .... ¶15,312
. . penalty .... ¶15,315

Borrowed money
. election to capitalize cost .... ¶3297

Paragraph

Borrowed money — continued
. expense .... ¶3277; ¶3282
. interest
. . deduction .... ¶3277
. . limitation .... ¶3277; ¶3300
. loss of source .... ¶3294
. premiums or expenses .... ¶3282

British Columbia
. de-harmonization .... ¶16,213
. logging tax credit .... ¶8675
. new PST 2013 .... ¶16,393

Brokers
. dividends received by, withholding
      of tax .... ¶12,185

Brothers
. dependants .... ¶15,405

Budget resolutions
. constitutionality .... ¶775

Buildings
. capital cost allowance
. . allocation of proceeds between
      land and building .... ¶4485
. . rate .... ¶4085

Business
. defined for GST .... ¶16,110

Business income
. accounts payable .... ¶17,665
. accounts receivable .... ¶17,670
. accrued, of corporations, etc. .... ¶3051
. advantages of incorporation .... ¶17,662
. amateur athletic trust fund
      payments .... ¶3068
. attribution rules .... ¶17,050
. capital cost allowance .... ¶17,690
. capital losses, limitation .... ¶3393
. deductions .... ¶3162
. . limitations on .... ¶3165
. depreciable assets in inventory .... ¶17,725
. determination of profit .... ¶3010
. forgiven indebtedness .... ¶17,730
. fuel tax rebates .... ¶3067
. home office expenses .... ¶17,685
. illegal business .... ¶3045
. incorporation
. . tax deferral .... ¶17,664
. inventory .... ¶17,675a
. manufacturing and processing .... ¶8405
. meals and entertainment
      expense .... ¶17,680
. proprietor .... ¶3033
. replacement property .... ¶17,720

Paragraph

Business income — continued
. reserves for proceeds not
    received .... ¶17,675
. self-employed individuals .... ¶17,740
. SR&ED incentives .... ¶17,700
. "tax" defined for foreign tax credit ...... ¶8590
. timing of asset acquisitions .... ¶17,676

Business losses
. considerations .... ¶17,810
. flexibility of use .... ¶17,805
. from property or business .... ¶17,801
. investment losses .... ¶17,370

Businesses
. carrying on
. . non-residents .... ¶15,425
. ceasing .... ¶3093
. . consideration for accounts
      receivable .... ¶3504
. . cumulative eligible capital
      deduction .... ¶3519
. . in Canada .... ¶3522
. . information returns .... ¶12,050
. changes in control or type, losses ..... ¶3390
. defined .... ¶3246
. divided .... ¶8640
. investment loss .... ¶5034
. profits
. . liquidation, from .... ¶3513
. sale of, including accounts
      receivable .... ¶3510
. taxation year .... ¶15,392

Buying groups
. GST/HST .... ¶16,330

Buy-sell agreements
. deceased person's property .... ¶2575

C

Canada Disability Savings Bond (CDSB)
. income test .... ¶10,428
. provincial payments .... ¶10,428a
. . carryover .... ¶10,428
. repayment .... ¶10,428

Canada Disability Savings Grant (CDSG)
. income test .... ¶10,428
. provincial payments .... ¶10,428a
. . carryover .... ¶10,428
. repayment .... ¶10,428

Canada Oil Substitution Program
. information returns .... ¶12,050

Canada Pension Plan
. appeal or objection expenses .... ¶2460

Paragraph

Canada Pension Plan — continued
. benefits, inclusion in income .... ¶2150
. foreign professors and teachers
. . part of earned income .... ¶10,372
. income splitting .... ¶17,070
. machine computation of
      deductions .... ¶12,125
. non-resident withholding .... ¶14,160
. overpayments of benefits repaid ....¶2455
. retroactive benefits .... ¶8022
. self-employed persons .... ¶2425
. tax credit for contributions paid .... ¶2425
. transfers to RRSP .... ¶2435; ¶10,357

Canada Savings Bonds
. cash bonus
. . information returns .... ¶12,050
. interest deduction .... ¶3024

Canada–U.K. Tax Convention
. capital gains .... ¶14,540
. dividends .... ¶14,555
. double taxation .... ¶14,570
. employment income .... ¶14,560
. immovable property, income .... ¶14,545
. industrial and commercial
      profits .... ¶14,520
. interest .... ¶14,555
. miscellaneous income .... ¶14,565
. pensions and annuities .... ¶14,550
. prevention, double taxation .... ¶14,515
. royalties .... ¶14,535
. ship or aircraft profits .... ¶14,530
. trust payments to Canadian
      beneficiaries .... ¶7337

Canada–U.S. Tax Convention
. avoidance, double taxation .... ¶14,490
. business profits .... ¶14,385
. charitable organizations .... ¶14,465
. compensation
. . artistes and athletes .... ¶14,440
. . dependent personal services .... ¶14,435
. . personal services .... ¶14,440
. diplomatic agents and consular
      officers .... ¶14,475
. dividends .... ¶14,470
. double taxation, elimination .... ¶14,490
. educational organization .... ¶14,465
. entry into force .... ¶14,505
. gains .... ¶14,450
. government compensation .... ¶14,415
. income from real property .... ¶14,390
. information exchange .... ¶14,500
. interest .... ¶14,470

Paragraph

Canada–U.S. Tax Convention — continued
. literary organizations ....¶14,465
. mutual agreement procedure .... ¶14,485
. non-discrimination rules ....¶14,495
. pensions and annuities .... ¶14,420
. permanent establishment ....¶14,400
. related persons ....¶14,405
. religious organizations ....¶14,465
. remittances, students and
    apprentices ....¶14,455
. residence ....¶14,395
. RRSP contributions and earned
    investment income ....¶14,425
. scientific organizations ....¶14,465
. ships, aircraft and motor
    vehicles ....¶14,410
. trust payments to Canadian
    beneficiaries ....¶7335
. U.S. social security benefits ....¶14,420
. withholding taxes, personal
    services .... ¶14,445

Canadian amateur athletic organizations
. information returns ....¶12,050
. qualifications ....¶3365

**Canadian Charter of Rights and
    Freedoms** ....¶770

Canadian development expenses
. Part IX tax ....¶13,375

Canadian Forces
. tax exemption for high-risk
    missions ....¶2487

Canadian home insulation program
. information returns ....¶12,050

Canadian investment income
. defined ....¶9039
. "designated property" defined ....¶9039

Canadian resource property
. disposition certificate ....¶14,040

**Canadian Wheat Board participation
    certificate**
. interest on tax .... ¶12,280

Canadian-controlled private corporation
. active business income ....¶8440
. defined ....¶8435
. small business deduction ....¶8430
. special reduction ....¶8480; ¶9186;
                                                            ¶9207

Capital
. dividends ....¶6050
. . payable simultaneously ....¶6155

Paragraph

Capital — continued
. expenditures, eligible ....¶3078
. paid-up
. . deficiency ....¶6150
. . defined ....¶6170
. . limit, defined ....¶6150
. . reduction, deemed dividend ....¶6195
. . shares, valuation ....¶6200

Capital contributions
. property
. . adjusted cost base ....¶5180

Capital cost
. depreciable property ....¶4010

Capital cost allowance
. aircraft ....¶2320; ¶4120
. allocation of proceeds between
    land and building ....¶4490
. alphabetical table of rates ....¶4505
. assets
. . acquired during the year ....¶4055–4062
. . election re grouping ....¶4035; ¶4037
. automobiles ....¶2320; ¶4120
. available-for-use rule ....¶4060
. bridges ....¶4014
. buildings ....¶4085
. . allocation of proceeds between
    land and building ....¶4485
. certified productions ....¶4275
. change in proportionate use of
    assets ....¶4420
. classes ....¶4025; ¶4030; ¶4035
. computer hardware and software ......¶4220
. computers software ....¶4282
. concessions ....¶4110
. . election to defer recapture ....¶4115
. . condominiums ....¶4085
. contractor's movable equipment ....¶4124
. data network infrastructure
    equipment ....¶4283
. death of taxpayer ....¶4067
. deductible ....¶3273
. depreciable property
. . deemed dispositions ....¶4430
. . non-arm's length transfers ....¶4425
. . disposition of assets ....¶4400
. electronic office equipment ....¶4283
. energy conservation equipment ....¶4215
. exchanges of property ....¶4460
. excluded property ....¶4340
. farm property transferred to child ......¶4375
. farming and fishing assets ....¶4350
. films ....¶8685

Cap

Paragraph

Capital cost allowance — continued
. franchises ....¶4110
. . election to defer recapture ....¶4115
. general rules ....¶4005
. government assistance ....¶4012
. half-year rule ....¶4062
. industrial mineral mines ....¶4150
. input tax credits ....¶4012
. investment tax credits ....¶4012
. leased property acquired by
　　lessee ....¶4450
. leaseholds ....¶4090
. leases
. . election by lessee ....¶4307
. leasing properties, restrictions ....¶4300
. licences ....¶4110
. . election to defer recapture ....¶4115
. list of bulletins and circulars ....¶4075
. logging assets ....¶4145
. manufacturing and processing
　　equipment ....¶4210
. mines ....¶3534
. mining assets ....¶4172
. misclassified property ....¶4040
. modems ....¶4282
. monitors ....¶4282
. motion picture films ....¶4275
. passenger vehicles ....¶4120
. patents ....¶4110
. pipelines ....¶4127
. pollution control equipment ....¶4190
. power-operated movable
　　machinery ....¶4124
. printers ....¶4282
. property
. . change in use ....¶4410
. . misclassified ....¶4040
. . multi-purpose ....¶4045; ¶4415
. . pre-1972 acquisition ....¶4015
. . received from trust ....¶7465
. . transferred to partnership ....¶7115
. property not eligible for ....¶4340
. railway property ....¶4165
. rates ....¶4025–4035
. . farming and fishing assets ....¶4355
. . tables ....¶4505
. recapture ....¶4385
. rental properties ....¶4290
. replacement property ....¶4460
. roads ....¶4014
. separate classes ....¶4045
. shares
. . adjusted cost base ....¶6095

Paragraph

Capital cost allowance — continued
. specified energy property ....¶4215
. specified leasing properties ....¶4305
. straight-line method
. . farming and fishing assets ....¶4355
. subsidies and inducements ....¶4012
. surface constructions ....¶4014
. systems software ....¶4220; ¶4282
. tax planning ....¶17,690
. taxation year less than 12
　　months ....¶4065
. terminal loss ....¶4475
. timber limits ....¶4135
. timber resource property ....¶4140
. townsite costs ....¶4014
. transfer between classes ....¶4040
. transitional provisions, property
　　held in 1971 ....¶4015
. trucks ....¶4122
. trust property ....¶7375
. undepreciated capital cost ....¶4387
. vessels ....¶4170
. video tapes ....¶4275

Capital equipment
. repairs and maintenance ....¶3174

Capital gains
. adjusted cost base
. . deemed ....¶5175
. . defined ....¶5080
. . negative ....¶7095
. . shares ....¶6095
. adjustments to cost base ....¶5170
. attribution rules ....¶2620; ¶2635
. bonds, purchased by issuer ....¶5235
. calculation of ....¶5145
. Canada–U.K. Tax Agreement ....¶14,540
. Canada–U.S. Tax Agreement ....¶14,450
. Canadian securities ....¶5240
. Canadian security
. . partnership election ....¶7040
. change of residence ....¶5380
. credit unions, allocation ....¶9213
. cultural property ....¶5065
. debts settled after 1971 ....¶3456
. deemed disposition of shares of
　　small business corporation ....¶5347
. deemed on intercorporate
　　dividend ....¶5350
. deferral for small business
　　investments ....¶5026–5029;
　　　　　　　　　　　　　　　　　　¶17,320
. defined ....¶5031
. depreciable property ....¶5060

Cap

	Paragraph
Capital gains — continued	
. distinguished from income	¶5105
. distribution by mutual funds	¶9103; ¶9121
. dividends	
. . mortgage investment corporations	¶9078
. . mutual fund corporations	¶9090
. . non-resident-owned investment corporations	¶9147
. . tax-free	¶17,365
. . electing	¶17,345
. eligible capital property	¶5045
. employee profit sharing plans	¶10,297
. exchanged property	¶5357
. exempt organizations	¶11,598
. farmer, on disposition of land	¶5280
. . child, to	¶2545; ¶2590
. foreign currency fluctuations	¶5230; ¶17,360
. general rules	¶17,305
. gifts	
. . ecologically sensitive land	¶5033
. . publicly traded securities	¶5033
. goodwill disposition	¶3088
. inclusion rate	¶5001; ¶5033
. income splitting tax	¶8085
. investment corporations	¶9057
. . dividends	¶9060
. . refund	¶9063
. life insurance policies	¶10,525
. listed personal property	¶5050; ¶5310; ¶5315
. median rule	¶5135
. minors	¶17,047
. mutual fund	
. . corporation	¶9090–9105
. . trust	¶9120
. non-competition clauses	¶5340
. non-resident owned investment corporation	¶9144
. . dividends	¶9147
. non-residents	¶14,035
. . property disposition	¶7325
. . tax agreements	¶14,125
. . taxable Canadian property	¶5095
. options	¶5415; ¶17,350
. partial disposition of property	¶5150
. partnership interest	
. . adjustment to cost base	¶7100
. . disposition to exempt person	¶7215
. . disposition to non-exempt person	¶7220

	Paragraph
Capital gains — continued	
. personal-use property	¶5055; ¶5305
. principal residence	¶5085; ¶5260; ¶5265;
. . effect of election	¶5014
. . transitional rules	¶5275
. proceeds of disposition	¶5075
. property	
. . transferred to spouse	¶2585
. real estate transactions	¶5110
. . farm land	¶5115
. realizations	¶17,355
. refund	¶9063; ¶9099
. reorganizations	¶5350
. replacement property	¶5357
. reserve	
. . future proceeds	¶5160
. . non-qualifying security gift	¶5162
. reserves	¶17,340
. restrictive covenants	¶5340
. superficial loss	¶5090
. taxable	¶5001; ¶5145
. . included in income	¶5002
. taxable Canadian property, disposition	¶5095
. taxable net	¶5315
. taxable trusts	¶7285
. tax-free dividends	¶17,365
. transitional rules	
. . non-arm's length transfers	¶5195
. trusts	
. . flow-through to beneficiary	¶7390
. valuation day	¶5130
. warranty	¶5340
Capital gains exemption	
. attribution rules	¶2635
. designation by trust	¶7390
. final capital gains election	¶5010
. flow-through entities	¶5011
. mechanism	¶5008
. qualified farm property	¶5021; ¶17,315
. qualified fishing property	¶5021; ¶17,315
. small business corporation shares	¶5022; ¶17,315
. withdrawal	¶5010
Capital losses	
. allowable	¶5001; ¶5145
. allowable business investment	¶5034
. attribution rules	¶2620; ¶2635
. bad debts	¶5425
. bonds, purchased by issuer	¶5235
. business (non-capital)	¶3384

	Paragraph
Capital losses	
. business (non-capital) — continued	
. . limitations	¶3390–3393
. business investment losses	¶17,370
. calculation of	¶5145
. carryover to other years	¶5002
. change of residence	¶5380
. control change in business	¶3381;
	¶3390
. cumulative net investment	
losses	¶17,325
. deduction rate	¶5033
. deemed on repayment of	
assistance	¶5342
. defined	¶5032
. disposition	¶3393
. . transferred to controlled	
corporation	¶6300
. foreign currency fluctuations	¶5230
. income splitting	¶17,056
. limitations	¶3393
. . changes in control or type of	
business	¶3390
. . dispositions to affiliated person	¶5217
. . provincial assistance	¶5220
. listed personal property	¶5315
. loss timing	¶17,330
. net	¶3381; ¶5002
. . year of death	¶3399
. non-residents	¶14,035
. options	¶5415
. partial disposition of property	¶5150
. warranty	¶5340
. winding up	¶17,366
Capital outlays	
. deduction	¶3165
Capital property	
. deceased taxpayer	¶2575
. definition and exceptions	¶5040
. eligible	
. . bad debt	¶5425
. . deceased taxpayer	¶2565
. . deemed dispositions	¶3099
. . "eligible capital property" defined	¶5045
. . partnership election	¶7040
. . replacement property	¶3090
. reduction in cost base	¶5185
. valuation of pre-1972	¶5130
Capital surplus on hand, post-1971	
. dividends	
. . paid	¶6080
. . simultaneous	¶6155

	Paragraph
Capital surplus on hand, post-1971	
. dividends — continued	
. . taxable, defined	¶6025
Capital surplus on hand, pre-1972	
. defined	¶6125
Capital tax	
. capital deduction	¶13,235
. capital of financial institution	¶13,220
. financial institutions	¶13,210
. payments of tax	¶13,240
. returns	¶13,240
. taxable capital employed in	
Canada	¶13,215
Carrybacks	
. losses	
. . assessments	¶12,090
. . effect	¶12,295
Carrying on business in Canada	
. agent, through	¶1045
. defined	¶1040
Carryovers	
. education, textbook and tuition	
credit	¶8124
. investment tax credit	¶8340
. losses	
. . year of death	¶3399
Carve-outs	
. special tax	¶13,600
Cash flow planning	
. GST/HST	¶17,867
Cemetery care trusts	
. exemption from tax	¶11,584
Certificates	
. Canadian resource property	
disposal	¶14,040
. legal representative	¶12,235
. non-resident property disposal	¶14,040
. unpaid taxes	¶15,035
Chambers of commerce	
. exemption from tax	¶11,300
Charitable donations	
. alter ego and joint partner trusts	¶17,170
. Canadian amateur athletic	
organizations	¶3365
. capital gains on qualifying	
securities	¶5033
. Corporations	
. . control acquisition	¶3376
. . order of deduction	¶3375
. deduction by corporations	¶3361

Paragraph

Charitable donations — continued
. eligible recipients .... ¶3362
. flow-through shares .... ¶3361; ¶5033
. gifts of capital property .... ¶3374
. gifts of cultural property .... ¶3369
. gifts of ecologically sensitive land ...... ¶3370
. gifts to Canada or provinces .... ¶3368
. granting of options by
　　corporations .... ¶3372
. meaning of "gift" .... ¶3363
. not deductible .... ¶3364
. receipts .... ¶3367
. registered charities .... ¶3365
. returned gifts .... ¶3373
. tax credit
. . individuals .... ¶8150
. wills .... ¶17,150

Charities
. GST/HST .... ¶16,310
. tax exemption
. . charities' political activities .... ¶11,625;
　　　　　　　　　　　　¶11,633; ¶11,640;
. . foreign charitable organizations
　　as qualified donees .... ¶11,618
. tax-receipting privileges .... ¶13,207

Chattels
. seizure .... ¶15,055

Cheques
. tax payment .... ¶15,020

Child support payments
. retroactive lump sums .... ¶8023

Children
. adoption
. . expenses giving rise to credit .... ¶8148
. arts tax credit .... ¶8114
. child care expenses .... ¶2405
. child fitness tax credit .... ¶8113
. child tax credit .... ¶8095
. defined .... ¶15,405
. farm property transferred to .... ¶2545;
　　　　　　　　　　¶2550; ¶2590; ¶2595
. income splitting
. . capital gains .... ¶8085
. . excluded amounts .... ¶8084
. . liability for tax .... ¶12,246
. . overview .... ¶8081
. . tax computation .... ¶8083
. . tax liability .... ¶8082
. ITC for child care spaces .... ¶8343
. tax benefit .... ¶8237
. transfers to parents on death .... ¶2600

Paragraph

Children — continued
. universal child care benefit
. . retroactive payments .... ¶8022

Class of shares
. presumption .... ¶15,350

Clawback
. eligible dividends .... ¶17,415
. family allowance and old age
　　security benefits .... ¶13,015
. labour-sponsored funds tax
　　credit .... ¶13,655
. . application .... ¶13,657
. . HBP or LLP withdrawals .... ¶13,658
. . refund .... ¶13,665; ¶15,075
. treaty-exempt income .... ¶13,016

Cleric's residence
. deduction .... ¶2330

Collection of taxes
. acquisition of debtor's property .... ¶15,050
. agreements with provinces .... ¶15,190
. debt to Crown .... ¶15,020
. GST/HST
. . imports .... ¶16,185
. restrictions .... ¶15,025
. taxpayer leaving Canada .... ¶15,060

Commercial activity
. GST/HST .... ¶16,110

Commission
. reinsurance, reserves .... ¶3060

Common-law spouses
. alimony and maintenance
　　payments .... ¶2180
. married credit .... ¶8095
. meaning .... ¶8095
. not considered spouses prior
　　to 1993 .... ¶8095
. same tax treatment as married
　　persons .... ¶8095

Communal organizations
. election
. . gifts .... ¶9285
. . taxable income .... ¶9283
. tax treatment .... ¶9282

Compensation
. damaged property
. repair .... ¶3042
. lost income or property .... ¶3039

Computation of income
. accrual method .... ¶2020
. . foreign investment entities .... ¶7395

Paragraph

Computation of income
. accrual method — continued
. . partnerships ....¶1095; ¶7005
. . professional businesses ....¶3552
. cash method ....¶2020
. death of taxpayer ....¶2560
. farmers and fishers cash method .....¶3573
. inadequate considerations ....¶2505
. income defined ....¶2005
. investment corporation, non-
    resident ....¶9138
. life insurance corporations ....¶9237
. limitation on expenses ....¶2495
. mark-to-market method
. . foreign investment entities ....¶7395
. mortgage foreclosures and
    conditional sales
    repossessions ....¶2690
. non-arm's length property transfers,
    price adjustment clause ....¶2530
. partial consideration for disposition
    of property ....¶2500
. partnership ....¶7035
. part-time residents ....¶14,015
. rules ....¶2495
. scientific research and
    experimental development
    corporations ....¶11,576
. security received for debts ....¶2670
. sources of income ....¶2010
. unpaid expenses or remuneration .....¶2680

Computation of tax
. credits
. . logging ....¶8670–8675
. provincial ....¶8630–8660
. rates
. . corporations ....¶8300–8330
. . individuals ....¶8005–8045
. . trusts ....¶8390
. small business deduction ....¶8430

Computation of taxable income
. business losses ....¶3384
. non-residents ....¶14,025–14,080

Computer software
. capital cost allowance ....¶4220; ¶4282

Computers
. capital cost allowance ....¶4220; ¶4282

Concessions
. capital cost allowance ....¶4110
. . election to defer recapture ....¶4115

Conditional sales contract
. repossession of property ....¶2690

Paragraph

Condominiums
. capital cost allowance ....¶4085

Connected corporations
. election by directors ....¶13,150
. special refundable tax on
    dividends ....¶13,150

Constructive residence
. time required ....¶1025

Contracts
. pension plan, under ....¶15,430

Controlled corporations
. change in control
. . date of ....¶15,555
. . deemed ....¶15,545
. control defined ....¶6030; ¶15,540
. . affiliated persons ....¶15,450
. controller defined ....¶15,530
. deduction for inter-company
    dividends ....¶6030
. definition ....¶15,500; ¶15,540
. goodwill transferred to ....¶3096
. special refundable tax on
    dividends ....¶13,150

Convention expenses
. deductibility ....¶3355

Convertible property
. defined ....¶5435
. exchange for capital stock ....¶5435

Co-operatives
. defined ....¶9186
. tax instalment requirement ....¶12,210

Corporate distributions tax
. application ....¶13,060
. exception to Part II.1 tax ....¶13,080
. indirect payments ....¶13,075
. Part II.1 ....¶13,055
. returns ....¶13,090
. share purchase
. . declared but unpaid dividends .....¶13,070
. stock dividends ....¶13,065

Corporations
. additional tax on investment
    income ....¶8323
. affiliated defined ....¶15,455
. . two corporations ....¶15,460
. affiliation to partnerships ....¶15,470
. aircraft, thinly capitalized
. . interest deduction ....¶3258
. amalgamation
. . general ....¶6340

Paragraph

Corporations
. amalgamation — continued
. . obligations issued by
    predecessor .... ¶6360
. amalgamations
. . affiliated persons .... ¶6345
. bankruptcy .... ¶9006
. . change in fiscal period .... ¶1015
. . dividend refund .... ¶9033
. branch assets rolled over to
    mother .... ¶6215
. branch assets to Canadian company
. . joint election .... ¶6225
. branch assets to mother corporation
. . rollover .... ¶6220
. Canadian currency tax reporting
    requirement .... ¶15,565
. capital dividend account .... ¶6120
. change in exempt status
. . deemed disposition .... ¶4430
. charter
. . lapsing, change in fiscal period ...... ¶1015
. connected, defined .... ¶13,150
. deemed disposition of shares on
    going public .... ¶5347
. deemed resident .... ¶1085; ¶6005
. departure tax .... ¶5395
. dividends
. . deductible .... ¶6030
. . distribution .... ¶6075; ¶6080
. . election .... ¶6080; ¶6115
. . eligible .... ¶6052
. . inter-corporate .... ¶6030
. . reduction of paid-up capital .... ¶6195
. . simultaneous .... ¶6155
. . subsidiary to parent
    on liquidation .... ¶6145; ¶6185
. . taxable .... ¶6050
. farm
. . *inter vivos* transfer .... ¶2550
. . transfer to child .... ¶2595
. fiscal period .... ¶1015
. Form T2 and T2S .... ¶8330
. functional currency reporting
. . conversion of tax attributes .... ¶15,580
. . conversion of tax results .... ¶15,575
. . transition .... ¶15,585
. functional currency reporting
    election .... ¶15,570
. housing, exemption for low-cost ...... ¶11,552
. individuals related to, defined .... ¶15,410
. information returns .... ¶13,165
. labour-sponsored venture capital ...... ¶9089

Paragraph

Corporations — continued
. liability for tax .... ¶1085
. loans to non-residents, interest as
    income .... ¶3156
. losses, limitations on .... ¶3393
. low-cost housing, tax exemption ..... ¶11,552
. lower taxes .... ¶17,405
. manufacturing and processing .... ¶8400
. not associated, deemed .... ¶15,530
. owned by public bodies performing
    governmental functions
. . tax exemption .... ¶11,200
. payment of tax
. . new corporation .... ¶12,215
. . regular instalments .... ¶12,210
. . small-CCPCs .... ¶12,211
. permanent establishment, defined ..... ¶8645
. personal-use property .... ¶15,330
. predecessor, option for shares .... ¶6355
. private
. . capital dividend distribution .... ¶6110
. . defined .... ¶6020; ¶9018
. . dividends tax-exempt .... ¶6050
. . excessive elections .... ¶13,100
. . reduction of instalment
    payments .... ¶12,225
. . refundable dividend tax on hand .....¶9036
. provincial tax credit
. . resident .... ¶6005
. public
. . defined .... ¶6010
. rates of tax — *see also* Rates of
    tax .... ¶8300–8330
. related .... ¶15,415
. . specified financial institutions .... ¶15,385
. reorganization, rollover
    provisions .... ¶6310–6315
. research and development
    exemption .... ¶11,575
. residence .... ¶1085; ¶8645
. returns .... ¶12,010
. . mandatory electronic filing .... ¶12,011
. shares
. . deemed dividends .... ¶6190
. . discount .... ¶6205
. . valuation on winding-up .... ¶6200
. small business deduction .... ¶8430
. subsidiary, winding-up .... ¶6375
. surtax .... ¶8320
. tax credit re provincial taxes .... ¶8630
. tax overpayments and underpayment
. . interest offset .... ¶12,267
. tax payable .... ¶8300

Cor

Paragraph

Corporations
. tax payable — continued
. . general reduction ....¶8475; ¶9186;
                                                          ¶9207
. . resource rate reduction ....¶8490
. . special CCPC reduction .....¶8480; ¶9186;
                                                          ¶9207
. tax rates ....¶8310
. tax treatment ....¶930
. taxable income
. . non-resident ....¶6005
. taxation year ....¶15,390
. thinly capitalized, interest
     deduction ....¶3258
. transfer or loan of property
. . attribution rules ....¶2655
. undistributed surplus
. . 1971, dividends ....¶6080
. wills ....¶17,145

Cost of capital
. defined for Canadian
     manufacturing and processing
     business ....¶8405

Cost of property
. adjustments to cost base ....¶5170

Credit unions
. capital gains, allocation ....¶9213
. deductions
. . additional ....¶9207
. . allocations in proportion to
     borrowing ....¶9204
. . reserves ....¶9207
. deemed not private corporation ....¶9198
. defined ....¶9195
. dividends, allocation ....¶9213
. members, income ....¶9210
. share distribution ....¶9209
. tax instalment requirement ....¶12,210

Creditor protection
. alter ego and joint partner trusts .....¶17,169

Credits
. adoption expenses ....¶8148
. age ....¶8100
. bankruptcy year ....¶8227
. Canada employment ....¶8111
. caregiver ....¶8147
. charitable donations
. . individuals ....¶8150
. child tax benefit ....¶8237
. corporations ....¶8300–8320
. deceased taxpayer ....¶8220
. dividend ....¶6052; ¶8280

Paragraph

Credits — continued
. education
. . full-time ....¶8120
. . part-time ....¶8121
. . student loans ....¶8123
. . textbook ....¶8121
. EI, CPP, QPP ....¶8105
. films
. . Canadian content ....¶8685
. . foreign content ....¶8710
. . qualified Canadian labour
      expenditures ....¶8715
. . qualified labour expenditures ....¶8687
. financial institutions
. . capital tax ....¶8380
. first-time home buyers ....¶8117
. foreign ....¶8550
. . business income tax ....¶8565
. . employees, international
      organizations ....¶8575
. . non-business income tax ....¶8555
. . portion of tax not included ....¶8580
. . tax other than income ....¶8585
. . trusts ....¶7405
. general ....¶920
. GST/HST ....¶8270
. home renovation ....¶8115
. indexing ....¶8230
. individuals
. . ordering ....¶8091
. . personal amounts ....¶8095
. . supplemental personal amounts .....¶8095
. investment ....¶8340
. . apprenticeship job creation ....¶8343
. . child care spaces ....¶8343
. . eligible property ....¶8343
. . refundable ....¶8350
. labour-sponsored funds ....¶8290
. . minimum holding period ....¶8294
. logging ....¶8670
. manufacturing and processing ....¶8400
. medical expenses ....¶8125
. . refundable supplement ....¶8260
. mental or physical impairment ....¶8145
. non-resident individuals ....¶8225
. non-residents ....¶14,081
. overseas employment ....¶2380; ¶8250
. pension ....¶8110
. political contributions ....¶8537
. provincial ....¶8630
. . Quebec abatement ....¶8020
. provincial logging tax rates ....¶8675
. provincial tax abatement ....¶8315

Paragraph

Credits — continued
. transfer
. . individuals ....¶8215
. transit passes ....¶8112
. tuition ....¶8119
. volunteer firefighters ....¶8118

Crown
. taxes, debt to ....¶15,020
. withholding provisions,
      applicable to ....¶15,095

Crown corporations
. liability for tax ....¶3639

Cultural property
. defined ....¶5065
. disposition of ....¶13,545
. gifts ....¶8190

Cumulative eligible capital
. amount, deductible ....¶3276
. business ceasing .... ¶3093; ¶3519
. deductions in computing ....¶3087

Cumulative offset account
. administrative provisions ....¶13,377
. Canadian development .... ¶13,375
. Canadian exploration expenses ......¶13,375
. returns .... ¶13,377

Currency fluctuations
. tax loss selling .... ¶17,655

D

Damages
. income ....¶3036
. wrongful dismissal .... ¶2040; ¶2110;
                                                              ¶2160

Death
. benefits
. . inclusion in income ....¶2165
. . payment to surviving spouse ....¶12,170
. capital cost allowance in year of ....¶4067
. duties
. . interest deductible from income ......¶2420
. occurrences as a
      consequence of ....¶15,360
. rollover of RRSP, RRIF, or RPP
      proceeds to RDSP ....¶2447

Death of taxpayer
. taxation upon ....¶2555

Debt forgiveness
. repossession of property ....¶3454
. reserves ....¶3451
. wills ....¶17,135

Paragraph

Debt obligations
. adjusted cost base ....¶5180

Debts
. adjusted cost base ....¶5185
. bad
. . deemed disposition of ....¶5425
. . recovery ....¶3498
. . reserves ....¶3453
. doubtful
. . defined ....¶3459
. . reserves ....¶3459
. foreclosure ....¶3454
. listed value excess, defined ....¶2585
. repossession of property ....¶3454
. security in satisfaction ....¶2670
. settlement
. . post-1971 ....¶3456
. testamentary, defined ....¶2585

Deceased persons
. computation of income ....¶2560
. depreciable and other capital
      property ....¶2575
. eligible capital property ....¶2565
. farm property transferred
      to child .... ¶2590; ¶2595
. . transfer on child's death ....¶2600
. information returns ....¶12,050
. property transferred to spouse or
      trust ....¶2580
. reserves in year of death ....¶2605
. resource properties and land
      inventories ....¶2570
. returns ....¶12,015
. rights or things ....¶2560
. separate return
. . tax credits ....¶8220
. separate returns
. . alternative fiscal period ....¶12,015

Deductions
. aircraft expenses ....¶2320
. alimony ....¶2180
. annuity contracts, payment
      received ....¶3357
. apprentice mechanics' tools ....¶2388
. artists' expenses ....¶2387
. attendant care expenses ....¶2410
. automobile ....¶3567
. automobile expenses ....¶2320
. bad debts ....¶3453
. business ....¶3087
. business income ....¶3162
. Canada Pension Plan contributions

	Paragraph
Deductions	
. Canada Pension Plan contributions — continued	
. . self-employed person	¶2425
. capital cost allowance	¶3273
. capital element, annuity payments	¶2415
. capital outlays	¶3165
. charitable donations, corporations	¶3361
. charitable donations receipts	¶3367
. child care expenses	¶2405
. clearing or levelling land	¶3582
. cleric's residence	¶2330
. contingent accounts	¶3207
. cost of property, capital	¶3567
. cumulative eligible capital	¶3276
. disability supports expenses	¶2410
. employee	
. . home office	¶2390
. . profit sharing plans contributions	¶10,300
. . trusts	¶7305
. employment	
. . expenses	
. . . general restriction	¶2300
. entertainment	¶3567
. estate tax paid	¶2450
. exchange fund contributions, teachers	¶2335
. exploration and development grants	¶3356
. farmers	¶3201
. forfeited amounts	¶2375
. general	¶915
. GST/HST	¶2391
. health insurance premiums	¶3358
. hobby farmer's restricted losses	¶3396
. income exempt under treaty	¶2470
. interest	
. . borrowed money	¶3303
. . death duties	¶2420
. . loss of source	¶3294
. . thin capitalization provisions	¶3258
. inventory adjustment	¶3486
. investment counsel	¶3339
. landscaping costs	¶3336
. lease cancellation payments, arm's length	¶3333
. legal expenses	¶2325
. life insurance corporations	¶9234
. life insurance premiums	¶3282
. limitations	¶2495
. maintenance payments	¶2180

	Paragraph
Deductions — continued	
. malpractice insurance	¶2315
. matchable expenditures	¶3254
. medical supplies, doctor or dentist	¶3567
. membership dues	¶2315
. metric conversion costs	¶3204
. mortgage sale, losses	¶3353
. moving expenses	¶2400
. musical instruments	¶2385
. net capital loss	¶3381
. non-capital loss	¶3384
. non-residents	¶14,080
. Northern area residents	¶2480
. Northern residents	¶2485
. obligations, discounted	¶3312
. order of	¶3411
. organizational expenses	¶3192
. over-accrued income	¶3051
. overpayments of benefits repaid	¶2455
. Part XII.6 tax	¶3350
. part-time residents	¶14,015
. payments or leased property	¶3330
. pension plans	
. . employer contribution	¶3321
. . employer's contribution	¶3567
. personal service business, limitation	¶3240
. post-death RRSP/RRIF losses	¶2430
. property, capital cost	¶3567
. provincial mining taxes	¶3546
. Quebec Parental Insurance Plan contributions	
. . self-employed person	¶2427
. Quebec Pension Plan contributions	
. . self-employed person	¶2425
. railway employees	¶2340
. registered pension plan contributions	¶2360; ¶3321
. registered retirement savings plan premiums	¶2430; ¶10,350
. . deduction limit	¶10,353
. . dollar limit	¶10,351
. . pension adjustment	¶10,352
. . pension adjustment, net past service	¶10,355
. . pension adjustment reversal	¶10,356
. . total pension adjustment reversal	¶10,354
. . unused deduction room	¶10,356
. repayment for undelivered goods	¶3438
. repayment of loans with borrowed money	¶3285

Ded

Paragraph

Deductions — continued
. retirement compensation
   arrangement contributions .... ¶3231
. salary deferrals .... ¶3228
. salary reimbursement .... ¶2370
. salesperson's expenses .... ¶2305
. scientific research, income
   inclusion .... ¶3066
. share transfer fees .... ¶3315
. SIFT trusts .... ¶7307
. sinking funds .... ¶3207
. site investigation cost .... ¶3351
. social assistance payments .... ¶2470
. succession duties .... ¶2450
. technological advancement
   repayments .... ¶3612
. tile drainage .... ¶3582
. top up disability payment .... ¶2373
. tradespersons' tools .... ¶2389
. transfers
. . registered pension plans .... ¶2445
. . registered retirement income
      funds .... ¶2445
. . registered retirement savings
      plans .... ¶2445
. . retiring allowance .... ¶2440
. . superannuation benefits .... ¶2435
. transport employees .... ¶2350
. travelling expenses .... ¶2310
. truck drivers meals .... ¶2353;
. trusts .... ¶7295
. . capital interest greater than
      income .... ¶7300
. . non-resident trusts .... ¶7315
. utility service connection costs .... ¶3345
. workers' compensation .... ¶2470

Deemed residence in the U.S.
. substantial presence test .... ¶17,593

Deferred profit sharing plans (DPSPs)
. acceptance of plan as deferred ...... ¶10,438
. acquisition of non-publicly-traded
   shares .... ¶13,525
. administration of Part X.1 tax .... ¶13,472
. amounts received .... ¶10,453
. benefits
. . included in income .... ¶2195
. contribution limits .... ¶10,441
. deductibility of employer
   contributions .... ¶10,447
. disposition of property to
. . limitation on losses .... ¶3393
. employee's contributions .... ¶2360
. employer contributions .... ¶3222

Paragraph

Deferred profit sharing plans (DPSPs) —
   continued
. excess contributions tax .... ¶13,455;
                                              ¶13,470
. . waiver .... ¶13,471
. inadequate consideration on
   purchase or sale .... ¶13,430
. inadequate consideration on trust
   transaction .... ¶10,465
. interest .... ¶13,445
. loss on transfer to .... ¶5210
. non-qualified investments
. . tax .... ¶13,525
. non-qualified investments,
   defined .... ¶13,405
. . tax .... ¶13,400
. Part X returns .... ¶13,440
. Part X tax .... ¶13,440
. principal features .... ¶10,432
. property appropriated by
   employer .... ¶10,456
. qualified investments, defined .... ¶13,405
. registration conditions .... ¶10,435
. revocation of registration .... ¶10,459
. revoked .... ¶10,462
. . taxation .... ¶13,395–13,445
. taxability of trust .... ¶10,444
. . assessment .... ¶13,445
. . taxation .... ¶13,395–13,445
. transfer to deduction from income
. . registered retirement
      savings plan .... ¶2435
. transferred .... ¶2435
. transfers out of .... ¶10,468

Definitions
. accumulating income .... ¶7345
. active business .... ¶8440
. adjusted cost base .... ¶5080
. . life insurance policies .... ¶10,519
. allowable capital loss .... ¶5033
. amalgamation .... ¶6325
. amount .... ¶2255
. amounts receivable .... ¶3555
. arm's length transaction .... ¶15,400
. at-risk amount
. . limited partnership .... ¶7065
. blood relationships .... ¶15,405
. bonus interest payment .... ¶9204
. buildings .... ¶4085
. business income tax .... ¶8590
. business investment loss .... ¶5034
. Canadian cultural property .... ¶5065
. Canadian investment income .... ¶9039

Def

	Paragraph			**Paragraph**

Definitions — continued

. Canadian partnership ....¶7240
. Canadian-controlled private
   corporation ....¶8435
. capital cost ....¶4010
. capital dividend account ....¶6120
. capital gain ....¶5031
. capital loss ....¶5032
. capital property ....¶5040
. carrying on business ....¶1040
. certified feature films ....¶4275
. certified productions ....¶4275
. child ....¶15,405
. class of shares ....¶15,350
. common-law partner ....¶2255
. connection by marriage ....¶15,405
. contributor ....¶15,483
. controller ....¶15,530
. co-operative corporations ....¶9186
. cost amount
. . trust capital interest ....¶7460
. cost of capital (manufacturing and
   processing) ....¶8405
. cost of labour (manufacturing and
   processing) ....¶8405
. credit union ....¶9195
. deposit insurance corporation ....¶9219
. depreciable property ....¶4005; ¶5060
. designated gift ....¶11,630
. designated person ....¶2650; ¶2655
. designated property ....¶9039
. disposition of property, capital
   gains and losses ....¶5070
. eligible amount ....¶10,395
. eligible capital property ....¶5045
. eligible dividend ....¶6052
. eligible funeral arrangement ....¶10,535
. employed ....¶1040
. employment ....¶2040
. exempt interest ....¶7075
. farming ....¶3576
. first instalment base ....¶12,210
. fiscal period ....¶1015; ¶15,390
. foreign investment income ....¶9039
. gift ....¶8175
. grandparent ....¶15,405
. gross cost, manufacturing and
   processing ....¶8405
. in Canada ....¶1060
. income ....¶2005
. . earned in a province ....¶8035; ¶8635
. income interest in trust ....¶7445
. individual ....¶1010

Definitions — continued

. insurance corporations ....¶9225
. interest in real property ....¶15,335
. inventory ....¶3477
. land ....¶3246
. life insurance corporation ....¶9228
. limited partner ....¶7070
. listed personal property ....¶5050
. majority interest beneficiary ....¶15,482
. majority interest group of
   beneficiaries ....¶15,483
. majority interest partner ....¶15,465
. majority-interest group of
   partners ....¶15,465
. negative amounts ....¶15,440
. non-business income tax ....¶8605
. non-qualifying
. . debt ....¶2585
. . investments ....¶13,405
. non-qualifying security ....¶5162
. non-resident investment fund ....¶14,037
. non-resident pension fund ....¶14,037
. non-resident-owned investment
   corporation ....¶9135
. office ....¶2040
. other remuneration ....¶2040
. parent ....¶15,405
. passenger vehicles ....¶3291
. payment ....¶9165
. permanent establishment ....¶8645
. person ....¶1010
. personal services business ....¶8450
. personal-use property ....¶5055
. preferred beneficiary ....¶7345
. principal residence ....¶5085; ¶5265
. private corporations ....¶9018
. proceeds of disposition ....¶4388; ¶5075;
                                                          ¶5357
. . life insurance policies ....¶10,519
. property ....¶5035
. public corporation ....¶6010
. qualified investment ....¶10,378; ¶13,405
. . TFSA ....¶13,515
. qualifying home ....¶10,395
. refundable capital gains tax
   on hand ....¶9120
. refundable dividend tax on hand ......¶9027
. registered education
   savings plan ....¶10,399
. registered retirement
   income fund ....¶10,414
. registered supplemental
   unemployment benefit plan ....¶10,325

Def

Paragraph

Definitions — continued
. related group ....¶15,420
. reportable transaction ....¶15,253
. residence ....¶1020
. salary ....¶2040
. scientific research and
  experimental development ....¶3618
. second instalment base ....¶12,210
. settlor ....¶7345
. shared-custody parent ....¶8237; ¶8270
. shareholder ....¶3114
. SIFT partnership ....¶13,385
. specified investment business ....¶8445
. specified partnership income
  and loss ....¶8460
. specified shareholder ....¶2655
. spouse ....¶15,405
. superficial loss ....¶5090
. tax payable ....¶15,325
. taxable
. . Canadian property ....¶5095; ¶9011
. . dividend ....¶10,306
. . obligation ....¶15,290
. taxable Canadian property ....¶14,035
. taxable capital gain ....¶5033
. taxation year ....¶1015; ¶15,390
. . of individual ....¶4390
. taxed capital gains ....¶9057
. taxpayer ....¶1010
. testamentary debts ....¶2585
. testamentary trusts ....¶7415
. TV commercial message ....¶4280
. undepreciated capital cost ....¶4387
. wages ....¶2040

De-harmonization
. British Columbia ....¶16,213

Departure from Canada
. checklist ....¶17,570
. deemed disposition on ....¶17,565

Departure tax
. change of residence ....¶5380
. corporation ....¶5395
. exceptions ....¶5385
. instalment payments ....¶12,240
. post-departure loss carryback ....¶5393
. trusts ceasing to be resident in
  Canada ....¶5400

Dependants
. brothers ....¶15,405
. tax credits ....¶8095

Depletion allowance
. deduction ....¶3543

Paragraph

Depletion allowance — continued
. earned depletion base ....¶3543
. trusts ....¶7375

Deposit insurance corporation
. computation of income ....¶9219
. defined ....¶9219
. tax liability ....¶9219

Depreciable property
. capital cost ....¶4010
. capital cost allowance
  rates ....¶4025–4035; ¶4505
. date of acquisition ....¶4055
. deceased taxpayer ....¶2575
. deemed disposition ....¶4430
. definition ....¶4005; ¶5060
. non-arm's-length transfers ....¶4425
. recapture provisions ....¶4385
. separate classes ....¶4045
. terminal loss ....¶4475
. transferred and misclassified ....¶4040
. undepreciated capital cost ....¶4387

Depreciation
. vessels, election by partnership ....¶7040

Designated beneficiary
. Part XII.2 taxes ....¶13,620

Designated income
. application of Part XII.2 ....¶13,615
. taxation of ....¶13,610

Designated persons
. filing returns ....¶12,030

Direct sellers
. GST/HST ....¶16,320

Directors
. fees
. . inclusion in income ....¶2075
. liability
. . offence ....¶15,280
. . withholding taxes ....¶15,085
. signing officers, authorization ....¶15,215

Disability
: building modifications in respect of
. . deductibility ....¶3349
. insurance plan
. . benefits, employee's income ....¶2095
. tax credit ....¶8145

Disability payments, top ups
. deductible ....¶2373

Discounts
. bonds
. . payments ....¶3210

Paragraph

Discounts — continued
. obligations issued
. . adjusted cost base .... ¶5180

Dispositions
. allocation of proceeds between
    land and building .... ¶4490
. assets .... ¶5345
. deemed proceeds .... ¶2535
. involuntary .... ¶5357
. land and building
. . reallocation of proceeds .... ¶5358
. life estates and remainder
    interests .... ¶5353
. of capital property
. . defined .... ¶5070
. of part of property .... ¶5150
. of pre-1972 assets .... ¶5135
. partnership interest .... ¶7160
. proceeds of
. . defined .... ¶5075
. shares
. . on corporation going public .... ¶5347

Dispositions of property
. adjustments to cost base .... ¶5170
. capital gains .... ¶5070
. certificates .... ¶14,040
. deemed .... ¶5070
. . emigration .... ¶9012a
. . immigration .... ¶9011
. . non-resident trust beneficiaries .... ¶7485
. deemed of trust .... ¶7290
. depreciable property by trust .... ¶7480
. exclusions .... ¶5070
. farm land .... ¶5280
. involuntary .... ¶3042; ¶5357
. land inventory by trust .... ¶7480
. limitations on losses .... ¶3393
. non-resident's .... ¶14,120
. option granted .... ¶5415
. part consideration .... ¶2500
. partial .... ¶5150
. partnership interest .... ¶7075; ¶7160
. principal residence .... ¶5260
. proceeds .... ¶4388
. "proceeds of disposition" defined .... ¶5075
. resource property by trust .... ¶7480
. superficial loss .... ¶5090
. taxpayer's gain or loss .... ¶5145
. terminal loss denied to affiliated
    persons .... ¶4495

Paragraph

Dispositions of property — continued
. uncollectible portion of proceeds .... ¶3352

Distribution of assets
. partnership ceasing .... ¶7150; ¶7200
. shareholders deemed to have
    received dividend .... ¶6160; ¶6185
. trust .... ¶7460;   ¶7465; ¶7475;
                                    ¶7477; ¶7480
. . accrued loss .... ¶7487
. . cost amount of property to
    beneficiary .... ¶7460
. . deemed realization at fair market
    value .... ¶7480
. . non-residents .... ¶7485
. . non-residents, after
    October 1, 1996 .... ¶7485

Distribution strategies
. small business deduction
    available .... ¶17,430
. small business deduction not
    available .... ¶17,445

Dividend tax credits
. individuals .... ¶8280
. large corporations .... ¶6050
. two rates .... ¶6052

Dividends
. brokers receiving, withholding
    of tax .... ¶12,185
. *Canada–U.K. Tax Convention* .... ¶14,555
. *Canada–U.S. Tax Convention* .... ¶14,470
. capital
. . account defined .... ¶6120
. . election procedure .... ¶6115
. . excessive election .... ¶13,110; ¶13,115;
                                        ¶13,120
. . private corporation .... ¶6050; ¶6110
. classification .... ¶6050
. corporate distributions tax .... ¶13,070
. corporate surplus, distribution
    out of .... ¶6075
. . more than one class, payable
    simultaneously .... ¶6155
. corporations
. . deemed, defined .... ¶6150
. . deemed, distribution .... ¶6145
. . inter-corporate deduction .... ¶6030;
                                            ¶6055
. credit unions, allocation .... ¶9213
. deductions from adjusted
    cost base .... ¶5185
. deemed
. . adjusted cost base .... ¶5180

Paragraph

Dividends
. deemed — continued
. . after December 31, 1978 ....¶6385
. . defined ....¶6150
. . net proceeds of distribution ....¶6160
. . provisions not applicable ....¶6205
. . received ....¶6055
. . reduction in paid-up capital ....¶6195
. . SIFT partnership ....¶7026
. . SIFT trust ....¶7357
. . winding-up by resident
    corporation ....¶6185
. eligible
. . gross-up ....¶8280
. . introduction ....¶17,405
. . planning ....¶17,415
. . tax credit ....¶8280
. . tax on excessive elections ....¶13,127
. employee profit sharing plans ....¶10,306
. gross-up ....¶6052; ¶8280
. income ....¶3015
. inter-company, deductibility ....¶3405;
                                          ¶6030¶6055
. life insurance policies ....¶10,525
. mortgage investment corporation,
    deductibility ....¶9075
. private corporation's portfolio,
    special tax ....¶9024
. refund of tax ....¶9027
. . bankrupt corporations ....¶9033
. remuneration ....¶17,435
. short-term preferred shares ....¶6040
. spouse, election ....¶6060
. stock, computation of future gains
    and losses ....¶6165
. surplus, out of, distribution .....¶6075; ¶6080
. tax credit ....¶6052; ¶8280
. taxable ....¶6050
. . corporation deduction ....¶6030
. . defined ....¶6025
. . private corporation
    receiving ....¶13,135–13,165
. . subject corporation receiving ....¶13,140
. taxes on ....¶13,175; ¶13,180; ¶13,250
. tax-exempt
. . adjusted cost base ....¶6095
. . paid out of capital surplus ....¶6050
. term preferred shares ....¶6035
. trusts
. . flow-through of non-taxable
    dividends ....¶7385
. . flow-through to beneficiary ....¶7380

Paragraph

Dividends — continued
. withholding tax, non-residents ....¶14,172

Documents
. copies of, evidence ....¶15,145
. proof ....¶15,300
. solicitor-client privilege ..... ¶15,175; ¶15,180

Domicile
. differentiated from residence ....¶1020

Donations
. individuals ....¶8150
. medicines to developing world ....¶3374

Drop shipments
. GST/HST ....¶16,315

Dues
. club, or expenses ....¶3225

E

Earned income
. defined ....¶10,372
. trust beneficiary ....¶7275

Ecological property
. disposition of ....¶13,545
. gifts ....¶8193

E-commerce transactions
. GST/HST planning ....¶17,887

Education
. allowances received ....¶2070
. savings plans
. . tax-exempt payments ....¶2030

Education credit
. carryforward ....¶8124
. entitlement
. . full-time ....¶8120
. . part-time ....¶8121

Election expenses
. tax credit for contributions ....¶8537

Elections
. accounts receivable ....¶3501
. borrowed money ....¶3297
. Canadian partnerships ....¶7240
. capital cost allowance
. . concessions ....¶4115
. . franchises ....¶4115
. . licences ....¶4115
. capital gains ....¶5010; ¶17,345
. . deadline ....¶5015
. . effect on principal residence
    exemption ....¶5014
. capital gains dividends

Paragraph

Elections
. capital gains dividends — continued
. . mortgage investment
corporations ....¶9078
. . mutual fund corporations ....¶9093
. . non-resident-owned investment
corporations ....¶9147
. classification of depreciable
assets ....¶4037
. communal organization
. . gifts ....¶9285
. . taxable income ....¶9283
. deferred-income plan trusts
. . look-through rule re qualified
investments ....¶15,340
. dividends received by spouse ....¶6060
. employee stock option of
deceased taxpayer ....¶12,366
. excessive
. . capital gains dividends ....¶13,122
. . eligible dividends ....¶13,127
. . penalty tax ....¶6080
. . private corporations ....¶13,100
. farm property transferred to child ......¶4375
. functional currency reporting ....¶15,570
. . conversion of tax attributes ....¶15,580
. . conversion of tax results ....¶15,575
. . transition ....¶15,585
. GST/HST
. . business transfer ....¶16,165
. . exempt supplies ....¶16,160
. . nil consideration ....¶16,155
. income computation, partnership
member ....¶7040
. late, amended or revoked ....¶15,008
. Part III tax, election to avoid ....¶13,120
. partners
. . effect ....¶7137
. partners', on rollover ....¶7120
. . example ....¶7137
. payments for others ....¶12,240
. professionals, re work in progress .....¶3558
. refundable dividend tax
on hand ....¶13,150
. rollovers to corporation ....¶6225
. termination of partnership ....¶7155
. unwind deemed disposition on
emigration ....¶9012b

Electronic Filing
. GST/HST Returns ....¶16,370

Electronic office equipment
. capital cost allowance ....¶4283

Paragraph

Eligible dividends
. introduction ....¶17,405
. planning ....¶17,415
. planning points ....¶17,405
. tax rates ....¶17,405

Eligible funeral arrangement
. accrual of income ....¶10,535
. contribution limit ....¶10,535
. definition ....¶10,535
. income inclusion ....¶2168
. return of funds ....¶10,540

Emigration
. corporations ....¶5395
. departure tax ....¶5380
. returning former residents ....¶9012b
. tax effects ....¶9012a
. trusts ....¶5400

Employee benefit plans
. allocations ....¶10,501
. deferred employment
compensation ....¶10,501
. defined ....¶10,501; ¶10,504
. employer contributions ....¶3237; ¶10,501;
¶10,504
. interest accrual rules ....¶3021
. property distributed by ....¶7490
. taxable benefit
to employee ....¶10,501; ¶10,504
. trust exempt from tax ....¶10,501

Employee Life and Health Trust (ELHT)
. employee benefits ....¶10,323
. employee contributions ....¶10,321
. employer contributions ....¶10,320
. employer contributions deduction ......¶3321
. history ....¶10,318
. non-resident withholding tax ....¶14,171
. qualification ....¶10,319
. taxation of trust ....¶10,322

Employee trusts
. deductions ....¶7305
. defined ....¶10,501
. employer contributions ....¶10,501
. exemption from tax ....¶10,501
. property distributed by ....¶7490
. taxable benefit ....¶10,501

Employees
. allowances and
reimbursements ....¶16,275
. automobile and aircraft expenses .....¶2320
. benefit, deemed on loans and
debts .... ¶3117

Paragraph

Employees — continued
. benefits under government
　assistance programs ....¶2175
. Canada employment tax credit ....¶8111
. GST on benefits ....¶16,300
. independent contractors v. ....¶2050;
　　　　　　　　　　　　　　　　¶8450
. international organizations ....¶8575
. loans, low or interest free ....¶2130
. overseas employment,
　tax relief ....¶2380; ¶8250
. payments from employers ....¶2110
. registered pension plan
　contributions ....¶10,489
. returns, filing ....¶12,150
. returns re withholding tax ....¶15,070
. salary deferral arrangements ....¶2105
. salary reimbursement ....¶2370
. special work site ....¶2120
. spouse ....¶2625
. stock options ....¶2135; ¶12,366
. . exchange of shares ....¶2140
. . reduction in adjusted cost base ......¶5185
. temporarily outside Canada ....¶1055
. travelling expenses and meals ....¶2310

Employees' profit sharing plans
. acceptance as deferred plan ....¶10,438
. allocations ....¶2080; ¶10,297
. beneficiary's receipts,
　deductions ....¶10,303
. contributions, deductible ....¶10,300
. dividends ....¶10,306
. employer contributions ....¶3222
. foreign tax deduction ....¶10,309
. forfeiture deduction ....¶10,312
. loss on transfer to ....¶5210
. Part XI.4 tax on excessive employer
　contributions ....¶13,577
. payments
. . profits, out of ....¶10,315
. requirements ....¶10,291
. taxation year ....¶10,316
. trust not subject to tax ....¶10,294

Employers
. contributions
. . employee life and health trust ....¶3322
. . employee life and health trusts ....¶3222
. . group sickness and accident
　　insurance plans ....¶2100
. . pension plans ....¶3321
. . profit sharing plans ....¶3222
. . registered pension plans ....¶3222;
　　　　　　　　　　　　　　　　¶3321

Paragraph

Employers
. contributions — continued
. . supplemental unemployment
　　benefit plans ....¶3222
. convention expenses ....¶3355
. liability
. . failure to withhold tax ....¶15,265
. . unpaid taxes of employees ....¶15,040
. payments to employees ....¶2110
. registered pension plan
　contributions ....¶10,486
. union
. . deemed single employer ....¶15,423

Employment
. employed defined ....¶1040
. employment defined ....¶2040
. expenses
. . apprentice mechanics' tools ....¶2388
. . deduction limit ....¶2300
. . home office ....¶2390
. . tradespersons' tools ....¶2389
. fringe benefits
. . administrative exclusion from
　　income ....¶2057
. . income inclusion ....¶2055
. income ....¶2040; ¶2050
. . court decisions ....¶2140
. outside Canada ....¶1020
. overseas, tax relief ....¶2380
. tax credit ....¶8111

Employment benefits
. aircraft used by employee ....¶2090
. automobile provided by employer .....¶2085
. board and lodging ....¶2055
. excluded from income ....¶2040
. health and welfare trusts ....¶2065
. housing cost/housing loss ....¶2060
. included in income ....¶2040
. income maintenance payments ....¶2095
. loans, low interest ....¶2130
. operating expenses of
　automobile ....¶2055
. personal or living expenses ....¶2070
. stock option plans ....¶2135
. . exchange of shares ....¶2140

Employment insurance
. appeal or objection expenses ....¶2460
. benefits included in income ....¶2170
. legal costs re objection or appeal .....¶2205
. premium deductions, machine
　computation ....¶12,125
. tax credit for premiums paid ....¶2355

Emp

Paragraph

Energy
. conservation equipment
. . capital cost allowance .... ¶4215
. conversion grants
. . included in income .... ¶2220; ¶3063
. savings programs
. . information returns .... ¶12,050

Entering Canada
. checklist .... ¶17,585

Entertainers and musicians
. deductibility of expenses .... ¶3171

Entertainment expenses
. limitation .... ¶3219; ¶3567; ¶7045

Estates and trusts
. administration tax .... ¶17,165
. capital interest
. . disposition .... ¶7455
. information returns .... ¶12,050
. joint tenancy .... ¶17,170
. legal representatives .... ¶7265
. liability for tax .... ¶1100
. realization date, deemed .... ¶7290
. residence .... ¶1100
. returns .... ¶12,020
. splits .... ¶17,120
. splitting .... ¶17,170
. spouse .... ¶7480
. tax
. . deductible from income .... ¶2450
. taxation year .... ¶1015
. . change in fiscal period .... ¶1015

Estimates
. tax .... ¶12,055

**Excise tax on insurance
  premiums** .... ¶16,425

Exempt corporations
. Part IV tax .... ¶13,160

Exempt supplies
. GST/HST .... ¶16,180

Exemptions
. agricultural organizations .... ¶11,300
. amounts not included in income .... ¶2030
. apportionment rule .... ¶11,603
. banks .... ¶13,135; ¶13,160
. benevolent societies .... ¶11,564
. Canadian Forces/Police on high-
    risk missions .... ¶2487
. cemetery care trust .... ¶11,584
. change of status .... ¶11,609
. charities' political activities .... ¶11,583

Paragraph

Exemptions
. charities' political activities .... ¶11,583
. corporations owned by public
    bodies performing governmental
    functions .... ¶11,200; ¶11,633; ¶11,640
. foreign charitable organizations as
    qualified donees .... ¶11,618
. foreign government officers and
    servants .... ¶11,000
. general .... ¶920
. government grants .... ¶3645
. Governor General's salary .... ¶2030
. housing corporations .... ¶11,567
. insurers, farmers and fishers .... ¶11,570
. interest payments to non-residents
. . certificate .... ¶14,115
. interest payments to non-residents
    (after 2007) .... ¶14,110
. interest payments to non-residents
    (before 2008) .... ¶14,111
. investment corporations .... ¶13,135;
                                                          ¶13,160
. labour organizations .... ¶11,564
. low-cost housing corporations .... ¶11,552
. municipal authorities .... ¶11,100
. municipal corporations .... ¶11,200
. mutual insurance corporations .... ¶11,566
. non-profit clubs .... ¶11,600
. non-profit corporations, scientific
    research and experimental
    development .... ¶11,575
. non-profit organizations .... ¶11,565
. overseas employment, partial .... ¶2380
. pension corporations .... ¶11,568
. principal residence, gains on sale ..... ¶5260
. provincial corporations .... ¶11,200
. registered charity .... ¶11,400
. scholarships and bursaries .... ¶2210
. scientific research and
    experimental development
    corporations .... ¶11,575
. small business corporations .... ¶11,569
. trust companies .... ¶13,135
. trusts
. . master .... ¶11,582
. . qualifying environmental trusts ...... ¶11,590
. . social environmental .... ¶11,595
. . vacation-with-pay trust .... ¶11,589
. universities .... ¶11,500

Expense allowances
. inclusion in income .... ¶2070

Expenses
. advertising

Paragraph

Expenses
. advertising — continued
. . non-Canadian publications ....¶3264
. aircraft, costs end interest ....¶2320
. appeals, assessments .... ¶2460
. artists' ....¶2387
. attendant care ....¶2410
. automobiles ....¶2320
. borrowing money ....¶3306
. . insurance premiums ....¶3282
. building modifications
. . disability related ....¶3349
. child care ....¶2405
. club dues ....¶3225
. conventions ....¶3355; ¶3567
. disability supports ....¶2410
. earning exempt income ....¶3195
. election contributions ....¶8537
. entertainers and musicians
. . deductibility ....¶3171
. entertainment ....¶3219
. exploring or developing resource
    properties ....¶7060
. exploring or developing resource
    property ....¶3534
. fines ....¶3180
. food and beverages ....¶3219
. forestry workers ....¶2345
. GST/HST ....¶2391
. home office ....¶2390; ¶3183
. illegal payments ....¶3184
. interest ....¶3291
. lawyer's disbursements ....¶3561
. lease of automobile ....¶2320
. legal costs ....¶3186; ¶3567
. limitations on deductibility ....¶2495
. losses
. . fire ....¶3189
. . theft ....¶3189
. metric conversion costs ....¶3204
. money, borrowing ....¶3306
. moving ....¶2400
. musical instruments ....¶2385
. objections ....¶2460
. organizational ....¶3192
. penalties ....¶3180
. power saws ....¶2345
. prepaid ....¶3252
. professional individuals ....¶3567
. prospectors ....¶3597
. recreational facilities ....¶3225
. repairs and maintenance ....¶3174

Paragraph

Expenses — continued
. representation costs ....¶3342
. . partnership, election to defer ....¶7040
. scientific research ....¶3609
. . incurred in Canada ....¶3603
. . outside Canada ....¶3606
. shares
. . issuing ....¶3306
. . transfer fees ....¶3315
. unpaid, non-arm's length ....¶2680
. unpaid salaries, cost of collecting .....¶2325
. upkeep, trust property ....¶7435

Exploration
. expenses
. . flow-through shares ....¶3540
. . mineral deposits ....¶3537
. . oil or gas ....¶3537
. grants, deduction ....¶3356

Exploration and development expenses
. adjusted cost base ....¶5185

Expropriation
. assets, adjusted cost base .... ¶5180;
                                                        ¶5185
. capital gain and recapture
    deferment ....¶5357
. replacement property ....¶5357

F

Family allowances
. clawbacks ....¶13,015
. information returns ....¶12,050
. overpayment ....¶2455
. returns ....¶13,020

Family income
. child tax benefit ....¶8237

Family trusts
. year-end strategies ....¶17,644b

Farmers and farming
. bequests of farm properties ....¶17,100
. farming defined ....¶3576
. real estate transactions ....¶5115
. restricted loss ....¶3579

Farmers and fishers
. capital gains exemption ..... ¶5021; ¶17,315
. computation of income ....¶3573
. depreciable assets with more than
    one use ....¶4370
. depreciable property
. . capital cost allowance .... ¶4355; ¶4360
. farm losses ....¶13,155
. farming defined ....¶3576

Far

Paragraph

Farmers and fishers — continued
. feeding operations ....¶3588
. fiscal period ....¶4365
. insurer's tax exemption ....¶11,570
. land
.. clearing or levelling ....¶3582
.. disposition, where principal
    residence included ....¶5280
. manufacturing and farming ....¶8400
. partnership engaged in ....¶7045
.. sale of basic herd, election in
    computing income ....¶7040
. payment of tax ....¶12,190
. restricted farm loss ....¶3579
. re-transfer on death of child ....¶2600
. transfer of farm property to child
.. capital cost allowance ....¶4375
. transfer of property, farmer to
    child ....¶2545; ¶2550; ¶2590; ¶2595

Federal Court of Canada
. appeals ....¶12,430
.. disposition ....¶12,440
.. special jurisdiction ....¶12,435
. jurisdiction ....¶12,420
. powers re penalties ....¶15,285

Federal Government of Germany
. compensation, tax exempt ....¶2030

Feedlot operations
. defined ....¶3588

Fees
. consultants ....¶3567
. inclusion in income ....¶2075
. investment counsel ....¶3339
. professional associations ....¶3567
. share transfer ....¶3315
. tuition ....¶3567

Filing
. GST/HST ....¶16,365

Filing of documents
. waiver ....¶15,006

Film productions
. limited partnerships
.. negative adjusted cost base ....¶7097

Films
. CCA terminated ....¶8685
. motion picture ....¶4275
. returns ....¶12,050
. tax credit
.. Canadian content ....¶8685
.. foreign content ....¶8710
.. qualified labour expenditures ....¶8687

Paragraph

Films — continued
. tax shelter eliminated ....¶8705

Financial corporations
. accrued interest ....¶3021

Financial counselling
. fees paid by employer ....¶2055

Financial institutions
. capital tax ....¶13,210; ¶13,225
.. deduction ....¶13,217
. GST/HST ....¶16,305
.. deemed financial institution ....¶17,890
. input tax credits ....¶16,225
. investment in related institution ....¶13,230
. mark-to-market property ....¶9277
. Selected Listed Financial
    Institution/HST ....¶16,205
. specified
.. related corporations ....¶15,385
. specified debt obligations ....¶9277
. tax credit
.. capital tax ....¶8380

First Nations People
. First Nations Taxes ....¶16,397
. Indian Bands & GST/HST ....¶16,165

First-time home buyers' tax credit
. eligibility ....¶8115

Fiscal period
. businesses ....¶15,392
. calendar year-end requirement ....¶1017
. change ....¶1015
.. single-tier alignment election ....¶1018
. corporate partnership structure ....¶15,393
. corporation ....¶1015; ¶15,390
. defined ....¶1015; ¶15,390
. farmers or fishers ....¶4365
. partner ....¶7205
. partnership ....¶15,390
.. corporations as members ....¶15,393
. partnerships ....¶1017–1018
. professional corporations ....¶1017
. self-employed individuals ....¶1017
. sole proprietorships ....¶1017
.. death ....¶12,015
. terminated partnership ....¶7195

Flow-through shares
. charitable donations ....¶3361; ¶5033
. general ....¶3540
. grace period for instalments ....¶12,292
. information returns ....¶12,050
. special tax ....¶13,675
. wills ....¶17,105

Paragraph

Food and beverages
. deductions of .... ¶3219

Foreign affiliates
. information reporting .... ¶15,134
. rules for non-resident trusts
. . adjusted cost base .... ¶5180

Foreign currency reporting
. conversion of tax attributes .... ¶15,580
. conversion of tax results .... ¶15,575
. conversion to Canadian
     currency .... ¶15,565
. election
. . transition .... ¶15,585
. election re functional currency .... ¶15,570
. requirements .... ¶15,570

Foreign exchange
. capital gains and losses,
     computation .... ¶5230
. conversion rates .... ¶5233

Foreign investment entities
. accrual regime .... ¶7395
. mark-to-market regime .... ¶7395
. offshore investment fund property
     rules reversing .... ¶7395
. prescribed rate of interest regime ..... ¶7395

Foreign investment income
. defined .... ¶9039

Foreign property
. former Part XI .... ¶13,497
. information returns .... ¶12,050
. . penalties .... ¶12,325
. reporting
. . requirements .... ¶17,640
. . year-end strategies .... ¶17,645b
. reporting rules .... ¶15,133
. . foreign affiliates .... ¶15,134
. . penalties .... ¶12,325

Foreign tax adjustment
. interest .... ¶12,290

Foreign tax credit
. business income tax .... ¶8565; ¶8590
. . limitation .... ¶8570
. carryover .... ¶8600
. denial where profit not material .... ¶8573
. determination of income
     sources .... ¶8595; ¶8610
. employees of international
     organizations .... ¶8575
. employees' profit sharing plan
     beneficiaries .... ¶10,309

Paragraph

Foreign tax credit — continued
. example of calculation .... ¶8620
. life insurance corporations .... ¶9246
. life insurance policies .... ¶10,525
. non-business income tax .... ¶8555
. . defined .... ¶8605
. . limitation .... ¶8560
. portion of tax not included .... ¶8580
. short-term securities acquisitions ...... ¶8572
. source of income .... ¶8595; ¶8610
. tax other than income .... ¶8585
. trusts, allocation .... ¶7405

Forestry workers
. expenses, deduction .... ¶2345

Forfeiture
. GST/HST .... ¶16,335

Forms
. employee to file, TD-1 .... ¶12,150
. general .... ¶820
. Home Buyers' Plan .... ¶10,395f
. request for tax deduction, TD-3 .... ¶12,145
. returns, corporations .... ¶8330

Franchises
. capital cost allowance .... ¶4110
. . election to defer recapture .... ¶4115

Freeze shares
. spouse trusts .... ¶17,155

Fringe benefits
. administrative exclusion from
     income .... ¶2057
. aircraft, use by employees .... ¶2090
. automobiles, use by employees .... ¶2085
. employees, use of employer's
     aircraft .... ¶2090
. income inclusion
. . included in income .... ¶2055

Fuel tax rebates
. business income .... ¶3067

Funds
. sinking .... ¶3207

Funeral arrangements
. exemption from tax .... ¶11,583
. income inclusion of eligible
     arrangement .... ¶3069
. non-resident withholding tax .... ¶14,170

G

Garnishment
. unpaid taxes .... ¶15,040

Gar

Paragraph

Generally accepted accounting principles (GAAP)
. general .... ¶840
. importance in determination of
   profit .... ¶3010

Gifts
. by partnership .... ¶8195
. charitable donations .... ¶3363
. . art .... ¶8165
. . capital property .... ¶8200
. . commuters .... ¶8170
. . member of religious order .... ¶8160
. . non-qualified securities .... ¶8203
. . partnership .... ¶7045
. . publicly-traded securities .... ¶8202
. crown .... ¶8185
. cultural .... ¶8190
. definition .... ¶8175
. designated
. . definition .... ¶11,630
. direct designation .... ¶8207
. ecological .... ¶8193
. election
. . communal organization .... ¶9285
. income-earning property .... ¶3048
. non-qualifying security .... ¶5162
. options .... ¶8204
. receipts .... ¶8155
. return .... ¶8205
. returned .... ¶3373
. . reassessments .... ¶12,095
. scientific research and
   experimental development
   organizations .... ¶11,577
. split-gift rules .... ¶8175
. tax credit not allowed .... ¶8180
. timing of on taxpayer's death .... ¶8210
. will .... ¶8206
. windfalls and prizes, capital gains ..... ¶5205

Gifts-in-kind
. year-end-strategies .... ¶17,645

GST/HST
. acting for non-residents .... ¶17,885
. agents .... ¶16,290
. amalgamation .... ¶16,345
. amount on which tax charged .... ¶16,135
. auctioneers .... ¶16,295
. bad debts .... ¶16,150
. business defined .... ¶16,110
. business transfer, election .... ¶16,165
. buying groups .... ¶16,330
. cash flow planning .... ¶17,867

Paragraph

GST/HST — continued
. commercial activity .... ¶16,110
. consideration .... ¶16,135
. contract wording .... ¶17,875
. Deemed Financial Institution .... ¶17,890
. direct sellers .... ¶16,320
. drop shipments .... ¶16,315
. e-commerce transactions .... ¶17,887
. election for exempt supplies .... ¶16,160
. election for nil consideration .... ¶16,155
. employee/partner rebates .... ¶17,865
. employee reimbursements and
   allowances .... ¶16,275
. employment income deductions
   rebate .... ¶2391
. exempt supplies .... ¶16,180
. filing .... ¶16,365
. Financial Institution
. . Selected Listed Financial
     Institution .... ¶16,205
. financial institutions .... ¶16,305
. forfeiture .... ¶16,335
. Harmonized Sales Tax ..... ¶16,200; ¶16,201
. . intangible property brought into
    participating province .... ¶16,210
. . Selected Listed Financial
    Institution .... ¶16,205
. . service brought into participating
    province .... ¶16,210
. . supply in a participating
    province .... ¶16,202
. . tangible property brought into
    participating province .... ¶16,207
. . transitional rules .... ¶16,203
. imported supplies
. . self-assessment .... ¶16,195
. imports .... ¶16,185
. Indian Bands .... ¶16,175
. input tax credit restrictions .... ¶17,863
. input tax credits (ITCs) .... ¶16,215
. . capital property .... ¶16,235
. . commercial use .... ¶16,220
. . documentary requirements .... ¶16,245
. . financial institutions .... ¶16,225
. . meals and entertainment .... ¶16,255
. . passenger vehicles and
    aircraft .... ¶16,240
. . personal-use restrictions .... ¶16,260
. . public service bodies .... ¶16,230
. . tax planning .... ¶17,860
. . time limits .... ¶16,250
. . vehicle restrictions .... ¶16,265
. insurance settlements .... ¶16,340

Paragraph

GST/HST — continued
. interest and penalties .... ¶16,385
. joint ventures .... ¶16,355
. Made in Canada ....¶16,125
. non-resident flow-through .... ¶16,190
. partnerships .... ¶16,350
. pricing and promotional
　adjustments ....¶16,145
. provincial governments ....¶16,177
. public sector ....¶16,310
. quick method accounting ....¶16,380
. real property supplies .... ¶16,170
. rebates ....¶16,145; ¶16,285
. registration
. . voluntary ....¶16,105
. registration required ....¶16,095
. reorganizations ....¶17,870
. reporting periods ....¶16,370
. seizures ....¶16,340
. self-assessment
. . imported supplies ....¶16,195
. simplified accounting ....¶16,375
. small supplier ....¶16,100
. supply defined ....¶16,120
. tax planning ....¶17,850
. taxable benefits ....¶16,300
. transactions with non-residents ....¶17,880
. trusts ....¶16,360
. value-added tax .... ¶16,085
. when due ....¶16,140
. wind-up ....¶16,345
. zero-rated supplies .... ¶16,180

GST/HST Rates
. Rates Chart ....¶16,085

Goodwill
. dispositions
. . capital gains ....¶3088
. . deemed ....¶3099
. eligible capital expenditure ....¶3078
. general ....¶3075
. non-eligible capital expenditures ....¶3081
. partnership interest, purchased by
　new partner ....¶7135
. replacement property .... ¶3090
. transfers
. . controlled corporation ....¶3096
. . rollover provisions ....¶6315

Government
. American system ....¶765
. Canadian system ....¶760
. German ....¶2030

Paragraph

Government — continued
. officials
. . liability for tax ....¶1065

Governor-General
. exempt from tax ....¶2030

Governor-in-Council
. powers, regulations ....¶15,010

Grandparents
. defined ....¶15,405

Grants
. additions to salary as income ....¶3645
. Canadian exploration rights ....¶15,435
. energy conversion ....¶2220; ¶3063
. . non-residents ....¶14,165
. exploration and development,
　deduction ....¶3356
. government ....¶3645
. . effect on capital cost allowance ......¶4012
. home insulation ....¶3063
. . non-residents ....¶14,165
. inclusion in income ....¶2210

Gratuities
. defined ....¶2040

Grubstaker
. defined ....¶3597

Guarantee of loan
. reserve ....¶3429

H

Half-year rule
. capital cost allowance ....¶4062

Harmonization
. B.C. De-Harmonization ....¶16,213
. elimination in British Columbia ....¶2391
. GST/HST ....¶16,200; ¶16,201
. intangible property brought into
　participating province ....¶16,210
. property brought into participating
　province ....¶16,210
. supply in a participating
　province ....¶16,202
. tax planning ....¶17,857
. TPP brought into participating
　province ....¶16,207
. transitional rules ....¶16,203

Health services plans
. health and wealth trusts ....¶2065

Hobbies
. income receipts ....¶2280

Hob

	Paragraph
Hobby farmers	
. losses	
. . effect on cost base of property	¶5180
. . restricted	¶3396
Holdbacks	
. reserve	¶3423
Home Buyers' Plan	
. acquisitions of property	
deadline	¶10,395a
. characteristics	¶10,393a
. deadline of acquisition	¶10,395a
. death	¶10,395e
. deemed acquisition date	¶10,395a
. definitions	¶10,395
. forms	¶10,395f
. income inclusion	¶2198
. joint property	¶10,395a
. limitation or RRSP	
contributions	¶10,393b
. non-residents	¶10,395d
. qualifying withdrawals	¶10,395
. replacement shares not eligible for	
Quebec LSVCC credit	¶13,658
. return of withdrawals not used	¶10,395b
. schedule of repayments	¶10,395c
Home insulation grants	
. income, included	¶3063
Home office	
. deduction of expenses	¶3183; ¶17,685
Home ownership savings plans	
. information returns	¶12,050
Home renovation tax credit	
. eligibility	¶8115
Housing benefits	
. northern residents deduction	¶2485
. subsidy for relocation cost	
or loss	¶2060
Housing corporations	
. low-cost housing, tax exemption	¶11,552
. tax exemption	¶11,567

I

Indian bands	
. First Nations Taxes	¶16,397
Input tax credits (ITCs)	
. capital property	¶16,235
. commercial use	¶16,220
. documentary requirements	¶16,245
. effect on capital cost allowance	¶4012
. financial institutions	¶16,225
. GST/HST	¶16,215

	Paragraph
Input tax credits (ITCs) — continued	
. passenger vehicles and aircraft	¶16,240
. personal-use restrictions	¶16,260
. public service bodies	¶16,230
. restrictions	
. . GST/HST	¶17,863
. tax planning	¶17,860
. time limits	¶16,250
. vehicle restrictions	¶16,265

J

Joint partner trusts	
. advantages	¶17,169
. disadvantages	¶17,170
. nature of	¶17,168
Joint tenancy	
. complications	¶17,172
Joint ventures	
. GST/HST	¶16,355
Judicial decisions	
. general	¶825

L

Labour Adjustment Benefits Act	
. benefits included in income	¶2175
. overpayments repaid	¶2455
Labour organizations	
. tax exemption	¶11,564
Labour-sponsored funds tax credit	
. entitlement	¶8290
. . minimum holding period	¶8294
. Quebec	
. . HBP or LLP withdrawals	¶13,658
. recovery tax	¶13,655
. . excess withheld	¶15,075
. . HBP or LLP withdrawals	¶13,658
. . refund	¶13,660; ¶15,075
. . remittance	¶13,660
. . withholding	¶13,660
Labour-sponsored venture capital	
corporations	
. investment requirements	¶13,487
. mutual fund corporations	¶9089
. Part X.3 tax	¶13,486
. penalties	¶13,489
. revocation	¶13,488
. year-end strategies	¶17,656
Land	
. adjusted cost base	¶5180
. allocation of proceeds between	
building and land	¶4485

Paragraph

Land — continued
. deceased taxpayer ....¶2570
. interest and property taxes on
vacant land ....¶3246
. interest on money borrowed to
acquire ....¶3477
. sale
. . reserves ....¶3420

Landscaping
. deductibility of cost ....¶3336

Large corporations
. capital deduction ....¶13,040
. returns ....¶13,045
. small business deduction
decrease ....¶8467
. tax ....¶13,030
. . deduction ....¶13,031
. taxable capital ....¶13,035

Lawyers
. accounting records ....¶15,120
. trust accounts and
disbursements ....¶3561

Leasehold interests
. capital cost allowance
. . rate ....¶4090
. interest in real property ....¶15,335
. principal residence ....¶5265

Lease-option agreements
. nature of agreement
. . sale or lease ....¶4450
. property acquired by lessee ....¶4450

Leases
. automobile
. . deductibility ....¶2320
. cancellation, payments deductible .....¶3333
. property, acquired by lessee ....¶4450

Leasing properties
. capital cost allowance restrictions .....¶4300
. deduction for lease payments ....¶3330
. lessee's position
. . election ....¶4307
. specified
. . capital cost allowance ....¶4305

Legal costs
. deduction from income ....¶2325; ¶3186
. . professionals ....¶3567
. inclusion in income ....¶2205

Legal representative
. liability for tax ....¶12,235

Paragraph

Liability for tax
. armed forces members ....¶1065
. Crown corporations ....¶3639
. employees temporarily outside
Canada ....¶1055
. estates ....¶1100
. government officials ....¶1065
. . international development
assistance programs,
employees ....¶1020
. legal representative ....¶12,235
. minimum income ....¶1075
. non-residents ....¶1040
. partnerships ....¶1095
. . property transferred to spouse,
minor or person not at arm's
length ....¶2645
. residence ....¶1020
. . constructive ....¶1025
. . corporations ....¶1085
. sojourners ....¶1025
. syndicates ....¶1095
. tax agreements ....¶1020
. taxability of income ....¶1005
. taxable income ....¶1005
. taxation year ....¶1015
. trusts ....¶1100

Libraries
. deductibility of cost ....¶3567

Licences
. capital cost allowance ....¶4110
. . election to defer recapture ....¶4115
. expense of obtaining ....¶3342

Life estates and remainder interests
. deemed dispositions ....¶5353

Life insurance
. death of insured ....¶17,110

Life insurance corporations
. amounts included in
income ....¶9252–9258
. . branch accounting election ....¶9265
. . real property ....¶9240
. Canada security ....¶9234
. conversion from provincial to
mutual ....¶9274
. deductions from income ....¶9234
. defined ....¶9228
. dividends deductions ....¶9243
. foreign tax credits ....¶9246
. foreign taxes paid ....¶9246
. information returns ....¶12,050
. non-allowable deductions ....¶9249

Lif

Paragraph

Life insurance corporations — continued
. non-resident insurer
. . transfers of business ....¶9270
. participating life insurance
  business ....¶9255
. policy loans, deductions ....¶9234
. policy reserves, deductions ....¶9237
. property not subject to capital cost
  allowance ....¶4340
. taxation of ....¶13,635

Life insurance policies
. disposition
. . "adjusted cost basis" defined ....¶10,519
. . defined ....¶10,519
. . included in income ....¶2200
. . proceeds ....¶10,516
. income from disposition ....¶10,522
. interest, dividend and capital gains
  from segregated fund ....¶10,525
. rollover ....¶10,516

Lifelong learning plan
. death ....¶10,396c
. eligibility ....¶10,396a
. non-residents ....¶10,396c
. repayment
. . shares not eligible for Quebec
   LSVCC credit ....¶13,658
. repayments ....¶10,396b

Limited partner
. defined
. . negative adjusted cost base ....¶7097

Limited partnerships
. at-risk amount ....¶7065
. at-risk rules ....¶7055
. definition of "limited partner" ....¶7070
. exempt interest
. . meaning ....¶7075
. loss deduction
. . limitation ....¶7060
. negative adjusted cost base ....¶7097
. non-recourse debt ....¶7098
. non-recourse financing defined ....¶7098

Livestock
. income from destruction of ....¶3591

Living expenses
. deductibility ....¶3213
. defined ....¶3216

Loans
. bonus to obtain mortgage loan ....¶3277
. corporations
. . attribution rules ....¶2655

Paragraph

Loans — continued
. housing ....¶3117; ¶3120
. included in income, not ....¶2040
. income splitting ....¶17,042
. low interest ....¶3111; ¶3117; ¶3120
. . benefit included in income ....¶2130
. minors
. . attribution rules ....¶2630; ¶2645
. non-arm's length attribution ....¶2260
. outstanding, deemed interest ....¶3156
. repayment with borrowed money ......¶3285
. shareholders receiving ....¶3111
. spouse receiving
. . attribution rules ....¶2620

Logging
. assets
. . capital cost allowance ....¶4145
. tax credit ....¶8670
. . provincial rates ....¶8675

Losses
. allowable business investment ....¶5034
. carrybacks
. . amended return ....¶3402
. . assessments ....¶12,090
. . effect ....¶12,295
. determination by Minister ....¶12,071
. farm ....¶13,155
. . restricted .....¶3396; ¶3579;   ¶5180
. fire ....¶3189
. limited partnership ....¶7060
. mortgage sale ....¶3353
. net capital ....¶3381
. non-capital (business) ....¶3384
. . application ....¶13,155
. . defined ....¶3387
. partnership interest
. . disposition ....¶7225
. . replacement of capital by former
   member ....¶7230
. personal-use property ....¶5300; ¶5305
. share transaction, deduction ....¶3408
. superficial
. . definition ....¶5090
. theft ....¶3189
. trust's beneficiary ....¶7487

Lottery prizes
. capital gain or loss ....¶5205
. income from annuity ....¶2185

Lump-sum payments
. retroactive ....¶8023
. withholding of tax ....¶12,170

Paragraph

Lump-sum payments
. withholding of tax

M

Machinery and equipment
. manufacturing and processing
  equipment ....¶4210
. power operated movable
  machinery ....¶4124

Made in Canada
. GST/HST ....¶16,125

Mail
. deemed receipt ....¶15,355

Manufacturing and processing business
. Canadian profits
. . calculation ....¶8405
. . resource activities ....¶8415
. machinery and equipment, capital
  cost allowance ....¶4210
. partnerships ....¶8410
. qualified activities ....¶8405
. small manufacturers ....¶8420
. tax reduction ....¶8400

Marital property protection
. alter ego and joint partner trusts .....¶17,169

Married persons
. connection by marriage defined .....¶15,405

Married status
. tax credit ....¶8095
. . married equivalent status ....¶8095

Master trusts
. tax exemption ....¶11,582

Matchable expenditures
. right to receive production ....¶3254

Meals and entertainment
. expense ....¶17,680
. input tax credits ....¶16,255
. transport employees ....¶2350
. truck drivers ....¶2353

Median rule
. capital gain or loss, valuation ......¶5135

Medical expenses
. prescribed expenses ....¶8135
. qualifying expenses ....¶8130
. refundable supplement ....¶8260
. tax credit ....¶8125
. . devices and equipment ....¶8135
. . services ....¶8130

Medicine donations
. to developing world ....¶3374

Paragraph

Membership dues
. deductions ....¶2315

Mental or physical impairment
. tax credit ....¶8145

Mergers
. cross-border ....¶9013
. mutual fund trusts ....¶9131

Metric conversion costs
. deductibility ....¶3204

Mines
. capital cost allowance ....¶4172
. depletion allowances ....¶3534
. industrial mineral, capital cost
  allowance ....¶4150
. interest, deductibility ....¶3277
. prospectors and grubstakers,
  tax deferment ....¶3597
. provincial mining tax, deduction ....¶3546

Minimum income
. liability for tax ....¶1075

Minimum tax ....¶8065
. calculation ....¶8070
. carryover ....¶8077
. planning considerations ....¶17,605
. special taxpayers ....¶8075

Mining reclamation trusts
. allocation of income of loss ....¶7497
. taxation of ....¶13,645
. taxation of beneficiaries ....¶7497

Minister
. administration of Act ....¶15,005
. allocation of tax collected under
  agreement ....¶8030; ¶15,190
. approval, fiscal period change .....¶1015
. assessment for tax withheld ......¶15,090
. books and records, disposal
  permission ....¶15,120
. certificate judgments ....¶15,035
. delegation of powers ....¶15,005
. demand for returns ....¶12,045
. information or complaint,
  authorization ....¶15,300
. inquiries ....¶15,140
. investigations ....¶15,125
. partnership income and loss
  allocations ....¶7250
. payment of tax where avoidance
  suspected ....¶15,035; ¶15,060
. receipt, considered discharge of
  liability ....¶15,100
. returns, extension of time ....¶15,005

Paragraph

Minister — continued
. security for payment of tax ....¶15,005
. social insurance number
    applications ....¶15,225
. withholding of tax ....¶12,050

Minors
. capital gains
.. attribution rules ....¶17,047
. designation, order in which
    dividends payable ....¶6155
. property income, attribution rule ....¶2630
. transfers and loans to, payment of
    tax on income ....¶2645
. transfers to, payment of tax on
    income ....¶12,245
. trusts ....¶7345
.. attribution of property transfers ....¶7365
.. income deemed payable ....¶7420

Miscellaneous receipts
. income ....¶2280

Misrepresentation
. information returns ....¶12,085

Money
. lenders
.. deduction ....¶3462
. worth, alternative form of income ....¶2010

Mortgage investment corporations
. capital dividend, excessive
    election ....¶13,110
. capital gains dividends ....¶9078
. characteristics ....¶9069
. income ....¶9075
. qualifications ....¶9072

Mortgages
. bonus to obtain ....¶3277
. foreclosures ....¶2690
. loss on sale ....¶3353; ¶4455
. transfer between spouses ....¶2645

Motion pictures
. capital cost allowance ....¶4275
. tax, non-residents ....¶14,180

Moving expenses
. deductible from income ....¶2400

Multiple-unit residential buildings
. capital cost allowance ....¶4290

Municipalities
. authorities, exemptions ....¶11,100
. officers, allowances exempt ....¶2030
. tax exemption ....¶11,200

Paragraph

Musical instruments
. deductibility ....¶2385

Mutual fund corporations
. capital dividend, excessive
    election ....¶13,115
. capital gains ....¶9090–9105
.. dividends ....¶9090
.. dividends, late-filed election ....¶9093
.. redemption of shares ....¶9096
.. refundable tax ....¶9099; ¶9105
. dividend refund ....¶9102
. qualifications ....¶9087
. reduction ....¶12,225
. tax instalments ....¶9108
. TCP gains distribution ....¶9103
. types ....¶9084

Mutual fund trusts
. application of trust provisions ....¶9123
. capital cost allowance
.. designations ....¶9129
. capital gains refundable tax ....¶9120
. December 15 year end ....¶9130
. instalments ....¶12,205
. merger ....¶9131
. overdistributions ....¶9130
. payment of tax ....¶12,205
. qualifying exchanges ....¶9131
. rates of tax ....¶9126
. requirements ....¶9117
. TCP gains distribution ....¶9121
. year ends ....¶17,645a

Mutual insurance corporations
. tax exemption ....¶11,566

N

National arts service organizations
. defined ....¶11,620

Negative amounts
. deemed to be nil ....¶15,440

Net income stabilization account
. farmers ....¶14,168
. interest accrual rules ....¶3021
. withholding tax ....¶14,168

Net worth method
. assessments ....¶12,100

Newspapers
. non-Canadian, limitation of
    advertising deduction ....¶3264

Non-profit clubs
. tax exemption ....¶11,600

Paragraph

Non-profit organizations
. exemption from tax ....¶11,565

Non-qualified investments
. deferred income plans
. . tax payable ....¶13,525–13,535
. defined ....¶13,405
. disposition, refund of tax ....¶13,410
. election by deferred income plan
    trusts ....¶15,340
. tax on deferred income plans ....¶13,525

Non-resident corporations
. additional tax ....¶14,275
. information returns ....¶12,050
. insurance ....¶14,300
. taxable income ....¶6005; ¶8640

Non-resident trusts ....¶7315
. beneficiaries ....¶7485
. deductions ....¶7315
. withholding tax ....¶7320

**Non-resident-owned investment
  corporations**
. capital gains ....¶9144
. . dividends ....¶9147
. . dividends, late-filed election ....¶9150
. computation of income ....¶9138
. deemed not private or Canadian ......¶9156
. defined ....¶9135
. instalment payments, reduction ....¶12,225
. special tax rate ....¶9141

Non-residents
. capital cost allowance
. . recapture ....¶4435
. . capital gains ....¶14,035
. . tax agreements ....¶14,125
. . withholding tax ....¶7325
. carrying on business in Canada ....¶1040
. . agent, through ....¶1045
. . deemed ....¶15,425
. . goods purchased to be
      processed elsewhere ....¶14,075
. credits restricted ....¶14,081
. deductions from income ....¶14,080
. departure tax ....¶1055
. disposition of property ....¶14,120
. employed in Canada ....¶1040
. employees ....¶14,060
. energy conversion grants ....¶14,165
. GST flow-through ....¶16,190
. home insulation grants ....¶14,165
. inadequate considerations ....¶2505
. income

Paragraph

Non-residents
. income — continued
. . amounts payable under
      agreement for services ....¶14,065
. . ships or aircraft ....¶2030
. . signing bonus ....¶14,065
. individuals
. . tax credits ....¶8225
. information returns ....¶12,050
. insurers ....¶14,245; ¶14,300
. investment funds ....¶14,037
. liability for tax ....¶1040
. mutual fund corporations shareholders
. . TCP gains distribution ....¶9103
. mutual fund trusts beneficiaries
. . TCP gains distribution ....¶9121
. non-arm's length
. . reporting requirement ....¶15,131
. . transfer pricing adjustment ....¶15,311
. non-arm's length sale of shares .....¶14,200
. pension funds ....¶14,037
. receipts for past service ....¶14,060
. rents, election re tax payment
      method ....¶14,255
. signing bonus ....¶14,065
. students ....¶14,070
. taxable Canadian property ......¶7325–7330
. . disposition ....¶14,040
. . transfer ....¶14,090
. taxable income ....¶14,025
. . effect of tax agreements ....¶14,030
. trust
. . deemed residence ....¶7394
. trust beneficiaries
. . deemed disposition ....¶7485
. withholding of tax ....¶12,175
. . excess refunded ....¶15,075

Northern area residents
. deductions ....¶2480
. housing benefit deduction ....¶2485

O

Objections
. assessments ....¶12,380
. awards as income ....¶2205
. expenses, deductible from
      income ....¶2460
. expenses reimbursed, income ....¶2205

Obligations
. discounted
. . adjusted cost base ....¶5180
. indexed
. . adjusted cost base ....¶5180; ¶5185

Obl

Paragraph

Obligations — continued
. predecessor corporation,
   on amalgamation .... ¶6360
. undischarged, reserves .... ¶3447

Off-calendar years
. year-end strategies .... ¶17,647a

Office
. defined .... ¶2040
. income .... ¶2040
. maintenance expenses
. . employee or officer .... ¶2315

Officers, corporations
. liability .... ¶15,280

Offshore investment fund property
. adjusted cost base .... ¶5180
. foreign investment entities rules
   reversed .... ¶7395

Old Age Security
. clawback .... ¶13,015
. . treaty-exempt income .... ¶13,016
. overpayments repaid .... ¶2455
. transfers to RRSP .... ¶2435; ¶10,357

Onus of proof
. general .... ¶865

Options
. acquired and disposed of .... ¶5415
. capital gains and losses .... ¶17,350
. charitable donations .... ¶3372
. gifts .... ¶8204
. predecessor corporation's shares ..... ¶6355
. U.S. citizens in Canada .... ¶17,585

Other sales taxes
. First Nations taxes .... ¶16,397
. other provinces .... ¶16,395
. Quebec sales tax .... ¶16,392

Overpayments
. interest .... ¶12,355
. . corporate offsetting
   mechanism .... ¶12,267
. repayments deductible from
   income .... ¶2455

Overseas employment tax credit ...... ¶8250
. phase-out .... ¶2380

Ownership certificates
. information returns .... ¶12,050
. obligation to complete .... ¶15,200
. penalties .... ¶15,205

P

Paid-up capital
. immigration
. . tax effects .... ¶9012

Parents
. defined .... ¶15,405

Part IV tax
. eligible dividends .... ¶17,415

Part XI.3 tax
. RCA advantages and prohibited
   investments .... ¶13,575

Part XI.4 tax
. excessive employer contributions
   to EPSPs .... ¶17,415

Participating province
. Harmonized Sales Tax .... ¶16,202

Partnership interest
. adjusted cost base .... ¶5175; ¶5190;
   ¶7100
. amalgamations .... ¶7183
. continuing, person retaining rights
   to receive property .... ¶7150
. deemed cost .... ¶7165
. disposition .... ¶7095; ¶7160; ¶7215;
   ¶7220
. . replacement of capital by former
   member .... ¶7230
. loss .... ¶7225
. partner's share, deemed cost .... ¶7165
. purchase by new partner .... ¶7135
. replacement of capital by former
   member .... ¶7230
. residual .... ¶7190

Partnerships
. accrual rules for corporate
   partners .... ¶1018
. accrued income .... ¶3051
. affiliation of two .... ¶15,480
. affiliation to corporation .... ¶15,470
. allocation
. . computation .... ¶1095; ¶7005–7020
. . election re computation .... ¶7040
. . allocation of income .... ¶7020
. . retiring partner .... ¶7025
. allocation of income and loss .... ¶7250
. assessments .... ¶12,073
. at-risk resource rules .... ¶7085
. Canadian, defined .... ¶7240
. capital gain
. . negative adjusted cost base .... ¶7095
. charitable donations of partner .... ¶7045
. continuation of former .... ¶7185

Paragraph

Partnerships — continued
. corporations as members .... ¶7015
. defined .... ¶7015
. disposition of personal-use
  property .... ¶5330
. dissolution .... ¶7150
. election on rollover .... ¶7120
. expenses of partner ....¶7045
. farm
. . interest, rollover .... ¶2550; ¶2595
. fiscal period .... ¶1017–1018; ¶7047
. fiscal period, partner .... ¶7205
. GST/HST ....¶16,350
. income computation .... ¶7035
. interest disposition
. . resident becoming partner .... ¶7107
. interest in, meaning .... ¶15,380
. liability for tax .... ¶1095
. majority interest partner
. . affiliation .... ¶15,475
. . defined .... ¶15,465
. . disposition of property .... ¶3393
. majority-interest group of partners
  defined .... ¶15,465
. manufacturing and processing .... ¶8410
. property
. . deemed disposition ....¶7145
. . right to receive
. . . adjusted cost .... ¶5185
. . rollovers to sole proprietorship .... ¶7180
. . transfers .... ¶7115–7135
. recapture of capital cost
  allowance .... ¶7130
. rollover ....¶6290
. SIFT
. . deemed dividend .... ¶7026
. . definition .... ¶13,385
. . returns .... ¶13,389
. . tax .... ¶13,385
. . taxable non-portfolio earnings
  defined .... ¶13,387
. small business deduction .... ¶8410
. spouse as partner .... ¶2625
. spouses as members .... ¶7015
. tax treatment ....¶930
. taxation year .... ¶15,390
. termination
. . election re tax-free rollover ....¶7155
. . fiscal period .... ¶7200
. . fiscal period, election .... ¶1015
. . recaptured depreciation ....¶7170
. transfer of eligible property
. . rollovers .... ¶6220

Paragraph

Partnerships — continued
. waivers of time limit for CRA's
  determination ....¶12,073

Part-time residents
. constructive residence ....¶1025
. taxable income .... ¶14,005
. . deductions .... ¶14,015

Passenger vehicles
. capital cost allowance ....¶4120
. definitions of ....¶3291
. input tax credit restrictions .... ¶16,265
. input tax credits .... ¶16,240
. restriction on expenses .... ¶2320

Patents
. capital cost allowance ....¶4110

Patronage dividends
. agricultural cooperatives .... ¶9181
. deduction .... ¶9161
. exemptions from tax .... ¶2030
. inclusion in income .... ¶9180
. . deferral .... ¶9181
. information returns .... ¶12,050
. non-member customer .... ¶9164
. payments withheld .... ¶9177
. qualifications .... ¶9168
. tax deferral .... ¶9181
. withholding tax, non-residents .... ¶14,155

Payment of tax
. administrator .... ¶12,235
. balance to be paid .... ¶12,180
. corporations
. . example .... ¶12,212
. . non small-CCPCs .... ¶12,210
. . small-CCPCs .... ¶12,211
. deferred profit sharing
  plans .... ¶13,440; ¶13,535
. departure .... ¶12,240
. dividends
. . broker receiving .... ¶12,185
. executor .... ¶12,235
. farmers and fishers .... ¶12,190
. federal–provincial transfers .... ¶12,160
. immediate where avoidance
  suspected .... ¶15,035
. legal representative .... ¶12,235
. liquidator .... ¶12,235
. loss carryback, effect .... ¶12,295
. machine computation .... ¶12,125
. provincial rates .... ¶12,135
. registered retirement savings
  plans .... ¶10,348
. remittance of amounts withheld ...... ¶12,115

Pay

Paragraph

Payment of tax — continued
. tax avoidance suspected .... ¶15,035
. TD1 forms .... ¶12,150
. transfers
. . minors .... ¶12,245
. . persons not at arm's length .... ¶2645
. . spouse .... ¶12,245
. transfers and loans
. . minors .... ¶2645
. . spouse .... ¶2645
. trustees liable for withholding .... ¶12,110
. underpayment, interest .... ¶12,255
. unpaid portion .... ¶12,230

Payments
. Canadian Wheat Board
    participation certificate .... ¶12,280
. defined .... ¶9165
. employer to employee .... ¶2110
. income maintenance .... ¶2095
. indirect .... ¶2250
. non-residents
. . inadequate considerations .... ¶2505
. . to, withholding tax .... ¶14,230
. lump-sum settlement .... ¶2095
. to farmers .... ¶3201

Penalties
. accounts not kept,
    withholding tax .... ¶15,265
. books and records, failure
    to keep .... ¶15,265
. communication of information
. . officials and authorized
    persons .... ¶15,275
. company officers, liability .... ¶15,280
. documentation of transfer pricing
    arrangements .... ¶15,315
. ecological gifts .... ¶8193
. failure to file return .... ¶12,310; ¶15,010
. . foreign information .... ¶12,325
. . individuals .... ¶15,265
. . trustee .... ¶12,315
. . withholding .... ¶15,080
. failure to report income .... ¶12,330
. . foreign property .... ¶12,325
. failure to report tax avoidance
    transaction .... ¶15,255
. failure to withhold tax .... ¶12,155; ¶15,265
. incomplete information .... ¶12,320
. interest on late payment of .... ¶12,300
. investigations, violations .... ¶15,265
. late or deficient instalments .... ¶12,335

Paragraph

Penalties — continued
. minimum not to be decreased .... ¶15,285
. misrepresentation by third
    parties .... ¶12,333
. ownership certificates, failure
    to file .... ¶15,205
. small amounts owing .... ¶12,337
. tax evasion .... ¶15,270
. transfer pricing adjustment .... ¶15,315
. waiver by Minister .... ¶945; ¶15,006
. withholding tax, failure to deduct or
    remit .... ¶14,095

Pension income
. income splitting .... ¶2437; ¶17,075

Pensions
. adjustments
. . registered pension plans .... ¶10,477
. . registered retirement savings
    plans .... ¶10,352; ¶10,355
. . registered retirement savings
    plans, PAR .... ¶10,356
. . registered retirement savings
    plans, total PAR .... ¶10,354
. benefits
. . Canada–U.K. Tax Convention .... ¶14,550
. . Canada–U.S. Tax Convention .... ¶14,420
. . inclusion in income .... ¶2150
. . withholding tax, non-residents .... ¶14,160
. corporations
. . tax exemption .... ¶11,568
. credit .... ¶8110
. . split-pension amount .... ¶2437
. current service contributions .... ¶2360
. employer's contributions .... ¶3321
. exempt from tax .... ¶2030
. income splitting .... ¶2437; ¶17,075
. . liability for tax .... ¶12,247
. non-resident funds .... ¶14,037
. past service contributions .... ¶2360
. retroactive lump sum payments .... ¶8023
. rights under contract .... ¶15,430
. transfers to RRSP .... ¶2435; ¶10,357
. trust tax exempt .... ¶11,581
. unregistered .... ¶10,504

Periodicals
. deduction .... ¶3264

Permanent establishment
. defined .... ¶8645

Person
. deemed to be resident .... ¶1020
. defined .... ¶1010

Paragraph

Personal injury awards
. excluded from taxpayer's income ...... ¶2290

Personal or living expenses
. deduction not allowed .... ¶3213
. income inclusion and exceptions ...... ¶2070

Personal service business
. deduction limitation .... ¶3240
. defined .... ¶8450

Personal tax credits .... ¶8095
. non-residents .... ¶14,081

Personal trusts
. principal residence designation .... ¶5260

Personal-use property
. definition .... ¶5055; ¶5300
. disposition .... ¶5305
. . losses, limitation .... ¶3393
. . sets of property .... ¶5325

Pipelines
. capital cost allowance .... ¶4127

Police
. tax exemption for high-risk
    missions .... ¶2487

Policy
. life insurance premiums,
    deductibility .... ¶3282

Policy reserves
. deductions .... ¶9237

Political contributions
. deductibility .... ¶3234
. partnerships .... ¶7045
. tax credit .... ¶8537

Pollution control equipment
. capital cost allowance .... ¶4190

Power saws
. expenses, deductibility .... ¶2345

Preferred shares
. tax on dividends .... ¶13,175

Premiums
. group term life insurance .... ¶2115
. health insurance, deductibility .... ¶3358
. life insurance, deductibility .... ¶3282
. registered retirement savings
    plans .... ¶2430; ¶10,350
. . refund of premiums .... ¶10,369
. unearned as reserves .... ¶3441

Prepaid expenses
. deduction .... ¶3252

Paragraph

Prescribed debt obligations
. income .... ¶3018

Price adjustment clause
. property transferred in non-arm's
    length transaction .... ¶2530

Principal residence
. change in use .... ¶5270
. defined .... ¶5085; ¶5265
. designation .... ¶5275
. exemption for gains on sale .... ¶5260;
                                                             ¶17,335
. . effect of capital gains election .... ¶5014
. farmer disposing of land
    including .... ¶5280
. option to acquire or dispose of .... ¶5415
. received from a trust .... ¶5290
. transfer to spouse or trust .... ¶5285

Principal residence exemption
. alter ego and joint partner trusts ..... ¶17,170
. capital gains and losses .... ¶17,335
. effect of capital gains election .... ¶5014
. joint tenancy .... ¶17,170
. trust beneficiary .... ¶7397
. wills .... ¶17,095

Printing and publishing
. printing
. . deductible expense .... ¶3306; ¶3315
. . separate from publishing .... ¶8400
. publishing
. . whether manufacturing and
    processing .... ¶8400

Private corporations
. attributions .... ¶9015
. bankrupt .... ¶13,160
. capital dividend distributions .... ¶6110
. defined .... ¶6020; ¶9018
. dividends tax exempt .... ¶6050
. investment income .... ¶9021
. . associated companies .... ¶9042
. portfolio dividends, special tax .... ¶9024
. refundable dividend tax on hand ...... ¶9027;
                                              ¶13,135–13,145
. . anti-avoidance measure .... ¶9030
. . bankruptcy .... ¶9033
. . procedure .... ¶9036
. "specified investment
    business" .... ¶9021; ¶9027

Private foundations
. excess corporate holdings
    regime .... ¶11,643

Paragraph

Privilege
. solicitor-client ....¶15,160
. . client's right to waive ......¶15,160; ¶15,165

Prizes
. achievement, for ....¶2210
. lottery ....¶2185; ¶5205

Probate tax ....¶17,165

Proceeds of disposition
. deemed ....¶2535
. defined ....¶4388; ¶5357
. income averaging annuity
    contracts ....¶2190
. life insurance policy ....¶2200
. part consideration ....¶2500
. Part II.1 tax ....¶13,060
. reallocation between land and
    building ....¶5358

Professional businesses
. computation of income
. . accrual method ....¶3552
. doubtful debts, reserve ....¶3555
. election re work-in-progress ....¶3558
. . partnership ....¶7040
. fiscal period ....¶1017
. lawyers' trust accounts and
    disbursements ....¶3561
. partnership member ....¶7040
. payment of tax ....¶3552
. . amounts receivable ....¶3555
. . deductions ....¶3567

Professionals
. incorporation
. . advantages ....¶17,630
. . CRA technical interpretation ....¶17,630
. . disadvantages ....¶17,630
. . rules ....¶17,620
. . technical interpretation ....¶17,630

Profit sharing plans
. allocations, included in income ....¶2080
. employer contributions ....¶3222
. information returns ....¶12,050

Profits
. Canadian manufacturing and
    processing
. . calculation .... ¶8405
. determination ....¶3010
. illegal ....¶3045
. real estate transactions ....¶5110

Property
. acquisition

Paragraph

Property
. acquisition — continued
. . deemed, upon becoming resident
    of Canada ....¶5405
. . trust beneficiary ....¶7465
. adjusted cost base
. . additions ....¶5180
. . deductions ....¶5185
. . deemed gain ....¶5175
. adjusted cost base defined ....¶5080
. annual value, as expense .... ¶3198
. appropriation, to shareholders
. . inadequate consideration ....¶2520
. . income ....¶3516
. capital cost
. . adjustments to cost base ....¶5170
. . deductible ....¶3567
. . deemed, to trust ....¶7285
. . on receipt by trust beneficiary ....¶7475
. . partnership interest, adjustments
    to cost base ....¶7100
. change in use ....¶5362
. . depreciable property ....¶4410
. . principal residence ....¶5270
. compensation for loss ....¶3039
. conditional sales repossession ....¶2690
. cost of
. . adjustments to cost base ....¶5170
. costs of surveying or valuing
. . adjusted cost bases ....¶5180
. damaged, compensation ....¶3042
. defined ....¶5035
. departure tax ....¶5380
. . elective deemed disposition ....¶5390
. . exceptions ....¶5385
. . post-departure loss carryback ....¶5393
. employee trust, distributed by ....¶7490
. exchanges ....¶4460; ¶5357
. . partnership election ....¶7040
. expenses of upkeep, trusts ....¶7435
. gross cost defined for
    manufacturing and processing ......¶8405
. identical — *see also* see also Identical
    properties ....¶5370
. income-earning, disposition ....¶3048
. involuntary disposition ....¶4460
. jointly held, partition ....¶5070
. life estates and remainder
    interests ....¶5353
. limited losses on dispositions to
    affiliated person ....¶5217
. listed personal, defined ....¶5050; ¶5310
. logging assets

Pri

Paragraph

Property
. logging assets — continued
. . capital cost allowance .... ¶4145
. loss or destruction .... ¶4460
. matrimonial
. . partition .... ¶15,387
. non-arm's length transactions
. . inadequate considerations .... ¶2505
. . price adjustment clause .... ¶2530
. . transitional rules .... ¶5195
. not eligible for capital cost
   allowance .... ¶4340
. partition .... ¶15,386
. . matrimonial .... ¶15,387
. partnership interest
. . adjusted cost base .... ¶5190
. personal use
. . transactions not at arm's length ...... ¶5325
. personal-use
. . business-owned .... ¶5330
. . debts .... ¶5425
. . defined .... ¶5055; ¶5300
. principal residence .... ¶5085
. prize .... ¶5205
. railway
. . capital cost allowance .... ¶4165
. real, interest in .... ¶15,335
. remainder interest
. . adjusted cost base .... ¶5180
. rental
. . capital cost allowance .... ¶4290
. replacement
. . CCA recapture deferred .... ¶4460
. . concessions .... ¶4115
. . franchises .... ¶4115
. . gain deferred .... ¶7040
. . licences .... ¶4115
. replacement, gain deferred .... ¶5357
. retirement compensation
   arrangement, distributed by .... ¶7495
. rollover to corporation
. . consideration .... ¶6230
. rules applicable to Quebec .... ¶15,330
. specified leasing
. . capital cost allowance .... ¶4305
. spouse .... ¶2580
. . spouse, tax liability .... ¶12,245
. . vacant land .... ¶3246
. substituted
. . adjusted cost base .... ¶5180
. . deemed, successive
   substitutions .... ¶15,345
. taxable Canadian

Paragraph

Property
. taxable Canadian — continued
. . adjusted cost base to
   non-resident .... ¶5180
. . capital interest in resident trust .... ¶7330
. . defined .... ¶5095
. . disposition .... ¶14,035
. . disposition by
   non-residents .... ¶14,035; ¶14,040
. . excluded property .... ¶14,045
. . non-resident .... ¶14,090
. timber limits .... ¶4135
. timber resource property .... ¶4140
. transfer
. . farmer to child .... ¶2550; ¶2590; ¶2595
. . inter vivos, to spouse .... ¶2540
. . minors .... ¶2545; ¶2630
. . non-residents .... ¶14,090
. undepreciated capital cost .... ¶4387
. valuation
. . inventory purposes .... ¶3477

Property income
. attribution rules
. . minors .... ¶2630
. . spouse .... ¶2620
. production or use .... ¶3027

Prospecting
. disposition of rights .... ¶3597
. exemptions .... ¶2030

Provinces
. corporate taxes .... ¶8630
. income earned in a province .... ¶8635
. . individuals .... ¶8035
. . special cases .... ¶8640
. income not earned in a province,
   additional tax .... ¶8037
. Quebec abatement for individuals ..... ¶8020
. tax rates .... ¶8025

Provincial corporations
. exemption from tax .... ¶11,200

Provincial governments
. chart .... ¶16,177
. payment of GST/HST .... ¶16,177

Provincial legislatures
. members' expense allowances .... ¶2030

Provincial sales tax
. B.C. new PST 2013 .... ¶16,393
. provinces other than Quebec .... ¶16,395
. Quebec sales tax .... ¶16,392

Provincial tax
. rates .... ¶8630; ¶12,135

Pro

Paragraph

Provincial tax credit
. amounts earned in province
. . salary and wages ....¶8660
. permanent establishment ....¶8645
. . gross revenue ....¶8650

Public sector
. GST/HST ....¶16,310

Public service bodies
. input tax credits ....¶16,230
. rebates with chart ....¶16,285

Publications
. regulations ....¶15,010

Q

Quadrennial surveys
. reserves ....¶3465

Qualified investments
. deferred profit sharing
    plans ....¶13,405; ¶13,525
. . disposition ....¶13,410
. defined ....¶10,378; ¶13,405
. information returns ....¶12,050
. non-resident investment funds ....¶14,037
. non-resident pension funds ....¶14,037
. registered education
    savings plan ....¶13,525
. registered investment ....¶13,480
. registered retirement
    income fund ....¶13,525
. registered retirement
    savings plan ....¶10,378; ¶13,525
. . disposition ....¶10,375
. tax-free savings account ....¶13,515

Qualifying environmental trusts
. allocation of income of loss ....¶7497
. exemption from tax ....¶11,590
. taxation of beneficiaries ....¶7497

Quebec
. labour-sponsored funds tax credit
. . HBP or LLP withdrawals ....¶13,658
. logging tax credit ....¶8675
. property
. . rules applicable ....¶15,330

Quebec Parental Insurance Plan
. self-employed persons ....¶2427
. tax credit for contributions paid ....¶2427

Quebec Pension Plan
. contribution and benefits
. . part of earned income ....¶10,372

Paragraph

Quebec Pension Plan — continued
. non-resident withholding ....¶14,160
. self-employed persons ....¶2425
. tax credit for contributions paid ....¶2425

Quebec sales tax ....¶16,392

Quick method accounting
. GST/HST ....¶16,380

R

Railway
. employees deduction ....¶2340
. property
. . capital cost allowance ....¶4165

Rates
. capital cost allowance ....¶4025–4035;
                                                    ¶4505
. . half-year rule ....¶4062
. capital gain inclusion ....¶5033
. capital loss deduction ....¶5033
. investment tax credit ....¶8342
. refundable investment tax credit ....¶8350

Rates of tax
. consumer price index affecting ....¶8005
. corporations ....¶8300; ¶8310
. . additional tax on investment
    income ....¶8323
. . general reduction ....¶8475; ¶9186;
                                                    ¶9207
. . resource rate reduction ....¶8490
. . special ....¶9282
. . special CCPC reduction .....¶8480; ¶9186;
                                                    ¶9207
. . surtax ....¶8320
. . tax credits ....¶8300–8320
. general ....¶935
. individuals ....¶8005
. . income not earned in a
    province ....¶8037
. . provincial ....¶8025
. . Quebec school allowances ....¶8020
. logging ....¶8675
. manufacturing and processing
    business ....¶8400
. mutual fund trust ....¶9126
. provincial ....¶12,135
. provincial rates for corporations ....¶8630
. small business deduction — *see also* Small
    business deduction ....¶8430
. tables ....¶8005
. . withholding ....¶12,130
. trusts ....¶7280; ¶8390

Paragraph

Rates of tax
. trusts — continued
. . SIFT .... ¶7282

Real estate
. brokerage, computation of
income .... ¶3552
. capital gains election
. . adjusted cost base .... ¶5185
. GST/HST .... ¶16,170
. soft costs capitalization .... ¶3249
. transactions
. . amounts receivable .... ¶3420
. . farm land, resale .... ¶5115
. . income or capital receipt .... ¶5110

Real property
. GST/HST .... ¶16,170

Reassessments
. excluded amounts .... ¶12,085
. notice available on line .... ¶15,301
. returned gifts .... ¶12,095
. time allowed .... ¶12,080

Rebates
. GST/HST .... ¶16,285
. PSB Rebates Chart .... ¶16,285

Recapture of capital cost allowance
. additions to class in the year .... ¶4395
. business assets used partly for
personal purposes .... ¶4410; ¶4415
. . change in proportionate use .... ¶4420
. general rules .... ¶4385
. leased property acquired by
lessee .... ¶4450
. non-residents .... ¶4435
. partnership interest .... ¶7215
. partnership property .... ¶7130; ¶7170
. property acquired for scientific
research .... ¶3624
. property acquired from trust .... ¶7470
. replacement property .... ¶4460
. . concessions .... ¶4115
. . franchises .... ¶4115
. . licences .... ¶4115
. representation costs .... ¶4465

Receipts
. capital distinguished from income ..... ¶5105
. real estate transactions .... ¶5110

Recreational facilities
. deductibility .... ¶3225

Redemption of shares
. corporation .... ¶6190
. shareholders, gain or loss .... ¶6160

Paragraph

Refundable capital gains tax on hand
. defined .... ¶9120

Refundable dividend tax on hand
. amount subject to tax .... ¶13,145
. corporations
. . connected .... ¶13,150
. . exempt .... ¶13,160
. . subject .... ¶13,140
. eligible dividends and .... ¶17,415
. interest .... ¶13,165
. losses, non-capital and farm .... ¶13,155
. private corporations .... ¶13,135–13,165
. returns .... ¶13,165

Refundable investment tax credit
. balance of investment tax credit .... ¶8372
. CPCC other than qualifying
corporations .... ¶8365
. filing of Form T2038 .... ¶8371
. individuals .... ¶8355
. other taxpayers .... ¶8370
. qualifying corporations .... ¶8355
. . definition .... ¶8360
. rates .... ¶8350
. taxpayers eligible .... ¶8350
. trusts .... ¶8355

Refundable medical expense supplement
. entitlement .... ¶8260

Refunds
. assignments .... ¶12,346
. capital gains .... ¶9063; ¶9099
. clawback of LSVCC tax credit .... ¶15,075
. disposition of employee stock
option of deceased taxpayer .... ¶12,366
. disposition of property of deceased
taxpayer .... ¶12,365
. dividend tax, private corporations ...... ¶9027
. . bankruptcy .... ¶9033
. . procedure .... ¶9036
. . excess .... ¶12,350
. excessive instalments .... ¶12,345
. non-qualified investment
. . dispositions, tax .... ¶13,410
. non-resident withholding tax .... ¶15,075
. non-residents, taxes on rentals .... ¶14,140
. overpayments .... ¶12,345
. . corporation .... ¶6075
. . CPP, QPP, and OAS .... ¶2455
. . interest .... ¶12,355
. . late-filed tax returns .... ¶12,345
. . loss carryback effect .... ¶12,360

Ref

Paragraph

Refunds — continued
. taxes in dispute ....¶12,347

Registered Canadian amateur athletic associations
. information returns ....¶12,050
. penalties
. . carrying on business ....¶13,208
. . delay of expenditures ....¶13,208
. . failure to file information
        returns ....¶13,208
. . false receipts ....¶13,208
. . incorrect receipts ....¶13,208
. . undue benefits ....¶13,208
. returns
. . failure to file penalty ....¶13,208

Registered charities
. accumulation of property ....¶11,645
. assessments ....¶13,205
. *Canada–U.S. Tax Convention* ....¶10,325
. charitable foundations
. . business activities ....¶11,636
. . defined ....¶11,633
. . disbursement quotas ....¶11,639
. . revocation of registration ....¶11,636
. charitable organizations
. . accumulation of property ....¶11,627
. . defined ....¶11,618
. . designated gifts ....¶11,630
. . disbursements ....¶11,627; ¶11,628
. . political activities ....¶11,625
. . related business ....¶11,624
. . revocation of registration ....¶11,630
. . revocation tax ....¶11,631
. defined ....¶11,615
. exempt status ....¶11,400
. income ....¶11,621
. interest ....¶13,205
. intermediate sanctions ....¶11,632
. non-qualified investments tax ....¶13,200
. Part V tax ....¶13,190
. penalties
. . assessment ....¶13,205
. . carrying on business ....¶13,207
. . delay of expenditures ....¶13,207
. . failure to file information
        returns ....¶13,207
. . false receipts ....¶13,207
. . incorrect receipts ....¶13,207
. . undue benefits ....¶13,207
. private foundations
. . excess corporate holdings
        regime ....¶11,643
. qualifications ....¶3365

Paragraph

Registered charities — continued
. returns ....¶11,648; ¶13,205
. . failure to file penalty ....¶13,207
. returns, records, receipts ....¶3366
. revocation tax ....¶11,631; ¶13,190
. transfer of property tax ....¶13,195

Registered disability savings plans (RDSPs)
. attribution rules ....¶2640
. Canada Disability Savings Bond
        (CDSB) ....¶10,428
. . repayment ....¶10,428
. Canada Disability Savings Grant
        (CDSG) ....¶10,428
. . repayment ....¶10,428
. concept ....¶10,425
. contributions ....¶10,425
. non-compliant plan ....¶10,429
. registration requirements ....¶10,426
. RESP rollover ....¶10,425
. rollover on death ....¶10,430
. RRSP rollover ....¶2447
. trust income ....¶10,427

Registered education savings plans (RESPs)
. acquisition of non-publicly-traded
        shares ....¶13,525
. benefits included in income ....¶2215
. Canada Education Savings
        Grant ....¶10,400
. Canada Learning Bond ....¶10,400
. definition ....¶10,399
. exempt status ....¶11,585
. non-qualified investments ....¶13,525
. provincial payments ....¶10,400
. registration ....¶10,401
. tax on income payments ....¶13,494
. tax on over-contributions ....¶13,491
. . deceased taxpayers ....¶13,492
. . marriage breakdown ....¶13,492
. . waiver ....¶13,492
. trust income ....¶10,402
. wills ....¶17,130

Registered home ownership savings plans (RHOSPs)
. disposition of property to
. . limitation on losses ....¶3393
. information returns ....¶12,050

Registered investments
. Part X.2 tax ....¶13,480

Registered pension plans (RPPs)
. annuity contracts ....¶10,493

Reg

Paragraph

Registered pension plans (RPPs)
. annuity contracts — continued
. . commencement after 69 .... ¶10,494
. business owner/manager .... ¶10,495
. contributions, deductible .... ¶2360
. defined benefit plans .... ¶10,477
. employee contributions .... ¶10,489
. employer contributions .... ¶3222
. employer contributions deduction ...... ¶3321
. employers contributions .... ¶10,486
. family .... ¶10,495
. individual .... ¶10,495
. investment limits in income
    trusts .... ¶10,475
. money purchase limits .... ¶2360
. money purchase plans .... ¶10,477
. past service benefits .... ¶10,480
. pension adjustment .... ¶10,477
. phased retirement .... ¶10,475
. pooled registered pension
    plans .... ¶10,475
. registration
. . requirements .... ¶10,474
. . revocation .... ¶10,483
. rollover on death .... ¶2445
. teachers .... ¶10,489
. transfers .... ¶10,492
. transfers to .... ¶2435; ¶2440

**Registered retirement income funds
(RRIFs)**
. acquisition of non-publicly-traded
    shares .... ¶13,525
. amount deductible .... ¶2445
. benefits taxable .... ¶10,417
. carriers .... ¶10,414
. consideration for .... ¶10,414
. death of annuitant .... ¶10,418
. definition .... ¶10,414
. definitions
. . advantage .... ¶13,518
. exemption from tax .... ¶11,588
. fund created from
    spousal RRSP .... ¶10,419
. information returns .... ¶12,050
. loss on transfer to .... ¶5210
. minimum amount .... ¶10,414
. . annuitant turning 70 or 71
    in 2007 .... ¶10,415
. non-qualified investments .... ¶10,423;
                                                         ¶13,525
. payments included in income .... ¶2225
. payments out of .... ¶10,418
. post-death losses deductible .... ¶2430

Paragraph

**Registered retirement income funds
(RRIFs)** — continued
. property as security .... ¶10,423
. qualified investments
. . tax .... ¶13,518
. registration .... ¶10,420
. . revocation .... ¶10,421
. roll-over by spouse and child .... ¶10,418
. tax
. . advantage extended .... ¶13,518
. . non-qualified investments .... ¶13,518
. . prohibited investments .... ¶13,518
. transfer .... ¶10,422
. transfers .... ¶10,411
. . provincial pension plans .... ¶10,392
. trust .... ¶10,423
. withholding tax .... ¶10,411

**Registered retirement savings plans
(RRSPs)**
. acquisition of non-publicly-traded
    shares .... ¶13,525
. advantages .... ¶17,185
. attribution rules .... ¶2640; ¶10,363
. benefits included in income .... ¶2195;
                                                         ¶10,387
. contributions
. . catch-up .... ¶17,225
. . deductible .... ¶2360
. . . where spouse annuitant .... ¶10,360
. . . withdrawals under Home
        Buyers' Plan .... ¶10,393b
. . deferred .... ¶17,235
. . in kind .... ¶17,215
. . last-chance .... ¶17,225
. death of annuitant .... ¶10,366
. . post-death growth .... ¶10,367
. . post-death loss .... ¶10,368
. definitions
. . advantage .... ¶13,518
. de-registration
. . amended plans .... ¶10,389
. direct beneficiary .... ¶17,125
. disposition, non-qualified
    investments .... ¶10,375
. disposition of property to
. . limitation on losses .... ¶3393
. earned income .... ¶10,372
. excess contributions .... ¶10,369
. excess contributions tax .... ¶13,455
. . waiver .... ¶13,471
. excess contributions tax
    after 1990 .... ¶13,465

Paragraph

Registered retirement savings plans (RRSPs)
. excess contributions tax after 1990 — continued
.. transition from $8,000 to $2,000 ....¶13,466
. excess contributions tax before 1991 ....¶13,465
. foreign investments ....¶10,381
. high tax investments ....¶17,200
. information returns ....¶12,050
. locked-in ....¶17,250
. losses after death ....¶10,368
. losses on transfer ....¶5210
. non-qualified investments ....¶13,525
. post death loss deduction ....¶10,368
. post-death losses deductible ....¶2430
. premiums
.. deductible ....¶2430; ¶10,350
.. deduction limit ....¶10,353
.. dollar limit ....¶10,351
.. pension adjustment ....¶10,352
.. pension adjustment, net past service ....¶10,355
.. pension adjustment reversal ....¶10,356
.. plan not registered ....¶10,391
.. refunds ....¶10,366; ¶10,369
.. refunds, deductible ....¶2445
.. total pension adjustment reversal ....¶10,354
.. unused deduction room ....¶10,356
. property as security, disposition ......¶10,384
. qualified investments ....¶10,378
.. tax ....¶13,518
. registration conditions ....¶10,345
. retirement income alternatives ....¶10,342
. spousal ....¶17,190
. spouse as annuitant ....¶10,360; ¶10,363
. tax
.. advantage extended ....¶13,518
.. non-qualified investments ....¶13,518
.. prohibited investments ....¶13,518
. taxability ....¶10,348; ¶10,363
. tax-free cash ....¶17,210
. transfers
.. provincial pension plans ....¶10,392
.. transfers to plan .....¶2435; ¶2440; ¶10,357
. types ....¶10,339
. U.S. citizens ....¶14,425; ¶17,585
. wills ....¶17,125
. withdrawal from spouse's plan ....¶10,363
. withdrawals

Paragraph

Registered retirement savings plans (RRSPs)
. withdrawals — continued
.. lifelong learning plan ....¶10,396a

Registered supplementary unemployment benefit plans
. defined ....¶10,325
. registration ....¶10,330
.. tax advantages ....¶10,327

Registration
. GST/HST
.. voluntary ....¶16,105

Registration required
. GST/HST ....¶16,095

Regulations
. authority of Governor-in-Council to make ....¶15,010
. effective date ....¶15,010
. failure to file returns, penalty ....¶15,010
. publication ....¶15,010

Reimbursements
. GST/HST input tax credits ....¶16,275

Related corporations
. deeming provision ....¶15,385

Related groups
. defined ....¶15,405; ¶15,420

Related persons
. corporations related to each other ....¶15,415
. individuals to corporations ....¶15,415
. shareholder, related to himself ....¶15,425

Remuneration
. corporate tax rates ....¶17,427
. distribution strategies ....¶17,430
. eligible dividends ....¶17,427
. integration ....¶17,425
. "other remuneration", defined ....¶2040
. salary vs. dividends ....¶17,435; ¶17,440
. unpaid
.. non-arm's length ....¶2680

Rentals
. buildings used for revenue, capital cost allowance ....¶4290
. non-residents ....¶4435
. reserves ....¶3444

Rents
. non-residents ....¶14,250
. professionals, business premises ......¶3567

Reorganizations
. GST/HST ....¶17,870

Paragraph

Repairs and maintenance
. deductibility ....¶3174

Repayments
. deductible ....¶3612

Replacement property
. deferring gains ....¶17,720
. deferring gains ....¶4460
. deferring recapture of capital cost
   allowance ....¶4460
. . concessions ....¶4115
. . franchises ....¶4115
. . licences ....¶4115

Reporting Periods
. GST/HST ....¶16,370

Repossession of property
. debt forgiveness ....¶3454

Representation costs
. allowance not included in income .....¶2070
. deductibility ....¶3342; ¶4465

Research grants
. inclusion in income ....¶2210

Reserves
. amounts receivable ....¶3417; ¶3450
. . sale of land ....¶3420
. bad debts ....¶3453
. . professionals ....¶3555
. capital gains
. . future proceeds ....¶5160
. . non-qualifying security gift ....¶5162
. debt forgiveness ....¶3451
. deduction ....¶3207
. doubtful debts ....¶3459; ¶3498
. indemnities ....¶3432
. insurance, unearned premiums ....¶3441
. loan guarantees ....¶3429
. mortgage lenders ....¶3462
. non-calendar year-end
. . death ....¶12,015
. proceeds not received ....¶17,675
. reinsurance commissions ....¶3060
. sale of land, special ....¶3450
. ships, quadrennial surveys ....¶3465
. special ....¶3462
. undelivered goods ....¶3423
. undischarged obligations ....¶3447
. unexpired rent ....¶3444
. . unearned commissions ....¶3432
. unrendered services ....¶3426

Paragraph

Reserves — continued
. warranties ....¶3432

Residence
. becoming resident in Canada
. . deemed acquisition of property ....¶5405
. change
. . deemed disposition ....¶5380
. . elective deemed disposition ....¶5390
. . emigration ....¶9012a
. . immigration ....¶9011
. . post-departure loss carryback ....¶5393
. considerations ....¶17,560
. constructive ....¶1025
. corporations ....¶1085
. deemed ....¶1020
. defined ....¶1020
. determination of ....¶1020
. estates ....¶1100
. general ....¶940
. trusts ....¶1100

Residents
. corporations, deemed resident ....¶6005
. definition ....¶14,010
. partnership deemed resident ....¶7240
. part-time ....¶1030; ¶14,005
. public corporation defined ....¶6010

Resource industries
. depletion allowances ....¶3543
. exploration or developing
   expenses ....¶3537
. . flow-through shares ....¶3540
. income ....¶3534
. manufacturing and processing ....¶8415
. provincial mining taxes, deduction .....¶3546
. tax rate reduction ....¶8490

Resource property
. deceased taxpayer ....¶2570
. disposition by partnership ....¶7100
. disposition by trust ....¶7480
. partnerships
. . at-risk rules ....¶7085
. . income computation ....¶7045
. reduced rate of tax ....¶13,585
. special tax on exempt persons ....¶13,585
. special tax payment ....¶13,590
. tax on carved-out income ....¶13,600

Restrictive covenants
. capital gains ....¶5340
. rules ....¶2112

Retirement compensation arrangements
. deduction for contribution ....¶3231

Ret

Paragraph

Retirement compensation arrangements —
continued
. generally ....¶13,555
. income ....¶2245
. interest accrual rules ....¶3021
. liability re contributions ....¶15,092
. Part XI.3 tax on advantages and
    prohibited investments ....¶13,575
. prescribed plan or arrangement .....¶13,571
. property distributed by ....¶7495
. refundable tax ....¶13,565
. . example ....¶13,567
. returns ....¶13,575
. special rules ....¶13,570
. taxes .... ¶13,560; ¶13,575
. transfers ....¶13,573

Retirement income
. defined ....¶10,342

Retiring allowances
. inclusion in income ....¶2160
. transfers to RRSP ....¶2440; ¶10,357

Returns
. amended ....¶3402
. capital tax ....¶13,240
. commercial tax preparers
. . mandatory electronic filing ....¶12,012
. corporate distributions tax ....¶13,090
. corporations ....¶12,010
. . excessive eligible dividends
    election ....¶13,128
. . mandatory electronic filing ....¶12,011
. cumulative offset account ....¶13,377
. deceased taxpayer ....¶12,015
. deferred profit sharing plan ....¶13,440
. demand by Minister ....¶12,045
. designated persons ....¶12,030
. estates ....¶12,020
. estimate of tax ....¶12,055
. excessive elections ....¶13,123
. failure to file ....¶15,265
. . penalties ....¶12,310
. family allowances and old age
    security benefits ....¶13,020
. filing ....¶12,005
. . electronic ....¶12,006; ¶12,011
. individuals ....¶12,025
. large corporations ....¶13,045
. Part XII.2 taxes ....¶13,625
. Part XI.01 tax ....¶13,513–13,517; ¶13,517
. refundable dividend tax
    on hand ....¶13,165

Paragraph

Returns — continued
. registered Canadian amateur
    athletic associations ....¶13,208
. . failure to file penalty ....¶13,208
. registered charities ....¶11,648; ¶13,207
. . failure to file penalty ....¶13,207
. retirement compensation
    arrangements ....¶13,575
. scientific research and
    experimental development
    corporations ....¶11,578
. SIFT partnerships ....¶13,389
. time for filing ....¶12,035
. . refunds of overpayments ....¶12,035
. trusts ....¶12,020
. voluntary disclosures ....¶12,040

RFI shares
. dividends
. . taxes on ....¶13,180

Right to receive production
. proceeds of disposition
. . income inclusion ....¶3026

Rights or things
. adjustment to partnership
    cost base ....¶7100
. election ....¶17,160
. included in income ....¶2560

Rollovers
. amalgamation of corporations ....¶6340
. capital gains on small business
    investments ....¶5026–5029
. capital, reorganization ....¶6310–6315
. definition ....¶6215
. farm property transferred to child ......¶2545;
                      ¶2550; ¶2590; ¶2595; ¶4375
. farm property transferred to parent
    on death of child ....¶2600
. inter vivos transfer of property ....¶2540
. insurance business ....¶9268
. life insurance policies ....¶10,516
. mutual funds merger ....¶9131
. partial, elective
. . property transferred to child ....¶2595
. partnership
. . continuation of former ....¶7185
. . election on dissolution ....¶7155
. . to partnership ....¶7120
. . to sole proprietorship ....¶7180
. partnership's property to
    corporation ....¶6285
. winding-up ....¶6290

	Paragraph
Rollovers — continued	
. property transferred to bare, protective trusts	¶7500
. property transferred to controlled corporation	¶6300
. property transferred to spouse	¶2585
. RPPs	¶2445
. . to RDSPs	¶2447
. RRIFs	¶2445
. . to RDSPs	¶2447
. RRSPs	¶2445
. . to RDSPs	¶2447
. shareholder's property to corporation	¶6230
. shares	
. . cost base	¶6315
. . exchange	¶6275
. . foreign affiliate, disposition	¶6275
. SIFT trusts	¶7486
. small business corporation shares	¶2595; ¶2600
. tax-free	¶6220
. to partnership	¶7100
. trust to beneficiary, employee profit sharing plans	¶10,303

Royalties
. Canada–U.K. tax convention	¶14,535
. Canada–U.S. tax convention	¶14,480

S

Safe income strips
. eligible dividends	¶17,415

Salaries and wages
. computing taxable income	¶8660
. garnishment for unpaid taxes	¶15,040
. professional assistants	¶3567
. reimbursement, deduction of	¶2370
. remuneration	¶17,440
. RRSP factor	¶17,442
. "salaries" defined	¶2040
. taxation of Governor General's salary	¶2030
. TFSA factor	¶17,442
. "wages" defined	¶2040
. withholding tax	
. . failure to remit	¶15,080
. . penalty	¶15,265

Salary deferral arrangements
. employer's deduction	¶3228
. forfeited amounts	¶2375
. income inclusion	¶2105; ¶2240
. interest accrual rules	¶3021

	Paragraph
Salary deferral arrangements — continued	
. receipt of benefits	¶10,510

Sale-leaseback agreements
. recapture of capital cost allowance	¶4450

Sales
. accounts receivable	¶3492
. income-earning property	¶3048

Salespeople
. expenses	
. . automobile	¶2320
. . deduction	¶2305

Scholarships and bursaries
. exemption	¶2210
. inclusion in income	¶2210

Scientific research and experimental development
. capital expenditures depreciable	¶3609
. corporations	
. . acquisition of control	¶11,579
. . computation of income	¶11,576
. . . gifts	¶11,577
. . exemption from tax	¶11,575
. . information returns	¶11,578
. deductible expenses	
. . incurred in Canada	¶3603
. . limitations	¶3627
. . outside Canada	¶3606
. deductions included in income	¶3066
. defined	¶3618
. forms to be filed	¶3628
. incentives	
. . filing deadline	¶17,710
. . proprietorship vs. incorporation	¶17,390
. interest, deductibility	¶3277
. investment tax credit	¶3615; ¶8343
. recapture of additional allowance	¶3624
. time limit for claims	¶3628

Scientific research tax credit
. information return	¶12,050

Securities
. Canadian, disposition	¶5240
. charitable donations	
. . non-qualified securities	¶8203
. . publicly-traded securities	¶8202
. convertible, cost base	¶6315
. debts, received for	¶2670
. foreign tax credit	
. . short-term acquisitions	¶8572
. sale between interest dates	¶3354
. term preferred shares	¶6035

	Paragraph
Securities — continued	
. valuation	
. . short term	¶14,220
. . withholding tax, non-residents	¶14,210
Seizures	
. books and records	¶15,135
. chattels	¶15,055
. GST/HST	¶16,340
. moneys seized by police	¶15,045
Selected Listed Financial Institution	
. Harmonized Sales Tax	¶16,205
Self-assessment	
. GST/HST	¶16,195
Self-employment	
. business income	¶17,740
. independent contractor vs. employee	¶17,385
. proprietorship vs incorporation	¶17,390
Service connections	
. deductibility	¶3345
Services	
. unrendered, reserves for	¶3417; ¶3426
Shareholders	
. capital gain or loss, on winding-up	¶6160
. deemed dividends	¶6145
. . allocation according to holdings	¶6195
. defined	¶3114
. indebtedness	¶3111
. property	
. . appropriation, inadequate consideration	¶2520
. . deemed income	¶3516
. . transferred to corporation	¶6225
. transfer of property to controlled corporation	
. . limitation on losses	¶3393
. transfer to corporation	
. . consideration	¶6230
Share-purchase tax credit	
. information returns	¶12,050
Shares	
. class of shares, presumptive	¶15,350
. cost base	
. . defined	¶6095
. . determination	¶6310–6315
. . disposition of property to corporation	¶5180
. deemed acquired	¶15,550
. deemed to be capital property	¶5345

	Paragraph
Shares — continued	
. discount	¶6205
. exchange	¶6275
. expenses of issuing	¶3306
. family farm corporation	
. . *inter vivos* transfer	¶2550
. . transfer to child	¶2595
. foreign affiliates	
. . rollover	¶6275
. non-resident's sale of	¶14,200
. of bankrupt corporation	¶5425
. paid-up capital	¶6170
. predecessor corporation, option	¶6355
. preferred	
. . term, dividends on	¶6035
. . protected	¶6045
. redemptions, acquisitions or cancellations	¶6190
. resource industry	
. . flow-through	¶3540
. right to acquire	¶3129
. short-term preferred	¶6040
. specified class, meaning of	¶15,495
. tax-free rollovers on amalgamation	¶6340–6350
. transactions, losses	¶3408
. transfer fees	¶3315
. valuation	¶6095; ¶6200
. worthless	¶5425
Short taxation years	
. small business deduction	¶8465
Sickness insurance plan	
. benefits, employee's income	¶2095
SIFT trusts	
. conversion	
. . loss trading	¶15,545
. deductions	¶7307
. deemed dividend	¶7357
. monthly instalment rules	¶12,220
. tax rates	¶7282
. wind-up rollover	¶7486
Signing officer	
. authorized by board of directors	¶15,215
Simplified accounting	
. B.C. de-harmonization	¶16,213
. GST/HST	¶16,375
Single status	
. tax credit	¶8095
Site investigation	
. deductibility of cost	¶3351

Paragraph

Small business corporations
. capital gains deferral .... ¶5026–5029
. capital gains exemption .... ¶5022
. shares
. . capital gains and losses .... ¶17,315
. tax exemption .... ¶11,569
. transfer of shares .... ¶2600

Small business deduction
. active business income .... ¶8440
. associated corporations .... ¶8465
. Canadian-controlled private
    corporation .... ¶8435
. computation .... ¶8455
. corporation member of more than
    one partnerships .... ¶8463
. defined .... ¶8430
. manufacturing and
    processing .... ¶8400; ¶8420
. partnerships .... ¶8460
. personal service business .... ¶8450
. reduction for large corporations .... ¶8467
. short taxation years .... ¶8465
. specified investment business .... ¶8445
. tax rate .... ¶8430; ¶8455

Small supplier
. GST/HST .... ¶16,100

Small CCPCs
. instalment payments .... ¶12,211

Social assistance payments
. deduction .... ¶2470
. included in income .... ¶2230

Social Insurance Number
. application for and assignment ...... ¶15,225
. improper use of .... ¶15,270

Social Security (U.S.)
. benefits .... ¶2055; ¶2155
. Canada–U.S. taxation .... ¶17,595

Sole proprietorship
. death of proprietor
. . change in fiscal year .... ¶1015
. fiscal period .... ¶1017
. . reserve for December 31, 1995
    income .... ¶12,015
. rollovers from partnership .... ¶7180

Solicitor-client privilege
. documents
. . production of .... ¶15,175
. . seizure .... ¶15,170
. . types .... ¶15,180

Paragraph

Solicitor-client privilege — continued
. prosecution under .... ¶15,165
. protection of communications .... ¶15,160

Special transaction taxes
. general .... ¶13,005

Special work site
. allowances excluded from
    income .... ¶2120

Specified investment business
. defined .... ¶8445

Specified member of partnership
. defined
. . negative adjusted cost base .... ¶7097

Specified partnership income and loss
. defined .... ¶8460

Spousal RRSP
. attribution rules .... ¶17,058
. three year rule .... ¶17,190

Spousal trusts
. deceased's property, transfer or
    distribution .... ¶2580
. distribution of property .... ¶7480
. farm property transferred
    to child .... ¶2590; ¶2595
. *inter vivos* transfer of property .... ¶2540
. special rules .... ¶2585
. wills .... ¶17,155

Spouses
. alimony .... ¶2180
. attribution rules .... ¶2620
. . non-application .... ¶2625
. deceased's property, transfer or
    distribution .... ¶2580
. deemed .... ¶15,405
. election on dividends received .... ¶6060
. employee .... ¶2625
. exemption for principal residence ...... ¶5285
. *inter vivos* transfer of property .... ¶2540
. maintenance payments .... ¶2180
. partners in business .... ¶2625; ¶7015
. property transfers .... ¶7365
. . minors .... ¶7365
. separation
. . attribution rules .... ¶2660
. surviving
. . pension fund payments .... ¶12,170
. transfer or loan to, payment of tax
    on income .... ¶2645
. transfer to, payment of tax on
    income .... ¶12,245

Spo

Paragraph

Spouses — continued
. trust beneficiaries ....¶7290

Standby charges
. automobile, inclusion in income ....¶2085
. selling or leasing automobiles ....¶2085

Statutory exemptions
. statutes exempting income tax ....¶2030

Stock options
. deceased taxpayer ....¶12,366
. inclusion in income ....¶2135
. . exchange of shares ....¶2140

Stocks
. dividend, future gains and losses ......¶6165
. dividends
. . corporate distributions tax ....¶13,065

Students
. credit for interest on loans ....¶8123
. education credit
. . full-time ....¶8120
. . part-time ....¶8121
. non-residents ....¶14,070
. textbook tax credit ....¶8122

Subject corporations
. refundable dividend tax
    on hand ....¶13,140

Subsidiaries
. deemed dividend
    on liquidation ....¶6145; ¶6185
. deemed proceeds of disposition ....¶3099
. dividends, simultaneous ....¶6155
. winding-up
. . corporation not a subsidiary ....¶6380
. . 90% or greater owned Canadian
    corporation ....¶6375

Subsidies
. capital loss on repayment ....¶5342
. deduction from adjusted
    cost base ....¶5185
. government
. . effect of capital cost allowance ....¶4012
. . taxability ....¶3645

Succession duties
. deductibility
. . income averaging annuity
    payments ....¶2450
. interest ....¶2420

Superannuation benefits
. inclusion in income ....¶2150
. transfers, deductible ....¶2435

Paragraph

Superficial loss
. definition ....¶5090

**Supplementary unemployment benefit
    plans**
. benefits included in income ....¶2195
. employer contributions ....¶3222

Supply
. defined for GST ....¶16,120

Supreme Court of Canada
. appeals ....¶12,450

Surtax
. corporations ....¶8320
. tobacco manufacturers ....¶13,048

Surveys
. quadrennial ....¶3465

Syndicates
. liability for tax ....¶1095

Systems software
. capital cost allowance ....¶4220; ¶4282

T

Tables
. withholding of tax ....¶12,130

Tax
. additional, excessive elections
. . assessments ....¶13,123
. . interest ....¶13,123
. . returns ....¶13,123
. additional, income not earned in a
    province ....¶8037
. allocation by Minister ....¶8030
. estimate ....¶12,055
. federal-provincial transfers ....¶12,160
. payable, defined ....¶15,325
. reduction
. . disposition of employee stock
    option of deceased
    taxpayer ....¶12,366
. . disposition of property of
    deceased taxpayer ....¶12,365
. refundable
. . connected corporation,
    dividends ....¶13,150
. . private corporations,
    dividends ....¶13,135–13,145
. . subject corporations,
    dividends ....¶13,140
. withholding tables ....¶12,130

Tax agreements
. liability for tax ....¶1020
. list ....¶14,310

Paragraph

Tax avoidance
. associated corporations ....¶15,525
. general anti-avoidance rule ....¶15,307
. meaning ....¶875
. payment immediate where
    suspected ....¶15,035
. reporting regime
. . background ....¶15,251
. . due diligence defence ....¶15,255
. . liability ....¶15,252
. . penalty for failure to report ....¶15,255
. . return to file ....¶15,254
. . transaction to report ....¶15,253

Tax Court of Canada
. appeals — *see also* see also
    Appeals ....¶12,375
. . disposition ....¶12,405
. . general procedure ....¶12,395
. . informal procedure ....¶12,390
. decisions re capital and income
    receipts ....¶5105
. documents as proof ....¶15,300
. special references ....¶12,400

Tax credits
. Canada employment ....¶8111
. child arts ....¶8114
. child fitness ....¶8113
. CPP/QPP contributions ....¶2425
. disability
. . determination ....¶12,072
. formerly deductions ....¶2400
. Quebec Parental Insurance Plan
    contributions ....¶2427
. transit passes ....¶8112
. unemployment insurance
    premiums ....¶2355

Tax deferral plans
. RRSPs ....¶17,185
. spousal RRSPs ....¶17,190

Tax deferrals and savings
. business income ....¶17,664
. Canadian-controlled private
    corporations ....¶17,390

Tax evasion
. meaning ....¶875
. penalties ....¶12,330
. . third parties ....¶12,333

Tax loss selling
. currency fluctuations ....¶17,655
. mutual fund losses ....¶17,653
. transfers to children ....¶17,652a

Paragraph

Tax loss selling — continued
. year-end strategies ....¶17,652

Tax payments
. capital tax ....¶13,240

Tax planning
. GST/HST ....¶17,850
. . employee/partner rebates ....¶17,865
. Harmonized Sales Tax ....¶17,857
. input tax credits ....¶17,860
. introduction ....¶17,010
. meaning ....¶875
. year-end strategies ....¶17,642

Tax rulings
. advance ....¶12,060

Tax shelters
. at-risk adjustment ....¶9305
. cost of investments ....¶9295
. enforcement provisions ....¶15,247
. evasion of reporting
    requirements ....¶15,270
. gifting arrangements ....¶9307
. identification number, failure to
    obtain ....¶15,245
. identification number required ....¶15,235
. information returns ....¶15,246
. limited-recourse debt ....¶9307
. meaning of ....¶15,240
. non-recourse debt ....¶9300

Tax treaties
. Canada–U.K. Tax Treaty ....¶14,510
. Canada–U.S. Tax Treaty ....¶14,380
. general ....¶14,305
. interpretation tool ....¶845
. non-resident corporations
. . information returns ....¶12,050

Taxable benefits
. GST on benefits ....¶16,300

Taxable dividend
. defined ....¶10,306

Taxable income
. corporations ....¶6005
. court decisions ....¶2140
. dividends ....¶6050
. earned in a province,
    corporations ....¶8635
. . liability for tax ....¶1005
. non-residents ....¶14,025
. . effect of tax agreements ....¶14,030
. . trusts end beneficiaries ....¶7315
. part-time residents ....¶14,005
. deductions ....¶14,015

Tax

Paragraph

Taxable income — continued
. trust benefits ....¶7430

Taxable obligation
. defined ....¶15,290

Taxable preferred shares
. dividends on ....¶13,250
. excluded dividends ....¶13,255

Taxation year
. employee profit sharing plan ....¶10,316
. fiscal period ....¶1015
. less than 12 months
. . capital cost allowance ....¶4065
. liability for tax ....¶1015
. partnerships ....¶7047
. "taxation year" defined ....¶1015
. "taxation year of individual"
   defined ....¶4390
. trust ....¶7275
. . arising on death ....¶7415

Taxes
. dividends from taxable preferred
   shares ....¶13,250
. dividends on preferred shares ....¶13,175
. Part I.2 ....¶13,015
. Part I.3 ....¶13,030
. Part II ....¶13,048
. Part II.1 ....¶13,055
. Part III ....¶13,100
. Part III.1 ....¶13,127
. Part IV ....¶13,135
. Part IV.1 ....¶13,175
. Part V ....¶13,190
. Part V.1 ....¶13,215
. Part VI.1 ....¶13,250
. Part IX ....¶13,375
. Part IX.1 ....¶13,385
. Part X ....¶13,395
. Part X.1 ....¶13,455
. Part X.2 ....¶13,480
. Part X.3 ....¶13,486
. Part X.4 ....¶13,491
. Part X.5 ....¶13,494
. Part XI.1 ....¶13,525–13,525
. Part XI.2 ....¶13,545
. Part XII ....¶13,585
. Part XII.1 ....¶13,600
. Part XII.2 ....¶13,625
. Part XII.3 ....¶13,635
. Part XII.4 ....¶13,645
. Part XII.5 ....¶13,655
. . application ....¶13,657

Paragraph

Taxes — continued
. Part XII.6
. . part-time residents ....¶13,675
. retirement compensation
   arrangements ....¶13,560; ¶13,575
. RFI shares ....¶13,180
. SIFT partnerships ....¶13,385
. . definitions ....¶13,387

Tax-free savings accounts (TFSAs)
. attribution rules ....¶2640
. concept ....¶10,404
. contribution limit
. . tax on excess ....¶13,513
. contributions ....¶10,404
. definitions
. . advantage ....¶13,516
. . allowable refund ....¶13,517
. . excess TFSA amount ....¶13,513
. . prohibited investment ....¶13,515
. . qualified investments ....¶13,515
. interest accrual rules ....¶3021
. non-resident withholding tax ....¶14,160
. overview ....¶17,262
. qualifications ....¶10,405
. qualified investments
. . tax ....¶13,515
. tax
. . advantage extended ....¶13,516
. . excess contributions ....¶13,513
. . non-qualified investments ....¶13,515
. . non-resident contributions ....¶13,514
. . prohibited investments ....¶13,515
. . return ....¶13,517
. TFSAs vs. RRSPs ....¶17,265
. trust income ....¶10,406

Tax-free zone
. valuation method ....¶5135

Taxpayers
. affected by Valuation Day ....¶5130
. bad debts, deductibility ....¶5425
. bonuses, as income ....¶2040
. borrowing money, election to
   capitalize cost ....¶3297
. business income, distinguished
   from capital receipts ....¶5105
. change of residence
. . deemed dispositions ....¶5380
. . elective deemed disposition ....¶5390
. . post-departure loss carryback ....¶5393
. conversion of capital stock ....¶5435
. deceased

Paragraph

Taxpayers
. deceased — continued
. . election re instalment
    payments ....¶12,240
. . eligible capital property ....¶2565
. . property transferred to spouse or
    trust ....¶2580
. . resource properties and land
    inventories ....¶2570
. . spousal trust, special rules ....¶2585
. defaulting, seizure of chattels ....¶15,055
. defined ....¶1010
. dividends, deemed received ....¶6055
. eligible property
. . transfer to corporation ....¶6220
. entering Canada
. . deemed acquisition of property ....¶5405
. fine, failure to file return ....¶15,265
. income interest in a trust ....¶7445
. leaving Canada ....¶15,060
. property
. . listed personal ....¶5310
. . personal-use, defined ....¶5300
. sale of principal residence ....¶5265

Teachers
. exchange
. . fund contributions, deductible ....¶2335
. past service contributions
    to RPP ....¶10,489

Technical notes and explanations
. information source ....¶835

Television
. "TV commercial message"
    defined ....¶4280

Tenants
. life
. . upkeep expenses incurred by
    trust ....¶7435

Terminal loss
. assets destroyed, lost or obsolete .....¶4480
. disposition of property ....¶4475
. dispositions to affiliated persons ....¶4495

Thin capitalization ....¶17,775
. interest deduction ....¶3258
. rules ....¶3258

Three-year rule
. spousal RRSPs ....¶17,190

Timber
. limits
. . capital cost allowance ....¶4135

Paragraph

Timber — continued
. resource property
. . capital cost allowance ....¶4140
. royalties
. . non-residents recapture of capital
    cost allowance ....¶4435
. . withholding tax, non-residents ....¶14,145;
                            ¶14,250; ¶14,255

Tobacco manufacturers
. Part II return ....¶13,049
. surtax ....¶13,048

Tools
. apprentice mechanics' deduction ......¶2388
. tradespersons' deduction ....¶2389

Transactions
. nature of, factor in defining
    income ....¶5105
. series of ....¶15,365
. shares, loss deductible ....¶3408

Transfer
. assets, partnership to a partner ....¶7145
. business
. . election re GST ....¶16,165
. capital property not at arm's length
. . transitional rules ....¶5195
. corporations
. . attribution rules ....¶2655
. deferred profit sharing plan ....¶10,468
. eligible property
. . corporations, to ....¶6220
. farmer to child ....¶2545; ¶2550; ¶2590;
                                      ¶2595
. . capital cost allowance ....¶4375
. fees deductible ....¶3315
. inter vivos
. . family farm corporation and
    partnership ....¶2550
. . farm property to child ....¶2545
. . property to spouse or trust ....¶2540
. minors
. . payment of tax ....¶2645; ¶12,245
. non-arm's length transactions
. . inadequate considerations ....¶2505
. . price adjustment clause ....¶2530
. non-arm's length
. . depreciable property ....¶4425
. non-residents, taxable Canadian
    property ....¶14,125
. partnership's property to corporation
. . rollover ....¶6290
. pension income ....¶2437
. property

Paragraph

Transfer
. property — continued
. . deceased to spouse or trust .... ¶2580
. . partnership .... ¶7115
. . spouse .... ¶2620
. . to parent on death of child .... ¶2600
. . trust beneficiaries .... ¶7365
. property income
. . minors .... ¶2630
. . spouse .... ¶2620
. registered pension plans .... ¶10,492
. registered retirement
　　income fund .... ¶10,422
. registered retirement savings plan
. . income receipts to plan .... ¶2435;
　　　　　　　　　　　　　　　　　　　　¶10,357
. . losses on transfer .... ¶5210
. rental property .... ¶4290
. retirement compensation
　　arrangements .... ¶13,573
. rights to income .... ¶2255
. spouses .... ¶7365
. spouses, between
. . mortgage on their residence .... ¶2645
. . payment of tax .... ¶2645
. superannuation benefits .... ¶2435
. tax, federal-provincial .... ¶12,160

Transitional provisions
. capital cost allowance .... ¶4015
. . farming and fishing assets .... ¶4350
. depreciable property .... ¶4015

Transitional rules
. B.C. de-harmonization .... ¶16,213
. Harmonized Sales Tax .... ¶16,203

Transport employees
. deduction .... ¶2350

Travel
. expenses
. . deductions .... ¶2310
. . income inclusion and
　　exceptions .... ¶2070
. transit passes tax credit .... ¶8112

Truck drivers
. meals deduction .... ¶2353

Trucks
. capital cost allowance .... ¶4122

Trust interest
. transfer of principal residence .... ¶5290

Trustee
. bankruptcy .... ¶9003

Paragraph

Trustee — continued
. deferred profit sharing plans
. . liability for tax .... ¶13,535
. liability for tax .... ¶7265
. withholding and payment of tax ...... ¶12,110

Trusts
. accrued income .... ¶3051
. accumulating income .... ¶7345
. adjusted cost base .... ¶5180
. affiliation of two .... ¶15,483
. amateur athlete trust .... ¶11,586
. amounts deemed not paid .... ¶7360
. amounts expended on upkeep .... ¶7435
. assets, revaluation .... ¶7285
. attribution of income .... ¶2650
. bare
. . rollover of property .... ¶7500
. capital assets, distribution .... ¶7460
. capital interest
. . disposition .... ¶7450
. . taxable Canadian property,
　　deemed .... ¶7330
. communal organizations .... ¶9282
. deductions
. . capital interest greater than
　　income .... ¶7300
. deemed dispositions and
　　realization .... ¶7285
. deferred income plans
. . look-through rule re qualified
　　investments .... ¶15,340
. deferred profit sharing
　　plans .... ¶10,432–10,468
. departure tax on leaving Canada ...... ¶5400
. depletion allowance .... ¶7375
. designated income .... ¶13,610
. disposition of
. . capital interest to beneficiary .... ¶7475
. . depreciable property .... ¶7480
. . eligible capital property to
　　beneficiary .... ¶7477
. . land inventory .... ¶7480
. . personal-use property .... ¶5330
. . resource property .... ¶7480
. earned income .... ¶7275
. employee profit sharing plans .... ¶10,294
. . rollover .... ¶10,303
. exempt status .... ¶11,580; ¶13,135
. family
. . year-end strategies .... ¶17,644b
. foreign
. . reporting requirement .... ¶15,132
. foreign tax allocation .... ¶7405

Tra

Paragraph

Trusts — continued
. foreign tax credit ....¶7405
. general treatment ....¶7260
. GST/HST ....¶16,360
. health and welfare, employees ....¶2065
. income
. . election re accumulating ....¶7345
. . investment limits for RPP ....¶10,475
. income interest, defined ....¶7445
. income splitting ....¶17,040
. income transferred to ....¶17,040
. information returns ....¶12,050
. *inter vivos*, tax rates ....¶7280
. interest in, meaning ....¶15,380
. liability for tax ....¶1100
. losses on transfers to ....¶5210
. maintenance expenses and
      beneficiary ....¶7295
. majority interest beneficiary
. . affiliation ....¶15,482
. . minors ....¶7420
. . beneficiaries ....¶7345
. . income payable ....¶7420
. non-resident
. . deemed residence ....¶7394
. pension
. . tax exemption ....¶11,581
. personal
. . principal residence designation ....¶5260
. preferred beneficiary election ....¶7345;
                                                                          ¶7355
. property transfers ....¶7365
. . bare, protective trusts ....¶7500
. protective
. . rollover of property ....¶7500
. reduction in cost base ....¶5185
. refundable investment tax credit ....¶8355
. registered investment ....¶13,480
. registered retirement savings
      plans .... ¶10,336–10,393
. residence .... ¶1100; ¶7260
. returns ....¶12,020
. revocable living
. . rollover of property ....¶7500
. segregated fund
. . life insurance policy ....¶5180; ¶5185
. SIFT
. . deductions ....¶7307
. . deemed dividend ....¶7357
. . tax rates ....¶7282
. social environmental
. . tax exemption ....¶11,595

Paragraph

Trusts — continued
. tax rates ....¶8390
. tax treatment ....¶930
. taxation of ....¶13,610
. taxation year .... ¶7275; ¶7415
. testamentary, taxation year ....¶7415
. testamentary trust, defined ....¶7415
. vacation-with-pay
. . tax exemption ....¶11,589
. withholding tax
. . non-residents ....¶7325; ¶7335; ¶7337

Tuition credit
. carryforward ....¶8124
. entitlement ....¶8119

Tuition fees
. deductibility ....¶3567

U

**Undistributed income and undistributed
      surplus**
. computation
. . designated surplus ....¶6075
. dividends
. . NRO corporations ....¶9156
. . paid ....¶6050; ¶6080
. . payable simultaneously ....¶6155
. . taxable, defined ....¶6025
. 1971
. . election ....¶6080
. . reduction ....¶6080

Union employer
. deemed single employer ....¶15,423

United States
. Canada–U.S. Tax Treaty ....¶14,380
. social security payments ....¶2055; ¶2155

Universal child care benefit
. retroactive payments ....¶8022

Universities
. tax exemption ....¶11,500

Unpaid remuneration
. income inclusion ....¶2685

U.S. citizens
. considerations for coming to
      Canada ....¶17,585
. U.S. estate tax ....¶17,590

Utilities
. corporations
. . information returns ....¶12,050
. . special tax rate ....¶9282
. cost of connection, deductible ....¶3345

Uti

Paragraph

Utilities
. cost of connection, deductible

V

Vacation-with-pay trusts
. exemption from tax .... ¶11,589

Valuation Day
. capital property .... ¶5130
. gain or loss
. . calculation for pre-1972 assets ...... ¶5135

Value-added tax
. GST/HST .... ¶16,085

Vendor
. accounts receivable, deductions .... ¶3495
. certificate, on disposition of taxable
    Canadian property .... ¶14,040
. election re accounts receivable
    deductions .... ¶7040

Venture capital corporations
. exclusion from private
    corporation .... ¶13,135
. limitation on losses .... ¶3393
. meaning .... ¶13,135

Vessels
. capital cost allowance .... ¶4170
. quadrennial surveys .... ¶3465
. recapture of depreciation, election ..... ¶7040

Videotapes
. capital cost allowance .... ¶4280
. certified, defined .... ¶4275
. returns .... ¶12,050

Visiting Forces Act
. members' residence status .... ¶1065

Voluntary disclosures
. income tax returns .... ¶12,040

W

Waiver
. filing of documents .... ¶15,006
. . scientific research and
        experimental development .... ¶3628
. interest .... ¶945; ¶15,006
. penalties .... ¶945; ¶15,006

War savings certificates
. not included in income .... ¶2030

Warranties
. capital gains treatment .... ¶5340
. reserves .... ¶3432

Paragraph

Western Grain Stabilization Act .... ¶3348

Wills
. association rules .... ¶17,140
. bequests of farm or fishing
    properties .... ¶17,100
. bequests to low income
    earners .... ¶17,115
. charitable gifts through .... ¶17,150
. corporation shares and partnership
    interest .... ¶17,145
. debt forgiveness in .... ¶17,135
. estate administration tax .... ¶17,165
. estate splits .... ¶17,120
. gifts .... ¶8206
. principal residence exemption .... ¶17,095
. probate tax .... ¶17,165
. RESPs .... ¶17,130
. RRSPs and RRIFs .... ¶17,125
. spouse as beneficiary .... ¶17,090
. spouse trusts .... ¶17,155
. substitutes .... ¶17,168
. tax planning .... ¶17,080
. treatment of flow-through
    shares .... ¶17,105

Winding-up
. change in fiscal year .... ¶1015
. deemed dividends .... ¶6145
. . after December 31, 1978 .... ¶6385
. property, appropriated to
    shareholder .... ¶3516
. property distribution, deemed
    dividend .... ¶6185;   ¶6200
. share valuation .... ¶6200
. subsidiary corporation
. . not 90% or greater owned .... ¶6380
. 90% or greater owned Canadian
    corporation .... ¶6375

Wind-up
. GST/HST .... ¶16,345

Withholding of tax
. amounts to withhold .... ¶12,120
. balance to be paid .... ¶12,180
. bonus .... ¶12,165
. dividends received by brokers .... ¶12,185
. information returns .... ¶12,050
. lump-sum payments .... ¶12,170
. machine computation .... ¶12,125
. not required .... ¶12,140
. payments subject to withholding ..... ¶12,110
. payments to non-residents .... ¶12,175
. penalties
. . failure to withhold .... ¶12,155

Paragraph

Withholding of tax — continued
. provincial rates ....¶12,135
. provincial tables ....¶12,130
. recovery of labour-sponsored funds
   tax credit ....¶13,660
. recovery of LSVCC
. . refund ....¶15,075
. remittance ....¶12,110; ¶12,115
. retroactive pay increase ....¶12,165
. tables ....¶12,130
. . provincial rates ....¶12,135
. TD1 forms ....¶12,150
. trustees ....¶12,110
. variations in deductions ....¶12,145

Withholding tax — Non-residents
. alternative .... ¶14,255
. business in Canada .... ¶14,197
. deductions from tax .... ¶14,230; ¶14,235
. deemed dividends .... ¶14,175
. dividends .... ¶14,172
. energy conversion grants .... ¶14,165
. estate or trust income .... ¶14,135
. exemptions ....¶14,110–14,215
. failure to deduct or remit .... ¶14,095
. guarantee fees and loans .... ¶14,225
. home insulation grants .... ¶14,165
. income and capital combined .... ¶14,205
. insurers .... ¶14,245
. interest .... ¶14,105
. . failure to deduct or remit .... ¶14,095
. . non-arm's length payments
    after 2007 .... ¶14,112
. liability for tax .... ¶14,240
. management fees .... ¶14,100
. mortgage interest .... ¶14,250
. motion picture film royalties .... ¶14,180
. non-resident trust beneficiaries .... ¶7320
. partnerships .... ¶14,195
. payments from deferred income
   plans .... ¶14,250
. payments to non-residents
. . patronage dividends .... ¶14,155
. . pension benefits .... ¶14,160
. . property transfer to spouse .... ¶14,190
. . refunds .... ¶14,140
. . rents .... ¶14,140; ¶14,250
. . retiring allowances .... ¶14,250
. . royalties .... ¶14,140
. . securities .... ¶14,210
. . timber royalties .... ¶14,145
. . transfer of obligations .... ¶14,220
. penalties, failure to deduct or
   remit .... ¶14,095

Paragraph

Withholding tax — Non-residents —
   continued
. retiring allowances .... ¶14,250
. RPP benefits .... ¶14,250
. . shares, sale of .... ¶14,200
. timber royalties .... ¶14,145; ¶14,250
. . transfer of obligations .... ¶14,220;
. trust income .... ¶7320–7335
. trust payments .... ¶7320; ¶7335; ¶7337

Withholding tax
. agreement not to withhold, void ...... ¶15,070
. amateur athlete trusts .... ¶14,169
. assessment .... ¶15,090
. Canada and Quebec Pension
   Plans .... ¶14,160
. Crown's liability .... ¶15,095
. directors' liability .... ¶15,085
. employee life and health trust .... ¶14,169
. funeral arrangements .... ¶14,170
. income-averaging annuity contract,
   dividends .... ¶14,175
. liability
. . failure to keep separate
    accounts .... ¶15,265
. . failure to withhold .... ¶15,265
. net income stabilization
   account .... ¶14,168
. partnership deemed person .... ¶15,110
. payment
. . administrator .... ¶15,083
. . assignee .... ¶15,083
. . executor .... ¶15,083
. . liquidator .... ¶15,083
. . receiver .... ¶15,083
. . secured creditor .... ¶15,083
. . trustee .... ¶15,083
. penalties
. . failure to remit .... ¶15,080
. . failure to withhold .... ¶15,080
. pensions .... ¶14,160
. refund of overpayments .... ¶15,075
. separate accounts .... ¶15,070
. TD1 forms .... ¶15,070

Workers' compensation
. deduction .... ¶2470
. included in income .... ¶2235

Working income tax benefit
. calculation .... ¶8243
. eligibility .... ¶8242
. overview .... ¶8241
. prepayment .... ¶8244

Wor

Paragraph

Work-in-progress

. election by professionals ....¶3558

. . partnership member ....¶7040

Y

Year of death

. disposition of property, reserves ....¶2605

Year-end strategies

. bad take-back mortgages ....¶17,651

. CRA prescribed rate ....¶17,644a

. defer tax on interest ....¶17,648

. employee auto benefits ....¶17,649

. expenses to pay ....¶17,643

. family trusts ....¶17,644b

. foreign property reporting ....¶17,645b

Paragraph

Year-end strategies — continued

. gifts-in-kind ....¶17,645

. income splitting ....¶17,651a

. increasing business expenses ....¶17,646

. lowering tax instalments ....¶17,645c

. mutual fund year ends ....¶17,645a

. off-calendar years ....¶17,647a

. real estate tax losses ....¶17,650

. RESP contributions ....¶17,648

. tax deadlines ....¶17,647

. tax loss selling ....¶17,652

Z

Zero-rated supplies

. GST/HST ....¶16,180

Wor